HARRAP

POCKET
SPANISH
DICTIONARY
English-Spanish/Spanish-English

HARRAP

First published in Great Britain 1992
by Chambers Harrap Publishers Ltd
7 Hopetoun Crescent, Edinburgh EH7 4AY

© Chambers Harrap Publishers Ltd 1997

ISBN 0 245 60633 5

Editors/Redactores:
Joaquín Blasco   Fernando León Solís   Hugh O'Donnell

Trademarks
Words considered to be trademarks have been designated
in this dictionary by ®. However, no judgement is implied
concerning the legal status of any trademark by virtue
of the presence or absence of such a designation.

Marcas Registradas
Las palabras consideradas marcas registradas vienen
distinguidas en este diccionario con una ®. Sin embargo, la presencia
o la ausencia de tal distintivo no implica juicio alguno acerca de la
situación legal de la marca registrada.

Reprinted 1997

Printed and bound in Great Britain by
Caledonian International Book Manufacturing Ltd, Glasgow

Preface

This dictionary is a shortened version of *Harrap's Concise Spanish and English Dictionary*. The selection of headwords and phrases - over 57,000 in total - is aimed at providing a broad coverage of modern English and Spanish, including a considerable number of important Latin American and North American terms.

The new system for Spanish alphabetical order has been adopted. In this system 'ch' and 'll' are no longer considered as separate letters of the alphabet, but are each incorporated at their respective alphabetical positions under 'c' and 'l' - 'ñ', however, is treated as a separate letter.

Entries are divided into grammatical categories by Roman numerals (I, II etc) and into sense categories by Arabic numerals (1, 2 etc). A lozenge ◆ has been used i) to highlight adverbs which have been placed directly after their related adjective (for example: happily/happy) and which are not always therefore in strict alphabetical order and ii) to identify phrasal verbs (give up, come out, send back etc).

A major feature of this dictionary is the systematic use of signposting to guide users and to enable them to identify the translation they require quickly and accurately. There are two main types of signpost: **field labels** (of which a complete list is given on pages vii-x) identify the area of usage of a word, for example: *Ftb* is for football, *Comput* is for computers. **Indicators** show, for example, what might be the typical subject or object of a verb or what might be the typical noun used with a certain adjective. These help the user to identify the correct translation for a particular word by showing the context in which a certain translation is appropriate.

Gender markers for Spanish translations are not given where the presence of an adjective makes the gender of a noun self-evident. For example 'centro deportivo' has no gender marker whereas 'centro *m* comercial' does.

Spanish verbs with irregular conjugations are coded ([12], [24] etc). By looking at the information in the introductory section on pages xii-xxi it is possible to work out the form of an irregular Spanish verb in any required tense or person. A list of irregular English verbs is given on pages (ii)-(iv) of the English-Spanish section.

Full IPA (International Phonetic Alphabet) pronunciation is given for English headwords in the English-Spanish part of the dictionary with a guide to IPA on pages (v)-(vi) of the introduction. There is also an introduction to Spanish pronunciation on pages xxii-xxiii of the Spanish-English part of the dictionary.

Prólogo

El presente diccionario es una versión abreviada del *Harrap's Concise Spanish and English Dictionary*. La selección de la entradas y frases idiomáticas - más de 57000 en total - tiene como objetivo ofrecer una amplia cobertura del inglés y del español actuales, incluído un número importante de términos usados en Latinoamérica y Norteamérica.

Se ha adoptado la nueva ordenación alfabética del español. Según ésta, los dígrafos "ch" y "ll" no se consideran letras independientes, sino que ocupan el lugar que les corresponde alfabéticamente dentro de la "c" y "l", respectivamente. La "ñ", sin embargo, se considera letra independiente.

Las diferentes categorías gramaticales de una misma entrada se señalan mediante números romanos (I, II, etc), mientras que la numeración árabe (1, 2, etc) indica las diferentes categorías semánticas. Se utilizan los rombos ◆ para i) resaltar los adverbios colocados justo después del adjetivo del que derivan (por ejemplo: justo/justamente) y que no siguen, por tanto, un riguroso orden alfabético y ii) para identificar los "phrasal verbs" (give up, come out, send back etc).

Una característica relevante de esta obra es el uso sistemático de señales indicadoras que orientan al usuario y le permiten identificar la traducción adecuada con rapidez y precisión. Hay dos tipos de señales indicadoras: las **abreviaturas de campo semántico** (de las que aparece una lista completa en las páginas vii-x) identifican el área de uso de una palabra, por ejemplo: *Ftb* es fútbol, *Inform* es informática. Los **indicadores** muestran, por ejemplo, un sujeto o un objeto típicos de un verbo, o un sustantivo que frecuentemente acompaña a determinado adjetivo. Estos ayudan al usuario a identificar la traducción correcta de una determinada palabra al mostrar el contexto adecuado para cada traducción.

Los indicadores de género de las traducciones españolas no aparecerán cuando la presencia de un adjetivo deje claro el género del sustantivo. Por ejemplo "centro deportivo" no lleva indicador de género, mientras que, por el contrario, sí aparece en "centro *m* comercial".

Los verbos españoles de conjugación irregular vienen seguidos de un número de referencia ([12], [24] etc). En la sección introductoria, en las páginas xii-xxi, viene dada la información necesaria para poder conjugar los verbos irregulares en español. Una lista de verbos irregulares del inglés aparece en las páginas (ii)-(iv) de la sección Inglés-Español.

Las entradas inglesas de la sección Inglés-Español del diccionario van acompañadas de una transcripción fonética basada en el Alfabeto Fonético Internacional (AFI). En la página (v)-(vi) de la introducción de la sección Inglés-Español aparece una guía explicativa de dicho alfabeto. También viene dada una guía introductoria de pronunciación española en las páginas xxii-xxiii de la sección Español-Inglés.

Abbreviations used in this dictionary
Abreviaturas usadas en este diccionario

abbreviation	*abbr, abr*	abreviatura
adjective	*adj*	adjetivo
adverb	*adv*	adverbio
agriculture	*Agr*	agricultura
chess	*Ajedrez*	
somebody, someone	*algn*	alguien
Latin American	*Am*	hispanoamericano
anatomy	*Anat*	anatomía
approximately	*approx, aprox*	aproximadamente
archaic	*arc, arch*	arcaico
architecture	*Archit*	arquitectura
slang	*arg*	argot
architecture	*Arquit*	arquitectura
article	*art*	artículo
art	*Art, Arte*	bellas artes
astronomy	*Astron*	astronomía
space travel	*Astronaut, Astronáut*	astronáutica
Australian	*Austral*	australiano
motoring	*Aut*	automóviles
auxiliary	*aux*	auxiliar
aviation	*Av*	aviación
biology	*Biol*	biología
bowling	*Bolos*	
botany	*Bot*	botánica
	Bowling	bolos
boxing	*Box*	boxeo
Canary Islands	*Can*	Canarias
	Cards	naipes
chemistry	*Chem*	químico
	Chess	ajedrez
cycling	*Cicl*	ciclismo
cinema	*Cin*	cine
commerce	*Com*	comercio
comparative	*comp*	comparativo
computers	*Comput*	informática
conditional	*cond*	condicional
conjunction	*conj*	conjunción
building industry	*Constr*	construcción
sewing	*Cost*	costura
cookery	*Culin*	cocina
cycling	*Cycl*	ciclismo
definite	*def*	definido
defective	*defect*	defectivo
demonstrative	*dem*	demostrativo
sport	*Dep*	deporte
ecology	*Ecol*	ecología
economics	*Econ*	economía
education	*Educ*	educación
electricity	*Elec*	electricidad
entomology	*Ent*	entomología
especially	*esp*	especialmente
only in Spain	*Esp*	solo en España
etcetera	*etc*	etcétera

vii

euphemism	*euf, euph*	eufemismo
exclamatory	*exclam*	exclamativo
feminine	*f*	femenino
familiar	*fam*	familiar
pharmacy	*Farm*	farmacia
railways	*Ferroc*	ferrocarriles
figurative use	*fig*	uso figurado
finance	*Fin*	finanzas
physics	*Fís*	física
	Fishing	pesca
formal use	*fml*	uso formal
photography	*Fot*	fotografía
feminine plural	*fpl*	plural femenino
football	*Ftb*	fútbol
future	*fut*	futuro
British	*GB*	británico
geography	*Geog*	geografía
geology	*Geol*	geología
geometry	*Geom*	geometría
present participle	*ger*	gerundio
gymnastics	*Gimn, Gym*	gimnasia
history	*Hist*	historia
humorous	*hum*	humorístico
imperative	*imperat*	imperativo
imperfect	*imperf*	imperfecto
impersonal	*impers*	impersonal
printing	*Impr*	imprenta
industry	*Ind*	industria
indefinite	*indef*	indefinido
indeterminate	*indet*	indeterminado
indicative	*indic*	indicativo
infinitive	*infin*	infinitivo
computers	*Inform*	informática
insurance	*Ins*	seguros
interjection	*interj*	interjección
interrogative	*interr*	interrogativo
invariable	*inv*	invariable
ironic	*iron*	irónico
irregular	*irreg*	irregular
law	*Jur*	derecho
linguistics	*Ling*	lingüística
literary	*lit*	literario
literature	*Lit*	literatura
phrase	*loc*	locución
masculine	*m*	masculino
mathematics	*Mat, Math*	matemáticas
medicine	*Med*	medicina
meteorology	*Meteor*	meteorología
military	*Mil*	militar
mining	*Min*	minas
masculine plural	*mpl*	plural masculino
music	*Mus, Mús*	música
noun	*n*	nombre
cards	*Naipes*	
swimming	*Natación*	
nautical	*Naut, Náut*	náutica
negative	*neg*	negativo

neuter	*neut*	neutro
feminine noun	*nf*	nombre femenino
plural feminine noun	*nfpl*	nombre femenino plural
masculine noun	*nm*	nombre masculino
masculine and feminine noun	*nmf/nm,f*	nombre masculino y femenino
plural masculine noun	*nmpl*	nombre masculino plural
plural noun	*npl*	nombre plural
obsolete	*obs*	obsoleto
offensive	*ofens, offens*	ofensivo
optics	*Opt*	óptica
ornithology	*Orn*	ornitología
Parliament	*Parl*	parlamento
pejorative	*pej*	peyorativo
personal	*pers*	personal
fishing	*Pesca*	
petroleum industry	*Petrol, Petról*	industria petrolera
pejorative	*pey*	peyorativo
pharmacy	*Pharm*	farmacia
photography	*Phot*	fotografía
physics	*Phys*	física
plural	*pl*	plural
politics	*Pol*	política
possessive	*pos, poss*	posesivo
past participle	*pp*	participio pasado
prefix	*pref*	prefijo
press	*Prensa*	
preposition	*prep*	preposición
present	*pres*	presente
present participle	*pres p*	gerundio
	Press	prensa
preterite	*pret*	pretérito
printing	*Print*	imprenta
pronoun	*pron*	pronombre
psychology	*Psic, Psych*	psicología
past tense	*pt*	pretérito
chemistry	*Quím*	químico
radio	*Rad*	radio
railways	*Rail*	ferrocarriles
relative	*rel*	relativo
religion	*Rel*	religión
somebody, someone	*sb*	alguien
Scottish	*Scot*	escocés
insurance	*Seg*	seguros
sewing	*Sew*	costura
singular	*sing*	singular
slang	*sl*	argot
Spanish	*Span*	español
something	*sth*	algo
subjunctive	*subj*	subjuntivo
suffix	*suf, suff*	sufijo
superlative	*superl*	superlativo
	Swimming	natación
also	*tamb*	también
bullfighting	*Taur*	tauromaquia

theatre	*Teat*	teatro
technical	*Téc, Tech*	técnica
telephones	*Tel*	teléfonos
telecommunications	*Telec*	telecomunicaciones
tennis	*Ten*	tenis
textiles	*Tex*	textiles
theatre	*Theat*	teatro
typography	*Tip*	tipografía
television	*TV*	televisión
typography	*Typ*	tipografía
university	*Univ*	universidad
United States	*US*	Estados Unidos
usually	*usu*	usualmente
verb	*v*	verbo
auxiliary verb	*v aux*	verbo auxiliar
veterinary medicine	*Vet*	veterinaria
intransitive verb	*vi*	verbo intransitivo
impersonal verb	*v impers*	verbo impersonal
reflexive verb	*vr*	verbo reflexivo
transitive verb	*vtr*	verbo transitivo
vulgar	*vulg*	vulgar
zoology	*Zool*	zoología
see	→	véase
cultural equivalent	≈	equivalencia cultural
registered trade mark	®	marca registrada

Spanish - English
Español - Inglés

SPANISH VERBS

Regular Spelling Changes

The rules of spelling in Spanish cause a number of verbs to have regular spelling changes. These are listed below.

Spanish verbs fall into three groups depending on whether their infinitive ends in **-ar**, **-er** or **-ir**. The stem of the verb is the part which is left when the **-ar**, **-er** or **-ir** is removed from the infinitive. For example, the stem of **tomar** is **tom**, the stem of **beber** is **beb**, and the stem of **salir** is **sal**.

In the lists given below, the following indicators are used:

> **(1)** = first person singular present indicative
> **(2)** = present subjunctive, all persons
> **(3)** = first person singular preterite

Verbs ending in -ar

Verbs with a stem ending in **c**, for example **buscar**

The **c** changes to **qu** in:

> **(2)** busque, busques, busque, busquemos, busquéis, busquen
> **(3)** busqué

Verbs with a stem ending in **g**, for example **cargar**

The **g** changes to **gu** in:

> **(2)** cargue, cargues, cargue, carguemos, carguéis, carguen
> **(3)** cargué

Verbs with a stem ending in **gu**, for example **averiguar**

The **gu** changes to **gü** in:

> **(2)** averigüe, averigües, averigüe, averigüemos, averigüéis, averigüen
> **(3)** averigüé

Verbs with a stem ending in **z**, for example **realizar**

The **z** changes to **c** in:

> **(2)** realice, realices, realice, realicemos, realicéis, realicen
> **(3)** realicé

Verbs ending in -er *or* -ir

Verbs with a stem ending in c, for example **esparcir**

The c changes to z in:

> (1) esparzo
> (2) esparza, esparzas, esparza, esparzamos, esparzáis, esparzan

Verbs with a stem ending in g, for example **coger**

The g changes to j in:

> (1) cojo
> (2) coja, cojas, coja, cojamos, cojáis, cojan

Verbs with a stem ending in qu, for example **delinquir**

The qu changes to c in:

> (1) delinco
> (2) delinca, delincas, delinca, delincamos, delincáis, delincan

Verbs with a stem ending in gu, for example **distinguir**

The gu changes to g in:

> (1) distingo
> (2) distinga, distingas, distinga, distingamos, distingáis, distingan

Models for regular conjugation

TOMAR to take

INDICATIVE

PRESENT	**FUTURE**	**CONDITIONAL**
1. tomo	tomaré	tomaría
2. tomas	tomarás	tomarías
3. toma	tomará	tomaría
1. tomamos	tomaremos	tomaríamos
2. tomáis	tomaréis	tomaríais
3. toman	tomarán	tomarían

IMPERFECT	**PRETERITE**	**PERFECT**
1. tomaba	tomé	he tomado
2. tomabas	tomaste	has tomado
3. tomaba	tomó	ha tomado
1. tomábamos	tomamos	hemos tomado
2. tomabais	tomasteis	habéis tomado
3. tomaban	tomaron	han tomado

FUTURE PERFECT	**CONDITIONAL PERFECT**	**PLUPERFECT**
1. habré tomado	habría tomado	había tomado
2. habrás tomado	habrías tomado	habías tomado
3. habrá tomado	habría tomado	había tomado
1. habremos tomado	habríamos tomado	habíamos tomado
2. habréis tomado	habríais tomado	habíais tomado
3. habrán tomado	habrían tomado	habían tomado

SUBJUNCTIVE

PRESENT	**IMPERFECT**	**PERFECT/PLUPERFECT**
1. tome	tom-ara/ase	haya/hubiera* tomado
2. tomes	tom-aras/ases	hayas/hubieras tomado
3. tome	tom-ara/ase	haya/hubiera tomado
1. tomemos	tom-áramos/ásemos	hayamos/hubiéramos tomado
2. toméis	tom-arais/aseis	hayáis/hubierais tomado
3. tomen	tom-aran/asen	hayan/hubieran tomado

IMPERATIVE	*INFINITIVE*	*PARTICIPLE*
(tú) toma	**PRESENT**	**PRESENT**
(Vd) tome	tomar	tomando
(nosotros) tomemos		
(vosotros) tomad	**PERFECT**	**PAST**
(Vds) tomen	haber tomado	tomado

* the alternative form 'hubiese' etc is also possible

xiv

COMER to eat

INDICATIVE

PRESENT	FUTURE	CONDITIONAL
1. como	comeré	comería
2. comes	comerás	comerías
3. come	comerá	comería
1. comemos	comeremos	comeríamos
2. coméis	comeréis	comeríais
3. comen	comerán	comerían

IMPERFECT	PRETERITE	PERFECT
1. comía	comí	he comido
2. comías	comiste	has comido
3. comía	comió	ha comido
1. comíamos	comimos	hemos comido
2. comíais	comisteis	habéis comido
3. comían	comieron	han comido

FUTURE PERFECT	CONDITIONAL PERFECT	PLUPERFECT
1. habré comido	habría comido	había comido
2. habrás comido	habrías comido	habías comido
3. habrá comido	habría comido	había comido
1. habremos comido	habríamos comido	habíamos comido
2. habréis comido	habríais comido	habíais comido
3. habrán comido	habrían comido	habían comido

SUBJUNCTIVE

PRESENT	IMPERFECT	PERFECT/PLUPERFECT
1. coma	com-iera/iese	haya/hubiera* comido
2. comas	com-ieras/ieses	hayas/hubieras comido
3. coma	com-iera/iese	haya/hubiera comido
1. comamos	com-iéramos/iésemos	hayamos/hubiéramos comido
2. comáis	com-ierais/ieseis	hayáis/hubierais comido
3. coman	com-ieran/iesen	hayan/hubieran comido

IMPERATIVE	*INFINITIVE*	*PARTICIPLE*
(tú) come	**PRESENT**	**PRESENT**
(Vd) coma	comer	comiendo
(nosotros) comamos		
(vosotros) comed	**PERFECT**	**PAST**
(Vds) coman	haber comido	comido

* the alternative form 'hubiese' etc is also possible

PARTIR to leave

INDICATIVE

PRESENT	**FUTURE**	**CONDITIONAL**
1. parto	partiré	partiría
2. partes	partirás	partirías
3. parte	partirá	partiría
1. partimos	partiremos	partiríamos
2. partís	partiréis	partiríais
3. parten	partirán	partirían

IMPERFECT	**PRETERITE**	**PERFECT**
1. partía	partí	he partido
2. partías	partiste	has partido
3. partía	partió	ha partido
1. partíamos	partimos	hemos partido
2. partíais	partisteis	habéis partido
3. partían	partieron	han partido

FUTURE PERFECT	**CONDITIONAL PERFECT**	**PLUPERFECT**
1. habré partido	habría partido	había partido
2. habrás partido	habrías partido	habías partido
3. habrá partido	habría partido	había partido
1. habremos partido	habríamos partido	habíamos partido
2. habréis partido	habríais partido	habíais partido
3. habrán partido	habrían partido	habían partido

SUBJUNCTIVE

PRESENT	**IMPERFECT**	**PERFECT/PLUPERFECT**
parta	parti-era/ese	haya/hubiera* partido
partas	parti-eras/eses	hayas/hubieras partido
parta	parti-era/ese	haya/hubiera partido
partamos	parti-éramos/ésemos	hayamos/hubiéramos partido
partáis	parti-erais/eseis	hayáis/hubierais partido
partan	parti-eran/esen	hayan/hubieran partido

IMPERATIVE	*INFINITIVE*	*PARTICIPLE*
(tú) parte	**PRESENT**	**PRESENT**
(Vd) parta	partir	partiendo
(nosotros) partamos		
(vosotros) partid	**PERFECT**	**PAST**
(Vds) partan	haber partido	partido

* the alternative form 'hubiese' etc is also possible

xvi

Models for irregular conjugation

[1] **pensar** *PRES* pienso, piensas, piensa, pensamos, pensáis, piensan; *PRES SUBJ* piense, pienses, piense, pensemos, penséis, piensen; *IMPERAT* piensa, piense, pensemos, pensad, piensen

[2] **contar** *PRES* cuento, cuentas, cuenta, contamos, contáis, cuentan; *PRES SUBJ* cuente, cuentes, cuente, contemos, contéis, cuenten; *IMPERAT* cuenta, cuente, contemos, contad, cuenten

[3] **perder** *PRES* pierdo, pierdes, pierde, perdemos, perdéis, pierden; *PRES SUBJ* pierda, pierdas, pierda, perdamos, perdáis, pierdan; *IMPERAT* pierde, pierda, perdamos, perded, pierdan

[4] **morder** *PRES* muerdo, muerdes, muerde, mordemos, mordéis, muerden; *PRES SUBJ* muerda, muerdas, muerda, mordamos, mordáis, muerdan; *IMPERAT* muerde, muerda, mordamos, morded, muerdan

[5] **sentir** *PRES* siento, sientes, siente, sentimos, sentís, sienten; *PRES SUBJ* sienta, sientas, sienta, sintamos, sintáis, sientan; *PRES P* sintiendo; *IMPERAT* siente, sienta, sintamos, sentid, sientan

[6] **vestir** *PRES* visto, vistes, viste, vestimos, vestís, visten; *PRES SUBJ* vista, vistas, vista, vistamos, vistáis, vistan; *PRES P* vistiendo; *IMPERAT* viste, vista, vistamos, vestid, vistan

[7] **dormir** *PRES* duermo, duermes, duerme, dormimos, dormís, duermen; *PRES SUBJ* duerma, duermas, duerma, durmamos, durmáis, duerman; *PRES P* durmiendo; *IMPERAT* duerme, duerma, durmamos, dormid, duerman

[8] **andar** *PRET* anduve, anduviste, anduvo, anduvimos, anduvisteis, anduvieron; *IMPERF SUBJ* anduviera/anduviese

[9] **caber** *PRES* quepo, cabes, cabe, cabemos, cabéis, caben; *PRES SUBJ* quepa, quepas, quepa, quepamos, quepáis, quepan; *FUT* cabré; *COND* cabría; *PRET* cupe, cupiste, cupo, cupimos, cupisteis, cupieron; *IMPERF SUBJ* cupiera/cupiese; *IMPERAT* cabe, quepa, quepamos, cabed, quepan

[10] **conducir** *PRES* conduzco, conduces, conduce, conducimos, conducís, conducen; *PRES SUBJ* conduzca, conduzcas, conduzca, conduzcamos, conduzcáis, conduzcan; *PRET* conduje, condujiste, condujo, condujimos, condujisteis, condujeron; *IMPERF SUBJ* condujera/condujese; *IMPERAT* conduce, conduzca, conduzcamos, conducid, conduzcan

[11] **dar** *PRES* doy, das, da, damos, dais, dan; *PRES SUBJ* dé, des, dé, demos, deis, den; *PRET* di, diste, dio, dimos, disteis, dieron; *IMPERF SUBJ* diera/diese; *IMPERAT* da, dé, demos, dad, den

[12] **decir** *PRES* digo, dices, dice, decimos, decís, dicen; *PRES SUBJ* diga, digas, diga, digamos, digáis, digan; *FUT* diré; *COND* diría; *PRET* dije, dijiste, dijo, dijimos, dijisteis, dijeron; *IMPERF SUBJ* dijera/dijese; *PRES P* diciendo; *PP* dicho; *IMPERAT* di, diga, digamos, decid, digan

[13] ESTAR to be

INDICATIVE

PRESENT	FUTURE	CONDITIONAL
1. estoy	estaré	estaría
2. estás	estarás	estarías
3. está	estará	estaría
1. estamos	estaremos	estaríamos
2. estáis	estaréis	estaríais
3. están	estarán	estarían

IMPERFECT	PRETERITE	PERFECT
1. estaba	estuve	he estado
2. estabas	estuviste	has estado
3. estaba	estuvo	ha estado
1. estábamos	estuvimos	hemos estado
2. estabais	estuvisteis	habéis estado
3. estaban	estuvieron	han estado

FUTURE PERFECT	CONDITIONAL PERFECT	PLUPERFECT
1. habré estado	habría estado	había estado
2. habrás estado	habrías estado	habías estado
3. habrá estado	habría estado	había estado
1. habremos estado	habríamos estado	habíamos estado
2. habréis estado	habríais estado	habíais estado
3. habrán estado	habrían estado	habían estado

SUBJUNCTIVE

PRESENT	IMPERFECT	PERFECT/PLUPERFECT
1. esté	estuv-iera/iese	haya/hubiera* estado
2. estés	estuv-ieras/ieses	hayas/hubieras estado
3. esté	estuv-iera/iese	haya/hubiera estado
1. estemos	estuv-iéramos/iésemos	hayamos/hubiéramos estado
2. estéis	estuv-ierais/ieseis	hayáis/hubierais estado
3. estén	estuv-ieran/iesen	hayan/hubieran estado

IMPERATIVE	INFINITIVE	PARTICIPLE
(tú) está	**PRESENT**	**PRESENT**
(Vd) esté	estar	estando
(nosotros) estemos		
(vosotros) estad	**PERFECT**	**PAST**
(Vds) estén	haber estado	estado

* the alternative form 'hubiese' etc is also possible

xviii

[14] HABER to have *(auxiliary)*

INDICATIVE

PRESENT	FUTURE	CONDITIONAL
1. he	habré	habría
2. has	habrás	habrías
3. ha/hay*	habrá	habría
1. hemos	habremos	habríamos
2. habéis	habréis	habríais
3. han	habrán	habrían

IMPERFECT	PRETERITE	PERFECT
1. había	hube	
2. habías	hubiste	
3. había	hubo	ha habido*
1. habíamos	hubimos	
2. habíais	hubisteis	
3. habían	hubieron	

FUTURE PERFECT	CONDITIONAL PERFECT	PLUPERFECT
1.		
2.		
3. habrá habido*	habría habido*	había habido*
1.		
2.		
3.		

SUBJUNCTIVE

PRESENT	IMPERFECT	PERFECT/PLUPERFECT
1. haya	hub-iera/iese	
2. hayas	hub-ieras/ieses	
3. haya	hub-iera/iese	haya/hubiera** habido*
1. hayamos	hub-iéramos/iésemos	
2. hayáis	hub-ierais/ieseis	
3. hayan	hub-ieran/iesen	

INFINITIVE	PARTICIPLE
PRESENT	**PRESENT**
haber	habiendo
PERFECT	**PAST**
haber habido*	habido

* 'haber' is an auxiliary verb used with the participle of another verb to form compound tenses (eg he bebido - I have drunk). 'hay' means 'there is/are' and all third person singular forms in their respective tenses have this meaning. The forms highlighted with an asterisk are used only for this latter construction.

** the alternative form 'hubiese' is also possible

[15] **hacer** *PRES* hago, haces, hace, hacemos, hacéis, hacen; *PRES SUBJ* haga, hagas, haga, hagamos, hagáis, hagan; *FUT* haré; *COND* haría; *PRET* hice, hiciste, hizo, hicimos, hicisteis, hicieron; *IMPERF SUBJ* hiciera/hiciese; *PP* hecho; *IMPERAT* haz, haga, hagamos, haced, hagan

[16] **ir** *PRES* voy, vas, va, vamos, vais, van; *PRES SUBJ* vaya, vayas, vaya, vayamos, vayáis, vayan; *IMPERF* iba, ibas, iba, íbamos, ibais, iban; *PRET* fui, fuiste, fue, fuimos, fuisteis, fueron; *IMPERF SUBJ* fuera/fuese; *PRES P* yendo; *IMPERAT* ve, vaya, vamos, id, vayan

[17] **oír** *PRES* oigo, oyes, oye, oímos, oís, oyen; *PRES SUBJ* oiga, oigas, oiga, oigamos, oigáis, oigan; *PRET* oí, oíste, oyó, oímos, oísteis, oyeron; *IMPERF SUBJ* oyera/oyese; *PRES P* oyendo; *PP* oído; *IMPERAT* oye, oiga, oigamos, oíd, oigan

[18] **poder** *PRES* puedo, puedes, puede, podemos, podéis, pueden; *PRES SUBJ* pueda, puedas, pueda, podamos, podáis, puedan; *FUT* podré; *COND* podría; *PRET* pude, pudiste, pudo, pudimos, pudisteis, pudieron; *IMPERF SUBJ* pudiera/pudiese; *PRES P* pudiendo; *IMPERAT* puede, pueda, podamos, poded, puedan

[19] **poner** *PRES* pongo, pones, pone, ponemos, ponéis, ponen; *PRES SUBJ* ponga, pongas, ponga, pongamos, pongáis, pongan; *FUT* pondré; *COND* pondría; *PRET* puse, pusiste, puso, pusimos, pusisteis, pusieron; *IMPERF SUBJ* pusiera/pusiese; *PP* puesto; *IMPERAT* pon, ponga, pongamos, poned, pongan

[20] **querer** *PRES* quiero, quieres, quiere, queremos, queréis, quieren; *PRES SUBJ* quiera, quieras, quiera, queramos, queráis, quieran; *FUT* querré; *COND* querría; *PRET* quise, quisiste, quiso, quisimos, quisisteis, quisieron; *IMPERF SUBJ* quisiera/quisiese; *IMPERAT* quiere, quiera, queramos, quered, quieran

[21] **saber** *PRES* sé, sabes, sabe, sabemos, sabéis, saben; *PRES SUBJ* sepa, sepas, sepa, sepamos, sepáis, sepan; *FUT* sabré; *COND* sabría; *PRET* supe, supiste, supo, supimos, supisteis, supieron; *IMPERF SUBJ* supiera/supiese; *IMPERAT* sabe, sepa, sepamos, sabed, sepan

[22] **salir** *PRES* salgo, sales, sale, salimos, salís, salen; *PRES SUBJ* salga, salgas, salga, salgamos, salgáis, salgan; *FUT* saldré; *COND* saldría; *IMPERAT* sal, salga, salgamos, salid, salgan

[23] **ser** *PRES* soy, eres, es, somos, sois, son; *PRES SUBJ* sea, seas, sea, seamos, seáis, sean; *IMPERF* era, eras, era, éramos, erais, eran; *PRET* fui, fuiste, fue, fuimos, fuisteis, fueron; *IMPERF SUBJ* fuera/fuese; *IMPERAT* sé, sea, seamos, sed, sean

[24] **tener** *PRES* tengo, tienes, tiene, tenemos, tenéis, tienen; *PRES SUBJ* tenga, tengas, tenga, tengamos, tengáis, tengan; *FUT* tendré; *COND* tendría; *PRET* tuve, tuviste, tuvo, tuvimos, tuvisteis, tuvieron; *IMPERF SUBJ* tuviera/tuviese; *IMPERAT* ten, tenga, tengamos, tened, tengan

[25] **traer** *PRES* traigo, traes, trae, traemos, traéis, traen; *PRES SUBJ* traiga, traigas, traiga, traigamos, traigáis, traigan; *PRET* traje, trajiste, trajo, trajimos, trajisteis, trajeron; *IMPERF SUBJ* trajera/trajese; *IMPERAT* trae, traiga, traigamos, traed, traigan

[26] **valer** *PRES* valgo, vales, vale, valemos, valéis, valen; *PRES SUBJ* valga, valgas, valga, valgamos, valgáis, valgan; *FUT* valdré; *COND* valdría; *IMPERAT* vale, valga, valgamos, valed, valgan

[27] **venir** *PRES* vengo, vienes, viene, venimos, venís, vienen; *PRES SUBJ* venga, vengas, venga, vengamos, vengáis, vengan; *FUT* vendré; *COND* vendría; *PRET* vine, viniste, vino, vinimos, vinisteis, vinieron; *IMPERF SUBJ* viniera/viniese; *PRES P* viniendo; *IMPERAT* ven, venga, vengamos, venid, vengan

[28] **ver** *PRES* veo, ves, ve, vemos, veis, ven; *PRES SUBJ* vea, veas, vea, veamos, veáis, vean; *IMPERF* veía, veías, veía, veíamos, veíais, veían; *PRET* vi, viste, vio, vimos, visteis, vieron; *IMPERF SUBJ* viera/viese; *IMPERAT* ve, vea, veamos, ved, vean

[29] **desviar** *PRES* desvío, desvías, desvía, desviamos, desviáis, desvían; *PRES SUBJ* desvíe, desvíes, desvíe, desviemos, desviéis, desvíen; *IMPERAT* desvía, desvíe, desviemos, desviéis, desvíen

[30] **continuar** *PRES* continúo, continúas, continúa, continuamos, continuáis, continúan; *PRES SUBJ* continúe, continúes, continúe, continuemos, continuéis, continúen; *IMPERAT* continúa, continúe, continuemos, continuad, continúen

[31] **adquirir** *PRES* adquiero, adquieres, adquiere, adquirimos, adquirís, adquieren; *PRES SUBJ* adquiera, adquieras, adquiera, adquiramos, adquiráis, adquieran; *IMPERAT* adquiere, adquiera, adquiramos, adquirid, adquieran

[32] **jugar** *PRES* juego, juegas, juega, jugamos, jugáis, juegan; *PRES SUBJ* juegue, juegues, juegue, juguemos, juguéis, jueguen; *IMPERAT* juega, juegue, juguemos, jugad, jueguen

[33] **agradecer** *PRES* agradezco, agradeces, agradece, agradecemos, agradecéis, agradecen; *PRES SUBJ* agradezca, agradezcas, agradezca, agradezcamos, agradezcáis, agradezcan; *IMPERAT* agradece, agradezca, agradezcamos, agradeced, agradezcan

[34] **conocer** *PRES* conozco, conoces, conoce, conocemos, conocéis, conocen; *PRES SUBJ* conozca, conozcas, conozca, conozcamos, conozcáis, conozcan; *IMPERAT* conoce, conozca, conozcamos, conoced, conozcan

[35] **lucir** *PRES* luzco, luces, luce, lucimos, lucís, lucen; *PRES SUBJ* luzca, luzcas, luzca, luzcamos, luzcáis, luzcan; *IMPERAT* luce, luzca, luzcamos, lucid, luzcan

[36] **leer** *PRET* leí, leíste, leyó, leímos, leísteis, leyeron; *IMPERF SUBJ* leyera/leycse; *PRES P* leyendo; *PP* leído; *IMPERAT* lee, lea, leamos, leed, lean

[37] **huir** *PRES* huyo, huyes, huye, huimos, huís, huyen; *PRES SUBJ* huya, huyas, huya, huyamos, huyáis, huyan; *PRET* huí, huiste, huyó, huimos, huisteis, huyeron; *IMPERF SUBJ* huyera/huyese; *PRES P* huyendo; *PP* huido; *IMPERAT* huye, huya, huyamos, huid, huyan

[38] **roer** *PRES* roo/roigo/royo, roes, roe, roemos, roéis, roen; *PRES SUBJ* roa/roiga/roya, roas, roa, roamos, roáis, roan; *PRET* roí, roíste, royó, roímos, roísteis, royeron; *IMPERF SUBJ* royera/royese; *PRES P* royendo; *PP* roído; *IMPERAT* roe, roa, roamos, roed, roan

[39] **caer** *PRES* caigo, caes, cae, caemos, caéis, caen; *PRES SUBJ* caiga, caigas, caiga, caigamos, caigáis, caigan; *PRES P* cayendo; *PP* caído; *IMPERAT* cae, caiga, caigamos, caed, caigan

Guide to the Pronunciation of Spanish

The following table is based on IPA (the International Phonetic Alphabet) with certain modifications and attempts to give an approximate idea of the Spanish sound system as compared with the British English one.

Letter	Phonetic symbol	Examples	Approximate British English equivalent
Vowels:			
a	[a]	gato, amar, mesa	as in father, but shorter
e	[e]	estrella, vez, firme	as in labour
i	[i]	inicuo, iris	as in see, but shorter
o	[o]	bolo, cómodo, oso	between lot and taught
u	[u]	turuta, puro, tribu	as in food, but shorter, but u in -que- or -qui- and -gue- or -gui- is silent (unless -güe- or -güe-)
y	[i]	y	as in see, but shorter
Diphthongs:			
ai, ay	[ai]	baile, hay	as in life, aisle
au	[au]	fauna	as in fowl, house
ei, ey	[ei]	peine, ley	as in hate, feign
eu	[eu]	feudo	pronounce each vowel separately
oi, oy	[oi]	boina, hoy	as in boy
Semi-consonants:			
u	[w]	buey, cuando, fuiste	as in wait
i	[j]	viernes, vicio, ciudad, ciar	as in yes
y	[j]	yermo, ayer, rey	as in yes
Consonants:			
b	[b]	boda, burro, ambos	as in be
	[β]	haba, traba	a very light b
c	[k]	cabeza, cuco, acoso, frac	as in car, keep
	[θ]	cecina, cielo	as in thing, but in Andalusia and all of Latin America as s in silly
ch	[tʃ]	chepa, ocho	as in chamber
d	[d]	dedo, andar	as in day
	[ð]	dedo, ánade, abad	as in this (often omitted in spoken Spanish when at the end of a word)
f	[f]	fiesta, afición	as in for
g	[g]	gas, rango, gula	as in get
	[γ]	agua, agosto, lagar	a very light g
	[x]	genio, legión	similar to Scottish [x] in loch
h	-	hambre, ahíto	Spanish h is silent
j	[x]	jabón, ajo, carcaj	similar to Scottish [x] in loch
k	[k]	kilo, kimono	as in car, keep
l	[l]	labio, hábil, elegante	as in law
ll	[ʎ]	lluvia, calle	similar to the sound in million
m	[m]	mano, amigo, hambre	as in man
n	[n]	nata, ratón, antes, enemigo	as in night

ñ	[ɲ]	año, ñoño	similar to the sound in o*ni*on
p	[p]	pipa, pelo	as in *p*oint
q	[k]	quiosco, querer, alambique	as in *c*ar
r(r)	[r]	pero, correr, padre	always pronounced, rolled as in Scots
	[rr]	reír, honrado, perro	**rr** is a lengthened **r** sound
s	[s]	sauna, asado, cortés	similar to the **s** in hi*ss*ing
t	[t]	teja, estén, atraco	as in *t*ime
v	[b]	verbena, vena	as in *b*e
	[β]	ave, vivo	a very light **b**
w	[b]	wagón, waterpolo	as in *b*e
x	[ks]	éxito, examen	as in e*x*ercise
	[s]	extensión	as in e*s*tate
z	[θ]	zorro, azul, caza, soez	as in *th*ing, but in Andalusia and in all of Latin America as **s** in *s*illy

Stress rules

If a word ends in a vowel, **-n** or **-s**, the stress should fall on the second last syllable, for example:

mano, examen, bocadillos

If a word has any other ending, the stress falls on the last syllable, for example:

hablar, Madrid, ayer

Exceptions to these rules carry a written accent on the stressed syllable, for example:

cómodo, legión, hábil

A

A, a |a| *nf* (*la letra*) A, a.

a *abr de* área.

a *prep* → **al. 1** (*dirección*) to; **ir a Colombia**, to go to Colombia; **llegar a Valencia**, to arrive in Valencia; **subir al tren**, to get on the train; **ir al cine**, to go to the cinema; **vete a casa**, go home. **2** (*lugar*) at, on; **a la derecha**, on the right; **a la entrada**, at the entrance; **a lo lejos**, in the distance; **a mi lado**, at *o* by my side, next to me; **al sol**, in the sun; **a la mesa**, at (the) table. **3** (*tiempo*) at; **a las doce**, at twelve o'clock; **a los sesenta años**, at the age of sixty; **a los tres meses/la media hora**, three months/half an hour later; **al final**, in the end; **al principio**, at first. **4** (*distancia*) away; **a cien kilómetros de aquí**, a hundred kilometres from here. **5** (*manera*) **a la inglesa**, (in) English fashion *o* manner *o* style; **escrito a máquina**, typed, typewritten; **a mano**, by hand. **6** (*proporción*) **a 90 kilómetros por hora**, at 90 kilometres an hour; **a 300 pesetas el kilo**, three hundred pesetas a kilo; **tres veces a la semana**, three times a week. **7** *Dep* **ganar cuatro a dos**, to win four (to) two. **8** (*complemento indirecto*) to; (*procedencia*) from; **díselo a Javier**, tell Javier; **te lo di a ti**, I gave it to you; **comprarle algo a algn**, to buy sth from sb; (*para algn*) to buy sth for sb; (*complemento directo de persona*) **saludé a tu tía**, I said hello to your aunt. **9** *fam* **ir a por algn/algo**, to go and fetch sb/sth. **10** (*verbo* + **a** + *infin*) to; **aprender a nadar**, to learn (how) to swim; **fueron a ayudarle**, they went to help him. **11** (*nombre* + **a** + *infin*) **distancia a recorrer**, distance to be covered. **12 a decir verdad**, to tell (you) the truth; **a no ser por ...**, if it were not for ...; **a no ser que**, unless; **a ver**, let's see; **¡a comer!**, lunch/dinner *etc* is ready!; **¡a dormir!**, bedtime!; **¿a que no lo haces?**, (*desafío*) I bet you don't do it!

abad *nm* abbot.

abadía *nf* abbey.

abajeño,-a *nm,f Am* lowlander, coastal dweller.

abajo I *adv* **1** (*en una casa*) downstairs; **el piso de a.**, the flat downstairs. **2** (*dirección*) down, downwards; **ahí/aquí a.**, down there/here; **la parte de a.**, the bottom (part); **más a.**, further down; **hacia a.**, down, downwards; **calle a.**, down the street; **echar algo a.**, to knock sth down; **venirse a.**, (*edificio*) to fall down; *fig* (*proyecto*) to fall through. **II** *interj* **¡a. la censura!**, down with censorship!

abalanzarse |4| *vr* **a. sobre/contra**, to

rush towards.

abalear *vtr Am* to shoot *o* fire at.

abalorio *nm* **1** (*cuenta*) glass bead. **2** (*baratija*) trinket.

abanderado,-a *nm,f* standard bearer.

abandonado,-a *adj* **1** abandoned; **tiene a su familia muy abandonada**, he takes absolutely no interest in his family. **2** (*desaseado*) untidy, unkempt.

abandonar I *vtr* **1** (*lugar*) to leave, quit; (*persona, cosa*) to abandon; (*proyecto, plan*) to give up. **2** *Dep* (*carrera*) to drop out of. **II abandonarse** *vr* to let oneself go.

abandono *nm* **1** (*acción*) abandoning, desertion. **2** (*de proyecto, idea*) giving up. **3** (*descuido*) neglect.

abanicarse *vr* to fan oneself.

abanico *nm* **1** fan. **2** (*gama*) range; **un amplio a. de posibilidades**, a wide range of possibilities.

abaratar I *vtr* to cut *o* reduce the price of. **II abaratarse** *vr* (*artículos*) to become cheaper, come down in price; (*precios*) to come down.

abarcar |1| *vtr* **1** to embrace. **2** *Am* (*acaparar*) to monopolize.

abarrotado,-a *adj* packed (**de**, with), crammed (**de**, with).

abarrotar *vtr* to pack, cram (**de**, with); **el público abarrotaba la sala**, the room was packed (with people).

abarrotes *nmpl Am* groceries.

abastecedor,-a *nm,f* supplier.

abastecer |33| **I** *vtr* to supply. **II abastecerse** *vr* **a. de**, to be supplied with.

abastecimiento *nm* supplying; **a. de agua**, water supply.

abasto *nm* **1** *fam* **no doy a.**, I can't cope, I can't keep up. **2 mercado de abastos**, wholesale food market.

abatible *adj* folding, collapsible; **asiento a.**, reclining seat.

abatido,-a *adj* downcast.

abatir I *vtr* **1** (*derribar*) to knock down, pull down. **2** (*matar*) to kill; **a. a tiros**, to shoot down. **3** (*desanimar*) to depress, dishearten. **II abatirse** *vr* (*desanimarse*) to lose heart, become depressed.

abdicación *nf* abdication.

abdicar |1| *vtr & vi* to abdicate.

abdomen *nm* abdomen.

abdominales *nmpl* sit-ups.

abecedario *nm* alphabet.

abedul *nm* birch.

abeja *nf* bee; **a. reina**, queen bee.

abejorro *nm* bumblebee.

aberración *nf* aberration.

aberrante *adj* deviant.

abertura *nf* (*hueco*) opening, gap; (*grieta*)

crack, slit.

abertzale *adj & nm,f* Basque nationalist.

abeto *nm Bot* fir (tree); **a. rojo**, spruce.

abierto,-a *adj* 1 open; *(grifo)* (turned) on; **a. de par en par**, wide open. 2 *(persona)* open- minded.

abigarrado,-a *adj (mezclado)* jumbled, mixed up.

abismal *adj* abysmal; *fig* **una diferencia a.**, a world of a difference.

abismo *nm* abyss; *fig* **al borde del a.**, on the brink of ruin; *fig* **entre ellos media un a.**, they are worlds apart.

ablandar I *vtr* to soften. II **ablandarse** *vr* 1 to soften, go soft *o* softer. 2 *fig (persona)* to mellow.

abnegación *nf* abnegation, self-denial.

abnegado,-a *adj* selfless, self-sacrificing.

abocado,-a *adj* 1 **está a. al fracaso**, it is doomed to failure. 2 *(vino)* medium dry.

abochornar *vtr* to shame, embarrass.

abofetear *vtr* to slap.

abogacía *nf* legal profession.

abogado,-a *nm,f* lawyer, solicitor; *(en tribunal supremo)* barrister; **a. de oficio**, legal aid lawyer; **a. defensor**, counsel for the defense; **a. del diablo**, devil's advocate; **a. laboralista**, union lawyer.

abogar |7| *vtr* to plead; **a. a favor de**, to plead for, defend; **a. por algo**, to advocate *o* champion sth.

abolengo *nm* ancestry, lineage.

abolición *nf* abolition.

abolir *vtr defect* to abolish.

abolladura *nf* dent.

abollar *vtr* to dent.

abominable *adj* abominable.

abominar *vi* **a. (de)**, to abominate, loathe.

abonado,-a I *nm,f* subscriber. II *adj Fin (pagado)* paid; **a. en cuenta**, credited.

abonar I *vtr* 1 *Agr* to fertilize. 2 *(pagar)* to pay (for). 3 *(subscribir)* to subscribe. II **abonarse** *vr* to subscribe (**a**, to).

abono *nm* 1 *Agr (producto)* fertilizer; *(estiércol)* manure. 2 *(pago)* payment. 3 *(a revista etc)* subscription; *(billete)* season ticket.

abordar *vtr (persona)* to approach; *(barco)* to board; **a. un asunto**, to tackle a subject.

aborigen *(pl aborígenes)* I *adj* native, indigenous; *esp Austral* aboriginal. II *nmf* native; *esp Austral* aborigine.

aborrecer |33| *vtr* to detest, loathe.

abortar I *vi (involuntariamente)* to miscarry, have a miscarriage; *(intencionadamente)* to abort, have an abortion. II *vtr* to abort.

abortista *nmf* abortionist.

aborto *nm* miscarriage; *(provocado)* abortion.

abotargado,-a *adj* swollen.

abotonar *vtr (ropa)* to button (up).

abovedado,-a *adj* vaulted, arched.

abracadabra *nm* abracadabra.

abrasador,-a *adj* scorching.

abrasar I *vtr & vi* to scorch. II **abrasarse** *vr* to burn.

abrazadera *nf* clamp.

abrazar |4| I *vtr* to embrace, hug; *fig (doctrina)* to embrace. II **abrazarse** *vr* **a. a algn**, to embrace sb; **se abrazaron**, they embraced each other.

abrazo *nm* embrace, hug; **un a., abrazos**, *(en carta)* best wishes.

abrecartas *nm inv* letter-opener, paper-knife.

abrefácil *nm Com* **caja con a.**, easy-open carton.

abrelatas *nm inv* tin-opener, *US* can opener.

abreviar |12| 1 *vtr* to shorten; *(texto)* to abridge; *(palabra)* to abbreviate. II *vi* to be quick *o* brief; **para a.**, to cut a long story short.

abreviatura *nf* abbreviation.

abridor *nm (de latas, botellas)* opener.

abrigado,-a *adj* wrapped up; **ir muy a.**, to be well wrapped-up.

abrigar |7| *vtr* 1 to keep warm; **esta chaqueta abriga mucho**, this cardigan is very warm. 2 *(proteger)* to protect, shelter. 3 *(esperanza)* to cherish; *(duda)* to have, harbour, *US* harbor.

abrigo *nm* 1 *(prenda)* coat, overcoat; **ropa de a.**, warm clothes *pl*. 2 **al a. de**, protected *o* sheltered from.

abril *nm* April.

abrillantador *nm* polish.

abrillantar *vtr* to polish.

abrir¹ *nm* **en un a. y cerrar de ojos**, in the twinkling of an eye.

abrir² *(pp abierto)* I *vi* to open. II *vtr* 1 to open; *(cremallera)* to undo. 2 *(gas, grifo)* to turn on. 3 *Jur* **a. (un) expediente**, to start proceedings. III **abrirse** *vr* 1 to open; *fig* **a. paso**, to make one's way. 2 *arg* **¡me abro!**, I'm off!

abrochar *vtr*, **abrocharse** *vr (botones)* to do up; *(camisa)* to button (up); *(cinturón)* to fasten; *(zapatos)* to tie up; *(cremallera)* to do up.

abrumado,-a *adj* overwhelmed.

abrumador,-a *adj* overwhelming.

abrumar *vtr* to overwhelm, crush; **tantos problemas me abruman**, all these problems are getting on top of me.

abrupto,-a *adj* 1 *(terreno)* steep, abrupt. 2 *fig* abrupt, sudden.

absceso *nm* abscess.

absentismo *nm* absenteeism; **a. laboral**, absenteeism from work.

absolución *nf* 1 *Rel* absolution. 2 *Jur* acquittal.

absoluto,-a *adj* absolute; **en a.**, not at all, by no means. ◆**absolutamente** *adv* absolutely, completely; **a. nada**, nothing at all.

absolutorio,-a *adj Jur* sentencia absolutoria, verdict of not guilty.

absolver |4| (*pp* **absuelto**) *vtr* 1 *Rel* to absolve. 2 *Jur* to acquit.

absorbente *adj* 1 (*papel*) absorbent. 2 *fig* absorbing, engrossing.

absorber *vtr* to absorb.

absorción *nf* absorption.

absorto,-a *adj* absorbed, engrossed (**en**, in).

abstemio,-a I *adj* teetotal, abstemious. II *nm,f* teetotaller.

abstención *nf* abstention.

abstenerse |24| *vr* to abstain (**de**, from); (*privarse*) to refrain (**de**, from).

abstinencia *nf* abstinence; **síndrome de a.**, withdrawal symptoms *pl*.

abstracción *nf* abstraction.

abstracto,-a *adj* abstract.

abstraer |25| I *vtr* to abstract. II **abstraerse** *vr* to become lost in thought.

abstraído,-a *adj* (*ensimismado*) absorbed, engrossed (**en**, in); (*distraído*) absentminded.

absuelto,-a *pp* → **absolver**.

absurdo,-a I *adj* absurd. II *nm* absurdity, absurd thing.

abuchear *vt* to boo, jeer at.

abucheo *nm* booing, jeering.

abuela *nf* grandmother; *fam* grandma, granny; *fig* old woman.

abuelo *nm* 1 grandfather; *fam* grandad, grandpa; *fig* old man. 2 **abuelos**, grandparents.

abulense I *adj* of *o* from Avila. II *nmf* native *o* inhabitant of Avila.

abulia *nf* apathy, lack of willpower.

abultado,-a *adj* bulky, big.

abultar I *vi* to be bulky; **abulta mucho**, it takes up a lot of space. II *vtr* to exaggerate.

abundancia *nf* abundance, plenty; *fig* **nadar en la a.**, to be rolling in money.

abundante *adj* abundant, plentiful.

abundar *vi* to abound, be plentiful.

abur *interj fam* cheerio!, see you!

aburrido,-a *adj* 1 **ser a.**, to be boring. 2 **estar a.**, to be bored; (*harto*) to be tired (**de**, of).

aburrimiento *nm* boredom; ¡qué **a.!**, how boring!, what a bore!

aburrir I *vtr* to bore. II **aburrirse** *vr* to get bored; **a. como una ostra**, to be bored stiff.

abusar *vi* 1 (*propasarse*) to go too far. 2 **a. de**, (*situación, persona*) to take (unfair) advantage of; (*poder, amabilidad*) to abuse; **a. de la bebida/del tabaco**, to drink/smoke too much *o* to excess; *Jur* **a. de un niño/una mujer**, to abuse a child/woman.

abusivo,-a *adj* (*precio*) exorbitant.

abuso *nm* abuse.

abyecto,-a *adj* abject.

a. C. *abr de* **antes de Cristo**, before Christ, BC.

a/c *Com abr de* **a cuenta**, on account.

acá *adv* 1 (*lugar*) here, over here; **más a.**, nearer; ¡**ven a.!**, come here! 2 **de entonces a.**, since then.

acabado,-a I *adj* 1 (*terminado*) finished. 2 *fig* (*persona*) worn-out, spent. II *nm* finish.

acabar I *vtr* to finish (off); (*completar*) to complete. II *vi* 1 to finish, end; **a. bien**, to have a happy ending; **a. con algo**, (*terminarlo*) to finish sth; (*romperlo*) to break sth. 2 **a. de ...**, to have just ...; **acaba de entrar**, he has just come in; **no acaba de convencerme**, I'm not quite convinced. 3 **acabaron casándose** *o* **por casarse**, they ended up getting married; **acabó en la cárcel**, he ended up in jail. III **acabarse** *vr* to finish, come to an end; **se nos acabó la gasolina**, we ran out of petrol; *fam* ¡**se acabó!**, that's that!

acabóse *nm fam* **esto es el a.**, this is the end.

acacia *nf* acacia.

academia *nf* academy.

académico,-a *adj & nm,f* academic.

acaecer |33| *v impers* to happen, occur.

acallar *vtr* to silence.

acalorado,-a *adj* 1 hot. 2 *fig* (*excitado*) worked up, excited; (*debate etc*) heated, angry.

acalorarse 1 to get warm *o* hot. 2 *fig* to get excited *o* worked up.

acampada *nf* camping; **ir de a.**, to go camping; **zona de a.**, camp site.

acampanado,-a *adj* bell-shaped; (*prendas*) flared.

acampar *vi* to camp.

acantilado *nm* cliff.

acantonar *vtr* (*tropas*) to billet, quarter (**en**, in).

acaparar *vtr* 1 (*productos*) to hoard; (*el mercado*) to corner. 2 *fig* to monopolize.

acaramelado,-a *adj* 1 (*color*) caramel-coloured, *US* caramel-colored. 2 (*pareja*) lovey-dovey, starry-eyed.

acariciar |12| *vtr* to caress; (*pelo, animal*) to stroke; (*esperanza*) to cherish.

acarrear *vtr* 1 (*transportar*) to carry, transport. 2 *fig* (*conllevar*) to entail.

acaso *adv* perhaps, maybe; ¿**a. no te lo dije?**, did I not tell you, by any chance?; **por si a.**, just in case; **si a. viene ...**, if he should come ....

acatamiento *nm* respect; (*de la ley*) observance.

acatar *vtr* to observe, comply with.

acatarrado,-a *adj* **estar a.**, to have a cold.

acatarrarse *vr* to catch a cold.

acaudalado,-a *adj* rich, wealthy.

acaudalar *vtr* to accumulate, amass.

acaudillar vtr to lead.
acceder vi a. a, (consentir) to accede to, consent to; (tener acceso) to gain admittance to; Inform to access.
accesible adj accessible; (persona) approachable.
acceso nm 1 (entrada) access, entry; Inform a. al azar, a. directo, random access; Univ prueba de a., entrance examination. 2 (carretera) approach, access. 3 Med & fig fit.
accesorio,-a adj & nm accessory.
accidentado,-a I adj (terreno) uneven, hilly; (viaje, vida) eventful. **II** nm,f casualty, accident victim.
accidental adj accidental; un encuentro a., a chance meeting.
accidente nm 1 accident; por a., by chance; a. laboral, industrial accident. 2 Geog accidentes geográficos, geographical features.
acción nf 1 action; (acto) act; poner en a., to put in action; ponerse en a., to go into action; campo de a., field of action; película de a., adventure film. 2 Fin share.
accionar vtr to drive.
accionista nmf shareholder.
acebo nm (hoja) holly; (árbol) holly tree.
acechar vtr to lie in wait for; un grave peligro nos acecha, great danger awaits us.
acecho nm estar al a. de, (esperar) to lie in wait for.
acedía nf (pez) dab.
aceite nm oil; a. de girasol/maíz/oliva, sunflower/corn/olive oil.
aceitera nf 1 Culin oil bottle; aceiteras, oil and vinegar set sing. 2 Aut oil can.
aceitero,-a I adj oil. **II** nm,f oil merchant.
aceitoso,-a adj oily.
aceituna nf olive; a. rellena, stuffed olive.
aceitunado,-a adj olive, olive-coloured.
aceitunero,-a nm,f 1 (recolector) olive picker o harvester. 2 (vendedor) olive seller.
acelerado,-a adj accelerated, fast.
acelerador nm Aut accelerator.
acelerar vtr to accelerate.
acento nm 1 accent; (de palabra) stress. 2 (énfasis) stress, emphasis.
acentuar |30| **I** vtr 1 to stress. 2 fig to emphasize, stress. **II** acentuarse vr fig to become more pronounced o noticeable.
aceña nf watermill.
acepción nf meaning, sense.
aceptable adj acceptable.
aceptación nf 1 acceptance. 2 tener poca a., to have little success, not to be popular.
aceptar vtr to accept.
acequia nf irrigation ditch o channel.
acera nf pavement, US sidewalk; fam pey

ser de la a. de enfrente, to be gay o queer.
acerado nm pavement.
acerbo,-a adj harsh, bitter.
acerca adv a. de, about.
acercamiento nm bringing together, coming together; Pol rapprochement.
acercar |1| **I** vtr to bring near o nearer, bring (over); fig to bring together; ¿te acerco a casa?, can I give you a lift home? **II** acercarse vr 1 to approach (a, -). 2 (ir) to go; (venir) to come.
acerico nm pincushion.
acero nm steel; a. inoxidable, stainless steel.
acérrimo,-a adj (partidario) staunch; (enemigo) bitter.
acertado,-a adj 1 (solución) right, correct; (decisión) wise. 2 no estuviste muy a. al decir eso, it wasn't very wise of you to say that.
acertante I nmf winner. **II** adj winning.
acertar |1| **I** vtr (pregunta) to get right; (adivinar) to guess correctly; a. las quinielas, to win the pools. **II** vi to be right; acertó con la calle que buscaba, she found the street she was looking for.
acertijo nm riddle.
acervo nm a. cultural, cultural tradition o heritage.
acetona nf acetone.
achacar |1| vtr (atribuir) to attribute.
achacoso,-a adj ailing, unwell.
achaque nm ailment, complaint.
achicar |1| **I** vtr 1 (amilanar) to intimidate. 2 (encoger) to reduce, make smaller. 3 (barco) to bale out. **II** achicarse vr 1 (amilanarse) to lose heart. 2 (encogerse) to get smaller.
achicharrar vtr to burn to a crisp.
achicoria nf chicory.
achinado,-a adj 1 (ojos) slanting. 2 Am with mestizo features.
acholado,-a adj Am half-caste.
achuchar vtr (empujar) to shove.
achuchón nm (empujón) push, shove.
aciago,-a adj ill-fated, fateful.
acicalado,-a adj well-dressed, smart.
acicalarse vr to dress up, smarten up.
acicate nm fig (aliciente) spur, incentive.
acidez nf (de sabor) sharpness, sourness; Quím acidity; Med a. de estómago, heartburn.
ácido,-a I adj (sabor) sharp, tart; Quím acidic; fig (tono) harsh. **II** nm Quím acid.
acierto nm (buena decisión) good choice o idea; con gran a., very wisely.
aclamación nf acclamation, acclaim.
aclamar vtr to acclaim.
aclaración nf explanation.
aclarado nm rinsing, rinse.
aclarar I vtr 1 (explicar) to clarify, explain; (color) to lighten, make lighter. 2 (enjuagar) to rinse. **II** v impers Meteor to

clear (up). **III aclararse** vr 1 (decidirse) to make up one's mind; (entender) to understand. 2 Meteor to clear (up).

aclaratorio,-a adj explanatory.

aclimatación nf acclimatization, US acclimation.

aclimatar I vtr to acclimatize, US acclimate (a, to). **II aclimatarse** vr fig **a. a algo**, to get used to sth.

acné nf acne.

acobardar I vtr to frighten. **II acobardarse** vr to become frightened, lose one's nerve, shrink back (ante, from).

acodarse vr to lean (en, on).

acogedor,-a adj cosy, warm.

acoger |5| **I** vtr 1 (recibir) to receive; (a invitado) to welcome. 2 (persona desvalida) to take in. **II acogerse** vr fig **a. a**, to take refuge in; (amnistía) to avail oneself of; **a. a la ley**, to have recourse to the law.

acogida nf reception, welcome.

acojonado,-a adj vulg shit-scared.

acojonante adj vulg bloody great o terrific.

acojonarse vr vulg (acobardarse) to shit oneself, be shit-scared.

acolchar vtr (rellenar) to pad; (prenda) to quilt.

acometer vtr 1 (emprender) to undertake. 2 (atacar) to attack.

acometida nf (ataque) attack; (de gas etc) connection.

acomodado,-a adj well-off, well-to-do.

acomodador,-a nm,f (hombre) usher; (mujer) usherette.

acomodar I vtr 1 (alojar) to lodge, accommodate. 2 (en cine etc) to find a place for. **II acomodarse** vr 1 to make oneself comfortable. 2 (adaptarse) to adapt.

acomodaticio,-a adj 1 accommodating, easy-going. 2 pey pliable.

acompañante I nmf companion. **II** adj accompanying.

acompañar vtr 1 to accompany; **le acompañó hasta la puerta**, she saw him to the door; **me acompañó al médico**, he came with me to see the doctor; **¿te acompaño a casa?**, can I walk you home?; fml **le acompaño en el sentimiento**, my condolences. 2 (adjuntar) to enclose.

acompasado,-a adj (rítmico) rhythmic.

acomplejado,-a adj **estar a.**, to have a complex (por, about).

acomplejar I vtr to give a complex. **II acomplejarse** vr **a. por**, to develop a complex about.

acondicionado,-a adj **aire a.**, air conditioning.

acondicionador nm conditioner.

acondicionar vtr to prepare, set up; (mejorar) to improve; (cabello) to condition.

acongojar vtr to distress.

aconsejable adj advisable.

aconsejar vtr to advise.

acontecer |33| v impers to happen, take place.

acontecimiento nm event.

acopio nm store, stock; **hacer a. de**, to store.

acoplar I vtr 1 to fit (together), join. 2 Téc to couple, connect. **II acoplarse** vr (nave espacial) to dock.

acorazado,-a I adj armoured, US armored, armour-plated, US armor-plated. **II** nm battleship.

acordado,-a adj agreed; **según lo a.**, as agreed.

acordar |2| **I** vtr to agree; (decidir) to decide. **II acordarse** vr to remember; **no me acuerdo (de Silvia)**, I can't remember (Silvia).

acorde I adj in agreement. **II** nm Mús chord.

acordeón nm accordion.

acordonado,-a adj cordoned off, sealed off.

acordonar vtr 1 (zona) to cordon off, seal off. 2 (atar) to lace up.

acorralar vtr to corner.

acortar vtr to shorten; **a. distancias**, to cut down the distance.

acosar vtr to harass; fig **a. a algn a preguntas**, to bombard sb with questions.

acoso nm harassment; **a. sexual**, sexual harassment.

acostar |2| **I** vtr to put to bed. **II acostarse** vr 1 to go to bed. 2 fam **a. con algn**, to sleep with sb, go to bed with sb.

acostumbrado,-a adj 1 usual, customary; **es lo a.**, it is the custom. 2 **a. al frío/calor**, used to the cold/heat.

acostumbrar I vi **a.**, (soler) to be in the habit of. **II** vtr **a. a algn a algo**, (habituar) to get sb used to sth. **III acostumbrarse** vr (habituarse) to become accustomed (a, to), get used (a, to).

acotación nf 1 (en escrito) (marginal) note; Teat stage direction. 2 (en mapa) elevation mark.

acotar vtr 1 (área) to enclose; fig (tema) to delimit. 2 (texto) to annotate. 3 (mapa) to mark with elevations.

acotejar vtr Am to arrange.

ácrata adj & nmf anarchist.

acre¹ adj 1 (sabor) sour, bitter; (olor) acrid. 2 fig (palabras) bitter, harsh; (crítica) biting.

acre² nm (medida) acre.

acrecentar |1| vtr to increase.

acreditar vtr 1 to be a credit to. 2 (probar) to prove. 3 (embajador) to accredit. 4 Fin to credit.

acreditativo,-a adj which proves, which gives proof.

acreedor,-a nm,f Com creditor.

acribillar *vtr* to riddle, pepper; **a. a algn a balazos,** to riddle sb with bullets.
acrílico,-a *adj* acrylic.
acriollarse *vr Am* to adopt local customs.
acritud *nf (mordacidad)* acrimony.
acrobacia *nf* acrobatics *sing.*
acróbata *nmf* acrobat.
acta *nf* 1 *(de reunión)* minutes *pl,* record. 2 *(certificado)* certificate, official document; **a. notarial,** affidavit.
actitud *nf* attitude.
activar *vtr* 1 to activate. 2 *(avivar)* to liven up.
actividad *nf* activity.
activista *nmf* activist.
activo,-a I *adj* active; **en a.,** on active service. II *nm Fin* assets *pl.*
acto *nm* 1 act, action; **a. sexual,** sexual intercourse; **en el a.,** at once; **a. seguido,** immediately afterwards; *Mil* **en a. de servicio,** in action; **hacer a. de presencia,** to put in an appearance. 2 *(ceremonia)* ceremony. 3 *Teat* act.
actor *nm* actor.
actriz *nf* actress.
actuación *nf* 1 performance. 2 *(intervención)* intervention, action.
actual *adj* current, present; *(al día)* up-to-date; **un tema muy a.,** a very topical subject. ◆**actualmente** *adv (hoy en día)* nowadays, these days; *(ahora)* at the moment, at present.
actualidad *nf* 1 present time; **en la a.,** at present; **estar de a.,** to be fashionable; **temas de a.,** topical subjects. 2 *(hechos)* current affairs *pl.*
actualizar |4| *vtr* to update, bring up to date.
actuar |30| *vi* 1 to act; **a. como** *o* **de,** to act as. 2 *Cin Teat* to perform, act.
acuarela *nf* watercolour, *US* watercolor.
Acuario *nm* Aquarius.
acuario *nm* aquarium.
acuartelar *vtr* to confine to barracks.
acuático,-a *adj* aquatic; **esquí a.,** water skiing.
acuchillar *vtr* to knife, stab.
acuciante *adj* urgent, pressing.
acuciar |12| *vtr* to urge on.
acudir *vi (ir)* to go; *(venir)* to come, arrive; **nadie acudió en su ayuda,** nobody came to help him; **no sé dónde a.,** I don't know where to turn.
acueducto *nm* aqueduct.
acuerdo *nm* agreement; **¡de a.!,** all right!, O.K.!; **de a. con,** in accordance with; **de común a.,** by common consent; **estar de a. en algo,** to agree on sth; **ponerse de a.,** to agree; **a. marco,** framework agreement.
acumular I *vtr* to accumulate. II **acumularse** *vr* 1 to accumulate, build up. 2 *(gente)* to crowd.
acunar *vtr* to rock.

acuñar *vtr (moneda)* to mint; *(frase)* to coin.
acuoso,-a *adj* watery; *(jugoso)* juicy.
acupuntura *nf* acupuncture.
acurrucarse |1| *vr* to curl up, snuggle up.
acusación *nf* 1 accusation. 2 *Jur* charge.
acusado,-a I *nm,f* accused, defendant. II *adj (marcado)* marked, noticeable.
acusar I *vtr* 1 to accuse (**de,** of); *Jur* to charge (**de,** with). 2 *(golpe etc)* to feel; *fig* **su cara acusaba el cansancio,** his face showed his exhaustion. 3 *Com* **a. recibo,** to acknowledge receipt. II **acusarse** *vr* 1 *(acentuarse)* to become more pronounced. 2 *fig (notarse)* to show.
acuse *nm* **a. de recibo,** acknowledgment of receipt.
acusica *adj & nmf fam* telltale.
acústica *nf* acoustics *sing.*
acústico,-a *adj* acoustic.
adán *nm fam* untidy *o* slovenly person.
adaptable *adj* adaptable.
adaptación *nf* adaptation.
adaptador *nm* adapter.
adaptar I *vtr* 1 to adapt. 2 *(ajustar)* to adjust. II **adaptarse** *vr* to adapt oneself (**a,** to).
adecentar *vtr* to tidy (up), clean (up).
adecuado,-a *adj* appropriate, suitable.
adecuar |10| *vtr* to adapt.
adefesio *nm (persona)* freak; *(cosa)* monstrosity.
a. de J.C. *abr de* **antes de Jesucristo,** before Christ, BC.
adelantado,-a *adj* 1 advanced; *(desarrollado)* developed; *(precoz)* precocious. 2 *(reloj)* fast. 3 **pagar por a.,** to pay in advance.
adelantamiento *nm* overtaking; **hacer un a.,** to overtake.
adelantar I *vtr* 1 to move *o* bring forward; *(reloj)* to put forward; *fig* to advance. 2 *Aut* to overtake. 3 *(fecha)* to bring forward; *fig* **a. (los) acontecimientos,** to get ahead of oneself. II *vi* 1 to advance. 2 *(progresar)* to make progress. 3 *(reloj)* to be fast. III **adelantarse** *vr* 1 *(ir delante)* to go ahead. 2 *(reloj)* to gain, be fast. 3 **el verano se ha adelantado,** we are having an early summer.
adelante I *adv* forward; **más a.,** *(lugar)* further on; *(tiempo)* later; **seguir a.,** to keep going, carry on; **llevar a. un plan,** to carry out a plan. II *interj* **¡a.!,** come in!
adelanto *nm* 1 advance; *(progreso)* progress. 2 **el reloj lleva diez minutos de a.,** the watch is ten minutes fast. 3 *(de dinero)* advance payment.
adelfa *nf* oleander, rosebay.
adelgazamiento *nm* slimming.
adelgazar |4| *vi* to slim, lose weight.
ademán *nm* 1 gesture. 2 **ademanes,** manners.

además *adv* moreover, furthermore; **a., no lo he visto nunca**, what's more, I've never seen him; **a. de él**, besides him.

adentrarse *vr* **a. en**, *(bosque)* to go deep into; *(asunto)* to study thoroughly.

adentro I *adv (dentro)* inside; **mar a.**, out to sea; **tierra a.**, inland. II *nmpl* **decir algo para sus adentros**, to say sth to oneself.

adepto,-a *nm,f* follower, supporter.

aderezar |4| *vtr (comida)* to season; *(ensalada)* to dress.

aderezo *nm (de comida)* seasoning; *(de ensalada)* dressing.

adeudar I *vtr* to owe. II **adeudarse** *vr* to get into debt.

adherencia *nf* adherence; *Aut* roadholding.

adherir |5| I *vtr* to stick on. II **adherirse** *vr* **a. a**, to adhere to; *(partido)* to join.

adhesión *nf* adhesion; *(a partido)* joining; *(a teoría)* adherence.

adhesivo,-a *adj & nm* adhesive.

adicción *nf* addiction; **crear a.**, to be addictive.

adición *nf* addition.

adicional *adj* additional.

adicto,-a I *nm,f* addict. II *adj* addicted (**a**, to).

adiestrar *vtr* to train.

adinerado,-a I *adj* wealthy, rich. II *nm,f* rich person.

adiós *(pl adioses)* I *interj* goodbye; *fam* bye-bye; *(al cruzarse)* hello. II *nm* goodbye.

aditivo,-a *adj & nm* additive.

adivinanza *nf* riddle, puzzle.

adivinar *vtr* to guess; **a. el pensamiento de algn**, to read sb's mind.

adivino,-a *nm,f* fortune-teller.

adjetivo,-a *nm* I adjective. II *adj* adjectival.

adjudicación *nf* award; *(en subasta)* sale.

adjudicar |15| I *vtr* 1 *(premio, contrato)* to award. 2 *(en subasta)* to sell. II **adjudicarse** *vr* to appropriate, take over.

adjuntar *vtr* to enclose.

adjunto,-a I *adj* 1 enclosed, attached. 2 *Educ* assistant. II *nm,f Educ* assistant teacher.

adm., admón., *abr de* **administración**, administration.

administración *nf* 1 *(gobierno)* administration, authorities *pl*; *Pol* **a. central**, central government; **a. pública**, civil service. 2 *(de empresa)* administration, management. 3 *(oficina)* (branch) office.

administrador,-a I *nm,f* administrator. I *adj* administrating.

administrar I *vtr* 1 to administer. 2 *(dirigir)* to run, manage. II **administrarse** *vr* to manage one's own money.

administrativo,-a I *adj* administrative. II *nm,f (funcionario)* official.

admirable *adj* admirable.

admiración *nf* 1 admiration; **causar a.**, to impress. 2 *Ling* exclamation mark.

admirador,-a *nm,f* admirer.

admirar I *vtr* 1 to admire. 2 *(sorprender)* to amaze, astonish. II **admirarse** *vr* to be amazed, be astonished.

admisible *adj* admissible, acceptable.

admisión *nf* admission; **'reservado el derecho de a.'**, 'the management reserves the right to refuse admission'.

admitir *vtr* 1 to admit, let in. 2 *(aceptar)* to accept; **'no se admiten cheques'**, 'no cheques accepted'. 3 *(tolerar)* to allow. 4 *(reconocer)* to admit, acknowledge; **admito que mentí**, I admit that I lied.

admonición *nf* warning.

ADN *nm abr de* **ácido desoxirribonucleico**, desoxyribonucleic acid, DNA.

adobar *vtr Culin* to marinate.

adobe *nm* adobe.

adobo *nm* marinade.

adoctrinar *vtr* to indoctrinate.

adolecer |33| *vi* **a. de**, *(carecer de)* to lack; *fig fml* to suffer from.

adolescencia *nf* adolescence.

adolescente *adj & nmf* adolescent.

adónde *adv interr* where (to)?

adonde *adv* where.

adondequiera *adv* wherever.

adopción *nf* adoption.

adoptar *vtr* to adopt.

adoptivo,-a *adj (hijo)* adopted; *(padres)* adoptive; *fig* **país a.**, country of adoption.

adoquín *nm* cobble, paving stone.

adorable *adj* adorable.

adorar *vtr* 1 *Rel* to worship. 2 *fig* to adore.

adormecer |33| I *vtr* to send to sleep, make sleepy. II **adormecerse** *vr* 1 *(dormirse)* to doze off. 2 *(brazo etc)* to go to sleep, go numb.

adormecido,-a *adj* sleepy, drowsy.

adormilarse *vr* to doze, drowse.

adornar *vtr* to adorn, decorate.

adorno *nm* decoration, adornment; **de a.**, decorative.

adosado,-a *adj* adjacent; *(casa)* semidetached.

adquirir |31| *vtr* to acquire; *(comprar)* to purchase.

adquisición *nf* acquisition; *(compra)* buy, purchase.

adquisitivo,-a *adj* **poder a.**, purchasing power.

adrede *adv* deliberately, on purpose.

adrenalina *nf* adrenalin.

adriático,-a *nm* **el (Mar) A.**, the Adriatic (Sea).

adscribir *(pp adscrito)* I *vtr* 1 *(atribuir)* to ascribe to. 2 *(a un trabajo)* to appoint to. II **adscribirse** *vr* to affiliate (**a**, to).

adscrito,-a *pp de* **adscribir**.

aduana *nf* customs *pl*.

aduanero,-a I *adj* customs. **II** *nm,f* customs officer.

aducir |10| *vtr* to adduce, allege.

adueñarse *vr* **a. de**, to take over; *(pánico etc)* to take hold of.

aduje *pt indef* → aducir.

adulación *nf* adulation.

adular *vtr* to adulate.

adulterar *vtr* to adulterate.

adulterio *nm* adultery.

adúltero,-a I *adj* adulterous. **II** *nm,f (hombre)* adulterer; *(mujer)* adulteress.

adulto,-a *adj & nm,f* adult.

adusto,-a *adj* harsh, severe.

aduzco *indic pres* → aducir.

advenedizo,-a *adj & nm,f* upstart.

advenimiento *nm* advent, coming.

adverbio *nm* adverb.

adversario,-a I *nm,f* adversary, opponent. **II** *adj* opposing.

adversidad *nf* adversity; *(revés)* setback.

adverso,-a *adj* adverse.

advertencia *nf* warning.

advertido,-a *adj* warned; *(informado)* informed; **estás** *o* **quedas a.**, you've been warned.

advertir |5| *vtr* **1** to warn; *(informar)* to inform, advise; *fam* **te advierto que yo tampoco lo vi**, mind you, I didn't see it either. **2** *(notar)* to realize, notice.

adviento *nm* Advent.

adyacente *adj* adjacent.

aéreo,-a *adj* **1** aerial. **2** *Av* air; **tráfico a.**, air traffic; **Com por vía aerea**, by air.

aero- *pref* aero-.

aeróbic *nm* aerobics *sing*.

aerodinámico,-a *adj* aerodynamic; **de línea aerodinámica**, streamlined.

aeródromo *nm* aerodrome.

aeromodelismo *nm* aeroplane modelling *o US* modeling.

aeromoza *nf Am* air hostess.

aeronáutica *nf* aeronautics *sing*.

aeronáutico,-a *adj* **la industria aeronáutica**, the aeronautics industry.

aeronave *nf* airship.

aeroplano *nm* light aeroplane.

aeropuerto *nm* airport.

aerosol *nm* aerosol.

aerostático,-a *adj* **globo a.**, hot-air balloon.

a/f *abr de* **a favor**, in favour *o US* favor.

afable *adj* affable.

afamado,-a *adj* famous, well-known.

afán *nm (pl* afanes) **1** *(esfuerzo)* effort. **2** *(celo)* zeal.

afanar I *vtr (robar)* to nick, pinch. **II afanarse** *vr* **a. por conseguir algo**, to do one's best to achieve sth.

afanoso,-a *adj* **1** *(persona)* keen, eager. **2** *(tarea)* hard, tough.

afección *nf* disease.

afectación *nf* affectation.

afectado,-a *adj* affected.

afectar *vtr* **a. a**, to affect; **le afectó mucho**, she was deeply affected; **nos afecta a todos**, it concerns all of us.

afecto,-a *nm* affection; **tomarle a. a algn**, to become fond of sb.

afectuoso,-a *adj* affectionate.

afeitado *nm* shave.

afeitar *vtr*, **afeitarse** *vr* to shave.

afeminado,-a *adj* effeminate.

aferrado,-a *adj* **a.**, a clinging to.

aferrar I *vtr Náut* to anchor, moor. **II aferrarse** *vr* to clutch, cling; *fig* **a. a una creencia**, to cling to a belief.

Afganistán *n* Afghanistan.

afgano,-a *adj & nm,f* Afghan.

afianzamiento *nm* strengthening, reinforcement.

afianzar |4| **I** *vtr* to strengthen, reinforce. **II afianzarse** *vr (persona)* to become established.

afición *nf* **1** liking; **tiene a. por la música**, he is fond of music. **2** *Dep* **la a.**, the fans *pl*.

aficionado,-a I *nm,f* **1** enthusiast; **un a. a la música**, a music lover. **2** *(no profesional)* amateur. **I** *adj* **1** keen, fond; **ser a. a algo**, to be fond of sth. **2** *(no profesional)* amateur.

aficionarse *vr* to become fond (a, of), take a liking (a, to).

afilado,-a *adj* sharp.

afilar *vtr* to sharpen.

afiliación *nf* affiliation.

afiliado,-a *nm,f* member.

afiliarse |12| *vtr* to become a member.

afín *adj (semejante)* kindred, similar; *(relacionado)* related.

afinar *vtr* **1** *(puntería)* to sharpen. **2** *(instrumento)* to tune.

afincarse |11| *vr* to settle down.

afinidad *nf* affinity.

afirmación *nf* affirmation; **afirmaciones**, *(declaracion)* statement.

afirmar 1 *vtr (aseverar)* to state, declare. **2** *(afianzar)* to strengthen, reinforce.

afirmativo,-a *adj* affirmative; **en caso a. ...**, if the answer is yes ...

aflicción *nf* affliction.

afligir |6| **I** *vtr* to afflict. **II afligirse** *vr* to grieve, be distressed.

aflojar I *vtr* to loosen. **II** *vi (viento etc)* to weaken, grow weak. **III aflojarse** *vr* to come *o* work loose; *(rueda)* to go down.

aflorar *vi* to come to the surface, appear.

afluencia *nf* inflow, influx; **gran a. de público**, great numbers of people.

afluente *nm* tributary.

afluir |37| *vi* to flow (a, into).

afónico,-a *adj* **estar a.**, to have lost one's voice.

aforismo *nm* aphorism.

aforo *nm (capacidad)* seating capacity.

afortunado,-a *adj* fortunate; **las Islas Afortunadas**, the Canaries.

afrenta *nf fml* affront.
Africa *n* Africa.
africano,-a *adj & nm,f* African.
afrodisíaco,-a *adj & nm* aphrodisiac.
afrontar *vtr* to confront, face; **a. las consecuencias,** to face the consequences.
afuera I *adv* outside; **la parte de a.,** the outside; **más a.,** further out; **salir a.,** to come *o* go out. II *nfpl* **afueras,** outskirts.
agachar I *vtr* to lower. II **agacharse** *vr* to duck.
agalla *nf* 1 *(de pez)* gill. 2 **tiene agallas,** she's got guts.
agarraderas *nfpl fam* **tener buenas a.,** to be well connected.
agarrado,-a *adj* 1 *fam* stingy, tight. 2 **baile a.,** cheek-to-cheek dancing.
agarrar I *vtr* 1 to grasp, seize; **agárralo fuerte,** hold it tight. 2 *Am* to take. 3 *fam (pillar)* to catch; **a. una borrachera,** to get drunk *o* pissed. II **agarrarse** *vr* to hold on; **agarraos bien,** hold tight.
agarrotarse *vr* 1 *(músculo)* to stiffen. 2 *(máquina)* to seize up.
agasajar *vtr* to smother with attentions.
ágata *nf* agate.
agazaparse *vr* to crouch (down).
agencia *nf* agency; *(sucursal)* branch; **a. de viajes,** travel agency; **a. de seguros,** insurance agency; **a. inmobiliaria,** estate agency.
agenciarse |12| *vr* 1 to get oneself; **se agenció una moto,** he got himself a motorbike. 2 **agenciárselas,** to manage.
agenda *nf* diary.
agente *nmf* agent; **a. de policía,** *(hombre)* policeman; *(mujer)* policewoman; **a. de bolsa,** stockbroker; **a. de seguros,** insurance broker.
agigantado,-a *adj* **a pasos agigantados,** by leaps and bounds.
ágil *adj* agile.
agilidad *nf* agility.
agilización *nf* speeding up.
agilizar |4| *vtr (trámites)* to speed up.
agitación *nf (intranquilidad)* restlessness; *(social, político)* unrest.
agitado,-a *adj* agitated; *(persona)* anxious; *(mar)* rough; **una vida muy agitada,** a very hectic life.
agitar I *vtr (botella)* to shake; *(multitud)* to agitate. II **agitarse** *vr (persona)* to become agitated; *(mar)* to become rough.
aglomeración *nf* agglomeration; *(de gente)* crowd.
aglomerar *vtr,* **aglomerarse** *vr* 1 *(agruparse)* to agglomerate, amass. 2 *(gente)* to crowd, form a crowd.
agnóstico,-a *adj & nm,f* agnostic.
agobiado,-a *adj fig* **a. de problemas,** snowed under with problems; *fig* **a. de trabajo,** up to one's eyes in work.
agobiante *adj (trabajo)* overwhelming; *(lugar)* claustrophobic; *(calor)* oppressive;

(persona) tiresome, tiring.
agobiar |12| I *vtr* to overwhelm. II **agobiarse** *vr (con problemas)* to be over-anxious; *(por el calor)* to suffocate.
agobio *nm* 1 *(angustia)* anxiety. 2 *(sofoco)* suffocation.
agolpamiento *nm* crowd, crush.
agolparse *vr* to crowd, throng.
agonía *nf* dying breath, last gasp.
agonizante *adj* dying.
agonizar |4| *vi* to be dying.
agosto *nm* August; *fam* **hacer su a.,** to make a packet.
agotado,-a *adj* 1 *(cansado)* exhausted, worn out. 2 *Com* sold out; *(existencias)* exhausted; *(libro)* out of print.
agotador,-a *adj* exhausting.
agotamiento *nm* exhaustion.
agotar I *vtr* 1 *(cansar)* to exhaust, wear out. 2 *(acabar)* to exhaust, use up (completely). II **agotarse** *vr* 1 *(acabarse)* to run out, be used up; *Com* to be sold out. 2 *(persona)* to become exhausted *o* tired out.
agraciado,-a *adj* 1 *(hermoso)* pretty. 2 *(ganador)* winning; **ser a. con,** to win.
agradable *adj* pleasant.
agradar *vi* to please; **no me agrada,** I don't like it.
agradecer |33| *vtr* 1 *(dar las gracias)* to thank for; **les agradezco su atención,** (I) thank you for your attention; **te lo agradezco mucho,** thank you very much. 2 *(estar agradecido)* to be grateful to; **te agradecería que vinieras,** I'd be grateful if you'd come. 3 *(uso impers)* **siempre se agradece un descanso,** a rest is always welcome.
agradecido,-a *adj* grateful; **le estoy muy a.,** I am very grateful to you.
agradecimiento *nm* gratitude.
agrado *nm* pleasure; **no es de su a.,** it isn't to his liking.
agrandar I *vtr* to enlarge, make larger. II **agrandarse** *vr* to enlarge, become larger.
agrario,-a *adj* agrarian; **política agraria,** agricultural policy.
agravamiento *nm* aggravation.
agravante I *adj Jur* aggravating. II *nm Jur* aggravating circumstance.
agravar I *vtr* to aggravate. II **agravarse** *vr* to worsen, get worse.
agraviar |12| *vtr* to offend, insult.
agravio *nm* offense, insult.
agredir *vtr* *defect* to assault.
agregación *nf* aggregation.
agregado,-a I *adj Educ* **profesor a.,** *(escuela)* secondary school teacher; *Univ* assistant teacher. II *nm,f Pol* attaché.
agregar |7| I *vtr* 1 *(añadir)* to add. 2 *(destinar)* to appoint. II **agregarse** *vr* **a. a,** to join.
agresión *nf* aggression.
agresividad *nf* aggressiveness.

agresivo,-a *adj* aggressive.

agresor,-a **I** *nm,f* aggressor, attacker. **II** *adj* attacking.

agriarse *vr* to turn sour.

agrícola *adj* agricultural.

agricultor,-a *nm,f* farmer.

agricultura *nf* agriculture.

agridulce *adj* bittersweet.

agrietar **I** *vtr* to crack; (*piel, labios*) to chap. **II agrietarse** *vr* to crack; (*piel*) to get chapped.

agringarse |7| *vr Am* to behave like a gringo.

agrio,-a **I** *adj* sour. **II** *nmpl* **agrios**, citrus fruits.

agrónomo,-a *nm,f* (**ingeniero**) **a.**, agronomist.

agropecuario,-a *adj* farming, agricultural.

agrupación *nf* association.

agrupar **I** *vtr* to group. **II agruparse** *vr* **1** (*congregarse*) to group together, form a group. **2** (*asociarse*) to associate.

agua *nf* water; **a. potable**, drinking water; **a. corriente/del grifo**, running/tap water; **a. dulce/salada**, fresh/salt water; **a. mineral sin/con gas**, still/fizzy *o* sparkling mineral water; **a. de colonia**, (eau de) cologne; *fig* **estar con el a. al cuello**, to be up to one's neck in it; **aguas jurisdiccionales**, territorial waters; **aguas residuales**, sewage *sing*.

aguacate *nm* (*árbol*) avocado; (*fruto*) avocado (pear).

aguacero *nm* shower, downpour.

aguado,-a *adj* watered down.

aguafiestas *nmf inv* spoilsport, wet blanket.

aguafuerte *nm* **1** *Arte* etching. **2** *Quím* nitric acid.

aguamarina *nf* aquamarine.

aguanieve *nf* sleet.

aguantar **I** *vtr* (*soportar*) to tolerate; **no lo aguanto más**, I can't stand it any longer. **2** (*sostener*) to support, hold; **aguanta esto**, hold this. **3 aguanta la respiración**, hold your breath. **II aguantarse** *vr* **1** (*contenerse*) to keep back; (*lágrimas*) to hold back; **no pude aguantarme la risa**, I couldn't help laughing. **2** (*resignarse*) to resign oneself.

aguante *nm* endurance; **tener mucho a.**, (*ser paciente*) to be very patient; (*tener resistencia*) to be strong, have a lot of stamina.

aguar |22| *vtr* to water down; *fig* **a. la fiesta a algn**, to spoil sb's fun.

aguardar **I** *vtr* to await. **II** *vi* to wait.

aguardiente *nm* liquor, brandy.

aguarrás *nm* turpentine.

aguatero,-a *nm,f Am* water carrier *o* seller.

agudeza *nf* **1** sharpness; (*del dolor*) acuteness. **2** *fig* (*ingenio*) witticism, witty saying.

agudización *nf* **1** sharpening. **2** (*empeoramiento*) worsening.

agudizar |4| **I** *vtr* to intensify, make more acute. **II agudizarse** *vr* to intensify, become more acute.

agudo,-a *adj* (*dolor*) acute; (*voz*) high-pitched; (*sonido*) treble, high; *fig* (*ingenioso*) witty; *fig* (*sentido*) sharp, keen.

agüero *nm* omen.

aguijón *nm* sting; *fig* (*estímulo*) spur.

águila *nf* eagle; **á. real**, golden eagle.

aguileño,-a *adj* aquiline; **nariz aguileña**, aquiline nose.

aguinaldo *nm* Christmas box; **pedir el a.**, to go carol singing.

aguja *nf* **1** needle; (*de reloj*) hand; (*de tocadiscos*) stylus. **2** *Arquit* spire. **3** *Ferroc* point, *US* switch.

agujerear *vtr* to make holes in.

agujero *nm* **1** hole; **a. negro**, black hole. **2** *Econ* deficit, shortfall.

agujetas *nfpl* stiffness *sing*; **tener a.**, to be stiff.

agur *interj fam* bye!, see you!

aguzar |4| **I** *vtr* (*afilar*) to sharpen. **2** *fig* **a. el oído**, to prick up one's ears; **a. la vista**, to look attentively; **aguzar el ingenio**, to sharpen one's wits.

ahí *adv* there; **a. está**, there he *o* she *o* it is; **ve por a.**, go that way; **está por a.**, it's over there; **setenta o por a.**, seventy or thereabouts; **de a.**, hence.

ahijado,-a *nm,f* godchild; (*niño*) godson; (*niña*) goddaughter; **ahijados**, godchildren.

ahínco *nm* eagerness; **con a.**, eagerly.

ahíto,-a *adj* (*de comida*) full, stuffed; (*harto*) fed up.

ahogado,-a **I** *adj* **1** (*en líquido*) drowned; **morir a.**, to drown. **2** (*asfixiado*) suffocated. **II** *nm,f* drowned person.

ahogar |7| **I** *vtr* **1** (*en líquido*) to drown. **2** (*asfixiar*) to suffocate. **II ahogarse** *vr* **1** (*en líquido*) to drown, be drowned; *fig* **a. en un vaso de agua**, to make a mountain out of a molehill. **2** (*asfixiarse*) to suffocate. **3** (*motor*) to be flooded.

ahondar *vtr* to deepen. **II** *vi* to go deep; *fig* **a. en un problema**, to go into a problem in depth.

ahora **I** *adv* **1** (*en este momento*) now; **a. mismo**, right now; **de a. en adelante**, from now on; **por a.**, for the time being. **2 a. voy**, I'm coming; **a. vuelvo**, I'll be back in a minute. **3 hasta a.**, (*hasta el momento*) until now, so far; (*hasta luego*) see you later. **II** *conj* **a. bien**, (*sin embargo*) however; (*y bueno*) well then.

ahorcado,-a *nm,f* hanged person. **II** *adj* hanged.

ahorcar |1| **I** *vtr* to hang. **II ahorcarse** *vr* to hang oneself.

ahorita *adv Am* right now.

ahorrador,-a *adj* thrifty.

ahorrar I *vtr* to save. **II ahorrarse** *vr* **ahórrate los comentarios,** keep your comments to yourself.

ahorrativo,-a *adj* thrifty.

ahorro *nm* **1** saving; **a. energético,** energy saving. **2 ahorros,** savings; *Fin* **caja de a.,** savings bank.

ahuecar |1| *vtr* **1** to hollow out; *fam* **a. el ala,** to clear off, beat it. **2** (*voz*) to deepen.

ahuevado *adj Am* stupid.

ahumado,-a *adj* (*cristal, jamón*) smoked; (*bacon*) smoky; **salmón a.,** smoked salmon.

ahumar |16| **I** *vtr* to smoke. **II** *vi* (*echar humo*) to smoke, give off smoke.

ahuyentar *vtr* to scare away.

aindiado,-a *adj Am* Indian-like.

airado,-a *adj* angry.

airar |15| **I** *vtr* to anger. **II airarse** *vr* to get angry.

aire *nm* **1** air; **a. acondicionado,** air conditioning; **al a.,** (*hacia arriba*) into the air; (*al descubierto*) uncovered; **al a. libre,** in the open air; **en el a.,** (*pendiente*) in the air; *Rad* on the air; **hacerse a.,** to fan oneself; **saltar por los aires,** to blow up; **tomar el a.,** to get some fresh air; **necesito un cambio de aires,** I need a change of scene. **2** *Aut* choke. **3** (*viento*) wind; **hace a.,** it's windy. **4** (*aspecto*) air, appearance. **5 él va a su a.,** he goes his own sweet way. **6 darse aires,** to put on airs.

airear *vtr* (*ropa, lugar*) to air; *fig* (*asunto*) to publicize.

airoso,-a *adj* graceful, elegant; *fig* **salir a. de una situación,** to come out of a situation with flying colours.

aislacionismo *nm* isolationism.

aislado,-a *adj* **1** isolated. **2** *Téc* insulated.

aislamiento *nm* **1** isolation. **2** *Téc* insulation.

aislante I *adj* **cinta a.,** insulating tape. **II** *nm* insulator.

aislar |15| *vtr* **1** to isolate. **2** *Téc* to insulate.

ajar *vtr* to wear out.

ajedrez *nm* **1** (*juego*) chess. **2** (*piezas y tablero*) chess set.

ajeno,-a *adj* belonging to other people; **los bienes ajenos,** other peoples' goods; **por causas ajenas a nuestra voluntad,** for reasons beyond our control.

ajetreado,-a *adj* (very) busy, hectic.

ajetreo *nm* activity, hard work, bustle.

ajillo *nm Culin* **al a.,** fried with garlic.

ajo *nm* garlic; **cabeza/diente de a.,** head/clove of garlic; *fam* **estar en el a.,** to be in on it.

ajonjolí *nm* sesame.

ajorca *nf* bracelet; (*en el tobillo*) anklet.

ajuar *nm* (*de novia*) trousseau.

ajustado,-a *adj* tight.

ajustador,-a *nm,f* fitter.

ajustar *vtr* **1** to adjust. **2** (*apretar*) to tighten. **3** *Fin* (*cuenta*) to settle; *fig* **ajustarle las cuentas a algn,** to settle a score with sb.

ajuste *nm* **1** adjustment; *Téc* assembly; *TV* **carta de a.,** test card. **2** (*de precio*) fixing; (*de cuenta*) settlement; *fig* **a. de cuentas,** settling of scores.

ajusticiar |12| *vtr* to execute.

al (*contracción de a & el*) **1** → **a. 2** (*al + infin*) **al salir,** on leaving; **está al caer,** it's about to happen; **al parecer,** apparently.

ala I *nf* **1** wing; *fig* **cortarle las alas a algn,** to clip sb's wings. **2** (*de sombrero*) brim. **II** *nmf Dep* winger.

alabanza *nf* praise.

alabar *vtr* to praise.

alabastro *nm* alabaster.

alacena *nf* (food) cupboard.

alacrán *nm* scorpion.

alambicado,-a *adj* intricate.

alambique *nm* still.

alambrada *nf,* **alambrado** *nm* wire fence.

alambrar *vtr* to fence with wire.

alambre *nm* wire; **a. de púas,** barbed wire.

alambrista *nmf* tightrope walker.

alameda *nf* **1** poplar grove. **2** (*paseo*) avenue, boulevard.

álamo *nm* poplar.

alano,-a *nm,f* (*perro*) **a.,** mastiff.

alarde *nm* (*ostentación*) bragging, boasting; **hacer a. de,** to show off.

alardear *vi* to brag, boast; **a. de rico** *o* **de riqueza,** to flaunt one's wealth.

alargadera *nf Elec* extension.

alargado,-a *adj* elongated.

alargar |7| **I** *vtr* **1** to lengthen; (*estirar*) to stretch; **ella alargó la mano para cogerlo,** she stretched out her hand to get it. **2** (*prolongar*) to prolong, extend. **3** (*dar*) to pass, hand over; **alárgame ese jersey,** can you pass me that jumper? **II alargarse** *vr* **1** to get longer. **2** (*prolongarse*) to go on. **3 ¿puedes a. a casa?,** can you give me a lift home?

alarido *nm* screech, shriek; **dar un a.,** to howl.

alarma *nf* alarm; **la a. saltó,** the alarm went off; **falsa a.,** false alarm; **señal de a.,** alarm (signal).

alarmado,-a *adj* alarmed.

alarmante *adj* alarming.

alarmar I *vtr* to alarm. **II alarmarse** *vr* to be alarmed.

alazán,-ana *adj* & *nm,f* (*caballo*) **a.,** chestnut.

alba *nf* dawn, daybreak.

albacea *nmf* (*hombre*) executor; (*mujer*) executrix.

albahaca *nf* basil.
albanés,-esa *adj & nm,f* Albanian.
Albania *n* Albania.
albañal *nm* sewer, drain.
albañil *nm* bricklayer.
albañilería *nf* bricklaying; **pared de a.,** (*obra*) brick wall.
albarán *nm Com* delivery note, despatch note.
albaricoque *nm* (*fruta*) apricot; (*árbol*) apricot tree.
albatros *nm inv* albatross.
albedrío *nm* will; **libre a.,** free will.
alberca *nf* (small) reservoir.
albergar |7| I *vtr* (*alojar*) to house, accommodate; *fig* (*sentimientos*) to cherish, harbour, *US* harbor. II **albergarse** *vtr* to stay.
albergue *nm* hostel; **a. juvenil,** youth hostel.
albino,-a *adj & nm,f* albino.
albóndiga *nf* meatball.
albores *nmpl* beginning *sing*; **en los a. de ...,** at the beginning of ...
albornoz *nm* bathrobe.
alborotado,-a *adj* 1 worked up, agitated. 2 (*desordenado*) untidy, messy. 3 (*mar*) rough; (*tiempo*) stormy.
alborotar I *vtr* 1 (*agitar*) to agitate, work up. 2 (*desordenar*) to make untidy, turn upside down. II *vi* to kick up a racket. III **alborotarse** *vr* 1 to get excited *o* worked up. 2 (*mar*) to get rough; (*tiempo*) to get stormy.
alboroto *nm* 1 (*jaleo*) din, racket. 2 (*desorden*) disturbance, uproar.
alborozo *nm* merriment, gaiety.
albufera *nf* lagoon.
álbum *nm* album.
alcachofa *nf* 1 *Bot* artichoke. 2 (*de tubo, regadera*) rose, sprinkler.
alcalde *nm* mayor.
alcaldesa *nf* mayoress.
alcaldía *nf* 1 (*cargo*) mayorship. 2 (*oficina*) mayor's office.
alcalino,-a *adj* alkaline.
alcance *nm* 1 reach; **al a. de cualquiera,** within everybody's reach; **dar a. a,** to catch up with; **fuera del a. de los niños,** out of the reach of children. 2 *fig* scope; (*de noticia*) importance.
alcancía *nf* money box; (*cerdito*) piggy bank.
alcanfor *nm* camphor.
alcantarilla *nf* sewer; (*boca*) drain.
alcantarillado *nm* sewer system.
alcanzar |4| I *vtr* 1 to reach; (*persona*) to catch up with; **la producción alcanza dos mil unidades,** production is up to two thousand units. 2 **alcánzame la sal,** (*pasar*) pass me the salt. 3 (*conseguir*) to attain, achieve. II *vi* (*ser suficiente*) to be sufficient; **con un kilo no alcanza para todos,** one kilo won't be enough for all

of us.
alcaparra *nf* (*fruto*) caper; (*planta*) caper bush.
alcatraz *nm Orn* gannet.
alcayata *nf* hook.
alcazaba *nf* fortress, citadel.
alcázar *nm* 1 (*fortaleza*) fortress, citadel. 2 (*castillo*) castle, palace.
alcista I *adj* (*bolsa*) rising, bullish; **tendencia a.,** upward tendency. II *nmf* (*bolsa*) bull.
alcoba *nf* bedroom.
alcohol *nm* alcohol.
alcoholemia *nf* blood alcohol level; **prueba de a.,** breath test.
alcohólico,-a *adj & nm,f* alcoholic.
alcoholímetro *nm* Breathalyzer®.
alcoholismo *nm* alcoholism.
alcoholizado,-a *adj & nm,f* alcoholic.
alcornoque *nm* cork oak.
alcurnia *nf* lineage, ancestry; **de alta a.,** of noble lineage.
alcuzcuz *nm* couscous.
aldaba *nf* (*llamador*) door knocker.
aldabonazo *nm* 1 loud knock. 2 (*advertencia*) warning.
aldea *nf* village.
aldeano,-a I *adj* village. II *nm,f* villager.
aleación *nf* alloy.
aleatorio,-a *adj* random.
aleccionador,-a *adj* (*instructivo*) instructive; (*ejemplar*) exemplary.
aleccionar *vtr* (*instruir*) to teach, instruct; (*adiestrar*) to train.
aledaño,-a I *adj* adjoining, adjacent. II *nmpl* **aledaños,** outskirts.
alegar |7| *vtr* 1 (*aducir*) to claim; *Jur* to allege. 2 (*presentar*) to put forward.
alegato *nm* argument.
alegoría *nf* allegory.
alegrar I *vtr* 1 (*complacer*) to make happy *o* glad; **me alegra que se lo hayas dicho,** I am glad you told her. 2 *fig* (*avivar*) to enliven, brighten up. II **alegrarse** *vr* to be glad, be happy; **me alegro de verte,** I am pleased to see you; **me alegro por ti,** I am happy for you.
alegre *adj* 1 (*contento*) happy, glad. 2 (*color*) bright; (*música*) lively; (*lugar*) pleasant, cheerful. 3 *fig* (*borracho*) tipsy, merry.
alegría *nf* joy, happiness.
alejado,-a *adj* far away, remote.
alejar I *vtr* to move further away. II **alejarse** *vr* to go away, move away; **no te alejes de mí,** keep close to me.
aleluya *nm & f* hallelujah, alleluia.
alemán,-ana I *adj & nm,f* German. II *nm* (*idioma*) German.
Alemania *n* Germany; **A. del Este/Oeste,** East/West Germany; **A. Occidental/ Oriental,** West/East Germany.
alentador,-a *adj* encouraging; **un panorama poco a.,** a rather bleak outlook.

alentar |1| *vtr fig* to encourage.

alergia *nf* allergy.

alérgico,-a *adj* allergic.

alero *nm* eaves *pl*.

alerón *nm Av* aileron.

alerta *nf & adj* alert; **estar en estado de a.**, to be (on the) alert.

alertar *vtr* to alert (**de**, to); **nos alertó del peligro**, he alerted us to the danger.

aleta *nf (de pez)* fin; *(de foca, de nadador)* flipper.

aletargado,-a *adj* lethargic.

aletargar |7| I *vtr* to make lethargic. II **aletargarse** *vr* to become lethargic.

aletear *vi* to flutter *o* flap its wings.

alevín *nm (pescado)* young fish; *fig (principiante)* beginner.

alevosía *nf (traición)* treachery; *(premeditación)* premeditation.

alevoso,-a *adj (persona)* treacherous; *(acto)* premeditated.

alfabético,-a *adj* alphabetic.

alfabetización *nf* teaching to read and write; **campaña de a.**, literacy campaign.

alfabeto *nm* alphabet.

alfalfa *nf* lucerne, alfalfa.

alfarería *nf* 1 *(arte)* pottery. 2 *(taller)* potter's workshop; *(tienda)* pottery shop.

alfarero,-a *nm,f* potter.

alféizar *nm* sill, windowsill.

alférez *nm* second lieutenant.

alfil *nm Ajedrez* bishop.

alfiler *nm* pin; *(broche)* pin, brooch; *(de corbata)* tiepin; *(para tender)* peg.

alfiletero *nm* pin box, pin case.

alfombra *nf* rug; *(moqueta)* carpet.

alfombrar *vtr* to carpet.

alfombrilla *nf* rug, mat.

alforja *nf (para caballos)* saddlebag; *(para hombro)* knapsack.

alga *nf* alga; *(marina)* seaweed.

algarabía *nf* hubbub, hullabaloo.

algarrobo *nm* carob tree.

algazara *nf* din, row.

álgebra *nf* algebra.

álgido,-a *adj* culminating, critical; **el punto a.**, the climax.

algo I *pron indef* 1 *(afirmativo)* something; *(interrogativo)* anything; **a. así**, something like that; **¿a. más?**, anything else?; **por a. será**, there must be a reason for it; *fam* **a. es a.**, it's better than nothing. 2 *(cantidad indeterminada)* some; **¿queda a. de pastel?**, is there any cake left? II *adv* *(un poco)* quite, somewhat; **se siente a. mejor**, she's feeling a bit better.

algodón *nm* cotton; **a. (hidrófilo)**, cotton wool; **a. de azúcar**, candy floss.

algodonero,-a I *nm,f* cotton grower. II *adj* cotton.

alguacil *nm* bailiff.

alguien *pron indef (afirmativo)* somebody, someone; *(interrogativo)* anybody, anyone.

algún *adj (delante de nombres masculinos)* → **alguno,-a**.

alguno,-a I *adj* 1 *(delante de nombre)* *(afirmativo)* some; *(interrogativo)* any; **algunos días**, some days; **algunas veces**, some times; **alguna que otra vez**, now and then; **¿has tomado alguna medicina?**, have you taken any medicine?; **¿le has visto alguna vez?**, have you ever seen him? 2 *(después de nombre)* not at all; **no vino persona alguna**, nobody came. II *pron indef* 1 someone, somebody; **a. dirá que ...**, someone might say that ...; **a. que otro**, some. 2 **algunos,-as**, some (people).

alhaja *nf* jewel.

alhelí *nm (pl alhelíes)* wallflower, stock.

aliado,-a I *adj* allied. II *nm,f* **los Aliados**, the Allies.

alianza *nf* 1 *(pacto)* alliance. 2 *(anillo)* wedding ring.

aliarse |29| *vr* to become allies, form an alliance.

alias *adv & nm inv* alias.

alicaído,-a *adj* 1 *fig (débil)* weak, feeble. 2 *fig (deprimido)* down, depressed.

alicatar *vtr* to tile.

alicates *nmpl* pliers.

aliciente *nm* 1 *(atractivo)* lure, charm. 2 *(incentivo)* incentive.

alienación *nf* alienation.

alienado,-a *adj* insane, deranged.

alienar *vtr* to alienate.

alienígena *adj & nmf* alien.

aliento *nm* 1 breath; **sin a.**, breathless. 2 *(ánimo)* encouragement.

aligerar I *vtr (acelerar)* to speed up; **a. el paso**, to quicken one's pace. II *vi fam* **¡aligera!**, hurry up!

alijo *nm* haul; **un a. de drogas**, a consignment of drugs.

alimaña *nf* vermin.

alimentación *nf (comida)* food; *(acción)* feeding; *Téc* supply.

alimentar I *vtr* 1 *(dar alimento)* to feed; *(ser nutritivo)* to be nutritious. 2 *fig (sentimientos)* to nourish. 3 *Inform* to feed; *Téc* to supply. II **alimentarse** *vr* **a. con** *o* **de**, to live on.

alimentario,-a *adj* food.

alimenticio,-a *adj* nutritious; **productos alimenticios**, food products, foodstuffs; **valor a.**, nutritional value.

alimento *nm* 1 *(comida)* food. 2 *fig* **tiene poco a.**, it is not very nourishing.

alimón *adv* **al a.**, together.

alineación *nf* 1 alignment. 2 *Dep (equipo)* line-up.

alineado,-a *adj* aligned, lined-up; **países no alineados**, non-aligned countries.

alineamiento *nm* alignment.

alinear I *vtr* to align, line up. II **alinearse** *vr* to line up.

aliñar *vtr* to season, flavour, *US* flavor; *(ensalada)* to dress.

aliño *nm* seasoning, dressing.

alioli *nm* garlic mayonnaise.

alisar *vtr*, **alisarse** *vr* to smooth.

alistar I *vtr Mil* to recruit, enlist. **II alistarse** *vr Mil* to enlist, enrol, *US* enroll.

aliviar |12| **I** *vtr* (*dolor*) to soothe, relieve; (*carga*) to lighten, make lighter. **II aliviarse** *vr* (*dolor*) to diminish, get better.

alivio *nm* relief.

aljibe *nm* cistern, tank.

allá *adv* 1 (*lugar alejado*) there, over there; **a. abajo/arriba,** down/up there; **¡a. voy!,** here I go!; **más a.,** further on; **más a. de,** beyond; **el más a.,** the beyond. 2 (*tiempo*) **a. por los años veinte,** back in the twenties. 3 **a. tú,** that's your problem.

allanamiento *nm Jur* **a. de morada,** unlawful entry.

allanar *vtr* 1 (*terreno*) to level, flatten; *fig* (*camino*) to smooth. 2 *Jur* to break into.

allegado,-a I *adj* close. **II** *nm,f* close friend.

allende *adv fml* beyond; **a. los mares,** overseas.

allí *adv* there, over there; **a. abajo/arriba,** down/up there; **de a.** para acá, back and forth; **por a.,** (*movimiento*) that way; (*posición*) over there.

alma *nf* soul; **no había ni un a.,** there was not a soul.

almacén *nm* 1 (*local*) warehouse; (*habitación*) storeroom. 2 *Com* (**grandes**) **almacenes,** department store *sing*.

almacenaje *nm* storage, warehousing.

almacenamiento *nm* storage, warehousing; *Inform* storage.

almacenar *vtr* to store.

almacenista *nmf* (*vendedor*) wholesaler; (*propietario*) warehouse owner.

almanaque *nm* calendar.

almeja *nf* clam; *vulg* cunt.

almena *nf* merlon.

almendra *nf* almond; **a. garapiñada,** sugared almond.

almendro *nm* almond tree.

almiar *nm* haystack.

almíbar *nm* syrup.

almidón *nm* starch.

almidonar *vtr* to starch.

alminar *nm* minaret.

almirante *nm* admiral.

almizcle *nm* musk.

almohada *nf* pillow; *fam* **consultarlo con la a.,** to sleep on it.

almohadilla *nf* (small) cushion.

almohadón *nm* large pillow, cushion.

almorrana *nf fam* pile.

almorzar |2| **I** *vi* to have lunch. **II** *vtr* to have for lunch.

almuerzo *nm* lunch.

alocado,-a *adj* thoughtless, rash.

alocución *nf* speech, address.

alojamiento *nm* accommodation; **dar a.,** to accommodate.

alojar I *vtr* to accommodate. **II alojarse** *vr* to stay.

aló *interj Am Tel* hello.

alondra *nf* lark; **a. común,** skylark.

alpaca *nf* alpaca.

alpargata *nf* canvas sandal, espadrille.

Alpes *npl* los **A.,** the Alps.

alpinismo *nm* mountaineering, climbing.

alpinista *nmf* mountaineer, climber.

alpino,-a *adj* Alpine; **esquí a.,** downhill skiing.

alquilar *vtr* to hire; (*pisos, casas*) to rent; **'se alquila',** 'to let'.

alquiler *nm* 1 (*de pisos, casas*) renting, letting; **a. de coches,** car hire; **de a.,** (*pisos, casas*) to let, rented; (*coche*) for hire; (*televisión*) for rent. 2 (*precio*) hire, rental; (*de pisos, casas*) rent.

alquimia *nf* alchemy.

alquitrán *nm* tar.

alrededor I *adv* (*lugar*) round, around; **mira a.,** look around; **a. de la mesa,** round the table; **a. de las dos,** around two o'clock; **a. de quince,** about fifteen; **II** *nmpl* **alrededores,** surrounding area *sing*; **en los alrededores de Murcia,** in the area round Murcia.

alta *nf* **dar de** *o* **el a.,** (*a un enfermo*) to discharge from hospital.

altanería *nf* arrogance.

altanero,-a *adj* arrogant.

altar *nm* altar.

altavoz *nm* loudspeaker.

alterable *adj* changeable.

alteración *nf* 1 (*cambio*) alteration. 2 (*alboroto*) quarrel, row; **a. del orden público,** disturbance of the peace. 3 (*excitación*) agitation.

alterar I *vtr* to alter, change; **a. el orden público,** to disturb the peace. **II alterarse** *vr* 1 (*cambiar*) to change. 2 (*inquietarse*) to be upset.

altercado *nm* quarrel, argument.

alternar I *vtr* to alternate. **II** *vi* (*relacionarse*) to meet people, socialize. **III alternarse** *vr* to alternate.

alternativa *nf* alternative.

alternativo,-a *adj* alternative.

alterno,-a *adj* alternate; **días alternos,** alternate days.

alteza *nf* Highness; **Su A. Real,** His *o* Her Royal Highness.

altibajos *nmpl fig* ups and downs.

altiplano *nm* high plateau.

altísimo,-a *nm* el **A.,** the Almighty.

altisonante *adj* grandiloquent.

altitud *nf* altitude.

altivez *nf* arrogance, haughtiness.

altivo,-a *adj* arrogant, haughty.

alto¹ *nm* 1 (*interrupción*) stop, break. 2 *Mil* halt; **dar el a.,** to order to halt; **un a. el fuego,** a cease-fire.

alto,-a² I *adj* 1 *(persona, árbol, edificio)* tall; *(montaña, techo, presión)* high; *(sonido)* loud; *fig (precio, tecnología)* high; *(tono)* high-pitched; **los pisos altos,** the top floors; **en lo a.,** at the top; **alta sociedad,** high society; **clase alta,** upper class; **en voz alta,** aloud, in a loud voice; **a altas horas de la noche,** late at night. II *adv* 1 high, high up. 2 *(sonar, hablar etc)* loud, loudly; **pon la radio más alta,** turn the radio up; **¡habla más a.!,** speak up. III *nm* 1 *(altura)* height; **¿cuánto tiene de a.?,** how tall/high is it?; *fig* **por todo lo a.,** in a grand way. 2 *(elevación)* hill. ◆**altamente** *adv* highly, extremely.

altoparlante *nm Am* loudspeaker.

altozano *nm* hillock, hill.

altramuz *nm* lupin.

altruista I *adj* altruistic. II *nmf* altruist.

altura *nf* 1 height; **de diez metros de a.,** ten metres high. 2 *(nivel)* level; **a la misma a.,** on the same level; *Geog* on the same latitude; **a la a. del cine,** by the cinema; *fig* **estar a la a. de las circunstancias,** to meet the challenge; *fig* **no está a su a.,** he does not measure up to him; *fig* **a estas alturas,** at this stage. 3 *Rel* **alturas,** heaven *sing*.

alubia *nf* bean.

alucinación *nf* hallucination.

alucinado,-a *adj arg* amazed.

alucinante *adj arg* brilliant, mind-blowing.

alucinar I *vtr* to hallucinate; *fig (encantar)* to fascinate. II *vi arg* to be amazed, be spaced out.

alucinógeno,-a I *adj* hallucinogenic. II *nm* hallucinogen.

alud *nm* avalanche.

aludido,-a *adj fig* **darse por a.,** to take it personally.

aludir *vi* to allude to, mention.

alumbrado,-a I *adj* lit. II *nm Elec* lighting; **a. público,** street lighting.

alumbrar I *vtr (iluminar)* to light, illuminate. II *vi (parir)* to give birth.

aluminio *nm* aluminium, *US* aluminum.

alumnado *nm (de colegio)* pupils *pl; Univ* student body.

alumno,-a *nm,f* 1 *(de colegio)* pupil; **a. externo,** day pupil; **a. interno,** boarder. 2 *Univ* student.

alusión *nf* allusion, mention.

aluvión *nm* downpour; *fig* **un a. de preguntas,** a barrage of questions.

alverja, alverjana *nf Am* pea.

alza *nf* 1 rise; **en a.,** rising; **jugar al a.,** *(bolsa)* to bull the market. 2 *Mil* sight.

alzado,-a I *adj* raised, lifted; **votación a mano alzada,** vote by a show of hands. II *nm Arquit* elevation.

alzamiento *nm (rebelión)* uprising.

alzar |4| I *vtr* to raise, lift; **a. el vuelo,** to take off; **a. los ojos/la vista,** to look up;

álzate el cuello, turn your collar up. II **alzarse** *vr* 1 *(levantarse)* to get up, rise. 2 *(rebelarse)* to rise, rebel. 3 **a. con la victoria,** to win, be victorious.

ama *nf (señora)* lady of the house; *(dueña)* owner; **a. de casa,** housewife; **a. de llaves,** housekeeper.

amabilidad *nf* kindness; *fml* **tenga la a. de esperar,** would you be so kind as to wait?

amable *adj* kind, nice; *fml* **¿sería usted tan a. de ayudarme?,** would you be so kind as to help me?

a.m. *adv* a.m.

amado,-a I *adj* loved, beloved. II *nm,f* sweetheart.

amaestrar *vtr* to train; *(domar)* to tame.

amagar |7| *vtr (amenazar)* to threaten; **amaga tormenta,** a storm is threatening.

amago *nm* 1 *(indicio)* first sign; **a. de infarto,** onset of a heart attack. 2 *(intento)* attempt. 3 *fig (amenaza)* threat.

amainar *vi (viento etc)* to drop, die down.

amalgama *nf* amalgam.

amalgamar *vtr* to amalgamate.

amamantar *vtr* to breast-feed; *Zool* to suckle.

amancay *nm Am* amaryllis.

amancebarse *vr* to cohabit.

amanecer |33| I *v impers* to dawn; **¿a qué hora amanece?,** when does it get light?; **amaneció lluvioso,** it was rainy at daybreak. II *vi* **amanecimos en Finlandia,** we were in Finland at daybreak; **amaneció muy enfermo,** he woke up feeling very ill. III *nm* dawn, daybreak; **al a.,** at dawn.

amanerado,-a *adj* mannered, affected.

amansar *vtr* 1 to tame. 2 *fig (apaciguar)* to tame, calm.

amante *nmf* lover; **a. del arte,** art lover.

amañar *vtr* to fix, fiddle; *(elecciones)* to rig.

amapola *nf* poppy.

amar I *vtr* to love. II **amarse** *vr* to love each other.

amaraje *nm Av* landing at sea.

amargado,-a I *adj (rencoroso)* embittered, bitter; *fam (agobiado)* pissed off; **estoy a. con los exámenes,** I'm pissed off with the exams. II *nm,f* bitter person.

amargar |7| I *vtr* to make bitter; *fig* to embitter, sour. II **amargarse** *vr fig* to become embittered *o* bitter; **no te amargues por eso,** don't let that make you bitter.

amargo,-a *adj* bitter.

amargor *nm,* **amargura** *nf* bitterness.

amarillento,-a *adj* yellowish.

amarillo,-a *adj & nm* yellow; **prensa amarilla,** gutter press.

amarilloso,-a *adj Am* yellowish.

amarra *nf* mooring rope; **soltar amarras,** to cast off, let go.

amarradero *nm* mooring.
amarrar *vtr Náut* to moor, tie up; *(atar)* to tie (up), bind.
amasar *vtr* 1 *Culin* to knead. 2 *fig (fortuna)* to amass.
amasijo *nm fam* hotchpotch, jumble.
amateur *adj & nmf* amateur.
amatista *nf* amethyst.
amazona *nf* 1 *(jinete)* horsewoman. 2 *(en mitología)* Amazon.
Amazonas *n* el A., the Amazon.
amazónico,-a *adj* Amazonian.
ambages *nmpl* hablar sin a., to go straight to the point.
ámbar *nm* amber.
Amberes *n* Antwerp.
ambición *nf* ambition.
ambicionar *vtr* to have as an ambition; ambiciona ser presidente, his ambition is to become president.
ambicioso,-a I *adj* ambitious. II *nm,f* ambitious person.
ambidextro,-a *nm,f* ambidextrous person.
ambientación *nf Cin Teat* setting.
ambientado,-a *adj (bar etc)* lively.
ambiental *adj* environmental.
ambientar I *vtr* 1 *(bar etc)* to liven up. 2 *Cin Teat* to set. II **ambientarse** *vr (adaptarse)* to get used to.
ambiente I *nm* environment; *fig (medio)* environment, milieu. II *adj* environmental; **temperatura a.**, room temperature.
ambigüedad *nf* ambiguity.
ambiguo,-a *adj* ambiguous.
ámbito *nm* field; empresa de a. nacional, nationwide company.
ambos,-as *adj pl fml* both; por a. lados, on both sides.
ambulancia *nf* ambulance.
ambulante *adj* travelling, *US* traveling, mobile; **biblioteca a.**, a mobile library.
ambulatorio *nm* surgery, clinic.
amedrentar *vtr* to frighten, scare.
amén[1] *nm* amen.
amén[2] *adv* a. de, in addition to.
amenaza *nf* threat.
amenazador,-a, amenazante *adj* threatening, menacing.
amenazar |4| *vtr* to threaten; a. de muerte a algn, to threaten to kill sb.
amenizar |4| *vtr* to liven up.
ameno,-a *adj* entertaining.
América *n* America; A. Central/del Norte/del Sur, Central/North/South America.
americana *nf (prenda)* jacket.
americano,-a *adj & nm,f* American.
amerindio,-a *adj & nm,f* Amerindian, American Indian.
amerizar |4| *vi* → amarar.
ametralladora *nf* machine gun.
ametrallar *vtr* to machine-gun.
amianto *nm* asbestos *sing*.

amigable *adj* friendly.
amígdala *nf* tonsil.
amigdalitis *nf* tonsillitis.
amigo,-a I *nm,f* friend; **hacerse a. de**, to make friends with; **hacerse amigos**, to become friends; **son muy amigos**, they are very good friends. II *adj (aficionado)* fond (de, of).
amilanar I *vtr* to frighten, scare. II **amilanarse** *vr* to be frightened.
aminorar *vtr* to reduce; a. el paso, to slow down.
amistad *nf* 1 friendship. 2 amistades, friends.
amistoso,-a *adj* friendly.
amnesia *nf* amnesia.
amnistía *nf* amnesty.
amo *nm* 1 *(dueño)* owner. 2 *(señor)* master.
amodorrarse *vr* to become sleepy *o* drowsy.
amoldar I *vtr* to adapt, adjust. II **amoldarse** *vr* to adapt oneself.
amonestación *nf* 1 rebuke, reprimand; *Dep* warning. 2 *Rel* amonestaciones, banns.
amonestar *vtr* 1 *(advertir)* to rebuke, reprimand; *Dep* to warn. 2 *Rel* to publish the banns of.
amoníaco, amoniaco *nm* ammonia.
amontonar I *vtr* to pile up, heap up. II **amontonarse** *vr* to pile up, heap up; *(gente)* to crowd together.
amor *nm* love; hacer el a., to make love; a. propio, self-esteem; ¡por el a. de Dios!, for God's sake!
amoral *adj* amoral.
amoratado,-a *adj (de frío)* blue with cold; *(de un golpe)* black and blue.
amordazar |4| *vtr (perro)* to muzzle; *(persona)* to gag.
amorfo,-a *adj* amorphous.
amorío *nm* love affair, flirtation.
amoroso,-a *adj* loving, affectionate.
amortajar *vtr* to shroud, wrap in a shroud.
amortiguador *nm Aut* shock absorber.
amortiguar |22| *vtr (golpe)* to cushion; *(ruido)* to muffle; *(luz)* to subdue.
amortización *nf* payment.
amortizar |4| *vtr* to pay off.
amotinado,-a *nm,f* rioter; *Mil* mutineer.
amotinamiento *nm* riot, rioting; *Mil* mutiny.
amotinar I *vtr* to incite to riot; *Mil* to incite to mutiny. 2 *Rel* to publish the banns of. II **amotinarse** *vr* to rise up; *Mil* to mutiny.
amparar I *vtr* to protect. II **ampararse** *vr* to seek refuge.
amparo *nm* protection, shelter; al a. de la ley, under the protection of the law.
amperio *nm* ampère, amp.
ampliación *nf* enlargement; *(de plazo, casa)* extension.
ampliar |29| *vtr* to enlarge; *(casa, plazo)*

to extend.

amplificador *nm* amplifier.

amplificar |1| *vtr* to amplify.

amplio,-a *adj* large, roomy; *(ancho)* wide, broad; **en el sentido más a. de la palabra**, in the broadest sense of the word.

amplitud *nf* 1 spaciousness; **a. de miras**, broad-mindedness. 2 *(de espacio)* room, space. 3 *Fis* amplitude.

ampolla *nf* 1 *Med* blister; *fig* **levantar ampollas**, to raise people's hackles. 2 *(de medicina)* ampoule.

ampuloso,-a *adj* pompous, bombastic.

amputar *vtr Med* to amputate; *fig* to cut out.

amueblar *vtr* to furnish.

amuermar *vtr fam* 1 *(atontar)* to make feel dopey *o* groggy. 2 *(aburrir)* to bore.

amuleto *nm* amulet; **a. de la suerte**, lucky charm.

amurallar *vtr* to wall, fortify.

anacronismo *nm* anachronism.

ánade *nm* duck; **á. real**, mallard.

anales *nmpl* annals.

analfabetismo *nm* illiteracy.

analfabeto,-a *nm,f* illiterate.

analgésico,-a *adj & nm* analgesic.

análisis *nm inv* analysis; **a. de sangre**, blood test.

analista *nmf* analyst.

analizar |4| *vtr* to analyze.

analogía *nf* analogy.

analógico,-a *adj* analog.

análogo,-a *adj* analogous, similar.

ananá *nm (pl ananaes)*, **ananás** *nm (pl ananases)* pineapple.

anaquel *nm* shelf.

anaranjado,-a *adj & nm* orange.

anarquía *nf* anarchy.

anarquismo *nm* anarchism.

anarquista *adj & nmf* anarchist.

anatomía *nf* anatomy.

anatómico,-a *adj* anatomical.

anca *nf* haunch; **ancas de rana**, frogs' legs.

ancestral *adj* ancestral.

ancho,-a I *adj* wide, broad; **a lo a.**, breadthwise; **te está muy a.**, it's too big for you. II *nm* 1 *(anchura)* width, breadth; **dos metros de a.**, two metres wide; **¿qué a. tiene?**, how wide is it? 2 *Cost* width. III *nfpl fam* **a mis o tus anchas**, at ease, comfortable.

anchoa *nf* anchovy.

anchura *nf* width, breadth.

anciano,-a I *adj* very old. II *nm,f* old person; **los ancianos**, old people.

ancla *nf* anchor.

anclar *vtr & vi* to anchor.

andadas *nfpl* **volver a las a.**, to go back to one's old tricks.

andaderas *nfpl* baby-walker *sing.*

andadura *nf* walking.

Andalucía *n* Andalusia.

andaluz,-a *adj & nm,f* Andalusian.

andamiaje, **andamio** *nm* scaffolding.

andanza *nf* adventure, happening.

andar *nm*, **andares** *nmpl* walk *sing*, gait *sing.*

andar |8| I *vi* 1 to walk. 2 *(coche etc)* to move; **este coche anda despacio**, this car goes very slowly. 3 *(funcionar)* to work; **esto no anda**, this doesn't work. 4 *fam* **anda por los cuarenta**, he's about forty; **anda siempre diciendo que ...**, he's always saying that ...; **¿cómo andamos de tiempo?**, how are we off for time?; **tu bolso debe a. por ahí**, your bag must be over there somewhere. II *vtr (recorrer)* to walk.

andariego,-a *adj* fond of walking.

andén *nm* platform.

Andes *npl* Andes.

andinismo *nm Am* mountaineering.

andino,-a *adj & nm,f* Andean.

andrajo *nm* rag, tatter.

andrajoso,-a *adj* ragged, tattered.

androide *nm* android.

andurriales *nmpl fam* out-of-the way place *sing.*

anécdota *nf* anecdote.

anecdótico,-a *adj* anecdotal.

anegar *vtr*, **anegarse** *vr* |7| to flood.

anejo,-a I *adj* attached, joined (**a**, to). II *nm* appendix.

anemia *nf* anaemia, *US* anemia.

anestesia *nf* anaesthesia, *US* anesthesia.

anestésico,-a *adj & nm* anaesthetic, *US* anesthetic.

anexar *vtr* to annex.

anexión *nf* annexation.

anexionar *vtr* to annex.

anexo,-a I *adj* attached, joined (**a**, to). II *nm* appendix.

anfetamina *nf* amphetamine.

anfibio,-a I *adj* amphibious. II *nm* amphibian.

anfiteatro *nm* 1 amphitheatre, *US* amphitheater. 2 *Cin Teat* gallery.

anfitrión,-ona I *nm* host. II *nf* hostess.

ángel *nm* 1 angel; **á. de la guarda**, guardian angel. 2 *Am (micrófono)* hand microphone.

angelical, **angélico,-a** *adj* angelic.

angina *nf* angina; **tener anginas**, to have tonsilitis; *Med* **a. de pecho**, angina pectoris.

anglófono,-a I *adj* English speaking. II *nm,f* English speaker.

anglosajón,-ona *adj & nm,f* Anglo-Saxon.

angosto,-a *adj fml* narrow.

anguila *nf* eel; **a. de mar**, conger eel.

angula *nf* elver.

angular *adj* angular; *Fot* **(objetivo) gran a.**, wide-angle lens; **piedra a.**, cornerstone.

ángulo *nm* angle; *(rincón)* corner.

angustia *nf* anguish.

angustiar |12| *vtr* to distress.

angustioso,-a *adj* distressing.

anhelar *vtr* to long for, yearn for.

anhelo *nm* longing, yearning.

anhídrido *nm* **a. carbónico**, carbon dioxide.

anidar *vi* to nest.

anilla *nf* ring; **carpeta de anillas**, ring-binder.

anillo *nm* ring; **a. de boda**, wedding ring.

ánima *nf* soul.

animación *nf* (*diversión*) entertainment.

animado,-a *adj* (*fiesta etc*) lively.

animador,-a *nm,f* 1 entertainer; *TV* presenter; **a. cultural**, cultural organiser. 2 *Dep* cheerleader.

animadversión *nf* ill feeling, animosity.

animal I *nm* animal; *fig* (*basto*) brute; (*necio*) dunce. **II** *adj* animal.

animar I *vtr* 1 (*alentar*) to encourage. 2 (*alegrar*) (*persona*) to cheer up; (*fiesta, bar*) to liven up, brighten up. **II animarse** *vr* 1 (*persona*) to cheer up; (*fiesta, reunión*) to brighten up. 2 ¿**te animas a venir?**, do you fancy coming along?

anímico,-a *adj* **estado a.**, frame o state of mind.

ánimo *nm* 1 (*espíritu*) spirit; **estado de á.**, frame o state of mind. 2 **con á. de**, (*intención*) with the intention of. 3 (*valor, coraje*) courage; **dar ánimos a**, to encourage; **¡a.!**, cheer up!.

animosidad *nf* animosity.

animoso,-a *adj* cheerful.

aniñado,-a *adj* childlike; *pey* childish.

aniquilación *nf* annihilation.

aniquilar *vtr* to annihilate.

anís *nm* 1 (*bebida*) anisette. 2 (*grano*) aniseed.

anisete *nm* anisette.

aniversario *nm* anniversary.

ano *nm* anus.

anoche *adv* last night; (*por la tarde*) yesterday evening; **antes de a.**, the night before last.

anochecer |33| **I** *v impers* to get dark; **cuando anochece**, at nightfall, at dusk. **II** *vi* to be somewhere at dusk; **anochecimos en Cuenca**, we were in Cuenca at dusk. **III** *nm* nightfall, dusk.

anodino,-a *adj* (*insustancial*) insubstantial; (*soso*) insipid, dull.

anomalía *nf* anomaly.

anómalo,-a *adj* anomalous.

anonadado,-a *adj* **me quedé/dejó a.**, I was astonished.

anonimato *nm* anonimity; **permanecer en el a.**, to remain anonymous o nameless.

anónimo,-a I *adj* 1 (*desconocido*) anonymous. 2 *Com* **sociedad anónima**, public liability company, *US* corporation. **II** *nm* (*carta*) anonymous letter.

anorak *nm* (*pl* **anoraks**) anorak.

anorexia *nf* anorexia.

anormal I *adj* 1 abnormal. 2 (*inhabitual*) unusual; **una situación a.**, an irregular situation. 3 *Med* subnormal. **II** *nmf Med* subnormal person.

anotación *nf* 1 annotation. 2 (*apunte*) note.

anotar *vtr* 1 to annotate. 2 (*apuntar*) to take down, make a note of.

anquilosado,-a *adj fig* fossilized; **a. en el pasado**, locked in the past.

anquilosarse *vr fig* to stagnate.

ansia *nf* 1 (*deseo*) longing, yearning. 2 (*ansiedad*) anxiety. 3 *Med* sick feeling.

ansiar |29| *vtr* to long for, yearn for.

ansiedad *nf* anxiety; **con a.**, anxiously.

ansioso,-a *adj* 1 (*deseoso*) eager (**por**, for). 2 (*avaricioso*) greedy.

antagónico,-a *adj* antagonistic.

antagonismo *nm* antagonism.

antagonista I *adj* antagonistic. **II** *nmf* antagonist.

antaño *adv* in the past, formerly.

antártico,-a I *adj* Antarctic. **II** *nm* **el A.**, the Antarctic.

Antártida *n* Antarctica.

ante[1] *nm* 1 *Zool* elk, moose. 2 (*piel*) suede.

ante[2] *prep* 1 before, in the presence of; *Jur* **a. notario**, in the presence of a notary; **a. todo**, most of all. 2 (*en vista de*) faced with, in view of; **a. la crisis energética**, faced with the energy crisis.

anteanoche *adv* the night before last.

anteayer *adv* the day before yesterday.

antecedente I *adj* previous. **II** *nm* antecedent. **III** *nmpl* 1 **antecedentes**, (*historial*) record *sing*; *Jur* **antecedentes penales**, criminal record *sing*. 2 *fig* **poner en antecedentes**, to put in the picture.

anteceder *vtr* to precede, go before.

antecesor,-a *nm,f* 1 (*en un cargo*) predecessor. 2 (*antepasado*) ancestor.

antedicho,-a *adj* abovementioned.

antelación *nf* notice; **con poca a.**, at short notice; **con un mes de a.**, a month beforehand, with a month's notice.

antemano *adv* **de a.**, beforehand, in advance.

antena *nf* 1 *Rad TV* aerial; **a. parabólica**, dish aerial; **en a.**, on the air. 2 *Zool* antenna, feeler.

anteojo *nm* 1 telescope. 2 **anteojos**, (*binoculares*) binoculars, field glasses; *Am* (*gafas*) glasses, spectacles.

antepasado,-a *nm,f* ancestor.

antepecho *nm* (*de ventana*) sill; (*pretil*) parapet, guardrail.

antepenúltimo,-a *adj* antepenultimate; **el capítulo a.**, the last chapter but two.

anteponer |19| (*pp* **antepuesto**) *vtr fig* to give preference to.

anteproyecto *nm* preliminary plan, draft;

Pol a. de ley, draft bill.
antepuesto,-a *pp* → **anteponer.**
antepuse *pt indef* → **anteponer.**
anterior *adj* 1 previous; **el día a.,** the day before. 2 (*delantero*) front; **parte a.,** front part. ◆**anteriormente** *adv* previously, before.
anterioridad *nf* **con a.,** before; **con a. a,** prior to, before.
antes *adv* 1 (*tiempo*) before; **a. de las tres,** before three o'clock; **mucho a.,** long before; **la noche a.,** the night before; **cuanto a.,** as soon as possible. 2 (*antaño*) in the past; **a. llovía más,** it used to rain more in the past. 3 (*lugar*) before; **a. del semáforo,** before the traffic lights. 4 **a. prefiero hacerlo yo,** I'd rather do it myself; **a. (bien),** on the contrary.
antesala *nf* antechamber, anteroom; *fig* **en la a. de,** on the eve of.
anti- *pref* anti-.
antiadherente *adj* nonstick.
antiaéreo,-a *adj* anti-aircraft.
antibiótico,-a *adj & nm* antibiotic.
anticaspa *adj* anti-dandruff.
anticiclón *nm* anticyclone, high pressure area.
anticipación *nf* bringing forward; **con a.,** in advance.
anticipado,-a *adj* brought forward; **elecciones anticipadas,** early elections; **gracias anticipadas,** thanks in advance; *Com* **por a.,** in advance. ◆**anticipadamente** *adv* in advance.
anticipar I *vtr* (*acontecimiento*) to bring forward; (*dinero*) to pay in advance; **no anticipemos acontecimientos,** we'll cross that bridge when we come to it. II **anticiparse** *vr* 1 (*adelantarse*) to beat to it; **iba a decírtelo, pero él se me anticipó,** I was going to tell you, but he beat me to it. 2 (*llegar pronto*) to arrive early; *fig* **a. a su tiempo,** to be ahead of one's time.
anticipo *nm* (*adelanto*) advance; **pedir un a.,** to ask for an advance (on one's wages).
anticonceptivo,-a *adj & nm* contraceptive.
anticongelante *adj & nm* (*de radiador*) antifreeze; (*de parabrisas*) de-icer.
anticonstitucional *adj* unconstitutional.
anticuado,-a *adj* antiquated.
anticuario,-a *nm,f* antique dealer.
anticuerpo *nm* antibody.
antídoto *nm* antidote.
antier *adv* the day before yesterday.
antiestético,-a *adj* ugly, unsightly.
antifaz *nm* mask.
antigás *adj* **careta/mascarilla a.,** gas mask.
antigualla *nf* old-fashioned thing.
antigüedad *nf* 1 (*período histórico*) antiquity; **en la a.,** in olden days, in for-

mer times. 2 (*en cargo*) seniority. 3 **tienda de antigüedades,** antique shop.
antiguo,-a *adj* 1 old, ancient. 2 (*pasado de moda*) old-fashioned. 3 (*en cargo*) senior. 4 (*anterior*) former.
antihigiénico,-a *adj* unhygienic, unhealthy.
antihistamínico,-a *adj & nm* antihistamine.
Antillas *npl* **las A.,** the West Indies, the Antilles.
antinatural *adj* unnatural, contrary to nature.
antiniebla *adj inv* **luces a.,** foglamps, *US* foglights.
antipatía *nf* antipathy, dislike; **tener a. a,** to dislike.
antipático,-a *adj* unpleasant; **Pedro me es a.,** I don't like Pedro.
antípodas *npl* **las A.,** the Antipodes.
antiquísimo,-a (*superl de* **antiguo**) *adj* very old, ancient.
antirrobo I *adj inv* antitheft; **alarma a.,** burglar alarm; (*para coche*) car alarm. II *nm* (*para coche*) car alarm; (*para casa*) burglar alarm.
antisemita I *adj* anti-Semitic. II *nmf* anti-Semite.
antiséptico,-a *adj & nm* antiseptic.
antítesis *nf inv* antithesis.
antojadizo,-a *adj* capricious, unpredictable.
antojarse *vr* 1 **cuando se me antoja,** when I feel like it; **se le antojó un helado,** he fancied an ice-cream. 2 (*suponer*) **se me antoja que no lo sabe,** I have the feeling that he doesn't know.
antojo *nm* 1 (*capricho*) whim, caprice; (*de embarazada*) craving; **a su a.,** in one's own way, as one pleases. 2 (*en la piel*) birthmark.
antología *nf* anthology.
antonomasia *nf* **por a.,** par excellence.
antorcha *nf* torch.
antro *nm* dump, hole; *fig* **a. de perdición,** den of vice.
antropología *nf* anthropology.
antropólogo,-a *nm,f* anthropologist.
anual *adj* annual; **ingresos anuales,** yearly income.
anualidad *nf* annual payment, annuity.
anuario *nm* yearbook.
anudar *vtr* 1 (*atar*) to knot, tie. 2 *fig* (*unir*) to join, bring together.
anulación *nf* cancellation; (*de matrimonio*) annulment; (*de ley*) repeal.
anular[1] *nm* ring finger.
anular[2] *vtr* 1 *Com* (*pedido*) to cancel; *Dep* (*gol*) to disallow; (*matrimonio*) to annul; *Jur* (*ley*) to repeal. 2 *Inform* to delete.
anunciador,-a *adj* **empresa anunciadora,** advertising company.
anunciante *nm* advertiser.
anunciar |12| I *vtr* 1 (*producto etc*) to

advertise. 2 (*avisar*) to announce. II
anunciarse *vr* to advertise oneself; **a. en
un periódico**, to put an advert in a newspaper.
anuncio *nm* 1 (*comercial*) advertisment,
advert, ad. 2 (*aviso*) announcement. 3
(*cartel*) notice, poster.
anzuelo *nm* (fish) hook.
añadidura *nf* addition; **por a.**, besides, on
top of everything else.
añadir *vtr* to add (**a**, to).
añejo,-a *adj* 1 (*vino, queso*) mature. 2 (*estropeado*) stale.
añicos *nmpl* smithereens; **hacer a.**, to
smash to smithereens.
añil I *adj* indigo, blue. II *nm* 1 *Bot* indigo
plant. 2 (*color*) indigo.
año *nm* 1 year; **el a. pasado**, last year; **el
a. que viene**, next year; **hace años**, a
long time ago, years ago; **los años noventa**, the nineties; **todo el a.**, all the
year (round); **a. luz**, light year. 2
¿cuántos años tienes?, how old are
you?; **tiene seis años**, he's six years old;
entrado en años, getting on.
añoranza *nf* longing, yearning.
añorar *vtr* (*pasado*) to long for, yearn for;
(*país*) to feel homesick for, miss.
apabullar *vtr* to bewilder.
apacentar |1| *vtr* to put out to pasture,
graze.
apacible *adj* mild, calm.
apaciguar |22| I *vtr* (*calmar*) to pacify,
appease. II **apaciguarse** *vr* (*persona*) to
calm down; (*tormenta*) to abate.
apadrinar *vtr* 1 (*en bautizo*) to act as
godfather to; (*en boda*) to be best man
for. 2 (*artista*) to sponsor.
apagado,-a *adj* 1 (*luz, cigarro*) out. 2 (*color*) dull; (*voz*) sad; (*mirada*) expression-
less, lifeless; (*carácter, persona*) spiritless.
apagar |7| *vtr* (*fuego*) to put out; (*luz, tele
etc*) to turn off, switch off; (*color*) to soften; (*sed*) to quench.
apagón *nm* power cut, blackout.
apaisado,-a *adj* 1 oblong. 2 (*papel*) landscape.
apalabrar *vtr* (*concertar*) to make a verbal
agreement on.
apalancar |1| I *vtr* to lever up. II **apa-
lancarse** *vr* *arg* to ensconce oneself, settle
down.
apalear[1] *vtr* to beat, thrash.
apalear[2] *vtr* *Agr* (*grano*) to winnow.
apañar I *vtr* to mend, fix. II **apañarse** *vr*
fam **apañárselas**, to manage.
apaño *nm* mend, repair.
aparador *nm* (*mueble*) sideboard; (*de
tienda*) shop window.
aparato *nm* 1 (piece of) apparatus; (*dispositivo*) device; (*instrumento*) instrument; **a.
de radio/televisión**, radio/television set;
a. digestivo, digestive system; **a. eléctrico**, thunder and lightning. 2 *Tel* **¿quién**

está al a.?, who's speaking? 3 (*ostentación*) display.
aparatoso,-a *adj* 1 (*pomposo*) ostentatious,
showy. 2 (*espectacular*) spectacular. 3
(*grande*) bulky.
aparcamiento *nm* (*en la calle*) parking
place; (*parking*) car park, *US* parking lot.
aparcar |1| *vtr* to park.
aparcería *nf* *Agr* sharecropping.
apareamiento *nm* 1 (*de cosas*) pairing off.
2 (*de animales*) mating.
aparear *vtr*, **aparearse** *vr* to mate.
aparecer |33| I *vi* 1 to appear; **no apare-
ce en mi lista**, it's not on my list. 2 to
turn up, show up; **¿apareció el dinero?**,
did the money turn up?; **no apareció nadie**, nobody turned up. II **aparecerse** *vr*
to appear.
aparejado,-a *adj* **llevar o traer a.**, to entail.
aparejador,-a *nm,f* quantity surveyor.
aparejar *vtr* 1 (*caballo*) to harness. 2
(*emparejar*) to pair off.
aparejo *nm* 1 (*equipo*) equipment. 2 (*de
caballo*) harness.
aparentar I *vtr* 1 (*fingir*) to affect. 2 (*tener
aspecto*) to look; **no aparenta esa edad**,
she doesn't look that age. II *vi* to show
off.
aparente *adj* 1 apparent; **sin motivo a.**,
for no apparent reason. 2 *fam* (*conveniente*) suitable.
aparición *nf* 1 appearance. 2 (*visión*)
apparition.
apariencia *nf* appearance; **en a.**,
apparently; *fig* **guardar las apariencias**,
to keep up appearances.
apartado,-a I *adj* (*lugar*) remote, isolated;
mantente a. de él, keep away from him.
II *nm* 1 (*párrafo*) section, paragraph. 2 **a.
de correos**, Post Office Box.
apartamento *nm* (small) flat, apartment.
apartar I *vtr* 1 (*alejar*) to move away, remove; **a. la mirada**, to look away. 2
(*guardar*) to put aside. II *vi* **¡aparta!**,
move out of the way! III **apartarse** *vr*
(*alejarse*) to move over, move away;
apártate de en medio, move out of the
way.
aparte I *adv* 1 aside; **ponlo a.**, put it
aside; **modestia/bromas a.**, modesty/
joking apart. 2 **eso hay que pagarlo a.**,
(*separadamente*) you have to pay for that
separately. 3 **a. de eso**, (*además*) besides
that; (*excepto*) apart from that. 4 **eso es
caso a.**, that's completely different. II
nm 1 *Teat* aside. 2 *Ling* **punto y a.**, full
stop, new paragraph.
apasionado,-a I *adj* passionate; **a. de la
música**, very fond of music. II *nm,f* enthusiast.
apasionante *adj* exciting.
apasionar *vtr* to excite, thrill; **le apasiona
el jazz**, he is mad about jazz.

apatía *nf* apathy.

apático,-a I *adj* apathetic. II *nm,f* apathetic person.

apátrida I *adj* stateless. II *nmf* stateless person.

apdo. *abr de* apartado, Post Office Box, P.O.B.

apeadero *nm* halt.

apearse *vi* (de un autobús, tren) to get off, alight; (de un coche) to get out; **se apeó en Jerez,** he got off in Jerez.

apechugar |7| *vi* **a. con,** to shoulder.

apedrear *vtr* to throw stones at.

apegado *adj* devoted, attached (a, to).

apegarse |7| *vr* to become devoted *o* attached (a, to).

apego *nm* love, affection; **tener a. a,** to be attached to.

apelación *nf* appeal; **interponer a.,** to lodge and appeal.

apelar *vi* 1 *Jur* to appeal. 2 (recurrir) to resort (a, to).

apellidarse *vr* to have as a surname, be called.

apellido *nm* surname; **a. de soltera,** maiden name.

apelmazado,-a *adj* stodgy.

apelotonar I *vtr* to pile up, put into a pile. II **apelotonarse** *vr* (gente) to crowd together.

apenar I *vtr* to grieve. II **apenarse** *vr* 1 to be grieved. 2 *Am* (avergonzarse) to be ashamed.

apenas *adv* 1 (casi no) hardly, scarcely; **a. come,** he hardly eats anything; **a. (si) hay nieve,** there is hardly any snow. 2 (tan pronto como) scarcely; **a. llegó, sonó el teléfono,** no sooner had he arrived than the phone rang.

apéndice *nm* appendix.

apendicitis *nf* appendicitis.

apercibir I *vtr* to warn. II **apercibirse** *vr* to notice (de, -).

aperitivo *nm* (bebida) apéritif; (comida) appetizer.

apero *nm* (usu pl) equipment, tools pl; **aperos de labranza,** farming implements.

apertura *nf* 1 (comienzo) opening. 2 *Pol* liberalization.

apestar I *vi* to stink (a, of). II *vtr* to infect with the plague.

apetecer |33| *vi* to appeal to; **¿qué te apetece para cenar?,** what would you like for supper?; **¿te apetece ir al cine?,** do you fancy going to the cinema?

apetecible *adj* tempting, inviting.

apetito *nm* appetite; **tengo mucho a.,** I'm really hungry.

apetitoso,-a *adj* appetizing, tempting; (comida) delicious, tasty.

apiadarse *vr* to take pity (de, on).

ápice *nm* 1 (punta) apex. 2 *fig* **ni un á.,** not a bit.

apicultura *nf* beekeeping, apiculture.

apilar *vtr,* **apilarse** *vr* to pile up, heap up.

apiñarse *vr* to crowd together.

apio *nm* celery.

apisonadora *nf* roadroller, steamroller.

apisonar *vtr* to roll.

aplacar |1| I *vtr* to placate, calm. II **aplacarse** *vr* to calm down.

aplanar *vtr* to level.

aplastante *adj* crushing; *Pol* **victoria a.,** landslide victory.

aplastar *vtr* 1 to flatten, squash. 2 *fig* (vencer) to crush.

aplatanarse *vr* *fam* to become lethargic.

aplaudir *vtr* 1 to clap, applaud. 2 *fig* to applaud.

aplauso *nm* applause.

aplazamiento *nm* postponement, adjournment; (de un pago) deferment.

aplazar |4| *vtr* to postpone, adjourn; *Fin* (pago) to defer.

aplicación *nf* application.

aplicado,-a *adj* hard-working.

aplicar |1| I *vtr* to apply. II **aplicarse** *vr* 1 (esforzarse) to apply oneself, work hard. 2 (norma, ley) to apply, be applicable.

aplique *nm* wall light, wall lamp.

aplomo *nm* aplomb.

apocado,-a *adj* shy, timid.

apocamiento *nm* timidity, lack of self-confidence.

apocarse |1| *vr* to become frightened.

apodar *vtr* to nickname.

apoderado,-a *nm,f* 1 agent, representative. 2 (de torero, deportista) manager.

apoderarse *vr* to take possession (de, of), seize; *fig* **el miedo se apoderó de ella,** she was seized by fear.

apodo *nm* nickname.

apogeo *nm* height; **estar en pleno a.,** (fama etc) to be at its height.

apolillarse *vr* to get moth-eaten.

apolítico,-a *adj* apolitical.

apología *nf* apology, defence, *US* defense.

apoltronarse *vr* *fam* to vegetate.

apoplejía *nf* apoplexy.

apoquinar *vtr* *fam* to cough up, fork out.

aporrear *vtr* to beat, hit, thrash; (puerta) to bang; *fam* **a. el piano,** to bang (away) on the piano.

aportación *nf* contribution.

aportar I *vtr* to contribute. II *vi* *Náut* to reach port.

aposentarse *vr* to stay, lodge.

aposento *nm* room.

aposta *adv* on purpose, intentionally.

apostar¹ |2| I *vtr* to bet; **te apuesto una cena a que no viene,** I bet you a dinner that he won't come. II *vi* to bet (por, on); **a. a los caballos,** to bet on horses; **apuesto a que sí viene,** I bet she will come. III **apostarse** *vr* to bet; **me apuesto lo que quieras,** I bet you anything.

apostar² *vtr (situar)* to post, station.

apostilla *nf* note.

apóstol *nm* apostle.

apóstrofo *nm* apostrophe.

apostura *nf* good bearing.

apoteósico,-a *adj* enormous, tremendous.

apoyacabezas *nm Aut* headrest.

apoyar I *vtr* **1** to lean. **2** *(causa)* to support. **II apoyarse** *vr* **1 a. en,** to lean on; **apóyate en mi brazo,** take my arm. **2 a. en,** *(opinión)* to be based on, rest on.

apoyo *nm* support.

apreciable *adj* appreciable, noticeable.

apreciación *nf* appreciation.

apreciar |12| **I** *vtr* **1** to appreciate. **2** *(percibir)* to notice, see. **II apreciarse** *vr* to be noticeable.

aprecio *nm* regard, esteem; **tener a. a algn,** to be fond of sb.

aprehender *vtr (alijo, botín)* to apprehend, seize.

aprehensión *nf* seizure.

apremiante *adj* urgent, pressing.

apremiar |12| *vtr* to be urgent; **el tiempo apremia,** time is at a premium.

aprender *vtr* to learn; **así aprenderás,** that'll teach you.

aprendiz,-a *nm,f* apprentice, trainee.

aprendizaje *nm* **1** learning. **2** *(instrucción)* apprenticeship, traineeship.

aprensión *nf* apprehension.

aprensivo,-a *adj* apprehensive.

apresar *vtr* to seize, capture.

aprestar I *vtr* to prepare, get ready. **II aprestarse** *vr* to get ready.

apresurado,-a *adj (persona)* in a hurry; *(cosa)* hurried.

apresuramiento *nm* haste, hurry.

apresurar I *vtr (paso etc)* to speed up. **II apresurarse** *vr* to hurry up.

apretado,-a *adj* **1** *(ropa, cordón)* tight; **íbamos todos apretados en el coche,** we were all squashed together in the car. **2** *(día, agenda)* busy.

apretar |11| **I** *vtr (botón)* to press; *(nudo, tornillo)* to tighten; **a. el gatillo,** to pull the trigger; **me aprietan las botas,** these boots are too tight for me. **II** *vi* **apretaba el calor,** it was really hot. **III apretarse** *vr* to squeeze together, cram together; *fig* **a. el cinturón,** to tighten one's belt.

apretón *nm* squeeze; **a. de manos,** handshake.

apretujar I *vtr* to squeeze, crush. **II apretujarse** *vr* to squeeze together, cram together.

aprieto *nm* tight spot, fix, jam; **poner a algn en un a.,** to put sb in an awkward position.

aprisa *adv* quickly.

aprisionar *vtr (atrapar)* to trap.

aprobación *nf* approval.

aprobado *nm Educ* pass.

aprobar |2| *vtr* **1** *(autorizar)* to approve. **2** *(estar de acuerdo con)* to approve of. **3** *Educ* to pass. **4** *Pol (ley)* to pass.

apropiado,-a *adj* suitable, appropriate.

apropiarse |12| *vr* to appropriate.

aprovechado,-a *adj* **1** mal a., *(recurso, tiempo)* wasted; **bien a.,** put to good use. **2** *(espacio)* well-planned. **3** *pey (egoísta)* self-seeking.

aprovechamiento *nm* use.

aprovechar I *vtr* **1** to make good use of, make the most of; **aprovechamos bien la tarde,** we've done lots of things this afternoon. **2** *(recursos etc)* to take advantage of; **a. la ocasión,** to seize the opportunity. **II** *vi* **¡que aproveche!,** enjoy your meal!, bon appétit!. **III aprovecharse** *vr* to use to one's advantage, take advantage; **a. de algn,** to take advantage of sb; **a. de algo,** to make the most of sth.

aprovisionar *vtr* to supply, provide; **a. las tropas,** to give supplies to the troops.

aproximación *nf* **1** approximation. **2** *(en lotería)* consolation prize.

aproximado,-a *adj* approximate; **un cálculo a.,** a rough estimate. ◆**aproximadamente** approximately, roughly.

aproximar I *vtr* to bring o put nearer. **II aproximarse** *vr* to approach **(a, -).**

aproximativo,-a *adj* approximate, rough.

aptitud *nf* aptitude; **prueba de a.,** aptitude test.

apto,-a *adj* **1** *(apropiado)* suitable, appropriate; *Cin* **a. para todos los públicos,** U-certificate film, *US* rated 'G'. **2** *(capacitado)* capable, able. **3** *Educ* passed.

apuesta *nf* bet, wager.

apuesto,-a *adj* good-looking; *(hombre)* handsome.

apuntador,-a *nm,f Teat* prompter.

apuntalar *vtr* to prop up, shore up, underpin.

apuntar I *vtr* **1** *(con arma)* to aim. **2** *(señalar)* to point out. **3** *(anotar)* to note down, make a note of. **4** *(indicar)* to indicate, suggest; **todo parece a. a ...,** everything seems to point to .... **II** *vi* **cuando apunta el día,** when day breaks. **III apuntarse** *vr* **1** *(en una lista)* to put one's name down. **2** *fam* **¿te apuntas?,** are you game?; **me apunto,** count me in.

apunte *nm (usu pl)* note; **tomar apuntes,** to take notes.

apuñalar *vtr* to stab.

apurado,-a I *adj* **1** *(necesitado)* in need; **a. de dinero,** hard up for money; **a. de tiempo,** in a hurry. **2** *(preocupado)* worried; *(avergonzado)* embarrassed. **3** *(situación)* awkward, difficult. **4** *(afeitado)* close. **II** *nm (afeitado)* close shave.

apurar I *vtr* **1** *(terminar)* to finish off, end. **2** *(preocupar)* to worry. **II apurarse** *vr* **1**

(*preocuparse*) to worry, get worried; **no te apures**, don't worry. 2 (*darse prisa*) to rush, hurry, pester; **apúrate**, get a move on.

apuro *nm* 1 (*situación difícil*) tight spot, fix, jam; **estar en un a.**, to be in a tight spot. 2 (*escasez de dinero*) hardship; **pasar apuros**, to be hard up. 3 (*vergüenza*) embarrassment; **¡qué a.!**, how embarrassing!

aquejado,-a *adj* suffering (**de**, from).

aquel,-ella *adj dem* 1 that; **a. niño**, that boy. 2 **aquellos,-as**, those; **aquellas niñas**, those girls.

aquél,-élla *pron dem m,f* 1 that one; (*el anterior*) the former; **aquél/-élla ... éste/ésta**, the former ... the latter. 2 **todo a. que**, anyone who, whoever. 3 **aquéllos, -as**, those; (*los anteriores*) the former.

aquella *adj dem f* → **aquel**.

aquélla *pron dem f* → **aquél**.

aquello *pron dem neut* that, it.

aquellos,-as *adj dem pl* → **aquel,-ella**.

aquéllos,-as *pron dem m,fpl* → **aquél, -élla**.

aquí *adv* 1 (*lugar*) here; **a. arriba/fuera**, up/out here; **a. está**, here it is; **a. mismo**, right here; **de a. para allá**, up and down, to and fro; **hasta a.**, this far; **por a., por favor**, this way please; **está por a.**, it's around here somewhere. 2 (*tiempo*) **de a. en adelante**, from now on; **de aquí a junio**, between now and June; **hasta a.**, up till now.

aquietar *vtr* to pacify, calm down.

ara *nf fml* **en aras de**, for the sake of.

árabe I *adj* (*de Arabia*) Arab. II *nmf* (*persona*) Arab. III *nm* (*idioma*) Arabic.

Arabia *n* Arabia; **A. Saudita**, Saudi Arabia.

arado *nm* plough, *US* plow.

Aragón *n* Aragon.

aragonés,-esa *adj & nm,f* Aragonese.

arancel *nm* tariff, customs duty.

arancelario,-a *adj* tariff, duty; **derechos arancelarios**, duties; **barreras arancelarias**, customs barriers.

arandela *nf Téc* washer; (*anilla*) ring.

araña *nf* 1 spider. 2 (*lámpara*) chandelier.

arañar *vtr* to scratch.

arañazo *nm* scratch.

arar *vtr* to plough, *US* plow.

araucaria *nf* araucaria, monkey puzzle tree.

arbitraje *nm* 1 arbitration. 2 *Dep* refereeing; *Ten* umpiring.

arbitrar *vtr* 1 to arbitrate. 2 *Dep* to referee; *Ten* umpire.

arbitrariedad *nf* 1 arbitrariness. 2 (*acto*) arbitrary action.

arbitrario,-a *adj* arbitrary.

arbitrio *nm* (*voluntad*) will; (*juicio*) judgement.

árbitro,-a *nm,f* 1 *Dep* referee; (*de tenis*) umpire. 2 (*mediador*) arbitrator.

árbol *nm* 1 *Bot* tree. 2 *Téc* shaft. 3 *Náut* mast. 4 (*gráfico*) tree (diagram); **á. genealógico**, family *o* genealogical tree.

arbolado,-a I *adj* wooded. II *nm* woodland.

arboleda *nf* grove.

arbusto *nm* bush, shrub.

arca *nf* 1 chest. 2 (*para caudales*) strongbox, safe; **arcas públicas**, Treasury *sing*.

arcada *nf* 1 arcade; (*de puente*) arch. 2 (*náusea*) retching.

arcaico,-a *adj* archaic.

arcén *nm* verge; (*de autopista*) hard shoulder.

archi- *pref* super-.

archiconocido,-a *adj* extremely well-known.

archipiélago *nm* archipelago.

archivador *nm* filing cabinet.

archivar *vtr* 1 (*documento etc*) to file (away). 2 (*caso, asunto*) to shelve. 3 *Inform* to save.

archivo *nm* 1 file. 2 (*archivador*) filing cabinet. 3 **archivos**, archives.

arcilla *nf* clay.

arco *nm* 1 *Arquit* arch. 2 *Mat Elec* arc. 3 (*de violín*) bow. 4 *Dep* bow; **tiro con a.**, archery. 5 **a. iris**, rainbow.

arder *vi* to burn; *fam* **la conversación está que arde**, the conversation is really heating up; **Juan está que arde**, Juan is really fuming.

ardid *nm* scheme, plot.

ardiente *adj* 1 (*encendido*) burning; **capilla a.**, chapel of rest. 2 *fig* (*fervoroso*) eager.

ardilla *nf* squirrel.

ardor *nm* 1 heat; *Med* **a. de estómago**, heartburn. 2 *fig* ardour, *US* ardor, fervour, *US* fervor.

ardoroso,-a *adj fig* ardent, passionate.

arduo,-a *adj* arduous.

área *nf* 1 area; *Dep* penalty area. 2 (*medida*) are (100 square metres).

arena *nf* 1 sand; **playa de a.**, sandy beach. 2 *Taur* bullring.

arengar |7| *vtr* to harangue.

arenisca *nf* sandstone.

arenoso,-a *adj* sandy.

arenque *nm* herring; *Culin* **a. ahumado**, kipper.

arete *nm* earring.

argamasa *nf* mortar.

Argel *n* Algiers.

Argelia *n* Algeria.

argelino,-a *adj & nm,f* Algerian.

Argentina *n* Argentina.

argentino,-a *adj & nm,f* Argentinean, Argentine.

argolla *nf* 1 (large) ring. 2 *Am* (*alianza*) wedding ring.

argot *nm* (*popular*) slang; (*técnico*) jargon.

argucia *nf* ruse.

argüir |37| *vtr* 1 (*deducir*) to deduce, conclude. 2 (*argumentar*) to argue.

argumentación *nf* argument.

argumentar *vtr* → **argüir**.

argumento *nm* 1 *Lit Teat* (*trama*) plot. 2 (*razonamiento*) argument.

arguyo *indic pres* → **argüir**.

aridez *nf* aridity; *fig* dryness.

árido,-a *adj* arid; *fig* dry.

Aries *nm* Aries.

ariete *nm Mil* battering ram.

ario,-a *adj & nm,f* Aryan.

arisco,-a *adj* (*persona*) unfriendly, stand-offish; (*animal*) unfriendly.

arista *nf* edge.

aristocracia *nf* aristocracy.

aristócrata *nmf* aristocrat.

aristocrático,-a *adj* aristocratic.

aritmética *nf* arithmetic.

arma *nf* weapon; **a. blanca,** knife; **a. de fuego,** firearm; **a. homicida,** murder weapon; **a. nuclear,** nuclear weapon; *fig* **a. de doble filo,** double-edged sword.

armada *nf* navy.

armado,-a *adj* armed; **ir a.,** to be armed; **lucha armada,** armed struggle.

armador,-a *nm,f* shipowner.

armadura *nf* 1 (*armazón*) frame. 2 *Hist* suit of armour *o US* armor.

armamentista *adj* arms; **la carrera a.,** the arms race.

armamento *nm* armaments *pl*; **a. nuclear,** nuclear weapons.

armar I *vtr* 1 (*tropa, soldado*) to arm. 2 (*piezas*) to fit *o* put together, assemble. 3 *fam* **armaron un escándalo,** they created a scandal. II **armarse** *vr* to arm oneself; *fig* **a. de paciencia,** to summon up one's patience; *fig* **a. de valor,** to pluck up courage; *fam* **se armó la gorda,** all hell broke loose.

armario *nm* (*para ropa*) wardrobe; (*de cocina*) cupboard; **a. empotrado,** built-in wardrobe *o* cupboard.

armatoste *nm* (*cosa*) monstrosity.

armazón *nm* frame; (*de madera*) timberwork; *Arquit* shell.

armería *nf* gunsmith's (shop).

armiño *nm* ermine.

armisticio *nm* armistice.

armonía *nf* harmony.

armonioso,-a *adj* harmonious.

armonizar |4| *vtr & vi* to harmonize.

aro *nm* hoop; (*servilletero*) serviette ring; *fam* **pasar por el a.,** to knuckle under.

aroma *nm* aroma; (*de vino*) bouquet.

aromático,-a *adj* aromatic.

arpa *nf* harp.

arpía *nf* (*en mitología*) harpy; *fig* harpy, old witch.

arpón *nm* harpoon.

arquear *vtr*, **arquearse** *vr* to bend, curve.

arqueología *nf* archaeology, *US* archeology.

arqueólogo,-a *nm,f* archaeologist, *US* archeologist.

arquero,-a *nm,f* archer.

arquetipo *nm* archetype.

arquitecto,-a *nm,f* architect.

arquitectónico,-a *adj* architectural.

arquitectura *nf* architecture.

arrabales *nmpl* slums.

arrabalero,-a *adj pey* coarse.

arraigado,-a *adj* deeply rooted.

arraigar |7| *vi* to take root.

arraigo *nm fig* roots *pl*; **una tradición con mucho a.,** a deeply-rooted tradition.

arrancar |1| I *vtr* 1 (*planta*) to uproot, pull up; **a. de raíz,** to uproot. 2 (*extraer*) to pull *o* tear off *o* out; (*diente, pelo*) to pull out; *fig* (*confesión etc*) to extract; **arranca una hoja del cuaderno,** tear a page out of the notebook. 3 (*coche, motor*) to start. II *vi* 1 *Aut Téc* to start. 2 (*empezar*) to begin; **a. a llorar,** to burst out crying.

arranque *nm* 1 *Aut Téc* starting. 2 (*comienzo*) start. 3 *fam* (*arrebato*) outburst, fit.

arrasar I *vtr* to devastate, destroy. II *vi* (*en elecciones etc*) to win by a landslide.

arrastrado,-a *fam* I *adj* wretched. II *nm,f* bad egg.

arrastrar I *vtr* to pull (along), drag (along); **vas arrastando el vestido,** your dress is trailing on the ground; **lo arrastró la corriente,** he was swept away by the current. II **arrastrarse** *vr* to drag oneself; *fig* (*humillarse*) to crawl.

arrastre *nm* 1 pulling, dragging; *fam* **para el a.,** (*persona*) on one's last legs; (*cosa*) done for. 2 (*pesca de*) a., trawling.

arrayán *nm* myrtle.

arre *interj* gee up!, giddy up!

arrear *fam vtr* 1 to spur on; (*caballos*) to urge on. 2 *fam* (*bofetada*) to give.

arrebatador,-a *adj fig* captivating, fascinating.

arrebatar I *vtr* (*coger*) to snatch, seize; *fig* (*cautivar*) to captivate, fascinate. II **arrebatarse** *vr* (*enfurecerse*) to become furious; (*exaltarse*) to get carried away.

arrebato *nm* outburst, fit.

arreciar |12| *vi* (*viento, tormenta*) to get worse.

arrecife *nm* reef.

arreglado,-a *adj* 1 (*reparado*) repaired, fixed. 2 (*solucionado*) settled. 3 (*habitación*) tidy, neat. 4 (*persona*) well-dressed, smart.

arreglar I *vtr* 1 to arrange; (*problema*) to sort out; (*habitación*) to tidy; (*papeles*) to put in order. 2 (*reparar*) to repair, fix. 3 (*vestir*) to get ready. II **arreglarse** *vr* 1 (*vestirse*) to get ready. 2 *fam* **arreglárselas,** to manage. 3 (*reconciliarse*) to make up.

arreglo *nm* 1 arrangement; (*acuerdo*) compromise. **2** *(reparación)* repair; **no tiene a.**, it is beyond repair; *fam* **¡no tienes a.!**, you're hopeless! **3** *fml* **con a. a**, in accordance with.

arrellanarse *vr* to sit back.

arremangarse |7| *vr* to roll one's sleeves *o* trousers up.

arremeter *vi* to attack.

arremolinarse *vr* to whirl about; *fig (gente)* to crowd together, cram together.

arrendamiento *nm* **1** *(alquiler)* renting. **2** *(precio)* rent.

arrendar |1| *vtr (piso)* to rent; *(dar en arriendo)* to let on lease; *(tomar en arriendo)* to take on lease.

arrendatario,-a *nm,f* leaseholder, lessee; *(inquilino)* tenant.

arreos *nmpl* **1** *(de caballería)* harness *sing*, trappings. **2** *(adornos)* adornments.

arrepentido,-a *adj* regretful.

arrepentimiento *nm* regret.

arrepentirse |5| *vr* **a. de**, to regret; *Rel* to repent.

arrestar *vtr* to arrest, detain; *(encarcelar)* to put in prison.

arresto *nm* arrest; *Jur* **a. domiciliario**, house arrest.

arriar |29| *vtr (bandera)* to strike; *(velas)* to lower.

arriba **I** *adv* up; *(encima)* on the top; **ahí a.**, up there; **de a. abajo**, from top to bottom; *fam* **mirar a algn de a. abajo**, to look sb up and down; **desde a.**, from above; **hacia a.**, upwards; **de un millón para a.**, from one million upwards; **más a.**, higher up, further up; **a. del todo**, r´´,ht on *o* at the top; **la parte de a.**, the top (part); **vive a.**, he lives upstairs; **véase más a.**, see above. **II** *interj* get up!, up you get!; **¡a. la República!**, long live the Republic!; **¡a. las manos!**, hands up! **III** *prep* *Am* on top of.

arribar *vi* to reach port, arrive.

arribeño,-a *Am* **I** *adj* highland. **II** *nm,f* highlander.

arribista *nmf* parvenu, social climber.

arriendo *nm* lease; *(de un piso)* renting; **dar en a.**, to let out on lease; **tomar en a.**, to take on lease.

arriesgado,-a *adj* **1** *(peligroso)* risky. **2** *(temerario)* fearless, daring.

arriesgar |7| **I** *vtr* to risk. **II arriesgarse** *vr* to risk; **se arriesga demasiado**, he's taking too many risks.

arrimar **I** *vtr* to move closer, bring near *o* nearer; *fam* **a. el hombro**, to lend a hand. **II arrimarse** *vr* to move *o* get close, come near *o* nearer.

arrinconar *vtr* **1** *(poner en un rincón)* to put in a corner. **2** *(abandonar)* to put away, lay aside. **3** *(acorralar)* to corner.

arrobo *nm* rapture, enthralment, *US* enthrallment.

arrocero,-a *adj* **la industria arrocera**, the

rice industry.

arrodillarse *vr* to kneel down.

arrogancia *nf* arrogance.

arrogante *adj* arrogant.

arrojadizo,-a *adj* **arma arrojadiza**, missile.

arrojado,-a *adj (osado)* bold, daring.

arrojar **I** *vtr* **1** *(tirar)* to throw, fling. **2** *Com (saldo)* to show. **II arrojarse** *vr* to throw oneself, fling oneself.

arrojo *nm* daring, courage.

arrollador,-a *adj fig* overwhelming; *(éxito)* resounding; *(personalidad)* captivating.

arrollar *vtr* **I** *(atropellar)* to run over, knock down. **II** *vi Dep Pol* to win easily.

arropar **I** *vtr* to wrap up; *(en la cama)* to tuck in. **II arroparse** *vr* to wrap oneself up.

arrostrar *vtr* to face.

arroyo *nm* brook, stream.

arroz *nm* rice; **a. con leche**, rice pudding.

arruga *nf (en la piel)* wrinkle; *(en la ropa)* crease.

arrugar |7| **I** *vtr (piel)* to wrinkle; *(ropa)* to crease; *(papel)* to crumple (up). **II arrugarse** *vr (piel)* to wrinkle; *(ropa)* to crease.

arruinado,-a *adj* bankrupt, ruined.

arruinar **I** *vtr* to ruin. **II arruinarse** *vr* to be ruined.

arrullar **I** *vtr (bebé)* to lull. **II** *vi (paloma)* to coo.

arrullo *nm* **1** *(de paloma)* cooing. **2** *(nana)* lullaby.

arrumaco *nm fam* kissing and hugging; *(halago)* flattery.

arsenal *nm* arsenal.

arsénico *nm* arsenic.

arte *nm & f* **1** art; **bellas artes**, fine arts; *fam* **por amor al a.**, for the love of it. **2** *(habilidad)* skill.

artefacto *nm* device; **a. explosivo**, explosive device.

arteria *nf* artery; *(carretera)* highway.

artesanal *adj* handmade.

artesanía *nf* **1** *(cualidad)* craftsmanship. **2** *(objetos)* crafts *pl*, handicrafts *pl*.

artesano,-a **I** *nm,f (hombre)* craftsman; *(mujer)* craftswoman. **II** *adj* handmade.

ártico,-a *adj* arctic; **el océano á.**, the Arctic Ocean. **II nm el Á.**, the Arctic.

articulación *nf* **1** *Anat* joint, articulation. **2** *Téc* joint.

articulado,-a *adj (tren etc)* articulated.

articular *vtr* to articulate.

artículo *nm* article; **a. de fondo**, leader (article).

artífice *nmf* author; *fig* **el a. del acuerdo**, the architect of the agreement.

artificial *adj* artificial; *Tex* man-made *o* synthetic.

artificio *nm* **1** artifice; **fuego de a.**, firework. **2** *(artimaña)* ruse.

artillería *nf* artillery; **a. antiaérea**, anti-aircraft guns pl.

artillero nm artilleryman.

artilugio nm gadget, device.

artimaña nf trick, ruse.

artista nmf artist; **a. de cine**, film star.

artístico,-a I adj artistic.

artritis nf arthritis.

arveja nf Am pea.

arzobispo nm archbishop.

as nm ace.

asa nf handle.

asado,-a I adj Culin roast; **pollo a.**, roast chicken; fig **a. de calor**, roasting, boiling hot. II nm Culin roast.

asaduras nfpl offal sing; (de ave) giblets.

asalariado,-a I adj salaried. II nm,f wage earner, salaried worker.

asaltador,-a nm,f, **asaltante** nmf attacker; (en un robo) robber.

asaltar vtr to assault, attack; (banco) to rob; fig to assail.

asalto nm 1 assault, attack; **a. a un banco**, bank robbery. 2 Box round.

asamblea nf meeting; **a. general**, general meeting.

asar I vtr to roast. II **asarse** vr fig to be roasting, be boiling hot.

ascendencia nf ancestry, ancestors pl; **de a. escocesa**, of Scottish descent.

ascender [3] I vtr (en un cargo) to promote. II vi 1 move upward; (temperatura) to rise; **la factura asciende a ...**, the bill adds up to ... 2 (al trono) to ascend. 3 (de categoría) to be promoted.

ascendiente nmf ancestor.

ascensión nf 1 climb. 2 (al trono) accession.

ascenso nm promotion; (subida) rise.

ascensor nm lift, US elevator.

asco nm disgust, repugnance; **me da a.**, it makes me (feel) sick; **¡qué a.!**, how disgusting o revolting.

ascua nf ember; fig **en ascuas**, on tenterhooks.

aseado,-a adj tidy, neat.

asear I vtr to clean, tidy up. II **asearse** vr to wash, get washed.

asediar [12] vtr to besiege.

asedio nm siege.

asegurado,-a adj 1 insured. 2 (indudable) secure.

asegurador,-a I adj insurance. II nm,f insurer.

asegurar I vtr 1 to insure. 2 (garantizar) **me aseguró que ...**, he assured me that ...; **a. el éxito de un proyecto**, to ensure the success of a project. 3 (cuerda) to fasten. II **asegurarse** vr 1 to make sure; **a. de que ...**, to make sure that .... 2 Seg to insure onself.

asemejarse vr **a. a**, to look like.

asentado,-a adj (establecido) established, settled.

asentamiento nm settlement.

asentar |1| I vtr **a. la cabeza**, to settle down. II **asentarse** vr 1 (establecerse) to settle down, establish oneself. 2 (té, polvo) to settle.

asentimiento nm assent, consent.

asentir |5| vi to assent, agree; **a. con la cabeza**, to nod.

aseo nm 1 cleanliness, tidiness. 2 **aseos** o (**cuarto de) a.**, bathroom; (retrete) toilet.

asequible adj affordable; (comprensible) easy to understand; (alcanzable) attainable.

aserrín nm sawdust.

asesinar vtr to murder; (rey, ministro) to assassinate.

asesinato nm murder; (de rey, ministro) assassination.

asesino,-a I adj murderous. II nm,f killer; (hombre) murderer; (mujer) murderess; Pol assassin.

asesor,-a I nm,f adviser; **a. fiscal**, tax advisor. II adj advisory.

asesoramiento nm 1 (acción) advising. 2 (consejo) advice.

asesorar I vtr 1 to advise, give (professional) advice to. 2 Com to act as consultant to. II **asesorarse** vr to consult.

asesoría nf consultant's office.

asestar vtr to deal; **a. un golpe a algn**, to deal sb a blow.

aseverar vtr to assert.

asfalto nm asphalt.

asfixia nf asphyxiation, suffocation.

asfixiante adj asphyxiating, suffocating; fam **hace un calor a.**, it's stifling.

asfixiar |12| vtr, **asfixiarse** vr to asphyxiate, suffocate.

así I adv 1 (de esta manera) like this o that, this way, thus; **ponlo a.**, put it this way; **a. de grande/alto**, this big/tall; **algo a.**, something like this o that; **¿no es a.?**, isn't that so o right?; **a. es la vida**, such is life; **a. a.**, so-so. 2 **a las seis o a.**, around six o'clock; **diez años o a.**, ten years more or less. 3 **a. como**, as well as. 4 **a. tenga que ...**, (aunque) even if I have to .... 5 **aun a.**, and despite that. 6 **a. pues**, so; **a. que ...**, so ... 7 **a. que llegues**, as soon as.

Asia n Asia; **A. Menor**, Asia Minor.

asiático,-a adj & nm,f Asian.

asidero nm (asa) handle; fig pretext, excuse.

asiduidad nf assiduity; **con a.**, frequently, regularly.

asiduo,-a I adj assiduous. II nm,f regular customer.

asiento nm 1 seat; **a. trasero/delantero**, front/back seat; **tome a.**, take a seat. 2 (poso) sediment. 3 Fin entry.

asignación nf 1 (de dinero) assignment, allocation. 2 (de puesto) appointment. 3 (paga) allowance.

asignar vtr 1 to assign, allocate. 2 (nom-

brar) to appoint.

asignatura *nf* subject; **a. pendiente,** failed subject.

asilado,-a *nm,f* refugee.

asilar *vtr* to grant *o* give political asylum to.

asilo *nm* asylum; **a. de ancianos,** old people's home; *Pol* **a. político,** political asylum.

asimilación *nf* assimilation.

asimilar *vtr* to assimilate.

asimismo *adv* also, as well.

asir |22| *vtr* to grasp, seize.

asistencia *nf* 1 (*presencia*) attendance; **falta de a.,** absence. 2 **a. médica/técnica,** medical/technical assistance. 3 (*público*) audience, public.

asistenta *nf* charlady, cleaning lady.

asistente I *adj* attending; **el público a.,** the audience. II *nmf* 1 (*ayudante*) assistant; **a. social,** social worker. 2 **los asistentes,** the public *sing*.

asistido,-a *adj* assisted; **a. por ordenador,** computer-assisted; *Aut* **dirección asistida,** power steering.

asistir I *vtr* to assist, help. II *vi* to attend (**a, -**), be present (**a, at**).

asma *nf* asthma.

asno *nm* donkey, ass.

asociación *nf* association.

asociado,-a I *adj* associated. III *nm,f* associate, partner.

asociar |12| I *vtr* to associate. II **asociarse** *vr* 1 to be associated. 2 *Com* to become partners.

asolar |2| *vtr* to devastate, destroy.

asomar I *vtr* to put out, stick out; **asomó la cabeza por la ventana,** he put his head out of the window. II *vi* to appear. III **asomarse** *vr* 1 to lean out; **a. a la ventana,** to lean out of the window. 2 (*entrar*) to pop in; (*salir*) to pop out.

asombrar I *vtr* to amaze, astonish. II **asombrarse** *vr* to be astonished; **a. de algo,** to be amazed at sth.

asombro *nm* amazement, astonishment.

asombroso,-a *adj* amazing, astonishing.

asomo *nm* trace, hint.

asonada *nf* putsch.

asorocharse *vr Am* to suffer from altitude sickness.

aspa *nf* 1 (*de molino*) arm; (*de ventilador*) blade. 2 (*cruz*) cross.

aspaviento *nm* **hacer aspavientos,** to wave one's arms about.

aspecto *nm* 1 look, appearance. 2 (*de un asunto*) aspect.

aspereza *nf* roughness; *fig* **limar asperezas,** to smooth things over.

áspero,-a *adj* rough; *fig* (*carácter*) surly.

aspersión *nf* sprinkling.

aspersor *nm* sprinkler.

aspiración *nf* 1 inhalation, breathing in. 2 (*pretensión*) aspiration.

aspiradora *nf* vacuum cleaner.

aspirante *nmf* candidate, applicant.

aspirar I *vtr* 1 (*respirar*) to inhale, breath in. 2 *Téc* (*absorber*) to suck in, draw in. II *vi fig* **a. a algo,** to aspire after sth.

aspirina *nf* aspirin.

asquear *vtr* to disgust.

asquerosidad *nf* filthy *o* revolting thing; **¡que a.!,** how revolting!

asqueroso,-a I *adj* (*sucio*) filthy; (*desagradable*) revolting, disgusting. II *nm,f* filthy *o* revolting person.

asta *nf* 1 (*de bandera*) staff, pole; **a media a.,** at half-mast. 2 *Zool* (*cuerno*) horn.

asterisco *nm* asterisk.

astilla *nf* splinter.

astillero *nm* shipyard.

astral *adj* astral; **carta a.,** birth chart.

astringente *adj & nm* astringent.

astro *nm* star.

astrología *nf* astrology.

astrólogo,-a *nm,f* astrologer.

astronauta *nmf* astronaut.

astronave *nf* spaceship.

astronomía *nf* astronomy.

astronómico,-a *adj* astronomical.

astrónomo,-a *nm,f* astronomer.

astucia *nf* shrewdness; (*artimaña*) ruse.

asturiano,-a *adj & nm,f* Asturian.

Asturias *n* Asturias.

astuto,-a *adj* astute, shrewd.

asumir *vtr* to assume.

asunción *nf* assumption.

asunto *nm* 1 subject; **no es a. tuyo,** it's none of your business. 2 **Asuntos Exteriores,** Foreign Affairs.

asustar I *vtr* to frighten, scare. II **asustarse** *vr* to be frightened, be scared.

atacante *nmf* attacker, assailant.

atacar |1| *vtr* to attack, assault; *fig* **me ataca los nervios,** he gets on my nerves.

atado *adj* tied; (*ocupado*) tied up.

atadura *nf fig* hindrance.

atajar *vi* to take a shortcut (**por,** across *o* through).

atajo *nm* 1 shortcut. 2 (*grupo*) bunch.

atalaya *nf* watchtower.

atañer |38| *v impers* to concern, have to do with; **eso no te atañe,** that has nothing to do with you.

ataque *nm* 1 attack, assault; **a. aéreo,** air raid. 2 *Med* fit; **a. cardíaco** *o* **al corazón,** heart attack; **a. de nervios/tos,** fit of hysterics/coughing.

atar I *vtr* 1 to tie; *fig* **a. cabos,** to put two and two together; *fam* **loco de a.,** as mad as a hatter. 2 *fig* to tie down. II **atarse** *vr fig* to get tied up; **átate los zapatos,** do your shoes up.

atardecer |33| I *v impers* to get *o* grow dark. II *nm* evening, dusk.

atareado,-a *adj* busy.

atascado,-a *adj* stuck.

atascar |1| I *vtr* (*bloquear*) to block, obstruct. II **atascarse** *vr* 1 (*bloquearse*) to become blocked, become blocked. 2 *fig* (*estancarse*) to get bogged down.

atasco *nm* traffic jam.

ataúd *nm* coffin.

ataviarse |29| *vr* to dress oneself up.

atavío *nm* dress, attire.

atemorizar |4| *vtr* to frighten, scare.

atemperar *vtr* to moderate, temper.

Atenas *n* Athens.

atención I *nf* attention; **llamar la a.**, to attract attention; **prestar/poner a.**, to pay attention (**a**, to). II *interj* attention!

atender [3] I *vtr* to attend to; (*petición*) to agree to. II *vi* (*alumno*) to pay attention (**a**, to).

atenerse |24| *vr* 1 (*a reglas etc*) to abide (**a**, by); **a. a las consecuencias**, to bear the consequences. 2 (*remitirse*) to go by; **me atengo a sus palabras**, I'm going by what he said; **no saber a qué a.**, not to know what to expect.

atentado *nm* attack; **a. terrorista**, terrorist attack.

atentar *vi* **a. a** *o* **contra**, to commit a crime against; **a. contra la vida de algn**, to make an attempt on sb's life.

atento,-a *adj* 1 attentive; **estar a. a**, to be mindful *o* aware of. 2 (*amable*) thoughtful, considerate; **atentos saludos de**, (*en carta*) yours faithfully. ◆**atentamente** *adv* **le saluda a.**, (*en carta*) yours sincerely *o* faithfully.

atenuante I *adj* attenuating. II *nm* *Jur* extenuating circumstance.

atenuar |30| *vtr* 1 to attenuate; *Jur* to extenuate. 2 (*importancia*) to lessen, diminish.

ateo,-a I *adj* atheistic. II *nm,f* atheist.

aterciopelado,-a *adj* velvety; (*vino*) smooth.

aterido,-a *adj* **a. de frío**, stiff with cold, numb.

aterrador,-a *adj* terrifying.

aterrar I *vtr* to terrify. II **aterrarse** *vr* to be terrified.

aterrizaje *nm* *Av* landing; **a. forzoso**, forced landing.

aterrizar |4| *vi* to land.

aterrorizar |4| I *vtr* to terrify; *Mil Pol* to terrorize. II **aterrorizarse** *vr* to be terrified.

atesorar *vtr* to accumulate; (*dinero*) to hoard.

atestado[1] *nm* *Jur* affidavit, statement; **atestados**, testimonials.

atestado,-a[2] *adj* packed, crammed; **estaba a. de gente**, it was full of people.

atestar[1] *vtr* *Jur* to testify.

atestar[2] |1| *vtr* (*abarrotar*) to pack, cram (**de**, with).

atestiguar |22| *vtr* 1 *Jur* to testify to. 2 *fig* to vouch for.

atiborrar I *vtr* to pack, stuff (**de**, with). II

atiborrarse *vr* *fam* to stuff oneself (**de**, with).

ático *nm* attic.

atinado,-a *adj* (*juicioso*) sensible; (*pertinente*) pertinent.

atinar *vi* to get it right; **a. a hacer algo**, to succeed in doing sth; **a. al blanco**, to hit the target; **atinó con la solución**, he found the solution.

atingencia *nf* *Am* connection, relation.

atípico,-a *adj* atypical.

atisbar *vtr* to make out.

atisbo *nm* *fig* slight sign, inkling.

atizar |4| *vtr* 1 (*fuego*) to poke, stoke. 2 *fig* (*rebelión*) to stir up; (*pasión*) to rouse, excite.

atlántico,-a I *adj* Atlantic. II *nm* **el (océano) A.**, the Atlantic (Ocean).

atlas *nm inv* atlas.

atleta *nmf* athlete.

atlético,-a *adj* athletic.

atletismo *nm* athletics *sing*.

atmósfera *nf* atmosphere.

atmosférico,-a *adj* atmospheric.

atolladero *nm* fix, jam; **estar en un a.**, to be in a jam.

atolondrado,-a *adj* stunned, bewildered; (*atontado*) stupid.

atolondrar I *vtr* to confuse, bewilder. II **atolondrarse** *vr* to be confused, bewildered.

atómico,-a *adj* atomic.

átomo *nm* atom.

atónito,-a *adj* amazed, astonished.

atontado,-a *adj* 1 (*tonto*) silly, foolish. 2 (*aturdido*) bewildered, amazed.

atontar I *vtr* to confuse, bewilder. II **atontarse** *vr* to be *o* get confused, bewildered.

atorarse *vr Am* to get stuck.

atormentar I *vtr* to torment. II **atormentarse** *vr* to torment oneself, suffer agonies.

atornillar *vtr* to screw on.

atosigar |7| *vtr* to harass.

atracador,-a *nm,f* (*de banco*) (bank) robber; (*en la calle*) attacker, mugger.

atracar |1| I *vtr* to hold up; (*persona*) to rob. II *vi* *Náut* to come alongside, tie up. III **atracarse** *vr* (*de comida*) to stuff oneself (**de**, with), gorge oneself (**de**, on).

atracción *nf* attraction; **parque de atracciones**, funfair.

atraco *nm* hold-up, robbery; **a. a mano armada**, armed robbery.

atracón *nm* *fam* binge, blowout; **darse un a. de comer**, to make a pig of oneself.

atractivo,-a I *adj* attractive, appealing. II *nm* attraction, appeal.

atraer |25| *vtr* to attract.

atragantarse *vr* to choke (**con**, on), swallow the wrong way; *fig* **esa chica se me ha atragantado**, I can't stand that girl.

atraigo *indic pres* → **atraer**.

atraje *pt indef* → **atraer**.

atrancar |1| I *vtr (puerta)* to bolt. II **atrancarse** *vr* to get stuck; *(al hablar, leer)* to get bogged down.

atrapar *vtr* to catch.

atrás I *adv* 1 *(lugar)* at the back, behind; **hacia/para a.**, backwards; **puerta de a.**, back *o* rear door; *fig* **echarse a.**, to back out. 2 *(tiempo)* previously, in the past, ago; **un año a.**, a year ago; **venir de muy a.**, to go *o* date back a long time.

atrasado,-a *adj* late, slow; *(pago)* overdue; *(reloj)* slow; *(país)* backward; *Prensa* **número a.**, back number.

atrasar I *vtr* to put back. II *vi (reloj)* to be slow. II **atrasarse** *vr* 1 to remain *o* stay behind, lag behind. 2 *(tren)* to be late.

atraso *nm* 1 delay. 2 *(de país)* backwardness. 3 *Fin* **atrasos**, arrears.

atravesado,-a *adj (cruzado)* lying crosswise; *(persona)* difficult; **lo tengo a.**, I can't stand him.

atravesar |1| I *vtr* 1 *(calle)* to cross. 2 *(muro)* to pierce, go through. 3 *(poner a través)* to lay across, put across, put crosswise. II **atravesarse** *vr* to get in the way; *fig* **se me ha atravesado Luis**, I can't stand Luis.

atrayente *adj* attractive.

atreverse *vr* to dare; **a. a hacer algo**, to dare to do sth.

atrevido,-a *adj* 1 *(osado)* daring, bold. 2 *(insolente)* insolent, impudent. 3 *(ropa etc)* daring, risqué.

atrevimiento *nm* 1 *(osadía)* daring, audacity. 2 *(insolencia)* insolence, impudence.

atribuir |37| I *vtr* to attribute, ascribe. II **atribuirse** *vr* to assume.

atribular *vtr* to afflict.

atributo *nm* attribute.

atril *nm* music stand.

atrochar *vi* to take a short cut.

atrocidad *nf* atrocity.

atrofiar |12| *vtr*, **atrofiarse** *vr* to atrophy.

atropellado,-a *adj* hasty, impetuous.

atropellar *vtr* to knock down, run over.

atropello *nm* 1 *Aut* knocking down, running over. 2 *(abuso)* abuse.

atroz *adj* 1 *(bárbaro)* atrocious. 2 *fam (hambre, frío)* enormous, tremendous.

ATS *nmf abr de* **ayudante técnico sanitario.**

atta. *abr de* **atenta.**

atto. *abr de* **atento.**

atuendo *nm* dress, attire.

atún *nm* tuna, tunny.

aturdido,-a *adj* stunned, dazed.

aturdimiento *nm* confusion, bewilderment.

aturdir *vtr* 1 *(con un golpe)* to stun, daze. 2 *(confundir)* to bewilder, confuse.

aturrullar *vtr* to confuse, bewilder.

atuve *pt indef* → **atenerse**.

audacia *nf* audacity.

audaz *adj* audacious, bold.

audible *adj* audible.

audición *nf* 1 hearing. 2 *Teat* audition.

audiencia *nf* 1 *(público)* audience; *TV Rad* **horas de máxima a.**, prime time; **índice de a.**, viewing figures, ratings. 2 *(entrevista)* audience. 3 *Jur* high court.

audiovisual *adj* audio-visual.

auditivo,-a I *adj* auditory; **comprensión auditiva**, listening comprehension. II *nm* receiver.

auditor *nm Fin* auditor.

auditorio *nm* 1 *(público)* audience. 2 *(sala)* auditorium, hall.

auge *nm* peak; *Econ* boom; *fig* **estar en a.**, to be thriving *o* booming.

augurar *vtr* to augur.

augurio *nm* omen.

aula *nf (en colegio)* classroom; *Univ* lecture room; **a. magna**, amphitheatre.

aulaga *nf* gorse.

aullar |16| *vtr* to howl, yell.

aullido *nm* howl, yell.

aumentar I *vtr* to increase; *(precios)* to put up; *(producción)* to step up; *Fot* to enlarge; *Opt* to magnify. II *vi (precios)* to go up, rise; *(valor)* to appreciate. III **aumentarse** *vr* to increase, be on the increase.

aumento *nm* increase; *Opt* magnification; **a. de precios**, rise in prices; **ir en a.**, to be on the increase.

aun *adv* even; **a. así**, even so, even then; **a. más**, even more.

aún *adv* still; *(en negativas)* yet; **a. está aquí**, he's still here; **ella no ha venido a.**, she hasn't come yet.

aunar |16| *vtr* to unite, join.

aunque *conj* although, though; *(enfático)* even if, even though; **a. no vengas**, even if you don't come.

aúpa *interj* up!, get up!

aura *nf* aura.

aureola *nf* halo.

auricular *nm* 1 *Tel* receiver. 2 **auriculares**, earphones, headphones.

aurora *nf* daybreak, dawn.

auscultar *vtr* to sound (with a stethoscope).

ausencia *nf* absence.

ausentarse *vr* to leave.

ausente I *adj* absent. II *nmf* absentee.

austeridad *nf* austerity.

austero,-a *adj* austere.

austral I *adj* southern. II *nm Fin* standard monetary unit of Argentina.

Australia *n* Australia.

australiano,-a *adj & nm,f* Australian.

Austria *n* Austria.

austríaco,-a *adj & nm,f* Austrian.

autenticidad *nf* authenticity.

auténtico,-a *adj* authentic.

autentificar |1| *vtr* to authenticate.

autismo *nm* autism.

autista *adj* autistic.

auto¹ *nm* car.

auto² *nm Jur* decree, writ; **autos,** *(pleito)* papers, documents.

autoadhesivo,-a *adj* self-adhesive.

autobiografía *nf* autobiography.

autobiográfico,-a *adj* autobiographical.

autobombo *nm fam* self-praise, blowing one's own trumpet.

autobús *nm* bus.

autocar *nm* coach.

autocrítica *nf* self-criticism.

autóctono,-a *adj* indigenous, autochthonous.

autodefensa *nf* self-defence, *US* self-defense.

autodisciplina *nf* self-discipline.

autoescuela *nf* driving school, school of motoring.

autogobierno *nm* self-government.

autógrafo *nm* autograph.

autómata *nm* automaton.

automático,-a *adj* automatic.

automatización *nf* automation.

automatizar |4| *vtr* to automate.

automotor,-a I *adj* self-propelled. II *nm Ferroc* diesel train.

automóvil *nm* car.

automovilismo *nm* motoring.

automovilista *nmf* motorist.

automovilístico,-a *adj* car; **accidente a.,** car accident.

autonomía *nf* 1 autonomy. 2 *(región)* autonomous region.

autonómico,-a *adj* autonomous, self-governing; **elecciones autonómicas,** elections for the autonomous parliament; **televisión autonómica,** regional television.

autónomo,-a *adj* autonomous.

autopista *nf* motorway.

autopsia *nf* autopsy, post mortem.

autor,-a *nm,f (hombre)* author; *(mujer)* authoress; *(de crimen)* perpetrator.

autoridad *nf* authority.

autoritario,-a *adj* authoritarian.

autorizado,-a *adj* authoritative, official.

autorizar |4| *vtr* to authorize.

autorretrato *nm* self-portrait.

autoservicio *nm* self-service; *(supermercado)* supermarket.

autostop *nm* hitch-hiking; **hacer a.,** to hitch-hike.

autostopista *nmf* hitch-hiker.

autosuficiencia *nf* self-sufficiency.

autosuficiente *adj* self-sufficient.

auxiliar |14| I *adj & nmf* auxiliary, assistant. II *vtr* to help, assist.

auxilio *nm* help, assistance; **primeros auxilios,** first aid *sing.*

Av., Avda. *abr de* **Avenida,** Avenue, Ave.

aval *nm Com Fin* endorsement.

avalancha *nf* avalanche.

avalar *vtr* to guarantee, endorse.

avance *nm* 1 advance. 2 *Fin* advance payment. 3 *TV* **a. informativo,** headlines, *US* news brief.

avanzado,-a *adj* advanced; **de avanzada edad,** advanced in years.

avanzar |4| *vtr* to advance.

avaricia *nf* avarice.

avaricioso *adj* greedy.

avaro,-a I *adj* avaricious, miserly. II *nm,f* miser.

avasallar *vtr* to subdue.

avatares *nmpl* quirks.

ave *nf* bird; **aves de corral,** poultry.

AVE *nf abr de* **Alta Velocidad Española,** High Speed Train.

avecinarse *vr* to approach, come near.

avellana *nf* hazelnut.

avellano *nm* hazelnut tree.

avena *nf* oats *pl.*

avendré *indic fut* → **avenir.**

avenencia *nf* compromise.

avengo *indic pres* → **avenir.**

avenida *nf* avenue.

avenido,-a *adj* **bien/mal avenidos,** on good/bad terms.

avenir |27| I *vtr* to reconcile. II **avenirse** *vr* to be on good terms; *(consentir)* to agree (**en,** to).

aventajado,-a *adj (destacado)* outstanding, exceptional; *(en cabeza)* in the lead.

aventajar *vtr* 1 to be ahead *o* in front (**a,** of). 2 *(superar)* to surpass, outdo.

aventar |1| *vtr* 1 *Agr* to winnow. 2 *(el fuego)* to blow (on), fan.

aventura *nf* 1 adventure. 2 *(amorosa)* (love) affair.

aventurado,-a *adj* risky.

aventurarse *vr* to venture.

aventurero,-a *adj* adventurous.

avergonzado,-a *adj* ashamed.

avergonzar |2| I *vtr* to shame. II **avergonzarse** *vr* to be ashamed (**de,** of).

avería *nf* breakdown.

averiado,-a *adj* out of order; *(coche)* broken down.

averiar |29| I *vtr* to break. II **averiarse** *vr* *(estropearse)* to malfunction, go wrong; *(coche)* to break down.

averiguación *nf* enquiry.

averiguar |22| *vtr* to ascertain.

aversión *nf* aversion.

avestruz *nm* ostrich.

aviación *nf* 1 aviation; **accidente de a.,** plane crash; **a. civil,** civil aviation. 2 *Mil* air force.

aviador,-a *nm,f* aviator, flier; *Mil (piloto)* air force pilot.

aviar |29| *vtr* *(preparar)* to prepare, get ready.

avícola *adj* poultry.

avicultura *nf* aviculture; *(de aves de corral)* poultry keeping.

avidez *nf* avidity, eagerness.

ávido,-a *adj* avid; **a. de,** eager for.

avinagrado,-a *adj* vinegary, sour; *fig* sour.

avinagrarse *vr* to turn sour; *fig* to become sour *o* bitter.

avión[1] *nm* aeroplane, *US* airplane, plane, aircraft; **viajar en a.,** to fly, go by plane; **por a.,** *(en carta)* airmail.

avión[2] *nm* *Orn* martin.

avioneta *nf* light aircraft *o* plane.

avíos *nmpl* *Culin* ingredients.

avisar *vtr* 1 *(informar)* to inform; **avísame cuando hayas acabado,** let me know when you finish. 2 *(advertir)* to warn; **ya te avisé,** I warned you. 3 *(llamar)* to call for; **a. a la policía,** to notify the police; **a. al médico,** to send for the doctor.

aviso *nm* 1 notice; *(advertencia)* warning; *(nota)* note; **hasta nuevo a.,** until further notice; **sin previo a.,** without notice. 2 **estar sobre a.,** to know what's going on, be in on it.

avispa *nf* wasp.

avispado,-a *adj* *fam* quick-witted.

avispero *nm* *(nido)* wasps' nest.

avistar *vtr* to see, sight.

avituallamiento *nm* provisioning.

avivar *vtr* *(fuego)* to stoke (up); *(pasión)* to intensify; *(paso)* to quicken.

avizor,-a *adj* **estar ojo a.,** to be on the alert *o* on the lookout.

axila *nf* armpit, axilla.

axioma *nm* axiom.

ay *interj* *(dolor)* ouch!

aya *nf* arc *(niñera)* nanny.

ayer I *adv* yesterday; **a. por la mañana/ por la tarde,** yesterday morning/ afternoon; **a. por la noche,** last night; **antes de a.,** the day before yesterday. II *nm* el a., yesteryear.

ayuda *nf* help, assistance; **ir en a. de algn,** to come to sb's assistance.

ayudante *nmf* assistant; *Med* **a. técnico-sanitario,** nurse.

ayudar I *vtr* to help; **¿en qué puedo ayudarle?,** (how) can I help you? II **ayu-**

darse *vr* 1 *(unos a otros)* to help. 2 **a. de,** to use, make use of.

ayunar *vi* to fast.

ayunas *nfpl* **en a.,** without having eaten breakfast.

ayuno *nm* fasting; **guardar/hacer a.,** to fast.

ayuntamiento *nm* *(institución)* town council; *(edificio)* town hall.

azabache *nm* jet; **negro a.,** jet black.

azada *nf* hoe.

azafata *nf* 1 *Av* air hostess. 2 *(de congresos)* stewardess; *(de concurso)* hostess.

azafrán *nm* saffron.

azahar *nm* *(del naranjo)* orange blossom; *(del limonero)* lemon blossom.

azar *nm* chance; **por a.,** by chance; **al a.,** at random; **juegos de a.,** games of chance; **los azares de la vida,** the ups and downs of life.

azaroso,-a *adj* hazardous, dangerous.

azogue *nm* mercury, quicksilver.

azorado,-a *adj* embarrassed.

azorar I *vtr* to embarrass. II **azorarse** *vr* to be embarrassed.

Azores *nfpl* **las (Islas) A.,** the Azores.

azotar *vtr* to beat; *(con látigo)* to whip, flog; *fig* to scourge.

azote *nm* 1 *(golpe)* smacking; *(latigazo)* lash, stroke (of the whip). 2 *fig* scourge.

azotea *nf* flat roof.

azteca *adj & nmf* Aztec.

azúcar *nm & f* sugar; **a. blanco,** refined sugar; **a. moreno,** brown sugar.

azucarado,-a *adj* sweetened.

azucarero,-a I *nm & f* sugar bowl. II *adj* sugar.

azucena *nf* white lily.

azufre *nm* sulphur, *US* sulfur.

azul *adj & nm* blue; **a. celeste,** sky blue; **a. marino,** navy blue; **a. turquesa,** turquoise; **sangre a.,** blue blood.

azulado,-a *adj* bluish.

azulejo *nm* *(glazed)* tile.

azuzar |4| *vtr* **a. los perros a algn,** to set the dogs on sb.

B

B, b |be| *nf* *(la letra)* B, b.

baba *nf* dribble; *fig* **se le caía la b.,** he was delighted.

babear *vi* *(niño)* to dribble; *(adulto, animal)* to slobber.

babel *nm & f* bedlam.

babero *nm* bib.

Babia *n* *fig* **estar en B.,** to be daydreaming.

babor *nm* *Náut* port, port side.

babosa *nf* slug.

baboso,-a *adj* *fam* slimy; *Am* fool, idiot.

babucha *nf* slipper.

baca *nf* *Aut* roof rack.

bacalao *nm* *(pez)* cod.

bache *nm* 1 *(en carretera)* pot hole. 2 *Av* air pocket. 3 *fig* bad patch; **pasar un b.,** to go through a bad patch.

bachillerato *nm* ≈ General Certificate of Secondary Education, *US* high school degree.

bacilo *nm* bacillus.

bacon *nm* bacon.

bacteria *nf* bacterium; **bacterias,** bacteria.

bacteriológico,-a *adj* bacteriological;

guerra bacteriológica, germ warfare.

báculo *nm* walking stick; *(de obispo)* crosier.

badén *nm Aut* bump.

bádminton *nm* badminton.

bafle *nm* loudspeaker.

bagaje *nm* baggage.

bagatela *nf (baratija)* knick-knack; *fig* trifle.

Bagdad *n* Baghdad.

Bahamas *npl* las (Islas) B., the Bahamas.

bahía *nf* bay.

baila(d)or,-a *nm,f* flamenco dancer.

bailar |15| *vtr & vi* to dance; *fig* b. al son que le tocan, to toe the line; *fam* ¡que me quiten lo baila(d)o!, but at least I had a good time!

bailarín,-ina *nm,f* dancer; *(clásico)* ballet dancer.

baile *nm* 1 *(danza)* dance. 2 *(fiesta popular)* dance; *(formal)* ball; b. de disfraces, fancy dress ball.

baja *nf* 1 drop, fall; *Fin* jugar a la b., to bear. 2 *Mil* loss, casualty. 3 dar de b. a algn, *(despedir)* to lay sb off; darse de b., *(por enfermedad)* to take sick leave; *(de un club)* to resign (de, from), drop out (de, of).

bajada *nf* 1 *(descenso)* descent. 2 *(cuesta)* slope. 3 b. de bandera, *(de taxi)* minimum fare.

bajamar *nf* low tide.

bajar I *vtr* 1 to come *o* go down; b. la escalera, to come *o* go downstairs. 2 *(descender)* to bring *o* get *o* take down; *(volumen)* to turn down; *(voz, telón)* to lower; *(precios etc)* to reduce, cut; *(persiana)* to let down; *(cabeza)* to bow *o* lower. II *vi* 1 to go *o* come down. 2 *(apearse)* to get off; *(de un coche)* to get out (de, of). 3 *(disminuir)* to fall, drop. III bajarse *vr* 1 to come *o* go down. 2 *(apearse)* to get off; *(de un coche)* to get out (de, of).

bajeza *nf* despicable action.

bajinis (por lo) *loc adv fam* on the sly.

bajío *nm* 1 sandbank. 2 *Am* lowland.

bajista I *adj Fin* bearish; tendencia b., downward trend. II *nmf* 1 *Fin* bear. 2 *Mús* bass guitarist.

bajo,-a I *adj* 1 low; *(persona)* short; *(sonido)* faint, soft; en voz baja, in a low voice; planta baja, ground floor; de baja calidad, of poor quality; la clase baja, the lower class. 2 *fig (vil)* base, contemptible. II *nm* 1 *Mús* bass. 2 *(planta baja)* ground floor. III *adv* low; hablar b., to speak quietly; *fig* por lo b., on the sly. IV *prep* 1 *(lugar)* under, underneath; b. tierra, underground; b. la lluvia, in the rain. 2 *Pol Hist* under; b. la República, under the Republic. 3 b. cero, *(temperatura)* below zero. 4 *Jur* under; b. juramento, under oath; b. pena de muerte,

on pain of death; b. fianza, on bail.

bajón *nm* 1 *(bajada)* sharp fall, decline. 2 *Com* slump. 3 *(de salud)* relapse, deterioration.

bajorrelieve *nm* bas-relief.

bajura *nf* pesca de b., coastal fishing.

bala *nf* bullet; *fig* como una b., like a shot.

balada *nf* ballad.

baladí *adj (pl baladíes)* trivial.

balance *nm* 1 *Fin* balance; *(declaración)* balance sheet; *fig* hacer b. de una situación, to take stock of a situation. 2 *(resultado)* outcome.

balancear I *vtr* to rock. II balancearse *vr (en mecedora)* to rock; *(en columpio)* to swing.

balanceo *nm* rocking, swinging.

balanza *nf* scales *pl*; *fig* estar en la b., to be in the balance *o* in danger; b. comercial, balance of trade; b. de pagos, balance of payments.

balar *vi* to bleat.

balaustrada *nf* balustrade, railing.

balazo *nm* 1 *(disparo)* shot; matar a algn de un b., to shoot sb dead. 2 *(herida)* bullet wound.

balboa *nm Fin* standard monetary unit of Panama.

balbucear *vi (adulto)* to stutter, stammer; *(niño)* to babble.

balbuceo *nm (de adulto)* stuttering, stammering; *(de niño)* babbling.

balbucir *vi defect* → balbucear.

Balcanes *npl* los B., the Balkans.

balcón *nm* balcony.

baldado,-a *adj fam* shattered.

baldar *vtr* to cripple, maim.

balde[1] *nm* pail, bucket.

balde[2] *loc adv* 1 de b., *(gratis)* free. 2 en b., *(en vano)* in vain.

baldío,-a *adj (terreno)* uncultivated, waste; *(esfuerzo)* vain, useless.

baldosa *nf (ceramic)* floor tile; *(para pavimentar)* flagstone, paving stone.

balear I *adj* Balearic. II *nmf* native *o* inhabitant of the Balearic Islands.

Baleares *npl* las (Islas) B., the Balearic Islands.

balido *nm* bleating, bleat.

balística *nf* ballistics *sing*.

balístico,-a *adj* ballistic.

baliza *nf* 1 *Náut* buoy. 2 *Av* beacon.

ballena *nf* whale.

ballet *nm* ballet.

balneario *nm* spa, health resort.

balompié *nm* football.

balón *nm* ball, football; *fig* b. de oxígeno, boost.

baloncesto *nm* basketball.

balonmano *nm* handball.

balonvolea *nm* volleyball.

balsa *nf* 1 *Náut* raft. 2 *fig* como una b. de aceite, very quiet.

bálsamo *nm* balsam, balm.
Báltico *nm* el (Mar) B., the Baltic (Sea).
baluarte *nm fig* stronghold.
bambas® *nfpl* trainers.
bambolear *vi*, **bambolearse** *vr* to swing; *(persona, árbol)* to sway; *(mesa, silla)* to wobble.
bambú *nm* (*pl* **bambúes**) bamboo.
banal *adj* banal, trivial.
banalidad *nf* triviality, banality.
banana *nf* banana.
banano *nm* (*fruto*) banana; (*árbol*) banana tree.
banca *nf* 1 (*asiento*) bench. 2 *Com Fin* (the) banks; (*actividad*) banking. 3 (*en juegos*) bank.
bancario,-a *adj* banking.
bancarrota *nf Fin* bankruptcy; **estar en b.**, to be bankrupt.
banco *nm* 1 bench. 2 *Com Fin* bank. 3 **b. de arena**, sandbank. 4 (*de peces*) shoal, school. 5 *Geol* layer.
banda *nf* 1 *Mús* band. 2 *Cin* **b. sonora**, sound track. 3 (*de pájaros*) flock. 4 (*cinta*) sash. 5 (*lado*) side; *Ftb* **línea de b.**, touchline; **saque de b.**, throw-in.
bandada *nf* flock.
bandazo *nm* **dar bandazos**, to lurch.
bandeja *nf* tray; *fig* **servir algo a algn en b.**, to hand sth to sb on a plate.
bandera *nf* flag.
banderín *nm* pennant, small flag.
bandido *nm* bandit, outlaw.
bando¹ *nm* 1 *Jur* (*edicto*) edict, proclamation. 2 **bandos**, banns.
bando² *nm* faction, side; **pasarse al otro b.**, to go over to the other side, change allegiances.
bandolero *nm* bandit, outlaw.
banquero,-a *nm,f* banker.
banqueta *nf* stool.
banquete *nm* banquet, feast; **b. de bodas**, wedding reception.
banquillo *nm* 1 *Jur* dock. 2 *Dep* bench.
bañador *nm* (*de mujer*) bathing o swimming costume; (*de hombre*) swimming trunks *pl*.
bañar I *vtr* 1 to bath. 2 (*cubrir*) to coat, cover; **b. en oro**, to goldplate. II **bañarse** *vr* (*en baño*) to have o take a bath; (*en mar, piscina*) to go for a swim.
bañera *nf* bath, bathtub.
bañista *nmf* bather, swimmer.
baño *nm* 1 bath; **tomar un b.**, to have o take a bath; *fig* **darse un b. de sol**, to sunbathe; **b. de sangre**, bloodbath. 2 (*de oro etc*) coat; (*de chocolate etc*) coating, covering. 3 (*cuarto de baño*) bathroom; (*lavabo*) toilet.
bar *nm* bar, pub.
barahúnda *nf* din, uproar.
baraja *nf* pack, deck.
barajar *vtr* (*cartas*) to shuffle; *fig* (*nombres, cifras*) to juggle with.

baranda, barandilla *nf* (*de escalera*) handrail, banister; (*de balcón*) handrail.
baratija *nf* trinket, knick-knack.
baratillo *nm* flea market.
barato,-a I *adj* cheap. II *adv* cheaply.
baraúnda *nf* din, uproar.
barba *nf* 1 *Anat* chin. 2 (*pelo*) beard; *fig* **cien pesetas por b.**, a hundred pesetas a head.
barbacoa *nf* barbecue.
barbaridad *nf* 1 atrocity. 2 (*disparate*) piece of nonsense; **no digas barbaridades**, don't talk nonsense. 3 **una b.**, a lot; **costar una b.**, to cost a fortune.
barbarie *nf* savagery, cruelty.
bárbaro,-a I *adj* 1 *Hist* barbarian. 2 (*cruel*) barbaric, barbarous. 3 *fam* (*enorme*) massive. 4 *fam* (*estupendo*) tremendous, terrific. II *nm,f Hist* barbarian.
barbecho *nm* fallow land; **dejar en b.**, to leave fallow.
barbería *nf* barber's (shop).
barbero *nm* barber.
barbilla *nf* chin.
barbitúrico *nm* barbiturate.
barbudo,-a *adj* with a heavy beard.
barca *nf* small boat.
barcaza *nf* lighter.
barcelonés,-esa I *adj* of o from Barcelona. II *nm,f* native o inhabitant of Barcelona.
barco *nm* boat, ship; **b. de pasajeros**, liner; **b. de vapor**, steamer.
baremo *nm* scale.
barítono *nm* baritone.
barlovento *nm* windward.
barman *nm* barman.
barniz *nm* 1 (*en madera*) varnish; (*en cerámica*) glaze. 2 *fig* veneer.
barnizar |4| *vtr* (*madera*) to varnish; (*cerámica*) to glaze.
barómetro *nm* barometer.
barón *nm* baron.
baronesa *nf* baroness.
barquero,-a *nm,f* (*hombre*) boatman; (*mujer*) boatwoman.
barquillo *nm* wafer.
barra *nf* 1 bar; **b. de pan**, French loaf, baguette; **b. de labios**, lipstick. 2 (*mostrador*) bar. 3 *Gimn* **b. fija**, horizontal bar.
barraca *nf* 1 (*caseta*) shack, hut. 2 (*en Valencia y Murcia*) thatched farmhouse.
barracón *nm Mil* prefabricated hut.
barranco *nm* (*despeñadero*) cliff, precipice; (*torrentera*) gully, ravine.
barrena *nf* twist drill.
barrenar *vtr Téc* to drill.
barrendero,-a *nm,f* sweeper, street sweeper.
barreno *nm* 1 (*taladro*) large drill. 2 *Min* charge.
barreño *nm* tub.
barrer I *vtr* to sweep. II *vi* (*en elecciones*)

to win by landslide.

barrera *nf* barrier.

barricada *nf* barricade.

barrida *nf* landslide victory.

barriga *nf* belly; *fam* tummy.

barrigón,-ona, barrigudo,-a *adj* potbellied.

barril *nm* barrel; **cerveza de b.**, draught beer.

barrillo *nm* pimple, spot.

barrio *nm* area, district; **del b.**, local; **el B. Gótico**, the Gothic Quarter; **b. chino**, red-light district; **barrios bajos**, slums.

barrizal *nm* mire, quagmire.

barro *nm* 1 (*lodo*) mud. 2 (*arcilla*) clay; **objetos de b.**, earthenware *sing*.

barroco,-a *adj* baroque.

barruntar *vtr* (*sospechar*) to suspect; (*presentir*) to have a feeling.

barrunto *nm* (*presentimiento*) feeling, presentiment; (*sospecha*) suspicion.

bartola (a la) *loc adv fam* **tenderse** *o* **tumbarse a la b.**, to laze around, idle away one's time.

bártulos *nmpl fam* things, bits and pieces.

barullo *nm* (*alboroto*) row, din; (*confusión*) confusion.

basar *vtr* to base (**en**, on). II **basarse** *vr* (*teoría, película*) to be based (**en**, on); **¿en qué te basas para decir eso?**, what grounds do you have for saying that?

basca *nf arg* people, crowd.

báscula *nf* scales *pl*; (*para camiones*) weighbridge.

bascular *vi* to tilt.

base *nf* 1 base; **sueldo b.**, minimum wage; *Inform* **b. de datos**, data base. 2 (*de argumento, teoría*) basis; **en b. a**, on the basis of; **a b. de estudiar**, by studying; **a b. de productos naturales**, using natural products. 3 (*de partido*) grass roots; **miembro de b.**, rank and file member. 4 (*nociones*) grounding.

básico,-a *adj* basic.

basílica *nf* basilica.

básquet *nm* basketball.

bastante I *adj* 1 (*suficiente*) enough; **b. tiempo/comida**, enough time/food; **bastantes platos**, enough plates. 2 (*abundante*) quite a lot of; **hace b. calor/frío**, it's quite hot/cold; **bastantes amigos**, quite a lot of friends. II *adv* 1 (*suficiente*) enough; **con esto hay b.**, that is enough; **no soy lo b. rico (como) para ...**, I am not rich enough to .... 2 (*considerablemente*) fairly, quite; **me gusta b.**, I quite like it; **vamos b. al cine**, we go to the cinema quite *o* fairly often.

bastar I *vi* to be sufficient *o* enough, suffice; **basta con tres**, three will be enough; **¡basta de tonterías!**, enough of this nonsense!; **basta con tocarlo para que se abra**, you only have to touch it and it opens; **¡basta (ya)!**, that's

enough!, that will do! II **bastarse** *vr* **b. a sí mismo**, to be self-sufficient, rely only on oneself.

bastardilla *nf Impr* italics *pl*.

bastardo,-a *adj & nm,f* bastard.

bastidor *nm* 1 frame. 2 *Teat* **bastidores**, wings; *fig* **entre b.**, behind the scenes.

bastión *nm* bastion.

basto,-a *adj* (*cosa*) rough, coarse; (*persona*) coarse, uncouth.

bastos *nm Naipes* ≈ clubs.

bastón *nm* stick, walking stick.

basura *nf* rubbish, *US* trash, garbage.

basurero *nm* 1 (*persona*) dustman, refuse collector, *US* garbage collector. 2 (*lugar*) rubbish dump, *US* garbage dump.

bata *nf* (*para casa*) dressing gown; (*de médico etc*) white coat; (*de científico*) lab coat.

batacazo *nm* 1 crash, bang. 2 *Am* fluke, stroke of luck.

batalla *nf* battle; **librar b.**, to do *o* join battle; **b. campal**, pitched battle.

batallar *vi* to fight, quarrel.

batallón *nm* battalion.

batata *nf* sweet potato.

batatazo *nm Am* → **batacazo**.

bate *nm Dep* bat.

batear I *vi* to bat. II *vtr* to hit.

batería I *nf* 1 battery. 2 *Mús* drums *pl*. 3 **b. de cocina**, pots and pans, set of pans. II *nmf* drummer.

batiburrillo *nm* jumble, mess.

batida *nf* 1 (*de la policía*) raid. 2 (*en caza*) beat.

batido,-a I *adj* 1 *Culin* whipped. 2 *Dep* **tierra batida**, clay. II *nm* milk shake.

batidora *nf Culin* beater, whisk.

batiente *adj* **reírse a mandíbula b.**, to laugh one's head off.

batín *nm* short dressing gown.

batir I *vtr* 1 to beat. 2 (*huevo*) to beat; (*nata*) to whip, whisk. 3 (*récord*) to break. 4 (*en caza*) to beat. II **batirse** *vr* to fight.

batuta *nf Mús* baton; *fig* **llevar la b.**, to be in charge.

baúl *nm* 1 trunk. 2 *Am Aut* boot, *US* trunk.

bautismo *nm* baptism, christening.

bautizar |4| *vtr* to baptize, christen; (*vino*) to water down.

bautizo *nm* baptism, christening.

Baviera *n* Bavaria.

baya *nf* berry.

bayeta *nf* floorcloth.

bayo,-a *adj* whitish yellow.

bayoneta *nf* bayonet.

baza *nf* trick; *fig* **meter b.**, to butt in.

bazar *nm* bazaar.

bazo *nm* spleen.

bazofia *nf pey* rubbish.

beatería *nf* sanctimoniousness.

beato,-a *adj* (*piadoso*) devout; *pey* prudish, sanctimonious.

bebé *nm* baby; **b. probeta,** test-tube baby.

bebedero *nm* drinking trough, water trough.

bebedor,-a *nm,f* (hard *o* heavy) drinker.

beber *vtr & vi* to drink.

bebible *adj* drinkable.

bebida *nf* drink; **darse a la b.,** to take to drink.

bebido,-a *adj* drunk.

beca *nf* grant.

becar |1| *vtr* to award a grant to.

becario,-a *nm,f* grant holder.

becerro *nm* calf.

bechamel *nf* bechamel; **salsa b.,** bechamel sauce, white sauce.

becuadro *nm Mús* natural sign.

bedel *nm* beadle.

begonia *nf* begonia.

beige *adj & nm inv* beige.

béisbol *nm* baseball.

Belén *n* Bethlehem.

belén *nm* nativity scene, crib.

belga *adj & nmf* Belgian.

Bélgica *n* Belgium.

Belgrado *n* Belgrade.

Belice *n* Belize.

bélico,-a *adj* warlike, bellicose; *(preparativos etc)* war; **material b.,** armaments *pl.*

belicoso,-a *adj* warlike, bellicose; *(agresivo)* aggressive.

beligerancia *nf* belligerence.

beligerante *adj* belligerent; **los países beligerantes,** the countries at war.

bellaco,-a I *adj* wicked, roguish. **II** *nm,f* scoundrel, rogue.

belleza *nf* beauty.

bello,-a *adj* beautiful.

bellota *nf Bot* acorn; *fig* **animal de b.,** blockhead.

bemol I *adj Mús* flat. **II** *nm* **esto tiene bemoles,** this is a tough one.

bencina *nf Am* petrol.

bendecir |12| *vtr* to bless; **b. la mesa,** to say grace; **¡Dios te bendiga!,** God bless you!

bendición *nf* blessing.

bendito,-a I *adj* blessed; *(maldito)* damned. **II** *nm,f (bonachón)* good sort, kind soul; *(tontorrón)* simple soul.

beneficencia *nf* beneficence, charity.

beneficiado,-a *adj* favoured, *US* favored; **salir b. de algo,** to do well out of sth.

beneficiar |12| **I** *vtr* to benefit. **II beneficiarse** *vr* **b. de o con algo,** to profit from *o* by sth.

beneficiario,-a *nm,f* beneficiary; **margen b.,** profit margin.

beneficio *nm* **1** *Com Fin* profit. **2** *(bien)* benefit; **en b. propio,** in one's own interest; **un concierto a b. de ...,** a concert in aid of ....

beneficioso,-a *adj* beneficial.

benéfico,-a *adj* charitable.

benemérita *nf* **la B.,** the Spanish Civil Guard.

beneplácito *nm fml* approval, consent.

benevolencia *nf* benevolence.

benevolente, benévolo,-a *adj* benevolent.

bengala *nf* flare.

benigno,-a *adj (persona)* gentle, benign; *(clima)* mild; *(tumor)* benign.

benjamín,-ina *nm,f* youngest child.

beodo,-a *adj* drunk.

berberecho *nm* (common) cockle.

berbiquí *nm Téc* drill.

berenjena *nf* aubergine, *US* eggplant.

Berlín *n* Berlin.

berlina *nf (coche)* saloon; *(carruaje)* sedan.

berlinés,-esa I *adj* of *o* from Berlin. **II** *nm,f* Berliner.

bermejo,-a *adj* reddish.

bermellón *nm* vermilion.

Bermudas I *nfpl* **las (Islas) B.,** Bermuda *sing.* **II** *nmpl* **bermudas,** *(prenda)* Bermuda shorts.

Berna *n* Bern.

berrear *vi* to bellow, low.

berrido *nm* bellowing, lowing.

berrinche *nm fam* rage, tantrum.

berro *nm* cress, watercress.

berza *nf* cabbage.

besar I *vtr* to kiss. **II besarse** *vr* to kiss.

beso *nm* kiss.

best-seller *nm* best-seller.

bestia I *nf* beast, animal; **b. de carga,** beast of burden. **II** *nmf fam fig* brute, beast. **III** *adj fig* brutish, boorish; **a lo b.,** rudely.

bestial *adj* bestial; *fam (enorme)* huge, tremendous; *(extraordinario)* fantastic, terrific.

bestialidad *nf* **1** *fam (estupidez)* stupidity. **2** *(crueldad)* act of cruelty. **3** *fam* **una b. de,** tons of, stacks of.

besugo *nm* **1** *(pez)* sea bream. **2** *(persona)* idiot, half-wit.

besuquear *fam* **I** *vtr* to kiss, cover with kisses. **II besuquearse** *vr* to smooch.

betún *nm (para el calzado)* shoe polish; *Quím* bitumen.

biberón *nm* baby's bottle, feeding bottle.

Biblia *nf* Bible.

bíblico,-a *adj* biblical.

bibliografía *nf* bibliography.

biblioteca *nf* library; **b. ambulante,** mobile library.

bibliotecario,-a *nm,f* librarian.

BIC *nf abr de* **Brigada de Investigación Criminal,** ≈ Criminal Investigation Department, CID.

bicameral *adj Pol* bicameral, two-chamber.

bicarbonato *nm* bicarbonate; **b. sódico,** bicarbonate of soda.

bicentenario *nm* bicentenary, *US* bicentennial.

bíceps *nm inv* biceps.

bicha *nf* snake.

bicho *nm* **1** bug, insect; **¿qué b. te ha picado?**, what's bugging you? **2** *Taur* bull. **3** *fam* **todo b. viviente**, every living soul; **un b. raro**, a weirdo, an oddball.

bici *nf fam* bike.

bicicleta *nf* bicycle; **montar en b.**, to ride a bicycle.

bicolor *adj* two-coloured; *Pol* **gobierno b.**, two-party government.

bidé *nm* bidet.

bidón *nm* drum.

biela *nf Aut* connecting rod.

bien[1] *adv* **1** *(correctamente)* well; **habla b. (el) inglés**, she speaks English well; **responder b.**, to answer correctly; **hiciste b. en decírmelo**, you were right to tell me; **las cosas le van b.**, things are going well for him; **¡b.!**, good!, great!; **¡muy b.!**, excellent, first class!; **¡qué b.!**, great!, fantastic! **2** *(de salud)* well; **sentirse/encontrarse/estar b.**, to feel well. **3 vivir b.**, to be comfortably off; **¡está b.!**, *(¡de acuerdo!)* fine!, all right!; **¡ya está b.!**, that's (quite) enough!; **aquí se está muy b.**, it's really nice here; **esta falda te sienta b.**, this skirt suits you; *fam* **ese libro está muy b.**, that book is very good; *fam* **su novia está muy b.**, his girlfriend is very nice. **4** *(intensificador)* very, quite; **b. temprano**, very early, nice and early; **b. caliente**, pretty hot; **b. es verdad que ...**, it's quite clear that .... **5 más b.**, rather, a little. **6 b. podía haberme avisado**, she might have let me know. **7** *(de buena gana)* willingly, gladly; **b. me tomaría una cerveza**, I'd really love a beer.

II *conj* **ahora b.**, now, now then; **o b.**, or, or else; **b. ... o b. ...**, either ... or ...; **no b.**, as soon as; **no b. llegó ...**, no sooner had she arrived than ...; **si b.**, although, even if.

III *adj* **la gente b.**, the wealthy, the upper classes.

bien[2] *nm* **1** *(bondad)* good; **el b. y el mal**, good and evil; **un hombre/familia de b.**, a good man/family. **2** *(bienestar)* **por el b. de**, for the good of; **lo hago por tu b.**, he does it for your sake. **3 bienes**, goods; **bienes de equipo**, capital goods; **bienes gananciales**, communal property; **bienes inmuebles**, real estate; **bienes de consumo**, consumer goods.

bienal *nf* biennial exhibition.

bienestar *nm* *(personal)* well-being, contentment; *(comodidad)* ease, comfort; **la sociedad del b.**, the affluent society.

bienhechor,-a *nm,f* *(hombre)* benefactor; *(mujer)* benefactress.

bienintencionado,-a *adj* well-meaning, well-intentioned.

bienio *nm* biennium, two-year period.

bienvenida *nf* welcome; **dar la b. a algn**, to welcome sb.

bienvenido,-a *adj* welcome.

bife *nm* steak.

bifocal *adj* bifocal; **gafas bifocales**, bifocals.

bifurcación *nf* bifurcation; *(de la carretera)* fork.

bifurcarse |1| *vr* to fork, branch off.

bigamia *nf* bigamy.

bígamo,-a **I** *adj* bigamous. **II** *nm,f* bigamist.

bigote *nm* *(de persona)* moustache, *US* mustache; *(de animal)* *(usu pl)* whiskers *pl*.

bilateral *adj* bilateral; **acuerdo b.**, bilateral agreement.

bilbaíno,-a **I** *adj* of *o* from Bilbao. **II** *nm,f* native *o* inhabitant of Bilbao.

bilingüe *adj* bilingual.

bilis *nf* bile.

billar *nm* **1** *(juego)* billiards *sing*; **b. americano**, pool; **b. ruso**, snooker. **2** *(mesa)* billiard table.

billete *nm* **1** ticket; **b. de ida y vuelta**, return (ticket), *US* round-trip ticket; **b. sencillo** *o* **de ida**, single (ticket). **2** *(de banco)* note, *US* bill; **un b. de mil pesetas**, a thousand peseta note.

billetera *nf*, **billetero** *nm* wallet, *US* billfold.

billón *nm* billion, *US* trillion.

bimensual *adj* twice-monthly, bi-monthly.

bimotor **I** *adj* twin-engined. **II** *nm* twin-engined plane.

binario,-a *adj* binary.

bingo *nm* **1** *(juego)* bingo. **2** *(sala)* bingo hall.

binomio *nm* binomial.

biodegradable *adj* biodegradable.

biofísica *nf* biophysics.

biografía *nf* biography.

biográfico,-a *adj* biographical.

biógrafo,-a *nm,f* biographer.

biología *nf* biology.

biológico,-a *adj* biological.

biólogo,-a *nm,f* biologist.

biombo *nm* (folding) screen.

biomasa *nf* bio-mass.

biopsia *nf* biopsy.

bioquímica *nf* biochemistry.

bioquímico,-a **I** *adj* biochemical. **II** *nm,f* biochemist.

bióxido *nm* dioxide; **b. de carbono**, carbon dioxide.

bipartidismo *nm* two-party system.

biquini *nm* bikini.

birlar *vtr fam* to pinch, nick.

Birmania *n* Burma.

birmano,-a *adj & nm,f* Burmese.

birrete *nm* cap, beret; *Rel* biretta; *Univ* mortar-board.

birria *nf fam* rubbish.

bis I *nm* encore. II *adv* twice.
bisabuela *nf* great-grandmother.
bisabuelo *nm* great-grandfather; **bisabuelos**, great-grandparents.
bisagra *nf* hinge; **partido b.**, party holding the balance of power.
bisbisar, bisbisear *vtr* to whisper.
bisexual *adj & nmf* bisexual.
bisiesto *adj* **año b.**, leap year.
bisnieto,-a *nm,f* (*niño*) great-grandson; (*niña*) great-granddaughter; **mis bisnietos**, my great-grandchildren.
bisonte *nm* bison, American buffalo.
bisoño,-a *adj* inexperienced.
bisté *nm* **bistec** *nm* steak.
bisturí *nm* scalpel.
bisutería *nf* imitation jewellery *o* US jewelry.
bit *nm Inform* bit.
bíter *nm* bitters *pl*.
bizantino,-a *adj fig* **discusiones bizantinas**, hair-splitting arguments.
bizco,-a I *adj* cross-eyed. II *nm,f* cross-eyed person.
bizcocho *nm* sponge cake.
biznieto,-a *nm,f* → **bisnieto,-a**.
blanca *nf fam* **estar sin b.**, to be flat broke.
blanco,-a¹ I *adj* white; (*tez*) fair. II *nm,f* (*hombre*) white man; (*mujer*) white woman; **los blancos**, whites.
blanco² *nm* 1 (*color*) white. 2 (*hueco*) blank; **dejó la hoja en b.**, he left the page blank; **votos en b.**, blank votes; *fig* **pasar la noche en b.**, to have a sleepless night; **me quedé en b.**, my mind went blank. 3 (*diana*) target; **dar en el b.**, to hit the target; *fig* **ser el b. de todas las miradas**, to be the centre of attention.
blancura *nf* whiteness.
blandengue *adj pey* weak, soft.
blandir *vtr* to brandish.
blando,-a *adj* soft.
blanquear *vtr* 1 to whiten. 2 (*encalar*) to whitewash. 3 (*dinero*) to launder.
blanquecino,-a *adj* whitish.
blanqueo *nm* 1 whitening. 2 (*encalado*) whitewashing. 3 (*de dinero*) laundering.
blasfemar *vi* to blaspheme (**contra**, against).
blasfemia *nf* blasphemy.
blasón *nm* coat of arms.
bledo *nm fam* **me importa un b.**, I couldn't give a damn.
blindado,-a *adj Mil* armoured, US armored, armour-plated, US armor-plated; (*antibalas*) bullet-proof; **coche b.**, bulletproof car; **puerta blindada**, reinforced door, security door.
blindaje *nm* armour, US armor; (*vehículo*) armour *o* US armor plating.
bloc *nm* pad; **b. de notas**, notepad.
bloque *nm* 1 block; **en b.**, en bloc; **b. de pisos**, (block of) flats. 2 *Pol* bloc; **el b.**

comunista, the Communist Bloc.
bloquear *vtr* 1 to block. 2 *Mil* to blockade.
bloqueo *nm* blockade; *Dep* block.
blues *nm* blues *pl*.
blusa *nf* blouse.
blusón *nm* loose blouse, smock.
boato *nm* show, ostentation.
bobada *nf* nonsense; **decir bobadas**, to talk nonsense.
bobalicón,-ona *fam* I *adj* simple, stupid. II *nm,f* simpleton, idiot.
bobería *nf* → **bobada**.
bobina *nf* 1 reel. 2 *Elec* coil.
bobo,-a I *adj* (*tonto*) stupid, silly; (*ingenuo*) naïve. II *nm,f* fool.
boca *nf* 1 mouth; **b. abajo**, face downward; **b. arriba**, face upward; *fig* **a pedir de b.**, in accordance with one's wishes; *fig* **andar de b. en b.**, to be the talk of the town; *fam* **¡cierra la b!**, shut up!; *fam* **con la b. abierta**, open-mouthed; *fam* **se le hizo la b. agua**, his mouth watered; **el b. a b.**, kiss of life, mouth-to-mouth respiration. 2 **la b. del metro**, the entrance to the tube *o* underground station; **b. de riego**, hydrant.
bocacalle *nf* entrance to a street.
bocadillo *nm* 1 sandwich; **un b. de jamón/tortilla**, a ham/omelette sandwich. 2 (*de cómic*) balloon.
bocado *nm* 1 (*mordedura*) bite. 2 (*de caballo*) bit.
bocajarro (a) *loc adv* point-blank.
bocanada *nf* 1 (*de vino*) mouthful. 2 (*de humo*) puff; **una b. de viento**, a gust of wind.
bocata *nm* sandwich.
bocazas *nmf inv fam* bigmouth, blabbermouth.
boceto *nm Arte* sketch, outline; (*esquema*) outline, plan.
bochinche *nm fam* uproar; **armar un b.**, to kick up a row.
bochorno *nm* 1 (*tiempo*) sultry *o* close weather; (*calor sofocante*) stifling heat. 2 *fig* (*vergüenza*) shame, embarrassment.
bochornoso,-a *adj* 1 (*tiempo*) sultry, close, muggy; (*calor*) stifling. 2 *fig* (*vergonzoso*) shameful, embarrassing.
bocina *nf* horn; **tocar la b.**, to blow *o* sound one's horn.
bocinazo *nm* hoot, toot.
boda *nf* wedding, marriage; **bodas de plata**, silver wedding *sing*.
bodega *nf* 1 wine cellar; (*tienda*) wine shop. 2 *Náut* hold. 3 (*almacén*) warehouse. 4 *Am* grocery store, grocer's.
bodegón *nm* still-life.
bodrio *nm fam* rubbish, trash.
body *nm* bodystocking, leotard.
BOE *nm abr de* **Boletín Oficial del Estado**, Official Gazette.
bofetada *nf*, **bofetón** *nm* slap on the

face; **dar una b./un b. a algn,** to slap sb's face.

boga nf fig **estar en b.,** to be in vogue.

bogar [7] vi 1 (remar) to row. 2 (navegar) to sail.

bogavante nm lobster.

bogotano,-a I adj of o from Bogotá. **II** n m,f native of Bogotá.

bohío nm Am hut, cabin.

boicot nm (pl **boicots**) boycott.

boicotear vtr to boycott.

boicoteo nm boycott.

boina nf beret.

bol nm bowl.

bola nf 1 ball; (canica) marble; **b. de nieve,** snowball; **no dar pie con b.,** to be unable to do anything right. 2 fam (mentira) fib, lie; **meter bolas,** to tell fibs. 3 Am (rumor) rumour.

bolchevique adj & nmf Bolshevik.

bolear vtr to throw.

bolera nf bowling alley.

boletería nf Am Dep Ferroc ticket office, GB booking office; Teat ticket office, box office.

boletín nm bulletin; **B. Oficial del Estado,** Official Gazette.

boleto nm ticket.

boli nm fam ball-point pen, biro®.

boliche nm 1 (juego) bowling, skittles. 2 (bola) jack. 3 (lugar) bowling alley.

bólido nm Aut racing car.

bolígrafo nm ballpoint (pen), biro®.

bolívar nm Fin standard monetary unit of Venezuela.

Bolivia n Bolivia.

boliviano,-a I adj & nm,f Bolivian.

bollar vtr to dent.

bollo nm 1 Culin bun, bread roll. 2 (abolladura) dent.

bolo nm 1 skittle, ninepin. 2 **bolos,** (juego) skittles.

bolsa[1] nf bag; Av **b. de aire,** air pocket; **b. de deportes,** sports bag; **b. de la compra,** shopping bag; **b. de viaje,** travel bag.

bolsa[2] nf Fin Stock Exchange; **jugar a la b.,** to play the market.

bolsillo nm (en prenda) pocket; **de b.,** pocket, pocket-size; **libro de b.,** paperback; **lo pagó de su b.,** he paid for it out of his own pocket.

bolso nm handbag, bag, US purse.

bomba[1] nf pump; **b. de aire,** air pump; **b. de incendios,** fire engine.

bomba[2] nf bomb; **b. atómica/de hidrógeno/de neutrones,** atomic/hydrogen/neutron bomb; **b. de relojería,** time bomb; **b. fétida,** stink bomb; fam **noticia b.,** shattering piece of news; fam **pasarlo b.,** to have a whale of a time.

bombardear vtr to bomb, shell; **b. a algn a preguntas,** to bombard sb with questions.

bombardeo nm bombing, bombardment.

bombardero nm Av bomber.

bombazo nm bomb blast.

bombear vtr 1 (agua etc) to pump. 2 (pelota) to blow up.

bombeo nm (de líquido) pumping; **estación de b.,** pumping station.

bombero,-a nm,f (hombre) fireman; (mujer) firewoman; US (ambos sexos) firefighter; **cuerpo de bomberos,** fire brigade; **parque de bomberos,** fire station.

bombilla nf (light) bulb.

bombín nm bowler hat.

bombo nm 1 Mús bass drum; fig **a b. y platillo(s),** with a great song and dance; fam **darse b.,** to blow one's own trumpet. 2 (de sorteo) lottery drum.

bombón nm chocolate.

bombona nf cylinder; **b. de butano,** butane gas cylinder.

bombonera nf chocolate box.

bonachón,-ona adj good-natured, easygoing.

bonaerense I adj of o from Buenos Aires. **II** nmf native o inhabitant of Buenos Aires.

bonanza nf 1 Náut (tiempo) fair weather; (mar) calm at sea. 2 fig (prosperidad) prosperity.

bondad nf goodness; fml **tenga la b. de esperar,** please be so kind as to wait.

bondadoso,-a adj kind, good-natured.

bonete nm Rel cap, biretta; Univ mortar-board.

boniato nm sweet potato.

bonificación nf bonus.

bonificar [1] vtr Com to give a bonus to.

bonito,-a[1] adj pretty, nice.

bonito[2] nm tuna.

bono nm 1 (vale) voucher. 2 Fin bond, debenture; **bonos del tesoro o del Estado,** Treasury bonds.

bono-bus nm bus pass.

boom nm boom.

boomerang nm boomerang.

boquerón nm anchovy.

boquete nm hole.

boquiabierto,-a adj open-mouthed; **se quedó b.,** he was flabbergasted.

boquilla nf 1 (de cigarro) tip; (de pipa) mouthpiece; **decir algo de b.,** to pay lip service to sth. 2 Mús mouthpiece. 3 (orificio) opening.

borbotar, borbotear vi to bubble.

borbotón nm bubbling; fig **salir a borbotones,** to gush forth.

borda nf Náut gunwale; **arrojar o echar por la b.,** to throw overboard; **fuera b.,** (motor) outboard motor.

bordado,-a I adj embroidered; **el examen me salió b.,** I made a good job of that exam. **II** nm embroidery.

bordar vtr 1 to embroider. 2 fig to do excellently.

borde¹ *nm* (*de mesa, camino*) edge; *Cost* hem, edge; (*de vasija*) rim, brim; **al b. de,** on the brink of, on the verge of; **al b. del mar,** at the seaside.

borde² *fam* **I** *adj* stroppy. **II** *nmf* stroppy person.

bordear *vtr* to go round the edge of, skirt.

bordillo *nm* kerb, *US* curb.

bordo **a un b.,** on board; **subir a b.,** to go on board.

borla *nf* tassel.

borne *nm Elec* terminal.

borra *nf* **1** (*pelusa*) fluff. **2** (*poso*) sediment, dregs *pl*.

borrachera *nf* (*embriaguez*) drunkenness; (*curda*) binge; **coger** *o* **pillar una b.,** to get drunk.

borracho,-a I *adj* **1** (*bebido*) drunk; **estar b.,** to be drunk. **2** (*bizcocho*) with rum. **II** *nm,f* drunkard, drunk.

borrador *nm* **1** (*escrito*) rough copy, *US* first draft. **2** (*croquis*) rough *o* preliminary sketch. **3** (*de pizarra*) duster.

borraja *nf* **quedar en agua de borrajas,** to come to nothing, fizzle *o* peter out.

borrar I *vtr* **1** (*con goma*) to erase, rub out; (*pizarra*) to clean. **2** *Inform* to delete. **II borrarse** *vr* (*de un club etc*) to drop out, withdraw.

borrasca *nf* area of low pressure.

borrascoso,-a *adj* stormy.

borrego,-a *nm,f* **1** yearling lamb. **2** *fam* (*persona*) sheep.

borrico *nm* ass, donkey; *fam fig* ass, dimwit.

borrón *nm* blot, smudge.

borroso,-a *adj* blurred; **veo b.,** I can't see clearly, everything's blurred.

bosque *nm* wood.

bosquejar *vtr* (*dibujo*) to sketch, outline; (*plan*) to draft, outline.

bosquejo *nm* (*de dibujo*) sketch, study; (*de plan*) draft, outline.

bostezar |4| *vi* to yawn.

bostezo *nm* yawn.

bota *nf* **1** boot; *fig* **ponerse las botas,** to make a killing. **2** (*de vino*) wineskin.

botana *nf Am* snack.

botánica *nf* botany.

botánico,-a I *adj* botanic; **jardín b.,** botanic gardens. **II** *nm,f* botanist.

botar I *vi* **1** (*saltar*) to jump. **2** (*pelota*) to bounce. **II** *vtr* **1** (*barco*) to launch. **2** (*pelota*) to bounce. **3** *Am* (*arrojar*) to throw *o* chuck out.

botarate *nmf* madcap, fool.

bote¹ *nm* **1** jump, bound; **dar botes,** to jump up and down; **de un b.,** with one leap. **2** (*de pelota*) bounce, rebound.

bote² *nm* (*lata*) can, tin; (*para propinas*) jar *o* box for tips; (*en lotería*) jackpot; *fam* **chupar del b.,** to scrounge.

bote³ *nm* (*lancha*) boat; **b. salvavidas,**
lifeboat.

bote *nm* **de b. en b.,** packed, full to bursting.

botella *nf* bottle.

botellín *nm* small bottle.

botepronto *nm fam* **a b.,** all of a sudden.

botica *nf* chemist's (shop), pharmacy, *US* drugstore; *fam* **hay de todo como en b.,** there's everything under the sun.

boticario,-a *nm,f* chemist, pharmacist, *US* druggist.

botijo *nm* earthenware pitcher (with spout and handle).

botín¹ *nm* (*de un robo*) loot, booty.

botín² *nm* (*calzado*) ankle boot.

botiquín *nm* **1** medicine chest *o* cabinet; (*portátil*) first aid kit. **2** (*enfermería*) first aid post.

botón *nm* button; **pulsar el b.,** to press the button; **b. de muestra,** sample.

botones *nm inv* (*en hotel*) bellboy, *US* bellhop; (*recadero*) messenger, errand boy.

boutique *nf* boutique.

bóveda *nf* vault.

bovino,-a *adj* bovine; **ganado b.,** cattle.

boxeador *nm* boxer.

boxear *vi* to box.

boxeo *nm* boxing.

boya *nf* **1** *Náut* buoy. **2** (*corcho*) float.

boyante *adj* buoyant.

boy-scout *nm* boy scout.

bozal *nm* muzzle.

bracero *nm* (*day*) labourer.

bragas *nfpl* panties *pl*, knickers *pl*.

bragueta *nf* (*de pantalón etc*) fly, flies *pl*.

braguetazo *nm vulg* **dar el b.,** to marry for money.

braille *nm* braille.

bramar *vi* to low, bellow.

bramido *nm* lowing, bellowing.

brandy *nm* brandy.

branquia *nf* gill.

brasa *nf* ember, red-hot coal; **chuletas a la b.,** barbecued chops.

brasero *nm* brazier.

Brasil *n* Brazil.

brasileño,-a, brasilero,-a *adj & nm,f* Brazilian.

bravata *nf* piece *o* act of bravado.

bravo,-a I *adj* **1** (*valiente*) brave, courageous. **2** (*feroz*) fierce, ferocious; **un toro b.,** a fighting bull. **3** (*mar*) rough, stormy. **II** *interj* **¡b.!,** well done!, bravo!

bravucón,-ona *nm,f* boaster, braggart.

bravura *nf* **1** (*de animal*) ferocity, fierceness. **2** (*de persona*) courage, bravery. **3** (*de toro*) fighting spirit.

braza *nf* **1** *Náut* fathom. **2** *Natación* breast stroke; **nadar a b.,** to do the breast stroke.

brazada *nf Natación* stroke.

brazalete *nm* **1** (*insignia*) armband. **2** (*pulsera*) bracelet.

brazo *nm* arm; *(de animal)* foreleg; *(de sillón, tocadiscos)* arm; **en brazos,** in one's arms; **ir del b.,** to walk arm in arm; *fig* **con los brazos abiertos,** with open arms; *fig* **no dar su b. a torcer,** not to give in, stand firm; **b. de gitano,** type of Swiss roll containing cream.

brea *nf* tar, pitch.

brebaje *nm* concoction, brew.

brecha *nf (en muro)* opening, gap; *Mil & fig* breach; *fig* **estar siempre en la b.,** to be always in the thick of things.

brécol *nm* broccoli.

bregar |7| *vi* to fight.

Bretaña *nf* 1 Brittany. 2 **Gran B.,** Great Britain.

brete *nm fig* **poner a algn en un b.,** to put sb in a tight spot.

breva *nf* early fig; *fam* **de higos a brevas,** once in a blue moon; *fam* **¡no caerá esa b.!,** no such luck!

breve *adj* brief; **en b., en breves momentos,** shortly, soon; **en breves palabras,** in short.

brevedad *nf* briefness; *(concision)* brevity; **con la mayor b. posible,** as soon as possible.

brezo *nm* heather.

bribón,-ona I *adj* roguish, dishonest. II *nm,f* rogue, rascal.

bricolaje *nm* do-it-yourself, DIY.

brida *nf* 1 *(rienda)* rein, bridle. 2 *Téc* flange.

bridge *nm Naipes* bridge.

brigada I *nf* 1 *Mil* brigade. 2 *(de policías)* squad; **b. antiterrorista,** anti-terrorist squad. II *nm Mil* sergeant major.

brigadier *nm* brigadier.

brillante I *adj* brilliant. II *nm* diamond.

brillantez *nf* brilliance.

brillantina *nf* brilliantine.

brillar *vi (resplandecer)* to shine; *(ojos, joyas)* to sparkle; *(lentejuelas etc)* to glitter; **b. por su ausencia,** to be conspicuous by one's absence.

brillo *nm (resplandor)* shine; *(del sol, de la luna)* brightness; *(de lentejuelas etc)* glittering; *(del cabello, tela)* sheen; *(de color)* brilliance; *(de pantalla)* brightness; *(de zapatos)* shine; **sacar b. a,** to shine, polish.

brincar |1| *vi* to skip.

brinco *nm* skip.

brindar I *vi* to drink a toast; **b. por algn/algo,** to drink to sb/sth. II *vtr* 1 *(oportunidad)* to offer, provide. 2 *Taur* to dedicate the bull **(a, to).** III **brindarse** *vr* to offer **(a, to),** volunteer **(a, to).**

brindis *nm* 1 toast. 2 *Taur* dedication (of the bull).

brío *nm* energy.

brioso,-a *adj* energetic, vigorous.

brisa *nf* breeze; **b. marina,** sea breeze.

británico,-a I *adj* British; **las Islas Británicas,** the British Isles. II *nm,f* Briton; **los británicos,** the British.

brizna *nf (de hierba)* blade; *(de carne)* string.

broca *nf Téc* bit.

brocha *nf (para pintar)* paintbrush; **b. de afeitar,** shaving brush.

broche *nm* 1 *(joya)* brooch; *fig* **poner el b. de oro,** to finish with a flourish. 2 *(de vestido)* fastener.

bróculi *nm* broccoli.

broma *nf (chiste)* joke; **bromas aparte,** joking apart; **en b.,** as a joke; **¡ni en b.!,** not on your life!; **b. pesada,** practical joke; **gastar una b.,** to play a joke.

bromear *vi* to joke.

bromista I *adj* fond of joking *o* playing jokes. II *nmf* joker, prankster.

bronca *nf* 1 *(riña)* quarrel, row. 2 **echar una b. a algn,** to bawl sb out.

bronce *nm* bronze.

bronceado,-a I *adj* suntanned, tanned. II *nm* suntan, tan.

bronceador,-a I *adj* **leche bronceadora,** suntan cream. II *nm* suntan cream *o* lotion.

broncearse *vr* to get a tan *o* a suntan.

bronco,-a *adj* rough, coarse.

bronquitis *nf inv* bronchitis.

brotar *vi (planta)* to sprout; *(agua)* to spring, gush; *(lágrimas)* to well up; *(epidemia)* to break out.

brote *nm* 1 *Bot (renuevo)* bud, shoot; *(de agua)* gushing. 2 *(de epidemia, violencia)* outbreak.

bruces (de) *loc adv* face downwards; **se cayó de b.,** he fell flat on his face.

bruja *nf* witch, sorceress.

brujería *nf* witchcraft, sorcery.

brújula *nf* compass.

bruma *nf* mist.

brumoso,-a *adj* misty.

bruñir *vtr* to polish.

brusco,-a *adj* 1 *(persona)* brusque, abrupt. 2 *(repentino)* sudden, sharp.

Bruselas *n* Brussels; **coles de B.,** Brussels sprouts.

brusquedad *nf* brusqueness, abruptness.

brutal *adj* brutal.

brutalidad *nf* brutality.

bruto,-a I *adj* 1 *(necio)* stupid, thick; *(grosero)* coarse, uncouth. 2 *Fin* gross; **peso b.,** gross weight. 3 **un diamante en b.,** an uncut diamond. II *nm,f* blockhead, brute.

búcaro *nm* earthenware jug.

bucear *vi* to swim under water.

buche *nm* maw; *(de ave)* craw; *fam (estómago)* belly, stomach.

bucle *nm* curl, ringlet.

budín *nm* pudding.

budismo *nm* Buddhism.

budista *adj* Buddhist.

buen *adj (delante de un nombre masculino*

singular) good; **¡b. viaje!**, have a good trip!; → **bueno,-a.**

buenaventura *nf* good fortune, good luck; **echar la b. a algn**, to tell sb's fortune.

bueno,-a I *adj* **1** good; **un alumno muy b.**, a very good pupil; **una buena película**, a good film; **lo b.**, the good thing. **2** *(amable) (con ser)* good, kind; **el b. de Carlos**, good old Carlos; **es muy buena persona**, he's a very kind soul. **3** *(sano) (con estar)* well, in good health. **4** *(tiempo)* good; **hoy hace buen tiempo**, it's fine today; **mañana hará b.**, it will be fine *o* a nice day tomorrow. **5** *(conveniente)* good; **no es b. comer tanto**, it's not good for you to eat so much; **sería b. que vinieras**, it would be a good idea if you came. **6** *(considerable)* considerable; **un buen número de**, a good number of; **una buena cantidad**, a considerable amount. **7** *(grande)* good, big; **un buen trozo de pastel**, a nice *o* good big piece of cake. **8** *fam (atractivo)* gorgeous, sexy; **Rosa está muy buena**, Rosa's a bit of all right!; **una buena chica**, a good-looking girl. **9** *irón* fine, real, proper; **¡en buen lío te has metido!**, that's a fine mess you've got yourself into! **10** **¡buenas!**, *(saludos)* hello!; **buenas tardes**, *(desde mediodía hasta las cinco)* good afternoon; *(desde las cinco)* good evening; **buenas noches**, *(al llegar)* good evening; *(al irse)* good night; **buenos días**, good morning. **11** *(locuciones)* **de buenas a primeras**, suddenly, all at once; **estar de buenas**, to be in a good mood; **los buenos tiempos**, the good old days; **por las buenas**, willingly; **por las buenas o por las malas**, willy-nilly; **¡buena la has hecho!**, that's done it!; **un susto de los buenos**, a real fright; *irón* **¡estaría b.!**, I should jolly well hope not!; *irón* **librarse de una buena**, to get off scot free. **II** *interj* **¡b.!**, *(vale)* all right, OK.

◆buenamente *adv* **haz lo que b. puedas**, just do what you can; **si b. puedes**, if you possibly can.

buey *nm* ox, bullock.

búfalo,-a *nm,f* buffalo.

bufanda *nf* scarf.

bufar *vi* **1** *(toro)* to snort; *(caballo)* to neigh. **2** *(persona)* to be fuming.

bufé *nm* buffet; **b. libre**, self-service buffet meal.

bufete *nm* *(despacho de abogado)* lawyer's office.

buffet *nm* *(pl buffets)* → **bufé.**

bufido *nm* *(de toro)* snort; *(de caballo)* neigh.

bufón,-ona *nm,f* clown, buffoon.

buhardilla *nf* attic, garret.

búho *nm* owl; **b. real**, eagle owl.

buhonero,-a *nm,f* pedlar, hawker.

buitre *nm* vulture.

bujía *nf* **1** *Aut* spark plug. **2** *Fís* candlepower.

bulbo *nm* bulb.

buldog *nm* bulldog.

bulevar *nm* boulevard.

Bulgaria *n* Bulgaria.

búlgaro,-a *adj & nm,f* Bulgarian.

bulla *nf* **1** *(muchedumbre)* crowd, mob. **2** *(ruido)* din; **armar b.**, to kick up a din.

bullicio *nm* din, hubbub.

bullir *vi* **1** *(hervir)* to boil, bubble (up). **2 b. de gente**, to be teeming with people.

bulto *nm* **1** *(cosa indistinta)* shape, form. **2** *(maleta, caja)* piece of luggage. **3** *Med* lump. **4 hacer mucho b.**, to be very bulky; *fam* **escurrir el b.**, to pass the buck.

bumerán, bumerang *nm* boomerang.

bungalow *nm* bungalow.

búnker *nm* bunker.

buñuelo *nm* doughnut.

BUP *nm abr de* **Bachillerato Unificado Polivalente**, ≈ GCSE studies.

buque *nm* ship; **b. de guerra**, warship; **b. de pasajeros**, liner, passenger ship; **b. insignia**, flagship.

burbuja *nf* bubble; **hacer burbujas**, to bubble, make bubbles.

burbujear *vi* to bubble.

burdel *nm* brothel.

Burdeos *n* Bordeaux.

burdo,-a *adj* coarse, rough.

burgalés,-a I *adj* of *o* from Burgos. **II** *nm,f* native *o* inhabitant of Burgos.

burgués,-a *adj & nm,f* bourgeois.

burguesía *nf* bourgeoisie.

burla *nf* gibe, jeer; **hacer b. de algo o algn**, to make fun of sth *o* sb; **hacer b. a algn**, to stick one's tongue out at sb.

burladero *nm* *Taur* refuge in bullring.

burlar I *vtr* **1** *(engañar)* to deceive. **2** *(eludir)* to dodge, evade. **II burlarse** *vr* to make fun *(de*, of*)*, laugh *(de*, at*)*.

burlón,-ona *adj* mocking.

buró *nm* **1** *Pol* executive committee. **2** *(escritorio)* bureau, desk.

burocracia *nf* bureaucracy.

burócrata *nmf* bureaucrat.

burocrático,-a *adj* bureaucratic.

buromática *nf* office automation.

burrada *nf* *(comentario)* stupid *o* foolish remark; *(hecho)* stupid *o* foolish act.

burro,-a I *nm,f* **1** donkey, ass; *fam fig* **bajarse del b.**, to climb *o* back down. **2** *fam (estúpido)* dimwit, blockhead. **3 b. de carga**, dogsbody, drudge. **II** *adj* **1** *fam (necio)* stupid, dumb. **2** *fam (obstinado)* stubborn.

bursátil *adj* stock-market.

bus *nm* bus.

busca *nf* search; **ir en b. de**, to go in search of.

buscapersonas *nm* pager.

buscapleitos *nmf inv* troublemaker.
buscar |1| **I** *vtr* **1** to look *o* search for; **b. una palabra en el diccionario**, to look up a word in the dictionary. **2 ir a b. algo**, to go and get sth, fetch sth; **fue a buscarme a la estación**, she picked me up at the station. **II buscarse** *vr fam* **b. la vida**, to try and earn one's living; *fam* **te la estás buscando**, you're asking for it; **se busca**, wanted.
búsqueda *nf* search, quest; *Inform* search.
busto *nm* bust.
butaca *nf* **1** (*sillón*) armchair, easy chair. **2** *Cin Teat* seat; **b. de platea** *o* **patio**, seat in the stalls.
butano *nm* butane; **(gas) b.**, butane gas.
butifarra *nf* sausage.
buzo *nm* diver.
buzón *nm* letter box, *US* mailbox; **echar una carta al b.**, to post a letter.
byte *nm Inform* byte.

C

C, c |θe| *nf* (*la letra*) C, c.
C 1 *abr de* **Celsius**, Celsius, C. **2** *abr de* **centígrado**, centigrade, C.
c/ 1 *abr de* **calle**, Street, St; Road, Rd. **2** *abr de* **cargo**, cargo, freight. **3** *abr de* **cuenta**, account, a/c.
C., Cª *abr de* **compañía**, Company, Co.
cabal I *adj* **1** (*exacto*) exact, precise. **2** (*honesto*) honest, upright. **II** *nmpl fam* **estar algn en sus cabales**, to be in full possession of one's faculties.
cábala *nf fig* **hacer cábalas sobre algo**, to speculate about sth.
cabalgadura *nf* mount.
cabalgar |7| *vtr & vi* to ride.
cabalgata *nf* cavalcade; **la c. de los Reyes Magos**, the procession of the Three Wise Men.
caballa *nf* mackerel.
caballar *adj* **ganado c.**, horses *pl.*
caballería *nf* **1** (*cabalgadura*) mount, steed. **2** *Mil* cavalry.
caballeriza *nf* stable.
caballero *nm* **1** gentleman; **¿qué desea, c.?**, can I help you, sir?; **ropa de c.**, menswear. **2** *Hist* knight. **3 caballeros**, (*en letrero*) gents.
caballeroso,-a *adj* gentlemanly, chivalrous.
caballete *nm* **1** (*de pintor*) easel. **2** *Téc* trestle. **3** (*de nariz*) bridge.
caballito *nm* **1 c. de mar**, sea-horse. **2 caballitos**, merry-go-round *sing*, *US* carousel *sing*.
caballo *nm* **1** horse; **a c.**, on horseback; **montar a c.**, to ride; *fig* **a c. entre ...**, halfway between .... **2** *Téc* **c. de vapor**, horse power. **3** *Ajedrez* knight. **4** *Naipes* queen. **5** *arg* (*heroína*) horse, smack.
cabaña *nf* cabin.
cabaret *nm* (*pl* **cabarets**) cabaret.
cabecear I *vi* to nod. **II** *vtr Dep* to head.
cabecera *nf* **1** top, head. **2** *Tip* headline.
cabecilla *nmf* leader.
cabellera *nf* head of hair.
cabello *nm* **1** hair. **2** *Culin* **c. de ángel**, sweet made of gourd and syrup.
cabelludo,-a *adj* **cuero c.**, scalp.

caber |9| *vi* **1** to fit, be (able to be) contained; **cabe en el maletero**, it fits in the boot; **¿cabemos todos?**, is there room for all of us?; **en este coche/jarro caben ...**, this car/jug holds ...; **no cabe por la puerta**, it won't go through the door; **no c. en sí de gozo**, to be beside oneself with joy; **no me cabe en la cabeza**, I can't understand it; **no cabe duda**, there is no doubt; **cabe la posibilidad de que ...**, there is a possibility *o* chance that ...; **no está mal dentro de lo que cabe**, it isn't bad, under the circumstances. **2 cabe señalar que ...**, we should point out that .... **3** *Mat* **doce entre cuatro caben a tres**, four into twelve goes three (times).
cabestrillo *nm* sling.
cabestro *nm* halter.
cabeza I *nf* head; **en c.**, in the lead; **por c.**, a head, per person; *fig* **a la c. de**, at the front *o* top of; *fig* **estar mal de la c.**, to be a mental case; **c. de turco**, scapegoat; **el** *o* **la c. de familia**, the head of the family. **II** *nm* **c. rapada**, skinhead.
cabezada *nf* **1** (*golpe*) butt, blow on the head. **2** *fam* **echar una c.**, to have a snooze; **dar cabezadas**, to nod.
cabezal *nm Téc* head; (*de tocadiscos*) pickup.
cabezota *fam* **I** *adj* pigheaded. **II** *nmf* pigheaded person.
cabezudo *nm* carnival figure with a huge head.
cabida *nf* capacity; **dar c. a**, to leave room for.
cabildo *nm Rel* chapter.
cabina *nf* cabin; **c. telefónica**, telephone box, *US* telephone booth.
cabizbajo,-a *adj* crestfallen.
cable *nm* cable; *arg* **echarle un c. a algn**, to give sb a hand.
cabo *nm* **1** (*extremo*) end; **al c. de**, after; **de c. a rabo**, from start to finish. **2** *Mil* corporal; (*policía*) sergeant. **3** *Náut* rope, cable; *fig* **atar cabos**, to put two and two together; *fig* **no dejar ningún c. suelto**, to leave no loose ends. **4** *Geog* cape; **Ciudad del C.**, Cape Town; **C. Verde**, Cape

Verde.

cabra *nf* goat; *fam* **estar como una c.,** to be off one's head.

cabré *indic fut* → **caber.**

cabreado,-a *adj vulg* pissed-off.

cabrear I *vtr vulg* to make angry. **II cabrearse** *vr* to get worked up.

cabreo *nm vulg* anger.

cabrío,-a *adj* **macho c.,** billy goat; **ganado c.,** goats *pl*.

cabriola *nf* skip.

cabrito *nm Zool* kid.

cabrón,-ona *nm,f ofens* (*hombre*) bastard; (*woman*) bitch.

cabronada *nf vulg* dirty trick.

cabuya *nf Am* agave, pita.

caca *nf fam* poopoo.

cacahuete *nm* peanut.

cacao *nm* **1** *Bot* cacao. **2** (*polvo, bebida*) cocoa. **3** *fam* (*lío*) mess, cockup.

cacarear I *vi* (*gallina*) to cluck. **II** *vtr fig* to boast about.

cacareo *nm* **1** (*de gallina*) clucking. **2** *fig* boasting, bragging.

cacatúa *nf* cockatoo.

cacereño,-a I *adj* of *o* from Cáceres. **II** *nm,f* native *o* inhabitant of Cáceres.

cacería *nf* **1** (*actividad*) hunting, shooting. **2** (*partida*) hunt, shoot.

cacerola *nf* saucepan.

cacha *nf fam* (*muslo*) thigh; **estar cachas,** to be really muscular.

cachalote *nm* sperm whale.

cacharro *nm* **1** earthenware pot *o* jar. **2** *fam* (*cosa*) thing, piece of junk. **3 cacharros,** (*de cocina*) pots and pans.

cachear *vtr* to frisk, search.

cachemir *nm,* **cachemira** *nf* cashmere.

cacheo *nm* frisk, frisking.

cachetada *nf Am* slap.

cachete *nm* **1** (*bofetada*) slap. **2** *Am* (*mejilla*) cheek.

cachimba *nf Am* pipe.

cachiporra *nf* club, truncheon.

cachivache *nm fam* thing, knick-knack.

cacho¹ *nm fam* (*pedazo*) bit; piece; *fig* **¡qué c. de animal!,** what a nasty piece of work!

cacho² *nm Am* (*cuerno*) horn.

cachondearse *vr fam* **c. de,** to take the mickey out of.

cachondeo *nm fam* laugh; **tomar algo a c.,** to take sth as a joke.

cachondo,-a *adj fam* **1** (*sexualmente*) randy. **2** (*divertido*) funny.

cachorro,-a *nm,f* (*de perro*) pup, puppy; (*de gato*) kitten; (*de otros animales*) cub, baby.

cacique *nm* (*jefe*) local boss.

caco *nm fam* thief.

cacofonía *nf* cacophony.

cacto *nm,* **cactus** *nm inv Bot* cactus *inv*.

cada *adj* (*de dos*) each; (*de varios*) each, every; **c. día,** every day; **c. dos días**

every second day; **c. vez más,** more and more; **¿c. cuánto?,** how often?; **c. dos por tres,** every other minute; **cuatro de c. diez,** four out of (every) ten; **¡tienes c. cosa!,** you come up with some fine ideas!

cadalso *nm* scaffold.

cadáver *nm* (*de persona*) corpse, (dead) body; (*de animal*) body, carcass; **ingresar c.,** to be dead on arrival.

cadena *nf* **1** chain; (*correa de perro*) lead, leash. **2** *TV* channel. **3** *Ind* line; **c. de montaje,** assembly line; **trabajo en c.,** assembly line work. **4** *Geog* **c. montañosa,** mountain range. **5** *Jur* **c. perpetua,** life imprisonment. **6** *Aut* **cadenas,** tyre *o* US tire chains.

cadencia *nf* rhythm; *Mús* cadenza.

cadera *nf* hip.

cadete *nm* cadet.

caducar |1| *vi* to expire.

caducidad *nf* expiry; **fecha de c.,** (*en alimentos*) ≈ sell-by date; (*en medicinas*) to be used before.

caduco,-a *adj* **1** *Bot* deciduous. **2** *pey* (*anticuado*) out-of-date.

caer [39] **I** *vi* **1** to fall; **dejar c.,** to drop; *fig* **está al c.,** (*llegar*) he'll arrive any minute now; (*ocurrir*) it's on the way. **2** (*fecha*) to be; **su cumpleaños cae en sábado,** his birthday falls on a Saturday. **3** (*entender*) to understand, see; **ya caigo,** I get it; **no caí,** I didn't twig. **4** (*hallarse*) to be; **cae por Granada,** it is somewhere near Granada. **5 me cae bien/mal,** I like/don't like her. **6 al c. el día,** in the evening; **al c. la noche,** at nightfall. **II caerse** *vr* to fall (down); **me caí de la moto,** I fell off the motorbike; **se le ha caído el pañuelo,** she dropped her handkerchief.

café *nm* **1** coffee; **c. solo/con leche,** black/white coffee. **2** (*cafetería*) café.

cafeína *nf* caffeine.

cafetal *nm* coffee plantation.

cafetera *nf* coffee-maker.

cafetería *nf* snack bar, coffee bar; *Ferroc* buffet car.

cafetero,-a *adj* **1** coffee. **2** *fam* **es muy c.,** (*persona*) he loves coffee.

cafre *nm,f* savage, beast.

cagado,-a *adj vulg* (*cobarde*) coward; **estar c. de miedo,** to be shit-scared.

cagar |7| *vulg* **I** *vi* **1** to (have a) shit. **2** (*estropear*) to ruin, spoil; **cagarla,** to cock it up. **II cagarse** *vr* to shit oneself; **c. de miedo,** to be shit-scared; **¡me cago en diez!,** damn it!

caída *nf* **1** fall; (*de pelo, diente*) loss. **2** (*de precios*) drop. **3** *Pol* downfall, collapse.

caído,-a I *adj* fallen. **III** *nmpl* **los caídos,** the fallen *pl*.

caigo *indic pres* → **caer.**

caimán *nm* alligator.

Cairo *n* **El C.,** Cairo.

caja *nf* 1 box; **c. fuerte**, safe; *fam TV* **la c. tonta**, the idiot box. 2 *(de leche etc)* carton. 3 *(de embalaje)* crate, case; **una c. de cerveza**, a crate of beer. 4 *Fin (en tienda)* cash desk; *(en banco)* cashier's desk. 5 *Aut* **c. de cambios**, gearbox. 6 *Com* **c. de ahorros** *o* **de pensiones**, savings bank. 7 *(féretro)* coffin, *US* casket.

cajero,-a *nm,f* cashier; **c. automático**, cash point, dispenser.

cajetilla *nf* packet, *US* pack.

cajón *nm* 1 *(en un mueble)* drawer; *fig* **c. de sastre**, jumble; *fam* **de c.**, obvious, self-evident. 2 *(caja grande)* crate, chest.

cal¹ *nf* lime; *fig* **a c. y canto**, hermetically; *fam* **una de c. y otra de arena**, six of one and half a dozen of the other.

cal² *abr de* **caloría(s)**, calorie(s), cal.

cala *nf* 1 *Geog* creek, cove. 2 *Náut* hold.

calabacín *nm Bot* 1 *(pequeño)* courgette, *US* zucchini. 2 *(grande)* marrow, *US* squash.

calabaza *nf* pumpkin, gourd.

calabobos *nm inv fam* drizzle.

calabozo *nm* 1 *(prisión)* jail, prison. 2 *(celda)* cell.

calada *nf fam (de cigarrillo)* drag, puff.

calado,-a I *adj* soaked. II *nm Náut* draught, *US* draft.

calamar *nm* squid *inv*; *Culin* **calamares a la romana**, squid fried in batter.

calambre *nm* 1 *Elec (descarga)* electric shock; **ese cable da c.**, that wire is live. 2 *(en músculo)* cramp.

calamidad *nf* calamity.

calaña *nf pey* kind, sort; **una persona de mala c.**, a bad sort.

calar I *vtr* 1 *(mojar)* to soak, drench. 2 *(agujerear)* to pierce, penetrate. 3 *fam (a alguien)* to rumble; **¡te hemos calado!**, we've got your number!. II *vi* 1 *(prenda)* to let in water. 2 *Náut* to draw. III **calarse** *vr* 1 *(prenda, techo)* to let in water; *(mojarse)* to get soaked. 2 *(el sombrero)* to pull down. 3 *Aut* to stall.

calavera I *nf* skull. II *nm* tearaway, madcap.

calcar |1| *vtr* 1 *(un dibujo)* to trace. 2 *fig (imitar)* to copy, imitate.

calceta *nf* 1 *(prenda)* stocking. 2 **hacer c.**, to knit.

calcetín *nm* sock.

calcinar *vtr* to burn.

calcio *nm* calcium.

calco *nm* tracing; **papel de c.**, carbon paper.

calcomanía *nf* transfer.

calculadora *nf* calculator.

calcular *vtr* 1 *Mat* to calculate. 2 *(evaluar)* to (make an) estimate. 3 *(suponer)* to figure, guess.

cálculo *nm* 1 calculation; **según mis cálculos**, by my reckoning. 2 *Med* gallstone. 3 *Mat* calculus.

caldear *vtr* to heat up.

caldera *nf* boiler.

caldereta *nf* stew.

calderilla *nf* small change.

caldo *nm* stock, broth; **c. de cultivo**, culture medium; *fig* breeding ground.

calé *adj & nm* gypsy.

calefacción *nf* heating; **c. central**, central heating.

calefactor *nm* heater.

caleidoscopio *nm* kaleidoscope.

calendario *nm* calendar.

calentador *nm* heater.

calentamiento *nm Dep* warm up.

calentar |1| *vtr* 1 *(agua, horno)* to heat; *(comida, habitación)* to warm up; *fig* **no me calientes la cabeza**, don't bug me. 2 *fam (pegar)* to smack. 3 *fam (excitar)* to arouse (sexually), turn on. II **calentarse** *vr* 1 to get hot *o* warm, heat up. 2 *fig* **se calentaron los ánimos**, people became very excited.

calentón,-ona, **calentorro,-a** *adj fam* randy.

calentura *nf* fever, temperature.

calibrar *vtr* to gauge, bore.

calibre *nm* 1 *(de arma)* calibre. 2 *fig (importancia)* importance.

calidad *nf* 1 quality; **de primera c.**, first-class; **un vino de c.**, good-quality wine. 2 **en c. de**, as.

cálido,-a *adj* warm; **una cálida acogida**, a warm welcome.

calidoscopio *nm → caleidoscopio*.

caliente *adj* 1 hot. 2 *fig (debate)* heated; **en c.**, in the heat of the moment. 3 *fam (cachondo)* hot, randy.

calificación *nf* 1 qualification. 2 *Educ* mark.

calificar |1| *vtr* 1 to describe (**de**, as); **le calificó de inmoral**, he called him immoral. 2 *(examen)* to mark, grade.

calificativo *nm* epithet.

caligrafía *nf* calligraphy; *(modo de escribir)* handwriting.

calima *nf* haze, mist.

calimocho *nm* drink made with wine and Coca-Cola.

calina *nf → calima*.

cáliz *nm* chalice.

caliza *nf* limestone.

calizo,-a *adj* lime.

callado,-a *adj* quiet; **te lo tenías muy c.**, you were keeping that quiet.

callar I *vi* 1 *(dejar de hablar)* to stop talking; **¡calla!**, be quiet!, *fam* shut up! 2 *(no hablar)* to keep quiet, say nothing. II *vtr* *(noticia)* not to mention, keep to oneself. III **callarse** *vr* to stop talking, be quiet; **¡cállate!**, shut up!

calle *nf* 1 street, road; **c. de dirección única**, one-way street; **c. mayor**, high street, *US* main street; **el hombre de la c.**, the man in the street. 2 *Dep* lane.

calleja *nf* narrow street.
callejero,-a I *nm* (*mapa*) street directory. II *adj* street; **gato c.**, alley cat.
callejón *nm* back alley *o* street; **c. sin salida**, cul-de-sac, dead end.
callejuela *nf* narrow street, lane.
callista *nmf* chiropodist.
callo *nm* 1 *Med* callus, corn; *fam* **dar el c.**, to slog. 2 *Culin* **callos**, tripe *sing*.
calma *nf* 1 calm; **¡c.!**, calm down!; **en c.**, calm; **tómatelo con c.**, take it easy. 2 *Meteor* calm weather; **c. chicha**, dead calm.
calmante *nm* painkiller.
calmar I *vtr* (*persona*) to calm (down); (*dolor*) to soothe, relieve. II **calmarse** *vr* 1 (*persona*) to calm down. 2 (*dolor, viento*) to ease off.
caló *nm* gypsy dialect.
calor *nm* 1 heat; **hace c.**, it's hot; **tengo c.**, I'm hot; **entrar en c.**, to warm up. 2 *fig* (*afecto*) warmth.
caloría *nf* calorie.
calumnia *nf* 1 calumny. 2 *Jur* slander.
calumniar |12| *vtr* 1 to calumniate. 2 *Jur* to slander.
caluroso,-a *adj* hot; (*acogida etc*) warm.
calva *nf* bald patch.
calvicie *nf* baldness.
calvinismo *nm* Calvinism.
calvo,-a I *adj* bald; **ni tanto ni tan c.**, neither one extreme nor the other. II *nm* bald man.
calza *nf* wedge.
calzada *nf* road, carriageway.
calzado *nm* shoes *pl*, footwear.
calzador *nm* shoehorn.
calzar |4| I *vtr* 1 (*poner calzado*) to put shoes on; **¿qué número calzas?**, what size do you take? 2 (*mueble*) to wedge. II **calzarse** *vr* **c. los zapatos**, to put on one's shoes.
calzones *nmpl* trousers.
calzonazos *nm inv fam* henpecked husband.
calzoncillos *nmpl* underpants, pants.
cama *nf* bed; **estar en** *o* **guardar c.**, to be confined to bed; **hacer la c.**, to make the bed; **irse a la c.**, to go to bed; **c. doble/sencilla**, double/single bed; **c. turca**, couch.
camada *nf* litter; (*de pájaros*) brood.
camafeo *nm* cameo.
camaleón *nm* chameleon.
cámara I *nf* 1 (*aparato*) camera; **a c. lenta**, in slow motion. 2 *Pol* Chamber, House; **C. Alta/Baja**, Lower/Upper House. 3 *Aut* inner tube. 4 (*habitación*) room, chamber; **c. de gas**, gas chamber; **c. frigorífica**, cold-storage room; **música de c.**, chamber music. II *nmf* (*hombre*) cameraman; (*mujer*) camerawoman.
camarada *nmf* comrade.
camaradería *nf* camaraderie.

camarera *nf* (*de hotel*) chambermaid.
camarero,-a *nm,f* 1 (*de restaurante*) (*hombre*) waiter; (*mujer*) waitress; (*trás la barra*) (*hombre*) barman; (*mujer*) barmaid. 2 (*de avión*) (*hombre*) steward; (*mujer*) stewardess.
camarilla *nf* clique.
camarón *nm* (common) prawn.
camarote *nm* cabin.
cambiante *adj* changing; (*carácter*) changeable.
cambiar |12| I *vtr* 1 to change; **c. algo de sitio**, to move sth. 2 (*intercambiar*) to swap, exchange. 3 (*dinero*) to change. II *vi* to change; **c. de casa**, to move (house); **c. de idea**, to change one's mind; **c. de trabajo**, to get another job; **c. de velocidad**, to change gear. III **cambiarse** *vr* 1 (*de ropa*) to change (clothes). 2 (*de casa*) to move (house).
cambiazo *nm fam* switch.
cambio *nm* 1 change; (*de impresiones*) exchange; **c. de planes**, change of plans; **un c. en la opinión pública**, a shift in public opinion; *fig* **a c. de**, in exchange for; **en c.**, on the other hand. 2 (*dinero*) change; **¿tienes c. de mil pesetas?**, have you got change for a thousand pesetas? 3 *Fin* (*de divisas*) exchange; (*de acciones*) price. 4 *Aut* gear change; **c. automático**, automatic transmission.
cambista *nmf* moneychanger.
Camboya *n* Cambodia.
camelar *vtr*, **camelarse** *vr fam* 1 to cajole. 2 (*galantear*) to win over.
camelia *nf* camellia.
camello,-a I *nm,f* camel. II *nm arg* (*traficante de drogas*) (drug) pusher.
camelo *nm fam* 1 (*engaño*) hoax. 2 (*trola*) cock-and-bull story.
camerino *nm* dressing room.
Camerún *n* Cameroon.
camilla *nf* 1 stretcher. 2 **mesa c.**, small round table under which a heater is placed.
caminante *nmf* walker.
caminar I *vi* to walk. II *vtr* to cover, travel; **caminaron diez kilómetros**, they walked for ten kilometres.
caminata *nf* long walk.
camino *nm* 1 (*ruta*) route, way; **ir c. de**, to be going to; **ponerse en c.**, to set off; *fig* **ir por buen/mal c.**, to be on the right/wrong track; **abrirse c.**, to break through; **a medio c.**, half-way; **en el c.**, on the way; **estar en c.**, to be on the way; **nos coge** *o* **pilla de c.**, it is on the way. 2 (*vía*) path, track. 3 (*modo*) way.
camión *nm* lorry, *US* truck; **c. cisterna**, tanker; **c. de la basura**, refuse lorry, *US* garbage truck; **c. frigorífico**, refrigerator lorry.
camionero,-a *nm,f* lorry *o US* truck

driver.

camioneta *nf* van.

camisa *nf* shirt; **en mangas de c.,** in one's shirtsleeves; *fig* **cambiar de c.,** to change sides; **c. de fuerza,** straightjacket.

camiseta *nf* 1 *(de uso interior)* vest, *US* undershirt. 2 *(de uso exterior)* T-shirt. 3 *Dep* shirt; **sudar la c.,** to run oneself into the ground.

camisón *nm* nightdress, *fam* nightie.

camomila *nf* camomile.

camorra *nf fam* trouble.

camorrista I *adj* quarrelsome, rowdy. II *nmf* troublemaker.

camote *nm Am* sweet potato.

campal *adj* **batalla c.,** pitched battle.

campamento *nm* camp.

campana *nf* bell; **pantalones de campana,** bell-bottom trousers.

campanada *nf* peal *o* ring of a bell.

campanario *nm* belfry, bell tower.

campanilla *nf* 1 small bell. 2 *Anat* uvula. 3 *Bot* bell flower.

campante *adj fam* **se quedó tan c.,** he didn't bat an eyelid.

campaña *nf* 1 campaign; **c. electoral,** election campaign; **c. publicitaria,** advertising campaign. 2 *Mil* expedition; **de c.,** field.

campar *vi fam* **c. por sus respetos,** to do as one pleases.

campechano,-a *adj* unpretentious.

campeón,-ona *nm,f* champion; **c. mundial,** world champion.

campeonato *nm* championship; **un tonto de c.,** an utter idiot.

campero,-a *adj* country, rural; *(botas)* **camperas,** leather boots.

campesino,-a *nm,f (hombre)* countryman; *(mujer)* countrywoman.

campestre *adj* rural.

camping *nm* campsite; **hacer** *o* **ir de c.,** to go camping.

campiña *nf* open country.

campista *nmf* camper.

campo *nm* 1 country, countryside; **a c. traviesa** *o* **través,** cross-country; **trabaja (en) el c.,** he works (on) the land; **trabajo de c.,** fieldwork. 2 *(parcela)* field. 3 *Fis Fot* field. 4 *(ámbito)* field; **c. de acción,** field of action; *Mil* **c. de batalla,** battlefield; **c. de concentración,** concentration camp; **c. de trabajo,** work camp. 5 *Dep* field; *(de fútbol)* pitch; *(de golf)* course.

camposanto *nm* cemetery.

camuflaje *nm* camouflage.

camuflar *vtr* to camouflage.

cana *nf (gris)* grey hair; *(blanco)* white hair; **tener canas,** to have grey hair; *fam* **echar una c. al aire,** to let one's hair down.

Canadá *n* Canada.

canadiense *adj & nmf* Canadian.

canal *nf* 1 *(artificial)* canal; *(natural)* channel; **C. de la Mancha,** English Channel. 2 *TV Elec Inform* channel.

canalizar |4| *vtr* to channel.

canalla *pey* I *nm* swine, rotter. II *nf* riff-raff, mob.

canallesco,-a *adj pey* rotten, despicable.

canalón *nm* gutter.

canalones *nmpl* canneloni.

canapé *nm* 1 *Culin* canapé. 2 *(sofá)* couch, sofa.

canario,-a I *adj & nm,f* Canarian; **Islas Canarias,** Canary Islands, Canaries. II *nm Orn* canary.

canasta *nf* basket.

canastilla *nf* small basket; *(de un bebé)* layette.

canasto *nm* big basket, hamper.

cancán *nm* frilly petticoat.

cancela *nf* wrought-iron gate.

cancelación *nf* cancellation.

cancelar *vtr* 1 *(acto etc)* to cancel. 2 *(deuda)* to pay off.

cáncer *nm* cancer; **c. de pulmón/mama,** lung/breast cancer.

cancerbero,-a *nm,f Ftb* goalkeeper.

cancerígeno,-a *adj* carcinogenic.

canceroso,-a *adj* cancerous.

cancha *nf* ground; *Ten* court.

canciller *nm* chancellor.

canción *nf* song.

candado *nm* padlock.

candela *nf* fire.

candelabro *nm* candelabrum.

candelero *nm* candlestick; *fig* **en el c.,** at the top.

candente *adj* red-hot; *fig* **tema c.,** topical issue.

candidato,-a *nm,f* candidate; *(a un puesto)* applicant.

candidatura *nf* 1 *(lista)* list of candidates. 2 **presentar su c.,** to submit one's application.

candidez *nf* candour, *US* candor.

cándido,-a *adj* candid.

candil *nm* oil lamp.

candilejas *nfpl Teat* footlights.

candor *nm* candour, *US* candor.

candoroso,-a *adj* innocent, pure.

canela *nf* cinnamon.

cangrejo *nm (de mar)* crab; *(de río)* freshwater crayfish.

canguro I *nm* kangaroo. II *nmf fam* baby-sitter.

caníbal *adj & nmf* cannibal.

canica *nf* marble.

canícula *nf* dog days, midsummer heat.

caniche *nm* poodle.

canijo,-a *adj fam* puny, weak.

canillera *nf Am (cobardía)* cowardice; *(miedo)* fear.

canillita *nm Am* newspaper boy.

canino,-a I *adj* canine; *fam* **tener un hambre canina,** to be starving. II *nm*

(colmillo) canine.
canjear *vtr* to exchange.
cano,-a *adj (blanco)* white; *(gris)* grey.
canoa *nf* canoe.
canódromo *nm* dog *o* greyhound track.
canon *nm* 1 canon, norm. 2 *Mús Rel* canon. 3 *Com* royalty.
canónigo. *nm* canon.
canonizar |4| *vtr* to canonize.
canoso,-a *adj (de pelo blanco)* white-haired; *(de pelo gris)* grey-haired; *(pelo)* white, grey.
cansado,-a *adj* 1 *(agotado)* tired, weary; estar c., to be tired. 2 ser c., *(pesado)* to be boring *o* tiresome.
cansancio *nm* tiredness, weariness; *fam* estoy muerto de c., I'm on my last legs.
cansar I *vtr* to tire. II *vi* to be tiring. III cansarse *vr* to get tired; se cansó de esperar, he got fed up (with) waiting.
Cantabria *n* Cantabria.
cantábrico,-a *adj* Cantabrian; Mar C., Bay of Biscay.
cántabro,-a *adj & nm,f* Cantabrian.
cantante I *nmf* singer. II *adj* singing; llevar la voz c., to rule the roost.
cantaor,-a *nm,f* flamenco singer.
cantar¹ *vtr & vi* 1 *Mús* to sing; fig en menos que canta un gallo, in a flash. 2 *arg (confesar)* to sing, spill the beans. 3 *arg (oler mal)* to hum.
cantar² *nm lit* song; *fam* ¡eso es otro c.!, that's a totally different thing!
cantarín,-ina *adj (voz)* sing-song.
cántaro *nm* pitcher; *fig* llover a cántaros, to rain cats and dogs.
cante *nm* 1 *(canto)* singing; *Esp* c. hondo, c. jondo, flamenco. 2 *arg* dar el c., to attract attention.
cantera *nf* 1 *(de piedra)* quarry. 2 *fig Ftb* young players.
cantero *nm* stonemason.
cantidad I *nf* quantity; *(de dinero)* amount, sum; en c., a lot; *fam* c. de gente, thousands of people. II *adv fam* a lot; me gusta c., I love it.
cantimplora *nf* water bottle.
cantina *nf* canteen.
cantinero,-a *nm,f* bar attendant.
canto¹ *nm* 1 *(arte)* singing. 2 *(canción)* song.
canto² *nm (borde)* edge; de c., on its side.
canto³ *nm (guijarro)* pebble, stone; c. rodado, *(grande)* boulder; *(pequeño)* pebble.
cantor,-a I *adj* singing; pájaro c., songbird. II *nm,f* singer.
canturrear *vi* to hum, croon.
canutas *nfpl fam* pasarlas c., to have a hard time.
canuto *nm* 1 *(tubo)* tube. 2 *arg (porro)* joint.
caña *nf* 1 *(vaso)* glass; *(de cerveza)* glass of draught *o* US draft beer. 2 *Bot* reed; *(tallo)* cane, stem; c. de azúcar, sugar cane.

3 *(de pescar)* rod. 4 *fam* darle c. al coche, to go at full speed.
cañada *nf* gully, ravine.
cáñamo *nm* hemp.
cañería *nf* (piece of) piping; cañerías, plumbing.
cañí *adj & nmf (pl cañís) fam* gypsy.
caño *nm (tubo)* tube; *(tubería)* pipe.
cañón *nm* 1 cannon; *fig* estar siempre al pie del c., to be always ready for a fight. 2 *(de fusil)* barrel. 3 *Geog* canyon.
cañonazo *nm* gunshot.
caoba *nf* mahogany.
caos *nm* chaos.
caótico,-a *adj* chaotic.
cap. *abr de* capítulo, chapter, ch.
capa *nf* 1 *(prenda)* cloak, cape; de c. caída, low-spirited. 2 *(de pintura)* layer, coat; *Culin* coating. 3 *Geol* stratum, layer.
capacidad *nf* 1 *(cabida)* capacity. 2 *(aptitud)* capacity, ability.
capacitación *nf* qualification.
capacitar *vtr (autorizar)* to authorize.
capar *vtr* to castrate.
caparazón *nm* shell.
capataz *nm,f (hombre)* foreman; *(mujer)* forewoman.
capaz *adj* 1 capable, able; ser c. de hacer algo, *(tener la habilidad de)* to be able to do sth; *(atreverse a)* to dare to do sth; si se entera es c. de despedirle, if he finds out he could quite easily sack him. 2 *Am* es c. que, it is likely that.
capcioso,-a *adj* captious; pregunta capciosa, catch question.
capea *nf* amateur bullfight.
capear *vtr (dificultad etc)* to dodge, shirk; *fig* c. el temporal, to weather the storm.
capellán *nm* chaplain.
caperuza *nf* hood.
capicúa *adj* número c., reversible number; palabra c., palindrome.
capilar *adj* hair; loción c., hair lotion.
capilla *nf* chapel; c. ardiente, chapel of rest.
capirote *nm fam* tonto de c., silly idiot.
capital I *nf* capital. II *nm Fin* capital; c. activo *o* social, working *o* share capital. III *adj* capital, main; de importancia c., of capital importance; pena c., capital punishment.
capitalismo *nm* capitalism.
capitalista *adj & nmf* capitalist.
capitalizar |4| *vtr* to capitalize.
capitán,-ana *nm,f* captain; c. general, field marshal, US general of the army.
capitanear *vtr* 1 *Mil Náut* to captain, command. 2 *(dirigir)* to lead; *Dep* to captain.
capitulación *nf* agreement; *Mil* capitulation; capitulaciones matrimoniales, marriage settlement.
capitular *vi* 1 *Mil* to capitulate,

surrender. 2 *(convenir)* to reach an agreement.

capítulo *nm* 1 *(de libro)* chapter. 2 *fig* **dentro del c. de ...,** *(tema)* under the heading of ....

capó *nm Aut* bonnet, *US* hood.

capón *nm* rap on the head with the knuckles.

capota *nf Aut* folding hood o top.

capote *nm* 1 *Taur* cape. 2 *Mil* greatcoat.

capricho *nm* 1 *(antojo)* whim, caprice. 2 *Mús* caprice, capriccio.

caprichoso,-a *adj* whimsical.

Capricornio *nm* Capricorn.

cápsula *nf* capsule.

captar *vtr* 1 *(ondas)* to receive, pick up. 2 *(comprender)* to understand, grasp. 3 *(interés etc)* to attract.

captura *nf* capture.

capturar *vtr (criminal)* to capture; *(caza, pescar)* to catch; *Mil* to seize.

capucha *nf* hood.

capuchino *nm (café)* capuccino.

capullo *nm* 1 *(de insecto)* cocoon. 2 *Bot* bud. 3 *vulg (prepucio)* foreskin. 4 *ofens (persona)* silly bugger.

caqui I *adj (color)* khaki. II *nm (fruto)* persimmon.

cara *nf* 1 face; **c. a c.,** face to face; **c. a la pared,** facing the wall; **poner mala c.,** to pull a long face; **tener buena/mala c.,** to look good/bad; *fig* **c. de circunstancias,** serious look; *fig* **dar la c.,** to face the consequences (of one's acts); *fig* **dar la c. por algn,** to stand up for sb; *fig* **(de) c. a,** with a view to; *fig* **echarle a algn algo en c.,** to reproach sb for sth; *fig* **plantar c. a algn,** to face up to sb. 2 *(lado)* side; *(de moneda)* right side; **¿c. o cruz?,** heads or tails?; **echar algo a c. o cruz,** to toss (a coin) for sth. 3 *fam (desfachatez)* cheek, nerve; **¡qué c. (más dura) tienes!,** what a cheek you've got!. II *nm fam (desvergonzado)* cheeky person.

carabela *nf* caravel.

carabina *nf* 1 *(arma)* carbine, rifle. 2 *(persona)* chaperon.

caracense I *adj* of o from Guadalajara. II *nmf* native o inhabitant of Guadalajara.

caracol I *nm* 1 *(de tierra)* snail; *Am* shell. 2 *(rizo)* kiss-curl. II *interj* **¡caracoles!,** good heavens!

caracola *nf* conch.

carácter *nm (pl* **caracteres)** 1 *(temperamento)* character; **de mucho c.,** with a strong character; **tener buen/mal c.,** to be good-natured/bad-tempered. 2 *fig (índole)* nature; **con c. de invitado,** as a guest. 3 *Impr* character.

característica *nf* characteristic.

característico,-a *adj* characteristic.

caracterizar |4| *vtr* to characterize.

caradura *nmf fam* cheeky devil; **¡qué c. eres!,** you're so cheeky!

carajillo *nm fam* coffee with a dash of brandy.

carajo *interj vulg* shit!; **¡vete al c.!,** go to hell!

caramba *interj fam (sorpresa)* good grief!; *(enfado)* damn it!

carámbano *nm* icicle.

carambola *nf* cannon, *US* carom.

caramelo *nm* 1 *(dulce)* sweet, *US* candy. 2 *(azúcar quemado)* caramel; *Culin* **a punto de c.,** syrupy.

carantoña *nf* caress.

caraqueño,-a I *adj* of o from Caracas. II *nm,f* native o inhabitant of Caracas.

carátula *nf* 1 *(cubierta)* cover. 2 *(máscara)* mask.

caravana *nf* 1 *(vehículo)* caravan. 2 *(de tráfico)* tailback.

caray *interj* God!, good heavens!

carbón *nm* coal; **c. vegetal,** charcoal; **c. mineral,** coal.

carboncillo *nm* charcoal.

carbonero,-a *nm* coal merchant.

carbónico,-a *adj* carbonic; **agua carbónica,** mineral water.

carbonilla *nf* coal dust.

carbonizar |4| I *vtr* to carbonize, char; **morir carbonizado,** to be burnt to death. II **carbonizarse** *vr* to carbonize, char.

carbono *nm* carbon.

carburador *nm* carburettor, *US* carburetor.

carburante *nm* fuel.

carburar *vi fam (funcionar)* to work properly.

carca *adj & nmf fam* old fogey; *Pol* reactionary.

carcaj *nm* quiver.

carcajada *nf* guffaw.

carcamal *nm fam* old fogey.

cárcel *nf* prison, jail.

carcelario,-a *adj* prison, jail.

carcelero,-a *nm,f* jailer, warder, *US* warden.

carcoma *nf* woodworm.

carcomer I *vtr* to eat away. II **carcomerse** *vr* to be consumed (**de,** with).

cardar *vtr* 1 *(lana, algodón)* to card. 2 *(pelo)* to backcomb.

cardenal *nm* 1 *Rel* cardinal. 2 *Med* bruise.

cárdeno,-a *adj* purple.

cardiaco,-a, cardíaco,-a I *adj* cardiac, heart; **ataque c.,** heart attack. II *nm,f* person with a heart condition.

cardinal *adj* cardinal; **punto/número c.,** cardinal point/number.

cardiólogo,-a *nm,f* cardiologist.

cardo *nm (con espinas)* thistle.

carear *vtr* 1 *Jur* to bring two people face to face. 2 *(cotejar)* to compare.

carecer |33| *vi* **c. de,** to lack.

carencia *nf* lack (**de,** of).

carente *adj* lacking; **c. de interés,** lacking

interest.

careo nm Jur confrontation.

carestía nf 1 (falta) lack, shortage. 2 Fin high price o cost.

careta nf mask; **c. antigás**, gas mask.

carey nm tortoiseshell.

carezco indic pres → **carecer**.

carga nf 1 (acción) loading. 2 (cosa cargada) load; (de avión, barco) cargo, freight; fig **c. afectiva**, emotional content. 3 Fin (gasto) debit; **c. fiscal**, tax charge. 4 fig (obligación) burden. 5 Elec charge.

cargado,-a adj 1 loaded. 2 (bebida) strong; **un café c.**, a strong coffee. 3 (ambiente) heavy; **atmósfera cargada**, stuffy atmosphere. 4 fig burdened; **c. de deudas**, up to one's eyes in debt. 5 Elec charged.

cargamento nm 1 (carga) load. 2 (mercancías) cargo, freight.

cargante adj fam annoying.

cargar [7] I vtr 1 to load; (mechero, pluma) to fill; (batería) to charge; fig **c. las culpas a algn**, to put the blame on sb. 2 Com to charge; **cárguelo a mi cuenta**, charge it to my account; fam Educ **me han cargado las matemáticas**, I failed maths. II vi 1 **c. con**, (llevar) to carry; fig **c. con la responsabilidad**, to take the responsibility; fig **c. con las consecuencias**, to suffer the consequences. 2 Mil **c. contra**, to charge. III **cargarse** vr 1 fam **te la vas a c.**, you're asking for trouble and you're going to get it. 2 fam (estropear) to smash, ruin. 3 fam (matar) to kill, bump off.

cargo nm 1 (puesto) post, position; **alto c.**, (puesto) top job, high ranking position; (persona) top person. 2 **estar al c. de**, to be in charge of; **correr a c. de**, (gastos) to be met by; **hacerse c. de**, to take charge of; **hazte c. de mi situación**, please try to understand my situation; **c. de conciencia**, weight on one's conscience. 3 Fin charge, debit; **con c. a mi cuenta**, charged to my account. 4 Jur charge, accusation.

carguero nm 1 (avión) transport plane. 2 (barco) freighter.

cariarse vr to decay.

caribe nm (idioma) Carib; **el (mar) C.**, the Caribbean Sea.

caricatura nf caricature.

caricaturizar [4] vtr to caricature.

caricia nf caress, stroke.

caridad nf charity.

caries nf inv decay, caries.

carilla nf page, side of a piece of paper.

cariño nm 1 (amor) affection; **coger/tener c. a algo/algn**, to grow/to be fond of sth/sb; **con c.**, (en carta) love. 2 (querido) darling; (abrazo) cuddle.

cariñoso,-a adj loving, affectionate.

carisma nm charisma.

carismático,-a adj charismatic.

caritativo,-a adj charitable.

cariz nm look.

carmesí adj & nm crimson.

carmín nm (de color) c., carmine; **c. (de labios)**, lipstick.

carnal adj 1 (de carne) carnal. 2 (pariente) first; **primo c.**, first cousin.

carnaval nm carnival.

carne nf 1 flesh; fam **ser de c. y hueso**, to be only human; fig **c. de cañón**, cannon fodder; **c. de gallina**, goose-pimples; **c. viva**, raw flesh. 2 (alimento) meat; **c. de cerdo/cordero/ternera/vaca**, pork/lamb/veal/beef. 3 (de fruta) pulp.

carné, carnet nm card; **c. de conducir**, driving licence; **c. de identidad**, identity card.

carnero nm ram; Culin mutton.

carnicería nf 1 butcher's (shop). 2 fig (masacre) slaughter.

carnicero,-a nm,f butcher.

cárnico,-a adj **productos cárnicos**, meat products.

carnívoro,-a I adj carnivorous. II nm,f carnivore.

carnoso,-a adj fleshy.

caro,-a I adj expensive, dear. II adv **salir c.**, to cost a lot; **te costará c.**, (amenaza) you'll pay dearly for this.

carpa nf 1 (pez) carp. 2 (de circo) big top, marquee. 3 Am (de camping) tent.

carpeta nf folder.

carpetazo nm **dar c. a un asunto**, to shelve a matter.

Cárpatos npl Carpathians.

carpintería nf 1 (oficio) carpentry; **c. metálica**, metalwork. 2 (taller) carpenter's (shop).

carpintero,-a nm,f carpenter.

carraca nf rattle.

carraspear vi to clear one's throat.

carraspeo nm clearing of the throat.

carraspera nf hoarseness.

carrera nf 1 run; (de media) run, ladder; **a la c.**, in a hurry. 2 (competición) race; **c. contra reloj**, race against the clock; **c. de coches**, rally, meeting; **echar una c. a algn**, to race sb; **c. de armamentos**, arms race. 3 (estudios) degree. 4 (profesión) career, profession.

carrerilla nf run; **tomar c.**, to take a run; **de c.**, parrot fashion.

carreta nf cart.

carrete nm (de hilo) reel; (de película) spool; (de cable) coil.

carretera nf road; **c. comarcal/nacional**, B/A road; **c. de circunvalación**, ring road; **c. de acceso**, access road; (en autopista) slip road.

carretilla nf wheelbarrow.

carricoche nm caravan.

carril nm 1 Ferroc rail. 2 Aut lane.

carrillo nm cheek; fam **comer a dos carri-**

llos, to devour, gobble up.

carro *nm* 1 (*carreta*) cart; *fam* ¡para el c.!, hold your horses! 2 *Mil* c. de combate, tank. 3 (*de máquina de escribir*) carriage. 4 *Am* car.

carrocería *nf Aut* bodywork.

carroña *nf* carrion.

carroza I *nf* 1 (*coche de caballos*) coach, carriage. 2 (*de carnaval*) float. II *nmf fam* old fogey.

carruaje *nm* carriage, coach.

carta *nf* 1 letter; c. **certificada/urgente**, registered/express letter. 2 (*menú*) menu; **a la c.**, à la carte; **c. de vinos**, wine list. 3 *Naipes* card; **echar las cartas a algn**, to tell sb's fortune; *fig* **poner las cartas sobre la mesa**, to lay one's cards on the table, come clean. 4 *Geog* (*mapa*) chart. 5 *fig* **adquirir c. de naturaleza**, to become widely accepted; **tomar cartas en un asunto**, to take part in an affair.

cartabón *nm* set square.

cartearse *vr* to correspond (**con**, with), exchange letters (**con**, with).

cartel *nm* poster; **pegar/fijar carteles**, to put *o* stick up bills.

cartél *nm Com* cartel.

cartelera *nf* hoarding, *US* billboard; *Prensa* c. **de espectáculos**, entertainments section *o* page.

cartera *nf* 1 (*de bolsillo*) wallet. 2 (*de mano*) handbag; (*para documentos etc*) briefcase; (*de colegial*) satchel, schoolbag. 3 *Pol* (*ministerio*) portfolio. 4 *Com* portfolio; c. **de pedidos**, order book. 5 *Am* (*bolso*) handbag, *US* purse.

carterista *nmf* pickpocket.

cartero,-a *nm,f* (*hombre*) postman; (*mujer*) postwoman.

cartilla *nf* 1 (*libreta*) book; c. **de ahorros**, savings book. 2 (*libro*) first reader; *fam* **leerle la c. a algn**, to tell sb off.

cartografía *nf* cartography.

cartón *nm* 1 (*material*) card, cardboard; c. **piedra**, papier mâché. 2 (*de cigarrillos*) carton.

cartucho *nm* 1 (*de balas*) cartridge. 2 (*de papel*) cone.

cartulina *nf* card.

casa *nf* 1 (*edificio*) house; c. **de huéspedes**, boarding house; c. **de socorro**, first aid post. 2 (*hogar*) home; **vete a c.**, go home; **en c. de Daniel**, at Daniel's; **de andar por c.**, everyday. 3 (*empresa*) company, firm; c. **matriz/principal**, head/central office.

casación *nf Jur* cassation, annulment.

casadero,-a *adj* of marrying age.

casado,-a I *adj* married. **II** *nm,f* married person; **los recién casados**, the newlyweds.

casamiento *nm* marriage; (*boda*) wedding.

casar¹ I *vtr* to marry. **II** *vi* to match, go *o*

fit together. **III casarse** *vr* to marry, get married; c. **por la iglesia/por lo civil**, to get married in church/in a registry office.

casar² *vtr Jur* to annul, quash.

cascabel *nm* bell.

cascada *nf* waterfall, cascade.

cascanueces *nm inv* nutcracker.

cascar [1] I *vtr* 1 to crack. 2 *fam* **cascarla**, to kick the bucket, snuff it. II *vi fam* (*charlar*) to chat away. III **cascarse** *vr* to crack.

cáscara *nf* shell; (*de fruta*) skin, peel; (*de grano*) husk.

cascarón *nm* eggshell.

cascarrabias *nmf inv fam* short-tempered person.

casco *nm* 1 (*para la cabeza*) helmet. 2 (*de caballo*) hoof. 3 (*envase*) empty bottle. 4 c. **urbano**, city centre. 5 (*de barco*) hull. 6 **cascos**, (*auriculares*) headphones.

cascote *nm* piece of rubble *o* debris.

caserío *nm* country house.

casero,-a I *adj* 1 (*hecho en casa*) homemade. 2 (*persona*) home-loving. **II** *nm,f* (*dueño*) (*hombre*) landlord; (*mujer*) landlady.

caseta *nf* hut, booth; (*de feria, exposición*) stand, stall.

casete I *nm* (*magnetófono*) cassette player *o* recorder. **II** *nf* (*cinta*) cassette (tape).

casi *adv* almost, nearly; c. **mil personas**, almost one thousand people; c. **ni me acuerdo**, I can hardly remember it; c. **nunca**, hardly ever; c. **nadie**, hardly anyone; c. **me caigo**, I almost fell.

casilla *nf* 1 (*de casillero*) pigeonhole. 2 (*recuadro*) box. 3 *Am* P.O. Box. 4 *fig* **sacar a algn de sus casillas**, to drive sb mad.

casillero *nm* pigeonholes *pl*.

casino *nm* casino.

caso *nm* case; **el c. es que ...**, the fact *o* thing is that ...; **el c. Mattei**, the Mattei affair; (**en**) c. **contrario**, otherwise; **en c. de necesidad**, if need be; **en cualquier c.**, in any case; **en el mejor/peor de los casos**, at best/worst; **en ese c.**, in such a case; **en todo c.**, in any case; **en un c. extremo**, in the last resort; **hacer c. a** *o* **de algn**, to pay attention to sb; **hacer c. omiso de**, to take no notice of; **no venir al c.**, to be beside the point; **pongamos por c.**, let's say.

caspa *nf* dandruff.

casquete *nm* 1 (*de bala*) case, shell. 2 *Geog* c. **polar**, polar cap.

casquillo *nm* (*de bala*) case.

cassette *nm & f* → **casete**.

casta *nf* 1 (*linaje*) lineage, descent. 2 (*animales*) breed; **de c.**, thoroughbred, purebred. 3 (*división social*) caste.

castaña *nf* chestnut; *fig* **sacarle a algn las castañas del fuego**, to save sb's bacon.

castañetear *vi* (*dientes*) to chatter.

castaño,-a I *adj* chestnut-brown; (*pelo,*

ojos) brown, dark. **II** *nm Bot* chestnut.

castañuela *nf* castanet.

castellano,-a I *adj* Castilian. **II** *nm,f* (*persona*) Castilian. **III** *nm* (*idioma*) Spanish, Castilian.

castidad *nf* chastity.

castigar [7] *vtr* **1** to punish. **2** (*dañar*) to harm, ruin. **3** *Jur Dep* to penalize.

castigo *nm* punishment; *Jur* penalty; *Dep* **área de c.**, penalty area.

Castilla *n* Castile.

castillo *nm* castle.

castizo,-a *adj* pure, authentic.

casto,-a *adj* chaste.

castor *nm* beaver.

castrar *vtr* to castrate.

castrense *adj* military.

casual I *adj* accidental, chance. **II** *nm fam* chance. ◆**casualmente** *adv* by chance.

casualidad *nf* chance, coincidence; **de** *o* **por c.**, by chance; **dió la c. que ...**, it so happened that ...; **¿tienes un lápiz, por c.?**, do you happen to have a pencil?; **¡que c.!**, what a coincidence!

cata *nf* tasting.

cataclismo *nm* cataclysm.

catador,-a *nm,f* taster.

catalán,-ana I *adj & nm,f* Catalan. **II** *nm* (*idioma*) Catalan.

catalejo *nm* telescope.

catalepsia *nf* catalepsy.

catalizador *nm* catalyst; *Aut* catalytic converter.

catalizar [4] *vtr fig* to act as a catalyst for.

catalogar [7] *vtr* **1** to catalogue, *US* catalog. **2** (*clasificar*) to classify.

catálogo *nm* catalogue, *US* catalog.

Cataluña *n* Catalonia.

cataplasma *nf* **1** *Farm* cataplasm, poultice. **2** *fam* (*pelmazo*) bore.

catapulta *nf* catapult; *fig* springboard.

catapultar *vtr* to catapult.

catar *vtr* to taste.

catarata *nf* **1** waterfall. **2** *Med* cataract.

catarro *nm* (common) cold.

catastral *adj* **valor c.**, rateable value.

catastro *nm* cadastre, cadaster.

catástrofe *nf* catastrophe.

catastrófico,-a *adj* catastrophic.

catear *vtr fam Educ* to fail, *US* flunk.

catecismo *nm* catechism.

cátedra *nf* (professorial) chair; **le han dado la c.**, they have appointed him professor.

catedral *nf* cathedral.

catedrático,-a *nm,f Educ* **1** *Univ* professor. **2** (*de instituto*) head of department.

categoría *nf* category; *fig* class; **de c.**, (*persona*) important; (*vino etc*) quality.

categórico,-a *adj* categoric; **un no c.**, a flat refusal.

cateto,-a *nm,f pey* yokel, bumpkin.

catolicismo *nm* Catholicism.

católico,-a *adj & nm,f* Catholic.

catorce *adj & nm inv* fourteen.

catre *nm fam* bed.

Cáucaso *n* Caucasus.

cauce *nm* **1** (*de un río*) bed. **2** *fig* (*canal*) channel; **cauces oficiales**, official channels.

caucho *nm* **1** rubber. **2** *Am* (*cubierta*) tyre, *US* tire.

caudal *nm* **1** (*de un río*) flow. **2** (*riqueza*) wealth, riches *pl*.

caudaloso,-a *adj* (*río*) plentiful.

caudillo *nm* leader, head.

causa *nf* **1** cause; **a** *o* **por c. de**, because of. **2** (*ideal*) cause. **3** *Jur* (*caso*) case; (*juicio*) trial.

causante I *adj* causal, causing. **II** *nm,f* **el c. del incendio**, the person who caused the fire.

causar *vtr* to cause, bring about; **me causa un gran placer**, it gives me great pleasure; **c. buena/mala impresión**, to make a good/bad impression.

cáustico,-a *adj* caustic.

cautela *nf* caution.

cautivar *vtr* **1** to capture, take prisoner. **2** *fig* (*fascinar*) to captivate.

cautiverio *nm*, **cautividad** *nf* captivity.

cautivo,-a *adj & nm,f* captive.

cauto,-a *adj* cautious, wary.

cava I *nf* (*bodega*) wine cellar. **II** *nm* (*vino espumoso*) cava, champagne.

cavar *vtr* to dig.

caverna *nf* cave; **hombre de las cavernas**, caveman.

cavernícola *nm,f* cave dweller.

caviar *nm* caviar.

cavidad *nf* cavity.

cavilar *vtr* to ponder.

cayado *nm* **1** (*de pastor*) crook. **2** (*de obispo*) crosier, crozier.

cayuco *nm Am* small flat-bottomed canoe.

caza I *nf* **1** hunting; **ir de c.**, to go hunting; **c. furtiva**, poaching. **2** (*animales*) game; **c. mayor/menor**, big/small game. **3** *fig* (*persecución*) hunt; **c. de brujas**, witch hunt. **II** *nm Av* fighter, fighter plane.

cazabombardero *nm Av* fighter bomber.

cazador,-a *nm,f* hunter; **c. furtivo**, poacher.

cazadora *nf* (waist-length) jacket.

cazar [4] *vtr* to hunt; *fam* **cazarlas al vuelo**, to be quick on the uptake.

cazatalentos *nmf inv* head-hunter.

cazo *nm* **1** (*cacerola*) saucepan. **2** (*cucharón*) ladle.

cazuela *nf* saucepan; (*guiso*) casserole, stew; **a la c.**, stewed.

c/c *abr de* **cuenta corriente**, current account, c/a.

CCOO *nfpl abr de* **Comisiones Obreras**.

CDS *nm Pol abr de* **Centro Democrático y Social**.

cebada *nf* barley.

cebar I *vtr* 1 (*animal*) to fatten; *fam* (*persona*) to feed up. 2 (*anzuelo*) to bait. II **cebarse** *vr* c. con, (*ensañarse*) to delight in tormenting.

cebo *nm* bait.

cebolla *nf* onion.

cebolleta *nf* 1 (*especie*) chives *pl*. 2 (*cebolla tierna*) spring onion.

cebra *nf* zebra; **paso de c.**, zebra crossing, *US* crosswalk.

cecear *vi* to lisp.

ceceo *nm* lisp.

cedazo *nm* sieve.

ceder I *vtr* 1 to give, hand over; *Aut* **c. el paso**, to give way. II *vi* 1 (*cuerda, cable*) to give way. 2 (*lluvia, calor*) to diminish, slacken. 3 (*consentir*) to give in.

cedro *nm* cedar.

cédula *nf* 1 document, certificate; *Am* **c. de identidad**, identity card. 2 *Com Fin* bond, certificate, warrant.

C(E)E *nf abr de* **Comunidad (Económica) Europea**, European (Economic) Community, E(E)C.

cegador,-a *adj* blinding.

cegar [1] *vtr* 1 to blind. 2 (*puerta, ventana*) to wall up.

ceguera *nf* blindness.

CEI *abr de* **Comunidad de Estados Independientes**, Commonwealth of Independent States, CIS.

Ceilán *n* Ceylon.

ceja *nf* eyebrow.

cejar *vi* c. en el empeño, to give up.

celada *nf* trap, ambush.

celador,-a *nm,f* attendant; (*de una cárcel*) warder.

celda *nf* cell; **c. de castigo**, punishment cell.

celebración *nf* 1 (*festejo*) celebration. 2 (*de juicio etc*) holding.

celebrar I *vtr* 1 to celebrate; **celebro que todo saliera bien**, I'm glad everything went well. 2 (*reunión, juicio, elecciones*) to hold. 3 (*triunfo*) to laud. II **celebrarse** *vr* to take place, be held.

célebre *adj* famous, well-known.

celebridad *nf* 1 celebrity, fame. 2 (*persona*) celebrity.

celeste I *adj* 1 (*de cielo*) celestial. 2 (*color*) sky-blue. II *nm* sky blue.

celestial *adj* celestial, heavenly.

celibato *nm* celibacy.

célibe *adj & nmf* celibate.

celo *nm* 1 zeal. 2 **en c.**, (*macho*) in rut; (*hembra*) on o in heat. 3 **celos**, jealousy *sing*; **tener celos (de algn)**, to be jealous (of sb).

celo® *nm fam* sellotape®, *US* Scotch tape®.

celofán *nm* cellophane.

celosía *nf* lattice.

celoso,-a *adj* 1 jealous. 2 (*cumplidor*) con-

scientious.

celta I *adj* Celtic. II *nm,f* Celt. III *nm* (*idioma*) Celtic.

célula *nf* cell.

celular *adj* 1 cellular. 2 **coche c.**, Black Maria.

celulitis *nf inv* cellulitis.

celuloide *nm* celluloid.

celulosa *nf* cellulose.

cementerio *nm* cemetery, graveyard; **c. de coches**, scrapyard.

cemento *nm* cement; **c. armado**, reinforced cement.

cena *nf* evening meal; (*antes de acostarse*) supper; **la Última C.**, the Last Supper.

cenagal *nm* marsh, swamp.

cenar I *vi* to have supper o dinner. II *vtr* to have for supper o dinner.

cencerro *nm* cowbell.

cenefa *nf* (*de ropa*) edging, trimming; (*de suelo, techo*) ornamental border, frieze.

cenetista I *adj* of o related to the CNT (Confederación Nacional del Trabajo). II *nmf* member of the CNT.

cenicero *nm* ashtray.

cenit *nm* zenith.

ceniza *nf* ash.

cenizo *nm fam* (*gafe*) jinx.

censo *nm* census; **c. electoral**, electoral roll.

censor *nm* censor.

censura *nf* 1 censorship. 2 *Pol* **moción de c.**, vote of no confidence.

censurar *vtr* 1 (*libro, película*) to censor. 2 (*criticar*) to censure, criticize.

centavo *nm Am Fin* cent, centavo.

centella *nf* spark.

centellear *vi* to flash, sparkle.

centelleo *nm* flashing, sparkling.

centena *nf*, **centenar** *nm* hundred; **a centenares**, in hundreds.

centenario *nm* centenary, hundredth anniversary.

centeno *nm* rye.

centésimo,-a *adj & nm,f* hundredth.

centígrado,-a *adj* centigrade.

centilitro *nm* centilitre, *US* centiliter.

centímetro *nm* centimetre, *US* centimeter.

céntimo *nm* cent.

centinela *nm* sentry.

centollo *nm* spider crab.

centrado,-a *adj* 1 centred, *US* centered. 2 (*equilibrado*) balanced.

central I *adj* central. II *nf* 1 *Elec* **c. nuclear/térmica**, nuclear/coal-fired power station. 2 (*oficina principal*) head office.

centralismo *nm* centralism.

centralita *nf Tel* switchboard.

centralizar [4] *vtr* to centralize.

centrar I *vtr* 1 to centre, *US* center. 2 (*esfuerzos, atención*) to concentrate, centre, *US* center. II **centrarse** *vr* 1 to be centred o *US* centered o based. 2

(*concentrarse*) to concentrate (**en,** on).
céntrico,-a *adj* centrally situated; **zona céntrica**, centrally situated area.
centrifugar |7| *vtr* to centrifuge; (*ropa*) to spin-dry.
centrista *Pol* **I** *adj* centre, *US* center; **partido c.,** centre party. **II** *nmf* centrist.
centro *nm* **1** middle, centre, *US* center; **c. de la ciudad,** town *o* city centre. **2** (*establecimiento*) institution, centre, *US* center; **c. comercial,** shopping centre.
Centroamérica *n* Central America.
centroamericano,-a *adj & nm,f* Central American.
centrocampista *nmf Ftb* midfield player.
centuria *nf* century.
ceñido,-a *adj* tight-fitting, clinging.
ceñirse |6| *vr* **1** (*atenerse, limitarse*) to limit oneself, stick (**a**, to); **c. al tema,** to keep to the subject; **ciñéndonos a este caso en concreto,** coming down to this particular case. **2** (*prenda*) to cling (**a**, to).
ceño *nm* scowl, frown; **con el c. fruncido,** frowning.
CEOE *nf abr de* **Confederación Española de Organizaciones Empresariales,** ≈ Confederation of British Industry, CBI.
cepa *nf* **1** (*de vid*) vine. **2** *fig* **vasco de pura c.,** (*origen*) Basque through and through.
cepillar I *vtr* **1** to brush. **2** (*en carpintería*) to plane (down). **3** *fam* (*robar*) to pinch. **II cepillarse** *vr* **1** (*con cepillo*) to brush. **2** *fam* (*matar*) to do in. **3** *vulg* to lay.
cepillo *nm* brush; (*en carpintería*) plane; **c. de dientes,** toothbrush; **c. del pelo,** hairbrush.
cepo *nm* **1** *Caza* trap. **2** *Aut* clamp.
cera *nf* wax; (*de abeja*) beeswax.
cerámica *nf* ceramics *sing.*
cerca¹ *adv* **1** near, close; **ven más c.,** come closer; **ya estamos c.,** we are almost there. **2 c. de,** (*al lado de*) near, close; **el colegio está c. de mi casa,** the school is near my house. **3 c. de,** (*casi*) nearly, around; **c. de cien personas,** about one hundred people. **4 de c.,** closely; **lo vi muy de c.,** I saw it close up.
cerca² *nf* fence, wall.
cercado *nm* **1** (*lugar cerrado*) enclosure. **2** (*valla*) fence, wall.
cercanía *nf* **1** proximity, nearness. **2** **cercanías,** outskirts, suburbs; **(tren de) c.,** suburban train.
cercano,-a *adj* nearby; **el C. Oriente,** the Near East.
cercar |1| *vtr* **1** (*tapiar*) to fence, enclose. **2** (*rodear*) to surround.
cercenar *vtr* to cut off, amputate.
cerciorar I *vtr* to assure. **II cerciorarse** *vr* to make sure.
cerco *nm* **1** circle, ring. **2** *Mil* (*sitio*) siege; **poner c. (a una ciudad),** to besiege (a town).

cerda *nf* **1** *Zool* sow. **2** (*pelo*) bristle; **cepillo de c.,** bristle brush.
Cerdeña *n* Sardinia.
cerdo *nm* **1** pig. **2** (*carne*) pork. **3** *fam* *pey* pig, arsehole.
cereal *nm* cereal.
cerebral *adj* **1** cerebral. **2** (*frío*) calculating.
cerebro *nm* brain; *fig* (*inteligencia*) brains *pl.*
ceremonia *nf* ceremony.
ceremonioso,-a *adj* ceremonious, formal; *pey* pompous, stiff.
cereza *nf* cherry.
cerezo *nm* cherry tree.
cerilla *nf* match.
cernerse |3| *fig* to loom (**sobre,** above).
cernícalo *nm* kestrel.
cernir |5| *vtr & vr* → **cerner.**
cero *nm* zero; *Dep* nil; *fig* **partir de c.,** to start from scratch; *fig* **ser un c. a la izquierda,** to be useless *o* a good-for-nothing.
cerrado,-a *adj* **1** closed, shut; **a puerta cerrada,** behind closed doors. **2** (*reservado*) reserved; (*intransigente*) uncompromising, unyielding; *fam* (*torpe*) thick; (*acento*) broad; (*curva*) tight, sharp. **3** (*barba*) bushy.
cerradura *nf* lock.
cerrajero,-a *nm,f* locksmith.
cerrar |1| **I** *vtr* to shut, close; (*grifo, gas*) to turn off; (*luz*) to turn off, switch off; (*cremallera*) to do up; (*negocio*) to close down; (*cuenta*) to close; (*carta*) to seal; (*puños*) to clench; **c. con llave,** to lock; **c. el paso a algn,** to block sb's way; *fam* **c. el pico,** to shut one's trap. **II** *vi* to close, shut. **III cerrarse** *vr* to close, shut; *fam* **c. en banda,** to stick to one's guns.
cerro *nm* hill; *fig* **irse por los cerros de Ubeda,** to beat around the bush.
cerrojo *nm* bolt; **echar el c. (de una puerta),** to bolt (a door).
certamen *nm* competition, contest.
certero,-a *adj* accurate.
certeza, certidumbre *nf* certainty; **saber (algo) con c.,** to be certain (of sth); **tener la c. de que ...,** to be sure *o* certain that ....
certificado,-a I *adj* **1** certified. **2** (*correo*) registered. **II** *nm* certificate.
certificar |1| *vtr* **1** to certify. **2** (*carta*) to register.
cervatillo *nm* fawn.
cervecería *nf* **1** (*bar*) pub, bar. **2** (*fábrica*) brewery.
cerveza *nf* beer; **c. de barril,** draught beer; **c. dorada** *o* **ligera,** lager; **c. negra,** stout.
cervical *adj* cervical.
cesar I *vi* to stop, cease (**de,** -); **sin c.,** incessantly. **II** *vtr* (*empleado*) to dismiss.
cesárea *nf* Caesarean (section), *US* Cesar-

ean (section).
cese *nm* 1 cessation, suspension. 2 *(despido)* dismissal.
CESID *nm Mil abr de* **Centro Superior de Información de la Defensa**.
césped *nm* lawn, grass.
cesta *nf* basket; **c. de Navidad**, Christmas hamper.
cesto *nm* basket.
cetáceo *nm* cetacean, whale.
cetrino,-a *adj* sallow.
cetro *nm* sceptre, *US* scepter.
Ceuta *n* Ceuta.
ceutí I *adj* of *o* from Ceuta. II *nmf* native *o* inhabitant of Ceuta.
chabacano,-a *adj* cheap.
chabola *nf* shack; **barrio de chabolas**, shanty town.
chacal *nm* jackal.
chacha *nf* maid.
cháchara *nf fam* small talk, chinwag; **estar de c.**, to have a yap.
chachi *adj* smashing.
chacinería *nf* pork bucher's shop.
chacra *nf Am* small farm *o* holding.
chafar *vtr* 1 *fam (plan etc)* to ruin, spoil. 2 *(aplastar)* to squash, flatten.
chal *nm* shawl.
chalado,-a *adj fam* crazy, nuts **(por,** about).
chalé *nm (pl* **chalés)** → **chalet**.
chaleco *nm* waistcoat, *US* vest; *(de punto)* sleeveless pullover; **c. antibalas**, bulletproof vest; **c. salvavidas**, life jacket.
chalet *nm* villa.
chalupa *nf* boat, launch.
chamarra *nf* sheepskin jacket.
chambelán *nm* chamberlain.
chambergo *nm* heavy coat.
chamizo *nm* thatched hut.
champán, champaña *nm* champagne.
champiñón *nm* mushroom.
champú *nm* shampoo.
chamuscar [1] *vtr* to singe, scorch.
chamusquina *nf* singeing, scorching; *fam* **esto me huele a c.**, there's something fishy going on here.
chancaca *nf Am* syrup cake.
chance *nm Am* opportunity.
chancear *vi Am* to joke, horse around.
chanchada *nf Am fam* dirty trick.
chancho,-a *nm,f Am* pig, hog.
chanchullo *nm fam* fiddle, wangle.
chancla *nf* flipflop.
chanclo *nm (zueco)* clog; *(de goma)* overshoe, galosh.
chándal *nm* track *o* jogging suit.
chantaje *nm* blackmail; **hacer c. a algn,** to blackmail sb.
chantajear *vtr* to blackmail.
chantajista *nmf* blackmailer.
chanza *nf* joke.
chapa *nf* 1 *(de metal)* sheet; *(de madera)* panel-board. 3 *(tapón)* bottle top, cap. 4

(de adorno) badge. 5 *Am* lock.
chapado,-a *adj (metal)* plated; **c. en oro,** gold-plated; *fig* **c. a la antigua,** old-fashioned.
chaparro *nm Bot* holm oak.
chaparrón *nm* downpour, heavy shower.
chapotear *vi* to splash about, paddle.
chapucero,-a *adj (trabajo)* slapdash, shoddy; *(persona)* bungling.
chapurrear *vtr* to speak badly *o* with difficulty; **sólo chapurreaba el francés,** he spoke only a few words of French.
chapuza *nf* 1 *(trabajo mal hecho)* shoddy piece of work. 2 *(trabajo ocasional)* odd job.
chapuzón *nm (baño corto)* dip; **darse un c.,** to have a dip.
chaqué *nm* morning coat.
chaqueta *nf* jacket; *Pol* **cambiar de c.,** to change sides.
chaquetero,-a *nm,f fam Pol* turncoat.
chaquetilla *nf* short jacket.
charanga *nf Mús* brass band.
charca *nf* pond, pool.
charco *nm* puddle.
charcutería *nf* delicatessen.
charla *nf (conversación)* talk, chat; *(conferencia)* informal lecture *o* address.
charlar *vi* to talk, chat.
charlatán,-ana I *adj (parlanchín)* talkative; *(chismoso)* gossipy. II *nm,f* 1 *(parlanchín)* chatterbox; *(chismoso)* gossip; *(bocazas)* bigmouth. 2 *(embaucador)* trickster, charmer.
charol *nm* patent leather; **zapatos de c.,** patent leather shoes.
charqui *nm Am (carne)* dried beef, cured meat; *(fruta)* dried fruit.
chárter *adj inv* **(vuelo) c.,** charter (flight).
chasca *nf Am* mop of hair, tangled hair.
chascar [1] *vtr (lengua)* to click; *(dedos)* to snap; *(látigo)* to crack.
chascarrillo *nm* shaggy dog story.
chasco *nm fam* disappointment; **llevarse un c.,** to be disappointed.
chasis *nm inv* chassis.
chasquear *vtr (lengua)* to click; *(dedos)* to snap; *(látigo)* to crack.
chasqui *nm Am* messenger, courier.
chasquido *nm (de la lengua)* click; *(de los dedos)* snap; *(de látigo, madera)* crack.
chatarra *nf* scrap (metal), scrap iron; *fam* junk.
chato,-a I *adj* 1 *(nariz)* snub; *(persona)* snub-nosed. 2 *(objeto)* flat, flattened. II *nm* (small) glass of wine.
chauvinista *adj & nmf* chauvinist.
chaval,-a *nm,f fam (chico)* boy, lad; *(chica)* girl.
checo,-a *adj* Czech.
checoslovaco,-a I *adj* Czechoslovakian, Czech. II *nm,f (persona)* Czechoslovakian, Czechoslovak, Czech.
Checoslovaquia *n* Czechoslovakia.

chelín *nm* shilling.

chepa *nf fam* hump.

cheque *nm* cheque, *US* check; **c. al portador,** cheque payable to bearer; **c. de viaje** *o* **(de) viajero,** traveller's cheque, *US* traveler's check.

chequeo *nm Med* checkup; *Aut* service.

chévere *adj Am fam* great, terrific, fantastic.

chic *adj inv* chic, elegant.

chicano,-a *adj & nm,f* chicano.

chicha[1] *nf Am* chicha, maize liquor.

chicha[2] *adj inv Náut* **calma c.,** dead calm.

chícharo *nm Am* pea.

chicharra *nf* cicada.

chichón *nm* bump, lump.

chichonera *nf* helmet.

chicle *nm* chewing gum.

chico,-a I *nm,f* (*muchacho*) boy, lad; (*muchacha*) girl. **II** *adj* small, little.

chicoria *nf* chicory.

chicote *nm Am* whip.

chiflado,-a *adj fam* mad, crazy (**por,** about).

chiflar *vtr* 1 (*silbar*) to hiss (at), boo (at). 2 *fam* **le chiflan las motos,** he's really into motorbikes.

chiflido *nm* whistle, whistling.

chiíta *adj & nmf* Shiite.

chile *nm* chili (pepper).

Chile *n* Chile.

chileno,-a *adj & nm,f* Chilean.

chillar *vi* (*persona*) to scream, shriek; (*ratón*) to squeak; (*frenos*) to screech, squeal; (*puerta*) to creak, squeak.

chillido *nm* (*de persona*) scream, shriek; (*de ratón*) squeak; (*de frenos*) screech, squeal; (*de puerta*) creaking, sweaking.

chillón,-ona *adj* 1 (*voz*) shrill, high-pitched; (*sonido*) harsh, strident. 2 (*color*) loud, gaudy.

chimenea *nf* 1 (*hogar abierto*) fireplace, hearth. 2 (*conducto*) chimney; (*de barco*) funnel, stack.

China *n* China.

china *nf* 1 pebble, small stone; *fam* **tocarle a uno la c.,** to get the short straw. 2 *arg* (*droga*) deal.

chinche I *nf* bug, bedbug; *fam* **caer como chinches,** to fall like flies. **II** *nm,f fam* nuisance, pest.

chincheta *nf* drawing pin, *US* thumbtack.

chinchín *interj* **¡c.!,** cheers!, (to) your (good) health!

chinesco,-a *adj* **sombras chinescas,** shadow theatre *sing*.

chingana *nf Am* bar.

chingar |7| *vtr* 1 (*fastidiar*) to annoy. 2 *vulg* (*estropear*) to fuck up. 3 *vulg* (*joder*) to fuck, screw.

chino[1] *nm* (*piedrecita*) pebble, stone.

chino,-a[2] *adj* (*de la China*) Chinese; *fam*

eso me suena a c., it's all Greek to me.

chip *nm* (*pl* **chips**) *Inform* chip.

chipirón *nm* baby squid.

Chipre *n* Cyprus.

chipriota *adj & nmf* Cypriot.

chiquillo,-a *nm,f* kid, youngster.

chiquito,-a *adj* tiny.

chirimiri *nm* drizzle, fine misty rain.

chirimoya *nf* custard apple.

chiringuito *nm* (*en playa etc*) refreshment stall; (*en carretera*) roadside snack bar.

chiripa *nf* fluke, lucky stroke; *fam* **fig de** *o* **por c.,** by a fluke, by chance; **cogió al tren por c.,** it was sheer luck that he caught the train.

chirla *nf* small clam.

chirona *nf arg* clink, nick.

chirriar |29| *vi* (*puerta etc*) to creak; (*frenos*) to screech, squeal.

chirrido *nm* (*de puerta etc*) crack, cracking; (*de frenos*) screech, squeal.

chisme *nm* 1 (*habladuría*) piece of gossip. 2 *fam* (*trasto*) knick-knack; (*cosa*) thing.

chismorrear *vi fam* to gossip.

chismorreo *nm fam* gossip, gossiping.

chismoso,-a I *adj* gossipy. **II** *nm,f* gossip.

chispa *nf* 1 spark; **echar chispas,** to fume. 2 *fam* (*un poco*) bit, tiny amount. 3 *fam* (*agudeza*) wit, sparkle; (*viveza*) liveliness.

chispear *vi* 1 to spark, throw out sparks. 2 (*lloviznar*) to spit.

chiste *nm* joke; **contar un c.,** to tell a joke; **c. verde,** blue joke, dirty joke.

chistera *nf* top hat.

chistoso,-a *adj* (*persona*) funny, witty; (*anécdota*) amusing, funny.

chivarse *vr fam* to tell tales.

chivatazo *nm fam* tip-off; **dar el c.,** to squeal.

chivato,-a *nm,f fam* (*delator*) squealer, grass; (*acusica*) telltale.

chivo,-a *nm,f Zool* kid, young goat; *fig* **c. expiatorio,** scapegoat.

chocante *adj* 1 (*persona*) off-putting. 2 (*sorprendente*) surprising, startling; (*raro*) strange.

chocar |11| **I** *vi* 1 (*topar*) to crash, collide; **c. con** *o* **contra,** to run into, collide with. 2 (*en discusión*) to clash. **II** *vtr* 1 to knock; (*la mano*) to shake; *fam* **¡chócala!, ¡choca esos cinco!,** shake (on it)!, put it there! 2 (*sorprender*) to surprise.

chochear *vi* 1 to be senile *o* in one's dotage. 2 **c. con algn,** to dote on sb.

chocho,-a I *adj* (*senil*) senile; **viejo c.,** old dodderer. **II** *nm* 1 (*altramuz*) lupin. 2 *vulg* cunt.

chocolate *nm* 1 chocolate; **c. con leche,** milk chocolate. 2 *arg* (*droga*) dope.

chocolatina *nf* bar of chocolate, chocolate bar.

chófer *nm* (*pl* **chóferes**) *Am,* **chofer** *nm* (*pl* **choferes**) driver; (*particular*) chauffeur.

chollo *nm fam (ganga)* bargain, snip.

chomba *nf Am* jumper, pullover.

chonta *nf Am* palm tree.

chopo *nm* poplar.

choque *nm* 1 impact; *(de coches etc)* crash, collision; **c. frontal**, head-on collision; **c. múltiple**, pile-up. 2 *fig (contienda)* clash.

choricear, chorizar *vtr fam* to pinch.

chorizo I *nm* 1 chorizo, highly-seasoned pork sausage. 2 *fam (ratero)* thief, pickpocket.

chorlito *nm Orn* plover; *fam fig* **cabeza de c.**, scatterbrain.

chorra I *nmf vulg (tonto)* idiot, fool. II *nf fam (suerte)* luck.

chorrada *nf fam* piece of nonsense.

chorrear *vi* to drip, trickle; *fam* **c. de sudor**, to pour with sweat; *fam* **tengo el abrigo chorreando**, my coat is dripping wet.

chorro *nm* 1 *(de agua etc)* spurt; *(muy fino)* trickle; **salir a chorros**, to gush forth. 2 *Téc* jet. 3 *fig* stream, flood.

chovinismo *nm* chauvinism.

chovinista I *adj* chauvinistic. II *nmf* chauvinist.

choza *nf* hut, shack.

christmas *nm* Christmas card.

chubasco *nm* heavy shower, downpour.

chubasquero *nm* raincoat.

chuchería *nf fam* sweet, *US* candy.

chufa *nf* groundnut.

chulear *vi* to strut around; **c. de**, to go on about.

chuleta *nf* 1 chop, cutlet; **c. de cerdo**, pork chop. 2 *Educ fam* crib (note), *US* trot.

chulo,-a *fam* I *nm,f* show off. II *nm (proxeneta)* pimp. III *adj (bonito)* smashing.

chungo,-a *adj fam* dodgy.

chupa *nf arg* short jacket.

chupachup® *nm* lollipop.

chupado,-a *adj* 1 *(flaco)* skinny, thin. 2 *fam* **está c.**, it's dead easy.

chupar I *vtr* 1 to suck. 2 *(lamer)* to lick. 3 *(absorber)* to soak up, absorb. II *vi* to suck. III **chuparse** *vr* 1 **está para c. los dedos**, it's really mouthwatering. 2 *fam* to put up with; **nos chupamos toda la película**, we sat through the whole film.

chupatintas *nm inv pey* penpusher.

chupete *nm* dummy, *US* pacifier.

chupi *adj fam* great, terrific, fantastic.

chupón *nm* 1 lollipop. 2 *(desatrancador)* plunger.

churrasco *nm* barbecued meat.

churrería *nf* fritter shop.

churrete *nm* dirty mark, grease spot.

churro *nm* 1 fritter, *US* cruller. 2 *fam (chapuza)* mess.

chusco *nm* chunk of stale bread; *Mil fam* ration bread.

chusma *nf* rabble, mob.

chutar I *vi* 1 *Dep (a gol)* to shoot. 2 *fam* **¡y vas que chutas!**, and then you're well away! II **chutarse** *vr arg (drogas)* to shoot up.

chute *nm* 1 *Dep* shot. 2 *arg (drogas)* fix.

CI *nm abr de* **coeficiente intelectual**, intelligence quotient, IQ.

Cía., cía *abr de* **compañía**, Company, Co.

cianuro *nm* cyanide.

cibernética *nf* cybernetics *sing*.

cicatero,-a I *adj* stingy, mean. II *nm,f* miser.

cicatriz *nf* scar.

cicatrizar |4| *vtr & vi Med* to heal.

cíclico,-a *adj* cyclical.

ciclismo *nm* cycling.

ciclista I *adj* cycling. II *nmf* cyclist.

ciclo *nm* cycle; *(de conferencias etc)* course, series.

ciclocróss *nm* cyclo-cross.

ciclomotor *nm* moped.

ciclón *nm* cyclone.

ciego,-a I *adj (persona)* blind; *fam (borracho)* blind drunk; *(de droga)* stoned; **a ciegas**, blindly. II *nm,f* blind person; **los ciegos**, the blind *pl*.

cielo *nm* 1 sky. 2 *Rel* heaven; *fig* **caído del c.**, *(oportuno)* heaven-sent; *(inesperado)* out of the blue; **¡c. santo!**, good heavens! 3 *Arquit* **c. raso**, ceiling. 4 **c. de la boca**, roof of the mouth.

ciempiés *nm inv* centipede.

cien *adj & nm inv* hundred; **c. libras**, a *o* one hundred pounds; **c. por c.**, one hundred per cent.

ciénaga *nf* marsh, bog.

ciencia *nf* 1 science; *fig* **saber algo a c. cierta**, to know something for certain; **c. ficción**, science fiction; **c. infusa**, intuition; **ciencias ocultas**, the occult *sing*. 2 *(conocimiento)* knowledge.

cieno *nm* mud, mire.

científico,-a I *adj* scientific. II *nm,f* scientist.

ciento *adj* hundred; **c. tres**, one hundred and three; **por c.**, per cent.

cierne *nm fig* **en ciernes**, budding.

cierre *nm* 1 *(acción)* closing, shutting; *(de fábrica)* shutdown; *TV* close-down; **c. patronal**, lockout. 2 *(de bolso)* clasp; *(de puerta)* catch; *(prenda)* fastener; **c. de seguridad**, safety lock; **c. centralizado**, central locking.

cierto,-a I *adj* 1 *(verdadero)* true; *(seguro)* certain; **estar en lo c.**, to be right; **lo c. es que ...**, the fact is that ...; **por c.**, by the way. 2 *(algún)* certain; **ciertas personas**, certain *o* some people. II *adv* certainly.

ciervo,-a *nm,f* deer; *(macho)* stag; *(hembra)* doe, hind.

cifra *nf* 1 *(número)* figure, number. 2 *(código)* cipher, code.

cifrar *vtr* to express in figures.

cigala *nf* Norway lobster.

cigarra *nf* cicada.

cigarrillo *nm* cigarette.

cigarro *nm* 1 (*puro*) cigar. 2 (*cigarrillo*) cigarette.

cigüeña *nf* 1 *Orn* stork. 2 *Téc* crank.

cigüeñal *nm* crankshaft.

cilindrada *nf* *Aut* cylinder capacity.

cilíndrico,-a *adj* cylindrical.

cilindro *nm* cylinder.

cima *nf* summit.

cimbrearse *vr* to sway.

cimentar *vtr* to lay the foundations of; *fig* (*amistad*) to strengthen.

cimientos *nmpl* foundations; **echar** *o* **poner los c.**, to lay the foundations.

cinc *nm* zinc.

cincel *nm* chisel.

cincelar *vtr* to chisel.

cinco *adj & nm inf* five.

cincuenta *adj & nm inf* fifty.

cine *nm* 1 (*local*) cinema, *US* movie theater. 2 (*arte*) cinema; **c. mudo/sonoro,** silent/talking films *pl.*

cineasta *nmf* film director, film maker.

cinéfilo,-a *nm,f* film lover, *US* movie fan.

cinematográfico,-a *adj* cinematographic; **la industria cinematográfica,** the film *o US* movie industry.

cíngaro,-a *adj & nm,f* gypsy.

cínico,-a I *adj* cynical. II *nm,f* cynic.

cinismo *nm* cynicism.

cinta *nf* 1 (*tira*) band, strip; (*para adornar*) ribbon; *Cost* braid, edging. 2 *Téc* tape; **c. adhesiva/aislante,** adhesive/insulating tape; **c. de vídeo,** video tape; **c. transportadora,** conveyor belt. 3 *Cin* film.

cinto *nm* belt.

cintura *nf* waist.

cinturón *nm* belt; *fig* **apretarse el c.,** to tighten one's belt; **c. de seguridad,** safety belt.

ciprés *nm* cypress.

circense *adj* circus.

circo *nm* circus.

circuito *nm* circuit.

circulación *nf* 1 circulation. 2 *Aut* (*tráfico*) traffic.

circular I *adj & nf* circular. II *vi* (*moverse*) to circulate; (*líquido*) to flow; (*tren, autobús*) to run; *fig* (*rumor*) to go round; **circule por la izquierda,** (*en letrero*) keep to the left.

circulatorio,-a *adj* circulatory; *Aut* **un caos c.,** traffic chaos.

círculo *nm* circle; *fig* **c. vicioso,** vicious circle.

circuncisión *nf* circumcision.

circundante *adj* surrounding.

circundar *vtr* to surround, encircle.

circunferencia *nf* circumference.

circunloquio *nm* circumlocution.

circunscribirse (*pp* **circunscrito**) *vr* to confine *o* limit oneself (**a, to**).

circunscripción *nf* district; **c. electoral,** constituency.

circunscrito,-a *adj* circumscribed.

circunspecto,-a *adj* circumspect.

circunstancia *nf* circumstance; **en estas circunstancias ...,** under the circumstances ....

circunstancial *adj* circumstancial.

cirio *nm* wax candle.

cirrosis *nf* cirrhosis.

ciruela *nf* plum; **c. claudia,** greengage; **c. pasa,** prune.

ciruelo *nm* plum tree.

cirugía *nf* surgery; **c. estética** *o* **plástica,** plastic surgery.

cirujano,-a *nm,f* surgeon.

cisma *nm* 1 *Rel* schism. 2 *Pol* split.

cisne *nm* swan.

cisterna *nf* cistern, tank.

cistitis *nf inv* cystitis.

cita *nf* 1 appointment; **darse c.,** to come together. 2 (*amorosa*) date. 3 (*mención*) quotation.

citación *nf* *Jur* citation, summons *sing.*

citado,-a *adj* aforementioned.

citar I *vtr* 1 (*dar cita*) to arrange to meet, make an appointment with. 2 (*mencionar*) to quote. 3 *Jur* to summon. II **citarse** *vr* to arrange to meet, make a date (**con, with**).

cítrico,-a I *adj* citric, citrus. II *nmpl* **cítricos,** citrus fruits.

ciudad *nf* town; (*capital*) city.

ciudadanía *nf* citizenship.

ciudadano,-a I *nm,f* citizen; **c. de a pie,** the man in the street. II *adj* civic.

cívico,-a *adj* civic.

civil I *adj* 1 civil; **matrimonio c.,** civil marriage. 2 *Mil* civilian. II *nm* member of the Guardia Civil.

civilización *nf* civilization.

civilizado,-a *adj* civilized.

civilizar |4| *vtr* to civilize.

civismo *nm* civility.

cizaña *nf* *Bot* bearded darnel; *fig* **sembrar c.,** to sow discord.

cl *abr de* **centilitro(s),** centilitre(s), *US* centiliter(s), cl.

clamar *vtr* to cry out for, clamour *o US* clamor for.

clamor *nm* clamour, *US* clamor.

clamoroso,-a *adj* resounding.

clan *nm* clan.

clandestinidad *nf* **en la c.,** underground.

clandestino,-a *adj* clandestine, underground; **aborto c.,** backstreet abortion.

clara *nf* (*de huevo*) white.

claraboya *nf* skylight.

clarear *vi* 1 (*amanecer*) to dawn. 2 (*despejar*) to clear up. 3 (*transparentar*) to wear thin, become transparent.

clarete *adj & nm* claret.

claridad *nf* 1 (*luz*) light, brightness. 2

(inteligibilidad) clarity; **con c.**, clearly.
clarificador,-a *adj* clarifying.
clarificar |1| *vtr* to clarify.
clarín *nm* bugle.
clarinete *nm* clarinet.
clarividente I *adj* 1 far-sighted. 2 *(lúcido)* lucid. **II** *nmf (persona)* clairvoyant.
claro,-a I *adj* 1 clear; **dejar algo c.**, to make sth clear. 2 *(líquido, salsa)* thin. 3 *(color)* light. **II** *interj* of course!; **¡c. que no!**, of course not!; **¡c. que sí!**, certainly!. **III** *nm* 1 *(espacio)* gap, space; *(en un bosque)* clearing. 2 *Meteor* bright spell. **IV** *adv* clearly.
clase *nf* 1 *(grupo)* class; **c. alta/media**, upper/middle class; **clases pasivas**, pensioners; **primera/segunda c.**, first/ second class. 2 *(tipo)* kind, sort; **toda c. de ...**, all kinds of .... 3 *Educ (curso)* class; *(aula)* classroom; **c. particular**, private class *o* lesson. 4 *(estilo)* class; **tener c.**, to have class.
clásico,-a I *adj* classical; *(típico)* classic; *(en el vestir)* classic. **II** *nm* classic.
clasificación *nf* 1 classification; *Dep* league table. 2 *(para campeonato, concurso)* qualification.
clasificar |1| **I** *vtr* to classify, class. **II clasificarse** *vr Dep* to qualify.
claudicar |1| *vi* to give in.
claustro *nm* 1 *Arquit* cloister. 2 *(reunión)* staff meeting.
claustrofobia *nf* claustrophobia.
cláusula *nf* clause.
clausura *nf* 1 *(cierre)* closure; **ceremonia de c.**, closing ceremony. 2 *Rel* enclosure.
clausurar *vtr* to close.
clavar I *vtr* 1 to nail; *(clavo)* to bang *o* hammer in; *(estaca)* to drive in. 2 *fam (timar)* to sting *o* fleece. **II clavarse** *vr* **c. una astilla**, to get a splinter.
clave I *nf* key; **la palabra c.**, the key word. **II** *nm* harpsichord.
clavel *nm* carnation.
clavícula *nf* collarbone.
clavija *nf Téc* jack.
clavo *nm* 1 nail; *fig* **dar en el c.**, to hit the nail on the head. 2 *Bot* clove.
claxon *nm (pl cláxones)* horn; **tocar el c.**, to sound the horn.
clemencia *nf* mercy, clemency.
clementina *nf* clementine.
cleptómano,-a *adj & nm,f* kleptomaniac.
clerical *adj* clerical.
clérigo *nm* priest.
clero *nm* clergy.
cliché *nm* 1 *fig (tópico)* cliché. 2 *Fot* negative. 3 *Impr* plate.
cliente *nmf* customer, client.
clientela *nf* clientele.
clima *nm* climate.
climatizado,-a *adj* air-conditioned.
climatizar |4| *vtr* to air-condition.
clímax *nm inv* climax.

clínica *nf* clinic.
clínico,-a *adj* clinical.
clip *nm* clip.
clítoris *nm inv* clitoris.
cloaca *nf* sewer, drain.
clorhídrico,-a *adj* hydrochloric.
cloro *nm* chlorine.
cloroformo *nm* chloroform.
cloruro *nm* chloride; **c. sódico**, sodium chloride.
club *nm (pl clubs o clubes)* club; **c. náutico**, yacht club.
cm *abr de* **centímetro(s)**, centimetre(s), *US* centimeter(s), cm.
CNT *nf abr de* **Confederación Nacional de Trabajadores.**
coacción *nf* coercion.
coaccionar *vtr* to coerce.
coactivo,-a *adj* coercive.
coadyuvar *vtr* to assist.
coagular *vtr & vi*, **coagularse** *vr* to coagulate; *(sangre)* to clot; *(leche)* to curdle.
coágulo *nm* coagulum, clot.
coalición *nf* coalition.
coartada *nf* alibi.
coartar *vtr* to restrict.
coba *nf fam* **dar c. a algn**, to soft-soap sb.
cobalto *nm* cobalt.
cobarde I *adj* cowardly. **II** *nmf* coward.
cobardía *nf* cowardice.
cobaya *nf* guinea pig.
cobertizo *nm* shed, shack.
cobertor *nm* bedspread.
cobertura *nf* cover; *(de noticia)* coverage.
cobija *nf Am* blanket.
cobijar I *vtr* to shelter. **II cobijarse** *vr* to take shelter.
cobijo *nm* shelter; *fig (protección)* protection.
cobra *nf* cobra.
cobrador,-a *nm,f* 1 *(de autobús) (hombre)* conductor; *(mujer)* conductress. 2 *(de luz, agua etc)* collector.
cobrar I *vtr* 1 *(dinero)* to charge; *(cheque)* to cash; *(salario)* to earn. 2 *fig (fuerza)* to gain, get; **c. ánimos**, to take courage *o* heart; **c. importancia**, to become important. **II** *vi fam* to catch it. **III cobrarse** *vr* ¿**se cobra?**, *(al pagar)* take it out of this, please.
cobre *nm* 1 copper. 2 *Am (moneda)* copper cent.
cobrizo,-a *adj* copper, copper-coloured, *US* copper-colored.
cobro *nm (pago)* collecting; *(de cheque)* cashing; *Tel* **llamada a c. revertido**, reverse-charge, *US* collect call.
coca *nf* 1 *Bot* coca. 2 *arg (droga)* cocaine, coke.
cocaína *nf* cocaine.
cocainómano,-a *nm,f* cocaine addict.
cocción *nf* cooking; *(en agua)* boiling; *(en horno)* baking.
cocer |4| **I** *vtr* to cook; *(hervir)* to boil;

(hornear) to bake. **II** *vi (hervir)* to boil. **III**
cocerse *vr* 1 *(comida)* to cook; *(hervir)* to
boil; *(hornear)* to bake. 2 *(tramarse)* to be
going on.

cochambroso,-a *adj* squalid.

coche *nm* 1 car; **en c.**, by car; **c. de carreras**, racing car; **c. de bomberos**, fire
engine; **c. fúnebre**, hearse. 2 *Ferroc*
carriage, coach; **c. cama**, sleeping car,
US sleeper. 3 *(de caballos)* carriage,
coach.

cochecito *nm (de niño)* pram, *US* baby
carriage.

cochera *nf* 1 garage. 2 *(de autobuses)* depot.

cochinillo *nm* suckling pig.

cochino,-a **I** *nm,f* 1 *(macho)* pig; *(hembra)*
sow. 2 *fam (persona)* filthy person, pig. **II**
adj (sucio) filthy, disgusting.

cocido *nm* stew.

cociente *nm* quotient.

cocina *nf* 1 kitchen. 2 *(aparato)* cooker,
US stove; **c. eléctrica/de gas**, electric/
gas cooker. 3 *(arte)* cooking; **c. casera**,
home cooking; **c. española**, Spanish
cooking *o* cuisine.

cocinar *vtr & vi* to cook.

cocinero,-a *nm,f* cook.

cocktail *nm* → **cóctel**.

coco[1] *nm* coconut; *arg (cabeza)* nut; **co-
merle el c. a algn**, to brainwash sb; **comerse el c.**, to get obsessed.

coco[2] *nm fam (fantasma)* bogeyman.

cocodrilo *nm* crocodile.

cocotero *nm* coconut palm.

cóctel *nm* cocktail; **c. Molotov**, Molotov
cocktail.

coctelera *nf* cocktail shaker.

codazo *nm* 1 *(señal)* nudge with one's
elbow. 2 *(golpe)* blow with one's elbow.

codearse *vr* to rub shoulders (**con**, with),
hobnob (**con**, with).

codeína *nf* codeine.

codicia *nf* greed.

codiciar [12] *vtr* to covet.

codicioso,-a *adj* covetous, greedy.

codificar [1] *vtr (ley)* to codify; *(mensajes)*
to encode.

código *nm* code; **c. de circulación**, highway code.

codo *nm* elbow; *fig* **c. con c.**, side by
side; *fam* **hablar por los codos**, to talk
nonstop.

codorniz *nf* quail.

coeficiente *nm* 1 coefficient. 2 *(grado)*
rate; **c. intelectual**, intelligence quotient.

coercitivo,-a *adj* coercive.

coetáneo,-a *adj & nm,f* contemporary.

coexistencia *nf* coexistence.

coexistir *vi* to coexist.

cofia *nf* bonnet.

cofradía *nf (hermandad)* brotherhood;
(asociación) association.

cofre *nm (arca)* trunk, chest; *(para joyas)*
box, casket.

coger [5] **I** *vtr* 1 to take; *(del suelo)* to
pick (up); *(fruta, flores)* to pick; *(asir)* to
seize, take hold of; *(bus, tren)* to take,
catch; *(pelota, ladrón, resfriado)* to catch;
(entender) to grasp; *(costumbre)* to pick
up; *(velocidad, fuerza)* to gather; *(atropellar)* to run over, knock down. 2 *Am vulg*
to fuck. **II** *vi fam* **cogió y se fue**, he
upped and left. **III** **cogerse** *vr (agarrarse)*
to hold on.

cogida *nf* goring.

cogollo *nm (de lechuga)* heart.

cogotazo *nm fam* blow on the back of the
neck.

cogote *nm* nape *o* back of the neck.

cohabitación *nf* cohabitation.

cohabitar *vi* to live together, cohabit.

cohecho *nm Jur* bribery.

coherencia *nf* coherence.

coherente *adj* coherent.

cohesión *nf* cohesion.

cohete *nm* rocket; **c. espacial**, space
rocket.

cohibido,-a *adj* inhibited.

cohibir [21] **I** *vtr* to inhibit. **II** **cohibirse**
vr to feel inhibited.

COI *nm Dep abr de* **Comité Olímpico
Internacional**, International Olympic
Committee, IOC.

coincidencia *nf* coincidence.

coincidir *vi* 1 to coincide. 2 *(concordar)* to
agree; **todos coincidieron en señalar
que**, everyone agreed that. 3 *(encontrarse)*
to meet by chance.

coito *nm* coitus, intercourse.

cojear *vi (persona)* to limp, hobble; *(mueble)* to wobble.

cojera *nf* limp.

cojín *nm* cushion.

cojinete *nm Téc* bearing; **c. de agujas/
bolas**, needle/ball bearing.

cojo,-a **I** *adj (persona)* lame; *(mueble)* rickety. **II** *nm,f* lame person.

cojón *nm vulg* ball; **de cojones**, *(estupendo)* fucking brilliant *o* good; *(pésimo)*
fucking awful *o* bad.

cojonudo,-a *adj vulg* fucking great.

col *nf* cabbage; **c. de Bruselas**, Brussels
sprout.

cola[1] *nf* 1 *(de animal)* tail; *(de vestido)*
train; *(de pelo)* ponytail; **a la c.**, at the
back *o* rear; *fam* **traer c.**, to have consequences. 2 *(fila)* queue, *US* line; **hacer
c.**, to queue (up), *US* stand in line.

cola[2] *nf (pegamento)* glue.

colaboración *nf* 1 collaboration. 2 *Prensa*
contribution.

colaboracionismo *nm Pol* collaboration.

colaborador,-a **I** *nm,f* 1 collaborator. 2
Prensa contributor. **II** *adj* collaborating.

colaborar *vi* to collaborate, cooperate.

colación *nf* **sacar** *o* **traer (algo) a c.**, to
bring (sth) up.

colada *nf* wash, laundry; **hacer la c.**, to do the washing *o* laundry.

colador *nm* colander, sieve; *(de té, café)* strainer.

colapsar I *vtr* to bring to a standstill. **II colapsarse** *vr* to come to a standstill.

colapso *nm* 1 *Med* collapse. 2 *Aut* **c. circulatorio**, traffic jam, hold-up.

colar |2| **I** *vtr* 1 *(líquido)* to strain, filter. 2 *(por agujero)* to slip. **II** *vi fam* **esa mentira no cuela**, that lie won't wash. **III colarse** *vr* 1 to slip in; *(a fiesta)* to gate-crash; *(en una cola)* to jump the queue. 2 *fam (pasarse)* to go too far.

colateral *adj* collateral.

colcha *nf* bedspread.

colchón *nm* mattress.

colchoneta *nf* air bed.

colear *vi* 1 to wag its tail; *fam* **vivito y coleando**, alive and kicking. 2 *fam* **el asunto aún colea**, we haven't heard the last of it yet.

colección *nf* collection.

coleccionable *adj & nm* collectable.

coleccionar *vtr* to collect.

coleccionista *nmf* collector.

colecta *nf* collection.

colectividad *nf* community.

colectivo,-a I *adj* collective. **II** *nm* 1 *(asociación)* association. 2 *Am* long-distance taxi.

colega *nmf* 1 colleague. 2 *arg (amigo)* buddy, mate.

colegiado,-a *nm Dep* referee.

colegial I *adj (escolar)* school. **II** *nmf* 1 *(alumno)* schoolboy; *(alumna)* schoolgirl; **los colegiales**, the schoolchildren.

colegio *nm* 1 *(escuela)* school; **c. privado**, *GB* public *o* independent school. 2 *(profesional)* association, college; **c. de abogados**, the Bar; *Pol* **c. electoral**, electoral college. 3 *Univ* **c. mayor** *o* **universitario**, hall of residence.

colegir |6| *vtr* to infer, deduce.

cólera[1] *nf* anger, rage.

cólera[2] *nm Med* cholera.

colérico,-a *adj* furious.

colesterol *nm* cholesterol.

coleta *nf* pigtail, ponytail; *fig* **cortarse la c.**, to retire.

coletazo *nm* **dar los últimos coletazos**, to be on one's last legs.

coletilla *nf* postcript.

colgado,-a *adj* 1 *arg* **dejar (a algn) c.**, to leave (sb) in the lurch. 2 *arg* weird; *(drogado)* high.

colgante I *nm (joya)* pendant. **II** *adj* hanging.

colgar |2| **I** *vtr* 1 to hang (up); *(colada)* to hang (out). 2 *(ahorcar)* to hang. **II** *vi* 1 to hang (**de**, from); *fig* **c. de un hilo**, to hang by a thread. 2 *Tel* to hang up. **III colgarse** *vr (ahorcarse)* to hang oneself.

colibrí *nm* humming bird.

cólico *nm* colic.

coliflor *nf* cauliflower.

colijo *indic pres* → **colegir**.

colilla *nf (cigarette)* end *o* butt.

colina *nf* hill.

colindante *adj* adjoining, adjacent.

colindar *vi* to be adjacent (**con**, to).

colirio *nm* eyedrops.

colisión *nf* collision, crash; *(de ideas)* clash.

colisionar *vi* to collide, crash.

colitis *nf* colitis.

collage *nm* collage.

collar *nm* 1 *(adorno)* necklace. 2 *(de perro)* collar.

colmado,-a *adj* full, filled; *(cucharada)* heaped.

colmar *vtr* 1 to fill (right up); *(vaso, copa)* to fill to the brim; *fig* to shower (**de**, with). 2 *(ambiciones)* to fulfil, satisfy.

colmena *nf* beehive.

colmillo *nm* eye *o* canine tooth; *Zool (de carnívoro)* fang; *(de jabalí, elefante)* tusk.

colmo *nm* height; **el c. de**, the height of; **¡eso es el c.!**, that's the last straw!; **para c.**, to top it all.

colocación *nf* 1 *(acto)* positioning. 2 *(disposición)* lay-out. 3 *(empleo)* job, employment.

colocado,-a *adj* 1 *(empleado)* employed. 2 *arg (drogado)* high.

colocar |1| **I** *vtr* 1 to place, put. 2 *Fin (invertir)* to invest. 3 *(emplear)* to give work to. 4 *arg (drogar)* to stone. **II colocarse** *vr* 1 *(situarse)* to put oneself. 2 *(emplearse)* to take a job (**de**, as). 3 *arg (drogarse)* to get high.

colofón *nm* 1 *(apéndice)* colophon. 2 *fig* climax.

Colombia *n* Colombia.

colombiano,-a *adj & nm,f* Colombian.

colón *nm Fin* standard monetary unit of Costa Rica and El Salvador.

Colón *n* Columbus.

colonia[1] *nf* colony; *(campamento)* summer camp.

colonia[2] *nf (perfume)* cologne.

colonial *adj* colonial.

colonialismo *nm* colonialism.

colonización *nf* colonization.

colonizar |4| *vtr* to colonize.

coloquial *adj* colloquial.

coloquio *nm* discussion, colloquium.

color *nm* colour, *US* color; **Cin Fot en c.**, in colour; **de colores**, multicoloured; **persona de c.**, coloured person.

colorado,-a I *adj* red; **ponerse c.**, to blush. **II** *nm* red.

colorante *nm* colouring, *US* coloring.

colorear *vtr* to colour, *US* color.

colorete *nm* rouge.

colorido *nm* colour, *US* color.

colorín *nm* goldfinch.

colosal *adj* colossal.

columna *nf* column; *Anat* **c. vertebral,** vertebral column, spinal column.

columpiar |12| I *vtr* to swing. II **columpiarse** *vr* to swing.

columpio *nm* swing.

coma[1] *nf* 1 *Ling Mús* comma. 2 *Mat* point; **tres c. cinco,** three point five.

coma[2] *nm Med* coma.

comadre *nf* godmother.

comadreja *nf* weasel.

comadreo *nm* gossip, gossiping.

comadrona *nf* midwife.

comandancia *nf* command.

comandante *nm* 1 *Mil* commander, commanding officer. 2 *Av* captain.

comandar *vtr* to command.

comando *nm* 1 *Mil* commando. 2 *Inform* command.

comarca *nf* region.

comarcal *adj* regional.

comba *nf* 1 (*curvatura*) curve, bend. 2 (*cuerda*) skipping rope; **saltar a la c.,** to skip.

combar *vtr* to bend.

combate *nm* combat; *Box* fight; *Mil* battle; **fuera de c.,** out for the count; (*eliminado*) out of action.

combatiente I *adj* fighting. II *nmf* combatant.

combatir I *vtr* to combat. II *vi* to fight (*contra,* against).

combativo,-a *adj* spirited, aggressive.

combinación *nf* 1 combination. 2 (*prenda*) slip.

combinado,-a I *adj* combined. III *nm* 1 (*cóctel*) cocktail. 2 *Dep* line-up.

combinar *vtr,* **combinarse** *vr* to combine.

combustible I *nm* fuel. II *adj* combustible.

combustión *nf* combustion.

comedia *nf* comedy.

comediante,-a *nm,f* (*hombre*) actor; (*mujer*) actress.

comedido,-a *adj* self-restrained, reserved.

comedor *nm* dining room.

comensal *nmf* companion at table.

comentar *vtr* **c. algo con algn,** to talk sth over with sb; **me han comentado que ...,** I've been told that ....

comentario *nm* 1 comment, remark; (*crítica*) commentary; **sin c.,** no comment. 2 **comentarios,** (*cotilleos*) gossip.

comentarista *nmf* commentator.

comenzar |1| *vtr & vi* to begin, start; **comenzó a llover,** it started raining *o* to rain; **comenzó diciendo que ...,** he started by saying that ....

comer I *vtr* 1 to eat. 2 (*en juegos*) to take, capture. II *vi* to eat; **dar de c. a algn,** to feed sb. III **comerse** *vr* 1 to eat. 2 *fig* (*saltarse*) to skip.

comercial *adj* commercial.

comercialización *nf* marketing.

comercializar |4| *vtr* to market.

comerciante *nmf* merchant.

comerciar |12| *vi* to trade; **comercia con oro,** he trades in gold.

comercio *nm* 1 commerce, trade; **c. exterior,** foreign trade. 2 (*tienda*) shop.

comestible I *adj* edible. II *nmpl* **comestibles,** food *sing*, foodstuff(s); **tienda de comestibles,** grocer's shop, *US* grocery store.

cometa I *nm Astron* comet. II *nf* (*juguete*) kite.

cometer *vtr* (*error, falta*) to make; (*delito, crimen*) to commit.

cometido *nm* 1 (*tarea*) task, assignment. 2 (*deber*) duty; **cumplir su c.,** to do one's duty.

comezón *nf* itch.

cómic *nm* comic.

comicios *nmpl* elections.

cómico,-a I *adj* 1 comical, funny. 2 *Teat* **actor c.,** comedian. II *nm,f* comic; (*hombre*) comedian; (*mujer*) comedienne.

comida *nf* 1 (*alimento*) food. 2 (*almuerzo, cena*) meal.

comidilla *nf fam* **la c. del pueblo,** the talk of the town.

comienzo *nm* beginning, start; **a comienzos de,** at the beginning of; **dar c.** (**a algo**), to begin *o* start (sth).

comilón,-ona I *adj* greedy, gluttonous. II *nm,f* big eater, glutton.

comilona *nf fam* big meal, feast.

comillas *nfpl* inverted commas; **entre c.,** in inverted commas.

comino *nm* cumin, cummin; *fam* **me importa un c.,** I don't give a damn (about it).

comisaría *nf* police station.

comisario *nm* 1 (*de policía*) police inspector. 2 (*delegado*) commissioner.

comisión *nf* 1 *Com* (*retribución*) commission; **a** *o* **con c.,** on a commission basis. 2 (*comité*) committee.

comité *nm* committee.

comitiva *nf* suite, retinue.

como I *adv* 1 (*manera*) how; **me gusta c. cantas,** I like the way you sing; **dilo c. quieras,** say it however you like. 2 (*comparación*) as; **blanco c. la nieve,** as white as snow; **habla c. su padre,** he talks like his father. 3 (*según*) as; **c. decíamos ayer,** as we were saying yesterday. 4 (*en calidad de*) as; **c. presidente,** as president; **lo compré c. recuerdo,** I bought it as a souvenir. 5 (*aproximadamente*) about; **c. a la mitad de camino,** halfway; **c. unos diez,** about ten.

II **conj** 1 **c.** + *subj*, (*si*) if; **c. no estudies vas a suspender,** if you don't study hard, you'll fail. 2 (*porque*) as, since; **c. no venías me marché,** as you didn't come I left. 3 **c. si,** as if; **c. si nada** *o* **tal cosa,** as if nothing had happened; *fam* **c.**

si lo viera, I can imagine perfectly well.

cómo I *adv* 1 *(¿c.?, (¿perdón?)* what? 2 *(interrogativo)* how; **¿c. estás?,** how are you?; **¿c. lo sabes?,** how do you know?; **¿c. es de grande/ancho?,** how big/wide is it?; **¿a c. están los tomates?,** how much are the tomatoes?; **¿c. es que no viniste a la fiesta?,** *(por qué)* how come you didn't come to the party?; *fam* **¿c. es eso?,** how come? 3 *(exclamativo)* how; **¡c. has crecido!,** you've really grown a lot!; **¡c. no!,** but of course!. II *nm* **el c. y el porqué,** the whys and wherefores.

cómoda *nf* chest of drawers.

comodidad *nf* 1 comfort. 2 *(convenciencia)* convenience.

comodín *nm Naipes* joker.

cómodo,-a *adj* 1 comfortable; **ponerse c.,** to make oneself comfortable. 2 *(útil)* handy, convenient.

comoquiera *adv* 1 however, whatever way; **c. que sea,** one way or another. 2 **c. que no estaba enterado,** *(puesto que)* as he didn't know.

compacto,-a *adj* compact; **disco c.,** compact disc.

compadecer [33] I *vtr* to feel sorry for, pity. II **compadecerse** *vr* to have *o* take pity (**de,** on).

compadre *nm* 1 *(padrino)* godfather. 2 *Am fam (amigo)* friend, mate.

compaginar *vtr* to combine.

compañerismo *nm* companionship, comradeship.

compañero,-a *nm,f* companion; **c. de colegio,** school friend; **c. de piso,** flatmate.

compañía *nf* company; **hacer c. (a algn),** to keep (sb) company; **c. de seguros/de teatro,** insurance/theatre company.

comparable *adj* comparable.

comparación *nf* comparison; **en c.,** comparatively; **en c. con,** compared to; **sin c.,** beyond compare.

comparar *vtr* to compare (**con,** with).

comparativo,-a *adj & nm* comparative.

comparecencia *nf* appearance.

comparecer [33] *vi Jur* to appear (**ante,** before).

comparsa *nf* band of revellers.

compartimento, compartimiento *nm* compartment; **c. de primera/segunda clase,** first-/second-class compartment.

compartir *vtr* to share.

compás *nm* 1 *Téc* (pair of) compasses. 2 *Náut* compass. 3 *Mús (división)* time; *(intervalo)* beat; *(ritmo)* rhythm; **c. de espera,** *Mús* bar rest; *fig (pausa)* delay; **al c. de,** in time to.

compasión *nf* compassion, pity; **tener c. (de algn),** to feel sorry (for sb).

compasivo,-a *adj* compassionate.

compatible *adj* compatible.

compatriota *nmf* compatriot; *(hombre)* fellow countryman; *(mujer)* fellow countrywoman.

compendiar [12] *vtr* to abridge, summarize.

compendio *nm* compendium.

compenetrarse *vr* to understand each other *o* one another.

compensación *nf* compensation.

compensar I *vtr (pérdida, error)* to make up for; *(indemnizar)* to compensate (for). II *vi* to be worthwhile; **este trabajo no compensa,** this job's not worth my time.

competencia *nf* 1 *(rivalidad, empresas rivales)* competition. 2 *(capacidad)* competence. 3 *(incumbencia)* field, province; **no es de mi c.,** it's not up to me.

competente *adj* competent.

competición *nf* competition, contest.

competido,-a *adj* hard-fought.

competidor,-a I *nm,f* 1 *Com Dep* competitor. 2 *(participante)* contestant. II *adj* competing.

competir [6] *vi* to compete (**con,** with *o* against; **en,** in; **por,** for).

competitividad *nf* competitivity.

competitivo,-a *adj* competitive.

compilar *vtr* to compile.

compinche *nmf* 1 *(compañero)* chum, pal. 2 *pey (cómplice)* accomplice.

complacencia *nf* 1 *(satisfacción)* satisfaction. 2 *(indulgencia)* indulgence.

complacer [33] I *vtr* to please; *fml* **me complace presentarles a ...,** it gives me great pleasure to introduce to you .... II **complacerse** *vr* to delight (**en,** in), take pleasure (**en,** in).

complaciente *adj* obliging.

complejidad *nf* complexity.

complejo,-a *adj & nm* complex.

complementar I *vtr* to complement. II **complementarse** *vr* to complement (each other), be complementary to (each other).

complementario,-a *adj* complementary.

complemento *nm* complement; *Ling* object.

completar *vtr* to complete.

completo,-a *adj* 1 *(terminado)* complete; **por c.,** completely. 2 *(lleno)* full; **al c.,** full up, to capacity. ◆**completamente** *adv* completely.

complexión *nf* build; **de c. fuerte,** wellbuilt.

complicación *nf* complication.

complicado,-a *adj* 1 *(complejo)* complicated. 2 *(implicado)* involved.

complicar [1] I *vtr* 1 to complicate. 2 *(involucrar)* to involve (**en,** in). II **complicarse** *vr* to get complicated; **c. la vida,** to make life difficult for oneself.

cómplice *nmf* accomplice.

complot *nm (pl complots)* conspiracy, plot.

componente I *adj* component. II *nm* 1

(pieza) component; *(ingrediente)* ingredient. 2 *(persona)* member.

componer |19| *(pp* **compuesto)** I *vtr* 1 *(formar)* to compose, make up. 2 *Mús Lit* to compose. 3 *(reparar)* to mend, repair. II **componerse** *vr* 1 *(consistir)* to be made up *(de, of),* consist *(de, of).* 2 *(arreglarse)* to dress up. 3 *fam* **componérselas,** to manage.

comportamiento *nm* behaviour, *US* behavior.

comportar I *vtr* to entail, involve. II **comportarse** *vr* to behave; **c. mal,** to misbehave.

composición *nf* composition.

compositor,-a *nm,f* composer.

compostelano,-a *adj* from Santiago de Compostela.

compostura *nf* composure.

compota *nf* compote.

compra *nf (acción)* buying; *(cosa comprada)* purchase, buy; **ir de c.,** to go shopping.

comprador,-a *nm,f* purchaser, buyer.

comprar *vtr* 1 to buy. 2 *fig (sobornar)* to bribe, buy off.

compraventa *nf* buying and selling; **contrato de c.,** contract of sale.

comprender *vtr* 1 *(entender)* to understand; **se comprende,** it's understandable. 2 *(contener)* to comprise, include.

comprensible *adj* understandable.

comprensión *nf* understanding.

comprensivo,-a *adj* understanding.

compresa *nf* 1 *(para mujer)* sanitary towel. 2 *Med* compress.

comprimido,-a I *nm Farm* tablet. II *adj* compressed; **escopeta de aire c.,** air rifle.

comprimir *vtr* to compress.

comprobante *nm (de compra etc)* voucher, receipt.

comprobar |2| *vtr* to check.

comprometer I *vtr* 1 *(arriesgar)* to compromise, jeopardize. 2 *(obligar)* to compel, force. II **comprometerse** *vr* 1 **c. a hacer algo,** to undertake to do sth. 2 *(novios)* to become engaged.

comprometido,-a *adj* 1 *(situación)* difficult. 2 *(para casarse)* engaged.

compromiso *nm* 1 *(obligación)* obligation, commitment; **sin c.,** without obligation; **por c.,** out of a sense of duty. 2 **poner a (algn) en un c.,** to put (sb) in a difficult *o* embarrassing situation. 3 *(acuerdo)* agreement; *fml* **c. matrimonial,** engagement; **soltero y sin c.,** single and unattached.

compuesto,-a I *adj* 1 compound. 2 **c. de,** composed of. II *nm* compound.

compulsar *vtr* to make a certified true copy of.

compungido,-a *adj (arrepentido)* remorseful; *(triste)* sorrowful, sad.

compuse *pt indef* → **componer.**

computadora *nf* computer.

cómputo *nm* calculation.

comulgar |7| *vi* 1 to receive Holy Communion. 2 *fig* **no comulgo con sus ideas,** I don't share his ideas.

común I *adj* 1 common; **de c. acuerdo,** by common consent; **hacer algo en c.,** to do sth jointly; **poco c.,** unusual; **por lo c.,** generally. 2 *(compartido)* shared, communal; **amigos comunes,** mutual friends. II *nm GB Pol* **los Comunes,** the Commons.

comunal *adj* communal.

comunicación *nf* 1 communication; **ponerse en c.** *(con algn),* to get in touch *(with sb).* 2 *(comunicado)* communication; **c. oficial,** communiqué. 3 *Tel* connection; **se nos cortó la c.,** we were cut off. 4 *(unión)* link, connection.

comunicado,-a I *adj* **una zona bien comunicada,** a well-served zone; **dos ciudades bien comunicadas,** two towns with good connections (between them). II *nm* communiqué; **c. de prensa,** press release.

comunicar |1| I *vtr* 1 to communicate; **comuníquenoslo lo antes posible,** let us know as soon as possible. II *vi* 1 to communicate. 2 *Tel* to be engaged; **está comunicando,** it's engaged. III **comunicarse** *vr* to communicate.

comunicativo,-a *adj* communicative.

comunidad *nf* community; **C. Europea,** European Community; **C. de Estados Independientes,** Commonwealth of Independent States.

comunión *nf* communion.

comunismo *nm* communism.

comunista *adj & nmf* communist.

comunitario,-a *adj* 1 of *o* relating to the community. 2 *(de CE)* of *o* relating to the EC; **la política agraria comunitaria,** the common agricultural policy.

con *prep* 1 with; **córtalo c. las tijeras,** cut it with the scissors; **voy cómodo c. este jersey,** I'm comfortable in this sweater. 2 *(compañía)* with; **vine c. mi hermana,** I came with my sister. 3 **c. ese frío/niebla,** in that cold/fog; **estar c. (la) gripe,** to have the flu. 4 *(contenido)* with; **una bolsa c. dinero,** a bag (full) of money. 5 *(a)* to; **habló c. todos,** he spoke to everybody; **sé amable c. ella,** be nice to her. 6 *(con infinitivo)* **c. llamar será suficiente,** it will be enough just to phone; *(+ que + subjuntivo)* **bastará c. que lo esboces,** a general idea will do. 7 **c. tal (de) que ...,** provided that ...; **c. todo (y eso),** even so.

conato *nm* attempt; **c. de asesinato,** attempted murder.

concebible *adj* conceivable, imaginable.

concebir |6| I *vtr* 1 *(plan, hijo)* to conceive. 2 *(entender)* to understand. II *vi*

(mujer) to become pregnant, conceive.
conceder *vtr* to grant; *(premio)* to award.
concejal,-a *nm,f* town councillor.
concejo *nm* council.
concentración *nf* concentration; *(de manifestantes)* gathering; *(de coches, motos)* rally; *(de equipo)* base.
concentrado *nm* concentrate.
concentrar I *vtr* to concentrate. II **concentrarse** *vr* 1 to concentrate (**en**, on). 2 *(reunirse)* to gather.
concepción *nf* conception.
concepto *nm* 1 *(idea)* concept; **tener buen/mal c. de**, to have a good/a bad opinion of; **bajo/por ningún c.**, under no circumstances. 2 **en c. de**, under the heading of. 3 *(en factura)* item.
concerniente *adj* concerning, regarding (**a, -**); *fml* **en lo c. a**, with regard to.
concernir |5| *v impers* 1 *(afectar)* to concern; **en lo que a mí concierne**, as far as I am concerned; **en lo que concierne a**, with regard/respect to. 2 *(corresponder)* to be up to.
concertación *nf* compromise.
concertar |1| I *vtr* 1 *(cita)* to arrange; *(precio)* to agree on; *(acuerdo)* to reach. 2 *(una acción etc)* to plan, co-ordinate. II *vi* to agree, tally.
concesión *nf* 1 concession. 2 *(de un premio, contrato)* awarding.
concesionario,-a *nm,f* dealer.
concha *nf* 1 *Zool (caparazón)* shell; *(carey)* tortoiseshell. 2 *Am vulg* cunt.
conchabarse *vr* to gang up.
conciencia *nf* 1 conscience; **tener la c. tranquila**, to have a clear conscience. 2 *(conocimiento)* consciousness, awareness; **a c.**, conscientiously; **tener/tomar c. (de algo)**, to be/become aware (of sth).
concienciar |12| I *vtr* to make aware (**de**, of). II **concienciarse** *vr* to become aware (**de**, of).
concienzudo,-a *adj* conscientious.
concierto *nm* 1 *Mús* concert; *(composición)* concerto. 2 *(acuerdo)* agreement.
conciliar |12| *vtr* to reconcile; **c. el sueño**, to get to sleep.
concilio *nm* council.
conciso,-a *adj* concise.
conciudadano,-a *nm,f* fellow citizen.
concluir |37| *vtr* to conclude.
conclusión *nf* conclusion; **sacar una c.**, to draw a conclusion.
concluyente *adj* conclusive.
concomerse *vr* to be consumed; **c. de envidia**, to be green with envy.
concordar |2| I *vi* to agree; **esto no concuerda con lo que dijo ayer**, this doesn't fit in with what he said yesterday. II *vtr* to bring into agreement.
concordia *nf* concord.
concretar *vtr (precisar)* to specify, state explicitly; *(fecha, hora)* to fix.

concreto,-a I *adj* 1 *(preciso, real)* concrete. 2 *(particular)* specific; **en c.**, specifically; **en el caso c. de ...**, in the specific case of .... II *nm Am* concrete.
◆**concretamente** *adv* specifically.
concurrencia *nf* 1 *(de dos cosas)* concurrence. 2 *(público)* audience.
concurrido,-a *adj* crowded, busy.
concurrir *vi* 1 *(gente)* to converge (**en**, on), meet (**en**, in). 2 *(coincidir)* to concur, coincide. 3 *(participar)* to compete; *(en elecciones)* to be a candidate.
concursante *nmf* 1 contestant, competitor. 2 *(para un empleo)* candidate.
concursar *vi* to compete, take part.
concurso *nm* 1 *(competición)* competition; *(de belleza etc)* contest; *TV* quiz show; **presentar (una obra) a c.**, to invite tenders (for a piece of work). 2 *fml (ayuda)* help.
condal *adj* of *o* relating to a count; **la Ciudad C.**, Barcelona.
conde *nm* count.
condecoración *nf* decoration.
condecorar *vtr* to decorate.
condena *nf* 1 *Jur* sentence. 2 *(desaprobación)* condemnation, disapproval.
condenado,-a I *adj* 1 *Jur* convicted; **c. a muerte**, condemned to death. 2 *Rel & fam* damned; **c. al fracaso**, doomed to failure. II *nm,f* 1 *Jur* convicted person; *(a muerte)* condemned person. 2 *Rel* damned.
condenar I *vtr* 1 *Jur* to convict, find guilty; **c. a algn a muerte**, to condemn sb to death. 2 *(desaprobar)* to condemn. II **condenarse** *vr Rel* to be damned.
condensado,-a *adj* condensed; **leche condensada**, condensed milk.
condensador *nm* condenser.
condensar *vtr*, **condensarse** *vr* to condense.
condesa *nf* countess.
condescender |3| *vi* 1 to condescend. 2 *(ceder)* to comply (with), consent (to).
condescendiente *adj* 1 *(displicente)* condescending. 2 *(complaciente)* complacent.
condición *nf* 1 condition; **en buenas/malas condiciones**, in good/bad condition; **condiciones de trabajo**, working conditions; **con la c. de que ...**, on the condition that .... 2 *(manera de ser)* nature, character. 3 **en su c. de director**, *(calidad)* in his capacity as director.
condicional *adj* conditional.
condicionar *vtr* 1 to condition. 2 **una cosa condiciona la otra**, one thing determines the other.
condimentar *vtr* to season, flavour, *US* flavor.
condimento *nm* seasoning, flavouring, *US* flavoring.
condolerse |4| *vr* **c. de**, to sympathize with.

condón *nm* condom.

condonar *vtr (ofensa)* to condone; *(deuda)* to cancel.

cóndor *nm* condor.

conducir |10| I *vtr (coche)* to drive; *(electricidad)* to conduct. II *vi* 1 *Aut* to drive; **permiso de c.**, driving licence, *US* driver's license. 2 *(camino, actitud)* to lead; **eso no conduce a nada**, this leads nowhere.

conducta *nf* behaviour, *US* behavior, conduct; **mala c.**, misbehaviour, misconduct.

conducto *nm* 1 *(tubería)* pipe; *fig* **por conductos oficiales**, through official channels. 2 *Anat* duct, canal.

conductor,-a I *nm,f* *Aut* driver. II *nm* *Elec* conductor.

conectar *vtr* 1 to connect up. 2 *Elec* to plug in, switch on.

coneja *nf* doe rabbit.

conejillo *nm* **c. de Indias**, guinea pig.

conejo *nm* rabbit.

conexión *nf* connection.

confabularse *vr* to conspire, plot.

confección *nf* 1 *Cost* dressmaking, tailoring; **la i. de la c.**, the rag trade. 2 *(de un plan etc)* making, making up.

confeccionar *vtr* to make (up).

confederación *nf* confederation.

conferencia *nf* 1 lecture; **dar una c. (sobre algo)**, to give a lecture (on sth). 2 **c. de prensa**, press conference. 3 *Tel* long-distance call.

conferenciante *nmf* lecturer.

conferir |5| *vtr fml (honor, privilegio)* to confer.

confesar |1| I *vtr* to confess, admit; *(crimen)* to own up to; *Rel (pecados)* to confess. II *vi Jur* to own up. III **confesarse** *vr* to confess; **c. culpable**, to admit one's guilt; *Rel* to go to confession.

confesión *nf* confession, admission; *Rel* confession.

confesionario *nm Rel* confessional.

confeti *nm (pl confetis)* confetti.

confiado,-a *adj* 1 *(seguro)* self-confident. 2 *(crédulo)* gullible, unsuspecting.

confianza *nf (seguridad)* confidence; **tener c. en uno mismo**, to be self-confident. 2 **de c.**, reliable. 3 **tener c. con algn**, to be on intimate terms with sb; **con toda c.**, in all confidence; **tomarse (demasiadas) confianzas**, to take liberties.

confiar |29| I *vtr (entregar)* to entrust; *(información, secreto)* to confide. II *vi* **c. en**, to trust; **confío en ella**, I trust her; **no confíes en su ayuda**, don't count on his help. III **confiarse** *vr* to confide (en *o* a, in); **c. demasiado**, to be overconfident.

confidencia *nf* confidence.

confidencial *adj* confidential.

confidente,-a *nm,f* 1 *(hombre)* confidant; *(mujer)* confidante. 2 *(de la policía)* informer.

configuración *nf* configuration; *Inform* configuration.

configurar *vtr* to shape, form.

confín *nm* limit, boundary.

confinar *vtr Jur* to confine.

confirmación *nf* confirmation.

confirmar *vtr* to confirm; *prov* **la excepción confirma la regla**, the exception proves the rule.

confiscar |1| *vtr* to confiscate.

confite *nm* sweet, *US* candy.

confitería *nf* 1 confectioner's (shop), *US* candy store. 2 *Am* café.

confitura *nf* preserve, jam.

conflagración *nf fig* **c. mundial**, world war.

conflictividad *nf* **c. laboral**, industrial unrest.

conflictivo,-a *adj (asunto)* controversial; *(época)* unsettled; **niño c.**, problem child.

conflicto *nm* conflict; **c. laboral**, industrial dispute.

confluencia *nf* confluence.

confluir |37| *vi* to converge; *(caminos, ríos)* to meet, come together.

conformar I *vtr* to shape. II **conformarse** *vr* to resign oneself, be content.

conforme I *adj* 1 *(satisfecho)* satisfied; **c.**, agreed, all right; **no estoy c.**, I don't agree. 2 **c. a**, in accordance *o* keeping with. II *conj* 1 *(según, como)* as; **c. lo vi/lo oí**, as I saw/heard it. 2 *(a medida que)* as; **la policía los detenía c. iban saliendo**, the police were arresting them as they came out.

conformidad *nf* 1 approval, consent. 2 **en c.**, in conformity (con, with).

conformismo *nm* conformity.

conformista *adj & nmf* conformist.

confort *nm (pl conforts)* comfort; **'todo c.'**, 'all mod cons'.

confortable *adj* comfortable.

confortar *vtr* to comfort.

confraternizar |4| *vi* to fraternize.

confrontación *nf* 1 *(enfrentamiento)* confrontation. 2 *(comparación)* contrast.

confrontar *vtr* 1 to confront. 2 *(cotejar)* to compare, collate.

confundir I *vtr* 1 to confuse (con, with); **c. a una persona con otra**, to mistake somebody for somebody else. 2 *(persona)* to mislead. 3 *(turbar)* to confound. II **confundirse** *vr* 1 *(equivocarse)* to be mistaken; *Tel* **se ha confundido**, you've got the wrong number. 2 *(mezclarse)* to mingle; **se confundió entre el gentío**, he disappeared into the crowd.

confusión *nf* confusion.

confuso,-a *adj* 1 confused; *(formas, recuerdo)* blurred, vague. 2 *(mezclado)* mixed up.

congelación *nf* 1 freezing. 2 *Fin* freeze. 3 *Med* frostbite.

congelado,-a I *adj* frozen; *Med* frostbitten. II *nmpl* **congelados,** frozen food *sing.*

congelador *nm* freezer.

congelar I *vtr* to freeze. II **congelarse** *vr* 1 to freeze; *fam* **me estoy congelando,** I'm freezing. 2 *Med* to get *o* become frostbitten.

congeniar |12| *vi* to get on (**con,** with).

congénito,-a *adj* congenital.

congestión *nf* congestion; *Med* **c. cerebral,** stroke.

congestionar *vtr* to congest.

conglomerado *nm* conglomerate.

conglomerar *vtr,* **conglomerarse** *vr* to conglomerate.

congoja *nf* sorrow, grief.

congraciarse |12| *vr* to ingratiate oneself (**con,** with).

congratular *vtr fml* to congratulate (**por,** on).

congregación *nf* congregation.

congregar |7| *vtr,* **congregarse** *vr* to congregate, assemble.

congresista *nmf* member of a congress.

congreso *nm* congress, conference; *Pol* **c. de los Diputados,** ≈ Parliament, *US* Congress.

congrio *nm* conger (eel).

congruente *adj* coherent, suitable.

conjetura *nf* conjecture; **por c.,** by guesswork.

conjeturar *vtr* to conjecture.

conjugación *nf* conjugation.

conjugar |7| *vtr* to conjugate; *fig (planes, opiniones)* to combine.

conjunción *nf* conjunction.

conjuntar *vtr* to co-ordinate.

conjuntivitis *nf* conjunctivitis.

conjunto,-a I *nm* 1 *(grupo)* collection, group. 2 *(todo)* whole; **de c.,** overall; **en c.,** on the whole. 3 *Mús (pop)* group, band. 4 *(prenda)* outfit, ensemble. 5 *Mat* set. 6 *Dep* team. II *adj* joint.

conjurar I *vtr* 1 to exorcise; *(peligro)* to ward off. II **conjurarse** *vr* to conspire, plot.

conjuro *nm* 1 *(exorcismo)* exorcism. 2 *(encantamiento)* spell, incantation.

conllevar *vtr* to entail.

conmemoración *nf* commemoration.

conmemorar *vtr* to commemorate.

conmigo *pron pers* with me; **vino c.,** he came with me; **él habló c.,** he talked to me.

conminar *vtr* to threaten, menace.

conmoción *nf* commotion, shock; **c. cerebral,** concussion.

conmocionar *vtr* to shock; *Med* to concuss.

conmovedor,-a *adj* touching; **una película conmovedora,** a moving film.

conmover |4| *vtr* to touch, move.

conmutador *nm* 1 *Elec* switch. 2 *Am Tel* switchboard.

conmutar *vtr* to exchange; *Jur* to commute; *Elec* to commutate.

connivencia *nf* connivance, collusion.

connotación *nf* connotation.

cono *nm* cone; **C. Sur,** South America.

conocedor,-a *adj & nm,f* expert; *(de vino, arte etc)* connoisseur.

conocer |34| I *vtr* 1 to know; **dar (algo/algn) a c.,** to make (sth/sb) known. 2 *(a una persona)* to meet. 2 *(reconocer)* to recognize; **te conocí por la voz,** I recognized you by your voice. II **conocerse** *vr (dos personas)* to know each other; *(por primera vez)* to meet.

conocido,-a I *adj* known; *(famoso)* well-known. II *nm,f* acquaintance.

conocimiento *nm* 1 knowledge; **con c. de causa,** with full knowledge of the facts. 2 *(conciencia)* consciousness; **perder/recobrar el c.,** to lose/regain consciousness. 3 **conocimientos,** knowledge.

conque *conj* so.

conquense I *adj* of *o* from Cuenca. II *nmf* native *o* inhabitant of Cuenca.

conquista *nf* conquest.

conquistador,-a *nm,f* conqueror.

conquistar *vtr (país, ciudad)* to conquer; *fig (puesto, título)* to win; *(a una persona)* to win over.

consabido,-a *adj* 1 *(bien conocido)* well-known. 2 *(usual)* familiar, usual.

consagración *nf* 1 *Rel* consecration. 2 *(de un artista)* recognition.

consagrar I *vtr* 1 *Rel* to consecrate. 2 *(artista)* to confirm. 3 *(tiempo, vida)* to devote. II **consagrarse** *vr* 1 *(dedicarse)* to devote oneself (**a,** to), dedicate oneself (**a,** to). 2 *(lograr fama)* to establish oneself.

consciente *adj* 1 conscious, aware; **ser c. de algo,** to be aware of sth. 2 *Med* conscious.

consecución *nf* 1 *(de un objetivo)* achievement. 2 *(obtención)* obtaining.

consecuencia *nf* 1 consequence; **a** *o* **como c. de,** as a consequence *o* result of; **en c.,** therefore; **tener** *o* **traer (malas) consecuencias,** to have (ill) effects; **sacar como** *o* **en c.,** to come to a conclusion. 2 *(coherencia)* consistency; **actuar en c.,** to be consistent.

consecuente *adj* consistent.

consecutivo,-a *adj* consecutive; **tres días consecutivos,** three days in a row.

conseguir |6| *vtr* 1 to get, obtain; *(objetivo)* to achieve. 2 **conseguí terminar,** I managed to finish.

consejero,-a *nm,f (asesor)* adviser. 2 *Pol* councillor. 3 *Com* **c. delegado,** managing director.

consejo *nm* 1 *(recomendación)* advice; **un**

c., a piece of advice. 2 (*junta*) council; **c. de ministros**, cabinet; (*reunión*) cabinet meeting; **c. de administración**, board of directors; **c. de guerra**, court martial.

consenso *nm* consensus.

consensuar *vtr* to approve by consensus.

consentido,-a *adj* spoiled.

consentimiento *nm* consent.

consentir |5| I *vtr* 1 (*tolerar*) to allow, permit; **no consientas que haga eso**, don't allow him to do that. 2 (*mimar*) to spoil. II *vi* to consent; **c. en**, to agree to.

conserje *nm* commissionaire; (*en escuela etc*) janitor.

conserva *nf* tinned *o* canned food.

conservación *nf* 1 preservation. 2 (*mantenimiento*) maintenance, upkeep.

conservador,-a I *adj & nm,f* conservative; *Pol* Conservative. II *nm* (*de museo*) curator.

conservadurismo *nm* conservatism.

conservante *nm* preservative.

conservar I *vtr* to conserve, preserve; (*mantener*) to keep up, maintain; (*alimentos*) to preserve. II **conservarse** *vr* 1 (*tradición etc*) to survive. 2 **c. bien**, (*persona*) to age well.

conservatorio *nm* conservatory.

considerable *adj* considerable.

consideración *nf* 1 consideration; **tomar algo en c.**, to take sth into account. 2 (*respeto*) regard. **3 de c.**, important, considerable; **herido de c.**, seriously injured.

considerado,-a *adj* 1 (*atento*) considerate, thoughtful. 2 **estar bien/mal c.**, to well/badly thought of.

considerar *vtr* to consider; **lo considero imposible**, I think it's impossible.

consigna *nf* 1 (*para maletas*) left-luggage office, *US* check-room. 2 *Mil* orders, instructions.

consignar *vtr* 1 (*puesto*) to allocate; (*cantidad*) to assign. 2 (*mercancía*) to ship, dispatch.

consigo[1] *pron pers* 1 (*tercera persona*) (*hombre*) with him; (*mujer*) with her; (*cosa, animal*) with it; (*plural*) with them; (*usted*) with you. 2 **hablar c. mismo**, to speak to oneself.

consigo[2] *indic pres* → **conseguir**.

consiguiente *adj* resulting, consequent; **por c.**, therefore, consequently.

consistencia *nf* 1 consistency. 2 (*de argumento*) soundness.

consistente *adj* 1 (*firme*) firm, solid. 2 (*teoría*) sound. 3 **c. en**, consisting of.

consistir *vi* to consist (**en**, of); **el secreto consiste en tener paciencia**, the secret lies in being patient.

consistorial *adj* **casa c.**, town hall.

consola *nf* console table; *Inform* console.

consolación *nf* consolation; **premio de c.**, consolation prize.

consolador,-a I *adj* consoling, comfort-ing. II *nm* dildo.

consolar |2| I *vtr* to console, comfort. II **consolarse** *vr* to console oneself, take comfort (**con**, from).

consolidar *vtr*, **consolidarse** *vr* to consolidate.

consomé *nm* clear soup, consommé.

consonancia *nf* **en c. con**, in keeping with.

consonante *adj & nf* consonant.

consorcio *nm* consortium.

consorte I *adj* **príncipe c.**, prince consort. II *nmf* (*cónyuge*) partner, spouse.

conspicuo,-a *adj* prominent, outstanding.

conspiración *nf* conspiracy, plot.

conspirar *vi* to conspire, plot.

constancia *nf* 1 constancy, perseverance. 2 (*testimonio*) proof, evidence; **dejar c. de algo**, to put sth on record.

constante I *adj* constant; (*persona*) steadfast. II *nf* constant feature; *Mat* constant.

◆**constantemente** *adv* constantly.

constar *vi* 1 (*figurar*) to figure in, be included (in); **c. en acta**, to be on record. 2 **me consta que ...**, I am absolutely certain that .... **3 c. de**, to be made up of, consist of.

constatar *vtr* to state; (*comprobar*) to check.

constelación *nf* constellation.

consternación *nf* consternation.

consternar *vtr* to dismay.

constipado,-a I *adj* **estar c.**, to have a cold *o* a chill. II *nm* cold, chill.

constiparse *vr* to catch a cold *o* a chill.

constitución *nf* constitution.

constitucional *adj* constitutional.

constituir |37| I *vtr* 1 (*formar*) to constitute; **estar constituido por**, to consist of. 2 (*suponer*) to represent. 3 (*fundar*) to constitute, set up. II **constituirse** *vr* to set oneself up (**en**, as).

constituyente *adj & nmf* constituent.

constreñir |6| I *vtr* 1 (*forzar*) to compel, force. 2 (*oprimir*) to restrict. 3 *Med* to constrict.

construcción *nf* 1 construction; (*sector*) the building industry; **en c.**, under construction. 2 (*edificio*) building.

constructivo,-a *adj* constructive.

constructor,-a I *nm,f* builder. II *adj* **empresa constructora**, builders *pl*, construction company.

construir |37| *vtr* to construct, build.

consuelo *nm* consolation.

cónsul *nmf* consul.

consulado *nm* consulate.

consulta *nf* 1 consultation; **obra de c.**, reference book. 2 *Med* surgery; (*despacho*) consulting room; **horas de c.**, surgery hours.

consultar *vtr* to consult, seek advice (**con**, from); (*libro*) to look up.

consultivo,-a *adj* consultative, advisory.

consultorio *nm* 1 *Med* medical center. 2 *Prensa* problem page, advice column.

consumado,-a *adj* 1 consummated; **hecho c.**, fait accompli, accomplished fact. 2 *fig (artista)* consummate.

consumar *vtr* to complete, carry out; *(crimen)* to commit.

consumición *nf* 1 consumption. 2 *(bebida)* drink.

consumidor,-a I *nm,f* consumer. II *adj* consuming.

consumir I *vtr* to consume. II **consumirse** *vr (al hervir)* to boil away; *fig (persona)* to waste away.

consumismo *nm* consumerism.

consumo *nm* consumption; **bienes de c.**, consumer goods; **sociedad de c.**, consumer society.

contabilidad *nf Com* 1 *(profesión)* accountancy. 2 *(de empresa, sociedad)* accounting, book-keeping.

contabilizar [4] *vtr Com* to enter in the books; *Dep* to score.

contable *nmf* accountant.

contactar *vi* **c. con**, to contact, get in touch with.

contacto *nm* contact; *Aut* ignition; **perder el c.**, to lose touch; **ponerse en c.**, to get in touch.

contado,-a I *adj* few and far between; **contadas veces**, very seldom; **tiene los días contados**, his days are numbered. II *nm* **pagar al c.**, to pay cash.

contador *nm* meter; **c. de agua**, water meter.

contagiar [12] I *vtr Med* to pass on. II **contagiarse** *vr* 1 *(persona)* to get infected. 2 *(enfermedad)* to be contagious.

contagio *nm* contagion.

contagioso,-a *adj* contagious; *fam (risa)* infectious.

contaminación *nf* contamination; *(del aire)* pollution.

contaminar *vtr* to contaminate; *(aire, agua)* to pollute.

contante *adj* **dinero c. (y sonante)**, hard *o* ready cash.

contar [2] I *vtr* 1 *(sumar)* to count. 2 *(narrar)* to tell. II *vi* 1 to count. 2 **c. con**, *(confiar en)* to count on; *(tener)* to have. III **contarse** *vr fam* **¿qué te cuentas?**, how's it going?

contemplación *nf* contemplation; *fam* **no andarse con contemplaciones**, to make no bones about it.

contemplar *vtr* to contemplate; *(considerar)* to consider; *(estipular)* to stipulate.

contemporáneo,-a *adj & nm,f* contemporary.

contención *nf* **muro de c.**, retaining wall; **c. salarial**, wage restraint.

contencioso,-a I *adj* contentious; *Jur* litigious. II *nm Jur* legal dispute.

contendiente *nmf* contender, contestant.

contenedor *nm* container.

contener [24] I *vtr* 1 to contain. 2 *(pasiones etc)* to restrain, hold back. II **contenerse** *vr* to control oneself, hold (oneself) back.

contenido *nm* content, contents *pl.*

contentar I *vtr* 1 *(satisfacer)* to please. 2 *(alegrar)* to cheer up. II **contentarse** *vr* 1 *(conformarse)* to make do (**con**, with), be satisfied (**con**, with). 2 *(alegrarse)* to cheer up.

contento,-a *adj* happy, pleased (**con**, with).

contestador *nm* **c. automático**, answering machine.

contestación *nf* answer; **dar c.**, to answer.

contestar *vtr* 1 to answer. 2 *fam (replicar)* to answer back.

contestatario,-a *adj* anti-establishment.

contexto *nm* context.

contienda *nf* struggle.

contigo *pron pers* with you.

contiguo,-a *adj* contiguous (**a**, to), adjoining.

continente *nm* 1 *Geog* continent. 2 *(compostura)* countenance.

contingencia *nf* limit, restriction.

contingente *nm* contingent.

continuación *nf* continuation; **a c.**, next.

continuar [30] *vtr & vi* to continue, carry on (with); **continúa en Francia**, he's still in France; **continuará**, to be continued.

continuidad *nf* continuity.

continuo,-a I *adj* 1 continuous; *Aut* **línea continua**, solid white line. 2 *(reiterado)* continual, constant. II *nm* continuum. ◆**continuamente** *adv* continuously.

contonearse *vr* to swing one's hips.

contorno *nm* 1 outline. 2 **contornos**, surroundings *pl*, environment.

contorsión *nf* contortion.

contorsionarse *vr* to contort *o* twist oneself.

contra I *prep* against; **en c. de**, against. II *nm* **los pros y los contras**, the pros and cons.

contraataque *nm* counterattack.

contrabajo *nm* double bass.

contrabandista *nmf* smuggler; **c. de armas**, gunrunner.

contrabando *nm* smuggling; **c. de armas**, gunrunning; **pasar algo de c.**, to smuggle sth in.

contracción *nf* contraction.

contracepción *nf* contraception.

contrachapado *nm* plywood.

contracorriente I *nf* crosscurrent. II *adv* **ir (a) c.**, to go against the tide.

contradecir [12] *(pp contradicho)* *vtr* to contradict.

contradicción *nf* contradiction.

contradictorio,-a *adj* contradictory.

contraer [25] I *vtr* to contract; **c. matri-**

monio con algn, to marry sb. **II contraerse** vr to contract.
contraigo indic pres → **contraer.**
contraindicación nf contraindication.
contraje pt indef → **contraer.**
contraluz nm view against the light; **a c.,**
against the light.
contramaestre nm foreman.
contramano (a) loc adv the wrong way o
direction.
contrapartida nf **en c.,** in return.
contrapelo (a) loc adv the wrong way; fig
against the grain.
contrapesar vtr 1 to counterbalance,
counterpoise. 2 fig (compensar) to offset,
balance.
contrapeso nm counterweight.
contraportada nf back page.
contraposición nf contrast.
contraproducente adj counterproductive.
contrapunto nm counterpoint.
contrariar [29] vtr 1 (oponerse a) to
oppose, go against. 2 (disgustar) to upset.
contrariedad nf 1 (contratiempo) obstacle,
setback. 2 (disgusto) annoyance.
contrario,-a I adj 1 opposite; **lo c. de,**
the opposite of; **en el lado/sentido c.,** on
the other side/in the other direction; **al
c., por el c.,** on the contrary; **de lo c.,**
otherwise; **todo lo c.,** quite the opposite.
2 (perjudicial) contrary **(a,** to). **II** nm,f
opponent, rival. **III** nf **llevar la contraria,** to be contrary. ◆**contrariamente**
adv **c. a ...,** contrary to ....
contrarrestar vtr to offset, counteract.
contrasentido nm contradiction.
contraseña nf password.
contrastar vtr to contrast **(con,** with).
contraste nm 1 contrast. 2 (en oro, plata)
hallmark.
contrata nf contract.
contratar vtr to hire, engage.
contratiempo nm setback, hitch.
contratista nmf contractor.
contrato nm contract; **c. de trabajo,** work
contract; **c. de alquiler,** lease, leasing
agreement.
contravenir [27] vtr to contravene, infringe.
contraventana nf shutter.
contribución nf 1 contribution. 2
(impuesto) tax.
contribuir [37] I vtr to contribute **(a,** to).
II vi 1 to contribute. 2 (pagar impuestos)
to pay taxes.
contribuyente nmf taxpayer.
contrincante nmf rival, opponent.
control nm 1 control; **c. a distancia,** remote control. 2 (inspección) check; (de policía etc) checkpoint.
controlador,-a nm,f **c. (aéreo),** air traffic
controller.
controlar I vtr 1 to control. 2 (comprobar)

to check. **II controlarse** vr to control
oneself.
controversia nf controversy.
controvertido,-a adj controversial.
contumaz adj obstinate.
contundente adj 1 (arma) blunt. 2 (argumento) forceful, convincing.
contusión nf contusion, bruise.
convalecencia nf convalescence.
convaleciente adj & nmf convalescent.
convalidar vtr to validate; (documento) to
ratify.
convencer [2] vtr to convince; **c. a algn
de algo,** to convince sb about sth.
convencimiento nm conviction; **tener el
c. de que ...,** to be convinced that ....
convención nf convention.
convencional adj conventional.
convenido,-a adj agreed; **según lo c.,** as
agreed.
conveniencia nf 1 (provecho) convenience. 2 **conveniencias sociales,** social
proprieties.
conveniente adj 1 (oportuno) convenient;
(aconsejable) advisable. 2 (precio) good,
fair.
convenio nm agreement; **c. laboral,**
agreement on salary and conditions.
convenir [27] vtr & vi 1 (acordar) to
agree; **c. una fecha,** to agree on a date;
sueldo a c., salary negotiable; **c. en,** to
agree on. 2 (ser oportuno) to suit, be good
for; **conviene recordar que ...,** it's as
well to remember that ....
convento nm (de monjas) convent; (de
monjes) monastery.
convergente adj convergent.
converger [5] vi to converge.
conversación nf conversation.
conversar vi to converse, talk.
conversión nf conversion.
converso,-a nm,f convert.
convertible adj convertible.
convertir [5] I vtr to change, convert. **II
convertirse** vr 1 **c. en,** to turn into, become. 2 Rel to be converted **(a,** to).
convexo,-a adj convex.
convicción nf conviction; **tengo la c. de
que ...,** I am convinced that ...
convicto,-a adj convicted.
convidado,-a adj & nm,f guest.
convidar vtr to invite.
convincente adj convincing.
convite nm reception.
convivencia nm life together; fig coexistence.
convivir vi to live together; fig to coexist
(con, with).
convocar [1] vtr to summon; (reunión,
elecciones) to call.
convocatoria nf 1 (a huelga etc) call. 2
Educ diet.
convulsión nf Med convulsion; (agitación
social) upheaval.

convulsivo,-a *adj* convulsive.

conyugal *adj* conjugal; **vida c.**, married life.

cónyuge *nmf* spouse; **cónyuges**, married couple *sing*, husband and wife.

coña *nf vulg* **estar de c.**, to be joking.

coñac *nm* brandy, cognac.

coñazo *nm vulg* pain, drag; **dar el c.**, to be a real pain.

coño I *nm vulg* cunt. II *interj vulg* for fuck's sake!

cooperación *nf* co-operation.

cooperador,-a *nm,f* collaborator, co-operator.

cooperar *vi* to co-operate (**a, en,** in; **con,** with).

cooperativa *nf* co-operative.

coordenada *nf* co-ordinate.

coordinación *nf* co-ordination.

coordinadora *nf* coordinating committee; **c. general**, joint committee.

coordinador,-a *nm,f* co-ordinator.

coordinar *vtr* to co-ordinate.

copa *nf* 1 glass; **tomar una c.**, to have a drink. 2 (*de árbol*) top. 3 *Dep* cup. 4 *Naipes* **copas**, hearts.

copar *vtr* to take up.

copartícipe *adj & nmf* (*socio*) partner; (*colaborador*) collaborator; (*copropietario*) joint owner, co-owner.

Copenhague *n* Copenhagen.

copia *nf* copy.

copiar [12] *vtr* to copy.

copiloto *nm Av* copilot; *Aut* co-driver.

copioso,-a *adj* abundant, copious.

copistería *nf* photocopying service.

copla *nf* verse, couplet.

copo *nm* flake; (*de nieve*) snowflake; **copos de maíz**, cornflakes.

coproducción *nf* co-production, joint production.

cópula *nf* 1 (*coito*) copulation, intercourse. 2 *Ling* conjunction.

copular *vtr* to copulate (**con,** with).

COPYME *nm abr de* Confederación de la Pequeña y Mediana Empresa.

coquetear *vi* to flirt (**con,** with).

coqueta *nf* dressing table.

coqueto,-a I *adj* coquettish. II *nm,f* flirt.

coraje *nm* 1 (*valor*) courage. 2 (*ira*) anger, annoyance; *fig* **dar c.** a algn, to infuriate sb; **¡qué c.!**, how maddening!

coral[1] *nm Zool* coral.

coral[2] *nf Mús* choral, chorale.

Corán *n* Koran.

coraza *nf* armour, *US* armor; *fig* protection.

corazón *nm* 1 heart; *fig* **de (todo) c.**, in all sincerity; *fig* **tener buen c.**, to be kind-hearted. 2 (*parte central*) heart; (*de fruta*) core. 3 *Naipes* **corazones**, hearts.

corazonada *nf* hunch, feeling.

corbata *nf* tie, *US* necktie; **con c.**, wearing a tie.

Córcega *n* Corsica.

corchete *nm* 1 *Impr* square bracket. 2 *Cost* hook and eye, snap fastener.

corcho *nm* cork; (*de pesca*) float.

cordel *nm* rope, cord.

cordero,-a *nm,f* lamb.

cordial *adj* cordial, warm.

cordialidad *nf* cordiality, warmth.

cordillera *nf* mountain chain *o* range.

córdoba *nm Fin* monetary unit of Nicaragua.

cordón *nm* string; (*de zapatos*) shoelace; *Anat* **c. umbilical**, umbilical cord; **c. policial**, police cordon.

cordura *nf* common sense.

Corea *n* Korea.

coreano,-a *adj & nm,f* Korean.

corear *vtr* 1 (*cantar a coro*) to sing in chorus. 2 (*aclamar*) to applaud.

coreografía *nf* choreography.

cornada *nf Taur* goring.

corneja *nf* crow.

córner *nm Ftb* corner (kick); **sacar un c.**, to take a corner.

corneta *nf* bugle; **c. de llaves**, cornet.

cornisa *nf* cornice.

cornudo,-a *nm ofens* cuckold.

coro *nm Mús* choir; *Teat* chorus; *fig* **a c.**, all together.

corona *nf* 1 crown. 2 (*de flores etc*) wreath, garland; **c. funeraria**, funeral wreath.

coronación *nf* 1 coronation. 2 *fig* (*culminación*) crowning point.

coronar *vtr* to crown.

coronel *nm* colonel.

coronilla *nf* crown of the head; *fam* **estar hasta la c.**, to be fed up (**de,** with).

corpiño *nm* bodice.

corporación *nf* corporation.

corporal *adj* corporal; **castigo c.**, corporal punishment; **olor c.**, body odour, BO.

corporativo,-a *adj* corporative.

corpulento,-a *adj* corpulent, stout.

corpus *nm* corpus.

corral *nm* farmyard, *US* corral; (*de casa*) courtyard.

correa *nf* 1 (*tira*) strap; (*de reloj*) watchstrap; (*de pantalón*) belt; (*de perro*) lead, *US* leash. 2 *Téc* belt.

corrección *nf* 1 (*rectificación*) correction. 2 (*urbanidad*) courtesy, politeness.

correcto,-a *adj* 1 (*sin errores*) correct. 2 (*educado*) polite, courteous (**con,** to); (*conducta*) proper.

corredera *nf* **puerta/ventana de c.**, sliding door/window.

corredizo,-a *adj* sliding; **nudo c.**, slipknot; **techo c.**, sunroof.

corredor,-a *nm,f* 1 *Dep* runner. 2 *Fin* **c. de bolsa**, stockbroker.

corregir [6] I *vtr* to correct. II **corregirse** *vr* to mend one's ways.

correo *nm* 1 post, *US* mail; **echar al c.**, to post; **por c.**, by post; **c. aéreo**, airmail; **c. certificado**, registered post; **(tren) c.**, mail train. **2 correos**, *(edificio)* post office *sing*.

correr I *vi* **1** to run; *(coche)* to go fast; *(conductor)* to drive fast; *(viento)* to blow; *fig* **no corras, habla más despacio**, don't rush, speak slower; **c. prisa**, to be urgent. **2 c. con los gastos**, to foot the bill; **corre a mi cargo**, I'll take care of it. **II** *vtr* **1** *(cortina)* to draw; *(cerrojo)* to close; *(aventura etc)* to have; **c. el riesgo o peligro**, to run the risk. **2** *(mover)* to pull up, draw up. **III correrse** *vr* **1** *(moverse)* to move over. **2** *fam* **c. una juerga**, to go on a spree. **3** *arg (tener orgasmo)* to come.

correspondencia *nf* **1** correspondence. **2** *Ferroc* connection.

corresponder I *vi* **1** to correspond (**a**, to; **con**, with). **2** *(incumbir)* to concern, be incumbent upon; **esta tarea te corresponde a ti**, it's your job to do this. **3** *(pertenecer)* to belong; **me dieron lo que me correspondía**, they gave me my share. **II corresponderse** *vr* **1** *(ajustarse)* to correspond. **2** *(dos cosas)* to tally; **no se corresponde con la descripción**, it does not match the description. **3** *(dos personas)* to love each other.

correspondiente *adj* corresponding (**a**, to).

corresponsal *nmf* correspondent.

corrida *nf* **c. (de toros)**, bullfight.

corrido,-a *adj* **1** *(avergonzado)* abashed. **2 de c.**, without stopping.

corriente I *adj* **1** *(común)* common. **2** *(agua)* running. **3** *(mes, año)* current, present; **el diez del c.**, the tenth of this month. **4** *Fin (cuenta)* current. **5 estar al c.**, to be up to date. **II** *nf* **1** current, stream; *fig* **ir** *o* **navegar contra c.**, to go against the tide; *fam* **seguirle** *o* **llevarle la c. a algn**, to humour sb; *Elec* **c. eléctrica**, (electric) current. **2** *(de aire)* draught, *US* draft. **3** *(tendencia)* trend, current.

corrijo *indic pres* → **corregir**.

corrillo *nm* small group of people talking; *fig* clique.

corro *nm* **1** circle, ring. **2** *(juego)* ring-a-ring-a-roses.

corroborar *vtr* to corroborate.

corroer [38] *vtr* to corrode; *fig* **la envidia le corroe**, envy eats away at him.

corromper I *vtr* **1** *(pudrir)* to turn bad, rot. **2** *(pervertir)* to corrupt, pervert. **II corromperse** *vr* **1** *(pudrirse)* to go bad, rot. **2** *(pervertirse)* to become corrupted.

corrosivo,-a *adj* corrosive; *fig (mordaz)* caustic.

corrupción *nf* **1** *(putrefacción)* rot, decay. **2** *fig* corruption; *Jur* **c. de menores**, corruption of minors.

corrupto,-a *adj* corrupt.

corsé *nm* corset.

cortacésped *nm & f* lawnmower.

cortado,-a *adj* **1** cut (up). **2** *(leche)* sour. **3** *(labios)* chapped. **4** *fam (tímido)* shy. **II** *nm* small coffee with a dash of milk.

cortafuego *nm* firebreak.

cortapisa *nf fig* restriction, limitation.

cortar I *vtr* **1** to cut; *(carne)* to carve; *(árbol)* to cut down; *fam* **c. por lo sano**, to take drastic measures; *fam* **cortó con su novio**, she split up with her boyfriend. **2** *(piel)* to chap, crack. **3** *(luz, teléfono)* to cut off. **4** *(paso, carretera)* to block. **II cortarse** *vr* **1** *(herirse)* to cut oneself. **2 c. el pelo**, to have one's hair cut. **3** *(leche etc)* to curdle. **4** *Tel* **se cortó la comunicación**, we were cut off. **5** *fam (aturdirse)* to become all shy.

cortaúñas *nm inv* nail clippers *pl*.

corte¹ *nm* **1** cut; **c. de pelo**, haircut; *TV* **c. publicitario**, commercial break; **c. de mangas**, ≈ V-sign. **2** *(sección)* section; **c. transversal**, cross section. **3** *fam* rebuff; **dar un c. a algn**, to cut sb dead.

corte² *nf* **1** *(real)* court. **2 Las Cortes**, (Spanish) Parliament *sing*.

cortejar *vtr* to court.

cortejo *nm* **1** *(galanteo)* courting. **2** *(comitiva)* entourage, retinue; **c. fúnebre**, funeral cortège.

cortés *adj* courteous, polite.

cortesía *nf* courtesy, politeness.

corteza *nf (de árbol)* bark; *(de queso)* rind; *(de pan)* crust.

cortijo *nm* Andalusian farm *o* farmhouse.

cortina *nf* curtain; **c. de humo**, smoke screen.

corto,-a I *adj* **1** *(distancia, tiempo)* short; *fam* **c. de luces**, dim-witted; **c. de vista**, short-sighted; *fam* **luz corta**, dipped headlights *pl*. **2** *fam* **quedarse c.**, *(calcular mal)* to underestimate. **3** *(apocado)* timid, shy. **II** *nm Cin* short (film).

cortocircuito *nm* short circuit.

cortometraje *nm* short (film).

corvo,-a *adj* curved, bent.

cosa *nf* **1** thing; **no he visto c. igual**, I've never seen anything like it; **no ser gran c.**, not to be up to much. **2** *(asunto)* matter, business; **eso es c. tuya**, that's your business *o* affair; **eso es otra c.**, that's different. **3 hace c. de una hora**, about an hour ago.

coscorrón *nm* knock *o* blow on the head.

cosecha *nf* **1** *Agr* harvest, crop. **2** *(año del vino)* vintage.

cosechadora *nf* combine harvester.

cosechar *vtr* to harvest, gather (in).

coser *vtr* **1** to sew; **fam es c. y cantar**, it's a piece of cake. **2** *Med* to stitch up.

cosmético,-a *adj & nm* cosmetic.

cósmico,-a *adj* cosmic.

cosmonauta *n mf* cosmonaut.

cosmopolita *adj & nmf* cosmopolitan.

cosmos *nm inv* cosmos.
coso *nm Taur* bullring.
cosquillas *nfpl* tickling *sing*; hacer c. a algn, to tickle sb; tener c., to be ticklish.
cosquilleo *nm* tickling.
costa¹ *nf* coast; (*litoral*) coastline; (*playa*) beach, seaside, *US* shore.
costa² *nf* a c. de, at the expense of; a toda c., at all costs, at any price; vive a c. mía, he lives off me.
costado *nm* side; de c., sideways; es catalana por los cuatro costados, she's Catalan through and through.
costal *nm* sack.
costar |2| *vi* 1 to cost; ¿cuánto cuesta?, how much is it?; c. barato/caro, to be cheap/expensive. 2 *fig* te va a c. caro, you'll pay dearly for this; c. trabajo *o* mucho, to be hard; me cuesta hablar francés, I find it difficult to speak French; cueste lo que cueste, at any cost.
costarricense, **costarriqueño,-a** *adj & nm,f* Costa Rican.
coste *nm* cost; a precio de c., (at) cost price; c. de la vida, cost of living.
costear I *vtr* to afford, pay for; c. los gastos, to foot the bill. II costearse *vr* to pay for.
costero,-a *adj* coastal; ciudad costera, seaside town.
costilla *nf* 1 *Anat* rib. 2 *Culin* cutlet.
costo¹ *nm* cost.
costo² *nm arg* (*hachís*) dope, shit, stuff.
costoso,-a *adj* costly, expensive.
costra *nf* crust; *Med* scab.
costumbre *nf* 1 (*hábito*) habit; como de c., as usual; tengo la c. de levantarme temprano, I usually get up early; tenía la c. de ..., he used to .... 2 (*tradición*) custom.
costura *nf* 1 sewing. 2 (*confección*) dressmaking; alta c., haute couture. 3 (*línea de puntadas*) seam.
costurera *nf* seamstress.
costurero *nm* sewing basket.
cota *nf Geog* height above sea level; *fig* rating.
cotejar *vtr* to compare.
cotidiano,-a *adj* daily; vida cotidiana, everyday life.
cotilla *nmf fam* busybody, gossip.
cotillear *vi fam* to gossip (de, about).
cotilleo *nm fam* gossip.
cotización *nf* 1 *Fin* (market) price, quotation. 2 (*cuota*) membership fees *pl*, subscription.
cotizar |4| I *vtr Fin* to quote. II *vi* to pay national insurance. III cotizarse *vr Fin* c. a, to sell at.
coto *nm* 1 enclosure, reserve; c. de caza, game reserve. 2 poner c. a, to put a stop to.
cotorra *nf* parrot; *fig* (*persona*) chatterbox.

COU *nm Educ abr de* Curso de Orientacion Universitaria, ≈ GCE A-level studies, sixth-form studies.
coyote *nm* coyote, prairie wolf.
coyuntura *nf* 1 *Anat* articulation, joint. 2 *fig* (*circunstancia*) juncture; la c. económica, the economic situation.
coz *nf* kick; dar una c., to kick.
C.P. *abr de* código postal, postcode.
crac(k) *nm* 1 *Fin* crash. 2 (*droga*) crack.
cráneo *nm* cranium, skull.
cráter *nm* crater.
creación *nf* creation.
creador,-a *nm,f* creator.
crear *vtr* to create.
creatividad *nf* creativity.
creativo,-a *adj* creative.
crecer |33| *vi* 1 to grow; c. en importancia, to become more important. 2 (*al tricotar*) to increase.
creces *nfpl* con c., fully, in full; devolver con c., to return with interest.
crecido,-a *adj* (*persona*) grown-up.
creciente *adj* growing, increasing; cuarto c., crescent.
crecimiento *nm* growth.
credencial *adj* credential; (*cartas*) credenciales, credentials.
credibilidad *nf* credibility.
crédito *nm* 1 *Com Fin* credit. 2 (*confianza*) belief; dar c. a, to believe.
credo *nm* creed.
crédulo,-a *adj* credulous, gullible.
creencia *nf* belief.
creer |36| I *vtr* 1 to believe. 2 (*pensar*) to think; creo que no, I don't think so; creo que sí, I think so; ya lo creo, I should think so. II *vi* to believe; c. en, to believe in. III creerse *vr* 1 to consider oneself to be; ¿qué te has creído?, what *o* who do you think you are? 2 no me lo creo, I can't believe it.
creíble *adj* credible, believable.
creído,-a I *adj* arrogant, vain. II *nm,f* big head.
crema *nf* cream.
cremallera *nf* zip (fastener), *US* zipper.
crematorio,-a *nm* (horno) c., crematorium.
cremoso,-a *adj* creamy.
crepe *nm* crêpe, pancake.
crepería *nf* creperie.
crepitar *vi* to crackle.
crepúsculo *nm* twilight.
crespo,-a *adj* frizzy.
crespón *nm* crepe.
cresta *nf* 1 crest; (*de gallo*) comb. 2 (*de punk*) mohican.
Creta *n* Crete.
cretino,-a I *adj* stupid, cretinous. II *nm,f* cretin.
creyente *nmf* believer.
crezco *indic pres* → crecer.
cría *nf* 1 (*cachorro*) young. 2 (*crianza*)

breeding, raising.
criada *nf* maid.
criadero *nm* nursery.
criadilla *nf Culin* bull's testicle.
criado,-a I *adj* mal c., spoilt. II *nm,f* servant.
crianza *nf (de animales)* breeding; *fig* **vinos de c.**, vintage wines.
criar [29] *vtr* 1 *(animales)* to breed, raise; *(niños)* to bring up, rear. 2 *(producir)* to have, grow.
criatura *nf* 1 (living) creature. 2 *(crío)* baby, child.
criba *nf* sieve.
cribar *vtr* to sieve, sift.
crimen *nm (pl crímenes)* murder.
criminal *nmf & adj* criminal.
crin *nf*, **crines** *nfpl* mane *sing*.
crío,-a I *nm fam* kid. II *adj* babyish.
criollo,-a *adj & nm,f* Creole.
críquet *nm* cricket.
crisantemo *nm* chrysanthemum.
crisis *nf inv* 1 crisis. 2 *(ataque)* fit, attack; **c. nerviosa**, nervous breakdown.
crispación *nf* tension.
crispar *vtr* to make tense; *fig* **eso me crispa los nervios**, that sets my nerves on edge.
cristal *nm* 1 crystal; **c. de roca**, rock crystal. 2 *(vidrio)* glass; *(de gafas)* lense; *(de ventana)* (window) pane.
cristalera *nf* window.
cristalería *nf (conjunto)* glassware; *(vasos)* glasses *pl*.
cristalino,-a *adj* crystal clear.
cristalizar [4] *vi* to crystallize.
cristiandad *nf* Christendom.
cristianismo *nm* Christianity.
cristiano,-a *adj & nm,f* Christian.
Cristo *nm* Christ.
criterio *nm* 1 *(pauta)* criterion. 2 *(opinión)* opinion. 3 *(discernimiento)* discretion; **lo dejo a tu c.**, I'll leave it up to you.
crítica *nf* 1 criticism. 2 *Prensa* review; **tener buena c.**, to get good reviews. 3 *(conjunto de críticos)* critics.
criticar [1] I *vtr* to criticize. II *vi (murmurar)* to gossip.
crítico,-a I *adj* critical. II *nm,f* critic.
criticón,-ona *nm,f fam* fault-finder.
croar *vi* to croak.
croché *nm* crochet.
croissant *nm* croissant.
crol *nm Natación* crawl.
cromo *nm* 1 *(metal)* chromium, chrome. 2 *(estampa)* picture card.
cromosoma *nm* chromosome.
crónica *nf* 1 account, chronicle. 2 *Prensa* feature, article.
crónico,-a *adj* chronic.
cronista *nmf Prensa* feature writer.
cronología *nf* chronology.
cronológico,-a *adj* chronological.
cronometrar *vtr* to time.

cronómetro *nm* stopwatch.
croqueta *nf* croquette.
croquis *nm inv* sketch.
cruce *nm* 1 crossing; *(de carreteras)* crossroads; *(de razas)* crossbreeding. 2 *Tel* crossed line.
crucero *nm Náut* cruise; *(barco)* cruiser.
crucial *adj* crucial.
crucificar [1] *vtr* to crucify.
crucifijo *nm* crucifix.
crucigrama *nm* crossword (puzzle).
crudeza *nf* crudeness, coarseness.
crudo,-a I *adj* 1 raw; *(comida)* underdone; *fam fig* **lo veo muy c.**, it doesn't look too good. 2 *(clima)* harsh. 3 *(color)* cream. II *nm (petróleo)* crude.
cruel *adj* cruel.
crueldad *nf* cruelty; *fig (del clima)* severity.
cruento,-a *adj* bloody.
crujido *nm (de puerta)* creak, creaking; *(de dientes)* grinding.
crujiente *adj* crunchy.
crujir *vi (madera)* to creak; *(comida)* to crunch; *(dientes)* to grind.
cruz *nf* 1 cross; **C. Roja**, Red Cross; **c. gamada**, swastika. 2 **¿cara o c.?**, ≈ heads or tails?
cruzada *nf* crusade.
cruzado,-a I *adj* 1 crossed; **con los brazos cruzados**, arms folded. 2 *Cost* double-breasted. 3 *(atravesado)* lying across. 4 *(animal)* crossbred. II *nm Hist* crusader.
cruzar [4] I *vtr* 1 to cross. 2 *(palabras, miradas)* to exchange. 3 *(animal, planta)* to cross, crossbreed. II *vi (atravesar)* to cross. III **cruzarse** *vr* to cross; **c. con algn**, to pass sb.
cta. *Com abr de* **cuenta**, account, a/c.
cta. cte. *Com abr de* **cuenta corriente**, current account, c/a.
CTNE *nf abr de* **Compañía Telefónica Nacional de España**, ≈ British Telecom.
c/u *abr de* **cada uno**, each, ea.
cuaderno *nm* notebook.
cuadra *nf* 1 *(establo)* stable. 2 *Am* block (of houses).
cuadrado,-a I *adj* 1 *Geom* square. 2 *(complexión física)* broad, stocky. 3 *fig (mente)* rigid. II *nm* 1 *Geom* square. 2 *Mat* square; **elevar (un número) al c.**, to square (a number).
cuadrar I *vtr Mat* to square. II *vi (coincidir)* to square, agree **(con,** with); *(sumas, cifras)* to tally. III **cuadrarse** *vr (soldado)* to stand to attention.
cuadriculado,-a *adj* **papel c.**, square paper.
cuadrilátero,-a I *adj* quadrilateral. II *nm Box* ring.
cuadrilla *nf (equipo)* gang, team; *Mil* squad; *Taur* bullfighter's team.
cuadro *nm* 1 *Geom* square; **tela a cua-**

dros, checked cloth. **2** *Arte* painting, picture. **3** *Teat* scene. **4** *Elec Téc* panel; **c. de mandos,** control panel. **5** *(gráfico)* chart, graph.

cuádruple *adj* quadruple, fourfold.

cuajada *nf* curd.

cuajar I *vtr (leche)* to curdle; *(sangre)* to clot. **II** *vi* **1** *(nieve)* to lie. **2** *(moda)* to catch on; *(plan, esfuerzo)* to get off the ground.

cual I *pron rel (precedido de artículo)* **1** *(persona) (sujeto)* who; *(objeto)* whom. **2** *(cosa)* which. **II** *pron* **1** tal **c.,** exactly as. **2** *arc (comparativo)* such as, like.

cuál I *pron interr* which (one)?, what?; ¿**c. quieres?,** which one do you want? **II** *adj interr* which. **III** *loc adv* a **c. más tonto,** each more stupid than the other.

cualidad *nf* quality.

cualificado,-a *adj* qualified.

cualquier *adj indef* any; **c. cosa,** anything; **en c. momento,** at any moment *o* time.

cualquiera *(pl* **cualesquiera) I** *adj indef* **1** *(indefinido)* any; **un profesor c.,** any teacher. **2** *(corriente)* ordinary. **II** *pron indef* **1** *(persona)* anybody; **c. te lo puede decir,** anybody can tell you. **2** *(cosa, animal)* anyone. **3 c. que sea,** whatever it is. **III** *nmf fig pey* **ser un c.,** to be a nobody; **es una c.,** she's a tart.

cuando I *adv (de tiempo)* when; **c. más,** at the most; **c. menos,** at least; **de c. en c.,** de vez **en c.,** from time to time. **II** *conj* **1** *(temporal)* when; **c. quieras,** whenever you want; **c. vengas,** when you come. **2** *(condicional) (si)* if. **3** *(concesiva) (aunque)* (aun) **c.,** even if. **III** *prep* during, at the time of; **c. la guerra,** during the war; **c. niño,** as a child.

cuándo *adv interr* when?; ¿**desde c.?,** since when?; ¿**para c. lo quieres?,** when do you want it for?

cuantía *nf* quantity, amount.

cuantioso,-a *adj* substantial, considerable.

cuanto,-a I *adj* all; **gasta c. dinero gana,** he spends all the money *o* as much as he earns; **unas cuantas niñas,** a few girls. **II** *pron rel* as much as; **coma c. quiera,** eat as much as you want; **regala todo c. tiene,** he gives away everything he's got. **III** *pron indef pl* **unos cuantos,** a few. **IV** *adv* **1** *(tiempo)* **c. antes,** as soon as possible; **en c.,** as soon as. **2** *(cantidad)* **c. más ... más,** the more ... the more; **c. más lo miro, más me gusta,** the more I look at it the more I like it; **cuantas más personas (haya) mejor,** the more the merrier. **3 en c. a,** with respect to, regarding; **en c. a Juan,** as for Juan, as far as Juan is concerned.

cuánto,-a I *adj & pron interr (sing)* how much?; *(pl)* how many?; ¿**cuántas ve-** ces?, how many times?; ¿**c. es?,** how much is it? **II** *adv* how, how much; ¡**cuánta gente hay!,** what a lot of people there are!

cuarenta *adj & nm inv* forty; *fam* **cantarle a algn las c.,** to give sb a piece of one's mind.

cuarentena *nf Med* quarantine.

cuarentón,-ona *nm,f* forty-year old.

cuaresma *nf* Lent.

cuartear *vtr* to quarter.

cuartel *nm Mil* barracks *pl*; **c. general,** headquarters; *fig* **no dar c.,** to give no quarter.

cuartelada *nf,* **cuartelazo** *nm* putsch, military uprising.

cuartelillo *nm Mil* post, station.

cuarteto *nm* quartet.

cuartilla *nf* sheet of paper.

cuarto,-a I *nm* **1** *(habitación)* room; **c. de baño,** bathroom; **c. de estar,** living room. **2** *(cuarta parte)* quarter; **c. de hora,** quarter of an hour; *Dep* **cuartos de final,** quarter finals. **3** *fam* **cuartos,** *(dinero)* dough, money. **II** *adj & nm,f* fourth.

cuarzo *nm* quartz.

cuatro I *adj & nm inv* four. **II** *nm fam* a few; **cayeron c. gotas,** it rained a little bit.

cuatrocientos,-as *adj & nm,f* four hundred.

Cuba *n* Cuba.

cuba *nf* cask, barrel; *fam* **como una c.,** (as) drunk as a lord.

cubalibre *nm* rum *o* gin and coke.

cubano,-a *adj & nm,f* Cuban.

cubata *nm fam* → **cubalibre.**

cubertería *nf* cutlery.

cúbico,-a *adj* cubic; *Mat* **raíz cúbica,** cube root.

cubierta *nf* **1** cover. **2** *(de rueda)* tyre, *US* tire. **3** *Náut* deck. **4** *(techo)* roof.

cubierto,-a I *adj* **1** covered; *(piscina)* indoors; *(cielo)* overcast. **2** *(trabajo, plaza)* filled. **II** *nm* **1** *(en la mesa)* place setting. **2** **cubiertos,** cutlery *sing.*

cubil *nm* lair.

cubismo *nm* cubism.

cubito *nm* little cube; **c. de hielo,** ice cube.

cubo *nm* **1** bucket; **c. de la basura,** rubbish bin. **2** *Mat* cube. **3** *(de rueda)* hub.

cubrecama *nm* bedspread.

cubrir *(pp* **cubierto) I** *vtr* to cover. **II** **cubrirse** *vr (cielo)* to become overcast.

cucaracha *nf* cockroach.

cuchara *nf* spoon.

cucharada *nf* spoonful; **c. rasa/colmada,** level/heaped spoonful.

cucharilla *nf* teaspoon; **c. de café,** coffee spoon.

cucharón *nm* ladle.

cuchichear *vi* to whisper.

cuchicheo *nm* whispering.

cuchilla *nf* blade; **c. de afeitar,** razor blade.

cuchillada *nf,* **cuchillazo** *nm* stab.

cuchillo *nm* knife.

cuchitril *nm fam* hovel, hole.

cuclillas *loc adv* **en c.,** crouching; **ponerse en c.,** to crouch down.

cuco,-a I *adj fam (astuto)* shrewd, crafty. **II** *adj fam (astuto)* shrewd, crafty.

cucurucho *nm* **1** *(para helado)* cornet. **2** *(de papel)* paper cone.

cuello *nm* **1** neck. **2** *(de camisa etc)* collar.

cuenca *nf* **1** *Geog* basin. **2** *(de los ojos)* socket.

cuenco *nm* earthenware bowl.

cuenta *nf* **1** *(factura)* bill. **2** *Fin (de banco)* account; **c. corriente,** current account. **3** *(cálculo)* count; **hacer cuentas,** to do sums; **c. atrás,** countdown. **4** *(de collar)* bead. **5** *(locuciones)* **caer en la c.,** **darse c.,** to realize; **dar c.,** to report; **tener en c.,** to take into account; **traer c.,** to be worthwhile; **más sillas de la c.,** too many chairs; **en resumidas cuentas,** in short; **pedir cuentas,** to ask for an explanation; **trabajar por c. propia,** to be self-employed.

cuentagotas *nm inv* dropper.

cuentakilómetros *nm inv (distancia)* milometer; *(velocidad)* speedometer.

cuento *nm* story; *Lit* short story; **contar un c.,** to tell a story; *fig* **eso no viene a c.,** that's beside the point; **c. chino,** tall story; **c. de hadas,** fairy story.

cuerda *nf* **1** *(cordel)* rope; *fig* **bajo c.,** dishonestly; **c. floja,** tightrope; **cuerdas vocales,** vocal chords. **2** *(de instrumento)* string. **3** *(del reloj)* spring; **dar c. al reloj,** to wind up a watch.

cuerdo,-a *adj* sane.

cuerno *nm* horn; *(de ciervo)* antler; *fam* **¡vete a c.!,** get lost!; *fam* **ponerle cuernos a algn,** to be unfaithful to sb.

cuero *nm* **1** leather; **chaqueta de c.,** leather jacket. **2** **c. cabelludo,** scalp; *fam* **en cueros (vivos),** (stark) naked.

cuerpo *nm* **1** body; **de c. entero,** full-length; *fig* **tomar c.,** to take shape. **2** *(cadáver)* corpse; **de c. presente,** lying in state. **3** *(parte)* section, part. **4** *(grupo)* corps, force; **c. de bomberos,** fire brigade; **c. diplomático,** diplomatic corps.

cuervo *nm* raven.

cuesta I *nf* slope; **c. abajo,** downhill; **c. arriba,** uphill. **II** *loc adv* **a cuestas,** on one's back *o* shoulders.

cuestión *nf* **1** *(asunto)* matter, question; **es c. de vida o muerte,** it's a matter of life or death; **en c. de unas horas,** in just a few hours. **2** *(pregunta)* question.

cuestionario *nm* questionnaire.

cueva *nf* cave.

cuezo *indic pres* → **cocer.**

cuidado,-a I *nm* **1** care; **con c.,** carefully; **tener c.,** to be careful; **estar al c. de,** *(cosa)* to be in charge of; *(persona)* to look after; **me trae sin c.,** I couldn't care less. **2** *Med* **cuidados intensivos,** intensive care *sing.* **II** *interj* **¡c.!,** look out!, watch out!; **¡c. con lo que dices!,** watch what you say!; **¡c. con el escalón!,** mind the step!

cuidadoso,-a *adj* careful.

cuidar I *vtr* to care for, look after; **c. de que todo salga bien,** to make sure that everything goes alright; **c. los detalles,** to pay attention to details. **II cuidarse** *vr* **cuídate,** look after yourself.

culata *nf* **1** *(de arma)* butt. **2** *Aut* cylinder head.

culebra *nf* snake.

culebrilla *nf Med* ringworm.

culebrón *nm* soap opera.

culinario,-a *adj* culinary.

culminación *nf* culmination.

culminante *adj (punto)* highest; *(momento)* culminating.

culminar *vi* to culminate.

culo *nm* **1** *fam (trasero)* backside; *ofens* **¡vete a tomar por c.!,** fuck off! **2** *(de recipiente)* bottom.

culpa *nf* **1** blame; **echar la c. a algn,** to put the blame on sb; **fue c. mía,** it was my fault; **por tu c.,** because of you. **2** *(culpabilidad)* guilt.

culpabilidad *nf* guilt, culpability.

culpable I *nmf* offender, culprit. **II** *adj* guilty; *Jur* **declararse c.,** to plead guilty.

culpar *vtr* to blame; **c. a algn de un delito,** to accuse sb of an offence.

cultivado,-a *adj* **1** *Agr* cultivated. **2** *(con cultura)* cultured, refined.

cultivar *vtr* **1** to cultivate. **2** *Biol* to culture.

cultivo *nm* **1** cultivation; *(planta)* crop. **2** *Biol* culture.

culto,-a I *adj* educated; *(palabra)* learned. **II** *nm* cult; *Rel* worship.

cultura *nf* culture.

cultural *adj* cultural.

culturismo *nm* body building.

culturista *nmf* body builder.

cumbre *nf* **1** *(de montaña)* summit, top; *(conferencia)* **c.,** summit conference. **2** *fig (culminación)* pinnacle.

cumple *nm fam* birthday.

cumpleaños *nm inv* birthday; **¡feliz c.!,** happy birthday!

cumplido,-a I *adj* **1** completed; *(plazo)* expired; **misión cumplida,** mission accomplished. **2** *(cortés)* polite. **II** *nm* compliment.

cumplidor,-a *adj* reliable, dependable.

cumplimiento *nm* fulfilment, *US* fulfillment; **c. de la ley,** observance of the law.

cumplir I *vtr* **1** to carry out, fulfil, *US*

fulfill; (*deseo*) to fulfil; (*promesa*) to keep; (*sentencia*) to serve. **2 ayer cumplí veinte años,** I was twenty (years old) yesterday. **II** *vi* **1** (*plazo*) to expire, end. **2 c. con el deber,** to do one's duty. **III cumplirse** *vr* **1** (*deseo, sueño*) to be fulfilled, come true. **2** (*plazo*) to expire.

cúmulo *nm* pile, load.

cuna *nf* **1** cot. **2** *fig* (*origen*) cradle.

cundir *vi* **1 me cunde mucho el trabajo** *o* **el tiempo,** I seem to get a lot done. **2** (*extenderse*) to spread; **cundió el pánico,** panic spread; **cundió la voz de que ...,** rumour had it that ....

cuneta *nf* (*de la carretera*) gutter; **quedarse en la c.,** to be left behind.

cuña *nf* wedge; **c. publicitaria,** commercial break.

cuñado,-a *nm,f* (*hombre*) brother-in-law; (*mujer*) sister-in-law.

cuño *nm* **de nuevo c.,** newly-coined.

cuota *nf* **1** (*de club etc*) membership fees *pl,* dues *pl.* **2** (*porción*) quota, share. **3** *Am* **carretera de c.,** toll road.

cupe *pt indef* → **caber.**

cupiera *subj imperf* → **caber.**

cupo *nm* ceiling; *Mil* **excedente de c.,** exempt from military service.

cupón *nm* coupon, voucher.

cúpula *nf* dome, cupola; (*líderes*) leadership.

cura I *nm Rel* priest. **II** *nf Med* cure; *fig* **no tiene c.,** there's no remedy.

curación *nf* cure, treatment.

curandero,-a *nm,f* quack.

curar I *vtr* **1** (*sanar*) to cure; (*herida*) to dress; (*enfermedad*) to treat. **2** (*carne, pescado*) to cure. **II** *vi & vr* **curar(se)** (*sanar*) to recover, get well; (*herida*) to heal up; **c. en salud,** to make sure.

curiosear *vi* to pry.

curiosidad *nf* curiosity; **tener c. de,** to be curious about.

curioso,-a I *adj* **1** (*indiscreto*) curious, in-

quisitive. **2** (*extraño*) strange, odd; **lo c. es que ...,** the strange thing is that .... **3** (*limpio*) neat, tidy. **II** *nm,f* **1** (*mirón*) onlooker. **2** *pey* (*chismoso*) nosey-parker, busybody.

currante *nmf arg* worker.

currar, currelar *vi arg* to graft, grind.

curriculum *nm* (*pl* **curricula**) **c. vitae,** curriculum vitae.

curro *nm arg* job, meal ticket.

cursar *vtr* (*estudiar*) to study; (*enviar*) to send.

cursi *adj pey* vulgar.

cursillo *nm* short course; **c. de reciclaje,** refresher course.

cursivo,-a *adj* **letra cursiva,** italics.

curso *nm* **1** (*año académico*) year; (*clase*) class. **2** *fig* **año** *o* **mes en c.,** current year *o* month; **en el c. de,** during. **3** (*de acontecimientos, río*) course. **4** *Fin* **moneda de c. legal,** legal tender.

cursor *nm* cursor.

curtido,-a *adj* **1** (*piel*) weatherbeaten; (*cuero*) tanned. **2** *fig* (*persona*) hardened.

curtir *vtr* **1** (*cuero*) to tan. **2** *fig* (*avezar*) to harden, toughen.

curva *nf* **1** curve. **2** (*en carretera*) bend; **c. cerrada,** sharp bend.

curvilíneo,-a *adj* curvaceous.

curvo,-a *adj* curved.

cuscús *nm* couscous.

cúspide *nf* summit, peak; *fig* peak.

custodia *nf* custody.

custodiar [12] *vtr* to watch over.

cutáneo,-a *adj* cutaneous, skin; *Med* **erupción cutánea,** rash.

cutícula *nf* cuticle.

cutis *nm* complexion.

cuyo,-a *pron rel & pos* (*de persona*) whose; (*de cosa*) of which; **en c. caso,** in which case.

cv *abr de* **caballos de vapor,** horse power, hp.

D

D, d |de| *nf* (*la letra*) D, d.

D. *abr de* **don,** Mister, Mr.

D.ª *abr de* **doña,** Mrs, Miss.

dactilar *adj* **huellas dactilares,** fingerprints.

dádiva *nf* (*regalo*) gift, present; (*donativo*) donation.

dadivoso,-a *adj* generous.

dado,-a[1] *adj* **1** given; **en un momento d.,** at a certain point. **2 ser d. a,** to be given to. **3 d. que,** since, given that.

dado[2] *nm* die, dice *pl.*

daga *nf* dagger.

dalia *nf* dahlia.

dálmata *nm* Dalmatian (dog).

daltónico,-a *adj* colour-blind *o US* colorblind.

dama *nf* **1** (*señora*) lady. **2** (*en damas*) king. **3 damas,** (*juego*) draughts, *US* checkers.

damasco *nm* damask.

damnificado,-a *nm,f* victim, injured person.

danés,-esa I *adj* Danish. **II** *nm,f* (*persona*) Dane. **III** *nm* **1** (*idioma*) Danish. **2 gran d.,** (*perro*) Great Dane.

Danubio *nm* **el D.,** the Danube.

danza *nf* dancing; (*baile*) dance.

danzar [4] *vtr & vi* to dance.

dañar *vtr* (*cosa*) to damage; (*persona*) to

hurt, harm.

dañino,-a *adj* harmful, damaging (**para**, to).

daño *nm* (*a cosa*) damage; (*a persona*) (*físico*) hurt; (*perjuicio*) harm; **se hizo d. en la pierna**, he hurt his leg; *Jur* **daños y perjuicios**, (legal) damages.

dar [11] I *vtr* 1 to give; (*recado, recuerdos*) to pass on, give; (*noticia*) to tell. 2 (*mano de pintura, cera*) to apply, put on. 3 (*película*) to show, screen; (*fiesta*) to throw, give. 4 (*cosecha*) to produce, yield; (*fruto, flores*) to bear; (*beneficio, interés*) to give, yield. 5 (*bofetada etc*) to deal; **d. a algn en la cabeza**, to hit sb on the head. 6 **dale a la luz**, switch the light on; **d. la mano a algn**, to shake hands with sb; **d. los buenos días/las buenas noches a algn**, to say good morning/good evening to sb; **me da lo mismo, me da igual**, it's all the same to me; **¿qué más da?**, what difference does it make? 7 (*hora*) to strike; **ya han dado las nueve**, it's gone nine (o'clock). 8 **d. de comer a**, to feed. 9 **d. a conocer**, (*noticia*) to release; **d. a entender a algn que ...**, to give sb to understand that .... 10 **d. por**, (*considerar*) to assume, consider; **lo dieron por muerto**, he was assumed dead, he was given up for dead; **d. por descontado/sabido**, to take for granted, to assume.
II *vi* 1 **me dio un ataque de tos/risa**, I had a coughing fit/an attack of the giggles. 2 **d. a**, (*ventana, habitación*) to look out onto, overlook; (*puerta*) to open onto, lead to. 3 **d. con**, (*persona*) to come across; **d. con la solución**, to hit upon the solution. 4 **d. de sí**, (*ropa*) to stretch, give. 5 **d. en**, to hit; **el sol me daba en los ojos**, the sun was (shining) in my eyes. 6 **d. para**, to be enough *o* sufficient for; **el presupuesto no da para más**, the budget will not stretch any further. 7 **le dio por nadar**, he took it into his head to go swimming. 8 **d. que hablar**, to set people talking; **el suceso dio que pensar**, the incident gave people food for thought.
III **darse** *vr* 1 **se dio un caso extraño**, something strange happened. 2 (*hallarse*) to be found, exist. 3 **d. a**, to take to; **se dio a la bebida**, he took to drink. 4 **d. con** *o* **contra**, to bump *o* crash into. 5 **dárselas de**, to consider oneself. 6 **d. por satisfecho**, to feel satisfied; **d. por vencido**, to give in. 7 **se le da bien/mal el francés**, she's good/bad at French.

dardo *nm* dart.

dársena *nf* dock.

datar I *vtr* to date. II *vi* **d. de**, to date back to *o* from.

dátil *nm* date.

dato *nm* 1 piece of information; **datos personales**, personal details. 2 *Inform* da-

tos, data.

d.C. *abr de* **después de Cristo**, Anno Domini, AD.

dcha. *abr de* **derecha**, right.

de *prep* 1 (*pertenencia*) of; **el título de la novela**, the title of the novel; **el coche/hermano de Sofía**, Sofía's car/brother; **las bicicletas de los niños**, the boys' bicycles. 2 (*procedencia*) from; **de Madrid a Valencia**, from Madrid to Valencia; **soy de Palencia**, I'm from *or* I come from Palencia. 3 (*descripción*) **el niño de ojos azules**, the boy with blue eyes; **el señor de la chaqueta**, the man in the jacket; **el bobo del niño**, the silly boy; **un reloj de oro**, a gold watch; **un joven de veinte años**, a young man of twenty. 4 (*contenido*) of; **un saco de patatas**, a sack of potatoes. 5 **gafas de sol**, sunglasses; **goma de borrar**, rubber, *US* eraser. 6 (*oficio*) **es arquitecto de profesión**, he's an architect by profession; **trabaja de secretaria**, she's working as a secretary. 7 (*acerca de*) about; **curso de informática**, computer course. 8 (*tiempo*) **a las tres de la tarde**, at three in the afternoon; **de día**, by day; **de noche**, at night; **de lunes a jueves**, from Monday to Thursday; **de pequeño**, as a child; **de año en año**, year in year out. 9 (*precio*) at; **patatas de treinta pesetas el kilo**, potatoes at thirty pesetas a kilo. 10 **una avenida de quince kilómetros**, an avenue fifteen kilometres long; **una botella de litro**, a litre bottle. 11 (*con superlativo*) in; **el más largo de España**, the longest in Spain. 12 (*causa*) **llorar de alegría**, to cry with joy; **morir de hambre**, to die of hunger. 13 (*condicional*) **de haber llegado antes**, if he had arrived before; **de no ser así**, if that wasn't *o* weren't the case; **de ser cierto**, if it was *o* were true. 14 **lo mismo de siempre**, the usual thing. 15 **de cuatro en cuatro**, in fours, four at a time.

deambular *vi* to saunter, stroll.

debajo *adv* underneath, below; **el mío es el de d.**, mine is the one below; **está d. de la mesa**, it's under the table; **por d. de lo normal**, below normal; **salió por d. del coche**, he came out from under the car.

debate *nm* debate.

debatir I *vtr* to debate. II **debatirse** *vr* to struggle; **d. entre la vida y la muerte**, to fight for one's life.

debe *nm Com* debit, debit side.

deber¹ *nm* 1 duty; **cumplir con su d.**, to do one's duty. 2 *Educ* **deberes**, homework *sing*.

deber² I *vtr* (*dinero, explicación*) to owe. II *vi* 1 **debe (de) comer**, he must eat; **debe (de) irse ahora**, she has to leave now; **la factura debe pagarse mañana**, the bill

must be paid tomorrow; **el tren debe llegar a las dos,** the train is expected to
arrive at two. 2 *(consejo)* **deberías visitar
a tus padres,** you ought to visit your
parents; **debería haber ido ayer,** I
should have gone yesterday; **no debiste
hacerlo,** you shouldn't have done it. 3
(suposición) **deben de estar fuera,** they
must be out. **III deberse** *vr* **d. a,** to be
due to; **esto se debe a la falta de agua,**
this is due to lack of water.

debido,-a *adj* 1 due; **a su d. tiempo,** in
due course; **con el d. respeto,** with due
respect. 2 *(adecuado)* proper; **más de lo
d.,** too much; **tomaron las debidas pre-
cauciones,** they took the proper precautions; **como es d.,** properly. 3 **d. a,** because of, due to; **d. a que,** because of the
fact that.

debidamente *adv* duly, properly.

débil *adj* weak; *(luz)* dim; **punto d.,** weak
spot.

debilidad *nm* weakness; *fig* **tener d. por,**
(persona) to have a soft spot for; *(cosa)* to
have a weakness for.

debilitamiento *nm* weakening.

debilitar **I** *vtr* to weaken, debilitate. **II
debilitarse** *vr* to weaken, grow weak.

débito *nm* 1 *(deuda)* debt. 2 *(debe)* debit.

debut *nm* début, debut.

debutar *vi* to make one's début *o* debut.

década *nf* decade; **en la d. de los noventa,** during the nineties.

decadencia *nf* decadence.

decadente *adj & nmf* decadent.

decaer |39| *vi* to deteriorate.

decaído,-a *adj* down.

decaimiento *nm* 1 *(debilidad)* weakness. 2
(desaliento) low spirits *pl.*

decano,-a *nm,f* *Univ* dean.

decantarse *vr* to lean towards; **d. por,** to
come down on the side of.

decapitar *vtr* to behead, decapitate.

decena *nf* (about) ten; **una d. de veces,**
(about) ten times; **por decenas,** in tens.

decencia *nf* 1 *(decoro)* decency. 2 *(honradez)* honesty.

decenio *nm* decade.

decente *adj* decent; *(decoroso)* modest.

decepción *nf* disappointment.

decepcionante *adj* disappointing.

decepcionar *vtr* to disappoint.

decidido,-a *adj* determined, resolute.

decididamente *adv* 1 *(resueltamente)* resolutely. 2 *(definitivamente)* definitely.

decidir **I** *vtr & vi* to decide. **II decidirse**
vr to make up one's mind; **d. a hacer
algo,** make up one's mind to do sth;
d. por algo, to decide on sth.

décima *nf* tenth.

decimal *adj & nm* decimal; **el sistema
métrico d.,** the decimal system.

décimo,-a **I** *adj & nm,f* tenth. **II** *nm* 1
(parte) tenth. 2 *(billete de lotería)* tenth

part of a lottery ticket.

decir[1] *nm* saying.

decir[2] |12| *(pp* **dicho) I** *vtr* 1 to say; **dice
que no quiere venir,** he says he doesn't
want to come. 2 **d. una mentira/la
verdad,** to tell a lie/the truth. 3 *Tel Esp*
dígame, hello. 4 **¿qué me dices del nuevo jefe?,** what do you think of the new
boss? 5 *(mostrar)* to tell, show; **su cara
dice que está mintiendo,** you can tell
from his face that he's lying. 6 *(sugerir)*
to mean; **esta película no me dice nada,**
this film doesn't appeal to me; **¿qué te
dice el cuadro?,** what does the picture
mean to you? 7 *(querer* **d.,** to mean. 8
(locuciones) **es d.,** that is (to say); **por así
decirlo,** as it were, so to speak; **digamos,**
let's say; **digo yo,** in my opinion; **el qué
dirán,** what people say; **ni que d. tiene,**
needless to say; **¡no me digas!,** really!; **¡y
que lo digas!,** you bet!
II decirse *vr* **¿cómo se dice 'mesa' en
inglés?,** how do you say 'mesa' in English?; **se dice que ...,** they say that ...;
sé lo que me digo, I know what I am
saying.

decisión *nf* 1 decision; **tomar una d.,** to
take *o* make a decision. 2 *(resolución)* determination; **con d.,** decisively.

decisivo,-a *adj* decisive.

decisorio *adj* decision-making.

declamar *vtr & vi* to declaim, recite.

declaración *nf* 1 declaration; **d. de (la)
renta,** tax declaration *o* return. 2 *(afirmación)* statement; **hacer declaraciones,** to
comment. 3 *Jur* **prestar d.,** to give evidence.

declarante *nmf Jur* witness.

declarar **I** *vtr* 1 to declare; **d. la guerra a,**
to declare war on. 2 *(afirmar)* to state. 2
Jur **d. culpable/inocente a algn,** to find
sb guilty/not guilty. **II** *vi* 1 to declare. 2
Jur to testify. **III declararse** *vr* 1 **d. a
favor/en contra de,** to declare oneself in
favour of/against; **d. en huelga,** to go on
strike; **d. a algn** to declare one's love for
sb. 2 *(guerra, incendio)* to start, break
out. 3 *Jur* **d. culpable,** to plead guilty.

declinar *vi & vtr* to decline.

declive *nm* 1 *(del terreno)* incline, slope. 2
(de imperio etc) decline.

decolorante *nm* bleaching agent.

decolorar **I** *vtr* to fade; *(pelo)* to bleach.
II decolorarse *vr* to fade.

decomisar *vtr* to confiscate, seize.

decoración *nf* decoration.

decorado *nm* scenery, set.

decorador,-a *nm,f* 1 decorator. 2 *Teat* set
designer.

decorar *vtr* to decorate.

decorativo,-a *adj* decorative.

decoro *nm* 1 *(respeto)* dignity, decorum. 2
(pudor) modesty, decency.

decoroso,-a *adj* 1 *(correcto)* seemly, de-

corous. 2 *(decente)* decent, modest.
decrecer [33] *vi* to decrease, diminish.
decrépito,-a *adj* decrepit.
decretar *vtr* to decree.
decreto *nm* decree; **d.-ley,** decree.
dedal *nm* thimble.
dedicación *nf* dedication.
dedicar [1] I *vtr* to dedicate; *(tiempo, esfuerzos)* to devote **(a,** to). II **dedicarse** *vr* **¿a qué se dedica Vd.?** what do you do for a living?; **los fines de semana ella se dedica a pescar,** at weekends she spends her time fishing.
dedicatoria *nf* dedication.
dedillo *nm* **saber algo al d.,** to have sth at one's fingertips, know sth very well.
dedo *nm* *(de la mano)* finger; *(del pie)* toe; **d. anular/ corazón/índice/meñique,** ring/middle/index/little finger; **d. pulgar, d. gordo,** thumb; **hacer d.,** to hitchhike; *fig* **elegir a algn a d.,** to hand-pick sb.
deducción *nf* deduction.
deducible *adj* *Com* deductible.
deducir [10] I *vtr* **1** to deduce, infer. **2** *Com* to deduct. II **deducirse** *vr* **de aquí se deduce que ...,** from this it follows that ....
deductivo,-a *adj* deductive.
defecar *vi* to defecate.
defecto *nm* defect, fault; **d. físico,** physical defect.
defectuoso,-a *adj* defective, faulty.
defender [3] I *vtr* to defend **(contra,** against; **de,** from); **d. del frío/viento,** to shelter from the cold/wind. II **defenderse** *vr* **1** to defend oneself. **2** *fam* **se defiende en francés,** he can get by in French.
defendido,-a *adj* *Jur* defendant.
defensa I *nf* defence, US defense; **en d. propia, en legítima d.,** in self-defence; **salir en d. de algn,** to come out in defence of sb. II *nm* *Dep* defender, back.
defensiva *nf* defensive; **estar/ponerse a la d.,** to be/go on the defensive.
defensivo,-a *adj* defensive.
defensor,-a *nm,f* defender; **abogado d.,** counsel for the defence; **el defensor del pueblo,** the ombudsman.
deferencia *nf* deference; **en** *o* **por d. a,** out of deference for.
deficiencia *nf* deficiency, shortcoming; **d. mental,** mental deficiency; **d. renal,** kidney failure.
deficiente I *adj* deficient. II *nmf* **d. mental,** mentally retarded person. III *nm* *Educ* fail.
déficit *nm* *(pl* **déficits)** deficit; *(carencia)* shortage.
deficitario,-a *adj* showing a deficit.
definición *nf* definition; **por d.,** by definition.
definido,-a *adj* clear; *Ling* definite.
definir *vtr* to define.
definitivo,-a *adj* definitive; **en definitiva,**

in short. ◆**definitivamente** *adv* **1** *(para siempre)* for good, once and for all. **2** *(con toda seguridad)* definitely.
deflación *nf* *Econ* deflation.
deflacionista *adj* *Econ* deflationary.
deformación *nf* deformation.
deformar I *vtr* to deform, put out of shape; *(cara)* to disfigure; *fig (la verdad, una imagen)* to distort. II **deformarse** *vr* to go out of shape, become distorted.
deforme *adj* deformed; *(objeto)* misshapen.
defraudación *nf* fraud; **d. fiscal,** tax evasion.
defraudar *vtr* **1** *(decepcionar)* to disappoint. **2** *(al fisco)* to defraud, cheat; **d. a Hacienda,** to evade taxes.
defunción *nf* *fml* decease, demise.
degeneración *nf* degeneration.
degenerado,-a *adj & nm,f* degenerate.
degenerar *vi* to degenerate.
degollar [2] *vtr* to behead.
degradación *nf* degradation.
degradante *adj* degrading.
degradar *vtr* to degrade.
degustación *nf* tasting.
degustar *vtr* to taste, sample.
dehesa *nf* pasture, meadow.
deificar [1] *vtr* to deify.
dejadez *nf* slovenliness.
dejado,-a *adj* **1** *(descuidado)* untidy, slovenly. **2** *(negligente)* negligent, careless. **3** *fam* **d. de la mano de Dios,** godforsaken.
dejar I *vtr* **1** to leave; **déjame en paz,** leave me alone; **d. dicho,** to leave word *o* a message. **2** *(prestar)* to lend. **3** *(abandonar)* to give up; **d. algo por imposible,** to give sth up; **dejé el tabaco y la bebida,** I gave up smoking and drinking. **4** *(permitir)* to let, allow; **d. caer,** to drop; **d. entrar/salir,** to let in/out. **5** *(omitir)* to leave out, omit. **6** *(ganancias)* to produce. **7** *(+ adj)* to make; **d. triste,** to make sad; **d. preocupado/sorprendido,** to worry/surprise. **8** *(posponer)* **dejaron el viaje para el verano,** they put the trip off until the summer.
II *v aux* **d. de + *inf*,** to stop, give up; **dejó de fumar el año pasado,** he gave up smoking last year; **no deja de llamarme,** she's always phoning me up.
III **dejarse** *vr* **1 me he dejado las llaves dentro,** I've left the keys inside. **2** *(locuciones)* **d. barba,** to grow a beard; **d. caer,** to flop down; **d. llevar por,** to be influenced by.
del *(contracción de de + el)* → **de.**
delantal *nm* apron.
delante *adv* **1** in front; **la entrada de d.,** the front entrance. **2 d. de,** in front of; *(en serie)* ahead of. **3 por d.,** in front; **se lo lleva todo por d.,** he destroys everything in his path; **tiene toda la vida por**

d., he has his whole life ahead of him.
delantera nf 1 (ventaja) lead; **tomar la d.**, take the lead. 2 Ftb forward line, the forwards pl.
delantero,-a I adj front. **II** nm Ftb forward; **d. centro**, centre forward.
delatar vtr 1 to inform against. 2 fig to give away.
delator,-a nm,f informer.
delegación nf 1 (acto, delegados) delegation. 2 (oficina) local office, branch; **D. de Hacienda**, Tax Office.
delegado,-a nm,f 1 delegate; **d. de Hacienda**, chief tax inspector. 2 Com representative.
delegar |7| vtr to delegate (**en**, to).
deleitar I vtr to delight. **II deleitarse** vr to delight in, take delight in.
deleite nm delight.
deletrear vtr to spell (out).
deleznable adj brittle.
delfín nm dolphin.
delgadez nf slimness.
delgado,-a adj slim; (capa) fine.
deliberación nf deliberation.
deliberado,-a adj deliberate.
deliberar vi to deliberate (on), consider.
delicadeza nf 1 (finura) delicacy, daintiness. 2 (tacto) tactfulness; **falta de d.**, tactlessness.
delicado,-a adj 1 delicate. 2 (exigente) fussy, hard to please. 3 (sensible) hypersensitive.
delicia nf delight; **hacer las delicias de algn**, to delight sb.
delicioso,-a adj (comida) delicious; (agradable) delightful.
delictivo,-a adj criminal, punishable.
delimitar vtr to delimit.
delincuencia nf delinquency.
delincuente adj & nmf delinquent; **d. juvenil**, juvenile delinquent.
delineante nmf (hombre) draughtsman; (mujer) draughtswoman.
delinear vtr to delineate, outline.
delinquir |9| vi to break the law, commit an offence o US offense.
delirante adj delirious.
delirar vi to be delirious.
delirio nm delirium; **delirios de grandeza**, delusions of grandeur.
delito nm crime, offence, US offense.
delta nm delta; **ala d.**, hang-glider.
demacrado,-a adj emaciated.
demagogia nf demagogy.
demagogo,-a nm,f demagogue.
demanda nf 1 Jur lawsuit. 2 Com demand.
demandado,-a I nm,f defendant. **II** adj in demand.
demandante nmf claimant.
demandar vtr to sue.
demarcar |1| vtr to demarcate.
demás I adj **los/las d.**, the rest of; **la d.**

gente, the rest of the people. **II** pron **lo/ los/las d.**, the rest; **por lo d.**, otherwise, apart from that; **y d.**, etcetera.
demasía nf **en d.**, excessively.
demasiado,-a I adj (singular) too much; (plural) too many; **hay demasiada comida**, there is too much food; **quieres demasiadas cosas**, you want too many things. **II** adv too (much); **es d. grande/ caro**, it is too big/dear; **fumas/trabajas d.**, you smoke/work too much.
demencia nf dementia, insanity.
demente I adj insane, mad. **II** nmf mental patient.
democracia nf democracy.
demócrata I adj democratic. **II** nmf democrat.
democrático,-a adj democratic.
democratizar |4| vtr to democratize.
demografía nf demography.
demográfico,-a adj demographic; **crecimiento d.**, population growth.
demoledor,-a adj fig devastating.
demoler |4| vtr to demolish.
demonio nm devil; demon; fam **¿cómo/ dónde demonios ...?**, how/where the hell ...?; fam **¡demonio(s)!**, hell!, damn!; fam **¡d. de niño!**, you little devil!
demora nf delay.
demorar I vtr to delay, hold up. **II demorarse** vr 1 (retrasarse) to be delayed, be held up. 2 (detenerse) to daily.
demostrable adj demonstrable.
demostración nf demonstration; **una d. de fuerza/afecto**, a show of strength.
demostrar |2| vtr 1 (mostrar) to show, demonstrate. 2 (evidenciar) to prove.
demudado,-a adj pale.
denegar |1| vtr to refuse; Jur **d. una demanda**, to dismiss a claim.
denigrante adj humiliating.
denigrar vtr to humiliate.
denominación nf denomination; **'d. de origen'**, (vinos) ≈ 'appellation d'origine'.
denominado,-a adj so-called.
denominador nm denominator.
denominar vtr to name, designate.
denotar vtr to denote.
densidad nf density; **d. de población**, population density.
denso,-a adj dense.
dentadura nf teeth, set of teeth; **d. postiza**, false teeth pl, dentures pl.
dental adj dental.
dentera nf **me da d.**, it sets my teeth on edge.
dentífrico,-a I adj **pasta/crema dentífrica**, toothpaste. **II** nm toothpaste.
dentista nmf dentist.
dentro adv 1 (en el interior) inside; **aquí d.**, in here; **por d.**, (on the) inside; **por d. está triste**, deep down (inside) he feels sad. 2 **d. de**, (lugar) inside. 3 **d. de poco**, shortly, soon; **d. de un mes**, in a

month's time; **d. de lo que cabe,** all
things considered.
denuncia *nf* **1** *Jur* report. **2** *(crítica)* denunciation.
denunciar |12| *vtr* **1** *(delito)* to report (**a,
to**). **2** *(criticar)* to denounce.
deparar *vtr* to give; **no sabemos qué nos
depara el destino,** we don't know what
fate has in store for us.
departamento *nm* **1** department. **2** *Ferroc*
compartment. **3** *(territorial)* province, district. **4** *Am (piso)* flat.
dependencia *nf* **1** dependence (**de,** on). **2
dependencias,** premises.
depender *vi* to depend (**de,** on); *(económicamente)* to be dependent (**de,** on).
dependienta *nf* shop assistant.
dependiente **I** *adj* dependent (**de,** on). **II**
nm shop assistant.
depilación *nf* depilation; **d. a la cera,**
waxing.
depilar *vtr* to remove the hair from; *(ce-
jas)* to pluck.
depilatorio,-a *adj & nm* depilatory; **crema depilatoria,** hair-remover, hair-
removing cream.
deplorable *adj* deplorable.
deplorar *vtr* to deplore.
deponer |19| *(pp depuesto) vtr* **1** *(desti-
tuir)* to remove from office; *(líder)* to depose. **2** *(actitud)* to abandon.
deportado,-a *nm,f* deportee, deported
person.
deportar *vtr* to deport.
deporte *nm* sport; **hacer d.,** to practise
sports.
deportista **I** *nmf (hombre)* sportsman;
(mujer) sportswoman. **II** *adj* sporty.
deportividad *nf* sportsmanship.
deportivo,-a **I** *adj* sports; **club/chaqueta
d.,** sports club/jacket. **II** *nm Aut* sports
car.
deposición *nf* removal from office; *(de un
líder)* deposition.
depositar **I** *vtr* **1** *Fin* to deposit. **2** *(colocar)* to place, put. **II depositarse** *vr* to
settle.
depósito *nm* **1** *Fin* deposit; **en d.,** on deposit. **2** *(de agua, gasolina)* tank. **3 d. de
basuras,** rubbish tip *o* dump; **d. de cadáveres,** mortuary, *US* morgue.
depravación *nf* depravity.
depravar *vtr* to deprave.
depre *nf fam* downer, depression.
depreciación *nf* depreciation.
depreciar |12| **I** *vtr* to reduce the value
of. **II depreciarse** *vr* to depreciate, lose
value.
depredador,-a **I** *adj* predatory. **II** *nm,f*
predator.
depresión *nf* depression; **d. nerviosa,**
nervous breakdown.
depresivo,-a *adj* depressive.
deprimente *adj* depressing.

deprimido,-a *adj* depressed.
deprimir **I** *vtr* to depress. **II deprimirse** *vr*
to get depressed.
deprisa *adv* quickly.
depuesto,-a *pp* → **deponer.**
depuración *nf* **1** *(del agua)* purification. **2**
(purga) purge.
depurador,-a *adj* **planta depuradora,**
purification plant.
depuradora *nf* purifier.
depurar *vtr* **1** *(agua)* to purify. **2** *(partido)*
to purge. **3** *(estilo)* to refine.
derecha *nf* **1** *(mano)* right hand. **2** *(lugar)*
right, right-hand side; **a la d.,** to *o* on
the right, on the right-hand side. **3** *Pol* **la
d.,** the right; **de derechas,** right-wing.
derechista *nmf* right-winger.
derecho,-a **I** *adj* **1** *(de la derecha)* right. **2**
(recto) upright, straight. **II** *nm* **1** *(privilegio)* right; **derechos civiles/humanos,**
civil/human rights; **tener d. a,** to be en-
titled to, have the right to; **estar en su
d.,** to be within one's rights; **no hay d.,**
it's not fair; **d. de admisión,** right to refuse admission. **2** *Jur* law; **d. penal/
político,** criminal/constitutional law. **3**
Com **derechos,** duties; **d. de autor,**
royalties; **d. de matrícula,** enrolment
fees. **III** *adv* **siga todo d.,** go straight
ahead.
deriva *nf* drift; **ir a la d.,** to drift.
derivado *nm (producto)* derivative, by-
product.
derivar **I** *vtr* **1** to divert; *(conversación)* to
steer. **II** *vi* **1** to drift. **2 d. de,** to derive
from. **III derivarse** *vr* **1** *(proceder)* to result *o* stem (**de,** from). **2** *Ling* to be der-
ived (**de,** from).
dermatitis *nf inv* dermatitis.
dermatólogo,-a *nm,f* dermatologist.
derogar |7| *vtr* to repeal.
derramamiento *nm* spilling; **d. de sangre,** bloodshed.
derramar **I** *vtr* to spill; *(lágrimas)* to shed.
II derramarse *vr* to spill.
derrame *nm Med* discharge; **d. cerebral,**
brain haemorrhage.
derrapar *vi* to skid.
derredor *nm* **en d. de,** round, around.
derretir |6| *vtr,* **derretirse** *vr* to melt;
(hielo, nieve) to thaw.
derribar *vtr* **1** *(edificio)* to pull down,
knock down. **2** *(avión)* to shoot down. **3**
(gobierno) to bring down.
derrocar |1| *vtr* to bring down; *(violenta-
mente)* to overthrow.
derrochador,-a **I** *adj* wasteful. **II** *nm,f*
wasteful person, squanderer.
derrochar *vtr* to waste, squander.
derroche *nm* **1** *(de dinero, energía)* waste,
squandering. **2** *(abundancia)* profusion,
abundance.
derrota *nf* **1** defeat. **2** *Náut* (ship's)
course.

derrotar *vtr* to defeat, beat.

derrotero *nm* 1 *fig* path, course *o* plan of action. 2 *Náut* sailing directions *pl.*

derrotista *adj & nmf* defeatist.

derruido,-a *adj* in ruins.

derruir [37] *vtr* to demolish.

derrumbar I *vtr* (*edificio*) to knock down, pull down. **II derrumbarse** *vr* to collapse, fall down; (*techo*) to fall in, cave in.

desabastecido,-a *adj* **d. de**, out of.

desaborido,-a I *adj* 1 (*comida*) tasteless. 2 *fig* (*persona*) dull. **II** *nm,f fig* dull person.

desabrido,-a *adj* 1 (*comida*) tasteless. 2 (*tiempo*) unpleasant. 3 *fig* (*tono*) harsh; (*persona*) moody, irritable.

desabrigado,-a *adj* ir/estar **d.**, to be lightly dressed.

desabrochar I *vtr* to undo. **II desabrocharse** *vr* 1 **desabróchate la camisa**, undo your shirt. 2 (*prenda*) to come undone.

desacatar *vtr* to disobey.

desacato *nm* lack of respect, disrespect (**a**, for); *Jur* **d. al tribunal**, contempt of court.

desacertado,-a *adj* unwise.

desacierto *nm* mistake, error.

desaconsejar *vtr* to advise against.

desacorde *adj* estar **d. con**, to be in disagreement with.

desacreditar *vtr* 1 (*desprestigiar*) to discredit, bring into discredit. 2 (*criticar*) to disparage.

desactivador,-a *nm,f* bomb disposal expert.

desactivar *vtr* (*bomba*) to defuse.

desacuerdo *nm* disagreement.

desafiante *adj* defiant.

desafiar [29] *vtr* to challenge.

desafinado,-a *adj* out of tune.

desafinar I *vi* to sing out of tune; (*instrumento*) to play out of tune. **II** *vtr* to put out of tune. **III desafinarse** *vr* to go out of tune.

desafío *nm* challenge.

desaforado,-a *adj* wild.

desafortunado,-a *adj* unlucky, unfortunate.

desagradable *adj* unpleasant, disagreeable.

desagradar *vi* to displease.

desagradecido,-a I *adj* ungrateful. **II** *nm,f* ungrateful person.

desagrado *nm* displeasure.

desagraviar [12] *vtr* to make amends for.

desaguar [22] *vtr* to drain.

desagüe *nm* (*vaciado*) drain; (*cañería*) waste pipe, drainpipe.

desaguisado *nm* mess.

desahogado,-a *adj* 1 (*acomodado*) well-off, well-to-do. 2 (*espacioso*) spacious, roomy.

desahogarse [7] *vr* to let off steam; **se**

desahogó de su depresión, he got his depression out of his system.

desahogo *nm* 1 (*alivio*) relief. 2 vivir con **d.**, to live comfortably.

desahuciado,-a *adj* 1 (*enfermo*) hopeless. 2 (*inquilino*) evicted.

desahuciar [12] *vtr* 1 (*desalojar*) to evict. 2 (*enfermo*) to deprive of all hope.

desahucio *nm* eviction.

desairado,-a *adj* 1 (*humillado*) spurned. 2 (*sin gracia*) awkward.

desairar *vtr* to slight, snub.

desaire *nm* slight, rebuff.

desajustar I *vtr* to upset. **II desajustarse** *vr* (*piezas*) to come apart.

desajuste *nm* upset; **d. económico**, economic imbalance; **un d. de horarios**, clashing timetables.

desalentador,-a *adj* discouraging, disheartening.

desalentar [1] **I** *vtr* to discourage, dishearten. **II desalentarse** *vr* to get discouraged, lose heart.

desaliento *nm* discouragement.

desaliñado,-a *adj* scruffy, untidy.

desaliño *nm* scruffiness, untidiness.

desalmado,-a *adj* cruel, heartless.

desalojamiento *nm* (*de inquilino*) eviction; (*de público*) removal; (*de lugar*) evacuation.

desalojar *vtr* 1 (*inquilino*) to evict; (*público*) to move on; (*lugar*) to evacuate. 2 (*abandonar*) to move out of, abandon.

desalojo *nm* → **desalojamiento**.

desamor *nm* lack of affection.

desamortizar [4] *vtr* to alienate, disentail.

desamparado,-a I *adj* (*persona*) helpless, unprotected; (*lugar*) abandoned, forsaken. **II** *nm,f* helpless *o* abandoned person.

desamparar *vtr* 1 to abandon, desert. 2 *Jur* to renounce, relinquish.

desamparo *nm* helplessness.

desamueblado,-a *adj* unfurnished.

desandar [8] *vtr* **d. lo andado**, to retrace one's steps.

desangrarse *vr* to lose (a lot of) blood.

desanimado,-a *adj* 1 (*persona*) downhearted, dejected. 2 (*fiesta etc*) dull, lifeless.

desanimar I *vtr* to discourage, dishearten. **II desanimarse** *vr* to lose heart, get discouraged.

desánimo *nm* discouragement, dejection.

desapacible *adj* unpleasant.

desaparecer [33] *vi* to disappear.

desaparecido,-a I *adj* missing. **II** *nm,f* missing person.

desaparición *nf* disappearance.

desapego *nm* indifference, lack of affection.

desapercibido,-a *adj* 1 (*inadvertido*) unnoticed; **pasar d.**, to go unnoticed. 2 (*desprevenido*) unprepared.

desaprensivo,-a I *adj* unscrupulous. **II** *nm,f* unscrupulous person.

desaprobar |2| *vtr* **1** (*no aprobar*) to disapprove of. **2** (*rechazar*) to reject.

desaprovechar *vtr* (*dinero, tiempo*) to waste; **d. una ocasión,** to fail to make the most of an opportunity.

desarmable *adj* that can be taken to pieces.

desarmar *vtr* **1** (*desmontar*) to dismantle, take to pieces. **2** *Mil* to disarm.

desarme *nm* disarmament; **d. nuclear,** nuclear disarmament.

desarraigado,-a *adj* rootless, without roots.

desarraigar |7| *vtr* to uproot.

desarraigo *nm* rootlessness.

desarreglado,-a *adj* **1** (*lugar*) untidy. **2** (*persona*) untidy, slovenly.

desarreglar *vtr* **1** (*desordenar*) to make untidy, mess up. **2** (*planes etc*) to spoil, upset.

desarreglo *nm* difference of opinion.

desarrollado,-a *adj* developed; **país d.,** developed country.

desarrollar I *vtr* to develop. **II desarrollarse** *vr* **1** (*persona, enfermedad*) to develop. **2** (*tener lugar*) to take place.

desarrollo *nm* development; **países en vías de d.,** developing countries.

desarticular *vtr* to dismantle; **d. un complot,** to foil a plot.

desaseado,-a *adj* unkempt.

desasir |22| **I** *vtr* to release. **II desasirse** *vr* to get loose; **d. de,** to free *o* rid oneself of.

desasosegar |1| *vtr* to make restless *o* uneasy.

desasosiego *nm* restlessness, uneasiness.

desastrado,-a I *adj* untidy, scruffy. **II** *nm,f* scruffy person.

desastre *nm* disaster; **eres un d.,** you're just hopeless.

desastroso,-a *adj* disastrous.

desatar I *vtr* to untie, undo; (*provocar*) to unleash. **II desatarse** *vr* **1** (*zapato, cordón*) to come undone. **2** (*tormenta*) to break; (*pasión*) to run wild.

desatascar |1| *vtr* to unblock, clear.

desatender |3| *vtr* to neglect, not pay attention to.

desatento,-a *adj* inattentive; (*descortés*) impolite, discourteous.

desatinado,-a *adj* unwise.

desatino *nm* blunder.

desatornillar *vtr* to unscrew.

desatrancar |1| *vtr* to unblock; (*puerta*) to unbolt.

desautorizar |4| *vtr* **1** to disallow. **2** (*huelga etc*) to ban, forbid. **3** (*desmentir*) to deny.

desavenencia *nf* disagreement.

desaventajado,-a *adj* at a disadvantage.

desayunar I *vi* to have breakfast; *fml* to

breakfast. **II** *vtr* to have for breakfast.

desayuno *nm* breakfast.

desazón *nf* malaise.

desazonar *vtr* to cause malaise.

desbancar |1| *vtr* to oust.

desbandada *nf* scattering; **hubo una d. general,** everyone scattered.

desbandarse *vr* to scatter, disperse.

desbarajuste *nm* confusion, disorder.

desbaratar *vtr* to ruin, wreck; (*jersey*) to unravel.

desbloquear *vtr* **1** (*negociaciones*) to get going again. **2** (*créditos, precios*) to unfreeze.

desbocado,-a *adj* (*caballo*) runaway.

desbocarse *vr* (*caballo*) to bolt, run away.

desbordante *adj* overflowing, bursting.

desbordar I *vtr* to overflow; *fig* to overwhelm. **II** *vi* to overflow (**de,** with). **II desbordarse** *vr* to overflow, flood.

descabalgar |7| *vi* to dismount.

descabellado,-a *adj* crazy, wild.

descafeinado,-a *adj* **1** (*café*) decaffeinated. **2** *fig* watered-down, diluted.

descalabrar *vtr* **1** to wound in the head. **2** *fig* to damage, harm.

descalabro *nm* setback, misfortune.

descalificar |1| *vtr* to disqualify.

descalzarse |4| *vr* to take one's shoes off.

descalzo,-a *adj* barefoot.

descambiar |12| *vtr* to exchange.

descaminado,-a *adj fig* **ir d.,** to be on the wrong track.

descampado *nm* waste ground.

descansado,-a *adj* **1** (*persona*) rested. **2** (*vida, trabajo*) restful.

descansar *vi* **1** to rest, have a rest; (*corto tiempo*) to take a break. **2** *euf* **que en paz descanse,** may he *o* she rest in peace.

descansillo *nm* landing.

descanso *nm* **1** rest, break; **un día de d.,** a day off. **2** *Cin Teat* interval; *Dep* half-time, interval. **3** (*alivio*) relief. **4** (*rellano*) landing.

descapotable *adj & nm* convertible.

descarado,-a I *adj* **1** (*insolente*) cheeky, insolent; (*desvergonzado*) shameless. **2** *fam* **d. que sí/no,** (*por supuesto*) of course/course not. **II** *nm,f* cheeky person.

descarga *nf* **1** unloading. **2** *Elec Mil* discharge.

descargar |7| **I** *vtr* **1** to unload. **2** *Elec* to discharge. **3** (*disparar*) to fire; (*golpe*) to deal. **II** *vi* (*tormenta*) to burst. **III descargarse** *vr* (*batería*) to go flat.

descargo *nm Jur* discharge; **testigo de d.,** witness for the defence.

descarnado,-a *adj* crude.

descaro *nm* cheek, nerve; **¡qué d.!,** what a cheek!

descarriar |29| **I** *vtr* to lead astray, put on the wrong road. **II descarriarse** *vr* to go astray, lose one's way.

descarrilar *vi* to go off the rails, be derailed.

descartar I *vtr* to rule out. **II descartarse** *vr Naipes* to discard, throw away.

descascarillarse *vr* to chip, peel.

descendencia *nf* descendants *pl*; **morir sin d.**, to die without issue.

descendente *adj* descending, downward.

descender [3] **I** *vi* 1 (*temperatura, nivel*) to fall, drop. 2 **d. de**, to descend from. **II** *vtr* to lower.

descendiente *nmf* descendant.

descenso *nm* 1 descent; (*de temperatura*) fall, drop. 2 *Dep* relegation.

descentrado,-a *adj* off-centre.

descentralizar [4] *vtr* to decentralize.

descifrar *vtr* to decipher; (*mensaje*) decode; (*misterio*) to solve; (*motivos, causas*) to figure out.

descojonarse *vr vulg* (*reírse*) to piss oneself laughing.

descolgar [2] **I** *vtr* (*el teléfono*) to pick up; (*cuadro, cortinas*) to take down. **II descolgarse** *vr* to let oneself down, slide down.

descolorido,-a *adj* faded.

descombros *nmpl* rubble, debris.

descompasado,-a *adj* inconsistent.

descomponer [19] (*pp descompuesto*) **I** *vtr* 1 to break down. 2 (*corromper*) to rot, decompose. **II descomponerse** *vi* (*corromperse*) to rot, decompose; (*ponerse nervioso*) to lose one's cool.

descomposición *nf* 1 (*de carne*) decomposition, rotting; (*de país*) disintegration. 2 *Quim* breakdown.

descompuesto,-a *adj* 1 (*podrido*) rotten, decomposed. 2 (*furioso*) furious.

descompuse *pt indef* → **descomponer**.

descomunal *adj* huge, massive.

desconcertante *adj* disconcerting.

desconcertar [1] **I** *vtr* to disconcert. **II desconcertarse** *vr* to be bewildered, be puzzled.

desconchón *nm* bare patch.

desconcierto *nm* chaos, confusion.

desconectar *vtr* to disconnect.

desconexión *nf* disconnection.

desconfiado,-a *adj* distrustful, wary.

desconfianza *nf* distrust, mistrust.

desconfiar [29] *vi* to distrust (**de, -**), mistrust (**de, -**).

descongelar *vtr* (*nevera*) to defrost; (*créditos*) to unfreeze.

descongestionar *vtr* to clear.

desconocer [34] *vtr* not to know, be unaware of.

desconocido,-a I *adj* unknown; (*irreconocible*) unrecognizable. **II** *nm* **lo d.**, the unknown. **III** *nm,f* stranger.

desconsiderado,-a I *adj* inconsiderate, thoughtless. **II** *nm,f* inconsiderate *o* thoughtless person.

desconsolado,-a *adj* disconsolate, grief-stricken.

desconsuelo *nm* grief, sorrow.

descontado,-a *adj fam* **dar por d.**, to take for granted; **por d.**, needless to say, of course.

descontar [2] *vtr* 1 to deduct. 2 *Dep* (*tiempo*) to add on.

descontento,-a I *adj* unhappy. **II** *nm* dissatisfaction.

descontrol *nm fam* lack of control; **había un d. total**, it was absolute chaos.

descontrolarse *vr* to lose control.

desconvocar *vtr* to call off.

descorchar *vtr* to uncork.

descornarse [2] *vr fam* (*trabajar*) to slave (away).

descorrer *vtr* to draw back.

descortés *adj* impolite, discourteous.

descortesía *nf* discourtesy, impoliteness.

descoser *vtr* to unstitch, unpick.

descosido *nm* (*en camisa etc*) open seam; *fam* **como un d.**, like mad, wildly.

descoyuntar *vtr* to dislocate.

descrédito *nm* disrepute, discredit.

descremado,-a *adj* skimmed.

describir (*pp descrito*) *vtr* to describe.

descripción *nf* description.

descriptivo,-a *adj* descriptive.

descrito,-a *pp* → **describir**.

descuajaringar [7] *vtr fam* to pull *o* take to pieces.

descuartizar [4] *vtr* to cut up, cut into pieces.

descubierto,-a I *adj* open, uncovered; **a cielo d.**, in the open. **II** *nm* 1 *Fin* overdraft. 2 **al d.**, in the open; **poner al d.**, to uncover, bring out into the open.

descubridor,-a *nm,f* discoverer.

descubrimiento *nm* discovery.

descubrir (*pp descubierto*) *vtr* to discover; (*conspiración*) to uncover; (*placa*) to unveil.

descuento *nm* discount.

descuidado,-a *adj* 1 (*desaseado*) untidy, neglected. 2 (*negligente*) careless, negligent. 3 (*desprevenido*) off one's guard.

descuidar I *vtr* to neglect, overlook. **II** *vi* **descuida, voy yo**, don't worry, I'll go. **III descuidarse** *vr* (*despistarse*) to be careless; **como te descuides, llegarás tarde**, if you don't watch out, you'll be late.

descuido *nm* 1 oversight, mistake; **por d.**, inadvertently, by mistake. 2 (*negligencia*) negligence, carelessness.

desde *adv* 1 (*tiempo*) since; **d. ahora**, from now on; **d. el lunes/entonces**, since Monday/then; **espero d. hace media hora**, I've been waiting for half an hour; **no lo he visto d. hace un año**, I haven't seen him for a year; **¿d. cuándo?**, since when?; **d. siempre**, always. 2 (*lugar*) from; **d. aquí**, from here; **d. arriba/abajo**, from above/below. 3 **d. luego**, of course. 4 **d. que**, ever since; **d. que lo**

conozco, ever since I've known him.
desdecir [12] (*pp* **desdicho**) I *vi* not to
live up (**de**, to). II **desdecirse** *vr* to go
back on one's word.
desdén *nm* disdain.
desdentado,-a *adj* toothless.
desdeñar *vtr* to disdain.
desdeñoso,-a *adj* disdainful.
desdibujarse *vr* to become blurred *o*
faint.
desdicha *nf* misfortune; **por d.**, unfortunately.
desdichado,-a I *adj* unfortunate. II *nm,f*
poor devil, wretch.
desdigo *indic pres* → **desdecir**.
desdiré *indic fut* → **desdecir**.
desdoblar *vtr* to unfold.
deseable *adj* desirable.
desear *vtr* 1 to desire; **deja mucho que
d.**, it leaves a lot to be desired. 2 (*querer*)
to want; **¿qué desea?**, can I help you?;
estoy deseando que vengas, I'm looking
forward to your coming. 3 **te deseo buena suerte/feliz Navidad**, I wish you good
luck/a merry Christmas.
desecar [1] *vtr* to dry up.
desechable *adj* disposable, throw-away.
desechar *vtr* 1 (*tirar*) to discard, throw
out *o* away. 2 (*oferta*) to turn down, refuse; (*idea, proyecto*) to drop, discard.
desechos *nmpl* waste *sing*.
desembalar *vtr* to unpack.
desembarcar [1] I *vtr* (*mercancías*) to un-
load; (*personas*) to disembark. II *vi* to disembark.
desembarco, desembarque *nm* (*de
mercancías*) unloading; (*de personas*) dis-
embarkation.
desembocadura *nf* mouth.
desembocar [1] *vi* (*río*) to flow (**en**, into);
(*calle, situación*) to lead (**en**, to).
desembolsar *vtr* to pay out.
desembolso *nm* expenditure.
desembragar [7] *vtr Aut* to declutch.
desembrollar *vtr fam* 1 (*aclarar*) to clarify, clear up. 2 (*desenredar*) to disentangle.
desembuchar *vtr fig* to blurt out; *fam*
¡desembucha!, out with it!
desempañar *vtr* to wipe the condensation
from; *Aut* to demist.
desempaquetar *vtr* to unpack, unwrap.
desempatar *vi Dep* to break the deadlock.
desempate *nm* play-off; **partido de d.**,
play-off, deciding match.
desempeñar *vtr* 1 (*cargo*) to hold, occupy; (*función*) to fulfil; (*papel*) to play. 2
(*recuperar*) to redeem.
desempleado,-a I *adj* unemployed, out
of work. II *nm,f* unemployed person; **los
desempleados**, the unemployed.
desempleo *nm* unemployment; **cobrar el
d.**, to be on the dole.
desempolvar *vtr* 1 to dust. 2 *fig* (*pasado*)

to revive.
desencadenar I *vtr* 1 to unchain. 2 (*provocar*) to unleash. II **desencadenarse** *vr* 1
(*prisionero*) to break loose; (*viento, pasión*)
to rage. 2 (*conflicto*) to start, break out.
desencajar I *vtr* (*pieza*) to knock out;
(*hueso*) to dislocate. II **desencajarse** *vr* 1
(*pieza*) to come out; (*hueso*) to become
dislocated. 2 (*cara*) to become distorted.
desencaminado,-a *adj* →
descaminado,-a.
desencanto *nm* disenchantment.
desenchufar *vtr* to unplug.
desenfadado,-a *adj* carefree, free and
easy.
desenfado *nm* ease.
desenfocado,-a *adj* out of focus.
desenfoque *nm* incorrect focusing; *fig* (*de
asunto*) wrong approach.
desenfrenado,-a *adj* frantic, uncontrolled; (*vicio, pasión*) unbridled.
desenfreno *nm* debauchery.
desenganchar *vtr* to unhook; (*vagón*) to
uncouple.
desengañar I *vtr* **d. a algn**, to open sb's
eyes. II **desengañarse** *vr* 1 to be disappointed. 2 *fam* **¡desengáñate!**, get real!
desengaño *nm* disappointment; **llevarse
o sufrir un d. con algo**, to be disappointed in sth.
desengrasar *vtr* to degrease, remove the
grease from.
desenlace *nm* 1 result, outcome; **un feliz
d.**, a happy end. 2 *Cin Teat* ending, dé-
nouement.
desenmarañar *vtr* (*pelo*) to untangle;
(*problema*) to unravel; (*asunto*) to sort
out.
desenmascarar *vtr* to unmask.
desenredar *vtr* to untangle, disentangle.
desenrollar *vtr* to unroll; (*cable*) to un-
wind.
desenroscar [1] *vtr* to unscrew.
desentenderse [3] *vr* **se desentendió de
mi problema**, he didn't want to have
anything to do with my problem.
desenterrar [1] *vtr* 1 (*cadáver*) to exhume,
disinter; (*tesoro etc*) to dig up. 2 (*recuerdo*)
to revive.
desentonar *vi* 1 *Mús* to sing out of tune,
be out of tune. 2 (*colores etc*) not to
match. 3 (*persona, comentario*) to be out
of place.
desentrañar *vtr* (*misterio*) to unravel, get
to the bottom of.
desentrenado,-a *adj* out of training *o*
shape.
desentumecer [33] *vtr* to put the feeling
back into.
desenvoltura *nf* ease.
desenvolver [4] (*pp* **desenvuelto**) I *vtr* to
unwrap. II **desenvolverse** *vr* 1 (*persona*)
to manage, cope. 2 (*hecho*) to develop.
desenvuelto,-a *adj* relaxed.

deseo *nm* wish; *(sexual)* desire; **formular un d.**, to make a wish.

deseoso,-a *adj* eager; **estar d. de**, be eager to.

desequilibrado,-a I *adj* unbalanced. **II** *nm,f* unbalanced person.

desequilibrar I *vtr* to unbalance, throw off balance. **II desequilibrarse** *vr* to become mentally disturbed.

desequilibrio *nm* imbalance; **d. mental**, mental disorder.

deserción *nf* desertion.

desertar *vi* to desert.

desértico,-a *adj* desert.

desertización *nf* desertification.

desertor,-a *nm,f* deserter.

desesperación *nf* *(desesperanza)* despair; *(exasperación)* desperation.

desesperado,-a *adj* 1 *(sin esperanza)* desperate, hopeless. 2 *(exasperado)* exasperated, infuriated.

desesperante *adj* exasperating.

desesperar I *vtr* to drive to despair; *(exasperar)* to exasperate. **II desesperarse** *vr* to despair.

desestabilizar [4] *vtr* to destabilize.

desestimar *vtr* to reject.

desfachatez *nf* cheek, nerve.

desfalco *nm* embezzlement, misappropriation.

desfallecer [33] *vi* 1 *(debilitarse)* to feel faint; *(desmayarse)* to faint. 2 *(desanimarse)* to lose heart.

desfasado,-a *adj* 1 outdated. 2 *(persona)* old-fashioned, behind the times. 3 *Téc* out of phase.

desfase *nm* gap; **d. horario**, time lag.

desfavorable *adj* unfavourable, *US* unfavorable.

desfigurar *vtr* *(cara)* to disfigure; *(verdad)* to distort.

desfiladero *nm* narrow pass.

desfilar *vi* 1 to march in single file. 2 *Mil* to march past, parade.

desfile *nm Mil* parade, march past; **d. de modas**, fashion show.

desfogar [7] **I** *vtr* to give vent to. **II desfogarse** *vr* to let off steam.

desgajar I *vtr* *(arrancar)* to rip *o* tear out; *(rama)* to tear off. **II desgajarse** *vr* to come off.

desgana *nf* 1 *(inapetencia)* lack of appetite. 2 *(apatía)* apathy, indifference; **con d.**, reluctantly, unwillingly.

desganado,-a *adj* 1 **estar d.**, *(inapetente)* to have no appetite. 2 *(apático)* apathetic.

desgañitarse *vr fam* to shout oneself hoarse.

desgarbado,-a *adj* ungraceful, ungainly.

desgarrador,-a *adj* bloodcurdling.

desgarrar *vtr* to tear.

desgarrón *nm* big tear, rip.

desgastar I *vtr* to wear out. **II desgastarse** *vr* *(consumirse)* to wear out; *(per-*

sona) to wear oneself out.

desgaste *nm* wear; **d. del poder**, wear and tear of power.

desgracia *nf* 1 misfortune; **por d.**, unfortunately. 2 *(deshonor)* disgrace. 3 **desgracias personales**, loss of life.

desgraciado,-a I *adj* unfortunate; *(infeliz)* unhappy. **II** *nm,f* unfortunate person; **un pobre d.**, a poor devil. ◆**desgraciadamente** *adv* unfortunately.

desgravable *adj* tax-deductible.

desgravación *nf* deduction; **d. fiscal**, tax deduction.

desgravar *vtr* to deduct.

desguazar [4] *vtr* *(un barco)* to break up; *Aut* to scrap.

deshabitado,-a *adj* uninhabited, unoccupied.

deshabitar *vtr* to abandon, vacate.

deshacer [15] *(pp deshecho)* **I** *vtr* 1 *(paquete)* to undo; *(maleta)* to unpack. 2 *(plan)* to destroy, ruin. 3 *(acuerdo)* to break off. 4 *(disolver)* to dissolve; *(derretir)* to melt. **II deshacerse** *vr* 1 to come undone *o* untied. 2 **d. de algn/algo**, to get rid of sb/sth. 3 *(afligirse)* to go to pieces; **d. en lágrimas**, to cry one's eyes out. 4 *(disolverse)* to dissolve; *(derretirse)* to melt. 5 *(niebla)* to fade away, disappear.

deshecho,-a *adj* 1 *(cama)* unmade; *(maleta)* unpacked; *(paquete)* unwrapped. 2 *(roto)* broken, smashed. 3 *(disuelto)* dissolved; *(derretido)* melted. 4 *(abatido)* devasted, shattered. 5 *(cansado)* exhausted, tired out.

desheredar *vtr* to disinherit.

deshidratar *vtr* to dehydrate.

deshielo *nm* thaw.

deshilachar *vtr* to fray.

deshilvanado,-a *adj fig* *(inconexo)* disjointed.

deshonesto,-a *adj* 1 dishonest. 2 *(indecente)* indecent, improper.

deshonor *nm*, **deshonra** *nf* dishonour, *US* dishonor.

deshonrar *vtr* 1 to dishonour, *US* dishonor. 2 *(a la familia etc)* to bring disgrace on.

deshora (a) *loc adv* at an inconvenient time; **comer a d.**, to eat at odd times.

deshuesar *vtr* *(carne)* to bone; *(fruta)* to stone.

deshumanizar [4] *vtr* to dehumanize.

desidia *nf* apathy.

desierto,-a I *nm* desert. **II** *adj* 1 *(deshabitado)* uninhabited. 2 *(vacío)* empty, deserted. 3 *(premio)* void.

designación *nf* designation.

designar *vtr* 1 to designate. 2 *(fecha, lugar)* to fix.

designio *nm* intention, plan.

desigual *adj* 1 uneven. 2 *(lucha)* unequal.

3 *(carácter)* changeable.

desigualdad *nf* **1** inequality. **2** *(del terreno)* unevenness.

desilusión *nf* disappointment, disillusionment.

desilusionar *vtr* to disappoint, disillusion.

desinfectante *adj & nm* disinfectant.

desinfectar *vtr* to disinfect.

desinflar I *vtr* to deflate; *(rueda)* to let down. **II desinflarse** *vr* to go flat.

desintegración *nf* disintegration.

desintegrar *vtr,* **desintegrarse** *vr* to disintegrate.

desinterés *nm* **1** *(indiferencia)* lack of interest, apathy. **2** *(generosidad)* unselfishness.

desinteresado,-a *adj* selfless, unselfish.

desintoxicar |1| **I** *vtr* to detoxicate; *(de alcohol)* to dry out. **II desintoxicarse** *vr Med* to detoxicate oneself; *(de alcohol)* to dry out.

desistir *vi* to desist.

deslavazado,-a *adj* disjointed.

desleal *adj* disloyal; *(competencia)* unfair.

deslealtad *nf* disloyalty.

deslenguado,-a *adj (insolente)* insolent, cheeky; *(grosero)* coarse, foul-mouthed.

desliar [29] *vtr* to unwrap.

desligar [7] **I** *vtr* **1** *(separar)* to separate. **2** *(desatar)* to untie, unfasten. **II desligarse** *vr* **d. de,** to disassociate oneself from.

desliz *nm* mistake, slip; **cometer** *o* **tener un d.,** to slip up.

deslizar |4| **I** *vi* to slide. **II deslizarse** *vr* **1** *(patinar)* to slide. **2** *(fluir)* to flow.

deslucir [35] *vtr* **1** *(espectáculo)* to spoil. **2** *(metal)* to make dull.

deslumbrador,-a, **deslumbrante** *adj* dazzling; *fig* stunning.

deslumbrar *vtr* to dazzle.

desmadrarse *vr fam* to go wild.

desmadre *nm fam* hullabaloo.

desmandarse *vr* to get out of hand, run wild; *(caballo)* to bolt.

desmano (a) *loc adv* out of the way; **me coge a d.,** it is out of my way.

desmantelar *vtr* **1** to dismantle. **2** *Náut* to dismast, unrig.

desmaquillador,-a I *nm* make-up remover. **II** *adj* **leche désmaquilladora,** cleansing cream.

desmaquillarse *vr* to remove one's make-up.

desmarcarse |1| *vr Dep* to lose one's marker.

desmayado,-a *adj* unconscious; **caer d.,** to faint.

desmayarse *vr* to faint.

desmayo *nm* faint, fainting fit; **tener un d.,** to faint.

desmedido,-a *adj* disproportionate, out of all proportion; *(ambición)* unbounded.

desmejorar(se) *vi & vr* to deteriorate, go downhill.

desmelenarse *vr fam* to let one's hair down.

desmembración *nf,* **desmembramiento** *nm* dismemberment.

desmemoriado,-a *adj* forgetful, absentminded.

desmentir |5| *vtr* to deny.

desmenuzar |4| *vtr* **1** *(deshacer)* to break into little pieces, crumble; *(carne)* to cut into little pieces. **2** *(asunto)* to examine in detail.

desmerecer [33] *vi* **1** to be unworthy (**de,** of). **2** *(deteriorarse)* to deteriorate.

desmesura *nf* excess.

desmesurado,-a *adj* excessive.

desmilitarizar |4| *vtr* to demilitarize.

desmontable *adj* that can be taken to pieces.

desmontar I *vtr* **1** *(desarmar)* to take to pieces, dismantle. **2** *(allanar)* to level. **II** *vi* to dismount (**de, -**), get off (**de, -**).

desmoralizar |4| *vtr* to demoralize.

desmoronarse *vr* to crumble, fall to pieces.

desnatado,-a *adj (leche)* skimmed.

desnivel *nm (en el terreno)* drop, difference in height.

desnivelar *vtr* to throw out of balance.

desnucarse |1| *vr* to break one's neck.

desnuclearizar *vtr* to denuclearize.

desnudar I *vtr* to undress. **II desnudarse** *vr* to get undressed.

desnudismo *nm* nudism.

desnudista *adj & nmf* nudist.

desnudo,-a I *adj* naked, nude. **II** *nm Arte* nude.

desnutrición *nf* malnutrition.

desnutrido,-a *adj* undernourished.

desobedecer |33| *vtr* to disobey.

desobediencia *nf* disobedience.

desobediente I *adj* disobedient. **II** *nmf* disobedient person.

desocupado,-a *adj* **1** *(vacío)* empty, vacant. **2** *(ocioso)* free, not busy. **3** *(sin empleo)* unemployed.

desocupar *vtr* to empty, vacate.

desodorante *adj & nm* deodorant.

desolación *nf* desolation.

desolar |2| *vtr* to devastate.

desollar |2| **I** *vtr* to skin. **II desollarse** *vr* to scrape; **me desollé el brazo,** I scraped my arm.

desorbitado,-a *adj (precio)* exhorbitant.

desorden *nm* untidiness, mess; **¡qué d.!,** what a mess!; **d. público,** civil disorder.

desordenado,-a *adj* messy, untidy.

desordenar *vtr* to make untidy, mess up.

desorganizar |4| *vtr* to disorganize, disrupt.

desorientación *nf* disorientation.

desorientar I *vtr* to disorientate. **II desorientarse** *vr* to lose one's sense of direction, lose one's bearings; *fig* to become disorientated.

despabilado,-a *adj* 1 *(sin sueño)* wide awake. 2 *(listo)* quick, smart.

despachar *vtr* 1 *(asunto)* to get through. 2 *(correo)* to send, dispatch. 3 *(en tienda)* to serve. 4 *fam (despedir)* to send packing, sack.

despacho *nm* 1 *(oficina)* office; *(en casa)* study. 2 *(venta)* sale. 3 *(comunicación)* dispatch.

despachurrar *vtr fam* to squash, flatten.

despacio *adv* 1 *(lentamente)* slowly. 2 *(en voz baja)* quietly.

despampanante *adj fam* stunning.

desparpajo *nm* self-assurance; **con d.**, in a carefree manner.

desparramar *vtr*, **desparramarse** *vr* to spread, scatter; *(líquido)* to spill.

despavorido,-a *adj* terrified.

despecho *nm* spite; **por d.**, out of spite.

despectivo,-a *adj* derogatory, disparaging.

despedazar |4| *vtr* to cut o tear to pieces.

despedida *nf* farewell, goodbye; **d. de soltera/soltero**, hen/stag party.

despedido,-a *adj* **salir d.**, to be off like a shot.

despedir |6| I *vtr* 1 *(empleado)* to sack, fire. 2 *(decir adiós)* to see off, say goodbye to. 3 *(olor, humo etc)* to give off. II **despedirse** *vr* 1 *(decir adiós)* to say goodbye (de, to). 2 *fig* to forget, give up; **ya puedes despedirte del coche**, you can say goodbye to the car.

despegado,-a *adj* 1 unstuck. 2 *(persona)* couldn't-care-less.

despegar |7| I *vtr* to take off, detach. II *vi Av* to take off. III **despegarse** *vr* to come unstuck.

despego *nm* detachment.

despegue *nm* takeoff.

despeinado,-a *adj* dishevelled, with untidy hair.

despejado,-a *adj* clear; *(cielo)* cloudless.

despejar I *vtr* to clear; *(misterio, dudas)* to clear up. II **despejarse** *vr* 1 *(cielo)* to clear. 2 *(persona)* to clear one's head.

despeje *nm Dep* clearance.

despellejar *vtr* to skin.

despelotarse *vr vulg* 1 *(desnudarse)* to strip. 2 **d. de risa**, to laugh one's head off.

despensa *nf* pantry, larder.

despeñadero *nm* cliff, precipice.

despeñarse *vr* to go over a cliff.

desperdiciar |12| *vtr* to waste; *(oportunidad)* to throw away.

desperdicio *nm* 1 *(acto)* waste. 2 **desperdicios**, *(basura)* rubbish *sing*; *(desechos)* scraps, leftovers.

desperdigar |7| *vtr*, **desperdigarse** *vr* to scatter, separate.

desperezarse |4| *vr* to stretch (oneself).

desperfecto *nm* 1 *(defecto)* flaw, imperfection. 2 *(daño)* damage.

despertador *nm* alarm clock; **reloj d.**, alarm watch.

despertar |1| I *vtr* to wake (up), awaken; *fig (sentimiento)* to arouse. II **despertarse** *vr* to wake (up).

despiadado,-a *adj* merciless.

despido *nm* dismissal, sacking.

despierto,-a *adj* 1 *(desvelado)* awake. 2 *(vivo)* quick, sharp.

despilfarrar *vtr* to waste, squander.

despilfarro *nm* wasting, squandering.

despintar *vi*, **despintarse** *vr* *(ropa)* to fade.

despistado,-a I *adj* 1 *(olvidadizo)* scatterbrained. 2 *(confuso)* confused. II *nm,f* scatterbrain.

despistar I *vtr* 1 *(hacer perder la pista a)* to lose, throw off one's scent. 2 *fig* to mislead. II **despistarse** *vr* 1 *(perderse)* to get lost. 2 *(distraerse)* to switch off.

despiste *nm* 1 *(cualidad)* absent-mindedness. 2 *(error)* slip-up.

desplazamiento *nm (viaje)* trip, journey; **dietas de d.**, travelling expenses.

desplazar |4| I *vtr* to displace. II **desplazarse** *vr* to travel.

desplegar |1| I *vtr* 1 to open (out), spread (out). 2 *(energías etc)* to use, deploy. II **desplegarse** *vr* 1 *(abrirse)* to open (out), spread (out). 2 *Mil* to deploy.

despliegue *nm* 1 *Mil* deployment. 2 *(de medios etc)* display.

desplomarse *vr* to collapse; *(precios)* to slump, fall sharply.

desplumar *vtr* to pluck.

despoblar |2| *vtr* to depopulate.

despojar *vtr* 1 to strip (de, of). 2 *fig* to divest, deprive (de, of).

despojo *nm* 1 stripping. 2 **despojos**, leftovers, scraps.

desposado,-a *adj fml* newly-wed.

desposar *vtr fml* to marry.

desposeer |36| *vtr* **d. de**, to dispossess of; *(autoridad)* to strip of.

desposeído *nm* **los desposeídos**, the have-nots.

déspota *nmf* despot.

despótico,-a *adj* despotic.

despotismo *nm* despotism.

despotricar |1| *vi* to rant and rave (**contra**, about).

despreciable *adj* despicable, contemptible; *(cantidad)* negligible.

despreciar |12| *vtr* 1 *(desdeñar)* to scorn, despise. 2 *(rechazar)* to reject, spurn.

desprecio *nm* 1 *(desdén)* scorn, disdain. 2 *(desaire)* slight, snub.

desprender I *vtr* 1 *(separar)* to remove, detach. 2 *(olor, humo etc)* to give off. II **desprenderse** *vr* 1 *(soltarse)* to come off o away. 2 **d. de**, to rid oneself (**de**, of), free oneself (**de**, from). 3 **de aquí se desprende que ...**, it can be deduced from this that ....

desprendido,-a *adj fig* generous, unselfish.

desprendimiento *nm* **1** loosening, detachment; **d. de tierras,** landslide. **2** *fig* (*generosidad*) generosity, unselfishness.

despreocupado,-a *adj* **1** (*tranquilo*) unconcerned. **2** (*descuidado*) careless; (*estilo*) casual.

despreocuparse *vr* **1** (*tranquilizarse*) to stop worrying. **2** (*desentenderse*) to be unconcerned, be indifferent (**de, to**).

desprestigiar |12| *vtr* to discredit, run down.

desprestigio *nm* discredit, loss of reputation; **campaña de d.,** smear campaign.

desprevenido,-a *adj* unprepared; **coger o pillar a algn d.,** to catch sb unawares.

desproporción *nf* disproportion, lack of proportion.

desproporcionado,-a *adj* disproportionate.

desprovisto,-a *adj* lacking (**de, -**), without (**de, -**), devoid (**de, of**).

después *adv* **1** afterwards, later; (*entonces*) then; (*seguidamente*) next; **una semana d.,** a week later; **poco d.,** soon after. **2** (*lugar*) next. **3** *d.* after; **d. de la guerra,** after the war; **mi calle está d. de la tuya,** my street is the one after yours; **d. de cenar,** after eating; **d. de todo,** after all. **4** **d. de que,** after; **d. de que viniera,** after he came.

despuntar **I** *vtr* to blunt, make blunt. **II** *vi* **1** (*día*) to dawn. **2** (*destacar*) to excel, stand out.

desquiciar |12| **I** *vtr* (*persona*) to unhinge. **II** desquiciarse *vr* (*persona*) to go crazy.

desquitarse *vr* to take revenge (**de, for**).

desquite *nm* revenge.

destacado,-a *adj* outstanding.

destacamento *nm* detachment.

destacar |1| **I** *vtr fig* to emphasize, stress. **II** destacar(se) *vi & vr* to stand out.

destajo *nm* piecework; **trabajar a d.,** to do piecework.

destapar **I** *vtr* to take the lid off; (*botella*) to open; *fig* (*asunto*) to uncover. **II** destaparse *vr* to get uncovered.

destartalado,-a *adj* rambling; (*desvencijado*) ramshackle.

destello *nm* flash, sparkle.

destemplado,-a *adj* **1** (*voz, gesto*) sharp, snappy; **con cajas destempladas,** rudely, brusquely. **2** (*tiempo*) unpleasant. **3** (*enfermo*) indisposed, out of sorts. **4** *Mús* out of tune, discordant.

desteñir |6| **I** *vi & vtr* to discolour, *US* discolor. **II** desteñirse *vr* to lose colour *o* *US* color, fade.

desternillarse *vi* **d. (de risa),** to split one's sides laughing.

desterrar |1| *vtr* to exile.

destiempo (a) *loc adv* at the wrong time *o* moment.

destierro *nm* exile.

destilado,-a *adj* distilled; **agua destilada,** distilled water.

destilar *vtr* to distil.

destilería *nf* distillery.

destinado,-a *adj* destined, bound; *fig* **d. al fracaso,** doomed to failure.

destinar *vtr* **1** (*dinero etc*) to set aside, assign. **2** (*empleado*) to appoint.

destinatario,-a *nm,f* **1** (*de carta*) addressee. **2** (*de mercancías*) consignee.

destino *nm* **1** (*rumbo*) destination; **el avión con d. a Bilbao,** the plane to Bilbao. **2** (*sino*) fate, fortune. **3** (*de empleo*) post.

destitución *nf* dismissal from office.

destituir |37| *vtr* to dismiss *o* remove from office.

destornillador *nm* screwdriver.

destornillar *vtr* to unscrew.

destreza *nf* skill.

destrozado,-a *adj* **1** (*roto*) torn-up, smashed. **2** (*cansado*) worn-out, exhausted. **3** (*abatido*) shattered.

destrozar |4| *vtr* **1** (*destruir*) to destroy; (*rasgar*) to tear to shreds *o* pieces. **2** (*afligir*) to shatter; (*vida, reputación*) to ruin.

destrozo *nm* **1** destruction. **2** destrozos, damage *sing.*

destrucción *nf* destruction.

destructivo,-a *adj* destructive.

destructor,-a **I** *adj* destructive. **II** *nm* *Náut* destroyer.

destruir |37| *vtr* to destroy.

desusado,-a *adj* old-fashioned, outdated.

desuso *nm* disuse; **caer en d.,** to fall into disuse; **en d.,** obsolete, outdated.

desvalido,-a *adj* defenceless.

desvalijar *vtr* (*robar*) to clean out, rob; (*casa, tienda*) to burgle.

desvalorizar |4| *vtr* to devalue.

desván *nm* attic, loft.

desvanecerse |33| *vr* **1** (*disiparse*) to vanish, fade away. **2** (*desmayarse*) to faint.

desvariar |29| *vi* to talk nonsense.

desvarío *nm* **1** (*delirio*) raving, delirium. **2** (*disparate*) nonsense.

desvelado,-a *adj* awake, wide awake.

desvelar **I** *vtr* to keep awake. **II** desvelarse *vr* **1** (*despabilarse*) to stay awake. **2** (*desvivirse*) to devote oneself (**por, to**).

desvencijar **I** *vtr* to take apart. **II** desvencijarse *vr* to fall apart.

desventaja *nf* **1** disadvantage; **estar en d.,** to be at a disadvantage. **2** (*inconveniente*) drawback.

desventura *nf* misfortune, bad luck.

desvergonzado,-a **I** *adj* **1** (*indecente*) shameless. **2** (*descaro*) insolent. **II** *nm,f* **1** (*sinvergüenza*) shameless person. **2** (*fresco*) insolent *o* cheeky person.

desvergüenza *nf* **1** (*indecencia*) shamelessness. **2** (*atrevimiento*) insolence; **tuvo la d. de negarlo,** he had the cheek to deny it.

3 *(impertinencia)* insolent *o* rude remark.

desvestir |6| I *vtr* to undress. II **desvestirse** *vr* to undress, get undressed.

desviación *nf* deviation; *(de carretera)* diversion, detour; *Med* **d. de columna**, slipped disc.

desviar |29| I *vtr (río, carretera)* to divert; *(golpe, conversación)* to deflect; **d. la mirada**, to look away. II **desviarse** *vr* to go off course; *(coche)* to turn off; *fig* **d. del tema**, to digress.

desvincular I *vtr* to separate. II **desvincularse** *vr* to separate, cut oneself off.

desvío *nm* diversion, detour.

desvirgar |7| *vtr* to deflower.

desvirtuar |30| *vtr* to distort.

desvivirse *vr* to bend over backwards.

detallado,-a *adj* detailed, thorough.
◆**detalladamente** *adv* in (great) detail.

detallar *vtr* to give the details of.

detalle *nm* 1 detail; **entrar en detalles**, to go into details. 2 *(delicadeza)* nice thought, nicety; ¡**qué d.!**, how nice!, how sweet! 3 *(toque decorativo)* touch, ornament.

detallista I *adj* perfectionist. II *nmf* Com retailer.

detectar *vtr* to detect.

detective *nmf* detective; **d. privado**, private detective *o* eye.

detector,-a *nm,f* detector; **d. de incendios**, fire detector.

detención *nf* 1 *Jur* detention, arrest. 2 **con d.**, carefully, thoroughly.

detener |24| I *vtr* 1 to stop, halt. 2 *Jur (arrestar)* to arrest, detain. II **detenerse** *vr* to stop.

detenido,-a I *adj* 1 *(parado)* standing still, stopped. 2 *(arrestado)* detained. 3 *(minucioso)* detailed, thorough. II *nm,f* detainee, person under arrest.
◆**detenidamente** *adv* carefully, thoroughly.

detenimiento *nm* **con d.**, carefully, thoroughly.

detentar *vtr* to hold.

detergente *adj & nm* detergent.

deteriorar I *vtr* to spoil, damage. II **deteriorarse** *vr* 1 *(estropearse)* to get damaged. 2 *(empeorar)* to get worse.

deterioro *nm* 1 *(empeoramiento)* deterioration, worsening. 2 *(daño)* damage; **ir en d. de**, to be to the detriment of.

determinación *nf* 1 determination; **con d.**, determinedly. 2 *(decisión)* decision.

determinado,-a *adj* 1 *(preciso)* definite, precise. 2 *(resuelto)* decisive, resolute. 3 *Ling* definite.

determinante *adj* decisive.

determinar I *vtr* 1 *(fecha etc)* to fix, set. 2 *(decidir)* to decide on. 3 *(condicionar)* to determine. 4 *(ocasionar)* to bring about. II **determinarse** *vr* to make up one's mind to.

detestable *adj* detestable, repulsive.

detestar *vtr* to detest, hate.

detonante *nm* detonator; *fig* trigger.

detonar *vtr* to detonate.

detractor,-a *nm,f* detractor.

detrás *adv* 1 behind, on *o* at the back (de, of). 2 **d. de**, behind.

detrimento *nm* detriment; **en d. de**, to the detriment of.

detuve *pt indef* → **detener**.

deuda *nf* debt; **estoy en d. contigo**, *(monetaria)* I am in debt to you; *(moral)* I am indebted to you; **d. del Estado**, public debt; **d. pública**, national debt.

deudor,-a I *adj* indebted. II *nm,f* debtor.

devaluación *nf* devaluation.

devaluar |30| *vtr* to devalue.

devanar I *vtr (hilo)* to wind; *(alambre)* to coil. II **devanarse** *vr fam* **d. los sesos**, to rack one's brains.

devaneo *nm* dabbling.

devastador,-a *adj* devastating.

devastar *vtr* to devastate, ravage.

devengar |7| *vtr* Com to earn, accrue.

devenir |27| *vi* to become.

devoción *nf* 1 *Rel* devoutness. 2 *(al trabajo etc)* devotion; *fam* **Juan no es santo de mi d.**, Juan isn't really my cup of tea.

devolución *nf* 1 giving back, return; *Com* refund, repayment. 2 *Jur* devolution.

devolver |4| *(pp* **devuelto***)* I *vtr* to give back, return; *(dinero)* to refund. II *vi (vomitar)* to vomit, throw *o* bring up. II **devolverse** *vr Am* to go *o* come back, return.

devorar *vtr* to devour.

devoto,-a I *adj* pious, devout. II *nm f* 1 *Rel* pious person. 2 *(seguidor)* devotee.

devuelto,-a *pp de* → **devolver**.

DF *nm abr de* **Distrito Federal**, Federal District.

DGS *nf* 1 *abr de* **Dirección General de Seguridad**, government department responsible for National Security. 2 *abr de* **Dirección General de Sanidad**, government department responsible for Public Health.

DGT *nf abr de* **Dirección General de Tráfico**, government department responsible for Traffic.

di 1 *pt indef* → **dar**. 2 *imperat* → **decir**.

día *nm* day; ¿**qué d. es hoy?**, what's the date today?; **d. a d.**, day by day; **de d.**, by day; **durante el d.**, during the daytime; **de un d. para otro**, overnight; **un d. sí y otro no**, every other day; **pan del d.**, fresh bread; **hoy (en) d.**, nowadays; **el d. de mañana**, in the future; *fig* **estar al d.**, to be up to date; *fig* **poner al d.**, to bring up to date; **d. festivo**, holiday; **d. laborable**, working day; **d. libre**, free day, day off; **es de d.**, it is daylight; **hace buen/mal d.**, it's a nice/bad day, the weather is nice/bad today.

diabetes *nf* diabetes.
diabético,-a *adj & nm,f* diabetic.
diablo *nm* devil; *fam* ¡al d. con ...!, to hell with ...!; *fam* vete al d., get lost; *fam* ¿qué/cómo diablos ...?, what/how the hell ...?
diablura *nf* mischief.
diácono *nm* deacon.
diadema *nf* tiara.
diáfano,-a *adj* clear.
diafragma *nm* diaphragm; *Fot* aperture; *Med* cap.
diagnosis *nf inv* diagnosis.
diagnosticar [1] *vtr* to diagnose.
diagnóstico *nm* diagnosis.
diagonal *adj & nf* diagonal; **en d.**, diagonally.
diagrama *nm* diagram; *Inform* **d. de flujo**, flowchart.
dial *nm* dial.
dialecto *nm* dialect.
dialogar [7] *vi* to have a conversation; *(para negociar)* to talk.
diálogo *nm* dialogue.
diamante *nm* diamond.
diámetro *nm* diameter.
diana *nf* 1 *Mil* reveille. 2 *(blanco)* bull's eye.
diapositiva *nf* slide.
diario,-a I *nm* 1 *Prensa* (daily) newspaper. 2 *(memorias)* diary; *Náut* **d. de a bordo**, **d. de navegación**, logbook. II *adj* daily; **a d.**, daily, every day. ◆**diariamente** *adv* daily, every day.
diarrea *nf* diarrhoea, *US* diarrhea.
diatriba *nf* diatribe.
dibujante *nmf* 1 drawer. 2 *(de cómic)* cartoonist. 3 *Téc (hombre)* draughtsman, *US* draftsman; *(mujer)* draughtswoman, *US* draftswoman.
dibujar *vtr* to draw.
dibujo *nm* 1 drawing; **dibujos animados**, cartoons. 2 *(arte)* drawing; **d. artístico**, artistic drawing; **d. lineal**, draughtsmanship.
diccionario *nm* dictionary; **buscar/mirar una palabra en el d.**, to look up a word in the dictionary.
dicha *nf* happiness.
dicharachero,-a *adj* talkative and witty.
dicho,-a *adj* 1 said; **mejor d.**, or rather; **d. de otro modo**, to put it another way; **d. sea de paso**, let it be said in passing; **d. y hecho**, no sooner said than done. 2 **dicha persona**, *(mencionado)* the above mentioned person.
dichoso,-a *adj* 1 *(feliz)* happy. 2 *fam* damned; ¡este d. trabajo!, this damned job!
diciembre *nm* December.
dictado *nm* dictation *fig* **dictados**, dictates.
dictador,-a *nm,f* dictator.
dictadura *nf* dictatorship.

dictáfono® *nm* Dictaphone®.
dictamen *nm (juicio)* ruling; *(informe)* report.
dictaminar *vi* to rule (**sobre,** on).
dictar *vtr* 1 to dictate. 2 *(ley)* to enact; *(sentencia)* to pass.
dictatorial *adj* dictatorial.
didáctico,-a *adj* didactic.
diecinueve *adj & nm inv* nineteen.
dieciocho *adj & nm inv* eighteen.
dieciséis *adj & nm inv* sixteen.
diecisiete *adj & nm inv* seventeen.
diente *nm* tooth; *Téc* cog; *(de ajo)* clove; **d. de leche**, milk tooth; **dientes postizos**, false teeth; *fig* **hablar entre dientes**, to mumble; *fig* **poner los dientes largos a algn**, to make sb green with envy.
diera *subj imperf* → **dar**.
diéresis *nf inv* diaeresis.
diesel *adj & nm* diesel.
diestra *nf* right hand.
diestro,-a I *adj* 1 *(hábil)* skilful, *US* skillful, clever. 2 **a d. y siniestro**, right, left and centre. II *nm* *Taur* bullfighter, matador.
dieta *nf* 1 diet; **estar a d.**, to be on a diet. 2 **dietas**, expenses *o* subsistence allowance.
dietética *nf* dietetics *sing*.
dietista *nmf* dietician.
diez *adj & nm inv* ten.
difamación *nf* defamation, slander; *(escrita)* libel.
difamar *vtr* to defame, slander; *(por escrito)* to libel.
diferencia *nf* difference; **a d. de**, unlike.
diferencial I *adj* distinguishing. II *nm* differential.
diferenciar [12] I *vtr* to differentiate, distinguish (**entre**, between). II **diferenciarse** *vr* to differ (**de**, from), be different (**de**, from).
diferente I *adj* different (**de**, from, *US* than). II *adv* differently.
diferido,-a *adj* *TV* **en d.**, recorded.
difícil *adj* difficult, hard; **d. de creer/hacer**, difficult to believe/do; **es d. que venga**, it is unlikely that she'll come.
dificultad *nf* difficulty; *(aprieto)* trouble, problem.
dificultar *vtr* to make difficult.
dificultoso,-a *adj* difficult, hard.
difuminar *vtr* to blur.
difundir *vtr*, **difundirse** *vr* to spread.
difunto,-a I *adj* late, deceased. II *nm,f* deceased.
difusión *nf* 1 *(de noticia)* spreading; **tener gran d.**, to be widely broadcast. 2 *Rad TV* broadcasting.
difuso,-a *adj* diffuse.
digerir [5] *vtr* to digest; *fig* to assimilate.
digestión *nf* digestion; **corte de d.**, sudden indigestion.
digestivo,-a *adj* easy to digest.

digital *adj* digital; **huellas digitales,** fingerprints; **tocadiscos d.,** CD player.

digitalizar *vtr* digitize.

dígito *nm* digit.

dignarse *vr* to deign (**a**, to), condescend (**a**, to).

dignidad *nf* dignity.

digno,-a *adj* 1 (*merecedor*) worthy; **d. de admiración,** worthy of admiration; **d. de mención/verse,** worth mentioning/seeing. 2 (*decoroso*) decent, good.

digo *indic pres* → **decir.**

dije *pt indef* → **decir.**

dilación *nf* delay, hold-up; **sin d.,** without delay.

dilatado,-a *adj* 1 (*agrandado*) dilated. 2 (*vasto*) vast, extensive.

dilatar I *vtr* 1 (*agrandar*) to expand. 2 (*pupila*) to dilate. II **dilatarse** *vr* 1 (*agrandarse*) to expand. 2 (*pupila*) to dilate.

dilema *nm* dilemma.

diligencia *nf* 1 diligence; **con d.,** diligently. 2 **diligencias,** formalities.

diligente *adj* diligent.

dilucidar *vtr* to elucidate, clarify.

diluir |37| I *vtr* to dilute. II **diluirse** *vr* to dilute.

diluviar |12| *v impers* to pour with rain.

diluvio *nm* flood; **el D. (Universal),** the Flood.

diluyo *indic pres* → **diluir.**

dimensión *nf* 1 dimension, size; **de gran d.,** very large. 2 *fig* (*importancia*) importance.

diminutivo,-a *adj & nm* diminutive.

diminuto,-a *adj* minute, tiny.

dimisión *nm* resignation; **presentar la d.,** to hand in one's resignation.

dimitir *vi* to resign (**de,** from); **d. de un cargo,** to give in *o* tender one's resignation.

Dinamarca *n* Denmark.

dinámica *nf* dynamics *sing.*

dinámico,-a *adj* dynamic.

dinamita *nf* dynamite.

dinamitar *vtr* to dynamite.

dinamo, dínamo *nf* dynamo.

dinar *nm Fin* dinar.

dinastía *nf* dynasty.

dineral *nm fam* fortune.

dinero *nm* money; **d. contante (y sonante),** cash; **d. efectivo *o* en metálico,** cash; **gente de d.,** wealthy people.

dinosaurio *nm* dinosaur.

diócesis *nf inv* diocese.

dios *nm* god; **¡D. mío!,** my God!; **¡por D.!,** for goodness sake!; **a la buena de D.,** any old how; **hacer algo como D. manda,** to do sth properly; *arg* **ni d.,** nobody; *arg* **todo d.,** everybody.

diosa *nf* goddess.

diploma *nm* diploma.

diplomacia *nf* diplomacy.

diplomarse *vr* to graduate.

diplomático,-a I *adj* diplomatic; **cuerpo d.,** diplomatic corps. II *nm,f* diplomat.

diptongo *nm* diphthong.

diputación *nf* **d. provincial,** ≈ county council.

diputado,-a *nm,f* ≈ Member of Parliament, M.P.; *US* (*hombre*) Congressman; (*mujer*) Congresswoman; **Congreso de Diputados,** ≈ House of Commons, *US* Congress; **d. provincial,** ≈ county councillor.

dique *nm* dike.

diré *fut* → **decir.**

dirección *nf* 1 direction; **d. prohibida,** no entry; **calle de d. única,** one-way street. 2 (*señas*) address. 3 *Cin Teat* direction. 4 (*destino*) destination. 5 *Aut Téc* steering. 6 (*dirigentes*) management; (*cargo*) directorship; (*de un partido*) leadership; (*de un colegio*) headship.

directa *nf Aut* top gear.

directiva *nf* board of directors, management.

directivo,-a *adj* directive; **junta directiva,** board of directors.

directo,-a *adj* direct; *TV Rad* **en d.,** live. ◆**directamente** *adv* directly, straight away.

director,-a *nm,f* director; (*de colegio*) (*hombre*) headmaster; (*mujer*) headmistress; (*de periódico*) editor; **d. de cine,** (film) director; **d. de orquesta,** conductor; **d. gerente,** managing director.

directorio *nm Inform* directory.

directriz *nf* directive; *Mat* directrix.

dirigente I *adj* leading; **clase d.,** ruling class. II *nmf* leader.

dirigir |6| I *vtr* to direct; (*empresa*) to manage; (*negocio, colegio*) to run; (*orquesta*) to conduct; (*partido*) to lead; (*periódico*) to edit; (*coche, barco*) to steer; **d. la palabra a algn,** to speak to sb. II **dirigirse** *vr* 1 **d. a** *o* **hacia,** to go to, make one's way towards. 2 (*escribir*) to write; **diríjase al apartado de correos 42,** write to P.O. Box 42. 3 (*hablar*) to speak.

discapacidad *nf* disability.

discernir |5| *vtr* to discern.

disciplina *nf* discipline.

disciplinado,-a *adj* disciplined.

discípulo,-a *nm,f* disciple.

disco *nm* 1 disc, *US* disk; **d. de freno,** brake disc. 2 *Mús* record; **d. compacto,** compact disc. 3 *Inform* disk; **d. duro** *o* **fijo/flexible,** hard/floppy disk. 4 *Dep* discus. 5 *Tel* dial.

discográfico,-a *adj* **casa/compañía discográfica,** record company.

disconforme *adj* **estar d. con,** to disagree with.

discontinuo,-a *adj* discontinuous; *Aut* **línea discontinua,** broken line.

discordante *adj* discordant; **ser la nota d.**, to be the odd man out.

discordia *nf* discord; **la manzana de la d.**, the bone of contention; **sembrar d.**, to sow discord.

discoteca *nf* 1 (*lugar*) discotheque. 2 (*colección*) record collection.

discreción *nf* 1 discretion. 2 **a d.**, at will.

discrecional *adj* optional; **servicio d.**, special service.

discrepancia *nf* (*desacuerdo*) disagreement; (*diferencia*) discrepancy.

discrepar *vi* (*disentir*) to disagree (**de**, with; **en**, on); (*diferenciarse*) to be different (**de**, from).

discreto,-a *adj* 1 discreet. 2 (*mediocre*) average.

discriminación *nf* discrimination.

discriminar *vtr* 1 to discriminate against. 2 *fml* (*diferenciar*) to discriminate between, distinguish.

disculpa *nf* excuse; **dar disculpas**, to make excuses; **pedir disculpas a algn**, to apologize to sb.

disculpar I *vtr* to excuse. II **disculparse** *vr* to apologize (**por**, for).

discurrir *vi* 1 (*reflexionar*) to think. 2 *fig* (*transcurrir*) to pass, go by. 3 *fml* (*río*) to wander.

discurso *nm* speech; **dar** *o* **pronunciar un d.**, to make a speech.

discusión *nf* argument.

discutir I *vi* to argue (**de**, about). II *vtr* to discuss, talk about.

disecar [1] *vtr* 1 (*animal*) to stuff. 2 (*planta*) to dry.

diseminar *vtr* to disseminate, spread.

disentir [5] *vi* to dissent, disagree (**de**, with).

diseñar *vtr* to design.

diseño *nm* design; **d. de interiores**, interior design.

disertar *vi* to expound (**sobre**, on, upon).

disfraz *nm* disguise; (*para fiesta*) fancy dress; **fiesta de disfraces**, fancy dress party.

disfrazar [4] I *vtr* to disguise. II **disfrazarse** *vr* to disguise oneself; **d. de pirata**, to dress up as a pirate.

disfrutar I *vi* 1 (*gozar*) to enjoy oneself. 2 (*poseer*) to enjoy (**de**, -). II *vtr* to enjoy.

disgregar [7] *vtr* 1 to disintegrate, break up. 2 (*dispersar*) to disperse.

disgustado,-a *adj* upset, displeased.

disgustar I *vtr* to upset. II **disgustarse** *vr* 1 (*molestarse*) to get upset, be annoyed. 2 (*dos amigos*) to quarrel.

disgusto *nm* 1 (*preocupación*) upset; **llevarse un d.**, to get upset; **dar un d. a algn**, to upset sb. 2 (*desgracia*) trouble; **a d.**, unwillingly; **sentirse** *o* **estar a d.**, to feel ill at ease. 3 (*desavenencia*) fall-out.

disidente *adj & nmf* dissident.

disimulado,-a *adj* 1 (*persona*) sly, crafty.

2 (*oculto*) hidden, concealed.

◆**disimuladamente** *adv* surreptitiously.

disimular *vtr* to conceal, hide.

disimulo *nm* pretence.

disipar I *vtr* (*niebla*) to drive away; (*temor, duda*) to dispel. II **disiparse** *vr* (*gaseosa*) to go flat; (*niebla, temor etc*) to disappear.

disketera *nf Inform* disk drive.

dislexia *nf* dyslexia.

dislocar [1] *vtr* to dislocate.

disminución *nf* decrease.

disminuir [37] I *vtr* to reduce. II *vi* to diminish.

disolución *nf* dissolution.

disolvente *adj & nm* solvent.

disolver [4] (*pp disuelto*) *vtr* to dissolve.

disparar I *vtr* (*pistola etc*) to fire; (*flecha, balón*) to shoot; **d. a algn**, to shoot at sb. II **dispararse** *vr* 1 (*arma*) to go off, fire. 2 (*precios*) to rocket.

disparatado,-a *adj* absurd.

disparate *nm* 1 (*dicho*) nonsense; **decir disparates**, to talk nonsense. 2 (*acto*) foolish act.

disparidad *nf* disparity.

disparo *nm* shot; *Dep* **d. a puerta**, shot.

dispensar *vtr* 1 (*disculpar*) to pardon, forgive. 2 (*eximir*) to exempt.

dispersar I *vtr* to disperse; (*esparcir*) to scatter. II **dispersarse** *vr* to disperse.

disperso,-a *adj* (*separado*) dispersed; (*esparcido*) scattered.

displicencia *nf* condescension.

displicente *adj* condescending.

disponer [19] (*pp dispuesto*) I *vtr* 1 (*arreglar*) to arrange, set out. 2 (*ordenar*) to order. II *vi* **d. de**, to have at one's disposal. III **disponerse** *vr* to prepare, get ready.

disponible *adj* available.

disposición *nf* 1 (*uso*) disposal; **a su d.**, at your disposal *o* service. 2 (*colocación*) arrangement, layout. 3 **no estar en d. de**, not to be prepared to. 4 (*orden*) order, law.

dispositivo *nm* device.

dispuesto,-a *adj* 1 (*ordenado*) arranged. 2 (*a punto*) ready. 3 (*decidido*) determined; **no estar d. a**, not to be prepared to. 4 **según lo d. por la ley**, in accordance with what the law stipulates.

disputa *nf* (*discusión*) argument; (*contienda*) contest.

disputar I *vtr* 1 (*premio*) to compete for. 2 *Dep* (*partido*) to play. II **disputarse** *vr* (*premio*) to compete for.

disquete *nm* *Inform* diskette, floppy disk.

disquetera *nf Inform* disk drive.

distancia *nf* distance; **a d.**, from a distance.

distanciamiento *nm* distancing.

distanciar [12] I *vtr* to separate. II **distanciarse** *vr* to become separated; (*de*

otra persona) to distance oneself.
distante *adj* distant, far-off.
distar *vi* to be distant *o* away; *fig* to be far from; **dista mucho de ser perfecto**, it's far from (being) perfect.
distender [3] *vtr fig* to ease, relax.
distensión *nf Pol* détente.
distinción *nf* distinction; **a d. de**, unlike; **sin d. de**, irrespective of.
distinguido,-a *adj* distinguished.
distinguir [8] I *vtr* 1 (*diferenciar*) to distinguish. 2 (*reconocer*) to recognize. 3 (*honrar*) to honour, *US* honor. II *vi* (*diferenciar*) to discriminate. III **distinguirse** *vr* to distinguish oneself.
distintivo,-a I *adj* distinctive, distinguishing. II *nm* distinctive sign *o* mark.
distinto,-a *adj* different.
distorsión *nf* 1 distortion. 2 *Med* sprain.
distracción *nf* 1 entertainment; (*pasatiempo*) pastime, hobby. 2 (*descuido*) distraction, absent-mindedness.
distraer [25] I *vtr* 1 (*atención*) to distract. 2 (*divertir*) to entertain, amuse. II **distraerse** *vr* 1 (*divertirse*) to amuse oneself. 2 (*abstraerse*) to let one's mind wander.
distraído,-a *adj* 1 (*divertido*) entertaining. 2 (*abstraído*) absent-minded.
distribución *nf* 1 distribution. 2 (*disposición*) layout.
distribuidor,-a I *adj* distributing. II *nm,f* 1 distributor. 2 *Com* wholesaler.
distribuir [37] *vtr* to distribute; (*trabajo*) to share out.
distrito *nm* district; **d. postal**, postal district.
disturbio *nm* riot, disturbance.
disuadir *vtr* to dissuade.
disuasión *nf* dissuasion.
disuelto,-a *pp* → **disolver**.
DIU *nm abr de* **dispositivo intrauterino**, intrauterine device, IUD.
diurético,-a *adj & nm* diuretic.
diurno,-a *adj* daytime.
divagar [7] *vi* to digress, wander.
diván *nm* divan, couch.
divergencia *nf* divergence.
divergente *adj* diverging.
diversidad *nf* diversity.
diversificar [1] I *vtr* to diversify. II **diversificarse** *vr* to be diversified *o* varied; (*empresa*) to diversify.
diversión *nf* fun.
diverso,-a *adj* different; **diversos**, several, various.
divertido,-a *adj* amusing, funny.
divertir [5] I *vtr* to amuse, entertain. II **divertirse** *vr* to enjoy oneself, have a good time; **¡que te diviertas!**, enjoy yourself!, have fun!
dividendo *nm* dividend.
dividir I *vtr* to divide (**en**, into); *Mat* 15 **dividido entre 3**, 15 divided by 3. II **dividirse** *vr* to divide, split up.

divinidad *nf* divinity.
divino,-a *adj* divine.
divisa *nf* 1 (*emblema*) symbol, emblem. 2 *Com* **divisas**, foreign currency *sing*.
divisar *vtr* to make out, discern.
división *nf* division.
divisorio,-a *adj* dividing.
divorciado,-a I *adj* divorced. II *nm,f* (*hombre*) divorcé; (*mujer*) divorcée.
divorciar [12] I *vtr* to divorce. II **divorciarse** *vr* to get divorced; **se divorció de él**, she divorced him, she got a divorce from him.
divorcio *nm* divorce.
divulgación *nf* disclosure.
divulgar [7] *vtr* to disclose; *Rad TV* to broadcast.
DNI *nm abr de* **Documento Nacional de Identidad**, Identity Card, ID card.
do *nm Mús* (*de solfa*) doh, do; (*de escala diatónica*) C; **do de pecho**, high C.
doberman *nm* Doberman (pinscher).
dobladillo *nm* hem.
doblaje *nm Cin* dubbing.
doblar I *vtr* 1 to double; **me dobla la edad**, he is twice as old as I am. 2 (*plegar*) to fold *o* turn up. 3 (*torcer*) to bend. 4 (*la esquina*) to go round. 5 (*película*) to dub. II *vi* 1 (*girar*) to turn; **d. a la derecha/izquierda**, to turn right/left. 2 (*campanas*) to toll. III **doblarse** *vr* 1 (*plegarse*) to fold. 2 (*torcerse*) to bend.
doble I *adj* double; **arma de d. filo**, double-edged weapon. II *nm* 1 double; **gana el d. que tú**, she earns twice as much as you do. 2 *Dep* **dobles**, doubles.
doblegar [7] I *vtr* to bend. II **doblegarse** *vr* to give in.
doblez [2] I *nm* (*pliegue*) fold. II *nm & f fig* two-facedness, hypocrisy.
doce *adj & nm inv* twelve.
docena *nf* dozen.
docencia *nf* teaching.
docente *adj* teaching; **centro d.**, educational centre.
dócil *adj* docile.
doctor,-a *nm,f* doctor.
doctorado *nm Univ* doctorate, PhD.
doctrina *nf* doctrine.
documentación *nf* documentation; (*DNI, de conducir etc*) papers *pl*.
documental *adj & nm* documentary.
documentar I *vtr* to document. II **documentarse** *vr* to research (**sobre**, -), get information (**sobre**, about *o* on).
documento *nm* document; **d. nacional de identidad**, identity card.
dogma *nm* dogma.
dogmático,-a *adj & nm,f* dogmatic.
dogo *nm* bulldog.
dólar *nm* dollar.
dolencia *nf* ailment.
doler [4] I *vi* 1 to hurt, ache; **me duele la cabeza**, I've got toothache/a headache;

me duele la mano, my hand is sore. II **dolerse** *vr* to be sorry *o* sad.

dolido,-a *adj* estar d., to be hurt.

dolor *nm* 1 *Med* pain; **d. de cabeza,** headache; **d. de muelas,** toothache. 2 *(pena)* grief, sorrow.

dolorido,-a *adj* 1 *(dañado)* sore, aching. 2 *(apenado)* hurt.

doloroso,-a *adj* painful.

domar *vtr* to tame; *(caballo)* to break in.

domesticar |1| *vtr* to domesticate; *(animal)* to tame.

doméstico,-a *adj* domestic; **animal d.,** pet.

domiciliación *nf* payment by standing order.

domiciliar |12| *vtr* 1 to house. 2 *Fin* to pay by standing order.

domiciliario,-a *adj* **arresto d.,** house arrest.

domicilio *nm* home, residence; *(señas)* address; **sin d. fijo,** of no fixed abode; **d. fiscal,** registered office.

dominación *nf* domination.

dominante *adj* 1 dominant. 2 *(déspota)* domineering.

dominar I *vtr* 1 to dominate, rule. 2 *(situación)* to control; *(idioma)* to speak very well; *(asunto)* to master; *(paisaje etc)* to overlook. II *vi* 1 to dominate. 2 *(resaltar)* to stand out. III **dominarse** *vr* to control oneself.

domingo *nm inv* Sunday; **D. de Resurrección** *o* **Pascua,** Easter Sunday.

dominguero,-a *nm,f fam (excursionista)* weekend tripper; *(conductor)* weekend driver.

dominical I *adj* Sunday. II *nm (suplemento)* Sunday supplement.

dominicano,-a *adj & nm,f* Dominican; **República Dominicana,** Dominican Republic.

dominio *nm* 1 *(poder)* control; *(de un idioma)* command; **d. de sí mismo,** self-control. 2 *(ámbito)* scope, sphere; **ser del d. público,** to be public knowledge. 3 *(territorio)* dominion.

dominó, dómino *nm* dominoes *pl.*

don¹ *nm* 1 *(habilidad)* gift, talent; **tener el d. de,** to have a knack for; **tener d. de gentes,** to get on well with people. 2 *(regalo)* present, gift.

don² *nm* Señor D. José García, Mr José García; **D. Fulano de Tal,** Mr So-and-So; **d. nadie,** a nobody.

donaire *nm* grace, elegance.

donante *nmf* donor; *Med* **d. de sangre,** blood donor.

donar *vtr fml* to donate; *(sangre)* to give.

donativo *nm* donation.

doncella *nf arc* 1 *(joven)* maid, maiden. 2 *(criada)* maid, housemaid.

dónde *adv interr* where; ¿**de d. eres?**, where are you from?; ¿**por d. se va a la** playa?, which way is it to the beach?

donde *adv rel* where; **a** *o* **en d.,** where; **de** *o* **desde d.,** from where; **está d. lo dejaste,** it is where you left it; *fam* **está d. su tía,** he's at his aunt's.

dondequiera *adv* everywhere; **d. que vaya,** wherever I go.

donostiarra I *adj* of *o* from San Sebastián. II *nmf* native of San Sebastián.

doña *nf* (Señora) D. Leonor Benítez, Mrs Leonor Benítez.

dopaje *nm Dep* drug taking.

dopar I *vtr (caballo etc)* to dope. II **doparse** *vr* to take drugs.

doping *nm Dep* drug taking.

doquier, doquiera *adv lit* **por d.,** everywhere.

dorada *nf (pez)* gilthead bream.

dorado,-a I *adj* golden. II *nm Téc* gilding.

dorar *vtr* 1 to gild. 2 *Culin* to brown.

dormido,-a *adj* 1 asleep; **quedarse d.,** to fall asleep; *(no despertarse)* to oversleep, sleep in. 2 *(pierna, brazo)* numb.

dormilón,-ona I *adj fam* sleepyheaded. II *nm,f* sleepyhead.

dormir |7| I *vi* to sleep; **tener ganas de d.,** to feel sleepy; II *vtr* **d. la siesta,** to have an afternoon nap. III **dormirse** *vr* to fall asleep; **se me ha dormido el brazo,** my arm has gone to sleep.

dormitar *vi* to doze, snooze.

dormitorio *nm* 1 *(de una casa)* bedroom. 2 *(de colegio, residencia)* dormitory; **ciudad d.,** dormitory town.

dorsal I *adj* **espina d.,** spine. II *nm Dep* number.

dorso *nm* back; **instrucciones al d.,** instructions over; **véase al d.,** see overleaf.

dos *adj & nm inv* two; **los d.,** both; **nosotros/vosotros d.,** both of us/you; *fam* **cada d. por tres,** every other minute; *fam* **en un d. por tres,** in a flash.

doscientos,-as *adj & nm,f* two hundred.

dosel *nm* canopy.

dosificación *nf* dosage.

dosificar |1| *vtr* 1 to dose. 2 *(esfuerzos, energías)* to measure.

dosis *nf inv* dose.

dossier *nm* dossier.

dotación *nf (dinero)* grant; *(personal)* personnel, staff; *(de barco)* crew.

dotado,-a *adj* 1 *(persona)* gifted. 2 *(equipado)* equipped; **d. de,** provided with.

dotar *vtr* **d. de,** to provide with.

dote *nf* 1 *(de novia)* dowry. 2 **dotes,** *(talento)* gift *sing*, talent *sing*.

doy *indic prec* → **dar.**

DP *nm abr de* **distrito postal,** postal district, PD.

dpt. *abr de* **departamento,** department, Dept.

Dr. *abr de* **doctor,** doctor, Dr.

Dra. *abr de* **doctora,** doctor, Dr.

dragar |7| *vtr* to dredge.

dragón *nm* dragon.
drama *nm* drama.
dramático,-a *adj* dramatic.
dramatismo *nm* drama.
dramaturgo,-a *nm,f* playwright, dramatist.
drástico,-a *adj* drastic.
drenar *vtr* to drain.
driblar *vi* to dribble.
droga *nf* drug; **d. blanda/dura,** soft/hard drug.
drogadicto,-a *nm,f* drug addict.
drogar [7] **I** *vtr* to drug. **II drogarse** *vr* to drug oneself, take drugs.
droguería *nf* hardware and household goods shop.
dto. *abr de* **descuento,** discount.
dual *adj* dual.
dualidad *nf* duality.
dubitativo,-a *adj* doubtful.
Dublín *n* Dublin.
dublinés,-esa **I** *adj* of *o* from Dublin. **II** *nm,f* Dubliner.
ducha *nf* shower; **darse/tomar una d.,** to take/have a shower.
ducharse *vr* to shower, have *o* take a shower.
ducho,-a *adj* expert; **ser d. en,** to be well versed in.
duda *nf* doubt; **sin d.,** without a doubt; **no cabe d.,** (there is) no doubt; **poner algo en d.,** to question sth; **sacar a algn de dudas,** to dispel sb's doubts.
dudar **I** *vi* 1 to doubt. 2 *(vacilar)* to hesitate (**en,** to); **dudaba entre ir o quedarme,** I hesitated whether to go *o* to stay. 3 **d. de algn,** *(desconfiar)* to suspect sb. **II** *vtr* to doubt.
dudoso,-a *adj* 1 **ser d.,** *(incierto)* to be uncertain *o* doubtful. 2 *(indeciso)* to be undecided. 3 *(poco honrado)* dubious.
duelo¹ *nm (combate)* duel.
duelo² *nm (luto)* mourning.

duende *nm* 1 *(espíritu)* goblin, elf. 2 *(encanto)* magic, charm.
dueña *nf* owner; *(de pensión)* landlady.
dueño *nm* owner; *(de casa etc)* landlord; *fig* **ser d. de sí mismo,** to be self-possessed.
Duero *n* **el D.,** the Douro.
dulce **I** *adj* 1 *(sabor)* sweet. 2 *(carácter, voz)* gentle. 3 *(metal)* soft. 4 **agua d.,** fresh water. **II** *nm* 1 *Culin (pastel)* cake. 2 *(caramelo)* sweet, *US* candy.
dulzura *nf* 1 sweetness. 2 *fig* gentleness, softness.
duna *nf* dune.
dúo *nm* duet.
duodécimo,-a *adj & nm,f* twelfth.
dúplex *nm* 1 *(piso)* duplex, duplex apartment. 2 *Telec* linkup.
duplicado,-a **I** *adj* **por d.,** in duplicate. **II** *nm* duplicate, copy.
duplicar [1] **I** *vtr* to duplicate; *(cifras)* to double. **II duplicarse** *vr* to double.
duplo,-a *adj & nm,f* double.
duque *nm* duke.
duquesa *nf* duchess.
duración *nf* duration, length; **disco de larga d.,** long-playing record.
duradero,-a *adj* durable, lasting.
durante *prep* during; **d. el día,** during the day; **d. todo el día,** all day long; **viví en La Coruña d. un año,** I lived in La Coruña for a year.
durar *vi* 1 to last. 2 *(ropa, calzado)* to wear well, last.
durazno *nm (fruto)* peach; *(árbol)* peach tree.
dureza *nf* 1 hardness; *(severidad)* harshness, severity. 2 *(callosidad)* corn.
duro,-a **I** *adj* 1 hard; *Dep* **juego d.,** rough play. 2 *(resistente)* tough; *(severo)* hard. 3 *(clima)* harsh. **II** *nm (moneda)* five-peseta coin. **III** *adv* hard; **trabajar d.,** to work hard.

E

E, e |e| *nf (la letra)* E, e.
E *abr de* **Este,** East, E.
e *conj (delante de palabras que empiecen por i o hi)* and; **verano e invierno,** summer and winter.
ebanista *nm* cabinet-maker.
ébano *nm* ebony.
ebrio,-a *adj* inebriated; **e. de dicha,** drunk with joy.
ebullición *nf* boiling; **punto de e.,** boiling point.
eccema *nm* eczema.
echar **I** *vtr* 1 *(lanzar)* to throw; *fig* **e. una mano,** to give a hand; *fig* **e. una mirada/una ojeada,** to have a look/a quick look *o*

glance. 2 *(carta)* to post; *(vino, agua)* to pour; **e. sal al estofado,** to put salt in the stew; **e. gasolina al coche,** to put petrol in the car. 3 *(expulsar)* to throw out; *(despedir)* to sack, fire. 4 *(humo, olor etc)* to give off. 5 *fam (película)* to show. 6 **le echó 37 años,** he reckoned she was about 37. 7 **e. de menos *o* en falta,** to miss. 8 **e. abajo,** *(edificio)* to demolish.
II *vi* (+ **a** + *infin) (empezar)* to begin to; **echó a correr,** he ran off.
III echarse *vr* 1 *(tumbarse)* to lie down; *(lanzarse)* to throw oneself; *fig* **la noche se nos echó encima,** it was night before we knew it. 2 **échate a un lado,** stand

aside; *fig* **e. atrás,** to get cold feet. **3** *fam*
e. novio/novia, to get a boyfriend/
girlfriend. **4** (+ **a** + *infin*) (*empezar*) to
begin to; **e. a llorar,** to burst into tears;
e. a reír, to burst out laughing; **e. a perder,** (*comida*) to go bad.

ecléctico,-a *adj & nm,f* eclectic.

eclesiástico,-a I *adj* ecclesiastical. **II** *nm*
clergyman.

eclipsar *vtr* to eclipse.

eclipse *nm* eclipse.

eco *nm* echo; *fig* **hacerse e. de una noticia,** to publish an item of news; **tener e.,**
to arouse interest.

ecografía *nf* scan.

ecología *nf* ecology.

ecológico,-a *adj* ecological.

ecologista I *adj* ecological; *Pol* **partido
e.,** ecology party. **II** *nmf* ecologist.

economía *nf* **1** economy; **con e.,** econo-
mically. **2** (*ciencia*) economics.

económico,-a *adj* **1** economic. **2** (*barato*)
economical, inexpensive. **3** (*persona*)
thrifty.

economista *nmf* economist.

economizar |4| *vtr & vi* to economize.

ecosistema *nm* ecosystem.

ecuación *nf* equation.

Ecuador *n* Ecuador.

ecuador *nm Geog* equator.

ecualizador *nm* graphic equalizer.

ecuánime *adj* **1** (*temperamento*) equable,
even-tempered. **2** (*juicio*) impartial.

ecuatorial *adj* equatorial; **Guinea E.,**
Ecuatorial Guinea.

ecuatoriano,-a *adj & nm,f* Ecuadorian.

ecuestre *adj* equestrian.

ecuménico,-a *adj* ecumenical.

eczema *nm* eczema.

edad *nf* age; **¿qué e. tienes?,** how old are
you?; **la tercera e.,** senior citizens *pl*; **E.
Media,** Middle Ages *pl*.

edición *nf* **1** (*publicación*) publication; (*de
sellos*) issue. **2** (*conjunto de ejemplares*) edition.

edicto *nm* edict, proclamation.

edificante *adj* edifying.

edificar |1| *vtr* to build.

edificio *nm* building.

edil,-a *nm,f* town councillor.

Edimburgo *n* Edinburgh.

editar *vtr* **1** (*libro, periódico*) to publish;
(*disco*) to release. **2** *Inform* to edit.

editor,-a I *adj* publishing. **II** *nm,f* publisher.

editorial I *adj* publishing. **II** *nf* publishers, publishing house. **III** *nm Prensa*
editorial, leader article.

edredón *nm* continental quilt, duvet, *US*
comforter.

educación *nf* **1** education. **2** (*formación*)
upbringing. **3 buena/mala e.,** (*modales*)
good/bad manners; **falta de e.,** bad manners.

educado,-a *adj* polite.

educador,-a I *adj* educating. **II** *nm,f* edu-
cationalist.

educar |1| *vtr* (*hijos*) to raise; (*alumnos*) to
educate; (*la voz*) to train.

educativo,-a *adj* educational; **sistema e.,**
education system.

edulcorante *nm* sweetener.

EE.UU. *abr de* **Estados Unidos,** United
States of America, USA.

efectista *adj* spectacular.

efectividad *nf* effectiveness.

efectivo,-a I *adj* effective; **hacer algo e.,**
to carry sth out; *Fin* **hacer e. un cheque,**
to cash a cheque. **II** *nm* **1** *Fin* **en e.,** in
cash. **2 efectivos,** *Mil* forces.
◆**efectivamente** *adv* quite!, yes indeed!

efecto *nm* **1** (*resultado*) effect; **efectos
especiales/sonoros,** special/sound
effects; **efectos personales,** personal belongings *o* effects; **a efectos de ...,** for
the purposes of ...; **en e.,** quite!, yes indeed! **2** (*impresión*) impression; **causar *o*
hacer e.,** to make an impression. **3** *Dep*
spin.

efectuar |30| *vtr* to carry out; (*viaje*) to
make; *Com* (*pedido*) to place.

efeméride *nf* event.

efervescente *adj* effervescent; **aspirina
e.,** soluble aspirin.

eficacia *nf* (*de persona*) efficiency; (*de remedio etc*) effectiveness.

eficaz *adj* (*persona*) efficient; (*remedio, medida etc*) effective.

eficiencia *nf* efficiency.

eficiente *adj* efficient.

efigie *nf* effigy.

efímero,-a *adj* ephemeral.

efusivo,-a *adj* effusive.

EGB *nf Educ abr de* **Enseñanza General
Básica,** ≈ Primary School Education.

Egeo *n* **el (Mar) E.,** the Aegean Sea.

egipcio,-a *adj & nm,f* Egyptian.

Egipto *n* Egypt.

egocéntrico,-a *adj* egocentric, self-
centred.

egoísmo *nm* egoism, selfishness.

egoísta I *adj* ego(t)istic, selfish. **II** *nmf*
ego(t)ist, selfish person.

egregio,-a *adj* eminent, illustrious.

egresar *vi Am* to leave school, *US* graduate.

Eire *n* Eire, Republic of Ireland.

ej. *abr de* **ejemplo,** example.

eje *nm* **1** *Téc* (*de rueda*) axle; (*de máquina*)
shaft. **2** *Mat* axis. **3** *Hist* **El E.,** the Axis.

ejecución *nf* **1** (*de orden*) carrying out. **2**
(*ajusticiamiento*) execution. **3** *Mús*
performance.

ejecutar *vtr* **1** (*orden*) to carry out. **2**
(*ajusticiar*) to execute. **3** *Mús* to perform,
play. **4** *Inform* to run.

ejecutiva *nf Pol* executive.

ejecutivo,-a I *adj* executive; *Pol* **el poder e.**, the government. **II** *nm* executive.

ejecutor,-a *nm,f* **1** *Jur* executor. **2** *(verdugo)* executioner.

ejemplar I *nm* **1** *(de libro)* copy; *(de revista, periódico)* number, issue. **2** *(especimen)* specimen. **II** *adj* exemplary, model.

ejemplificar [1] *vtr* to exemplify.

ejemplo *nm* example; **por e.**, for example; **dar e.**, to set an example.

ejercer [2] **I** *vtr* **1** *(profesión etc)* to practise. **2** *(influencia)* to exert. **3 e. el derecho de/a ...**, to exercise one's right to .... **II** *vi* to practise **(de, as)**.

ejercicio *nm* **1** exercise; *(de profesión)* practice; **hacer e.**, to take *o* do exercise. **2** *Fin* tax year; **e. económico**, financial *o* fiscal year.

ejercitar *vtr* to practise.

ejército *nm* army.

el I *art def m* **1** the. **2** *(no se traduce)* **el Sr. García**, Mr. Garcia; **el hambre/destino**, hunger/fate. **3** *(con partes del cuerpo, prendas de vestir)* **me he cortado el dedo**, I've cut my finger; **métetelo en el bolsillo**, put it in your pocket. **4** *(con días de la semana)* **el lunes**, on Monday. **II** *pron* **1** the one; **el de las once**, the eleven o'clock one; **el que tienes en la mano**, the one you've got in your hand; **el que quieras**, whichever one you want. **2** *(no se traduce)* **el de tu amigo**, your friend's.

él *pron pers* **1** *(sujeto)* *(persona)* he; *(animal, cosa)* it. **2** *(complemento)* *(persona)* him; *(animal, cosa)* it.

elaboración *nf* **1** *(de un producto)* manufacture, production. **2** *(de una idea)* working out, development.

elaborar *vtr* **1** *(producto)* to manufacture, produce. **2** *(teoría)* to develop.

elasticidad *nf* elasticity; *fig* flexibility.

elástico,-a *adj & nm* elastic.

elección *nf* choice; *Pol* election.

elector,-a *nm,f* elector.

electorado *nm* electorate *pl.*

electoral *adj* electoral; **campaña e.**, election campaign; **colegio e.**, polling station.

electoralismo *nm* electioneering.

electricidad *nf* electricity.

electricista *nmf* electrician.

eléctrico,-a *adj* electric.

electrificar [1] *vtr* to electrify.

electrizar [4] *vtr* to electrify.

electrochoque *nm* electric shock therapy.

electrocutar *vtr* to electrocute.

electrodo *nm* electrode.

electrodoméstico *nm* (domestic) electrical appliance.

electroimán *nm* electromagnet.

electromagnético,-a *adj* electromagnetic.

electrón *nm* electron.

electrónica *nf* electronics *sing.*

electrónico,-a *adj* electronic.

elefante *nm* elephant.

elegancia *nf* elegance.

elegante *adj* elegant.

elegía *nf* elegy.

elegir [6] *vtr* **1** to choose. **2** *Pol* to elect.

elemental *adj* **1** *(fundamental)* basic, fundamental. **2** *(simple)* elementary.

elemento *nm* **1** element. **2** *(componente)* component, part. **3** *(individuo)* type, individual. **4 elementos**, elements; *(fundamentos)* rudiments.

elepé *nm* LP (record).

elevación *nf* elevation; **e. de precios**, rise in prices; **e. del terreno**, rise in the ground.

elevado,-a *adj* **1** high; *(edificio)* tall. **2** *(pensamiento etc)* lofty, noble.

elevalunas *nm inv Aut* **e. eléctrico**, electric windows.

elevar I *vtr* to raise. **II elevarse** *vr* **1** *(subir)* to rise; *(edificio)* to stand. **2 e. a**, *(cantidad)* to amount *o* come to.

elijo *indic pres* → **elegir**.

eliminación *nf* elimination.

eliminar *vtr* to eliminate.

eliminatoria *nf Dep* heat, qualifying round.

eliminatorio,-a *adj* qualifying, eliminatory.

élite *nf* elite, élite.

elitista *adj* elitist.

elixir *nm* *(enjuage bucal)* mouthwash; *Lit* elixir.

ella *pron pers f* **1** *(sujeto)* she; *(animal, cosa)* it, she. **2** *(complemento)* her; *(animal, cosa)* it, her.

ellas *pron pers fpl* → **ellos**.

ello *pron pers neut* it; **por e.**, for that reason.

ellos *pron pers mpl* **1** *(sujeto)* they. **2** *(complemento)* them.

elocuencia *nf* eloquence.

elocuente *adj* eloquent; **los hechos son elocuentes**, the facts speak for themselves.

elogiar [12] *vtr* to praise.

elogio *nm* praise.

elote *nm Am* tender corncob.

El Salvador *n* El Salvador.

elucidar *vtr* to elucidate.

eludir *vtr* to avoid.

emanar *vi* to emanate; *fig* *(derivar)* to derive *o* come (**de**, from).

emancipar I *vtr* to emancipate. **II emanciparse** *vr* to become emancipated.

embadurnar *vtr* to daub, smear (**de**, with).

embajada *nf* embassy.

embajador,-a *nm,f* ambassador.

embalaje *nm* packing, packaging.

embalar *vtr* to pack.

embalarse *vr* to speed up; *fig* **no te embales**, hold your horses.

embalsamar *vtr* to embalm.

embalsar I *vtr* to dam; *(problema)* to contain. **II embalsarse** *vr* to form a pool.

embalse *nm* dam, reservoir.

embarazada I *adj* pregnant; **dejar e.,** to get pregnant. **II** *nf* pregnant woman, expectant mother.

embarazar |4| *vtr fig* to hinder.

embarazo *nm* **1** *(preñez)* pregnancy. **2** *(obstáculo)* obstacle. **3** *(turbación)* embarrassment.

embarazoso,-a *adj* awkward, embarrassing.

embarcación *nf* **1** *(nave)* boat, craft. **2** *(embarco)* embarkation.

embarcadero *nm* quay.

embarcar |1| **I** *vtr* to ship. **II** *vi* to embark, go on board. **III embarcarse** *vr* **1** *Naut* to go on board (**en,** -); *Av* to board (**en,** -). **2 e. en un proyecto,** to embark on a project.

embarco *nm* embarkation.

embargar |7| *vtr* **1** *Jur* to seize, impound. **2** *fig* **le embarga la emoción,** he's overwhelmed with joy.

embargo *nm* **1** *Jur* seizure of property. **2** *Com Pol* embargo. **3 sin e.,** however, nevertheless.

embarque *nm (de persona)* boarding; *(de mercancías)* loading; **tarjeta de e.,** boarding card.

embarrancar(se) |1| *vi & vr Náut* to run aground.

embaucador,-a I *adj* deceitful. **II** *nm,f* swindler, cheat.

embaucar |1| *vtr* to swindle, cheat.

embeber I *vtr* to soak up. **II embeberse** *vr* to become absorbed *o* engrossed.

embelesar *vtr* to fascinate.

embellecer |33| *vtr* to embellish.

embestida *nf* **1** onslaught. **2** *Taur* charge.

embestir |6| *vtr* **1** *Taur* to charge. **2** *(atacar)* to attack.

emblandecer |33| **I** *vtr* to soften. **II emblandecerse** *vr fig* to relent.

emblema *nm* emblem.

embobado,-a *adj* fascinated.

embobarse *vr* to be fascinated *o* besotted (**con, de,** by).

embolia *nf* embolism.

émbolo *nm* piston.

embolsar *vtr,* **embolsarse** *vr* to pocket.

emborrachar *vtr,* **emborracharse** *vr* to get drunk.

emboscada *nf* ambush; **tender una e.,** to lay an ambush.

embotar *vtr* to blunt; *fig (sentidos)* to dull; *(mente)* to befuddle.

embotellado *nm* bottling.

embotellamiento *nm Aut* traffic jam.

embotellar *vtr* **1** to bottle. **2** *(tráfico)* to block.

embragar |7| *vi Aut* to engage the clutch.

embrague *nm* clutch.

embravecerse |33| *vr* **1** *(enfadarse)* to become enraged. **2** *(mar)* to become rough.

embriagador,-a *adj* intoxicating.

embriagar |7| **I** *vtr* to intoxicate; *fig* to enrapture. **II embriagarse** *vr* to get drunk; *fig* to be enraptured.

embriaguez *nf* intoxication.

embridar *vtr* to bridle.

embrión *nm* embryo.

embrollar I *vtr* to confuse, muddle. **II embrollarse** *vr* to get muddled *o* confused.

embrollo *nm* **1** *(lío)* muddle, confusion. **2** *(aprieto)* fix, jam.

embrujado,-a *adj (persona)* bewitched; *(sitio)* haunted.

embrujo *nm* spell, charm; *fig* attraction, fascination.

embrutecer |33| *vtr* to stultify..

embuchar *vtr* to stuff.

embudo *nm* funnel.

embuste *nm* lie, trick.

embustero,-a *nm,f* cheater, liar.

embutido *nm* sausage.

embutir I *vtr* **1** *(carne)* to stuff. **2** *(meter)* to stuff *o* cram *o* squeeze (**en,** into). **3** *(incrustar)* to inlay.

emergencia *nf* emergency; **salida de e.,** emergency exit; **en caso de e.,** in an emergency.

emerger |5| *vi* to emerge.

emigración *nf* emigration; *(de pájaros)* migration.

emigrado,-a *nm,f* emigrant; *Pol* émigré.

emigrante *adj & nmf* emigrant.

emigrar *vi* to emigrate; *(pájaros)* to migrate.

eminencia *nf* eminence; *(genio)* genius.

eminente *adj* eminent.

emirato *nm* emirate.

emisario,-a *nm,f* emissary.

emisión *nf* **1** emission. **2** *(de bonos, sellos)* issue. **3** *Rad TV* broadcasting.

emisora *nf* radio *o* television station.

emitir *vtr* **1** to emit; *(luz, calor)* to give off. **2** *(opinión, juicio)* to express. **3** *Rad TV* to transmit. **4** *(bonos, sellos)* to issue.

emoción *nf* **1** emotion. **2** *(excitación)* excitement; **¡qué e.!,** how exciting!

emocionado,-a *adj* deeply moved *o* touched.

emocionante *adj* **1** *(conmovedor)* moving, touching. **2** *(excitante)* exciting, thrilling.

emocionar I *vtr* **1** *(conmover)* to move, touch. **2** *(excitar)* to thrill. **II emocionarse** *vr* **1** *(conmoverse)* to be moved. **2** *(excitarse)* to get excited.

emotivo,-a *adj* emotional.

empacar |1| *vtr* **1** *(mercancías)* to pack. **2** *Am* to annoy.

empachar *vtr* to give indigestion to.

empacho *nm (de comida)* indigestion, upset stomach; *fig* surfeit.

empadronar *vtr,* **empadronarse** *vr* to register.

empalagar [7] *vi* to pall.
empalagoso,-a *adj* 1 *(dulce)* sickly sweet. 2 *fig (persona)* smarmy.
empalizada *nf* fence.
empalmar I *vtr* 1 *(unir)* to join; *(cuerdas, cables)* to splice. 2 *Ftb* to volley. II *vi* to converge; *Ferroc* to connect. III **empalmarse** *vr vulg* to get a hard-on.
empalme *nm* 1 connection. 2 *Ferroc* junction; *(en carretera)* intersection, T-junction.
empanada *nf* pie.
empanadilla *nf* pasty.
empanado,-a *adj (filete etc)* breaded, in breadcrumbs.
empantanarse *vr* 1 *(inundarse)* to become flooded. 2 *fig* to be bogged down.
empañar *vtr*, **empañarse** *vr (cristales)* to steam up.
empapado,-a *adj* soaked.
empapar I *vtr* 1 *(mojar)* to soak. 2 *(absorber)* to soak up. II **empaparse** *vr* 1 *(persona)* to get soaked. 3 *fam fig* to take in (**de**, -).
empapelar *vtr* to wallpaper.
empaque *nm* bearing, presence.
empaquetar *vtr* to pack.
emparedado *nm* sandwich.
emparejar *vtr (cosas)* to match; *(personas)* to pair off.
empastar *vtr (diente)* to fill.
empaste *nm (de diente)* filling.
empatado,-a *adj* drawn; **estar/ir empatados**, to be drawing.
empatar I *vi Dep* to tie, draw. II *vtr* 1 *Dep* **e. el partido**, to equalize. 2 *Am (unir)* to join.
empate *nm Dep* draw, tie.
empecinarse *vr* to dig one's heels in.
empedernido,-a *adj (fumador, bebedor)* hardened.
empedrado,-a I *adj* cobbled. III *nm* 1 *(adoquines)* cobblestones *pl*. 2 *(acción)* paving.
empeine *nm* instep.
empellón *nm* push, shove.
empeñar I *vtr* to pawn, *US* hock. II **empeñarse** *vr* 1 *(insistir)* to insist (**en**, on), be determined (**en**, to). 2 *(endeudarse)* to get into debt.
empeño *nm* 1 *(insistencia)* insistence; **poner e. en algo**, to put a lot of effort into sth. 2 *(deuda)* pledge; **casa de empeños**, pawnshop.
empeoramiento *nm* deterioration, worsening.
empeorar I *vi* to deteriorate, worsen. II *vtr* to make worse. III **empeorarse** *vr* to deteriorate, worsen.
empequeñecer [33] *vtr fig* to belittle.
emperador *nm* emperor.
emperatriz *nf* empress.
emperifollarse *vr fam* to get dolled up.
emperrarse *vr* to dig one's heels in, be-come stubborn.

empezar [1] *vtr & vi (a hacer algo)* to be-gin; *(algo)* to start, commence.
empinado,-a *adj (cuesta)* steep.
empinar I *vtr* to raise; *fam* **e. el codo**, to drink. II **empinarse** *vr (persona)* to stand on tiptoe.
empírico,-a *adj* empirical.
emplasto *nm* poultice.
emplazamiento *nm* 1 *(colocación)* site, lo-cation. 2 *Jur* summons *sing*.
emplazar¹ [4] *vtr* to locate, situate.
emplazar² [4] *vtr* 1 *Jur* to summons. 2 *(a una reunión etc)* to call.
empleado,-a *nm,f* employee; *(de oficina, banco)* clerk; **empleada del hogar**, servant, maid.
emplear *vtr* 1 *(usar)* to use; *(contratar)* to employ. 2 *(dinero, tiempo)* to spend.
empleo *nm* 1 *(oficio)* job; *Pol* employ-ment. 2 *(uso)* use; **modo de e.**, instruc-tions for use.
emplomar *vtr Am (diente)* to fill.
empobrecer [33] I *vi* to impoverish. II **empobrecerse** *vr* to become impover-ished *o* poor.
empobrecimiento *nm* impoverishment.
empollar *vtr* 1 *(huevos)* to sit on. 2 *fam (estudiar)* to swot (up), *US* bone up on.
empollón,-ona *fam* I *adj* swotty. II *nm,f* swot.
empolvar I *vtr* to cover in dust. II **empolvarse** *vr (la cara)* to powder.
emponzoñar *vtr* to poison.
emporcar [1] *vtr* to foul, dirty.
emporio *nm* 1 *Com* emporium, trading *o* commercial centre. 2 *Am* department store.
emporrarse *vr arg* to get high.
empotrado,-a *adj* fitted.
emprendedor,-a *adj* enterprising.
emprender *vtr* to undertake; *fam* **em-prenderla con algn**, to pick on sb.
empresa *nf* 1 *Com Ind* firm, company. 2 *Pol* **la libre e.**, free enterprise. 3 *(tarea)* undertaking.
empresariado *nm* employers *pl*.
empresarial *adj* 1 *(de empresa)* business; **(ciencias) empresariales**, business stu-dies. 2 *(espíritu) entrepreneurial*; **organiza-ción e.**, employers' organization.
empresario,-a *nm,f* 1 *(hombre)* business-man; *(mujer)* businesswoman. 2 *(patrón)* employer.
empréstito *nm Fin* debenture loan.
empujar *vtr* to push, shove.
empuje *nm* push; *fig (brío)* verve, get-up-and-go.
empujón *nm* push, shove; **dar empujo-nes**, to push and shove.
empuñadura *nf (de espada)* hilt.
empuñar *vtr* to grasp, seize.
emular *vtr* to emulate.
emulsión *nf* emulsion.

en prep 1 (posición) in, on, at; **en Madrid/ Bolivia**, in Madrid/Bolivia; **en la mesa**, on the table; **en el bolso**, in the bag; **en casa/el trabajo**, at home/work. 2 (movimiento) into; **entró en el cuarto**, he went into the room. 3 (tiempo) in, on, at; **en 1940**, in 1940; **en verano**, in summer; **Am en la mañana**, in the morning; **cae en martes**, it falls on a Tuesday; **en ese momento**, at that moment. 3 (transporte) by, in; **en coche/tren**, by car/train; **en avión**, by air. 4 (modo) **en español**, in Spanish; **en broma**, jokingly; **en serio**, seriously. 5 (reducción, aumento) by; **los precios aumentaron en un diez por ciento**, the prices went up by ten percent. 6 (tema, materia) at, in; **bueno en deportes**, good at sports; **experto en política**, expert in politics. 7 (división, separación) in; **lo dividió en tres partes**, he divided it in three. 8 (con infinitivo) **fue rápido en responder**, he was quick to answer; **la conocí en el andar**, I recognized her by her walk; **ser sobrio en el vestir**, to dress simply.

enaguas nfpl underskirt sing, petticoat sing.

enajenación nf, **enajenamiento** nm alienation; **e. mental**, mental derangement, insanity.

enajenar I vtr 1 Jur to alienate. 2 (turbar) to drive insane. II **enajenarse** vr (enloquecer) to go insane.

enaltecer [33] vtr 1 (alabar) to praise, extol. 2 (ennoblecer) to do credit to.

enamorado,-a I adj in love. II nm,f person in love.

enamorar I vtr to win the heart of. II **enamorarse** vr to fall in love (**de**, with).

enano,-a adj & nm,f dwarf.

enardecer [33] I vtr (sentimientos) to rouse, stir up; (persona) to fill with enthusiasm. II **enardecerse** vr fig to become excited.

encabezamiento nm (de carta) heading; (de periódico) headline; (preámbulo) foreword, preamble.

encabezar [4] vtr 1 (carta, lista) to head; (periódico) to lead. 2 (rebelión, carrera, movimiento) to lead.

encabritarse vr 1 (caballo) to rear (up). 2 fig (persona) to get cross.

encadenar vtr to chain.

encajar I vtr 1 (ajustar) to insert; **e. la puerta**, to push the door to. 2 fam (asimilar) to take. 3 (comentario) to get in; **e. un golpe a algn**, to land sb a blow. II vi 1 (ajustarse) to fit. 2 fig **e. con**, to fit (in) with, square with.

encaje nm lace.

encalar vtr to whitewash.

encallar vi 1 Náut to run aground. 2 fig to flounder, fail.

encaminado,-a adj **estar bien/mal e.**, to be on the right/wrong track.

encaminar I vtr to direct. II **encaminarse** vr to head (**a**, for; **hacia**, towards).

encandilar vtr to dazzle.

encantado,-a adj 1 (contento) delighted; **e. de conocerle**, pleased to meet you. 2 (embrujado) enchanted.

encantador,-a I adj charming, delightful. II nm,f magician.

encantamiento nm spell.

encantar vtr (hechizar) to bewitch, cast a spell on; fig **me encanta nadar**, I love swimming.

encanto nm 1 (atractivo) charm; **ser un e.**, to be charming. 2 (hechizo) spell.

encapricharse vr to set one's mind (**con**, on); (encariñarse) to take a fancy (**con**, to); (enamorarse) to get a crush (**con**, on).

encapuchado,-a adj hooded.

encaramarse vr to climb up.

encarar I vtr to face, confront. II **encararse** vr **e. con**, to face up to.

encarcelar vtr to imprison, jail.

encarecer [33] I vtr to put up the price of. II **encarecerse** vr to go up (in price).

encarecidamente adv earnestly, insistently; **le rogamos e. que ...**, we would earnestly request you to ....

encarecimiento nm increase o rise in price.

encargado,-a I nm,f Com (hombre) manager; (mujer) manager, manageress; (responsable) person in charge. II adj in charge.

encargar [7] I vtr 1 to put in charge of, entrust with. 2 Com (mercancías) to order, place an order for; (encuesta) to commission. II **encargarse** vr **e. de**, to see to, deal with.

encargo nm 1 Com order; **hecho de e.**, (a petición) made to order. 2 (recado) errand. 3 (tarea) job, assignment.

encariñarse vr to become fond (**con**, of), get attached (**con**, to).

encarnación nf incarnation, embodiment.

encarnado,-a adj (rojo) red.

encarnar vtr to personify, embody.

encarnizado,-a adj fierce.

encarrilar vtr (coche, tren) to put on the road o rails; fig to put on the right track.

encasillar vtr to pigeonhole.

encausar vtr to prosecute.

encauzar [4] vtr to channel.

encenagarse [7] vr to get covered in mud.

encendedor nm lighter.

encender [3] I vtr 1 (luz, radio, tele) to switch on, put on; (cigarro, vela, fuego) to light; (cerilla) to strike, light. 2 fig to inflame, stir up. II **encenderse** vr 1 (fuego) to catch; (luz) to go o come on. 2 (cara) to blush, go red.

encendido nm ignition.

encerado nm (pizarra) blackboard.

encerar *vtr* to wax, polish.

encerrar |1| I *vtr* 1 to shut in; *(con llave)* to lock in. 2 *fig (contener)* to contain, include. II **encerrarse** *vr* to shut oneself up *o* in; *(con llave)* to lock oneself in.

encestar *vi Dep* to score (a basket).

enchaquetado,-a *adj* smartly dressed.

encharcar |1| I *vtr* to flood, swamp. II **encharcarse** *vr* to get flooded.

enchilada *nf Culin* stuffed corn pancake seasoned with chili.

enchironar *vtr arg* to put away.

enchufado,-a I *adj fam* estar e., to have good connections *o* contacts. III *nm,f fam (favorito)* pet.

enchufar *vtr* 1 *Elec* to plug in. 2 *(unir)* to join, connect. 3 *fam (para un trabajo)* to pull strings for.

enchufe *nm* 1 *Elec (hembra)* socket; *(macho)* plug. 2 *fam* contact.

enchufismo *nm fam* string-pulling.

encía *nf* gum.

enciclopedia *nf* encyclopaedia, encyclopedia.

encierro *nm Pol (protesta)* sit-in.

encima *adv* 1 on top; *(arriba)* above; *(en el aire)* overhead; **déjalo e.**, put it on top; **¿llevas cambio e.?**, do you have any change on you?; *fig* **quitarse algo de e.**, to get rid of sth; **ahí e.**, up there. 2 *(además)* besides. 3 **e. de**, *(sobre)* on; *(en el aire)* above; *fig (además)* besides; **e. de la mesa**, on the table. 4 **por e.**, above; *fig* **por e. de sus posibilidades**, beyond his abilities; **leer un libro por e.**, to skip through a book.

encimera *nf (de cocina)* worktop.

encina *nf* holm *o* evergreen oak, ilex.

encinta *adj* pregnant.

enclaustrarse *vr* to shut oneself up.

enclave *nm* enclave.

enclenque *adj (débil)* puny; *(enfermizo)* sickly.

encoger [5] I *vi (contraerse)* to contract; *(prenda)* to shrink. II *vtr* to contract; *(prenda)* to shrink. III **encogerse** *vr (contraerse)* to contract; *(prenda)* to shrink; **e. de hombros**, to shrug (one's shoulders).

encolar *vtr (papel)* to paste; *(madera)* to glue.

encolerizar [4] I *vtr* to infuriate, anger. II **encolerizarse** *vr* to become furious.

encomendar |1| I *vtr* to entrust with, put in charge of. II **encomendarse** *vr* to entrust oneself (a, to).

encomienda 1 *nf* assignment, mission. 2 *(paquete postal)* parcel.

encomio *nm* praise.

enconado,-a *adj (discusión)* bitter, fierce. 2 *Med* inflamed, sore.

enconarse *vr* 1 *(exasperarse)* to get angry *o* irritated. 2 *Med (herida)* to become inflamed *o* sore.

encono *nm* spitefulness, ill feeling.

encontrado,-a *adj (contrario)* conflicting.

encontrar |2| I *vtr* 1 *(hallar)* to find; **no lo encuentro**, I can't find it; **lo encuentro muy agradable**, I find it very pleasant. 2 *(dar con)* to meet; *(problema)* to run into, come up against. II **encontrarse** *vr* 1 *(persona)* to meet. 2 *(sentirse)* to feel, be; **e. a gusto**, to feel comfortable. 3 *(estar)* to be.

encontronazo *nm* 1 *(choque)* collision, crash. 2 *fig (de ideas etc)* clash.

encorvar I *vtr* to bend. II **encorvarse** *vr* to stoop *o* bend (over).

encrespar I *vtr* 1 *(pelo)* to curl. 2 *(mar)* to make choppy *o* rough. 3 *fig (enfurecer)* to infuriate. II **encresparse** *vr* 1 *(mar)* to get rough. 2 *fig (enfurecerse)* to get cross *o* irritated.

encrucijada *nf* crossroads.

encrudecer |33| *vi*, **encrudecerse** *vr* to get worse.

encuadernación *nf* 1 *(oficio)* bookbinding. 2 *(cubierta)* binding.

encuadernador,-a *nm,f* bookbinder.

encuadernar *vtr* to bind.

encuadrar *vtr* 1 *(imagen etc)* to frame. 2 *fig (encajar)* to fit, insert.

encuadre *nm Cin TV* framing.

encubierto,-a *adj (secreto)* hidden; *(operación)* covert.

encubridor,-a *nm,f Jur* accessory (after the fact), abettor.

encubrir *vtr* to conceal.

encuentro *nm* 1 encounter, meeting. 2 *Dep* meeting; match; **e. amistoso**, friendly match.

encuesta *nf* 1 *(sondeo)* (opinion) poll, survey. 2 *(investigación)* investigation, inquiry.

encuestador,-a *nm,f* pollster.

encuestar *vtr* to poll.

encumbrar I *vtr* to exalt. II **encumbrarse** *vr* to rise to a high (social) position.

ende (por) *loc adv* therefore.

endeble *adj* weak, feeble.

endeblez *nf* weakness, feebleness.

endémico,-a *adj Med* endemic; *fig* chronic.

endemoniado,-a *adj* 1 *(poseso)* possessed. 2 *fig (travieso)* mischievous.

enderezar [4] I *vtr (poner derecho)* to straighten out; *(poner vertical)* to set upright. II **enderezarse** *vr* to straighten up.

endeudarse *vr* to get *o* fall into debt.

endiablado,-a *adj* 1 *(poseso)* possessed. 2 *(travieso)* mischievous, devilish.

endibia *nf* endive.

endiosar *vtr* to deify.

endomingarse |7| *vr fam* to put on one's Sunday best.

endosar *vtr* 1 *(cheque)* to endorse. 2 *fam (tarea)* to lumber with.

endrina *nf Bot* sloe.

endrogarse |7| *vr Am* to take drugs, use drugs.

endulzar |4| *vtr* to sweeten.

endurecer |33| I *vtr* to harden. II **endurecerse** *vr* to harden, become hard.

enebro *nm* juniper.

enema *nm* enema.

enemigo,-a I *adj* enemy; **soy e. de la bebida**, I'm against drink. II *nm,f* enemy.

enemistad *nf* hostility, enmity.

enemistar I *vtr* to set at odds, cause a rift between. II **enemistarse** *vr* to become enemies; **e. con algn**, to fall out with sb.

energético,-a *adj* energy.

energía *nf* energy; **e. hidráulica/nuclear**, hydro-electric/nuclear power; *fig* **e. vital**, vitality.

enérgico,-a *adj* energetic; *(decisión)* firm; *(tono)* emphatic.

energúmeno,-a *nm,f fam (hombre)* madman; *(mujer)* mad woman; **ponerse como un e.**, to go up the wall.

enero *nm* January.

enervante *adj* enervating.

enervar *vtr* to enervate.

enésimo,-a *adj* 1 *Mat* nth. 2 *fam* umpteenth; **por enésima vez**, for the umpteenth time.

enfadado,-a *adj* angry, annoyed, *US* mad; **estamos enfadados**, we've fallen out with each other.

enfadar I *vtr* to make angry *o* annoyed. II **enfadarse** *vr* 1 to get angry (**con**, with). 2 *(dos personas)* to fall out.

enfado *nm* anger; *(desavenencia)* fall-out.

enfangarse |7| *vr* to get muddy; *fig* to get involved (in dirty business).

énfasis *nm inv* emphasis, stress; **poner e. en algo**, to lay stress on sth.

enfático,-a *adj* emphatic.

enfatizar |4| *vtr* to emphasize, stress.

enfermar *vi*, **enfermarse** *vr* to become *o* fall ill, be taken ill.

enfermedad *nf* illness; *(contagiosa)* disease.

enfermería *nf* infirmary.

enfermero,-a *nm,f (mujer)* nurse; *(hombre)* male nurse.

enfermizo,-a *adj* unhealthy, sickly.

enfermo,-a I *adj* ill; **caer e.**, to be taken ill; *fam* **esa gente me pone e.**, those people make me sick. II *nm,f* ill person; *(paciente)* patient.

enfervorizar |4| *vtr* to enthuse.

enfilar *vi* **e. hacia**, to make for.

enflaquecer |33| *vtr (adelgazar)* to make thin; *(debilitar)* to weaken.

enfocado,-a *adj Fot* **bien/mal enfocado**, in/out of focus.

enfocar |1| *vtr* 1 *(imagen)* to focus; *(persona)* to focus on. 2 *(tema)* to approach. 3 *(con linterna)* to shine a light on.

enfoque *nm* 1 focus; *(acción)* focusing. 2 *(de un tema)* approach.

enfrentamiento *nm* clash.

enfrentar I *vtr* 1 *(situación, peligro)* to confront. 2 *(enemistar)* to set at odds. II **enfrentarse** *vr* 1 **e. con** *o* **a**, to face up to, confront. 2 *Dep (rival)* to face (**a**, -), meet (**a**, -).

enfrente *adv* 1 opposite, facing; **la casa de e.**, the house opposite *o* across the road. 2 **e. de.**, opposite (to); facing; **e. del colegio**, opposite the school.

enfriamiento *nm* 1 *(proceso)* cooling. 2 *Med (catarro)* cold, chill.

enfriar |29| I *vtr* to cool (down), chill. II *vi* to cool down. III **enfriarse** *vr* 1 to get *o* go cold. 2 *(resfriarse)* to get *o* catch a cold. 3 *fig (pasión)* to cool down.

enfurecer |33| I *vtr* to enrage, enfuriate. II **enfurecerse** *vr* to get furious, lose one's temper.

enfurruñarse *vr fam* to sulk.

engalanar I *vtr* to deck out, adorn. II **engalanarse** *vr* to dress up, get dressed up.

enganchado,-a *adj arg* **estar e. (a la droga)**, to be hooked (on drugs).

enganchar I *vtr* 1 to hook; *Ferroc* to couple. 2 *fam (pillar)* to nab. II **engancharse** *vr* to get caught *o* hooked; *arg (a la droga)* to get hooked.

enganche *nm (gancho)* hook; *Ferroc* coupling.

engañabobos *nm inv (persona)* con man, confidence trickster; *(truco)* con trick.

engañar I *vtr* to deceive, mislead; *(estafar)* to cheat, trick; *(mentir a)* to lie to; *(al marido, mujer)* to be unfaithful to. II **engañarse** *vr* to deceive oneself.

engañifa *nf fam* swindle.

engaño *nm* 1 deceit; *(estafa)* fraud, swindle; *(mentira)* lie. 2 *(error)* mistake, misunderstanding.

engañoso,-a *adj (palabras)* deceitful; *(apariencias)* deceptive; *(consejo)* misleading.

engarzar |4| *vtr* 1 *(unir)* to link. 2 *(engastar)* to mount, set.

engastar *vtr* to set, mount.

engatusar *vtr fam* to coax; **e. a algn para que haga algo**, to coax sb into doing sth.

engendrar *vtr* 1 *Biol* to engender. 2 *fig* to give rise to, cause.

engendro *nm* freak.

englobar *vtr* to include.

engomar *vtr* to gum, glue.

engordar I *vtr* to fatten (up), make fat. II *vi* 1 to put on weight, get fat; **he engordado tres kilos**, I've put on three kilos. 2 *(comida, bebida)* to be fattening.

engorro *nm fam* bother, nuisance.

engorroso,-a *adj fam* bothersome, tiresome.

engranaje *nm* 1 *Téc* gearing. 2 *fig* machinery.

engranar *vtr Téc* to engage.

engrandecer |33| *vtr* to exalt.
engrasar *vtr* 1 (*lubricar*) to lubricate, oil. 2 (*manchar*) to make greasy, stain with grease.
engrase *nm* lubrication.
engreído,-a *adj* vain, conceited.
engreírse |6| *vr* to become vain *o* conceited.
engrosar |2| *vtr* (*incrementar*) to enlarge; (*cantidad*) to increase, swell.
engrudo *nm* paste.
enguatar *vtr* to pad.
engullir *vtr* to gobble up.
enharinar *vtr* to cover with flour.
enhebrar *vtr* to thread.
enhorabuena *nf* congratulations *pl*; **dar la e. a algn**, to congratulate sb.
enigma *nm* enigma.
enigmático,-a *adj* enigmatic.
enjabonar *vtr* to soap.
enjalbegar |7| *vtr* to whitewash.
enjambre *nm* swarm.
enjaular *vtr* 1 (*animal*) to cage. 2 *fam* to put inside, put in jail.
enjuagar |7| *vtr* to rinse.
enjuague *nm* rinse; **e. bucal**, mouthwash.
enjugar |7| *vtr*, **enjugarse** *vr* 1 (*secar*) to mop up; (*lágrimas*) to wipe away. 2 (*deuda, déficit*) to clear, wipe out.
enjuiciamiento *nm* 1 (*opinión*) judgement. 2 *Jur* (*civil*) lawsuit; (*criminal*) trial, prosecution.
enjuiciar |12| *vtr* 1 (*juzgar*) to judge, examine. 2 *Jur* (*criminal*) to indict, prosecute.
enjundia *nf fig* (*sustancia*) substance; (*importancia*) importance.
enjuto,-a *adj* lean, skinny.
enlace *nm* 1 (*unión*) link, connection; **e. químico**, chemical bond. 2 *Ferroc* connection. 3 (*casamiento*) marriage. 4 (*persona*) liaison officer; **e. sindical**, shop steward, *US* union delegate.
enlatado,-a *adj* canned, tinned.
enlatar *vtr* to can, tin.
enlazar |4| *vtr & vi* to link, connect (**con**, with).
enlodar *vtr* 1 (*enfangar*) to muddy, cover with mud. 2 *fig* (*reputación*) to stain, besmirch.
enloquecedor,-a *adj* maddening.
enloquecer |33| I *vi* to go mad. II *vtr* 1 (*volver loco*) to drive mad. 2 *fam* **me enloquecen las motos**, I'm mad about motorbikes. III **enloquecerse** *vr* to go mad, go out of one's mind.
enlosar *vtr* to tile.
enlucir |35| *vtr* (*pared*) to plaster; (*plata, oro*) to polish.
enlutado,-a *adj* in mourning.
enmadrado,-a *adj* **estar e.**, to be tied to one's mother's apron strings.
enmarañar I *vtr* 1 (*pelo*) to tangle. 2 *fig* (*complicar*) to complicate, confuse. II

enmarañarse *vr* 1 (*pelo*) to get tangled. 2 *fig* (*situación*) to get confused, get into a mess *o* a muddle.
enmarcar |1| *vtr* to frame.
enmascarar I *vtr* 1 to mask. 2 (*problema, la verdad*) to mask, disguise. II **enmascararse** *vr* to put on a mask.
enmendar |1| I *vtr* (*corregir*) to correct, put right; *Jur* to amend. II **enmendarse** *vr* (*persona*) to reform, mend one's ways.
enmienda *nf* correction; *Jur Pol* amendment.
enmohecerse |33| *vr* (*metal*) to rust, get rusty; *Bot* to go mouldy *o* *US* moldy.
enmoquetar *vtr* to carpet.
enmudecer |33| *vi* (*callar*) to fall silent; *fig* to be dumbstruck.
ennegrecer |33| *vtr*, **ennegrecerse** *vr* to blacken, turn black.
ennoblecer *vtr* to ennoble.
enojado,-a *adj* angry, cross.
enojadizo *adj* irritable, touchy.
enojar I *vtr* to anger, annoy. II **enojarse** *vr* to get angry, lose one's temper.
enojo *nm* anger, annoyance.
enorgullecer |33| I *vtr* to fill with pride. II **enorgullecerse** *vtr* to be *o* feel proud (**de**, of).
enorme *adj* enormous.
enormidad *nf* enormity; *fam* **una e.**, loads.
enraizado,-a *adj* rooted.
enraizar |24| *vi*, **enraizarse** *vr* (*persona*) to put down roots; (*planta, costumbre*) to take root.
enrarecerse |33| *vr* (*aire*) to become rarefied.
enredadera *nf* climbing plant, creeper.
enredar I *vtr* 1 (*pelo*) to entangle, tangle up. 2 *fig* (*asunto*) to confuse, complicate. 3 *fig* (*implicar*) to involve (**en**, in). 4 (*confundir*) to mix up. II **enredarse** *vr* 1 (*pelo*) to get entangled, get tangled (up) *o* in a tangle. 2 *fig* (*asunto*) to get complicated *o* confused. 3 *fig* (*involucrarse*) to get involved (**con**, with). 4 (*confundirse*) to get mixed up.
enredo *nm* 1 (*maraña*) tangle. 2 *fig* (*lío*) muddle, mess.
enrejado *nm* (*de ventana*) lattice.
enrevesado,-a *adj* complicated, difficult.
enriquecer |33| *vtr* to make rich; *fig* to enrich. II **enriquecerse** *vr* to get *o* become rich, prosper; *fig* to become enriched.
enrocar |1| *vi Ajedrez* to castle.
enrojecer |33| I *vtr* to redden, turn red. II **enrojecer(se)** *vi & vr* (*ruborizarse*) to blush.
enrolarse *vr* to enrol, *US* enroll, sign on; *Mil* to enlist, join up.
enrollado,-a *adj* 1 rolled up. 2 (*persona*) great. 3 *fam* **estar e. con algn**, (*estar saliendo con*) to go out with sb.

enrollar I *vtr* to roll up; *(cable)* to coil; *(hilo)* to wind up. **II enrollarse** *vr* **1** *fam (hablar)* to chatter, go on and on. **2** *fam* **e. con algn,** *(tener relaciones)* to have an affair with sb.

enroque *nm Ajedrez* castling.

enroscar |1| **I** *vtr* **1** to coil (round), wind. **2** *(tornillo, tapón)* to screw in *o* on. **II enroscarse** *vr* to coil, wind.

ensaimada *nf* kind of spiral pastry from Majorca.

ensalada *nf* salad.

ensaladera *nf* salad bowl.

ensaladilla *nf* **e. rusa,** Russian salad.

ensalzar |4| *vtr (enaltecer)* to exalt; *(elogiar)* to praise, extol, *US* extoll.

ensamblador *nm Inform* assembler.

ensamblaje *nm Téc* assembly.

ensamblar *vtr* to assemble.

ensanchar I *vtr* to enlarge, widen; *Cost* to let out. **II ensancharse** *vr* to get wider.

ensanche *nm* enlargement, widening; *(de ciudad)* urban development.

ensangrentado,-a *adj* bloodstained, covered in blood.

ensangrentar |1| *vtr* to stain with blood, cover in blood.

ensañarse *vr* to be brutal (**con,** with); *(cebarse)* to delight in tormenting (**con,** -).

ensartar *vtr* **1** *(perlas etc)* to string together. **2** *(mentiras etc)* to reel off, rattle off.

ensayar *vtr* to test, try out; *Teat* to rehearse; *Mús* to practise.

ensayista *nmf* essayist.

ensayo *nm* **1** *(prueba)* test, trial. **2** *Teat* rehearsal; **e. general,** dress rehearsal. **3** *(escrito)* essay.

enseguida, en seguida *adv (inmediatamente)* at once, straight away; *(poco después)* in a minute, soon; **e. voy,** I'll be right there.

ensenada *nf* inlet, cove.

enseña *nf* ensign, standard.

enseñanza *nf* **1** *(educación)* education. **2** *(de idioma etc)* teaching. **3 enseñanzas,** teachings.

enseñar *vtr* **1** to teach; **e. a algn a hacer algo,** to teach sb how to do sth. **2** *(mostrar)* to show; *(señalar)* to point out.

enseres *nmpl (bártulos)* belongings, goods; *(de trabajo)* tools.

ensillar *vtr* to saddle (up).

ensimismado,-a *adj (en la lectura etc)* engrossed; *(abstraído)* lost in thought.

ensimismarse *vr (en la lectura etc)* to become engrossed; *(abstraerse)* to be lost in thought.

ensombrecer |33| **I** *vtr* to cast a shadow over. **II ensombrecerse** *vr* to darken.

ensopar *vtr Am* to soak.

ensordecedor,-a *adj* deafening.

ensordecer |33| **I** *vtr* to deafen. **II** *vi* to go deaf.

ensortijado,-a *adj* curly.

ensuciar |12| **I** *vtr* **1** to get dirty. **2** *fig (reputación)* to harm, damage. **II ensuciarse** *vr* to get dirty.

ensueño *nm* dream; **una casa de e.,** a dream house.

entablado *nm* **1** *(entarimado)* planking, planks *pl.* **2** *(suelo)* wooden floor.

entablar *vtr* **1** *(conversación)* to open, begin; *(amistad)* to strike up; *(negocios)* to start. **2** *Ajedrez* to set up. **3** *(pleito)* to initiate.

entablillar *vtr Med* to splint.

entallado,-a *adj (vestido)* close-fitting; *(camisa)* fitted.

entallar I *vtr* to take in at the waist. **II** *vi* to fit at the waist.

entarimado *nm* parquet floor.

entarimar *vtr* to cover with parquet.

ente *nm* **1** *(institución)* organization, body; **e. público,** public service organization. **2** *(ser)* being.

entendederas *nfpl fam* brains; **ser duro de e.,** to be slow on the uptake.

entender |3| **I** *vtr (comprender)* to understand; **a mi e.,** to my way of thinking; **dar a algn a e. que ...,** to give sb to understand that .... **II** *vi* **1** *(comprender)* to understand. **2 e. de,** *(saber)* to know about. **III entenderse** *vr* **1** *(comprenderse)* to be understood, be meant. **2** *fam* **e. (bien) con,** to get on (well) with.

entendido,-a I *nm,f* expert. **II** *adj* **tengo entendido que ...,** I understand that ....

entendimiento *nm* understanding.

enterado,-a I *adj* knowledgeable, well-informed; **estar e.,** to be in the know; **estar e. de ...,** to be aware of .... **II** *nm,f (listillo)* know-all.

enterar I *vtr* to inform (**de,** about, of). **II enterarse** *vr* to find out; **me he enterado de que ...,** I understand ...; **ni me enteré,** I didn't even realize it.

entereza *nf* strength of character.

enternecedor,-a *adj* moving, touching.

enternecer |33| **I** *vtr* to move, touch. **II enternecerse** *vr* to be moved *o* touched.

entero,-a I *adj* **1** *(completo)* entire, whole; **por e.,** completely. **2** *fig (íntegro)* honest, upright. **3** *fig (firme)* strong. **II** *nm* **1** *Mat* whole number. **2** *Fin* point. ◆**enteramente** *adv* entirely, completely.

enterrador *nm* gravedigger.

enterramiento *nm* burial.

enterrar |1| *vt* to bury.

entidad *nf* organization; **e. comercial,** company, firm.

entierro *nm* **1** burial. **2** *(ceremonia)* funeral.

entomología *nf* entomology.

entonación *nf* intonation.

entonar I *vtr* **1** *(canto)* to sing. **2** *Med* to

tone up. **II** *vi* to be in harmony, be in tune (**con**, with).

entonces *adv* then; **por aquel e.**, at that time; **el e. ministro**, the then minister.

entornar *vtr (ojos etc)* to half-close; *(puerta)* to leave ajar.

entorno *nm* environment.

entorpecer [33] *vtr (obstaculizar)* to hinder, impede.

entrada *nf* 1 entrance. 2 *(billete)* ticket; *(recaudación)* takings *pl*. 3 **de e.**, for a start. 4 *Culin* entrée. 5 *Com* entry; *(pago inicial)* down payment, deposit; **e. de capital**, capital inflow. 6 *Com* **entradas**, *(ingresos)* receipts, takings. 7 *(en la frente)* receding hairline.

entrado,-a *adj* **e. en años**, advanced in years; **hasta bien entrada la noche**, well into the night.

entramado *nm* framework; *(de sistema etc)* network.

entramparse *vr fam* to get into debt.

entrante **I** *adj* coming; **el mes e.**, next month; **el ministro e.**, the incoming minister. **II** *Culin* starter.

entrañable *adj* 1 *(lugar)* intimate, close. 2 *(persona)* affectionate, warm-hearted.

entrañar *vtr* to entail.

entrañas *nfpl* bowels.

entrar **I** *vi* 1 to come in, go in, enter; *fig* **no me entran las matemáticas**, I can't get the hang of maths. 2 *(encajar)* to fit. 3 **el año que entra**, next year, the coming year. 4 *(venir)* to come over; **me entró dolor de cabeza**, I got a headache; **me entraron ganas de reír**, I felt like laughing. **II** *vtr* 1 to introduce. 2 *Inform* to enter.

entre *prep* 1 *(dos)* between. 2 *(más de dos)* among(st).

entreabierto,-a *adj (ojos etc)* half-open; *(puerta)* ajar.

entreacto *nm* interval, intermission.

entrecejo *nm* space between the eyebrows; **fruncir el e.**, to frown, knit one's brow.

entrecortado,-a *adj (voz)* faltering, hesitant.

entrecot *nm* fillet steak.

entrecruzar *vtr*, **entrecruzarse** [4] *vr* to entwine.

entredicho *nm* 1 *Jur* injunction. 2 **estar en e.**, to be suspect; **poner algo en e.**, to bring sth into question.

entrega *nf* 1 *(de productos)* delivery; *(de premios)* presentation. 2 *(fascículo)* part, instalment, *US* installment. 3 *(devoción)* selflessness.

entregar [7] **I** *vtr* to hand over; *(deberes etc)* to give in, hand in; *Com* to deliver. **II entregarse** *vr* 1 *(rendirse)* to give in, surrender. 2 **e. a**, to devote oneself to; *pey* to indulge in.

entreguismo *nm Pol* appeasement.

entrelazar [4] *vtr*, **entrelazarse** *vr* to entwine.

entremedias *adv* in between; *(mientras tanto)* meanwhile, in the meantime.

entremés *nm Culin* hors d'oeuvres.

entremeterse *vr* → **entrometerse**.

entremezclarse *vr* to mix, mingle.

entrenador,-a *nm,f* trainer, coach.

entrenamiento *nm* training.

entrenar *vi*, **entrenarse** *vr* to train.

entrepierna *nf* crotch, crutch.

entresacar [1] *vtr* to pick out, select.

entresijos *nmpl* nooks and crannies.

entresuelo *nm* mezzanine.

entretanto **I** *adv* meanwhile. **II** *nm* **en el e.**, in the meantime.

entretejer *vtr* to interweave.

entretención *nf Am* amusement, entertainment.

entretener [24] **I** *vtr* 1 *(divertir)* to entertain, amuse. 2 *(retrasar)* to delay; *(detener)* to hold up, detain. **II entretenerse** *vr* 1 *(distraerse)* to amuse oneself, while away the time. 2 *(retrasarse)* to be delayed, be held up.

entretenido,-a *adj* enjoyable, entertaining.

entretenimiento *nm* entertainment, amusement.

entretiempo *adj* **ropa de e.**, lightweight clothing.

entrever [28] *vtr* to glimpse, catch sight of; *fig* **dejó e. que ...**, she hinted that ....

entrevista *nf* interview.

entrevistador,-a *nm,f* interviewer.

entrevistar **I** *vtr* to interview. **II entrevistarse** *vr* **e. con algn**, to have an interview with sb.

entristecer [33] **I** *vtr* to sadden, make sad. **II entristecerse** *vr* to be sad (**por**, about).

entrometerse *vr* to meddle, interfere (**en**, in).

entrometido,-a **I** *nm,f* meddler, busybody. **II** *adj* interfering.

entroncar *vi* to connect.

entumecer [33] **I** *vtr* to numb. **II entumecerse** *vr* to go numb.

entumecido,-a *adj* numb.

enturbiar [12] **I** *vtr* 1 *(agua)* to make cloudy. 2 *fig (asunto)* to cloud, obscure. **II enturbiarse** *vr* to become cloudy.

entusiasmar **I** *vtr* to fill with enthusiasm. **II entusiasmarse** *vr* to get excited *o* enthusiastic (**con**, about).

entusiasmo *nm* enthusiasm; **con e.**, enthusiastically.

entusiasta **I** *adj* enthusiastic, keen (**de**, on). **II** *nmf* enthusiast.

enumerar *vtr* to enumerate.

enunciado *nm (de teoría, problema)* wording.

envainar *vtr* to sheathe.

envanecer [33] **I** *vtr* to make proud *o*

vain. II **envanecerse** vr to become conceited o proud, give oneself airs.

envasado,-a I nm (en botella) bottling; (en paquete) packing; (en lata) canning. II adj **e. al vacío,** vacuum-packed.

envasar vtr (embotellar) to bottle; (empaquetar) to pack; (enlatar) to can, tin.

envase nm 1 (acto) packing; (de botella) bottling; (de lata) canning. 2 (recipiente) container. 3 (botella vacía) empty.

envejecer [33] I vi to grow old. II vtr to age.

envejecimiento nm ageing.

envenenar vtr to poison.

envergadura nf 1 (importancia) importance, scope; **de gran e.,** large-scale. 2 (de pájaro, avión) span, wingspan; Náut breadth (of sail).

envés nm other side.

envestidura nf investiture.

enviado nm,f envoy; Prensa **e. especial,** special correspondent.

enviar [29] vtr to send.

enviciarse [12] vr to become addicted (con, to).

envidia nf envy; **tener e. de algn,** to envy sb.

envidiable adj enviable.

envidiar [12] vtr to envy; **no tener nada que e.,** to be in no way inferior (a, to).

envidioso,-a adj envious.

envilecer [33] vtr to degrade, debase.

envío nm sending; (remesa) consignment; (paquete) parcel; **gastos de e.,** postage and packing; **e. contra reembolso,** cash on delivery.

enviudar vi (hombre) to become a widower, lose one's wife; (mujer) to become a widow, lose one's husband.

envoltorio nm, **envoltura** nf wrapper, wrapping.

envolver [4] (pp **envuelto**) I vtr 1 (con papel) to wrap. 2 (cubrir) to envelope. 3 (en complot etc) to involve (en, in). II **envolverse** vr 1 to wrap oneself up (en, in). 2 (implicarse) to become involved (en, in).

enyesar vtr to plaster; Med to put in plaster.

enzima nf enzyme.

épica nf epic poetry.

epicentro nm epicentre, US epicenter.

épico,-a adj epic.

epidemia nf epidemic.

epilepsia nf epilepsy.

epílogo nm epilogue, US epilog.

episcopal adj episcopal.

episodio nm episode.

epístola nf epistle.

epitafio nm epitaph.

epíteto nm epithet.

época nf time; Hist period, epoch; Agr season; **en esta é. del año,** at this time of the year; **hacer é.,** to be a landmark;

mueble de é., period furniture.

equidad nf equity.

equilátero nm equilateral.

equilibrar vtr to balance.

equilibrio nm balance.

equilibrismo nm balancing act.

equilibrista nmf 1 tightrope walker. 2 Am Pol opportunist.

equipaje nm luggage; **hacer el e.,** to pack, do the packing.

equipar vtr to equip, furnish (con, de, with).

equiparable adj comparable (a, to; con, with).

equiparar vtr to compare (con, with), liken (con, to).

equipo nm 1 (de expertos, jugadores) team. 2 (aparatos) equipment; **e. de alta fidelidad,** hi-fi stereo system. 3 (ropas) outfit.

equis nf name of the letter X in Spanish.

equitación nf horse o US horseback riding.

equitativo,-a adj equitable, fair.

equivalente adj equivalent.

equivaler [26] vi to be equivalent (to, a).

equivocación nf error, mistake.

equivocado,-a adj mistaken, wrong.

equivocar [1] I vtr to mix up. II **equivocarse** vr to make a mistake; Tel **se equivocó de número,** he dialled the wrong wrong; **se equivocó de fecha,** he got the wrong date.

equívoco,-a I adj equivocal, misleading. II nm misunderstanding.

era[1] nf (época) era, age.

era[2] nf Agr threshing floor.

era[3] pt indef → ser.

erario nm exchequer, treasury.

eras pt indef → ser.

erección nf erection.

`**erecto,-a** adj upright; (pene) erect.

eres indic pres → ser.

erguir [5] I vtr to erect. II **erguirse** vr to straighten up, stand o sit up straight.

erial nm uncultivated land.

erigir [6] I vtr to erect. II **erigirse** vr **e. en algo,** to set oneself up in sth.

erizado,-a adj bristly, prickly.

erizarse [4] vr to bristle, stand on end.

erizo nm hedgehog; **e. de mar** o **marino,** sea urchin.

ermita nf hermitage, shrine.

ermitaño,-a nm,f hermit.

erosión nf erosion.

erosionar vtr to erode.

erótico,-a adj erotic.

erotismo nm eroticism.

erradicar [1] vtr to eradicate.

errante adj wandering.

errar [1] I vtr to miss, get wrong. II vi 1 (vagar) to wander, roam. 2 (fallar) to err.

errata nf erratum, misprint; **fe de erratas,** errata.

erre nf **e. que e.,** stubbornly, pigheadedly.

erróneo,-a adj erroneous, wrong.

error nm error, mistake; Inform bug; **por e.**, by mistake, in error; Impr **e. de imprenta**, misprint; **caer en un e.**, to make a mistake.

Ertzaintza nf Basque police force.

eructar vi to belch, burp.

eructo nm belch, burp.

erudición nf erudition.

erudito,-a I adj erudite, learned. **II** nm,f scholar.

erupción nf 1 (de volcán) eruption. 2 (en la piel) rash.

es indic pres → **ser**.

esa adj dem → **ese**.

ésa adj dem → **ése**.

esbelto,-a adj slender.

esbirro nm henchman.

esbozar |4| vi to sketch, outline.

esbozo nm sketch, outline, rough draft.

escabeche nm brine.

escabechina nf massacre.

escabroso,-a adj 1 (espinoso) tricky. 2 (indecente) crude.

escabullirse vr to slip away, scuttle o scurry off.

escacharrar vtr fam to break.

escafandra nf diving helmet or suit; **e. espacial,** spacesuit.

escala nf 1 scale; (de colores) range; **e. musical,** scale; **en gran e.,** on a large scale. 2 (parada) Náut port of call; Av stopover; **hacer e. en,** to call in at, stop over in. 3 (escalera) ladder, stepladder.

escalada nf 1 climb. 2 fig (de violencia) escalation; (de precios) rise.

escalador,-a nm,f climber, mountaineer.

escalafón nm (graduación) rank; (de salarios) salary o wage scale.

escalar vtr to climb, scale.

escaldar vtr to scald.

escalera nf 1 stair; **e. de incendios,** fire escape; **e. mecánica,** escalator; **e. de caracol,** spiral staircase. 2 (escala) ladder. 3 Naipes run.

escalerilla nf (de piscina) steps pl; Náut gangway; Av (boarding) ramp.

escalfar vtr to poach.

escalinata nf stoop.

escalofriante adj hair-raising, bloodcurdling.

escalofrío nm shiver; **me dió un e.,** it made me shiver.

escalón nm step; **e. lateral** (en letrero) ramp.

escalonar vtr to place at intervals, space out.

escalope nm escalope.

escalpelo nm scalpel.

escama nf Zool scale; (de jabón) flake.

escamarse vr to smell a rat, become suspicious.

escamotear vtr fam to diddle out of, do out of.

escampar vi to stop raining, clear up.

escanciar |12| vtr (vino) to pour out, serve.

escandalizar |4| **I** vtr to scandalize, shock. **II escandalizarse** vr to be shocked (**de,** at, by).

escándalo nm 1 (alboroto) racket, din; **armar un e.,** to kick up a fuss. 2 (desvergüenza) scandal.

escandaloso,-a adj 1 (ruidoso) noisy, rowdy. 2 (ofensivo) scandalous.

Escandinavia n Scandinavia.

escandinavo,-a adj & nm,f Scandinavian.

escáner nf scanner.

escaño nm Parl seat.

escapada nf 1 (de prisión) escape; Dep breakaway. 2 (viaje rápido) flying visit, quick trip.

escapar I vi to escape, run away. **II escaparse** vr 1 to escape, run away; **se me escapó de las manos,** it slipped out of my hands; **se me escapó el tren,** I missed the train. 2 (gas etc) to leak, escape.

escaparate nm shop window.

escapatoria nf escape; **no tener e.,** to have no way out.

escape nm 1 (de gas etc) leak, escape. 2 Téc exhaust; **tubo de e.,** exhaust (pipe). 3 (huida) escape; (escapatoria) way out.

escaquearse vr fam to shirk, skive off.

escarabajo nm beetle.

escaramuza nf Mil skirmish; fig (riña) squabble, brush.

escarbar vtr 1 (suelo) to scratch; (fuego) to poke. 2 fig to inquire into, investigate.

escarceo nm attempt.

escarcha nf hoarfrost, frost.

escarchado,-a adj (fruta) crystallized, candied.

escardar vtr to hoe.

escardillo nm weeding hoe.

escarlata adj scarlet.

escarlatina nf scarlet fever.

escarmentar |1| vi to learn one's lesson.

escarmiento nm punishment, lesson.

escarnio nm derision, mockery.

escarola nf curly endive, US escarole.

escarpado,-a adj (paisaje) craggy; (pendiente) steep.

escasear vi to be scarce.

escasez nf scarcity.

escaso,-a adj scarce; (dinero) tight; (conocimientos) scant; **e. de dinero,** short of money.

escatimar vtr to skimp on; **no escatimó esfuerzos para ...,** he spared no efforts to ....

escayola nf 1 plaster of Paris, stucco. 2 Med plaster.

escayolar vtr Med to put in plaster.

escena nf 1 scene. 2 (escenario) stage; **poner en e.,** to stage.

escenario nm 1 Teat stage. 2 (entorno) scenario; (de crimen) scene; (de película) setting.

escénico,-a adj scenic.

escenografía nf Cin set design; Teat stage design.

escepticismo nm scepticism, US skepticism.

escéptico,-a adj & nm,f sceptic, US skeptic.

escindirse vr to split (off) (en, into).

escisión nf split.

esclarecer [33] vtr to shed light on.

esclavitud nf slavery.

esclavizar [4] vtr to enslave.

esclava nf bangle.

esclavo,-a adj & nm,f slave.

esclusa nf lock, sluicegate.

escoba nf brush, broom.

escocer [4] I vi to sting, smart. II **escocerse** vr (piel) to chafe.

escocés,-a I adj Scottish, Scots; **falda escocesa**, kilt. II nm,f (hombre) Scotsman; (mujer) Scotswoman.

Escocia n Scotland.

escoger [5] vtr to choose.

escogido,-a adj chosen, selected; (producto) choice, select; Lit **obras escogidas**, selected works.

escolar I adj (curso, año) school. II nm,f (niño) schoolboy; (niña) schoolgirl.

escolaridad nf schooling.

escollo nm reef; fig pitfall.

escolta nf escort.

escoltar vtr to escort.

escombros nmpl rubbish sing, debris sing.

esconder I vtr to hide (de, from), conceal (de, from). II **esconderse** vr to hide (de, from).

escondidas adv a e., secretly.

escondite nm 1 (lugar) hiding place, hide-out. 2 (juego) hide-and-seek.

escondrijo nm hiding place, hide-out.

escopeta nf shotgun; e. de aire comprimido, air gun; e. de cañones recortados, sawn-off shotgun.

escopetazo nm gunshot.

escorbuto nm scurvy.

escoria nf 1 (de metal) slag. 2 fig pey scum, dregs pl.

Escorpio nm Scorpio.

escorpión nm scorpion.

escotado,-a adj low-cut.

escote nm low neckline.

escotilla nf hatch, hatchway.

escozor nm stinging, smarting.

escribano,-a nm,f Jur court clerk.

escribiente nmf clerk.

escribir (pp escrito) I vtr to write; e. a mano, to write in longhand; e. a máquina, to type. II **escribirse** vr 1 (dos personas) to write to each other, correspond. 2 se escribe con h, it is spelt with an h.

escrito,-a I adj written; e. a mano, handwritten, in longhand; por e., in writing. II nm writing.

escritor,-a nm,f writer.

escritorio nm (mueble) writing desk, bureau; (oficina) office.

escritura nf 1 Jur deed, document; e. de propiedad, title deed. 2 Rel **Sagradas Escrituras**, Holy Scriptures.

escrúpulo nm 1 scruple; **una persona sin escrúpulos**, an unscrupulous person. 2 (esmero) care. 3 me da e., (asco) it makes me feel squeamish.

escrupuloso,-a adj 1 (honesto) scrupulous. 2 (meticuloso) painstaking. 3 (delicado) squeamish.

escrutar vtr 1 to scrutinize. 2 (votos) to count.

escrutinio nm 1 scrutiny. 2 (de votos) count.

escuadra nf 1 (intrumento) square. 2 Mil squad; Naut squadron; Dep team; (de coches) fleet.

escuadrilla nf squadron.

escuadrón nm squadron.

escuálido,-a adj emaciated.

escucha nf listening; **escuchas telefónicas**, phone tapping sing; estar a la e., to be listening out (de, for).

escuchar I vtr to listen to; (oír) to hear. II vi to listen; (oír) to hear.

escudarse vr fig e. en algo, to hide behind sth.

escudería nf Aut racing team.

escudilla nf bowl.

escudo nm 1 (arma defensiva) shield. 2 (blasón) coat of arms.

escudriñar vtr to scrutinize.

escuela nf school; e. de Bellas Artes, Art School; e. de conducir/de idiomas, driving/language school.

escueto,-a adj plain, unadorned.

escuezo indic pres → escocer.

esculcar [1] vtr Am to search.

esculpir vtr to sculpt; (madera) to carve; (metal) to engrave.

escultor,-a nm,f (hombre) sculptor; (mujer) sculptress; (de madera) woodcarver; (de metales) engraver.

escultura nf sculpture.

escultural adj sculptural; (persona) statuesque.

escupidera nf 1 (recipiente) spittoon, US cuspidor. 2 (orinal) chamberpot.

escupir I vi to spit. II vtr to spit out.

escupitajo nm vulg spit.

escurreplatos nm inv dish rack.

escurridizo,-a adj 1 (resbaladizo) slippery. 2 fig (huidizo) elusive, slippery.

escurridor nm colander; (escurreplatos) dish rack.

escurrir I vtr (plato, vaso) to drain; (ropa) to wring out; e. el bulto, to wriggle out. II **escurrirse** vr 1 (platos etc) to drip. 2

(escaparse) to run *o* slip away. 3 *(resbalarse)* to slip.

escúter *nm* (motor) scooter.

ese,-a *adj dem* **1** that. **2 esos,-as,** those.

ése,-a *pron dem m,f* **1** that one. **2 ésos,-as,** those (ones); *fam* ¡ni por ésas!, no way!; *fam* ¡no me vengas con ésas!, come off it!

esencia *nf* essence.

esencial *adj* essential; **lo e.,** the main thing. ◆**esencialmente** *adv* essentially.

esfera *nf* **1** sphere; *fig* sphere, field. **2** *(de reloj de pulsera)* dial; *(de reloj de pared)* face.

esférico,-a I *adj* spherical. **II** *nm Ftb* ball.

esfinge *nf* sphinx.

esforzarse [2] *vr* to endeavour **(por,** to).

esfuerzo *nm* effort.

esfumarse *vr fam* to beat it.

esgrima *nf Dep* fencing.

esgrimir *vtr* to wield.

esguince *nm* sprain.

eslabón *nm* link.

eslavo,-a I *adj* Slav, Slavonic. **II** *nm,f (persona)* Slav. **III** *nm (idioma)* Slavonic.

eslip *nm (pl eslips)* men's briefs *pl,* underpants *pl.*

eslogan *nm (pl eslóganes)* slogan; **e. publicitario,** advertising slogan.

eslora *nf Náut* length.

esmaltar *vtr* to enamel.

esmalte *nm* enamel; *(de uñas)* nail polish *o* varnish.

esmerado,-a *adj* painstaking, careful.

esmeralda *nf* emerald.

esmerarse *vr* to be careful; *(esforzarse)* to go to great lengths.

esmero *nm* great care.

esmoquin *nm (pl esmóquines)* dinner jacket, *US* tuxedo.

esnifar *vtr arg (drogas)* to sniff.

esnob *(pl esnobs)* **I** *adj (persona)* snobbish; *(restaurante etc)* posh. **II** *nmf* snob.

esnobismo *nm* snobbery, snobbishness.

eso *pron dem neut* that; ¡e. es!, that's it!; **por e.,** that's why; *fam* a e. de las diez, around ten; *fam* e. de las Navidades sale muy caro, this whole Christmas thing costs a fortune.

esófago *nm* oesophagus, *US* esophagus.

esos,-as *adj dem pl* → ese,-a.

ésos,-as *pron dem m,fpl* → ése,-a.

esotérico,-a *adj* esoteric.

espabilado,-a *adj* **1** *(despierto)* wide awake. **2** *(niño)* bright.

espabilar I *vtr* to wake up. **II espabilarse** *vr* to wake up, waken up.

espachurrar *vtr* to squash.

espacial *adj* spatial, spacial; **nave e.,** space ship.

espaciar [12] *vtr* to space out.

espacio *nm* **1** space; *(de tiempo)* length; **a doble e.,** double-spaced. **2** *Rad TV* programme, *US* program.

espacioso,-a *adj* spacious, roomy.

espada I *nf* **1** sword; **estar entre la e. y la pared,** to be between the devil and the deep blue sea; **pez e.,** swordfish. **2** *Naipes* spade. **II** *nm Taur* matador.

espadaña *nf* belfry.

espaguetis *nmpl* spaghetti *sing.*

espalda *nf* **1** *Anat* back; **espaldas,** back *sing;* **a espaldas de algn,** behind sb's back; **por la e.,** from behind; **volver la e. a algn,** to turn one's back on sb; *fam* **e. mojada,** *US* wetback. **2** *Natación* backstroke.

espaldar *nm (de silla)* back.

espaldilla *nf* shoulder blade.

espantapájaros *nm inv* scarecrow.

espantar I *vtr* **1** *(asustar)* to frighten, scare. **2** *(ahuyentar)* to frighten away. **II espantarse** *vr* to get *o* feel frightened **(de,** of), get *o* feel scared **(de,** of).

espanto *nm* fright; *fam* **de e.,** dreadful, shocking.

espantoso,-a *adj* dreadful.

España *n* Spain.

español,-a I *adj* Spanish. **II** *nm,f* Spaniard; **los españoles,** the Spanish. **III** *nm (idioma)* Spanish.

esparadrapo *nm* sticking plaster.

esparcimiento *nm (relajación)* relaxation.

esparcir [3] **I** *vtr (papeles, semillas)* to scatter; *fig (rumor)* to spread. **II esparcirse** *vr* **1** to be scattered. **2** *(relajarse)* to relax.

espárrago *nm* asparagus.

espartano,-a *adj fig* spartan.

espasmo *nm* spasm.

espástico,-a *adj* spastic.

espátula *nf Culin* spatula; *Art* palette knife; *Téc* stripping knife; *(de albañil)* trowel.

especia *nf* spice.

especial *adj* special; **en e.,** especially; **e. para ...,** suitable for .... ◆**especialmente** *adv (exclusivamente)* specially; *(muy)* especially.

especialidad *nf* speciality, *US* specialty; *Educ* main subject.

especialista *nmf* specialist.

especializarse [4] *vr* to specialize **(en,** in).

especie *nf* **1** *Biol* species *inv.* **2** *(clase)* kind; **una e. de salsa,** a kind of sauce. **3** *Com* **en e.,** in kind.

especificar [1] *vtr* to specify.

específico,-a *adj* specific; **peso e.,** specific gravity. ◆**específicamente** *adv* specifically.

espécimen *nm (pl especímenes)* specimen.

espectacular *adj* spectacular.

espectacularidad *nf* **de gran e.,** really spectacular.

espectáculo *nm* **1** *(escena)* spectacle,

sight; *fam* **dar un e.**, to make a spectacle of oneself. 2 *Teat Cin* TV show; **montar un e.**, to put on a show.

espectador,-a *nm,f Dep* spectator; *(de accidente)* onlooker; *Teat Cin* member of the audience; **los espectadores**, the audience *sing*; *TV* viewers.

espectro *nm* 1 *Fís* spectrum. 2 *(fantasma)* spectre, *US* specter. 3 *(gama)* range.

especulación *nf* speculation; **e. del suelo**, land speculation.

especulador,-a *nm,f Fin* speculator.

especular *vi* to speculate.

especulativo,-a *adj* speculative.

espejismo *nm* mirage.

espejo *nm* mirror; *Aut* **e. retrovisor**, rear-view mirror.

espeleología *nf* potholing, speleology.

espeluznante *adj* hair-raising, horrifying.

espera *nf* wait; **en e. de ...**, waiting for ...; **a la e. de**, expecting; **sala de e.**, waiting room.

esperanza *nf* hope; **tener la e. puesta en algo**, to have one's hopes pinned on sth; **e. de vida**, life expectancy; **en estado de buena e.**, expecting, pregnant.

esperanzador,-a *adj* encouraging.

esperanzar *vtr* to give hope to.

esperar I *vi* 1 *(aguardar)* to wait. 2 *(tener esperanza de)* to hope. II *vtr* 1 *(aguardar)* to wait for; **espero a mi hermano**, I'm waiting for my brother. 2 *(tener esperanza de)* to hope for; **espero que sí**, I hope so; **espero que vengas**, I hope you'll come. 3 *(estar a la espera de)* to expect; **te esperábamos ayer**, we were expecting you yesterday. 4 *fig (bebé)* to expect.

esperma 1 *nm Biol* sperm. 2 *Am (vela)* candle.

espermaticida *nm* spermicide.

espermatozoide *nm* spermatozoid.

esperpéntico,-a *adj fam* grotesque.

espesar I *vtr* to thicken. II **espesarse** *vr* to thicken, get thicker.

espeso,-a *adj (bosque, niebla)* dense; *(líquido)* thick; *(masa)* stiff.

espesor *nm* thickness; **tres metros de e.**, three metres thick.

espesura *nf* denseness.

espetar *vtr fig* to spit out.

espía *nmf* spy.

espiar [29] I *vi* to spy. II *vtr* to spy on.

espichar *vi vulg (morir)* to snuff it; **espicharla**, to kick the bucket.

espiga *nf* 1 *(de trigo)* ear. 2 *Téc* pin.

espigado,-a *adj* slender.

espina *nf* 1 *Bot* thorn. 2 *(de pescado)* bone. 3 *Anat* **e. dorsal**, spinal column, spine. 4 *fig* **ése me da mala e.**, there's something fishy about that one.

espinaca *nf* spinach.

espinal *adj* spinal; **médula e.**, spinal marrow.

espinazo *nm* spine, backbone.

espinilla *nf* 1 *Anat* shin. 2 *(en la piel)* spot.

espinillera *nf Dep* shin pad.

espino *nm* hawthorn; **alambre de e.**, barbed wire.

espionaje *nm* spying, espionage; **novela de e.**, spy story.

espiral *adj & nf* spiral.

espirar *vi* to breathe out, exhale.

espiritismo *nm* spiritualism.

espíritu *nm* 1 spirit; **e. deportivo**, sportsmanship. 2 *Rel (alma)* soul; **el E. Santo**, the Holy Ghost.

espiritual *adj* spiritual.

espléndido,-a *adj* 1 *(magnífico)* splendid. 2 *(generoso)* lavish, generous.

esplendor *nm* splendour, *US* splendor.

esplendoroso,-a *adj* magnificent.

espliego *nm* lavender.

espolear *vtr* to spur on.

espolio *nm* → **expolio**.

espolvorear *vtr* to sprinkle (**de**, with).

esponja *nf* sponge.

esponjoso,-a *adj* spongy; *(bizcocho)* light.

esponsales *nmpl* betrothal *sing*, engagement *sing*.

espontaneidad *nf* spontaneity; **con e.**, naturally.

espontáneo,-a I *adj* spontaneous. II *nm Taur* spectator who spontaneously joins in the bullfight.

esporádico,-a *adj* sporadic.

esposado,-a *adj* 1 *(recién casado)* newly married. 2 *(con esposas)* handcuffed.

esposar *vtr* to handcuff.

esposas *nfpl* handcuffs.

esposo,-a *nm,f* spouse; *(hombre)* husband; *(mujer)* wife.

esprint *nm* sprint.

esprintar *vi* to sprint.

espuela *nf* spur.

espuerta *nf* hod.

espuma *nf* foam; *(de olas)* surf; *(de cerveza)* froth, head; *(de jabón)* lather; **e. de afeitar**, shaving foam.

espumoso,-a *adj* frothy; *(vino)* sparkling.

esputo *nm* spit.

esquela *nf* notice, announcement; **e. mortuoria**, announcement of a death.

esquelético,-a *adj* 1 *Anat* skeletal. 2 *(flaco)* skinny.

esqueleto *nm* 1 skeleton. 2 *Constr* framework.

esquema *nm* diagram.

esquemático,-a *adj (escueto)* schematic; *(con diagramas)* diagrammatic.

esquí *nm* 1 *(objeto)* ski. 2 *(deporte)* skiing; **e. acuático**, water-skiing.

esquiador,-a *nm,f* skier.

esquiar [29] *vi* to ski.

esquilar *vtr* to shear.

esquimal *adj & nmf* Eskimo.

esquina *nf* corner; *Dep* **saque de e.**, corner kick.

esquinazo *nm* **dar e. a algn,** to give sb the slip.

esquirla *nf* splinter.

esquirol *nm Ind* blackleg, scab.

esquivar *vtr (a una persona)* to avoid; *(un golpe)* to dodge.

esquivo,-a *adj* cold, aloof.

esquizofrenia *nf* schizophrenia.

esquizofrénico,-a *adj & nm,f* schizophrenic.

esta *adj dem* → **este,-a.**

está *indic pres* → **estar.**

ésta *pron dem f* → **éste.**

estabilidad *nf* stability.

estabilizar |4| *vtr* to stabilize.

estable *adj* stable.

establecer |33| **I** *vtr* to establish; *(fundar)* to set up, found; *(récord)* to set. **II establecerse** *vr* to settle.

establecimiento *nm* establishment.

establo *nm* cow shed.

estaca *nf* stake, post; *(de tienda de campaña)* peg.

estacada *nf* fence; *fig* **dejar a algn en la e.,** to leave sb in the lurch.

estacazo *nm* blow with a stick.

estación *nf* 1 station; **e. de servicio,** service station; **e. de esquí,** ski resort. 2 *(del año)* season.

estacional *adj* seasonal.

estacionamiento *nm Aut (acción)* parking; *(lugar)* car park, *US* parking lot.

estacionar *vtr,* **estacionarse** *vr Aut* to park.

estacionario,-a *adj* stationary.

estada *nf,* **estadía** *nf Am* stay.

estadio *nm* 1 *Dep* stadium. 2 *(fase)* stage, phase.

estadista *nmf Pol (hombre)* statesman; *(mujer)* stateswoman.

estadística *nf* statistics *sing;* **una e.,** a statistic.

estado *nm* 1 *Pol* state. 2 *(situación)* state, condition; **en buen e.,** in good condition; **e. de salud,** condition, state of health; **e. de excepción,** state of emergency; **estar en e.,** to be pregnant; **e. civil,** marital status; *Com* **e. de cuentas,** statement of accounts. 3 *Mil* **e. mayor,** general staff.

Estados Unidos *npl* the United States.

estadounidense **I** *adj* United States, American. **II** *nmf* United States citizen.

estafa *nf* swindle.

estafador,-a *nm,f* swindler.

estafar *vtr* to swindle.

estafeta *nf* **e. de Correos,** sub post office.

estalactita *nf* stalactite.

estalagmita *nf* stalagmite.

estallar *vi* 1 to burst; *(bomba)* to explode, go off; *(guerra)* to break out. 2 *fig (de cólera etc)* to explode; **e. en sollozos,** to burst into tears.

estallido *nm* explosion; *(de guerra)* outbreak.

estambre *nm Bot* stamen.

Estambul *n* Istanbul.

estamento *nm Hist* estate; *fig (grupo)* group.

estampa *nf* illustration.

estampado,-a I *adj (tela)* printed. **II** *nm* 1 *(tela)* print. 2 *(proceso)* printing.

estampar *vtr* 1 *(tela)* to print. 2 *(dejar impreso)* to imprint. 3 *fig (bofetada, beso)* to plant, place.

estampida *nf* 1 *(estampido)* bang. 2 *(carrera rápida)* stampede; **de e.,** suddenly.

estampido *nm* bang.

estampilla *nf Am* (postage) stamp.

estancado,-a *adj (agua)* stagnant; *fig* static, at a standstill; **quedarse e.,** to get stuck *o* bogged down.

estancar |1| **I** *vtr* 1 *(agua)* hold back. 2 *fig (asunto)* to block; *(negociaciones)* to bring to a standstill. **II estancarse** *vr* to stagnate; *fig* to get bogged down.

estancia *nf* 1 *(permanencia)* stay. 2 *(habitación)* room. 3 *Am (hacienda)* ranch, farm.

estanco,-a I *nm* tobacconist's. **II** *adj* watertight.

estándar *(pl estándares)* *adj & nm* standard.

estandarizar |4| *vtr* to standardize.

estandarte *nm* standard, banner.

estanque *nm* pool, pond.

estanquero,-a *nm,f* tobacconist.

estante *nm* shelf; *(para libros)* bookcase.

estantería *nf* shelves *pl,* shelving.

estaño *nm* tin.

estar |13| **I** *vi* 1 to be; **está en la playa,** he is at the beach; **e. en casa,** to be in, be at home; **estamos en Caracas,** we are in Caracas; **¿está tu madre?,** is your mother in?; **¿cómo estás?** how are you?; **los precios están bajos,** prices are low; **el problema está en el dinero,** the problem is money; **e. en lo cierto,** to be right; **e. en todo,** not to miss a trick. 2 *(+ adj)* to be; **está cansado/enfermo,** he's tired/ill; **está vacío,** it's empty. 3 *(+ adv)* to be; **está bien/mal,** it's all right/wrong; **e. mal de dinero,** he's short of money; **estará enseguida,** it'll be ready in a minute. 4 *(+ ger)* to be; **está escribiendo,** she is writing; **estaba comiendo,** he was eating. 5 *(+ a + fecha)* to be; **¿a cuántos estamos?,** what's the date (today)?; **estamos a 2 de Noviembre,** it is the 2nd of November. 6 *(+ precio)* to be at; **están a 100 pesetas el kilo,** they're at 100 pesetas a kilo. 7 *(locuciones)* **e. al caer,** to be just round the corner; **¿estamos?,** OK? 8 *(+ de)* **e. de más,** not to be needed; **e. de paseo,** to be out for a walk; **e. de vacaciones/viaje,** to be (away) on holiday/a trip; **estoy de jefe hoy,** I'm the boss today. 9 *(+ para)* **esta-**

rá para las seis, it will be finished by six; **hoy no estoy para bromas,** I'm in no mood for jokes today; **el tren está para salir,** the train is just about to leave. **10** (+ **por**) **está por hacer,** it has still to be done; **eso está por ver,** it remains to be seen; **estoy por esperar,** *(a favor de)* I'm for waiting. **11** (+ **con**) to have; **e. con la gripe,** to have the flu, be down with flu; **estoy con Jaime,** *(de acuerdo con)* I agree with Jaime. **12** (+ **sin**) to have no; **e. sin luz/agua,** to have no light/water. **13** (+ **que**) **está que se duerme,** he is nearly asleep; *fam* **está que rabia,** he's hopping mad.
II estarse *vr* ¡estáte quieto!, keep still!, stop fidgeting!

statal *adj* state; **enseñanza e.,** state education.

stático,-a *adj* static.

statua *nf* statue.

statura *nf* **1** height; **¿cuál es tu e.?,** how tall are you? **2** *(renombre)* stature.

status *nm* status; **e. quo,** status quo.

statutario *adj* statutory.

statuto *nm Jur* statute; *(de ciudad)* by-law; *(de empresa etc)* rules.

ste I *adj* eastern; *(dirección)* easterly. **II** *nm* east; **al e. de,** to the east of.

sté *subj pres* → **estar.**

ste,-a *adj dem* **1** this. **2 estos,-as,** these.

ste,-a *pron dem m,f* **1** this one; **aquél ... é.,** the former ... the latter. **2 éstos,-as,** these (ones); **aquéllos ... é.,** the former ... the latter.

stela *nf* *(de barco)* wake; *(de avión)* vapour trail; *(de cometa)* tail.

stelar *adj* **1** *Astron* stellar. **2** *fig Cin Teat* star.

stentóreo,-a *adj* stentorian, thundering.

stepa *nf* steppe.

stera *nf* rush mat.

stercolero *nm* dunghill; *fig* pigsty.

stéreo *nm & adj* stereo.

stereofónico,-a *adj* stereophonic, stereo.

stereotipar *vtr* to stereotype.

stereotipo *nm* stereotype.

stéril *adj* **1** sterile. **2** *fig (esfuerzo)* futile.

sterilidad *nf* **1** sterility. **2** *fig* futility, uselessness.

sterilizar [4] *vtr* to sterilize.

sterilla *nf* small mat.

sterlina *adj & nf* sterling; **libra e.,** pound (sterling).

sternón *nm* sternum, breastbone.

stero *nm Am* marsh, swamp.

stertor *nm* death rattle.

stética *nf* aesthetics, *US* esthetics *sing.*

steticienne, esteticista *nf* beautician.

stético,-a *adj* aesthetic, *US* esthetic; **cirugía estética,** plastic surgery.

stibador *nm* docker, stevedore.

stiércol *nm* manure, dung.

stigma *nm* stigma; *Rel* stigmata.

estilarse *vr* to be in vogue, be fashionable.

estilete *nm (punzón)* stylus; *(puñal)* stiletto.

estilístico,-a *adj* stylistic.

estilizar [4] *vtr* to stylize.

estilo *nm* **1** style; *(modo)* manner, fashion; **algo por el e.,** something like that; **e. de vida,** way of life. **2** *Natación* stroke. **3** *Ling* **e. directo/indirecto,** direct/indirect speech.

estilográfica *nf* **(pluma) e.,** fountain pen.

estima *nf* esteem, respect.

estimación *nf* **1** *(estima)* esteem, respect. **2** *(valoración)* evaluation; *(cálculo aproximado)* estimate.

estimado,-a *adj* esteemed, respected; **E. Señor,** *(en carta)* Dear Sir.

estimar *vtr* **1** *(apreciar)* to esteem. **2** *(considerar)* to consider, think; **lo estimo conveniente,** I think it appropriate. **3** *(valorar)* to value.

estimativo,-a *adj* approximate, estimated.

estimulante I *adj* stimulating. **II** *nm* stimulant.

estimular *vtr* **1** to stimulate. **2** *fig* to encourage.

estímulo *nm Biol Fís* stimulus; *fig* encouragement.

estío *nm* summer.

estipendio *nm* stipend, fee.

estipular *vtr* to stipulate.

estirado,-a *adj* stiff.

estirar I *vtr* to stretch; *fig (dinero)* to spin out; *fig* **e. la pata,** to kick the bucket. **II estirarse** *vr* to stretch.

estirón *nm* pull, jerk, tug; *fam* **dar** *o* **pegar un e.,** to shoot up *o* grow quickly.

estirpe *nf* stock, pedigree.

estival *adj* summer; **época e.,** summertime.

esto *pron dem neut* this, this thing, this matter; *fam* **e. de la fiesta,** this business about the party.

estocada *nf Taur* stab.

Estocolmo *n* Stockholm.

estofado *nm* stew.

estoico,-a I *adj* stoical. **II** *nm,f* stoic.

estómago *nm* stomach; **dolor de e.,** stomach ache.

estoque *nm Taur* sword.

estorbar I *vtr* **1** *(dificultar)* to hinder, get in the way of. **2** *(molestar)* to disturb. **II** *vi* to be in the way.

estorbo *nm* **1** *(obstáculo)* obstruction, obstacle. **2** *(molestia)* nuisance.

estornino *nm* starling.

estornudar *vi* to sneeze.

estornudo *nm* sneeze.

estos,-as *adj dem pl* → **este,-a.**

éstos,-as *pron dem m,fpl* → **éste,-a.**

estoy *indic pres* → **estar.**

estrabismo *nm* squint.

estrado *nm* platform; *Mús* bandstand; *Jur*

stand.

estrafalario,-a *adj fam* outlandish.

estragos *nmpl* **hacer e. en,** to wreak havoc with *o* on.

estrambótico,-a *adj fam* outlandish, eccentric.

estrangulador,-a *nm,f* strangler.

estrangular *vtr* to strangle; *Med* to strangulate.

estraperlo *nm* black market; **tabaco de e.,** black market cigarettes.

Estrasburgo *n* Strasbourg.

estratagema *nf Mil* stratagem; *fam* trick, ruse.

estratega *nmf* strategist.

estrategia *nf* strategy.

estratégico,-a *adj* strategic.

estratificar [1] *vtr* to stratify.

estrato *nm* stratum.

estraza *nf* **papel de e.,** brown paper.

estrechamiento *nm* 1 narrowing; 'e. de calzada', *(en letrero)* 'road narrows'. 2 *(de amistad etc)* tightening.

estrechar I *vtr* 1 to make narrow. 2 *(mano)* to shake; *(lazos de amistad)* to tighten; **me estrechó entre sus brazos,** he hugged me. II **estrecharse** *vr* to narrow, become narrower.

estrechez *nf* 1 narrowness; *fig* **e. de miras,** narrow-mindedness. 2 *fig (dificultad económica)* want, need; **pasar estrecheces,** to be hard up.

estrecho,-a I *adj* 1 narrow; *(ropa, zapato)* tight; *(amistad, relación)* close, intimate. 2 *fig* **e. de miras,** narrow-minded. II *nm Geog* strait, straits *pl*. ◆**estrechamente** *adv (intimamente)* closely, intimately; **e. relacionados,** closely related.

estregar *vtr* to scrub.

estrella *nf* star; **e. de cine,** film star; *Zool* **e. de mar,** starfish; **e. fugaz,** shooting star.

estrellado,-a *adj* 1 *(en forma de estrella)* star-shaped. 2 *(cielo)* starry. 3 *(huevos)* scrambled.

estrellar I *vtr fam* to smash. II **estrellarse** *vr Aut Av (chocar)* to crash (**contra,** into); *(morir)* to die in a car crash.

estrellato *nm* stardom.

estremecedor,-a *adj* bloodcurdling.

estremecer [33] *vtr*, **estremecerse** *vr* to shake.

estrenar *vtr* 1 to use for the first time; *(ropa)* to wear for the first time. 2 *Teat Cin* to premiere.

estreno *nm Teat* first performance; *Cin* premiere.

estreñido,-a *adj* constipated.

estreñimiento *nm* constipation.

estrépito *nm* din, racket.

estrepitoso,-a *adj* deafening; *fig (fracaso)* spectacular.

estrés *nm* stress.

estresante *adj* stressful.

estría *nf* 1 *(en la piel)* stretch mark. 2 *Arquit* flute, fluting.

estribar *vi* **e. en,** to lie in, be based on.

estribillo *nm (en canción)* chorus; *(en poema)* refrain.

estribo *nm* 1 stirrup; *fig* **perder los estribos,** to lose one's temper, lose one' head. 2 *Arquit* buttress; *(de puente)* pier support.

estribor *nm* starboard.

estricto,-a *adj* strict.

estridente *adj* strident.

estrofa *nf* verse.

estropajo *nm* scourer.

estropear I *vtr (máquina, cosecha)* to damage; *(fiesta, plan)* to spoil, ruin; *(pelo, manos)* to ruin. II **estropearse** *vr* to be ruined; *(máquina)* to break down.

estropicio *nm fam (destrozo)* damage; *(ruido)* crash, clatter.

estructura *nf* structure; *(armazón)* frame framework.

estructurar *vtr* to structure.

estruendo *nm* roar.

estrujar I *vtr (limón etc)* to squeeze; *(ropa)* to wring; *(apretar)* to crush. II **estrujarse** *vr fam* **e. los sesos** *o* **el cerebro,** to rack one's brains.

estrujón *nm* tight squeeze, big hug.

estuche *nm* case; *(para lápices)* pencil case.

estuco *nm* stucco.

estudiante *nmf* student.

estudiantil *adj* student.

estudiar [12] *vtr & vi* to study.

estudio *nm* 1 study; *(encuesta)* survey *Com* **e. de mercado,** market research. 2 *(sala)* studio; **e. cinematográfico/de grabación,** film/recording studio. 3 *(apartamento)* studio (flat). 4 **estudios,** studies.

estudioso,-a I *adj* studious. II *nm,f* specialist.

estufa *nf (calentador)* heater; *(de leña)* stove.

estupefaciente *nm* drug, narcotic.

estupefacto,-a *adj* astounded, flabbergasted.

estupendo,-a *adj* super, marvellous, *US* marvelous; ¡e.!, great! ◆**estupendamente** *adv* marvellously, *US* marvelously, wonderfully.

estupidez *nf* stupidity.

estúpido,-a I *adj* stupid. II *nm,f* berk, idiot.

estupor *nm* amazement, astonishment.

estupro *nm* *Jur* rape (of a minor).

estuve *pt indef* → **estar.**

esvástica *nf* swastika.

ETA *nf abr de* **Euzkadi Ta Askatasuna** *(Patria Vasca y Libertad)*, ETA.

etapa *nf* stage; **por etapas,** in stages.

etarra *nmf* member of ETA.

etc. *abr de* **etcétera,** etcetera, etc.

etcétera *adv* etcetera.

éter *nm* ether.
etéreo,-a *adj* ethereal.
eternidad *nf* eternity; *fam* **una e.**, ages.
eterno,-a *adj* eternal.
ética *nf* ethic; *(ciencia)* ethics *sing*.
ético,-a *adj* ethical.
etílico,-a *adj* ethylic; **alcohol e.**, ethyl alcohol; **en estado e.**, intoxicated; **intoxicación etílica**, alcohol poisoning.
etimología *nf* etymology.
etimológico,-a *adj* etymological.
etíope, etíope *adj & nmf* Ethiopian.
Etiopía *nf* Ethiopia.
etiqueta *nf* 1 *(de producto)* label. 2 *(ceremonia)* etiquette; **de e.**, formal.
etiquetar *vtr* to label.
etnia *nf* ethnic group.
étnico,-a *adj* ethnic.
eucalipto *nm* eucalyptus.
eucaristía *nf* eucharist.
eufemismo *nm* euphemism.
euforia *nf* euphoria.
eufórico,-a *adj* euphoric.
eureka *interj* eureka!
eurocomunismo *nm* Eurocommunism.
eurodiputado,-a *nm,f* Euro MP.
euromisil *nm* Euromissile.
Europa *n* Europe.
europeísmo *nm* Europeanism.
europeizar |26| *vtr* to europeanize.
europeo,-a *adj & nm,f* European.
euscalduna I *adj* Basque; *(que habla vasco)* Basque-speaking. II *nmf* Basque speaker.
euskera *adj & nm* Basque.
eutanasia *nf* euthanasia.
evacuación *nf* evacuation.
evacuar |10| *vtr* to evacuate.
evadir I *vtr (respuesta, peligro, impuestos)* to avoid; *(responsabilidad)* to shirk. II **evadirse** *vr* to escape.
evaluación *nf* evaluation; *Educ* assessment; **e. continua**, continuous assessment.
evaluar |30| *vtr* to evaluate, assess.
evangélico,-a *adj* evangelical.
evangelio *nm* gospel.
evangelista *nm* evangelist.
evaporación *nf* evaporation.
evaporar I *vtr* to evaporate. II **evaporarse** *vr* to evaporate; *fig* to vanish.
evasión *nf (fuga)* escape; *fig* evasion; **e. fiscal** *o* **de impuestos**, tax evasion.
evasiva *nf* evasive answer.
evasivo,-a *adj* evasive.
evento *nm* 1 *(acontecimiento)* event. 2 *(incidente)* contingency, unforeseen event.
eventual I *adj* 1 *(posible)* possible; *(gastos)* incidental. 2 *(trabajo, obrero)* casual, temporary. ◆**eventualmente** *adv* by chance; **los problemas que e. surjan**, such problems as may arise.
eventualidad *nf* contingency.
evidencia *nf* obviousness; **poner a algn en e.**, to show sb up.
evidenciar |12| *vtr* to show, demonstrate.
evidente *adj* obvious. ◆**evidentemente** *adv* obviously.
evitar *vtr* to avoid; *(prevenir)* to prevent; *(desastre)* to avert.
evocador,-a *adj* evocative.
evocar |1| *vtr (traer a la memoria)* to evoke; *(acordarse de)* to recall.
evolución *nf* evolution; *(desarrollo)* development.
evolucionar *vi* to develop; *Biol* to evolve; **el enfermo evoluciona favorablemente**, the patient is improving.
ex *pref* former, ex-; ex alumno, former pupil, ex-student; **ex combatiente**, ex-serviceman, *US veteran*; **ex marido**, ex-husband; *fam* **mi ex**, my ex.
exabrupto *nm* sharp comment.
exacerbar I *vtr* 1 *(agravar)* to exacerbate, aggravate. 2 *(irritar)* to exasperate, irritate. II **exacerbarse** *vr (irritarse)* to feel exasperated.
exactitud *nf* accuracy; **con e.**, precisely.
exacto,-a *adj* exact; **¡e.!**, precisely!; **para ser e.**, to be precise. ◆**exactamente** *adv* exactly, precisely.
exageración *nf* exaggeration.
exagerado,-a *adj* exaggerated; *(excesivo)* excessive.
exagerar I *vtr* to exaggerate. II *vi* to overdo it.
exaltado,-a *adj* I *(persona)* excitable, hotheaded. II *nm,f fam* fanatic.
exaltar I *vtr* 1 to praise, extol. II **exaltarse** *vr (acalorarse)* to get overexcited, get carried away.
examen *nm* examination, exam; **e. de conducir**, driving test; *Med* **e. médico**, checkup.
examinador,-a *nm,f* examiner.
examinar I *vtr* to examine. II **examinarse** *vr* to take *o* sit an examination.
exasperante *adj* exasperating.
exasperar I *vtr* to exasperate. II **exasperarse** *vr* to become exasperated.
Exc., Exca., Exc.ª *abr de* **Excelencia**, Excellency.
excavación *nf* excavation; *(en arqueología)* dig.
excavadora *nf* digger.
excavar *vtr* to excavate, dig.
excedencia *nf* leave (of absence).
excedente *adj & nm* excess, surplus.
exceder I *vtr* to exceed, surpass. II **excederse** *vr* to go too far.
excelencia *nf* 1 excellence; **por e.**, par excellence. 2 *(título)* **Su E.**, His *o* Her Excellency.
excelente *adj* excellent.
excelso,-a *adj* sublime, lofty.
excentricidad *nf* eccentricity.
excéntrico,-a *adj* eccentric.
excepción *nf* exception; **a e. de**, with the

exception of, except for; **de e.**, exceptional; *Pol* **estado de e.**, state of emergency.

excepcional *adj* exceptional.

excepto *adv* except (for), apart from.

exceptuar [30] *vtr* to except, exclude.

excesivo,-a *adj* excessive.

exceso *nm* excess; **en e.**, in excess, excessively; **e. de equipaje**, excess baggage; **e. de velocidad**, speeding.

excitable *adj* excitable.

excitación *nf (sentimiento)* excitement.

excitante I *adj* exciting; *Med* stimulating. II *nm* stimulant.

excitar I *vtr* to excite. II **excitarse** *vr* to get excited.

exclamación *nf* exclamation.

exclamar *vtr & vi* to exclaim, cry out.

excluir [37] *vtr* to exclude; *(rechazar)* to reject.

exclusión *nf* exclusion.

exclusiva *nf Prensa* exclusive; *Com* sole right.

exclusive *adv (en fechas)* exclusive.

exclusivo,-a *adj* exclusive.

Excma. *abr de* **Excelentísima**, Most Excellent.

Excmo. *abr de* **Excelentísimo**, Most Excellent.

excomulgar [7] *vtr Rel* to excommunicate.

excomunión *nf* excommunication.

excremento *nm* excrement.

exculpar *vtr* to exonerate.

excursión *nf* excursion.

excursionista *nmf* tripper; *(a pie)* hiker.

excusa *nf (pretexto)* excuse; *(disculpa)* apology.

excusado *nm (retrete)* toilet.

excusar I *vtr* 1 *(justificar)* to excuse. 2 *(eximir)* to exempt (**de**, from). II **excusarse** *vr (disculparse)* to apologize.

execrar *vtr* to execrate, abhor.

exención *nf* exemption; **e. de impuestos**, tax exemption.

exento,-a *adj* exempt, free (**de**, from).

exequias *nfpl* funeral rites.

exhalar *vtr* to exhale, breathe out; *(gas)* to give off, emit; *(suspiro)* to heave.

exhaustivo,-a *adj* exhaustive.

exhausto,-a *adj* exhausted.

exhibición *nf* exhibition.

exhibicionista *nmf* exhibitionist.

exhibir I *vtr* 1 *(mostrar)* to exhibit, display. 2 *(lucir)* to show off. II **exhibirse** *vr* to show off, make an exhibition of oneself.

exhortar *vtr* to exhort.

exhumar *vtr* to exhume.

exigencia *nf* 1 demand. 2 *(requisito)* requirement.

exigente *adj* demanding, exacting.

exigir [6] *vtr* to demand.

exiguo,-a *adj* minute.

exilado,-a I *adj* exiled, in exile. II *nm,f* exile.

exilar I *vtr* to exile, send into exile. II **exilarse** *vr* to go into exile.

exiliado,-a *adj & nm,f* → **exilado,-a**.

exiliar [12] *vtr*, **exiliarse** *vr* → **exilar**.

exilio *nm* exile.

eximio,-a *adj* distinguished, eminent.

eximir *vtr* to exempt (**de**, from).

existencia *nf* 1 *(vida)* existence. 2 *Com* **existencias**, stock *sing*, stocks.

existente *adj* existing; *Com* in stock.

existir *vi* to exist, be (in existence).

éxito *nm* success; **con é.**, successfully; **tener é.**, to be successful.

exitoso,-a *adj* successful.

éxodo *nm* exodus.

exonerar *vtr* to exonerate.

exorbitante *adj* exorbitant, excessive.

exorcista *nmf* exorcist.

exorcizar [4] *vtr* to exorcize.

exótico,-a *adj* exotic.

expandir I *vtr* to expand. II **expandirse** *(gas etc)* to expand; *(noticia)* to spread.

expansión *nf* 1 expansion; *(de noticia)* spreading. 2 *(diversión)* relaxation, recreation.

expansionarse *vr fig (divertirse)* to relax, let one's hair down.

expatriado,-a *adj & nm,f* expatriate.

expatriar [19] I *vtr* to exile, banish. II **expatriarse** *vr* to leave one's country.

expectación *nf* excitement.

expectativa *nf* expectancy; **estar a la e. de**, to be on the lookout for.

expectorante *nm* expectorant.

expedición *nf* expedition.

expedientar *vtr* to place under enquiry.

expediente *nm* 1 *(informe)* dossier, record; *(ficha)* file; *Educ* **e. académico**, student's record; **abrirle e. a algn**, to place sb under enquiry. 2 *Jur* proceedings *pl*, action.

expedir [6] *vtr* 1 *(carta)* to send, dispatch. 2 *(pasaporte etc)* to issue.

expedito,-a *adj* free, clear.

expendedor,-a I *nm,f* seller. II *nm* **e. automático**, vending machine.

expendeduría *nf* tobacconist's.

expensas *nfpl* **a e. de**, at the expense of.

experiencia *nf* 1 experience; **por e.**, from experience. 2 *(experimento)* experiment.

experimentado,-a *adj* experienced.

experimental *adj* experimental.

experimentar I *vi* to experiment. II *vtr* to undergo; *(aumento)* to show; *(pérdida)* to suffer; *(sensación)* to experience, feel; *Med* **e. una mejoría**, to improve, make progress.

experimento *nm* experiment.

experto,-a *nm,f* expert.

expiar [29] *vtr* to expiate, atone for.

expirar *vi* to expire.

explanada *nf* esplanade.

explayarse *vr* to talk at length (about).

explicación *nf* explanation.

explicar [1] I *vtr* to explain. II **explicarse** *vr* (persona) to explain (oneself); **no me lo explico**, I can't understand it.

explicativo,-a *adj* explanatory.

explícito,-a *adj* explicit.

exploración *nf* exploration; *Téc* scanning; *Med* probe; *Mil* reconnaissance.

explorador,-a *nm,f* 1 (persona) explorer. 2 *Med* probe; *Téc* scanner.

explorar *vtr* to explore; *Med* to probe; *Téc* to scan; *Mil* to reconnoitre.

explosión *nf* explosion, blast; **hacer e.**, to explode; **motor de e.**, internal combustion engine; **e. demográfica**, population explosion.

explosionar *vtr & vi* to explode, blow up.

explosivo,-a *adj & nm* explosive.

explotación *nf* 1 (abuso) exploitation. 2 (uso) exploitation, working; *Agr* cultivation (of land); (granja) farm.

explotador,-a *nm,f pey* exploiter.

explotar I *vi* (bomba) to explode, go off. II *vtr* 1 (aprovechar) to exploit; (recursos) to tap; (tierra) to cultivate. 2 (abusar de) to exploit.

expoliar [12] *vtr* to plunder, pillage.

exponente *nmf* exponent.

exponer [19] (pp **expuesto**) I *vtr* 1 (mostrar) to exhibit, display. 2 (explicar) to expound, put forward. 3 (arriesgar) to expose. II **exponerse** *vr* to expose oneself (a, to); **te expones a perder el trabajo**, you run the risk of losing your job.

exportación *nf* export.

exportador,-a I *adj* exporting. II *nm,f* exporter.

exportar *vtr* to export.

exposición *nf* 1 *Arte* exhibition; **e. universal**, world fair; **sala de exposiciones**, gallery. 2 (de hechos, ideas) exposé. 3 *Fot* exposure.

exprés *adj* express; (olla) **e.**, pressure cooker; (café) **e.**, espresso (coffee).

expresar I *vtr* to express; (manifestar) to state. II **expresarse** *vr* to express oneself.

expresión *nf* expression; **la mínima e.**, the bare minimum.

expresivo,-a *adj* expressive.

expreso,-a I *adj* express; **con el fin e. de**, with the express purpose of. II *nm Ferroc* express (train). III *adv* on purpose, deliberately. ◆**expresamente** *adv* specifically, expressly.

exprimidor *nm* squeezer, *US* juicer.

exprimir *vtr* (limón) to squeeze; (zumo) to squeeze out; *fig* (persona) to exploit, bleed dry.

expropiar [12] *vtr* to expropriate.

expuesto,-a *adj* 1 (sin protección) exposed; **estar e. a**, to be exposed to. 2 (peligroso) risky, dangerous. 3 (exhibido) on display, on show.

expulsar *vtr* 1 to expel, throw out; *Dep* (jugador) to send off. 2 (gas etc) to belch out.

expulsión *nf* expulsion; *Dep* sending off.

expurgar [7] *vtr* to expurgate; *fig* to purge.

expuse *pt indef* → **exponer**.

exquisito,-a *adj* exquisite; (comida) delicious; (gusto) refined.

extasiado,-a *adj* ecstatic; **quedarse e.**, to go into ecstasies o raptures.

extasiarse [29] *vr* to go into ecstasies o raptures.

éxtasis *nm inv* ecstasy.

extender [3] I *vtr* 1 to extend; (agrandar) to enlarge. 2 (mantel, mapa) to spread (out), open (out); (mano, brazo) to stretch (out). 3 (crema, mantequilla) to spread. 3 (cheque) to make out; (documento) to draw up; (certificado) to issue. II **extenderse** *vr* 1 (en el tiempo) to extend, last. 2 (en el espacio) to spread out, stretch. 3 (rumor, noticia) to spread, extend. 4 *fig* (hablar demasiado) to go on.

extendido,-a *adj* 1 extended; (mapa, plano) spread out, open; (mano, brazo) outstretched. 2 (costumbre, rumor) widespread.

extensible *adj* extending.

extensión *nf* (de libro etc) length; (de cuerpo) size; (de terreno) area, expanse; (edificio anexo) extension; **en toda la e. de la palabra**, in every sense of the word; **por e.**, by extension.

extensivo,-a *adj* hacer **e.**, to extend; ser **e. a**, to cover.

extenso,-a *adj* (terreno) extensive; (libro, película) long.

extenuar [30] I *vtr* to exhaust. II **extenuarse** *vr* to exhaust oneself.

exterior I *adj* 1 (de fuera) outer; (puerta) outside. 2 (política, deuda) foreign; *Pol* **Ministerio de Asuntos Exteriores**, Ministry of Foreign Affairs, *GB* Foreign Office, *US* State Department. II *nm* 1 (parte de fuera) exterior, outside. 2 (extranjero) abroad. 3 **exteriores**, *Cin* location *sing*. ◆**exteriormente** *adv* outwardly.

exteriorizar [4] *vtr* to show.

exterminar *vtr* to exterminate.

exterminio *nm* extermination.

externo,-a I *adj* external; *Farm* **de uso e.**, for external use only. II *nm,f Educ* day pupil.

extinción *nf* extinction.

extinguir [8] I *vtr* (fuego) to exinguish, put out; (raza) to wipe out. II **extinguirse** *vr* (fuego) to go out; (especie) to become extinct, die out.

extinto,-a *adj* extinct.

extintor *nm* fire extinguisher.

extirpar *vtr* 1 *Med* to remove. 2 *fig* to

eradicate, stamp out.

extorsión *nf* extortion.

extorsionar *vtr* to extort.

extra¹ I *adj* **1** *(suplementario)* extra; **horas e.**, overtime; **paga e.**, bonus. **2** *(superior)* top quality. **II** *nm* extra. **III** *nm,f Cin Teat* extra.

extra² *pref* extra; **extramatrimonial**, extramarital.

extracción *nf* **1** extraction. **2** *(en lotería)* draw.

extracto *nm* **1** extract; **e. de fresa**, strawberry extract; **e. de regaliz**, liquorice; *Fin* **e. de cuenta**, statement of account. **2** *(resumen)* summary.

extractor *nm* extractor.

extradición *nf* extradition.

extraer |25| *vtr* to extract, take out.

extraescolar *adj (actividad etc)* extracurricular.

extrafino,-a *adj* superfine.

extralimitarse *vr* to overstep the mark.

extranjería *nf* ley de e., law on aliens.

extranjero,-a I *adj* foreign. **II** *nm,f* foreigner. **III** *nm* abroad; **en el e.**, abroad.

extrañar I *vtr* **1** *(sorprender)* to surprise; **no es de e.**, it's hardly surprising. **2** *Am (echar de menos)* to miss. **II extrañarse** *vr* **e. de**, to be surprised at.

extrañeza *nf* **1** *(sorpresa)* surprise, astonishment. **2** *(singularidad)* strangeness.

extraño,-a I *adj* strange; *Med* **cuerpo e.**, foreign body. **II** *nm,f* stranger.

extraoficial *adj* unofficial.

extraordinaria *nf (paga)* bonus.

extraordinario,-a *adj* extraordinary; *Prensa* **edición extraordinaria**, special edition.

extrarradio *nm* outskirts *pl*, suburbs *pl*.

extraterrestre *nmf* alien.

extravagancia *nf* extravagance.

extravagante *adj* odd, outlandish.

extravertido,-a *adj* → extrovertido,-a.

extraviado,-a *adj* lost, missing.

extraviar |29| **I** *vtr* to mislay, lose. **II extraviarse** *vr* to be missing, get mislaid.

extremado,-a *adj* extreme. ◆**extremadamente** *adv* extremely.

Extremadura *n* Estremadura.

extremar I *vtr* **e. la prudencia**, to be extremely careful. **II extremarse** *vr* to take great pains, do one's utmost.

extremaunción *nf* extreme unction.

extremeño,-a I *adj* of *o* from Estremadura. **II** *nm,f* native of Estremadura.

extremidad *nf* **1** *(extremo)* end, tip. **2** *Anat (miembro)* limb, extremity.

extremista *adj & nmf* extremist.

extremo,-a I *nm (de calle, cable)* end; *(máximo)* extreme; **en e.**, very much; **en último e.**, as a last resort. **II** *nm,f Dep* winger; *Ftb* **e. derecha/izquierda**, outside-right/-left. **III** *adj* extreme; **E. Oriente**, Far East.

extrovertido,-a *adj & nm,f* extrovert.

exuberante *adj* exuberant; *(vegetación)* lush, abundant.

eyaculación *nf* ejaculation; **e. precoz**, premature ejaculation.

eyacular *vi* to ejaculate.

eyectable *adj* **asiento e.**, ejector seat.

F

F, f |'efe| *nf (la letra)* F, f.

F *abr de* Fahrenheit, Fahrenheit, F.

fa *nm Mús* F.

fabada *nf* stew of beans, pork sausage and bacon.

fábrica *nf* factory; **marca de f.**, trademark; **precio de f.**, factory *o* ex-works price.

fabricación *nf* manufacture; **de f. casera**, home-made; **de f. propia**, our own make; **f. en cadena**, mass production.

fabricante *nmf* manufacturer.

fabricar |1| *vtr* **1** *Ind* to manufacture. **2** *fig (mentiras etc)* to fabricate.

fabril *adj* manufacturing.

fábula *nf* fable.

fabuloso,-a *adj* fabulous.

faca *nf* large curved knife.

facción *nf* **1** *Pol* faction. **2** **facciones**, *(rasgos)* features.

faccioso,-a I *adj* seditious. **II** *nm,f* rebel.

faceta *nf* facet.

facha¹ *nf fam* appearance, look.

facha² *nmf pey* fascist.

fachada *nf* façade.

facial *adj* facial.

fácil *adj* **1** easy; **f. de comprender**, easy to understand. **2** *(probable)* likely, probable; **es f. que ...**, it's (quite) likely that .... ◆**fácilmente** *adv* easily.

facilidad *nf* **1** *(sencillez)* easiness. **2** *(soltura)* ease. **3** *(servicio)* facility; **dar facilidades**, to make things easy; *Com* **facilidades de pago**, easy terms. **4** **f. para los idiomas**, gift for languages.

facilitar *vtr (proporcionar)* to provide, supply (**a**, with).

facineroso,-a *adj* criminal.

facsímil, facsímile *nm* facsimile.

factible *adj* feasible.

fáctico,-a *adj* **poderes fácticos**, vested interests.

factor *nm* **1** factor. **2** *Ferroc* luggage clerk.

factoría *nf (fábrica)* factory.

factura *nf Com* invoice.

facturación *nf* **1** *Com* invoicing. **2** *(de*

equipajes) (en aeropuerto) check-in; *(en estación)* registration.

facturar *vtr* 1 *Com* to invoice. 2 *(en aeropuerto)* to check in; *(en estación)* to register.

facultad *nf* faculty; **facultades mentales,** faculties.

facultativo,-a I *adj* optional. II *nm,f* doctor.

faena *nf* 1 *(tarea)* task. 2 *fam (mala pasada)* dirty trick. 3 *Taur* performance.

faenar *vi* to fish.

fagot *Mús* bassoon.

faisán *nm* pheasant.

faja *nf* 1 *(corsé)* girdle, corset. 2 *(banda)* sash. 3 *(de terreno)* strip.

fajo *nm (de ropa etc)* bundle; *(de billetes)* wad.

falacia *nf* fallacy.

falaz *adj* 1 *(erróneo)* fallacious. 2 *(engañoso)* deceitful.

falda *nf* 1 *(prenda)* skirt; **f. pantalón,** culottes *pl.* 2 *(de montaña)* slope, hillside. 3 *(de mesa)* cover. 4 *(regazo)* lap.

faldero,-a *adj* **perro f.,** lapdog.

falla¹ *nf Am (defecto)* defect, fault.

falla² *nf Geol* fault.

fallar¹ I *vi Jur* to rule. II *vtr (premio)* to award.

fallar² I *vi* to fail; **le falló la puntería,** he missed his aim; *fig* **no me falles,** don't let me down. II *vtr* to miss.

fallecer [33] *vi fml* to pass away, die.

fallecido,-a *adj* deceased.

fallecimiento *nm* demise.

fallido,-a *adj* unsuccessful, vain.

fallo¹ *nm* 1 *(error)* mistake; **f. humano,** human error. 2 *(del corazón, de los frenos)* failure.

fallo² *nm* 1 *Jur* judgement, sentence. 2 *(en concurso)* awarding.

falo *nm* phallus.

falsear *vtr* 1 *(informe etc)* to falsify; *(hechos, la verdad)* to distort. 2 *(moneda)* to forge.

falsedad *nf* 1 falseness, *(doblez)* hypocrisy. 2 *(mentira)* falsehood.

falsificar [1] *vtr* to falsify; *(cuadro, firma, moneda)* to forge.

falso,-a *adj* 1 false; **dar un paso en f.,** *(tropezar)* to trip, stumble; *fig* to make a blunder; **jurar en f.,** to commit perjury. 2 *(persona)* insincere.

falta *nf* 1 *(carencia)* lack; **por f. de,** for want *o* lack of; **sin f.,** without fail; **f. de educación,** bad manners. 2 *(escasez)* shortage. 3 *(ausencia)* absence; **echar algo/a algn en f.,** to miss sth/sb. 4 *(error)* mistake; *(defecto)* fault, defect; **f. de ortografía,** spelling mistake; **sacar faltas a algo/a algn,** to find fault with sth/sb. 5 *Jur* misdemeanour. 6 *Dep (fútbol)* foul; *(tenis)* fault. 7 **hacer f.,** to be necessary; **(nos) hace f. una escalera,** we need a

ladder; **harán f. dos personas para mover el piano,** it'll take two people to move the piano; **no hace f. que ...,** there is no need for ....

faltar *vi* 1 *(no estar)* to be missing; **¿quién falta?,** who is missing? 2 *(escasear)* to be lacking *o* needed; **le falta confianza en sí mismo,** he lacks confidence in himself; **¡lo que me faltaba!,** that's all I needed!; **¡no faltaría o faltaba más!,** *(por supuesto)* (but) of course! 3 *(quedar)* to be left; **¿cuántos kilómetros faltan para Managua?,** how many kilometres is it to Managua?; **ya falta poco para las vacaciones,** it won't be long now till the holidays; **faltó poco para que me cayera,** I very nearly fell. 4 **f. a la verdad,** not to tell the truth; **f. al deber,** to fail in one's duty; **f. a su palabra/promesa,** to break one's word/promise; **f. al respeto a algn,** to treat sb with disrespect.

falto,-a *adj* **f. de,** lacking in.

fama *nf* 1 fame, renown; **de f. mundial,** world-famous. 2 *(reputación)* reputation.

famélico,-a *adj* starving, famished.

familia *nf* family; **estar en f.,** to be among friends; **f. numerosa,** large family.

familiar I *adj* 1 *(de la familia)* family; **empresa f.,** family business. 2 *(conocido)* familiar. II *nmf* relation, relative.

familiaridad *nf* familiarity.

familiarizarse [4] *vr* to familiarize oneself *(con,* with).

famoso,-a I *adj* famous. II *nm* famous person.

fan *nmf* fan.

fanático,-a I *adj* fanatical. II *nm,f* fanatic.

fanatismo *nm* fanaticism.

fanfarrón,-ona *fam* I *adj* boastful. II *nm,f* show-off.

fanfarronear *vi fam (chulear)* to show off; *(bravear)* to brag, boast.

fango *nm* 1 *(barro)* mud. 2 *fig* degradation.

fantasear *vi* to daydream, dream.

fantasía *nf* fantasy; **joya de f.,** imitation jewellery.

fantasioso,-a *adj* imaginative.

fantasma *nm* 1 *(espectro)* ghost. 2 *fam (fanfarrón)* braggart, show-off.

fantasmal *adj* ghostly.

fantástico,-a *adj* fantastic.

fantoche *nm pey* nincompoop, ninny.

faraón *nm* Pharaoh.

fardar *vi arg* to show off.

fardo *nm* bundle.

farfullar *vtr* to jabber.

faringe *nf* pharynx.

faringitis *nf* pharyngitis.

fariseo,-a *nm,f (falso)* hypocrite.

farmacéutico,-a I *adj* pharmaceutical. II *nm,f* pharmacist.

farmacia *nf* 1 *(tienda)* chemist's (shop),

US pharmacy. 2 (*ciencia*) pharmacology.

fármaco *nm* medicine, medication.

faro *nm* 1 (*torre*) lighthouse. 2 (*de coche*) headlight, headlamp.

farol *nm* 1 lantern; (*en la calle*) streetlight, streetlamp. 2 *arg* (*fanfarronada*) bragging; **tirarse un f.**, to brag. 3 (*en naipes*) bluff.

farola *nf* streetlight, streetlamp.

farolear *vi arg* to brag.

farolillo *nm fig* **ser el f. rojo**, to bring up the rear.

farragoso,-a *adj* confused, rambling.

farruco,-a *adj fam* cocky.

farsa *nf* farce.

farsante *nmf* fake, impostor.

fascículo *nm Impr* instalment, US installment.

fascinador,-a, fascinante *adj* fascinating.

fascinar *vtr* to fascinate.

fascismo *nm* fascism.

fascista *adj & nmf* fascist.

fase *nf* 1 (*etapa*) phase, stage. 2 *Elec Fís* phase.

fastidiado,-a *adj fam* 1 (*roto*) broken. 2 (*enfermo*) sick; **tiene el estómago f.**, he's got a bad stomach.

fastidiar [12] I *vtr* 1 (*molestar*) to annoy, bother; (*dañar*) to hurt; *fam* ¡**no fastidies!**, you're kidding! 2 *fam* (*estropear*) to damage, ruin; (*planes*) to spoil. II **fastidiarse** *vr* 1 (*aguantarse*) to put up with it, resign oneself; **que se fastidie**, that's his tough luck. 2 *fam* (*estropearse*) to get damaged, break down. 3 **me he fastidiado el tobillo**, I've hurt my ankle.

fastidio *nm* nuisance.

fastuoso,-a *adj* 1 (*acto*) splendid, lavish. 2 (*persona*) lavish, ostentatious.

fatal I *adj* 1 *fam* (*muy malo*) awful, dreadful. 2 (*mortal*) deadly, fatal. 3 (*inexorable*) fateful, inevitable. II *adv fam* awfully, terribly; **lo pasó f.**, he had a rotten time.

fatalidad *nf* 1 (*destino*) fate. 2 (*desgracia*) misfortune.

fatalista I *adj* fatalistic. II *nmf* fatalist.

fatiga *nf* 1 (*cansancio*) fatigue. 2 **fatigas**, (*dificultades*) troubles, difficulties.

fatigar [7] I *vtr* to tire, weary. II **fatigarse** *vr* to tire, become tired.

fatigoso,-a *adj* tiring, exhausting.

fatuo,-a *adj* 1 (*envanecido*) vain, conceited. 2 (*necio*) fatuous, foolish.

fauces *nfpl fig* jaws.

fauna *nf* fauna.

favor *nm* favour, US favor; **por f.**, please; ¿**puedes hacerme un f.?**, can you do me a favour?; **estar a f. de**, to be in favour of; **haga el f. de sentarse**, please sit down.

favorable *adj* favourable, US favorable; **f. a**, in favour of.

favorecedor,-a *adj* flattering.

favorecer [33] *vtr* 1 to favour, US favor. 2 (*sentar bien*) to flatter.

favoritismo *nm* favouritism, US favoritism.

favorito,-a *adj & nm,f* favourite, US favorite.

faz *nf* (*pl* **faces**) *lit* (*cara*) face.

fe *nf* 1 faith; **de buena/mala fe**, with good/dishonest intentions. 2 (*certificado*) certificate; **fe de bautismo/matrimonio**, baptism/marriage certificate. 3 *Impr* **fe de erratas**, list of errata.

fealdad *nf* ugliness.

febrero *nm* February.

febril *adj* 1 *Med* feverish. 2 (*actividad*) hectic.

fecha *nf* 1 date; **f. límite** *o* **tope**, deadline; **f. de caducidad**, sell-by date; **hasta la f.**, so far; **en f. próxima**, at an early date. 2 **fechas**, (*época*) time *sing*; **el año pasado por estas fechas**, this time last year.

fechar *vtr* to date.

fechoría *nf* (*de niños*) mischief; *arc* misdeed.

fécula *nf* starch.

fecundación *nf* fertilization; **f. in vitro**, in vitro fertilization.

fecundar *vtr* to fertilize.

fecundo,-a *adj* fertile.

federación *nf* federation.

federal *adj & nmf* federal.

fehaciente *adj* 1 *fml* authentic, reliable. 2 *Jur* irrefutable; **documento** *o* **prueba f.**, irrefutable proof.

felicidad *nf* happiness; (**muchas**) **felicidades**, (*en cumpleaños*) many happy returns.

felicitación *nf* **tarjeta de f.** greetings card.

felicitar *vtr* to congratulate (**por**, on); ¡**te felicito!**, congratulations!

feligrés,-a *nm,f* parishioner.

felino,-a *adj & nm* feline.

feliz *adj* 1 (*contento*) happy; ¡**felices Navidades!**, Happy *o* Merry Christmas! 2 (*decisión etc*) fortunate.

felonía *nf* treachery.

felpa *nf* 1 *Tex* plush; **oso** *o* **osito de f.**, teddy bear. 2 (*para el pelo*) hairband.

felpudo *nm* mat, doormat.

femenino,-a *adj* feminine; (*equipo, ropa*) women's; **sexo f.**, female sex.

feminismo *nm* feminism.

feminista *adj & nmf* feminist.

fémur *nm* femur.

fenecer [33] *vi euf* to pass away, die.

fenomenal I *adj* 1 phenomenal. 2 *fam* (*fantástico*) great, terrific. II *adv fam* wonderfully, marvellously; **lo pasamos f.**, we had a fantastic time.

fenómeno,-a I *nm* 1 phenomenon. 2 (*prodigio*) genius. 3 (*monstruo*) freak. II *adj fam* fantastic, terrific. III *interj* fantastic!, terrific!

feo,-a I *adj* ugly; (*asunto etc*) nasty. II *nm fam* **hacerle un f. a algn**, to offend sb.

féretro *nm* coffin.

feria nf fair; f. **de muestras/del libro,** trade/book fair.
feriado,-a adj día f., holiday.
ferial adj recinto f., (de exposiciones) exhibition centre; (de fiestas) fairground.
ferina adj tos f., whooping cough.
fermentar vi to ferment.
fermento nm ferment.
ferocidad nf ferocity, fierceness.
feroz adj fierce, ferocious; **el lobo f.,** the big bad wolf.
férreo,-a adj ferreous; fig iron.
ferretería nf ironmonger's (shop), hardware store.
ferrocarril nm railway, US railroad.
ferroviario,-a adj railway, rail.
ferry nm ferry.
fértil adj fertile.
fertilidad nf fertility.
fertilizante I adj fertilizing. II nm fertilizer.
fertilizar [4] vtr to fertilize.
ferviente adj fervent.
fervor nm fervour, US fervor.
fervoroso,-a adj fervent.
festejar vtr to celebrate.
festejos nmpl festivities.
festín nm feast, banquet.
festival nm festival.
festividad nf festivity.
festivo,-a I adj 1 (ambiente etc) festive. 2 día f., holiday. II nm holiday.
fetal adj foetal, US fetal.
fetiche nm fetish.
fétido,-a adj stinking, fetid.
feto nm foetus, US fetus.
feudalismo nm feudalism.
feudo nm fief; Pol stronghold.
FEVE nmpl abr de **Ferrocarriles Españoles de Vía Estrecha.**
FF.AA. nfpl abr de **Fuerzas Armadas,** Armed Forces.
FF.CC. nmpl abr de **ferrocarriles,** railways.
fiabilidad nf reliability, trustworthiness.
fiable adj reliable, trustworthy.
fiador,-a nm,f guarantor; **salir** o **ser f. de algn,** (pagar fianza) to stand bail for sb; (avalar) to vouch for sb.
fiambre nm 1 Culin cold meat. 2 fam (cadáver) stiff, corpse.
fiambrera nf lunch box.
fianza nf (depósito) deposit; Jur bail; **en libertad bajo f.,** on bail.
fiar [29] I vtr 1 (avalar) to guarantee. 2 (vender sin cobrar) to sell on credit. II **fiarse** vr to trust (de, -).
fiasco nm fiasco.
fibra nf fibre, US fiber; (de madera) grain; **f. de vidrio,** fibreglass.
ficción nf fiction.
ficha nf 1 (tarjeta) filing card; **f. técnica,** specifications pl, technical data; Cin credits pl. 2 (en juegos) counter; (de ajedrez) piece, man; (de dominó) domino.

fichado,-a adj está f. **por la policía,** he has a police record.
fichaje nm Dep signing.
fichar I vtr 1 to put on file. 2 Dep to sign up. II vi 1 (en el trabajo) (al entrar) to clock in; (al salir) to clock out. 2 Dep to sign.
fichero nm card index.
ficticio,-a adj fictitious.
fidedigno,-a adj reliable, trustworthy; **fuentes fidedignas,** reliable sources.
fidelidad nf faithfulness; **alta f.,** high fidelity, hi-fi.
fideo nm noodle.
fiebre nf fever; **tener f.,** to have a temperature.
fiel I adj 1 (leal) faithful, loyal. 2 (exacto) accurate, exact. II nm 1 (de balanza) needle, pointer. 2 Rel **los fieles,** the congregation.
fieltro nm felt.
fiera nf 1 wild animal; fam **estaba hecho una f.,** he was hopping mad. 2 Taur bull.
fiero,-a adj (salvaje) wild; (feroz) fierce, ferocious.
fierro nm Am 1 (hierro) iron. 2 (navaja) knife.
fiesta nf 1 (entre amigos) party. 2 día de f., holiday. 3 Rel feast; **f. de guardar,** holy day of obligation. 4 (festividad) celebration, festivity.
figura nf figure.
figurado,-a adj figurative; **en sentido f.,** figuratively.
figurar I vi (en lista) to figure. II **figurarse** vr 1 to imagine, suppose; **ya me lo figuraba,** I thought as much. 2 **¡figúrate!,** **¡figúrese!,** just imagine!
figurinista nmf Teat Cin costume designer.
fijador nm 1 (gomina) gel. 2 Fot fixative.
fijar I vtr to fix; **prohibido f. carteles,** (en letrero) post no bills. II **fijarse** vr 1 (darse cuenta) to notice. 2 (poner atención) to pay attention, watch.
fijo,-a adj fixed; **sin domicilio f.,** of no fixed abode. 2 (trabajo) steady. ◆**fijamente** adv mirar f., to stare.
fila nf 1 file; **en f. india,** in single file; **poner en f.,** to line up. 2 (de cine, teatro) row. 3 Mil **filas,** ranks; **llamar a algn a f.,** to call sb up; **¡rompan f.!,** fall out!, dismiss!
filamento nm filament.
filantropía nf philanthropy.
filántropo,-a nm,f philanthropist.
filarmónico,-a adj philharmonic.
filatelia nf philately, stamp collecting.
filete nm (de carne, pescado) fillet.
filiación nf Pol affiliation.
filial I adj 1 (de hijos) filial. 2 Com subsidiary. II nf Com subsidiary.
filigrana nf 1 filigree. 2 fig **filigranas,** intricacy sing, intricate work sing.

Filipinas *npl* (las) F., (the) Philippines.
filipino,-a *adj & nm,f* Philippine, Filipino.
filmar *vtr* to film, shoot.
film(e) *nm* film.
fílmico,-a *adj* film.
filmoteca *nf (archivo)* film library.
filo *nm* (cutting) edge; **al f. de la medianoche**, on the stroke of midnight; *fig* **de doble f.**, double-edged.
filón *nm* 1 *Min* seam, vein. 2 *fig (buen negocio)* gold mine.
filoso,-a *adj Am* sharp-edged.
filosofal *adj* **piedra f.**, philosopher's stone.
filosofía *nf* philosophy; *fig* **con f.**, philosophically.
filosófico,-a *adj* philosophical.
filósofo,-a *nm,f* philosopher.
filtración *nf* filtration; *(de información)* leak.
filtrar I *vtr* 1 to filter. 2 *(información)* to leak. **II filtrarse** *vr* 1 *(líquido)* seep. 2 *(información)* to leak out.
filtro *nm* filter.
fin *nm* 1 *(final)* end; **dar** *o* **poner f. a**, to put an end to; **llegar** *o* **tocar a su f.**, to come to an end; **en f.**, anyway; **¡por** *o* **al f.!**, at last!; **f. de semana**, weekend; **al f. y al cabo**, when all's said and done; **noche de F. de Año**, New Year's Eve. 2 *(objetivo)* purpose, aim; **a f. de**, in order to, so as to; **a f. de que**, in order that, so that; **con el f. de**, with the intention of.
final I *adj* final. **II** *nm* end; **al f.**, in the end; **f. de línea**, terminal; **f. feliz**, happy ending; **a finales de octubre**, at the end of October. **III** *nf Dep* final.
◆finalmente *adv* finally.
finalidad *nf* purpose, aim.
finalista I *nmf* finalist. **II** *adj* in the final.
finalizar [4] *vtr & vi* to end, finish.
financiación *nf* financing.
financiar [12] *vtr* to finance.
financiero,-a I *adj* financial. **II** *nm,f* financier.
financista *nmf Am* financier, financial expert.
finanzas *nfpl* finances.
finca *nf (inmueble)* property; *(de campo)* country house.
finés,-a *adj & nm,f* → **finlandés,-esa.**
fingido,-a *adj* feigned, false; **nombre f.**, assumed name.
fingir [6] **I** *vtr* to feign. **II fingirse** *vr* to pretend to be.
finlandés,-a I *adj* Finnish. **II** *nm,f (persona)* Finn. **III** *nm (idioma)* Finnish.
Finlandia *n* Finland.
fino,-a I *adj* 1 *(hilo, capa)* fine. 2 *(flaco)* thin. 3 *(educado)* refined, polite. 4 *(oído)* sharp, acute; *(olfato)* keen. 5 *(humor, ironía)* subtle. **II** *nm (vino)* type of dry sherry.

finta *nf (en boxeo)* feint; *(en fútbol)* dummy.
finura *nf* 1 *(refinamiento)* refinement, politeness. 2 *(sutileza)* subtlety.
firma *nf* 1 signature. 2 *(empresa)* firm, company.
firmamento *nm* firmament.
firmante *adj & nmf* signatory; **el** *o* **la abajo f.**, the undersigned.
firmar *vtr* to sign.
firme I *adj* 1 firm; *fig* **mantenerse f.**, to hold one's ground; **tierra f.**, terra firma. 2 *Mil* **¡firmes!**, attention!. **II** *nm (de carretera)* road surface. **III** *adv* hard.
◆firmemente *adv* firmly.
firmeza *nf* firmness.
fiscal I *adj* fiscal, tax. **II** *nmf Jur* public prosecutor, *US* district attorney.
fisco *nm* treasury, exchequer.
fisgar [7] *vi fam* to snoop, pry.
fisgón,-ona *nm,f* snooper.
fisgonear *vi* to snoop, pry.
física *nf* physics *sing.*
físico,-a I *adj* physical. **II** *nm,f (profesión)* physicist. **III** *nm* physique.
fisión *nf* fission.
fisioterapeuta *nmf* physiotherapist.
fisioterapia *nf Med* physiotherapy.
fisonomía *nf* physiognomy.
fisonomista *nmf fam* **ser buen/mal f.**, to be good/no good at remembering faces.
fisura *nf* fissure.
flácido,-a *adj* flaccid, flabby.
flaco,-a I *adj* 1 *(delgado)* skinny. 2 *fig* **punto f.**, weak spot.
flagelar *vtr* to flagellate.
flagelo *nm (látigo)* whip; *fig* scourge.
flagrante *adj* flagrant; **en f. delito**, redhanded.
flamante *adj* 1 **nuevecito f.**, *(nuevo)* brand-new. 2 *(vistoso)* splendid, brilliant.
flamenco,-a I *adj* 1 *Mús* flamenco. 2 *(de Flandes)* Flemish. **II** *nm* 1 *Mús* flamenco. 2 *Orn* flamingo. 3 *(idioma)* Flemish.
flan *nm* caramel custard.
flanco *nm* flank, side.
flanquear *vtr* to flank.
flaquear *vi (fuerzas, piernas)* to weaken, give way.
flaqueza *nf* weakness.
flash *nm Fot* flash.
flato *nm* wind, flatulence.
flatulencia *nf* flatulence.
flauta *nf* flute; **f. dulce**, recorder.
flautín *nm (instrumento)* piccolo.
flautista *nmf Mús* flautist, *US* flutist, flute player.
flecha *nf* arrow.
flechazo *nm fig (enamoramiento)* love at first sight.
fleco *nm* fringe.
flema *nf* phlegm.
flemático,-a *adj* phlegmatic.
flemón *nm* gumboil, abscess.

flequillo *nm* fringe, *US* bangs.
fletar *vtr* to charter.
flete *nm* 1 (*alquiler*) charter. 2 (*carga*) freight.
flexibilidad *nf* flexibility.
flexible *adj* flexible.
flexión *nf* 1 flexion. 2 *Ling* inflection. 3 *Gimn* flexiones, press-ups, *US* push-ups.
flexionar *vtr* to bend; (*músculo*) to flex.
flexo *nm* reading lamp.
flipante *adj fam* great, cool.
flipar *vtr fam* **le flipan las motos**, he's crazy about motorbikes.
flirtear *vi* to flirt.
flirteo *nm* flirting.
flojear *vi* (*ventas etc*) to fall off, go down; (*piernas*) to weaken, grow weak; (*memoria*) to fail.
flojedad *nf* weakness.
flojera *nf fam* weakness, faintness.
flojo,-a I *adj* 1 (*tornillo, cuerda etc*) loose, slack. 2 (*perezoso*) lazy, idle; (*exámen, trabajo, resultado*) poor.
flor *nf* 1 flower; **en f.**, in blossom; *fig* **en la f. de la vida**, in the prime of life; *fig* **la f. y nata**, the cream (of society). 2 **a f. de piel**, skin-deep.
flora *nf* flora.
floreado,-a *adj* flowery.
florecer [33] *vi* 1 (*plantas*) to flower. 2 *fig* (*negocio*) to flourish, thrive.
floreciente *adj fig* flourishing, prosperous.
Florencia *n* Florence.
florero *nm* vase.
floricultura *nf* flower growing, floriculture.
florido,-a *adj* 1 (*con flores*) flowery. 2 (*estilo*) florid.
floripondio *nm pey* (*adorno*) heavy ornamentation.
florista *nmf* florist.
floristería *nf* florist's (shop).
flota *nf* fleet.
flotador *nm* 1 (*de pesca*) float. 2 (*para nadar*) rubber ring.
flotar *vi* to float.
flote *nm* floating; **a f.**, afloat; **sacar a f. un negocio**, to put a business on a sound footing.
flotilla *nf* flotilla.
fluctuación *nf* fluctuation.
fluctuar [30] *vi* to fluctuate.
fluidez *nf* fluency.
fluido,-a I *adj* fluid; (*estilo etc*) fluent. II *nm* fluid; **f. eléctrico**, current.
fluir [37] *vi* to flow.
flujo *nm* 1 flow. 2 rising tide; **f. y reflujo**, ebb and flow. 3 *Fís* flux. 4 *Med* discharge. 5 *Inform* stream.
flúor *nm* fluorine.
fluorescente *adj* fluorescent.
fluvial *adj* river.
FM *nf abr de* **Frecuencia Modulada**, frequency modulation, FM.

FMI *nm abr de* **Fondo Monetario Internacional**, International Monetary Fund, IMF.
fobia *nf* phobia (a, about).
foca *nf* seal.
foco *nm* 1 *Elec* spotlight, floodlight. 2 (*de ideas, revolución etc*) centre, *US* center, focal point. 2 *Am* (*bombilla*) (electric light) bulb; (*de coche*) (car) headlight; (*farola*) street light.
fofo,-a *adj* soft; (*persona*) flabby.
fogata *nf* bonfire.
fogón *nm* (*de cocina*) ring.
fogonazo *nm* flash.
fogosidad *nf* ardour, *US* ardor, fire.
fogoso,-a *adj* fiery, spirited.
fogueo *nm* **cartucho de f.**, blank cartridge.
folio *nm* sheet of paper.
folklore *nm* folklore.
folklórico,-a *adj* **m. folklórica**, folk music.
follaje *nm* foliage.
follar *vulg* I *vi* to fuck, screw. II *vtr* (*suspender*) to fail. III **follarse** *vr* **f. a algn**, to fuck sb, screw sb.
folletín *nm* 1 (*relato*) newspaper serial. 2 *fig* melodrama.
folleto *nm* leaflet; (*turístico*) brochure.
follón *nm fam* 1 (*alboroto*) rumpus, shindy; **armar (un) f.**, to kick up a rumpus. 2 (*enredo, confusión*) mess, trouble; **meterse en un f.**, to get into a mess. 3 **un f. de**, (*montón*) a load of.
follonero,-a *nm,f* troublemaker.
fomentar *vtr* to promote.
fomento *nm* promotion.
fonda *nf* inn.
fondear *vi* to anchor.
fondista *nmf Dep* long-distance runner.
fondo¹ *nm* 1 (*parte más baja*) bottom; **a f.**, thoroughly; **al f. de la calle**, at the bottom of the street; **tocar f.**, *Náut* to touch bottom; *fig* to reach rock bottom; *fig* **en el f. es bueno**, deep down he's kind; **bajos fondos**, dregs of society; **doble f.**, false bottom. 2 (*de habitación*) back; (*de pasillo*) end. 3 (*segundo término*) background; **música de f.**, background music. 4 *Prensa* **artículo de f.**, leading article. 5 *Dep* **corredor de f.**, long-distance runner; **esquí de f.**, cross-country skiing.
fondo² *Fin* fund; **cheque sin fondos**, bad cheque; *fam* **f. común**, kitty.
fonendoscopio *nm* stethoscope.
fonética *nf* phonetics *sing*.
fonético,-a *adj* phonetic.
fontanería *nf* plumbing.
fontanero,-a *nm,f* plumber.
footing *nm* jogging; **hacer f.**, to go jogging.
forajido,-a *nm,f* outlaw.
foral *adj* **Comunidad F.**, Navarre.

foráneo,-a *adj* foreign.
forastero,-a *nm,f* outsider, stranger.
forcejear *vi* to wrestle, struggle.
forcejeo *nm* struggle.
fórceps *nm inv* forceps *pl*.
forense I *adj* forensic. **II** *nmf* (**médico**) f., forensic surgeon.
forestal *adj* forest; **repoblación f.**, re-afforestation.
forjado,-a *adj* wrought.
forjar *vtr* (*metal*) to forge; *fig* to create, make.
forma *nf* 1 form, shape; **en f. de L**, L-shaped; **¿qué f. tiene?**, what shape is it? 2 (*manera*) way; **de esta f.**, in this way; **de f. que**, so that; **de todas formas**, anyway, in any case; **no hubo f. de convencerla**, there was no way we could convince her; **f. de pago**, method of payment. 3 *Dep* form; **estar en f.**, to be on form; **estar en baja f.**, to be off form. 4 *Rel* **Sagrada F.**, Host. 5 **formas**, (*modales*) manners.
formación *nf* 1 formation. 2 (*educación*) upbringing. 3 (*enseñanza*) training; **f. profesional**, vocational training.
formal *adj* formal; (*serio*) serious, serious-minded; (*fiable*) reliable, dependable.
formalidad *nf* 1 formality. 2 (*seriedad*) seriousness. 3 (*fiabilidad*) reliability. 4 **formalidades**, (*trámites*) formalities.
formalizar [4] **I** *vtr* to formalize. **II formalizarse** *vr* to settle down.
formar I *vtr* 1 to form; **f. parte de algo**, to be a part of sth. 2 (*educar*) to bring up; (*enseñar*) to educate, train. **II formarse** *vr* 1 to be formed, form; **se formó un charco**, a puddle formed; **f. una impresión de algo**, to get an impression of sth. 2 (*educarse*) to be educated *o* trained.
formato *nm* format; (*del papel*) size.
formica® *nf* Formica®.
formidable *adj* 1 (*estupendo*) wonderful, terrific. 2 (*espantoso*) formidable.
fórmula *nf* formula; *Aut* **f. uno**, formula one.
formular *vtr* (*quejas*, *peticiones*) to make; (*deseo*) to express; (*pregunta*) to ask; (*una teoría*) to formulate.
formulario *nm* form.
fornicación *nf* fornication.
fornicar [1] *vi* to fornicate.
fornido,-a *adj* strapping, hefty.
foro *nm* 1 forum. 2 (*mesa redonda*) round table. 3 *Teat* back (of the stage). 4 *Jur* law court, court of justice.
forofo,-a *nm,f fam* fan, supporter.
forrado,-a *adj* lined; *fam* **estar f.**, to be well-heeled, be well-off.
forraje *nm* fodder.
forrar I *vtr* (*por dentro*) to line; (*por fuera*) to cover. **II forrarse** *vr fam* (*de dinero*) to make a packet.

forro *nm* (*por dentro*) lining; (*por fuera*) cover, case.
fortalecer [33] *vtr* to fortify, strengthen.
fortaleza *nf* 1 strength; (*de espíritu*) fortitude. 2 *Mil* fortress, stronghold.
fortificante I *adj* fortifying. **II** *nm* tonic.
fortificar [1] *vtr* to fortify.
fortísimo,-a *adj* very strong.
fortuito,-a *adj* fortuitous.
fortuna *nf* 1 (*destino*) fortune, fate. 2 (*suerte*) luck; **por f.**, fortunately. 3 (*capital*) fortune.
forzado,-a *adj* forced; **a marchas forzadas**, at a brisk pace; **trabajos forzados**, hard labour *sing*.
forzar [2] *vtr* 1 (*obligar*) to force; **f. a algn a hacer algo**, to force sb to do sth. 2 (*puerta*, *candado*) to force, break open.
forzoso,-a *adj* obligatory, compulsory; *Av* **aterrizaje f.**, forced landing.
◆**forzosamente** *adv* necessarily.
fosa *nf* 1 (*sepultura*) grave. 2 (*hoyo*) pit. 3 *Anat* **fosas nasales**, nostrils.
fosforescente *adj* phosphorescent.
fósforo *nm* (*cerilla*) match.
fósil *adj* & *nm* fossil.
fosilizarse [4] *vr* to fossilize, become fossilized.
foso *nm* 1 (*hoyo*) pit. 2 (*de fortificación*) moat. 3 (*en garage*) inspection pit.
foto *nf fam* photo; **sacar/echar una f.**, to take a photo.
fotocopia *nf* photocopy.
fotocopiadora *nf* photocopier.
fotocopiar [12] *vtr* to photocopy.
fotogénico,-a *adj* photogenic.
fotografía *nf* 1 photograph; **echar** *o* **hacer** *o* **sacar fotografías**, to take photographs. 2 (*arte*) photography.
fotografiar [29] *vtr* to photograph, take a photograph of.
fotográfico,-a *adj* photographic.
fotógrafo,-a *nm,f* photographer.
fotograma *nm* still, shot.
fotomatón *nm* automatic coin-operated photo machine.
fotómetro *nm* light meter, exposure meter.
FP *nf Educ abr de* **Formación Profesional**, vocational training.
frac *nm* (*pl* **fracs** *o* **fraques**) (*prenda*) dress coat, tails *pl*.
fracasado,-a I *adj* unsuccessful. **II** *nm,f* (*persona*) failure.
fracasar *vi* to fail.
fracaso *nm* failure.
fracción *nf* 1 fraction. 2 *Pol* faction.
fraccionar *vtr*, **fraccionarse** *vr* to break up, split up.
fraccionario,-a *adj* fractional; **moneda fraccionaria**, small change.
fractura *nf* fracture.
fracturar *vtr*, **fracturarse** *vr* to fracture, break.

fragancia *nf* fragrance.
fragata *nf* frigate.
frágil *adj* **1** (*quebradizo*) fragile. **2** (*débil*) frail.
fragmentar I *vtr* to fragment. **II fragmentarse** *vr* to break up.
fragmento *nm* fragment; (*de novela etc*) passage.
fragor *nm* din.
fragua *nf* forge.
fraguar |22| *vtr* **1** (*metal*) to forge. **2** (*plan*) to think up, fabricate; (*conspiración*) to hatch.
fraile *nm* friar, monk.
frailecillo *nm* puffin.
frambuesa *nf* raspberry.
francés,-a I *adj* French; *Culin* **tortilla francesa**, plain omelette. **II** *nm,f* (*hombre*) Frenchman; (*mujer*) Frenchwoman. **III** *nm* (*idioma*) French.
Francfort, Francfurt *n* Frankfurt; *Culin* **salchicha estilo f.**, frankfurter.
Francia *n* France.
francmasón,-ona *nm,f* freemason.
franco,-a¹ *adj* **1** (*persona*) frank. **2** *Com* **f. a bordo**, free on board; **f. fábrica**, ex-works; **puerto f.**, free port. ◆**francamente** *adv* frankly.
franco² *nm Fin* (*moneda*) franc.
francotirador,-a *nm,f* sniper.
franela *nf* flannel.
franja *nf* (*de terreno*) strip; (*de bandera*) stripe; *Cost* fringe, border.
franquear *vtr* **1** (*atravesar*) to cross; *fig* (*dificultad, obstáculo*) to overcome. **2** (*carta*) to frank. **3** (*camino, paso*) to free, clear.
franqueo *nm* postage.
franqueza *nf* frankness.
franquicia *nf* exemption; *Com* franchise.
franquismo *nm Hist* **1** (*ideología*) Francoism. **2** (*régimen*) the Franco regime.
franquista *adj&* *nmf* Francoist.
frasco *nm* small bottle, flask.
frase *nf* (*oración*) sentence; (*expresión*) phrase; **f. hecha**, set phrase *o* expression.
fraternidad *nf* brotherhood, fraternity.
fraternizar |4| *vi* to fraternize.
fraterno,-a *adj* fraternal, brotherly.
fraude *nm* fraud; **f. fiscal**, tax evasion.
fraudulento,-a *adj* fraudulent.
fray *nm Rel* brother.
frecuencia *nf* frequency; **con f.**, frequently, often.
frecuentar *vtr* to frequent.
frecuente *adj* frequent. ◆**frecuentemente** *adv* frequently, often.
fregadero *nm* (kitchen) sink.
fregado¹ *nm* **1** (*lavado*) washing. **2** *fam* (*follón*) racket.
fregado,-a² *adj Am* tiresome, annoying.
fregar |1| *vtr* **1** (*lavar*) to wash; (*suelo*) to mop. **2** *Am vulg* to annoy, irritate.

fregona *nf* mop.
fregón,-ona *adj Am* annoying.
freidora *nf* (deep) fryer.
freír |5| (*pp* **frito**) **I** *vtr* to fry. **II freírse** *vr* to fry; *fig* **f. de calor**, to be roasting.
frenar *vtr* to brake; *fig* (*inflación etc*) to slow down; (*impulsos*) to restrain.
frenazo *nm* sudden braking; **dar un f.**, to jam on the brakes.
frenesí *nm* frenzy.
frenético,-a *adj* frantic.
freno *nm* **1** brake; **pisar/soltar el f.**, to press/release the brake; **f. de disco/tambor**, disc/drum brake; **f. de mano**, handbrake. **2** (*de caballería*) bit. **3** *fig* curb, check; **poner f. a algo**, to curb sth.
frente I *nm* **1** front; **al f. de**, at the head of; **chocar de f.**, to crash head on; **hacer f. a algo**, to face sth, stand up to sth. **II** *nf Anat* forehead; **f. a f.**, face to face. **III** *adv* **f. a**, in front of, opposite.
fresa *nf* **1** strawberry. **2** *Téc* milling cutter.
fresca *nf fam* cheeky remark.
fresco,-a I *adj* **1** (*frío*) cool. **2** (*comida, fruta*) fresh. **3** (*reciente*) fresh, new. **4** (*descarado*) cheeky, shameless; **se quedó tan f.**, he didn't bat an eyelid; **¡qué f.!**, what a nerve!. **II** *nm* **1** (*frescor*) fresh air, cool air; **al f.**, in the cool; **hace f.**, it's chilly. **2** *Arte* fresco.
frescor *nm* freshness.
frescura *nf* **1** freshness. **2** (*desvergüenza*) cheek, nerve.
fresno *nm* ash tree.
fresón *nm* (large) strawberry.
frialdad *nf* coldness.
fricción *nf* **1** friction. **2** (*masaje*) massage.
friega *nf* rub.
friegaplatos *nmf inv* (*persona*) dishwasher.
frígido,-a *adj* frigid.
frigorífico,-a I *nm* refrigerator, fridge. **II** *adj* **cámara frigorífica**, coldstorage room.
frijol, fríjol *nm* kidney bean.
frío,-a I *adj* **1** cold. **2** (*indiferente*) cold, cool, indifferent. **3** **su comentario me dejó f.**, I was stunned by her remark. **II** *nm* cold; **hace f.**, it's cold. ◆**fríamente** *adv* coolly.
friolera *nf fam* **la f. de diez mil pesetas/dos horas**, a mere ten thousand pesetas/two hours.
friolero,-a *adj* sensitive to the cold.
fritanga *nf* **1** *Am* fried food. **2** *Esp* greasy food.
frito,-a I *adj* **1** *Culin* fried. **2** *fam* exasperated, fed up; **me tienes f.**, I'm sick to death of you. **II** *nm* fry, piece of fried food.
frívolo,-a *adj* frivolous.
frondoso,-a *adj* leafy, luxuriant.
frontera *nf* frontier.
fronterizo,-a *adj* frontier, border; **países fronterizos**, neighbouring countries.

frontón *nm Dep* pelota.

frotar I *vtr* to rub. **II frotarse** *vr* to rub; **f. las manos,** to rub one's hands together.

fructífero,-a *adj* (*árbol*) fruit-bearing; (*esfuerzo*) fruitful.

frugal *adj* frugal.

fruncir [3] *vtr* **1** *Cost* to gather. **2** (*labios*) to purse, pucker; **f. el ceño,** to frown, knit one's brow.

frustración *nf* frustration.

frustrado,-a *adj* frustrated; **intento f.,** unsuccessful attempt.

frustrante *adj* frustrating.

frustrar I *vtr* to frustrate; (*defraudar*) to disappoint. **II frustrarse** *vr* **1** (*esperanza*) to fail, go awry. **2** (*persona*) to be frustrated *o* disappointed.

fruta *nf* fruit; **f. del tiempo,** fresh fruit.

frutería *nf* fruit shop.

frutero,-a I *nm,f* fruiterer. **II** *nm* fruit dish *o* bowl.

frutilla *nf Am* (large) strawberry.

fruto *nm* fruit; **frutos secos,** nuts; **dar f.,** to bear fruit; *fig* (*dar buen resultado*) to be fruitful; **sacar f. de algo,** to profit from sth.

fu *interj* **ni fu ni fa,** so-so.

fucsia *nf* fuchsia.

fuego *nm* **1** fire; **fuegos artificiales,** fireworks. **2** (*lumbre*) light; **¿me da f., por favor?,** have you got a light, please? **3** *Culin* **a f. lento,** on a low flame; (*al horno*) in a slow oven.

fuel, fuel-oil *nm* diesel.

fuente *nf* **1** fountain. **2** (*recipiente*) dish, serving dish. **3** (*de información*) source.

fuera¹ *adv* **1** outside, out; **quédate f.,** stay outside; **sal f.,** go out; **desde f.,** from (the) outside; **por f.,** on the outside; **la puerta de f.,** the outer door. **2 f. de,** out of; **f. de serie,** extraordinary; *fig* **estar f. de sí,** to be beside oneself. **3** *Dep* **el equipo de f.,** the away team; **jugar f.,** to play away; **f. de juego,** offside.

fuera² **I** *subj imperf* → **ir.** **II** *subj imperf* → **ser.**

fuero *nm* **1** *Hist* code of laws. **2** *fig* **en tu f. interno,** deep down, in your heart of hearts.

fuerte I *adj* **1** strong; (*dolor*) severe; (*sonido*) loud; (*comida*) heavy; **el plato f.,** the main course; *fig* the most important event. **II** *nm* **1** (*fortaleza*) fort. **2** (*punto fuerte*) forte, strong point. **III** *adv* **¡abrázame f.!,** hold me tight!; **comer f.,** to eat a lot; **¡habla más f.!,** speak up!; **¡pégale f.!,** hit him hard!

fuerza I *nf* **1** (*fortaleza*) strength; *fig* **a f. de,** by dint of. **2** (*violencia*) force; **a la f.,** (*por obligación*) of necessity; (*con violencia*) by force; **por f.,** of necessity; **f. mayor,** force majeure. **3** *Fís* force. **4** (*cuerpo*) force; **las fuerzas del orden,** the forces of law and order; **Fuerzas Aéreas,**

≈ *GB* Royal Air Force; **Fuerzas Armadas,** Armed Forces.

fuese I *subj imperf* → **ir.** **II** *subj imperf* → **ser.**

fuete *nm Am* whip.

fuga *nf* **1** (*huida*) escape; **darse a la f.,** to take flight. **2** (*de gas etc*) leak.

fugarse [7] *vr* to escape; **f. de casa,** to run away from home.

fugaz *adj* fleeting, brief.

fugitivo,-a *nm,f* fugitive.

fui I *pt indef* → **ir.** **II** *pt indef* → **ser.**

fulana *nf pey* whore, tart.

fulano,-a **I** *nm,f* so-and-so; (*hombre*) what's his name; (*mujer*) what's her name; **Doña Fulana de tal,** Mrs So-and-so. **II** *nf fam pey* tart, slag.

fular *nm* foulard, scarf.

fulgor *nm lit* brilliance, glow.

fullería *nf* cheating; **hacer fullerías,** to cheat.

fullero,-a I *adj* cheating. **II** *nm,f* cheat.

fulminante *adj* (*cese*) summary; (*muerte, enfermedad*) sudden; (*mirada*) withering.

fulminar *vtr fig* to strike dead; **f. a algn con la mirada,** to look daggers at sb.

fumada *nf Am* (*calada*) pull, drag.

fumado,-a *adj arg* (*colocado*) stoned.

fumador,-a *nm,f* smoker; **los no fumadores,** nonsmokers.

fumar I *vtr & vi* to smoke; **no f.,** (*en letrero*) no smoking. **II fumarse** *vr* to smoke; **f. un cigarro,** to smoke a cigarette.

fumigar [7] *vtr* to fumigate.

funambulista *nmf,* **funámbulo,-a** *nm,f* tightrope walker.

función *nf* **1** function; **en f. de,** according to. **2** (*cargo*) duties *pl*; **entrar en funciones,** to take up one's duties; **presidente en funciones,** acting president. **3** *Cin Teat* performance.

funcionamiento *nm* operation; **poner/entrar en f.,** to put/come into operation.

funcionar *vi* to work; **no funciona,** (*en letrero*) out of order.

funcionario,-a *nm,f* civil servant; **f. público,** public official.

funda *nf* cover; (*de gafas etc*) case; (*de espada*) sheath; **f. de almohada,** pillowcase.

fundación *nf* foundation.

fundador,-a *nm,f* founder.

fundamental *adj* fundamental.

fundamentar *vtr* to base (**en,** on).

fundamento *nm* basis, grounds; **sin f.,** unfounded.

fundar I *vtr* **1** (*empresa*) to found. **2** (*teoría*) to base, found. **II fundarse** *vr* **1** (*empresa*) to be founded. **2** (*teoría*) to be based; (*persona*) to base oneself.

fundición *nf* **1** (*de metales*) smelting. **2** (*fábrica*) foundry.

fundir I *vtr* **1** to melt; (*bombilla, plomos*) to blow. **2** (*unir*) to unite, join. **II**

fundirse *vr* 1 (*derretirse*) to melt. 2 (*bombilla, plomos*) to blow. 3 (*unirse*) to merge.

fúnebre *adj* 1 (*mortuorio*) funeral; **coche f.**, hearse. 2 (*lúgubre*) mournful, lugubrious.

funeral *nm* funeral.

funeraria *nf* undertaker's, *US* funeral parlor.

funesto,-a *adj* ill-fated, fatal; (*consecuencias*) disastrous.

fungir *vi Am* to act (**de**, as).

funicular *nm* funicular (railway).

furcia *nf ofens* whore, tart.

furgón *nm Aut* van.

furgoneta *nf* van.

furia *nf* fury; **ponerse hecho una f.**, to become furious, fly into a rage.

furibundo,-a *adj* furious, enraged.

furioso,-a *adj* furious; **ponerse f.**, to get furious.

furor *nm* fury, rage; *fig* **hacer f.**, to be all the rage.

furtivo,-a *adj* furtive, stealthy; **caza/pesca furtiva**, poaching; **cazador/pescador f.**, poacher.

furúnculo *nm Med* boil.

fuselaje *nm* fuselage.

fusible *nm* fuse.

fusil *nm* gun, rifle.

fusilamiento *nm* shooting, execution.

fusilar *vtr* to shoot, execute.

fusión *nf* 1 (*de metales*) fusion; (*del hielo*) thawing, melting; **punto de f.**, melting point. 2 *Com* merger.

fusionar *vtr*, **fusionarse** *vr* 1 *Fis* to fuse. 2 *Com* to merge.

fútbol *nm* football, soccer.

futbolín *nm* table football.

futbolista *nmf* footballer, football *o* soccer player.

fútil *adj* futile, trivial.

futilidad *nf* futility, triviality.

futurista *adj* futuristic.

futuro,-a I *adj* future. **II** *nm* future; **en un f. próximo**, in the near future.

G

G, g |xe| *nf* (*la letra*) G, g.

gabán *nm* overcoat.

gabardina *nf* (*prenda*) raincoat.

gabinete *nm* 1 (*despacho*) study; **g. de abogados**, lawyers' office. 2 *Pol* cabinet.

gaceta *nf* gazette.

gachas *nfpl* porridge *sing*.

gacho,-a *adj* **con la cabeza gacha**, hanging one's head.

gaditano,-a I *adj* of *o* from Cadiz. **II** *nm,f* inhabitant *o* native of Cadiz.

gafas *nfpl* glasses, spectacles; **g. de sol**, sunglasses.

gafar *vtr fam* to put a jinx on, bring bad luck to.

gafe *adj & nm fam* **ser g.**, to be a jinx.

gaita *nf* bagpipes *pl*.

gajes *nmpl fam irón* **g. del oficio**, occupational hazards.

gajo *nm* 1 (*de naranja, pomelo etc*) segment. 2 (*rama desprendida*) torn-off branch.

gala *nf* 1 (*vestido*) full dress; **de g.**, dressed up; (*ciudad*) decked out. 2 (*espectáculo*) gala; **hacer g. de**, to glory in. 3 **galas**, finery *sing*.

galán *nm* 1 handsome young man; *hum* ladies' man. 2 *Teat* leading man.

galante *adj* gallant.

galantear *vtr* to court.

galanteo *nm* courtship.

galantería *nf* gallantry.

galápago *nm* turtle.

galardón *nm* prize.

galardonado,-a *nm,f* prizewinner.

galardonar *vtr* to award a prize to.

galaxia *nf* galaxy.

galeón *nm* galleon.

galeote *nm* galley slave.

galera *nf* 1 *Náut* galley. 2 (*carro*) covered wagon. 3 *Impr* galley proof.

galería *nf* 1 *Arquit* covered balcony. 2 (*museo*) art gallery. 3 *Teat* gallery, gods *pl*.

Gales *n* (**el país de**) G., Wales.

galés,-esa I *adj* Welsh. **II** *nm,f* (*hombre*) Welshman; (*mujer*) Welshwoman; **los galeses**, the Welsh. **III** *nm* (*idioma*) Welsh.

galgo *nm* greyhound.

Galicia *n* Galicia.

galimatías *nm inv fam* gibberish.

gallardo *adj* 1 (*apuesto*) smart. 2 (*valeroso*) brave.

gallego,-a I *adj* 1 Galician. 2 *Am pey* Spanish. **II** *nm,f* 1 Galician, native of Galicia. 2 *Am pey* Spaniard. **III** *nm* (*idioma*) Galician.

galleta *nf* 1 *Culin* biscuit. 2 *fam* (*cachete*) slap.

gallina I *nf* hen. **II** *nmf fam* coward, chicken.

gallinero *nm* 1 hen run. 2 *Teat* **el g.**, the gods *pl*.

gallito *nm fam* (*peleón*) bully.

gallo *nm* 1 cock, rooster; *fam fig* **en menos que un canto de g.**, before you could say Jack Robinson. 2 *Mús fam* off-key note.

galón¹ *nm Mil* stripe.

galón² *nm* (*medida*) gallon; *GB* 4.55 litres, *US* 3.79 litres.

galopante *adj fig* (*inflación etc*) galloping.

galopar *vi* to gallop.
galope *nm* gallop; **a g. tendido,** flat out.
gama *nf* range; *Mús* scale.
gamba *nf* prawn.
gamberrismo *nm* hooliganism.
gamberro,-a I *nm,f* hooligan. II *adj* uncouth.
gamo *nm* fallow deer.
gamuza *nf* 1 *Zool* chamois. 2 *(trapo)* chamois *o* shammy leather.
gana *nf* 1 *(deseo)* wish (**de,** for); **de buena g.,** willingly; **de mala g.,** reluctantly; *fam* **no me da la g.,** I don't feel like it. 2 **tener ganas de (hacer) algo,** to feel like (doing) sth; **quedarse con las ganas,** not to manage. 3 *(apetito)* appetite; **comer con ganas,** to eat heartily.
ganadería *nf* 1 *(crianza)* livestock farming. 2 *(conjunto de ganado)* livestock.
ganadero,-a *nm,f* livestock farmer.
ganado *nm* 1 livestock. 2 *fam fig (gente)* crowd.
ganador,-a I *adj* winning. II *nm,f* winner.
ganancia *nf* profit.
ganar I *vtr* 1 *(sueldo)* to earn. 2 *(victoria)* to win. 3 *(aventajar)* to beat. 4 *(alcanzar)* to reach. II **ganarse** *vr* 1 to earn; **g. el pan,** to earn one's daily bread. 2 *(merecer)* to deserve; **se lo ha ganado,** he deserves it.
ganchillo *nm* crochet work.
gancho *nm* 1 hook. 2 *fam fig (gracia, atractivo)* charm. 3 *Am (horquilla)* hairpin.
gandul,-a *nm,f* loafer.
ganga *nf* bargain.
gangoso,-a *adj* nasal.
gangrena *nf* gangrene.
gansada *nf fam* silly thing to say *o* do.
ganso,-a I *nm,f* 1 goose; *(macho)* gander. 2 *fam* dolt. II *adj fam* ginormous; **pasta gansa,** bread, dough.
ganzúa *nf* picklock.
gañán *nm (obrero)* farmhand; *fam (bribón)* cheat.
garabatear *vtr & vi* to scribble.
garabato *nm* scrawl.
garaje *nm* garage.
garante *nmf Fin* guarantor.
garantía *nf* 1 guarantee. 2 *Jur (fianza)* bond, security.
garantizar [4] *vtr* to guarantee.
garbanzo *nm* chickpea.
garbeo *nm arg (paseo)* stroll; **darse un g.,** to go for a stroll.
garbo *nm* grace.
garfio *nm* hook, grappling iron.
gargajo *nm* spit.
garganta *nf* 1 throat. 2 *(desfiladero)* narrow pass.
gargantilla *nf* short necklace.
gárgaras *nfpl* 1 gargling *sing*; *fam* **¡vete a hacer g.!,** get lost! 2 *Am (licor)* gargling solution *sing*.

gárgola *nf* gargoyle.
garita *nf (caseta)* hut; *Mil* sentry box.
garito *nm arg* joint.
garra *nf* 1 *Zool* claw; *(de ave)* talon. 2 *fig (fuerza)* force; **tener g.,** to be compelling.
garrafa *nf* carafe.
garrafal *adj* monumental.
garrapata *nf Ent* tick.
garrote *nm* 1 *(porra)* club. 2 *Jur* garrotte.
garrucha *nf* pulley.
gárrulo,-a *adj fig* garrulous.
garza *nf* heron.
gas *nm* 1 gas; **g. ciudad,** town gas; **gases (nocivos),** fumes; **g. de escape,** exhaust fumes. 2 *(en bebida)* fizz; **agua con g.,** fizzy water. 3 *Med* gases, flatulence *sing*.
gasa *nf* gauze.
gaseosa *nf* lemonade.
gasoducto *nm* gas pipeline.
gasoil, gasóleo *nm* diesel oil.
gasolina *nf* petrol, *US* gasoline.
gasolinera *nf* petrol *o US* gas station.
gastado,-a *adj (zapatos etc)* worn-out; *fig (frase)* hackneyed.
gastar I *vtr* 1 *(consumir) (dinero, tiempo)* to spend; *(gasolina, electricidad)* to consume. 2 *fig (malgastar)* to waste. 3 *(ropa)* to wear; **¿qué número gastas?,** what size do you take? 4 **g. una broma a algn,** to play a practical joke on sb. II **gastarse** *vr* 1 *(zapatos etc)* to wear out. 2 *(gasolina etc)* to run out.
gasto *nm* expenditure; **gastos,** expenses; **gastos de viaje,** travelling expenses.
gatas (a) *loc adv* on all fours.
gatear *vi* 1 to crawl. 2 *(trepar)* to climb.
gatillo *nm (de armas)* trigger; **apretar el g.,** to pull the trigger.
gato *nm* 1 cat. 2 *Aut Téc* jack.
gaveta *nf* 1 *(cajón)* drawer. 2 *Am Aut (guantera)* glove compartment.
gavilán *nm Orn* sparrowhawk.
gavilla *nf (de ramillas etc)* sheaf.
gaviota *nf* seagull.
gay *adj inv & nm (pl gays)* homosexual, gay.
gazapo *nm* 1 *(error)* misprint. 2 *Zool* young rabbit.
gaznate *nm* gullet.
gazpacho *nm Culin* gazpacho.
gel *nm* gel; **g. (de ducha),** shower gel.
gelatina *nf (ingrediente)* gelatin; *Culin* jelly.
gema *nf Min* gem.
gemelo,-a I *adj & nm,f (identical)* twin. II *nmpl* **gemelos** 1 *(de camisa)* cufflinks. 2 *(anteojos)* binoculars.
gemido *nm* groan.
Géminis *nm* Gemini.
gemir [6] *vi* to groan.
generación *nf* generation.
general I *adj* general; **por lo *o* en g.,** in general, generally; II *nm Mil Rel* general.
◆**generalmente** *adv* generally.

Generalitat *nf* Catalan/Valencian/Balearic parliament.

generalización *nf* 1 generalization. 2 *(extensión)* spread.

generalizar |4| I *vtr* 1 to generalize. 2 *(extender)* to spread. II **generalizarse** *vr* to become widespread *o* common.

generar *vtr* to generate.

género *nm* 1 *(clase)* kind, sort. 2 *Arte Lit* genre. 3 *(mercancía)* article. 4 *Ling* gender. 5 *Biol* genus; **el g. humano,** mankind.

generosidad *nf* generosity.

generoso,-a *adj* 1 generous (**con, para,** to). 2 *(vino)* full-bodied.

Génesis *nm Rel* Genesis.

genética *nf* genetics *sing.*

genético,-a *adj* genetic.

genial *adj* brilliant; *fam* terrific.

genio *nm* 1 *(carácter)* temperament; *(mal carácter)* temper; **estar de mal g.,** to be in a bad mood. 2 *(facultad)* genius.

genocidio *nm* genocide.

Génova *n* Genoa.

gente *nf* 1 people *pl.* 2 *(familia)* folks *pl.* 3 *Am* respectable people.

gentil *adj* 1 *(amable)* kind. 2 *(pagano)* pagan.

gentileza *nf* kindness; *fml* **por g. de,** by courtesy of.

gentío *nm* crowd.

gentuza *nf pey* riffraff.

genuino,-a *adj* *(puro)* genuine; *(verdadero)* authentic.

geografía *nf* geography.

geología *nf* geology.

geometría *nf* geometry.

geranio *nm* geranium.

gerencia *nf* management.

gerente *nmf* manager.

germano,-a I *adj* German, Germanic. II *nm,f* German.

gérmen *nm* 1 *Biol* germ. 2 *fig (inicio)* germ; *(fuente)* origin.

germinar *vi* to germinate.

gerundio *nm* gerund.

gesta *nf arc* heroic exploit.

gestación *nf* gestation.

gestar *vtr* to gestate.

gesticular *vi* to gesticulate.

gestión *nf* 1 *(administración)* management. 2 **gestiones,** *(negociaciones)* negotiations; *(trámites)* formalities.

gestionar *vtr* to take steps to acquire *o* obtain; *(negociar)* to negotiate.

gesto *nm* 1 *(mueca)* face. 2 *(con las manos)* gesture.

gestor,-a *nm,f* ≈ solicitor.

giba *nf* hump.

gibar *vtr fam* to annoy.

Gibraltar *n* Gibraltar; **el peñón de G.,** the Rock of Gibraltar.

gibraltareño,-a I *adj* of *o* from Gibraltar. II *nm,f* Gibraltarian.

gigante,-a I *nm,f* giant. II *adj* giant, enormous.

gigantesco-a *adj* gigantic.

gigoló *nm* gigolo.

gili, gili *nm arg ofens* → **gilipollas**.

gilipollas *nmf ofens* bloody fool *o* idiot.

gimnasia *nf* gymnastics *pl.*

gimnasio *nm* gymnasium.

gimotear *vi* to whine.

Ginebra *n* Geneva.

ginebra *nf (bebida)* gin.

ginecología *nf* gynaecology, *US* gynecology.

ginecólogo,-a *nm,f* gynaecologist, *US* gynecologist.

gira *nf Teat Mus* tour.

girar I *vi* 1 *(dar vueltas)* to spin. 2 **g. a la derecha/izquierda,** to turn right/left. 3 *Fin (expedir)* to draw. II *vtr Fin (dinero)* to send by giro.

girasol *nm* sunflower.

giratorio,-a *adj* revolving.

giro *nm* 1 *(vuelta)* turn. 2 *(de acontecimientos)* direction. 3 *(frase)* turn of phrase. 4 *Fin* draft; **g. telegráfico,** giro *o* money order; **g. postal,** postal *o* money order.

gitano,-a *adj & nm,f* gypsy, gipsy.

glacial *adj* icy.

glaciar *nm* glacier.

glándula *nf* gland.

glasear *vtr Culin* to glaze.

global *adj* comprehensive; **precio g.,** all-inclusive price. ◆**globalmente** *adv* as a whole.

globo *nm* 1 balloon. 2 *(esfera)* globe. 3 *(lámpara)* globe, glass lampshade.

glóbulo *nm* globule.

gloria *nf* 1 *(fama)* glory. 2 *Rel* heaven; *fam fig* **estar en la g.,** to be in seventh heaven. 3 *fam (delicia)* delight.

glorieta *nf* 1 *(plazoleta)* small square. 2 *(encrucijada de calles)* roundabout, *US* traffic circle. 3 *(en un jardín)* arbour, *US* arbor.

glorificar |1| *vtr* to glorify.

glorioso,-a *adj* glorious.

glosa *nf* 1 gloss. 2 *Lit (comentario)* notes *pl,* commentary.

glosar *vtr* 1 *(explicar)* to gloss; *(texto)* to interpret. 2 *(comentar)* to comment on.

glosario *nm* glossary.

glotón,-ona I *adj* greedy. II *nm,f* glutton.

glotonería *nf* gluttony.

glucosa *nf Quím* glucose.

gobernación *nf* government; *Pol Hist* **Ministerio de la G.,** ≈ *GB* Home Office, *US* Department of the Interior.

gobernador,-a *nm,f* governor.

gobernante *adj* ruling.

gobernar |1| I *vtr* to govern; *(un país)* to rule. II *vi Náut* to steer.

gobierno *nm* 1 *Pol* government. 2 *(mando)* running. 3 *Náut* steering. 4 *Náut*

(timón) rudder.
goce *nm* enjoyment.
gofio *nm Am Can* roasted maize meal.
gol *nm* goal.
goleada *nf* lots of goals; **ganar por g.**, to win by a barrowload.
golear *vtr* to hammer.
golf *nm* golf; **palo de g.**, golf club.
golfista *nmf* golfer.
golfo,-a¹ I *nm,f* good-for-nothing. II *nf fam pey* tart.
golfo² *nm Geog* gulf; **el g. Pérsico**, the Persian Gulf.
golondrina *nf* swallow.
golosina *nf* sweet, *US* candy.
goloso,-a *adj* sweet-toothed.
golpe *nm* 1 blow; *(llamada)* knock; *(puñetazo)* punch; **de g.**, all of a sudden; **g. de estado**, coup d'état; **g. de suerte**, stroke of luck; **no dar ni g.**, not to lift a finger. 2 *Aut* bump. 3 *(desgracia)* blow; **un duro g.**, a great blow. 4 *(de humor)* witticism.
golpear *vtr* to hit; *(con el puño)* to punch; *(puerta, cabeza)* to bang.
goma *nf* 1 rubber; **g. de pegar**, glue; **g. de borrar**, rubber, *US* eraser. 2 *(elástica)* rubber band. 3 *arg (preservativo)* condom.
gomaespuma *nf* foam rubber.
gomal *nm Am Agr* rubber plantation.
gomero *nm Am* 1 *Bot* gum tree. 2 *(recolector)* rubber collector.
gomina *nf* hair cream.
góndola *nf* gondola.
gordo,-a I *adj* 1 *(carnoso)* fat. 2 *(grueso)* thick. 3 *(importante)* big; **me cae g.**, I can't stand him; **de g.**, in a big way. II *nm,f* fat person; *fam* fatty. III *nm* **el g.**, *(de lotería)* the jackpot.
gordura *nf* fatness.
gorgorito *nm* trill.
gorila *nm* 1 gorilla. 2 *fig (en discoteca etc)* bouncer.
gorjear I *vi* to chirp. II **gorjearse** *vr Am* **g. de algn**, to laugh at sb's expense.
gorjeo *nm* chirping.
gorra *nf* cap; *(con visera)* peaked cap; *fam* **de g.**, free.
gorrión *nm* sparrow.
gorro *nm* 1 cap. 2 *fam* **estar hasta el g.**, to be up to here *(de*, with).
gorrón,-ona *nm,f* sponger.
gota *nf* 1 drop; *(de sudor)* bead; **g. a g.**, drop by drop; **ni g.**, not a bit. 2 *Med* gout.
gotear *v impers* to drip; **el techo gotea**, there's a leak in the ceiling.
gotera *nf* leak.
gótico,-a *adj* Gothic.
gozar [4] I *vtr* to enjoy. II *vi (disfrutar)* to enjoy *(de, -)*.
gozne *nm* hinge.
gozo *nm* pleasure.
grabación *nf* recording.
grabado,-a *nm* 1 *(arte)* engraving. 2 *(dibu-*

jo) drawing.
grabadora *nf* tape recorder.
grabar *vtr* 1 *(sonidos, imágenes)* to record. 2 *Inform* to save. 3 *Arte* to engrave.
gracia *nf* 1 *(atractivo)* grace. 2 *(chiste)* joke; **hacer o tener g.**, to be funny. 3 *(indulto)* pardon.
gracias *nfpl (agradecimiento)* thanks; **g. a Dios**, thank God, thank goodness; **g. a**, thanks to; **muchas o muchísimas g.**, thank you very much.
gracioso,-a I *adj* 1 *(divertido)* funny. 2 *(garboso)* graceful. II *nm,f Teat* comic character.
grada *nf* 1 *(peldaño)* step. 2 **gradas**, flight *sing* of steps, *US* forecourt *sing*; *(en estadio)* terracing.
gradación *nf* 1 gradation. 2 *Mús* scale.
graderío *nm* tiers *pl* of seats; *Dep* terracing, *US* bleachers *pl*.
gradiente I *nm* gradient, *US* grade. II *nf Am* slope.
grado *nm* 1 degree. 2 *Mil* rank. 3 **de buen g.**, willingly, gladly.
graduable *adj* adjustable.
graduación *nf* 1 gradation. 2 *Mil* rank.
graduado,-a *nmf* graduate.
gradual *adj* gradual. ◆**gradualmente** *adv* gradually.
graduar [30] I *vtr* 1 *Educ Mil* to confer a degree *o* a rank on. 2 *(regular)* to regulate. II **graduarse** *vr* 1 *Educ Mil* to graduate. 2 **g. la vista**, to have one's eyes tested.
gráfico,-a I *adj* graphic; **diseño g.**, graphic design. II *nm,f* graph.
grafista *nmf* graphic designer.
gragea *nf Med* pill.
grajo,-a I *nm,f Orn* rook. II *nm Am* body odour.
gral. *abr de* **General**, General, gen.
gramática *nf* grammar.
gramo *nm* gram, gramme.
gran *adj* → **grande**.
grana *adj* scarlet.
granada *nf* 1 *(fruto)* pomegranate. 2 *Mil* grenade.
granate I *adj inv (color)* maroon. II *nm (color)* maroon.
Gran Bretaña *n* Great Britain.
grande *adj (before singular noun* **gran** *is used)* 1 *(tamaño)* big, large; *fig (persona)* great. 2 *(cantidad)* large; **vivir a lo g.**, to live in style; *fig* **pasarlo en g.**, to have a great time.
grandeza *nf* 1 *(importancia)* greatness. 2 *(grandiosidad)* grandeur; **delirios de g.**, delusions of grandeur.
grandioso,-a *adj* grandiose.
granel (a) *loc adv (sin medir exactamente)* loose.
granero *nm Agr* granary.
granito *nm* granite.
granizada *nf*, **granizado** *nm* iced drink.

granizar |4| *v impers* to hail.

granizo *nm* hail.

granja *nf* farm.

granjear(se) *vtr & vr* to gain.

granjero,-a *nm,f* farmer.

grano *nm* 1 grain; *(de café)* bean; **ir al g.**, to get to the point. 2 *(espinilla)* spot.

granuja *nm* 1 *(pilluelo)* ragamuffin. 2 *(estafador)* con-man.

grapa *nf* 1 staple. 2 *Constr* cramp.

grapadora *nf* stapler.

grapar *vtr* to staple.

grasa *nf* grease.

grasiento *adj* greasy.

graso,-a *adj (pelo)* greasy; *(materia)* fatty.

gratificar |1| *vtr* 1 *(satisfacer)* to gratify. 2 *(recompensar)* to reward.

gratinar *vtr Culin* to cook in a sauce until golden brown.

gratis *adv inv* free.

gratitud *nf* gratitude.

grato,-a *adj* pleasant.

gratuito,-a *adj* 1 *(de balde)* free (of charge). 2 *(arbitrario)* gratuitous.

grava *nf (guijas)* gravel; *(en carretera)* chippings.

gravamen *nm Jur* 1 *(carga)* burden. 2 *(impuesto)* tax.

gravar *vtr Jur* 1 *(cargar)* to burden. 2 *(impuestos)* to tax.

grave *adj* 1 *(importante)* serious. 2 *(muy enfermo)* seriously ill. 3 *(voz, nota)* low.

gravedad *nf* 1 *(seriedad, importancia)* seriousness. 2 *Fís* gravity.

gravilla *nf* chippings.

gravitar *vi* 1 *Fís* to gravitate. 2 **g. sobre**, to rest on.

gravoso,-a *adj* 1 *(costoso)* costly. 2 *(molesto)* burdensome.

graznar *vi* to squawk; *(de pato)* to quack; *(de cuervo)* to caw.

graznido *nm (un sonido)* squawk; *(varios)* squawking; *(de pato)* quack; *(de cuervo)* caw.

Grecia *n* Greece.

gregario,-a *adj* gregarious; **instinto g.**, herd instinct.

gremio *nm* 1 *Hist* guild. 2 *(profesión)* profession.

greña *nf* lock of entangled hair; *fam* **andar a la g.**, to squabble.

gres *nm* **artículos de g.**, stoneware.

gresca *nf* 1 *(bulla)* racket. 2 *(riña)* row.

griego,-a *adj & nm,f* Greek.

grieta *nf* crack; *(en la piel)* chap.

grifo *nm* tap, *US* faucet.

grillete *nm* shackle.

grillo *nm Ent* cricket.

gringo,-a *I adj* foreign; *Am* yankee. **II** *nm,f* foreigner; *Am* yankee, gringo.

gripe *nf* flu.

gris *adj & nm* grey, *US* gray.

grisáceo,-a *adj* greyish.

gritar *vtr & vi* to shout.

grito *nm* shout; **a voz en g.**, at the top of one's voice.

grosella *nf (fruto)* redcurrant; **g. negra**, blackcurrant; **g. silvestre**, gooseberry.

grosería *nf* 1 *(ordinariez)* rude word *o* expression. 2 *(rusticidad)* rudeness.

grosero,-a *adj (tosco)* coarse; *(maleducado)* rude.

grosor *nm* thickness.

grotesco,-a *adj* grotesque.

grúa *nf* 1 *Constr* crane. 2 *Aut* breakdown van, *US* tow truck.

grueso,-a **I** *adj* thick; *(persona)* stout. **II** *nm (parte principal)* bulk.

grulla *nf Orn* crane.

grumo *nm* lump; *(de leche)* curd.

gruñido *nm* grunt.

gruñir *vi* to grunt.

gruñón,-ona *adj* grumpy.

grupa *nf* hindquarters.

grupo *nm* 1 group. 2 *Téc* unit, set.

gruta *nf* cave.

guacamayo,-a *nm,f Orn* macaw.

guacamol, guacamole *nm Am Culin* guacamole, avocado sauce.

guachafita *nf Am* uproar.

guacho,-a *adj & nm,f Am* orphan.

guadaña *nf* scythe.

guagua[1] *nf* 1 *(perro)* bow-wow. 2 *Can Cuba* bus.

guagua[2] *nf Am* baby.

guantazo *nm* slap.

guante *nm* glove.

guantera *nf Aut* glove compartment.

guapo,-a I *adj* 1 good-looking, *US* cute; *(mujer)* beautiful, pretty; *(hombre)* handsome. 2 *Am (matón)* bully.

guaraca *nf Am* sling.

guarango,-a *adj Am* rude.

guarda *nm,f* guard; **g. jurado**, security guard.

guardabarros *nm inv Aut* mudguard, *US* fender.

guardabosque *nmf* gamekeeper.

guardacoches *nmf inv* parking attendant.

guardacostas *nm inv (persona)* coastguard; *(embarcación)* coastguard vessel.

guardaespaldas *nmf inv* bodyguard.

guardameta *nmf Dep* goalkeeper.

guardapolvo *nm* overalls *pl*.

guardar **I** *vtr* 1 *(conservar)* to keep. 2 *(un secreto)* to keep; **g. silencio**, to remain silent; **g. cama**, to stay in bed. 3 *(poner en un sitio)* to put away. 4 *(reservar)* to keep. 5 *Inform* to save. **II guardarse** *vr* **g. de hacer algo**, *(abstenerse)* to be careful not to do sth; **guardársela a algn**, to have it in for sb.

guardarropa *nm* 1 *(cuarto)* cloakroom. 2 *(armario)* wardrobe.

guardería *nf* **g. infantil**, nursery (school).

guardia **I** *nf* 1 *(vigilancia)* watch. 2 **la G. Civil**, the civil guard. 3 *(turno de servicio)* duty; *Mil* guard duty; **de g.**, on duty;

farmacia de g., duty chemist. II *nmf* policeman; *(mujer)* policewoman.
guardián,-ana *nm,f* watchman.
guarecer [33] I *vtr* to shelter. II **guare-cerse** *vr* to take shelter *o* refuge (**de**, from).
guarida *nf (de animal)* lair; *(refugio)* hide-out.
guarismo *nm* digit.
guarnecer [33] *vtr* 1 *Culin* to garnish. 2 *(dotar)* to provide (**de**, with). 3 *Mil* to garrison.
guarnición *nf* 1 *Culin* garnish. 2 *Mil* garrison.
guarro,-a I *adj* filthy. II *nm,f* pig.
guasa *nf* mockery.
guasearse *vr fam* **g. de**, to make fun of.
guaso,-a *adj Am* peasant.
guasón,-ona I *adj* humorous. II *nm,f* jo-ker.
guata *nf* 1 *(relleno)* padding. 2 *Am (barri-ga)* paunch.
guay *adj inv fam* brilliant, terrific.
guayabera *nf* short jacket.
guayabo,-a *nm,f Am fig (chica bonita)* pretty young girl; *(chico guapo)* good-looking boy.
guepardo *nm* cheetah.
guerra *nf* war; **en g.**, at war; **g. bacterio-lógica**, germ warfare; **g. civil/fría/mundial/nuclear**, civil/cold/world/nuclear war; *fam* **dar g.**, to be a real nuisance.
guerrero,-a I *nm,f* warrior. II *adj* warlike.
guerrilla *nf* 1 *(partida armada)* guerrilla force *o* band. 2 *(lucha)* guerrilla warfare.
guía I *nmf (persona)* guide. II *nf* 1 *(norma)* guideline. 2 *(libro)* guide; *(lista)* directory; **g. de teléfonos**, telephone directory.
guiar [29] I *vtr* 1 *(indicar el camino)* to guide. 2 *Aut* to drive; *Náut* to steer; *(ca-ballo, bici)* to ride. II **guiarse** *vr* to be guided, to go (**por**, by).
guija *nf* pebble.
guijarro *nm* pebble.

guinda *nf (fruto)* morello (cherry).
guindilla *nf* chilli.
guiñapo *nm* 1 *(andrajo)* rag. 2 *fig (persona)* wreck; **poner a algn como un g.**, to tear sb to pieces.
guiñar *vtr* to wink.
guiño *nm* wink.
guión *nm* 1 *Cin TV* script. 2 *Ling* hyphen, dash. 3 *(esquema)* sketch.
guionista *nmf* scriptwriter.
guiri *nmf arg* foreigner.
guirigay *nm* hubbub.
guirnalda *nf* garland.
guisa *nf* way, manner; **a g. de**, as, by way of.
guisado *nm Culin* stew.
guisante *nm* pea.
guisar *vtr* to cook.
guiso *nm* dish; *(guisado)* stew.
guita *nf* 1 *(cuerda)* rope. 2 *arg* dough.
guitarra I *nf* guitar. II *nmf* guitarist.
guitarrista *nmf* guitarist.
gula *nf* gluttony.
gusano *nm* worm; *(oruga)* caterpillar; **g. de seda**, silkworm.
gustar I *vtr* 1 **me gusta el vino**, I like wine; **me gustaban los caramelos**, I used to like sweets; **me gusta nadar**, I like swimming; **me gustaría ir**, I would like to go. 2 *fml* **¿gustas?**, would you like some?; **cuando gustes**, whenever you like. II *vi* **g. de**, to enjoy.
gusto *nm* 1 *(sentido)* taste. 2 *(en fórmulas de cortesía)* pleasure; **con (mucho) g.**, with (great) pleasure; **tanto g.**, pleased to meet you. 3 **estar a g.**, to feel comfort-able *o* at ease; **por g.**, for the sake of it; **ser de buen/mal g.**, to be in good/bad taste; **tener buen/mal g.**, to have good/bad taste; **tenemos el gusto de comuni-carle que ...**, we are pleased to inform you that ....
gutural *adj* guttural.

H

H, h |atʃe| *nf (la letra)* H,h; **bomba H**, H-bomb.
ha *indic pres* → **haber**.
haba *nf* broad bean.
Habana *nf* **La H.**, Havana.
habano *nm* Havana cigar.
haber [14] I *v aux* 1 *(en tiempos com-puestos)* to have; **lo he visto**, I have seen it; **ya lo había hecho**, he had already done it. 2 **h. de** + *infin*, *(obligación)* to have to; **has de ser bueno**, you must be good.
II *v impers (special form of present tense:* **hay)** 1 *(existir, estar) (singular used also with plural nouns)* hay, there is *o* are; **ha-bía**, there was *o* were; **había un gato en**

el tejado, there was a cat on the roof; **había muchos libros**, there were a lot of books; **hay 500 kilómetros entre Madrid y Granada**, it's 500 kilometers from Na-drid to Granada. 2 **h. que** + *infin*, it is necessary to; **hay que trabajar**, you've got to *o* you must work; **habrá que com-probarlo**, I/you/we *etc* will have to check it. 3 *(tener lugar)* **habrá una fiesta**, there will be a party; **hoy hay partido**, there's a match today; **los accidentes habidos en esta carretera**, the accidents which have happened on this road. 4 **había una vez ...**, once upon a time ...; **no hay de qué**, you're welcome, don't mention it; **¿qué hay?**, how are things?

III *nm* **1** *Fin* credit; **haberes,** assets. **2 en su h.,** in his possession.

habichuela *nf* kidney bean.

hábil *adj* **1** *(diestro)* skilful, *US* skillful. **2** *(astuto)* smart. **3 días hábiles,** working days.

habilidad *nf* **1** *(destreza)* skill. **2** *(astucia)* cleverness.

habilitar *vtr* **1** *(espacio)* to fit out. **2** *(persona)* to entitle. **3** *Fin (financiar)* to finance.

habitación *nf* *(cuarto)* room; *(dormitorio)* bedroom; **h. individual/doble,** single/ double room.

habitante *nmf* inhabitant.

habitar I *vtr* to live in, inhabit. **II** *vi* to live.

hábitat *nm* *(pl* **hábitats)** habitat.

hábito *nm* **1** *(costumbre)* habit. **2** *Rel* habit.

habitual *adj* usual, habitual; *(cliente, lector)* regular.

habituar [30] **I** *vtr* to accustom (**a,** to). **II habituarse** *vr* to get used (**a,** to), become accustomed (**a,** to).

habla *nf* **1** *(idioma)* language; **países de h. española,** Spanish-speaking countries. **2** *(facultad de hablar)* speech; **quedarse sin h.,** to be left speechless. **3** *Tel* **¡al h.!,** speaking!

hablado,-a *adj* spoken; **el inglés h.,** spoken English; **mal h.,** coarse, foul-mouthed.

hablador,-a *adj* *(parlanchín)* talkative; *pey (chismoso)* gossipy.

habladuría *nf* *(rumor)* rumour, *US* rumor; *(chisme)* piece of gossip.

hablante *nmf* speaker.

hablar I *vi* **1** to speak, talk; **h. con algn,** to speak to sb. **2** **¡ni h.!,** certainly not!; *fam* **¡quién fue a h.!,** look who's talking! **II** *vtr* *(idioma)* to speak; **habla alemán,** he speaks German. **2** *(tratar un asunto)* to talk over, discuss. **III hablarse** *vr* **1** to speak *o* talk to one another. **2 'se habla español',** *(en letrero)* 'Spanish spoken'.

habré *indic fut* → **haber.**

hacendoso,-a *adj* hardworking.

hacer [15] **I** *vtr* **1** *(crear, producir, fabricar)* to make; **h. una casa,** to build a house. **2** *(obrar, ejecutar)* to do; **eso no se hace,** it isn't done; **hazme un favor,** do me a favour; **¿qué haces?,** *(en este momento)* what are you doing?; *(para vivir)* what do you do (for a living)?; **tengo mucho que h.,** I have a lot to do; **h. deporte,** to do sports; **h. una carrera/medicina,** to do a degree/medicine. **3** *(conseguir)* *(amigos, dinero)* to make. **4** *(obligar)* to make; **hazle callar/trabajar,** make him shut up/work. **5** *(arreglar)* to make; **h. la cama,** to make the bed. **6** *Mat (sumar)* to make; **y con éste hacen cien,** and that makes a hundred. **7** *(dar aspecto)* to make look; **el negro le hace más delgado,** black makes

him look slimmer. **8** *(sustituyendo a otro verbo)* to do; **ya no puedo leer como solía hacerlo,** I can't read as well as I used to. **9** *(representar)* to play; **h. el bueno,** to play the (part of the) goody. **10 ¡bien hecho!,** well done!

II *vi* **1** *(actuar)* to play; **hizo de Desdémona,** she played Desdemona. **2 h. por** *o* **para** + *infin,* to try to; **hice por venir,** I tried to come. **3** *(fingir)* to pretend; **h. como si,** to act as if. **4** *(convenir)* to be suitable; **a las ocho si te hace,** will eight o'clock be all right for you?

III *v impers* **1** **hace calor/frío,** it's hot/ cold. **2** *(tiempo transcurrido)* ago; **hace mucho (tiempo),** a long time ago; **hace dos días que no le veo,** I haven't seen him for two days; **hace dos años que vivo en Glasgow,** I've been living in Glasgow for two years.

IV hacerse *vr* **1** *(volverse)* to become, grow; **h. viejo,** to grow old. **2** *(simular)* to pretend; **h. el dormido,** to pretend to be sleeping. **3 h. con,** *(apropiarse)* to get hold of. **4** *(habituarse)* to get used (**a,** to); **enseguida me hago a todo,** I soon get used to anything.

hacha *nf* **1** *(herramienta)* axe, *US* ax. **2** *fam* **ser una h. en algo,** to be an ace *o* a wizard at sth.

hachís *nm* hashish.

hacia *prep* **1** *(dirección)* towards, to; **h. abajo,** down, downwards; **h. adelante,** forwards; **h. arriba,** up, upwards; **h. atrás,** back, backwards. **2** *(tiempo)* at about, at around; **h. las tres,** at about three o'clock.

hacienda *nf* **1** *(finca agrícola)* estate, *US* ranch. **2** *Fin* Treasury; **h. pública,** public funds *o* finances *pl*; **Ministerio de H.,** = Exchequer, Treasury.

hacinamiento *nm* **1** *Agr* stacking; *fig (montón)* piling. **2** *(de gente)* overcrowding.

hacinar I *vtr* *Agr* to stack; *fig (amontonar)* to pile up, heap up. **II hacinarse** *vr* *(gente)* to be packed (**en,** into).

hada *nf* fairy; **cuento de hadas,** fairy tale; **h. madrina,** fairy godmother.

hado *nm* destiny.

hago *indic pres* → **hacer.**

halagar [7] *vtr* to flatter.

halago *nm* flattery.

halagüeño,-a *adj* *(noticia, impresión)* promising.

halcón *nm* falcon; **h. peregrino,** peregrine (falcon).

hálito *nm* **1** *(aliento)* breath. **2** *(vapor)* vapour, *US* vapor.

hallar I *vtr* *(encontrar)* to find; *(averiguar)* to find out; *(descubrir)* to discover. **II hallarse** *vr* *(estar)* to be, find oneself; *(estar situado)* to be situated.

hallazgo *nm* **1** *(descubrimiento)* discovery.

2 (*cosa encontrada*) find.
hamaca *nf* hammock; (*mecedora*) rocking chair.
hambre *nf* (*apetito*) hunger; (*inanición*) starvation; (*catástrofe*) famine; **tener h.**, to be hungry.
hambriento,-a *adj* starving.
hamburguesa *nf* hamburger.
hampa *nf* underworld.
han *indic pres* → **haber**.
harapo *nm* rag; **hecho un h.**, in tatters.
haré *indic fut* → **hacer**.
harén *nm* (*pl harenes*) harem.
harina *nf* flour.
hartar I *vtr* 1 (*cansar, fastidiar*) to annoy. 2 (*atiborrar*) to satiate; **el dulce harta enseguida**, sweet things soon fill you up. II **hartarse** *vr* 1 (*saciar el apetito*) to eat one's fill. 2 (*cansarse*) to get fed up (**de**, with), grow tired (**de, of**).
harto,-a *adj* 1 (*de comida*) full. 2 (*cansado*) fed up; **¡me tienes h.!**, I'm fed up with you!; **estoy h. de trabajar**, I'm fed up working. ◆**harto** *adv* (*muy*) very.
hartura *nf* bellyful; **¡qué h.!**, what a drag!
has *indic pres* → **haber**.
hasta I *prep* 1 (*lugar*) up to, as far as, down to. 2 (*tiempo*) until, till, up to; **h. el domingo**, until Sunday; **h. el final**, right to the end; **h. la fecha**, up to now; **h. luego**, see you later. 3 (*con cantidad*) up to, as many as. 4 (*incluso*) even. II *conj* **h. que**, until.
hastiado,-a *adj* sick, tired (**de, of**).
hastiar [29] *vtr* to sicken.
hastío *nm* weariness.
hato *nm* bundle.
hay *indic pres* → **haber**.
Haya (La) *nf* The Hague.
haya¹ *nf* 1 *Bot* (*árbol*) beech. 2 (*madera*) beech (wood).
haya² *subj pres* → **haber**.
haz¹ *nm* 1 *Agr* sheaf. 2 (*de luz*) shaft.
haz² *nf* (*de hoja*) top side.
haz³ *imperat* → **hacer**.
hazaña *nf* deed, exploit.
hazmerreír *nm* laughing stock.
he¹ *adv* **he ahí/aquí ...**, there/here you have ....
he² *indic pres* → **haber**.
hebilla *nf* buckle.
hebra *nf* thread; (*de carne*) sinew; (*de madera*) grain; **pegar la h.**, to chat.
hebreo,-a I *adj* Hebrew. II *nm,f* Hebrew.
hecatombe *nf* disaster.
hechicería *nf* witchcraft.
hechicero,-a I *adj* bewitching. II *nm,f* (*hombre*) wizard, sorcerer; (*mujer*) witch, sorceress.
hechizar [4] *vtr* 1 (*embrujar*) to cast a spell on. 2 *fig* (*fascinar*) to bewitch, charm.
hechizo *nm* 1 (*embrujo*) spell. 2 *fig* (*fascinación*) fascination, charm.
hecho,-a I *adj* 1 made, done; **¡bien h.!**,

well done! 2 (*carne*) done. 3 (*persona*) mature. 4 (*frase*) set; (*ropa*) ready-made. II *nm* 1 (*realidad*) fact; **de h.**, in fact; **el h. es que ...**, the fact is that .... 2 (*acto*) act, deed. 3 (*suceso*) event, incident.
hechura *nf* (*forma*) shape; *Cost* cut.
hectárea *nf* hectare.
hectolitro *nm* hectolitre, *US* hectoliter.
heder [3] *vi* to stink, smell foul.
hediondo,-a *adj* foul-smelling.
hedor *nm* stink, stench.
hegemonía *nf* hegemony.
helada *nf* frost.
heladería *nf* ice-cream parlour.
helado,-a I *nm* ice cream. II *adj* 1 (*muy frío*) frozen, freezing cold; **estoy h. (de frío)**, I'm frozen. 2 *fig* **quedarse h.**, (*atónito*) to be flabbergasted.
helar [1] I *vtr* (*congelar*) to freeze. II *v impers* to freeze; **anoche heló**, there was a frost last night. III **helarse** *vr* (*congelarse*) to freeze.
helecho *nm Bot* fern.
hélice *nf* 1 *Av Náut* propeller. 2 *Anat Arquit Mat* helix.
helicóptero *nm Av* helicopter.
helipuerto *nm Av* heliport.
hematoma *nm Med* haematoma, *US* hematoma.
hembra *nf* 1 *Bot Zool* female. 2 (*mujer*) woman. 3 *Téc* female; (*de tornillo*) nut; (*de enchufe*) socket.
hemiciclo *nm fam* (Spanish) parliament.
hemisferio *nm* hemisphere.
hemorragia *nf Med* haemorrhage, *US* hemorrhage.
hemos *indic pres* → **haber**.
henchir [6] *vtr* to stuff.
hender [3] *vtr* (*resquebrajar*) to crack, split; *fig* (*olas*) to cut.
hendidura *nf* crack.
hendir [5] *vtr* → **hender**.
heno *nm* hay.
heráldica *nf* heraldry.
herbicida *nm* weedkiller, herbicide.
herbívoro,-a I *adj* herbivorous, grass-eating. II *nm,f Zool* herbivore.
herbolario *nm* herbalist's (shop).
herboso,-a *adj* grassy.
hercio *nm* Herz.
heredad *nf* 1 (*finca*) country estate. 2 (*conjunto de bienes*) private estate.
heredar *vtr* 1 *Jur* to inherit. 2 **ha heredado la sonrisa de su madre**, she's got her mother's smile.
heredero,-a *nm,f* (*hombre*) heir; (*mujer*) heiress; **príncipe h.**, crown prince.
hereditario,-a *adj* hereditary.
hereje *nmf Rel* heretic.
herejía *nf Rel* heresy.
herencia *nf* 1 *Jur* inheritance, legacy. 2 *Biol* heredity.
herida *nf* (*lesión*) injury; (*corte*) wound.
herido,-a *n* injured person; **no hubo heri-**

dos, there were no casualties.
herir [5] **I** *vtr* **1** *(físicamente) (lesionar)* to injure; *(cortar)* to wound. **2** *(emocionalmente)* to hurt, wound. **3** *(vista)* to offend. **II herirse** *vr* to injure *o* hurt oneself.
hermana 1 sister. **2** *Rel (monja)* sister (→ **hermano**).
hermanado,-a *adj* twinned; **ciudad hermanada,** twin town.
hermanar I *vtr* **1** *(personas)* to unite spiritually. **2** *(ciudades)* to twin. **3** *(unir)* to unite, combine. **II hermanarse** *vr* **1** *(ciudades)* to twin. **2** *(combinar)* to combine.
hermanastro,-a *nm,f (hombre)* stepbrother; *(mujer)* stepsister.
hermandad *nf* **1** *(grupo)* fraternity, brotherhood, sisterhood. **2** *(relación)* brotherhood, sisterhood.
hermano *nm* **1** brother; **h. político,** brother-in-law; **primo h.,** first cousin. **2** *Rel (fraile)* brother. **3 hermanos,** brothers and sisters.
hermético,-a *adj* **1** *(cierre)* hermetic, airtight. **2** *fig (abstruso)* secretive. ◆**herméticamente** *adv* **h. cerrado,** hermetically sealed.
hermetismo *nm* hermeticism; *fig* impenetrability.
hermoso,-a *adj* beautiful, lovely; *(grande)* fine.
hermosura *nf* beauty.
héroe *nm* hero.
heroico,-a *adj* heroic.
heroína *nf* **1** *(mujer)* heroine. **2** *(droga)* heroin.
heroinómano,-a *nm,f* heroin addict.
heroísmo *nm* heroism.
herrador *nm* blacksmith.
herradura *nf* horseshoe.
herramienta *nf* *Téc* tool; **caja de herramientas,** toolbox.
herrar [1] *vtr* **1** *(caballo)* to shoe. **2** *(ganado)* to brand.
herrería *nf* forge, smithy.
herrero *nm* blacksmith, smith.
herrumbre *nf* rust.
hervidero *nm* *fig (lugar)* hotbed.
hervir [5] **I** *vtr (hacer bullir)* to boil. **II** *vi* **1** *Culin* to boil; **romper a h.,** to come to the boil. **2** *(abundar)* to swarm, seethe (**de,** with).
heterodoxo,-a *adj* unorthodox.
heterogéneo,-a *adj* heterogeneous.
hez *nf* **1** *(usu pl) (poso)* sediment, dregs *pl*. **2 heces,** faeces.
hiato *nm* *Ling* hiatus.
híbrido,-a *adj & nm,f* hybrid.
hice *pt indef* → **hacer.**
hiciste *pt indef* → **hacer.**
hidalgo *nm* *Hist* nobleman, gentleman.
hidalguía *nf* nobility; *fig* chivalry, gentlemanliness.
hidratación *nf* **1** *Quím* hydration. **2** *(de la piel)* moisturizing.

hidratante *adj* moisturizing; **crema/leche h.,** moisturizing cream/cream.
hidráulico,-a *adj* hydraulic; **energía hidráulica,** hydro-electric energy.
hidroavión *nm* seaplane, *US* hydroplane.
hidrocarburo *nm* hydrocarbon.
hidrófilo-a *adj* absorbent; **algodón h.,** cotton wool.
hidrógeno *nm* *Quím* hydrogen.
hidroterapia *nf* *Med* hydrotherapy.
hiedra *nf* ivy.
hiel *nf* **1** *Anat* bile. **2** *fig* bitterness, gall.
hielo *nm* ice; *fig* **romper el h.,** to break the ice.
hiena *nf* hyena.
hierba *nf* **1** grass; **mala h.,** *Bot* weed; *fig (persona)* bad lot; *fam* **hum ... y otras hierbas,** ... among others. **2** *Culin* herb; **h. luisa,** lemon verbena. **3** *sl (marihuana)* grass.
hierbabuena *nf* mint.
hierro *nm* **1** *(metal)* iron; **h. forjado,** wrought iron. **2** *(punta de arma)* head, point. **3** *(marca en el ganado)* brand.
hígado *nm* **1** *Anat* liver. **2** *euf* guts *pl*.
higiene *nf* hygiene.
higiénico,-a *adj* hygienic; **papel h.,** toilet paper.
higo *nm* *fam fig* **hecho un h.,** wizened, crumpled.
higuera *nf* *Bot* fig tree.
hija *nf* daughter (→ **hijo**).
hijastro,-a *nm,f (hombre)* stepson; *(mujer)* stepdaughter.
hijo *nm* **1** son, child; *pey* **h. de papá,** daddy's boy; *vulg* **h. de puta,** bastard, son of a bitch. **2 hijos,** children.
hijoputa *nm* *vulg ofens* bastard.
hilacha *nf*, **hilacho** *nm* loose *o* hanging thread.
hilandería *nf* mill; *(de algodón)* cotton mill.
hilandero,-a *nm,f* spinner.
hilar *vtr & vi* **1** to spin. **2** *fig (idea, plan)* to work out; **h. muy fino,** to split hairs.
hilaridad *nf* hilarity, mirth.
hilera *nf* line, row.
hilo *nm* **1** *Cost* thread; *(grueso)* yarn. **2** *fig (de historia, discurso)* thread; *(de pensamiento)* train; **perder el h.,** to lose the thread; **h. musical,** background music. **3** *Tex* linen.
hilvanar *vtr* **1** *Cost* to tack, baste. **2** *fig (ideas etc)* to outline.
himno *nm* hymn; **h. nacional,** national anthem.
hincapié *nm* **hacer h. en,** *(insistir)* to insist on; *(subrayar)* to emphasize, stress.
hincar [1] **I** *vtr (clavar)* to drive (in); **h. el diente a,** to sink one's teeth into. **II hincarse** *vr* **h. de rodillas,** to kneel (down).
hincha *fam* **I** *nmf* *Ftb* fan, supporter. **II** *nf*

(*antipatía*) grudge, dislike; **me tiene h.**, he's got it in for me.

hinchada *nf Ftb fam* fans *pl*, supporters *pl*.

hinchado,-a *adj* 1 inflated, blown up. 2 *Med* (*cara etc*) swollen, puffed up; (*estómago*) bloated. 3 *fig* (*estilo*) bombastic, pompous.

hinchar I *vtr* 1 (*inflar*) to inflate, blow up. 2 *fig* (*exagerar*) to inflate, exaggerate. II **hincharse** *vr* 1 *Med* to swell (up). 2 *fam* **me hinché de comida**, I stuffed myself; **me hinché de llorar**, I cried for all I was worth.

hinchazón *nf Med* swelling.

hindú *adj & nmf* Hindu.

hipermercado *nm* hypermarket.

hipertensión *nf* high blood pressure.

hípica *nf* (horse) riding.

hípico,-a *adj* horse; **club h.**, riding club.

hipnotizar |4| *vtr* to hypnotize.

hipo *nm* hiccups, hiccough; **me ha dado h.**, it's given me the hiccups.

hipocondríaco,-a *adj & nm,f* hypochondriac.

hipocresía *nf* hypocrisy.

hipócrita I *adj* hypocritical. II *nmf* hypocrite.

hipódromo *nm* racetrack, racecourse.

hipopótamo *nm* hippopotamus.

hipoteca *nf Fin* mortgage.

hipotecar |1| *vtr* 1 *Fin* to mortgage. 2 *fig* to jeopardize.

hipótesis *nf inv* hypothesis.

hipotético,-a *adj* hypothetical.

hiriente *adj* offensive, wounding; (*palabras*) cutting.

hirsuto,-a *adj* hirsute, hairy; (*cerdoso*) bristly.

hispánico,-a *adj* Hispanic, Spanish.

hispanidad *nf* **el Día de la H.**, Columbus Day (12 October).

hispano,-a I *adj* (*español*) Spanish; (*español y sudamericano*) Hispanic; (*sudamericano*) Spanish American. II *nm,f* Spanish American, *US* Hispanic.

Hispanoamérica *nf* Latin America.

hispanoamericano,-a *adj & nm,f* Latin American.

hispanohablante I *adj* Spanish-speaking. II *nmf* Spanish speaker.

histeria *nf* hysteria; **un ataque de h.**, hysterics *pl*.

histérico,-a *adj* hysterical; *fam fig* **me pones h.**, you're driving me mad.

historia *nf* 1 history; **this will go down in history.** 2 (*narración*) story, tale; *fam* **¡déjate de historias!**, don't give me that!

historiador,-a *nm,f* historian.

historial *nm* 1 *Med* medical record, case history. 2 (*currículum*) curriculum vitae. 3 (*antecedentes*) background.

historiar |29| *vtr* to recount.

histórico,-a *adj* 1 historical. 2 (*auténtico*) factual, true; **hechos históricos**, true facts. 3 (*de gran importancia*) historic, memorable.

historieta *nf* 1 (*cuento*) short story, tale. 2 (*tira cómica*) comic strip.

hito *nm* milestone; **mirar de h. en h.**, to stare at.

hizo *indic indef* → **hacer**.

hnos. *abr de* **Hermanos**, Brothers, Bros.

hocico *nm* 1 (*de animal*) snout. 2 *pey* (*de persona*) mug, snout; *fam* **meter los hocicos en algo**, to stick *o* poke one's nose into sth.

hogar *nm* 1 (*casa*) home. 2 (*de la chimenea*) hearth, fireplace. 3 *fig* **formar** *o* **crear un h.**, (*familia*) to start a family.

hogareño,-a *adj* (*vida*) home, family; (*persona*) home-loving, stay-at-home.

hoguera *nf* bonfire.

hoja *nf* 1 *Bot* leaf. 2 (*pétalo*) petal. 3 (*de papel*) sheet, leaf; **h. de cálculo**, spreadsheet. 4 (*de libro*) leaf, page. 5 (*de metal*) sheet. 6 (*de cuchillo, espada*) blade. 7 (*impreso*) hand-out, printed sheet. 8 (*de puerta o ventana*) leaf.

hojalata *nf* tin, tin plate.

hojaldre *nm Culin* puff pastry.

hojarasca *nf* fallen *o* dead leaves *pl*.

hojear *vtr* to leaf through, flick through.

hola *interj* hello!, hullo!, hi!

Holanda *n* Holland.

holandés,-esa I *adj* Dutch. II *nm,f* (*hombre*) Dutchman; (*mujer*) Dutchwoman. III *nm* (*idioma*) Dutch.

holding *nm Fin* holding company.

holgado,-a *adj* 1 (*ropa*) loose, baggy. 2 (*económicamente*) comfortable. 3 (*espacio*) roomy; **andar h. de tiempo**, to have plenty of time.

holgar |2| *vi* 1 (*no trabajar*) to be idle. 2 (*sobrar*) **huelga decir que ...**, it goes without saying that ....

holgazán,-ana I *adj* lazy, idle. II *nm,f* layabout *inv*, layabout.

holgura *nf* 1 (*ropa*) looseness. 2 (*espacio*) space, roominess; *Téc* play, give. 3 (*bienestar económico*) affluence, comfort; **vivir con h.**, to be comfortably off, be well-off.

hollar |2| *vtr fig* to walk on; **terrenos jamás hollados**, uncharted territory.

hollín *nm* soot.

hombre I *nm* 1 man; **de h. a h.**, man-to-man; **¡pobre h.!**, poor chap!; **ser muy h.**, to be every inch a man; **h. de estado**, statesman; **h. de negocios**, businessman. 2 (*especie*) mankind, man. II *interj* 1 (*saludo*) hey!, hey there!; **¡h., Juan!**, hey, Juan! 2 **¡sí h.!**, **¡h. claro!**, (*enfático*) sure!, you bet!; **¡anda, h.!**, (*incredulidad*) oh come on!

hombrera *nf* shoulder pad.

hombría *nf* manliness, virility.

hombro *nm* shoulder; **a hombros**, on one's shoulders; **encogerse de hombros**, to shrug one's shoulders; **mirar a algn por encima del h.**, to look down one's nose at sb.

hombruno,-a *adj* mannish, butch.

homenaje *nm* homage, tribute; **rendir h. a algn**, to pay homage *o* tribute to sb.

homenajear *vtr* to pay tribute to.

homicida I *nmf (hombre)* murderer; *(mujer)* murderess. II *adj* homicidal; **el arma h.**, the murder weapon.

homicidio *nm* homicide.

homogéneo,-a *adj* homogeneous, uniform.

homologable *adj* comparable (**con**, with).

homologar [7] *vtr* to give official approval *o* recognition to.

homólogo,-a I *adj (equiparable)* comparable. II *nm,f (persona con mismas condiciones)* counterpart.

homosexual *adj & nmf* homosexual.

homosexualidad *nf* homosexuality.

honda *nf (arma)* sling.

hondo,-a *adj* 1 *(profundo)* deep; **plato h.**, soup dish. 2 *fig (pesar)* profound, deep.

hondonada *nf Geog* hollow, depression.

hondura *nf* depth; *fig* **meterse en honduras**, *(profundizar)* to go into too much detail.

Honduras *n* Honduras.

hondureño,-a *adj & nm,f* Honduran.

honestidad *nf* 1 *(honradez)* honesty, uprightness. 2 *(decencia)* modesty.

honesto,-a *adj* 1 *(honrado)* honest, upright. 2 *(decente)* modest.

hongo *nm* 1 *Bot* fungus; **h. venenoso**, toadstool. 2 *(sombrero)* bowler, bowler hat.

honor *nm* 1 *(virtud)* honour, *US* honor; **palabra de h.**, word of honour. 2 **en h. a la verdad ...**, to be fair ...; **es un h. para mí**, it's an honour for me. 3 **hacer h. a**, to live up to.

honorable *adj* honourable, *US* honorable; *Pol* **el h.**, head of the Catalan government.

honorario,-a I *adj* honorary. II *nmpl* **honorarios**, fees, fee *sing*.

honorífico,-a *adj* honorary.

honra *nf* 1 *(dignidad)* dignity, self-esteem. 2 *(fama)* reputation, good name. 3 *(honor)* honour, *US* honor; **me cabe la h. de ...**, I have the honour of ...; **¡a mucha h.!**, and proud of it!

honradez *nf* honesty, integrity.

honrado,-a *adj* 1 *(de fiar)* honest. 2 *(decente)* upright, respectable.

honrar *vtr* 1 *(respetar)* to honour, *US* honor. 2 *(enaltecer)* to be a credit to.

honrilla *nf* self-respect, pride.

honroso,-a *adj* *(loable)* honourable, *US* honorable.

hora *nf* 1 hour; **media h.**, half an hour; **a altas horas de la madrugada**, in the small hours; **dar la h.**, to strike the hour; **(trabajo) por horas**, (work) paid by the hour; **h. punta**, rush hour; **horas extra**, overtime (hours). 2 *fig* time; **¿qué h. es?**, what time is it?; **a su h.**, at the proper time; **a última h.**, at the last moment; **la h. de la verdad**, the moment of truth. 3 *(cita)* appointment; **pedir h.**, *(al médico etc)* to ask for an appointment.

horadar *vtr (perforar)* to drill *o* bore a hole in.

horario-a I *nm* timetable, *US* schedule. II *adj* time; *Rad* **señal horaria**, pips.

horca *nf* gallows *pl*.

horcajada *nf* **a horcajadas**, astride.

horchata *nf Culin* sweet milky drink made from chufa nuts or almonds.

horda *nf* horde, mob.

horizonte *nm* horizon.

horma *nf (de zapato)* last.

hormiga *nf* ant.

hormigón *nm Constr* concrete; **h. armado**, reinforced concrete.

hormiguear *vi* to itch, tingle; **me hormigueaba la pierna**, I had pins and needles in my leg.

hormigueo *nm* 1 pins and needles *pl*, tingling *o* itching sensation. 2 *fig* anxiety.

hormiguero *nm* 1 anthill. 2 *fig* **ser un h.**, *(lugar)* to be swarming (with people).

hormona *nf* hormone.

hornada *nf* 1 *(pan)* batch. 2 *fig* set, batch.

hornillo *nm (de cocinar)* stove; *(placa)* hotplate.

horno *nm (cocina)* oven; *Téc* furnace; *(para cerámica, ladrillos)* kiln; *Culin* **pescado al h.**, baked fish; *fam fig* **esta habitación es un h.**, this room is boiling hot.

Hornos *n* **Cabo de H.**, Cape Horn.

horóscopo *nm* horoscope.

horquilla *nf* 1 *(del pelo)* hair-grip, hairpin, *US* bobby pin. 2 *(estadística)* chart. 3 **h. de precios**, price range.

horrendo-a *adj* horrifying, horrible.

hórreo *nm Agr* granary.

horrible *adj* horrible, dreadful, awful.

horripilante *adj* hair-raising, scary.

horror *nm* 1 horror, terror; **¡qué h.!**, how awful!; *fam* **tengo h. a las motos**, I hate motorbikes. 2 *fam fig* **me gusta horrores**, *(muchísimo)* I like it an awful lot.

horrorizar [4] *vtr* to horrify, terrify.

horroroso,-a *adj* 1 *(que da miedo)* horrifying, terrifying. 2 *fam (muy feo)* hideous, ghastly. 3 *fam (malísimo)* awful, dreadful.

hortaliza *nf* vegetable.

hortelano *nm,f* market gardener, *US* truck farmer.

hortensia *nf Bot* hydrangea.

hortera *adj arg (persona)* flashy; *(cosa)* tacky, kitsch.

horterada *nf arg* tacky thing *o* act.
hosco,-a *adj* 1 *(poco sociable)* surly, sullen. 2 *(tenebroso)* dark, gloomy. 3 *(difícil)* tough.
hospedaje *nm* lodgings *pl*, accommodation, *US* accommodations.
hospedar I *vtr* to put up, lodge. II **hospedarse** *vr* to stay (**en**, at).
hospicio *nm* orphanage.
hospital *nm* hospital.
hospitalario,-a *adj* 1 *(acogedor)* hospitable. 2 *Med* hospital; **instalaciones hospitalarias**, hospital facilities.
hospitalidad *nf* hospitality.
hospitalizar [4] *vtr* to take *o* send into hospital, hospitalize.
hostal *nm* guest house.
hostelería *nf (negocio)* catering business; *(estudios)* hotel management.
hostelero,-a *nm,f (hombre)* landlord; *(mujer)* landlady.
hostería *nf Am* inn, lodging house.
hostia I *nf* 1 *Rel* host. 2 *vulg (tortazo)* bash. 3 **estar de mala h.**, to be in a foul mood; **ser la h.**, *(fantástico)* to be bloody amazing *o* fantastic; *(penoso)* to be bloody useless. II *interj* damn! bloody hell!
hostiar *vtr vulg* to bash, sock.
hostigar [7] *vtr* 1 to harass. 2 *(caballerías)* to whip.
hostil *adj* hostile.
hostilidad *nf* hostility.
hotel *nm* hotel.
hotelero,-a I *adj* hotel; **el sector h.**, the hotel sector. II *nm,f* hotel-keeper, hotelier.
hoy *adv* 1 *(día)* today. 2 *fig (presente)* now; **h. (en) día**, nowadays; **h. por h.**, at the present time.
hoya *nf Geog* dale, valley.
hoyo *nm* 1 *(agujero)* hole, pit. 2 *(sepultura)* grave. 3 *Golf* hole.
hoyuelo *nm* dimple.
hoz *nf Agr* sickle; **la h. y el martillo**, the hammer and sickle.
HR *nm abr de* **Hostal Residencia**.
hube *pt indef* → **haber**.
hubiera *subj imperf* → **haber**.
hucha *nf* piggy bank.
hueco,-a I *adj* 1 *(vacío)* empty, hollow. 2 *(sonido)* resonant. II *nm* 1 *(cavidad)* hollow, hole. 2 *(sitio no ocupado)* empty space. 3 *(rato libre)* free time.
huele *indic pres* → **oler**.
huelga *nf* strike; **estar en** *o* **de h.**, to be on strike; **h. de brazos caídos**, go-slow; **h. de celo**, work- to-rule.
huelguista *nmf* striker.
huella *nf* 1 *(del pie)* footprint; *(coche)* track; **h. dactilar**, fingerprint. 2 *fig (vestigio)* trace, sign; **dejar h.**, to leave one's mark.
huérfano,-a *nmf* orphan.
huero,-a *adj fig* empty.

huerta *nf Agr* 1 *(parcela)* market *o US* truck garden. 2 *(región)* irrigated area used for cultivation.
huerto *nm (de verduras)* vegetable garden, kitchen garden; *(de frutales)* orchard.
hueso *nm* 1 *Anat* bone; **estar en los huesos**, to be all skin and bones. 2 *(de fruto)* stone, *US* pit. 3 *fig (difícil)* hard work; *(profesor)* hard nut. 4 *Am (enchufe)* contact.
huésped,-a *nm,f (invitado)* guest; *(en hotel etc)* lodger, boarder; **casa de huéspedes**, guesthouse.
hueste *nf Mil* army, host.
huesudo,-a *adj* bony.
huevera *nf* 1 *(caja)* egg box. 2 *vulg (suspensorio)* jockstrap.
huevo *nm* 1 egg; **h. duro**, hard-boiled egg; **h. escalfado**, poached egg; **h. frito**, fried egg; **h. pasado por agua**, *Am* **h. tibio**, soft-boiled egg; **huevos revueltos**, scrambled eggs. 2 *vulg (usu pl)* balls *pl*; **hacer algo por huevos**, to do sth even if it kills you; **tener huevos**, to have guts.
huida *nf* flight, escape.
huidizo,-a *adj* elusive.
huir [37] *vi* to run away (**de**, from); flee; **h. de la cárcel**, to escape from prison; **h. de algn**, to avoid sb.
hule *nm* 1 *(tela impermeable)* oilcloth, oilskin. 2 *(de mesa)* tablecloth. 3 *Am* rubber.
hulla *nf Min* coal.
humanidad *nf* 1 *(género humano)* humanity, mankind. 2 *(cualidad)* humanity, humaneness. 3 *(bondad)* compassion, kindness.
humanitario,-a *adj* humanitarian.
humano,-a I *adj* 1 *(relativo al hombre)* human. 2 *(compasivo)* humane. II *nm* human (being); **ser h.**, human being.
humear *vi (echar humo)* to smoke; *(arrojar vapor)* to steam, be steaming hot.
humedad *nf (atmosférica)* humidity; *(de lugar)* dampness; **a prueba de h.**, dampproof.
humedecer [33] I *vtr* to moisten, dampen. II **humedecerse** *vr* to become damp *o* wet *o* moist.
húmedo,-a *adj (casa, ropa)* damp; *(clima)* humid, damp, moist.
humildad *nf* humility; *(pobreza)* humbleness.
humilde *adj* humble, modest; *(pobre)* poor.
humillación *nf* humiliation.
humillante *adj* humiliating, humbling.
humillar I *vtr (rebajar)* to humiliate, humble. II **humillarse** *vr* **h. ante algn**, to humble oneself before sb.
humo *nm* 1 smoke; *(gas)* fumes *pl*; *(vapor)* vapour, *US* vapor, steam. 2 **¡qué humos tiene!**, she thinks a lot of herself.
humor *nm* 1 *(genio)* mood; **estar de buen**

o **mal h.**, to be in a good *o* bad mood. **2** (*carácter*) temper; **es persona de mal h.**, he's bad tempered. **3** (*gracia*) humour, *US* humor; **sentido del h.**, sense of humour.

humorismo *nm* humour, *US* humor.
humorista *nmf* humorist; **h. gráfico**, cartoonist.
humorístico,-a *adj* humorous, funny.
hundido,-a *adj* **1** (*barco*) sunken; (*ojos*) deep-set. **2** *fig* (*abatido*) down, demoralized.
hundimiento *nm* **1** (*de edificio*) collapse. **2** (*de barco*) sinking. **3** (*de tierra*) subsidence. **4** *fig Fin* crash, slump; (*ruina*) downfall.
hundir I *vtr* **1** (*barco*) to sink. **2** (*edificio*) to bring *o* knock down. **3** *fig* (*desmoralizar*) to demoralize. II **hundirse** *vr* **1** (*barco*) to sink. **2** (*edificio*) to collapse. **3** *fig* (*empresa*) to collapse, crash.

húngaro,-a I *adj* Hungarian. II *nm,f* (*persona*) Hungarian. III *nm* (*idioma*) Hungarian.
Hungría *n* Hungary.
huracán *nm* hurricane.
huraño,-a *adj pey* unsociable.
hurgar |7| I *vi* (*fisgar*) to poke one's nose in. II *vtr* (*fuego etc*) to poke, rake. III **hurgarse** *vr* **h. las narices**, to pick one's nose.
hurón,-ona I *nm Zool* ferret. II *nm,f fam fig* (*fisgón*) busybody, nosey-parker.
hurraca *nf Orn* → **urraca**.
hurtadillas *adv* **a h.**, stealthily, on the sly.
hurtar *vtr* to steal, pilfer.
hurto *nm* petty theft, pilfering.
husmear I *vtr* (*olfatear*) to sniff out, scent. II *vi fig* (*curiosear*) to snoop, pry.
huyo *indic pres* → **huir**.

I

I, i |i| *nf* (*la letra*) I, i; **i griega**, Y, y.
ib. *abr de* **ibídem**, ibidem, ibid., ib.
IB *nm Educ abr de* **Instituto de Bachillerato**, ≈ state secondary school.
ibérico,-a *adj* Iberian.
Iberoamérica *n* Latin America.
iberoamericano,-a *adj & nm,f* Latin American.
iceberg *nm* (*pl* **icebergs**) iceberg.
ICONA *nm abr de* **Instituto para la Conservación de la Naturaleza**.
icono *nm* icon; *Inform* icon.
iconoclasta I *adj* iconoclastic. II *nmf* iconoclast.
iconografía *nf* iconography.
ictericia *nf Med* jaundice.
íd. *abr de* **ídem**, idem, id.
I+D *abr de* **Investigación más Desarrollo**, Research and Development, R&D.
ida *nf* **billete de i. y vuelta**, return ticket; **idas y venidas**, comings and goings.
idea *nf* **1** idea; **i. fija**, fixed idea. **2** (*noción*) idea; **hacerse a la i. de**, to get used to the idea of; *fam* **ni i.**, no idea, not a clue. **3** (*opinión*) opinion; **cambiar de i.**, to change one's mind. **4** (*intención*) intention; **a mala i.**, on purpose.
ideal *adj & nm* ideal.
idealismo *nm* idealism.
idealista I *adj* idealistic. II *nmf* idealist.
idealizar |4| *vtr* to idealize, glorify.
idear *vtr* **1** (*inventar*) to devise, invent. **2** (*concebir*) to think up, conceive.
ídem *adv* idem, ditto; *fam* **í. de í.**, exactly the same.
idéntico,-a *adj* identical.
identidad *nf* **1** identity; **carnet de i.**, identity card. **2** (*semejanza*) identity, sameness.
identificación *nf* identification.
identificar |1| I *vtr* to identify. II **identificarse** *vr* to identify oneself; *fig* **i. con**, to identify with.
ideología *nf* ideology.
ideológico,-a *adj* ideological.
idílico,-a *adj* idyllic.
idilio *nm* **1** *Lit* idyll. **2** *fig* (*romance*) romance, love affair.
idioma *nm* language.
idiomático,-a *adj* idiomatic.
idiosincrasia *nf* idiosyncrasy.
idiota I *adj* idiotic, stupid. II *nmf* idiot, fool.
idiotez *nf* idiocy, stupidity.
ido,-a *adj* **1** (*distraído*) absent-minded. **2** *fam* (*chiflado*) crazy, nuts.
idólatra I *adj* idolatrous. II *nmf* (*hombre*) idolater; (*mujer*) idolatress.
idolatrar *vtr* to worship; *fig* to idolize.
idolatría *nf* idolatry.
ídolo *nm* idol.
idóneo,-a *adj* suitable, fit.
iglesia *nf* **1** (*edificio*) church. **2 la I.**, (*institución*) the Church.
ignominia *nf* ignominy.
ignominioso,-a *adj* ignominious, shameful.
ignorancia *nf* ignorance.
ignorante I *adj* **1** (*sin instrucción*) ignorant. **2** (*no informado*) ignorant, unaware (**de**, of). II *nmf* ignoramus.
ignorar I *vtr* **1** (*algo*) not to know. **2** (*a algn*) to ignore. II **ignorarse** *vr* to be unknown.
ignoto,-a *adj* unknown.
igual I *adj* **1** (*idéntico*) the same, alike;

son todos iguales, they're all the same; **es i.,** it doesn't matter; **i. que,** the same as. **2** *(equivalente)* equal; **a partes iguales,** fifty-fifty. **3** *Dep (empatados)* even; **treinta iguales,** thirty all. **4** *Mat* equal; **tres más tres i. a seis,** three plus three equals six. **5 al i. que,** just like. **6 por i.,** equally. **II** *nm* equal; **de i. a i.,** on an equal footing; **sin i.,** unique, unrivalled. **III** *adv* **1 lo haces i. que yo,** you do it the same way I do. **2** *(probablemente)* probably; **i. vengo,** I'll probably come. ◆**igualmente** *adv* equally; *(también)* also, likewise; *fam* **¡gracias! - ¡i.!,** thank you! - the same to you!

igualar I *vtr* **1** to make equal. **2** *(nivelar)* to level; **3** *Dep* **i. el partido,** to equalize, square the match. **II igualarse** *vr* **1** to be equal. **2 i. con algn,** to place oneself on an equal footing with sb.

igualdad *nf* **1** equality; **i. ante la ley,** equality before the law. **2** *(identidad)* sameness; **en i. de condiciones,** on equal terms.

igualitario,-a *adj* egalitarian.

ijada *nf,* **ijar** *nm Anat* flank.

ikastola *nf* Basque language school.

ikurriña *nf* Basque flag.

ilegal *adj* illegal. ◆**ilegalmente** *adv* illegally.

ilegalidad *nf* illegality.

ilegible *adj* illegible, unreadable.

ilegítimo,-a *adj* illegitimate.

ileso,-a *adj* unhurt, unharmed.

ilícito,-a *adj* illicit, unlawful.

ilimitado,-a *adj* unlimited, limitless.

Ilmo. *abr de* **Ilustrísimo,** His Excellence *o* Excellency.

ilógico,-a *adj* illogical.

iluminación *nf (alumbrado)* illumination, lighting.

iluminar *vtr* **1** to illuminate, light (up). **2** *fig (a persona)* to enlighten; *(tema)* to throw light upon.

ilusión *nf* **1** *(esperanza)* hope; *(esperanza vana)* illusion, delusion; **hacerse ilusiones,** to build up one's hopes. **2** *(sueño)* dream. **3** *(emoción)* excitement, thrill; **me hace i. verla,** I'm looking forward to seeing her; **¡qué i.!,** how exciting!

ilusionar I *vtr* **1** *(esperanzar)* to build up sb's hopes. **2** *(entusiasmar)* to excite, thrill. **II ilusionarse** *vr* **1** *(esperanzarse)* to build up one's hopes. **2** *(entusiasmarse)* to be excited *o* thrilled *(con,* about).

iluso,-a *adj* easily deceived, gullible.

ilusorio,-a *adj* illusory, unreal.

ilustración *nf* **1** *(grabado)* illustration, picture; *(ejemplo)* illustration. **2** *(erudición)* learning, erudition; *Hist* **la I.,** the Enlightenment.

ilustrado,-a *adj* **1** *(con dibujos, ejemplos)* illustrated. **2** *(erudito)* learned, erudite.

ilustrar I *vtr* **1** to illustrate. **2** *(aclarar)* to

explain, make clear. **II ilustrarse** *vr* to acquire knowledge **(sobre,** of), learn.

ilustrativo,-a *adj* illustrative.

ilustre *adj* illustrious, distinguished.

imagen *nf* **1** image; **ser la viva i. de algn,** to be the spitting image of sb; **tener buena i.,** to have a good image. **2** *Rel* image, statue. **3** *TV* picture.

imaginación *nf* imagination; **eso son imaginaciones tuyas,** you're imagining things.

imaginar I *vtr* to imagine. **II imaginarse** *vr* to imagine; **me imagino que sí,** I suppose so.

imaginario,-a *adj* imaginary.

imaginativo,-a *adj* imaginative.

imán *nm* magnet.

imbatible *adj* unbeatable.

imbatido,-a *adj* unbeaten, undefeated.

imbécil I *adj* stupid, silly. **II** *nmf* idiot, imbecile.

imbecilidad *nf* stupidity, imbecility.

imborrable *adj* indelible.

imbuir |37| *vtr fml* to imbue.

imitación *nf* imitation.

imitar *vtr* to imitate; *(gestos)* to mimic; **este collar imita al oro,** this necklace is imitation gold.

impaciencia *nf* impatience.

impacientar I *vtr* **i. a algn,** to make sb lose patience, exasperate sb. **II impacientarse** *vr* to get *o* grow impatient **(por,** at).

impaciente *adj (deseoso)* impatient; *(intranquilo)* anxious.

impactar *vtr* to shock, stun.

impacto *nm* impact; *Mil* hit.

impactante *adj* **una noticia i.,** a sensational piece of news.

impar *adj Mat* odd; **número i.,** odd number.

imparable *adj Dep* unstoppable.

imparcial *adj* impartial, unbiased.

imparcialidad *nf* impartiality.

impartir *vtr (clases)* to give.

impasible *adj* impassive.

impávido,-a *adj* fearless.

impecable *adj* impeccable.

impedido,-a I *adj* disabled, handicapped. **II** *nm,f* disabled *o* handicapped person.

impedimento *nm* impediment; *(obstáculo)* hindrance, obstacle.

impedir |6| *vtr (obstaculizar)* to impede, hinder; *(imposibilitar)* to prevent, stop; **i. el paso,** to block the way.

impeler *vtr Téc* to drive, propel; *fig* to drive, impel.

impenetrable *adj* impenetrable.

impenitente *adj Rel* impenitent, unrepentant.

impensable *adj* unthinkable.

impepinable *adj fam* dead sure, certain.

imperante *adj (gobernante)* ruling; *(predominante)* prevailing.

imperar vi (gobernar) to rule; (predominar) to prevail.

imperativo,-a I adj imperative. **II** nm Ling imperative.

imperceptible adj imperceptible.

imperdible nm safety pin.

imperdonable adj unforgivable, inexcusable.

imperecedero,-a adj imperishable; fig enduring.

imperfección nf 1 imperfection. 2 (defecto) defect, fault.

imperfecto,-a adj 1 imperfect, fallible. 2 (defectuoso) defective, faulty. 3 Ling imperfect.

imperial adj imperial.

imperialismo nm imperialism.

impericia nf incompetence.

imperio nm empire; **el i. de la ley,** the rule of law.

imperioso,-a adj 1 (autoritario) imperious. 2 (ineludible) urgent, imperative; **una necesidad imperiosa,** a pressing need.

impermeable I adj impermeable, impervious; (ropa) waterproof. **II** nm raincoat, mac.

impersonal adj impersonal.

impertérrito,-a adj undaunted, fearless.

impertinencia nf impertinence.

impertinente I adj (insolente) impertinent; (inoportuno) irrelevant. **II** nmpl **impertinentes,** lorgnette sing.

imperturbable adj imperturbable, unruffled.

ímpetu nm 1 (impulso) impetus, momentum. 2 (violencia) violence. 3 (energía) energy.

impetuosidad nf 1 (violencia) violence. 2 (fogosidad) impetuosity, impulsiveness.

impetuoso,-a adj 1 (violento) violent. 2 (fogoso) impetuous, impulsive.

impío,-a adj ungodly, irreligious.

implacable adj relentless, implacable.

implantar vtr (costumbres) to implant, instil; (reformas) to introduce; Med to implant.

implicación nf (participación) involvement; (significado) implication.

implicar [1] vtr 1 (involucrar) to involve, implicate (**en,** in). 2 (conllevar) to imply.

implícito,-a adj implicit, implied.

implorar vtr to implore, beg.

impoluto,-a adj pure, spotless.

imponente adj 1 (impresionante) imposing, impressive. 2 (sobrecogedor) stunning. 2 fam (atractivo) terrific, tremendous, smashing.

imponer [19] (pp **impuesto**) **I** vtr 1 to impose. 2 (impresionar) to be impressive; (respeto) to inspire respect. 3 Fin to deposit. **II imponerse** vr 1 (infundir respeto) to command respect. 2 (prevalecer) to prevail. 3 (ser necesario) to be necessary.

imponible adj Fin taxable.

impopular adj unpopular, disliked.

importación nf (mercancía) import; (acción) importing; **artículos de i.,** imported goods.

importancia nf importance, significance; **dar i. a,** to attach importance to; **sin i.,** unimportant.

importante adj important, significant; **una suma i.,** a considerable sum.

importar¹ I vi 1 (atañer) **eso no te importa a tí,** that doesn't concern you, that's none of your business. 2 (tener importancia) to be important; **no importa,** it doesn't matter; fam **me importa un bledo** o **un pito,** I couldn't care less. 3 (molestar) **¿te importaría repetirlo?,** would you mind repeating it?; **¿te importa si fumo?,** do you mind if I smoke? **II** vtr (valer) to amount to; **los libros importan dos mil pesetas,** the books come to two thousand pesetas.

importar² vtr to import.

importe nm Com Fin amount, total.

importunar vtr to bother, pester.

imposibilidad nf impossibility.

imposibilitar vtr 1 (impedir) to make impossible, prevent. 2 (incapacitar) to disable, cripple.

imposible adj impossible; **me es i. hacerlo,** I can't (possibly) do it.

imposición nf 1 (disciplina, condiciones) imposing. 2 Fin deposit; (impuesto) taxation.

impostor,-a nm,f (farsante) impostor.

impotencia nf powerlessness, helplessness; Med impotence.

impotente adj powerless, helpless; Med impotent.

impracticable adj 1 (inviable) impracticable, unviable. 2 (camino) impassable.

imprecar [1] vtr to imprecate, curse.

imprecisión nf imprecision, vagueness.

impreciso,-a adj imprecise, vague.

impregnar I vtr to impregnate (**en, de,** with). **II impregnarse** vr to become impregnated.

imprenta nf 1 (taller) printer's, print works. 2 (aparato) printing press. 3 **libertad de i.,** freedom of the press.

imprescindible adj essential, indispensable.

impresentable adj unpresentable.

impresión nf 1 fig (efecto) impression; **causar i.,** to make an impression. 2 fig (opinión) impression; **cambiar impresiones,** to exchange impressions. 3 Impr (acto) printing; (edición) edition. 4 (huella) impression, imprint.

impresionable adj impressionable.

impresionante adj impressive, striking; fam **un error i.,** (tremendo) a terrible mistake.

impresionar vtr 1 (causar admiración) to impress; (sorprender) to stun, shock. 2 Fot

to expose.
impresionismo *nm Arte* impressionism.
impresionista *adj & nmf* impressionist.
impreso,-a I *adj* printed. **II** *nm* **1** (*papel, folleto*) printed matter. **2** (*formulario*) form; **i. de solicitud,** application form. **3 impresos,** (*de correos*) printed matter *sing.*
impresora *nf Inform* printer; **i. láser,** laser printer.
imprevisible *adj* unforeseeable, unpredictable.
imprevisión *nf* lack of foresight.
imprevisto,-a I *adj* unforeseen, unexpected. **II** *nm* (*incidente*) unforeseen event.
imprimir *vtr* (*pp* **impreso**) **1** *Impr Inform* to print. **2** (*marcar*) to stamp.
improbable *adj* improbable, unlikely.
ímprobo,-a *adj* (*inmoral*) dishonest, corrupt.
improcedente *adj* **1** inappropriate, unsuitable. **2** *Jur* inadmissible.
improductivo,-a *adj* unproductive.
improperio *nm* insult, offensive remark.
impropio,-a *adj* (*inadecuado*) inappropriate, unsuitable; **i. de,** uncharacteristic of.
improvisación *nf* improvisation; *Mús* extemporization.
improvisado,-a *adj* (*espontáneo*) improvised, impromptu, ad lib; (*provisional*) makeshift; **discurso i.,** impromptu speech.
improvisar *vtr* to improvise; *Mús* to extemporize.
improviso *adj* **de i.,** unexpectedly, suddenly; *fam* **coger** *o* **pillar a algn de i.,** to catch sb unawares.
imprudencia *nf* imprudence, rashness; (*indiscreción*) indiscretion.
imprudente *adj* imprudent, unwise; (*indiscreto*) indiscreet.
impudicia *nf* (*falta de pudor*) immodesty; (*desvergüenza*) shamelessness.
impudor *nm* immodesty; (*desvergüenza*) shamelessness.
impuesto,-a I *nm Fin* tax; **i. sobre la renta,** income tax; **libre de impuestos,** tax-free; **i. sobre el valor añadido,** value added tax. **II** *adj* imposed.
impugnar *vtr* (*teoría*) to refute, disprove; (*decisión*) to challenge, contest.
impulsar *vtr* to impel, drive.
impulsivo,-a *adj* impulsive.
impulso *nm* impulse, thrust; *Dep* **tomar i.,** to take a run up.
impune *adj* unpunished.
◆**impunemente** *adv* with impunity.
impunidad *nf* impunity.
impureza *nf* impurity.
impuro,-a *adj* impure.
impuse *pt indef* → **imponer**.
imputar *vtr* to impute, attribute.
inabarcable *adj* unfathomable.
inabordable *adj* unapproachable, inaccessible.

inacabable *adj* interminable, endless.
inaccesible *adj* inaccessible.
inaceptable *adj* unacceptable.
inactividad *nf* inactivity; *Fin* lull, stagnation.
inactivo,-a *adj* inactive.
inadaptación *nf* maladjustment.
inadaptado,-a I *adj* maladjusted. **II** *nm,f* misfit.
inadecuado,-a *adj* unsuitable, inappropriate.
inadmisible *adj* inadmissible.
inadvertido,-a *adj* (*desapercibido*) unnoticed, unseen; **pasar i.,** to escape notice, pass unnoticed.
inagotable *adj* **1** (*recursos etc*) inexhaustible. **2** (*persona*) tireless, indefatigable.
inaguantable *adj* unbearable, intolerable.
inalámbrico,-a I *adj* cordless. **II** *nm* cordless telephone.
inalcanzable *adj* unattainable, unachievable.
inalterable *adj* **1** unalterable. **2** (*persona*) impassive, imperturbable.
inamovible *adj* immovable, fixed.
inanición *nf* starvation; *Med* inanition.
inanimado,-a *adj* inanimate.
inapreciable *adj* **1** (*valioso*) invaluable, inestimable. **2** (*insignificante*) insignificant, trivial.
inasequible *adj* **1** (*producto*) unaffordable. **2** (*meta*) unattainable, unachievable. **3** (*persona*) unapproachable, inaccessible. **4** (*cuestión*) incomprehensible.
inaudito,-a *adj* **1** (*sin precedente*) unprecedented. **2** *fig* (*escandaloso*) outrageous.
inauguración *nf* inauguration, opening.
inaugural *adj* inaugural, opening; **ceremonia i.,** inaugural ceremony.
inaugurar *vtr* to inaugurate, open.
inca *adj & nmf* Inca.
incalculable *adj* incalculable, indeterminate.
incandescente *adj* white hot, incandescent.
incansable *adj* tireless, indefatigable.
incapacidad *nf* **1** incapacity, inability; **i. física,** physical disability. **2** (*incompetencia*) incompetence, inefficiency.
incapacitado,-a *adj* (*imposibilitado*) incapacitated, disabled; (*desautorizado*) incapacitated.
incapacitar *vtr* **1** to incapacitate, disable. **2** (*inhabilitar*) to disqualify, make unfit (**para,** for).
incapaz *adj* **1** unable (**de,** to), incapable (**de,** of); **soy i. de continuar,** I can't go on. **2** *Jur* unfit.
incautación *nf Jur* seizure, confiscation.
incautarse *vr Jur* **i. de,** to seize, confiscate.
incauto,-a *adj* **1** (*imprudente*) incautious, unwary. **2** (*crédulo*) gullible.

incendiar |12| I *vtr* to set fire to, set alight. II **incendiarse** *vr* to catch fire.

incendiario,-a I *adj* incendiary; *fig (discurso etc)* inflammatory. II *nm,f (persona)* arsonist, fire-raiser.

incendio *nm* fire; i. **forestal**, forest fire.

incentivar *vtr* to give an incentive to.

incentivo *nm* incentive.

incertidumbre *nf* uncertainty, doubt.

incesante *adj* incessant, never-ending.

incesto *nm* incest.

incestuoso,-a *adj* incestuous.

incidencia *nf* 1 *(repercusión)* impact, effect; **la huelga tuvo escasa i.**, the strike had little effect. 2 *(hecho)* incident. 3 *Fís* incidence.

incidente *nm* incident.

incidir *vi* 1 *(incurrir)* to fall (**en**, into). 2 **i. en**, *(afectar)* to affect, influence.

incienso *nm* incense.

incierto,-a *adj (inseguro)* uncertain.

incineración *nf (de basuras)* incineration; *(de cadáveres)* cremation.

incinerar *vtr (basura)* to incinerate; *(cadáveres)* to cremate.

incipiente *adj* incipient, budding.

incisión *nf* incision, cut.

incisivo,-a I *adj (mordaz)* incisive, cutting; *(cortante)* sharp. II *nm Anat* incisor.

inciso *nm (paréntesis)* digression; **a modo de i.**, in passing, incidentally.

incitación *nf* incitement.

incitante *adj* 1 *(instigador)* inciting. 2 *(provocativo)* provocative.

incitar *vtr* to incite, urge.

incivil *adj* uncivil, rude.

inclemencia *nf* inclemency, harshness.

inclemente *adj* inclement, harsh.

inclinación *nf* 1 *(de terreno)* slope, incline; *(del cuerpo)* stoop. 2 *(reverencia)* bow. 3 *fig (tendencia)* tendency, inclination, penchant.

inclinado,-a *adj* inclined, slanting; *fig* **me siento i. a creerle**, I feel inclined to believe him.

inclinar I *vtr* 1 to incline, bend; *(cabeza)* to nod. 2 *fig (persuadir)* to persuade, induce. II **inclinarse** *vr* 1 to lean, slope, incline. 2 *(al saludar)* to bow; **i. ante**, to bow down to. 3 *fig (optar)* **i. a**, to be *o* feel inclined to; **me inclino por éste**, I'd rather have this one, I prefer this one.

incluido,-a *adj* 1 *(después del sustantivo)* included; *(antes del sustantivo)* including; **servicio no i.**, service not included; **i. I.V.A.**, including VAT; **todos pagan, incluidos los niños**, everyone has to pay, including children. 2 *(adjunto)* enclosed.

incluir |37| *vtr* 1 to include. 2 *(contener)* to contain, comprise. 3 *(adjuntar)* to enclose.

inclusión *nf* inclusion.

inclusive *adv* 1 *(incluido)* inclusive; **de martes a viernes i.**, from Tuesday to Friday inclusive; **hasta la lección ocho i.**, up to and including lesson eight. 2 *(incluso)* even.

incluso *adv* even; **i. mi madre**, even my mother.

incoar *vtr defect Jur* to initiate.

incógnita *nf* 1 *Mat* unknown quantity, unknown. 2 *(misterio)* mystery.

incógnito *nm* **de i.**, incognito.

incoherencia *nf* incoherence.

incoherente *adj* incoherent.

incoloro,-a *adj* colourless.

incólume *adj fml* unharmed; **salir i.**, to escape unharmed.

incombustible *adj* incombustible, fireproof.

incomodar I *vtr* 1 *(causar molestia)* to inconvenience, put out. 2 *(fastidiar)* to bother, annoy. II **incomodarse** *vr* 1 *(tomarse molestias)* to put oneself out, go out of one's way. 2 *(disgustarse)* to get annoyed *o* angry.

incomodidad *nf (falta de comodidad)* discomfort; *(molestia)* inconvenience.

incómodo,-a *adj* uncomfortable; **sentirse i.**, to feel uncomfortable *o* awkward.

incompatibilidad *nf* incompatibility; *Jur* **i. de caracteres**, mutual incompatibility.

incompatible *adj* incompatible.

incompetencia *nf* incompetence.

incompetente *adj & nmf* incompetent.

incompleto,-a *adj* incomplete; *(inacabado)* unfinished.

incomprensible *adj* incomprehensible.

incomprensión *nf* lack of understanding, failure to understand; *(indiferencia)* lack of sympathy.

incomunicado,-a *adj* 1 *(aislado)* isolated; **el pueblo se quedó i.**, the town was cut off. 2 *(en la cárcel)* in solitary confinement.

incomunicar |1| *vtr* 1 *(ciudad)* to isolate, cut off. 2 *(recluso)* to place in solitary confinement.

inconcebible *adj* inconceivable, unthinkable.

inconcluso,-a *adj* unfinished.

incondicional I *adj* unconditional; *(apoyo)* wholehearted; *(amigo)* faithful; *(partidario)* staunch. II *nm* diehard.

inconexo,-a *adj (incoherente)* incoherent, confused.

inconformismo *nm* nonconformity.

inconformista *adj & nmf* nonconformist.

inconfundible *adj* unmistakable, obvious.

incongruencia *nf* incongruity.

incongruente *adj* incongruous.

inconmensurable *adj* immeasurable, vast.

inconsciencia *nf Med* unconsciousness; *fig (irreflexión)* thoughtlessness; *(irresponsabilidad)* irresponsibility.

inconsciente I *adj* 1 *(con estar)* *(desmaya-*

do) unconscious. 2 *(con* ser) *(despreocupado)* unaware (de, of); *fig (irreflexivo)* thoughtless, irresponsible.

inconsecuente *adj* inconsistent.

inconsistente *adj* flimsy; *(argumento)* weak.

inconstancia *nf* inconstancy, fickleness.

inconstante *adj* inconstant, fickle.

incontable *adj* countless, innumerable.

incontenible *adj* uncontrollable, irrepressible.

incontestable *adj* indisputable, unquestionable.

incontinencia *nf* incontinence.

incontrolable *adj* uncontrollable.

incontrolado,-a I *adj* uncontrolled. II *nmf* troublemaker.

inconveniencia *nf* 1 inconvenience. 2 *(impropiedad)* unsuitability.

inconveniente I *adj* 1 inconvenient. 2 *(inapropiado)* unsuitable. II *nm* 1 *(objeción)* objection; **poner inconvenientes**, to raise objections. 2 *(desventaja)* disadvantage, drawback; *(problema)* difficulty; **¿tienes i. en acompañarme?**, would you mind coming with me?

incordiar |12| *vtr fam* to bother, pester.

incordio *nm fam* nuisance, pain.

incorporación *nf* incorporation.

incorporar I *vtr* 1 to incorporate (en, into). 2 *(levantar)* to help to sit up. II **incorporarse** *vr* 1 i. a, *(sociedad)* to join; *(trabajo)* to start; *Mil* i. a filas, to join up. 2 *(en la cama)* to sit up.

incorrección *nf* 1 *(falta)* incorrectness, inaccuracy; *(gramatical)* mistake. 2 *(descortesía)* discourtesy, impropriety.

incorrecto,-a *adj* 1 *(equivocado)* incorrect, inaccurate. 2 *(grosero)* impolite, discourteous.

incorregible *adj* incorrigible.

incrédulo,-a I *adj* 1 incredulous, disbelieving. 2 *Rel* unbelieving. II *nm,f* 1 disbeliever. 2 *Rel* unbeliever.

increíble *adj* incredible, unbelievable.

incrementar I *vtr* to increase. II **incrementarse** *vr* to increase.

incremento *nm (aumento)* increase; *(crecimiento)* growth; **i. de la temperatura**, rise in temperature.

increpar *vtr fml* to rebuke, reprimand.

incruento,-a *adj* bloodless.

incrustar *vtr* 1 *(insertar)* to encrust o incrust. 2 *(embutir)* to inlay; **incrustado con perlas**, inlaid with pearls.

incubadora *nf* incubator.

incubar *vtr* to incubate.

incuestionable *adj* unquestionable, indisputable.

inculcar |1| *vtr (principios, ideas)* to instil (en, into).

inculpado,-a *nm,f* the accused.

inculpar *vtr* to accuse (de, of), blame (de, for); *Jur* to charge (de, with).

inculto,-a I *adj (ignorante)* uneducated, uncouth. II *nm,f* ignoramus.

incultura *nf (ignorancia)* ignorance, lack of culture.

incumbencia *nf* **no es de mi i.**, it doesn't come within my province, it isn't my concern.

incumbir *vi* be incumbent (a, upon); **esto no te incumbe**, this is none of your business.

incumplimiento *nm (de un deber)* nonfulfilment; *(de una orden)* failure to execute; **i. de contrato**, breach of contract.

incumplir *vtr* not to fulfil; *(deber)* fail to fulfil; *(promesa, contrato)* to break; *(orden)* to fail to carry out.

incurrir *vi (cometer)* to fall (en, into); **i. en delito**, to commit a crime; **i. en (un) error**, to fall into error.

incursión *nf* raid, incursion.

indagar |7| *vtr* to investigate, inquire into.

indebido,-a *adj* 1 *(desconsiderado)* improper, undue. 2 *(ilegal)* unlawful, illegal.

indecencia *nf* indecency, obscenity.

indecente *adj* 1 *(impúdico)* indecent. 2 *(impresentable)* dreadful.

indecible *adj* unspeakable; *(inefable)* indescribable; **sufrir lo i.**, to suffer agonies.

indecisión *nf* indecision, hesitation.

indeciso,-a *adj* 1 *(vacilante)* hesitant, irresolute. 2 *(resultados etc)* inconclusive.

indefenso,-a *adj* defenceless, helpless.

indefinido,-a *adj* 1 *(indeterminado)* indefinite; *(impreciso)* undefined, vague. 2 *Ling* indefinite. ◆**indefinidamente** *adv* indefinitely.

indeleble *adj* indelible.

indemne *adj (persona)* unharmed, unhurt; *(cosa)* undamaged.

indemnización *nf* 1 *(acto)* indemnification. 2 *Fin (compensación)* indemnity, compensation; **i. por despido**, redundancy payment.

indemnizar |4| *vtr* to indemnify, compensate (de, por, for).

independencia *nf* independence.

independiente *adj (libre)* independent; *(individualista)* self-reliant. ◆**independientemente** *adv* 1 independently (de, of). 2 *(aparte de)* regardless, irrespective (de, of).

independizar |4| I *vtr* to make independent, grant independence to. II **independizarse** *vr* to become independent.

indescifrable *adj* indecipherable.

indescriptible *adj* indescribable.

indeseable *adj & nmf* undesirable.

indeterminación *nf* indecision, irresolution.

indeterminado,-a *adj* 1 indefinite; *(impreciso)* vague. 2 *(persona)* irresolute. 3 *Ling* indefinite.

India *nf* (la) I., India.

Indias *nfpl* (las) I., the Indies; **las I. Orientales/Occidentales,** the East/West Indies.

indicación *nf* 1 *(señal)* indication, sign. 2 *(instrucción)* instruction, direction; **por i. de algn.,** at sb's suggestion.

indicado,-a *adj* right, suitable; **a la hora indicada,** at the specified time; **en el momento menos i.,** at the worst possible moment.

indicador,-a *nm* 1 indicator. 2 *Téc* gauge, dial, meter; *Aut* **i. del nivel de aceite,** (oil) dipstick; *Aut* **i. de velocidad,** speedometer.

indicar [1] *vtr (señalar)* to indicate, show, point out; **¿me podría i. el camino?,** could you show me the way?

indicativo,-a *adj* 1 indicative **(de,** of). 2 *Ling* **(modo) i.,** indicative (mode).

índice *nm* 1 *(de libro)* index, table of contents. 2 *(relación)* rate. **í. de natalidad/ mortalidad,** birth/death rate; *Fin* **í. de precios,** price index. 3 *Anat (dedo)* **í.,** index finger, forefinger.

indicio *nm* 1 *(señal)* indication, sign, token **(de,** of). 2 *Jur* **indicios,** *(prueba)* evidence *sing.*

índico,-a *adj* Indian; **Océano I.,** Indian Ocean.

indiferencia *nf* indifference, apathy.

indiferente *adj* 1 *(no importante)* unimportant; **me es i.,** it makes no difference to me. 2 *(apático)* indifferent.

indígena *adj* indigenous, native **(de,** to). II *nmf* native **(de,** of).

indigencia *nf fml* poverty, indigence.

indigente *fml adj* needy, poverty-stricken.

indigestarse *vr* 1 **se le indigestó la comida,** the meal gave her indigestion. 2 *(sufrir indigestión)* to get indigestion.

indigestión *nf* indigestion.

indigesto,-a *adj (comida)* indigestible, difficult to digest; **me siento i.,** I've got indigestion.

indignación *nf* indignation.

indignado,-a *adj* indignant **(por,** at, about).

indignante *adj* outrageous, infuriating.

indignar I *vtr* to infuriate, make angry. II **indignarse** *vr* to be *o* feel indignant **(por,** at, about).

indigno,-a *adj* 1 unworthy **(de,** of). 2 *(despreciable)* wretched, dreadful.

indio,-a *adj & nm,f* Indian; **en fila india,** in single file; *fam* **hacer el i.,** to act the fool.

indirecta *nf fam (insinuación)* hint, insinuation; **tirar** *o* **lanzar una i.,** to drop a hint; **coger la i.,** to get the message.

indirecto,-a *adj* indirect; *Ling* **estilo i.,** indirect *o* reported speech.

indisciplinado,-a *adj* undisciplined, unruly.

indiscreción *nf* indiscretion; *(comentario)* tactless remark.

indiscreto,-a *adj* indiscreet, tactless.

indiscutible *adj* indisputable, unquestionable.

indispensable *adj* indispensable, essential.

indisponer [19] *(pp* **indispuesto)** I *vtr* to upset, make unwell. II **indisponerse** *vr* 1 to fall ill, become unwell. 2 *fig* **i. con algn,** to fall out with sb.

indispuesto,-a *adj* indisposed, unwell.

indispuse *pt indef* → **indisponer.**

indistinto,-a *adj (indiferente)* immaterial, inconsequential; ◆**indistintamente** *adv* **pueden escribir en inglés o en español i.,** you can write in English or Spanish, it doesn't matter which.

individual I *adj* individual; **habitación i.,** single room. II *nmpl Dep* **individuales,** singles.

individualismo *nm* individualism.

individualista I *adj* individualistic. II *nmf* individualist.

individuo *nm* 1 individual. 2 *(tío)* bloke, guy.

índole *nf* 1 *(carácter)* character, nature. 2 *(clase, tipo)* kind, sort.

indolencia *nf* indolence, laziness.

indolente I *adj* indolent, lazy. II *nmf* idler.

indomable *adj* 1 *(animal)* untameable. 2 *(pueblo)* ungovernable, unruly; *(niño)* uncontrollable; *(pasión)* indomitable.

indómito,-a *adj* 1 *(no domado)* untamed; *(indomable)* untamable. 2 *(pueblo)* unruly; *(persona)* uncontrollable.

inducir [10] *vtr* 1 *(incitar, mover)* to lead, induce; **i. a error,** to lead into error, mislead. 2 *Elec (corriente)* to induce.

inductivo,-a *adj* inductive.

indudable *adj* indubitable, unquestionable; **es i. que,** there is no doubt that.

induje *pt indef* → **inducir.**

indulgencia *nf* indulgence, leniency.

indulgente *adj* indulgent **(con,** towards), lenient **(con,** with).

indultar *vtr Jur* to pardon.

indulto *nm Jur* pardon, amnesty.

indumentaria *nf* clothing, clothes *pl.*

industria *nf* industry.

industrial I *adj* industrial. II *nmf* industrialist.

industrialización *nf* industrialization.

industrializar [4] *vtr* to industrialize.

induzco *indic pres* → **inducir.**

INE *nm abr de* **Instituto Nacional de Estadística.**

inédito,-a *adj* 1 *(libro, texto)* unpublished. 2 *(nuevo)* completely new; *(desconocido)* unknown.

inefable *adj* ineffable, indescribable.

ineficacia *nf (ineptitud)* inefficiency; *(inutilidad)* ineffectiveness.

ineficaz *adj (inepto)* inefficient; *(inefectivo)* ineffective.

ineludible *adj* inescapable, unavoidable.

INEM *nm abr de* **Instituto Nacional de Empleo**.

ineptitud *nf* ineptitude, incompetence.

inepto,-a I *adj* inept, incompetent. **II** *nm,f* incompetent person.

inequívoco,-a *adj* unmistakable, unequivocal.

inercia *nf* 1 *Fís* inertia. 2 *fig (pasividad)* inertia, passivity; **hacer algo por i.**, to do sth out of habit.

inerte *adj (inanimado)* inert; *(inmóvil)* motionless.

inesperado,-a *adj (fortuito)* unexpected, unforeseen; *(imprevisto)* sudden.

inestabilidad *nf* instability.

inestable *adj* unstable, unsteady.

inestimable *adj* inestimable, invaluable.

inevitable *adj* inevitable, unavoidable.

inexistente *adj* non-existent.

inexorable *adj* inexorable.

inexperiencia *nf* lack of experience.

inexperto,-a *adj (inexperto)* inexpert; *(sin experiencia)* inexperienced.

inexplicable *adj* inexplicable.

inexpugnable *adj Mil* impregnable.

infalible *adj* infallible.

infamar *vtr* to defame, slander.

infame *adj (vil)* infamous, vile; *(despreciable)* dreadful, awful.

infamia *nf* disgrace, infamy.

infancia *nf* childhood, infancy.

infanta *nf* infanta, princess.

infante *nm* 1 infante, prince. 2 *Mil* infantryman.

infantería *nf Mil* infantry; **la i. de marina**, the marines.

infantil *adj* 1 literatura i., *(para niños)* children's literature. 2 *(aniñado)* childlike; *pey* childish, infantile.

infarto *nm Med* infarction, infarct; **i. (de miocardio)**, heart attack, coronary thrombosis; *fam* **de i.**, thrilling, stunning.

infatigable *adj* indefatigable, tireless.

infección *nf* infection.

infeccioso,-a *adj* infectious.

infectar I *vtr* to infect. **II infectarse** *vr* to become infected **(de, with)**.

infeliz I *adj* unhappy; *(desdichado)* unfortunate. **II** *nmf fam* simpleton; **es un pobre i.**, he is a poor devil.

inferior I *adj* 1 *(más bajo)* lower. 2 *(calidad)* inferior; **de calidad i.**, of inferior quality. 3 *(cantidad)* lower, less; **i. a la media**, below average. **II** *nmf (persona)* subordinate, inferior.

inferioridad *nf* inferiority; **estar en i. de condiciones**, to be at a disadvantage; **complejo de i.**, inferiority complex.

inferir [5] *vtr lit (deducir)* to infer, deduce **(de, from)**.

infernal *adj* infernal, hellish; *fig* **había un ruido i.**, there was a hell of a noise.

infestar *vtr* 1 **infestado de**, *(parásitos)* infested with; *(plantas)* overgrown with. 2 *fig (llenar)* to overrun, invade; **infestado de turistas**, swarming with tourists. 3 *(infectar)* to infect.

infidelidad *nf* infidelity, unfaithfulness.

infiel I *adj (desleal)* unfaithful. **II** *nmf Rel* infidel.

infierno *nm* 1 *Rel* hell. 2 *fig (tormento)* hell; **su vida es un i.**, his life is sheer hell. 3 *(horno)* inferno; **en verano esto es un i.**, in summer it's like an inferno here; *fam* **¡vete al i.!**, go to hell!, get lost!

infiltración *nf (de agua)* infiltration; *(de noticia)* leak.

infiltrado,-a *nm,f* infiltrator.

infiltrar I *vtr* to infiltrate; *(noticia)* to leak. **II infiltrarse** *vr* to infiltrate **(en, into)**.

ínfimo,-a *adj fml (mínimo)* extremely low; **detalle í.**, smallest detail; **ínfima calidad**, very poor quality.

infinidad *nf* 1 infinity; 2 *(sinfín)* great number; **en i. de ocasiones**, on countless occasions.

infinitivo,-a *adj & nm Ling* infinitive.

infinito,-a I *adj* infinite, endless. **II** *nm* infinity. ◆**infinito** *adv fam (muchísimo)* infinitely, immensely.

inflación *nf Econ* inflation.

inflacionario,-a, **inflacionista** *adj Econ* inflationary.

inflamable *adj* flammable.

inflamación *nf Med* inflammation.

inflamar I *vtr* 1 *Med* to inflame. 2 *(encender)* to set on fire, ignite. **II inflamarse** *vr* 1 *Med* to become inflamed. 2 *(incendiarse)* to catch fire.

inflar I *vtr* 1 *(hinchar)* to inflate, blow up; *Náut (vela)* to swell. 2 *fig (exagerar)* to exaggerate. **II inflarse** *vr* 1 to inflate; *Náut (vela)* to swell. 2 *fam* **i. de**, to overdo; **se inflaron de macarrones**, they stuffed themselves with macaroni.

inflexible *adj* inflexible.

infligir [6] *vtr* to inflict.

influencia *nf* influence; **ejercer** *o* **tener i. sobre algn**, to have an influence on *o* upon sb; **tener influencias**, to be influential; **tráfico de influencias**, old boy network.

influenciar [12] *vtr* to influence.

influir [37] **I** *vtr* to influence. **II** *vi* 1 to have influence. 2 **i. en** *o* **sobre**, to influence, have an influence on.

influjo *nm* influence.

influyente *adj* influential.

información *nf* 1 information; **oficina de i.**, information bureau. 2 **una i.**, *(noticia)* a piece of news, news *sing*. 3 *Tel* directory enquiries *pl*. 4 *(referencias)* references *pl*.

informado,-a *adj* informed; **de fuentes bien informadas,** from well-informed sources.

informal *adj* 1 *(reunión, cena)* informal. 2 *(comportamiento)* casual. 3 *(persona)* unreliable, untrustworthy.

informalidad *nf (incumplimiento)* unreliability; *(desenfado)* informality.

informar I *vtr* to inform (**de,** of); *(dar informes)* to report. II **informarse** *vr (procurarse noticias)* to find out (**de,** about); *(enterarse)* to enquire (**de,** about).

informática *nf* information technology, IT; **ley de i.,** data protection act.

informático,-a I *adj* computer, computing. II *nm,f* (computer) technician.

informativo,-a I *adj* 1 *Rad TV* news; **boletín i.,** news (broadcast). 2 **(explicativo)** informative, explanatory. II *nm Rad TV* news bulletin.

informe *nm* 1 report. 2 **informes,** references; **pedir i. sobre algn,** to make enquiries about sb.

infracción *nf (de ley)* infringement, breach (**de,** of).

infractor,-a *nm,f* offender.

infraestructura *nf* infrastructure.

in fraganti *loc adv* in the act; **coger** *o* **pillar a algn in f.,** to catch sb red-handed.

infrahumano-o *adj* subhuman.

infranqueable *adj* impassable; *fig* insurmountable.

infrarrojo-a *adj* infra-red.

infrautilizar *vtr* to under-utilise.

infringir |6| *vtr* to infringe, contravene; **i. una ley,** to break a law.

infructuoso,-a *adj* fruitless, unsuccessful.

infundado-a *adj* unfounded, groundless.

infundir *vtr* to infuse; *fig* to instil; **i. dudas,** to give rise to doubt; **i. respeto,** to command respect.

infusión *nf* infusion.

infuso,-a *adj fam irón* **ciencia infusa,** sheer genius.

ingeniar |12| I *vtr* to invent, devise. II **ingeniarse** *vr* **ingeniárselas para hacer algo,** to manage to do sth.

ingeniería *nf* engineering.

ingeniero,-a *nm,f* engineer; **i. agrónomo,** agricultural engineer; **i. de caminos,** civil engineer; **i. de minas/montes,** mining/forestry engineer; **i. de telecomunicaciones,** telecommunications engineer; **i. técnico,** technician.

ingenio *nm* 1 *(talento)* talent; *(inventiva)* inventiveness, creativeness; *(agudeza)* wit. 2 *(aparato)* device.

ingenioso,-a *adj* ingenious, clever; *(vivaz)* witty.

ingente *adj* huge, enormous.

ingenuidad *nf* ingenuousness, naïveté.

ingenuo,-a I *adj* ingenuous, naïve. II *nm,f* naïve person.

ingerir |5| *vtr (comida)* to ingest, consume; *(líquidos, alcohol)* to drink, consume.

Inglaterra *n* England.

ingle *nf Anat* groin.

inglés,-esa I *adj* English. II *nm,f (hombre)* Englishman; *(mujer)* Englishwoman; **los ingleses,** the English. III *nm (idioma)* English.

ingratitud *nf* ingratitude, ungratefulness.

ingrato,-a I *adj* 1 *(persona)* ungrateful. 2 *(noticia)* unpleasant. 3 *(trabajo)* thankless, unrewarding. 4 *(tierra)* unproductive. II *nm,f* ungrateful person.

ingrediente *nm* ingredient.

ingresar I *vtr* 1 *Fin* to deposit, pay in. 2 *Med* to admit; **la ingresaron en el hospital,** she was admitted to hospital. II *vi* 1 to enter; **i. en el ejército,** to enlist in the army, join the army; **i. en un club,** to join a club. 2 **i. cadáver,** to be dead on arrival.

ingreso *nm* 1 *Fin* deposit; **hacer un i. en una cuenta,** to pay money into an account. 2 *(entrada)* entry (**en,** into); *(admisión)* admission (**en,** to). 3 **ingresos,** *(sueldo, renta)* income *sing*; *(beneficios)* revenue *sing*.

inhábil *adj* 1 *(incapaz)* unfit; **i. para el trabajo,** unfit for work. 2 **día i.,** non-working day.

inhabilitación *nf* 1 *fml (incapacidad)* disablement. 2 *Jur* disqualification.

inhabilitar *vtr* 1 *fml (incapacitar)* to disable; **inhabilitado para el trabajo,** unfit for work. 2 *Jur* to disqualify.

inhabitable *adj* uninhabitable.

inhalación *nf* inhalation.

inhalador *nm Med* inhaler.

inhalar *vtr* to inhale.

inherente *adj* inherent (**a,** in).

inhibición *nf* inhibition.

inhibir I *vtr* to inhibit. II **inhibirse** *vr* 1 *(cohibirse)* to be *o* feel inhibited. 2 *(abstenerse)* to refrain (**de,** from).

inhóspito,-a *adj* inhospitable.

inhumación *nf* burial.

inhumano,-a *adj* inhumane; *(cruel)* inhuman.

inhumar *vtr* to bury.

INI *nm abr de* **Instituto Nacional de Industria.**

inicial *adj & nf* initial; **punto i.,** starting point.

iniciar |12| I *vtr* 1 *(empezar)* to begin, start; *(discusión)* to initiate; *(una cosa nueva)* to pioneer. 2 *(introducir)* to initiate. II **iniciarse** *vr* 1 **i. en algo,** *(aprender)* to start to study sth. 2 *(empezar)* to begin, start.

iniciativa *nf* initiative; **i. privada,** private enterprise; **por i. propia,** on one's own initiative.

inicio *nm* beginning, start; **a inicios de,** at the beginning of.

inimitable *adj* inimitable.
ininterrumpido,-a *adj* uninterrupted, continuous.
iniquidad *nf* iniquity.
injerencia *nf* interference, meddling (**en**, in).
injerirse *vr* to interfere, meddle (**en**, in).
injertar *vtr Agr Med* to graft.
injerto *nm* graft.
injuria *nf* (*insulto*) insult, affront; (*agravio*) outrage.
injuriar |12| *vtr* (*insultar*) to insult; (*ultrajar*) to outrage.
injusticia *nf* injustice, unfairness.
injustificado,-a *adj* unjustified.
injusto,-a *adj* unjust, unfair.
inmaculado,-a *adj* immaculate.
inmadurez *nf* immaturity.
inmaduro,-a *adj* immature.
inmediaciones *nfpl* neighbourhood *sing*.
inmediato,-a *adj* 1 (*en el tiempo*) immediate; **de i.**, at once. 2 (*en el espacio*) next (**a**, to), adjoining. ◆**inmediatamente** *adv* immediately, at once.
inmejorable *adj* (*trabajo*) excellent; (*precio*) unbeatable.
inmemorial *adj* immemorial; **desde tiempos inmemoriales**, since time immemorial.
inmensidad *nf* immensity, enormity.
inmenso,-a *adj* immense, vast.
inmerecido,-a *adj* undeserved, unmerited.
inmersión *nf* immersion; (*de submarino*) dive.
inmerso,-a *adj* immersed (**en**, in).
inmigración *nf* immigration.
inmigrante *adj & nm,f* immigrant.
inmigrar *vi* to immigrate.
inminente *adj* imminent, impending.
inmiscuirse |37| *vr* to interfere, meddle (**en**, in).
inmobiliaria *nf* estate agency, *US* real estate company.
inmobiliario,-a *adj* property, real-estate; **agente i.**, estate agent, *US* realtor.
inmolar *vtr fml* to immolate, sacrifice.
inmoral *adj* immoral.
inmoralidad *nf* immorality.
inmortal *adj & nmf* immortal.
inmortalidad *nf* immortality.
inmortalizar |4| *vtr* to immortalize.
inmóvil *adj* motionless, immobile.
inmovilista *adj* ultra-conservative.
inmovilizar |4| *vtr* 1 (*persona, cosa*) to immobilize. 2 *Fin* (*capital*) to immobilize, tie up.
inmueble I *adj* **bienes inmuebles**, real estate. II *nm* building.
inmundicia *nf* 1 (*suciedad*) dirt, filth; *fig* dirtiness. 2 (*basura*) rubbish, refuse.
inmundo,-a *adj* dirty, filthy; *fig* nasty.
inmune *adj* immune (**a**, to), exempt (**de**, from).

inmunidad *nf* immunity (**contra**, against); **i. diplomática/parlamentaria**, diplomatic/parliamentary immunity.
inmunizar |4| *vtr* to immunize (**contra**, against).
inmutarse *vr* to change countenance; **ni se inmutó**, he didn't turn a hair.
innato,-a *adj* innate, inborn.
innecesario,-a *adj* unnecessary.
innegable *adj* undeniable.
innovación *nf* innovation.
innovar *vtr & vi* to innovate.
innumerable *adj* innumerable, countless.
inocencia *nf* 1 innocence. 2 (*ingenuidad*) naïveté.
inocentada *nf fam* ≈ April Fool's joke; **hacer una i. a algn**, to play an April Fool's joke on sb.
inocente I *adj* innocent. II *nmf* innocent; **día de los Inocentes**, Holy Innocents' Day, 28th December, ≈ April Fools' Day.
inocuo,-a *adj* innocuous.
inodoro,-a I *adj* odourless. II *nm* toilet, lavatory.
inofensivo,-a *adj* harmless.
inolvidable *adj* unforgettable.
inoperante *adj* ineffective.
inopia *nf fig* **estar en la i.**, to be in the clouds, be miles away.
inopinado,-a *adj* unexpected.
inoportuno,-a *adj* inappropriate; **llegó en un momento muy i.**, he turned up at a very awkward moment.
inorgánico,-a *adj* inorganic.
inoxidable *adj* **acero i.**, stainless steel.
INP *nm abr de* **Instituto Nacional de Previsión**.
inquebrantable *adj fig* unshakeable; (*persona*) unyielding.
inquietante *adj* worrying.
inquietar I *vtr* to worry. II **inquietarse** *vr* to worry (**por**, about).
inquieto,-a *adj* 1 (*preocupado*) worried, (**por**, about). 2 (*intranquilo*) restless. 3 (*emprendedor*) eager.
inquietud *nf* 1 (*preocupación*) worry. 2 (*agitación*) restlessness. 3 (*anhelo*) eagerness.
inquilino,-a *nm,f* tenant.
inquirir |31| *vtr* to investigate.
inquisitivo,-a *adj* inquisitive.
inri *nm fam* insult; **para más o mayor i.**, to make matters worse.
insaciable *adj* insatiable.
insalubre *adj* unhealthy.
insano,-a *adj* 1 (*loco*) insane, mad. 2 (*insalubre*) unhealthy.
insatisfecho,-a *adj* dissatisfied.
inscribir (*pp* **inscrito**) I *vtr* 1 (*registrar*) to register; **i. a un niño en el registro civil**, to register a child's birth. 2 (*matricular*) to enrol, *US* enroll. 3 (*grabar*) to inscribe. II **inscribirse** *vr* 1 (*registrarse*) to

register; *(hacerse miembro)* to join. 2 *(matricularse)* to enrol, US enroll.
inscripción *nf* 1 *(matriculación)* enrolment, US enrollment, registration. 2 *(escrito etc)* inscription.
insecticida *nm* insecticide.
insecto *nm* insect.
inseguridad *nf* 1 *(falta de confianza)* insecurity. 2 *(duda)* uncertainty. 3 *(peligro)* lack of safety; **la i. ciudadana,** the breakdown of law and order.
inseguro,-a *adj* 1 *(poco confiado)* insecure. 2 *(dubitativo)* uncertain. 3 *(peligroso)* unsafe.
inseminar *vtr* to inseminate.
insensatez *nf* foolishness.
insensato,-a I *adj* foolish. II *nm,f* fool.
insensibilidad *nf* insensitivity.
insensible *adj* 1 *(indiferente)* insensitive (a, to), unfeeling. 2 *(imperceptible)* imperceptible. 3 *Med* numb.
inseparable *adj* inseparable.
insertar *vtr* to insert.
inservible *adj* useless.
insidia *nf* 1 *(trampa)* malicious ploy. 2 *(malicia)* maliciousness.
insidioso,-a *adj* insidious.
insigne *adj* distinguished.
insignia *nf* 1 *(emblema)* badge. 2 *(bandera)* flag.
insignificancia *nf* 1 *(intrascendencia)* insignificance. 2 *(nadería)* trifle.
insignificante *adj* insignificant.
insinuación *nf* insinuation.
insinuante *adj* insinuating; *(atrevido)* forward.
insinuar [30] I *vtr* to insinuate. II **insinuarse** *vr* **i. a algn,** to make advances to sb.
insípido,-a *adj* insipid; *fig* dull, flat.
insistencia *nf* insistence; **con i.,** insistently.
insistente *adj* insistent.
insistir *vi* to insist (**en,** on); **insistió en ese punto,** he stressed that point.
insociable *adj* unsociable.
insolación *nf Med* sunstroke; **coger una i.,** to get sunstroke.
insolencia *nf* insolence.
insolente *adj* insolent.
insolidaridad *nf* unsupportive stance.
insólito,-a *adj (poco usual)* unusual; *(extraño)* strange, odd.
insoluble *adj* insoluble.
insolvencia *nf Fin* insolvency.
insolvente *adj Fin* insolvent.
insomnio *nm* insomnia; **noche de i.,** sleepless night.
insondable *adj* unfathomable.
insonorizado,-a *adj* soundproof.
insonorizar [4] *vtr* to soundproof.
insoportable *adj* unbearable.
insospechado,-a *adj* unsuspected.
insostenible *adj* untenable.

inspección *nf* inspection.
inspeccionar *vtr* to inspect.
inspector,-a *nm,f* inspector; **i. de Hacienda,** tax inspector.
inspiración *nf* 1 inspiration. 2 *(inhalación)* inhalation.
inspirado,-a *adj* inspired.
inspirar I *vtr* 1 to inspire. 2 *(inhalar)* to inhale, breathe in. II **inspirarse** *vr* **i. en,** to be inspired by.
instalación *nf* installation; **instalaciones deportivas,** sports facilities.
instalar I *vtr* 1 to instal, US install. 2 *(puesto, tienda)* to set up. II **instalarse** *vr (persona)* to settle (down).
instancia *nf* 1 *(solicitud)* request; **a instancia(s) de,** at the request of. 2 *(escrito)* application form. 3 *Jur* **tribunal de primera i.,** court of first instance. 4 **en primera i.,** first of all; **en última i.,** as a last resort.
instantánea *nf* snapshot.
instantáneo,-a *adj* instantaneous; **café i.,** instant coffee. ◆**instantáneamente** *adv* instantly.
instante *nm* instant, moment; **a cada i.,** constantly; **al i.,** immediately, right away; **por instantes,** with every second; **¡un i.!,** just a moment!
instar *vtr* to urge.
instauración *nf* founding.
instaurar *vtr* to found.
instigador,-a *nm,f* instigator.
instigar [7] *vtr* to instigate; **i. a la rebelión,** to incite a rebellion.
instintivo,-a *adj* instinctive.
instinto *nm* instinct; **por i.,** instinctively; **i. de conservación,** instinct of self-preservation.
institución *nf* institution.
instituir [37] *vtr* to institute.
instituto *nm* 1 institute. 2 *Educ* state secondary school, US high school.
institutriz *nf* governess.
instituyo *indic pres* → **instituir**.
instrucción *nf* 1 *(educación)* education. 2 *(usu pl) (indicación)* instruction; **instrucciones para el o de uso,** directions for use. 3 *Jur* preliminary investigation; **la i. del sumario,** proceedings *pl;* **juez de i.,** examining magistrate. 4 *Mil* drill.
instructivo,-a *adj* instructive.
instruido,-a *adj* educated, well-educated.
instruir [37] *vtr* 1 to instruct. 2 *(enseñar)* to educate. 3 *Mil* to drill. 4 *Jur* to investigate.
instrumental *adj* instrumental.
instrumento *nm* instrument.
insubordinación *nf* insubordination.
insubordinado-a *adj* insubordinate.
insubordinarse *vr (sublevarse)* to rebel (**contra,** against).
insuficiencia *nf* insufficiency.
insuficiente I *adj* insufficient. II *nm Educ*

(nota) fail.

insufrible *adj* insufferable.

insular I *adj* insular, island. **II** *nmf* islander.

insulso,-a *adj* insipid.

insultante *adj* insulting.

insultar *vtr* to insult.

insulto *nm* insult.

insumisión *nf* refusal to do military service.

insumiso,-a I *adj* unsubmissive. **II** *nm* person who refuses to do military service.

insuperable *adj* 1 *(inmejorable)* unsurpassable. 2 *(problema)* insurmountable.

insurgente *adj & nmf* insurgent.

insurrección *nf* insurrection.

intacto,-a *adj* intact.

intachable *adj* irreproachable; **conducta i.**, impeccable behaviour.

integral I *adj* integral; *Culin* **pan i.**, wholemeal bread; **arroz i.**, brown rice. **II** *nf Mat* integral.

integrante I *adj* integral; **ser parte i. de**, to be an integral part of. **II** *nmf* member.

integrar I *vtr (formar)* to compose, make up; **el equipo lo integran once jugadores**, there are eleven players in the team. **II integrarse** *vr* to integrate (**en**, with).

integridad *nf* integrity.

íntegro,-a *adj* 1 *(entero)* whole, entire; *Cin Lit* **versión íntegra**, unabridged version. 2 *(honrado)* upright.

intelecto *nm* intellect.

intelectual *adj & nmf* intellectual.

inteligencia *nf (intelecto)* intelligence; **cociente de i.**, intelligence quotient, IQ.

inteligente *adj* intelligent.

inteligible *adj* intelligible.

intemperie *nf* bad weather; **a la i.**, in the open (air).

intempestivo,-a *adj* untimely.

intención *nf* intention; **con i.**, deliberately, on purpose; **con segunda/doble i.**, with an ulterior motive; **tener la i. de hacer algo**, to intend to do sth.

intencionado,-a *adj* deliberate.

intencional *adj* intentional.

◆intencionadamente *adv* on purpose.

intensidad *nf* intensity; *(del viento)* force.

intensificar [1] *vtr*, **intensificarse** *vr* to intensify; *(amistad)* to strengthen.

intensivo,-a *adj* intensive; *Agr* **cultivo i.**, intensive farming; *Educ* **curso i.**, crash course.

intenso,-a *adj* intense.

intentar *vtr* to try, attempt; *fam* **¡inténtalo!**, give it a go!.

intento *nm* attempt; **i. de suicidio**, attempted suicide.

intentona *nf* putsch.

inter- *pref* inter-.

intercalar *vtr* to insert.

intercambiar [12] *vtr* to exchange.

intercambio *nm* exchange; **i. comercial**, trade.

interceder *vi* to intercede.

interceptar *vtr* 1 *(detener)* to intercept. 2 *(carretera)* to block; *(tráfico)* to hold up.

intercesión *nf* intercession.

intercontinental *adj* intercontinental.

interdicto *nm* prohibition.

interés *nm* 1 interest; **poner i. en**, to take an interest in; **tener i. en** *o* **por**, to be interested in. 2 *(provecho personal)* self-interest; **hacer algo (sólo) por i.**, to do sth out of self-interest; **intereses creados**, vested interests. 3 *Fin* interest; **con un i. del 11%**, at an interest of 11%; **tipos de i.**, interest rates.

interesado,-a I *adj* 1 interested (**en**, in); **las partes interesadas**, the interested parties. 2 *(egoísta)* selfish. **II** *nm,f* interested person; **los interesados**, those interested *o* concerned.

interesante *adj* interesting.

interesar I *vtr* 1 *(tener interés)* to interest; **la poesía no me interesa nada**, poetry doesn't interest me at all. 2 *(concernir)* to concern. **II** *vi (ser importante)* to be of interest, to be important; **interesaría llegar pronto**, it is important to get there early. **III interesarse** *vr* **i. por** *o* **en**, to be interested in; **se interesó por ti**, he asked about *o* after you.

interferencia *nf* interference; *Rad TV* jamming.

interferir [5] *vtr* 1 to interfere with; *(plan)* to upset. 2 *Rad TV* to jam.

interfono *nm Tel* intercom.

interinidad *nf* 1 *(temporalidad)* temporariness. 2 *(empleo)* temporary employment.

interino,-a I *adj (persona)* acting. **II** *nm,f (trabajador temporal)* temporary worker.

interior I *adj* 1 inner, inside, interior; **habitación i.**, inner room; **ropa i.**, underwear. 2 *Pol* domestic, internal. 3 *Geog* inland. **II** *nm* 1 inside, interior; *fig* **en su i. no estaba de acuerdo**, deep down she disagreed. 2 *Geog* interior; *Pol* **Ministerio del I.**, Home Office, *US* Department of the Interior.

interiorizar [4] *vtr* to internalize.

interjección *nf Ling* interjection.

interlocutor,-a *nm,f* speaker; *(negociador)* negotiator.

intermediario *nm Com* middleman.

intermedio,-a I *adj* intermediate. **II** *nm TV (intervalo)* break.

interminable *adj* endless.

intermitente I *adj* intermittent. **II** *nm Aut* indicator.

internacional *adj* international.

internado,-a I *nm,f* inmate. **II** *(colegio)* boarding school.

internar I *vtr (en hospital)* to confine. **II internarse** *vr* 1 *(penetrar)* to advance (**en**, into). 2 *Dep* to break through.

interno,-a I *adj* 1 internal; **por vía**

interna, internally. **2** *Pol* domestic. **II** *nm,f (alumno)* boarder; *Med (enfermo)* patient; *(preso)* inmate.

interponer |19| *(pp interpuesto)* **I** *vtr* to insert; *Jur* **i. un recurso,** to give notice of appeal. **II interponerse** *vr* to intervene.

interpretación *nf* **1** interpretation. **2** *Mús Teat* performance.

interpretar *vtr* **1** to interpret. **2** *Teat (papel)* to play; *(obra)* to perform; *Mús (concierto)* to play, perform; *(canción)* to sing.

intérprete *nmf* **1** *(traductor)* interpreter. **2** *Teat* performer; *Mús (cantante)* singer; *(músico)* performer.

interpuse *pt indef* → **interponer.**

interrogación *nf* interrogation; *Ling* **(signo de) i.,** question *o* interrogation mark.

interrogante *nf fig* question mark.

interrogar |7| *vtr* to question; *(testigo etc)* to interrogate.

interrogatorio *nm* interrogation.

interrumpir *vtr* to interrupt; *(tráfico)* to block.

interrupción *nf* interruption; **i. del embarazo,** termination of pregnancy.

interruptor *nm Elec* switch.

intersección *nf* intersection.

interurbano,-a *adj* intercity; *Tel* **conferencia interurbana,** long-distance call.

intervalo *nm* interval; **habrá intervalos de lluvia,** there will be periods of rain.

intervención *nf* **1** *(participación)* intervention, participation **(en,** in); *(aportación)* contribution **(en,** to). **2** *Med* intervention.

intervenir |27| **I** *vi (mediar)* to intervene **(en,** in); *(participar)* to take part **(en,** in); *(contribuir)* to contribute **(en,** to). **II** *vtr* **1** *(confiscar)* to confiscate, seize. **2** *Tel (teléfono)* to tap. **3** *Med* to operate on.

interventor,-a *nm,f (supervisor)* inspector; *Fin* **i. (de cuentas),** auditor.

interviú *nm (pl interviús)* interview.

intestino,-a **I** *adj (luchas)* internal. **II** *nm Anat* intestine.

intimar *vi* to become close **(con,** to).

intimidad *nf (amistad)* intimacy; *(vida privada)* private life; *(privacidad)* privacy; **en la i.,** privately, in private.

intimidar *vtr* to intimidate.

íntimo,-a **I** *adj* **1** intimate. **2** *(vida)* private; **una boda íntima,** a quiet wedding. **3** *(amistad)* close. **II** *nm,f* close friend, intimate.

intolerable *adj* intolerable.

intolerancia *nf* intolerance.

intolerante **I** *adj* intolerant. **II** *nmf* intolerant person.

intoxicación *nf* poisoning; **i. alimentaria,** food poisoning.

intoxicar |1| *vtr* to poison.

intra- *pref* intra-.

intranquilidad *nf* worry.

intranquilizarse *vr* to get worried.

intranquilo,-a *adj (preocupado)* worried; *(agitado)* restless.

intransigente *adj* intransigent.

intransitable *adj* impassable.

intransitivo,-a *adj Ling* intransitive.

intratable *adj* **1** *(problema)* intractable. **2** *(persona)* unsociable.

intrépido,-a *adj* intrepid.

intriga *nf* intrigue; *Cin Teat* plot.

intrigante **I** *adj* **1** *(interesante)* intriguing, interesting. **2** *pey (maquinador)* scheming. **II** *nmf (persona)* schemer.

intrigar |7| **I** *vtr (interesar)* to intrigue, interest. **II** *vi (maquinar)* to plot.

intrincado,-a *adj* **1** *(cuestión, problema)* intricate. **2** *(bosque)* dense.

intrínseco,-a *adj* intrinsic.

introducción *nf* introduction.

introducir |10| **I** *vtr* **1** to introduce. **2** *(meter)* to insert, put in.

intromisión *nf (injerencia)* meddling; **perdón por la i.,** forgive the intrusion.

introspectivo,-a *adj* introspective.

introvertido,-a **I** *adj* introverted. **II** *nm,f* introvert.

intruso,-a **I** *adj* intrusive. **II** *nm,f* intruder; *Jur* trespasser.

intuición *nf* intuition.

intuir |37| *vtr* to know by intuition.

intuitivo,-a *adj* intuitive.

inundación *nf* flood.

inundar *vtr* to flood; *fig (de trabajo etc)* to swamp.

inusitado,-a *adj* unusual.

inútil **I** *adj* **1** useless; *(esfuerzo, intento)* vain, pointless. **2** *Mil* unfit (for service). **II** *nmf fam* good-for-nothing.

inutilidad *nf* uselessness.

inutilizar |4| *vtr* to make *o* render useless; *(máquina etc)* to put out of action.

invadir *vtr* to invade; *fig* **los estudiantes invadieron la calle,** students poured out onto the street.

invalidar *vtr* to invalidate.

invalidez *nf* **1** *Jur (nulidad)* invalidity. **2** *Med (minusvalía)* disability.

inválido,-a **I** *adj* **1** *Jur (nulo)* invalid. **2** *Med (minusválido)* disabled, handicapped. **II** *nm,f Med* disabled *o* handicapped person.

invariable *adj* invariable.

invasión *nf* invasion.

invasor,-a **I** *adj* invading. **II** *nm,f* invader.

invencible *adj* **1** *(enemigo)* invincible. **2** *(obstáculo)* insurmountable.

invención *nf (invento)* invention; *(mentira)* fabrication.

inventar *vtr* to invent; *(excusa, mentira)* to make up, concoct.

inventario *nm* inventory.

inventiva *nf* inventiveness; *(imaginación)* imagination.

invento *nm* invention.

inventor,-a *nm,f* inventor.

invernadero *nm* greenhouse; **efecto i.**, greenhouse effect.

invernal *adj* winter, wintry.

invernar [1] *vi* to hibernate.

inverosímil *adj* unlikely, improbable.

inversión *nf* 1 inversion. 2 *Fin* investment.

inverso,-a *adj* opposite; **en sentido i.**, in the opposite direction; **en orden i.**, in reverse order.

inversor,-a *nm,f Fin* investor.

invertebrado,-a *adj & nm Zool* invertebrate.

invertido,-a I *adj* inverted, reversed. II *nm,f* homosexual.

invertir [5] *vtr* 1 (*orden*) to invert, reverse. 2 (*dinero*) to invest (**en**, in); (*tiempo*) to spend (**en**, on).

investidura *nf* investiture; *Pol* vote of confidence.

investigación *nf* 1 (*policial etc*) investigation. 2 (*científica*) research.

investigador,-a *nm,f* 1 (*detective*) investigator. 2 (*científico*) researcher, research worker.

investigar [7] *vtr* to research; (*indagar*) to investigate.

investir [6] *vtr* to invest.

invidente I *adj* unsighted. II *nmf* unsighted person.

invierno *nm* winter.

invisible *adj* invisible.

invitación *nf* invitation.

invitado,-a I *adj* invited; **artista i.**, guest artist. II *nm,f* guest.

invitar *vtr* to invite; **hoy invito yo**, it's on me today; **me invitó a una copa**, he treated me to a drink.

invocar [1] *vtr* to invoke.

involucrar I *vtr* to involve (**en**, in). II **involucrarse** *vr* to get involved (**en**, in).

involuntario,-a *adj* involuntary; (*impremeditado*) unintentional.

invulnerable *adj* invulnerable.

inyección *nf* injection; **poner una i.**, to give an injection.

inyectar *vtr* to inject (**en**, into); **i. algo a algn**, to inject sb with sth.

IPC *abr de* **Indice de Precios al Consumo**, Retail Price Index, RPI.

ir [16] I *vi* 1 to go; **¡vamos!**, let's go!; **voy a Lima**, I'm going to Lima; **¡ya voy!**, (I'm) coming! 2 (*río, camino*) to lead; **esta carretera va a la frontera**, this road leads to the border. 3 (*funcionar*) to work (properly); **el ascensor no va**, the lift is out of order. 4 (*desenvolverse*) **¿cómo le va el nuevo trabajo?**, how is he getting on in his new job?; **¿cómo te va?**, how are things?, how are you doing? 5 (*sentar bien*) to suit; **el verde te va mucho**, green really suits you. 6 (*combinar*) to

match; **el rojo no va con el verde**, red doesn't go with green. 7 (*vestir*) to wear; **ir con falda**, to wear a skirt; **ir de blanco/de uniforme**, to be dressed in white/in uniform. 8 *fam* (*importar, concernir*) to concern; **eso va por ti también**, and the same goes for you; **ni me va ni me viene**, I don't care one way or the other. 9 *fam* (*comportarse*) to act; **ir de guapo por la vida**, to be a flash Harry. 10 **va para abogado**, he's studying to be a lawyer. 11 (*ir + por*) **ir por la derecha**, to keep (to the) right; (*ir a buscar*) **ve (a) por agua**, go and fetch some water; (*haber llegado*) **voy por la página noventa**, I've got as far as page ninety. 12 (*locuciones*) **a eso iba**, I was coming to that; **¡ahí va!**, catch!; **en lo que va de año**, so far this year; **ir a parar**, to end up; **¡qué va!**, of course not!, nothing of the sort!; **va a lo suyo**, he looks after his own interests; **¡vamos a ver!**, let's see!; **¡vaya!**, fancy that; **¡vaya moto!**, what a bike!

II *v aux* 1 (*ir + gerundio*) **ir andando**, to go on foot; **va mejorando**, she's improving. 2 (*ir + pp*) **ya van rotos tres**, three (of them) have already been broken. 3 (*ir a + inf*) **iba a decir que**, I was going to say that; **va a llover**, it's going to rain; **vas a caerte**, you'll fall.

III **irse** *vr* 1 (*marcharse*) to go away, leave; **me voy**, I'm off; **¡vámonos!**, let's go!; **¡vete!**, go away!; **vete a casa**, go home. 2 (*líquido, gas*) (*escaparse*) to leak. 3 (*direcciones*) **¿por dónde se va a ...?** which is the way to ...? **por aquí se va al río**, this is the way to the river.

ira *nf* wrath, rage, anger.

iracundo,-a *adj* 1 (*irascible*) irascible. 2 (*enfadado*) irate, angry.

Irak *n* Irak.

Irán *n* Iran.

iraní *adj & nmf* (*pl* **iraníes**) Iranian.

Iraq *n →* **Irak**.

iraquí *adj & nmf* (*pl* **iraquíes**) Iraqi.

irascible *adj* irascible, irritable.

iris *nm inv Anat* iris; **arco i.**, rainbow.

Irlanda *n* Ireland; **I. del Norte**, Northern Ireland.

irlandés,-esa I *adj* Irish. II *nm,f* (*hombre*) Irishman; (*mujer*) Irishwoman; **los irlandeses**, the Irish. III *nm* (*idioma*) Irish.

ironía *nf* irony.

irónico,-a *adj* ironic.

IRPF *nm Econ abr de* **impuesto sobre la renta de las personas físicas**, income tax.

irracional *adj* irrational.

irradiar [12] *vtr* 1 (*emitir*) to radiate. 2 *Am fig* (*expulsar*) to expel.

irreal *adj* unreal.

irrealizable *adj* unattainable, unfeasible;

fig unreachable.
irreconocible *adj* unrecognizable.
irregular *adj* irregular.
irregularidad *nf* irregularity.
irremediable *adj* irremediable, incurable.
irremplazable *adj* irreplaceable.
irreparable *adj* irreparable.
irreprochable *adj* irreproachable, blameless.
irresistible *adj* 1 (*impulso, persona*) irresistible. 2 (*insoportable*) unbearable.
irresoluto,-a *adj* irresolute.
irresponsable *adj* irresponsible.
irreverente *adj* irreverent.
irrigación *nf* irrigation.
irrigar |7| *vtr* to irrigate, water.
irrisorio,-a *adj* derisory, ridiculous.
irritación *nf* irritation.
irritante *adj* irritating.
irritar I *vtr* 1 (*enfadar*) to irritate, exasperate. 2 *Med* to irritate. **II irritarse** *vr* 1 (*enfadarse*) to lose one's temper, get angry. 2 *Med* to become irritated.
irrompible *adj* unbreakable.
irrumpir *vi* to burst (**en**, into).
isla *nf* island, isle.
islam *nm Rel* Islam.
islámico,-a *adj* Islamic.
islandés,-esa I *adj* Icelandic. **II** *nm,f* (*persona*) Icelander. **III** *nm* (*idioma*) Icelandic.
Islandia *n* Iceland.
isleño,-a I *adj* island. **II** *nm,f* islander.
islote *nm* small *o* rocky island.
ismo *nm fam* ism.
Israel *n* Israel.
israelí *adj & nmf* (*pl israelíes*) Israeli.
istmo *nm Geog* isthmus.
Italia *n* Italy.
italiano,-a I *adj* Italian. **II** *nm,f* (*persona*) Italian. **III** *nm* (*idioma*) Italian.
itinerante *adj* itinerant, itinerating.
itinerario *nm* itinerary, route.
IVA *nm Econ abr de* **impuesto sobre el valor añadido,** value-added tax, VAT.
izar |4| *vtr* to hoist, raise.
izqda., izqdª *abr de* izquierda, left.
izqdo., izqdº *abr de* izquierdo, left.
izquierda *nf* 1 left; **a la i.,** on the left; **girar a la i.,** to turn left. 2 (*mano*) left hand. 3 *Pol* **la i.,** the left; **de izquierdas,** left-wing.
izquierdista *Pol* **I** *adj* leftist, left-wing. **II** *nmf* leftist, left-winger.
izquierdo,-a *adj* 1 left; **brazo i.,** left arm. 2 (*zurdo*) left-handed.
izquierdoso,-a *adj fam* leftish.

J

J, j |'xota| *nf* (*la letra*) J,j.
jabalí *nm* (*pl jabalíes*) wild boar.
jaɪ .lina *nf Dep* javelin.
jabón *nm* soap; **j. de afeitar/tocador,** shaving/toilet soap.
jabonera *nf* soapdish.
jaca *nf* gelding.
jacaré *nm Am Zool* caiman.
jacinto *nm Bot* hyacinth.
jactancia *nf* boastfulness.
jactancioso,-a I *adj* boastful. **II** *nm,f* braggart.
jactarse *vr* to boast, brag (**de**, about).
jadeante *adj* panting, breathless.
jadear *vi* to pant, gasp.
jadeo *nm* panting, gasping.
jaez *nm pey* (*ralea*) kind, sort.
jalar I *vtr fam* (*comer*) to wolf down. **II jalarse** *vr fam* (*comerse*) to wolf down, scoff.
jalbegar |7| *vtr* to whitewash.
jalea *nf* jelly; **j. real,** royal jelly.
jalear *vtr* (*animar*) to cheer (on).
jaleo *nm* (*alboroto*) din, racket; (*riña*) row; (*confusión*) muddle; **armar j.,** to make a racket.
jalón¹ *nm* (*estaca*) stake; *fig* (*hito*) milestone.
jalón² *nm* 1 (*tirón*) pull, tug. 2 *Am Aut* lift.

jamaicano,-a *adj & nm,f* Jamaican.
jamar *vtr fam* to scoff, eat.
jamás *adv* 1 never; **j. he estado allí,** I have never been there. 2 ever; **el mejor libro que j. se ha escrito,** the best book ever written. 3 **nunca j.,** never again; **por siempre j.,** for ever (and ever).
jamba *nf Arquit* jamb.
jamón *nm* ham; **j. de York/serrano,** boiled/cured ham.
jamona *fam adj* buxom.
Japón *n* (el) J., Japan.
japonés,-esa I *adj* Japanese. **II** *nm,f* (*persona*) Japanese; **los japoneses,** the Japanese. **III** *nm* (*idioma*) Japanese.
japuta *nf* (*pez*) Ray's bream.
jaque *nm Ajedrez* check; **dar j. a,** to check; **j. mate,** checkmate; **j. al rey,** check; *fig* **estar en j.,** to be stymied.
jaqueca *nf* migraine.
jara *nf Bot* rockrose.
jarabe *nm* syrup; **j. para la tos,** cough mixture.
jarana *nf fam* 1 (*juerga*) wild party, spree; **ir de j.,** to go on a spree *o* a binge. 2 (*jaleo*) racket, din.
jaranero,-a I *adj* fun-loving, party-loving. **II** *nm,f* pleasure seeker, party-lover.
jardín *nm* garden; **j. botánico,** botanical garden; **j. de infancia,** nursery school,

kindergarten.

jardinería nf gardening.

jardinero nm gardener.

jarra nf pitcher; **j. de cerveza**, beer mug; *fig* **de** o **en jarras**, arms akimbo, hands on hips.

jarro nm *(recipiente)* jug; *(contenido)* jugful; *fig* **echar un j. de agua fría a**, to pour cold water on.

jarrón nm vase; *(en arqueología)* urn.

jaspe nm *Min* jasper; **como el j.**, spotless, like a new pin.

Jauja nf *fig* promised land; **¡esto es J.!**, this is the life!

jaula nf *(para animales)* cage.

jauría nf pack of hounds.

jazmín nm *Bot* jasmine.

J.C. *abr de* **Jesucristo**, Jesus Christ, J.C.

jeep nm *Aut* jeep.

jefa nf female boss, manageress.

jefatura nf 1 *(cargo, dirección)* leadership. 2 *(sede)* central office; **j. de policía**, police headquarters.

jefe nm 1 head, chief, boss; *Com* manager; **j. de estación**, stationmaster; **j. de redacción**, editor-in-chief; **j. de ventas**, sales manager. 2 *Pol* leader; **J. de Estado**, Head of State. 3 *Mil* officer in command; **comandante en j.**, commander-in-chief.

Jehová nm Jehovah; **testigos de J.**, Jehovah's Witnesses.

jején nm *Am Ent* black fly.

jengibre nm *Bot* ginger.

jeque nm sheik, sheikh.

jerarquía nf 1 hierarchy. 2 *(categoría)* rank.

jerárquico,-a adj hierarchical.

jeremías nmf inv whiner, whinger.

jerez nm sherry.

jerga nf *(argot)* *(técnica)* jargon; *(vulgar)* slang; **la j. legal**, legal jargon.

jerigonza nf 1 *(extravagancia)* oddness. 2 *(galimatías)* gibberish.

jeringa nf *Med* syringe; *Aut* **j. de engrase**, grease gun.

jeringar [7] vtr fam 1 *(molestar)* to pester, annoy. 2 *(romper)* to break.

jeringuilla nf (hypodermic) syringe.

jeroglífico,-a I adj hieroglyphic. II nm 1 *Ling* hieroglyph, hieroglyphic. 2 *(juego)* rebus.

jersey nm *(pl jerseis)* sweater, pullover, jumper.

Jerusalén n Jerusalem.

Jesucristo nm Jesus Christ.

jesuita adj & nmf Jesuit.

Jesús I nm Jesus. II interj 1 *(expresa sorpresa)* good heavens! 2 *(al estornudar)* bless you!

jet nf jet set.

jeta nf fam 1 *(descaro)* cheek; **tener j.**, to be cheeky, have a nerve. 2 *(cara)* mug, face. 3 *(hocico)* snout.

jet-set nf jet set.

jíbaro,-a nm,f *Am* peasant.

jícara nf *(bol)* small cup; *Am* gourd.

jilguero,-a nm,f *Orn* goldfinch.

jilipollas nmf inv fam ofens → **gilipollas**.

jinete nm rider, horseman.

jiñar vi vulg to shit.

jirafa nf 1 giraffe. 2 *(de micrófono)* boom.

jirón nm *(trozo desgarrado)* shred, strip; *(pedazo suelto)* bit, scrap; **hecho jirones**, in shreds o tatters.

JJOO nmpl *abr de* **Juegos Olímpicos**, Olympic Games.

jocoso,-a adj funny, humorous.

joder vulg ofens I interj bloody hell!, shit! II vtr 1 *(fastidiar)* to piss off; **¡no me jodas!**, come on, don't give me that! 2 *(copular)* to fuck. 3 *(echar a perder)* to screw up; **¡la jodiste!**, you screwed it up! 4 *(romper)* to bugger. II **joderse** vr 1 *(aguantarse)* to put up with it; **¡hay que j.!**, you'll just have to grin and bear it. 2 *(echarse a perder)* to get screwed up; **¡se jodió el invento!**, that's really screwed things up. **¡que se joda!**, to hell with him! 3 *(romperse)* to go bust.

jodido,-a adj vulg ofens 1 *(maldito)* bloody, damned. 2 *(molesto)* annoying. 3 *(enfermo)* in a bad way; *(cansado)* knackered, exhausted. 4 *(estropeado, roto)* bust, kaput, buggered. 5 *(difícil)* shitty.

jodienda nf vulg ofens 1 *(coito)* fuck. 2 *(molestia)* pain in the arse.

jofaina nf washbasin.

jolgorio nm fam *(juerga)* binge; *(algazara)* fun.

jolín, jolines interj fam *(sorpresa)* go~\!, good grief!; *(enfado)* blast!, damn!

Jordania n Jordan.

jornada nf 1 **j. (laboral)**, *(día de trabajo)* working day; **j. intensiva**, continuous working day; **j. partida**, working day with a lunch break; **trabajo de media j./j. completa**, part-time/full-time work. 2 **jornadas**, conference sing.

jornal nm *(paga)* day's wage; **trabajar a j.**, to be paid by the day.

jornalero,-a nm,f day labourer o US laborer.

joroba I nf *(jiba)* hump. II interj drat!

jorobado,-a I adj hunchbacked. II nm,f hunchback.

jorobar fam I vtr 1 *(fastidiar)* to annoy, bother; **me joroba**, it really gets up my nose; **¡no jorobes!**, *(incredulidad)* pull the other one! 2 *(estropear)* to ruin, wreck. II **jorobarse** vr 1 *(fastidiarse)* to grin and bear it. 2 *(estropearse)* to break.

jota¹ nf 1 name of the letter J in Spanish. 2 *(cantidad mínima)* jot, scrap; **ni j.**, not an iota; **no entiendo ni j.**, I don't understand a thing.

jota² nf *Mús* Spanish dance and music.

joven I adj young; **de aspecto j.**, young-looking. II *nmf (hombre)* youth, young man; *(mujer)* girl, young woman; **de j.**, as a young man o woman; **los jóvenes**, young people, youth.

jovial *adj* jovial, good-humoured.

joya *nf* 1 jewel, piece of jewellery; **joyas de imitación**, imitation jewellery *sing.* 2 *fig* **ser una j.**, *(persona)* to be a real treasure o gem.

joyería *nf (tienda)* jewellery shop, jeweller's (shop).

joyero,-a I *nm,f* jeweller. II *nm* jewel case o box.

juanete *nm (en el pie)* bunion.

jubilación *nf* 1 *(acción)* retirement; **j. anticipada**, early retirement. 2 *(pensión)* pension.

jubilado,-a I *adj* retired. II *nm,f* retired person, pensioner; **los jubilados**, retired people.

jubilar I *vtr (retirar)* to retire, pension off; *fam fig* to get rid of, ditch. II **jubilarse** *vr (retirarse)* to retire, go into retirement.

júbilo *nm* jubilation, joy.

jubón *nm* doublet, jerkin.

judería *nf (barrio)* Jewish quarter.

judía *nf* bean; **j. verde**, French bean, green bean.

judicial *adj* judicial; **vía j.**, legal channels.

judío,-a I *adj* Jewish. II *nm,f* Jew.

judo *nm Dep* judo.

juego *nm* 1 game; **j. de azar**, game of chance; **j. de cartas**, card game; *fig* **j. de manos**, sleight of hand; *fig* **j. de palabras**, play on words, pun; *fig* **j. limpio/sucio**, fair/foul play; 2 *Dep* game; **Juegos Olímpicos**, Olympic Games; **terreno de j.**, *Ten* court; *Ftb* field; **fuera de j.**, offside. 3 *(apuestas)* gambling; *fig* **poner algo en j.**, to put sth at stake. 4 *(conjunto de piezas)* set; **j. de café/té**, coffee/tea service; *fig* **ir a j. con**, to match.

juerga *nf fam* binge, rave-up; **ir de j.**, to go on a binge.

juerguista I *adj* fun-loving. II *nmf* fun-loving person, raver.

jueves *nm inv* Thursday; **J. Santo**, Maundy Thursday.

juez *nmf* judge; **j. de instrucción**, examining magistrate; **j. de paz**, justice of the peace; *Dep* **j. de salida**, starter; **j. de línea**, linesman.

jugada *nf* 1 move; *(en billar)* shot. 2 *fam* dirty trick.

jugador,-a player; *(apostador)* gambler.

jugar [32] I *vi* 1 to play; **a(l) fútbol/tenis**, to play football/tennis; *fig* **j. sucio**, to play dirty. 2 **j. con**, *(no tomar en serio)* to toy with. II *vtr* 1 to play. 2 *(apostar)* to bet, stake. III **jugarse** *vr* 1 *(arriesgar)* to risk; *fam* **j. el pellejo**, to risk one's neck. 2 *(apostar)* to bet, stake.

jugarreta *nf fam* dirty trick.

jugo *nm* juice; *fig* **sacar el j. a**, *(aprove-*

char) to make the most of; *(explotar)* to squeeze dry.

jugoso,-a *adj* 1 juicy; **un filete j.**, a juicy steak. 2 *fig (sustancioso)* substantial, meaty; **un tema j.**, a meaty topic.

juguete *nm* toy; **pistola de j.**, toy gun; *fig* **ser el j. de algn**, to be sb's plaything.

juguetear *vi* to play.

juguetón,-ona *adj* playful.

juicio *nm* 1 *(facultad mental)* judgement, discernment; *(opinión)* opinion, judgement; **a j. de**, in the opinion of; **a mi j.**, in my opinion. 2 *(sensatez)* reason, common sense; **en su sano j.**, in one's right mind; **perder el j.**, to go mad o insane. 3 *Jur* trial, lawsuit; **llevar a algn a j.**, to take legal action against sb, sue sb.

juicioso,-a *adj* judicious, wise.

julio *nm* July.

junco *nm Bot* rush.

jungla *nf* jungle.

junio *nm* June.

júnior *adj Dep* junior; **campeonato j. de golf**, junior golf championship.

junta *nf* 1 *(reunión)* meeting, assembly; *Pol* **j. de gobierno**, cabinet meeting. 2 *(dirección)* board, committee; **j. directiva**, board of directors. 3 *Mil* junta; **j. militar**, military junta. 4 *(parlamento regional)* regional parliament. 5 *Téc* joint.

juntar I *vtr* 1 *(unir)* to join, put together; *(piezas)* to assemble. 2 *(reunir) (sellos)* to collect; *(dinero)* to raise. II **juntarse** *vr* 1 *(unirse)* to join; *(ríos, caminos)* to meet; *(personas)* to gather. 2 *(amancebarse)* to live together.

junto,-a I *adj* together; **dos mesas juntas**, two tables side by side; **todos juntos**, all together. II *junto adv* **j. con**, together with; **j. a**, next to.

juntura *nf* 1 *Téc* joint, seam. 2 *Anat* joint.

jura *nf (acción)* oath; *(ceremonia)* swearing in; **j. de bandera**, oath of allegiance to the flag.

jurado *nm* 1 *(tribunal)* jury; *(en un concurso)* panel of judges, jury. 2 *(miembro del tribunal)* juror, member of the jury.

juramento *nm* 1 *Jur* oath; **bajo j.**, under oath. 2 *(blasfemia)* swearword, curse.

jurar I *vi Jur Rel* to swear, take an oath. II *vtr* to swear; **j. el cargo**, to take the oath of office; **j. por Dios**, to swear to God. III **jurarse** *vr fam* **jurársela(s) a algn**, to have it in for sb.

jurel *nm (pez)* scad, horse mackerel.

jurídico,-a *adj* legal.

jurisdicción *nf* jurisdiction.

jurisdiccional *adj* jurisdictional; **aguas jurisdiccionales**, territorial waters.

jurista *nmf* jurist, lawyer.

justicia *nf* justice; **tomarse la j. por su mano**, to take the law into one's own hands.

justiciero,-a *adj* severe.
justificable *adj* justifiable.
justificación *nf* justification.
justificado,-a *adj* justified, well-grounded.
justificante *nm* written proof; **j. de pago,** proof of payment.
justificar |1| I *vtr* to justify. II **justificarse** *vr* to clear oneself, justify oneself.
justo,-a I *adj* 1 just, fair, right; **un trato j.,** a fair deal. 2 *(apretado) (ropa)* tight; **estamos justos de tiempo,** we're pressed for time. 3 *(exacto)* right, accurate; **la palabra justa,** the right word. 4 *(preciso)* **llegamos en el momento j. en que salían,** we arrived just as they were leav-

ing. 5 **lo j.,** just enough. II *nm,f* just *o* righteous person; **los justos,** the just, the righteous. III **justo** *adv (exactamente)* exactly, precisely; **j. al lado,** right beside. ◆**justamente** *adv* |j.!, precisely!; **j. detrás de,** right behind.
juvenil I *adj (aspecto)* youthful, young; **ropa j.,** young people's clothes; **delincuencia j.,** juvenile delinquency. II *nmf* **los juveniles,** the juveniles.
juventud *nf* 1 *(edad)* youth. 2 *(jóvenes)* young people.
juzgado *nm* court, tribunal; **j. de guardia,** police court.
juzgar |7| *vtr* to judge; **a j. por ...,** judging by ....

K

K, k |ka| *nf (la letra)* K, k.
ka *nf* name of the letter K in Spanish.
kárate *nm Dep* karate.
karateka *nmf Dep* person who does karate.
Kg, kg *abr de* **kilogramo(s),** kilograms, kilogrammes, kg.
kilo *nm* 1 *(medida)* kilo; *fam* **pesa un k.,** it weighs a ton. 2 *arg (millón)* a million pesetas.
kilogramo *nm* kilogram, kilogramme.
kilolitro *nm* kilolitre, *US* kiloliter.
kilometraje *nm* ≈ mileage.

kilométrico,-a *adj* kilometric, kilometrical; **billete k.,** multiple-journey ticket.
kilómetro *nm* kilometre, *US* kilometer.
kilovatio *nm* kilowatt; **k. hora,** kilowatt-hour.
kiosco *nm* → **quiosco.**
kiwi *nm* 1 *Orn* kiwi. 2 *(fruto)* kiwi (fruit), Chinese gooseberry.
Kleenex® *nm* Kleenex®, tissue.
Km, km *abr de* **kilómetro(s),** kilometre, kilometres, km, kms.
Kw, kw *abr de* **kilovatio(s),** kilowatt, kilowatts, kW, kw.

L

L, l |'ele| *nf (la letra)* L, l.
l *abr de* **litro(s),** litre, litres, *US* liter, liters, l.
la¹ *art def f* I the; **la mesa,** the table. II *pron dem* the one; **la del vestido azul,** the one in the blue dress; **la que vino ayer,** the one who came yesterday; → **el.**
la² *pron pers f (persona)* her; *(usted)* you; *(cosa)* it; **la invitaré,** I'll invite her along; **no la dejes abierta,** don't leave it open; **ya la avisaremos, señora,** we'll let you know, madam; → **le.**
la³ *nm Mús* la, A.
laberinto *nm* labyrinth.
labia *nf fam* loquacity; *pey* glibness; **tener mucha l.,** to have the gift of the gab.
labio *nm* lip.
labor *nf* 1 job, task; **l. de equipo,** teamwork; *(de profesión)* **sus labores,** housewife. 2 *Agr* farmwork. 3 *(de costura)* needlework, sewing.
laborable *adj* 1 **día l.,** *(no festivo)* working day. 2 *Agr* arable.
laboral *adj* industrial; **accidente l.,** industrial accident; **conflictividad l.,** in-

dustrial unrest; **jornada l.,** working day; **Universidad L.,** technical training college.
laboratorio *nm* laboratory.
laborioso,-a *adj* 1 *(persona)* hardworking. 2 *(tarea)* laborious.
laborista *Pol* I *adj* Labour; **partido l.,** Labour Party. II *nmf* Labour (Party) member *o* supporter.
labrado,-a *adj Arte* carved.
labrador,-a *nm,f (granjero)* farmer; *(trabajador)* farm worker.
labranza *nf* farming.
labrar I *vtr* 1 *Agr* to till. 2 *(madera)* to carve; *(piedra)* to cut; *(metal)* to work. II **labrarse** *vr fig* **l. un porvenir,** to build a future for oneself.
laca *nf* 1 hair lacquer, hairspray; **l. de uñas,** nail polish *o* varnish. 2 *Arte* lacquer.
lacio,-a *adj* 1 *(pelo)* lank, limp. 2 **qué l.!,** *(soso)* what a weed!
lacónico,-a *adj* laconic; *(conciso)* terse.
lacra *nf* evil, curse; **una l. social,** a scourge of society.

lacrar *vtr* to seal with wax.

lacre *nm* sealing wax.

lacrimógeno,-a *adj* 1 **gas l.**, tear gas. 2 *fig* **una película lacrimógena**, a tear-jerker.

lactar *vi* to breastfeed.

lácteo,-a *adj* **productos lácteos**, milk *o* dairy products; *Astron* **Vía Láctea**, Milky Way.

ladear I *vtr* (*inclinar*) to tilt; (*cabeza*) to lean. II **ladearse** *vr* 1 (*inclinarse*) to lean, tilt. 2 (*desviarse*) to go off to one side.

ladera *nf* slope.

ladino,-a *adj* (*astuto*) cunning, crafty.

lado *nm* 1 side; **a un l.**, aside; **al l.**, close by, nearby; **al l. de**, next to, beside; **ponte de l.**, stand sideways. 2 (*en direcciones*) direction; **por todos lados**, on *o* from all sides. 3 *fig* **dar de l. a algn**, to cold-shoulder sb; **por otro l.**, (*además*) moreover; **por un l. ...**, **por otro l. ...**, on the one hand ..., on the other hand ....

ladrar *vi* to bark.

ladrillo *nm* 1 *Constr* brick. 2 *fam* (*pesado*) bore, drag.

ladrón,-ona I *nm,f* thief, robber; **¡al l.!**, stop thief!. II *nm Elec* multiple socket.

lagartija *nf* small lizard.

lagarto *nm* lizard.

lago *nm* lake.

lágrima *nf* 1 tear; **llorar a l. viva**, to cry one's eyes out. 2 (*en lámpara*) teardrop.

lagrimoso,-a *adj* tearful.

laguna *nf* 1 small lake. 2 *fig* (*hueco*) gap.

La Haya *n* The Hague.

laico,-a I *adj* lay. II *nm,f* lay person; (*hombre*) layman; (*mujer*) laywoman.

lameculos *nmf inv ofens* bootlicker, arse-licker.

lamentable *adj* regrettable; (*infame*) lamentable.

lamentar I *vtr* to regret; **lo lamento**, I'm sorry. II **lamentarse** *vr* to complain.

lamento *nm* moan, wail.

lamer *vtr* to lick.

lámina *nf* 1 sheet, plate; **l. de acero**, steel sheet. 2 *Impr* plate.

laminado,-a I *adj* 1 laminated. 2 (*metales*) rolled; **acero l.**, rolled steel. II *nm* lamination.

laminar *vtr* (*metal*) to roll.

lámpara *nf* 1 lamp; **l. de pie**, standard lamp. 2 *Elec* (*bombilla*) bulb. 3 *Rad* valve.

lamparón *nm fam* oil *o* grease stain.

lana *nf* wool; **pura l. virgen**, pure new wool.

lanar *adj* **ganado l.**, sheep.

lance *nm lit* (*episodio*) incident.

lancha *nf* motorboat, launch; **l. motora**, speedboat; **l. neumática**, rubber dinghy; **l. salvavidas**, lifeboat.

langosta *nf* 1 lobster. 2 (*insecto*) locust.

langostino *nm* king prawn.

languidecer |33| *vi* to languish.

lánguido,-a *adj* languid; (*sin vigor*) listless.

lanudo,-a *adj* woolly, fleecy; (*peludo*) furry.

lanza *nf* spear, lance; **punta de l.**, spearhead; *fig* **romper una l. en favor de algn/de algo**, to defend sb/sth.

lanzadera *nf* shuttle; **l. espacial**, space shuttle.

lanzado,-a *adj fam* reckless; **ir l.**, to tear along.

lanzagranadas *nm inv Mil* grenade launcher.

lanzamiento *nm* 1 throwing, hurling. 2 *Dep* (*de disco, jabalina*) throw; (*de peso*) put. 3 *Mil* (*de cohete etc*) launching. 4 *Com* launch; **precio de l.**, launch price. 5 *Náut* launch.

lanzar |4| I *vtr* 1 (*arrojar*) to throw, fling. 2 *fig* (*grito*) to let out. 3 *Náut Com Mil* to launch. II **lanzarse** *vr* 1 (*arrojarse*) to throw *o* hurl oneself; **l. al suelo**, to throw oneself to the ground. 2 (*emprender*) to embark on; **l. a los negocios**, to go into business. 3 (*irse, largarse*) *fam* to scram.

lapa *nf* 1 *Zool* limpet. 2 *pey* **es una verdadera l.**, he/she sticks to you like glue.

lapicero *nm* pencil-case.

lápida *nf* headstone.

lapidario,-a *adj* lapidary.

lápiz *nm* pencil; **l. labial** *o* **de labios**, lipstick; **l. de ojos**, eyeliner.

lapso *nm* 1 (*periodo de tiempo*) period. 2 (*error*) lapse, slip.

lapsus *nm* slip; **l. linguae**, slip of the tongue.

largas *nfpl* **dar l. a un asunto**, to put a matter off.

largar |7| I *vtr* 1 *fam* (*golpe, discurso, dinero*) to give. 2 *Náut* **l. amarras**, to cast off. II **largarse** *vr fam* to clear off, split; **¡lárgate!**, beat it!

largo,-a I *adj* 1 (*espacio*) long; (*tiempo*) long, lengthy; **pasamos un mes l. allí**, we spent a good month there; **a lo l. de**, (*espacio*) along; (*tiempo*) through; **a la larga**, in the long run. 2 (*excesivo*) too long; **se hizo l. el día**, the day dragged on. 3 **largos años**, many years. II *nm* 1 (*longitud*) length; **¿cuánto tiene de l.?**, how long is it? 2 *Mús* largo. III *largo adv* **l. y tendido**, at length; *fam* **¡l. (de aquí)!**, clear off!; **esto va para l.**, this is going to last a long time.

largometraje *nm* feature film, full-length film.

laringe *nf* larynx.

laringitis *nf* laryngitis.

las[1] *art def fpl* 1 the; **l. sillas**, the chairs; **lávate l. manos**, wash your hands; (*no se traduce*) **me gustan l. flores**, I like flowers. 2 l. que, *(personas)* the ones who, those who; *(objetos)* the ones that, those that; **toma l. que quieras**, take whichever ones you want; → **la y los**.

las² *pron pers fpl (ellas)* them; *(ustedes)* you; **l. llamaré mañana (a ustedes)**, I'll call you tomorrow; **no l. rompas**, don't break them; **Pepa es de l. mías**, Pepa thinks the way I do; → **los**.

lasaña *nf* lasagna, lasagne.

lascivo,-a *adj* lewd, lecherous.

láser *nm inv* laser; **impresora l.**, laser printer.

lástima *nf* pity; **¡qué l.!**, what a pity!, what a shame!; **es una l. que ...**, it's a pity (that) ...; **estar hecho una l.**, to be a sorry sight; **tener l. a algn**, to feel sorry for sb.

lastimar *vtr* to hurt, injure.

lastre *nm* 1 *(peso)* ballast. 2 *fig* dead weight.

lata¹ *nf* 1 *(envase)* tin, *US* can; **en l.**, tinned *o US* canned. 2 *(hojalata)* tin(plate); **hecho de l.**, made of tin.

lata² *nf fam* nuisance, drag; **dar la l.**, to be a nuisance *o* a pest.

latente *adj* latent.

lateral I *adj* side, lateral; **salió por la puerta l.**, he went out by the side door; **escalón l.**, *(en letrero)* ramp. II *nm* side passage; *Aut (carril)* l., side lane.

latido *nm (del corazón)* beat.

latifundio *nm* large landed estate.

latigazo *nm* 1 lash. 2 *arg (trago)* drink, swig.

látigo *nm* whip.

latín *nm* Latin.

latino,-a I *adj* Latin; **América Latina**, Latin America. II *nm,f* Latin American.

Latinoamérica *nf* Latin America.

latinomericano,-a *adj & nm,f* Latin American.

latir *vi* to beat.

latitud *nf* 1 *Geog* latitude. 2 **latitudes**, region *sing*, area *sing*.

latón *nm* brass.

latoso,-a *adj fam* annoying.

laucha *nf Am* mouse.

laúd *nm* lute.

laurel *nm Bot* laurel, (sweet) bay; *Culin* bay leaf; *fig* **dormirse en los laureles**, to rest on one's laurels.

lava *nf* lava.

lavable *adj* washable.

lavabo *nm* 1 *(pila)* washbasin. 2 *(cuarto de aseo)* washroom. 3 *(retrete)* lavatory, toilet.

lavadero *nm (de coches)* carwash.

lavado *nm* wash, washing; *fig* **l. de cerebro**, brainwashing; **l. en seco**, dry-cleaning.

lavadora *nf* washing machine.

lavanda *nf* lavender.

lavandería *nf* 1 *(automática)* launderette,

US laundromat. 2 *(atendida por personal)* laundry.

lavaplatos *nm inv* dishwasher.

lavar *vtr* to wash; **l. en seco**, to dry-clean.

lavativa *nf* enema.

lavavajillas *nm inv* dishwasher.

laxante *adj & nm* laxative.

laxar *vtr (vientre)* to loosen.

laxitud *nf* laxity, laxness.

lazada *nf (nudo)* bow.

lazarillo *nm* **perro l.**, guide dog, *US* Seeing Eye dog.

lazo *nm* 1 *(adorno)* bow. 2 *(nudo)* knot; **l. corredizo**, slipknot. 3 *(para reses)* lasso. 4 *fig (usu pl) (vínculo)* tie, bond.

le **I** *pron pers mf (objeto indirecto) (a él)* (to *o* for) him; *(a ella)* (to *o* for) her; *(a cosa)* (to *o* for) it; *(a usted)* (to *o* for) you; **lávale la cara**, wash his face; **le compraré uno**, I'll buy one for her; **¿qué le pasa (a usted)?**, what's the matter with you? **II** *pron pers m (objeto directo) (él)* him; *(usted)* you; **no le oigo**, I can't hear him; **no quiero molestarle**, I don't wish to disturb you.

leal I *adj* loyal, faithful. **II** *nmf* loyalist.

lealtad *nf* loyalty, faithfulness.

lebrel *nm* greyhound.

lección *nf* lesson; *fig* **dar una l. a algn**, to teach sb a lesson; *fig* **te servirá de l.**, let that be a lesson to you.

leche *nf* 1 milk; *Anat* **dientes de l.**, milk teeth; **l. descremada** *o* **desnatada**, skim *o* skimmed milk. 2 *fam* **mala l.**, badness. 3 **l.!**, damn! 4 *arg (golpe)* knock; **dar** *o* **pegar una l. a algn**, to clobber sb. 5 *vulg* semen.

lechera *nf* 1 *(vasija)* churn. 2 *arg* police car.

lechería *nf* dairy, creamery.

lechero,-a I *adj* milk, dairy; **central lechera**, dairy co-operative; **vaca lechera**, milk cow. II *nm* milkman.

lecho *nm Lit* bed; **l. del río**, river-bed; **l. mortuorio**, deathbed.

lechón *nm* sucking pig.

lechoso,-a *adj* milky.

lechuga *nf* lettuce.

lechuza *nf* owl.

lectivo,-a *adj* school; **horas lectivas**, teaching hours.

lector,-a I *nm,f* 1 *(persona)* reader. 2 *Univ* lector, (language) assistant. **II** *nm* **l. de microfichas**, *(aparato)* microfile reader.

lectura *nf* reading.

leer |36| *vtr* to read; **léenos el menú**, read out the menu for us; *fig* **l. entre líneas**, to read between the lines.

legado *nm (herencia)* legacy.

legajo *nm* bundle (of papers).

legal *adj* 1 *Jur* legal, lawful; **requisitos legales**, legal formalities. 2 *fam (persona)* honest, trustworthy.

legalidad *nf* legality, lawfulness.

legalizar |4| *vtr* to legalize; *(documento)* to authenticate.

legaña *nf* sleep.

legar |7| *vtr (propiedad etc)* to bequeath; *fig (tradiciones etc)* to hand down, pass on.

legendario,-a *adj* legendary.

legión *nf* legion.

legionela *nf* legionnaire's disease.

legislación *nf* legislation.

legislar *vi* to legislate.

legislativo,-a *adj* legislative; **el poder l.,** parliament.

legislatura *nf* legislature.

legitimar *vtr* to legitimize; *(legalizar)* to legalize.

legitimidad *nf* Jur legitimacy; *(licitud)* justice.

legítimo,-a *adj* 1 Jur legitimate; **en legítima defensa,** in self-defence. 2 *(auténtico)* authentic, real; **oro l.,** pure gold.

lego,-a I *adj* Rel lay. II *nm* 1 layman; **ser l. en la materia,** to be a layman in the subject. 2 *Rel* lay brother.

legua *nf (medida)* league; *fig* **se nota a la l.,** it stands out a mile.

legumbres *nfpl* pulses.

lejanía *nf* distance.

lejano,-a *adj* distant, far-off; **parientes lejanos,** distant relatives; **el L. Oriente,** the Far East.

lejía *nf* bleach.

lejos *adv* far (away); **a lo l.,** in the distance; **de l.,** from a distance; *fig* **ir demasiado l.,** to go too far; *fig* **llegar l.,** to go a long way; *fig* **sin ir más l.,** to take an obvious example.

lelo,-a *fam* I *adj* stupid, silly. II *nm,f* ninny.

lema *nm* 1 *(divisa)* motto, slogan. 2 *(contraseña)* code name.

lencería *nf* 1 *(prendas)* lingerie. 2 *(ropa blanca)* linen *(goods pl).*

lendakari *nm* head of the Basque government.

lengua *nf* 1 tongue; *fig* **malas lenguas,** gossips; *fam* **irse de la l.,** to spill the beans; *fam fig* **tirarle a algn de la l.,** to try to draw sth out of sb. 2 *Ling* language; **l. materna,** native *o* mother tongue.

lenguado *nm (pez)* sole.

lenguaje *nm* language; *Inform* language; **l. corporal,** body language.

lengüeta *nf* 1 *(de zapato)* tongue. 2 *Mús* reed.

lente *nmf* lens; *Opt* **l. de contacto,** contact lenses.

lenteja *nf* lentil.

lentejuela *nf* sequin, spangle.

lentilla *nf* contact lens.

lentitud *nf* slowness; **con l.,** slowly.

lento,-a *adj* slow; **a fuego l.,** on a low heat.

leña *nf* 1 firewood; *fig* **echar l. al fuego,** to add fuel to the fire. 2 *fam (golpes)* knocks *pl.*

leñazo *nm arg (golpe)* blow, smash.

leñe *interj fam* damn it!

leño *nm* 1 log. 2 *fam (persona)* blockhead, half-wit.

león *nm* lion.

leona *nf* lioness.

leonera *nf* lion's den; *fig (habitación)* den.

leopardo *nm* leopard.

leotardos *nmpl* thick tights.

lepra *nf* leprosy.

leproso,-a I *adj* leprous. II *nm,f* leper.

les I *pron pers mfpl (objeto indirecto)* *(a ellos,-as)* them; *(a ustedes)* you; **dales el dinero,** give them the money; **les he comprado un regalo,** I've bought you a present. II *pron pers mpl (objeto directo) (ellos)* them; *(ustedes)* you; **l. esperaré,** I shall wait for you; **no quiero molestarles,** I don't wish to disturb you.

lesbiana *nf* lesbian.

lesión *nf* 1 *(corporal)* injury. 2 *Jur (perjuicio)* damage.

lesionar *vtr* to injure.

leso,-a *adj* Jur **crimen de lesa humanidad,** crime against humanity.

letal *adj* lethal, deadly.

letanía *nf* litany.

letargo *nm* lethargy.

letón,-ona I *adj* Latvian. II *nm,f* Latvian. III *nm (idioma)* Latvian, Lettish.

Letonia *n* Latvia.

letra *nf* 1 letter; **l. de imprenta,** block capitals; **l. mayúscula** capital letter; **l. minúscula** small letter; **l. pequeña,** small print. 2 *(escritura)* (hand)writing. 3 *Mús (texto)* lyrics *pl,* words *pl.* 4 *Fin* **l. (de cambio),** bill of exchange, draft. 5 *Univ* **letras,** arts.

letrado,-a *nm,f* lawyer.

letrero *nm (aviso)* notice, sign; *(cartel)* poster; **l. luminoso,** neon sign.

leucemia *nf* leukaemia, *US* leukemia.

levadizo,-a *adj* **puente l.,** drawbridge.

levadura *nf* yeast; **l. en polvo,** baking powder.

levantamiento *nm* 1 raising, lifting; *Dep* **l. de pesos,** weightlifting. 2 *(insurrección)* uprising, insurrection.

levantar I *vtr* 1 to raise, lift; *(mano, voz)* to raise; *(edificio)* to erect; *fig (ánimos)* to raise; **l. los ojos,** to look up. 2 *(castigo)* to suspend. II *vr* 1 *(ponerse de pie)* to stand up, rise. 2 *(salir de la cama)* to get up. 3 *(concluir)* to finish; **se levanta la sesión,** the meeting is closed. 4 *Pol* to rise, revolt; **l. en armas,** to rise up in arms. 5 *(viento)* to come up; *(tormenta)* to gather.

levante *nm* 1 *(el) L.,* Levante, the regions of Valencia and Murcia. 2 *(viento)* east wind, Levanter.

levar *vtr* **l. ancla,** to weigh anchor.

leve adj (ligero) light; fig (de poca importancia) slight. ◆**levemente** adv slightly.

levedad nf (ligereza) lightness; fig slightness; fig (de ánimo) levity; **heridas de l.**, minor injuries.

levitar vi to levitate.

léxico Ling I nm (diccionario) lexicon; (vocabulario) vocabulary, word list. II adj lexical.

ley nf 1 law; Parl bill, act; **aprobar una l.**, to pass a bill. 2 **oro de l.**, pure gold; **plata de l.**, sterling silver.

leyenda nf 1 (relato) legend. 2 (en un mapa) legend; (en una moneda) inscription; (bajo ilustración) caption.

liar [29] I vtr 1 (envolver) to wrap up; (un cigarrillo) to roll. 2 (enredar) to muddle up; (confundir) to confuse. II **liarse** vr 1 (embarullarse) to get muddled up. 2 fam (salir con) to get involved; (besarse) to neck. 3 **l. a bofetadas**, to come to blows.

libanés,-esa adj & nm,f Lebanese.

Líbano n el L., the Lebanon.

libelo nm (difamación) lampoon, satire.

libélula nf dragonfly.

liberación nf (de país) liberation; (de rehén) release, freeing.

liberal I adj 1 liberal; (carácter) open-minded; Pol **Partido L.**, Liberal Party; **profesión l.**, profession. 2 (generoso) generous, liberal. II nmf liberal.

liberalizar [4] vtr to liberalize.

liberar vtr (país) to liberate; (prisionero) to free, release.

líbero nm Ftb sweeper.

libertad nf freedom, liberty; **en l.**, free; Jur (en) **l. bajo palabra/fianza**, (on) parole/bail; Jur (en) **l. condicional**, (on) parole; **l. de comercio**, free trade; **l. de expresión**, freedom of speech.

libertador,-a nm,f liberator.

libertar vtr to set free, release.

libertinaje nm licentiousness.

libertino,-a adj & nm,f libertine.

Libia n Libya.

libio,-a adj & nm,f Libyan.

libra nf (moneda, peso) pound; **l. esterlina**, pound sterling.

librador,-a nm,f Fin drawer.

librar I vtr 1 (de un peligro) to free, release. 2 Com (una letra) to draw. 3 **l. batalla**, to do o join battle. II vi **libro los martes**, (no ir a trabajar) I have Tuesdays off. III **librarse** vr to escape; **l. de algn**, to get rid of sb.

libre adj free; **entrada l.**, (gratis) admission free; (sin restricción) open to the public; **l. cambio**, free trade; **l. de impuestos**, tax-free.

librecambio, librecambismo nm free trade.

librería nf 1 (tienda) bookshop, US bookstore. 2 (estante) bookcase.

librero,-a nm,f bookseller.

libreta nf notebook; **l. (de ahorro)**, savings book.

libro nm book; **l. de texto**, textbook; Com **l. de caja**, cashbook; Fin **l. mayor**, ledger.

licencia nf 1 (permiso) permission; (documentos) permit, licence, US license; **l. de armas/caza**, gun/hunting licence. 2 (libertad abusiva) licence, US license, licentiousness. 3 Am Aut driving licence, US driver's license.

licenciado,-a nm,f 1 Univ graduate; **l. en Ciencias**, Bachelor of Science. 2 Am lawyer.

licenciar [12] I vtr 1 Mil to discharge. 2 Univ to confer a degree on. II **licenciarse** vr Univ to graduate.

licenciatura nf Univ (título) (bachelor's) degree (course); (carrera) degree (course).

liceo nm 1 (sociedad literaria) literary society. 2 (escuela) secondary school.

licitar vtr Com (pujar) to bid for.

lícito,-a adj (permisible) allowed; Jur lawful.

licor nm liquor, spirits pl, US licor.

licuadora nf liquidizer.

licuar [10] vtr to liquidize.

lid nf (combate) contest.

líder nmf leader.

liderar vtr to lead, head.

liderato, liderazgo nm leadership; Dep top o first position.

lidia nf bullfight, bullfighting.

lidiador nm bullfighter.

lidiar [12] I vtr Taur to fight. II vi to fight; **l. con**, to contend with, fight against.

liebre nf 1 hare. 2 Dep pacemaker.

liendre nf nit.

lienzo nm 1 Tex linen. 2 Arte canvas.

lifting nm facelift.

liga nf 1 Dep Pol league; **hacer buena l.**, to get on well together. 2 (prenda) garter.

ligamento nm ligament.

ligar [7] I vtr 1 to join; fig (dos personas) to unite. 2 fam (coger) to get. II vi fam (seducir) to get off with sb. III **ligarse** vr (vincularse) to become attached (a, to).

ligazón nf bond, tie.

ligereza nf 1 lightness; (de tela, argumento) flimsiness. 2 (frivolidad) flippancy; (acto) indiscretion; (dicho) indiscreet remark. 3 (rapidez) speed.

ligero,-a I adj 1 (peso) light, lightweight; **l. de ropa**, lightly clad. 2 (ágil) light on one's feet; (veloz) swift, quick. 3 (leve) slight; **brisa/comida ligera**, light breeze/meal. 4 **a la ligera**, lightly. II adv ligero (rápido) fast, swiftly. ◆**ligeramente** adv 1 (levemente) lightly. 2 (un poco) slightly.

light adj inv (tabaco) mild; fig (persona) lightweight.

ligón,-ona *adj & nm,f fam (hombre)* ladies' man; **es muy ligona**, she's hot stuff.

ligue *nm* pick-up.

liguero,-a I *adj Dep* league; **partido l.,** league match. **II** *nm* suspenders *pl, US* garter belt.

lija *nf* sandpaper; **papel de l.,** sandpaper.

lijar *vtr* to sand *o* sandpaper (down).

lila¹ *adj inv & nf* lilac.

lila² *fam* **I** *adj (tonto)* dumb, stupid. **II** *nmf (tonto)* twit.

lima¹ *nf (fruto)* lime.

lima² *nf (herramienta)* file; **l. de uñas,** nailfile.

limar *vtr* to file; *fig* **l. asperezas,** to smooth things over.

limbo *nm* limbo.

limitación *nf* limitation; **l. de velocidad,** speed limit.

limitar I *vtr* to limit, restrict. **II** *vi* to border; **l. con,** to border on.

límite *nm* limit; *Geog Pol* boundary, border; **caso l.,** borderline case; **fecha l.,** deadline; **velocidad l.,** maximum speed.

limítrofe *adj* neighbouring, *US* neighboring.

limo *nm* slime.

limón *nm* lemon.

limonada *nf* lemon squash.

limonero *nm* lemon tree.

limosna *nf* alms; **pedir l.,** to beg.

limpiabotas *nm inv* bootblack, shoeshine.

limpiacristales *nm inv* window cleaner.

limpiador,-a I *adj* cleansing. **II** *nm,f (persona)* cleaner. **III** *nm (producto)* cleaner.

limpiaparabrisas *nm inv* windscreen *o US* windshield wiper.

limpiar [12] *vtr* **1** to clean; *(con un trapo)* to wipe; *(zapatos)* to polish; *fig* to cleanse. **2** *fam (hurtar)* to pinch, nick.

limpieza *nf (calidad)* cleanliness; *(acción)* cleaning; *fig (integridad)* integrity; **con l.,** cleanly.

limpio,-a I *adj* **1** *(aseado)* clean. **2** *Dep* **juego l.,** fair play. **3** *Fin (neto)* net; **beneficios en l.,** net profit. **4** *fam* **pasar algo a l.** to produce a fair copy of sth. **II** **limpio** *adv* fairly; **jugar l.,** to play fair.

linaje *nm* lineage.

linaza *nf* **aceite de l.,** linseed oil.

lince *nm* lynx; **tiene ojos de l.,** he's eagle-eyed.

linchar *vtr* to lynch; *fam (pegar)* to beat up.

lindante *adj* bordering.

lindar *vi* **l. con,** to border on.

linde *nmf* boundary, limit.

lindero,-a I *adj* bordering, adjoining. **II** *nm* boundary, limit.

lindo,-a I *adj (bonito)* pretty, lovely; **de lo l.,** a great deal. **II** *adv Am (bien)* nicely.

línea *nf* **1** line; **l. aérea,** airline; **en líneas generales,** roughly speaking; *Inform* **fuera de l.,** off-line; **en l.,** on-line. **2**

guardar la l., to watch one's figure.

lineal *adj* linear; **dibujo l.,** line drawing.

lingote *nm* ingot; *(de oro, plata)* bar.

lingüista *nmf* linguist.

lino *nm* **1** *Bot* flax. **2** *Tex* linen.

linterna *nf* torch.

lío *nm* **1** *(paquete)* bundle. **2** *fam (embrollo)* mess, muddle; **hacerse un l.,** to get mixed up; **meterse en líos,** to get into trouble; **armar un l.,** to kick up a fuss. **3** *fam (relación amorosa)* affair.

lioso,-a *adj fam (asunto)* confusing.

lipotimia *nf* fainting fit.

liquidación *nf* **1** *Com (saldo)* clearance sale. **2** *Fin* liquidation.

liquidar **I** *vtr Com (deuda, cuenta)* to settle; *(mercancías)* to sell off. **II** *vr* **1** *fam (gastar)* to spend. **2** *fam* **l. a algn,** *(matar)* to bump sb off.

liquidez *nf Fin* liquidity.

líquido,-a I *adj* **1** liquid. **2** *Fin* net. **II** *nm* **1** *(fluido)* liquid. **2** *Fin* liquid assets *pl*; **l. imponible,** taxable income.

lira *nf (moneda)* lira.

lírico,-a *adj* lyrical.

lirio *nm* iris.

lirismo *nm* lyricism.

lirón *nm* dormouse; *fig* **dormir como un l.,** to sleep like a log.

Lisboa *n* Lisbon.

lisiado,-a I *adj* crippled. **II** *nm,f* cripple.

lisiar [12] *vtr* to maim, cripple.

liso,-a *adj* **1** *(superficie)* smooth, even; *Dep* **los cien metros lisos,** the one hundred metres sprint. **2** *(pelo, falda)* straight. **3** *(tela)* self-coloured. **4** *Am (desvergonzado)* rude. **II** *adv* **lisa y llanamente,** purely and simply.

lisonjero,-a I *adj* flattering. **II** *nm,f* flatterer.

lista *nf* **1** *(relación)* list; **l. de espera,** waiting list; *(en avión)* standby; **pasar l.,** to call the register *o* the roll. **2** *(franja)* stripe; **de/a listas,** striped.

listado,-a I *adj* striped. **II** *nm* list; *Inform* listing.

listín *nm* **l. telefónico,** telephone directory.

listo,-a *adj* **1** ser **l.,** *(inteligente)* to be clever, smart. **2** estar **l.,** *(a punto)* to be ready.

listón *nm Dep* bar; *fig* **subir el l.,** to raise the requirements level.

litera *nf (cama)* bunk bed; *(en tren)* couchette.

literal *adj* literal.

literario,-a *adj* literary.

literato,-a *nm,f* writer, man *o* woman of letters.

literatura *nf* literature.

litigar |7| *vi Jur* to litigate.

litigio *nm Jur* lawsuit; *fig* dispute; **en l.,** in dispute.

litografía *nf* **1** *(técnica)* lithography. **2**

(imagen) lithograph.
litoral I *nm* coast, seaboard. **II** *adj coastal.*
litro *nm* litre, *US* liter.
liturgia *nf* liturgy.
liviano,-a *adj (de poco peso)* lightweight.
lívido,-a *adj* livid.
liza *nf* contest.
llaga *nf* sore; *(herida)* wound.
llama *nf* flame; **en llamas**, in flames, ablaze.
llamada *nf* call; *Tel* **l. interurbana**, long-distance call; **señal de l.**, ringing tone.
llamado,-a *adj* so-called.
llamamiento *nm* appeal.
llamar I *vtr* 1 to call; **l. (por teléfono)**, to ring up, call. 2 *(atraer)* to draw, attract; **l. la atención**, to attract attention. **II** *vi (a la puerta)* to knock. **III llamarse** *vr* to be called; **¿cómo te llamas?**, what's your name?
llamarada *nf* blaze.
llamativo,-a *adj* 1 *(color, ropa)* loud, flashy. 2 *(persona)* striking.
llaneza *nf (sencillez)* simplicity.
llano,-a I *adj* 1 *(superficie)* flat, level. 2 *(claro)* clear. 3 *(sencillo)* simple; **el pueblo l.**, the common people. **II** *nm* plain.
llanta *nf* 1 *(de rueda)* wheel rim. 2 *Am (neumático)* tyre, *US* tire.
llanto *nm* crying, weeping.
llanura *nf* plain.
llave *nf* 1 key; **cerrar con l.**, to lock; **llaves en mano**, *(en anuncio)* available for immediate occupation; *Aut* **l. de contacto**, ignition key. 2 *Téc* spanner; **l. inglesa**, adjustable spanner. 3 *(interruptor)* switch; **l. de paso**, stopcock. 4 *(en lucha)* lock. 5 *Tip* brace.
llavero *nm* key ring.
llegada *nf* arrival; *Dep* finish.
llegar [7] **I** *vi* 1 to arrive; **l. a Madrid**, to arrive in Madrid. 2 *(ser bastante)* to be enough. 3 *(alcanzar)* to reach; **¿llegas al techo?**, can you reach the ceiling? 4 *fig* **l. a las manos**, to come to blows; **l. a presidente.**, to become president. 5 **l. a +** *inf.*, to go so far as to. 6 **l. a ser**, to become. **II llegarse** *vr* to stop by.
llenar I *vtr* 1 to fill; *(cubrir)* to cover. 2 *(satisfacer)* to satisfy. **II** *vi (comida)* to be filling. **III llenarse** *vr* to fill (up), become full.
lleno,-a I *adj* full (up); *fig* **de l.**, fully. **II** *nm Teat* full house.
llevadero,-a *adj* bearable, tolerable.
llevar I *vtr* 1 to take; *(hacia el oyente)* to bring; **adónde llevas eso?**, where are you taking that?; **te llevaré un regalo**, I'll bring you a present. 2 *(transportar)* to carry; **dejarse l.**, to get carried away. 3 *(prenda)* to wear; **llevaba falda**, she was wearing a skirt. 4 *(soportar)* to bear; **¿cómo lleva lo de su enfermedad?**, how's he bearing up? 5 *(tiempo)* **llevo dos**

años aquí, I've been here for two years; **esto lleva mucho tiempo**, this takes a long time. 6 *(negocio)* to be in charge of. **II** *v aux* 1 **l.** + *gerundio*, to have been + present participle; **llevo dos años estudiando español**, I've been studying Spanish for two years. 2 **l.** + *participio pasado*, to have + past participle; **llevaba escritas seis cartas**, I had written six letters. **III llevarse** *vr* 1 to take away; *(premio)* to win; *(recibir)* to get. 2 *(arrastrar)* to carry away. 3 *(estar de moda)* to be fashionable. 4 **l. bien con algn**, to get on well with sb.
llorar *vi* to cry; *Lit* weep.
llorica *nmf fam* crybaby.
lloriquear *vi* to whimper, snivel.
llorón,-ona *adj* **un bebé l.**, a baby which cries a lot.
lloroso,-a *adj* tearful.
llover [4] *v impers* to rain.
llovizna *nf* drizzle.
lloviznar *v impers* to drizzle.
lluvia *nf* rain; **una l. de**, lots of; **l. radiactiva**, fallout; **l. ácida**, acid rain.
lluvioso,-a *adj* rainy.
lo¹ *art det neut* the; **lo mejor**, the best (part); **lo mismo**, the same thing; **lo mío**, mine; **lo tuyo**, yours.
lo² *pron pers m & neut* 1 *(cosa)* it; **debes hacerlo**, you must do it; **no lo creo**, I don't think so; *(no se traduce)* **no se lo dije**, I didn't tell her; → **le.** 2 **lo que ...**, what ...; **no sé lo que pasa**, I don't know what's going on. 3 **lo cual ...**, which ... 4 **lo de ...**, the business of ...; **cuéntame lo del juicio**, tell me about the trial.
loable *adj* praiseworthy, laudable.
loar *vtr* to praise.
lobo *nm* wolf; **como boca de l.**, pitch-dark; *fam* **¡menos lobos!**, pull the other one!
lóbrego,-a *adj* gloomy.
lóbulo *nm* lobe.
local I *adj* local. **II** *nm (recinto)* premises *pl*, site.
localidad *nf* 1 *(pueblo)* locality; *(en impreso)* place of residence. 2 *Cin Teat (asiento)* seat; *(entrada)* ticket.
localizar [4] *vtr* 1 *(encontrar)* to find. 2 *(fuego, dolor)* to localize.
loción *nf* lotion.
loco,-a I *adj* mad, crazy; **a lo l.**, crazily; **l. por**, crazy about; **volverse l.**, to go mad; *fam* **¡ni l.!**, I'd sooner die! **II** *nm,f* madman, madwoman; **hacerse el l.**, to act the fool.
locomotora *nf* locomotive.
locomotriz *adj* locomotive.
locuaz *adj* loquacious, talkative.
locución *nf* phrase.
locura *nf (enfermedad)* madness, insanity; **con l.**, madly; *fam* **esto es una l.**, this is

crazy.
locutor,-a *nm,f TV Rad* presenter.
locutorio *nm* telephone booth.
lodo *nm* mud.
logaritmo *nm* logarithm.
lógica *nf* logic; **no tiene l.**, there's no logic to it.
lógico,-a *adj* logical; **era l. que ocurriera**, it was bound to happen.
logística *nf* logistics *sing o pl*.
logotipo *nm* logo.
lograr *vtr* **1** to get, obtain; *(premio)* to win; *(ambición)* to achieve. **2 l. hacer algo**, to manage to do something.
logro *nm* achievement.
loma *nf* hillock, rise.
lombriz *nf* worm, earthworm.
lomo *nm* **1** back; **a lomo(s)**, on the back. **2** *Culin* loin. **3** *(de libro)* spine.
lona *nf* canvas.
loncha *nf* slice; **l. de bacon**, rasher.
lonchería *nf Am* snack bar.
londinense I *adj* of *o* from London. **II** *nmf* native *o* inhabitant of London.
Londres *n* London.
longaniza *nf* spicy (pork) sausage.
longevo,-a *adj* long lived.
longitud *nf* **1** length; **dos metros de l.**, two metres long; **l. de onda**, wavelength; *Dep* **salto de l.**, long jump. **2** *Geog* longitude.
lonja[1] *nf (loncha)* slice; **l. de bacon**, rasher.
lonja[2] *nf* **l. de pescado**, fish market.
loquería *nf Am* mental asylum, mental hospital.
lord *nm (pl lores)* lord; *GB Parl* **Cámara de los Lores**, House of Lords.
loro *nm* parrot.
los[1] **I** *art def mpl* the; **l. libros**, the books; **cierra l. ojos**, close your eyes; **l. García**, the Garcías; → **el, las y lo**. **II** *pron* **l. que**, *(personas)* those who; *(cosas)* the ones (that); **toma l. que quieras**, take whichever ones you want; **esos son l. míos/tuyos**, these are mine/yours; → **les**.
los[2] *pron pers mpl* them; **¿l. has visto?**, have you seen them?
losa *nf* (stone) slab, flagstone.
lote *nm* **1** set. **2** *Com* lot. **3** *Inform* batch. **4** *fam* **darse el l.**, to pet.
lotería *nf* lottery; **me tocó la l.**, I won a prize in the lottery.
loto *nf* **1** *Bot* lotus. **2** *(lotería)* lottery.
loza *nf* **1** *(material)* earthenware. **2** *(de cocina)* crockery.
lozano,-a *adj* **1** *(persona)* healthy looking. **2** *(plantas)* lush, luxuriant.
Ltda. *abr de* **Limitada**, Limited, Ltd.
lubricante *nm* lubricant.
lubricar |1| *vtr* to lubricate.
lucero *nm* (bright) star.
lucidez *nf* lucidity.
lúcido,-a *adj* lucid, clear.

luciérnaga *nf* glow-worm.
lucir |35| **I** *vi* **1** *(brillar)* to shine. **2** *fam (compensar)* **no le luce lo que estudia**, his studies don't get him anywhere. **II** *vtr (ropas)* to sport; *(talento)* to display. **III lucirse** *vr* **1** *(hacer buen papel)* to do very well. **2** *(pavonearse)* to show off.
lucrativo,-a *adj* lucrative, profitable.
lucro *nm* profit, gain; **afán de l.**, greed for money.
lucha *nf* **1** fight, struggle; **l. de clases**, class struggle. **2** *Dep* wrestling; **l. libre**, free-style wrestling.
luchador,-a *nm,f* **1** fighter. **2** *Dep* wrestler.
luchar *vi* **1** to fight, struggle. **2** *Dep* to wrestle.
lúdico,-a *adj* relating to games, recreational.
luego I *adv* **1** *(después)* then, next, afterwards. **2** *(más tarde)* later (on); **¡hasta l.!**, so long!; *Am* **l. de**, after. **3 desde l.**, of course. **II** *conj* therefore.
lugar *nm* **1** place; **en primer l.**, in the first place; **en l. de**, instead of; **sin l. a dudas**, without a doubt; **tener l.**, to take place. **2 dar l. a**, to cause, give rise to.
lugareño,-a *adj & nm,f* local.
lugarteniente *nmf* lieutenant.
lúgubre *adj* gloomy, lugubrious.
lujo *nm* luxury; **productos de l.**, luxury products; **no puedo permitirme ese l.**, I can't afford that.
lujoso,-a *adj* luxurious.
lujuria *nf* lechery, lust.
lujurioso,-a *adj* lecherous, lustful.
lumbre *nf* fire.
lumbrera *nf* luminary.
luminoso,-a *adj* luminous; *fig* bright.
luna *nf* **1** moon; *fig* **estar en la l.**, to have one's head in the clouds; **l. creciente/llena**, crescent/full moon; *fig* **l. de miel**, honeymoon. **2** *(de escaparate)* pane; *(espejo)* mirror.
lunar *nm (redondel)* dot; *(en la piel)* mole, beauty spot; **vestido de lunares**, spotted dress.
lunar *adj* lunar.
lunático,-a *nm,f* lunatic.
lunes *nm inv* Monday; **vendré el l.**, I'll come on Monday.
lupa *nf* magnifying glass.
luso,-a *adj & nm,f* Portuguese.
lustrar *vtr* to polish; *(zapatos)* to shine.
lustre *nm (brillo)* shine, lustre, *US* luster; *fig (esplendor)* splendour, *US* splendor, glory; **dar *o* sacar l. a algo**, to polish sth.
lustro *nm* five-year period.
lustroso,-a *adj* shiny, glossy.
luto *nm* mourning.
Luxemburgo *n* Luxembourg.
luz *nf* **1** light; **apagar la l.**, to put out the light; **a la l. de**, in the light of; **a todas luces**, obviously; *fig* **dar a l.**, *(parir)* to

give birth to; *fig* dar l. verde a, to give the green light to. 2 *Aut* light; **luces de cruce**, dipped headlights; **luces de posición**, sidelights; **l. larga**, headlights *pl*. 3

luces, *(inteligencia)* intelligence *sing*; **corto de l.**, dim-witted. 4 **traje de luces**, bullfighter's costume.

luzco *indic pres* → **lucir**.

M

M, m |'eme| *nf (la letra)* M, m.

m 1 *abr de* **metro(s)**, metre, metres, *US* meter, meters, m. 2 *abr de* **minuto(s)**, minute, minutes, min. 3 *abr de* **milla(s)**, mile, miles.

macabro,-a *adj* macabre.

macana *nf* 1 *Am (palo)* club. 2 *(trasto)* rubbish.

macanear *vtr Am (paparruchas)* to make up.

macanudo,-a *adj fam* great, terrific.

macarra *nm arg* yob.

macarrón *nm* 1 macaroon. 2 *Elec* sheath.

macarrones *nmpl* macaroni *sing*.

macedonia *nf* fruit salad.

macerar *vtr* to macerate.

maceta *nf (tiesto)* plant pot, flowerpot.

machacar |1| I *vtr* 1 to crush; *Dep* to smash. 2 *fam (estudiar con ahínco)* to swot up on, *US* grind away at. 3 *fam (insistir en)* to harp on about, go on about. II *vi* 1 *fam (insistir mucho)* to harp on, go on. 2 *fam (estudiar con ahínco)* to swot, cram, *US* grind. 3 *(en baloncesto)* to smash.

machacón,-ona *fam* I *adj (repetitivo)* repetitious; *(pesado)* boring, tiresome. II *nm,f (muy estudioso)* swot, *US* grind.

machamartillo (a) *loc adv (con firmeza)* firmly; *(con obstinación)* obstinately.

machete *nm* machete.

machismo *nm* machismo, male chauvinism.

machista *adj & nm* male chauvinist.

macho I *adj* 1 *(animal, planta)* male. 2 *fam (viril)* manly, virile, macho. II *nm* 1 *(animal, planta)* male. 2 *Téc (pieza)* male piece *o* part; *(de enchufe)* plug. 3 *fam (hombre viril)* macho, he-man, tough guy.

machote *nm Am (borrador)* rough draft.

macilento,-a *adj* gaunt.

macizo,-a I *adj* 1 *(sólido)* solid; **de oro m.**, of solid gold. 2 *(robusto)* solid, robust; *fam (atractivo)* well built. II *nm (masa sólida)* mass.

macramé *nm* macramé.

macro- *pref* macro-.

macro *nf Inform* macro.

macroeconomía *nf* macroeconomics *sing*.

macuto *nm (morral)* knapsack, haversack.

madeja *nf (de lana etc)* hank, skein.

madera *nf* 1 wood; *(de construcción)* timber, *US* lumber; **de m.**, wood, wooden. 2 *fig* **tiene m. de líder**, he has all the makings of a leader.

madero *nm* 1 *(de construcción)* timber; *(le-*

ño) log. 2 *arg (policía)* cop; **los maderos**, the fuzz *pl*.

madrastra *nf* stepmother.

madre I *nf* 1 mother; **es m. de tres hijos**, she is a mother of three (children); **m. adoptiva**, adoptive mother; **m. alquilada**, surrogate mother; **m. de familia**, mother, housewife; **m. política**, mother-in-law; **m. soltera**, unmarried mother; *fig* **la m. patria**, one's motherland. 2 *(de río)* bed. II *interj* **¡m. de Dios!**, **¡m. mía!**, good heavens!

madreperla *nf (nácar)* mother-of-pearl.

madreselva *nf* honeysuckle.

Madrid *n* Madrid.

madriguera *nf* burrow, hole.

madrileño,-a I *adj* of *o* from Madrid. II *nm,f* native *o* inhabitant of Madrid.

madrina *nf* 1 *(de bautizo)* godmother. 2 *(de boda)* ≈ bridesmaid. 3 *fig (protectora)* protectress.

madrugada *nf* 1 dawn; **de m.**, in the wee small hours. 2 early morning; **las tres de la m.**, three o'clock in the morning.

madrugador,-a I *adj* early rising. II *nm,f* early riser.

madrugar |7| *vi* to get up early.

madurar I *vtr fig (un plan)* to think out. II *vi* 1 *(persona)* to mature. 2 *(fruta)* to ripen.

madurez *nf* 1 maturity. 2 *(de la fruta)* ripeness.

maduro,-a *adj* 1 mature; **de edad madura**, middle-aged. 2 *(fruta)* ripe.

maestría *nf* mastery; **con m.**, masterfully.

maestro,-a I *nm,f* 1 *Educ* teacher; **m. de escuela**, schoolteacher. 2 *(especialista)* master; **m. de obras**, foreman. 3 *Mús* maestro. II *adj* **obra maestra**, masterpiece; **llave maestra**, master key.

mafia *nf* mafia.

mafioso,-a I *adj* of *o* relating to the mafia. II *nm,f* member of the mafia, mafioso.

magdalena *nf* bun, cake.

magia *nf* magic; **por arte de m.**, as if by magic.

mágico,-a *adj* 1 magic. 2 *fig (maravilloso)* magical, wonderful.

magisterio *nm* teaching.

magistrado,-a *nm,f* judge; *Am* **primer m.**, prime minister.

magistral *adj (excelente)* masterly; **una jugada m.**, a master stroke.

magistratura *nf* magistracy.

magnánimo,-a *adj* magnanimous.

magnate *nm* magnate, tycoon.

magnesio *nm* magnesium.

magnético,-a *adj* magnetic.

magnetizar [4] *vtr* **1** (*imantar*) to magnetize. **2** *fig* (*hipnotizar*) to hypnotize.

magnetofón, magnetófono *nm* tape recorder.

magnetofónico,-a *adj* magnetic.

magnífico,-a *adj* magnificent, splendid.

magnitud *nf* magnitude, dimension; **de primera m.**, of the first order.

magno,-a *adj lit* great; **aula magna**, main amphitheatre.

mago,-a *nm,f* wizard, magician; **los tres Reyes Magos**, the Three Wise Men, the Three Kings.

magrear *vtr vulg* to grope.

magro,-a I *nm* (*de cerdo*) lean meat. **II** *adj* (*sin grasa*) lean.

magullar I *vtr* to bruise, damage. **II magullarse** *vr* to get bruised, get damaged.

mahometano,-a *adj* & *nm,f Rel* Mohammedan, Muslim.

mahonesa *nf* mayonnaise.

maillot *nm* (*malla*) leotard; *Dep* shirt.

maíz *nm* maize, *US* corn.

maizal *nm* field of maize *o US* corn.

majadería *nf* silly thing, absurdity.

majadero,-a *nm,f* fool, idiot.

majara, majareta *adj fam* loony, nutty.

majestad *nf* majesty.

majestuosidad *nf* majesty.

majestuoso,-a *adj* majestic, stately.

majo,-a *adj* (*bonito*) pretty, nice; *fam* (*simpático*) nice; **tiene un hijo muy m.**, she's got a lovely little boy; *fam* **ven aquí, m.**, come here, dear.

mal I *nm* **1** evil, wrong. **2** (*daño*) harm; **no le deseo ningún m.**, I don't wish him any harm. **3** (*enfermedad*) illness, disease. **II** *adj* bad; **un m. año**, a bad year; → **malo,-a**. **III** *adv* badly, wrong; **lo hizo muy m.**, he did it very badly; **menos m. que ...**, it's a good job (that) ...; **no está (nada) m.**, it is not bad (at all); **te oigo/ veo (muy) m.**, I can hardly hear/see you; **tomar a m.**, (*enfadarse*) to take badly.

malabar *adj* (*juegos*) malabares, juggling *sing*.

malabarista *nmf* juggler.

malapata *nf fam* (*mala suerte*) bad luck.

malaria *nf* malaria.

malcriado,-a I *adj* ill-mannered, ill-bred. **II** *nm,f* ill-mannered *o* uncivil person.

malcriar [29] *vtr* to spoil.

maldad *nf* **1** badness, evil. **2** (*acción perversa*) evil *o* wicked thing.

maldecir [12] **I** *vtr* to curse. **II** *vi* **1** (*blasfemar*) to curse. **2** (*criticar*) to speak ill (**de**, of).

maldición I *nf* curse. **II** *interj* damnation!

maldito,-a *adj* **1** *fam* (*molesto*) damned, bloody. **2** (*endemoniado*) damned, cursed;

¡maldita sea!, damn it!

maleante *adj* & *nmf* delinquent, criminal.

malear I *vtr fig* to corrupt, pervert. **II malearse** *vr* to go bad.

maleducado,-a I *adj* bad-mannered. **II** *nm,f* bad-mannered person.

maleficio *nm* (*hechizo*) curse, spell.

maléfico,-a *adj* evil, harmful.

malentendido *nm* misunderstanding.

malestar *nm* **1** (*molestia*) discomfort. **2** *fig* (*inquietud*) uneasiness; **tengo m.**, I feel uneasy.

maleta I *nf* suitcase, case; **hacer la m.**, to pack one's things *o* case. **II** *nm fam* (*persona*) bungler.

maletero *nm Aut* boot, *US* trunk.

maletín *nm* briefcase.

malévolo,-a *adj* malevolent.

maleza *nf* **1** (*arbustos*) thicket, undergrowth. **2** (*malas hierbas*) weeds *pl*.

malgastar *vtr* & *vi* to waste, squander.

malhablado,-a I *adj* foul-mouthed. **II** *nm,f* foulmouthed person.

malhechor,-a *nm,f* wrongdoer, criminal.

malhumor *nm* bad temper *o* mood; **de m.**, in a bad temper *o* mood.

malicia *nf* **1** (*mala intención*) malice, maliciousness. **2** (*astucia*) cunning, slyness. **3** (*maldad*) badness, evil.

malicioso,-a I *adj* malicious, spiteful. **II** *nm,f* malicious *o* spiteful person.

maligno,-a *adj* malignant.

malintencionado,-a I *adj* ill-intentioned. **II** *nm,f* ill-intentioned person.

malla *nf* **1** (*prenda*) leotard. **2** (*red*) mesh. **3** *Am* (*bañador*) swimsuit, swimming costume.

Mallorca *n* Majorca.

mallorquín,-ina *adj* & *nm,f* Majorcan.

malo,-a I *adj* → **mal**. **1** bad; **un año m.**, a bad year; **estar a malas**, to be on bad terms; **por las malas**, by force. **2** (*persona*) (*malvado*) wicked, bad; (*travieso*) naughty. **3** (*de poca calidad*) bad, poor; **una mala canción/comida**, a poor song/ meal. **4** (*perjudicial*) harmful; **el tabaco es m.**, tobacco is harmful. **5** **lo m. es que ...**, the problem is that .... **6** (*enfermo*) ill, sick. **II** *nm,f fam* **el m.**, the baddy *o* villain.

malograr I *vtr* to upset. **II malograrse** *vr* to fail, fall through.

maloliente *adj* foul-smelling.

malparado,-a *adj* **salir m.**, to end up in a sorry state.

malpensado,-a I *adj* nasty-minded. **II** *nm,f* nasty-minded person.

malsonante *adj* (*grosero*) rude, offensive; **palabras malsonantes**, foul language.

malta *nf* (*cebada*) malt.

maltratado,-a *adj* battered.

maltratar *vtr* to ill-treat, mistreat.

maltrecho,-a *adj* in a sorry state, wrecked.

malva I *adj inv* mauve. **II** *nm* (*color*) mauve. **III** *nf Bot* mallow.
malvado,-a I *adj* evil, wicked. **II** *nm,f* villain, evil person.
malvender *vtr* to sell at a loss.
malversar *vtr* to misappropriate, embezzle.
Malvinas *npl* las (**Islas M.**), the Falkland Islands.
malvivir *vi* to live very badly.
mamá *nf fam* mum, mummy.
mama *nf* **1** (*de mujer*) breast; (*de animal*) teat. **2** *fam* (*mamá*) mum, mummy.
mamada *nf* **1** (*bebé*) feed. **2** *vulg* (*felatio*) blow job.
mamadera *nf Am* feeding bottle.
mamar *vtr* (*leche*) to suck; *fig* (*adquirir*) to absorb.
mamarracho,-a *nm,f fam* (*persona*) ridiculous-looking person, mess, sight; (*cosa*) mess.
mameluco *nm fig* **1** fool, idiot, dim-wit. **2** *Am* boiler-suit.
mamífero,-a *nm,f* mammal.
mamón *nm vulg ofens* prick.
mampara *nf* screen.
mamporro *nm fam* wallop.
mampostería *nf* masonry.
mamut *nm* mammoth.
manada *nf* **1** *Zool* (*de vacas, elefantes*) herd; (*de ovejas*) flock; (*de lobos, perros*) pack; (*de leones*) pride. **2** *fam* (*multitud*) crowd, mob; **en manada(s)**, in crowds.
manager *nmf Dep Mús* manager.
manantial *nm* spring.
manar I *vi* to flow, run (**de**, from). **II** *vtr* to run with, flow with; **la herida manaba sangre**, blood flowed from his wound.
manazas *nmf inv fam* ham-fisted person.
mancebo *nm* **1** (*de farmacia*) assistant. **2** *arc* (*muchacho*) young man.
Mancha (La)[1] *n* La Mancha.
Mancha[2] *n* **el Canal de la M.**, the English Channel.
mancha *nf* stain, spot; **m. solar**, sunspot; **m. de tinta/vino**, ink/wine stain.
manchado,-a *adj* dirty, stained; **leche manchada**, milky coffee.
manchar I *vtr* to stain, dirty; *fig* to stain, blemish. **II mancharse** *vr* to get dirty.
manchego,-a *adj* of *o* from La Mancha.
manco,-a I *adj* **1** (*de un brazo*) one-armed; (*sin brazos*) armless. **2** (*de una mano*) one-handed; (*sin manos*) handless. **II** *nm,f* **1** (*de brazos*) one-armed *o* armless person. **2** (*de manos*) one-handed *o* handless person.
mancomunidad *nf* community, association.
mancornas *nfpl Am* cufflinks.
mandado *nm* (*recado*) order, errand; **hacer un m.**, to run an errand.
mandamás *nmf* (*pl* **mandamases**) *fam* bigwig, boss.

mandamiento *nm* **1** (*orden*) order, command. **2 los Diez Mandamientos**, the Ten Commandments.
mandar *vtr* **1** to order; *fam* **¿mande?**, pardon? **2** (*grupo*) to lead, be in charge *o* command of; *Mil* to command. **3** (*enviar*) to send; **m. (a) por**, to send for; **m. algo por correo**, to post sth, send sth by the post; **m. recuerdos**, to send regards.
mandarina *nf* mandarin (orange), tangerine.
mandatario,-a *nm,f Pol* president.
mandato *nm* **1** (*orden*) order, command. **2** *Jur* writ, warrant. **3** *Pol* (*legislatura*) mandate, term of office.
mandíbula *nf* jaw; *fam* **reír a m. batiente**, to laugh one's head off.
mandil *nm* apron.
mando *nm* **1** (*autoridad*) command, control. **2 los altos mandos del ejército**, high-ranking army officers. **3** *Téc* (*control*) controls *pl*; *Aut* **cuadro** *o* **tablero de mandos**, dashboard; **m. a distancia**, remote control; **palanca de m.**, *Téc* control lever; (*de avión, videojuego*) joystick.
mandón,-ona I *adj fam* bossy, domineering. **II** *nm,f fam* bossy *o* domineering person. **III** *nm Am* (mine) foreman.
manecilla *nf* (*de reloj*) hand.
manejable *adj* manageable; (*herramienta*) easy-to-use; (*coche*) manoeuvrable, *US* maneuvrable.
manejar I *vtr* **1** (*máquina*) to handle, operate; (*situación*) to handle. **2** (*negocio*) to run, manage. **3** *fig* (*a otra persona*) to domineer, boss about. **4** (*coche*) to drive. **II manejarse** *vr* to manage.
manejo *nm* **1** (*uso*) handling, use; **de fácil m.**, easy-to-use. **2** *fig* (*de un negocio*) management; (*de un coche*) driving. **3** *fig* tricks *pl*.
manera *nf* **1** way, manner; **a mi/tu m.**, (in) my/your way; **de cualquier m.**, (*mal*) carelessly, any old how; (*en cualquier caso*) in any case; **de esta m.**, in this way; **de ninguna m.**, in no way, certainly not; **de todas maneras**, anyway, at any rate, in any case; **es mi m. de ser**, that's the way I am; **no hay m.**, it's impossible. **2 de m. que**, so; **de tal m. que**, in such a way that. **3 maneras**, manners; **de buenas maneras**, politely.
manga *nf* **1** sleeve; **de m. corta/larga**, short-/long-sleeved; **sin mangas**, sleeveless; *fig* **hacer un corte de mangas a algn**, ≈ to give sb the fingers; *fig* **m. por hombro**, messy and untidy; *fig* **sacarse algo de la m.**, to pull sth out of one's hat. **2** (*de riego*) hose. **3** (*del mar*) arm. **4** *Dep* leg, round; *Ten* set.
mangante *arg nmf* thief.
mangar [7] *vtr arg* to pinch, nick, swipe.
mango *nm* handle.
mangonear *vi* **1** *fam* (*entrometerse*) to

meddle. 2 *fam (dar órdenes)* to throw one's weight around.

manguera *nf* hose.

mangui *nmf arg* thief.

manguito *nm* 1 *(para las mangas)* over-sleeve; *(para flotar)* armband. 2 *Téc* sleeve.

maní *nm (pl* manises*)* peanut.

manía *nf* 1 dislike, ill will; **me tiene m.**, he has it in for me. 2 *(costumbre)* habit; **tiene la m. de llegar tarde**, he's always arriving late. 3 *(afición exagerada)* craze; **la m. de las motos**, the motorbike craze. 4 *Med* mania.

maniaco,-a, maníaco,-a *adj & nm,f Psic* manic; *fam (obseso)* maniac.

maniatar *vtr* to tie the hands of.

maniático,-a I *adj* fussy. II *nm,f* fusspot.

manicomio *nm* mental hospital.

manicura *nf* manicure.

manido,-a *adj* 1 *(comida)* off. 2 *(asunto)* trite, hackneyed.

manifestación *nf* 1 demonstration. 2 *(expresión)* manifestation, expression.

manifestante *nmf* demonstrator.

manifestar [1] I *vtr* 1 *(declarar)* to state, declare. 2 *(mostrar)* to show, display. II **manifestarse** *vr* 1 *(por la calle)* to demonstrate. 2 *(declararse)* to declare oneself; **se manifestó contrario a ...**, he spoke out against ...

manifiesto,-a I *adj* clear, obvious; **poner de m.**, *(revelar)* to reveal, show; *(hacer patente)* to make clear. II *nm* manifesto.

manigua *nf Am Geog* scrubland.

manilla *nf* 1 *(de reloj)* hand. 2 *Am (palanca)* lever.

manillar *nm* handlebar.

maniobra *nf* manoeuvre, *US* maneuver.

maniobrar *vi* to manoeuvre, *US* maneuver.

manipulación *nf* manipulation.

manipular *vtr* to manipulate; *(máquina)* to handle.

maniquí *nm (muñeco)* dummy.

manitas *nmf inv fam* 1 **ser un m.**, to be handy, be very good with one's hands. 2 **hacer m.**, to hold hands.

manivela *nf Téc* crank.

manjar *nm* dish, food.

mano *nf* 1 hand; **a m.**, *(sin máquina)* by hand; *(asequible)* at hand; **escrito a m.**, hand-written; **hecho a m.**, hand-made; **a m. armada**, armed; **estrechar la m. a algn**, to shake hands with sb; **de segunda m.**, second-hand; **echar una m. a algn**, to give sb a hand; **¡manos a la obra!**, shoulders to the wheel!; **meter m.**, *(a un problema)* to tackle; *vulg* to touch up; **traerse algo entre manos**, to be up to sth; **equipaje de m.**, hand luggage. 2 *(lado)* side; **a m. derecha/izquierda**, on the right/left(-hand side). 3 **m. de pintura**, coat of paint. 4 **m. de**

obra, labour (force).

manojo *nm* bunch; **ser un m. de nervios**, to be a bundle of nerves.

manopla *nf* mitten.

manoseado,-a *adj (objeto)* worn(-out); *(tema)* hackneyed.

manosear *vtr* to touch repeatedly, finger; *fam* to paw.

manotazo *nm* cuff, slap.

mansalva (a) *loc adv (en gran cantidad)* galore.

mansedumbre *nf* 1 *(de persona)* meek-ness, gentleness. 2 *(de animal)* tameness, docility.

manso,-a *adj* 1 *(persona)* gentle, meek. 2 *(animal)* tame, docile.

manta I *nf* 1 blanket; **m. eléctrica**, elec-tric blanket. 2 *(zurra)* beating, hiding. II *nmf fam* lazy person, idler.

manteca *nf (de animal)* fat; **m. de cacao/ cacahuete**, cocoa/peanut butter; **m. de cerdo**, lard.

mantecado *nm* shortcake.

mantel *nm* tablecloth.

mantener [24] I *vtr* 1 *(conservar)* to keep; **mantén el fuego encendido**, keep the fire burning; **m. la línea**, to keep in trim. 2 *(entrevista, reunión)* to have; **m. correspondencia con algn**, to correspond with sb. 3 *(ideas, opiniones)* to defend, maintain. 4 *(familia)* to support, feed. 5 *(peso)* to support, hold up. II **mantenerse** *vr* 1 *(sostenerse)* to stand. 2 **m. firme**, *(perseverar)* to hold one's ground. 3 *(sustentarse)* to live (**de**, on).

mantenimiento *nm* 1 *Téc* maintenance, upkeep; **servicio de m.**, maintenance service. 2 *(alimento)* sustenance, support. 3 **gimnasia y m.**, keep-fit.

mantequilla *nf* butter.

manto *nm* cloak.

mantón *nm* shawl.

mantuve *pt indef* → **mantener**.

manual I *adj* manual; **trabajo m.**, manual labour; *Educ* **trabajos manuales**, hand-icrafts. II *nm* manual, handbook.

manufactura *nf* 1 *(fabricación)* man-ufacture. 2 *(fábrica)* factory.

manufacturar *vtr* to manufacture.

manuscrito,-a *nm* manuscript.

manutención *nf* maintenance.

manzana *nf* 1 apple. 2 *(de edificios)* block.

manzanilla *nf* 1 *Bot* camomile. 2 *(infusión)* camomile tea. 3 *(vino)* manzanilla.

maña *nf* 1 *(astucia)* cunning. 2 *(habilidad)* skill.

mañana I *nf* morning; **a las dos de la m.**, at two in the morning; **de m.**, early in the morning; **por la m.**, in the morning. II *nm* tomorrow, the future. III *adv* tomorrow; **¡hasta m.!**, see you tomorrow! **m. por la m.**, tomorrow morning; **pasado m.**, the day after tomorrow.

mañoso,-a *adj* skilful, *US* skillful.

mapa *nm* map; **m. mudo**, blank map; *fam* **borrar del m.**, to wipe out.

maqueta *nf* 1 (*miniatura*) scale model, maquette. 2 *Mús* demo (tape).

maquiavélico,-a *adj* Machiavellian.

maquillaje *nm* make-up.

maquillar I *vtr* to make up. II **maquillarse** *vr* 1 (*ponerse maquillaje*) to put one's make-up on, make (oneself) up. 2 (*usar maquillaje*) to wear make-up.

máquina *nf* 1 machine; **escrito a m.**, typewritten; **hecho a m.**, machine-made; *fam* **a toda m.**, at full speed. **m. de afeitar (eléctrica)**, (electric) razor *o* shaver; **m. de coser**, sewing machine; **m. de escribir**, typewriter; **m. fotográfica** *o* **de fotos**, camera; **m. tragaperras**, slot machine, one-armed bandit. 2 *fam* (*coche*) car.

maquinar *vtr* to machinate, plot.

maquinaria *nf* 1 machinery, machines *pl.* 2 (*de reloj etc*) (*mecanismo*) mechanism, works *pl.*

maquinilla *nf* **m. de afeitar**, safety razor.

maquinista *nmf* (*de tren*) engine driver.

mar I *nm & f* 1 sea; **en alta m.**, on the high seas; **m. adentro**, out to sea; **por m.**, by sea; **m. gruesa**, heavy sea; **m. picada**, rough sea. 2 *fam* **está la m. de guapa**, she's looking really beautiful; **llover a mares**, to rain cats and dogs. II *nm* sea. **M. del Norte**, North Sea; **M. Muerto/Negro**, Dead/Black Sea.

maraña *nf* tangle.

maratón *nm* marathon.

maratoniano,-a *adj* marathon.

maravilla *nf* marvel, wonder; **de m.**, wonderfully; **¡qué m. de película!**, what a wonderful film!; *fam* **a las mil maravillas**, marvellously.

maravillar I *vtr* to amaze, astonish. II **maravillarse** *vr* to marvel (**con**, at), wonder (**con**, at).

maravilloso,-a *adj* wonderful, marvellous, *US* marvelous.

marca *nf* 1 mark, sign. 2 *Com* brand, make; **ropa de m.**, brand-name clothes; **m. de fábrica**, trademark; **m. registrada**, registered trademark. 3 *Dep* (*récord*) record; **batir la m. mundial**, to break the world record.

marcador,-a *nm* 1 marker. 2 *Dep* (*tablero*) scoreboard; (*persona*) scorer.

marcaje *nm Dep* marking.

marcapasos *nm inv Med* pacemaker.

marcar [1] I *vtr* 1 to mark. 2 *Tel* to dial. 3 (*indicar*) to indicate, show; **el contador marca 1.327**, the meter reads 1,327. 4 *Dep* (*gol, puntos*) to score; (*a jugador*) to mark. 5 (*cabello*) to set. II **marcarse** *vr fam* **m. un farol**, to show off, boast.

marcha *nf* 1 march; **hacer algo sobre la m.**, to do sth as one goes along; **a marchas forzadas**, against the clock. 2 *estar*

en m., (*vehículo*) to be in motion; (*máquina*) to be working; (*proyecto etc*) to be under way; **poner en m.**, to start. 3 *Aut* gear; **m. atrás**, reverse (gear). 4 *Mús* march. 5 *fam* (*juerga*) **hay mucha m.**, there's lots going on; **ella tiene mucha m.**, she likes a good time.

marchar I *vi* 1 (*ir*) to go, walk; *fam* **¡marchando!**, on your way!; **¡una cerveza! - ¡marchando!**, a beer, please! - coming right up! 2 (*aparato*) to be on; **m. bien**, (*negocio*) to be going well. 3 *Mil* to march. II **marcharse** *vr* (*irse*) to leave, go away.

marchitar *vtr*, **marchitarse** *vr* to shrivel, wither.

marchito,-a *adj* shrivelled, *US* shriveled, withered.

marchoso,-a *fam* I *adj* (*persona*) fun-loving, wild. II *nm,f* raver, fun lover.

marcial *adj* martial; **artes marciales**, martial arts.

marcianitos *nmpl* (*juego*) space invaders.

marciano,-a *adj & nm,f* Martian.

marco *nm* 1 (*de cuadro etc*) frame. 2 *fig* (*ámbito*) framework; **acuerdo m.**, framework agreement. 3 *Fin* (*moneda*) mark.

marea *nf* 1 tide; **m. alta/baja**, high/low tide; **m. negra**, oil slick. 2 *fig* (*multitud*) crowd, mob.

mareado,-a *adj* 1 sick; (*en un avión*) airsick; (*en un coche*) carsick, travel-sick; (*en el mar*) seasick. 2 *euf* (*bebido*) tipsy. 3 (*aturdido*) dizzy.

marear I *vtr* 1 to make sick; (*en el mar*) to make seasick; (*en un avión*) to make airsick; (*en un coche*) to make carsick *o* travel-sick. 2 (*aturdir*) to make dizzy. 3 *fam* (*fastidiar*) to annoy, pester. 4 *Culin* to stir. II **marearse** *vr* 1 to get sick/seasick/airsick/carsick *o* travel-sick. 2 (*quedar aturdido*) to get dizzy. 3 *euf* (*emborracharse*) to get tipsy.

mareo *nm* 1 (*náusea*) sickness; (*en el mar*) seasickness; (*en un avión*) airsickness; (*en un coche*) carsickness, travel-sickness; (*aturdimiento*) dizziness, lightheadedness.

marfil *nm* ivory.

margarina *nf* margarine.

margarita *nf* daisy.

margen *nmf* 1 border, edge; (*de río*) bank; *fig* **dejar algn/algo al m.**, to leave sb/sth out; *fig* **mantenerse al m.**, not to get involved; **al margen de**, leaving aside. 2 (*del papel*) margin. 3 *Com* **m. beneficiario**, profit margin.

marginación *nf* (*exclusión*) exclusion.

marginado,-a I *adj* excluded. II *nm,f* dropout.

marginal *adj* 1 marginal. 2 *Pol* fringe.

marginar *vtr* (*de un grupo, sociedad*) to leave out, exclude.

maría *nf arg* 1 (*droga*) marijuana, pot. 2 *Educ arg* (*asignatura fácil*) easy subject. 3

fam *(ama de casa)* housewife.
marica *nm vulg ofens* queer, poof.
maricón *nm vulg ofens* queer, poof.
marido *nm* husband.
mariguana, marihuana, marijuana *nf* marijuana.
marimacho *nm vulg* mannish woman, butch woman.
marimandón,-ona *nm,f fam* domineering person.
marimorena *nf fam* row, fuss; *fam* **armar(se) la m.**, to kick up a racket.
marina *nf* 1 *Náut* seamanship. 2 *Mil* navy; **m. de guerra**, navy; **m. mercante**, merchant navy. 3 *Geog (zona costera)* seacoast.
marinero,-a I *nm* sailor, seaman. II *adj* seafaring.
marino,-a I *adj* marine; **brisa marina**, sea breeze. II *nm* sailor.
marioneta *nf* marionette, puppet.
mariposa *nf* 1 *Ent* butterfly. 2 *(lamparilla)* oil lamp. 3 *Natación* butterfly.
mariposear *vi fig* 1 *(flirtear)* to flirt. 2 *(ser inconstante)* to be fickle.
mariposón *nm* 1 *(galanteador)* flirt. 2 *ofens (marica)* queer, pansy, poof.
mariquita I *nf Ent* ladybird. II *nm fam ofens (marica)* queer, pansy, poof.
mariscal *nm Mil* marshal; **m. de campo**, field marshal.
marisco *nm* shellfish; **mariscos**, seafood.
marisma *nf* marsh.
marisquería *nf* seafood restaurant, shellfish bar.
marítimo,-a *adj* maritime, sea; **ciudad marítima**, coastal town; **paseo m.**, promenade.
mármol *nm* marble.
marmóreo,-a *adj* marble.
maroma *nf* 1 *Náut* cable. 2 *(cuerda)* thick rope.
marqués *nm* marquis.
marquesa *nf* marchioness.
marquesina *nf* canopy; **m. (del autobús)**, bus shelter.
marquetería *nf* marquetry, inlaid work.
marrano,-a I *adj (sucio)* filthy, dirty. II *nm,f* 1 *fam (persona)* dirty pig, slob. 2 *(animal)* pig.
marras (de) *loc adv* **el individuo de m.**, the man in question.
marrón I *adj (color)* brown. II *nm* 1 *(color)* brown. 2 *arg (condena)* sentence.
marroquí *adj & nmf* Moroccan.
marroquinería *nf* leather goods.
Marruecos *n* Morocco.
marrullero,-a I *adj* cajoling, wheedling. II *nm,f* cajoler, wheedler.
Marte *n* Mars.
martes *nm inv* Tuesday; **m. y trece**, ≈ Friday the thirteenth.
martillo *nm* hammer.
mártir *nmf* martyr.

martirio *nm* 1 martyrdom. 2 *fig (fastidio)* torment.
martirizar [4] *vtr* 1 to martyr. 2 *fig (fastidiar)* to torture, torment.
marxista *adj & nmf* Marxist.
marzo *nm* March.
mas *conj lit* but.
más I *adv* 1 *(adicional)* more; **no tengo m.**, I haven't got any more. 2 *(comparativo)* more; **es m. alta/inteligente que yo**, she's taller/more intelligent than me; **tengo más dinero que tú**, I've more money than you; **más gente de la que esperas**, more people than you're expecting; **m. de**, *(con numerales, cantidad)* more than, over. 3 *(superlativo)* most; **es el m. bonito/caro**, it's the prettiest/most expensive. 4 *exclam* so ..., what a ...; **¡qué casa m. bonita!**, what a lovely house! **¡está m. guapa!**, she looks so beautiful! 6 *(después de pron interr e indef)* else; **¿algo m.?**, anything else?; **no, nada m.**, no, nothing else; **¿quién m.?**, who else?; **nadie/alguien m.**, nobody/somebody else. 7 **cada día** *o* **vez m.**, more and more; **estar de m.**, to be unnecessary; **traje uno de m.**, I brought a spare one; **es m.**, what's more, furthermore; **lo m. posible**, as much as possible; **m. bien**, rather; **m. o menos**, more or less; **m. aún**, even more; **¿qué m. da?**, what's the difference?; **todo lo m.**, at the most. 8 **por m.** + *(adj/adv +)* **que** + *subj*, however (much), no matter how (much); **por m. fuerte que sea**, however strong he may be; **por m. que grites no te oirá nadie**, no matter how much you shout nobody will hear you.
II *nm inv* **los/las m.**, the majority, most people; **sus m. y sus menos**, its pros and cons.
III *prep Mat* plus; **dos m. dos**, two plus *o* and two.
masa *nf* 1 mass. 2 *(de cosas)* bulk, volume; **m. salarial**, total wage bill. 3 *(gente)* mass; **en m.**, *en masse*; **medios de comunicación de masas**, mass media. 4 *Culin* dough. 5 *Constr* mortar.
masacrar *vtr* to massacre.
masacre *nf* massacre.
masaje *nm* massage; **dar masaje(s) (a)**, to massage.
masajista *nmf (hombre)* masseur; *(mujer)* masseuse.
mascar [1] *vtr & vi* to chew, masticate.
máscara *nf* mask; **m. de gas**, gas mask; **traje de m.**, fancy dress.
mascarilla *nf* 1 mask; **m. de oxígeno**, oxygen mask. 2 *Med* face mask. 3 *(cosmética)* face pack.
mascota *nf* mascot.
masculino,-a *adj* 1 *Zool Bot* male. 2 *(de hombre)* male, manly; **una voz masculina**, a manly voice. 3 *(para hombre)*

men's; **ropa masculina,** men's clothes, menswear. **4** *Ling* masculine.

mascullar *vtr* to mumble.

masificación *nf* overcrowding.

masificado,-a *adj* overcrowded.

masilla *nf* putty.

masivo,-a *adj* massive.

masón *nm* freemason, mason.

masonería *nf* freemasonry, masonry.

masoquista I *adj* masochistic. **II** *nmf* masochist.

máster *nm* master's degree.

masticar |1| *vt* to chew.

mástil *nm* **1** (*asta*) mast, pole. **2** *Náut* mast. **3** (*de guitarra*) neck.

mastín *nm* mastiff.

masturbación *nf* masturbation.

masturbar *vtr,* **masturbarse** *vr* to masturbate.

mata *nf* **1** (*matorral*) bush, shrub; **m. de pelo,** head of hair. **2** (*ramita*) sprig.

matadero *nm* slaughterhouse, abattoir.

matador *nm* matador, bullfighter.

matadura *nf* sore.

matamoscas *nm inv* (*pala*) fly swat.

matanza *nf* slaughter.

matar *vtr* **1** to kill; *fam* **m. el hambre/el tiempo,** to kill one's hunger/the time; *fam* **que me maten si ...,** I'll be damned if **....** **2** (*cigarro, bebida*) to finish off. **3** (*sello*) to frank.

matasellos *nm inv* postmark.

matasuegras *nm inv* party blower.

mate[1] *adj* (*sin brillo*) matt.

mate[2] *nm* *Ajedrez* mate; **jaque m.,** checkmate.

matemática *nf,* **matemáticas** *nfpl* mathematics *sing.*

matemático,-a I *adj* mathematical. **II** *nm,f* mathematician.

materia *nf* **1** matter; **m. prima,** raw material. **2** (*tema*) matter, question; **índice de materias,** table of contents. **3** *Educ* (*asignatura*) subject.

material I *adj* material, physical; **daños materiales,** damage to property. **II** *nm* **1** material; **m. escolar/de construcción,** teaching/building material *o* materials *pl.* **2** (*equipo*) equipment; **m. de oficina,** office equipment. ◆**materialmente** *adv* physically.

materialista *adj & nmf* materialist.

maternal *adj* maternal, motherly.

maternidad *nf* maternity, motherhood.

materno,-a *adj* maternal; **abuelo m.,** maternal grandfather; **lengua materna,** native *o* mother tongue.

mates *nfpl fam* maths *sing,* US math *sing.*

matinal *adj* morning; **televisión m.,** breakfast television.

matiz *nm* **1** (*de color*) shade. **2** (*de palabra*) shade of meaning, nuance; **un m. irónico,** a touch of irony.

matización *nf* hacer una m., to add a

rider.

matizar |1| *vtr* **1** *fig* (*precisar*) to be more precise *o* explicit about. **2** *Arte* to blend, harmonize. **3** *fig* (*palabras, discurso*) to tinge; (*voz*) to vary, modulate.

matón,-ona *nm,f fam* thug, bully.

matorral *nm* brushwood, thicket.

matraca *nf* (*ruido*) rattle; *fam* **dar la m. a algn,** to pester *o* bother sb.

matrero,-a *nm,f Am* (*bandolero*) bandit, brigand.

matriarcado *nm* matriarchy.

matrícula *nf* **1** registration; **derechos de m.,** registration fee; **m. de honor,** distinction; **plazo de m.,** registration period. **2** *Aut* (*número*) registration number; (*placa*) number *o* US license plate.

matriculación *nf* registration.

matricular *vtr,* **matricularse** *vr* to register.

matrimonial *adj* matrimonial; **agencia m.,** marriage bureau; **enlace m.,** wedding; **vida m.,** married life.

matrimonio *nm* **1** marriage; **m. civil/religioso,** registry office/church wedding; **contraer m.,** to marry; **cama de m.,** double bed. **2** (*pareja casada*) married couple; **el m. y los niños,** the couple and their children; **el m. Romero,** Mr and Mrs Romero, the Romeros.

matriz *nf* **1** *Anat* womb, uterus. **2** *Mat* matrix. **3** (*de documento*) (*original*) original, master copy. **4** *Téc* mould, *US* mold. **5** **casa m.,** parent company.

matrona *nf* midwife.

matutino,-a *adj* morning; **prensa matutina,** morning papers.

maullar |16| *vi* to miaow.

maullido *nm* miaowing, miaow.

maxilar *nm* jaw, jawbone.

máxima *nf* **1** *Meteor* maximum temperature. **2** (*aforismo*) maxim.

máxime *adv* especially, all the more so.

máximo,-a I *adj* maximum, highest; **la máxima puntuación,** the highest score. **II** *nm* maximum; **al m.,** to the utmost; **como m.,** (*como mucho*) at the most; (*lo más tarde*) at the latest.

mayo *nm* May.

mayonesa *nf* mayonnaise.

mayor I *adj* **1** (*comparativo*) (*tamaño*) larger, bigger (**que,** than); (*edad*) older, elder; **m. que yo,** older than me. **2** (*superlativo*) (*tamaño*) largest, biggest; (*edad*) oldest, eldest; **la m. parte,** the majority; **la m. parte de las veces,** most often. **3** (*adulto*) grown-up; **ser m. de edad,** to be of age. **4** (*maduro*) elderly, mature. **5** (*principal*) major, main; *Educ* **colegio m.,** hall of residence. **6** *Mús* major. **7** *Com* **al por m.,** wholesale; *fig* (*en abundancia*) by the score, galore. **II** *nm* **1** *Mil* major. **2** **mayores,** (*adultos*) grown-ups, adults.

mayordomo *nm* butler.

mayoría *nf* majority; **en su m.**, in the main; **la m. de los niños**, most children; **m. absoluta/relativa**, absolute/relative majority; **m. de edad**, majority.

mayorista I *adj* wholesale. II *nmf* wholesaler; **precios de m.**, wholesale prices.

mayoritario,-a *adj* majority; **un gobierno m.**, a majority government.

mayúscula *nf* capital letter.

mayúsculo,-a *adj* 1 *Ling (letra)* capital. 2 *(error)* very big, enormous.

mazacote *nm* 1 *Culin* solid mass, stodge. 2 *(mezcla confusa)* hotch-potch.

mazapán *nm* marzipan.

mazmorra *nf* dungeon.

mazo *nm* mallet.

mazorca *nf Agr* cob.

me *pron pers* 1 *(objeto directo)* me; **no me mires**, don't look at me. 2 *(objeto indirecto)* me, to me, for me; **¿me das un caramelo?**, will you give me a sweet?; **me lo dio**, he gave it to me; **me es difícil hacerlo**, it is difficult for me to do it. 3 *(pron reflexivo)* myself; **me he cortado**, I've cut myself; **me voy/muero**, *(no se traduce)* I'm off/dying.

meada *nf vulg* piss; **echar una m.**, to have a piss.

meadero *nm vulg* bog.

meandro *nm* meander.

mear I *vi vulg* to (have a) piss. II **mearse** *vr* to wet oneself; *fig* **m. de risa**, to piss oneself (laughing).

MEC *nm abr de* **Ministerio de Educación y Ciencia**, Department of Education and Science.

mecachis *fam interj* darn it!, damn it!

mecánica *nf* 1 *(ciencia)* mechanics *sing*. 2 *(mecanismo)* mechanism, works *pl*.

mecánico,-a I *adj* mechanical. II *nm,f* mechanic.

mecanismo *nm* mechanism.

mecanizar |4| *vtr* to mechanize.

mecanografía *nf* typewriting, typing.

mecanografiar [29] *vtr* to type.

mecanógrafo,-a *nm,f* typist.

mecedora *nf* rocking chair.

mecenas *nmf inv* patron.

mecer |2| I *vtr* to rock. II **mecerse** *vr* to swing, rock.

mecha *nf* 1 *(de vela)* wick. 2 *Mil Min* fuse; *fam* **aguantar m.**, to grin and bear it. 3 *(de pelo)* streak; **hacerse mechas**, to have one's hair streaked.

mechar *vtr (carne)* to lard.

mechero,-a *nm (cigarette)* lighter.

mechón *nm* 1 *(de pelo)* lock. 2 *(de lana)* tuft.

medalla I *nf* medal. II *nmf Dep (campeón)* medallist, *US* medalist.

medallón *nm* medallion.

media *nf* 1 stocking; *Am (calcetín)* sock. 2

(promedio) average; *Mat* mean; **m. aritmética/geométrica**, arithmetic/geometric mean. 3 **a medias**, *(incompleto)* unfinished; *(entre dos)* half and half; **ir a medias**, to go halves.

mediación *nf* mediation, intervention; **por m. de un amigo**, through a friend.

mediado,-a *adj* half-full, half-empty; **a mediados de mes/semana**, about the middle of the month/week.

mediador,-a *nm,f* mediator.

medialuna *nf* 1 *(símbolo musulmán)* crescent. 2 *Am Culin (pasta)* croissant.

mediano,-a *adj* 1 middling, average. 2 *(tamaño)* medium-sized.

medianoche *nf* midnight.

mediante *prep* by means of, with the help of, using; **Dios m.**, God willing.

mediar |12| *vi* 1 *(intervenir)* to mediate, intervene; **m. en favor de o por algn**, to intercede on behalf of sb. 2 *(tiempo)* to pass; **mediaron tres semanas**, three weeks passed.

mediático,-a *adj* media.

medicación *nf* medication, medical treatment.

medicamento *nm* medicine, medicament.

medicina *nf* medicine; **estudiante de m.**, medical student, medic.

médico,-a I *nm,f* doctor; **m. de cabecera**, family doctor, general practitioner, GP. II *adj* medical.

medida *nf* 1 measure; **a (la) m.**, *(ropa)* made-to-measure; **a m. que avanzaba**, as he advanced; **en gran m.**, to a great extent. 2 *(dimensión)* measurement. 3 *(disposición)* measure; **adoptar o tomar medidas**, to take steps; **m. represiva**, deterrent.

medieval *adj* medieval.

medievo *nm* Middle Ages *pl*.

medio,-a I *adj* 1 half; **a m. camino**, halfway; **m. kilo**, half a kilo; **una hora y media**, one and a half hours, an hour and a half. 2 *(intermedio)* middle; **a media mañana/tarde**, in the middle of the morning/afternoon; **clase media**, middle class; **punto m.**, middle ground. 3 *(normal)* average; **salario m.**, average wage. II *adv* half; **está m. muerta**, she is half dead. III *nm* 1 *(mitad)* half. 2 *(centro)* middle; **en m. (de)**, *(en el centro)* in the middle (of); *(entre dos)* in between. 3 **medios de transporte**, means of transport; **por m. de ...**, by means of ...; **medios económicos**, means; **medios de comunicación**, (mass) media. 4 **m. ambiente**, environment. 5 *Dep (jugador)* halfback.

medioambiental *adj* environmental.

medioambientalista *nmf* environmentalist.

mediocre *adj* mediocre.

mediocridad *nf* mediocrity.

mediodía *nm* 1 *(hora exacta)* midday,

noon. 2 (*período aproximado*) early afternoon, lunchtime. 3 (*sur*) south.

medir |6| I *vtr* 1 (*distancia, superficie, temperatura*) to measure. 2 (*moderar*) to weigh; **mide tus palabras**, weigh your words. II *vi* to measure, be; **¿cuánto mides?**, how tall are you?; **mide dos metros**, he is two metres tall; **mide dos metros de alto/ancho/largo**, it is two metres high/wide/long.

meditar *vtr & vi* to meditate, ponder; **m. sobre algo**, to ponder over sth.

mediterráneo,-a I *adj* Mediterranean. II *nm* **el M.**, the Mediterranean.

medrar *vi* to climb the social ladder.

medroso,-a *adj* 1 (*temeroso*) fearful, fainthearted. 2 (*que causa miedo*) frightening.

médula *nf* 1 marrow; **m. ósea**, bone marrow. 2 *fig* (*lo más profundo*) marrow, pith; **hasta la m.**, to the marrow.

medusa *nf* jellyfish.

megafonía *nf* public-address system, PA system.

megáfono *nm* megaphone.

megalito *nm* megalith.

megalómano,-a *adj* megalomaniac.

mejicano,-a *adj & nm,f* Mexican.

Méjico *n* Mexico; **ciudad de M.**, Mexico City; **Nuevo M.**, New Mexico.

mejilla *nf* cheek.

mejillón *nm* mussel.

mejor I *adj* 1 (*comparativo*) better (**que**, than); **el m. de los dos**, the better of the two; **es m. no decírselo**, it's better not to tell her; **es m. que vayas**, you'd better go. 2 (*superlativo*) best; **el m. de los tres**, the best of the three; **tu m. amiga**, your best friend; **lo m.**, the best thing. II *adv* 1 (*comparativo*) better (**que**, than); **cada vez m.**, better and better; **ella conduce m.**, she drives better; **m. dicho**, or rather; **¡mucho o tanto m.!**, so much the better! 2 (*superlativo*) best; **es el que m. canta**, he is the one who sings the best; **a lo m.**, (*quizás*) perhaps; (*ojalá*) hopefully.

mejora *nf* improvement.

mejorar I *vtr* to improve; **m. la red vial**, to improve the road system; **m. una marca o un récord**, to break a record. II *vi* to improve, get better. III **mejorarse** *vr* to get better; **¡que te mejores!**, get well soon!

mejoría *nf* improvement.

melancolía *nf* melancholy.

melancólico,-a *adj* melancholic, melancholy.

melé *nf Dep* scrum.

melena *nf* (head of) hair; (*de león*) mane.

Melilla *n* Melilla.

melindroso,-a I *adj* affected, fussy, finicky. II *nm,f* affected o finicky person.

mella *nf* 1 (*hendedura*) nick, notch; (*en plato, taza etc*) chip. 2 (*en dentadura*) gap.

3 *fig* impression; **hacer m. en algn**, to make an impression on sb.

mellado,-a *adj* (*sin dientes*) gap-toothed.

mellizo,-a *adj & nm,f* twin.

melocotón *nm* peach.

melodía *nf* melody, tune.

melodrama *nm* melodrama.

melón *nm* 1 (*fruto*) melon. 2 *fam* (*tonto*) ninny. 3 *vulg* **melones**, (*tetas*) boobs.

melopea *nf fam* **coger o agarrar/llevar una m.**, to get/be drunk o pissed.

meloso,-a *adj* sweet, honeyed.

membrana *nf* membrane.

membrete *nm* letterhead.

membrillo *nm* 1 *Bot* quince; (*árbol*) quince tree; (*dulce*) quince preserve o jelly. 2 *fam* (*tonto*) dimwit.

memo,-a *fam* I *adj* silly, stupid. II *nm,f* nincompoop, ninny.

memorable *adj* memorable.

memorándum *nm* (*pl* **memorándums**) memorandum.

memoria *nf* 1 memory; **aprender/saber algo de m.**, to learn/know sth by heart; **irse de la m.**, to slip one's mind. 2 (*informe*) report, statement; **m. anual**, annual report. 3 (*recuerdo*) memory, recollection. 4 **memorias**, (*biografía*) memoirs.

memorístico *adj* acquired by memory.

memorizar |4| *vtr* to memorize.

menaje *nm* furniture and furnishing *pl*; **m. de cocina**, kitchen equipment o utensils.

mención *nf* mention; **m. honorífica**, honourable mention.

mencionar *vtr* to mention.

mendicidad *nf* begging.

mendigar |7| *vtr & vi* to beg.

mendigo,-a *nm,f* beggar.

mendrugo *nm* 1 crust o chunk (of stale bread). 2 (*tonto*) dimwit.

menear I *vtr* to shake, move; (*cola*) to wag, waggle; *fam* (*culo*) to wiggle. II **menearse** *vr* to move, shake; *fam* **una tormenta de no te menees**, a hell of a storm; *vulg* **meneársela**, to wank.

meneo *nm* shake; (*de cola*) wag, waggle; (*de culo*) wiggle.

menester *nm* 1 **es m.**, it is necessary. 2 **menesteres**, (*deberes*) jobs.

menestra *nf* vegetable stew.

mengano,-a *nm,f fam* so-and-so, what's-his o her-name.

menguante *adj* waning, on the wane; **cuarto m.**, last quarter.

menguar |22| I *vtr* 1 to diminish, reduce. 2 (*en labor de punto*) to decrease. II *vi* 1 to diminish, decrease. 2 (*la luna*) to wane.

meñique *adj & nm* (**dedo**) **m.**, little finger.

menopausia *nf Med* menopause.

menor I *adj* 1 (*comparativo*) (*de tamaño*)

smaller (**que**, than); (*de edad*) younger (**que**, than); **mal m.**, the lesser of two evils; **el m. de los dos**, the smaller of the two; **ser m. de edad**, to be a minor o under age. **2** (*superlativo*) (*de tamaño*) smallest; (*de intensidad*) least, slightest; **al m. ruido**, at the slightest noise; (*de edad*) youngest; **el m. de los tres**, the youngest of the three; **es la m.**, she's the youngest child. **3** *Mús* minor. **4** *Com* **al por m.**, retail. II *nmf* minor; *Jur* **tribunal de menores**, juvenile court.

menos I *adj* **1** (*comparativo*) (*con singular*) less; (*con plural*) fewer; **m. dinero/leche/tiempo que**, less money/milk/time than; **m. libros/pisos que**, fewer books/flats than; (*con cláusula*) **tiene m. años de lo que parece**, he's younger than he looks. **2** (*superlativo*) **fui el que perdí m. dinero**, I lost the least money. II *adv* **1 m. de**, (*con singular*) less than; **m. de media hora**, less than a half hour; (*con plural*) fewer than, less than. **2** (*superlativo*) (*con singular*) least; (*con plural*) the fewest; **el m. inteligente de la clase**, the least intelligent boy in the class; **ayer fue cuando vinieron m. personas**, yesterday was when the fewest people came; (*con cantidad*) the least. III (*locuciones*) **a m. que + *subj***, unless; **al o por lo m.** at least; **echar a algn de m.**, to miss sb; **eso es lo de m.**, that's the least of it; **¡m. mal!**, just as well!; **nada m. que**, no less o no fewer than; **ni mucho m.**, far from it. IV *prep* **1** but, except; **todo m. eso**, anything but that. **2** *Mat* minus; **tres m. uno**, three minus one.

menoscabar *vtr* **1** (*perjudicar*) to damage. **2** *fig* (*desacreditar*) to discredit.

menoscabo *nm* harm, damage; **ir en m. de algo**, to be to the detriment of sth.

menospreciar [12] *vtr* to scorn, disdain.

menosprecio *nm* contempt, scorn, disdain.

mensáfono *nm* ansaphone.

mensaje *nm* message.

mensajero,-a *nm,f* messenger, courier.

menstruación *nf* menstruation.

mensual *adj* monthly; **dos visitas mensuales**, two visits a month.

mensualidad *nf* (*pago*) monthly payment; (*sueldo*) monthly salary o wage.

menta *nf* **1** *Bot* mint. **2** (*licor*) crème de menthe.

mental *adj* mental.

mentalidad *nf* mentality; **de m. abierta/cerrada**, open-/narrow-minded.

mentalizar I *vtr* (*concienciar*) to make aware. II **mentalizarse** *vr* **1** (*concienciarse*) to become aware. **2** (*hacerse a la idea*) to come to terms (**a**, with).

mentar [1] *vtr* to mention, name.

mente *nf* mind; **se me quedó la m. en blanco**, my mind went blank; **m.**

abierta/tolerante/cerrada, open/broad/closed mind.

mentecato,-a *nm,f* fool, idiot.

mentir [5] *vi* to lie, tell lies.

mentira *nf* lie; **aunque parezca m.**, strange as it may seem; **parece m.**, it is unbelievable.

mentiroso,-a I *adj* lying. II *nm,f* liar.

mentís *nm* denial.

mentón *nm* *Anat* chin.

menú *nm* menu.

menudillos *nmpl* giblets.

menudo,-a I *adj* minute, tiny; (*irónico*) tremendous; **la gente menuda**, the little ones *pl*; **¡m. lío/susto!**, what a mess/fright! II *adv* **a m.**, often.

meollo *nm* **1** *fig* (*quid*) essence. **2** (*miga*) crumb.

mercado *nm* market; **M. Común**, Common Market; **m. negro**, black market; **sacar algo al m.**, to put sth on the market.

mercadotecnia *nf* marketing.

mercancía *nf* commodity, goods *pl*.

mercante *adj* merchant; **barco/marina m.**, merchant ship/navy.

mercantil *adj* mercantile, commercial.

merced *nf fml* favour, *US* favor, grace; **a m. de**, at the mercy of.

mercenario,-a *adj & nm,f* mercenary.

mercería *nf* haberdasher's (shop), *US* notions store.

mercurio *nm* **1** *Quím* mercury, quicksilver. **2** **M.**, Mercury.

merecer [33] I *vtr* **1** to deserve. **2** (*uso impers*) **no merece la pena hacerlo**, it's not worth while doing it. II **merecerse** *vr* to deserve.

merecido,-a I *adj* deserved; **ella lo tiene m.**, (*recompensa*) she deserves it; (*castigo*) it serves her right. II *nm* just deserts *pl*.

merendar [1] I *vtr* to have as an afternoon snack, have for tea. II *vi* to have an afternoon snack, have tea.

merendero *nm* (*establecimiento*) tearoom, snack bar; (*en el campo*) picnic spot.

merengue *nm* *Culin* meringue.

merezco *indic pres* → **merecer**.

meridiano,-a *nm* meridian.

meridional I *adj* southern. II *nmf* southerner.

merienda *nf* afternoon snack, tea.

mérito *nm* merit, worth; **hacer méritos para algo**, to strive to deserve sth.

merluza *nf* (*pez*) hake.

merma *nf* decrease, reduction.

mermar I *vtr* to cause to decrease o diminish. II *vi* to decrease, diminish. III **mermarse** *vr* to decrease, diminish.

mermelada *nf* **1** jam; **m. de fresa**, strawberry jam. **2** (*de agrios*) marmalade; **m. de naranja**, orange marmalade.

mero,-a *adj* mere, pure; **por el m. hecho de**, through the mere fact of.

merodear *vi* to prowl.

mes *nm* 1 month; **el m. pasado/que viene,** last/next month. 2 *(cobro)* monthly salary *o* wages *pl*; *(pago)* monthly payment. 3 *fam (menstruación)* period.

mesa *nf* 1 table; **poner/recoger la m.,** to set/clear the table; *(de despacho etc)* desk; **m. redonda,** round table. 2 *(junta directiva)* board, executive; **el presidente de la m.,** the chairman; **m. electoral,** electoral college.

meseta *nf* plateau, tableland, meseta; **la M.,** the plateau of Castile.

mesilla *nf* **m. de noche,** bedside table.

mesón *nm* old-style tavern.

mesonero,-a *nm,f* innkeeper.

mestizo,-a *adj & nm,f* half-breed, half-caste, mestizo.

mesura *nf fml* moderation, restraint.

meta *nf* 1 *(objetivo)* goal, aim, objective. 2 *(de carrera)* finish, finishing line. 3 *Ftb (portería)* goal.

metafísica *nf* metaphysics.

metáfora *nf* metaphor.

metal *nm* 1 metal; **metales preciosos,** precious metals. 2 *(timbre de la voz)* timbre. 3 *Mús* brass.

metálico,-a *adj* 1 metallic. II *nm* cash; **pagar en m.,** to pay (in) cash.

metalizado-a *adj* metallic.

metalúrgico,-a I *adj* metallurgical. II *nm,f* metallurgist.

metedura *nf fam* **m. de pata,** blunder.

meteorito *nm* meteorite.

meteorología *nf* meteorology.

meteorológico,-a *adj* meteorological; **parte m.,** weather report.

meter I *vtr* 1 *(poner)* to put (en, in); *fig* **m. las narices en algo,** to poke one's nose into sth. 2 *(comprometer)* to involve (en, in), to get mixed up (en, in). 3 *fam fig (dar)* to give; **m. un rollo,** to go on and on; **m. prisa a algn,** to hurry sb up. 4 *(hacer)* to make; **m. ruido,** to make a noise. II **meterse** *vr* 1 *(entrar)* to go *o* come in, get into. 2 *(estar)* to be; **¿dónde te habías metido?,** where have you been (all this time)? 3 *(entrometerse)* to meddle. 4 **m. con algn,** *(en broma)* to get at sb.

meticuloso,-a *adj* meticulous.

metido,-a *adj fam* **estar muy m. en algo,** to be deeply involved in sth; **m. en años,** getting on (in years).

metódico,-a *adj* methodical.

método *nm* 1 method. 2 *Educ* course.

metodología *nf* methodology.

metomentodo *nmf inv fam* busybody.

metralleta *nf* sub machine-gun.

métrico,-a *adj* metric; **sistema m.,** metric system.

metro *nm* 1 *(medida)* metre, *US* meter. 2 *(tren)* underground, tube, *US* subway.

metrópoli *nf* metropolis.

metropolitano,-a I *adj* metropolitan. II

nm fml underground, tube, *US* subway.

mexicano,-a *adj & nm,f* Mexican.

México *nm* Mexico.

mezcla *nf* 1 *(acción)* mixing, blending; *Rad Cin* mixing. 2 *(producto)* mixture, blend.

mezclar I *vtr* 1 *(dos o más cosas)* to mix, blend. 2 *(desordenar)* to mix up. 3 *(involucrar)* to involve, mix up. II **mezclarse** *vr* 1 *(cosas)* to get mixed up; *(gente)* to mingle. 2 *(relacionarse)* to get involved (con, with).

mezcolanza *nf fml* strange mixture, hotch-potch.

mezquino,-a *adj* 1 *(persona)* mean, stingy. 2 *(sueldo)* miserable.

mezquita *nf* mosque.

m/g *abr de* **miligramo,** milligramme, milligram, mg.

mi¹ *adj* my; **mi casa/trabajo,** my house/job; **mis cosas/libros,** my things/books.

mi² *nm Mús* E; **mi menor,** E minor.

mí *pron pers* me; **a mí me dio tres,** he gave me three; **compra otro para mí,** buy one for me too; **por mí mismo,** just by myself.

mía *adj & pron pos f* → **mío.**

miaja *nf* crumb; *fig* bit.

michelín *nm fam* spare tyre.

mico,-a *nm* 1 *Zool* long-tailed monkey. 2 *fam (pequeñajo)* little kid.

micra *nf (medida)* micron.

micro *nm fam* mike, microphone.

microbio *nm* microbe.

microbús *nm* minibus.

microchip *nm (pl microchips) Inform* microchip.

microficha *nf* microfiche.

micrófono *nm* microphone.

microonda *nf* **un (horno) microondas,** a microwave (oven).

microscopio *nm* microscope.

miedica *nmf fam* scaredy-cat.

miedo *nm (pavor)* fear; *(temor)* aprehension; **una película de m.,** a horror film; **tener m. de algo/algn,** to be afraid of sth/sb; *fam* **lo pasamos de m.,** we had a fantastic time; **un calor de m.,** sizzling heat.

miedoso,-a *adj* fearful.

miel *nf* honey; **luna de m.,** honeymoon.

miembro *nm* 1 *(socio)* member; **estado m.,** member state. 2 *Anat* limb; **m. viril,** penis.

mientras I *conj* 1 *(al mismo tiempo que)* while. 2 *(durante el tiempo que)* when, while; **m. viví en Barcelona,** when I lived in Barcelona. 3 **m. que,** *(por el contrario)* whereas. 4 *fam (cuanto más que)* **más/menos ...,** the more/less ... II *adv* **m. (tanto),** meanwhile, in the meantime.

miércoles *nm inv* Wednesday; **M. de Ceniza,** Ash Wednesday.

mierda *nf vulg* 1 shit; **ese libro es una**

m., that book is crap; ¡vete a la m.!, piss off! 2 *fig (porquería)* dirt, filth. 3 *(borrachera)* bender.

miga *nf (de pan etc)* crumb; *fig* hacer buenas migas con algn, to get on well with sb.

migaja *nf* 1 *(de pan)* crumb. 2 *fig* bit, scrap. 3 migajas, *(del pan)* crumbs; *fig* leftovers.

migraña *nf Med* migraine.

mil *adj & nm* thousand; **m. pesetas**, a *o* one thousand pesetas.

milagro *nm* miracle.

milagroso,-a *adj* miraculous.

milano *nm Orn* kite; **m. real**, red kite.

milenario,-a I *adj* millenarian, millenial. II *nm* millenium.

milenio *nm* millenium.

milésimo,-a *adj & nm,f* thousandth.

mili *nf fam* military *o* national service; **hacer la m.**, to do one's military service.

milicia *nf (ejército)* militia; *(servicio militar)* military service.

milímetro *nm* millimetre, *US* millimeter.

militar I *adj* military. II *nm* military man, soldier. III *vi Pol (en un partido)* to be a member.

milla *nf* mile.

millar *nm* thousand.

millón *nm* million.

millonario,-a *adj & nm,f* millionaire.

mimar *vtr* to spoil, pamper.

mimbre *nm* wicker.

mimetismo *nm* mimicry.

mímica *nf* mimicry.

mimo *nm* 1 *(delicadeza)* care. 2 *fig (zalamería)* pampering. 3 *Teat (actor)* mime.

mina *nf* 1 mine; **ingeniero de minas**, mining engineer. 2 *(explosivo)* mine; **campo de minas**, minefield. 3 *(de lápiz)* lead; **lápiz de m.**, propelling pencil. 4 *fig (ganga)* gold mine.

minar *vtr* 1 *Mil Min* to mine. 2 *fig (desgastar)* to undermine.

mineral I *adj* mineral. II *nm* ore.

minería *nf* 1 *Min* mining. 2 *Ind* mining industry.

minero,-a I *nm,f* miner. II *adj* mining.

miniatura *nf* miniature.

minifalda *nf* miniskirt.

minifundio *nm* smallholding.

mínima *nf* minimum temperature.

minimizar *vtr* to minimize.

mínimo,-a I *adj* 1 *(muy pequeño)* minute, tiny. 2 *Mat Téc* minimum, lowest; **m. común múltiplo**, lowest common denominator. II *nm* minimum; **como m.**, at least; **ni lo más m.**, not in the least.

minipímer® *nm o f* liquidizer, blender.

ministerio *nm* 1 *Pol* ministry, *US* department. 2 *Rel* ministry.

ministro,-a *nm,f* 1 *Pol* minister; **primer m.**, Prime Minister. 2 *Rel* minister.

minoría *nf* minority; *Jur* **m. de edad,**

minority.

minoritario,-a *adj* minority.

minucioso,-a *adj* 1 *(persona)* meticulous. 2 *(informe, trabajo etc)* minute, detailed.

minúsculo,-a *adj* miniscule, minute; **letra minúscula**, lower-case *o* small letter.

minusválido,-a I *adj* handicapped, disabled. II *nm,f* handicapped person, disabled person.

minuta *nf* 1 *(cuenta)* lawyer's bill. 2 *(menú)* menu.

minutero *nm* minute hand.

minuto *nm* minute.

mío,-a I *adj pos* of mine; **un amigo m.**, a friend of mine; **no es asunto m.**, it is none of my business. II *pron pos* mine; **ese libro es m.**, that book is mine; **lo m. es el tenis**, tennis is my strong point; *fam* **los míos**, my people *o* folks.

miope *nmf* myopic *o* short-sighted person.

miopía *nf* myopia, short-sightedness.

mira *nf* 1 *Téc* sight. 2 *fig (objetivo)* aim, target; **con miras a**, with a view to; **amplitud de miras**, broad-mindedness.

mirada *nf* look; **lanzar** *o* **echar una m.**, to glance at *o* over; **levantar la m.**, to raise one's eyes; **m. fija**, stare.

mirador *nm* 1 *(lugar con vista)* viewpoint. 2 *(balcón)* bay window, windowed balcony.

mirar *vtr* 1 to look at. 2 *(observar)* to watch. 3 **m. por algn/algo**, *(cuidar)* to look after sb/sth. 4 *(procurar)* to see; **mira que no le pase nada**, see that nothing happens to him. 5 *(dar a)* to look, face; **la casa mira al sur**, the house faces south.

mirilla *nf* spyhole, peephole.

mirlo *nm* blackbird.

misa *nf* mass.

misántropo,-a I *adj* misanthropic. II *nm,f* misanthrope, misanthropist.

miserable I *adj* 1 *(mezquino) (persona)* despicable; *(sueldo etc)* miserable. 2 *(pobre)* wretched, poor; **una vida m.**, a wretched life. II *nmf* 1 *(mezquino)* miser. 2 *(canalla)* wretch.

miseria *nf* 1 *(pobreza extrema)* extreme poverty. 2 *(insignificancia)* pittance; **ganar una m.**, to earn next to nothing. 3 *(tacañería)* miserliness, meanness.

misericordia *nf* mercy, compassion.

mísero,-a *adj* miserable, wretched.

misil *nm* missile; **m. tierra-aire**, surface-to-air missile.

misión *nf* mission; **m. cumplida**, mission accomplished.

misionero,-a *nm,f* missionary.

mismísimo,-a *adj superl fam* 1 *(preciso)* very; **en el m. centro**, right in the centre. 2 *(en persona)* in person.

mismo,-a I *adj* 1 same. 2 *(uso enfático)* yo m., I myself; **aquí m.**, right here. II *pron* same; **es el m. de ayer**, it's the same one as yesterday; **estamos en las mismas,** we're back to square one; **lo m.,** the same (thing); **dar** *o* **ser lo m.,** to make no difference; **por eso m.,** that is why; **por uno** *o* **sí m.,** by oneself. **III** *adv* **1** *(por ejemplo)* for instance; **que venga algn, Juan m.,** ask one of them to come, Juan, for instance. **2 así m.,** likewise.

misógino,-a I *adj* misogynous. **II** *nm,f* misogynist.

miss *nf* beauty queen.

míster *nm Ftb* coach, trainer.

misterio *nm* mystery.

misterioso,-a *adj* mysterious.

MIT *nm abr de* **Ministerio de Información y Turismo.**

mitad *nf* **1** half; **a m. de camino,** halfway there; **a m. de precio,** half price. **2** *(centro)* middle; **en la m. del primer acto,** half way through the first act; *fam* **eso me parte por la m.,** that really screws things up for me.

mítico,-a *adj* mythical.

mitigar [7] *vtr fml* to mitigate, palliate; *(luz)* to reduce.

mitin *nm Pol* meeting, rally.

mito *nm* myth.

mitología *nf* mythology.

mitote *nm Am (bulla)* uproar.

mixto *adj* mixed.

mobiliario *nm* furniture.

moca *nm* mocha, coffee.

mochila *nf* rucksack, backpack.

mochuelo *nm Zool* little owl.

moción *nf* motion; **m. de censura,** vote of censure.

moco *nm* snot; **sonarse los mocos,** to blow one's nose.

mocoso,-a *nm,f fam* brat.

moda *nf* **1** fashion; **a la m., de m.,** in fashion; **pasado de m.,** old-fashioned. **2** *(furor pasajero)* craze.

modales *nmpl* manners.

modalidad *nf* form, category; *Com* **m. de pago,** method of payment; *Dep* **m. deportiva,** sport.

modelar *vtr* to model, shape.

modélico,-a *adj* model.

modelo I *adj inv & nm* model. **II** *nmf* (fashion) model; **desfile de modelos,** fashion show.

modem *nm Inform Tel* modem.

moderación *nf* moderation.

moderado,-a *adj* moderate; **un m. aumento de temperatura,** a mild increase in temperature.

moderador,-a *nm,f* chairperson; *(hombre)* chairman; *(mujer)* chairwoman.

moderar I *vtr* **1** to moderate; *(velocidad)* to reduce. **2** *(debate)* to chair. **II moderarse** *vr* to be moderate.

modernizar [4] *vtr*, **modernizarse** *vr* to modernize.

moderno,-a *adj* modern.

modestia *nf* modesty; **m. aparte,** without wishing to be immodest.

modesto,-a *adj* modest.

módico,-a *adj* moderate; **una módica suma,** a modest *o* small sum.

modificar [1] *vtr* to modify.

modismo *nm* idiom.

modisto,-a *nm,f* **1** *(diseñador)* fashion designer. **2** *(sastre) (hombre)* couturier; *(mujer)* couturière.

modo *nm* **1** *(manera)* way, manner; **m. de empleo,** instructions for use; → **manera.** **2 modos,** manners. **3** *Ling* mood.

modorra *nf (somnolencia)* drowsiness.

modoso,-a *adj* **1** *(educado)* well-behaved. **2** *(recatado)* modest.

modulación *nf* modulation.

modular *vtr* to modulate.

módulo *nm* module.

mofa *nf* mockery; **en tono de m.,** in a gibing tone.

mofarse *vr* to laugh (de, at), make fun (de, of).

moflete *nm* chubby cheek.

mogollón *nm arg* **1 m. de,** loads of; **me gusta un m.,** I like it loads. **2** *(confusión)* commotion; *(ruido)* racket.

moho *nm* **1** *Bot* mould, *US* mold. **2** *(de metales)* rust.

mohoso,-a *adj* **1** mouldy, *US* moldy. **2** *(oxidado)* rusty.

mojado,-a *adj (empapado)* wet; *(húmedo)* damp.

mojar I *vtr* **1** to wet; *(humedecer)* to damp; **m. pan en la leche,** to dip *o* dunk bread in one's milk. **2** *arg* **mojarla** to have it off. **II mojarse** *vr* to get wet.

mojón *nm* **1 m. kilométrico,** ≈ milestone. **2** *arg (mierda)* shit.

moka *nm* mocha.

molar I *vi fam* **me mola cantidad,** I really love it, it's brilliant. **II** *adj & nm Anat* molar.

molde *nm* mould, *US* mold; **letras de m.,** printed letters; **pan de m.,** ≈ sliced bread.

moldeador *nm (del pelo)* wave.

moldear *vtr* to mould, *US* mold.

mole *nf* mass, bulk.

molécula *nf* molecule.

moler [4] *vtr* **1** *(triturar)* to grind. **2 m. a algn a golpes,** to beat sb up.

molestar I *vtr* **1** *(incomodar)* to disturb, bother. **2** *fml* to bother; **¿le molestaría esperar fuera?,** would you mind waiting outside? **3** *(causar malestar)* to hurt. **II molestarse** *vr* **1** *(tomarse la molestia)* to bother. **2** *(ofenderse)* to take offence *o US* offense, get upset.

molestia *nf* **1** bother; **no es ninguna m.,** it is no trouble at all; **perdone las molestias,** forgive the inconvenience. **2** *Med (dolor)* trouble, slight pain.

molesto,-a *adj* **1** *(irritante)* annoying,

upsetting. **2 estar m. con algn,** (enfadado) to be annoyed o upset with sb.

molinillo nm grinder.

molino nm mill; **m. de agua,** watermill; **m. de viento,** windmill.

mollera nf fam brains pl; **duro de m.,** (tonto) dense, thick; (testarudo) pigheaded.

molón,-ona adj arg flashy, showy.

momentáneo,-a adj momentary.

momento nm 1 (instante) moment; **al m.,** at once; **por momentos,** by the minute. 2 (periodo) time; **de m.,** for the time being; **en cualquier m.,** at any time.

momia nf mummy.

mona nf fam **coger una m.,** to get drunk; **dormir la m.,** to sleep it off.

monada nf fam **¡qué m.!,** how cute!

monaguillo nm Rel altar boy.

monarca nmf monarch.

monarquía nf monarchy.

monasterio nm Rel monastery.

monda nf 1 (piel) peel, skin. 2 fam **ser la m.,** (divertido) to be a scream.

mondadientes nm inv toothpick.

mondar I vtr to peel. II **mondarse** vr fam **m. (de risa),** to laugh one's head off.

moneda nf 1 (pieza) coin; **m. suelta,** small change; **acuñar m.,** to mint money. 2 Fin currency.

monedero nm purse.

monería nf → monada.

monetario,-a adj monetary.

mongol I adj Mongolian. II nmf (persona) Mongolian. II nm (idioma) Mongolian.

mongólico,-a Med I adj Down's syndrome. II nm,f **ser m.,** to have Down's syndrome.

monigote nm 1 pey (persona) wimp. 2 (dibujo) rough drawing o sketch (of a person).

monitor,-a nm,f monitor; (profesor) instructor.

monja nf nun.

monje nm monk.

mono,-a I nm 1 monkey. 2 (prenda) (de trabajo) boiler suit, overalls pl; (de vestir) catsuit. 3 arg (droga) cold turkey. II adj fam (bonito) pretty, cute.

monográfico,-a I adj monographic. II nm monograph.

monólogo nm monologue.

monopolio nm monopoly.

monopolizar [4] vtr to monopolize.

monótono,-a adj monotonous.

monserga nf fam drag.

monstruo nm 1 monster. 2 (genio) genius.

monstruoso,-a adj 1 (repugnante) monstrous. 2 (enorme) massive, huge.

monta nf fig **de poca m.,** of little importance.

montacargas nm inv service lift, US freight elevator.

montado-a I adj (nata) whipped. II nm sandwich.

montador,-a nm,f 1 (operario) fitter. 2 Cin TV film editor. 3 Teat producer.

montaje nm 1 Téc (instalación) fitting; (ensamblaje) assembling; **cadena de m.,** assembly line. 2 Cin editing and mounting. 3 Teat staging. 4 Fot montage. 5 fam (farsa) farce.

montaña nf mountain; **m. rusa,** big dipper.

montañismo nm mountaineering.

montañoso,-a adj mountainous.

montante nm 1 Fin amount. 2 (de puerta) post.

montar I vi 1 (subirse) to get in; (en bici, a caballo) to ride. 2 Fin (ascender) **m. a,** to amount to, come to. II vtr 1 (colocar) to put on. 2 (máquina etc) to assemble, (negocio) to set up, start. 3 Culin to whip. 4 Cin Fot (película) to edit, mount; (fotografía) to mount. 5 Teat (obra) to stage, mount. 6 Zool (cubrir) to mount. III **montarse** vr 1 (subirse) to get on; (en coche) to get in (en, to). 2 fam (armarse) to break out. 3 arg **montárselo bien,** to have things (nicely) worked out o set up.

monte nm 1 (montaña) mountain; (con nombre propio) mount; **de m.,** wild. 2 **el m.,** (zona) the hills.

montés,-a adj (animal) wild.

monto nm total.

montón nm heap, pile; **un m. de,** a load of; arg **me gusta un m.,** I really love it; fam **del m.,** run-of-the-mill, nothing special.

montura nf 1 (cabalgadura) mount. 2 (de gafas) frame.

monumento nm monument.

monzón nm monsoon.

moño nm (de pelo) bun.

MOPU nm abr de **Ministerio de Obras Públicas y Urbanismo,** ≈ Ministry of Public Works.

moquear vi to have a runny nose.

moqueta nf fitted carpet.

mora nf (zarzamora) blackberry.

morado,-a I adj purple; fam **pasarlas moradas,** to have a tough time; **ponerse m.,** to stuff oneself. II nm purple.

moral I adj moral. II nf 1 (ética) morals pl. 2 (ánimo) morale, spirits pl; **levantar la m. a algn,** raise sb's spirits.

moraleja nf moral.

moralista I adj moralistic. II nmf moralist.

moratoria nf moratorium.

morbo nm fam (interés malsano) morbid curiosity.

morboso,-a adj (malsano) morbid.

morcilla nf black pudding; fam **que le den m.,** he can drop dead for all I care.

mordaz adj biting.

mordaza nf gag.

mordedura nf bite.

morder [4] vtr to bite; **me ha mordido,** it

has bitten me; *fig* **m. el anzuelo**, to take
the bait.

mordida *nf Am (soborno)* bribe.

mordisco *nm* bite.

mordisquear *vtr* to nibble (at).

moreno,-a I *adj* 1 *(pelo)* dark-haired;
(piel) dark-skinned. 2 *(bronceado)* tanned;
ponerse m., to get a suntan; **pan/azúcar
m.**, brown bread/sugar. II *nm,f (persona)
(de pelo)* dark-haired person; *(de piel)*
dark-skinned person.

morera *nf Bot* white mulberry.

moretón *nm fam* bruise.

morfina *nf* morphine.

morfinómano,-a I *nm,f* morphine addict.
II *adj* addicted to morphine.

morgue *nf Am* morgue.

moribundo,-a *adj & nm,f* moribund.

morir [7] 1 *vi* 1 to die; **m. de frío/
hambre/cáncer**, to die of cold/hunger/
cancer; **m. de amor** *o* **pena**, to die from
a broken heart. II **morirse** *vr* to die; **m.
de hambre**, to starve to death; *fig* to be
starving; **m. de aburrimiento**, to be
bored to death; **m. de ganas (de hacer
algo)**, to be dying (to do sth); **m. de
risa**, to die laughing.

mormón,-ona *adj & nm,f* Mormon.

moro,-a *adj nm,f* 1 *Hist* Moor; *fam* **no
hay moros en la costa**, the coast is clear.
2 *pey (musulmán)* Muslim; *(árabe)* Arab.

morocho,-a *adj Am (moreno)* swarthy.

moroso,-a *nm,f* bad debtor.

morral *nm* 1 *(para pienso)* nosebag. 2 *Mil*
haversack; *(de cazador)* gamebag.

morralla *nf* 1 *(cosas sin valor)* rubbish,
junk. 2 *(chusma)* scum.

morrear *vtr*, **morrearse** *vr vulg* to snog.

morreo *nm vulg* snog.

morro *nm* 1 *(de animal) (hocico)* snout. 2
fam (de persona) mouth, (thick) lips;
caerse de m., to fall flat on one's face;
por los morros, without so much as a by
your leave; *fam* **¡vaya m.!**, what a cheek!
3 *(de coche)* nose.

morrón *adj* **pimiento m.**, (fleshy) red
pepper.

morsa *nf* walrus.

morse *nm* morse.

mortadela *nf* mortadella.

mortaja *nf* shroud.

mortal I *adj* 1 mortal. 2 *(mortífero)* fatal;
un accidente m., a fatal accident. II *nmf*
mortal.

mortalidad *nf* mortality; **índice de m.**,
death rate.

mortandad *nf* death toll.

mortecino,-a *adj* colourless, *US* color-
less.

mortero *nm Culin Mil* mortar.

mortífero,-a *adj* deadly, lethal.

mortificar [1] *vtr* to mortify.

mortuorio,-a *adj* death; **lecho m.**,
deathbed.

moruno,-a *adj* Moorish; *Culin* **pincho
m.**, ≈ kebab.

mosaico *nm* mosaic.

mosca *nf* fly; **peso m.**, flyweight; *fam*
estar m., *(suspicaz)* to be suspicious; *(borracho)* to be pissed; *fam* **por si las
moscas**, just in case; *fam* **¿qué m. te ha
picado?**, what's biting you?

moscada *adj* **nuez m.**, nutmeg.

moscardón *nm* 1 *Ent* blowfly. 2 *fam (pesado)* pest.

moscovita *adj & nmf* Muscovite.

Moscú *n* Moscow.

mosquearse *vr fam* 1 *(enfadarse)* to get
cross. 2 *(sospechar)* to smell a rat.

mosquetero *nm Hist* musketeer.

mosquitero *nm (red)* mosquito net.

mosquito *nm* mosquito.

mostaza *nf Bot Culin* mustard.

mosto *nm (bebida)* grape juice; *(del vino)*
must.

mostrador *nm* 1 *(de tienda)* counter. 2 *(de
bar)* bar.

mostrar I *vtr* to show; **muéstramelo**,
show it to me. II **mostrarse** *vr* to be; **se
mostró muy comprensiva**, she was very
understanding.

mostrenco,-a I *nm,f* 1 *(ignorante)* blockhead. 2 *(gordo)* very fat person. II *adj (sin
dueño)* ownerless; **bienes mostrencos**,
ownerless property.

mota *nf* speck.

mote¹ *nm (apodo)* nickname; **poner m. a
algn**, to give sb a nickname.

mote² *nm Am* boiled salted maize *o US*
corn.

moteado,-a *adj* dotted.

motín *nm (amotinamiento)* mutiny; *(disturbio)* riot.

motivación *nf* motivation.

motivar *vtr* 1 *(causar)* to cause, give rise
to. 2 *(inducir)* to motivate.

motivo *nm* 1 *(causa)* reason; *(usu pl)*
grounds *pl*; **con este** *o* **tal m.**, for this
reason; **con m. de**, on the occasion of;
sin m., for no reason at all; **bajo ningún
m.**, under no circumstances. 2 *Art Mús*
motif, leitmotif.

moto *nf Aut* motorbike.

motocicleta *nf* motorbike.

motociclismo *nm* motorcycling.

motociclista *nmf* motorcyclist.

motocross *nm* motocross.

motor,-a I *nm (grande)* engine; *(pequeño)*
motor; **m. de reacción**, jet engine; **m. de
explosión**, internal combustion engine;
m. eléctrico, electric motor. II *adj Téc*
motive.

motora *nf* motorboat.

motorista *nmf* motorcyclist.

motorizar [4] I *vtr* to motorize. II **moto-
rizarse** *vr fam* to get oneself a car *o*
motorbike.

motosierra *nf* power saw.

motriz *adj* **fuerza m.**, motive power.
movedizo,-a *adj* **arenas movedizas**, quicksand *sing*.
mover |4| I *vtr* 1 to move; **m. algo de su sitio**, to move sth out of its place. 2 *(hacer funcionar)* to drive; **el motor mueve el coche**, the engine drives the car. II **moverse** *vr* 1 to move. 2 *fam (gestionar)* to do everything possible. 3 *(darse prisa)* to hurry up; **¡muévete!**, get a move on!
movida *nf arg* **hay mucha m.**, there's a lot going on.
movido,-a *adj* 1 *Fot* blurred. 2 *(ocupado)* busy.
móvil I *adj* mobile; *TV Rad* **unidad m.**, outside broadcast unit. II *nm (de delito)* motive.
movilización *nf* mobilization.
movilizar |4| *vtr* to mobilize.
movimiento *nm* 1 *gen* movement; *Fís Téc* motion; **(poner algo) en m.**, (to set sth) in motion; **m. sísmico**, earth tremor. 2 *(actividad)* activity. 3 *Com Fin (entradas y salidas)* operations. 4 *Esp Hist* **el M.**, the Falangist Movement.
moviola *nf Cin TV* 1 *(cámara)* editing projector. 2 *(repetición)* action replay.
moza *nf* lass, young girl.
mozo *nm* 1 lad, boy. 2 *(de estación)* porter; *(de hotel)* bellboy, *US* bellhop. 3 *Mil* conscript.
mucamo,-a *nm,f Am* servant.
muchacha *nf* girl.
muchacho *nm* boy.
muchedumbre *nf (de gente)* crowd.
mucho,-a I *adj* 1 *sing (usu en frases afirmativas)* a lot of, lots of; *(usu en frases neg)* much; **m. tiempo**, a long time; **tengo m. sueño/mucha sed**, I am very sleepy/thirsty; **hay m. tonto suelto**, there are lots of idiots around; **¿bebes m. café?** - **no, no m.**, do you drink a lot of coffee?; - no, not much. 2 *(demasiado)* **es m. coche para mí**, this car is a bit too much for me. 3 **muchos,-as**, *(usu en frases afirmativas)* a lot of, lots of; *(usu en frases neg)* many; **tiene m. años**, he is very old. II *pron* 1 a lot, a great deal; **¿cuánta leche queda?** - **mucha**, how much milk is there left? - a lot. 2 **muchos,-as**, a lot, lots, many; **¿cuántos libros tienes?** - **muchos**, how many books have you got? - lots *o* a lot; **muchos creemos que ...**, many of us believe that ...
III *adv* 1 a lot, very much; **lo siento m.**, I'm very sorry; **como m.**, at the most; **con m.**, by far; **m. antes/después**, long before/after; **¡ni m. menos!**, no way!; **por m. (que)** + *subj*, however much. 2 *(tiempo)* **hace m. que no viene por aquí**, he has not been to see us for a long time. 3 *(a menudo)* often; **vamos m. al cine**, we go to the cinema quite often.
muda *nf (de ropa)* change of clothes.

mudanza *nf* move; **estar de m.**, to be moving; **camión de m.**, removal van.
mudar I *vtr* 1 *(ropa)* to change. 2 *(plumas, pelo)* to moult, *US* molt; *(piel)* to shed, slough. II **mudarse** *vr* **m. de casa/ropa** to move house/to change one's clothes.
mudo,-a I *adj* 1 *(que no habla)* dumb; **cine m.**, silent films *pl*. 2 *fig (callado)* speechless. II *nm,f* mute.
mueble I *nm* piece of furniture; **muebles**, furniture *sing*; **con/sin muebles**, furnished/unfurnished; **m. bar**, cocktail cabinet. II *adj* movable.
mueca *nf* 1 *(de burla)* mocking face; **hacer muecas**, to pull faces. 2 *(de dolor, asco)* grimace.
muela *nf* 1 *Anat* molar; **dolor de muelas**, toothache; **m. del juicio**, wisdom tooth. 2 *Téc (de molino)* millstone.
muelle¹ *nm* spring.
muelle² *nm Náut* dock.
muermo *nm fam (tedio)* boredom; *(rollo)* drag.
muerte *nf* death; **m. natural**, natural death; **dar m. a algn**, to kill sb; **odiar a algn a m.**, to loathe sb; *fam* **un susto de m.**, the fright of one's life.
muerto,-a I *adj* dead; **caer m.**, to drop dead; **m. de hambre**, starving; **m. de frío**, frozen to death; **m. de miedo**, scared stiff; **m. de risa**, laughing one's head off; **horas muertas**, spare time; *Aut* **(en) punto m.**, (in) neutral. II *nm,f* 1 *(difunto)* dead person; **hacerse el m.**, to pretend to be dead; *fam* **cargar con el m.**, to do the dirty work. 2 *(víctima)* fatality; **hubo dos muertos**, two (people) died.
muesca *nf* notch.
muestra *nf* 1 *(espécimen)* sample, specimen. 2 *(modelo a copiar)* model. 3 *(prueba, señal)* sign; **dar muestras de**, to show signs of; **m. de cariño/respeto**, token of affection/respect; **una m. más de ...**, yet another example of ...
muestral *adj* **error m.**, margin of error.
muestreo *nm* sampling.
mugido *nm (de vaca)* moo; *(de toro)* bellow.
mugir |6| *vi (vaca)* to moo, low; *(toro)* to bellow.
mugre *nf* filth.
mugriento,-a *adj* filthy.
mujer *nf* 1 woman; **dos mujeres**, two women; **m. de la limpieza**, cleaner; **m. de su casa**, houseproud woman. 2 *(esposa)* wife; **su futura m.**, his bride-to-be.
mujeriego I *adj* woman-chasing. II *nm* womanizer, woman chaser.
muleta *nf* 1 *(prótesis)* crutch. 2 *Taur* muleta.
muletilla *nf* pet word *o* phrase.
mullido,-a *adj* soft.

mulo *nm* mule.
multa *nf* fine; *Aut* ticket.
multar *vtr* to fine.
multi- *pref* multi-.
multicolor *adj* multicoloured, *US* multicolored.
multicopista *nf* duplicator.
multilateral *adj* multilateral.
multinacional *adj & nf* multinational.
múltiple *adj* 1 multiple; **accidente m., pile up.** 2 múltiples, (*muchos*) many.
multiplicación *nf Mat* multiplication.
multiplicar ||1|| I *vtr & vi* to multiply (**por**, by). II **multiplicarse** *vr* (*reproducirse, aumentar*) to multiply.
múltiplo,-a *adj & nm* multiple.
multirriesgo *adj inv* **póliza m.,** multiple risk policy.
multitud *nf* 1 (*de personas*) crowd. 2 (*de cosas*) multitude.
mundano,-a *adj* mundane.
mundial I *adj* worldwide; **campeón m.,** world champion; **de fama m.,** world-famous. II *nm* world championship.
◆**mundialmente** *adv* **m. famoso,** world-famous, famous worldwide.
mundo *nm* world; **todo el m.,** everyone; **correr** *o* **ver m.,** to travel widely; **nada del otro m.,** nothing special; **el otro m.,** the hereafter.
muñeca *nf* 1 wrist. 2 (*juguete, muchacha*) doll.
muñeco *nm* (*juguete*) (little) boy doll; **m. de trapo,** rag doll; **m. de nieve,** snowman.
muñequera *nf* wristband.
munición *nf* ammunition.
municipal I *adj* municipal. II *nm* (*municipal*) policeman.
municipio *nm* 1 (*territorio*) municipality. 2 (*ayuntamiento*) town council.
muñón *nm Anat* stump.
muralla *nf* wall.
Murcia *n* Murcia.
murciélago *nm Zool* bat.

murmullo *nm* murmur.
murmuración *nf* gossip.
murmurar *vi* 1 (*criticar*) to gossip. 2 (*susurrar*) to whisper; (*refunfuñar*) to grumble. 3 *fig* (*río*) to murmur.
muro *nm* wall.
murrio,-a *adj fam* sad, blue.
musa *nf* muse.
musaraña *nf fam* **estar mirando a** *o* **pensando en las musarañas,** to be daydreaming *o* in the clouds.
musculatura *nf* musculature; **desarrollar la m.,** to develop one's muscles.
músculo *nm* muscle.
musculoso,-a *adj* muscular.
museo *nm* museum; **m. de arte** *o* **pintura,** art gallery.
musgo *nm* moss.
música *nf* music; **m. clásica,** classical music; **m. de fondo,** background music.
musical I *adj* musical. II *nm* musical.
músico,-a I *adj* musical. II *nm,f* musician.
muslo *nm* thigh.
mustio,-a *adj* 1 (*plantas*) wilted, withered. 2 (*persona*) sad, gloomy.
musulmán,-ana *adj & nm,f* Muslim, Moslem.
mutación *nf Biol* mutation.
mutilación *nf* mutilation.
mutilado,-a *nm,f* disabled person; **m. de guerra,** disabled serviceman.
mutilar *vtr* to mutilate.
mutis *nm Teat* exit.
mutua *nf* mutual benefit society.
mutualidad *nf* 1 (*reciprocidad*) mutuality. 2 (*asociación*) mutual benefit society.
mutuo,-a *adj* mutual.
muy *adv* very; **m. bueno/malo,** very good/bad; **¡m. bien!,** very good!; *fam* **m. mucho,** very much; **M. señor mío,** Dear Sir; **m. de los andaluces,** typically Andalusian; **m. de mañana/noche,** very early/late.

N

N, n |'ene| *nf* (*la letra*) N, n.
N *abr de* **Norte,** North, N.
n/ *abr de* **nuestro,-a,** our.
nabo *nm* 1 *Bot* turnip. 2 *vulg* (*pene*) prick.
nácar *nm* mother-of-pearl.
nacer |33| *vi* 1 to be born; **al n.,** at birth; **nací en Montoro,** I was born in Montoro; *fam fig* **n. de pie,** to be born under a lucky star. 2 (*pájaro*) to hatch (out). 3 (*pelo*) to begin to grow. 4 (*río*) to rise.
nacido,-a *adj* born; **n. de padre español,** born of a Spanish father; **recién n.,** newborn; *fig* **mal n.,** despicable, mean.
naciente *adj* (*nuevo*) new, recent; (*sol*)

rising.
nacimiento *nm* 1 birth; **sordo de n.,** deaf from birth; **lugar de n.,** birthplace, place of birth. 2 *fig* (*principio*) origin, beginning; (*de río*) source. 3 (*belén*) Nativity scene, crib.
nación *nf* nation; **las Naciones Unidas,** the United Nations.
nacional I *adj* 1 national. 2 (*producto, mercado*) domestic; **vuelos nacionales,** domestic flights. II *nmf* national; *Hist* **los nacionales,** the Francoist forces.
nacionalidad *nf* nationality.
nacionalismo *nm* nationalism.

nacionalista *adj & nmf* nationalist.
nacionalizar |4| I *vtr* 1 *Econ (banca, industria)* to nationalize. 2 *(naturalizar)* to naturalize. II **nacionalizarse** *vr* to become naturalized; **n. español,** to take up Spanish citizenship.
nada I *pron* 1 *(como respuesta)* nothing; **qué quieres? - n.,** what do you want? - nothing. 2 *(con verbo)* not ... anything; *(enfático)* nothing; **no sé n.,** I don't know anything; **yo no digo n.,** I'm saying nothing. 3 *(con otro negativo)* anything; **no hace nunca n.,** he never does anything; **nadie sabía n.,** nobody knew anything. 4 *(en ciertas construcciones)* anything; **más que n.,** more than anything; **sin decir n.,** without saying anything; **casi n.,** hardly anything. 5 **gracias, - de n.,** thanks, - don't mention it; *fam* **para n.,** not at all; **casi n.,** almost nothing; **como si n.,** just like that; **un rasguño de n.,** an insignificant little scratch; **n. de eso,** nothing of the kind; **n. de n.,** nothing at all; **n. más verla,** as soon as he saw her. II *adv* not at all; **no me gusta n.,** I don't like it at all; **no lo encuentro n. interesante,** I don't find it remotely interesting. III *nf* nothingness; **salir de la n.,** to come out of nowhere.
nadar *vi* 1 *Dep* to swim; **n. a braza,** to do the breaststroke. 2 *(flotar)* to float.
nadador,-a *nm,f* swimmer.
nadie I *pron* 1 *(como respuesta)* no-one, nobody; **quién vino? - n.,** who came? - no-one. 2 *(con verbo)* not ... anyone, anybody; *(enfático)* no-one, nobody; **no conozco a n.,** I don't know anyone *o* anybody; **no vi a n.,** I saw no-one. 3 *(con otro negativo)* anyone, anybody; **nunca habla con n.,** he never speaks to anybody. 4 *(en ciertas construcciones)* anybody, anyone; **más que n.,** more than anyone; **sin decírselo a n.,** without telling anyone; **casi n.,** hardly anyone. II *nm* nobody; **ser un don n.,** to be a nobody.
nado (a) *loc adv* swimming; **cruzar** *o* **pasar a n.,** to swim across.
nafta *nf Am (gasolina)* petrol, *US* gasoline.
nailon *nm* nylon; **medias de n.,** nylons *pl*.
naipe *nm* playing card.
nalga *nf* buttock; **nalgas,** bottom *sing*, buttocks.
nana *nf* lullaby.
napalm *nm* napalm.
napias *nfpl fam* snout *sing*.
Nápoles *n* Naples.
napolitano,-a *adj & nm,f* Neapolitan.
naranja I *nf* orange; **fig mi media n.,** my better half. II *adj & nm (color)* orange.
naranjada *nf* orangeade.
naranjo *nm* orange tree.
narciso *nm* 1 *(blanco)* narcissus; *(amarillo)* daffodil. 2 *fig (hombre)* narcissist.

narcótico *nm* narcotic; *(droga)* drug.
narcotizar |4| *vtr (drogar)* to drug.
narcotraficante *nmf* drug trafficker.
narcotráfico *nm* drug trafficking.
nariz *nf* 1 nose; *fam* **me da en la n. que ...,** I've got this feeling that .... 2 *fam* **narices,** nose *sing*; *fam* **en mis (propias) narices,** right under my very nose; *fam* **estar hasta las narices de,** to be totally fed up with; *fam* **meter las narices en algo,** to poke one's nose into sth; *fam* **por narices,** because I say so; *fam* **tocarle a algn las narices,** to get on sb's wick.
narración *nf* narration.
narrar *vtr* to narrate, tell.
narrativo,-a *adj & nf* narrative.
nata *nf* 1 cream; **n. batida/montada,** whipped cream. 2 *(de leche hervida)* skin. 3 *fig* cream, best.
natación *nf Dep* swimming.
natal *adj* **mi país n.,** my native country; **su pueblo n.,** his home town.
natalicio *nm fml* birthday.
natalidad *nf* birth rate; **control de n.,** birth control.
natillas *nfpl Culin* custard *sing*.
natividad *nf* Nativity.
nativo,-a *adj & nm,f* native.
nato,-a *adj* born.
natura *nf lit* nature; **contra n.,** against nature.
natural I *adj* natural; *(fruta, flor)* fresh; **de tamaño n.,** life-size; **en estado n.,** in its natural state; *Jur* **hijo n.,** illegitimate child. II *nmf* native.
naturaleza *nf* 1 nature; **en la n.,** in the wild, in unspoilt countryside; *Arte* **n. muerta,** still life. 2 *(complexión)* physical constitution.
naturalidad *nf (sencillez)* naturalness; **con n.,** naturally, straightforwardly.
naturalismo *nm* naturalism.
naturalista I *adj* naturalistic. II *nmf* naturalist.
naturalización *nf* naturalization.
naturalizar |4| I *vtr* to naturalize. II **naturalizarse** *vr* to become naturalized.
naturalmente *adv* naturally; **¡n.!,** of course!
naturismo *nm* naturism.
naturista *nmf* naturist.
naufragar |7| *vi (barco)* to sink, be wrecked; *(persona)* to be shipwrecked.
naufragio *nm Náut* shipwreck.
náufrago,-a *nm,f* shipwrecked person, castaway.
náusea *nf (usu pl)* nausea, sickness; **me da n.,** it makes me sick; **sentir náuseas,** to feel sick.
nauseabundo,-a *adj* nauseating, sickening.
náutico,-a *adj* nautical.
navaja *nf* 1 *(cuchillo)* penknife, pocket-

knife; **n. de afeitar**, razor. 2 (*molusco*) razor-shell.

navajada *nf*, **navajazo** *nm* stab, gash.

navajero *nm fam* thug.

naval *adj* naval.

Navarra *n* Navarre.

navarro,-a I *adj* Navarrese, of *o* from Navarre. II *nm,f* native *o* inhabitant of Navarre.

nave *nf* 1 ship; **n. (espacial)**, spaceship, spacecraft. 2 *Ind* plant, building. 3 (*de iglesia*) nave; **n. lateral**, aisle.

navegable *adj* navigable.

navegación *nf* navigation; **n. costera**, coastal shipping.

navegar [7] *vi* 1 to navigate, sail. 2 *Av* to navigate, fly.

Navidad(es) *nf(pl)* Christmas; **árbol de Navidad**, Christmas tree; **Feliz Navidad/Felices Navidades**, Merry Christmas.

navideño,-a *adj* Christmas.

navío *nm* ship.

nazi *adj & nmf* Nazi.

nazismo *nm* Nazism.

n/c., n/cta. *abr de* **nuestra cuenta**, our account, our acct.

neblina *nf* mist, thin fog.

nebulosa *nf Astron* nebula.

nebuloso,-a *adj* 1 *Meteor* cloudy, hazy. 2 *fig* nebulous, vague.

necedad *nf* 1 (*estupidez*) stupidity, foolishness. 2 (*tontería*) stupid thing to say *o* to do.

necesario,-a *adj* necessary; **es n. hacerlo**, it has to be done; **es n. que vayas**, you must go; **no es n. que vayas**, there is no need for you to go; **si fuera n.**, if need be.

neceser *nm* (*de aseo*) toilet bag; (*de maquillaje*) make-up bag.

necesidad *nf* 1 necessity, need; **artículos de primera n.**, essentials; **por n.**, of necessity; **tener n. de**, to need. 2 (*pobreza*) poverty, hardship. 3 **hacer sus necesidades**, to relieve oneself.

necesitado,-a I *adj* (*pobre*) needy, poor; **n. de**, in need of. II *npl* **los necesitados**, the needy.

necesitar *vtr* to need; '**se necesita chico**', (*en anuncios*) 'boy wanted'.

necio,-a I *adj* silly, stupid. II *nm,f* fool, idiot.

necrología *nf* obituary.

néctar *nm* nectar.

nectarina *nf* nectarine.

neerlandés,-esa I *adj* Dutch, of *o* from the Netherlands. II *nm,f* (*persona*) (*hombre*) Dutchman; (*mujer*) Dutchwoman; **los neerlandeses**, the Dutch. III *nm* (*idioma*) Dutch.

nefasto,-a *adj* 1 (*perjudicial*) harmful. 2 (*funesto*) unlucky, ill-fated. 3 (*inútil*) hopeless.

negación *nf* 1 negation. 2 (*negativa*) denial; (*rechazo*) refusal. 3 *Ling* negative.

negado,-a I *adj* **ser n. para algo**, to be hopeless *o* useless at sth. II *nm,f* no-hoper.

negar [1] I *vtr* 1 to deny; **negó haberlo robado**, he denied stealing it. 2 (*rechazar*) to refuse, deny; **le negaron la beca**, they refused him the grant. II **negarse** *vr* to refuse (**a**, to).

negativa *nf* denial.

negativo,-a *adj & nm* negative.

negligencia *nf* negligence.

negociación *nf* negotiation.

negociador,-a *adj* negotiating; **comité n.**, negotiating commitee.

negociante *nmf* dealer; (*hombre*) businessman; (*mujer*) businesswoman.

negociar [12] I *vtr Fin Pol* to negotiate. II *vi* (*comerciar*) to do business, deal.

negocio *nm Com Fin* business; (*transacción*) deal, transaction; (*asunto*) affair; **hombre de negocios**, businessman; **mujer de negocios**, businesswoman.

negra *nf* 1 *fig* (*mala suerte*) bad luck; **tener la n.**, to be very unlucky. 2 *Mús* crotchet, *US* quarter note.

negrilla, **negrita** *adj & nf Impr* bold (face).

negro,-a I *adj* 1 black; **estar n.**, (*bronceado*) to be suntanned. 2 *fig* (*suerte*) awful; (*desesperado*) desperate; (*furioso*) furious; **verlo todo n.**, to be very pessimistic; **vérselas negras para hacer algo**, to have a tough time doing sth. II *nm,f* (*hombre*) black; (*mujer*) black (woman). III *nm* (*color*) black.

nene,-a *nm,f* (*niño*) baby boy; (*niña*) baby girl.

nenúfar *nm Bot* water lily.

neocelandés,-esa I *adj* of *o* from New Zealand. II *nm,f* New Zealander.

neoclásico,-a *adj Arte Lit* neoclassic, neoclassical.

neologismo *nm* neologism.

neón *nm* neon.

neoyorkino,-a I *adj* of *o* from New York. II *nm,f* New Yorker.

neozelandés,-esa *adj & nm,f* → **neocelandés,-esa**.

nepotismo *nm* nepotism.

Neptuno *n* Neptune.

nervio *nm* 1 *Anat Bot* nerve; (*de la carne*) sinew. 2 *fig* (*fuerza, vigor*) nerve, courage. 3 **nervios**, nerves; **ataque de n.**, a fit of hysterics; **ser un manojo de n.**, to be a bundle of nerves; **tener los nervios de acero**, to have nerves of steel.

nerviosismo *nm* nerves *pl*.

nervioso,-a *adj* 1 nervous; **poner n. a algn**, to get on sb's nerves. 2 (*inquieto*) fidgety.

neto,-a *adj* 1 (*peso, cantidad*) net. 2 (*nítido*) neat, clear.

neumático,-a I adj pneumatic. **II** nm tyre, US tire; **n. de recambio,** spare tyre.

neumonía nf pneumonia.

neurálgico,-a adj neuralgic; fig **punto n.,** nerve centre.

neurólogo,-a nm,f neurologist.

neurosis nf neurosis.

neurótico,-a adj & nm,f neurotic.

neutral adj neutral.

neutralidad nf neutrality.

neutralizar [4] vtr to neutralize.

neutro,-a adj 1 (imparcial) neutral. 2 Ling neuter.

neutrón nm Fís neutron; **bomba de neutrones,** neutron bomb.

nevada nf snowfall.

nevar [1] v impers to snow.

nevera nf 1 (frigorífico) refrigerator, fam fridge. 2 (portátil) cool box.

nexo nm connection, link.

ni conj 1 **no ... ni, ni ... ni,** neither ... nor, not ... or; **no tengo tiempo ni dinero,** I have got neither time nor money; **ni ha venido ni ha llamado,** he hasn't come or phoned; **no vengas ni hoy ni mañana,** don't come today or tomorrow. 2 (ni siquiera) not even; **ni por dinero,** not even for money; **ni se te ocurra,** don't even think about it; **¡ni hablar!,** no way!

Nicaragua nf Nicaragua.

nicaragüense, nicaragüeño,-a adj & nm,f Nicaraguan.

nicho nm niche.

nicotina nf nicotine.

nido nm nest.

niebla nf fog; **hay mucha n.,** it is very foggy.

nieto,-a nm,f (niño) grandson; (niña) granddaughter; **mis nietos,** my grandchildren.

nieve nf 1 Meteor snow; Culin **a punto de n.,** (beaten) stiff. 2 arg (cocaína) snow.

nigeriano,-a adj & nm,f Nigerian.

nigerino,-a adj & nm,f Nigerien.

Nilo n el N., the Nile.

nilón nm Tex nylon.

nimio,-a adj (insignificante) insignificant, petty.

ninfómana nf nymphomaniac.

ningún adj (delante de nm sing) → ninguno,-a.

ninguno,-a I adj 1 (con verbo) not ... any; **no leí ninguna revista,** I didn't read any magazines; **no tiene ninguna gracia,** it is not funny at all. 2 **en ninguna parte,** nowhere; **de ningún modo,** no way. **II** pron 1 (persona) nobody, no one; **n. lo vio,** no one saw it; **n. de los dos,** neither of the two; **n. de ellos,** none of them. 2 (cosa) not ... any of them; (enfático) none of them; **me gusta n.,** I don't like any of them; **no vi n.,** I saw none of them.

niña nf 1 girl; → niño,-a. 2 Anat pupil;

fig **es la n. de sus ojos,** she's the apple of his eye.

niñera nf nursemaid, nanny.

niñez nf infancy; (a partir de los cuatro años) childhood.

niño,-a nm,f 1 child; (muchacho) (small) boy; (muchacha) (little) girl; **de n.,** as a child; **n. prodigio,** child prodigy; pey **n. bien** o **de papá,** rich boy, rich kid; pey **n. bonito** o **mimado,** mummy's o daddy's boy. 2 (bebé) baby. 3 **niños,** children; fig **juego de niños,** child's play.

nipón,-ona adj & nm,f Japanese; **los nipones,** the Japanese.

níquel nm nickel.

niqui nm T-shirt.

níspero nm (fruto) medlar; (árbol) medlar tree.

nítido,-a adj (claro) clear; (imagen) sharp.

nitrógeno nm nitrogen.

nitroglicerina nf nitroglycerine.

nivel nm 1 (altura) level; **a n. del mar,** at sea level. 2 (categoría) standard; **n. de vida,** standard of living. 3 (instrumento) level; **n. de aire,** spirit level. 4 Ferroc **paso a n.,** level crossing, US grade crossing.

nivelar vtr 1 to level out o off. 2 (equilibrar) to balance out.

nº abr de **número,** number, n.

no I adv 1 (como respuesta) no; **te gusta? - no.,** do you like it? - no. 2 (en otros contextos) not; **n. vi a nadie,** I didn't see anyone; **aún no,** not yet; **ya no,** no longer, not any more. **no es así ...,** not without first ...; **¿por qué no?,** why not? 3 **no fumar/aparcar,** (en letrero) no smoking/parking. 4 **no sea que** + subj, in case. 5 **es rubia, ¿no?,** she's blonde, isn't she? **llegaron anoche, no?,** they arrived yesterday, didn't they? 6 (como prefijo negativo) non; **la no violencia,** non-violence. **II** nm no; **un no rotundo,** a definite no.

noble I adj noble. **II** nmf (hombre) nobleman; (mujer) noblewoman; **los nobles,** the nobility sing.

nobleza nf nobility.

noche nf evening; (después de las diez) night, night-time; **de n., por la n.,** at night; **esta n.,** tonight; **mañana por la n.,** tomorrow night o evening; **buenas noches,** (saludo) good evening; (despedida) good night; **son las nueve de la noche,** it's nine p.m.

nochebuena nf Christmas Eve.

nochevieja nf New Year's Eve.

noción nf 1 notion, idea. 2 **nociones,** smattering sing, basic knowledge sing; **n. de español,** a smattering of Spanish.

nocivo,-a adj noxious, harmful.

noctámbulo,-a nm,f sleepwalker; fam night-bird.

nocturno,-a adj 1 night; **vida nocturna,**

night life; **clases nocturnas,** evening classes. **2** *Bot Zool* nocturnal.

nodriza *nf* **1** *(ama)* wet nurse. **2 buque n.,** supply ship.

nogal *nm Bot* walnut (tree).

nómada I *adj* nomadic. **II** *nmf* nomad.

nombrado,-a *adj (célebre)* famous, well-known.

nombramiento *nm* appointment.

nombrar *vtr* **1** *(designar)* to name, appoint; **n. a algn director,** to appoint sb director. **2** *(mencionar)* to name, mention.

nombre *nm* **1** name; **n. de pila,** Christian name; **n. y apellidos,** full name; **a n. de,** addressed to; **en n. de,** on behalf of. **2** *Ling* noun; **n. propio,** proper noun.

nómina *nf* **1** *(de sueldo)* pay slip. **2** *(plantilla)* payroll.

nominar *vtr* to nominate.

nominativo,-a *adj* **cheque n. a,** cheque made out to.

non *nm* **1** *Mat* odd number; **pares y nones,** odds and evens. **2** *fam* **nones,** *(negación)* no; **decir (que) nones,** to refuse.

nono,-a *adj* → **noveno,-a.**

norcoreano,-a *adj & nm,f* North Korean.

nordeste *nm* → **noreste.**

nórdico,-a I *adj* **1** *(del norte)* northern. **2** *(escandinavo)* Nordic. **II** *nm,f* Nordic person.

noreste *nm* northeast.

noria *nf* **1** *(de feria)* big wheel. **2** *(para agua)* water-wheel.

norirlandés,-esa I *adj* Northern Irish. **II** *nm,f (persona) (hombre)* Northern Irishman; *(mujer)* Northern Irishwoman; **los norirlandeses,** the Northern Irish.

norma *nf* norm; **n. de seguridad,** safety standard.

normal *adj* normal, usual; **lo n.,** the normal thing, what usually happens.

normalidad *nf* normality; **volver a la n.,** to return to normal.

normalizar |4| **I** *vtr* to normalize, restore to normal. **II normalizarse** *vr* to return to normal.

normativa *nf* rules *pl.*

noroeste *nm* northwest.

norte *nm* **1** north; **al n. de,** to the north of. **2** *fig* aim, goal.

norteafricano,-a *adj & nm,f* North African.

Norteamérica *n* North America.

norteamericano,-a *adj & nm,f* (North) American.

norteño,-a I *adj* northern. **II** *nm,f* Northerner.

Noruega *n* Norway.

noruego,-a I *adj* Norwegian. **II** *nm,f* Norwegian. **III** *nm (idioma)* Norwegian.

nos I *pron pers (directo)* us; *(indirecto)* us; **n. ha visto,** he has seen us; **n. trajo un regalo,** he brought us a present; **n. lo dio,** he gave it to us. **II** *pron (reflexivo)* ourselves; *(recíproco)* each other; **n. hemos divertido mucho,** we enjoyed ourselves a lot; **n. queremos mucho,** we love each other very much.

nosotros,-as *pron pers pl* **1** *(sujeto)* we; **n. lo vimos,** we saw it; **somos n.,** it is us. **2** *(complemento)* us; **con n.,** with us.

nostalgia *nf* nostalgia; *(morriña)* homesickness.

nostálgico,-a *adj* nostalgic; *(con morriña)* homesick.

nota *nf* **1** *(anotación)* note. **2** *Educ* mark, grade; **sacar buenas notas,** to get good marks. **3** *fig (detalle)* element, quality; **la n. dominante,** the prevailing quality. **4** *Mús* note; *fam* **dar la n.,** to make oneself noticed.

notable I *adj (apreciable)* noticeable; *(destacado)* outstanding, remarkable. **II** *nm (nota)* very good.

notar I *vtr (percibir)* to notice, note. **II notarse** *vr* **1** to be noticeable *o* evident, show; **no se nota,** it doesn't show; **se nota que ...,** one can see that ....

notaría *nf (despacho)* notary's office.

notarial *adj* notarial; **acta n.,** affidavit.

notario,-a *nm,f* notary (public), solicitor.

noticia *nf* news *sing*; **una n.,** a piece of news; **una buena n.,** good news; **no tengo n. de esto,** I don't know anything about it.

notificación *nf* notification; **sin n. previa,** without (previous) notice; *Jur* **n. judicial,** summons *sing.*

notificar |1| *vtr* to notify.

notorio,-a *adj* **1** *(evidente)* noticeable, evident. **2** *(famoso)* famous, well-known.

novatada *nf (broma)* rough joke, rag. **2 pagar la n.,** to learn the hard way.

novato,-a I *adj (persona)* inexperienced; *fam* green. **II** *nm,f* **1** *(principiante)* novice, beginner. **2** *Univ* fresher.

novecientos,-as *adj & nm,f* nine hundred.

novedad *nf* **1** *(cosa nueva)* novelty; **últimas novedades,** latest arrivals. **2** *(cambio)* change, development. **3** *(cualidad)* newness.

novedoso,-a *adj* **1** *(nuevo)* new, full of novelties. **2** *(innovador)* innovative.

novel *adj* new, inexperienced. **II** *nmf* beginner, novice.

novela *nf Lit* novel; **n. corta,** short story; **n. policíaca,** detective story.

novelero,-a *adj* **1** fond of new things. **2** *(fantasioso)* highly imaginative.

novelesco,-a *adj* **1** *(de novela)* novelistic, fictional. **2** *(extraordinario)* bizarre, fantastic.

novelista *nmf* novelist.

noveno,-a *adj & nm* ninth; **novena parte,** ninth.

noventa *adj & nm inv* ninety.

novia *nf* **1** *(amiga)* girlfriend. **2** *(prometida)*

fiancée. **3** (*en boda*) bride.
noviazgo *nm* engagement.
noviembre *nm* November.
novillada *nf Taur* bullfight with young bulls.
novillero,-a *nm,f Taur* apprentice matador.
novillo,-a *nm,f* **1** (*toro*) young bull; (*vaca*) young cow. **2** *fam Educ* **hacer novillos**, to play truant *o US* hooky.
novio *nm* **1** (*amigo*) boyfriend. **2** (*prometido*) fiancé. **3** (*en boda*) bridegroom; **los novios**, the bride and groom.
nubarrón *nm fam* storm cloud.
nube *nf* cloud; *fig* **vivir en las nubes**, to have one's head in the clouds; *fig* **poner a algn por las nubes**, to praise sb to the skies.
nublado,-a *adj* cloudy, overcast.
nublarse *vr* to become cloudy, cloud over; *fig* **se le nubló la vista**, his eyes clouded over.
nuboso,-a *adj* cloudy.
nuca *nf* nape, back of the neck.
nuclear *adj* nuclear; **central n.**, nuclear power station.
núcleo *nm* nucleus; (*parte central*) core; **n. urbano**, city centre.
nudillo *nm* (*usu pl*) knuckle.
nudista *adj & nmf* nudist.
nudo *nm* **1** knot; **hacer un n.**, to tie a knot; *fig* **se me hizo un n. en la garganta**, I got a lump in my throat. **2** (*punto principal*) crux, core. **3** (*de comunicaciones*) centre, *US* center.
nuera *nf* daughter-in-law.
nuestro,-a I *adj pos* **1** our; **nuestra familia**, our family. **2** (*después del sustantivo*) of ours; **un amigo n.**, a friend of ours. **II** *pron pos* ours; **este libro es n.**, this book is ours.
nueve *adj & nm inv* nine.
nuevo,-a I *adj* **1** new; *fam* **¿qué hay de n.?**, what's new?; **de n.**, again; **N. York**, New York; **N. Zelanda**, New Zealand. **2**

(*adicional*) further. **II** *nm,f* newcomer; (*principiante*) beginner. ◆**nuevamente** *adv* again.
nuez *nf* **1** walnut; **n. moscada**, nutmeg. **2** *Anat* n. **(de Adán)**, Adam's apple.
nulidad *nf* **1** (*ineptitud*) incompetence. **2** *Jur* nullity.
nulo,-a *adj* **1** (*inepto*) useless, totally incapable. **2** (*sin valor*) null and void, invalid; **voto n.**, invalid vote. **3 crecimiento n.**, zero growth.
núm. *abr de* **número**, number, n.
numeral *adj & nm* numeral.
numerar *vtr* to number.
numerario,-a I *adj* **profesor no n.**, teacher on a temporary contract. **II** *nm* **1** (*miembro*) full member. **2** (*dinero*) cash.
numérico,-a *adj* numerical.
número *nm* **1** number; **n. de matrícula**, registration number, *US* license number; **n. de serie**, serial number; *fig* **sin n.**, countless. **2** *Prensa* number, issue; **n. atrasado**, back number. **3** (*de zapatos*) size. **4** (*en espectáculo*) sketch, act; *fam* **montar un n.**, to make a scene.
numeroso,-a *adj* numerous.
nunca *adv* **1** (*como respuesta*) never; **cuándo volverás? - n.**, when will you come back? - never. **2** (*con verbo*) never; (*enfático*) not ... ever; **no he estado n. en España**, I've never been to Spain; **yo no haría n. eso**, I wouldn't ever do that. **3** (*en ciertas construcciones*) ever; **casi n.**, hardly ever; **más que n.**, more than ever. **4 n. jamás**, never ever; (*futuro*) never again.
nupcial *adj* wedding, nuptial; **marcha n.**, wedding march.
nupcias *nfpl fml* wedding *sing*, nuptials; **casarse en segundas n.**, to marry again.
nutrición *nf* nutrition.
nutrir I *vtr* to nourish, feed. **II nutrirse** *vr* to feed (**de**, **con**, on).
nutritivo,-a *adj* nutritious, nourishing; **valor n.**, nutritional value.

Ñ

Ñ, ñ [ˈeɲe] *nf* (*la letra*) Ñ, ñ.
ñam *interj fam* **¡ñ., ñ.!**, yum-yum!, yummy!
ñame *nm Am* yarn.
ñapa *nf Am* bonus, little extra.
ñato,-a *adj Am* snub-nosed.
ñiquiñaque *nm fam* **1** (*objeto*) junk,

rubbish. **2** (*persona*) good-for-nothing.
ñoñería, ñoñez *nf* **1** (*sosería*) insipidness, bore. **2** (*melindrería*) fussiness.
ñoño,-a I *adj* **1** (*soso*) insipid, dull. **2** (*melindroso*) fussy. **II** *nm,f* dull *or* spineless person.
ñu *nm* gnu.

O

O, o |o| *nf (la letra)* O, o.

o *conj* or; **jueves o viernes**, Thursday or Friday; **o ... o**, either ... or; **o sea**, that is (to say), in other words.

O. *abr de* **Oeste**, West, W.

oasis *nm inv* oasis.

obcecado,-a *adj fig* stubborn.

obcecar |1| I *vtr fig* to blind; **la ira lo obceca**, he is blinded by anger. II **obcecarse** *vr fig* to refuse to budge; *(obsesionarse)* to become obsessed.

obedecer |33| I *vtr* to obey. II *vi* **o. a**, *(provenir)* to be due to; **¿a qué obedece esa actitud?**, what's the reason behind this attitude?

obediencia *nf* obedience.

obediente *adj* obedient.

obertura *nf* overture.

obesidad *nf* obesity.

obeso,-a *adj* obese.

óbice *nm* obstacle; **eso no es ó. para que yo no ...**, it won't prevent me from ....

obispo *nm* bishop.

objeción *nf* objection; **poner una o.**, to raise an objection, object.

objetar I *vtr* **no tengo nada que o.**, I've got no objections. II *vi Mil* to be a conscientious objector.

objetividad *nf* objectivity.

objetivo,-a I *nm* **1** *(fin, meta)* objective, aim. **2** *Mil* target. **3** *Cin Fot* lens; **o. zoom**, zoom lens. II *adj* objective.

objeto *nm* **1** object; **objetos perdidos**, lost property *sing*; **mujer o.**, sex object. **2** *(fin)* aim, purpose; **con o. de ...**, in order to ...; **tiene por o. ...**, it is designed to .... **3** *Ling* object.

objetor,-a I *nm,f* objector; **o. de conciencia**, conscientious objector. II *adj* objecting, dissenting.

obligación *nf* **1** *(deber)* obligation; **por o.**, out of a sense of duty; **tengo o. de ...**, I have to .... **2** *Fin* bond, debenture.

obligado,-a *adj* obliged; **verse** *o* **estar o. a**, to be obliged to.

obligar |7| *vtr* to compel, force.

obligatorio,-a *adj* compulsory, obligatory.

obra *nf* **1** *(trabajo)* (piece of) work; **por o. de**, thanks to. **2** *Arte* work; **o. maestra**, masterpiece. **3** *(acto)* deed. **4** *Constr* building site. **5 obras**, *(arreglos)* repairs; **'carretera en o.'**, 'roadworks'; **'cerrado por o.'**, 'closed for repairs'.

obrar I *vi* **1** *(proceder)* to act, behave; **o. bien/mal**, to do the right/wrong thing. **2** *fml* **obra en nuestro poder ...**, we are in receipt of .... II *vtr* *(milagro)* to work.

obrero,-a I *nm,f* worker, labourer, *US* laborer. II *adj* working; **clase obrera**, working class; **movimiento o.**, labour movement.

obscenidad *nf* obscenity.

obsceno,-a *adj* obscene.

obscurecer |33| I *vi impers* to get dark. II *vtr* to darken. III **obscurecerse** *vr (nublarse)* to become cloudy.

obscuridad *nf* darkness; *fig* obscurity.

obscuro,-a *adj* **1** dark. **2** *fig (origen, idea)* obscure; *(futuro)* uncertain, gloomy; *(asunto)* shady; *(nublado)* overcast.

obsequiar |12| *vtr* to give away.

obsequio *nm* gift, present.

observación *nf* observation.

observador,-a I *nm,f* observer. II *adj* observant.

observancia *nf* observance.

observar *vtr* **1** *(mirar)* to observe, watch. **2** *(notar)* to notice. **3** *(cumplir)* to observe.

observatorio *nm* observatory.

obsesión *nf* obsession.

obsesionar I *vtr* to obsess; **estoy obsesionado con eso**, I can't get it out of my mind. II **obsesionarse** *vr* to get obsessed.

obsesivo,-a *adj* obsessive.

obseso,-a *nm,f* obsessed person; **un o. sexual**, a sex maniac.

obsoleto,-a *adj* obsolete.

obstaculizar |4| *vtr* to obstruct, get in the way of.

obstáculo *nm* obstacle.

obstante (no) *loc adv* nevertheless; *prep* notwithstanding.

obstetricia *nf* obstetrics *sing*.

obstinación *nf* obstinacy.

obstinado,-a *adj* obstinate.

obstinarse *vr* to persist **(en**, in).

obstrucción *nf* obstruction; *Med* blockage.

obstruir |37| I *vtr* **1** *(salida, paso)* to block, obstruct. **2** *(progreso)* to impede, block. II **obstruirse** *vr* to get blocked up.

obtención *nf* obtaining.

obtener |24| I *vtr* *(alcanzar)* to obtain, get. II **obtenerse** *vr* **o. de**, *(provenir)* to come from.

obturador *nm Fot* shutter.

obtuso,-a *adj* obtuse.

obús *nm* shell.

obviar |12| *vtr* *(problema)* to get round.

obvio,-a *adj* obvious.

oca *nf* goose.

ocasión *nf* **1** *(momento)* occasion; **con o. de ...**, on the occasion of ...; **en cierta o.**, once. **2** *(oportunidad)* opportunity, chance; **aprovechar la o.**, to make the most of an opportunity. **3** *Com* bargain; **de o.**, cheap; **precios de o.**, bargain prices.

ocasional *adj* **1** *(eventual)* occasional; **tra-**

bajo o., casual work; **de forma o.**, occasionally. 2 *(fortuito)* accidental, chance.

ocasionar *vtr* to cause, bring about.

ocaso *nm (anochecer)* sunset; *fig (declive)* fall, decline.

occidental *adj* western, occidental.

occidente *nm* west; **el O.**, the West.

OCDE *nf abr de* **Organización para la Cooperación y el Desarrollo Económico,** Organization for Economic Co-operation and Development, OECD.

Oceanía *n* Oceania.

oceánico,-a *adj* oceanic.

océano *nm* ocean.

ochenta *adj & nm inv* eighty.

ocho *adj & nm inv* eight.

ochocientos,-as *adj & nm,f* eight hundred.

ocio *nm* leisure; **en mis ratos de o.**, in my spare *o* leisure time.

ocioso,-a *adj* 1 *(inactivo)* idle. 2 *(inútil)* pointless.

ocre *nm* ochre, *US* ocher.

octavilla *nf (panfleto)* hand-out, leaflet.

octavo,-a *adj & nm,f* eighth.

octogenario,-a *adj & nm,f* octogenarian.

octogésimo,-a *adj & nm,f* eightieth.

octubre *nm* October.

ocular *adj* **testigo o.**, eye witness.

oculista *nmf* ophthalmologist.

ocultar I *vtr* to conceal, hide; **o. algo a algn**, to hide sth from sb. **II ocultarse** *vr* to hide.

oculto,-a *adj* concealed, hidden.

ocupación *nf* occupation.

ocupado,-a *adj (persona)* busy; *(asiento)* taken; *(aseos, teléfono)* engaged; *(puesto de trabajo)* filled.

ocupante *nmf (de casa)* occupant, occupier; *(ilegal)* squatter; *(de vehículo)* occupant.

ocupar I *vtr* 1 to occupy. 2 *(espacio, tiempo)* to take up; *(cargo)* to hold, fill. **II ocuparse** *vr* **o. de,** *(cuidar)* to look after; *(encargarse)* to see to.

ocurrencia *nf (agudeza)* witty remark, wisecrack; *(idea)* idea.

ocurrente *adj* witty.

ocurrir I *v impers* to happen, occur; **¿qué ocurre?,** what's going on?; **¿qué te ocurre?,** what's the matter with you? **II ocurrirse** *vr* **no se me ocurre nada,** I can't think of anything; **se me ocurre que ...,** it occurs to me that ....

odiar |12| *vtr* to detest, hate; **odio tener que ...,** I hate having to ....

odio *nm* hatred, loathing; **mirada de o.,** hateful look.

odioso,-a *adj* hateful.

odontología *nf* dentistry, odontology.

odontólogo,-a *nm,f* dental surgeon, odontologist.

odre *nm* wineskin.

OEA *nf abr de* **Organización de Estados**

Americanos, Organization of American States, OAS.

oeste *nm* west.

ofender I *vtr* to offend. **II ofenderse** *vr* to get offended **(con, por,** by), take offence *o US* offense **(con, por,** at).

ofensa *nf* offence, *US* offense.

ofensiva *nf* offensive.

ofensivo,-a *adj* offensive.

oferta *nf* offer; *Fin Ind* bid, tender, proposal; *Com* **de/en o.,** on (special) offer; **o. y demanda,** supply and demand.

ofertar *vtr* to offer.

off *adj* **voz en o.,** *Cin TV* voice-over; *Teat* voice offstage.

offset *nm Impr* offset.

oficial,-a I *adj* official. **II** *nm* 1 *Mil Náut* officer. 2 *(empleado)* clerk. 3 *(obrero)* skilled worker.

oficialismo *nm Am (gobierno)* government.

oficina *nf* office; **o. de empleo,** job centre, *US* job office; **o. de turismo,** tourist office; **o. de correos,** post office; **horas/horario de o.,** business hours.

oficinista *nmf* office worker, clerk.

oficio *nm* 1 *(ocupación)* job, occupation; *(profesión)* trade; **ser del o.,** to be in the trade. 2 *(comunicación oficial)* official letter *o* note; **de o.,** ex-officio; **abogado de o.,** state-appointed lawyer. 3 *Rel* service.

oficioso,-a *adj (noticia, fuente)* unofficial.

ofimática *nf* office automation.

ofimático,-a *adj Inform* **paquete o.,** business package.

ofrecer |33| **I** *vtr* 1 to offer. 2 *(aspecto)* to present. **II ofrecerse** *vr* 1 *(prestarse)* to offer, volunteer. 2 *(situación)* to present itself. 3 *fml* **¿qué se le ofrece?,** what can I do for you?

ofrecimiento *nm* offering.

ofrendar *vtr Rel* to make offerings *o* an offering.

ofrezco *indic pres* → **ofrecer.**

oftalmología *nf* ophthalmology.

oftalmólogo,-a *nm,f* ophthalmologist.

ofuscación *nf*, **ofuscamiento** *nm* blinding, dazzling.

ofuscar |1| *vtr* 1 *fig (confundir)* to blind. 2 *(deslumbrar)* to dazzle.

oídas (de) *loc adv* by hearsay.

oído *nm* 1 *(sentido)* hearing. 2 *(órgano)* ear; **aprender de o.,** to learn by ear; *fig* **hacer oídos sordos,** to turn a deaf ear.

oír |17| *vtr* to hear; **¡oye!, hey!; ¡oiga!,** excuse me!; *fam* **como lo oyes,** believe it or not.

OIT *nf abr de* **Organización Internacional del Trabajo,** International Labour Organization, ILO.

ojal *nm* buttonhole.

ojalá I *interj* let's hope so!, I hope so! **II** *conj (+ subj)* **¡o. sea cierto!,** I hope it's true!

ojeada *nf* echar una o., to have a quick look.

ojeras *nfpl* rings *o* bags under the eyes.

ojeriza *nf* dislike.

ojo I *nm* **1** eye; **o. morado** black eye; **ojos saltones,** bulging eyes; *fig* **a ojos vista,** clearly, openly; *fig* **calcular a o.,** to guess; *fam* **no pegué o.,** I didn't sleep a wink. **2** *(de aguja)* eye; *(de cerradura)* keyhole. **3** *(de un puente)* span. **II** *interj* careful!, look out!

ojota *nf Am* sandal.

okupa *nmf* squatter.

ola *nf* wave; **o. de calor,** heatwave.

ole, olé *interj* bravo!

oleada *nf* wave; *fig* **o. de turistas,** influx of tourists.

oleaje *nm* swell.

óleo *nm Arte* oil; **pintura** *o* **cuadro al ó.,** oil painting.

oleoducto *nm* pipeline.

oler [4] **I** *vtr* **1** *(percibir olor)* to smell. **2** *fig* *(adivinar)* to smell, feel. **II** *vi* **1** *(exhalar)* to smell; **o. a,** to smell of; **o. bien/mal,** to smell good/bad. **2** *fig* *(parecer)* to smack (a, of). **III olerse** *vr fig* *(adivinar)* to feel, sense; **me lo olía,** I thought as much.

olfatear *vtr* **1** *(oler)* to sniff. **2** *fig* *(indagar)* to pry into.

olfato *nm* sense of smell; *fig* good nose, instinct.

oligarquía *nf* oligarchy.

olimpiada *nf Dep* Olympiad, Olympic Games *pl*; **las olimpiadas,** the Olympic Games.

olímpico,-a *adj* Olympic; **Juegos Olímpicos,** Olympic Games.

olímpicamente *adv* **paso o. de estudiar,** I couldn't give a damn about studying.

oliva *nf* olive; **aceite de o.,** olive oil.

olivar *nm* olive grove.

olivo *nm* olive (tree).

olmo *nm* smooth-leaved elm.

olor *nm* smell; **o. corporal,** body odour.

oloroso,-a *adj* fragant, sweet-smelling.

OLP *nf abr de* **Organización para la Liberación de Palestina,** Palestine Liberation Organization, PLO.

olvidadizo,-a *adj* forgetful.

olvidar I *vtr* **1** to forget; *fam* **¡olvídame!,** leave me alone! **2 olvidé el paraguas allí,** I left my umbrella there. **II olvidarse** *vr* to forget; **se me ha olvidado hacerlo,** I forgot to do it.

olvido *nm* **1** *(desmemoria)* oblivion. **2** *(lapsus)* oversight.

olla *nf* saucepan, pot; **o. exprés** *o* **a presión,** pressure cooker.

ombligo *nm* navel.

ominoso,-a *adj* shameful.

omisión *nf* omission.

omiso,-a *adj* **hacer caso o. de,** to take no

notice of.

omitir *vtr* to omit, leave out.

omnipotente *adj* omnipotent, almighty.

omnipresente *adj* omnipresent.

omnisciente *adj* omniscient, all-knowing.

omnívoro,-a I *adj* omnivorous. **II** *nm,f* omnivore.

omóplato, omoplato *nm* shoulder blade.

OMS *nf abr de* **Organización Mundial de la Salud,** World Health Organization, WHO.

once I *adj inv* eleven. **II** *nm inv* eleven; *Ftb* eleven, team.

ONCE *nf abr de* **Organización Nacional de Ciegos Españoles,** ≈ Royal National Institute for the Blind, RNIB.

onda *nf* **1** *Fís* wave; *fam fig* **estar en la o.,** to be with it; **o. expansiva,** shock wave; *Rad* **o. larga/media/corta,** long/medium/short wave. **2** *(en el agua)* ripple. **3** *(de pelo)* wave.

ondear *vi* **1** *(bandera)* to flutter. **2** *(de agua)* to ripple.

ondulación *nf* undulation; *(de agua)* ripple.

ondulado,-a *adj* *(pelo)* wavy; *(paisaje)* rolling.

ondulante *adj* undulating.

ondular I *vtr* *(el pelo)* to wave. **II** *vi* *(moverse)* to undulate.

oneroso,-a *adj* *(impuesto)* heavy.

onomástica *nf* saint's day.

onomatopeya *nf* onomatopoeia.

ONU *nf abr de* **Organización de las Naciones Unidas,** United Nations (Organization), UN(O).

onubense I *adj* of *o* from Huelva. **II** *nmf* native *o* inhabitant of Huelva.

onza *nf* *(medida)* ounce.

OPA *abr de* **Oferta Pública de Adquisición,** takeover bid.

opaco,-a *adj* opaque.

ópalo *nm* opal.

opción *nf* **1** *(elección)* option, choice; *(alternativa)* alternative. **2** *(posibilidad)* opportunity, chance.

opcional *adj* optional.

open *nm Golf* open.

OPEP *nf abr de* **Organización de los Países Exportadores de Petróleo,** Organization of Petroleum Exporting Countries, OPEC.

ópera *nf Mús* opera.

operación *nf* **1** *Med* operation; **o. quirúrgica,** surgical operation. **2** *Fin* transaction, deal; **operaciones bursátiles,** stock exchange transactions. **3** *Mat* operation.

operador,-a *nm,f* **1** *(técnico)* operator. **2** *Cin (de cámara)* *(hombre)* cameraman; *(mujer)* camerawoman; *(del proyector)* projectionist. **3** *Tel* operator.

operante *adj* operative.

operar I *vtr* **1** *Med* to operate (a, on). **2** *(cambio etc)* to bring about. **II** *vi Fin* to

deal, do business (**con**, with). **III ope-
rarse** *vr* **1** *Med* to have an operation (**de**,
for). **2** (*producirse*) to occur, come about.
operario,-a *nm,f* operator; (*obrero*) worker.
operativo,-a *adj* operative.
opereta *nf* operetta.
opinar *vi* **1** (*pensar*) to think. **2** (*declarar*)
to give one's opinion, be of the opinion.
opinión *nf* **1** (*juicio*) opinion; **cambiar de
o.**, to change one's mind.
opio *nm* opium.
oponente *nmf* opponent.
oponer [19] (*pp* **opuesto**) **I** *vtr* (*resistencia*)
to offer. **II oponerse** *vr* (*estar en contra*)
to be opposed, be against; **se opone a
aceptarlo**, he refuses to accept it.
oporto *nm* (*vino*) port.
oportunidad *nf* opportunity, chance.
oportunista *adj & nmf* opportunist.
oportuno,-a *adj* **1** (*adecuado*) timely; **¡qué
o.!**, what good timing! **2** (*conveniente*) appropriate; **si te parece o.**, if you think it
appropiate.
oposición *nf* **1** opposition. **2** (*examen*)
competitive examination.
opositar *vi* to sit a competitive examination.
opositor,-a *nm,f* **1** (*candidato*) candidate
for a competitive examination. **2** *Am Pol*
opponent.
opresión *nf* oppression; **o. en el pecho**,
tightness of the chest.
opresivo,-a *adj* oppressive.
opresor,-a I *nm,f* oppressor. **II** *adj* oppressive, oppressing.
oprimir *vtr* **1** (*pulsar*) to press. **2** (*subyugar*) to oppress.
oprobio *nm* ignominy, opprobrium.
optar *vi* **1** (*elegir*) to choose (**entre**,
between); **opté por ir yo mismo**, I decided to go myself. **2** (*aspirar*) to apply
(**a**, for); **puede o. a medalla**, he's in with
a chance of winning a medal.
optativo,-a *adj* optional.
óptica *nf* **1** (*tienda*) optician's (shop). **2**
(*punto de vista*) angle.
óptico,-a I *adj* optical. **II** *nm,f* optician.
optimismo *nm* optimism.
optimista I *adj* optimistic. **II** *nmf* optimist.
óptimo,-a *adj* optimum, excellent.
opuesto,-a *adj* **1** (*contrario*) contrary; **en
direcciones opuestas**, in opposite directions; **gustos opuestos**, conflicting tastes.
2 (*de enfrente*) opposite; **el extremo o.**,
the other end.
opulencia *nf* opulence.
opulento,-a *adj* opulent.
opuse *pt indef* → **oponer**.
oración *nf* **1** *Rel* prayer. **2** *Ling* clause,
sentence.
oráculo *nm* oracle.
orador,-a *nm,f* speaker, orator.

oral *adj* oral; *Med* **por vía o.**, to be taken
orally.
orangután *nm* orang-outang, orang-utan.
orar *vi Rel* to pray.
oratoria *nf* oratory.
órbita *nf* **1** orbit. **2** *Anat* eye socket.
orden I *nm* order; **o. público**, law and
order; **por o. alfabético**, in alphabetical
order; **de primer o.**, first-rate; **o. del día**,
agenda; **del o. de**, approximately. **II** *nf* **1**
(*mandato*) order; *Mil* **¡a la o.!**, sir! **2** *Jur*
warrant, order; **o. de registro**, search
warrant; **o. judicial**, court order.
ordenado,-a *adj* tidy.
ordenador,-a *nm* computer; **o. personal**,
personal computer.
ordenamiento *nm* ordering.
ordenanza I *nm* (*empleado*) office boy. **II**
nf regulations; **o. municipal**, by-laws.
ordenar I *vtr* **1** (*organizar*) to put in
order; (*habitación*) to tidy up. **2** (*mandar*)
to order. **II ordenarse** *vr Rel* to be
ordained (**de**, as), take holy orders.
ordeñar *vtr* to milk.
ordinario,-a *adj* **1** (*corriente*) ordinary,
common. **2** (*grosero*) vulgar, common.
orégano *nm* oregano, marjoram.
oreja *nf* ear; (*de sillón*) wing.
orejero,-a *adj Am* (*soplón*) grass.
orfanato *nm* orphanage.
orfebre *nm* (*del oro*) goldsmith; (*de la plata*) silversmith.
orfebrería *nf* gold o silver work.
orfelinato *nm* orphanage.
orgánico,-a *adj* organic.
organigrama *nm* organization chart;
Inform flow chart.
organismo *nm* **1** (*ser vivo*) organism. **2**
(*institución*) organization, body.
organista *nmf* organist.
organización *nf* organization.
organizado,-a *adj* organized; **viaje o.**,
package tour.
organizador,-a I *adj* organizing. **II** *nm,f*
organizer.
organizar [4] **I** *vtr* to organize. **II organi-
zarse** *vr fig* (*armarse*) to happen.
órgano *nm* organ.
orgasmo *nm* orgasm.
orgía *nf* orgy.
orgullo *nm* **1** (*propia estima*) pride. **2** (*arrogancia*) arrogance.
orgulloso,-a *adj* **1 estar o.**, (*satisfecho*) to
be proud. **2 ser o.**, (*arrogante*) to be arrogant, haughty.
orientación *nf* **1** (*dirección*) orientation,
direction. **2** (*guía*) guidance; **curso de o.**,
induction course.
oriental I *adj* eastern, oriental. **II** *nmf* Oriental.
orientar I *vtr* **1** (*enfocar*) to aim (**a**, at), intend (**a**, for); **orientado al consumo**, intended for consumption. **2** (*indicar camino*) to give directions to; *fig* (*aconsejar*) to

advise. **3** *una casa orientada al sur*, a house facing south. **4** *(esfuerzo)* to direct. **II orientarse** *vr (encontrar el camino)* to get one's bearings, find one's way about.

oriente *nm* East, Orient; **el Extremo** *o* **Lejano/Medio/Próximo O.**, the Far/Middle/Near East.

orificio *nm* hole, opening; *Anat Téc* orifice; **o. de entrada**, inlet; **o. de salida**, outlet.

origen *nm* origin; **país de o.**, country of origin; **dar o. a**, to give rise to.

original *adj & nmf* original.

originalidad *nf* originality.

originar **I** *vtr* to cause, give rise to. **II originarse** *vr* to originate.

originario,-a *adj* native.

◆**originariamente** *adv* originally.

orilla *nf (borde)* edge; *(del río)* bank; *(del mar)* shore.

orillero,-a *adj Am (persona)* suburban.

orín[1] *nm (herrumbre)* rust.

orín[2] *nm (usu pl) (orina)* urine.

orina *nf* urine.

orinal *nm* chamberpot; *fam* potty.

orinar **I** *vi* to urinate. **II orinarse** *vr* to wet oneself.

oriundo,-a *adj* native of; **ser o. de**, to come from.

orla *nf Univ* graduation photograph.

ornamentar *vtr* to adorn, embellish.

ornamento *nm* ornament.

ornar *vt* to adorn, embellish.

ornato *nm (atavío)* finery; *(adorno)* decoration.

ornitología *nf* ornithology.

ornitólogo,-a *nm,f* ornithologist.

oro *nm* **1** gold; **de o.**, gold, golden; **o. de ley**, fine gold. **2** *Naipes* **oros**, *(baraja española)* ≈ diamonds.

orquesta *nf* orchestra; *(de verbena)* dance band.

orquestar *vtr* to orchestrate.

orquídea *nf* orchid.

ortiga *nf (stinging)* nettle.

ortodoxia *nf* orthodoxy.

ortodoxo,-a *adj & nm,f* orthodox.

ortografía *nf* orthography, spelling; **faltas de o.**, spelling mistakes.

ortográfico,-a *adj* orthographic, orthographical; **signos ortográficos**, punctuation *sing*.

ortopédico,-a *adj* orthopaedic, *US* orthopedic; **pierna ortopédica**, artificial leg.

oruga *nf* caterpillar.

orzuelo *nm Med* sty, stye.

os *pron pers pl* **1** *(complemento directo)* you; **os veo mañana**, I'll see you tomorrow. **2** *(complemento indirecto)* you, to you; **os daré el dinero**, I'll give you the money; **os escribiré**, I'll write to you. **3** *(con verbo reflexivo)* yourselves. **4** *(con verbo recíproco)* each other; **os queréis mucho**, you love each other very much.

osa *nf* **O. Mayor**, Great Bear, *US* Big Dipper; **O. Menor**, Little Bear, *US* Little Dipper.

osadía *nf* **1** *(audacia)* daring. **2** *(desvergüenza)* impudence.

osado,-a *adj* **1** *(audaz)* daring. **2** *(desvergonzado)* shameless.

osar *vi* to dare.

osario *nm* ossuary.

oscilación *nf* **1** oscillation. **2** *(de precios)* fluctuation.

oscilante *adj* **1** oscillating. **2** *(precios)* fluctuating.

oscilar *vi* **1** *Fís* to oscillate. **2** *(variar)* to vary, fluctuate.

oscuras (a) *loc adv* in the dark; **nos quedamos a o.**, we were left in darkness.

oscurecer [33] *vi impers & vtr & vr* → obscurecer.

oscuridad *nf* → obscuridad.

oscuro,-a *adj* → obscuro,-a.

óseo,-a *adj* osseous, bony; **tejido ó.**, bone tissue.

osito *nm fam* **o. (de peluche)**, teddy bear.

ósmosis, osmosis *nf inv* osmosis.

oso *nm* bear; **o. polar**, polar bear; **o. hormiguero**, anteater; **o. marino**, fur seal; *fam fig* **hacer el o.**, to play the fool.

ostensible *adj* ostensible.

ostentación *nf* ostentation; **hacer o. de algo**, to show sth off.

ostentar *vtr* **1** *(lucir)* to flaunt. **2** *(cargo)* to hold.

ostentoso,-a *adj* ostentatious.

osteópata *nmf* osteopath.

osteopatía *nf* osteopathy.

ostra *nf* oyster; *fig* **aburrirse como una o.**, to be bored stiff; *fam* **¡ostras!**, crikey!, *US* gee!

ostracismo *nm* ostracism.

OTAN *nf abr de* **Organización del Tratado del Atlántico Norte**, North Atlantic Treaty Organization, NATO.

otear *vtr (horizonte)* to scan, search.

OTI *nf abr de* **Organización de la Televisión Iberoamericana**.

otitis *nf inv* infection and inflammation of the ear, otitis.

otoñal *adj* autumnal, autumn, *US* fall.

otoño *nm* autumn, *US* fall.

otorgamiento *nm (concesión)* granting; *(de un premio)* award.

otorgar [7] *vtr* **1** *(premio)* to award (**a**, to); **o. un indulto**, to grant pardon. **2** *(permiso)* to grant (**a**, to).

otorrinolaringólogo,-a *nm,f* ear, nose and throat specialist.

otro,-a **I** *adj indef* **1** *(sin artículo)* *(sing)* another; *(pl)* other; **o. coche**, another car; **otras personas**, other people. **2** *(con artículo definido)* other; **el o. coche**, the other car. **3 otra cosa**, something else; **otra vez**, again. **II** *pron indef* **1** *(sin artículo)* *(sing)* another (one); *(pl)* *(personas)*

others; (cosas) other ones; **dame o.**, give
me another (one); **no es mío, es de o.**,
it's not mine, it's somebody else's. **2** (con
artículo definido) (sing) the other (one);
(pl) (personas) the others; (cosas) the other
ones. **3 hacer o. tanto**, to do likewise.
ovación nf ovation.
ovacionar vtr to give an ovation to, applaud.
oval, ovalado,-a adj oval.
óvalo nm oval.
ovario nm ovary.
oveja nf **1** sheep; (hembra) ewe; fig **la o.
negra**, the black sheep.
overol nm Am overalls pl.
ovillo nm ball (of wool); fig **hacerse un
o.**, to curl up into a ball.
ovino,-a adj ovine; **ganado o.**, sheep pl.
OVNI nm abr de **objeto volador no
identificado**, unidentified flying object,
UFO.
ovular I adj ovular. II vi to ovulate.
óvulo nm ovule.
oxidación nf (metal) rusting.
oxidado,-a adj (metal) rusty; fig **su inglés
está un poco o.**, her English is a bit
rusty.
oxidar I vtr Quím to oxidize; (metales) to
rust. II **oxidarse** vr Quím to oxidize; (metales) to rust, go rusty.
óxido nm **1** oxide; **ó. de carbono**, carbon
monoxide. **2** (orín) rust.
oxigenado,-a adj oxygenated; **agua oxi-
genada**, (hydrogen) peroxide.
oxígeno nm oxygen; **bomba de o.**, oxygen cylinder o tank.
oye indic pres & imperat → **oír**.
oyente nmf **1** Rad listener. **2** Univ occasional student.

ozono nm ozone; **capa de o.**, ozone layer.

P

P, p [pe] nf (la letra) P, p.
pabellón nm **1 p. de deportes**, sports
centre. **2** (en feria) stand. **3** (bloque)
wing. **4** (bandera) flag.
pábulo nm fml fig fuel; **dar p. a**, to encourage.
pacer [33] vtr & vi to graze, pasture.
pachá nm fam fig **vivir como un p.**, to
live like a king.
pachanguero,-a adj fam pey (música)
catchy.
pachón,-ona nm,f (perro) pointer.
pachorra nf fam sluggishness; **tener p.**, to
be phlegmatic.
paciencia nf patience; **armarse de p.**, to
grin and bear it.
paciente adj & nmf patient.
pacificación nf pacification.
pacificador,-a I adj pacifying. II nm,f
peacemaker.
pacificar [1] I vtr to pacify; fig (apaciguar)
to appease, calm. II **pacificarse** vr to
calm down.
pacífico,-a adj peaceful.
Pacífico nm el (océano) **P.**, the Pacific
(Ocean).
pacifismo nm pacifism.
pacifista adj & nmf pacifist.
paco nm Am fam (policía) policeman.
pacotilla nf fam **de p.**, second-rate.
pactar vtr to agree.
pacto nm pact; **el P. de Varsovia**, the
Warsaw Pact; **p. de caballeros**, gentlemen's agreement.
padecer [33] vtr & vi to suffer; **padece
del corazón**, he suffers from heart
trouble.
padecimiento nm suffering.
padrastro nm **1** stepfather. **2** (pellejo)
hangnail.
padrazo nm easy-going o indulgent father.
padre I nm **1** father; **p. de familia**, family
man. **2 padres**, parents. II adj fam huge;
pegarse la vida p., to live like a king.
padrenuestro nm Lord's Prayer.
padrino nm **1** (de bautizo) godfather; (de
boda) best man; **padrinos**, godparents. **2**
(espónsor) sponsor.
padrón nm census.
paella nf paella (rice dish made with vegetables, meat and/or seafood).
paellera nf paella pan.
pág abr de **página**, page, p.
paga nf (salario) wage; (de niños) pocket
money; **p. extra**, bonus.
pagadero,a adj payable; Fin **cheque p. al
portador**, cheque payable to bearer.
pagador,-a nm,f payer.
pagano,-a adj & nm,f pagan, heathen.
pagar [7] vtr **1** to pay; **p. en metálico** o **al
contado**, to pay cash; **p. por**, (producto,
mala acción) to pay for; fig **(ella) lo ha
pagado caro**, she's paid dearly for it. **2**
(recompensar) repay.
pagaré nm Fin promissory note, IOU; **p.
del tesoro**, treasury note.
página nf page; **en la p. 3**, on page 3; fig
una p. importante de la historia, an
important chapter in history.
pago nm payment; **p. adelantado** o **anticipado**, advance payment; **p. contra
reembolso**, cash on delivery; **p. inicial**,
down payment.
paila nf Am (frying) pan.
paipái, paipay nm (pl paipáis) large palm
fan.
país nm country, land; **vino del p.**, local
wine; **P. Vasco**, Basque Country; **P. Va-**

lenciano, Valencia.

paisaje *nm* landscape, scenery.

paisano,-a I *adj* of the same country. II *nm,f* (*compatriota*) fellow countryman *o* countrywoman, compatriot; **en traje de p.**, in plain clothes.

Países Bajos *npl* (los) P. B., the Netherlands, the Low Countries.

paja *nf* 1 straw. 2 *fam fig* (*bazofia*) padding, waffle. 3 *vulg* **hacerse una p.**, to wank.

pajar *nm* (*almacén*) straw loft; (*en el exterior*) straw rick.

pajarita *nf* 1 bow tie. 2 (*de papel*) paper bird.

pájaro *nm* 1 bird; **Madrid a vista de p.**, a bird's-eye view of Madrid; **p. carpintero**, woodpecker. 2 *fam* **tener pájaros**, to have daft ideas.

Pakistán *n* Pakistan.

pakistaní *adj & nmf* Pakistani.

pala *nf* 1 shovel; (*de jardinero*) spade; (*de cocina*) *Dep* (*de ping-pong, frontón*) bat; (*de remo*) blade.

palabra *nf* 1 word; **de p.**, by word of mouth; **dirigir la p. a algn**, to address sb; **juego de palabras**, pun. 2 (*promesa*) word; **p. de honor**, word of honour. 3 (*turno para hablar*) right to speak; **tener la p.**, to have the floor.

palabrería *nf* palaver.

palabrota *nf* swearword.

palacio *nm* (*grande*) palace; (*pequeño*) mansion; **P. de Justicia**, Law Courts.

paladar *nm* 1 palate. 2 (*sabor*) taste.

paladear *vtr* to savour, *US* savor, relish.

palanca *nf* 1 lever. 2 (*manecilla*) handle, stick; *Aut* **p. de cambio**, gearstick, *US* gearshift; **p. de mando**, control lever. 3 *Dep* (*trampolín*) diving board.

palangana *nf* washbasin.

palco *nm* box.

paleolítico *adj* palaeolithic, paleolithic.

paleontología *nf* palaeontology, paleontology.

Palestina *n* Palestine.

palestino,-a *adj & nm,f* Palestinian.

palestra *nf* arena; *fig* **salir** *o* **saltar a la p.**, to enter the fray, take the field.

paleta *nf* 1 (*espátula*) slice. 2 (*de pintor*) palette; (*de albañil*) trowel. 3 *Dep* (*de cricket, pingpong*) bat.

paletilla *nf* 1 shoulder blade. 2 *Culin* shoulder.

paleto,-a I *adj fam pey* unsophisticated, boorish. II *nm,f fam pey* country bumpkin, yokel.

paliar [12] *vtr* to alleviate, palliate.

paliativo,-a *adj & nm* palliative.

palidecer [33] *vi* 1 (*persona*) to turn pale. 2 *fig* (*disminuir*) to diminish, be on the wane.

palidez *nf* paleness, pallor.

pálido,-a *adj* pale.

palillero *nm* toothpick case.

palillo *nm* 1 (*mondadientes*) toothpick; **palillos chinos**, chopsticks. 2 *Mús* drumstick.

palio *nm* 1 canopy. 2 *Rel* pallium.

palique *nm fam* chat, small talk.

paliza *nf* 1 (*zurra*) thrashing, beating; **darle a algn una p.**, to beat sb up. 2 (*derrota*) beating. 3 *fam* (*pesadez*) bore, pain (in the neck).

palma *nf* 1 *Anat* palm. 2 *Bot* palm tree. 3 **hacer palmas**, to applaud.

palmada *nf* 1 (*golpe*) slap. 2 **palmadas**, applause, clapping.

palmar *vtr fam* **palmarla**, to snuff it, kick the bucket.

palmarés *nm* 1 (*historial*) service record. 2 (*vencedores*) list of winners.

palmatoria *nf* candlestick.

palmera *nf* palm tree.

palmo *nm* (*medida*) span; *fig* **p. a p.**, inch by inch.

palo *nm* 1 stick; (*vara*) rod; (*de escoba*) broomstick; *fig* **a p. seco**, on its own. 2 (*golpe*) blow; *fig* **dar un p. a algn**, to let sb down. 3 **de p.**, wooden. 4 *Dep* (*de portería*) woodwork. 5 *Golf* club. 6 *Naipes* suit.

paloma *nf* pigeon; *Lit* dove; **p. mensajera**, homing *o* carrier pigeon.

palomar *nm* pigeon house, dovecote.

palomilla *nf* 1 grain moth. 2 (*tuerca*) wing *o* butterfly nut.

palomitas (de maíz) *nfpl* popcorn *sing*.

palpable *adj* palpable.

palpar *vtr* to touch, feel; *Med* to palpate.

palpitación *nf* palpitation, throbbing.

palpitante *adj* palpitating, throbbing; (*asunto*) burning.

palpitar *vi* to palpitate, throb.

palúdico,-a *adj* malarial.

paludismo *nm* malaria.

palurdo,-a *adj* uncouth, boorish.

pamela *nf* broad-brimmed hat.

pampa *nf* pampa, pampas *pl*.

pamplina *nf fam* nonsense.

pan *nm* bread; **p. de molde**, loaf of bread; **p. integral**, wholemeal *o* wholewheat bread; **p. rallado**, breadcrumbs *pl*; *fam fig* **más bueno que el p.**, as good as gold; *fam fig* **es p. comido**, it's a piece of cake.

pana *nf* corduroy.

panacea *nf* panacea.

panadería *nf* baker's (shop), bakery.

panadero,-a *nm,f* baker.

panal *nm* honeycomb.

Panamá *n* Panama.

panamá *nm* (*sombrero*) Panama hat.

panameño,-a *adj & nm,f* Panamanian.

pancarta *nf* placard; (*en manifestación*) banner.

páncreas *nm inv* pancreas.

panda¹ *nm* panda.

panda² *nf* gang.

pandereta *nf* tambourine.
pandilla *nf fam* gang.
panecillo *nm* bread roll.
panel *nm* panel.
panera *nf* breadbasket.
pánfilo,-a *adj fam (bobo)* silly, stupid; *(crédulo)* gullible.
panfleto *nm* lampoon, political pamphlet.
pánico *nm* panic; **sembrar el p.**, to cause panic.
panocha *nf Bot* corncob; *(de trigo etc)* ear.
panoli *nmf fam* idiot.
panorama *nm (vista)* panorama, view; *fig* panorama.
panorámico,-a *adj* panoramic.
pantaletas *nfpl Am* panties.
pantalón *nm (usu pl)* trousers *pl*; **p. vaquero**, jeans *pl*.
pantalla *nf* 1 *Cin TV Inform* screen. 2 *(de lámpara)* shade. 3 *fig* **servir de p.**, to act as a decoy.
pantano *nm Geog* 1 *(natural)* marsh, bog. 2 *(artificial)* reservoir.
panteón *nm* pantheon, mausoleum; **p. familiar**, family vault.
pantera *nf* panther.
pantomima *nf Teat* pantomime, mime; *pey (farsa)* farce.
pantorrilla *nf Anat* calf.
pantufla *nf* slipper.
panty *nm* (pair of) tights *pl*.
panza *nf fam* belly, paunch.
panzada *nf fam* bellyful.
panzudo,-a, **panzón,-ona**, *adj* potbellied, paunchy.
pañal *nm* nappy, *US* diaper; *fig* **estar en pañales**, to be in one's infancy.
paño *nm* 1 cloth material; *(de lana)* woollen o *US* woolen cloth; *(para polvo)* duster, rag; *(de cocina)* dishcloth; *fig* **paños calientes**, half measures. 2 **paños**, *(ropa)* clothes; **en p. menores**, in one's underclothes.
pañoleta *nf* 1 shawl. 2 *Taur* bullfighter's tie.
pañuelo *nm* handkerchief; *(pañoleta)* shawl.
papa *nf* potato; *fam* **no saber ni p. (de algo)**, not to have the faintest idea (about sth).
Papa *nm* **el P.**, the Pope.
papá *nm fam* dad, daddy.
papada *nf* double chin.
papagayo *nm* parrot.
papamoscas *nm inv* flycatcher.
papanatas *nmf inv* sucker, twit.
paparrucha(da) *nf* (piece of) nonsense.
papaya *nf* papaya o papaw fruit.
papear *vi arg* to eat.
papel *nm* 1 paper; *(hoja)* piece o sheet of paper; **papeles**, *(documentos)* documents, identification papers; **p. higiénico**, toilet paper; **p. carbón**, carbon paper; **p. de carta**, writing paper, stationery; **p. de**

alumimio/de estraza, aluminium foil/brown paper; **p. de fumar**, cigarette paper; **p. de lija**, sandpaper; *Fin* **p. moneda**, paper money, banknotes *pl*; **p. pintado**, wallpaper; **p. secante**, blotting paper. 2 *Cin Teat* role, part.
papeleo *nm fam* paperwork.
papelera *nf (en despacho)* wastepaper basket; *(en calle)* litter bin.
papelería *nf (tienda)* stationer's.
papeleta *nf* 1 *(de rifa)* ticket; *(de votación)* ballot paper; *(de resultados)* report. 2 *fam (dificultad)* tricky problem, difficult job.
papeo *nm arg* grub.
paperas *nfpl Med* mumps.
papilla *nf* pap, mush; *(de niños)* baby food.
papista *nmf* papist.
Papúa Nueva Guinea *n* Papua New Guinea.
paquete *nm* 1 *(de cigarrillos etc)* packet; *(postal)* parcel, package. 2 *(conjunto)* set, package; *Fin* **p. de acciones**, share package. 3 *Inform* software package. 4 *arg (castigo)* punishment. 5 *arg (pene)* prick.
Paquistán *n* Pakistan.
paquistaní *adj & nmf* Pakistani.
par **I** *adj Mat* even. **II** *nm* 1 *(pareja)* pair; *(dos)* couple. 2 *Mat* even number; **pares y nones**, odds and evens. 3 *(noble)* peer. 4 *(locuciones)* **a la p.**, *(a la vez)* at the same time; **de p. en p.**, wide open; *fig* **sin p.**, matchless.
para *prep* 1 for; **bueno p. la salud**, good for your health; **¿p. qué?**, what for?; **p. ser inglés habla muy bien español**, for an Englishman he speaks very good Spanish. 2 *(finalidad)* to, in order to; **p. terminar antes**, to o in order to finish earlier; **p. que lo disfrutes**, for you to enjoy. 3 *(tiempo)* by; **p. entonces**, by then. 4 *(a punto de)* **está p. salir**, it's about to leave. 5 *(locuciones)* **decir p. sí**, to say to oneself; **ir p. viejo**, to be getting old; **no es p. tanto**, it's not as bad as all that; **p. mí**, in my opinion.
parábola *nf* 1 *Geom* parabola. 2 *Rel* parable.
parabólico,-a *adj* parabolic; *TV* **antena parabólica**, satellite dish.
parabrisas *nm inv Aut* windscreen, *US* windshield.
paraca *nm fam* para(chutist).
paracaídas *nm inv* parachute.
paracaidista *nmf Dep* parachutist; *Mil* paratrooper.
parachoques *nm inv* bumper, *US* fender.
parada *nf* 1 stop; **p. de autobús**, bus stop; **p. de taxis**, taxi stand o rank. 2 *Ftb* save, stop.
paradero *nm (lugar)* whereabouts *pl*. 2 *Am (apeadero)* stop.
parado,-a **I** *adj* 1 stopped, stationary; *(quieto)* still; *(fábrica)* at a standstill; *fig*

salir bien/mal p., to come off well/badly.
2 *(desempleado)* unemployed, out of
work. 3 *fig (lento)* slow. 4 *Am (de pie)*
standing. II *nm,f* unemployed person.
paradoja *nf* paradox.
paradójico,-a *adj* paradoxical.
parador *nm* roadside inn; **p. nacional** *o*
de turismo,state-run hotel.
parafernalia *nf* paraphernalia *pl.*
parafrasear *vtr* to paraphrase.
paráfrasis *nf inv* paraphrase.
paraguas *nm inv* umbrella.
Paraguay *n* Paraguay.
paragüero *nm* umbrella stand.
paraíso *nm* 1 paradise; **p. terrenal,** heaven on earth; *Fin* **p. fiscal,** tax haven. 2
Teat gods *pl,* gallery.
paraje *nm* spot, place.
paralelo,-a *adj & nm* parallel.
parálisis *nm inv* paralysis; **p. infantil,** po-
liomylitis.
paralítico,-a *adj & nm,f* paralytic.
paralización *nf* 1 *Med* paralysis. 2 *(detención)* halting, stopping.
paralizar [1] I *vtr* to paralyse; *(circulación)*
to stop. II **paralizarse** *vr fig* to come to a
standstill.
parámetro *nm* parameter.
paramilitar *adj* paramilitary.
páramo *nm* bleak plain *o* plateau, moor.
parangón *nm fml* comparison; **sin p.,** incomparable.
paranoia *nf* paranoia.
paranoico,-a *adj & nm,f* paranoiac, paranoid.
parapeto *nm* 1 parapet. 2 *(de defensa)*
barricade.
parapléjico,-a *adj & nm,f* paraplegic.
parar I *vtr* 1 to stop. 2 *Dep* to save. II *vi*
1 to stop; **p. de hacer algo,** to stop doing
sth; **sin p.,** nonstop, without stopping;
fam **no p.,** to be always on the go. 2 *(alojarse)* to stay. 3 *(acabar)* **fue a p. a la
cárcel,** he ended up in jail. III **pararse**
vtr 1 to stop; **p. a pensar,** to stop to
think. 2 *Am (ponerse en pie)* to stand up.
pararrayos *nm inv* lightning conductor,
US lightning rod.
parásito,-a *adj nm* parasite.
parasol *nm* sunshade, parasol.
parcela *nf* plot.
parche *nm* 1 patch. 2 *(emplasto)* plaster. 3
pey (chapuza) botched up *o* slapdash job.
parchís *nm* ludo.
parcial I *adj* 1 *(partidario)* biased. 2 *(no
completo)* partial; **a tiempo p.,** part-time.
II *adj & nm* **(examen) p.,** class examination.
parcialmente *adv* partially, partly.
parco,-a *adj (moderado)* sparing; *(frugal)*
scant.
pardillo,-a I *nm,f pey* yokel, bumpkin. II
nm Orn linnet.
pardo,-a *adj (marrón)* brown; *(gris)* dark

grey.
parecer¹ *nm* 1 *(opinión)* opinion. 2
(aspecto) appearance.
parecer² [33] I *vi* to seem, look (like);
parece difícil, it seems *o* looks difficult;
parecía (de) cera, it looked like wax;
(uso impers) **parece que no arranca,** it
looks as if it won't start; **como te parezca,** whatever you like; **¿te parece?,** is
that okay with you?; **parece que sí/no,** I
think/don't think so; **¿qué te parece?,**
what do you think of it? II **parecerse**
vr to be alike; **no se parecen,** they're not
alike. 2 **p. a,** to look like, resemble; **se
parecen a su madre,** they look like their
mother.
parecido,-a *adj* 1 alike, similar. 2 **bien
p.,** good-looking. II *nm* likeness, resemblance; **tener p. con algn,** to bear a
resemblance to sb.
pared *nf* wall.
paredón *nm* 1 thick wall. 2 *fam* **le llevaron al p.,** he was shot by firing squad.
pareja *nf* 1 pair; **por parejas,** in pairs. 2
(hombre y mujer) couple; *(hijo e hija)* boy
and girl; **hacen buena p.,** they make a
nice couple, they're well matched. 3 *(en
naipes)* pair; **doble p.,** two pairs. 4 *(de
baile, juego)* partner.
parejo,-a *adj* 1 *(parecido)* similar, alike. 2
ir parejos, to be neck and neck.
parentela *nf fam* relations *pl,* relatives *pl.*
parentesco *nm* relationship, kinship.
paréntesis *nm inv* 1 parenthesis, bracket;
entre p., in parentheses *o* brackets. 2
(descanso) break, interruption; *(digresión)*
digression.
parezco *indic pres* → **parecer.**
paria *nmf* pariah.
parida *nf fam* silly thing.
pariente *nmf* relative, relation.
parir *vtr & vi* to give birth (to).
París *n* Paris.
parking *nm* car park, *US* parking lot.
parlamentario,-a I *adj* parliamentary. II
nm,f member of parliament, MP, *US*
congressman.
parlamento *nm* parliament.
parlanchín,-ina *adj fam* talkative, chatty.
parné *nm arg* dough, cash.
paro *nm* 1 *(huelga)* strike, stoppage. 2
(desempleo) unemployment; **estar en p.,**
to be unemployed; **cobrar el p.,** to be on
the dole.
parodia *nf* parody.
parodiar [12] *vtr* to parody.
parpadear *vi (ojos)* to blink; *fig (luz)* to
flicker.
parpadeo *nm (de ojos)* blinking; *fig (de
luz)* flickering.
párpado *nm* eyelid.
parque *nm* 1 park; **p. de atracciones,**
funfair; **p. zoológico,** zoo; **p. nacional/
natural,** national park/nature reserve. 2

(de niños) playpen. **3 p. móvil,** total number of cars.

parqué nm parquet.

parquear vtr Am to park.

parquet nm → **parqué.**

parquímetro nm Aut parking meter.

parra nf grapevine.

párrafo nm paragraph.

parranda nf fam spree.

parricidio nm parricide.

parrilla nf **1** Culin grill; **pescado a la p.,** grilled fish. **2** Téc grate. **3** Aut Dep starting grid.

párroco nm parish priest.

parroquia nf parish; (iglesia) parish church.

parroquiano,-a nm,f (regular) customer.

parsimonia nf phlegm, calmness.

parte I nf **1** (sección) part. **2** (en una repartición) share. **3** (lugar) place, spot; **en** o **por todas partes,** everywhere; **se fue por otra p.,** he went another way. **4** Jur party. **5** (bando) side; **estoy de tu p.,** I'm on your side. **6** euf **partes,** (genitales) private parts. **7** (locuciones) **por mi p.,** as far as I am concerned; **de p. de ...,** on behalf of ...; Tel **¿de p. de quién?,** who's calling?; **en gran p.,** to a large extent; **en p.,** partly; **la mayor p.,** the majority; **por otra p.,** on the other hand; **tomar p. en,** to take part in. **II** nm (informe) report.

partición nf (reparto) division, sharing out; (de herencia) partition; (de territorio) partition.

participación nf **1** participation. **2** Fin (acción) share, US stock; **p. en los beneficios,** profit-sharing. **3** (en lotería) part of a lottery ticket. **4** (notificación) notice, notification.

participante I adj participating. **II** nmf participant.

participar I vi **1** to take part, participate (en, in). **2** Fin to have shares in. **3** fig **p. de,** to share. **II** vtr (notificar) to notify.

partícipe I nmf participant; **hacer p. de algo,** (notificar) to inform about sth. **2** Com Fin partner.

participio nm Ling participle.

partícula nf particle.

particular I adj **1** (concreto) particular. **2** (privado) private, personal. **3** (raro) peculiar. **II** nmf (individuo) private individual. **III** nm (asunto) subject, matter.

particularidad nf special feature.

partida nf **1** (salida) departure. **2** Com (remesa) batch, consignment. **3** (juego) game. **4** Fin (entrada) item. **5** Jur (certificado) certificate; **p. de nacimiento,** birth certificate.

partidario,-a I adj ser/no ser p. de algo, to be for/against sth. **II** nm,f supporter, follower; **es p. del aborto,** he is in favour of abortion.

partidista adj biased, partisan.

partido,-a nm **1** Pol party. **2** Dep match, game; **p. amistoso,** friendly game; **p. de vuelta,** return match. **3** (provecho) advantage; **sacar p. de,** to profit from. **4** Jur (distrito) district. **5** tomar p. por, to side with. **6** ser un buen p., to be a good catch.

partir I vtr to break; (dividir) to split, divide; (cortar) to cut; **p. a algn por la mitad,** to mess things up for sb. **II** vi **1** (marcharse) to leave, set out o off. **2 a p. de,** from. **III** partirse vr to split (up), break (up); fam **p. de risa,** to split one's sides laughing.

partisano,-a nm,f partian.

partitura nf Mús score.

parto nm childbirth, labour, US labor; **estar de p.,** to be in labour.

parvulario nm nursery school, kindergarten.

párvulo,-a nm,f infant.

pasa nf raisin; **p. de Corinto,** currant.

pasable adj passable, tolerable.

pasada nf **1 de p.,** in passing. **2** (jugarreta) dirty trick. **3** fam **eso es una p.,** it's too much!

pasadizo nm corridor, passage.

pasado,-a I adj **1** (último) last; **el año/lunes p.,** last year/Monday. **2** (anticuado) dated, old-fashioned; **p. (de moda),** out of date o fashion. **3** (alimento) bad. **4** Culin cooked; **lo quiero muy p.,** I want it well done. **5 p. mañana,** the day after tomorrow. **II** nm past.

pasador nm **1** (prenda) pin, clasp; (para el pelo) (hair) slide, hairpin. **2** (pestillo) bolt, fastener.

pasaje nm **1** passage. **2** (calle) alley. **3** (pasajeros) passengers pl. **4** (billete) ticket.

pasajero,-a I adj passing, temporary; **aventura pasajera,** fling. **II** nm,f passenger.

pasamanos nm inv (barra) handrail; (de escalera) banister, bannister.

pasamontañas nm inv balaclava.

pasaporte nm passport.

pasapurés nm inv Culin potato masher.

pasar I vtr **1** to pass; (objeto) to pass, give; (mensaje) to give; (página) to turn; (trasladar) to move; **p. algo a limpio,** to make a clean copy of sth. **2** (tiempo) to spend, pass; **p. el rato,** to kill time. **3** (padecer) to suffer, endure; **p. hambre,** to go hungry. **4** (río, calle) to cross; (barrera) to pass through o over; (límite) to go beyond. **5** (perdonar) to forgive, tolerate; **p. algo (por alto),** to overlook sth. **6** (introducir) to insert, put through. **7** (examen) to pass. **8** Cin to run, show.

II vi **1** to pass; **¿ha pasado el autobús?,** has the bus gone by?; **ha pasado un hombre,** a man has gone past; **p. de largo,** to go by (without stopping); **el tren pasa por Burgos,** the train goes via

Burgos; **pasa por casa mañana**, come round to my house tomorrow. **2 p. a**, (*continuar*) to go on to; **p. a ser**, to become. **3** (*entrar*) to come in. **4** (*tiempo*) to pass, go by. **5 p. sin**, to do without; *fam* **paso de tí**, I couldn't care less about you; *fam* **yo paso**, count me out.
III v impers (*suceder*) to happen; **¿qué pasa aquí?**, what's going on here?; **¿qué te pasa?**, what's the matter?; *fam* **¿qué pasa?**, (*saludo*) how are you?; **pase lo que pase**, whatever happens, come what may.
IV pasarse vr **1 se me pasó la ocasión**, I missed my chance; **se le pasó llamarme**, he forgot to phone me. **2** (*gastar tiempo*) to spend o pass time; **pasárselo bien/mal**, to have a good/bad time. **3** (*comida*) to go off. **4** *fam* (*excederse*) to go too far; **no te pases**, don't overdo it. **5 pásate por mi casa**, call round to my place.
pasarela nf (*puente*) footbridge; (*de barco*) gangway; (*de moda*) catwalk.
pasatiempo nm pastime, hobby.
pascua nf **1** Easter. **2 pascuas**, (*Navidad*) Christmas *sing*; **¡felices Pascuas!**, Merry Christmas!
pase nm **1** pass, permit. **2** *Cin* showing.
pasear I vi to go for a walk, take a walk. **II** vt **1** (*persona*) to take for a walk; (*perro*) to walk. **2** *fig* (*exhibir*) to show off. **III pasearse** vr to go for a walk.
paseíllo nm *Taur* opening parade.
paseo nm **1** walk; (*en bicicleta, caballo*) ride; (*en coche*) drive; **dar un p.**, to go for a walk o a ride. **2** (*avenida*) avenue.
pasillo nm corridor; *Av* **p. aéreo**, air corridor.
pasión nf passion.
pasional adj passionate; **crimen p.**, crime of passion.
pasividad nf passivity, passiveness.
pasivo,-a I adj passive; (*inactivo*) inactive. **II** nm *Com* liabilities pl.
pasmado,-a adj (*asombrado*) astounded, amazed; (*atontado*) flabbergasted; **dejar p.**, to astonish; **quedarse p.**, to be amazed.
pasmo nm astonishment, amazement.
paso,-a¹ adj **ciruela pasa**, prune; **uva pasa**, raisin.
paso² nm 1 step; (*modo de andar*) gait, walk; (*ruido al andar*) footstep; *Mil* **llevar el p.**, to keep in step; *fig* **a dos pasos**, a short distance away; *fig* **seguir los pasos de algn**, to follow in sb's footsteps. **2** (*camino*) passage, way; **abrirse p.**, to force one's way through; *Aut* **'ceda el p.'**, 'give way'; **'prohibido el p.'**, 'no entry'; **p. a nivel**, level o US grade crossing; **p. de cebra**, zebra crossing; **p. de peatones**, pedestrian crossing, US crosswalk; **p. elevado**, flyover, US overpass; **p. subterráneo**, (*para peatones*) subway; (*para co-*

ches) underpass. **3** (*acción*) passage, passing; **a su p. por la ciudad**, when he was in town; **el p. del tiempo**, the passage of time; **estar de p.**, to be just passing through. **4 p. de montaña**, mountain pass.
pasodoble nm paso doble.
pasota nmf *fam* waster.
pasta nf **1** paste; **p. de dientes** o **dentífrica**, toothpaste. **2** (*de pan, pasteles*) dough; (*italiana*) pasta. **3** (*galleta*) biscuit. **4** *fam* (*dinero*) dough, bread.
pastar vtr & vi to graze, pasture.
pastel nm **1** cake; (*de carne, fruta*) pie. **2** *Arte* pastel. **3** *fam* **descubrir el p.**, to spill the beans.
pastelería nf **1** (*tienda*) confectioner's (shop). **2** (*dulces*) confectionery.
pastelero,-a nm,f pastrycook, confectioner.
pastiche nm **1** pastiche. **2** *fam* (*chapuza*) botch(-up).
pastilla nf **1** tablet, pill; **pastillas para la tos**, cough drops. **2** (*de jabón*) bar. **3** *fam* **a toda p.**, at full speed.
pastizal nm grazing land, pasture.
pasto nm **1** (*hierba*) grass. **2** (*alimento*) fodder; **ser p. de**, to fall prey to.
pastor,-a I nm,f shepherd; (*mujer*) shepherdess; **perro p.**, sheepdog; **p. alemán**, Alsatian. **II** nm *Rel* pastor, minister.
pastoreo nm shepherding.
pastoso,-a adj pasty; (*lengua*) furry.
pata nf leg; *fig* **patas arriba**, upside down; **estirar la p.**, to kick the bucket; **mala p.**, bad luck; **meter la p.**, to put one's foot in it; **p. de gallo**, crow's foot.
patada nf (*puntapié*) kick, stamp.
patalear vi to stamp one's feet (with rage).
pataleo nm kicking; (*de rabia*) stamping.
patán nm bumpkin, yokel.
patata nf potato; **patatas fritas**, chips, US French fries; (*de bolsa*) crisps, US potato chips.
patatús nm inv *fam* dizzy spell, queer turn.
paté nm pâté.
patear I vtr (*pelota*) to kick; (*pisotear*) to stamp on. **II** vi (*patalear*) to stamp (one's foot with rage).
patentar vtr to patent.
patente I nf (*autorización*) licence, US license; (*de invención*) patent. **II** adj (*evidente*) patent, obvious.
pateo nm stamping; (*abucheo*) boo(ing), jeer(ing).
paternal adj paternal, fatherly.
paternalista adj paternalistic.
paternidad nf paternity, fatherhood.
paterno,a adj paternal.
patético,-a adj moving.
patíbulo nm scaffold, gallows pl.

patidifuso,-a *adj fam* dumbfounded, flabbergasted.

patilla *nf* 1 (*de gafas*) leg. 2 **patillas**, (*pelo*) sideboards, *US* sideburns.

patín *nm* 1 skate; (*patinete*) scooter; **p. de ruedas/de hielo**, roller/ice skate. 2 *Náut* pedal boat.

patinaje *nm* skating; **p. artístico**, figure skating; **p. sobre hielo/ruedas**, ice-/roller skating.

patinar *vi* 1 to skate; (*sobre ruedas*) to roller-skate; (*sobre hielo*) to ice-skate. 2 (*deslizarse*) to slide; (*resbalar*) to slip; (*vehículo*) to skid. 3 *fam* (*equivocarse*) to put one's foot in it, slip up.

patinazo *nm* 1 skid. 2 *fam* (*equivocación*) blunder, boob.

patinete *nm* scooter.

patio *nm* 1 (*de una casa*) yard, patio; (*de recreo*) playground. 2 *Teat Cin* **p. de butacas**, stalls.

pato *nm* duck; *fam* **pagar el p.**, to carry the can.

patochada *nf* blunder, boob.

patógeno,-a *adj* pathogenic.

patología *nf* pathology.

patológico,-a *adj* pathological.

patoso,-a *adj* clumsy, awkward.

patraña *nf* nonsense.

patria *nf* fatherland, native country; **madre p.**, motherland; **p. chica**, one's home town *o* region.

patriarca *nm* patriarch.

patrimonio *nm* (*bienes*) wealth; (*herencia*) inheritance.

patriota *nmf* patriot.

patriótico,-a *adj* patriotic.

patriotismo *nm* patriotism.

patrocinador,-a I *adj* sponsoring. II *nm,f* sponsor.

patrocinar *vtr* to sponsor.

patrocinio *nm* sponsorship, patronage.

patrón,-ona I *nm,f* 1 (*jefe*) boss. 2 (*de pensión*) (*hombre*) landlord; (*mujer*) landlady. 3 *Rel* patron saint. II *nm* 1 pattern. 2 (*medida*) standard.

patronal I *adj* employers'; **cierre p.**, lockout; **clase p.**, managerial class. II *nf* (*dirección*) management.

patronato, patronazgo *nm* 1 (*institución benéfica*) foundation. 2 (*protección*) patronage.

patrono,-a *nm,f* 1 boss; (*empresario*) employer. 2 *Rel* patron saint.

patrulla *nf* 1 patrol; **estar de p.**, to be on patrol; **coche p.**, patrol car. 2 (*grupo*) group, band; **p. de rescate**, rescue party; **p. ciudadana**, vigilante group.

patrullar I *vtr* to patrol. II *vi* to be on patrol.

paulatino,-a *adj* gradual.

paupérrimo,-a (*adj superl de* **pobre**) extremely poor, poverty-stricken.

pausa *nf* pause, break; *Mús* rest.

pausado,-a *adj* unhurried, calm.

pauta *nf* guidelines *pl*.

pava *nf fam* **pelar la p.**, to chat.

pavesa *nf* ash.

pavimentar *vtr* to pave.

pavimento *nm* (*de calle*) paving; (*de habitación*) flooring.

pavo *nm* 1 turkey; *fam* **no ser moco de p.**, to be nothing to scoff at. 2 *fam* (*tonto*) twit; *fam* **estar en la edad del p.**, to be growing up.

pavonearse *vr fam* to show off, strut.

pavoneo *nm fam* showing off, strutting.

pavor *nm* terror, dread.

payaso *nm* clown; **hacer el p.**, to act the clown.

payés,-a *nm,f* Catalan *o* Balearic peasant.

payo,-a *nm,f* non-Gipsy person.

paz *nf* peace; (*sosiego*) peacefulness; *fam* ¡déjame en p.!, leave me alone!, **hacer las paces**, to make (it) up.

pazguato,-a *adj* 1 (*estúpido*) silly, stupid. 2 (*mojigato*) prudish.

PCE *nm Pol abr de* **Partido Comunista de España**, Spanish Communist party.

pe *nf fam* **de pe a pa**, from A to Z.

peaje *nf* toll; **autopista de p.**, toll motorway, *US* turnpike.

peatón *nm* pedestrian.

peca *nf* freckle.

pecado *nm Rel* sin; **p. capital** *o* **mortal**, deadly sin.

pecador,-a *nm,f* sinner.

pecaminoso,-a *adj* sinful.

pecar [1] *vi* to sin; *fig* **p. por defecto**, to fall short of the mark.

pecera *nf* fishbowl, fishtank.

pecho *nm* chest; (*de mujer*) breast, bust; (*de animal*) breast; **dar el p. (a un bebé)**, to breast-feed (a baby); *fig* **tomar(se) (algo) a p.**, to take (sth) to heart.

pechuga *nf* 1 (*de ave*) breast. 2 *fam pey* (*de mujer*) boob.

pectoral *adj* pectoral, chest.

peculiar *adj* (*raro*) peculiar; (*característico*) characteristic.

peculiaridad *nf* peculiarity.

pedagogía *nf* pedagogy.

pedagógico,-a *adj* pedagogical.

pedal *nm* pedal.

pedalear *vi* to pedal.

pedante I *adj* pedantic. II *nmf* pedant.

pedantería *nf* pedantry.

pedazo *nm* piece, bit; **a pedazos**, in pieces; **caerse a pedazos**, to fall apart *o* to pieces; **hacer pedazos**, to break *o* tear to pieces, smash (up); *fam* ¡qué p. de coche!, what a terrific car!

pederasta *nm* pederast.

pedernal *nm* flint.

pedestal *nm* pedestal.

pediatra *nmf* paediatrician, *US* pediatrician.

pediatría *nf* paediatrics *sing*, *US* pediatrics *sing.*

pedicuro,-a *nm,f* chiropodist.

pedido *nm* 1 *Com* order; **hacer un p. a,** to place an order with. 2 *(petición)* request.

pedigrí *nm* pedigree.

pedir [6] *vtr* 1 to ask (for); **p. algo a algn,** to ask sb for sth; **te pido que te quedes,** I'm asking you to stay; **p. prestado,** to borrow; *fig* **p. cuentas,** to ask for an explanation. 2 *Com & (en bar etc)* to order. 3 *(mendigar)* to beg.

pedo *nm vulg* 1 fart; **tirarse un p.,** to fart. 2 *(borrachera)* bender.

pedrada *nf (golpe)* blow from a stone; *(lanzamiento)* throw of a stone.

pedrea *nf (en lotería)* small prizes *pl.*

pedregoso,-a *adj* stony, rocky.

pedrería *nf* precious stones *pl,* gems *pl.*

pedrisco *nm* hailstorm.

pega *nf* 1 *fam (objeción)* objection; **poner pegas,** to find fault. 2 **de p.,** *(falso)* sham.

pegadizo,-a *adj* catchy.

pegado,-a *adj* 1 *(adherido)* stuck. 2 *(quemado)* burnt.

pegajoso,-a *adj (pegadizo)* sticky; *fig (persona)* tiresome, hard to get rid of.

pegamento *nm* glue.

pegar [7] I *vtr* 1 *(adherir)* to stick; *(con pegamento)* to glue; *(coser)* to sew on; *fam* **no pegó ojo,** he didn't sleep a wink; **p. fuego a,** to set fire to. 2 *(golpear)* to hit. 3 **p. un grito,** to shout; **p. un salto,** to jump. 4 *fam (contagiar)* to give; **me ha pegado sus manías,** I've caught his bad habits. 5 *(arrimar)* to put against, lean against. II *vi* 1 *(adherirse)* to stick. 2 *(armonizar)* to match, go; **el azul no pega con el verde,** blue and green don't go together *o* don't match; *fig* **ella no pegaría aquí,** she wouldn't fit in here. 3 *(sol)* to beat down. III **pegarse** *vr* 1 *(adherirse)* to stick; *(pelearse)* to fight. 2 *fam (darse)* to have, get; **p. un tiro,** to shoot oneself. 3 *(comida)* to get burnt; **se me ha pegado el sol,** I've got a touch of the sun. 4 *fam* **pegársela a algn,** to trick *o* deceive sb. 5 *(arrimarse)* to get close. 6 *fam fig* to stick. 7 *Med (enfermedad)* to be catching *o* contagious; *fig (melodía)* to be catchy.

pegatina *nf* sticker.

peinado,-a *nm* hairstyle, *fam* hairdo.

peinar I *vtr* 1 *(pelo)* to comb. 2 *(registrar)* to comb. II **peinarse** *vr* to comb one's hair.

peine *nm* comb.

peineta *nf* ornamental comb.

pela *nf fam* peseta.

pelado,-a I *adj* 1 *(cabeza)* shorn; *(piel, fruta)* peeled; *(terreno)* bare. 2 *fam* **saqué un cinco p.,** *(en escuela)* I just scraped a pass; **a grito p.,** shouting and bawling. 3 *fam (arruinado)* broke, penniless. 4 *(des-*

vergonzado) impudent, insolent. II *nm fam* haircut.

peladura *nf* peeling.

pelagatos *nmf inv fam* poor devil, nobody.

pelaje *nm* 1 fur, hair. 2 *pey (apariencia)* looks *pl,* appearance.

pelambrera *nf fam* mop (of hair), long *o* thick hair.

pelapatatas *nm inv* potato peeler.

pelar I *vtr (cortar el pelo a)* to cut the hair of; *(fruta, patata)* to peel; *fam* **hace un frío que pela,** it's brass monkey weather. II *vi (despellejar)* to peel. II **pelarse** *vr* 1 *(cortarse el pelo)* to get one's hair cut. 2 *fam* **pelárselas,** to do sth fast.

peldaño *nm* step; *(de escalera de mano)* rung.

pelea *nf* fight; *(riña)* row, quarrel; **buscar p.,** to look for trouble.

peleado,-a *adj* **estar p. (con algn),** not to be on speaking terms (with sb).

pelear I *vi* to fight; *(reñir)* to quarrel. II **pelearse** *vr* 1 to fight; *(reñir)* to quarrel. 2 *(enemistarse)* to fall out.

pelele *nm (muñeco)* straw puppet; *fig* puppet.

peleón,-ona *adj* 1 quarrelsome, aggressive. 2 *(vino)* cheap.

peletería *nf* furrier's; *(tienda)* fur shop.

peletero,-a *nm,f* furrier.

peliagudo,-a *adj* difficult, tricky.

pelícano *nm* pelican.

película *nf* 1 *Cin* film, picture, *US* movie; **p. de miedo** *o* **terror,** horror film; **p. del Oeste,** Western; *fam* **de p.,** fabulous. 2 *Fot* film.

peligrar *vi* to be in danger, be threatened; **hacer p.,** to endanger, jeopardize.

peligro *nm* danger; *(riesgo)* risk; **con p. de ...,** at the risk of ...; **correr (el) p. de ...,** to run the risk of ...; **poner en p.,** to endanger.

peligroso,-a *adj* dangerous, risky.

pelirrojo,-a I *adj* red-haired; *(anaranjado)* ginger-haired. II *nm,f* redhead.

pellejo *nm* 1 *(piel)* skin. 2 *(odre)* wineskin. 3 *fam* **arriesgar** *o* **jugarse el p.,** to risk one's neck.

pelliza *nf* fur jacket.

pellizcar [1] *vtr* to pinch, nip.

pellizco *nm* pinch, nip.

pelma *nmf,* **pelmazo,-a** *nm,f (persona)* bore, drag.

pelo *nm* 1 hair; **cortarse el p.,** *(uno mismo)* to cut one's hair; *(en la peluquería)* to have one's hair cut; *fig* **no tiene ni un p. de tonto,** he's no fool; *fig* **no tener pelos en la lengua,** to be very outspoken; *fig* **tomar el p. a algn,** to pull sb's leg, take the mickey out of sb; *fam* **con pelos y señales,** in full detail; *fam* **por los pelos,** by the skin of one's teeth; *fam* **me puso el p. de punta,** it gave me the creeps. 2 (*de animal*) fur, coat, hair. 3 *Tex* (*de una tela*) nap, pile. 4 (*cerda*) bristle.

pelón,-ona *adj* (*sin pelo*) bald.

pelota I *nf* 1 ball; *fam* **devolver la p.**, to give tit for tat. 2 *Dep* pelota. 3 *fam* (*cabeza*) nut. 4 **hacer la p. a algn**, to toady to sb, butter sb up. 5 *vulg* **pelotas**, (*testiculos*) balls; **en p.**, starkers. II *nmf fam* (*pelotillero*) crawler.

pelotari *nm* pelota player.

pelotear *vi Dep* to kick a ball around; *Ten* to knock up.

peloteo *nm Ten* knock-up.

pelotilla *nf fam* **hacer la p. (a algn)**, to fawn on (sb).

pelotillero,-a *nm,f fam* crawler.

pelotón *nm* 1 *Mil* squad. 2 *fam* (*grupo*) small crowd, bunch; (*en ciclismo*) pack. 3 (*amasijo*) bundle.

pelotudo,-a *adj Am* slack, sloppy.

peluca *nf* wig.

peluche *nm* **osito de p.**, teddy bear.

peludo,-a *adj* hairy, furry.

peluquería *nf* hairdresser's (shop).

peluquero,-a *nm,f* hairdresser.

peluquín *nm* toupee.

pelusa, pelusilla *nf* 1 fluff; (*de planta*) down. 2 *fam* jealousy (among children).

pelvis *nf inv* pelvis.

pena *nf* 1 (*tristeza*) grief, sorrow; *fig* **me da p. de ella**, I feel sorry for her; **¡qué p.!**, what a pity! 2 (*dificultad*) hardships *pl*, trouble; **no merece** *o* **vale la p.** (**ir**), it's not worth while (going); **a duras penas**, with great difficulty. 3 (*castigo*) punishment, penalty; **p. de muerte** *o* **capital**, death penalty.

penacho *nm* 1 (*de ave*) crest, tuft. 2 *Mil* (*de plumas*) plume.

penal I *adj* penal; *Jur* **código p.**, penal code. II *nm* prison, jail.

penalidad *nf* (*usu pl*) hardships *pl*, troubles *pl*.

penalización *nf* penalization; *Dep* penalty.

penalizar [4] *vtr* to penalize.

penalti *nm* (*pl* **penaltis**) *Dep* penalty; *fam* **casarse de p.**, to have a shotgun wedding.

penar I *vtr* to punish. II *vi* to be in torment, suffer.

pendejo *nm Am* (*tonto*) jerk, dummy.

pendenciero,-a *adj* quarrelsome, argumentative.

pendiente I *adj* 1 (*por resolver*) pending; *Educ* **asignatura p.**, failed subject; *Com* **p. de pago**, unpaid. 2 **estar p. de**, (*esperar*) to be waiting for; (*vigilar*) to be on the lookout for. 3 (*colgante*) hanging (**de**, from). II *nm* (*joya*) earring. III *nf* slope; (*de tejado*) pitch.

pendón *nm* 1 (*bandera*) banner. 2 *pey* (*mujer*) slut, whore; (*hombre*) playboy.

péndulo *nm* pendulum.

pene *nm* penis.

penetración *nf* penetration; (*perspicacia*) insight, perception.

penetrante *adj* penetrating; (*frío, voz, mirada*) piercing; *fig* (*inteligencia*) sharp, acute.

penetrar I *vtr* to penetrate; **p. un misterio**, to get to the bottom of a mystery. II *vi* (*entrar*) to go *o* get (**en**, in).

penicilina *nf* penicillin.

península *nf* peninsula.

penique *nm* penny, *pl* pence.

penitencia *nf* penance.

penitenciaría *nf* prison.

penitenciario,-a *adj* penitentiary, prison.

penoso,-a *adj* 1 (*lamentable*) sorry, distressing. 2 (*laborioso*) laborious, difficult.

pensado,-a *adj* 1 thought out; **bien p.**, ... on reflection, ...; **en el momento menos p.**, when least expected; **mal p.**, twisted; **tener algo p.**, to have sth planned, have sth in mind; **tengo p. ir**, I intend to go. 2 (*concebido*) designed.

pensamiento *nm* 1 thought. 2 (*máxima*) saying, motto. 3 *Bot* pansy.

pensar [1] I *vi* to think (**en**, of, about; **sobre**, about, over); *fig* **sin p.**, (*con precipitación*) without thinking; (*involuntariamente*) involuntarily. II *vtr* 1 to think (**de**, of); (*considerar*) to think over *o* about; **piénsalo bien**, think it over; *fam* **¡ni pensarlo!**, not on your life! 2 (*proponerse*) to intend; **pienso quedarme**, I plan to stay. 3 (*concebir*) to make; **p. un plan**, to make a plan; **p. una solución**, to find a solution.

pensativo,-a *adj* pensive, thoughtful.

pensión *nf* 1 (*residencia*) boarding house; (*hotel*) guesthouse; **media p.**, half board; **p. completa**, full board. 2 (*paga*) pension, allowance; **p. vitalicia**, life annuity.

pensionista *nmf* pensioner.

pentágono *nm* pentagon.

pentagrama *nm* staff, stave.

penúltimo,-a *adj & nm,f* next to the last, penultimate.

penumbra *nf* penumbra, half-light.

penuria *nf* scarcity, shortage.

peña *nf* 1 rock, crag. 2 (*de amigos*) club. 3 *fam* (*gente*) people.

peñasco *nm* rock, crag.

peñón *nm* rock; **el P. de Gibraltar**, the Rock of Gibraltar.

peón *nm* 1 unskilled labourer *o US* laborer; **p. agrícola**, farmhand. 2 *Ajedrez* pawn.

peonada *nf* day's work.

peonza *nf* (spinning) top.

peor I *adj* 1 (*comparativo*) worse. 2 (*superlativo*) worst; **en el p. de los casos**, if the worst comes to the worst; **lo p. es que**, the worst of it is that. II *adv* 1 (*comparativo*) worse; **¡p. para mí** *o* **ti!**, too

bad! 2 *(superlativo)* worst.
pepinillo *nm* gherkin.
pepino *nm* cucumber; *fam* **me importa un p.,** I don't give a hoot.
pepita *nf (de fruta)* pip, seed; *(de metal)* nugget.
pepitoria *nf* fricassee; **pollo en p.,** fricassee of chicken.
peque *nm fam (niño)* kid.
pequeño,-a I *adj* small, little; *(bajo)* short. II *nm,f* child; **de p.,** as a child.
Pequín *n* Peking.
pera I *nf* 1 *Bot* pear; **p. de agua,** juicy pear. 2 *vulg (pene)* prick.
peral *nm* pear tree.
percance *nm* mishap, setback.
percatarse *vr* **p. de,** to realise.
percepción *nf* perception.
perceptible *adj* 1 perceptible. 2 *Fin* receivable, payable.
percha *nf (colgador)* (coat) hanger; *(de gallina)* perch.
perchero *nm* clothes rack.
percibir *vtr* 1 *(notar)* to perceive, notice. 2 *(cobrar)* to receive.
percusión *nf* percussion.
perdedor,-a I *adj* losing. II *nm,f* loser.
perder [3] I *vtr* 1 to lose. 2 *(tren, autobús)* to miss; *(tiempo)* to waste; *(oportunidad)* to miss. 3 *(pervertir)* to be the ruin *o* downfall of. II *vi* to lose; **echar (algo) a p.,** to spoil (sth); **echarse a p.,** to be spoilt; **salir perdiendo,** to come off worst. III **perderse** *vr* 1 *(extraviarse) (persona)* to get lost; **se me ha perdido la llave,** I've lost my key; **no te lo pierdas,** don't miss it. 2 *(pervertirse)* to go to rack and ruin.
perdición *nf* undoing, downfall.
pérdida *nf* 1 loss; **no tiene p.,** you can't miss it. 2 *(de tiempo, esfuerzos)* waste. 3 *Mil* **pérdidas,** losses.
perdido,-a *adj* 1 *(extraviado)* lost. 2 *fam (sucio)* filthy. 3 *fam* **loco p.,** mad as a hatter. 4 **estar p. por algn,** *(enamorado)* to be crazy about sb. 5 *(acabado)* finished; **¡estoy p.!,** I'm a goner!
perdigón *nm* pellet.
perdiguero,-a *adj* partidge-hunting; **perro p.,** setter.
perdiz *nf* partridge.
perdón *nm* pardon, forgiveness; **¡p.!,** sorry!; **pedir p.,** to apologize.
perdonar *vtr* 1 *(remitir)* to forgive. 2 **perdone!,** sorry!; **perdone que le moleste,** sorry for bothering you. 3 *(eximir)* to pardon; **perdonarle la vida a algn,** to spare sb's life; **p. una deuda,** to write off a debt.
perdurable *adj* 1 *(eterno)* everlasting. 2 *(duradero)* durable, long-lasting.
perdurar *vi* 1 *(durar)* to endure, last. 2 *(persistir)* to persist, continue to exist.
perecedero,-a *adj* perishable; **artículos**

perecederos, perishables.
perecer [33] *vi* to perish, die.
peregrinación *nf,* **peregrinaje** *nm* pilgrimage.
peregrino,-a I *nm,f* pilgrim. II *adj* **ideas peregrinas,** crazy ideas.
perejil *nm* parsley.
perenne *adj* perennial, everlasting.
perentorio,-a *adj* peremptory, urgent.
pereza *nf* laziness, idleness.
perezoso,-a *adj (vago)* lazy, idle.
perfección *nf* perfection; **a la p.,** to perfection.
perfeccionamiento *nm* 1 *(acción)* perfecting. 2 *(mejora)* improvement.
perfeccionar *vtr* to perfect; *(mejorar)* improve, make better.
perfeccionista *adj & nmf* perfectionist.
perfecto,-a *adj* perfect.
◆**perfectamente** *adv* perfectly; **¡p.!,** *(de acuerdo)* agreed!, all right!
perfidia *nf* perfidy, treachery.
perfil *nm* 1 profile; *(contorno)* outline, contour; **de p.,** in profile. 2 *Geom* cross section.
perfilar I *vtr (dar forma)* to shape, outline. II **perfilarse** *vr (tomar forma)* to take shape.
perforación, perforado *nm* perforation; *Min* drilling, boring; *Inform (de tarjetas)* punching.
perforadora punch; *Min* drill; *Inform* **p. de teclado,** keypunch.
perforar *vtr* to perforate; *Min* to drill, bore; *Inform* to punch.
perfumar I *vtr & vi* to perfume. II **perfumarse** *vr* to put on perfume.
perfume *nm* perfume, scent.
pergamino *nm* parchment.
pericia *nf* expertise, skill.
periferia *nf* periphery; *(alrededores)* outskirts *pl.*
periférico,-a *adj & nm* peripheral.
perífrasis *nf inv* periphrasis, long-winded explanation.
perilla *nf (barba)* goatee; *fam* **de perilla(s),** *(oportuno)* at the right moment; *(útil)* very handy.
perímetro *nm* perimeter.
periódico,-a I *nm* newspaper. II *adj* periodic; *Quím* **tabla periódica,** periodic table.
periodismo *nm* journalism.
periodista *nmf* journalist, reporter.
periodo, período *nm* period.
peripecia *nf* sudden change, vicissitude.
periplo *nm* voyage, tour.
periquete *nm fam* **en un p.,** in a jiffy.
periquito *nm* budgerigar, *fam* budgie.
periscopio *nm* periscope.
peritaje *nm (estudios)* technical studies *pl.*
perito,-a *nm,f* technician, expert; **p. industrial/agrónomo,** ≈ industrial/agricultural expert.

peritonitis *nf* peritonitis.
perjudicar [1] *vtr* to harm, injure; *(intereses)* to prejudice.
perjudicial *adj* prejudicial, harmful.
perjuicio *nm* harm, damage; **en p. de,** to the detriment of; **sin p. de,** without prejudice to.
perjurar *vi* to commit perjury.
perjurio *nm* perjury.
perla *nf* pearl; *fig (persona)* gem, jewel; *fam* **me viene de perlas,** it's just the ticket.
permanecer [33] *vi* to remain, stay.
permanencia *nf* 1 *(inmutabilidad)* permanence. 2 *(estancia)* stay.
permanente I *adj* permanent. II *nf (de pelo)* permanent wave, perm; **hacerse la p.,** to have one's hair permed.
permisivo,-a *adj* permissive.
permiso *nm* 1 *(autorización)* permission. 2 *(licencia)* licence, *US* license, permit; **p. de conducir,** driving licence, *US* driver's license; **p. de residencia/trabajo,** residence/work permit. 3 *Mil* leave; **estar de p.,** to be on leave.
permitir I *vtr* to permit, allow; **¿me permite?,** may I? II **permitirse** *vr* 1 to permit *o* allow oneself; **me permito recordarle que,** let me remind you that. 2 'no se permite fumar', 'no smoking'.
permutar *vtr* to exchange.
pernicioso,-a *adj* pernicious.
pernil *nm (de pantalón)* leg; *(jamón)* leg of pork.
pernocta *nf Mil (pase de)* **p.,** overnight pass.
pero I *conj* but; **p., ¿qué pasa aquí?,** now, what's going on here? II *nm* objection.
perogrullada *nf* truism, platitude.
perol *nm* large saucepan, pot.
perorata *nf* boring speech.
perpendicular *adj & nf* perpendicular.
perpetrar *vtr* to perpetrate, commit.
perpetuar [30] *vtr* to perpetuate.
perpetuo,-a *adj* perpetual, everlasting; *Jur* **cadena perpetua,** life imprisonment.
perplejidad *nf* perplexity, bewilderment.
perplejo,-a *adj* perplexed, bewildered.
perra *nf* 1 bitch. 2 *fam (moneda)* penny; **estar sin una p.,** to be broke.
perrera *nf* kennel, kennels *pl.*
perrería *nf fam* dirty trick.
perro,-a I *nm* dog; *fam* **un día de perros,** a lousy day; *fam* **vida de perros,** dog's life; *Culin* **p. caliente,** hot dog. II *adj fam (vago)* lazy.
persecución *nf* 1 pursuit. 2 *Pol (represión)* persecution.
perseguir [6] *vtr* 1 to pursue, chase; *(correr trás)* to run after, follow. 2 *(reprimir)* to persecute.
perseverante *adj* persevering.
perseverar *vi* 1 to persevere, persist. 2

(durar) to last.
persiana *nf* blinds *pl.*
pérsico,-a *adj* Persian; **golfo P.,** Persian Gulf.
persignarse *vr* to cross oneself.
persistencia *nf* persistence.
persistente *adj* persistent.
persistir *vi* to persist.
persona *nf* person; **algunas personas,** some people; *fam* **p. mayor,** grown-up.
personaje *nm* 1 *Cin Lit Teat* character. 2 *(celebridad)* celebrity, important person.
personal I *adj* personal, private. II *nm* 1 *(plantilla)* staff, personnel. 2 *fam (gente)* people.
personalidad *nf* personality.
personarse *vr* to present oneself, appear in person.
personificar [1] *vtr* to personify.
perspectiva *nf* 1 perspective. 2 *(futuro)* prospect.
perspicacia *nf* insight, perspicacity.
perspicaz *adj* sharp, perspicacious.
persuadir *vtr* to persuade; **estar persuadido de que,** to be convinced that.
persuasión *nf* persuasion.
persuasivo,-a *adj* persuasive, convincing.
pertenecer [33] *vi* to belong (**a,** to).
perteneciente *adj* belonging.
pertenencia *nf* 1 possessions *pl*, property. 2 *(a un partido etc)* affiliation, membership.
pértiga *nf* pole; *Dep* **salto con p.,** pole vault.
pertinaz *adj* 1 persistent. 2 *(obstinado)* obstinate, stubborn.
pertinente *adj* 1 pertinent, relevant. 2 *(apropiado)* appropriate.
perturbación *nf* disturbance; **p. del orden público,** breach of the peace; *Med* **p. mental,** mental disorder.
perturbado,-a *adj (mentally)* deranged *o* unbalanced.
perturbador,-a I *adj* disturbing. II *nm,f* unruly person.
perturbar *vtr (el orden)* to disturb.
Perú (el) *n* Peru.
peruano,-a *adj & nm,f* Peruvian.
perversión *nf* perversion.
perverso,-a *adj* perverse, evil.
pervertir [5] *vtr* to pervert, corrupt.
pervivir *vi* to survive.
pesa *nf* weight; **levantamiento de pesas,** weightlifting.
pesadez *nf* 1 heaviness; *(de estómago)* fullness. 2 *fam (fastidio)* drag, nuisance.
pesadilla *nf* nightmare; **de p.,** nightmarish.
pesado,-a I *adj* 1 heavy. 2 *(aburrido)* tedious, dull; **¡qué p.!,** what a drag!. II *nm,f* bore.
pesadumbre *nf* grief, affliction.
pésame *nm* condolence, sympathy; **dar el p.,** to offer one's condolences; **mi más**

sentido p., my deepest sympathy.

pesar I *vtr* to weigh; *fig (entristecer)* to grieve. II *vi* 1 to weigh; ¿cuánto pesas?, how much do you weigh? 2 *(ser pesado)* to be heavy. 3 *fig (tener importancia)* este factor pesa mucho, this is a very important factor. III *nm* 1 *(pena)* sorrow, grief. 2 *(arrepentimiento)* regret; a su p., to his regret. 3 a p. de, in spite of.

pesaroso,-a *adj* 1 *(triste)* sorrowful, sad. 2 *(arrepentido)* regretful, sorry.

pesca *nf* fishing; *fam* y toda la p., and all that.

pescadería *nf* fish shop, fishmonger's (shop).

pescadero,-a *nm,f* fishmonger.

pescadilla *nf* young hake.

pescado *nm* fish.

pescador,-a I *adj* fishing. II *nm,f (hombre)* fisherman; *(mujer)* fisherwoman.

pescante *nm* 1 *(de carruaje)* coachman's seat. 2 *Constr* jib, boom. 3 *Náut* davit.

pescar [1] I *vi* to fish. II *vtr* 1 to fish. 2 *fam (coger)* to catch.

pescozada *nf*, **pescozón** *nm* slap on the neck o head.

pescuezo *nm fam* neck.

pese a (que) *loc adv* in spite of (the fact that).

pesebre *nm* manger, stall.

peseta *nf* peseta; *fam* hacer la p. a algn, to give sb the fingers.

pesetero,-a *nm,f* skinflint.

pesimismo *nm* pessimism.

pesimista I *adj* pessimistic. II *nmf* pessimist.

pésimo,-a *adj* very bad, awful, terrible.

peso *nm* 1 weight; al p., by weight; p. bruto/neto, gross/net weight; *fig* me quité un p. de encima, it took a load off my mind; *Box* p. mosca/pesado, flyweight/heavyweight. 2 *(importancia)* importance; de p., *(persona)* influential; *(razón)* convincing.

pespunte *nm* backstitch.

pesquero,-a I *adj* fishing. II *nm* fishing boat.

pesquisa *nf* inquiry.

pestaña *nf* 1 eyelash, lash. 2 *Téc* flange; *(de neumático)* rim.

pestañear *vi* to blink; sin p., without batting an eyelid.

peste *nf* 1 *(hedor)* stench, stink. 2 *Med* plague; *Hist* la p. negra, the Black Death. 3 decir o echar pestes, to curse.

pesticida *nm* pesticide.

pestilencia *nf* stench, stink.

pestilente *adj* stinking, foul.

pestillo *nm* bolt, latch.

petaca *nf* 1 *(para cigarrillos)* cigarette case; *(para bebidas)* flask. 2 *Am (maleta)* suitcase.

petaco *nm (de juego)* flipper; máquina de petacos, pinball machine.

pétalo *nm* petal.

petardo *nm* 1 firecracker, firework; *Mil* petard. 2 *fam (persona aburrida)* bore. 3 *(droga)* joint.

petate *nm Mil* luggage.

petición *nf* request; *Jur* petition, plea.

peto *nm* pantalón de p., dungarees *pl*.

petrificar [1] *vtr*, **petrificarse** *vr* to petrify.

petróleo *nm* petroleum, oil.

petrolero *nm* oil tanker.

petulante *adj* arrogant, vain.

petunia *nf* petunia.

peyorativo,-a *adj* pejorative, derogatory.

pez[1] *nm* fish; ella está como p. en el agua, she's in her element; p. gordo, big shot.

pez[2] *nf* pitch, tar.

pezón *nm* nipple.

pezuña *nf* hoof.

piadoso,-a *adj* 1 *(devoto)* pious. 2 *(compasivo)* compassionate; mentira piadosa, white lie.

pianista *nmf* pianist, piano player.

piano *nm* piano.

piar [29] *vi* to chirp, tweet.

piara *nf* herd of pigs.

PIB *nm Fin abr de producto interior bruto*, gross domestic product, GDP.

pibe,-a *nm,f Am (niño)* kid.

picadero *nm* riding school.

picadillo *nm (de carne)* minced meat; *(de verduras)* vegetable salad.

picado,-a I *adj* 1 *(carne)* minced. 2 *(fruta)* bad; *(diente)* decayed. 3 *(mar)* choppy. 4 *fam (enfadado)* narked. 5 estar p. con, *(en competición)* to be at loggerheads with. II *nm Av* dive; caer en p., to plummet.

picador *nm Taur* mounted bullfighter, picador.

picadora *nf* mincer.

picadura *nf* 1 *(mordedura)* bite; *(de avispa, abeja)* sting. 2 *(en fruta)* spot; *Med (de viruela)* pockmark; *(en diente)* decay, caries *sing*; *(en metalurgia)* pitting.

picajoso,-a I *adj* touchy. II *nm,f* touchy person.

picante *adj* 1 *Culin* hot, spicy. 2 *fig (chiste etc)* risqué, spicy.

picapica *nf* polvos p., itching powder *sing*.

picaporte *nm (aldaba)* door knocker; *(pomo)* door handle.

picar [1] I *vtr* 1 *(de insecto, serpiente)* to bite; *(de avispas, abejas)* to sting; *(barba)* to prick. 2 *(comer) (aves)* to peck (at); *(persona)* to nibble, pick at. 3 *Pesca* to bite. 4 *(perforar)* to prick, puncture. 5 *Culin (carne)* to mince. 6 *(incitar)* to incite, goad; p. la curiosidad (de algn), to arouse (sb's) curiosity. II *vi* 1 *(escozer)* to itch; *(herida)* to smart; *(el sol)* to burn. 2 *Culin* to be hot. 3 *Pesca* to bite. 4 *fig (dejarse engañar)* to swallow it. III **picarse** *vr*

1 (*hacerse rivales*) to be at loggerheads. 2 (*fruta*) to spot, rot; (*ropa*) to become moth-eaten; (*dientes*) to decay. 3 (*enfadarse*) to get cross. 4 (*drogadicto*) to shoot up.

picardía *nf* 1 (*astucia*) craftiness. 2 (*palabrota*) swear word. 3 (*prenda*) baby-doll pyjamas.

pícaro,-a I *adj* 1 (*travieso*) naughty, mischievous; (*astuto*) sly, crafty. 2 (*procaz*) risqué. II *nm,f* rascal, rogue.

picatoste *nm* crouton.

pichi *nm* pinafore dress.

pichón *nm* young pigeon; **tiro al** *o* **de p.**, pigeon shooting.

pico *nm* 1 (*de ave*) beak, bill; *fam* (*boca*) mouth; **tener un p. de oro**, to have the gift of the gab. 2 (*punta*) corner. 3 *Geog* peak. 4 (*herramienta*) pick, pickaxe, *US* pickax. 5 (*cantidad*) odd amount; **cincuenta y p.**, fifty odd; **las dos y p.**, just after two. 6 (*drogas*) fix.

picoleto *nm fam* civil guard.

picor *nm* itch, tingling.

picotazo *nm* peck.

picotear *vtr & vi* 1 (*pájaro*) to peck. 2 (*comer*) to nibble.

pictórico,-a *adj* pictorial.

pídola *nf* leapfrog.

pie *nm* 1 foot; **pies**, feet; **a p.**, on foot; **de p.**, standing up; **de pies a cabeza**, from head to foot; **en p.**, standing; **el acuerdo sigue en p.**, the agreement still stands; **hacer p.**, to touch the bottom; **perder p.**, to get out of one's depth; *fig* **a p.** *o* **pies juntillas**, blindly; *fig* **al p. de la letra**, to the letter, word for word; *fig* **con buen/mal p.**, on the right/wrong footing; *fig* **con pies de plomo**, gingerly, cautiously; *fig* **dar p. a**, to give cause for. 2 (*de instrumento*) stand; (*de copa*) stem. 3 foot; (*de una ilustración*) caption; **p. de página**, foot of the page. 4 (*medida*) foot. 5 *Teat* cue. 6 *Lit* foot.

piedad *nf* 1 devoutness, piety. 2 (*compasión*) compassion, pity.

piedra *nf* stone; (*de mechero*) flint; **poner la primera p.**, to lay the foundation stone; *fam fig* **me dejó** *o* **me quedé de p.**, I was flabbergasted.

piel *nf* 1 skin; **p. de gallina**, goose pimples *pl*. 2 (*de fruta, de patata*) skin, peel. 3 (*cuero*) leather; (*con pelo*) fur.

pienso *nm* fodder, feed; **piensos compuestos**, mixed feed *sing*.

pierna *nf* leg.

pieza *nf* 1 piece, part; **p. de recambio**, spare part; *fig* **me dejó** *o* **me quedé de una p.**, I was speechless *o* dumbfounded *o* flabbergasted. 2 (*habitación*) room. 3 *Teat* play.

pigmento *nm* pigment.

pigmeo,-a I *adj* pigmy; *fig* pygmean. II *nm,f* Pygmy, Pigmy; *fig* pygmy, pigmy.

pijama *nm* pyjamas *pl*.

pijo,-a *fam* I *adj* posh; **un barrio p.**, a posh area. II *nm,f* (*chico*) poor little rich boy; (*chica*) poor little rich girl. III *nm* (*pene*) willy.

pila *nf* 1 *Elec* battery. 2 (*montón*) pile, heap; *fig* (*muchos*) piles *pl*, heaps *pl*, loads *pl*. 3 (*lavadero*) basin. 4 *fig* **nombre de p.**, Christian name.

pilar *nm* 1 *Arquit* pillar. 2 (*fuente*) waterhole.

píldora *nf* pill; **p. abortiva**, morning-after pill; *fig* **dorar la p. a algn**, to butter sb up.

pileta *nf* 1 (*pila*) sink. 2 *Am* (*piscina*) swimming pool.

pililla *nf fam* willy.

pillaje *nm* looting, pillage.

pillar I *vtr* 1 (*robar*) to plunder, loot. 2 (*coger*) to catch; (*alcanzar*) to catch up with; **lo pilló un coche**, he was run over by a car. 3 *fam* to be; **me pilla un poco lejos**, it's a bit far for *o* from me. II **pillarse** *vr* to catch; **p. un dedo/una mano**, to catch one's finger/hand.

pillo,-a I *adj* 1 (*travieso*) naughty. 2 (*astuto*) sly, cunning. II *nm,f* rogue.

pilotar *vtr* *Av* to pilot, fly; *Aut* to drive; *Náut* to pilot, steer.

piloto *nm* 1 *Av* *Náut* pilot; *Aut* driver; **piso p.**, show flat; **programa p.**, pilot programme. 2 (*luz*) pilot lamp, light.

piltrafa *nf* 1 *fam* weakling; **estar hecho una p.**, to be on one's last legs. 2 (*desecho*) scraps.

pimentón *nm* paprika, red pepper.

pimienta *nf* pepper.

pimiento *nm* (*fruto*) pepper; (*planta*) pimiento; **p. morrón**, sweet pepper; *fam* **me importa un p.**, I don't give a damn, I couldn't care less.

pimpollo *nm* 1 *Bot* shoot. 2 *fam* (*hombre*) handsome young man; (*mujer*) elegant young woman.

pinacoteca *nf* art gallery.

pináculo *nm* pinnacle.

pinar *nm* pine grove, pine wood.

pincel *nm* brush, paintbrush.

pincelada *nf* brushstroke, stroke of a brush.

pinchadiscos *nmf inv fam* disc jockey, DJ.

pinchar I *vtr* 1 (*punzar*) to jag; (*balón, globo*) to burst; (*rueda*) to puncture. 2 *fam* (*incitar*) to prod; (*molestar*) to get at, nag. 3 *Med* (*inyectar*) to give an injection to. 4 *Tel* to bug. II *vi* 1 *Aut* to get a puncture. 2 *fam* **ni pincha ni corta**, he cuts no ice.

pinchazo *nm* 1 (*punzadura*) prick; *Aut* puncture, blowout. 2 (*de dolor*) sudden *o* sharp pain.

pinche *nm* 1 **p. de cocina**, kitchen assistant. 2 *Am* (*bribón*) rogue.

pinchito *nm* (*de carne*) type of kebab.

pincho nm 1 (púa) barb. 2 p. moruno, shish kebab; **p. de tortilla**, small portion of omelette.

ping-pong® nm table tennis, ping-pong.

pingüe adj abundant, plentiful; **pingües beneficios**, fat profits.

pingüino nm penguin.

pino nm pine; fig **hacer el p.**, to do a handstand; fam **en el quinto p.**, in the back of beyond.

pinole nm Am maize drink.

pinta I nf 1 fam (aspecto) look; **tiene p. de ser interesante**, it looks interesting. 2 (mota) dot; (lunar) spot. 3 (medida) pint. II nmf fam shameless person.

pintada nf graffiti.

pintado,-a adj 'recién p.', 'wet paint'; fam fig **nos viene que ni p.**, it is just the ticket; fam fig **te está que ni p.**, it suits you to a tee.

pintar I vtr 1 (dar color) to paint. 2 (dibujar) to draw, sketch. II vi (importar) to count; fig **yo aquí no pinto nada**, I am out of place here. III **pintarse** vr 1 (maquillarse) to put make-up on. 2 fam **pintárselas**, to manage.

pintarraj(e)ar vtr to daub.

pintor,-a nm,f painter.

pintoresco,-a adj 1 (lugar) picturesque. 2 (raro) eccentric, bizarre.

pintura nf 1 painting; **p. rupestre**, cave painting; fam fig **no la puedo ver ni en p.**, I can't stand the sight of her. 2 (materia) paint.

pinza nf (para depilar) tweezers pl; (para tender) clothes peg; (de animal) pincer, nipper; Téc tongs pl.

piña nf 1 (de pino) pine cone; (ananás) pineapple. 2 fig (grupo) clan, clique. 3 fam (golpe) thump.

piñón nm 1 pine seed o nut. 2 Téc pinion.

pío[1] nm fam **no dijo ni p.**, there wasn't a cheep out of him.

pío,-a[2] adj pious.

piojo nm louse.

pionero,-a nm,f pioneer.

pipa[1] nf 1 (de fumar) pipe; **fumar en p.**, to smoke a pipe. 2 (de fruta) pip; (de girasol) sunflower seed.

pipí nm fam pee, wee-wee; **hacer p.**, to pee, wee-wee.

pique nm 1 resentment. 2 (rivalidad) needle. 3 **a p. de**, on the point of. 4 **irse a p.**, Náut to sink; (un plan) to fall through; (un negocio) to go bust.

piqueta nf pickaxe, US pickax.

piquete nm 1 (de huelga) picket. 2 Mil **p. de ejecución**, firing squad.

pira nf pyre.

pirado,-a adj arg crazy.

piragua nf canoe.

piragüismo nm canoeing.

piragüista nmf canoeist.

pirámide nf pyramid.

piraña nf piranha.

pirarse, pirárselas vr arg to clear off, hop it.

pirata adj & nmf pirate.

piratear vtr fig to pirate.

Pirineo(s) nmpl Pyrenees.

pirita nf pyrite.

pirómano,-a nm,f Med pyromaniac; Jur arsonist.

piropo nm **echar un p.**, to pay a compliment.

pirueta nf pirouette; fig Pol **hacer una p.**, to do a U-turn.

pirulí nm lollipop; TV television tower.

pis nm fam wee-wee, pee; **hacer p.**, to wee-wee, have a pee.

pisada nf step, footstep; (huella) footprint.

pisapapeles nm inv paperweight.

pisar vtr to tread on, step on.

piscifactoría nf fish farm.

piscina nf swimming pool.

piscolabis nm inv fam snack.

piso nm 1 flat, apartment; Pol **p. franco**, safe house. 2 (planta) floor; (de carretera) surface.

pisotear vtr (aplastar) to stamp on; (pisar) to trample on.

pisotón nm **me dio un p.**, he stood on my foot.

pista nf 1 track; **p. de baile**, dance floor; Dep **p. de esquí**, ski run o slope; Dep **p. de patinaje**, ice rink; Dep **p. de tenis**, tennis court; **p. de aterrizaje**, landing strip; **p. de despegue**, runway. 2 (rastro) trail, track. 3 **dame una p.**, give me a clue.

pistacho nm pistachio nut.

pisto nm Culin ≈ ratatouille.

pistola nf 1 gun, pistol. 2 (para pintar) spray gun.

pistolero,-a nm gunman, gangster.

pistón nm 1 Téc (émbolo) piston. 2 (de arma) cartridge cap. 3 Mús key.

pita nf agave.

pitada nf booing, hissing.

pitar I vtr 1 (silbato) to blow. 2 Dep **el árbitro pitó un penalti**, the referee awarded a penalty. II vi 1 to whistle. 2 Aut to toot one's horn. 3 Dep to referee. 4 fam **salir pitando**, to fly off.

pitido nm whistle.

pitillera nf cigarette case.

pitillo nm cigarette, fag.

pito nm 1 whistle; Aut horn; fam **me importa un p.**, I don't give a hoot. 2 fam (cigarrillo) fag. 3 fam (pene) prick, willie.

pitón nm 1 (serpiente) python. 2 (de toro) horn.

pitorreo nm fam scoffing, teasing; **hacer algo de p.**, to do sth for a laugh.

pivot, pivote nmf pivot.

pizarra nf 1 (encerado) blackboard. 2 Min slate.

pizca *nf* little bit, tiny piece; **ni p.**, not a bit; **una p. de sal**, a pinch of salt.

placa *nf* 1 plate. 2 *(conmemorativa)* plaque.

placaje *nm Dep* tackle.

placentero,-a *adj* pleasant, agreeable.

placer *nm* pleasure; **ha sido un p. (conocerle)**, it's been a pleasure (meeting you); *fml* **tengo el p. de**, it gives me great pleasure to; **un viaje de p.**, a holiday trip.

placer [33] *vtr* to please.

placidez *nf* placidity.

plácido,-a *adj* placid, easy-going.

plaga *nf* 1 plague. 2 *Agr* pest, blight.

plagar [7] *vtr* to cover, fill.

plagiar [12] *vtr* 1 *(copiar)* to plagiarize. 2 *Am (secuestrar)* to kidnap.

plagiario,-a *nm,f Am* *(secuestrador)* kidnapper.

plagio *nm* plagiarism.

plan *nm* 1 *(proyecto)* plan. 2 *(programa)* scheme, programme; *Educ* **p. de estudios**, syllabus; **estar a p.** to be on a diet. 3 *fam* **en p. de broma**, for a laugh; **si te pones en ese p.**, if you're going to be like that (about it); **en p. barato**, cheaply. 4 *fam (cita)* date.

plana *nf* 1 page; **a toda p.**, full page; **primera p.**, front page. 2 *Mil* **p. mayor**, staff.

plancha *nf* 1 iron; *(de metal)* plate. 2 *Culin* hotplate; **sardinas a la p.**, grilled sardines. 3 *Impr* plate.

planchado *nm* ironing.

planchar *vtr* to iron.

planchazo *nm fam* blunder, boob.

planeador *nm* glider.

planear I *vtr* to plan. II *vi* to glide.

planeta *nm* planet.

planetario,-a I *adj* planetary. II *nm* planetarium.

planicie *nf* plain.

planificación *nf* planning; **p. familiar**, family planning.

planificar [1] *vtr* to plan.

planilla *nf Am* application form.

plano,-a I *nm* 1 *(de ciudad)* map; *Arquit* plan, draft. 2 *Cin* shot; **un primer p.**, a close-up; *fig* **estar en primer/segundo p.**, to be in the limelight/in the background. 3 *Mat* plane. II *adj* flat, even.

planta *nf* 1 plant. 2 *(del pie)* sole. 3 *(piso)* floor, storey; **p. baja**, ground floor.

plantación *nf* 1 plantation. 2 *(acción)* planting.

plantado,-a *fam* **dejar a algn p.**, to stand sb up.

plantar I *vtr* 1 *(árboles, campo)* to plant. 2 *(poner)* to put, place; **p. cara a algn**, to stand up to sb. 3 *fam* **p. a algn en la calle**, to throw sb out; **le ha plantado su novia**, his girlfriend has ditched him. II **plantarse** *vr* 1 to stand. 2 *(llegar)* to

arrive; **en cinco minutos se plantó aquí**, he got here in five minutes flat.

planteamiento *nm (enfoque)* approach.

plantear I *vtr* 1 *(problema)* to pose, raise. 2 *(planear)* to plan. 3 *(proponer)* to put forward. 4 *(exponer)* to present. II **plantearse** *vtr & vr* 1 *(considerar)* to consider. 2 *(problema)* to arise.

plantel *nm fig* cadre, clique.

plantilla *nf* 1 *(personal)* staff, personnel. 2 *(de zapato)* insole. 3 *(patrón)* model, pattern.

plantón *nm fam* **dar un p. a algn**, to stand sb up.

plañir *vi* to mourn.

plasmar I *vtr* 1 *(reproducir)* to capture. 2 *(expresar)* to express. II **plasmarse** *vr* **p. en**, to take the shape of.

plasta *nmf fam* bore.

plástico,-a I *adj* plastic. II *nm* 1 plastic. 2 *(disco)* record.

plastificar [1] *vtr* to coat *o* cover with plastic.

plastilina® *nf* Plasticine®.

plata *nf* 1 silver; *(objetos de plata)* silverware; *fam* **hablar en p.**, to lay (it) on the line; **p. de ley**, sterling silver. 2 *Am* money.

plataforma *nm* platform.

plátano *nm* 1 *(fruta)* banana. 2 *(árbol)* plane tree; **falso p.**, sycamore.

platea *nf Cin Teat* stalls *pl, US* ground floor.

platear *vtr* to silver-plate.

platense I *adj* of *o* from the River Plate. II *nmf* native *o* inhabitant of the River Plate.

plática *nf* chat, talk.

platicar [1] *vi* to chat, talk.

platillo *nm* 1 saucer; **p. volante**, flying saucer. 2 *Mús* cymbal.

platina *nf (de tocadiscos)* deck; **doble p.**, double deck.

platino *nm* 1 platinum. 2 *Aut* **platinos**, contact breaker *sing*, points.

plato *nm* 1 plate, dish. 2 *(parte de una comida)* course; **de primer p.**, for starters; **p. fuerte**, main course; **p. combinado**, one-course meal. 3 *(guiso)* dish. 4 *(de balanza)* pan, tray. 5 *(de tocadiscos)* turntable.

plató *nm Cin* TV *(film)* set.

plausible *adj* 1 *(admisible)* plausible, acceptable. 2 *(loable)* commendable.

playa *nf* 1 beach; *(costa)* seaside. 2 *Am* **p. de estacionamiento**, car park, *US* parking lot.

playera *nf* 1 *(zapatilla)* sandshoe, *US* sneaker. 2 *Am (camiseta)* teeshirt.

plaza *nf* 1 square. 2 *(mercado)* market, marketplace. 3 *Aut* seat. 4 *(laboral)* post, position. 5 **p. de toros**, bullring.

plazo *nm* 1 *(periodo)* time, period; *(término)* deadline; **a corto/largo p.**, in the short term/in the long run; **el p. termina el viernes**, Friday is the deadline. **2** *Fin* **comprar a plazos**, to buy on hire purchase, *US* buy on an installment plan; **en seis plazos**, in six instalments.

pleamar *nf* high tide.

plebe *nf* masses *pl*, plebs *pl*.

plebeyo,-a I *adj* plebeian. **II** *nm,f* plebeian, pleb.

plebiscito *nm* plebiscite.

plegable *adj* folding, collapsible.

plegar |1| **I** *vtr* to fold. **II plegarse** *vr* to give way, bow.

plegaria *nf* prayer.

pleitear *vi* to conduct a lawsuit, plead.

pleito *nm* *Jur* lawsuit, litigation; **poner un p. (a algn)**, to sue (sb).

plenilunio *nm* full moon.

plenitud *nf* plenitude, fullness; **en la p. de la vida**, in the prime of life.

pleno,-a I *adj* full; **en plena noche**, in the middle of the night; **los empleados en p.**, the entire staff. **II** *nm* plenary meeting.

pletórico,-a *adj* abundant.

plexiglás® *nm* *(plástico)* Perspex®, *US* Plexiglass®.

pliego *nm* 1 *(hoja)* sheet *o* piece of paper; **p. de condiciones**, bidding specifications. **2** *(carta)* sealed letter.

pliegue *nm* 1 fold. **2** *(de vestido)* pleat.

plinto *nm* *Gimn* horse.

plisar *vtr* to pleat.

plomero,-a *nm* *Am* plumber.

plomizo,-a *adj* lead, leaden; *(color)* lead-colored, *US* lead-colored.

plomo *nm* 1 *(en metalurgia)* lead. **2** *Elec (fusible)* fuse. **3** *(bala)* slug, pellet.

pluma *nf* 1 feather. **2** *(de escribir)* fountain pen.

plumaje *nm* plumage.

plumazo *nm* **de un p.**, at a stroke.

plumero *nm* 1 *(para el polvo)* feather duster. **2** *fam* **se te ve el p.**, I can see through you.

plumier *nm* pencil box.

plural *adj & nm* plural.

pluralismo *nm* pluralism.

pluriempleo *nm* moonlighting.

plus *nm* bonus, bonus payment.

plusmarca *nf* record.

plusmarquista *nmf* record breaker.

plusvalía *nf* capital gain.

población *nf* 1 *(ciudad)* town; *(pueblo)* village. **2** *(habitantes)* population.

poblado,-a *adj* 1 populated; *fig* **p. de**, full of. **2** *(barba)* bushy, thick.

poblador,-a *nm,f* settler.

poblar |2| *vtr* 1 *(con gente)* to settle, people; *(con plantas)* to plant. **2** *(vivir)* to inhabit.

pobre I *adj* poor; **¡p.!**, poor thing!; **un hombre p.**, a poor man; **un p. hombre**, a poor devil. **II** *nmf* poor person; **los po-**

bres, the poor.

pobreza *nf* poverty; *fig (de medios, recursos)* lack.

pocilga *nf* pigsty.

pocillo *nm* *Am* cup.

pócima, poción *nf* potion; *pey* concoction, brew.

poco,-a I *nm* 1 **un p.**, *(con adj o adv)* a little; **un p. tarde/frío**, a little late/cold. **2 un p.**, *(con sustantivo)* a little; **un p. de azúcar**, a little sugar. **II** *adj* 1 not much, little; **p. sitio/tiempo**, not much *o* little space/time; **poca cosa**, not much. **2 pocos,-as**, not many, few; **pocas personas**, not many *o* few people. **3 unos-as pocos-as**, a few. **III** *pron* 1 not much; **queda p.**, there isn't much left. **2 pocos,-as**, *(cosas)* few, not many; **tengo muy pocos**, I have very few, I don't have very many. **3 pocos,-as**, *(personas)* few people, not many people; **vinieron pocos**, few people came, not many people came. **IV** *adv* 1 *(con verbo)* not (very) much, little; **ella come p.**, she doesn't eat much, she eats little. **2** *(con adj)* not very; **es p. probable**, it's not very likely. **V** *(locuciones)* **a p. de**, shortly *o* a little after; **dentro de p.**, soon; **p. a p.**, little by little, gradually; **p. antes/después**, shortly *o* a little before/afterwards; **por p.**, almost.

pocho,-a *adj* 1 *(fruta)* bad, overripe. **2** *fig (persona)* *(débil)* off-colour, *US* off-color; *(triste)* depressed, down.

podar *vtr* to prune.

poder[1] *nm* power; *Econ* **p. adquisitivo**, purchasing power.

poder[2] |18| **I** *vtr* 1 *(capacidad)* to be able to; **no puede hablar**, she can't speak; **no podré llamarte**, I won't be able to phone; **no puedo más**, I can't take anymore; **guapa a más no p.**, unbelievably pretty. **2** *(permiso)* may, might; **¿puedo pasar?**, can *o* may I come in?; **¿se puede (entrar)?**, may I (come in)?; **aquí no se puede fumar**, you can't smoke here. **3** *(uso impers)* *(posibilidad)* may, might; **puede que no lo sepan**, they may *o* might not know; **no puede ser**, that's impossible; **puede (ser) (que sí)**, maybe, perhaps. **4** *(deber)* **podrías haberme advertido**, you might have warned me. **II** *vi* 1 to cope *(con,* with); **no puede con tanto trabajo**, he can't cope with so much work. **2** *(batir)* to be stronger than; **les puede a todos**, he can take on anybody.

poderoso,-a *adj* powerful.

podio, pódium *nm* *Dep* podium.

podré *indic fut* → **poder**.

podrido,-a *adj* 1 *(putrefacto)* rotten, putrid. **2** *(corrupto)* corrupt; *fam* **p. de dinero**, stinking rich.

podrir *vtr defect* → **pudrir**.

poema *nm* poem.
poesía *nf* 1 (*género*) poetry. 2 (*poema*) poem.
poeta *nmf* poet.
poético,-a *adj* poetic.
póker *nm* poker.
polaco,-a I *adj* Polish. II *nm,f* Pole. III *nm* (*idioma*) Polish.
polaridad *nf* polarity.
polarizar [4] *vtr* 1 *Fís* to polarize. 2 *fig* (*ánimo, atención*) to concentrate.
polea *nf* pulley.
polémica *nf* controversy.
polémico,-a *adj* controversial.
polemizar [4] *vi* to argue, debate.
polen *nm* pollen.
poli- *pref* poly-.
poli *fam* I *nmf* cop. II *nf* la p., the fuzz *pl*.
policía I *nf* police (force). II *nmf* (*hombre*) policeman; (*mujer*) policewoman.
policíaco,-a, policiaco,-a, policial *adj* police; novela/película policíaca, detective story/film.
polideportivo *nm* sports centre *o US* center *o* complex.
poliéster *nm* polyester.
polietileno *nm* polythene, *US* polyethylene.
polifacético,-a *adj* versatile, many-sided; es un hombre muy p., he's a man of many talents.
poligamia *nf* polygamy.
políglota *adj & nm,f* polyglot.
polígono *nm* polygon; p. industrial, industrial estate.
polilla *nf* moth.
poliomielitis *nf* polio, poliomyelitis.
politécnico,-a *adj & nm* polytechnic.
política *nf* 1 politics *sing*. 2 (*estrategia*) policy.
político,-a I *adj* 1 political. 2 (*pariente*) in-law; hermano p., brother-in-law; su familia política, her in-laws. II *nm,f* politician.
póliza *nf* 1 (*sello*) stamp. 2 p. de seguros, insurance policy.
polizón *nm* stowaway.
polo *nm* 1 *Elec Geog* pole; P. Norte/Sur, North/South Pole. 2 (*helado*) ice lolly, *US* Popsicle®. 2 (*prenda*) sports shirt, polo neck (sweater). 3 *Dep* polo.
Polonia *n* Poland.
polución *nf* pollution.
poltrona *nf* easy chair.
polvareda *nf* cloud of dust.
polvera *nf* powder compact.
polvo *nm* 1 dust; limpiar *o* quitar el p., to dust; en p., powdered; polvo(s) de talco, talcum powder. 2 *fam* estar hecho p., (*cansado*) to be knackered; (*deprimido*) to be depressed. 3 *vulg* echar un p., to have a screw.
pólvora *nf* gunpowder.

polvoriento,-a *adj* dusty.
polvorín *nm* gunpowder arsenal; *fig* powder keg.
polvorón *nm* sweet pastry.
polla *nf* 1 *vulg* (*pene*) prick. 2 *Orn* p. de agua, moorhen.
pollo *nm* 1 chicken. 2 *fam* (*joven*) lad.
pomada *nf* ointment.
pomelo *nm* (*fruto*) grapefruit; (*árbol*) grapefruit tree.
pómez *adj inv* piedra p., pumice (stone).
pomo *nm* (*de puerta*) knob.
pompa *nf* 1 bubble. 2 (*ostentación*) pomp.
pompis *nm inv fam* botty.
pomposo,-a *adj* pompous.
pómulo *nm* cheekbone.
ponche *nm* punch.
poncho *nm* poncho.
ponderar *vtr* 1 (*asunto*) to weigh up *o* consider. 2 (*alabar*) to praise.
pondré *indic fut* → **poner**.
ponencia *nf* paper.
poner [19] (*pp* **puesto**) I *vtr* 1 to put; (*mesa, huevo*) to lay; (*gesto*) to make; (*multa*) to impose; (*telegrama*) to send; (*negocio*) to set up. 2 (*tele, radio etc*) to turn *o* switch on. 3 (+ *adj*) to make; p. triste a algn, to make sb sad; p. colorado a algn, to make sb blush. 4 ¿qué llevaba puesto?, what was he wearing? 5 (*decir*) ¿qué pone aquí?, what does it say here? 6 (*suponer*) to suppose; pongamos que Ana no viene, supposing Ana doesn't turn up. 7 *TV Cin* to put on, show; ¿qué ponen en la tele?, what's on the telly? 8 *Tel* ponme con Manuel, put me through to Manuel. 9 (*nombrar*) le pondremos (de nombre) Pilar, we are going to call her Pilar.
II **ponerse** *vr* 1 to put oneself; ponte en mi lugar, put yourself in my place; ponte más cerca, come closer. 2 (*vestirse*) to put on; ella se puso el jersey, she put her jumper on. 3 (+ *adj*) to become; p. furioso/malo, to become furious/ill. 4 (*sol*) to set. 5 *Tel* p. al teléfono, to answer the phone. 6 p. a, to start to; p. a trabajar, to get down to work.
poney *nm* pony.
pongo *indic pres* → **poner**.
poniente *nm* 1 (*occidente*) West. 2 (*viento*) westerly (wind).
pontífice *nm* Pontiff; el Sumo P., His Holiness the Pope.
ponzoña *nf* 1 venom, poison. 2 tener p., (*tristeza*) to be down in the dumps.
ponzoñoso,-a *adj* 1 venomous, poisonous. 2 (*triste*) down in the dumps.
popa *nf* stern; *fig* ir viento en p., to go full speed ahead.
populacho *nm pey* plebs *pl*, masses *pl*.
popular *adj* 1 folk; arte/música p., folk art/music. 2 (*medida*) popular. 3 (*actor*) well-known.

popularidad *nf* popularity.
popularizar [4] *vtr* to popularize.
populoso,-a *adj* densely populated.
popurrí *nm* *Mús* medley.
póquer *nm* poker.
por *prep* **1** *(agente)* by; **pintado p. Picasso**, painted by Picasso. **2 p. qué**, why. **3** *(causa)* because of; **p. sus ideas**, because of her ideas; **p. necesidad/amor**, out of need/love; **suspendió p. no estudiar**, he failed because he didn't study. **4** *(tiempo)* **p. la mañana/noche**, in the morning/at night; **p. ahora**, for the time being; **p. entonces**, at that time. **5** *(en favor de)* for; **lo hago p. mi hermano**, I'm doing it for my brother('s sake). **6** *(lugar)* **pasamos p. Córdoba**, we went through Córdoba; **p. ahí**, over there; **¿p. dónde vamos?**, which way are we taking?; **p. la calle**, in the street; **mirar p. la ventana**, to look out the window; **entrar p. la ventana**, to get in through the window. **7** *(medio)* by; **p. avión/correo**, by plane/post. **8** *(a cambio de)* for; **cambiar algo p. otra cosa**, to exchange sth for sth else. **9** *(distributivo)* **p. cabeza**, a head, per person; **p. hora/mes**, per hour/month. **10** *Mat* **dos p. tres, seis**, two times three is six; **un diez p. ciento**, ten per cent. **11** *(con infinitivo)* in order to, so as to; **hablar p. hablar**, to talk for the sake of it. **12** *(locuciones)* **p. así decirlo**, so to speak; **p. más/muy ... que sea**, no matter how ... he *o* she is; **p. mí**, as far as I'm concerned.
porcelana *nf* porcelain.
porcentaje *nm* percentage.
porcino,-a *adj* **ganado p.**, pigs.
porción *nf* portion, part.
porche *nm* porch.
pordiosero,-a *nm,f* tramp.
porfía *nf* *(obstinación)* obstinacy, stubbornness.
porfolio *nm* portfolio.
pormenor *nm* detail; **venta al p.**, retail.
porno *adj inv fam* porn.
pornografía *nf* pornography.
pornográfico,-a *adj* pornographic.
poro *nm* pore.
poroso,-a *adj* porous.
porque *conj* **1** *(causal)* because; **¡p. no!**, just because. **2** *(final)* (+ *subj*) so that, in order that.
porqué *nm* reason.
porquería *nf* **1** *(suciedad)* dirt, filth. **2** *(birria)* rubbish. **3** *fam* *(chuchería)* rubbish, *US* junk food.
porra *nf* **1** *(de policía)* truncheon, baton. **2** *fam* *(locuciones)* **¡una p.!**, rubbish!; **¡vete a la p.!**, get lost!
porrazo *nm* thump.
porro *nm* *arg* joint.
porrón *nm* glass bottle with a spout coming out of its base, used for drinking wine.

porta(a)viones *nm inv* aircraft carrier.
portada *nf* **1** *(de libro etc)* cover; *(de periódico)* front page; *(de disco)* sleeve. **2** *(fachada)* front, facade.
portador,-a *nm,f* *Com* bearer; *Med* carrier.
portaequipajes *nm inv* **1** *Aut* *(maletero)* boot, *US* trunk; *(baca)* roof rack. **2** *(carrito)* luggage trolley.
portafolios *nm inv* briefcase.
portal *nm* **1** *(zaguán)* porch, entrance hall. **2** *(puerta de la calle)* main door. **3 p. de Belén**, Nativity scene.
portamaletas *nm inv* → **portaequipajes**.
portaminas *nm inv* propelling pencil.
portamonedas *nm inv* purse.
portarse *vr* to behave; **p. mal**, to misbehave.
portátil *adj* portable.
portavoz *nmf* spokesperson; *(hombre)* spokesman; *(mujer)* spokeswoman.
portazo *nm* slam of a door; **dar un p.**, to slam the door.
porte *nm* **1** *(aspecto)* bearing. **2** *(transporte)* carriage.
portento *nm* **1** *(cosa)* wonder, marvel. **2** *(persona)* genius.
portentoso,-a *adj* extraordinary, prodigious.
porteño,-a **I** *adj* *o* from Buenos Aires. **II** *nm,f* native *o* inhabitant of Buenos Aires.
portería *nf* **1** porter's lodge. **2** *Dep* goal.
portero,-a *nm,f* **1** *(de vivienda)* porter, caretaker; *(de edificio público)* doorman; **p. automático**, entryphone. **2** *Dep* goalkeeper.
pórtico *nm* **1** *(portal)* portico, porch. **2** *(con arcadas)* arcade.
portorriqueño,-a *adj* & *nm,f* Puerto Rican.
portuario,-a *adj* harbour, *US* harbor, port.
Portugal *n* Portugal.
portugués,-a **I** *adj* Portuguese. **II** *nm* *(idioma)* Portuguese.
porvenir *nm* future; **sin p.**, with no prospects.
pos- *pref* post-.
pos *adv* **en p. de**, after.
posada *nf* inn.
posaderas *nfpl fam* buttocks.
posadero,-a *nm,f* innkeeper.
posar **I** *vi* *(para retrato etc)* to pose. **II** *vtr* to put *o* lay down. **III posarse** *vr* to settle, alight.
posdata *nf* postscript.
pose *nf* **1** *(postura)* pose. **2** *(afectación)* posing.
poseedor,-a *nm,f* possessor.
poseer [36] *vtr* to possess, own.
poseído,-a *adj* possessed.
posesión *nf* possession; **estar en p. de**, to

have; **tomar p.**, **(de un cargo)** to take up
(a post).
posesivo,-a *adj* possessive.
poseso,-a *adj & nm,f* possessed.
posguerra *nf* postwar period.
posibilidad *nf* possibility; *(oportunidad)*
chance.
posibilitar *vtr* to make possible.
posible I *adj* possible; **de ser p.**, if
possible; **en (la medida de) lo p.**, as far
as possible; **haré todo lo p.**, I'll do
everything I can; **lo antes p.**, as soon as
possible; **es p. que venga**, he might
come. **II** *nmpl* **posibles**, means.
posición *nf* position.
positivo,-a *adj* positive.
poso *nm* dregs *pl*, sediment.
posponer [19] *vtr* **1** *(aplazar)* to postpone,
put off. **2** *(relegar)* to put in second place
o behind, relegate.
post- *pref* post-.
posta *nf* **a p.**, on purpose.
postal I *adj* postal. **II** *nf* postcard.
poste *nm* pole; *Dep (de portería)* post.
póster *nm* poster.
postergar [7] *vtr* **1** *(relegar)* to relegate. **2**
(retrasar) to delay; *(aplazar)* to postpone.
posteridad *nf* posterity; **pasar a la p.**, to
go down in history.
posterior *adj* **1** *(lugar)* posterior, rear. **2**
(tiempo) later (**a**, than), subsequent (**a**,
to). ◆**posteriormente** *adv* subsequently, later.
posterioridad *nf* posteriority; **con p.**, later.
postgraduado,-a *adj & nm,f* postgraduate.
postigo *nm* *(de puerta)* wicket; *(de ventana)* shutter.
postín *nm* *fam* boasting, showing-off;
darse p., to show off, swank; **de p.**,
posh, swanky.
postizo,-a I *adj* false, artificial; **dentadura
postiza**, false teeth, dentures. **II** *nm* hairpiece.
postor *nm* bidder.
postrarse *vr* to prostrate oneself, kneel
down.
postre *nm* dessert, sweet.
postrero,-a *adj* *(delante de nm sing, pos-
trer)* last.
postrimería *nf* *(usu pl)* last part *o* period.
postular *vtr* to collect.
póstumo,-a *adj* posthumous.
postura *nf* **1** position, posture. **2** *fig (actitud)* attitude.
pos(t)venta *adj* **servicio p.**, after-sales
service.
potable *adj* drinkable; **agua p./no p.**,
drinking water/not drinking water.
potaje *nm* hotpot, stew.
pote *nm* pot; *(jarra)* jug.
potencia *nf* power; **en p.**, potential.

potencial I *adj* potential. **II** *nm* **1** potential; **p. eléctrico**, voltage; **p. humano**,
manpower. **2** *Ling* conditional (tense).
potenciar [12] *vtr* to promote, strengthen.
potente *adj* powerful, strong.
potestad *nf* power, authority.
potingue *nm* *fam pey* **1** *(bebida)* concoction. **2** *(maquillaje)* make-up, face cream
o lotion.
potra *nf* *fam* luck.
potro *nm* *Zool* colt; *(de gimnasia)* horse.
poyo *nm* stone bench.
pozo *nm* well; *Min* shaft, pit.
PP *nm* *Pol abr de* **Partido Popular**.
práctica *nf* **1** practice; **en la p.**, in
practice. **2** *(formación)* placement; **período de prácticas**, practical training
period.
practicante I *adj* *Rel* practising, *US*
practicing. **II** *nmf* *Med* medical assistant.
practicar [1] **I** *vtr* to practise, *US*
practice; *(operación)* to carry out. **II** *vi* to
practise, *US* practice.
práctico,-a *adj* practical; *(útil)* handy,
useful.
pradera *nf* meadow.
prado *nm* meadow, field.
Praga *n* Prague.
pragmático,-a I *adj* pragmatic. **II** *nm,f*
pragmatist.
pre- *pref* pre-.
preámbulo *nm* **1** *(introducción)* preamble.
2 *(rodeo)* circumlocution.
preaviso *nm* previous warning, notice.
precalentamiento *nm* warm-up.
precalentar [1] *vtr* to preheat.
precario,-a *adj* precarious.
precaución *nf* **1** *(cautela)* caution; **con p.**,
cautiously. **2** *(medida)* precaution.
precaver I *vtr* to guard against. **II preca-
verse** *vr* to take precautions (**de, contra**,
against).
precavido,-a *adj* cautious, prudent.
precedencia *nf* precedence, priority.
precedente I *adj* preceding. **II** *nmf* predecessor. **III** *nm* precedent; **sin p.**, unprecedented.
preceder *vtr* to precede.
precepto *nm* precept.
preciarse [12] *vr* to fancy oneself (**de**, as).
precintar *vtr* to seal.
precinto *nm* seal.
precio *nm* price; **p. de coste**, cost price; **a
cualquier p.**, at any price.
preciosidad *nf* **1** *(hermosura) (cosa)* lovely
thing; *(persona)* darling. **2** *fml (cualidad)*
preciousness.
precioso,-a *adj* **1** *(hermoso)* lovely, beautiful. **2** *(valioso)* precious, valuable.
precipicio *nm* precipice.
precipitación *nf* **1** *(prisa)* haste. **2** *(lluvia)*
rainfall.
precipitado,-a *adj* *(apresurado)* hasty,
hurried; *(irreflexivo)* rash.

precipitar I *vtr* **1** (*acelerar*) to hurry, rush. **2** (*arrojar*) to throw, hurl down. **II precipitarse** *vr* **1** (*persona*) to hurl oneself; (*acontecimientos*) to gather speed. **2** (*actuar irreflexivamente*) to hurry, rush.

precisar *vtr* **1** (*determinar*) to determine, give full details of; (*especificar*) to specify. **2** (*necesitar*) to require, need.

precisión *nm* **1** (*exactitud*) precision, accuracy; **con p.**, precisely, accurately. **2** (*aclaración*) clarification.

preciso,-a *adj* **1** (*necesario*) necessary, essential. **2** (*exacto*) accurate, exact; **en este p. momento**, at this very moment. **3** (*claro*) concise, clear. ◆**precisamente** *adv* (*con precisión*) precisely; (*exactamente*) exactly; **p. por eso**, for that very reason.

preconizar [4] *vtr* to advocate.

precoz *adj* **1** (*persona*) precocious. **2** (*fruta*) early.

precursor,-a *nm,f* precursor.

predecesor,-a *nm,f* predecessor.

predecir [12] (*pp* **predicho**) *vtr* to foretell, predict.

predestinado,-a *adj* predestined.

predeterminar *vtr* to predetermine.

predicador,-a *nm,f* preacher.

predicado *nm* predicate.

predicar [1] *vtr* to preach.

predicción *nf* prediction, forecast.

predice *indic pres* → **predecir**.

predije *pt indef* → **predecir**.

predilección *nf* predilection.

predilecto,-a *adj* favourite, *US* favorite, preferred.

predisponer [19] (*pp* **predispuesto**) *vtr* to predispose.

predisposición *nf* predisposition.

predominante *adj* predominant.

predominar *vi* to predominate.

predominio *nm* predominance.

preescolar *adj* preschool; **en p.**, in the nursery school.

prefabricado,-a *adj* prefabricated.

prefacio *nm* preface.

preferencia *nf* preference.

preferente *adj* preferable, preferential.

preferible *adj* preferable; **es p. que no vengas**, you'd better not come.

preferido,-a *nm,f* favourite, *US* favorite.

preferir [5] *vtr* to prefer.

prefijo *nm* **1** *Tel* code, *US* area code. **2** *Ling* prefix.

pregonar *vtr* (*anunciar*) to announce publicly; *fig* (*divulgar*) to reveal, disclose.

pregunta *nf* question; **hacer una p.** to ask a question.

preguntar I *vtr* to ask; **p. algo a algn**, to ask sb sth; **p. por algn**, to ask after *o* about sb. **II preguntarse** *vr* to wonder; **me pregunto si ...,** I wonder whether ....

preguntón,-ona *nm,f fam* busybody.

prehistoria *nf* prehistory.

prehistórico,-a *adj* prehistoric.

prejuicio *nm* prejudice; **tener prejuicios**, to be prejudiced, be biased.

preliminar *adj & nm* preliminary.

preludio *nm* prelude.

prematrimonial *adj* premarital.

prematuro,-a *adj* premature.

premeditación *nf* premeditation; **con p.**, deliberately.

premeditado,-a *adj* premeditated, deliberate.

premiado,-a *adj* prize-winning.

premiar [12] *vtr* **1** to award a prize (**a**, to). **2** (*recompesar*) to reward.

premio *nm* prize, award; (*recompensa*) reward.

premisa *nf* premise.

premonición *nf* premonition.

premura *nf* (*urgencia*) urgency; **p. de tiempo**, haste.

prenatal *adj* antenatal, prenatal.

prenda *nf* **1** (*prenda*) garment. **2** (*garantía*) token, pledge.

prendar I *vtr* to captivate, delight. **II prendarse** *vr* (*enamorarse*) to fall in love (**de**, with).

prendedor *nm* brooch, pin.

prender I *vtr* **1** (*sujetar*) to fasten, attach; (*con alfileres*) to pin. **2 p. fuego a**, to set fire to. **3** (*arrestar*) to arrest. **II vi** (*fuego*) to catch; (*madera*) to catch fire; (*planta*) to take root. **III prenderse** *vr* to catch fire.

prensa *nf* press; *fig* **tener buena/mala p.**, to have a good/bad press.

prensar *vtr* to press.

preñado,-a *adj* **1** pregnant. **2** *fig* (*lleno*) pregnant (**de**, with), full (**de**, of).

preñar *vtr* (*mujer*) to make pregnant; (*animal*) to impregnate.

preocupación *nf* worry, concern.

preocupado,-a *adj* worried, concerned.

preocupar I *vtr* to worry; **me preocupa que llegue tan tarde**, I'm worried about him arriving so late. **II preocuparse** *vr* to worry, get worried (**por**, about); **no te preocupes**, don't worry; **p. de algn/algo**, to look after sb/to see to sth.

preparación *nf* preparation; (*formación*) training.

preparado,-a I *adj* **1** (*dispuesto*) ready, prepared; **comidas preparadas**, ready-cooked meals. **2** (*capacitado*) trained, qualified. **II** *nm Farm* preparation.

preparador,-a *nm,f* coach, trainer.

preparar I *vtr* **1** to prepare, get ready; **p. un examen**, to prepare for an exam. **2** *Dep* (*entrenar*) to train, coach. **II prepararse** *vr* **1** to prepare oneself, get ready. **2** *Dep* (*entrenarse*) to train.

preparativo *nm* preparation.

preparatorio,-a *adj* preparatory.

preponderante *adj* preponderant.

preposición *nf Ling* preposition.

prepotente *adj* domineering; (*arrogante*)

overbearing.
prerrogativa *nf* prerogative.
presa *nf* 1 prey; *fig* **ser p. de**, to be a victim of; **p. del pánico**, panic-stricken. 2 *(embalse)* dam.
presagiar |12| *vtr* to predict, foretell.
presagio *nm* 1 *(señal)* omen; **buen/mal p.**, good/bad omen. 2 *(premonición)* premonition.
presbiteriano,-a *adj & nm,f* Presbyterian.
presbítero *nm* priest.
prescindir *vi* **p. de**, to do without.
prescribir *(pp* prescrito*)* *vtr* to prescribe.
prescripción *nf* prescription; **p. facultativa**, medical prescription.
presencia *nm* presence; **hacer acto de p.**, to put in an appearance; **p. de ánimo**, presence of mind.
presencial *adj* **testigo p.**, eyewitness.
presenciar |12| *vtr (ver)* to witness.
presentable *adj* presentable; **no estoy p.**, I'm not dressed for the occasion.
presentación *nf* presentation; *(aspecto)* appearance; *(de personas)* introduction.
presentador,-a *nm,f* Rad TV presenter, host, hostess.
presentar I *vtr* 1 to present; *(mostrar)* to show, display; *(ofrecer)* to offer. 2 *(una persona a otra)* to introduce; **le presento al doctor Ruiz**, may I introduce you to Dr Ruiz. II **presentarse** *vr* 1 *(comparecer)* to present oneself; *(inesperadamente)* to turn *o* come up. 2 *(ocasión, oportunidad)* to present itself, arise. 3 *(candidato)* to stand; **p. a unas elecciones**, to stand for election, *US* run for office; **p. a un examen**, to sit an examination. 4 *(darse a conocer)* to introduce oneself (a, to).
presente I *adj* present; **la p. (carta)**, this letter; **hacer p.**, to declare, state; **tener p.**, *(tener en cuenta)* to bear in mind; *(recordar)* to remember. II *nm* present.
presentimiento *nm* presentiment, premonition; **tengo el p. de que ...**, I have the feeling that ....
presentir [5] *vtr* to have a presentiment *o* premonition of; **presiento que lloverá**, I've got the feeling that it's going to rain.
preservación *nf* preservation, protection.
preservar *vtr* to preserve, protect (**de**, from; **contra**, against).
preservativo,-a *nm* sheath, condom.
presidencia *nf* 1 *Pol* presidency; *(de una reunión) (hombre)* chairmanship; *(mujer)* chairwomanship.
presidencial *adj* presidential.
presidente,-a *nm,f* 1 *Pol* president; **p. del gobierno**, Prime Minister, Premier. 2 *(de una reunión)* chairperson.
presidiario,-a *nm,f* prisoner, convict.
presidio *nm* prison, penitentiary.
presidir *vtr* 1 *Pol* to rule, head. 2 *(reunión)* to chair, preside over.
presión *nf* pressure; **a** *o* **bajo p.**, under

pressure; **grupo de p.**, pressure group, lobby; **p. arterial** *o* **sanguínea**, blood pressure; **p. atmosférica**, atmospheric pressure.
presionar *vtr* to press; *fig* to pressurize, put pressure on.
preso,-a I *adj* imprisoned. II *nm,f* prisoner.
prestación *nf* 1 service. 2 **prestaciones**, *(de coche etc)* performance.
prestado,-a *adj* **dejar p.**, to lend; **pedir p.**, to borrow; **vivir de p.**, to scrounge.
prestamista *nmf* moneylender.
préstamo *nm* loan.
prestar I *vtr* 1 to lend, loan; **¿me prestas tu pluma?**, can I borrow your pen? 2 *(atención)* to pay; *(ayuda)* to give; *(servicio)* to do. II **prestarse** *vr* 1 *(ofrecerse)* to offer oneself (a, to). 2 **p. a**, *(dar motivo)* to cause; **se presta a (crear) malentendidos**, it makes for misunderstandings.
presteza *nf* promptness; **con p.**, promptly.
prestidigitador,-a *nm,f* conjuror, magician.
prestigiar |12| *vtr* to give prestige to.
prestigio *nm* prestige.
prestigioso,-a *adj* prestigious.
presto,-a *adj* *fml* 1 *(dispuesto)* ready, prepared. 2 *(rápido)* swift, prompt.
presumible *adj* probable, likely.
presumido,-a I *adj* vain, conceited. II *nm,f* vain person.
presumir I *vtr (suponer)* to presume, suppose. II *vi* 1 *(ser vanidoso)* to show off. 2 **presume de guapo**, he thinks he's good-looking.
presunción *nf* 1 *(suposición)* presumption, supposition. 2 *(vanidad)* vanity, conceit.
presunto,-a *adj* supposed; *Jur* alleged.
presuntuoso,-a *adj* 1 *(vanidoso)* vain, conceited. 2 *(pretencioso)* pretentious, showy.
presuponer |19| *(pp* presupuesto*)* *vtr* to presuppose.
presupuestar *vtr* to budget for; *(importe)* to estimate for.
presupuestario,-a *adj* budgetary.
presupuesto,-a *nm* 1 *Fin* budget; *(cálculo)* estimate. 2 *(supuesto)* supposition, assumption.
presuroso,-a *adj* *(rápido)* quick; *(con prisa)* in a hurry.
pretencioso,-a *adj* pretentious.
pretender *vtr* 1 *(intentar)* to try; **¿qué pretendes insinuar?**, what are you getting at? 2 *(afirmar)* to claim. 3 *(aspirar a)* to try for. 4 *(cortejar)* to court, woo.
pretendiente,-a *nm,f* 1 *(al trono)* pretender. 2 *(a un cargo)* applicant, candidate. 3 *(amante)* suitor.
pretensión *nf* 1 *(aspiración)* aim, aspiration. 2 *(presunción)* pretentiousness.
pretérito,-a I *adj* past, former. II *nm Ling*

preterite, simple past tense.
pretextar *vtr* to plead, allege.
pretexto *nm* pretext, excuse.
pretil *nm* parapet.
prevalecer [33] *vi* to prevail.
prevaler [26] *vi* → **prevalecer**.
prevención *nf* 1 (*precaución*) prevention; **en p. de**, as a prevention against. 2 (*medida*) precaution.
prevenir [27] *vtr* 1 (*preparar*) to prepare, get ready. 2 (*prever*) to prevent, forestall; (*evitar*) to avoid; **para p. la gripe**, to prevent flu; *prov* **más vale p. que curar**, prevention is better than cure. 3 (*advertir*) to warn.
preventivo,-a *adj* preventive; (*medidas*) precautionary; *Jur* **detención** *o* **prisión preventiva**, remand in custody.
prever [28] (*pp previsto*) *vtr* 1 (*prevenir*) to foresee, forecast. 2 (*preparar de antemano*) to cater for.
previo,-a *adj* previous, prior; **p. pago de su importe**, only on payment; **sin p. aviso**, without prior notice.
previsible *adj* predictable.
previsión *nf* 1 (*predicción*) forecast; **p. del tiempo**, weather forecast. 2 (*precaución*) precaution; **en p. de**, as a precaution against.
previsor,-a *adj* careful, far-sighted.
previsto,-a *adj* foreseen, forecast; **según lo p.**, as expected.
prima *nf* 1 (*gratificación*) bonus; **p. de seguro**, insurance premium. 2 (*persona*) → **primo,-a**.
primacía *nf* primacy.
primar I *vi* to have priority, prevail. II *vtr* to give a bonus to.
primario,-a *adj* primary.
primavera *nf* spring.
primer *adj* (*delante de nm*) → **primero,-a**.
primera *nf* 1 (*en tren*) first class. 2 *Aut* (*marcha*) first gear. 3 **a la p.**, at the first attempt; *fam* **de p.**, great, first class.
primero,-a I *adj* first; **a primera hora de la mañana**, first thing in the morning; **primera página/plana**, front page; **de primera necesidad**, basic. II *nm,f* first; **a primero(s) de mes**, at the beginning of the month. III *adv* 1 first. 2 (*más bien*) rather, sooner; → **primera**.
primicia *nf* novelty; **p. informativa**, scoop; **p. mundial**, world premiere.
primitivo,-a *adj* 1 primitive. 2 (*tosco*) coarse, rough.
primo,-a I *nm,f* 1 cousin; **p. hermano**, first cousin. 2 *fam* (*tonto*) fool, drip, dunce. II *adj* 1 **materia prima**, raw material. 2 (*número*) prime.
primogénito,-a *adj & nm,f* first-born.
primor *nm* 1 (*delicadeza*) delicacy. 2 (*belleza*) beauty.
primordial *adj* essential, fundamental.
primoroso,-a *adj* delicate, exquisite.

princesa *nf* princess.
principado *nm* principality.
principal *adj* main, principal; **lo p. es que ...**, the main thing is that ...; **puerta p.**, front door.
príncipe *nm* prince.
principiante I *adj* novice. II *nmf* beginner, novice.
principio *nm* 1 beginning, start; **a principio(s) de**, at the beginning of; **al p., en un p.**, at first, in the beginning. 2 (*fundamento*) principle; **en p.**, in principle. 3 **principios**, rudiments, basics.
pringar [7] I *vtr* (*ensuciar*) to make greasy *o* dirty. II *vi arg* (*trabajar*) to work hard. III **pringarse** *vr* 1 (*ensuciarse*) to get greasy *o* dirty. 2 *fam* (*meterse de lleno*) to get involved.
pringoso,-a *adj* (*grasiento*) greasy; (*sucio*) dirty.
pringue *nm* (*grasa*) grease.
prior,-a *nm,f* (*hombre*) prior; (*mujer*) prioress.
priori (a) *adv* a priori.
prioridad *nf* priority.
prioritario,-a *adj* priority.
prisa *nf* 1 (*rapidez*) hurry; **date p.**, hurry up; **tener p.**, to be in a hurry; **de/a p.**, in a hurry. 2 **correr p.**, to be urgent; **me corre mucha p.**, I need it right away.
prisión *nf* prison, jail.
prisionero,-a *nm,f* prisoner.
prisma *nm* prism.
prismáticos *nmpl* binoculars, field glasses.
priva *nf arg* booze.
privación *nf* deprivation.
privado,-a *adj* private.
privar I *vtr* (*despojar*) to deprive (**de**, of). II *vi* 1 *arg* (*gustar*) to like; (*estar de moda*) to be fashionable *o* popular. 2 *fam* (*beber*) to booze. III **privarse** *vr* (*abstenerse*) to deprive oneself (**de**, of), go without.
privativo,-a *adj* exclusive (**de**, of).
privilegiado,-a I *adj* privileged. II *nm,f* privileged person.
privilegio *nm* privilege.
pro I *nm* advantage; **los pros y los contras**, the pros and cons; **en p. de**, in favour of. II *prep* in favour *o US* favor of; **campaña p. desarme**, campaign for disarmament, disarmament campaign.
pro- *pref* pro-.
proa *nf* prow, bows *pl*.
probabilidad *nf* probability, likelihood; **tiene pocas probabilidades**, he stands little chance.
probable *adj* probable, likely; **es p. que llueva**, it'll probably rain.
probador *nm* fitting room.
probar [2] I *vtr* 1 (*comida, bebida*) to try. 2 (*comprobar*) to test, check. 3 (*intentar*) to try. 4 (*demostrar*) to prove, show. II *vi* to try; **p. a**, to attempt *o* try to. III **pro-**

barse *vr (ropa)* to try on.
probeta *nf* test tube; **niño p.,** test-tube baby.
problema *nm* problem.
problemático,-a *adj* problematic.
procedencia *nf* origin, source.
procedente *adj* 1 *(originario)* coming (**de,** from). 2 *(adecuado)* appropriate; *Jur* proper.
proceder I *vi* 1 **p. de,** *(provenir)* to come from. 2 *(actuar)* to act. 3 *(ser oportuno)* to be advisable *o* appropriate; *Jur* **la protesta no procede,** objection overruled. 4 **p. a,** *(continuar)* to go on to. II *nm (comportamiento)* behaviour, *US* behavior.
procedimiento *nm* 1 *(método)* procedure. 2 *Jur (trámites)* proceedings *pl.*
procesado,-a I *nm,f* accused. II *nm Inform* processing.
procesador *nm* processor; **p. de textos,** word processor.
procesamiento *nm* 1 *Jur* prosecution. 2 *Inform* **p. de datos/textos,** data/word processing.
procesar *vtr* 1 *Jur* to prosecute. 2 *(elaborar, transformar)* to process; *Inform* to process.
procesión *nf* procession.
proceso *nm* 1 process; *Inform* **p. de datos,** data processing. 2 *Jur* trial.
proclamación *nf* proclamation.
proclamar *vtr* to proclaim.
proclive *adj* prone, inclined.
procreación *nf* procreation.
procrear *vtr* to procreate.
procurador,-a *nm,f Jur* attorney.
procurar *vtr* 1 *(intentar)* to try, attempt; **procura que no te vean,** make sure they don't see you. 2 *(proporcionar)* (to manage) to get.
prodigar [7] *fml* I *vtr (dar generosamente)* to lavish. II **prodigarse** *vr* **p. en,** to be lavish in.
prodigio *nm* prodigy, miracle; **hacer prodigios,** to work wonders; **niño p.,** child prodigy.
prodigioso,-a *adj (sobrenatural)* prodigious; *(maravilloso)* wonderful, marvellous, *US* marvelous.
pródigo,-a *adj* generous, lavish; **ella es pródiga en regalos,** she's very generous with presents.
producción *nf (acción)* production; *(producto)* product; *Cin* production; **p. en cadena/serie,** assembly-line/mass production.
producir [10] I *vtr* 1 to produce; *(fruto, cosecha)* to yield, bear; *(ganancias)* to yield. 2 *fig (originar)* to cause, bring about. II **producirse** *vr* to take place, happen.
productividad *nf* productivity.
productivo,-a *adj* productive; *(beneficioso)* profitable.

producto *nm* product; *Agr (producción)* produce.
productor,-a I *adj* producing. II *nm,f* producer.
proeza *nf* heroic deed, exploit.
profanación *nf* desecration, profanation.
profanar *vtr* to desecrate, profane.
profano,-a I *adj* profane, secular. II *nm,f (hombre)* layman; *(mujer)* laywoman.
profecía *nf* prophecy.
proferir [5] *vtr* to utter; **p. insultos,** to hurl insults.
profesar *vtr* to profess.
profesión *nf* profession; **de p.,** by profession.
profesional *adj & nmf* professional.
profeso *adv* **ex p.,** intentionally.
profesor,-a *nm,f* teacher; *Univ* lecturer.
profesorado *nm (profesión)* teaching; *(grupo de profesores)* staff.
profeta *nm* prophet.
profetizar [4] *vtr* to prophesy, foretell.
profiláctico,-a I *adj* prophylactic. II *nm* condom, *US* prophylactic.
prófugo,-a I *adj & nm,f* fugitive. II *nm Mil* deserter.
profundidad *nf* depth; **un metro de p.,** one metre deep *o* in depth; *fig (de ideas etc)* profundity, depth.
profundizar [4] *vtr & vi (cavar)* to deepen; *fig (examinar)* to study in depth.
profundo,-a *adj* deep; *fig (idea, sentimiento)* profound.
profusión *nf* profusion.
progenitor,-a *nm,f (antepasado)* ancestor, progenitor; **progenitores,** *(padres)* parents.
programa *nm* programme, *US* program; *Inform* program; *Educ* syllabus.
programación *nf Rad TV* programme planning.
programador,-a *nm,f Inform* programmer.
programar *vtr* to programme, *US* program; *Inform* to program.
progre *adj & nmf fam* trendy, lefty.
progresar *vi* to progress, make progress.
progresista *adj & nmf* progressive.
progresivo,-a *adj* progressive.
progreso *nm* progress; **hace grandes progresos,** he's making great progress.
prohibición *nf* prohibition, ban.
prohibido,-a *adj* forbidden, prohibited; **'prohibida la entrada',** 'no admittance'; **p. aparcar/fumar,** no parking/smoking.
prohibir [21] *vtr* to forbid, prohibit; **'se prohíbe pasar',** 'no admittance *o* entry'.
prohibitivo,-a, prohibitorio,-a *adj* prohibitive.
prójimo,-a *nm,f* one's fellow man, one's neighbour *o US* neighbor.
proletariado *nm* proletariat.
proletario,-a *adj & nm,f* proletarian.
proliferar *vi* to proliferate.

prolífico,-a *adj* prolific.
prolijo,-a *adj* verbose, long-winded.
prólogo *nm* prologue, *US* prolog.
prolongación *nf* prolonging, extension, prolongation.
prolongado,-a *adj* long.
prolongar [7] I *vtr (alargar)* to prolong, extend. II **prolongarse** *vr (continuar)* to carry on.
promedio *nm* average; **como p.,** on average.
promesa *nf* promise; *fig* **la joven p. de la música,** the promising young musician.
prometedor,-a *adj* promising.
prometer I *vtr* to promise; **te lo prometo,** I promise. II *vi* to be promising. III **prometerse** *vr (pareja)* to get engaged.
prometido,-a I *adj* promised. II *nm,f (hombre)* fiancé; *(mujer)* fiancée.
prominente *adj (elevado)* protruding, projecting; *(importante)* prominent.
prosmicuo,-a *adj* promiscuous.
promoción *nf* promotion; *Educ* **p. universitaria,** class *o* year.
promocionar *vtr (cosas)* to promote; *(personas)* to give promotion to.
promotor,-a I *adj* promoting. II *nm,f* promoter.
promover [4] *vtr* 1 *(cosas, personas)* to promote; *(juicio, querella)* to initiate. 2 *(causar)* to cause, give rise to.
promulgar [7] *vtr* to promulgate.
pronombre *nm* pronoun.
pronosticar [1] *vtr* to predict, forecast; *Med* to make a prognosis of.
pronóstico *nm (del tiempo)* forecast; *Med* prognosis.
pronto,-a I *adj* quick, prompt; *fml (dispuesto)* prepared. II *nm (impulso)* sudden impulse. III *adv* 1 *(deprisa)* quickly, rapidly; **al p.,** at first; **de p.,** suddenly; **por de** *o* **lo p.,** *(para empezar)* to start with. 2 *(temprano)* soon, early; **hasta p.,** see you soon!
pronunciación *nf* pronunciation.
pronunciamiento *nm* 1 *Mil* uprising, insurrection. 2 *Jur* pronouncement.
pronunciar [12] I *vtr* to pronounce; *(discurso)* to deliver. II **pronunciarse** *vr* 1 *(opinar)* to declare oneself. 2 *(sublevarse)* to rise up.
propagación *nf* propagation, spreading.
propagador,-a *nm,f* propagator.
propaganda *nf (política)* propaganda; *(comercial)* advertising, publicity.
propagar [7] I *vtr* to propagate, spread. II **propagarse** *vr* to spread.
propano *nm* propane.
propasarse *vr* to go too far.
propensión *nf* tendency, inclination.
propenso,-a *adj* 1 *(inclinado)* prone, inclined. 2 *Med* susceptible.
propiciar [12] *vtr* 1 *(causar)* to cause. 2 *Am (patrocinar)* to sponsor.

propicio,-a *adj* propitious, suitable; **ser p. a,** to be inclined to.
propiedad *nf* 1 *(posesión)* ownership; *(cosa poseída)* property. 2 *(cualidad)* property, quality; *fig* **con p.,** properly, appropriately.
propietario,-a *nm,f* owner.
propina *nf* tip; **dar p. (a algn),** to tip (sb).
propinar *vtr* to give.
propio,-a *adj* 1 *(de uno)* own; **en su propia casa,** in his own house. 2 *(correcto)* suitable, appropriate; **juegos propios para su edad,** games suitable for their age. 3 *(característico)* typical, peculiar. 4 *(mismo) (hombre)* himself; *(mujer)* herself; *(animal, cosa)* itself; **el p. autor,** the author himself. 5 **propios,-as,** themselves; **los propios inquilinos,** the tenants themselves. 6 *Ling* proper.
◆**propiamente** *adv* **p. dicho,** strictly speaking.
proponer [19] *(pp* **propuesto)** I *vtr* to propose, suggest. II **proponerse** *vr* to intend.
proporción *nf* 1 proportion; **en p. con,** in proportion to. 2 **proporciones,** *(tamaño)* size *sing.*
proporcionado,-a *adj (mesurado)* proportionate, in proportion.
proporcional *adj* proportional.
proporcionar *vtr (dar)* to give; to supply *o* provide.
proposición *nf* 1 *(propuesta)* proposal. 2 *(oración)* clause.
propósito *nm* 1 *(intención)* intention. 2 **a p.,** *(por cierto)* by the way; *(adrede)* on purpose, intentionally; **a p. de viajes ...,** speaking of travelling ....
propuesta *nf* suggestion, proposal.
propuesto,-a *pp* → **proponer.**
propugnar *vtr* to advocate.
propulsar *vtr (vehículo)* to drive; *fig (idea)* to promote.
propulsión *nf* propulsion.
propulsor,-a *nm,f, fig (persona)* promoter.
propuse *pt indef* → **proponer.**
prórroga *nf* 1 *(prolongación)* extension; *Dep* extra time, *US* overtime. 2 *(aplazamiento)* postponement; *Mil* deferment.
prorrogar [7] *vtr* 1 *(prolongar)* to extend. 2 *(aplazar)* to postpone; *Mil* to defer.
prorrumpir *vi* to burst **(en,** into).
prosa *nf* prose.
proscrito,-a I *adj (persona)* exiled, banished; *(cosa)* banned. II *nm,f* exile, outlaw.
proseguir [6] *vtr & vi* to carry on, continue.
prospección *nf* 1 *Min* prospect. 2 *Com* survey.
prospecto *nm* leaflet, prospectus.
prosperar *vi (negocio, país)* to prosper, thrive; *(propuesta)* to be accepted.

prosperidad *nf* prosperity.

próspero,-a *adj* prosperous, thriving; **p. año nuevo,** Happy New Year.

prostíbulo *nm* brothel.

prostitución *nf* prostitution.

prostituir [37] **I** *vtr* to prostitute. **II prostituirse** *vr* to prostitute oneself.

prostituta *nf* prostitute.

protagonista *nmf* 1 main character, leading role; **¿quién es el p.?,** who plays the lead? 2 *fig (centro)* centre *o US* center of attraction.

protagonizar [4] *vtr* to play the lead in, star in.

protección *nf* protection.

proteccionismo *nm* protectionism.

protector,-a I *adj* protecting, protective. **II** *nm,f* protector.

proteger [5] *vtr* to protect, defend.

protegido,-a *nm,f (hombre)* protégé; *(mujer)* protégée.

proteína *nf* protein.

prótesis *nf inv* prosthesis.

protesta *nf* protest; *Jur* objection.

protestante *adj & nmf Rel* Protestant.

protestar *vi* 1 to protest; *Jur* to object. 2 *fam (quejarse)* to complain.

protestón,-ona *nm,f* moaner, grumbler.

protocolo *nm* protocol.

protón *nm* proton.

prototipo *nm* prototype.

protuberancia *nf* protuberance.

protuberante *adj* protuberant, bulging.

prov. *abr de* **provincia,** province, prov.

provecho *nm* profit, benefit; **¡buen p.!,** enjoy your meal!; **sacar p. de algo,** to benefit from sth.

provechoso,-a *adj* beneficial.

proveedor,-a *nm,f* supplier, purveyor.

proveer [36] *(pp* **provisto)** *vtr* to supply, provide.

proveniente *adj (procedente)* coming; *(resultante)* arising, resulting.

provenir [27] *vi* **p. de,** to come from.

proverbio *nm* proverb.

providencia *nf* providence.

provincia *nf* province.

provincial *adj* provincial.

provinciano,-a *adj & nm,f pey* provincial.

provisión *nf* provision.

provisional *adj* provisional.

provisto,-a *adj* **p. de,** equipped with.

provocación *nf* provocation.

provocado,-a *adj* provoked, caused; **incendio p.,** arson.

provocador,-a I *nm,f* instigator, agent provocateur. **II** *adj* provocative.

provocar [1] *vtr* 1 *(causar)* to cause; **p. un incendio,** to start a fire. 2 *(instigar)* to provoke. 3 *Am* **si no le provoca,** if he doesn't feel like it.

provocativo,-a *adj* provocative.

proxeneta *nmf* procurer, pimp.

proximidad *nf* proximity, closeness; **en las proximidades de,** close to, in the vicinity of.

próximo,-a *adj* 1 *(cercano)* near, close. 2 *(siguiente)* next. ◆**próximamente** *adv (pronto)* soon; *Cin Teat* 'coming soon'.

proyección *nf* 1 projection. 2 *Cin* showing.

proyectar *vtr* 1 *(luz)* to project. 2 *(planear)* to plan. 3 *Cin* to show.

proyectil *nm* projectile.

proyecto *nm (plan)* project, plan; **tener algo en p.,** to be planning sth; **p. de ley,** bill.

proyector *nm Cin* projector.

prudencia *nf* prudence, discretion; *(moderación)* care.

prudente *adj* prudent, sensible; *(conductor)* careful; **a una hora p.,** at a reasonable time.

prueba *nf* 1 proof; **en p. de,** as a sign of. 2 *(examen etc)* test; **a p.,** on trial; **a p. de agua/balas,** waterproof/bullet-proof; **haz la p.,** try it. 3 *Dep* event.

pseudo *adj* pseud, pseudo.

psicoanálisis *nm inv* psychoanalysis.

psicodélico,-a *adj* psychedelic.

psicología *nf* psychology.

psicológico,-a *adj* psychological.

psicólogo,-a *nm,f* psychologist.

psicópata *nmf* psychopath.

psicosis *nf inv* psychosis.

psicotécnico,-a *adj* psychometric.

psicoterapia *nf* psychotherapy.

psique *nf* psyche.

psiquiatra *nmf* psychiatrist.

psiquiatría *nf* psychiatry.

psiquiátrico,-a I *adj* psychiatric; **hospital p.,** psychiatric hospital. **II** *nm* psychiatric hospital.

psíquico,-a *adj* psychic.

PSOE *nm Pol abr de* **Partido Socialista Obrero Español,** Socialist Workers' Party.

pta(s). *abr de* **peseta(s),** peseta(s).

pts *abr de* **pesetas.**

púa *nf* 1 *(de planta)* thorn; *(de animal)* quill, spine; *(de peine)* tooth; **alambre de púas,** barbed wire. 2 *Mús* plectrum.

pub *nm (pl* **pubs, pubes)** pub.

pubertad *nf* puberty.

publicación *nf* publication.

publicar [1] *vtr* 1 *(libro etc)* to publish. 2 *(secreto)* to publicize.

publicidad *nf* 1 *Com* advertising. 2 *(conocimiento público)* publicity.

publicitario,-a *adj* advertising.

público,-a I *adj* public. **II** *nm* public; *Teat* audience; *Dep* spectators *pl.*

pucherazo *nm* rigging of an election.

puchero *nm* 1 *(olla)* cooking pot; *(cocido)* stew. 2 **hacer pucheros,** to pout.

pucho *nm Am* dog-end.

pude *pt indef* → **poder.**

pudendo,-a *adj* **partes pudendas,** private

parts.

púdico,-a *adj* modest.

pudiente *adj* rich, wealthy.

pudor *nm* modesty.

pudoroso,-a *adj* modest.

pudrir *vtr* defect, **pudrirse** *vr* to rot, decay.

pueblerino,-a *adj pey* (*provinciano*) countrified, provincial.

pueblo *nm* 1 village; (small) town. 2 (*gente*) people; **el p. español,** the Spanish people.

puente *nm* 1 bridge; *Av* **p. aéreo,** (*civil*) air shuttle service; *Mil* airlift; **p. colgante,** suspension bridge; **p. levadizo,** drawbridge. 2 (*entre dos fiestas*) long weekend.

puerco,-a I *adj* filthy. **II** *nm,f* pig; **p. espín,** porcupine.

puericultura *nf* paediatrics *sing*, *US* pediatrics *sing*.

pueril *adj* childish, puerile.

puerro *nm* leek.

puerta *nf* door; (*verja, en aeropuerto*) gate; *Dep* goal; **p. corredera/giratoria,** sliding/revolving door; *fig* **a las puertas, en puertas,** imminent; *fig* **a p. cerrada,** behind closed doors.

puerto *nm* 1 (*de mar*) port, harbour, *US* harbor; **p. deportivo,** marina. 2 (*de montaña*) (mountain) pass.

Puerto Rico *n* Puerto Rico.

puertorriqueño,-a *adj & nm,f* Puerto Rican.

pues *conj* 1 (*puesto que*) as, since. 2 (*por lo tanto*) therefore. 3 (*entonces*) so. 4 (*para reforzar*) ¡**p. claro que sí!,** but of course!; **p. como iba diciendo,** well, as I was saying; ¡**p. mejor!,** so much the better!; ¡**p. no!,** certainly not! 5 (*como pregunta*) ¿**p.?,** why?

puesta *nf* 1 **p. de sol,** sunset. 2 *fig* **p. a punto,** tuning, adjusting; *fig* **p. al día,** updating; *Teat* **p. en escena,** staging; **p. en marcha,** starting-up, start-up; → **puesto,-a.**

puestero,-a *nm,f Am* stallholder.

puesto,-a I *conj* **p. que,** since, as. **II** *nm* 1 (*lugar*) place; (*asiento*) seat. 2 (*empleo*) position, post, job; **p. de trabajo,** job, post. 3 (*tienda*) stall. 4 *Mil* post. **III** *adj* 1 (*colocado*) set, put. 2 **llevar p.,** (*ropa*) to have on; *fam* **ir muy p.,** to be all dressed up. 3 *fam* (*borracho*) drunk. 4 *fam* **estar p. en una materia,** to be well up in a subject.

púgil *nm* boxer.

pugilato *nm* boxing.

pugna *nf* battle, fight.

pugnar *vi* to fight, struggle (**por,** for).

puja *nf* (*acción*) bidding; (*cantidad*) bid.

pujante *adj* thriving, prosperous.

pujanza *nf* strength, vigour, *US* vigor.

pujar *vtr* 1 (*pugnar*) to struggle. 2 (*en una subasta*) to bid higher.

pulcro,-a *adj* (extremely) neat.

pulga *nf* flea; *fam* **tener malas pulgas,** to be nasty, have a nasty streak.

pulgada *nf* inch.

pulgar *nm* thumb.

pulimentar *vtr* to polish.

pulir *vtr* 1 (*metal, madera*) to polish. 2 (*mejorar*) to polish up.

pulmón *nm* lung.

pulmonía *nf* pneumonia.

pulpa *nf* pulp.

pulpería *nf Am* store.

púlpito *nm* pulpit.

pulpo *nm* octopus.

pulsación *nf* pulsation; (*en mecanografía*) stroke, tap; **pulsaciones por minuto,** ≈ keystrokes per minute.

pulsar *vtr* (*timbre, botón*) to press; (*tecla*) to hit, strike.

pulsera *nf* (*aro*) bracelet; (*de reloj*) watchstrap; **reloj de p.,** wristwatch.

pulso *nm* 1 pulse; *fig* **tomar el p. a la opinión pública,** to sound out opinion. 2 (*mano firme*) steady hand; **a p.,** freehand; **ganarse algo a p.,** to deserve sth. 3 *fig* trial of strength; **echarse un p.,** to armwrestle.

pulverizador,-a *nm* spray, atomizer.

pulverizar [4] *vtr* (*sólidos*) to pulverize; (*líquidos*) to spray; (*un récord*) to smash.

pulla *nf* dig.

puma *nm* puma.

puna *nf Am* 1 high moor. 2 (*mal*) mountain *o* altitude sickness.

pundonor *nm* self-respect, self-esteem.

punta *nf* 1 (*extremo*) tip; (*extremo afilado*) point; (*de cabello*) end; **sacar p. a un lápiz,** to sharpen a pencil; **tecnología p.,** state-of-the-art technology; **me pone los nervios de p.,** he makes me very nervous. 2 (*período*) peak; **hora p.,** rush hour. 3 (*pequeña cantidad*) bit; **una p. de sal,** a pinch of salt. 4 (*clavo*) nail.

puntal *nm* prop; (*travesaño*) beam; *fig* (*soporte*) pillar, support.

puntapié *nm* kick.

puntear *vtr* 1 (*dibujar*) to dot. 2 *Mús* (*guitarra*) to pluck.

punteo *nm* plucking.

puntería *nf* aim; **tener buena/mala p.,** to be a good/bad shot.

puntero,-a *adj* leading.

puntiagudo,-a *adj* pointed, sharp.

puntilla *nf* 1 (*encaje*) lace. 2 **dar la p.,** *Taur* to finish (the bull) off; *fig* (*liquidar*) to finish off. 3 **de puntillas,** on tiptoe.

puntilloso,-a *adj* touchy.

punto *nm* 1 point; **a p.,** ready; *Culin* **en su p.,** just right; **a p. de,** on the point of; **hasta cierto p.,** to a certain *o* some extent; **p. muerto,** *Aut* neutral; *fig* (*impasse*) deadlock; **p. de vista,** point of view. 2 (*marca*) dot; **línea de puntos,** dotted line. 3 (*lugar*) place, point. 4 **p. y seguido,**

full stop; **p. y coma,** semicolon; **dos puntos,** colon; **p. y aparte,** full stop, new paragraph. 5 *(tiempo)* **en p.,** sharp, on the dot. 6 *Dep (tanto)* point. 7 *Cost Med* stitch; **hacer p.,** to knit.

puntuable *adj Dep* **una prueba p. para,** a race counting towards.

puntuación *nf* 1 *Ling* punctuation. 2 *Dep* score. 3 *Educ* mark.

puntual I *adj* 1 punctual. 2 *(exacto)* accurate, precise. 3 *(caso)* specific. II *adv* punctually.

puntualidad *nf* punctuality.

puntualizar |4| *vtr* to make it clear.

puntuar |30| I *vtr* 1 *(al escribir)* to punctuate. 2 *Educ (calificar)* to mark. II *vi Dep* 1 *(marcar)* to score. 2 *(ser puntuable)* to count.

punzada *nf (de dolor)* sudden sharp pain.

punzante *adj (objeto)* sharp; *(dolor)* acute, piercing.

punzar |4| *vtr Téc* to punch.

puñado *nm* handful; *fam* **a puñados,** by the score, galore.

puñal *nm* dagger.

puñalada *nf* stab; *fig* **p. trapera,** stab in the back.

puñeta *nf fam* **hacer la p. a algn,** to pester sb, annoy sb; **¡puñetas!,** damn!; **¡vete a hacer puñetas!,** go to hell!

puñetazo *nm* punch.

puño *nm* 1 fist. 2 *(de camisa etc)* cuff. 3 *(de herramienta)* handle.

pupa *nf* 1 *(herida)* cold sore. 2 *fam (daño)* pain.

pupila *nf* pupil.

pupilo,-a *nm,f* pupil.

pupitre *nm* desk.

purasangre *adj & nm* thoroughbred.

puré *nm* purée; **p. de patata,** mashed potatoes; **p. de verduras,** thick vegetable soup.

pureta *nmf* old fogey.

pureza *nf* 1 purity. 2 *(castidad)* chastity.

purga *nf Med* purgative; *fig* purge.

purgante *adj & nm* purgative.

purgar |7| *vtr Med & fig* to purge.

purgatorio *nm* purgatory.

purificación *nf* purification.

purificar |1| *vtr* to purify.

purista *nmf* purist.

puritano,-a I *adj* puritanical. II *nm,f* puritan, Puritan.

puro,-a I *adj* 1 *(sin mezclas)* pure; **aire p.,** fresh air; **la pura verdad,** the plain truth; *Pol* **p. y duro,** hardline. 2 *(mero)* sheer, mere; **por pura curiosidad,** out of sheer curiosity. 3 *(casto)* chaste, pure. II *nm (cigarro)* cigar.

púrpura *adj inv* purple.

purpúreo,-a *adj* purple.

pus *nm* pus.

puse *pt indef* → **poner.**

pusilánime *adj* faint-hearted.

pústula *nf* sore, pustule.

puta *nf ofens* whore; **de p. madre,** great, terrific; **de p. pena,** bloody awful; **no tengo ni p. idea,** I haven't (got) a bloody clue; **pasarlas putas,** to go through hell, have a rotten time.

putada *nf vulg* dirty trick.

putear *vtr* to fuck o piss around.

puticlub *nm fam* brothel.

puto,-a I *adj ofens* bloody. II *nm* male prostitute, stud.

putrefacto,-a, pútrido,-a *adj* putrefied, rotten.

puzzle *nm* jigsaw puzzle.

P.V.P. *nm abr de* **precio de venta al público,** recommended retail price, RRP.

Pza., Plza. *abr de* **plaza,** square, Sq.

Q

Q, q |ku| *nf (la letra)* Q, q.

que¹ *pron rel* 1 *(sujeto) (persona)* who; *(cosa)* that, which; **el hombre q. vino,** the man who came; **la bomba q. estalló,** the bomb that o which went off. 2 *(complemento) (persona) no se traduce* o that o who o *fml* whom; *(cosa) no se traduce* o that, which; **la chica q. conocí,** the girl (that o who o whom) I met; **el coche q. compré,** the car (that o which) I bought. 3 **lo q., which; lo q. más me gusta,** what I like best. 4 *(con infinitivo) no se traduce;* **hay mucho q. hacer,** there's a lot to do.

que² *conj* 1 *no se traduce* o that; **dijo que llamaría,** he said (that) he would call; **quiero q. vengas,** I want you to come. 2 *(consecutivo) no se traduce* o that; *(en comparativas)* than; **habla tan bajo q. no**

se le oye, he speaks so quietly (that) he can't be heard; **más alto q. yo,** taller than me. 3 *(causal) no se traduce* **date deprisa q. no tenemos mucho tiempo,** hurry up, we haven't got much time. 4 *(enfático) no se traduce* **¡q. no!,** no!; **¡q. te calles!,** I said be quiet! 5 *(deseo, mandato)* (+ *subj*) *no se traduce* **¡q. te diviertas!,** enjoy yourself! 6 *(final)* so that; **ven q. te dé un beso,** come and let me give you a kiss. 7 *(disyuntivo)* whether; **me da igual que suba o no,** I couldn't care whether he comes up or not. 8 *(locuciones)* **¿a q. no ...?,** I bet you can't ...!; **q. yo sepa,** as far as I know; **yo q. tú,** if I were you.

qué I *pron interr* 1 what; **¿q. quieres?,** what do you want?; *fam* **¡y q.!,** so what? 2 *(exclamativo)* (+ *adj*) how; **¡q. bonito!,**

how pretty! 3 (+ *n*) what a; ¡q. lástima!,
what a pity! 4 *fam* ¡q. de ...!, what a lot
of ...!. II *adj interr* which; ¿q. libro quieres?, which book do you want?

quebrada *nf Am* stream.

quebradero *nm fig* q. de cabeza, headache.

quebradizo,-a *adj* (*débil*) fragile; (*cabello,
hielo*) brittle.

quebrado *nm Mat* fraction.

quebradura *nf* 1 (*grieta*) crack. 2 *Med*
hernia, rupture.

quebrantamiento *nm* (*de una ley*) violation, infringement.

quebrantar I *vtr* (*promesa, ley*) to break.
II **quebrantarse** *vr* to break down.

quebrar [1] I *vtr* (*romper*) to break. II *vi
Fin* to go bankrupt. III **quebrarse** *vr* to
break; *Med* to rupture oneself.

queda *nf* toque de q., curfew.

quedar I *vi* 1 (*restar*) to be left, remain;
quedan dos, there are two left. 2 (*en un
lugar*) to arrange to meet; **quedamos en
el bar**, I'll meet you in the bar. 3 **me
queda corta**, (*ropa*) it is too short for me;
quedaría muy bien allí, (*objeto*) it would
look very nice there. 4 (*acordar*) to agree
(en, to); ¿en qué quedamos?, so what's
it to be? 5 (*estar situado*) to be; ¿dónde
queda la estación?, where's the station?
6 (*terminar*) to end; ¿en qué quedó la película?, how did the film, end? 7 (*locuciones*) q. en ridículo, to make a fool of
oneself; q. bien/mal, to make a good/bad
impression. II **quedarse** *vr* 1 (*permanecer*)
to stay; **se quedó en casa**, she stayed
home; q. sin dinero/pan, to run out of
money/bread; q. con hambre, to still be
hungry. 2 q. (con), (*retener*) to keep;
quédese (con) el cambio, keep the
change. 3 *fam* q. con algn, to make a
fool of sb.

quedo *adv* softly, quietly.

quehacer *nm* task, chore.

queja *nf* complaint; (*de dolor*) groan,
moan.

quejarse *vr* to complain (de, about).

quejica *fam* I *adj* grumpy. II *nmf* moaner.

quejido *nm* groan, cry.

quemado,-a *adj* 1 burnt, burned; (*del sol*)
sunburnt. 2 *fig* (*agotado*) burnt-out.

quemador *nm* (*de cocina etc*) burner.

quemadura *nf* burn.

quemar I *vtr* to burn; *fig* (*agotar*) to burn
out. II *vi* to be burning hot; **este café
quema**, this coffee's boiling hot. III **quemarse** *vr fig* to burn oneself out.

quemarropa *loc adv* a q., point-blank.

quemazón *nf* smarting.

quepo *indic pres* → **caber**.

querella *nf Jur* lawsuit.

querer [20] I *vtr* 1 (*amar*) to love. 2 (*desear*) to want; ¿cuánto quiere por la
casa?, how much does he want for the

house?; sin q., without meaning to; que-
riendo, on purpose; ¡por lo que más
quieras!, for heaven's sake!; ¿quiere pa-
sarme el pan?, would you pass me the
bread? 3 q. decir, to mean. 4 no quiso
darme permiso, he refused me permission. II **quererse** *vr* to love each other.
III *nm* love, affection.

querido,-a I *adj* dear, beloved; q. amigo,
(*en carta*) dear friend. II *nm,f* (*amante*)
lover; (*mujer*) mistress.

queroseno *nm* kerosene, kerosine.

querré *indic fut* → **querer**.

queso *nm* cheese; q. rallado, grated
cheese; q. de cerdo, brawn, *US* head-
cheese.

quetzal *nm* (*moneda*) standard monetary
unit of Guatemala.

quicio *nm* 1 (*de puerta*) doorpost. 2 *fig*
fuera de q., beside oneself; sacar de q.,
(*a algn*) to infuriate; (*algo*) to take too
far.

quid *nm* crux; has dado en el q., you've
hit the nail on the head.

quiebra *nf Fin* (*bancarrota*) bankruptcy;
(*crack*) crash.

quiebro *nm* (*con el cuerpo*) dodge; *Ftb*
dribbling.

quien *pron rel* 1 (*con prep*) *no se traduce o
fml* whom; **el hombre con q. vino**, the
man she came with; *fml* the man with
whom she came. 2 (*indefinido*) whoever,
anyone who; q. quiera venir que venga,
whoever wants to can come; hay q. dice
lo contrario, some people say the opposite; *fig* q. más q. menos, everybody.

quién *pron interr* 1 (*sujeto*) who?; ¿q. es?,
who is it? 2 (*complemento*) who; *fml*
whom; ¿para q. es?, who is it for?; ¿de
q. es esa bici?, whose bike is that?

quienquiera *pron indef* (*pl* **quienesquiera**)
whoever.

quieto,-a *adj* still; (*mar*) calm; ¡estáte q.!,
keep still!, don't move!

quietud *nf* stillness; (*calma*) calm.

quijada *nf* jawbone.

quilate *nm* carat.

quilo *nm* → **kilo**.

quilla *nf* keel.

quimera *nf fig* fantasy, pipe dream.

química *nf* chemistry.

químico,-a I *adj* chemical. II *nm,f* chemist.

quimioterapia *nf* chemotherapy.

quimono *nm* kimono.

quincalla *nf* metal pots and pans *pl*, tin-
ware.

quince *adj & nm inv* fifteen.

quinceañero,-a *adj & nm,f* fifteen-year-
old.

quincena *nf* fortnight, two weeks.

quincenal *adj* fortnightly.

quiniela *nf* football pools *pl*.

quinientos,-as *adj & nm,f* five

hundred.
quinina *nf* quinine.
quinqué *nm* oil lamp.
quinquenal *adj* quinquennial, five-year.
quinqui *nm fam* delinquent, petty criminal.
quinta *nf* 1 (*casa*) country house. 2 *Mil* conscription, *US* draft.
quintaesencia *nf* quintessence.
quintal *nm* (*medida*) 46 kg; **q. métrico,** ≈ 100 kg.
quinteto *nm* quintet.
quinto,-a I *adj & nm,f* fifth. **II** *nm Mil* conscript, recruit.
quiosco *nm* kiosk; **q. de periódicos,** newspaper stand.
quirófano *nm* operating theatre.
quiromancia *nf* palmistry.
quirúrgico,-a *adj* surgical.
quise *indic fut* → **querer**.
quisque, quisqui *pron fam* **todo** *o* **cada q.,** everyone, everybody.
quisquilloso,-a I *adj* fussy, finicky. **II** *nm,f* fusspot.
quiste *nm* cyst.

quitaesmalte(s) *nm inv* nail varnish *o* polish remover.
quitamanchas *nm inv* stain remover.
quitanieves *nm* (*máquina*) **q.,** snowplough, *US* snowplow.
quitar I *vtr* 1 to remove; (*ropa*) to take off; (*la mesa*) to clear; (*mancha*) to remove; (*dolor*) to relieve; (*hipo*) to stop; (*sed*) quench; (*hambre*) to take away. 2 (*apartar*) to take away, take off; *fig* **q. importancia a algo,** to play sth down; *fig* **q. las ganas a algn,** to put sb off. 3 (*robar*) to steal, take; *fig* (*tiempo*) to take up; (*sitio*) to take. 4 (*descontar*) to take off. 5 *fam* (*apagar*) to turn off. **6 eso no quita para que ...,** that's no reason not to be .... 7 **¡quita!,** go away! **II quitarse** *vr* 1 (*apartarse*) to move away. 2 (*mancha*) to come out; (*dolor*) to go away; **se me han quitado las ganas,** I don't feel like it any more. 3 (*ropa, gafas*) to take off. **4 q. de beber/fumar,** to give up drinking/ smoking. **5 q. a algn de encima,** to get rid of sb.
quizá(s) *adv* perhaps, maybe.

R

R, r ['erre] *nf* (*la letra*) R, r.
rábano *nm* radish; *fam* **me importa un r.,** I couldn't care less.
rabia *nf* 1 *fig* (*ira*) fury, rage; **¡qué r.!,** how annoying!; **me da r.,** it gets up my nose; **me tiene r.,** he's got it in for me. 2 *Med* rabies *sing*.
rabiar [12] *vi* 1 *fig* (*sufrir*) to be in great pain. 2 *fig* (*enfadar*) to rage; **hacer r. a algn,** to make sb see red. 3 *Med* to have rabies.
rabieta *nf fam* tantrum; **coger una r.,** to throw a tantrum.
rabillo *nm* (*del ojo*) corner.
rabino *nm* rabbi.
rabioso,-a *adj* 1 *Med* rabid; **perro r.,** rabid dog. 2 *fig* (*enfadado*) furious. 3 **de rabiosa actualidad,** up-to-the-minute.
rabo *nm* tail; (*de fruta etc*) stalk.
racanear *vi fam* (*ser tacaño*) to be stingy.
rácano,-a *adj fam* 1 (*tacaño*) stingy, mean. 2 *pey* (*novato*) fresher.
racha *nf* (*de viento*) gust, squall; *fam* (*período*) spell, patch; **a rachas,** in fits and starts.
racial *adj* **discriminación r.,** racial discrimination; **disturbios raciales,** race riots.
racimo *nm* bunch, cluster.
raciocinio *nm* reason.
ración *nf* portion.
racional *adj* rational.
racionalizar [4] *vtr* to rationalize.
racionamiento *nm* rationing; **cartilla de r.,** ration book.

racionar *vtr* (*limitar*) to ration; (*repartir*) to ration out.
racismo *nm* racism.
racista *adj & nmf* racist.
radar *nm* (*pl* **radares**) *Téc* radar.
radiación *nf* radiation.
radiactividad *nf* radioactivity.
radiactivo,-a *adj* radioactive.
radiador *nm* radiator.
radiante *adj* radiant (**de,** with).
radiar [12] *vtr* to broadcast, transmit.
radical *adj* radical.
radicalizar [4] *vtr*, **radicalizarse** *vr* (*conflicto*) to intensify; (*postura*) to harden.
radicar [1] *vi* (*estar*) to be (situated) (**en,** in), be rooted (**en,** in).
radio I *nf* radio, wireless; (*aparato*) radio (set). **II** *nm* 1 radius; **r. de acción,** field of action, scope. 2 (*de rueda*) spoke.
radioactividad *nf* radioactivity.
radioactivo,-a *adj* radioactive.
radioaficionado,-a *nm,f* radio ham.
radiocasete *nm* (*pl* **radiocasetes**) radio cassette.
radioescucha *nmf* listener.
radiografía *nf* (*imagen*) X-ray.
radioyente *nmf* listener.
ráfaga *nf* (*de viento*) gust, squall; (*de disparos*) burst.
raído,-a *adj* 1 (*gastado*) worn. 2 *fam* (*desvergonzado*) insolent.
raigambre *nf* roots *pl*.
raíl *nm* rail.

raíz *nf* (*pl* **raíces**) root; **r. cuadrada**, square root; *fig* **a r. de**, as a result of.

raja *nf* (*corte*) cut, slit; (*hendidura*) crack, split.

rajar I *vtr* (*hender*) to crack, split; *arg* (*acuchillar*) to cut up. **II** *vi fam* to backbite. **III rajarse** *vr* 1 (*partirse*) to crack, split. 2 *fam* (*echarse atrás*) to back out. 3 *Am* (*acobardarse*) to chicken out.

rajatabla (a) *loc adv* strictly.

ralea *nf pey* type, sort.

ralentí *nm* neutral; **estar al r.**, to be ticking over.

ralentizar *vtr* to slow down.

rallado,-a *adj* **queso r.**, grated cheese; **pan r.**, breadcrumbs.

rallador *nm* grater.

ralladura *nf* gratings *pl*.

rallar *vtr* to grate.

ralo,-a *adj* sparse, thin.

rama *nf* branch; *fam* **andarse** *o* **irse por las ramas**, to beat about the bush.

ramaje *nm* branches *pl*.

ramalazo *nm fam* (*toque*) touch.

rambla *nf* (*avenida*) boulevard, avenue.

ramera *nf* prostitute, whore.

ramificación *nf* ramification.

ramificarse [1] *vr* to ramify, branch (out).

ramillete *nm* (*de flores*) posy.

ramo *nm* 1 (*de flores*) bunch, bouquet. 2 (*sector*) branch.

rampa *nf* ramp; **r. de lanzamiento**, launch pad.

ramplón,-ona *adj* coarse, vulgar.

rana *nf* frog; *fam* **salir r.**, to be a disappointment.

ranchero,-a *nm,f* (*granjero*) rancher, farmer.

rancho *nm* 1 (*granja*) ranch. 2 *Mil* (*comida*) mess.

rancio,-a *adj* 1 (*comida*) stale. 2 (*antiguo*) ancient.

rango *nm* rank; (*jerarquía elevada*) high social standing.

ranura *nf* slot.

rapar *vtr* (*afeitar*) to shave; (*pelo*) to crop.

rapaz *I adj* predatory; **ave r.**, bird of prey. **II** *nm,f* (*muchacho*) lad; (*muchacha*) lass.

rape *nm* 1 (*pez*) angler fish. 2 *fam* **cortado al r.**, close-cropped.

rapidez *nf* speed, rapidity.

rápido,-a I *adj* quick, fast, rapid. **II** *adv* quickly. **III** *nm* 1 (*tren*) fast train. 2 **rápidos**, (*de un río*) rapids.

rapiña *nf* robbery, theft; **ave de r.**, bird of prey.

raptar *vtr* to kidnap, abduct.

rapto *nm* 1 (*secuestro*) kidnapping, abduction. 2 *fig* (*arrebato*) outburst, fit.

raqueta *nf* 1 (*de tenis*) racket; (*de pingpong*) bat, *US* paddle. 2 (*de nieve*) snowshoe.

raquítico,-a *adj fam* (*escaso*) small,

meagre, *US* meager; (*delgado*) emaciated.

raquitismo *nm* rickets *pl*.

rareza *nf* 1 rarity, rareness. 2 (*extravagancia*) eccentricity.

raro,-a *adj* 1 rare; **rara vez**, seldom. 2 (*extraño*) odd, strange.

ras *nm* level; **a r. de**, (on a) level with; **a r. de tierra**, at ground level.

rasante I *nf Aut* **cambio de r.**, brow of a hill. **II** *adj* (*vuelo*) low.

rasar *vtr* (*nivelar*) to level.

rasca *nf fam* (*frío*) cold.

rascacielos *nm inv* skyscraper.

rascar [1] **I** *vtr* (*con las uñas*) to scratch; (*guitarra*) to strum. **II** *vi* to chafe.

rasero *nm fig* **medir con el mismo r.**, to treat impartially.

rasgado,-a *adj* (*ojos*) slit, almond-shaped.

rasgar [7] *vtr* to tear, rip.

rasgo *nm* (*característica*) characteristic, feature; (*de la cara*) feature; *fig* **a grandes rasgos**, broadly speaking.

rasgón *nm* tear, rip.

rasguñar *vtr* to scratch, scrape.

rasguño *nm* scratch, scrape.

rasilla *nf* (*ladrillo*) tile.

raso,-a I *adj* (*llano*) flat, level; (*vuelo*) low; (*cielo*) clear, cloudless; **soldado r.**, private. **II** *nm* satin.

raspa *nf* (*de pescado*) bone, backbone.

raspador *nm* scraper.

raspadura *nf* (*ralladura*) scraping, scrapings *pl*.

raspar I *vtr* (*limar*) to scrape (off). **II** *vi* (*ropa etc*) to chafe.

rasposo,-a *adj* rough, sharp.

rastra *nf Agr* harrow; **a la r.**, **a rastras**, dragging; *fig* (*de mal grado*) grudgingly.

rastreador *nm* tracker.

rastrear *vtr* (*zona*) to comb.

rastreo *nm* search.

rastrero,-a *adj* creeping; *fig* (*despreciable*) vile, base.

rastrillo *nm* 1 rake. 2 *fam* (*mercadillo*) flea market.

rastro *nm* 1 trace, sign; (*en el suelo*) track, trail. 2 **el R.**, the Madrid flea market.

rastrojo *nm* stubble.

rasurar *vtr*, **rasurarse** *vr* to shave.

rata I *nf* rat. **II** *nm fam* (*tacaño*) mean *o* stingy person.

ratero,-a *nm,f* pickpocket.

raticida *nm* rat poison.

ratificar [1] *vtr* to ratify.

rato *nm* 1 (*momento*) while; time; **a ratos**, at times; **al poco r.**, shortly after; **hay para r.**, it'll take a while; **pasar un buen/mal r.**, to have a good/bad time; **ratos libres**, free time *sing*. 2 *fam* **un r.**, (*mucho*) very, a lot.

ratón *nm* mouse; *Inform* mouse.

ratonera *nf* mousetrap.

raudal *nm* torrent, flood; *fig* **a raudales**, in abundance.

raya *nf* 1 (*línea*) line; (*del pantalón*) crease; (*del pelo*) parting; **camisa a rayas**, striped shirt. 2 *fig* **tener a r.**, to keep at bay; **pasarse de la r.**, to go over the score. 3 (*de droga*) fix, dose.

rayano,-a *adj* bordering (**en**, on).

rayar I *vtr* (*arañar*) to scratch. **II** *vi* **r. en/con**, to border on.

rayo *nm* 1 ray, beam. 2 (*relámpago*) (flash of) lightning; **¡mal r. la parta!**, to hell with her!

rayón *nm* rayon.

rayuela *nf Am* hopscotch.

raza *nf* 1 (*humana*) race. 2 (*de animal*) breed.

razón *nf* 1 (*facultad*) reason; **uso de r.**, power of reasoning. 2 (*motivo*) reason; **r. de más para**, all the more reason to. 3 (*justicia*) rightness, justice; **dar la r. a algn**, to say that sb is right; **tienes r.**, you're right. 4 (*proporción*) ratio, rate; **a r. de**, at the rate of. 5 '**r. aquí**', 'enquire within', 'apply within'.

razonable *adj* reasonable.

razonado,-a *adj* reasoned, well-reasoned.

razonamiento *nm* reasoning.

razonar I *vtr* (*argumentar*) to reason out. **II** *vi* (*discurrir*) to reason.

RDA *nf Hist abr de* **República Democrática Alemana** *o* **de Alemania**, GDR.

re- *pref* re-.

reacción *nf* reaction; **avión de r.**, jet (plane); **r. en cadena**, chain reaction.

reaccionar *vi* to react.

reaccionario,-a *adj & nm,f* reactionary.

reacio,-a *adj* reluctant, unwilling.

reactor *nm* reactor; (*avión*) jet (plane).

readaptación *nf* rehabilitation; **r. profesional**, industrial retraining.

reafirmar *vtr* to reaffirm, reassert.

reagrupar *vtr*, **reagruparse** *vr* to regroup.

reajuste *nm* readjustment; **r. ministerial**, cabinet reshuffle.

real¹ *adj* (*efectivo*, *verdadero*) real; **en la vida r.**, in real life. ◆**realmente** *adv* really; (*en realidad*) actually, in fact.

real² *adj* (*regio*) royal.

realce *nm* (*relieve*) relief; *fig* (*esplendor*) splendour, *US* splendor.

realeza *nf* royalty.

realidad *nf* reality; **en r.**, in fact, actually; **la r. es que ...**, the fact of the matter is that ....

realismo *nm* realism.

realista I *adj* realistic. **II** *nmf* realist.

realizable *adj* feasible.

realización *nf* (*ejecución*) carrying out; *Cin TV* production.

realizador,-a *nm,f Cin TV* producer.

realizar |4| **I** *vtr* 1 (*hacer*) to carry out; (*ambición*) to achieve fulfil, *US* fulfill. 2 *Cin TV* to produce. 3 *Fin* to realize. **II** **realizarse** *vr* (*persona*) to fulfil *o US*

fulfill oneself; (*sueño*) to come true.

realzar |4| *vtr* (*recalcar*) to highlight; *fig* (*belleza*, *importancia*) to enhance, heighten.

reanimación *nf* revival.

reanimar *vtr*, **reanimarse** *vr* to revive.

reanudación *nf* renewal, resumption, reestablishment; **r. de las clases**, return to school.

reanudar I *vtr* to renew, resume; **r. el paso** *o* **la marcha**, to set off again; **r. las clases**, to go back to school. **II** **reanudarse** *vr* to start again, resume.

reaparición *nf* reappearance, recurrence; (*de artista etc*) comeback.

reapertura *nf* reopening.

rearme *nm* rearmament.

reaseguro *nm* reinsurance.

reavivar *vtr* to revive.

rebaja *nf* (*descuento*) reduction, discount; **rebajas**, sales; **precio de r.**, sale price.

rebajar I *vtr* 1 (*precio*) to cut, reduce; (*cantidad*) to take off. 2 (*color*) to tone down, soften; (*intensidad*) to diminish. 3 (*trabajador*) to excuse, exempt (**de**, from). 4 (*humillar*) to humiliate. **II** **rebajarse** *vr* (*humillarse*) to humble oneself.

rebanada *nf* slice.

rebanar *vtr* to slice, cut into slices.

rebañar *vtr* (*plato etc*) to finish off.

rebaño *nm* (*de ovejas*) flock; (*de otros animales*) herd.

rebasar *vtr* 1 (*exceder*) to exceed, go beyond. 2 *Aut* to overtake.

rebatir *vtr* to refute.

rebeca *nf* cardigan.

rebelarse *vr* to rebel, revolt.

rebelde I *nmf* rebel. **II** *adj* rebellious; *fig* **una tos r.**, a persistent cough.

rebeldía *nf* 1 rebelliousness. 2 *Jur* default.

rebelión *nf* rebellion, revolt.

rebenque *nm Am* whip.

reblandecer |33| *vtr* to soften.

rebobinar *vtr* to rewind.

rebosante *adj* overflowing (**de**, with), brimming (**de**, with).

rebosar I *vi* to overflow, brim over; *fig* **r. de**, to be overflowing *o* brimming with. **II** *vtr* (*irradiar*) to radiate.

rebotar *vi* (*pelota*) to bounce, rebound; (*bala*) to ricochet.

rebote *nm* (*de pelota*) bounce, rebound; (*de bala*) ricochet; **de r.**, on the rebound.

rebozar |4| *vtr* to coat in breadcrumbs *o* batter.

rebullir *vi*, **rebullirse** *vr* to stir.

rebuscado,-a *adj* recherché.

rebuznar *vi* to bray.

recabar *vtr* (*información*) to obtain, manage to get.

recado *nm* (*mandado*) errand; (*mensaje*) message; **dejar un r.**, to leave a message.

recaer |39| *vi* 1 *Med* to relapse. 2 (*culpa*,

responsabilidad) to fall (**sobre,** on).

recaída *nf* relapse.

recalcar [1] *vtr* to stress, emphasize.

recalcitrante *adj* recalcitrant.

recalentar [1] *vtr (comida)* to reheat, warm up; *(calentar demasiado)* to overheat.

recámara *nf* **1** *(de rueda)* tube. **2** *Am (habitación)* dressing room.

recambiar [12] *vtr* to change (over).

recambio *nm* **1** *(repuesto)* spare (part); **rueda de r.,** spare wheel. **2** *(de pluma etc)* refill.

recapacitar *vi* to think over.

recargable *adj (pluma)* refillable; *(mechero)* rechargeable.

recargado,-a *adj* overloaded; *fig (estilo)* overelaborate, affected.

recargar [7] *vtr* **1** *Elec* to recharge. **2** *(sobrecargar)* to overload; *(adornar mucho)* to overelaborate. **3** *Fin* to increase.

recargo *nm* extra charge, surcharge.

recatado,-a *adj (prudente)* prudent, cautious; *(modesto)* modest, decent.

recato *nm (cautela)* caution, prudence; *(pudor)* modesty.

recaudación *nf (cobro)* collection; *(cantidad recaudada)* takings *pl*; *Dep* gate.

recaudador,-a *nm,f* tax collector.

recaudar *vtr* to collect.

recaudo *nm* **estar a buen r.,** to be in safekeeping.

recelar *vtr* **r. de,** to distrust.

recelo *nm* suspicion, distrust.

receloso,-a *adj* suspicious, distrustful.

recepción *nf* reception; *(en hotel)* reception (desk).

recepcionista *nmf* receptionist.

receptivo,-a *adj* receptive.

receptor,-a I *nm,f (persona)* recipient. **II** *nm Rad TV* receiver.

recesión *nf* recession.

receta *nf* recipe; *Med* prescription.

recetar *vtr Med* to prescribe.

rechache *nm Dep* rebound.

rechazar [4] *vtr* to reject, turn down; *Mil* to repel, drive back.

rechazo *nm* rejection.

rechiflar *vtr* **1** *(silbar)* to hiss, boo. **2** *(mofarse)* to mock, jeer at.

rechinar *vi (madera)* to creak; *(metal)* to squeak, screech; *(dientes)* to chatter.

rechistar *vi* **sin r.,** that's final.

rechoncho,-a *adj fam* chubby, tubby.

rechupete (de) *loc fam* **me sé el tema de r.,** I know the subject inside out; **la comida estaba de r.,** the food was mouthwateringly good.

recibidor *nm* entrance hall.

recibimiento *nm* reception, welcome.

recibir I *vtr* to receive; *(en casa)* to welcome; *(en la estación etc)* to meet. **II recibirse** *vr Am* **r. de,** to qualify as.

recibo *nm* **1** *(factura)* invoice; bill;

(resguardo) receipt; **r. de la luz,** electricity bill. **2 acusar r. de,** to acknowledge receipt of.

reciclado,-a I *adj* recycled. **II** *nm (reciclaje)* recycling.

reciclaje *nm (de residuos)* recycling; *fig (renovación)* retraining; **curso de r.,** refresher course.

reciclar *vtr (residuos)* to recycle; *fig (profesores etc)* to retrain.

recién *adv* **1** *(recientemente) (antes de pp)* recently, newly; **café r. hecho,** freshlymade coffee; **r. casados,** newlyweds; **r. nacido,** newborn baby. **2** *Am (hace poco)* recently. ◆**recientemente** *adv* recently, lately.

reciente *adj* recent.

recinto *nm (cercado)* enclosure; **r. comercial,** shopping precinct.

recio,-a I *adj (robusto)* strong, sturdy; *(grueso)* thick; *(voz)* loud. **II** *adv* hard.

recipiente *nm* receptacle, container.

recíproco,-a *adj* reciprocal.

recital *nm Mús* recital; *Lit* reading.

recitar *vtr* to recite.

reclamación *nf* **1** *(demanda)* claim, demand. **2** *(queja)* complaint.

reclamar I *vtr* to claim, demand. **II** *vi* **1** to protest (**contra,** against). **2** *Jur* to appeal.

reclamo *nm* **1** *(publicitario)* appeal. **2** *(en caza)* decoy bird, lure; *fig* inducement.

reclinar I *vtr* to lean (**sobre,** on). **II reclinarse** *vr* to lean back, recline.

recluir [37] *vtr* to shut away, lock away; *(encarcelar)* to imprison, intern.

reclusión *nf* seclusion; *(encarcelamiento)* imprisonment, internment.

recluso,-a *nm,f* prisoner, inmate.

recluta *nmf* recruit.

reclutamiento *nm (voluntario)* recruitment; *(obligatorio)* conscription.

recobrar I *vtr* to recover, retrieve; *(conocimiento)* to regain; **r. el aliento,** to get one's breath back. **II recobrarse** *vr* to recover, recuperate.

recochineo *nm fam* mockery.

recodo *nm (de río)* twist, turn; *(de camino)* bend.

recogedor *nm* dustpan.

recoger [5] **I** *vtr* **1** *(del suelo etc)* to pick up. **2** *(datos etc)* to gather, collect. **3** *(ordenar, limpiar)* to clean; **r. la mesa,** to clear the table. **4** *(ir a buscar)* to pick up, fetch. **5** *(cosecha)* to gather, pick. **II recogerse** *vr* **1** *(irse a casa)* to go home. **2** *(pelo)* to lift up.

recogida *nf* collection; *Agr (cosecha)* harvest, harvesting.

recolección *nf Agr* harvest, harvesting; *(recogida)* collection, gathering.

recomendable *adj* recommendable.

recomendación *nf* recommendation, reference.

recomendar [1] *vtr* to recommend.
recompensa *nf* reward.
recompensar *vtr* to reward.
recomponer [19] *(pp recompuesto) vtr* to repair, mend.
reconciliación *nf* reconciliation.
reconciliar [12] I *vtr* to reconcile. II **reconciliarse** *vr* to be reconciled.
recóndito,-a *adj* hidden, secret.
reconfortante *adj* comforting.
reconfortar *vtr* to comfort.
reconocer [34] *vtr* 1 to recognize. 2 *(admitir)* to recognize, admit. 3 *Med (paciente)* to examine.
reconocimiento *nm* 1 recognition. 2 *Med* examination, checkup.
reconquista *nf* reconquest.
reconstituyente *nm* tonic.
reconstruir [37] *vtr* to reconstruct.
reconversión *nf* reconversion; **r. industrial**, industrial redeployment.
reconvertir [5] *vtr* to reconvert; *Ind* to modernize.
recopilación *nf* 1 *(resumen)* summary, resumé. 2 *(compendio)* compilation, collection.
recopilar *vtr* to compile, collect.
récord *nm* record.
recordar [2] I *vtr* 1 *(rememorar)* to remember. 2 **r. algo a algn**, to remind sb of sth. II *vi* to remember.
recordatorio *nm (aviso)* reminder; *(de defunción)* notice of death.
recordman *nmf* record holder.
recorrer *vtr (distancia)* to cover, travel; *(país)* to tour, travel through *o* round; *(ciudad)* to visit, walk round.
recorrido *nm (distancia)* distance travelled; *(trayecto)* trip, journey; *(itinerario)* itinerary, route.
recortable *adj & nm* cutout.
recortar *vtr* to cut out.
recorte *nm (acción, de periódico)* cutting; *(de pelo)* trim, cut; *fig (de salarios etc)* cut.
recostado,-a *adj* reclining, leaning.
recostar [2] I *vtr* to lean. II **recostarse** *vr (tumbarse)* to lie down.
recoveco *nm (curva)* turn, bend; *(rincón)* nook, corner.
recreación *nf* recreation.
recrear I *vtr* 1 *(divertir)* to amuse, entertain. 2 *(crear de nuevo)* to recreate. II **recrearse** *vr* to amuse oneself, enjoy oneself; **r. con**, to take pleasure *o* delight in.
recreativo,-a *adj* recreational.
recreo *nm* 1 *(diversión)* recreation. 2 *(en el colegio)* break, recreation.
recriminar *vtr* to recriminate; *(reprochar)* to reproach.
recrudecer(se) [33] *vtr & vr* to worsen.
recrudecimiento *nm* worsening.
recta *nf Geom* straight line; *(de carretera)* straight stretch; *Dep* **la r. final**, the home straight.

rectangular *adj* rectangular.
rectángulo *nm* rectangle.
rectificación *nf* rectification; *(corrección)* correction.
rectificar [1] *vtr* to rectify; *(corregir)* to correct, remedy.
rectilíneo,-a *adj* straight.
rectitud *nf* straightness; *fig* uprightness, rectitude.
recto,-a I *adj* 1 *(derecho)* straight. 2 *(honesto)* upright, honest. 3 *Geom* right. II *nm Anat* rectum. III *adv* straight (on).
rector,-a I *adj (principio)* guiding, ruling. II *nm,f* rector.
recua *nf fig* string, series.
recuadro *nm Prensa* box.
recubrir *(pp recubierto) vtr* to cover.
recuento *nm* count; **hacer (el) r. de**, to count.
recuerdo *nm* 1 *(memoria)* memory. 2 *(regalo etc)* souvenir. 3 **recuerdos**, regards.
recuperación *nf* recovery; *(examen)* resit.
recuperar I *vtr (salud)* to recover; *(conocimiento)* to regain; *(tiempo, clases)* to make up. II **recuperarse** *vr* to recover.
recurrir *vi* 1 *Jur* to appeal. 2 **r. a**, *(a algn)* to turn to; *(a algo)* to make use of, resort to.
recurso *nm* 1 resource; **recursos naturales**, natural resources; **como último r.**, as a last resort. 2 *Jur* appeal.
recusar *vtr* to challenge, object to.
red *nf* net; *(sistema)* network; *Com (cadena)* chain of supermarkets; *fig (trampa)* trap.
redacción *nf (escrito)* composition, essay; *(acción)* writing; *Prensa* editing; *(redactores)* editorial staff.
redactar *vtr* to draft; *Prensa* to edit.
redactor,-a *nm,f Prensa* editor.
redada *nf* **r. policial**, *(en un solo sitio)* raid; *(en varios lugares a la vez)* round-up.
redentor,-a *nm,f* redeemer.
redicho,-a *adj fam* affected, pretentious.
redil *nm* fold, sheepfold.
redimir *vtr* to redeem.
rédito *nm* yield, interest.
redivivo *adj* revived.
redoblar I *vtr* to redouble. II *vi (tambor)* to roll.
redoble *nm* roll; *(de campanas)* peal.
redomado,-a *adj* utter, out-and-out.
redonda *nf* **a la r.**, around.
redondear *vtr (objeto)* to round, make round; *(cantidad)* to round up.
redondel *nm fam (círculo)* circle, ring; *Taur* ring, arena.
redondo,-a *adj* 1 round; *fig* **caer r.**, to collapse. 2 *(rotundo)* categorical; *(perfecto)* perfect.
reducción *nf* reduction.
reducido,-a *adj (disminuido)* reduced, decreased; *(pequeño)* limited, small.
reducir [10] I *vtr (disminuir)* to reduce. II

reducirse vr 1 (disminuirse) to be reduced, diminish. 2 (limitarse) to confine oneself.

redundancia nf redundancy, superfluousness; **valga la r.**, if I might say so again.

redundante adj redundant.

redundar vi r. **en**, (resultar) to result in, lead to.

reduplicar [1] vtr to redouble.

reembolsar vtr to reimburse; (deuda) to repay; (importe) to refund.

reembolso nm reimbursement; (de deuda) repayment; (devolución) refund; **contra r.**, cash on delivery.

reemplazar [4] vtr to replace (**con**, with).

reemplazo nm replacement; Mil call-up.

reestructuración nf restructuring.

reestructurar vtr to restructure.

ref. abr de **referencia**, reference, ref.

refaccionar vtr Am to repair, do up.

refectorio nm refectory, canteen.

referencia nf reference; **con r. a**, with reference to.

referéndum nm (pl **referéndums**) referendum.

referente adj r. **a**, concerning, regarding.

referir [5] I vtr to tell, relate. II **referirse** vr (aludir) to refer (**a**, to); **¿a qué te refieres?**, what do you mean?

refilón (de) loc adv (de pasada) briefly.

refinado,-a adj refined.

refinamiento nm refinement.

refinar vtr to refine.

refinería nf refinery.

reflector,-a I adj reflecting. II nm Elec spotlight, searchlight.

reflejar I vtr to reflect. II **reflejarse** vr to be reflected (**en**, in).

reflejo,-a I nm 1 (imagen) reflection. 2 (destello) gleam, glint. 3 Anat reflex. 4 reflejos, (en el cabello) streaks, highlights. II adj (movimiento) reflex.

reflexión nf reflection.

reflexionar vi to reflect (**sobre**, on), think (**sobre**, about).

reflexivo,-a adj 1 (persona) thoughtful. 2 Ling reflexive.

reflujo nm ebb (tide).

reforma nf 1 reform; **r. fiscal**, tax reform. 2 (reparación) repair.

reformador,-a nm,f reformer.

reformar I vtr to reform; (edificio) to renovate. II **reformarse** vr to reform.

reformatorio nm reformatory, reform school.

reforzar [2] vtr to reinforce, strengthen.

refractario,-a adj 1 Téc heat-resistant. 2 (persona) unwilling, reluctant.

refrán nm proverb, saying.

refregar [1] vtr to rub vigorously; fig **no me lo refriegues**, don't rub it in.

refrenar I vtr (contener) to restrain, curb. II **refrenarse** vr to restrain oneself.

refrendar vtr (firmar) to endorse, counter-

sign; (aprobar) to approve.

refrescante adj refreshing.

refrescar [1] I vtr to refresh. II vi 1 (tiempo) to turn cool. 2 (bebida) to be refreshing. III **refrescarse** vr to cool down.

refresco nm soft drink, refreshments pl.

refriega nf (lucha) scuffle, brawl; (escaramuza) skirmish.

refrigeración nf (enfriamento) refrigeration; (aire acondicionado) air conditioning.

refrigerado,-a adj air-conditioned.

refrigerador nm refrigerator, fridge.

refrigerar vtr to refrigerate; (habitación) to air-condition.

refrigerio nm snack, refreshments pl.

refuerzo nm reinforcement, strengthening.

refugiado,-a adj & nm,f refugee.

refugiarse [12] vr to shelter, take refuge.

refugio nm refuge.

refulgente adj radiant, brilliant.

refulgir [6] vi (brillar) to shine; (resplandecer) to glitter, sparkle.

refunfuñar vi to grumble, moan.

refutar vtr to refute.

regadera nf watering can; fam **estar como una r.**, to be as mad as a hatter.

regadío nm (tierra) irrigated land.

regalado,-a adj 1 (gratis) free; (muy barato) dirt cheap. 2 **una vida regalada**, an easy life.

regalar vtr 1 (dar) to give (as a present); (en ofertas etc) to give away. 2 r. **el oído a algn**, to flatter sb.

regaliz nm liquorice, US licorice.

regalo nm 1 gift, present; **de r.**, as a present. 2 (comodidad) pleasure, comfort.

regañadientes (a) loc adv reluctantly, unwillingly.

regañar I vtr fam to scold, tell off. II vi to nag.

regañina nf scolding, telling-off.

regañón,-ona nm,f adj nag.

regar [1] vtr to water.

regata nf boat race.

regatear I vi 1 to haggle, bargain. 2 Dep to dribble. II vtr **no r. esfuerzos**, to spare no effort.

regateo nm 1 (de precios) haggling. 2 Dep dribbling.

regazo nm lap.

regeneración nf regeneration.

regenerar vtr to regenerate.

regentar vtr to rule, govern; (cargo) to hold.

regente I nmf Pol regent. II nm (director) manager.

régimen nm (pl **regímenes**) 1 Pol regime. 2 Med diet; **estar a r.**, to be on a diet.

regimiento nm regiment.

regio,-a adj 1 (real) royal, regal. 2 (suntuoso) sumptuous, luxurious; Am (magnífico) splendid, majestic.

región nf region.

regional *adj* regional.

regionalista *adj & nmf* regionalist.

regir |6| I *vtr* to govern. II *vi* to be in force. III **regirse** *vr* to be guided, go (**por**, by).

registrado,-a *adj* **marca registrada**, registered trademark.

registrador,-a *adj* **caja registradora**, cash register.

registrar I *vtr* 1 *(examinar)* to inspect; *(cachear)* to frisk. 2 *(inscribir)* to register. 3 *(grabar)* to record. II **registrarse** *vr* 1 *(inscribirse)* to register, enrol. 2 *(detectarse)* to be recorded.

registro *nm* 1 inspection. 2 *(inscripción)* registration, recording; *(oficina)* registry office. 3 *Mús* register.

regla *nf* 1 *(norma)* rule; **en r.**, in order; **por r. general**, as a (general) rule; **r. de oro**, golden rule. 2 *(instrumento)* ruler. 3 *Mat* rule. 4 *Med (periodo)* period.

reglamentación *nf* 1 *(acción)* regulation. 2 *(reglamento)* regulations *pl*, rules *pl*.

reglamentar *vtr* to regulate.

reglamentario,-a *adj* statutory; *Mil* **arma reglamentaria**, regulation gun.

reglamento *nm* regulations *pl*, rules *pl*.

reglar *vtr* to regulate.

regocijar I *vtr* to delight, amuse. II **regocijarse** *vr* to be delighted, rejoice.

regocijo *nm (placer)* delight, joy; *(alborozo)* rejoicing, merriment.

regodearse *vr fam* to delight (**con**, in).

regodeo *nm fam* delight.

regordete,-a *adj fam* plump, chubby.

regresar *vi* to return.

regresión *nf* regression; *(decaimiento)* deterioration, decline.

regreso *nm* return.

reguero *nm (corriente)* trickle; *(de humo)* trail.

regulable *adj* adjustable.

regular I *vtr* 1 to regulate, control. 2 *(ajustar)* to adjust. II *adj* 1 regular; **por lo r.**, as a rule; **vuelo r.**, scheduled flight. 2 *fam (mediano)* average, so-so. III *adv* so-so.

regularidad *nf* regularity; **con r.**, regularly.

regularizar |4| *vtr* to regularize.

regusto *nm* aftertaste.

rehabilitar *vtr* to rehabilitate; *(edificio)* to convert.

rehacer |15| *(pp rehecho)* I *vtr* to redo. II **rehacerse** *vr (recuperarse)* to recover, recuperate.

rehén *nm* hostage.

rehogar |7| *vtr* to brown.

rehuir |37| *vtr* to shun, avoid.

rehusar |18| *vtr* to refuse.

reina *nf* queen.

reinado *nm* reign.

reinante *adj (que reina)* reigning, ruling; *(prevaleciente)* prevailing.

reinar *vi* to reign.

reincidente *nmf Jur* recidivist.

reincidir *vi* to relapse, fall back (**en**, into).

reincorporarse *vr* **r. al trabajo**, to return to work.

reino *nm* kingdom; **el R. Unido**, the United Kingdom.

reinserción *nf* reintegration.

reinsertar(se) *vtr & vr* to reintegrate.

reintegrar *vtr* 1 *(trabajador)* to reinstate. 2 *(dinero)* to reimburse, refund.

reintegro *nm (en lotería)* winning of one's stake.

reír |6| I *vi* to laugh. II **reírse** *vr* 1 to laugh. 2 *(mofarse)* to laugh (**de**, at), make fun (**de**, of).

reiterar *vtr* to reiterate, repeat.

reivindicación *nf* claim, demand.

reivindicar |1| *vtr* to claim, demand; **el atentado fue reivindicado por los terroristas**, the terrorists claimed responsibility for the attack.

reivindicativo,-a *adj* protest.

reja *nf* 1 *(de ventana)* grill, grating; *fam* **estar entre rejas**, to be behind bars. 2 *Agr* ploughshare, *US* plowshare.

rejilla *nf (de ventana, ventilador, radiador)* grill; *(de horno)* gridiron; *(para equipaje)* luggage rack.

rejoneador,-a *nm,f Taur* bullfighter on horseback.

rejonear *vtr Taur* to fight on horseback.

rejuvenecer |33| *vtr* to rejuvenate.

relación *nf* 1 relationship; *(conexión)* connection, link; **con** *o* **en r. a**, with regard to; **relaciones públicas**, public relations. 2 *(lista)* list. 3 *(relato)* account. 4 *Mat Téc* ratio.

relacionado,-a *adj* related (**con**, to), connected (**con**, with).

relacionar I *vtr* to relate (**con**, to), connect (**con**, with). II **relacionarse** *vr* 1 to be related, be connected. 2 *(alternar)* to mix, get acquainted.

relajación *nf* relaxation.

relajante *adj* relaxing.

relajar I *vtr* to relax. II **relajarse** *vr* to relax; *(moral)* to deteriorate.

relamerse *vr* to lick one's lips.

relamido,-a *adj (afectado)* affected; *(pulcro)* prim and proper.

relámpago *nm* flash of lightning; *fig* **pasó como un r.**, he flashed past; *fig* **visita r.**, flying visit.

relampaguear *vi impers* to flash.

relanzar *vtr* to relaunch.

relatar *vtr* to narrate, relate.

relatividad *nf* relativity.

relativo,-a *adj* relative (**a**, to); **en lo r. a**, with regard to, concerning.

relato *nm (cuento)* tale, story.

relax *nm fam* relaxation.

relegar |7| *vtr* to relegate.

relente *nm* dew.

relevante *adj* important.
relevancia *nf* importance.
relevar I *vtr* to relieve, take over from; **fue relevado del cargo,** he was relieved of his duties. **II relevarse** *vr* *(turnarse)* to relieve one another.
relevo *nm* relief; *Dep* relay.
relieve *nm* *Arte* relief; *fig* **poner de r.,** to emphasize.
religión *nf* religion.
religioso,-a I *adj* religious. **II** *nm,f* *(hombre)* monk; *(mujer)* nun.
relinchar *vi* to neigh, whinny.
relincho *nm* neigh, whinny.
reliquia *nf* relic.
rellamada *nf* *Tel* redial.
rellano *nm* landing.
rellenar *vtr* 1 *(impreso etc)* to fill in. 2 *(un ave)* to stuff; *(un pastel)* to fill.
relleno,-a I *nm* *(de aves)* stuffing; *(de pasteles)* filling. **II** *adj* stuffed.
reloj *nm* clock; *(de pulsera)* watch; **r. de arena,** hourglass; **r. de sol,** sundial; **r. despertador,** alarm clock.
relojería *nf* *(tienda)* watchmaker's, clockmaker's; **bomba de r.,** time bomb.
relojero,-a *nm,f* watchmaker, clockmaker.
reluciente *adj* shining, gleaming.
relucir [35] *vi* *(brillar)* to shine, gleam; **sacar a r. un tema,** to bring up a subject.
relumbrar *vi* to shine, gleam.
reluzco *indic pres* → **relucir**.
remachar *vtr* to drive home, hammer home.
remache *nm* rivet.
remanente *nm* *(restos)* remainder; *(extra)* surplus.
remangar(se) [7] *vtr & vr* *(mangas, pantalones)* to roll up; *(camisa)* to tuck up.
remanso *nm* pool; *(lugar tranquilo)* quiet place.
remar *vi* to row.
remarcar [1] *vtr* to stress, underline.
rematadamente *adv* **r. loco,** as mad as a hatter.
rematar *vtr* 1 to finish off, put the finishing touches to. 2 *Com* to sell off cheaply. 3 *Dep* to shoot.
remate *nm* 1 *(final)* end, finish; **para r.,** to crown it all. 2 *Dep* shot at goal. 3 **de r.,** utter, utterly.
rembolsar *vtr* → **reembolsar**.
rembolso *nm* → **reembolso**.
remedar *vtr* to imitate, copy.
remediar [12] *vtr* 1 to remedy; *(enmendar)* to repair, make good. 2 *(evitar)* to avoid, prevent; **no pude remediarlo,** I couldn't help it.
remedio *nm* *(cura)* remedy, cure; *(solución)* solution; **¡qué r.!,** what else can I do!; **no hay más r.,** there's no choice; **sin r.,** without fail; *fam* **¡no tienes r.!,** you're hopeless!

remedo *nm* *(imitación)* imitation, copy; *(parodia)* parody.
rememorar *vtr* to remember, recall.
remendar [1] *vtr* *(ropa)* to patch.
remero,-a *nm,f* rower.
remesa *nf* *(de mercancías)* consignment, shipment; *(de dinero)* remittance.
remiendo *nm* *(parche)* patch.
remilgado,-a *adj* *(afectado)* affected; *(melindroso)* fussy, finicky; *(gazmoño)* prudish.
remilgo *nm* affectation; *(gazmoñería)* prudishness.
reminiscencia *nf* reminiscence.
remiso,-a *adj* reluctant.
remite *nm* *(en carta)* sender's name and address.
remitente *nmf* sender.
remitir I *vtr* 1 *(enviar)* to send. 2 *(referir)* to refer. **II** *vi* *(fiebre, temporal)* to subside. **III remitirse** *vr* **si nos remitimos a los hechos,** if we look at the facts; **remítase a la página diez,** see page ten.
remo *nm* oar; *(deporte)* rowing.
remodelación *nf* *(modificación)* reshaping; *(reorganización)* reorganization; *Pol* **r. ministerial** *o* **del gobierno,** cabinet reshuffle.
remodelar *vtr* to reshape; *(reorganizar)* to reorganize.
remojar *vtr* to soak **(en,** in).
remojo *nm* **dejar** *o* **poner en r.,** to soak, leave to soak.
remojón *nm* *fam* **darse un r.,** to go for a dip.
remolacha *nf* beetroot.
remolcador *nm* 1 *Náut* tug, tugboat. 2 *Aut* breakdown truck, *US* tow truck.
remolcar [1] *vtr* to tow.
remolino *nm* *(de agua)* whirlpool, eddy; *(de aire)* whirlwind.
remolón,-ona *adj* **hacerse el r.,** to shirk, slack.
remolonear *vi* to shirk, slack.
remolque *nm* *(acción)* towing; *(vehículo)* trailer; *fig* **ir a r. de algn,** to trundle along behind sb.
remontar I *vtr* 1 *(subir)* to go up. 2 *(superar)* to overcome. **II remontarse** *vr* 1 *(pájaros, aviones)* to soar. 2 *(datar)* to go back, date back **(a,** to).
remorder [4] *vtr* to trouble; **me remuerde la conciencia por ...,** I've got a bad conscience about ....
remordimiento *nm* remorse.
remoto,-a *adj* remote, faraway; **no tengo la más remota idea,** I haven't got the faintest idea.
remover [4] *vtr* 1 *(trasladar)* to move over. 2 *(tierra)* to turn over; *(líquido)* to shake up; *(comida etc)* to stir; *(asunto)* to stir up.
remozar [4] *vtr* to modernize.
remplazar [4] *vtr* → **reemplazar**.

remplazo *nm* → **reemplazo**.

remuneración *nf* remuneration.

remunerar *vtr* to remunerate.

renacer [33] *vi* to be reborn; *fig (revivir)* to revive, come back to life.

renacentista *adj* Renaissance.

renacimiento *nm* el R., the Renaissance.

renacuajo *nm* tadpole; *fam (niño pequeño)* shrimp.

renal *adj* kidney; **insuficiencia r.**, kidney failure.

rencilla *nf* quarrel.

rencor *nm* rancour, *US* rancor; *(resentimiento)* resentment; **guardar r. a algn**, to have a grudge against sb.

rencoroso,-a *adj (hostil)* rancorous; *(resentido)* resentful.

rendición *nf* surrender.

rendido,-a *adj (muy cansado)* exhausted, worn out.

rendija *nf* crack, split.

rendimiento *nm (producción)* yield, output; *(de máquina, motor)* efficiency, performance.

rendir [6] I *vtr* 1 *(fruto, beneficios)* to yield, produce. 2 *(cansar)* to exhaust, wear out. 3 **r. culto a**, to worship; **r. homenaje a**, to pay homage to. II *vi (dar beneficios)* to pay, be profitable. III **rendirse** *vr* 1 to surrender, give in; **¡me rindo!**, I give up! 2 *(cansarse)* to wear oneself out.

renegado,-a *adj & nm,f* renegade.

renegar [1] *vtr* **r. de**, to renounce, disown.

renegrido,-a *adj* blackened.

RENFE *abr de* **Red Nacional de los Ferrocarriles Españoles**.

renglón *nm* line; **a r. seguido**, immediately afterwards.

reno *nm* reindeer.

renombrado,-a *adj* renowned, famous.

renombre *nm* renown, fame.

renovable *adj* renewable.

renovación *nf (de contrato, pasaporte)* renewal; *(de una casa)* renovation.

renovar [2] *vtr* to renew; *(edificio)* to renovate.

renta *nf* 1 *Fin (ingresos)* income; *(beneficio)* interest, return; **r. per cápita**, per capita income; **r. fija**, fixed interest security. 2 *(alquiler)* rent.

rentable *adj* profitable.

rentar *vtr* to produce, yield.

renuncia *nf* 1 renunciation. 2 *(dimisión)* resignation.

renunciar [12] *vi* 1 **r. a**, to renounce, give up; *(no aceptar)* to decline. 2 *(dimitir)* to resign.

reñido,-a *adj (disputado)* tough, hard-fought.

reñir [6] I *vtr (regañar)* to scold, tell off. II *vi (discutir)* to quarrel, argue; *(pelear)* to fight; **r. con algn**, to fall out with sb.

reo *nmf (acusado)* defendant, accused;

(culpable) culprit.

reojo (de) *loc adv* **mirar algo de r.**, to look at sth out of the corner of one's eye.

reparación *nf* repair; *(compensación)* reparation, amends *pl*.

reparar I *vtr* to repair; *(ofensa, injuria)* to make amends for; *(daño)* to make good. II *vi* **r. en**, *(darse cuenta de)* to notice; *(reflexionar sobre)* to think about.

reparo *nm* **no tener reparos en**, not to hesitate to; **me da r.**, I feel embarrassed.

repartidor,-a *nm,f* distributor.

repartir *vtr* 1 *(dividir)* to distribute, share out. 2 *(regalo, premio)* to give out, hand out; *(correo)* to deliver; *Naipes* to deal.

reparto *nm* 1 distribution, sharing out. 2 *(distribución)* handing out; *(de mercancías)* delivery. 3 *Cin Teat* cast.

repasar *vtr* 1 to revise, go over. 2 *(ropa)* to mend.

repaso *nm* revision.

repatear *vtr fam* to annoy, turn off.

repatriar [14] *vtr* to repatriate.

repecho *nm* short steep slope.

repelente *adj* repulsive, repellent; *fam* **niño r.**, little know-all.

repeler *vtr (rechazar)* to repel, repulse; *(repugnar)* to disgust.

repente *nm fam (arrebato)* fit, outburst; **de r.**, suddenly, all of a sudden.

repentino,-a *adj* sudden.

repercusión *nm* repercussion.

repercutir *vi* 1 *(sonido)* to resound, reverberate; *(objeto)* to rebound. 2 *fig* **r. en**, to have repercussions on, affect.

repertorio *nm* repertoire, repertory.

repesca *nf fam* second chance; *(examen)* resit.

repetición *nf* repetition; **r. de la jugada**, action replay.

repetido,-a *adj* **repetidas veces**, repeatedly.

repetidor,-a I *adj* repeating. II *nm,f fam Educ* student who is repeating a year.

repetir [6] I *vtr* 1 to repeat. 2 *(plato)* to have a second helping. II *vi Educ* to repeat a year. III **repetirse** *vr* 1 *(persona)* to repeat oneself. 2 *(hecho)* to recur. 3 **el pepino se repite**, cucumber repeats (on me/you/him etc).

repicar [1] *vtr (las campanas)* to peal, ring out.

repipi *adj fam* **niño r.**, little know-all.

repique *nm (de campanas)* peal, ringing.

repiquetear *vtr & vi (campanas)* to ring; *(tambor)* to beat.

repisa *nf* shelf, ledge.

replantear, replantearse *vr* to reconsider, rethink.

replegarse [1] *vr* to fall back, retreat.

repleto,-a *adj* full (up), jam-packed; **r. de**, packed with, crammed with.

réplica *nf* 1 answer, reply. 2 *(copia)* replica.

replicar |1| **I** *vtr* to answer back. **II** *vi* **1** to reply, retort. **2** *(objetar)* to argue. **3** *Jur* to answer.

repliegue *nm Mil* withdrawal, retreat.

repoblación *nf* repopulation; **r. forestal,** reafforestation.

repoblar |2| *vtr* to repopulate; *(bosque)* to reafforest.

repollo *nm* cabbage.

reponer |19| **I** *vtr* **1** to put back, replace. **2** *Teat (obra)* to put on again; *Cin (película)* to rerun; *TV (programa)* to repeat. **II reponerse** *vr* **r. de,** to recover from, get over.

reportaje *nm Prensa Rad* report; *(noticias)* article, news item.

reportar *vtr (beneficios etc)* to bring.

reportero,-a *nm,f* reporter.

reposar I *vtr* to rest **(en,** on). **II** *vi (descansar)* to rest, take a rest; *(té)* to infuse; *(comida)* to stand.

reposición *nf TV* repeat; *Cin* rerun, re-showing.

reposo *nm* rest; **en r.,** at rest.

repostar *vtr (provisiones)* to stock up with; *Aut (gasolina)* to fill up.

repostería *nf* confectionery; *(tienda)* confectioner's (shop).

repostero,-a *nm,f* confectioner.

reprender *vtr* to reprimand, scold.

represalia *nf (usu pl)* reprisals *pl,* retaliation.

representación *nf* **1** representation. **2** *Teat* performance.

representante *nmf* representative.

representar **1** to represent. **2** *(significar)* to mean, represent. **3** *Teat (obra)* to perform.

representativo,-a *adj* representative.

represión *nf* repression.

represivo,-a *adj* repressive.

reprimenda *nf* reprimand.

reprimir *vtr* to repress.

reprobar |2| *vtr (cosa)* to condemn; *(a persona)* to reproach, reprove.

réprobo,-a *adj & nm,f* reprobate.

reprochable *adj* reproachable.

reprochar *vtr* to reproach; **r. algo a algn,** to reproach sb for sth.

reproche *nm* reproach.

reproducción *nf* reproduction.

reproducir |10| **I** *vtr* to reproduce. **II reproducirse** *vr* **1** to reproduce, breed. **2** *(repetirse)* to recur, happen again.

reproductor,-a *adj* reproductive.

reptar *vi* to slither.

reptil *nm* reptile.

república *nf* republic.

republicano,-a *adj & nm,f* republican.

repudiar |12| *vtr* to repudiate.

repuesto *nm (recambio)* spare part, spare; *Aut* **rueda de r.,** spare wheel.

repugnancia *nf* loathing, disgust.

repugnante *adj* disgusting, revolting.

repugnar *vtr* to disgust, revolt.

repujar *vtr* to emboss.

repulsa *nf* rebuff.

repulsión *nf* repulsion, repugnance.

repulsivo,-a *adj* repulsive, revolting.

repuse *pt indef →* **reponer.**

reputación *nf* reputation.

reputar *vtr* to consider, deem.

requemar *vtr* to scorch.

requerimiento *nm* **1** *(súplica)* request. **2** *Jur (aviso)* summons *pl.*

requerir |5| *vtr* **1** to require. **2** *(solicitar)* to request. **3** *Jur (avisar)* to summon.

requesón *nm* cottage cheese.

requete- *pref fam* really, very, incredibly; **requetebueno,** brilliant.

réquiem *nm (pl* **réquiems)** requiem.

requisa *nf* **1** *(inspección)* inspection. **2** *Mil* requisition.

requisar *vtr* to requisition.

requisito *nm* requirement, requisite.

res *nf* animal.

resabiado,-a *adj pey* pedantic.

resabio *nm* **1** *(mal sabor)* unpleasant *o* bad aftertaste. **2** *(vicio)* bad habit.

resaca *nf* **1** hangover. **2** *Náut* undertow, undercurrent.

resaltar *vi* **1** *(sobresalir)* to project, jut out. **2** *fig* to stand out.

resarcir |3| *vtr* to compensate.

resbaladizo,-a *adj* slippery.

resbalar(se) *vi & vr* to slip; *Aut* to skid.

resbalón *nm* slip.

rescatar *vtr (persona)* to rescue; *(objeto)* to recover.

rescate *nm* **1** *(salvamento)* rescue; *(recuperación)* recovery. **2** *(suma)* ransom.

rescindir *vtr* to rescind, annul; *(contrato)* to cancel.

rescisión *nf* rescission, annulment.

rescoldo *nm* **1** embers *pl.* **2** *fig (recelo)* lingering doubt.

resecarse |1| *vr* to dry up, become parched.

reseco,-a *adj* very dry, parched.

resentido,-a *adj* resentful.

resentimiento *nm* resentment.

resentirse |5| *vr* **1** **r. de,** to suffer from, feel the effects of. **2** *(ofenderse)* to feel offended; **r. por algo,** to take offence at sth, feel bitter about sth.

reseña *nf* review; *Prensa* write-up.

reserva I *nf* **1** *(de entradas etc)* reservation, booking. **2** *(provisión)* reserve, stock; **un vino de r.,** a vintage wine. **3** *Mil* reserve, reserves *pl.* **4** *(duda)* reservation. **II** *nmf Dep* reserve, substitute.

reservado,-a I *adj (persona)* reserved, quiet. **II** *nm* private room.

reservar I *vtr* **1** *(billetes etc)* to reserve, book. **2** *(dinero, tiempo etc)* to keep, save. **II reservarse** *vr* **1** to save oneself **(para,** for). **2** *(sentimientos)* to keep to oneself. **3 r. el derecho de,** to reserve the right to.

resfriado,-a I nm (catarro) cold; **coger un r.**, to catch (a) cold. **II** adj **estar r.**, to have a cold.

resfriarse vr to catch (a) cold.

resguardar vtr (proteger) to protect, shelter (**de**, from).

resguardo nm 1 (recibo) receipt. 2 (protección) protection, shelter.

residencia nf residence; **r. de ancianos**, old people's home.

residencial adj residential.

residente adj & nmf resident.

residir vi to reside, live (**en**, in); fig to lie (**en**, in).

residuo nm 1 residue. 2 **residuos**, waste sing.

resignación nf resignation.

resignado,-a adj resigned.

resignarse vr to resign oneself (**a**, to).

resina nf resin.

resistencia nf 1 resistance. 2 (aguante) endurance, stamina. 3 Elec element.

resistente adj 1 resistant (**a**, to). 2 (fuerte) tough, hardy.

resistir I vi 1 to resist. 2 (aguantar) to hold (out). **II** vtr (situación, persona) to put up with; (tentación) to resist. **III resistirse** vr to resist; (oponerse) to offer resistance; (negarse) to refuse.

resolución nf 1 (solución) solution. 2 (decisión) resolution.

resolver [4] (pp **resuelto**) **I** vtr (problema) to solve; (asunto) to settle. **II** vi (decidir) to resolve, decide. **III resolverse** vr 1 (solucionarse) to be solved. 2 (decidirse) to resolve, make up one's mind (**a**, to).

resollar [7] vi to breathe heavily; (con silbido) to wheeze.

resonancia nf 1 (sonora) resonance. 2 (repercusión) repercussions pl.

resonar [6] vi to resound; (tener eco) to echo.

resoplar vi (respirar) to breathe heavily; (de cansancio) to puff and pant; (de enfado) to huff and puff.

resoplido nm (silbido) wheezing; (de cansancio) panting; (de enfado) snort.

resorte nm 1 (muelle) spring. 2 fig means pl.

respaldar vtr to support, back (up).

respaldo nm (de silla etc) back; fig (apoyo) support, backing.

respectar vtr to concern, regard; **por lo que a mí respecta**, as far as I'm concerned.

respectivo,-a adj respective; **en lo r. a**, with regard to, regarding.

respecto nm **al r.**, **a este r.**, in this respect; **con r. a**, **r. a**, **r. de**, with regard to; **r. a mí**, as for me, as far as I am concerned.

respetable I adj respectable. **II** nm fam **el r.**, the audience.

respetar vtr to respect; **hacerse r. de todos**, to command everyone's respect.

respeto nm 1 respect; **por r.**, out of consideration. 2 (recelo) fear.

respetuoso,-a adj respectful.

respingar [7] vi to shy.

respingo nm start, jump.

respingón,-ona adj (nariz) snub, upturned.

respiración nf (acción) breathing, respiration; (aliento) breath; **r. artificial**, artificial resuscitation.

respirar vi to breathe; **¡por fin respiro!**, well, that's a relief!

respiratorio,-a adj respiratory.

respiro nm 1 breathing. 2 (descanso) breather, break.

resplandecer [33] vi to shine.

resplandeciente adj (brillante) shining; (esplendoroso) resplendent, radiant.

resplandor nm (brillo) brightness; (muy intenso) brilliance; (de fuego) glow, blaze.

responder I vtr to answer. **II** vi 1 (una carta) to reply. 2 (reaccionar) to respond. 3 (protestar) to answer back. 4 **r. de algn**, to be responsible for sb; **r. por algn**, to vouch for sb.

respondón,-ona adj fam argumentative, cheeky.

responsabilidad nf responsibility.

responsabilizar [4] **I** vtr to make o hold responsible (**de**, for). **II responsabilizarse** vr to assume o claim responsibility (**de**, for).

responsable I adj responsible. **II** nmf **el/la r.**, (encargado) the person in charge; (de robo etc) the perpetrator.

respuesta nf answer, reply; (reacción) response.

resquebrajarse vr to crack.

resquemor nm resentment, ill feeling.

resquicio nm crack, chink.

resta nf subtraction.

restablecer [33] **I** vtr to re-establish; (el orden) to restore. **II restablecerse** vr Med to recover.

restablecimiento nm 1 re-establishment; (del orden etc) restoration. 2 Med recovery.

restante adj remaining; **lo r.**, the rest, the remainder.

restar I vtr 1 Mat to subtract, take away. 2 **r. importancia a algo**, to play sth down. **II** vi (quedar) to be left, remain.

restauración nf restoration.

restaurador,-a I nm,f restorer. **II** adj restoring.

restaurante nm restaurant.

restaurar vtr to restore.

restitución nf restitution.

restituir [37] vtr (restablecer) to restore; (devolver) to return, give back.

resto nm 1 rest, remainder; Mat remainder. 2 **restos**, remains; (de comida) leftovers.

restregar |1| *vtr* to rub hard, scrub.
restricción *nf* restriction.
restrictivo,-a *adj* restrictive.
restringir |6| *vtr* to restrict, limit.
resucitar *vtr & vi* to resuscitate.
resuelto,-a *adj (decidido)* resolute, determined.
resuello *nm* breath, gasp.
resultas *nfpl* **a r. de**, as a result of.
resultado *nm* result; *(consecuencia)* outcome; **dar buen r.**, to work, give results.
resultante *adj* resulting.
resultar *vi* 1 *(ser)* to turn *o* work out; **así
resulta más barato**, it works out cheaper
this way; **me resultó fácil**, it turned out
to be easy for me. 2 *(ocurrir)* **resulta que
...**, the thing is ...; **y ahora resulta que
no puede venir**, and now it turns out
that she can't come. 3 *(tener éxito)* to be
successful; **la fiesta no resultó**, the party
wasn't a success.
resumen *nm* summary; **en r.**, in short, to
sum up.
resumir I *vtr* to sum up; *(recapitular)* to
summarize. II **resumirse** *vr (reducirse)* to
be reduced to.
resurgir |6| *vi* to reappear.
resurrección *nf* resurrection.
retablo *nm* altarpiece.
retaguardia *nf* rearguard.
retahíla *nf* series *sing*, string.
retal *nm (pedazo)* scrap.
retar *vtr* to challenge.
retardarse *vr* to be delayed.
retardo *nm* delay.
retazo *nm (pedazo)* scrap; *(fragmento)* fragment, piece.
rete- *pref fam Am* very.
retención *nf* retention; *Fin* withholding;
r. de tráfico, (traffic) hold-up, traffic
jam.
retener |24| *vtr* 1 *(conservar)* to retain. 2
Fin (descontar) to deduct. 3 *(detener)* to
detain.
reticencia *nf* reticence, reserve.
reticente *adj* reticent, reserved.
retina *nf* retina.
retintín *nm (tono irónico)* innuendo,
sarcastic tone.
retirada *nf* retreat, withdrawal.
retirado,-a I *adj* 1 *(alejado)* remote. 2 *(jubilado)* retired. II *nm,f* retired person,
US retiree.
retirar I *vtr* to take away, remove; *(dinero)*
to withdraw; *(ofensa)* to take back. II **retirarse** *vr* 1 *(apartarse)* to withdraw, draw
back; *(irse)* to retire. 2 *(jubilarse)* to retire. 3 *Mil* to retreat, withdraw.
retiro *nm* 1 *(jubilación)* retirement;
(pensión) pension. 2 *(lugar tranquilo)* retreat. 3 *Rel* retreat.
reto *nm* challenge.
retocar |1| *vtr* to touch up.
retoño *nm (rebrote)* shoot, sprout; *fig (ni-*

ño) kid.
retoque *nm* retouching, touching up; **los
últimos retoques**, the finishing touches.
retorcer |4| I *vtr (cuerda, hilo)* to twist;
(ropa) to wring (out). II **retorcerse** *vr* to
twist, become twisted; **r. de dolor**, to
writhe in pain.
retorcido,-a *adj fig* twisted.
retórica *nf* rhetoric.
retórico,-a *adj* rhetorical.
retornable *adj* returnable; **'envase no r.'**,
'nondeposit bottle'.
retornar I *vtr* to return, give back. II *vi*
to return, come back, go back.
retorno *nm* return.
retortijón *nm (dolor)* stomach cramp.
retozar |4| *vi* to frolic, romp.
retracción *nf* retraction.
retractar I *vtr* to retract. II **retractarse** *vr*
to retract, take back **(de, -)**.
retraerse *vr (retirarse)* to withdraw; *(por
miedo)* to shy away.
retraído,-a *adj* shy, reserved.
retraimiento *nm (timidez)* shyness.
retransmisión *nf* broadcast, transmission.
retransmitir *vtr* to broadcast.
retrasado,-a I *adj* 1 *(tren)* late; *(reloj)*
slow; **voy r.**, I'm behind schedule. 2 *(país)* backward, underdeveloped. 3 *(mental)*
retarded, backward. II *nm,f* **r. (mental)**,
mentally retarded person.
retrasar I *vtr* 1 *(retardar)* to slow down. 2
(atrasar) to delay, postpone. 3 *(reloj)* to
put back. II **retrasarse** *vr* to be late, be
delayed; *(reloj)* to be slow.
retraso *nm* delay; **con r.**, late; **una hora
de r.**, an hour behind schedule; **r.
mental**, mental deficiency.
retratar I *vtr (pintar)* to paint a portrait
of; *Fot* to take a photograph of; *fig (describir)* to describe, depict. II **retratarse** *vr*
Fot to have one's photograph taken.
retrato *nm (pintura)* portrait; *Fot* photograph; **r. robot**, identikit picture,
photofit picture; **ser el vivo r. de**, to be
the spitting image of.
retreta *nf* retreat.
retrete *nm* lavatory, toilet.
retribución *nf (pago)* pay, payment; *(recompensa)* reward.
retribuir *vtr (pagar)* to pay; *(recompensar)*
to reward.
retro *adj inv fam (retrógrado)* reactionary;
(antiguo) old-fashioned.
retroactivo,-a *adj* retroactive; **con efecto
r.**, retrospectively.
retroceder *vi* to move back, back away.
retroceso *nm* 1 *(movimiento)* backward
movement. 2 *Med* deterioration, worsening. 3 *Econ* recession.
retrógrado,-a *adj & nm,f (reaccionario)*
reactionary.
retropropulsión *nf Av* jet propulsion.
retrospectivo,-a *adj & nf* retrospective.

retrovisor *nm Aut* rear-view mirror.

retumbar *vi* (*resonar*) to resound, echo; (*tronar*) to thunder, boom.

retuve *pt indef* → **retener**.

reúma, reumatismo *nm* rheumatism.

reumático,-a *adj & nm,f* rheumatic.

reunión *nf* meeting; (*reencuentro*) reunion.

reunir [19] **I** *vtr* to gather together; (*dinero*) to raise; (*cualidades*) to have, possess; (*requisitos*) to fulfil. **II reunirse** *vr* to meet, gather; **r. con algn**, to meet sb.

revalidar *vtr* to ratify, confirm; *Dep* (*título*) to retain.

revalorizar [4] *vtr,* **revalorizarse** *vr* (*moneda*) to revalue.

revancha *nf* revenge; *Dep* return match.

revanchista *adj* vengeful, vindictive.

revelación *nf* revelation.

revelado *nm Fot* developing.

revelar *vtr* **1** to reveal, disclose. **2** *Fot* (*película*) to develop.

revender *vtr* (*entradas*) to tout.

reventa *nf* (*de entradas*) touting.

reventado,-a *adj fam* (*cansado*) knackered.

reventar [1] **I** *vtr* **1** to burst. **2** (*romper*) to break, smash. **3** (*fastidiar*) to annoy, bother. **II** *vi* (*estallar*) to burst; **r. de ganas de hacer algo**, to be dying to do sth; **está que revienta**, he's bursting at the seams. **III reventarse** *vr* (*estallar*) to burst, explode.

reventón *nm* (*de neumático*) blowout, puncture, flat tyre *o US* tire.

reverberación *nf* reverberation.

reverberar *vi* to reverberate.

reverencia *nf* **1** (*respeto*) reverence. **2** (*inclinación*) (*de hombre*) bow; (*de mujer*) curtsy.

reverenciar [12] *vtr* to revere, venerate.

reverendo,-a *adj & nm,f* reverend.

reversible *adj* reversible.

reverso *nm* reverse, back.

revertido,-a *adj* **llamada a cobro r.,** reverse-charge call, *US* collect call.

revertir [5] *vi* to result (**en**, in).

revés *nm* **1** (*reverso*) reverse; **al** *o* **del r.,** (*al contrario*) the other way round; (*la parte interior en el exterior*) inside out; (*boca abajo*) upside down; (*la parte de detrás delante*) back to front; **al r. de lo que dicen**, contrary to what they say. **2** (*bofetada*) slap; *Ten* backhand (stroke). **3** *fig* (*contrariedad*) setback, reverse; **los reveses de la vida**, life's misfortunes; **reveses de fortuna**, setbacks, blows of fate.

revestimiento *nm Téc* covering, coating.

revestir [6] *vtr* **1** (*recubrir*) to cover (**de**, with), coat (**de**, with), line (**de**, with). **2** *fig* **la herida no reviste importancia**, the wound is not serious.

revisar *vtr* to check; (*coche*) to service.

revisión *nf* checking; (*de coche*) service, overhaul; **r. médica**, checkup.

revisor,-a *nm,f* ticket inspector.

revista *nf* **1** magazine. **2 pasar r. a**, to inspect, review. **3** *Teat* revue.

revitalizar [4] *vtr* to revitalize.

revivir *vi & vtr* to revive.

revocar [1] *vtr* to revoke, repeal.

revolcar [2] **I** *vtr fam* (*oponente*) to floor, crush. **II revolcarse** *vr* to roll about.

revolcón *nm* fall, tumble; *vulg* (*sexual*) romp.

revolotear *vi* to fly about, flutter about.

revoltijo, revoltillo *nm* mess, jumble.

revoltoso,-a *adj* (*travieso*) mischievous, naughty.

revolución *nf* revolution.

revolucionar *vtr* to revolutionize.

revolucionario,-a *adj & nm,f* revolutionary.

revolver [4] (*pp* **revuelto**) **I** *vtr* (*desordenar*) to mess up, disturb; **me revuelve el estómago**, it turns my stomach. **II revolverse** *vr* **1** (*agitarse*) to roll. **2** *fig* **r. contra algn**, to turn against sb. **3** (*el tiempo*) to turn stormy; (*el mar*) to become rough.

revólver *nm* (*pl* **revólveres**) revolver.

revuelo *nm fig* stir, commotion.

revuelta *nf* **1** (*insurrección*) revolt. **2** (*curva*) bend, turn.

revuelto,-a *adj* **1** (*desordenado*) jumbled, in a mess. **2** (*tiempo*) stormy, unsettled; (*mar*) rough. **3** (*agitado*) excited.

revulsivo,-a *adj & nm* revulsive.

rey *nm* king; *Rel* (**el día de) Reyes,** (the) Epiphany, 6 January.

reyerta *nf* quarrel, dispute.

rezagado,-a *nm,f* straggler, latecomer.

rezagarse *vr* to lag *o* fall behind.

rezar [4] **I** *vi* **1** (*orar*) to pray. **2** (*decir*) to say, read. **II** *vtr* (*oración*) to say.

rezo *nm* prayer.

rezumar *vtr* to ooze; *fig* to exude.

RFA *nf Hist abr de* **República Federal de Alemania,** Federal Republic of Germany, FRG.

ría *nf* estuary.

riada *nf* flood.

ribera *nf* (*de río*) bank; (*zona*) riverside, waterfront.

ribete *nm* edging, border.

ribetear *vtr* to edge, border.

rico,-a **I** *adj* **1 ser r.,** (*adinerado*) to be rich, wealthy; (*abundante*) to be rich; (*bonito*) to be lovely *o* adorable; (*fértil*) to be rich *o* fertile. **2 estar r.,** (*delicioso*) to be delicious. **II** *nm,f* rich person. ◆**ricamente** *adv fam* **tan r.,** very well.

rictus *nm inv* grin.

ridiculez *nf* ridiculous thing; (*cualidad*) ridiculousness.

ridiculizar [4] *vtr* to ridicule.

ridículo,-a I *adj* ridiculous. **II** *nm* ridicule; **hacer el r., quedar en r.,** to make a fool of oneself; **poner a algn en r.,** to make a fool of sb.

riego *nm* watering, irrigation; **r. sanguíneo**, blood circulation.

riel *nm* rail.

rienda *nf* rein; *fig* **dar r. suelta a**, to give free rein to; *fig* **llevar las riendas**, to hold the reins, be in control.

riesgo *nm* risk; **correr el r. de**, to run the risk of; **seguro a todo r.**, fully-comprehensive insurance.

rifa *nf* raffle.

rifar *vtr* to raffle (off).

rifle *nm* rifle.

rigidez *nf* rigidity, stiffness; *fig* *(severidad)* strictness, inflexibility.

rígido,-a *adj* rigid, stiff; *fig (severo)* strict, inflexible.

rigor *nm* rigour, *US* rigor; *(severidad)* severity; **con r.**, rigorously; **de r.**, indispensable.

riguroso,-a *adj* rigorous; *(severo)* severe, strict. ◆**rigurosamente** *adv* rigorously; *(meticulosamente)* meticulously; *(severamente)* severely; **r. cierto**, absolutely true.

rijo *indic pres* → **regir**.

rima *nf* rhyme.

rimar *vtr & vi* to rhyme (**con**, with).

rimbombante *adj (lenguaje)* pompous, pretentious.

rímel *nm* mascara.

Rin *n* **el R.**, the Rhine.

rincón *nm* corner; *fam (lugar remoto)* nook.

rinoceronte *nm* rhinoceros.

riña *nf (pelea)* fight; *(discusión)* row, quarrel.

riñón *nm* kidney; *fam* **costar un r.**, to cost an arm and a leg; *Med* **r. artificial**, kidney machine.

río *nm* river; **r. abajo**, downstream; **r. arriba**, upstream.

Rioja *n* Rioja.

rioplatense *adj* from *o* of Buenos Aires.

ripio *nm (palabras de relleno)* waffle; *fam* **no perder r.**, not to miss a trick.

riqueza *nf* 1 wealth. 2 *(cualidad)* wealthiness.

risa *nf* laugh; *(carcajadas)* laughter; **es (cosa) de r.**, it's laughable; **me da r.**, it makes me laugh; **tomarse algo a r.**, to laugh sth off; *fig* **morirse** *o* **mondarse de r.**, to die *o* fall about laughing; *fam* **mi hermano es una r.**, my brother is a laugh; *fam fig* **tener algo muerto de r.**, to leave sth lying around.

risco *nm* crag, cliff.

risible *adj* laughable.

risilla, risita *nf* giggle, titter; *(risa falsa)* false laugh.

risotada *nf* guffaw.

ristra *nf* string.

ristre *nm* **en r.**, at the ready.

risueño,-a *adj* smiling.

rítmico,-a *adj* rhythmic; **gimnasia rítmi-**

ca, eurhythmics *sing*, *US* eurythmics *sing*.

ritmo *nm* 1 rhythm. 2 *(paso)* rate; **llevar un buen r. de trabajo**, to work at a good pace.

rito *nm* 1 rite. 2 *(ritual)* ritual.

ritual *adj & nm* ritual.

rival *adj & nmf* rival.

rivalidad *nf* rivalry.

rivalizar [4] *vi* to rival (**en**, in).

rizado,-a *adj* 1 *(pelo)* curly. 2 *(mar)* choppy.

rizar [4] **I** *vtr (pelo)* to curl; *(tela, papel)* to crease; **r. el rizo**, *fig* to make things even more complicated. **II rizarse** *vr (pelo)* to curl, go curly.

rizo *nm* 1 *(de pelo)* curl. 2 *(en el agua)* ripple.

RNE *nf abr de* **Radio Nacional de España**.

robalo *nm (pez)* bass.

robar *vtr* 1 *(objeto)* to steal; *(banco, persona)* to rob; *(casa)* to burgle; *fig* **en aquel supermercado te roban**, they really rip you off in that supermarket. 2 *Naipes* to draw.

roble *nm* oak (tree).

robledal, robledo *nm* oak grove *o* wood.

robo *nm* robbery, theft; *(en casa)* burglary; *fam (timo)* rip-off.

robot *nm (pl* robots*)* robot; **r. de cocina**, food processor.

robótica *nf* robotics *sing*.

robustecer [33] *vtr* to strengthen.

robusto,-a *adj* robust, sturdy.

roca *nf* rock.

rocalla *nf* pebbles *pl*, stone chippings *pl*.

rocambolesco,-a *adj* incredible, farfetched.

roce *nm* 1 *(fricción)* rubbing; *(en la piel)* chafing. 2 *(marca) (en la pared etc)* scuff mark; *(en la piel)* chafing mark, graze. 3 *(contacto ligero)* brush, light touch. 4 *fam (trato entre personas)* contact. 5 *fam (discusión)* brush.

rociar [29] *vtr (salpicar)* to spray, sprinkle.

rocín *nm (nag, hack.*

rocío *nm* dew.

Rocosas *npl* **las R.**, the Rockies.

rocoso,-a *adj* rocky, stony.

rodaballo *nm (pez)* turbot.

rodado,-a *adj* 1 *(piedra)* smooth, rounded; **canto r.**, boulder. 2 **tráfico r.**, road traffic, vehicular traffic.

rodaja *nf* slice; **en rodajas**, sliced.

rodaje *nm* 1 *(filmación)* filming, shooting. 2 *Aut* running in.

Ródano *n* **el R.**, the Rhone.

rodante *adj* rolling.

rodar [2] **I** *vtr (película etc)* to film, shoot. **II** *vi* to roll, turn.

rodear **I** *vtr* to surround, encircle. **II rodearse** *vr* to surround oneself (**de**, with).

rodeo *nm* 1 *(desvío)* detour. 2 *(al hablar)*

evasiveness; **andarse con rodeos,** to beat about the bush; **no andarse con rodeos,** to get straight to the point. **3** *Am* rodeo.

rodilla *nf* knee; **de rodillas,** *(arrodillado)* kneeling; **hincarse/ponerse de rodillas,** to kneel down, go down on one's knees.

rodillera *nf (de pantalón)* knee patch; *Dep* knee pad.

rodillo *nm* roller; **r. de cocina,** rolling pin.

rododendro *nm* rhododendron.

roedor *nm* rodent.

roer [38] *vtr (hueso)* to gnaw; *(galleta)* to nibble at; *fig (conciencia)* to gnaw at, nag at; *fig* **un hueso duro de r.,** a hard nut to crack.

rogar [2] *vtr (pedir)* to request, ask; *(implorar)* to beg; **hacerse de r.,** to play hard to get; **'se ruega silencio',** 'silence please'; **rogamos disculpen la molestia,** please forgive the inconvenience.

roído,-a *adj* gnawed, eaten away.

rojizo,-a *adj* reddish.

rojo,-a **I** *adj* **1** red; *Fin* **estar en números rojos,** to be in the red. **2** *Pol (comunista)* red. **II** *nm (color)* red; **al r. vivo,** *(caliente)* red-hot; *fig (tenso)* very tense. **III** *nm,f Pol (comunista)* red.

rol *nm* role; **juego de r.,** role play.

rollizo,-a *adj* chubby, plump.

rollo *nm* **1** *(de papel etc)* roll. **2** *fam (pesadez)* drag, bore; **es el mismo r. de siempre,** it's the same old story; **un r. de libro,** a boring book. **3** *fam (amorío)* affair.

Roma *n* Rome.

romana *nf* calamares a la r., squid in batter.

romance *nm* **1** *(aventura amorosa)* romance. **2** *(idioma)* Romance; *fig* **hablar en r.,** to speak plainly. **3** *Lit* narrative poem, ballad.

románico,-a *adj & nf* Romanesque.

romanticismo *nm* romanticism.

romántico,-a *adj & nm,f* romantic.

rombo *nm* rhombus.

romería *nf Rel* pilgrimage.

romero *nm Bot* rosemary.

romo,-a *adj* **1** blunt. **2** *(nariz)* snub.

rompecabezas *nm inv (juego)* (jigsaw) puzzle; *fig (problema)* riddle, puzzle.

rompeolas *nm inv* breakwater, jetty.

romper *(pp* roto*)* **I** *vtr* **1** to break; *(papel, tela)* to tear; *(vajilla, cristal)* to smash, shatter. **2** *(relaciones)* to break off. **II** *vi* **1** *(olas, día)* to break. **2** *(acabar)* to break **(con,** with); **rompió con su novio,** she broke it off with her boyfriend. **3 r. a llorar,** to burst out crying; **r. en llanto,** to burst into tears. **III romperse** *vr* to break; *(papel, tela)* to tear; **se rompió por la mitad,** it broke *o* split in half; *fig* **r. la cabeza,** to rack one's brains.

ron *nm* rum.

roncar |1| *vi* to snore.

roncha *nf (en la piel)* swelling, lump.

ronco,-a *adj* hoarse; **quedarse r.,** to lose one's voice.

ronda *nf* **1** round; *(patrulla)* patrol. **2** *(carretera)* ring road; *(paseo)* avenue. **3 pagar una r.,** to pay for a round of drinks.

rondar **I** *vtr* **1** *(vigilar)* to patrol, do the rounds of. **2** *pey (merodear)* to prowl around, hang about. **3** *(estar cerca de)* to be about *o* approximately; **ronda los cuarenta,** she is about forty. **II** *vi* **1** *(vigilar)* to patrol. **2** *(merodear)* to prowl around, roam around.

ronquera *nf* hoarseness.

ronquido *nm* snore.

ronronear *vi* to purr.

ronroneo *nm* purring.

roña *nf* **1** *(mugre)* filth, dirt. **2** *Vet (sarna)* mange.

roñica *fam* **I** *adj* mean, stingy. **II** *nmf* scrooge, miser.

roñoso,-a *adj* **1** *(mugriento)* filthy, dirty. **2** *Vet (sarnoso)* mangy. **3** *fam (tacaño)* mean, stingy.

ropa *nf* clothes *pl,* clothing; *fig* **a quema r.,** point-blank; **r. blanca,** (household) linen; **r. interior,** underwear.

ropaje *nm* clothes.

ropero *nm (armario)* r., *US* (clothes) closet.

roque *nm* **1** *(en ajedrez)* rook. **2** *fam* **quedarse r.,** to fall fast asleep.

rosa **I** *adj inv (color)* pink; **novela r.,** romantic novel. **II** *nf Bot* rose; *(en la piel)* birthmark; **r. de los vientos,** compass (rose). **III** *nm (color)* pink.

rosáceo,-a *adj* rose-coloured, rosy.

rosado,-a **I** *adj (color)* pink, rosy; *(vino)* rosé. **II** *nm (vino)* rosé.

rosal *nm* rosebush.

rosaleda *nf* rose garden.

rosario *nm Rel* rosary; *(sarta)* string, series *sing.*

rosbif *nm* roast beef.

rosca *nf* **1** *(de tornillo)* thread; **tapón de r.,** screw top; *fig* **pasarse de r.,** to go too far. **2** *(espiral)* spiral, coil.

rosco *nm (pastel)* ring-shaped roll *o* pastry; *arg* **no comerse un r.,** not to get one's oats.

rosetón *nm* rose window.

rosquilla *nf* ring-shaped pastry; *fam fig* **venderse como rosquillas,** to sell like hot cakes.

rostro *nm* face; *fam* **tener mucho r.,** to have a lot of nerve; *fam* **¡vaya r.!,** what cheek!

rotación *nf* rotation.

rotativo,-a **I** *adj* rotary, revolving. **II** *nm* newspaper.

roto,-a **I** *adj* broken; *(papel)* torn; *(ropa)* in tatters, tattered. **II** *nm (agujero)* hole, tear.

rótula *nf* **1** *Anat* kneecap. **2** *Téc* ball-and-socket joint.

rotulador *nm* felt-tip pen.

rotular *vtr* to letter, label.

rótulo *nm* (*letrero*) sign, notice; (*titular*) title, heading.

rotundo,-a *adj* categorical; **éxito r.,** resounding success; **un no rotundo,** a flat refusal.

rotura *nf* (*ruptura*) breaking; *Med* fracture.

roturar *vtr* to plough, *US* plow.

roulotte *nf* caravan.

rozadura *nf* scratch, abrasion.

rozamiento *nm* rubbing, friction.

rozar |4| **I** *vtr* to touch, rub against, brush against. **II** *vi* to rub. **III rozarse** *vr* to rub, brush (**con**, against).

Rte. *abr de* **remite, remitente,** sender.

RTVE *nf abr de* **Radio Televisión Española.**

rubéola *nf* German measles *pl*, rubella.

rubí *nm* (*pl* **rubíes**) ruby.

rubicundo,-a *adj* rosy, reddish.

rubio,-a I *adj* (*pelo, persona*) fair, blond; **r. de bote,** peroxide blonde; **tabaco r.,** Virginia tobacco. **II** *nm,f* blond.

rublo *nm* rouble.

rubor *nm* blush, flush.

ruborizarse |4| *vr* to blush, go red.

ruboroso,-a *adj* blushing, bashful.

rúbrica *nf* 1 (*firma*) flourish added to a signature. 2 (*título*) title, heading.

rubricar |1| *vtr* 1 (*firmar*) to sign with a flourish. 2 (*respaldar*) to endorse, ratify.

rudeza *nf* roughness, coarseness.

rudimentario,-a *adj* rudimentary.

rudimento *nm* rudiment.

rudo,-a *adj* rough, coarse.

rueda *nf* 1 wheel; *Aut* **r. de recambio,** spare wheel; *Aut* **r. delantera/trasera,** front/rear wheel; **r. de prensa,** press conference; *fam* **ir sobre ruedas,** to go very smoothly. 2 (*rodaja*) round slice.

ruedo *nm* 1 *Taur* bullring, arena. 2 (*de falda*) hem.

ruego *nm* request.

rufián *nm* villain, scoundrel.

rugby *nm* rugby.

rugido *nm* (*de animal*) roar; (*del viento*) howl; (*de tripas*) rumbling *sing*.

rugir |6| *vi* to roar; (*viento*) to howl.

rugoso,-a *adj* rough.

ruibarbo *nm* rhubarb.

ruido *nm* noise; (*sonido*) sound; (*jaleo*) din, row; *fig* stir, commotion; **hacer r.,** to make a noise.

ruidoso,-a *adj* noisy, loud.

ruin *adj* 1 (*vil*) vile, despicable. 2 (*tacaño*) mean, stingy.

ruina *nf* ruin; (*derrumbamiento*) collapse; (*de persona*) downfall.

ruindad *nf* vileness, meanness; (*acto*) mean act, low trick.

ruinoso,-a *adj* dilapidated, tumbledown.

ruiseñor *nm* nightingale.

ruleta *nf* roulette.

rulo *nm* 1 (*para el pelo*) curler, roller. 2 *Culin* rolling pin.

rulot(a) *nf* (*pl* **rulots**) caravan.

Rumania *n* Rumania, Roumania.

rumba *nf* rhumba, rumba.

rumbo *nm* direction, course; (**con**) **r. a,** bound for, heading for.

rumiante *nm* ruminant.

rumiar |12| **I** *vtr* 1 (*mascar*) to chew. 2 *fig* (*pensar*) to ruminate, reflect on, chew over. **II** *vi* to ruminate, chew the cud.

rumor *nm* 1 rumour, *US* rumor. 2 (*murmullo*) murmur.

rumorearse *v impers* to be rumoured, *US* be rumored.

runrún, runruneo *nm* buzz, noise.

rupestre *adj* **pintura r.,** cave painting.

ruptura *nf* breaking; (*de relaciones*) breaking-off.

rural *adj* rural, country.

Rusia *n* Russia.

ruso,-a *adj & nm,f* Russian.

rústico,-a *adj* rustic, rural.

ruta *nf* route, road.

rutilar *vi* to sparkle.

rutina *nf* routine; **por r.,** as a matter of course.

rutinario,-a *adj* routine.

S

S, s |'ese| *nf* (*la letra*) S,s.

S *abr de* **Sur,** South, S.

S. *abr de* **San o Santo,** Saint, St.

s. *abr de* **siglo,** century, c.

S.A. *abr de* **Sociedad Anónima,** PLC, plc.

sábado *nm* Saturday.

sabana *nf* savannah.

sábana *nf* sheet; *fam* **se me pegaron las sábanas,** I overslept.

sabandija *nf* (*insecto*) creepy-crawly; (*persona*) creep.

sabañón *nm* chilblain.

sabático,-a *adj* sabbatical.

sabelotodo *nmf inv* know-all.

saber¹ *nm* knowledge.

saber² |21| **I** *vtr* 1 to know; **hacer s.,** to inform; **para que lo sepas,** for your information; **que yo sepa,** as far as I know; **vete tú a s.,** goodness knows; **¡y yo qué sé!,** how should I know!; *fig* **a s.,** namely. 2 (*tener habilidad*) to be able to; **¿sabes cocinar?,** can you cook?; **¿sabes hablar inglés?,** can you speak English? 3 (*enterarse*) to learn, find out; **lo supe**

ayer, I found this out yesterday. **II** *vi* 1 (*tener sabor a*) to taste (**a**, of); **sabe a fresa**, it tastes of strawberries; *fig* **me sabe mal**, I feel guilty o bad about that. 2 *Am* (*soler*) to be accustomed to.

sabido,-a *adj* known; **como es s.**, as everyone knows.

sabiduría *nf* wisdom.

sabiendas (a) *loc adv* **lo hizo a s.**, he did it in the full knowledge of what he was doing; **a s. de que ...**, knowing full well that ....

sabihondo,-a *fam nm,f* (*sabelotodo*) know-all; (*pedante*) pedant.

sabio,-a I *adj* (*prudente*) wise. **II** *nm,f* scholar.

sabiondo,-a *adj fam* → **sabihondo,-a**.

sable *nm* sabre, *US* saber.

sabor *nm* (*gusto*) taste, flavour, *US* flavor; **con s. a limón**, lemon-flavoured; **sin s.**, tasteless; **me deja mal s. de boca**, it leaves a bad taste in my mouth.

saborear *vtr* (*degustar*) to taste; *fig* (*apreciar*) to savour, *US* savor.

sabotaje *nm* sabotage.

saboteador,-a *nm,f* saboteur.

sabotear *vtr* to sabotage.

sabré *indic fut* → **saber**.

sabroso,-a *adj* 1 tasty; (*delicioso*) delicious. 2 (*agradable*) delightful.

sabueso *nm* bloodhound.

sacacorchos *nm inv* corkscrew.

sacamuelas *nmf inv fam* dentist.

sacapuntas *nm inv* pencil sharpener.

sacar [1] *vtr* 1 to take out; (*con más fuerza*) to pull out; **s. dinero del banco**, to withdraw money from the bank; **s. la lengua**, to stick one's tongue out; *fig* **s. faltas a algo**, to find fault with sth; *fig* **s. adelante**, to help to get on; **s. provecho de algo**, to benefit from sth; **s. algo en claro o en limpio**, to make sense of sth. 2 (*obtener*) to get; (*dinero*) to get, make; (*conclusiones*) to draw, reach; (*entrada*) to get, buy. 3 (*producto*) to bring out; (*nueva moda*) to bring in; (*libro, disco*) to bring out. 4 (*fotografía*) to take; (*fotocopia*) to make. 5 *Ten* to serve; *Ftb* to kick off.

sacarina *nf* saccharin.

sacerdotal *adj* priestly.

sacerdote *nm* priest; **sumo s.**, high priest.

saciar [12] *vtr* to satiate; (*sed*) to quench; (*deseos, hambre*) to satisfy; (*ambiciones*) to fulfil, *US* fulfill.

saciedad *nf* satiety; **repetir algo hasta la s.**, to repeat sth ad nauseam.

saco *nm* 1 sack; **s. de dormir**, sleeping bag. 2 *Mil* **entrar a s. en una ciudad**, to pillage a town. 3 *Am* (*chaqueta*) jacket.

sacralizar [4] *vtr* to consecrate.

sacramento *nm* sacrament.

sacrificar [1] **I** *vtr* to sacrifice. **II** **sacrificarse** *vr* to make a sacrifice o sacrifices.

sacrificio *nm* sacrifice.

sacrilegio *nm* sacrilege.

sacrílego,-a *adj* sacrilegious.

sacristán *nm* verger, sexton.

sacristía *nf* vestry, sacristy.

sacro,-a *adj* sacred.

sacudida *nf* 1 shake; (*espasmo*) jolt, jerk; **s. eléctrica**, electric shock. 2 (*de terremoto*) tremor.

sacudir *vtr* 1 (*agitar*) to shake; (*alfombra, sábana*) to shake out; (*arena, polvo*) to shake off. 2 (*golpear*) to beat. 3 (*conmover*) to shock, stun.

sádico,-a I *adj* sadistic. **II** *nm,f* sadist.

sadismo *nm* sadism.

sadomasoquista I *adj* sadomasochistic. **II** *nmf* sadomasochist.

saeta *nf* 1 (*dardo*) dart. 2 (*canción*) popular religious song.

safari *nm* (*cacería*) safari; (*parque*) safari park.

sagacidad *nf fml* (*listeza*) cleverness; (*astucia*) astuteness, shrewdness.

sagaz *adj* (*listo*) clever; (*astuto*) astute, shrewd.

Sagitario *nm* Sagittarius.

sagrado,-a *adj* sacred.

sagrario *nm* tabernacle.

Sáhara *n* Sahara.

saharaui *adj & nmf* Saharan.

sahariana *nf* safari jacket.

sainete *nm Teat* comic sketch, one-act farce.

sajón,-ona *adj & nm,f* Saxon.

sal *nf* 1 salt; **s. fina**, table salt; **s. gema**, salt crystals; **s. gorda**, cooking salt. 2 *fig* (*gracia*) wit.

sal *imperat* → **salir**.

sala *nf* room; (*en un hospital*) ward; *Jur* courtroom. **s. de estar**, lounge, living room; **s. de espera**, waiting room; **s. de exposiciones**, exhibition hall; **s. de fiestas**, nightclub, discotheque; **s. de lectura**, reading room.

salado,-a *adj* 1 (*con sal*) salted; (*con exceso de sal*) salty; **agua salada**, salt water. 2 *fig* (*encantador*) charming. 3 *Am* (*infortunado*) unlucky.

salamandra *nf* salamander.

salamanquesa *nf* gecko.

salame, salami *nm* salami.

salar *vtr* to salt, add salt to.

salarial *adj* salary, wage.

salario *nm* salary, wages *pl*; **s. mínimo**, minimum wage.

salazón *nm* salted meat o fish.

salchicha *nf* sausage.

salchichón *nm* (*salami-type*) sausage.

saldar *vtr* 1 *Fin* (*cuenta*) to settle; (*deuda*) to pay off. 2 *Com* (*vender barato*) to sell off. 3 *fig* (*diferencias*) to settle, resolve.

saldo *nm* 1 **saldos**, sales; **a precio de s.**, at bargain prices. 2 *Fin* balance. 3 (*de* *una deuda)* liquidation, settlement. 4 *(resto de mercancía)* remainder, leftover.

saldré *indic fut* → salir.

saledizo,-a *adj* projecting.

salero *nm* 1 *(recipiente)* saltcellar. 2 *fig (gracia)* charm.

salgo *indic pres* → salir.

salida *nf* 1 *(partida)* departure; *(puerta etc)* exit, way out; **callejón sin s.**, dead end; **s. de emergencia**, emergency exit. 2 *Dep* start; **línea de s.**, starting line; **s. nula**, false start. 3 **te vi a la s. del cine**, I saw you leaving the cinema. 4 *(de un astro)* rising; **s. del sol**, sunrise. 5 *(profesional)* opening; *Com* outlet. 6 *(recurso)* solution, way out; **no tengo otra s.**, I have no other option. 7 *fam (ocurrencia)* witty remark, witticism. 8 *Inform* output.

salido,-a *adj* 1 prominent, projecting. 2 *vulg (persona)* horny.

saliente *adj* 1 projecting, prominent; *fig* outstanding. 2 *(cesante)* outgoing.

salina *nf* salt mine.

salino,-a *adj* saline.

salir [22] **I** *vi* 1 *(de un sitio)* to go out, leave; *(venir de dentro)* to come out; **salió de la habitación**, she left the room; **s. de la carretera**, to turn off the road. 2 *(tren etc)* to depart. 3 *(novios)* to go out *(con, with)*. 4 *(aparecer)* to appear; *(revista, disco)* to come out; *(ley)* to come in; *(trabajo, vacante)* to come up. 5 *(resultar)* to turn out, turn out to be; **el pequeño les ha salido muy listo**, their son has turned out to be very clever; **¿cómo te salió el examen?**, how did your exam go?; **s. ganando**, to come out ahead or on top; **salió presidente**, he was elected president. 6 **s. a,** *(precio)* to come to, to work out at; **s. barato/caro**, to work out cheap/ expensive. 7 **ha salido al abuelo**, she takes after her grandfather. 8 *(problema)* to work out; **esta cuenta no me sale**, I can't work this sum out. 8 **¡con qué cosas sales!**, the things you come out with! **II salirse** *vr* 1 *(líquido, gas)* to leak (out); *fig* **s. de lo normal**, to be out of the ordinary; **se salió de la carretera**, he went off the road. 2 *fam* **s. con la suya**, to get one's own way.

saliva *nf* saliva.

salivar *vi* to salivate.

salivazo *nm* spit.

salmantino,-a I *adj* of *o* from Salamanca. **II** *nm,f* native *o* inhabitant of Salamanca.

salmo *nm* psalm.

salmón I *nm (pescado)* salmon. **II** *adj inv (color)* salmon pink, salmon.

salmonete *nm (pescado)* red mullet.

salmorejo *nm (salsa)* sauce made from vinegar, water, pepper and salt.

salmuera *nf* brine.

salobre *adj (agua)* brackish; *(gusto)* salty, briny.

salón *nm* 1 *(en una casa)* lounge, sitting room. 2 **s. de actos**, assembly hall; **s. de baile**, dance hall. 3 **s. de belleza**, beauty salon; **s. de té**, tearoom, teashop. 4 **s. del automóvil**, motor show.

salpicadura *nf* splashing.

salpicar [1] *vtr* 1 *(rociar)* to splash; **me salpicó el abrigo de barro**, he splashed mud on my coat. 2 *fig (esparcir)* to sprinkle.

salpicón *nm* 1 splash. 2 *Culin* cocktail.

salpimentar [1] *vtr* to season.

salpullido *nm* rash.

salsa *nf n* sauce; *(de carne)* gravy; *fig* **en su (propia) s.**, in one's element.

saltador,-a *nm,f Dep* jumper.

saltamontes *nm inv* grasshopper.

saltar I *vtr (obstáculo, valla)* to jump (over). **II** *vi* 1 to jump; *fig* **s. a la vista**, to be obvious. 2 *(cristal etc)* to break, shatter; *(plomos)* to go, blow. 3 *(desprenderse)* to come off. 4 *(encolerizarse)* to explode, blow up; **por menos de nada salta**, the smallest thing makes him explode. **III saltarse** *vr* 1 *(omitir)* to skip, miss out; **s. el semáforo/turno**, to jump the lights/the queue. 2 *(botón)* to come off; **se me saltaron las lágrimas**, tears came to my eyes.

salteado,-a *adj* 1 *(espaciado)* spaced out. 2 *Culin* sauté, sautéed.

saltear *vtr Culin* to sauté.

saltimbanqui *nmf* acrobat, tumbler.

salto *nm* 1 *(acción)* jump, leap; *fig (paso adelante)* leap forward; **a saltos**, in leaps and bounds; **dar** *o* **pegar un s.**, to jump, leap; **de un s.**, in a flash; *fig* **a s. de mata**, every now and then; **s. de agua**, waterfall; **s. de cama**, negligée. 2 *Dep* jump; **s. de altura**, high jump; **s. de longitud**, long jump; **s. mortal**, somersault.

saltón,-ona *adj* prominent; **ojos saltones**, bulging eyes.

salubre *adj* salubrious.

salubridad *nf* healthiness; **por razones de s.**, for health reasons.

salud *nf* health; **beber a la s. de algn**, to drink to sb's health; *fam* **¡s.!**, cheers!

saludable *adj* 1 *(sano)* healthy, wholesome. 2 *fig (beneficioso)* good, beneficial.

saludar *vtr* 1 *(decir hola a)* to say hello to, to greet; **saluda de mi parte a**, give my regards to; **le saluda atentamente**, *(en una carta)* yours faithfully. 2 *Mil* to salute.

saludo *nm* 1 greeting; **un s. de**, best wishes from. 2 *Mil* salute.

salva *nf Mil* salvo, volley.

salvación *nf* salvation.

salvado *nm* bran.

salvador,-a I *nm,f* saviour; *(rescatador)* rescuer. **II** *nm* **El S.**, El Salvador.

salvadoreño,-a *adj & nm,f* Salvadoran,

Salvadorian.
salvaguarda *nf* → **salvaguardia**.
salvaguardar *vtr* to safeguard (**de**, from), protect (**de**, from).
salvajada *nf* brutal act.
salvaje *adj* **1** *Bot* wild, uncultivated; *Zool* wild; (*pueblo, tribu*) savage, uncivilized. **2** *fam* (*violento*) savage, wild.
salvajismo *nm* savagery.
salvamento, salvamiento *nm* rescue.
salvar I *vtr* **1** to save, rescue (**de**, from). **2** (*obstáculo*) to clear; (*dificultad*) to get round, overcome. **3** (*exceptuar*) to exclude, except; **salvando ciertos errores**, except for a few mistakes. **II salvarse** *vr* **1** (*sobrevivir*) to survive, come out alive; *fam* (*escaparse*) to escape (**de**, from); **¡sálvese quien pueda!**, every man for himself!; *fam* **s. por los pelos**, to have a narrow escape. **2** *Rel* to be saved, save one's soul.
salvavidas *nm inv* life belt.
salvedad *nf* **1** (*excepción*) exception. **2** (*reserva*) proviso.
salvia *nf Bot* sage.
salvo,-a I *adj* unharmed, safe; **a s.**, safe. **II** *adv* (*exceptuando*) except (for); **s. que**, unless.
salvoconducto *nm* safe-conduct.
san *adj* saint; → **santo,-a**.
sanar I *vtr* (*curar*) to cure, heal. **II** *vi* **1** (*persona*) to recover, get better. **2** (*herida*) to heal.
sanatorio *nm* sanatorium.
sanción *nf* **1** sanction. **2** (*aprobación*) sanction, approval. **3** *Jur* penalty.
sancionar *vtr* **1** (*castigar*) to penalize. **2** (*aprobar*) to sanction.
sancochar *vtr* to parboil; *Am* to boil meat in water and salt.
sandalia *nf* sandal.
sándalo *nm* sandalwood.
sandez *nf* piece of nonsense.
sandía *nf* watermelon.
sandwich *nm* sandwich.
sandwichera *nf* toasted sandwich maker.
saneamiento *nm* (*de terreno*) drainage, draining; (*de una empresa*) reorganisation.
sanear *vtr* (*terrenos*) to drain; (*empresa*) to reorganise.
sangrar I *vtr* **1** to bleed. **2** *fam* (*sacar dinero*) to bleed dry. **II** *vi* to bleed.
sangre *nf* blood; **donar s.**, to give blood; **s. fría**, sang-froid; **a s. fría**, in cold blood.
sangría *nf* **1** *Med* bleeding, bloodletting; *fig* drain. **2** (*timo*) rip-off. **3** (*bebida*) sangría.
sangriento,-a *adj* (*guerra etc*) bloody.
sanguijuela *nf* leech, bloodsucker.
sanguinario,-a *adj* bloodthirsty.
sanguíneo,-a *adj* blood; **grupo s.**, blood group.
sanidad *nf* health; **Ministerio de S.**,

Department of Health.
sanitario,-a I *adj* health. **II** *nm* toilet.
sano,-a *adj* **1** (*bien de salud*) healthy; **s. y salvo**, safe and sound. **2** (*comida*) healthy, wholesome. **3** **en su s. juicio**, in one's right mind.
santiamén *nm fam* **en un s.**, in a flash, in no time at all.
santidad *nf* saintliness, holiness.
santificar [1] *vtr* to sanctify.
santiguarse [22] *vr* to cross oneself.
santo,-a I *adj* **1** holy, sacred. **2** (*bueno*) saintly; **un s. varón**, a saint. **II** *nm,f* **1** saint; *fam* **¡por todos los santos!**, for heaven's sake!; *fig* **se me fue el s. al cielo**, I clean forgot. **2** (*día onomástico*) saint's day; *fig* **¿a s. de qué?**, why on earth?
santuario *nm* sanctuary, shrine.
saña *nf* fury; **con s.**, furiously.
sapo *nm* toad; *fam* **echar sapos y culebras**, to rant and rave.
saque *nm* **1** *Ftb* **s. inicial**, kick-off; **s. de banda**, throw-in; **s. de esquina**, corner kick. **2** *Ten* service.
saquear *vtr* (*ciudad*) to sack, plunder; (*casas, tiendas*) to loot.
saqueo *nm* (*de ciudades*) sacking, plundering; (*de casa, tienda*) looting.
S.A.R. *abr de* **Su Alteza Real**, His o Her Royal Highness, H.R.H.
sarampión *nm* measles *pl*.
sarao *nm* knees-up.
sarcasmo *nm* sarcasm.
sarcástico,-a *adj* sarcastic.
sarcófago *nm* sarcophagus.
sardana *nf* sardana (Catalan dance and music).
sardina *nf* sardine.
sardónico,-a *adj* sardonic.
sargento *nm* sergeant.
sarmiento *nm* vine shoot.
sarna *nf Med* scabies *sing*; *Zool* mange.
sarpullido *nm* rash.
sarracina *nf* massacre.
sarro *nm* (*sedimento*) deposit; (*en los dientes*) tartar; (*en la lengua*) fur.
sarta *nf* string.
sartén *nf* frying pan, *US* skillet; *fig* **tener la s. por el mango**, to have the upper hand.
sastre *nm* tailor.
Satanás *nm* Satan.
satánico,-a *adj* satanic.
satélite *nm* satellite; *fig* **país s.**, satellite state; **televisión vía s.**, satellite TV.
satén *nm* satin.
satinar *vtr* to gloss, make glossy.
sátira *nf* satire.
satírico,-a *adj* satirical.
satirizar [4] *vtr* to satirize.
satisfacción *nf* satisfaction; **s. de un deseo**, fulfilment of a desire.
satisfacer [15] (*pp* **satisfecho**) *vtr* **1** (*de-*

seos, necesidades) to satisfy. **2** (*requisitos*) to meet, satisfy. **3** (*deuda*) to pay.

satisfactorio,-a *adj* satisfactory.

satisfecho,-a *adj* satisfied; **me doy por s.**, that's good enough for me; **s. de sí mismo**, self-satisfied, smug.

saturar *vtr* to saturate.

Saturno *nm* Saturn.

sauce *nm* willow; **s. llorón**, weeping willow.

saudí, saudita *adj & nmf* Saudi; **Arabia Saudita**, Saudi Arabia.

sauna *nf* sauna.

savia *nf* sap.

saxo *nm Mús fam* sax.

saxofón *nm* saxophone.

saxofonista *nmf* saxophonist.

sayo *nm* cassock, smock.

sazonar *vtr* to season, flavour, *US* flavor.

s/c. *abr de* **su cuenta**, your account.

Sdad. *abr de* **sociedad**, Society, Soc.

se¹ *pron* **1** (*reflexivo*) (*objeto directo*) (*a él mismo*) himself; (*animal*) itself; (*a ella misma*) herself; (*animal*) itself; (*a usted mismo*) yourself; (*a ellos mismos*) themselves; (*a ustedes mismos*) yourselves. **2** (*objeto indirecto*) (*a él mismo*) (to o for) himself; (*animal*) (to o for) itself; (*a ella misma*) (to o for) herself; (*animal*) (to o for) itself; (*a usted mismo*) (to o for) yourself; (*a ellos mismos*) (to o for) themselves; (*a ustedes mismos*) (to o for) yourselves; **se compró un nuevo coche**, he bought himself a new car; **todos los días se lava el pelo**, she washes her hair every day. **3** (*recíproco*) one another, each other. **4** (*voz pasiva*) **el vino se guarda en cubas**, wine is kept in casks. **5** (*impersonal*) **nunca se sabe**, you never know; **se habla inglés**, English spoken; **se dice que ...**, it is said that ....

se² *pron pers* (*a él*) (to o for) him; (*a ella*) (to o for) her; (*a usted o ustedes*) (to o for) you; (*a ellos*) (to o for) them; **se lo diré en cuanto los vea**, I'll tell them as soon as I see them; **¿se lo explico?**, shall I explain it to you?; **¿se lo has dado ya?**, have you given it to him yet?

sé¹ *indic pres* → **saber**.

sé² *imperat* → **ser**.

S.E. *abr de* **Su Excelencia**, His o Her Excellency, HE.

sea *subj pres* → **ser**.

sebo *nm* (*grasa*) fat.

secado *nm* drying.

secador,-a **I** *nm* dryer, drier; **s. de pelo**, hairdryer. **II** *nf* tumble dryer.

secano *nm* dry land.

secante *adj* **papel s.**, blotting paper.

secar [1] **I** *vtr* to dry. **II secarse** *vr* **1** to dry; **sécate**, dry yourself; **s. las manos**, to dry one's hands. **2** (*marchitarse*) to dry up, wither.

sección *nf* section.

seco,-a *adj* **1** dry; **frutos secos**, dried fruit; **limpieza en s.**, dry-cleaning; *fig* **a palo s.**, on its own; *fig* **a secas**, just, only. **2** (*tono*) curt, sharp; (*golpe, ruido*) sharp; *fig* **frenar en s.**, to pull up sharply; *fig* **parar en s.**, to stop dead. **3** (*delgado*) skinny.

secreción *nf* secretion.

secretaría *nf* (*oficina*) secretary's office; **S. de Estado**, State Department.

secretariado *nm* **1** (*oficina*) secretariat. **2** *Educ* secretarial course.

secretario,-a *nm,f* secretary.

secreto,-a **I** *adj* secret; **en s.**, in secret, secretly. **II** *nm* secret; **guardar un s.**, to keep a secret; **con mucho s.**, in great secrecy.

secta *nf* sect.

sectario,-a *adj* sectarian.

sector *nm* **1** sector. **2** (*zona*) area; **un s. de la ciudad**, an area of the city.

sectorial *adj* sectoral.

secuela *nf* consequence.

secuencia *nf* sequence.

secuestrador,-a *nm,f* **1** (*de persona*) kidnapper; (*de un avión*) hijacker. **2** *Jur* sequestrator.

secuestrar *vtr* **1** (*persona*) to kidnap; (*aviones*) to hijack. **2** *Jur* to confiscate.

secuestro *nm* **1** (*de persona*) kidnapping; (*de un avión*) highjacking. **2** *Jur* confiscation.

secular *adj* **1** *Rel* secular, lay. **2** (*antiquísimo*) ancient, age-old.

secundar *vtr* to back.

secundario,-a *adj* secondary.

secuoya *nf Bot* redwood, sequoia; **s. gigante**, giant sequoia.

sed *nf* thirst; **tener s.**, to be thirsty.

seda *nf* silk.

sedal *nm* fishing line.

sedante *adj & nm* sedative.

sede *nf* **1** headquarters, head office; (*de gobierno*) seat. **2 la Santa S.**, the Holy See.

sedentario,-a *adj* sedentary.

sedición *nf* sedition.

sedicioso,-a **I** *adj* rebellious. **II** rebel.

sediento,-a *adj* thirsty; *fig* **s. de poder**, hungry for power.

sedimentarse *vr* to settle.

sedimentario,-a *adj* sedimentary.

sedimento *nm* sediment, deposit.

sedoso,-a *adj* silky, silken.

seducción *nf* seduction.

seducir [10] *vtr* to seduce; (*persuadir*) to tempt.

seductor,-a **I** *adj* seductive; (*persuasivo*) tempting. **II** *nm,f* seducer.

segadora *nf* (*máquina*) reaper, harvester.

segar [1] *vtr* to reap, cut.

seglar **I** *adj* secular, lay. **II** *nmf* lay person; (*hombre*) layman; (*mujer*) laywoman.

segmento *nm* segment.
segregación *nf* 1 (*separación*) segregation. 2 (*secreción*) secretion.
segregar |7| *vtr* 1 (*separar*) to segregate. 2 (*secretar*) to secrete.
seguida *nf* en s., immediately, straight away.
seguido,-a *adj* 1 (*continuo*) continuous. 2 (*consecutivo*) consecutive, successive; **tres veces seguidas**, on three consecutive occasions; **tres lunes seguidos**, three Mondays in a row.
seguido *adv* straight; **todo s.**, straight on, straight ahead.
seguidor,-a *nm,f* follower.
seguimiento *nm* 1 pursuit. 2 *Prensa* in-depth coverage. 3 **estación de s.** (*espacial*), tracking station.
seguir |6| I *vtr* 1 to follow. 2 (*camino*) to continue. 3 (*perseguir*) to chase. II *vi* 1 to follow. 2 s. + ger, (*continuar*) to continue, go on, keep on; **siguió hablando**, he continued *o* went on *o* kept on speaking. 3 s. + adj/pp, to continue to be, be still; **sigo resfriado**, I've still got the cold; **sigue con vida**, he's still alive. III **seguirse** *vr* to follow, ensue.
según I *prep* 1 according to; **s. la Biblia**, according to the Bible. 2 (*en función de*) depending on; **varía s. el tiempo (que haga)**, it varies depending on the weather. II *adv* 1 depending on; **s. estén las cosas**, depending on how things stand; **¿vendrás mañana? - s.**, will you come tomorrow? - it depends. 2 (*tal como*) just as; **estaba s. lo dejé**, it was just as I had left it. 3 (*a medida que*) as; **s. iba leyendo ...**, as I read on ....
segundero *nm* second hand.
segundo,-a¹ I *adj* second; *fig* **decir algo con segundas (intenciones)**, to say sth with a double meaning. II *nm,f* (*de una serie*) second (one).
segundo² *nm* (*tiempo*) second; **sesenta segundos**, sixty seconds.
seguramente *adv* 1 (*seguro*) surely. 2 (*probablemente*) most probably; **s. no lloverá**, it isn't likely to rain.
seguridad *nf* 1 security; **cerradura de s.**, security lock. 2 (*física*) safety; **s. en carretera**, road safety; **para mayor s.**, to be on the safe side. 3 (*confianza*) confidence; **s. en sí mismo**, self-confidence. 4 (*certeza*) sureness; **con toda s.**, most probably; **tener la s. de que ...**, to be certain that .... 5 **S. Social**, ≈ Social Security, *GB* National Health Service. 6 (*fiabilidad*) reliability.
seguro,-a I *adj* 1 (*cierto*) sure; **estoy s. de que ...**, I am sure that ...; **dar algo por s.**, to take sth for granted. 2 (*libre de peligro*) safe; *fig* **ir sobre s.**, to play safe. 3 (*protegido*) secure. 4 (*fiable*) reliable. 5 **está segura de ella misma**, she has self-

confidence. 6 (*firme*) steady, firm. II *nm* 1 *Seg* insurance; **s. a todo riesgo**, fully comprehensive insurance; **s. contra terceros**, third party insurance; **s. de vida**, life insurance. 2 (*dispositivo*) safety catch *o* device. III *adv* for sure, definitely.
seis *adj & nm inv* six.
seiscientos,-as *adj & nm,f* six hundred.
seísmo *nm* (*terremoto*) earthquake; (*temblor de tierra*) earth tremor.
selección *nf* 1 selection. 2 *Dep* team.
seleccionador,-a *nm,f* 1 selector. 2 *Dep* manager.
seleccionar *vtr* to select.
selectividad *nf* selectivity; *Univ* (**prueba de**) **s.**, entrance examination.
selectivo,-a *adj* selective.
selecto,-a *adj* select; **ambiente s.**, exclusive atmosphere.
self-service *nm* self-service cafeteria.
selva *nf* jungle.
sellar *vtr* (*documento*) to seal; (*carta*) to stamp.
sello *nm* 1 (*de correos*) stamp; (*para documentos*) seal. 2 (*precinto*) seal.
semáforo *nm* traffic lights *pl*.
semana *nf* week; **entre s.**, during the week; **S. Santa**, Holy Week.
semanal *adj & nm* weekly.
semanario *nm* weekly magazine.
semblante *nm* *lit* (*cara*) face; *fig* (*aspecto*) look.
sembrado *nm* sown field.
sembrar |26| *vtr* 1 *Agr* to sow. 2 *fig* **s. el pánico**, to spread panic.
semejante I *adj* 1 (*parecido*) similar; **nunca he visto nada s.**, I've never seen anything like it. 2 *pey* (*comparativo*) such; **s. desvergüenza**, such insolence. II *nm* (*prójimo*) fellow being.
semejanza *nf* similarity, likeness.
semen *nm* semen.
semental *nm* stud.
semestral *adj* half-yearly.
semestre *nm* six-month period, semester.
semicírculo *nm* semicircle.
semifinal *nf* semifinal.
semifinalista *nmf* semifinalist.
semilla *nf* seed.
semillero *nm* seedbed.
seminario *nm* 1 *Educ* seminar. 2 *Rel* seminary.
sémola *nf* semolina.
Sena *n el* **S.**, the Seine.
senado *nm* senate.
senador,-a *nm,f* senator.
sencillez *nf* simplicity.
sencillo,-a *adj* 1 (*fácil*) simple, easy. 2 (*natural*) natural, unaffected. 3 (*billete*) single. 4 (*sin adornos*) simple, plain.
senda *nf*, **sendero** *nm* path.
sendos,-as *adj pl* one each; **con sendas carteras**, each carrying a briefcase.

senil adj senile.

seno nm 1 (pecho) breast. 2 fig bosom, heart; **en el s. de**, within. 3 Mat sine.

sensación nf 1 sensation, feeling; **tengo la s. de que ...**, I have a feeling that .... 2 (impresión) sensation; **causar s.**, to cause a sensation.

sensacional adj sensational.

sensacionalista adj sensationalist; **prensa s.**, gutter press.

sensato,-a adj sensible.

sensibilizar [4] vtr to make aware; **s. a la opinión pública**, to increase public awareness.

sensible adj 1 sensitive. 2 (perceptible) perceptible. ◆**sensiblemente** adv noticeably, considerably.

sensiblero,-a adj over-sentimental, mawkish.

sensitivo,-a adj sense; **órgano s.**, sense organ.

sensorial, sensorio,-a adj sensory.

sensual adj sensual.

sensualidad nf sensuality.

sentada nf 1 sitting. 2 fam (protesta) sit-in (demonstration).

sentado,-a adj (establecido) established, settled; **dar algo por s.**, to take sth for granted; **dejar s. que ...**, to make it clear that ....

sentar [1] I vtr 1 to sit. 2 (establecer) to establish; **s. las bases**, to lay the foundations. II vi 1 (color, ropa etc) to suit; **el pelo corto le sienta mal**, short hair doesn't suit you. 2 **s. bien/mal a**, (comida) to agree/disagree with; **la sopa te sentará bien**, the soup will do you good. 3 **le sentó mal la broma**, she didn't like the joke. II **sentarse** vr to sit, sit down.

sentencia nf 1 sentence; **visto para s.**, ready for judgement. 2 (aforismo) maxim, saying.

sentenciar [12] vtr Jur to sentence (a, to).

sentido,-a I nm 1 sense; **los cinco sentidos**, the five senses; **s. común**, common sense; **s. del humor**, sense of humour. 2 (significado) meaning; **doble s.**, double meaning; **no tiene s.**, it doesn't make sense. 3 (dirección) direction; **(de) s. único**, one-way. 4 (conciencia) consciousness; **perder el s.**, to faint. II adj deeply felt; fml **mi más s. pésame**, my deepest sympathy.

sentimental I adj sentimental; **vida s.**, love life. II nmf sentimental person.

sentimiento nm 1 feeling. 2 (pesar) sorrow, grief; fml **le acompaño en el s.**, my deepest sympathy.

sentir[1] nm 1 (sentimiento) feeling. 2 (opinión) opinion, view.

sentir[2] [5] I vtr 1 to feel; **s. hambre/calor**, to feel hungry/hot. 2 (lamentar) to regret, be sorry about; **lo siento (mu-** cho), I'm (very) sorry; **siento molestarle**, I'm sorry to bother you. II **sentirse** vr to feel; **me siento mal**, I feel ill; **s. con ánimos de hacer algo**, to feel like doing sth.

senyera nf Catalan flag.

seña nf 1 mark. 2 (gesto) sign; **hacer señas a algn**, to signal to sb. 3 (indicio) sign. 3 **señas**, (dirección) address sing.

señal nf 1 (indicio) sign, indication; **en s. de**, as a sign of, as a token of. 2 (placa) sign; **s. de tráfico**, road sign. 3 (gesto etc) signal, sign. 4 (marca) mark; (vestigio) trace. 5 Tel tone; **s. de llamada**, dialling o US dial tone. 6 Com deposit.

señalado,-a adj (importante) important; **un día s.**, a red-letter day.

señalar I vtr 1 (indicar) to mark, indicate; **s. con el dedo**, to point at. 2 (resaltar) to point out. 3 (precio, fecha) to fix, arrange.

señor nm 1 (hombre) man; (caballero) gentleman. 2 Rel **El S.**, the Lord. 3 (con apellido) Mr; (tratamiento de respeto) sir; **el Sr. Gutiérrez**, Mr Gutiérrez; **muy s. mío**, (en carta) Dear Sir. 4 (con título) (no se traduce) **el s. ministro**, the Minister.

señora nf 1 (mujer) woman; fml lady; **¡señoras y señores!**, ladies and gentlemen! 2 Rel **Nuestra S.**, Our Lady. 3 (con apellido) Mrs; (tratamiento de respeto) madam; **la Sra. Salinas**, Mrs Salinas; **muy s. mía**, (en carta) Dear Madam. 4 (con título) (no se traduce) **la s. ministra**, the Minister. 5 (esposa) wife.

señoría nf 1 Jur (hombre) lordship; (mujer) ladyship. 2 Pol **sus señorías**, the honourable gentlemen.

señorita nf 1 (joven) young woman; fml young lady. 2 (tratamiento de respeto) Miss; **S. Padilla**, Miss Padilla. 3 Educ **la s.**, the teacher, Miss.

señuelo nm (en caza) decoy.

sepa subj pres → **saber**.

separación nf 1 separation. 2 Jur **s. conyugal**, legal separation. 2 (espacio) space, gap.

separado,-a adj 1 separate; **por s.**, separately, individually. 2 (divorciado) separated.

separar I vtr 1 to separate. 2 (desunir) to detach, remove. 3 (dividir) to divide, separate. 4 (apartar) to move away. II **separarse** vr 1 to separate, part company. 2 (matrimonio) to separate. 3 (apartarse) to move away (**de**, from).

separata nf offprint.

separatismo nm separatism.

separatista adj & nmf separatist.

sepia I nf (pez) cuttlefish. II adj & nm (color) sepia.

septentrional adj northern.

septiembre[*] nm September; **el 5 de s.**, the 5th of September; **en s.**, in September.

séptimo,-a *adj & nm,f* seventh; **la** *o* **una séptima parte**, a seventh.

sepulcral *adj (silencio)* deathly.

sepulcro *nm* tomb.

sepultura *nf* grave.

sepulturero,-a *nm,f* gravedigger.

sequía *nf* drought.

séquito *nm* entourage, retinue.

SER *nf Rad TV abr de* **Sociedad Española de Radiodifusión**.

ser[1] *nm* being; **s. humano**, human being; **s. vivo**, living being.

ser[2] [23] *vi* **1** (+ *adj*) to be; **es alto y rubio**, he is tall and fair; **el edificio es gris**, the building is grey. **2** (+ *profesión*) to be a(n); **Rafael es músico**, Rafael is a musician. **3 s. de**, *(procedencia)* to be *o* come from; **¿de dónde eres?**, where are you from?, where do you come from? **4 s. de**, (+ *material*) to be made of. **5 s. de**, (+ *poseedor*) to belong to; **el perro es de Miguel**, the dog belongs to Miguel; **¿de quién es este abrigo?**, whose coat is this? **6 s. para**, *(finalidad)* to be for; **esta agua es para lavar**, this water is for washing. **7** (+ *día, hora*) to be; **hoy es dos de noviembre**, today is the second of November; **son las cinco de la tarde**, it's five o'clock. **8** (+ *cantidad*) **¿cuántos estaremos en la fiesta?** how many of us will there be at the party? **9** *(costar)* to be, cost; **¿cuánto es?**, how much is it? **10** *(tener lugar)* to be; **el estreno será mañana**, tomorrow is the opening night. **11 ¿qué es de Gonzalo?**, what has become of Gonzalo? **12** *(auxiliar en pasiva)* to be; **fue asesinado**, he was murdered. **13** *(locuciones)* **¿cómo es eso?**, **¿cómo puede s.?**, how can that be?; **es más**, furthermore; **es que ...**, it's just that ...; **como sea**, anyhow; **lo que sea**, whatever; **o sea**, that is (to say); **por si fuera poco**, to top it all; **sea como sea**, in any case, be that as it may; **a no s. que**, unless; **de no s. por ...**, had it not been for ...; **eso era de esperar**, it was to be expected.

serenarse *vr* to calm down.

serenidad *nf* serenity.

sereno[1] *nm (vigilante)* night watchman.

sereno,-a[2] *adj* **1** calm. **2** *fam* **estar s.**, *(sobrio)* to be sober.

serial *nm Rad TV* serial.

serie *nf* **1** series *sing*; **fabricación en s.**, mass production; **lleva ABS de s.**, it has ABS fitted as standard; **fuera de s.**, out of the ordinary. **2** *Rad TV* series *sing*.

seriedad *nf* **1** seriousness. **2** *(formalidad)* reliability, dependability; **falta de s.**, irresponsibility.

serio,-a *adj* **1** *(severo)* serious; **en s.**, seriously. **2** *(formal)* reliable, responsible.

sermón *nm* sermon.

sermonear *vi & vtr fam* to lecture.

seropositivo,-a *adj* HIV-positive.

serpentear *vi (zigzaguear)* to wind one's way, meander.

serpentina *nf (de papel)* streamer.

serpiente *nf* snake; **s. de cascabel**, rattlesnake; **s. pitón**, python.

serranía *nf* mountainous area *o* country.

serrar [1] *vtr* to saw.

serrín *nm* sawdust.

serrucho *nm* handsaw.

servicial *adj* helpful, obliging.

servicio *nm* **1** service; **s. a domicilio**, delivery service. **2** *Mil* service; **s. militar**, military service; **estar de s.**, to be on duty. **3 servicios**, *(retrete)* toilet *sing*, *US* rest room *sing*.

servidor,-a *nm,f* servant; *fam* **un s.**, yours truly.

servil *adj* servile.

servilleta *nf* serviette, napkin.

servilletero *nm* serviette ring, napkin ring.

servio,-a *adj & nm,f* Serbian.

servir [6] **I** *vtr* to serve; **¿en qué puedo servirle?**, what can I do for you?, may I help you?; **¿te sirvo una copa?**, will I pour you a drink? **II** *vi* **1** to serve. **2** *(valer)* to be useful, be suitable; **no sirve de nada llorar**, it's no use crying; **ya no sirve**, it's no use; **¿para qué sirve esto?**, what is this (used) for? **3 s. de**, to serve as, act as. **III servirse** *vr* **1** *(comida etc)* to help oneself. **2** *fml* **sírvase comunicarnos su decisión**, please inform us of your decision.

sésamo *nm* sesame.

sesenta *adj & nm inv* sixty.

sesgar [7] *vtr* **1** *(cortar)* to cut diagonally. **2** *(torcer)* to slant.

sesgo *nm fig* slant, turn; **tomar un s. favorable**, to take a turn for the better.

sesión *nf* **1** *(reunión)* meeting, session; *Jur* session, sitting. **2** *Cin* showing.

seso *nm* brain.

set *nm Ten* set.

seta *nf (comestible)* mushroom; **s. venenosa**, toadstool.

setecientos,-as *adj & nm inv* seven hundred.

setenta *adj & nm inv* seventy.

setiembre *nm* September.

seto *nm* hedge.

seudónimo *nm* pseudonym; *(de escritores)* pen name.

severidad *nf* severity.

severo,-a *adj* severe.

Sevilla *n* Seville.

sexismo *nm* sexism.

sexista *adj* sexist.

sexo *nm* **1** sex. **2** *(órgano)* genitals *pl*.

sexólogo,-a *nm,f* sexologist.

sexto,-a *adj & nm,f* sixth.

sexual *adj* sexual; **vida s.**, sex life.

sexualidad *nf* sexuality.

sexy *adj* sexy.

s/f. *abr de* **su favor,** your favour *o US* favor.

shock *nm* shock.

show *nm* show.

si[1] *conj* 1 *(condicional)* if; **como si,** as if; **si no,** if not; **si quieres,** if you like, if you wish. 2 *(pregunta indirecta)* whether, if; **me preguntó si me gustaba,** he asked me if I liked it; **no sé si ir o no,** *(disyuntivo)* I don't know whether to go or not. 3 *(sorpresa)* **¡si está llorando!,** but she's crying!

si[2] *nm (pl* **sis***) Mús* B; *(en solfeo)* ti.

sí[1] *pron pers* 1 *(singular)* *(él)* himself; *(ella)* herself; *(cosa)* itself; *(plural)* themselves; **de por sí, en sí,** in itself; **hablaban entre sí,** they were talking among themselves *o* to each other; **por sí mismo,** by himself. 2 *(uno mismo)* oneself; **decir para sí,** to say to oneself.

sí[2] **I** *adv* 1 yes; **dije que sí,** I said yes, I accepted, I agreed; **porque sí,** just because; **¡que sí!,** yes, I tell you!; **un día sí y otro no,** every other day. 2 *(uso enfático)* *(no se traduce)* **sí que me gusta,** of course I like it; **¡eso sí que no!,** certainly not! **II** *nm (pl* **síes***)* yes; **los síes,** *(en parlamento)* the ayes.

siamés,-esa *nm,f* Siamese twin.

sibarita *nmf* sybarite.

sicario *nm* hired gunman; *fam* hitman.

Sicilia *n* Sicily.

sico- → **psico-.**

sicómoro *nm* sycamore.

SIDA *nm abr de* **síndrome de inmuno-deficiencia adquirida,** acquired immune deficiency syndrome, AIDS.

sidecar *nm* sidecar.

siderurgia *nf* iron and steel industry.

siderúrgico,-a *adj* iron and steel; **la industria siderúrgica,** the iron and steel industry.

sidra *nf* cider.

siempre *adv* always; **s. pasa lo mismo,** it's always the same; **como s.,** as usual; **a la hora de s.,** at the usual time; **eso es así desde s.,** it has always been like that; **para s.,** for ever; **s. que,** *(cada vez que)* whenever; *(a condición de que)* provided, as long as; **s. y cuando,** provided, as long as.

sien *nf* temple.

sierra *nf* 1 saw; **s. mecánica,** power saw. 2 *Geog* mountain range, sierra.

siervo,-a *nm,f* slave.

siesta *nf* siesta, nap; **dormir la s.,** to have a siesta *o* an afternoon nap.

siete *adj & nm inv* seven.

sietemesino,-a *nm,f* seven-month baby, premature baby.

sífilis *nf inv* syphilis.

sifón *nm* siphon; **whisky con s.,** whisky and soda.

sig. *abr de* **siguiente,** following.

sigilo *nm* secrecy; **entrar con mucho s.,** to tiptoe in.

sigiloso,-a *adj* secretive.

◆**sigilosamente** *adv (secretamente)* secretly; **entró s. en la habitación,** she crept *o* slipped into the room.

sigla *nf* acronym.

siglo *nm* century; **el s. veintiuno,** the twenty-first century; *fam* **hace siglos que no le veo,** I haven't seen him for ages.

signatario,-a *adj & nm,f* signatory.

significación *nf* 1 *(sentido)* meaning. 2 *(importancia)* significance.

significado *nm* meaning.

significar [1] *vtr* to mean.

significativo,-a *adj* significant; *(expresivo)* meaningful.

signo *nm* 1 sign; **s. del zodiaco,** zodiac sign. 2 *Ling* mark; **s. de interrogación,** question mark.

sigo *indic pres* → **seguir.**

siguiente *adj* following, next; **¡el s.!,** next, please!; **al día s.,** the following day.

sílaba *nf* syllable.

silbar *vi* to whistle; *(abuchear)* to hiss, boo.

silbato *nm* whistle.

silbido *nm* whistle, whistling; *(agudo)* hiss.

silenciador *nm (de arma)* silencer; *(de coche, moto)* silencer, *US* muffler.

silenciar [12] *vtr* 1 *(un sonido)* to muffle. 2 *(noticia)* to hush up.

silencio *nm* silence; **imponer s. a algn,** to make sb be quiet.

silencioso,-a *adj (persona)* quiet; *(motor etc)* silent.

silicio *nm* silicon.

silicona *nf* silicone.

silla *nf* 1 chair; **s. de ruedas,** wheelchair; **s. giratoria,** swivel chair. 2 *(de montura)* saddle.

sillín *nm* saddle.

sillón *nm* armchair.

silo *nm* silo.

silueta *nf* silhouette; *(de cuerpo)* figure.

silvestre *adj* wild.

simbólico,-a *adj* symbolic; **precio s.,** token price.

simbolizar [4] *vtr* to symbolize.

símbolo *nm* symbol.

simetría *nf* symmetry.

simétrico,-a *adj* symmetrical.

simiente *nf* seed.

similar *adj* similar.

similitud *nf* similarity.

simio *nm* monkey.

simpatía *nf* liking, affection; **le tengo mucha s.,** I am very fond of him.

simpático,-a *adj (amable)* nice, likeable; **me cae s.,** I like him.

simpatizante *nmf* sympathizer.

simpatizar [4] *vi* 1 to sympathise (**con**, with). 2 (*llevarse bien*) to hit it off (**con**, with).

simple I *adj* 1 simple. 2 (*fácil*) simple, easy. 3 (*mero*) mere. 4 (*persona*) simple, simple-minded. **II** *nm* (*persona*) simpleton.

simpleza *nf* simple-mindedness; (*tontería*) nonsense.

simplificar [1] *vtr* to simplify.

simposio *nm* symposium.

simulacro *nm* sham, pretence; **un s. de ataque,** a mock attack.

simular *vtr* to simulate.

simultanear *vtr* to combine; **simultanea el trabajo y los estudios,** he's working and studying at the same time.

simultáneo,-a *adj* simultaneous.

sin *prep* 1 without; **s. dinero/ti,** without money/you; **estamos s. pan,** we're out of bread; **s. hacer nada,** without doing anything; **cerveza s.,** alcohol-free beer; **s. más ni más,** without further ado. 2 (+ *inf*) **está s. secar,** it hasn't been dried.

sinagoga *nf* synagogue.

sincerarse *vr* to open one's heart (**con**, to).

sinceridad *nf* sincerity; **con toda s.,** in all sincerity.

sincero,-a *adj* sincere.

sincronizar [4] *vtr* to synchronize.

sindical *adj* trade union, union.

sindicalista *nmf* trade unionist.

sindicato *nm* union, trade union.

síndrome *nm* syndrome.

sinfín *nm* endless number; **un s. de,** lots of.

sinfonía *nf* symphony.

single *nm* single, 7-inch.

singular I *adj* 1 singular. 2 (*excepcional*) exceptional, unique. 3 (*raro*) peculiar, odd. **II** *nm Ling* singular; **en s.,** in the singular.

siniestrado,-a *adj* stricken.

siniestro,-a I *adj* sinister, ominous. **II** *nm* disaster, catastrophe.

sino¹ *nm fml* fate, destiny.

sino² *conj* 1 but; **no fui a Madrid, s. a Barcelona,** I didn't go to Madrid but to Barcelona. 3 (*excepto*) **nadie s. él,** no-one but him; **no quiero s. que me oigan,** I only want them to listen (to me).

sinónimo,-a I *adj* synonymous. **II** *nm* synonym.

sinóptico,-a *adj* **cuadro s.,** diagram, chart.

sinsabor *nm* (*usu pl*) trouble, worry.

sintético,-a *adj* synthetic.

sintetizador *nm* synthesizer.

sintetizar [4] *vtr* to synthesize.

síntoma *nm* symptom.

sintonía *nf* 1 *Elec Rad* tuning. 2 *Mús Rad* (*de programa*) signature tune. 3 *fig* harmony.

sintonizador *nm Rad* tuning knob.

sintonizar [4] *vtr* 1 *Rad* to tune in. 2 (*simpatizar*) to be in tune (**con**, with).

sinuoso,-a *adj* (*camino*) winding.

sinvergüenza I *adj* (*desvergonzado*) shameless; (*descarado*) cheeky. **II** *nmf* (*desvergonzado*) rogue; (*caradura*) cheeky devil.

sionismo *nm* Zionism.

siquiera I *adv* (*por lo menos*) at least; **ni s.,** not even. **II** *conj fml* (*aunque*) although, even though.

sirena *nf* 1 siren, mermaid. 2 (*señal acústica*) siren.

Siria *n* Syria.

sirimiri *nm* fine drizzle.

sirio,-a *adj & nm,f* Syrian.

sirviente,-a *nm,f* servant.

sisar *vtr* (*hurtar*) to pilfer, filch.

sisear *vi* to hiss.

sísmico,-a *adj* seismic.

sismógrafo *nm* seismograph.

sistema *nm* system; **por s.,** as a rule; **s. nervioso,** nervous system; **s. montañoso,** mountain chain.

sistemático,-a *adj* systematic.

sitiar [12] *vtr* to besiege.

sitio¹ *nm* 1 (*lugar*) place; **en cualquier s.,** anywhere; **en todos los sitios,** everywhere; *fig* **quedarse en el s.,** to die. 2 (*espacio*) room; **hacer s.,** to make room.

sitio² *nm* siege; **estado de s.,** state of emergency.

sito,-a *adj fml* situated, located.

situación *nf* 1 situation; **su s. económica es buena,** his financial position is good. 2 (*ubicación*) situation, location.

situado,-a *adj* situated; *fig* **estar bien s.,** to have a good position.

situar [30] **I** *vtr* to locate. **II situarse** *vr* to be situated *o* located.

sketch *nm Cin Teat* sketch.

s/l *abr de* **su letra (de crédito).**

S.L. *abr de* **Sociedad Limitada,** limited company, Ltd.

slip *nm* underpants *pl*.

slogan *nm* slogan.

S.M. *abr de* **Su Majestad,** (*rey*) His Majesty; (*reina*) Her Majesty.

smoking *nm* dinner jacket, *US* tuxedo.

s/n. *abr de* **sin número.**

snob *adj & nmf* → **esnob.**

snobismo *nm* → **esnobismo.**

so¹ *prep* (*bajo*) under; **so pena de,** under penalty of.

so² *nm fam* **¡so imbécil!,** you damned idiot!

sobaco *nm* armpit.

sobar *vtr* 1 *fam* (*dormir*) to sleep. 2 *vulg* (*manosear*) to fondle, paw.

soberanía *nf* sovereignty.

soberano,-a I *adj* 1 sovereign. 2 *fam* huge, great. **II** *nm,f* (*monarca*) sovereign.

soberbia *nf* pride.

soberbio,-a *adj* 1 proud. 2 *(magnífico)* splendid, magnificent.

sobón,-ona *nm,f fam* **ser un s.**, to be fresh *o* all hands.

sobornar *vtr* to bribe.

soborno *nm (acción)* bribery; *(dinero etc)* bribe.

sobra *nf* 1 **de s.**, *(no necesario)* superfluous; **tener de s.**, to have plenty; **estar de s.**, not to be needed; **saber algo de s.**, to know sth only too well. 2 **sobras**, *(restos)* leftovers.

sobrado,-a *adj (que sobra)* abundant, more than enough; **sobradas veces**, repeatedly; **andar s. de tiempo/dinero**, to have plenty of time/money. ◆**sobradamente** *adv* only too well.

sobrante I *adj* remaining, spare. II *nm* surplus, excess.

sobrar *vi* 1 to be more than enough, *(sing)* be too much, *(pl)* to be too many; **sobran tres sillas**, there are three chairs too many; **sobran comentarios**, I've nothing further to add; *fam* **tú sobras aquí**, you are not wanted here. 2 *(quedar)* to be left over; **ha sobrado carne**, there's still some meat left.

sobrasada *nf* sausage spread.

sobre¹ *nm* 1 *(para carta)* envelope. 2 *(de sopa etc)* packet.

sobre² *prep* 1 *(encima de)* on, upon, on top of. 2 *(por encima de)* over, above. 3 *(acerca de)* about, on. 4 *(aproximadamente)* about; **vendré s. las ocho**, I'll come at about eight o'clock. 5 **s. todo**, especially, above all.

sobre- *pref* super-, over-.

sobrealimentado,-a *adj* overfed.

sobrecarga *nf* overload.

sobrecargar [7] *vtr* to overload.

sobrecogedor,-a *adj* dramatic, awesome.

sobrecoger [5] *vtr (conmover)* to shock.

sobredosis *nf inv* overdose.

sobreentenderse *vr* **se sobreentiende**, that goes without saying.

sobrehumano,-a *adj* superhuman.

sobregiro *nm* overdraft.

sobreimpresión *nf Fot Cin* superimposing.

sobrellevar *vtr* to endure, bear.

sobremesa¹ *nf* afternoon.

sobremesa² *nf* **ordenador de s.**, desktop computer.

sobrenatural *adj* supernatural.

sobrenombre *nm* nickname.

sobrepasar I *vtr* to exceed, surpass; *(rival)* to beat. II **sobrepasarse** *vr* to go too far.

sobrepeso *nm (de carga)* overload, excess weight; *(de persona)* excess weight.

sobreponerse *vr* 1 **s. a**, *(superar)* to overcome; **s. al dolor**, to overcome pain. 2 *(animarse)* to pull oneself together.

sobreproducción *nf* overproduction.

sobresaliente I *nm (nota)* A. II *adj (que destaca)* outstanding, excellent.

sobresalir [22] *vi* stick out, protrude; *fig (destacar)* to stand out, excel.

sobresaltar I *vtr* to startle. II **sobresaltarse** *vr* to be startled, start.

sobresalto *nm (movimiento)* start; *(susto)* fright.

sobreseer [36] *vtr Jur* to stay; **s. una causa**, to stay proceedings.

sobretodo *nm (abrigo)* overcoat; *(guardapolvo)* overalls *pl*.

sobrevalorar *vtr* to overestimate.

sobrevenir [27] *vi* to happen unexpectedly.

sobreviviente I *adj* surviving. II *nmf* survivor.

sobrevivir *vi* to survive.

sobrevolar [2] *vtr* to fly over.

sobriedad *nf* sobriety; *(en la bebida)* soberness.

sobrina *nf* niece.

sobrino *nm* nephew.

sobrio,-a *adj* sober.

socarrón,-ona *nm,f* 1 *(sarcástico)* sarcastic. 2 *(astuto)* sly, cunning.

socavar *vtr fig* to undermine.

socavón *nm (bache)* pothole.

sociable *adj* sociable, friendly.

social *adj* social.

socialdemócrata I *adj* social democratic. II *nmf* social democrat.

socialismo *nm* socialism.

socialista *adj & nmf* socialist.

socializar [4] *vtr* to socialize.

sociedad *nf* 1 society; **s. de consumo**, consumer society. 2 *(asociación)* association, society. 3 *Com* company; **s. anónima**, public liability company; **s. limitada**, limited company.

socio,-a *nm,f* 1 *(miembro)* member; **hacerse s. de un club**, to become a member of a club, join a club. 2 *Com (asociado)* partner.

sociología *nf* sociology.

sociológico,-a *adj* sociological.

sociólogo,-a *nm,f* sociologist.

socorrer *vtr* to help, assist.

socorrido,-a *adj* handy, useful.

socorrista *nmf* life-saver, lifeguard.

socorro *nm* help, assistance; **¡s.!**, help!; **puesto de s.**, first-aid post.

soda *nf* soda water.

soez *adj* vulgar, crude.

sofá *nm (pl* **sofás)** sofa, settee; **s. cama**, sofa bed, studio couch.

Sofía *n* Sophia.

sofisticado,-a *adj* sophisticated.

sofocado,-a *adj* suffocated.

sofocante *adj* suffocating, stifling; **hacía un calor s.**, it was unbearably hot.

sofocar [1] I *vtr* 1 *(ahogar)* to suffocate, smother. 2 *(incendio)* to extinguish, put out. II **sofocarse** *vr* 1 *(ahogarse)* to suffocate, stifle. **2** *fam* (*irritarse*) to get upset.

sofoco *nm fig* (*vergüenza*) embarrassment; **le dio un s.**, (*disgusto*) it gave her quite a turn.

sofocón *nm fam* shock; **llevarse un s.**, to get upset.

sofreír |6| *vtr* to fry lightly, brown.

sofrito *nm* fried tomato and onion sauce.

software *nm* software.

soga *nf* rope; *fig* **estar con la s. al cuello**, to be in dire straits.

soja *nf* soya bean, *US* soybean.

sojuzgar |7| *vtr* to subjugate.

sol[1] *nm* **1** sun. **2** (*luz*) sunlight; (*luz y calor*) sunshine; **hace s.**, it's sunny, the sun is shining; **tomar el s.**, to sunbathe; **al** *o* **bajo el s.**, in the sun; **de s. a s.**, from sunrise to sunset. **3** *Fin* standard monetary unit of Perú.

sol[2] *nm Mús* G; (*solfeo*) so.

solamente *adv* only; **no s.**, not only; **s. con mirarte lo sé**, I know just by looking at you; **s. que ...**, except that ....

solapa *nf* (*de chaqueta*) lapel; (*de sobre, bolsillo, libro*) flap.

solapado,-a *adj* (*persona*) sly. ◆ **solapadamente** *adv* stealthily, in an underhand way.

solapamiento *nm* overlap.

solapar **I** *vtr fig* to conceal, cover up. **II** *vi* to overlap.

solar[1] *adj* solar; **luz s.**, sunlight.

solar[2] *nm* (*terreno*) plot; (*en obras*) building site.

solario, **solárium** *nm* sunbed.

solaz *nm fml* (*descanso*) rest, relaxation; (*esparcimiento*) recreation, entertainment.

solazarse |4| *vr* (*relajar*) to relax; (*divertir*) to entertain oneself, amuse oneself.

soldado *nm* soldier; **s. raso**, private.

soldador,-a **I** *nm,f* welder. **II** *nm* soldering iron.

soldar |2| *vtr* (*cable*) to solder; (*chapa*) to weld.

soleado,-a *adj* sunny.

soledad *nf* (*estado*) solitude; (*sentimiento*) loneliness.

solemne *adj* **1** (*majestuoso*) solemn. **2** *pey* downright.

solemnidad *nf* solemnity.

soler |4| *vi defect* **1** (*en presente*) to be in the habit of; **solemos ir en coche**, we usually go by car; **sueles equivocarte**, you are usually wrong. **2** (*en pasado*) to use to; **solía pasear por aquí**, he used to walk round here.

solera *nf fig* tradition; **de s.**, old-established; **vino de s.**, vintage wine.

solfa *nf* **1** *Mús* solfa; *fam* **poner en s.**, to ridicule. **2** *fam* (*paliza*) thrashing, beating.

solicitar *vtr* (*información etc*) to request, ask for; (*trabajo*) to apply for.

solícito,-a *adj* obliging, attentive.

solicitud *nf* (*petición*) request; (*de trabajo*) application.

solidaridad *nf* solidarity.

solidario,-a *adj* **1** supportive; **una sociedad solidaria**, a caring society. **2** *Jur* jointly responsible.

solidarizarse *vr* to show one's solidarity (*con*, with).

solidez *nf* solidity, strength.

sólido,-a *adj* solid, strong.

soliloquio *nm* soliloquy.

solista *nmf* soloist.

solitario,-a **I** *adj* **1** (*que está solo*) solitary, lone; (*que se siente solo*) lonely. **II** *nm* **1** (*diamante*) solitaire. **2** *Naipes* solitaire, patience.

soliviantar *vtr* (*irritar*) to irritate.

sollozar |4| *vi* to sob.

sollozo *nm* sob.

solo,-a **I** *adj* **1** only, single; **ni un s. día**, not a single day; **una sola vez**, just once, just once. **2** (*solitario*) lonely. **3** **hablar s.**, to talk to oneself; **se enciende s.**, it switches itself on automatically; **a solas**, alone, by oneself. **II** *nm Mús* solo.

sólo *adv* only; **tan s.**, only; **no s. ... sino** (**también**), not only ... but (also); **con s.**, (**tan**) **s. con**, just by.

solomillo *nm* sirloin.

soltar |2| **I** *vtr* **1** (*desasir*) to let go of; **¡suéltame!**, let me go! **2** (*prisionero*) to release. **3** (*humo, olor*) to give off. **4** (*bofetada*) to deal; (*carcajada*) to let out; **me soltó un rollo**, he bored me to tears. **II** **soltarse** *vr* **1** (*desatarse*) to come loose. **2** (*perro etc*) to get loose, break loose. **3** (*desprenderse*) to come off.

soltero,-a **I** *adj* single, unmarried. **II** *nm* (*hombre*) bachelor, single man. **III** *nf* (*mujer*) single woman, spinster.

solterón,-ona *pey* **I** *nm* (*hombre*) old bachelor. **II** *nf* (*mujer*) old maid.

soltura *nf* (*agilidad*) agility; (*seguridad*) confidence, assurance; **habla italiano con s.**, he speaks Italian fluently.

soluble *adj* soluble; **café s.**, instant coffee.

solución *nf* solution.

solucionar *vtr* to solve; (*arreglar*) to settle.

solvencia *nf* **1** *Fin* solvency. **2** (*fiabilidad*) reliability; **fuentes de toda s.**, completely reliable sources.

solventar *vtr* (*problema*) to solve, resolve; (*deuda, asunto*) to settle.

solvente *adj* **1** *Fin* solvent. **2** (*fiable*) reliable.

sombra *nf* **1** shade. **2** (*silueta proyectada*) shadow; **s. de ojos**, eyeshadow; **sin s. de duda**, beyond a shadow of doubt. **3 tener buena s.**, (*tener suerte*) to be lucky.

sombrero *nm* hat; **s. de copa**, top hat; **s. hongo**, bowler hat.

sombrilla *nf* parasol, sunshade.

sombrío,-a *adj* (*oscuro*) dark; (*tenebroso*)

sombre, gloomy; *fig (persona)* gloomy, sullen.

somero,-a *adj* superficial, shallow.

someter I *vtr* 1 to subject; **s. a prueba,** to put to the test; **s. algo a votación,** to put sth to the vote. 2 *(rebeldes)* to subdue, put down. **II someterse** *vr* 1 *(subordinarse)* to submit. 2 *(rendirse)* to surrender, yield. **3 s. a un tratamiento,** to undergo treatment.

somier *nm (pl* **somieres)** spring mattress.

somnífero *nm* sleeping pill.

somnoliento,-a *adj* sleepy, drowsy.

son *nm* sound; **al s. del tambor,** to the sound of the drum; **venir en s. de paz,** to come in peace.

sonado,-a *adj* 1 much talked of. 2 *(trastocado)* mad, crazy.

sonajero *nm* baby's rattle.

sonámbulo,-a *nm,f* somnambulist, sleepwalker.

sonar [2] **I** *vi* 1 to sound; **s. a,** to sound like; **suena bien,** it sounds good. 2 *(timbre, teléfono)* to ring; **sonaron las cinco,** the clock struck five. **3 tu nombre/cara me suena,** your name/face rings a bell. **II sonarse** *vr* **s. (la nariz),** to blow one's nose.

sonda *nf* 1 *Med* sound, probe. 2 **s. espacial,** space probe.

sondear *vtr* 1 *(opinión)* to test, sound out. 2 *Med* to sound, probe. 3 *Náut* to sound.

sondeo *nm* 1 *(encuesta)* poll. 2 *Med* sounding, probing. 3 *Náut* sounding.

soneto *nm Lit* sonnet.

sonido *nm* sound.

sonoro,-a *adj Cin* sound; **banda sonora,** soundtrack. 2 *(resonante)* loud, resounding. 3 *Ling* voiced.

sonreír [6] *vi,* **sonreírse** *vr* to smile; **me sonrió,** he smiled to me.

sonriente *adj* smiling.

sonrisa *nf* smile.

sonrojarse *vr* to blush.

sonrojo *nm* blush.

sonsacar [1] *vtr* to wheedle; *(secreto)* to worm out.

soñador,-a *nm,f* dreamer.

soñar [2] *vtr & vi* 1 to dream; **s. con,** to dream of *o* about; *fig* **¡ni soñarlo!,** not on your life! 2 *(fantasear)* to daydream, dream.

soñoliento,-a *adj* sleepy, drowsy.

sopa *nf* soup; **s. juliana,** spring vegetable soup; *fig* **quedar hecho una s.,** to get soaked to the skin.

sopera *nf* soup tureen.

sopero,-a *adj* **cucharada sopera,** soup spoon.

sopesar *vtr* to try the weight of; *fig* to weigh up.

sopetón *nm fam* slap; **de s.,** all of a sudden.

soplado *nm* glass-blowing.

soplar I *vi (viento)* to blow. **II** *vtr* 1 *(polvo etc)* to blow away; *(para enfriar)* to blow on. 2 *(para apagar)* to blow out. 3 *(para inflar)* to blow up. 4 *(en examen etc)* to whisper *o* tell the answer.

soplete *nm* blowlamp, blowtorch.

soplido *nm* blow, puff.

soplillo *nm* fan; *fam* **orejas de s.,** cauliflower ears.

soplo *nm* 1 *(acción)* blow, puff; *(de viento)* gust. 2 *Med* murmur.

soplón,-ona *nm,f fam (niño)* telltale, sneak; *(delator)* informer, squealer.

soporífero,-a *adj* 1 *(que adormece)* soporific, sleep-inducing. 2 *(aburrido)* boring, dull.

soportable *adj* bearable.

soportal *nm* porch; **soportales,** arcade *sing.*

soportar *vtr* 1 *(peso)* to support, bear. 2 *fig (calor, ruido)* to bear, endure; *(situación)* to put up with, to bear; **no te soporto,** I can't stand you.

soporte *nm* support; **s. publicitario,** advertising medium.

soprano *nmf* soprano.

sorber *vtr* 1 *(beber)* to sip. 2 *(absorber)* to soak up, absorb.

sorbete *nm* sorbet, sherbet.

sorbo *nm* sip; *(trago)* gulp; **de un s.,** in one gulp.

sordera *nf* deafness.

sórdido,-a *adj* squalid, sordid.

sordo,-a I *adj* 1 *(persona)* deaf; **s. como una tapia,** stone-deaf. 2 *(golpe, ruido, dolor)* dull. **II** *nm,f* deaf person; **los sordos,** the deaf *pl;* *fam fig* **hacerse el s.,** to turn a deaf ear.

sordomudez *nf* deaf-muteness.

sordomudo,-a I *adj* deaf and dumb, deaf-mute. **II** *nm,f* deaf and dumb person, deaf-mute.

sorprendente *adj* surprising.

sorprender *vtr* 1 *(extrañar)* to surprise. 2 *(coger desprevenido)* to catch unawares, take by surprise.

sorpresa *nf* surprise; **coger de** *o* **por s.,** to take by surprise.

sorpresivo,-a *adj Am* unexpected, surprising.

sortear *vtr* 1 to draw *o* cast lots for; *(rifar)* to raffle (off). 2 *(evitar)* to avoid, get round.

sorteo *nm* draw; *(rifa)* raffle.

sortija *nf* ring.

sortilegio *nm* spell.

S.O.S. *nm* SOS.

sosa *nf* soda; **s. cáustica,** caustic soda.

sosegado,-a *adj (tranquilo)* calm, quiet; *(pacífico)* peaceful.

sosegar [1] **I** *vtr* to calm, quieten. **II sosegarse** *vr* to calm down.

sosiego *nm (calma)* calmness; *(paz)* peace, tranquility.

soslayo (al, de) *loc adv* **mirar de s.**, to look sideways (at).

soso,-a *adj* lacking in salt; *fig (persona)* insipid, dull.

sospecha *nf* suspicion.

sospechar I *vi (desconfiar)* to suspect; **s. de algn**, to suspect sb. II *vtr (pensar)* to suspect.

sospechoso,-a *adj* suspicious; **s. de**, suspected of. II *nm,f* suspect.

sostén *nm* 1 *(apoyo)* support. 2 *(sustento)* sustenance. 3 *(prenda)* bra, brassière.

sostener [24] I *vtr* 1 *(sujetar)* to support, hold up. 2 *(con la mano)* to hold. 3 *fig (teoría etc)* to defend, uphold; **s. que ...**, to maintain that .... 4 *(conversación)* to hold, sustain. 5 *(familia)* to support. II **sostenerse** *vr* 1 *(mantenerse)* to support oneself. 2 *(permanecer)* to stay, remain.

sostenido,-a *adj* 1 *(continuado)* sustained. 2 *Mús* sharp.

sostuve *pt indef* → **sostener**.

sota *nf Naipes* jack, knave.

sotana *nf* cassock, soutane.

sótano *nm* basement, cellar.

soto *nm* grove.

soviético,-a *adj & nm,f* Soviet; *Hist* **la Unión Soviética**, the Soviet Union.

soy *indic pres* → **ser**.

S.P. *abr de* **Servicio Público**.

sport (de) *loc adj* casual, sports; **chaqueta s.**, sports jacket.

spot *nm (pl spots) TV* commercial, advert, ad.

spray *nm (pl sprays)* spray.

sprint *nm* sprint.

Sr. *abr de* **Señor**, Mister, Mr.

Sra. *abr de* **Señora**, Mrs.

S.R.C., s.r.c. *abr de* **se ruega contestación**, please reply, R.S.V.P.

Srta. *abr de* **Señorita**, Miss.

SS *nf abr de* **Seguridad Social**, ≈ National Health Service, NHS.

SS.AA. *abr de* **Sus Altezas**, Their Royal Highnesses.

Sta., sta. *abr de* **Santa**, Saint, St.

stand *nm Com* stand.

standard *adj & nm* standard.

status *nm inv* status.

Sto., sto. *abr de* **Santo**, Saint, St.

su *adj pos (de él)* his; *(de ella)* her; *(de usted, ustedes)* your; *(de animales o cosas)* its; *(impersonal)* one's; *(de ellos)* their; **su coche**, his *o* her *o* your *o* their car; **su pata**, its leg; **sus libros**, his *o* her *o* your *o* their books; **sus patas**, its legs.

suave *adj* 1 smooth; *(luz, voz etc)* soft. 2 *Meteor (templado)* mild.

suavidad *nf* 1 smoothness; *(dulzura)* softness. 2 *Meteor* mildness.

suavizante *nm (para el pelo)* (hair) conditioner; *(para la ropa)* fabric softener.

suavizar [4] I *vtr* to smooth (out). II **suavizarse** *vr (temperatura)* to get milder;

(persona) to calm down.

subacuático,-a *adj* underwater.

subalimentado,-a *adj* undernourished, underfed.

subalterno,-a *adj & nm,f* subordinate, subaltern.

subarrendar [1] *vtr Com* to sublet, sublease.

subasta *nf* auction.

subastar *vtr* to auction (off), sell at auction.

subcampeón *nm Dep* runner-up.

subconsciente *adj & nm* subconscious.

subdesarrollado,-a *adj* underdeveloped.

subdesarrollo *nm* underdevelopment.

subdirector,-a *nm,f* assistant director *o* manager.

súbdito,-a *nm,f* subject, citizen; **s. francés**, French citizen.

subdividir *vtr* to subdivide.

subestimar *vtr* to underestimate.

subida *nf* 1 *(de temperatura)* rise; *(de precios, salarios)* rise, increase. 2 *(ascenso)* ascent, climb. 3 *(pendiente)* slope, hill. 4 *fam (drogas)* high.

subido,-a *adj* **s. de tono**, daring, risqué.

subir I *vtr* 1 to go up. 2 *(llevar arriba)* to take up, bring up. 3 *(cabeza, mano)* to lift, raise. 4 *(precio, salario)* to raise, put up. 5 *(volumen)* to turn up; *(voz)* to raise. II *vi* 1 *(ir arriba)* to go up, come up. 2 **s. a**, *(un coche)* to get into; *(un autobús)* to get on; *(un barco, avión, tren)* to board, get on. 3 *(aumentar)* to rise, go up. III **subirse** *vr* 1 to climb up; *fig* **el vino se le subió a la cabeza**, the wine went to his head. 2 **s. a**, *(un coche)* to get into; *(un autobús, avión, tren)* to get on, board; *(caballo, bici)* to get on. 3 *(cremallera)* to do up; *(mangas)* to roll up.

súbito,-a *adj* sudden. ◆**súbitamente** *adv* suddenly.

subjetivo,-a *adj* subjective.

sublevación *nf* rising, rebellion.

sublevar I *vtr fig (indignar)* to infuriate, enrage. II **sublevarse** *vr* to rebel, revolt.

sublime *adj* sublime.

submarinismo *nm* skin-diving.

submarino,-a I *adj* submarine, underwater. II *nm* submarine.

subnormal I *adj* mentally handicapped. II *nmf* mentally handicapped person.

suboficial *nm* 1 *Mil* noncommissioned officer. 2 *Náut* petty officer.

subordinado,-a *adj & nm,f* subordinate.

subordinar *vtr* to subordinate.

subproducto *nm* by-product.

subrayar *vtr* to underline; *fig (recalcar)* to emphasize, stress.

subrepticio,-a *adj* surreptitious.

subrutina *nf* subroutine.

subsanar *vtr (error)* to rectify, put right; *(daño)* to make up for.

subscribir *(pp subscrito) vtr* → **suscribir**.

subscripción *nf* subscription.
subscrito,-a *adj & nm,f* → **suscrito,-a**.
subsecretario,-a *nm,f* undersecretary.
subsidiario,-a *adj* subsidiary.
subsidio *nm* allowance, benefit; **s. de desempleo,** unemployment benefit.
subsistencia *nf* subsistence.
subsistir *vi* to subsist, remain; *(vivir)* to live on, survive.
subsuelo *nm* subsoil.
subterráneo,-a I *adj* underground. II *nm* *(túnel)* tunnel, underground passage.
subtítulo *nm* subtitle.
suburbano,-a *adj* suburban.
suburbio *nm* *(barrio pobre)* slums *pl*; *(barrio periférico)* suburb.
subvención *nf* subsidy.
subvencionar *vtr* to subsidize.
subversión *nf* subversion.
subversivo,-a *adj* subversive.
subyacente *adj* underlying.
subyugar [7] *vtr* to subjugate.
succionar *vtr* to suck (in).
sucedáneo,-a *adj & nm* substitute.
suceder I *vi* 1 *(ocurrir)* (*uso impers*) to happen, occur; **¿qué sucede?,** what's going on?, what's the matter? 2 *(seguir)* to follow, succeed. II **sucederse** *vr* to follow one another, come after the other.
sucesión *nf* 1 *(serie)* series *sing*, succession. 2 *(al trono)* succession. 3 *(descendencia)* issue, heirs *pl*.
sucesivo,-a *adj* following, successive; **en lo s.,** from now on. ◆**sucesivamente** *adv* **y así s.,** and so on.
suceso *nm* *(hecho)* event, occurrence; *(incidente)* incident; *Prensa* **sección de sucesos,** accident and crime reports.
sucesor,-a *nm,f* successor.
suciedad *nf* 1 dirt. 2 *(calidad)* dirtiness.
sucinto,-a *adj* concise, succinct.
sucio,-a I *adj* dirty; **en s.,** in rough; *fig* **juego s.,** foul play; *fig* **negocio s.,** shady business. II *adv* **jugar s.,** to play dirty.
sucre *nm* *Fin* standard monetary unit of Ecuador.
suculento,-a *adj* succulent, juicy.
sucumbir *vi* to succumb, yield.
sucursal *nf* *Com Fin* branch, branch office.
sudaca *nmf* *pey* South American.
sudadera *nf* sweatshirt.
Sudáfrica *n* South Africa.
sudafricano,-a *adj & nm,f* South African.
Sudamérica *n* South America.
sudamericano,-a *adj & nm,f* South American.
sudar *vtr & vi* to sweat; *fam fig* **s. la gota gorda,** to sweat blood.
sudeste *nm* southeast.
sudoeste *nm* southwest.
sudor *nm* sweat; *fig* **con el s. de mi frente,** by the sweat of my brow.
sudoroso,-a *adj* sweaty.

Suecia *n* Sweden.
sueco,-a I *adj* Swedish. II *nm,f* *(persona)* Swede. III *nm* *(idioma)* Swedish.
suegra *nf* mother-in-law.
suegro *nm* father-in-law; **mis suegros,** my in-laws.
suela *nf* *(de zapato)* sole.
sueldo *nm* salary, wages *pl*.
suelo *nm* 1 *(superficie)* ground; *(de interior)* floor; *fig* **estar por los suelos,** *(precios)* to be rock-bottom. 2 *(territorio)* soil, land. 3 *(campo, terreno)* land; **s. cultivable,** arable land. 4 *(de carretera)* surface.
suelto,-a I *adj* 1 loose; *(desatado)* undone. 2 *fig* **dinero s.,** loose change; **hojas sueltas,** loose sheets (of paper); **se venden sueltos,** they are sold singly *o* separately *o* loose. 3 *(en libertad)* free; *(huido)* at large. 4 *(vestido, camisa)* loose, loose-fitting. II *nm* *(dinero)* (loose) change.
sueño *nm* 1 sleep; *(ganas de dormir)* sleepiness; **tener s.,** to feel *o* be sleepy. 2 *(cosa soñada)* dream.
suero *nm* *Med* serum; *(de la leche)* whey.
suerte *nf* 1 *(fortuna)* luck; **por s.,** fortunately; **probar s.,** to try one's luck; **tener s.,** to be lucky; **¡que tengas s.!,** good luck! 2 **echar algo a suertes,** to draw lots for sth. 3 *(destino)* fate, destiny. 4 *fml* *(género)* kind, sort, type.
suéter *nm* sweater.
suficiencia *nf* 1 *(engreimiento)* smugness, complacency. 2 *Educ* **prueba de s.,** final exam.
suficiente I *adj* *(bastante)* sufficient, enough. II *nm* *Educ* pass. ◆**suficientemente** *adv* sufficiently; **no es lo s. rico como para ...** he isn't rich enough to ....
sufijo *nm* suffix.
sufragar [7] I *vtr* *(gastos)* to pay, defray. II *vi* *Am* to vote (**por,** for).
sufragio *nm* *Pol* suffrage; *(voto)* vote.
sufrido,-a *adj* *(persona)* long-suffering.
sufrimiento *nm* suffering.
sufrir I *vi* to suffer; **s. del corazón,** to have a heart condition. II *vtr* 1 *(accidente)* to have; *(operación)* to undergo; *(dificultades, cambios)* to experience; **s. dolores de cabeza,** to suffer from headaches. 2 *(aguantar)* to bear, put up with.
sugerencia *nf* suggestion.
sugerente *adj* suggestive.
sugerir [5] *vtr* to suggest.
sugestión *nf* suggestion.
sugestionar *vtr* to influence, persuade.
sugestivo,-a *adj* suggestive; *(atractivo)* alluring.
suicida I *nmf* *(persona)* suicide. II *adj* suicidal.
suicidarse *vr* to commit suicide, kill oneself.
suicidio *nm* suicide.
suite *nf* suite.

Suiza *n* Switzerland.

suizo,-a I *adj* Swiss. II *nm,f (persona)* Swiss. III *nm Culin* eclair.

sujetador *nm (prenda)* bra, brassière.

sujetar I *vtr* 1 *(agarrar)* to hold. 2 *(fijar)* to hold down, hold in place. 3 *fig (someter)* to restrain. II **sujetarse** *vr (agarrarse)* to hold on.

sujeto,-a I *nm* subject; *(individuo)* fellow, individual. II *adj (atado)* fastened, secure; **s. a,** *(sometido)* subject to, liable to.

sulfato *nm* sulphate.

sulfurar I *vtr fam (exasperar)* to exasperate, infuriate. II **sulfurarse** *vr fam* to lose one's temper, blow one's top.

sultán *nm* sultan.

suma *nf* 1 *(cantidad)* sum, amount. 2 *Mat* sum, addition; **s. total,** sum total. 3 **en s.,** in short.

sumamente *adv* extremely, highly.

sumar I *vtr Mat* to add, add up. II **sumarse** *vr* **s. a,** *(huelga)* to join; *(propuesta)* to support.

sumario,-a I *adj* summary, brief; *Jur* juicio **s.,** summary proceedings *pl.* II *nm Jur* summary.

sumarísimo,-a *adj Jur* swift, expeditious.

sumergible *adj & nm* submersible.

sumergir [6] I *vtr* to submerge, submerse; *(hundir)* to sink, plunge. II **sumergirse** *vr* to submerge, go underwater; *(hundirse)* to sink.

sumidero *nm* drain, sewer.

suministrar *vtr* to supply, provide; **s. algo a algn,** to supply sb with sth.

suministro *nm* supply.

sumir *vtr (hundir)* to sink, plunge; *fig* to plunge.

sumiso,-a *adj* submissive, obedient.

sumo,-a *adj (supremo)* supreme; **con s. cuidado,** with extreme care; **a lo s.,** at (the) most.

suntuoso,-a *adj* sumptuous, magnificent.

supe *pt indef* → **saber.**

supeditar *vtr* to subject (**a,** to).

super- *pref* super-.

súper *fam* I *adj* super, great. II *nm* 1 *(supermercado)* supermarket. 2 *(gasolina)* 4 star.

superado,-a *adj* outdated, obsolete.

superar I *vtr* 1 *(obstáculo etc)* to overcome, surmount; *(prueba)* pass. 2 *(aventajar)* to surpass, excel. II **superarse** *vr* to improve o better oneself.

superávit *nm* surplus.

superdotado,-a I *adj* exceptionally gifted. II *nm,f* genius.

superficial *adj* superficial.

superficialidad *nf* superficiality.

superficie *nf* surface; *(área)* area; *Com* **grandes superficies,** hypermarkets.

superfluo,-a *adj* superfluous.

superhombre *nm* superman.

superior I *adj* 1 *(posición)* top, upper. 2 *(cantidad)* greater, higher, larger (**a,** than). 3 *(calidad)* superior; **calidad s.,** top quality. 4 *Educ* higher. II *nm (jefe)* superior.

superioridad *nf* superiority.

supermán *nm (pl* **supermanes)** superman.

supermercado *nm* supermarket.

superpoblación *nf* overpopulation.

superponer [19] *vtr* to superimpose.

superpotencia *nf* superpower.

superproducción *nf* 1 *Ind* overproduction. 2 *Cin* mammoth production.

supersónico,-a *adj* supersonic.

superstición *nf* superstition.

supersticioso,-a *adj* superstitious.

supervisar *vtr* to supervise.

supervisor,-a *nm,f* supervisor.

supervivencia *nf* survival.

supino,-a *adj* 1 *(boca arriba)* supine, face up. 2 *fig (absoluto)* total absolute.

súpito,-a *adj Am* sudden.

suplantar *vtr* to supplant, take the place of.

suplementario,-a *adj* supplementary, additional.

suplemento *nm* supplement; **sin s.,** without extra charge.

suplente *adj & nmf (sustituto)* substitute, deputy; *Dep* substitute.

supletorio,-a *adj* supplementary, additional; **cama supletoria,** extra bed; **teléfono s.,** extension.

súplica *nf* entreaty, plea.

suplicar [1] *vtr* to beseech, beg.

suplicio *nm (tortura)* torture; *fig (tormento)* torment.

suplir *vtr* 1 *(reemplazar)* to replace, substitute. 2 *(compensar)* to make up for.

suponer [19] *(pp* **supuesto)** *vtr* 1 *(significar)* to mean. 2 *(implicar)* to entail. 3 *(representar)* to account for. 4 *(pensar)* to suppose; **supongo que sí,** I suppose so; **supongamos que ...,** let's assume that .... 5 *(adivinar)* to guess; (**me) lo suponía,** I guessed as much.

suposición *nf* supposition.

supositorio *nm* suppository.

supremacía *nf* supremacy.

supremo,-a *adj* supreme.

supresión *nf (de una ley etc)* abolition; *(de restricciones)* lifting; *(de una palabra)* deletion; *(de una rebelión)* suppression; *(omisión)* omission.

suprimir *vtr* 1 *(ley, impuesto)* to abolish; *(restricción)* to lift; *(palabra)* to delete, take o leave out; *(rebelión)* to suppress. 2 *(omitir)* to omit.

supuesto,-a I *adj* 1 *(asumido)* supposed, assumed; **¡por s.!,** of course!; **dar algo por s.,** to take sth for granted. 2 *(presunto)* alleged. II *nm* assumption; **en el s. de que,** on the assumption that.

supurar *vi* to suppurate, fester.

supuse *pt indef* → **suponer.**

sur *nm* south.
Suramérica *nf* South America.
suramericano,-a *adj & nm,f* South American.
surcar |1| *vtr Agr* to plough; *fig (olas)* to cut through.
surco *nm Agr* furrow; *(en un disco)* groove.
sureño,-a I *adj* southern. **II** *nm,f* southerner.
sureste *adj & nm →* **sudeste.**
surf(ing) *nm Dep* surfing.
surfista *nmf* surfer.
surgir |6| *vi (aparecer)* to arise, emerge, appear; *(problema, dificultad)* to crop up.
suroeste *adj & nm →* **sudoeste.**
surrealista *adj & nmf* surrealist.
surtido,-a I *adj* 1 *(variado)* assorted. 2 **bien s.,** well stocked. **II** *nm* selection, assortment.
surtidor *nm* spout; **s. de gasolina,** petrol *o US* gas pump.
surtir *vtr* 1 to supply, provide. 2 **s. efecto,** to have the desired effect.
susceptible *adj* susceptible; *(quisquilloso)* oversensitive, touchy.
suscitar *vtr (provocar)* to cause, provoke; *(rebelión)* to stir up, arouse; *(interés etc)* to arouse.
suscribir *(pp suscrito)* **I** *vtr* 1 to subscribe to, endorse. 2 *fml (firmar)* to sign. **II suscribirse** *vr* to subscribe **(a,** to).
suscripción *nf* subscription.
susodicho,-a *adj* above-mentioned, aforesaid.
suspender I *vtr* 1 *(ley)* to suspend; *(reunión)* to adjourn. 2 *(examen)* to fail; **me han suspendido,** I've failed (the exam). 3 *(colgar)* to hang, suspend. **II** *vi Educ* **he suspendido,** I've failed.
suspense *nm* suspense; **novela/película de s.,** thriller.
suspensión *nf* 1 hanging (up), suspension. 2 *Aut* suspension. 3 *Fin Jur* **s. de pagos,** suspension of payments.
suspensivo,-a *adj* **puntos suspensivos,** suspension points.
suspenso *nm* 1 *Educ* fail. 2 **en s.,** *(asunto, trabajo)* pending; **estar en s.,** to be pending.
suspicacia *nf* suspiciousness.
suspicaz *adj* suspicious; *(desconfiado)* distrustful.
suspirar *vi* to sigh.
suspiro *nm* sigh.
sustancia *nf* substance.
sustancial *adj* 1 substantial. 2 *(fundamental)* essential, fundamental.
sustantivo,-a I *adj* substantive. **II** *nm Ling* noun.
sustentar *vtr* 1 *(peso)* to support. 2 *(familia)* to maintain, support. 3 *(teoría)* to support, defend.
sustento *nm* 1 *(alimento)* sustenance, food. 2 *(apoyo)* support.
sustitución *nf* substitution, replacement.
sustituir |37| *vtr* to substitute, replace.
sustituto,-a *nm,f* substitute, stand-in.
susto *nm* fright, scare; **llevarse** *o* **darse un s.,** to get a fright.
sustraer |25| *vtr* 1 *Mat* to subtract. 2 *(robar)* to steal, remove.
sustrato *nm* substratum.
susurrar *vtr* to whisper.
susurro *nm* whisper.
sutil *adj* 1 *(diferencia, pregunta)* subtle. 2 *(delgado)* thin, fine. 3 *(aroma)* delicate.
sutileza *nf* 1 *(dicho)* subtlety. 2 *(finura)* fineness.
suyo,-a *adj & pron pos (de él)* his; *(de ella)* hers; *(de usted, ustedes)* yours; *(de animal o cosa)* its; *(de ellos, ellas)* theirs; **los zapatos no son suyos,** the shoes aren't hers; **varios amigos suyos,** several friends of his *o* hers *o* yours *o* theirs; *fam* **es muy s.,** he's very aloof; *fam* **hacer de las suyas,** to be up to one's tricks; *fam* **ir (cada uno) a lo s.,** to mind one's own business; *fam* **salirse con la suya,** to get one's way.
svástica *nf* swastika.

T

T, t |te| *nf (la letra)* T, t.
t *abr de* **tonelada(s),** ton, tons.
tabacalero,-a I *nm,f (vendedor)* tobacco trader. **II** *nf* **La Tabacalera,** Spanish state tobacco monopoly.
tabaco *nm* 1 *(planta, hoja)* tobacco; **t. rubio,** Virginia tobacco. 2 *(cigarrillos)* cigarettes *pl.*
tábano *nm* horsefly.
tabaquismo *nm* nicotine poisoning.
tabarra *nf fam* nuisance, bore; **dar la t.,** to go on and on.
tabasco *nm* tabasco sauce.
taberna *nf* pub, bar; *(antiguamente)* tavern.
tabernero,-a *nm,f* publican; *(hombre)* landlord; *(mujer)* landlady.
tabique *nm* 1 *(pared)* partition (wall). 2 *Anat* **t. nasal,** nasal wall.
tabla *nf* 1 board; *Dep* **t. de surf,** surfboard; *Dep* **t. de windsurf,** sailboard. 2 *(de vestido)* pleat. 3 *Mat* table. 4 *Ajedrez* **tablas,** stalemate *sing,* draw *sing;* **quedar en t.,** *(juego)* to end in a draw. 5 *Taur* **tablas,** fence *sing.* 6 *Teat* **las tablas,** the stage *sing; fig* **tener (muchas) t.,** to be an old hand.
tablado *nm* 1 *(plataforma)* wooden plat-

form. 2 *Teat* stage.

tablao *nm fam* flamenco bar *o* show.

tablero *nm* 1 (*tablón*) panel, board; **t. de mandos**, (*de coche*) dash(board). 2 (*en juegos*) board; **t. de ajedrez**, chessboard.

tableta *nf* (*de chocolate*) bar.

tablón *nm* plank; (*en construcción*) beam; **t. de anuncios**, notice *o* US bulletin board.

tabú *adj & nm* (*pl* **tabúes**) taboo.

tabular *vtr* to tabulate.

taburete *nm* stool.

tacaño,-a I *adj* mean, stingy. II *nm,f* miser.

tacatá, tacataca *nm* baby-walker.

tacha *nf* (*defecto*) flaw, defect; **sin t.**, flawless, without blemish.

tachar *vtr* 1 to cross out. 2 *fig* **t. de**, to accuse of.

tacho *nm Am* bucket.

tachón *nm* (*borrón*) crossing out.

tachuela *nf* tack, stud.

tácito,-a *adj* tacit.

taciturno,-a *adj* 1 (*callado*) taciturn. 2 (*triste*) sullen.

taco *nm* 1 plug; (*de billetes*) wad; *Culin* (*de jamón, queso*) cube, piece; (*de bota de fútbol*) stud; (*en billar*) cue. 2 *Culin* taco, rolled-up tortilla pancake. 3 *fam* (*palabrota*) swearword. 4 *fam* (*lío*) mess, muddle; **armarse o hacerse un t.**, to get all mixed up. 5 **me gusta un t.**, I like it a lot. 6 *fam* **tacos**, (*años*) years.

tacón *nm* heel; **zapatos de t.**, high-heeled shoes.

taconeo *nm* (*pisada*) heel tapping; (*golpe*) stamping with the heels.

táctica *nf* tactics *pl*.

táctil *adj* tactile; **pantalla t.**, touch screen.

táctico,-a *adj* tactical.

tacto *nm* 1 (*sentido*) touch. 2 *fig* (*delicadeza*) tact; **tener t.**, to be tactful.

taekwondo *nm* tae kwon do.

tafetán *nm* taffeta.

tahur *nm* cardsharp.

Tailandia *n* Thailand.

tailandés,-esa I *adj* Thai. II *nm,f* (*persona*) Thai; **los tailandeses**, the Thai *o* Thais. III *nm* (*idioma*) Thai.

taimado,-a *adj* sly, crafty.

tajada *nf* 1 slice; *fig* **sacar o llevarse t.**, to take one's share. 2 *fam* (*borrachera*) drunkenness.

tajante *adj* incisive.

Tajo *n* **el T.**, the Tagus.

tal I *adj* 1 (*semejante*) such; (*más sustantivo singular contable*) such a; **en tales condiciones**, in such conditions; **nunca dije t. cosa**, I never said such a thing. 2 (*indeterminado*) such and such; **t. día y a t. hora**, on such a day and at such and such a time. 3 (*persona*) person called …; **te llamó una t. Amelia**, someone called Amelia phoned you. 4 (*locuciones*)

t. vez, perhaps, maybe; **como si t. cosa**, as if nothing had happened. II *adv* 1 (*así*) just; **t. cual**, just as it is; **t. (y) como**, just as. 2 **¿qué t.?**, how are things?; **¿qué t. ese vino?**, how do you find this wine? III *conj so* **con t. (de) que**, so long as, provided. IV *pron* (*cosa*) something; (*persona*) someone, somebody; **t. para cual**, two of a kind; **y t. y cual**, and so on.

tala *nf* tree felling.

taladradora *nf* drill.

taladrar *vtr* to drill; (*pared*) to bore through; (*papeles*) to punch.

taladro *nm* 1 (*herramienta*) drill. 2 (*agujero*) hole.

talante *nm* 1 (*carácter*) disposition. 2 (*voluntad*) **de buen t.**, willingly; **de mal t.**, unwillingly, reluctantly.

talar *vtr* (*árboles*) to fell, cut down.

talco *nm* talc; **polvos de t.**, talcum powder.

talega *nf* bag, sack.

talego *nm* 1 long bag, long sack. 2 *arg* (*cárcel*) clink, hole. 3 *arg* (*mil pesetas*) one thousand peseta note.

talento *nm* talent.

Talgo *nm* fast passenger train.

talismán *nm* talisman, lucky charm.

talla *nf* 1 (*de prenda*) size; **¿qué t. usas?**, what size are you? 2 (*estatura*) height; *fig* stature; *fig* **dar la t.**, to make the grade. 3 (*escultura*) carving, sculpture. 4 (*tallado*) cutting, carving.

tallado,-a *nm* (*de madera*) carving; (*de piedras preciosas*) cutting; (*de metales*) engraving.

tallar *vtr* 1 (*madera, piedra*) to carve, shape; (*piedras preciosas*) to cut; (*metales*) to engrave. 2 (*medir*) to measure the height of.

tallarines *nmpl* tagliatelle *sing*.

talle *nm* 1 (*cintura*) waist. 2 (*cuerpo*) (*de hombre*) build, physique; (*de mujer*) figure, shape.

taller *nm* 1 (*obrador*) workshop; *Aut* **t. de reparaciones**, garage. 2 *Ind* factory, mill.

tallo *nm* stem, stalk.

talón *nm* 1 (*del pie*) heel. 2 (*cheque*) cheque, *US* check.

talonario *nm* (*de cheques*) cheque *o US* check book; (*de billetes*) book of tickets.

tamaño *nm* size; **de gran t.**, large; **del t. de**, as large as, as big as.

tamaño,-a *adj* such a big, so big a.

tamarindo *nm* tamarind.

tambalearse *vr* (*persona*) to stagger; (*mesa*) to wobble; *fig* to teeter.

tambero *nm Am* (*mesonero*) innkeeper, landlord.

también *adv* (*igualmente*) too, also, as well; **tú t. puedes venir**, you can come too; **¿lo harás?, yo t.**, are you going to do it?, so am I.

tambor *nm* 1 (*Mús, de lavadora, de freno*) drum. 2 *Anat* eardrum.

Támesis *n* el T., the Thames.

tamiz *nm* sieve.

tamizar [1] *vtr* to sieve.

tampoco *adv* 1 (*en afirmativas*) nor, neither; **Juan no vendrá y María t.,** Juan won't come and neither will Maria; **no lo sé, - yo t.,** I don't know, - neither do I. 2 (*en negativas*) either, nor ... either; **la Bolsa no sube, pero t. baja,** the stock market isn't going up, but it's not going down either.

tampón *nm* tampon.

tan *adv* 1 such; (*más sustantivo singular contable*) such a; **es t. listo,** he's such a clever fellow; **no me gusta t. dulce,** I don't like it so sweet; **¡qué gente t. agradable!,** such nice people!; **¡qué vestido t. bonito!,** what a beautiful dress! 2 (*comparativo*) **t. ... como,** as ... as; **t. alto como tú,** as tall as you (are). 3 (*consecutivo*) so ... (that); **iba t. deprisa que no lo ví,** he was going so fast that I couldn't see him. 4 **t. siquiera,** at least; **t. sólo,** only.

tanda *nf* (*conjunto*) batch, lot; (*serie*) series *sing*; **por tandas,** in groups.

tándem *nm* tandem.

tanga *nm* tanga.

tangente *nf* tangent; *fig* **salirse** *o* **escaparse por la t.,** to go off at a tangent.

Tánger *n* Tangier.

tangible *adj* tangible.

tango *nm* tango.

tanque *nm* tank.

tantear I *vtr* 1 *fig* **t. a algn,** to sound sb out; **t. el terreno,** to see how the land lies. 2 (*calcular*) to estimate, guess. II *vi* *Dep* to (keep) score.

tanteo *nm* 1 (*cálculo*) estimate, guess. 2 *Dep* score.

tanto,-a I *nm* 1 (*punto*) point. 2 (*cantidad imprecisa*) so much, a certain amount; **t. por ciento,** percentage. 3 **un t.,** a bit; **la casa es un t. pequeña,** the house is rather *o* somewhat small. 4 **estar al t.,** (*informado*) to be informed; (*pendiente*) to be on the lookout.

II *adj* 1 (+ *singular*) so much; (+ *plural*) so many; **no le des t. dinero,** don't give him so much money; **¡ha pasado t. tiempo!,** it's been so long!; **no comas tantas manzanas,** don't eat so many apples. 2 **cincuenta y tantas personas,** fifty odd people; **en el año sesenta y tantos,** in nineteen sixty something. 3 **t. como,** as much as; **tantos,-as como,** as many as.

III *pron* 1 (+ *singular*) so much; **otro t.,** as much again, the same again; **no es** *o* **hay para t.,** it's not that bad. 2 (+ *plural*) so many; **otros tantos,** as many again; **uno de tantos,** run-of-the-mill; *fam* **a las tantas,** very late, at an un-

earthly hour.

IV *adv* 1 (*cantidad*) so much; **t. mejor/peor,** so much the better/worse; **t. más cuanto que,** all the more so because. 2 (*tiempo*) so long. 3 (*frecuencia*) so often. 4 **t. ... como,** both ... and; **t. tú como yo,** both you and I; **t. si vienes como si no,** whether you come or not. 5 (*locuciones*) **por lo t.,** therefore; **¡y t.!,** oh yes!, and how!

tañer [38] *vtr* to play.

tapa *nf* 1 (*cubierta*) lid; (*de botella*) cap, top; (*de libro*) cover; (*de zapato*) heelplate; *Aut* (*de cilindro*) head. 2 (*aperitivo*) appetizer.

tapadera *nf* (*tapa*) cover, lid; *fig* cover, front.

tapadillo *nm* **hacer algo de t.,** to do sth secretly.

tapar I *vtr* 1 to cover; (*botella etc*) to put the lid *o* top on; (*con ropas o mantas*) to wrap up. 2 (*ocultar*) to hide; (*vista*) to block. 3 (*encubrir*) to cover up for sb. II **taparse** *vr* (*cubrirse*) to cover oneself; (*abrigarse*) to wrap up.

taparrabos *nm inv* loincloth.

tapete *nm* (table) cover; *fig* **poner algo sobre el t.,** to table sth.

tapia *nf* garden wall.

tapiar [12] *vtr* 1 (*área*) to wall off. 2 (*puerta, ventana etc*) to wall, close up.

tapicería *nf* 1 tapestry; (*de muebles, coche*) upholstery. 2 (*tienda*) upholsterer's shop *o* workshop.

tapioca *nf* tapioca.

tapiz *nm* tapestry.

tapizar [4] *vtr* to upholster.

tapón *nm* 1 (*de lavabo etc*) stopper, plug; (*de botella*) cap, cork; **t. de rosca,** screw-on cap. 2 (*de oídos*) earplug. 3 (*en baloncesto*) block. 4 *Aut* traffic jam.

taponar I *vtr* 1 (*tubería, hueco*) to plug. 2 *Med* (*herida*) to tampon. II **taponarse** *vr* **se me han taponado los oídos,** my ears are blocked up.

taquigrafía *nf* shorthand.

taquígrafo,-a *nm,f* shorthand writer.

taquilla *nf* 1 ticket office, booking office; *Cin Teat* box-office; **un éxito de t.,** a box-office success. 2 (*recaudación*) takings *pl.* 3 (*armario*) locker.

taquillero,-a I *adj* popular; **película taquillera,** box office hit. II *nm,f* booking *o* ticket clerk.

tara *nf* 1 (*peso*) tare. 2 (*defecto*) defect, fault.

tarántula *nf* tarantula.

tararear *vtr* to hum.

tardanza *nf* delay.

tardar I *vtr* to take time; **¿cuánto va a t.?,** how long will it take?; **tardé dos horas en venir,** it took me two hours to get here. II *vi* (*demorar*) to take long; **si tarda mucho me voy,** if it takes much longer, I'm going; **no tardes,** don't be long; **a más t.,** at the latest. **III tardarse** *vr* ¿**cuánto se tarda en llegar?,** how long does it take to get there?

tarde I *nf* **1** *(hasta las cinco)* afternoon. **2** *(después de las cinco)* evening. **3 la t.- noche,** late evening. **II** *adv* **1** late; **siento llegar t.,** sorry I'm late. **2** *(locuciones)* **de t. en t.,** very rarely, not very often; **(más) t. o (más) temprano,** sooner or later.

tardío,-a *adj* late, belated.

tardo,-a *adj* slow.

tarea *nf* job, task; **tareas,** *(de ama de casa)* housework *sing*; *(de estudiante)* homework *sing*.

tarifa *nf* **1** *(precio)* tariff, rate; *(en transportes)* fare. **2** *(lista de precios)* price list.

tarima *nf* platform, dais.

tarjeta *nf* card; **t. postal,** postcard; **t. de crédito,** credit card; **t. de visita,** visiting *o* US calling card; *Inform* **t. perforada,** punch *o* punched card.

tarraconense I *adj* of *o* from Tarragona. **II** *nmf* native *o* inhabitant of Tarragona.

tarro *nm* **1** *(vasija)* jar, pot, tub. **2** *fam* *(cabeza)* bonce. **3** *Am* *(lata)* tin, can.

tarta *nf* tart, pie.

tartamudear *vi* to stutter, stammer.

tartamudo,-a I *adj* stuttering, stammering. **II** *nm,f* stutterer, stammerer.

tartana *nf fam* *(coche viejo)* banger, heap.

tártaro,-a *adj* **salsa tártara,** tartar sauce.

tartera *nf* **1** *(fiambrera)* lunch box. **2** *(cazuela)* baking tin.

tarugo *nm* **1** *(de madera)* lump of wood. **2** *fam* *(persona)* blockhead.

tarumba *adj fam* crazy, mad; **estar t.,** to be bonkers.

tasa *nf* **1** *(precio)* fee; **tasas académicas,** course fees. **2** *(impuesto)* tax. **3** *(índice)* rate; **t. de natalidad/mortalidad,** birth/death rate. **4** *(valoración)* valuation, appraisal.

tasación *nf* valuation.

tasador,-a *nm,f* valuer.

tasar *vtr* **1** *(valorar)* to value; **t. una casa en diez millones de pesetas,** to value a house at ten million pesetas. **2** *(poner precio)* to set *o* fix the price of.

tasca *nf fam* bar, pub.

tata *nf fam* nanny.

tatarabuelo,-a *nm,f* *(hombre)* great-great-grandfather; *(mujer)* great-great-grandmother; **tatarabuelos,** great-great grandparents.

tataranieto,-a *nm,f* *(hombre)* great-great-grandson; *(mujer)* great-great-granddaughter; **tataranietos,** great-great-grandchildren.

tatuaje *nm* tattoo.

tatuar [10] *vtr* to tattoo.

taurino,-a *adj* of *o* relating to bullfighting.

Tauro *nm* Taurus.

tauromaquia *nf* tauromachy, (art of)

bullfighting.

TAV *abr de* **Tren de Alta Velocidad.**

taxativo,-a *adj* categorical.

taxi *nm* taxi.

taxímetro *nm* taximeter, clock.

taxista *nmf* taxi driver.

taza *nf* **1** cup; **una t. de café,** *(recipiente)* coffee cup; *(contenido)* a cup of coffee. **2** *(de retrete)* bowl.

tazón *nm* bowl.

te *pron pers* **1** *(complemento directo)* you; *(complemento indirecto)* (to *o* for) you; **no quiero verte,** I don't want to see you; **te compraré uno,** I'll buy one for you, I'll buy you one; **te lo dije,** I told you so. **2** *(reflexivo)* yourself; **lávate,** wash yourself; *(sin traducción)* **bébetelo todo,** drink it up; **no te vayas,** don't go.

té *nm* *(pl* **tés)** tea; **t. con limón,** lemon tea.

tea *nf* torch.

teatral *adj* **1** **grupo t.,** theatre company; **obra t.,** play. **2** *fig* *(teatrero)* theatrical.

teatrero,-a *adj* theatrical.

teatro *nm* **1** theatre, *US* theater; **obra de t.,** play; **autor de t.,** playwright. **2** *Lit* drama.

tebeo *nm* children's comic.

techar *vtr* to roof.

techo *nm* *(de habitación)* ceiling; *(tejado)* roof; *Aut* **t. corredizo,** sun roof.

tecla *nf* key; *fig* **dar en la t.,** to get it right.

teclado *nm* keyboard; *Inform* **t. expandido,** expanded keyboard.

teclear I *vtr* to key in. **II** *vi* to drum with one's fingers.

técnica *nf* **1** *(tecnología)* technology. **2** *(método)* technique. **3** *(habilidad)* skill.

técnico,-a I *adj* technical. **II** *nm,f* technician, technical expert.

tecnicolor *nm* Technicolor.

tecno- *pref* techno-.

tecnócrata *nmf* technocrat.

tecnología *nf* technology.

tecnológico,-a *adj* technological.

tedio *nm* tedium, boredom.

tedioso,-a *adj* tedious, boring.

teja *nf Constr* tile; *fam fig* **a toca t.,** on the nail.

tejado *nm* roof.

tejanos *nmpl* jeans.

tejemaneje *nm fam* **1** *(actividad)* bustle, fuss. **2** *(maquinación)* intrigue, scheming.

tejer *vtr* *(en el telar)* to weave; *(hacer punto)* to knit; *(telaraña)* to spin; *fig* *(plan)* to plot, to scheme.

tejido *nm* **1** fabric; **t. de punto,** knitted fabric. **2** *Anat* tissue.

tejo *nm fam* **tirar los tejos a algn,** to make a play for sb.

tejón *nm* badger.

tel. *abr de* **teléfono,** telephone, tel.

tela *nf* **1** *Tex* material, fabric, cloth; *(de la*

leche) skin; **t. de araña,** cobweb; **t. metá-**
lica, gauze. **2** *fam (dinero)* dough. **3** *Arte*
canvass. **4** *fig* **poner en t. de juicio,** to
question; *fig* **tiene mucha t.,** it's not an
easy thing.

telar *nm Tex* loom.

telaraña *nf* cobweb, spider's web.

tele *nf fam* telly, TV.

telearrastre *nm* ski lift.

telecabina *nm* cable car.

telecomunicaciones *nfpl* telecommunications.

telediario *nm TV* television news bulletin.

teledirigido,-a *adj* remote-controlled.

telefax *nm* telefax, fax.

teleférico *nm* cable car *o* railway.

telefilm, telefilme *nm* TV film.

telefonazo *nm* **dar un t. (a algn),** to give
(sb) a ring.

telefonear *vt & vi* to telephone, phone.

telefónica *nf* **Compañía T.,** ≈ British
Telecom.

telefónico,-a *adj* telephone; **llamada telefó-**
nica, telephone call.

telefonista *nmf* (telephone) operator.

teléfono *nm* telephone, phone; **t. portátil,**
portable telephone; **t. móvil,** car phone;
está hablando por t., she's on the
phone; **te llamó por t.,** she phoned you.

telegrafiar [29] *vtr* to telegraph, wire.

telegráfico,-a *adj* telegraphic; **giro t.,**
giro, money order.

telégrafo *nm* **1** telegraph. **2 telégrafos,**
post office *sing*.

telegrama *nm* telegram, cable.

teleimpresor *nm,* **teleimpresora** *nf* teleprinter.

telele *nm fam* **darle a uno un t.,** to have a
fit.

telemando *nm* remote control (unit).

telenovela *nf* television serial.

teleobjetivo *nm* telephoto lens *sing*.

telepático,-a *adj* telepathic.

telescopio *nm* telescope.

teleserie *nf* television series.

telesilla *nm* chair lift.

telespectador,-a *nm,f TV* viewer.

telesquí *nm* ski lift.

teletexto *nm* teletext.

teletipo *nm* teleprinter.

televidente *nm,f TV* viewer.

televisar *vtr* to televise.

televisión *nf* **1** *(sistema)* television. **2** *fam*
(aparato) television set; **t. en color/en**
blanco y negro, colour/black and white
television; **ver la t.,** to watch television.

televisivo,-a *adj* television; **espacio t.,**
television programme.

televisor *nm* television set.

télex *nm inv* telex.

telón *nm Teat* curtain; *Pol Hist* **t. de ace-**
ro, iron curtain; **t. de fondo,** *Teat* backdrop; *fig* background.

telonero,-a *adj* **(grupo) t.,** support band.

tema *nm* **1** *(asunto)* topic, subject; *(de exa-*
men) subject; **temas de actualidad,**
current affairs. **2** *Mús* theme.

temario *nm (de examen)* programme.

temática *nf* subject matter.

temático,-a *adj* thematic.

temblar [1] *vi (de frío)* to shiver; *(de mie-*
do) to tremble **(de,** with); *(voz)* to quiver;
(pulso) to shake.

tembleque *nm fam* shaking fit.

temblón,-ona *adj fam* trembling, shaky.

temblor *nm* tremor, shudder; **t. de tierra,**
earth tremor.

tembloroso,-a, tembloso,-a *adj* shaking; *(voz)* quivering, *(de frío)* shivering;
(de miedo) trembling; **manos temblo-**
sas, shaky hands.

temer I *vtr* to fear, be afraid; **temo que**
esté muerto, I fear he's dead; **temo que**
no podrá recibirte, I'm afraid (that) he
won't be able to see you. **II** *vi* to be
afraid. **III temerse** *vr* to fear, be afraid;
¡me lo temía!, I was afraid this would
happen!

temerario,-a *adj* reckless, rash.

temeridad *nf* **1** *(actitud)* temerity, rashness. **2** *(acto temerario)* reckless act.

temeroso,-a *adj* **1** fearful, timid. **2** *(temi-*
ble) frightful.

temible *adj* fearful, frightful.

temor *nm* **1** fear. **2** *(recelo)* worry, apprehension.

témpano *nm* ice floe.

temperamental *adj* temperamental.

temperamento *nm* temperament; **tener**
t., to have a strong character.

temperatura *nf* temperature.

tempestad *nf* storm; *fig* turmoil, uproar.

tempestuoso,-a *adj* stormy, tempest-
uous.

templado,-a *adj* **1** *(agua)* lukewarm; *(cli-*
ma) mild, temperate. **2** *Mús (afinado)*
tuned.

templanza *nf* moderation, restraint.

templar *vtr* **1** to moderate. **2** *(algo frío)* to
warm up; *(algo caliente)* to cool down. **3**
Mús (instrumento) to tune. **4** *Téc (metal)* to
temper.

temple *nm* **1** *(fortaleza)* boldness, courage.
2 *Arte* tempera.

templete *nm* bandstand.

templo *nm* temple.

temporada *nf* **1** season; **t. alta,** high *o*
peak season; **t. baja,** low *o* off season. **2**
(período) period, time; **por temporadas,**
on and off.

temporal I *adj* temporary, provisional. **II**
nm storm.

temporero,-a *nm,f* seasonal *o* temporary
worker.

tempranero,-a *adj* **1** *(persona)* early-
rising. **2** *(cosecha)* early.

temprano,-a *adj & adv* early.

tenacidad *nf* **1** *(perseverancia)* tenacity,

perseverance. 2 *(de metal)* tensile
strength.

tenacillas *nfpl (para pelo)* curling tongs.

tenaz *adj* tenacious.

tenaza *nf*, **tenazas** *nfpl (herramienta)*
pliers, pincers; *(para el fuego)* tongs.

tendedero *nm* clothesline, drying place.

tendencia *nf* tendency.

tendencioso,-a *adj* tendentious, biased.

tender [3] **I** *vtr* 1 *(mantel etc)* to spread
out; *(para secar)* to hang out. 2 *(red)* to
cast; *(puente)* to build; *(vía, cable)* to lay;
(trampa) to lay, set. 3 *(mano)* to stretch *o*
hold out. 4 *(tumbar)* to lay. **II** *vi* to tend
(**a**, to), have a tendency (**a**, to). **III**
tenderse *vr* to lie down, stretch out.

tenderete *nm (puesto)* market stall.

tendero,-a *nm,f* shopkeeper.

tendido *nm* 1 *(de vía, cable)* laying; *(de
puente)* construction; **t. eléctrico**, electrical installation. 2 *Taur (asientos)* front
tiers *pl* of seats, *US* bleachers *pl*.

tendón *nm* tendon, sinew.

tenebroso,-a *adj (sombrío)* dark, gloomy;
(siniestro) sinister, shady.

tenedor,-a *nm* fork.

teneduría *nf* **t. de libros**, book-keeping.

tenencia *nf Jur* **t. ilícita de armas**, illegal
possession of arms.

tener [24] **I** *vtr* 1 to have, have got; **tenemos un examen**, we've got *o* we have an
exam; **va a t. un niño**, she's going to
have a baby, she's expecting; **¡ahí (lo)
tienes!**, here you are! 2 *(poseer)* to own,
possess. 3 *(sostener)* to hold; **tenme el
bolso un momento**, hold my bag a minute; **ten, es para ti**, take this *o* here you
are, it's for you. 4 **t. calor/frío**, to be
hot/cold; **t. cariño a algn**, to be fond of
sb; **t. miedo**, to be frightened. 5 *(edad)*
to be; **tiene dieciocho (años)**, he's eighteen (years old). 6 *(medida)* **la casa tiene
cien metros cuadrados**, the house is 100
square metres. 7 *(contener)* to hold, contain. 8 *(mantener)* to keep; **me tuvo despierto toda la noche**, he kept me up all
night. 9 **t. por**, *(considerar)* to consider,
think; **me tienen por estúpido**, they
think I'm a fool; **ten por seguro que lloverá**, you can be sure it'll rain. 10 **t.
que**, to have (got) to; **tengo que irme**, I
must leave; **tienes/tendrías que verlo**,
you must/should see it.
II tenerse *vr* 1 **t. en pie**, to stand (up). 2
t. por, *(considerarse)* to think *o* consider
oneself; **se tiene por muy inteligente**, he
thinks he's very intelligent.

tenga *subj pres* → **tener**.

tengo *indic pres* → **tener**.

teniente *nm* 1 *Mil* lieutenant. 2 **t. (de)
alcalde**, deputy mayor.

tenis *nm* tennis.

tenista *nmf* tennis player.

tenor¹ *nm Mús* tenor.

tenor² *nm* **a t. de**, according to.

tensar *vtr (cable etc)* to tighten; *(arco)* to
draw.

tensión *nf* 1 tension; **en t.**, tense. 2 *Elec*
tension, voltage. 3 *Med* **t. arterial**, blood
pressure; **t. nerviosa**, nervous strain. 4
Téc stress.

tenso,-a *adj* 1 *(cuerda, cable)* tense, taut.
2 *(persona)* tense; *(relaciones)* strained.

tentación *nf* temptation.

tentáculo *nm* tentacle.

tentador,-a *adj* tempting.

tentar [1] *vtr* 1 *(palpar)* to feel, touch. 2
(incitar) to tempt.

tentativa *nf* attempt; *Jur* **t. de asesinato**,
attempted murder.

tentempié *nm fam (pl* **tentempiés)** 1
(comida) snack, bite. 2 *(juguete)* tumbler.

tenue *adj* 1 *(luz, sonido)* subdued, faint. 2
(delgado) thin, light.

teñir [6] **I** *vtr* 1 *(pelo etc)* to dye. 2 *fig* to
tinge with. **II teñirse** *vr* **t. el pelo**, to dye
one's hair.

teología *nf* theology.

teorema *nm* theorem.

teoría *nf* theory; **en t.**, theoretically.

teórico,-a *adj* theoretical.

teorizar [4] *vi* to theorize (**sobre**, on).

tequila *nm* tequila.

terapeuta *nmf* therapist.

terapia *nf* therapy.

tercer *adj* third; **el t. mundo**, the third
world.

tercermundista *adj* third-world.

tercero,-a **I** *adj* third. **II** *nm,f* 1 *(de una
serie)* third; **a la tercera va la vencida**,
third time lucky. **III** *nm (mediador)*
mediator; *Jur* third party.

terceto *nm Mús* trio.

terciar [12] **I** *vi* 1 *(mediar)* to mediate,
arbitrate. 2 *(participar)* to take part,
participate. **II terciarse** *vr* **si se tercia**,
should the occasion arise.

terciario,-a *adj* tertiary.

tercio *nm* 1 *(parte)* (one) third. 2 *(de cerveza)* medium-size bottle of beer. 3 *Taur*
stage, part (of a bullfight).

terciopelo *nm* velvet.

terco,-a *adj* stubborn, obstinate.

tergiversar *vtr (verdad)* to distort; *(palabras)* to twist.

termal *adj* thermal.

termas *nfpl (baños)* spa *sing*, hot baths *o*
springs *pl*.

térmico,-a *adj* thermal; **central térmica**,
coal-fired power station.

terminación *nf* completion.

terminal **I** *adj* terminal. **II** *nf* 1 *(de aeropuerto)* terminal; *(de autobús)* terminus. 2
Elec Inform terminal.

terminante *adj* 1 *(categórico)* categorical,
final. 2 *(dato, resultado)* conclusive.
◆**terminantemente** *adv* categorically;
t. prohibido, strictly forbidden.

terminar I *vtr* (*acabar*) to finish, complete; (*completamente*) to finish off. II *vi* 1 (*acabarse*) to finish, end; **termina en seis,** it ends with a six; **no termina de convencerse,** he still isn't quite convinced. 2 (*ir a parar*) to end up (**en,** in); **terminó por comprarlo,** he ended up buying it. 3 **t. con,** (*eliminar*) to put an end to. III **terminarse** *vr* 1 to finish, end, be over. 2 (*vino, dinero etc*) to run out.

término *nm* 1 (*final*) end, finish. 2 (*palabra*) term, word; **en otros términos,** in other words; **en términos generales,** generally speaking. 3 **t. municipal,** district. 4 **por t. medio,** on average. 5 *fig* **en último t.,** as a last resort.

terminología *nf* terminology.

termo *nm* thermos (flask), flask.

termodinámico,-a *adj* thermodynamic.

termómetro *nm* thermometer.

termonuclear *adj* thermonuclear.

termostato *nm* thermostat.

ternera *nf* calf; (*carne*) veal.

ternero *nm* calf.

ternura *nf* tenderness.

terquedad *nf* stubbornness, obstinacy.

terracota *nf* terracotta.

Terranova *n* Newfoundland.

terraplén *nm* embankment.

terráqueo,-a *adj* **globo t.,** (*tierra*) (the) earth; (*esfera*) globe.

terrateniente *nmf* landowner.

terremoto *nm* earthquake.

terrenal *adj* **un paraíso t.,** a heaven on earth.

terreno *nm* 1 (*tierra*) (piece of) land, ground; *Geol* terrain; (*campo*) field; **ganar/perder t.,** to gain/lose ground. 2 *Dep* field, ground. 3 *fig* field, sphere.

terrestre *adj* 1 (*de la tierra*) terrestrial, earthly. 2 (*por tierra*) by land; **por vía t.,** by land.

terrible *adj* terrible, awful.

terrícola *nmf* (*en ciencia ficción*) earthling.

terrier *nm* terrier.

territorio *nm* territory.

terrón *nm* (*de azúcar*) lump; (*de tierra*) clod.

terror *nm* terror; *Cin* horror.

terrorífico,-a *adj* terrifying, frightening.

terrorismo *nm* terrorism.

terrorista *adj & nmf* terrorist.

terroso,-a *adj* (*color*) earth-coloured, *US* earth-colored.

terruño *nm* (*terreno*) piece of land; (*patria chica*) homeland, native land.

terso,-a *adj* smooth.

tersura *nf* smoothness.

tertulia *nf* get-together; **t. literaria,** literary gathering.

tesina *nf* first degree dissertation.

tesis *nf inv* thesis; (*opinión*) view, theory.

tesón *nm* tenacity, firmness.

tesorero,-a *nm,f* treasurer.

tesoro *nm* 1 treasure. 2 (*erario*) exchequer; **T. Público,** Treasury.

test *nm* test.

testaferro *nm* front man.

testamentario,-a *Jur* I *adj* testamentary. II *nm,f* executor.

testamento *nm* 1 *Jur* will; **hacer** *o* **otorgar t.,** to make *o* draw up one's will. 2 *Rel* Testament.

testar *vi* to make *o* draw up one's will.

testarudo,-a *adj* stubborn, obstinate.

testículo *nm* testicle.

testificar [1] *vtr* to testify.

testigo *nmf* witness; *Jur* **t. de cargo/descargo,** witness for the prosecution/defence; *Jur* **t. ocular/presencial,** eyewitness; *Rel* **Testigos de Jehová,** Jehovah's Witnesses. II *nm Dep* baton.

testimoniar [12] *vtr* 1 (*dar testimonio*) to testify to, attest to. 2 (*mostrar*) to show.

testimonio *nm* *Jur* testimony; (*prueba*) evidence, proof.

teta *nf fam* 1 tit, boob; **niño de t.,** breastfeeding baby. 2 (*de vaca*) udder.

tétano *nm* tetanus.

tetera *nf* teapot.

tetilla *nf* 1 *Anat* man's nipple. 2 (*de biberón*) (rubber) teat.

tetina *nf* (rubber) teat.

tétrico,-a *adj* gloomy, dull.

textil *adj & nm* textile.

texto *nm* text; **libro de t.,** textbook.

textual *adj* textual; (*exacto*) literal; **en palabras textuales,** literally.

textura *nf* *Tex* texture; (*en minerales*) structure.

tez *nf* complexion.

ti *pron pers* you; **es para ti,** it's for you; **hazlo por ti,** do it for your own sake; **piensas demasiado en ti mismo,** you think too much about yourself.

tía *nf* 1 (*pariente*) aunt. 2 *arg* (*mujer*) girl, woman.

tibieza *nf* tepidity; *fig* lack of enthusiasm.

tibio,-a *adj* tepid, lukewarm; *fam* **ponerse t. de cerveza,** to get pissed.

tiburón *nm* shark.

tic *nm* (*pl* **tiques**) tic, twitch; **t. nervioso,** nervous tic *o* twitch.

ticket *nm* (*pl* **tickets**) (*billete*) ticket; (*recibo*) receipt.

tictac *nm* tick-tock, ticking.

tiempo *nm* 1 time; **a t.,** in time; **a su** (**debido**) **t.,** in due course; **a un t.,** **al mismo t.,** at the same time; **al poco t.,** soon afterwards; **antes de t.,** (too) early *o* soon; **con el t.,** in the course of time, with time; **con t.,** in advance; **¿cuánto t.?,** how long?; **¿cuánto t. hace?,** how long ago?; **demasiado t.,** too long; **estar a t. de,** to still have time to; **hacer t.,** to kill time; **¿nos da t. de llegar?,** have we got (enough) time to get there?; **t. libre,** free time; *fig* **dar t. al t.,** to let matters take their course. 2 (*meteorológico*) weather; ¿**qué t. hace?**, what's the weather like?; **hace buen/mal t.**, the weather is good/bad. 3 (*edad*) age; ¿**cuánto** o **qué t. tiene tu niño?**, how old is your baby o child? 4 *Mús* movement. 5 *Dep* half. 6 *Ling* tense.

tienda *nf* 1 shop, *US* store; **ir de tiendas**, to go shopping. 2 **t. (de campaña)**, tent.

tienta *nf* **a tientas**, by touch; **andar a tientas**, to feel one's way; **buscar (algo) a tientas**, to grope (for sth).

tiento *nm* tact; **con t.**, tactfully.

tierno,-a *adj* 1 (*blando*) tender, soft. 2 (*reciente*) fresh.

tierra *nf* 1 (*planeta*) earth. 2 *Agr* land, soil. 3 (*continente*) land; **tocar t.**, to land. 4 (*país*) country; **t. de nadie**, no-man's-land. 5 (*suelo*) ground; *fig* **echar** o **tirar por t.**, to spoil. 6 *Elec* earth, *US* ground.

tierral *nm Am* cloud of dust.

tieso,-a *adj* (*rígido*) stiff, rigid; (*erguido*) upright, erect.

tiesto *nm* flowerpot.

tifoidea *nf* (*fiebre*) **t.**, typhoid (fever).

tifón *nm* typhoon.

tifus *nm inv* typhus (fever).

tigre *nm* tiger; *Am* jaguar.

tijeras *nf* (pair of) scissors *pl*.

tijereta *nf* 1 (*insecto*) earwig. 2 *Dep* scissors *pl*.

tila *nf* (*flor*) lime o linden blossom; (*infusión*) lime o linden blossom tea.

tildar *vtr* to call, brand; **me tildó de ladrón**, he called me a thief.

tilde *nm & f* written accent.

tilín *nm* (*sonido*) ting-a-ling; *fig* **José le hace t.**, she fancies José.

tilo *nm* lime tree.

timar *vtr* to swindle; **me han timado**, they did me.

timbal *nm* kettledrum.

timbrar *vtr* (*carta*) to stamp; (*documento*) to seal.

timbre *nm* 1 (*de la puerta*) bell. 2 (*sello*) stamp, seal; *Fin* fiscal o revenue stamp. 3 *Mús* (*sonido*) timbre.

timidez *nf* shyness, timidity.

tímido,-a *adj* shy, timid; *fig* (*mejoría*) light; (*intento*) cautious.

timo *nm* swindle, fiddle; **es un t.**, it's a rip-off.

timón *nm* 1 *Náut Av* rudder; **golpe de t.**, U-turn. 2 *Am Aut* steering wheel.

timonel *nm* helmsman.

tímpano *nm Anat* eardrum.

tinaja *nf* large earthenware jar.

tinerfeño,-a I *adj* of o from to Tenerife. II *nm,f* native o inhabitant of Tenerife.

tinglado *nm* 1 (*intriga*) intrigue. 2 (*cobertizo*) shed.

tinieblas *nfpl* darkness *sing*.

tino *nm* 1 (*puntería*) (good) aim; **tener buen t.**, to be a good shot. 2 (*tacto*) (common) sense, good judgement.

tinta *nf* 1 ink; **t. china**, Indian ink; **t. simpática**, invisible ink. 2 *fig* **medias tintas**, ambiguities, half measures.

tintar *vtr* to dye.

tinte *nm* 1 dye. 2 *fig* (*matiz*) shade, overtone.

tintero *nm* inkpot, inkwell; *fig* **se quedó en el t.**, it wasn't said.

tintinear *vi* (*vidrio*) to clink; (*campana*) to jingle, tinkle.

tintineo *nm* (*de vidrio*) clinking; (*de campana*) jingling.

tinto I *adj* (*vino*) red. II *nm* (*vino*) red wine.

tintorería *nf* dry-cleaner's.

tintura *nf* 1 (*colorante*) dye. 2 *Quím* tincture; **t. de yodo**, iodine.

tío *nm* 1 (*pariente*) uncle; **mis tíos**, my uncle and aunt. 2 *fam* fellow, bloke, *US* guy.

tiovivo *nm* roundabout, merry-go-round.

tipazo *nm fam* good figure.

típico,-a *adj* 1 typical; **eso es t. de Antonio**, that's just like Antonio. 2 (*baile, traje*) traditional.

tipificar [1] *vtr* 1 (*normalizar*) to standardize. 2 (*caracterizar*) to typify.

tipismo *nm* local colour.

tipo *nm* 1 (*clase*) type, kind. 2 *fam* (*persona*) guy, fellow, bloke, *US* guy; **t. raro**, weirdo. 3 *Anat* (*de hombre*) build, physique; (*de mujer*) figure; (*de mujer*) **jugarse el t.**, to risk one's neck; **aguantar el t.**, to keep one's cool o head. 4 *Fin* rate; **t. bancario** o **de descuento**, bank rate; **t. de cambio/interés**, rate of exchange/interest. 5 **el político t. de la izquierda**, the typical left-wing politician.

tipografía *nf* typography.

tipográfico,-a *adj* typographic; **error t.**, printing error.

tipógrafo,-a *nm,f* typographer.

tiquismiquis *fam* I *nmf inv* fusspot. II *nmpl* 1 (*escrúpulos*) silly scruples. 2 (*rencillas*) bickering *sing*.

tira *nf* 1 (*banda, cinta*) strip. 2 (*de dibujos*) comic strip. 3 *fam* **la t. de gente**, a lot o loads of people. 4 **t. y afloja**, tug of war.

tirabuzón *nm* ringlet.

tirachinas *nm inv* catapult, *US* slingshot.

tirada *nf* (*impresión*) printing; (*edición*) edition.

tirado,-a *adj fam* 1 (*precio*) dirt cheap. 2 (*examen*) dead easy. 3 *fam* **dejar t.** (a algn), to let (sb) down.

tirador *nm* 1 (*persona*) marksman. 2 (*pomo*) knob, handle; (*cordón*) bell pull. 3 (*tirachinas*) catapult, *US* slingshot.

tiralíneas *nm inv* tracer, drawing o ruling pen.

tiranía *nf* tyranny.

tiránico,-a *adj* tyrannical.

tiranizar [4] *vtr* to tyrannize.

tirano,-a *nm,f* tyrant.
tirante I *adj (cable etc)* tight, taut; *(situación, relación)* tense. II *nm* 1 *(de vestido etc)* strap; **tirantes**, braces, *US* suspenders. 2 *Téc* brace, stay.
tirar I *vtr* 1 *(echar)* to throw, fling. 2 *(dejar caer)* to drop. 3 *(desechar)* to throw away; *fig (dinero)* to squander. 4 *(derribar)* to knock down; **t. la puerta (abajo)**, to smash the door in. 5 *(foto)* to take. 6 *Impr* to print. 7 *(beso)* to blow. II *vi* 1 **t. de**, *(cuerda, puerta)* to pull. 2 *(chimenea, estufa)* to draw. 3 *(funcionar)* to work, run. 4 **ir tirando**, to get by. 5 **t. a**, to tend towards; **tira a rojo**, it's reddish. 6 **tira a la izquierda**, turn left; **¡venga, tira ya!**, come on, get going! 7 *(disparar)* to shoot, fire; *Ftb* **t. a puerta**, to shoot at goal. III **tirarse** *vr* 1 *(lanzarse)* to throw *o* hurl oneself; **t. de cabeza al agua**, to dive into the water. 2 *(tumbarse)* to lie down. 3 *fam (tiempo)* to spend; **me tiré una hora esperando**, I waited (for) a good hour. 4 *vulg* **t. a algn**, to lay sb.
tirita® *nf* Elastoplast®, Band-aid®, plaster.
tiritar *vi* to shiver, to shake.
tiro *nm* 1 *(lanzamiento)* throw. 2 *(disparo, ruido)* shot; *Ftb* **t. a gol**, shot at goal; **t. al blanco**, target shooting; **t. al plato**, clay pigeon shooting; **t. con arco**, archery. 3 *(de vestido)* shoulder width. 4 *(de chimenea)* draught, *US* draft; **animal de t.**, draught animal.
tirón *nm* pull, tug; *(del bolso)* snatch; *fam* **de un t.**, in one go.
tirotear *vtr* to shoot, snipe.
tiroteo *nm* shooting, firing to and fro.
tirria *nf fam* dislike; **le tengo t.**, I dislike him, I can't stand him.
tísico,-a *adj* tubercular, consumptive.
tisis *nf inv* tuberculosis, consumption.
tisú *nm* tissue, paper hankie.
títere *nm (marioneta)* puppet; **no dejar t. con cabeza**, to spare no-one.
titilar *vi (luz)* to flicker; *(estrella)* to twinkle.
titiritero,-a *nm,f* 1 puppeteer. 2 *(acróbata)* travelling acrobat.
titubeante *adj (indeciso)* hesitant; *(al hablar)* stammering.
titubear *vi* 1 *(dudar)* to hesitate, waver. 2 *(al hablar)* to stammer.
titubeo *nm* 1 *(duda)* hesitation. 2 *(al hablar)* stammering.
titulación *nf* qualifications *pl.*
titulado,-a *adj (licenciado)* graduate; *(diplomado)* qualified.
titular¹ I *nmf (persona)* holder. II *nm Prensa* headline. III *adj* appointed, official.
titular² I *vtr (poner título)* to call. II **titularse** *vr* 1 *(película etc)* to be called; **¿cómo se titula?**, what is it called? 2 *Educ* to graduate (**en**, in).

titulariedad *nf Educ* tenure.
titulitis I *nf* obsession with qualifications. II *nm fam* certificate.
título *nm* 1 title. 2 *Educ* degree; *(diploma)* diploma. 3 *Prensa (titular)* headline. 4 **a t. de ejemplo**, by way of example.
tiza *nf* chalk; **una t.**, a piece of chalk.
tiznada *nf Am* **hijo de la t.**, son of a bitch.
tiznar *vtr* to blacken (with soot).
tizne *nm* soot.
tizón *nm* half-burnt stick, brand.
toalla *nf* towel; **tirar la t.**, to throw in the towel.
toallero *nm* towel rack *o* rail.
tobera *nf* nozzle.
tobillo *nm* ankle.
tobogán *nm* slide, chute.
toca *nf (sombrero)* headdress; *(de monja)* wimple..
tocadiscos *nm inv* record player; **t. digital** *o* **compacto**, CD player.
tocado¹ *nm* 1 *(peinado)* coiffure, hairdo. 2 *(prenda)* headdress.
tocado,-a² *adj fam* crazy, touched.
tocador *nm* 1 *(mueble)* dressing table. 2 *(habitación)* dressing room; **t. de señoras**, powder room.
tocante a *loc adv* **en lo t. a ...**, with reference to ....
tocar [1] I *vtr* 1 to touch; *fam fig* **toca madera**, touch wood. 2 *(instrumento, canción)* to play; *(timbre, campana)* to ring; *(puerta)* to knock; *(bocina)* to blow. 3 *(tema, asunto)* to touch on. 4 *(afectar)* to concern; **por lo que a mí me toca**, as far as I am concerned. II *vi* 1 **¿a quién le toca?**, *(en juegos)* whose turn is it? 2 **me tocó el gordo**, *(en rifa)* I won the jackpot. 3 **t. con**, to be next to; *fig* **t. a su fin**, to be coming to an end. III **tocarse** *vr (una cosa con otra)* to touch each other; **¿os tocáis algo?**, *(ser parientes)* are you related?
tocarse *vr (cubrirse)* to cover one's head.
tocata I *nf Mús* toccata. II *nm fam* record player.
tocateja (a) *loc adv* **pagar a t.**, to pay on the nail.
tocayo,-a *nm,f* namesake.
tocho *nm fam (libro) (grande)* tome.
tocino *nm* lard; **t. ahumado**, smoked bacon; **t. de cielo**, sweet made with egg yolk.
tocólogo,-a *nm* tocologist, obstetrician.
tocuyo *nm Am* coarse cotton cloth.
todavía *adv* 1 *(aún)* still; *(en negativas)* yet; **t. la quiere**, he still loves her; **t. no**, not yet; **no mires t.**, don't look yet. 2 *(para reforzar)* even, still; **t. más/menos**, even more/less.
todo,-a I *adj* 1 all; **t. el pan**, all the bread; **t. el mundo**, (absolutely) everybody; **t. el día**, all day, the whole *o* en-

tire day; *fam* **t. quisqui**, every Tom, Dick and Harry. **2** *(cada)* every; **t. ciudadano de más de dieciocho años**, every citizen over eighteen years of age. **3** *(entero)* complete, thorough; **es toda una mujer**, she is every inch a woman. **4 todos,-as**, all; *(con expresiones de tiempo)* every; **t. los niños**, all the children; **t. los martes**, every Tuesday.
II *nm (totalidad)* whole.
III *pron* **1** *(sin excluir nada)* all, everything; **ante t.**, first of all; **con t.**, in spite of everything; **del t.**, completely; **después de t.**, after all; **eso es t.**, that's all, that's it; **estar en t.**, to be really with it; **hay de t.**, there are all sorts; **lo sé t.**, I know all about it; **t. lo contrario**, quite the contrary *o* opposite; **t. lo más**, at the most. **2** *(cualquiera)* anybody; **t. aquél** *o* **el que quiera**, anybody who wants (to). **3 todos,-as**, *(cada uno)* **t. aprobamos**, we all passed; **t. fueron**, they all went.
IV *adv* completely, totally; **volvió t. sucio**, he was all dirty when he got back.
todopoderoso,-a *adj* all-powerful, almighty.
todoterreno *nm* all-terrain vehicle.
toga *nf* **1** gown, robe. **2** *Hist* toga.
Tokio *n* Tokyo.
toldo *nm* **1** *(cubierta)* awning. **2** *Am (cabaña)* tent, teepee.
tolerancia *nf* tolerance.
tolerante *adj* tolerant.
tolerar *vtr* to tolerate; *(situación)* to stand; *(gente)* to put up with.
toma *nf* **1** *(acción)* taking; *Elec* **t. de corriente**, plug, socket. **2** *Med* dose. **3** *Mil* capture. **4** *Cin* take, shot. **5 t. de posesión**, swearing-in. **6** *fam fig* **toma y daca**, give and take.
tomado,-a *adj* **1** *(voz)* hoarse. **2** *Am (borracho)* drunk. **3 tenerla tomada con algn**, to have it in for sb.
tomadura *nf fam* **t. de pelo**, leg-pull; *(timo)* rip-off.
tomar **I** *vtr* **1** *(coger)* to take; *(autobús, tren)* to catch; *(decisión)* to make, take; **toma**, here (you are); **t. el sol**, to sunbathe; *Av* **t. tierra**, to land; *fam* **tomarla con algn**, to have it in for sb. **2** *(comer, beber)* to have. **3 t. algo a mal**, to take sth badly; **t. en serio/broma**, to take seriously/as a joke. **4** *(confundir)* to take *(por,* for*)*. **5** *Mil* to take. **II tomarse** *vr* **1** *(comer)* to eat; *(beber)* to drink. **2** *fam* **no te lo tomes así**, don't take it like that.
tomate *nm* tomato; **salsa de t.**, *(de lata)* tomato sauce; *(de botella)* ketchup.
tomavistas *nm inv* cine *o* US movie camera.
tómbola *nf* tombola.
tomillo *nm* thyme.
tomo *nm* volume; *fam* **de t. y lomo**, utter, out-and-out.

ton *nm* **sin t. ni son**, without rhyme or reason.
tonada *nf* **1** *Mús* tune, song. **2** *Am (acento)* accent.
tonalidad *nf* tonality.
tonel *nm* barrel, cask.
tonelada *nf* ton; **t. métrica**, tonne.
tonelaje *nm* tonnage.
tonelero,-a *nm,f* cooper.
tongo *nm* fix.
tónico,-a **I** *nm* *Med* tonic; *(cosméticos)* skin tonic. **II** *nf* **1** *(tendencia)* tendency, trend; **tónica general**, overall trend. **2** *(bebida)* tonic (water). **3** *Mús* tonic. **III** *adj* **1** *Ling* tonic, stressed. **2** *Mús Med* tonic.
tonificante *adj* invigorating.
tonificar [1] *vtr* to tone up, invigorate.
tono *nm* tone; **a t. con**, in tune *o* harmony with; **subir de t.** *o* **el t.**, to speak louder; **un t. alto/bajo**, a high/low pitch; *fig* **darse t.**, to put on airs; *fig* **fuera de t.**, inappropiate, out of place; **dar el t.**, to set the tone.
tontear *vi* **1** to act the clown, fool about. **2** *(galantear)* to flirt.
tontería *nf* **1** stupidity, silliness. **2** *(dicho, hecho)* silly *o* stupid thing. **3** *(insignificancia)* trifle.
tonto,-a **I** *adj* silly, dumb. **II** *nm,f* fool, idiot; **t. de remate** *o* **de capirote**, prize idiot.
topacio *nm* topaz.
toparse *vr* **t. con**, to bump into; *(dificultades)* to run up against, encounter; **t. con algo**, to come across sth.
tope **I** *nm* **1** *(límite)* limit, end; *fam* **a t.**, *(al máximo)* flat out; *fig* **estar hasta los topes**, to be full up; **fecha t.**, deadline. **2** *Téc* stop, check. **3** *Ferroc* buffer. **II** *adv fam* incredibly; **t. difícil**, really difficult.
tópico,-a **I** *nm* commonplace, cliché. **II** *adj Med Farm* for external use.
topo *nm* mole.
topografía *nf* topography.
topónimo *nm* place name.
toque *nm* **1** touch; *fam* **dar un t. a algn**, *(avisar)* to let sb know; *(advertir)* to warn sb. **2** *(de campanas)* peal; *fig* warning; **t. de queda**, curfew.
toquetear *vtr* to fiddle with, finger.
toquilla *nf* (knitted) shawl.
tórax *nm* thorax.
torbellino *nm* **1** *(de viento)* whirlwind. **2** *fig (confusión)* whirl, turmoil.
torcedura *nf (acción)* twist, twisting; *Med* sprain.
torcer [4] **I** *vtr* **1** *(metal)* to bend; *(cuerda, hilo)* to twist; *Med* to sprain; *fig (esquina)* to turn. **2** *(inclinar)* to slant. **II** *vi* to turn (left *o* right). **III torcerse** *vr* **1** *(doblarse)* to twist, bend. **2** *Med* **se me torció el tobillo**, I sprained my ankle. **3** *(plan)* to fall through. **4** *(desviarse)* to go off to the side.

torcido,-a adj twisted; (ladeado) slanted, lopsided; (corbata) crooked.

tordo,-a I adj dapple-grey. II nm Orn thrush.

torear I vtr to fight; fam **t. a algn**, to tease o confuse sb; fam **t. un asunto**, to tackle a matter skilfully. II vi to fight.

toreo nm bullfighting.

torero,-a nm,f bullfighter.

tormenta nf storm.

tormento nm (tortura) torture; (padecimiento) torment.

tormentoso,-a adj stormy.

tornado nm tornado.

tornar fml I vtr (convertir) to transform, to turn (en, into). II vi (regresar) to return, go back; **t. en sí**, to regain consciousness. III **tornarse** vr to become, turn.

tornasolado,-a adj iridescent.

torneo nm 1 Dep tournament. 2 Hist tourney, joust.

tornillo nm screw.

torniquete nm 1 turnstile. 2 Med tourniquet.

torno nm 1 Téc lathe; (de alfarero) wheel. 2 **en t. a**, (alrededor de) around; (acerca de) about.

toro nm bull; ¿te gustan los toros?, do you like bullfighting?

toronja nf grapefruit.

torpe adj 1 (sin habilidad) clumsy. 2 (tonto) dim, thick. 3 (movimiento) slow, awkward.

torpedear vtr to torpedo.

torpedo nm torpedo.

torpeza nf 1 (física) clumsiness; (mental) dimness, stupidity. 2 (lentitud) slowness, heaviness. 3 (error) blunder.

torre nf 1 tower. 2 Mil Náut turret. 3 Ajedrez rook, castle.

torrefacto,-a adj roasted; **café t.**, high roast coffee.

torrencial adj torrential.

torrente nm 1 (de agua) torrent. 2 fig **t. de voz**, strong o powerful voice.

torrezno nm rasher of fried bacon.

tórrido,-a adj torrid.

torrija nf French toast.

torsión nf 1 (torcedura) twist, twisting. 2 Téc torsion.

torso nm 1 Anat torso. 2 Arte bust.

torta nf 1 Culin cake; 2 fam (golpe) slap, punch.

tortazo nm fam 1 (bofetada) slap, punch. 2 (golpe) whack, thump.

tortícolis nf inv crick in the neck.

tortilla nf 1 (egg) omelette, US omelet; **t. francesa/española**, (plain)/potato omelette. 2 Am tortilla.

tortillera nf vulg dyke, lesbian.

tórtola nf dove.

tortuga nf (de tierra) tortoise, US turtle; (de mar) turtle.

tortuoso,-a adj tortuous.

tortura nf torture.

torturar vtr to torture.

tos nf cough; **t. ferina**, whooping cough.

tosco,-a adj (basto) rustic, rough; (persona) uncouth.

toser vi to cough.

tosquedad nf roughness.

tostada nf (slice of) toast.

tostado,-a adj 1 (pan) toasted. 2 (moreno) tanned, brown.

tostador nm toaster.

tostar [2] vtr (pan) to toast; (café) to roast; (carne, pescado) to brown; fig (la piel) to tan.

tostón nm 1 Culin (pan frito) crouton. 2 fam (tabarra) bore, drag.

total I adj (completo) total. II nm 1 (todo) whole; **en t.**, in all. 2 Mat total. III adv so, in short; ¿**t. para qué?**, what's the point anyhow?; fam **t. que ...**, so ...; **t., tampoco te hará caso**, he won't listen to you, anyway.

totalidad nf whole, totality; **la t. de**, all of; **en su t.**, as a whole.

totalitario,-a adj totalitarian.

totalizar [4] I vtr to total. II vi to amount to.

tóxico,-a I adj toxic, poisonous. II nm poison.

toxicología nf toxicology.

toxicólogo,-a nm,f toxicologist.

toxicomanía nf drug addiction.

toxicómano,-a Med I adj addicted to drugs. II nm drug addict.

tozudo,-a adj obstinate, stubborn.

traba nf 1 (de rueda) chock; (enlace) bond, tie. 2 fig (obstáculo) hindrance, obstacle.

trabajador,-a I nm,f worker, labourer, US laborer. II adj hard-working.

trabajar I vi to work; **trabaja mucho**, he works hard; **t. de camarera**, to work as a waitress. II vtr 1 to work (on); (la tierra) to till. 2 (asignatura etc) to work on. 3 fam (convencer) to (try to) persuade.

trabajo nm 1 (ocupación) work; **t. a destajo**, piecework; **t. eventual**, casual labour; **trabajos manuales**, arts and crafts. 2 (empleo) employment, job. 3 (tarea) task, job. 4 Educ (redacción) report, paper. 5 (esfuerzo) effort; **cuesta t. creerlo**, it's hard to believe.

trabajoadicto nm,f workaholic.

trabajoso,-a adj (laborioso) hard, laborious; (difícil) difficult.

trabalenguas nm inv tongue twister.

trabar I vtr 1 (sujetar) to lock, fasten; (un plan) to obstruct. 2 (conversación, amistad) to start, to strike up. 3 Culin to thicken. II **trabarse** vr 1 (cuerdas) to get tangled up. 2 fig **se le trabó la lengua**, he got tongue-tied.

trabazón nf (de ideas) link.

trabilla nf (de pantalón) belt loop.

trabuco nm blunderbuss.

tracción *nf* traction; *Aut* **t. delantera/ trasera,** front-/rear-wheel drive; *Aut* **t. en las cuatro ruedas,** four-wheel drive.

tractor *nm* tractor.

tradición *nf* tradition.

tradicional *adj* traditional.

traducción *nf* translation; **t. directa/ inversa,** translation from/into a foreign language.

traducir [10] **I** *vtr* to translate (**a,** into). **II traducirse** *vr fig* to result (**en,** in).

traductor,-a *nm,f* translator.

traer [25] **I** *vtr* **1** to bring; **trae,** give it to me. **2** (*llevar puesto*) to wear. **3** (*llevar consigo*) to carry. **4** (*problemas*) to cause; **traerá como consecuencia ...,** it will result in .... **II traerse** *vr* (*llevar consigo*) to bring along; *fig* **¿qué se trae entre manos?,** what is he up to?

traficante *nmf* (*de drogas etc*) trafficker, pusher.

traficar [1] *vi* (*ilegalmente*) to traffic (**con,** in).

tráfico *nm* **1** *Aut* traffic; **t. rodado,** road traffic. **2** *Com* traffic, trade; **t. de drogas,** drug traffic.

tragaluz *nm* skylight.

tragaperras *nf inv* (*máquina*) t., slot machine.

tragar [7] **I** *vtr* **1** (*ingerir*) to swallow. **2** *fam* (*engullir*) to gobble up, tuck away. **3** *fig* (*a una persona*) to stand, stomach. **4** *fig* (*creer*) to believe, swallow. **II tragarse** *vr* **1** (*ingerir*) to swallow. **2** *fig* (*creer*) to believe, swallow.

tragedia *nf* tragedy.

trágico,-a *adj* tragic.

trago *nm* **1** (*bebida*) swig; **de un t.,** in one go. **2 pasar un mal t.,** to have a bad time of it.

tragón,-ona *nm,f* glutton, big eater.

traición *nf* treason, betrayal; **a t.,** treacherously; **alta t.,** high treason.

traicionar *vtr* to betray; (*delatar*) to give away, betray.

traicionero,-a *adj* treacherous.

traidor,-a **I** *adj* treacherous. **II** *nm,f* traitor.

traigo *indic pres* → **traer.**

tráiler *nm* (*pl* **tráilers**) **1** *Cin* trailer, *US* preview. **2** *Aut* articulated lorry, *US* trailer truck.

traje¹ *nm* **1** (*de hombre*) suit; **t. de baño,** bathing suit o costume, swimsuit; **t. de paisano,** civilian clothes *pl*; **t. de luces,** bullfighter's costume. **2** (*de mujer*) dress; **t. de chaqueta,** two-piece suit; **t. de novia,** wedding dress.

traje² *pt indef* → **traer.**

trajeado,-a *adj fam* sharp, dapper.

trajearse *vr* to dress up.

trajín *nm fam* comings and goings *pl*, hustle and bustle.

trajinar *vi* to run o bustle about.

trama *nf* **1** *Tex* weft, woof. **2** *Lit* plot.

tramar *vtr* to plot, cook up; **¿qué tramas?,** what are you up to?

tramitar *vtr* **1** (*gestionar*) to take the necessary (legal) steps to obtain. **2** *fml* (*despachar*) to convey, transmit. **3** *Com Jur Fin* to carry out, to process.

trámite *nm* (*paso*) step; (*formalidad*) formality; *Com Jur Fin* procedures *pl*, proceeding.

tramo *nm* (*de carretera*) section, stretch; (*de escalera*) flight.

tramoya *nf* (*maquinaria*) stage machinery; (*trama*) plot, scheme.

trampa *nf* **1** (*de caza*) trap, snare. **2** (*puerta*) trap door. **3** (*engaño*) fiddle; **hacer trampa(s),** to cheat. **4** (*truco*) trick.

trampilla *nf* trap door, hatch.

trampolín *nm* **1** *Natación* diving board. **2** *Esquí* ski jump.

tramposo,-a **I** *adj* deceitful. **II** *nm,f* cheat; *Naipes* cardsharp.

tranca *nf* **1** (*garrote*) cudgel; *fam* **a trancas y barrancas,** with great difficulty. **2** (*en puerta, ventana*) bar.

trance *nm* **1** (*coyuntura*) (critical) moment; **estar en t. de ...,** to be on the point of ... **2** (*éxtasis*) trance.

tranquilidad *nf* calmness, tranquillity, *US* tranquility; **con t.,** calmly; **pídemelo con toda t.,** don't hesitate to ask me.

tranquilizante *nm* tranquillizer, *US* tranquilizer.

tranquilizar [4] **I** *vtr* to calm down; **lo dijo para tranquilizarme,** he said it to reassure me. **II tranquilizarse** *vr* (*calmarse*) to calm down.

tranquilo,-a *adj* **1** (*persona, lugar*) calm; (*agua*) still; (*conciencia*) clear; *fam* **tú t.,** don't you worry. **2** (*despreocupado*) placid, easy-going.

tranquillo *nm fig* knack; **coger el t. a algo,** to get the knack of sth.

transacción *nf* transaction, deal.

transatlántico,-a **I** *nm* *Náut* (ocean) liner. **II** *adj* transatlantic.

transbordador *nm* (car) ferry; **t. espacial,** space shuttle.

transbordar **I** *vtr* to transfer; *Náut* (*mercancías*) to transship. **II** *vi* *Ferroc* to change trains, *US* transfer.

transbordo *nm* **1** *Ferroc* change, *US* transfer; **hacer t.,** to change o transfer. **2** *Náut* transshipment.

transcurrir *vi* **1** (*tiempo*) to pass, to go by. **2** (*acontecer*) to take place.

transcurso *nm* course o passing (of time); **en el t. de,** in the course of, during.

transeúnte *nmf* **1** (*peatón*) passer-by. **2** (*residente temporal*) temporary resident, *US* transient.

transferencia *nf* transference; *Fin* transfer; **t. bancaria,** banker's order.

transferible *adj* transferable.

transferir [5] *vtr* to transfer.

transformación *nf* transformation.

transformador *nm Elec* transformer.

transformar I *vtr* to transform, change. II **transformarse** *vr* to change, to turn (**en**, into); (*algo plegable*) to convert.

tránsfuga *nmf* 1 *Mil* deserter. 2 *Pol* turncoat.

transfusión *nf* transfusion.

transgredir *vtr defect* to transgress, break.

transgresor,-a *nm,f* transgressor, lawbreaker.

transición *nf* transition.

transido,-a *adj fml* t. de angustia, overcome by anxiety; t. de dolor, racked with pain.

transigente *adj* tolerant.

transigir [6] *vi* to compromise.

transistor *nm* transistor.

transitable *adj* passable.

transitado,-a *adj* (*carretera*) busy.

transitar *vi* to pass.

transitivo,-a *adj* transitive.

tránsito *nm* 1 *Aut* traffic. 2 (*movimiento*) movement, passage; **pasajeros en t.**, passengers in transit.

transitorio,-a *adj* transitory.

translucir [35] *vtr* → **traslucir**.

transmisión *nf* 1 transmission. 2 *Téc* drive; t. delantera/trasera, front-/rear-wheel drive. 3 *Rad TV* transmission, broadcast.

transmisor *nm* transmitter.

transmitir *vtr* 1 to transmit, pass on. 2 *Rad TV* to transmit, broadcast. 3 *Jur* to transfer, hand down.

transparencia *nf* 1 transparency; *Pol* openness. 2 *Fot* slide.

transparentarse *vr* to be transparent; **esta tela se transparenta**, this is see-through material; **se le transparentaban las bragas**, you could see her underpants.

transparente I *adj* transparent; *Pol* open. II *nm* 1 (*visillo*) net curtain. 2 (*pantalla*) shade, blind.

transpiración *nf* perspiration.

transpirar *vi* to perspire.

transplante *nm* transplant; *Med* t. de corazón/córnea, heart/eye transplant.

transponer [19] I *vtr* (*mudar de sitio*) to transpose, move about. II **transponerse** *vr* (*desmayarse*) to faint.

transportar *vtr* to transport; (*pasajeros*) to carry; (*mercancías*) to ship.

transporte *nm* 1 transport. 2 *Com* freight; t. de mercancías, freight transport; t. marítimo, shipment.

transportista *nmf* carrier.

transvase *nm* 1 (*de líquidos*) decanting. 2 (*de ríos*) transfer.

transversal *adj* transverse, cross.

tranvía *nm* tram, tramcar, *US* streetcar.

trapecio *nm* trapeze.

trapecista *nmf* trapeze artiste.

trapero,-a I *nm* rag-and-bone man, *US* junkman. II *adj* **puñalada trapera**, stab in the back.

trapichear *vi* to be up to something.

trapicheo *nm* jiggery-pokery.

trapo *nm* 1 (*viejo, roto*) rag. 2 (*bayeta*) cloth; t. de cocina, dishcloth; t. del polvo, duster; *fam* poner (a algn) como un t. (sucio), to tear sb apart.

tráquea *nf* trachea, windpipe.

traqueteo *nm* rattle, clatter.

tras *prep* 1 (*después de*) after; **uno t. otro**, one after the other. 2 (*detrás*) behind; **sentados uno t. oto**, sitting one behind the other. 3 **andar/ir t.**, to be after; **la policía iba t. ella**, the police were after her.

trasatlántico,-a *adj & nm* → **transatlántico,-a**.

trasbordador *nm* → **transbordador**.

trasbordar *vtr & vi* → **transbordar**.

trasbordo *nm* → **transbordo**.

trascendencia *nf* 1 (*importancia*) importance, significance. 2 (*en filosofía*) transcendence.

trascendental, trascendente *adj* 1 significant, far-reaching. 2 (*en filosofía*) transcendental.

trascender [3] *vtr vi* 1 (*noticia*) to become known, leak out. 2 (*tener consecuencias*) to have far-reaching consequences. 3 t. de, to go beyond.

trascribir *vtr* → **transcribir**.

trascripción *nf* → **transcripción**.

trascurrir *vi* → **transcurrir**.

trascurso *nm* → **transcurso**.

trasero,-a I *adj* back, rear; **en la parte trasera**, at the back. II *nm euf* bottom, bum.

trasferencia *nf* → **transferencia**.

trasferible *adj* → **transferible**.

trasferir [5] *vtr* → **transferir**.

trasfondo *nm* background.

trasformación *nf* → **transformación**.

trasformador *adj & nm* → **transformador**.

trasformar *vtr* → **transformar**.

trásfuga *nmf* → **tránsfuga**.

trasfusión *nf* → **transfusión**.

trasgredir *vtr* → **transgredir**.

trasgresión *nf* → **transgresión**.

trasgresor,-a *nm,f* → **transgresor,-a**.

trashumancia *nf* seasonal movement of livestock.

trasiego *nm* comings and goings *pl*, hustle and bustle.

trasladar I *vtr* (*cosa*) to move; (*persona*) to move, transfer. II **trasladarse** *vr* to go, move.

traslado *nm* (*de casa*) move, removal; (*de personal*) transfer; *Educ* t. de expediente, transfer of student record.

traslucirse *vr* to show (through).

trasluz *nm* mirar algo al t., to hold sth against the light.

trasmano *nm* a t., out of reach; (me) coge a t., it's out of my way.

trasmisión *nf* → transmisión. .

trasmisor,-a *adj & nm* → transmisor,-a.

trasmitir *vtr* → transmitir.

trasnochado,-a *adj* (*desfasado*) old, hackneyed.

trasnochador,-a I *adj* given to staying up late. II *nm,f* night bird, nighthawk.

trasnochar *vi* to stay up (very) late.

traspapelarse *vr* to get mislaid *o* misplaced.

trasparencia *nf* → transparencia.

trasparentar *vtr* → transparentar.

trasparente *adj & nm* → transparente.

traspasar *vtr* 1 (*atravesar*) to go through; (*río*) to cross. 2 (*negocio, local*) to transfer; 'se traspasa', 'for sale'. 3 *fig* (*exceder*) to exceed, go beyond.

traspaso *nm* 1 (*de propiedad etc*) transfer. 2 *Com* (*venta*) sale.

traspié *nm* (*pl traspiés*) stumble, trip; dar un t., to trip; *fig* to slip up.

traspiración *nf* → transpiración.

traspirar *vi* → transpirar.

trasplantar *vtr* → transplantar.

trasplante *nm* → transplante.

trasponer [19] *vtr* → transponer.

trasportador,a *adj & nm adj* → transportador,-a.

trasportar *vtr* → transportar.

trasporte *nm* → transporte.

traspuesto,-a *adj* quedarse t., to faint.

trasquilar *vtr* (*oveja*) to shear; (*pelo*) to crop.

trastabillar *vi* (*tambalearse*) to stagger, totter.

trastada *nf fam* hacer trastadas, to be up to mischief.

trastazo *nm fam* wallop, thump.

traste[1] *nm Mús* fret.

traste[2] *nm* 1 (*trasto*) piece of junk. 2 *fig* dar al t. (con un plan), to spoil (a plan); irse al t., to fall through.

trastear *vi* (*revolver*) to rummage about.

trastero *nm* (*cuarto*) t., junk room.

trastienda *nf* back shop.

trasto *nm* (*objeto cualquiera*) thing; (*cosa inservible*) piece of junk.

trastocar [2] *vtr* → trastornar.

trastornado,-a *adj* (*loco*) mad, unhinged.

trastornar I *vtr* 1 (*planes*) to disrupt. 2 *fig* (*persona*) to unhinge. II **trastornarse** *vr* (*enloquecer*) to go out of one's mind, go mad.

trastorno *nm* (*molestia*) trouble, inconvenience; t. mental, mental disorder *o* disturbance.

trasvasar *vtr* → transvasar.

trasvase *nm* → transvase.

trasversal *adj* → transversal.

trasverso,-a *adj* → transverso,-a.

trata *nf* slave trade *o* traffic; t. de blancas, white slave trade.

tratable *adj* easy to get along with, congenial.

tratado *nm* 1 (*pacto*) treaty. 2 (*estudio*) treatise.

tratamiento *nm* 1 treatment. 2 *Téc* processing, treatment. 3 *Inform* processing.

tratar I *vtr* 1 (*atender*) to treat; t. bien/mal, to treat well/badly. 2 *Med* to treat. 3 (*asunto*) to discuss. 4 *Inform Téc* to process. 5 me trata de tú, he addresses me as 'tu'. II *vi* 1 t. de, (*intentar*) to try. 2 t. de *o* sobre *o* acerca, to be about; ¿de qué trata?, what is it about? 3 t. con, (*tener tratos*) to deal with; (*negociar*) to negotiate with; (*relacionarse*) to move among. 4 *Com* t. en, to deal in. III **tratarse** *vr* 1 (*relacionarse*) to be on speaking terms. 2 se trata de, (*es cuestión de*) it's a question of; se trata de un caso excepcional, it's an exceptional case.

trato *nm* 1 (*de personas*) manner; (*contacto*) contact; malos tratos, ill-treatment *sing*. 2 (*acuerdo*) agreement; ¡t. hecho!, it's a deal! 3 *Com* deal.

trauma *nm* trauma.

traumático,-a *adj* traumatic.

traumatizar *vtr Med* to traumatize; *fam* to shock.

través I *prep* 1 a t. de, (*superficie*) across, over; (*agujero etc*) through; a t. del río, across the river; a t. del agujero, through the hole. 2 *fig* a t. de, through; a t. del periódico, through the newspaper. II *adv* de t., (*transversalmente*) crosswise; (*de lado*) sideways. III *nm* (*pl traveses*) *fig* (*desgracia*) misfortune.

travesaño *nm Ftb* crossbar.

travesía *nf* (*viaje*) crossing.

travestí, travesti *nmf* transvestite.

travesura *nf* mischief, childish prank.

travieso,-a *adj* mischievous.

trayecto *nm* 1 (*distancia*) distance; (*recorrido*) route; (*trecho*) stretch. 2 (*viaje*) journey.

trayectoria *nf* 1 (*de proyectil, geométrica*) trajectory. 2 *fig* (*orientación*) line, course.

traza *nf* 1 (*apariencia*) looks *pl*, appearance; no lleva trazas de curarse, it doesn't look as if he's going to get better. 2 *Arquit* plan, design.

trazado,-a *nm* 1 (*plano*) layout, plan. 2 (*de carretera, ferrocarril*) route.

trazar [4] *vtr* (*línea*) to draw; (*plano*) to design; *fig* (*plan*) to draw up the broad lines of.

trazo *nm* 1 (*línea*) line. 2 (*de letra*) stroke.

trébol *nm* 1 trefoil. 2 *Naipes* club.

trece *inv* I *adj* thirteen. II *nm* thirteen; *fig* estar *o* mantenerse *o* seguir en sus t., to stick to one's guns.

trecho *nm* distance, way; (*tramo*) stretch; de t. en t., from time to time.

tregua *nf Mil* truce; *fig* respite.
treinta *adj & nm inv* thirty.
treintena *nf* **una t. de,** (about) thirty.
treintavo,-a *adj & nm* thirtieth.
tremendista *adj* over the top.
tremendo,-a *adj* **1** *(terrible)* terrible, dreadful. **2** *(muy grande)* enormous; *fig* tremendous.
trementina *nf* turpentine.
trémulo,-a *adj lit (vacilante)* quivering, tremulous; *(luz)* flickering.
tren *nm* **1** train. **2** *Av* **t. de aterrizaje,** undercarriage; **t. de lavado,** car wash. **3** **t. de vida,** life style.
trenca *nf* duffle coat.
trenza *nf (de pelo)* plait, *US* braid.
trepador,-a *adj* climbing.
trepar *vtr & vi* to climb.
trepidante *adj* vibrating, shaking; *fig* **lleva un ritmo de vida t.,** he leads a hectic *o* frantic life.
trepidar *vi* to vibrate, shake.
tres I *adj inv (cardinal)* three; *(ordinal)* third; *fam* **de t. al cuarto,** cheap, of little value. **II** *nm (pl* **treses)** three; **t. en raya,** noughts and crosses, *US* tick-tack-toe.
trescientos,-as *adj & nm,f* three hundred.
tresillo *nm* **1** *(mueble)* (three-piece) suite. **2** *Mús* triplet.
treta *nf* trick, ruse.
triángulo *nm* triangle; *fig* **t. amoroso,** eternal triangle.
tribal *adj* tribal.
tribu *nf* tribe.
tribuna *nf* **1** *(plataforma)* rostrum, dais; **t. de (la) prensa,** press box. **2** *Dep* stand.
tribunal *nm* **1** *Jur* court; **t. de apelación,** court of appeal; **T. Supremo,** High Court, *US* Supreme Court; **t. (tutelar) de menores,** juvenile court. **2** *(de examen)* board of examiners.
tributar *vtr* to pay.
tributario,-a *adj* **sistema t.,** tax system.
tributo *nm* **1** *Com* tax. **2 pagar t. a,** *(homenaje)* to pay tribute to.
triciclo *nm* tricycle.
tricornio *nm* three-cornered hat.
tridimensional *adj* three-dimensional.
trienio *nm* three year period.
trifásico,-a I *adj Elec* three-phase. **II** *nm* adapter.
trigésimo,-a *adj & nm,f* thirtieth; **t. primero,** thirty-first.
trigo *nm* wheat.
trilogía *nf* trilogy.
trilla *nf* threshing.
trillado,-a *adj fig* well-worn.
trilladora *nf* threshing machine; **t. segadora,** combine harvester.
trillar *vtr* to thresh.
trimestral *adj* quarterly, three-monthly.
trimestre *nm* quarter; *Educ* term.
trinar *vi* **1** to warble. **2** *fam* to rage, fume;

Santiago está que trina, Santiago is really fuming.
trincar¹ |1| *vtr fam (capturar)* to catch.
trincar² *vtr fam* to drink.
trinchar *vtr (carne)* to carve, slice (up).
trinchera *nf* trench.
trineo *nm* sledge, sleigh.
trinidad *nf* **la Santísima T.,** the Holy Trinity.
trino *nm* **1** warble, trill. **2** *Mús* trill.
trío *nm* trio.
tripa *nf* **1** *(intestino)* gut, intestine; *fam* tummy; **dolor de t.,** stomach ache. **2 tripas,** innards.
triple *adj & nm* triple.
triplicado,-a *adj* triplicate; **por t.,** in triplicate.
triplicar |1| *vtr* to triple, treble.
trípode *nm* tripod.
tríptico *nm* **1** *(cuadro)* triptych. **2** *(folleto)* leaflet.
tripulación *nf* crew.
tripulante *nmf* crew member.
tripular *vtr* to man.
trip(y) *nm arg (droga)* trip.
triquiñuela *nf fam* trick, dodge.
tris *nm* **estar en un t. de,** to be on the verge of.
triste *adj* **1** *(persona, situación)* sad. **2** *(lugar)* gloomy.
tristeza *nf* sadness.
triturar *vtr (machacar)* to grind (up).
triunfador,-a I *adj* winning. **II** *nm,f* winner.
triunfal *adj* triumphant.
triunfar *vi* to triumph.
triunfo *nm* **1** *(victoria)* triumph, victory; *Dep* win. **2** *(éxito)* success.
trivial *adj* trivial.
trivialidad *nf* triviality.
trivializar *vtr* to trivialize, minimize.
triza *nf* bit, fragment; **hacer trizas,** to tear to shreds.
trocar |2| *vtr* to barter.
trocear *vtr* to cut up (into bits *o* pieces).
trochemoche (a) *loc adv fam* haphazardly.
trofeo *nm* trophy.
trola *nf fam* fib.
trolebús *nm* trolley bus.
tromba *nf* **t. de agua,** violent downpour.
trombón *nm* trombone.
trombosis *nf inv* thrombosis.
trompa *nf* **1** *Mús* horn. **2** *(de elefante)* trunk. **3** *Anat* tube. **4** *fam* **estar t.,** to be sloshed *o* plastered.
trompazo *nm fam* bump; **darse *o* pegarse un t.,** to have a bump.
trompeta *nf* trumpet.
trompetista *nmf* trumpet player, trumpeter.
trompicón *nm* trip, stumble; **hacer algo a trompicones,** to do sth in fits and starts.

trompo *nm* spinning top.

tronar [2] **I** *vi* to thunder. **II** *vtr Am* to shoot.

tronchar I *vtr (rama, tronco)* to cut down, fell; *fig (esperanzas etc)* to destroy. **II troncharse** *vr* **t. de risa,** to split one's sides with laughter.

troncho *nm* stem, stalk.

tronco *nm* **1** *Anat* trunk, torso. **2** *Bot (de árbol)* trunk; *(leño)* log; *fam fig* **dormir como un t.,** to sleep like a log.

tronera *nf* **1** *(de billar)* pocket. **2** *(ventana)* small window; *(de fortificación)* loophole; *Náut* porthole.

trono *nm* throne.

tropa *nf* **1** squad. **2 tropas,** troops *pl.*

tropel *nm* throng, mob; **en t.,** in a mad rush.

tropezar [1] *vi* **1** to trip, stumble **(con,** on). **2 t. con algo,** to come across sth; **t. con algn/dificultades,** to run into sb/ difficulties.

tropezón *nm* **1** *(traspié)* trip, stumble; **dar un t.,** to trip. **2** *(error)* slip-up, faux pas. **3** *(de comida)* chunk of meat.

tropical *adj* tropical.

trópico *nm* tropic.

tropiezo I *nm* **1** *(obstáculo)* trip. **2** *fig (error)* blunder, faux pas. **II** *indic pres* → **tropezar.**

trotamundos *nmf inv* globe-trotter.

trotar *vi* to trot.

trote *nm* **1** trot; **al t.,** at a trot. **2** *fam* **ya no está para esos trotes,** he cannot keep up the pace any more.

trovador *nm* troubadour.

trozo *nm* piece.

trucar [1] *vtr* to doctor, alter.

truco *nm* **1** *(ardid)* trick; **aquí hay t.,** there's something fishy going on here. **2 coger el t. (a algo),** to get the knack *o* hang (of sth).

truculento,-a *adj* cruel.

trucha *nf* trout.

trueno *nm* thunder; **un t.,** a thunderclap.

trueque *nm* barter.

trufa *nf* truffle.

truhán,-ana *nm,f* rogue, crook.

truncar [1] *vtr* to truncate; *fig (vida etc)* to cut short; *fig (esperanzas)* to shatter.

trust *nm (pl* **trusts)** trust, cartel.

tu *adj pos* your; **tu libro,** your book; **tus libros,** your books.

tú *pron* you; **de tú a tú,** on equal terms.

tuba *nf* tuba.

tubérculo *nm* **1** *Bot* tuber. **2** *Med* tubercle.

tuberculosis *nf inv* tuberculosis.

tubería *nf* **1** *(de agua)* piping, pipes *pl.* **2** *(de gas)* pipeline.

tubo *nm* **1** tube; **t. de ensayo,** test tube. **2** *(tubería)* pipe; *Aut* **t. de escape,** exhaust (pipe).

tucán *nm* toucan.

tuerca *nf* nut.

tuerto,-a I *adj* one-eyed, blind in one eye. **II** *nm,f* one-eyed person.

tuerzo *indic pres* → **torcer.**

tuétano *nm* marrow; **hasta el t.,** to one's fingertips.

tufo *nm* foul odour *o US* odor *o* smell.

tugurio *nm* hovel.

tul *nm* tulle.

tulipa *nf* small tulip.

tulipán *nm* tulip.

tullido,-a *adj* crippled, disabled.

tullir *vtr* to cripple.

tumba *nf* grave, tomb.

tumbar I *vtr* to knock down *o* over. **II tumbarse** *vr (acostarse)* to lie down, to stretch out.

tumbo *nm* **dar tumbos,** to reel.

tumbona *nf* easy chair; *(de lona)* deck chair.

tumor *nm* tumour, *US* tumor.

tumulto *nm* tumult, commotion.

tumultuoso,-a *adj* tumultuous, riotous.

tuna *nf* student folkloric music group.

tunante,-a *nm,f* rogue, crook.

túnel *nm* tunnel; **el t. del Canal de la Mancha,** the Channel Tunnel.

Túnez *n* **1** *(país)* Tunisia. **2** *(ciudad)* Tunis.

túnica *nf* tunic.

tuno,-a I *nm,f (bribón)* rogue, crook. **II** *nm* member of a **tuna.**

tuntún (al) *nm* haphazardly, any old how.

tupé *nm (pl* **tupés)** *(flequillo)* quiff.

tupido,-a *adj* thick, dense.

turba¹ *nf (combustible)* peat.

turba² *nf (muchedumbre)* mob, crowd.

turbado,-a *adj* **1** *(alterado)* disturbed. **2** *(preocupado)* worried, anxious. **3** *(desconcertado)* confused.

turbante *nm* turban.

turbar I *vtr* **1** *(alterar)* to unsettle. **2** *(preocupar)* to upset *o* worry. **3** *(desconcertar)* to baffle, put off. **II turbarse** *vr* **1** *(preocuparse)* to be *o* become upset. **2** *(desconcertarse)* to be *o* become confused *o* baffled.

turbina *nf* turbine.

turbio,-a *adj (agua)* cloudy; *pey (negocio etc)* shady, dubious.

turborreactor *nm* turbojet (engine).

turbulencia *nf* turbulence.

turbulento,-a *adj* turbulent.

turco,-a I *adj* Turkish. **II** *nm,f (persona)* Turk; *fig* **cabeza de t.,** scapegoat. **III** *nm (idioma)* Turkish.

turismo *nm* **1** tourism; **ir de t.,** to go touring. **2** *Aut* car.

turista *nmf* tourist.

turístico,-a *adj* tourist; **de interés t.,** of interest to tourists.

turnarse *vr* to take turns.

turno *nm* **1** *(en juegos etc)* turn, go. **2** *(de trabajo)* shift; **estar de t.,** to be on duty;

t. de día/noche, day/night shift.
turquesa *adj & nf* turquoise.
Turquía *n* Turkey.
turrón *nm* nougat.
tute *nm fam* **darse un t. de algo**, to go to town doing sth.
tutear I *vtr* to address as **tú**. II **tutearse** *vr* to address (each other *o* one another) as **tú**.
tutela *nf* 1 *Jur* guardianship, tutelage. 2 *fig (protección)* protection, guidance.
tuteo *nm* use of the **tú** form of address.

tutor *nm* 1 *Jur* guardian. 2 *Educ* tutor.
tuve *pt indef* → **tener**.
tuyo,-a I *adj pos (con personas)* of yours; *(con objetos)* one of your; **¿es amigo t.?**, is he a friend of yours?; **unas amigas tuyas**, some friends of yours; **un libro t.**, one of your books. II *pron pos* yours; **éste es t.**, this one is yours; *fam* **los tuyos**, *(familiares)* your family.
TV *abr de* **televisión**, television, TV.
TVE *nf abr de* **Televisión Española**.

U

U, u [u] *nf (la letra)* U, u.
u *conj (delante de palabras que empiecen por o o ho)* or; **siete u ocho**, seven or eight; **ayer u hoy**, yesterday or today.
ubicación *nf* location, position.
ubicar [1] I *vtr Am (situar)* to locate, situate. II **ubicarse** *vr* to be situated *o* located.
ubicuo,-a *adj* ubiquitous.
ubre *nf* udder.
Ucrania *n* Ukraine.
ucraniano,-a *adj & nm,f* Ukrainian.
Ud. *abr de* **usted**, you.
Uds. *abr de* **ustedes**, you.
ufanarse *vr* to boast (de, of).
ufano,-a *adj* conceited.
UGT *nf abr de* **Unión General de Trabajadores**.
ugetista *adj* relating to the UGT.
ujier *nm* usher.
úlcera *nf* ulcer.
ulcerar *vtr*, **ulcerarse** *vr* to ulcerate.
ulterior *adj (siguiente)* subsequent.
ultimar *vtr* 1 *(terminar)* to finalize. 2 *Am (matar)* to kill, finish off.
ultimátum *nm (pl* **ultimátums)** ultimatum.
último,-a *adj* 1 last; **el u. día**, the last day; **llegar el ú.**, to arrive last; **por ú.**, finally; **a últimos de mes**, at the end of the month; **en las últimas**, on one's last legs. 2 *(más reciente)* latest; **últimas noticias**, latest news; *fam* **a la última**, up to the minute. 3 *(más alto)* top; **el u. piso**, the top flat. 4 *(más bajo)* lowest; **el u. de la lista**, the lowest in the list. 5 *(más lejano)* back, last; **la última fila**, the back row. 6 *(definitivo)* final. ◆**últimamente** *adv* lately, recently.
ultra *nmf* extreme right-winger; **los ultras**, the extreme right *sing*.
ultra- *pref* ultra-.
ultraderecha *nf Pol* extreme right.
ultraderechista *Pol* I *adj* extreme right-wing. II *nmf* extreme right-winger.
ultraizquierda *nf* extreme left.
ultrajar *vtr* to outrage, offend.

ultraje *nm* outrage, offence.
ultramar *nm* overseas (countries), abroad; **del o en u.**, overseas.
ultramarinos *nm* groceries; **tienda de u.**, greengrocer.
ultranza (a) *loc adv* 1 *(a todo trance)* at all costs, at any price; **defender algo a u.**, to defend sth to the death. 2 *(acérrimo)* out-and-out, extreme.
ultrasónico,-a *adj* ultrasonic.
ultratumba *nf* afterlife.
ultravioleta *adj inv* ultraviolet.
ulular *vi (viento)* to howl; *(búho)* to hoot.
umbral *nm* threshold.
umbrío,-a, umbroso,-a *adj* shady.
un,-a I *art indet* 1 a; *(antes de vocal)* an; **un coche**, a car; **un huevo**, an egg; **una flor**, a flower. 2 *unos,-as*, some; **unas flores**, some flowers. II *adj (delante de nm sing)* one; **un chico o dos chicas**, one boy and two girls; → *tamb* **uno,-a** I.
unánime *adj* unanimous.
unanimidad *nf* unanimity; **por u.**, unanimously.
unción *nf* unction.
undécimo,-a *adj* eleventh.
UNED *nf abr de* **Universidad Nacional de Educación a Distancia**, ≈ Open University, OU.
ungir [6] *vtr Rel* to anoint.
ungüento *nm* ointment.
único,-a *adj* 1 *(solo)* only; **es el ú. que tengo**, it's the only one I've got; **hijo ú.**, only child; **lo ú. que quiero**, the only thing I want; **el Mercado Ú.**, the Single Market; **el Acta Única**, the Single European Act. 2 *(extraordinario)* unique. ◆**únicamente** *adv* only, solely.
unidad *nf* 1 unit. 2 *(cohesión)* unity.
unido,-a *adj* united; **están muy unidos**, they are very attached to one another; **una familia muy unida**, a very close family.
unifamiliar *adj* **vivienda u.**, detached house.
unificación *nf* unification.
unificar [1] *vtr* to unify.

uniformar *vtr* 1 (*igualar*) to make uniform, standardize. 2 (*poner un uniforme a*) to put into uniform, give a uniform to.
uniforme I *nm* (*prenda*) uniform. II *adj* 1 (*igual*) uniform. 2 (*superficie*) even.
uniformidad *nf* 1 (*igualdad*) uniformity. 2 (*de superficie*) evenness.
unilateral *adj* unilateral.
unión *nf* union.
Unión Soviética *n* Soviet Union.
unir I *vtr* (*juntar*) to unite, join (together); **esta carretera une las dos comarcas**, this road links both districts. II **unirse** *vr* (*juntarse*) to unite, join.
unisex *adj inv* unisex.
unísono *nm* unison; **al u.**, in unison.
unitario,-a *adj* unitary; **precio u.**, unit price.
universal *adj* universal; **historia u.**, world history.
universidad *nf* university; **u. a distancia**, ≈ Open University; **u. laboral**, technical college.
universitario,-a I *adj* university. II *nm,f* university student.
universo *nm* universe.
uno,-a I *nm inv* one; **el u.**, (number) one; **el u. de mayo**, the first of May. II *nf* (*hora*) **es la una**, it's one o'clock. III *adj* **unos,-as**, some; **unas cajas**, some boxes; **habrá unos o unas veinte**, there must be around twenty. IV *pron* 1 one; **u. (de ellos)**, **una (de ellas)**, one of them; **unos cuantos**, a few; **se miraron el u. al otro**, they looked at each other; **de u. en u.**, one by one; **un trás otro**, one after the other; **una de dos**, one of the two. 2 (*persona*) someone, somebody; **u. que pasaba por allí**, some passer-by; **vive con u.**, she's living with some man. **unos ... otros**, some people ... others. 3 (*impers*) you, one; **u. tiene que ...**, you have to ....
untar *vtr* to grease, smear; (*mantequilla*) to spread.
untura *nf* ointment.
uña *nf* 1 nail; **morderse** *o* **comerse las uñas** to bite one's fingernails; *fig* **ser u. y carne**, to be hand in glove. 2 *Zool* (*garra*) claw; (*pezuña*) hoof.
uperizado,-a *adj* **leche uperizada**, UHT milk.
Urales *nmpl* **los U.**, the Urals.
uranio *nm* uranium.
Urano *nm* Uranus.
urbanidad *nf* urbanity, politeness.
urbanismo *nm* town planning.
urbanístico,-a *adj* town-planning.
urbanización *nf* 1 (*barrio*) housing development *o* estate. 2 (*proceso*) urbanization.
urbanizar *vtr* to build up.

urbano,-a *adj* urban, city; **guardia u.**, (traffic) policeman.
urbe *nf* large city.
urdimbre *nf* 1 *Tex* warp. 2 (*trama*) intrigue.
urdir *vtr* 1 *Tex* to warp. 2 (*tramar*) to plot, scheme.
urgencia *nf* 1 urgency. 2 (*emergencia*) emergency.
urgente *adj* urgent; **correo u.**, express mail.
urgir [6] *vi* to be urgent *o* pressing; **me urge (tenerlo)**, I need it urgently.
urinario *nm* urinal.
urna *nf* 1 *Pol* ballot box. 2 (*vasija*) urn.
urólogo,-a *nm,f* *Med* urologist.
urraca *nf* magpie.
URSS *nf* *Hist abr de* **Unión de Repúblicas Socialistas Soviéticas**, Union of Socialist Soviet Republics, USSR.
urticaria *nf* *Med* hives.
Uruguay *n* **(el) U.**, Uruguay.
uruguayo,-a *adj & nm,f* Uruguayan.
usado,-a *adj* (*ropa*) second-hand, used.
usanza *nf* *lit* **a la antigua u.**, in the old style.
usar I *vtr* 1 to use. 2 (*prenda*) to wear. II **usarse** *vr* to be used *o* in fashion.
usina *nf* *Am* (*central eléctrica*) power station.
USO *nf abr de* **Unión Sindical Obrera**.
uso *nm* 1 use; *Farm* **u. externo/tópico**, external/local application. 2 (*de poder, privilegio*) exercise. 3 (*de prenda*) wearing; **haga u. del casco**, wear a helmet. 4 (*costumbre*) usage, custom; **al u.**, conventional.
usted, *pl* **ustedes** *pron pers fml* you; **¿quién es u.?**, **¿quiénes son ustedes?**, who are you?
usual *adj* usual, common.
usuario,-a *nm,f* user.
usura *nf* usury.
usurero,-a *nm,f* usurer.
usurpar *vtr* to usurp.
utensilio *nm* utensil; (*herramienta*) tool.
útero *nm* uterus, womb.
útil I *adj* useful; (*día*) working. II *nm* (*herramienta*) tool, instrument.
utilidad *nf* usefulness, utility; (*beneficio*) profit.
utilitario,-a I *nm* (*coche*) utility vehicle. II *adj* utilitarian.
utilización *nf* use, utilization.
utilizar [4] *vtr* to use, utilize.
utopía *nf* utopia.
utópico,-a *adj & nm,f* utopian.
uva *nf* grape; **u. blanca**, green grape.
UVI *nf abr de* **unidad de vigilancia intensiva**, intensive care unit, ICU.
úvula *nf* uvula.

V

V, v ['uβe] *nf* (*la letra*) V, v.
V *Elec abr de* **voltio(s),** volt, volts, V.
vaca *nf* 1 cow. 2 (*carne*) beef.
vacaciones *nfpl* holidays *pl*, *US* vacation; (*viaje*) holiday; **durante las v.,** during the holidays; **estar/irse de v.,** to be/go on holiday.
vacante I *adj* vacant. **II** *nf* vacancy.
vaciar [29] **I** *vtr* 1 (*recipiente*) to empty; (*contenido*) to empty out. 2 (*terreno*) to hollow out. 3 *Arte* to cast, mould, *US* mold. **II vaciarse** *vr* to empty.
vacilación *nf* hesitation.
vacilante *adj* 1 (*persona*) hesitant, irresolute. 2 (*voz*) hesitant, faltering. 3 (*luz*) flickering.
vacilar *vi* 1 (*dudar*) to hesitate; **sin v.,** without hesitation. 2 (*voz*) to falter. 3 (*luz*) to flicker. 4 *fam* (*jactarse*) to show off.
vacío,-a I *adj* 1 empty; (*hueco*) hollow. 2 (*sin ocupar*) vacant, unoccupied. **II** *nm* 1 emptiness, void. 2 (*hueco*) gap; (*espacio*) (empty) space. 3 *Fís* vacuum; **envasado al v.,** vacuum-packed.
vacuna *nf* vaccine; *Vet* cowpox.
vacunación *nf* vaccination.
vacunar I *vtr* to vaccinate (**contra,** against); *fig* to inure. **II vacunárse** *vr* to get oneself vaccinated.
vacuno,-a *adj* bovine; **ganado v.,** cattle.
vacuo,-a *adj* vacuous, empty.
vadear *vtr* (*río*) to ford; *fig* (*dificultad*) to overcome.
vado *nm* 1 (*de un río*) ford. 2 *Aut* 'v. permanente', 'keep clear'.
vagabundear *vi* to wander, roam.
vagabundo,-a I *adj* (*errante*) wandering; *pey* vagrant; **perro v.,** stray dog. **II** *nm,f* wanderer; (*sin casa*) tramp, *US* hobo; *pey* vagrant, tramp.
vagancia *nf* idleness, laziness.
vagar [7] *vi* to wander about, roam about.
vagido *nm* cry of a newborn baby.
vagina *nf* vagina.
vago,-a I *adj* 1 (*perezoso*) lazy. 2 (*indefinido*) vague. **II** *nm,f* 1 (*holgazán*) layabout. 2 *Jur* vagrant.
vagón *nm* (*para pasajeros*) carriage, coach, *US* car; (*para mercancías*) truck, wagon, *US* freight car, *US* boxcar.
vaguedad *nf* vagueness.
vaho *nm* (*de aliento*) breath; (*vapor*) vapour, *US* vapor.
vaina I *nf* 1 (*de espada*) sheath, scabbard. 2 *Bot* pod. 3 *Am fam* (*molestia*) bother, nuisance. II *nmf* (*persona*) dimwit.
vainilla *nf* vanilla.
vaivén *nm* 1 (*oscilación*) swinging, to-and-fro movement. 2 (*de gente*) coming and going, bustle; *fig* **vaivenes,** ups and downs.
vajilla *nf* crockery, dishes *pl*; **una v.,** a set of dishes, a dinner service.
valdré *indic fut* → **valer.**
vale¹ *interj* all right, O.K.
vale² *nm* 1 (*comprobante*) voucher. 2 (*pagaré*) promissory note, IOU (I owe you).
valedero,-a *adj* valid.
valenciano,-a *adj* Valencian; **Comunidad Valenciana,** Valencia.
valentía *nf* courage, bravery.
valentón,-ona *pey* **I** *adj* bragging, boastful. **II** *nm,f* braggart.
valer [26] **I** *vtr* 1 to be worth; **no vale nada,** it is worthless; **vale una fortuna,** it is worth a fortune; **no vale la pena (ir),** it's not worth while (going). 2 (*costar*) to cost; **¿cuánto vale?,** how much is it? 3 (*proporcionar*) to earn. **II** *vi* 1 (*servir*) to be useful, be of use. 2 (*ser válido*) to be valid, count; **no vale hacer trampa,** cheating isn't on. 3 **más vale,** it is better; **más vale que te vayas ya,** you had better leave now. **III valerse** *vr* to use, make use (**de,** of); **v. por sí mismo,** to be able to manage on one's own.
valeroso,-a *adj* brave, courageous.
valgo *indic pres* → **valer.**
valía *nf* value, worth.
validez *nf* validity.
válido,-a *adj* valid.
valiente *adj* 1 (*valeroso*) brave, courageous. 2 *irón* **¡v. amigo eres tú!,** a fine friend you are!
valija *nf* (*de correos*) mailbag; **v. diplomática,** diplomatic bag.
valioso,-a *adj* valuable.
valor *nm* 1 (*valía*) value, worth; (*precio*) price; **objetos de v.,** valuables; **sin v.,** worthless; **v. alimenticio,** food value. 2 (*valentía*) courage. 3 *Fin* **valores,** securities, bonds.
valoración *nf* valuation.
valorar *vtr* to value, calculate the value of.
valorización *nf* 1 (*tasación*) valuation. 2 (*revalorización*) appreciation.
valorizar [4] *vtr* 1 (*tasar*) to value. 2 (*revalorizar*) to raise the value of.
vals *nm* waltz; **bailar el v.,** to waltz.
válvula *nf* valve; **v. de seguridad,** safety valve.
valla *nf* 1 (*cerca*) fence; (*muro*) wall; **v. publicitaria,** hoarding, *US* billboard. 2 *Dep* hurdle; **los 100 metros vallas,** the 100 metres hurdle race.
vallado *nm* fence.
vallar *vtr* to fence (in).
valle *nm* valley.
vallisoletano,-a I *adj* of *o* from Vallado-

lid. **II** *nm,f* native *o* inhabitant of Valladolid.

vampiro *nm* vampire.

vanagloriarse [12] *vr* to boast (**de,** of).

vandalismo *nm* vandalism.

vándalo,-a *nm,f* vandal.

vanguardia *nf* 1 avant-garde, vanguard; *fig* ir a la v. de, to be at the forefront of. 2 *Mil* vanguard, van.

vanguardista I *adj* avant-garde. **II** *nm,f* avant-gardist.

vanidad *nf* vanity.

vanidoso,-a *adj* vain, conceited.

vano,-a *adj* 1 (*vanidoso*) vain, conceited. 2 (*esfuerzo, esperanza*) vain, futile; **en v.,** in vain.

vapor *nm* 1 (*de agua hirviendo*) steam; *Culin* al v., steamed. 2 (*gas*) vapour, *US* vapor; **v. de agua,** water vapour.

vaporizador *nm* vaporizer, spray.

vaporizar [4] **I** *vtr* to vaporize. **II vaporizarse** *vr* to vaporize, become vaporized, evaporate.

vaporoso,-a *adj* vaporous.

vapulear *vtr* (*físicamente*) to shake; (*con palabras*) to slate.

vaqueriza *nf* cowshed.

vaquero,-a I *nm* cowherd, *US* cowboy. **II** *adj* pantalón v., jeans *pl*, pair *sing* of jeans. **III** *nmpl* **vaqueros,** (*prenda*) jeans, pair *sing* of jeans.

vara *nf* pole, rod.

varar I *vtr* to beach, dock. **II** *vi* to run aground.

variable *adj & nf* variable.

variación *nf* variation.

variado,-a *adj* varied; **galletas variadas,** assorted biscuits.

variante *nf* variant; *Aut* detour.

variar [29] **I** *vtr* to vary, change. **II** *vi* to vary, change; *irón* para v., as usual, just for a change.

varice, várice *nf* → **variz.**

varicela *nf* chickenpox.

variedad *nf* 1 variety. 2 *Teat* **variedades,** variety show *sing*.

varilla *nf* (*vara*) rod, stick; (*de abanico, paraguas*) rib.

varios,-as *adj* several.

variopinto,-a *adj* diverse, assorted; **un público v.,** a varied audience.

varita *nf* v. mágica, magic wand.

variz *nf* varicose vein.

varón *nm* (*hombre*) man; (*chico*) boy; **hijo v.,** male child; **sexo v.,** male sex.

varonil *adj* manly, virile.

Varsovia *n* Warsaw.

vas *indic pres* → **ir.**

vasallo,-a *nm,f Hist* vassal.

vasco,-a *adj* Basque; **el País V.,** the Basque Country.

vascuence *nm* (*idioma*) Basque.

vasectomía *nf* vasectomy.

vaselina *nf* vaseline®.

vasija *nf* pot.

vaso *nm* 1 (*para beber*) glass. 2 (*florero*) vase. 3 *Anat* vessel.

vástago *nm* 1 *Bot* shoot. 2 *fig* (*hilo*) offspring. 3 *Téc* rod, stem.

vasto,-a *adj* vast.

Vaticano *nm* el V., Vatican.

vaticinar *vtr* to prophesy, predict.

vaticinio *nm* prophesy, prediction.

vatio *nm* watt.

vaya¹ *interj* ¡v. lío!, what a mess!

vaya² *subj pres* → **ir.**

Vd. Vds. *abr de* **usted, ustedes,** you.

ve I *imperat* → **ir. II** *indic pres* → **ver.**

vecinal *adj* local.

vecindad *nf*, **vecindario** *nm* 1 (*área*) neighbourhood, *US* neighborhood, vicinity. 2 (*vecinos*) community, residents *pl*.

vecino,-a I *nm,f* 1 (*persona*) neighbour, *US* neighbor; **el v. de al lado,** the next-door neighbour. 2 (*residente*) resident. **II** *adj* neighbouring, *US* neighboring, nearby.

veda *nf* (*de caza*) close season, *US* closed season; **levantar la v.,** to open the season.

vedado *adj* coto v. de caza, private hunting ground.

vedar *vtr* to forbid, prohibit.

vega *nf* fertile plain *o* low.

vegetación *nf* 1 *Bot* vegetation. 2 *Med* **vegetaciones,** adenoids.

vegetal *nm* vegetable.

vegetar *vi fig* to vegetate.

vegetariano,-a *adj & nm,f* vegetarian.

vehemencia *nf* vehemence.

vehemente *adj* vehement.

vehículo *nm* vehicle.

veinte *adj & nm inv* twenty.

veintena *nf* (*veinte*) twenty; **una v. de,** about twenty.

vejación *nf* humiliation.

vejar *vtr* to humiliate.

vejatorio,-a *adj* humiliating.

vejez *nf* old age.

vejiga *nf* bladder.

vela¹ *nf* 1 candle. 2 *fam* **quedarse a dos velas,** to be in the dark. 3 **pasar la noche en v.,** to have a sleepless night.

vela² *nf Náut* sail.

velada *nf* evening (party).

velado,-a *adj* 1 (*oculto*) veiled, hidden. 2 *Fot* blurred.

velador *nm* 1 (*mesa*) table. 2 *Am* (*mesilla de noche*) bedside table.

velar¹ *vi* 1 v. por, to watch over. 2 (*hacer guardia*) to keep watch.

velar² *Fot* **I** *vtr* to blur. **II velarse** *vr* to become blurred.

velatorio *nm* vigil, wake.

veleidad *nf* fickleness.

veleidoso,-a *adj* fickle.

velero *nm* sailing boat *o* ship.

veleta I *nf* weather vane, weathercock. **II**

nmf fam fickle *o* changeable person.
velo *nm* veil.
velocidad *nf* 1 *(rapidez)* speed; *(de proyectil etc)* velocity; *Aut* **v. máxima,** speed limit; *Inform* **v. de transmisión,** bit rate; *Inform* **v. operativa,** operating speed. 2 *Aut (marcha)* gear.
velocímetro *nm* speedometer.
velocista *nmf* sprinter.
velódromo *nm* cycle track, *US* velodrome.
veloz I *adj* swift, rapid. **II** *adv* quickly, fast.
vello *nm* hair.
vellón *nm* fleece.
velloso,-a, velludo,-a *adj* downy.
vena *nf* vein.
venado *nm* deer, stag; *Culin* venison.
vencedor,-a I *nm,f* winner. **II** winning.
vencejo *nm* Orn swift.
vencer [2] **I** *vtr* 1 *(al enemigo)* to defeat; *(al contrincante)* to beat. 2 *(dificultad)* to overcome, surmount. **II** *vi* 1 *(pago, deuda)* to fall due, be payable. 2 *(plazo)* to expire. **III vencerse** *vr (torcerse)* to warp.
vencido,-a *adj Mil (derrotado)* defeated; *Dep* beaten; *fig* **darse por v.,** to give up, accept defeat. 2 *(pago, deuda)* due, payable. 3 *(plazo)* expired. 4 *fam* **a la tercera va la vencida,** third time lucky.
vencimiento *nm* 1 *Com* maturity. 2 *(de un plazo)* expiry.
venda *nf* bandage.
vendaje *nm* dressing.
vendar *vtr* to bandage; *fig* **v. los ojos a algn,** to blindfold sb.
vendaval *nm* gale.
vendedor,-a *nm,f* seller; *(hombre)* salesman; *(mujer)* saleswoman.
vender I *vtr* to sell; **v. a plazos/al contado,** to sell on credit/for cash; **v. al por mayor/menor,** to (sell) wholesale/retail. **II venderse** *vr* 1 to sell; **este disco se vende bien,** this record is selling well; **for sale.** 2 *(claudicar)* to sell out.
vendimia *nf* grape harvest.
vendré *indic fut* → **venir.**
Venecia *n* Venice.
veneno *nm* poison; *(de serpiente)* venom.
venenoso,-a *adj* poisonous.
venerable *adj* venerable.
veneración *nf* veneration.
venerar *vtr* to venerate, revere.
venéreo,-a *adj* venereal.
venero *nm* spring.
venezolano,-a *adj & nm,f* Venezuelan.
Venezuela *n* Venezuela.
venga *subj pres* → **venir.**
venganza *nf* vengeance, revenge.
vengar [7] **I** *vtr* to avenge. **II vengarse** *vr* to avenge oneself; **v. de algn,** to take revenge on sb.
vengativo,-a *adj* vengeful, vindictive.
vengo *indic pres* → **venir.**

venia *nf* 1 *fml (permiso)* permission. 2 *(perdón)* pardon.
venial *adj* venial.
venida *nf* coming, arrival.
venidero,-a *adj* future, coming.
venir [27] **I** *vi* 1 to come; *fig* **v. a menos,** to come down in the world; *fig* **v. al mundo,** to be born; **el año que viene,** next year; *fig* **v. a la memoria,** to remember; *fam* **¡venga ya!,** *(vamos)* come on!; *(expresa incredulidad)* come off it! 2 **v. grande/pequeño,** *(ropa)* to be too big/small; **v. mal/bien,** to be inconvenient/convenient; **el metro me viene muy bien,** I find the underground very handy. 3 *(en pasivas)* **esto vino provocado por ...,** this was brought about by .... 4 **esto viene ocurriendo desde hace mucho tiempo,** this has been going on for a long time now. **II venirse** *vr* **v. abajo,** to collapse.
venta *nf* 1 sale; **en v.,** for sale; **a la v.,** on sale; **v. a plazos/al contado,** credit/cash sale; **v. al por mayor/al por menor,** wholesale/retail. 2 *(posada)* country inn.
ventaja *nf* advantage; **llevar v. a,** to have the advantage over; **le sacó dos metros de v. a,** he beat him by two metres.
ventajoso,-a *adj* advantageous.
ventana *nf* 1 window. 2 *(de la nariz)* nostril.
ventanal *nm* large window.
ventanilla *nf* 1 window. 2 *(de la nariz)* nostril.
ventanuco *nm* small window.
ventilación *nf* ventilation; **sin v.,** unventilated.
ventilador *nm* ventilator; *(de coche)* fan.
ventilar I *vtr* 1 *(habitación)* to ventilate, air. 2 *fig (opinión)* to air. **II ventilarse** *vr* *fam (terminar)* to finish off.
ventisca *nf* blizzard; *(de nieve)* snowstorm.
ventosa *nf* sucker; *Med* cupping glass.
ventosear *vi* to break wind.
ventoso,-a *adj* windy.
ventrílocuo,-a *nm,f* ventriloquist.
ventura *nf* 1 *(felicidad)* happiness. 2 *(suerte)* luck; *(casualidad)* chance.
venturoso,-a *adj* lucky, fortunate.
Venus *nm* Venus.
veo-veo *nm fam* **el (juego del) v.-v.,** I-spy.
ver¹ *nm* **de buen v.,** good-looking.
ver² [28] **I** *vtr* 1 to see; *(televisión)* to watch; **a v.,** let me see, let's see; **a v. si escribes,** I hope you'll write; **(ya) veremos,** we'll see; *fam* **había un jaleo que no veas,** you should have seen the fuss that was made; **no veo por qué,** I can't see why; **a mi modo de v.,** as I see it. 2 **no tener nada que v. con,** to have nothing to do with. **II verse** *vr* 1 *(imagen etc)* to be seen. 2 *(encontrarse con algn)* to

meet, see each other; ¡**nos vemos!**, see you later! **3 no se pueden ni v.**, *(soportarse)* they can't stand (the sight of) each other. **4** *Am* **te ves divina**, you look divine.

vera *nf* edge, border; **a la v. de**, beside, next to.

veracidad *nf* veracity, truthfulness.

veraneante *nmf* holidaymaker, *US* (summer) vacationist.

veranear *vi* to spend one's summer holiday.

veraneo *nm* summer holiday.

veraniego,-a *adj* summer.

verano *nm* summer.

veras *nfpl* **de v.**, really, seriously.

veraz *adj* veracious, truthful.

verbal *adj* verbal.

verbena *nf* street party.

verbo *nm* verb.

verborrea *nf fam* verbosity, verbal diarrhoea.

verdad *nf* **1** truth; **es v.**, it is true; **a decir v.**, to tell the truth; ¡**de v!.**, really, truly; **un amigo de v.**, a real friend. **2** *(en frase afirmativa)* **está muy bien, ¿(no es) v.?**, it is very good, isn't it?; *(en frase negativa)* **no te gusta, ¿v.?**, you don't like it, do you?.

verdadero,-a *adj* true, real.
◆**verdaderamente** *adv* truly, really.

verde **I** *adj* **1** green. **2** *(fruta)* unripe. **3** *fam (chiste, película)* blue; **viejo v.**, dirty old man. **4** *fam fig* **poner v. a algn**, to call sb every name under the sun. **II** *nm* **1** *(color)* green. **2** *Pol* **los verdes**, the Greens.

verdear *vi* to turn green.

verdor *nm (color)* greenness; *(de plantas)* verdure.

verdoso,-a *adj* greenish.

verdugo,-a **I** *nm* executioner. **II** *nmf fig* tyrant.

verdulería *nf* greengrocer's (shop).

verdulero,-a *nm,f* greengrocer.

verdura *nf* vegetables *pl*, greens *pl*.

vereda *nf* **1** *(camino)* path, lane. **2** *Am (acera)* pavement, *US* sidewalk.

veredicto *nm* verdict.

verga *nf* penis.

vergonzoso,-a *adj* **1** *(penoso)* shameful, disgraceful. **2** *(tímido)* shy, bashful.

vergüenza *nf* **1** shame; ¿**no te da v.?**, aren't you ashamed?, have you no shame?; **es una v.**, it's a disgrace. **2** *(timidez)* shyness, bashfulness; **tener v.**, to be shy; **me da v.**, I'm too embarrassed.

vericueto *nm* winding path; *fig* **los vericuetos**, the ins and outs.

verídico,-a *adj* truthful, true.

verificar [1] **I** *vtr (comprobar)* to check. **II verificarse** *vr* to take place, occur.

verja *nf (reja)* grating; *(cerca)* railing, railings *pl*; *(puerta)* iron gate.

vermut, vermú *nm (pl* **vermús)** vermouth.

verosímil *adj* probable, likely; *(creíble)* credible.

versado,-a *adj* well-versed **(en**, in).

versar *vi* **v. sobre**, to be about, deal with.

versátil *adj* **1** versatile. **2** *(voluble)* changeable, inconstant.

versatilidad *nf* **1** versatility. **2** *(volubilidad)* changeableness, inconstancy.

versículo *nm* verse.

versión *nf* version; **película en v. original**, film in the original language.

verso *nm* **1** *(poesía)* verse. **2** *(línea)* line.

vértebra *nf* vertebra.

vertebrado,-a *adj* & *nm* vertebrate.

vertedero *nm (de basura)* rubbish dump, tip.

verter [3] **I** *vtr* **1** to pour (out). **2** *(basura)* to dump. **II** *vi (río)* to flow, run **(a**, into).

vertical *adj* vertical.

vértice *nm* vertex.

vertiente *nf* **1** *(de una montaña, un tejado)* slope; *fig* aspect. **2** *Am (manantial)* spring.

vertiginoso,-a *adj* dizzy, giddy; *fig (velocidad)* breakneck.

vértigo *nm* vertigo; **me da v.**, it makes me dizzy.

vesícula *nf* vesicle; **v. biliar**, gall bladder.

vespa® *nf* (motor) scooter.

vespertino,-a **I** *adj* evening. **II** *nm Prensa* evening newspaper.

vespino® *nm* moped.

vestíbulo *nm (de casa)* hall; *(de edificio público)* foyer.

vestido,-a **I** *nm (ropa)* clothes *pl*; *(de mujer)* dress. **II** *adj* dressed; **policía v. de paisano**, plain clothes policeman.

vestidura *nf* clothing, clothes *pl*.

vestigio *nm* vestige, trace.

vestimenta *nf* clothes *pl*, garments *pl*.

vestir [6] **I** *vtr* **1** *(a alguien)* to dress. **2** *(llevar puesto)* to wear. **II** *vi* **1** to dress; **ropa de (mucho) v.**, formal dress. **2** *fam* **la seda viste mucho**, silk always looks very elegant. **III vestirse** *vr* **1** to get dressed, dress. **2 v. de**, to wear, dress in; *(disfrazarse)* to disguise oneself as, to dress up as.

vestuario *nm* **1** *(conjunto de vestidos)* clothes *pl*, wardrobe; *Teat* wardrobe, costumes *pl*. **2** *(camerino)* dressing room. **3** *Dep* changing room *sing*.

veta *nf Min* vein, seam; *(de carne)* streak.

vetar *vtr* to veto.

veterano,-a *adj* & *nm,f* veteran.

veterinario,-a **I** *nm,f* veterinary surgeon, vet, *US* veterinarian. **II** *nf* veterinary medicine *o* science.

veto *nm* veto; **derecho a v.**, power *o* right of veto.

vetusto,-a *adj fml* ancient.

vez *nf* 1 time; **una v.**, once; **dos veces**, twice; **cinco veces**, five times; **a** *o* **algunas veces**, sometimes; **cada v.**, each *o* every time; **cada v. más**, more and more; **de v. en cuando**, now and again, every now and then; **¿le has visto alguna v.?**, have you ever seen him?; **otra v.**, again; **a la v.**, at the same time; **tal v.**, perhaps, maybe; **de una v.**, in one go; **de una v. para siempre**, once and for all; **en v. de**, instead of; **érase** *o* **había una v.**, *(en cuentos etc)* once upon a time. **2** *(turno)* turn. **3 hacer las veces de**, to do duty as.

v.g(r). *abr de* verbigracia, for example, eg.

vía I *nf* 1 *Ferroc* track, line. 2 *(camino)* road; **v. pública**, public thoroughfare; **V. Láctea**, Milky Way. 3 *Anat* passage, tract; *Farm* **(por) v. oral**, to be taken orally. 4 *fig* **por v. oficial**, through official channels; **por v. aérea/marítima**, by air/sea. 5 **en vías de**, in the process of; **países en vías de desarrollo**, developing countries. **II** *prep (a través de)* via, through; **v. París**, via Paris; **transmisión v. satélite**, satellite transmission.

viable *adj* viable.

viaducto *nm* viaduct.

viajante *nmf* commercial traveller, travelling salesman *o* saleswoman.

viajar *vi* to travel.

viaje *nm (recorrido)* journey, trip; *(largo, en barco)* voyage; **¡buen v.!**, bon voyage!, have a good trip!; **estar de v.**, to be away (on a trip); **irse** *o* **marcharse de v.**, to go on a journey *o* trip; **v. de negocios**, business trip; **v. de novios**, honeymoon.

viajero,-a I *nm,f* 1 traveller. 2 *(en transporte público)* passenger. **II** *adj* **cheque v.**, travellers cheque.

viandante *nmf* passer-by.

viario,-a *adj* road, highway; **red viaria**, road network.

víbora *nf* viper.

vibración *nf* vibration.

vibrador *nm* vibrator.

vibrar *vtr & vi* to vibrate.

vicario,-a *nm,f* vicar.

vicepresidente,-a *nm,f* 1 *Pol* vice president. 2 *(de compañía, comité)* vicechairperson; *(hombre)* vice-chairman; *(mujer)* vice-chairwoman.

vicesecretario,-a *nm,f* assistant secretary.

viceversa *adv* vice versa.

viciado,-a *adj* 1 *(corrompido)* corrupt. 2 *(aire)* foul.

viciar [12] **I** *vtr* 1 *(corromper)* to corrupt. 2 *(estropear)* to waste. **II viciarse** *vr* 1 *(deformarse)* to go out of shape. 2 *(corromperse)* to become corrupted.

vicio *nm* 1 vice. 2 *(mala costumbre)* bad habit. 3 *fam (destreza)* skill.

vicioso,-a I *adj* 1 *(persona)* depraved,

perverted. 2 **círculo v.**, vicious circle. **II** *nm,f* depraved person; **v. del trabajo**, workaholic.

vicisitud *nf (usu pl)* vicissitude.

víctima *nf* victim.

victoria *nf* victory.

victorioso,-a *adj* victorious.

vicuña *nf* vicuna.

vid *nf* vine, grapevine.

vida *nf* life; *(período)* lifetime; **de toda la v.**, life-long; **en mi v.**, never in my life; **de por v.**, for life; **ganarse la v.**, to earn one's living; **¿qué es de tu v.?**, how's life?; **estar con/sin v.**, to be alive/dead.

vidente *nmf* clairvoyant.

vídeo *nm* video; **grabar en v.**, to videotape.

videoclub *nm* video club.

videocámara *nf* video camera.

videoconferencia *nf* videoconferencing; *(sesión)* videoconference.

videojuego *nm* video game.

vidriera *nf* 1 stained-glass window. 2 *Am (escaparate)* shop window.

vidrio *nm* glass.

viejo,-a I *adj* old; **hacerse v.**, to grow old; **un v. amigo**, an old friend. **II** *nm,f (hombre, padre)* old man; *(mujer, madre)* old woman; **los viejos**, old people; *fam* **mis viejos**, my parents.

Viena *n* Vienna.

vienés,-esa *adj & nm,f* Viennese.

viento *nm* wind; **hace** *o* **sopla mucho v.**, it is very windy; *fam fig* **vete a tomar v.**, get lost.

vientre *nm* 1 belly; **hacer de v.**, to have a bowel movement. 2 *(útero)* womb.

viernes *nm inv* Friday; **V. Santo**, Good Friday.

Vietnam *n* Vietnam.

vietnamita *adj & nmf* Vietnamese.

viga *nf (de madera)* beam; *(de hierro)* girder.

vigencia *nf* validity; **entrar en v.**, to come into force *o* effect.

vigente *adj* in force.

vigésimo,-a *adj & nm,f* twentieth.

vigía I *nf* watchtower, lookout post. **II** *nmf* lookout; *(hombre)* watchman; *(mujer)* watchwoman.

vigilancia *nf* vigilance, watchfulness; *Med* **unidad de v. intensiva**, intensive care unit.

vigilante *nm* watchman; *(de banco)* guard.

vigilar I *vtr* to watch; *(un lugar)* to guard; **vigila que no entren**, make sure they don't get in. **II** *vi (gen)* to keep watch.

vigilia *nf* 1 vigil. 2 *(víspera)* eve. 3 *Rel (abstinencia)* abstinence.

vigor *nm* 1 vigour, *US* vigor; *(fuerza)* strength. 2 **en v.**, in force.

vigoroso,-a *adj* vigorous.

VIH *abr de* **Virus de Inmunodeficiencia Humana**, Human Immunodeficiency

Virus, HIV.

vikingo *nm* Viking.

vil *adj fml* vile, base.

vileza *nf* 1 vileness, baseness. 2 *(acto)* vile act, despicable deed.

vilipendiar [12] *vtr fml* to vilify, revile.

vilo (en) *loc adv (persona)* on tenterhooks; *(cosa)* up in the air.

villa *nf* 1 *(población)* town. 2 *(casa)* villa, country house.

villancico *nm* (Christmas) carol.

vinagre *nm* vinegar.

vinagrera *nf* **vinagreras,** oil and vinegar cruets, cruet (stand) *sing.*

vinagreta *nf* vinaigrette sauce.

vinajeras *nfpl* cruets.

vincha *nf Am* headband.

vinculante *adj* binding.

vincular *vtr* to link, bind; *(relacionar)* to relate, connect.

vínculo *nm* link.

vine *pt indef* → **venir.**

vinícola *adj* wine-producing.

vinicultor,-a *nm,f* wine producer.

vinicultura *nf* wine production *o* growing.

vinilo *nm* vinyl.

vino *nm* wine; **tomar un v.,** to have a glass of wine; **v. blanco/tinto/dulce/seco,** white/red/sweet/dry wine; **v. rosado,** rosé.

viña *nf* vineyard.

viñedo *nm* vineyard.

viñeta *nf* illustration.

viola *nf* viola.

violación *nf* 1 *(de una persona)* rape. 2 *(de ley, derecho)* violation, infringement.

violador,-a *n* rapist.

violar *vtr* 1 *(persona)* to rape. 2 *(ley, derecho)* to violate, infringe.

violencia *nf* 1 violence; **la no v.,** non-violence. 2 *(incomodidad)* embarrassment.

violentar *vtr* 1 *(forzar)* to force, break open; *(sitio)* to break into, enter by force. 2 *(enojar)* to infuriate.

violento,-a *adj* 1 violent. 2 *(situación)* embarrassing, awkward. 3 **sentirse v.,** *(incómodo)* to feel embarrassed *o* awkward.

violeta *adj & nm & nf* violet.

violín *nm* violin; *fam* fiddle.

violinista *nmf* violinist.

violón *nm* double bass.

violoncelista, violonchelista *nmf* cellist.

violoncelo, violonchelo *nm* violoncello, cello.

viraje *nm* 1 turn. 2 *fig* about-face, U-turn.

virar *vi* 1 *(girar)* to turn round. 2 *fig* to change.

virgen I *adj* 1 *(persona, selva)* virgin. 2 *(aceite, lana)* pure; *(cinta)* blank. II *nmf* virgin; *fam* **ser un viva la v.,** to be a devil-may-care person.

virginidad *nf* virginity.

virgo *nm* hymen.

Virgo *nm* Virgo.

virguería *nf arg* gem, marvel; **hacer virguerías,** to work wonders, be a dab hand.

virguero,-a *adj arg* smart, great; **esta camisa es muy virguera,** that shirt is the business.

vírico,-a *adj* viral.

viril *adj* virile, manly; **miembro v.,** penis.

virilidad *nf* virility.

virtual *adj* virtual.

virtud *nf* 1 virtue; *fig* **en v. de,** by virtue of. 2 *(propiedad)* property, quality.

virtuoso,-a I *adj* virtuous. II *nm,f* 1 virtuous person. 2 *(músico)* virtuoso.

viruela *nf* smallpox; **viruelas,** pockmarks *pl.*

virulé (a la) *loc adv fam* 1 *(torcido)* crooked, twisted. 2 **un ojo a la v.,** a black eye.

virulencia *nf* virulence.

virulento,-a *adj* virulent.

virus *nm inv* virus.

visa *nf Am* visa.

visado *nm* visa.

víscera *nf* 1 internal organ. 2 **vísceras,** viscera, entrails.

visceral *adj* 1 *Anat* visceral. 2 *fig* profound, deep-rooted.

viscoso,-a *adj* viscous.

visera *nf (de gorra)* peak; *(de casco)* visor.

visibilidad *nf* visibility; **curva con mala v.,** blind corner.

visible *adj* visible; *(evidente)* evident.

visillo *nm* small lace *o* net curtain.

visión *nf* 1 vision. 2 *(vista)* sight; *fig* **v. de conjunto,** overall view; **con v. de futuro,** forward-looking. 3 *(aparición)* vision.

visionario,-a *nm,f* visionary; *(iluso)* person who imagines things.

visita *nf* 1 *(acción)* visit; **hacer una v.,** to pay a visit; **estar de v.,** to be visiting. 2 *(invitado)* visitor, guest.

visitador,-a *nm,f Farm* pharmaceutical salesman *o* saleswoman.

visitante I *nmf* visitor. II *adj (equipo)* away.

visitar *vtr* to visit.

vislumbrar *vtr* to glimpse.

viso *nm* 1 *(reflejo)* sheen. 2 *fig* **tener visos de,** to seem, appear.

visón *nm* mink.

visor *nm Fot* viewfinder.

víspera *nf (día anterior)* day before; *(de festivo)* eve; **en vísperas de,** in the period leading up to.

vista *nf* 1 sight; **a la v.,** visible; **a primera** *o* **simple v.,** at first sight, on the face of it; **con vistas a,** with a view to; **en v. de,** in view of, considering; **corto de v.,** short-sighted; **conocer a algn de v.,** to know sb by sight; **perder de v. a,** to lose sight of; **quítalo de mi v.,** take it away;

fig **tener mucha v. para**, to have a good eye for; *fig* **volver la v. atrás**, to look back; *fam* **¡hasta la v.!**, goodbye!, see you!; *fam* **hacer la v. gorda**, to turn a blind eye. **2** *(panorama)* view; **con vista(s) al mar**, overlooking the sea. **3** *Jur* trial, hearing.

vistazo *nm* glance; **echar un v. a algo**, *(ojear)* to have a (quick) look at sth; *(tener cuidado de)* to keep an eye on sth.

visto,-a I *adj* **1 está v. que ...**, it is obvious that ...; **por lo v.**, evidently, apparently; **v. que**, in view of the fact that, seeing *o* given that. **2 estar bien v.**, to be well looked upon, be considered acceptable; **estar mal v.**, to be frowned upon. **3 estar muy v.**, to be old hat. **II** *nm* **v. bueno**, approval, O.K.

vistoso,-a *adj* eye-catching.

visual *adj* visual; **campo v.**, field of vision.

visualizar [4] *vtr* to visualize; *(película)* to view.

vital *adj* **1** vital. **2** *(persona)* full of vitality.

vitalicio,-a *adj* life, for life; **pensión/cargo v.**, life pension/permanent post.

vitalidad *nf* vitality.

vitamina *nf* vitamin.

vitamínico,-a *adj* vitamin; **complejo v.**, multivitamins.

viticultura *nf* wine growing.

viticultor,-a *nmf* wine grower.

vitorear *vtr* to cheer.

vítreo,-a *adj* vitreous.

vitrina *nf* *(aparador)* glass *o* display cabinet; *(de exposición)* glass case, showcase; *Am* *(escaparate)* shop window.

vituallas *nfpl* provisions.

vituperar *vtr* to condemn.

vituperio *nm* condemnation.

viudo,-a *nm,f* *(hombre)* widower; *(mujer)* widow.

viva *interj* **¡v.!**, hurrah!

vivacidad *nf* vivacity.

vivaracho,-a *adj fam* lively, sprightly.

vivaz *adj* **1** lively, vivacious. **2** *(perspicaz)* sharp, quick-witted.

vivencias *nfpl* personal experience.

víveres *nmpl* provisions, supplies.

vivero *nm* *(de plantas)* nursery; *(de peces)* fish farm *o* hatchery; *fig* breeding ground, hotbed.

viveza *nf* **1** liveliness, vivacity; *(en los ojos)* sparkle. **2** *(agudeza)* sharpness, quick-wittedness.

vividor,-a *nm,f pey* sponger, scrounger.

vivienda *nf* **1** housing. **2** *(casa)* house; *(piso)* flat.

vivir I *vi* to live; **vive de sus ahorros**, she lives off her savings; **viven de la pesca**, they make their living by fishing. **II** *vtr* to live through. **III** *nm* life.

vivito,-a *adj fam* **v. y coleando**, alive and kicking.

vivo,-a I *adj* **1** alive; **de viva voz**, verbally, by word of mouth; **en v.**, *(programa)* live; *fam* **es el v. retrato** *o* **la viva imagen de**, she is the spitting image of. **2 al rojo v.**, red-hot. **3** *(vivaz)* lively, vivacious. **4** *(listo)* sharp, clever. **5** *(color)* vivid, bright. **6** *(descripción)* lively, graphic. **II** *nm* **los vivos**, the living.

Vizcaya *n* **el golfo de V.**, the Bay of Biscay.

VºBº *abr de* **visto bueno**.

vocablo *nm* word, term.

vocabulario *nm* vocabulary.

vocación *nf* vocation, calling; **con v. europea**, with leanings towards Europe.

vocacional *adj* vocational.

vocal I *nf Ling* vowel. **II** *nmf* member.

vocalista *nmf Mús* vocalist, singer.

vocalizar [4] *vtr & vi* to vocalize.

voceador,-a *nm,f Am* vendor.

vocerío *nm* shouting.

vocero,-a *nm,f Am* spokesperson; *(hombre)* spokesman; *(mujer)* spokeswoman.

vociferante *adj* vociferous.

vociferar *vtr & vi* to vociferate.

vodka *nm* vodka.

vol. *abr de* **volumen**, volume, vol.

volado,-a *adj fam* **estar v.**, to have a screw loose.

volador,-a *adj* flying.

volandas (en) *loc adv (por el aire)* in the air, flying through the air.

volante I *nm* **1** *Aut* steering wheel; **ir al v.**, to be driving; **un as del v.**, a motor-racing champion. **2** *Cost* frill, ruffle. **3** *Med* note. **II** *adj* flying; **platillo v.**, flying saucer.

volantín *nm Am (cometa)* small kite.

volar [2] **I** *vi* **1** to fly; *fig* **lo hizo volando**, he did it in a flash. **2** *fam (desaparecer)* to disappear, vanish. **II** *vtr (edificios)* to blow up; *(caja fuerte)* to blow open; *Min* to blast. **III volarse** *vr (papel etc)* to be blown away.

volátil *adj* volatile.

volatinero,-a *nm,f* acrobat.

volcán *nm* volcano.

volcánico,-a *adj* volcanic.

volcar [2] **I** *vtr* **1** *(cubo etc)* to knock over; *(barco, bote)* to capsize. **2** *(vaciar)* to empty out. **3** *(tiempo)* to invest. **II** *vi (coche)* to turn over; *(barco)* to capsize. **III volcarse** *vr* **1** *(vaso, jarra)* to fall over, tip over; *(coche)* to turn over; *(barco)* to capsize. **2** *fig* **v. con**, to do one's utmost for.

voleibol *nm* volleyball.

voleo *nm fig* **a(l) v.**, at random, haphazardly.

voltaje *nm* voltage.

voltear I *vtr* to turn upside down. **II** *vi* to turn over, roll over.

voltereta *nf* somersault.

voltio *nm* volt.

voluble *adj* fickle, changeable.
volumen *nm* volume.
voluminoso,-a *adj* voluminous; *(enorme)* massive, bulky.
voluntad *nf* will; **fuerza de v.,** willpower; **tiene mucha v.,** he is very strong-willed; **a v.,** at will.
voluntario,-a I *adj* voluntary; **ofrecerse v.,** to volunteer. II *nm,f* volunteer.
voluntarioso,-a *adj* willing.
voluptuoso,-a *adj* voluptuous.
volver [4] *(pp* vuelto) I *vi* 1 to return; *(venir)* to come back; *(ir)* to go back; **v. en sí,** to come round, recover consciousness. 2 **v. a hacer algo,** to do sth again. II *vtr* 1 *(convertir)* to turn, make; **me vas a v. loco,** you are driving me mad. 2 *(dar vuelta a)* to turn; *(boca abajo)* to turn upside down; *(de fuera adentro)* to turn inside out; *(de atrás adelante)* to turn back to front; *(dar la vuelta a)* to turn over; **volverle la espalda a algn,** to turn one's back on sb; *fig* **v. la vista atrás,** to look back; **al v. la esquina,** on turning the corner. III **volverse** *vr* 1 to turn. 2 *(regresar) (venir)* to come back; *(ir)* to go back. 3 *(convertirse)* to become; **v. loco -a,** to go mad.
vomitar I *vi* to vomit, be sick; **tengo ganas de v.,** I feel sick, I want to be sick. II *vtr* to vomit, bring up.
vómito *nm (lo vomitado)* vomit; *(acción)* vomiting.
vomitona *nf fam* vomit.
voracidad *nf* voracity, voraciousness.
vorágine *nf* whirlpool; *fig* maelstrom.
voraz *adj* voracious; *fig* raging, fierce.
vórtice *nm* vortex.
vos *pron pers* 1 *arc (usted)* ye, you. 2 *Am (tú)* you.
vosotros,-as *pron pers pl* 1 *(sujeto)* you. 2 *(con prep)* you; **entre v.,** among yourselves; **sin vosotras,** without you.
votación *nf* 1 *(voto)* vote, ballot. 2 *(acción)* voting.
votante *nmf* voter.
votar *vi* to vote; **v. a algn,** to vote (for) sb.
voto *nm* 1 vote; **tener v.,** to have the right to vote; **v. secreto,** secret ballot. 2 *Rel* vow.
vox *nf* esto es **v. populi,** this is common knowledge.

voy *indic pres →* **ir.**
voz *nf* 1 voice; **en v. alta,** aloud; **en v. baja,** in a low voice; **a media v.,** in a low voice, softly; **de viva v.,** verbally. 2 *(grito)* shout; **a voces,** shouting; **dar voces,** to shout; *fig* **estar pidiendo algo a voces,** to be crying out for sth; *fig* **secreto a voces,** open secret; **a v. en grito,** at the top of one's voice. 3 **no tener ni v. ni voto,** to have no say in the matter; *fig* **llevar la v. cantante,** to rule the roost. 4 *Gram* **v. pasiva,** passive voice.
vudú *nm* voodoo.
vuelco *nm* upset, tumble; **dar un v.,** *(coche)* to overturn; *fig* **me dio un v. el corazón,** my heart missed a beat.
vuelo *nm* 1 flight; **v. chárter/regular,** charter/scheduled flight; **v. sin motor,** gliding; *fig* **cazarlas** *o* **cogerlas al v.,** to be quick on the uptake. 2 *Cost* **una falda de v.,** a full skirt.
vuelta *nf* 1 *(regreso)* return; *(viaje)* return journey; **a v. de correo,** by return post; **estar de v.,** to be back; *Dep* **partido de v.,** return match. 2 *(giro)* turn; *(en carreras)* lap; *Dep (ciclista)* tour; **dar media v.,** to turn round; *fig* **la cabeza me da vueltas,** my head is spinning; *fig* **no le des más vueltas,** stop worrying about it; **v. de campana,** somersault. 3 *(dinero)* change. 4 **dar una v.,** *(a pie)* to go for a walk *o* stroll; *(en coche)* to go for a drive *o* a spin (in the car). 5 *fig* **no tiene v. de hoja,** there's no doubt about it.
vuelto,-a I *adj* **jersey de cuello v.,** roll-neck sweater. II *nm Am* change.
vuestro,-a I *adj pos (antes del sustantivo)* your; *(después del sustantivo)* of yours; **v. libro,** your book; **un amigo v.,** a friend of yours. II *pron pos* yours; **éstos son los vuestros,** these are yours; **lo v.,** what is yours, what belongs to you.
vulgar *adj* 1 vulgar. 2 **el término v.,** the everyday term. ◆**vulgarmente** *adv* **v. llamado,** commonly known as.
vulgaridad *nf* vulgarity.
vulgarizar [4] *vtr (popularizar)* to popularize.
vulgo *nm* **el v.,** the common people *pl*; *pey* the masses.
vulnerable *adj* vulnerable.
vulnerar *vtr (ley, acuerdo)* to violate.
vulva *nf* vulva.

W

W, w [uβe'δoβle] *nf (la letra)* W, w.
W *abr de* vatio(s), Watt, Watts, W.
walkie-talkie *nm* walkie-talkie.
walkman® *nm* walkman®.
wáter *nm (pl wáteres) fam* toilet.

waterpolo *nm* water polo.
whisky *nm (escocés)* whisky; *(irlandés, US)* whiskey.
windsurf, windsurfing *nm* windsurfing.
windsurfista *nmf* windsurfer.

X

X, x [ˈekis] *nf (la letra)* X, x.
xenofobia *nf* xenophobia.
xenófobo,-a I *adj* xenophobic. **II** *nm,f* xe-
nophobe.
xerografía *nf* xerography.
xilófono *nm* xylophone.

Y

Y, y [iɣriˈeɣa] *nf (la letra)* Y, y.
y *conj* 1 and; **una chica alta y morena,** a
tall, dark-haired girl; **son las tres y
cuarto,** it's a quarter past three. 2 *¿y
qué?,* so what?; **¿y si no llega a tiempo?,**
what if he doesn't arrive in time?; **¿y tú?,**
what about you?; **¿y eso?,** how come?; **y
eso que,** although, even though; **¡y
tanto!,** you bet!, and how!; → **e.**
ya I *adv* 1 already; **ya lo sabía,** I already
knew; **ya en la Edad Media,** as far back
as the Middle Ages. 2 *(ahora mismo)* now;
es preciso actuar ya, it is vital that we
act now; **¡hazlo ya!,** do it at once!; **ya
mismo,** right away. 3 *(en el futuro)* **ya hablaremos luego,** we'll talk about it later;
ya nos veremos, see you!; **ya verás,**
you'll see. 4 **ya no,** no longer; **ya no viene por aquí,** he doesn't come round here
any more. 5 *(refuerza el verbo)* **ya era
hora,** about time too; **ya lo creo,** of
course, I should think so; **¡ya voy!,** coming!; **¡ya está!,** that's it!. **II** *conj* **ya que,**
since.
yacaré *nm Am* alligator, cayman.
yacer [33] *vi* to lie, be lying.
yacimiento *nm* bed, deposit; **yacimientos
petrolíferos,** oilfields.
yaguar *nm* jaguar.
yanqui *pey* **I** *adj* Yankee. **II** *nmf* Yankee,
Yank.
yarará *nm Am* large poisonous snake.
yaraví *nm Am* Quechuan song.
yarda *nf* yard.
yate *nm* yacht.
yaya *nf Am Bot* lancewood; *fam (abuela)*
granny.
yedra *nf* → **hiedra.**
yegua *nf* mare.
yema *nf* 1 *(de huevo)* yolk. 2 *Bot* bud. 3

y. del dedo, fingertip. 4 *Culin* sweet
made from sugar and egg yolk.
Yemen *n* Yemen.
yen *nm (moneda)* yen.
yendo *ger* → **ir.**
yerba *nf* 1 → **hierba.** 2 *Am* maté.
yerbatero,-a *Am* **I** *nm,f (curandero)* witch
doctor who uses herbs. **II** *adj* maté.
yermo,-a *adj* 1 *(baldío)* barren, uncultivated. 2 *(despoblado)* deserted, uninhabited.
yerno *nm* son-in-law.
yerro *indic pres* → **errar.**
yeso *nm* 1 *Geol* gypsum. 2 *Constr* plaster.
Yibuti *n* Djibouti.
yiu-yitsu *nm* jujitsu.
yo *pron pers* I; **entre tú y yo,** between you
and me; **¿quién es? - soy yo,** who is it? -
it's me; **yo no,** not me; **yo que tú,** if I
were you; **yo mismo,** I myself.
yodo *nm* iodine.
yoga *nm* yoga.
yogur *nm* yogurt, yoghurt.
yogurtera *nf* yoghurt maker.
yonqui *nmf arg* junkie, drug addict.
yoyo, yoyó *nm* yo-yo.
yuca *nf* yucca.
Yucatán *n* Yucatan.
yudo *nm* judo.
yudoka *nmf* judoka.
yugo *nm* yoke.
Yugoslavia *n* Yugoslavia.
yugoslavo,-a, yugoeslavo,-a *adj & nm,f*
Yugoslav, Yugoslavian.
yugular *nf* jugular.
yunque *nm* anvil.
yunta *nf* yoke *o* team of oxen.
yuxtaponer [19] *(pp yuxtapuesto) vtr* to
juxtapose.
yuxtaposición *nf* juxtaposition.

Z

Z, z [ˈθeta] *nf (la letra)* Z, z.
zafarse *vr (librarse)* to get away **(de,**
from), escape **(de,** from).
zafio,-a *adj* uncouth.
zafiro *nm* sapphire.
zaga *nf* **a la z.,** behind, at the rear.
zaguán *nm* hall, hallway.

zaherir [5] *vtr* to hurt.
zahúrda *nf* pigsty.
zaino,-a *adj (caballo)* chestnut; *(toro)*
black.
Zaire *n* Zaire.
zalamería *nf* flattery.
zalamero,-a **I** *nm,f* flatterer, fawner. **II**

adj flattering, fawning.
zamarra *nf (prenda)* sheepskin jacket.
Zambia *n* Zambia.
zambo,-a I *adj* 1 *(patizambo)* knock-kneed. 2 *Am (persona)* half Indian and half Negro. II *nm,f Am (persona)* person who is half Indian and half Negro.
zambomba *nf* kind of primitive drum.
zambullida *nf* plunge.
zambullirse *vr* to plunge.
zamparse *vr fam* to gobble down.
zanahoria *nf* carrot.
zancada *nf* stride.
zancadilla *nf* ponerle la z. a algn, to trip sb up.
zanco *nm* stilt.
zancudo,-a I *adj* 1 long-legged. 2 *Orn* wading; **ave zancuda,** wading bird, wader. II *nm Am* mosquito.
zángano,-a I *nm (insecto)* drone. II *nm,f fam (persona)* idler, lazybones *inv*.
zanja *nf* ditch, trench.
zanjar *vtr (asunto)* to settle.
zapallo *nm Am* pumpkin, calabash.
zapata *nf* 1 *(cuña)* wedge. 2 *Téc* shoe.
zapatear *vi* to tap one's feet.
zapatería *nf* shoe shop.
zapatero,-a *nm,f (vendedor)* shoe dealer; *(fabricante)* shoemaker, cobbler.
zapatilla *nf* slipper; **zapatillas de deporte,** trainers.
zapato *nm* shoe; **zapatos de tacón,** high-heeled shoes.
zar *nm* czar, tsar.
Zaragoza *n* Saragossa.
zaragozano,-a I *adj* of *o* from Saragossa. II *nm,f* native *o* inhabitant of Saragossa.
zarandear *vtr* to shake.
zarandeo *nm* shaking.
zarcillo *nm* 1 *(pendiente)* earring. 2 *Bot* tendril.
zarina *nf* czarina, tsarina.
zarpa *nf* claw.
zarpar *vi* to weigh anchor, set sail.
zarpazo *nm* clawing; **dar** *o* **pegar un z. a,** to claw.
zarza *nf* bramble, blackberry bush.
zarzal *nm* bramble patch.

zarzamora *nf (zarza)* blackberry bush; *(fruto)* blackberry.
zarzuela *nf* 1 Spanish operetta. 2 **la Z.,** royal residence in Madrid. 3 *Culin* fish stew.
zenit *nm* zenith.
zigzag *nm (pl* **zigzags** *o* **zigzagues)** zigzag.
zigzaguear *vi* to zigzag.
Zimbabwe *n* Zimbabwe.
zinc *nm* zinc.
zócalo *nm* 1 *(de pared)* skirting board. 2 *(pedestal)* plinth.
zodiaco, zodíaco *nm* zodiac; **signo del z.,** sign of the zodiac.
zona *nf* zone; *(región)* region; **z. verde,** park.
zoo *nm* zoo.
zoología *nf* zoology.
zoológico,-a I *adj* zoological; **parque z.,** zoo. II *nm* zoo.
zoom *nm Cin Fot* zoom.
zopenco,-a *nm,f fam* dope, half-wit.
zopilote *nm Am* buzzard.
zoquete *nmf fam* blockhead.
zorra *nf* 1 vixen. 2 *fam* slut.
zorro,-a I *nm* fox. II *adj fam* 1 *(astuto)* cunning, sly. 2 *vulg* **no tener ni zorra (idea),** not to have the slightest idea.
zorzal *nm Orn* thrush.
zozobrar *vi* to be in danger of going under.
zueco *nm* clog.
zumbado,-a *adj fam* crazy, mad.
zumbar I *vi* to buzz, hum; **me zumban los oídos,** my ears are buzzing; *fam* **salir zumbando,** to zoom off. II *vtr fam* to thrash.
zumbido *nm* buzzing, humming.
zumo *nm* juice.
zurcir [3] *vtr Cost* to darn; *fam* **¡que te zurzan!,** go to hell!
zurda *nf (mano)* left hand.
zurdo,-a I *nm,f (persona)* left-handed person. II *adj* left-handed.
zurrar *vtr (pegar)* to beat, flog.
zutano,-a *nm,f fam* so-and-so; *(hombre)* what's-his-name; *(mujer)* what's-her-name.

English - Spanish
Inglés - Español

TABLA DE VERBOS IRREGULARES INGLESES

American forms have been indicated by *. Unusual, archaic or literary forms are given in brackets.

infinitive	past tense	past participle
abide	abided, (abode)	abided
arise	arose	arisen
be	was, were	been
awake	awoke, awaked	awoken, (awaked)
bear	bore	borne
beat	beat	beaten
become	became	become
befall	befell	befallen
begin	began	begun
behold	beheld	beheld
bend	bent	bent
beseech	besought	besought
bet	bet, betted	bet, betted
bid *(offer)*	bid	bid
bid *(command)*	bade	bidden
bind	bound	bound
bite	bit	bitten
bleed	bled	bled
blow	blew	blown
break	broke	broken
breed	bred	bred
bring	brought	brought
broadcast	broadcast	broadcast
build	built	built
burn	burnt, burned	burnt, burned
burst	burst	burst
buy	bought	bought
cast	cast	cast
catch	caught	caught
choose	chose	chosen
cling	clung	clung
clothe	clothed, (clad)	clothed, (clad)
come	came	come
cost	cost	cost
creep	crept	crept
crow	crowed, (crew)	crowed
cut	cut	cut
deal	dealt	dealt
dig	dug	dug
dive	dived, dove*	dived
do	did	done
draw	drew	drawn
dream	dreamt, dreamed	dreamt, dreamed
drink	drank	drunk
drive	drove	driven
dwell	dwelt, dwelled	dwelt, dwelled
eat	ate	eaten
fall	fell	fallen
feed	fed	fed
feel	felt	felt
fight	fought	fought
find	found	found

fit	fit*, fitted	fit*, fitted
flee	fled	fled
fling	flung	flung
fly	flew	flown
forbid	forbad(e)	forbidden
forget	forgot	forgotten
forgive	forgave	forgiven
forsake	forsook	forsaken
freeze	froze	frozen
get	got	got, gotten*
give	gave	given
go	went	gone
grind	ground	ground
grow	grew	grown
hang	hung, hanged	hung, hanged
have	had	had
hear	heard	heard
hide	hid	hidden
hit	hit	hit
hold	held	held
hurt	hurt	hurt
keep	kept	kept
kneel	knelt, kneeled	knelt, kneeled
know	knew	known
lay	laid	laid
lead	led	led
lean	leant, leaned	leant, leaned
leap	leapt, leaped	leapt, leaped
learn	learnt, learned	learnt, learned
leave	left	left
lend	lent	lent
let	let	let
lie	lay	lain
light	lit, lighted	lit, lighted
lose	lost	lost
make	made	made
mean	meant	meant
meet	met	met
mow	mowed	mown, mowed
pay	paid	paid
plead	pled*, pleaded	pled*, pleaded
put	put	put
quit	quit, (quitted)	quit, (quitted)
read	read [red]	read [red]
rend	rent	rent
rid	rid	rid
ride	rode	ridden
ring	rang	rung
rise	rose	risen
run	ran	run
saw	sawed	sawn, sawed
say	said	said
see	saw	seen
seek	sought	sought
sell	sold	sold
send	sent	sent
set	set	set
sew	sewed	sewn, sewed

shake	shook	shaken
shear	sheared	shorn, sheared
shed	shed	shed
shine	shone	shone
shoe	shod, shoed	shod, shoed
shoot	shot	shot
show	showed	shown, showed
shrink	shrank, shrunk	shrunk
shut	shut	shut
sing	sang	sung
sink	sank	sunk
sit	sat	sat
slay	slew	slain
sleep	slept	slept
slide	slid	slid
sling	slung	slung
slink	slunk	slunk
slit	slit	slit
smell	smelt, smelled	smelt, smelled
sneak	snuck*, sneaked	snuck*, sneaked
sow	sowed	sown, sowed
speak	spoke	spoken
speed	sped, speeded	sped, speeded
spell	spelt, spelled	spelt, spelled
spend	spent	spent
spill	spilt, spilled	spilt, spilled
spin	spun	spun
spit	spat, spit*	spat, spit*
split	split	split
spoil	spoilt, spoiled	spoilt, spoiled
spread	spread	spread
spring	sprang	sprung
stand	stood	stood
steal	stole	stolen
stick	stuck	stuck
sting	stung	stung
stink	stank	stunk
strew	strewed	strewn, strewed
stride	strode	stridden
strike	struck	struck
string	strung	strung
strive	strove	striven
swear	swore	sworn
sweat	sweat*, sweated	sweat*, sweated
sweep	swept	swept
swell	swelled	swollen, swelled
swim	swam	swum
swing	swung	swung
take	took	taken
teach	taught	taught
tear	tore	torn
tell	told	told
think	thought	thought
thrive	thrived, (throve)	thrived, (thriven)
throw	threw	thrown
thrust	thrust	thrust
tread	trod	trodden
understand	understood	understood

undertake	undertook	undertaken
wake	woke	woken
wear	wore	worn
weave	wove	woven
weep	wept	wept
wet	wet, wetted	wet, wetted
win	won	won
wind	wound	wound
wring	wrung	wrung
write	wrote	written

Fonética Inglesa

En este diccionario la transcripción fonética de las palabras inglesas se basa en el sistema de la Asociación Fonética Internacional (AFI) con algunas modificaciones. Cada entrada viene seguida de su correspondiente transcripción fonética entre corchetes ([ ]). El acento primario se indica mediante un ' delante de la sílaba acentuada.

Las consonantes

[p]	*p*en
[b]	*b*ill
[t]	*t*en*t*
[d]	*d*esk
[k]	*c*ar
[g]	*g*oal
[tʃ]	tea*ch*er
[dʒ]	a*g*e
[f]	*f*ish
[v]	ha*v*e
[θ]	me*th*od
[ð]	mo*th*er
[s]	i*c*y
[z]	ea*s*y
[ʃ]	*sh*oe
[ʒ]	mea*s*ure
[h]	*h*at
[m]	*m*ilk
[n]	*n*ame
[ŋ]	si*ng*
[l]	*l*ight
[r]	*r*ead
[j]	*y*oghurt
[w]	*w*atch
[x]	lo*ch* (como en legión)
[ʳ]	se llama '*linking r*' y se encuentra únicamente a final de palabra. Se pronuncia sólo cuando la palabra siguiente empieza por una vocal: mother ['mʌðəʳ]

Las vocales y los diptongos

[iː]	sh*ee*p
[ɪ]	sh*i*p, hous*e*s
[e]	b*e*d
[æ]	c*a*t
[ɑː]	*fa*ther
[ɒ]	d*o*g
[ɔː]	h*o*rse
[ʊ]	w*o*man
[uː]	bl*ue*
[ʌ]	c*u*p
[ɜː]	*ea*rth
[ə]	*a*bout
[ə]	opcional. En algunos casos se pronuncia y en otros se omite: trifle ['traɪfəl]
[eɪ]	t*a*ble
[əʊ]	g*o*
[aɪ]	t*i*me
[aʊ]	h*ou*se
[ɔɪ]	b*oy*
[ɪə]	f*ie*rce
[eə]	c*a*re
[ʊə]	d*u*ring

A

A, a [eɪ] n 1 (the letter) A, a f. 2 Mus la m.

a [eɪ, unstressed ə] indef art (before vowel or silent h an) 1 un, una; **a man/a woman**, un hombre/una mujer; **he has a big nose**, tiene la nariz grande. 2 (omitted in Span) **half a litre/an hour**, medio litro/ media hora; **a hundred/thousand people**, cien/mil personas; **let's have a drink**, vamos a beber algo; **he's a teacher**, es profesor; **what a pity**, qué pena. 3 (each) **60 pence a kilo**, 60 peniques el kilo; **to eat grapes two at a time**, comer las uvas de dos en dos; **three times a week**, tres veces a la semana. 4 (a certain) un or una tal; **a Mr Rees phoned**, llamó un tal Sr. Rees.

AA [eɪ'eɪ] 1 abbr of **Alcoholics Anonymous**, Alcohólicos Anónimos, AA. 2 abbr of **Automobile Association**, ≈ Automóvil Club m, AC.

AAA [eɪeɪ'eɪ] 1 GB abbr of **Amateur Athletic Association**, Asociación Atlética Amateur, AAA. 2 US abbr of **Automobile Association of America**, ≈ Automóvil Club m, AC.

aback [ə'bæk] adv **to be taken a.**, quedarse de una pieza (**by**, por).

abandon [ə'bændən] I n desenfreno m; **with reckless a.**, desenfrenadamente. II vtr (child) abandonar; (job) dejar; (project) renunciar a.

abase [ə'beɪs] vtr **to a. oneself**, humillarse.

abashed [ə'bæʃt] adj desconcertado,-a.

abate [ə'beɪt] vi (anger) apaciguarse; (storm) amainar.

abattoir [æbə'twɑːr] n matadero m.

abbey ['æbɪ] n abadía f.

abbot ['æbət] n abad m.

abbreviate [ə'briːvɪeɪt] vtr abreviar.

abbreviation [əbriːvɪ'eɪʃən] n abreviatura f.

abdicate ['æbdɪkeɪt] vtr & vi abdicar.

abdication [æbdɪ'keɪʃən] n abdicación f.

abdomen ['æbdəmən] n abdomen m.

abduct [æb'dʌkt] vtr raptar, secuestrar.

aberration [æbə'reɪʃən] n aberración f.

abet [ə'bet] vtr **to aid and a. sb**, ser cómplice de algn.

abeyance [ə'beɪəns] n **to be in a.**, estar en desuso.

abhor [əb'hɔːr] vtr aborrecer.

abhorrent [əb'hɒrənt] adj aborrecible.

abide [ə'baɪd] vtr aguantar; **I can't a. it**, no lo aguanto. ◆**abide by** vtr (promise) cumplir con; (rules) atenerse a.

ability [ə'bɪlɪtɪ] n (capability) capacidad f, aptitud f; (talent) talento m.

abject ['æbdʒekt] adj (state) miserable; (apology) rastrero,-a.

ablaze [ə'bleɪz] adj & adv en llamas, ardiendo.

able ['eɪbəl] adj (capable) capaz; **will you be a. to come on Tuesday?**, ¿podrás venir el martes?

able-bodied [eɪbəl'bɒdɪd] adj sano,-a; **a.-b. seaman**, marinero m de primera.

abnormal [æb'nɔːməl] adj anormal. ◆**abnormally** adv anormalmente; (large) extraordinariamente.

aboard [ə'bɔːd] I adv a bordo; **to go a.**, (ship) embarcarse; (train) subir. II prep a bordo de.

abode [ə'bəʊd] n Jur **of no fixed a.**, sin domicilio fijo.

abolish [ə'bɒlɪʃ] vtr abolir.

abolition [æbə'lɪʃən] n abolición f.

abominable [ə'bɒmɪnəbəl] adj abominable; (dreadful) terrible.

aborigine [æbə'rɪdʒɪnɪ] n aborigen mf australiano,-a.

abort [ə'bɔːt] I vtr Med hacer abortar; fig (plan etc) archivar. II vi Med abortar.

abortion [ə'bɔːʃən] n Med aborto m; **a. law**, ley f del aborto; **to have an a.**, abortar.

abortive [ə'bɔːtɪv] adj (plan) fracasado,-a; (attempt) frustrado,-a.

abound [ə'baʊnd] vi **to a. in** or **with**, abundar en.

about [ə'baʊt] adv & prep 1 (concerning) acerca de, sobre; **a programme a. Paris**, un programa sobre París; **to be worried a. sth**, estar preocupado,-a por algo; **to speak a. sth**, hablar de algo; **what's it all a.?**, (what's happening?) ¿qué pasa?; (story etc) ¿de qué se trata?; fam **how a. a game of tennis?**, ¿qué te parece un partido de tenis? 2 (around) por todas partes; **don't leave things lying a.**, no dejes las cosas por medio; **there's nobody a.**, no hay nadie; **to look a.**, mirar alrededor; **to rush a.**, correr de un lado para otro; **we went for a walk a. the town**, dimos una vuelta por el pueblo. 3 (approximately) más o menos; **it's a. 3 o'clock**, son más o menos las 3; **it's a. time you got up**, ya es hora de que te levantes; **it's just a. finished**, está casi terminado; **she's a. 40**, tiene unos 40 años. 4 **it's a. to start**, está a punto de empezar; **not to be a. to do sth**, no estar dispuesto,-a a hacer algo.

about-turn [əbaʊt'tɜːn, əbaʊt'feɪs], US **about-face** n media vuelta f; **to do an a.-t.**, dar media vuelta; fig cambiar de idea por completo.

above [ə'bʌv] adv & prep 1 (higher than) encima de, sobre, arriba; **100 metres a. sea level**, 100 metros sobre el nivel del mar; **it's a. the door**, está encima de la puerta; **the flat a.**, el piso de arriba. **2** *(greater than)* superior (a); **amounts a. £10**, cantidades superiores a las 10 libras; *fig* **a policy imposed from a.**, una política impuesta desde arriba. **3 a. all**, sobre todo; **he's not a. stealing**, es capaz incluso de robar. **4** *(in book etc)* más arriba.

above-board [ə'bʌvbɔːd] *adj* *(scheme)* legítimo,-a.

above-mentioned [ə'bʌvmenʃənd] *adj* susodicho,-a.

abrasive [ə'breɪsɪv] **I** *adj* *(substance)* abrasivo,-a; *fig* *(voice, wit etc)* cáustico,-a. **II** *n* abrasivo *m*.

abreast [ə'brest] *adv* **to walk 3 a.**, ir de 3 en fondo; *fig* **to keep a. of things**, mantenerse al día.

abridged [ə'brɪdʒd] *adj* *(book)* abreviado,-a.

abroad [ə'brɔːd] *adv* **to be a.**, estar en el extranjero; **to go a.**, irse al extranjero.

abrupt [ə'brʌpt] *adj* *(manner)* brusco,-a; *(tone)* áspero,-a; *(change)* súbito,-a. ◆**abruptly** *adv* *(act)* bruscamente; *(speak)* con aspereza; *(change)* repentinamente.

abscess ['æbses] *n* absceso *m*; *(on gum)* flemón *m*.

abscond [əb'skɒnd] *vi* huir.

absence ['æbsəns] *n* *(of person)* ausencia *f*; *(of thing)* falta *f*.

absent ['æbsənt] *adj* ausente; *fig* **an a. look**, una mirada distraída. ◆**absently** *adv* distraídamente.

absentee [æbsən'tiː] *n* ausente *mf*.

absenteeism [æbsən'tiːɪzəm] *n* absentismo *m*.

absent-minded [æbsənt'maɪndɪd] *adj* distraído,-a.

absolute ['æbsəluːt] *adj* absoluto,-a; *(failure)* total; *(truth)* puro,-a; **it's an a. disgrace**, es una auténtica vergüenza. ◆**absolutely I** *adv* *(completely)* completamente; **a. wrong**, totalmente equivocado,-a; **a. not**, en absoluto; **you're a. right**, tienes toda la razón. **II** *interj* **a.!**, ¡desde luego!

absolve [əb'zɒlv] *vtr* absolver **(from**, de).

absorb [əb'zɔːb] *vtr* *(liquid)* absorber; *(sound, blow)* amortiguar; *fig* **to be absorbed in sth**, estar absorto,-a en algo.

absorbing [əb'zɔːbɪŋ] *adj* *(book, work)* absorbente.

abstain [əb'steɪn] *vi* abstenerse **(from**, de).

abstemious [əb'stiːmɪəs] *adj* abstemio,-a.

abstention [əb'stenʃən] *n* abstención *f*.

abstinence ['æbstɪnəns] *n* abstinencia *f*.

abstract ['æbstrækt] **I** *adj* abstracto,-a. **II** *n* *(of thesis etc)* resumen *m*.

abstruse [əb'struːs] *adj* abstruso,-a.

absurd [əb'sɜːd] *adj* absurdo,-a.

abundance [ə'bʌndəns] *n* abundancia *f*.

abundant [ə'bʌndənt] *adj* abundante,

rico,-a **(in**, en).

abuse [ə'bjuːs] **I** *n* **1** *(ill-treatment)* malos tratos; *(misuse)* abuso *m*. **2** *(insults)* injurias *fpl*. **II** [ə'bjuːz] *vtr* **1** *(ill-treat)* maltratar; *(misuse)* abusar de. **2** *(insult)* injuriar.

abusive [əb'juːsɪv] *adj* *(insulting)* insultante.

abysmal [ə'bɪzməl] *adj* *(conditions)* extremo,-a; *fam* *(very bad)* fatal, pésimo,-a.

abyss [ə'bɪs] *n* abismo *m*; *fig* extremo *m*.

AC ['eɪsiː] *abbr of* **alternating current**, corriente alterna, CA.

academic [ækə'demɪk] **I** *adj* académico, -a; *(career)* universitario,-a; *(discussion)* teórico,-a; **a. year**, año *m* escolar. **II** *n* académico,-a *m,f*.

academy [ə'kædəmɪ] *n* *(society)* academia *f*; *Educ* instituto *m* de enseñanza media; **a. of music**, conservatorio *m*.

accede [æk'siːd] *vi* acceder **(to**, a).

accelerate [æk'seləreɪt] **I** *vtr* *(engine)* acelerar; *(step)* aligerar. **II** *vi* *(car, engine)* acelerar.

acceleration [ækselə'reɪʃən] *n* aceleración *f*.

accelerator [æk'seləreɪtəʳ] *n* acelerador *m*.

accent ['æksənt] *n* acento *m*.

accentuate [æk'sentʃueɪt] *vtr* subrayar.

accept [ək'sept] *vtr & vi* aceptar; *(theory)* admitir; **do you a. that ...?**, ¿estás de acuerdo en que ...?

acceptable [ək'septəbəl] *adj* *(satisfactory)* aceptable; *(tolerable)* admisible.

acceptance [ək'septəns] *n* *(act of accepting)* aceptación *f*; *(good reception)* aprobación *f*.

access ['ækses] *n* acceso *m*; **a. road**, carretera *f* de acceso; **to have a. to sth**, tener libre acceso a algo.

accessible [ək'sesəbəl] *adj* *(place, position)* accesible; *(person)* asequible.

accession [ək'seʃən] *n* subida *f* (al trono).

accessory [ək'sesərɪ] *n* **1** *Jur* cómplice *mf*. **2 accessories**, accesorios *mpl*; *(for outfit)* complementos *mpl*.

accident ['æksɪdənt] *n* accidente *m*; *(coincidence)* casualidad *f*; **it was an a. on my part**, lo hice sin querer; **car a.**, accidente *m* de carretera; **by a.**, por casualidad.

accidental [æksɪ'dentəl] *adj* fortuito,-a; *(unintended)* imprevisto,-a. ◆**accidentally** *adv* *(by chance)* por casualidad; **he did it a.**, lo hizo sin querer.

accident-prone ['æksɪdəntprəʊn] *adj* propenso,-a a los accidentes.

acclaim [ə'kleɪm] **I** *n* aclamación *f*. **II** *vtr* aclamar.

acclimatize [ə'klaɪmətaɪz] *vtr* aclimatar.

acclimatized [ə'klaɪmətaɪzd] *adj* aclimatado,-a; **to become a.**, aclimatarse.

accolade |'ækəleɪd| *n* elogio *m*.

accommodate |ə'kɒmədeɪt| *vtr* 1 (*guests*) alojar. 2 **to a. sb's wishes**, complacer a algn.

accommodating |ə'kɒmədeɪtɪŋ| *adj* (*obliging*) complaciente; (*understanding*) comprensivo,-a.

accommodation |əkɒmə'deɪʃən| *n* (*US also* **accommodations**) (*lodgings*) alojamiento *m*.

accompany |ə'kʌmpənɪ| *vtr* acompañar.

accomplice |ə'kʌmplɪs| *n* cómplice *mf*.

accomplish |ə'kʌmplɪʃ| *vtr* (*aim*) conseguir; (*task, mission*) llevar a cabo.

accomplished |ə'kʌmplɪʃt| *adj* dotado,-a, experto,-a.

accomplishment |ə'kʌmplɪʃmənt| *n* 1 (*of task*) realización *f*; (*of duty*) cumplimiento *m*. 2 **accomplishments**, (*talents*) dotes *fpl*.

accord |ə'kɔːd| I *n* (*agreement*) acuerdo *m*; **of her** *or* **his own a.**, espontáneamente. II *vtr* (*honour etc*) conceder.

accordance |ə'kɔːdəns| *n* **in a. with**, de acuerdo con.

according |ə'kɔːdɪŋ| *prep* **a. to**, según; **everything went a. to plan**, todo salió conforme a los planes.

accordingly |ə'kɔːdɪŋlɪ| *adv* 1 **to act a.**, (*appropriately*) obrar según y conforme. 2 (*therefore*) así pues.

accordion |ə'kɔːdɪən| *n* acordeón *m*.

account |ə'kaʊnt| *n* 1 (*report*) informe *m*; **by all accounts**, al decir de todos. 2 **I was fearful on her a.**, sufría por ella; **it's of no a.**, no tiene importancia; **on a. of**, a causa de; **on no a.**, bajo ningún concepto; **to take a. of, to take into a.**, tener en cuenta. 3 *Com* cuenta *f*; **to keep the accounts**, llevar las cuentas; **accounts department**, servicio *m* de contabilidad; **to open/close an a.**, abrir/cancelar una cuenta; **current a.**, cuenta corriente; **a. number**, número *m* de cuenta. ◆**account for** *vtr* (*explain*) explicar.

accountable |ə'kaʊntəbəl| *adj* **to be a. to sb for sth**, ser responsable ante algn por algo.

accountancy |ə'kaʊntənsɪ| *n* contabilidad *f*.

accountant |ə'kaʊntənt| *n* contable *mf*.

accredited |ə'kredɪtɪd| *adj* acreditado,-a.

accrue |ə'kruː| *vi* (*interest*) acumularse.

accumulate |ə'kjuːmjʊleɪt| I *vtr* acumular; (*fortune*) amasar. II *vi* acumularse.

accuracy |'ækjʊrəsɪ| *n* (*of number etc*) exactitud *f*; (*of shot, criticism*) certeza *f*.

accurate |'ækjərɪt| *adj* (*number*) exacto,-a; (*shot, criticism*) certero,-a; (*answer*) correcto,-a; (*observation*) acertado,-a; (*instrument*) de precisión; (*translation*) fiel.

accusation |ækjʊ'zeɪʃən| *n* acusación *f*.

accuse |ə'kjuːz| *vtr* acusar.

accused |ə'kjuːzd| *n* **the a.**, el/la acusado,-a.

accustom |ə'kʌstəm| *vtr* acostumbrar; **to be accustomed to doing sth**, estar acostumbrado,-a a hacer algo.

ace |eɪs| *n* 1 *Cards & fig* as *m*. 2 **Ten** ace *m*.

acetate |'æsɪteɪt| *n* acetato *m*.

acetone |'æsɪtəʊn| *n* acetona *f*.

ache |eɪk| I *n* dolor *m*; **aches and pains**, achaques *mpl*. II *vi* doler; **my back aches**, me duele la espalda.

achieve |ə'tʃiːv| *vtr* (*attain*) conseguir, alcanzar; (*accomplish*) llevar a cabo, realizar.

achievement |ə'tʃiːvmənt| *n*. (*attainment*) logro *m*; (*completion*) realización *f*; (*feat*) hazaña *f*.

acid |'æsɪd| I *adj* ácido,-a; (*taste*) agrio,-a; (*remark*) mordaz; **a. rain**, lluvia ácida; *fig* **a. test**, prueba decisiva. II *n* ácido *m*.

acknowledge |ək'nɒlɪdʒ| *vtr* 1 (*recognize*) reconocer; (*claim, defeat*) admitir; (*present*) agradecer; (*letter*) acusar recibo de. 2 (*greet*) saludar.

acknowledgement |ək'nɒlɪdʒmənt| *n* 1 (*recognition*) reconocimiento *m*; (*of letter*) acuse *m* de recibo. 2 **acknowledgements**, (*in preface*) menciones *fpl*.

acne |'æknɪ| *n* acné *m*.

acorn |'eɪkɔːn| *n* bellota *f*.

acoustic |ə'kuːstɪk| I *adj* acústico,-a. II *npl* **acoustics**, acústica *f sing*.

acquaint |ə'kweɪnt| *vtr* **to a. sb with the facts**, informar a algn de los detalles; **to be acquainted with the procedure**, estar al corriente de como se procede; **to be acquainted with sb**, conocer a algn.

acquaintance |ə'kweɪntəns| *n* 1 conocimiento *m*; **to make sb's a.**, conocer a algn. 2 (*person*) conocido,-a *m,f*.

acquiesce |ækwɪ'es| *vi* consentir (**in**, en).

acquiescent |ækwɪ'esənt| *adj* conforme.

acquire |ə'kwaɪər| *vtr* adquirir.

acquisition |ækwɪ'zɪʃən| *n* adquisición *f*.

acquisitive |ə'kwɪzɪtɪv| *adj* codicioso,-a.

acquit |ə'kwɪt| *vtr* 1 *Jur* **to a. sb of sth**, absolver a algn de algo. 2 **to a. oneself well**, defenderse bien.

acquittal |ə'kwɪtəl| *n* absolución *f*.

acre |'eɪkər| *n* acre *m* (*aprox* 40,47 áreas).

acrid |'ækrɪd| *adj* (*smell, taste*) acre.

acrimonious |ækrɪ'məʊnɪəs| *adj* (*remark*) cáustico,-a; (*dispute*) enconado,-a.

acrobat |'ækrəbæt| *n* acróbata *mf*.

across |ə'krɒs| I *adv* a través; **the river is 30 metres a.**, el río mide 30 metros de ancho; **to go a.**, atravesar; **to run a.**, atravesar corriendo. II *prep* 1 a través de; **they live a. the road**, viven enfrente; **to go a. the street**, cruzar la calle. 2 (*at the other side of*) al otro lado de.

acrylic |ə'krɪlɪk| *adj* acrílico,-a.

act |ækt| I *n* 1 (*action*) acto *m*, acción *f*; **a.**

of God, caso *m* de fuerza mayor. 2 *Parl* ley *f,* decreto *m.* 3 *Theat* acto *m; (turn in show)* número *m.* II *vtr Theat (part)* interpretar; *(character)* representar; *fig* **to a. the fool,** hacer el tonto. III *vi* 1 *Theat* hacer teatro; *Cin* hacer cine; *fig (pretend)* fingir. 2 *(behave)* comportarse. 3 *(take action)* actuar, obrar; **to a. on sb's advice,** seguir el consejo de algn. 4 *(work)* funcionar; *(drug etc)* actuar; **to a. as a deterrent,** servir de disuasivo. 5 **to a. as director,** hacer de director. ◆**act out** *vtr* exteriorizar. ◆**act up** *vi fam (machine)* funcionar mal; *(child)* dar guerra.

acting ['æktɪŋ] I *adj* interino,-a. II *n (profession)* teatro *m;* **he's done some a.,** ha hecho algo de teatro.

action ['ækʃən] *n* 1 *(deed)* acción *f; Mil* acción de combate; **to be out of a.,** *(person)* estar fuera de servicio; *(machine)* estar estropeado,-a; **to take a.,** tomar medidas. 2 *Jur* demanda *f.* 3 *TV* **a. replay,** repetición *f.*

activate ['æktɪveɪt] *vtr* activar.

active ['æktɪv] *adj* activo,-a; *(energetic)* vigoroso,-a; *(interest)* vivo,-a; *Ling* **a. voice,** voz activa.

activist ['æktɪvɪst] *n* activista *mf.*

activity [æk'tɪvɪtɪ] *n (of person)* actividad *f; (on street etc)* bullicio *m.*

actor ['æktər] *n* actor *m.*

actress ['æktrɪs] *n* actriz *f.*

actual ['æktʃʊəl] *adj* real, verdadero,-a.

actually ['æktʃʊəlɪ] *adv (really)* en efecto, realmente; *(even)* incluso, hasta; *(in fact)* de hecho.

acumen ['ækjʊmən] *n* perspicacia *f.*

acupuncture ['ækjʊpʌŋktʃər] *n* acupuntura *f.*

acute [ə'kjuːt] *adj* agudo,-a; *(pain)* intenso,-a; *(hearing)* muy fino,-a; *(shortage)* grave; *(mind)* perspicaz.

ad [æd] *n fam* anuncio *m.*

AD [eɪ'diː] *abbr of* **Anno Domini,** después de Cristo, d.d.C.

adamant ['ædəmənt] *adj* firme, inflexible.

adapt [ə'dæpt] I *vtr* adaptar (**to, a**); **to a. oneself to sth,** adaptarse a algo. II *vi* adaptarse.

adaptable [ə'dæptəbəl] *adj (instrument)* ajustable; **he's very a.,** se amolda fácilmente a las circunstancias.

adaptation [ædəp'teɪʃən] *n* adaptación *f.*

adapter, adaptor [ə'dæptər] *n Elec* ladrón *m.*

add [æd] I *vtr (numbers)* sumar; *(one thing to another)* añadir. II *vi (count)* sumar. ◆**add to** *vtr* aumentar. ◆**add up** I *vtr* sumar. II *vi (numbers)* sumar; *fig* **it doesn't a. up,** no tiene sentido; **it doesn't a. up to much,** no es gran cosa.

added ['ædɪd] *adj* adicional.

adder ['ædər] *n* víbora *f.*

addict ['ædɪkt] *n* adicto,-a *m,f; fam* **television a.,** teleadicto,-a *m,f.*

addicted [ə'dɪktɪd] *adj* adicto,-a; **to become a. to sth,** enviciarse con algo.

addiction [ə'dɪkʃən] *n (to gambling etc)* vicio *m; (to drugs)* adicción *f.*

addictive [ə'dɪktɪv] *adj* que crea adicción.

addition [ə'dɪʃən] *n Math* adición *f; (increase)* aumento *m;* **an a. to the family,** un nuevo miembro de la familia; **in a. to,** además de.

additional [ə'dɪʃənəl] *adj* adicional.

additive ['ædɪtɪv] *n* aditivo *m.*

address [ə'dres] I *n* 1 *(on letter)* dirección *f,* señas *fpl.* 2 *(speech)* discurso *m.* II *vtr* 1 *(letter)* dirigir. 2 *(speak to)* dirigirse (**to, a**); **to a. the floor,** tomar la palabra. 3 *(use form of address to)* tratar de.

adenoids ['ædɪnɔɪdz] *npl* vegetaciones *fpl* (adenoideas).

adept [ə'dept] I *adj* experto,-a, (**at, en**). II *n* experto,-a.

adequate ['ædɪkwɪt] *adj (enough)* suficiente; *(satisfactory)* adecuado,-a.

adhere [əd'hɪər] *vi (stick)* pegarse (**to, a**). ◆**adhere to** *vtr (policy)* adherirse a; *(contract)* cumplir con.

adherent [əd'hɪərənt] *n* partidario,-a *m,f.*

adhesive [əd'hiːsɪv] I *adj* adhesivo,-a; *(sticky)* pegajoso,-a; **a. tape,** cinta adhesiva. II *n* adhesivo *m.*

ad hoc [æd'hɒk] *adj (remark)* improvisado,-a; **an ad h. committee,** un comité especial.

ad infinitum [ædɪnfɪ'naɪtəm] *adv* hasta el infinito.

adjacent [ə'dʒeɪsənt] *adj (building)* contiguo,-a; *(land)* colindante; **a. to,** contiguo,-a a.

adjective ['ædʒɪktɪv] *n* adjetivo *m.*

adjoining [ə'dʒɔɪnɪŋ] *adj* contiguo,-a; *(land)* colindante; **the a. room,** la habitación de al lado.

adjourn [ə'dʒɜːn] I *vtr (postpone)* aplazar; *(court)* levantar. II *vi* aplazarse (**until,** hasta).

adjudicate [ə'dʒuːdɪkeɪt] *vtr* juzgar.

adjudicator [ə'dʒuːdɪkeɪtər] *n* juez,-a *m,f.*

adjust [ə'dʒʌst] I *vtr (machine etc)* ajustar; *fig (methods)* variar. II *vi (person)* adaptarse (**to, a**).

adjustable [ə'dʒʌstəbəl] *adj* ajustable.

adjustment [ə'dʒʌstmənt] *n* 1 *(to machine etc)* ajuste *m; (by person)* adaptación *f.* 2 *(change)* modificación *f.*

ad lib [æd'lɪb] I *adv (speak)* sin preparación; *(continue)* a voluntad. II *adj (speech)* improvisado,-a. III **ad-lib** *vi* improvisar.

administer [əd'mɪnɪstər] *vtr (country)* gobernar; *(justice)* administrar.

administration [ədmɪnɪ'streɪʃən] *n (of country)* gobierno *m; (of justice)* administración *f; (governing body)* dirección *f.*

administrative [əd'mɪnɪstrɪtɪv] *adj*

adm_istrativo,-a.
admirable [ædmərəbəl] *adj* admirable.
admiral ['ædmərəl] *n* almirante *m*.
admiration [ædmə'reɪʃən] *n* admiración
f.
admire [əd'maɪər] *vtr* admirar.
admirer [əd'maɪərər] *n* admirador,-a *m,f*.
admissible [əd'mɪsəbəl] *adj* admisible.
admission [əd'mɪʃən] *n* 1 (*to school etc*)
ingreso *m*; (*price*) entrada *f*. 2 (*of fact*)
reconocimiento *m*; (*confession*) confesión
f.
admit [əd'mɪt] *vtr* 1 (*person*) dejar entrar;
to be admitted to hospital, ser
ingresado,-a en el hospital. 2
(*acknowledge*) reconocer; (*crime, guilt*)
confesar.
admittance [əd'mɪtəns] *n* (*entry*) entrada
f.
admittedly [əd'mɪtɪdlɪ] *adv* la verdad es
que ....
admonish [əd'mɒnɪʃ] *vtr* amonestar.
ad nauseam [æd'nɔːzɪæm] *adv* hasta la
saciedad.
ado [ə'duː] *n* **without further a.**, sin más.
adolescence [ædə'lesəns] *n* adolescencia
f.
adolescent [ædə'lesənt] *n* adolescente *mf*.
adopt [ə'dɒpt] *vtr* adoptar; (*suggestion*)
aceptar.
adopted [ə'dɒptɪd] *adj* **a. child**, hijo,-a
m,f adoptivo,-a.
adoption [ə'dɒpʃən] *n* adopción *f*; **country of a.**, país adoptivo.
adore [ə'dɔːr] *vtr* adorar.
adorn [ə'dɔːn] *vtr* adornar.
adornment [ə'dɔːnmənt] *n* adorno *m*.
adrenalin [ə'drenəlɪn] *n* adrenalina *f*.
Adriatic [eɪdrɪ'ætɪk] *adj* **the A. (Sea)**, el
(Mar) Adriático.
adrift [ə'drɪft] *adv* **to come a.**, (*boat*) irse
a la deriva; (*rope*) soltarse; *fig* **to go a.**,
(*plans*) ir a la deriva.
adult ['ædʌlt] I *adj* (*person*) adulto,-a, mayor; (*film, education*) para adultos. II *n*
adulto,-a *m,f*.
adulterate [ə'dʌltəreɪt] *vtr* adulterar.
adulterer [ə'dʌltərər] *n* adúltero *m*.
adulteress [ə'dʌltrɪs] *n* adúltera *f*.
adultery [ə'dʌltərɪ] *n* adulterio *m*.
advance [əd'vɑːns] I *n* 1 (*movement*)
avance *m*; *fig* (*progress*) progreso *m*; **to
have sth ready in a.**, tener algo preparado de antemano; **to make advances**, (*to a
person*) insinuarse (**to**, a). 2 (*loan*) anticipo *m*. II *adj* (*before time*) adelantado,-a;
Cin Theat **a. bookings**, reservas *fpl* por
adelantado. III *vtr* 1 (*troops*) avanzar;
(*time, date*) adelantar. 2 (*idea*) proponer;
(*opinion*) dar. 3 *Fin* (*sum of money*) anticipar. IV *vi* (*move forward*) avanzar, a-
delantarse; (*make progress*) hacer progresos; (*gain promotion*) ascender.
advanced [əd'vɑːnst] *adj* (*developed*)

avanzado,-a; (*student*) adelantado,-a;
(*course*) superior; *Educ* **A. level**, examen
m superior de segunda enseñanza, ≈
COU *m*.
advancement [əd'vɑːnsmənt] *n* (*progress*)
adelanto *m*; (*promotion*) ascenso *m*.
advantage [əd'vɑːntɪdʒ] *n* ventaja *f*; *Ten*
a. Velasco, ventaja para Velasco; **to take
a. of sb/sth**, abusar de algn/aprovechar
algo.
advantageous [ædvən'teɪdʒəs] *adj*
ventajoso,-a.
advent ['ædvent] *n* (*arrival*) llegada *f*; (*of
Christ*) advenimiento *m*; **A.**, Adviento *m*.
adventure [əd'ventʃər] *n* aventura *f*.
adventurous [əd'ventʃərəs] *adj*
aventurero,-a.
adverb ['ædvɜːb] *n* adverbio *m*.
adversary ['ædvəsərɪ] *n* adversario,-a *m,f*.
adverse ['ædvɜːs] *adj* (*effect*) desfavorable; (*conditions*) adverso,-a; (*winds*)
contrario,-a.
adversity [əd'vɜːsɪtɪ] *n* adversidad *f*.
advert ['ædvɜːt] *n fam* anuncio *m*.
advertise ['ædvətaɪz] I *vtr* anunciar. II *vi*
hacer publicidad; (*in newspaper*) poner un
anuncio; **to a. for sth/sb**, buscar algo/a
algn mediante un anuncio.
advertisement [əd'vɜːtɪsmənt] *n* anuncio
m; **advertisements**, publicidad *f sing*.
advertiser ['ædvətaɪzər] *n* anunciante *mf*.
advertising ['ædvətaɪzɪŋ] I *n* publicidad
f, propaganda *f*; (*in newspaper*) anuncios
mpl. II *adj* publicitario,-a; **a. agency**,
agencia *f* de publicidad.
advice [əd'vaɪs] *n* consejos *mpl*; **a piece
of a.**, un consejo; **to take legal a. on a
matter**, consultar el caso con un abogado; **to take sb's a.**, seguir los consejos de
algn.
advisable [əd'vaɪzəbəl] *adj* aconsejable.
advise [əd'vaɪz] *vtr* aconsejar; (*on business
etc*) asesorar; **I a. you to do it**, te aconse-
jo que lo hagas.
adviser [əd'vaɪzər] *n* consejero,-a *m,f*; (*in
business etc*) asesor,-a *m,f*.
advisory [əd'vaɪzərɪ] *adj* asesor,-a.
advocate ['ædvəkɪt] I *n Scot Jur*
abogado,-a *m,f*; (*supporter*) defensor,-a
m,f. II ['ædvəkeɪt] *vtr* (*reform*) abogar
por; (*plan*) apoyar.
aerial ['eərɪəl] I *adj* aéreo,-a. II *n* antena
f.
aerobics [eə'rəʊbɪks] *n* aerobic *m*.
aerodrome ['eərədrəʊm] *n GB* aeródromo *m*.
aerodynamics [eərəʊdaɪ'næmɪks] *n* aerodinámica *f*.
aeroplane ['eərəpleɪn] *n* avión *m*.
aerosol ['eərəsɒl] *n* aerosol *m*.
aerospace ['eərəʊspeɪs] *adj* aeroespacial.
aesthetic [iːs'θetɪk] *adj* estético,-a.
afar [ə'fɑːr] *adv* lejos; **from a.**, desde lejos.

affair [ə'feəʳ] n (matter) asunto m; (event) acontecimiento m; **that's my a.,** eso es asunto mío; **business affairs,** negocios mpl; **foreign affairs,** asuntos exteriores; **love a.,** aventura f amorosa.

affect [ə'fekt] vtr (person, health) afectar; (prices, future) influir en; (touch emotionally) conmover.

affected [ə'fektɪd] adj 1 (unnatural) afectado,-a. 2 (influenced) influido,-a. 3 (touched emotionally) conmovido,-a. 4 (pretended) fingido,-a.

affection [ə'fekʃən] n afecto m, cariño m.

affectionate [ə'fekʃənɪt] adj cariñoso,-a.

affidavit [æfɪ'deɪvɪt] n declaración escrita y jurada.

affiliated [ə'fɪlɪeɪtɪd] adj afiliado,-a; **to be or become a.,** afiliarse (**to, with,** a).

affinity [ə'fɪnɪtɪ] n afinidad f; (liking) simpatía f.

affirm [ə'fɜːm] vtr afirmar, sostener.

affirmation [æfə'meɪʃən] n afirmación f.

affirmative [ə'fɜːmətɪv] I adj afirmativo,-a. II n **he answered in the a.,** contestó que sí.

affix [ə'fɪks] vtr (stamp) pegar.

afflict [ə'flɪkt] vtr afligir.

affluence [ˈæfluəns] n opulencia f.

affluent [ˈæfluənt] adj (society) opulento, -a; (person) rico,-a.

afford [ə'fɔːd] vtr 1 (be able to buy) permitirse el lujo de; **I can't a. a new car,** no puedo pagar un coche nuevo. 2 (be able to do) permitirse; **you can't a. to miss the opportunity,** no puedes perderte la ocasión.

affront [ə'frʌnt] I n afrenta f. II vtr afrentar.

afield [ə'fiːld] adv **far a.,** muy lejos.

afloat [ə'fləʊt] adv **to keep a.,** mantenerse a flote.

afoot [ə'fʊt] adv **there's a plan a.,** hay un proyecto en marcha; **there's something strange a.,** se está tramando algo.

aforementioned [ə'fɔːmenʃənd], **aforesaid** [ə'fɔːsed] adj susodicho,-a.

afraid [ə'freɪd] adj 1 **to be a.,** tener miedo (**of sb,** a algn; **of sth,** de algo); **I'm a. of it,** me da miedo. 2 **I'm a. not,** me temo que no; **I'm a. so,** me temo que sí; **I'm a. you're wrong,** me temo que estás equivocado,-a.

afresh [ə'freʃ] adv de nuevo.

Africa [ˈæfrɪkə] n Africa.

African [ˈæfrɪkən] adj & n africano,-a (m,f).

Afro [ˈæfrəʊ] n & adj fam (hairstyle) afro (m).

aft [ɑːft] adv en popa; **to go a.,** ir en popa.

after [ˈɑːftəʳ] I adv después; **soon a.,** poco después; **the day a.,** el día siguiente. II prep 1 (later) después de; US **it's ten a. five,** son las cinco y diez; **soon**

a. arriving, al poco rato de llegar; **the day a. tomorrow,** pasado mañana. 2 (behind) detrás de, tras; **a. you!,** ¡pase usted!; **they went in one a. the other,** entraron uno tras otro; **the police are a. them,** la policía anda tras ellos. 3 (about) por; **they asked a. you,** preguntaron por ti; **what's he a.?,** ¿qué pretende? 4 **he takes a. his uncle,** se parece a su tío; **she was named a. her grandmother,** le llamaron como su abuela. III conj después (de) que; **a. it happened,** después de que ocurriera.

after-effect [ˈɑːftərɪfekt] n efecto m secundario.

afterlife [ˈɑːftəlaɪf] n vida f después de la muerte.

aftermath [ˈɑːftəmæθ] n secuelas fpl.

afternoon [ɑːftə'nuːn] n tarde f; **good a.!,** ¡buenas tardes!; **in the a.,** por la tarde.

afters [ˈɑːftəz] npl fam postre m.

after-sales service [ɑːftəseɪlz'sɜːvɪs] n Com servicio m posventa.

aftershave (lotion) [ˈɑːftəʃeɪv('ləʊʃən)] n loción f para después del afeitado.

afterthought [ˈɑːftəθɔːt] n ocurrencia f tardía.

afterwards [ˈɑːftəwədz] adv después, más tarde.

again [ə'gen] adv 1 otra vez, de nuevo; **I tried a. and a.,** lo intenté una y otra vez; **to do sth a.,** volver a hacer algo; **never a.!,** ¡nunca más!; **now and a.,** de vez en cuando; **once a.,** otra vez. 2 (besides) además; **then a.,** por otra parte.

against [ə'genst] prep 1 (touching) contra. 2 (opposing) contra, en contra (de); **a. the grain,** a contrapelo; **it's a. the law,** es ilegal. 3 **as a.,** en contraste con, comparado con.

age [eɪdʒ] I n 1 edad f; **she's 18 years of a.,** tiene 18 años; **to be under a.,** ser menor de edad; **to come of a.,** llegar a la mayoría de edad; **a. limit,** límite m de edad; **old a.,** vejez f. 2 (period) época f; **the Iron A.,** la Edad de Hierro. 3 fam (long time) eternidad f; **it's ages since I last saw her,** hace siglos que no la veo. II vtr & vi envejecer.

aged¹ [eɪdʒd] adj de or a la edad de.

aged² [ˈeɪdʒɪd] npl **the a.,** los ancianos.

agency [ˈeɪdʒənsɪ] n 1 Com agencia f. 2 **by the a. of,** por medio de.

agenda [ə'dʒendə] n orden m del día.

agent [ˈeɪdʒənt] n agente mf; (representative) representante mf.

aggravate [ˈægrəveɪt] vtr (worsen) agravar; (annoy) molestar.

aggregate [ˈægrɪgɪt] n conjunto m; **on a.,** en conjunto.

aggression [ə'greʃən] n agresión f.

aggressive [ə'gresɪv] adj (violent) agresivo,-a, violento,-a; (dynamic)

dinámico,-a.
aggrieved [ə'gri:vd] *adj* apenado,-a.
aghast [ə'gɑ:st] *adj* espantado,-a.
agile ['ædʒaɪl] *adj* ágil.
agitate ['ædʒɪteɪt] I *vtr* (*shake*) agitar; *fig* (*worry*) perturbar. II *vi Pol* to a. against sth, hacer campaña en contra de algo.
agitator ['ædʒɪteɪtər] *n Pol* agitador,-a *m,f*.
AGM [eɪdʒi:'em] *abbr of* annual general meeting, junta *f* general anual.
agnostic [æg'nɒstɪk] *n* agnóstico,-a *m,f*.
ago [ə'gəʊ] *adv* a long time a., hace mucho tiempo; **as long a. as** 1910, ya en 1910; **a week a.**, hace una semana; how long a.?, ¿hace cuánto tiempo?
agog [ə'gɒg] *adj* ansioso,-a.
agonizing ['ægənaɪzɪŋ] *adj* (*pain*) atroz; (*decision*) desesperante.
agony ['ægənɪ] *n* dolor *m* muy fuerte; (*anguish*) angustia *f*; **he was in a. with his back**, tenía un dolor insoportable de espalda.
agree [ə'gri:] I *vi* 1 (*be in agreement*) estar de acuerdo; (*reach agreement*) ponerse de acuerdo; (*consent*) consentir; **to a. to do sth**, consentir en hacer algo; **to a. with sb**, estar de acuerdo con algn. 2 (*harmonize*) (*things*) concordar; (*people*) congeniar; **onions don't a. with me**, la cebolla no me sienta bien. II *vtr* acordar.
agreeable [ə'gri:əbəl] *adj* (*pleasant*) agradable; (*person*) simpático,-a; (*in agreement*) de acuerdo.
agreement [ə'gri:mənt] *n* (*arrangement*) acuerdo *m*; *Com* contrato *m*; **to reach an a.**, llegar a un acuerdo.
agricultural [ægrɪ'kʌltʃərəl] *adj* agrícola; (*college*) de agricultura.
agriculture ['ægrɪkʌltʃər] *n* agricultura *f*.
aground [ə'graʊnd] *adv* to run a., encallar, varar.
ahead [ə'hed] *adv* delante; (*early*) antes; **go a.!**, ¡adelante!; **to be a.**, llevar la ventaja; **to go a.**, ir adelante; *fig* **to go a. with sth**, llevar algo adelante; (*start*) comenzar algo; **to get a.**, triunfar; **to look a.**, pensar en el futuro.
aid [eɪd] I *n* ayuda *f*; (*rescue*) auxilio *m*; **in a. of**, a beneficio de; **to come to the a. of sb**, acudir en ayuda de algn. II *vtr* ayudar; **to a. and abet sb**, ser cómplice de algn.
aide [eɪd] *n* ayudante *mf*.
Aids [eɪdz] *n* (*abbr of* **Acquired Immune Deficiency Syndrome**) SIDA *m* (Síndrome *m* de Inmunodeficiencia Adquirida).
ailing ['eɪlɪŋ] *adj* achacoso,-a.
ailment ['eɪlmənt] *n* enfermedad *f* (leve), achaque *m*.
aim [eɪm] I *n* (*with weapon*) puntería *f*; (*target*) propósito *m*. II *vtr* (*gun*) apuntar (**at, a**, hacia); (*attack, action*) dirigir (**at, a**, hacia). ◆**aim at** *vtr* (*target*) tirar para;

to a. at doing sth, tener pensado hacer algo. ◆**aim to** *vtr* to a. to do sth, tener la intención de hacer algo.
aimless ['eɪmlɪs] *adj* sin objeto, sin propósito. ◆**aimlessly** *adv* (*wander*) sin rumbo fijo.
air [eər] I *n* 1 aire *m*; **to travel by a.**, viajar en avión; **to throw sth up in the a.**, lanzar algo al aire; *fig* **it's still in the a.**, todavía queda por resolver; **a. base**, base aérea; **a. bed**, colchón *m* hinchable; **a. conditioning**, aire acondicionado; **A. Force**, Fuerzas Aéreas; **a. freshener**, ambientador *m*; **a. gun**, pistola *f* de aire comprimido; **a. hostess**, azafata *f*; **a. letter**, carta aérea; **a. pocket**, bache *m*; **a. pressure**, presión atmosférica; **a. raid**, ataque aéreo; **a. terminal**, terminal aérea; **a. traffic control**, control *m* de tráfico aéreo; **a. traffic controller**, controlador,-a *m,f* aéreo,-a. 2 *Rad TV* **to be on the a.**, (*programme*) estar emitiendo; (*person*) estar transmitiendo. 3 (*appearance*) aspecto *m*. II *vtr* (*bed, clothes*) airear; (*room*) ventilar; *fig* (*grievance*) airear; (*knowledge*) hacer alarde de.
airborne ['eəbɔ:n] *adj* (*aircraft*) en vuelo; (*troops*) aerotransportado,-a.
air-conditioned ['eəkɒndɪʃənd] *adj* climatizado,-a.
aircraft ['eəkrɑ:ft] *n inv* avión *m*; **a. carrier**, portaviones *m inv*.
airfield ['eəfi:ld] *n* campo *m* de aviación.
airlift ['eəlɪft] *n* puente aéreo.
airline ['eəlaɪn] *n* línea aérea.
airlock ['eəlɒk] *n* (*in pipe*) bolsa *f* de aire; (*in spacecraft*) esclusa *f* de aire.
airmail ['eəmeɪl] *n* correo *m* aéreo; **by a.**, por avión.
airplane ['eəpleɪn] *n US* avión *m*.
airport ['eəpɔ:t] *n* aeropuerto *m*.
airsick ['eəsɪk] *adj* to be a., marearse en avión.
airstrip ['eəstrɪp] *n* pista *f* de aterrizaje.
airtight ['eətaɪt] *adj* hermético,-a.
airy ['eərɪ] *adj* (**airier, airiest**) (*well-ventilated*) bien ventilado,-a; (*vague, carefree*) ligero,-a.
aisle [aɪl] *n* (*in church*) nave *f*; (*in theatre*) pasillo *m*.
ajar [ə'dʒɑ:r] *adj & adv* entreabierto,-a.
akin [ə'kɪn] *adj* semejante.
alacrity [ə'lækrɪtɪ] *n* with a., con presteza.
alarm [ə'lɑ:m] I *n* 1 alarma *f*; **a. clock**, despertador *m*. 2 (*fear*) inquietud *f*; **to cause a.**, provocar temor. II *vtr* alarmar.
alas [ə'læs] *interj* ¡ay!, ¡ay de mí!
albatross ['ælbətrɒs] *n* albatros *m*.
albeit [ɔ:l'bi:ɪt] *conj* aunque, no obstante.
album ['ælbəm] *n* álbum *m*.
alcohol ['ælkəhɒl] *n* alcohol *m*.
alcoholic [ælkə'hɒlɪk] *adj & n* alcohólico,-a (*m,f*).

alcove ['ælkəʊv] n hueco m.

ale [eɪl] n cerveza f; **brown/pale a.**, cerveza negra/rubia.

alert [ə'lɜːt] I adj alerta; (lively) despabilado,-a. II n alerta m; **to be on the a.**, estar alerta. III vtr **to a. sb to sth**, avisar a algn de algo.

A-level ['eɪlevəl] n GB Educ abbr of **Advanced level**, ≈ Curso m de Orientación Universitaria, COU m.

algae ['ældʒiː] npl algas fpl.

algebra ['ældʒɪbrə] n álgebra f.

Algeria [æl'dʒɪərɪə] n Argelia.

Algerian [æl'dʒɪərɪən] adj & n argelino,-a (m,f).

Algiers [æl'dʒɪəz] n Argel.

alias ['eɪlɪəs] I n alias m. II adv alias.

alibi ['ælɪbaɪ] n coartada f.

alien ['eɪlɪən] I adj (foreign) extranjero,-a; (from space) extraterrestre; **a. to**, ajeno a. II n (foreigner) extranjero,-a m,f; (from space) extraterrestre mf.

alienate ['eɪlɪəneɪt] vtr 1 **to a. sb**, ofender a algn; **to a. oneself from sb**, alejarse de algn. 2 Jur enajenar.

alight¹ [ə'laɪt] adj (on fire) ardiendo,-a.

alight² [ə'laɪt] vi (get off) apearse (from, de).

align [ə'laɪn] vtr alinear.

alike [ə'laɪk] I adj (similar) parecidos,-as; (the same) iguales. II adv (in the same way) de la misma manera, igualmente; **dressed a.**, vestidos,-as iguales.

alimony ['ælɪmənɪ] n Jur pensión alimenticia.

alive [ə'laɪv] adj vivo,-a; fig (teeming) lleno,-a (with, de); **to be a.**, estar vivo, -a.

alkaline ['ælkəlaɪn] adj alcalino,-a.

all [ɔːl] I adj todo,-a, todos,-as; **a. year**, (durante) todo el año; **a. kinds of things**, todo tipo de cosas; **at a. hours**, a todas horas; **at a. times**, siempre; **she works a. the time**, siempre está trabajando; **all six of us were there**, los seis estábamos allí. II pron todo,-a, todos,-as; **after a.**, al fin y al cabo; **a. of his work**, toda su obra; **a. of us**, todos,-as nosotros,-as; **a. who saw it**, todos los que lo vieron; **a. you can do is wait**, lo único que puedes hacer es esperar; **I don't like it at a.**, no me gusta en absoluto; **is that a.?**, ¿eso es todo?; **most of or above a.**, sobre todo; **once and for a.**, de una vez por todas; **thanks - not at a.**, gracias - de nada; **in a.**, en conjunto; **that's a.**, ya está; **the score was one a.**, empataron a uno. III adv **a. by myself**, completamente solo,-a; **a. at once**, (suddenly) de repente; (altogether) de una vez; **a. the better**, tanto mejor; **a. the same**, de todos modos; **he knew a. along**, lo sabía desde el principio; **if it's a. the same to you**, si no te importa; **it's a. but impossible**, es

casi imposible; **I'm not a. that tired**, no estoy tan cansado,-a como eso.

IV n **to give one's a.**, darse por completo.

Allah ['ælə] n Alá m.

allay [ə'leɪ] vtr (fears, doubts) apaciguar.

allegation [ælɪ'geɪʃən] n alegato m.

allege [ə'ledʒ] vtr sostener, pretender (that, que).

allegedly [ə'ledʒɪdlɪ] adv supuestamente.

allegiance [ə'liːdʒəns] n lealtad f.

allergic [ə'lɜːdʒɪk] adj alérgico,-a (to, a).

allergy ['ælədʒɪ] n alergia f.

alleviate [ə'liːvɪeɪt] vtr (pain) aliviar.

alley ['ælɪ] n callejón m.

alliance [ə'laɪəns] n alianza f.

allied ['ælaɪd] adj aliado,-a.

alligator ['ælɪgeɪtər] n caimán m.

all-in ['ɔːlɪn] adj (price) todo incluido; Sport **a.-in wrestling**, lucha f libre.

alliteration [əlɪtə'reɪʃən] n aliteración f.

all-night ['ɔːlnaɪt] adj (café etc) abierto,-a toda la noche; (vigil) que dura toda la noche.

allocate ['æləkeɪt] vtr destinar (to, para).

allocation [ælə'keɪʃən] n 1 (distribution) asignación f. 2 (amount allocated) cuota f.

allot [ə'lɒt] vtr asignar.

allotment [ə'lɒtmənt] n 1 (distribution) asignación f. 2 (land) parcela f.

all-out ['ɔːlaʊt] I adj (effort) supremo,-a; (attack) concentrado,-a. II **all out** adv **to go a. o. to do sth**, emplearse a fondo para hacer algo.

allow [ə'laʊ] vtr 1 (permit) permitir; (a request) acceder a. **to a. sb to do sth**, permitir que algn haga algo. 2 (allot) (time) dejar; (money) destinar. ◆**allow for** vtr tener en cuenta.

allowance [ə'laʊəns] n (payment) pensión f, subvención f; (discount) descuento m; **to make allowances for sb/sth**, disculpar a algn/tener algo en cuenta; **tax a.**, desgravación f fiscal; **travel a.**, dietas fpl de viaje.

alloy ['ælɔɪ] n aleación f.

all right [ɔːl'raɪt] I adj (okay) bien; **thank you very much - that's a. r.**, muchas gracias - de nada. II adv 1 (well) bien. 2 (definitely) sin duda. 3 (okay) de acuerdo, vale.

all-round [ɔːl'raʊnd] adj (athlete etc) completo,-a.

all-terrain [ɔːltə'reɪn] adj **a.-t. vehicle**, todoterreno m.

all-time ['ɔːltaɪm] adj **an a.-t. low**, una baja sin antecedente; **the a.-t. greats**, los grandes de siempre.

allude [ə'luːd] vi **to a. to**, aludir a.

alluring [ə'ljʊərɪŋ] adj atractivo,-a.

allusion [ə'luːʒən] n alusión f.

ally ['ælaɪ] I n aliado,-a m,f. II vtr **to a. oneself to/with sb**, aliarse a/con algn.

almighty [ɔːl'maɪtɪ] I adj (all-powerful)

todopoderoso,-a. II *n* **the A.**, El Todopoderoso.

almond ['ɑ:mənd] *n* almendra *f*.

almost ['ɔ:lməust] *adv* casi.

alms [ɑ:mz] *npl* limosna *f sing*.

aloft [ə'lɒft] *adv* arriba.

alone [ə'ləun] I *adj* solo,-a; **can I speak to you a.?**, ¿puedo hablar contigo a solas?; **let a.**, ni mucho menos; **leave it a.!**, ¡no lo toques!; **leave me a.**, déjame en paz; **to be a.**, estar solo,-a. II *adv* solamente, sólo.

along [ə'lɒŋ] I *adv* **come a.!**, ¡anda, ven!; **he'll be a. in 10 minutes**, llegará dentro de 10 minutos; **a. with**, junto con. II *prep* (*the length of*) a lo largo de; **to walk a. the street**, andar por la calle; **it's just a. the street**, está un poco más abajo.

alongside [ə'lɒŋsaɪd] I *adv* *Naut* de costado. II *prep* al lado de.

aloof [ə'lu:f] I *adj* (*person*) distante. II *adv* **to keep oneself a.**, mantenerse a distancia (*from*, de).

aloud [ə'laud] *adv* en voz alta.

alphabet ['ælfəbet] *n* alfabeto *m*.

alphabetical [ælfə'betikəl] *adj* alfabético,-a. ◆**alphabetically** *adv* por orden alfabético.

alpine ['ælpaɪn] *adj* alpino,-a.

Alps [ælps] *npl* **the A.**, los Alpes.

already [ɔ:l'redɪ] *adv* ya.

alright [ɔ:l'raɪt] *adj & adv* → **all right**.

Alsatian [æl'seɪʃən] *n* pastor *m* alemán.

also ['ɔ:lsəu] *adv* también, además.

also-ran ['ɔ:lsəuræn] *n* *fam* (*person*) segundón,-ona *m,f*.

altar ['ɔ:ltə'] *n* altar *m*.

alter ['ɔ:ltə'] I *vtr* (*plan*) cambiar, retocar; (*project*) modificar; (*clothing*) arreglar; (*timetable*) revisar. II *vi* cambiar, cambiarse.

alteration [ɔ:ltə'reɪʃən] *n* (*to plan*) cambio *m*; (*to project*) modificación *f*; (*to clothing*) arreglo *m*; (*to timetable*) revisión *f*; **alterations**, (*to building*) reformas *fpl*.

alternate [ɔ:l'tɜ:nɪt] I *adj* alterno,-a; **on a. days**, cada dos días. II ['ɔ:ltəneɪt] *vtr* alternar. ◆**alternately** *adv* **a. hot and cold**, ahora caliente, ahora frío.

alternative [ɔ:l'tɜ:nətɪv] I *adj* alternativo,-a. II *n* alternativa *f*; **I have no a. but to accept**, no tengo más remedio que aceptar. ◆**alternatively** *adv* o bien; **a. you could walk**, o bien podrías ir andando.

alternator ['ɔ:ltəneɪtə'] *n* *Aut* alternador *m*.

although [ɔ:l'ðəu] *conj* aunque.

altitude ['æltɪtju:d] *n* altitud *f*.

alto ['æltəu] *adj & n* (*male singer, instrument*) alto (*m*); (*female singer*) contralto (*f*).

altogether [ɔ:ltə'geðə'] *adv* (*in total*) en conjunto, en total; (*completely*) completamente, del todo.

altruism ['æltru:ɪzəm] *n* altruismo *m*.

aluminium [ælju'mɪnɪəm], *US* **aluminum** [ə'lu:mɪnəm] *n* aluminio *m*.

always ['ɔ:lweɪz] *adv* siempre.

AM [eɪ'em] *Rad abbr of* **amplitude modulation**, AM.

am [æm] *1st person sing pres* → **be**.

a.m. [eɪ'em] *abbr of* **ante meridiem**, de la mañana.

amalgamate [ə'mælgəmeɪt] I *vtr* (*metals*) amalgamar. II *vi* (*metals*) amalgamarse; (*companies*) fusionarse.

amalgamation [əmælgə'meɪʃən] *n* fusión *f*.

amass [ə'mæs] *vtr* (*money*) amontonar; (*information*) acumular.

amateur ['æmətə'] I *n* amateur *mf*, aficionado,-a *m,f*. II *adj* aficionado,-a; (*work etc*) *pej* chapucero,-a.

amateurish ['æmətərɪʃ] *adj* chapucero,-a.

amaze [ə'meɪz] *vtr* asombrar, pasmar; **to be amazed at sth**, quedarse pasmado,-a de algo.

amazement [ə'meɪzmənt] *n* asombro *m*, sorpresa *f*.

amazing [ə'meɪzɪŋ] *adj* asombroso,-a, increíble.

ambassador [æm'bæsədə'] *n* embajador,-a *m,f*.

amber ['æmbə'] I *n* ámbar *m*. II *adj* ambarino,-a; (*traffic light*) amarillo,-a.

ambiguity [æmbɪ'gju:ɪtɪ] *n* ambigüedad *f*.

ambiguous [æm'bɪgjuəs] *adj* ambiguo,-a.

ambition [æm'bɪʃən] *n* ambición *f*.

ambitious [æm'bɪʃəs] *adj* ambicioso,-a.

ambivalent [æm'bɪvələnt] *adj* ambivalente.

amble ['æmbəl] *vi* deambular.

ambulance ['æmbjuləns] *n* ambulancia *f*; **a. man**, ambulanciero *m*.

ambush ['æmbuʃ] I *n* emboscada *f*. II *vtr* tender una emboscada a; *fig* atacar por sorpresa.

amen [ɑ:'men] *interj* amén.

amenable [ə'mi:nəbəl] *adj* **I'd be quite a. to doing that**, no me importaría nada hacer eso; **a. to reason**, razonable.

amend [ə'mend] *vtr* (*law*) enmendar; (*error*) subsanar.

amendment [ə'mendmənt] *n* enmienda *f*.

amends [ə'mendz] *npl* **to make a. to sb for sth**, compensar a algn por algo.

amenities [ə'mi:nɪtɪz] *npl* comodidades *fpl*.

America [ə'merɪkə] *n* (*continent*) América *f*; (*USA*) (los) Estados *mpl* Unidos; **South A.**, América del Sur, Sudamérica *f*.

American [ə'merɪkən] *adj & n* americano,-a (*m,f*); (*of USA*) norteamericano,-a (*m,f*), estadounidense (*mf*).

amiable ['eɪmɪəbəl] *adj* amable, afable.

amicable ['æmɪkəbəl] *adj* amistoso,-a.

amid(st) [ə'mɪd(st)] *prep* entre, en medio de.

amiss [ə'mɪs] *adj & adv* mal; **there's sth a.**, algo anda mal; **to take sth a.**, tomar algo a mal.

ammonia [ə'məʊnɪə] *n* amoníaco *m*.

ammunition [æmjʊ'nɪʃən] *n* municiones *fpl*.

amnesia [æm'niːʒə] *n* amnesia *f*.

amnesty ['æmnɪstɪ] *n* amnistía *f*.

amok [ə'mɒk] *adv fig* **to run a.**, *(child)* desmadrarse; *(inflation etc)* dispararse.

among(st) [ə'mʌŋ(st)] *prep* entre.

amoral [eɪ'mɒrəl] *adj* amoral.

amorous ['æmərəs] *adj* cariñoso,-a.

amorphous [ə'mɔːfəs] *adj* amorfo,-a.

amount [ə'maʊnt] *n* cantidad *f*; *(of money)* suma *f*; *(of bill)* importe *m*. ◆**amount to** *vtr* ascender a; *fig* equivaler a.

amp [æmp], **ampère** ['æmpeə^r] *n* amperio *m*.

amphetamine [æm'fetəmiːn] *n* anfetamina *f*.

amphibian [æm'fɪbɪən] *adj & n* anfibio,-a *(m)*.

amphibious [æm'fɪbɪəs] *adj* anfibio,-a.

amphitheatre ['æmfɪθɪətə^r] *n* anfiteatro *m*.

ample ['æmpəl] *adj (enough)* bastante; *(more than enough)* abundante; *(large)* amplio,-a.

amplifier ['æmplɪfaɪə^r] *n* amplificador *m*.

amputate ['æmpjʊteɪt] *vtr* amputar.

amuck [ə'mʌk] *adv →* amok.

amuse [ə'mjuːz] *vtr* divertir, entretener.

amusement [ə'mjuːzmənt] *n (enjoyment)* diversión *f*; *(laughter)* risa *f*; *(pastime)* pasatiempo *m*; **a. arcade**, salón *m* de juegos; **a. park**, parque *m* de atracciones.

amusing [ə'mjuːzɪŋ] *adj* divertido,-a.

an [æn, *unstressed* ən] *indef art → a*.

anabolic steroid [ænəbɒlɪk'stiːrɔɪd] *n* esteroide *m* anabolizante.

anaemia [ə'niːmɪə] *n* anemia *f*.

anaemic [ə'niːmɪk] *adj* anémico,-a; *fig (weak)* débil.

anaesthetic [ænɪs'θetɪk] *n* anestesia *f*.

anaesthetist [ə'niːsθətɪst] *n* anestesista *mf*.

analog(ue) ['ænəlɒg] *n* análogo *m*; **a. computer**, ordenador analógico; **a. watch**, reloj *m* de agujas.

analogy [ə'nælədʒɪ] *n* analogía *f*.

analyse ['ænəlaɪz] *vtr* analizar.

analysis [ə'nælɪsɪs] *n (pl analyses* [ə'nælɪsiːz]) análisis *m inv*.

analyst ['ænəlɪst] *n* analista *mf*; *(psychoanalyst)* psicoanalista *mf*.

analyze ['ænəlaɪz] *vtr US →* analyse.

analytic(al) [ænə'lɪtɪk(əl)] *adj* analítico,-a.

anarchist ['ænəkɪst] *n* anarquista *mf*.

anarchy ['ænəkɪ] *n* anarquía *f*.

anathema [ə'næθəmə] *n* the very idea was a. to him, le repugnaba sólo de pensarlo.

anatomy [ə'nætəmɪ] *n* anatomía *f*.

ancestor ['ænsestə^r] *n* antepasado *m*.

anchor ['æŋkə^r] **I** *n Naut* ancla *f*; *fig* áncora *f*; **to drop a.**, echar el ancla; **to weigh a.**, zarpar. **II** *vtr Naut* anclar; *fig (fix securely)* sujetar. **III** *vi* anclar.

anchovy ['æntʃəvɪ] *n* anchoa *f*.

ancient ['eɪnʃənt] *adj* antiguo,-a.

ancillary [æn'sɪlərɪ] *adj & n* auxiliar *(mf)*.

and [ænd, *unstressed* ənd, ən] *conj* y; *(before i-, hi-)* e; **a hundred a. one**, ciento uno; **a. so on** etcétera; **Bill a. Pat**, Bill y Pat; **Chinese a. Indian**, chino e indio; **come a. see us**, ven a vernos; **four a. a half**, cuatro y medio; **she cried a. cried**, no paró de llorar; **try a. help me**, trata de ayudarme; **wait a. see**, espera a ver; **worse a. worse**, cada vez peor.

Andalusia [ændə'luːzɪə] *n* Andalucía.

Andalusian [ændə'luːzɪən] *adj* andaluz,-a.

Andes ['ændiːz] *npl* **the A.**, los Andes.

Andorra [æn'dɔːrə] *n* Andorra.

anecdote ['ænɪkdəʊt] *n* anécdota *f*.

anemia [ə'niːmɪə] *n US →* anaemia.

anesthetic [ænɪs'θetɪk] *n US →* anaesthetic.

angel ['eɪndʒəl] *n* ángel *m*.

anger ['æŋgə^r] **I** *n* cólera *f*. **II** *vtr* enojar.

angina [æn'dʒaɪnə] *n* angina *f* (de pecho).

angle ['æŋgəl] *n* ángulo *m*; *fig* punto *m* de vista.

angler ['æŋglə^r] *n* pescador,-a *m,f* de caña.

Anglican ['æŋglɪkən] *adj & n* anglicano,-a *(m,f)*.

Anglo-Saxon [æŋgləʊ'sæksən] *adj & n* anglosajón,-ona *(m,f)*.

Angola [æŋ'gəʊlə] *n* Angola.

angry ['æŋgrɪ] *adj (angrier, angriest) (person etc)* enfadado,-a; *(voice)* airado,-a; **to get a. with sb about sth**, enfadarse con algn por algo. ◆**angrily** *adv* furiosamente.

anguish ['æŋgwɪʃ] *n* angustia *f*.

angular ['æŋgjʊlə^r] *adj (shape)* angular; *(face)* anguloso,-a.

animal ['ænɪməl] **I** *adj* animal. **II** *n* animal *m*; *fig* bestia *f*.

animate ['ænɪmɪt] **I** *adj* vivo,-a. **II** ['ænɪmeɪt] *vtr* animar; *fig* estimular.

animated ['ænɪmeɪtɪd] *adj (lively)* animado,-a.

animosity [ænɪ'mɒsɪtɪ] *n* animosidad *f*.

aniseed ['ænɪsiːd] *n* anís *m*.

ankle ['æŋkəl] *n* tobillo *m*; **a. boots**, botines *mpl*; **a. socks**, calcetines cortos.

annex [æ'neks] *vtr (territory)* anexionar.

annexe, *US* **annex** ['æneks] *n (building)* *(edificio m)* anexo *m*.

annihilate [ə'naɪəleɪt] *vtr* aniquilar.

anniversary [ænɪ'vɜːsərɪ] n aniversario m; **wedding a.**, aniversario de bodas.

announce [ə'naʊns] vtr anunciar; (news) comunicar; (fact) hacer saber.

announcement [ə'naʊnsmənt] n anuncio m; (news) comunicación f; (statement) declaración f.

announcer [ə'naʊnsər] n TV Rad locutor,-a m,f.

annoy [ə'nɔɪ] vtr molestar, fastidiar; **to get annoyed**, enfadarse, molestarse.

annoyance [ə'nɔɪəns] n (feeling) enojo m; (thing) molestia f, fastidio m.

annoying [ə'nɔɪɪŋ] adj molesto,-a, fastidioso,-a.

annual ['ænjʊəl] I adj anual. II n (book) anuario m; (plant) anual m. ◆**annually** adv anualmente.

annul [ə'nʌl] vtr anular.

annulment [ə'nʌlmənt] n anulación f.

anomaly [ə'nɒmǝlɪ] n anomalía f.

anonymity [ænə'nɪmɪtɪ] n anonimato m.

anonymous [ə'nɒnɪməs] adj anónimo,-a.

anorak ['ænəræk] n anorak m.

anorexia [ænə'reksɪə] n anorexia f.

another [ə'nʌðər] I adj otro,-a; **a. one**, otro,-a; **without a. word**, sin más. II pron otro,-a; **have a.**, toma otro,-a; **to love one a.**, quererse el uno al otro.

ansaphone ['ɑːnsəfəʊn] n mensáfono m.

answer ['ɑːnsər] I n (to letter etc) contestación f; (to question) respuesta f; (to problem) solución f; **in a. to your letter**, contestando a su carta; **there's no a.**, (on telephone) no contestan; (at door) no abren. II vtr contestar a; (problem) resolver; (door) abrir; (phone) contestar. III vi contestar, responder. ◆**answer back** vi replicar; **don't a. back!**, ¡no seas respondón! ◆**answer for** vtr responder de; **he's got a lot to a. for**, es responsable de muchas cosas. ◆**answer to** vtr (name) responder a; (description) corresponder a.

answerable ['ɑːnsərəbəl] adj **to be a. to sb for sth**, ser responsable ante algn de algo.

answering machine ['ɑːnsərɪŋməʃiːn] n contestador automático.

ant [ænt] n hormiga f; **a. hill**, hormiguero m.

antagonism [æn'tægənɪzəm] n antagonismo m (**between**, entre), hostilidad f (**towards**, hacia).

antagonize [æn'tægənaɪz] vtr enemistar, malquistar.

Antartic [ænt'ɑːktɪk] I adj antártico,-a; **A. Ocean**, océano Antártico. II n the A., La Antártica.

Antarctica [ænt'ɑːktɪkə] n Antártida.

antecedent [æntɪ'siːdənt] n antecedente m.

antelope ['æntɪləʊp] n antílope m.

antenatal [æntɪ'neɪtəl] adj antenatal; (clinic) prenatal.

antenna [æn'tenə] n 1 (pl antennae [æn'teniː]) (of animal, insect) antena f. 2 (pl antennas) TV Rad antena f.

anthem ['ænθəm] n motete m; **national a.**, himno m nacional.

anthology [æn'θɒlədʒɪ] n antología f.

anthracite ['ænθrəsaɪt] n antracita f.

anthropology [ænθrə'pɒlədʒɪ] n antropología f.

anti-aircraft [æntɪ'eəkrɑːft] adj antiaéreo,-a.

antibiotic [æntɪbaɪ'ɒtɪk] n antibiótico m.

antibody ['æntɪbɒdɪ] n anticuerpo m.

anticipate [æn'tɪsɪpeɪt] vtr 1 (expect) esperar. 2 (predict) prever; (get ahead of) anticiparse a, adelantarse a.

anticipation [æntɪsɪ'peɪʃən] n (expectation) esperanza f; (expectancy) ilusión f.

anticlimax [æntɪ'klaɪmæks] n (disappointment) decepción f.

anticlockwise [æntɪ'klɒkwaɪz] adv en sentido contrario a las agujas del reloj.

antics ['æntɪks] npl payasadas fpl; (naughtiness) travesuras fpl.

anticyclone [æntɪ'saɪkləʊn] n anticiclón m.

antidote ['æntɪdəʊt] n antídoto m.

antifreeze ['æntɪfriːz] n anticongelante m.

antihistamine [æntɪ'hɪstəmɪn] n antihistamínico m.

antinuclear [æntɪ'njuːklɪər] adj antinuclear.

antipathy [æn'tɪpəθɪ] n antipatía f (**to**, a).

antiquated ['æntɪkweɪtɪd] adj anticuado,-a.

antique [æn'tiːk] I adj antiguo,-a. II n antigüedad f; **a. dealer**, anticuario,-a m,f; **a. shop**, tienda f de antigüedades.

antiquity [æn'tɪkwɪtɪ] n antigüedad f.

anti-Semitism [æntɪ'semɪtɪzəm] n antisemitismo m.

antiseptic [æntɪ'septɪk] adj & n antiséptico,-a (m).

antisocial [æntɪ'səʊʃəl] adj (delinquent) antisocial; (unsociable) insociable.

antithesis [æn'tɪθɪsɪs] n antítesis f.

antler ['æntlər] n cuerna f; **antlers**, cornamenta f.

Antwerp ['æntwɜːp] n Amberes.

anus ['eɪnəs] n ano m.

anvil ['ænvɪl] n yunque m.

anxiety [æŋ'zaɪɪtɪ] n (concern) inquietud f; (worry) preocupación f; (fear) angustia f; (eagerness) ansia f.

anxious ['æŋkʃəs] adj (concerned) inquieto,-a; (worried) preocupado,-a; (fearful) angustiado,-a; (eager) ansioso,-a; **to be a. about sth**, estar preocupado,-a por algo.

any ['enɪ] I adj (in questions, conditionals) algún,-una; (in negative clauses) ningún, -una; (no matter which) cualquier,-a; (every) todo,-a; **a. doctor will say the**

same, cualquier médico te dirá lo mismo; **are there a. seats left?,** ¿quedan plazas?; **at a. moment,** en cualquier momento; **have you a. apples?,** ¿tienes manzanas?; **have you a. money?,** ¿tienes (algo de) dinero?; **I don't have a. time,** no tengo tiempo; **in a. case,** de todas formas.
II *pron (in questions)* alguno,-a; *(in negative clauses)* ninguno,-a; *(no matter which)* cualquiera; **do they have a.?,** ¿tienen alguno?; **I don't want a.,** no quiero ninguno,-a; **I need some paper, have you a.?,** ¿necesito papel, ¿tienes?; **you can have a. (one),** coge el *or* la que quieras.
III *adv* **is there a. more?,** ¿hay más?; **I used to like it but not a. more/longer,** antes me gustaba pero ya no; **is he a. better?,** ¿está mejor?

anybody ['enibɒdi] *pron (in questions, conditionals)* alguien, alguno,-a; *(in negative clauses)* nadie, ninguno,-a; *(no matter who)* cualquiera; **a. but me,** cualquiera menos yo; **bring a. you like,** trae a quien quieras; **do you see a. over there?,** ¿ves a alguien allí?; **I can't find a.,** no encuentro a nadie.

anyhow ['enihau] *adv* 1 *(in spite of that)* en todo caso, de todas formas; *(changing the subject)* bueno, pues. 2 *(carelessly)* desordenadamente, de cualquier modo *or* forma.

anyone ['eniwʌn] *pron* → **anybody.**

anything ['eniθiŋ] **I** *pron (in questions, conditionals)* algo, alguna cosa; *(in negative clauses)* nada; *(no matter what)* cualquier cosa; **a. but that,** cualquier cosa menos eso; **a. else?,** ¿algo más?; **can I do a. for you?,** ¿puedo ayudarte en algo?; **hardly a.,** casi nada; **if a., I'd buy the big one,** de comprar uno compraría el grande; **to run/work like a.,** correr/trabajar a más no poder. **II** *adv* **is this a. like what you wanted?,** ¿viene a ser éste lo que querías?

anyway ['eniwei] *adv* → **anyhow.**

anywhere ['eniweər] *adv* 1 *(in questions, conditionals)* *(situation)* en alguna parte; *(movement)* a alguna parte; **could it be a. else?,** ¿podría estar en otro sitio? 2 *(in negative clauses)* *(situation)* en ninguna parte; *(movement)* a ninguna parte; *(no matter where)* dondequiera, en cualquier parte; **go a. you like,** ve a donde quieras; **we aren't a. near finished,** no hemos terminado ni mucho menos.

apart [ə'pɑːt] *adv* 1 aparte; **to fall a.,** deshacerse; **to take sth a.,** desmontar algo. 2 *(distant)* alejado,-a; *(separate)* separado,-a; **to be poles a.,** ser polos opuestos; **you can't tell the twins a.,** no se puede distinguir los mellizos el uno del otro. 3 **a. from,** aparte de.

apartheid [ə'pɑːtheit] *n* apartheid *m.*

apartment [ə'pɑːtmənt] *n (large room)* salón *m; US (flat)* piso *m,* apartamento *m;* **a. block,** bloque *m* de pisos.

apathetic [æpə'θetik] *adj* apático,-a.

apathy ['æpəθi] *n* apatía *f.*

ape [eip] **I** *n* mono *m.* **II** *vtr* imitar, copiar.

apéritif [ə'peritiːf] *n* aperitivo *m.*

aperture ['æpətʃər] *n (hole, crack)* resquicio *m,* rendija *f; Phot* abertura *f.*

apex ['eipeks] *n (of triangle)* vértice *m; fig* cumbre *f.*

aphrodisiac [æfrə'diziæk] *n* afrodisíaco *m.*

apiece [ə'piːs] *adv* cada uno,-a.

aplomb [ə'plɒm] *n* aplomo *m.*

apocalypse [ə'pɒkəlips] *n* apocalipsis *m inv.*

apolitical [eipə'litikəl] *adj* apolítico,-a.

apologetic [əpɒlə'dʒetik] *adj (remorseful)* de disculpa; **he was very a.,** pidió mil perdones. ◆**apologetically** *adv* disculpándose, pidiendo perdón.

apologize [ə'pɒlədʒaiz] *vi (say sorry)* disculparse; **they apologized to us for the delay,** se disculparon con nosotros por el retraso.

apology [ə'pɒlədʒi] *n* disculpa *f,* excusa *f; fam* **what an a. for a meal!,** ¡vaya birria de comida!

apoplectic [æpə'plektik] *adj Med* apopléctico,-a; *fam* **to be a. with rage,** estar furioso,-a.

apostle [ə'pɒsəl] *n* apóstol *m.*

apostrophe [ə'pɒstrəfi] *n* apóstrofo *m.*

appal, *US* **appall** [ə'pɔːl] *vtr* horrorizar; **to be appalled by sth,** quedar horrorizado,-a por algo.

appalling [ə'pɔːliŋ] *adj (horrifying)* horroroso,-a; *fam (very bad)* pésimo,-a, fatal.

apparatus [æpə'reitəs] *n* aparato *m; (equipment)* equipo *m.*

apparent [ə'pærənt] *adj (obvious)* evidente; *(seeming)* aparente; **to become a.,** ponerse de manifiesto. ◆**apparently** *adv (seemingly)* por lo visto.

apparition [æpə'riʃən] *n* aparición *f.*

appeal [ə'piːl] **I** *n* 1 *(request)* solicitud *f; (plea)* súplica *f.* 2 *(attraction)* atractivo *m; (interest)* interés *m.* 3 *Jur* apelación *f.* **II** *vi* 1 *(plead)* rogar, suplicar (**to,** a); **to a. for help,** solicitar ayuda. 2 *(attract)* atraer; *(interest)* interesar; **it doesn't a. to me,** no me dice nada. 3 *Jur* apelar.

appealing [ə'piːliŋ] *adj (moving)* conmovedor,-a; *(attractive)* atractivo,-a; *(tempting)* atrayente.

appear [ə'piər] *vi* 1 *(become visible)* aparecer; *(publicly)* presentarse; *(on stage)* actuar; **to a. before a court,** comparecer ante un tribunal; **to a. on television,** salir en la televisión. 2 *(seem)* parecer; **he**

appears relaxed, parece relajado; **so it appears,** según parece.

appearance |ə'pɪərəns| n 1 (becoming visible) aparición f; (publicly) presentación f; (on stage) actuación f; (before court) comparecencia f; (of book etc) publicación f; **to put in an a.,** hacer acto de presencia. 2 (look) apariencia f, aspecto m; **to all appearances,** al parecer.

appease |ə'pi:z| vtr apaciguar; (curiosity) satisfacer.

appeasement |ə'pi:zmənt| n Pol entreguismo m.

appendicitis |əpendi'saitis| n apendicitis f.

appendix |ə'pendiks| n (pl appendices |ə'pendisi:z|) apéndice m.

appetite |'æpɪtaɪt| n apetito m; fig deseo m.

appetizer |'æpɪtaɪzər| n (drink) aperitivo m; (snack) tapa f, pincho m.

applaud |ə'plɔːd| vtr & vi aplaudir.

applause |ə'plɔːz| n aplausos mpl.

apple |'æpəl| n manzana f; **a. tree,** manzano m.

appliance |ə'plaɪəns| n dispositivo m.

applicable |ə'plɪkəbəl| adj aplicable.

applicant |'æplɪkənt| n (for post) candidato,-a m,f; (to court, for tickets) solicitante mf.

application |æplɪ'keɪʃən| n 1 (of cream) aplicación f. 2 (for post etc) solicitud f; **a. form,** solicitud f; **job a.,** solicitud de empleo. 3 (effort) aplicación f; **she lacks a.,** no se aplica.

applied |ə'plaɪd| adj aplicado,-a.

apply |ə'plaɪ| I vtr aplicar; (brake) echar; (law) recurrir a; (force) usar; **to a. oneself to,** dedicarse a. II vi 1 (refer) aplicarse (to, a). 2 (for job) presentar una solicitud; (for information, to court) presentar una petición. ◆**apply for** vtr (post, information) solicitar; (tickets) pedir.

appoint |ə'pɔɪnt| vtr (person) nombrar; (time, place etc) fijar, señalar.

appointment |ə'pɔɪntmənt| n 1 (to post) nombramiento m; (post) cargo m. 2 (meeting) cita f; **to make an a. with,** citarse con; (at doctor's) pedir hora a.

apportion |ə'pɔːʃən| vtr fig (blame) echar.

appraisal |ə'preɪzəl| n evaluación f.

appreciable |ə'priːʃəbəl| adj (difference) apreciable; (sum) importante.

appreciate |ə'priːʃɪeɪt| I vtr 1 (be thankful for) agradecer. 2 (understand) entender. 3 (value) apreciar, valorar. II vi (increase in value) apreciarse.

appreciation |əpriːʃɪ'eɪʃən| n 1 (of help, advice) agradecimiento m; (of difficulty) comprensión f; (of wine etc) aprecio m; (appraisal) evaluación f. 2 (increase in value) apreciación f.

appreciative |ə'priːʃɪətɪv| adj (thankful) agradecido,-a; (responsive) apreciativo,-a.

apprehend |æprɪ'hend| vtr (arrest) detener.

apprehension |æprɪ'henʃən| n 1 (arrest) detención f. 2 (fear) aprensión f.

apprehensive |æprɪ'hensɪv| adj (fearful) aprensivo,-a.

apprentice |ə'prentɪs| n aprendiz,-a m,f.

apprenticeship |ə'prentɪsʃɪp| n aprendizaje m.

approach |ə'prəʊtʃ| I n 1 (coming near) acercamiento m; (to town) acceso m; **a. road,** vía f de acceso. 2 (to problem) enfoque m. II vtr (come near to) acercarse a; (be similar to) aproximarse a; fig (problem) abordar; (person) dirigirse a; **to a. sb about sth,** dirigirse a algn a propósito de algo. III vi acercarse.

approachable |ə'prəʊtʃəbəl| adj (person) accesible.

appropriate¹ |ə'prəʊprɪɪt| adj (suitable) apropiado,-a, adecuado,-a; (convenient) oportuno,-a.

appropriate² |ə'prəʊprɪeɪt| vtr (allocate) asignar; (steal) apropiarse de.

approval |ə'pruːvəl| n aprobación f, visto m bueno; Com **to get sth on a.,** adquirir algo sin compromiso de compra.

approve |ə'pruːv| vtr aprobar; **approved school,** reformatorio m. ◆**approve of** vtr aprobar.

approving |ə'pruːvɪŋ| adj (look etc) aprobatorio,-a.

approx |ə'prɒks| abbr of **approximately,** aprox.

approximate |ə'prɒksɪmɪt| I adj aproximado,-a. II |ə'prɒksɪmeɪt| vtr aproximar a. ◆**approximately** adv aproximadamente.

apricot |'eɪprɪkɒt| n albaricoque m.

April |'eɪprəl| n abril m; **A. Fools' Day,** día m uno de abril, ≈ día de los Inocentes (28 de diciembre).

apron |'eɪprən| n delantal m; (for workman) mandil m.

apt |æpt| adj 1 (suitable) apropiado,-a; (remark) acertado,-a, oportuno,-a; (name) justo,-a; (description) exacto,-a. 2 **to be a. to do sth,** ser propenso,-a a hacer algo. ◆**aptly** adv acertadamente.

aptitude |'æptɪtjuːd| n capacidad f; **a. test,** prueba f de aptitud.

aqualung |'ækwəlʌŋ| n botella f de oxígeno.

aquamarine |ækwəmə'riːn| I n Min aguamarina f. II adj de color de aguamarina.

aquarium |ə'kweərɪəm| n acuario m.

Aquarius |ə'kweərɪəs| n Acuario m.

aquatic |ə'kwætɪk| adj acuático,-a.

aqueduct |'ækwɪdʌkt| n acueducto m.

Arab |'ærəb| adj & n árabe (mf).

Arabian |ə'reɪbɪən| adj árabe.

Arabic |'ærəbɪk| I adj árabe, arábigo,-a; **A. numerals,** numeración f arábiga. II n (language) árabe m.

arable ['ærəbəl] *adj* cultivable.
Aragon ['ærəgən] *n* Aragón.
arbitrary ['ɑ:bɪtrərɪ] *adj* arbitrario,-a.
arbitrate ['ɑ:bɪtreɪt] *vtr & vi* arbitrar.
arbitration [ɑ:bɪ'treɪʃən] *n* arbitraje *m*.
arc [ɑ:k] *n* arco *m*; **a. lamp**, arco voltaico.
arcade [ɑ:'keɪd] *n* arcada *f*; (passageway) pasaje *m*; **shopping a.**, galerías *fpl* (comerciales).
arch [ɑ:tʃ] **I** *n* **1** *Archit* arco *m*; (vault) bóveda *f*. **2** *Anat* empeine *m*. **II** *vtr* (back) arquear.
archaeologist [ɑ:kɪ'ɒlədʒɪst] *n* arqueólogo,-a *m,f*.
archaeology [ɑ:kɪ'ɒlədʒɪ] *n* arqueología *f*.
archaic [ɑ:'keɪɪk] *adj* arcaico,-a.
archbishop [ɑ:tʃ'bɪʃəp] *n* arzobispo *m*.
arched [æ:tʃt] *adj* arqueado,-a.
archeology [ɑ:kɪ'ɒlədʒɪ] *n US* → **archaeology**.
archer ['ɑ:tʃər] *n* arquero,-a *m,f*.
archery ['ɑ:tʃərɪ] *n* tiro *m* con arco.
archetypal ['ɑ:kɪtaɪpəl] *adj* arquetípico, -a.
archipelago [ɑ:kɪ'pelɪgəʊ] *n* archipiélago *m*.
architect ['ɑ:kɪtekt] *n* arquitecto,-a *m,f*.
architectural [ɑ:kɪ'tektʃərəl] *adj* arquitectónico,-a.
architecture ['ɑ:kɪtektʃər] *n* arquitectura *f*.
archives ['ɑ:kaɪvz] *npl* archivos *mpl*.
archway ['ɑ:tʃweɪ] *n* (arch) arco *m*; (vault) bóveda *f*; (in church) atrio *m*; (passage) pasaje *m*.
arctic ['ɑ:ktɪk] **I** *adj* ártico,-a; **A. Circle**, círculo *m* polar Ártico. **II** *n* the A., el Ártico.
ardent ['ɑ:dənt] *adj* (supporter etc) apasionado,-a; (desire) ardiente.
ardour, *US* **ardor** ['ɑ:dər] *n* pasión *f*, ardor *m*.
arduous ['ɑ:djʊəs] *adj* arduo,-a, penoso, -a.
are [ɑ:r] *2nd person sing pres, 1st, 2nd, 3rd person pl pres* → **be**.
area ['eərɪə] *n* (surface) área *f*, superficie *f*; (space) extensión *f*; (region) región *f*; (of town) zona *f*; fig (field) campo *m*; *US Tel* **a. code**, prefijo *m* local.
arena [ə'ri:nə] *n* (stadium) estadio *m*; (bullring) plaza *f*; (circus) pista *f*; fig (stage) campo *m* de batalla.
Argentina [ɑ:dʒən'ti:nə] *n* Argentina.
Argentinian [ɑ:dʒən'tɪnɪən] *adj & n* argentino,-a (m,f).
arguable [ɑ:gjʊəbəl] *adj* discutible.
◆**arguably** *adv* it's a. the best, hay quienes dicen que es el mejor.
argue ['ɑ:gju:] **I** *vtr* (reason) discutir; (point of view) mantener. **II** *vi* (quarrel) discutir; (reason) argumentar, razonar; **to a. for**, abogar por; **to a. against sth**, po-

nerse en contra de algo.
argument ['ɑ:gjʊmənt] *n* (reason) argumento *m* (for, a favor de; against, en contra de); (quarrel) discusión *f*, disputa *f*; **for the sake of a.**, por decir algo.
argumentative [ɑ:gjʊ'mentətɪv] *adj* she's very a., le gusta discutir por todo.
aria ['ɑ:rɪə] *n* aria *f*.
arid ['ærɪd] *adj* árido,-a.
Aries ['eərɪz] *n* Aries *m*.
arise [ə'raɪz] *vi* (pt arose; pp arisen [ə'rɪzən]) (get up) levantarse; (happen) surgir; **should the occasion a.**, si se presenta la ocasión.
aristocracy [ærɪ'stɒkrəsɪ] *n* aristocracia *f*.
aristocrat ['ærɪstəkræt] *n* aristócrata *mf*.
arithmetic [ə'rɪθmətɪk] *n* aritmética *f*.
ark [ɑ:k] *n* arca *f*; Noah's A., el arca de Noé.
arm [ɑ:m] **I** *n* **1** brazo *m*; (of garment) manga *f*; **to walk a. in a.**, ir cogidos,-as del brazo. **2** *Mil* arms, armas *fpl*; arms race, carrera armamentística; coat of arms, escudo *m*. **II** *vtr* armar; **to a. oneself against sth**, armarse contra algo.
armaments ['ɑ:məmənts] *npl* armamentos *mpl*.
armchair ['ɑ:mtʃeər] *n* sillón *m*.
armed ['ɑ:md] *adj* armado,-a; **a. forces**, fuerzas armadas; **a. robbery**, robo *m* a mano armada.
armistice ['ɑ:mɪstɪs] *n* armisticio *m*.
armour, *US* **armor** ['ɑ:mər] *n* (on vehicle) blindaje *m*; (suit of) a., armadura *f*.
armoured car, *US* **armored car** [ɑ:məd'kɑ:r] *n* coche *m* blindado.
armour-plated ['ɑ:məpleɪtɪd] *adj* acorazado,-a.
armoury, *US* **armory** ['ɑ:mərɪ] *n* arsenal *m*.
armpit ['ɑ:mpɪt] *n* axila *f*, sobaco *m*.
army ['ɑ:mɪ] *n* ejército *m*.
aroma [ə'rəʊmə] *n* aroma *m*.
arose [ə'rəʊz] *pt* → **arise**.
around [ə'raʊnd] **I** *adv* alrededor; **all a.**, por todos los lados; **are the children a.?**, ¿están los niños por aquí?; **he looked a.**, miró (a su) alrededor. **II** *prep* **1** alrededor de; **a. the corner**, a la vuelta de la esquina; **a. here**, por aquí. **2** (approximately) aproximadamente.
arouse [ə'raʊz] *vtr* despertar; (sexually) excitar.
arrange [ə'reɪndʒ] **I** *vtr* **1** (order) ordenar; (hair, flowers) arreglar; *Mus* adaptar. **2** (plan) organizar; (agree on) quedar en; **to a. a time**, fijar una hora; **arranged marriage**, boda arreglada. **II** *vi* I shall a. for him to be there, lo arreglaré para que pueda asistir.
arrangement [ə'reɪndʒmənt] *n* **1** (display) colocación *f*; *Mus* adaptación *f*. **2** (agreement) acuerdo *m*. **3** arrangements, (plans) planes *mpl*; (preparations) preparativos

mpl.

array |ə'reɪ| *n* colección *f*; **a great a. of goods,** un gran surtido de productos.

arrears |ə'rɪəz| *npl* atrasos *mpl*; **to be in a. with the rent,** estar atrasado,-a con el alquiler; **to be paid in a.,** cobrar con retraso.

arrest |ə'rest| **I** *n* detención *f*; **to be under a.,** estar detenido,-a. **II** *vtr* (*criminal*) detener; *fig* (*progress*) frenar.

arresting |ə'restɪŋ| *adj* llamativo,-a.

arrival |ə'raɪvəl| *n* llegada *f*; **a new a.,** un,-a recién llegado,-a.

arrive |ə'raɪv| *vi* llegar (**at, in, a**).

arrogance |'ærəɡəns| *n* arrogancia *f*.

arrogant |'ærəɡənt| *adj* arrogante.

arrow |'ærəʊ| *n* flecha *f*.

arse |'ɑːs| *n vulg* culo *m*.

arsenal |'ɑːsənəl| *n* arsenal *m*.

arsenic |'ɑːsənɪk| *n* arsénico *m*.

arson |'ɑːsən| *n* incendio *m* provocado.

art |ɑːt| *n* **1** arte *m*; (*drawing*) dibujo *m*; **the arts,** las bellas artes; **arts and crafts,** artes *fpl* y oficios *mpl*; **a. gallery,** galería *f* de arte. **2 arts,** (*branch of knowledge*) letras *fpl*.

artefact |'ɑːtɪfækt| *n* artefacto *m*; (*in archaelogy*) objeto *m* de arte.

artery |'ɑːtərɪ| *n* arteria *f*.

artful |'ɑːtfʊl| *adj* (*cunning*) ladino,-a.

arthritis |ɑː'θraɪtɪs| *n* artritis *f*.

artichoke |'ɑːtɪtʃəʊk| *n* alcachofa *f*.

article |'ɑːtɪkəl| *n* **1** artículo *m*; *Press* artículo; **a. of clothing,** prenda *f* de vestir. *Jur* **articles,** contrato *n sing* de aprendizaje.

articulate¹ |ɑː'tɪkjʊlɪt| *adj* (*speech*) claro,-a; (*person*) que se expresa bien.

articulate² |ɑː'tɪkjʊleɪt| *vtr & vi* articular; (*words*) pronunciar; **articulated lorry,** camión articulado.

artificial |ɑːtɪ'fɪʃəl| *adj* artificial; (*limb*) postizo,-a; **a. intelligence,** inteligencia *f* artificial.

artillery |ɑː'tɪlərɪ| *n* artillería *f*.

artisan |'ɑːtɪzæn| *n* artesano,-a *m,f*.

artist |'ɑːtɪst| *n* artista *mf*; (*painter*) pintor,-a *m,f*.

artistic |ɑː'tɪstɪk| *adj* artístico,-a.

artistry |'ɑːtɪstrɪ| *n* arte *m*, talento artístico.

as |æz. *unstressed* əz| **I** *adv & conj* **1** (*comparison*) **as ... as ...,** tan ... como ...; **as far as,** hasta; *fig* **as far as I'm concerned,** por lo que a mí respecta; **as many as,** tantos,-as como; **as much as,** tanto,-a como; **as tall as me,** tan alto,-a como yo; **as opposed to,** a diferencia de; **as little as £5,** tan sólo cinco libras ; **as soon as they arrive,** en cuanto lleguen; **I'll stay as long as I can,** quedaré todo el tiempo que pueda; **just as big,** igual de grande; **three times as fast,** tres veces más rápido; **the same as,** igual que. **2**

(*manner*) como; **as a rule,** por regla general; **as you know,** como ya sabéis; **as you like,** como quieras; **do as I say,** haz lo que yo te digo; **he's working as a doctor,** está trabajando de médico; **I thought as much,** ya me lo suponía; **it serves as a table,** sirve de mesa; **leave it as it is,** déjalo tal como está; **he was dressed as a pirate,** iba vestido de pirata. **3** (*while, when*) mientras (que); **as a child,** de niño,-a; **as I was eating,** mientras comía; **as we were leaving we saw Pat,** al salir vimos a Pat. **4** (*though*) aunque; **be that as it may,** por mucho que así sea; **young as he is,** aunque es joven. **5** (*because*) como, ya que. **6** (*and so*) igual que; **as do I,** igual que yo; **as well,** también. **7** (*purpose*) para; **so as to do sth,** para hacer algo. **8 as for my brother,** en cuanto a mi hermano. **9 as from, as of,** a partir de. **10 to act as if,** actuar como si + *subj*; **it looks as if the concert is off,** parece ser que no habrá concierto. **11 it's late enough as it is,** ya es muy tarde; **as it were,** por así decirlo. **12 as long as,** (*only if*) siempre que, con tal de que. **13 as regards,** en cuanto a, por lo que se refiere a; **as usual,** como siempre; **as yet,** aún, todavía.

II *rel pron* **such as,** tal(es) como.

asbestos |æz'bestəs| *n* amianto *m*, asbesto *m*.

ascend |ə'send| *vi* subir, ascender.

ascendancy |ə'sendənsɪ| *n* dominio *m*, influencia *f*.

ascendant |ə'sendənt| *n* **to be in the a.,** estar en auge.

ascent |ə'sent| *n* subida *f*.

ascertain |æsə'teɪn| *vtr* averiguar, enterarse de.

ascribe |ə'skraɪb| *vtr* **to a. sth to,** imputar algo a.

aseptic |ə'septɪk| *adj* aséptico,-a.

ash¹ |æʃ| *n Bot* fresno *m*.

ash² |æʃ| *n* ceniza *f*; **a. bin,** *US* **a. can,** cubo *m* de la basura; *Rel* **A. Wednesday,** miércoles *m inv* de ceniza.

ashamed |ə'ʃeɪmd| *adj* avergonzado,-a; **you ought to be a. of yourself!,** ¡debería dar vergüenza!

ashen |'æʃən| *adj* (*face*) pálido,-a.

ashore |ə'ʃɔːr| *adv* (*position*) en tierra; **to go a.,** desembarcar; **to swim a.,** nadar hacia tierra.

ashtray |'æʃtreɪ| *n* cenicero *m*.

Asia |'eɪʒə| *n* Asia; **A. Minor,** Asia Menor.

Asian |'eɪʒən| *adj & n* asiático,-a (*m,f*).

aside |ə'saɪd| **I** *adv* al lado, aparte; **to cast a.,** echar a un lado; **to stand a.,** apartarse. **II** *prep* **a. from,** (*apart from*) aparte de; (*as well as*) además de. **III** *n Theat* aparte *m*.

ask |ɑːsk| **I** *vtr* **1** preguntar; **to a. sb a**

question, hacer una pregunta a algn. 2 (*request*) pedir, solicitar; **she asked me to post it,** me pidió que lo echara al buzón. 3 (*invite*) invitar. **II** *vi* (*inquire*) preguntar; (*request*) pedir. ◆**ask after** *vtr* to a. after sb, preguntar por algn. ◆**ask for** *vtr* (*help*) pedir, solicitar; (*person*) preguntar por. ◆**ask out** *vtr* to a. sb out, invitar a algn a salir.

askance |əˈskæns| *adv* to look a. at sb, mirar a algn con recelo.

askew |əˈskjuː| **I** *adj* ladeado,-a. **II** *adv* de lado.

asleep |əˈsliːp| *adj* (*person*) dormido,-a; (*limb*) adormecido,-a; **to fall a.,** quedarse dormido,-a.

asparagus |əˈspærəgəs| *n inv* espárragos *mpl.*

aspect |ˈæspɛkt| *n* **1** (*of question*) aspecto *m.* **2** (*of building*) orientación *f.*

aspersions |əˈspɜːʃənz| *npl* to cast a. on sb, difamar a algn.

asphalt |ˈæsfælt| *n* asfalto *m.*

asphyxiation |æsfɪksɪˈeɪʃən| *n* asfixia *f.*

aspiration |æspəˈreɪʃən| *n* aspiración *f.*

aspire |əˈspaɪər| *vi* to a. to, aspirar a.

aspirin® |ˈæsprɪn| *n* aspirina® *f.*

ass¹ |æs| *n Zool* asno,-a *m,f,* burro,-a *m,f; fam fig* burro,-a.

ass² |æs| *n US vulg* culo *m.*

assailant |əˈseɪlənt| *n* agresor,-a *m,f,* atacante *mf.*

assassin |əˈsæsɪn| *n* asesino,-a *m,f.*

assassinate |əˈsæsɪneɪt| *vtr* asesinar.

assassination |əsæsɪˈneɪʃən| *n* asesinato *m.*

assault |əˈsɔːlt| **I** *n Mil* ataque *m* (**on,** a); *Jur* agresión *f.* **II** *vtr Mil* asaltar, atacar; *Jur* agredir; (*sexually*) violar.

assemble |əˈsɛmbəl| **I** *vtr* (*people*) reunir, juntar; (*furniture*) montar. **II** *vi* (*people*) reunirse, juntarse.

assembly |əˈsɛmblɪ| *n* reunión *f,* asamblea *f;* *Tech* montaje *m;* *Ind* a. line, cadena *f* de montaje; *Educ* morning a., servicio *m* matinal.

assent |əˈsɛnt| **I** *n* (*agreement*) asentimiento *m;* (*consent*) consentimiento *m;* (*approval*) aprobación *f.* **II** *vi* asentir, consentir (**to,** en).

assert |əˈsɜːt| *vtr* afirmar; **to a. oneself,** imponerse; **to a. one's rights,** hacer valer sus derechos.

assertive |əˈsɜːtɪv| *adj* enérgico,-a.

assess |əˈsɛs| *vtr* (*estimate value*) valorar; (*damages, price*) calcular; (*tax*) gravar; *fig* (*effect*) evaluar.

assessment |əˈsɛsmənt| *n* (*of value*) valoración *f;* (*of damages etc*) cálculo *m;* (*of taxes*) gravamen *m;* *fig* juicio *m.*

assessor |əˈsɛsər| *n* asesor,-a *m,f.*

asset |ˈæsɛt| *n* **1** ventaja *f;* **to be an a.,** (*person*) ser de gran valor. **2** *Fin* assets, bienes *mpl;* **fixed assets,** bienes raíces.

assiduous |əˈsɪdjʊəs| *adj* asiduo,-a.

assign |əˈsaɪn| *vtr* (*task*) asignar; (*property etc*) ceder; **to a. sb to a job,** designar a algn para un trabajo.

assignment |əˈsaɪnmənt| *n* (*allocation*) asignación *f;* (*task*) tarea *f;* (*mission*) misión *f;* (*appointment*) cita *f.*

assimilate |əˈsɪmɪleɪt| *vtr* asimilar.

assist |əˈsɪst| *vtr & vi* ayudar.

assistance |əˈsɪstəns| *n* ayuda *f,* auxilio *m.*

assistant |əˈsɪstənt| *n* ayudante *mf;* **a. manager,** subdirector,-a *m,f;* **shop a.,** dependiente,-a *m,f;* (**language**) a., lector,-a *m,f.*

associate¹ |əˈsəʊʃɪeɪt| **I** *vtr* (*ideas*) relacionar; (*companies*) asociar; **to be associated with sth,** estar relacionado,-a con algo. **II** *vi* a. with, tratar con.

associate² |əˈsəʊʃɪɪt| **I** *adj* asociado,-a. **II** *n* (*colleague*) colega *mf;* (*partner*) socio,-a *m,f;* (*accomplice*) cómplice *mf.*

association |əsəʊsɪˈeɪʃən| *n* asociación *f;* (*company*) sociedad *f.*

assorted |əˈsɔːtɪd| *adj* surtido,-a, variado,-a.

assortment |əˈsɔːtmənt| *n* surtido *m,* variedad *f.*

assume |əˈsjuːm| **I** *vtr* (*power*) asumir; (*attitude, name*) adoptar; **an assumed name,** un nombre falso. **II** *vi* (*suppose*) suponer.

assumption |əˈsʌmpʃən| *n* **1** (*of power*) toma *f;* **a. of office,** toma de posesión. **2** (*supposition*) suposición *f.*

assurance |əˈʃʊərəns| *n* **1** (*guarantee*) garantía *f.* **2** (*confidence*) confianza *f.* **3** (*insurance*) seguro *m.*

assure |əˈʃʊər| *vtr* asegurar.

asterisk |ˈæstərɪsk| *n* asterisco *m.*

astern |əˈstɜːn| *adv* a popa.

asthma |ˈæsmə| *n* asma *f.*

astonish |əˈstɒnɪʃ| *vtr* asombrar, pasmar; **I was astonished,** me quedé pasmado,-a.

astonishing |əˈstɒnɪʃɪŋ| *adj* asombroso, -a, pasmoso,-a.

astonishment |əˈstɒnɪʃmənt| *n* asombro *m;* **to my a.,** para gran sorpresa mía.

astound |əˈstaʊnd| *vtr* asombrar, pasmar.

astray |əˈstreɪ| *adv* **to go a.,** extraviarse; (*fig*) equivocarse; **to lead sb a.,** llevar a algn por mal camino.

astride |əˈstraɪd| *prep* a horcajadas sobre.

astrology |əˈstrɒlədʒɪ| *n* astrología *f.*

astronaut |ˈæstrənɔːt| *n* astronauta *mf.*

astronomer |əˈstrɒnəmər| *n* astrónomo,-a *m,f.*

astronomical |æstrəˈnɒmɪkəl| *adj* astronómico,-a.

astronomy |əˈstrɒnəmɪ| *n* astronomía *f.*

Asturias |æˈstʊərɪæs| *n* Asturias.

astute |əˈstjuːt| *adj* astuto,-a.

asylum |əˈsaɪləm| *n* **1** (*protection*) asilo *m;* **to seek political a.,** pedir asilo político.

2 mental a., manicomio m.
at [æt] *prep* 1 *(position)* a, en; **at school/
work,** en el colegio/trabajo; **at the
window,** a la ventana; **at the top,** en lo
alto. 2 *(direction)* a; **to be angry at sb/
sth,** enfadarse con algn/por algo; **to laugh
at sb,** reírse de algn; **to look at sth/sb,**
mirar algo/a algn; **to shout at sb,** gritarle
a algn. 3 *(time)* a; **at Easter/Christmas,**
en Semana Santa/Navidad; **at six
o'clock,** a las seis; **at first,** al principio;
at last, por fin; **at once,** enseguida; **at
that time,** entonces; **at the moment,** ahora. 4 *(manner)* a, en; **at best/worst,** en el
mejor/peor de los casos; **at hand,** a
mano; **at least,** por lo menos; **not at all,**
en absoluto; *(don't mention it)* de nada. 5
(rate) a; **they retail at 100 pesetas each,**
se venden a 100 pesetas la unidad; **two at
a time,** de dos en dos.
ate [et, eɪt] *pt* → **eat.**
atheist ['eɪθɪɪst] *n* ateo,-a *m,f.*
Athens ['æθɪnz] *n* Atenas.
athlete ['æθliːt] *n* atleta *mf.*
athletic [æθ'letɪk] **I** *adj* atlético,-a; *(sporty)*
deportista. **II** *npl* **athletics** atletismo *m
sing.*
Atlantic [ət'læntɪk] *adj* **the A. (Ocean),** el
(océano) Atlántico.
atlas ['ætləs] *n* atlas *m.*
atmosphere ['ætməsfɪər] *n* atmósfera *f*;
fig (ambience) ambiente m.
atmospheric [ætməs'ferɪk] *adj*
atmosférico,-a.
atom ['ætəm] *n* átomo *m*; **a. bomb,**
bomba atómica.
atomic [ə'tɒmɪk] *adj* atómico,-a.
atone [ə'təʊn] *vi* to a. for, expiar.
atrocious [ə'trəʊʃəs] *adj* atroz.
attach [ə'tætʃ] *vtr (stick)* pegar; *(fasten)*
sujetar; *(document)* adjuntar; **to a.
importance to sth,** dar importancia a
algo; *fig* **to be attached to,** *(be fond of)*
tener cariño a.
attaché [ə'tæʃeɪ] *n* agregado,-a *m,f*; **a.
case,** maletín *m.*
attachment [ə'tætʃmənt] *n* 1 *Tech* accesorio *m*; *(action)* acoplamiento *m.* 2
(fondness) apego *m* (**to,** por).
attack [ə'tæk] **I** *n* 1 *(assault)* ataque *m*,
asalto *m*; **an a. on sb's life,** un atentado
contra la vida de algn. 2 *Med* ataque *m.*
II *vtr (assault)* atacar, asaltar; *fig (problem)*
abordar, *(job)* emprender; *fig (criticize)*
atacar.
attacker [ə'tækər] *n* asaltante *mf*,
agresor,-a *m,f.*
attain [ə'teɪn] *vtr (aim)* lograr; *(rank, age)*
llegar a.
attainment [ə'teɪnmənt] *n (achievement)*
logro *m*; *(skill)* talento *m.*
attempt [ə'tempt] **I** *n* intento *m*, tentativa
f; **at the second a.,** a la segunda; **an a.
on sb's life,** un atentado contra la vida

de algn. **II** *vtr* intentar; **to a. to do sth,**
tratar de *or* intentar hacer algo; *Jur*
attempted murder/rape, intento *m* de
asesinato/violación.
attend [ə'tend] **I** *vtr (be present at)* asistir
a; *(care for, wait on)* atender. **II** *vi (be
present)* asistir; *(pay attention)* prestar
atención. ◆**attend to** *vtr (business)* ocuparse de; *(in shop)* atender a.
attendance [ə'tendəns] *n* asistencia *f.*
attendant [ə'tendənt] *n (in cinema etc)*
acomodador,-a *m,f*; *(in museum)* guía *mf*;
(in car park) vigilante,-a *m,f.*
attention [ə'tenʃən] *n* 1 atención *f*; **for
the a. of Miss Jones,** a la atención de la
Srta. Jones; **pay a.!,** ¡atiende!; **to pay a.
to sb/sth,** prestar atención a algn/algo. 2
Mil **a.!,** ¡firmes!; **to stand to a.,** estar
firmes.
attentive [ə'tentɪv] *adj (listener)* atento,-a;
(helpful) solícito,-a.
attest [ə'test] *vi* to a. to, dar testimonio
a.
attic ['ætɪk] *n* ático *m.*
attire [ə'taɪər] *n fml* traje *m.*
attitude ['ætɪtjuːd] *n* actitud *f*; *(position of
body)* postura *f*; **an a. of mind,** un estado
de ánimo.
attorney [ə'tɜːnɪ] *n* 1 *US (lawyer)*
abogado,-a *m,f*; **A. General,** ≈
Ministro,-a *m,f* de Justicia; **district a.,**
fiscal *mf.* 2 *Jur* **power of a.,** poderes *mpl.*
attract [ə'trækt] *vtr* atraer; **to a. attention,** llamar la atención; **to a. a waiter's
attention,** llamar a un camarero.
attraction [ə'trækʃən] *n* 1 *(power)*
atracción *f.* 2 *(attractive thing)* atractivo
m; *(charm)* encanto *m*; *(incentive)* aliciente
m; **the main a.,** el número fuerte.
attractive [ə'træktɪv] *adj* atractivo,-a;
(good-looking) guapo,-a; *(idea, proposition)*
atrayente.
attribute¹ ['ætrɪbjuːt] *n (quality)* atributo
m.
attribute² [ə'trɪbjuːt] *vtr* atribuir.
attrition [ə'trɪʃən] *n* **war of a.,** guerra *f*
de desgaste.
aubergine ['əʊbəʒiːn] *n* berenjena *f.*
auburn ['ɔːbən] *adj* castaño rojizo *inv.*
auction ['ɔːkʃən] **I** *n* subasta *f.* **II** *vtr* subastar.
auctioneer [ɔːkʃə'nɪər] *n* subastador,-a
m,f.
audacious [ɔː'deɪʃəs] *adj (daring)* audaz;
(bold) atrevido,-a; *(impudent)* descarado,
-a.
audible ['ɔːdɪbəl] *adj* audible.
audience ['ɔːdɪəns] *n* 1 *(spectators)* público *m*; *(at concert, conference)* auditorio *m*;
(television) telespectadores *mpl.* 2 *(meeting)* audiencia *f.*
audio-visual [ɔːdɪəʊ'vɪzjʊəl] *adj* audiovisual; **a.-v. aids,** apoyo *m* audiovisual.
audit ['ɔːdɪt] **I** *n* revisión *f* de cuentas. **II**

vtr revisar, intervenir.

audition |ɔː'dɪʃən| **I** *n* prueba *f*. **II** *vtr* **to a. sb for a part**, probar a algn para un papel.

auditor |'ɔːdɪtər| *n* revisor,-a *m,f* de cuentas.

auditorium |ɔːdɪ'tɔːrɪəm| *n* auditorio *m*.

augment |ɔːg'ment| *vtr* aumentar.

augur |'ɔːgər| *vi* **to a. well**, ser de buen agüero.

August |'ɔːgəst| *n* agosto *m*.

aunt |ɑːnt| *n* (*also fam* **auntie, aunty** |'ɑːntɪ|) tía *f*.

au pair |əʊ'peər| *n* **au p. (girl)**, au pair *f*.

aura |'ɔːrə| *n* aura *f*; *Rel* aureola *f*.

aural |'ɔːrəl| *adj* auditivo,-a, del oído.

auspices |'ɔːspɪsɪz| *npl* **under the a. of**, bajo los auspicios de.

auspicious |ɔː'spɪʃəs| *adj* de buen augurio.

austere |ɒ'stɪər| *adj* austero,-a.

austerity |ɒ'sterɪtɪ| *n* austeridad *f*.

Australia |ɒ'streɪlɪə| *n* Australia.

Australian |ɒ'streɪlɪən| *adj & n* australiano,-a (*m,f*).

Austria |'ɒstrɪə| *n* Austria.

Austrian |'ɒstrɪən| *adj & n* austríaco,-a (*m,f*).

authentic |ɔː'θentɪk| *adj* auténtico,-a.

author |'ɔːθər| *n* autor,-a *m,f*.

authoritarian |ɔːθɒrɪ'teərɪən| *adj* autoritario,-a.

authoritative |ɔː'θɒrɪtətɪv| *adj* (*reliable*) autorizado,-a; (*authoritarian*) autoritario,-a.

authority |ɔː'θɒrɪtɪ| *n* autoridad *f*; **local a.**, ayuntamiento *m*.

authorize |'ɔːθəraɪz| *vtr* autorizar; (*payment etc*) aprobar; **to a. sb to do sth**, autorizar a algn a hacer algo.

auto |'ɔːtəʊ| *n US* coche *m, Am* carro *m*.

autobiography |ɔːtəʊbaɪ'ɒgrəfɪ| *n* autobiografía *f*.

autograph |'ɔːtəgrɑːf| **I** *n* autógrafo *m*. **II** *vtr* (*sign*) firmar; (*book, photo*) dedicar.

automatic |ɔːtə'mætɪk| **I** *adj* automático,-a. **II** *n* (*car*) coche automático; (*gun*) pistola automática. ◆**automatically** *adv* automáticamente.

automation |ɔːtə'meɪʃən| *n* automatización *f*; office a., ofimática *f*.

automaton |ɔː'tɒmətən| *n* (*pl* **automata** |ɔː'tɒmətə|) autómata *m*.

automobile |'ɔːtəməbiːl| *n US* coche *m*, automóvil *m, Am* carro *m*.

autonomous |ɔː'tɒnəməs| *adj* autónomo,-a.

autonomy |ɔː'tɒnəmɪ| *n* autonomía *f*.

autopsy |'ɔːtəpsɪ| *n* autopsia *f*.

autumn |'ɔːtəm| *n* otoño *m*.

auxiliary |ɔːg'zɪljərɪ| *adj* auxiliar.

Av., av. *abbr of* **Avenue**, avenida *f*, Av., Avda.

avail |ə'veɪl| **I** *n* **to no a.**, en vano. **II** *vtr*

to a. oneself of sth, aprovecharse de algo.

available |ə'veɪləbəl| *adj* (*thing*) disponible; (*person*) libre.

avalanche |'ævəlɑːnʃ| *n* avalancha *f*.

avarice |'ævərɪs| *n* avaricia *f*.

Ave *abbr of* **Avenue**, Avenida *f*, Av., Avda.

avenge |ə'vendʒ| *vtr* vengar.

avenue |'ævɪnjuː| *n* avenida *f*; *fig* vía *f*.

average |'ævərɪdʒ| **I** *n* promedio *m*, media *f*; **on a.**, por término medio. **II** *adj* medio,-a; (*condition*) regular. **III** *vtr* sacar la media de; **he averages 8 hours' work a day**, trabaja una media de 8 horas al día. ◆**average out** *vtr* salir a una media de.

averse |ə'vɜːs| *adj* **to be a. to sth**, ser reacio,-a a algo.

aversion |ə'vɜːʃən| *n* (*feeling*) aversión *f*; (*thing*) bestia negra.

avert |ə'vɜːt| *vtr* (*eyes, thoughts*) apartar (*from*, de); (*accident*) impedir; (*danger*) evitar.

avid |'ævɪd| *adj* (*reader*) voraz. ◆**avidly** *adv* vorazmente.

avocado |ævə'kɑːdəʊ| *n* (*also* **avocado pear**) aguacate *m*.

avoid |ə'vɔɪd| *vtr* evitar; (*question*) eludir.

avoidable |ə'vɔɪdəbəl| *adj* evitable.

await |ə'weɪt| *vtr* esperar, aguardar.

awake |ə'weɪk| **I** *adj* despierto,-a; **to be a.**, estar despierto,-a. **II** *vtr* (*pt* **awoke, awaked;** *pp* **awoken, awaked**) despertar.

awaken |ə'weɪkən| *vtr & vi* (*pt* **awakened;** *pp* **awoken**) → **awake II.**

awakening |ə'weɪkənɪŋ| *n* despertar *m*.

award |ə'wɔːd| **I** *n* (*prize*) premio *m*; (*medal*) condecoración *f*; *Jur* indemnización *f*; (*grant*) beca *f*. **II** *vtr* (*prize*) conceder, otorgar; (*medal*) dar; (*damages*) adjudicar.

aware |ə'weər| *adj* (*informed*) enterado,-a; **not that I'm a. of**, que yo sepa no; **to be a. of sth**, ser consciente de algo; **to become a. of sth**, darse cuenta de algo.

awareness |ə'weənɪs| *n* conciencia *f* (**of**, de).

awash |ə'wɒʃ| *adj* inundado,-a (**with**, de).

away |ə'weɪ| *adv* far a., lejos; **go a.!**, ¡lárgate!; **it's 3 miles a.**, está a 3 millas (de distancia); **keep a. from the fire!**, ¡no te acerques al fuego!; **right a.**, en seguida; **to be a.**, (*absent*) estar ausente; (*out*) estar fuera; **to die a.**, desvanecerse; **to give sth a.**, regalar algo; (*secret*) revelar algo; **to go a.**, irse; *Sport* **to play a.**, jugar fuera; **to turn a.**, volver la cara; **to work a.**, trabajar.

awe |ɔː| *n* (*fear*) temor *m*; (*amazement*) asombro *m*; **he was in a. of his father**, le intimidaba su padre.

awe-inspiring |'ɔːɪnspaɪərɪŋ| *adj* impresionante, imponente.

awesome |'ɔːsəm| *adj* impresionante.

awful ['ɔːful] *adj fam* espantoso,-a; **an a. lot of work,** muchísimo trabajo.
◆**awfully** *adv fam* terriblemente.
awkward ['ɔːkwəd] *adj* (*clumsy*) torpe; (*difficult*) pesado,-a; (*object*) incómodo,-a; (*moment*) inoportuno,-a; (*situation*) embarazoso,-a; (*problem*) difícil.
awning ['ɔːnɪŋ] *n* (*on ship*) toldo *m*; (*on shop*) marquesina *f*.

awoke [ə'wəʊk] *pt* → **awake**.
awoken [ə'wəʊkən] *pp* → **awake**.
axe, *US* **ax** [æks] **I** *n* hacha *f*. **II** *vtr fig* (*jobs*) eliminar; (*costs*) reducir; (*plan*) cancelar; (*person*) despedir.
axis ['æksɪs] *n* (*pl* **axes** ['æksiːz]) eje *m*.
axle ['æksəl] *n* eje *m*; *Tech* árbol *m*.
ayatollah [aɪə'tɒlə] *n* ayatolá *m*.
Aztec ['æztek] *adj & n* azteca (*mf*).

B

B, b [biː] *n* **1** (*the letter*) B, b *f*; *Aut* **B road,** carretera secundaria. **2** *Mus* si *m*; **B flat,** si *m* bemol.
BA [biː'eɪ] *abbr of* **Bachelor of Arts,** Licenciado en Filosofía y Letras.
babble ['bæbəl] *vi* (*baby*) balbucear; (*brook*) murmurar.
babe [beɪb] *n* **1** (*baby*) bebé *m*. **2** *US fam* **hi, b.!,** ¡hola, guapa!
baboon [bə'buːn] *n* zambo *m*.
baby ['beɪbɪ] *n* **1** bebé *m*; (*young child*) niño,-a *m/f*; **b. buggy,** *US* **b. carriage,** cochecito *m* de niño; **b. face,** cara *f* de niño. **2** (*animal*) cría *f*. **3** *fam* (*darling*) querido,-a *m,f*.
baby-sit ['beɪbɪsɪt] *vi* hacer de canguro.
baby-sitter ['beɪbɪsɪtər] *n* canguro *mf*.
baby-walker ['beɪbɪwɔːkər] *n* tacataca *m*.
bachelor ['bætʃələr] *n* **1** soltero *m*. **2** *Univ* licenciado,-a *m/f*; **B. of Arts/Science,** licenciado,-a *m,f* en Filosofía y Letras/ Ciencias.
back [bæk] **I** *n* **1** (*of person*) espalda *f*; (*of animal*) lomo *m*; **b. to front,** al revés; *fig* **to get sb's b. up,** poner negro a algn; *fig* **to have one's b. to the wall,** estar en un aprieto. **2** (*of book*) lomo *m*; (*of chair*) respaldo *m*; (*of coin*) reverso *m*; (*of hand*) dorso *m*; (*of house, car*) parte *f* de atrás; *fig* **he knows Leeds like the b. of his hand,** se conoce Leeds como la palma de la mano. **3** (*of stage, cupboard*) fondo *m*; *fam* **at the b. of beyond,** en el quinto pino. **4** *Ftb* defensa *mf*.
II *adj* **1** trasero,-a, de atrás; **b. door,** puerta *f* de atrás; **b. seat,** asiento *m* de detrás; *fig* **to take a b. seat,** pasar al segundo plano; *Aut* **b. wheel,** rueda trasera. **2** **b. rent,** alquiler atrasado; **b. pay,** atrasos *mpl*; *Press* **b. number,** número *m* atrasado.
III *adv* **1** (*to the rear*) atrás; (*towards the rear*) hacia atrás; **b. and forth,** de acá para allá. **2** *some years b.,* hace unos años.
IV *vtr* **1** (*support*) apoyar, respaldar. **2** *Fin* financiar. **3** (*bet on*) apostar por. **4** (*car etc*) dar marcha atrás.
V *vi* **1** (*move backwards*) retroceder. **2** (*car etc*) dar marcha atrás.

◆**back away** *vi* retirarse. ◆**back down** *vi* echarse atrás. ◆**back off** *vi* desistir. ◆**back out** *vi* (*withdraw*) retractarse, volverse atrás. ◆**back up I** *vtr* apoyar. **II** *vi Aut* ir marcha atrás.
backache ['bækeɪk] *n* dolor *m* de espalda.
backbencher ['bækbentʃər] *n* diputado,-a *m,f* que no es ministro.
backbiting ['bækbaɪtɪŋ] *n* murmuración *f*.
backbone ['bækbəʊn] *n Anat* columna *f*.
backcloth ['bækklɒθ] *n* telón *m* de fondo.
backdate [bæk'deɪt] *vtr* antedatar.
backdated [bæk'deɪtɪd] *adj* con efecto retroactivo.
backdrop ['bækdrɒp] *n* telón *m* de fondo.
backer ['bækər] *n* **1** *Fin* promotor,-a *m,f*. **2** *Pol* partidario, -a *m,f*. **3** (*person who bets*) apostante *mf*.
backfire [bæk'faɪər] *vi* **1** *Aut* petardear. **2** *fig* **our plan backfired,** nos salió el tiro por la culata.
background ['bækgraʊnd] *n* **1** fondo *m*; **to stay in the b.,** quedarse en segundo plano; **b. music,** música de fondo. **2** (*origin*) origen *m*; (*past*) pasado *m*; (*education*) formación *f*. **3** (*circumstances*) antecedentes *mpl*. **4** (*atmosphere*) ambiente *m*.
backhand ['bækhænd] *n Sport* revés *m*.
backhanded ['bækhændɪd] *adj* equívoco,-a, ambiguo,-a.
backhander ['bækhændər] *n sl* (*bribe*) soborno *m*.
backing ['bækɪŋ] *n* **1** (*support*) apoyo *m*; *Com Fin* respaldo financiero. **2** *Mus* acompañamiento *m*.
backlash ['bæklæʃ] *n* reacción violenta y repentina.
backlog ['bæklɒg] *n* **to have a b. of work,** tener un montón de trabajo atrasado.
backpack ['bækpæk] *n* mochila *f*.
backpedal ['bækpedəl] *vi fam* dar marcha atrás.
backside [bæk'saɪd] *n fam* trasero *m*, culo *m*.
backstage [bæk'steɪdʒ] *adv* entre bastidores.
backstroke ['bækstrəʊk] *n* espalda *f*.
backtrack ['bæktræk] *vi fig* volverse atrás.

backup ['bækʌp] n apoyo m; respaldo m; Comput b. (file), fichero m de apoyo.

backward ['bækwəd] I adj 1 (movement) hacia atrás. 2 (country) subdesarrollado, -a; (child) retrasado,-a. II adv esp US hacia atrás.

backwards ['bækwədz] adv hacia atrás; to walk b., andar de espaldas.

backyard [bæk'jɑːd] n patio trasero; US jardín trasero.

bacon ['beɪkən] n tocino m, beicon m.

bacteria [bæk'tɪərɪə] npl bacterias fpl.

bad [bæd] I adj (worse, worst) 1 (poor) malo,-a; to go from b. to worse, ir de mal en peor. 2 (decayed) podrido,-a; to go b., echarse a perder. 3 that's too b.!, ¡qué pena! 4 (wicked) malo,-a; to use b. language, ser mal hablado,-a. 5 (accident) grave; (headache) fuerte. 6 (ill) enfermo, -a. 7 b. debt, deuda f incobrable. II n lo malo. ◆badly adv 1 mal; he did b. in the exam, le salió mal el examen; to be b. off, andar mal de dinero. 2 (seriously) gravemente. 3 (very much) mucho; to miss sb b., echar mucho de menos a algn; we need it b., nos hace mucha falta.

bade [beɪd] pt → **bid**.

badge [bædʒ] n insignia f; (metal disc) chapa f.

badger ['bædʒər] I n tejón m. II vtr acosar.

badminton ['bædmɪntən] n bádminton m.

bad-tempered [bæd'tempəd] adj to be b.-t., (temperament) tener mal genio; (temporarily) estar de mal humor.

baffle ['bæfəl] I vtr desconcertar. II n Tech pantalla acústica.

baffling ['bæflɪŋ] adj incomprensible, enigmático,-a.

bag [bæg] I n 1 (large) bolsa f; (handbag) bolso m; fam bags of, montones de; travel b., bolsa de viaje. 2 (hunting) caza f; fam it's in the b., es cosa hecha. 3 pej old b., (woman) bruja f. 4 bags, (under eyes) ojeras fpl. II vtr 1 (put into sacks) meter en sacos. 2 fam coger.

baggage ['bægɪdʒ] n 1 equipaje m. 2 Mil bagaje m.

baggy ['bægɪ] adj (baggier, baggiest) holgado,-a; b. trousers, pantalones anchos.

bagpipes ['bægpaɪps] npl gaita f sing.

Bahamas [bə'hɑːməz] npl the B., las Bahamas.

bail¹ [beɪl] n Jur fianza f; on b., bajo fianza; to stand b. for sb, salir fiador por algn. ◆**bail out** vtr fig (person) sacar de un apuro.

bail² [beɪl] vi Naut to b. (out), achicar.

bailiff ['beɪlɪf] n 1 Jur alguacil m. 2 (steward) administrador m.

bait [beɪt] I n cebo m; to rise to the b.,

tragar el anzuelo, picar. II vtr 1 Fishing cebar. 2 (torment) hostigar.

baize [beɪz] n bayeta f; green b., tapete m verde.

bake [beɪk] I vtr 1 cocer al horno. 2 (harden) endurecer. II vi fam hacer mucho calor.

baked [beɪkt] adj al horno; b. potato, patata f al horno.

baker ['beɪkər] n panadero,-a m,f.

bakery ['beɪkərɪ] n panadería f.

baking ['beɪkɪŋ] n cocción f; b. dish, fuente f para horno; b. powder, levadura f en polvo; b. tin, molde m.

balaclava [bælə'klɑːvə] n pasamontañas m inv.

balance ['bæləns] I n 1 (scales) balanza f; fig to hang in the b., estar en juego. 2 (equilibrium) equilibrio m; Pol b. of power, equilibrio de fuerzas. 3 Fin saldo m; b. of payments, balanza f de pagos; b. sheet, balance m; credit b., saldo acreedor. 4 (remainder) resto m. II vtr 1 poner en equilibrio (on, en). 2 (budget) equilibrar; to b. the books, hacer el balance. 3 (weigh up) sopesar. III vi guardar el equilibrio. ◆**balance out** vi (figures) corresponderse.

balanced ['bælənst] adj equilibrado,-a.

balcony ['bælkənɪ] n balcón m; Theat anfiteatro m.

bald [bɔːld] adj 1 (person) calvo,-a. 2 (tyre) desgastado,-a. 3 (style) escueto,-a.

baldness ['bɔːldnɪs] n 1 (of person) calvicie f. 2 (of tyre) desgaste m. 3 (of style) sencillez f.

bale¹ [beɪl] I n fardo m. II vtr embalar.

bale² [beɪl] vtr → **bail²**. ◆**bale out** I vi Av saltar en paracaídas de un avión. II vtr fig (person) sacar de apuros a.

Balearic [bælɪ'ærɪk] adj the B. Islands, las Islas Baleares.

baleful ['beɪlful] adj funesto,-a, siniestro,-a.

Balkan ['bɔːlkən] adj the Balkans, los Balcanes.

ball¹ [bɔːl] n 1 (in cricket, tennis etc) pelota f; Ftb balón m; (in billiards, golf etc) bola f; fig the b. is in your court, ahora te toca a tí; fig to play b. with sb, cooperar con algn; fam to be on the b., ser un espabilado; Tech b. bearing, rodamiento m de bolas. 2 (of paper) bola f; (of wool) ovillo m. 3 US béisbol m; fig it's a whole new b. game, es otra historia. 4 vulg offens balls, cojones mpl.

ball² [bɔːl] n baile m.

ballad ['bæləd] n balada f.

ballast ['bæləst] n Naut lastre m.

ballerina [bælə'riːnə] n bailarina f.

ballet ['bæleɪ] n ballet m; b. dancer, bailarín,-ina m,f.

ballistic [bə'lɪstɪk] adj balístico,-a.

ballistics [bə'lɪstɪks] n balística f.

balloon [bə'lu:n] I n 1 globo m. 2 (in cartoon) bocadillo m. II vi hincharse; fig aumentar rápidamente.

ballot ['bælət] I n votación f; b. box, urna f; b. paper, papeleta f. II vtr someter a votación.

ballpoint (pen) ['bɔ:lpɔint ('pen)] n bolígrafo m.

ballroom ['bɔ:lru:m] n salón m de baile.

ballyhoo ['bælɪ'hu:] n fam (fuss) jaleo m.

balm [bɑ:m] n bálsamo m.

balmy ['bɑ:mɪ] adj (balmier, balmiest) (weather) suave.

Baltic ['bɔ:ltɪk] adj báltico,-a; the B. (Sea), el Mar Báltico.

balustrade ['bæləstreɪd] n barandilla f.

bamboo [bæm'bu:] n bambú m.

bamboozle [bæm'bu:zəl] vtr fam 1 (puzzle) dejar perplejo. 2 (trick) engañar, embaucar.

ban [bæn] I n prohibición f. II vtr 1 (prohibit) prohibir. 2 (exclude) excluir.

banal [bə'nɑ:l] adj banal, trivial.

banana [bə'nɑ:nə] n plátano m, Am banana f; fam to go bananas, volverse loco, -a.

band [bænd] I n 1 (strip) tira f; (ribbon) cinta f. 2 (stripe) raya f. 3 Rad banda f. 4 (group) grupo m; (of youths) pandilla f; (of thieves) banda f. 5 Mus banda f. II vi to b. together, unirse, juntarse.

bandage ['bændɪdʒ] I n venda f. II vtr vendar.

Band-Aid® ['bænderd] n US tirita® f.

B & B [bi:ən'bi:] n abbr of bed and breakfast.

bandit ['bændɪt] n bandido m.

bandstand ['bændstænd] n quiosco m de música.

bandwagon ['bændwægən] n fig to jump on the b., subirse al tren.

bandy ['bændɪ] I vtr (words, ideas) intercambiar. II adj (bandier, bandiest) torcido,-a hacia fuera. ◆bandy about vtr (ideas) propagar, difundir.

bandy-legged ['bændɪleg(ɪ)d] adj patizambo,-a.

bang [bæŋ] I n 1 (blow) golpe m. 2 (noise) ruido m; (explosion) estallido m; (of gun) estampido m; to shut the door with a b., dar un portazo. II vtr golpear; to b. sth shut, cerrar algo de golpe. III vi golpear; to b. shut, cerrarse de golpe. IV interj (blow) ¡zas!; b., b.!, (of gun) ¡pum, pum! V adv fam justo.

banger ['bæŋər] n 1 (firework) petardo m. 2 fam (sausage) salchicha f. 3 fam old b., (car) tartana f.

bangle ['bæŋgəl] n brazalete m.

banish ['bænɪʃ] vtr desterrar.

banister ['bænɪstər] n pasamanos m inv.

bank1 [bæŋk] I n 1 Com Fin banco m; b. account, cuenta bancaria; b. card, tarjeta bancaria; b. clerk, empleado, -a m,f de

banca; b. draft, letra bancaria; b. holiday, fiesta f nacional; b. statement, extracto m de cuenta. 2 (in gambling) banca f. 3 (store) banco m. II vtr Com Fin depositar, ingresar. III vi Com Fin to b. with, tener una cuenta en. ◆bank on vtr contar con.

bank2 [bæŋk] I n 1 (mound) loma f; (embankment) terraplén m. 2 (of river) ribera f; (edge) orilla f. II vtr & vi Av ladearse.

bankbook ['bæŋkbʊk] n libreta f de ahorros.

banker ['bæŋkər] n banquero,-a m,f.

banking ['bæŋkɪŋ] n banca f.

banknote ['bæŋknəʊt] n billete m de banco.

bankrupt ['bæŋkrʌpt] I adj en quiebra; to go b., quebrar. II vtr llevar a la bancarrota.

bankruptcy ['bæŋkrʌptsɪ] n quiebra f, bancarrota f.

banner ['bænər] n (in demonstration) pancarta f; (flag) bandera f.

banns [bænz] npl amonestaciones fpl.

banquet ['bæŋkwɪt] n banquete m.

banter ['bæntər] I n bromas fpl. II vi bromear.

bap [bæp] n bollo m, panecillo m.

baptism ['bæptɪzəm] n bautismo m.

baptize [bæp'taɪz] vtr bautizar.

bar [bɑ:r] I n 1 (of gold) barra f; (of chocolate) tableta f; (of soap) pastilla f; Com b. code, código m de barras. 2 (of cage) barrote m; fam to be behind bars, estar en la cárcel. 3 (obstacle) obstáculo m. 4 Jur (dock) banquillo m; (court) tribunal m. 5 Jur the B., (profession) abogacía f; (body of lawyers) colegio m de abogados. 6 (pub) bar m; (counter) barra f. 7 Mus compás m. II vtr (door) atrancar; (road) cortar. 2 (exclude) excluir (from, de). 3 (prohibit) prohibir. III prep salvo; b. none, sin excepción.

barbarian [bɑ:'beərɪən] adj & n bárbaro,-a m,f.

barbaric [bɑ:'bærɪk] adj bárbaro,-a.

barbecue ['bɑ:bɪkju:] I n barbacoa f. II vtr asar a la parrilla.

barbed [bɑ:bd] adj 1 b. wire, alambre m de púas. 2 fig (remark) mordaz.

barber ['bɑ:bər] n barbero,-a m,f; b.'s (shop), barbería f.

barbiturate [bɑ:'bɪtjʊrɪt] n barbitúrico m.

bare [beər] I adj 1 desnudo,-a; (head) descubierto,-a; (foot) descalzo,-a; (room) sin muebles; to lay b., poner al descubierto; with his b. hands, sólo con las manos. 2 (basic) mero,-a; the b. minimum, lo mínimo. II vtr desnudar; (uncover) descubrir.

bareback(ed) ['beəbæk(t)] adj & adv to ride b., montar un caballo a pelo.

barefaced ['beəfeɪst] adj desvergonzado,

-a.

barefoot ['beəfʊt] adj & adv descalzo,-a.

barely ['beəlɪ] adv apenas.

bargain ['bɑːgɪn] I n 1 (agreement) pacto m; (deal) negocio m; **into the b.,** por añadidura, además; **to drive a hard b.,** imponer condiciones duras; **to strike a b.,** cerrar un trato. 2 (cheap purchase) ganga f; **b. price,** precio m de oferta. II vi 1 negociar. 2 (haggle) regatear. ◆**bargain for** vtr esperar, contar con.

barge [bɑːdʒ] I n gabarra f. II vtr fam **to b. into,** (room) irrumpir en; (person) tropezar con. ◆**barge in** vi fam 1 (go in) entrar sin permiso. 2 (interfere) entrometerse.

baritone ['bærɪtəʊn] adj & n barítono (m).

bark¹ [bɑːk] I n ladrido m. II vi (dog) ladrar.

bark² [bɑːk] n Bot corteza f.

barley ['bɑːlɪ] n cebada f; **b. sugar,** azúcar m cande.

barmaid ['bɑːmeɪd] n camarera f.

barman ['bɑːmən] n camarero m, barman m.

barn [bɑːn] n granero m; **b. dance,** baile m popular.

barnacle ['bɑːnəkəl] n percebe m.

barometer [bəˈrɒmɪtər] n barómetro m.

baron ['bærən] n barón m.

baroness ['bærənɪs] n baronesa f.

baroque [bəˈrɒk] adj barroco,-a.

barrack ['bærək] vtr abuchear.

barracks ['bærəks] n Mil cuartel m sing.

barrage ['bærɑːdʒ] n 1 (dam) presa f. 2 Mil barrera f de fuego. 3 fig (of questions) lluvia f.

barrel ['bærəl] n 1 (of wine) tonel m; (of beer, oil) barril m. 2 (of firearm) cañón m.

barren ['bærən] adj estéril; (land) yermo,-a.

barricade [bærɪˈkeɪd] I n barricada f. II vtr levantar barricadas; **to b. oneself in,** parapetarse.

barrier ['bærɪər] n barrera f.

barrister ['bærɪstər] n GB abogado,-a m,f (capacitado,-a para ejercer ante tribunales superiores).

barrow ['bærəʊ] n carretilla f.

bartender ['bɑːtendər] n US camarero m, barman m.

barter ['bɑːtər] vtr trocar (**for,** por).

base [beɪs] I n 1 (foot) pie m; (of column) basa f; Sport (of team) concentración f; **air/naval b.,** base f aérea/naval. II vtr 1 basar, fundar (**on,** en). 2 (troops) estacionar. III adj 1 (despicable) bajo,-a, despreciable. 2 (metals) común.

baseball ['beɪsbɔːl] n béisbol m.

baseline ['beɪslaɪn] n Ten línea f de saque.

basement ['beɪsmənt] n sótano m.

bash [bæʃ] I n (heavy blow) golpetazo m;

(dent) bollo m; fam (attempt) intento m. II vtr golpear.

bashful ['bæʃfʊl] adj tímido,-a.

basic ['beɪsɪk] I adj básico,-a; **b. pay,** sueldo m base. II npl **basics,** lo fundamental. ◆**basically** adv fundamentalmente.

basil ['bæzəl] n albahaca f.

basin ['beɪsən] n 1 (washbowl) palangana f; (for washing up) barreño m; (in bathroom) lavabo m; (dish) cuenco m. 2 (of river) cuenca f.

basis ['beɪsɪs] n (pl bases ['beɪsiːz]) base f; **on the b. of,** en base a.

bask [bɑːsk] vi tostarse; **to b. in the sun,** tomar el sol.

basket ['bɑːskɪt] n cesta f, cesto m.

basketball ['bɑːskɪtbɔːl] n baloncesto m.

Basque [bæsk, bɑːsk] I adj vasco,-a; **B. Country,** País Vasco, Euskadi; **B. flag,** ikurriña f; **B. nationalist,** abertzale mf. II n 1 (person) vasco,-a m,f. 2 (language) vasco m, euskera m.

bass¹ [bæs] n inv (seawater) lubina f; (freshwater) perca f.

bass² [beɪs] I n 1 (singer) bajo m. 2 (notes) graves mpl; **b. drum,** bombo m; **b. guitar,** bajo m. II adj bajo,-a.

bassoon [bəˈsuːn] n fagot m.

bastard ['bɑːstəd, 'bæstəd] I n 1 bastardo,-a m,f. 2 offens cabrón m, hijo m de puta; **poor b.!,** ¡el pobre! II adj bastardo,-a.

baste [beɪst] vtr Culin untar.

bastion ['bæstɪən] n baluarte m, bastión m.

bat¹ [bæt] I n (in cricket, baseball) bate m; (in table tennis) pala f; fig **to do sth off one's own b.,** hacer algo por cuenta propia. II vi (in cricket, baseball) batear.

bat² [bæt] n Zool murciélago m.

bat³ [bæt] vtr fam **without batting an eyelid,** sin pestañear.

batch [bætʃ] n (of bread) hornada f; (of goods) lote m; Comput **b. processing,** procesamiento m por lotes.

bated ['beɪtɪd] adj **with b. breath,** sin respirar.

bath [bɑːθ] I n 1 baño m; **to have a b.,** bañarse; **b. towel,** toalla f de baño. 2 (tub) bañera f. 3 **baths,** piscina f municipal. II vtr bañar.

bathe [beɪð] I vi bañarse. II vtr 1 (wound) lavar. 2 **he was bathed in sweat,** (covered) estaba empapado de sudor.

bather ['beɪðər] n bañista mf.

bathing ['beɪðɪŋ] n baño m; **b. cap,** gorro m de baño; **b. costume,** traje m de baño; **b. trunks,** bañador m de hombre.

bathrobe ['bɑːθrəʊb] n albornoz m.

bathroom ['bɑːθruːm] n cuarto m de baño.

bathtub ['bɑːθtʌb] n bañera f.

baton ['bætən, 'bætɒn] n 1 Mus batuta f.

2 *(truncheon)* porra *f*. 3 *Sport* testigo *m*.

battalion |bə'tæljən| *n* batallón *m*.

batter¹ |'bætər| *vtr* aporrear, apalear.

batter² |'bætər| *n (in cricket, baseball)* bateador-a, *m,f*.

batter³ |'bætər| *Culin* I *n* pasta *f* (para rebozar); **fish in b.**, pescado rebozado. II *vtr* rebozar.

battered |'bætəd| *adj (car)* abollado,-a; *(person)* maltratado,-a.

battering |'bætərɪŋ| *n* paliza *f*; **to take a b.**, recibir una paliza; *Mil* **b. ram**, ariete *m*.

battery |'bætərɪ| *n* 1 *(for torch, radio)* pila *f*; *Aut* batería *f*. 2 *Jur* **assault and b.**, lesiones *fpl*.

battle |'bætəl| I *n* batalla *f*; *fig* lucha *f*; **to do b.**, librar batalla; *fig* **b. cry**, lema *m*. II *vi* luchar.

battlefield |'bætəlfiːld| *n* campo *m* de batalla.

battleship |'bætəlʃɪp| *n* acorazado *m*.

bauble |'bɔːbəl| *n* chuchería *f*.

bawdy |'bɔːdɪ| *adj (joke etc)* verde.

bawl |bɔːl| *vi* gritar, chillar.

bay¹ |beɪ| *n Geog* bahía *f*; *(large)* golfo *m*; **B. of Biscay**, golfo de Vizcaya; **B. of Bengal**, golfo de Bengala.

bay² |beɪ| *n* 1 *(recess)* hueco *m*; **b. window**, ventana salediza. 2 *(in factory)* nave *f*; **cargo b.**, bodega *f* de carga.

bay³ |beɪ| *n* laurel *m*.

bay⁴ |beɪ| I *vi (dog)* aullar. II *n* ladrido *m*; *fig* **at b.**, acorralado,-a; *fig* **to keep sb at b.**, mantener a algn a raya.

bayonet |'beɪənɪt| *n* bayoneta *f*.

bazaar |bə'zɑːr| *n* 1 *(market)* bazar *m*. 2 *(Church)*, *(charity sale)* rastrillo benéfico.

BBC |biːbiːˈsiː| *abbr of* **British Broadcasting Corporation**, Compañía británica de radiofusión, BBC *f*.

BC |biːˈsiː| *abbr of* **before Christ**, antes de Jesucristo, a.d.C.

be |biː|, *unstressed* bɪ| I *vi (pres 1st person sing* **am**; *3rd person sing* **is**; *2nd person sing & all persons pl* **are**; *pt 1st & 3rd persons sing* **was**; *2nd person sing & all persons pl* **were**; *pp* **been**) 1 ser; **he is very tall**, es muy alto; **Madrid is the capital**, Madrid es la capital; **sugar is sweet**, el azúcar es dulce. 2 *(nationality, occupation)* ser; **he's Italian**, es italiano. 3 *(origin, ownership)* ser; **the car is Domingo's**, el coche es de Domingo; **this painting is by Goya**, este cuadro es de Goya. 4 *(price)* costar; *(total)* ser; **a return ticket is £24**, un billete de ida y vuelta cuesta £24; **how much is a kilo of cod?**, ¿a cuánto está el kilo de bacalao?; **how much is it?**, ¿cuánto es? 5 *(temporary state)* estar; **how are you?** - **I'm very well**, ¿cómo estás? - estoy muy bien; **this soup is cold**, esta sopa está fría; **to be cold/afraid/hungry**, tener frío/miedo/hambre; **to be lucky**, tener

suerte. 6 *(location)* estar; **Aberdeen is in Scotland**, Aberdeen está en Escocia; **Birmingham is two hundred miles from London**, Birmingham está a doscientas millas de Londres. 7 *(age)* tener; **she is thirty (years old)**, tiene treinta años.
II *v aux* 1 *(with pres p)* estar; **he is writing a letter**, está escribiendo una carta; **she was singing**, estaba cantando; **they are leaving next week**, se van la semana que viene; **we have been waiting for a long time**, hace mucho que estamos esperando; **he is coming**, *(emphatic)* es seguro que viene. 2 *(passive)* ser; **he was murdered**, fue asesinado; **she is allowed to smoke**, se le permite fumar. 3 *(obligation)* **I am to see him this afternoon**, debo verle esta tarde; **you are not to smoke here**, no se puede fumar aquí.
III *v impers* 1 *(with there)* haber; **there is, there are, hay; there was, there were**, había; **there will be**, habrá; **there would be**, habría; **there have been a lot of complaints**, ha habido muchas quejas; **there were ten of us**, éramos diez. 2 *(with it)* **it's late**, es tarde; **it is said that**, se dice que; **who is it?** - **it's me**, ¿quién es? - soy yo; **what is it?**, ¿qué pasa? 3 *(weather)* **it's foggy**, hay niebla; **it's cold/hot**, hace frío/calor. 4 *(time)* ser; **it's one o'clock**, es la una; **it's four o'clock**, son las cuatro. 5 *(date)* **it's the 11th/Tuesday today**, hoy es 11/martes. 6 *(tag questions)* ¿verdad?, ¿no?; **it's lovely, isn't it?**, es bonito, ¿no?; **you're happy, aren't you?**, estás contento, ¿verdad? **he's not very clever, is he?**, no es muy listo, ¿verdad? 7 *(unreal conditions)* **if I was/were you ...**, yo en tu lugar ...; **if you were a millionaire ...**, si fueras millonario .... 8 *pres & past perfect (visit, go)* estar, ir; **I've been to Paris**, he estado en París.

beach |biːtʃ| I *n* playa *f*. II *vtr* varar.

beacon |'biːkən| *n* 1 *Av Naut* baliza *f*. 2 *(lighthouse)* faro *m*.

bead |biːd| *n* 1 *(of necklace etc)* cuenta *f*; **glass b.**, abalorio *m*. 2 *(of liquid)* gota *f*.

beady |'biːdɪ| *adj (beadier, beadiest) (eyes)* pequeños y brillantes.

beagle |'biːɡəl| *n* beagle *m*.

beak |biːk| *n* 1 *(of bird)* pico *m*. 2 *fam (nose)* nariz ganchuda.

beaker |'biːkər| *n (tumbler)* taza alta, jarra *f*.

beam |biːm| I *n* 1 *Archit* viga *f*. 2 *(of light)* rayo *m*; *Phys* haz *m*. 3 *Gymn* barra fija. 4 *(smile)* sonrisa *f* radiante. II *vi* 1 *(sun)* brillar. 2 *(smile)* sonreír. III *vtr* 1 *(broadcast)* difundir, emitir. 2 *(transmit)* transmitir.

beaming |'biːmɪŋ| *adj (smiling)* radiante.

bean |biːn| *n* alubia *f*, judía *f*, frijol *m*; *fam* **to spill the beans**, descubrir el pastel; **baked beans**, alubias cocidas en salsa de tomate; **broad b.**, haba *f*; **butter b.**, judía *f*; **coffee b.**, grano *m* de café; **green/runner b.**, judía verde; **haricot b.**, alubia; **kidney b.**, frijol.

beansprout ['biːnspraʊt] *n* brote *m* de soja.

bear¹ [beə^r] (*pt* bore; *pp* borne) I *vtr* 1 (*carry*) llevar. 2 (*support*) sostener. 3 (*endure*) soportar, aguantar; **I can't b. him**, no lo soporto. 4 (*fruit*) dar; *Fin* (*interest*) devengar. 5 **to b. a resemblance to**, parecerse a. 6 **to b. a grudge against sb**, guardar rencor a algn; **to b. in mind**, tener presente. 7 **to b. witness**, atestiguar. 8 (*pp born passive only, not followed by by*) (*give birth to*) dar a luz; **he was born in Wakefield**, nació en Wakefield. II *vi* (*turn*) girar, torcer; **to b. left**, girar a la izquierda. ◆**bear down** *vi* (*approach*) correr (**on**, sobre). ◆**bear out** *vtr* (*confirm*) confirmar. ◆**bear up** *vi* (*endure*) resistir. ◆**bear with** *vtr* tener paciencia con.

bear² [beə^r] *n* 1 oso *m*; **b. cub**, osezno *m*; *Astr* **Great B.**, Osa *f* Mayor; **Little B.**, Osa Menor. 2 *Fin* bajista *mf*.

beard [bɪəd] *n* barba *f*.

bearer ['beərə^r] *n* portador,-a *m,f*; (*of passport, office*) titular *mf*.

bearing ['beərɪŋ] *n* 1 (*posture*) porte *m*. 2 (*relevance*) relación *f*; **to have a b. on**, estar relacionado,-a con. 3 *Tech* cojinete *m*. 4 *Naut* **bearings**, posición *f*, orientación *f*; **to get one's bearings**, orientarse; **to lose one's bearings**, desorientarse.

beast [biːst] *n* 1 bestia *f*; **b. of burden**, bestia de carga. 2 *fig* bestia *f*, bruto *m*. 3 **beasts**, (*cattle*) reses *fpl*.

beastly ['biːstlɪ] *adj* (*beastlier, beastliest*) *fam* asqueroso,-a.

beat [biːt] I *vtr* (*pt* beat; *pp* beaten) ['biːtən] 1 (*hit*) pegar, golpear; (*clothes*) sacudir; (*drum*) tocar; **off the beaten track**, en un lugar muy apartado; *sl* **b. it!**, ¡lárgate! 2 *Culin* batir. 3 (*defeat*) batir, vencer; **we b. them 5-2**, les ganamos 5 a 2. 4 **to b. a retreat**, batirse en retirada. 5 *Mus* (*time*) marcar. 6 **to b. the traffic**, evitar los embotellamientos de tráfico. 7 *sl* (*puzzle*) extrañar; **it beats me**, no lo entiendo. II *vi* 1 (*heart*) latir. 2 (*strike*) dar golpes; *fig* **to b. about the bush**, andarse por las ramas. III *n* 1 (*of heart*) latido *m*. 2 *Mus* ritmo *m*, compás *m*. 3 (*of policeman*) ronda *f*. IV *adj fam* (*exhausted*) agotado,-a. ◆**beat down** *vi* (*sun*) apretar. ◆**beat off** *vtr* rechazar. ◆**beat up** *vtr fam* dar una paliza a.

beating ['biːtɪŋ] *n* 1 (*thrashing*) paliza *f*. 2 (*defeat*) derrota *f*. 3 (*of drum*) toque *m*. 4 (*of heart*) latido *m*.

beautician [bjuː'tɪʃən] *n* esteticista *mf*.

beautiful ['bjuːtɪfʊl] *adj* hermoso,-a,

bello,-a; (*delicious*) delicioso,-a; **b. people**, gente *f* guapa.

beauty ['bjuːtɪ] *n* belleza *f*, hermosura *f*; **b. contest**, concurso *m* de belleza; **b. queen**, miss *f*; **b. salon**, salón *m* de belleza; **b. spot**, (*on face*) lunar *m*; (*place*) lugar pintoresco.

beaver ['biːvə^r] I *n* castor *m*. II *vi* **to b. away at sth**, meterse de lleno en algo.

became [bɪ'keɪm] *pt* → **become**.

because [bɪ'kɒz] I *conj* porque. II *prep* **b. of**, a causa de, debido a.

beckon ['bekən] *vtr & vi* llamar (con la mano); **to b. to sb**, llamar a algn con señas.

becoming [bɪ'kʌmɪŋ] *adj* 1 (*dress*) favorecedor,-a. 2 (*behaviour*) conveniente, apropiado,-a.

bed [bed] *n* 1 cama *f*; **to get out of b.**, levantarse de la cama; **to go to b.**, acostarse; **to make the b.**, hacer la cama; *GB* **b. and breakfast**, (*service*) cama y desayuno *m*; (*sign*) 'pensión'; **b. linen**, ropa *f* de cama. 2 (*of river*) lecho *m*; (*of sea*) fondo *m*. 3 *Geol* capa *f*. 4 (*flower*) **b.**, arriate *m*.

bedbug ['bedbʌg] *n* chinche *mf*.

bedclothes ['bedkləʊðz] *npl*, **bedding** ['bedɪŋ] *n* ropa *f* de cama.

bedlam ['bedləm] *n* algarabía *f*, alboroto *m*.

bedraggled [bɪ'drægəld] *adj* (*wet*) mojado,-a; (*dirty*) ensuciado,-a.

bedridden ['bedrɪdən] *adj* postrado,-a en cama.

bedroom ['bedruːm] *n* dormitorio *m*.

bedside ['bedsaɪd] *n* **at sb's b.**, junto a la cama de algn; **b. table**, mesilla *f* de noche.

bedsit ['bedsɪt] *n* *fam*, **bedsitter** [bed'sɪtə^r] *n* estudio *m*.

bedspread ['bedspred] *n* colcha *f*.

bedtime ['bedtaɪm] *n* hora *f* de acostarse.

bee [biː] *n* abeja *f*.

beech [biːtʃ] *n* haya *f*.

beef [biːf] *n* carne *f* de vaca, *Am* carne de res; **roast b.**, rosbif *m*. ◆**beef up** *vtr fam* reforzar.

beefburger ['biːfbɜːgə^r] *n* hamburguesa *f*.

beefsteak ['biːfsteɪk] *n* bistec *m*.

beehive ['biːhaɪv] *n* colmena *f*.

beeline ['biːlaɪn] *n* *fam* **to make a b. for sth**, ir directo hacia algo.

been [biːn, bɪn] *pp* → **be**.

beep [biːp] *n* (*of apparatus*) pitido *m*; (*of horn*) pito *m*.

beer [bɪə^r] *n* cerveza *f*; **a glass of b.**, una caña.

beet [biːt] *n* remolacha *f*; *US* **red b.**, remolacha.

beetle ['biːtəl] *n* escarabajo *m*.

beetroot ['biːtruːt] *n* remolacha *f*.

befit [bɪ'fɪt] *vtr* convenir a, corresponder a.

before [bɪ'fɔːr] I *conj* 1 (*earlier than*) antes de que (+ *subj*), antes de (+ *infin*); **b. she goes**, antes de que se vaya; **b. leaving**, antes de salir. 2 (*rather than*) antes que (+ *infin*). II *prep* 1 (*place*) delante de; (*in the presence of*) ante. 2 (*order, time*) antes de; **b. Christ**, antes de Cristo; **b. long**, dentro de poco; **b. 1950**, antes de 1950; **I saw it b. you**, lo vi antes que tú. III *adv* 1 (*time*) antes; **I have met him b.**, ya lo conozco; **not long b.**, poco antes; **the night b.**, la noche anterior. 2 (*place*) delante, por delante.

beforehand [bɪ'fɔːhænd] *adv* 1 (*earlier*) antes. 2 (*in advance*) de antemano, con anticipación.

befriend [bɪ'frend] *vtr* trabar amistad con.

beg [beg] I *vtr* 1 (*money etc*) pedir. 2 (*beseech*) rogar, suplicar; **I b. your pardon!**, ¡perdone usted!; **I b. your pardon?**, ¿cómo ha dicho usted? II *vi* 1 (*solicit*) mendigar; (*dog*) pedir; **to b. for money**, pedir limosna. 2 **to b. for help/mercy**, (*beseech*) implorar ayuda/compasión.

began [bɪ'gæn] *pt* → **begin**.

beggar ['begər] *n* 1 mendigo,-a *m,f*. 2 *fam euph* (*chap*) tío *m*.

begin [bɪ'gɪn] *vtr & vi* (*pt* **began**; *pp* **begun**) empezar, comenzar; **to b. again**, volver a empezar; **to b. at the beginning**, empezar por el principio; **to b. doing** or **to do sth**, empezar a hacer algo; **to b. with ...**, (*initially*) para empezar ....

beginner [bɪ'gɪnər] *n* principiante *mf*.

beginning [bɪ'gɪnɪŋ] *n* 1 principio *m*, comienzo *m*; **at the b. of May**, a principios de mayo; **from the b.**, desde el principio; **in the b.**, al principio. 2 (*origin*) origen *m*.

begonia [bɪ'gəʊnjə] *n* begonia *f*.

begrudge [bɪ'grʌdʒ] *vtr* dar de mala gana; (*envy*) envidiar.

beguile [bɪ'gaɪl] *vtr* (*charm*) seducir.

begun [bɪ'gʌn] *pp* → **begin**.

behalf [bɪ'hɑːf] *n* **on b. of**, *US* **in b. of**, en nombre de, de parte de; **don't worry on my b.**, no te preocupes por mí.

behave [bɪ'heɪv] *vi* 1 (*person*) portarse, comportarse; **b. yourself!**, ¡pórtate bien!; **to b. well/badly**, portarse bien/mal. 2 (*machine*) funcionar.

behaviour, *US* **behavior** [bɪ'heɪvjər] *n* 1 (*of person*) comportamiento *m*, conducta *f*. 2 (*of machine*) funcionamiento *m*.

behead [bɪ'hed] *vtr* decapitar.

beheld [bɪ'held] *pt & pp* → **behold**.

behind [bɪ'haɪnd] I *prep* 1 detrás de; **b. sb's back**, a espaldas de algn; **b. the scenes**, entre bastidores; **to be b. sb**, apoyar a algn; **what motive was there b. the crime?**, ¿cuál fue el móvil del crimen? 2 **b. the times**, (*less advanced than*) anticuado,-a. II *adv* 1 (*in the rear*) detrás,

atrás; **I've left my umbrella b.**, se me ha olvidado el paraguas. 2 **to be b. with one's payments**, (*late*) estar atrasado,-a en los pagos. III *n fam* trasero *m*.

behold [bɪ'həʊld] *vtr* (*pt & pp* **beheld**) *arch* contemplar.

beige [beɪʒ] *adj & n* beige (*m*).

being ['biːɪŋ] *n* 1 ser *m*. 2 (*existence*) existencia *f*; **to come into b.**, nacer.

belated [bɪ'leɪtɪd] *adj* tardío,-a.

belch [beltʃ] I *vi* (*person*) eructar. II *vtr* (*smoke, flames*) vomitar, arrojar. III *n* eructo *m*.

beleaguered [bɪ'liːgəd] *adj* asediado,-a.

belfry ['belfrɪ] *n* campanario *m*.

Belgian ['beldʒən] *adj & n* belga (*mf*).

Belgium ['beldʒəm] *n* Bélgica.

Belgrade [bel'greɪd] *n* Belgrado.

belie [bɪ'laɪ] *vtr* desmentir.

belief [bɪ'liːf] *n* 1 creencia *f*; **beyond b.**, increíble. 2 (*opinion*) opinión *f*. 3 (*faith*) fe *f*. 4 (*confidence*) confianza *f* (**in**, en).

believe [bɪ'liːv] I *vi* 1 (*have faith*) creer. 2 **to b. in**, (*be in favour of*) ser partidario,-a de. 3 (*think*) creer; **I b. so**, creo que sí. II *vtr* creer.

believer [bɪ'liːvər] *n* 1 *Rel* creyente *mf*. 2 partidario,-a *m,f* (**in**, de).

belittle [bɪ'lɪtl] *vtr* (*person*) menospreciar; (*problem*) minimizar.

bell [bel] *n* (*of church*) campana *f*; (*small*) campanilla *f*; (*of school, door, bicycle etc*) timbre *m*; (*on cat*) cascabel *m*; (*on cow*) cencerro *m*; *fig* **that rings a b.**, eso me suena; **b. jar**, campana *f*; **b. tower**, campanario *m*.

bell-bottoms ['belbɒtəmz] *npl* pantalones *mpl* de campana.

belligerent [bɪ'lɪdʒərənt] *adj* agresivo,-a.

bellow ['beləʊ] *vi* (*bull*) bramar; (*person*) rugir.

bellows ['beləʊz] *npl* (**pair of**) **b.**, fuelle *m sing*.

belly ['belɪ] *n* 1 (*of person*) barriga *f*; **b. flop**, panzazo *m*. 2 (*of animal*) panza *f*.

bellyache ['belɪeɪk] *n fam* dolor *m* de vientre.

belong [bɪ'lɒŋ] *vi* 1 pertenecer (**to**, a). 2 (*be a member*) ser socio,-a (**to**, de); *Pol* **to b. to a party**, ser miembro de un partido. 3 (*have a proper place*) corresponder; **this chair belongs here**, esta silla va aquí.

belongings [bɪ'lɒŋɪŋz] *npl* efectos *mpl* personales.

beloved [bɪ'lʌvɪd, bɪ'lʌvd] I *adj* amado, -a, querido,-a. II *n* amado,-a *m,f*.

below [bɪ'ləʊ] I *prep* debajo de; **b. average**, por debajo de la media; **ten degrees b. zero**, diez grados bajo cero. II *adv* abajo; **above and b.**, arriba y abajo; **see b.**, véase más abajo.

belt [belt] I *n* 1 cinturón *m*; **blow below the b.**, golpe *m* bajo. 2 *Tech* correa *f*, cinta *f*. 3 *(area)* zona *f*. II *vtr sl* pegar una paliza a. ◆**belt along** *vi fam* ir a todo gas. ◆**belt out** *vtr fam (song)* cantar a voz en grito. ◆**belt up** *vi fam* callarse.

bemused [bɪˈmjuːzd] *adj* perplejo,-a.

bench [bentʃ] *n* 1 *(seat)* banco *m*. 2 *Parl* escaño *m*. 3 *Jur* the b., *(judges)* la magistratura. 4 *Sport* banquillo *m*. 5 b. mark, *Geol* cota *f* de referencia; *fig* punto *m* de referencia.

bend [bend] I *vtr (pt & pp bent)* doblar; *(back)* encorvar; *(head)* inclinar; **fam to b. the rules,** hacer una excepción. II *vi* 1 doblarse; *(road)* torcerse. 2 **to b. (over),** inclinarse; *fam* **he bends over backwards to please her,** hace lo imposible por complacerla. III *n* 1 *(in river, road)* curva *f*; *(in pipe)* recodo *m*; *GB sl* **round the b.,** loco,-a perdido,-a. ◆**bend down** *vi* inclinarse.

beneath [bɪˈniːθ] I *prep (below)* bajo, debajo de; *fig* **it's b. him,** es indigno de él. II *adv* debajo.

benefactor [ˈbenɪfæktər] *n* bienhechor,-a *m,f*.

beneficial [benɪˈfɪʃəl] *adj* 1 *(doing good)* benéfico,-a. 2 *(advantageous)* beneficioso,-a.

beneficiary [benɪˈfɪʃərɪ] *n* beneficiario,-a *m,f*.

benefit [ˈbenɪfɪt] I *vtr* beneficiar. II *vi* sacar provecho *(from or by, de)*. III *n* 1 *(advantage)* beneficio *m*, provecho *m*; **for the b. of,** en beneficio de; **I did it for your b.,** lo hice por tu bien. 2 *(allowance)* subsidio *m*; **unemployment b.,** subsidio de desempleo. 3 *(event)* función *f* benéfica.

benevolent [bɪˈnevələnt] *adj* benévolo,-a.

Bengal [beŋˈɡɔːl] *n* Bengala.

benign [bɪˈnaɪn] *adj* benigno,-a.

bent [bent] I *adj* 1 *(curved)* curvado,-a. 2 **to be b. on doing sth,** *(determined)* estar empeñado,-a en hacer algo. 3 *sl (corrupt)* deshonesto,-a. 4 *sl (homosexual)* gay. II *n (inclination)* inclinación *f (towards,* hacia).

benzine [ˈbenziːn] *n Chem* bencina *f*.

bequeath [bɪˈkwiːð] *vtr Jur* legar.

bequest [bɪˈkwest] *n Jur* legado *m*.

bereaved [bɪˈriːvd] *npl* **the b.,** los familiares del/de un difunto.

bereavement [bɪˈriːvmənt] *n (mourning)* duelo *m*.

bereft [bɪˈreft] *adj* **b. of,** privado,-a de.

beret [ˈbereɪ] *n* boina *f*.

Berlin [bɜːˈlɪn] *n* Berlín.

Bermuda [bəˈmjuːdə] *n* las (Islas) Bermudas; **B. shorts,** bermudas *fpl*.

Bern [bɜːn] *n* Berna.

berry [ˈberɪ] *n* baya *f*.

berserk [bəˈsɜːk, bəˈzɜːk] *adj* **to go b.,** volverse loco,-a.

berth [bɜːθ] *Naut* I *n* 1 *(mooring)* amarra-

dero *m*; *fig* **to give sb a wide b.,** evitar a algn. 2 *(bed)* litera *f*. II *vi* atracar.

beseech [bɪˈsiːtʃ] *vtr* suplicar, implorar.

beset [bɪˈset] *vtr (pt & pp beset)* acosar; **it is b. with dangers,** está plagado de peligros.

beside [bɪˈsaɪd] *prep* 1 *(next to)* al lado de, junto a. 2 *(compared with)* comparado con. 3 **he was b. himself with joy,** estaba loco de alegría; **that's b. the point,** eso no viene al caso; **to be b. oneself,** estar fuera de sí.

besides [bɪˈsaɪdz] I *prep* 1 *(in addition to)* además de. 2 *(except)* excepto, menos; **no one b. me,** nadie más que yo. II *adv* además.

besiege [bɪˈsiːdʒ] *vtr (city)* sitiar; *fig* asediar.

besought [bɪˈsɔːt] *pt & pp →* **beseech.**

best [best] I *adj (superl of good)* mejor; **b. man,** ≈ padrino *m* de boda; **her b. friend,** su mejor amiga; **the b. thing would be to phone them,** lo mejor sería llamarles; **we had to wait the b. part of a year,** tuvimos que esperar casi un año; **with b. wishes from Mary,** *(in letter)* con mis mejores deseos, Mary. II *adv (superl of well)* mejor; **as b. I can,** lo mejor que pueda; **I like this one b.,** éste es el que más me gusta; **the world's b. dressed man,** el hombre mejor vestido del mundo. III *n* lo mejor; **all the b.!,** que te vaya bien!; **at b.,** a lo más; **to be at one's b.,** estar en plena forma; **to do one's b.,** hacer todo lo posible; **to make the b. of sth,** sacar el mejor partido de algo; **to the b. of my knowledge,** que yo sepa.

bestiality [bestɪˈælɪtɪ] *n* bestialidad *f*.

bestow [bɪˈstəʊ] *vtr (favour etc)* conceder; *(honours, power)* otorgar *(on,* a); *(title etc)* conferir *(on,* a).

best-seller [bestˈselər] *n* best-seller *m*.

best-selling [ˈbestselɪŋ] *adj* **a b.-s. author,** un autor de superventas.

bet [bet] I *n* apuesta *f*. II *vtr (pt & pp bet or betted)* apostar. III *vi* apostar *(on,* por); *fam* **you b.!,** ¡y tanto!

Bethlehem [ˈbeθlɪhem] *n* Belén.

betray [bɪˈtreɪ] *vtr* 1 traicionar. 2 *(be unfaithful to)* engañar. 3 *(reveal)* revelar.

betrayal [bɪˈtreɪəl] *n* traición *f*.

better [ˈbetər] I *adj* 1 *(comp of good)* mejor; **that's b.!,** ¡así está mejor!; **the weather is b. than last week,** hace mejor tiempo que la semana pasada; **to be no b. than ...,** no ser más que ...; **to get b.,** mejorar. 2 *(healthier)* mejor (de salud). 3 **b. off,** *(better)* mejor; *(richer)* más rico,-a; **you'd be b. off going home,** lo mejor es que te vayas a casa. 4 **the b. part of the day,** la mayor parte del día. II *adv (comp of well)* 1 mejor; **all the b., so much the b.,** tanto mejor; **b. and b.,** cada vez mejor; *prov* b. late than never, más vale tarde que nunca. 2 we had b. leave, más vale que nos vayamos. 3 to think b. of, *(plan)* cambiar de. III *n* mejor; a change for the b., una mejora; to get the b. of sb, vencer a algn. IV *vtr* 1 *(improve)* mejorar. 2 *(surpass)* superar.

betting ['betɪŋ] *n* apuestas *fpl*; GB b. shop, quiosco *m* de apuestas.

between [bɪ'twiːn] I *prep* entre; b. you and me, entre nosotros; closed b. 1 and 2, cerrado de 1 a 2. II *adv* in b., *(position)* en medio; *(time)* entretanto, mientras (tanto).

beverage ['bevərɪdʒ] *n* bebida *f*.

bevy ['bevɪ] *n* bandada *f*.

beware [bɪ'weər] *vi* tener cuidado (of, con); b.!, ¡cuidado!; 'b. of the dog', *(sign)* 'cuidado con el perro'.

bewildered [bɪ'wɪldəd] *adj* desconcertado,-a.

bewilderment [bɪ'wɪldəmənt] *n* desconcierto *m*.

bewitching [bɪ'wɪtʃɪŋ] *adj* fascinador,- a.

beyond [bɪ'jɒnd] I *prep* más allá de; b. belief, increíble; b. doubt, sin lugar a dudas; it is b. me why ..., no comprendo por qué ...; it's b. a joke, eso ya no tiene gracia; she is b. caring, ya no le importa; this task is b. me, no puedo con esta tarea. II *adv* más allá, más lejos.

bias ['baɪəs] *n* *(tendency)* tendencia *f* (towards, hacia); *(prejudice)* prejuicio *m*.

bias(s)ed ['baɪəst] *adj* parcial; to be b. against sth/sb, tener prejuicio en contra de algo/algn.

bib [bɪb] *n* *(for baby)* babero *m*; *(of apron)* peto *m*.

Bible ['baɪbəl] *n* Biblia *f*; *sl* B. basher, B. thumper, evangelista *mf*.

bibliography [bɪblɪ'ɒgrəfɪ] *n* bibliografía *f*.

bicarbonate [baɪ'kɑːbənɪt] *n* bicarbonato *m*; b. of soda, bicarbonato sódico.

biceps ['baɪseps] *n* bíceps *m*.

bicker ['bɪkər] *vi* reñir.

bicycle ['baɪsɪkəl] *n* bicicleta *f*; b. pump, bomba *f* (de aire); to go by b., ir en bicicleta.

bid [bɪd] I *vtr* (*pt* bid *or* bade; *pp* bid *or* bidden) ['bɪdən]) 1 *(say)* decir; to b. sb farewell, despedirse de algn. 2 *(command)* mandar, ordenar; she bade him be quiet, le mandó que se callase. 3 *(invite)* invitar; he bade me sit down, me invitó a sentarme. 4 *(at auction)* (*pt* & *pp* bid) pujar. II *vi* *(at auction)* pujar (for, por). III *n* 1 *(offer)* oferta *f*. 2 *(at auction)* puja *f*. 3 *(attempt)* intento *m*, tentativa *f*.

bidder ['bɪdər] *n* the highest b., el mejor postor.

bidding ['bɪdɪŋ] *n* 1 *(at auction)* puja *f*. 2 *(order)* orden *f*; to do sb's b., cumplir la orden de algn.

bide [baɪd] *vtr* (*pt* bided *or* bode; *pp* bided) esperar; to b. one's time, esperar el momento oportuno.

bidet ['biːdeɪ] *n* bidé *m*.

bifocal [baɪ'fəʊkəl] I *adj* bifocal. II *npl* bifocals lentes *fpl* bifocales.

big [bɪg] I *adj* (bigger, biggest) grande (gran *before sing noun*); a b. clock, un reloj grande; a b. surprise, una gran sorpresa; my b. brother, mi hermano mayor; *fam iron* b. deal!, ¿y qué?; b. business, los grandes negocios; b. dipper, montaña rusa; *Astron US* B. Dipper, Osa *f* Mayor; b. toe, dedo gordo del pie; *fam* b. gun, b. shot, pez gordo; *fam* to make the b. time, tener éxito; *fam* b. top, carpa *f*. II *adv* 1 *(on a grand scale)* a lo grande. 2 *(well)* de manera excepcional.

bigamy ['bɪgəmɪ] *n* bigamia *f*.

bighead ['bɪghed] *n* *fam* creído,-a *m,f*, engreído,-a *m,f*.

bigheaded [bɪg'hedɪd] *adj* creído,-a, engreído,-a.

bigot ['bɪgət] *n* intolerante *mf*.

bigoted ['bɪgətɪd] *adj* intolerante.

bigotry ['bɪgətrɪ] *n* intolerancia *f*.

bigwig ['bɪgwɪg] *n* *fam* pez gordo.

bike [baɪk] *fam* *(abbr of bicycle or motorbike)* *n* *(bicycle)* bici *f*; *(motorcycle)* moto *f*; *sl* on your b.!, ¡vete de aquí!

bikini [bɪ'kiːnɪ] *n* bikini *m*.

bilateral [baɪ'lætərəl] *adj* bilateral.

bile [baɪl] *n* bilis *f*.

bilingual [baɪ'lɪŋgwəl] *adj* bilingüe.

bill¹ [bɪl] I *n* 1 *(for gas etc)* factura *f*, recibo *m*. 2 *esp GB* *(in restaurant)* cuenta *f*. 3 *Parl* proyecto *m* de ley. 4 *US* *(banknote)* billete *m* de banco. 5 *(poster)* cartel *m*; on the b., en cartel; 'post no bills', 'prohibido fijar carteles'; *Theat* to top the b., encabezar el reparto; b. of exchange, letra *f* de cambio; *Pol* B. of Rights, declaración *f* de derechos. II *vtr* 1 *(send bill to)* facturar. 2 *Theat* programar.

bill² [bɪl] *n* *(of bird)* pico *m*.

Bill [bɪl] *n* *dimin of* William; GB *sl* the Old B., la poli.

billboard ['bɪlbɔːd] *n* *US* *(hoarding)* cartelera *f*.

billet ['bɪlɪt] I *n* alojamiento *m*. II *vtr* alojar.

billfold ['bɪlfəʊld] *n* *US* cartera *f*, billetero *m*.

billiards ['bɪljədz] *n* billar *m*.

billion ['bɪljən] *n* *US* mil millones *mpl*; GB *(former use)* billón *m*.

billionaire [bɪljə'neər] *n* multimillonario,-a *m,f*.

billow ['bɪləʊ] I *n* *(of water)* ola *f*; *(of smoke)* nube *f*. II *vi* *(sea)* ondear; *(sail)* hincharse.

billy goat ['bɪlɪgəʊt] *n* macho cabrío.

bin [bɪn] *n* *(for storage)* cajón *m*; bread b., panera *f*; (rubbish) b., cubo *m* de la basura.

binary ['baɪnərɪ] *adj* **b. number**, número binario.

bind [baɪnd] *vtr* (*pt & pp* **bound**) 1 (*tie up*) atar. 2 *Med* (*bandage*) vendar. 3 (*book*) encuadernar. 4 (*require*) obligar. 5 (*join etc*) unir. ◆**bind over** *vtr Jur* obligar legalmente.

binder ['baɪndər] *n* (*file*) carpeta *f*.

binding ['baɪndɪŋ] *adj* (*promise*) comprometedor,-a; (*contract*) vinculante.

binge [bɪndʒ] *n fam* borrachera *f*; **to go on a b.**, irse de juerga.

bingo ['bɪŋgəʊ] *n* bingo *m*.

binoculars [bɪ'nɒkjʊləz] *npl* prismáticos *mpl*, gemelos *mpl*.

biochemistry [baɪəʊ'kemɪstrɪ] *n* bioquímica *f*.

biodegradable [baɪəʊdɪ'greɪdəbəl] *adj* biodegradable.

biography [baɪ'ɒgrəfɪ] *n* biografía *f*.

biological [baɪə'lɒdʒɪkəl] *adj* biológico, -a; **b. warfare**, guerra biológica.

biologist [baɪ'ɒlədʒɪst] *n* biólogo,-a *m,f*.

biology [baɪ'ɒlədʒɪ] *n* biología *f*.

biorhythm ['baɪəʊrɪðəm] *n* biorritmo *m*.

biosphere ['baɪəsfɪər] *n* biosfera *f*.

birch [bɜ:tʃ] **I** *n* 1 *Bot* abedul *m*. 2 (*rod*) vara *f* (de abedul). **II** *vtr* azotar.

bird [bɜ:d] *n* 1 pájaro *m*, ave *f*; *fig* **to kill two birds with one stone**, matar dos pájaros de un tiro; **they're birds of a feather**, son tal para cual; **b. of prey**, ave de rapiña. 2 *GB sl* (*girl*) tía *f*, chica *f*.

birdcage ['bɜ:dkeɪdʒ] *n* jaula *f*.

birdie ['bɜ:dɪ] *n Golf* birdie *m*.

bird's-eye view [bɜ:dzaɪ'vju:] *n* vista *f* de pájaro.

bird-watcher ['bɜ:dwɒtʃər] *n* ornitólogo,-a *m,f*.

Biro® ['baɪrəʊ] *n fam* boli *m*.

birth [bɜ:θ] *n* 1 nacimiento *m*; (*childbirth*) parto *m*; **by b.**, de nacimiento; **to give b. to a child**, dar a luz a un niño; **b. certificate**, partida *f* de nacimiento; **b. control**, (*family planning*) control *m* de la natalidad; (*contraception*) métodos anticonceptivos; **b. rate**, índice *m* de natalidad. 2 **of noble b.**, (*parentage*) de noble linaje.

birthday ['bɜ:deɪ] *n* cumpleaños *m inv*.

birthmark ['bɜ:θmɑ:k] *n* antojo *m*.

birthplace ['bɜ:θpleɪs] *n* lugar *m* de nacimiento.

Biscay ['bɪskeɪ] *n* Vizcaya; **the Bay of B.**, el golfo de Vizcaya.

biscuit ['bɪskɪt] *n* galleta *f*; (*muffin*) bollo *m*, bizcocho *m*; *fam* **that really takes the b.!**, ¡eso ya es el colmo!

bisect [baɪ'sekt] *vtr* bisegmentar; *Geom* bisecar.

bisexual [baɪ'seksjʊəl] *adj* bisexual.

bishop ['bɪʃəp] *n* 1 *Rel* obispo *m*. 2 *Chess* alfil *m*.

bison ['baɪsən] *n inv* bisonte *m*.

bit¹ [bɪt] *n* 1 (*small piece*) trozo *m*, pedazo *m*; **to smash sth to bits**, hacer añicos algo; *fig* **thrilled to bits**, muy emocionado,-a; *fig* **to do one's b.**, poner de su parte. 2 (*small quantity*) poco *m*; **a b. of sugar**, un poco de azúcar; **a b. of advice**, un consejo; **a b. of news**, una noticia; **bits and pieces**, trastos *mpl*; *fig* **b. by b.**, poco a poco. 3 **a b.**, (*slightly*) un poco; **a b. longer**, un ratito más; **a b. worried**, un poco preocupado. 4 (*coin*) moneda *f*.

bit² [bɪt] *n* (*of tool*) broca *f*.

bit³ [bɪt] *n Comput* bit *m*.

bit⁴ [bɪt] *pt* → **bite**.

bitch [bɪtʃ] **I** *n* 1 *Zool* (*female*) hembra *f*; (*dog*) perra *f*. 2 *fam* (*spiteful woman*) bruja *f*. **II** *vi fam* **to b. (about)**, (*criticize*) criticar.

bitchy ['bɪtʃɪ] *adj fam* (*spiteful*) maldiciente; (*malicious*) malicioso,-a; (*malevolent*) malintencionado,-a.

bite [baɪt] **I** *n* 1 (*act*) mordisco *m*. 2 (*wound*) mordedura *f*; (*insect*) **b.**, picadura *f*. 3 (*mouthful*) bocado *m*. 4 *fam* (*snack*) bocado *m*. **II** *vtr* (*pt* **bit**; *pp* **bitten**) morder; (*insect*) picar; **to b. one's nails**, morderse las uñas; *fig* **to b. the dust**, (*suffer defeat*) morder el polvo; (*die*) palmarla; *fam* **to b. sb's head off**, echarle una bronca a algn. **III** *vi* 1 morder; (*insect*) picar. 2 *fig* (*take effect*) surtir efecto. 3 *Fishing* picar.

biting ['baɪtɪŋ] *adj* (*wind*) cortante; *fig* (*criticism*) mordaz.

bitten ['bɪtən] *pp* → **bite**.

bitter ['bɪtər] **I** *adj* 1 amargo,-a. 2 (*weather*) glacial; (*wind*) cortante. 3 (*person*) amargado,-a. 4 (*struggle*) enconado,-a; (*hatred*) implacable. **II** *n* 1 (*beer*) cerveza amarga. 2 **bitters**, bíter *m*. ◆**bitterly** *adv* **she was b. disappointed**, sufrió una terrible decepción.

bitterness ['bɪtənɪs] *n* 1 amargura *f*. 2 (*of weather*) crudeza *f*. 3 (*of person*) rencor *m*.

bittersweet [bɪtə'swi:t] *adj* agridulce.

bitumen ['bɪtjʊmɪn] *n* betún *m*.

bizarre [bɪ'zɑ:r] *adj* (*odd*) extraño,-a; (*eccentric*) estrafalario,-a.

blab [blæb] *vi fam* parlotear; (*let out a secret*) chivarse.

black [blæk] **I** *adj* 1 (*colour*) negro,-a; **a b. and white television**, un televisor en blanco y negro; *fig* **b. and blue**, amoratado,-a; **to put sth down in b. and white**, poner algo por escrito; *Av* **b. box**, caja negra; **b. coffee**, café solo; **b. eye**, ojo morado; **b. hole**, agujero negro; **b. humour**, humor negro; **b. magic**, magia negra; **b. market**, mercado negro; **b. pudding**, morcilla *f*; **B. Sea**, Mar Negro; *Aut* **b. spot**, punto negro; *GB* **the B. Country**, la región de los Midlands; *fig* **b.**

sheep, oveja negra. **2** (*gloomy*) negro,-a; *fig* **a b. day,** un día aciago. **II** *n* **1** (*colour*) negro *m*. **2** (*person*) negro,-a *m,f*. **III** *vtr* **1** (*make black*) ennegrecer. **2** (*polish*) lustrar. **3** (*boycott*) boicotear. ◆**black out I** *vtr* **1** (*extinguish lights in*) apagar las luces de. **2** (*censor*) censurar. **II** *vi* (*faint*) desmayarse.

blackberry ['blækbərɪ] *n* zarzamora *f*.

blackbird ['blækbɜːd] *n* mirlo *m*.

blackboard ['blækbɔːd] *n* pizarra *f*, encerado *m*.

blackcurrant [blæk'kʌrənt] *n* grosella negra.

blacken ['blækən] *vtr* **1** (*make black*) ennegrecer. **2** *fig* (*defame*) manchar.

blackhead ['blækhed] *n* espinilla *f*.

blackjack ['blækdʒæk] *n* *Cards* veintiuna *f*.

blackleg ['blækleg] *n* esquirol *m*.

blacklist ['blæklɪst] *n* lista negra.

blackmail ['blækmeɪl] **I** *n* chantaje *m*. **II** *vtr* chantajear.

blackout ['blækaʊt] *n* **1** (*of lights*) apagón *m*. **2** *Rad TV* censura *f*. **3** (*fainting*) pérdida *f* de conocimiento.

blacksmith ['blæksmɪθ] *n* herrero *m*.

bladder ['blædər] *n* vejiga *f*; **gall b.,** vesícula *f* biliar.

blade [bleɪd] *n* **1** (*of grass*) brizna *f*. **2** (*of knife etc*) hoja *f*. **3** (*of propeller, oar*) pala *f*.

blame [bleɪm] **I** *n* culpa *f*; **to take the b. for sth,** asumir la responsabilidad de algo. **II** *vtr* echar la culpa a; **he is to b.,** él tiene la culpa.

blameless ['bleɪmlɪs] *adj* (*person*) inocente; (*conduct*) intachable.

blancmange [blə'mɒnʒ] *n* tipo de budín *m* dulce.

bland [blænd] *adj* (*climate*) suave; (*food*) soso,-a.

blank [blæŋk] **I** *adj* **1** (*without writing*) en blanco; *Fin* **b. cheque,** cheque *m* en blanco. **2** (*empty*) vacío,-a; **a. b. look,** una mirada inexpresiva; **a b. refusal,** (*absolute*) una negativa rotunda. **II** *n* **1** (*space*) espacio *m* en blanco; **to draw a b.,** no tener éxito. **2** *Mil* cartucho *m* de fogueo. **3** *US* (*form*) impreso *m*.

blanket ['blæŋkɪt] **I** *n* manta *f*; *fig* capa *f*. **II** *adj* general.

blare [bleər] *vi* resonar. ◆**blare out** *vtr* pregonar.

blasé ['blɑːzeɪ] *adj* de vuelta (de todo).

blasphemous ['blæsfɪməs] *adj* blasfemo,-a.

blasphemy ['blæsfɪmɪ] *n* blasfemia *f*.

blast [blɑːst] **I** *n* **1** (*of wind*) ráfaga *f*. **2** (*of horn etc*) toque *m*; **at full b.,** a toda marcha. **3** (*explosion*) explosión *f*; **b. furnace,** alto horno. **4** (*shock wave*) onda *f* de choque. **II** *vtr* **1** (*blow up*) volar; *fam* **b. (it)!,** ¡maldito sea! **2** *fig* (*destroy*) arruinar. **3** *fig*

(*criticize*) criticar.

blasted ['blɑːstɪd] *adj* maldito,-a.

blast-off ['blɑːstɒf] *n* despegue *m*.

blatant ['bleɪtənt] *adj* (*very obvious*) evidente; (*shameless*) descarado,-a; **a b. lie,** una mentira patente.

blaze¹ [bleɪz] **I** *n* **1** (*burst of flame*) llamarada *f*. **2** (*fierce fire*) incendio *m*. **3** (*of sun*) resplandor *m*. **4** *fig* (*of anger*) arranque *m*. **II** *vi* **1** (*fire*) arder. **2** (*sun etc*) brillar.

blaze² [bleɪz] *vtr* **to b. a trail,** abrir un camino.

blazer ['bleɪzər] *n* chaqueta *f* sport.

bleach [bliːtʃ] **I** *n* (*household*) lejía *f*. **II** *vtr* **1** (*whiten*) blanquear; (*fade*) descolorir. **2** (*hair*) decolorar.

bleachers ['bliːtʃəz] *npl* *US* *Sport* (*seats*) gradas *fpl*.

bleak [bliːk] *adj* **1** (*countryside*) desolado, -a. **2** (*weather*) desapacible. **3** (*future*) poco prometedor,-a.

bleary ['blɪərɪ] *adj* (**blearier, bleariest**) (*eyes*) (*due to tears*) lloroso,-a; (*due to tiredness*) cansado,-a.

bleary-eyed [blɪərɪ'aɪd] *adj* con los ojos llorosos *or* cansados.

bleat [bliːt] **I** *n* balido *m*. **II** *vi* (*animal*) balar.

bled [bled] *pt & pp* → **bleed.**

bleed [bliːd] **I** *vi* (*pt & pp* **bled**) sangrar. **II** *vtr* *Med* sangrar; *fam* **to b. sb dry,** sacarle a algn hasta el último céntimo.

bleeding ['bliːdɪŋ] **I** *n* (*loss of blood*) pérdida *f* de sangre. **II** *adj* **1** *Med* sangrante. **2** *sl offens* puñetero,-a.

bleep [bliːp] **I** *n* bip *m*, pitido *m*. **II** *vi* pitar.

bleeper ['bliːpər] *n* *fam* busca *m*, buscapersonas *m inv*.

blemish ['blemɪʃ] *n* (*flaw*) defecto *m*; (*on fruit*) maca *f*; *fig* mancha *f*; *fig* **without b.,** sin tacha.

blend [blend] **I** *n* mezcla *f*. **II** *vtr* (*mix*) mezclar; (*colours*) armonizar. **III** *vi* (*mix*) mezclarse; (*colours*) armonizar.

blender ['blendər] *n* licuadora *f*.

bless [bles] *vtr* (*pt & pp* **blessed** *or* **blest**) **1** bendecir; **b. you!,** (*after a sneeze*) ¡Jesús! **2** **blessed with good eyesight,** dotado,-a de buena vista.

blessing ['blesɪŋ] *n* bendición *f*; (*advantage*) ventaja *f*; **a mixed b.,** una ventaja relativa.

blew [bluː] *pt* → **blow.**

blight [blaɪt] **I** *n* plaga *f*. **II** *vtr* *fig* (*spoil*) arruinar; (*frustrate*) frustrar.

blimey ['blaɪmɪ] *interj* *fam* ¡caramba!, ¡caray!

blind [blaɪnd] **I** *adj* ciego,-a; **a b. man,** un ciego; **a b. woman,** una ciega; *fig* **b. faith,** fe ciega; *fig* **to turn a b. eye,** hacer la vista gorda; **b. alley,** callejón *m* sin salida; *Aut* **b. corner,** curva *f* sin visibilidad; **b. spot,** ángulo muerto; *fam* **b.**

date, cita *f* a ciegas. **II** *adv* a ciegas; *fam* **to get b. drunk**, agarrar una curda. **III** *n* 1 (*on window*) persiana *f*. 2 *pl* **the b.**, los ciegos. **IV** *vtr* 1 cegar, dejar ciego; *fig* **blinded by ambition**, cegado por la ambición. 2 (*dazzle*) deslumbrar.

blinders ['blaɪndəz] *npl US* anteojeras *fpl*.

blindfold ['blaɪndfəʊld] **I** *n* venda *f*. **II** *vtr* vendar los ojos a.

blinding ['blaɪndɪŋ] *adj* cegador,-a, deslumbrante.

blindly ['blaɪndlɪ] *adv* a ciegas, ciegamente.

blindness ['blaɪndnɪs] *n* ceguera *f*.

blink [blɪŋk] *vi* (*eyes*) pestañear; (*lights*) parpadear.

blinkered ['blɪŋkəd] *adj fig* de miras estrechas.

blinkers ['blɪŋkəz] *npl* (*on horse*) anteojeras *fpl*.

bliss [blɪs] *n* felicidad *f*; **it was b.!**, ¡fue maravilloso!

blissful ['blɪsfʊl] *adj* (*happy*) feliz; (*marvellous*) maravilloso,-a.

blister ['blɪstər] **I** *n* (*on skin*) ampolla *f*; (*on paint*) burbuja *f*. **II** *vi* ampollarse.

blithe [blaɪð] *adj* alegre. ◆**blithely** *adv* alegremente.

blitz [blɪts] **I** *n* bombardeo aéreo. **II** *vtr* bombardear.

blizzard ['blɪzəd] *n* ventisca *f*.

bloated ['bləʊtɪd] *adj* hinchado,-a.

blob [blɒb] *n* (*drop*) gota *f*; (*spot*) mancha *f*.

bloc [blɒk] *n Pol* bloque *m*.

block [blɒk] **I** *n* 1 bloque *m*; (*of wood*) taco *m*; **in b. capitals**, en mayúsculas. 2 **a b. of flats**, un bloque de pisos. 3 (*group of buildings*) manzana *f*. 4 (*obstruction*) bloqueo *m*. 5 *Fin* **a b. of shares**, un paquete de acciones. 6 *fam* (*head*) coco *m*. **II** *vtr* 1 (*obstruct*) obstruir; *Aut* '**road blocked**', 'carretera cortada'; **to b. the way**, cerrar el paso. 2 *Sport* (*player*) obstaculizar. 3 *Fin Parl* bloquear. ◆**block up** *vtr* bloquear, obstruir; **to get blocked up**, (*pipe*) obstruirse.

blockade [blɒ'keɪd] *n* bloqueo *m*.

blockage ['blɒkɪdʒ] *n* bloqueo *m*, obstrucción *f*; (*traffic jam*) atasco *m*.

blockbuster ['blɒkbʌstər] *n fam* exitazo *m*; *Cin TV* gran éxito *m* de taquilla; (*book*) éxito de ventas.

bloke [bləʊk] *n fam* tío *m*, tipo *m*.

blond [blɒnd] *adj & n* rubio (*m*).

blonde [blɒnd] *adj & n* rubia (*f*).

blood [blʌd] *n* 1 sangre *f*; **b. bank**, banco *m* de sangre; **b. cell**, glóbulo *m*; **b. donor**, donante *mf* de sangre; **b. group**, grupo sanguíneo; **b. pressure**, tensión *f* arterial; **b. test**, análisis *m* de sangre; **b. transfusion**, transfusión *f* de sangre; **b. vessel**, vaso sanguíneo; **blue b.**, sangre azul; **high/low b. pressure**, hipertensión *f*/hipotensión *f*. 2 (*race*) sangre *f*, raza *f*.

bloodbath ['blʌdbɑːθ] *n fig* baño *m* de sangre.

bloodhound ['blʌdhaʊnd] *n* sabueso *m*.

bloodshed ['blʌdʃed] *n* derramamiento *m* de sangre.

bloodshot ['blʌdʃɒt] *adj* inyectado,-a de sangre.

bloodstream ['blʌdstriːm] *n* corriente *f* sanguínea.

bloodthirsty ['blʌdθɜːstɪ] *adj* sanguinario,-a.

bloody ['blʌdɪ] **I** *adj* (**bloodier, bloodiest**) 1 (*battle*) sangriento,-a. 2 (*bloodstained*) manchado,-a de sangre. 3 *sl* (*damned*) condenado,-a, puñetero,-a. **II** *adv sl* **it's b. difficult**, ¡joder, qué difícil!; **not b. likely!**, ¡ni de coña!

bloody-minded [blʌdɪ'maɪndɪd] *adj fam* terco,-a.

bloom [bluːm] **I** *n* 1 (*flower*) flor *f*; **in full b.**, en flor. 2 (*on fruit*) vello *m*. **II** *vi* (*blossom*) florecer.

blooming ['bluːmɪŋ] *adj* 1 (*blossoming*) floreciente. 2 *fam euph* (*damned*) maldito,-a, condenado,-a.

blossom ['blɒsəm] **I** *n* (*flower*) flor *f*. **II** *vi* florecer; *fig* **to b. out**, alcanzar la plenitud.

blot [blɒt] **I** *n* (*of ink*) borrón *m*; *fig* mancha *f*. **II** *vtr* 1 (*with ink*) emborronar. 2 (*dry*) secar. **III** *vi* (*ink*) correrse. ◆**blot out** *vtr* (*memories*) borrar; (*view*) ocultar.

blotchy ['blɒtʃɪ] *adj* (*skin etc*) enrojecido,-a; (*paint etc*) cubierto,-a de manchas.

blotting-paper ['blɒtɪŋpeɪpər] *n* papel *m* secante.

blouse [blaʊz] *n* blusa *f*.

blow[1] [bləʊ] *n* golpe *m*; **to come to blows**, llegar a las manos; **it came as a terrible b.**, fue un duro golpe.

blow[2] [bləʊ] **I** *vi* (*pt* **blew**, *pp* **blown**) 1 (*wind*) soplar; **to b. shut**, cerrarse de golpe. 2 (*fuse*) fundirse. 3 (*tyre*) reventar. **II** *vtr* 1 (*kiss*) mandar. 2 (*trumpet etc*) tocar; *fig* **to b. one's own trumpet**, darse bombo. 3 (*one's nose*) sonarse. 4 (*fuse*) fundir. 5 *fam* (*waste*) despilfarrar. 6 *fam* (*chances*) dar al traste con. 7 (*explode*) volar; *fig* **to b. sb's cover**, descubrir la tapadera de algn; *fam* **to b. one's top**, salirse de sus casillas. ◆**blow away** → **blow off**. ◆**blow down** *vtr* derribar. ◆**blow off** I *vtr* (*by wind*) llevarse. II *vi* (*hat*) salir volando. ◆**blow out** I *vtr* apagar. II *vi* apagarse. ◆**blow over** *vi* (*storm*) calmarse; (*scandal*) olvidarse. ◆**blow up** I *vtr* 1 (*building*) volar. 2 (*inflate*) inflar. 3 *Phot* ampliar. II *vi* (*explode*) explotar.

blowlamp ['bləʊlæmp] *n* soplete *m*.

blown [bləʊn] *pp* → **blow**.

blowout ['bləʊaʊt] *n Aut* reventón *m*; *sl* comilona *f*.

blowtorch ['bləʊtɔːtʃ] *n US* soplete *m*.

blow-up ['bləʊʌp] *n Phot* ampliación *f*.

blubber ['blʌbər] I *n* grasa *f* de ballena. II *vi fam* llorar a moco tendido.

bludgeon ['blʌdʒən] *vtr* aporrear; *fig* to **b. sb into doing sth,** forzar a algn a hacer algo.

blue [bluː] I *adj* 1 (*colour*) azul; *fig* **once in a b. moon,** de higos a brevas; *fam* **to scream b. murder,** gritar como un loco; **b. jeans,** vaqueros *mpl*, tejanos *mpl*. 2 (*sad*) triste; **to feel b.,** sentirse deprimido. 3 (*obscene*) verde; **b. joke,** chiste *m* verde. II *n* 1 (*colour*) azul *m*; *fam* **the boys in b.,** los maderos. 2 **out of the b.,** (*suddenly*) de repente; (*unexpectedly*) como llovido del cielo.

bluebell ['bluːbel] *n* campanilla *f*.

blueberry ['bluːbərɪ] *n* arándano *m*.

bluebottle ['bluːbɒtəl] *n* moscarda *f*, mosca *f* azul.

blue-collar ['bluːkɒlər] *adj* **b.-c. worker,** obrero,-a *m,f*.

blueprint ['bluːprɪnt] *n* anteproyecto *m*.

blues [bluːz] *n* 1 *Mus* **the b.,** el blues. 2 *fam* (*sadness*) tristeza *f*, melancolía *f*; **to have the b.,** sentirse deprimido.

bluetit ['bluːtɪt] *n* herrerillo *m* común.

bluff [blʌf] I *n* (*trick*) farol *m*; **to call sb's b.,** hacer que algn ponga sus cartas encima de la mesa. II *adj* (*abrupt*) brusco,-a; (*forthright*) francote,-a. III *vi* tirarse un farol; **to b. one's way through sth,** hacer colar algo.

blunder ['blʌndər] I *n* metedura *f* de pata; *fam* patinazo *m*. II *vi* meter la pata, pegar un patinazo.

blunt [blʌnt] I *adj* 1 (*knife*) desafilado,-a; (*pencil*) despuntado,-a; **b. instrument,** instrumento *m* contundente. 2 (*frank*) directo,-a, francote,-a; (*statement*) tajante. II *vtr* (*pencil*) despuntar; (*knife*) desafilar. ◆**bluntly** *adv* francamente.

blur [blɜːr] I *n* aspecto borroso. II *vtr* (*windows*) empañar; (*shape*) desdibujar; (*memory*) enturbiar.

blurb [blɜːb] *n* (*in book*) resumen *m*.

blurred [blɜːd] *adj* borroso,-a.

blurt [blɜːt] *vtr* to **b. out,** dejar escapar.

blush [blʌʃ] I *n* rubor *m*. II *vi* ruborizarse.

blusher ['blʌʃər] *n* colorete *m*.

blustery ['blʌstərɪ] *adj* borrascoso,-a.

boar [bɔːr] *n* verraco *m*; **wild b.,** jabalí *m*.

board [bɔːd] I *n* 1 (*plank*) tabla *f*. 2 (*work surface*) mesa *f*; (*blackboard*) pizarra *f*; (*for games*) tablero *m*. 3 (*meals*) pensión *f*; **full b.,** pensión completa; **b. and lodging,** casa *f* y comida. 4 (*committee*) junta *f*, consejo *m*; **b. of directors,** consejo de administración; **b. room,** sala *f* del consejo. 5 *Naut* **on b.,** a bordo. 6 *fig* **above b.,**

en regla; **across-the-b.,** general; **to let sth go by the b.,** abandonar algo. II *vtr* (*ship, plane etc*) embarcarse en, subir a. III *vi* 1 (*lodge*) alojarse. 2 (*at school*) estar interno,-a. ◆**board up** *vtr* tapar.

boarder ['bɔːdər] *n* 1 (*in boarding house*) huésped *mf*. 2 (*at school*) interno,-a *m,f*.

boarding ['bɔːdɪŋ] *n* 1 (*embarkation*) embarque *m*; **b. card, b. pass,** tarjeta *f* de embarque. 2 (*lodging*) alojamiento *m*, pensión *f*; **b. house,** pensión *f*; **b. school,** internado *m*.

boast [bəʊst] I *n* jactancia *f*, alarde *m*. II *vi* jactarse, alardear (**about,** de). III *vtr* presumir de, alardear de; **the town boasts an Olympic swimming pool,** la ciudad disfruta de una piscina olímpica.

boat [bəʊt] *n* barco *m*; (*small*) barca *f*, bote *m*; (*launch*) lancha *f*; (*large*) buque *m*; *fig* **we're all in the same b.,** todos estamos en el mismo barco; **fishing b.,** barco de pesca.

boater ['bəʊtər] *n* canotié *m*, canotier *m*.

boatswain ['bəʊsən] *n* contramaestre *m*.

boatyard ['bəʊtjɑːd] *n* astillero *m*.

bob [bɒb] I *n* 1 (*haircut*) pelo *m* a lo chico. 2 *fam inv* (*shilling*) chelín *m*. II *vi* to **b. up and down,** subir y bajar.

bobbin ['bɒbɪn] *n* (*of sewing machine*) canilla *f*; (*for lace-making*) bolillo *m*.

bobby ['bɒbɪ] *n fam* (*policeman*) poli *m*.

bobsleigh ['bɒbsleɪ] *n* bobsleigh *m*.

bode¹ [bəʊd] *pt → bide*.

bode² [bəʊd] *vtr & vi* presagiar; **to b. well/ill,** ser de buen/mal agüero.

bodice ['bɒdɪs] *n* 1 (*sleeveless undergarment*) corpiño *m*. 2 (*of dress*) cuerpo *m*.

bodily ['bɒdɪlɪ] I *adj* físico,-a; **b. harm,** daños *mpl* corporales. II *adv* **to carry sb b.,** llevar a algn en brazos.

body ['bɒdɪ] *n* 1 cuerpo *m*; **b. language,** expresión *f* corporal; **b. odour,** olor *m* corporal. 2 (*corpse*) cadáver *m*. 3 (*main part*) parte *f* principal. 4 *Aut* carrocería *f*; *Naut* casco *m*. 5 (*organization*) organismo *m*; (*profession*) cuerpo *m*; **the b. politic,** el estado. 6 (*group of people*) conjunto *m*, grupo *m*.

body-blow ['bɒdɪbləʊ] *n fig* duro golpe *m*.

body-builder ['bɒdɪbɪldər] *n* culturista *mf*.

body-building ['bɒdɪbɪldɪŋ] *n* culturismo *m*.

bodyguard ['bɒdɪgɑːd] *n* guardaespaldas *mf inv*.

bodywork ['bɒdɪwɜːk] *n Aut* carrocería *f*.

Boer ['bəʊər] *adj* **the B. War,** la guerra del Transvaal.

bog [bɒg] *n* 1 ciénaga *f*. 2 *sl* (*lavatory*) meódromo *m*. ◆**bog down** *vtr* **to get bogged down,** atascarse.

bogey ['bəʊgɪ] *n* 1 (*spectre*) espectro *m*, fantasma *m*. 2 (*bugbear*) pesadilla *f*. 3

Golf bogey *m.* **4** *sl (mucus)* moco *m.*

boggle ['bɒgəl] *vi fam* **the mind boggles,** ¡es alucinante!

bogus ['bəʊgəs] *adj* falso,-a; **b. company,** compañía fantasma.

boil¹ [bɔɪl] **I** *n* **to come to the b.,** empezar a hervir. **II** *vtr (water)* hervir; *(food)* cocer; *(egg)* cocer, pasar por agua. **III** *vi* hervir; *fig* **to b. with rage,** estar furioso. ◆**boil down** *vi* reducirse (**to,** a). ◆**boil over** *vi (milk)* salirse.

boil² [bɔɪl] *n Med* furúnculo *m.*

boiled [bɔɪld] *adj* **b. egg,** huevo cocido *or* pasado por agua.

boiler ['bɔɪlər] *n* caldera *f;* **b. suit,** mono *m.*

boiling ['bɔɪlɪŋ] *adj* **b. water,** agua hirviendo; **it's b. hot,** *(food)* quema; *(weather)* hace un calor agobiante; **b. point,** punto *m* de ebullición.

boisterous ['bɔɪstərəs] *adj* **1** *(person, party)* bullicioso,-a. **2** *(weather)* borrascoso,-a.

bold [bəʊld] *adj* **1** *(brave)* valiente. **2** *(daring)* audaz. **3** *(features)* marcado,-a; *Typ* **b. type,** negrita *f.* **4** *(impudent)* descarado,-a.

Bolivia [bə'lɪvɪə] *n* Bolivia.

Bolivian [bə'lɪvɪən] *adj & n* boliviano,-a *(m,f).*

bollard ['bɒlɑːd] *n Aut* baliza *f.*

bollocks ['bɒləks] *npl vulg* cojones *mpl;* **b.!,** *(disagreement)* ¡y un huevo!

Bolshevik ['bɒlʃəvɪk] *adj & n* bolchevique *(mf).*

bolster ['bəʊlstər] **I** *n (pillow)* cabezal *m,* travesaño *m.* **II** *vtr (strengthen)* reforzar; *(support)* apoyar.

bolt [bəʊlt] **I** *n* **1** *(on door)* cerrojo *m;* *(small)* pestillo *m.* **2** *Tech* perno *m,* tornillo *m.* **3** *(of lightning)* rayo *m.* **4** *(crossbow)* flecha *f.* **II** *vtr* **1** *(lock)* cerrar con cerrojo. **2** *Tech* sujetar con pernos. **3** *fam (food)* engullir. **III** *vi (person)* largarse; *(horse)* desbocarse. **IV** *adv* **b. upright,** derecho.

bomb [bɒm] **I** *n* bomba *f; GB sl* **to cost a b.,** costar un ojo de la cara; **b. disposal squad,** brigada *f* de artificieros; **b. scare,** amenaza *f* de bomba; **car b.,** cochebomba *m;* **letter b.,** carta-bomba *f.* **II** *vtr (city etc)* bombardear; *(by terrorists)* volar. **III** *vi fam* **to b. (along),** *(car)* ir a toda pastilla.

bombard [bɒm'bɑːd] *vtr* bombardear.

bombardment [bɒm'bɑːdmənt] *n* bombardeo *m.*

bombastic [bɒm'bæstɪk] *adj* rimbombante.

bomber ['bɒmər] *n* **1** *Av* bombardero *m;* **b. jacket,** cazadora *f.* **2** terrorista *mf* que coloca bombas.

bombshell ['bɒmʃel] *n* **1** *Mil* obús *m.* **2** *fig (surprise)* bomba *f.* **3** *fam* **a blonde b.,** una rubia explosiva.

bona fide [bəʊnə'faɪdɪ] *adj* **1** *(genuine)* auténtico,-a. **2** *(in good faith)* bienintencionado,-a.

bond [bɒnd] **I** *n* **1** *(link)* lazo *m,* vínculo *m.* **2** *Fin* bono *m.* **3** *Jur (bail)* fianza *f.* **4** *(binding agreement)* acuerdo *m.* **5** *(warehouse)* depósito *m;* **in b.,** en depósito. **6** *US (guarantee)* garantía *f.* **7 bonds,** *(shackles)* cadenas *fpl.* **II** *vtr* **1** *(join)* pegar. **2** *(merchandise)* poner en depósito.

bondage ['bɒndɪdʒ] *n* esclavitud *f.*

bone [bəʊn] **I** *n* hueso *m;* *(in fish)* espina *f; fig* **b. of contention,** manzana *f* de la discordia; *fig* **to make no bones about sth,** no andarse con rodeos en un asunto; **b. china,** porcelana fina. **2 bones,** *(remains)* restos *mpl;* **the bare bones,** lo esencial. **II** *vtr (meat)* deshuesar; *(fish)* quitar las espinas a. ◆**bone up on** *vtr fam* empollar.

bone-dry [bəʊn'draɪ] *adj* completamente seco,-a.

bone-idle [bəʊn'aɪdəl] *adj* gandul,-a.

bonfire ['bɒnfaɪər] *n* hoguera *f,* fogata *f;* **B. Night,** noche *f* del cinco de noviembre.

bonkers ['bɒŋkəz] *adj GB sl* chalado,-a.

bonnet ['bɒnɪt] *n* **1** *(child's)* gorra *f.* **2** *Aut* capó *m.*

bonus ['bəʊnəs] *n* **1** *(on wages)* prima *f.* **2** *Fin (on shares)* dividendo *m* extraordinario. **3** *GB Ins* beneficio *m.*

bony ['bəʊnɪ] *adj* (**bonier, boniest**) *(person)* huesudo,-a; *(fish)* lleno,-a de espinas.

boo [buː] **I** *interj* ¡bu!. **II** *n* abucheo *m.* **III** *vtr* abuchear.

boob [buːb] *n GB sl* **1** *(silly mistake)* patinazo *m.* **2 boobs,** *(breasts)* tetas *fpl.*

booby ['buːbɪ] *n* **b. prize,** premio *m* de consolación; **b. trap,** trampa *f;* *Mil* trampa explosiva.

boogie ['buːgɪ] *vi fam* bailar.

book [bʊk] **I** *n* **1** libro *m; fig* **in my b.,** según mi punto de vista; *fig* **by the b.,** según las reglas; **b. end,** sujetalibros *m inv; GB* **b. token,** vale *m* para comprar libros; **savings b.,** libreta *f* de ahorros. **2** *(of stamps)* carpeta *f;* *(of matches)* cajetilla *f.* **3** *Com* **books,** cuentas *fpl;* **to keep the books,** llevar las cuentas. **II** *vtr* **1** *(reserve)* reservar; *(return flight)* cerrar. **2** *(engage)* contratar. **3** *(by police)* poner una multa a. **4** *Ftb* amonestar. ◆**book into** *vtr (hotel)* reservar una habitación en. ◆**book out** *vi (of hotel)* marcharse. ◆**book up** *vtr* booked up, completo.

booking ['bʊkɪŋ] *n esp GB (reservation)* reserva *f;* **b. office,** taquilla *f.*

bookmaker ['bʊkmeɪkər] *n* corredor,-a *m,f* de apuestas.

bookseller ['bʊkselər] *n* librero,-a *m,f.*

bookshelf ['bʊkʃelf] *n* **bookshelves,** estantería *f sing.*

bookshop ['bʊkʃɒp] n librería f.
bookstall ['bʊkstɔːl] n quiosco m.
bookstore ['bʊkstɔːr] n US librería f.
bookworm ['bʊkwɜːm] n fam ratón m de biblioteca.
boom¹ [buːm] I n 1 (noise) estampido m, trueno m. 2 (sudden prosperity) boom m, auge m. II vi 1 (thunder) retumbar; (cannon) tronar. 2 (prosper) estar en auge.
boom² [buːm] n (of microphone) jirafa f.
boomerang ['buːməræŋ] n bumerang m, bumerán m.
booming ['buːmɪŋ] adj 1 (voice, thunder) que retumba. 2 (prosperous) en auge.
boon [buːn] n (blessing) bendición f.
boost [buːst] I n estímulo m, empujón m. II vtr 1 (increase) aumentar. 2 to b. sb's confidence, subirle la moral a algn. 3 (tourism, exports) fomentar. 4 (voltage) elevar.
booster ['buːstər] n 1 Elec elevador m de voltaje. 2 Rad TV (amplifier) amplificador m. 3 Med b. (shot), revacunación f.
boot¹ [buːt] I n 1 bota f; (short) botín m; fig he's too big for his boots, es muy creído; fam to put the b. in, pisotear; fam she got the b., la echaron (del trabajo); b. polish, betún m. 2 GB Aut maletero m. II vtr fam 1 Ftb (ball) chutar. 2 to b. (out), echar a patadas.
boot² [buːt] n to b., además.
bootblack ['buːtblæk] n esp US limpiabotas mf inv.
booth [buːð, buːθ] n 1 (in language lab etc) cabina f; telephone b., cabina telefónica. 2 (at fair) puesto m.
bootleg ['buːtleg] adj de contrabando.
bootlegger ['buːtlegər] n contrabandista m.
booty ['buːtɪ] n botín m.
booze [buːz] fam I n priva f. II vi privar.
bop [bɒp] I n 1 Mus be-bop m. 2 fam (dance) baile m. II vi fam (dance) bailar.
Bordeaux [bɔːˈdəʊ] n 1 (city) Burdeos. 2 (wine) burdeos m.
border ['bɔːdər] I n 1 borde m, margen m. 2 Sew ribete m. 3 (frontier) frontera f; b. town, pueblo fronterizo. 4 (flower bed) arriate m. II vtr Sew ribetear. ◆border on vtr 1 Geog lindar con. 2 fig rayar en.
borderline ['bɔːdəlaɪn] I n 1 (border) frontera f. 2 (dividing line) línea divisoria. II adj 1 (on the border) fronterizo,-a. 2 fig (case etc) dudoso,-a.
bore¹ [bɔːr] I vtr Tech taladrar, perforar. II n 1 Tech (hole) taladro m. 2 (of gun) calibre m.
bore² [bɔːr] I vtr aburrir. II n (person) pesado,-a m,f, pelma mf; (thing) lata f, rollo m; what a b.!, ¡qué rollo!
bore³ [bɔːr] pt → bear¹.
bored [bɔːd] adj aburrido,-a; to be b. stiff or to tears, estar aburrido,-a como una ostra.

boredom ['bɔːdəm] n aburrimiento m.
boring ['bɔːrɪŋ] adj (uninteresting) aburrido,-a; (tedious) pesado,-a, latoso,-a.
born [bɔːn] I pp → bear¹; to be b., nacer; I wasn't b. yesterday, no nací ayer. II adj (having natural ability) nato,-a; b. poet, poeta nato.
born-again ['bɔːnəgen] adj Rel converso,-a.
borne [bɔːn] pp → bear¹.
borough ['bʌrə] n 1 (town) ciudad f; US (municipality) municipio m. 2 esp GB (constituency) distrito m electoral.
borrow ['bɒrəʊ] I vtr 1 pedir or tomar prestado; can I b. your pen?, ¿me dejas tu bolígrafo? 2 (ideas etc) apropiarse. II vi pedir or tomar prestado.
borstal ['bɔːstəl] n GB fam reformatorio m.
bosom ['bʊzəm] n 1 (breast) pecho m; (breasts) pechos mpl; b. friend, amigo,-a m,f del alma. 2 fig seno m.
boss [bɒs] I n 1 (head) jefe,-a m,f; (factory owner etc) patrón,-ona m,f. 2 esp US Pol jefe m; pej cacique m. II vtr to b. sb about or around, mandar sobre algn.
bossy ['bɒsɪ] adj (bossier, bossiest) fam mandón,-ona.
bosun ['bəʊsən] n contramaestre m.
botanic(al) [bəˈtænɪk(əl)] adj botánico,-a; b. garden, jardín botánico.
botany ['bɒtənɪ] n botánica f.
botch [bɒtʃ] I vtr chapucear; a botched job, una chapuza. II n chapuza f.
both [bəʊθ] I adj ambos,-as, los dos, las dos; b. men are teachers, ambos son profesores; hold it with b. hands, sujétalo con las dos manos. II pron b. (of them), ambos,-as, los dos, las dos; b. of you, vosotros dos. III conj a la vez; b. England and Spain are in Europe, tanto Inglaterra como España están en Europa.
bother ['bɒðər] I vtr 1 (disturb) molestar; (be a nuisance to) dar la lata a. 2 (worry) preocupar; fam I can't be bothered, no tengo ganas. II vi molestarse; don't b. about me, no te preocupes por mí; he didn't b. shaving, no se molestó en afeitarse. III n 1 (disturbance) molestia f; (nuisance) lata f. 2 (trouble) problemas mpl. IV interj GB ¡maldito sea!
bothersome ['bɒðəsəm] adj molesto,-a.
bottle ['bɒtəl] I n 1 botella f; (of perfume, ink) frasco m; fam to hit the b., darle a la bebida; baby's b., biberón m. b. opener, abrebotellas m inv. 2 GB sl to have a lot of b., (nerve) tener muchas agallas. II vtr (wine) embotellar; (fruit) enfrascar. ◆bottle out vi GB sl encogerse. ◆bottle up vtr reprimir.
bottle-bank ['bɒtəlbæŋk] n contenedor m de vidrio.
bottled ['bɒtəld] adj (beer, wine) en botella, embotellado,-a; (fruit) envasado,-a.

bottle-green ['bɒtəlgriːn] *adj* verde botella.

bottleneck ['bɒtəlnek] *n Aut* embotellamiento *m*, atasco *m*.

bottom ['bɒtəm] **I** *adj* **1** (*lowest*) más bajo,-a; (*drawer, shelf*) de abayo; *Aut* **b. gear**, primera *f*. **2** (*last*) último,-a; **b. line**, *Fin* saldo *m* final; *fig* resultado *m* final. **II** *n* **1** parte *f* inferior; (*of sea, garden, street, box*) fondo *m*; (*of bottle*) culo *m*; (*of page, kill*) pie *m*; *Educ* **to be** (**at**) **the b. of the class**, ser el último *or* la última de la clase; *fam* **bottoms up!**, ¡salud! **2 to get to the b.** of a matter, llegar al meollo de una cuestión; **who is at the b. of all this?**, ¿quién está detrás de todo esto? **3** (*buttocks*) trasero *m*. ◆**bottom out** *vi Fin* tocar fondo.

bottomless ['bɒtəmlɪs] *adj* (*pit*) sin fondo; (*mystery*) insondable.

boudoir ['buːdwɑːʳ] *n* tocador *m*.

bough [baʊ] *n* rama *f*.

bought [bɔːt] *pt & pp* → **buy**.

bouillon ['buːjɒn] *n* caldo *m*.

boulder ['bəʊldəʳ] *n* canto rodado.

boulevard ['buːlvɑːʳ] *n* bulevar *m*.

bounce [baʊns] **I** *vi* **1** (*ball*) rebotar. **2** (*jump*) saltar. **3** *sl* (*cheque*) ser rechazado (por el banco). **II** *vtr* (*ball*) botar. **III** *n* **1** (*of ball*) bote *m*. **2** (*jump*) salto *m*. **3** (*energy*) vitalidad *f*. ◆**bounce back** *vi* (*recover health*) recuperarse, recobrarse.

bouncer ['baʊnsəʳ] *n sl* gorila *m*.

bound¹ [baʊnd] *adj* **1** (*tied up*) atado,-a. **2** (*book*) encuadernado,-a. **3** (*obliged*) obligado,-a. **4 b.** (**up**), (*linked*) vinculado,-a (**with**, a). **5 it's b. to happen**, sucederá con toda seguridad; **it was b. to fail**, estaba destinado al fracaso.

bound² [baʊnd] **I** *vi* saltar. **II** *n* salto *m*.

bound³ [baʊnd] *adj* **b. for**, con destino a, rumbo a; **to be b. for**, dirigirse a.

boundary ['baʊndərɪ] *n* límite *m*.

boundless ['baʊndlɪs] *adj* ilimitado,-a, sin límites.

bounds [baʊndz] *npl* **beyond the b. of reality**, más allá de la realidad; **her ambition knows no b.**, su ambición no conoce límites; **the river is out of b.**, está prohibido bajar al río.

bounty ['baʊntɪ] *n* prima *f*, gratificación *f*.

bouquet [buːˈkeɪ, bəʊˈkeɪ] *n* **1** (*of flowers*) ramillete *m*. **2** [buːˈkeɪ] (*of wine*) aroma *m*, buqué *m*.

bourbon ['bɜːbən] *n* bourbon *m*.

bourgeois ['bʊəʒwɑː] *adj & n* burgués, -esa (*m,f*).

bourgeoisie [bʊəʒwɑːˈziː] *n* burguesía *f*.

bout [baʊt] *n* **1** (*of work*) turno *m*; (*of illness*) ataque *m*. **2** *Box* combate *m*.

boutique [buːˈtiːk] *n* boutique *f*, tienda *f*.

bow¹ [baʊ] **I** *vi* **1** hacer una reverencia. **2** (*give in*) ceder. **II** *n* (*with head, body*) reverencia *f*. ◆**bow out** *vi* retirarse (**of**, de).

bow² [bəʊ] **1** *n Sport & Mus* arco *m*; *fig* **to have more than one string to one's b.**, ser una persona de recursos. **2** (*knot*) lazo *m*; **b. tie**, pajarita *f*.

bow³ [baʊ] *n esp Naut* proa *f*.

bowel ['baʊəl] *n* **1** intestino *m*. **2 bowels**, entrañas *fpl*.

bowl¹ [bəʊl] *n* **1** (*dish*) cuenco *m*; (*for soup*) tazón *m*; (*for washing hands*) palangana *f*; (*for washing clothes, dishes*) barreño *m*; (*of toilet*) taza *f*. **2** *Geol* cuenca *f*.

bowl² [bəʊl] **I** *n* bola *f*. **II** *vtr* (*in cricket*) lanzar. **III** *vi* **1** (*play bowls*) jugar a los bolos. **2** (*in cricket*) lanzar la pelota. ◆**bowl along** *vi fam* (*car*) ir volando. ◆**bowl out** *vtr* (*in cricket*) eliminar. ◆**bowl over** *vtr* **1** (*knock down*) derribar. **2** *fig* (*astonish*) desconcertar.

bow-legged ['bəʊleg(ɪ)d] *adj* patizambo,-a.

bowler¹ ['bəʊləʳ] *n* (*in cricket*) lanzador,-a *m,f*.

bowler² ['bəʊləʳ] *n* (*hat*) bombín *m*.

bowling ['bəʊlɪŋ] *n* (*game*) bolos *mpl*; **b. alley**, bolera *f*; **b. green**, campo *m* de bolos.

bowls [bəʊlz] *npl Sport* bolos *mpl*.

box¹ [bɒks] *n* **1** caja *f*; (*large*) cajón *m*; (*of matches*) cajetilla *f*; **jewellery b.**, joyero *m*; *Theat* **b. office**, taquilla *f*; **b. office success**, éxito taquillero. **2** *Press* recuadro *m*. **3** *Jur* (*witness*) **b.**, barra *f* de los testigos. **4** *Theat* palco *m*. **5** *GB fam* (*television*) caja tonta *f*. **II** *vtr* (*pack*) embalar.

box² [bɒks] *Sport* **I** *vi* boxear. **II** *vtr* (*hit*) pegar; **to b. sb's ears**, dar un cachete a algn.

boxer ['bɒksəʳ] *n* **1** *Box* boxeador *m*. **2** (*dog*) bóxer *m*.

boxing ['bɒksɪŋ] *n* boxeo *m*; **b. ring**, cuadrilátero *m*.

Boxing Day ['bɒksɪŋdeɪ] *n GB* el día de San Esteban (26 de diciembre).

boxroom ['bɒksruːm] *n* trastero *m*.

boy [bɔɪ] *n* **1** (*child*) niño *m*, chico *m*; (*youth*) joven *m*; *fam* **oh b.!**, ¡vaya! **2** (*son*) hijo *m*.

boycott ['bɔɪkɒt] *n* **I** *n* boicot *m*. **II** *vtr* boicotear.

boyfriend ['bɔɪfrend] *n* novio *m*; (*live-in*) compañero *m*.

boyhood ['bɔɪhʊd] *n* niñez *f*, juventud *f*.

boyish ['bɔɪʃ] *adj* juvenil, de muchacho.

bra [brɑː] *n abbr of* **brassiere**.

brace [breɪs] *n* **1** (*clamp*) abrazadera *f*; (*of drill*) berbiquí *m*; (*for teeth*) aparato *m*. **2** (*of wood*) puntal *m*. **3** (*pair*) par *m*. **4** *GB* **braces**, tirantes *mpl*. **II** *vtr* **1** (*wall*) apuntalar. **2** (*strengthen*) reforzar. **3 to b. oneself**, prepararse (**for**, para). ◆**brace**

up *vi* cobrar ánimo.

bracelet |'breislit| *n* pulsera *f*.

bracing |'breisiŋ| *adj* (*wind*) fresco,-a; (*stimulating*) tonificante.

bracken |'brækən| *n* helecho *m*.

bracket |'brækit| I *n* 1 *Typ* (*round*) paréntesis *m*; (*square*) corchete *m*; (*curly*) llave *f*; **in brackets**, entre paréntesis. 2 (*support*) soporte *m*; (*for lamp*) brazo *m*; (*shelf*) repisa *f*. 3 (*for tax*) sector *m*. II *vtr* 1 *Ling* (*phrase etc*) poner entre paréntesis. 2 (*group together*) agrupar, juntar.

brag |bræg| *vi* jactarse (**about**, de).

braggart |'brægət| *n* fanfarrón,-ona *m,f*.

braid |breid| I *vtr* trenzar. II *n* 1 *Sew* galón *m*. 2 *esp US* (*plait*) trenza *f*.

Braille |breil| *n* Braille *m*.

brain |brein| *n* 1 cerebro *m*; **she's got cars on the b.**, está obsesionada por los coches; *Med* **b. death**, muerte *f* cerebral; *fig* **b. drain**, fuga *f* de cerebros; **b. wave**, idea *f* genial. 2 *fam* **brains**, inteligencia *f*; **to have brains**, ser inteligente; **b. trust**, grupo *m* de expertos. 3 *Culin* **brains**, sesos *mpl*.

brainchild |'breintʃaild| *n* invento *m*, idea *f* genial.

brainpower |'breinpauər| *n* capacidad *f* intelectual.

brainstorm |'breinstɔːm| *n* 1 (*outburst*) arranque *m*. 2 (*brain wave*) genialidad *f*, lluvia *f* de ideas.

brainwash |'breinwɒʃ| *vtr* lavar el cerebro a.

brainy |'breini| *adj* (**brainier, brainiest**) *fam* listo,-a.

braise |breiz| *vtr* cocer a fuego lento.

brake |breik| I *n* *Aut* (*also pl*) freno *m*; **b. drum**, tambor *m* del freno; **b. fluid**, líquido *m* de frenos; **b. light**, luz *f* de freno. II *vi* frenar, echar el freno.

bramble |'bræmbəl| *n* zarza *f*, zarzamora *f*.

bran |bræn| *n* salvado *m*.

branch |brɑːntʃ| I *n* (*of tree*) rama *f*; (*of road*) bifurcación *f*; (*of science etc*) ramo *m*; *Com* **b.** (*office*), sucursal *f*. II *vi* (*road*) bifurcarse. ◆**branch off** *vi* desviarse. ◆**branch out** *vi* diversificarse.

brand |brænd| I *n* 1 *Com* marca *f*; **b. name**, marca de fábrica. 2 (*type*) clase *f*. 3 (*on cattle*) hierro *m*. II *vtr* 1 (*animal*) marcar con hierro candente. 2 (*label*) tildar.

brandish |'brændiʃ| *vtr* blandir.

brand-new |brænd'njuː| *adj* flamante.

brandy |'brændi| *n* coñac *m*, brandy *m*.

brash |bræʃ| *adj* 1 (*impudent*) descarado, -a. 2 (*reckless*) temerario,-a. 3 (*loud, showy*) chillón,-ona.

brass |brɑːs| I *n* latón *m*; *sl* (*money*) pasta *f*; *Mus* instrumentos *mpl* de metal; **b. band**, banda *f* de metal.

brassiere |'bræziər| *n* sostén *m*, sujetador

m.

brat |bræt| *n* *fam* mocoso,-a *m,f*.

bravado |brə'vɑːdəʊ| *n* bravuconería *f*.

brave |breiv| I *adj* valiente, valeroso,-a. II *n* *US* (**Indian**) **b.**, guerrero *m* indio. III *vtr* 1 (*face*) hacer frente a. 2 (*defy*) desafiar. ◆**bravely** *adv* valientemente.

bravery |'breivəri| *n* valentía *f*, valor *m*.

bravo |brɑː'vəʊ| *interj* ¡bravo!

brawl |brɔːl| I *n* reyerta *f*. II *vi* pelearse.

brawn |brɔːn| *n* 1 (*strength*) fuerza física. 2 *Culin GB* carne *f* de cerdo adobada.

bray |brei| I *n* (*of donkey*) rebuzno *m*. II *vi* rebuznar.

brazen |'breizən| *adj* descarado,-a.

brazil |brə'zil| *n* **b. nut**, nuez *f* del Brasil.

Brazil |brə'zil| *n* (el) Brasil.

Brazilian |brə'ziliən| *adj & n* brasileño,-a (*m,f*).

breach |briːtʃ| I *n* 1 (*in wall*) brecha *f*. 2 (*violation*) incumplimiento *m*; **b. of confidence**, abuso *m* de confianza; **b. of contract**, incumplimiento de contrato; **b. of the law**, violación *f* de la ley; **b. of the peace**, alteración *f* del orden público. 3 (*in relations*) ruptura *f*. II *vtr* violar.

bread |bred| *n* 1 pan *m*; **b. and butter**, pan con mantequilla; *fig* **our daily b.**, el pan nuestro de cada día. 2 *sl* (*money*) pasta *f*, *Am* plata *f*.

breadboard |'bredbɔːd| *n* tabla *f* (para cortar el pan).

breadcrumb |'bredkrʌm| *n* miga *f* de pan; **breadcrumbs**, pan *m sing* rallado.

breadline |'bredlain| *n* *fam* miseria *f*; **to be on the b.**, vivir en la miseria.

breadth |bredθ| *n* 1 (*width*) anchura *f*; **it is two metres in b.**, tiene dos metros de ancho. 2 (*extent*) amplitud *f*.

breadwinner |'bredwinər| *n* cabeza *mf* de familia.

break |breik| I *vtr* (*pt* **broke**; *pp* **broken**) 1 romper; **to b. a leg**, romperse la pierna; **to b. a record**, batir un récord; **to b. even**, no tener ni ganancias ni pérdidas; *fig* **to b. one's back**, trabajar a tragajar; *fig* **to b. sb's heart**, partirle el corazón a algn; *fig* **to b. the ice**, romper el hielo. 2 (*fail to keep*) faltar a; **to b. a contract**, romper un contrato; **to b. the law**, violar la ley. 3 (*destroy*) destrozar; *Fin* arruinar. 4 (*interrupt*) interrumpir. 5 (*code*) descifrar. 6 (*fall*) amortiguar. 7 **she broke the news to him**, le comunicó la noticia.

II *vi* 1 romperse; (*clouds*) dispersarse; (*waves*) romper. 2 (*storm*) estallar. 3 (*voice*) cambiar. 4 (*health*) resentirse. 5 **when day breaks**, al rayar el alba. 6 (*story*) divulgarse.

III *n* 1 (*fracture*) rotura *f*; (*crack*) grieta *f*; (*opening*) abertura *f*. 2 (*in relationship*) ruptura *f*. 3 (*pause*) pausa *f*, descanso *m*; (*at school*) recreo *m*; **to take a b.**, descansar un rato; (holiday) tomar unos días libres; **without a b.**, sin parar. 4 fam (chance) oportunidad f; **a lucky b.**, un golpe de suerte.

◆**break away** vi 1 (become separate) desprenderse (from, de). 2 (escape) escaparse. ◆**break down** I vtr 1 (door) derribar. 2 (resistance) acabar con. 3 (costs) desglosar. II vi 1 Aut tener una avería. 2 (resistance) ceder. 3 (health) debilitarse. 4 (weep) ponerse a llorar. ◆**break in** I vtr acostumbrar; **to b. in a pair of shoes,** cogerle la forma a los zapatos. II vi (burglar) entrar por la fuerza. ◆**break into** vtr 1 (burgle) (house) allanar; (safe) forzar. 2 **to b. into song,** empezar a cantar. ◆**break off** I vtr partir. II vi 1 (become detached) desprenderse. 2 (talks) interrumpirse. 3 (stop) pararse. ◆**break out** vi 1 (prisoners) escaparse. 2 (war etc) estallar; **to b. out in a rash,** salirle a uno una erupción. ◆**break through** I vtr 1 (crowd) abrirse paso por; (cordon) romper. 2 (clouds) atravesar. II vi 1 (crowd) abrirse paso. 2 (sun) salir. ◆**break up** I vtr (object) romper; (car) desguazar; (crowd) disolver. II vi 1 (object) romperse. 2 (crowd) disolverse; (meeting) levantarse. 3 (relationship) fracasar; (couple) separarse. 4 Educ terminar. ◆**break with** vtr (past) romper con.

breakable ['breɪkəbəl] adj frágil.

breakage ['breɪkɪdʒ] n (breaking) rotura f.

breakaway ['breɪkəweɪ] adj disidente.

breakdown ['breɪkdaʊn] n 1 Aut avería f; **b. truck,** grúa f. 2 (nervous) **b.,** crisis f nerviosa. 3 (in communications) ruptura f. 4 (analysis) análisis m; Fin desglose m.

breaker ['breɪkər] n 1 (wave) ola f grande. 2 Tech trituradora f. 3 (switch) interruptor automático.

breakfast ['brekfəst] I n desayuno m; **to have b.,** desayunar. II vi desayunar.

break-in ['breɪkɪn] n robo m (con allanamiento de morada).

breaking ['breɪkɪŋ] n 1 rotura f; **b. point,** punto m de ruptura. 2 Jur **b. and entering,** allanamiento m de morada.

breakthrough ['breɪkθruː] n paso m adelante, avance m.

breakwater ['breɪkwɔːtər] n rompeolas m inv.

breast [brest] n (chest) pecho m; (of woman) pecho m, seno m; (of chicken etc) pechuga f; fig **to make a clean b. of it,** dar la cara.

breast-feed ['brestfiːd] vtr dar el pecho a, amamantar a.

breaststroke ['breststrəʊk] n braza f.

breath [breθ] n 1 aliento m; (breathing) respiración f; **in the same b.,** al mismo tiempo; **out of b.,** sin aliento; **to catch one's b.,** recobrar el aliento; **to draw b.,**

respirar; **under one's b.,** en voz baja; fig **to take sb's b. away,** dejar pasmado a algn; Aut **b. test,** alcoholemia f. 2 **to go out for a b. of fresh air,** salir a tomar el aire.

Breathalyzer® ['breθəlaɪzər] n GB alcoholímetro m.

breathe [briːð] I vtr respirar; **to b. a sigh of relief,** dar un suspiro de alivio. II vi respirar; **to b. in,** aspirar; **to b. out,** espirar; **to b. heavily,** resoplar.

breather ['briːðər] n fam (rest) descanso m.

breathing ['briːðɪŋ] n respiración f; **b. space,** pausa f, respiro m.

breathless ['breθlɪs] adj sin aliento, jadeante.

breathtaking ['breθteɪkɪŋ] adj impresionante.

breeches ['brɪtʃɪz, 'briːtʃɪz] npl bombachos mpl; **knee b., riding b.,** pantalones mpl de montar.

breed [briːd] I n (of animal) raza f; fig (class) clase f. II vtr (pt & pp bred) (animals) criar; fig (ideas) engendrar. III vi (animals) reproducirse.

breeder ['briːdər] n 1 (person) criador,-a m,f. 2 (fast) **b. reactor,** reactor m generador.

breeding ['briːdɪŋ] n 1 (of animals) cría f; fig **b. ground,** caldo m de cultivo. 2 (of person) educación f.

breeze [briːz] I n brisa f; Constr **b. block,** bloque m de cemento. II vi **to b. in/out,** entrar/salir despreocupadamente.

breezy ['briːzɪ] adj (breezier, breeziest) 1 (weather) ventoso,-a. 2 (person) despreocupado,-a.

brevity ['brevɪtɪ] n brevedad f.

brew [bruː] I vtr (beer) elaborar; (hot drink) preparar. II vi (tea) reposar; fig **a storm is brewing,** se prepara una tormenta; fam **something's brewing,** algo se está cociendo. III n 1 (of tea) infusión f; fam (of beer) birra f. 2 (magic potion) brebaje m.

brewer ['bruːər] n cervecero,-a m,f.

brewery ['bruːərɪ] n cervecería f.

brewing ['bruːɪŋ] I adj cervecero,-a. II n (of beer) elaboración f de la cerveza.

briar ['braɪər] n brezo m.

bribe [braɪb] I vtr sobornar. II n soborno m.

bribery ['braɪbərɪ] n soborno m.

bric-a-brac ['brɪkəbræk] n baratijas fpl.

brick [brɪk] n ladrillo m; fam (reliable person) persona f de confianza.

bricklayer ['brɪkleɪər] n albañil m.

brickwork ['brɪkwɜːk] n ladrillos mpl.

bridal ['braɪdəl] adj nupcial.

bride [braɪd] n novia f; **the b. and groom,** los novios.

bridegroom ['braɪdgruːm] n novio m.

bridesmaid ['braɪdzmeɪd] n dama f de

honor.

bridge¹ [brɪdʒ] **I** n puente m; (of nose) caballete m; (of ship) puente de mando. **II** vtr 1 (river) tender un puente sobre. 2 (gap) llenar; Fin **bridging loan**, crédito m a corto plazo.

bridge² [brɪdʒ] n Cards bridge m.

bridle ['braɪdəl] **I** n brida f; (bit) freno m; **b. path**, camino m de herradura. **II** vtr (horse) embridar.

brief [briːf] **I** adj 1 (short) breve. 2 (concise) conciso,-a. **II** n 1 (report) informe m; **in b.**, en resumen. 2 Mil instrucciones fpl. 4 **briefs**, (for men) calzoncillos mpl; (for women) bragas fpl. **III** vtr 1 (inform) informar. 2 (instruct) dar instrucciones a. ◆**briefly** adv brevemente; **as b. as possible**, con la mayor brevedad (posible).

briefcase ['briːfkeɪs] n cartera f, portafolios mpl.

briefing ['briːfɪŋ] n (meeting) reunión informativa.

brigade [brɪ'geɪd] n brigada f.

brigadier [brɪgə'dɪər] n general m de brigada.

bright [braɪt] adj 1 (light, sun, eyes) brillante; (colour) vivo,-a; (day) claro,-a. 2 (cheerful) alegre; **to look on the b. side**, mirar el lado bueno. 3 (clever) listo,-a, espabilado,-a. 4 (promising) prometedor, -a. ◆**brightly** adv brillantemente.

brighten ['braɪtən] vi (prospects) mejorarse; (face) iluminarse. ◆**brighten up** **I** vtr (room etc) alegrar. **II** vi (weather) despejarse; (person) animarse.

brightness ['braɪtnɪs] n 1 (of sun) resplandor m; (of day) claridad f; (of colour) viveza f. 2 (cleverness) inteligencia f.

brilliance ['brɪljəns] n 1 (of light) brillo m; (of colour) viveza f. 2 (of person) brillantez f.

brilliant ['brɪljənt] **I** adj brillante; (idea) genial; fam (very good) estupendo,-a. **II** n brillante m.

brim [brɪm] **I** n borde m; (of hat) ala f; **full to the b.**, lleno hasta el borde. **II** vi rebosar (with, de). ◆**brim over** rebosar.

brine [braɪn] n salmuera f.

bring [brɪŋ] vtr (pt & pp **brought**) 1 (carry sth to sb, take sth or sb with you) traer; **could you b. that book?**, ¿podrías traerme el libro? 2 (take to a different position) llevar; **the war brought hunger to many homes**, la guerra llevó el hambre a muchos hogares. 3 (cause) provocar; **he brought it upon himself**, se lo buscó. 4 (persuade) convencer; **how did they b. themselves to do it?**, ¿cómo llegaron a hacerlo? 5 (lead) llevar. 6 **to b. an action against**, acusar. ◆**bring about** vtr provocar. ◆**bring along** vtr traer. ◆**bring back** vtr 1 (return) devolver. 2 (reintroduce) volver a introducir. 3 (make one remember) traerle a la memoria. ◆**bring down** vtr 1 (from upstairs) bajar. 2 (government) derribar; Theat **to b. the house down**, echar el teatro abajo con los aplausos. 3 (reduce) rebajar. ◆**bring forward** vtr 1 (meeting etc) adelantar. 2 (present) presentar. 3 Fin **brought forward**, suma y sigue. ◆**bring in** vtr 1 (yield) dar. 2 (show in) hacer entrar. 3 (law etc) introducir; (fashion) lanzar. ◆**bring off** vtr lograr, conseguir. ◆**bring on** vtr provocar. ◆**bring out** vtr 1 (publish) publicar. 2 (reveal) recalcar; **he brings out the worst in me**, despierta lo peor que hay en mí. ◆**bring round** vtr 1 (revive) hacer volver en sí. 2 (persuade) convencer. ◆**bring to** vtr reanimar. ◆**bring up** vtr 1 (educate) criar, educar. 2 (subject) plantear. 3 (vomit) devolver.

brink [brɪŋk] n (edge) borde m; fig **on the b. of ruin**, al borde de la ruina; **on the b. of tears**, a punto de llorar.

brisk [brɪsk] adj enérgico,-a; (pace) rápido,-a; (trade) activo,-a; (weather) fresco,-a.

bristle ['brɪsəl] **I** n cerda f. **II** vi 1 erizarse. 2 (show anger) enfurecer (at, con). ◆**bristle with** vtr (be full of) estar lleno,-a de.

Brit [brɪt] n fam británico,-a m,f.

Britain ['brɪtən] n (Great) **B.**, Gran Bretaña.

British ['brɪtɪʃ] **I** adj británico,-a; **the B. Isles**, las Islas Británicas. **II** npl **the B.**, los británicos.

brittle ['brɪtəl] adj quebradizo,-a, frágil.

broach [brəʊtʃ] vtr (subject) abordar.

broad [brɔːd] **I** adj 1 (wide) ancho,-a; (large) extenso,-a. 2 **a b. hint**, (clear) una indirecta clara. 3 (daylight) pleno,-a. 4 (not detailed) general. 5 (accent) marcado,-a, cerrado,-a. **II** n US sl (woman) tía f. ◆**broadly** adv en términos generales.

broadcast ['brɔːdkɑːst] Rad TV **I** n emisión f. **II** vtr (pt & pp **broadcast**) emitir, transmitir.

broadcaster ['brɔːdkɑːstər] n locutor,-a m,f.

broadcasting ['brɔːdkɑːstɪŋ] n Rad radiodifusión f; TV transmisión f; Rad **b. station**, emisora f.

broaden ['brɔːdən] vtr ensanchar.

broad-minded [brɔːd'maɪndɪd] adj liberal, tolerante.

broadsheet ['brɔːdʃiːt] n folleto m.

broccoli ['brɒkəlɪ] n brécol m.

brochure ['brəʊʃər, 'brəʊʃjʊər] n folleto m.

broil [brɔɪl] vtr US asar a la parrilla.

broke [brəʊk] adj fam **to be (flat) b.**, estar sin blanca.

broken ['brəʊkən] adj 1 roto,-a; (machinery) averiado,-a; (leg) fracturado,-a. 2 (home) deshecho,-a; (person) destrozado, -a; (ground) accidentado,-a; to speak b. English, chapurrear el inglés.

broken-hearted [brəʊkən'hɑːtɪd] adj fig con el corazón destrozado.

broker ['brəʊkəʳ] n corredor m, agente mf de Bolsa.

brolly ['brɒlɪ] n fam paraguas m inv.

bronchitis [brɒŋ'kaɪtɪs] n bronquitis f.

bronze [brɒnz] I n bronce m. II adj (material) de bronce; (colour) bronceado,-a.

bronzed [brɒnzd] adj (suntanned) bronceado,-a.

brooch [brəʊtʃ] n broche m.

brood [bruːd] I n (birds) cría f; hum (children) prole m. II vi (hen) empollar; fig (ponder) rumiar; fig to b. over a problem, darle vueltas a un problema.

broody ['bruːdɪ] adj 1 fam (woman) con ganas de tener hijos. 2 (pensive) pensativo,-a. 3 (moody) melancólico,-a.

brook¹ [brʊk] n arroyo m.

brook² [brʊk] vtr (usu in negative) soportar, aguantar.

broom [bruːm] n 1 escoba f. 2 Bot retama f.

broomstick ['bruːmstɪk] n palo m de escoba.

Bros Com abbr of **Brothers**, Hermanos mpl, Hnos.

broth [brɒθ] n caldo m.

brothel ['brɒθəl] n burdel m.

brother ['brʌðəʳ] n hermano m; **brothers and sisters**, hermanos.

brotherhood ['brʌðəhʊd] n hermandad f.

brother-in-law ['brʌðərɪnlɔː] n cuñado m.

brotherly ['brʌðəlɪ] adj fraternal.

brought [brɔːt] pt & pp → **bring**.

brow [braʊ] n 1 (forehead) frente f. 2 (eyebrow) ceja f. 3 (of hill) cima f.

brown [braʊn] I adj 1 marrón; (hair, eyes) castaño,-a; **b. bread**, pan m integral; **b. paper**, papel m de estraza; **b. sugar**, azúcar moreno. 2 (tanned) moreno,-a. II n marrón m. III vtr Culin dorar; (tan) broncear.

Brownie ['braʊnɪ] n niña exploradora.

brownish ['braʊnɪʃ] adj pardusco,-a.

browse [braʊz] I vi (person in shop) mirar; (through book) hojear. II n to have a b., dar un vistazo (in, a).

bruise [bruːz] I n morado m, cardenal m. II vtr (body) contusionar; (fruit) estropear. III vi (body) magullarse; (fruit) estropearse.

brunch [brʌntʃ] n combinación f de desayuno y almuerzo.

brunette [bruː'net] adj & n morena (f).

brunt [brʌnt] n lo peor; **to bear the b.**, llevar el peso.

brush¹ [brʌʃ] n 1 (for hair, teeth) cepillo

m; Art pincel m; (for house-painting) brocha f. 2 (with the law) roce m. II vtr 1 cepillar; **to b. one's hair**, cepillarse el pelo; **to b. one's teeth**, cepillarse los dientes. 2 (touch lightly) rozar. III vi to b. against, rozar al pasar. ◆**brush aside** vtr dejar de lado. ◆**brush off** vtr ignorar. ◆**brush up** vtr repasar.

brush² [brʌʃ] n (undergrowth) broza f, maleza f.

brushwood ['brʌʃwʊd] n maleza f.

brusque [bruːsk, brʊsk] adj brusco,-a; (words) áspero,-a.

Brussels ['brʌsəlz] n Bruselas.

brutal ['bruːtəl] adj brutal, cruel.

brute [bruːt] I adj bruto,-a; **b. force**, fuerza bruta. II n (animal) bruto m; (person) bestia f.

BSc [biːes'siː] abbr of **Bachelor of Science**.

bubble ['bʌbəl] I n burbuja f; **b. bath**, espuma f de baño; **b. gum**, chicle m; **soap b.**, pompa f de jabón. II vi burbujear; Culin borbotear.

bubbly ['bʌblɪ] I adj (bubblier, bubbliest) efervescente. II n fam champán m, cava m.

buck¹ [bʌk] I n 1 Zool macho m; (male deer) ciervo m; (male goat) macho cabrío; fam to pass the b. to sb, echarle el muerto a algn. II vi (horse) corcovear. ◆**buck up** I vtr fam **b. your ideas up!**, ¡espabílate!. II vi (cheer up) animarse.

buck² [bʌk] n US fam dólar m.

bucket ['bʌkɪt] I n cubo m; fam **it rained buckets**, llovía a cántaros. II vi fam (rain) llover a cántaros.

buckle ['bʌkəl] I n hebilla f. II vtr abrochar con hebilla. III vi 1 (wall, metal) combarse. 2 (knees) doblarse.

bud [bʌd] I n (shoot) brote m; (flower) capullo m. II vi brotar; fig florecer.

Buddhism ['bʊdɪzəm] n budismo m.

budding ['bʌdɪŋ] adj en ciernes.

buddy ['bʌdɪ] n US fam amigote m, compinche m.

budge [bʌdʒ] vi 1 (move) moverse. 2 (yield) ceder.

budgerigar ['bʌdʒərɪgɑːʳ] n periquito m.

budget ['bʌdʒɪt] I n presupuesto m; Pol **the B.**, los presupuestos del Estado. II vi hacer un presupuesto (for, para).

budgie ['bʌdʒɪ] n fam → **budgerigar**.

buff¹ [bʌf] I & n (colour) color (m) de ante. II vtr dar brillo a.

buff² [bʌf] n fam (enthusiast) aficionado,-a m,f.

buffalo ['bʌfələʊ] n (pl **buffaloes** or **buffalo**) búfalo m.

buffer ['bʌfəʳ] I n 1 (device) amortiguador m; Rail tope m; **b. zone**, zona f de seguridad. 2 Comput memoria intermedia. II vtr amortiguar.

buffet¹ ['bʊfeɪ] n 1 (snack bar) bar m; (at

railway station) cantina *f*; *Rail* **b. car**, coche *m* restaurante. **2** (*self-service meal*) bufet *m* libre. **3** (*item of furniture*) aparador *m*.

buffet² ['bʌfɪt] *vtr* golpear.

buffoon [bə'fuːn] *n* bufón *m*, payaso *m*.

bug [bʌg] **I** *n* **1** (*insect*) bicho *m*. **2** *fam* (*microbe*) microbio *m*; **the flu b.**, el virus de la gripe. **3** (*hidden microphone*) micrófono oculto. **4** *Comput* error *m*. **II** *vtr fam* **1** **to b. a room**, ocultar micrófonos en una habitación; **to b. a phone**, pinchar un teléfono. **2** (*annoy*) fastidiar, molestar.

bugger ['bʌgə'] **I** *n* **1** sodomita *m*. **2** *sl offens* (*person*) gilipollas *mf inv*; (*thing*) coñazo *m*; **poor b.!**, ¡el pobre! **II** *interj sl offens* ¡joder!. **III** *vtr* sodomizar.
◆**bugger about** *vulg* **I** *vi* hacer chorradas. **II** *vtr* **they really buggered him about**, se las hicieron pasar canutas. ◆**bugger off** *vi sl offens* pirarse; **b. off!**, ¡vete a la mierda! ◆**bugger up** *vtr sl vulg* jorobar.

buggy ['bʌgɪ] *n* (*baby's pushchair*) cochecito *m* de niño.

bugle ['bjuːgəl] *n* bugle *m*.

build [bɪld] **I** *vtr* (*pt & pp* **built**) construir. **II** *n* (*physique*) tipo *m*, físico *m*. ◆**build up** *vtr* (*accumulate*) acumular; **to b. up a reputation**, labrarse una buena reputación.

builder ['bɪldə'] *n* constructor,-a *m,f*; (*contractor*) contratista *mf*.

building ['bɪldɪŋ] *n* edificio *m*, construcción *f*; **b. site**, obra *f*; **b. society**, sociedad hipotecaria.

build-up ['bɪldʌp] *n* **1** (*accumulation*) aumento *m*; (*of gas*) acumulación *f*. **2** (*publicity*) propaganda *f*.

built [bɪlt] *pt & pp* → **build**.

built-in [bɪlt'ɪn] *adj* **1** (*cupboard*) empotrado,-a. **2** (*incorporated*) incorporado,-a.

built-up [bɪlt'ʌp] *adj* urbanizado,-a.

bulb [bʌlb] *n* **1** *Bot* bulbo *m*. **2** (*lightbulb*) bombilla *f*.

Bulgaria [bʌl'geərɪə] *n* Bulgaria.

Bulgarian [bʌl'geərɪən] **I** *adj* búlgaro,-a. **II** *n* **1** (*person*) búlgaro,-a *m,f*. **2** (*language*) búlgaro *m*.

bulge [bʌldʒ] **I** *n* protuberancia *f*; (*in pocket*) bulto *m*. **II** *vi* (*swell*) hincharse; (*be full*) estar repleto,-a.

bulk [bʌlk] *n* **1** (*mass*) masa *f*, volumen *m*; *Com* **in b.**, a granel; **to buy in b.**, comprar algo al por mayor. **2** (*greater part*) mayor parte *f*.

bulky ['bʌlkɪ] *adj* (**bulkier, bulkiest**) **1** (*large*) voluminoso,-a. **2** **this crate is rather b.**, esta caja es un armatoste.

bull [bʊl] *n* **1** toro *m*; *fig* **to take the b. by the horns**, coger al toro por los cuernos. **2** *Fin* alcista *mf*.

bulldog ['bʊldɒg] *n* buldog *m*.

bulldoze ['bʊldəʊz] *vtr* (*land*) nivelar; (*building*) derribar.

bulldozer ['bʊldəʊzə'] *n* bulldozer *m*.

bullet ['bʊlɪt] *n* bala *f*; **b. wound**, balazo *m*.

bulletin ['bʊlɪtɪn] *n* boletín *m*; *Rad TV* **news b.**, boletín de noticias.

bullet-proof ['bʊlɪtpruːf] *adj* a prueba de balas; **b.-p. vest**, chaleco *m* antibalas.

bullfight ['bʊlfaɪt] *n* corrida *f* de toros.

bullfighter ['bʊlfaɪtə'] *n* torero,-a *m,f*.

bullfighting ['bʊlfaɪtɪŋ] *n* los toros *mpl*; (*art*) tauromaquia *f*.

bullion ['bʊljən] *n* (*gold, silver*) lingote *m*.

bullish ['bʊlɪʃ] *adj* *Fin* (*market*) en alza.

bullock ['bʊlək] *n* buey *m*.

bullring ['bʊlrɪŋ] *n* plaza *f* de toros.

bull's-eye ['bʊlzaɪ] *n* (*of target*) blanco *m*.

bully ['bʊlɪ] **I** *n* matón *m*. **II** *vtr* (*terrorize*) intimidar; (*bulldoze*) tiranizar. **III** *interj iron* **b. for you!**, ¡bravo!

bulwark ['bʊlwək] *n* baluarte *m*.

bum¹ [bʌm] *n fam* (*bottom*) culo *m*.

bum² [bʌm] *fam* **I** *n* **1** *US* (*tramp*) vagabundo *m*. **2** (*idler*) holgazán,-ana *m,f*. **II** *vi* gorronear. ◆**bum around** *vi fam* vaguear.

bumblebee ['bʌmbəlbiː] *n* abejorro *m*.

bumbling ['bʌmblɪŋ] *adj* torpe.

bump [bʌmp] **I** *n* **1** (*swelling*) chichón *m*; (*lump*) abolladura *f*; (*on road*) bache *m*. **2** (*blow*) choque *m*, golpe *m*. **3** (*jolt*) sacudida *f*. **II** *vtr* golpear; **to b. one's head**, darse un golpe en la cabeza. **III** *vi* chocar (*into*, contra). ◆**bump into** *vtr* (*meet*) tropezar con. ◆**bump off** *vtr sl* liquidar.

bumper ['bʌmpə'] **I** *adj* abundante; **b. edition**, edición *f* especial. **II** *n* *Aut* parachoques *m inv*.

bumptious ['bʌmpʃəs] *adj* presuntuoso, -a, engreído,-a.

bumpy ['bʌmpɪ] *adj* (**bumpier, bumpiest**) con muchos baches.

bun [bʌn] *n* **1** (*bread*) panecillo *m*; (*sweet*) bollo *m*; *fig vulg* **she's got a b. in the oven**, esta preñada. **2** (*of hair*) moño *m*.

bunch [bʌntʃ] **I** *n* (*of keys*) manojo *m*; (*of flowers*) ramo *m*; (*of grapes*) racimo *m*; (*of people*) grupo *m*; (*gang*) pandilla *f*. **II** *vi* **to b. together**, juntarse, agruparse.

bundle ['bʌndəl] **I** *n* (*of clothes*) bulto *m*, fardo *m*; (*of papers*) fajo *m*; (*of wood*) haz *m*. **II** *vtr* **1** (*make a bundle of*) liar, atar. **2** (*push*) empujar.

bung [bʌŋ] **I** *n* tapón *m*. **II** *vtr fam* **1** (*throw*) arrojar. **2** (*put*) meter. ◆**bung up** *vtr fam* atascar.

bungalow ['bʌŋgələʊ] *n* chalé *m*, bungalow *m*.

bungle ['bʌŋgəl] *vtr* chapucear.

bunion ['bʌnjən] *n* juanete *m*.

bunk [bʌŋk] *n* (*bed*) litera *f*.

bunker |'bʌŋkər| n 1 (coal) carbonera. 2 Mil búnker m. 3 Golf bunker m.
bunny |'bʌnɪ| n fam (baby talk) b. (rabbit), conejito m.
bunting |'bʌntɪŋ| n (material) lanilla f; (flags) banderines mpl; Naut empavesada f.
buoy |bɔɪ| I n boya f. II vtr mantener a flote (up, a). ◆**buoy up** vtr fig alentar, animar.
buoyancy |'bɔɪənsɪ| n 1 (of object) flotabilidad f. 2 Fin tendencia f alcista. 3 (optimism) optimismo m.
buoyant |'bɔɪənt| adj 1 (object) flotante. 2 Fin con tendencia alcista. 3 (optimistic) optimista.
burble |'bɜːbəl| vi 1 (stream) murmurar; (baby) balbucear. 2 (talk quickly) farfullar.
burden |'bɜːdən| I n carga f; fig to be a b. to sb, ser una carga para algn. II vtr cargar (with, con).
bureau |'bjʊərəʊ| n (pl bureaux) 1 (desk) escritorio m. 2 (office) agencia f, oficina f. 3 US (chest of drawers) cómoda f. 4 US Pol departamento m del Estado.
bureaucracy |bjʊə'rɒkrəsɪ| n burocracia f.
bureaucrat |'bjʊərəkræt| n burócrata mf.
bureaucratic |bjʊərə'krætɪk| adj burocrático,-a.
burgeon |'bɜːdʒən| vi florecer.
burger |'bɜːgər| n fam abbr of hamburger.
burglar |'bɜːglər| n ladrón,-ona m,f; b. alarm, alarma f antirrobo.
burglary |'bɜːglərɪ| n robo m con allanamiento de morada.
burial |'berɪəl| n entierro m.
burly |'bɜːlɪ| adj (burlier, burliest) fornido,-a, fuerte.
Burma |'bɜːmə| n Birmania.
Burmese |bɜː'miːz| I adj birmano,-a. II n 1 (person) birmano,-a m,f. 2 (language) birmano m.
burn |bɜːn| I n quemadura f. II vtr (pt & pp burnt or burned) quemar. III vi 1 (fire) arder; (building, food) quemarse. 2 (lamp) estar encendido,-a. 3 (sore) escocer. ◆**burn down** I vtr incendiar. II vi incendiarse. ◆**burn out** vi (people) quemarse. ◆**burn up** vtr (energy, calories) quemar.
burner |'bɜːnər| n quemador m.
burning |'bɜːnɪŋ| adj 1 (on fire) incendiado,-a; (hot) abrasador,-a. 2 (passionate) ardiente. 3 a b. question, una cuestión candente.
burnt |bɜːnt| adj quemado,-a; b. almonds, almendras tostadas.
burp |bɜːp| I n eructo m. II vi eructar.
burrow |'bʌrəʊ| I n madriguera f; (for rabbits) conejera f. II vi 1 hacer una madriguera. 2 (search) hurgar.

bursar |'bɜːsər| n tesorero,-a m,f.
bursary |'bɜːsərɪ| n beca f.
burst |bɜːst| I n 1 (explosion) estallido m; (of tyre) reventón m. 2 (of applause) arranque m; (rage) arrebato m; b. of gunfire, ráfaga f de tiros; b. of laughter, carcajadas fpl. II vtr (pt & pp burst) (balloon) reventar; fig the river b. its banks, el río se salió de madre. III vi 1 reventarse; (shell) estallar. 2 (enter suddenly) irrumpir (into, en). ◆**burst into** vi to b. into laughter/tears, echarse a reír/allorar. ◆**burst open** vi abrirse violentamente. ◆**burst out** vi to b. out laughing, echarse a reír.
bursting |'bɜːstɪŋ| adj the bar was b. with people, el bar estaba atestado de gente; fam to be b. to do sth, reventar por hacer algo.
bury |'berɪ| vtr 1 enterrar; to be buried in thought, estar absorto en pensamientos. 2 (hide) ocultar.
bus |bʌs| n (pl buses, US busses) autobús m; b. conductor, revisor m; b. driver, conductor,-a m,f; b. stop, parada f de autobús.
bush |bʊʃ| n 1 (shrub) arbusto m. 2 Austral the b., el monte; fam b. telegraph, radio f macuto.
bushy |'bʊʃɪ| adj espeso,-a, tupido,-a.
business |'bɪznɪs| n 1 (commerce) negocios mpl; how's b.?, ¿cómo andan los negocios?; to be away on b., estar en viaje de negocios; b. deal, negocio m; b. hours, horas fpl de oficina; b. trip, viaje m de negocios. 2 (firm) empresa f. 3 (matter) asunto m; I mean b., estoy hablando en serio; it's no b. of mine, no es asunto mío; to make it one's b. to ..., encargarse de ...; to get down to b., ir al grano; to go about one's b., ocuparse de sus asuntos.
businesslike |'bɪznɪslaɪk| adj (practical) eficiente; (methodical) metódico,-a; (serious) serio,-a.
businessman |'bɪznɪsmən| n hombre m de negocios.
businesswoman |'bɪznɪswʊmən| n mujer f de negocios.
busker |'bʌskər| n fam músico,-a m,f callejero,-a.
bust¹ |bʌst| n 1 (of woman) pecho m. 2 Art busto m.
bust² |bʌst| I vtr 1 fam estropear. 2 sl (person) trincar; (place) hacer una redada. II adj fam 1 (damaged) estropeado,-a. 2 to go b., (bankrupt) quebrar.
bustle |'bʌsəl| I n (activity, noise) bullicio m. II vi to b. about, ir y venir.
bustling |'bʌslɪŋ| adj bullicioso,-a.
bust-up |'bʌstʌp| n fam riña f, pelea f.
busy |'bɪzɪ| I adj 1 ocupado,-a, atareado,-a; (life) ajetreado,-a; (street) concurrido,-a. 2 esp US Tel ocupado,-a;

b. signal, señal *f* de comunicando. II *vtr* **to b. oneself doing sth,** ocuparse haciendo algo.

busybody ['bɪzɪbɒdɪ] *n* entrometido,-a *m,f.*

but [bʌt] I *conj* 1 pero; **b. yet,** a pesar de todo. 2 *(after negative)* sino; **not two b. three,** no dos sino tres; **she's not Spanish b.** Portuguese, no es española sino portuguesa. II *adv* **had we b. known,** de haberlo sabido; **we can b. try,** al menos podemos intentarlo; **b. for her we would have drowned,** si no hubiera sido por ella, nos habríamos ahogado. III *prep* salvo, menos; **everyone b. her,** todos menos ella; **he's anything b. handsome,** es todo menos guapo. IV *npl* **ifs and buts,** pegas *fpl.*

butane ['bjuːteɪn] *n* butano *m*; **b. gas,** gas butano.

butcher ['butʃər] I *n* carnicero,-a *m,f*; **b.'s (shop),** carnicería *f.* II *vtr (animals)* matar; *(people)* masacrar.

butler ['bʌtlər] *n* mayordomo *m.*

butt[1] [bʌt] *n* 1 *(end)* extremo *m*; *(of rifle)* culata *f*; *(of cigarette)* colilla *f.* 2 **he was the b. of all the jokes,** era el blanco de todas las bromas. 3 *US fam (bottom)* culo *m.*

butt[2] [bʌt] I *n (with head)* cabezazo *m.* II *vtr* 1 *(strike with head)* dar un cabezazo a. 2 **to b. way through,** *(shove)* abrirse paso. ◆**butt in** *vi* entrar en la conversación.

butt[3] [bʌt] *n (barrel)* tonel *m.*

butter ['bʌtər] I *n* mantequilla *f*; **b. dish,** mantequera *f.* II *vtr* untar con mantequilla.

buttercup ['bʌtəkʌp] *n* ranúnculo *m*, botón *m* de oro.

butterfingers ['bʌtəfɪŋgəz] *n fam* manazas *mf inv.*

butterfly ['bʌtəflaɪ] *n* mariposa *f.*

buttock ['bʌtək] *n* nalga *f*; **buttocks,** nalgas *fpl.*

button ['bʌtən] I *n* botón *m.* II *vtr* **to b. (up),** abrochar(se), abotonar(se).

buttonhole ['bʌtənhəʊl] *n* ojal *m.*

buttress ['bʌtrɪs] I *n* 1 contrafuerte *m.* 2 *(support)* apoyo *m.* II *vtr* apuntalar; *fig* reforzar, apoyar.

buxom ['bʌksəm] *adj (woman)* pechugona.

buy [baɪ] I *n* compra *f*; **a good b.,** una ganga. II *vtr (pt & pp* **bought)** 1 comprar; **she bought that car from a neighbour,** compró ese coche a un vecino. 2 *sl (believe)* tragar. ◆**buy off** *vtr* sobornar. ◆**buy out** *vtr* adquirir la parte de. ◆**buy up** *vtr* comprar en grandes cantidades.

buyer ['baɪər] *n* comprador,-a *m,f.*

buzz [bʌz] I *n* 1 *(of bee)* zumbido *m*; *(of conversation)* rumor *m.* 2 *fam (telephone call)* telefonazo *m.* II *vi* zumbar.

buzzer ['bʌzər] *n* timbre *m.*

by [baɪ] I *prep* 1 *(indicating agent)* por; **composed by Bach,** compuesto,-a por Bach; **a film by Almodóvar,** una película de Almodóvar. 2 *(via)* por; **he left by the back door,** salió por la puerta trasera. 3 *(manner)* por; **by car/train,** en coche/tren; **by credit card,** con tarjeta de crédito; **by chance,** por casualidad; **by oneself,** solo,-a; **made by hand,** hecho a mano; **you can obtain a ticket by filling in the coupon,** puede conseguir una entrada llenando el cupón. 4 *(amount)* por; **little by little,** poco a poco; **they are sold by the dozen,** se venden por docenas; **to be paid by the hour,** cobrar por horas. 5 **by far,** con mucho; **he won by a foot,** ganó por un pie. 6 *(beside)* al lado de, junto a; **side by side,** juntos. 7 **to walk by a building,** *(pass)* pasar por delante de un edificio. 8 *(time)* para; **by now,** ya; **by then,** para entonces; **we have to be there by nine,** tenemos que estar allí para las nueve; **by the time we arrive,** (para) cuando lleguemos; **by this time next year,** el año que viene por estas fechas. 9 *(during)* de; **by day/night,** de día/noche. 10 *(in an oath)* por; **by God!,** ¡por Dios! 11 *Math* por. 12 *(according to)* según; **is that O.K by you?,** ¿te viene bien? 13 **he had two children by his first wife,** tuvo dos hijos con su primera esposa. 14 *(phrases)* **bit by bit,** poco a poco; **day by day,** día a día; **what do you mean by that?,** ¿qué quieres decir con eso?; **by the way,** a propósito.

II *adv* 1 **to go by,** *(past)* pasar; **she just walked by,** pasó de largo. 2 **by and by,** con el tiempo; **by and large,** en conjunto.

bye [baɪ] *n* 1 *fam* ¡hasta luego! 2 **by the b.** por cierto.

bye-bye ['baɪbaɪ] *n fam* ¡adiós!, ¡hasta luego!

by-election ['baɪɪlekʃən] *n* elección *f* parcial.

bygone ['baɪgɒn] I *adj* pasado,-a. II *npl* **let bygones be bygones,** lo pasado pasado está.

by-law ['baɪlɔː] *n* ley *f* municipal.

bypass ['baɪpɑːs] I *n* 1 *(road)* carretera *f* de circunvalación. 2 *Med* **surgery,** cirugía *f* de by-pass. II *vtr* evitar.

by-product ['baɪprɒdʌkt] *n Chem Ind* derivado *m*, subproducto *m*; *fig* consecuencia *f.*

by-road ['baɪrəʊd] *n* carretera secundaria.

bystander ['baɪstændər] *n* testigo *mf.*

byte [baɪt] *n Comput* byte *m*, octeto *m.*

byword ['baɪwɜːd] *n* **it became a b. for modernity,** se convirtió en sinónimo de modernidad.

C

C, c |siː| n 1 (*the letter*) C, c f. 2 *Mus* do m.

C 1 *abbr of* **Celsius,** C. 2 *abbr of* **Centigrade,** C.

cab |kæb| n *US* taxi m; **c. driver,** taxista mf.

cabaret |'kæbəreɪ| n cabaret m.

cabbage |'kæbɪdʒ| n col f, berza f; **red c.,** (col) lombarda f.

cabin |'kæbɪn| n 1 (*hut*) choza f; **log c.,** cabaña f. 2 *Naut* camarote m. 3 (*of lorry, plane*) cabina f.

cabinet |'kæbɪnɪt| n 1 (*item of furniture*) armario m; (*glassfronted*) vitrina f; **c. maker,** ebanista mf. 2 *Pol* gabinete m, consejo m de ministros.

cable |'keɪbəl| I n cable m; **c. car,** teleférico m; **c. TV,** televisión f por cable. II vtr & vi cablegrafiar, telegrafiar.

cache |kæʃ| n alijo m.

cackle |'kækəl| vi cacarear.

cactus |'kæktəs| n (*pl* **cacti** |'kæktaɪ|) cactus m.

CAD |kæd| *abbr of* **computer-aided** *or* **-assisted design** *or* **draughting,** diseño m con ayuda de ordenador.

cad |kæd| n *GB fam* canalla m.

caddie |'kædɪ| n *Golf* cadi m.

cadet |kə'det| n *Mil* cadete m.

cadge |kædʒ| *fam* vtr & vi gorronear.

Caesarean |siː'zeərɪən| n *Med* **she had a c.,** le hicieron una cesárea; **C. section,** operación f cesárea.

café |'kæfeɪ| n, **cafeteria** |kæfɪ'tɪərɪə| n cafetería f.

caffeine |'kæfiːn| n cafeína f.

cage |keɪdʒ| I n jaula f. II vtr enjaular.

cagey |'keɪdʒɪ| adj (**cagier, cagiest**) *fam* reservado,-a.

cagoule |kə'guːl| n (*garment*) canguro m.

Cairo |'kaɪrəʊ| n (el) Cairo.

cajole |kə'dʒəʊl| vtr engatusar.

cake |keɪk| I n 1 pastel m, tarta f; *fam fig* **it's a piece of c.,** está chupado; **birthday c.,** pastel de cumpleaños; **c. shop,** pastelería f. 2 (*of soap*) pastilla f. II vi (*mud*) endurecerse. II vtr **caked with ...,** cubierto,-a de ....

calamity |kə'læmɪtɪ| n calamidad f.

calcium |'kælsɪəm| n calcio m.

calculate |'kælkjʊleɪt| vtr calcular.

calculated |'kælkjʊleɪtɪd| adj intencionado,-a.

calculating |'kælkjʊleɪtɪŋ| adj 1 **c. machine,** calculadora f. 2 *pej* (*person*) calculador,-a.

calculation |kælkjʊ'leɪʃən| n cálculo m.

calculator |'kælkjʊleɪtəʳ| n calculadora f.

calendar |'kælɪndəʳ| n calendario m; **c. year,** año m civil.

calf¹ |kɑːf| n (*pl* **calves** |kɑːvz|) (*of cattle*) becerro,-a m,f, ternero,-a m,f; (*of other animals*) cría f.

calf² |kɑːf| n (*pl* **calves** |kɑːvz|) *Anat* pantorilla f.

calfskin |'kɑːfskɪn| n piel f de becerro.

caliber |'kælɪbəʳ|, **calibre** |'kælɪbəʳ| n calibre m.

call |kɔːl| I vtr 1 llamar; **to c. sb names,** poner verde a algn; **what's he called?,** ¿cómo se llama? 2 (*meeting etc*) convocar; **to c. sth to mind,** traer algo a la memoria.

II vi 1 llamar; *Tel* **who's calling?,** ¿de parte de quién? 2 **to c. at sb's (house),** pasar por casa de algn; **to c. for sth/sb,** pasar a recoger algo/a algn. 3 (*trains*) parar. 4 **to c. for,** (*require*) exigir; **that wasn't called for,** eso no estaba justificado.

III n 1 llamada f, grito m. 2 (*visit*) visita f; **to pay a c. on sb,** visitar a algn. 3 *Tel* (*phone*) **c.,** llamada f; **c. box,** cabina telefónica. 4 *Med* **to be on c.,** estar de guardia. 5 **there's no c. for you to worry,** no hay motivo para que te preocupes.

◆**call away** vtr **to be called away on business,** tener que ausentarse por motivos de trabajo. ◆**call back** vi (*phone again*) llamar otra vez; (*visit again*) volver. ◆**call in** I vtr (*doctor*) llamar. II vi 1 **I'll c. in tomorrow,** (*visit*) mañana me paso. 2 *Naut* hacer escala (at, en). ◆**call off** vtr suspender. ◆**call on** vtr 1 visitar. 2 **to c. on sb for support,** recurrir a algn en busca de apoyo. ◆**call out** I vtr 1 (*shout*) gritar. 2 (*doctor*) hacer venir; (*workers*) convocar a la huelga. II vi gritar. ◆**call up** vtr 1 *Tel* llamar (por teléfono). 2 *Mil* llamar a filas, reclutar.

caller |'kɔːləʳ| n visita mf; *Tel* persona f que llama.

calling |'kɔːlɪŋ| n *esp Rel* llamada f, vocación f.

callous |'kæləs| adj insensible, duro,-a.

call-up |'kɔːlʌp| n llamamiento m a filas.

calm |kɑːm| I adj 1 (*weather, sea*) en calma. 2 (*relaxed*) tranquilo,-a; **keep c.!,** ¡tranquilo,-a!. II n 1 (*of weather, sea*) calma f. 2 (*tranquility*) tranquilidad f. III vtr calmar, tranquilizar. IV vi **to c. (down),** calmarse, tranquilizarse.

Calor Gas® |'kæləgæs| n (*gas* m) butano m.

calorie, calory |'kælərɪ| n caloría f.

calve |kɑːv| vi (*cow*) parir (un becerro).

calves |kɑːvz| *npl* → **calf¹, calf².**

Cambodia |kæm'bəʊdɪə| n Camboya.

came |keɪm| *pt* → **come.**

camel ['kæməl] *n* camello,-a *m,f*.
cameo ['kæmɪəʊ] *n* camafeo *m*.
camera ['kæmərə] *n* 1 cámara *f or* máquina *f* fotográfica; *Cin TV* cámara. 2 *Jur* in c., a puerta cerrada.
cameraman ['kæmərəmən] *n* cámara *mf*.
Cameroon [kæmə'ruːn] *n* Camerún.
camomile ['kæməmaɪl] *n* camomila *f*; c. tea, (infusión *f* de) manzanilla *f*.
camouflage ['kæməflɑːʒ] I *n* camuflaje *m*. II *vtr* camuflar.
camp¹ [kæmp] I *n* campamento *m*; c. bed, cama *f* plegable; c. site, camping *m*. II *vi* to go camping, ir de camping.
camp² [kæmp] *adj fam* afeminado,-a; *(affected)* amanerado,-a.
campaign [kæm'peɪn] I *n* campaña *f*. II *vi* to c. for sb/sth, hacer una campaña a favor de algn/de algo.
campaigner [kæm'peɪnər] *n* defensor,-a *m,f* (for, de).
camper ['kæmpər] *n* 1 *(person)* campista *mf*. 2 *US (vehicle)* caravana *f*.
camping ['kæmpɪŋ] *n* c. ground, c. site, camping *m*.
campus ['kæmpəs] *n* campus *m*, ciudad *f* universitaria.
can¹ [kæn] *v aux (pt could)* 1 *(be able to)* poder; **he could have come**, podría haber venido; **I'll phone you as soon as I c.**, te llamaré en cuanto pueda; **she can't do it**, no puede hacerlo; **I cannot understand why**, *(fml & emphatic)* no entiendo por qué. 2 *(know how to)* saber; c. **you ski?**, ¿sabes esquiar?; **I can't speak English**, no sé hablar inglés. 3 *(be permitted to)* poder; **they can't go out tonight**, no le dejan salir esta noche. 4 *(be possible)* poder; **she could have forgotten**, puede (ser) que lo haya olvidado; **they can't be very poor**, no deben ser muy pobres; **what c. it be?**, ¿qué será?
can² [kæn] I *n* 1 *(of oil)* bidón *m*. 2 *US (tin)* lata *f*, bote *m*. II *vtr* 1 *(fish, fruit)* envasar, enlatar. 2 *US fam* desestimar.
Canada ['kænədə] *n* Canadá.
Canadian [kə'neɪdɪən] *adj & n* canadiense *(mf)*.
canal [kə'næl] *n* canal *m*.
canary [kə'neərɪ] *n* canario *m*.
Canary Islands [kə'neərɪaɪləndz] *npl* (Islas *fpl*) Canarias *fpl*.
cancel ['kænsəl] *vtr* anular *(train, contract)* cancelar; *Com* anular; *(permission)* retirar; *(decree)* revocar.
cancellation [kænsɪ'leɪʃən] *n* cancelación *f*; *Com* anulación *f*.
cancer ['kænsər] *n* 1 *Med* cáncer *m*; breast c., cáncer de mama; c. research, cancerología *f*. 2 C., *(in astrology)* Cáncer *m*.
candelabra [kændɪ'lɑːbrə] *n* candelabro *m*.
candid ['kændɪd] *adj* franco,-a, sincero,-a.

candidate ['kændɪdeɪt, 'kændɪdɪt] *n* candidato,-a *m,f*; *(in exam)* opositor,-a *m,f*.
candle ['kændəl] *n* vela *f*; *(in church)* cirio *m*.
candlelight ['kændəllaɪt] *n* luz *f* de vela; **by c.**, a la luz de las velas.
candlestick ['kændəlstɪk] *n* candelero *m*, palmatoria *f*; *(in church)* cirial *m*.
candour, *US* **candor** ['kændər] *n* franqueza *f*.
candy ['kændɪ] *n US* caramelo *m*.
candyfloss ['kændɪflɒs] *n GB* algodón *m* dulce.
cane [keɪn] I *n* 1 *Bot* caña *f*; c. **sugar**, azúcar *m* de caña. 2 *(wicker)* mimbre *m*. 3 *(walking stick)* bastón *m*; *(for punishment)* palmeta *f*. II *vtr* castigar con la palmeta.
canine ['keɪnaɪn] *adj Zool* canino,-a; c. **tooth**, colmillo *m*.
canister ['kænɪstər] *n* bote *m*.
canned [kænd] *adj* enlatado,-a; c. **foods**, conservas *fpl*.
cannibal ['kænɪbəl] *adj & n* caníbal *(mf)*.
cannon ['kænən] I *n (pl* **cannons** *or* **cannon)** cañón *m*; *fig* c. **fodder**, carne *f* de cañón. II *vi* chocar (**into**, contra).
cannonball ['kænənbɔːl] *n* bala *f* de cañón.
cannot ['kænɒt, kæ'nɒt] *v aux → can¹*.
canoe [kə'nuː] *n* canoa *f*; *Sport* piragua *f*.
canon ['kænən] *n Rel* canon *m*.
canopy ['kænəpɪ] *n* 1 *(on throne)* dosel *m*. 2 *(awning)* toldo *m*.
can't [kɑːnt] *v aux → can¹*.
Cantabria *n* Cantabria.
cantankerous [kæn'tæŋkərəs] *adj* intratable.
canteen [kæn'tiːn] *n* 1 *(restaurant)* cantina *f*. 2 *(set of cutlery)* juego *m* de cubiertos. 3 *(flask)* cantimplora *f*.
canter ['kæntər] I *n* medio galope. II *vi* ir a medio galope.
canvas ['kænvəs] *n* 1 *Tex* lona *f*. 2 *(painting)* lienzo *m*.
canvass ['kænvəs] *vi* 1 *Pol* hacer propaganda electoral. 2 *Com* hacer promoción, buscar clientes.
canvasser ['kænvəsər] *n Pol* persona *f* que hace propaganda electoral de puerta en puerta.
canyon ['kænjən] *n* cañón *m*; **the Grand C.**, el Gran Cañón.
cap [kæp] I *n* 1 gorro *m*; *(soldier's)* gorra *f*. 2 *GB Sport* **to win a c. for England**, ser seleccionado,-a para el equipo de Inglaterra. 3 *(of pen)* capuchón *m*; *(of bottle)* chapa *f*. II *vtr* 1 *(bottle)* poner la chapa a; *fig* **to c. it all**, para colmo. 2 *GB Sport* seleccionar.
capability [keɪpə'bɪlɪtɪ] *n* habilidad *f*.
capable ['keɪpəbəl] *adj* 1 *(skilful)* hábil. 2 *(able)* capaz (**of**, de).
capacity [kə'pæsɪtɪ] *n* 1 capacidad *f*. 2

(position) puesto *m*; **in her c. as management**, en calidad de gerente.
cape¹ [keɪp] *n (garment)* capa *f*.
cape² [keɪp] *n Geog* cabo *m*, promontorio *m*; **C. Horn,** Cabo de Hornos; **C. Town,** Ciudad del Cabo; **C. Verde,** Cabo Verde.
caper ['keɪpər] *n (prank)* travesura *f*.
capital ['kæpɪtəl] **I** *n* **1** *(town)* capital *f*. **2** *Fin* capital *m*; **c. expenditure,** inversión *f* de capital. **3** *(letter)* mayúscula *f*. **II** *adj* **1** *(city)* capital. **2 c. punishment,** pena *f* capital. **3** *(primary)* primordial. **4 c. letter,** mayúscula *f*.
capitalism ['kæpɪtəlɪzəm] *n* capitalismo *m*.
capitalist ['kæpɪtəlɪst] *adj & n* capitalista *(mf)*.
capitalize ['kæpɪtəlaɪz] *vi Fin* capitalizar; *fig* **to c. on sth,** sacar provecho *or* beneficio de algo.
capitulate [kə'pɪtjuleɪt] *vi* capitular.
Capricorn ['kæprɪkɔːn] *n* Capricornio *m*.
capsicum ['kæpsɪkəm] *n* pimiento *m*.
capsize [kæp'saɪz] **I** *vtr* hacer zozobrar. **II** *vi* zozobrar.
capsule ['kæpsjuːl] *n* cápsula *f*.
captain ['kæptɪn] **I** *n* capitán *m*. **II** *vtr* capitanear.
caption ['kæpʃən] *n (under picture)* leyenda *f; Cin* subtítulo *m*.
captivating ['kæptɪveɪtɪŋ] *adj* seductor, -a.
captive ['kæptɪv] **I** *n* cautivo,-a *m,f*. **II** *adj* cautivo,-a.
captivity [kæp'tɪvɪtɪ] *n* cautiverio *m*.
capture ['kæptʃər] **I** *vtr* **1** capturar, apresar; *Mil (town)* tomar. **2** *(market)* acaparar. **3** *fig (mood)* captar. **II** *n (of fugitive)* captura *f; (of town)* toma *f*.
car [kɑːr] *n* **1** coche *m, Am* carro *m*; **c. ferry,** transbordador *m* para coches; *GB* **c. park,** parking *m*, aparcamiento *m*; **c. wash,** túnel *m* de lavado. **2** *GB Rail* coche *m*.
carafe [kə'ræf, kə'rɑːf] *n* garrafa *f*.
caramel ['kærəmel] *n* azúcar *m* quemado; *(sweet)* caramelo *m*.
carat [US **karat** ['kærət] *n* kilate *m*.
caravan ['kærəvæn] *n* **1** *(vehicle)* remolque *m*, caravana *f*. **2** *(in the desert)* caravana *f*.
carbohydrate [kɑːbəʊ'haɪdreɪt] *n* hidrato *m* de carbono, carbohidrato *m*.
carbon ['kɑːbən] *n* carbono *m*; **c. copy,** copia *f* al papel carbón; *fig* copia exacta; **c. dioxide,** dióxido *m* de carbono; **c. paper,** papel *m* carbón.
carburettor [kɑːbju'retər], *US* **carburetor** ['kɑːbjʊreɪtər] *n* carburador *m*.
carcass ['kɑːkəs] *n* res *f* muerta.
card [kɑːd] *n* **1** tarjeta *f; (of cardboard)* cartulina *f;* **birthday/visiting c.,** tarjeta de cumpleaños/de visita. **2** *(in file)* ficha *f; (identity)* carnet *m*; **c. index,** fichero *m*. **3 pack of cards,** baraja *f*, cartas *fpl; (play-*

ing) **c.,** naipe *m*, carta *f; fig* **on the cards,** previsto.
cardboard ['kɑːdbɔːd] *n* cartón *m*; **c. box,** caja *f* de carton; **c. cutout,** recortable *m*.
cardiac ['kɑːdɪæk] *adj* cardíaco,-a; **c. arrest,** paro cardíaco.
cardigan ['kɑːdɪgən] *n* rebeca *f*.
cardinal ['kɑːdɪnəl] **I** *n Rel* cardenal *m*. **II** *adj* cardinal; **c. numbers,** números *mpl* cardinales.
care [keər] **I** *vi (be concerned)* preocuparse *(about,* por); **I don't c.,** no me importa; *fam* **for all I c.,** me trae sin cuidado; *fam* **he couldn't c. less,** le importa un bledo. **II** *n* **1** *(attention, protection)* cuidado *m*, atención *f;* **'c. of...',** *(on letter)* 'al cuidado de...'; *medical* **c.,** asistencia *f* médica; **to take c. of,** cuidar; *(business)* ocuparse de. **2** *(carefulness)* cuidado *m;* **take c.,** *(be careful)* ten cuidado; *(as farewell)* ¡cuídate! **3** *(worry)* preocupación *f*. ◆**care for** *vtr* **1** *(look after)* cuidar. **2** *(like)* gustar, interesar; **would you c. for a coffee?,** ¿te apetece un café?
career [kə'rɪər] **I** *n* carrera *f*. **II** *vi* correr a toda velocidad.
carefree ['keəfriː] *adj* despreocupado,-a.
careful ['keəfʊl] *adj* cuidadoso,-a; *(cautious)* prudente; **be c.!,** ¡ojo!; **to be c.,** tener cuidado. ◆**carefully** *adv (painstakingly)* cuidadosamente; *(cautiously)* con cuidado.
careless ['keəlɪs] *adj* descuidado,-a; *(about clothes)* desaliñado,-a; *(driving)* negligente; **a c. mistake,** un descuido. ◆**carelessly** *adv* descuidadamente, a la ligera.
carelessness ['keəlɪsnɪs] *n* descuido *m*.
caress [kə'res] **I** *n* caricia *f*. **II** *vtr* acariciar.
caretaker ['keəteɪkər] *n (in school etc)* bedel *mf; (in block of flats)* portero,-a *m,f*.
cargo ['kɑːgəʊ] *n (pl* **cargoes** *or* **cargos)** carga *f*, cargamento *m; Naut* **c. boat,** buque *m* de carga, carguero *m*.
Caribbean [kærɪ'bɪən, *US* kə'rɪbɪən] *adj* caribe, caribeño,-a; **the C. (Sea),** el (Mar) Caribe.
caricature ['kærɪkətjʊər] *n* caricatura *f*.
caring ['keərɪŋ] *adj* solidario,-a.
carnage ['kɑːnɪdʒ] *n fig* carnicería *f*.
carnal ['kɑːnəl] *adj* carnal.
carnation [kɑː'neɪʃən] *n* clavel *m*.
carnival ['kɑːnɪvəl] *n* carnaval *m*.
carnivorous [kɑː'nɪvərəs] *adj* carnívoro, -a.
carol ['kærəl] *n* villancico *m*.
carp¹ [kɑːp] *n (fish)* carpa *f*.
carp² [kɑːp] *vi* refunfuñar.
carpenter ['kɑːpɪntər] *n* carpintero,-a *m,f*.
carpentry ['kɑːpɪntrɪ] *n* carpintería *f*.
carpet ['kɑːpɪt] **I** *n* moqueta *f*. **II** *vtr fig* **carpeted with,** cubierto,-a de.

carriage |'kærɪdʒ| n 1 (horse-drawn) carruaje m; Rail vagón m, coche m; (of gun) cureña f; (of typewriter) carro m. 2 (of goods) porte m, transporte m.

carriageway |'kærɪdʒweɪ| n GB carril m, autovía f; dual c., autovía.

carrier |'kærɪər| n 1 (company) transportista mf; GB c. bag, bolsa f de plástico; c. pigeon, paloma mensajera. 2 Med portador,-a m,f.

carrot |'kærət| n zanahoria f.

carry |'kærɪ| I vtr 1 llevar; (goods) transportar. 2 (stock) tener; (responsibility, penalty) conllevar, implicar. 3 the motion was carried, se aprobó la moción. 4 (disease) ser portador,-a de. II vi (sound) oírse. ◆carry away vtr llevarse; to get carried away, entusiasmarse. ◆carry forward vtr Fin carried forward, suma y sigue. ◆carry off vtr (prize) llevarse; fam to c. it off, salir airoso,-a. ◆carry on I vtr continuar; (conversation) mantener. II vi 1 continuar, seguir adelante; c. on!, ¡adelante! 2 fam (make a fuss) hacer una escena; don't c. on about it, ¡no te enrolles! 3 fam (have an affair) estar liado,-a con algn. ◆carry out vtr (plan) llevar a cabo, realizar; (test) verificar.

carrycot |'kærɪkɒt| n cuna f portátil.

carsick |'kɑːsɪk| adj mareado,-a (en el coche).

cart |kɑːt| I n (horse-drawn) carro m; (handcart) carretilla f. II vtr carretear.

cartel |kɑː'tel| n cártel m.

carton |'kɑːtən| n (of cream etc) caja f.

cartoon |kɑː'tuːn| n (strip) tira cómica, historieta f; Art cartón m; (animated) dibujos mpl animados.

cartoonist |kɑː'tuːnɪst| n caricaturista mf.

cartridge |'kɑːtrɪdʒ| n 1 cartucho m. 2 (for pen) recambio m; c. paper, papel guarro.

carve |kɑːv| vtr 1 (wood) tallar; (stone, metal) cincelar, esculpir. 2 (meat) trinchar.

cascade |kæs'keɪd| n cascada f.

case¹ |keɪs| n 1 caso m; a c. in point, un buen ejemplo; in any c., en cualquier caso, de todas formas; in c. of doubt, en caso de duda; just in c., por si acaso. 2 Med caso m; c. history, historial clínico. 3 Jur causa f.

case² |keɪs| I n 1 (suitcase) maleta f; (small) estuche m; (soft) funda f. 2 a c. of wine, una caja de botellas de vino. 3 Typ lower c., minúscula f; upper c., mayúscula f.

cash |kæʃ| I n dinero efectivo; to pay c., pagar al contado or en efectivo; c. desk, caja f; c. on delivery, entrega f contra reembolso; c. dispenser, cajero automático; c. register, caja registradora. II vtr (cheque) cobrar. ◆cash in I vi fam fig to c. in on sth, sacar provecho de algo. II vtr hacer efectivo,-a.

cash-and-carry |kæʃən'kærɪ| adj & adv de venta al por mayor y pago al contado.

cashew |'kæʃuː| n c. (nut), anacardo m.

cashier |kæ'ʃɪər| n cajero,-a m,f.

cashmere |'kæʃmɪər| n cachemira f.

casino |kə'siːnəʊ| n casino m.

cask |kɑːsk| n tonel m, barril m.

casket |'kɑːskɪt| n (box) cofre m; (coffin) ataúd m.

casserole |'kæsərəʊl| n 1 (container) cacerola f. 2 Culin guisado m.

cassette |kæ'set| n cassette f; c. recorder, cassette m.

cast |kɑːst| I vtr (pt & pp cast) 1 (net, fishing line) echar, arrojar; (light) proyectar; (glance) lanzar; (anchor) echar; (vote) emitir; (skin) mudar. 2 fig to c. doubts on sth, poner algo en duda; to c. suspicion on sb, levantar sospechas sobre algn. 3 (metal) moldear; c. iron, hierro fundido. 4 Theat (play) hacer el reparto de. II n 1 (mould) molde m; (product) pieza f. 2 Med (plaster) c., escayola f. 3 Theat reparto m. ◆cast off vi Naut soltar (las) amarras.

castanets |kæstə'nets| npl castañuelas fpl.

castaway |'kɑːstəweɪ| n náufrago,-a m,f.

caste |kɑːst| n casta f.

caster |'kɑːstər| n c. sugar, azúcar molido muy fino.

Castile |kæ'stiːl| n Castilla.

Castilian |kæ'stɪljən| I adj castellano,-a. II n C. (Spanish), (language) castellano m.

casting |'kɑːstɪŋ| n c. vote, voto m de calidad.

cast-iron |'kɑːstaɪən| adj de hierro fundido.

castle |'kɑːsəl| I n 1 castillo m. 2 Chess torre f. II vi Chess enrocar.

castor¹ |'kɑːstər| n c. oil, aceite m de ricino.

castor² |'kɑːstər| n (on furniture) ruedecilla f.

castrate |kæ'streɪt| vtr castrar.

casual |'kæʒjʊəl| adj 1 (meeting etc) fortuito,-a. 2 (worker) eventual. 3 (clothes) (de) sport. 4 (visit) de paso. 5 (person, attitude) despreocupado,-a, informal.

casualty |'kæʒjʊəltɪ| n 1 Mil baja f; casualties, pérdidas fpl. 2 (injured) herido,-a m,f.

cat |kæt| n gato,-a m,f; fig to let the c. out of the bag, descubrir el pastel.

Catalan |'kætələn| I adj catalán,-ana; C. flag, senyera f. II n 1 (person) catalán, -ana m,f. 2 (language) catalán m.

catalogue, US **catalog** |'kætəlɒg| I n catálogo m. II vtr catalogar.

Catalonia |kætə'ləʊnɪə| n Cataluña.

catalyst |'kætəlɪst| n catalizador m.

catapult |'kætəpʌlt| n tirachinas m inv.

catarrh |kə'tɑː| n catarro m.

catastrophe |kə'tæstrəfɪ| n catástrofe f.

catastrophic |kætə'strɒfɪk| adj

catastrófico,-a.

catch [kætʃ] **I** *vtr* (*pt & pp* **caught**) **1** (*ball, thief*) coger; (*fish*) pescar; (*mouse etc*) atrapar; (*train, bus*) coger, *Am* agarrar; **to c. a cold,** coger un resfriado; **to c. fire,** (*log*) prenderse; (*building*) incendiarse; **to c. hold of,** agarrar; **to c. sb's eye,** captar la atención de algn; **to c. sight of,** entrever. **2** (*surprise*) pillar, sorprender. **3** (*hear*) entender. **4 to c. one's breath,** (*hold*) sostener la respiración; (*recover*) recuperar el aliento. **II** *vi* (*sleeve etc*) · engancharse (**on,** en); (*fire*) encenderse. **III** *n* **1** (*of ball*) parada *f*; (*of fish*) presa *f*. **2** (*on door*) pestillo *m*. **3** (*drawback*) pega *f*; **c. question,** pregunta *f* con pega. **4 c. phrase,** slogan *m*. ◆**catch on** *vi fam* **1** (*become popular*) ganar popularidad. **2** (*understand*) caer en la cuenta. ◆**catch out** *vtr fam* **to c. sb out,** pillar a algn cometiendo una falta. ◆**catch up** *vi* **1 to c. up with sb,** (*reach*) alcanzar a algn. **2** (*with news*) ponerse al corriente (**on,** de); **to c. up on sleep,** recuperar el sueño perdido; **to c. up with work,** ponerse al día de trabajo.

catching [ˈkætʃɪŋ] *adj* (*disease*) contagioso,-a.

catchment [ˈkætʃmənt] *n* **c. area,** zona *f* de captación.

catchword [ˈkætʃwɜːd] *n* lema *m*.

catchy [ˈkætʃɪ] *adj* (**catchier, catchiest**) *fam* (*tune*) pegadizo,-a.

categoric(al) [kætɪˈgɒrɪk(əl)] *adj* categórico,-a.

categorize [ˈkætɪgəraɪz] *vtr* clasificar.

category [ˈkætɪgərɪ] *n* categoría *f*.

cater [ˈkeɪtər] *vi* **1 to c. for,** (*wedding etc*) proveer comida para. **2 to c. for,** (*taste*) atender a.

caterer [ˈkeɪtərər] *n* proveedor,-a *m,f*.

catering [ˈkeɪtərɪŋ] *n* abastecimiento *m* (de comidas por encargo).

caterpillar [ˈkætəpɪlər] *n* **1** oruga *f*. **2 c. (tractor),** tractor *m* de oruga.

cathedral [kəˈθiːdrəl] *n* catedral *f*.

Catholic [ˈkæθəlɪk] *adj & n* católico,-a (*m,f*).

catholic [ˈkæθəlɪk] *adj* católico,-a.

Catholicism [kəˈθɒlɪsɪzəm] *n* catolicismo *m*.

Catseye® [ˈkætsaɪ] *n GB* catafaro *m*.

cattle [ˈkætəl] *npl* ganado *m* (vacuno).

catty [ˈkætɪ] *adj* (**cattier, cattiest**) *fam* (*remark*) malintencionado,-a; (*person*) malicioso,-a.

catwalk [ˈkætwɔːk] *n* pasarela *f*.

Caucasian [kɔːˈkeɪzɪən] *adj & n* caucásico,-a (*m,f*), blanco,-a (*m,f*).

caucus [ˈkɔːkəs] *n* comité *m* central, ejecutiva *f*.

caught [kɔːt] *pt & pp* → **catch.**

cauliflower [ˈkɒlɪflaʊər] *n* coliflor *f*.

cause [kɔːz] **I** *n* **1** (*origin*) causa *f*. **2** (*reason*) motivo *m*. **3 for a good c.,** por una buena causa. **II** *vtr* causar; **to c. sb to do sth,** hacer que algn haga algo.

caustic [ˈkɔːstɪk] *adj* cáustico,-a; *fig* mordaz.

caution [ˈkɔːʃən] **I** *n* **1** (*care*) cautela *f*, prudencia *f*. **2** (*warning*) aviso *m*, advertencia *f*. **3** *GB Jur* reprensión *f*. **II** *vtr* advertir, amonestar.

cautious [ˈkɔːʃəs] *adj* cauteloso,-a, prudente.

cavalcade [kævəlˈkeɪd] *n* cabalgata *f*.

cavalier [kævəˈlɪər] **I** *adj* arrogante. **II** *n* caballero *m*.

cavalry [ˈkævəlrɪ] *n* caballería *f*.

cave [keɪv] *n* cueva *f*. ◆**cave in** *vi* (*roof etc*) derrumbarse, hundirse.

caveman [ˈkeɪvmæn] *n* hombre *m* de las cavernas.

cavern [ˈkævən] *n* caverna *f*.

caviar(e) [ˈkævɪɑːr] *n* caviar *m*.

cavity [ˈkævɪtɪ] *n* **1** (*hole*) cavidad *f*. **2** (*in tooth*) caries *f inv*.

cavort [kəˈvɔːt] *vi* retozar, brincar.

CB [siːˈbiː] *abbr* **Citizens' Band,** banda ciudadana, CB.

CBI [siːbiːˈaɪ] *GB abbr of* **Confederation of British Industry,** ≈ CEOE *f*.

cc [siːˈsiː] *abbr of* **cubic centimetre(s),** cc.

CD [siːˈdiː] *abbr of* **compact disc,** CD *m*; **CD player,** tocadiscos *m* digital *o* compacto.

cease [siːs] **I** *vtr* cesar; **to c. doing** *or* **to do sth,** dejar de hacer algo. **II** *vi* terminar.

cease-fire [siːsˈfaɪər] *n* alto *m* el fuego.

ceaseless [ˈsiːslɪs] *adj* incesante.

cedar [ˈsiːdər] *n* cedro *m*.

cede [siːd] *vtr* ceder.

ceiling [ˈsiːlɪŋ] *n* techo *m*.

celebrate [ˈselɪbreɪt] **I** *vtr* (*occasion*) celebrar. **II** *vi* divertirse.

celebrated [ˈselɪbreɪtɪd] *adj* célebre.

celebration [selɪˈbreɪʃən] *n* **1** celebración *f*. **2 celebrations,** festividades *fpl*.

celebrity [sɪˈlebrɪtɪ] *n* celebridad *f*.

celery [ˈselərɪ] *n* apio *m*.

celibate [ˈselɪbɪt] *adj & n* célibe (*mf*).

cell [sel] *n* **1** (*in prison*) celda *f*. **2** *Biol Pol* célula *f*. **3** *Elec* pila *f*.

cellar [ˈselər] *n* sótano *m*; (*for wine*) bodega *f*.

cello [ˈtʃeləʊ] *n* violoncelo *m*.

cellophane [ˈseləfeɪn] *n* celofán *m*.

celluloid [ˈseljʊlɔɪd] *n* celuloide *m*.

cellulose [ˈseljʊləʊs] *n* celulosa *f*.

Celsius [ˈselsɪəs] *adj* Celsio.

Celt [kelt, selt] *n* celta *mf*.

Celtic [ˈkeltɪk, ˈseltɪk] **I** *n* (*language*) celta *m*. **II** *adj* celta.

cement [sɪˈment] **I** *n* cemento *m*; **c. mixer,** hormigonera *f*. **II** *vtr Constr* unir con cemento; *fig* (*friendship*) cimentar.

cemetery [ˈsemɪtrɪ] *n* cementerio *m*.

censor ['sensər] I *n* censor,-a *m,f.* II *vtr* censurar.

censorship ['sensəʃɪp] *n* censura *f.*

censure ['senʃər] I *n* censura *f.* II *vtr* censurar.

census ['sensəs] *n* censo *m.*

cent [sent] *n* 1 centavo *m*, céntimo *m.* 2 **per c.**, por ciento.

centenary [sen'tiːnəri] *n* centenario *m.*

center ['sentər] *n & vtr US* → **centre**.

centigrade ['sentɪgreɪd] *adj* centígrado, -a.

centilitre, *US* **centiliter** ['sentɪliːtər] *n* centilitro *m.*

centimetre, *US* **centimeter** ['sentɪmiːtər] *n* centímetro *m.*

centipede ['sentɪpiːd] *n* ciempiés *m inv.*

central ['sentrəl] *adj* central; **c. heating**, calefacción *f* central; **C. America**, Centroamérica; **C. American**, centroamericano,-a *m,f.* ◆**centrally** *adv* **c. heated**, con calefacción central; **c. situated**, céntrico,-a.

centralize ['sentrəlaɪz] *vtr* centralizar.

centre ['sentər] I *n* centro *m*; **town c.**, centro de la ciudad; **Ftb c. forward**, delantero centro; **Ftb c. half**, medio centro; *Pol* **c. party**, partido *m* centrista; **sports c.**, centro deportivo. II *vtr (attention etc)* centrar (**on**, en).

century ['sentʃəri] *n* siglo *m*; **the nineteenth c.**, el siglo diecinueve.

ceramic [sɪ'ræmɪk] I *n* cerámica *f.* II *adj* de cerámica.

ceramics [sɪ'ræmɪks] *n sing* cerámica *f.*

cereal ['sɪərɪəl] *n* cereal *m.*

cerebral ['serɪbrəl, sɪ'riːbrəl] *adj* cerebral; **c. palsy**, parálisis *f* cerebral.

ceremony ['serɪmənɪ] *n* ceremonia *f.*

certain ['sɜːtən] I *adj* 1 *(sure)* seguro,-a; **to be c.**, estar seguro,-a; **to make c. of sth**, asegurarse de algo. 2 **to a c. extent**, hasta cierto punto. 3 *(not known)* cierto, -a; **a c. Miss Ward**, una tal señorita Ward. 4 *(true)* cierto,-a. II *adv* **for c.**, a ciencia cierta. ◆**certainly** *adv* desde luego; **c. not**, de ninguna manera.

certainty ['sɜːtəntɪ] *n* certeza *f*; *(assurance)* seguridad *f.*

certificate [sə'tɪfɪkɪt] *n* certificado *m*; *Educ* diploma *m.*

certified ['sɜːtɪfaɪd] *adj* certificado,-a; *(copy)* compulsado,-a.

certify ['sɜːtɪfaɪ] *vtr* certificar.

cervical ['sɜːvɪkəl, sə'vaɪkəl] *adj* **c. cancer**, cáncer *m* del útero; **c. smear**, frotis *m* cervical.

cervix ['sɜːvɪks] *n* 1 *(uterus)* cuello *m* del útero. 2 *(neck)* cerviz *f*, cuello *m.*

cessation [se'seɪʃən] *n* cese *m.*

cesspit ['sespɪt] *n* pozo negro.

Ceuta *n* Ceuta.

Ceylon [sɪ'lɒn] *n* Ceilán.

cf *abbr of* **confer,** *(compare)* compárese,

cfr.

chafe [tʃeɪf] I *vtr (make sore)* rozar. II *vi (skin)* irritarse; *(item of clothing)* rozar.

chaffinch ['tʃæfɪntʃ] *n* pinzón *m* vulgar.

chagrin ['ʃægrɪn] *n* disgusto *m*, desilusión *f.*

chain [tʃeɪn] I *n* cadena *f*; *fig (of events)* serie *f*; **c. of mountains**, cordillera *f*; **c. reaction**, reacción *f* en cadena; **c. saw**, sierra mecánica. II *vtr* **to c. (up)**, encadenar.

chain-smoke ['tʃeɪnsməʊk] *vi* fumar un pitillo tras otro.

chair [tʃeər] I *n* 1 silla *f*; *(with arms)* sillón *m*; **c. lift**, telesilla *m.* 2 *(position)* presidencia *f*; *Univ* cátedra *f.* II *vtr* presidir.

chairman ['tʃeəmən] *n* presidente *m.*

chairperson ['tʃeəpɜːsən] *n* presidente,-a *m,f.*

chalet ['ʃæleɪ] *n* chalet *m*, chalé *m.*

chalk [tʃɔːk] I *n (for writing)* tiza *f.* II ◆**chalk up** *vtr fam (victory etc)* apuntarse.

challenge ['tʃælɪndʒ] I *vtr* 1 retar, desafiar; **to c. sb to do sth**, retar a algn a que haga algo. 2 *(authority etc)* poner a prueba; *(statement)* poner en duda. 3 *Mil* dar el alto a. II *n* 1 reto *m*, desafío *m.* 2 *Mil* quién vive *m.*

challenging ['tʃælɪndʒɪŋ] *adj (idea)* desafiante; *(task)* que presenta un desafío.

chamber ['tʃeɪmbər] *n* 1 *(hall)* cámara *f*; **C. of Commerce**, Cámara de Comercio. 2 *Mus* **c. music**, música *f* de cámara. 3 *GB Jur* **chambers**, gabinete *m sing.*

chambermaid ['tʃeɪmbəmeɪd] *n* camarera *f.*

chameleon [kə'miːlɪən] *n* camaleón *m.*

champagne [ʃæm'peɪn] *n (French)* champán *m*; *(from Catalonia)* cava *m.*

champion ['tʃæmpɪən] *n* campeón,-ona *m,f*; *fig* **c. of human rights**, defensor,-a de los derechos humanos.

championship ['tʃæmpɪənʃɪp] *n* campeonato *m.*

chance [tʃɑːns] I *n* 1 *(fortune)* casualidad *f*, azar *m*; **by c.**, por casualidad; **to take a c.**, arriesgarse; **c. meeting**, encuentro *m* casual. 2 *(likelihood)* posibilidad *f*; **(the) chances are that ...**, lo más posible es que .... 3 *(opportunity)* oportunidad *f.* II *vtr* **to c. upon**, encontrar por casualidad. III *vtr* arriesgar.

chancellor ['tʃɑːnsələr] *n* 1 *(head of state, in embassy)* canciller *m.* 2 *GB Univ* rector,-a *m,f.* 3 *GB* **C. of the Exchequer**, ministro,-a *m,f* de Hacienda.

chandelier [ʃændɪ'lɪər] *n* araña *f* (de luces).

change [tʃeɪndʒ] I *vtr* cambiar; **to c. gear**, cambiar de marcha; **to c. one's mind/the subject**, cambiar de opinión/de tema; **to c. trains**, hacer trasbordo; **to get changed**, cambiarse de ropa; *fig* **to c.**

hands, cambiar de dueño,-a. II *vi* cambiar, cambiarse; **to c. for the better/ worse,** mejorar/empeorar; **to c. into,** convertirse en. III *n* 1 cambio *m;* **for a c.,** para variar; **c. of heart,** cambio de parecer; **c. of scene,** cambio de aires. 2 *(money)* cambio *m; (after purchase)* vuelta *f;* **small c.,** suelto *m.* ◆**change over** *vi* cambiarse.

changeable ['tʃeɪndʒəbəl] *adj (weather)* variable; *(person)* inconstante.

changeover ['tʃeɪndʒəʊvər] *n* conversión *f.*

changing ['tʃeɪndʒɪŋ] I *n* 1 **c. room,** vestuario *m.* 2 *Mil* relevo *m* (de la guardia). II *adj* cambiante.

channel ['tʃænəl] I *n* 1 *Geog* canal *m; (of river)* cauce *m;* **the C. Islands,** las Islas Anglonormandas; **the English C.,** el Canal de la Mancha. 2 *(administrative)* vía *f.* 3 *TV Rad* canal *m,* cadena *f.* II *vtr fig (ideas etc)* canalizar, encauzar.

chant [tʃɑːnt] I *n Rel* cántico *m; (of demonstrators)* slogan *m.* II *vtr & vi Rel* cantar; *(demonstrators)* corear.

chaos ['keɪɒs] *n* caos *m.*

chaotic [keɪ'ɒtɪk] *adj* caótico,-a.

chap [tʃæp] *n fam* chico *m,* tío *m.*

chapel ['tʃæpəl] *n* capilla *f.*

chaperon(e) ['ʃæpərəʊn] *n* carabina *f.*

chaplain ['tʃæplɪn] *n* capellán *m.*

chapter ['tʃæptər] *n* 1 capítulo *m.* 2 *Rel* cabildo *m.*

char [tʃɑːr] *vtr* chamuscar, carbonizar.

character ['kærɪktər] *n* 1 carácter *m.* 2 *fam (person)* tipo *m.* 3 *Theat* personaje *m.*

characteristic [kærɪktə'rɪstɪk] I *n* característica *f.* II *adj* característico,-a.

characterize ['kærɪktəraɪz] *vtr* caracterizar.

charcoal ['tʃɑːkəʊl] *n Min* carbón *m* vegetal; *Art* **c. drawing,** carboncillo *m;* **c. grey,** gris marengo *u* oscuro.

charge [tʃɑːdʒ] I *vtr* 1 cobrar; **c. it to my account,** cárguelo en mi cuenta. 2 **to c. sb with a crime,** acusar a algn de un crimen. 3 *Mil* cargar contra. 4 *Elec* cargar. II *vi Elec Mil* cargar; **to c. about,** andar a lo loco. III *n* 1 *(cost)* precio *m;* **bank charges,** comisión *f;* **free of c.,** gratis; **service c.,** servicio *m;* **c. account,** cuenta *f* corriente. 2 **to be in c. of,** estar a cargo de; **to take c. of,** hacerse cargo de. 3 *Jur* cargo *m,* acusación *f.* 4 *(explosive)* carga explosiva. 5 *Elec* carga *f.*

charged [tʃɑːdʒd] *adj fig* emotivo,-a.

charismatic [kærɪz'mætɪk] *adj* carismático,-a.

charitable ['tʃærɪtəbəl] *adj (person)* caritativo,-a; *(organization)* benéfico,-a.

charity ['tʃærɪtɪ] *n* caridad *f; (organization)* institución benéfica.

charlady ['tʃɑːleɪdɪ] *n GB* mujer *f* de la limpieza.

charlatan ['ʃɑːlətən] *n (doctor)* curandero,-a *m,f.*

charm [tʃɑːm] I *n* 1 *(quality)* encanto *m.* 2 *(spell)* hechizo *m;* **lucky c.,** amuleto *m.* II *vtr* encantar.

charming ['tʃɑːmɪŋ] *adj* encantador,-a.

chart [tʃɑːt] I *n* 1 *(giving information)* tabla *f; (graph)* gráfico *m.* 2 *(map)* carta *f* de navegación. 3 *Mus* **the charts,** la lista de éxitos. II *vtr Av Naut (on map)* trazar.

charter ['tʃɑːtər] I *n* 1 *(of institution)* estatutos *mpl; (of rights)* carta *f.* 2 **c. flight,** vuelo *m* chárter. II *vtr (plane, boat)* fletar.

chartered accountant [tʃɑːtədə 'kaʊntənt] *n GB* contable *mf* diplomado,-a.

charwoman ['tʃɑːwʊmən] *n GB* → **charlady.**

chase [tʃeɪs] I *vtr* perseguir; *(hunt)* cazar. II *n* persecución *f; (hunt)* caza *f.*

chasm ['kæzəm] *n Geog* sima *f; fig* abismo *m.*

chassis ['ʃæsɪ] *n* chasis *m inv.*

chastise [tʃæs'taɪz] *vtr* castigar.

chastity ['tʃæstɪtɪ] *n* castidad *f.*

chat [tʃæt] I *n* charla *f; GB* **c. show,** coloquio *m.* II *vi* charlar. ◆**chat up** *vtr fam* (intentar) ligar con algn.

chatter ['tʃætər] I *vi (person)* parlotear; *(bird)* piar; *(teeth)* castañetear. II *n (of person)* parloteo *m; (of birds)* gorjeo *m; (of teeth)* castañeteo *m.*

chatterbox ['tʃætəbɒks] *n fam* parlanchín,-ina *m,f.*

chatty ['tʃætɪ] *adj* (**chattier, chattiest**) hablador,-a.

chauffeur ['ʃəʊfər, ʃəʊ'fɜːr] *n* chófer *mf.*

chauvinism ['ʃəʊvɪnɪzəm] *n* chovinismo *m;* **male c.,** machismo *m.*

chauvinist ['ʃəʊvɪnɪst] *adj & n* chovinista *(mf);* **male c.,** machista *m.*

cheap [tʃiːp] I *adj* barato,-a; *(fare)* económico,-a; *(joke)* de mal gusto; *(contemptible)* bajo,-a; *fam* **dirt c.,** tirado,-a. II *n GB* **fam on the c.,** en plan barato. III *adv* barato. ◆**cheaply** *adv* barato, en plan económico.

cheapen ['tʃiːpən] *vtr fig* degradar.

cheat [tʃiːt] I *vtr* engañar; **to c. sb out of sth,** estafar algo a algn. II *vi* 1 *(at games)* hacer trampa; *(in exam etc)* copiar(se). 2 *fam (husband, wife)* poner cuernos (**on,** a). III *n (trickster)* tramposo,-a.

check [tʃek] I *vtr* repasar; *(facts)* comprobar; *(tickets)* controlar; *(tyres, oil)* revisar. 2 *(impulse)* refrenar; *(growth)* retardar. 3 *(stop)* detener. 4 *Chess* dar jaque a. II *vi* comprobar. III *n* 1 *(of documents etc)* revisión *f; (of facts)* comprobación *f.* 2 *Chess* jaque *m.* 3 *(pattern)* cuadro *m.* 4 **to keep in c.,** *(feelings)* contener; *(enemy)* mantener a raya. 5 *US* → **cheque.** ◆**check in** *vi (at airport)* facturar; *(at hotel)* registrarse (**at,** en). ◆**check out** I *vi (of ho-*

tel) dejar el hotel. **II** *vtr (facts)* verificar.
◆**check up** *vi* to c. up on sb, hacer averiguaciones sobre algn; **to c. up on sth**, comprobar algo.
checked [tʃekt] *adj* a cuadros.
checker [ˈtʃekər] *n US (cashier)* cajero,-a *m,f*.
checkered [ˈtʃekəd] *adj US →* **chequered**.
checkers [ˈtʃekəz] *n US (game)* damas *fpl*.
check-in [ˈtʃekɪn] *n* **c.-in desk**, *(at airport)* mostrador *m* de facturación.
checkmate [ˈtʃekmeɪt] **I** *n Chess* jaque mate *m*. **II** *vtr Chess* dar (jaque) mate a; *fig* poner en un callejón sin salida.
checkout [ˈtʃekaʊt] *n (counter)* caja *f*.
checkpoint [ˈtʃekpɔɪnt] *n* control *m*.
checkup [ˈtʃekʌp] *n Med* chequeo *m*, examen médico.
cheek [tʃiːk] *n* **1** mejilla *f*. **2** *fam (nerve)* cara *f*; **what c.!**, ¡vaya jeta!
cheekbone [ˈtʃiːkbəʊn] *n* pómulo *m*.
cheeky [ˈtʃiːkɪ] *adj (cheekier, cheekiest) fam* fresco,-a, descarado,-a.
cheep [tʃiːp] **I** *n (of bird)* pío *m*. **II** *vi* piar.
cheer [tʃɪər] *vi* aplaudir, aclamar. **II** *vtr* **1** *(applaud)* vitorear, aclamar. **2** *(make hopeful)* animar. **III** *n* viva *m*; **cheers**, aplausos *mpl*; *fam* **cheers!**, *(thank you)* gracias; *(before drinking)* ¡salud! ◆**cheer up I** *vi* animarse. **II** *vtr* to c. sb up, alegrar *or* animar a algn.
cheerful [ˈtʃɪəfʊl] *adj* alegre.
cheerio [tʃɪərɪˈəʊ] *interj GB fam* ¡hasta luego!
cheese [tʃiːz] *n* queso *m*.
cheesecake [ˈtʃiːzkeɪk] *n* tarta *f* de queso.
cheetah [ˈtʃiːtə] *n* guepardo *m*.
chef [ʃef] *n* chef *m*.
chemical [ˈkemɪkəl] **I** *n* sustancia química, producto químico. **II** *adj* químico,-a.
chemist [ˈkemɪst] *n* **1** químico,-a *m,f*. **2** *GB* **c.'s (shop)**, farmacia *f*; **dispensing c.**, farmacéutico,-a *m,f*.
chemistry [ˈkemɪstrɪ] *n* química *f*.
cheque [tʃek] *n* cheque *m*; **to pay by c.**, pagar con (un) cheque; **c. book**, talonario *m* (de cheques); **c. card**, tarjeta *f* de identificación bancaria.
chequered [ˈtʃekəd] *adj* a cuadros; *fig* **a c. career**, una carrera con altibajos.
cherish [ˈtʃerɪʃ] *vtr* **1** *(person)* tenerle mucho cariño a. **2** *fig (hopes etc)* abrigar.
cherry [ˈtʃerɪ] *n* cereza *f*.
chess [tʃes] *n* ajedrez *m*.
chessboard [ˈtʃesbɔːd] *n* tablero *m* de ajedrez.
chesspiece [ˈtʃespiːs] *n* pieza *f* de ajedrez.
chest [tʃest] *n* **1** *Anat* pecho *m*. **2** *(for linen)* arca *f*; *(for valuables)* cofre *m*; **c. of**

drawers, cómoda *f*.
chestnut [ˈtʃesnʌt] *n (tree, colour)* castaño *m*; *(nut)* castaña *f*.
chew [tʃuː] *vtr* masticar, mascar.
chewing gum [ˈtʃuːɪŋɡʌm] *n* chicle *m*.
chic [ʃiːk] *adj* elegante.
chick [tʃɪk] *n* pollito *m*.
chicken [ˈtʃɪkɪn] **I** *n* **1** pollo *m*. **2** *sl (coward)* gallina *m*. **II** *vi fam* **to c. out**, rajarse (por miedo).
chickenpox [ˈtʃɪkɪnpɒks] *n* varicela *f*.
chickpea [ˈtʃɪkpiː] *n* garbanzo *m*.
chicory [ˈtʃɪkərɪ] *n* achicoria *f*.
chief [tʃiːf] **I** *n* jefe *m*. **II** *adj* principal. ◆**chiefly** *adv (above all)* sobre todo; *(mainly)* principalmente.
chiffon [ʃɪˈfɒn, ˈʃɪfɒn] *n* gasa *f*.
chilblain [ˈtʃɪlbleɪn] *n* sabañón *m*.
child [tʃaɪld] *n (pl children)* niño,-a *m,f*; *(son)* hijo *m*; *(daughter)* hija *f*; **c. minder**, persona *f* que cuida niños en su propia casa.
childbirth [ˈtʃaɪldbɜːθ] *n* parto *m*.
childhood [ˈtʃaɪldhʊd] *n* infancia *f*, niñez *f*.
childish [ˈtʃaɪldɪʃ] *adj* pueril, aniñado.
childlike [ˈtʃaɪldlaɪk] *adj* infantil.
children [ˈtʃɪldrən] *npl →* **child**.
Chile [ˈtʃɪlɪ] *n* Chile.
Chilean [ˈtʃɪlɪən] *adj & n* chileno,-a *(m,f)*.
chill [tʃɪl] **I** *n* **1** *Med* resfriado *m*. **2** *(coldness)* fresco *m*. **II** *adj* frío,-a. **III** *vtr (meat)* refrigerar; *(wine)* enfriar.
chil(l)i [ˈtʃɪlɪ] *n* chile *m*.
chilly [ˈtʃɪlɪ] *adj (chillier, chilliest)* frío, -a.
chime [tʃaɪm] **I** *n (peal)* campanada *f*. **II** *vtr* **to c. five o'clock**, *(of clock)* dar las cinco. **III** *vi* sonar. ◆**chime in** *vi fam* intervenir.
chimney [ˈtʃɪmnɪ] *n* chimenea *f*; **c. sweep**, deshollinador *m*.
chimpanzee [tʃɪmpænˈziː] *n* chimpancé *m*.
chin [tʃɪn] *n* barbilla *f*, mentón *m*; **double c.**, papada *f*.
china [ˈtʃaɪnə] *n* loza *f*.
China [ˈtʃaɪnə] *n* China.
Chinese [tʃaɪˈniːz] **I** *adj* chino,-a. **II** *n* **1** *(person)* chino,-a *m,f*. **2** *(language)* chino *m*.
chink¹ [tʃɪŋk] *n (opening)* resquicio *m*; *(crack)* grieta *f*.
chink² [tʃɪŋk] **I** *vi* tintinear. **II** *n* tintineo *m*.
chip [tʃɪp] **I** *n* **1** *(of wood)* astilla *f*; *(of stone)* lasca *f*; *(in cup)* mella *f*. **2** *GB Culin* **chips**, patatas fritas. **3** *Comput* chip *m*. **4** *(in gambling)* ficha *f*. **II** *vtr (wood)* astillar; *(stone)* resquebrajar; *(china, glass)* mellar. **III** *vi (wood)* astillarse; *(china, glass)* mellarse; *(paint)* desconcharse. ◆**chip in** *vi fam* **1** meterse. **2** *(with money)* poner algo (de dinero).

chiropodist [kɪ'rɒpədɪst] *n* pedicuro,-a *m,f*.

chirp [tʃɜːp] *vi (birds)* gorjear.

chisel ['tʃɪzəl] *n* cincel *m*.

chit [tʃɪt] *n* nota *f*; *(small invoice)* vale *m*.

chitchat ['tʃɪttʃæt] *n fam* palique *m*.

chivalry ['ʃɪvəlrɪ] *n* caballerosidad *f*.

chives [tʃaɪvz] *npl* cebolleta *f sing*.

chlorine ['klɔːriːn] *n* cloro *m*.

chock-a-block [tʃɒkə'blɒk], **chock-full** [tʃɒk'ful] *adj fam* (lleno,-a) hasta los topes.

chocolate ['tʃɒkəlɪt] **I** *n* chocolate *m*; **chocolates**, bombones *mpl*. **II** *adj* de chocolate.

choice [tʃɔɪs] **I** *n* elección *f*; **a wide c.**, un gran surtido; **by c.**, por gusto. **II** *adj* selecto,-a.

choir ['kwaɪər] *n* coro *m*, coral *f*.

choirboy ['kwaɪəbɔɪ] *n* niño *m* de coro.

choke [tʃəuk] **I** *vtr* **1** *(person)* ahogar. **2** *(obstruct)* obstruir. **II** *vi* ahogarse; **to c. on food**, atragantarse con la comida. **III** *n Aut* estárter *m*. ◆**choke back** *vtr (emotions)* tragarse.

cholera ['kɒlərə] *n* cólera *m*.

cholesterol [kə'lestərɒl] *n* colesterol *m*.

choose [tʃuːz] **I** *vtr (pt chose; pp chosen)* escoger, elegir; *(decide on)* optar por. **II** *vi* escoger, elegir.

choos(e)y ['tʃuːzɪ] *adj (choosier, choosiest) fam* exigente.

chop [tʃɒp] **I** *vtr* **1** *(wood)* cortar; *(tree)* talar. **2** *Culin* cortar a pedacitos. **II** *n* **1** *(blow)* tajo *m*; *(with axe)* hachazo *m*. **2** *Culin* chuleta *f*.

chopper ['tʃɒpər] *n fam* helicóptero *m*.

choppy ['tʃɒpɪ] *adj (choppier, choppiest) (sea)* picado,-a.

chopsticks ['tʃɒpstɪks] *npl* palillos *mpl*.

chord [kɔːd] *n Mus* acorde *m*; *fig* **it strikes a c.**, (me) suena.

chore [tʃɔːr] *n* quehacer *m*, tarea *f*.

chortle ['tʃɔːtəl] *vi* reír con ganas.

chorus ['kɔːrəs] *n Mus Theat* coro *m*; *(in a song)* estribillo *m*; **c. girl**, corista *f*.

chose [tʃəuz] *pt →* **choose**.

chosen ['tʃəuzən] *pp →* **choose**.

Christ [kraɪst] *n* Cristo *m*, Jesucristo *m*.

christen ['krɪsən] *vtr* bautizar.

christening ['krɪsənɪŋ] *n* bautizo *m*.

Christian ['krɪstʃən] **I** *adj* cristiano,-a; **c. name**, nombre *m* de pila. **II** *n* cristiano,-a *m,f*.

Christianity [krɪstɪ'ænɪtɪ] *n* cristianismo *m*.

Christmas ['krɪsməs] *n* Navidad *f*; **merry C.**, feliz Navidad; **C. card**, tarjeta *f* de Navidad; **C. carol**, villancico *m*; **C. Day**, día *m* de Navidad; **C. Eve**, Nochebuena *f*.

chrome [krəum] *n* cromo *m*.

chromium ['krəumɪəm] *n* cromo *m*; **c. plating**, cromado *m*.

chromosome ['krəuməsəum] *n* cromosoma *m*.

chronic ['krɒnɪk] *adj* crónico,-a.

chronicle ['krɒnɪkəl] **I** *n* crónica *f*. **II** *vtr* hacer la crónica de.

chronological [krɒnə'lɒdʒɪkəl] *adj* cronológico,-a.

chrysanthemum [krɪ'sænθəməm] *n* crisantemo *m*.

chubby ['tʃʌbɪ] *adj (chubbier, chubbiest)* rellenito,-a.

chuck [tʃʌk] *vtr fam* tirar; **to c. one's job in** *or* **up**, dejar el trabajo; **to c. sb out**, echar a algn; **to c. sth away** *or* **out**, tirar algo.

chuckle ['tʃʌkəl] **I** *vi* reír entre dientes. **II** *n* sonrisita *f*.

chug [tʃʌg] *vi* traquetear.

chum [tʃʌm] *n* compinche *mf*, compañero,-a *m,f*.

chunk [tʃʌŋk] *n fam* cacho *m*, pedazo *m*.

church [tʃɜːtʃ] *n* iglesia *f*; **to go to c.**, ir a misa; **C. of England**, Iglesia Anglicana.

churchyard ['tʃɜːtʃjɑːd] *n* cementerio *m*, campo santo.

churlish ['tʃɜːlɪʃ] *adj* grosero,-a.

churn [tʃɜːn] **I** *n (for butter)* mantequera *f*; *GB (for milk)* lechera *f*. **II** *vtr (butter)* hacer. **III** *vi* revolverse, agitarse. ◆**churn out** *vtr fam* producir en serie.

chute [ʃuːt] *n (channel)* conducto *m*; *(slide)* tobogán *m*.

chutney ['tʃʌtnɪ] *n* conserva *f* (de frutas) picante.

CIA [siːaɪ'eɪ] *US abbr of* **Central Intelligence Agency**, Agencia *f* Central de Información, CIA *f*.

CID [siːaɪ'diː] *GB abbr of* **Criminal Investigation Department**, ≈ Brigada *f* de Investigación Criminal, BIC.

cider ['saɪdər] *n* sidra *f*.

cigar [sɪ'gɑːr] *n* puro *m*.

cigarette [sɪgə'ret] *n* cigarrillo *m*; **c. case**, pitillera *f*; **c. end**, colilla *f*; **c. holder**, boquilla *f*; **c. lighter**, mechero *m*.

Cinderella [sɪndə'relə] *n* Cenicienta *f*.

cine camera ['sɪnɪkæmərə] *n GB* cámara cinematográfica.

cinema ['sɪnɪmə] *n* cine *m*.

cinnamon ['sɪnəmən] *n* canela *f*.

cipher ['saɪfər] *n (numeral)* cifra *f*.

circle ['sɜːkəl] **I** *n* **1** círculo *m*; *(of people)* corro *m*; **in business circles**, en el mundo de los negocios. **2** *Theat* anfiteatro *m*. **II** *vtr (surround)* rodear; *(move round)* dar la vuelta a. **III** *vi* dar vueltas.

circuit ['sɜːkɪt] *n* **1** *(journey)* recorrido *m*. **2** *Elec* circuito *m*. **3** *Sport (events)* liga *f*; *GB (track)* circuito *m*. **4** *GB Jur* **c. judge**, juez *mf* de distrito.

circular ['sɜːkjulər] *adj & n* circular (*f*).

circulate ['sɜːkjuleɪt] **I** *vtr (news)* hacer circular. **II** *vi* circular.

circulation [sɜːkju'leɪʃən] *n* **1** *(of blood)*

circulación f. 2 (of newspaper) tirada f.
circumcise ['sɜːkəmsaɪz] vtr circuncidar.
circumference [sə'kʌmfərəns] n circunferencia f.
circumspect ['sɜːkəmspekt] adj prudente.
circumstance ['sɜːkəmstəns] n (usu pl) circunstancia f; **under no circumstances**, en ningún caso; **economic circumstances**, situación económica.
circumvent [sɜːkəm'vent] vtr fig burlar.
circus ['sɜːkəs] n circo m.
cirrhosis [sɪ'rəʊsɪs] n cirrosis f.
CIS [siːaɪ'es] n abbr of **Commonwealth of Independent States**, CEI.
cistern ['sɪstən] n cisterna f.
cite [saɪt] vtr (quote) citar.
citizen ['sɪtɪzən] n ciudadano,-a m,f.
citizenship ['sɪtɪzənʃɪp] n ciudadanía f.
citr(o)us ['sɪtrəs] adj c. **fruit**, agrios mpl.
city ['sɪtɪ] n 1 ciudad f. 2 Fin **the C.**, el centro financiero de Londres.
civic ['sɪvɪk] adj cívico,-a; GB c. **centre**, centro cívico; c. **duties**, obligaciones cívicas.
civil ['sɪvəl] adj 1 civil; c. **defence**, defensa f civil; c. **rights**, derechos mpl civiles; c. **servant**, funcionario,-a m,f; Pol c. **service**, administración pública. 2 (polite) cortés, educado,-a.
civilian [sɪ'vɪljən] adj & n civil (mf); c. **clothing** traje m de paisano.
civilization [sɪvɪlaɪ'zeɪʃən] n civilización f.
civilized ['sɪvɪlaɪzd] adj civilizado,-a.
clad [klæd] adj lit vestido,-a.
claim [kleɪm] I vtr 1 (benefits, rights) reclamar; Jur (compensation) exigir. 2 (assert) afirmar. II n 1 (demand) reclamación f; Jur demanda f; **to put in a c.**, reclamar una indemnización. 2 (right) derecho m. 3 (assertion) pretensión f.
claimant ['kleɪmənt] n Jur demandante mf.
clairvoyant [kleə'vɔɪənt] n clarividente mf.
clam [klæm] n almeja f. ◆**clam up** vi fam callarse.
clamber ['klæmbər] vi trepar (**over**, por).
clammy ['klæmɪ] adj (clammier, clammiest) (weather) bochornoso,-a; (hand) pegajoso,-a.
clamor ['klæmər] n US → **clamour**.
clamour ['klæmər] I n clamor m. II vi clamar; **to c. for**, pedir a gritos.
clamp [klæmp] I n (for carpentry) tornillo m de banco; Tech abrazadera f; **wheel c.**, cepo m. II vtr sujetar con abrazaderas. ◆**clamp down on** vtr aumentar los esfuerzos contra.
clan [klæn] n clan m.
clandestine [klæn'destɪn] adj clandestino,-a.
clang [klæŋ] I vi sonar. II n sonido metálico.

clap [klæp] I vi aplaudir. II n 1 palmada f. 2 a c. **of thunder**, un trueno.
clapping ['klæpɪŋ] n aplausos mpl.
claret ['klærət] n GB (wine) clarete m; (colour) burdeos m.
clarify ['klærɪfaɪ] vtr aclarar.
clarinet [klærɪ'net] n clarinete m.
clarity ['klærɪtɪ] n claridad f.
clash [klæʃ] I vi 1 (cymbals) sonar; (swords) chocar; fig (disagree) estar en desacuerdo. 2 (colours) desentonar. 3 (dates) coincidir. II n 1 (sound) sonido m. 2 (fight) choque m; fig (conflict) conflicto m.
clasp [klɑːsp] I n 1 (on belt) cierre m; (on necklace) broche m. 2 (grasp) apretón m; c. **knife**, navaja f. II vtr (object) agarrar; **to c. hands**, juntar las manos.
class [klɑːs] I n 1 clase f; c. **struggle**, lucha f de clases; Educ c. **of '84**, promoción f de 1984; Rail **second c. ticket**, billete m de segunda (clase). II vtr clasificar.
classic ['klæsɪk] I adj clásico,-a. II n 1 (author) autor clásico; (work) obra clásica. 2 **the classics**, (literature) las obras clásicas; (languages) clásicas fpl.
classical ['klæsɪkəl] adj clásico,-a.
classified ['klæsɪfaɪd] adj (information) secreto,-a; c. **advertisements**, anuncios mpl por palabras.
classify ['klæsɪfaɪ] vtr clasificar.
classless ['klɑːslɪs] adj sin clases.
classmate ['klɑːsmeɪt] n compañero,-a m,f de clase.
classroom ['klɑːsruːm] n aula f, clase f.
clatter ['klætər] I vi hacer ruido; (things falling) hacer estrépito. II n ruido m, estrépito m.
clause [klɔːz] n 1 Jur cláusula f. 2 Ling oración f.
claw [klɔː] I n (of bird, lion) garra f; (of cat) uña f; (of crab) pinza f. II vtr agarrar, arañar; (tear) desgarrar. ◆**claw at** vtr agarrar, arañar.
clay [kleɪ] n arcilla f; c. **pigeon shooting**, tiro m al plato.
clean [kliːn] I adj 1 limpio,-a. 2 (unmarked, pure) sin defecto; a c. **copy**, una copia en limpio; **to have a c. record**, no tener antecedentes (penales). 3 (not obscene) decente. 4 fig **to make a c. sweep of it**, arrasar. II adv 1 **to play c.**, jugar limpio; fam **to come c.**, confesarlo todo. 2 fam por completo; **it went c. through the middle**, pasó justo por el medio. III vtr (room) limpiar; **to c. one's teeth**, lavarse los dientes. ◆**clean out** vtr (room) limpiar a fondo. ◆**clean up** vtr & vi limpiar.
clean-cut ['kliːnkʌt] adj (person) limpio, -a, pulcro,-a.
cleaner ['kliːnər] n limpiador,-a m,f.
cleaning ['kliːnɪŋ] n limpieza f.
cleanliness ['klenlɪnɪs] n limpieza f.

cleanse [klenz] *vtr* limpiar.

cleansing ['klenzɪŋ] *n* **c. lotion,** leche limpiadora.

clear [klɪəʳ] **I** *adj* **1** claro,-a; *(road, day)* despejado,-a; **c. conscience,** conciencia tranquila. **2** *(obvious)* claro,-a; **to make sth c.,** aclarar algo. **3** *(majority)* absoluto; *(profit)* neto; **three c. days,** tres días completos. **4** *(free)* libre. **II** *adv* **1** *fig* **loud and c.,** claramente. **2 stand c.!,** ¡apártese!; **to stay c. of,** evitar. **III** *vtr* **1** *(room)* vaciar; *Com* liquidar; **to c. one's throat,** aclararse la garganta; **to c. the table,** quitar la mesa. **2** *(authorize)* autorizar. **3** *(hurdle)* salvar. **4 to c. sb of a charge,** exculpar a algn de un delito. ◆**clear away** *vtr* quitar. ◆**clear off** *vi fam* largarse; **c. off!,** ¡largo! ◆**clear out** *vtr* *(room)* limpiar a fondo; *(cupboard)* vaciar. ◆**clear up I** *vtr* **1** *(tidy)* recoger; *(arrange)* ordenar. **2** *(mystery)* resolver; *(misunderstanding)* aclarar. **II** *vi* *(weather)* despejarse; *(problem)* desaparecer. ◆**clearly** *adv* **1** claramente. **2** *(at start of sentence)* evidentemente.

clearance ['klɪərəns] *n* **1** *(of area)* despeje *m*; *Com* **c. sale,** liquidación *f* (de existencias). **2** *(space)* espacio *m* libre. **3** *(authorization)* autorización *f*.

clear-cut [klɪə'kʌt] *adj* claro,-a.

clearing ['klɪərɪŋ] *n* **1** *(in wood)* claro *m*. **2** *(of rubbish)* limpieza *f*. **3** *(of cheque)* compensación *f*.

clearway ['klɪəweɪ] *n GB* carretera *f* donde está prohibido parar.

cleaver ['kliːvəʳ] *n* cuchillo *f* de carnicero.

clef [klef] *n* clave *f*; **bass/treble c.,** clave de fa/de sol.

cleft [kleft] *n* hendidura *f*, grieta *f*.

clementine ['kleməntaɪn] *n* clementina *f*.

clench [klentʃ] *vtr* *(teeth, fist)* apretar.

clergy ['klɜːdʒɪ] *n* clero *m*.

clergyman ['klɜːdʒɪmən] *n* clérigo *m*.

clerical ['klerɪkəl] *adj* **1** *Rel* clerical. **2** *(staff, work)* de oficina.

clerk [klɑːk, *US* klɜːrk] *n* **1** *(office worker)* oficinista *mf*; *(civil servant)* funcionario,-a *m,f*. **2** *US Com* dependiente,-a *m,f*, vendedor,-a *m,f*.

clever ['klevəʳ] *adj* **1** *(person)* inteligente, listo,-a; **to be c. at sth,** tener aptitud para algo; *fam* **c. Dick,** sabiondo,-a *m,f*. **2** *(argument)* ingenioso,-a.

cliché ['kliːʃeɪ] *n* cliché *m*.

click [klɪk] **I** *n* *(sound)* clic *m*. **II** *vtr* *(tongue)* chasquear. **III** *vi* **it didn't c.,** *(I didn't realize)* no me di cuenta.

client ['klaɪənt] *n* cliente *mf*.

clientele [kliːɒn'tel] *n* clientela *f*.

cliff [klɪf] *n* acantilado *m*.

climate ['klaɪmɪt] *n* clima *m*.

climax ['klaɪmæks] *n* **1** *(peak)* clímax *m*, punto *m* culminante. **2** *(sexual)* orgasmo *m*.

climb [klaɪm] **I** *vtr* *(ladder)* subir a; *(mountain)* escalar; *(tree)* trepar a. **II** *vi* *(plants)* trepar; *Av* subir; *fig* *(socially)* ascender. **III** *n* subida *f*, ascensión *f*. ◆**climb down** *vi* bajar; *fig* volverse atrás.

climber ['klaɪməʳ] *n* alpinista *mf*, *Am* andinista *mf*.

climbing ['klaɪmɪŋ] *n Sport* montañismo *m*, alpinismo *m*, *Am* andinismo *m*.

clinch [klɪntʃ] **I** *vtr* resolver; *(deal)* cerrar. **II** *n sl* abrazo apasionado.

cling [klɪŋ] *vi* *(pt & pp* **clung)** *(hang on)* agarrarse; *(clothes)* ajustarse; *(smell)* pegarse; **to c. together,** unirse.

clinic ['klɪnɪk] *n* *(in state hospital)* ambulatorio *m*; *(specialized)* clínica *f*.

clinical ['klɪnɪkəl] *adj* **1** *Med* clínico,-a. **2** *(detached)* frío,-a.

clink [klɪŋk] **I** *vi* tintinear. **II** *n* tintineo *m*.

clip¹ [klɪp] **I** *vtr* *(cut)* cortar; *(ticket)* picar. **II** *n* **1** *(of film)* extracto *m*. **2** *(with scissors)* tijeretada *f*.

clip² [klɪp] **I** *n* *(for hair)* pasador *m*; *(for paper)* clip *m*, sujetapapeles *m inv*; *(brooch)* clip. **II** *vtr* sujetar.

clippers ['klɪpəz] *npl* *(for hair)* maquinilla *f* para rapar; *(for nails)* cortauñas *m inv*; *(for hedge)* tijeras *fpl* de podar.

clipping ['klɪpɪŋ] *n* recorte *m*.

clique [kliːk, klɪk] *n pej* camarilla *f*.

cloak [kləʊk] **I** *n* *(garment)* capa *f*. **II** *vtr* encubrir.

cloakroom ['kləʊkruːm] *n* guardarropa *m*; *euph* *(toilets)* servicios *mpl*.

clock [klɒk] **I** *n* reloj *m*. **II** *vtr* *(race)* cronometrar. ◆**clock in, clock on** *vi* fichar. ◆**clock off, clock out** *vi* fichar a la salida. ◆**clock up** *vtr* *(mileage)* hacer.

clockwise ['klɒkwaɪz] *adj & adv* en el sentido de las agujas del reloj.

clockwork ['klɒkwɜːk] *n* mecanismo *m*; **c. toy,** juguete *m* de cuerda.

clog [klɒg] **I** *vtr* obstruir; *(pipe)* atascar; **to get clogged up,** atascarse. **II** *n* *(footwear)* zueco *m*.

cloister ['klɔɪstəʳ] *n* claustro *m*.

close¹ [kləʊs] **I** *adj* **1** *(in space, time)* cercano,-a; *(print, weave)* compacto,-a; *(encounter)* cara a cara; *(contact)* directo,-a; **c. to,** cerca de; **c. together,** juntos; *fig* **we had a c. shave,** nos libramos por los pelos. **2** *(relationship)* estrecho,-a; *(friend)* íntimo,-a. **3** *(inspection)* detallado,-a; *(watch)* atento,-a. **4** *(contest)* reñido,-a; **a c. resemblance,** un gran parecido. **5** *(air)* cargado,-a; *(weather)* bochornoso,-a. **6** *(secretive)* reservado,-a. **7 c. season,** *(in hunting)* veda *f*. **II** *adv* cerca; **they live c. by** or **c. at hand,** viven cerca; **to stand c. together,** estar apretados,-as. ◆**closely** *adv* **1** *(tightly)* estrechamente, muy; **c.**

contested, muy reñido,-a; **they are c. related**, *(people)* son parientes próximos. **2** *(attentively)* con atención; **to follow (events) c.**, seguir de cerca (los acontecimientos).

close² [kləʊz] I *vtr* **1** cerrar; **closing time**, hora *f* de cierre. **2** *(end)* concluir, terminar; *(meeting)* levantar. II *vi* **1** *(shut)* cerrar, cerrarse. **2** *(end)* concluirse, terminarse. III *n* fin *m*, final *m*. ◆**close down** *vi (business)* cerrar para siempre; *Rad TV* cerrar. ◆**close in** *vi* to c. in on sb, rodear a algn.

closed [kləʊzd] *adj* cerrado,-a; *Ind* c. **shop**, empresa *f* que emplea solamente a miembros de un sindicato.

close-knit [kləʊs'nɪt] *adj fig* unido,-a.

closet ['klɒzɪt] *n US* armario *m*.

close-up ['kləʊsʌp] *n* primer plano *m*.

closure ['kləʊʒər] *n* cierre *m*.

clot [klɒt] I *n* **1** *(of blood)* coágulo *m*; *Med* **c. on the brain**, embolia *f* cerebral. **2** *GB fam* tonto,-a *m,f*. II *vi* coagularse.

cloth [klɒθ] *n* tela *f*, paño *m*; *(rag)* trapo *m*; *(tablecloth)* mantel *m*.

clothe [kləʊð] *vtr (pt & pp clothed or clad)* vestir (in, with, de); *fig* revestir, cubrir (in, with, de).

clothes [kləʊðz] *npl* ropa *f sing*, vestidos *mpl*; **c. brush**, cepillo *m* de la ropa; **c. hanger**, percha *f*; **c. horse**, tendedero *m* plegable; **c. line**, tendedero *m*; **c. peg**, pinza *f*.

clothing ['kləʊðɪŋ] *n* ropa *f*.

cloud [klaʊd] I *n* nube *f*. II *vtr* nublar; *fig* **to c. the issue**, complicar el asunto. III *vi* **to c. over**, nublarse.

cloudy ['klaʊdɪ] *adj (cloudier, cloudiest)* **1** *(sky)* nublado,-a. **2** *(liquid)* turbio,-a.

clout [klaʊt] *fam* I *n* **1** *(blow)* tortazo *m*. **2** *(influence)* influencia *f*. II *vtr* dar un tortazo a.

clove¹ [kləʊv] *n (spice)* clavo *m*.

clove² [kləʊv] *n (of garlic)* diente *m*.

clover ['kləʊvər] *n* trébol *m*.

clown [klaʊn] I *n* payaso *m*. II *vi* **to c.** *(about or around)*, hacer el payaso.

cloying ['klɔɪɪŋ] *adj* empalagoso,-a.

club [klʌb] I *n* **1** *(society)* club *m*; **sports c.**, club deportivo. **2** *(heavy stick)* garrote *m*, porra *f*; *Golf* palo *m*. **3** *Cards* trébol *m*. **4** *Culin* **c. sandwich**, sandwich *m* doble. II *vtr* aporrear. III *vi* **to c. together**, pagar entre varios.

clubhouse ['klʌbhaʊs] *n* sede *f* de un club.

cluck [klʌk] I *n* cloqueo *m*. II *vi* cloquear.

clue [kluː] *n (sign)* indicio *m*; *(to mystery)* pista *f*; *(in crossword)* clave *f*; *fam* I **haven't a c.**, no tengo ni idea.

clump [klʌmp] *n (of trees)* grupo *m*; *(of plants)* mata *f*.

clumsy ['klʌmzɪ] *adj (clumsier, clumsiest)* desmañado,-a, torpe; *(awkward)*

tosco,-a.

clung [klʌŋ] *pt & pp* → **cling**.

cluster ['klʌstər] I *n* grupo *m*; *(of grapes)* racimo *m*. II *vi* agruparse.

clutch [klʌtʃ] I *vtr* agarrar. II *vi fig* **to c. at straws**, aferrarse a cualquier cosa. III *n* **1** *Aut* embrague *m*. **2** *fig* **to fall into sb's clutches**, caer en las garras de algn.

clutter ['klʌtər] *vtr* **to c.** (up), llenar, atestar.

cm *abbr of* **centimetre(s)**, centímetro(s), cm.

CND [siːen'diː] *GB abbr of* **Campaign for Nuclear Disarmament**, campaña *f* para el desarme nuclear.

Co 1 *Com abbr of* **Company**, C., Cª, Cía. **2** *abbr of* **County**.

c/o [siː'əʊ] *abbr of* **care of**, en casa de, c/ d.

coach [kəʊtʃ] I *n* **1** *Aut* autocar *m*; *(carriage)* carruaje *m*; **c. tour**, excursión *f* en autocar. **2** *Rail* coche *m*, vagón *m*. **3** *Sport* entrenador,-a *m,f*; *Educ* dar clases particulares a. II *vtr Sport* entrenar; *Educ* dar clases particulares a.

coagulate [kəʊˈægjʊleɪt] *vi* coagularse.

coal [kəʊl] *n* carbón *m*, hulla *f*; **c. bunker**, carbonera *f*; **c. merchant**, carbonero *m*; **c. mine**, mina *f* de carbón.

coalfield ['kəʊlfiːld] *n* yacimiento *m* de carbón.

coalition [kəʊəˈlɪʃən] *n* coalición *f*.

coarse [kɔːs] *adj (material)* basto,-a; *(skin)* áspero,-a; *(language)* grosero,-a, ordinario,-a.

coast [kəʊst] I *n* costa *f*, litoral *m*; *fam fig* **the c. is clear**, no hay moros en la costa. II *vi Aut* ir en punto muerto.

coastal ['kəʊstəl] *adj* costero,-a.

coaster ['kəʊstər] *n (mat)* salvamanteles *m inv*.

coastguard ['kəʊstɡɑːd] *n* guardacostas *m inv*.

coastline ['kəʊstlaɪn] *n* litoral *m*, costa *f*.

coat [kəʊt] I *n* **1** *(overcoat)* abrigo *m*; *(short)* chaquetón *m*; **c. hanger**, percha *f*. **2** *(of animal)* pelo *m*. **3** *(of paint)* mano *f*, capa *f*. **4 c. of arms**, escudo *m* de armas. II *vtr* cubrir (with, de); *(with liquid)* bañar (with, en).

coating ['kəʊtɪŋ] *n* capa *f*, baño *m*.

coax [kəʊks] *vtr* engatusar.

cob [kɒb] *n* mazorca *f*.

cobble ['kɒbəl] *n* adoquín *m*.

cobbler ['kɒblər] *n* zapatero *m*.

cobweb ['kɒbweb] *n* telaraña *f*.

cocaine [kəˈkeɪn] *n* cocaína *f*.

cock [kɒk] I *n* **1** *Orn* gallo *m*; *(male bird)* macho *m*. **2** *(on gun)* percutor *m*. **3** *sl vulg (penis)* polla *f*. II *vtr (gun)* amartillar; *(ears)* erguir. ◆**cock up** *vtr GB sl* chapucear.

cocker ['kɒkər] *n* **c. spaniel**, cocker *m*.

cockerel ['kɒkərəl] *n* gallo *m* joven.

cockeyed ['kɒkaɪd] *adj fam (lopsided)*

torcido,-a; *(scheme)* disparatado,-a.
cockle ['kɒkəl] *n* berberecho *m*.
cockney ['kɒknɪ] **I** *adj* del East End londinense. **II** *n* persona *f* del East End londinense.
cockpit ['kɒkpɪt] *n* cabina *f* del piloto.
cockroach ['kɒkrəʊtʃ] *n* cucaracha *f*.
cocktail ['kɒkteɪl] *n* cóctel *m*; **c. lounge,** bar *m*; **c. party,** cóctel; **prawn c.,** cóctel de gambas; **Molotov c.,** cóctel Molotov.
cocky ['kɒkɪ] *adj* **(cockier, cockiest)** *fam* creído,-a.
cocoa ['kəʊkəʊ] *n* cacao *m*.
coconut ['kəʊkənʌt] *n* coco *m*.
cocoon [kə'kuːn] *n* capullo *m*.
COD [siːəʊ'diː] *GB abbr of* **cash on delivery, CAE.**
cod [kɒd] *n* bacalao *m*; **c. liver oil,** aceite *m* de hígado de bacalao.
code [kəʊd] **I** *n* código *m*; *(symbol)* clave *f*; *Tel* prefijo *m*. **II** *vtr (message)* cifrar, poner en clave.
co-ed [kəʊ'ed] *fam* **I** *adj* mixto,-a. **II** *n* colegio mixto.
coerce [kəʊ'ɜːs] *vtr* coaccionar.
coercion [kəʊ'ɜːʃən] *n* coacción *f*.
coexist [kəʊɪg'zɪst] *vi* coexistir.
coffee ['kɒfɪ] *n* café *m*; **c. bar/shop,** cafetería *f*; **c. break,** descanso *m*; **c. table,** mesita *f* de café.
coffeepot ['kɒfɪpɒt] *n* cafetera *f*.
coffer ['kɒfər] *n* arca *f*.
coffin ['kɒfɪn] *n* ataúd *m*.
cog [kɒg] *n* diente *m*.
cognac ['kɒnjæk] *n* coñac *m*.
coherent [kəʊ'hɪərənt] *adj* coherente.
coil [kɔɪl] **I** *vtr* **to c. (up),** enrollar. **II** *vi* enroscarse. **III** *n* **1** *(loop)* vuelta *f*; *(of rope)* rollo *m*; *(of hair)* rizo *m*. **2** *(contraceptive)* espiral *f*. **3** *Elec* carrete *m*, bobina *f*.
coin [kɔɪn] **I** *n* moneda *f*. **II** *vtr* **1** *(money)* acuñar. **2** *fig* **to c. a phrase,** por así decirlo.
coinage ['kɔɪnɪdʒ] *n* moneda *f*, sistema *m* monetario.
coincide [kəʊɪn'saɪd] *vi* coincidir (**with,** con).
coincidence [kəʊ'ɪnsɪdəns] *n* coincidencia *f*.
coincidental [kəʊɪnsɪ'dentəl] *adj* casual.
◆**coincidentally** *adv* por casualidad *or* coincidencia.
Coke® [kəʊk] *n (abbr of* **Coca-Cola®**) *fam* coca-cola *f*.
coke [kəʊk] *n (coal)* coque *m*.
colander ['kɒləndər] *n* colador *m*.
cold [kəʊld] **I** *adj* frío,-a; **I'm c.,** tengo frío; **it's c.,** *(weather)* hace frío; *(thing)* está frío,-a; *fig* **to get c. feet (about doing sth),** entrarle miedo a algn (de hacer algo); **c. cream,** crema *f* hidratante; *fig* **it leaves me c.,** no me dice nada; **c. war,** guerra fría. **II** *n* **1** frío *m*. **2** *Med* res-

friado *m*; **to catch a c.,** resfriarse, acatarrarse; *(cave in)* resfriado,-a; **c. sore,** herpes *m* (en el labio).
cold-blooded [kəʊld'blʌdɪd] *adj* **1** *(animal)* de sangre fría. **2** *fig (person)* frío,-a; *(crime)* a sangre fría.
coleslaw ['kəʊlslɔː] *n* ensalada *f* de col.
collaborate [kə'læbəreɪt] *vi* colaborar (**with,** con).
collaborator [kə'læbəreɪtər] *n Pol* colaboracionista *mf*.
collapse [kə'læps] **I** *vi (break down)* derrumbarse; *(cave in)* hundirse; *fig (prices)* caer en picado; *Med* sufrir un colapso. **II** *vtr (table)* plegar. **III** *n (breaking down)* derrumbamiento *m*; *(caving in)* hundimiento *m*; *Med* colapso *m*.
collapsible [kə'læpsəbəl] *adj* plegable.
collar ['kɒlər] **I** *n (of garment)* cuello *m*; *(for dog)* collar *m*. **II** *vtr fam* pescar, agarrar.
collarbone ['kɒləbəʊn] *n* clavícula *f*.
collateral [kɒ'lætərəl] **I** *n Fin* garantía subsidiaria. **II** *adj* colateral.
colleague ['kɒliːg] *n* colega *mf*.
collect [kə'lekt] **I** *vtr* **1** *(gather)* recoger. **2** *(stamps etc)* coleccionar. **3** *(taxes)* recaudar. **II** *vi* **1** *(people)* reunirse. **2** *(for charity)* hacer una colecta (**for,** para). **III** *adv US Tel* **to call c.,** llamar a cobro revertido.
collection [kə'lekʃən] *n* **1** *(of mail)* recogida *f*; *(of money)* colecta *f*. **2** *(of stamps)* colección *f*. **3** *(of taxes)* recaudación *f*. **4** *(of people)* grupo *m*.
collective [kə'lektɪv] **I** *adj* colectivo,-a; **c. bargaining,** negociación colectiva. **II** *n* colectivo *m*.
collector [kə'lektər] *n* **1** *(of stamps)* coleccionista *mf*. **2** **tax c.,** recaudador,-a *m,f* de impuestos.
college ['kɒlɪdʒ] *n* colegio *m*; *(of university)* colegio mayor.
collide [kə'laɪd] *vi* chocar, colisionar.
collie ['kɒlɪ] *n* perro *m* pastor escocés.
colliery ['kɒljərɪ] *n GB* mina *f* de carbón.
collision [kə'lɪʒən] *n* choque *m*.
colloquial [kə'ləʊkwɪəl] *adj* coloquial.
collusion [kə'luːʒən] *n* conspiración *f*.
cologne [kə'ləʊn] *n* (agua *f* de) colonia *f*.
Colombia [kə'lɒmbɪə] *n* Colombia.
Colombian [kə'lɒmbɪən] *adj & n* colombiano,-a *(m,f)*.
colon¹ ['kəʊlən] *n Typ* dos puntos *mpl*.
colon² ['kəʊlən] *n Anat* colon *m*.
colonel ['kɜːnəl] *n* coronel *m*.
colonial [kə'ləʊnɪəl] *adj* colonial.
colonize ['kɒlənaɪz] *vtr* colonizar.
colony ['kɒlənɪ] *n* colonia *f*.
color ['kʌlər] *n & vtr & vi US →* **colour.**
colossal [kə'lɒsəl] *adj* colosal.
colour ['kʌlər] **I** *n* **1** color *m*; **what c. is it?,** ¿de qué color es?; **c. film/television,** película *f*/televisión *f* en color; **c.**

scheme, combinación f de colores. 2 (*race*) color m; **c. bar**, discriminación f racial. 3 **colours**, GB Sport colores mpl; Mil (*flag*) bandera f sing. II vtr colorear. III vi to c. (up), ruborizarse.

colour-blind ['kʌləblaɪnd] adj daltónico, -a.

Coloured ['kʌləd] adj de color.

coloured ['kʌləd] adj (*photograph*) en color.

colourful ['kʌləful] adj 1 con muchos colores; fig lleno,-a de color; (*person*) pintoresco,-a.

colouring ['kʌlərɪŋ] n (*colour*) colorido m.

colourless ['kʌlələs] adj incoloro,-a; fig soso,-a.

colt [kəult] n potro m.

column ['kɒləm] n columna f.

columnist ['kɒləmnɪst] n columnista mf.

coma ['kəumə] n coma m; **to go into a c.**, entrar en coma.

comb [kəum] I n peine m. II vtr 1 peinar; **to c. one's hair**, peinarse.

combat ['kɒmbæt] I n combate m. II vtr (*enemy, disease*) combatir. III vi combatir (*against*, contra).

combination [kɒmbɪ'neɪʃən] n combinación f.

combine [kəm'baɪn] I vtr combinar. II vi combinarse; (*companies*) asociarse. III ['kɒmbaɪn] n 1 Com asociación f. 2 **c. harvester**, cosechadora f.

combustion [kəm'bʌstʃən] n combustión f.

come [kʌm] vi (pt **came**; pp **come**) 1 venir; (*arrive*) llegar; **coming!**, ¡voy!; **to c. and go**, ir y venir; fig **in years to c.**, en el futuro. 2 **to c. apart/undone**, desatarse/ soltarse. 3 (*happen*) suceder; **that's what comes of being too impatient**, es lo que pasa por ser demasiado impaciente; fam **how c.?**, ¿y eso? 4 **I came to believe that ...**, llegué a creer que .... 5 fig **c. what may**, pase lo que pase. 6 sl (*have orgasm*) correrse. ◆**come about** vi ocurrir, suceder. ◆**come across** I vtr (*thing*) encontrar por casualidad; **to c. across sb**, tropezar con algn. II vi fig **to c. across well**, causar buena impresión. ◆**come along** vi 1 (*arrive*) venir; **c. along!**, ¡venga! 2 (*make progress*) progresar. ◆**come away** vi (*leave*) salir; (*part*) desprenderse (**from**, de). ◆**come back** vi (*return*) volver. ◆**come before** vtr 1 preceder. 2 (*court*) comparecer ante. ◆**come by** vtr adquirir. ◆**come down** vi bajar; (*rain*) caer; (*building*) ser derribado,-a; **to c. down with the flu**, coger la gripe. ◆**come forward** vi (*advance*) avanzar; (*volunteer*) ofrecerse. ◆**come in** vi 1 (*enter*) entrar; **c. in!**, ¡pase! 2 (*arrive*) (*train*) llegar; (*tide*) subir; fam fig **where do I c. in?**, y yo ¿qué pinto? 3 **to c. in handy**, venir

bien. 4 **to c. in for**, ser objeto de. ◆**come into** vtr 1 (*enter*) entrar en. 2 (*inherit*) heredar. ◆**come off** I vtr (*fall from*) caerse de; fam **c. off it!**, ¡venga ya! II vi 1 (*fall*) caerse; (*stain*) quitarse; (*button*) caerse. 2 fam (*take place*) pasar; (*succeed*) salir bien; **to c. off badly**, salir mal. ◆**come on** vi 1 **c. on!**, (*hurry*) ¡venga! 2 (*make progress*) progresar. 3 (*rain, illness*) comenzar. ◆**come out** vi 1 salir (**of**, de); (*book*) aparecer; (*product*) estrenarse; (*facts*) revelarse. 2 (*stain*) quitarse; (*colour*) desteñir. 3 **to c. out against/in favour of sth**, declararse en contra/a favor de algo; GB Ind **to c. out (on strike)**, declararse en huelga. 4 (*turn out*) salir. ◆**come over** I vi venir. II vtr 1 (*hill*) aparecer en lo alto de. 2 fam **what's c. over you?**, ¿qué te pasa? ◆**come round** I vtr (*corner*) dar la vuelta a. II vi 1 (*visit*) venir. 2 (*regain consciousness*) volver en sí. 3 **to c. round to sb's way of thinking**, dejarse convencer por algn. ◆**come through** I vtr 1 (*cross*) cruzar. 2 (*illness*) recuperarse de; (*accident*) sobrevivir. II vi (*message*) llegar. ◆**come to** vi 1 (*regain consciousness*) volver en sí. II vtr 1 **to c. to one's senses**, fig recobrar la razón. 2 (*amount to*) costar. 3 (*arrive at*) llegar a; **to c. to an end**, terminar; fam **c. to that**, a propósito. ◆**come under** vtr fig **to c. under fire from sb**, ser criticado,-a por algn; ◆**come up** vi 1 (*rise*) subir; (*approach*) acercarse (**to**, a). 2 (*difficulty, question*) surgir; **to c. up with a solution**, encontrar una solución; **to c. up against problems**, encontrarse con problemas. 3 (*sun*) salir. 4 **to c. up to**, igualar; **to c. up to sb's expectations**, satisfacer a algn. 5 fam **three chips, coming up!**, ¡van tres de patatas fritas! ◆**come upon** vtr → **come across**.

comeback ['kʌmbæk] n fam 1 (*of person*) reaparición f; **to make a c.**, reaparecer. 2 (*answer*) réplica f.

comedian [kə'miːdɪən] n cómico m.

comedienne [kəmiːdɪ'en] n cómica f.

comedown ['kʌmdaun] n fam desilusión f, revés m.

comedy ['kɒmɪdɪ] n comedia f.

comet ['kɒmɪt] n cometa m.

comeuppance [kʌm'ʌpəns] n fam **to get one's c.**, llevarse su merecido.

comfort ['kʌmfət] I n comodidad f; US **c. station**, servicios mpl. 2 (*consolation*) consuelo m; **to take c. in or from sth**, consolarse con algo. II vtr consolar.

comfortable ['kʌmfətəbəl] adj (*chair, person, margin*) cómodo,-a; (*temperature*) agradable. ◆**comfortably** adv (*win*) con facilidad; **to be c. off**, vivir cómodamente.

comforter ['kʌmfətəʳ] n 1 GB (*scarf*) bufanda f. 2 (for baby) chupete m. 3 US edredón m.

comforting ['kʌmfətɪŋ] adj consolador,-a.

comic ['kɒmɪk] I adj cómico,-a; **c. strip**, tira cómica, historieta f. II n 1 (person) cómico,-a m,f. 2 Press tebeo m, comic m.

coming ['kʌmɪŋ] I adj (year) próximo,-a; (generation) futuro,-a. II n venida f, llegada f; **comings and goings**, idas y venidas; fig **c. and going**, ajetreo m.

comma ['kɒmə] n coma f.

command [kə'mɑːnd] I vtr 1 mandar. 2 (respect) infundir; (sympathy) merecer; (money etc) disponer de. II n 1 (order) orden f; (authority) mando m; **to be at sb's c.**, estar a las órdenes de algn. 2 (of language) dominio m. 3 (disposal) disposición f.

commandeer [kɒmən'dɪəʳ] vtr requisar.

commander [kə'mɑːndəʳ] n comandante m.

commanding [kə'mɑːndɪŋ] adj dominante; Mil **c. officer**, comandante m.

commandment [kə'mɑːndmənt] n mandamiento m.

commando [kə'mɑːndəʊ] n comando m.

commemorate [kə'meməreɪt] vtr conmemorar.

commence [kə'mens] vtr & vi fml comenzar.

commend [kə'mend] vtr 1 (praise) alabar, elogiar. 2 (entrust) encomendar. 3 (recommend) recomendar.

commensurate [kə'menʃərət] adj proporcional; **c. to or with**, en proporción con.

comment ['kɒment] I n comentario m; **no c.**, sin comentario. II vi hacer comentarios.

commentary ['kɒməntərɪ] n comentario m.

commentator ['kɒmənteɪtəʳ] n comentarista mf.

commerce ['kɒmɜːs] n comercio m.

commercial [kə'mɜːʃəl] I adj comercial; TV **c. break**, corte publicitario. II n TV anuncio m.

commiserate [kə'mɪzəreɪt] vi compadecerse (with, de).

commission [kə'mɪʃən] I n 1 Mil despacho m (de oficial); **out of c.**, fuera de servicio. 2 (of enquiry) comisión f; (job) encargo m. 3 (payment) comisión f. II vtr 1 Mil nombrar. 2 (order) encargar. 3 Naut poner en servicio.

commissionaire [kəmɪʃə'neəʳ] n GB portero m.

commissioner [kə'mɪʃənəʳ] n (official) comisario m; **c. of police**, comisario de policía.

commit [kə'mɪt] vtr 1 (crime) cometer; **to c. suicide**, suicidarse. 2 **to c. oneself (to do sth)**, comprometerse (a hacer algo). 3

to c. sth to sb's care, confiar algo a algn.

commitment [kə'mɪtmənt] n compromiso m.

committee [kə'mɪtɪ] n comisión f, comité m.

commode [kə'məʊd] n (chair) silla f con orinal; (chest of drawers) cómoda f.

commodity [kə'mɒdɪtɪ] n artículo m.

common ['kɒmən] I adj 1 común; **that's c. knowledge**, eso lo sabe todo el mundo; **c. law**, derecho consuetudinario; **C. Market**, Mercado m Común; GB **c. room**, sala f de profesores or de estudiantes. 2 (ordinary) corriente. 3 (vulgar) ordinario,-a, maleducado,-a. II n (land) campo m or terreno m comunal.

commonplace ['kɒmənpleɪs] adj corriente.

Commons ['kɒmənz] npl GB **the (House of) C.**, (la Cámara de) los Comunes.

Commonwealth ['kɒmənwelθ] n GB **the C.**, la Commonwealth; **C. of Independent States**, Comunidad f de Estados Independientes.

commotion [kə'məʊʃən] n alboroto m.

commune¹ [kə'mjuːn] vi (converse) conversar íntimamente; (with nature) estar en comunión (with, con).

commune² ['kɒmjuːn] n comuna f.

communicate [kə'mjuːnɪkeɪt] I vi comunicarse (with, con). II vtr comunicar.

communication [kəmjuːnɪ'keɪʃən] n 1 comunicación f. 2 GB Rail **c. cord**, timbre m de alarma.

communion [kə'mjuːnjən] n comunión f; **to take c.**, comulgar.

communiqué [kə'mjuːnɪkeɪ] n comunicado m oficial.

communism ['kɒmjʊnɪzəm] n comunismo m.

communist ['kɒmjʊnɪst] adj & n comunista (mf).

community [kə'mjuːnɪtɪ] n comunidad f; (people) colectividad f; **c. centre**, centro m social.

commute [kə'mjuːt] I vi viajar diariamente al lugar de trabajo. II vtr Jur conmutar.

commuter [kə'mjuːtəʳ] n persona f que viaja diariamente al lugar de trabajo.

compact¹ [kəm'pækt] I adj compacto,-a; (style) conciso,-a; **c. disc**, disco compacto. II ['kɒmpækt] n (for powder) polvera f.

compact² ['kɒmpækt] n Pol pacto m.

companion [kəm'pænjən] n compañero, -a m,f.

companionship [kəm'pænjənʃɪp] n compañerismo m.

company ['kʌmpənɪ] n 1 compañía f; **to keep sb c.**, hacer compañía a algn. 2 Com empresa f, compañía f.

comparable ['kɒmpərəbəl] adj comparable (**to, with,** con).

comparative [kəm'pærətɪv] **I** adj comparativo,-a; (relative) relativo,-a. **II** n Ling comparativo m. ◆**comparatively** adv relativamente.

compare [kəm'peəʳ] **I** vtr comparar (**to, with,** con); (**as**) **compared with,** en comparación con. **II** vi compararse.

comparison [kəm'pærɪsən] n comparación f; **by c.,** en comparación; **there's no c.,** no se puede comparar.

compartment [kəm'pɑːtmənt] n (section) compartimiento m; Rail departamento m.

compass ['kʌmpəs] n 1 brújula f. 2 (pair of) **compasses,** compás m. 3 fig (range) límites mpl.

compassion [kəm'pæʃən] n compasión f.

compassionate [kəm'pæʃənət] adj compasivo,-a.

compatible [kəm'pætəbəl] adj compatible.

compel [kəm'pel] vtr 1 (oblige) obligar; **to c. sb to do sth,** obligar a algn a hacer algo. 2 (admiration) despertar.

compelling [kəm'pelɪŋ] adj irresistible.

compensate ['kɒmpenseɪt] **I** vtr compensar; **to c. sb for sth,** indemnizar a algn de algo. **II** vi compensar.

compensation [kɒmpen'seɪʃən] n compensación f; (for loss) indeminización f.

compere ['kɒmpeəʳ] GB n animador,-a m,f.

compete [kəm'piːt] vi competir.

competence ['kɒmpɪtəns] n 1 (ability) aptitud f. 2 (of court etc) competencia f.

competent ['kɒmpɪtənt] adj competente.

competition [kɒmpɪ'tɪʃən] n 1 (contest) concurso m. 2 Com competencia f.

competitive [kəm'petɪtɪv] adj competitivo,-a.

competitor [kəm'petɪtəʳ] n competidor,-a m,f.

compilation [kɒmpɪ'leɪʃən] n recopilación f.

compile [kəm'paɪl] vtr compilar, recopilar.

complacency [kəm'pleɪsənsɪ] n complacencia f.

complacent [kəm'pleɪsənt] adj autocomplaciente.

complain [kəm'pleɪn] vi quejarse (**of, about,** de).

complaint [kəm'pleɪnt] n 1 queja f; Com reclamación f. 2 Jur demanda f. 3 Med enfermedad f.

complement ['kɒmplɪmənt] **I** n 1 complemento m. 2 Naut dotación f. **II** vtr complementar.

complementary [kɒmplɪ'mentərɪ] adj complementario,-a.

complete [kəm'pliːt] **I** adj 1 (entire) completo,-a. 2 (absolute) total. **II** vtr completar; **to c. a form,** rellenar un formulario. ◆**completely** adv completamente,

por completo.

completion [kəm'pliːʃən] n terminación f; **near c.,** casi terminado,-a; **on c.,** en cuanto se termine.

complex ['kɒmpleks] **I** adj complejo,-a. **II** n complejo m; **inferiority c.,** complejo de inferioridad.

complexion [kəm'plekʃən] n tez f; fig aspecto m.

compliance [kəm'plaɪəns] n conformidad f; **in c. with,** de acuerdo con.

complicate ['kɒmplɪkeɪt] vtr complicar.

complicated ['kɒmplɪkeɪtɪd] adj complicado,-a.

complication [kɒmplɪ'keɪʃən] n complicación f.

complicity [kəm'plɪsɪtɪ] n complicidad f.

compliment ['kɒmplɪmənt] **I** n 1 cumplido m; **to pay sb a c.,** hacerle un cumplido a algn. 2 **compliments,** saludos mpl. **II** ['kɒmplɪment] vtr felicitar; **to c. sb on sth,** felicitar a algn por algo.

complimentary [kɒmplɪ'mentərɪ] adj 1 (praising) elogioso,-a. 2 (free) gratis.

comply [kəm'plaɪ] vi obedecer; **to c. with,** (order) cumplir con; (request) acceder a.

component [kəm'pəʊnənt] **I** n componente m. **II** adj componente; **c. part,** parte f.

compose [kəm'pəʊz] vtr & vi 1 componer; **to be composed of,** componerse de. 2 **to c. oneself,** calmarse.

composed [kəm'pəʊzd] adj (calm) sereno,-a.

composer [kəm'pəʊzəʳ] n compositor,-a m,f.

composite ['kɒmpəzɪt] adj compuesto,-a.

composition [kɒmpə'zɪʃən] n composición f; (essay) redacción f.

compost ['kɒmpɒst] n abono m.

composure [kəm'pəʊzəʳ] n calma f, serenidad f.

compound¹ ['kɒmpaʊnd] **I** n compuesto m. **II** [kəm'paʊnd] vtr (problem) agravar. **III** ['kɒmpaʊnd] adj compuesto,-a; (fracture) complicado,-a.

compound² ['kɒmpaʊnd] n (enclosure) recinto m.

comprehend [kɒmprɪ'hend] vtr comprender.

comprehensible [kɒmprɪ'hensəbəl] adj comprensible.

comprehension [kɒmprɪ'henʃən] n comprensión f.

comprehensive [kɒmprɪ'hensɪv] **I** adj 1 (knowledge) amplio,-a; (study) detallado,-a. 2 Ins a todo riesgo. 2 **GB c. school,** ≈ instituto m de segunda enseñanza.

compress [kəm'pres] **I** vtr comprimir. **II** ['kɒmpres] n compresa f.

comprise [kəm'praɪz] vtr comprender; (consist of) constar de.

compromise ['kɒmprəmaɪz] **I** n término

medio; **to reach a c.,** llegar a un acuerdo. **II** vi *(two people)* llegar a un acuerdo; *(individual)* transigir. **III** vtr *(person)* comprometer.

compulsion [kəm'pʌlʃən] n obligación f.

compulsive [kəm'pʌlsɪv] adj compulsivo,-a.

compulsory [kəm'pʌlsərɪ] adj obligatorio,-a.

computer [kəm'pju:tər] n ordenador m, computadora f; **c. programmer,** programador,-a m,f de ordenadores; **c. science,** informática f; **personal c.,** ordenador personal.

computerize [kəm'pju:təraɪz] vtr informatizar.

computing [kəm'pju:tɪŋ] n informática f.

comrade ['kɒmreɪd] n 1 *(companion)* compañero,-a m,f. 2 *Pol* camarada mf.

comradeship ['kɒmreɪdʃɪp] n camaradería f.

con [kɒn] sl **I** vtr estafar, timar. **II** n estafa f, camelo m; **c. man,** estafador m.

concave ['kɒnkeɪv] adj cóncavo,-a.

conceal [kən'si:l] vtr ocultar; *(emotions)* disimular.

concede [kən'si:d] vtr conceder.

conceit [kən'si:t] n presunción f, vanidad f.

conceited [kən'si:tɪd] adj presuntuoso,-a.

conceivable [kən'si:vəbəl] adj concebible.

conceive [kən'si:v] vtr & vi concebir.

concentrate ['kɒnsəntreɪt] **I** vtr concentrar. **II** vi **to c. on sth,** concentrarse en algo.

concentration [kɒnsən'treɪʃən] n concentración f; **c. camp,** campo m de concentración.

concept ['kɒnsept] n concepto m.

conception [kən'sepʃən] n Med concepción f; *(understanding)* concepto m, idea f.

concern [kən'sɜ:n] **I** vtr 1 concernir, afectar; **as far as I'm concerned,** por lo que a mí se refiere. 2 *(worry)* preocupar. **II** n 1 **it's no c. of mine,** no es asunto mío. 2 *(worry)* preocupación f. 3 *Com* negocio m.

concerned [kən'sɜ:nd] adj 1 *(affected)* afectado,-a. 2 *(worried)* preocupado,-a *(about,* por).

concerning [kən'sɜ:nɪŋ] prep con respecto a, en cuanto a.

concert ['kɒnsət, 'kɒnsɜ:t] n Mus concierto m; **c. hall,** sala f de conciertos.

concerted [kən'sɜ:tɪd] adj concertado,-a.

concertina [kɒnsə'ti:nə] n concertina f.

concerto [kən'tʃeətəu] n concierto m.

concession [kən'seʃən] n 1 concesión f; **tax c.,** privilegio m fiscal. 2 *Com* reducción f.

concise [kən'saɪs] adj conciso,-a.

conclude [kən'klu:d] vtr & vi concluir.

conclusion [kən'klu:ʒən] n conclusión f; **to reach a c.,** llegar a una conclusión.

conclusive [kən'klu:sɪv] adj concluyente.

concoct [kən'kɒkt] vtr *(dish)* confeccionar; *fig (plan)* fraguar; *(excuse)* inventar.

concoction [kən'kɒkʃən] n *(mixture)* mezcolanza f; *pej (brew)* brebaje m.

concourse ['kɒŋkɔːs] n explanada f.

concrete ['kɒnkri:t] **I** n hormigón m; **c. mixer,** hormigonera f. **II** adj 1 *(definite)* concreto,-a. 2 *(made of concrete)* de hormigón.

concur [kən'kɜ:r] vi 1 **to c. with,** *(agree)* estar de acuerdo con. 2 *(coincide)* coincidir.

concurrent [kən'kʌrənt] adj simultáneo, -a.

concussion [kən'kʌʃən] n conmoción f cerebral.

condemn [kən'dem] vtr condenar.

condemnation [kɒndem'neɪʃən] n condena f.

condensation [kɒnden'seɪʃən] n condensación f.

condense [kən'dens] **I** vtr condensar. **II** vi condensarse.

condensed [kən'denst] adj **c. milk,** leche condensada.

condescending [kɒndɪ'sendɪŋ] adj condescendiente.

condition [kən'dɪʃən] **I** n condición f; **to be in good c.,** estar en buen estado; **on c. that ...,** a condición de que ...; **on one c.,** con una condición; **heart c.,** enfermedad cardíaca; **conditions,** *(circumstances)* circunstancias fpl. **II** vtr condicionar.

conditional [kən'dɪʃənəl] adj condicional.

conditioner [kən'dɪʃənər] n acondicionador m.

condolences [kən'dəulənsɪz] npl pésame m sing; **please accept my c.,** le acompaño en el sentimiento.

condom ['kɒndəm] n preservativo m.

condone [kən'dəun] vtr perdonar, consentir.

condor ['kɒndɔːr] n cóndor m.

conducive [kən'dju:sɪv] adj conducente.

conduct ['kɒndʌkt] **I** n *(behaviour)* conducta f, comportamiento m. **II** [kən'dʌkt] vtr *(lead)* guiar; *(business, orchestra)* dirigir; **conducted tour,** visita acompañada; **to c. oneself,** comportarse. **III** vi Mus dirigir.

conductor [kən'dʌktər] n 1 *(on bus)* cobrador m. 2 *US Rail* revisor,-a m,f. 3 *Mus* director,-a m,f. 4 *Phys* conductor m.

conductress [kən'dʌktrɪs] n *(on bus)* cobradora f.

cone [kəun] n 1 cono m; **ice-cream c.,** cucurucho m. 2 *Bot* piña f.

confectioner [kən'fekʃənər] n confitero,-a m,f; **c.'s (shop),** confitería f.

confectionery [kən'fekʃənərɪ] n dulces

mpl.

confederate [kən'fedərɪt] **I** *adj*
confederado,-a. **II** *n* confederado,-a *m,f*;
Jur cómplice *mf*.
confer [kən'fɜ:r] **I** *vtr* to c. a title on sb,
conferir un título a algn. **II** *vi* consultar.
conference ['kɒnfərəns] *n* conferencia *f*.
confess [kən'fes] **I** *vi* confesar; *Rel* confe-
sarse. **II** *vtr* confesar.
confession [kən'feʃən] *n* confesión *f*.
confessional [kən'feʃənəl] *n* confesionario *m*.
confetti [kən'fetɪ] *n* confeti *m*.
confide [kən'faɪd] *vi* to c. in sb, confiar
en algn.
confidence ['kɒnfɪdəns] *n* **1** confianza *f*;
vote of c./no c., voto *m* de confianza/de
censura; **c. trick**, camelo *m*. **2** *(secret)*
confidencia *f*; **in c.**, en confianza.
confident ['kɒnfɪdənt] *adj* seguro,-a.
confidential [kɒnfɪ'denʃəl] *adj* *(secret)*
confidencial; *(entrusted)* de confianza.
confine [kən'faɪn] *vtr* encerrar; *fig* limitar.
confinement [kən'faɪnmənt] *n* **1** *(prison)*
prisión *f*; **to be in solitary c.**, estar
incomunicado,-a. **2** *Med* parto *m*.
confirm [kən'fɜ:m] *vtr* confirmar.
confirmation [kɒnfə'meɪʃən] *n* confirmación *f*.
confirmed [kən'fɜ:md] *adj*
empedernido,-a.
confiscate ['kɒnfɪskeɪt] *vtr* confiscar.
conflict ['kɒnflɪkt] **I** *n* conflicto *m*. **II**
[kən'flɪkt] *vi* chocar (**with**, con).
conflicting [kən'flɪktɪŋ] *adj*
contradictorio,-a.
conform [kən'fɔ:m] *vi* conformarse; **to c.
to** *or* **with**, *(customs)* amoldarse a; *(rules)*
someterse a.
confound [kən'faʊnd] *vtr* confundir, desconcertar.
confront [kən'frʌnt] *vtr* hacer frente a.
confrontation [kɒnfrʌn'teɪʃən] *n* confrontación *f*.
confuse [kən'fju:z] *vtr* *(person)* despistar;
(thing) confundir (**with**, con); **to get confused**, confundirse.
confused [kən'fju:zd] *adj* *(person)*
confundido,-a; *(mind, ideas)* confuso,-a.
confusing [kən'fju:zɪŋ] *adj* confuso,-a.
confusion [kən'fju:ʒən] *n* confusión *f*.
congeal [kən'dʒi:l] *vi* coagularse.
congenial [kən'dʒi:njəl] *adj* agradable.
congenital [kən'dʒenɪtəl] *adj* congénito,
-a.
congested [kən'dʒestɪd] *adj* **1** *(street)*
repleto,-a de gente; *(city)* superpoblado,
-a. **2** *Med* congestionado,-a.
congestion [kən'dʒestʃən] *n* congestión
f.
conglomeration [kənglɒmə'reɪʃən] *n*
conglomeración *f*.
congratulate [kən'grætjʊleɪt] *vtr* felicitar.
congratulations [kəngrætjʊ'leɪʃənz] *npl*

felicitaciones *fpl*; **c.!**, ¡enhorabuena!
congregate ['kɒngrɪgeɪt] *vi* congregarse.
congregation [kɒngrɪ'geɪʃən] *n* *(group)*
congregación *f*; *Rel* fieles *mpl*.
congress ['kɒngres] *n* congreso *m*.
Congressman ['kɒngresmən] *n* congresista *m*.
conifer ['kɒnɪfər] *n* conífera *f*.
conjecture [kən'dʒektʃər] **I** *n* conjetura *f*.
II *vtr* conjeturar. **III** *vi* hacer conjeturas.
conjugal ['kɒndʒʊgəl] *adj* conyugal.
conjugate ['kɒndʒʊgeɪt] *vtr* conjugar.
conjunction [kən'dʒʌŋkʃən] *n*
conjunción *f*; *fig* **in c. with**, conjuntamente con.
conjunctivitis [kəndʒʌŋktɪ'vaɪtɪs] *n*
conjuntivitis *f*.
conjure ['kʌndʒər] **I** *vtr* to c. (**up**), *(magician)* hacer aparecer; *(memories)* evocar. **II**
vi hacer juegos de manos.
conjurer ['kʌndʒərər] *n* prestidigitador,-a
m,f.
conker ['kɒŋkər] *n fam* castaña *f*.
connect [kə'nekt] **I** *vtr* *(join)* juntar, unir;
(wires) empalmar; *fig* **to be connected by
marriage**, estar emparentado,-a por matrimonio. **2** *(instal)* instalar; *Elec* conectar. **3** *Tel (person)* poner. **4** *fig (associate)* asociar. **II** *vi* unirse; *(rooms)* comunicarse; *(train, flight)* enlazar *or* empalmar
(**with**, con).
connected [kə'nektɪd] *adj* unido,-a;
(events) relacionado,-a; *fig* **to be well c.**,
(person) *fam* tener enchufe.
connection [kə'nekʃən] *n* **1** *(joint)* juntura *f*, unión *f*; *Elec* conexión *f*; *Tel* instalación *f*. **2** *Rail* correspondencia *f*. **3** *fig (of
ideas)* relación *f*; **in c. with**, *(regarding)*
con respecto a. **4** *(person)* contacto *m*.
connive [kə'naɪv] *vi* to c. at, hacer la
vista gorda con.
connoisseur [kɒnɪ'sɜ:r] *n* conocedor,-a
m,f.
connotation [kɒnə'teɪʃən] *n* connotación
f.
conquer ['kɒŋkər] *vtr* *(enemy, bad habit)*
vencer; *(country)* conquistar.
conqueror ['kɒŋkərər] *n* conquistador *m*.
conquest ['kɒŋkwest] *n* conquista *f*.
conscience ['kɒnʃəns] *n* conciencia *f*; **to
have a clear c.**, tener la conciencia
tranquila; **to have a guilty c.**, sentirse
culpable.
conscientious [kɒnʃɪ'enʃəs] *adj*
concienzudo,-a; **c. objector**, objetor,-a
m,f de conciencia.
conscious ['kɒnʃəs] *adj* *(aware)*
consciente; *(choice etc)* deliberado,-a.
consciousness ['kɒnʃəsnɪs] *n Med* conocimiento *m*; *(awareness)* consciencia *f*.
conscript ['kɒnskrɪpt] *n* recluta *m*.
conscription [kən'skrɪpʃən] *n* servicio *m*
militar obligatorio.
consecrate ['kɒnsɪkreɪt] *vtr* consagrar.

consecutive [kən'sekjʊtɪv] *adj* consecutivo,-a.

consensus [kən'sensəs] *n* consenso *m*.

consent [kən'sent] I *n* consentimiento *m*; **by common c.**, de común acuerdo. II *vi* consentir (**to**, en).

consequence ['kɒnsɪkwəns] *n* consecuencia *f*.

consequent ['kɒnsɪkwənt] *adj* consiguiente. ◆**consequently** *adv* por consiguiente.

conservation [kɒnsə'veɪʃən] *n* conservación *f*.

conservative [kən'sɜ:vətɪv] I *adj* cauteloso,-a. II *adj & n Pol* **C.**, conservador,-a (*m,f*).

conservatory [kən'sɜ:vətrɪ] *n* 1 (*greenhouse*) invernadero *m*. 2 *Mus* conservatorio *m*.

conserve [kən'sɜ:v] I *vtr* conservar. II ['kɒnsɜ:v] *n* conserva *f*.

consider [kən'sɪdər] *vtr* 1 (*ponder on, regard*) considerar; **to c. doing sth**, pensar hacer algo. 2 (*keep in mind*) tener en cuenta.

considerable [kən'sɪdərəbəl] *adj* considerable. ◆**considerably** *adv* bastante.

considerate [kən'sɪdərɪt] *adj* considerado,-a.

consideration [kənsɪdə'reɪʃən] *n* consideración *f*; **without due c.**, sin reflexión.

considering [kən'sɪdərɪŋ] *prep* teniendo en cuenta.

consign [kən'saɪn] *vtr Com* consignar; *fig* entregar.

consignment [kən'saɪnmənt] *n* envío *m*.

consist [kən'sɪst] *vi* **to c. of**, consistir en.

consistency [kən'sɪstənsɪ] *n* 1 (*of actions*) consecuencia *f*. 2 (*of mixture*) consistencia *f*.

consistent [kən'sɪstənt] *adj* consecuente; **c. with**, de acuerdo con.

consolation [kɒnsə'leɪʃən] *n* consuelo *m*; **c. prize**, premio *m* de consolación.

console¹ [kən'səʊl] *vtr* consolar.

console² ['kɒnsəʊl] *n* consola *f*.

consolidate [kən'sɒlɪdeɪt] I *vtr* consolidar. II *vi* consolidarse.

consonant ['kɒnsənənt] *n* consonante *f*.

consortium [kən'sɔ:tɪəm] *n* consorcio *m*.

conspicuous [kən'spɪkjʊəs] *adj* (*striking*) llamativo,-a; (*easily seen*) visible; (*mistake*) evidente.

conspiracy [kən'spɪrəsɪ] *n* conjura *f*.

conspire [kən'spaɪər] *vi* conspirar.

constable ['kʌnstəbəl] *n* policía *m*, guardia *m*; **chief c.**, jefe *m* de policía.

constabulary [kən'stæbjʊlərɪ] *n GB* comisaría *f*.

constant ['kɒnstənt] I *adj* constante; (*continuous*) incesante; (*loyal*) fiel, leal. II *n* constante *f*.

constellation [kɒnstɪ'leɪʃən] *n* constelación *f*.

consternation [kɒnstə'neɪʃən] *n* consternación *f*.

constipated ['kɒnstɪpeɪtɪd] *adj* **to be c.**, estar estreñido,-a.

constipation [kɒnstɪ'peɪʃən] *n* estreñimiento *m*.

constituency [kən'stɪtjʊənsɪ] *n* circunscripción *f* electoral.

constituent [kən'stɪtjʊənt] I *adj* (*component*) constituyente. II *n* 1 (*part*) componente *m*. 2 *Pol* votante *mf*.

constitute ['kɒnstɪtjuːt] *vtr* constituir.

constitution [kɒnstɪ'tjuːʃən] *n* constitución *f*.

constitutional [kɒnstɪ'tjuːʃənəl] *adj* constitucional.

constrained [kən'streɪnd] *adj* **to feel c. to do sth**, sentirse obligado,-a a hacer algo.

constraint [kən'streɪnt] *n* coacción *f*; **to feel c. in sb's presence**, sentirse cohibido,-a ante algn.

construct [kən'strʌkt] *vtr* construir.

construction [kən'strʌkʃən] *n* construcción *f*.

constructive [kən'strʌktɪv] *adj* constructivo,-a.

construe [kən'struː] *vtr* interpretar.

consul ['kɒnsəl] *n* cónsul *mf*.

consulate ['kɒnsjʊlɪt] *n* consulado *m*.

consult [kən'sʌlt] *vtr & vi* consultar (**about**, sobre).

consultant [kən'sʌltənt] *n Med* especialista *mf*; *Com Ind* asesor,-a *m,f*.

consultation [kɒnsəl'teɪʃən] *n* consulta *f*.

consulting [kən'sʌltɪŋ] *adj* **c. room**, consulta *f*.

consume [kən'sjuːm] *vtr* consumir.

consumer [kən'sjuːmər] *n* consumidor,-a *m,f*; **c. goods**, bienes *mpl* de consumo.

consummate I ['kɒnsəmeɪt] I *vtr* consumar. II ['kɒnsəmɪt] *adj* consumado,-a.

consumption [kən'sʌmpʃən] *n* 1 (*of food*) consumo *m*; **fit for c.**, apto,-a para el consumo. 2 *Med* tisis *f*.

cont. *abbr of* **continued**, sigue.

contact ['kɒntækt] I *n* contacto *m*; **c. lenses**, lentes *fpl* de contacto. II *vtr* ponerse en contacto con.

contagious [kən'teɪdʒəs] *adj* contagioso,-a.

contain [kən'teɪn] *vtr* contener; **to c. oneself**, contenerse.

container [kən'teɪnər] *n* 1 (*box, package*) recipiente *m*; (*bottle*) envase *m*. 2 *Naut* contenedor *m*.

contaminate [kən'tæmɪneɪt] *vtr* contaminar.

contamination [kəntæmɪ'neɪʃən] *n* contaminación *f*.

contd. *abbr of* **continued**, sigue.

contemplate ['kɒntempleɪt] *vtr* 1 (*consider*) considerar, pensar en. 2 (*look at*) contemplar.

contemporary [kən'temprərɪ] *adj & n* contemporáneo,-a *(m,f).*

contempt [kən'tempt] *n* desprecio *m*; **to hold in c.**, despreciar; **c. of court**, desacato *m* a los tribunales.

contemptible [kən'temptəbəl] *adj* despreciable.

contemptuous [kən'temptjuəs] *adj* despectivo,-a.

contend [kən'tend] **I** *vi* competir; *fig* **there are many problems to c. with**, se han planteado muchos problemas. **II** *vtr* afirmar.

contender [kən'tendər] *n* contendiente *mf.*

content[1] ['kɒntent] *n* contenido *m*; **table of contents**, índice *m* de materias.

content[2] [kən'tent] **I** *adj* contento,-a. **II** *vtr* contentar. **III** *n* contento *m*; **to one's heart's c.**, todo lo que uno quiera.

contented [kən'tentɪd] *adj* contento,-a, satisfecho,-a.

contention [kən'tenʃən] *n* **1** *(dispute)* controversia *f*. **2** *(point)* punto *m* de vista.

contentment [kən'tentmənt] *n* contento *m.*

contest ['kɒntest] **I** *n* concurso *m*; *Sport* prueba *f*. **II** [kən'test] *vtr* **1** *(matter)* rebatir; *(verdict)* impugnar; *fig (will)* disputar. **2** *Pol (seat)* luchar por.

contestant [kən'testənt] *n* concursante *mf.*

context ['kɒntekst] *n* contexto *m.*

continent ['kɒntɪnənt] *n* continente *m*; **(on) the C.**, (en) Europa.

continental [kɒntɪ'nentəl] *adj* **1** continental; **c. shelf**, plataforma *m* continental. **2** *GB* **C.**, europeo,-a; **c. quilt**, edredón *m* de pluma.

contingency [kən'tɪndʒənsɪ] *n* contingencia *f*; **c. plans**, planes *mpl* para casos de emergencia.

contingent [kən'tɪndʒənt] *adj & n* contingente *(m).*

continual [kən'tɪnjuəl] *adj* continuo,-a, constante.

continuation [kəntɪnju'eɪʃən] *n* *(sequel etc)* continuación *f*; *(extension)* prolongación *f.*

continue [kən'tɪnjuː] *vtr & vi* continuar, seguir; **to c. to do sth**, seguir *or* continuar haciendo algo.

continuous [kən'tɪnjuəs] *adj* continuo,-a.

contort [kən'tɔːt] *vtr* retorcer.

contortion [kən'tɔːʃən] *n* contorsión *f.*

contour ['kɒntuər] *n* contorno *m*; **c. line**, línea *f* de nivel.

contraband ['kɒntrəbænd] *n* contrabando *m.*

contraception [kɒntrə'sepʃən] *n* anticoncepción *f.*

contraceptive [kɒntrə'septɪv] *adj & n* anticonceptivo *(m,f).*

contract [kən'trækt] **I** *vi Phys* contraerse.

II *vtr* **1** contraer. **2** **to c. to do sth**, *(make agreement)* comprometerse por contrato a hacer algo. **III** ['kɒntrækt] *n* contrato *m*; **to enter into a c.**, hacer un contrato.

contraction [kən'trækʃən] *n* contracción *f.*

contractor [kən'træktər] *n* contratista *mf.*

contradict [kɒntrə'dɪkt] *vtr* contradecir.

contradiction [kɒntrə'dɪkʃən] *n* contradicción *f*; **it's a c. in terms**, no tiene lógica.

contradictory [kɒntrə'dɪktərɪ] *adj* contradictorio,-a.

contraption [kən'træpʃən] *n fam* cacharro *m.*

contrary ['kɒntrərɪ] **I** *adj* **1** contrario,-a. **2** [kən'treərɪ] terco,-a. **II** *n* **on the c.**, todo lo contrario; **unless I tell you to the c.**, a menos que te diga lo contrario. **III** *adv* **c. to**, en contra de.

contrast [kən'trɑːst] **I** *vi* contrastar. **II** ['kɒntrɑːst] *n* contraste *m.*

contrasting [kən'trɑːstɪŋ] *adj* opuesto,-a.

contravene [kɒntrə'viːn] *vtr* contravenir.

contribute [kən'trɪbjuːt] **I** *vtr (money)* contribuir con; *(ideas, information)* aportar. **II** *vi* **1** contribuir; *(in discussion)* participar. **2** *Press* colaborar **(to, en).**

contribution [kɒntrɪ'bjuːʃən] *n* **1** *(of money)* contribución *f*; *(of ideas etc)* aportación *f*. **2** *Press* colaboración *f.*

contributor [kən'trɪbjutər] *n (to newspaper)* colaborador,-a *m,f.*

contrive [kən'traɪv] *vtr* inventar, idear; **to c. to do sth**, buscar la forma de hacer algo.

contrived [kən'traɪvd] *adj* artificial, forzado,-a.

control [kən'trəul] **I** *vtr* controlar; *(person, animal)* dominar; *(vehicle)* manejar; **to c. one's temper**, controlarse. **II** *n* **1** *(power)* control *m*, dominio *m*; *(authority)* autoridad *f*; **out of c.**, fuera de control; **to be in c.**, estar al mando; **to be under c.**, *(situation)* estar bajo control; **to go out of c.**, descontrolarse; **to lose c.**, perder los estribos. **2** *Aut Av (device)* mando *m*; *Rad TV* botón *m* de control; **c. panel**, tablero *m* de instrumentos; **c. room**, sala *f* de control; *Av* **c. tower**, torre *f* de control.

controversial [kɒntrə'vɜːʃəl] *adj* controvertido,-a, polémico,-a.

controversy ['kɒntrəvɜːsɪ, kən'trɒvəsɪ] *n* polémica *f.*

conurbation [kɒnɜː'beɪʃən] *n* conurbación *f.*

convalesce [kɒnvə'les] *vi* convalecer.

convalescence [kɒnvə'lesəns] *n* convalecencia *f.*

convalescent [kɒnvə'lesənt] *adj* convaleciente; **c. home**, clínica *f* de reposo.

convene [kən'viːn] **I** *vtr* convocar. **II** *vi* reunirse.

convenience [kən'viːnɪəns] *n* conveniencia f, comodidad f; **all modern conveniences,** todas las comodidades; **at your c.,** cuando le convenga; **c. food,** comida precocinada; *GB euph* **public conveniences,** aseos públicos.

convenient [kən'viːnɪənt] *adj (time, arrangement)* conveniente, oportuno,-a; *(place)* bien situado,-a.

convent ['kɒnvənt] *n* convento *m*.

convention [kən'venʃən] *n* convención *f*.

conventional [kən'venʃənəl] *adj* clásico,-a; *(behaviour)* convencional.

converge [kən'vɜːdʒ] *vi* convergir.

conversant [kən'vɜːsənt] *adj fml* **to be c. with a subject,** ser versado,-a en una materia.

conversation [kɒnvə'seɪʃən] *n* conversación *f*.

conversational [kɒnvə'seɪʃənəl] *adj* coloquial.

converse¹ [kən'vɜːs] *vi* conversar.

converse² ['kɒnvɜːs] *n* **the c.,** lo opuesto. ◆**conversely** *adv* a la inversa.

conversion [kən'vɜːʃən] *n Math Rel* conversión *f* **(to,** a; **into,** en).

convert [kən'vɜːt] I *vtr* convertir. II ['kɒnvɜːt] *n* converso,-a *m,f*.

convertible [kən'vɜːtəbəl] I *adj* convertible. II *n Aut* descapotable *m*.

convex ['kɒnveks, kɒn'veks] *adj* convexo,-a.

convey [kən'veɪ] *vtr* 1 *(carry)* transportar. 2 *(sound)* transmitir; *(idea)* comunicar.

conveyor [kən'veɪər] *n* **c. belt,** cinta transportadora.

convict [kən'vɪkt] I *vtr* declarar culpable a, condenar. II ['kɒnvɪkt] *n* presidiario,-a *m,f*.

conviction [kən'vɪkʃən] *n* 1 *(belief)* creencia f, convicción f. 2 *Jur* condena *f*.

convince [kən'vɪns] *vtr* convencer.

convincing [kən'vɪnsɪŋ] *adj* convincente.

convoluted ['kɒnvəluːtɪd] *adj* intrincado,-a.

convoy ['kɒnvɔɪ] *n* convoy *m*.

convulse [kən'vʌls] *vtr* convulsionar; *fam* **to be convulsed with laughter,** troncharse de risa.

convulsion [kən'vʌlʃən] *n* convulsión *f*.

coo [kuː] *vi (pigeon)* arrullar.

cook [kʊk] I *vtr* cocinar, guisar; *(dinner)* preparar; *sl* **to c. the books,** falsificar las cuentas. II *vi (person)* cocinar, guisar; *(food)* cocerse. III *n* cocinero,-a *m,f*.

cookbook ['kʊkbʊk] *n US* libro *m* de cocina.

cooker ['kʊkər] *n* cocina *f*.

cookery ['kʊkərɪ] *n* cocina f; **c. book,** libro *m* de cocina.

cookie ['kʊkɪ] *n US* galleta *f*.

cooking ['kʊkɪŋ] *n* cocina *f*.

cool [kuːl] I *adj* 1 fresco,-a; **it's c.,** *(weather)* hace fresquito. 2 *fig (calm)* tranquilo,-a; *(reserved)* frío,-a. II *n* 1

(coolness) fresco *m*. 2 *sl* **to lose one's c.,** perder la calma. III *vtr (air)* refrescar; *(drink)* enfriar. IV *adv fam* **to play it c.,** hacer como si nada. ◆**cool down, cool off** *vi fig* calmarse; *(feelings)* enfriarse.

coolness ['kuːlnɪs] *n* 1 *fig (calmness)* calma f; *(composure)* aplomo *m*. 2 *fam (nerve, cheek)* frescura *f*.

coop [kuːp] I *n* gallinero *m*. II *vtr* **to c. (up),** encerrar.

co-operate [kəʊ'ɒpəreɪt] *vi* cooperar.

co-operation [kəʊɒpə'reɪʃən] *n* cooperación *f*.

co-operative [kəʊ'ɒpərətɪv] I *adj (helpful)* cooperador,-a. II *n* cooperativa *f*.

co-ordinate [kəʊ'ɔːdɪneɪt] I *vtr* coordinar. II [kəʊ'ɔːdɪnɪt] *n* 1 *Math* coordenada f. 2 **co-ordinates,** *(clothes)* conjunto *m sing*.

co-ordination [kəʊɔːdɪ'neɪʃən] *n* coordinación *f*.

cop [kɒp] *sl* I *n (policeman)* poli *m*. II *vtr* **you'll c. it,** te vas a ganar una buena. ◆**cop out** *vi* rajarse.

cope [kəʊp] *vi* arreglárselas; **to c. with,** *(person, work)* poder con; *(problem)* hacer frente a.

Copenhagen [kəʊpən'heɪgən] *n* Copenhague.

copious ['kəʊpɪəs] *adj* copioso,-a, abundante.

copper¹ ['kɒpər] *n Min* cobre *m*. II *adj (colour)* cobrizo,-a.

copper² ['kɒpər] *n sl* poli *mf*.

coppice ['kɒpɪs], **copse** [kɒps] *n* arboleda f, bosquecillo *m*.

copulate ['kɒpjʊleɪt] *vi* copular.

copy ['kɒpɪ] I *n* 1 copia *f*. 2 *(of book)* ejemplar *m*. 3 *Print* manuscrito *m*. 4 *Press fam* asunto *m*. II *vtr & vi* copiar.

copycat ['kɒpɪkæt] *n fam* copión,-ona *m,f*.

copyright ['kɒpɪraɪt] *n* derechos *mpl* de autor.

coral ['kɒrəl] *n* coral *m*; **c. reef,** arrecife *m* de coral.

cord [kɔːd] *n* 1 *(string)* cuerda f; *Elec* cordón *m*. 2 *Tex (corduroy)* pana f; **cords,** pantalones *mpl* de pana.

cordial ['kɔːdɪəl] I *adj* cordial. II *n* licor *m*.

cordon ['kɔːdən] I *n* cordón *m*. II *vtr* **to c. off a street,** acordonar una calle.

corduroy ['kɔːdərɔɪ] *n* pana *f*.

core [kɔːr] I *n (of fruit)* corazón *m*; *Elec* núcleo *m*; *fig* **hard c.,** los incondicionales. II *vtr* quitarle el corazón a.

coriander [kɒrɪ'ændər] *n* culantro *m*.

cork [kɔːk] *n* corcho *m*; **c. oak,** alcornoque *m*.

corkscrew ['kɔːkskruː] *n* sacacorchos *m inv*.

corn¹ [kɔːn] *n* cereal m; *(grain)* granos *mpl*; *(maize)* maíz *m*; **c. on the cob,** ma-

zorca f de maíz.
corn² [kɔːn] n Med callo m.
cornea [ˈkɔːnɪə] n córnea f.
corner [ˈkɔːnər] n 1 (of street) esquina f; (bend in road) curva f; **round the c.**, a la vuelta de la esquina; Ftb **c. kick**, córner m; **c. shop**, tienda pequeña de barrio. 2 (of room) rincón m. II vtr 1 (enemy) arrinconar. 2 Com acaparar. III vi Aut tomar una curva.
cornerstone [ˈkɔːnəstəʊn] n piedra f angular.
cornet [ˈkɔːnɪt] n 1 Mus corneta f. 2 GB (for ice cream) cucurucho m.
cornflakes [ˈkɔːnfleɪks] npl copos mpl de maíz, cornflakes mpl.
cornflour [ˈkɔːnflaʊər] n harina f de maíz.
cornstarch [ˈkɔːnstɑːtʃ] n US → **cornflour**.
Cornwall [ˈkɔːnwəl] n Cornualles.
corny [ˈkɔːnɪ] adj (cornier, corniest) fam gastado,-a.
corollary [kəˈrɒlərɪ] n corolario m.
coronary [ˈkɒrənərɪ] adj coronario,-a; **c. thrombosis**, trombosis coronaria.
coronation [kɒrəˈneɪʃən] n coronación f.
coroner [ˈkɒrənər] n juez mpf de instrucción.
corporal¹ [ˈkɔːpərəl] adj corporal; **c. punishment**, castigo m corporal.
corporal² [ˈkɔːpərəl] n Mil cabo m.
corporate [ˈkɔːpərɪt] adj corporativo,-a.
corporation [kɔːpəˈreɪʃən] n 1 (business) sociedad anónima. 2 (of city) ayuntamiento m.
corps [kɔːr] n (pl corps [kɔːz]) cuerpo m.
corpse [kɔːps] n cadáver m.
corpulent [ˈkɔːpjʊlənt] adj corpulento,-a.
corpuscle [ˈkɔːpʌsəl] n corpúsculo m.
corral [kəˈrɑːl] n US corral m.
correct [kəˈrekt] I vtr 1 (mistake) corregir. 2 (child) reprender. II adj correcto,-a, exacto,-a; (behaviour) formal.
correction [kəˈrekʃən] n corrección f.
correlation [kɒrɪˈleɪʃən] n correlación f.
correspond [kɒrɪˈspɒnd] vi 1 corresponder; **to c. to**, equivaler a. 2 (by letter) escribirse.
correspondence [kɒrɪˈspɒndəns] n correspondencia f; **c. course**, curso m por correspondencia.
correspondent [kɒrɪˈspɒndənt] n Press corresponsal mpf; **special c.**, enviado,-a m,f especial.
corridor [ˈkɒrɪdɔːr] n pasillo m.
corroborate [kəˈrɒbəreɪt] vtr corroborar.
corrode [kəˈrəʊd] I vtr corroer. II vi corroerse.
corrosion [kəˈrəʊʒən] n corrosión f.
corrugated [ˈkɒrʊgeɪtəd] adj **c. iron**, hierro ondulado.
corrupt [kəˈrʌpt] I adj (person) corrompido,-a, corrupto,-a; (actions) deshonesto,-a. II vtr & vi corromper.

corruption [kəˈrʌpʃən] n corrupción f.
corset [ˈkɔːsɪt] n (garment) faja f.
Corsica [ˈkɔːsɪkə] n Córcega.
cortège [kɔːˈteɪʒ] n cortejo m, comitiva f.
cosh [kɒʃ] n GB porra f.
cosmetic [kɒzˈmetɪk] I n cosmético m. II adj cosmético,-a; **c. surgery**, cirugía plástica.
cosmic [ˈkɒzmɪk] adj cósmico,-a.
cosmonaut [ˈkɒzmənɔːt] n cosmonauta mf.
cosmopolitan [kɒzməˈpɒlɪtən] adj cosmopolita.
cosset [ˈkɒsɪt] vtr mimar.
cost [kɒst] I n (price) precio m, coste m; **c. of living**, coste de la vida; **to count the c.**, considerar las desventajas; **at all costs**, a toda costa. II vtr & vi (pt & pp cost) costar, valer; **how much does it c.?**, ¿cuánto cuesta?; **whatever it costs**, cueste lo que cueste. III vtr (pt & pp costed) Com Ind calcular el coste de.
co-star [ˈkəʊstɑːr] n Cin Theat coprotagonista mf.
Costa Rica [kɒstəˈriːkə] n Costa Rica.
Costa Rican [kɒstəˈriːkən] adj & n costarricense (mf).
cost-effective [kɒstɪˈfektɪv] adj rentable.
costly [ˈkɒstlɪ] adj (costlier, costliest) costoso,-a.
costume [ˈkɒstjuːm] n traje m; **swimming c.**, bañador m; **c. jewellery**, bisutería f.
cosy [ˈkəʊzɪ] adj (cosier, cosiest) (atmosphere) acogedor,-a; (bed) calentito,-a; **it's c. in here**, aquí se está bien.
cot [kɒt] n cuna f.
cottage [ˈkɒtɪdʒ] n casa f de campo; **c. cheese**, requesón m; **c. industry**, industria casera; GB **c. pie**, pastel m de carne picada con puré de patatas.
cotton [ˈkɒtən] n 1 Bot algodonero m; Tex algodón m; **c. wool**, algodón hidrófilo. 2 (thread) hilo m. ◆**cotton on** vi fam **to c. on to sth**, caer en la cuenta de algo.
couch [kaʊtʃ] n sofá m; (in surgery) camilla f.
couchette [kuːˈʃet] n Rail litera f.
cough [kɒf] I vi toser. II n tos f; **c. drop**, pastilla f para la tos; **c. mixture**, jarabe m para la tos. ◆**cough up** vtr fam **to c. up the money**, soltar la pasta.
could [kʊd] v aux → **can¹**.
council [ˈkaʊnsəl] n (body) consejo m; GB **c. house**, vivienda f de protección oficial; **town c.**, consejo m municipal, ayuntamiento m.
councillor, US councilor [ˈkaʊnsələr] n concejal mf.
counsel [ˈkaʊnsəl] I n 1 (advice) consejo m. 2 Jur abogado,-a m,f. II vtr aconsejar.
counsellor, US counselor [ˈkaʊnsələr] n 1 (adviser) asesor,-a m,f. 2 US Jur abogado,-a m,f.

count¹ [kaʊnt] **I** vtr **1** contar. **2** fig to c. oneself lucky, considerarse afortunado, -a. **II** vi contar; that doesn't c., eso no vale; to c. to ten, contar hasta diez. **III** n **1** cuenta f; (total) recuento m. **2** Jur cargo m. ♦count on vtr contar con.

count² [kaʊnt] n (nobleman) conde m.

countdown ['kaʊntdaʊn] n cuenta f atrás.

countenance ['kaʊntɪnəns] **I** n semblante m, rostro m. **II** vtr aprobar.

counter¹ ['kaʊntər] n **1** (in shop) mostrador m; (in bank) ventanilla f. **2** (in board games) ficha f.

counter² ['kaʊntər] n contador m.

counter³ ['kaʊntər] **I** adv c. to, en contra de. **II** vtr (attack) contestar a; (trend) contrarrestar. **III** vi contestar.

counteract [kaʊntər'ækt] vtr contrarrestar.

counterattack ['kaʊntərətæk] n contraataque m.

counterfeit ['kaʊntəfɪt] **I** adj falsificado, -a; c. coin, moneda falsa. **II** n falsificación f. **III** vtr falsificar.

counterfoil ['kaʊntəfɔɪl] n GB (of cheque) matriz f.

countermand [kaʊntə'mɑːnd] vtr (command) revocar; Com (order) anular.

counterpart ['kaʊntəpɑːt] n homólogo,-a m,f.

counterproductive [kaʊntəprə'dʌktɪv] adj contraproducente.

countersign ['kaʊntəsaɪn] vtr refrendar.

countess ['kaʊntɪs] n condesa f.

countless ['kaʊntlɪs] adj innumerable, incontable.

country ['kʌntrɪ] n **1** (state) país m; native c., patria f. **2** (rural area) campo m; c. dancing, baile m popular.

countryman ['kʌntrɪmən] n **1** (rural) hombre m del campo. **2** (compatriot) compatriota m.

countryside ['kʌntrɪsaɪd] n (area) campo m; (scenery) paisaje m.

county ['kaʊntɪ] n condado m.

coup [kuː] n golpe m; c. d'état, golpe de estado.

couple ['kʌpəl] **I** n **1** (of people) pareja f; a married c., un matrimonio. **2** (of things) par m; fam a c. of times, un par de veces. **II** vtr (wagons) enganchar.

coupling ['kʌplɪŋ] n Rail enganche m.

coupon ['kuːpɒn] n **1** cupón m. **2** GB Ftb quiniela f.

courage ['kʌrɪdʒ] n coraje m, valentía f.

courageous [kə'reɪdʒəs] adj valeroso,-a, valiente.

courgette [kʊə'ʒet] n calabacín m.

courier ['kʊərɪər] n **1** (messenger) mensajero,-a m,f. **2** (guide) guía mf turístico,-a.

course [kɔːs] n **1** (of river) curso m; Naut Av rumbo m. **2** fig desarrollo m; in the c.

of construction, en vías de construcción; in the c. of time, con el tiempo. **3** (series) ciclo m; a c. of treatment, un tratamiento. **4** Educ curso m; Univ asignatura f. **5** (for golf) campo m; (for horse-racing) hipódromo m. **6** Culin plato m. **7** of c., claro, por supuesto; of c. not!, ¡claro que no!.

court [kɔːt] **I** n **1** Jur tribunal m; c. martial, consejo m de guerra; c. order, orden f judicial. **2** (royal) corte f. **3** Sport pista f, cancha f. **II** vtr (woman) hacer la corte a; fig to c. danger, buscar el peligro; fig to c. disaster, exponerse al desastre. **III** vi (couple) tener relaciones.

courteous ['kɜːtɪəs] adj cortés.

courtesy ['kɜːtɪsɪ] n **1** cortesía f, educación f. **2** by c. of, por cortesía de.

courthouse ['kɔːthaʊs] n palacio m de justicia.

courtier ['kɔːtɪər] n cortesano,-a m,f.

court-martial ['kɔːtmɑːʃəl] vtr someter a consejo de guerra.

courtroom ['kɔːtruːm] n sala f de justicia.

courtyard ['kɔːtjɑːd] n patio m.

cousin ['kʌzən] n primo,-a m,f; first c., primo,-a hermano,-a.

cove [kəʊv] n cala f, ensenada f.

covenant ['kʌvənənt] n convenio m, pacto m.

cover ['kʌvər] **I** vtr **1** cubrir (with, de); (furniture) revestir (with, de); (with lid) tapar. **2** (hide) disimular. **3** (protect) abrigar. **4** (distance) recorrer. **5** Journ investigar. **6** (deal with) abarcar. **7** (include) incluir. **8** Sport marcar. **II** vi to c. for sb, sustituir a algn. **III** n **1** cubierta f; (lid) tapa f; (on bed) manta f; (of chair etc) funda f; (of book) tapa f; (of magazine) portada f; c. girl, modelo f de revista. **2** (in restaurant) cubierto m. **4** under separate c., por separado. **5** Ins full c., cobertura completa; GB c. note, seguro m provisional. **6** (protection) abrigo m; to take c., abrigarse; under c., al abrigo; (indoors) bajo techo. ♦cover up vtr **1** cubrir. **2** (crime) encubrir. **II** vi **1** (person) abrigarse. **2** to c. up for sb, encubrir a algn.

coverage ['kʌvərɪdʒ] n cobertura f.

coveralls ['kʌvərɔːlz] npl US mono m sing.

covering ['kʌvərɪŋ] **I** n cubierta f, envoltura f. **II** adj (letter) explicatorio,-a.

covert ['kʌvət] adj disimulado,-a, secreto,-a.

cover-up ['kʌvərʌp] n encubrimiento m.

covet ['kʌvɪt] vtr codiciar.

cow¹ [kaʊ] n vaca f; pej (woman) arpía f, bruja f.

cow² [kaʊ] vtr intimidar.

coward ['kaʊəd] n cobarde mf.

cowardice ['kaʊədɪs] n cobardía f.

cowardly ['kauədlı] *adj* cobarde.
cowboy ['kaubɔı] *n* vaquero *m*.
cower ['kauər] *vi (with fear)* encogerse.
cox [kɒks] *n* timonel *m*.
coy [kɔı] *adj (shy)* tímido,-a; *(demure)* coquetón,-ona.
cozy ['kəuzı] *adj US* → **cosy**.
crab [kræb] *n* **1** cangrejo *m*. **2 c. apple**, manzana *f* silvestre.
crack [kræk] **I** *vtr* **1** *(cup)* partir; *(bone)* fracturar; *(nut)* cascar; *(safe)* forzar. **2** *(whip)* hacer restallar. **3** *fig (problem)* dar con la solución de; *(joke)* contar. **II** *vi* **1** *(glass)* partirse; *(wall)* agrietarse. **2** *(whip)* restallar. **3** *fam* **to get cracking on sth**, ponerse a hacer algo. **III** *n* **1** *(in cup)* raja *f*; *(in wall, ground)* grieta *f*. **2** *(of whip)* restallido *m*; *(of gun)* detonación *f*. **3** *fam (blow)* golpetazo *m*. **4** *fam* **to have a c. at sth**, *(attempt)* intentar hacer algo. **5** *sl (wisecrack)* réplica aguda. **6** *sl (drug)* crack *m*. **IV** *adj sl* de primera. ◆**crack down on** *vtr* atajar con mano dura. ◆**crack up** *vi fam fig (go mad)* desquiciarse; *(with laughter)* partirse de risa.
cracker ['krækər] *n* **1** *(biscuit)* galleta salada. **2** *(firework)* petardo *m*.
crackle ['krækəl] *vi* crujir; *(fire)* crepitar.
cradle ['kreıdəl] *n (baby's)* cuna *f*.
craft ['krɑːft] *n* **1** *(occupation)* oficio *m*; *(art)* arte *m*; *(skill)* destreza *f*. **2** *(cunning)* maña *f*. **3** *Naut* embarcación *f*.
craftsman ['krɑːftsmən] *n* artesano *m*.
craftsmanship ['krɑːftsmənʃıp] *n* arte *f*.
crafty ['krɑːftı] *adj* **(craftier, craftiest)** astuto,-a.
crag [kræg] *n* peña *f*, peñasco *m*.
cram [kræm] **I** *vtr* atiborrar; **crammed with**, atestado,-a, de. **II** *vi Educ fam* empollar.
cramp¹ [kræmp] *n Med* calambre *m*; **cramps**, retortijones *mpl*.
cramp² [kræmp] *vtr (development etc)* poner trabas a.
cramped [kræmpt] *adj* atestado,-a; *(writing)* apretado,-a.
cranberry ['krænbərı] *n* arándano *m*.
crane [kreın] **I** *n* **1** *Zool* grulla *f* común. **2** *(device)* grúa *f*. **II** *vtr* estirar.
crank [kræŋk] *n* **1** *Tech* manivela *f*. **2** *fam (eccentric)* tío raro.
crankshaft ['kræŋkʃɑːft] *n* árbol *m* del cigüeñal.
cranny ['krænı] *n fig* **in every nook and c.**, en todos los rincones.
crap [kræp] *n fam* mierda *f*.
crash [kræʃ] **I** *vtr* **to c. one's car**, tener un accidente con el coche. **II** *vi* **1** *(car, plane)* estrellarse; *(collide)* chocar; **to c. into**, estrellarse contra. **2** *Com* quebrar. **III** *n* **1** *(noise)* estrépito *m*. **2** *(collision)* choque *m*; **car/plane c.**, accidente *m* de coche/avión; *fig* **c. course**, curso intensivo; **c. helmet**, casco *m* protector. **3** *Com*

quiebra *f*.
crash-land [kræʃ'lænd] *vi* hacer un aterrizaje forzoso.
crass [kræs] *adj (person)* grosero,-a; *(error)* garrafal.
crate [kreıt] *n* caja *f*, cajón *m* (para embalaje).
crater ['kreıtər] *n* cráter *m*.
cravat [krə'væt] *n* pañuelo *m* (de hombre).
crave [kreıv] *vi* **to c. for sth**, ansiar algo.
craving ['kreıvıŋ] *n* ansia *f*; *(in pregnancy)* antojo *m*.
crawfish ['krɔːfıʃ] *n* langosta *f*.
crawl [krɔːl] **I** *vi (baby)* gatear; *(vehicle)* avanzar lentamente; *fig* **to c. to sb**, arrastrarse a los pies de algn. **II** *n (swimming)* crol *m*.
crayfish ['kreıfıʃ] *n* cangrejo *m* de río.
crayon ['kreıɒn] *n* cera *f*.
craze [kreız] *n* manía *f*; *(fashion)* moda *f*; **it's the latest c.**, es el último grito.
crazy ['kreızı] *adj* **(crazier, craziest)** *fam* loco,-a, chalado,-a; *GB* **c. paving**, pavimento *m* en mosaico.
creak [kriːk] *vi (floor)* crujir; *(hinge)* chirriar.
cream [kriːm] **I** *n* **1** *(of milk)* nata *f*; **c. coloured**, color crema; *fig* **the c.**, la flor y nata; **c. cheese**, queso *m* crema. **2** *(cosmetic)* crema *f*. **II** *vtr* **1** *(milk)* desnatar. **2** *Culin* batir; **creamed potatoes**, puré *m* de patatas.
creamy ['kriːmı] *adj* **(creamier, creamiest)** cremoso,-a.
crease [kriːs] **I** *n (wrinkle)* arruga *f*; *(fold)* pliegue *m*; *(on trousers)* raya *f*. **II** *vtr (clothes)* arrugar. **III** *vi* arrugarse.
create [kriː'eıt] *vtr* crear.
creation [kriː'eıʃən] *n* creación *f*.
creative [kriː'eıtıv] *adj (person)* creativo, -a.
creativity [kriːeı'tıvıtı] *n* creatividad *f*.
creator [kriː'eıtər] *n* creador,-a *m,f*.
creature ['kriːtʃər] *n (animal)* criatura *f*.
crèche [kreıʃ, kreʃ] *n* guardería *f*.
credence ['kriːdəns] *n* **to give c. to**, dar crédito a.
credentials [krı'denʃəlz] *npl* credenciales *fpl*.
credible ['kredıbəl] *adj* creíble.
credit ['kredıt] **I** *n* **1** *Com* crédito *m*; **on c.**, a crédito; **c. card**, tarjeta *f* de crédito. **2 to give c. to sb for sth**, reconocer algo a algn. **3** *(benefit)* honor *m*; **to be a c. to**, hacer honor a. **4** *Cin TV* **credits**, créditos *mpl*. **II** *vtr* **1** *Com* abonar. **2** *(believe)* creer. **3** *fig* atribuir; **he is credited with having ...**, se le atribuye haber ....
creditor ['kredıtər] *n* acreedor,-a *m,f*.
creed [kriːd] *n* credo *m*.
creek [kriːk] *n* **1** *GB* cala *f*. **2** *US Austral* riachuelo *m*.
creep [kriːp] **I** *vi (pt & pp crept)* andar si-

lenciosamente; (insect) arrastrarse; (plant) trepar; to c. up on sb, sorprender a algn. II n fam (person) pelotillero,-a m,f.

creeper ['kri:pər] n Bot trepadora f.

creepy ['kri:pɪ] adj (creepier, creepiest) fam espeluznante.

cremate [krɪ'meɪt] vtr incinerar.

crematorium [kremə'tɔ:rɪəm] n crematorio m.

crepe [kreɪp] n 1 Tex crepé m. 2 c. paper, papel m crespón.

crept [krept] pt & pp → **creep**.

crescendo [krɪ'ʃendəu] n crescendo m.

crescent ['kresənt] I n (shape) medialuna f; GB (street) calle f en medialuna. II adj creciente.

cress [kres] n berro m.

crest [krest] n 1 (of cock, wave) cresta f; (on helmet) penacho m; (of hill) cima f. 2 (heraldic) blasón m.

crestfallen ['krestfɔ:lən] adj abatido,-a.

Crete [kri:t] n Creta.

cretin ['kretɪn] n cretino,-a m,f.

crevasse [krɪ'væs] n grieta f, fisura f.

crevice ['krevɪs] n grieta f, hendedura f.

crew [kru:] n Av Naut tripulación f; c. cut, corte m al rape; c.-neck sweater, jersey m con cuello redondo.

crib [krɪb] n (manger) pesebre m; (for baby) cuna f. II vtr fam 1 (copy) copiar. 2 (steal) quitar.

crick [krɪk] n fam a c. in the neck, una tortícolis.

cricket¹ ['krɪkɪt] n Ent grillo m.

cricket² ['krɪkɪt] n Sport cricket m.

crime [kraɪm] n delincuencia f; (offence) delito m.

criminal ['krɪmɪnəl] adj & n criminal (mf); c. law, derecho m penal; c. record, antecedentes mpl penales.

crimson ['krɪmzən] adj & n carmesí (m).

cringe [krɪndʒ] vi adularse, encogerse.

crinkle ['krɪŋkəl] vtr fruncir, arrugar.

cripple ['krɪpəl] I n lisiado,-a m,f, mutilado,-a m,f. II vtr mutilar, dejar cojo,-a; fig paralizar.

crisis ['kraɪsɪs] n (pl **crises** ['kraɪsi:z]) crisis f inv.

crisp [krɪsp] I adj crujiente; (lettuce) fresco,-a; (banknote) nuevo,-a; (weather) frío,-a y seco,-a; (style) directo,-a. II n GB (potato) c., patata frita.

crisscross ['krɪskrɒs] n líneas fpl entrecruzadas.

criterion [kraɪ'tɪərɪən] n (pl **criteria** [kraɪ'tɪərɪə]) criterio m.

critic ['krɪtɪk] n Art Theat crítico,-a m,f.

critical ['krɪtɪkəl] adj crítico,-a. ◆**critically** adv críticamente; c. ill, gravemente enfermo,-a.

criticism ['krɪtɪsɪzəm] n crítica f.

criticize ['krɪtɪsaɪz] vtr criticar.

croak [krəuk] vi (frog) croar; (raven) graznar; (person) hablar con voz ronca.

crochet ['krəuʃeɪ] n ganchillo m.

crockery ['krɒkərɪ] n loza f.

crocodile ['krɒkədaɪl] n cocodrilo m.

crocus ['krəukəs] n azafrán m.

crony ['krəunɪ] n compinche mf.

crook [kruk] I n 1 (of shepherd) cayado m. 2 fam caco m. II vtr (arm) doblar.

crooked ['krukɪd] adj 1 (stick, picture) torcido,-a; (path) tortuoso,-a. 2 fam (dishonest) deshonesto,-a.

crop [krɒp] I n 1 cultivo m; (harvest) cosecha f; (of hair) mata f. 2 (whip) fusta f. II vtr (hair) rapar; (grass) cortar. ◆**crop up** vi fam surgir, presentarse.

croquet ['krəukeɪ] n croquet m.

cross [krɒs] I n 1 cruz f. 2 (breeds) cruce m. 3 c. **section**, sección f transversal. II vtr 1 cruzar. 2 Rel to c. oneself, hacer la señal de la cruz; fam c. my heart!, ¡te lo juro! 3 (thwart) contrariar. III vi cruzar; (roads) cruzarse; to c. over, cruzar. IV adj 1 fig they are at c. purposes, hay un malentendido entre ellos. 2 (angry) enfadado,-a. ◆**cross off, cross out** vtr tachar, rayar.

crossbar ['krɒsbɑ:r] n travesaño m.

cross-country ['krɒskʌntrɪ] I n c.-c. race, cros m. II [krɒs'kʌntrɪ] adv campo través.

cross-examine [krɒsɪg'zæmɪn] vtr interrogar.

cross-eyed ['krɒsaɪd] adj bizco,-a.

crossfire ['krɒsfaɪər] n fuego cruzado.

crossing ['krɒsɪŋ] n cruce m; pedestrian c., paso m de peatones; sea c., travesía f.

cross-legged [krɒs'legɪd] adj con las piernas cruzadas.

cross-reference [krɒs'refərəns] n remisión f.

crossroads ['krɒsrəudz] n cruce m; fig encrucijada f.

crosswind ['krɒswɪnd] n viento m lateral.

crossword ['krɒswɜ:d] n c. (**puzzle**), crucigrama m.

crotch [krɒtʃ] n entrepierna f.

crotchet ['krɒtʃɪt] n Mus negra f.

crotchety ['krɒtʃɪtɪ] adj fam gruñón,-ona.

crouch [krautʃ] vi to c. (**down**), agacharse.

crow¹ [krəu] n cuervo m; fig as the c. flies, en línea recta; c.'s-feet, patas fpl de gallo.

crow² [krəu] I vi (cock) cantar; fig to c. over sth, jactarse de algo. 2 (baby) balbucir. II n (of cock) canto m.

crowbar ['krəubɑ:r] n palanca f.

crowd [kraud] I n muchedumbre f; the c., el populacho; fam (gang) pandilla f. II vtr (streets) llenar. III vi apiñarse; to c. in/out, entrar/salir en tropel.

crowded ['kraudɪd] adj atestado,-a, lleno,-a.

crown [kraun] I n 1 corona f; (garland) guirnalda f; the c. jewels, las joyas de la corona; *GB Jur* c. **court**, tribunal *m* superior; **C. Prince**, príncipe heredero. 2 *Anat* coronilla *f*; *(of hat, tree)* copa *f*. II *vtr* coronar; *fam fig* **to c. it all**, y para más inri.

crucial ['kru:ʃəl] *adj* decisivo,-a.

crucifix ['kru:sɪfɪks] *n* crucifijo *m*.

crucifixion [kru:sɪ'fɪkʃən] *n* crucifixión *f*.

crucify ['kru:sɪfaɪ] *vtr* crucificar.

crude [kru:d] *adj* 1 *(manners, style)* tosco,-a, grosero,-a; *(tool)* primitivo,-a. 2 **c. oil**, crudo *m*.

cruel [kru:əl] *adj* cruel (**to**, con).

cruelty ['kru:əltɪ] *n* crueldad *f* (**to**, hacia).

cruet ['kru:ɪt] *n* **c. set**, vinagreras *fpl*.

cruise [kru:z] I *vi* 1 *Naut* hacer un crucero. 2 *Aut* viajar a velocidad constante; *Av* viajar a velocidad de crucero. II *n* 1 *Naut* crucero *m*. 2 **c. missile**, misil teledirigido.

cruiser ['kru:zər] *n* (barco *m*) crucero *m*.

crumb [krʌm] *n* miga *f*, migaja *f*.

crumble ['krʌmbəl] I *vtr* desmigar. II *vi* *(wall)* desmoronarse; *fig (hopes)* desvanecerse.

crumbly ['krʌmblɪ] *adj* (**crumblier, crumbliest**) que se desmigaja.

crumpet ['krʌmpɪt] *n GB* clase *f* de crepe grueso que se puede tostar.

crumple ['krʌmpəl] *vtr* arrugar.

crunch [krʌntʃ] I *vtr (food)* ronchar; *(with feet)* hacer crujir. II *n fam* **when it comes to the c.**, a la hora de la verdad.

crunchy ['krʌntʃɪ] *adj* (**crunchier, crunchiest**) crujiente.

crusade [kru:'seɪd] *n* cruzada *f*.

crush [krʌʃ] I *vtr* aplastar; *(wrinkle)* arrugar; *(grind)* moler; *(squeeze)* exprimir. II *n* 1 *(of people)* gentío *m*. 2 **orange c.**, naranjada *f*.

crushing ['krʌʃɪŋ] *adj fig (defeat, reply)* aplastante.

crust [krʌst] *n* corteza *f*.

crutch [krʌtʃ] *n Med* muleta *f*; *fig* apoyo *m*.

crux [krʌks] *n* **the c. of the matter**, el quid de la cuestión.

cry [kraɪ] I *vi* *(pt & pp* **cried**) 1 gritar. 2 *(weep)* llorar. II *vtr* gritar; *fig* **to c. wolf**, dar una falsa alarma. III *n* 1 grito *m*. 2 *(weep)* llanto *m*. ◆**cry off** *vi fam* rajarse. ◆**cry out** *vi* gritar; **to c. out for sth**, pedir algo a gritos.

crying ['kraɪɪŋ] *adj* **it's a c. shame**, es una vergüenza.

cryptic ['krɪptɪk] *adj* enigmático,-a.

crystal ['krɪstəl] *n* cristal *m*.

crystal-clear [krɪstəl'klɪər] *adj* claro,-a como el agua.

crystallize ['krɪstəlaɪz] I *vtr* cristalizar. II *vi* cristalizarse.

cub [kʌb] *n* 1 *(animal)* cachorro *m*. 2 *(junior scout)* niño *m* explorador.

Cuba ['kju:bə] *n* Cuba.

Cuban ['kju:bən] *adj & n* cubano,-a (*m,f*).

cubbyhole ['kʌbɪhəʊl] *n* cuchitril *m*.

cube [kju:b] I *n* cubo *m*; *(of sugar)* terrón *m*; **c. root**, raíz cúbica. II *vtr Math* elevar al cubo.

cubic ['kju:bɪk] *adj* cúbico,-a.

cubicle ['kju:bɪkəl] *n* cubículo *m*; *(at swimming pool)* caseta *f*.

cuckoo ['kʊku:] I *n* cuco *m*; **c. clock**, reloj *m* de cuco. II *adj fam* lelo,-a.

cucumber ['kju:kʌmbər] *n* pepino *m*.

cuddle ['kʌdəl] I *vtr* abrazar. II *vi* abrazarse.

cuddly ['kʌdlɪ] *adj* **c. toy**, muñeco *m* de peluche.

cue[1] [kju:] *n Theat* pie *m*.

cue[2] [kju:] *n (in billiards)* taco *m*; **c. ball**, bola blanca.

cuff[1] [kʌf] *n (of sleeve)* puño *m*; *US (of trousers)* dobladillo *m*; *fig* **to do sth off the c.**, improvisar algo.

cuff[2] [kʌf] I *vtr* abofetear. II *n* bofetada *f*.

cufflinks ['kʌflɪŋks] *npl* gemelos *mpl*.

cul-de-sac ['kʌldəsæk] *n* callejón *m* sin salida.

cull [kʌl] *vtr* 1 *(choose)* escoger. 2 *(animals)* eliminar.

culminate ['kʌlmɪneɪt] *vi* **to c. in**, terminar en.

culmination [kʌlmɪ'neɪʃən] *n* culminación *f*, punto *m* culminante.

culottes [kju:'lɒts] *npl* falda-pantalón *f sing*.

culprit ['kʌlprɪt] *n* culpable *mf*.

cult [kʌlt] *n* culto *m*; **c. figure**, ídolo *m*.

cultivate ['kʌltɪveɪt] *vtr* cultivar.

cultivated ['kʌltɪveɪtɪd] *adj (person)* culto,-a.

cultivation [kʌltɪ'veɪʃən] *n* cultivo *m* (de la tierra).

cultural ['kʌltʃərəl] *adj* cultural.

culture ['kʌltʃər] *n* cultura *f*.

cultured ['kʌltʃəd] *adj* → **cultivated**.

cumbersome ['kʌmbəsəm] *adj (awkward)* incómodo,-a; *(bulky)* voluminoso,-a.

cum(m)in ['kʌmɪn] *n* comino *m*.

cumulative ['kju:mjʊlətɪv] *adj* acumulativo,-a.

cunning ['kʌnɪŋ] I *adj* astuto,-a. II *n* astucia *f*.

cup [kʌp] I *n* taza *f*; *Sport* copa *f*; **C. Final**, final *f* de copa; **c. tie**, partido *m* de copa. II *vtr (hands)* ahuecar.

cupboard ['kʌbəd] *n* armario *m*; *(on wall)* alacena *f*.

curate ['kjʊərɪt] *n* cura *m* coadjutor.

curator [kjʊə'reɪtər] *n* conservador,-a *m,f*.

curb [kɜ:b] I *n (kerb)* bordillo *m*. II *vtr (horse)* refrenar; *fig (public spending)* contener.

curd [kɜ:d] *n* cuajada *f*.

curdle ['kɜ:dəl] *vi* cuajarse.

cure [kjuə^r] I *vtr* curar. II *n* (*remedy*) cura *f*, remedio *m*.
curfew ['kɜːfjuː] *n* toque *m* de queda.
curiosity [kjuərɪ'ɒsɪtɪ] *n* curiosidad *f*.
curious ['kjuərɪəs] *adj* 1 (*inquisitive*) curioso,-a. 2 (*odd*) extraño,-a.
curl [kɜːl] I *vtr* (*hair*) rizar; (*lip*) fruncir. II *vi* rizarse. III *n* (*of hair*) rizo *m*; (*of smoke*) espiral *f*. ◆**curl up** *vi* enroscarse.
curly ['kɜːlɪ] *adj* (**curlier, curliest**) rizado,-a.
currant ['kʌrənt] *n* pasa *f* (de Corinto).
currency ['kʌrənsɪ] *n* 1 moneda *f*; **foreign c.**, divisa *f*. 2 **to gain c.**, cobrar fuerza.
current ['kʌrənt] I *adj* 1 (*opinion*) general; (*word*) en uso; (*year*) en curso; **c. account**, cuenta *f* corriente; **c. affairs**, actualidad *f sing* (política); *Fin* **c. assets**, activo *m sing* disponible. 2 **the c. issue**, (*of magazine, newspaper*) el último número. II *n* corriente *f*. ◆**currently** *adv* actualmente.
curriculum [kə'rɪkjʊləm] *n* (*pl* **curricula** [kə'rɪkjʊlə]) plan *m* de estudios; **c. vitae**, curriculum *m* (vitae).
curry[1] ['kʌrɪ] *n* curry *m*; **chicken c.**, pollo *m* al curry.
curry[2] ['kʌrɪ] *vtr* **to c. favour with**, congraciarse con.
curse [kɜːs] I *n* maldición *f*; (*oath*) palabrota *f*; *fig* azote *m*. II *vtr* maldecir. III *vi* blasfemar.
cursor ['kɜːsə^r] *n* cursor *m*.
cursory ['kɜːsərɪ] *adj* rápido,-a.
curt [kɜːt] *adj* brusco,-a, seco,-a.
curtail [kɜː'teɪl] *vtr* (*expenses*) reducir; (*text*) acortar.
curtain ['kɜːtən] *n* cortina *f*; *Theat* telón *m*; *fig* velo *m*.
curts(e)y ['kɜːtsɪ] I *n* reverencia *f*. II *vi* hacer una reverencia (**to**, a).
curve [kɜːv] I *n* curva *f*. II *vtr* encorvar. III *vi* torcerse, describir una curva.
cushion ['kʊʃən] I *n* cojín *m*; (*large*) almohadón *m*; (*of billiard table*) banda *f*. II *vtr fig* amortiguar; (*person*) proteger.
cushy ['kʊʃɪ] *adj* (**cushier, cushiest**) *fam* cómodo,-a.
custard ['kʌstəd] *n* natillas *fpl*; **c. powder**, polvos *mpl* para natillas.
custodian [kʌs'təʊdɪən] *n* conserje *mf*, guarda *mf*.
custody ['kʌstədɪ] *n* custodia *f*; **to take into c.**, detener.
custom ['kʌstəm] *n* 1 (*habit*) costumbre *f*. 2 *Com* clientela *f*.
customary ['kʌstəmərɪ] *adj* habitual.
customer ['kʌstəmə^r] *n* cliente *mf*.
customize ['kʌstəmaɪz] *vtr* hacer por encargo.
custom-made [kʌstəm'meɪd] *adj* hecho,-a a la medida.
customs ['kʌstəmz] *n sing* or *pl* aduana *f*;

c. duty, derechos *mpl* de aduana; **c. officer**, agente *mf* de aduana.
cut [kʌt] I *vtr* (*pt* & *pp* **cut**) 1 cortar; (*stone*) tallar; (*record*) grabar; **he's cutting a tooth**, le está saliendo un diente; **to c. one's finger**, cortarse el dedo; *fig* **to c. a long story short**, en resumidas cuentas; *fig* **to c. corners**, recortar presupuestos. 3 (*reduce*) reducir. 3 (*divide up*) dividir (**into**, en).
II *n* 1 corte *m*; (*in skin*) cortadura *f*; (*wound*) herida *f*; (*with knife*) cuchillada *f*. 2 (*of meat*) clase *f* de carne. 3 (*reduction*) reducción *f*. 4 *fig* **to be a c. above sb**, estar por encima de algn.
III *adj* cortado,-a; (*price*) reducido,-a; *fig* **c. and dried**, convenido,-a de antemano; **c. glass**, cristal tallado.
IV *vi* 1 cortar; *fam fig* **to c. loose**, romper con todo. 2 *Cin* **c.!**, ¡corten! ◆**cut back** *vtr* (*expenses*) reducir; (*production*) disminuir. ◆**cut down** *vtr* (*tree*) talar; **to c. down on**, reducir. ◆**cut in** *vi* (*driver*) adelantar bruscamente. ◆**cut off** *vtr* (*water etc*) cortar; (*place*) aislar; (*heir*) excluir; *Tel* **I've been c. off**, me han cortado (la comunicación). ◆**cut out** I *vtr* 1 (*from newspaper*) recortar; (*person*) **to be c. out for sth**, estar hecho,-a para algo. 2 (*delete*) suprimir. II *vi* (*engine*) calarse. ◆**cut up** *vtr* cortar en pedazos.
cutback ['kʌtbæk] *n* reducción *f* (**in**, de).
cute [kjuːt] *adj* mono,-a, lindo,-a; *US fam pej* listillo,-a.
cuticle ['kjuːtɪkəl] *n* cutícula *f*.
cutlery ['kʌtlərɪ] *n* cubiertos *mpl*.
cutlet ['kʌtlɪt] *n* chuleta *f*.
cut-price [kʌt'praɪs] *adj* (*article*) a precio rebajado.
cutthroat ['kʌtθrəʊt] I *n* asesino,-a *m,f*, matón *m*. II *adj* (*cruel*) cruel; (*competition*) feroz.
cutting ['kʌtɪŋ] I *n* (*from newspaper*) recorte *m*; *Rail* tajo *m*. II *adj* cortante; (*remark*) mordaz.
CV, cv [siː'viː] *abbr of* **curriculum vitae**.
cwt. *abbr of* **hundredweight**, quintal *m*.
cyanide ['saɪənaɪd] *n* cianuro *m*.
cycle ['saɪkəl] I *n* 1 ciclo *m*. 2 (*bicycle*) bicicleta *f*; (*motorcycle*) moto *f*. II *vi* ir en bicicleta.
cycling ['saɪklɪŋ] *n* ciclismo *m*.
cyclist ['saɪklɪst] *n* ciclista *mf*.
cyclone ['saɪkləʊn] *n* ciclón *m*.
cygnet ['sɪgnɪt] *n* pollo *m* de cisne.
cylinder ['sɪlɪndə^r] *n* 1 cilindro *m*. 2 (*for gas*) bombona *f*.
cymbal ['sɪmbəl] *n* címbalo *m*, platillo *m*.
cynic ['sɪnɪk] *n* cínico,-a *m,f*.
cynical ['sɪnɪkəl] *adj* cínico,-a.
cynicism ['sɪnɪsɪzəm] *n* cinismo *m*.
cypress ['saɪprəs] *n* ciprés *m*.

Cypriot ['sɪprɪət] *adj & n* chipriota (*mf*).
Cyprus ['saɪprəs] *n* Chipre.
cyst [sɪst] *n* quiste *m*.
cystitis [sɪ'staɪtɪs] *n* cistitis *f*.
czar [zɑːr] *n* zar *m*.

Czech [tʃek] **I** *adj* checo,-a. **II** *n* **1** (*person*) checo,-a *m,f*. **2** (*language*) checo *m*.
Czechoslovakia [tʃekəʊsləʊ'vækɪə] *n* Checoslovaquia.

D

D, d [diː] *n* **1** (*the letter*) D, d *f*. **2** *Mus* re *m*.
D.A. [diː'eɪ] *US abbr of* **District Attorney**.
dab [dæb] **I** *n* (*small quantity*) toque *m*. **II** *vt* **1** (*apply*) aplicar. **2** (*touch lightly*) tocar ligeramente.
dabble ['dæbəl] *vi* to d. in politics, meterse en política.
dachshund ['dækshʊnd] *n* perro *m* salchicha.
dad [dæd], **daddy** ['dædɪ] *n fam* papá *m*, papi *m*.
daddy-longlegs [dædɪ'lɒŋlegz] *n inv GB fam* típula *f*.
daffodil ['dæfədɪl] *n* narciso *m*.
daft [dɑːft] *adj GB fam* chalado,-a; (*idea*) tonto,-a.
dagger ['dægər] *n* puñal *m*, daga *f*.
dahlia ['deɪljə] *n* dalia *f*.
daily ['deɪlɪ] **I** *adj* diario,-a, cotidiano,-a. **II** *adv* diariamente; **three times d.**, tres veces al día. **III** *n* **1** (*newspaper*) diario *m*. **2** *GB fam* (*cleaning lady*) asistenta *f*.
dainty ['deɪntɪ] *adj* (**daintier, daintiest**) (*flower*) delicado,-a; (*child*) precioso,-a; (*food*) exquisito,-a.
dairy ['deərɪ] *n* (*on farm*) vaquería *f*; (*shop*) lechería *f*; **d. farming**, industria lechera; **d. produce**, productos lácteos.
dais ['deɪɪs] *n* (*in hall*) tarima *f*; (*in ceremony*) estrado *m*.
daisy ['deɪzɪ] *n* margarita *f*.
daisywheel ['deɪzɪwiːl] *n* (*printer*) margarita *f*.
dale [deɪl] *n* valle *m*, hondonada *f*.
Dalmatian [dæl'meɪʃən] *n* (perro *m*) dálmata *m*.
dam [dæm] **I** *n* (*barrier*) dique *m*; (*lake*) presa *f*. **II** *vtr* (*water*) represar. ◆**dam up** *vtr fig* (*emotion*) contener.
damage ['dæmɪdʒ] **I** *n* **1** daño *m*; (*to health, reputation*) perjuicio *m*; (*to relationship*) deterioro *m*. **2** *Jur* **damages**, daños *mpl* y perjuicios *mpl*. **II** *vtr* (*harm*) dañar, hacer daño a; (*spoil*) estropear; (*undermine*) perjudicar.
damaging ['dæmɪdʒɪŋ] *adj* perjudicial.
damn [dæm] **I** *vtr* condenar. **II** *interj fam* **d. (it)!**, ¡maldito,-a sea!; **well, I'll be damned!**, ¡vaya por Dios!. **III** *n fam* **I don't give a d.**, me importa un bledo. **IV** *adj fam* maldito,-a. **V** *adv fam* muy, sumamente.

damned [dæmd] **I** *adj* → **damn IV**. **II** *adv* → **damn V**.
damnedest ['dæmdɪst] *n fam* to do one's d. to ..., hacer todo lo posible para ....
damning ['dæmɪŋ] *adj* (*evidence*) irrefutable; (*criticism*) mordaz.
damp [dæmp] **I** *adj* húmedo,-a; (*wet*) mojado,-a. **II** *n* humedad *f*. **III** *vtr* **1** (*for ironing*) humedecer. **2 to d. (down)**, (*fire*) sofocar; *fig* (*violence*) frenar.
dampen ['dæmpən] *vtr* humedecer; *fig* frenar.
damper ['dæmpər] *n fig* to put a d. on sth, poner freno a algo.
damsel ['dæmzəl] *n lit* doncella *f*.
damson ['dæmzən] *n* ciruela damascena.
dance [dɑːns] **I** *n* baile *m*; (*classical, tribal*) danza *f*; **d. band**, orquesta *f* de baile; **d. floor**, pista *f* de baile; **d. hall**, salón *m* de baile. **II** *vi & vtr* bailar.
dancer ['dɑːnsər] *n* (*by profession*) bailarín,-ina *m,f*.
dandelion ['dændɪlaɪən] *n* diente *m* de león.
dandruff ['dændrəf] *n* caspa *f*.
Dane [deɪn] *n* danés,-esa *m,f*.
danger ['deɪndʒər] *n* **1** (*risk*) riesgo *m*; (*of war etc*) amenaza *f*. **2** (*peril*) peligro *m*; **'d.'**, 'peligro'; **out of d.**, fuera de peligro.
dangerous ['deɪndʒərəs] *adj* peligroso,-a; (*risky*) arriesgado,-a; (*harmful*) nocivo,-a; (*illness*) grave. ◆**dangerously** *adv* peligrosamente.
dangle ['dæŋgəl] **I** *vi* (*hang*) colgar; (*swing*) balancearse. **II** *vtr* (*legs*) colgar; (*bait*) dejar colgado,-a; (*swing*) balancear en el aire.
Danish ['deɪnɪʃ] **I** *adj* danés,-esa; **D. pastry**, pastel *m* de hojaldre. **II** *n* (*language*) danés *m*.
dapper ['dæpər] *adj* pulcro,-a.
dappled ['dæpəld] *adj* (*shade*) moteado,-a.
dare [deər] **I** *vi* atreverse, osar; **he doesn't d. be late**, no se atreve a llegar tarde; **how d. you!**, ¿cómo te atreves?; *esp GB* **I d. say**, quizás; *iron* ya (lo creo). **II** *vtr* (*challenge*) desafiar. **III** *n* desafío *m*.
daredevil ['deədevəl] *adj & n* atrevido,-a (*m,f*), temerario,-a (*m,f*).
daring ['deərɪŋ] **I** *adj* **1** (*bold*) audaz, osado,-a. **2** (*clothes*) atrevido,-a. **II** *n* atrevimiento *m*, osadía *f*.
dark [dɑːk] **I** *adj* **1** (*room, colour*) oscuro, -a; (*hair, complexion*) moreno,-a; (*eyes, fu-*

ture) negro,-a. 2 *fig (gloomy)* triste. 3 *fig* **to be a d. horse,** ser una incógnita; *(discreet)* ser una caja de sorpresas. 4 *fig (sinister)* siniestro,-a. II *n* 1 *(darkness)* oscuridad *f*, tinieblas *fpl*; **after d.,** después del anochecer. 2 *fig* **to be in the d.** *(about),* estar a oscuras (sobre).

darken ['dɑːkən] I *vtr (sky)* oscurecer; *(colour)* hacer más oscuro,-a. II *vi* oscurecerse; *(sky)* nublarse; *fig (face)* ensombrecerse.

darkness ['dɑːknɪs] *n* oscuridad *f*, tinieblas *fpl*.

darkroom ['dɑːkruːm] *n* cuarto oscuro.

darling ['dɑːlɪŋ] *adj & n* querido,-a *(m,f)*.

darn [dɑːn] *vtr* zurcir. II *n* zurcido *m*.

dart [dɑːt] I *n* 1 *(missile)* dardo *m*. 2 **darts,** *sing* dardos *mpl*. II *vi (fly about)* revolotear; **to d. in/out,** entrar/salir corriendo.

dartboard ['dɑːtbɔːd] *n* diana *f*.

dash [dæʃ] I *n* 1 *(rush)* carrera *f*. 2 *esp US (race)* sprint *m*. 3 *(small amount)* poquito *m*; *(of salt)* pizca *f*; *(of liquid)* gota *f*. 4 *Typ (hyphen)* guión largo; *(hyphen)* guión. 5 *(vitality)* brío *m*. II *vtr* 1 *(throw)* arrojar. 2 *(smash)* estrellar; *fig* **to d. sb's hopes,** desvanecer las esperanzas de algn. III *vi (rush)* correr; **to d. around,** correr de un lado a otro; **to d. out,** salir corriendo; *fam* **I must d.!,** ¡me voy pitando! ◆**dash off** *vi* salir corriendo.

dashboard ['dæʃbɔːd] *n Aut* salpicadero *m*.

dashing ['dæʃɪŋ] *adj (appearance)* garboso,-a.

data ['deɪtə, 'dɑːtə] *npl* datos *mpl*; **d. bank** *or* **base,** banco *m* de datos; **d. processing,** *(act)* proceso *m* de datos; *(science)* informática *f*; **d. protection act,** ley *f* de informática.

date¹ [deɪt] I *n* 1 fecha *f*; **what's the d. today?** ¿qué día es hoy?; **out of d.,** *(ideas)* anticuado,-a; *(expression)* desusado,-a; *(invalid)* caducado,-a; **to d.,** hasta la fecha; *fig* **to be up to d.,** estar al día; **d. of birth,** fecha de nacimiento. 2 *(social event)* compromiso *m*; *fam (with girl, boy)* cita *f*. 3 *US fam (person dated)* ligue *m*. II *vtr (ruins)* datar. III *vi (ideas)* quedar anticuado,-a. ◆**d. back to, date from** *vtr* remontar a, datar de.

date² [deɪt] *n (fruit)* dátil *m*; **d. palm,** datilera *f*.

dated ['deɪtɪd] *adj (idea)* anticuado,-a; *(fashion)* pasado,-a de moda; *(expression)* desusado,-a.

daub [dɔːb] *vtr* embadurnar; *(with oil, grease)* untar.

daughter ['dɔːtər] *n* hija *f*.

daughter-in-law ['dɔːtərɪnlɔː] *n* nuera *f*, hija política.

daunting ['dɔːntɪŋ] *adj* desalentador,-a.

dawdle ['dɔːdəl] *vi fam (walk slowly)*

andar despacio; *(waste time)* perder el tiempo.

dawn [dɔːn] I *n* alba *f*, amanecer *m*. II *vi* 1 *(day)* amanecer. 2 *fig (age, hope)* comenzar. 3 *fig* **it suddenly dawned on him that ...,** de repente cayó en la cuenta de que ....

day [deɪ] *n* 1 día *m*; **d. in, d. out,** día tras día; **d. by d.,** diariamente; **good d.!,** ¡buenos días!; **once a d.,** una vez al día; **one of these days,** un día de éstos; **(on) the next** *or* **following d.,** el *or* al día siguiente; **the d. after tomorrow,** pasado mañana; **the d. before yesterday,** anteayer; **the other d.,** el otro día; *fig* **to live from d. to d.,** vivir al día; *fig* **to win the d.,** llevarse la palma; *fam* **to call it a d.,** *(finish)* dar por acabado un trabajo; *(give up)* darse por vencido,-a; *fam* **to make sb's d.,** alegrarle a algn el día; *GB Rail* **d. return (ticket),** billete *m* de ida y vuelta para el mismo día; **d. trip,** excursión *f* de un día. 2 *(daylight)* día *m*; **by d.,** de día; **d. and night,** de día y de noche; *GB* **d. shift,** turno *m* de día. 3 *(period of work)* jornada *f*; **an eight-hour d.,** una jornada de ocho horas; **paid by the d.,** pagado,-a a jornal; **d. off,** día de fiesta; **I'll take a d. off tomorrow,** mañana me tomaré el día libre. 4 *(era)* época *f*; **in those days,** en aquellos tiempos; **these days, in this d. and age,** hoy (en) día.

daybreak ['deɪbreɪk] *n* amanecer *m*.

daydream ['deɪdriːm] I *n* ensueño *m*; *(vain hope)* fantasía *f*. II *vi* soñar despierto,-a; *(hope vainly)* hacerse ilusiones.

daylight ['deɪlaɪt] *n* luz *f* del día; **in broad d.,** en pleno día; **to scare the (living) daylights out of sb,** pegarle a algn un susto de muerte.

daytime ['deɪtaɪm] *n* día *m*; **in the d.,** de día.

day-to-day ['deɪtədeɪ] *adj* cotidiano,-a, diario,-a.

daze [deɪz] *n* aturdimiento *m*; **in a d.,** aturdido,-a.

dazed [deɪzd] *adj* aturdido,-a, atontado,-a.

dazzle ['dæzəl] *vtr* deslumbrar.

D-day ['diːdeɪ] *n* día *m* D.

deacon ['diːkən] *n* diácono *m*.

dead [ded] I *adj* 1 muerto,-a; **he was shot d.,** le mataron a tiros; **d. man,** muerto *m*; *fam fig* **over my d. body!,** ¡sobre mi cadáver!; **d. man,** muerto *m*. 2 *(machine)* averiado,-a; *(phone)* cortado,-a. 3 *(numb)* entumecido,-a; *(limb)* adormecido,-a; **my leg's gone d.,** se me ha dormido la pierna. 4 *(silence, secrecy)* total; **d. end,** callejón *m* sin salida; *Sport* **d. heat,** empate *m*; *fam* **d. loss,** inútil *m*, birria *f*. II *adv* 1 *(exactly)* justo; **d. on time,** a la hora en punto. 2 **to stop d.,**

pararse en seco. **3** (*very*) muy; *fam* **d. beat, d. tired**, rendido,-a; *fam* **it's d. easy!**, ¡está chupado,-a!; *Aut* **'d. slow'**, 'al paso'; *fam* **you're d. right**, tienes toda la razón. **III** *n* **1** the **d.**, (*pl*) los muertos. **2** at **d. of night**, a altas horas de la noche.

deaden ['dedən] *vtr* (*impact, noise*) amortiguar; *fig* (*pain, feeling*) calmar, aliviar.

deadline ['dedlaın] *n* (*date*) fecha *f* tope; (*time*) hora *f* tope; **we have to meet the d.**, tenemos que hacerlo dentro del plazo.

deadlock ['dedlɒk] *n* punto muerto.

deadly ['dedlı] **I** *adj* (**deadlier, deadliest**) mortal; (*weapon*) mortífero,-a; (*aim*) certero,-a. **II** *adv* (*extremely*) terriblemente, sumamente.

deadpan ['dedpæn] *adj fam* (*face*) sin expresión; (*humour*) guasón,-ona.

deaf [def] **I** *adj* sordo,-a; *fig* **to turn a d. ear**, hacerse el sordo; **d. mute**, sordomudo,-a *m,f*. **II** *npl* **the d.**, los sordos; **the d. and dumb**, los sordomudos.

deafen ['defən] *vtr* ensordecer.

deafening ['defənıŋ] *adj* ensordecedor,-a.

deafness ['defnıs] *n* sordera *f*.

deal [diːl] **I** *n* **1** *Com Pol* trato *m*, pacto *m*; **business d.**, negocio *m*, transacción *f*; **to do a d. with sb**, (*transaction*) cerrar un trato con algn; (*agreement*) pactar algo con algn; *fam* **it's a d.!**, ¡trato hecho! **2** (*amount*) cantidad *f*; **a good d. of criticism**, muchas críticas; **a good d. slower**, mucho más despacio. **3** *Cards* reparto *m*. **II** *vtr* (*pt & pp* **dealt**) **1** *Cards* dar (to, a). **2** **to d. sb a blow**, asestarle un golpe a algn. ◆**deal in** *vtr* (*goods*) comerciar en, tratar en; (*drugs*) traficar con. ◆**deal out** *vtr* repartir. ◆**deal with** *vtr* (*firm, person*) tratar con; (*subject, problem*) abordar, ocuparse de; (*in book etc*) tratar de.

dealer ['diːlər] *n* **1** *Com* (*in goods*) comerciante *mf*; (*in drugs*) traficante *mf*. **2** *Cards* repartidor,-a *m,f*.

dealings ['diːlıŋz] *npl* **1** (*relations*) trato *m sing*. **2** *Com* negocios *mpl*.

dealt [delt] *pt & pp* → **deal**.

dean [diːn] *n* **1** *Rel* deán *m*. **2** *Univ* decano *m*.

dear [dıər] **I** *adj* **1** (*loved*) querido,-a; **to hold sth/sb d.**, apreciar mucho algo/a algn. **2** (*in letter*) Querido,-a; *fam* **D. Andrew**, Querido Andrew; *fml* **D. Madam**, Estimada señora; *fml* **D. Sir(s)**, Muy señor(es) mío(s). **3** **it is very d. to me**, (*precious*) le tengo un gran cariño. **4** *GB* (*expensive*) caro,-a. **II** *n* querido,-a *m,f*; **my d.**, mi vida. **III** *interj* **oh d.!**, **d. me!**, (*surprise*) ¡caramba!; (*disappointment*) ¡qué pena! ◆**dearly** *adv* muchísimo; *fig* **he paid d. for his mistake**, su error le costó

caro.

dearth [dɜːθ] *n fml* escasez *f*.

death [deθ] *n* **1** muerte *f*; *fml* fallecimiento *m*; **to put sb to d.**, dar muerte a algn; *fam* **to be bored to d.**, aburrirse como una ostra; *fam* **to be scared to d.**, estar muerto,-a de miedo; *fam fig* **to be sick to d. of**, estar hasta la coronilla de; **d. certificate**, certificado *m* de defunción; **d. penalty, d. sentence**, pena *f* de muerte; **d. rate**, índice *m* de mortalidad; **d. squad**, escuadrón *m* de la muerte. **2** *fig* (*end*) fin *m*.

deathbed ['deθbed] *n* **to be on one's d.**, estar en el lecho de muerte.

deathly ['deθlı] *adj* (**deathlier, deathliest**) (*silence*) sepulcral; **d. pale**, pálido,-a como un muerto.

debacle [deı'baːkəl] *n* debacle *f*.

debar [dı'baːr] *vtr fml* excluir, prohibir.

debase [dı'beıs] *vtr fig* envilecer; **to d. oneself**, humillarse.

debate [dı'beıt] **I** *n* debate *m*; **a heated d.**, una discusión acalorada. **II** *vtr* **1** (*discuss*) discutir. **2** (*wonder about*) dar vueltas a. **III** *vi* discutir.

debat(e)able [dı'beıtəbəl] *adj* discutible.

debauchery [dı'bɔːtʃərı] *n* libertinaje *m*.

debilitating [dı'bılıteıtıŋ] *adj* debilitante; (*heat, climate*) agotador,-a.

debit ['debıt] **I** *n* débito *m*; **d. balance**, saldo negativo. **II** *vtr* **d. Mr Jones with £20**, cargar la suma de veinte libras en la cuenta del Sr. Jones.

debris ['debriː, 'deıbriː] *n sing* escombros *mpl*.

debt [det] *n* deuda *f*; **to be deeply in d.**, estar cargado,-a de deudas; *fig* **to be in sb's d.**, estar en deuda con algn.

debtor ['detər] *n* deudor,-a *m,f*.

debug [diː'bʌg] *vtr Comput* eliminar fallos de.

debunk [diː'bʌŋk] *vtr fam* desacreditar, desprestigiar.

debut ['deıbjuː, 'deıbjuː] *n* debut *m*; **to make one's d.**, debutar.

debutante ['debjʊtɑːnt] *n* debutante *f*.

decade [de'keıd, 'dekeıd] *n* decenio *m*, década *f*.

decadence ['dekədəns] *n* decadencia *f*.

decadent ['dekədənt] *adj* decadente.

decaffeinated [diː'kæfıneıtıd] *adj* descafeinado,-a.

decanter [dı'kæntər] *n* jarra *f*, jarro *m*.

decapitate [dı'kæpıteıt] *vtr* decapitar.

decay [dı'keı] **I** *n* (*of food, body*) descomposición *f*; (*of teeth*) caries *f inv*; (*of buildings*) desmoronamiento *m*; *fig* decadencia *f*. **II** *vi* descomponerse; (*teeth*) cariarse; (*building*) deteriorarse; *fig* corromperse.

deceased [dı'siːst] *fml adj* difunto,-a, fallecido,-a.

deceit [dı'siːt] *n* **1** (*dishonesty*) falta *f* de

honradez, falsedad *f*. 2 *(trick)* engaño *m*, mentira *f*.

deceitful [dɪˈsiːtful] *adj* falso,-a.

deceive [dɪˈsiːv] *vtr (mislead)* engañar; *(lie to)* mentir.

December [dɪˈsembər] *n* diciembre *m*.

decency [ˈdiːsənsɪ] *n* decencia *f*; *(modesty)* pudor *m*; *(morality)* moralidad *f*.

decent [ˈdiːsənt] *adj* decente; *(person)* honrado,-a; *fam (kind)* simpático,-a.

decentralize [diːˈsentrəlaɪz] *vtr* descentralizar.

deception [dɪˈsepʃən] *n* engaño *m*.

deceptive [dɪˈseptɪv] *adj* engañoso,-a.
◆**deceptively** *adv* **it looks d. simple**, parece engañosamente sencillo,-a.

decibel [ˈdesɪbel] *n* decibelio *m*.

decide [dɪˈsaɪd] **I** *vtr* 1 decidir; **to d. to do sth**, decidir hacer algo. 2 *(matter, question)* resolver, determinar. **II** *vi (reach decision)* decidirse; **to d. against sth**, decidirse en contra de algo. ◆**decide on** *vtr (choose)* optar por.

decided [dɪˈsaɪdɪd] *adj* 1 *(noticeable)* marcado,-a. 2 *(resolute)* decidido,-a; *(views)* categórico,-a. ◆**decidedly** *adv fml (clearly)* indudablemente. 2 *(resolutely)* decididamente.

deciding [dɪˈsaɪdɪŋ] *adj* decisivo,-a.

deciduous [dɪˈsɪdjuːəs] *adj* de hoja caduca.

decimal [ˈdesɪməl] **I** *adj* decimal; **d. point**, coma *f* (de fracción decimal). **II** *n* decimal *m*.

decimate [ˈdesɪmeɪt] *vtr* diezmar.

decipher [dɪˈsaɪfər] *vtr* descifrar.

decision [dɪˈsɪʒən] *n* 1 decisión *f*; *Jur* fallo *m*; **to come to a d.**, llegar a una decisión; **to make a d.**, tomar una decisión. 2 *(resolution)* resolución *f*.

decisive [dɪˈsaɪsɪv] *adj* 1 *(resolute)* decidido,-a, resuelto,-a. 2 *(conclusive)* decisivo,-a.

deck [dek] **I** *n* 1 *(of ship)* cubierta *f*; **on/below d.**, en/bajo cubierta; **d. chair**, tumbona *f*. 2 *(of bus)* piso *m*; **top d.**, piso de arriba. 3 *esp US (of cards)* baraja *f*. 4 *(of record player)* plato *m*. **II** *vtr* **to d. out**, adornar.

declaration [dekləˈreɪʃən] *n* declaración *f*.

declare [dɪˈkleər] *vtr* declarar; *(winner, innocence)* proclamar; *(decision)* manifestar.

declared [dɪˈkleəd] *adj (opponent)* declarado,-a; *(intention)* manifiesto,-a.

decline [dɪˈklaɪn] **I** *n* 1 *(decrease)* disminución *f*. 2 *(deterioration)* deterioro *m*; *(of health)* empeoramiento *m*; **to fall into d.**, empezar a decaer. **II** *vi* 1 *(decrease)* disminuir; *(amount)* bajar; *(business)* decaer. 2 *(deteriorate)* deteriorarse; *(health)* empeorar. 3 *(refuse)* negarse. **III** *vtr* 1 *(refuse)* rechazar. 2 *Ling* declinar.

declutch [dɪˈklʌtʃ] *vi* soltar el embrague.

decode [diːˈkəʊd] *vtr* descifrar.

decompose [diːkəmˈpəʊz] *vi* descomponerse.

décor [ˈdeɪkɔːr] *n* decoración *f*; *Theat* decorado *m*.

decorate [ˈdekəreɪt] *vtr* 1 *(adorn)* decorar, adornar (**with**, con). 2 *(paint)* pintar; *(wallpaper)* empapelar. 3 *(honour)* condecorar.

decoration [dekəˈreɪʃən] *n* 1 *(decor)* decoración *f*; **Christmas decorations**, adornos navideños. 2 *(medal)* condecoración *f*.

decorative [ˈdekərətɪv] *adj* decorativo,-a.

decorator [ˈdekəreɪtər] *n* decorador,-a *m,f*; *(painter)* pintor,-a *m,f*; *(paperhanger)* empapelador,-a *m,f*.

decorum [dɪˈkɔːrəm] *n* decoro *m*.

decoy [ˈdiːkɔɪ] *n* fig señuelo *m*.

decrease [ˈdiːkriːs] **I** *n* disminución *f*; *(in speed, size, price)* reducción *f*. **II** [dɪˈkriːs] *vi* disminuir; *(strength)* menguar; *(price, temperature)* bajar; *(speed, size)* reducir. **III** *vtr* disminuir, reducir; *(price, temperature)* bajar.

decree [dɪˈkriː] **I** *n* 1 *Pol Rel* decreto *m*. 2 *esp US Jur* sentencia *f*; **d. absolute**, sentencia definitiva de divorcio; **d. nisi**, sentencia provisional de divorcio. **II** *vtr Pol Rel* decretar, pronunciar.

decrepit [dɪˈkrepɪt] *adj* decrépito,-a.

dedicate [ˈdedɪkeɪt] *vtr* consagrar, dedicar.

dedicated [ˈdedɪkeɪtɪd] *adj* ardiente; **d. to**, entregado,-a a.

dedication [dedɪˈkeɪʃən] *n (act)* dedicación *f*; *(commitment)* entrega *f*; *(in book)* dedicatoria *f*.

deduce [dɪˈdjuːs] *vtr* deducir (**from**, de).

deduct [dɪˈdʌkt] *vtr* descontar (**from**, de).

deduction [dɪˈdʌkʃən] *n* 1 *(conclusion)* conclusión *f*. 2 *(subtraction)* descuento *m*.

deed [diːd] *n* 1 *(act)* acto *m*; *(feat)* hazaña *f*. 2 *Jur* escritura *f*; **title deeds**, título *m sing* de propiedad.

deem [diːm] *vtr fml* estimar.

deep [diːp] **I** *adj* 1 profundo,-a; *(breath, sigh)* hondo,-a; **it's ten metres d.**, tiene diez metros de profundidad. 2 *(voice)* grave; *(shame)* grande; *(interest)* vivo,-a. 3 *(colour)* oscuro,-a. 4 *(serious)* grave. **II** *adv* **to dig d.**, cavar hondo; **to be d. in thought**, estar absorto,-a; **to look d. into sb's eyes**, penetrar a algn con la mirada; *fig* **nine d.**, de nueve en fondo. ◆**deeply** *adv* profundamente; *(breathe)* hondo; **to be d. in debt**, estar cargado,-a de deudas.

deepen [ˈdiːpən] **I** *vtr (well)* profundizar, ahondar; *fig (knowledge)* aumentar. **II** *vi (river etc)* hacerse más hondo *or* profundo; *fig (knowledge)* aumentar; *(colour, emotion)* intensificarse; *(sound, voice)* hacerse más grave.

deep-freeze [di:p'fri:z] I *n* congelador *m*. II *vtr* congelar.

deep-fry [di:p'fraɪ] *vtr* freír en mucho aceite.

deep-rooted [di:p'ru:tɪd] *adj fig* arraigado,-a.

deep-seated [di:p'si:tɪd] *adj fig* arraigado,-a.

deep-set [di:p'set] *adj (eyes)* hundido,-a.

deer [dɪər] *n inv* ciervo *m*.

deface [dɪ'feɪs] *vtr (book, poster)* garabatear.

de facto [deɪ'fæktəʊ] *adj & adv fml* de hecho.

defamation [defə'meɪʃən] *n* difamación *f*.

default [dɪ'fɔ:lt] I *vi* 1 *(not act)* faltar a sus compromisos. 2 *Jur* estar en rebeldía. 3 *(not pay)* suspender pagos. II *n* 1 *(failure to act)* omisión *f*. 2 *(failure to pay)* incumplimiento *m* de pago. 3 *Jur* rebeldía *f*; **in d. of**, a falta de; **to win by d.**, ganar por incomparecencia del adversario.

defaulter [dɪ'fɔ:ltər] *n (on loan)* moroso,-a *mf*; *Jur Mil* rebelde *mf*.

defeat [dɪ'fi:t] I *vtr* 1 derrotar, vencer; *(motion)* rechazar. 2 *fig* frustrar. II *n* 1 *(of army, team)* derrota *f*; *(of motion)* rechazo *m*. 2 *fig* fracaso *m*.

defeatist [dɪ'fi:tɪst] *adj & n* derrotista *(mf)*.

defect ['di:fekt] I *n* defecto *m*; *(flaw)* desperfecto *m*. II [dɪ'fekt] *vi* desertar **(from, de)**; *(from country)* huir.

defective [dɪ'fektɪv] *adj (faulty)* defectuoso,-a; *(flawed)* con desperfectos; *(lacking)* incompleto,-a.

defector [dɪ'fektər] *n Pol* tránsfuga *mf*, trásfuga *mf*.

defence [dɪ'fens] *n* 1 defensa *f*; **the Ministry of D.**, el Ministerio de Defensa; **to come to sb's d.**, salir en defensa de algn. 2 *usu sing Jur* defensa *f*. 3 *Sport GB* [dɪ'fens], *US* ['di:fens] **the d.**, la defensa.

defenceless [dɪ'fenslɪs] *adj* indefenso,-a.

defend [dɪ'fend] *vtr* defender.

defendant [dɪ'fendənt] *n Jur* acusado,-a *m,f*.

defender [dɪ'fendə] *n* defensor,-a *m,f*; *Sport* defensa *mf*.

defending [dɪ'fendɪŋ] *adj Sport* defensor,-a; **d. champion**, campeón,-ona *m,f* titular.

defense [dɪ'fens, 'di:fens] *n US* → **defence**.

defensive [dɪ'fensɪv] I *adj* defensivo,-a. II *n* **to be on the d.**, estar a la defensiva.

defer¹ [dɪ'fɜ:] *vtr* aplazar, retrasar.

defer² [dɪ'fɜ:] *vi* **to d. to**, deferir a.

deference ['defərəns] *n fml* deferencia *f*, respeto *m*; **out of** *or* **in d. to**, por respeto *or* por deferencia a.

defiance [dɪ'faɪəns] *n* 1 *(challenge)* desafío *m*; **in d. of**, a despecho de. 2 *(resistance)* resistencia *f*.

defiant [dɪ'faɪənt] *adj (challenging)* desafiante; *(bold)* insolente.

deficiency [dɪ'fɪʃənsɪ] *n* 1 *(lack)* falta *f*, carencia *f*. 2 *(shortcoming)* defecto *m*.

deficient [dɪ'fɪʃənt] *adj* deficiente; **to be d. in sth**, carecer de algo.

deficit ['defɪsɪt] *n* déficit *m*.

defile [dɪ'faɪl] *vtr fml* 1 *(mind)* corromper; *(honour)* manchar; *(woman)* deshonrar. 2 *(desecrate)* profanar.

define [dɪ'faɪn] *vtr* definir; *(duties, powers)* delimitar.

definite ['defɪnɪt] *adj* 1 *(clear)* claro,-a; *(progress)* notable. 2 *(date, place)* determinado,-a; **is it d.?**, ¿es seguro? **◆definitely** I *adv* sin duda; **he was d. drunk**, no cabe duda de que estaba borracho. II *interj* ¡desde luego!

definition [defɪ'nɪʃən] *n* definición *f*; **by d.**, por definición.

definitive [dɪ'fɪnɪtɪv] *adj* definitivo,-a.

deflate [dɪ'fleɪt] *vtr* 1 *(tyre etc)* desinflar. 2 *fig* rebajar; **to d. sb**, hacer bajar los humos a algn. 3 **to d. the economy**, tomar medidas deflacionistas.

deflationary [dɪ'fleɪʃənərɪ] *adj Econ* deflacionista.

deflect [dɪ'flekt] *vtr* desviar.

deflection [dɪ'flekʃən] *n* desviación *f*.

deforestation [di:fɒrɪs'teɪʃən] *n* deforestación *f*.

deformed [dɪ'fɔ:md] *adj* deforme.

deformity [dɪ'fɔ:mɪtɪ] *n* deformidad *f*.

defraud [dɪ'frɔ:d] *vtr* estafar.

defrost [di:'frɒst] *vtr* 1 *(freezer, food)* descongelar. 2 *(windscreen)* desempañar.

deft [deft] *adj* hábil, diestro,-a.

defunct [dɪ'fʌŋkt] *adj (person)* difunto,-a; *(thing)* en desuso.

defuse [di:'fju:z] *vtr (bomb)* desactivar; *fig* **to d. a situation**, reducir la tensión de una situación.

defy [dɪ'faɪ] *vtr* 1 *(person)* desafiar; *(law, order)* contravenir. 2 *(challenge)* retar, desafiar.

degenerate [dɪ'dʒenəreɪt] I *vi* degenerar **(into, en)**. II [dɪ'dʒenərɪt] *adj & n* degenerado,-a *(m,f)*.

degrading [dɪ'greɪdɪŋ] *adj* degradante.

degree [dɪ'gri:] *n* 1 grado *m*; **to some d.**, hasta cierto punto. 2 *(stage)* etapa *f*; **by degrees**, poco a poco. 3 *(qualification)* título *m*; *(doctorate)* doctorado *m*; **to have a d. in science**, ser licenciado en ciencias.

dehydrated [di:haɪ'dreɪtɪd] *adj (person)* deshidratado,-a; *(vegetables)* seco,-a.

de-ice [di:'aɪs] *vtr* quitar el hielo a, deshelar.

de-icer [di:'aɪsər] *n* anticongelante *m*.

deign [deɪn] *vi* dignarse.

deity ['deɪtɪ] *n* deidad *f*.

dejected |dɪ'dʒektɪd| *adj* desalentado,-a, abatido,-a.

delay |dɪ'leɪ| **I** *vtr* **1** *(flight, train)* retrasar; *(person)* entretener; **delayed action**, acción retardada. **2** *(postpone)* aplazar. **II** *vi* **don't d.**, no lo deje para más tarde. **III** *n* retraso *m.*

delectable |dɪ'lektəbəl| *adj* delicioso,-a.

delegate |'delɪgɪt| **I** *n* delegado,-a *m,f.* **II** |'delɪgeɪt| *vtr* delegar (**to, en**); **to d. sb to do sth**, encargar a algn que haga algo.

delegation |delɪ'geɪʃən| *n* delegación *f.*

delete |dɪ'li:t| *vtr* tachar, suprimir.

deliberate |dɪ'lɪbərɪt| **I** *adj* *(intentional)* deliberado,-a, intencionado,-a; *(studied)* premeditado,-a; *(careful)* prudente; *(unhurried)* pausado,-a. **II** *vtr* |dɪ'lɪbəreɪt| deliberar. **III** *vi* deliberar (**on, about**, sobre). ◆**deliberately** *adv* *(intentionally)* a propósito; *(unhurriedly)* pausadamente.

deliberation |dɪlɪbə'reɪʃən| *n* **1** *esp pl* *(consideration)* deliberación *f.* **2** *(care)* cuidado *m*; *(unhurriedness)* pausa *f.*

delicacy |'delɪkəsɪ| *n* **1** delicadeza *f.* **2** *(food)* manjar *m* (exquisito).

delicate |'delɪkɪt| *adj* delicado,-a; *(handiwork)* fino,-a; *(instrument)* sensible; *(flavour)* sutil.

delicious |dɪ'lɪʃəs| *adj* delicioso,-a.

delight |dɪ'laɪt| **I** *n* **1** *(pleasure)* placer *m*; **he took d. in it**, le encantó. **2** *(source of pleasure)* encanto *m*, delicia *f.* **II** *vtr* encantar.

delighted |dɪ'laɪtɪd| *adj* encantado,-a; *(smile)* de alegría; **I'm d. to see you**, me alegro mucho de verte.

delightful |dɪ'laɪtful| *adj* encantador,-a; *(view, person)* muy agradable; *(meal, weather)* delicioso,-a.

delinquency |dɪ'lɪŋkwənsɪ| *n* delincuencia *f*; **juvenile d.**, delincuencia juvenil.

delinquent |dɪ'lɪŋkwənt| *adj & n* delincuente *(mf).*

delirious |dɪ'lɪrɪəs| *adj* delirante.

deliver |dɪ'lɪvər| *vtr* **1** *(goods)* repartir, entregar; *(message)* dar; *(order)* despachar; *fig* **to d. the goods**, cumplir con la obligación. **2** *(blow)* asestar; *(speech, verdict)* pronunciar. **3** *Med* ayudar en el nacimiento de. **4** *fml (rescue)* liberar.

delivery |dɪ'lɪvərɪ| *n* **1** *(of goods)* reparto *m*, entrega *f*; **to take d. of an order**, recibir un pedido; **d. note**, albarán *m* de entrega; *GB* **d. van**, furgoneta *f* de reparto. **2** *(of speech)* declamación *f.* **3** *(of baby)* parto *m.*

delta |'deltə| *n Geog* delta *m.*

delude |dɪ'lu:d| *vtr* engañar; **don't d. yourself**, no te hagas ilusiones.

deluge |'delju:dʒ| **I** *n* *(flood)* inundación *f*; *(rain)* diluvio *m*; *fig (of letters etc)* avalancha *f.* **II** *vtr fml* inundar.

delusion |dɪ'lu:ʒən| *n* **1** *(state, act)* enga-

ño *m.* **2** *(false belief)* ilusión *f* (vana); **delusions of grandeur**, delirios *mpl* de grandeza.

de luxe |də'lʌks, də'lʊks| *adj* de lujo *inv.*

delve |delv| *vi* **to d. into**, *(pocket)* hurgar en; *(subject)* profundizar en.

demand |dɪ'mɑ:nd| **I** *n* **1** solicitud *f*; *(for pay rise, rights)* reclamación *f*; *(need)* necesidad *f*; **on d.**, a petición. **2** *(claim)* exigencia *f*; **to be in d.**, ser solicitado,-a. **3** *Econ* demanda *f.* **II** *vtr* **1** exigir; *(rights)* reclamar; **to d. that ...**, insistir en que ... (+ *subj*). **2** *(need)* requerir.

demanding |dɪ'mɑ:ndɪŋ| *adj* **1** *(person)* exigente. **2** *(job)* agotador,-a.

demean |dɪ'mi:n| *vtr fml* **to d. oneself**, rebajarse.

demeaning |dɪ'mi:nɪŋ| *adj fml* humillante.

demeanour, *US* **demeanor** |dɪ'mi:nər| *n fml* **1** *(behaviour)* comportamiento *m*, conducta *f.* **2** *(bearing)* porte *m.*

demented |dɪ'mentɪd| *adj Med* demente; *fam* loco,-a.

demise |dɪ'maɪz| *n (death) fml* fallecimiento *m*; *fig (of institution)* desaparición *f*; *(of ambition etc)* fracaso *m.*

demist |di:'mɪst| *vtr Aut* desempañar.

demo |'deməʊ| *n fam* manifestación *f*; **d. tape**, maqueta *f.*

demobilize |di:'məʊbɪlaɪz| *vtr* desmovilizar.

democracy |dɪ'mɒkrəsɪ| *n* democracia *f.*

democrat |'deməkræt| *n* demócrata *mf*; *Pol* **Christian D.**, democratacristiano,-a *m,f*; **Social D.**, socialdemócrata *mf.*

democratic |demə'krætɪk| *adj* democrático,-a; *US Pol* **D. party**, partido *m* demócrata.

demographic |demə'græfɪk| *adj* demográfico,-a.

demolish |dɪ'mɒlɪʃ| *vtr (building)* derribar, demoler; *fig (theory, proposal)* echar por tierra.

demolition |demə'lɪʃən| *n* demolición *f.*

demon |'di:mən| *n* demonio *m.*

demonstrate |'demənstreɪt| **I** *vtr* demostrar. **II** *vi Pol* manifestarse.

demonstration |demən'streɪʃən| *n* **1** *(proof)* demostración *f*, prueba *f.* **2** *(explanation)* explicación *f.* **3** *Pol* manifestación *f.*

demonstrative |dɪ'mɒnstrətɪv| *adj* expresivo.

demonstrator |'demənstreɪtər| *n* manifestante *mf.*

demoralize |dɪ'mɒrəlaɪz| *vtr* desmoralizar.

demoralizing |dɪ'mɒrəlaɪzɪŋ| *adj* desmoralizador,-a, desmoralizante.

demote |dɪ'məʊt| *vtr* rebajar de graduación a.

demure |dɪ'mjʊər| *adj (person)* recatado, -a.

den [den] n **1** (of animal) guarida f. **2** fam (study) estudio m.

denial [dɪ'naɪəl] n **1** (of charge) desmentido m. **2** (of rights) denegación f; (of request) negativa f.

denim ['denɪm] n dril m; **d. skirt,** falda tejana;. **denims,** tejanos mpl, vaqueros mpl.

Denmark ['denmɑːk] n Dinamarca.

denomination [dɪnɒmɪ'neɪʃən] n **1** Rel confesión f. **2** Fin (of coins) valor m.

denominator [dɪ'nɒmɪneɪtəʳ] n denominador m.

denote [dɪ'nəʊt] vtr (show) indicar; (mean) significar.

denounce [dɪ'naʊns] vtr denunciar; (criticize) censurar.

dense [dens] adj **1** denso,-a; (crowd) numeroso,-a. **2** fam (stupid) torpe.
◆**densely** adv densamente.

density ['densɪtɪ] n densidad f.

dent [dent] I n abolladura f. II vtr (car) abollar.

dental ['dentəl] adj dental; **d. floss,** hilo m dental; **d. surgeon,** odontólogo,-a m,f; **d. surgery,** (place) clínica f dental; (treatment) cirugía f dental.

dentist ['dentɪst] n dentista mf.

dentistry ['dentɪstrɪ] n odontología f.

denture ['dentʃəʳ] n (usu pl) dentadura postiza.

denunciation [dɪnʌnsɪ'eɪʃən] n denuncia f, condena f.

deny [dɪ'naɪ] vtr **1** (repudiate) negar; (rumour, report) desmentir; (charge) rechazar. **2** (refuse) negar.

deodorant [diː'əʊdərənt] n desodorante m.

depart [dɪ'pɑːt] vi marcharse, irse; fig (from subject) desviarse (**from,** de).

department [dɪ'pɑːtmənt] n sección f; (in university) departamento m; (in government) ministerio m; **d. store,** grandes almacenes mpl .

departure [dɪ'pɑːtʃəʳ] n partida f; Av Rail salida f; Av **d. lounge,** sala f de embarque.

depend [dɪ'pend] I vi (rely) fiarse (**on, upon,** de). II v impers (be determined by) depender (**on, upon,** de); **it depends on the weather,** según el tiempo que haga; **that depends,** según.

dependable [dɪ'pendəbəl] adj (person) responsable, fiable; (income) seguro,-a; (machine) fiable.

dependant, US **dependent** [dɪ'pendənt] n dependiente mf.

dependence [dɪ'pendəns] n dependencia f.

dependent [dɪ'pendənt] I adj dependiente; **to be d. on sth,** depender de algo. II n US → **dependant.**

depict [dɪ'pɪkt] vtr Art representar; fig describir.

deplete [dɪ'pliːt] vtr reducir.

deplorable [dɪ'plɔːrəbəl] adj lamentable.

deplore [dɪ'plɔːʳ] vtr deplorar.

deploy [dɪ'plɔɪ] vtr Mil desplegar; fig utilizar.

depopulate [diː'pɒpjʊleɪt] vtr despoblar.

deport [dɪ'pɔːt] vtr expulsar (**from,** de; **to,** a).

deportation [diːpɔː'teɪʃən] n expulsión f.

deportment [dɪ'pɔːtmənt] n fml porte m.

depose [dɪ'pəʊz] vtr deponer.

deposit [dɪ'pɒzɪt] I n **1** sedimento m; Min yacimiento m; (in wine) poso m. **2** (in bank) depósito m; **d. account,** cuenta f de ahorros. **3** Com (on purchase) señal f; (on rented car, flat) depósito m; (on house) entrada f. II vtr depositar; (into account) ingresar.

deposition [depə'zɪʃən] n **1** (of leader) destitución f. **2** Jur (of witness) declaración f.

depositor [dɪ'pɒzɪtəʳ] n depositante mf.

depot ['depəʊ] n almacén m; Mil depósito m; (bus garage) garaje m (de autobuses).

depraved [dɪ'preɪvd] adj (person) depravado,-a.

deprecate ['deprɪkeɪt] vtr desaprobar, censurar.

depreciate [dɪ'priːʃɪeɪt] vi depreciarse.

depreciation [dɪpriːʃɪ'eɪʃən] n depreciación f.

depress [dɪ'pres] vtr **1** (person) deprimir. **2** Econ (profits) reducir; (trade) dificultar. **3** fml (switch, lever etc) presionar; (clutch, piano pedal) pisar.

depressed [dɪ'prest] adj **1** (person) deprimido,-a; **to get d.,** deprimirse. **2** (market) en crisis. **3** (surface) hundido,-a.

depressing [dɪ'presɪŋ] adj deprimente.

depression [dɪ'preʃən] n depresión f.

deprivation [deprɪ'veɪʃən] n (hardship) privación f; (loss) pérdida f.

deprive [dɪ'praɪv] vtr privar (**of,** de).

deprived [dɪ'praɪvd] adj necesitado,-a.

Dept abbr of **Department,** dpt, dpto; (in store) sección f.

depth [depθ] n **1** profundidad f. **2** fig (of emotion) intensidad f; (of thought) complejidad f; **to be in the depths of despair,** estar completamente desesperado,-a; **in d.,** a fondo.

deputation [depjʊ'teɪʃən] n delegación f.

deputy ['depjʊtɪ] n **1** (substitute) suplente mf; **d. chairman,** vicepresidente m; **d. head,** subdirector,-a m,f. **2** Pol diputado,-a m,f.

derail [dɪ'reɪl] vtr hacer descarrilar.

deranged [dɪ'reɪndʒd] adj trastornado,-a.

derby ['dɑːbɪ] n **1** Sport prueba f. **2** ['dɜːrbɪ] US sombrero hongo.

derelict ['derɪlɪkt] adj abandonado,-a, en ruinas.

deride [dɪ'raɪd] vtr ridiculizar, burlarse de.

derisive [dɪ'raɪsɪv] *adj* burlón,-ona.
derisory [dɪ'raɪsərɪ] *adj* irrisorio,-a.
derivative [de'rɪvətɪv] **I** *adj* (*art, writing*) sin originalidad. **II** *n* (*of word, substance*) derivado *m*.
derive [dɪ'raɪv] **I** *vtr* sacar. **II** *vi* (*word*) derivarse (**from**, de); (*skill*) provenir (**from**, de).
derogatory [dɪ'rɒgətərɪ] *adj* (*remark, article*) despectivo,-a; (*meaning*) peyorativo,-a.
derrick ['derɪk] *n Petrol* torre *f* de perforación.
descend [dɪ'send] **I** *vi* 1 descender; **to d. from**, (*be related to*) descender de. **II** *vtr* (*stairs*) bajar.
descendant [dɪ'sendənt] *n* descendiente *mf*.
descent [dɪ'sent] *n* 1 descenso *m*. 2 *fig* (*into madness, poverty*) caída *f*. 3 (*slope*) declive *m*. 4 (*ancestry*) ascendencia *f*.
describe [dɪ'skraɪb] *vtr* 1 describir. 2 (*circle*) trazar.
description [dɪ'skrɪpʃən] *n* 1 descripción *f*; **to defy d.**, superar la descripción. 2 (*type*) clase *f*.
desecrate ['desɪkreɪt] *vtr* profanar.
desert[1] ['dezət] *n* desierto *m*.
desert[2] [dɪ'zɜːt] **I** *vtr* (*place, family*) abandonar. **II** *vi Mil* desertar (**from**, de).
deserter [dɪ'zɜːtər] *n* desertor,-a *m,f*.
desertion [dɪ'zɜːʃən] *n* abandono *m*; *Pol* defección *f*; *Mil* deserción *f*.
deserts [dɪ'zɜːts] *npl* **to get one's just d.**, llevarse su merecido.
deserve [dɪ'zɜːv] *vtr* (*rest, punishment*) merecer; (*prize, praise*) ser digno,-a de.
deservedly [dɪ'zɜːvɪdlɪ] *adv* con (toda) razón.
deserving [dɪ'zɜːvɪŋ] *adj* (*person*) de valía; (*cause*) meritorio,-a.
design [dɪ'zaɪn] **I** *n* 1 diseño *m*. 2 (*drawing, blueprint*) plano *m*. 3 (*layout*) disposición *f*. 4 (*pattern*) dibujo *m*. 5 *fig* (*scheme*) intención *f*; **by d.**, a propósito; *fam* **to have designs on**, tener puestas las miras en. **II** *vtr* diseñar.
designate ['dezɪgneɪt] **I** *vtr* 1 (*appoint*) designar, nombrar. 2 *fml* (*boundary*) señalar. **II** ['dezɪgnɪt] *adj* designado,-a.
designer [dɪ'zaɪnər] *n Art* diseñador,-a *m,f*; **d. jeans**, pantalones *mpl* de marca.
desirable [dɪ'zaɪərəbəl] *adj* deseable; (*asset, offer*) atractivo,-a.
desire [dɪ'zaɪər] **I** *n* deseo *m*; **I haven't the slightest d. to go**, no me apetece nada ir. **II** *vtr* desear.
desist [dɪ'zɪst] *vi fml* desistir (**from**, de).
desk [desk] *n* (*in school*) pupitre *m*; (*in office*) escritorio *m*; *US* **d. clerk**, recepcionista *mf*; **d. job**, trabajo *m* de oficina; **news d.**, redacción *f*; **reception d.**, recepción *f*.
desktop ['desktɒp] *n* **d. computer**, orde-

nador *m* de sobremesa; **d. publishing**, autoedición *f*.
desolate ['desəlɪt] *adj* 1 (*uninhabited*) desierto,-a; (*barren*) yermo,-a. 2 (*person*) desconsolado,-a.
desolation [desə'leɪʃən] *n* 1 (*of place*) desolación *f*; (*by destruction*) asolamiento *m*. 2 (*of person*) desconsuelo *m*.
despair [dɪ'speər] **I** *n* desesperación *f*; **to drive sb to d.**, desesperar a algn. **II** *vi* desesperar(se) (**of**, de).
despairing [dɪ'speərɪŋ] *adj* desperado,-a.
despatch [dɪ'spætʃ] *n & vtr* → **dispatch**.
desperate ['despərɪt] *adj* 1 desesperado, -a; (*struggle*) encarnizado,-a. 2 (*need*) apremiante. ◆**desperately** *adv* (*recklessly*) desesperadamente; (*struggle*) encarnizadamente; (*ill*) gravemente; (*in love*) locamente; (*difficult*) sumamente.
desperation [despə'reɪʃən] *n* desesperación *f*; **in d.**, a la desesperada.
despicable [dɪ'spɪkəbəl] *adj* despreciable; (*behaviour*) indigno,-a.
despise [dɪ'spaɪz] *vtr* despreciar, menospreciar.
despite [dɪ'spaɪt] *prep fml* a pesar de.
despondent [dɪ'spɒndənt] *adj* abatido,-a.
despot ['despɒt] *n* déspota *mf*.
dessert [dɪ'zɜːt] *n* postre *m*; **d. wine**, vino *m* dulce.
dessertspoon [dɪ'zɜːtspuːn] *n* 1 cuchara *f* de postre. 2 **d.(ful)**, (*measure*) cucharada *f* de postre.
destination [destɪ'neɪʃən] *n* destino *m*.
destined ['destɪnd] *adj* 1 **d. to fail**, condenado,-a al fracaso. 2 (*bound*) con destino (**for**, a).
destiny ['destɪnɪ] *n* destino *m*.
destitute ['destɪtjuːt] *adj* indigente.
destroy [dɪ'strɔɪ] *vtr* destruir; (*vehicle, old furniture*) destrozar.
destroyer [dɪ'strɔɪər] *n Naut* destructor *m*.
destruction [dɪ'strʌkʃən] *n* destrucción *f*; *fig* ruina *f*.
destructive [dɪ'strʌktɪv] *adj* (*gale etc*) destructor,-a; (*tendency, criticism*) destructivo,-a.
detach [dɪ'tætʃ] *vtr* (*remove*) separar.
detachable [dɪ'tætʃəbəl] *adj* separable (**from**, de).
detached [dɪ'tætʃt] *adj* 1 (*separated*) separado,-a; **d. house**, casa *f* independiente. 2 (*impartial*) objetivo,-a.
detachment [dɪ'tætʃmənt] *n* 1 (*impartiality*) objetividad *f*; (*aloofness*) despego *m*. 2 *Mil* destacamento *m*.
detail ['diːteɪl] **I** *n* 1 detalle *m*, pormenor *m*; **without going into detail(s)**, sin entrar en detalles; **details**, (*information*) información *f sing*. 2 *Mil* destacamento *m*. **II** *vtr* 1 (*list*) detallar, enumerar. 2 *Mil* (*appoint*) destacar.
detailed ['diːteɪld] *adj* detallado,-a,

minucioso,-a.
detain |dɪ'teɪn| *vtr* 1 *Jur* detener. 2 (*delay*) retener.
detainee |diːteɪ'niː| *n Pol* preso,-a *m,f*.
detect |dɪ'tekt| *vtr* 1 (*error, movement*) advertir; (*difference*) notar; (*smell, sound*) percibir. 2 (*discover*) descubrir; (*enemy ship*) detectar; (*position*) localizar.
detection |dɪ'tekʃən| *n* 1 descubrimiento *m*; (*of smell, sound*) percepción *f*. 2 (*discovery*) (*of enemy ship*) detección *f*.
detective |dɪ'tektɪv| *n* detective *mf*; d. story, novela policíaca.
detector |dɪ'tektər| *n* aparato *m* detector.
detention |dɪ'tenʃən| *n* detención *f*, arresto *m*; *Educ* to get d., quedarse castigado,-a.
deter |dɪ'tɜːr| *vtr* (*dissuade*) disuadir (**from**, de); (*stop*) impedir.
detergent |dɪ'tɜːdʒənt| *n* detergente *m*.
deteriorate |dɪ'tɪərɪəreɪt| *vi* deteriorarse.
deterioration |dɪtɪərɪə'reɪʃən| *n* empeoramiento *m*; (*of substance, friendship*) deterioro *m*.
determination |dɪtɜːmɪ'neɪʃən| *n* (*resolution*) resolución *f*.
determine |dɪ'tɜːmɪn| *vtr* determinar.
determined |dɪ'tɜːmɪnd| *adj* (*person*) decidido,-a; (*effort*) enérgico,-a.
deterrent |dɪ'terənt| I *adj* disuasivo,-a. II *n* fuerza disuasoria.
detest |dɪ'test| *vtr* detestar, odiar.
detonate |'detəneɪt| *vtr & vi* detonar.
detonation |detə'neɪʃən| *n* detonación *f*.
detour |'diːtʊər| *n* desvío *m*.
detract |dɪ'trækt| *vi* quitar mérito (**from**, a).
detractor |dɪ'træktər| *n* detractor,-a *m,f*.
detriment |'detrɪmənt| *n* perjuicio *m* (**to**, de).
detrimental |detrɪ'mentəl| *adj* perjudicial (**to**, para).
deuce |djuːs| *n Ten* cuarenta iguales *mpl*.
devaluation |diːvæljuː'eɪʃən| *n* devaluación *f*.
devastate |'devəsteɪt| *vtr* (*city, area*) asolar; *fig* (*person*) desolar.
devastating |'devəsteɪtɪŋ| *adj* (*fire*) devastador,-a; (*wind, flood*) arrollador,-a.
devastation |devə'steɪʃən| *n* asolación *f*.
develop |dɪ'veləp| I *vtr* 1 desarrollar; (*trade*) fomentar; (*skill*) perfeccionar; (*plan*) elaborar; (*habit*) contraer; (*interest*) mostrar. 2 (*natural resources*) aprovechar; *Constr* (*site*) urbanizar. 3 *Phot* revelar. II *vi* 1 (*body, industry*) desarrollarse; (*system*) perfeccionarse; (*interest*) crecer. 2 (*appear*) crearse; (*evolve*) evolucionar.
developer |dɪ'veləpər| *n* (**property**) d., inmobiliaria *f*.
development |dɪ'veləpmənt| *n* 1 desarrollo *m*; (*of trade*) fomento *m*; (*of skill*) perfección *f*; (*of character*) formación *f*. 2 (*advance*) avance *m*. 3 there are no new

developments, no hay ninguna novedad. 4 (*exploitation*) explotación *f*. 5 *Constr* urbanización *f*.
deviate |'diːvɪeɪt| *vi* desviarse (**from**, de).
deviation |diːvɪ'eɪʃən| *n* (*from norm, route*) desviación *f* (**from**, de); (*from truth*) alejamiento *m*.
device |dɪ'vaɪs| *n* 1 aparato *m*; (*mechanism*) mecanismo *m*. 2 (*trick, scheme*) ardid *m*.
devil |'devəl| *n* diablo *m*, demonio *m*; **d.'s advocate**, abogado,-a *m,f* del diablo; *fam* **where the d. did you put it?**, ¿dónde demonios lo pusiste?; **you lucky d.!**, ¡vaya suerte que tienes!
devious |'diːvɪəs| *adj* 1 (*winding*) tortuoso,-a. 2 *esp pej* (*person*) taimado,-a.
devise |dɪ'vaɪz| *vtr* idear, concebir.
devoid |dɪ'vɔɪd| *adj* desprovisto,-a (**of**, de).
devolution |diːvə'luːʃən| *n Pol* transmisión *f* de poderes a las regiones.
devote |dɪ'vəʊt| *vtr* dedicar; **she devoted her life to helping the poor**, consagró su vida a la ayuda de los pobres.
devoted |dɪ'vəʊtɪd| *adj* fiel, leal (**to**, a).
devotee |devə'tiː| *n* (*of religion*) devoto,-a *m,f*; (*of theatre, sport*) aficionado,-a *m,f*; *Pol* partidario,-a *m,f*.
devotion |dɪ'vəʊʃən| *n* devoción *f*; (*to cause*) dedicación *f*.
devour |dɪ'vaʊər| *vtr* devorar.
devout |dɪ'vaʊt| *adj* devoto,-a.
dew |djuː| *n* rocío *m*.
dexterity |dek'sterɪtɪ| *n* destreza *f*.
dext(e)rous |'dekstrəs| *adj* diestro,-a.
diabetes |daɪə'biːtiːz, daɪə'biːtɪs| *n* diabetes *f*.
diabetic |daɪə'betɪk| *adj & n* diabético,-a (*m,f*).
diabolical |daɪə'bɒlɪkəl| *adj* 1 (*evil*) diabólico,-a. 2 *fam* (*unbearable*) espantoso,-a.
diagnose |'daɪəgnəʊz| *vtr* diagnosticar.
diagnosis |daɪəg'nəʊsɪs| *n* (*pl* **diagnoses** |daɪəg'nəʊsiːz|) diagnóstico *m*.
diagonal |daɪ'ægənəl| *adj & n* diagonal (*f*). ◆**diagonally** *adv* en diagonal, diagonalmente.
diagram |'daɪəgræm| *n* diagrama *m*; (*of process, system*) esquema *m*; (*of workings*) gráfico *m*.
dial |'daɪəl, daɪl| I *n* (*of clock*) esfera *f*; (*of radio*) cuadrante *m*; (*of telephone*) disco *m*; (*of machine*) botón *m* selector. II *vi & vtr Tel* marcar; **dialling code**, prefijo *m*; **dialling tone**, señal *f* de marcar.
dialect |'daɪəlekt| *n* dialecto *m*.
dialogue, *US* **dialog** |'daɪəlɒg| *n* diálogo *m*.
diameter |daɪ'æmɪtər| *n* diámetro *m*.
diametrically |daɪə'metrɪkəlɪ| *adv* diametralmente.
diamond |'daɪəmənd| *n* 1 diamante *m*. 2

(shape) rombo *m*.

diaper ['daɪəpəʳ] *n US* pañal *m*.

diaphragm ['daɪəfræm] *n* diafragma *m*.

diarrhoea, *US* **diarrhea** [daɪə'rɪə] *n* diarrea *f*.

diary ['daɪərɪ] *n* **1** diario *m*; **to keep a d.**, llevar un diario. **2** *GB (for appointments)* agenda *f*.

dice [daɪs] **I** *npl* dados *mpl*. **II** *vtr* Culin cortar en cuadritos.

dichotomy [daɪ'kɒtəmɪ] *n* dicotomía *f*.

dictate [dɪk'teɪt] **I** *vtr (letter, order)* dictar. **II** *vi* **to d. to sb**, dar órdenes a algn. **III** ['dɪkteɪt] *n* *fig* **the dictates of conscience**, los dictados de la conciencia.

dictation [dɪk'teɪʃən] *n* dictado *m*.

dictator [dɪk'teɪtəʳ] *n* dictador,-a *m,f*.

dictatorship [dɪk'teɪtəʃɪp] *n* dictadura *f*.

diction ['dɪkʃən] *n* dicción *f*.

dictionary ['dɪkʃənərɪ] *n* diccionario *m*.

did [dɪd] *pt* → **do**.

die [daɪ] *vi* **1** morir, morirse; *fam fig* **to be dying for sth/to do sth**, morirse por algo/de ganas de hacer algo. **2** *fig (flame)* extinguirse; *fig* **to d. hard**, *(habit)* tardar en desaparecer. **3** *(engine)* calarse; *(battery)* agotarse. ◆**die away** *vi* desvanecerse. ◆**die down** *vi (fire)* extinguirse; *(wind)* amainar; *(noise, excitement)* disminuir. ◆**die off** *vi* morir uno por uno. ◆**die out** *vi* extinguirse.

die-hard ['daɪhɑːd] *n* reaccionario,-a *m,f*.

diesel ['diːzəl] *n* **1** *(oil)* gasoil *m*. **2**. **engine**, motor *m* diesel. **2** *fam (vehicle)* vehículo *m* diesel.

diet ['daɪət] **I** *n (normal food)* dieta *f*; *(selected food)* régimen *m*; **to be on a d.**, estar a régimen. **II** *vi* estar a régimen.

dietician [daɪə'tɪʃən] *n* especialista *mf* en dietética.

differ ['dɪfəʳ] *vi (be unlike)* ser distinto,-a; *(disagree)* discrepar.

difference ['dɪfərəns] *n* **1** *(dissimilarity)* diferencia *f*; **it makes no d. (to me)**, (me) da igual; **what d. does it make?**, ¿qué más da? **2** *(disagreement)* desacuerdo *m*.

different ['dɪfərənt] *adj* diferente, distinto,-a; **you look d.**, pareces otro,-a. ◆**differently** *adv* de otra manera.

differentiate [dɪfə'renʃɪeɪt] **I** *vtr* distinguir, diferenciar *(from*, de*)*. **II** *vi* distinguir *(between*, entre*)*.

difficult ['dɪfɪkəlt] *adj* difícil.

difficulty ['dɪfɪkəltɪ] *n* dificultad *f*; *(problem)* problema *m*; **to be in difficulties**, estar en un apuro.

diffident ['dɪfɪdənt] *adj* tímido,-a.

diffuse [dɪ'fjuːs] **I** *adj (light)* difuso,-a; *fig* vago,-a. **II** [dɪ'fjuːz] *vtr* difundir; *(heat)* desprender.

dig [dɪg] **I** *n* **1** *(poke)* codazo *m*. **2** *fam (gibe)* pulla *f*. **3** *(archeological)* excavación

f. **3** *GB* **digs**, *(lodgings)* alojamiento *m sing*; *(room)* habitación *f sing* alquilada. **II** *vtr (pt & pp* **dug**) **1** *(earth)* cavar; *(tunnel)* excavar. **2** *fam fig* **to d. one's heels in**, mantenerse en sus trece. **III** *vi (person)* cavar; *(animal)* escarbar; *(excavate)* excavar. ◆**dig in** *vi Mil* atrincherarse. ◆**dig out** *vtr fig (old suit)* sacar; *(information)* descubrir. ◆**dig up** *vtr (weeds)* arrancar; *(buried object)* desenterrar; *(road)* levantar; *fig* sacar a relucir.

digest ['daɪdʒest] **I** *n (summary)* resumen *m*. **II** [dɪ'dʒest] *vtr (food)* digerir; *fig (facts)* asimilar.

digestion [dɪ'dʒestʃən] *n* digestión *f*.

digestive [dɪ'dʒestɪv] *adj* digestivo,-a; *GB* **d. biscuit**, galleta *f* integral.

digger ['dɪgəʳ] *n* excavadora *f*.

digit ['dɪdʒɪt] *n* **1** *Math* dígito *m*. **2** *fml Anat* dedo *m*.

digital ['dɪdʒɪtəl] *adj* digital.

dignified ['dɪgnɪfaɪd] *adj (manner)* solemne, serio,-a; *(appearance)* majestuoso,-a.

dignitary ['dɪgnɪtərɪ] *n* dignatario *m*.

dignity ['dɪgnɪtɪ] *n* dignidad *f*.

digress [daɪ'gres] *vi* apartarse del tema.

dike [daɪk] *n US* → **dyke**.

dilapidated [dɪ'læpɪdeɪtɪd] *adj* en mal estado.

dilemma [daɪ'lemə, dɪ'lemə] *n* dilema *m*.

diligent ['dɪlɪdʒənt] *adj (worker)* diligente; *(inquiries, search)* esmerado,-a.

dilute [daɪ'luːt] **I** *vtr* diluir; *(wine, milk)* aguar; *fig (effect, influence)* atenuar. **II** *vi* diluirse.

dim [dɪm] **I** *adj (dimmer, dimmest)* **1** *(light)* débil, tenue; *(room)* oscuro,-a; *(outline)* borroso,-a; *(eyesight)* defectuoso,-a; *fig (memory)* vago,-a; *fig (future)* sombrío,-a. **2** *fam (stupid)* torpe. **II** *vtr (light)* bajar. **III** *vi (light)* bajarse; *(sight)* nublarse; *fig (joy)* extinguirse. ◆**dimly** *adv* vagamente.

dime [daɪm] *n US* moneda *f* de diez centavos.

dimension [daɪ'menʃən] *n* dimensión *f*.

diminish [dɪ'mɪnɪʃ] *vtr & vi* disminuir.

diminutive [dɪ'mɪnjʊtɪv] **I** *adj* diminuto,-a. **II** *n Ling* diminutivo *m*.

dimmer ['dɪməʳ] *n* **d. (switch)**, regulador *m* de voltaje.

dimple ['dɪmpəl] *n* hoyuelo *m*.

din [dɪn] *n (of crowd)* alboroto *m*; *(of machinery)* estruendo *m*.

dine [daɪn] *vi fml* cenar; **to d. out**, cenar fuera.

diner ['daɪnəʳ] *n* **1** *(person)* comensal *mf*. **2** *US (restaurant)* restaurante barato.

dinghy ['dɪŋɪ] *n* bote *m*; *(rubber)* **d.**, bote neumático.

dingy ['dɪndʒɪ] *adj (dingier, dingiest)* **1** *(dark)* oscuro,-a. **2** *(dirty)* sucio,-a. **3** *(colour)* desteñido,-a.

dining car |'daınıŋkɑ:r| n vagón m restaurante.

dining room |'daınıŋru:m| n comedor m.

dinner |'dınər| n (at midday) comida f; (in evening) cena f; **d. jacket**, smoking m; **d. service**, vajilla f; **d. table**, mesa f de comedor.

dinosaur |'daınəsɔ:r| n dinosaurio m.

dint |dınt| n **by d. of**, a fuerza de.

diocese |'daıəsıs| n diócesis f inv.

dioxide |daı'nksaıd| n bióxido m.

dip |dıp| I n 1 fam (bathe) chapuzón m. 2 (of road) pendiente f; (in ground) depresión f. 3 Culin salsa f. II vtr 1 bañar; (spoon, hand) meter. 2 GB Aut **to d. one's lights**, poner luces de cruce. III vi (road) bajar. ◆**dip into** vtr 1 (savings) echar mano de. 2 (book) hojear.

diphthong |'dıfθɒŋ| n diptongo m.

diploma |dı'pləʊmə| n diploma m.

diplomacy |dı'pləʊməsı| n diplomacia f.

diplomat |'dıpləmæt| n diplomático,-a m,f.

diplomatic |dıplə'mætık| adj diplomático,-a.

dipstick |'dıpstık| n indicador m de nivel del aceite.

dire |daıər| adj (urgent) extremo,-a; (serious) grave.

direct |dı'rekt, 'daırekt| I adj 1 directo, -a; **d. current**, corriente continua. 2 the **d. opposite**, todo lo contrario. II adv directamente. III vtr 1 dirigir; **can you d. me to a bank?**, ¿me puede indicar dónde hay un banco? 2 fml (order) mandar.

direction |dı'rekʃən, daı'rekʃən| n 1 dirección f; **sense of d.**, sentido m de la orientación. 2 **directions**, (to place) señas fpl; **d. for use**, modo m de empleo. 3 Theat puesta f en escena.

directive |dı'rektıv, daı'rektıv| n directiva f.

directly |dı'rektlı, daı'rektlı| I adv 1 (above etc) exactamente, justo. 2 (speak) francamente. 3 (descend) directamente. 4 (come) en seguida. II conj fam en cuanto.

director |dı'rektər, daı'rektər| n director,-a m,f.

directory |dı'rektərı, daı'rektərı| n Tel guía telefónica; **d. enquiries**, (servicio m de) información f.

dirt |dɜ:t| n suciedad f.

dirt-cheap |dɜ:t'tʃi:p| adv & adj fam tirado,-a.

dirty |'dɜ:tı| I adj (dirtier, dirtiest) 1 sucio,-a. 2 **to give sb a d. look**, fulminar a algn con la mirada. 3 (joke) verde; (mind) pervertido,-a; **d. word**, palabrota f; **d. old man**, viejo m verde. II vtr ensuciar.

disability |dısə'bılıtı| n incapacidad f, discapacidad f; **d. pension**, pensión f por invalidez.

disabled |dı'seıbəld| I adj minusválido,

-a. II npl **the d.**, los minusválidos.

disadvantage |dısəd'vɑ:ntıdʒ| n desventaja f; (obstacle) inconveniente m.

disaffection |dısə'fekʃən| n descontento m.

disagree |dısə'gri:| vi 1 (differ) no estar de acuerdo (with, con); **to d. on or over sth**, reñir por algo. 2 (not match) discrepar (with, de, con). 3 **garlic disagrees with me**, el ajo no me sienta bien.

disagreeable |dısə'grıəbəl| adj desagradable.

disagreement |dısə'gri:mənt| n 1 desacuerdo m; (argument) riña f. 2 (non-correspondence) discrepancia f.

disallow |dısə'laʊ| vtr (goal) anular; (objection) rechazar.

disappear |dısə'pıər| vi desaparecer.

disappearance |dısə'pıərəns| n desaparición f.

disappoint |dısə'pɔınt| vtr (person) decepcionar, defraudar; (hope, ambition) frustrar.

disappointed |dısə'pɔıntıd| adj decepcionado,-a.

disappointing |dısə'pɔıntıŋ| adj decepcionante.

disappointment |dısə'pɔıntmənt| n decepción f.

disapproval |dısə'pru:vəl| n desaprobación f.

disapprove |dısə'pru:v| vi **to d. of**, desaprobar.

disarm |dıs'ɑ:m| I vtr desarmar. II vi desarmarse.

disarmament |dıs'ɑ:məmənt| n desarme m.

disarray |dısə'reı| n fml **in d.**, (room, papers) en desorden; (hair) desarreglado,-a; (thoughts) confuso,-a.

disaster |dı'zɑ:stər| n desastre m.

disastrous |dı'zɑ:strəs| adj desastroso,-a.

disband |dıs'bænd| I vtr disolver. II vi disolverse.

disbelief |dısbı'li:f| n incredulidad f.

disc |dısk| n disco m; Comput disquete m; **d. jockey**, disc-jockey mf, pinchadiscos mf inv.

discard |dıs'kɑ:d| vtr (old things) deshacerse de; (plan) descartar.

discern |dı'sɜ:n| vtr (shape, difference) percibir; (truth) darse cuenta de.

discerning |dı'sɜ:nıŋ| adj (person) perspicaz; (taste) refinado,-a.

discharge |dıs'tʃɑ:dʒ| fml I vtr 1 (smoke) emitir; (liquid) echar; (cargo) descargar. 2 (prisoner) soltar; (patient) dar de alta a; (soldier) licenciar; (employee) despedir. 3 (debt) saldar. 4 (fulfil) cumplir. II |'dıstʃɑ:dʒ| n 1 (of current, load) descarga f; (of gases) escape m. 2 (of prisoner) liberación f; (of patient) alta f; (of soldier) licencia f. 3 (of debt) descargo m. 4 (of duty) cumplimiento m.

disciple [dɪˈsaɪpəl] *n* discípulo,-a *m,f*.

discipline [ˈdɪsɪplɪn] I *n* disciplina *f*. II *vtr* (*child*) castigar; (*worker*) sancionar; (*official*) expedientar.

disclaim [dɪsˈkleɪm] *vtr fml* negar tener.

disclose [dɪsˈkləʊz] *vtr* revelar.

disclosure [dɪsˈkləʊʒəʳ] *n* revelación *f*.

disco [ˈdɪskəʊ] *n* (*abbr of* **discotheque**) *fam* disco *f*.

discolour, *US* **discolor** [dɪsˈkʌləʳ] *vtr* descolorir.

discomfort [dɪsˈkʌmfət] *n* **1** (*lack of comfort*) incomodidad *f*. **2** (*pain*) malestar *m*. **3** (*unease*) inquietud *f*.

disconcert [dɪskənˈsɜːt] *vtr* desconcertar.

disconcerting [dɪskənˈsɜːtɪŋ] *adj* desconcertante.

disconnect [dɪskəˈnekt] *vtr* desconectar (**from**, de); (*gas, electricity*) cortar.

disconnected [dɪskəˈnektɪd] *adj* inconexo,-a.

disconsolate [dɪsˈkɒnsəlɪt] *adj* desconsolado,-a.

discontent [dɪskənˈtent] *n* descontento *m*.

discontented [dɪskənˈtentɪd] *adj* descontento,-a.

discontinue [dɪskənˈtɪnjuː] *vtr fml* abandonar; (*work*) interrumpir.

discord [ˈdɪskɔːd] *n* **1** *fml* discordia *f*. **2** *Mus* disonancia *f*.

discordant [dɪsˈkɔːdənt] *adj* discordante.

discotheque [ˈdɪskətek] *n* discoteca *f*.

discount [ˈdɪskaʊnt] I *n* descuento *m*. II [dɪsˈkaʊnt] *vtr* **1** (*price*) rebajar. **2** (*view, suggestion*) descartar.

discourage [dɪsˈkʌrɪdʒ] *vtr* (*dishearten*) desanimar; (*advances*) rechazar.

discouraging [dɪsˈkʌrɪdʒɪŋ] *adj* desalentador,-a.

discover [dɪsˈkʌvəʳ] *vtr* descubrir; (*missing person, object*) encontrar.

discovery [dɪsˈkʌvərɪ] *n* descubrimiento *m*.

discredit [dɪsˈkredɪt] I *n* descrédito *m*. II *vtr* (*person, régime*) desacreditar; (*theory*) poner en duda.

discreet [dɪsˈkriːt] *adj* discreto,-a; (*distance, silence*) prudente; (*hat, house*) modesto,-a.

discrepancy [dɪˈskrepənsɪ] *n* diferencia *f*.

discretion [dɪˈskreʃən] *n* discreción *f*; (*prudence*) prudencia *f*; **at the d. of ...,** a juicio de ....

discriminate [dɪˈskrɪmɪneɪt] *vi* discriminar (**between**, entre); **to d. against sth/ sb,** discriminar algo/a algn.

discriminating [dɪˈskrɪmɪneɪtɪŋ] *adj* (*person*) entendido,-a; (*taste*) refinado,-a.

discrimination [dɪskrɪmɪˈneɪʃən] *n* **1** (*bias*) discriminación *f*. **2** (*distinction*) diferenciación *f*.

discuss [dɪˈskʌs] *vtr* discutir; (*in writing*) tratar de.

discussion [dɪˈskʌʃən] *n* discusión *f*.

disdain [dɪsˈdeɪn] *fml* I *n* desdén *m*. II *vtr* desdeñar.

disdainful [dɪsˈdeɪnfʊl] *adj fml* desdeñoso,-a.

disease [dɪˈziːz] *n* enfermedad *f*; *fig* mal *m*.

disembark [dɪsɪmˈbɑːk] *vtr & vi* desembarcar.

disenchanted [dɪsɪnˈtʃɑːntɪd] *adj* desencantado,-a, desilusionado,-a.

disengage [dɪsɪnˈgeɪdʒ] *vtr* soltar; *Aut* **to d. the clutch,** soltar el embrague, desembragar.

disentangle [dɪsɪnˈtæŋgəl] *vtr* desenredar.

disfigure [dɪsˈfɪgəʳ] *vtr* desfigurar.

disgrace [dɪsˈgreɪs] I *n* **1** desgracia *f*; **to be in d.,** estar desacreditado,-a; **to fall into d.,** caer en desgracia. **2** (*shame*) vergüenza *f*, escándalo *m*. II *vtr* deshonrar, desacreditar.

disgraceful [dɪsˈgreɪsfʊl] *adj* vergonzoso,-a.

disgruntled [dɪsˈgrʌntəld] *adj* contrariado,-a, disgustado,-a.

disguise [dɪsˈgaɪz] I *n* disfraz *m*; **in d.,** disfrazado,-a. II *vtr* **1** (*person*) disfrazar (**as**, de). **2** (*feelings*) disimular.

disgust [dɪsˈgʌst] I *n* **1** (*loathing*) repugnancia *f*, asco *m*. **2** (*strong disapproval*) indignación *f*. II *vtr* **1** (*revolt*) repugnar, dar asco a. **2** (*offend*) indignar.

disgusting [dɪsˈgʌstɪŋ] *adj* asqueroso,-a, repugnante; (*behaviour, state of affairs*) intolerable.

dish [dɪʃ] *n* (*for serving*) fuente *f*; (*course*) plato *m*; **to wash** *or* **do the dishes,** fregar los platos. ◆**dish out** *vtr fam* (*food*) servir; (*books, advice*) repartir; **to d. it out** (**to sb**), (*criticize*) criticar (a algn). ◆**dish up** *vtr* (*meal*) servir.

dishcloth [ˈdɪʃklɒθ] *n* trapo *m* de fregar.

dishearten [dɪsˈhɑːtən] *vtr* desanimar.

dishevelled, *US* **disheveled** [dɪˈʃevəld] *adj* (*hair*) despeinado,-a; (*appearance*) desaliñado,-a.

dishonest [dɪsˈɒnɪst] *adj* (*person*) poco honrado,-a; (*means*) fraudulento,-a.

dishonesty [dɪsˈɒnɪstɪ] *n* (*of person*) falta *f* de honradez.

dishonour, *US* **dishonor** [dɪsˈɒnəʳ] I *n fml* deshonra *f*. II *vtr* (*name*) deshonrar.

dishonourable [dɪsˈɒnərəbəl] *adj* deshonroso,-a.

dishtowel [ˈdɪʃtaʊəl] *n US* trapo *m* de cocina.

dishwasher [ˈdɪʃwɒʃəʳ] *n* lavaplatos *m inv*; (*person*) lavaplatos *mf inv*.

disillusion [dɪsɪˈluːʒən] *vtr* desilusionar.

disincentive [dɪsɪnˈsentɪv] *n* freno *m*.

disinfect [dɪsɪnˈfekt] *vtr* desinfectar.

disinfectant [dɪsɪnˈfektənt] *n* desinfectante *m*.

disinherit [dɪsɪnˈherɪt] *vtr* desheredar.

disintegrate [dɪs'ɪntɪgreɪt] *vi* desintegrarse.

disintegration [dɪsɪntɪ'greɪʃən] *n* desintegración *f*.

disinterested [dɪs'ɪntrɪstɪd] *adj* desinteresado,-a.

disjointed [dɪs'dʒɔɪntɪd] *adj* inconexo,-a.

disk [dɪsk] *n US* disco *m*; *Comput* disquete *m*; **d. drive**, disquetera *f*, disketera *f*.

diskette [dɪs'ket] *n Comput* disquete *m*.

dislike [dɪs'laɪk] **I** *n* antipatía *f*, aversión *f* (**for, of**, a, hacia). **II** *vtr* tener antipatía *or* aversión a *or* hacia.

dislocate ['dɪsləkeɪt] *vtr* (*joint*) dislocar.

dislodge [dɪs'lɒdʒ] *vtr* sacar.

disloyal [dɪs'lɔɪəl] *adj* desleal.

dismal ['dɪzməl] *adj* 1 (*prospect*) sombrío,-a; (*place, weather*) deprimente; (*person*) triste. 2 (*failure*) lamentable.

dismantle [dɪs'mæntəl] *vtr* desmontar.

dismay [dɪs'meɪ] **I** *n* consternación *f*. **II** *vtr* consternar.

dismiss [dɪs'mɪs] *vtr* 1 (*idea*) descartar. 2 (*employee*) despedir; (*official*) destituir. 3 **to d. sb**, (*from room, presence*) dar permiso a algn para retirarse. 4 (*reject*) rechazar; *Jur* desestimar; (*case*) sobreseer.

dismissal [dɪs'mɪsəl] *n* 1 (*of employee*) despido *m*; (*of official*) destitución *f*. 2 (*of claim*) rechazo *m*; *Jur* desestimación *f*.

dismount [dɪs'maʊnt] *vi fml* apearse (**from**, de).

disobedience [dɪsə'biːdɪəns] *n* desobediencia *f*.

disobedient [dɪsə'biːdɪənt] *adj* desobediente.

disobey [dɪsə'beɪ] *vtr & vi* desobedecer; (*law*) violar.

disorder [dɪs'ɔːdər] *n* 1 (*untidiness*) desorden *m*. 2 (*riot*) disturbio *m*. 3 (*of organ, mind*) trastorno *m*; (*of speech*) defecto *m*.

disorderly [dɪs'ɔːdəlɪ] *adj* 1 (*untidy*) desordenado,-a. 2 (*meeting*) alborotado,-a; (*conduct*) escandaloso,-a.

disorganized [dɪs'ɔːgənaɪzd] *adj* desorganizado,-a.

disorient [dɪs'ɔːrɪənt], **disorientate** [dɪs'ɔːrɪənteɪt] *vtr* desorientar.

disown [dɪs'əʊn] *vtr* desconocer.

disparaging [dɪ'spærɪdʒɪŋ] *adj* despectivo,-a.

disparity [dɪ'spærɪtɪ] *n fml* disparidad *f*.

dispassionate [dɪs'pæʃənɪt] *adj* desapasionado,-a.

dispatch [dɪ'spætʃ] **I** *n* 1 (*official message*) despacho *m*; (*journalist's report*) reportaje *m*; (*military message*) parte *m*. 2 (*of mail*) envío *m*; (*of goods*) consignación *f*. **II** *vtr* 1 (*mail*) enviar; (*goods*) expedir. 2 *fam* (*food*) zamparse; (*job*) despachar.

dispel [dɪ'spel] *vtr* disipar.

dispensary [dɪ'spensərɪ] *n* dispensario *m*.

dispense [dɪ'spens] *vtr* (*supplies*) repartir; (*justice*) administrar. ◆**dispense with** *vtr* (*do without*) prescindir de.

dispenser [dɪ'spensər] *n* máquina expendedora; **cash d.**, cajero automático; **soap d.**, dosificador *m* de jabón.

dispensing chemist [dɪspensɪŋ'kemɪst] *n GB* farmacéutico,-a *m,f*.

dispersal [dɪ'spɜːsəl] *n* dispersión *f*.

disperse [dɪ'spɜːs] **I** *vtr* dispersar. **II** *vi* dispersarse; (*fog*) disiparse.

dispirited [dɪ'spɪrɪtɪd] *adj* abatido,-a.

displace [dɪs'pleɪs] *vtr* 1 desplazar; **displaced person**, desterrado,-a *m,f*. 2 (*supplant*) sustituir.

display [dɪ'spleɪ] **I** *n* (*exhibition*) exposición *f*; *Comput* visualización *f*; (*of feelings, skills*) demostración *f*; (*of force*) despliegue *m*; **d. window**, escaparate *m*; **military d.**, desfile *m* militar. **II** *vtr* 1 mostrar; (*goods*) exponer; *Comput* visualizar. 2 (*feelings*) manifestar.

displease [dɪs'pliːz] *vtr* disgustar; (*offend*) ofender.

displeasure [dɪs'pleʒər] *n* disgusto *m*.

disposable [dɪ'spəʊzəbəl] *adj* 1 (*throwaway*) desechable. 2 (*available*) disponible.

disposal [dɪ'spəʊzəl] *n* 1 (*removal*) eliminación *f*. 2 (*availability*) disponibilidad *f*; **at my d.**, a mi disposición. 3 *fml* (*arrangement*) disposición *f*. 4 (*sale*) venta *f*; (*of property*) traspaso *m*.

dispose [dɪ'spəʊz] **I** *vi* **to d. of**, (*remove*) eliminar; (*rubbish*) tirar; (*unwanted object*) deshacerse de; (*matter*) resolver; (*sell*) vender; (*property*) traspasar. **II** *vtr fml* (*arrange*) disponer.

disposed [dɪ'spəʊzd] *adj* (*inclined*) dispuesto,-a.

disposition [dɪspə'zɪʃən] *n* 1 (*temperament*) genio *m*. 2 *fml* (*arrangement*) disposición *f*.

disproportionate [dɪsprə'pɔːʃənɪt] *adj* desproporcionado,-a (**to**, a).

disprove [dɪs'pruːv] *vtr* refutar.

dispute ['dɪspjuːt] **I** *n* (*disagreement*) discusión *f*; (*quarrel*) disputa *f*; **industrial d.**, conflicto *m* laboral. **II** *vtr* (*claim*) refutar; (*territory*) disputar; (*matter*) discutir. **III** *vi* discutir (**about, over**, de, sobre).

disqualify [dɪs'kwɒlɪfaɪ] *vtr* 1 *Sport* descalificar. 2 (*make ineligible*) incapacitar.

disquiet [dɪs'kwaɪət] *n* preocupación *f*, inquietud *f*.

disregard [dɪsrɪ'gɑːd] **I** *n* indiferencia *f*; (*for safety*) despreocupación *f*. **II** *vtr* descuidar; (*ignore*) ignorar.

disrepair [dɪsrɪ'peər] *n* mal estado *m*; **in (a state of) d.**, en mal estado; **to fall into d.**, deteriorarse.

disreputable [dɪs'repjʊtəbəl] *adj* (*person, area*) de mala fama; (*behaviour*) vergonzoso,-a.

disrepute |dɪsrɪ'pjuːt| *n* mala fama *f*, oprobio *m*.
disrespectful |dɪsrɪ'spektful| *adj* irrespetuoso,-a.
disrupt |dɪs'rʌpt| *vtr (meeting, traffic)* interrumpir; *(schedule etc)* desbaratar.
disruption |dɪs'rʌpʃən| *n (of meeting, traffic)* interrupción *f*; *(of schedule etc)* desbaratamiento *m*.
dissatisfaction |dɪssætɪs'fækʃən| *n* descontento *m*, insatisfacción *f*.
dissatisfied |dɪs'sætɪsfaɪd| *adj* descontento,-a.
dissect |dɪ'sekt, daɪ'sekt| *vtr* disecar.
disseminate |dɪ'semɪneɪt| *vtr fml* diseminar, difundir.
dissent |dɪ'sent| I *n* disentimiento *m*. II *vi* disentir.
dissertation |dɪsə'teɪʃən| *n* disertación *f*; *Univ* tesina *f* (**on**, sobre).
disservice |dɪs'sɜːvɪs| *n* perjuicio *m*; **to do sth/sb a d.**, perjudicar algo/a algn.
dissident |'dɪsɪdənt| *adj & n* disidente (*mf*).
dissimilar |dɪ'sɪmɪlər| *adj* distinto,-a.
dissipate |'dɪsɪpeɪt| I *vtr* 1 disipar. 2 *(waste)* derrochar. II *vi* disiparse.
dissociate |dɪ'səʊʃɪeɪt| *vtr* **to d. oneself,** distanciarse.
dissolute |'dɪsəluːt| *adj* disoluto,-a.
dissolution |dɪsə'luːʃən| *n* disolución *f*; *(of agreement)* rescisión *f*.
dissolve |dɪ'zɒlv| I *vtr* disolver. II *vi* disolverse.
dissuade |dɪ'sweɪd| *vtr* disuadir (**from**, de).
distance |'dɪstəns| I *n* distancia *f*; **in the d.,** a lo lejos; *fam* **to stay the d.,** completar la prueba. II *vtr* distanciarse.
distant |'dɪstənt| *adj* 1 *(place, time)* lejano,-a; *(look)* distraído,-a. 2 *(aloof)* distante, frío,-a.
distaste |dɪs'teɪst| *n* aversión *f*.
distasteful |dɪs'teɪstful| *adj* desagradable.
distend |dɪ'stend| *fml* I *vtr* dilatar. II *vi* dilatarse.
distil, *US* **distill** |dɪs'tɪl| *vtr* destilar.
distillery |dɪ'stɪlərɪ| *n* destilería *f*.
distinct |dɪ'stɪŋkt| *adj* 1 *(different)* diferente; **as d. from,** a diferencia de. 2 *(smell, change)* marcado,-a; *(idea, intention)* claro,-a.
distinction |dɪ'stɪŋkʃən| *n* 1 *(difference)* diferencia *f*. 2 *(excellence)* distinción *f*. 3 *Educ* sobresaliente *m*.
distinctive |dɪ'stɪŋktɪv| *adj* distintivo,-a.
distinguish |dɪ'stɪŋgwɪʃ| *vtr* distinguir.
distinguished |dɪ'stɪŋgwɪʃt| *adj* distinguido,-a.
distinguishing |dɪ'stɪŋgwɪʃɪŋ| *adj* distintivo,-a, característico,-a.
distort |dɪ'stɔːt| *vtr (misrepresent)* deformar; *(words)* tergiversar.
distortion |dɪ'stɔːʃən| *n* deformación *f*;

(of sound, image) distorsión *f*.
distract |dɪ'strækt| *vtr* distraer.
distracted |dɪ'stræktɪd| *adj* distraído,-a.
distraction |dɪ'strækʃən| *n (interruption)* distracción *f*; *(confusion)* confusión *f*; **to drive sb to d.,** sacar a algn de quicio.
distraught |dɪ'strɔːt| *adj (anguished)* afligido,-a.
distress |dɪ'stres| I *n (mental)* angustia *f*; *(physical)* dolor *m*; **d. signal,** señal *f* de socorro. II *vtr (upset)* apenar.
distressing |dɪ'stresɪŋ| *adj* penoso,-a.
distribute |dɪ'strɪbjuːt| *vtr* distribuir, repartir.
distribution |dɪstrɪ'bjuːʃən| *n* distribución *f*.
distributor |dɪ'strɪbjʊtər| *n* 1 *Com* distribuidor,-a *m,f*. 2 *Aut* delco *m*.
district |'dɪstrɪkt| *n (of country)* región *f*; *(of town)* barrio *m*; *US* **d. attorney,** fiscal *m*; **d. council,** corporación *f* local; **d. nurse,** practicante *mf*.
distrust |dɪs'trʌst| I *n* recelo *m*. II *vtr* desconfiar de.
disturb |dɪ'stɜːb| *vtr* 1 *(inconvenience)* molestar. 2 *(silence)* romper; *(sleep)* interrumpir. 3 *(worry)* perturbar. 4 *(papers)* desordenar.
disturbance |dɪ'stɜːbəns| *n* 1 *(of routine)* alteración *f*. 2 *(commotion)* disturbio *m*, alboroto *m*.
disturbed |dɪ'stɜːbd| *adj (mentally)* inestable.
disturbing |dɪ'stɜːbɪŋ| *adj* inquietante.
disuse |dɪs'juːs| *n* desuso *m*.
disused |dɪs'juːzd| *adj* abandonado,-a.
ditch |dɪtʃ| I *n* zanja *f*; *(at roadside)* cuneta *f*; *(for irrigation)* acequia *f*. II *vtr fam (plan, friend)* abandonar.
dither |'dɪðər| *vi GB fam* vacilar, titubear.
ditto |'dɪtəʊ| *n* ídem, lo mismo.
dive |daɪv| I *n* 1 *(into water)* salto *m* de cabeza; *(of submarine)* inmersión *f*; *(of plane)* picado *m*; *Sport* salto *m*. 2 *fam (bar)* antro *m*. II *vi* tirarse de cabeza; *(submarine)* sumergirse; *(plane)* bajar en picado; *Sport* saltar. 3 **he dived for the phone,** se precipitó hacia el teléfono.
diver |'daɪvər| *n (person)* buceador,-a *m,f*; *(professional)* buzo *m*; *Sport* saltador,-a *m,f*.
diverge |daɪ'vɜːdʒ| *vi* divergir.
diverse |daɪ'vɜːs| *adj (varied)* diverso,-a, variado,-a; *(different)* distinto,-a, diferente.
diversion |daɪ'vɜːʃən| *n* 1 *(distraction)* distracción *f*. 2 *GB (detour)* desvío *m*.
divert |daɪ'vɜːt| *vtr* desviar.
divide |dɪ'vaɪd| I *vtr* dividir. II *vi (road, stream)* bifurcarse. III *n* división *f*, diferencia *f*.
dividend |'dɪvɪdend| *n Com* dividendo *m*;

fig beneficio *m*.
divine [dɪ'vaɪn] *adj* divino,-a.
diving board ['daɪvɪŋbɔːd] *n* trampolín *m*.
divinity [dɪ'vɪnɪtɪ] *n* 1 divinidad *f*. 2 *(subject)* teología *f*.
division [dɪ'vɪʒən] *n* 1 división *f*. 2 *(sharing)* reparto *m*. 3 *(of organization)* sección *f*.
divorce [dɪ'vɔːs] I *n* divorcio *m*. II *vtr* **she divorced him,** se divorció de él. III *vi* divorciarse.
divorcé [dɪ'vɔːseɪ], **divorcée** [dɪvɔː'siː] *n* divorciado,-a *m,f*.
divulge [daɪ'vʌldʒ] *vtr fml* divulgar, revelar.
DIY [diːaɪ'waɪ] *n GB abbr of* **do-it-yourself,** bricolaje *m*.
dizziness ['dɪzɪnɪs] *n* vértigo *m*.
dizzy ['dɪzɪ] *adj* (**dizzier, dizziest**) 1 *(person) (unwell)* mareado,-a. 2 *(height, pace)* vertiginoso,-a.
DJ ['diːdʒeɪ] *n abbr of* **disc jockey.**
DNA [diːen'eɪ] *n abbr of* **deoxyribonucleic acid,** ácido *m* desoxirribonucleico, ADN *m*.
do [duː, *unstressed* dʊ, də] I *v aux (3rd person sing pres* **does;** *pt* **did;** *pp* **done**) 1 *(in negatives and questions) (not translated in Span)* **do you want some coffee?** ¿quieres café?; **do you drive?,** ¿tienes carnet de conducir?; **don't you want to come?,** ¿no quieres venir?; **he doesn't smoke,** no fuma. 2 *(emphatic) (not translated in Span)* **do come with us!,** ¡ánimo, vente con nosotros!; **I do like your bag,** me encanta tu bolso. 3 *(substituting main verb) (in sentence) (not translated in Span)* **I don't believe him - neither do I,** no le creo - yo tampoco; **I'll go if you do,** si vas tú, voy yo; **I think it's dear, but he doesn't,** a mí me parece caro pero a él no; **who went? - I did,** ¿quién asistió? - yo. 4 *(in question tags)* **he refused, didn't he?,** dijo que no, ¿verdad?; **I don't like it, do you?,** a mí no me gusta, ¿y a ti?
II *vtr* 1 hacer; *(task) (duty)* cumplir con; **to do one's best,** hacer todo lo posible; **to do sth again,** volver a hacer algo; **to do sth for sb,** hacer algo por algn; **to do the cooking/cleaning,** cocinar/limpiar; **to do the dishes,** lavar los platos; **what can I do for you?,** ¿en qué puedo servirle?; **what do you do (for a living)?,** ¿a qué te dedicas?; **what's to be done?,** ¿qué se puede hacer?; *fam* **he's done it!,** ¡lo ha conseguido! 2 **do you do sportswear?,** *(make, offer)* ¿(aquí) tienen ropa de deporte? 3 *(distance)* recorrer; *(speed)* **we were doing eighty,** íbamos a ochenta; **this car can do a hundred and twenty,** este coche puede alcanzar los ciento veinte.

III *vi* 1 *(act)* hacer; **do as I tell you,** haz lo que te digo; **you did right,** hiciste bien. 2 **he did badly in the exams,** los exámenes le salieron mal; **how are you doing?,** ¿qué tal?; **how do you do?,** *(greeting)* ¿cómo está usted?; *(answer)* mucho gusto; **to do well,** *(person)* tener éxito; *(business)* ir bien. 3 **five pounds will do,** *(suffice)* con cinco libras será suficiente; *fam* **that will do!,** ¡basta ya! 4 **this cushion will do as a pillow,** *(be suitable)* este cojín servirá de almohada; **this won't do,** esto no puede ser.
IV *n fam* 1 *GB (party)* fiesta *f*; *(event)* ceremonia *f*. 2 **do's and don'ts,** reglas *fpl* de conducta.
◆**do away with** *vtr* 1 *(abolish)* abolir; *(discard)* deshacerse de. 2 *(kill)* asesinar. ◆**do down** *vtr fam (humiliate)* hacer quedar mal. ◆**do for** *fam vtr (destroy, ruin)* arruinar; *fig* **I'm done for if I don't finish this,** estoy perdido,-a si no acabo esto. ◆**do in** *vtr sl* 1 *(kill)* cargarse. 2 **I'm done in,** *(exhausted)* estoy hecho,-a polvo. ◆**do over** *vtr fam* 1 *US (repeat)* repetir. 2 *GB (thrash)* dar una paliza a. ◆**do up** *vtr* 1 *(wrap)* envolver. 2 *(belt etc)* abrochar; *(laces)* atar. 3 *(dress up)* arreglar. 4 *fam (redecorate)* renovar. ◆**do with** *vtr* 1 **I could do with a rest,** *(need)* un descanso no me vendría nada mal. 2 **to have or be to do with,** *(concern)* tener que ver con. ◆**do without** *vtr* pasar sin, prescindir de.
docile ['dəʊsaɪl] *adj* dócil; *(animal)* manso,-a.
dock¹ [dɒk] I *n Naut* the docks, el muelle. II *vi* 1 *(ship)* atracar. 2 *(spacecraft)* acoplarse.
dock² [dɒk] *vtr (reduce)* descontar.
dock³ [dɒk] *n Jur* banquillo *m* (de los acusados).
docker ['dɒkəʳ] *n* estibador *m*.
dockland ['dɒklænd] *n* zona *f* del puerto.
dockyard ['dɒkjɑːd] *n* astillero *m*.
doctor ['dɒktəʳ] I *n* 1 *Med* médico,-a *m,f*. 2 *Univ* doctor,-a *m,f*; **D. of Law,** doctor en derecho. II *vtr pej (figures)* falsificar; *(text)* arreglar; *(drink etc)* adulterar.
doctorate ['dɒktərɪt] *n* doctorado *m*.
doctrine ['dɒktrɪn] *n* doctrina *f*.
document ['dɒkjʊmənt] I *n* documento *m*; **documents,** documentación *f*. II *vtr* documentar.
documentary [dɒkjʊ'mentərɪ] *adj & n* documental *m*.
dodge [dɒdʒ] I *vtr* 1 *(blow)* esquivar; *(pursuer)* despistar; *fig* eludir. 2 *fam* **to d. one's taxes,** engañar a Hacienda. II *vi (move aside)* echarse a un lado. III *n* 1 *(movement)* regate *m*. 2 *fam (trick)* truco *m*.
dodgem® ['dɒdʒəm] *n fam* **d. (car),** coche *m* de choque.

dodgy ['dɒdʒɪ] adj (dodgier, dodgiest) GB fam (risky) arriesgado,-a; (tricky) difícil; (dishonest, not working properly) chungo,-a.

doe [dəʊ] n inv (of deer) gama f; (of rabbit) coneja f.

does [dʌz] 3rd person sing pres → do.

doesn't ['dʌzənt] = does not.

dog [dɒg] I n 1 perro,-a m,f; fam fig a d.'s life, una vida de perros; d. collar, (of dog) collar m de perro; Rel fam alzacuello m. 2 (male canine) macho m; (fox) zorro m; (wolf) lobo m. 3 fam dirty d., canalla m. 4 US fam (disappointment) desastre m. II vtr acosar; to d. sb's footsteps, seguir los pasos de algn; fig dogged by bad luck, perseguido,-a por la mala suerte.

dog-eared ['dɒgɪəd] adj (book) con los bordes de las páginas doblados; (shabby) sobado,-a.

dogged ['dɒgɪd] adj obstinado,-a, tenaz.

doghouse ['dɒghaʊs] n US fam perrera f; fig to be in the d., estar castigado,-a.

dogma ['dɒgmə] n dogma m.

dogmatic [dɒg'mætɪk] adj dogmático,-a.

dogsbody ['dɒgzbɒdɪ] n GB fam (drudge) burro m de carga.

doh [dəʊ] n Mus do m.

doing ['duːɪŋ] n 1 (action) obra f; it was none of my d., yo no tuve nada que ver; fig it took some d., costó trabajo hacerlo. 2 doings, (activities) actividades fpl.

do-it-yourself [duːɪtjəˈself] n bricolaje m.

doldrums ['dɒldrəmz] npl fam fig to be in the d., (person) estar abatido,-a; (trade) estar estancado,-a.

dole [dəʊl] I n GB fam the d., el paro; to be or go on the d., estar en el paro; fig d. queue, los parados. II vtr to d. (out), repartir.

doleful ['dəʊlfʊl] adj triste, afligido,-a.

doll [dɒl] I n (toy) muñeca f. 2 US fam (girl) muñeca f. II vtr fam to d. oneself up, ponerse guapa.

dollar ['dɒlər] n dólar m.

dolphin ['dɒlfɪn] n delfín m.

domain [dəˈmeɪn] n 1 (sphere) campo m, esfera f; that's not my d., no es de mi competencia. 2 (territory) dominio m.

dome [dəʊm] n (roof) cúpula f; (ceiling) bóveda f.

domestic [dəˈmestɪk] adj 1 (appliance, pet) doméstico,-a; d. science, economía doméstica. 2 (home-loving) casero,-a. 3 (flight, news) nacional; (trade, policy) interior.

domesticate [dəˈmestɪkeɪt] vtr (make home-loving) volver hogareño,-a or casero,-a.

domicile ['dɒmɪsaɪl] n domicilio m.

dominant ['dɒmɪnənt] adj dominante.

dominate ['dɒmɪneɪt] vtr & vi dominar.

domineering [dɒmɪˈnɪərɪŋ] adj domi-

nante.

Dominican [dəˈmɪnɪkən] adj & n (of Dominica) dominicano,-a (m,f); D. Republic, República Dominicana.

dominion [dəˈmɪnjən] n dominio m.

domino ['dɒmɪnəʊ] n (pl dominoes) (piece) ficha f de dominó; **dominoes**, (game) dominó m sing.

don [dɒn] n GB Univ catedrático,-a m,f.

donate [dəʊˈneɪt] vtr donar.

donation [dəʊˈneɪʃən] n donativo m.

done [dʌn] adj 1 (finished) terminado,-a; it's over and d. with, se acabó. 2 fam (tired) rendido,-a. 3 (meat) hecho,-a; (vegetables) cocido,-a.

donkey ['dɒŋkɪ] n burro,-a m,f.

donor ['dəʊnər] n donante m.

don't [dəʊnt] = do not.

doodle ['duːdəl] vi fam (write) garabatear; (draw) hacer dibujos.

doom [duːm] I n 1 (fate) destino m (funesto); (ruin) perdición f; (death) muerte f. II vtr usu pass (destine) destinar; doomed to failure, condenado,-a al fracaso.

doomsday ['duːmzdeɪ] n día m del juicio final.

door [dɔːr] n puerta f; **front/back d.**, puerta principal/trasera; fig behind closed doors, a puerta cerrada; d. handle, manilla f (de la puerta); d. knocker, picaporte m; next d. (to), (en) la casa de al lado (de).

doorbell ['dɔːbel] n timbre m (de la puerta).

doorknob ['dɔːnɒb] n pomo m.

doorman ['dɔːmən] n portero m.

doormat ['dɔːmæt] n felpudo m, esterilla f; fam fig (person) trapo m.

doorstep ['dɔːstep] n peldaño m; fig on one's d., a la vuelta de la esquina.

door-to-door [dɔːtəˈdɔːr] adj a domicilio.

doorway ['dɔːweɪ] n portal m, entrada f.

dope [dəʊp] I n 1 sl (drug) chocolate m. 2 fam (person) imbécil mf. II vtr (food, drink) adulterar con drogas; Sport dopar.

dop(e)y ['dəʊpɪ] adj (dopier, dopiest) fam 1 (sleepy) medio dormido,-a; (fuddled) atontado,-a. 2 sl (silly) torpe.

dormant ['dɔːmənt] adj inactivo,-a; fig (rivalry) latente.

dormitory ['dɔːmɪtərɪ] n 1 (in school) dormitorio m. 2 US (in university) colegio m mayor.

dosage ['dəʊsɪdʒ] n fml (amount) dosis f inv.

dose [dəʊs] I n dosis f inv. II vtr (patient) medicar.

doss [dɒs] vi GB sl sobar.

dosshouse ['dɒshaʊs] n GB sl pensión f de mala muerte.

dossier ['dɒsɪeɪ] n expediente m.

dot [dɒt] I n punto m; on the d., en punto. II vtr 1 fam to d. one's i's and

cross one's t's, poner los puntos sobre las íes. 2 (*scatter*) esparcir, salpicar.

dote [dǝʊt] *vi* to d. on sb, chochear con algn.

double ['dʌbǝl] **I** *adj* doble; **it's d. the price,** cuesta dos veces más; **d. bass,** contrabajo *m*; **d. bed,** cama *f* de matrimonio; **d. bill,** programa *m* doble; *GB* **d. cream,** nata *f* para montar; **d. glazing,** ventana *f* doble. **II** *adv* doble; **folded d.,** doblado,-a por la mitad. **III** *n* 1 vivo retrato *m*; *Cin Theat* doble *m*. **2** to earn d., ganar el doble; *fam* **at** *or* **on the d.,** corriendo. 3 *Ten* doubles, (partido *m sing de*) dobles *mpl*. **IV** *vtr* doblar; *fig* (*efforts*) redoblar. **V** *vi* 1 (*increase*) doblarse. **2** to d. as, (*serve*) hacer las veces de.
◆**double back** *vi* to d. back on one's tracks, volver sobre sus pasos.
◆**double up I** *vtr* (*bend*) doblar. **II** *vi* 1 (*bend*) doblarse. **2** (*share room*) compartir la habitación (**with**, con).

double-barrelled ['dʌbǝlbærǝld] *adj* 1 (*gun*) de dos cañones. **2** *GB* (*surname*) compuesto,-a.

double-breasted ['dʌbǝlbrestɪd] *adj* cruzado,-a.

double-check [dʌbǝl'tʃek] *vtr & vi* repasar dos veces.

double-cross [dʌbǝl'krɒs] *fam* **I** *vtr* engañar, traicionar. **II** *n* engaño *m*, traición *f*.

double-decker [dʌbǝl'dekǝr] *n GB* d.-d. (**bus**), autobús *m* de dos pisos.

double-edged [dʌbǝl'edʒd] *adj* de doble filo.

doubt [daʊt] **I** *n* duda *f*; **beyond (all) d.,** sin duda alguna; **no d.,** sin duda; **there's no d. about it,** no cabe la menor duda; **to be in d. about sth,** dudar algo; **to be open to d.,** (*fact*) ser dudoso,-a; (*outcome*) ser incierto,-a. **II** *vtr* (*distrust*) desconfiar de. **2** (*not be sure of*) dudar; **I d. if** *or* **whether he'll come,** dudo que venga.

doubtful ['daʊtfʊl] *adj* 1 (*future*) dudoso,-a, (*look*) dubitativo,-a; **I'm a bit d. about it,** no me convence del todo; **it's d. whether ...,** no se sabe seguro si .... **2** (*questionable*) sospechoso,-a.

doubtless ['daʊtlɪs] *adv* sin duda, seguramente.

dough [dǝʊ] *n* 1 (*for bread*) masa *f*; (*for pastries*) pasta *f*. **2** *sl* (*money*) pasta *f*.

doughnut ['dǝʊnʌt] *n* rosquilla *f*, dónut® *m*.

douse [daʊs] *vtr* 1 (*soak*) mojar. 2 (*extinguish*) apagar.

dove [dʌv] *n* paloma *f*.

dovetail ['dʌvteɪl] *vtr fig* (*plans*) sincronizar.

dowdy ['daʊdɪ] *adj* (*dowdier, dowdiest*) poco elegante.

down¹ [daʊn] **I** *prep* 1 (*to* or *at a lower level*) the river, río abajo; **to go d. the road,** bajar la calle. **2** (*along*) por. **II** *adv*

1 (*to lower level*) (hacia) abajo; (*to floor*) al suelo; (*to ground*) a tierra; **to fall d.,** caerse; **to go d.,** (*price, person*) bajar; (*sun*) ponerse. **2** (*at lower level*) abajo; **d. there,** allí abajo; **face d.,** boca abajo; *fig* **to be d. with a cold,** estar resfriado,-a; *fam fig* **to feel d.,** estar deprimido,-a; *fam fig* **d. under,** Australia *f*, Nueva Zelanda *f*. **3** I'm d. to my last stamp, no me queda más que un solo sello; **sales are d. by five percent,** las ventas han bajado un cinco por ciento. **4** to take sth d., (*in writing*) apuntar algo. **5** d. through the ages, a través de los siglos. **III** *adj* (*payment*) al contado; (*on property*) de entrada. **IV** *vtr fam* (*drink*) tomarse de un trago; (*food*) zamparse. **V** *n* ups and downs, altibajos *mpl*. **VI** *interj* d. with taxes!, ¡abajo los impuestos!

down² [daʊn] *n* 1 (*on bird*) plumón *m*. 2 (*on cheek, peach*) pelusa *f*; (*on body*) vello *m*.

down-and-out ['daʊnǝnaʊt] **I** *adj* en las últimas. **II** *n* vagabundo,-a *m,f*.

downbeat ['daʊnbiːt] *adj fam* (*gloomy*) deprimido,-a.

downcast ['daʊnkɑːst] *adj* abatido,-a.

downfall ['daʊnfɔːl] *n* (*of régime*) caída *f*; (*of person*) perdición *f*.

downgrade ['daʊngreɪd] *vtr* degradar.

downhearted [daʊn'hɑːtɪd] *adj* desalentado,-a.

downhill [daʊn'hɪl] **I** *adj* (*skiing*) de descenso; *fam* **after his first exam, the rest were all d.,** después del primer examen, los demás le fueron sobre ruedas. **II** *adv* **to go d.,** ir cuesta abajo; *fig* (*standards*) deteriorarse.

down-market [daʊn'mɑːkɪt] **I** *adj* barato,-a. **II** *adv* **to move d.,** (*of company*) producir artículos más asequibles.

downpour ['daʊnpɔːr] *n* chaparrón *m*.

downright ['daʊnraɪt] *fam* **I** *adj* (*blunt*) tajante; (*categorical*) categórico,-a; **it's a d. lie,** es una mentira y gorda. **II** *adv* (*totally*) completamente.

downstairs [daʊn'steǝz] **I** *adv* abajo; (*to ground floor*) a la planta baja; **to go d.,** bajar la escalera. **II** *adj* (*on ground floor*) de la planta baja.

downstream [daʊn'striːm] *adv* río abajo.

down-to-earth [daʊntʊ'ɜːθ] *adj* realista.

downtown [daʊn'taʊn] *adv US* en el centro (de la ciudad).

downturn ['daʊntɜːn] *n* baja *f*.

downward ['daʊnwǝd] *adj* (*slope*) descendente; (*look*) hacia abajo; *Fin* (*tendency*) a la baja.

downward(s) ['daʊnwǝd(z)] *adv* hacia abajo.

dowry ['daʊǝrɪ] *n* dote *f*.

doz *abbr of* **dozen,** docena *f*, doc.

doze [dǝʊz] **I** *vi* dormitar. **II** *n* cabezada *f*; **to have a d.,** echar una cabezada.

◆**doze off** vi quedarse dormido,-a.

dozen ['dʌzən] n docena f; **half a d./a d. eggs,** media docena/una docena de huevos; **fam dozens of,** un montón de.

Dr abbr of **Doctor,** Doctor,-a m,f, Dr., Dra.

drab [dræb] adj (drabber, drabbest) 1 (ugly) feo,-a; (dreary) monótono,-a, gris. 2 (colour) pardo,-a.

draft [drɑːft] I n 1 borrador m. 2 (bill of exchange) giro m. 3 US servicio militar obligatorio. 4 US → **draught.** II vtr 1 hacer un borrador de. 2 US Mil reclutar.

draftsman ['drɑːftsmən] n US → **draughtsman.**

drag [dræg] I vtr 1 (pull) arrastrar; fig **to d. one's heels (over sth),** dar largas (a algo). 2 (lake) rastrear. II vi 1 (trail) arrastrarse. 2 (person) rezagarse. III n 1 Tech resistencia f (aerodinámica). 2 fam (nuisance) lata f. 3 fam (on cigarette) calada f. 4 sl **to be in d.,** ir vestido de mujer. ◆**drag off** vtr llevarse arrastrando. ◆**drag on** vi (of war, strike) hacerse interminable. ◆**drag out** vtr (speech etc) alargar.

dragon ['drægən] n dragón m.

dragonfly ['drægənflaɪ] n libélula f.

drain [dreɪn] I n 1 (for water) desagüe m; (for sewage) alcantarilla f. 2 (grating) sumidero m. 3 fig **the boys are a d. on her strength,** los niños la dejan agotada. II vtr 1 (marsh etc) avenar; (reservoir) desecar. 2 (crockery) escurrir. 3 (empty) (glass) apurar; fig (capital etc) agotar. III vi 1 (crockery) escurrirse. 2 **to d. (away),** (liquid) irse.

drainage ['dreɪnɪdʒ] n (of marsh) drenaje m; (of reservoir, building) desagüe m; (of town) alcantarillado m.

drainpipe ['dreɪnpaɪp] n tubo m de desagüe.

dram [dræm] n fam trago m (de whisky).

drama ['drɑːmə] n 1 (play) obra f de teatro; fig drama. 2 Lit (subject) teatro m.

dramatic [drə'mætɪk] adj 1 (change) impresionante; (moment) emocionante. 2 Theat dramático,-a, teatral.

dramatist ['dræmətɪst] n dramaturgo,-a m,f.

dramatization [dræmətaɪ'zeɪʃən] n adaptación f teatral.

dramatize ['dræmətaɪz] vtr 1 (adapt) hacer una adaptación teatral de. 2 (exaggerate) dramatizar.

drank [dræŋk] pt → **drink.**

drape [dreɪp] I vtr **to d. sth over sth,** colgar algo sobre algo; **draped with,** cubierto,-a de. II n 1 (of fabric) caída f. 2 US cortina f.

draper ['dreɪpər] n GB pañero,-a m,f.

drastic ['dræstɪk] adj 1 (measures) drástico,-a, severo,-a. 2 (change) radical.

draught [drɑːft] I n 1 (of cold air) co-

rriente f (de aire). 2 (of liquid) trago m. **d. (beer),** cerveza f de barril. 4 GB **draughts,** (game) damas fpl. 5 Naut calado m. II adj (animal) de tiro.

draughtboard ['drɑːftbɔːd] n GB tablero m de damas.

draughtsman ['drɑːftsmən] n delineante mf.

draw [drɔː] I vtr (pt drew; pp drawn) 1 (picture) dibujar; (line) trazar. 2 (pull) tirar de; (train, carriage) arrastrar; (curtains) (open) descorrer; (close) correr; (blinds) bajar. 3 (remove) sacar; (salary) cobrar; (cheque) librar. 4 (attract) atraer; (attention) llamar. 5 fig (strength) sacar. 6 **to d. breath,** respirar. 7 **to d. lots,** echar suertes. 8 (comparison) hacer; (conclusion) sacar. II vi 1 (sketch) dibujar. 2 (move) **the train drew into/out of the station,** el tren entró en/salió de la estación; **to d. apart (from),** separarse (de); **to d. to an end,** acabarse. 3 Sport **they drew two all,** empataron a dos. III n 1 (raffle) sorteo m. 2 Sport empate m. 3 fig (attraction) atracción f. ◆**draw in** vi (days) acortarse. ◆**draw on** vtr (savings) recurrir a; (experience) aprovecharse de. ◆**draw out** vtr 1 (make long) alargar. 2 (encourage to speak) desatar la lengua a. 3 (from pocket, drawer etc) sacar. ◆**draw up** vtr (contract) preparar; (plan) esbozar.

drawback ['drɔːbæk] n desventaja f, inconveniente m.

drawbridge ['drɔːbrɪdʒ] n puente levadizo.

drawer ['drɔːər] n cajón m.

drawing ['drɔːɪŋ] n dibujo m; fam fig **to go back to the d. board,** volver a empezar; GB **d. pin,** chincheta f; fml **d. room,** sala f de estar.

drawl [drɔːl] I vi hablar arrastrando las palabras. II n voz cansina; US **a Southern d.,** un acento sureño.

drawn [drɔːn] adj (tired) ojeroso,-a.

dread [dred] I vtr temer a, tener pavor a. II n temor m.

dreadful ['dredfʊl] adj 1 (shocking) espantoso,-a. 2 fam (awful) fatal; **how d.!,** ¡qué horror! ◆**dreadfully** adv fam (horribly) terriblemente; (very) muy, sumamente.

dream [driːm] I n 1 sueño m. 2 (daydream) ensueño m. 3 fam (marvel) maravilla f. II vtr (pt & pp dreamed or dreamt) soñar. III vi soñar (of, about, con).

dreamer ['driːmər] n soñador,-a m,f.

dreamy ['driːmɪ] adj (dreamier, dreamiest) (absent-minded) distraído,-a; (wonderful) de ensueño.

dreary ['drɪərɪ] adj (drearier, dreariest) 1 (gloomy) triste. 2 fam (boring) aburrido,-a, pesado,-a.

dredge [dredʒ] vtr & vi dragar, rastrear. ◆**dredge up** vtr 1 (body) sacar del

agua. **2** *fam fig* sacar a relucir.
dregs |dregz| *npl* poso *m sing*.
drench |drentʃ| *vtr* empapar.
dress |dres| **I** *n* **1** *(frock)* vestido *m*. **2**
(clothing) ropa *f*; **d. rehearsal,** ensayo *m*
general; **d. shirt,** camisa *f* de etiqueta. **II**
vtr **1** *(person)* vestir; **he was dressed in a**
grey suit, llevaba (puesto) un traje gris. **2**
(salad) aliñar. **3** *(wound)* vendar. **III** *vi*
vestirse. ◆**dress up I** *vi* **1** *(in disguise)*
disfrazarse (**as,** de). **2** *(in best clothes)*
vestirse elegante. **II** *vtr fig* disfrazar.
dresser |'dresər| *n* **1** *GB (in kitchen)* aparador *m*. **2** *US (in bedroom)* tocador *m*. **3**
Theat ayudante *mf* de camerino.
dressing |'dresɪŋ| *n* **1** *(bandage)* vendaje
m. **2** (**salad**) **d.,** aliño *m*. **3 d. gown,** bata
f; **d. room,** *Theat* camerino *m*; *Sport*
vestuario *m*; **d. table,** tocador *m*.
dressmaker |'dresmeɪkər| *n* modista *mf*.
dressy |'dresɪ| *adj* (**dressier, dressiest**)
vistoso,-a.
drew |dru:| *pt* → **draw.**
dribble |'drɪbəl| **I** *vi* **1** *(baby)* babear. **2**
(liquid) gotear. **II** *vtr Sport (ball)* driblar.
III *n* *(saliva)* saliva *f*; *(of water, blood)* gotas *fpl*.
dried |draɪd| *adj (fruit)* seco,-a; *(milk)* en
polvo.
drier |'draɪər| *n* → **dryer.**
drift |drɪft| **I** *vi* **1** *(boat)* ir a la deriva; *fig*
(person) ir sin rumbo, vagar; **they drifted**
away, se marcharon poco a poco. **2**
(snow) amontonarse. **II** *n* **1** *(flow)* flujo *m*.
2 *(of snow)* ventisquero *m*; *(of sand)*
montón *m*. **3** *fig (meaning)* idea *f*.
driftwood |'drɪftwʊd| *n* madera *f* flotante.
drill |drɪl| **I** *n* **1** *(handtool)* taladro *m*; *Min*
barrena *f*; **dentist's d.,** fresa *f*; **pneu**
matic d., martillo neumático. **II** *vtr* **1**
(wood etc) taladrar. **2** *(soldiers, children)* instruir. **III** *vi* *(by*
hand) taladrar; *(for oil, coal)* perforar,
sondar.
drink |drɪŋk| **I** *vtr (pt* **drank;** *pp* **drunk)**
beber. **II** *vi* beber; **to have sth to d.,** tomarse algo; **to d. to sth/sb,** brindar por
algo/algn. **III** *n* bebida *f*; *(alcoholic)* copa
f.
drinker |'drɪŋkər| *n* bebedor,-a *m,f*.
drinking |'drɪŋkɪŋ| *n* **d. water,** agua *f* potable.
drip |drɪp| **I** *n* **1** *(goteo m.* **2** *Med* gota a
gota *m inv*. **3** *fam (person)* necio,-a *m,f*. **II**
vi gotear; **he was dripping with sweat,** el
sudor le caía a gotas.
drip-dry |'drɪpdraɪ| *adj* que no necesita
planchado.
dripping |'drɪpɪŋ| *n Culin* pringue *f*.
drive |draɪv| **I** *vtr (pt* **drove;** *pp* **driven) 1**
(vehicle) conducir, *Am* manejar; *(person)*
llevar. **2** *(power)* impulsar. **3** *(enemy)* acosar; *(ball)* mandar. **4** *(stake)* hincar; *(nail)*

clavar. **5** *(compel)* forzar, obligar; **to d. sb**
mad, volver loco,-a a algn. **6 to d. (off),**
rechazar. **II** *vi Aut* conducir, *Am* manejar. **III** *n* **1** *(trip)* paseo *m* en coche; **to go**
for a d., dar una vuelta en coche. **2** *(to*
house) camino *m* de entrada. **3** *(transmis*
sion) transmisión *f*; *Aut* tracción *f*; *Aut*
left-hand d., conducción *f* por la
izquierda. **4** *Golf* golpe *m* inicial. **5**
(campaign) campaña *f*. **6** *(need)* necesidad
f; *(energy)* energía *f*, vigor *m*; **sex d.,**
instinto *m* sexual.
drive-in |'draɪvɪn| *n US (cinema)* autocine
m.
driven |'drɪvən| *pp* → **drive.**
driver |'draɪvər| *n (of car, bus)*
conductor,-a *m,f*; *(of train)* maquinista
mf; *(of lorry)* camionero,-a *m,f*; *(of racing*
car) piloto *mf*; *US* **d.'s license,** carnet *m*
de conducir.
driveway |'draɪvweɪ| *n (to house)* camino
m de entrada.
driving |'draɪvɪŋ| **I** *n* **1 d. licence,** carnet
m de conducir; **d. school,** autoescuela *f*;
d. test, examen *m* de conducir. **II** *adj* **1**
(rain) intenso,-a. **2 d. force,** fuerza *f* motriz.
drizzle |'drɪzəl| **I** *n* llovizna *f*. **II** *vi* lloviznar.
droll |drəʊl| *adj* gracioso,-a.
dromedary |'drɒmədərɪ| *n* dromedario
m.
drone |drəʊn| *vi (bee etc)* zumbar.
droop |dru:p| *vi (flower)* marchitarse;
(eyelids) caerse.
drop |drɒp| **I** *n* **1** *(of liquid)* gota *f*; **eye**
drops, colirio *m sing*. **2** *(sweet)* pastilla *f*.
3 *(descent)* desnivel *m*. **4** *(in price)* bajada
f; *(in temperature)* descenso *m*. **II** *vtr* **1** *(let*
fall) dejar caer; *(lower)* bajar; *(reduce)* disminuir; **to d. a hint,** soltar una indirecta.
2 *(abandon) (subject, charge etc)* abandonar, dejar; *Sport* **he was dropped from**
the team, le echaron del equipo. **3** *(omit)*
(spoken syllable) comerse. **III** *vi (object)*
caerse; *(person)* tirarse; *(voice, price,*
temperature) bajar; *(wind)* amainar; *(speed)*
disminuir. ◆**drop by, drop in, drop**
round *vi fam (visit)* pasarse (**at,** por).
◆**drop off I** *vi fam (fall asleep)* quedarse dormido,-a. **II** *vtr (deliver)* dejar.
◆**drop out** *vi (from college)* dejar los
estudios; *(from society)* marginarse; *(from*
competition) retirarse.
dropout |'drɒpaʊt| *n fam pej*
automarginado,-a *m,f*.
dropper |'drɒpər| *n* cuentagotas *m inv*.
droppiings |'drɒpɪŋz| *npl* excrementos
mpl.
drought |draʊt| *n* sequía *f*.
drove |drəʊv| *n (of cattle)* manada *f*.
drown |draʊn| **I** *vtr* **1** ahogar. **2** *(place)*
inundar. **II** *vi* ahogarse; **he (was)**
drowned, murió ahogado.

drowsy ['draʊzı] *adj* (*drowsier, drowsiest*) soñoliento,-a; **to feel d.,** tener sueño.

drudgery ['drʌdʒərı] *n* trabajo duro y pesado.

drug [drʌg] **I** *n* **1** (*medicine*) medicamento *m*. **2** (*narcotic*) droga *f*, estupefaciente *m*; **to be on drugs,** drogarse; **d. addict,** drogadicto,-a *m,f*; **d. addiction,** drogadicción *f*; **d. squad,** brigada *f* antidroga. **II** *vtr* (*person*) drogar; (*food, drink*) adulterar con drogas.

druggist ['drʌgıst] *n* US farmacéutico,-a *m,f*.

drugstore ['drʌgstɔ:r] *n* US establecimiento *m* donde se compran medicamentos, periódicos etc.

drum [drʌm] **I** *n* **1** tambor *m*; **to play the drums,** tocar la batería. **2** (*container*) bidón *m*. **II** *vi fig* (*with fingers*) tabalear. **III** *vtr fig* **to d. sth into sb,** enseñar algo a algn a machamartillo. ◆**drum up** *vtr fam* solicitar.

drummer ['drʌmər] *n* (*in band*) tambor *mf*; (*in pop group*) batería *mf*.

drumstick ['drʌmstık] *n Mus* baqueta *f*, *fam* palillo *m*.

drunk [drʌŋk] **I** *adj* borracho,-a; **to get d.,** emborracharse. **II** *n* borracho,-a *m,f*.

drunkard ['drʌŋkəd] *n* borracho,-a *m,f*.

dry [draı] **I** *adj* (*drier, driest or dryer, dryest*) **1** seco,-a. **2** (*wry*) socarrón,-ona. **II** *vtr* (*pt & pp* **dried**) secar. **II** *vi* **to d.** (**off**), secarse.

dry-clean [draı'kli:n] *vtr* limpiar *or* lavar en seco.

dryer ['draıər] *n* secadora *f*.

dub¹ [dʌb] *vtr* (*subtitle*) doblar (**into,** a).

dub² [dʌb] *vtr* **1** (*give nickname to*) apodar. **2** (*knight*) armar.

dubious ['dju:bıəs] *adj* **1** (*morals etc*) dudoso,-a; (*compliment*) equívoco,-a. **2** (*doubting*) indeciso,-a.

Dublin ['dʌblın] *n* Dublín.

duchess ['dʌtʃıs] *n* duquesa *f*.

duck¹ [dʌk] *n* pato,-a *m,f*; *Culin* pato *m*.

duck² [dʌk] **I** *vtr* **1** (*submerge*) dar una ahogadilla a. **2** (*evade*) esquivar. **II** *vi* **1** (*evade blow*) esquivar. **2** *fam* **to d.** (**out**), rajarse.

duckling ['dʌklıŋ] *n* patito *m*.

duct [dʌkt] *n* (*for fuel etc*) conducto *m*; *Anat* canal *m*.

dud [dʌd] *fam* **I** *adj* **1** (*useless*) inútil; (*defective*) estropeado,-a. **2** (*banknote*) falso, -a; (*cheque*) sin fondos. **II** *n* (*useless thing*) engañifa *f*; (*person*) desastre *m*.

due [dju:] **I** *adj* **1** (*expected*) esperado,-a; **the train is d.** (**to arrive**) **at ten,** el tren debe llegar a las diez. **2** *fml* (*proper*) debido,-a; **in d. course,** a su debido tiempo. **3** (*owing*) pagadero,-a; **how much are you d.?,** (*owed*) ¿cuánto te deben? **4** **to be d. to,** (*caused by*) deberse a;

d. to, (*because of*) debido de. **II** *adv* (*north etc*) derecho hacia. **III** *n* **1** **to give sb their d.,** dar a algn su merecido. **2** **dues,** (*fee*) cuota *f sing*.

duel ['dju:əl] *n* duelo *m*.

duet [dju:'et] *n* dúo *m*.

duffel ['dʌfəl] *n* **d. bag,** petate *m*; **d. coat,** trenca *f*.

dug [dʌg] *pt & pp →* **dig.**

duke [dju:k] *n* duque *m*.

dull [dʌl] **I** *adj* **1** (*boring*) pesado,-a; (*place*) sin interés. **2** (*light*) apagado,-a; (*weather*) gris. **3** (*sound, ache*) sordo,-a. **4** *fig* (*slow-witted*) torpe. **II** *vtr* **1** (*pain*) aliviar. **2** *fig* (*faculty*) embotar.

duly ['dju:lı] *adv fml* (*properly*) debidamente; (*as expected*) como era de esperar; (*in due course*) a su debido tiempo.

dumb [dʌm] **I** *adj* **1** *Med* mudo,-a. **2** *fam* (*stupid*) tonto,-a. **II** *npl* **the d.,** los mudos.

dumbbell ['dʌmbel] *n Sport* pesa *f*.

dumbfounded [dʌm'faʊndıd], **dumbstruck** ['dʌmstrʌk] *adj* pasmado,-a.

dummy ['dʌmı] *n* **1** (*sham*) imitación *f*. **2** (*in shop window*) maniquí *m*; (*of ventriloquist*) muñeco *m*. **3** GB (*for baby*) chupete *m*.

dump [dʌmp] **I** *n* **1** (*tip*) vertedero *m*; (*for old cars*) cementerio *m* (de coches). **2** *fam pej* (*place*) estercolero *m*; (*town*) poblacho *m*; (*dwelling*) tugurio *m*. **3** *Mil* depósito *m*. **II** *vtr* **1** (*rubbish*) verter. **2** (*truck contents*) descargar. **2** (*person*) dejar; *Com* inundar el mercado con. **3** *Comput* (*transfer*) copiar de memoria interna.

dumping ['dʌmpıŋ] *n* vertido *m*.

dumpling ['dʌmplıŋ] *n Culin* bola *f* de masa hervida.

dumpy ['dʌmpı] *adj* (*dumpier, dumpiest*) *fam* rechoncho,-a.

dunce [dʌns] *n fam* tonto,-a *m,f*.

dune [dju:n] *n* (*sand*) **d.,** duna *f*.

dung [dʌŋ] *n* estiércol *m*.

dungarees [dʌŋgə'ri:z] *npl* mono *m sing*.

dungeon ['dʌndʒən] *n* calabozo *m*, mazmorra *f*.

duo ['dju:əʊ] *n Mus* dúo *m*; *fam* pareja *f*.

dupe [dju:p] **I** *vtr* engañar. **II** *n* ingenuo, -a *m,f*.

duplex ['dju:pleks] *n US* (*house*) casa adosada; *US* **d. apartment,** dúplex *m inv*.

duplicate ['dju:plıkeıt] **I** *vtr* **1** (*copy*) duplicar; (*film, tape*) reproducir. **2** (*repeat*) repetir. **II** ['dju:plıkıt] *n* duplicado *m*; **in d.,** por duplicado.

durable ['djʊərəbəl] *adj* duradero,-a.

duration [djʊ'reıʃən] *n fml* duración *f*.

duress [djʊ'res] *n fml* coacción *f*.

during ['djʊərıŋ] *prep* durante.

dusk [dʌsk] *n fml* crepúsculo *m*; **at d.,** al anochecer.

dust [dʌst] **I** *n* polvo *m*; **d. cloud,** polvareda *f*; **d. jacket,** sobrecubierta *f*. **II** *vtr* **1**

(furniture) quitar el polvo a. 2 *(cake)* espolvorear.

dustbin ['dʌstbɪn] *n GB* cubo *m* de la basura.

duster ['dʌstəʳ] *n (for housework)* trapo *m* or paño *m* (del polvo); **feather d.**, plumero *m*.

dustman ['dʌstmən] *n GB* basurero *m*.

dustpan ['dʌstpæn] *n* recogedor *m*.

dusty ['dʌstɪ] *adj (dustier, dustiest)* polvoriento,-a.

Dutch [dʌtʃ] **I** *adj* holandés,-esa; *fig* **D. cap**, diafragma *m*. **II** *n* **1** *pl* **the D.**, los holandeses. 2 *(language)* holandés *m*; **it's double D.** to me, me suena a chino. **III** *adv fig* **to go D.** (with sb), pagar cada uno lo suyo.

Dutchman ['dʌtʃmən] *n* holandés *m*.

Dutchwoman ['dʌtʃwumən] *n* holandesa *f*.

duty ['djuːtɪ] *n* **1** deber *m*; **to do one's d.**, cumplir con su deber. 2 *(task)* función *f*. **3 to be on d.**, estar de servicio; *Med Mil* estar de guardia; **d. chemist**, farmacia *f* de guardia. 4 *(tax)* impuesto *m*; **customs d.**, derechos *mpl* de aduana.

duty-free ['djuːtɪfriː] **I** *adj* libre de impuestos. **II** *adv* sin pagar impuestos. **III** *n* duty-free *m*.

duvet ['duːveɪ] *n* edredón *m*.

dwarf [dwɔːf] **I** *n (pl* **dwarves** [dwɔːvz]) *(person)* enano,-a *m,f*. **II** *vtr* hacer parecer pequeño,-a a.

dwell [dwel] *vi (pt & pp* **dwelt**) *fml* morar. ◆**dwell on** *vtr* hablar extensamente de; **let's not d. on it**, olvidémoslo.

dwelling ['dwelɪŋ] *n fml & hum* morada *f*, vivienda *f*.

dwindle ['dwɪndəl] *vi* menguar, disminuir.

dye [daɪ] **I** *n* tinte *m*. **II** *vtr (pres p* **dyeing**; *pt & pp* **dyed**) teñir; **to d. one's hair black**, teñirse el pelo de negro.

dying ['daɪɪŋ] *adj (person)* moribundo,-a *m,f*, agonizante *mf*; *fig (custom)* en vías de desaparición.

dyke [daɪk] *n* **1** *(bank)* dique *m*; *(causeway)* terraplén *m*. 2 *offens sl* tortillera *f*.

dynamic [daɪ'næmɪk] *adj* dinámico,-a.

dynamics [daɪ'næmɪks] *n* dinámica *f*.

dynamism ['daɪnəmɪzəm] *n fig* dinamismo *m*.

dynamite ['daɪnəmaɪt] *n* dinamita *f*.

dynamo ['daɪnəməʊ] *n* dínamo *f*.

dynasty ['dɪnəstɪ] *n* dinastía *f*.

dysentery ['dɪsəntrɪ] *n* disentería *f*.

dyslexia [dɪs'leksɪə] *n* dislexia *f*.

E

E, e [iː] *n* **1** *(the letter)* E, e *f*. 2 *Mus* mi *m*.

E *abbr of* **East**, Este, E.

each [iːtʃ] **I** *adj* cada; **e. day/month**, todos los días/meses; **e. person**, cada cual; **e. time I see him**, cada vez que lo veo. **II** *pron* **1** cada uno,-a; **two pounds e.**, dos libras cada uno; **we bought one e.**, nos compramos uno cada uno. 2 **e. other**, el uno al otro; **they hate e. other**, se odian.

eager ['iːgəʳ] *adj (anxious)* impaciente; *(desirous)* deseoso,-a; **e. to begin**, impaciente por empezar; **to be e. for success**, codiciar el éxito. ◆**eagerly** *adv (anxiously)* con impaciencia; *(keenly)* con ilusión.

eagle ['iːgəl] *n* águila *f*.

ear [ɪəʳ] *n* **1** oreja *f*; *(sense of hearing)* oído *m*. 2 *(of corn etc)* espiga *f*.

earache ['ɪəreɪk] *n* dolor *m* de oídos.

eardrum ['ɪədrʌm] *n* tímpano *m*.

earl [ɜːl] *n* conde *m*.

earlobe ['ɪələʊb] *n* lóbulo *m*.

early ['ɜːlɪ] *(earlier, earliest)* **I** *adj* **1** *(before the usual time)* temprano,-a; **to have an e. night**, acostarse pronto; **you're e.!**, ¡qué pronto has venido! 2 *(at first stage, period)* **at an e. age**, siendo joven; **e. on**, al principio; **e. work**, obra de juventud; **in her e. forties**, a los cuarenta y pocos;

it's still e. days, aún es pronto. 3 *(in the near future)* **an e. reply**, una respuesta pronta; **at the earliest**, cuanto antes. **II** *adv* **1** *(before the expected time)* temprano, pronto; **earlier on**, antes; **five minutes e.**, con cinco minutos de adelanto; **to leave e.**, irse pronto. 2 *(near the beginning)* **as e. as 1914**, ya en 1914; **as e. as possible**, tan pronto como sea posible; **to book e.**, reservar con tiempo; **in e. July**, a principios de julio.

earmark ['ɪəmɑːk] *vtr* destinar (**for**, para, a).

earn [ɜːn] *vtr* **1** *(money)* ganar; **to e. one's living**, ganarse la vida. 2 *(reputation)* ganarse. **3 to e. interest**, cobrar interés *or* intereses.

earnest ['ɜːnɪst] **I** *adj* serio,-a, formal. **II** *n* **in e.**, de veras, en serio.

earnings ['ɜːnɪŋz] *npl* ingresos *mpl*.

earring ['ɪərɪŋ] *n* pendiente *m*.

earshot ['ɪəʃɒt] *n* **out of e.**, fuera del alcance del oído; **within e.**, al alcance del oído.

earth [ɜːθ] **I** *n* **1** tierra *f*; *fig* **to be down to e.**, ser práctico; *fam* **where/why on e. ...?**, ¿pero dónde/por qué demonios ...? 2 *Elec* toma *f* de tierra. **II** *vtr Elec* conectar a tierra.

earthenware ['ɜːðənweəʳ] **I** *n* loza *f*. **II**

adj de barro.
earthquake ['ɜːθkweɪk] *n* terremoto *m*.
earthshattering ['ɜːθʃætərɪŋ] *adj* trascendental; **e. news**, noticia bomba.
earthworm ['ɜːθwɜːm] *n* lombriz *f* de tierra.
earthy ['ɜːθɪ] *adj* (**earthier, earthiest**) 1 (*taste*) terroso,-a. 2 (*bawdy*) tosco,-a.
earwig ['ɪəwɪg] *n* tijereta *f*.
ease [iːz] I *n* 1 (*freedom from discomfort*) tranquilidad *f*; *Mil* posición *f* de descanso; **at e.**, relajado,-a. 2 (*lack of difficulty*) facilidad *f*. 3 (*affluence*) comodidad *f*. 4 **e. of manner**, naturalidad *f*. II *vtr* 1 (*pain*) aliviar. 2 (*move gently*) deslizar con cuidado. ◆**ease off, ease up** *vi* 1 (*decrease*) disminuir. 2 (*slow down*) ir más despacio.
easel ['iːzəl] *n* caballete *m*.
east [iːst] I *n* este *m*; **the Middle E.**, el Oriente Medio. II *adj* del este, oriental; **E. Germany**, Alemania Oriental. III *adv* al *or* hacia el este.
Easter ['iːstər] *n* Semana Santa, Pascua *f*; **E. egg**, huevo *m* de Pascua; **E. Sunday**, Domingo *m* de Resurrección.
easterly ['iːstəlɪ] *adj* (*from the east*) del este; (*to the east*) hacia al este.
eastern ['iːstən] *adj* oriental, del este.
eastward(s) ['iːstwəd(z)] *adv* hacia el este.
easy ['iːzɪ] (**easier, easiest**) I *adj* 1 (*simple*) fácil, sencillo,-a. 2 (*unworried, comfortable*) cómodo,-a, tranquilo,-a; *fam* **I'm e.!**, me da lo mismo; **e. chair**, butacón *m*. II *adv* **go e. on the wine**, no te pases con el vino; *fam* **to take things e.**, tomarse las cosas con calma; *fam* **take it e.!**, ¡tranquilo! ◆**easily** *adv* fácilmente; **e. the best**, con mucho el mejor.
easy-going [iːzɪˈgəʊɪŋ] *adj* (*calm*) tranquilo,-a; (*lax*) despreocupado,-a; (*undemanding*) poco exigente.
eat [iːt] (*pt* **ate** [et, eɪt]; *pp* **eaten**) *vtr* comer. ◆**eat away** *vtr* desgastar; (*metal*) corroer. ◆**eat into** *vtr* 1 (*wood*) roer. 2 *fig* (*savings*) consumir. ◆**eat out** *vi* comer fuera. ◆**eat up** *vtr* 1 (*meal*) terminar. 2 *fig* (*petrol*) consumir; (*miles*) recorrer rápidamente.
eatable ['iːtəbəl] *adj* comestible.
eaten ['iːtən] *pp* → **eat**.
eau de Cologne [əʊdəkəˈləʊn] *n* colonia *f*.
eaves [iːvz] *npl* alero *m sing*.
eavesdrop ['iːvzdrɒp] *vi* escuchar disimuladamente.
ebb [eb] I *n* reflujo *m*; **e. and flow**, flujo y reflujo; *fig* **to be at a low e.**, estar decaído. II *vi* 1 (*tide*) bajar; **to e. and flow**, subir y bajar. 2 *fig* **to e. away**, decaer.
ebony ['ebənɪ] I *n* ébano *m*. II *adj* de ébano.
eccentric [ɪkˈsentrɪk] *adj & nm,f*

excéntrico,-a.
ecclesiastic [ɪkliːzɪˈæstɪk] *adj & nm,f* eclesiástico,-a.
echelon ['eʃəlɒn] *n* escalafón *m*.
echo ['ekəʊ] I *n* (*pl* **echoes**) eco *m*. II *vtr* (*repeat*) repetir. III *vi* resonar, hacer eco.
eclectic [ɪˈklektɪk] *adj* ecléctico,-a.
eclipse [ɪˈklɪps] I *n* eclipse *m*. II *vtr* eclipsar.
ecological [iːkəˈlɒdʒɪkəl] *adj* ecológico, -a.
ecology [ɪˈkɒlədʒɪ] *n* ecología *f*.
economic [iːkəˈnɒmɪk] *adj* económico,-a; (*profitable*) rentable.
economical [iːkəˈnɒmɪkəl] *adj* económico,-a.
economics [iːkəˈnɒmɪks] *n sing* (*science*) economía *f*; *Educ* (ciencias *fpl*) económicas *fpl*.
economist [ɪˈkɒnəmɪst] *n* economista *mf*.
economize [ɪˈkɒnəmaɪz] *vi* economizar.
economy [ɪˈkɒnəmɪ] *n* 1 *Pol* **the e.**, la economía. 2 (*saving*) ahorro *m*; **e. class**, clase *f* turista.
ecosystem ['iːkɒsɪstəm] *n* ecosistema *m*.
ecstasy ['ekstəsɪ] *n* éxtasis *m*.
ecstatic [ek'stætɪk] *adj* extático,-a.
Ecuador ['ekwədɔːr] *n* Ecuador.
eczema ['eksɪmə] *n* eczema *m*.
eddy ['edɪ] I *n* remolino *m*. II *vi* arremolinarse.
edge [edʒ] I *n* borde *m*; (*of knife*) filo *m*; (*of coin*) canto *m*; (*of water*) orilla *f*; **on the e. of town**, en las afueras de la ciudad; **to have the e. on sb**, llevar ventaja a algn; *fig* **to be on e.**, tener los nervios de punta. II *vtr* *Sew* ribetear. III *vi* **to e. closer**, acercarse lentamente; **to e. forward**, avanzar poco a poco.
edgeways ['edʒweɪz] *adv* de lado; *fig* **I couldn't get a word in e.**, no pude decir ni pío.
edging ['edʒɪŋ] *n* borde *m*; *Sew* ribete *m*.
edgy ['edʒɪ] *adj* (**edgier, edgiest**) nervioso,-a.
edible ['edɪbəl] *adj* comestible.
edict ['iːdɪkt] *Hist n* edicto *m*; *Jur* decreto *m*.
Edinburgh ['edɪnbrə] *n* Edimburgo.
edit ['edɪt] *vtr* 1 (*prepare for printing*) preparar para la imprenta. 2 (*rewrite*) corregir; **to e. sth out**, suprimir algo. 3 *Press* ser redactor,-a de. 4 *Cin Rad TV* montar; (*cut*) cortar.
edition [ɪˈdɪʃən] *n* edición *f*.
editor ['edɪtər] *n* (*of book*) editor,-a *m,f*; *Press* redactor, -a *m,f*; *Cin TV* montador,-a *m,f*.
editorial [edɪˈtɔːrɪəl] I *adj* editorial; **e. staff**, redacción *f*. II *n* editorial *m*.
educate ['edjʊkeɪt] *vtr* educar.
educated ['edjʊkeɪtɪd] *adj* culto,-a.
education [edjʊˈkeɪʃən] *n* 1 (*schooling*) enseñanza *f*; **adult e.**, educación *f* de

adultos; **Ministry of E.**, Ministerio *m* de Educación. **2** *(training)* formación *f*. **3** *(studies)* estudios *mpl*. **4** *(culture)* cultura *f*.

educational [edjʊ'keɪʃənəl] *adj* educativo,-a, educacional.

eel [iːl] *n* anguila *f*.

eerie ['ɪərɪ] *adj* (**eerier**, **eeriest**) siniestro,-a.

efface [ɪ'feɪs] *vtr* borrar.

effect [ɪ'fekt] **I** *n* **1** efecto *m*; **in e.**, efectivamente; **to come into e.**, entrar en vigor; **to have an e. on**, afectar a; **to no e.**, sin resultado alguno; **to take e.**, *(drug)* surtir efecto; *(law)* entrar en vigor. **2** *(impression)* impresión *f*. **3** effects, *(possessions)* efectos *mpl*. **II** *vtr fml* provocar.

effective [ɪ'fektɪv] *adj* **1** *(successful)* eficaz. **2** *(real)* efectivo,-a. **3** *(impressive)* impresionante. ◆**effectively** *adv* **1** *(successfully)* eficazmente. **2** *(in fact)* en efecto.

effeminate [ɪ'femɪnɪt] *adj* afeminado,-a.

effervescent [efə'vesənt] *adj* efervescente.

efficiency [ɪ'fɪʃənsɪ] *n* (of person) eficacia *f*; (of machine) rendimiento *m*.

efficient [ɪ'fɪʃənt] *adj* eficaz, eficiente; *(machine)* de buen rendimiento.

effigy ['efɪdʒɪ] *n* efigie *f*.

effluent ['efluənt] *n* vertidos *mpl*.

effort ['efət] *n* **1** esfuerzo *m*; **to make an e.**, hacer un esfuerzo, esforzarse. **2** *(attempt)* intento *m*.

effortless ['efətlɪs] *adj* sin esfuerzo.

effrontery [ɪ'frʌntərɪ] *n* desfachatez *f*.

effusive [ɪ'fjuːsɪv] *adj* efusivo,-a.

eg [iː'dʒiː] *abbr* of **exempli gratia**, p. ej.

egalitarian [ɪgælɪ'teərɪən] *adj* igualitario,-a.

egg [eg] **I** *n* huevo *m*; *fam fig* **to put all one's eggs in one basket**, jugárselo todo a una carta; **e. cup**, huevera *f*; **e. timer**, reloj *m* de arena; **e. white**, clara *f* de huevo. **II** *vtr* **to e. sb on (to do sth)**, empujar a algn (a hacer algo).

eggplant ['egplɑːnt] *n US* berenjena *f*.

eggshell ['egʃel] *n* cáscara *f* de huevo.

ego ['iːgəʊ, 'egəʊ] *n* **1** ego *m*; *fam* **e. trip**, autobombo *m*. **2** *fam* amor propio.

egocentric(al) [iːgəʊ'sentrɪk(əl)] *adj* egocéntrico,-a.

egoism ['iːgəʊɪzəm] *n* egoísmo *m*.

egoist ['iːgəʊɪst] *n* egoísta *mf*.

egotistic(al) [iːgəʊ'tɪstɪk(əl)] *adj* egotista.

Egypt ['iːdʒɪpt] *n* Egipto.

Egyptian [ɪ'dʒɪpʃən] *adj & n* egipcio,-a *(m,f)*.

eiderdown ['aɪdədaʊn] *n* edredón *m*.

eight [eɪt] *adj & n* ocho *(m)* inv.

eighteen [eɪ'tiːn] *adj & n* dieciocho *(m)* inv.

eighteenth [eɪ'tiːnθ] **I** *adj & n* decimoctavo *(m,f)*. **II** *n* *(fraction)* decimoctavo *m*.

eighth [eɪtθ] **I** *adj & n* octavo,-a *(m,f)*. **II** *n* *(fraction)* octavo *m*.

eighty ['eɪtɪ] *adj & n* ochenta *(m)* inv.

Eire ['eərə] *n* Eire.

either ['aɪðər, 'iːðər] **I** *pron* **1** *(affirmative)* cualquiera; **e. of them**, cualquiera de los dos; **e. of us**, cualquiera de nosotros dos. **2** *(negative)* ninguno, ninguna, ni el uno ni el otro, ni la una ni la otra; **I don't want e. of them**, no quiero ninguno de los dos. **II** *adj* *(both)* cada, los dos, las dos; **on e. side**, en ambos lados; **in e. case**, en cualquier de los dos casos. **III** *conj* o; **e. ... or ...**, o ... o ...; **e. Friday or Saturday**, o (bien) el viernes o el sábado. **IV** *adv* *(after negative)* tampoco; **I don't want to do it e.**, yo tampoco quiero hacerlo.

ejaculate [ɪ'dʒækjʊleɪt] *vi (man)* eyacular.

eject [ɪ'dʒekt] **I** *vtr* expulsar. **II** *vi Av* eyectarse.

eke [iːk] *vtr* **to e. out a living**, ganarse la vida a duras penas.

elaborate [ɪ'læbəreɪt] **I** *vtr* **1** *(devise)* elaborar. **2** *(explain)* explicar detalladamente. **II** *vi* explicarse; **to e. on sth**, explicar algo con más detalles. **III** [ɪ'læbərɪt] *adj* **1** *(complicated)* complicado,-a. **2** *(detailed)* detallado,-a; *(style)* esmerado,-a.

elapse [ɪ'læps] *vi* transcurrir, pasar.

elastic [ɪ'læstɪk] **I** *adj* elástico,-a; *fig* flexible; **e. band**, goma elástica. **II** *n* elástico *m*.

Elastoplast® [ɪ'lɑːstəplɑːst] *n* tirita *f*.

elated [ɪ'leɪtɪd] *adj* eufórico,-a.

elation [ɪ'leɪʃən] *n* regocijo *m*.

elbow ['elbəʊ] **I** *n* **1** codo *m*; *fig* **e. room**, espacio *m*. **2** *(bend)* recodo *m*. **II** *vtr* **to e. sb**, dar un codazo a algn.

elder¹ ['eldər] **I** *adj* mayor. **II** *n* the elders, los ancianos.

elder² ['eldər] *n Bot* saúco *m*.

elderly ['eldəlɪ] **I** *adj* anciano,-a. **II** *npl* the e., los ancianos.

eldest ['eldɪst] **I** *adj* mayor. **II** *n* el *or* la mayor.

elect [ɪ'lekt] **I** *vtr* **1** *Pol* elegir. **2** **to e. to do sth**, *(choose)* decidir hacer algo. **II** *adj* the president e., el presidente electo.

election [ɪ'lekʃən] **I** *n* elección *f*; **general e.**, elecciones *fpl* generales. **II** *adj* electoral.

electioneering [ɪlekʃə'nɪərɪŋ] *n* electoralismo *m*.

elector [ɪ'lektər] *n* elector,-a *m,f*.

electoral [ɪ'lektərəl] *adj* electoral.

electorate [ɪ'lektərɪt] *n* electorado *m*.

electric [ɪ'lektrɪk] *adj* **1** eléctrico,-a; **e. blanket**, manta eléctrica; **e. chair**, silla eléctrica; **e. shock**, electrochoque *m*. **2** *fig* electrizante.

electrical [ɪ'lektrɪkəl] *adj* eléctrico,-a.
electrician [ɪlek'trɪʃən] *n* electricista *mf*.
electricity [ɪlek'trɪsɪtɪ] *n* electricidad *f*; **e. bill**, recibo *m* de la luz.
electrify [ɪ'lektrɪfaɪ] *vtr* **1** (*railway line*) electrificar. **2** *fig* (*excite*) electrizar.
electrocute [ɪ'lektrəkjuːt] *vtr* electrocutar.
electron [ɪ'lektrɒn] *n* electrón *m*.
electronic [ɪlek'trɒnɪk] *adj* electrónico,-a.
electronics [ɪlek'trɒnɪks] *n* **1** (*science*) electrónica *f*. **2** (*of machine*) componentes *mpl* electrónicos.
elegant ['elɪgənt] *adj* elegante.
element ['elɪmənt] *n* **1** elemento *m*. **2** (*part*) parte *f*. **3** (*electrical*) resistencia *f*. **4** *fam fig* **to be in one's e.**, estar en su salsa.
elementary [elɪ'mentərɪ] *adj* (*basic*) elemental; (*not developed*) rudimentario,-a; (*easy*) fácil; **e. school**, escuela primaria.
elephant ['elɪfənt] *n* elefante *m*.
elevate ['elɪveɪt] *vtr* elevar; (*in rank*) ascender.
elevation [elɪ'veɪʃən] *n* **1** elevación *f*. **2** *Archit* alzado *m*. **3** (*above sea level*) altitud *f*.
elevator ['elɪveɪtər] *n US* ascensor *m*.
eleven [ɪ'levən] *adj & once* (*m*) *inv*.
elevenses [ɪ'levənzɪz] *npl fam* bocadillo *m* de las once.
eleventh [ɪ'levənθ] **I** *adj & nm,f* undécimo,-a. **II** *n* (*fraction*) undécimo *m*.
elicit [ɪ'lɪsɪt] *vtr* obtener.
eligible ['elɪdʒəbəl] *adj* apto,-a; **he isn't e. to vote**, no tiene derecho al voto.
eliminate [ɪ'lɪmɪneɪt] *vtr* eliminar.
elite [ɪ'liːt] *n* elite *f*.
elitist [ɪ'liːtɪst] *adj* elitista.
elm [elm] *n* olmo *m*.
elocution [elə'kjuːʃən] *n* elocución *f*.
elongate ['iːlɒngeɪt] *vtr* alargar.
elope [ɪ'ləʊp] *vi* fugarse para casarse.
eloquent ['eləkwənt] *adj* elocuente.
else [els] *adv* **1** **anyone e.**, alguien más; **anything e.**?, ¿algo más?; **everything e.**, todo lo demás; **no-one e.**, nadie más; **someone e.**, otro,-a; **something e.**, otra cosa, algo más; **somewhere e.**, en otra parte; **what e.**?, ¿qué mas?; **where e.**?, ¿en qué otro sitio? **2** **or e.**, (*otherwise*) si no.
elsewhere [els'weər] *adv* en otra parte.
elucidate [ɪ'luːsɪdeɪt] *vtr* aclarar.
elude [ɪ'luːd] *vtr* **1** (*escape*) eludir; **his name eludes me**, no consigo acordarme de su nombre. **2** (*avoid*) esquivar.
elusive [ɪ'luːsɪv] *adj* esquivo,-a; (*evasive*) evasivo,-a.
emaciated [ɪ'meɪsɪeɪtɪd] *adj* demacrado,-a.
emanate ['eməneɪt] *vi* provenir (*from*, de).
emancipate [ɪ'mænsɪpeɪt] *vtr* emancipar.

emancipation [ɪmænsɪ'peɪʃən] *n* emancipación *f*.
embankment [ɪm'bæŋkmənt] *n* **1** (*made of earth*) terraplén *m*. **2** (*of river*) dique *m*.
embargo [em'bɑːgəʊ] *n* (*pl* **embargoes**) embargo *m*.
embark [em'bɑːk] **I** *vtr* (*merchandize*) embarcar. **II** *vi* embarcar, embarcarse; *fig* **to e. upon**, emprender; (*sth difficult*) embarcarse en.
embarkation [embɑː'keɪʃən] *n* embarque *m*.
embarrass [ɪm'bærəs] *vtr* avergonzar.
embarrassed [ɪm'bærəst] *adj* avergonzado,-a.
embarrassing [ɪm'bærəsɪŋ] *adj* embarazoso,-a.
embarrassment [ɪm'bærəsmənt] *n* vergüenza *f*.
embassy ['embəsɪ] *n* embajada *f*.
embed [ɪm'bed] *vtr* (*jewels*) incrustar; *fig* grabar.
embellish [ɪm'belɪʃ] *vtr* embellecer; (*story*) exagerar.
ember ['embər] *n* ascua *f*, rescoldo *m*.
embezzle [ɪm'bezəl] *vtr* desfalcar, malversar.
embezzlement [ɪm'bezəlmənt] *n* malversación *f*.
embitter [ɪm'bɪtər] *vtr* amargar.
embittered [ɪm'bɪtəd] *adj* amargado,-a, resentido,-a.
emblem ['embləm] *n* emblema *m*.
embody [ɪm'bɒdɪ] *vtr* **1** (*include*) abarcar. **2** (*personify*) encarnar.
embossed [ɪm'bɒst] *adj* en relieve.
embrace [ɪm'breɪs] **I** *vtr* **1** abrazar. **2** (*accept*) adoptar. **3** (*include*) abarcar. **II** *vi* abrazarse. **III** *n* abrazo *m*.
embroider [ɪm'brɔɪdər] *vtr* **1** *Sew* bordar. **2** *fig* (*story, truth*) adornar, embellecer.
embroidery [ɪm'brɔɪdərɪ] *n* bordado *m*.
embryo ['embrɪəʊ] *n* embrión *m*.
emerald ['emərəld] *n* esmeralda *f*.
emerge [ɪ'mɜːdʒ] *vi* salir; (*problem*) surgir; **it emerged that ...**, resultó que ....
emergence [ɪ'mɜːdʒəns] *n* aparición *f*.
emergency [ɪ'mɜːdʒənsɪ] *n* emergencia *f*; *Med* urgencia *f*; **in an e.**, en caso de emergencia; **e. exit**, salida *f* de emergencia; **e. landing**, aterrizaje forzoso; **e. measures**, medidas *fpl* de urgencia; *Aut* **e. stop**, frenazo *m* en seco; *Pol* **state of e.**, estado *m* de excepción.
emery ['emərɪ] *n* **e. board**, lima *f* de uñas.
emigrant ['emɪgrənt] *n* emigrante *mf*.
emigrate ['emɪgreɪt] *vi* emigrar.
emigration [emɪ'greɪʃən] *n* emigración *f*.
eminent ['emɪnənt] *adj* eminente.
emission [ɪ'mɪʃən] *n* emisión *f*.
emit [ɪ'mɪt] *vtr* (*signals*) emitir; (*smells*) despedir; (*sound*) producir.

emotion |ɪ'məʊʃən| n emoción f.
emotional |ɪ'məʊʃənəl| adj 1 emocional.
2 (moving) conmovedor,-a.
emotive |ɪ'məʊtɪv| adj emotivo,-a.
emperor |'empərər| n emperador m.
emphasis |'emfəsɪs| n (pl **emphases**
|'emfəsiːz|) énfasis m; **to place e. on sth,**
hacer hincapié en algo.
emphasize |'emfəsaɪz| vtr subrayar, hacer hincapié en; (insist) insistir; (highlight)
hacer resaltar.
emphatic |em'fætɪk| adj (forceful)
enfático,-a; (convinced) categórico,-a.
◆**emphatically** adv categóricamente.
empire |'empaɪər| n imperio m.
employ |ɪm'plɔɪ| vtr emplear; (time) ocupar.
employee |em'plɔɪiː, emplɔɪ'iː| n
empleado,-a m, f.
employer |ɪm'plɔɪər| n patrón,-ona m, f.
employment |ɪm'plɔɪmənt| n empleo m;
e. agency, agencia f de colocaciones; **full
e.,** pleno empleo.
empower |ɪm'paʊər| vtr autorizar.
empress |'emprɪs| n emperatriz f.
emptiness |'emptɪnɪs| n vacío m.
empty |'emptɪ| I adj (emptier, emptiest)
vacío,-a; **an e. house,** una casa deshabitada; **e. promises,** promesas fpl vanas. II
vtr vaciar. III vi 1 vaciarse. 2 (river) desembocar (into, en). IV npl **empties,**
envases vacíos.
empty-handed |emptɪ'hændɪd| adj con
las manos vacías.
emulate |'emjʊleɪt| vtr emular.
emulsion |ɪ'mʌlʃən| n emulsión f; **e.
paint,** pintura f mate.
enable |ɪn'eɪbəl| vtr permitir.
enact |ɪn'ækt| vtr (play) representar; (law)
promulgar.
enamel |ɪ'næməl| n esmalte m.
enamoured, US **enamored** |ɪ'næməd|
adj enamorado,-a; **to be e. of** or **by sth,**
encantarle algo a algn.
encase |ɪn'keɪs| vtr **encased in,** revestido
de.
enchant |ɪn'tʃɑːnt| vtr encantar.
enchanting |ɪn'tʃɑːntɪŋ| adj
encantador,-a.
encircle |ɪn'sɜːkəl| vtr rodear.
enclave |'enkleɪv| n enclave m.
enclose |ɪn'kləʊz| vtr 1 (surround) rodear.
2 (fence in) cercar. 3 (in envelope) adjuntar; **please find enclosed,** le enviamos
adjunto.
enclosure |ɪn'kləʊʒər| n 1 (fenced area)
cercado m. 2 (in envelope) documento adjunto. 3 (of racecourse) recinto m.
encompass |ɪn'kʌmpəs| vtr abarcar.
encore |'ɒŋkɔːr| I interj ¡otra!, ¡bis! II n
repetición f, bis m.
encounter |ɪn'kaʊntər| I n (meeting)
encuentro m. II vtr encontrar, encontrarse con; (problems) tropezar con.

encourage |ɪn'kʌrɪdʒ| vtr 1 (person) animar. 2 (tourism, trade) fomentar.
encouragement |ɪn'kʌrɪdʒmənt| n estímulo m.
encroach |ɪn'krəʊtʃ| vi **to e. on,** (territory) invadir; (rights) usurpar; (time, freedom) quitar.
encrusted |ɪn'krʌstɪd| adj incrustado,-a
(with, de).
encumber |ɪn'kʌmbər| vtr estorbar; (with
debts) gravar.
encyclop(a)edia |ensaɪkləʊ'piːdɪə| n
enciclopedia f.
end |end| I n 1 (of stick) punta f; (of
street) final m; (of table) extremo m; fig **to
make ends meet,** llegar a final de mes;
fig **it makes my hair stand on e.,** me
pone el pelo de punta. 2 (conclusion) fin
m, final m; **in the e.,** al final; **for hours
on e.,** hora tras hora; **no e. of,** un sinfín
de; **to bring an e. to sth,** poner fin a
algo; **to put an e. to,** acabar con. 3 (aim)
objetivo m, fin m; **to no e.,** en vano. II
vtr acabar, terminar. III vi acabarse,
terminarse. ◆**end up** vi terminar; **it
ended up in the dustbin,** fue a parar al
cubo de la basura; **to e. up doing sth,**
terminar por hacer algo.
endanger |ɪn'deɪndʒər| vtr poner en peligro.
endangered |ɪn'deɪndʒəd| adj en peligro.
endearing |ɪn'dɪərɪŋ| adj simpático,-a.
endeavour, US **endeavor** |ɪn'devər| I n
esfuerzo m. II vtr intentar, procurar.
ending |'endɪŋ| n final m.
endive |'endaɪv| n Bot 1 endibia f. 2 US
escarola f.
endless |'endlɪs| adj interminable.
endorse |ɪn'dɔːs| vtr 1 Fin endosar. 2
(approve) aprobar; (support) apoyar.
endorsement |ɪn'dɔːsmənt| n   1   Fin
endoso m. 2 Aut nota f de sanción. 3 (approval) aprobación f.
endow |ɪn'daʊ| vtr dotar; **to be endowed
with,** estar dotado,-a de.
endurance |ɪn'djʊərəns| n resistencia f.
endure |ɪn'djʊər| I vtr (bear) aguantar, soportar. II vi perdurar.
enemy |'enəmɪ| adj & n enemigo,-a
(m,f).
energetic |enə'dʒetɪk| adj enérgico,-a.
energy |'enədʒɪ| n energía f.
enforce |ɪn'fɔːs| vtr (law) hacer cumplir.
enforcement |ɪn'fɔːsmənt| n aplicación f.
engage |ɪn'geɪdʒ| vtr 1 (hire) contratar. 2
(attention) llamar. 3 (in conversation) entablar. 4 Tech engranar; Aut **to e. the
clutch,** pisar el embrague.
engaged |ɪn'geɪdʒd| adj 1 (betrothed)
prometido,-a; **to get e.,** prometerse. 2
(busy) ocupado,-a; Tel **it's e.,** está comunicando.
engagement |ɪn'geɪdʒmənt| n 1 (betrothal) petición f de mano; (period) no-

viazgo *m*; **e. ring,** anillo *m* de compromiso. **2** (*appointment*) cita *f*. **3** *Mil* combate *m*.

engaging [ɪnˈɡeɪdʒɪŋ] *adj* simpático,-a, agradable.

engender [ɪnˈdʒendər] *vtr* engendrar.

engine [ˈendʒɪn] *n* motor *m*; *Rail* locomotora *f*; **e. room,** sala *f* de máquinas; **e. driver,** maquinista *mf*.

engineer [endʒɪˈnɪər] **I** *n* **1** ingeniero,-a *m, f*; **civil e.,** ingeniero de caminos. **2** *US Rail* maquinista *mf*. **II** *vtr fig* (*contrive*) maquinar.

engineering [endʒɪˈnɪərɪŋ] *n* ingeniería *f*; **electrical e.,** electrotecnia *f*; **civil e.,** ingeniería civil.

England [ˈɪŋɡlənd] *n* Inglaterra *f*.

English [ˈɪŋɡlɪʃ] **I** *adj* inglés,-esa. **II** *n* **1** (*language*) inglés *m*. **2** *pl* the **E.,** los ingleses.

Englishman [ˈɪŋɡlɪʃmən] *n* inglés *m*.

English-speaking [ˈɪŋɡlɪʃspiːkɪŋ] *adj* de habla inglesa.

Englishwoman [ˈɪŋɡlɪʃwumən] *n* inglesa *f*.

engraving [ɪnˈɡreɪvɪŋ] *n* grabado *m*.

engrossed [ɪnˈɡrəust] *adj* absorto,-a (**in,** en).

engulf [ɪnˈɡʌlf] *vtr* tragarse.

enhance [ɪnˈhɑːns] *vtr* (*beauty*) realzar; (*power, chances*) aumentar.

enigma [ɪˈnɪɡmə] *n* enigma *m*.

enjoy [ɪnˈdʒɔɪ] **I** *vtr* **1** disfrutar de; **to e. oneself,** pasarlo bien. **2** (*benefit from*) gozar de.

enjoyable [ɪnˈdʒɔɪəbəl] *adj* agradable; (*amusing*) divertido,-a.

enjoyment [ɪnˈdʒɔɪmənt] *n* placer *m*, gusto *m*.

enlarge [ɪnˈlɑːdʒ] **I** *vtr* extender, ampliar; *Phot* ampliar. **II** *vi* to e. **upon a subject,** extenderse sobre un tema.

enlargement [ɪnˈlɑːdʒmənt] *n* *Phot* ampliación *f*.

enlighten [ɪnˈlaɪtən] *vtr* iluminar.

enlightened [ɪnˈlaɪtənd] *adj* **1** (*learned*) culto,-a; (*informed*) bien informado,-a. **2** *Hist* ilustrado,-a.

enlightenment [ɪnˈlaɪtənmənt] *n* **the Age of E.,** el Siglo de las Luces.

enlist [ɪnˈlɪst] **I** *vtr Mil* reclutar; **to e. sb's help,** conseguir ayuda de algn. **II** *vi Mil* alistarse.

enmity [ˈenmɪtɪ] *n* enemistad *f*, hostilidad *f*.

enormous [ɪˈnɔːməs] *adj* enorme. ◆**enormously** *adv* enormemente; **I enjoyed myself e.,** lo pasé genial.

enough [ɪˈnʌf] **I** *adj* bastante, suficiente; **e. books,** bastantes libros; **e. money,** bastante dinero; **have we got e. petrol?,** ¿tenemos suficiente gasolina? **II** *adv* bastante; **oddly e. ...,** lo curioso es que ...; **sure e.,** en efecto. **III** *n* lo bastante,

lo suficiente; **e. to live on,** lo suficiente para vivir; **it isn't e.,** no basta; **more than e.,** más que suficiente; *fam* **e. is e.,** ya está!; *fam* **I've had e.!,** estoy harto!

enquire [ɪnˈkwaɪər] *vi* preguntar.

enquiry [ɪnˈkwaɪərɪ] *n* **1** (*question*) pregunta *f*; **to make an e.,** preguntar; **enquiries,** información *f*. **2** (*investigation*) investigación *f*.

enrage [ɪnˈreɪdʒ] *vtr* enfurecer.

enrich [ɪnˈrɪtʃ] *vtr* enriquecer.

enrol, *US* **enroll** [ɪnˈrəul] **I** *vtr* matricular. **II** *vi* matricularse, inscribirse.

enrolment [ɪnˈrəulmənt] *n* matrícula *f*.

en route [ɒnˈruːt] *adv* en or por el camino.

ensign [ˈensaɪn] *n* (*flag*) bandera *f*; *Naut* pabellón *m*.

enslave [ɪnˈsleɪv] *vtr* esclavizar.

ensue [ɪnˈsjuː] *vi* **1** (*follow*) seguir. **2** (*result*) resultar (**from,** de).

ensure [ɪnˈʃuər] *vtr* asegurar.

entail [ɪnˈteɪl] *vtr* (*involve*) suponer.

entangle [ɪnˈtæŋɡəl] *vtr* enredar.

enter [ˈentər] **I** *vtr* **1** (*go into*) entrar en; *fig* (*join*) ingresar en. **2** (*write down*) apuntar, anotar. **3** **to e. one's name for a course,** (*register*) matricularse en un curso. **4** *Comput* dar entrada a. **II** *vi* entrar. ◆**enter into** *vtr* (*agreement*) firmar; (*negotiations*) iniciar; (*bargain*) cerrar. **2** (*relations*) establecer; (*conversation*) entablar.

enterprise [ˈentəpraɪz] *n* empresa *f*; **free e.,** libre empresa; **private e.,** iniciativa privada; (*as a whole*) el sector privado; **public e.,** el sector público.

enterprising [ˈentəpraɪzɪŋ] *adj* emprendedor,-a.

entertain [entəˈteɪn] **I** *vtr* **1** (*amuse*) divertir. **2** (*consider*) considerar; **to e. an idea,** abrigar una idea. **II** *vi* tener invitados.

entertainer [entəˈteɪnər] *n* artista *mf*.

entertaining [entəˈteɪnɪŋ] *adj* divertido, -a.

entertainment [entəˈteɪnmənt] *n* **1** diversión *f*. **2** *Theat* espectáculo *m*.

enthralling [ɪnˈθrɔːlɪŋ] *adj* fascinante.

enthuse [ɪnˈθjuːz] *vi* entusiasmarse (**over,** por).

enthusiasm [ɪnˈθjuːzɪæzəm] *n* entusiasmo *m*.

enthusiast [ɪnˈθjuːzɪæst] *n* entusiasta *mf*.

enthusiastic [ɪnθjuːzɪˈæstɪk] *adj* entusiasta; (*praise*) caluroso,-a; **to be e. about sth,** entusiasmarse por algo.

entice [ɪnˈtaɪs] *vtr* seducir, atraer.

enticing [ɪnˈtaɪsɪŋ] *adj* atractivo,-a, tentador,-a.

entire [ɪnˈtaɪər] *adj* entero,-a, todo,-a. ◆**entirely** *adv* **1** (*completely*) totalmente. **2** (*solely*) exclusivamente.

entirety [ɪnˈtaɪərɪtɪ] *n* **in its e.,** en su totalidad.

entitle |ɪnˈtaɪtəl| vtr 1 dar derecho a; **to be entitled to,** tener derecho a. 2 *(book etc)* titular.

entity |ˈentɪtɪ| n entidad f.

entourage |ɒntʊˈrɑːʒ| n séquito m.

entrails |ˈentreɪlz| npl tripas fpl; fig entrañas fpl.

entrance¹ |ˈentrəns| n 1 entrada f; **e. fee,** *(to museum etc)* entrada; *(to organization)* cuota f. 2 *(admission)* ingreso m; **e. examination,** examen m de ingreso.

entrance² |ɪnˈtrɑːns| vtr encantar.

entrant |ˈentrənt| n *(in competition)* participante mf; *(applicant)* aspirante mf.

entreat |ɪnˈtriːt| vtr fml suplicar, rogar.

entrenched |ɪnˈtrentʃt| adj firmemente enraizado,-a.

entrepreneur |ɒntrəprəˈnɜːr| n empresario, -a m,f.

entrust |ɪnˈtrʌst| vtr encargar (**with,** de); **to e. sth to sb,** dejar algo al cuidado de algn.

entry |ˈentrɪ| n 1 *(entrance)* entrada f; **no e.,** dirección prohibida. 2 *(in competition)* participante mf.

enumerate |ɪˈnjuːməreɪt| vtr enumerar.

enunciate |ɪˈnʌnsɪeɪt| vtr *(words)* articular; *(ideas)* formular.

envelop |ɪnˈveləp| vtr envolver.

envelope |ˈenvələʊp| n sobre m.

envious |ˈenvɪəs| adj envidioso,-a; **to feel e.,** tener envidia.

environment |ɪnˈvaɪərənmənt| n medio m ambiente.

environmental |ɪnvaɪərənˈmentəl| adj medioambiental.

envisage |ɪnˈvɪzɪdʒ| vtr *(imagine)* imaginarse; *(foresee)* prever.

envoy |ˈenvɔɪ| n enviado,-a m,f.

envy |ˈenvɪ| I n envidia f. II vtr envidiar, tener envidia de.

enzyme |ˈenzaɪm| n enzima m.

ephemeral |ɪˈfemərəl| adj efímero,-a.

epic |ˈepɪk| I n epopeya f. II adj épico,-a.

epidemic |epɪˈdemɪk| n epidemia f; fig *(of crime etc)* ola f.

epilepsy |ˈepɪlepsɪ| n epilepsia f.

epilogue, US **epilog** |ˈepɪlɒg| n epílogo m.

episode |ˈepɪsəʊd| n episodio m.

epistle |ɪˈpɪsəl| n epístola f.

epitaph |ˈepɪtɑːf| n epitafio m.

epitome |ɪˈpɪtəmɪ| n fml personificación f.

epitomize |ɪˈpɪtəmaɪz| vtr fml personificar.

epoch |ˈiːpɒk| n época f.

equable |ˈekwəbəl| adj 1 *(person)* ecuánime. 2 *(climate)* uniforme.

equal |ˈiːkwəl| I adj igual; **to be e. to the occasion,** estar a la altura de las circunstancias; **e. pay,** igualdad f de salarios. II n igual mf; **to treat sb as an e.,** tratar a algn de igual a igual. III vtr 1 Math equivaler. 2 *(match)* igualar.
◆**equally** adv igualmente; **e. pretty,** igual de bonito; **to share sth e.,** dividir algo en partes iguales.

equality |iːˈkwɒlɪtɪ| n igualdad f.

equalize |ˈiːkwəlaɪz| I vi Ftb empatar. II vtr igualar.

equalizer |ˈiːkwəlaɪzər| n Ftb gol m del empate; *(of sound)* ecualizador m.

equanimity |ekwəˈnɪmɪtɪ| n ecuanimidad f.

equate |ɪˈkweɪt| vtr equiparar, comparar (**to, a, con**).

equation |ɪˈkweɪʒən, ɪˈkweɪʃən| n Math ecuación f.

equator |ɪˈkweɪtər| n ecuador m.

equatorial |ekwəˈtɔːrɪəl| adj ecuatorial.

equestrian |ɪˈkwestrɪən| adj ecuestre.

equilibrium |iːkwɪˈlɪbrɪəm| n equilibrio m.

equinox |ˈiːkwɪnɒks| n equinoccio m.

equip |ɪˈkwɪp| vtr *(with tools, machines)* equipar; *(with food)* proveer.

equipment |ɪˈkwɪpmənt| n *(materials)* equipo m; **office e.,** material m de oficina.

equipped |ɪˈkwɪpt| adj *(with tools, machines)* equipado,-a; *(with skills)* dotado,-a.

equitable |ˈekwɪtəbəl| adj equitativo,-a.

equities |ˈekwɪtɪz| npl acciones ordinarias.

equivalent |ɪˈkwɪvələnt| adj & n equivalente *(m)*; **to be e. to,** equivaler a, ser equivalente a.

equivocal |ɪˈkwɪvəkəl| adj equívoco,-a.

era |ˈɪərə| n era f.

eradicate |ɪˈrædɪkeɪt| vtr erradicar.

erase |ɪˈreɪz| vtr borrar.

eraser |ɪˈreɪzər| n goma f de borrar.

erect |ɪˈrekt| I adj 1 *(upright)* erguido,-a. 2 *(penis)* erecto,-a. II vtr *(monument)* levantar, erigir.

erection |ɪˈrekʃən| n 1 *(of building)* construcción f. 2 *(penis)* erección f.

ermine |ˈɜːmɪn| n armiño m.

erode |ɪˈrəʊd| vtr 1 *(rock, soil)* erosionar. 2 *(metal)* corroer, desgastar; fig *(power, confidence)* hacer perder.

erosion |ɪˈrəʊʒən| n Geol erosión f.

erotic |ɪˈrɒtɪk| adj erótico,-a.

err |ɜːr| vi errar; **to e. on the side of ...,** pecar por exceso de ....

errand |ˈerənd| n recado m; **e. boy,** recadero m.

erratic |ɪˈrætɪk| adj *(performance, behaviour)* irregular; *(weather)* muy variable; *(person)* caprichoso,-a.

erroneous |ɪˈrəʊnɪəs| adj erróneo,-a.

error |ˈerər| n error m, equivocación f.

erupt |ɪˈrʌpt| vi 1 *(volcano)* entrar en erupción; *(violence)* estallar. 2 **his skin erupted in a rash,** le salió una erupción.

eruption [ɪ'rʌpʃən] n erupción f.

escalate ['eskəleɪt] vi (war) intensificarse; (prices) aumentar; (change) convertirse (into, en).

escalation [eskə'leɪʃən] n (of war) intensificación f, escalada f; (of prices) subida f.

escalator ['eskəleɪtər] n escalera mecánica.

escalope ['eskələp] n escalope m.

escapade ['eskəpeɪd] n aventura f.

escape [ɪs'keɪp] I n huída f, fuga f; (of gas) escape m; e. route, vía f de escape. II vi escaparse. III vtr 1 (avoid) evitar, huir de; to e. punishment, librarse del castigo. 2 fig his name escapes me, no recuerdo su nombre.

escapism [ɪ'skeɪpɪzəm] n evasión f.

escort ['eskɔːt] I n 1 (companion) acompañante mf. 2 Mil escolta f. II [ɪs'kɔːt] vtr 1 (accompany) acompañar. 2 (protect) escoltar.

Eskimo ['eskɪməʊ] adj & n esquimal (mf).

esoteric [esəʊ'terɪk] adj esotérico,-a.

especial [ɪ'speʃəl] adj especial.
◆**especially** adv especialmente, sobre todo.

espionage ['espɪənɑːʒ] n espionaje m.

esplanade [esplə'neɪd] n paseo marítimo.

espouse [ɪ'spaʊz] vtr fml (cause) abrazar, adoptar.

espresso [e'spresəʊ] n e. (coffee), café m exprés.

esquire [ɪ'skwaɪər] n GB señor m; Timothy Whiteman E., Sr. Don Timothy Whiteman.

essay ['eseɪ] n Educ redacción f.

essence ['esəns] n esencia f; in e., esencialmente.

essential [ɪ'senʃəl] I adj esencial, imprescindible. II n necesidad básica; the essentials, lo fundamental.
◆**essentially** adv esencialmente.

establish [ɪ'stæblɪʃ] vtr 1 (found) establecer; (business) montar. 2 Jur to e. a fact, probar un hecho; to e. the truth, demostrar la verdad.

established [ɪ'stæblɪʃt] adj (person) establecido,-a; (fact) conocido,-a.

establishment [ɪ'stæblɪʃmənt] n establecimiento m; the E., el sistema.

estate [ɪ'steɪt] n 1 (land) finca f; GB e. agent, agente mf inmobiliario,-a; GB e. car, coche m modelo familiar. 2 (housing) e., zona urbanizada. 3 (property) bienes mpl. 4 (inheritance) herencia f.

esteem [ɪ'stiːm] I n to hold sb in great e., apreciar mucho a algn. II vtr estimar.

esthetic [es'θetɪk] adj US estético,-a.

estimate ['estɪmɪt] I n (calculation) cálculo m; (likely cost of work) presupuesto m; rough e., cálculo aproximado. II ['estɪmeɪt] vtr calcular; fig pensar, creer.

estimation [estɪ'meɪʃən] n 1 (opinion) juicio m, opinión f. 2 (esteem) estima f.

estrange [ɪ'streɪndʒ] vtr to become estranged, alejarse (from, de).

Estremadura [estreɪmə'dʊrə] n Extremadura.

estuary ['estjʊərɪ] n estuario m.

etching ['etʃɪŋ] n aguafuerte m.

eternal [ɪ'tɜːnəl] adj eterno,-a, incesante; e. triangle, triángulo amoroso.

eternity [ɪ'tɜːnɪtɪ] n eternidad f.

ether ['iːθər] n éter m.

ethereal [ɪ'θɪərɪəl] adj etéreo,-a.

ethical ['eθɪkəl] adj ético,-a.

ethics ['eθɪks] n ética f.

Ethiopia [iːθɪ'əʊpɪə] n Etiopía.

ethnic ['eθnɪk] adj étnico,-a.

ethos ['iːθɒs] n carácter distintivo.

etiquette ['etɪket] n protocolo m, etiqueta f.

etymology [etɪ'mɒlədʒɪ] n etimología f.

eucalyptus [juːkə'lɪptəs] n eucalipto m.

euphemism ['juːfɪmɪzəm] n eufemismo m.

euphoria [juː'fɔːrɪə] n euforia f.

Eurocheque ['jʊərəʊtʃek] n eurocheque m.

Eurocrat ['jʊərəʊkræt] n eurócrata mf.

Euro-MP ['jʊərəʊempiː] n eurodiputado, -a m,f.

Europe ['jʊərəp] n Europa.

European [jʊərə'pɪən] adj & n europeo,-a (m,f); E. Economic Community, Comunidad Económica Europea.

euthanasia [juːθə'neɪzɪə] n eutanasia f.

evacuate [ɪ'vækjʊeɪt] vtr evacuar.

evacuation [ɪvækjʊ'eɪʃən] n evacuación f.

evade [ɪ'veɪd] vtr evadir.

evaluate [ɪ'væljʊeɪt] vtr evaluar.

evaluation [ɪvæljʊ'eɪʃən] n evaluación f.

evangelical [iːvæn'dʒelɪkəl] adj evangélico,-a.

evangelist [ɪ'vændʒɪlɪst] n evangelista mf.

evaporate [ɪ'væpəreɪt] I vtr evaporar; evaporated milk, leche condensada sin endulzar. II vi evaporarse; fig desvanecerse.

evasion [ɪ'veɪʒən] n 1 evasión f. 2 (evasive answer) evasiva f.

evasive [ɪ'veɪsɪv] adj evasivo,-a.

eve [iːv] n víspera f; on the e. of, en vísperas de.

even ['iːvən] I adj 1 (smooth) liso,-a; (level) llano,-a. 2 (regular) uniforme. 3 (equally balanced) igual; Sport to be e., ir empatados,-as; to get e. with sb, desquitarse con algn. 4 (number) par. 5 (at the same level) a nivel. 6 (quantity) exacto,-a. II adv 1 incluso, hasta, aun; e. now, incluso ahora; e. so, aun así; e. the children knew, hasta los niños lo sabían. 2 (negative) even more, siquiera; she can't e. write her name, ni siquiera sabe escribir su nombre; without e. speaking, sin hablar siquiera. **3** *(before comparative)* aun, todavía; **e. worse**, aun peor. **4 e. as**, mientras; **e. if**, incluso si; **e. though**, aunque. **III** *vtr* igualar.

evening ['i:vnɪŋ] *n* **1** *(early)* tarde *f*; *(late)* noche *f*; **in the e.**, por la tarde; **tomorrow e.**, mañana por la tarde; **e. class**, clase nocturna; **e. dress**, *(man)* traje *m* de etiqueta; *(woman)* traje de noche; **e. paper**, periódico vespertino. **2** *(greeting)* **good e.!**, *(early)* ¡buenas tardes!; *(late)* ¡buenas noches!

event [ɪ'vent] *n* **1** *(happening)* suceso *m*, acontecimiento *m*. **2** *(case)* caso *m*; **at all events**, en todo caso; **in the e. of fire**, en caso de incendio. **3** *Sport* prueba *f*.

eventful [ɪ'ventful] *adj* **an e. day**, *(busy)* un día agitado; *(memorable)* un día memorable.

eventual [ɪ'ventʃʊəl] *adj* *(ultimate)* final; *(resulting)* consiguiente. ◆**eventually** *adv* finalmente.

eventuality [ɪventʃʊ'ælɪtɪ] *n* eventualidad *f*.

ever ['evər] *adv* **1** nunca, jamás; **stronger than e.**, más fuerte que nunca. **2** *(interrogative)* alguna vez; **have you e. been there?**, ¿has estado allí alguna vez? **3** *(always)* siempre; **for e.**, para siempre; **for e. and e.**, para siempre jamás. **4** *(emphasis)* **how e. did you manage it?**, ¿cómo diablos lo conseguiste?; **why e. not?**, ¿por qué no?; *fam* **e. so, e. such**, muy; **thank you e. so much**, muchísimas gracias.

evergreen ['evəgri:n] **I** *adj* de hoja perenne. **II** *n* árbol *m* or planta *f* de hoja perenne.

everlasting [evə'lɑːstɪŋ] *adj* eterno,-a.

evermore [evə'mɔːr] *adv* **for e.**, para siempre jamás.

every ['evrɪ] *adj* **1** *(each)* cada; **e. now and then**, de vez en cuando; **e. day**, todos los días; **e. other day**, cada dos días; **e. one of you**, todos,-as vosotros,-as; **e. citizen**, todo ciudadano. **2 you had e. right to be angry**, tenías toda la razón para estar enfadado.

everybody ['evrɪbɒdɪ] *pron* todo el mundo, todos,-as.

everyday ['evrɪdeɪ] *adj* diario,-a, de todos los días; **an e. occurrence**, un suceso cotidiano.

everyone ['evrɪwʌn] *pron* todo el mundo, todos,-as.

everything ['evrɪθɪŋ] *pron* todo; **he eats e.**, come de todo; **she means e. to me**, ella lo es todo para mí.

everywhere ['evrɪweər] *adv* en todas partes, por todas partes.

evict [ɪ'vɪkt] *vtr* desahuciar.

evidence ['evɪdəns] *n* **1** *(proof)* evidencia *f*. **2** *Jur* testimonio *m*; **to give e.**, prestar declaración. **3** *(sign)* indicio *m*, señal *f*; **to be in e.**, dejarse notar.

evident ['evɪdənt] *adj* evidente, manifiesto,-a. ◆**evidently** *adv* evidentemente, al parecer.

evil ['i:vəl] **I** *adj* *(wicked)* malo,-a, malvado,-a; *(harmful)* nocivo,-a; *(unfortunate)* aciago,-a. **II** *n* mal *m*.

evocative [ɪ'vɒkətɪv] *adj* evocador,-a.

evoke [ɪ'vəʊk] *vtr* evocar.

evolution [i:və'lu:ʃən] *n* evolución *f*; *Biol* desarrollo *m*.

evolve [ɪ'vɒlv] **I** *vi* *(species)* evolucionar; *(ideas)* desarrollarse. **II** *vtr* desarrollar.

ewe [ju:] *n* oveja *f*.

ex [eks] *n* **her e.**, su ex marido; **his e.**, su ex mujer.

ex- [eks] *pref* ex, antiguo,-a; **ex-minister**, ex ministro *m*.

exacerbate [ɪg'zæsəbeɪt] *vtr* exacerbar.

exact [ɪg'zækt] **I** *adj* *(accurate)* exacto,-a; *(definition)* preciso,-a; **this e. spot**, ese mismo lugar. **II** *vtr* exigir. ◆**exactly** *adv* exactamente; precisamente; **e.!**, ¡exacto!

exacting [ɪg'zæktɪŋ] *adj* exigente.

exaggerate [ɪg'zædʒəreɪt] *vi & vtr* exagerar.

exaggeration [ɪgzædʒə'reɪʃən] *n* exageración *f*.

exalt [ɪg'zɔːlt] *vtr fml* exaltar.

exam [ɪg'zæm] *n fam* examen *m*.

examination [ɪgzæmɪ'neɪʃən] *n* **1** *Educ* examen *m*; **to sit an e.**, hacer un examen. **2** *Med* reconocimiento *m*. **3** *Jur* interrogatorio *m*.

examine [ɪg'zæmɪn] *vtr* *Educ* examinar; *(customs)* registrar; *Med* hacer un reconocimiento médico a; *Jur* interrogar.

examiner [ɪg'zæmɪnər] *n* examinador,-a *m,f*.

example [ɪg'zɑːmpəl] *n* ejemplo *m*; *(specimen)* ejemplar *m*; **for e.**, por ejemplo.

exasperate [ɪg'zɑːspəreɪt] *vtr* exasperar.

exasperation [ɪgzɑːspə'reɪʃən] *n* exasperación *f*.

excavate ['ekskəveɪt] *vtr* excavar.

excavation [ekskə'veɪʃən] *n* excavación *f*.

exceed [ek'si:d] *vtr* exceder, sobrepasar. ◆**exceedingly** *adv* extremadamente, sumamente.

excel [ɪk'sel] **I** *vi* sobresalir. **II** *vtr* superar.

excellency ['eksələnsɪ] *n* **His E.**, Su Excelencia.

excellent ['eksələnt] *adj* excelente.

except [ɪk'sept] **I** *prep* excepto, salvo; **e. for the little ones**, excepto los pequeños; **e. that ...**, salvo que .... **II** *vtr* exceptuar.

exception [ɪk'sepʃən] *n* **1** excepción *f*; **with the e. of**, a excepción de; **without e.**, sin excepción. **2** *(objection)* objeción *f*; **to take e. to sth**, ofenderse por algo.

exceptional [ɪk'sepʃənəl] *adj* excepcional.

excerpt [ek'sɜːpt] *n* extracto *m*.

excess [ɪk'ses] **I** *n* exceso *m*. **II** *adj* ['ekses] excedente; **e. baggage,** exceso *m* de equipaje; **e. fare,** suplemento *m*.

excessive [ɪk'sesɪv] *adj* excesivo,-a. ◆**excessively** *adv* excesivamente, en exceso.

exchange [ɪks'tʃeɪndʒ] **I** *n* 1 cambio *m*; **e. of ideas,** intercambio *m* de ideas; **in e. for,** a cambio de. 2 *Fin* **e. rate,** tipo *m* de cambio. 3 **(telephone) e.,** central telefónica. **II** 1 *vtr* intercambiar; **to e. blows,** golpearse. 2 *(prisoners)* canjear.

exchequer [ɪks'tʃekər] *n GB* **the E.,** Hacienda *f*; **Chancellor of the E.,** Ministro *m* de Hacienda.

excise ['eksaɪz] *n* impuesto *m* sobre el consumo; **e. duty,** derechos *mpl* de aduana.

excitable [ɪk'saɪtəbəl] *adj* excitable.

excite [ɪk'saɪt] *vtr (stimulate)* excitar; *(move)* emocionar; *(enthuse)* entusiasmar; *(arouse)* provocar.

excitement [ɪk'saɪtmənt] *n (stimulation)* excitación *f*; *(emotion)* emoción *f*; *(commotion)* agitación *f*.

exciting [ɪk'saɪtɪŋ] *adj* apasionante, emocionante.

exclaim [ɪk'skleɪm] **I** *vi* exclamar. **II** *vtr* gritar.

exclamation [eksklə'meɪʃən] *n* exclamación *f*; **e. mark,** *US* **e. point,** signo *m* de admiración.

exclude [ɪk'skluːd] *vtr* excluir; *(from club)* no admitir.

excluding [ɪk'skluːdɪŋ] *prep* excepto.

exclusion [ɪk'skluːʒən] *n* exclusión *f*.

exclusive [ɪk'skluːsɪv] **I** *adj* exclusivo,-a; *(neighbourhood)* selecto,-a; *(club)* cerrado, -a. **II** *n Press* exclusiva *f*. ◆**exclusively** *adv* exclusivamente.

excommunicate [ekskə'mjuːnɪkeɪt] *vtr* excomulgar.

excrement ['ekskrɪmənt] *n* excremento *m*.

excruciating [ɪk'skruːʃieɪtɪŋ] *adj* insoportable. ◆**excruciatingly** *adv* horriblemente.

excursion [ɪk'skɜːʃən] *n* excursión *f*.

excusable [ɪk'skjuːzəbəl] *adj* perdonable.

excuse [ɪk'skjuːz] **I** *vtr* 1 perdonar, disculpar; **e. me!,** con permiso; **may I be excused for a moment?,** ¿puedo salir un momento? 2 *(exempt)* dispensar. 3 *(justify)* justificar. **II** [ɪk'skjuːs] *n* excusa *f*; **to make an e.,** dar excusas.

ex-directory [eksdɪ'rektərɪ] *adj Tel* que no se encuentra en la guía telefónica.

execute ['eksɪkjuːt] *vtr* 1 *(order)* cumplir; *(task)* realizar. 2 *Jur* cumplir. 3 *(person)* ejecutar.

execution [eksɪ'kjuːʃən] *n* 1 *(of order)* cumplimiento *m*; *(of task)* realización *f*. 2 *Jur* cumplimiento *m*. 3 *(of person)* ejecución *f*.

executioner [eksɪ'kjuːʃənər] *n* verdugo *m*.

executive [ɪg'zekjutɪv] **I** *adj* ejecutivo,-a. **II** *n* ejecutivo,-a *m,f*.

executor [ɪg'zekjutər] *n* albacea *m*.

exemplary [ɪg'zemplərɪ] *adj* ejemplar.

exemplify [ɪg'zemplɪfaɪ] *vtr* ejemplificar.

exempt [ɪg'zempt] **I** *vtr* eximir (from, de). **II** *adj* exento,-a; **e. from tax,** libre de impuesto.

exemption [ɪg'zempʃən] *n* exención *f*.

exercise ['eksəsaɪz] **I** *n* ejercicio *m*; **e. book,** cuaderno *m*. **II** *vtr* 1 *(rights, duties)* ejercer. 2 *(dog)* sacar de paseo. **III** *vi* hacer ejercicio.

exert [ɪg'zɜːt] *vtr (influence)* ejercer; **to e. oneself,** esforzarse.

exertion [ɪg'zɜːʃən] *n* esfuerzo *m*.

exhale [eks'heɪl] **I** *vtr (breathe)* exhalar. **II** *vi* espirar.

exhaust [ɪg'zɔːst] **I** *vtr* agotar. **II** *n (gas)* gases *mpl* de combustión; **e. pipe,** tubo *m* de escape.

exhausted [ɪg'zɔːstɪd] *adj* agotado,-a.

exhaustion [ɪg'zɔːstʃən] *n* agotamiento *m*.

exhaustive [ɪg'zɔːstɪv] *adj* exhaustivo,-a.

exhibit [ɪg'zɪbɪt] **I** *n Art* objeto expuesto; *Jur* prueba *f* instrumental. **II** *vtr Art* exponer; *(surprise etc)* mostrar.

exhibition [eksɪ'bɪʃən] *n* exposición *f*.

exhibitionist [eksɪ'bɪʃənɪst] *adj & n* exhibicionista *(mf)*.

exhilarating [ɪg'zɪləreɪtɪŋ] *adj* estimulante.

exhilaration [ɪgzɪlə'reɪʃən] *n* regocijo *m*.

exhume [eks'hjuːm] *vtr* exhumar.

exile ['eksaɪl] **I** *n* 1 *(banishment)* exilio *m*. 2 *(person)* exiliado,-a *m,f*. **II** *vtr* exiliar.

exist [ɪg'zɪst] *vi* existir; *(have little money)* malvivir.

existence [ɪg'zɪstəns] *n* existencia *f*.

existing [ɪg'zɪstɪŋ] *adj* existente, actual.

exit ['eksɪt] **I** *n* 1 salida *f*. 2 *Theat* mutis *m*. **II** *vi Theat* hacer mutis.

exodus ['eksədəs] *n* éxodo *m*.

exonerate [ɪg'zɒnəreɪt] *vtr fml* exonerar (from, de).

exorbitant [ɪg'zɔːbɪtənt] *adj* exorbitante, desorbitado,-a.

exotic [ɪg'zɒtɪk] *adj* exótico,-a.

expand [ɪk'spænd] **I** *vtr (enlarge)* ampliar; *(gas, metal)* dilatar. **II** *vi (grow)* ampliarse; *(metal)* dilatarse; *(become more friendly)* abrirse. ◆**expand on** *vtr* ampliar.

expanse [ɪk'spæns] *n* extensión *f*.

expansion [ɪk'spænʃən] *n (in size)* expansión *f*; *(of gas, metal)* dilatación *f*.

expatriate [eks'pætriːt] **I** *adj & n* expatriado,-a *(m,f)*. **II** [eks'pætrieɪt] *vtr* expatriar.

expect [ɪk'spekt] **I** *vtr* **1** *(anticipate)* esperar; **I half-expected that to happen**, suponía que iba a ocurrir. **2** *(demand)* contar con. **3** *(suppose)* suponer. **II** *vi fam* **to be expecting**, estar embarazada.

expectancy [ɪk'spektənsɪ] *n* expectación *f*.

expectant [ɪk'spektənt] *adj* ilusionado,-a; **e. mother**, mujer embarazada.

expectation [ekspek'teɪʃən] *n* esperanza *f*; **contrary to e.**, contrariamente a lo que se esperaba.

expedient [ɪk'spiːdɪənt] **I** *adj* conveniente, oportuno,-a. **II** *n* expediente *m*, recurso *m*.

expedition [ekspɪ'dɪʃən] *n* expedición *f*.

expel [ɪk'spel] *vtr* expulsar.

expend [ɪk'spend] *vtr* gastar.

expendable [ɪk'spendəbəl] *adj* prescindible.

expenditure [ɪk'spendɪtʃəʳ] *n* desembolso *m*.

expense [ɪk'spens] *n* gasto *m*; **all expenses paid**, con todos los gastos pagados; **to spare no e.**, no escatimar gastos; *fig* **at the e. of**, a costa de; **e. account**, cuenta *f* de gastos de representación.

expensive [ɪk'spensɪv] *adj* caro,-a, costoso,-a.

experience [ɪk'spɪərɪəns] **I** *n* experiencia *f*. **II** *vtr* *(sensation)* experimentar; *(difficulty, loss)* sufrir.

experienced [ɪk'spɪərɪənst] *adj* experimentado,-a.

experiment [ɪk'sperɪmənt] **I** *n* experimento *m*. **II** *vi* experimentar, hacer experimentos **(on, with**, con).

experimental [ɪksperɪ'mentəl] *adj* experimental.

expert ['ekspɜːt] **I** *adj* experto,-a. **II** *n* experto,-a *m,f*, especialista *mf*.

expertise [ekspɜː'tiːz] *n* pericia *f*.

expire [ɪk'spaɪəʳ] *vi* **1** *(die)* expirar; *(mandate)* terminar. **2** *Com Ins* vencer; *(ticket)* caducar.

expiry [ɪk'spaɪərɪ] *n* vencimiento *m*; **e. date**, fecha *f* de caducidad.

explain [ɪk'spleɪn] **I** *vtr* explicar; *(clarify)* aclarar; **to e. oneself**, justificarse. **II** *vi* explicarse.

explanation [eksplə'neɪʃən] *n* explicación *f*; *(clarification)* aclaración *f*.

explanatory [ɪk'splænətərɪ] *adj* explicativo,-a, aclaratorio,-a.

explicit [ɪk'splɪsɪt] *adj* explícito,-a.

explode [ɪk'spləʊd] **I** *vtr* **1** *(bomb)* hacer explotar. **2** *fig (theory)* echar por tierra. **II** *vi* **1** *(bomb)* estallar, explotar; *fig* **to e. with** *or* **in anger**, montar en cólera.

exploit ['eksplɔɪt] **I** *n* proeza *f*, hazaña *f*. **II** [ɪk'splɔɪt] *vtr* explotar.

exploitation [eksplɔɪ'teɪʃən] *n* explotación *f*.

exploratory [ek'splɒrətərɪ] *adj* exploratorio,-a.

explore [ɪk'splɔːʳ] *vtr* explorar.

explorer [ɪk'splɔːrəʳ] *n* explorador,-a *m,f*.

explosion [ɪk'spləʊʒən] *n* explosión *f*.

explosive [ɪk'spləʊsɪv] **I** *adj* explosivo,-a; **e. issue**, asunto delicado. **II** *n* explosivo *m*.

exponent [ɪk'spəʊnənt] *n* exponente *m*; *(supporter)* defensor,-a *m,f*.

export [ɪk'spɔːt] **I** *vtr* exportar. **II** ['ekspɔːt] *n* **1** *(trade)* exportación *f*. **2** *(commodity)* artículo *m* de exportación.

exporter [eks'pɔːtəʳ] *n* exportador,-a *m,f*.

expose [ɪk'spəʊz] *vtr* *(uncover)* exponer; *(secret)* revelar; *(plot)* descubrir; **to e. oneself**, exhibirse desnudo.

exposed [ɪk'spəʊzd] *adj* expuesto,-a.

exposure [ɪk'spəʊʒəʳ] *n* **1** *(to light, cold, heat)* exposición *f*; **to die of e.**, morir de frío. **2** *Phot* fotografía *f*; **e. meter**, fotómetro *m*. **3** *(of criminal)* descubrimiento *m*.

expound [ɪk'spaʊnd] *vtr* exponer.

express [ɪk'spres] **I** *adj* **1** *(explicit)* expreso,-a. **2** *GB (letter)* urgente; **e. train**, expreso *m*. **II** *n Rail* expreso *m*. **III** *vtr* expresar. **IV** *adv* **send it e.**, mándalo urgente. ◆**expressly** *adv fml* expresamente.

expression [ɪk'spreʃən] *n* expresión *f*.

expulsion [ɪk'spʌlʃən] *n* expulsión *f*.

exquisite [ɪk'skwɪzɪt] *adj* exquisito,-a.

extend [ɪk'stend] **I** *vtr* **1** *(enlarge)* ampliar; *(lengthen)* alargar; *(increase)* aumentar; *fig* **the prohibition was extended to cover cigarettes**, extendieron la prohibición a los cigarrillos. **2** *(give)* rendir, dar; **to e. a welcome to sb**, recibir a algn. **3** *(prolong)* prolongar. **II** *vi* **1** *(stretch)* extenderse. **2** *(last)* prolongarse.

extension [ɪk'stenʃən] *n* **1** extensión *f*; *(of time)* prórroga *f*. **2** *Constr* anexo *m*.

extensive [ɪk'stensɪv] *adj* extenso,-a.

extent [ɪk'stent] *n* **1** *(area)* extensión *f*. **2** **to some e.**, hasta cierto punto; **to a large e.**, en gran parte; **to a lesser e.**, en menor grado; **to such an e.**, hasta tal punto.

extenuating [ɪk'stenjʊeɪtɪŋ] *adj* atenuante.

exterior [ɪk'stɪərɪəʳ] **I** *adj* exterior, externo,-a. **II** *n* exterior *m*.

exterminate [ɪk'stɜːmɪneɪt] *vtr* exterminar.

extermination [ɪkstɜːmɪ'neɪʃən] *n* exterminación *f*, exterminio *m*.

external [ek'stɜːnəl] *adj* externo,-a, exterior.

extinct [ɪk'stɪŋkt] *adj* extinguido,-a.

extinction [ɪk'stɪŋkʃən] *n* extinción *f*.

extinguish [ɪk'stɪŋgwɪʃ] *vtr* extinguir, apagar.

extinguisher [ɪk'stɪŋgwɪʃəʳ] *n* extintor *m*.

extol, *US* **extoll** [ɪk'stəʊl] *vtr* ensalzar,

alabar.

extort [ɪk'stɔːt] *vtr* arrancar; *(money)* sacar.

extortion [ɪk'stɔːʃən] *n* extorsión *f*.

extortionate [ɪk'stɔːʃənɪt] *adj* desorbitado,-a.

extra ['ekstrə] I *adj* extra; *(spare)* de sobra. II *adv* extra; e. fine, extra fino. III *n* *(additional charge)* suplemento *m*; Cin extra *mf*; *(newspaper)* edición *f* especial.

extract ['ekstrækt] I *n* extracto *m*. II [ɪk'strækt] *vtr (tooth, information)* extraer; *(confession)* arrancar.

extraction [ɪk'strækʃən] *n* extracción *f*.

extracurricular [ekstrəkə'rɪkjʊlər] *adj* extracurricular.

extradite ['ekstrədaɪt] *vtr* extraditar.

extramarital [ekstrə'mærɪtəl] *adj* extramatrimonial.

extramural [ekstrə'mjʊərəl] *adj* e. course, curso *m* para estudiantes libres.

extraordinary [ɪk'strɔːdənərɪ] *adj (meeting)* extraordinario,-a; *(behaviour etc)* extraño,-a.

extravagance [ɪk'strævɪgəns] *n (with money)* derroche *m*; *(of behaviour)* extravagancia *f*.

extravagant [ɪk'strævɪgənt] *adj (wasteful)* derrochador,-a; *(excessive)* exagerado,-a; *(luxurious)* lujoso,-a.

extreme [ɪk'striːm] I *adj* extremo,-a; an e. case, un caso excepcional; to hold e. views, tener opiniones radicales. II *n* extremo *m*; in the e., en sumo grado.
◆**extremely** *adv* extremadamente; I'm e. sorry, lo siento de veras.

extremist [ɪk'striːmɪst] *n* extremista *mf*.

extremity [ɪk'stremɪtɪ] *n* extremidad *f*.

extricate ['ekstrɪkeɪt] *vtr* sacar; to e. one-

self, lograr salir (from, de).

extrovert ['ekstrəvɜːt] *adj & n* extrovertido,-a *(m,f)*.

exuberant [ɪg'zjuːbərənt] *adj* exuberante.

exude [ɪg'zjuːd] *vtr & vi (moisture, sap)* exudar; *fig* rebosar.

exultant [ɪg'zʌltənt] *adj* jubiloso,-a.

eye [aɪ] I *n* ojo *m*; *fig* I couldn't believe my eyes, no podía creerlo; *fig* in the eyes of, según; *fig* not to take one's eyes off sb/sth, no quitar la vista de encima a algn/algo; *fig* to catch sb's e., llamar la atención a algn; *fig* to have an e. for, tener buen ojo para; *fig* to make eyes at sb, echar miraditas a algn; *fig* to see e. to e. with sb, estar de acuerdo con algn; *fig* to turn a blind e., hacer la vista gorda (to, a); *fig* with an e. to, con miras a; to keep an e. on sb/sth, vigilar a algn/algo; to keep an e. out for, estar pendiente de; black e., ojo morado. II *vtr* observar.

eyeball ['aɪbɔːl] *n* globo *m* ocular.

eyebrow ['aɪbraʊ] *n* ceja *f*.

eyecatching ['aɪkætʃɪŋ] *adj* llamativo,-a.

eyelash ['aɪlæʃ] *n* pestaña *f*.

eyelid ['aɪlɪd] *n* párpado *m*.

eyeliner ['aɪlaɪnə] *n* lápiz *m* de ojos.

eye-opener ['aɪəʊpənə'] *n* revelación *f*, gran sorpresa *f*.

eyeshadow ['aɪʃædəʊ] *n* sombra *f* de ojos.

eyesight ['aɪsaɪt] *n* vista *f*.

eyesore ['aɪsɔː'] *n* monstruosidad *f*.

eyestrain ['aɪstreɪn] *n* vista cansada.

eyewash ['aɪwɒʃ] *n* colirio *m*; *fig* it's all e., eso son disparates.

eyewitness ['aɪwɪtnɪs] *n* testigo *mf* ocular.

F

F, f [ef] *n* 1 *(the letter)* F, f *f*. 2 Mus fa *m*.

F [ef] *abbr of* **Fahrenheit**, Fahrenheit, F.

fable ['feɪbəl] *n* fábula *f*.

fabric ['fæbrɪk] *n* 1 Tex tela *f*, tejido *m*. 2 Constr estructura *f*.

fabricate ['fæbrɪkeɪt] *vtr* fabricar.

fabrication [fæbrɪ'keɪʃən] *n fig* fabricación *f*.

fabulous ['fæbjʊləs] *adj* fabuloso,-a.

façade *n* [fə'sɑːd, fæ'sɑːd] *n* fachada *f*.

face [feɪs] I *n* 1 cara *f*, rostro *m*; f. to f., cara a cara; I told him to his f., se lo dije en la cara; she slammed the door in my f., me dió con la puerta en las narices; to look sb in the f., mirarle a algn a la cara; f. cloth, paño *m*; f. cream, crema *f* facial; f. pack, mascarilla *f* facial. 2 *(expression)* cara *f*, expresión *f*; to pull a long f., poner cara larga; to pull faces, hacer muecas. 3 *(surface)* superficie *f*; *(of*

card, coin)* cara *f*; *(of watch)* esfera *f*; f. down/up, boca abajo/arriba; *fig* in the f. of danger, ante el peligro; f. value, valor *m* nominal; to take sth at f. value, entender algo sólo en su sentido literal. 4 *(appearance)* aspecto *m*; on the f. of it, a primera vista; to lose f., desprestigiarse; to save f., salvar las apariencias.
II *vtr* 1 *(look onto)* dar a; *(be opposite)* estar enfrente de. 2 to f. the wall/window, *(of person)* estar de cara a la pared/ventana. 3 *(problem)* hacer frente a; let's f. it, hay que reconocerlo; to f. up to, hacer cara a. 4 *(tolerate)* soportar, aguantar.
III *vi* to f. on to, dar a; to f. towards, mirar hacia; f. this way, vuélvase de este lado.

facelift ['feɪslɪft] *n* Med lifting *m*; *fig* renovación *f*.

facet ['fæsɪt] *n* faceta *f*.

facetious [fə'si:ʃəs] *adj* bromista.

facial ['feɪʃəl] *adj* facial.

facile ['fæsaɪl] *adj* superficial.

facilitate [fə'sɪlɪteɪt] *vtr* facilitar.

facility [fə'sɪlɪtɪ] *n* 1 (*ease*) facilidad *f*. 2 **facilities**, (*means*) facilidades *fpl*; **credit f.**, facilidades de crédito. 3 **facilities**, (*rooms, equipment*) instalaciones *fpl*; **cooking f.**, derecho *m* a cocina.

facing ['feɪsɪŋ] *adj* de enfrente.

facsimile [fæk'sɪmɪlɪ] *n* 1 (*copy*) facsímil *m*. 2 (*message*) telefax *m*. 3 (*machine*) facsímil *m*.

fact [fækt] *n* hecho *m*; **as a matter of f.**, de hecho; **the f. that he confessed**, el hecho de que confesara; **in f.**, en realidad.

fact-finding ['fæktfaɪndɪŋ] *adj* investigador,-a.

faction ['fækʃən] *n* (*group*) facción *f*.

factor ['fæktər] *n* factor *m*.

factory ['fæktərɪ] *n* fábrica *f*.

factual ['fæktʃʊəl] *adj* **a f. error**, un error de hecho.

faculty ['fækəltɪ] *n* 1 facultad *f*. 2 *US Univ* profesorado *m*, cuerpo *m* docente.

fad [fæd] *n fam* (*craze*) moda pasajera; (*whim*) capricho *m*.

fade [feɪd] *vi* (*colour*) desteñirse; (*flower*) marchitarse; (*light*) apagarse. ◆**fade away** *vi* desvanecerse. ◆**fade in, fade out** *vtr Cin TV* fundir.

faded ['feɪdɪd] *adj* (*colour*) desteñido,-a; (*flower*) marchito,-a.

fag [fæg] *n sl* 1 *GB fam* (*cigarette*) pitillo *m*. 2 *US sl* (*homosexual*) marica *m*.

fail [feɪl] I *n* 1 *Educ* suspenso *m*. 2 **without f.**, sin falta. II *vtr* **I don't f. me**, no me falles; **words f. me**, no encuentro palabras. 2 (*exam*) suspender. 3 (*to be unable*) no lograr; **he failed to score**, no logró marcar. 4 (*neglect*) dejar de; **don't f. to come**, no deje de venir. 5 (*of health*) deteriorarse. III *vi* 1 (*show, film*) fracasar; (*brakes*) fallar. 2 (*business*) quebrar; *Educ* suspender.

failing ['feɪlɪŋ] I *n* 1 (*shortcoming*) defecto *m*. 2 (*weakness*) punto *m* débil. II *prep* a falta de.

failure ['feɪljər] *n* 1 fracaso *m*. 2 *Com* quiebra *f*. 3 *Educ* suspenso *m*. 4 (*person*) fracasado,-a *m,f*. 5 (*breakdown*) avería *f*; **brake f.**, fallo *m* de los frenos; **power f.**, apagón *m*; *Med* **heart f.**, paro cardíaco. 6 **her f. to answer**, (*neglect*) el hecho de que no contestara.

faint [feɪnt] I *adj* 1 (*sound*) débil; (*colour*) pálido,-a; (*outline*) borroso,-a; (*recollection*) vago,-a; **I haven't the faintest idea**, no tengo la más mínima idea. 2 (*giddy*) mareado,-a. II *n* desmayo *m*. III *vi* desmayarse.

faint-hearted [feɪnt'hɑːtɪd] *adj*

temeroso,-a.

fair¹ [feər] I *adj* 1 (*impartial*) imparcial; (*just*) justo,-a; **it's not f.**, no hay derecho; **fam f. enough!**, ¡vale! 2 (*hair*) rubio,-a. 3 (*weather*) bueno,-a. 4 (*beautiful*) bello,-a. 5 **a f. number**, un buen número; **he has a f. chance**, tiene bastantes probabilidades. II *adv* **to play f.**, jugar limpio. ◆**fairly** *adv* 1 (*justly*) justamente. 2 (*moderately*) bastante.

fair² [feər] *n* feria *f*; **trade f.**, feria de muestras.

fairground ['feəgraʊnd] *n* real *m* de la feria.

fairness ['feənɪs] *n* justicia *f*, equidad *f*; **in all f.**, para ser justo,-a.

fairy ['feərɪ] *n* 1 hada *f*; **f. godmother**, hada madrina; **f. tale**, cuento *m* de hadas. 2 *sl offens* marica *m*.

fait accompli [feɪtə'kɒmpli:] *n fml* hecho consumado.

faith [feɪθ] *n* 1 *Rel* fe *f*. 2 (*trust*) confianza *f*; **in good f.**, de buena fe.

faithful ['feɪθfʊl] I *adj* fiel. II *npl* **the f.**, los fieles. ◆**faithfully** *adv* fielmente; **yours f.**, (*in letter*) le saluda atentamente.

fake [feɪk] I *adj* falso,-a. II *n* 1 (*object*) falsificación *f*. 2 (*person*) impostor,-a *m,f*. III *vtr* 1 (*forge*) falsificar. 2 (*feign*) fingir. IV *vi* (*pretend*) fingir.

falcon ['fɔːlkən] *n* halcón *m*.

Falklands ['fɔːlkləndz] *npl* **the F.**, las (Islas) Malvinas.

fall [fɔːl] I *n* 1 caída *f*. 2 (*of rock*) desprendimiento *m*; **f. of snow**, nevada *f*. 3 (*decrease*) baja *f*. 4 *US* otoño *m*. 5 (*usu pl*) cascada *f*; **Niagara Falls**, las cataratas del Niágara. II *vi* (*pt* fell; *pp* fallen) 1 caer, caerse; **they f. into two categories**, se dividen en dos categorías; *fig* **night was falling**, anochecía; *fig* **to f. into line**, aceptar las reglas; *fig* **to f. short**, no alcanzar (**of**, -). 2 (*in battle*) caer. 3 (*temperature, prices*) bajar. 4 **to f. asleep**, dormirse; **to f. ill**, caer enfermo,-a; **to f. in love**, enamorarse. ◆**fall back** *vi* replegarse. ◆**fall back on** *vtr* echar mano a, recurrir a. ◆**fall behind** *vi* (*in race*) quedarse atrás; **to f. behind with one's work**, retrasarse en el trabajo. ◆**fall down** *vi* 1 (*picture etc*) caerse. 2 (*building*) derrumbarse. 3 (*argument*) fallar. ◆**fall for** *vtr* 1 (*person*) enamorarse de. 2 (*trick*) dejarse engañar por. ◆**fall in** *vi* 1 (*roof*) desplomarse. 2 *Mil* formar filas. ◆**fall off** I *vi* 1 (*drop off*) caerse. II *vtr* **to f. off sth**, caerse de algo. 2 (*part*) desprenderse. 3 (*diminish*) disminuir. ◆**fall out** *vi* 1 (*hair*) caerse. 2 *Mil* romper filas. 3 (*quarrel*) pelearse. ◆**fall over** *vi* caerse. ◆**fall through** *vi* (*plan*) fracasar.

fallacy ['fæləsɪ] *n* falacia *f*.

fallen ['fɔːlən] *pp* → **fall**.

fallible ['fælɪbəl] *adj* falible.

fall-out ['fɔːlaut] *n* (**radioactive**) f., lluvia radioactiva; f. **shelter**, refugio antiatómico.

fallow ['fæləu] *adj* Agr en barbecho.

false [fɔːls] *adj* falso,-a; f. **step**, paso *m* en falso; f. **start**, salida nula; f. **teeth**, dentadura postiza; f. **alarm**, falsa alarma.

falsehood ['fɔːlshud] *n* falsedad *f*.

falsify ['fɔːlsɪfaɪ] *vt* (**records**, **accounts**) falsificar; (**story**) falsear.

falter ['fɔːltər] *vi* vacilar; (**voice**) fallar.

faltering ['fɔːltərɪŋ] *adj* vacilante.

fame [feɪm] *n* fama *f*.

familiar [fə'mɪlɪər] *adj* 1 (**common**) familiar, conocido,-a; **his face is f.**, su cara me suena. 2 (**aware**, **knowledgeable**) enterado,-a, al corriente (**with**, de). 3 **to be on f. terms with sb**, (**know well**) tener confianza con algn.

familiarity [fəmɪlɪ'ærɪtɪ] *n* 1 (**awareness**, **knowledge**) familiaridad (**with**, con). 2 (**intimacy**) confianza *f*.

familiarize [fə'mɪljəraɪz] *vtr* 1 (**become acquainted**) familiarizarse (**with**, con). 2 (**make understandable**) popularizar.

family ['fæmɪlɪ] *n* familia *f*; f. **allowance**, subsidio *m* familiar; f. **doctor**, médico *m* de cabecera; f. **man**, hombre hogareño; f. **planning**, planificación *f* familiar; f. **tree**, árbol genealógico.

famine ['fæmɪn] *n* hambre *f*, escasez *f* de alimentos.

famished ['fæmɪʃt] *adj* fam muerto,-a de hambre.

famous ['feɪməs] *adj* célebre, famoso,-a (**for**, por). ◆**famously** *adv* fam estupendamente.

fan [fæn] **I** *n* 1 abanico *m*; Elec ventilador *m*. 2 (**person**) aficionado,-a *m*,*f*; (**of pop star etc**) fan *m*,*f*; f. **club**, club *m* de fans; **football f.**, hincha *mf*. **II** *vtr* 1 abanicar. 2 (**fire**, **passions**) avivar. ◆**fan out** *vi* (**troops**) desplegarse en abanico.

fanatic [fə'nætɪk] *adj & n* fanático,-a (*m*,*f*).

fanatical [fə'nætɪkəl] *adj* fanático,-a.

fanciful ['fænsɪful] *adj* 1 (**person**) caprichoso,-a. 2 (**idea**) fantástico,-a.

fancy ['fænsɪ] **I** *adj* (**fancier**, **fanciest**) de fantasía; f. **dress**, disfraz *m*; f. **dress ball**, baile *m* de disfraces; f. **prices**, precios *mpl* exorbitantes. **II** *n* 1 (**imagination**) fantasía *f*. 2 (**whim**) capricho *m*, antojo *m*; **to take a f. to sb**, cogerle cariño a algn; **to take a f. to sth**, encapricharse con algo; **what takes your f.?**, ¿qué se le antoja? **III** *vtr* 1 (**imagine**) imaginarse; **fam f. that!**, ¡fíjate!; **fam f. seeing you here!**, ¡qué casualidad verte por aquí! 2 (**like**, **want**) apetecer; **do you f. a drink?**, ¿te apetece una copa?; **fam I f. her**, ella me gusta; **fam to f. oneself**, ser creído,-a *or* presumido,-a.

fanfare ['fænfeər] *n* fanfarria *f*.

fang [fæŋ] *n* colmillo *m*.

fantasize ['fæntəsaɪz] *vi* fantasear.

fantastic [fæn'tæstɪk] *adj* fantástico,-a.

fantasy ['fæntəsɪ] *n* fantasía *f*.

far [fɑːr] (**farther** *or* **further**, **farthest** *or* **furthest**) **I** *adj* 1 (**distant**) lejano,-a; **the F. East**, el Lejano Oriente. 2 **at the f. end**, en el otro extremo. 3 **the f. left**, la extrema izquierda. **II** *adv* 1 (**distant**) lejos; f. **and wide**, por todas partes; f. **off**, a lo lejos; **farther back**, más atrás; **farther north**, más al norte; **how f. is it to Cardiff?**, ¿cuánto hay de aquí a Cardiff?; *fig* **as f. as I can**, en lo que puedo; **as f. as I know**, que yo sepa; **as f. as possible**, en lo posible; *fig* f. **from complaining**, **he seemed pleased**, lejos de quejarse, parecía contento; *fig* **he went so f. as to swear**, llegó a jurar; *fig* **I'm f. from satisfied**, no estoy satisfecho,-a ni mucho menos; *fig* **in so f. as ...**, en la medida en que ...; *fam* **to go too f.**, pasarse de la raya. 2 (**in time**) **as f. back as the fifties**, ya en los años cincuenta; f. **into the night**, hasta muy entrada la noche; **so f.**, hasta ahora. 3 (**much**) mucho; **by f.**, con mucho; f. **cleverer**, mucho más listo,-a; f. **too much**, demasiado; **you're not f. wrong**, casi aciertas.

faraway ['fɑːrəweɪ] *adj* lejano,-a, remoto,-a.

farce [fɑːs] *n* farsa *f*.

farcical ['fɑːsɪkəl] *adj* absurdo,-a.

fare [feər] **I** *n* 1 (**ticket price**) tarifa *f*, precio *m* del billete; (**for boat**) pasaje *m*; **half f.**, media tarifa. 2 (**passenger**) pasajero,-a *m*,*f*. 3 (**food**) comida *f*. **II** *vi* **how did you f.?**, ¿qué tal te fue?

farewell [feə'wel] **I** *interj* arch ¡adiós! **II** *n* despedida *f*.

far-fetched [fɑː'fetʃt] *adj* rebuscado,-a.

farm [fɑːm] **I** *n* 1 granja *f*, Am hacienda *f*. **II** *vtr* cultivar, labrar. ◆**farm out** *vtr* encargar fuera.

farmer ['fɑːmər] *n* granjero,-a *m*,*f*, Am hacendado,-a *m*,*f*.

farmhand ['fɑːmhænd] *n* peón *m*, labriego,-a *m*,*f*.

farmhouse ['fɑːmhaus] *n* granja *f*, Am hacienda *f*.

farming ['fɑːmɪŋ] **I** *n* 1 (**agriculture**) agricultura *f*. 2 (**of land**) cultivo *m*, labranza *f*. **II** *adj* agrícola.

farmyard ['fɑːmjɑːd] *n* corral *m*.

far-reaching [fɑː'riːtʃɪŋ] *adj* de gran alcance.

far-sighted [fɑː'saɪtɪd] *adj* 1 (**person**) con visión de futuro. 2 (**plan**) con miras al futuro.

fart [fɑːt] *vulg* **I** *n* pedo *m*. **II** *vi* echarse un pedo.

farther ['fɑːðər] *adj & adv comp* → **far**.

farthest ['fɑːðɪst] *adj & adv superl* → **far**.

fascinate ['fæsɪneɪt] *vtr* fascinar.
fascinating ['fæsɪneɪtɪŋ] *adj* fascinante.
fascination [fæsɪ'neɪʃən] *n* fascinación *f.*
fascism ['fæʃɪzəm] *n* fascismo *m.*
fascist ['fæʃɪst] *adj & n* fascista (*mf*).
fashion ['fæʃən] **I** *n* **1** (*manner*) manera *f,* modo *m;* **after a f.,** más o menos. **2** (*latest style*) moda *f;* **to go/be out of f.,** pasar/no estar de moda; **f. designer,** diseñador,-a *m,f* de modas; **f. parade,** desfile *m* de modelos. **II** *vtr* (*metal*) labrar; (*clay*) formar.
fashionable ['fæʃənəbəl] *adj* **1** de moda. **2** (*area, hotel*) elegante.
fast¹ [fɑːst] **I** *adj* **1** (*quick*) rápido,-a. **2** **hard and f. rules,** reglas estrictas. **3** (*clock*) adelantado,-a. **II** *adv* **1** rápidamente, deprisa; **how f.?,** ¿a qué velocidad? **2** (*securely*) firmemente; **f. asleep,** profundamente dormido,-a.
fast² [fɑːst] **I** *n* ayuno *m.* **II** *vi* ayunar.
fasten ['fɑːsən] **I** *vtr* **1** (*attach*) sujetar; (*fix*) fijar. **2** (*belt*) abrochar; (*bag*) asegurar; (*shoe laces*) atar. **II** *vi* (*dress*) abrocharse.
fastener ['fɑːsənər] *n* cierre *m.*
fastidious [fæ'stɪdɪəs] *adj* quisquilloso,-a.
fat [fæt] **I** *adj* (*fatter, fattest*) **1** gordo,-a. **2** (*book, file*) grueso,-a. **3** (*meat*) que tiene mucha grasa. **II** *n* grasa *f;* **cooking f.,** manteca *f* de cerdo.
fatal ['feɪtəl] *adj* **1** (*accident, illness*) mortal. **2** (*ill-fated*) fatal, funesto,-a. **3** (*fateful*) fatídico,-a. ◆**fatally** *adv* **f. wounded,** mortalmente herido,-a.
fatalistic [feɪtə'lɪstɪk] *adj* fatalista.
fatality [fə'tælɪtɪ] *n* víctima *f* mortal.
fate [feɪt] *n* destino *m,* suerte *f.*
fateful ['feɪtful] *adj* fatídico,-a, aciago,-a.
father ['fɑːðər] *n* **1** padre *m;* **my f. and mother,** mis padres; **F. Christmas,** Papá *m* Noel. **2** *Rel* padre *m.*
father-in-law ['fɑːðərɪnlɔː] *n* suegro *m.*
fatherland ['fɑːðəlænd] *n* patria *f.*
fatherly ['fɑːðəlɪ] *adj* paternal.
fathom ['fæðəm] **I** *n* *Naut* braza *f.* **II** *vtr* comprender. ◆**fathom out** *vtr* comprobar; **I can't f. it out,** no me lo explico.
fatigue [fə'tiːɡ] *n* **1** (*tiredness*) fatiga *f.* **2** *Mil* faena *f;* **f. dress,** traje *m* de faena.
fatten ['fætən] *vtr* engordar.
fattening ['fætənɪŋ] *adj* que engorda.
fatty ['fætɪ] **I** *adj* (*food*) graso,-a; *Anat* (*tissue*) adiposo,-a. **II** *n* *fam* (*person*) gordinflón,-ona *m,f.*
fatuous ['fætjʊəs] *adj* necio,-a.
faucet ['fɔːsɪt] *n* *US* grifo *m.*
fault [fɔːlt] **I** *n* **1** (*defect*) defecto *m.* **2** (*in merchandise*) desperfecto *m;* **to find f. with,** poner reparos a. **3** (*blame*) culpa *f;* **to be at f.,** tener la culpa. **4** (*mistake*) error *m.* **5** *Geol* falla *f.* **6** *Ten* falta *f.* **II** *vtr* criticar.
faultless ['fɔːltlɪs] *adj* intachable.

faulty ['fɔːltɪ] *adj* defectuoso,-a.
fauna ['fɔːnə] *n* fauna *f.*
faux pas [fəʊ'pɑː] *n inv fml* (*mistake*) paso *m* en falso; (*blunder*) metedura *f* de pata.
favour, *US* **favor** ['feɪvər] **I** *n* **1** favor *m;* **in f. of,** a favor de; **to be in f. with sb,** gozar del favor de algn; **to ask sb a f.,** pedirle un favor a algn. **2** **1-0 in our f.,** (*advantage*)1-0 a favor nuestro. **II** *vtr* **1** (*person*) favorecer a. **2** (*approve*) estar a favor de.
favourable ['feɪvərəbəl] *adj* favorable.
favourite ['feɪvərɪt] *adj & n* favorito,-a *m,f.*
favouritism ['feɪvərɪtɪzəm] *n* favoritismo *m.*
fawn¹ [fɔːn] **I** *adj* (de) color café claro. **II** *n* **1** *Zool* cervato *m.* **2** color *m* café claro.
fawn² [fɔːn] *vi* adular (**on,** a).
fax [fæks] **I** *n* (*machine, message*) fax *m.* **II** *vtr* mandar por fax.
fear [fɪər] **I** *n* miedo *m,* temor *m;* **for f. of,** por temor a; *fam* **no f.!,** ¡ni pensarlo!. **II** *vtr* temer; **I f. it's too late,** me temo que ya es tarde. **III** *vi* temer (**for,** por).
fearful ['fɪəfʊl] *adj* **1** (*person*) temeroso,-a. **2** (*frightening*) espantoso,-a.
fearless ['fɪəlɪs] *adj* intrépido,-a.
feasible ['fiːzəbəl] *adj* (*practicable*) factible; (*possible*) viable.
feasibility [fiːzə'bɪlɪtɪ] *n* viabilidad *f.*
feast [fiːst] *n* **1** banquete *m,* *fam* comilona *f.* **2** *Rel* **f. day,** fiesta *f* de guardar.
feat [fiːt] *n* hazaña *f.*
feather ['feðər] **I** *n* pluma *f;* **f. duster,** plumero *m.* **II** *vtr* *fam* **to f. one's nest,** hacer su agosto.
feature ['fiːtʃər] **I** *n* **1** (*of face*) rasgo *m,* facción *f.* **2** (*characteristic*) característica *f.* **3** **f. film,** largometraje *m.* **4** *Press* crónica *f* especial. **II** *vtr* **1** poner de relieve. **2** *Cin* tener como protagonista a. **III** *vi* figurar.
February ['februərɪ] *n* febrero *m.*
fed [fed] *adj* *fam* **f. up,** harto,-a (**with,** de).
federal ['fedərəl] *adj* federal.
federation [fedə'reɪʃən] *n* federación *f.*
fee [fiː] *n* (*of lawyer, doctor*) honorarios *mpl; Ftb* **transfer f.,** prima *f* de traslado; *Univ* **tuition fees,** derechos *mpl* de matrícula.
feeble ['fiːbəl] *adj* débil.
feed [fiːd] **I** *vtr* (*pt & pp* **fed**) **1** (*give food to*) dar de comer a; *fig* (*fire*) alimentar; **to f. a baby,** (*breast-feed*) amamantar a un bebé; (*with bottle*) dar el biberón a un bebé. **2** *Elec* alimentar. **3** (*insert*) introducir. **II** *vi* comer (**on,** -); (*cows, sheep*) pacer. **III** *n* **1** (*food*) comida *f;* **cattle f.,** pienso *m.* **2** *Tech* alimentación *f.* ◆**feed up** *vtr* cebar.
feedback ['fiːdbæk] *n* **1** *Tech* feedback *m.* **2** *fig* reacción *f.*
feeder ['fiːdər] *n* *Tech* alimentador *m.*

feeding ['fiːdɪŋ] *n* f. **bottle**, biberón *m*.
feel [fiːl] I *vi* (*pt & pp* **felt**) 1 (*emotion, sensation*) sentir; **how do you f.?**, ¿qué tal te encuentras?; **I f. bad about it**, me da pena; **I f. (sorry) for him**, le compadezco; **to f. happy/uncomfortable**, sentirse feliz/incómodo; **to f. cold/sleepy**, tener frío/sueño; ●**m to f. up to sth**, sentirse con ánimos para hacer algo. 2 (*seem*) **your hand feels cold**, tienes la mano fría; **it feels like summer**, parece verano. 3 (*opinion*) opinar; **I f. sure that ...**, estoy seguro,-a de que ... 4 **I f. like an ice cream**, me apetece un helado; **to f. like doing sth**, tener ganas de hacer algo. II *vtr* 1 (*touch*) tocar. 2 **she feels a failure**, se siente inútil. 3 (*notice, be aware of*) notar. III *n* 1 (*touch, sensation*) tacto *m*; *fig* **to get the f. for sth**, cogerle el truco a algo. 2 (*atmosphere*) ambiente *m*. ◆**feel for** *vtr* 1 (*search for*) buscar. 2 (*have sympathy for*) compadecer.
feeler ['fiːlər] *n* *Ent* antena *f*; *fig* **to put one's feelers out**, tantear el terreno.
feeling ['fiːlɪŋ] I *n* 1 (*emotion*) sentimiento *m*; **ill f.**, rencor *m*. 2 (*compassion*) compasión *f*. 3 **I had the f. that ...**, (*impression*) tuve la impresión de que ... 4 (*sensitivity*) sensibilidad *f*. 5 (*opinion*) opinión *f*; **to express one's feelings**, expresar sus opiniones. II *adj* sensible, compasivo,-a.
feet [fiːt] *npl* → **foot**.
feign [feɪn] *vtr* fingir.
feint [feɪnt] *Sport* I *n* finta *f*. II *vi* fintar.
fell¹ [fel] *pt* → **fall**.
fell² [fel] *vtr* (*trees*) talar; *fig* (*enemy*) derribar.
fellow ['feləʊ] *n* 1 (*companion*) compañero,-a *m,f*; **f. citizen**, conciudadano,-a *m,f*; **f. countryman/countrywoman**, compatriota *mf*; **f. men**, prójimos *mpl*; **f. passenger/student**, compañero,-a *m,f*, de viaje/estudios. 2 *fam* (*chap*) tipo *m*, tío *m*. 3 (*of society*) socio,-a *m,f*.
fellowship ['feləʊʃɪp] *n* 1 (*comradeship*) camaradería *f*. 2 *Univ* beca *f* de investigación.
felony ['felənɪ] *n* crimen *m*, delito *m* mayor.
felt¹ [felt] *pt & pp* → **feel**.
felt² [felt] *n* *Tex* fieltro *m*.
felt-tip(ped) ['felttɪp(t)] *adj* **f.-t. pen**, rotulador *m*.
female ['fiːmeɪl] I *adj* 1 *Zool* hembra. 2 femenino,-a. II *n* 1 *Zool* hembra *f*. 2 (*woman*) mujer *f*; (*girl*) chica *f*.
feminine ['femɪnɪn] *adj* femenino,-a.
feminism ['femɪnɪzəm] *n* feminismo *m*.
feminist ['femɪnɪst] *adj & n* feminista (*mf*).
fence [fens] I *n* cerca *f*, valla *f*; *fig* **to sit on the f.**, ver los toros desde la barrera. II *vi* *Sport* practicar la esgrima. ◆**fence**

in *vtr* meter en un cercado.
fencing ['fensɪŋ] *n* *Sport* esgrima *f*.
fend [fend] *vi* **to f. for oneself**, valerse por sí mismo. ◆**fend off** *vtr* (*blow*) parar; (*question*) rehuir; (*attack*) rechazar.
fender ['fendər] *n* 1 (*fireplace*) pantalla *f*. 2 *US Aut* parachoques *m inv*. 3 *Naut* defensa *f*.
ferment ['fɜːment] I *n* *fig* **in a state of f.**, agitado,-a. II [fə'ment] *vtr & vi* fermentar.
fern [fɜːn] *n* helecho *m*.
ferocious [fə'rəʊʃəs] *adj* feroz.
ferocity [fə'rɒsɪtɪ] *n* ferocidad *f*.
ferret ['ferɪt] *n* hurón *m*. II *vi* huronear, husmear. ◆**ferret out** *vtr* descubrir.
ferry ['ferɪ] I *n* 1 (*small*) barca *f* de pasaje. 2 (*large, for cars*) transbordador *m*, ferry *m*. II *vtr* transportar.
fertile ['fɜːtaɪl] *adj* fértil.
fertility [fə'tɪlɪtɪ] *n* (*of soil*) fertilidad *f*.
fertilize ['fɜːtɪlaɪz] *vtr* 1 (*soil*) abonar. 2 (*egg*) fecundar.
fertilizer ['fɜːtɪlaɪzər] *n* abono *m*.
fervent ['fɜːvənt] *adj* ferviente.
fervour, *US* **fervor** ['fɜːvər] *n* fervor *m*.
fester ['festər] *vi* supurar.
festival ['festɪvəl] *n* (*event*) festival *m*; (*celebration*) fiesta *f*.
festive ['festɪv] *adj* festivo,-a; **the f. season**, las fiestas de Navidad.
festivity [fes'tɪvɪtɪ] *n* **the festivities**, las fiestas.
festoon [fe'stuːn] *vtr* adornar.
fetch [fetʃ] I *vtr* 1 (*go for*) ir a buscar. 2 (*bring*) traer. 3 **how much did it f.?**, (*sell for*) ¿por cuánto se vendió?
fetching ['fetʃɪŋ] *adj* atractivo,-a.
fete [feɪt] I *n* fiesta *f*. II *vtr* festejar.
fetish ['fetɪʃ, 'fiːtɪʃ] *n* fetiche *m*.
fetus ['fiːtəs] *n* *US* → **foetus**.
feud [fjuːd] I *n* enemistad duradera. II *vi* pelear.
feudal ['fjuːdəl] *adj* feudal.
fever ['fiːvər] *n* fiebre *f*.
feverish ['fiːvərɪʃ] *adj* febril.
few [fjuː] I *adj* 1 (*not many*) pocos,-as; **as f. as**, solamente. 2 (*some*) algunos,-as, unos,-as cuantos,-as; **a f. books**, unos or algunos libros; **she has fewer books than I thought**, tiene menos libros de lo que pensaba; **for the past f. years**, durante estos últimos años; **in the next f. days**, dentro de unos días; **quite a f.**, bastantes. II *pron* 1 (*not many*) pocos,-as; **there are too f.**, no hay suficientes; **the fewer the better**, cuantos menos mejor. 2 **a f.**, (*some*) algunos,-as, unos,-as cuantos,-as; **the chosen f.**, los elegidos; **who has the fewest?**, ¿quién tiene menos?
fiancé [fɪ'ɒnseɪ] *n* prometido *m*.
fiancée [fɪ'ɒnseɪ] *n* prometida *f*.
fiasco [fɪ'æskəʊ] *n* fiasco *m*.

fib [fɪb] *fam* **I** *n* trola *f*. **II** *vi* contar trolas.

fibre, *US* **fiber** ['faɪbər] *n* fibra *f*.

fibreglass, *US* **fiberglass** ['faɪbəglɑːs] *n* fibra *f* de vidrio.

fickle ['fɪkəl] *adj* inconstante, voluble.

fiction ['fɪkʃən] *n* ficción *f*.

fictional ['fɪkʃənəl] *adj* **1** *Lit* novelesco,-a. **2** *(imaginative)* ficticio,-a.

fictitious [fɪk'tɪʃəs] *adj* ficticio,-a.

fiddle ['fɪdəl] *fam* **I** *n* **1** *Mus* violín *m*. **2** *(shady deal)* trampa *f*. **II** *vtr* estafar; *(accounts)* falsificar. **III** *vi* juguetear (**with,** con). ◆**fiddle about** *vi* perder tiempo.

fiddly ['fɪdlɪ] *adj fam* laborioso,-a.

fidelity [fɪ'delɪtɪ] *n* fidelidad *f*.

fidget ['fɪdʒɪt] *vi* **1** moverse; **stop fidgeting!,** ¡estáte quieto! **2** jugar (**with,** con).

field [fiːld] *n* **1** campo *m*; **f. glasses,** gemelos *mpl*; **f. marshal,** mariscal *m* de campo. **2** *Geol Min* yacimiento *m*. **3** **f. trip,** viaje *m* de estudios; **f. work,** trabajo *m* de campo. **II** *vtr Sport* **1** *(ball)* parar y devolver. **2** *(team)* presentar.

fiend [fiːnd] *n* **1** demonio *m*; *fam (fanatic)* fanático,-a *m,f*.

fiendish ['fiːndɪʃ] *adj fam* diabólico,-a.

fierce [fɪəs] *adj (animal)* feroz; *(argument)* acalorado,-a; *(heat, competition)* intenso, -a; *(wind)* violento,-a.

fiery ['faɪərɪ] *adj (temper)* fogoso,-a; *(speech)* acalorado,-a; *(colour)* encendido,-a.

fifteen [fɪf'tiːn] *adj & n* quince *(m) inv*.

fifteenth [fɪf'tiːnθ] **I** *adj & n* decimoquinto,-a *(m,f)*. **II** *n (fraction)* quinzavo *m*.

fifth [fɪfθ] *adj & n* quinto,-a *(m,f)*. **II** *n (fraction)* quinto *m*.

fifty ['fɪftɪ] **I** *adj* cincuenta *inv*; *fam* **a f.-f. chance,** una probabilidad del cincuenta por ciento; *fam* **to go f.-f.,** ir a medias. **II** *n* cincuenta *m inv*.

fig¹ [fɪg] *n (fruit)* higo *m*.

fig² [fɪg] *abbr of* **figure,** fig.

fight [faɪt] **I** *vtr (pt & pp* **fought)** **1** pelear(se) con, luchar con; *(of boxer)* enfrentarse a, luchar con; *Taur* lidiar; *fig (corruption)* combatir (**against,** contra). **2** *(battle)* librar; *(war)* hacer. **3** *(decision)* recurrir contra. **II** *vi* **1** pelear(se), luchar. **2** *(quarrel)* reñir; **to f. over sth,** disputarse la posesión de algo. **3** *fig (struggle)* luchar (**for/against,** por/contra). **III** *n* **1** pelea *f*, lucha *f*; *Box* combate *m*. **2** *(quarrel)* riña *f*. **3** *fig (struggle)* lucha *f*. **4** *(spirit)* combatividad *f*. ◆**fight back I** *vtr (tears)* contener. **II** *vi* contraatacar. ◆**fight off** *vtr* **1** *(attack)* rechazar. **2** *(illness)* cortar. ◆**fight out** *vtr* discutir.

fighter ['faɪtər] *n* **1** *(person)* combatiente *mf*; *Box* púgil *m*. **2** *fig* luchador,-a *m,f*; **f. (plane),** *(avión m de)* caza *m*; **f. bomber,** cazabombardero *m*.

fighting ['faɪtɪŋ] **I** *adj* **he's got a f.**

chance, tiene verdaderas posibilidades. **II** *n* lucha *f*.

figment ['fɪgmənt] *n* **it's a f. of your imagination,** es un producto de tu imaginación.

figurative ['fɪgərətɪv] *adj* figurado,-a.

figure ['fɪgər, *US* 'fɪgjər] **I** *n* **1** *(form, outline)* forma *f*, silueta *f*. **2** *(shape, statue, character)* figura *f*; **she has a good f.,** tiene buen tipo. **3** *(in book)* dibujo *m*. **4** **f. of speech,** figura retórica. **5** *Math* cifra *f*. **II** *vtr US fam* imaginarse. **III** *vi* **1** *(appear)* figurar. **2** *US fam* **that figures,** eso tiene sentido. ◆**figure out** *vtr fam* comprender; **I can't f. it out,** no me lo explico.

figurehead ['fɪgəhed] *n fig* figura decorativa.

filament ['fɪləmənt] *n* filamento *m*.

filch [fɪltʃ] *vtr sl* mangar, birlar.

file [faɪl] **I** *n* **1** *(tool)* lima *f*. **2** *(folder)* carpeta *f*. **3** *(archive, of computer)* archivo *m*; **on f.,** archivado,-a. **4** *(line)* fila *f*; **in single f.,** en fila india. **II** *vtr* **1** *(smooth)* limar. **2** *(put away)* archivar. **III** *vi* **to f. past,** desfilar.

filing ['faɪlɪŋ] *n* clasificación *f*; **f. cabinet,** archivador *m*; *(for cards)* fichero *m,f*.

Filipino [fɪlɪ'piːnəu] *n* filipino,-a *m,f*.

fill [fɪl] **I** *vtr* **1** *(space, time)* llenar (**with,** de). **2** *(post, requirements)* cubrir. **3** *Culin* rellenar. **II** *vi* llenarse (**with,** de). **III** *n* **to eat one's f.,** comer hasta hartarse. ◆**fill in** *vtr* **1** *(space, time)* llenar; *(form)* rellenar. **2** *(inform) fam* poner al corriente (**on,** de). **3** *(time)* pasar. **II** *vi* **to f. in for sb,** sustituir a algn. ◆**fill out** *vtr US (form)* llenar. **II** *vi fam* engordar. ◆**fill up I** *vtr* llenar hasta arriba; *Aut fam* **f. her up!,** ¡llénelo!. **II** *vi* llenarse.

fillet ['fɪlɪt] *n* filete *m*; **f. steak,** filete.

filling ['fɪlɪŋ] **I** *adj* que llena mucho. **II** *n* **1** *(stuffing)* relleno *m*. **2** *(in tooth)* empaste *m*. **3** *GB* **f. station,** gasolinera *f*.

fillip ['fɪlɪp] *n fam* estímulo *m*.

film [fɪlm] **I** *n* **1** *Cin, Phot* película *f*; **f. star,** estrella *f* de cine. **2** *(layer)* capa *f*. **II** *vtr Cin* filmar. **III** *vi Cin* rodar.

film-strip ['fɪlmstrɪp] *n* cortometraje *m*.

filter ['fɪltər] **I** *n* filtro *m*; *Aut* **f. lane,** carril *m* de acceso. **II** *vtr* filtrar. **III** *vi Aut* **to f. to the right,** girar a la derecha. ◆**filter through** *vi fig* filtrarse (**to,** a).

filter-tip ['fɪltətɪp] *n (cigarette)* cigarrillo *m* con filtro.

filth [fɪlθ] *n (dirt)* porquería *f*; *fig* porquerías *fpl*.

filthy ['fɪlθɪ] *adj (filthier, filthiest)* **1** *(dirty)* asqueroso,-a. **2** *(obscene)* obsceno, -a.

fin [fɪn] *n Zool Av* aleta *f*.

final ['faɪnəl] **I** *adj* **1** *(last)* último,-a, final. **2** *(definitive)* definitivo,-a. **II** *n* **1** *Sport* final *f*. **2** *Univ* **finals,** exámenes *mpl* de

fin de carrera. ◆**finally** *adv* (*lastly*) por último; (*at last*) por fin.
finale |fı'nɑːlı| *n* final *m*.
finalist |'faınəlıst| *n* finalista *mf*.
finalize |'faınəlaız| *vtr* ultimar; (*date*) fijar.
finance |'faınæns, fı'næns| I *n* 1 finanzas *fpl*. 2 **finances**, fondos *mpl*. II *vtr* financiar.
financial |faı'nænʃəl, fı'nænʃəl| *adj* financiero,-a; **f. crisis**, crisis económica; **f. year**, año económico.
financier |faı'nænsıə', fı'nænsıə'| *n* financiero,-a *m,f*.
finch |fıntʃ| *n* pinzón *m*.
find |faınd| I *vtr* (*pt & pp* found) 1 (*locate*) encontrar. 2 (*think*) encontrar. 3 **this found its way into my bag**, esto vino a parar a mi bolso. 4 (*discover*) descubrir; **it has been found that ...**, se ha comprobado que ... 5 *Jur* **to f. sb guilty/not guilty**, declarar culpable/inocente a algn. 6 **I can't f. the courage to tell him**, no tengo valor para decírselo; **I found it impossible to get away**, me resultó imposible irme. II *n* hallazgo *m*. ◆**find out** I *vtr* 1 (*enquire*) averiguar. 2 (*discover*) descubrir. II *vi* 1 **to f. out about sth**, informarse sobre algo. 2 (*discover*) enterarse.
findings |'faındıŋz| *npl* conclusiones *fpl*.
fine¹ |faın| I *n* multa *f*. II *vtr* multar.
fine² |faın| I *adj* 1 (*delicate etc*) fino,-a. 2 (*subtle*) sutil. 3 (*excellent*) excelente. 4 (*weather*) bueno; **it was f.**, hacía buen tiempo. 5 **the f. arts**, las bellas artes. 6 (*all right*) bien. II *adv fam* muy bien. III *interj* ¡vale! ◆**finely** *adv* 1 finamente; **f. chopped**, picado fino. 2 **f. tuned**, a punto.
finery |'faınərı| *n* galas *fpl*.
finesse |fı'nes| *n* (*delicacy*) finura *f*; (*cunning*) astucia *f*; (*tact*) sutileza *f*.
finger |'fıŋgə'| I *n* dedo *m* (de la mano); *fam* **to keep one's fingers crossed**, esperar que todo salga bien; *fam* **you've put your f. on it**, has dado en el clavo; **middle f.**, dedo corazón. II *vtr* tocar; *pej* manosear.
fingernail |'fıŋgəneıl| *n* uña *f*.
fingerprint |'fıŋgəprınt| *n* huella *f* dactilar.
fingertip |'fıŋgətıp| *n* punta *f* or yema *f* del dedo.
finicky |'fınıkı| *adj* (*person*) quisquilloso, -a.
finish |'fınıʃ| I *n* 1 fin *m*; (*of race*) llegada *f*. 2 (*surface*) acabado *m*. II *vtr* 1 (*complete*) acabar, terminar; **to f. doing sth**, terminar de hacer algo. 2 (*use up*) agotar. III *vi* acabar, terminar; **to f. second**, quedar el segundo. ◆**finish off** *vtr* 1 (*complete*) terminar completamente. 2 (*kill*) *fam* rematar. ◆**finish up** I *vtr* aca-

bar, agotar. II *vi* **to f. up in jail**, ir a parar a la carcel.
finished |'fınıʃt| *adj* 1 (*product*) acabado, -a. 2 *fam* (*exhausted*) rendido,-a.
finishing |'fınıʃıŋ| *adj* **to put the f. touch(es) to sth**, darle los últimos toques a algo; **f. line**, (línea *f* de) meta *f*; **f. school**, escuela privada de modales para señoritas.
finite |'faınaıt| *adj* finito,-a; (*verb*) conjugable.
Finland |'fınlənd| *n* Finlandia.
Finn |fın| *n* finlandés,-esa *m,f*.
Finnish |'fınıʃ| I *adj* finlandés,-esa. II *n* (*language*) finlandés *m*.
fir |fɜː| *n* abeto *m*.
fire |'faıə'| I *n* 1 fuego *m*. 2 (*accident etc*) incendio *m*; **to be on f.**, estar en llamas; **to catch f.**, incendiarse; **f. alarm**, alarma *f* de incendios; **f. brigade**, (cuerpo *m* de) bomberos *mpl*; **f. engine**, coche *m* de bomberos; **f. escape**, escalera *f* de incendios; **f. exit**, salida *f* de emergencia; **f. extinguisher**, extintor *m*; **f. fighting**, extinción *f* de incendios; **f. station**, parque *m* de bomberos. 3 (*heater*) estufa *f*. 4 *Mil* fuego *m*; **to open f.**, abrir fuego; *fig* **to come under f.**, ser el blanco de las críticas. II *vtr* 1 (*gun*) disparar (**at**, a); (*rocket*) lanzar; *fig* **to f. questions at sb**, bombardear a algn a preguntas. 2 *fam* (*dismiss*) despedir. III *vi* (*shoot*) disparar (**at**, sobre).
firearm |'faıərɑːm| *n* arma *f* de fuego.
fire-fighter |'faıəfaıtə'| *n* US bombero *m*.
fireman |'faıəmən| *n* bombero *m*.
fireplace |'faıəpleıs| *n* chimenea *f*; (*hearth*) hogar *m*.
fireside |'faıəsaıd| *n* hogar *m*; **by the f.**, al calor de la lumbre.
firewood |'faıəwʊd| *n* leña *f*.
fireworks |'faıəwɜːks| *npl* fuegos *mpl* artificiales.
firing |'faıərıŋ| *n* *Mil* tiroteo *m*; **f. line**, línea *f* de fuego; **f. squad**, pelotón *m* de fusilamiento.
firm |fɜːm| I *adj* firme; **to be f. with sb**, (*strict*) tratar a algn con firmeza. II *n* *Com* empresa *f*, firma *f*. ◆**firmly** *adv* firmemente.
firmness |'fɜːmnıs| *n* firmeza *f*.
first |fɜːst| I *adj* primero,-a; (*before masculine singular noun*) primer; **Charles the F.**, Carlos Primero; **for the f. time**, por primera vez; **in the f. place**, en primer lugar; **f. floor**, primer piso *m*, US planta baja; **f. name**, nombre *m* de pila. II *adv* (*before anything else*) primero; **f. and foremost**, ante todo; **f. of all**, en primer lugar. III *n* 1 **the f.**, el primero, la primera; **the f. of April**, el uno or el primero de abril; **f. aid**, primeros auxilios; **f. aid box**, botiquín *m*. 2 **at f.**, al principio; **from the (very) f.**, desde el principio. 3

Aut primera *f*. 4 *Univ* to get a f., sacar un sobresaliente. ◆**firstly** *adv* en primer lugar.

first-class ['fɜːstklɑːs] I *adj* de primera clase. II **first class** *adv* to travel f. c., viajar en primera.

first-hand ['fɜːsthænd] *adv & adj* de primera mano.

first-rate ['fɜːstreɪt] *adj* de primera.

fiscal ['fɪskəl] *adj* fiscal.

fish [fɪʃ] I *n* (*pl* **fish**) 1 pez *m*; f. shop, pescadería *f*. 2 *Culin* pescado *m*; f. and chips, pescado frito con patatas fritas; *US* f. stick, palito *m* de pescado. II *vi* pescar; fig to f. in one's pocket for sth, buscar algo en el bolsillo.

fishbone ['fɪʃbəʊn] *n* espina *f*, raspa *f*.

fisherman ['fɪʃəmən] *n* pescador *m*.

fishfinger [fɪʃ'fɪŋgər] *n* palito *m* de pescado.

fishing ['fɪʃɪŋ] *n* pesca *f*; to go f., ir de pesca; f. net, red *f* de pesca; f. rod, caña *f* de pescar; f. tackle, aparejo *m* de pescar.

fishmonger ['fɪʃmʌŋgər] *n* GB pescadero,-a *m,f*; **fishmonger's** (shop), pescadería *f*.

fishy ['fɪʃɪ] *adj* (**fishier, fishiest**) de pescado; *fam fig* there's something f. going on, aquí hay gato encerrado.

fist [fɪst] *n* puño *m*.

fit¹ [fɪt] I *vtr* 1 ir bien a; that suit doesn't f. you, ese traje no te entalla. 2 *Sew* probar. 3 the key doesn't f. the lock, la llave no es de esta cerradura. 4 (*install*) colocar; a car fitted with a radio, un coche provisto de radio. 5 *fig* she doesn't f. the description, no responde a la descripción. II *vi* 1 (*be of right size*) caber. 2 (*facts etc*) cuadrar. III *adj* 1 (*suitable*) apto,-a, adecuado,-a (**for**, para); are you f. to drive?, ¿estás en condiciones de conducir? 2 (*healthy*) en (plena) forma; to keep f., mantenerse en forma. IV *n* ajuste *m*; *Sew* corte *m*; to be a good f., encajar bien. ◆**fit in** I *vi* 1 he didn't f. in with his colleagues, no encajó con sus compañeros de trabajo. 2 (*tally*) cuadrar (**with**, con). II *vtr* (*find time for*) encontrar un hueco para. ◆**fit out** *vtr* equipar.

fit² [fɪt] *n* 1 *Med* ataque *m*. 2 *fig* arrebato *m*; f. of anger, arranque *m* de cólera; *fig* by fits and starts, a trompicones.

fitful ['fɪtfʊl] *adj* discontinuo,-a.

fitness ['fɪtnɪs] *n* 1 (*aptitude*) aptitud *f*, capacidad *f*. 2 (*health*) (buen) estado físico.

fitted ['fɪtɪd] *adj* empotrado,-a; f. carpet, moqueta *f*; f. cupboard, armario empotrado.

fitter ['fɪtər] *n* ajustador,-a *m,f*.

fitting ['fɪtɪŋ] I *adj* apropiado,-a. II *n* 1 (*of dress*) prueba *f*; f. room, probador *m*. 2 (*usu pl*) accesorio *m*; light fittings, apli-

ques eléctricos.

five [faɪv] *adj & n* cinco (*m*) *inv*.

fiver ['faɪvər] *n fam* billete *m* de cinco libras *or* dólares.

fix [fɪks] I *n* 1 *fam* to be in a f., estar en un apuro. 2 (*drugs*) *sl* chute *m*. II *vtr* 1 (*fasten*) fijar, asegurar. 2 (*date, price*) fijar; (*limit*) señalar. 3 he'll f. it with the boss, (*arrange*) se las arreglará con el jefe. 4 (*repair*) arreglar. 5 *US* (*food, drink*) preparar. ◆**fix up** *vtr* (*arrange*) arreglar; to f. sb up with sth, proveer a algn de algo.

fixation [fɪk'seɪʃən] *n* idea fija.

fixed [fɪkst] *adj* 1 fijo,-a. 2 *fam* (*match etc*) amañado,-a.

fixture ['fɪkstʃər] *n* 1 *Sport* encuentro *m*. 2 fixtures, (*in building*) accesorios *mpl*.

fizz [fɪz] I *n* burbujeo *m*. II *vi* burbujear. ◆**fizzle out** ['fɪzəlaʊt] *vi* quedar en nada.

fizzy ['fɪzɪ] *adj* (**fizzier, fizziest**) (*water*) con gas.

flabbergasted ['flæbəgɑːstɪd] *adj* pasmado,-a.

flabby ['flæbɪ] *adj* (**flabbier, flabbiest**) fofo,-a.

flag [flæg] I *n* bandera *f*; *Naut* pabellón *m*. II *vtr fig* to f. down a car, hacer señales a un coche para que pare. III *vi* (*interest*) decaer; (*conversation*) languidecer.

flagpole ['flægpəʊl] *n* asta *f* de bandera.

flagrant ['fleɪgrənt] *adj* flagrante.

flagship ['flægʃɪp] *n* buque insignia *m*.

flagstone ['flægstəʊn] *n* losa *f*.

flair [fleər] *n* facilidad *f*.

flak [flæk] *n* 1 *Mil* fuego antiaéreo. 2 *fam* críticas *fpl*.

flake [fleɪk] I *n* (*of snow*) copo *m*; (*of skin, soap*) escama *f*; (*of paint*) desconchón *m*. II *vi* (*skin*) descamarse; (*paint*) desconcharse.

flamboyant [flæm'bɔɪənt] *adj* extravagante.

flame [fleɪm] *n* llama *f*; to go up in flames, incendiarse.

flameproof ['fleɪmpruːf] *adj* ininflamable.

flamingo [flə'mɪŋgəʊ] *n* flamenco *m*.

flammable ['flæməbəl] *adj* inflamable.

flan [flæn] *n* tarta rellena; fruit f., tarta de fruta.

flank [flæŋk] I *n* 1 (*of animal*) ijada *f*. 2 *Mil* flanco *m*. II *vtr* flanquear.

flannel ['flænəl] *n* 1 *Tex* franela *f*. 2 GB (*face cloth*) toallita *f*.

flap [flæp] I *vtr* (*wings, arms*) batir. II *vi* (*wings*) aletear; (*flag*) ondear. III *n* 1 (*of envelope, pocket*) solapa *f*; (*of tent*) faldón *m*. 2 (*of wing*) aletazo *m*. 3 *fam* to get into a f., ponerse nervioso,-a.

flare [fleər] I *n* 1 (*flame*) llamarada *f*. 2 *Mil Naut* bengala *f*. II *vi* to f. (up), (*fire*) llamear; *fig* (*person*) encolerizarse; (*trouble*) estallar.

flared [fleəd] *adj* (*trousers etc*)

acampanado,-a.

flash [flæʃ] **I** n 1 (of light) destello m; (of lightning) relámpago m; fig in a f., en un santiamén; fig **a f. in the pan**, un éxito fugaz. 2 **news f.**, noticia f de última hora. 3 Phot flash m. **II** adj sl chulo,-a. **III** vtr 1 (torch) dirigir. 2 Rad TV transmitir. 3 **he flashed his card**, enseñó rápidamente su carnet. **IV** vi 1 (light) destellar. 2 **a car flashed past**, un coche pasó como un rayo.

flashback ['flæʃbæk] n flashback m.

flashcube ['flæʃkjuːb] n cubo m flash.

flashlight ['flæʃlaɪt] n US linterna f.

flashy ['flæʃɪ] adj (flashier, flashiest) fam chillón,-a.

flask [flɑːsk, flæsk] n frasco m; (thermos) f., termo m.

flat [flæt] **I** adj (flatter, flattest) 1 (surface) llano,-a. 2 (beer) sin gas. 3 (battery) descargado,-a; (tyre) desinflado,-a. 4 (rate) fijo,-a. 5 (categorical) rotundo,-a. 6 (dull) soso,-a. 7 Mus B f., si m bemol. **II** adv 1 **to fall f. on one's face**, caerse de bruces. 2 **in ten seconds f.**, en diez segundos justos. 3 fam **to go f. out**, ir a todo gas. **III** n 1 (appartment) piso m. 2 US Aut pinchazo m. 3 **mud flats**, marismas fpl. ◆**flatly** adv rotundamente.

flatmate ['flætmeɪt] n GB compañero,-a m,f de piso.

flatten ['flætən] vtr 1 (make level) allanar. 2 (crush) aplastar.

flatter ['flætər] vtr 1 adular, halagar. 2 (clothes, portrait) favorecer. 3 **to f. oneself**, hacerse ilusiones.

flattering ['flætərɪŋ] adj 1 (words) halagador,-a. 2 (dress, portrait) favorecedor,-a.

flattery ['flætərɪ] n adulación f, halago m.

flaunt [flɔːnt] vtr hacer alarde de.

flavour, US **flavor** ['fleɪvər] **I** n 1 sabor m. **II** vtr Culin sazonar (**with**, con).

flavoured, US **flavored** ['fleɪvəd] adj **strawberry f.**, con sabor a fresa.

flavouring, US **flavoring** ['fleɪvərɪŋ] n condimento m; **artificial f.**, aroma m artificial.

flaw [flɔː] n (failing) defecto m; (fault) desperfecto m.

flawless ['flɔːlɪs] adj perfecto,-a.

flax [flæks] n lino m.

flaxen ['flæksən] adj (hair) rubio pajizo.

flea [fliː] n pulga f; **f. market**, rastro m.

fleck [flek] n (speck) mota f, punto m.

fledg(e)ling ['fledʒlɪŋ] adj fig novato,-a.

flee [fliː] **I** vtr (pt & pp **fled**) huir de. **II** vi huir (**from**, de).

fleece [fliːs] **I** n 1 (sheep's coat) lana f. 2 (sheared) vellón m. **II** vtr fam (cheat) sangrar.

fleet [fliːt] n flota f.

fleeting ['fliːtɪŋ] adj fugaz.

Flemish ['flemɪʃ] **I** adj flamenco,-a. **II** n

(language) flamenco m.

flesh [fleʃ] n 1 carne f; fig **in the f.**, en persona; fig **to be of f. and blood**, ser de carne y hueso; **f. wound**, herida f superficial. 2 (of fruit) pulpa f.

flew [fluː] pt → **fly**.

flex [fleks] **I** n GB Elec cable m. **II** vtr (muscles) flexionar.

flexible ['fleksɪbəl] adj flexible.

flexibility [fleksɪ'bɪlɪtɪ] n flexibilidad f.

flick [flɪk] **I** n movimiento rápido; (of finger) capirotazo m. **II** vtr (with finger) dar un capirotazo a. ◆**flick through** vtr (book) hojear.

flicker ['flɪkər] **I** n 1 parpadeo m; (of light) titileo m. 2 fig **a f. of hope**, un destello de esperanza. **II** vi (eyes) parpadear; (flame) vacilar.

flier ['flaɪər] n aviador,-a m,f.

flight [flaɪt] n 1 vuelo m; **f. path**, trayectoria f de vuelo; **f. recorder**, registrador m de vuelo. 2 (of ball) trayectoria f. 3 (escape) huida f, fuga f; **to take f.**, darse a la fuga. 4 (of stairs) tramo m.

flight-deck ['flaɪtdek] n (cockpit) cabina f del piloto.

flimsy ['flɪmzɪ] adj (flimsier, flimsiest) (cloth) ligero,-a; (paper) fino,-a; (structure) poco sólido,-a; (excuse) poco convincente.

flinch [flɪntʃ] vi (wince) estremecerse.

fling [flɪŋ] **I** vtr (pt & pp **flung**) arrojar. **II** n fam **to have a f.**, echar una cana al aire.

flint [flɪnt] n 1 (stone) pedernal m. 2 (in lighter) piedra f de mechero.

flip [flɪp] **I** n (flick) capirotazo m. **II** vtr (toss) tirar (al aire); **to f. a coin**, echar a cara o cruz.

flip-flop ['flɪpflɒp] n 1 Comput báscula f biestable. 2 (footwear) chancleta f.

flippant ['flɪpənt] adj frívolo,-a.

flipper ['flɪpər] n aleta f.

flirt [flɜːt] **I** n coqueto,-a m,f. **II** vi flirtear, coquetear; **to f. with death**, jugar con la muerte.

flirtation [flɜː'teɪʃən] n flirteo m, coqueteo m.

flit [flɪt] vi revolotear.

float [fləʊt] **I** n 1 flotador m. 2 (money) cambio m. 3 (in procession) carroza f. **II** vtr 1 poner a flote. 2 (shares) emitir; (currency, business) hacer flotar. **III** vi flotar.

floating ['fləʊtɪŋ] adj flotante; (voter) indeciso,-a.

flock [flɒk] **I** n Zool rebaño m; Orn bandada f; Rel grey f; (crowd) multitud f. **II** vi acudir en masa.

flog [flɒg] vtr 1 azotar; fam fig **flogged to death**, (idea) trillado. 2 sl (sell) vender.

flood [flʌd] **I** n 1 inundación f; (of river) riada f; fig torrente m. **II** vtr inundar. **III** vi (river) desbordarse; fig **to f. in**, entrar a raudales.

flooding |'flʌdɪŋ| n inundaciones fpl.

floodlight |'flʌdlaɪt| n foco m.

floor |flɔːr| I n 1 (of room) suelo m; dance f., pista f de baile. 2 (of ocean, forest) fondo m. 3 (storey) piso m; first f., GB primer piso m, US planta baja; GB ground f., planta baja. II vtr fig dejar perplejo,-a.

floorboard |'flɔːbɔːd| n tabla f (del suelo).

flop |flɒp| I n fam fracaso m. II vi 1 to f. down on the bed, tumbarse en la cama. 2 fam fracasar.

floppy |'flɒpɪ| adj (floppier, floppiest) flojo,-a; Comput f. disk, disco m flexible.

flora |'flɔːrə| n flora f.

florid |'flɒrɪd| adj (style) florido,-a.

florist |'flɒrɪst| n florista mf; f.'s, floristería f.

flounce¹ |flaʊns| vi to f. in/out, entrar/salir airadamente.

flounce² |flaʊns| n Sew volante m.

flounder¹ |'flaʊndər| n (fish) platija f.

flounder² |'flaʊndər| vi 1 (struggle) forcejear; fig enredarse. 2 (be at a loss) no saber que decir or hacer.

flour |'flaʊər| n harina f.

flourish |'flʌrɪʃ| I n 1 (gesture) ademán m (teatral). 2 (under signature) rúbrica f. II vtr (brandish) agitar. III vi (thrive) florecer; (plant) crecer.

flourishing |'flʌrɪʃɪŋ| adj floreciente.

flout |flaʊt| vtr Jur desacatar.

flow |fləʊ| I n flujo m; (of river) corriente f; (of traffic) circulación f; (of capital) movimiento m; (of people, goods) afluencia f; f. chart, diagrama m de flujo; Comput organigrama m. II vi (blood, river) fluir; (sea) subir; (traffic) circular.

flower |'flaʊər| I n flor f; f. bed, arriate m. II vi florecer.

flowerpot |'flaʊəpɒt| n maceta f.

flowery |'flaʊrɪ| adj fig florido,-a.

flowing |'fləʊɪŋ| adj (hair) suelto,-a; (dress) de mucho vuelo; (style) fluido,-a; (shape, movement) natural.

flown |fləʊn| pp → fly.

flu |fluː| n (abbr of influenza) gripe f.

fluctuate |'flʌktjʊeɪt| vi fluctuar.

fluctuation |flʌktjʊ'eɪʃən| n fluctuación f.

flue |fluː| n conducto m de humos; (chimney) cañón m.

fluent |'fluːənt| adj 1 he speaks f. German, habla el alemán con soltura. 2 (eloquent) fluido,-a.

fluff |flʌf| I n (down) pelusa f. II vtr fam to f. sth, hacer algo mal.

fluffy |'flʌfɪ| adj (fluffier, fluffiest) (pillow) mullido,-a; (toy) de peluche; (cake) esponjoso,-a.

fluid |'fluːɪd| I adj (movement) natural; (style, prose) fluido,-a; (situation) incierto,-a. II n fluido m, líquido m.

fluke |fluːk| n fam chiripa f; by a f., por chiripa.

flummox |'flʌməks| vtr fam desconcertar.

flung |flʌŋ| pt & pp → fling.

fluorescent |flʊə'resənt| adj fluorescente.

fluoride |'flʊəraɪd| n fluoruro m.

flurry |'flʌrɪ| n 1 (of wind) ráfaga f; (of snow) nevasca f. 2 fig (bustle) agitación f.

flush |flʌʃ| I adj f. with, (level) a ras de. II n (blush) rubor m. III vtr to f. the lavatory, tirar de la cadena. IV vi 1 the loo won't f., la cisterna del wáter no funciona. 2 (blush) ruborizarse.

flushed |flʌʃt| adj (cheeks) rojo,-a, encendido,-a; fig f. with success, emocionado,-a ante el éxito.

fluster |'flʌstər| vtr to get flustered, ponerse nervioso,-a.

flute |fluːt| n flauta f.

flutter |'flʌtər| I vi (leaves, birds) revolotear; (flag) ondear. II n fam (bet, gambling) apuesta pequeña.

flux |flʌks| n (flow) flujo m; (instability) inestabilidad f; fig to be in a state of f., estar cambiando constantemente.

fly¹ |flaɪ| I vtr (pt flew; pp flown) 1 Av pilotar. 2 (merchandize, troops) transportar. 3 (distance) recorrer. 4 (kite) hacer volar. II vi 1 (bird, plane) volar. 2 (go by plane) ir en avión. 3 (flag) ondear. 4 to f. into a rage, montar en cólera. 5 the train flew past, el tren pasó volando. 6 fam to go flying, (fall) caerse. III n flies, braguета f sing.

fly² |flaɪ| n (insect) mosca f; f. spray, spray m matamoscas.

flying |'flaɪɪŋ| I adj volador,-a; (rapid) rápido,-a; a f. visit, una visita relámpago; fig to come out of an affair with f. colours, salir airoso,-a de un asunto; fig to get off to a f. start, empezar con buen pie; f. picket, piquete m (informativo); f. saucer, platillo m volante. II n 1 (action) vuelo m. 2 (aviation) aviación f.

flyleaf |'flaɪliːf| n (of book) guarda f.

flyover |'flaɪəʊvər| n paso elevado.

flypast |'flaɪpɑːst| n GB Av desfile aéreo.

flyweight |'flaɪweɪt| n Box peso m mosca.

foal |fəʊl| n potro,-a m,f.

foam |fəʊm| I n espuma f. f. bath, espuma de baño; f. rubber, goma espuma. II vi hacer espuma.

fob |fɒb| vtr fam to f. sb off with excuses, darle largas a algn. ◆fob off vtr fam he fobbed off his old radio on a stranger, le colocó su radio vieja a un desconocido.

focus |'fəʊkəs| I vtr centrarse (on, en). II vi enfocar; to f. on sth, Phot enfocar algo; fig centrarse en algo. III n (pl focuses) foco m; to be in f./out of f., estar enfocado,-a/desenfocado,-a.

fodder |'fɒdər| n pasto seco.

foe |fəʊ| n fml enemigo,-a m,f.

foetus |'fiːtəs| n feto m.

fog [fɒg] n niebla f; (at sea) bruma f.

fogey ['fəʊgɪ] n fam old f., cascarrabias mf inv.

foggy ['fɒgɪ] adj (foggier, foggiest) it is f., hay niebla; fam I haven't the foggiest (idea), no tengo la más mínima idea.

foghorn ['fɒghɔːn] n sirena f (de niebla).

foglamp ['fɒglæmp], US **foglight** ['fɒglaɪt] n faro m antiniebla.

foil [fɔɪl] I n 1 aluminium f., papel m de aluminio. 2 (in fencing) florete m. II vtr (plot) desbaratar.

fold [fəʊld] I n (crease) pliegue m. II vtr plegar, doblar; to f. one's arms, cruzar los brazos. III vi to f. (up), (chair etc) plegarse; Com quebrar.

folder ['fəʊldər] n carpeta f.

folding ['fəʊldɪŋ] adj (chair etc) plegable.

foliage ['fəʊlɪɪdʒ] n follaje m.

folk [fəʊk] I npl 1 (people) gente f. 2 fam **folks**, (family) padres mpl; one's f., la familia. II adj popular; f. music, música f folk; f. song, canción f popular.

folklore ['fəʊklɔːr] n folklore m.

follow ['fɒləʊ] I vtr seguir; (pursue) perseguir; (understand) comprender; (way of life) llevar. II vi 1 (come after) seguir; as **follows**, como sigue. 2 (result) resultar; that doesn't f., eso no es lógico. 3 (understand) entender. ◆**follow through, follow up** vtr (idea) llevar a cabo; (clue) investigar.

follower ['fɒləʊər] n seguidor,-a m,f.

following ['fɒləʊɪŋ] I adj siguiente. II n seguidores mpl.

folly ['fɒlɪ] n locura f, desatino m.

fond [fɒnd] adj (loving) cariñoso,-a; to be f. of sb, tenerle mucho cariño a algn; to be f. of doing sth, ser aficionado,-a a hacer algo.

fondness ['fɒndnɪs] n (love) cariño m (for, a); (liking) afición f (for, a).

fondle ['fɒndəl] vtr acariciar.

font [fɒnt] n Rel pila f.

food [fuːd] n comida f; f. chain, cadena trófica; f. poisoning, intoxicación alimenticia.

foodstuffs ['fuːdstʌfs] npl productos alimenticios.

fool [fuːl] I n 1 tonto,-a m,f, imbécil mf; to make a f. of sb, poner a algn en ridículo; to play the f., hacer el tonto. 2 Culin ≈ mousse f de fruta. II vtr (deceive) engañar. III vi (joke) bromear; to f. about or around, hacer el tonto.

foolhardy ['fuːlhɑːdɪ] adj (foolhardier, foolhardiest) temerario,-a; (person) intrépido,-a.

foolish ['fuːlɪʃ] adj estúpido,-a.

foolproof ['fuːlpruːf] adj infalible.

foot [fʊt] I n (pl feet [fiːt]) pie m; Zool pata f; on f., a pie, andando; fig to find one's feet, acostumbrarse; fam fig to put one's f. down, (control) imponerse; (in

car) pisar a fondo; fam fig to put one's f. in it, meter la pata; fam fig to put one's feet up, descansar. II vtr to f. the bill, (pay) pagar la cuenta.

footage ['fʊtɪdʒ] n Cin metraje m.

football ['fʊtbɔːl] n 1 (soccer) fútbol m; bar f., futbolín m; f. ground, campo m de fútbol; f. match, partido m de fútbol; f. pools, quinielas fpl. 2 (ball) balón m.

footballer ['fʊtbɔːlər] n futbolista mf.

footbridge ['fʊtbrɪdʒ] n puente m para peatones.

foothills ['fʊthɪlz] npl estribaciones fpl.

foothold ['fʊthəʊld] n fig to gain a f., afianzarse en una posición.

footing ['fʊtɪŋ] n to lose one's f., perder el equilibrio; on a friendly f., en plan amistoso; on an equal f., en pie de igualdad.

footlights ['fʊtlaɪts] npl candilejas fpl.

footman ['fʊtmən] n lacayo m.

footnote ['fʊtnəʊt] n nota f a pie de página.

footpath ['fʊtpɑːθ] n (track) sendero m.

footprint ['fʊtprɪnt] n pisada f.

footsore ['fʊtsɔːr] adj con los pies doloridos.

footstep ['fʊtstep] n paso m.

footwear ['fʊtweər] n calzado m.

for [fɔːr] I prep 1 (intended) para; curtains f. the bedroom, cortinas para el dormitorio; f. sale, en venta; it's time f. bed, es hora de acostarse. 2 (representing) por; a cheque f. ten pounds, un cheque de diez libras; J f. John, J de Juan; what's the Spanish f. 'rivet'?, ¿cómo se dice 'rivet' en español? 3 (purpose) para; it's good f. the digestion, es bueno para la digestión; what's this f.?, ¿para qué sirve esto? 4 (because of) por; famous f. its cuisine, famoso,-a por su cocina; to jump f. joy, saltar de alegría. 5 (on behalf of) por; the campaign f. peace, la campaña por la paz; will you do it f. me?, ¿lo harás por mí? 6 (during) por, durante; I lent it to her f. a year, se lo presté por un año; I shall stay f. two weeks, me quedaré dos semanas; I was ill f. a month, estuve enfermo,-a durante un mes; I've been here f. three months, hace tres meses que estoy aquí. 7 (distance) I walked f. ten kilometres, caminé diez kilómetros. 8 (at a point in time) para; I can do it f. next Monday, puedo hacerlo para el lunes que viene; f. the last time, por última vez. 9 (destination) para. 10 (amount of money) por; I got the car f. five hundred pounds, conseguí el coche por quinientas libras. 11 (in favour of) a favor de; are you f. or against?, ¿estás a favor o en contra?; to vote f. sb, votar a algn. 12 (to obtain) para; to run f. the bus, correr para coger el autobús; to send sb f. water, mandar a algn a por agua. 13

(with respect to) en cuanto a; **as f. him,** en cuanto a él; **f. all I care,** por mí; **f. all I know,** que yo sepa; **f. one thing,** para empezar. **14** *(despite)* a pesar de; **f. all that,** aún así; **he's tall f. his age,** está muy alto para su edad. **15** *(instead of)* por; **can you go f. me?,** ¿puede ir por mí? **16** *(towards)* hacia, por; **affection f. sb,** cariño hacia algn; **his love f. you,** su amor por ti. **17** *(as)* por; **to leave sb f. dead,** dar a algn por muerto,-a; **what do you use f. fuel?,** ¿qué utilizan como combustible? **18** *(in exchange)* por; **to exchange one thing f. another,** cambiar una cosa por otra; **how much did you sell it f.?,** ¿por cuánto lo vendiste? **19** *(+ object + infin)* **there's no reason f. us to quarrel,** no hay motivo para que riñamos; **it's time f. you to go,** es hora de que os marchéis; **it's easy f. him to say that,** le es fácil decir eso.
II *conj (since, as)* ya que, puesto que.
forage ['fɒrɪdʒ] **I** *n* forraje *m.* **II** *vi* hurgar.
foray ['fɒreɪ] *n* incursión *f.*
forbearance [fɔːˈbeərəns] *n* paciencia *f.*
forbid [fəˈbɪd] *vtr (pt* **forbade;** *pp* **forbidden** [fəˈbɪdən]*)* prohibir; **to f. sb to do sth,** prohibirle a algn hacer algo.
forbidding [fəˈbɪdɪŋ] *adj (stern)* severo,-a; *(bleak)* inhóspito,-a.
force [fɔːs] **I** *n* **1** fuerza *f;* **by f.,** por la fuerza; **to come into f.,** entrar en vigor. **2** *Mil* cuerpo *m;* **the (armed) forces,** las fuerzas armadas; **the police f.,** la policía. **II** *vtr* forzar; **to f. sb to do sth,** forzar a algn a hacer algo.
forced [fɔːst] *adj* forzado,-a; **f. landing,** aterrizaje forzoso.
force-feed ['fɔːsfiːd] *vtr* alimentar a la fuerza.
forceful ['fɔːsfʊl] *adj* **1** *(person)* enérgico, -a. **2** *(argument)* convincente.
forcible ['fɔːsəbəl] *adj* **f. entry,** allanamiento *m* de morada. ◆**forcibly** *adv* a *or* por la fuerza.
forceps ['fɔːseps] *npl* fórceps *m sing.*
ford [fɔːd] **I** *n* vado *m.* **II** *vtr* vadear.
fore [fɔːr] *fig* **to come to the f.,** empezar a destacar.
forearm ['fɔːrɑːm] *n* antebrazo *m.*
foreboding [fɔːˈbəʊdɪŋ] *n* presentimiento *m.*
forecast ['fɔːkɑːst] **I** *n* pronóstico *m.* **II** *vtr (pt & pp* **forecast** *or* **forecasted***)* pronosticar.
forecourt ['fɔːkɔːt] *n (of garage)* área *f* de servicio.
forefathers ['fɔːfɑːðəz] *npl* antepasados *mpl.*
forefront ['fɔːfrʌnt] *n* **in the f.,** a la vanguardia.
forego [fɔːˈɡəʊ] *vtr fml (pt* **forewent;** *pp* **foregone***)* sacrificar.

foregone ['fɔːɡɒn] *adj* **a f. conclusion,** un resultado inevitable.
foreground ['fɔːɡraʊnd] *n* primer plano *m.*
forehead ['fɒrɪd, 'fɔːhed] *n* frente *f.*
foreign ['fɒrɪn] *adj* extranjero,-a; *(trade, policy)* exterior; **f. exchange,** divisas *fpl;* **the F. Office,** el Ministerio de Asuntos Exteriores; **f. body,** cuerpo extraño.
foreigner ['fɒrɪnər] *n* extranjero,-a *m,f.*
foreman ['fɔːmən] *n* **1** *Ind* capataz *m.* **2** *Jur* presidente *m* del jurado.
foremost ['fɔːməʊst] *adj* principal; **first and f.,** ante todo.
forename ['fɔːneɪm] *n* nombre *m* de pila.
forensic [fəˈrensɪk] *adj* forense.
forerunner ['fɔːrʌnər] *n* precursor,-a *m,f.*
foresee [fɔːˈsiː] *vtr (pt* **foresaw** *pp* **foreseen***)* prever.
foreseeable [fɔːˈsiːəbəl] *adj* previsible; **in the f. future,** en un futuro próximo.
foreshadow [fɔːˈʃædəʊ] *vtr* presagiar.
foresight ['fɔːsaɪt] *n* previsión *f.*
forest ['fɒrɪst] *n* bosque *m.*
forestall [fɔːˈstɔːl] *vtr (plan)* anticiparse a; *(danger)* prevenir.
forestry ['fɒrɪstrɪ] *n* silvicultura *f.*
foretaste ['fɔːteɪst] *n* anticipo *m* (**of,** de).
foretell [fɔːˈtel] *vtr (pt & pp* **foretold***)* presagiar.
forever [fəˈrevər] *adv* **1** *(eternally)* siempre. **2** *(for good)* para siempre. **3** *fam (ages)* siglos *mpl.*
foreword ['fɔːwɜːd] *n* prefacio *m.*
forfeit ['fɔːfɪt] **I** *n (penalty)* pena *f;* *(in games)* prenda *f.* **II** *vtr* perder.
forgave [fɔːˈɡeɪv] *pt →* **forgive.**
forge [fɔːdʒ] **I** *n* **1** *(furnace)* fragua *f.* **2** *(blacksmith's)* herrería *f.* **II** *vtr* **1** *(counterfeit)* falsificar. **2** *(metal)* forjar. **III** *vi* **to f. ahead,** hacer grandes progresos.
forger ['fɔːdʒər] *n* falsificador,-a *m,f.*
forgery ['fɔːdʒərɪ] *n* falsificación *f.*
forget [fəˈɡet] **I** *vtr (pt* **forgot;** *pp* **forgotten***)* olvidar, olvidarse de; **I forgot to close the window,** se me olvidó cerrar *or* me olvidé de cerrar la ventana; **I've forgotten my key,** he olvidado la llave. **II** *vi* olvidarse.
forgetful [fəˈɡetfʊl] *adj* olvidadizo,-a.
forget-me-not [fəˈɡetmɪnɒt] *n* nomeolvides *f inv.*
forgive [fəˈɡɪv] *vtr (pt* **forgave** *pp* **forgiven** [fəˈɡɪvən]*)* perdonar; **to f. sb for sth,** perdonarle algo a algn.
forgiveness [fəˈɡɪvnɪs] *n* perdón *m.*
forgo [fɔːˈɡəʊ] *vtr →* **forego.**
forgot [fəˈɡɒt] *pt,* **forgotten** [fəˈɡɒtən] *pp → * **forget.**
fork [fɔːk] **I** *n* **1** *Agr* horca *f.* **2** *(cutlery)* tenedor *m.* **3** *(in road)* bifurcación *f.* **II** *vi (roads)* bifurcarse. ◆**fork out** *vtr fam (money)* soltar.
fork-lift truck [fɔːklɪftˈtrʌk] *n* carretilla *f*

elevadora de horquilla.

forlorn [fə'lɔːn] *adj* (*forsaken*) abandonado,-a; (*desolate*) triste; (*without hope*) desesperado,-a.

form [fɔːm] I *n* 1 (*shape*) forma *f*. 2 (*type*) clase *f*. 3 **for f.'s sake**, para guardar las formas. 4 (*document*) formulario *m*. 5 **on/on top/off f.**, en/en plena/en baja forma. 6 *Educ* clase *f*; **the first f.**, el primer curso. II *vtr* formar; **to f. an impression**, formarse una impresión. III *vi* formarse.

formal ['fɔːməl] *adj* 1 (*official*) oficial; **a f. application**, una solicitud en forma. 2 (*party*, *dress*) de etiqueta. 3 (*ordered*) formal. 4 (*person*) formalista. ◆**formally** *adv* oficialmente.

formality [fɔː'mælɪtɪ] *n* formalidad *f*.

format ['fɔːmæt] I *n* formato *m*. II *vtr Comput* formatear.

formation [fɔː'meɪʃən] *n* formación *f*.

formative ['fɔːmətɪv] *adj* formativo,-a.

former ['fɔːmər] *adj* 1 (*time*) anterior. 2 (*one-time*) antiguo,-a; (*person*) ex; **the f. champion**, el excampeón. 3 (*first*) aquél, aquélla; **Peter and Lisa came, the f. wearing a hat**, vinieron Peter y Lisa, aquél llevaba sombrero. ◆**formerly** *adv* antiguamente.

formidable ['fɔːmɪdəbəl] *adj* (*prodigious*) formidable; (*daunting*) terrible.

formula ['fɔːmjʊlə] *n* fórmula *f*.

forsake [fə'seɪk] *vtr* (*pt* **forsook** [fɔː'sʊk] *pp* **forsaken** [fɔː'seɪkən]) *Lit* 1 (*abandon*, *desert*) abandonar. 2 (*give up*) renunciar a.

fort [fɔːt] *n* fortaleza *f*.

forte ['fɔːteɪ] *n* fuerte *m*.

forth [fɔːθ] *adv fml* **and so f.**, y así sucesivamente; **to go back and f.**, ir de acá para allá.

forthcoming [fɔːθ'kʌmɪŋ] *adj* 1 (*event*) próximo,-a. 2 **no money was f.**, no hubo oferta de dinero. 3 (*communicative*) comunicativo,-a.

forthright ['fɔːθraɪt] *adj* franco,-a.

fortify ['fɔːtɪfaɪ] *vtr* fortificar.

fortitude ['fɔːtɪtjuːd] *n* fortaleza *f*, fuerza *f*.

fortnight ['fɔːtnaɪt] *n GB* quincena *f*.

fortnightly ['fɔːtnaɪtlɪ] *GB* I *adj* quincenal. II *adv* cada quince días.

fortress ['fɔːtrɪs] *n* fortaleza *f*.

fortunate ['fɔːtʃənɪt] *adj* afortunado,-a; **it was f. that he came**, fue una suerte que viniera. ◆**fortunately** *adv* afortunadamente.

fortune ['fɔːtʃən] *n* 1 (*luck*, *fate*) suerte *f*; **to tell sb's f.**, echar la buenaventura a algn. 2 (*money*) fortuna *f*.

fortune-teller ['fɔːtʃəntelər] *n* adivino,-a *m,f*.

forty ['fɔːtɪ] *adj & n* cuarenta (*m*) *inv*.

forum ['fɔːrəm] *n* foro *m*.

forward ['fɔːwəd] I *adv* 1 (*also* **forwards**) (*direction and movement*) hacia adelante. 2

fig **to come f.**, ofrecerse. 3 **from this day f.**, de ahora en adelante. II *adj* 1 (*movement*) hacia adelante; (*position*) delantero,-a. 2 (*person*) fresco,-a. III *n Sport* delantero,-a *m,f*. IV *vtr* 1 (*send on*) remitir. 2 *fml* (*send goods*) expedir. 3 *fml* (*further*) fomentar.

forwent [fɔː'went] *pt* → **forego**.

fossil ['fɒsəl] *n* fósil *m*; **f. fuel**, combustible *m* fósil.

foster ['fɒstər] I *vtr* 1 (*child*) criar. 2 *fml* (*hopes*) abrigar; (*relations*) fomentar. II *adj* **f. child**, hijo,-a adoptivo,-a; **f. father** padre adoptivo; **f. mother**, madre adoptiva; **f. parents**, padres adoptivos.

fought [fɔːt] *pt & pp* → **fight**.

foul [faʊl] I *adj* 1 (*smell*) fétido,-a; (*taste*) asqueroso,-a. 2 (*deed*) atroz; (*weather*) de perros. 3 (*language*) grosero,-a. 4 **to fall f. of**, tener problemas con; *Sport* **f. play**, juego sucio; *Jur* **f. play is suspected**, se sospecha que se haya cometido un acto criminal. II *n Sport* falta *f*. III *vtr* 1 (*dirty*) ensuciar; (*air*) contaminar. 2 *Sport* cometer una falta contra.

found¹ [faʊnd] *pt & pp* → **find**.

found² [faʊnd] *vtr* (*establish*) fundar.

foundation [faʊn'deɪʃən] *n* 1 (*establishment*) fundación *f*. 2 (*basis*) fundamento *m*. 3 **f. (cream)**, maquillaje *m* de fondo. 4 *Constr* **foundations**, cimientos *mpl*.

founder¹ ['faʊndər] *n* fundador,-a *m,f*.

founder² ['faʊndər] *vi* 1 *fml* (*sink*) hundirse. 2 *fig* (*plan*, *hopes*) fracasar.

foundry ['faʊndrɪ] *n* fundición *f*.

fountain ['faʊntɪn] *n* (*structure*) fuente *f*; (*jet*) surtidor *m*; **f. pen**, pluma estilográfica.

four [fɔːr] *adj & n* cuatro (*m*) *inv*; **on all fours**, a gatas.

four-door ['fɔːdɔːr] *adj Aut* de cuatro puertas.

four-poster [fɔː'pəustər] *n* **f.-p. (bed)**, cama *f* con dosel.

foursome ['fɔːsəm] *n* grupo *m* de cuatro personas.

fourteen [fɔː'tiːn] *adj & n* catorce (*m*) *inv*.

fourteenth [fɔː'tiːnθ] I *adj & n* decimocuarto,-a (*m,f*). II *n* (*fraction*) catorceavo *m*.

fourth [fɔːθ] I *adj & n* cuarto,-a (*m,f*). II *n* 1 (*fraction*) cuarto *m*. 2 *Aut* cuarta *f* (*velocidad*).

fowl [faʊl] *n* aves *fpl* de corral.

fox [fɒks] I *n* zorro,-a *m,f*. II *vtr* 1 (*perplex*) dejar perplejo,-a. 2 (*deceive*) engañar.

foyer ['fɔɪeɪ, 'fɔɪə] *n* vestíbulo *m*.

fracas ['frækɑː] *n* gresca *f*, reyerta *f*.

fraction ['frækʃən] *n* fracción *f*.

fracture ['fræktʃər] I *n* fractura *f*. II *vtr* fracturar.

fragile ['frædʒaɪl] *adj* frágil.

fragment ['frægmənt] *n* fragmento *m*.

fragrance ['freigrəns] *n* fragancia *f*, perfume *m*.

fragrant ['freigrənt] *adj* fragante, aromático,-a.

frail [freil] *adj* frágil, delicado,-a.

frame [freim] **I** *n* 1 (*of window, door, picture*) marco *m*; (*of machine*) armazón *m*; (*of bicycle*) cuadro *m*; (*of spectacles*) montura *f*; *fig* f. of mind, estado *m* de ánimo. 2 *Cin TV* fotograma *m*. **II** *vtr* 1 (*picture*) enmarcar. 2 (*question*) formular. 3 *fam* (*innocent person*) incriminar.

framework ['freimwɜːk] *n fig* within the f. of ..., dentro del marco de ...

franc [fræŋk] *n* franco *m*.

France [frɑːns] *n* Francia.

franchise ['fræntʃaɪz] *n* 1 *Pol* derecho *m* al voto. 2 *Com* concesión *f*, licencia *f*.

frank [fræŋk] **I** *adj* franco,-a. **II** *vtr* (*mail*) franquear. ◆**frankly** *adv* francamente.

frankness ['fræŋknɪs] *n* franqueza *f*.

frantic ['fræntɪk] *adj* (*anxious*) desesperado,-a; (*hectic*) frenético,-a.

fraternal [frə'tɜːnəl] *adj* fraterno,-a.

fraternity [frə'tɜːnɪtɪ] *n* (*society*) asociación *f*; *Rel* cofradía *f*; *US Univ* club *m* de estudiantes.

fraud [frɔːd] *n* 1 fraude *m*. 2 (*person*) impostor,-a *m,f*.

fraught [frɔːt] *adj* 1 (*full*) cargado,-a (with, de). 2 (*tense*) nervioso,-a.

fray¹ [freɪ] *vi* 1 (*cloth*) deshilacharse. 2 (*nerves*) crisparse; his temper frequently frayed, se irritaba a menudo.

fray² [freɪ] *n* combate *m*.

freak [friːk] **I** *n* 1 (*monster*) monstruo *m*. 2 *fam* (*eccentric*) estrafalario,-a *m,f*. 3 *fam* (*fan*) fanático,-a *m,f*. **II** *adj* 1 (*unexpected*) inesperado,-a. 2 (*unusual*) insólito,-a.

freckle ['frekəl] *n* peca *f*.

free [friː] **I** *adj* 1 libre; to set sb f., poner en libertad a algn; f. kick, tiro *m* libre; f. speech, libertad *f* de expresión; f. will, libre albedrío *m*; f. trade, libre cambio *m*; f. time, tiempo *m* libre. 2 f. (of charge), (*gratis*) gratuito,-a; f. gift, obsequio *m*. 3 (*generous*) generoso,-a. 4 (for) f., gratis. 2 (*loose*) suelto,-a. **III** *vtr* 1 (*liberate*) poner en libertad. 2 (*let loose, work loose*) soltar. 3 (*untie*) desatar. 4 (*exempt*) eximir (from, de). ◆**freely** *adv* 1 libremente. 2 (*openly*) abiertamente.

freedom ['friːdəm] *n* 1 (*liberty*) libertad *f*; f. of the press, libertad de prensa. 2 (*exemption*) exención *f*.

free-for-all ['friːfərɔːl] *n* pelea *f*.

freehold ['friːhəʊld] *adj* en propiedad absoluta.

freelance ['friːlɑːns] *adj* independiente.

freemason ['friːmeɪsən] *n* francmasón, -ona *m,f*.

free-range ['friːreɪndʒ] *adj* GB de granja.

free-style ['friːstaɪl] *n Swimming* estilo *m*

libre.

freeway ['friːweɪ] *n US* autopista *f*.

freewheel [friː'wiːl] *vi* ir en punto muerto.

freeze [friːz] **I** *vtr* (*pt* froze; *pp* frozen) congelar. **II** *n Meteor* helada *f*; price f., congelación *f* de precios; *TV Cin* f. frame, imagen congelada. **III** *vi* (*liquid*) helarse; (*food*) congelarse.

freeze-dried ['friːzdraɪd] *adj* liofilizado,-a.

freezer ['friːzər] *n* congelador *m*.

freezing ['friːzɪŋ] *adj* 1 glacial. 2 f. point, punto *m* de congelación; above/below f. point, sobre/bajo cero.

freight [freɪt] *n* 1 (*transport*) transporte *m*. 2 (*goods, price*) flete *m*; f. train, tren *m* de mercancías.

French [frentʃ] **I** *adj* francés,-esa; F. bean, judía *f* verde; F. dressing, vinagreta *f*; *US* F. fries, patatas *fpl* fritas; F. window, puerta *f* vidriera. **II** *n* 1 (*language*) francés *m*. 2 *pl* the F., los franceses.

Frenchman ['frentʃmən] *n* francés *m*.

Frenchwoman ['frentʃwʊmən] *n* francesa *f*.

frenetic [frɪ'netɪk] *adj* frenético,-a.

frenzy ['frenzɪ] *n* frenesí *m*.

frequency ['friːkwənsɪ] *n* frecuencia *f*.

frequent ['friːkwənt] **I** *adj* frecuente. **II** [frɪ'kwent] *vtr* frecuentar. ◆**frequently** *adv* frecuentemente, a menudo.

fresh [freʃ] *adj* 1 fresco,-a; f. water, agua *f* dulce; f. bread, pan del día. 2 (*new*) nuevo,-a; open a f. packet, abrir otro paquete. 3 (*air*) puro,-a; in the f. air, al aire libre. ◆**freshly** *adv* recién, recientemente.

freshen ['freʃən] *vi* (*wind*) refrescar. ◆**freshen up** *vi* asearse.

fresher ['freʃər], **freshman** ['freʃmən] *n Univ* estudiante *mf* de primer año, novato,-a *m,f*.

freshness ['freʃnɪs] *n* frescura *f*.

freshwater ['freʃwɔːtər] *adj* de agua dulce.

fret [fret] *vi* preocuparse (about, por).

FRG [efɑː'dʒiː] *n Hist abbr of* Federal Republic of Germany, República Federal de Alemania, RFA.

friar ['fraɪər] *n* fraile *m*.

friction ['frɪkʃən] *n* fricción *f*.

Friday ['fraɪdɪ] *n* viernes *m*.

fridge [frɪdʒ] *n fam* nevera *f*, frigorífico *m*.

friend [frend] *n* amigo,-a *m,f*; a f. of mine, un,-a amigo,-a mío,-a; to make friends with sb, hacerse amigo,-a de algn; to make friends again, hacer las paces.

friendliness ['frendlɪnɪs] *n* amabilidad *f*, simpatía *f*.

friendly ['frendlɪ] *adj* (friendlier, friendliest) (*person*) simpático,-a; (at-

mosphere) acogedor,-a; **f. advice,** consejo *m* de amigo; **f. nation,** nación amiga.
friendship ['frendʃɪp] *n* amistad *f.*
frieze [fri:z] *n* friso *m.*
frigate ['frɪgɪt] *n* fragata *f.*
fright [fraɪt] *n* 1 *(fear)* miedo *m*; **to take f.,** asustarse. 2 *(shock)* susto *m*; **to get a f.,** pegarse un susto.
frighten ['fraɪtən] *vtr* asustar. ◆**frighten away, frighten off** *vtr* ahuyentar.
frightened ['fraɪtənd] *adj* asustado,-a; **to be f. of sb,** tenerle miedo a algn.
frightening ['fraɪtənɪŋ] *adj* espantoso,-a.
frightful ['fraɪtful] *adj* espantoso,-a, horroroso,-a. ◆**frightfully** *adv* tremendamente, terriblemente.
frigid ['frɪdʒɪd] *adj* frígido,-a.
frill [frɪl] *n (on dress)* volante *m*; *fig* **frills,** *(decorations)* adornos *mpl.*
fringe [frɪndʒ] *n* 1 *(of hair)* flequillo *m.* 2 *(edge)* borde *m*; *fig* **on the f. of society,** al margen de la sociedad; **f. theatre,** teatro *m* experimental; **f. benefits,** extras *mpl.*
Frisbee® ['frɪzbɪ] *n* platillo *m.*
frisk [frɪsk] *vtr fam (search)* registrar.
frisky ['frɪskɪ] *adj (friskier, friskiest)* 1 *(children, animals)* juguetón,-a. 2 *(adult)* vivo,-a.
fritter ['frɪtər] *n* buñuelo *m.* ◆**fritter away** *vtr* malgastar.
frivolous ['frɪvələs] *adj* frívolo,-a.
frizzy ['frɪzɪ] *adj (frizzier, frizziest)* crespo,-a.
frock [frɒk] *n* vestido *m*; **f. coat,** levita *f.*
frog [frɒg] *n* rana *f*; **frogs' legs,** ancas *fpl* de rana; *fig* **to have a f. in one's throat,** tener carraspera.
frogman ['frɒgmən] *n* hombre *m* rana.
frolic ['frɒlɪk] *vi* retozar, juguetear.
from [frɒm, *unstressed* frəm] *prep* 1 *(time)* desde, a partir de; **f. now on,** a partir de ahora; **f. Monday to Friday,** de lunes a viernes; **the eighth to the seventeenth,** desde el ocho hasta el diecisiete; **f. time to time,** de vez en cuando. 2 *(price, number)* desde, de; **dresses f. five pounds,** vestidos desde cinco libras; **a number f. one to ten,** un número del uno a diez. 3 *(origin)* de; **a letter f. her father,** una carta de su padre; **f. English into Spanish,** del inglés al español; **he's f. Malaga,** es de Málaga; **the train f. Bilbao,** el tren procedente de Bilbao; **to go f. door to door,** ir de puerta en puerta; **her eyes were red f. crying,** tenía los ojos rojos de llorar. 4 *(distance)* de; **the town is four miles f. the coast,** el pueblo está a cuatro millas de la costa. 5 *(out of)* de; **bread is made f. flour,** el pan se hace con harina. 6 *(remove, subtract)* a; **he took the book f. the child,** le quitó el libro al niño; **take three f. five,** restar tres a cinco. 7 *(according to)* según,

por; **f. what the author said,** según lo que dijo el autor; **speaking f. my own experience,** hablando por experiencia propia. 8 *(position)* desde, de; **f. here,** desde aquí. 9 **can you tell margarine f. butter?,** ¿puedes distinguir entre la margarina y la mantequilla?
front [frʌnt] **I** *n* 1 parte delantera; **in f.** *(of),* delante (de). 2 *(of building)* fachada *f.* 3 *Mil Pol Meteor* frente *m.* 4 *(seaside)* paseo marítimo. 5 *fig* **she put on a brave f.,** hizo de tripas corazón. **II** *adj* delantero,-a, de delante; *Parl* **f. bench,** primera fila de escaños donde se sientan los ministros del Gobierno o de la Oposición; **f. door,** puerta *f* principal; **f. room,** salón *m*; **f. seat,** asiento *m* de delante.
frontier ['frʌntɪər] *n* frontera *f.*
front-page ['frʌntpeɪdʒ] *adj* de primera página.
frost [frɒst] **I** *n* 1 *(covering)* escarcha *f.* 2 *(freezing)* helada *f.* **II** *vt US Culin* recubrir con azúcar glas. ◆**frost over** *vi* escarchar.
frostbite ['frɒstbaɪt] *n* congelación *f.*
frosted ['frɒstɪd] *adj* 1 *(glass)* esmerilado,-a. 2 *US Culin* recubierto,-a de azúcar glas.
frosty ['frɒstɪ] *adj (frostier, frostiest)* 1 **it will be a f. night tonight,** esta noche habrá helada. 2 *fig* glacial.
froth [frɒθ] **I** *n* espuma *f*; *(from mouth)* espumarajos *mpl.* **II** *vi* espumar.
frothy ['frɒθɪ] *adj (frothier, frothiest)* espumoso,-a.
frown [fraʊn] *vi* fruncir el ceño. ◆**frown upon** *vtr* desaprobar.
froze [frəʊz] *pt* → **freeze.**
frozen ['frəʊzən] *adj (liquid, feet etc)* helado,-a; *(food)* congelado,-a.
frugal ['fru:gəl] *adj* frugal.
fruit [fru:t] *n* 1 *Bot* fruto *m.* 2 *(apple, orange etc)* fruta *f*; **f. cake,** pastel *m* con fruto seco; **f. machine,** máquina *f* tragaperras; **f. salad,** macedonia *f* de frutas. 3 **fruits,** *(rewards)* frutos *mpl.*
fruitful ['fru:tful] *adj fig* provechoso,-a.
fruition [fru:'ɪʃən] *n fml* **to come to f.,** realizarse.
frustrate [frʌ'streɪt] *vtr* frustrar.
frustrated [frʌ'streɪtɪd] *adj* frustrado,-a.
frustration [frʌ'streɪʃən] *n* frustración *f.*
fry¹ [fraɪ] **I** *vtr (pt & pp* **fried)** freír. **II** *vi fig* asarse.
fry² [fraɪ] *npl* **small f.,** gente *f* de poca monta.
frying pan ['fraɪɪŋpæn], *US* **fry-pan** ['fraɪpæn] *n* sartén *f.*
ft *abbr* of **foot,** pie *m*; *abbr* of **feet,** pies *mpl.*
fuck [fʌk] *vulg offens vtr & vi* joder; **f. (it)!,** ¡joder! ◆**fuck off** *vi* **f. off!,** ¡vete a la mierda! ◆**fuck up** *vtr* joder.
fucking ['fʌkɪŋ] *vulg* I *adj* **f. idiot!,** ¡gili-

pollas!; **where are my f. keys?**, ¿dónde
coño están las llaves? **II** *adv* **a f. good
film**, una película de puta madre.
fuddy-duddy ['fʌdɪdʌdɪ] *n* persona cha-
pada a la antigua.
fudge [fʌdʒ] **I** *n Culin* dulce *m* hecho con
azúcar, leche y mantequilla. **II** *vtr*
(figures) amañar.
fuel ['fjuəl] **I** *n* **1** combustible *m*; *(for
engines)* carburante *m*; **f. tank**, depósito *m*
de combustible. **II** *vtr fig (ambition)* estimular; *(difficult situation)* empeorar.
fugitive ['fjuːdʒɪtɪv] *n fml* fugitivo,-a *m,f*.
fulfil, *US* **fulfill** [fʊl'fɪl] *vtr* **1** *(task, ambition)* realizar; *(promise)* cumplir; *(role)*
desempeñar. **2** *(wishes)* satisfacer.
fulfilment, *US* **fulfillment** [fʊl'fɪlmənt] *n*
1 *(of ambition)* realización *f*. **2** *(of duty,
promise)* cumplimiento *m*.
full [fʊl] **I** *adj* **1** lleno,-a; **f. of**, lleno,-a de;
I'm f. (up), no puedo más. **2** *(complete)*
completo,-a; **at f. speed**, a toda velocidad; **f. text**, texto íntegro; *fam* **in f.
swing**, en plena marcha; **f. board**,
pensión completa; **f. employment**, pleno
empleo *m*; **f. house**, lleno total; **f. moon**,
luna llena; **f. stop**, punto *m*. **II** *n* **in f.**,
en su totalidad; **name in f.**, nombre y
apellidos completos. **III** *adv* **f. well**, perfectamente. **◆fully** *adv* completamente.
full-blown ['fʊlbləʊn] *adj* auténtico,-a.
fullness ['fʊlnɪs] *n* **in the f. of time**, con
el tiempo.
full-scale ['fʊlskeɪl] *adj* **1** *(model)* de tamaño natural. **2** **f.-s. search**, registro *m* a
fondo; **f.-s. war**, guerra generalizada *or*
total.
full-time ['fʊltaɪm] **I** *adj* de jornada completa. **II** *adv* **to work f. t.**, trabajar a
tiempo completo.
fully-fledged ['fʊlɪfledʒd] *adj* hecho,-a y
derecho,-a.
fulsome ['fʊlsəm] *adj* excesivo,-a,
exagerado,-a.
fumble ['fʌmbəl] *vi* hurgar; **to f. for sth**,
buscar algo a tientas; **to f. with sth**, manejar algo con torpeza.
fume [fjuːm] **I** *n (usu pl)* humo *m*. **II** *vi*
echar humo.
fun [fʌn] **I** *n (amusement)* diversión *f*; **in** *or*
for f., en broma; **to have f.**, divertirse,
pasarlo bien; **to make f. of sb**, reírse de
algn. **II** *adj* divertido,-a.
function ['fʌŋkʃən] **I** *n* **1** función *f*. **2**
(ceremony) acto *m*; *(party)* recepción *f*. **II**
vi funcionar.
functional ['fʌŋkʃənəl] *adj* funcional.
fund [fʌnd] **I** *n* **1** *Com* fondo *m*. **2** **funds**,
fondos *mpl*. **II** *vtr (finance)* patrocinar.
fundamental [fʌndə'mentəl] **I** *adj* fundamental. **II** *npl* **fundamentals**, los fundamentos.
funeral ['fjuːnərəl] *n* funeral *m*; **f. march**,
marcha *f* fúnebre; *US* **f. parlor**, funeraria

f; **f. service**, misa *f* de cuerpo presente.
funfair ['fʌnfeəʳ] *n GB* parque *m* de
atracciones.
fungus ['fʌŋgəs] *n (pl* **fungi** ['fʌŋgaɪ])* **1**
Bot hongo *m*. **2** *Med* fungo *m*.
funnel ['fʌnəl] **I** *n* **1** *(for liquids)* embudo
m. **2** *Naut* chimenea *f*. **II** *vtr fig (funds,
energy)* encauzar.
funny ['fʌnɪ] *adj* **(funnier, funniest) 1** *(peculiar)* raro,-a, extraño,-a; **that's f.!**, ¡qué
raro! **2** *(amusing)* divertido,-a, gracioso,
-a; **I found it very f.**, me hizo mucha
gracia. **3** *fam (ill)* mal. **4** *fam (dishonest)*
dudoso,-a. **◆funnily** *adv fam* **f. enough**,
aunque parezca extraño.
fur [fɜːʳ] **I** *n* **1** *(of living animal)* pelo *m*. **2**
(of dead animal) piel *f*. **3** *(in kettle, on
tongue)* sarro *m*. **II** *adj* de piel; **f. coat**,
abrigo *m* de pieles.
furious ['fjʊərɪəs] *adj* **1** *(angry)* furioso,-a.
2 *(vigorous)* violento,-a.
furlong ['fɜːlɒŋ] *n (measurement)* = *aprox*
201 metros.
furnace ['fɜːnɪs] *n* horno *m*.
furnish ['fɜːnɪʃ] *vtr* **1** *(house)* amueblar. **2**
fml (food) suministrar; *(details)* facilitar.
furnishings ['fɜːnɪʃɪŋz] *npl* **1** muebles
mpl. **2** *(fittings)* accesorios *mpl*.
furniture ['fɜːnɪtʃəʳ] *n* muebles *mpl*; **a
piece of f.**, un mueble.
furrow ['fʌrəʊ] *n Agr* surco *m*; *(on forehead)* arruga *f*.
furry ['fɜːrɪ] *adj* **(furrier, furriest) 1**
(hairy) peludo,-a. **2** *(tongue, kettle)*
sarroso,-a.
further ['fɜːðəʳ] **I** *adj* → **far**. **1** *(new)*
nuevo,-a; **until f. notice**, hasta nuevo aviso. **2** *(additional)* otro,-a, adicional. **3**
(later) posterior; **f. education**, estudios
mpl superiores. **II** *adv* **1** *(more)* más; **f.
back**, más atrás; **f. along**, más adelante;
she heard nothing f., no volvió a saber
nada más. **2** *fml (besides)* además. **III** *vtr*
fomentar.
furthermore ['fɜːðəmɔːʳ] *adv fml* además.
furthest ['fɜːðɪst] *adj* → **far**; más lejano,
-a.
furtive ['fɜːtɪv] *adj* furtivo,-a.
fury ['fjʊərɪ] *n* furia *f*, furor *m*.
fuse [fjuːz] **I** *n* **1** *Elec* fusible *m*; **f. box**,
caja *f* de fusibles. **2** *(of bomb)* mecha *f*. **II**
vi **1** *Elec* **the lights fused**, se fundieron
los plomos. **2** *fig (merge)* fusionarse. **3**
(melt) fundirse. **III** *vtr* **1** *Elec* fundir los
plomos de. **2** *fig (merge)* fusionar. **3** *(melt)*
fundir.
fuselage ['fjuːzɪlɑːʒ] *n* fuselaje *m*.
fuss [fʌs] **I** *n (commotion)* jaleo *m*; **to kick
up a f.**, armar un escándalo; **stop making
a f.**, *(complaining)* deja ya de quejarte; **to
make a f. of**, *(pay attention to)* mimar a.
II *vi* preocuparse **(about**, por).

fussy ['fʌsɪ] *adj* (**fussier, fussiest**) exigente; (*nitpicking*) quisquilloso,-a.

futile ['fju:taɪl] *adj* inútil, vano,-a.

futility [fju:'tɪlɪtɪ] *n* inutilidad *f*.

future ['fju:tʃər] I *n* futuro *m*, porvenir *m*; in the near f., en un futuro próximo; in f., de aquí en adelante. II *adj* futuro,-a.

futuristic [fju:tʃə'rɪstɪk] *adj* futurista.

fuzzy ['fʌzɪ] *adj* (**fuzzier, fuzziest**) 1 (*hair*) muy rizado,-a. 2 (*blurred*) borroso,-a.

G

G, g [dʒi:] *n* 1 (*the letter*) G, g *f*. 2 *Mus* G, sol *m*.

g [dʒi:] *abbr of* **gram(s), gramme(s)**, g.

gabble ['gæbəl] I *n* chapurreo *m*. II *vi* hablar atropelladamente.

gable ['geɪbəl] *n* aguilón *m*.

gadget ['gædʒɪt] *n* artilugio *m*, aparato *m*.

Gaelic ['geɪlɪk] I *adj* gaélico,-a. II *n* (*language*) gaélico *m*.

gaffe [gæf] *n* metedura *f* de pata, plancha *f*; **to make a g.**, meter la pata, patinar.

gag [gæg] I *n* 1 mordaza *f*. 2 *fam* (*joke*) chiste *m*. II *vtr* amordazar.

gage [geɪdʒ] *n & vtr US* → **gauge**.

gaiety ['geɪətɪ] *n* regocijo *m*.

gaily ['geɪlɪ] *adv* alegremente.

gain [geɪn] I *n* ganancia *f*, beneficio *m*; (*increase*) aumento *m*. II *vtr* ganar; *fig* **to g. ground**, ganar terreno; **to g. speed**, ganar velocidad, acelerar; **to g. weight**, aumentar de peso.

gait [geɪt] *n* (manera *f* de) andar *m*.

gal (*pl* **gal** *or* **gals**) *abbr of* **gallon**.

gala ['gɑ:lə, 'geɪlə] *n* gala *f*, fiesta *f*.

galaxy ['gæləksɪ] *n* galaxia *f*.

gale [geɪl] *n* vendaval *m*.

Galicia [gə'lɪʃə] *n* Galicia.

Galician [gə'lɪʃɪən, gə'lɪʃən] I *adj* gallego,-a. II *n* 1 (*person*) gallego,-a *m,f*. 2 (*language*) gallego *m*.

gall [gɔ:l] I *n* *fam* descaro *m*. II *vtr* molestar, irritar.

gallant ['gælənt] *adj* (*brave*) valiente; (*also* [gə'lænt]) (*chivalrous*) galante.

gallantry ['gæləntrɪ] *n* (*bravery*) gallardía *f*; (*politeness*) galantería *f*.

galleon ['gælɪən] *n* galeón *m*.

gallery ['gælərɪ] *n* 1 galería *f*. 2 *Theat* gallinero *m*. 3 (*court*) tribuna *f*.

galley ['gælɪ] *n* 1 (*ship*) galera *f*; **g. slave**, galeote *m*. 2 (*kitchen*) cocina *f*.

Gallicism ['gælɪsɪzəm] *n* galicismo *m*.

gallivant ['gælɪvænt] *vi* *fam* callejear.

gallon ['gælən] *n* galón *m* (≈ 4,55 litros; *US* 3,79 litros).

gallop ['gæləp] I *n* galope *m*. II *vi* galopar.

gallows ['gæləʊz] *npl* horca *f* *sing*, patíbulo *m* *sing*.

gallstone ['gɔ:lstəʊn] *n* cálculo *m* biliar.

galore [gə'lɔ:r] *adv* *fam* en cantidad, en abundancia.

galvanize ['gælvənaɪz] *vtr* (*metal*) galvanizar; *fig* **to g. sb into action**, galvanizar a

algn.

galvanized ['gælvənaɪzd] *adj* galvanizado,-a.

gambit ['gæmbɪt] *n* *Chess* gambito *m*; *fig* táctica *f*.

gamble ['gæmbəl] I *n* (*risk*) riesgo *m*; (*risky undertaking*) empresa arriesgada; (*bet*) apuesta *f*. II *vi* (*bet*) jugar; (*take a risk*) arriesgarse.

gambler ['gæmblər] *n* jugador,-a *m,f*.

gambling ['gæmblɪŋ] *n* juego *m*.

gambol ['gæmbəl] *vi* brincar.

game [geɪm] I *n* 1 juego *m*; **g. of chance**, juego de azar. 2 (*match*) partido *m*; (*of bridge*) partida *f*. 3 **games**, *Sport* juegos *mpl*; *GB Educ* educación física. 4 (*hunting*) caza *f*; *fig* presa *f*; **g. reserve**, coto *m* de caza. II *adj* **g. for anything**, dispuesto,-a a todo. ◆**gamely** *adv* resueltamente.

gamekeeper ['geɪmki:pər] *n* guardabosque *m*.

gammon ['gæmən] *n* *GB* jamón ahumado *or* curado.

gamut ['gæmət] *n* gama *f*; **to run the g. of ...**, experimentar todas las posibilidades de ....

gang [gæŋ] *n* (*of criminals*) banda *f*; (*of youths*) pandilla *f*; (*of workers*) cuadrilla *f*. ◆**gang up** *vi* *fam* confabularse (**on**, contra).

gangplank ['gæŋplæŋk] *n* plancha *f*.

gangrene ['gæŋgri:n] *n* gangrena *f*.

gangster ['gæŋstər] *n* gángster *m*.

gangway ['gæŋweɪ] *n* *Naut* pasarela *f*; *Theat* pasillo *m*.

gantry ['gæntrɪ] *n* puente *m* transversal.

gaol [dʒeɪl] *n & vtr* *GB* → **jail**.

gap [gæp] *n* 1 abertura *f*, hueco *m*; (*blank space*) blanco *m*; (*in traffic*) claro *m*; **to bridge a g.**, rellenar un hueco. 2 (*in time*) intervalo *m*; (*emptiness*) vacío *m*. 3 (*gulf*) diferencia *f*. 4 (*deficiency*) laguna *f*.

gape [geɪp] *vi* (*person*) quedarse boquiabierto,-a, mirar boquiabierto,-a; (*thing*) estar abierto,-a.

gaping ['geɪpɪŋ] *adj* *fig* profundo,-a.

garage ['gærɑ:ʒ, 'gærɪdʒ] *n* garaje *m*; (*for repairs*) taller mecánico; (*filling station*) gasolinera *f*.

garbage ['gɑ:bɪdʒ] *n* *US* basura *f*; *fig* tonterías *fpl*. **g. can**, cubo *m* de la basura; **g. truck**, camión *m* de la basura.

garbled ['gɑ:bəld] *adj* embrollado,-a; **g.**

account, relato confuso.
garden ['gɑ:dən] n jardín m; **g. centre,** centro m de jardinería; **g. party,** recepción f al aire libre.
gardener ['gɑ:dənər] n jardinero,-a m,f.
gardening ['gɑ:dənɪŋ] n jardinería f; **his mother does the g.,** su madre es la que cuida el jardín.
gardenia [gɑ:'di:nɪə] n gardenia f.
gargle ['gɑ:gəl] vi hacer gárgaras.
gargoyle ['gɑ:gɔɪl] n gárgola f.
garish ['geərɪʃ] adj chillón,-ona.
garland ['gɑ:lənd] n guirnalda f.
garlic ['gɑ:lɪk] n ajo m.
garment ['gɑ:mənt] n prenda f.
garnish ['gɑ:nɪʃ] vtr guarnecer.
garrison ['gærɪsən] n guarnición f.
garrulous ['gærʊləs] adj locuaz.
garter ['gɑ:tər] n liga f.
gas [gæs] I n 1 gas m; **g. chamber,** cámara f de gas; **g. cooker,** cocina f de gas; **g. fire,** estufa f de gas; **g. mask,** careta f antigás; **g. ring,** hornillo m de gas. 2 US gasolina f; **g. station,** gasolinera f. II vtr (asphyxiate) asfixiar con gas. III vi fam (talk) charlotear.
gash [gæʃ] I n herida profunda. II vtr hacer un corte en; **he gashed his forehead,** se hizo una herida en la frente.
gasket ['gæskɪt] n junta f.
gasoline ['gæsəli:n] n US gasolina f.
gasp [gɑ:sp] I n (cry) grito sordo; (breath) bocanada f; fig to be at one's last g., estar en las últimas. II vi (in surprise) quedar boquiabierto,-a; (breathe) jadear.
gassy ['gæsɪ] adj (gassier, gassiest) gaseoso,-a.
gastric ['gæstrɪk] adj gástrico,-a.
gastronomic [gæstrə'nɒmɪk] adj gastronómico,-a.
gate [geɪt] n 1 puerta f. 2 (at football ground) entrada f; **g. (money),** taquilla f. 3 (attendance) entrada f.
gateau ['gætəʊ] n pastel m con nata.
gatecrash ['geɪtkræʃ] I vtr colarse en. II vi colarse.
gateway ['geɪtweɪ] n puerta f; fig pasaporte m.
gather ['gæðə] I vtr 1 (collect) juntar; (pick) coger; (pick up) recoger. 2 (bring together) reunir. 3 (harvest) cosechar. 4 to **g. speed,** ir ganando velocidad; to **g. strength,** cobrar fuerzas. 5 (understand) suponer; **I g. that ...,** tengo entendido que .... 6 Sew fruncir. II vi 1 (come together) reunirse. 2 (form) formarse. ◆**gather round** vi agruparse.
gathering ['gæðərɪŋ] I adj creciente. II n reunión f.
gauche [gəʊʃ] adj (clumsy) torpe; (tactless) sin tacto.
gaudy ['gɔ:dɪ] adj (gaudier, gaudiest) chillón,-ona.
gauge [geɪdʒ] n 1 medida f estándar; (of

gun, wire) calibre m. 2 Rail ancho m de vía. 3 (calibrator) indicador m. 4 fig (indication) indicación f. II vtr 1 (measure) medir, calibrar. 2 fig (judge) juzgar.
gaunt [gɔ:nt] adj (lean) demacrado,-a; (desolate) lúgubre.
gauntlet ['gɔ:ntlɪt] n guantelete m; fig to **run the g. of ...,** estar sometido,-a a ...; fig to **throw down the g.,** arrojar el guante.
gauze [gɔ:z] n gasa f.
gave [geɪv] pt → **give.**
gawky ['gɔ:kɪ] adj (gawkier, gawkiest) desgarbado,-a.
gay [geɪ] adj 1 (homosexual) gay. 2 (happy) alegre.
gaze [geɪz] I n mirada fija. II vi mirar fijamente.
gazelle [gə'zel] n gacela f.
gazette [gə'zet] n gaceta f; US periódico m.
gazump [gə'zʌmp] vi GB fam romper un compromiso de venta para vender a un precio más alto.
GB [dʒi:'bi:] abbr of **Great Britain.**
GCE [dʒi:si:'i:] abbr of **General Certificate of Education (A-Level),** ≈ COU m.
GCSE [dʒi:si:es'i:] abbr of **General Certificate of Secondary Education,** ≈ BUP m.
GDP [dʒi:di:'pi:] abbr of **gross domestic product,** producto m interior bruto, PIB m.
GDR [dʒi:di:'ɑ:r] n Hist abbr of **German Democratic Republic,** RDA.
gear [gɪər] I n 1 (equipment) equipo m. 2 fam (belongings) bártulos mpl. 3 fam (clothing) ropa f. 4 Tech engranaje m. 5 Aut velocidad f, marcha f; **first g.,** primera f (velocidad f); **g. lever,** palanca f de cambio. II vtr ajustar, adaptar.
gearbox ['gɪəbɒks] n caja f de cambios.
gearstick ['gɪəstɪk], US **gearshift** ['gɪəʃɪft] n palanca f de cambio.
geese [gi:s] npl → **goose.**
gel [dʒel] I n gel m; (for hair) gomina f. II vi fig (ideas etc) cuajar. III vtr (hair) engominar.
gelatin ['dʒelətɪn] n gelatina f.
gelignite ['dʒelɪgnaɪt] n gelignita f.
gem [dʒem] n piedra preciosa; fig (person) joya f.
Gemini ['dʒemɪnaɪ] n Géminis m sing.
gen [dʒen] n fam to get the **g. on sth,** informarse sobre algo.
gender ['dʒendə] n género m.
gene [dʒi:n] n gene m, gen m.
general ['dʒenərəl] I adj general; **g. knowledge,** conocimientos generales; **in g.,** en general; **the g. public,** el público; **g. practitioner (GP),** médico m de cabecera. II n Mil general m. ◆**generally** adv generalmente, en general.

generalization [dʒenərəlaɪˈzeɪʃən] *n* generalización *f*.

generalize [ˈdʒenərəlaɪz] *vtr & vi* generalizar.

generate [ˈdʒenəreɪt] *vtr* generar.

generation [dʒenəˈreɪʃən] *n* generación *f*; **g. gap**, abismo *m or* conflicto *m* generacional.

generator [ˈdʒenəreɪtər] *n* generador *m*.

generosity [dʒenəˈrɒsɪtɪ] *n* generosidad *f*.

generous [ˈdʒenərəs] *adj* generoso,-a; (*plentiful*) copioso,-a.

genetic [dʒɪˈnetɪk] *adj* genético,-a; **g. engineering**, ingeniería genética.

genetics [dʒɪˈnetɪks] *n* genética *f*.

Geneva [dʒɪˈniːvə] *n* Ginebra.

genial [ˈdʒiːnɪəl, ˈdʒiːnjəl] *adj* cordial.

genie [ˈdʒiːnɪ] *n* duende *m*, genio *m*.

genitals [ˈdʒenɪtəlz] *npl* órganos *mpl* genitales.

genius [ˈdʒiːnjəs, ˈdʒiːnɪəs] *n* 1 (*person*) genio *m*. 2 (*gift*) don *m*.

genre [ˈʒɑːnrə] *n* género *m*.

gent [dʒent] *n* (*abbr of gentleman*) *fam* señor *m*, caballero *m*; **the gents**, los servicios (de caballeros).

genteel [dʒenˈtiːl] *adj* fino,-a, distinguido,-a.

gentle [ˈdʒentəl] *adj* dulce, tierno,-a; (*breeze*) suave. ◆**gently** con cuidado.

gentleman [ˈdʒentəlmən] *n* caballero *m*; **g.'s agreement**, pacto *m* de caballeros.

gentry [ˈdʒentrɪ] *n* pequeña nobleza, alta burguesía.

genuine [ˈdʒenjuɪn] *adj* auténtico,-a, genuino,-a; (*sincere*) sincero,-a. ◆**genuinely** *adv* auténticamente.

geographic(al) [dʒɪəˈɡræfɪk(əl)] *adj* geográfico,-a.

geography [dʒɪˈɒɡrəfɪ, ˈdʒɒɡrəfɪ] *n* geografía *f*.

geologic(al) [dʒɪəˈlɒdʒɪk(əl)] *adj* geológico,-a.

geology [dʒɪˈɒlədʒɪ] *n* geología *f*.

geometric(al) [dʒɪəˈmetrɪk(əl)] *adj* geométrico,-a.

geometry [dʒɪˈɒmɪtrɪ] *n* geometría *f*.

geopolitical [dʒiːəʊpəˈlɪtɪkəl] *adj* geopolítico,-a.

geranium [dʒɪˈreɪnɪəm] *n* geranio *m*.

geriatric [dʒerɪˈætrɪk] *adj* geriátrico,-a.

germ [dʒɜːm] *n* 1 *Biol & fig* germen *m*. 2 *Med* microbio *m*.

German [ˈdʒɜːmən] **I** *adj* alemán,-ana; **G. measles**, rubeola *f*. **II** *n* 1 alemán,-ana *m,f*. 2 (*language*) alemán *m*.

Germany [ˈdʒɜːmənɪ] *n* Alemania.

germinate [ˈdʒɜːmɪneɪt] *vi* germinar.

gestation [dʒeˈsteɪʒən] *n* gestación *f*.

gesticulate [dʒeˈstɪkjuleɪt] *vi* gesticular.

gesture [ˈdʒestʃər] **I** *n* gesto *m*, ademán *m*; **it's an empty g.**, es pura formalidad. **II** *vi* gesticular, hacer gestos.

get [get] **I** *vtr* (*pt & pp* **got**, *pp* US *also*

gotten) 1 (*obtain*) obtener, conseguir; **to g. one's own way**, salirse con la suya. 2 (*earn*) ganar. 3 (*fetch*) (*something*) traer; (*somebody*) ir a por; **g. the police!**, ¡llama a la policía! *Tel* **g. me Mr Brown**, póngame con el Sr. Brown. 4 (*receive*) recibir; *fam* **he got the sack**, le despidieron. 5 (*bus, train, thief etc*) *Span* coger; *Am* agarrar. 6 (*prepare*) preparar; **can I g. you something to eat?**, ¿quieres comer algo? 7 (*ask*) pedir; **g. him to call me**, dile que me llame. 8 **to g. sb to agree to sth**, conseguir que algn acepte algo. 9 **when did you g. the house painted?** ¿cuándo os pintaron la casa?; **to g. one's hair cut**, cortarse el pelo. 10 **they got him in the chest**, le dieron en el pecho. 11 **have got, have got to** → **have**. 12 *fam* (*understand*) entender. 13 (*record*) (*in writing*) apuntar; (*on tape*) grabar.

II *vi* 1 (*become*) ponerse; **to g. dark**, anochecer; **to g. dressed**, vestirse; **to g. drunk**, emborracharse; **to g. late**, hacerse tarde; **to g. married**, casarse; **to g. used to doing sth**, acostumbrarse a hacer algo; **to get paid**, cobrar. 2 *fig* **we are not getting anywhere**, así no vamos a ninguna parte. 3 (*arrive*) llegar. 4 **to g. to**, (*come to*) llegar a; **to g. to know sb**, llegar a conocer a algn.

◆**get about** *vi* (*person*) salir; (*news*) difundirse. ◆**get across** *vtr* (*idea etc*) hacer comprender. ◆**get ahead** *vi* progresar. ◆**get along** *vi* 1 (*leave*) marcharse. 2 (*manage*) arreglárselas. 3 (*two people*) llevarse bien. ◆**get around** *vi* (*person*) salir; (*travel*) viajar; (*news*) difundirse. ◆**get at** *vtr* 1 (*reach*) alcanzar. 2 (*ascertain*) descubrir. 3 (*insinuate*) insinuar; **what are you getting at?**, ¿a dónde quieres llegar? 4 (*criticize*) criticar. ◆**get away** *vi* escaparse. ◆**get away with** *vtr* salir impune de. ◆**get back I** *vi* 1 (*return*) regresar, volver. 2 **g. back!**, (*move backwards*) ¡atrás!. **II** *vtr* (*recover*) recuperar; *fam* **to g. one's own back on sb**, vengarse de algn. ◆**get by** *vi* 1 (*manage*) arreglárselas; **she can g. by in French**, sabe defenderse en francés. 2 (*pass*) pasar. ◆**get down I** *vtr* (*depress*) deprimir. **II** *vi* (*descend*) bajar. ◆**get down to** *vi* ponerse a; **to g. down to the facts**, ir al grano. ◆**get in I** *vi* 1 (*arrive*) llegar. 2 *Pol* ser elegido,-a. **II** *vtr* 1 (*buy*) comprar. 2 (*collect*) recoger; *fam* **he couldn't g. a word in edgeways**, no pudo decir ni pío. ◆**get into** *vtr fig* **to g. into bad habits**, adquirir malas costumbres; **to g. into trouble**, meterse en un lío. ◆**get off I** *vtr* 1 (*bus etc*) bajarse de. 2 (*remove*) quitarse. **II** *vi* 1 bajarse; *fam* **g. off!**, ¡fuera! 2 **to g. off to a good start**, (*begin*) empezar bien. 3 (*escape*) escaparse; **to g. off lightly**, salir bien librado,-a. ◆**get off with** *vtr fam* ligar. ◆**get on I** *vtr (board)* subir a. **II** *vi* 1 *(board)* subirse. 2 *(make progress)* hacer progresos; **how are you getting on?,** ¿cómo te van las cosas? 3 **to g. on (well with sb),** llevarse bien (con algn). 4 *(continue)* seguir; **to g. on with one's work,** seguir trabajando. 5 **it's getting on for eleven,** son casi las once; **time's getting on,** se está haciendo tarde. ◆**get on to** *vtr* 1 *(find a person)* localizar; *(find out)* descubrir. 2 *(continue)* pasar a. ◆**get out I** *vtr (object)* sacar. **II** *vi* 1 *(room etc)* salir **(of,** de); *(train)* bajar **(of,** de). 2 *(escape)* escaparse **(of,** de); **to g. out of an obligation,** librarse de un compromiso. 3 *(news)* difundirse; *(secret)* hacerse público. ◆**get over** *vtr* 1 *(illness)* recuperarse; **I can't g. over him,** no le puedo olvidar. 2 *(difficulty)* vencer. 3 *(convey)* hacer comprender. ◆**get round** *vtr* 1 *(problem)* salvar; *(difficulty)* vencer. 2 *(rule)* soslayar. 3 *(win over)* persuadir. ◆**get round to** *vi* **if I g. round to it, si tengo tiempo. ◆get through I** *vi* 1 *(message)* llegar. 2 *Educ* aprobar. 3 *Tel* **to g. through to sb,** conseguir comunicar con algn. **II** *vtr* 1 **to g. through a lot of work,** trabajar mucho. 2 *(consume)* consumir. 3 *Educ* aprobar. ◆**get together I** *vi (people)* juntarse. reunirse. **II** *vtr (people)* juntar, reunir. ◆**get up I** *vi (rise)* levantarse. **II** *vtr* 1 *(wake)* despertar. 2 *(disguise)* **to g. oneself up as …,** disfrazarse de …. ◆**get up to** *vi* hacer; **to g. up to mischief,** hacer de las suyas.

getaway |'getəweɪ| *n* fuga *f*; **to make one's g.,** fugarse.

get-together |'getəgeðər| *n* reunión *f*.

geyser |'giːzə, *US* 'gaɪzə| *n* 1 *Geog* géiser *m*. 2 *(water heater)* calentador de agua.

ghastly |'gɑːstlɪ| *adj (ghastlier, ghastliest)* horrible, espantoso,-a.

gherkin |'gɜːkɪn| *n* pepinillo *m*.

ghetto |'getəʊ| *n* gueto *m*.

ghost |gəʊst| *n* fantasma *m*; **g. story,** cuento *m* de fantasmas; **g. town,** pueblo *m* fantasma.

ghost-writer |'gəʊstraɪtər| *n* negro,-a, *m,f*.

ghoulish |'guːlɪʃ| *adj* macabro,-a.

giant |'dʒaɪənt| *adj & n* gigante *m*.

gibberish |'dʒɪbərɪʃ| *n* galimatías *m inv*.

gibe |dʒaɪb| **I** *n* mofa *f*. **II** *vi* mofarse (at, de).

giblets |'dʒɪblɪts| *npl* menudillos *mpl*.

Gibraltar |dʒɪ'brɔːltər| *n* Gibraltar.

Gibraltarian |dʒɪbrɔːl'teərɪən| *adj & n* gibraltareño,-a *(m,f)*.

giddiness |'gɪdɪnɪs| *n* mareo *m*; *(vertigo)* vértigo *m*.

giddy |'gɪdɪ| *adj (giddier, giddiest)* mareado,-a; **it makes me g.,** me da vérti-

go; **to feel g.,** sentirse mareado,-a.

gift |gɪft| *n* 1 regalo *m*; *Com* obsequio *m*; **g. token,** vale *m*. 2 *(talent)* don *m*; **to have a g. for music,** estar muy dotado,-a para la música.

gifted |'gɪftɪd| *adj* dotado,-a.

gig |gɪg| *n sl Mus* actuación *f*.

gigantic |dʒaɪ'gæntɪk| *adj* gigantesco,-a.

giggle |'gɪgəl| **I** *n* 1 risita *f*. 2 *(lark)* broma *f*, diversión *f*. **II** *vi* reírse tontamente.

gild |gɪld| *vtr* dorar.

gill[1] |dʒɪl| *n (measurement)* medida *f* de líquidos (≈ 0,142 litro).

gill[2] |gɪl| *n (of fish)* branquia *f*, agalla *f*.

gilt |gɪlt| **I** *adj* dorado,-a. **II** *n (colour)* dorado *m*.

gilt-edged |'gɪltedʒd| *adj* **g.-e. securities,** valores *mpl* de máxima garantía.

gimmick |'gɪmɪk| *n* 1 truco *m*; *(in advertising)* reclamo *m*.

gin |dʒɪn| *n* ginebra *f*; **g. and tonic,** gin tonic *m*.

ginger |'dʒɪndʒər| **I** *n* jengibre *m*; **g. ale,** ginger ale *m*. **II** *adj* 1 de jengibre. 2 *(hair)* pelirrojo,-a.

gingerbread |'dʒɪndʒəbred| *n* pan *m* de jengibre.

gingerly |'dʒɪndʒəlɪ| *adv* cautelosamente.

gipsy |'dʒɪpsɪ| *adj & n* gitano,-a *(m,f)*.

giraffe |dʒɪ'rɑːf| *n* jirafa *f*.

girder |'gɜːdər| *n* viga *f*.

girdle |'gɜːdəl| *n* faja *f*.

girl |gɜːl| *n* 1 chica *f*, joven *f*; *(child)* niña *f*; **g. guide,** *US* **g. scout,** exploradora *f*. 2 *(daughter)* hija *f*. 3 *(sweetheart)* novia *f*.

girlfriend |'gɜːlfrend| *n* 1 *(lover)* novia *f*. 2 *(female friend)* amiga *f*.

girlhood |'gɜːlhʊd| *n* niñez *f*.

girlish |'gɜːlɪʃ| *adj* 1 de niña. 2 *(effeminate)* afeminado,-a.

giro |'dʒaɪrəʊ| *n GB* giro *m* (postal); **g. (cheque),** cheque *m* de giros postales.

gist |dʒɪst| *n* esencia *f*, lo esencial; **did you get the g. of what he was saying?,** ¿cogiste la idea de lo que decía?

give |gɪv| **I** *n (elasticity)* elasticidad *f*. **II** *vtr (pt* **gave***; pp* **given)** 1 dar; **to g. sth to sb,** dar algo a algn; **to g. a start,** pegar un salto; **to g. sb a present,** regalar algo a algn. 2 *(provide)* suministrar; **to g. sb sth to eat,** dar de comer a algn. 3 *(pay)* pagar. 4 *(concert)* dar; *(speech)* pronunciar. 5 *(dedicate)* dedicar. 6 *(grant)* otorgar; **to g. sb one's attention,** prestar atención a algn. 7 **to g. sb to understand that …,** dar a entender a algn que …. 8 *(yield)* ceder; **to g. way,** *Aut* ceder el paso; *fig* ceder; *(of legs)* flaquear. **III** *vi* 1 **to g. as good as one gets,** devolver golpe por golpe. 2 *(yield)* ceder; *(fabric)* dar de sí. ◆**give away** *vtr* 1 repartir; *(present)* regalar. 2 *(disclose)* revelar; **to g. the game away,** descubrir el pastel. 3 *(betray)* trai-

cionar. ◆**give back** *vtr* devolver.
◆**give in** I *vi* 1 (*admit defeat*) darse por
vencido,-a; (*surrender*) rendirse. 2 **to g. in
to**, ceder ante. II *vtr* (*hand in*) entregar.
◆**give off** *vtr* (*smell etc*) despedir.
◆**give out** *vtr* distribuir, repartir.
◆**give over** I *vtr* (*hand over*) entregar;
(*devote*) dedicar. II *vi fam* **g. over!**, ¡basta
ya! ◆**give up** I *vtr* 1 (*idea*) abandonar;
to g. up smoking, dejar de fumar. 2 (*betray*) traicionar. 3 (*hand over*) entregar; **to
g. oneself up**, entregarse. II *vi* (*admit defeat*) darse por vencido,-a, rendirse.
◆**give up on** *vtr* darse por vencido con.

given ['gɪvən] I *adj* 1 (*particular*) dado,-a;
at a g. time, en un momento dado. 2 **g.
to**, dado,-a a. II *conj* 1 (*considering*)
dado,-a. 2 (*if*) si.

glacial ['gleɪsɪəl] *adj Geol* glaciar. 2 (*icy*)
glacial; *fig* **g. look**, mirada *f* glacial.

glacier ['glæsɪər] *n* glaciar *m*.

glad [glæd] *adj* (**gladder, gladdest**)
contento,-a; (*happy*) alegre; **he'll be only
too g. to help you**, tendrá mucho gusto
en ayudarle; **to be g.**, alegrarse.
◆**gladly** *adv* con mucho gusto.

gladiator ['glædɪeɪtər] *n Hist* gladiador *m*.

glamor ['glæmər] *n US* → **glamour**.

glamorous ['glæmərəs] *adj* atractivo,-a,
encantador,-a.

glamour ['glæmər] *n* atractivo *m*; (*charm*)
encanto *m*; **a g. girl**, una belleza.

glance [glɑːns] I *n* mirada *f*, vistazo *m*; **at
a g.**, de un vistazo; **at first g.**, a primera
vista. II *vi* echar un vistazo (**at**, a).
◆**glance off** *vtr* (*ball etc*) rebotar de.

glancing ['glɑːnsɪŋ] *adj* (*blow*) oblicuo,-a.

gland [glænd] *n* glándula *f*.

glandular ['glændjʊlər] *adj* glandular; **g.
fever**, mononucleosis infecciosa.

glare [gleər] I *n* (*light*) luz *f* deslumbrante;
(*dazzle*) deslumbramiento *m*; (*look*) mirada *f* feroz. II *vi* (*dazzle*) deslumbrar;
(*look*) lanzar una mirada furiosa (**at**, a).

glaring ['gleərɪŋ] *adj* (*light*) deslumbrante;
(*colour*) chillón,-ona; (*obvious*) evidente.

glass [glɑːs] *n* 1 (*material*) vidrio *m*; **pane
of g.**, cristal *m*. 2 (*drinking vessel*) vaso *m*;
wine g., copa *f* (para vino). 3 **glasses**,
gafas *fpl*; **to wear g.**, llevar gafas.

glasshouse ['glɑːshaʊs] *n* invernadero *m*.

glassware ['glɑːsweər] *n* cristalería *f*.

glassy ['glɑːsɪ] *adj* (**glassier, glassiest**)
(*water*) cristalino,-a; (*eyes*) vidrioso,-a.

glaze [gleɪz] I *n* (*varnish*) barniz *m*; (*for
pottery*) vidriado *m*. II *vtr* 1 (*windows*)
acristalar; 2 (*varnish*) barnizar; (*ceramics*)
vidriar. 3 *Culin* glasear.

glazed [gleɪzd] *adj* (*eyes*) de mirada ausente.

glazier ['gleɪzɪər] *n* vidriero,-a *m,f*.

gleam [gliːm] I *n* 1 destello *m*. 2 *fig*
(*glimmer*) rayo *m*. II *vi* brillar, relucir.

gleaming ['gliːmɪŋ] *adj* brillante, relu-

ciente.

glean [gliːn] *vtr fig* recoger, cosechar.

glee [gliː] *n* gozo *m*.

gleeful ['gliːfʊl] *adj* gozoso,-a.

glen [glen] *n* cañada *f*.

glib [glɪb] *adj* (**glibber, glibbest**) *pej* de
mucha labia.

glide [glaɪd] *vi* 1 (*slip*, *slide*) deslizarse. 2
Av planear.

glider ['glaɪdər] *n* planeador *m*.

gliding ['glaɪdɪŋ] *n* vuelo *m* sin motor.

glimmer ['glɪmər] *n* 1 (*light*) luz *f* tenue.
2 *fig* (*trace*) destello *m*.

glimpse [glɪmps] I *n* atisbo *m*. II *vtr*
atisbar.

glint [glɪnt] I *n* destello *m*, centelleo *m*; **he
had a g. in his eye**, le brillaban los ojos.
II *vi* destellar, centellear.

glisten ['glɪsən] *vi* relucir, brillar.

glitter ['glɪtər] I *n* brillo *m*. II *vi* relucir.

gloat [gləʊt] *vi* jactarse; **to g. over
another's misfortune**, recrearse con la
desgracia de otro.

global ['gləʊbəl] *adj* 1 (*of the world*)
mundial. 2 (*overall*) global.

globe [gləʊb] *n* globo *m*, esfera *f*.

gloom [gluːm] *n* (*obscurity*) penumbra *f*;
(*melancholy*) melancolía *f*; (*despair*) desolación *f*.

gloomy ['gluːmɪ] *adj* (**gloomier, gloomi-
est**) (*dark*) oscuro,-a; (*weather*) gris; (*dismal*) deprimente; (*despairing*) pesimista;
(*sad*) triste.

glorify ['glɔːrɪfaɪ] *vtr* glorificar.

glorious ['glɔːrɪəs] *adj* (*momentous*)
glorioso,-a; (*splendid*) magnífico,-a,
espléndido,-a.

glory ['glɔːrɪ] *n* gloria *f*; *fig* (*splendour*) esplendor *m*; *fig* (*triumph*) triunfo *m*.

gloss [glɒs] I *n* 1 (*explanation*) glosa *f*. 2
(*sheen*) brillo *m*; **g. (paint)**, pintura *f* brillante. II *vi* glosar. ◆**gloss over** *vtr fig*
encubrir.

glossary ['glɒsərɪ] *n* glosario *m*.

glossy ['glɒsɪ] *adj* (**glossier, glossiest**)
lustroso,-a; **g. magazine**, revista *f* de
lujo.

glove [glʌv] *n* guante *m*; *Aut* **g. compartment**, guantera *f*.

glow [gləʊ] I *n* brillo *m*; (*of fire*)
incandescencia *f*; (*of sun*) arrebol *m*;
(*heat*) calor *m*; (*light*) luz *f*; (*in cheeks*) rubor *m*. II *vi* brillar; (*fire*) arder; *fig* rebosar de.

glower ['glaʊər] *vi* poner cara de
enfadado,-a.

glowing ['gləʊɪŋ] *adj* 1 (*fire*)
incandescente; (*colour*) vivo,-a; (*light*) brillante. 2 (*cheeks*) encendido,-a. 3 *fig* (*report*) entusiasta.

glucose ['gluːkəʊz] *n* glucosa *f*.

glue [gluː] I *n* pegamento *m*, cola *f*. II *vtr*
pegar (**to**, a).

glum [glʌm] *adj* (**glummer, glummest**)

alicaído,-a.

glut |glʌt| *n* superabundancia *f*, exceso *m*.

glutton |'glʌtən| *n* glotón,-ona *m,f*; *fam fig* **a g. for punishment**, masoquista *m,f*.

GMT |dʒiːem'tiː| *abbr of* **Greenwich Mean Time**, Hora media de Greenwich, GMT.

gnarled |nɑːld| *adj* nudoso,-a.

gnash |næʃ| *vtr* rechinar.

gnat |næt| *n* mosquito *m*.

gnaw |nɔː| *vtr & vi* (*chew*) roer.

GNP |dʒiːen'piː| *abbr of* **gross national product**, producto nacional bruto, PNB *m*.

gnome |nəʊm| *n* gnomo *m*.

go |gəʊ| I *vi* (*3rd person sing pres* **goes**; *pt* **went**; *pp* **gone**) 1 ir; **to go by car/on foot**, ir en coche/a pie; **to go for a walk**, (ir a) dar un paseo; **to g. on a journey**, ir de viaje; **to go shopping**, ir de compras; *fig* **to go too far**, pasarse (de la raya). 2 (*depart*) irse, marcharse; (*bus*) salir. 3 (*disappear*) desaparecer. 4 (*function*) funcionar; *fig* **to get things going**, poner las cosas en marcha. 5 (*sell*) venderse; **shoes going cheap**, zapatos a precios de rebaja. 6 (*become*) quedarse, volverse; **to go blind**, quedarse ciego,-a; **to go mad**, volverse loco,-a. 7 (*progress*) ir, marchar; **everything went well**, todo salió bien; **how's it going?**, qué tal (te van las cosas)? 8 **to be going to**, (*in the future*) ir a; (*on the point of*) estar a punto de. 9 (*fit*) caber. 10 (*be kept*) guardarse. 11 (*be available*) quedar; **I'll take whatever's going**, me conformo con lo que hay. 12 (*be acceptable*) valer; **anything goes**, todo vale. 13 (*break*) romperse; (*yield*) ceder. 14 **how does that song go?**, ¿cómo es aquella canción? 15 (*time*) pasar; **there are only two weeks to go**, sólo quedan dos semanas. 16 (*be inherited*) pasar (**to**, a). 17 (*say*) decir; **as the saying goes**, según el dicho. 18 **to let sth go**, soltar algo.
II *vtr* 1 (*travel*) hacer, recorrer. 2 **to go it alone**, apañárselas solo.
III *n* 1 (*energy*) energía *f*, dinamismo *m*. 2 (*try*) intento *m*; **to have a go at sth**, probar suerte con algo. 3 (*turn*) turno *m*; **it's your go**, te toca a ti. 4 **to make a go of sth**, tener éxito en algo. 5 **I knew from the word go**, lo sabía desde el principio. 6 **to have a go at sb**, criticar a algn. ◆**go about** I *vtr* 1 (*task*) emprender; **how do you go about it?**, ¿cómo hay que hacerlo? 2 **to go about one's business**, ocuparse de sus asuntos. II *vi* (*rumour*) correr. ◆**go after** *vtr* (*pursue*) andar tras. ◆**go against** *vtr* (*oppose*) ir en contra de; (*verdict*) ser desfavorable a. ◆**go ahead** *vi* 1 (*proceed*) proceder. 2 **we'll go on ahead**, iremos delante. ◆**go along** I *vtr* (*street*) pasar por. II *vi*

(*progress*) progresar. ◆**go along with** *vtr* 1 (*agree with*) estar de acuerdo con. 2 (*accompany*) acompañar. ◆**go around** *vi* 1 (*rumour*) correr. 2 **there's enough to go around**, hay para todos. ◆**go away** *vi* marcharse. ◆**go back** *vi* 1 (*return*) volver, regresar. 2 *fig* **to go back to**, (*date from*) datar de. ◆**go back on** *vtr* **to go back on one's word**, faltar a su palabra. ◆**go back to** *vtr* volver a. ◆**go by** *vi* pasar; **as time goes by**, con el tiempo. ◆**go down** *vi* 1 (*descend*) bajar; (*sun*) ponerse; (*ship*) hundirse. 2 (*diminish*) disminuir; (*temperature*) bajar. 3 (*be received*) ser acogido,-a. ◆**go down with** *vtr* (*contract*) coger. ◆**go for** *vtr* 1 (*attack*) lanzarse sobre; *fam fig* **go for it!**, ¡a por ello! 2 (*fetch*) ir por. 3 *fam* (*like*) gustar. ◆**go in** *vi* entrar. ◆**go in for** *vtr* (*exam*) presentarse a; (*hobby*) dedicarse a. ◆**go into** *vtr* 1 (*enter*) entrar en; **to go into journalism**, dedicarse al periodismo. 2 (*study*) examinar; (*matter*) investigar. 3 (*energy, money*) invertir en. ◆**go off** I *vi* 1 (*leave*) irse, marcharse. 2 (*bomb*) explotar; (*gun*) dispararse; (*alarm*) sonar. 3 (*food*) pasarse. 4 (*event*) resultar. II *vtr fam* **to go off sth**, perder el gusto or el interés por algo. ◆**go on** *vi* 1 (*continue*) seguir, continuar; **to go on talking**, seguir hablando; *fam* **to go on and on about sth**, no parar de hablar sobre algo; (*complain*) quejarse constantemente de algo. 2 (*happen*) ocurrir. 3 (*time*) transcurrir, pasar. 4 (*light*) encenderse. ◆**go out** *vi* 1 (*leave*) salir; **to go out for a meal**, comer or cenar fuera. 2 (*boy and girl*) salir juntos. 3 (*fire, light*) apagarse. 4 (*tide*) bajar. 5 *TV Rad* transmitirse. 6 **to go (all) out**, ir a por todas. 7 (*in competition*) perder la eliminatoria. ◆**go over** *vtr* (*revise*) repasar. ◆**go over to** *vtr* 1 acercarse a; **to go over to the enemy**, pasarse al enemigo. 2 (*switch to*) pasar a. ◆**go round** *vi* 1 (*revolve*) dar vueltas. 2 **to go round to sb's house**, pasar por casa de algn. ◆**go through** I *vi* (*bill*) ser aprobado,-a. II *vtr* 1 (*examine*) examinar; (*search*) registrar. 2 (*rehearse*) ensayar. 3 (*spend*) gastar. 4 (*list etc*) explicar. 5 (*endure*) sufrir. ◆**go through with** *vtr* llevar a cabo. ◆**go under** *vi* 1 (*ship*) hundirse. 2 (*business*) fracasar. ◆**go up** *vi* 1 (*price etc*) subir. 2 **to go up to sb**, acercarse a algn. 3 (*in a lift*) subir. 4 **to go up in flames**, quemarse. 5 *Sport* (*be promoted*) subir. ◆**go with** *vtr* 1 (*accompany*) ir con. 2 (*colours*) hacer juego con. ◆**go without** I *vtr* pasarse sin, prescindir de. 2 *fam* **that goes without saying**, eso es evidente. II *vi* (*not have*) aguantarse sin nada.

goad |gəʊd| *vtr* aguijonear.

go-ahead |'gəʊəhed| *fam n* **to give sb the**

go-a., dar luz verde a algn.

goal [gəʊl] *n* 1 *Sport* gol *m*; **g. kick**, saque *m* de puerta; **(g.) post**, poste *m*; **g. scorer**, goleador,-a *m,f*. 2 *(aim, objective)* meta *f*, objetivo *m*.

goalkeeper ['gəʊlkiːpər] *n* portero,-a *m,f*.

goat [gəʊt] *n (female)* cabra *f*; *(male)* macho cabrío.

gob [gɒb] *n GB sl* boca *f*.

gobble ['gɒbəl] *vtr* engullir.

go-between ['gəʊbɪtwiːn] *n* intermediario,-a *m,f*.

goblet ['gɒblɪt] *n* copa *f*.

god [gɒd] *n* dios *m*; **for G.'s sake!**, ¡por Dios!; **G., Dios; (my) G.!**, ¡Dios mío!; **G. forbid**, ¡Dios no lo quiera!; **G. only knows**, sabe Dios.

godchild ['gɒdtʃaɪld] *n* ahijado,-a *m,f*.

goddaughter ['gɒdɔːtər] *n* ahijada *f*.

goddess ['gɒdɪs] *n* diosa *f*.

godfather ['gɒdfɑːðər] *n* padrino *m*.

godforsaken ['gɒdfəseɪkən] *adj (place)* remoto,-a.

godmother ['gɒdmʌðər] *n* madrina *f*.

godparents ['gɒdpeərənts] *npl* padrinos *mpl*.

godsend ['gɒdsend] *n* regalo inesperado.

godson ['gɒdsʌn] *n* ahijado *m*.

goggles ['gɒgəlz] *npl* gafas protectoras.

going ['gəʊɪŋ] **I** *adj* 1 *(price)* corriente; **the g. rate**, el precio medio. 2 **a g. concern**, un negocio que marcha bien. 3 **to get** *or* **be g.**, marcharse. 4 **to keep g.**, resistir. **II** *n* 1 **that was good g.!**, ¡qué rápido! 2 *fig* **to get out while the g. is good**, retirarse antes que sea demasiado tarde.

goings-on [gəʊɪŋz'ɒn] *npl fam* tejemanejes *mpl*.

go-kart ['gəʊkɑːt] *n Sport* kart *m*.

gold [gəʊld] **I** *n* oro *m*; **g. leaf**, pan *m* de oro; **g. medal**, medalla *f* de oro; **g. mine**, mina *f* de oro. **II** *adj* de oro; *(colour)* oro, dorado,-a.

golden ['gəʊldən] *adj* de oro; *(colour)* dorado,-a; *fig* **a g. opportunity**, una excelente oportunidad; *Orn* **g. eagle**, águila *f* real; *fig* **g. handshake**, indemnización *f* por despido; **g. wedding**, bodas *fpl* de oro.

goldfish ['gəʊldfɪʃ] *n* pez *m* de colores.

gold-plated [gəʊld'pleɪtɪd] *adj* chapado, -a en oro.

goldsmith ['gəʊldsmɪθ] *n* orfebre *m*.

golf [gɒlf] *n* golf *m*; **g. ball**, pelota *f* de golf; **g. club**, *(stick)* palo *m* de golf; *(place)* club *m* de golf; **g. course**, campo *m* de golf.

golfer ['gɒlfər] *n* golfista *mf*.

golly ['gɒlɪ] *interj* ¡vaya!.

gone [gɒn] *adj* desaparecido,-a.

gong [gɒŋ] *n* gong *m*.

good [gʊd] **I** *adj (better, best)* 1 *(before noun)* buen,-a; *(after noun)* bueno,-a; **a g.**

book, un buen libro; **g. afternoon, g. evening**, buenas tardes; **g. morning**, buenos días; **g. night**, buenas noches; **it looks g.**, tiene buena pinta; **to be as g. as new**, estar como nuevo,-a; **to feel g.**, sentirse bien; **to have a g. time**, pasarlo bien; **to smell g.**, oler bien; **G. Friday**, Viernes *m* Santo. 2 *(kind)* amable; *(generous)* generoso,-a. 3 *(healthy)* sano,-a. 4 *(morally correct)* correcto,-a; **be g.!**, ¡pórtate bien! 5 **he's g. at languages**, tiene facilidad para los idiomas. 6 *(attractive)* bonito,-a; **red looks g. on you**, el rojo te favorece mucho; **g. looks**, atractivo *m sing*, belleza *f sing*. 7 **it's as g. as an offer**, equivale a una oferta; **it's as g. a way as any**, es una manera como otra cualquiera. 8 *(at least)* como mínimo. 9 *(sufficient)* bastante. 10 **to make g.**, *(injustice)* reparar; *(loss)* compensar; *(succeed in life)* triunfar. 11 *(reliable)* de confianza. 12 *(propitious)* propicio,-a. 13 **she comes from a g. family**, es de buena familia. 14 *(character)* agradable; **he's in a g. mood**, está de buen humor.

II *n* 1 bien *m*; **g. and evil**, el bien y el mal; **to do g.**, hacer el bien. 2 *(advantage)* bien *m*, provecho *m*; **for your own g.**, para tu propio bien; **it's no g. waiting**, no sirve de nada esperar; **it will do you g.**, te hará bien. 3 **goods**, *(possessions)* bienes *mpl*. 4 *Com* **goods**, artículos *mpl*, géneros *mpl*; **g. train**, tren *m* de mercancías.

III *adv* **she's gone for g.**, se ha ido para siempre.

IV *interj* **g.!**, ¡muy bien!

goodbye ['gʊdbaɪ] **I** *interj* ¡adiós!. **II** *n* adiós *m*, despedida *f*; **to say g. to sb**, despedirse de algn.

good-for-nothing ['gʊdfənʌθɪŋ] *adj & n* inútil *mf*.

good-hearted [gʊd'hɑːtɪd] *adj* de buen corazón.

good-looking [gʊd'lʊkɪŋ] *adj* guapo,-a.

good-natured [gʊd'neɪtʃəd] *adj* amable, bondadoso,-a.

goodness ['gʊdnɪs] *n* bondad *f*; **my g.!**, ¡Dios mío!; **thank g.!**, ¡gracias a Dios!; **for g. sake!**, ¡por Dios!

good-tempered [gʊd'tempəd] *adj* apacible.

goodwill [gʊd'wɪl] *n* 1 buena voluntad *f*. 2 *Com (reputation)* buen nombre *m*.

goose [guːs] *n (pl geese* [giːs]) ganso *m*, oca *f*.

gooseberry ['gʊzbərɪ, 'guːsbərɪ] *n* uva espina, grosella espinosa; *fam* **to play g.**, hacer de carabina.

gooseflesh ['guːsfleʃ] *n*, **goosepimples** ['guːspɪmpəlz] *npl* carne *f* de gallina.

goose-step ['guːsstep] *vi* ir a paso de la oca.

gore¹ [gɔːr] *n* sangre derramada.

gore² [gɔːʳ] *vtr Taur* cornear, dar cornadas a.

gorge [gɔːdʒ] **I** *n* desfiladero *m*. **II** *vtr & vi* **to g.** (oneself), atiborrarse (on, de).

gorgeous ['gɔːdʒəs] *adj* magnífico,-a, estupendo,-a; (person) atractivo,-a, guapo,-a.

gorilla [gə'rɪlə] *n* gorila *m*.

gorse [gɔːs] *n* aulaga *f*.

gory ['gɔːrɪ] *adj* (gorier, goriest) sangriento,-a.

gosh [gɒʃ] *interj fam* ¡cielos!, ¡caray!

go-slow [gəʊ'sləʊ] *n* huelga *f* de celo.

gospel ['gɒspəl] *n* the G., el Evangelio; *fam* it's the g. truth, es la pura verdad.

gossip ['gɒsɪp] **I** *n* **1** (rumour) cotilleo *m*; **g. column**, ecos *mpl* de sociedad. **2** (person) chismoso,-a *m,f*, cotilla *mf*. **II** *vi* (natter) cotillear, chismorrear.

got [gɒt] *pt & pp* → **get.**

Gothic ['gɒθɪk] *adj* gótico,-a.

gotten ['gɒtən] *pp US* → **get.**

gourmet ['gʊəmeɪ] *n* gourmet *mf*.

gout [gaʊt] *n* gota *f*.

govern ['gʌvən] *vtr* **1** gobernar. **2** (determine) determinar.

governess ['gʌvənɪs] *n* institutriz *f*.

governing ['gʌvənɪŋ] *adj* gobernante; **g. body**, consejo *m* de administración.

government ['gʌvənmənt] *n* gobierno *m*.

governmental [gʌvən'mentəl] *adj* gubernamental.

governor ['gʌvənəʳ] *n* (ruler) gobernador,-a *m,f*; (of prison) director,-a *m,f*; (of school) administrador,-a *m,f*.

gown [gaʊn] *n* (dress) vestido largo; *Jur Univ* toga *f*.

GP [dʒiː'piː] *abbr* of **general practioner.**

GPO [dʒiːpiː'əʊ] *GB abbr* of **General Post Office.**

grab [græb] **I** *n* agarrón *m*; *fam* **to be up for grabs**, estar disponible. **II** *vtr* **1** agarrar; **to g. hold of sb**, agarrarse a algn. **2** *fig* **a bottle of wine**, píllate una botella de vino. **3** *fig* **how does that g. you?**, ¿qué te parece?

grace [greɪs] **I** *n* **1** gracia *f*; *fig* **to fall from g.**, caer en desgracia. **2** **to say g.**, bendecir la mesa. **3** **to do sth with good g.**, hacer algo de buena gana. **4** **five days' g.**, (reprieve) un plazo de cinco días. **5** (elegance) elegancia *f*. **6** **Your G.**, (Su) Excelencia. **II** *vtr* **1** (adorn) adornar. **2** (honour) honrar.

graceful ['greɪsfʊl] *adj* elegante; (movement) garboso,-a. ◆**gracefully** *adv* **1** (beautifully) con gracia, con elegancia. **2** (accept) con cortesía.

gracious ['greɪʃəs] *adj* **1** (elegant) elegante. **2** (courteous) cortés. **3** (kind) amable. **II** *interj* **good g. (me)!**, **goodness g.!**, ¡santo cielo!

grade [greɪd] **I** *n* **1** (quality) grado *m*; (rank) categoría *f*; *Mil* rango *m*. **2** *Educ* (mark) nota *f*. **3** *US Educ* (class) clase *f*; *US* **g. school**, escuela primaria. **4** (level) nivel *m*; **to make the g.**, llegar al nivel deseado. **5** *US* (slope) pendiente *f*. **6** *US* **g. crossing**, paso *m* a nivel. **II** *vtr* clasificar.

gradient ['greɪdɪənt] *n* (graph) declive *m*; (hill) cuesta *f*, pendiente *f*.

gradual ['grædjʊəl] *adj* gradual, progresivo,-a. ◆**gradually** *adv* poco a poco.

graduate ['grædjʊɪt] **I** *n Educ* titulado,-a *m,f*; *Univ* licenciado,-a *m,f*; *US* **g. school**, escuela *f* para graduados. **II** *vi* ['grædjʊeɪt] **1** *Educ* sacarse el título; *Univ* licenciarse (in, en). **2** **to g. to**, pasar a.

graduation [grædjʊ'eɪʃən] *n* graduación *f*; *Univ* **g. ceremony**, ceremonia *f* de entrega de los títulos.

graffiti [grə'fiːtiː] *npl* grafiti *mpl*.

graft [grɑːft] **I** *n* **1** *Med* injerto *m*. **2** *fam* (work) trabajo *m*. **3** *US* (bribery) soborno *m*. **II** *vtr Med* injertar (on to, en). **III** *vi fam* trabajar duro.

grain [greɪn] *n* **1** (cereals) cereales *mpl*. **2** (particle) grano *m*; *fig* **there's not a g. of truth in it**, no tiene ni pizca de verdad. **3** (in wood) fibra *f*; (in stone) veta *f*; (in leather) flor *f*; *fig* **to go against the g.**, ir a contrapelo.

gram [græm] *n* gramo *m*.

grammar ['græməʳ] *n* gramática *f*; **g. (book)**, libro *m* de gramática; **g. school**, instituto estatal de segunda enseñanza al que se ingresa por examen selectivo.

grammatical [grə'mætɪkəl] *adj* gramatical.

gramme [græm] *n* gramo *m*.

gramophone ['græməfəʊn] *n* gramófono *m*.

granary ['grænərɪ] *n* granero *m*.

grand [grænd] **I** *adj* **1** grande; (before sing noun) gran; **g. piano**, piano *m* de cola; **G. Prix**, Gran Premio *m*. **2** (splendid) grandioso,-a, magnífico,-a; (impressive) impresionante. **3** **g. total**, total *m*. **4** *fam* (wonderful) estupendo,-a. **II** *n sl* mil libras *fpl*, *US* mil dólares *mpl*.

grandchild ['græntʃaɪld] *n* nieto,-a *m,f*.

granddad ['grændæd] *n fam* abuelo *m*.

granddaughter ['grændɔːtəʳ] *n* nieta *f*.

grandeur ['grændʒəʳ] *n* grandeza *f*, grandiosidad *f*.

grandfather ['grænfɑːðəʳ] *n* abuelo *m*; **g. clock**, reloj *m* de caja.

grandiose ['grændɪəʊs] *adj* grandioso,-a.

grandma ['grænmɑː] *n fam* abuelita *f*.

grandmother ['grænmʌðəʳ] *n* abuela *f*.

grandpa ['grænpɑː] *n fam* abuelito *m*.

grandparents ['grænpeərənts] *npl* abuelos *mpl*.

grandson ['grænsʌn] *n* nieto *m*.

grandstand ['grænstænd] *n* tribuna *f*.

granite ['grænɪt] n granito m.
granny ['grænɪ] n fam abuelita f.
grant [grɑːnt] I vtr 1 (allow) conceder, otorgar. 2 (admit) admitir; **to take sb for granted**, no apreciar a algn en lo que vale; **to take sth for granted**, dar algo por sentado. II n Educ beca f; (subsidy) subvención f.
granulated ['grænjʊleɪtɪd] adj granulado,-a.
granule ['grænjuːl] n gránulo m.
grape [greɪp] n uva f; **g. juice**, mosto m.
grapefruit ['greɪpfruːt] n pomelo m.
grapevine ['greɪpvaɪn] n Bot vid f; (against wall) parra f; fam **I heard it on or through the g.**, me enteré por ahí.
graph [grɑːf, græf] n gráfica f.
graphic ['græfɪk] adj gráfico,-a; **g. arts**, artes fpl gráficas; **g. designer**, grafista mf.
graphics ['græfɪks] n 1 (study) grafismo m. 2 pl Comput gráficas fpl.
grapple ['græpəl] I vi (struggle) luchar cuerpo a cuerpo (with, con); fig **to g. with a problem**, intentar resolver un problema. II n (hook) garfio m.
grasp [grɑːsp] I vtr 1 agarrar. 2 (understand) comprender. II n 1 (grip) agarrón m. 2 (understanding) comprensión f; **within sb's g.**, al alcance de algn.
grasping ['grɑːspɪŋ] adj avaro,-a.
grass [grɑːs] I n 1 hierba f; (lawn) césped m; (pasture) pasto m; **'keep off the g.'**, 'prohibido pisar el césped'; **g. court**, pista f de hierba; **g. roots**, base f; **g. snake**, culebra f. 2 sl (drug) hierba f. II vi GB sl chivarse (on, a). ◆**grass over** vi cubrirse de hierba.
grasshopper ['grɑːshɒpər] n saltamontes m inv.
grassland ['grɑːslænd] n pradera f.
grass-roots ['grɑːsruːts] adj de base; **at g.-r. level**, a nivel popular.
grassy ['grɑːsɪ] adj (grassier, grassiest) cubierto,-a de hierba.
grate¹ [greɪt] I vtr Culin rallar. II vi chirriar.
grate² [greɪt] n 1 (in fireplace) rejilla f. 2 (fireplace) chimenea f. 3 Constr rejilla f, reja f.
grateful ['greɪtfʊl] adj agradecido,-a; **to be g. for**, agradecer.
grater ['greɪtər] n Culin rallador m.
gratification [grætɪfɪ'keɪʃən] n (pleasure) placer m, satisfacción f.
gratify ['grætɪfaɪ] vtr 1 (please) complacer. 2 (yield to) sucumbir a.
gratifying ['grætɪfaɪɪŋ] adj grato,-a.
grating¹ ['greɪtɪŋ] n rejilla f, reja f.
grating² ['greɪtɪŋ] adj chirriante; (tone) áspero,-a.
gratis ['greɪtɪs, 'grætɪs] adv gratis.
gratitude ['grætɪtjuːd] n agradecimiento m.
gratuitous [grə'tjuːɪtəs] adj gratuito,-a.

gratuity [grə'tjuːɪtɪ] n gratificación f.
grave¹ [greɪv] n sepultura f, tumba f.
grave² [greɪv] adj (look etc) serio,-a; (situation) grave.
gravel ['grævəl] n grava f, gravilla f.
gravestone ['greɪvstəʊn] n lápida f sepulcral.
graveyard ['greɪvjɑːd] n cementerio m.
gravity ['grævɪtɪ] n gravedad f.
gravy ['greɪvɪ] n salsa f, jugo m (de la carne).
gray [greɪ] adj & n US → **grey**.
graze¹ [greɪz] vi pacer, pastar.
graze² [greɪz] I vtr (scratch) rasguñar; (brush against) rozar. II n rasguño m.
grease [griːs, griːz] I n grasa f. II vtr engrasar.
greaseproof ['griːspruːf] adj **g. paper**, papel graso.
greasy ['griːsɪ, 'griːzɪ] adj (greasier, greasiest) 1 (oily) grasiento,-a; (hair, food) graso,-a. 2 (slippery) resbaladizo,-a. 3 fam (ingratiating) pelotillero,-a.
great [greɪt] I adj 1 grande; (before sing noun) gran; (pain, heat) fuerte; **a g. many**, muchos,-as; **G. Britain**, Gran Bretaña. 2 fam (excellent) estupendo,-a, magnífico,-a; **to have a g. time**, pasarlo en grande. II adv fam muy bien, estupendamente. ◆**greatly** adv muy, mucho.
great-aunt [greɪt'ɑːnt] n tía abuela.
great-grandchild [greɪt'græntʃaɪld] n bisnieto,-a m,f.
great-grandfather [greɪt'grænfɑːðər] n bisabuelo m.
great-grandmother [greɪt'grænmʌðər] n bisabuela f.
greatness ['greɪtnɪs] n grandeza f.
great-uncle [greɪt'ʌŋkəl] n tío abuelo.
Greece [griːs] n Grecia f.
greed [griːd], **greediness** ['griːdɪnɪs] n (for food) gula f; (for money) codicia f, avaricia f.
greedy ['griːdɪ] adj (greedier, greediest) (for food) glotón,-ona; (for money) codicioso,-a (for, de).
Greek [griːk] I adj griego,-a. II n 1 (person) griego,-a m,f. 2 (language) griego m.
green [griːn] I n 1 (colour) verde m. 2 Golf campo m; **village g.**, plaza f (del pueblo). 3 **greens**, verdura f sing, verduras fpl. II adj 1 verde; **g. bean**, judía f verde; **g. belt**, zona f verde; **g. pepper**, pimiento m verde; **she was g. with envy**, se la comía la envidia. 2 (inexperienced) verde, novato,-a; (gullible) crédulo,-a. 3 Pol **G. Party**, Partido m Verde.
greenery ['griːnərɪ] n follaje m.
greenfly ['griːnflaɪ] n pulgón m.
greengage ['griːngeɪdʒ] n ciruela claudia.
greengrocer ['griːngrəʊsər] n GB verdulero,-a m,f.

greenhouse ['gri:nhaʊs] n invernadero m;
g. effect, efecto invernadero.

greenish ['gri:nɪʃ] adj verdoso,-a.

Greenland ['gri:nlənd] n Groenlandia.

greet [gri:t] vtr (wave at) saludar; (receive)
recibir; (welcome) dar la bienvenida a.

greeting ['gri:tɪŋ] n 1 saludo m; greetings
card, tarjeta f de felicitación. 2 (reception)
recibimiento m; (welcome) bienvenida f.

gregarious [grɪ'geərɪəs] adj gregario,-a,
sociable.

Grenada [gre'neɪdə] n Granada.

grenade [grɪ'neɪd] n granada f.

grew [gru:] pt → grow.

grey [greɪ] I adj (colour) gris; (hair)
cano,-a; (sky) nublado,-a; g. matter, materia f gris. II n 1 (colour) gris m. 2
(horse) caballo tordo.

grey-haired ['greɪheəd] adj canoso,-a.

greyhound ['greɪhaʊnd] n galgo m.

greyish ['greɪɪʃ] adj grisáceo,-a.

grid [grɪd] n 1 (on map) cuadrícula f. 2
(of electricity etc) red f nacional. 3 → gridiron.

gridiron ['grɪdaɪən] n Culin parrilla f.

grief [gri:f] n dolor m, pena f; fam to
come to g., (car, driver) sufrir un accidente; (plans) irse al traste.

grievance ['gri:vəns] n (wrong) agravio m;
(resentment) queja f.

grieve [gri:v] I vtr apenar, dar pena a. II
vi apenarse, afligirse; to g. for sb, llorar
la muerte de algn.

grievous ['gri:vəs] adj (offence) grave; g.
bodily harm, lesiones fpl corporales graves.

grill [grɪl] I vtr 1 Culin asar a la parrilla. 2
fam (interrogate) interrogar duramente. II
n parrilla f; (dish) parrillada f.

grill(e) [grɪl] n (grating) reja f.

grim [grɪm] adj (grimmer, grimmest) 1
(sinister) macabro,-a; (landscape) lúgubre;
(smile) sardónico,-a. 2 (manner) severo,-a;
(person) ceñudo,-a. 3 (resolute) inexorable.
4 fam (unpleasant) desagradable; g. reality, la dura realidad.

grimace [grɪ'meɪs] I n mueca f. II vi hacer una mueca.

grimy ['graɪmɪ] adj (grimier, grimiest)
mugriento,-a.

grin [grɪn] I vi sonreír abiertamente. II n
sonrisa abierta.

grind [graɪnd] I vtr (pt & pp ground)
(mill) moler; (crush) triturar; (sharpen)
afilar; to g. one's teeth, hacer rechinar
los dientes. II vi rechinar; fig to g. to a
halt, (vehicle) pararse lentamente; (production etc) pararse poco a poco. III n fam
the daily g., la rutina cotidiana; what a
g.!, ¡qué rollo! ◆grind down vtr fig to
g. down the opposition, acabar con la
oposición.

grip [grɪp] I n 1 (hold) agarrón m; (handshake) apretón m; (of tyre) adherencia f;

get a g. on yourself!, ¡tranquilízate!; to
get to grips with a problem, superar un
problema. 2 (handle) asidero m. 3 (travel
bag) maletín m. 4 (hairgrip) pasador m.
II vtr 1 agarrar, asir; (hand) apretar. 2 fig
(of film, story) captar la atención de; to be
gripped by fear, ser presa del miedo.

gripe [graɪp] I vi fam (complain) quejarse.
II n 1 Med (pain) retortijón m. 2 fam
(complaint) queja f.

gripping ['grɪpɪŋ] adj (film, story) apasionante.

grisly ['grɪzlɪ] adj (grislier, grisliest) espeluznante.

gristle ['grɪsəl] n cartílago m, ternilla f.

grit [grɪt] I n 1 (gravel) grava f. 2 fam
(courage) valor m. II vtr fig to g. one's
teeth, apretar los dientes.

gritty ['grɪtɪ] adj (grittier, grittiest) valiente.

grizzly ['grɪzlɪ] adj g. bear, oso pardo.

groan [grəʊn] I n 1 (of pain) gemido m. 2
fam (of disapproval) gruñido m. II vi 1 (in
pain) gemir. 2 fam (complain) quejarse
(about, de).

grocer ['grəʊsər] n tendero,-a m,f.

groceries ['grəʊsərɪz] npl comestibles
mpl.

grocery ['grəʊsərɪ] n (shop) tienda f de ultramarinos; US g. store, supermercado
m.

groggy ['grɒgɪ] adj (groggier, groggiest)
fam Box grogui; fig (unsteady) atontado,
-a; (weak) débil.

groin [grɔɪn] n 1 ingle f. 2 US → groyne.

groom [gru:m] I n 1 mozo m de cuadra. 2
(bridegroom) novio m. II vtr (horse) almohazar; (clothes, appearance) cuidar.

groove [gru:v] n (furrow etc) ranura f; (of
record) surco m.

grope [grəʊp] vi 1 (search about) andar a
tientas; to g. for sth, buscar algo a
tientas. 2 sl (fondle) meter mano.

gross [grəʊs] I adj 1 grosero,-a; (joke)
verde. 2 (fat) obeso,-a. 3 (flagrant) flagrante; (ignorance) craso,-a. 4 Com Econ
bruto,-a; g. national product, producto
nacional bruto. II vtr Com recaudar (en
bruto). ◆grossly adv enormemente.

grotesque [grəʊ'tesk] adj grotesco,-a.

grotto ['grɒtəʊ] n gruta f.

ground[1] [graʊnd] I n 1 suelo m, tierra f;
at g. level, al nivel del suelo; Av to get
off the g., despegar; Av g. control, control m de tierra; g. floor, planta baja; Av
g. staff, personal m de tierra; fig g. swell,
marejada f. 2 (terrain) terreno m; to
gain/lose g., ganar/perder terreno; fig to
stand one's g., mantenerse firme; football g., campo m de fútbol. 3 US Elec
tierra f. 4 grounds, (gardens) jardines
mpl. 5 grounds, (reason) motivo m sing. 6
grounds, (sediment) poso m sing. II vtr 1
Av obligar a quedarse en tierra; Naut va-

rar. **2** *US Elec* conectar con tierra.

ground² [graʊnd] *adj* (*coffee*) molido,-a; *US* (*meat*) picado,-a.

grounding ['graʊndɪŋ] *n* base *f*; **to have a good g. in**, tener buenos conocimientos de.

groundless ['graʊndlɪs] *adj* infundado,-a.

groundsheet ['graʊndʃiːt] *n* tela *f* impermeable.

groundsman ['graʊndzmən] *n* encargado *m* de campo.

groundwork ['graʊndwɜːk] *n* trabajo preparatorio.

group [gruːp] **I** *n* grupo *m*, conjunto *m*. **II** *vtr* agrupar, juntar (**into**, en). **III** *vi* **to g.** (**together**), agruparse, juntarse.

grouse¹ [graʊs] *n Orn* urogallo *m*.

grouse² [graʊs] *fam vi* quejarse (**about**, de). **II** *n* queja *f*.

grove [grəʊv] *n* arboleda *f*.

grovel ['grɒvəl] *vi* humillarse (**to**, ante); (*crawl*) arrastrarse (**to**, ante).

grow [grəʊ] **I** *vtr* (*pt* **grew**; *pp* **grown**) (*cultivate*) cultivar; **to g. a beard**, dejarse (crecer) la barba. **II** *vi* **1** crecer; (*increase*) aumentar. **2** (*become*) hacerse, volverse; **to g. accustomed to**, acostumbrarse a; **to g. dark**, oscurecer; **to g. old**, envejecer. ◆**grow out of** *vtr* **1 he's grown out of his shirt**, se le ha quedado pequeña la camisa. **2** *fig* (*phase etc*) superar. ◆**grow up** *vi* crecer, hacerse mayor.

grower ['grəʊər] *n* cultivador,-a *m,f*.

growing ['grəʊɪŋ] *adj* (*child*) que crece; (*problem etc*) creciente; **he's a g. boy**, está dando el estirón.

growl [graʊl] **I** *vi* gruñir. **II** *n* gruñido *m*.

grown [grəʊn] *adj* crecido,-a, adulto,-a.

grown-up ['grəʊnʌp] *adj & n* adulto,-a (*m,f*); **the g.-ups**, los mayores.

growth [grəʊθ] *n* **1** crecimiento *m*; (*increase*) aumento *m*; (*development*) desarrollo *m*. **2** *Med* bulto *m*.

groyne [grɔɪn] *n* espigón *m*.

grub [grʌb] *n* **1** (*larva*) gusano *m*. **2** *sl* (*food*) papeo *m*.

grubby ['grʌbɪ] *adj* (**grubbier**, **grubbiest**) sucio,-a.

grudge [grʌdʒ] **I** *n* rencor *m*; **to bear sb a g.**, guardar rencor a algn. **II** *vtr* (*give unwillingly*) dar a regañadientes; **he grudges me my success**, me envidia el éxito.

grudgingly ['grʌdʒɪŋlɪ] *adv* a regañadientes.

gruelling, *US* **grueling** ['gruːəlɪŋ] *adj* penoso,-a.

gruesome ['gruːsəm] *adj* espantoso,-a, horrible.

gruff [grʌf] *adj* (*manner*) brusco,-a; (*voice*) áspero,-a.

grumble ['grʌmbəl] **I** *vi* refunfuñar. **II** *n* queja *f*.

grumpy ['grʌmpɪ] *adj* (**grumpier**, **grumpiest**) gruñón,-ona.

grunt [grʌnt] **I** *vi* gruñir. **II** *n* gruñido *m*.

guarantee [gærənˈtiː] **I** *n* garantía *f*; (*certificate*) certificado *m* de garantía. **II** *vtr* garantizar; (*assure*) asegurar.

guard [gɑːd] **I** *vtr* **1** (*protect*) defender, proteger; (*keep watch over*) vigilar. **2** (*control*) guardar. **II** *vi* protegerse (**against**, de, contra). **III** *n* **1 to be on one's g.**, estar en guardia; **to catch sb off his g.**, coger desprevenido a algn. **2** (*sentry*) guardia *mf*; **g. of honour**, guardia de honor; **to stand g.**, montar la guardia; **g. dog**, perro *m* guardián. **3** *GB Rail* jefe *m* de tren; **g.'s van**, furgón *m* de cola. **4** (*on machine*) dispositivo *m* de seguridad; **fire g.**, pantalla *f*.

guarded ['gɑːdɪd] *adj* cauteloso,-a, precavido,-a.

guardhouse ['gɑːdhaʊs] *n Mil* **1** (*headquarters*) cuerpo *m* de guardia. **2** (*prison*) prisión *f* militar.

guardian ['gɑːdɪən] *n* **1** guardián,-ana *m,f*; **g. angel**, ángel *m* de la guarda. **2** *Jur* (*of minor*) tutor,-a *m,f*.

Guatemala [gwɑːtəˈmɑːlə] *n* Guatemala.

Guatemalan [gwɑːtəˈmɑːlən] *adj & n* guatemalteco,-a (*m,f*).

guava ['gwɑːvə] *n Bot* guayaba *f*; **g. tree**, guayabo *m*.

guer(r)illa [gəˈrɪlə] *n* guerrillero,-a *m,f*; **g. warfare**, guerra *f* de guerrillas.

guess [ges] **I** *vtr & vi* **1** adivinar; **I guessed as much**, me lo imaginaba; **to g. right/wrong**, acertar/no acertar. **2** *US fam* pensar, suponer; **I g. so**, supongo que sí. **II** *n* conjetura *f*, (*estimate*) cálculo *m*; **at a rough g.**, a ojo de buen cubero; **to have o make a g.**, intentar adivinar.

guesswork ['geswɜːk] *n* conjetura *f*.

guest [gest] *n* (*at home*) invitado,-a *m,f*; (*in hotel*) cliente,-a *m,f*, huésped,-a *m,f*; **g. artist**, artista *mf* invitado,-a; **g. room**, cuarto *m* de los invitados.

guesthouse ['gesthaʊs] *n* casa *f* de huéspedes.

guffaw [gʌˈfɔː] *vi* reírse a carcajadas.

guidance ['gaɪdəns] *n* orientación *f*, consejos *mpl*; **for your g.**, a título de información.

guide [gaɪd] **I** *vtr* guiar, dirigir. **II** *n* (*person*) guía *mf*; *GB* **girl g.**, exploradora *f*; **g. dog**, perro *m* lazarillo. **2** (*guidebook*) guía *f*.

guidebook ['gaɪdbʊk] *n* guía *f*.

guided ['gaɪdɪd] *adj* dirigido,-a; **g. tour**, visita con guía; **g. missile**, misil teledirigido.

guideline ['gaɪdlaɪn] *n* pauta *f*.

guild [gɪld] *n* gremio *m*.

guile [gaɪl] *n* astucia *f*.

guillotine ['gɪlətiːn] *n* guillotina *f*.

guilt [gɪlt] *n* **1** culpa *f*. **2** *Jur* culpabilidad *f*.

guilty ['gɪltɪ] *adj* (**guiltier**, **guiltiest**)

culpable (of, de); **to have a g. conscience,** remorderle a uno la conciencia.

guinea¹ ['gɪnɪ] *n* **g. pig,** conejillo *m* de Indias, cobayo *m; fig* **to act as a g. pig,** servir de conejillo de Indias.

guinea² ['gɪnɪ] *n (coin)* guinea *f (approx* 21 chelines).

guise [gaɪz] *n* **under the g. of,** so pretexto de.

guitar [gɪ'tɑ:r] *n* guitarra *f.*

guitarist [gɪ'tɑ:rɪst] *n* guitarrista *mf.*

gulf [gʌlf] *n* 1 golfo *m;* **G. of Mexico,** Golfo de Méjico; **G. Stream,** corriente *f* del Golfo de Méjico. 2 *fig* abismo *m.*

gull [gʌl] *n* gaviota *f.*

gull(e)y ['gʌlɪ] *n* barranco *m,* hondonada *f.*

gullible ['gʌləbəl] *adj* crédulo,-a.

gulp [gʌlp] **I** *n* trago *m.* **II** *vtr* tragar; **to g. sth down,** *(drink)* tomarse algo de un trago; *(food)* engullir algo. **III** *vi* 1 *(swallow air)* tragar aire. 2 *fig (with fear)* tragar saliva.

gum¹ [gʌm] **I** *n* goma *f.* **II** *vtr* pegar con goma.

gum² [gʌm] *n Anat* encía *f.*

gumboots ['gʌmbuːts] *npl* botas *fpl* de agua.

gun [gʌn] *n* arma *f* de fuego; *(handgun)* pistola *f,* revólver *m;* *(rifle)* fusil *m,* escopeta *f; (cannon)* cañón *m; fam* **the big guns,** los peces gordos. ◆**gun down** *vtr* matar a tiros.

gunboat ['gʌnbəʊt] *n* cañonero *m.*

gunfire ['gʌnfaɪər] *n* tiros *mpl.*

gunman ['gʌnmən] *n* pistolero *m,* gángster *m.*

gunpoint ['gʌnpɔɪnt] *n* **at g.,** a punta de pistola.

gunpowder ['gʌnpaʊdər] *n* pólvora *f.*

gunrunner ['gʌnrʌnər] *n* traficante *mf* de armas.

gunshot ['gʌnʃɒt] *n* disparo *m,* tiro *m.*

gunsmith ['gʌnsmɪθ] *n* armero *m.*

gurgle ['gɜːgəl] *vi (baby)* gorjear; *(liquid)* gorgotear; *(stream)* murmurar.

guru ['guruː, 'guːruː] *n* gurú *m.*

gush [gʌʃ] **I** *vi* 1 brotar. 2 *fig* **to g. over sb,** enjabonar a algn. **II** *n (of water)* chorro *m; (of words)* torrente *m.*

gushing ['gʌʃɪŋ] *adj fig (person)* efusivo, -a.

gusset ['gʌsɪt] *n* escudete *m.*

gust [gʌst] *n (of wind)* ráfaga *f,* racha *f.*

gusto ['gʌstəʊ] *n* entusiasmo *m.*

gut [gʌt] **I** *n* 1 *Anat* intestino *m.* 2 *(catgut)* cuerda *f* de tripa. 3 **guts,** *(entrails)* tripas *fpl; sl* **to have g.,** tener agallas. **II** *vtr* 1 *(fish)* destripar. 2 *(destroy)* destruir por dentro. **III** *adj fam* **g. reaction,** reacción *f* visceral.

gutter ['gʌtər] *n (in street)* arroyo *m; (on roof)* canalón *m; fig* **g. press,** prensa amarilla.

guttural ['gʌtərəl] *adj* gutural.

guy¹ [gaɪ] *n fam* tipo *m,* tío *m.*

guy² [gaɪ] *n (rope)* viento *m,* cuerda *f.*

guzzle ['gʌzəl] *vtr & vi fam (food etc)* zamparse; *(car)* tragar mucho.

gym [dʒɪm] *fam* 1 *(gymnasium)* gimnasio *m.* 2 *(gymnastics)* gimnasia *f;* **g. shoes,** zapatillas *fpl* de deporte.

gymnasium [dʒɪm'neɪzɪəm] *n* gimnasio *m.*

gymnast ['dʒɪmnæst] *n* gimnasta *mf.*

gymnastics [dʒɪm'næstɪks] *n* gimnasia *f.*

gynaecologist, *US* **gynecologist** [gaɪnɪ'kɒlədʒɪst] *n* ginecólogo,-a *m,f.*

gypsy ['dʒɪpsɪ] *adj & n* gitano,-a *(m,f).*

gyrate [dʒaɪ'reɪt] *vi* girar.

H

H, h [eɪtʃ] *n (the letter)* H, h *f.*

haberdashery [hæbə'dæʃərɪ] *n* 1 *GB* artículos *mpl* de mercería. 2 *US* ropa masculina.

habit ['hæbɪt] *n* 1 costumbre *f.* 2 *(garment)* hábito *m.*

habitable ['hæbɪtəbəl] *adj* habitable.

habitat ['hæbɪtæt] *n* hábitat *m.*

habitual [hə'bɪtjuəl] *adj* habitual; *(drinker, liar)* empedernido,-a. ◆**habitually** *adv* por costumbre.

hack¹ [hæk] **I** *n (cut)* corte *m; (with an axe)* hachazo *m.* **II** *vtr (with knife, axe)* cortar; *(kick)* dar un puntapié a.

hack² [hæk] *n fam (writer)* escritorzuelo,-a *m,f; (journalist)* gacetillero,-a *m,f.*

hackneyed ['hæknɪd] *adj* trillado,-a.

hacksaw ['hæksɔ:] *n* sierra *f* para metales.

had [hæd] *pt & pp →* **have.**

haddock ['hædək] *n* abadejo *m.*

haemophilia [hiːməʊ'fɪlɪə] *n* hemofilia *f.*

haemophiliac [hiːməʊ'fɪlɪæk] *adj & n* hemofílico,-a *(m,f).*

haemorrhage ['hemərɪdʒ] *n* hemorragia *f.*

haemorrhoids ['hemərɔɪdz] *npl* hemorroides *fpl.*

hag [hæg] *n pej* bruja *f,* arpía *f.*

haggard ['hægəd] *adj* ojeroso,-a.

haggle ['hægəl] *vi* regatear.

Hague [heɪg] *n* **The H.,** La Haya.

hail¹ [heɪl] **I** *n* granizo *m; fig* **a h. of bullets/insults,** una lluvia de balas/ insultos. **II** *vi* granizar.

hail² [heɪl] **I** *vtr* 1 *(taxi etc)* parar. 2 *(acclaim)* aclamar. **II** *vi* **to h. from,** *(origi-*

nate) ser nativo,-a de.

hailstone ['heɪlstəʊn] *n* granizo *m*.

hailstorm ['heɪlstɔːm] *n* granizada *f*.

hair [heəʳ] *n* (*strand*) pelo *m*, cabello *m*; (*mass*) pelo *m*, cabellos *mpl*; (*on arm, leg*) vello *m*; **to have long h.**, tener el pelo largo.

hairbrush ['heəbrʌʃ] *n* cepillo *m* (para el pelo).

haircut ['heəkʌt] *n* corte *m* de pelo; **to have a h.**, cortarse el pelo.

hairdo ['heədu:] *n fam* peinado *m*.

hairdresser ['heədresəʳ] *n* peluquero,-a *m,f*; **h.'s (shop)**, peluquería *f*.

hairdryer, hairdrier ['heədraɪəʳ] *n* secador *m* (de pelo).

hair-grip ['heəgrɪp] *n* horquilla *f*, pasador *m*.

hairline ['heəlaɪn] I *adj* muy fino,-a. II *n* nacimiento *m* del pelo; **receding h.**, entradas *fpl*.

hairnet ['heənet] *n* redecilla *f*.

hairpiece ['heəpi:s] *n* postizo *m*.

hairpin ['heəpɪn] *n* horquilla *f*; **h. bend**, curva muy cerrada.

hair-raising ['heəreɪzɪŋ] *adj* espeluznante.

hair-remover ['heərɪmu:vəʳ] *n* depilatorio *m*.

hairspray ['heəspreɪ] *n* laca *f* (para el pelo).

hairstyle ['heəstaɪl] *n* peinado *m*, corte *m* de pelo.

hairy ['heərɪ] *adj* (**hairier, hairiest**) 1 (*with hair*) peludo,-a. 2 *fig* (*frightening*) enervante, espantoso,-a.

hake [heɪk] *n* merluza *f*; (*young*) pescadilla *f*.

half [hɑːf] I *n* (*pl* **halves**) mitad *f*; *Sport* (*period*) parte *f*; **he's four and a h.**, tiene cuatro años y medio; **to cut in h.**, cortar por la mitad. II *adj* medio,-a; **h. a dozen/an hour**, media docena/hora; **h. board**, media pensión; **h. fare**, media tarifa; **h. term**, medio trimestre; **h. year**, semestre *m*. III *adv* medio, a medias; **h. asleep**, medio dormido,-a.

half-caste ['hɑːfkɑːst] *adj & n* mestizo,-a (*m,f*).

half-day [hɑːf'deɪ] *n* media jornada.

half-hearted [hɑːf'hɑːtɪd] *adj* poco entusiasta.

half-hour [hɑːf'aʊəʳ] *n* media hora.

half-life ['hɑːflaɪf] *n* media vida.

half-mast [hɑːf'mɑːst] *n* **at h.**, a media asta.

half-price [hɑːf'praɪs] *adv* a mitad de precio.

half-time [hɑːf'taɪm] *n* descanso *m*.

half-way [hɑːf'weɪ] I *adj* intermedio,-a. II **halfway** [hɑːf'weɪ] *adv* a medio camino, a mitad de camino.

half-yearly ['hɑːfjɪəlɪ] *adj* semestral.

halibut ['hælɪbət] *n* mero *m*.

hall [hɔːl] *n* 1 (*lobby*) vestíbulo *m*. 2

(*building*) sala *f*; *Univ* **h. of residence**, colegio *m* mayor.

hallmark ['hɔːlmɑːk] *n* 1 (*on gold, silver*) contraste *m*. 2 *fig* sello *m*.

hallo [hə'ləʊ] *interj* ¡hola!

hallowed ['hæləʊd] *adj* santificado,-a.

Hallowe('en [hæləʊ'i:n] *n* víspera *f* de Todos los Santos.

hallucinate [hə'lu:sɪneɪt] *vi* alucinar.

hallucination [həlu:sɪ'neɪʃən] *n* alucinación *f*.

hallucinogenic [həlu:sɪnəʊ'dʒenɪk] *adj* alucinógeno,-a.

hallway ['hɔːlweɪ] *n* vestíbulo *m*.

halo ['heɪləʊ] *n* 1 *Rel* aureola *f*. 2 *Astron* halo *m*.

halt [hɔːlt] I *n* (*stop*) alto *m*, parada *f*; **to call a h. to sth**, poner fin a algo. II *vtr* parar. III *vi* pararse.

halting ['hɔːltɪŋ] *adj* vacilante.

halve [hɑːv] *vtr* 1 partir por la mitad; (*reduce by half*) reducir a la mitad. 2 (*share*) compartir.

halves [hɑːvz] *pl* → **half**.

ham [hæm] *n* jamón *m*; **boiled h.**, jamón de York; **Parma** or **cured h.**, jamón serrano.

hamburger ['hæmbɜːgəʳ] *n* hamburguesa *f*.

hamlet ['hæmlɪt] *n* aldea *f*.

hammer ['hæməʳ] I *n* 1 martillo *m*; **the h. and sickle**, la hoz y el martillo. 2 (*of gun*) percusor *m*. 3 *Sport* lanzamiento *m* de martillo. II *vtr* 1 martillar; (*nail*) clavar; *fig* **to h. home**, insistir sobre. 2 *fam* (*defeat*) dar una paliza a. III *vi* martillar, dar golpes.

hammering ['hæmərɪŋ] *n fam* paliza *f*.

hammock ['hæmək] *n* hamaca *f*; *Naut* coy *m*.

hamper¹ ['hæmpəʳ] *n* cesta *f*.

hamper² ['hæmpəʳ] *vtr* estorbar, dificultar.

hamster ['hæmstəʳ] *n* hámster *m*.

hamstring ['hæmstrɪŋ] *n* tendón *m* de la corva.

hand [hænd] I *n* 1 mano *f*; **by h.**, a mano; (*close*) **at h.**, a mano; **hands up!**, ¡manos arriba!; **on the one/other h.**, por una/otra parte; *fig* **to get out of h.**, descontrolarse; *fig* **to be on h.**, estar a mano; *fig* **to have a h. in**, intervenir en; *fig* **to have time in h.**, sobrarle a uno tiempo; *fig* **to wash one's hands of sth**, lavarse las manos de algo; *fig* **to give sb a h.**, echarle una mano a algn; **h. grenade**, granada *f* de mano. 2 (*worker*) trabajador,-a *m,f*; *Naut* tripulante *m*. 3 (*of clock*) aguja *f*. 4 **to give sb a big h.**, (*applause*) dedicar a algn una gran ovación. 5 (*handwriting*) letra *f*.

II *vtr* (*give*) dar, entregar; *fam fig* **I have to h. it to you**, tengo que reconocerlo.

◆**hand back** *vtr* devolver. ◆**hand**

down *vtr* dejar en herencia. ◆**hand in** *vtr (homework)* entregar; *(resignation)* presentar. ◆**hand out** *vtr* repartir. ◆**hand over** *vtr* entregar. ◆**hand round** *vtr* repartir.

handbag ['hændbæg] *n* bolso *m*.

handball ['hændbɔːl] *n Sport* balonmano *m*.

handbook ['hændbʊk] *n* manual *m*.

handbrake ['hændbreɪk] *n* freno *m* de mano.

handcuff ['hændkʌf] I *vtr* esposar. II *npl* **handcuffs**, esposas *fpl*.

handful ['hændfʊl] *n* puñado *m*.

handicap ['hændɪkæp] *n* I *n* 1 *Med* minusvalía *f*. 2 *(Sport)* hándicap *m*, desventaja *f*. II *vtr* impedir.

handicapped ['hændɪkæpt] *adj* 1 *(physically)* minusválido,-a; *(mentally)* retrasado,-a. 2 *Sport* en desventaja. 3 *fig* desfavorecido,-a.

handicraft ['hændɪkrɑːft] *n* artesanía *f*.

handiwork ['hændɪwɜːk] *n (work)* obra *f*; *(craft)* artesanía *f*.

handkerchief ['hæŋkətʃiːf] *n* pañuelo *m*.

handle ['hændəl] I *n (of knife)* mango *m*; *(of cup)* asa *f*; *(of door)* pomo *m*; *(of lever)* palanca *f*; *(of drawer)* tirador *m*. II *vtr* 1 manejar; '**h. with care**', 'frágil'. 2 *(problem)* encargarse de; *(people)* tratar; *fam (put up with)* soportar. III *vi (car)* comportarse.

handlebar ['hændəlbɑːr] *n* manillar *m*.

handmade [hænd'meɪd] *adj* hecho,-a a mano.

hand-out ['hændaʊt] *n* 1 *(leaflet)* folleto *m*; *Press* nota *f* de prensa. 2 *(charity)* limosna *f*.

hand-picked [hænd'pɪkt] *adj* selecto,-a.

handrail ['hændreɪl] *n* pasamanos *m sing inv*.

handshake ['hændʃeɪk] *n* apretón *m* de manos.

handsome ['hænsəm] *adj* 1 *(person)* guapo,-a. 2 *(substantial)* considerable.

handwriting ['hændraɪtɪŋ] *n* letra *f*.

handy ['hændɪ] *adj* (**handier, handiest**) 1 *(useful)* útil, práctico,-a; *(nearby)* a mano. 2 *(dextrous)* diestro,-a.

hang [hæŋ] I *vtr* (*pt & pp* **hung**) 1 colgar. 2 *(head)* bajar. 3 (*pt & pp* **hanged**) ahorcar. II *vi* 1 colgar (**from**, de); *(in air)* flotar. 2 *(criminal)* ser ahorcado,-a; **to h. oneself**, ahorcarse. ◆**hang about**, **hang round** *vi fam* 1 perder el tiempo. 2 *fam (wait)* esperar. ◆**hang around** *vi fam* 1 esperar. 2 *fam* frecuentar; **where does he h. around?**, ¿a qué lugares suele ir? ◆**hang on** *vi* 1 agarrarse. 2 *(wait)* esperar. ◆**hang out** I *vtr (washing)* tender. II *vi fam (frequent)* frecuentar. ◆**hang together** *vi (ideas)* ser coherente. ◆**hang up** *vtr (picture, telephone)* colgar.

hangar ['hæŋər] *n* hangar *m*.

hanger ['hæŋər] *n* percha *f*.

hang-glider ['hæŋglaɪdər] *n* ala delta.

hang-gliding ['hæŋglaɪdɪŋ] *n* vuelo *m* libre.

hangman ['hæŋmən] *n* verdugo *m*.

hangover ['hæŋəʊvər] *n* resaca *f*.

hang-up ['hæŋʌp] *n fam (complex)* complejo *m*.

hanker ['hæŋkər] *vi* **to h. after sth**, anhelar algo.

hankie, **hanky** ['hæŋkɪ] *n fam* pañuelo *m*.

haphazard [hæp'hæzəd] *adj* caótico,-a, desordenado,-a.

happen ['hæpən] *vi* suceder, ocurrir; **it so happens that**, lo que pasa es que; **if you h. to see my friend**, si por casualidad ves a mi amigo.

happening ['hæpənɪŋ] *n* acontecimiento *m*.

happiness ['hæpɪnɪs] *n* felicidad *f*.

happy ['hæpɪ] *adj* (**happier, happiest**) *(cheerful)* feliz, contento,-a; *(fortunate)* afortunado,-a; **h. birthday!**, ¡feliz cumpleaños! ◆**happily** *adv (with pleasure)* felizmente; *(fortunately)* afortunadamente.

happy-go-lucky [hæpɪgəʊ'lʌkɪ] *adj* despreocupado,-a; **a h.-go-l. fellow**, un viva la virgen.

harangue [hə'ræŋ] I *vtr* arengar. II *n* arenga *f*.

harass ['hærəs] *vtr* acosar.

harassment ['hærəsmənt, hə'ræsmənt] *n* hostigamiento *m*, acoso *m*.

harbour, *US* **harbor** ['hɑːbər] I *n* puerto *m*. II *vtr* 1 *(criminal)* encubrir. 2 *(doubts)* abrigar.

hard [hɑːd] I *adj* 1 duro,-a; *(solid)* sólido,-a; **h. court**, pista (de tenis) rápida; *Comput* **h. disk**, disco duro; **h. shoulder**, arcén *m*. 2 *(difficult)* difícil; **h. of hearing**, duro,-a de oído; *fam fig* **to be h. up**, estar sin blanca. 3 *(harsh)* severo, -a; *(strict)* estricto,-a; **to take a h. line**, tomar medidas severas; **h. drugs**, droga dura; *Pol* **h. left**, extrema izquierda; **h. porn**, pornografía dura; **h. sell**, promoción *f* de venta agresiva. 4 **a h. drinker**, un bebedor inveterado; **a h. worker**, un trabajador concienzudo. 5 **h. luck!**, ¡mala suerte! 6 **h. evidence**, pruebas definitivas; *Com* **h. cash**, dinero *m* en metálico; **h. currency**, divisa *f* fuerte. II *adv* 1 *(hit)* fuerte. 2 *(work)* mucho, concienzudamente; *fig* **to be h. on sb's heels**, pisar los talones a algn. 3 **to be h. done by**, ser tratado,-a injustamente.

hardback ['hɑːdbæk] *n* edición *f* de tapas duras.

hard-boiled ['hɑːdbɔɪld] *adj* duro,-a.

hard-core ['hɑːdkɔːr] *adj* irreductible.

harden ['hɑːdən] I *vtr* endurecer. II *vi* endurecerse.

hardened ['hɑːdənd] *adj fig* habitual.

hard-headed |haːdˈhedɪd| adj realista.
hard-hearted |haːdˈhaːtɪd| adj insensible.
hardliner |haːdˈlaɪnər| n duro,-a m,f.
hardly |ˈhaːdlɪ| adv apenas; **h. anyone/ ever**, casi nadie/nunca; **he had h. begun when ...**, apenas había comenzado cuando ...; **I can h. believe it**, apenas lo puedo creer.
hardship |ˈhaːdʃɪp| n privación f, apuro m.
hardware |ˈhaːdweər| n 1 (goods) ferretería f; **h. shop**, ferretería. 2 Comput hardware m.
hardwearing |haːdˈweərɪŋ| adj duradero,-a.
hardworking |ˈhaːdwɜːkɪŋ| adj muy trabajador,-a.
hardy |ˈhaːdɪ| adj (hardier, hardiest) (person) robusto,-a, fuerte; (plant) resistente.
hare |heər| I n liebre f. II vi correr muy de prisa.
haricot |ˈhærɪkəʊ| n **h. (bean)**, alubia f.
harm |haːm| I n daño m, perjuicio m; **to be out of h.'s way**, estar a salvo. II vtr hacer daño a, perjudicar.
harmful |ˈhaːmfʊl| adj perjudicial (**to**, para).
harmless |ˈhaːmlɪs| adj inofensivo,-a.
harmonica |haːˈmɒnɪkə| n armónica f.
harmonize |ˈhaːmənaɪz| vtr & vi armonizar.
harmony |ˈhaːmənɪ| n armonía f.
harness |ˈhaːnɪs| I n (for horse) arreos mpl. II vtr 1 (horse) enjaezar. 2 fig (resources etc) aprovechar.
harp |haːp| n arpa f. ◆**harp on** vi fam hablar sin parar.
harpoon |haːˈpuːn| I n arpón m. II vtr arponear.
harrowing |ˈhærəʊɪŋ| adj angustioso,-a.
harsh |haːʃ| adj severo,-a; (voice) áspero,-a; (sound) discordante.
harvest |ˈhaːvɪst| I n cosecha f; (of grapes) vendimia f. II vtr cosechar, recoger.
harvester |ˈhaːvɪstər| n 1 (person) segador,-a m,f. 2 (machine) cosechadora f.
has |hæz| 3rd person sing pres → **have**
hash¹ |hæʃ| n Culin sofrito m de carne; fam fig **to make a h. of sth**, estropear algo.
hash² |hæʃ| n sl hachís m.
hashish |ˈhæʃiːʃ| n hachís m.
hassle |ˈhæsəl| fam I n 1 (nuisance) rollo m. 2 (problem) lío m. 3 (wrangle) bronca f. II vtr fastidiar.
haste |heɪst| n fml prisa f; **to make h.**, darse prisa.
hasten |ˈheɪsən| vi apresurarse.
hasty |ˈheɪstɪ| adj (hastier, hastiest) apresurado,-a; (rash) precipitado,-a. ◆**hastily** adv (quickly) de prisa.
hat |hæt| n sombrero m.
hatch¹ |hætʃ| n escotilla f; **serving h.**,

ventanilla f.
hatch² |hætʃ| vtr 1 (eggs) empollar. 2 fig (plan) tramar. ◆**hatch out** vi salirse del huevo.
hatchback |ˈhætʃbæk| n coche m de 3 or 5 puertas.
hatchet |ˈhætʃɪt| n hacha f; fam **h. man**, matón m.
hate |heɪt| I n odio m. II vtr odiar.
hateful |ˈheɪtfʊl| adj odioso,-a.
hatred |ˈheɪtrɪd| n odio m.
haughty |ˈhɔːtɪ| adj (haughtier, haughtiest) altanero,-a, arrogante.
haul |hɔːl| I n 1 (journey) trayecto m. 2 Fishing redada f. 3 (loot) botín m. II vtr 1 tirar; (drag) arrastrar. 2 (transport) acarrear. ◆**haul up** vtr fam (to court) llevar.
haulage |ˈhɔːlɪdʒ| n transporte m.
haulier |ˈhɔːljər| n transportista mf.
haunch |hɔːntʃ| n cadera f; Culin pernil m.
haunt |hɔːnt| I n guarida f. II vtr 1 (of ghost) aparecerse en. 2 fig atormentar. 3 (frequent) frecuentar.
haunted |ˈhɔːntɪd| adj encantado,-a, embrujado,-a.
Havana |həˈvænə| n La Habana; **H. cigar**, habano m.
have |hæv| I n (3rd person sing pres **has**) (pt & pp **had**) 1 (possess) tener; **h. you got a car?**, ¿tienes coche? 2 (get, experience, suffer) tener; **to h. a holiday**, tomarse unas vacaciones. 3 (partake of) tomar; **to h. a cigarette**, fumarse un cigarrillo; **to h. breakfast/lunch/tea/dinner**, desayunar/comer/merendar/cenar. 4 **to h. a bath/shave**, bañarse/afeitarse; **to h. a nap**, echar la siesta. 5 **to h. to**, (obligation) tener que, deber. 6 (make happen) hacer que; **I'll h. someone come round**, haré que venga alguien. 7 (receive) recibir; **to h. people round**, invitar a gente. 8 **can I h. your pen a moment?**, (borrow) ¿me dejas tu bolígrafo un momento? 9 (party, meeting) hacer, celebrar. 10 **to h. a baby**, tener un niño. 11 **we won't h. it**, (allow) no lo consentiremos. 12 (hold) tener; fig **to h. sth against sb**, tener algo en contra de algn. 13 **legend has it that ...**, según la leyenda .... 14 fam (deceive) engañar. 15 **you'd better stay**, más vale que te quedes.
II v aux 1 (compound) haber; **I had been waiting for half an hour**, hacía media hora que esperaba; **he hasn't eaten yet**, no ha comido aún; **she had broken the window**, había roto el cristal; **we h. lived here for ten years**, hace diez años que vivimos aquí; **so I h.!**, (emphatic) ¡ay, sí!, es verdad; **yes I h.!**, ¡que sí! 2 (tag questions) **you haven't seen my book, h. you?**, no has visto mis gafas, ¿verdad?; **he's been to France, hasn't he?**, ha estado en Francia, ¿verdad? o ¿no? 3 (have

+ *just*) acabar de.
◆**have on** *vtr* **1** (*wear*) vestir. **2** *fam* **to h. sb on**, tomarle el pelo a algn. ◆**have out** *vtr fam* **to h. it out with sb**, ajustar cuentas con algn. ◆**have over** *vtr* (*invite*) recibir.

haven ['heɪvən] *n* puerto *m*; *fig* refugio *m*.

haversack ['hævəsæk] *n* mochila *f*.

havoc ['hævək] *n* **to play h. with**, hacer estragos en.

hawk [hɔːk] *n Orn Pol* halcón *m*.

hawker ['hɔːkər] *n* vendedor,-a *m,f* ambulante.

hawthorn ['hɔːθɔːn] *n* espino *m* albar.

hay [heɪ] *n* heno *m*; **h. fever**, fiebre *f* del heno.

haystack ['heɪstæk] *n* almiar *m*.

haywire ['heɪwaɪər] *adj fam* en desorden; **to go h.**, (*machine etc*) estropearse; (*person*) volverse loco,-a.

hazard ['hæzəd] **I** *n* peligro *m*, riesgo *m*; *Golf* obstáculo *m*. **II** *vtr fml* arriesgar; **to h. a guess**, intentar adivinar.

hazardous ['hæzədəs] *adj* arriesgado,-a, peligroso,-a.

haze [heɪz] *n* (*mist*) neblina *f*; *fig* (*blur*) confusión *f*.

hazel ['heɪzəl] *adj* (de color) avellana.

hazelnut ['heɪzəlnʌt] *n* avellana *f*.

hazy ['heɪzɪ] *adj* (**hazier, haziest**) nebuloso,-a.

he [hiː] *pers pron* él; **he did it**, ha sido él; **he who**, el que.

head [hed] **I** *n* **1** cabeza *f*; (*mind*) mente *f*; *fig* **three pounds a h.**, tres libras por cabeza; *fig* **to be h. over heels in love**, estar locamente enamorado,-a; *fig* **to keep one's h.**, mantener la calma; *fig* **to lose one's h.**, perder la cabeza; **success went to his h.**, se le subió el éxito a cabeza; **h. start**, ventaja *f*. **2** (*of nail*) cabeza *f*; (*of beer*) espuma *f*; (*of tape recorder*) cabezal *m*; (*of steam*) presión *f*; *fig* **to come to a h.**, llegar a un momento decisivo. **3** (*boss*) cabeza *m*; (*of company*) director,-a *m,f*; **h. teacher**, director,-a *m,f*. **4** (*of coin*) cara *f*; **heads or tails**, cara o cruz. **II** *adj* principal; **h. office**, oficina *f* central. **III** *vtr* **1** (*list etc*) encabezar. **2** *Ftb* cabecear. ◆**head for** *vtr* dirigirse hacia. ◆**head off** **I** *vi* irse. **II** *vtr* (*avert*) evitar.

headache ['hedeɪk] *n* dolor *m* de cabeza; *fig* quebradero *m* de cabeza.

header ['hedər] *n Ftb* cabezazo *m*.

head-first [hed'fɜːst] *adv* de cabeza.

head-hunter ['hedhʌntər] *n fig* cazatalentos *mf inv*.

heading ['hedɪŋ] *n* título *m*; (*of letter*) membrete *m*.

headlamp ['hedlæmp] *n* faro *m*.

headland ['hedlənd] *n* punta *f*, cabo *m*.

headlight ['hedlaɪt] *n* faro *m*.

headline ['hedlaɪn] *n* titular *m*.

headlong ['hedlɒŋ] *adj & adv* de cabeza;

to rush h. into sth, lanzarse a hacer algo sin pensar.

headmaster [hed'mɑːstər] *n* director *m*.

headmistress [hed'mɪstrɪs] *n* directora *f*.

head-on ['hedɒn] *adj* **a h.-on collision**, un choque frontal.

headphones ['hedfəʊnz] *npl* auriculares *mpl*.

headquarters ['hedkwɔːtəz] *npl* **1** oficina *f* central, sede *f*. **2** *Mil* cuartel *m* general.

headrest ['hedrest] *n Aut* apoyacabezas *m*.

headroom ['hedruːm] *n* altura *f* libre.

headscarf ['hedskɑːf] *n* pañuelo *m*.

headstrong ['hedstrɒŋ] *adj* testarudo,-a.

headway ['hedweɪ] *n* **to make h.**, avanzar, progresar.

headwind ['hedwɪnd] *n* viento *m* de proa.

heady ['hedɪ] *adj* (**headier, headiest**) embriagador,-a.

heal [hiːl] **I** *vi* cicatrizar. **II** *vtr* (*illness*) curar.

health [helθ] *n* salud *f*; *fig* prosperidad *f*; **to be in good/bad h.**, estar bien/mal de salud; **your good h.!**, ¡salud!; **h. foods**, alimentos *mpl* naturales; **h. food shop**, tienda *f* de alimentos naturales; **h. service**, ≈ Insalud *m*.

healthy ['helθɪ] *adj* (**healthier, healthiest**) sano,-a; (*good for health*) saludable; (*thriving*) próspero,-a.

heap [hiːp] **I** *n* montón *m*. **II** *vtr* amontonar; *fig* (*praises*) colmar de; **a heaped spoonful**, una cucharada colmada.

hear [hɪər] **I** *vtr* (*pt & pp* **heard** [hɜːd]) **1** oír. **2** (*listen to*) escuchar. **3** **I won't h. of it!**, ¡ni hablar! **4** (*find out*) enterarse. **5** *Jur* ver; (*evidence*) oír. **II** *vi* **to h. from sb**, tener noticias de algn.

hearing ['hɪərɪŋ] *n* **1** oído *m*; **h. aid**, audífono *m*. **2** *Jur* audiencia *f*; *fig* **to give sb a fair h.**, escuchar a algn.

hearsay ['hɪəseɪ] *n* rumores *mpl*.

hearse [hɜːs] *n* coche *m* fúnebre.

heart [hɑːt] *n* **1** corazón *m*; **h. attack**, infarto *m* de miocardio; **h. transplant**, trasplante *m* de corazón; **a broken h.**, un corazón roto; **at h.**, en el fondo; **to take sth to h.**, tomarse algo a pecho; **to have a good h.**, (*be kind*) tener buen corazón. **2** (*courage*) valor *m*; **his h. wasn't in it**, no ponía interés en ello; **to lose h.**, desanimarse. **3** (*core*) meollo *m*; (*of lettuce*) cogollo *m*.

heartbeat ['hɑːtbiːt] *n* latido *m* del corazón.

heart-breaking ['hɑːtbreɪkɪŋ] *adj* desgarrador,-a.

heart-broken ['hɑːtbrəʊkən] *adj* hundido,-a; **he's h.-b.**, tiene el corazón destrozado.

heartburn ['hɑːtbɜːn] *n* acedía *f*.

heartening ['hɑːtənɪŋ] *adj* alentador,-a.

heartfelt ['hɑːtfelt] *adj* sincero,-a.

hearth [hɑːθ] n 1 (fireplace) chimenea f. 2 fml (home) hogar m.

heartless ['hɑːtlɪs] adj cruel, insensible.

heart-throb ['hɑːtθrɒb] n ídolo m.

hearty ['hɑːtɪ] adj (heartier, heartiest) (person) francote; (meal) abundante; (welcome) cordial; **to have a h. appetite**, ser de buen comer.

heat [hiːt] **I** n 1 calor m. 2 Sport eliminatoria f. 3 Zool **on h.**, en celo. **II** vtr calentar. ◆**heat up** vi 1 (warm up) calentarse. 2 (increase excitement) acalorarse.

heated ['hiːtɪd] adj fig (argument) acalorado,-a.

heater ['hiːtər] n calentador m.

heath [hiːθ] n (land) brezal m.

heathen ['hiːðən] adj & n pagano,-a (m,f).

heather ['heðər] n brezo m.

heating ['hiːtɪŋ] n calefacción f.

heatwave ['hiːtweɪv] n ola f de calor.

heave [hiːv] **I** n (pull) tirón m; (push) empujón m. **II** vtr 1 (lift) levantar; (haul) tirar; (push) empujar. 2 (throw) arrojar. **III** vi subir y bajar.

heaven ['hevən] **I** n 1 cielo m; **for heaven's sake!**, ¡por Dios!; **h. on earth**, un paraíso en la tierra. 2 heavens, cielo m sing. **II** interj **good heavens!**, ¡por Dios!

heavenly ['hevənlɪ] adj celestial.

heavy ['hevɪ] **I** adj (heavier, heaviest) pesado,-a; (rain, meal) fuerte; (traffic) denso,-a; (loss) grande; **h. going**, duro,-a; **is it h.?**, ¿pesa mucho?; **a h. drinker/ smoker**, un,-a bebedor,-a/fumador,-a empedernido,-a; Mus **h. metal**, heavy metal m. **II** n sl gorila m. ◆**heavily** adv **it rained h.**, llovió mucho; **to sleep h.**, dormir profundamente.

heavyweight ['heviweit] n Box peso pesado.

Hebrew ['hiːbruː] **I** adj hebreo,-a m,f. **II** n (language) hebreo m.

Hebrides ['hebridiːz] npl **the H.**, las (Islas) Hébridas.

heckle ['hekəl] vtr interrumpir.

heckler ['heklər] n altercador,-a m,f.

hectare ['hektɑːr] n hectárea f.

hectic ['hektɪk] adj agitado,-a.

hedge [hedʒ] **I** n seto m. **II** vtr cercar con un seto; fig **to h. one's bets**, cubrirse.

hedgehog ['hedʒhɒg] n erizo m.

hedgerow ['hedʒrəʊ] n seto vivo.

heed [hiːd] n **to take h. of**, hacer caso de.

heedless ['hiːdlɪs] adj desatento,-a.

heel [hiːl] n talón m; (of shoe) tacón m; (of palm) pulpejo m; fig **to be on sb's heels**, pisarle los talones a algn; **high heels**, zapatos mpl de tacón alto.

heeled [hiːld] adj fam fig **well-h.**, adinerado,-a.

hefty ['heftɪ] adj (heftier, heftiest) 1 (person) fornido,-a; (package) pesado,-a. 2 (large) grande.

height [haɪt] n 1 altura f; (of person) estatura f; Av **to gain/lose h.**, subir/bajar; **what h. are you?**, ¿cuánto mides?; fig **the h. of ignorance**, el colmo de la ignorancia. 2 Geog cumbre f.

heighten ['haɪtən] vtr (intensify) realzar; (increase) aumentar.

heir [eər] n heredero m.

heiress ['eərɪs] n heredera f.

heirloom ['eəluːm] n reliquia f or joya f de familia.

held [held] pt & pp → **hold**.

helicopter ['helɪkɒptər] n helicóptero m.

helium ['hiːlɪəm] n helio m.

hell [hel] n infierno m; fam **what the h. are you doing?**, ¿qué diablos estás haciendo?; offens **go to h.!**, ¡vete a hacer puñetas!; fam **a h. of a party**, una fiesta estupenda; fam **she's had a h. of a day**, ha tenido un día fatal.

hellish ['helɪʃ] adj fam infernal.

hello [hə'ləʊ, 'heləʊ] interj ¡hola!; Tel ¡diga!; (showing surprise) ¡hala!

helm [helm] n timón m; **to be at the h.**, llevar el timón.

helmet ['helmɪt] n casco m.

help [help] **I** n 1 ayuda f; **h.!**, ¡socorro! 2 (daily) **h.**, asistenta f. **II** vtr 1 ayudar; **can I h. you?**, (in shop) ¿qué desea? 2 (alleviate) aliviar. 3 **h. yourself!**, ¡sírvete! 4 (avoid) evitar; **I can't h. it**, no lo puedo remediar. ◆**help out** vtr **to h. sb out**, echarle una mano a algn.

helper ['helpər] n ayudante,-a m,f.

helpful ['helpfʊl] adj (person) amable; (thing) útil.

helping ['helpɪŋ] n ración f; **who wants a second h.?**, ¿quién quiere repetir?

helpless ['helplɪs] adj (defenceless) desamparado,-a; (powerless) incapaz. ◆**helplessly** adv inútilmente, en vano.

helter-skelter [heltə'skeltər] **I** n tobogán m. **II** adj atropellado,-a. **III** adv atropelladamente.

hem [hem] **I** n Sew dobladillo m. **II** vtr Sew hacer un dobladillo a. ◆**hem in** vtr cercar, rodear.

hemisphere ['hemɪsfɪər] n hemisferio m.

hemophilia [hiːməʊ'fɪlɪə] n US → **haemophilia**.

hemorrhage ['hemərɪdʒ] n US → **haemorrhage**.

hen [hen] n gallina f; fam **h. party**, reunión f de mujeres.

hence [hens] adv fml 1 **six months h.**, (from now) de aquí a seis meses. 2 (consequently) por lo tanto.

henceforth [hens'fɔːθ] adv fml de ahora en adelante.

henchman ['hentʃmən] n pej secuaz m.

henna ['henə] n Bot alheña f; (dye) henna f.

henpecked ['henpekt] adj fam **a h. husband**, un calzonazos.

hepatitis [hepə'taɪtɪs] *n* hepatitis *f*.
her [hɜːʳ, *unstressed* hə] **I** *poss adj (one thing)* su; *(more than one)* sus; *(to distinguish)* de ella; **are they h. books or his?**, ¿los libros son de ella o de él?; **she has cut h. finger**, se ha cortado el dedo. **II** *object pron* **1** *(direct object)* la; **I saw h. recently**, la vi hace poco. **2** *(indirect object)* le; *(with other third person pronouns)* se; **he gave h. money**, le dio dinero; **they handed it to h.**, se lo entregaron. **3** *(after prep)* ella; **for h.**, para ella. **4** *(as subject) fam* ella; **look, it's h.!**, ¡mira, es ella!
herald ['herəld] **I** *n* heraldo *m*. **II** *vtr* anunciar.
heraldry ['herəldrɪ] *n* heráldica *f*.
herb [hɜːb] *n* hierba *f*; **h. tea**, infusión *f*.
herbal ['hɜːbəl] *adj* herbario,-a; **h. remedies**, curas *fpl* de hierbas.
herd [hɜːd] *n (of cattle)* manada *f*; *(of goats)* rebaño *m*; *fig (large group)* multitud *f*.
here [hɪəʳ] *adv* aquí; **come h.**, ven aquí; **h.!**, ¡presente!; **h. goes!**, ¡vamos a ver!; **here's to success!**, ¡brindemos por el éxito!; **h. you are!**, ¡toma!. **II** *interj* **look h., you can't do that!**, ¡oiga, que no se permite hacer eso!
hereafter [hɪər'ɑːftəʳ] *fml* **I** *adv* de ahora en adelante. **II** *n* **the h.**, la otra vida, el más allá.
hereby [hɪə'baɪ] *adv fml* por la presente.
hereditary [hɪ'redɪtərɪ] *adj* hereditario,-a.
heresy ['herəsɪ] *n* herejía *f*.
heretic ['herətɪk] *n* hereje *mf*.
heritage ['herɪtɪdʒ] *n* patrimonio *m*; *Jur* herencia *f*.
hermetically [hɜː'metɪklɪ] *adv* **h. sealed**, herméticamente cerrado.
hermit ['hɜːmɪt] *n* ermitaño,-a *m,f*.
hermitage ['hɜːmɪtɪdʒ] *n* ermita *f*.
hernia ['hɜːnɪə] *n* hernia *f*.
hero ['hɪərəʊ] *n (pl heroes)* héroe *m*; *(in novel)* protagonista *m*; **h. worship**, idolatría *f*.
heroic [hɪ'rəʊɪk] *adj* heroico,-a.
heroin ['herəʊɪn] *n* heroína *f*.
heroine ['herəʊɪn] *n* heroína *f*; *(in novel)* protagonista *f*.
heron ['herən] *n* garza *f*.
herring ['herɪŋ] *n* arenque *m*.
hers [hɜːz] *poss pron* **1** *(attribute) (one thing)* suyo,-a; *(more than one)* suyos,-as; *(to distinguish)* de ella; **they are h. not his**, son de ella, no de él. **2** *(noun reference) (one thing)* el suyo, la suya; *(more than one)* los suyos, las suyas; **my car is blue and h. is red**, mi coche es azul y el suyo es rojo.
herself [hɜː'self] *pers pron* **1** *(reflexive)* se; **she dressed h.**, se vistió. **2** *(alone)* ella misma; **she was by h.**, estaba sola. **3** *(emphatic)* **she told me so h.**, eso dijo ella.

hesitant ['hezɪtənt] *adj* vacilante.
hesitate ['hezɪteɪt] *vi* vacilar.
hesitation [hezɪ'teɪʃən] *n* indecisión *f*.
heterogeneous [hetərəʊ'dʒiːnɪəs] *adj* heterogéneo,-a.
heterosexual [hetərəʊ'seksjʊəl] *adj & n* heterosexual *(mf)*.
hey [heɪ] *interj* ¡oye!, ¡oiga!
heyday ['heɪdeɪ] *n* auge *m*, apogeo *m*.
HGV [eɪtʃdʒiː'viː] *GB abbr of* **heavy goods vehicle**, vehículo *m* de carga pesada.
hi [haɪ] *interj fam* ¡hola!
hiatus [haɪ'eɪtəs] *n fml* laguna *f*.
hibernate ['haɪbəneɪt] *vi* hibernar.
hibernation [haɪbə'neɪʃən] *n* hibernación *f*.
hibiscus [haɪ'bɪskəs] *n* hibisco *m*.
hiccough ['hɪkʌp] *n & vi* → **hiccup**.
hiccup ['hɪkʌp] *n* hipo *m*; *fam (minor problem)* problemilla *m*; **to have hiccups**, tener hipo.
hide¹ [haɪd] **I** *vtr (pt hid* [hɪd] *pp hidden* ['hɪdən]) *(conceal)* esconder; *(obscure)* ocultar. **II** *vi* esconderse, ocultarse. **III** *n* puesto *m*.
hide² [haɪd] *n (of animal)* piel *f*.
hide-and-seek [haɪdən'siːk] *n* escondite *m*.
hideous ['hɪdɪəs] *adj (horrific)* horroroso,-a; *(extremely ugly)* espantoso,-a.
hide-out ['haɪdaʊt] *n* escondrijo *m*, guarida *f*.
hiding¹ ['haɪdɪŋ] *n* **to go into h.**, esconderse.
hiding² ['haɪdɪŋ] *n fam* paliza *f*.
hierarchy ['haɪərɑːkɪ] *n* jerarquía *f*.
hi-fi ['haɪfaɪ] *n* hifi *m*; **hi-fi equipment**, equipo *m* de alta fidelidad.
high [haɪ] **I** *adj* **1** alto,-a; **how h. is that wall?**, ¿qué altura tiene esa pared?; **it's three feet h.**, tiene tres pies de alto; **h. chair**, silla alta para niños; **h. jump**, salto *m* de altura. **2** *(elevated)* elevado,-a; **h. blood pressure**, tensión alta; **h. prices**, precios elevados; **to be in h. spirits**, estar de buen humor. **3** *(important)* importante; **h. wind**, viento *m* fuerte; **to have a h. opinion of sb**, tener muy buena opinión de algn; **H. Court**, Tribunal Supremo; **h. fidelity**, alta fidelidad *f*; **h. road**, carretera *f* principal; **h. school**, instituto *m* de enseñanza media; **the H. Street**, la Calle Mayor. **4** *sl (drugged)* colocado,-a. **II** *adv* alto; **to fly h.**, volar a gran altura. **III** *n (high point)* punto máximo.
highbrow ['haɪbraʊ] *adj & n* intelectual *(mf)*.
high-class ['haɪklɑːs] *adj* de alta categoría.
higher ['haɪəʳ] *adj* superior; **h. education**, enseñanza *f* superior.

high-flier, high-flyer [haɪ'flaɪəʳ] *n fig* persona dotada y ambiciosa.
high-handed [haɪ'hændɪd] *adj* despótico,-a.
high-heeled ['haɪhiːld] *adj* de tacón alto.
highlands ['haɪləndz] *npl* tierras altas.
highlight ['haɪlaɪt] I *n* 1 (*in hair*) reflejo *m.* 2 (*of event*) atracción *f* principal. II *vtr* 1 hacer resaltar. 2 (*a text*) marcar con un rotulador fosforescente.
highly ['haɪlɪ] *adv* (*very*) sumamente; **to speak h. of sb**, hablar muy bien de algn.
highly-strung [haɪlɪ'strʌn] *adj* muy nervioso,-a.
Highness ['haɪnɪs] *n* alteza *mf*; **Your H.,** Su Alteza.
high-pitched ['haɪpɪtʃt] *adj* estridente.
high-powered ['haɪpaʊəd] *adj* (*person*) dinámico,-a.
high-ranking ['haɪræŋkɪŋ] *adj* **h. official,** alto funcionario.
high-rise ['haɪraɪz] *adj* **h.-r. building,** rascacielos *m inv.*
high-speed ['haɪspiːd] *adj & adv* **h.-s. lens,** objetivo ultrarrápido; **h.-s. train,** tren *m* de alta velocidad.
highway ['haɪweɪ] *n US* carretera *f*, autopista *f*; *GB* **H. Code,** código *m* de la circulación.
highwayman ['haɪweɪmən] *n* salteador *m* de caminos.
hijack ['haɪdʒæk] I *vtr* secuestrar. II *n* secuestro *m.*
hijacker ['haɪdʒækəʳ] *n* secuestrador,-a *m,f*; (*of planes*) pirata *mf* del aire.
hike [haɪk] I *n* 1 (*walk*) excursión *f.* 2 **price h.,** aumento *m* de precio. II *vi* ir de excursión.
hiker ['haɪkəʳ] *n* excursionista *mf.*
hilarious [hɪ'leərɪəs] *adj* graciosísimo,-a.
hill [hɪl] *n* colina *f*; (*slope*) cuesta *f.*
hillside ['hɪlsaɪd] *n* ladera *f.*
hilltop ['hɪltɒp] *n* cima *f* de una colina.
hilly ['hɪlɪ] *adj* (**hillier, hilliest**) accidentado,-a.
hilt [hɪlt] *n* puño *m*, empuñadura *f*; **I'll support you up to the h.,** te daré mi apoyo total.
him [hɪm] *object pron* 1 (*direct object*) lo, le; **hit h.!,** ¡pégale!; **she loves h.,** lo quiere. 2 (*indirect object*) le; (*with other third person pronouns*) se; **give h. the money,** dale el dinero; **give it to h.,** dáselo. 3 (*after prep*) él; **it's not like h. to say that,** no es propio de él decir eso. 4 (*as subject*) *fam* él; **it's h.,** es él.
himself [hɪm'self] *pers pron* 1 (*reflexive*) se; **he hurt h.,** se hizo daño. 2 (*alone*) solo, por sí mismo; **by h.,** solo. 3 (*emphatic*) él mismo.
hind[1] [haɪnd] *adj* trasero,-a; **h. legs,** patas traseras.
hind[2] [haɪnd] *n Zool* cierva *f.*
hinder ['hɪndəʳ] *vtr* dificultar, estorbar; **to**

h. sb from doing sth, impedir a algn hacer algo.
hindrance ['hɪndrəns] *n* estorbo *m.*
hindsight ['haɪndsaɪt] *n* retrospectiva *f.*
Hindu [hɪn'duː, 'hɪnduː] *adj & n* hindú (*mf*).
Hinduism ['hɪnduːɪzəm] *n* hinduismo *m.*
hinge [hɪndʒ] I *n* bisagra *f*; *fig* eje *m.* II *vtr* engoznar. ◆**hinge on** *vtr* depender de.
hint [hɪnt] I *n* 1 indirecta *f*; **to take the h.,** coger la indirecta. 2 (*clue*) pista *f.* 3 (*trace*) pizca *f.* 4 (*advice*) consejo *m.* II *vi* 1 lanzar indirectas. 2 (*imply*) insinuar algo.
hip[1] [hɪp] *n* cadera *f*; **h. flask,** petaca *f.*
hip[2] [hɪp] *adj sl* en la onda.
hippie ['hɪpɪ] *adj & n fam* hippy (*mf*).
hippopotamus [hɪpə'pɒtəməs] *n* hipopótamo *m.*
hire ['haɪəʳ] I *n* alquiler *m*; **bicycles for h.,** se alquilan bicicletas; **taxi for h.,** taxi *m* libre; **h. purchase,** compra *f* a plazos. II *vtr* 1 (*rent*) alquilar. 2 (*employ*) contratar. ◆**hire out** *vtr* (*car*) alquilar; (*people*) contratar.
his [hɪz] I *poss adj* (*one thing*) su; (*more than one*) sus; (*to distinguish*) de él; **he washed h. face,** se lavó la cara; **is it h. dog or hers?,** ¿el perro es de él o de ella? II *poss pron* 1 (*attribute*) (*one thing*) suyo, -a; (*more than one*) suyos,-as; (*to distinguish*) de él. 2 (*noun reference*) (*one thing*) el suyo, la suya; (*more than one*) los suyos, las suyas; **my car is blue and h. is red,** mi coche es azul y el suyo es rojo.
Hispanic [hɪ'spænɪk] I *adj* hispánico,-a. II *n US* hispano,-a *m,f*, latino,-a *m,f.*
hiss [hɪs] I *n* siseo *m*; *Theat* silbido *m.* II *vtr & vi* silbar.
historian [hɪ'stɔːrɪən] *n* historiador,-a *m,f.*
historic [hɪ'stɒrɪk] *adj* histórico,-a.
historical [hɪ'stɒrɪkəl] *adj* histórico,-a; **h. novel,** novela histórica.
history ['hɪstərɪ] *n* historia *f.*
hit [hɪt] I *n* 1 (*blow*) golpe *m*; **direct h.,** impacto directo; *fam* **h. list,** lista negra; *fam* **h. man,** asesino *m* a sueldo. 2 (*success*) éxito *m*; **h. parade,** lista *f* de éxitos. II *vtr* (*pt & pp* **hit**) 1 (*strike*) golpear, pegar; **he was h. in the leg,** le dieron en la pierna; **the car h. the kerb,** el coche chocó contra el bordillo; *fam* **fig to h. the roof,** poner el grito en el cielo. 2 (*affect*) afectar. 3 **to h. the headlines,** ser noticia. ◆**hit back** *vi* (*reply to criticism*) replicar. ◆**hit on, hit upon** *vtr* dar con; **we h. on the idea of ...,** se nos ocurrió la idea de .... ◆**hit out** *vi* **to h. out at sb,** atacar a algn.
hit-and-run [hɪtən'rʌn] *adj* **h.-and-r. driver,** conductor que atropella a algn y no para.

hitch [hɪtʃ] **I** n dificultad f. **II** vtr (fasten) atar. **II** vi fam (hitch-hike) hacer autostop.
◆**hitch up** vtr remangarse.

hitch-hike ['hɪtʃhaɪk] vi hacer autostop or dedo.

hitch-hiker ['hɪtʃhaɪkəʳ] n autostopista mf.

hitherto [hɪðə'tuː] adv fml hasta la fecha.

HIV [eɪtʃaɪ'viː] abbr of **human immunodeficiency virus**, virus m de immunodeficiencia humano, VIH; **to be diagnosed HIV positive/negative**, dar seropositivo,-a/seronegativo,-a en la prueba del SIDA.

hive [haɪv] n colmena f; fig lugar muy activo.

HM abbr of **His** or **Her Majesty**, Su Majestad mf, SM.

hoard [hɔːd] **I** n (provisions) reservas fpl; (money etc) tesoro m. **II** vtr (objects) acumular; (money) atesorar.

hoarding ['hɔːdɪŋ] n (billboard) valla publicitaria; (temporary fence) valla.

hoarfrost ['hɔːfrɒst] n escarcha f.

hoarse [hɔːs] adj ronco,-a; **to be h.**, tener la voz ronca.

hoax [həʊks] n (joke) broma pesada; (trick) engaño m.

hob [hɒb] n (of cooker) encimera f.

hobble ['hɒbəl] vi cojear.

hobby ['hɒbɪ] n pasatiempo m, afición f.

hobbyhorse ['hɒbɪhɔːs] n (toy) caballito m de juguete; fig (fixed idea) idea fija, manía f.

hobo ['həʊbəʊ] n US vagabundo,-a m,f.

hockey ['hɒkɪ] n hockey m.

hog [hɒg] **I** n cerdo m, puerco m; fam **to go the whole h.**, liarse la manta a la cabeza. **II** vtr fam acaparar.

hoist [hɔɪst] **I** n (crane) grúa f; (lift) montacargas m inv. **II** vtr levantar, subir; **to h. the flag**, izar la bandera.

hold [həʊld] **I** vtr (pt & pp **held**) **1** (keep in hand) aguantar, tener (en la mano); (grip) agarrar; (support) (weight) soportar; (opinion) sostener; **to h. sb**, abrazar a algn; **to h. sb's hand**, cogerle la mano a algn; fig **she can h. her own in French**, se defiende en francés. **2** (contain) dar cabida a; **the jug holds a litre**, en la jarra cabe un litro. **3** (meeting) celebrar; (conversation) mantener. **4** (reserve) guardar. **5** **to h. office**, ocupar un puesto. **6** (consider) considerar. **7** **he was held for two hours at the police station**, estuvo detenido durante dos horas en la comisaría; **to h. one's breath**, contener la respiración; **to h. sb hostage**, retener a algn como rehén. **8** Tel **to h. the line**, no colgar.

II vi **1** (rope) aguantar. **2** fig (offer) ser válido,-a.

III n **1** **to get h. of**, (grip) coger, agarrar; fig localizar; **can you get h. of a newspa-**

per?, ¿puedes conseguir un periódico? **2** (control) control m. **3** Naut bodega f. **4** (in wrestling) llave f.
◆**hold back I** vtr (crowd) contener; (feelings) reprimir; (truth) ocultar; **I don't want to h. you back**, (delay) no quiero entretenerte. **II** vi (hesitate) vacilar.
◆**hold down** vtr **1** (control) dominar. **2** fam (job) desempeñar. ◆**hold off** vtr mantener a distancia. ◆**hold on** vi **1** (keep a firm grasp) agarrarse bien. **2** (wait) esperar; Tel **h. on!**, ¡no cuelgue! ◆**hold out I** vtr (hand) tender. **II** vi **1** (last) (things) durar; (person) resistir. **2 to h. out for**, insistir en. ◆**hold up** vtr **1** (rob) (train) asaltar; (bank) atracar. **2** (delay) retrasar; **we were held up for half an hour**, sufrimos media hora de retraso. **3** (raise) levantar. **4** (support) apuntalar.

holdall ['həʊldɔːl] n GB bolsa f de viaje.

holder ['həʊldəʳ] n **1** (receptacle) recipiente m. **2** (owner) poseedor,-a m,f; (bearer) portador,-a m,f; (of passport) titular mf; **record h.**, plusmarquista mf.

holding ['həʊldɪŋ] n **1** (property) propiedad f. **2** Fin valor m en cartera; **h. company**, holding m.

hold-up ['həʊldʌp] n **1** (robbery) atraco m. **2** (delay) retraso m; (in traffic) atasco m.

hole [həʊl] n **1** agujero m; (large) hoyo m; (in the road) bache m. **2** Golf hoyo m. **3** sl (of place) antro m.

holiday ['hɒlɪdeɪ] **I** n (one day) día m de fiesta; GB (several days) vacaciones fpl; **to be/go on h.**, estar/ir de vacaciones; **h. resort**, lugar turístico. **II** vi GB pasar las vacaciones; (in summer) veranear.

holiday-maker ['hɒlɪdeɪmeɪkəʳ] n GB turista mf; (in summer) veraneante mf.

holiness ['həʊlɪnɪs] n santidad f.

Holland ['hɒlənd] n Holanda.

hollow ['hɒləʊ] **I** adj **1** hueco,-a. **2** (cheeks, eyes) hundido,-a. **3** fig (insincere) falso,-a; (empty) vacío,-a. **II** n hueco m; Geog hondonada f. **III** vtr **to h. (out)**, hacer un hueco en.

holly ['hɒlɪ] n acebo m.

holocaust ['hɒləkɔːst] n holocausto m.

holster ['həʊlstəʳ] n pistolera f.

holy ['həʊlɪ] adj sagrado,-a, santo,-a; (blessed) bendito,-a; **H. Ghost**, Espíritu Santo; **H. Land**, Tierra Santa; **H. See**, Santa Sede.

homage ['hɒmɪdʒ] n homenaje m; **to pay h. to sb**, rendir homenaje a algn.

home [həʊm] **I** n **1** casa f, hogar m; **at h.**, en casa; fig **make yourself at h.!**, ¡estás en tu casa!; fig **to feel at h.**, estar a gusto. **2** (institution) asilo m; **old people's h.**, asilo de ancianos. **3** (country) patria f. **4** Sport **to play at h.**, jugar en casa; US **h. base**, (in baseball) base f del bateador; **h. run**, carrera completa. **II** adj **1** (domestic) del hogar; GB **h. help**, asistenta f. **2**

Pol interior; **h. affairs,** asuntos *mpl* interiores; *GB* **H. Office,** Ministerio *m* del Interior; *GB* **H. Secretary,** Ministro,-a *m,f* del Interior. **3** *(native)* natal. **III** *adv* en casa; **to go h.,** irse a casa; **to leave h.,** irse de casa.

homeland ['həʊmlænd] *n* patria *f*; *(birthplace)* tierra *f* natal.

homeless ['həʊmlɪs] **I** *adj* sin techo. **II** *npl* **the h.,** los sin techo.

homely ['həʊmlɪ] *adj* **(homelier, homeliest) 1** *GB (person)* casero,-a; *(atmosphere)* familiar. **2** *US (unattractive)* sin atractivo.

home-made ['həʊmmeɪd] *adj* casero,-a.

homeopathy [həʊmɪ'ɒpəθɪ] *n US* → **homoeopathy.**

homesick ['həʊmsɪk] *adj* **to be h.,** tener morriña.

homeward(s) ['həʊmwəd(z)] *adv* hacia casa.

homework ['həʊmwɜːk] *n* deberes *mpl.*

homicide ['hɒmɪsaɪd] *n* homicidio *m.*

homing ['həʊmɪŋ] *adj* **1 h. device,** cabeza buscadora. **2 h. pigeon,** paloma mensajera.

homoeopathy [həʊmɪ'ɒpəθɪ] *n* homeopatía *f.*

homogeneous [hɒmə'dʒiːnɪəs] *adj* homogéneo,-a.

homosexual [həʊməʊ'seksjʊəl] *adj & n* homosexual *(mf).*

Honduran [hɒn'djʊərən] *adj & n* hondureño,-a *(m,f).*

Honduras [hɒn'djʊərəs] *n* Honduras.

honest ['ɒnɪst] *adj* honrado,-a; *(sincere)* sincero,-a, franco,-a; *(fair)* justo,-a; **the h. truth,** la pura verdad; ◆**honestly** *adv* honradamente; *(question)* ¿de verdad?; *(exclamation)* ¡hay que ver!; **h., it doesn't matter,** de verdad, no tiene importancia.

honesty ['ɒnɪstɪ] *n* honradez *f.*

honey ['hʌnɪ] *n* miel *f*; *US fam (endearment)* cariño *m.*

honeycomb ['hʌnɪkəʊm] *n* panal *m.*

honeymoon ['hʌnɪmuːn] *n* luna *f* de miel.

honeysuckle ['hʌnɪsʌkəl] *n* madreselva *f.*

honk [hɒŋk] *vi Aut* tocar la bocina.

honor ['ɒnər] *n & vtr US* → **honour.**

honorary ['ɒnərərɪ] *adj (member)* honorario,-a; *(duties)* honorífico,-a.

honour ['ɒnər] **I** *n* **1** honor *m.* **2** *US Jur* Her H., His H., Your H., Su Señoría *f.* **3** *Mil* **honours,** honores *mpl.* **4 Honours degree,** licenciatura *f* superior. **II** *vtr* **1** *(respect)* honrar. **2** *(obligation)* cumplir con.

honourable ['ɒnərəbəl] *adj (person)* honrado,-a; *(action)* honroso,-a.

hood [hʊd] *n* **1** *(of garment)* capucha *f.* **2** *(of car)* capota *f*; *US (bonnet)* capó *m.*

hoodlum ['huːdləm] *n* matón *m.*

hoodwink ['hʊdwɪŋk] *vtr* engañar.

hoof [huːf] *n (pl* **hoofs** *or* **hooves** [huːvz]) *(of horse)* casco *m*; *(of cow, sheep)* pezuña *f.*

hook [hʊk] **I** *n* **1** gancho *m*; *Fishing* anzuelo *m*; *Sew* **hooks and eyes,** corchetes *mpl*; **to take the phone off the h.,** descolgar el teléfono. **2** *Box* gancho *m.* **II** *vtr* **1** enganchar. **2** *Box* hacer un gancho a. ◆**hook up** *vtr & vi Rad TV Comput* conectar *(with,* con).

hooked [hʊkt] *adj* **1** *(nose)* aguileño,-a. **2** *sl (addicted)* enganchado,-a *(on,* a); **to get h.,** engancharse.

hook-up ['hʊkʌp] *n* **1** *Comput* conexión *f.* **2** *Rad TV* emisión *f* múltiple.

hooligan ['huːlɪgən] *n sl* gamberro,-a *m,f.*

hoop [huːp] *n* aro *m*; *(of barrel)* fleje *m.*

hooray [huː'reɪ] *interj* ¡hurra!

hoot [huːt] **I** *n* **1** ululato *m*; *fam* **hoots of laughter,** carcajadas *fpl*; *fam* **I don't care a h.,** me importa un pepino. **2** *(of car horn)* bocinazo *m.* **II** *vi* **1** *(owl)* ulular. **2** *(car)* dar un bocinazo; *(train)* silbar; *(siren)* pitar.

hooter ['huːtər] *n esp GB (of car)* bocina *f*; *(siren)* sirena *f.*

Hoover® ['huːvər] *GB* **I** *n* aspiradora *f.* **II** *vtr* **to h.,** pasar la aspiradora por.

hop¹ [hɒp] **I** *vi* saltar; **to h. on one leg,** andar a la pata coja. **II** *n (small jump)* brinco *m.*

hop² [hɒp] *n Bot* lúpulo *m.*

hope [həʊp] **I** *n* esperanza *f*; *(false)* ilusión *f*; **to have little h. of doing sth,** tener pocas posibilidades de hacer algo. **II** *vtr & vi* esperar; **I h. so/not,** espero que sí/no; **we h. you're well,** esperamos que estés bien.

hopeful ['həʊpfʊl] *adj (confident)* optimista; *(promising)* prometedor,-a. ◆**hopefully** *adv* **1** *(confidently)* con optimismo. **2 h. the weather will be fine,** *(it is hoped)* esperemos que haga buen tiempo.

hopeless ['həʊplɪs] *adj* desesperado,-a; *fam* **to be h. at sports,** ser negado,-a para los deportes. ◆**hopelessly** *adv* desesperadamente; **h. lost,** completamente perdido,-a.

horde [hɔːd] *n* multitud *f.*

horizon [hə'raɪzən] *n* horizonte *m.*

horizontal [hɒrɪ'zɒntəl] *adj* horizontal.

hormone ['hɔːməʊn] *n* hormona *f.*

horn [hɔːn] *n* **1** cuerno *m.* **2** *Mus fam* trompeta *f*; **French h.,** trompa *f*; **hunting h.,** cuerno *m* de caza. **3** *Aut* bocina *f.*

hornet ['hɔːnɪt] *n* avispón *m.*

horny ['hɔːnɪ] *adj* **(hornier, horniest) 1** *(hands)* calloso,-a. **2** *sl (sexually aroused)* caliente, cachondo,-a.

horoscope ['hɒrəskəʊp] *n* horóscopo *m.*

horrendous [hɒ'rendəs] *adj* horrendo,-a.

horrible ['hɒrəbəl] *adj* horrible.

horrid ['hɒrɪd] *adj* horrible.

horrific [hə'rɪfɪk] *adj* horrendo,-a.

horrify ['hɒrɪfaɪ] *vtr* horrorizar.

horror ['hɒrəʳ] *n* horror *m*; *fam* **a little h.**, un diablillo; **h. film**, película *f* de miedo *or* de terror.

hors d'oeuvre [ɔː'dɜːvr] *n* entremés *m*.

horse [hɔːs] *n* 1 caballo *m*; **h. race**, carrera *f* de caballos. 2 *Gymn* potro *m*. 3 *Tech* caballete *m*. 4 **h. chestnut**, (*tree*) castaño *m* de Indias.

horseback ['hɔːsbæk] *n* **on h.**, a caballo.

horseman ['hɔːsmən] *n* jinete *m*.

horseplay ['hɔːspleɪ] *n* payasadas *fpl*.

horsepower ['hɔːspauəʳ] *n* caballo *m* (de vapor).

horseradish ['hɔːsrædɪʃ] *n* rábano rusticano.

horseshoe ['hɔːsʃuː] *n* herradura *f*.

horsewoman ['hɔːswumən] *n* amazona *f*.

horticulture ['hɔːtɪkʌltʃəʳ] *n* horticultura *f*.

hose [həuz] *n* (*pipe*) manguera *f*.

hosiery ['həuzɪərɪ] *n* medias *fpl* y calcetines *mpl*.

hospice ['hɒspɪs] *n* residencia *f* para enfermos terminales.

hospitable ['hɒspɪtəbəl, hɒ'spɪtəbəl] *adj* hospitalario,-a; **h. atmosphere**, ambiente acogedor.

hospital ['hɒspɪtəl] *n* hospital *m*.

hospitality [hɒspɪ'tælɪtɪ] *n* hospitalidad *f*.

host¹ [həust] I *n* 1 (*at home*) anfitrión *m*. 2 *Theat TV* presentador *m*. 3 *Biol* huésped *m*. II *vtr Theat TV* presentar.

host² [həust] *n* (*large number*) montón *m*.

Host [həust] *n Rel* hostia *f*.

hostage ['hɒstɪdʒ] *n* rehén *m*.

hostel ['hɒstəl] *n* hostal *m*.

hostess ['həustɪs] *n* 1 (*at home etc*) anfitriona *f*. 2 *Theat TV* presentadora *f*. 3 (**air**) **h.**, azafata *f*.

hostile ['hɒstaɪl] *adj* hostil.

hostility [hɒ'stɪlɪtɪ] *n* hostilidad *f*.

hot [hɒt] *adj* (**hotter, hottest**) 1 caliente; *fig* **h. line**, teléfono rojo; **h. spot**, (*nightclub*) club nocturno. 2 (*weather*) caluroso,-a; **it's very h.**, hace mucho calor; **to feel h.**, tener calor. 3 (*spicy*) picante; **h. dog**, perrito *m* caliente. 4 (*temper*) fuerte. 5 *fam* (*fresh*) de última hora. 6 *fam* (*good*) bueno,-a; **it's not so h.**, no es nada del otro mundo. 7 (*popular*) popular. 8 (*dangerous*) peligroso,-a; *fig* **to get oneself into h. water**, meterse en un lío; *fam* **h. seat**, primera fila. ◆**hot up** *vi fam* **things are hotting up**, la cosa se está poniendo al rojo vivo.

hotbed ['hɒtbed] *n fig* hervidero *m*.

hotel [həu'tel] *n* hotel *m*.

hotelier [həu'telɪeɪ] *n* hotelero,-a *m,f*.

hot-headed [hɒt'hedɪd] *adj* impetuoso,-a.

hothouse ['hɒthaus] *n* invernadero *m*.

hotplate ['hɒtpleɪt] *n* (*cooker*) placa *f* de cocina; (*to keep food warm*) calientaplatos *m inv*.

hotshot ['hɒtʃɒt] *n fam* as *m*.

hot-water ['hɒtwɔːtəʳ] *adj* **h.-w. bottle**, bolsa *f* de agua caliente.

hound [haund] I *n* perro *m* de caza. II *vtr* acosar.

hour ['auəʳ] *n* hora *f*; **60 miles an h.**, 60 millas por hora; **by the h.**, por horas; **h. hand**, manecilla *f*.

hourly ['auəlɪ] I *adj* cada hora. II *adv* por horas.

house [haus] I *n* 1 casa *f*; **at my h.**, en mi casa; *fig* **on the h.**, cortesía de la casa; **h. arrest**, arresto domiciliario; **h. plant**, planta *f* de interior. 2 *Pol* **H. of Commons**, Cámara *f* de los Comunes; **H. of Lords**, Cámara de los Lores; *US* **H. of Representatives**, Cámara de Representantes; **Houses of Parliament**, Parlamento *m*. 3 (*company*) empresa *f*; **publishing h.**, editorial *f*. 4 *Theat* sala *f*. II [hauz] *vtr* alojar; (*store*) guardar.

houseboat ['hausbəut] *n* casa *f* flotante.

housebreaking ['hausbreɪkɪŋ] *n* allanamiento *m* de morada.

housecoat ['hauskəut] *n* bata *f*.

household ['haushəuld] *n* hogar *m*; **h. products**, productos domésticos.

housekeeper ['hauskiːpəʳ] *n* ama *f* de llaves.

housekeeping ['hauskiːpɪŋ] *n* administración doméstica; **h. money**, dinero *m* para los gastos domésticos.

house-train ['haustreɪn] *vtr* (*pet*) educar.

house-warming ['hauswɔːmɪŋ] *n* **h.-w.** (**party**), fiesta *f* que se da al estrenar casa.

housewife ['hauswaɪf] *n* ama *f* de casa.

housework ['hauswɜːk] *n* trabajo *m* doméstico.

housing ['hauzɪŋ] *n* vivienda *f*; **h. estate**, urbanización *f*.

hovel ['hʌvəl, 'hɒvəl] *n* casucha *f*.

hover ['hɒvəʳ] *vi* (*bird*) cernerse; (*aircraft*) permanecer inmóvil (en el aire).

hovercraft ['hɒvəkrɑːft] *n* aerodeslizador *m*.

how [hau] *adv* 1 (*direct question*) ¿cómo?; **h. are you?**, ¿cómo estás?; *fam* **h. come?**, ¿por qué? 2 (*indirect question*) cómo; **I don't know h. to tell you**, no sé cómo decírtelo. 3 (*very*) qué; **h. funny!**, ¡qué divertido! 4 **h. about going to the cinema?**, (*suggestion*) ¿te apetece ir al cine?; **h. about a stroll?**, ¿qué te parece un paseo? 5 (*quantity*) cuánto; **h. old is she?**, ¿cuántos años tiene?; **h. tall are you?**, ¿cuánto mides? 6 **h. many?**, ¿cuántos,-as?; **h. much?**, ¿cuánto,-a?; **I don't know h. many people there were**, no sé cuánta gente había.

however [hau'evəʳ] *adv* 1 (*nevertheless*) no obstante, sin embargo. 2 (*with adjective*)

h. difficult it may be, por difícil que sea; **h. much,** por mucho que (+ *subj*).

howl [haʊl] I *n* aullido *m*. II *vi* aullar.

howler ['haʊlər] *n fam* despiste *m*.

HP, hp [eɪtʃ'piː] 1 *GB abbr of* **hire purchase.** 2 *abbr of* **horsepower,** cv *mpl*.

HQ [eɪtʃ'kjuː] *Mil abbr of* **headquarters.**

hub [hʌb] *n Aut* cubo *m*; *fig* eje *m*.

hubbub ['hʌbʌb] *n* alboroto *m*.

hubcap ['hʌbkæp] *n Aut* tapacubos *m inv*.

huddle ['hʌdəl] I *n* grupo *m*. II *vi* to **h. (up** or **together),** acurrucarse.

hue[1] [hjuː] *n (colour)* tinte *m*; *(shade)* matiz *m*.

hue[2] [hjuː] *n* **h. and cry,** fuerte protesta *f*.

huff [hʌf] *n* to be in a **h.,** estar de mala uva.

hug [hʌg] I *vtr* abrazar. II *n* abrazo *m*.

huge [hjuːdʒ] *adj* enorme. ◆**hugely** *adv* enormemente.

hulk [hʌlk] *n* 1 *Naut* casco *m*. 2 *(thing, person)* armatoste *m*.

hull [hʌl] *n Naut* casco *m*.

hullabal(l)oo [hʌləbə'luː] *n fam* follón *m*.

hullo [hʌ'ləʊ] *interj GB* ¡hola!

hum [hʌm] I *vtr (tune)* tararear. II *vi (bees, engine)* zumbar; *(sing)* tararear. III *n (of bees)* zumbido *m*.

human ['hjuːmən] I *adj* humano,-a; **h. race,** raza humana; **h. being,** ser humano. II *n* ser humano.

humane [hjuː'meɪn] *adj* humano,-a.

humanitarian [hjuːmænɪ'teərɪən] *adj* humanitario,-a.

humanity [hjuː'mænɪtɪ] *n* 1 humanidad *f*. 2 *Univ* **the humanities,** las humanidades.

humble ['hʌmbəl] I *adj* humilde. II *vtr* humillar.

humbug ['hʌmbʌg] *n* 1 *fam* tonterías *fpl*. 2 *GB* (mint) **h.,** caramelo *m* de menta.

humdrum ['hʌmdrʌm] *adj* monótono,-a, aburrido,-a.

humid ['hjuːmɪd] *adj* húmedo,-a.

humidity [hjuː'mɪdɪtɪ] *n* humedad *f*.

humiliate [hjuː'mɪlɪeɪt] *vtr* humillar.

humiliation [hjuːmɪlɪ'eɪʃən] *n* humillación *f*.

humility [hjuː'mɪlɪtɪ] *n* humildad *f*.

humor ['hjuːmər] *n US* → **humour.**

humorous ['hjuːmərəs] *adj (writer)* humorístico,-a; *(person, story)* gracioso,-a, divertido,-a.

humour ['hjuːmər] I *n* humor *m*. II *vtr* seguir la corriente a.

hump [hʌmp] I *n* 1 *(on back)* joroba *f*. 2 *(small hill)* montículo *m*. II *vtr GB sl* cargar (a la espalda).

humus ['hjuːməs] *n* mantillo *m*, humus *m*.

hunch [hʌntʃ] *n fam* corazonada *f*.

hunchback ['hʌntʃbæk] *n* jorobado,-a *m,f*.

hundred ['hʌndrəd] I *n* cien *m*, ciento *m*;

(rough number) centenar *m*; **a h. and twenty-five,** ciento veinticinco; **five h.,** quinientos. II *adj* cien; **a h. people,** cien personas; **a h. per cent,** cien por cien; **two h. chairs,** doscientas sillas.

hundredth ['hʌndrədθ] *adj* & *n* centésimo,-a *(m)*.

hundredweight ['hʌndrədweɪt] *n* ciento doce libras *fpl* (≈ quintal *m*).

hung [hʌŋ] *adj* 1 *fam* **h. over,** con resaca. 2 *fam* **h. up,** acomplejado,-a.

Hungarian [hʌŋ'geərɪən] *adj* & *n* húngaro,-a *(m,f)*.

Hungary ['hʌŋgərɪ] *n* Hungría.

hunger ['hʌŋgər] I *n* hambre *f*; **h. strike,** huelga *f* de hambre. II *vi fig* tener hambre (**for,** de).

hungry ['hʌŋgrɪ] *adj (hungrier, hungriest)* hambriento,-a; **to be h.,** tener hambre; **to go h.,** pasar hambre.

hunk [hʌŋk] *n* 1 *(piece)* buen pedazo *m*. 2 *sl (man)* machote *m*.

hunt [hʌnt] I *vtr* cazar. II *vi (for game)* cazar; *(search)* buscar. III *n* caza *f*; *(search)* búsqueda *f*. ◆**hunt down** *vtr* perseguir.

hunter ['hʌntər] *n* cazador,-a *m,f*.

hunting ['hʌntɪŋ] *n* caza *f*; *(expedition)* cacería *f*.

hurdle ['hɜːdəl] *n Sport* valla *f*; *fig* obstáculo *m*.

hurl [hɜːl] *vtr* arrojar, lanzar.

hurrah [hʊ'rɑː], **hurray** [hʊ'reɪ] *interj* ¡hurra!; **h. for John!,** ¡viva John!

hurricane ['hʌrɪkən, 'hʌrɪkeɪn] *n* huracán *m*.

hurried ['hʌrɪd] *adj* apresurado,-a; *(action etc)* hecho,-a de prisa. ◆**hurriedly** *adv* deprisa, apresuradamente.

hurry ['hʌrɪ] I *vi* darse prisa a. II *vtr* meter prisa a. III *n* to be in a **h.,** tener prisa.

hurt [hɜːt] I *vtr (pt* & *pp* **hurt)** hacer daño a; *(wound)* herir; *(feelings)* ofender. II *vi* doler; **my arm hurts,** me duele el brazo; *fam* **it doesn't h. to go out once in a while,** no viene mal salir de vez en cuando. III *adj (physically)* herido,-a; *(mentally)* dolido,-a.

hurtful ['hɜːtfʊl] *adj* hiriente.

hurtle ['hɜːtəl] *vi* lanzarse; **to h. down,** desplomarse.

husband ['hʌzbənd] *n* marido *m*, esposo *m*.

hush [hʌʃ] I *vtr* callar; **to h. sth up,** echar tierra a un asunto. II *n* silencio *m*. III *interj* ¡silencio!

hush-hush [hʌʃ'hʌʃ] *adj* *fam* confidencial.

husky[1] ['hʌskɪ] *adj (huskier, huskiest)* ronco,-a.

husky[2] ['hʌskɪ] *n (dog)* perro *m* esquimal.

hustings ['hʌstɪŋz] *npl Pol* 1 *(platform)* tribuna *f sing* electoral. 2 *(election)* elecciones *fpl*.

hustle ['hʌsəl] **I** *vtr* **1** (*jostle*) empujar. **2** *fam* meter prisa a. **II** *n* bullicio *m*; **h. and bustle**, ajetreo *m*.

hut [hʌt] *n* cabaña *f*; (*shed*) cobertizo *m*; *Mil* barraca *f*.

hutch [hʌtʃ] *n* jaula *f*; **rabbit h.**, conejera *f*.

hyacinth ['haɪəsɪnθ] *n* jacinto *m*.

hybrid ['haɪbrɪd] *adj* & *n* híbrido,-a (*m,f*).

hydrant ['haɪdrənt] *n* **fire h.**, boca *f* de incendio.

hydraulic [haɪ'drɒlɪk] *adj* hidráulico,-a.

hydrocarbon [haɪdrəʊ'ka:bən] *n* hidrocarburo *m*.

hydrochloric [haɪdrəʊ'klɒrɪk] *adj* **h. acid**, ácido clorhídrico.

hydroelectric [haɪdrəʊɪ'lektrɪk] *adj* hidroeléctrico,-a.

hydrofoil ['haɪdrəfɔɪl] *n* hidroala *f*.

hydrogen ['haɪdrɪdʒən] *n* hidrógeno *m*.

hyena [haɪ'iːnə] *n* hiena *f*.

hygiene ['haɪdʒiːn] *n* higiene *f*.

hygienic [haɪ'dʒiːnɪk] *adj* higiénico,-a.

hymn [hɪm] *n* himno *m*; **h. book**, cantoral *m*.

hype [haɪp] *n* *fam* campaña publicitaria, movida *f*.

hyper- ['haɪpər] *pref* hiper-; **hyperactive,**

hiperactivo,-a.

hypermarket ['haɪpəma:kɪt] *n* *GB* hipermercado *m*.

hypersensitive [haɪpə'sensɪtɪv] *adj* hipersensible.

hyphen ['haɪfən] *n* guión *m*.

hypnosis [hɪp'nəʊsɪs] *n* hipnosis *f*.

hypnotist ['hɪpnətɪst] *n* hipnotizador,-a *m,f*.

hypnotize ['hɪpnətaɪz] *vtr* hipnotizar.

hypochondriac [haɪpə'kɒndrɪæk] *adj* & *n* hipocondríaco,-a (*m,f*).

hypocrisy [hɪ'pɒkrəsɪ] *n* hipocresía *f*.

hypocrite ['hɪpəkrɪt] *n* hipócrita *mf*.

hypocritical [hɪpə'krɪtɪkəl] *adj* hipócrita.

hypodermic [haɪpə'dɜːmɪk] *adj* *Med* hipodérmico,-a; **h. needle**, aguja hipodérmica.

hypothesis [haɪ'pɒθɪsɪs] *n* (*pl* **hypotheses** [haɪ'pɒθɪsiːz]) hipótesis *f*.

hypothetic(al) [haɪpə'θetɪk(əl)] *adj* hipotético,-a.

hysteria [hɪ'stɪərɪə] *n* histeria *f*.

hysterical [hɪ'sterɪkəl] *adj* histérico,-a.

hysterics [hɪ'sterɪks] *n or npl* **1** ataque *m* de histeria. **2** *fam* (*of laughter*) ataque *m* de risa.

I

I, i [aɪ] *n* (*the letter*) I, i *f*.

I [aɪ] *pers pron* yo; **I know her**, (yo) la conozco.

ICBM [aɪsiːbiː'em] *abbr of* **intercontinental ballistic missile, MBI** *m*.

ice [aɪs] **I** *n* hielo *m*; **i. axe**, pico *m* (de alpinista); **i. cream**, helado *m*; **i. cube**, cubito *m* de hielo; **i. hockey**, hockey *m* sobre hielo; **i. lolly**, polo *m*; **i. rink**, pista *f* de patinaje; **i. skate**, patín *m* de cuchilla. **II** *vtr* (*cake*) alcorzar. ◆**ice over, ice up** *vi* (*pond etc*) helarse; (*windscreen, plane wings*) cubrirse de hielo.

iceberg ['aɪsbɜːg] *n* iceberg *m*.

icebox ['aɪsbɒks] *n* **1** (*compartment of fridge*) congelador *m*. **2** *US* (*fridge*) nevera *f*, frigorífico *m*.

icecap ['aɪskæp] *n* casquete *m* glaciar.

Iceland ['aɪslənd] *n* Islandia.

ice-skating ['aɪsskeɪtɪŋ] *n* patinaje *m* sobre hielo.

icicle ['aɪsɪkəl] *n* carámbano *m*.

icing ['aɪsɪŋ] *n* alcorza *f*; **i. sugar**, azúcar *m* glas.

icon ['aɪkɒn] *n* icono *m*.

icy ['aɪsɪ] *adj* (*icier, iciest*) (*road etc*) helado,-a; *fig* (*smile*) glacial.

ID [aɪ'diː] *US abbr of* **identification, identity; ID card**, documento *m* nacional de identidad, DNI *m*.

I'd [aɪd] = **I would; I had.**

idea [aɪ'dɪə] *n* **1** idea *f*. **2** (*aim*) intención *f*. **3** (*impression*) impresión *f*.

ideal [aɪ'dɪəl] *adj* & *n* ideal (*m*). ◆**ideally** *adv* **1** (*perfectly*) perfectamente. **2** (*in the best conditions*) de ser posible.

idealist [aɪ'dɪəlɪst] *n* idealista *mf*.

idealistic [aɪdɪə'lɪstɪk] *adj* idealista.

idealize [aɪ'dɪəlaɪz] *vtr* idealizar.

identical [aɪ'dentɪkəl] *adj* idéntico,-a.

identification [aɪdentɪfɪ'keɪʃən] *n* **1** identificación *f*. **2** (*papers*) documentación *f*.

identify [aɪ'dentɪfaɪ] **I** *vtr* (*body*) identificar; (*cause*) descubrir. **II** *vi* identificarse (**with**, con).

Identikit® [aɪ'dentɪkɪt] *n* **I. picture**, retrato *m* robot.

identity [aɪ'dentɪtɪ] *n* identidad *f*; **i. card**, carné *m* de identidad; **proof of i.**, prueba *f* de identidad.

ideological [aɪdɪə'lɒdʒɪkəl] *adj* ideológico,-a.

ideology [aɪdɪ'ɒlədʒɪ] *n* ideología *f*.

idiom ['ɪdɪəm] *n* modismo *m*; *fig* (*style*) lenguaje *m*.

idiomatic [ɪdɪə'mætɪk] *adj* idiomático,-a.

idiosyncrasy [ɪdɪəʊ'sɪŋkrəsɪ] *n* idiosincrasia *f*.

idiot ['ɪdɪət] *n* idiota *mf*, tonto,-a *m,f*.

idiotic [ɪdɪ'ɒtɪk] *adj* (*behaviour*) idiota,

tonto,-a; (joke, plan) estúpido,-a.

idle ['aɪdəl] **I** adj holgazán,-ana; (not working) (person) desempleado,-a; (machinery) parado,-a; (gossip) frívolo,-a; (threat) vano,-a. **II** vi (engine) funcionar en vacío. ◆**idle away** vtr (time) desperdiciar.

idleness ['aɪdəlnɪs] n (laziness) holgazanería f; (unemployment) desempleo m; (stoppage) paro m.

idol ['aɪdəl] n ídolo m.

idolize ['aɪdəlaɪz] vtr idolatrar.

idyllic [ɪ'dɪlɪk] adj idílico,-a.

i.e. abbr of id est (that is to say), esto es, a saber, i.e.

if [ɪf] **I** conj 1 si; **if at all**, si acaso; rarely, **if ever**, raras veces; **if I were rich**, si fuera rico,-a; **if necessary**, (en) caso de que sea necesario; **if not**, si no; **if so**, de ser así; **if I were you**, yo en tu lugar. 2 (whenever) si; **if you need help, ask**, siempre que necesites ayuda, pídela. 3 (although) aunque, si bien. 4 (exclamations) **if only I'd known!**, ¡de haberlo sabido!; **if only she were here!**, ¡ojalá estuviera aquí!. **II** n **ifs and buts**, pegas fpl.

igloo ['ɪgluː] n iglú m.

ignite [ɪg'naɪt] **I** vtr encender. **II** vi encenderse.

ignition [ɪg'nɪʃən] n ignición f; Aut encendido m; **i. key**, llave f de contacto.

ignorance ['ɪgnərəns] n ignorancia f.

ignorant ['ɪgnərənt] adj ignorante (**of**, de); **to be i. of the facts**, ignorar or desconocer los hechos.

ignore [ɪg'nɔːr] vtr (warning, remark) no hacer caso de; (behaviour, fact) pasar por alto.

ill [ɪl] **I** adj 1 enfermo,-a; **to be taken i.**, caer enfermo,-a; **to feel i.**, encontrarse mal. 2 (bad) malo,-a; **i. feeling**, resentimiento m; **i. will**, mala voluntad. **II** n mal m. **III** adv difícilmente.

I'll [aɪl] = **I shall; I will**.

ill-advised [ɪləd'vaɪzd] adj (person) imprudente; (act) desatinado,-a; **you'd be i.-a. to go**, harías mal en ir.

ill-disposed [ɪldɪ'spəʊzd] adj poco dispuesto,-a.

illegal [ɪ'liːgəl] adj ilegal.

illegible [ɪ'ledʒɪbəl] adj ilegible.

illegitimate [ɪlɪ'dʒɪtɪmɪt] adj ilegítimo,-a.

ill-fated [ɪl'feɪtɪd] adj abocado,-a al fracaso.

ill-founded [ɪl'faʊndɪd] adj infundado,-a.

illicit [ɪ'lɪsɪt] adj ilícito,-a.

illiteracy [ɪ'lɪtərəsɪ] n analfabetismo m.

illiterate [ɪ'lɪtərɪt] adj (person) analfabeto,-a; fam (uneducated) inculto,-a.

illness ['ɪlnɪs] n enfermedad f.

illogical [ɪ'lɒdʒɪkəl] adj ilógico,-a.

ill-treat [ɪl'triːt] vtr maltratar.

illuminate [ɪ'luːmɪneɪt] vtr 1 (light up) iluminar, alumbrar; fig (clarify) aclarar. 2

(manuscript) iluminar.

illuminating [ɪ'luːmɪneɪtɪŋ] adj (experience, book) instructivo,-a; (remark) revelador,-a.

illumination [ɪluːmɪ'neɪʃən] n 1 iluminación f; fig (clarification) aclaración f. 2 GB **illuminations**, iluminación f sing.

illusion [ɪ'luːʒən] n ilusión f; **to be under the i. that ...**, engañarse pensando que ....

illusory [ɪ'luːsərɪ] adj ilusorio,-a.

illustrate ['ɪləstreɪt] vtr ilustrar.

illustration [ɪlə'streɪʃən] ilustración f; (example) ejemplo m.

illustrious [ɪ'lʌstrɪəs] adj ilustre.

I'm [aɪm] = **I am**.

image ['ɪmɪdʒ] n imagen f.

imagery ['ɪmɪdʒərɪ] n Lit imágenes fpl.

imaginary [ɪ'mædʒɪnərɪ] adj imaginario,-a.

imagination [ɪmædʒɪ'neɪʃən] n imaginación f; (inventiveness) inventiva f.

imaginative [ɪ'mædʒɪnətɪv] adj imaginativo,-a.

imagine [ɪ'mædʒɪn] vtr (visualize) imaginar; (think) suponer, imaginarse; **just i.!**, ¡imagínate!

imbalance [ɪm'bæləns] n desequilibrio m.

imbecile ['ɪmbɪsɪl] n imbécil mf.

imitate ['ɪmɪteɪt] vtr imitar.

imitation [ɪmɪ'teɪʃən] **I** n imitación f, copia f; pej remedo m. **II** adj de imitación.

immaculate [ɪ'mækjʊlɪt] adj (clean) inmaculado,-a; (tidy) perfectamente ordenado,-a; (clothes) impecable; (work) perfecto,-a; **the I. Conception**, la Inmaculada Concepción.

immaterial [ɪmə'tɪərɪəl] adj irrelevante; **it's i. to me whether ...**, me trae sin cuidado si ....

immature [ɪmə'tjʊər] adj inmaduro,-a.

immediate [ɪ'miːdɪət] adj 1 inmediato,-a; (urgent) urgente. 2 (close) cercano,-a; (danger) inminente. 3 (cause) primero,-a. ◆**immediately I** adv 1 inmediatamente. 2 (directly) directamente. **II** conj en cuanto.

immense [ɪ'mens] adj inmenso,-a, enorme. ◆**immensely** adv (rich) enormemente; (interesting, difficult) sumamente.

immerse [ɪ'mɜːs] vtr sumergir (**in**, en); fig **to be immersed in sth**, estar absorto,-a en algo.

immersion [ɪ'mɜːʃən] n inmersión f; GB **i. heater**, calentador m de inmersión; **i. course**, cursillo intensivo.

immigrant ['ɪmɪgrənt] adj & n inmigrante (mf).

immigration [ɪmɪ'greɪʃən] n inmigración f.

imminent ['ɪmɪnənt] adj inminente.

immobile [ɪ'məʊbaɪl] adj inmóvil.

immobilize [ɪ'məʊbɪlaɪz] vtr inmovilizar.

immodest [ɪ'mɒdɪst] *adj* indecente.
immoral [ɪ'mɒrəl] *adj* inmoral.
immortal [ɪ'mɔːtəl] *adj* inmortal.
immortality [ɪmɔː'tælɪtɪ] *n* inmortalidad *f*.
immortalize [ɪ'mɔːtəlaɪz] *vtr* inmortalizar.
immune [ɪ'mjuːn] *adj* inmune; *(exempt)* exento,-a.
immunity [ɪ'mjuːnɪtɪ] *n* inmunidad *f*.
immunize ['ɪmjunaɪz] *vtr* inmunizar *(against, contra)*.
impact ['ɪmpækt] *n* impacto *m*; *(crash)* choque *m*.
impair [ɪm'peər] *vtr* perjudicar; *(sight etc)* dañar.
impart [ɪm'pɑːt] *vtr fml (news)* comunicar; *(knowledge)* transmitir.
impartial [ɪm'pɑːʃəl] *adj* imparcial.
impassable [ɪm'pɑːsəbəl] *adj (road, ground)* intransitable; *(barrier)* infranqueable.
impasse [æm'pɑːs] *n* punto muerto.
impassive [ɪm'pæsɪv] *adj* impasible.
impatience [ɪm'peɪʃəns] *n* impaciencia *f*.
impatient [ɪm'peɪʃənt] *adj* impaciente; *(fretful)* irritable; **to get i.,** perder la paciencia.
impeccable [ɪm'pekəbəl] *adj* impecable.
impede [ɪm'piːd] *vtr (prevent)* impedir; *(hinder)* estorbar; *(obstruct)* poner trabas a.
impediment [ɪm'pedɪmənt] *n* impedimento *m*; *(obstacle)* estorbo *m*; **speech i.,** defecto *m* del habla.
impending [ɪm'pendɪŋ] *adj fml* inminente.
impenetrable [ɪm'penɪtrəbəl] *adj* impenetrable; *fig (mystery, thoughts)* insondable.
imperative [ɪm'perətɪv] **I** *adj fml* imperativo,-a; *(tone)* imperioso,-a; *(urgent)* urgente. **II** *n Ling* imperativo *m*.
imperceptible [ɪmpə'septəbəl] *adj* imperceptible.
imperfect [ɪm'pɜːfɪkt] **I** *adj* imperfecto,-a; *(goods)* defectuoso,-a. **II** *n Ling* imperfecto *m*.
imperfection [ɪmpə'fekʃən] *n* defecto *m*.
imperial [ɪm'pɪərɪəl] *adj* 1 imperial. 2 *(measure)* **i. gallon,** galón británico *(approx 4,543 litres)*.
imperialism [ɪm'pɪərɪəlɪzəm] *n* imperialismo *m*.
imperialist [ɪm'pɪərɪəlɪst] *adj & n* imperialista *(mf)*.
imperious [ɪm'pɪərɪəs] *adj* imperioso,-a.
impersonal [ɪm'pɜːsənəl] *adj* impersonal.
impersonate [ɪm'pɜːsəneɪt] *vtr* hacerse pasar por; *(famous people)* imitar.
impersonation [ɪmpɜːsə'neɪʃən] *n* imitación *f*.
impertinent [ɪm'pɜːtɪnənt] *adj* impertinente.

impervious [ɪm'pɜːvɪəs] *adj (rock)* impermeable; *fig* **to be i. to reason,** no atender a razones.
impetuous [ɪm'petjuəs] *adj* impetuoso,-a.
impetus ['ɪmpɪtəs] *n* ímpetu *m*; *fig* impulso *m*.
impinge [ɪm'pɪndʒ] *vi fml* afectar *(on, a)*.
implant [ɪm'plɑːnt] *Med* **I** *vtr* implantar. **II** ['ɪmplɑːnt] *n* implantación *f*.
implement ['ɪmplɪmənt] **I** *n (tool)* herramienta *f*; *(instrument)* instrumento *m*; **farm implements,** aperos *mpl* de labranza. **II** ['ɪmplɪment] *vtr (decision, plan)* llevar a cabo; *(law, policy)* aplicar.
implicate ['ɪmplɪkeɪt] *vtr* implicar *(in, en)*.
implication [ɪmplɪ'keɪʃən] *n* implicación *f*; *(consequence)* consecuencia *f*.
implicit [ɪm'plɪsɪt] *adj (implied)* implícito,-a; *(trust)* absoluto,-a; *(faith)* incondicional.
implore [ɪm'plɔːr] *vtr* implorar, suplicar.
imply [ɪm'plaɪ] *vtr* 1 *(involve)* implicar. 2 *(hint)* dar a entender; *(mean)* significar.
impolite [ɪmpə'laɪt] *adj* maleducado,-a.
import ['ɪmpɔːt] **I** *n* 1 *Com (usu pl)* importación *f*; **i. duty,** derechos *mpl* de importación. 2 *fml (meaning)* sentido *m*. **II** [ɪm'pɔːt] *vtr Com* importar.
importance [ɪm'pɔːtəns] *n* importancia *f*; *(standing)* envergadura *f*; **of little i.,** de poca monta.
important [ɪm'pɔːtənt] *adj* importante; **it's not i.,** no importa.
importer [ɪm'pɔːtər] *n Com* importador,-a *m,f*.
impose [ɪm'pəʊz] **I** *vtr* imponer *(on, upon, a)*. **II** *vi* **to i. on** *or* **upon,** *(take advantage of)* abusar de.
imposing [ɪm'pəʊzɪŋ] *adj* imponente, impresionante.
imposition [ɪmpə'zɪʃən] *n (of tax etc)* imposición *f*; *(unfair demand)* abuso *m*; **would it be an i. if ...?,** ¿le molestaría si ...?
impossibility [ɪmpɒsə'bɪlɪtɪ] *n* imposibilidad *f*.
impossible [ɪm'pɒsəbəl] **I** *adj* imposible; *(person)* insoportable. **II** *n* **to do the i.,** hacer lo imposible. ◆**impossibly** *adv* de manera insoportable; **i. difficult,** de una dificultad insuperable.
impostor [ɪm'pɒstər] *n* impostor,-a *m,f*.
impotent ['ɪmpətənt] *adj* impotente.
impound [ɪm'paʊnd] *vtr* incautarse de.
impoverished [ɪm'pɒvərɪʃt] *adj (person, country)* empobrecido,-a; *(soil)* agotado,-a.
impracticable [ɪm'præktɪkəbəl] *adj* impracticable, irrealizable.
impractical [ɪm'præktɪkəl] *adj (person)* poco práctico,-a; *(project, solution etc)* poco viable.
imprecise [ɪmprɪ'saɪs] *adj* impreciso,-a.
impregnable [ɪm'pregnəbəl] *adj*

inexpugnable.

impregnate ['ɪmpregneɪt] *vtr* 1 *(soak)* impregnar *(with,* de*)*. 2 *fml (fertilize)* fecundar.

impress [ɪm'pres] *vtr* 1 impresionar; **to i. sb favourably/unfavourably,** dar a algn buena/mala impresión. 2 *(mark)* imprimir *(on,* en*)*; *(pattern)* estampar *(on,* en*)*; *fig* **to i. sth on sb,** convencer a algn de la importancia de algo.

impression [ɪm'preʃən] *n* 1 impresión *f*; **to be under the i. that ...,** tener la impresión de que ...; **to give the i. of ...,** dar la impresión de .... 2 *(imprint)* marca *f*; *(in snow)* huella *f*. 3 *(imitation)* imitación *f*. 4 *Print (number of copies)* edición *f*.

impressionist [ɪm'preʃənɪst] *adj & n* impresionista *(mf)*.

impressive [ɪm'presɪv] *adj* impresionante.

imprint [ɪm'prɪnt] I *vtr (mark)* dejar huella *(on,* en*)*. II ['ɪmprɪnt] *n* 1 *(mark)* marca *f*; *(left by foot etc)* huella *f*. 2 *(publisher's name)* pie *m* de imprenta.

imprison [ɪm'prɪzən] *vtr* encarcelar.

imprisonment [ɪm'prɪzənmənt] *n* encarcelamiento *m*.

improbable [ɪm'prɒbəbəl] *adj (event)* improbable; *(story)* inverosímil.

impromptu [ɪm'prɒmptjuː] I *adj (speech)* improvisado,-a; *(visit)* imprevisto,-a. II *adv* de improviso.

improper [ɪm'prɒpər] *adj* 1 impropio,-a; *(method)* inadecuado,-a. 2 *(indecent)* indecente; *(behaviour)* deshonesto,-a. 3 *(wrong)* incorrecto,-a.

improve [ɪm'pruːv] I *vtr* mejorar; *(knowledge)* perfeccionar; *(mind)* cultivar; *(increase)* aumentar. II *vi* mejorarse; *(increase)* aumentar. ◆**improve on** *vtr* superar; *(offer, bid)* sobrepujar.

improvement [ɪm'pruːvmənt] *n* mejora *f*; *(in skill)* perfeccionamiento *m*; *(increase)* aumento *m*.

improvise ['ɪmprəvaɪz] *vtr & vi* improvisar.

imprudent [ɪm'pruːdənt] *adj* imprudente.

impudence ['ɪmpjudəns] *n* insolencia *f*.

impudent ['ɪmpjudənt] *adj* insolente.

impulse ['ɪmpʌls] *n* impulso *m*; **to act on (an) i.,** dejarse llevar por un impulso.

impulsive [ɪm'pʌlsɪv] *adj* irreflexivo,-a.

impunity [ɪm'pjuːnɪtɪ] *n* impunidad *f*.

impure [ɪm'pjʊər] *adj* 1 *(act)* impuro,-a; *(thought)* impúdico,-a. 2 *(air)* contaminado,-a.

impurity [ɪm'pjʊərɪtɪ] *n* 1 *(of act)* deshonestidad *f*. 2 *(usu pl) (in air, substance)* impureza *f*.

in [ɪn] I *prep* 1 *(place)* en; *(within)* dentro de; **in bed,** en la cama; **in England/Brazil/China,** en Inglaterra/Brasil/China; **in prison,** en la cárcel; **in the distance,** a lo lejos. 2 *(motion)* en; **I threw it in the fire,** lo eché al fuego; **she arrived in Paris,** llegó a París. 3 *(time) (during)* en, durante; **I haven't seen her in years,** hace años que no la veo; **in May/1945,** en mayo/1945; **in spring,** en primavera; **in the daytime,** durante el día; **in the morning,** por la mañana; **at ten in the morning,** a las diez de la mañana. 4 *(time) (within)* dentro de; **I arrived in time,** llegué a tiempo. 5 *(time) (after)* al cabo de. 6 *(manner)* en; **in alphabetical order,** en orden alfabético; **in a loud/quiet voice,** en voz alta/baja; **in fashion,** de moda; **in French,** en francés; **in an odd way,** de una manera rara; **in writing,** por escrito; **write in pencil,** escribe con lápiz. 7 *(wearing)* en; **dressed in blue,** vestido,-a de azul; **in uniform,** de uniforme. 8 *(weather etc)* a, en; **in the rain,** bajo la lluvia; **in the sun,** al sol; **in darkness,** en la oscuridad; **in daylight,** a la luz del día; **in the shade,** a la sombra. 9 *(state, emotion)* en; **carved in wood,** tallado,-a en madera; **in bloom/danger/public/silence,** en flor/peligro/público/silencio; **in love,** enamorado,-a; **in tears,** llorando. 10 *(ratio, numbers)* de; **cut in half,** cortado,-a por la mitad; **in threes,** de tres en tres; **one in six,** uno de cada seis; **two metres in length,** dos metros de largo. 11 *(profession)* en; **to be in insurance,** trabajar en seguros. 12 *(person)* en; **he has it in him to win,** es capaz de ganar. 13 *(after superlative)* de; **the smallest car in the world,** el coche más pequeño del mundo. 14 *(before present participle)* **in behaving this way,** con su comportamiento; **in so doing,** con ello. 15 *(phrases)* **in all,** en total; **in itself/himself/herself,** en sí; **in that ...,** dado que ....

II *adv* **in here/there,** aquí/allí dentro; **let's go in,** vamos adentro; **to be in,** *(at home)* estar (en casa); *(at work)* estar; *(tide)* estar alta; *fam (in fashion)* estar de moda; **the bus is in,** el autobús ha llegado; **to invite sb in,** invitar a algn a entrar; *fam* **to be in on sth,** estar enterado,-a de algo; *fam* **we're in for a storm,** vamos a tener tormenta.

III *adj fam* 1 *(fashionable) (place)* de moda; *(clothes)* del último grito. 2 **an in joke,** una broma privada.

IV *n fam* **ins and outs,** detalles *mpl*.

inability [ɪnə'bɪlɪtɪ] *n* incapacidad *f*.

inaccessible [ɪnæk'sesəbəl] *adj* inaccesible.

inaccurate [ɪn'ækjʊrɪt] *adj* inexacto,-a; *(statement)* erróneo,-a; *(figures, total)* incorrecto,-a.

inactivity [ɪnæk'tɪvɪtɪ] *n* inactividad *f*.

inadequate [ɪn'ædɪkwɪt] *adj* 1 *(lacking)* insuficiente. 2 *(not capable)* incapaz; *(un-*

suitable) inadecuado,-a. **3** *(defective)* defectuoso,-a.

inadvertent [ɪnəd'vɜːtənt] *adj* involuntario,-a. ◆**inadvertently** *adv* involuntariamente.

inadvisable [ɪnəd'vaɪzəbəl] *adj* imprudente.

inane [ɪ'neɪn] *adj* necio,-a, fatuo,-a.

inanimate [ɪn'ænɪmɪt] *adj* inanimado,-a.

inappropriate [ɪnə'prəʊprɪɪt] *adj* inoportuno,-a; *(behaviour)* poco apropiado,-a.

inarticulate [ɪnɑː'tɪkjʊlɪt] *adj (cry, sound)* inarticulado,-a; *(words)* mal pronunciado,-a.

inasmuch as [ɪnəz'mʌtʃəz] *conj fml* **1** *(since)* puesto que, ya que. **2** *(in so far as)* en la medida en que.

inattentive [ɪnə'tentɪv] *adj* desatento,-a.

inaudible [ɪn'ɔːdəbəl] *adj* inaudible.

inaugural [ɪn'ɔːgjʊrəl] *adj* inaugural.

inaugurate [ɪn'ɔːgjʊreɪt] *vtr (building)* inaugurar; *(president)* investir.

inauguration [ɪnɔːgjʊ'reɪʃən] *n (of building)* inauguración *f*; *(of president)* investidura *f*.

inauspicious [ɪnɔː'spɪʃəs] *adj (start)* poco prometedor,-a; *(circumstances)* desfavorable.

inborn ['ɪnbɔːn] *adj* innato,-a.

inbred ['ɪnbred] *adj* **1** *(quality)* innato,-a. **2** *(family)* endogámico,-a.

Inc, inc *US Com abbr of* **Incorporated,** ≈ S.A.

incalculable [ɪn'kælkjʊləbəl] *adj* incalculable.

incapable [ɪn'keɪpəbəl] *adj* incapaz.

incapacitate [ɪnkə'pæsɪteɪt] *vtr fml* incapacitar.

incapacity [ɪnkə'pæsɪtɪ] *n* incapacidad *f*.

incarcerate [ɪn'kɑːsəreɪt] *vtr fml* encarcelar.

incarnation [ɪnkɑː'neɪʃən] *n* encarnación *f*.

incendiary [ɪn'sendɪərɪ] **I** *adj* incendiario,-a. **II** *n* bomba incendiaria.

incense[1] ['ɪnsens] *n* incienso *m*.

incense[2] [ɪn'sens] *vtr* enfurecer, sacar de quicio.

incentive [ɪn'sentɪv] *n* incentivo *m*.

incessant [ɪn'sesənt] *adj* incesante; *(demands)* constante. ◆**incessantly** *adv* sin cesar.

incest ['ɪnsest] *n* incesto *m*.

inch [ɪntʃ] *n* pulgada *f (approx* 2,54 cm); **fig i. by i.,** poco a poco; **she wouldn't give an i.,** no quería ceder ni un ápice. ◆**inch forward** *vtr & vi* avanzar poco a poco.

incidence ['ɪnsɪdəns] *n* frecuencia *f*.

incident ['ɪnsɪdənt] *n* incidente *m*.

incidental [ɪnsɪ'dentəl] *adj (accessory)* incidental, accesorio,-a; *(risk)* inherente **(to,** a); **i. music,** música *f* de fondo.

◆**incidentally** *adv* a propósito.

incinerator [ɪn'sɪnəreɪtə[r]] *n* incinerador *m*.

incipient [ɪn'sɪpɪənt] *adj fml* incipiente.

incision [ɪn'sɪʒən] *n* incisión *f*.

incisive [ɪn'saɪsɪv] *adj (comment)* incisivo,-a; *(reply)* tajante; *(mind)* penetrante.

incite [ɪn'saɪt] *vtr* incitar; **to i. sb to do sth,** incitar a algn a hacer algo.

inclination [ɪnklɪ'neɪʃən] *n* inclinación *f*; **my i. is to stay,** yo prefiero quedarme.

incline [ɪn'klaɪn] **I** *vtr* **1** **I'm inclined to believe him,** me inclino a creerlo; **if you feel so inclined,** si quieres; **she's inclined to be aggressive,** tiende a ser agresiva. **2** *(head etc)* inclinar. **II** *vi (slope)* inclinarse. **III** [ɪn'klaɪn, 'ɪnklaɪn] *n (slope)* pendiente *f*; **steep i.,** cuesta empinada.

include [ɪn'kluːd] *vtr* incluir **(in,** en); *(in price)* comprender **(in,** en); *(in list)* figurar **(in,** en).

including [ɪn'kluːdɪŋ] *prep* incluso, inclusive.

inclusion [ɪn'kluːʒən] *n* inclusión *f*.

inclusive [ɪn'kluːsɪv] *adj* inclusivo,-a; **pages six to ten i.,** de la página seis a la diez, ambas inclusive; **the rent is i. of bills,** el alquiler incluye las facturas.

incognito [ɪnkɒg'niːtəʊ] *adv* de incógnito.

incoherent [ɪnkəʊ'hɪərənt] *adj* incoherente.

income ['ɪnkʌm] *n* ingresos *mpl*; *(from investment)* réditos *mpl*; **i. tax,** impuesto *m* sobre la renta; **i. tax return,** declaración *f* de la renta.

incoming ['ɪnkʌmɪŋ] *adj (flight, train)* de llegada; *(tide)* ascendente; *(mail, message, call)* recibido,-a.

incomparable [ɪn'kɒmpərəbəl] *adj* incomparable, sin par.

incompatible [ɪnkəm'pætəbəl] *adj* incompatible **(with,** con).

incompetence [ɪn'kɒmpɪtəns] *n* incompetencia *f*.

incompetent [ɪn'kɒmpɪtənt] *adj* incompetente.

incomplete [ɪnkəm'pliːt] *adj* incompleto,-a.

incomprehensible [ɪnkɒmprɪ'hensəbəl] *adj* incomprensible.

inconceivable [ɪnkən'siːvəbəl] *adj* inconcebible.

inconclusive [ɪnkən'kluːsɪv] *adj (vote)* no decisivo,-a; *(proof)* no concluyente.

incongruous [ɪn'kɒŋgrʊəs] *adj* incongruente.

inconsiderate [ɪnkən'sɪdərɪt] *adj* desconsiderado,-a; **how i. of you!,** ¡qué falta de consideración por tu parte!

inconsistency [ɪnkən'sɪstənsɪ] *n* inconsecuencia *f*; *(contradiction)* contradicción *f*.

inconsistent [ɪnkənˈsɪstənt] *adj* inconse-cuente; *(contradictory)* contradictorio,-a; **your evidence is i. with the facts**, su testimonio no concuerda con los hechos.

inconspicuous [ɪnkənˈspɪkjuəs] *adj* que pasa desapercibido,-a; *(discrete)* discreto, -a.

incontrovertible [ɪnkɒntrəˈvɜːtəbəl] *adj fml* incontrovertible.

inconvenience [ɪnkənˈviːnɪəns] **I** *n* inconveniente *f*; *(annoyance)* molestia *f*. **II** *vtr (annoy)* molestar; *(cause difficulty to)* incomodar.

inconvenient [ɪnkənˈviːnɪənt] *adj* molesto,-a; *(time)* inoportuno,-a; *(design)* poco práctico,-a.

incorporate [ɪnˈkɔːpəreɪt] *vtr* incorporar (**in, into**, a); *(include)* incluir; *(contain)* contener.

incorporated [ɪnˈkɔːpəreɪtɪd] *adj US Com* **i. company**, sociedad anónima.

incorrect [ɪnkəˈrekt] *adj* incorrecto,-a.

incorrigible [ɪnˈkɒrɪdʒəbəl] *adj* incorregi-ble.

increase [ˈɪnkriːs] **I** *n* aumento *m*; *(in number)* incremento *m*; *(in price etc)* su-bida *f*. **II** [ɪnˈkriːs] *vtr* aumentar; *(price etc)* subir. **III** *vi* aumentar.

increasing [ɪnˈkriːsɪŋ] *adj* creciente.
◆**increasingly** *adv* cada vez más.

incredible [ɪnˈkredəbəl] *adj* increíble.

incredulous [ɪnˈkredjʊləs] *adj* incrédulo,-a.

increment [ˈɪnkrɪmənt] *n* incremento *m*.

incriminate [ɪnˈkrɪmɪneɪt] *vtr* incriminar.

incriminating [ɪnˈkrɪmɪneɪtɪŋ] *adj* incriminatorio,-a.

incubation [ɪnkjʊˈbeɪʃən] *n* incubación *f*.

incubator [ˈɪnkjʊbeɪtər] *n* incubadora *f*.

incumbent [ɪnˈkʌmbənt] **I** *n* titular *mf*. **II** *adj fml* **to be i. on sb to do sth**, ser la obligación de algn hacer algo.

incur [ɪnˈkɜːr] *vtr (blame)* incurrir en; *(risk)* correr; *(debt)* contraer; *(loss)* sufrir.

incurable [ɪnˈkjʊərəbəl] *adj* incurable.

indebted [ɪnˈdetɪd] *adj* endeudado,-a; *fig (grateful)* agradecido,-a; *fig* **to be i. to sb**, estar en deuda con algn.

indecent [ɪnˈdiːsənt] *adj* indecente; **i. assault**, atentado *m* contra el pudor; **i. exposure**, exhibicionismo *m*.

indecision [ɪndɪˈsɪʒən] *n* indecisión *f*.

indecisive [ɪndɪˈsaɪsɪv] *adj (person)* indeciso,-a; *(evidence)* poco concluyente; *(victory)* no decisivo,-a.

indeed [ɪnˈdiːd] *adv* **1** *fml (in fact)* efecti-vamente, en realidad. **2** **I'm very sorry i.**, lo siento de veras; **it's very hard i.**, es verdaderamente difícil; **thank you very much i.**, muchísimas gracias.

indefinite [ɪnˈdefɪnɪt] *adj* indefinido,-a.

indelible [ɪnˈdeləbəl] *adj* indeleble.

indemnify [ɪnˈdemnɪfaɪ] *vtr* indemnizar (**for**, por).

indemnity [ɪnˈdemnɪtɪ] *n* **1** *(insurance)* indemnidad *f*. **2** *(compensation)* indemni-zación *f*.

indentation [ɪndenˈteɪʃən] *n* **1** *Typ* san-gría *f*. **2** *(of edge)* muesca *f*; *(of surface)* depresión *f*.

independence [ɪndɪˈpendəns] *n* inde-pendencia *f*; *US* **I. Day**, día *m* de la Independencia *(4 julio)*.

independent [ɪndɪˈpendənt] *adj* inde-pendiente; *GB* **i. school**, colegio *m* no subvencionado por el estado; **to become i.**, independizarse.

in-depth [ˈɪndepθ] *adj* minucioso,-a, exhaustivo,-a.

indestructible [ɪndɪˈstrʌktəbəl] *adj* indes-tructible.

indeterminate [ɪndɪˈtɜːmɪnɪt] *adj* indeterminado,-a.

index [ˈɪndeks] **I** *n (pl* **indexes** *or* **indices**) **1** *(in book)* índice *m*; *(in library)* catálogo *m*; **i. card**, ficha *f*. **2** *Math* exponente *m*; *Econ* índice *m*. **3** **i. finger**, dedo *m* índi-ce. **II** *vtr* catalogar.

index-linked [ˈɪndekslɪŋkt] *adj* sujeto,-a al aumento de la inflación.

India [ˈɪndɪə] *n* (la) India.

Indian [ˈɪndɪən] *adj & n (of America)* indio,-a *(m,f)*; *(of India)* hindú *(m,f)*; **I. Ocean**, Océano Indico; **I. Summer**, vera-nillo *m* de San Martín.

indicate [ˈɪndɪkeɪt] **I** *vtr* indicar. **II** *vi Aut* poner el intermitente.

indication [ɪndɪˈkeɪʃən] *n* indicio *m*.

indicative [ɪnˈdɪkətɪv] **I** *adj* indicativo,-a. **II** *n Ling* indicativo *m*.

indicator [ˈɪndɪkeɪtər] *n* indicador *m*; *Aut* intermitente *m*.

indices [ˈɪndɪsiːz] *npl* → **index**.

indict [ɪnˈdaɪt] *vtr* acusar (**for**, de).

indictment [ɪnˈdaɪtmənt] *n Jur* acusación *f*; *fig* **a damning i. of his books**, una crí-tica feroz de sus libros.

indifference [ɪnˈdɪfərəns] *n* indiferencia *f*.

indifferent [ɪnˈdɪfərənt] *adj* **1** *(uninter-ested)* indiferente. **2** *(mediocre)* regular.

indigenous [ɪnˈdɪdʒɪnəs] *adj* indígena.

indigestion [ɪndɪˈdʒestʃən] *n* indigestión *f*; **to suffer from i.**, tener un empacho.

indignant [ɪnˈdɪgnənt] *adj* indignado,-a; *(look)* de indignación; **to get i. about sth**, indignarse por algo.

indignity [ɪnˈdɪgnɪtɪ] *n* indignidad *f*.

indigo [ˈɪndɪɡəʊ] **I** *n* añil *m*. **II** *adj* (de color) añil.

indirect [ɪndɪˈrekt, ɪndaɪˈrekt] *adj* indirecto,-a.

indiscreet [ɪndɪˈskriːt] *adj* indiscreto,-a.

indiscretion [ɪndɪˈskreʃən] *n* indiscreción *f*.

indiscriminate [ɪndɪˈskrɪmɪnɪt] *adj (punishment, shooting)* indiscriminado,-a; *(praise, reading)* sin criterio.

indispensable [ɪndɪˈspensəbəl] *adj*

indispensable, imprescindible.

indisposed |ɪndɪˈspəʊzd| *adj fml* indispuesto,-a.

indisputable |ɪndɪˈspjuːtəbəl| *adj* indiscutible, incontestable.

indistinct |ɪndɪˈstɪŋkt| *adj* indistinto,-a; *(memory)* confuso,-a, vago,-a; *(shape etc)* borroso,-a.

indistinguishable |ɪndɪˈstɪŋgwɪʃəbəl| *adj* indistinguible.

individual |ɪndɪˈvɪdjʊəl| I *adj* 1 *(separate)* individual; *(for one)* particular; *(personal)* personal. 2 *(characteristic)* particular; *(original)* original. II *n (person)* individuo *m*; private i., particular *m*.

individualist |ɪndɪˈvɪdjʊəlɪst| *n* individualista *mf*.

indoctrinate |ɪnˈdɒktrɪneɪt| *vtr* adoctrinar.

indoctrination |ɪndɒktrɪˈneɪʃən| *n* adoctrinamiento *m*.

indolent |ˈɪndələnt| *adj fml* indolente.

Indonesia |ɪndəʊˈniːzɪə| *n* Indonesia.

Indonesian |ɪndəʊˈniːzɪən| I *adj* indonesio,-a. II *n* 1 *(person)* indonesio,-a *m,f*. 2 *(language)* indonesio *m*.

indoor |ˈɪndɔːr| *adj (plant)* de interior; i. football, fútbol *m* sala; i. pool, piscina cubierta.

indoors |ɪnˈdɔːz| *adv (inside)* dentro (de casa); *(at home)* en casa; let's go i., vamos adentro.

induce |ɪnˈdjuːs| *vtr* 1 *(persuade)* inducir, persuadir. 2 *(cause)* producir; *Med (labour)* provocar.

inducement |ɪnˈdjuːsmənt| *n* incentivo *m*, aliciente *m*.

induction |ɪnˈdʌkʃən| *n* 1 *Med (of labour)* provocación *f*. 2 *Elec* inducción *f*. 3 *Educ* introducción *f*.

indulge |ɪnˈdʌldʒ| I *vtr* 1 *(child)* consentir; *(person)* complacer; to i. oneself, darse gusto. 2 *(whim)* ceder a, satisfacer. II *vi* darse el gusto (in, de).

indulgence |ɪnˈdʌldʒəns| *n* 1 *(of child)* mimo *m*; *(of attitude)* indulgencia *f*. 2 *(of whim)* satisfacción *f*.

indulgent |ɪnˈdʌldʒənt| *adj* indulgente.

industrial |ɪnˈdʌstrɪəl| *adj* industrial; *(accident)* laboral; *(disease)* profesional; *GB* to take i. action, declararse en huelga; *GB* i. dispute, conflicto *m* laboral; i. estate, polígono *m* industrial; i. relations, relaciones *fpl* laborales.

industrialist |ɪnˈdʌstrɪəlɪst| *n* industrial *mf*.

industrialize |ɪnˈdʌstrɪəlaɪz| *vtr* industrializar; to become industrialized, industrializarse.

industrious |ɪnˈdʌstrɪəs| *adj* trabajador, -a.

industry |ˈɪndəstrɪ| *n* 1 industria *f*. 2 *(diligence)* aplicación *f*.

inebriated |ɪnˈiːbrɪeɪtɪd| *adj* embriagado,-a.

inedible |ɪnˈedəbəl| *adj* incomible.

ineffective |ɪnɪˈfektɪv| *adj* ineficaz.

ineffectual |ɪnɪˈfektʃʊəl| *adj (aim, protest)* ineficaz; *(person)* incompetente.

inefficiency |ɪnɪˈfɪʃənsɪ| *n* ineficacia *f*; *(of person)* incompetencia *f*.

inefficient |ɪnɪˈfɪʃənt| *adj* ineficaz; *(person)* inepto,-a.

ineligible |ɪnˈelɪdʒəbəl| *adj* no apto (for, para).

inept |ɪnˈept| *adj (person)* inepto,-a; *(remark)* estúpido,-a.

inequality |ɪnɪˈkwɒlɪtɪ| *n* desigualdad *f*.

inert |ɪnˈɜːt| *adj* inerte.

inertia |ɪnˈɜːʃə| *n* inercia *f*.

inescapable |ɪnɪˈskeɪpəbəl| *adj* ineludible.

inevitability |ɪnevɪtəˈbɪlɪtɪ| *n* inevitabilidad *f*.

inevitable |ɪnˈevɪtəbəl| *adj* inevitable.

inexcusable |ɪnɪkˈskjuːzəbəl| *adj* inexcusable, imperdonable.

inexhaustible |ɪnɪgˈzɔːstəbəl| *adj* inagotable.

inexorable |ɪnˈeksərəbəl| *adj fml* inexorable.

inexpensive |ɪnɪkˈspensɪv| *adj* económico,-a.

inexperience |ɪnɪkˈspɪərɪəns| *n* inexperiencia *f*.

inexperienced |ɪnɪkˈspɪərɪənst| *adj* inexperto,-a.

inexplicable |ɪnɪkˈsplɪkəbəl| *adj* inexplicable.

infallible |ɪnˈfæləbəl| *adj* infalible.

infamous |ˈɪnfəməs| *adj* infame.

infancy |ˈɪnfənsɪ| *n* infancia *f*.

infant |ˈɪnfənt| *n* niño,-a *m,f*; *GB* i. school, parvulario *m*.

infantile |ˈɪnfəntaɪl| *adj* infantil.

infantry |ˈɪnfəntrɪ| *n* infantería *f*.

infatuated |ɪnˈfætjʊeɪtɪd| *adj* encaprichado,-a.

infatuation |ɪnfætjʊˈeɪʃən| *n* encaprichamiento *m*.

infect |ɪnˈfekt| *vtr (cut)* infectar; *(water)* contaminar; *(person)* contagiar.

infection |ɪnˈfekʃən| *n (of cut)* infección *f*; *(of water)* contaminación *f*; *(with illness)* contagio *m*.

infectious |ɪnˈfekʃəs| *adj (disease)* infeccioso,-a; *fig* contagioso,-a.

infer |ɪnˈfɜːr| *vtr* inferir (from, de).

inference |ˈɪnfərəns| *n* inferencia *f*.

inferior |ɪnˈfɪərɪər| I *adj* inferior (to, a). II *n pej* inferior *mf*.

inferiority |ɪnfɪərɪˈɒrɪtɪ| *n* inferioridad *f*.

inferno |ɪnˈfɜːnəʊ| *n lit* infierno *m*; *fig* the house was a raging i., la casa ardía en llamas.

infertile |ɪnˈfɜːtaɪl| *adj* estéril.

infertility |ɪnfəˈtɪlɪtɪ| *n* esterilidad *f*.

infest |ɪnˈfest| *vtr* infestar, plagar (with,

de).

infighting ['ɪnfaɪtɪŋ] *n fig* luchas *fpl* internas.

infiltrate ['ɪnfɪltreɪt] *vtr* infiltrarse (**into**, en).

infinite ['ɪnfɪnɪt] *adj* infinito,-a.

infinitive [ɪn'fɪnɪtɪv] *n* infinitivo *m*.

infinity [ɪn'fɪnɪtɪ] *n* infinidad *f*; *Math* infinito *m*.

infirm [ɪn'fɜːm] I *adj* (*ailing*) enfermizo,-a; (*weak*) débil. II *npl* **the i.**, los inválidos.

infirmary [ɪn'fɜːmərɪ] *n* hospital *m*.

infirmity [ɪn'fɜːmɪtɪ] *n fml* (*ailment*) enfermedad *f*; (*weakness*) debilidad *f*.

inflame [ɪn'fleɪm] *vtr* (*passion*) encender; (*curiosity*) avivar; (*crowd*) excitar; **to be inflamed with rage**, rabiar.

inflamed [ɪn'fleɪmd] *adj* inflamado,-a; **to become i.**, inflamarse.

inflammable [ɪn'flæməbəl] *adj* (*material*) inflamable; *fig* (*situation*) explosivo,-a.

inflammation [ɪnfləˈmeɪʃən] *n* inflamación *f*.

inflatable [ɪn'fleɪtəbəl] *adj* inflable.

inflate [ɪn'fleɪt] I *vtr* inflar. II *vi* inflarse.

inflated [ɪn'fleɪtɪd] *adj* 1 *fig* (*prices*) inflacionista. 2 *pej* (*view, idea*) exagerado,-a.

inflation [ɪn'fleɪʃən] *n* inflación *f*.

inflexible [ɪn'fleksəbəl] *adj* inflexible.

inflict [ɪn'flɪkt] *vtr* (*blow*) asestar (**on**, a); (*damage*) causar (**on**, a); (*defeat*) infligir (**on**, a).

in-flight ['ɪnflaɪt] *adj* durante el vuelo.

influence ['ɪnfluəns] I *n* influencia *f*; *fam* **to be under the i.**, llevar una copa de más. II *vtr* influir en.

influential [ɪnfluˈenʃəl] *adj* influyente.

influenza [ɪnflu'enzə] *n* gripe *f*.

influx ['ɪnflʌks] *n* afluencia *f*.

inform [ɪn'fɔːm] I *vtr* informar (**of, about**, de, sobre); (*police*) avisar (**of, about**, de). II *vi* **to i. against** *or* **on**, denunciar.

informal [ɪn'fɔːməl] *adj* 1 (*occasion, behaviour*) informal; (*language, treatment*) familiar. 2 (*unofficial*) no oficial.

informality [ɪnfɔːˈmælɪtɪ] *n* (*of occasion, behaviour*) sencillez *f*; (*of treatment*) familiaridad *f*.

informant [ɪn'fɔːmənt] *n* informante *mf*.

information [ɪnfəˈmeɪʃən] *n* información *f*; (*details*) detalles *mpl*; (*facts*) datos *mpl*; (*knowledge*) conocimientos *mpl*; (*news*) noticias *fpl*; **a piece of i.**, un dato; **i. bureau**, centro *m* de información; **i. technology**, informática *f*.

informative [ɪn'fɔːmətɪv] *adj* informativo,-a.

informed [ɪn'fɔːmd] *adj* enterado,-a; **keep me i.**, téngame al corriente.

informer [ɪn'fɔːmər] *n* delator,-a *m,f*; (*to the police*) soplón,-ona *m,f*.

infrared [ɪnfrəˈred] *adj* infrarrojo,-a.

infrastructure ['ɪnfrəstrʌktʃər] *n* infraes-

tructura *f*.

infringe [ɪn'frɪndʒ] I *vtr* (*law, rule*) infringir; (*copyright*) no respetar. II *vi* **to i. on** *or* **upon**, (*rights*) violar; (*privacy*) invadir.

infringement [ɪn'frɪndʒmənt] *n* (*of law, rule*) infracción *f*; (*of rights*) violación *f*.

infuriate [ɪn'fjʊərɪeɪt] *vtr* poner furioso, -a.

infuriating [ɪn'fjʊərɪeɪtɪŋ] *adj* exasperante.

infusion [ɪn'fjuːʒən] *n* infusión *f*.

ingenious [ɪn'dʒiːnɪəs] *adj* ingenioso,-a.

ingenuity [ɪndʒɪˈnjuːɪtɪ] *n* ingenio *m*.

ingenuous [ɪn'dʒenjʊəs] *adj* ingenuo,-a.

ingot ['ɪŋɡət] *n* lingote *m*.

ingrained [ɪn'ɡreɪnd] *adj fig* arraigado,-a.

ingratiate [ɪn'ɡreɪʃɪeɪt] *vtr pej* **to i. oneself with sb**, congraciarse con.

ingratiating [ɪn'ɡreɪʃɪeɪtɪŋ] *adj* zalamero,-a.

ingratitude [ɪn'ɡrætɪtjuːd] *n* ingratitud *f*.

ingredient [ɪn'ɡriːdɪənt] *n* ingrediente *m*.

inhabit [ɪn'hæbɪt] *vtr* vivir en, ocupar.

inhabitant [ɪn'hæbɪtənt] *n* habitante *mf*.

inhale [ɪn'heɪl] I *vtr* (*gas*) inhalar; (*air*) aspirar. II *vi* aspirar; (*smoker*) tragar el humo.

inherent [ɪn'hɪərənt] *adj* inherente.

inherit [ɪn'herɪt] *vtr* heredar (**from**, de).

inheritance [ɪn'herɪtəns] *n* herencia *f*.

inhibit [ɪn'hɪbɪt] *vtr* (*freedom*) limitar; (*person*) cohibir; **to i. sb from doing sth**, impedir a algn hacer algo.

inhibited [ɪn'hɪbɪtɪd] *adj* cohibido,-a.

inhibition [ɪnhɪˈbɪʃən] *n* cohibición *f*.

inhospitable [ɪnhɒˈspɪtəbəl] *adj* inhospitalario,-a; (*climate, place*) inhóspito,-a.

inhuman [ɪn'hjuːmən] *adj* inhumano,-a.

iniquity [ɪ'nɪkwɪtɪ] *n fml* iniquidad *f*.

initial [ɪ'nɪʃəl] I *adj* inicial, primero,-a. II *n* 1 inicial *f*. 2 **initials**, (*of name*) iniciales *fpl*; (*of abbreviation*) siglas *fpl*. III *vtr* firmar con las iniciales. ◆**initially** *adv* al principio.

initiate [ɪ'nɪʃɪeɪt] *vtr* 1 iniciar; (*reform*) promover; (*lawsuit*) entablar. 2 (*into society*) admitir (**into**, en); (*into knowledge*) iniciar (**into**, en).

initiation [ɪnɪʃɪ'eɪʃən] *n* 1 (*start*) principio *m*. 2 (*admission*) iniciación *f*.

initiative [ɪ'nɪʃətɪv] *n* iniciativa *f*.

inject [ɪn'dʒekt] *vtr* 1 (*drug etc*) inyectar. 2 *fig* (*capital*) invertir; (*life, hope*) infundir.

injection [ɪn'dʒekʃən] *n* 1 inyección *f*. 2 *fig* (*of capital*) inversión *f*.

injunction [ɪn'dʒʌŋkʃən] *n* interdicto *m*.

injure ['ɪndʒər] *vtr* herir; **to i. oneself**, hacerse daño; *fig* (*health, reputation*) perjudicar.

injured ['ɪndʒəd] I *adj* herido,-a; *fig* (*look, tone*) ofendido,-a. II *npl* **the i.**, los heridos.

injury ['ɪndʒərɪ] n (hurt) herida f; fig (harm) daño m; Sport i. time, (tiempo m de) descuento m.

injustice [ɪn'dʒʌstɪs] n injusticia f.

ink [ɪŋk] n tinta f; **invisible i.**, tinta simpática.

inkling ['ɪŋklɪŋ] n (idea) idea f; (suspicion) sospecha f; (sign) señal f.

inkwell ['ɪŋkwel] n tintero m.

inlaid [ɪn'leɪd] adj (wood) taraceado,-a; (ivory, gems) incrustado,-a.

inland ['ɪnlənd] I adj (del) interior; GB I. **Revenue**, Hacienda f. II [ɪn'lænd] adv (travel) tierra adentro.

in-laws ['ɪnlɔːz] npl fam familia f sing política.

inlet ['ɪnlet] n 1 (in coastline) ensenada f, cala f. 2 (in pipe, machine) entrada f, admisión f.

inmate ['ɪnmeɪt] n (of prison) preso,-a m,f; (of hospital) enfermo,-a m,f; (of asylum, camp) internado,-a m,f.

inn [ɪn] n (with lodging) posada f, mesón m.

innate [ɪ'neɪt] adj innato,-a.

inner ['ɪnər] adj 1 (region) interior; (structure) interno,-a; **i. city**, zona urbana desfavorecida; **i. tube**, cámara f de aire. 2 fig (thoughts) íntimo,-a; (peace etc) interior.

innermost ['ɪnəməʊst] adj (room) más interior; fig (thoughts) más íntimo,-a.

innings ['ɪnɪŋz] n (in cricket) entrada f, turno m.

innocence ['ɪnəsəns] n inocencia f.

innocent ['ɪnəsənt] adj & n inocente (mf).

innocuous [ɪ'nɒkjʊəs] adj inocuo,-a.

innovation [ɪnə'veɪʃən] n novedad f.

innuendo [ɪnjʊ'endəʊ] n indirecta f.

inoculate [ɪ'nɒkjʊleɪt] vtr inocular.

inoculation [ɪnɒkjʊ'leɪʃən] n inoculación f.

inoffensive [ɪnə'fensɪv] adj inofensivo,-a.

inopportune [ɪn'ɒpətjuːn, ɪnɒpə'tjuːn] adj inoportuno,-a.

inordinate [ɪ'nɔːdɪnɪt] adj desmesurado,-a.

inpatient ['ɪnpeɪʃənt] n interno,-a m,f.

input ['ɪnpʊt] n (of resources) inversión f; (of power) entrada f; Comput (of data) input m, entrada.

inquest ['ɪnkwest] n investigación f judicial.

inquire [ɪn'kwaɪər] I vtr preguntar; (find out) averiguar. II vi preguntar (**about**, por); (find out) informarse (**about**, de).
  ◆**inquire after** vtr preguntar por.
  ◆**inquire into** vtr investigar, indagar.

inquiry [ɪn'kwaɪərɪ] n 1 pregunta f; 'inquiries', 'información'. 2 (investigation) investigación f.

inquisitive [ɪn'kwɪzɪtɪv] adj (curious) curioso,-a; (questioning) preguntón,-ona.

inroads ['ɪnrəʊdz] npl **the firm is making i. into the market**, la empresa está ganando terreno en el mercado; **to make i. into one's capital**, reducir su capital.

insane [ɪn'seɪn] adj loco,-a; (act) insensato,-a; fig **to drive sb i.**, volver loco,-a a algn.

insanity [ɪn'sænɪtɪ] n demencia f, locura f.

insatiable [ɪn'seɪʃəbəl] adj insaciable.

inscribe [ɪn'skraɪb] vtr fml inscribir; (book) dedicar.

inscription [ɪn'skrɪpʃən] n (on stone, coin) inscripción f; (in book, on photo) dedicatoria f.

inscrutable [ɪn'skruːtəbəl] adj inescrutable, insondable.

insect ['ɪnsekt] n insecto m; **i. bite**, picadura f.

insecticide [ɪn'sektɪsaɪd] n insecticida m.

insecure [ɪnsɪ'kjʊər] adj inseguro,-a.

insecurity [ɪnsɪ'kjʊərɪtɪ] n inseguridad f.

insemination [ɪnsemɪ'neɪʃən] n inseminación f.

insensible [ɪn'sensəbəl]   adj   fml inconsciente.

insensitive [ɪn'sensɪtɪv] adj insensible.

inseparable [ɪn'sepərəbəl] adj inseparable.

insert ['ɪnsɜːt] I n encarte m. II [ɪn'sɜːt] vtr introducir.

insertion [ɪn'sɜːʃən] n introducción f; (of clause, text) inserción f.

inshore ['ɪnʃɔːr] I adj (fishing) de bajura. II [ɪn'ʃɔːr] adv cerca de la costa.

inside [ɪn'saɪd] I n 1 interior m; **on the i.**, por dentro; **to turn sth i. out**, volver algo al revés. 2 fam **insides**, tripas fpl. II ['ɪnsaɪd] adj interior; Sport **i. forward**, interior mf; Aut **i. lane**, carril m interior. III [ɪn'saɪd] adv (be) dentro, adentro; (run etc) (hacia) adentro; **to come i.**, entrar; GB fam **he spent a year i.**, pasó un año en chirona. IV prep 1 (place) dentro de. 2 fam **i. (of)**, (time) en menos de.

insider [ɪn'saɪdər] n **i. dealing**, uso indebido de información privilegiada y confidencial para operaciones comerciales.

insidious [ɪn'sɪdɪəs] adj insidioso,-a.

insight ['ɪnsaɪt] n perspicacia f.

insignia [ɪn'sɪgnɪə] n inv insignia f.

insignificant   [ɪnsɪg'nɪfɪkənt]   adj insignificante.

insincere [ɪnsɪn'sɪər] adj poco sincero,-a.

insinuate [ɪn'sɪnjʊeɪt] vtr insinuar.

insipid [ɪn'sɪpɪd] adj soso,-a, insulso,-a.

insist [ɪn'sɪst] I vi insistir (**on**, en); (argue) obstinarse (**on**, en). II vtr **to i. that ...**, insistir en que ....

insistence [ɪn'sɪstəns] n insistencia f.

insistent [ɪn'sɪstənt] adj insistente.

in so far as [ɪnsəʊ'fɑːrəz] adv en tanto que.

insole ['ɪnsəʊl] *n (of shoe)* plantilla *f*.
insolent ['ɪnsələnt] *adj* insolente.
insoluble [ɪn'sɒljʊbəl] *adj* insoluble.
insomnia [ɪn'sɒmnɪə] *n* insomnio *m*.
insomniac [ɪn'sɒmnɪæk] *n* insomne *mf*.
inspect [ɪn'spekt] *vtr* inspeccionar, examinar; *(troops)* pasar revista a.
inspection [ɪn'spekʃən] *n* inspección *f*; *(of troops)* revista *f*.
inspector [ɪn'spektər] *n* inspector,-a *m,f*; *(on bus, train)* revisor,-a *m,f*.
inspiration [ɪnspɪ'reɪʃən] *n* inspiración *f*; **to get i. from sb/sth,** inspirarse en algn/algo.
inspire [ɪn'spaɪər] *vtr* 1 inspirar; **to i. respect in sb,** infundir respeto a algn. 2 **to i. sb to do sth,** animar a algn a hacer algo.
inspired [ɪn'spaɪəd] *adj* inspirado,-a.
instability [ɪnstə'bɪlɪtɪ] *n* inestabilidad *f*.
install, *US* **instal** [ɪn'stɔːl] *vtr* instalar.
installation [ɪnstə'leɪʃən] *n* instalación *f*.
instalment, *US* **installment** [ɪn'stɔːlmənt] *n* 1 *(of payment)* plazo *m*; **to pay by instalments,** pagar a plazos; *US* **i. plan,** venta *f* or compra *f* a plazos. 2 *(of novel, programme)* entrega *f*; *(of journal)* fascículo *m*.
instance ['ɪnstəns] *n* ejemplo *m*, caso *m*; **for i.,** por ejemplo; **in the first i.,** en primer lugar.
instant ['ɪnstənt] I *n (moment)* instante *m*, momento *m*; **in an i.,** en un instante. II *adj* inmediato,-a; *(coffee, meal)* instantáneo,-a. ◆**instantly** *adv* inmediatamente.
instead [ɪn'sted] I *adv* en cambio. II *prep* **i. of,** en vez de, en lugar de.
instep ['ɪnstep] *n* empeine *m*.
instigation [ɪnstɪ'geɪʃən] *n* instigación *f*.
instil, *US* **instill** [ɪn'stɪl] *vtr (idea, habit)* inculcar (**in, a, en**); *(courage, respect)* infundir (**in, a**).
instinct ['ɪnstɪŋkt] *n* instinto *m*.
instinctive [ɪn'stɪŋktɪv] *adj* instintivo,-a.
institute ['ɪnstɪtjuːt] I *n* instituto *m*; *(centre)* centro *m*; *(professional body)* colegio *m*. II *vtr fml* 1 *(system)* establecer. 2 *(start)* iniciar; *(proceedings)* entablar.
institution [ɪnstɪ'tjuːʃən] *n* 1 institución *f*. 2 *(home)* asilo *m*; *(asylum)* manicomio *m*.
instruct [ɪn'strʌkt] *vtr* instruir; *(order)* mandar; **I am instructed to say that ...,** me han encargado decir que ....
instruction [ɪn'strʌkʃən] *n* 1 instrucción *f*. 2 **instructions,** instrucciones *fpl*; 'instructions for use', 'modo de empleo'.
instructive [ɪn'strʌktɪv] *adj* instructivo,-a.
instructor [ɪn'strʌktər] *n* instructor,-a *m,f*; *(of driving)* profesor,-a *m,f*.
instrument ['ɪnstrəmənt] *n* instrumento *m*; **i. panel,** tablero *m* de mandos.
instrumental [ɪnstrə'mentəl] *adj* 1 *Mus*

instrumental. 2 **to be i. in sth,** contribuir decisivamente a algo.
insubordinate [ɪnsə'bɔːdɪnɪt] *adj* insubordinado,-a.
insubstantial [ɪnsəb'stænʃəl] *adj* insubstancial; *(structure)* poco sólido,-a.
insufferable [ɪn'sʌfərəbəl] *adj* insoportable.
insufficient [ɪnsə'fɪʃənt] *adj* insuficiente.
insular ['ɪnsjʊlər] *adj* 1 *Geog* insular. 2 *fig pej* estrecho,-a de miras.
insulate ['ɪnsjʊleɪt] *vtr* aislar (**against, from,** de).
insulating tape ['ɪnsjʊleɪtɪŋteɪp] *n* cinta *f* aislante.
insulation [ɪnsjʊ'leɪʃən] *n* aislamiento *m*.
insulin ['ɪnsjʊlɪn] *n* insulina *f*.
insult ['ɪnsʌlt] I *n (words)* insulto *m*; *(action)* afrenta *f*, ofensa *f*. II [ɪn'sʌlt] *vtr* insultar, ofender.
insulting [ɪn'sʌltɪŋ] *adj* insultante, ofensivo,-a.
insuperable [ɪn'suːpərəbəl] *adj* insuperable.
insurance [ɪn'ʃʊərəns] *n* seguro *m*; **fire i.,** seguro contra incendios; **i. broker,** agente *mf* de seguros; **i. company,** compañía *f* de seguros; **i. policy,** póliza *f* (de seguros); **private health i.,** seguro médico privado.
insure [ɪn'ʃʊər] *vtr* asegurar (**against,** contra).
insurgent [ɪn'sɜːdʒənt] *adj & n* insurrecto,-a, *(m,f)*.
insurmountable [ɪnsə'maʊntəbəl] *adj* *(problem etc)* insuperable; *(barrier)* infranqueable.
intact [ɪn'tækt] *adj* intacto,-a.
intake ['ɪnteɪk] *n* 1 *(of air, water)* entrada *f*; *(of electricity etc)* toma *f*. 2 *(of food, calories)* consumo *m*. 3 *(of students, recruits)* número *m* de admitidos.
integral ['ɪntɪgrəl] I *adj* 1 *(intrinsic)* integrante. 2 *(whole)* íntegro,-a. 3 *Math* integral. II *n Math* integral *f*.
integrate ['ɪntɪgreɪt] I *vtr* integrar. II *vi* integrarse.
integration [ɪntɪ'greɪʃən] *n* integración *f*.
integrity [ɪn'tegrɪtɪ] *n* integridad *f*, honradez *f*.
intellect ['ɪntɪlekt] *n* intelecto *m*.
intellectual [ɪntɪ'lektʃʊəl] *adj & n* intelectual *(mf)*.
intelligence [ɪn'telɪdʒəns] *n* 1 inteligencia *f*. 2 *(information)* información *f*.
intelligent [ɪn'telɪdʒənt] *adj* inteligente.
intelligentsia [ɪntelɪ'dʒentsɪə] *n* intelectualidad *f*.
intelligible [ɪn'telɪdʒəbəl] *adj* inteligible.
intend [ɪn'tend] *vtr* 1 *(mean)* tener la intención de. 2 **to i. sth for sb,** destinar algo a algn.
intended [ɪn'tendɪd] *adj* *(planned)* previsto,-a.

intense |ɪn'tens| *adj* intenso,-a; *(person)* muy serio,-a. ◆**intensely** *adv (extremely)* enormemente, sumamente.

intensify |ɪn'tensɪfaɪ| *vtr (search)* intensificar; *(effort)* redoblar; *(production, pollution)* aumentar.

intensity |ɪn'tensɪtɪ| *n* intensidad *f*.

intensive |ɪn'tensɪv| *adj* intensivo,-a; *Med* **i. care unit,** unidad *f* de vigilancia intensiva.

intent |ɪn'tent| **I** *adj (absorbed)* absorto,-a; *(gaze etc)* atento,-a; **to be i. on doing sth,** estar resuelto,-a a a hacer algo. **II** *n fml* intención *f*, propósito *m*; **to all intents and purposes,** a todos los efectos.

intention |ɪn'tenʃən| *n* intención *f*.

intentional |ɪn'tenʃənəl| *adj* deliberado, -a. ◆**intentionally** *adv* a propósito.

interact |ɪntər'ækt| *vi (people)* interrelacionarse.

interaction |ɪntər'ækʃən| *n* interacción *f*.

interactive |ɪntər'æktɪv| *adj* interactivo, -a.

intercede |ɪntə'siːd| *vi* interceder (**with,** ante).

intercept |ɪntə'sept| *vtr* interceptar.

interchange |'ɪntətʃeɪndʒ| **I** *n* **1** *(exchange)* intercambio *m*. **2** *(on motorway)* cruce *m*. **II** |ɪntə'tʃeɪndʒ| *vtr* intercambiar (**with,** con).

interchangeable |ɪntə'tʃeɪndʒəbəl| *adj* intercambiable.

intercity |ɪntə'sɪtɪ| *adj* Rail de largo recorrido.

intercom |'ɪntəkɒm| *n* portero automático.

intercontinental |ɪntəkɒntɪ'nentəl| *adj* **i. ballistic missile,** misil balístico intercontinental.

intercourse |'ɪntəkɔːs| *n* **1** *(dealings)* trato *m*. **2** *(sexual)* relaciones *fpl* sexuales.

interest |'ɪntrɪst| **I** *n* **1** interés *m*. **2** *(advantage)* provecho *m*; **in the i. of,** en pro de. **3** *Com (share)* participación *f*. **4** *Fin* interés *m*; **i. rate,** tipo *m* de interés. **II** *vtr* interesar; **he's interested in politics,** le interesa la política.

interesting |'ɪntrɪstɪŋ| *adj* interesante.

interface |'ɪntəfeɪs| *n* interface *f*.

interfere |ɪntə'fɪər| *vi* **1** *(meddle)* entrometerse (**in,** en); **to i. with,** *(hinder)* dificultar; *(spoil)* estropear; *(prevent)* impedir. **2** *Rad TV* interferir (**with,** con).

interference |ɪntə'fɪərəns| *n (meddling)* intromisión *f*; *(hindrance)* estorbo *m*; *Rad TV* interferencia *f*.

interim |'ɪntərɪm| **I** *n fml* **in the i.,** en el ínterin. **II** *adj* interino,-a, provisional.

interior |ɪn'tɪərɪər| **I** *adj* interior. **II** *n* interior *m*; **i. design,** diseño *m* de interiores.

interlock |ɪntə'lɒk| *vi* encajarse; *(fingers)* entrelazarse; *(cogs)* engranarse.

interloper |'ɪntələʊpər| *n* intruso,-a *m,f*.

interlude |'ɪntəluːd| *n (break)* intervalo *m*; *Cin Theat* intermedio *m*; *Mus* interludio *m*.

intermediary |ɪntə'miːdɪərɪ| *n* intermediario,-a *m,f*.

intermediate |ɪntə'miːdɪɪt| *adj* intermedio,-a.

interminable |ɪn'tɜːmɪnəbəl| *adj* interminable.

intermission |ɪntə'mɪʃən| *n Cin Theat* intermedio *m*.

intermittent |ɪntə'mɪtənt| *adj* intermitente.

intern |ɪn'tɜːn| **I** *vtr* internar. **II** |'ɪntɜːn| *n US Med* interno,-a *m,f*.

internal |ɪn'tɜːnəl| *adj* interior; *(dispute, injury)* interno,-a; *US* **I. Revenue,** ≈ Hacienda *f*. ◆**internally** *adv* interiormente; **'not to be taken i.',** 'uso externo'.

international |ɪntə'næʃənəl| **I** *adj* internacional. **II** *n Sport (player)* internacional *mf*; *(match)* partido *m* internacional.

interplay |'ɪntəpleɪ| *n* interacción *f*.

interpret |ɪn'tɜːprɪt| **I** *vtr* interpretar. **II** *vi* actuar de intérprete.

interpretation |ɪntɜːprɪ'teɪʃən| *n* interpretación *f*.

interpreter |ɪn'tɜːprɪtər| *n* intérprete *mf*.

interrelated |ɪntərɪ'leɪtɪd| *adj* estrechamente relacionado,-a.

interrogate |ɪn'terəgeɪt| *vtr* interrogar.

interrogation |ɪnterə'geɪʃən| *n* interrogatorio *m*.

interrogative |ɪntə'rɒgətɪv| *Ling* **I** *adj* interrogativo,-a. **II** *n (word)* palabra interrogativa.

interrupt |ɪntə'rʌpt| *vtr & vi* interrumpir.

interruption |ɪntə'rʌpʃən| *n* interrupción *f*.

intersect |ɪntə'sekt| **I** *vtr* cruzar. **II** *vi* cruzarse.

intersection |ɪntə'sekʃən| *n* **1** *(crossroads)* cruce *m*. **2** *(of two lines)* intersección *f*.

intersperse |ɪntə'spɜːs| *vtr* esparcir.

intertwine |ɪntə'twaɪn| **I** *vtr* entrelazar (**with,** con). **II** *vi* entrelazarse (**with,** con).

interval |'ɪntəvəl| *n* **1** *(of time, space)* intervalo *m*; **at intervals,** *(time, space)* a intervalos; *(time)* de vez en cuando. **2** *GB Cin Theat* intermedio *m*.

intervene |ɪntə'viːn| *vi* **1** *(person)* intervenir (**in,** en). **2** *(event)* sobrevenir. **3** *(time)* transcurrir.

intervention |ɪntə'venʃən| *n* intervención *f*.

interview |'ɪntəvjuː| **I** *n* entrevista *f*; **to give an i.,** conceder una entrevista. **II** *vtr* entrevistar.

interviewer |'ɪntəvjuːər| *n* entrevistador,-a *m,f*.

intestine |ɪn'testɪn| *n (usu pl)* intestino *m*; **large/small i.,** intestino grueso/delgado.

intimacy |'ɪntɪməsɪ| *n (closeness)* intimidad *f*; *euph (sex)* relación íntima; **intimacies**, intimidades *fpl*.

intimate¹ ['ıntımıt] *adj* íntimo,-a; *(knowledge)* profundo,-a.

intimate² ['ıntımeıt] *vtr fml* dar a entender.

intimidate [ın'tımıdeıt] *vtr* intimidar.

intimidating [ın'tımıdeıtıŋ] *adj* atemorizante.

into ['ıntu:, *unstressed* 'ıntə] *prep* 1 *(motion)* en, a, con; **he fell i. the water**, se cayó al agua; **I bumped i. a friend**, me topé con un amigo; **to get i. a car**, subir a un coche; **to go i. a house**, entrar en una casa. 2 *(state)* en, a; **he grew i. a man**, se hizo un hombre; **to burst i. tears**, echarse a llorar; **to change pounds i. pesetas**, cambiar libras en *or* por pesetas; **to translate sth i. French**, traducir algo al francés. 3 **to work i. the night**, trabajar hasta muy avanzada la noche. 4 **to divide sth i. three**, dividir algo en tres. 5 *fam* **to be i. sth**, ser aficionado,-a a algo.

intolerable [ın'tɒlərəbəl] *adj* intolerable.

intolerant [ın'tɒlərənt] *adj* intolerante.

intonation [ıntəʊ'neıʃən] *n* entonación *f*.

intoxicated [ın'tɒksıkeıtıd] *adj* borracho,-a.

intoxicating [ın'tɒksıkeıtıŋ] *adj* embriagador,-a; **i. liquor**, bebida alcohólica.

intoxication [ıntɒksı'keıʃən] *n* embriaguez *f*.

intractable [ın'træktəbəl] *adj fml (person)* intratable; *(problem)* insoluble.

intransigent [ın'trænsıdʒənt] *adj fml* intransigente, intolerante.

intransitive [ın'trænsıtıv] *adj* intransitivo,-a.

intravenous [ıntrə'vi:nəs] *adj* intravenoso,-a.

in-tray ['ıntreı] *n* bandeja *f* de asuntos pendientes.

intrepid [ın'trepıd] *adj* intrépido,-a, audaz.

intricate ['ıntrıkıt] *adj* intrincado,-a.

intrigue [ın'tri:g, 'ıntri:g] **I** *n* intriga *f*. **II** [ın'tri:g] *vtr* intrigar. **III** *vi* intrigar, conspirar.

intriguing [ın'tri:gıŋ] *adj* intrigante.

intrinsic [ın'trınsık] *adj fml* intrínseco,-a.

introduce [ıntrə'dju:s] *vtr* 1 *(person, programme)* presentar (**to**, a). 2 *(bring in)* introducir (**into, to**, en); *Com* lanzar (**into, to**, a); *(topic)* proponer.

introduction [ıntrə'dʌkʃən] *n* 1 *(of person, programme)* presentación *f*; *(in book)* introducción *f*. 2 *(bringing in)* introducción *f*; *Com (of product)* lanzamiento *m*.

introductory [ıntrə'dʌktərı] *adj* introductorio,-a; *(remarks)* preliminar; *Com* de lanzamiento.

introspective [ıntrə'spektıv] *adj* introspectivo,-a.

introvert ['ıntrəvɜ:t] *n* introvertido,-a *m,f*.

intrude [ın'tru:d] *vi* entrometerse (**into, on**, en); *(disturb)* molestar.

intruder [ın'tru:dər] *n* intruso,-a *m,f*.

intrusion [ın'tru:ʒən] *n* incursión *f*.

intuition [ıntju'ıʃən] *n* intuición *f*.

inundate ['ınʌndeıt] *vtr* inundar (**with**, de).

invade [ın'veıd] *vtr* invadir.

invader [ın'veıdər] *n* invasor,-a *m,f*.

invalid¹ ['ınvəlıd] *n (disabled person)* minusválido,-a *m,f*; *(sick person)* enfermo,-a *m,f*.

invalid² [ın'vælıd] *adj* inválido,-a, nulo, -a.

invalidate [ın'vælıdeıt] *vtr* invalidar.

invaluable [ın'væljʊəbəl] *adj* inestimable.

invariable [ın'veərıəbəl] *adj* invariable.

invasion [ın'veıʒən] *n* invasión *f*.

invent [ın'vent] *vtr* inventar.

invention [ın'venʃən] *n* invento *m*; *(creativity)* inventiva *f*; *(lie)* mentira *f*.

inventive [ın'ventıv] *adj* inventivo,-a.

inventor [ın'ventər] *n* inventor,-a *m,f*.

inventory ['ınvəntərı] *n* inventario *m*.

invert [ın'vɜ:t] *vtr* invertir.

invertebrate [ın'vɜ:tıbrıt] **I** *adj* invertebrado,-a. **II** *n* invertebrado *m*.

inverted [ın'vɜ:tıd] *adj* **(in) i. commas**, (entre) comillas *fpl*.

invest [ın'vest] **I** *vtr* invertir (**in, en**); **to i. sb with sth**, conferir algo a algn. **II** *vi* invertir (**in**, en).

investigate [ın'vestıgeıt] *vtr (crime, subject)* investigar; *(cause, possibility)* estudiar.

investigation [ınvestı'geıʃən] *n (of crime)* investigación *f*; *(of cause)* examen *m*.

investigator [ın'vestıgeıtər] *n* investigador,-a *m,f*; **private i.**, detective privado.

investment [ın'vestmənt] *n* inversión *f*.

investor [ın'vestər] *n* inversor,-a *m,f*.

inveterate [ın'vetərıt] *adj* empedernido, -a.

invidious [ın'vıdıəs] *adj (task)* ingrato,-a; *(comparison)* injusto,-a.

invigilator [ın'vıdʒıleıtər] *n GB* vigilante *mf*.

invigorating [ın'vıgəreıtıŋ] *adj* vigorizante.

invincible [ın'vınsəbəl] *adj* invencible.

invisible [ın'vızəbəl] *adj* invisible.

invitation [ınvı'teıʃən] *n* invitación *f*.

invite [ın'vaıt] *vtr* 1 invitar (**to**, a). 2 *(comments etc)* solicitar; *(criticism)* provocar; **to i. trouble**, buscarse problemas.

inviting [ın'vaıtıŋ] *adj (attractive)* atractivo,-a; *(food)* apetitoso,-a.

invoice ['ınvɔıs] **I** *n* factura *f*. **II** *vtr* facturar.

invoke [ɪn'vəʊk] *vtr fml* invocar.
involuntary [ɪn'vɒləntərɪ] *adj* involuntario,-a.
involve [ɪn'vɒlv] *vtr* 1 (*concern*) implicar (**in, en**); **the issues involved,** las cuestiones en juego; **to be involved in an accident,** sufrir un accidente. 2 (*entail*) suponer, implicar; (*trouble, risk*) acarrear.
involved [ɪn'vɒlvd] *adj* (*complicated*) complicado,-a; *fam* (*romantically attached*) enredado,-a, liado,-a.
involvement [ɪn'vɒlvmənt] *n* (*participation*) participación *f*; (*in crime*) implicación *f*.
inward ['ɪnwəd] I *adj* interior. II *adv* → **inwards.** ◆**inwardly** *adv* interiormente, por dentro.
inwards ['ɪnwədz] *adv* hacia dentro.
iodine ['aɪədiːn] *n* yodo *m*.
iota [aɪ'əʊtə] *n* pizca *f*, ápice *m*.
IOU [aɪəʊ'juː] *abbr of* **I owe you,** pagaré *m*.
IQ [aɪ'kjuː] *abbr of* **intelligence quotient,** coeficiente *m* intelectual, CI *m*.
IRA [aɪɑː'reɪ] *abbr of* **Irish Republican Army,** Ejército *m* Republicano irlandés, IRA *m*.
Iran [ɪ'rɑːn] *n* Irán.
Iranian [ɪ'reɪnɪən] *adj & n* iraní (*mf*).
Iraq [ɪ'rɑːk] *n* Irak.
Iraqi [ɪ'rɑːkɪ] *adj & n* iraquí (*mf*).
irascible [ɪ'ræsɪbəl] *adj fml* irascible.
irate [aɪ'reɪt] *adj* airado,-a, furioso,-a.
Ireland ['aɪələnd] *n* Irlanda; **Republic of I.,** República de Irlanda.
iris ['aɪərɪs] *n* 1 *Anat* iris *m inv.* 2 *Bot* lirio *m*.
Irish ['aɪrɪʃ] I *adj* irlandés,-esa; **I. coffee,** café *m* irlandés; **I. Sea,** Mar *m* de Irlanda. II *n* 1 (*language*) irlandés *m*. 2 *pl* **the I.,** los irlandeses.
Irishman ['aɪrɪʃmən] *n* irlandés *m*.
Irishwoman ['aɪrɪʃwʊmən] *n* irlandesa *f*.
irksome ['ɜːksəm] *adj* fastidioso,-a.
iron ['aɪən] I *n* 1 hierro *m*; **the i. and steel industry,** la industria siderúrgica; **I. Curtain,** Telón *m* de Acero; **i. ore,** mineral *m* de hierro. 2 (*for clothes*) plancha *f*. 3 (*for golf*) hierro *m*. 4 **irons,** (*chains*) grillos *mpl*. II *vtr* (*clothes*) planchar. ◆**iron out** *vtr* 1 (*crease*) planchar. 2 *fam fig* (*problem*) resolver.
ironic(al) [aɪ'rɒnɪk(əl)] *adj* irónico,-a.
ironing ['aɪənɪŋ] *n* 1 **to do the i.,** planchar; **i. board,** mesa *f* de la plancha. 2 (*clothes to be ironed*) ropa *f* para planchar; (*clothes ironed*) ropa planchada.
ironmonger ['aɪənmʌŋgər] *n* *GB* ferretero,-a *m,f*; **i.'s (shop),** ferretería *f*.
irony ['aɪrənɪ] *n* ironía *f*.
irrational [ɪ'ræʃənəl] *adj* irracional.
irreconcilable [ɪrekən'saɪləbəl] *adj* irreconciliable.
irrefutable [ɪrɪ'fjuːtəbəl] *adj fml* irrefuta-

ble.
irregular [ɪ'regjʊlər] *adj* 1 irregular; (*abnormal*) anormal. 2 (*uneven*) desigual.
irrelevant [ɪ'reləvənt] *adj* no pertinente.
irreparable [ɪ'repərəbəl] *adj* irreparable.
irreplaceable [ɪrɪ'pleɪsəbəl] *adj* irremplazable.
irrepressible [ɪrɪ'presəbəl] *adj* incontenible.
irresistible [ɪrɪ'zɪstəbəl] *adj* irresistible.
irresolute [ɪ'rezəluːt] *adj fml* indeciso,-a.
irrespective [ɪrɪ'spektɪv] *adj* **i. of,** sin tener en cuenta.
irresponsible [ɪrɪ'spɒnsəbəl] *adj* irresponsable.
irreverent [ɪ'revərənt] *adj* irreverente.
irrevocable [ɪ'revəkəbəl] *adj* irrevocable.
irrigate ['ɪrɪgeɪt] *vtr* regar.
irrigation [ɪrɪ'geɪʃən] *n* riego *m*; **i. channel,** acequia *f*; **i. system,** sistema *m* de regadío.
irritable ['ɪrɪtəbəl] *adj* irritable.
irritate ['ɪrɪteɪt] *vtr* (*annoy*) fastidiar; *Med* irritar.
irritating ['ɪrɪteɪtɪŋ] *adj* irritante.
irritation [ɪrɪ'teɪʃən] *n* 1 (*annoyance*) fastidio *m*; (*ill humour*) mal humor *m*. 2 *Med* irritación *f*.
is [ɪz] *3rd person sing pres* → **be.**
Islam ['ɪzlɑːm] *n* Islam *m*.
Islamic [ɪz'læmɪk] *adj* islámico,-a.
island ['aɪlənd] *n* isla *f*; (*traffic*) **i,** isleta *f*.
islander ['aɪləndər] *n* isleño,-a *m,f*.
isle [aɪl] *n* isla *f*.
isn't ['ɪzənt] = **is not.**
isolate ['aɪsəleɪt] *vtr* aislar (**from,** de).
isolated ['aɪsəleɪtɪd] *adj* aislado,-a.
isolation [aɪsə'leɪʃən] *n* aislamiento *m*.
Israel ['ɪzreɪəl] *n* Israel.
Israeli [ɪz'reɪlɪ] I *adj* israelí. II *n* israelí *mf*.
issue ['ɪʃjuː] I *n* 1 (*matter*) cuestión *f*; **to take i. with sb (over sth),** manifestar su desacuerdo con algn (en algo). 2 (*of banknotes etc*) emisión *f*; (*of passport*) expedición *f*. 3 (*of journal etc*) ejemplar *m*. 4 (*of supplies*) reparto *m*. 5 *fml* (*outcome*) resultado *m*. 6 *Jur* (*offspring*) descendencia *f*. II *vtr* 1 (*book*) publicar; (*banknotes etc*) emitir; (*passport*) expedir. 2 (*supplies*) repartir. 3 (*order, instructions*) dar; (*warrant*) dictar. III *vi fml* (*blood*) brotar (**from,** de); (*smoke*) salir (**from,** de).
isthmus ['ɪsməs] *n* istmo *m*.
it [ɪt] *pers pron* 1 (*subject*) él, ella, ello (*often omitted*); **it's here,** está aquí. 2 (*direct object*) lo, la; **I don't believe it,** no me lo creo; **I liked the house and bought it,** me gustó la casa y la compré. 3 (*indirect object*) le; **give it a kick,** dale una patada. 4 (*after prep*) él, ella, ello; **I saw the beach and ran towards it,** vi la playa y fui corriendo hacia ella; **we'll talk about**

it later, ya hablaremos de ello. **5** (*abstract*) ello; **let's get down to it!,** ¡vamos a ello! **6** (*impersonal*) **it's late,** es tarde; **it's me,** soy yo; **it's raining,** está lloviendo; **it's said that ...,** se dice que ...; **it's two miles to town,** hay dos millas de aquí al pueblo; **that's it!,** (*agreeing*) ¡precisamente!; (*finishing*) ¡se acabó!; **this is it!,** ¡ha llegado la hora!; **who is it?,** ¿quién es?

Italian [ɪ'tæljən] **I** *adj* italiano,-a. **II** *n* **1** (*person*) italiano,-a *m,f.* **2** (*language*) italiano *m.*

italic [ɪ'tælɪk] *n* cursiva *f.*

Italy ['ɪtəlɪ] *n* Italia.

itch [ɪtʃ] **I** *n* picor *m; fig* **an i. to travel,** unas ganas locas de viajar. **II** *vi* **1** (*skin*) picar. **2** *fig* anhelar; *fam* **to be itching to do sth,** tener muchas ganas de hacer algo.

itchy ['ɪtʃɪ] *adj* (*itchier, itchiest*) que pica.

item ['aɪtəm] *n* **1** (*in list*) artículo *m; (in collection*) pieza *f; (in show*) número *m; news* **i., noticia *f.* **2** (*on agenda*) asunto *m; (of clothing*) prenda *f* de vestir.

itemize ['aɪtəmaɪz] *vtr* detallar.

itinerant [ɪ'tɪnərənt] *adj fml* itinerante.

itinerary [aɪ'tɪnərərɪ] *n* itinerario *m.*

it'll ['ɪtəl] = **it will.**

its [ɪts] *poss adj* (*one thing*) su; (*more than one*) sus.

itself [ɪt'self] *pers pron* **1** (*reflexive*) se; **the cat scratched i.,** el gato se arañó. **2** (*emphatic*) él *or* ella *or* ello mismo,-a; (*after prep*) sí (mismo,-a); **in i.,** en sí.

ITV [aɪtiː'viː] *GB abbr of* **Independent Television,** televisión *f* independiente, ITV *f.*

IUD [aɪjuː'diː] *abbr of* **intrauterine** (**contraceptive**) **device,** dispositivo intrauterino, DIU *m.*

ivory ['aɪvərɪ] *n* marfil *m.*

ivy ['aɪvɪ] *n* hiedra *f.*

J

J, j [dʒeɪ] *n* (*the letter*) J, j *f.*

jab [dʒæb] **I** *n* pinchazo *m; (poke*) golpe seco. **II** *vtr* pinchar; (*with fist*) dar un puñetazo a.

jabber ['dʒæbər] *fam vi* (*chatter*) charlotear; (*speak quickly*) hablar atropelladamente.

jack [dʒæk] *n* **1** *Aut* gato *m.* **2** *Cards* sota *f.* **3** (*bowls*) boliche *m.* ◆**jack in** *vtr GB fam* dejar. ◆**jack up** *vtr Aut* levantar (con el gato); *fig* (*prices*) aumentar.

jackal ['dʒækɔːl] *n* chacal *m.*

jackdaw ['dʒækdɔː] *n Orn* grajilla *f.*

jacket ['dʒækɪt] *n* **1** chaqueta *f; (of suit*) americana *f; (bomber jacket*) cazadora *f.* **2** (*of book*) sobrecubierta *f; US* (*of record*) funda *f.* **3** **j. potatoes,** patatas *fpl* al horno.

jack-knife ['dʒæknaɪf] **I** *n* navaja *f.* **II** *vi* colear.

jack-of-all-trades [dʒækəv'ɔːltreɪdz] *n* persona *f* mañosa *or* de muchos oficios.

jackpot ['dʒækpɒt] *n* (premio *m*) gordo *m.*

Jacuzzi® [dʒə'kuːzɪ] *n* jacuzzi® *m.*

jade [dʒeɪd] *n* jade *m.*

jaded ['dʒeɪdɪd] *adj* (*tired*) agotado,-a; (*palate*) hastiado,-a.

jagged ['dʒægɪd] *adj* dentado,-a.

jaguar ['dʒægjʊər] *n* jaguar *m.*

jail [dʒeɪl] **I** *n* cárcel *f,* prisión *f.* **II** *vtr* encarcelar.

jailbreak ['dʒeɪlbreɪk] *n* fuga *f,* evasión *f.*

jailer ['dʒeɪlər] *n* carcelero,-a *m,f.*

jam¹ [dʒæm] *n Culin* mermelada *f.*

jam² [dʒæm] **I** *n* **1** (*blockage*) atasco *m; fam* (*fix*) apuro *m.* **2** *Mus* improvisación *f.* **II** *vtr* **1** (*cram*) meter a la fuerza. **2** (*block*) atascar; *Rad* interferir. **III** *vi* (*door*) atrancarse; (*brakes*) agarrotarse.

Jamaica [dʒə'meɪkə] *n* Jamaica *f.*

jam-packed [dʒæm'pækt] *adj fam* (*with people*) atestado,-a; (*with things*) atiborrado,-a.

jangle ['dʒæŋgəl] *vi* tintinear.

janitor ['dʒænɪtər] *n* portero *m,* conserje *m.*

January ['dʒænjʊərɪ] *n* enero *m.*

Japan [dʒə'pæn] *n* (el) Japón.

Japanese [dʒæpə'niːz] **I** *adj* japonés,-esa. **II** *n* (*person*) japonés,-esa *m,f; (language*) japonés *m.*

jar¹ [dʒɑːr] *n* (*glass*) tarro *m; (earthenware*) tinaja *f; (jug*) jarra *f; GB fam* **to have a j.,** tomar una copa.

jar² [dʒɑːr] *vi* (*sounds*) chirriar; (*appearance*) chocar; (*colours*) desentonar; *fig* **to j. on one's nerves,** ponerle a uno los nervios de punta.

jargon ['dʒɑːgən] *n* jerga *f,* argot *m.*

jasmin(e) ['dʒæzmɪn] *n* jazmín *m.*

jaundice ['dʒɔːndɪs] *n* ictericia *f.*

jaundiced ['dʒɔːndɪst] *adj Med* ictérico, -a; *fig* (*bitter*) amargado,-a.

jaunt [dʒɔːnt] *n* (*walk*) paseo *m; (trip*) excursión *f.*

jaunty ['dʒɔːntɪ] *adj* (*jauntier, jauntiest*) (*sprightly*) garboso,-a; (*lively*) vivaz.

javelin ['dʒævəlɪn] *n* jabalina *f.*

jaw [dʒɔː] **I** *n* mandíbula *f.* **II** *vi fam* estar de palique.

jay [dʒeɪ] *n Orn* arrendajo *m* (común).

jaywalker ['dʒeɪwɔːkər] *n* peatón *m* imprudente.

jazz [dʒæz] *n* jazz *m.* ◆**jazz up** *vtr* alegrar; *(premises)* arreglar.

jazzy ['dʒæzı] *adj (jazzier, jazziest) fam (showy)* llamativo,-a; *(brightly coloured)* de colores chillones.

jealous ['dʒeləs] *adj* celoso,-a; *(envious)* envidioso,-a; **to be j. of ...**, tener celos de ....

jealousy ['dʒeləsı] *n* celos *mpl*; *(envy)* envidia *f*.

jeans [dʒi:nz] *npl* vaqueros *mpl*, tejanos *mpl*.

jeep [dʒi:p] *n* jeep *m*, todo terreno *m inv*.

jeer [dʒıər] **I** *n (boo)* abucheo *m*; *(mocking)* mofa *f*. **II** *vi (boo)* abuchear; *(mock)* burlarse.

jeering ['dʒıərıŋ] *adj* burlón,-ona.

Jehovah [dʒı'həʊvə] *n* **J.'s Witness**, testigo *mf* de Jehová.

jelly ['dʒelı] *n* gelatina *f*.

jellyfish ['dʒelıfıʃ] *n* medusa *f*.

jeopardize ['dʒepədaız] *vtr* poner en peligro; *(agreement etc)* comprometer.

jeopardy ['dʒepədı] *n* riesgo *m*, peligro *m*.

jerk [dʒɜːk] **I** *n* **1** *(jolt)* sacudida *f*; *(pull)* tirón *m*. **2** *pej (idiot)* imbécil *mf*. **II** *vtr (shake)* sacudir; *(pull)* dar un tirón a. **III** *vi (move suddenly)* dar una sacudida; **the car jerked forward,** el coche avanzaba a tirones.

jerkin ['dʒɜːkın] *n* chaleco *m*.

jersey ['dʒɜːzı] *n* jersey *m*, suéter *m*.

jest [dʒest] **I** *n* broma *f*. **II** *vi* bromear.

Jesuit ['dʒezjʊıt] *adj & n* jesuita *(m)*.

Jesus ['dʒi:zəs] *n* Jesús *m*; **J. Christ,** Jesucristo *m*.

jet¹ [dʒet] **I** *n* **1** *(stream of water)* chorro *m*. **2** *(spout)* surtidor *m*. **3** *Av* reactor *m*; **j. engine,** reactor *m*; **j. lag,** cansancio debido al desfase horario. **II** *vi fam* volar.

jet² [dʒet] *n* **j. black,** negro,-a como el azabache.

jet-set ['dʒetset] *n* **the j.-s.,** la alta sociedad, la jet.

jettison ['dʒetısən] *vtr* echar al mar; *fig* deshacerse de; *(project etc)* abandonar.

jetty ['dʒetı] *n* muelle *m*, malecón *m*.

Jew [dʒu:] *n* judío,-a *m,f*.

jewel ['dʒu:əl] *n* joya *f*; *(stone)* piedra preciosa; *(in watch)* rubí *m*; *fig (person)* joya.

jeweller, jeweler ['dʒu:ələr] *n* joyero,-a *m,f*; **j.'s (shop),** joyería *f*.

jewellery, jewelry ['dʒu:əlrı] *n* joyas *fpl*, alhajas *fpl*.

Jewess ['dʒu:ıs] *n* judía *f*.

Jewish ['dʒu:ıʃ] *adj* judío,-a.

jibe [dʒaıb] *n & vi* → **gibe**.

jiffy ['dʒıfı] *n fam* momento *m*; **in a j.,** en un santiamén; **just a j.!,** ¡un momento!

jig [dʒıg] *n Mus* giga *f*.

jigsaw ['dʒıgsɔ:] *n (puzzle)* rompecabezas *m inv*.

jilt [dʒılt] *vtr fam* dejar plantado,-a.

jingle ['dʒıŋgəl] **I** *n Rad TV* canción *f*

que acompaña un anuncio. **II** *vi* tintinear.

jingoistic [dʒıŋgəʊ'ıstık] *adj* patriotero, -a.

jinx [dʒıŋks] **I** *n (person)* gafe *mf*. **II** *vtr* gafar.

jitters ['dʒıtəz] *npl fam* **to get the j.,** tener canguelo.

jive [dʒaıv] **I** *n* swing *m*. **II** *vi* bailar el swing.

job [dʒɒb] *n* **1** trabajo *m*; *(task)* tarea *f*; **to give sth up as a bad j.,** darse por vencido,-a; *fam* **just the j.!,** ¡me viene de perlas! **2** *(occupation)* *(puesto m de)* trabajo *m*, empleo *m*; *(trade)* oficio *m*; *GB fam* **jobs for the boys,** enchufismo *m*; **j. centre,** oficina *f* de empleo; **j. hunting,** búsqueda *f* de empleo; **j. sharing,** trabajo compartido a tiempo parcial. **3** *fam* **we had a j. to ...,** nos costó (trabajo) .... **4** *(duty)* deber *m*. **5** *fam* **it's a good j. that ...,** menos mal que ....

jobless ['dʒɒblıs] *adj* parado,-a.

jockey ['dʒɒkı] **I** *n* jinete *m*, jockey *m*. **II** *vi* **to j. for position,** luchar para conseguir una posición aventajada.

jocular ['dʒɒkjʊlər] *adj* jocoso,-a.

jog [dʒɒg] **I** *n* trote *m*. **II** *vtr (memory)* refrescar. **III** *vi Sport* hacer footing; *fig* **to j. along,** *(progress slowly)* avanzar poco a poco; *(manage)* ir tirando.

jogging ['dʒɒgıŋ] *n* footing *m*.

join [dʒɔın] **I** *vtr* **1** juntar; **to j. forces with sb,** unir fuerzas con algn. **2** *(road)* empalmar con; *(river)* desembocar en. **3** *(meet)* reunirse con. **4** *(group)* unirse a; *(institution)* entrar; *(army)* alistarse a. **5** *(party)* afiliarse a; *(club)* hacerse socio,-a de. **II** *vi* **1** unirse. **2** *(roads)* empalmar; *(rivers)* confluir. **3** *(become a member of political party)* afiliarse; *(become member of club)* hacerse socio,-a. **III** *n* juntura *f*. ◆**join in I** *vi* participar, tomar parte; *(debate)* intervenir. **II** *vtr* participar en, tomar parte en. ◆**join up I** *vtr* juntar. **II** *vi (of roads)* unirse; *Mil* alistarse.

joiner ['dʒɔınər] *n GB* carpintero,-a *m,f*.

joinery ['dʒɔınərı] *n* carpintería *f*.

joint [dʒɔınt] **I** *n* **1** juntura *f*, unión *f*; *Tech Anat* articulación *f*; **out of j.,** dislocado,-a. **2** *Culin* corte *m* de carne para asar; *(once roasted)* asado *m*. **3** *sl (nightclub etc)* garito *m*. **4** *sl (drug)* porro *m*. **II** *adj* colectivo,-a; **j. (bank) account,** cuenta conjunta; **j. venture,** empresa conjunta. ◆**jointly** *adv* conjuntamente, en común.

joist [dʒɔıst] *n* vigueta *f*.

joke [dʒəʊk] *n* chiste *m*; *(prank)* broma *f*; **to play a j. on sb,** gastarle una broma a algn; **to tell a j.,** contar un chiste; *fam (person, thing)* hazmerreír *m*, payaso,-a *m,f*. **II** *vi* estar de broma; **you must be joking!,** ¡no hablarás en serio!

joker ['dʒəʊkər] n 1 bromista mf. 2 Cards comodín m.

jolly ['dʒɒlɪ] I adj (jollier, jolliest) alegre. II adv fam (very) muy; **she played j. well**, jugó muy bien.

jolt [dʒəʊlt] I n 1 sacudida f; (pull) tirón m. 2 fig (fright) susto m. II vi moverse a sacudidas. III vtr sacudir.

Jordan ['dʒɔːdən] n 1 (river) Jordán m. 2 (country) Jordania.

joss-stick ['dʒɒstɪk] n varita f de incienso.

jostle ['dʒɒsəl] I vi dar empujones. II vtr dar empujones a.

jot [dʒɒt] n jota f, pizca f; **not a j.**, ni jota. ◆**jot down** vtr apuntar.

jotter ['dʒɒtər] n GB bloc m.

journal ['dʒɜːnəl] n 1 revista f. 2 (diary) diario m. 3 (newspaper) periódico m.

journalism ['dʒɜːnəlɪzəm] n periodismo m.

journalist ['dʒɜːnəlɪst] n periodista mf.

journey ['dʒɜːnɪ] I n viaje m; (distance) trayecto m. II vi fml viajar.

jovial ['dʒəʊvɪəl] adj jovial.

jowl [dʒaʊl] n quijada f.

joy [dʒɔɪ] n alegría f; (pleasure) placer m.

joyful ['dʒɔɪfʊl] adj alegre, contento,-a.

joyous ['dʒɔɪəs] adj lit alegre.

joyride ['dʒɔɪraɪd] n fam paseo m en un coche robado.

joystick ['dʒɔɪstɪk] n Av palanca f de mando; (of video game) joystick m.

JP [dʒeɪ'piː] abbr of **Justice of the Peace**.

Jr abbr of junior.

jubilant ['dʒuːbɪlənt] adj jubiloso,-a.

jubilation [dʒuːbɪ'leɪʃən] n júbilo m.

jubilee ['dʒuːbɪliː] n festejos mpl; **golden j.**, quincuagésimo aniversario.

judge [dʒʌdʒ] I n juez mf, jueza f; (in competition) jurado m. II vtr 1 Jur juzgar. 2 (estimate) considerar. 3 (competition) actuar de juez de. 4 (assess) juzgar. III vi juzgar; **judging from what you say**, a juzgar por lo que dices.

judg(e)ment ['dʒʌdʒmənt] n 1 Jur sentencia f, fallo m; **to pass j.**, dictar sentencia. 2 (opinion) juicio m; **to pass j.**, opinar (on, sobre); **to reserve j.**, no opinar (on, sobre). 3 (ability) buen juicio m. 4 (trial) juicio m.

judicial [dʒuː'dɪʃəl] adj judicial.

judiciary [dʒuː'dɪʃɪərɪ] n magistratura f.

judicious [dʒuː'dɪʃəs] adj fml juicioso,-a.

judo ['dʒuːdəʊ] n judo m.

jug [dʒʌg] n GB jarra f; **milk j.**, jarra de leche.

juggernaut ['dʒʌgənɔːt] n GB camión pesado.

juggle ['dʒʌgəl] vi (perform) hacer juegos malabares (with, con); fig (responsibilities) ajustar.

juggler ['dʒʌglər] n malabarista mf.

juice [dʒuːs] n jugo m; (of citrus fruits) zumo m.

juicy ['dʒuːsɪ] adj (juicier, juiciest) 1 jugoso,-a. 2 fam fig picante.

jukebox ['dʒuːkbɒks] n rocola f.

July [dʒuː'laɪ, dʒə'laɪ] n julio m.

jumble ['dʒʌmbəl] I n revoltijo m; **j. sale**, mercadillo m de caridad. II vtr revolver.

jumbo ['dʒʌmbəʊ] n j. (jet), jumbo m.

jump [dʒʌmp] I n salto m; (sudden increase) subida repentina; **j. leads**, cables mpl de emergencia; **j. suit**, mono m. II vi 1 saltar, dar un salto; fig **to j. to conclusions**, sacar conclusiones precipitadas. 2 fig (start) sobresaltarse. 3 (increase) aumentar de golpe. III vtr saltar; fam fig **to j. the gun**, precipitarse; GB **to j. the queue**, colarse; **to j. the lights**, saltarse el semáforo. ◆**jump at** vtr aceptar sin pensarlo.

jumper ['dʒʌmpər] I n 1 GB (sweater) jersey m. 2 US (dress) pichi m, falda f con peto. 3 US Aut **j. cables**, cables mpl de emergencia.

jumpy ['dʒʌmpɪ] adj (jumpier, jumpiest) fam nervioso,-a.

junction ['dʒʌŋkʃən] n (of roads) cruce m; Rail Elec empalme m.

juncture ['dʒʌŋktʃər] n fml **at this j.**, en esta coyuntura.

June [dʒuːn] n junio m.

jungle ['dʒʌŋgəl] n jungla f, selva f; fig laberinto m; **the concrete j.**, la jungla de asfalto.

junior ['dʒuːnjər] I adj 1 (son of) hijo; **David Hughes j.**, David Hughes hijo. 2 **j. school**, escuela f de EGB (Enseñanza General Básica); **j. team**, equipo m juvenil. 3 (lower in rank) subalterno,-a. II n 1 (person of lower rank) subalterno,-a m,f. 2 (younger person) menor mf.

junk [dʒʌŋk] n 1 fam trastos mpl; **j. food**, comida basura; **j. mail**, propaganda f (por correo); **j. shop**, tienda f de segunda mano. 2 (boat) junco m.

junkie ['dʒʌŋkɪ] n sl yonqui mf.

junta ['dʒʌntə, 'dʒʊntə, US 'hʊntə] n junta f militar.

jurisdiction [dʒʊərɪs'dɪkʃən] n fml jurisdicción f.

juror ['dʒʊərər] n jurado,-a m,f.

jury ['dʒʊərɪ] n jurado m.

just [dʒʌst] I adj (fair) justo,-a; fml (well-founded) justificado,-a. II adv 1 **he had j. arrived**, acababa de llegar. 2 (at this very moment) ahora mismo, en este momento; **he was j. leaving when Rosa arrived**, estaba a punto de salir cuando llegó Rosa; **I'm j. coming!**, ¡ya voy!; **j. as ...**, cuando ..., justo al ...; **j. as I thought**, me lo figuraba. 3 (only) solamente; **j. in case**, por si acaso; **j. a minute!**, ¡un momento! 4 (barely) por poco; **j. caught the bus**, cogí el autobús por los pelos; **j. about**, casi; **j. enough**, justo lo suficiente. 5 *(emphatic)* it's j. fantastic!, ¡es sencillamente fantástico!; **you'll j. have to wait,** tendrás que esperar. 6 *(exactly)* exactamente, justo; **that's j. it!,** ¡precisamente! 7 *(equally)* **j. as fast as,** tan rápido como.

justice ['dʒʌstɪs] *n* 1 justicia *f*; **he was brought to j.,** lo llevaron ante los tribunales; **you didn't do yourself j.,** no diste lo mejor de ti. 2 *US (judge)* juez *mf*; *GB* **J. of the Peace,** juez de paz.

justifiable ['dʒʌstɪfaɪəbəl] *adj* justificable.

justification [dʒʌstɪfɪ'keɪʃən] *n* justifica-

ción *f*.

justified ['dʒʌstɪfaɪd] *adj* **to be j. in doing sth,** tener razón en hacer algo.

justify ['dʒʌstɪfaɪ] *vtr* justificar.

jut [dʒʌt] *vi* sobresalir; **to j. out over,** proyectarse sobre.

juvenile ['dʒuːvənaɪl] **I** *adj* 1 juvenil; **j. court,** tribunal *m* de menores; **j. delinquent,** delincuente *mf* juvenil. 2 *(immature)* infantil. **II** *n* menor *mf*, joven *mf*.

juxtapose [dʒʌkstə'pəuz] *vtr* yuxtaponer.

K

K, k [keɪ] *n (the letter)* K, k *f*.

kaleidoscope [kə'laɪdəskəup] *n* caleidoscopio *m*.

Kampuchea [kæmpu'tʃɪə] *n* Kampuchea.

kangaroo ['kæŋgə'ruː] *n* canguro *m*.

karat ['kærət] *n US* quilate *m*.

karate [kə'rɑːtɪ] *n* kárate *m*.

kebab [kə'bæb] *n Culin* pincho moruno, brocheta *f*.

keel [kiːl] *n* quilla *f*; *fig* **to be on an even k.,** estar en calma. ◆**keel over** *vi fam* desmayarse.

keen [kiːn] *adj* 1 *(eager)* entusiasta. 2 *(intense)* profundo,-a. 3 *(mind, senses)* agudo,-a; *(look)* penetrante; *(blade)* afilado,-a; *(competition)* fuerte.

keep [kiːp] **I** *n* 1 **to earn one's k.,** ganarse el pan. 2 *(tower)* torreón *m*. 3 *fam* **for keeps,** para siempre.
II *vtr (pt & pp kept)* 1 guardar; **to k. one's room tidy,** mantener su cuarto limpio; **to k. sb informed,** tener a algn al corriente; **to k. sth in mind,** tener algo en cuenta. 2 *(not give back)* quedarse con. 3 *(detain)* detener; **to k. sb waiting,** hacer esperar a algn. 4 *(maintain)* mantener; *(animals)* criar. 5 *(the law)* observar; *(a promise)* cumplir. 6 *(a secret)* guardar. 7 *(diary, accounts)* llevar. 8 *(prevent)* **to k. sb from doing sth,** impedir a algn hacer algo. 9 *(own, manage)* tener; *(shop, hotel)* llevar. 10 *(stock)* tener.
III *vi* 1 *(remain)* seguir; **k. still!,** ¡estáte quieto,-a!; **to k. fit,** mantenerse en forma; **to k. going,** seguir adelante; **to k. in touch,** no perder el contacto. 2 *(do frequently)* no dejar de; **she keeps forgetting her keys,** siempre se olvida las llaves. 3 *(food)* conservarse.
◆**keep at** *vi* perseverar en. ◆**keep away** *I* *vtr* mantener a distancia. **II** *vi* mantenerse a distancia. ◆**keep back** *vtr (information)* ocultar, callar; *(money etc)* retener. ◆**keep down** *vtr* **to k. prices down,** mantener los precios bajos. ◆**keep off** *vtr* **k. off the grass,** prohibi-

do pisar la hierba. ◆**keep on** *I* *vtr* 1 *(clothes etc)* no quitarse; **to k. an eye on sth/sb,** vigilar algo/a algn. 2 *(continue to employ)* no despedir a. **II** *vi (continue to do)* seguir. ◆**keep out** *I* *vtr* no dejar pasar. **II** *vi* no entrar; **k. out!,** ¡prohibida la entrada! ◆**keep to** *vtr (subject)* limitarse a; **to k. to one's room,** quedarse en el cuarto; **k. to the point!,** ¡cíñete a la cuestión!; **to k. to the left,** circular por la izquierda. ◆**keep up** *vtr* 1 mantener; **to k. up appearances,** guardar las apariencias. 2 **k. it up!,** ¡sigue así! 3 *(prevent from sleeping)* mantener despierto,-a. ◆**keep up with** *vtr* **to k. up with the times,** estar al día.

keeper ['kiːpər] *n (in zoo)* guarda *mf*; *(in record office)* archivero,-a *m,f*; *(in museum)* conservador,-a *m,f*.

keeping ['kiːpɪŋ] *n* 1 *(care)* cuidado *m*. 2 **in k. with,** en armonía con; **out of k. with,** en desacuerdo con.

keepsake ['kiːpseɪk] *n* recuerdo *m*.

keg [keg] *n* barril *m*.

kennel ['kenəl] *n* caseta *f* para perros; **kennels,** hotel *m sing* de perros.

Kenya ['kenjə, 'kiːnjə] *n* Kenia.

Kenyan ['kenjən, 'kiːnjən] *adj & n* keniano,-a *(m,f)*.

kept [kept] *pt & pp* → **keep.**

kerb [kɜːb] *n* bordillo *m*.

kernel ['kɜːnəl] *n (of fruit, nut)* pepita *f*; *(of wheat)* grano *m*; *fig* meollo *m*.

kerosene, kerosine ['kerəsiːn] *n US* queroseno *m*.

ketchup ['ketʃəp] *n* ketchup *m*, salsa *f* de tomate.

kettle ['ketəl] *n* hervidor *m*; **that's a different k. of fish,** eso es harina de otro costal.

key [kiː] **I** *n* 1 *(for lock)* llave *f*; **k. ring,** llavero *m*. 2 *(to code)* clave *f*. 3 *(of piano, typewriter)* tecla *f*. 4 *Mus* tono *m*. **II** *adj* clave. **III** *n Comput* teclear. ◆**key in** *vtr Comput* introducir.

keyboard ['kiːbɔːd] *n* teclado *m*.

keyed up [ki:d'ʌp] *adj* nervioso,-a.
keyhole ['ki:həʊl] *n* ojo *m* de la cerradura.
keynote ['ki:nəʊt] *n Mus* tónica *f*; *fig* nota *f* dominante.
kg *abbr of* **kilogram(s)**, kilogramo(s) *m* (*pl*), **kg**.
khaki ['ka:kı] *adj & n* caqui (*m*).

kick [kık] I *n* 1 (*from person*) patada *f*, puntapié *m*; (*from horse etc*) coz *f*; (*from gun*) culatazo *m*. 2 *fam* I get a k. out of it, eso me encanta; **to do sth for kicks**, hacer algo por gusto. II *vi* (*animal*) cocear; (*person*) dar patadas; (*gun*) dar un culatazo. III *vtr* dar un puntapié a. ◆**kick off** *vi fam* empezar; *Ftb* sacar. ◆**kick out** *vtr* echar a patadas. ◆**kick up** *vtr fam* (*fuss*) armar.
kick-off ['kıkɒf] *n Ftb* saque *m* inicial.
kid¹ [kıd] *n* 1 *Zool* cabrito *m*; *fig* **to handle sb with k. gloves**, tratar a algn con guante blanco. 2 *fam* niño,-a *m,f*, chiquillo,-a *m,f*; **the kids**, los críos.
kid² [kıd] I *vi fam* tomar el pelo; **no kidding!**, ¡va en serio!. II *vtr* tomar el pelo a; **to k. oneself**, (*fool*) hacerse ilusiones.
kidnap ['kıdnæp] *vtr* secuestrar.
kidnapper ['kıdnæpər] *n* secuestrador,-a *m,f*.
kidnapping ['kıdnæpıŋ] *n* secuestro *m*.
kidney ['kıdnı] *n* riñón *m*.
kill [kıl] *vtr* matar; *fig* **to k. time**, pasar el rato; *fam* **my feet are killing me**, ¡cómo me duelen los pies! ◆**kill off** *vtr* exterminar.
killer ['kılər] *n* asesino,-a *m,f*; **k. whale**, orca *f*.
killing ['kılıŋ] *n* asesinato *m*; *fig* **to make a k.**, forrarse de dinero.
killjoy ['kıldʒɔı] *n* aguafiestas *mf inv*.
kiln [kıln] *n* horno *m*.
kilo ['ki:ləʊ] *n* kilo *m*.
kilogram(me) ['kıləʊɡræm] *n* kilogramo *m*.
kilometre, *US* **kilometer** [kı'lɒmıtər] *n* kilómetro *m*.
kilowatt ['kıləʊwɒt] *n* kilovatio *m*.
kilt [kılt] *n* falda escocesa, kilt *m*.
kin [kın] *n* familiares *mpl*, parientes *mpl*.
kind¹ [kaınd] I *n* tipo *m*, clase *f*; **they are two of a k.**, son tal para cual; **in k.**, (*payment*) en especie; (*treatment*) con la misma moneda. II *adv fam* **k. of**, en cierta manera.
kind² [kaınd] *adj* amable, simpático,-a; *fml* **would you be so k. as to ...?**, ¿me haría usted el favor de ...?
kindergarten ['kındəga:tən] *n* jardín *m* de infancia.
kind-hearted [kaınd'ha:tıd] *adj* bondadoso,-a.
kindle ['kındəl] *vtr* encender.
kindly ['kaındlı] I *adj* (**kindlier, kindliest**)

amable, bondadoso,-a. II *adv fml* (*please*) por favor; **k. remit a cheque**, sírvase enviar cheque; **to look k. on**, aprobar.
kindness ['kaındnıs] *n* bondad *f*, amabilidad *f*.
kindred ['kındrıd] *adj* **k. spirits**, almas gemelas.
kinetic [kı'netık] *adj* cinético,-a.
king [kıŋ] *n* rey *m*; (*draughts*) dama *f*.
kingdom ['kıŋdəm] *n* reino *m*.
kingfisher ['kıŋfıʃər] *n Orn* martín *m* pescador.
king-size ['kıŋsaız] *adj* extralargo,-a.
kink [kıŋk] *n* (*in rope*) coca *f*; (*in hair*) rizo *m*.
kinky ['kıŋkı] *adj* (**kinkier, kinkiest**) *fam* raro,-a; (*sexually*) pervertido,-a.
kiosk ['kıɒsk] *n* quiosco *m*.
kiss [kıs] I *n* beso *m*. II *vtr* besar. III *vi* besarse.
kit [kıt] *n* 1 (*gear*) equipo *m*; *Mil* avíos *mpl*. 2 (*clothing*) ropa *f*. 3 (*toy model*) maqueta *f*. ◆**kit out** *vtr* equipar.
kitchen ['kıtʃın] *n* cocina *f*; **k. sink**, fregadero *m*.
kite [kaıt] *n* 1 (*toy*) cometa *f*. 2 *Orn* milano *m*.
kitten ['kıtən] *n* gatito,-a *m,f*.
kitty ['kıtı] *n* (*money*) fondo *m* común; *Cards* bote *m*.
kiwi ['ki:wi:] *n Bot Orn* kiwi *m*.
km (*pl* **km** *or* **kms**) *abbr of* **kilometre(s)**, **km**.
knack [næk] *n* **to get the k. of doing sth**, cogerle el truquillo a algo.
knapsack ['næpsæk] *n* mochila *f*.
knead [ni:d] *vtr* dar masaje a; (*bread etc*) amasar.
knee [ni:] I *n* rodilla *f*. II *vtr* dar un rodillazo a.
kneecap ['ni:kæp] I *n* rótula *f*. II *vtr* romper la rótula a.
kneel [ni:l] *vi* (*pt & pp* **knelt**) **to k. (down)**, arrodillarse.
knell [nel] *n lit* toque *m* de difuntos.
knelt [nelt] *pt & pp* → **kneel**.
knew [nju:] *pt* → **know**.
knickers ['nıkəz] *npl* bragas *fpl*.
knife [naıf] I *n* (*pl* **knives** [naıvz]) cuchillo *m*. II *vtr* apuñalar, dar una puñalada a.
knight [naıt] I *n Hist* caballero *m*; *Chess* caballo *m*. II *vtr* armar caballero.
knighthood ['naıthʊd] *n* (*rank*) título *m* de caballero.
knit [nıt] I *vtr* (*pt & pp* **knit**) 1 tejer. 2 (*join*) juntar (*together*, -); *fig* **to k. one's brow**, fruncir el ceño. II *vi* 1 tejer, hacer punto. 2 (*bone*) soldarse.
knitting ['nıtıŋ] *n* punto *m*; **k. machine**, máquina *f* de tejer; **k. needle**, aguja *f* de tejer.
knit-wear ['nıtweər] *n* géneros *mpl* de punto.
knob [nɒb] *n* 1 (*of stick*) puño *m*; (*of*

drawer) tirador *m*; (*button*) botón *m*. 2 (*small portion*) trozo *m*.

knock [nɒk] I *n* golpe *m*; *fig* revés *m*. II *vtr* 1 golpear. 2 *fam* (*criticize*) criticar. III *vi* chocar (**against, into**, contra); (*at door*) llamar (**at, a**). ◆**knock down** *vtr* 1 (*demolish*) derribar. 2 *Aut* atropellar. 3 (*price*) rebajar. ◆**knock off** I *vtr* 1 tirar. 2 *fam* (*steal*) birlar. 3 *sl* (*kill*) liquidar. II *vi fam* **they k. off at five**, se piran a las cinco. ◆**knock out** *vtr* 1 (*make unconscious*) dejar sin conocimiento; *Box* poner fuera de combate, derrotar por K.O. 2 (*surprise*) dejar pasmado,-a. ◆**knock over** *vtr* (*cup*) volcar; (*with car*) atropellar.

knocker ['nɒkəʳ] *n* (*on door*) aldaba *f*.

knock-kneed [nɒk'niːd] *adj* patizambo,-a.

knockout ['nɒkaʊt] *n* 1 *Box* K.O. *m*, knock-out *m*. 2 *fam* maravilla *f*.

knot [nɒt] I *n* nudo *m*; (*group*) grupo *m*. II *vtr* anudar.

knotty ['nɒtɪ] *adj* (**knottier, knottiest**) nudoso,-a; *fig* **a k. problem**, un problema espinoso.

know [nəʊ] *vtr & vi* (*pt* **knew**; *pp* **known**) 1 saber; **as far as I k.**, que yo sepa; **she knows how to ski**, sabe esquiar; **to get to k. sth**, enterarse de algo; **to let sb k.**,

avisar al algn. 2 (*be acquainted with*) conocer; **we got to k. each other at the party**, nos conocimos en la fiesta.

know-all ['nəʊɔːl] *n fam* sabelotodo *mf*.

know-how ['nəʊhaʊw] *n fam* conocimiento práctico.

knowing ['nəʊɪŋ] *adj* (*deliberate*) deliberado,-a; **a k. smile**, una sonrisa de complicidad. ◆**knowingly** *adv* (*shrewd*) a sabiendas; (*deliberately*) deliberadamente.

knowledge ['nɒlɪdʒ] *n* 1 conocimiento *m*; **without my k.**, sin saberlo yo. 2 (*learning*) conocimientos *mpl*.

knowledgeable ['nɒlɪdʒəbəl] *adj* erudito,-a; **k. about**, muy entendido,-a en.

known [nəʊn] *adj* conocido,-a.

knuckle ['nʌkəl] *n Anat* nudillo *m*; *Culin* hueso *m*. ◆**knuckle down** *vi fam* ponerse a trabajar en serio.

KO [keɪ'əʊ] *fam abbr of* **knockout**, K.O. *m*.

Koran [kɔː'rɑːn] *n* Corán *m*.

Korea [kə'riːə] *n* Corea.

Korean [kə'riːən] *adj & n* coreano,-a (*m,f*).

Kurd [kɜːd] *n* curdo,-a *m,f*.

Kuwait [kʊ'weɪt] *n* Kuwait.

L

L, l [el] *n* (*the letter*) L, l *f*.

lab [læb] *n fam abbr of* **laboratory**.

label ['leɪbəl] I *n* etiqueta *f*; **record l.**, ≈ casa discográfica. II *vtr* poner etiqueta a.

labor ['leɪbəʳ] *n & vi US* → **labour**.

laboratory [lə'bɒrətərɪ, *US* 'læbrətɔːrɪ] *n* laboratorio *m*.

laborious [lə'bɔːrɪəs] *adj* penoso,-a.

labour ['leɪbəʳ] I *n* 1 (*work*) trabajo *m*; (*task*) tarea *f*. 2 (*workforce*) mano *f* de obra. 3 **labours**, esfuerzos *mpl*. 4 **L**. (**Party**), el Partido Laborista. 5 (*childbirth*) parto *m*; **to be in l.**, estar de parto. II *adj* laboral. III *vi* 1 (*work*) trabajar (duro). 2 (*move with difficulty*) avanzar penosamente. IV *vtr* (*stress, linger on*) machacar; (*a point*) insistir en.

laboured ['leɪbəd] *adj* (*breathing*) fatigoso,-a; (*style*) forzado,-a.

labourer ['leɪbərəʳ] *n* peón *m*; **farm l.**, peón *m* agrícola.

labour-saving ['leɪbəseɪvɪŋ] *adj* **l.-s. devices**, electrodomésticos *mpl*.

labyrinth ['læbərɪnθ] *n* laberinto *m*.

lace [leɪs] I *n* 1 (*fabric*) encaje *m*. 2 **laces**, cordones *mpl*. II *vtr* 1 (*shoes*) atarse los cordones. 2 (*add spirits to*) echar licor (**with, a**). ◆**lace up** *vtr* atar con cordones.

lacerate ['læsəreɪt] *vtr* lacerar.

lack [læk] I *n* falta *f*, escasez *f*; **for l. of**, por falta de. II *vtr* carecer de. III *vi* carecer (**in, de**).

lackadaisical [lækə'deɪzɪkəl] *adj* (*lazy*) perezoso,-a; (*indifferent*) indiferente.

lacklustre, *US* **lackluster** ['læklʌstəʳ] *adj* (*eyes*) apagado,-a; (*performance*) anodino, -a.

laconic [lə'kɒnɪk] *adj* lacónico,-a.

lacquer ['lækəʳ] I *n* laca *f*. II *vtr* (*hair*) poner laca en.

lad [læd] *n fam* chaval *m*, muchacho *m*; *fam* **the lads**, los amigotes; (*stable*) **l.**, mozo *m* de cuadra.

ladder ['lædəʳ] I *n* 1 escalera *f* (de mano); *fig* escala *f*. 2 (*in stocking*) carrera *f*. II *vtr* **I've laddered my stocking**, me he hecho una carrera en las medias.

laden ['leɪdən] *adj* cargado,-a (**with**, de).

ladle ['leɪdəl] *n* cucharón *n*.

lady ['leɪdɪ] *n* señora *f*; *Pol* **First L.**, primera dama; (*WC*) '**Ladies**', 'Señoras'; **ladies and gentlemen!**, ¡señoras y señores!; **L. Brown**, Lady Brown.

ladybird ['leɪdɪbɜːd], *US Canada* **ladybug** ['leɪdɪbʌg] *n* mariquita *f*.

lady-in-waiting [leɪdɪɪn'weɪtɪŋ] *n* dama *f* de honor.

ladylike ['leɪdɪlaɪk] *adj* elegante.

ladyship ['leɪdɪʃɪp] *n* **Her L., Your L.,**

su señoría.

lag [læg] **I** *n* time l., demora *f*. **II** *vi* to l. (behind), quedarse atrás, retrasarse. **III** *vtr Tech* revestir.

lager ['lɑːgər] *n* cerveza rubia.

lagoon [lə'guːn] *n* laguna *f*.

laid [leɪd] *pt & pp* lay.

laid-back [leɪd'bæk] *adj fam* tranquilo,-a.

lain [leɪn] *pp* of lie.

lair [leər] *n* guarida *f*.

lake [leɪk] *n* lago *m*.

lamb [læm] *n* cordero *m*; (meat) carne *f* de cordero; l. chop, chuleta *f* de cordero; l.'s wool, lana *f* de cordero.

lame [leɪm] *adj* 1 cojo,-a. 2 *fig* (excuse) poco convincente; (argument) flojo,-a.

lament [lə'ment] **I** *n Mus* elegia *f*. **II** *vtr* (death) llorar, lamentar. **III** *vi* llorar (for, a), lamentarse (over, de).

lamentable ['læmentəbəl] *adj* lamentable.

laminated ['læmɪneɪtɪd] *adj* (metal) laminado,-a; (glass) inastillable; (paper) plastificado,-a.

lamp [læmp] *n* lámpara *f*; Aut faro *m*.

lampoon [læm'puːn] **I** *n* sátira *f*. **II** *vtr* satirizar.

lamp-post ['læmppəʊst] *n* farola *f*.

lampshade ['læmpʃeɪd] *n* pantalla *f*.

lance [lɑːns] **I** *n* lanza *f*; GB Mil l. corporal, cabo interino; Med lanceta *f*. **II** *vtr Med* abrir con lanceta.

land [lænd] **I** *n* 1 tierra *f*; (soil) suelo *m*; by l., por tierra; farm l., tierras *fpl* de cultivo. 2 (country) país *m*. 3 (property) tierras *fpl*; (estate) finca *f*; piece of l., terreno *m*. **II** *vtr* 1 (plane) hacer aterrizar. 2 (disembark) desembarcar. 3 Fishing pescar. 4 *fam* (obtain) conseguir; (contract) ganar. 5 *fam* she got landed with the responsibility, tuvo que cargar con la responsabilidad. 6 *fam* (blow) asestar. **III** *vi* 1 (plane) aterrizar. 2 (disembark) desembarcar. 3 (after falling) caer (in, sobre). ◆**land up** *vi fam* ir a parar.

landing ['lændɪŋ] *n* 1 (of staircase) rellano *m*. 2 (of plane) aterrizaje *m*; l. strip, pista *f* de aterrizaje. 3 (of passengers) desembarco *m*; l. stage, desembarcadero *m*.

landlady ['lændleɪdɪ] *n* (of flat) dueña *f*, propietaria *f*; (of boarding house) patrona *f*; (of pub) dueña.

landlord ['lændlɔːd] *n* (of flat) dueño *m*, propietario *m*; (of pub) patrón *m*, dueño.

landmark ['lændmɑːk] *n* 1 señal *f*, marca *f*; (well-known place) lugar muy conocido. 2 *fig* hito *m*.

landowner ['lændəʊnər] *n* terrateniente *mf*.

landscape ['lændskeɪp] **I** *n* paisaje *m*. **II** *vtr* ajardinar.

landslide ['lændslaɪd] *n* desprendimiento *m* de tierras; l. victory, victoria arrolladora.

lane [leɪn] *n* (in country) camino *m*; (in town) callejón *m*; (of motorway) carril *m*; Sport calle *f*; Naut ruta *f*.

language ['læŋgwɪdʒ] *n* 1 lenguaje *m*; bad l., palabrotas *fpl*. 2 (of a country) idioma *m*, lengua *f*; l. laboratory, laboratorio *m* de idiomas.

languid ['læŋgwɪd] *adj* lánguido,-a.

languish ['læŋgwɪʃ] *vi* languidecer; (project, plan etc) quedar abandonado,-a; (in prison) pudrirse.

lank [læŋk] *adj* (hair) lacio,-a.

lanky ['læŋkɪ] *adj* (lankier, lankiest) larguirucho,-a.

lantern ['læntən] *n* farol *m*.

lap¹ [læp] *n Anat* regazo *m*.

lap² [læp] **I** *n* (circuit) vuelta *f*; fig etapa *f*. **II** *vtr* (overtake) doblar.

lap³ [læp] **I** *vtr* (pt & pp lapped) (cat) beber a lengüetadas. **II** *vi* (waves) lamer, besar. ◆**lap up** *vtr* 1 (cat) beber a lengüetadas. 2 *fig* (wallow in) disfrutar con; (flattery) recibir con estusiasmo. 3 *fig* (believe) tragar.

lapel [lə'pel] *n* solapa *f*.

Lapland ['læplænd] *n* Laponia *f*.

lapse [læps] **I** *n* 1 (of time) lapso *m*. 2 (error) error *m*, desliz *m*; (of memory) fallo *m*. **II** *vi* 1 (time) pasar, transcurrir. 2 (expire) caducar. 3 (err) cometer un error; (fall back) caer (into, en). 4 Rel perder la fe.

larceny ['lɑːsənɪ] *n* GB latrocinio *m*; US hurto *m*.

larch [lɑːtʃ] *n* alerce *m*.

lard [lɑːd] *n* manteca *f* de cerdo.

larder ['lɑːdər] *n* despensa *f*.

large [lɑːdʒ] **I** *adj* grande; (amount) importante; (extensive) amplio,-a; by and l., por lo general. **II** *n* to be at l., andar suelto,-a; the public at l., el público en general. ◆**largely** *adv* (mainly) en gran parte; (chiefly) principalmente.

large-scale ['lɑːdʒskeɪl] *adj* (project, problem etc) de gran envergadura; (map) a gran escala.

lark¹ [lɑːk] *n Orn* alondra *f*.

lark² [lɑːk] *n fam* (joke) broma *f*; what a l.!, qué risa! ◆**lark about, lark around** *vi fam* hacer el tonto.

larva ['lɑːvə] *n* larva *f*.

laryngitis [lærɪn'dʒaɪtɪs] *n* laringitis *f*.

larynx ['lærɪŋks] *n Anat* laringe *f*.

laser ['leɪzər] *n* láser *m*; l. printer, impresora *f* láser.

lash [læʃ] **I** *n* 1 (eyelash) pestaña *f*. 2 (blow with whip) latigazo *m*. **II** *vtr* 1 (beat) azotar. 2 (rain) caer con fuerza. 3 (tie) atar. ◆**lash out** *vi* 1 (with fists) repartir golpes a diestro y siniestro; (verbally) criticar (at, a). 2 *fam* (spend money) tirar la casa por la ventana.

lass [læs] *n fam* chavala *f*, muchacha *f*.

lasso [læ'suː] **I** *n* lazo *m*. **II** *vtr* coger con el lazo.

last [lɑ:st] I *adj* 1 *(final)* último,-a, final; *fam* the l. straw, el colmo. 2 *(most recent)* último,-a. 3 *(past)* pasado,-a; *(previous)* anterior; l. but one, penúltimo,-a; l. month, el mes pasado; l. night, anoche; the night before l., anteanoche. II *adv* 1 when I l. saw her, la última vez que la vi. 2 *(at the end)* en último lugar; *(in race etc)* último; at (long) l., por fin; l. but not least, el último en orden pero no en importancia. III *n* el último, la última. IV *vi* 1 *(time)* durar; *(hold out)* aguantar. 2 *(be enough for)* llegar, alcanzar. ◆**lastly** *adv* por último, finalmente.

last-ditch ['lɑ:stdɪtʃ] *adj* *(effort, attempt)* último,-a y desesperado,-a.

lasting ['lɑ:stɪŋ] *adj* duradero,-a.

last-minute ['lɑ:stmɪnɪt] *adj* de última hora.

latch [lætʃ] *n* picaporte *m*, pestillo *m*.

late [leɪt] I *adj* 1 *(not on time)* tardío,-a; *(hour)* avanzado,-a; to be five minutes l., llegar con cinco minutos de retraso. 2 *(far on in time)* tarde; in l. autumn, a finales del otoño; in the l. afternoon, a última hora de la tarde; she's in her l. twenties, ronda los treinta. 3 *(dead)* difunto,-a. II *adv* 1 *(not on time)* tarde; to arrive l., llegar tarde. 2 *(far on in time)* tarde; l. at night, a altas horas de la noche; l. in life, a una edad avanzada. 3 as l. as 1950, todavía en 1950; of l., últimamente. ◆**lately** *adv* últimamente, recientemente.

latecomer ['leɪtkʌmər] *n* tardón,-ona *m,f*.

latent ['leɪtənt] *adj* 1 latente. 2 *(desire)* oculto,-a.

later ['leɪtər] I *adj* *(comp of late)* 1 *(subsequent)* más tarde; in her l. novels, en sus novelas posteriores. 2 *(more recent)* más reciente. II *adv* *(comp of late)* más tarde, después; l. on, más adelante, más tarde.

lateral ['lætərəl] *adj* lateral.

latest ['leɪtɪst] I *adj* *(superl of late)* *(most recent)* último,-a, más reciente. II *n* 1 lo último; have you heard the l.?, ¿te enteraste de lo último?; Friday at the l., el viernes a más tardar.

lathe [leɪð] *n Tech* torno *m*.

lather ['lɑ:ðər] I *n* *(of soap)* espuma *f*; *(horse's sweat)* sudor *m*. II *vtr* *(with soap)* enjabonar.

Latin ['lætɪn] I *adj & n* latino,-a *(m,f)*; L. America, América Latina, Latinoamérica *f*; L. American, latinoamericano,-a *(m,f)*. II *n* *(language)* latín *m*.

latitude ['lætɪtjuːd] *n* latitud *f*.

latrine [lə'triːn] *n* letrina *f*.

latter ['lætər] I *adj* 1 *(last)* último,-a. 2 *(second of two)* segundo,-a. II *pron* éste,-a; the former ... the l., aquél ... éste, aquélla ... ésta.

lattice ['lætɪs] *n* enrejado *m*, rejilla *f*.

laudable ['lɔːdəbəl] *adj* loable.

laugh [lɑːf] I *n* risa *f*; *(guffaw)* carcajada *f*; for a l., para divertirse. II *vi* reír, reírse. ◆**laugh at** *vi* to l. at sb/sth, reírse de algn/algo. ◆**laugh about** *vi* to l. about sb/sth, reírse de algn/algo. ◆**laugh off** *vtr* tomar a risa.

laughable ['lɑːfəbəl] *adj* *(situation, suggestion)* ridículo,-a; *(amount, offer)* irrisorio,-a.

laughing-stock ['lɑːfɪŋstɒk] *n* hazmerreír *m inv*.

laughter ['lɑːftər] *n* risa *f*.

launch [lɔːntʃ] I *n* 1 *(vessel)* lancha *f*. 2 → launching. II *vtr* 1 *(attack, rocket, new product)* lanzar. 2 *(ship)* botar. 3 *(film, play)* estrenar. 4 *(company)* fundar. 5 *fig* *(scheme)* iniciar.

launching ['lɔːntʃɪŋ] *n* 1 *(of rocket, new product)* lanzamiento *m*. 2 *(of ship)* botadura *f*. 3 *(of film, play)* estreno *m*. 4 *(of new company)* fundación *f*.

launchpad ['lɔːntʃpæd] *n* plataforma *f* de lanzamiento.

launder ['lɔːndər] *vtr* lavar y planchar; *fig* *(money)* blanquear.

launderette [lɔːndə'ret], *US* **Laundromat®** ['lɔːndrəmæt] *n* lavandería automática.

laundry ['lɔːndrɪ] *n* 1 *(place)* lavandería *f*. 2 *(dirty clothes)* ropa sucia; to do the l., lavar la ropa.

laurel ['lɒrəl] *n* laurel *m*; *fam fig* to rest on one's laurels, dormirse en los laureles.

lava ['lɑːvə] *n* lava *f*.

lavatory ['lævətərɪ] *n* 1 excusado *m*, retrete *m*. 2 *(room)* baño *m*; public l., servicios *mpl*, aseos *mpl*.

lavender ['lævəndər] *n* lavanda *f*.

lavish ['lævɪʃ] I *adj* 1 *(generous)* pródigo, -a. 2 *(abundant)* abundante. 3 *(luxurious)* lujoso,-a. II *vtr* *(praise)* colmar de (on, a); *(care, attention)* prodigarse en (on, con).

law [lɔː] *n* 1 ley *f*; by l., según la ley; l. and order, el orden público; to lay down the l., dictar la ley. 2 *(as subject)* derecho *m*; l. court, tribunal *m* de justicia. 3 *fam* the l., los maderos.

law-abiding ['lɔːəbaɪdɪŋ] *adj* respetuoso,-a de la ley.

lawful ['lɔːful] *adj* legal; *(permitted by law)* lícito,-a; *(legitimate)* legítimo,-a.

lawn [lɔːn] *n* césped *m*; l. tennis, tenis *m* sobre hierba.

lawnmower ['lɔːnməʊər] *n* cortacésped *m*.

lawsuit ['lɔːsjuːt] *n* pleito *m*.

lawyer ['lɔːjər] *n* abogado,-a *m,f*; l.'s office, bufete *m* de abogados.

lax [læks] *adj* *(not strict)* relajado,-a; *(not demanding)* poco exigente; *(careless)* descuidado,-a.

laxative ['læksətɪv] *adj & n* laxante *(m)*.

laxity ['læksɪtɪ] *n* relajamiento *m*; *(careless-*

ness) descuido *m; (negligence)* negligencia
f.

lay¹ [leɪ] *adj* **1** *Rel* laico,-a. **2** *(non-specialist)* lego,-a.

lay² [leɪ] *vtr (pt & pp* **laid)** **1** *(place)* poner, colocar; *(cable, trap)* tender; *(foundations)* echar. **2** *(fire)* preparar; *(table)* poner. **3** *(leave)* dejar. **4** *(eggs)* poner. **5** *vulg* follar. **6** *(set down)* asentar; *(blame)* echar.
◆**lay aside** *vtr* dejar a un lado. ◆**lay by** *vtr (save)* guardar; *(money)* ahorrar. ◆**lay down** *vtr (put down)* poner; *(let go)* dejar; **to l. down one's arms,** rendir las armas. **2** *(plan)* formular. **3** *(establish)* fijar, imponer; *(principles)* sentar. ◆**lay into** *vtr fam (physically)* dar una paliza a; *(verbally)* arremeter contra. ◆**lay off** **I** *vtr* **1** *(dismiss)* despedir. **2** *fam* dejar en paz. **II** *vi* **l. off!,** ¡para ya! ◆**lay on** *vtr* **1** *(provide)* proveer de; *(food)* preparar. **2** *(spread)* aplicar; *fam* **to l. it on (thick),** cargar las tintas. ◆**lay out** *vtr* **1** *(open out)* extender. **2** *(arrange)* disponer. **3** *(ideas)* exponer. **4** *(plan)* trazar. **5** *fam (spend)* gastar. **6** *fam (knock out)* derribar. ◆**lay up** *vtr* **1** *(store)* guardar. **2** *(accumulate)* almacenar. **3** *fam* **to be laid up,** tener que guardar cama.

lay³ [leɪ] *pt of* **lie².**

layabout ['leɪəbaut] *n fam* vago,-a *m,f.*

lay-by ['leɪbaɪ] *n* área *f* de descanso.

layer ['leɪər] *n* capa *f.*

layman ['leɪmən] *n* lego,-a *m,f.*

layout ['leɪaut] *n (arrangement)* disposición *f; (presentation)* presentación *f; Typ* composición *f; (plan)* diseño *m,* trazado *m.*

laze [leɪz] *vi* holgazanear, gandulear.

laziness ['leɪzɪnɪs] *n* pereza *f,* holgazanería *f.*

lazy ['leɪzɪ] *adj* **(lazier, laziest)** perezoso, -a, holgazán,-ana; **at a l. pace,** a paso lento.

lb *abbr of* **pound,** libra *f.*

lead¹ [led] *n* **1** *(metal)* plomo *m.* **2** *(in pencil)* mina *f.*

lead² [li:d] **I** *n* **1** *(front position)* delantera *f; (advantage)* ventaja *f;* **to take the l.,** *(in race)* tomar la delantera; *(score)* adelantarse. **2** *(clue)* pista *f.* **3** *Theat* primer papel *m;* **l. singer,** cantante *mf* principal. **4** *(leash)* correa *f.* **5** *Elec* cable *m.* **II** *vtr (pt & pp* **led)** **1** *(conduct)* llevar, conducir. **2** *(be the leader of)* dirigir, encabezar. **3** *(influence)* llevar a; **this leads me to believe that,** esto me lleva a creer que; **she's easily led,** se deja llevar fácilmente. **4** *(life)* llevar. **III** *vi* **1** *(road)* llevar, conducir **(to,** a). **2** *(go first)* ir delante; *(in race)* llevar la delantera. **3** **to l. to,** llevar a. ◆**lead away** *vtr* llevar. ◆**lead on** **I** *vi (go ahead)* ir adelante. **II** *vtr (deceive)* engañar, timar. ◆**lead up to** *vtr* llevar a.

leaden ['ledən] *adj (sky)* plomizo,-a; *(food)* pesado,-a.

leader ['li:dər] *n* **1** jefe,-a *m,f,* líder *mf; (in race)* líder. **2** *Press* editorial *m,* artículo *m* de fondo.

leadership ['li:dəʃɪp] *n* **1** *(command)* dirección *f,* mando *m; Pol* liderazgo *m.* **2** *(leaders)* dirigentes *mpl,* cúpula *f.*

lead-free ['ledfri:] *adj* sin plomo.

leading ['li:dɪŋ] *adj* **1** *(main)* principal. **2** *(outstanding)* destacado,-a.

leaf [li:f] *n (pl* **leaves** [li:vz]) hoja *f;* **to turn over a new l.,** hacer borrón y cuenta nueva. ◆**leaf through** *vtr* hojear.

leaflet ['li:flɪt] *n* folleto *m.*

league [li:g] *n* **1** *(alliance)* alianza *f; (association)* sociedad *f; fam* **to be in l. with sb,** estar conchabado,-a con algn. **2** *Sport* liga *f.*

leak [li:k] **I** *n* **1** *(hole)* agujero *m; (in roof)* gotera *f.* **2** *(of gas, liquid)* fuga *f,* escape *m; (of information)* filtración *f.* **II** *vi* **1** *(container)* tener un agujero; *(pipe)* tener un escape; *(roof)* gotear; *(boat)* hacer agua. **2** *(gas, liquid)* escaparse; *(information)* filtrarse; *(news)* trascender. **III** *vtr (information)* filtrar **(to,** a).

leaky ['li:kɪ] *adj* **(leakier, leakiest)** *(container)* agujereado,-a; *(roof)* que tiene goteras; *(ship)* que hace agua.

lean¹ [li:n] *adj (meat)* magro,-a; *(person)* flaco,-a; *(harvest)* escaso,-a.

lean² [li:n] **I** *vi (pt & pp* **leaned** or **leant)** **1** inclinarse. **2** **to l. on/against,** apoyarse en/contra; *fig* **to l. on sb,** *(pressurize)* presionar a algn; *(depend)* depender de algn. **II** *vtr* apoyar **(on,** en). ◆**lean back** *vi* reclinarse. ◆**lean forward** *vi* inclinarse hacia delante. ◆**lean out** *vi* asomarse. ◆**lean over** *vi* inclinarse.

leaning ['li:nɪŋ] **I** *adj* inclinado,-a. **II** *n fig (tendency)* inclinación *f,* tendencia *f.*

leant [lent] *pt & pp* → **lean².**

lean-to ['li:ntu:] *n (hut)* cobertizo *m.*

leap [li:p] **I** *n (jump)* salto *m; fig* paso *m;* **l. year,** año bisiesto. **II** *vi (pt & pp* **leaped** or **leapt)** saltar; *fig* **her heart leapt,** su corazón dio un vuelco. ◆**leap at** *vtr (chance)* no dejar escapar.

leapfrog ['li:pfrɒg] *n* pídola *f.*

leapt [lept] *pt & pp* → **leap.**

learn [lɜ:n] **I** *vtr (pt & pp* **learned** or **learnt)** **1** aprender; **to l. (how) to ski,** aprender a esquiar. **2** **to l. that,** enterarse de que. **II** *vi* **1** aprender. **2** **to l. about** o **of,** *(find out)* enterarse de.

learned ['lɜ:nɪd] *adj* erudito,-a.

learner ['lɜ:nər] *n (beginner)* principiante *mf;* **l. driver,** aprendiz,-a *m,f* de conductor.

learning ['lɜ:nɪŋ] *n (knowledge)* conocimientos *mpl; (erudition)* saber *m.*

learnt [lɜ:nt] *pt & pp* → **learn.**

lease [li:s] **I** n contrato m de arrendamiento; fig **to give sb a new l. of life**, dar nueva vida a algn. **II** vtr arrendar.

leasehold ['li:shəuld] **I** n derechos mpl de arrendamiento. **II** adj (property) arrendado,-a.

leash [li:ʃ] n correa f.

least [li:st] (superl of little) **I** adj menor, mínimo,-a; **he has the l. time**, él es quien menos tiempo tiene. **II** adv menos; **l. of all him**, él menos que nadie. **III** n lo menos; **at l.**, por lo menos, al menos; **not in the l.!**, ¡en absoluto!; **to say the l.**, por no decir más.

leather ['leðər] **I** n piel f, cuero m. **II** adj de piel.

leave¹ [li:v] **I** vtr (pt & pp **left**) **1** dejar; (go away from) abandonar; (go out of) salir de. **2 l. him alone!**, ¡déjale en paz!; fam **l. it to me**, yo me encargo. **3** (bequeath) legar. **4** (forget) dejarse, olvidarse. **5 I have two biscuits left**, me quedan dos galletas. **6 to be left over**, sobrar. **II** vi (go away) irse, marcharse; (go out) salir; **the train leaves in five minutes**, el tren sale dentro de cinco minutos. ◆**leave behind** vtr **1** dejar atrás. **2** (forget) olvidarse. ◆**leave on** vtr **1** (clothes) dejar puesto,-a. **2** (lights, radio) dejar encendido,-a. ◆**leave out** vtr (omit) omitir; fig **to feel left out**, sentirse excluido,-a.

leave² [li:v] n **1** (permission) permiso m. **2** (time off) vacaciones fpl; Mil **on l.**, de permiso; **l. of absence**, excedencia f. **3 to take one's l. of sb**, despedirse de algn.

leaves [li:vz] npl → leaf.

Lebanon ['lebənən] n (the) L., (el) Líbano.

lecherous ['letʃərəs] adj lascivo,-a.

lecture ['lektʃər] **I** n **1** conferencia f; Univ clase f; **to give a l.**, dar una conferencia (on, sobre); **l. hall**, **l. room**, **l. theatre**, sala f de conferencias; Univ aula f. **2** (rebuke) sermón m. **II** vi dar una conferencia; Univ dar clases. **III** vtr (reproach) sermonear.

lecturer ['lektʃərər] n conferenciante mf; Univ profesor,-a m,f.

led [led] pt & pp → lead².

ledge [ledʒ] n **1** (shelf) repisa f; (of window) alféizar m. **2** (on mountain) saliente m.

ledger ['ledʒər] n libro m mayor.

lee [li:] n **1** Naut sotavento m. **2** fig abrigo m.

leech [li:tʃ] n sanguijuela f.

leek [li:k] n puerro m.

leer [lɪər] vi mirar con lascivia.

leeway ['li:weɪ] n libertad f; **this gives me a certain amount of l.**, esto me da cierto margen de libertad.

left¹ [left] **I** adj izquierdo,-a; Pol **l. wing**,

izquierda f. **II** adv a la izquierda. **III** n **1** izquierda f; **on the l.**, a mano izquierda. **2** Pol **to be on the l.**, ser de izquierdas.

left² [left] pt & pp → leave¹.

left-hand ['lefthænd] adj **l.-h. drive**, con el volante a la izquierda; **on the l.-h. side**, a mano izquierda.

left-handed [left'hændɪd] adj zurdo,-a.

left-luggage [left'lʌgɪdʒ] n GB **l.-l. office**, consigna f.

leftovers ['leftəʊvəz] npl sobras fpl.

left-wing ['leftwɪŋ] adj de izquierdas, izquierdista.

leg [leg] n **1** (of person) pierna f; (of animal, table) pata f; Culin (of lamb) pierna f; (of trousers) pernera f. **2** (stage) etapa f.

legacy ['legəsɪ] n herencia f, legado m.

legal ['li:gəl] adj **1** legal; (permitted by law) lícito,-a; **l. tender**, moneda f de curso legal. **2** (relating to the law) jurídico,-a; **l. aid**, asesoramiento jurídico gratuito; **l. dispute**, contencioso m; US **l. holiday**, fiesta f nacional. ◆**legally** adv legalmente.

legalize ['li:gəlaɪz] vtr legalizar.

legend ['ledʒənd] n leyenda f.

legendary ['ledʒəndərɪ] adj legendario,-a.

leggings ['legɪŋz] npl polainas fpl.

legible ['ledʒəbəl] adj legible.

legion ['li:dʒən] n legión f.

legislation [ledʒɪs'leɪʃən] n legislación f.

legislative ['ledʒɪslətɪv] adj legislativo,-a.

legislator ['ledʒɪsleɪtər] n legislador,-a m,f.

legislature ['ledʒɪsleɪtʃər] n asamblea legislativa.

legitimate [lɪ'dʒɪtɪmɪt] adj legítimo,-a.

legroom ['legru:m] n espacio m para las piernas.

leisure ['leʒər, US 'li:ʒər] n ocio m, tiempo m libre; **at l.**, con calma; **do it at your l.**, hazlo cuando tengas tiempo; **l. activities**, pasatiempos mpl; **l. centre**, centro recreativo.

leisurely ['leʒəlɪ, US 'li:ʒəlɪ] adj (unhurried) tranquilo,-a; (slow) lento,-a.

lemon ['lemən] n limón m; **l. curd**, crema f de limón; **l. juice**, zumo m de limón; **l. tea**, té m con limón.

lemonade [lemə'neɪd] n limonada f.

lend [lend] vtr (pt & pp **lent**) prestar; **to l. oneself or itself to sth**, prestarse a or para algo.

lending ['lendɪŋ] n **l. library**, biblioteca pública.

length [leŋkθ, leŋθ] n **1** longitud f, largo m; **it is five metres in l.**, tiene cinco metros de largo. **2** (duration) duración f. **3** (of string) trozo m; (of cloth) retal m. **4** (of swimming pool) largo m; fig **to go to any lengths to achieve sth**, hacer lo que sea para conseguir algo. **5 at l.**, (finally) finalmente; (in depth) a fondo.

lengthen ['leŋkθən, 'leŋθən] **I** vtr alargar;

(lifetime) prolongar. II *vi* alargarse; *(lifetime)* prolongarse.

lengthways ['leŋθweɪz] *adv* a lo largo.

lengthy ['leŋkθɪ, 'leŋθɪ] *adj* (**lengthier, lengthiest**) largo,-a; *(film, illness)* de larga duración; *(meeting, discussion)* prolongado,-a.

lenient ['liːnɪənt] *adj* indulgente.

lens [lenz] *n (of eye)* cristalino *m*; *(of spectacles)* lente *f*; *Phot* objetivo *m*.

Lent [lent] *n* Cuaresma *f*.

lent [lent] *pt & pp →* **lend**.

lentil ['lentɪl] *n* lenteja *f*.

Leo ['liːəʊ] *n* Leo *m*.

leopard ['lepəd] *n* leopardo *m*.

leotard ['liːətɑːd] *n* leotardo *m*.

leper ['lepər] *n* leproso,-a *m,f*.

leprosy ['leprəsɪ] *n* lepra *f*.

lesbian ['lezbɪən] *adj & n* lesbiana *(f)*.

less [les] I *adj (comp of little)* menos. II *pron* menos; **the l. said about it, the better**, cuanto menos se hable de eso mejor. III *adv* menos; **l. and l.**, cada vez menos; **still l.**, menos aún. IV *prep* menos; **a year l. two days**, un año menos dos días.

lessen ['lesən] *vtr & vi* disminuir.

lesser ['lesər] *adj* menor; **to a l. extent**, en menor grado.

lesson ['lesən] *n* 1 clase *f*; *(in book)* lección *f*; **Spanish lessons**, clases de español. 2 *Rel* lectura *f*.

lest [lest] *conj fml* 1 para (que) no; **l. we forget**, para que no lo olvidemos. 2 *(for fear that)* por miedo a que.

let [let] I *vtr (pt & pp* **let***)* 1 dejar, permitir; **to l. go of sth**, soltar algo; **to l. sb know**, avisar a algn; *fig* **to l. oneself go**, dejarse ir. 2 *(rent out)* alquilar; **'to l.'**, 'se alquila'. 3 **l. alone**, ni mucho menos. II *v aux* **l. him wait**, que espere; **l. me go!**, ¡suéltame!; **l.'s go!**, ¡vamos!, ¡vámonos!; **l.'s see**, a ver. ◆**let down** *vtr* 1 *(lower)* bajar; *(lengthen)* alargar; *fam fig* **to l. one's hair down**, desmelenarse. 2 *(deflate)* desinflar. 3 *(fail)* fallar, defraudar. ◆**let in** *vtr* 1 *(admit)* dejar entrar. 2 **to l. oneself in for**, meterse en. ◆**let off** *vtr* 1 *(bomb)* hacer explotar; *(fireworks)* hacer estallar. 2 *(liquid, air)* soltar. 3 *fam* **to l. sb off**, *(pardon)* perdonar. ◆**let on** *vi fam* **don't l. on**, *(reveal information)* no se lo digas. ◆**let out** *vtr* 1 *(release)* soltar; *(news)* divulgar; *(secret)* revelar. 2 *(air, water)* dejar salir. 3 *(cry)* soltar. 4 *Sew* ensanchar. ◆**let up** *vi* cesar, parar.

letdown ['letdaʊn] *n* decepción *f*.

lethal ['liːθəl] *adj* letal.

lethargic [lɪ'θɑːdʒɪk] *adj* aletargado,-a.

letter ['letər] *n* 1 *(of alphabet)* letra *f*; *fig* **to the l.**, al pie de la letra. 2 *(written message)* carta *f*; *GB* **l. box**, buzón *m*; *Com* **l. of credit**, carta de crédito.

letterhead ['letəhed] *n* membrete *m*.

lettering ['letərɪŋ] *n* rótulo *m*.

lettuce ['letɪs] *n* lechuga *f*.

let-up ['letʌp] *n fam* descanso *m*, respiro *m*.

leukaemia, *US* **leukemia** [luː'kiːmɪə] *n* leucemia *f*.

level ['levəl] I *adj* 1 *(flat)* llano,-a; *(even)* nivelado,-a; *(equal)* igual, parejo,-a; **a l. spoonful of**, una cucharada rasa de; **to be l. with**, estar a nivel de; *GB* **l. crossing**, paso *m* a nivel. 2 *(steady)* estable; *(tone)* uniforme. II *vtr* 1 nivelar, allanar. 2 *(building)* arrasar. 3 *(stare, criticism)* dirigir. III *n* nivel *m*; **to be on a l. with**, estar al mismo nivel que; *fam* **to be on the l.**, *(be honest)* ser de fiar; *(be truthful)* decir la verdad. ◆**level off, level out** *vi* estabilizarse. ◆**level with** *vtr fam* ser franco,-a con.

level-headed [levəl'hedɪd] *adj* sensato,-a.

lever ['liːvər] I *n* palanca *f*. II *vtr* apalancar; **to l. sth out**, sacar algo con palanca.

leverage ['liːvərɪdʒ] *n fig* influencia *f*.

levy ['levɪ] I *vtr (tax)* recaudar; *(fine)* imponer. II *n (of tax)* recaudación *f*; *(of fine)* imposición *f*.

lewd [luːd] *adj (person)* lascivo,-a; *(story)* obsceno,-a.

liability [laɪə'bɪlɪtɪ] *n* 1 *Jur* responsabilidad *f*. 2 *(handicap)* estorbo *m*. 3 *Fin* **liabilities**, pasivo *m sing*.

liable ['laɪəbəl] *adj* 1 *Jur* responsable; *(susceptible)* sujeto,-a; **to be l. for**, ser responsable de. 2 **to be l. to do sth**, ser propenso,-a a hacer algo; **it's l. to happen**, es muy probable que *(así)* suceda.

liaise [lɪ'eɪz] *vi* comunicarse *(with*, con).

liaison [lɪ'eɪzɒn] *n* 1 enlace *m*; **l. officer**, oficial *mf* de enlace. 2 *(love affair)* amorío *m*.

liar ['laɪər] *n* mentiroso,-a *m,f*, embustero,-a *m,f*.

libel ['laɪbəl] I *n* libelo *m*. II *vtr* difamar, calumniar.

liberal ['lɪbərəl] I *adj* 1 liberal; **L. Party**, Partido *m* Liberal. 2 *(abundant)* abundante. II *n Pol* **L.**, liberal *mf*.

liberate ['lɪbəreɪt] *vtr* liberar; *(prisoner etc)* poner en libertad; **liberated woman**, mujer liberada.

liberation [lɪbə'reɪʃən] *n* liberación *f*.

liberty ['lɪbətɪ] *n* libertad *f*; **to be at l. to say sth**, ser libre de decir algo; **to take liberties**, tomarse libertades.

Libra ['liːbrə] *n* Libra *f*.

librarian [laɪ'breərɪən] *n* bibliotecario,-a *m,f*.

library ['laɪbrərɪ] *n* biblioteca *f*.

Libya ['lɪbɪə] *n* Libia.

Libyan ['lɪbɪən] *adj & n* libio,-a *(m,f)*.

lice [laɪs] *npl →* **louse**.

licence ['laɪsəns] *n* 1 *(permit)* licencia *f*, permiso *m*; *Aut* **l. number**, matrícula *f*. 2

(freedom) libertad *f*; *(excessive freedom)* libertinaje *m*.

license ['laɪsəns] I *vtr* dar licencia a, autorizar. II *n US* → **licence**.

licensed ['laɪsənst] *adj* autorizado,-a; **l. premises**, local autorizado para la venta de bebidas alcohólicas.

licentious [laɪ'senʃəs] *adj* licencioso,-a.

lichen ['laɪkən, 'lɪtʃən] *n* liquen *m*.

lick [lɪk] I *vtr* lamer; **to l. one's lips**, relamerse. II *n* lamedura *f*; *fam* **a l. of paint**, una mano de pintura.

licorice ['lɪkərɪs, 'lɪkərɪʃ] *n US* → **liquorice**.

lid [lɪd] *n* 1 *(cover)* tapa *f*. 2 *(of eye)* párpado *m*.

lie1 [laɪ] I *vi* mentir. II *n* mentira *f*.

lie2 [laɪ] I *vi* (*pt* **lay**; *pp* **lain**) 1 *(act)* echarse, acostarse. 2 *(state)* estar echado,-a, estar acostado,-a. *(be buried)* yacer. 2 *(be situated)* encontrarse, hallarse; **the valley lay before us**, el valle se extendía ante nosotros. 3 *(remain)* quedarse. II *n* *(position)* situación *f*; *(direction)* orientación *f*. ◆**lie about, lie around** *vi* *(person)* estar tumbado,-a; *(things)* estar tirado,-a. ◆**lie down** *vi* acostarse, echarse.

lie-in ['laɪɪn] *n fam* **to have a l.-in**, levantarse tarde.

lieu [ljuː, luː] *n* **in l. of**, en lugar de.

lieutenant [lef'tenənt, *US* luː'tenənt] *n* 1 *Mil* teniente *m*. 2 *(non-military)* lugarteniente *m*.

life [laɪf] *n* (*pl* **lives** [laɪvz]) 1 vida *f*; **to come to l.**, cobrar vida; **to take one's own l.**, suicidarse; *fam* **how's l.?**, ¿qué tal?; **l. belt**, cinturón *m* salvavidas; **l. imprisonment**, cadena perpetua; **l. insurance**, seguro *m* de vida; **l. jacket**, chaleco *m* salvavidas; **l. style**, estilo *m* de vida; **l. story**, biografía *f*. 2 *(liveliness)* vitalidad *f*; *fam fig* **to be the l. (and soul) of the party**, ser el alma de la fiesta.

lifeboat ['laɪfbəʊt] *n* *(on ship)* bote *m* salvavidas; *(on shore)* lancha *f* de socorro.

lifeguard ['laɪfgɑːd] *n* socorrista *mf*.

lifeless ['laɪflɪs] *adj* sin vida.

lifelike ['laɪflaɪk] *adj* natural; *(portrait)* fiel.

lifeline ['laɪflaɪn] *n fig* cordón *m* umbilical.

lifelong ['laɪflɒŋ] *adj* de toda la vida.

life-size(d) ['laɪfsaɪz(d)] *adj* (de) tamaño natural.

lifetime ['laɪftaɪm] *n* vida *f*; **in his l.**, durante su vida; **it's the chance of a l.**, es una ocasión única.

lift [lɪft] I *vtr* 1 levantar; *(head etc)* alzar; *(pick up)* coger. 2 *(troops)* transportar. 3 *fam* *(steal)* birlar; *(plagiarize)* plagiar. II *vi* *(clouds, mist)* disiparse. III *n* 1 *GB* *(elevator)* ascensor *m*. 2 **to give sb a l.**, llevar a algn en coche. 3 *fig* *(boost)* estímulo *m*. ◆**lift up** *vtr* levantar, alzar.

lift-off ['lɪftɒf] *n* despegue *m*.

light1 [laɪt] I *n* 1 luz *f*; *fig* **in the l. of**, en vista de; *fig* **to bring sth to l.**, sacar algo a la luz; *fig* **to come to l.**, salir a la luz; **l. bulb**, bombilla *f*; **l. meter**, fotómetro *m*; **l. pen**, lápiz óptico; **l. year**, año *m* luz. 2 *(lamp)* luz *f*, lámpara *f*; *(traffic light)* semáforo *m*; *(headlight)* faro *m*. 3 *(flame)* lumbre *f*; **to set l. to sth**, prender fuego a algo; *fam* **have you got a l.?**, ¿tiene fuego? II *vtr* (*pt* & *pp* **lighted** or **lit**) 1 *(illuminate)* iluminar, alumbrar. 2 *(ignite)* encender. III *adj* claro,-a; *(hair)* rubio,-a. ◆**light up** I *vtr* iluminar, alumbrar. II *vi* 1 iluminarse. 2 *fam* encender un cigarrillo.

light2 [laɪt] I *adj* ligero,-a; *(rain)* fino,-a; *(breeze)* suave; *fig* *(sentence etc)* leve; *fig* **to make l. of sth**, dar poca importancia a algo. II *adv* **to travel l.**, ir ligero,-a de equipaje. ◆**lightly** *adv* 1 ligeramente. 2 **to get off l.**, salir casi indemne.

lighten1 ['laɪtən] I *vtr* 1 *(colour)* aclarar. 2 *(illuminate)* iluminar. II *vi* aclararse.

lighten2 ['laɪtən] *vtr* 1 *(weight)* aligerar. 2 *fig* *(mitigate)* aliviar; *(heart)* alegrar.

lighter1 ['laɪtər] *n* *(cigarette)* l., encendedor *m*, mechero *m*.

light-headed [laɪt'hedɪd] *adj* 1 *(dizzy)* mareado,-a. 2 *(frivolous)* frívolo,-a.

light-hearted [laɪt'hɑːtɪd] *adj* alegre.

lighthouse ['laɪthaʊs] *n* faro *m*.

lighting ['laɪtɪŋ] *n* 1 *(act)* iluminación *f*. 2 *(system)* alumbrado *m*.

lightness1 ['laɪtnɪs] *n* luminosidad *f*, claridad *f*.

lightness2 ['laɪtnɪs] *n* *(of weight)* ligereza *f*.

lightning ['laɪtnɪŋ] *n* *(flash)* relámpago *m*; *(stroke)* rayo *m*; **l. conductor**, **l. rod**, pararrayos *m inv*; **l. strike**, huelga *f* relámpago.

lightweight ['laɪtweɪt] *adj* *(suit etc)* ligero,-a; *Box* de peso ligero; *fig* *(person)* light.

like1 [laɪk] I *adj* 1 parecido,-a, semejante. 2 *(equal)* igual. II *adv* (as) **l. as not**, a lo mejor. III *prep* 1 *(similar to)* como, parecido,-a a; *(the same as)* igual que; **it's not l. her to do that**, no es propio de ella hacer eso; **I've never seen anything l. it**, nunca he visto cosa igual; **l. that**, así; **people l. that**, ese tipo de gente; **what's he l.?**, ¿cómo es?; *fam* **that's more l. it!**, ¡así se hace! 2 **to feel l.**, *(want)* tener ganas de; **I feel l. a change**, me apetece un cambio. IV *n* **brushes, combs and the l.**, cepillos, peines y cosas por el estilo.

like2 [laɪk] I *vtr* 1 **do you l. chocolate?**, ¿te gusta el chocolate?; **he likes dancing**, le gusta bailar; **she likes children**, le gustan los niños. 2 *(want)* querer; **whether you l. it or not**, quieras o no

(quieras); **would you l. a drink?**, ¿te apetece tomar algo? II *vi* querer, gustar; **as you l.**, como quieras; **whenever you l.**, cuando quieras. III *n* gusto *m*.
likeable ['laɪkəbəl] *adj* simpático,-a.
likelihood ['laɪklɪhʊd] *n* probabilidad *f*.
likely ['laɪklɪ] I *adj* (**likelier**, **likeliest**) probable; **he's l. to cause trouble**, es probable que cause problemas; **where are you l. to be this afternoon?**, ¿dónde piensas estar esta tarde? II *adv* probablemente; **not l.!**, ¡ni hablar!
likeness ['laɪknɪs] *n* 1 semejanza *f*, parecido *m*. 2 (*portrait*) retrato *m*.
likewise ['laɪkwaɪz] *adv* 1 (*also*) también, asimismo. 2 (*the same*) lo mismo, igual.
liking ['laɪkɪŋ] *n* (*for thing*) afición *f*; (*for person*) simpatía *f*; (*for friend*) cariño *m*; **to take a l. to sth**, cogerle el gusto a algo; **to take a l. to sb**, coger cariño a algn.
lilac ['laɪlək] I *n* 1 *Bot* lila *f*. 2 (*colour*) lila *m*. II *adj* lila, de color lila.
lilt [lɪlt] *n* melodía *f*.
lily ['lɪlɪ] *n* lirio *m*, azucena *f*; **l. of the valley**, lirio de los valles.
limb [lɪm] *n* miembro *m*; *fig* **to be out on a l.**, (*in danger*) estar en peligro; *GB* (*isolated*) estar aislado,-a.
limber up ['lɪmbər] *vi Sport* entrar en calor; *fig* prepararse (**for**, para).
limbo ['lɪmbəʊ] *n* limbo *m*; *fig* olvido *m*; **to be in l.**, caer en el olvido.
lime¹ [laɪm] *n Chem* cal *f*.
lime² [laɪm] *n* (*fruit*) lima *f*; (*tree*) limero *m*.
limelight ['laɪmlaɪt] *n fig* **to be in the l.**, estar en el candelero.
limerick ['lɪmərɪk] *n* quintilla humorística.
limestone ['laɪmstəʊn] *n* piedra caliza.
limit ['lɪmɪt] I *n* límite *m*; (*maximum*) máximo *m*; (*minimum*) mínimo *m*. II *vtr* (*restrict*) limitar.
limitation [lɪmɪ'teɪʃən] *n* limitación *f*.
limited ['lɪmɪtɪd] *adj* limitado,-a; **l. edition**, edición limitada; *GB* **l. (liability) company**, sociedad anónima.
limitless ['lɪmɪtlɪs] *adj* ilimitado,-a.
limousine ['lɪməzɪːn, lɪmə'zɪːn] *n* limusina *f*.
limp¹ [lɪmp] I *vi* cojear. II *n* cojera *f*.
limp² [lɪmp] *adj* 1 (*floppy*) flojo,-a. 2 (*weak*) débil.
limpet ['lɪmpɪt] *n* lapa *f*.
linchpin ['lɪntʃpɪn] *n Tech* pezonera *f*; *fig* eje *m*.
line¹ [laɪn] *n* 1 línea *f*; (*straight*) raya *f*; **to be on the right lines**, ir por buen camino; *US* **State l.**, límite *m* de un Estado. 2 (*of writing*) renglón *m*; (*of poetry*) verso *m*; *Theat* **to learn one's lines**, aprenderse el papel. 3 (*row*) fila *f*; (*of trees*) hilera *f*; *US* (*queue*) cola *f*; *Mil* **l. of fire**, línea *f*

de fuego; *Mil* **to be in the front l.**, estar en primera línea; *fig* **to be in l.**, coincidir (**with**, con); *fam* **to bring sb into l.**, pararle los pies a algn; *fam* **to step out of l.**, salirse de las reglas; *fig* **sth along these lines**, algo por el estilo. 4 (*rope*) cuerda *f*; (*wire*) cable *m*; **fishing l.**, sedal *m*. 5 *Tel* línea *f*; **hold the l.!**, ¡no cuelgue! 6 *GB Rail* vía *f*. 7 (*range of goods*) surtido *m*; **a new l.**, una nueva línea. 8 (*of descent*) linaje *m*.
line² [laɪn] I *vtr* (*pipe etc*) revestir; *Sew* forrar; *fam* **to l. one's pockets**, forrarse. ◆**line up** I *vtr* 1 (*arrange in rows*) poner en fila. 2 **he has something lined up for this evening**, tiene algo organizado para esta noche. II *vi* (*people*) ponerse en fila; (*troops*) formar; (*in queue*) hacer cola.
linear ['lɪnɪər] *adj* lineal.
lined [laɪnd] *adj* 1 (*paper*) rayado,-a; (*face*) arrugado,-a. 2 (*garment*) forrado,-a.
linen ['lɪnɪn] *n* 1 (*cloth*) lino *m*. 2 (*clothes*) ropa *f*; (*sheets etc*) ropa blanca.
liner ['laɪnər] *n* transatlántico *m*.
linesman ['laɪnzmən] *n Sport* juez *m* de línea.
line-up ['laɪnʌp] *n Sport* alineación *f*.
linger ['lɪŋgər] *vi* tardar; (*dawdle*) rezagarse; (*smell, doubt*) persistir; *fig* (*memory*) perdurar.
lingerie ['læŋʒəriː] *n fml* ropa *f* interior (de mujer).
lingering ['lɪŋgərɪŋ] *adj* (*doubt*) persistente; (*look*) fijo,-a.
lingo ['lɪŋgəʊ] *n* (*pl* **lingoes**) *fam* 1 (*language*) lengua *f*, idioma *m*. 2 (*jargon*) jerga *f*.
linguist ['lɪŋgwɪst] *n* lingüista *mf*; **he's a good l.**, se le dan bien los idiomas.
linguistic [lɪŋ'gwɪstɪk] *adj* lingüístico,-a.
linguistics [lɪŋ'gwɪstɪks] *n* lingüística *f*.
lining ['laɪnɪŋ] *n* forro *m*.
link [lɪŋk] I *n* 1 (*of chain*) eslabón *m*. 2 (*connection*) conexión *f*; *fig* vínculo *m*; *rail* **l.**, enlace ferroviario. 3 **links**, campo *m sing* de golf. II *vtr* unir. ◆**link up** *vi* unirse; (*meet*) encontrarse; (*spaceships*) acoplarse.
link-up ['lɪŋkʌp] *n Tel TV* conexión *f*; (*meeting*) encuentro *m*; (*of spaceships*) acoplamiento *m*.
lino ['laɪnəʊ] *n fam* linóleo *m*.
linoleum [lɪ'nəʊlɪəm] *n* linóleo *m*, linóleum *m*.
lion ['laɪən] *n* león *m*.
lioness ['laɪənɪs] *n* leona *f*.
lip [lɪp] *n* 1 labio *m*. 2 (*of jug*) pico *m*.
lip-read ['lɪpriːd] *vtr & vi* leer en los labios.
lip-service ['lɪpsɜːvɪs] *n* palabrería *f*.
lipstick ['lɪpstɪk] *n* lápiz *m* de labios.
liqueur [lɪ'kjʊər] *n* licor *m*.
liquid ['lɪkwɪd] *adj & n* líquido,-a (*m*).
liquidate ['lɪkwɪdeɪt] *vtr* liquidar.

liquidation |lɪkwɪ'deɪʃən| n liquidación f; **to go into l.**, entrar en liquidación.
liquidize ['lɪkwɪdaɪz] vtr licuar.
liquidizer ['lɪkwɪdaɪzə'] n licuadora f.
liquor ['lɪkə'] n US alcohol m, bebidas alcohólicas.
liquorice ['lɪkərɪs, 'lɪkərɪʃ] n regaliz m.
Lisbon ['lɪzbən] n Lisboa.
lisp |lɪsp| I n ceceo m. II vi cecear.
list¹ |lɪst| I n lista f; (catalogue) catálogo m. II vtr (make a list of) hacer una lista de; (put on a list) poner en una lista; **it is not listed**, no figura en la lista.
list² |lɪst| Naut I n escora f. II vi escorar.
listen ['lɪsən] vi escuchar; (pay attention) prestar atención. ◆**listen out for** vtr estar atento,-a a.
listener ['lɪsənə'] n oyente mf.
listless ['lɪstlɪs] adj apático,-a.
lit |lɪt| pt & pp → **light¹**.
liter ['liːtə'] n US → **litre**.
literacy ['lɪtərəsɪ] n alfabetización f.
literal ['lɪtərəl] adj literal. ◆**literally** adv literalmente.
literary ['lɪtərərɪ] adj literario,-a.
literate ['lɪtərɪt] adj alfabetizado,-a.
literature ['lɪtərɪtʃə'] n 1 literatura f. 2 fam (documentation) folleto informativo.
lithe |laɪð| adj fml ágil.
Lithuania [lɪθjʊ'eɪnɪə] n Lituania.
Lithuanian [lɪθjʊ'eɪnɪən] I adj lituano,-a. II n (person) lituano,-a m,f; (language) lituano m.
litigation [lɪtɪ'geɪʃən] n litigio m.
litmus ['lɪtməs] n fig **l. test**, prueba f contundente.
litre ['liːtə'] n litro m.
litter ['lɪtə'] I n 1 (rubbish) basura f; (papers) papeles mpl; **l. bin**, papelera f. 2 (offspring) camada f. 3 arch (stretcher) camilla f. II vtr ensuciar.
littered ['lɪtəd] adj cubierto,-a (with, de).
little ['lɪtəl] I adj 1 pequeño,-a; **a l. dog**, un perrito; **a l. house**, una casita; **l. finger**, dedo m meñique. 2 (not much) poco,-a; **a l. cheese**, un poco de queso. II pron poco m; **save me a l.**, guárdame un poco. III adv poco; **l. by l.**, poco a poco; **as l. as possible**, lo menos posible; **they were a l. surprised**, se quedaron algo sorprendidos.
live¹ |lɪv| I vi vivir; **long l. the King!**, ¡viva el Rey!. II vtr vivir; **to l. an interesting life**, vivir una vida interesante. ◆**live down** vtr conseguir que se olvide. ◆**live for** vtr vivir para. ◆**live off** vtr vivir de. ◆**live on** I vtr (food, money) vivir de. II vi (memory) persistir. ◆**live through** vi vivir (durante). ◆**live together** vi vivir juntos. ◆**live up** vtr fam **to l. it up**, pegarse la gran vida. ◆**live up to** vtr (promises) cumplir con; **it didn't l. up to expectations**, no fue lo

que se esperaba. ◆**live with** vtr 1 vivir con. 2 fig (accept) aceptar.
live² |laɪv| adj 1 (living) vivo,-a. 2 TV Rad en directo, en vivo. 3 (ammunition) real; (bomb) sin explotar; Elec con corriente; fam **he's a real l. wire!**, ¡éste no para nunca!
livelihood ['laɪvlɪhʊd] n sustento m.
lively ['laɪvlɪ] adj (livelier, liveliest) (person) vivo,-a; (place) animado,-a; fig (interest) entusiástico,-a.
liven ['laɪvən] vtr **to l. (up)**, animar.
liver ['lɪvə'] n hígado m.
livery ['lɪvərɪ] n librea f.
livestock ['laɪvstɒk] n ganado m.
livid ['lɪvɪd] adj lívido,-a; fam (angry) furioso,-a.
living ['lɪvɪŋ] I adj vivo,-a. II n vida f; **l. conditions**, condiciones fpl de vida; **l. expenses**, dietas fpl; **to earn** or **make one's l.**, ganarse la vida; **l. room**, sala f de estar; **l. standards**, nivel m de vida; **l. wage**, sueldo mínimo.
lizard ['lɪzəd] n (large) lagarto m; (small) lagartija f.
llama ['lɑːmə] n llama f.
load |ləʊd| I n (cargo) carga f; (weight) peso m; Elec Tech carga; fam **loads (of)**, montones de; fam **that's a l. of rubbish!**, ¡no son más que tonterías!. II vtr cargar. ◆**load up** vi & vtr cargar.
loaded ['ləʊdɪd] adj cargado,-a (with, de); fig **a l. question**, una pregunta intencionada. 2 fam **to be l.**, (rich) estar forrado,-a. 3 (dice) trucado,-a.
loading ['ləʊdɪŋ] n carga f; **l. bay**, cargadero m.
loaf¹ |ləʊf| n (pl loaves) pan m; (French stick) barra f de pan; (sliced) pan de molde.
loaf² |ləʊf| vi **to l. (about** or **around)**, holgazanear.
loan |ləʊn| I n préstamo m; Fin empréstito m; **on l.**, prestado,-a; (footballer) cedido,-a. II vtr prestar.
loath |ləʊθ| adj **to be l. to do sth**, ser reacio,-a a hacer algo.
loathe |ləʊð| vtr aborrecer, odiar.
loathing ['ləʊðɪŋ] n aborrecimiento m, odio m.
loathsome ['ləʊðsəm] adj odioso,-a, repugnante.
loaves |ləʊvz| npl → **loaf**.
lob |lɒb| vi Ten hacer un lob.
lobby ['lɒbɪ] I n 1 (hall) vestíbulo m. 2 (pressure group) grupo m de presión, lobby m. II vtr presionar. III vi ejercer presiones.
lobe |ləʊb| n lóbulo m.
lobster ['lɒbstə'] n langosta f.
local ['ləʊkəl] I adj local; (person) del pueblo; Med **l. anaesthetic**, anestesia f local; Tel **l. call**, llamada urbana; **l. government**, gobierno m municipal. II n fam 1

the locals, los vecinos. 2 *GB (pub)* bar *m* del barrio. ◆**locally** *adv* en or de la localidad.

locality [ləʊ'kælɪtɪ] *n* localidad *f*.

locate [ləʊ'keɪt] *vtr (situate)* situar, ubicar; *(find)* localizar.

location [ləʊ'keɪʃən] *n* 1 lugar *m*, situación *f*. 2 *Cin* l. **shots**, exteriores *mpl*; **they're on l. in Australia**, están rodando en Australia.

loch [lɒx, lɒk] *n Scot* lago *m*.

lock¹ [lɒk] I *n* 1 *(on door etc)* cerradura *f*; *(bolt)* cerrojo *m*; *(padlock)* candado *m*. 2 *(on canal)* esclusa *f*. II *vtr* cerrar con llave or cerrojo or candado. III *vi (door etc)* cerrarse; *(wheels)* trabarse. ◆**lock up** *vtr (house)* cerrar; *(jail)* meter en la cárcel.

lock² [lɒk] *n lit (of hair)* mechón *m*.

locker [lɒkər] *n (cupboard)* armario ropero; **l. room**, vestuario *m* con armarios roperos.

locket ['lɒkɪt] *n* medallón *m*.

lockout ['lɒkaʊt] *n* cierre *m* patronal.

locksmith ['lɒksmɪθ] *n* cerrajero *m*.

lockup ['lɒkʌp] *n (garage)* garaje alejado de la casa; *US (prison)* cárcel *f*.

locomotive [ləʊkə'məʊtɪv] *n* locomotora *f*.

locust ['ləʊkəst] *n* langosta *f*.

lodge [lɒdʒ] I *n* 1 *(gamekeeper's)* casa *f* del guarda; *(porter's)* portería *f*; *(hunter's)* refugio *m*. 2 *(masonic)* logia *f*. 3 *(beaver's den)* madriguera *f*. II *vtr* 1 *(accommodate)* alojar. 2 *(complaint)* presentar. III *vi* 1 *(live)* alojarse. 2 *(get stuck)* meterse *(in, en)*.

lodger ['lɒdʒər] *n* huésped,-a *m,f*.

lodging ['lɒdʒɪŋ] *n* alojamiento *m*; **l. house**, casa *f* de huéspedes.

loft [lɒft] *n* desván *m*.

lofty ['lɒftɪ] *adj (loftier, loftiest)* lit *(high)* alto,-a, *pej (haughty)* altivo,-a.

log [lɒg] I *n* 1 tronco *m*; *(for fuel)* leño *m*; **l. cabin**, cabaña *f* de troncos. 2 *Naut* diario *m* de a bordo. II *vtr (record)* registrar. ◆**log in**, **log on** *vi Comput* entrar (en sistema). ◆**log out**, **log off** *vi Comput* salir (del sistema).

logarithm ['lɒgərɪðəm] *n* logaritmo *m*.

log-book ['lɒgbʊk] *n Naut* diario *m* de a bordo; *Av* diario *m* de vuelo; *Aut* documentación *f* (del coche).

loggerheads ['lɒgəhedz] *npl* **to be at l. with sb**, estar a mal con algn.

logic ['lɒdʒɪk] *n* lógica *f*.

logical ['lɒdʒɪkəl] *adj* lógico,-a.

logistics [lə'dʒɪstɪks] *npl* logística *f*.

logo ['ləʊgəʊ] *n* logotipo *m*.

loin [lɔɪn] *n (of animal)* ijada *f*; *Culin (of pork)* lomo *m*; *(of beef)* solomillo *m*.

loiter ['lɔɪtər] *vi (hang about)* holgazanear; *(lag behind)* rezagarse; *(prowl)* merodear.

loll [lɒl] *vi (tongue, head)* colgar. ◆**loll about**, **loll around** *vi* repantigarse.

lollipop ['lɒlɪpɒp] *n* pirulí *m*, chupachup® *m*; **ice(d) l.**, polo *m*; *GB fam* **l. lady** or **man**, guardia *mf* (que para el tráfico para que crucen los colegiales).

lolly ['lɒlɪ] *n fam* 1 *(sweet)* pirulí *m*, chupachup® *m*; **ice(d) l.**, polo *m*. 2 *fam (money)* pasta *f*.

London ['lʌndən] *n* Londres.

Londoner ['lʌndənər] *n* londinense *mf*.

lone [ləʊn] *adj (solitary)* solitario,-a; *(single)* solo,-a.

loneliness ['ləʊnlɪnɪs] *n* soledad *f*.

lonely ['ləʊnlɪ] *adj (lonelier, loneliest)* solo,-a, solitario,-a.

long¹ [lɒŋ] I *adj* 1 *(size)* largo,-a; **how l. is the table?**, ¿cuánto tiene de largo la mesa?; **it's three metres l.**, tiene tres metros de largo; **l. jump**, salto *m* de longitud. 2 *(time)* mucho,-a; **at l. last**, por fin; **how l. is the film?**, ¿cuánto tiempo dura la película? II *adv* mucho, mucho tiempo; **all day l.**, todo el día; **as l. as the exhibition lasts**, mientras dure la exposición; **as l. as** or **so l. as you don't mind**, con tal de que no te importe; **before l.**, dentro de poco; **how l. have you been here?**, ¿cuánto tiempo llevas aquí?

long² [lɒŋ] *vi* añorar; **to l. for**, anhelar.

long-distance ['lɒŋdɪstəns] *adj* de larga distancia; **l.-d. call**, conferencia interurbana; **l.-d. runner**, corredor,-a *m,f* de fondo.

longhand ['lɒŋhænd] *n* escritura *f* a mano.

longing ['lɒŋɪŋ] *n (desire)* anhelo *m*; *(nostalgia)* nostalgia *f*.

longitude ['lɒndʒɪtjuːd] *n* longitud *f*.

long-playing ['lɒŋpleɪɪŋ] *adj* de larga duración; **l.-p. record**, elepé *m*.

long-range ['lɒŋreɪndʒ] *adj (missile etc)* de largo alcance; *(weather forecast)* de largo plazo.

long-sighted [lɒŋ'saɪtɪd] *adj* 1 *Med* présbita. 2 *fig* previsor,-a.

long-standing ['lɒŋstændɪŋ] *adj* antiguo,-a, de mucho tiempo.

long-suffering ['lɒŋsʌfrɪŋ] *adj* sufrido,-a.

long-term ['lɒŋtɜːm] *adj* a largo plazo.

long-winded [lɒŋ'wɪndɪd] *adj* prolijo,-a.

loo [luː] *n GB fam* water *m*.

look [lʊk] I *n* 1 *(glance)* mirada *f*; **to take a l. at**, *(peep)* echar un vistazo a; *(examine)* examinar. 2 *(appearance)* aspecto *m*, apariencia *f*; **I don't like the l. of it**, me da mala espina. 3 *(fashion)* moda *f*. 4 *(good)* **looks**, belleza *f*.
II *vi* 1 mirar. 2 *(seem)* parecer; **he looks well**, tiene buena cara; **it looks delicious**, tiene un aspecto buenísimo; **she looks like her father**, *(resembles)* se parece a su padre.
III *vtr* mirar.
◆**look after** *vtr* cuidar a, ocuparse de.

◆**look at** *vtr* mirar; *fig* **whichever way you l. at it,** desde cualquier punto de vista. ◆**look away** *vi* apartar la mirada. ◆**look back** *vi* 1 mirar hacia atrás; *fig* **since then he has never looked back,** desde entonces ha ido prosperando. 2 *(remember)* recordar. ◆**look down** *vi fig* to l. down on sth/sb, despreciar algo/a algn. ◆**look for** *vtr* buscar. ◆**look forward to** *vtr* esperar con ansia; **I l. forward to hearing from you,** *(in letter)* espero noticias suyas. ◆**look into** *vtr* examinar, investigar. ◆**look on** I *vtr (consider)* considerar. II *vi* quedarse mirando. ◆**look onto** *vtr* dar a. ◆**look out** *vi* 1 **the bedroom looks out onto the garden,** el dormitorio da al jardín. 2 l. out!, *(take care)* ¡cuidado!, ¡ojo! ◆**look over** *vtr (examine)* revisar; *(place)* inspeccionar. ◆**look round** I *vi* mirar alrededor; *(turn head)* volver la cabeza. II *vtr (house, shop)* ver. ◆**look through** *vtr* 1 *(window)* mirar por. 2 *(leaf through)* hojear; *(examine)* revisar; *(check)* registrar. ◆**look to** *vtr* 1 *(take care of)* velar por. 2 *(turn to)* recurrir a. ◆**look up** I *vi* 1 *(glance upwards)* alzar la vista. 2 *fam (improve)* mejorar. II *vtr* 1 *(look for)* buscar. 2 *(visit)* ir a visitar. ◆**look upon** *vtr* considerar. ◆**look up to** *vtr* respetar.

lookout ['lʊkaʊt] *n (person)* centinela *mf*; *(place)* mirador *m*; **to be on the l. for,** estar al acecho de; *fam* **that's his l.!,** ¡eso es asunto suyo!

loom[1] [luːm] *n* telar *m*.

loom[2] [luːm] *vi* alzarse; *fig (threaten)* amenazar.

loony ['luːnɪ] *adj (loonier, looniest) fam* loco,-a.

loop [luːp] I *n* 1 lazo *m*. 2 *Comput* bucle *m*. II *vtr* 1 encordar. 2 *Av* **to l. the loop,** rizar el rizo.

loophole ['luːphəʊl] *n fig* escapatoria *f*.

loose [luːs] *adj* 1 *(not secure)* flojo,-a; *(papers, hair, clothes)* suelto,-a; *(tongue)* desatado,-a; *(baggy)* holgado,-a; **to set sb l.,** soltar a algn; *fam* **to be at a l. end,** no saber qué hacer. 2 *(not packaged)* a granel; **l. tobacco,** tabaco *m* en hebras; **l. change,** suelto *m*. 3 *(not exact)* vago,-a; *(translation)* libre. 4 *(lax)* relajado,-a; **a l. woman,** una mujer fácil. ◆**loosely** *adv* 1 *(approximately)* aproximadamente. 2 *(vaguely)* vagamente.

loosen ['luːsən] I *vtr* aflojar; *(belt)* desabrochar; *fig (restrictions)* flexibilizar. II *vi (slacken)* aflojarse.

loot [luːt] I *n* botín *m*. II *vtr* saquear.

lop [lɒp] *vtr* podar. ◆**lop off** *vtr* cortar.

lope [ləʊp] *vi* andar a zancadas.

lopsided [lɒp'saɪdɪd] *adj* ladeado,-a.

lord [lɔːd] *n* 1 señor *m*; *(British peer)* lord *m*; **the House of Lords,** la Cámara de los Lores; **the L. Mayor,** el señor alcalde. 2 *Rel* **the L.,** El Señor; **good L.!,** ¡Dios mío!; **the L.'s Prayer,** el Padrenuestro. 3 *(judge)* señoría *mf*.

lordship ['lɔːdʃɪp] *n GB* **His L., Your L.,** su señoría.

lorry ['lɒrɪ] *n GB* camión *m*; **l. driver,** camionero,-a *m,f*; **l. load,** carga *f*.

lose [luːz] I *vtr (pt & pp lost)* perder; **to l. time,** *(of clock)* atrasarse. II *vi* perder; **to l. to sb,** perder contra algn; **to l. out,** salir perdiendo.

loser ['luːzər] *n* perdedor,-a *m,f*.

loss [lɒs] *n* pérdida *f*; **to make a l.,** perder; *fig* **to be at a l. for words,** quedarse de una pieza; **to be at a l. what to do,** no saber qué hacer.

lost [lɒst] *adj* 1 perdido,-a; **to get l.,** perderse; *fam* **get l.!,** ¡vete a la porra!; **l. property office,** *US* **l. and found department,** oficina *f* de objetos perdidos. 2 *(disoriented)* desorientado,-a; *(distracted)* distraído,-a; **l. in thought,** ensimismado,-a.

lot [lɒt] *n* 1 *(fate)* suerte *f*. 2 **to cast lots for sth,** echar algo a suertes. 3 *US (plot of land)* parcela *f*. 4 *(in an auction)* lote *m*. 5 *(everything)* todo *m*; **he ate the l.,** se lo comió todo. 6 **a l. of,** *(much)* mucho, -a; *(many)* muchos,-as; **he feels a l. better,** se encuentra mucho mejor; **she reads a l.,** lee mucho; *fam* **lots of,** montones de, cantidad de.

lotion ['ləʊʃən] *n* loción *f*.

lottery ['lɒtərɪ] *n* lotería *f*; **l. ticket,** ≈ décimo *m* de lotería.

loud [laʊd] I *adj* 1 *(voice)* alto,-a; *(noise)* fuerte; *(laugh)* estrepitoso,-a; *(applause)* clamoroso,-a; *(protests, party)* ruidoso,-a. 2 *(flashy)* chillón,-ona. 3 *(vulgar)* hortera. II *adv* **to read/think out l.,** leer/pensar en voz alta.

loud-hailer [laʊd'heɪlər] *n* megáfono *m*.

loudspeaker [laʊd'spiːkər] *n* altavoz *m*.

lounge [laʊndʒ] I *n GB* salón *m*, sala *f* de estar. II *vi* hacer el vago.

louse [laʊs] *n (pl lice* [laɪs]*)* piojo *m*.

lousy ['laʊzɪ] *adj (lousier, lousiest) fam* fatal; **a l. trick,** una cochinada.

lout [laʊt] *n* gamberro *m*.

lovable ['lʌvəbəl] *adj* adorable.

love [lʌv] I *n* 1 amor *m* (**for**, por); *(passion)* pasión *f* (**for**, por); **to be in l. with sb,** estar enamorado,-a de algn; **to fall in l.,** enamorarse; **to make l.,** hacer el amor; (**with**) **l.** (**from**) **Mary,** *(in letter)* un abrazo, Mary; **l. affair,** amorío *m*; **l. letter/story,** carta *f*/historia *f* de amor; **l. life,** vida *f* sentimental. 2 *(person)* amor *m*, cariño *m*; *fam* chato,-a *m,f*; **my l.,** mi amor. 3 *Ten* **forty l.,** cuarenta a cero. II *vtr (person)* querer a, amar a; **he loves cooking/football,** le encanta cocinar/el fútbol.

lovely ['lʌvlɪ] *adj (lovelier, loveliest)*

(charming) encantador,-a; *(beautiful)* hermoso,-a, precioso,-a; *(delicious)* riquísimo,-a.

lover ['lʌvər] *n* 1 *(sexual partner)* amante *mf.* 2 *(enthusiast)* aficionado,-a *m,f*, amigo,-a *m,f*.

loving ['lʌvɪŋ] *adj* cariñoso,-a.

low¹ [ləʊ] I *adj* 1 bajo,-a; *(neckline)* escotado,-a; **the L. Countries**, los Países Bajos. 2 *(in quantity)* bajo,-a. 3 *(poor)* pobre. 4 *(battery)* gastado,-a; **l. frequency**, baja frecuencia. 5 **to feel l.**, sentirse deprimido,-a. 6 *(reprehensible)* malo,-a. II *adv* bajo. III *n* 1 *Meteor* área *f* de baja presión. 2 *(low point)* punto más bajo; **to reach an all-time l.**, tocar fondo.

low² [ləʊ] *vi (cow)* mugir.

lowdown ['ləʊdaʊn] *n fam* pormenores *mpl.*

lower ['ləʊər] I *adj (comp of low)* inferior; *Typ* **l. case**, minúscula *f*; **l. class**, clase baja. II *adv comp* → **low**. III *vtr* bajar; *(flag)* arriar; *(reduce)* reducir; *(price)* rebajar.

lower-class ['ləʊəklɑːs] *adj* de clase baja.

lowest ['ləʊɪst] I *adj (superl of low)* más bajo,-a; *(price, speed)* mínimo,-a. II *n* **at the l.**, como mínimo.

low-key [ləʊ'kiː] *adj* sin ceremonia.

lowlands ['ləʊləndz] *npl* tierras bajas.

lowly ['ləʊlɪ] *adj (lowlier, lowliest)* humilde.

low-necked ['ləʊnekt] *adj* escotado,-a.

loyal ['lɔɪəl] *adj* leal, fiel.

loyalty ['lɔɪəltɪ] *n* lealtad *f*, fidelidad *f*.

lozenge ['lɒzɪndʒ] *n* pastilla *f*.

LP [el'piː] *abbr of* **long-playing record**, LP *m*.

L-plate ['elpleɪt] *n GB* (placa *f* de) la ele.

LSD [eles'diː] *abbr of* **lysergic acid diethylamide**, dietilamida *f* del ácido lisérgico, LSD *m*.

Ltd *GB Com abbr of* **Limited (Liability)**, Sociedad Anónima, S.A..

lubricant ['luːbrɪkənt] *n* lubricante *m*.

lubricate ['luːbrɪkeɪt] *vtr* lubricar; *(engine)* engrasar.

lubrication [luːbrɪ'keɪʃən] *n* engrase *m*.

lucid ['luːsɪd] *adj* lúcido,-a.

luck [lʌk] *n* suerte *f*; **bad l.!**, ¡mala suerte!; **good l.!**, ¡(buena) suerte!; **to be in l.**, estar de suerte; **to be out of l.**, no tener suerte; *fig* **to push one's l.**, tentar la suerte; *fig* **to try one's l.**, probar fortuna.

lucky ['lʌkɪ] *adj (luckier, luckiest) (person)* afortunado,-a; *(day)* de suerte; *(move)* oportuno,-a; *(charm)* de la suerte; **a l. break**, una oportunidad. ◆**luckily** *adv* por suerte, afortunadamente.

lucrative ['luːkrətɪv] *adj* lucrativo,-a.

ludicrous ['luːdɪkrəs] *adj* absurdo,-a, ridículo,-a.

lug [lʌg] *vtr fam* arrastrar.

luggage ['lʌgɪdʒ] *n* equipaje *m*; **l. rack**, *Aut* baca *f*; *Rail* portaequipajes *m inv.*

lukewarm ['luːkwɔːm] *adj (water etc)* tibio,-a; *fig (reception etc)* poco entusiasta.

lull [lʌl] I *n (in storm)* calma chicha; *(in fighting)* tregua *f*. II *vtr (cause to sleep)* adormecer; **to l. sb into a false sense of security**, infundir una falsa seguridad a algn.

lullaby ['lʌləbaɪ] *n* canción *f* de cuna, nana *f*.

lumbago [lʌm'beɪgəʊ] *n* lumbago *m*.

lumber ['lʌmbər] I *n* 1 *GB (junk)* trastos viejos. 2 *US (timber)* maderos *mpl.* II *vtr fam* cargar (**with**, de).

lumberjack ['lʌmbədʒæk] *n* leñador *m*.

luminous ['luːmɪnəs] *adj* luminoso,-a.

lump [lʌmp] I *n (of coal etc)* trozo *m*; *(of sugar, earth)* terrón *m*; *(in sauce)* grumo *m*; *(swelling)* bulto *m*; *fam fig (in throat)* nudo *m*; **l. sum**, cantidad *f* global. II *vtr fam (endure)* aguantar. ◆**lump together** *vtr* apelotonar.

lumpy ['lʌmpɪ] *adj (lumpier, lumpiest) (bed)* lleno,-a de bultos; *(sauce)* grumoso,-a.

lunacy ['luːnəsɪ] *n* locura *f*.

lunar ['luːnər] *adj* lunar.

lunatic ['luːnətɪk] *adj & n* loco,-a *(m,f)*; **l. asylum**, manicomio *m*.

lunch [lʌntʃ] I *n* comida *f*, almuerzo *m*; **l. hour**, hora *f* de comer. II *vi* comer, almorzar.

luncheon ['lʌntʃən] *n arch fml* almuerzo *m*; **l. voucher**, vale *m* de comida; *(pork)* **l. meat**, carne *f* de cerdo troceada, chopped *m*.

lunchtime ['lʌntʃtaɪm] *n* hora *f* de comer.

lung [lʌŋ] *n* pulmón *m*.

lunge [lʌndʒ] I *n* arremetida *f*. II *vi (also* **l. forward)** arremeter; **to l. (out) at sb**, arremeter contra algn.

lurch [lɜːtʃ] I *n* 1 *(of vehicle)* sacudida *f*; *(of person)* tambaleo *m*. 2 *fam* **to leave sb in the l.**, dejar a algn en la cuneta. II *vi (vehicle)* dar sacudidas; *(person)* tambalearse.

lure [lʊər] I *n (decoy)* señuelo *m*; *(bait)* cebo *m*; *fig (charm)* aliciente *m*. II *vtr* atraer con engaños.

lurid ['lʊərɪd] *adj* 1 *(gruesome)* espeluznante; *(sensational)* sensacionalista. 2 *(gaudy)* chillón,-ona.

lurk [lɜːk] *vi (lie in wait)* estar al acecho; *(hide)* esconderse.

luscious ['lʌʃəs] *adj (food)* delicioso,-a.

lush [lʌʃ] *adj (vegetation)* exuberante.

lust [lʌst] I *n (sexual desire)* lujuria *f*; *(craving)* ansia *f*; *(greed)* codicia *f*. II *vi* **to l. after sth/sb**, codiciar algo/desear a algn.

luster ['lʌstər] *n US* → **lustre**.

lustre ['lʌstər] *n* lustre *m*.

lusty ['lʌstɪ] *adj (lustier, lustiest)* robusto,-a.

lute [luːt] *n* laúd *m*.

Luxembourg ['lʌksəmbɜːg] *n* Luxemburgo.

luxuriant [lʌg'zjuərɪənt] *adj (plants)* exuberante; *(hair etc)* abundante.

luxurious [lʌg'zjuərɪəs] *adj* lujoso,-a.

luxury ['lʌkʃərɪ] *n* lujo *m*; **l. flat**, piso *m* de lujo.

lychee ['laɪtʃiː] *n* lichi *m*.

lying ['laɪɪŋ] **I** *adj* mentiroso,-a. **II** *n* mentiras *fpl*.

lynch [lɪntʃ] *vtr* linchar.

lyre [laɪər] *n Mus* lira *f*.

lyric ['lɪrɪk] **I** *adj* lírico,-a. **II** *n* **1** *(poem)* poema *m* lírico. **2 lyrics,** *(words of song)* letra *f sing*.

lyrical ['lɪrɪkəl] *adj* lírico,-a.

M

M, m [em] *n (the letter)* M, m *f*.

m 1 *abbr of* metre(s), m. **2** *abbr of* million(s), m.

macabre [mə'kɑːbrə] *adj* macabro,-a.

mac(c)aroni [mækə'rəʊnɪ] *n* macarrones *mpl*.

mace¹ [meɪs] *n (club, ceremonial staff)* maza *f*.

mace² [meɪs] *n (spice)* macis *f inv*.

machine [mə'ʃiːn] **I** *n* máquina *f*; **m. gun,** ametralladora *f*; **m. language,** lenguaje *m* máquina. **II** *vtr* trabajar a máquina.

machine-gun [mə'ʃiːngʌn] *vtr* ametrallar.

machine-readable [məʃiːn'riːdəbəl] *adj Comput* legible,-a por ordenador.

machinery [mə'ʃiːnərɪ] *n (machines)* maquinaria *f*; *(workings of machine)* mecanismo *m*; *fig* **the bureaucratic m.,** la maquinaria burocrática.

mac [mæk] *n GB fam abbr of* mackintosh.

mackerel ['mækrəl] *n (pl mackerel)* caballa *f*.

mac(k)intosh ['mækɪntɒʃ] *n* impermeable *m*.

macroeconomics [mækrəʊiːkə'nɒmɪks] *n* macroeconomía *f*.

mad [mæd] *adj (madder, maddest)* **1** loco,-a; *(animal)* furioso,-a; *(dog)* rabioso,-a; **to be m.,** estar loco,-a; **to drive sb m.,** volver loco,-a a algn; **to go m.,** volverse loco,-a; **you must be m.!,** ¿estás loco? **2** *(idea, plan)* disparatado,-a. **3** *fam* **to be m. about sth/sb,** estar loco, -a por algo/algn. **4** *fam* **to be m. at sb,** estar enfadado,-a con algn. **5** *(gallop, race etc)* desenfrenado,-a. ◆**madly** *adv fam (extremely)* terriblemente; **to be m. in love with sb,** estar locamente enamorado,-a de algn.

madam ['mædəm] *n* **1** señora *f*; **Dear M.,** *(in letter)* Muy señora mía, Estimada señora. **2** *(brothelkeeper)* madam *f*.

madden ['mædən] *vtr* volver loco,-a.

maddening ['mædənɪŋ] *adj* exasperante.

made [meɪd] *pt & pp →* make.

Madeira [mə'dɪərə] *n* **1** *(island)* Madeira. **2** *(wine)* madeira *m*; **M. cake,** bizcocho *m*.

made-to-measure [meɪdtə'meʒər] *adj* hecho,-a a (la) medida.

made-up ['meɪdʌp] *adj* **1** *(face, person)* maquillado,-a; *(eyes, lips)* pintado,-a. **2** *(story, excuse)* inventado,-a.

madman ['mædmən] *n* loco *m*.

madness ['mædnɪs] *n* locura *f*.

Madrid [mə'drɪd] *n* Madrid.

Mafia ['mæfɪə] *n* mafia *f*.

magazine [mægə'ziːn] *n* **1** *(periodical)* revista *f*. **2** *(in rifle)* recámara *f*. **3** *Mil (storehouse)* almacén *m*; *(for explosives)* polvorín *m*.

maggot ['mægət] *n* larva *f*, gusano *m*.

magic ['mædʒɪk] **I** *n* magia *f*. **II** *adj* **1** mágico,-a; **m. wand,** varita mágica. **2** *fam (wonderful)* estupendo,-a.

magical ['mædʒɪkəl] *adj* mágico,-a.

magician [mə'dʒɪʃən] *n* **1** *(wizard)* mago,-a *m,f*. **2** *(conjuror)* prestidigitador,-a *m,f*.

magistrate ['mædʒɪstreɪt] *n* juez *mf* de paz; **magistrates' court,** juzgado *m* de paz.

magnanimous [mæg'nænɪməs] *adj* magnánimo,-a.

magnet ['mægnɪt] *n* imán *m*.

magnetic [mæg'netɪk] *adj* magnético,-a; *fig (personality)* carismático,-a; **m. tape,** cinta magnetofónica.

magnetism ['mægnɪtɪzəm] *n* magnetismo *m*.

magnificence [mæg'nɪfɪsəns] *n* magnificencia *f*.

magnificent [mæg'nɪfɪsənt] *adj* magnífico,-a.

magnify ['mægnɪfaɪ] *vtr* **1** *(enlarge)* aumentar. **2** *fig (exaggerate)* exagerar.

magnifying glass ['mægnɪfaɪɪŋglɑːs] *n* lupa *f*.

magnitude ['mægnɪtjuːd] *n* magnitud *f*.

magpie ['mægpaɪ] *n* urraca *f*.

mahogany [mə'hɒgənɪ] **I** *n* caoba *f*. **II** *adj* de caoba.

maid [meɪd] *n* **1** criada *f*, *Am* mucama *f*. **2** *pej* **old m.,** solterona *f*.

maiden ['meɪdən] **I** *n lit* doncella *f*. **II** *adj* **1** *(unmarried)* soltera; **m. aunt,** tía soltera;

m. name, apellido *m* de soltera. **2** (*voyage, flight*) inaugural.

mail [meɪl] **I** *n* correo *m*; **by m.,** por correo; **m. order,** venta *f* por correo; **m. train,** (tren *m*) correo. **II** *vtr* (*post*) echar al buzón; (*send*) enviar por correo.

mailbox ['meɪlbɒks] *n US* buzón *m*.

mailing list ['meɪlɪŋlɪst] *n* lista *f* de direcciones.

mailman ['meɪlmæn] *n US* cartero *m*.

maim [meɪm] *vtr* lisiar.

main [meɪn] **I** *adj* (*problem, door etc*) principal; (*square, mast, sail*) mayor; (*office*) central; **the m. thing is to keep calm,** lo esencial es mantener la calma; *Culin* **m. course,** plato *m* principal; **m. road,** carretera *f* principal. **II** *n* **1** (*pipe, wire*) conducto *m* principal; **the mains,** (*water or gas system*) la cañería maestra; *Elec* la red eléctrica; **a radio that works on battery or mains,** una radio que funciona con pilas o con corriente. **2 in the m.,** por regla general. ◆**mainly** *adv* principalmente, sobre todo; (*for the most part*) en su mayoría.

mainframe ['meɪnfreɪm] *n* **m. computer,** unidad *f*, central *f*.

mainland ['meɪnlənd] *n* continente *m*.

mainstay ['meɪnsteɪ] *n fig* sustento *m*, sostén *m*.

mainstream ['meɪnstriːm] *n* corriente *f* principal.

maintain [meɪnˈteɪn] *vtr* mantener; (*conversation*) sostener; (*silence, appearances*) guardar; (*road, machine*) conservar en buen estado.

maintenance ['meɪntənəns] *n* **1** mantenimiento *m*. **2** (*divorce allowance*) pensión *f*.

maisonette [meɪzəˈnet] *n* dúplex *m*.

maize [meɪz] *n* maíz *m*.

majestic [məˈdʒestɪk] *adj* majestuoso,-a.

majesty ['mædʒɪstɪ] *n* majestad *f*.

major ['meɪdʒər] **I** *adj* **1** principal, mayor; (*contribution, operation*) importante. **2** *Mus* mayor. **II** *n* **1** *Mil* comandante *m*. **2** *US Univ* especialidad *f*. **III** *vi US Univ* **to m. in,** especializarse en.

Majorca [məˈjɔːkə] *n* Mallorca.

Majorcan [məˈjɔːkən] *adj & n* mallorquín,-ina (*m,f*).

majority [məˈdʒɒrɪtɪ] *n* mayoría *f*; **to be in the m.,** ser (la) mayoría.

make [meɪk] (*pt & pp made*) **I** *vtr* **1** hacer; (*manufacture*) fabricar; (*create*) crear; (*clothes, curtains*) confeccionar; (*meal*) preparar; (*payment*) efectuar; (*speech*) pronunciar; (*decision*) tomar; (*mistake*) cometer; **to be made of,** ser de; **to m. a noise,** hacer ruido. **2** (*render*) poner, volver; (*convert*) convertir (**into,** en); (*appoint*) nombrar; **he made it clear that ...,** dejó claro que .... **3** (*force, compel*) obligar; (*cause*) causar; **to m. do with sth,** arreglárselas con algo. **4** (*earn*) ga-

nar; **to m. a living,** ganarse la vida; **to m. a name for oneself,** hacerse famoso, -a; *fig* **to m. the best of sth,** sacar partido de algo. **5 7 and 5 m. 12,** 7 y 5 son 12. **6** (*calculate, reckon*) calcular; **what time do you m. it?,** ¿qué hora tienes? **7** (*think*) opinar; **I don't know what to m. of it,** no sé qué pensar de eso; **it doesn't m. sense,** no tiene sentido. **8** (*achieve*) alcanzar, conseguir. **9 it will m. or break her,** será su consagración o su ruina. **10 to m. a fresh start,** volver a empezar. **II** *vi* **1** hacer; **to m. sure of sth,** asegurarse de algo. **2 she made as if to leave,** hizo como si quisiera marcharse. **III** *n* **1** (*brand*) marca *f*. **2** *fam* **to be on the m.,** andar tras el dinero. ◆**make for** *vtr* **1** (*move towards*) dirigirse hacia; (*attack*) atacar a. **2 this makes for less work,** esto ahorra trabajo. ◆**make out I** *vtr* **1** (*list, receipt*) hacer; (*cheque*) extender. **2** (*perceive*) distinguir; (*writing*) descifrar. **3** (*understand*) entender. **4** (*claim*) pretender. **5 to m. out a case for doing sth,** exponer los argumentos para hacer algo. **II** *vi* **how did you m. out?,** ¿qué tal te fue? ◆**make up I** *vtr* **1** (*parcel, list*) hacer; (*prescription*) preparar; (*assemble*) montar. **2** (*story*) inventar. **3** (*apply cosmetics to*) maquillar; (*one's face*) maquillarse. **4** (*loss*) compensar; (*lost time*) recuperar. **5** (*constitute*) componer. **6 to m. it up (with sb),** hacer las paces (con algn). **7 to m. up one's mind,** decidirse. **II** *vi* maquillarse. ◆**make up to** *vtr* **1 to m. up to sb,** congraciarse con algn. **2 to m. it up to sb for sth,** compensar a algn por algo.

make-believe ['meɪkbɪliːv] *n* (*fantasy*) fantasía *f*; (*pretence*) fingimiento *m*; **to live in a world of m.-b.,** vivir en un mundo de ensueño.

maker ['meɪkər] *n* fabricante *mf*.

makeshift ['meɪkʃɪft] *adj* (*improvised*) improvisado,-a; (*temporary*) provisional.

make-up ['meɪkʌp] *n* **1** (*cosmetics*) maquillaje *m*; **m.-up remover,** desmaquillador *m*. **2** (*composition*) composición *f*; (*character*) carácter *m*.

making ['meɪkɪŋ] *n* **1** (*manufacture*) fabricación *f*; (*preparation*) preparación *f*. **2 he has the makings of a politician,** tiene madera de político.

malaise [mæˈleɪz] *n* malestar *m*.

malaria [məˈleərɪə] *n* malaria *f*.

Malay [məˈleɪ] **I** *adj* malayo,-a. **II** *n* **1** (*person*) malayo,-a *m,f*. **2** (*language*) malayo *m*.

Malaysia [məˈleɪzɪə] *n* Malasia.

male [meɪl] **I** *adj* (*animal, plant*) macho; (*person*) varón; (*sex*) masculino; *pej* **m. chauvinism,** machismo *m*. **II** *n* (*person*) varón *m*; (*animal, plant*) macho *m*.

malevolent [məˈlevələnt] *adj* malévolo,

-a.

malfunction [mæl'fʌŋkʃən] I *n* mal funcionamiento *m*. II *vi* funcionar mal.

malice ['mælɪs] *n* malicia *f*; *Jur* **with m. aforethought**, con premeditación.

malicious [mə'lɪʃəs] *adj* malévolo,-a.

malign [mə'laɪn] I *adj* maligno,-a; (*influence*) perjudicial. II *vtr* calumniar, difamar.

malignant [mə'lɪgnənt] *adj* 1 (*person*) malvado,-a. 2 *Med* maligno,-a.

mall [mɔːl, mæl] *n US* centro *m* comercial.

malleable ['mælɪəbəl] *adj* maleable.

mallet ['mælɪt] *n* mazo *m*.

malnutrition [mælnjuː'trɪʃən] *n* desnutrición *f*.

malpractice [mæl'præktɪs] *n* procedimiento *m* ilegal; *Med* negligencia *f*.

malt [mɔːlt] *n* malta *f*.

Malta ['mɔːltə] *n* Malta *f*.

mammal ['mæməl] *n* mamífero *m*.

mammary ['mæmərɪ] *adj* **m. gland**, mama *f*.

mammoth ['mæməθ] I *n* *Zool* mamut *m*. II *adj* gigantesco,-a.

man [mæn] I *n* (*pl* **men**) 1 hombre *m*; **old m.**, viejo *m*; **young m.**, joven *m*; *fig* **he's a m. of his word**, es hombre de palabra; *fig* **the m. in the street**, el hombre de la calle; **m. Friday**, factótum *m*; *fam* **dirty old m.**, viejo verde. 2 (*humanity*) el hombre; (*human being*) el humano. 3 (*husband*) marido *m*; (*partner*) pareja *f*. 4 **our m. in Madrid**, nuestro representante en Madrid. 5 *Chess* pieza *f*. II *vtr* (*boat, plane*) tripular; (*post*) servir; **manned flight**, vuelo tripulado.

manage ['mænɪdʒ] I *vtr* 1 (*company, household*) llevar; (*money, affairs, person*) manejar. 2 (*succeed*) conseguir; **to m. to do sth**, lograr hacer algo. II *vi* (*cope physically*) poder; (*esp financially*) arreglárselas; **we're managing**, vamos tirando.

manageable ['mænɪdʒəbəl] *adj* manejable.

management ['mænɪdʒmənt] *n* dirección *f*.

manager ['mænɪdʒər] *n* 1 (*of company, bank*) director,-a *m,f*; (*head of department*) jefe,-a *m,f*. 2 (*of pop group etc*) mánager *m*. 3 *Sport* entrenador *m*.

manageress [mænɪdʒə'res] *n* (*of shop, restaurant*) encargada *f*; (*of company*) directora *f*.

managerial [mænɪ'dʒɪərɪəl] *adj* directivo,-a.

managing ['mænɪdʒɪŋ] *adj* directivo,-a; **m. director**, director,-a *m,f*, gerente.

mandarin ['mændərɪn] *n* **m. (orange)**, mandarina *f*.

mandate ['mændeɪt] *n* mandato *m*.

mandatory ['mændətərɪ] *adj* *fml* obligatorio,-a.

mane [meɪn] *n* (*of horse*) crin *f*; (*of lion*) melena *f*.

maneuver [mə'nuːvər] *n* & *vtr* *US* → **manoeuvre**.

manfully ['mænfʊlɪ] *adv* valientemente.

manger ['meɪndʒər] *n* pesebre *m*.

mangle[1] ['mæŋgəl] *n* (*for wringing*) rodillo *m*.

mangle[2] ['mæŋgəl] *vtr* (*crush*) aplastar; (*destroy by cutting*) despedazar.

mango ['mæŋgəʊ] *n* (*pl* **mangoes**) mango *m*.

mangy ['meɪndʒɪ] *adj* (**mangier, mangiest**) (*animal*) sarnoso,-a; *fam* (*carpet*) raído,-a.

manhandle ['mænhændəl] *vtr* maltratar.

manhole ['mænhəʊl] *n* boca *f* de acceso.

manhood ['mænhʊd] *n* 1 (*age*) mayoría *f* de edad; **to reach m.**, llegar a la edad viril. 2 (*manly qualities*) virilidad *f*.

mania ['meɪnɪə] *n* manía *f*.

maniac ['meɪnɪæk] *n* maníaco,-a *m,f*; *fam* loco,-a *m,f*.

manic ['mænɪk] *adj* maníaco,-a.

manic-depressive [mænɪkdɪ'presɪv] *adj* & *n* maníaco,-a (*m,f*) depresivo,-a.

manicure ['mænɪkjʊər] I *n* manicura *f*. II *vtr* **to m. one's nails**, hacerse la manicura.

manifest ['mænɪfest] *fml* I *adj* manifiesto,-a. II *vtr* manifestar.

manifesto [mænɪ'festəʊ] *n* programa *m* electoral.

manifold ['mænɪfəʊld] *adj* *fml* (*many*) múltiples; (*varied*) diversos,-as.

manipulate [mə'nɪpjʊleɪt] *vtr* 1 manipular. 2 *fig* (*accounts etc*) falsificar.

mankind [mæn'kaɪnd] *n* la humanidad, el género humano.

manly ['mænlɪ] *adj* (**manlier, manliest**) varonil, viril.

man-made ['mænmeɪd] *adj* (*lake*) artificial; (*fibres, fabric*) sintético,-a.

manner ['mænər] *n* 1 (*way, method*) manera *f*, modo *m*; **in this m.**, de esta manera. 2 (*way of behaving*) forma *f* de ser. 3 *fml* (*type, class*) clase *f*. 4 (**good**) **manners**, buenos modales; **bad manners**, falta *f sing* de educación.

mannerism ['mænərɪzəm] *n* (*gesture*) gesto *m*; (*affectation*) amaneramiento *m*.

manoeuvre [mə'nuːvər] I *n* maniobra *f*. II *vtr* maniobrar; (*person*) manejar. III *vi* maniobrar.

manor ['mænər] *n* **m. house**, casa solariega.

manpower ['mænpaʊər] *n* mano *f* de obra.

mansion ['mænʃən] *n* casa *f* grande; (*in country*) casa solariega.

manslaughter ['mænslɔːtər] *n* homicidio involuntario.

mantelpiece ['mæntəlpiːs] *n* (*shelf*) repisa *f* de chimenea; (*fireplace*) chimenea *f*.

mantle ['mæntəl] *n fig (of snow)* manto *m*, capa *f*.

manual ['mænjʊəl] *adj & n* manual (*m*).

manufacture [mænjʊ'fæktʃər] **I** *vtr* fabricar. **II** *n* fabricación *f*.

manufacturer [mænjʊ'fæktʃərər] *n* fabricante *mf*.

manure [mə'njʊər] *n* abono *m*, estiércol *m*.

manuscript ['mænjʊskrɪpt] *n* manuscrito *m*.

many ['menɪ] **I** *adj* (*more, most*) mucho,-a, muchos,-as; **a great m.**, muchísimos,-as; **as m. ... as ...**, tantos, -as ... como ...; **how m. days?**, ¿cuántos días?; **m. a time**, muchas veces; **so m. flowers!**, ¡cuántas flores!; **too m.**, demasiados,-as. **II** *pron* muchos,-as.

map [mæp] **I** *n (of country)* mapa *m*; *(of town, bus route)* plano *m*. **II** *vtr* trazar un mapa de. ◆**map out** *vtr (route)* trazar en un mapa; *fig (future etc)* planear.

maple ['meɪpəl] *n* arce *m*.

mar [mɑːr] *vtr* estropear; **to m. sb's enjoyment**, aguarle la fiesta a algn.

marathon ['mærəθɒn] *n* maratón *m*.

marble ['mɑːbəl] **I** *n* 1 *(stone)* mármol *m*. 2 *(glass ball)* canica *f*. **II** *adj* de mármol.

March [mɑːtʃ] *n* marzo *m*.

march [mɑːtʃ] **I** *n* 1 *Mil* marcha *f*; *fig* **to steal a m. on sb**, tomar la delantera a algn. 2 *(demonstration)* manifestación *f*. **II** *vi* 1 marchar. 2 *(demonstrate)* manifestarse. **III** *vtr Mil* hacer marchar.

march past ['mɑːtʃpɑːst] *n* desfile *m*.

mare [meər] *n* yegua *f*.

margarine [mɑːdʒə'riːn] *n* margarina *f*.

margin ['mɑːdʒɪn] *n* margen *m*; *fig* **to win by a narrow m.**, ganar por escaso margen; **m. of error**, *(in statistics)* error muestral.

marginal ['mɑːdʒɪnəl] *adj* marginal; *Pol* **m. seat**, escaño *m* pendiente. ◆**marginally** *adv* ligeramente.

marigold ['mærɪɡəʊld] *n* caléndula *f*.

marijuana, marihuana [mærɪ'hwɑːnə] *n* marihuana *f*, marijuana *f*.

marinate ['mærɪneɪt] *vtr* adobar.

marine [mə'riːn] **I** *adj* marino,-a. **II** *n* soldado *m* de infantería de marina; *GB* **the Marines**, *US* **the M. Corps**, la infantería de marina.

marital ['mærɪtəl] *adj* matrimonial; **m. status**, estado *m* civil.

maritime ['mærɪtaɪm] *adj* marítimo,-a.

marjoram ['mɑːdʒərəm] *n* mejorana *f*.

mark¹ [mɑːk] **I** *n* 1 *(left by blow etc)* señal *f*; *(stain)* mancha *f*; *fig* **to make one's m.**, distinguirse. 2 *(sign, token)* señal *f*; *(indication)* indicio *m*. 3 *(in exam etc)* nota *f*; **to get high marks**, sacar buenas notas. 4 *fig* **to hit the m.**, dar en el clavo; *fig* **to be wide of the m.**, estar lejos de la verdad. **II** *vtr* 1 *(stain)* manchar. 2 *(with*

tick, cross) señalar. 3 *(exam)* corregir; *(student)* dar notas a. 4 **'10% off marked price'**, 'descuento del 10% sobre el precio indicado'. 5 **m. my words**, fíjate en lo que te digo. 6 *Sport* marcar. 7 **to m. time**, *Mil* marcar el paso; *fig* hacer tiempo. ◆**mark out** *vtr* 1 *(area)* delimitar. 2 **to m. sb out for**, destinar a algn a.

mark² [mɑːk] *n (unit of currency)* marco *m*.

marked [mɑːkt] *adj* (*noticeable*) marcado,-a, acusado,-a.

marker ['mɑːkər] *n* 1 *(bookmark)* registro *m*. 2 *Sport* marcador,-a *m,f*. 3 *(pen)* rotulador *m* fluorescente.

market ['mɑːkɪt] **I** *n* mercado *m*; **m. garden**, *(small)* huerto *m*; *(large)* huerta *f*; **on the m.**, en venta; **m. forces**, tendencias *fpl* del mercado; **m. price**, precio *m* de mercado; **m. research**, estudio *m* de mercado. **II** *vtr (sell)* poner en venta; *(promote)* promocionar.

marketable ['mɑːkɪtəbəl] *adj* comerciable.

marketing ['mɑːkɪtɪŋ] *n* marketing *m*, mercadotecnia *f*.

marketplace ['mɑːkɪtpleɪs] *n* mercado *m*.

marksman ['mɑːksmən] *n* tirador *m*.

marmalade ['mɑːməleɪd] *n* mermelada *f* (de cítricos).

maroon [mə'ruːn] *adj (of colour)* granate.

marooned [mə'ruːnd] *adj* bloqueado,-a.

marquee [mɑː'kiː] *n* carpa *f*, entoldado *m*.

marquess, marquis ['mɑːkwɪs] *n* marqués *m*.

marriage ['mærɪdʒ] *n (state)* matrimonio *m*; *(wedding)* boda *f*; **m. bureau**, agencia *f* matrimonial; **m. certificate**, certificado *m* de matrimonio.

married ['mærɪd] *adj* casado,-a; **m. life**, vida *f* conyugal.

marrow ['mærəʊ] *n* 1 (bone) **m.**, médula *f*. 2 *Bot* calabacín *m*.

marry ['mærɪ] *vtr (take in marriage)* casarse con; *(give in marriage)* casar (**to**, con); *(unite in marriage)* casar; **to get married**, casarse.

Mars [mɑːz] *n* Marte *m*.

marsh [mɑːʃ] *n* pantano *m*; **salt m.**, marisma *f*.

marshal ['mɑːʃəl] **I** *n* 1 *Mil* mariscal *m*. 2 *GB (at sports event etc)* oficial *mf*. 3 *US (sheriff)* alguacil *m*. 4 *US (of police or fire department)* jefe *m*. **II** *vtr* 1 *Mil* formar. 2 *(facts etc)* ordenar.

marshy ['mɑːʃɪ] *adj* (**marshier, marshiest**) pantanoso,-a.

martial ['mɑːʃəl] *adj* marcial; **m. arts**, artes *fpl* marciales; **m. law**, ley *f* marcial.

martyr ['mɑːtər] **I** *n* mártir *mf*. **II** *vtr* martirizar.

martyrdom ['mɑːtədəm] *n* martirio *m*.

marvel ['mɑːvəl] **I** *n* maravilla *f*. **II** *vi* to

m. at, maravillarse de.
marvellous, *US* **marvelous** ['mɑːvələs] *adj* maravilloso,-a.
Marxism ['mɑːksɪzəm] *n* marxismo *m*.
Marxist ['mɑːksɪst] *adj & n* marxista *(mf)*.
marzipan ['mɑːzɪpæn] *n* mazapán *m*.
mascara [mæ'skɑːrə] *n* rímel *m*.
mascot ['mæskət] *n* mascota *f*.
masculine ['mæskjʊlɪn] *adj* masculino,-a; *(woman)* hombruna.
mash [mæʃ] I *n (for animals)* afrecho *m*. II *vtr* to m. (up), machacar; **mashed potatoes,** puré *m* de patatas.
mask [mɑːsk] I *n* máscara *f*; *(of doctor, dentist etc)* mascarilla *f*. II *vtr* enmascarar; *fig (conceal)* ocultar (**from,** de).
masochist ['mæsəkɪst] *adj & n* masoquista *(mf)*.
mason ['meɪsən] *n* 1 *(builder)* albañil *m*. 2 *(freemason)* masón *m*, francmasón *m*.
masonic [mə'sɒnɪk] *adj* masónico,-a.
masonry ['meɪsənrɪ] *n (stonework)* albañilería *f*.
masquerade [mæskə'reɪd] I *n (pretence)* farsa *f*. II *vi* to m. as, hacerse pasar por.
mass¹ [mæs] *n Rel* misa *f*; to say m., decir misa.
mass² [mæs] I *n* 1 masa *f*. 2 *(large quantity)* montón *m*; *(of people)* multitud *f*. 3 **the masses,** las masas. II *adj* masivo,-a; **m. media,** medios *mpl* de comunicación (de masas); **m. production,** fabricación *f* en serie. III *vi (people)* congregarse; *Mil* concentrarse.
massacre ['mæsəkər] I *n* masacre *f*. II *vtr* masacrar.
massage ['mæsɑːʒ, mæ'sɑːdʒ] I *n* masaje *m*. II *vtr* 1 dar masajes a. 2 *fig (figures)* amañar.
masseur [mæ'sɜːr] *n* masajista *m*.
masseuse [mæ'sɜːz] *n* masajista *f*.
massive ['mæsɪv] *adj* enorme; *(heart attack)* grave.
mast [mɑːst] *n* 1 *Naut* mástil *m*. 2 *Rad TV* torre *f*.
master ['mɑːstər] I *n* 1 *(of dog, servant)* amo *m*; *(of household)* señor *m*. 2 *GB (teacher)* profesor *m*. 3 *Univ* **m.'s degree,** ≈ máster *m*. 4 *(expert)* maestro *m*. 5 *(boy)* **M. James Brown,** el señor James Brown. II *adj* 1 **m. copy,** original *m*; **m. key,** llave *f* maestra. 2 *(expert)* maestro,-a. III *vtr* 1 *(person, situation)* dominar. 2 *(subject, skill)* llegar a dominar.
masterful ['mɑːstəfʊl] *adj* autoritario,-a; *(imperious)* imperioso,-a; *(personality)* dominante.
masterly ['mɑːstəlɪ] *adj* magistral.
mastermind ['mɑːstəmaɪnd] I *n (person)* cerebro *m*. II *vtr* ser el cerebro de.
masterpiece ['mɑːstəpiːs] *n* obra *f* maestra.
mastery ['mɑːstərɪ] *n* 1 *(control)* dominio *m* (**of,** de). 2 *(skill, expertise)* maestría *f*.

masturbate ['mæstəbeɪt] *vi* masturbarse.
mat¹ [mæt] *n (rug)* alfombrilla *f*; *(doormat)* felpudo *m*; *(rush mat)* estera *f*; *Sport* colchoneta *f*.
mat² [mæt] *adj* mate.
match¹ [mætʃ] *n* cerilla *f*, fósforo *m*.
match² [mætʃ] I *n* 1 *Sport* partido *m*; *Box* combate *m*. 2 *fig* **to meet one's m.,** *(equal)* encontrar uno la horma de su zapato. II *vtr* 1 *(equal, be the equal of)* igualar. 2 *(be in harmony with)* armonizar; **they are well matched,** *(teams)* van iguales; *(couple)* hacen buena pareja. 3 *(colours, clothes)* hacer juego con; *(pair of socks, gloves)* ser el compañero de. III *vi (harmonize)* hacer juego.
matchbox ['mætʃbɒks] *n* caja *f* de cerillas.
matching ['mætʃɪŋ] *adj* que hace juego.
mate [meɪt] I *n* 1 *(at school, work)* compañero,-a *m,f*, colega *mf*; *GB fam (friend)* amigo,-a *m,f*. 2 *Zool (male)* macho *m*; *(female)* hembra *f*. 3 *(assistant)* ayudante *mf*. 4 *Naut* **first/second m.,** primer/segundo oficial. II *vtr Zool* aparear. III *vi Zool* aparearse.
material [mə'tɪərɪəl] I *n* 1 *(substance)* materia *f*. 2 *(cloth)* tejido *m*, tela *f*. 3 *(information)* material *m*. 4 **materials,** *(ingredients, equipment)* materiales *mpl*. II *adj* 1 substancial. 2 *(not spiritual)* material.
materialistic [mətɪərɪə'lɪstɪk] *adj* materialista.
materialize [mə'tɪərɪəlaɪz] *vi* 1 *(hopes)* realizarse; *(plan, idea)* concretarse. 2 *(show up)* presentarse.
maternal [mə'tɜːnəl] *adj* maternal; *(uncle etc)* materno,-a.
maternity [mə'tɜːnɪtɪ] *n* maternidad *f*; **m. dress,** vestido *m* premamá; **m. hospital,** maternidad.
math [mæθ] *n US* → **maths.**
mathematical [mæθə'mætɪkəl] *adj* matemático,-a.
mathematician [mæθəmə'tɪʃən] *n* matemático,-a *m,f*.
mathematics [mæθə'mætɪks] *n* matemáticas *fpl*.
maths [mæθs] *n fam* matemáticas *fpl*.
matinée ['mætɪneɪ] *n Cin* sesión *f* de tarde; *Theat* función *f* de tarde.
mating ['meɪtɪŋ] *n* apareamiento *m*; **m. call,** reclamo *m*; **m. season,** época *f* de celo.
matriculation [mətrɪkjʊ'leɪʃən] *n Univ* matriculación *f*.
matrimonial [mætrɪ'məʊnɪəl] *adj* matrimonial.
matrimony ['mætrɪmənɪ] *n* matrimonio *m*; *(married life)* vida *f* conyugal.
matrix ['meɪtrɪks] *n (pl* **matrices** ['meɪtrɪsiːz]) matriz *f*.
matron ['meɪtrən] *n (in hospital)* enfermera *f* jefe.

matronly ['meɪtrənlɪ] *adj* madura y recia.
matt [mæt] *adj* mate.
matted ['mætɪd] *adj* enmarañado,-a.
matter ['mætər] *n* 1 (*affair, question*) asunto *m*; **as a m. of course**, por rutina; **as a m. of fact**, en realidad; **that's another m.**, eso es otra cosa. 2 (*problem*) **what's the m.?**, ¿qué pasa? 3 **no m. what he does**, haga lo que haga; **no m. when**, no importa cuando; **no m. where you go**, dondequiera que vayas; **no m. how clever he is**, por muy inteligente que sea; **no m. how**, como sea. 4 (*substance*) materia *f*, sustancia *f*. 5 (*content*) contenido *m*; (*subject*) tema *m*. 6 *Med* (*pus*) pus *m*. II *vi* importar; **it doesn't m.**, no importa, da igual.
matter-of-fact ['mætərəvfækt] *adj* (*person*) práctico,-a; (*account*) realista; (*style*) prosaico,-a.
mattress ['mætrɪs] *n* colchón *f*.
mature [məˈtʃʊər] I *adj* maduro,-a; *Fin* vencido,-a. II *vi* madurar; *Fin* vencer. III *vtr* madurar.
maturity [məˈtʃʊərɪtɪ] *n* madurez *f*.
maul [mɔːl] *vtr* 1 (*wound*) agredir. 2 (*handle roughly*) maltratar. 3 (*touch in unpleasant way*) sobar.
mauve [məʊv] *adj & n* malva (*m*).
max [mæks] *abbr of* **maximum**, máximo *m*, max.
maxim ['mæksɪm] *n* máxima *f*.
maximize ['mæksɪmaɪz] *vtr* maximizar.
maximum ['mæksɪməm] I *n* (*pl* **maxima** ['mæksɪmə]) máximo *m*. II *adj* máximo, -a.
may [meɪ] *v aux* (*pt* **might**) 1 (*possibility, probability*) poder, ser posible; **be that as it m.**, sea como sea; **come what m.**, pase lo que pase; **he m. or might come**, puede que venga; **you m. or might as well stay**, más vale que te quedes. 2 (*permission*) poder; **m. I?**, ¿me permite?; **you m. smoke**, pueden fumar. 3 (*wish*) ojalá (+ *subj*); **m. you always be happy!**, ¡ojalá seas siempre feliz!
May [meɪ] *n* mayo *m*; **M. Day**, el Primero *or* el Uno de Mayo.
maybe ['meɪbiː] *adv* quizá(s), tal vez.
mayhem ['meɪhem] *n* (*disturbance*) alboroto *m*; (*havoc*) estragos *mpl*.
mayonnaise [meɪəˈneɪz] *n* mayonesa *f*, mahonesa *f*.
mayor [meər] *n* (*man*) alcalde *m*; (*woman*) alcaldesa *f*.
mayoress ['meərɪs] *n* alcaldesa *f*.
maze [meɪz] *n* laberinto *m*.
MD [em'diː] 1 *abbr of* **Doctor of Medicine**, Dr. en Medicina. 2 *fam abbr of* **Managing Director**.
me [miː] *pron* 1 (*as object*) me; **he gave it to me**, me lo dio; **listen to me**, escúchame; **she knows me**, me conoce. 2 (*after prep*) mí; **it's for me**, es para mí; **with**

me, conmigo. 3 (*emphatic*) yo; **it's me**, soy yo; **what about me?**, ¿y yo, qué?
meadow ['medəʊ] *n* prado *m*, pradera *f*.
meagre, *US* **meager** ['miːgər] *adj* exiguo,-a.
meal¹ [miːl] *n* (*flour*) harina *f*.
meal² [miːl] *n* (*food*) comida *f*.
mealtime ['miːltaɪm] *n* hora *f* de comer.
mean¹ [miːn] *vtr* (*pt & pp* **meant**) 1 (*signify*) significar, querer decir; **what do you m. by that?**, ¿qué quieres decir con eso? 2 (*intend*) pensar, tener la intención de; **I m. it**, (te) lo digo en serio; **she was meant to arrive on the 7th**, tenía que *or* debía llegar el día 7; **they m. well**, tienen buenas intenciones; **she didn't m. to do it**, lo hizo sin querer. 3 (*entail*) suponer. 4 (*refer to*) referirse a. 5 (*destine*) destinar (**for**, a, para).
mean² [miːn] *adj* (*meaner, meanest*) 1 (*miserly*) tacaño,-a. 2 (*unkind*) malo,-a; (*petty*) mezquino,-a; *US* (*bad-tempered*) malhumorado,-a; **to be m.** **to sb**, tratar mal a algn. 3 (*inferior*) mediocre; (*origins*) humilde. 4 **it was no m. feat**, fue toda una hazaña.
mean³ [miːn] I *adj* (*average*) medio,-a. II *n* (*average*) promedio *m*; *Math* media *f*.
meander [mɪˈændər] *vi* (*river*) serpentear; (*person*) vagar; *fig* (*digress*) divagar.
meaning ['miːnɪŋ] *n* sentido *m*, significado *m*.
meaningful ['miːnɪŋfʊl] *adj* significativo,-a.
meaningless ['miːnɪŋlɪs] *adj* sin sentido.
meanness ['miːnnɪs] *n* 1 (*miserliness*) tacañería *f*. 2 (*nastiness*) maldad *f*.
means [miːnz] *n* 1 *sing or pl* (*method*) medio *m*, manera *f*; **by m. of**, por medio de, mediante. 2 *pl* (*resources, wealth*) medios *mpl* (de vida), recursos *mpl* (económicos); **to live beyond one's m.**, vivir por encima de sus posibilidades. 3 **by all m.!**, ¡por supuesto!; **by no m.**, de ninguna manera.
meant [ment] *pt & pp* → **mean¹**.
meantime ['miːntaɪm] I *adv* mientras tanto. II *n* **in the m.**, mientras tanto.
meanwhile ['miːnwaɪl] *adv* mientras tanto.
measles ['miːzəlz] *n* sarampión *m*.
measure ['meʒər] I *n* 1 (*action, step*) medida *f*. 2 (*ruler*) regla *f*. 3 **in some m.**, hasta cierto punto. 4 *Mus* compás *m*. II *vtr* (*object, area*) medir; (*person*) tomar las medidas de. ◆**measure up** *vi* **to m.** **(up) to sth**), estar a la altura (de algo).
measurement ['meʒəmənt] *n* medida *f*.
meat [miːt] *n* carne *f*; *Culin* **m. pie**, empanada *f* de carne.
meatball ['miːtbɔːl] *n* albóndiga *f*.
meaty ['miːtɪ] *adj* (*meatier, meatiest*) 1 carnoso,-a. 2 *fig* (*story*) jugoso,-a.

Mecca ['mekə] *n* la Meca.
mechanic [mɪ'kænɪk] *n* (*person*) mecánico,-a *m,f.*
mechanical [mɪ'kænɪkəl] *adj* mecánico, -a.
mechanics [mɪ'kænɪks] *n* **1** *sing* (*science*) mecánica *f.* **2** *pl* (*technical aspects*) mecanismo *m sing.*
mechanism ['mekənɪzəm] *n* mecanismo *m.*
medal ['medəl] *n* medalla *f.*
medallion [mɪ'dæljən] *n* medallón *m.*
medallist, *US* **medalist** ['medəlɪst] *n* medalla *f.*
meddle ['medəl] *vi* entrometerse (**in**, en); **to m. with sth**, manosear algo.
media ['miːdɪə] *npl* medios *mpl* de comunicación; **m. coverage**, cobertura periodística.
median ['miːdɪən] **I** *adj* mediano,-a. **II** *n Geom* mediana *f; Math* valor mediano.
mediate ['miːdɪeɪt] *vi* mediar.
mediator ['miːdɪeɪtər] *n* mediador,-a *m,f.*
medical ['medɪkəl] **I** *adj* (*treatment*) médico,-a; (*book*) de medicina. **II** *n fam* reconocimiento médico.
medicated ['medɪkeɪtɪd] *adj* medicinal.
medicine ['medsɪn, 'medɪsɪn] *n* (*science*) medicina *f;* (*drugs etc*) medicamento *m.*
medieval [medɪ'iːvəl] *adj* medieval.
mediocre [miːdɪ'əʊkər] *adj* mediocre.
meditate ['medɪteɪt] *vi* meditar (**on**, sobre).
meditation [medɪ'teɪʃən] *n* meditación *f.*
Mediterranean [medɪtə'reɪnɪən] **I** *adj* mediterráneo,-a. **II** *n* **the M.**, el Mediterráneo.
medium ['miːdɪəm] **I** *adj* (*average*) mediano,-a; *Rad* **m. wave**, onda media. **II** *n* **1** (*pl* **media**) (*means*) medio *m.* **2** (*pl* **mediums**) (*spiritualist*) médium *mf.*
medley ['medlɪ] *n* (*mixture*) mezcla *f; Mus* popurrí *m.*
meek [miːk] *adj* manso,-a, sumiso,-a; (*humble*) humilde.
meet [miːt] **I** *vtr* (*pt & pp* **met**) **1** (*by chance*) encontrar, encontrarse con; (*by arrangement*) reunirse con; (*in formal meeting*) entrevistarse con. **2** (*get to know*) conocer; **I'd like you to m. my mother**, quiero presentarle a mi madre; **the first time I met him**, cuando lo conocí; **pleased to m. you!**, ¡mucho gusto! **3** (*await arrival of*) esperar; (*collect*) ir a buscar. **4** (*danger*) encontrar; (*opponent*) enfrentarse con. **5** (*satisfy*) satisfacer; (*obligations*) cumplir con; (*expenses*) hacer frente a. **II** *vi* (*by chance*) encontrarse; (*by arrangement*) reunirse; (*formal meeting*) entrevistarse; (*get to know each other*) conocerse; *Sport* enfrentarse; (*join*) unirse; (*rivers*) confluir; **their eyes met**, cruzaron las miradas. **III** *n* (*hunting*) partida *f* de caza. ◆**meet with** *vtr* (*difficulty*) trope-

zar con; (*loss*) sufrir; (*success*) tener; *esp US* (*person*) reunirse con.
meeting ['miːtɪŋ] *n* (*chance encounter*) encuentro *m;* (*prearranged*) cita *f;* (*formal*) entrevista *f;* (*of committee etc*) reunión *f;* (*of assembly*) sesión *f;* (*of shareholders*) junta *f;* (*rally*) mitin *m; Sport* encuentro *m;* (*of rivers*) confluencia *f.*
megabyte ['megəbaɪt] *n Comput* megabyte *m.*
megaphone ['megəfəʊn] *n* megáfono *m.*
melancholy ['melənkəlɪ] **I** *n* melancolía *f.* **II** *adj* melancólico,-a.
Melilla [me'liːjə] *n* Melilla.
mellow ['meləʊ] **I** *adj* maduro,-a; (*wine*) añejo,-a; (*colour, voice*) suave; (*person*) apacible. **II** *vi* (*fruit*) madurar; (*colour, voice*) suavizarse.
melodramatic [melədrə'mætɪk] *adj* melodramático,-a.
melody ['melədɪ] *n* melodía *f.*
melon ['melən] *n* melón *m.*
melt [melt] **I** *vtr* (*metal*) fundir; *fig* (*sb's heart*) ablandar. **II** *vi* (*snow*) derretirse; (*metal*) fundirse; *fig* ablandarse. ◆**melt away** *vi* (*snow*) derretirse; *fig* (*money*) desaparecer; *fig* (*confidence*) desvanecerse. ◆**melt down** *vtr* (*metal*) fundir.
melting ['meltɪŋ] *n* fundición *f;* **m. point**, punto *m* de fusión; **m. pot**, crisol *m.*
member ['membər] *n* miembro *mf;* (*of a society*) socio,-a *m,f;* (*of party, union*) afiliado,-a *m,f;* **M. of Parliament**, diputado,-a *m,f.*
membership ['membəʃɪp] *n* (*state*) calidad *f* de socio; (*entry*) ingreso *m; Pol* afiliación *f;* (*number of members*) número *m* de socios; **m. card**, carnet *m* de socio.
memento [mə'mentəʊ] *n* recuerdo *m.*
memo ['meməʊ] *n* (*official note*) memorándum *m;* (*personal note*) nota *f,* apunte *m.*
memoirs ['memwɑːz] *npl* memorias *fpl.*
memorable ['memərəbəl] *adj* memorable.
memorandum [memə'rændəm] *n* (*pl* **memoranda**) (*official note*) memorándum *m;* (*personal note*) nota *f,* apunte *m.*
memorial [mɪ'mɔːrɪəl] **I** *adj* (*plaque etc*) conmemorativo,-a. **II** *n* monumento conmemorativo.
memorize ['meməraɪz] *vtr* memorizar, aprender de memoria.
memory ['memərɪ] *n* memoria *f;* (*recollection*) recuerdo *m.*
men [men] *npl* → **man**.
menace ['menɪs] **I** *n* (*threat*) amenaza *f;* (*danger*) peligro *m; fam* (*person*) pesado,-a *m,f.* **II** *vtr* amenazar.
menacing ['menɪsɪŋ] *adj* amenazador,-a.
menagerie [mɪ'nædʒərɪ] *n* casa *f* de fieras.
mend [mend] **I** *vtr* reparar, arreglar; (*clothes*) remendar; (*socks etc*) zurcir. **II** *vi*

(ill person) reponerse. **III** n *(patch)* remiendo m; *(darn)* zurcido m; *fig* **to be on the m.**, ir mejorando.

mending ['mendɪŋ] n *(repair)* reparación f; *(darning)* zurcido m; *(clothes for mending)* ropa f para remendar.

menial ['miːnɪəl] adj *(task)* servil, bajo,-a.

menopause ['menəpɔːz] n menopausia f.

menstrual ['menstruəl] adj menstrual.

menstruation [menstru'eɪʃən] n menstruación f.

mental ['mentəl] adj 1 mental; **m. home**, **m. hospital**, hospital psiquiátrico; **m. illness**, enfermedad f mental. 2 fam *(crazy)* chalado,-a. ◆**mentally** adv **m. ill**, enfermo,-a mental; **to be m. handicapped**, ser un,-a disminuido,-a psíquico,-a.

mentality [men'tælɪtɪ] n mentalidad f.

mention ['menʃən] **I** n mención f. **II** vtr mencionar; **don't m. it!**, ¡de nada!

mentor ['mentɔːr] n mentor m.

menu ['menjuː] n 1 *(card)* carta f; *(fixed meal)* menú m; **today's m.**, menú del día. 2 *Comput* menú m.

MEP [emiː'piː] abbr of **Member of the European Parliament**, eurodiputado,-a mf.

mercenary ['mɜːsɪnərɪ] adj & n mercenario,-a *(m,f)*.

merchandise ['mɜːtʃəndaɪz] n mercancías fpl, géneros mpl.

merchant ['mɜːtʃənt] n *Com Fin* comerciante mf; *(retailer)* detallista mf; **m. bank**, banco m comercial; **m. navy**, marina f mercante.

merciful ['mɜːsɪful] adj clemente, compasivo,-a **(towards**, con).

merciless ['mɜːsɪlɪs] adj despiadado,-a.

mercury ['mɜːkjurɪ] n mercurio m.

Mercury ['mɜːkjurɪ] n Mercurio m.

mercy ['mɜːsɪ] n misericordia f, compasión f; **at the m. of**, a la merced de; **to have m. on**, tener compasión de.

mere [mɪər] adj mero,-a, simple. ◆**merely** adv simplemente.

merge [mɜːdʒ] **I** vtr *(blend)* unir **(with**, con); *Com* fusionar. **II** vi unirse; *(roads)* empalmar; *Com* fusionarse.

merger ['mɜːdʒər] n *Com* fusión f.

meringue [mə'ræŋ] n merengue m.

merit ['merɪt] **I** n *(of person)* mérito m; *(of plan etc)* ventaja f. **II** vtr merecer.

mermaid ['mɜːmeɪd] n sirena f.

merry ['merɪ] adj *(merrier, merriest)* alegre; fam *(tipsy)* achispado,-a; **m. Christmas!**, ¡felices Navidades!

merry-go-round ['merɪgəuraund] n tiovivo m.

mesh [meʃ] **I** n *Tex* malla f; *Tech* engranaje m; fig red f. **II** vtr *Tech* engranar.

mesmerize ['mezməraɪz] vtr hipnotizar.

mess [mes] **I** n 1 *(confusion)* confusión f; *(disorder)* desorden m; **to be in a m.**, *(of room etc)* estar desordenado,-a. 2 *(in life, affairs)* lío m; **to get into a m.**, meterse en un lío. 3 *(dirt)* suciedad f. 4 *Mil (food)* rancho m. 5 *Mil (room)* comedor m. ◆**mess about**, **mess around** fam **I** vtr fastidiar. **II** vi *(act the fool)* hacer el primo; *(idle)* gandulear; *(kill time)* pasar el rato. ◆**mess about with** vtr fam *(fiddle with)* manosear; **to m. about with sb**, tener un lío con algn. ◆**mess up** vtr fam *(make untidy)* desordenar; *(dirty)* ensuciar; *(spoil)* estropear.

message ['mesɪdʒ] n *(communication)* recado m; *(of story etc)* mensaje m; fam **to get the m.**, comprender.

messenger ['mesɪndʒər] n mensajero,-a m,f.

Messrs ['mesəz] *Com* abbr of pl of **Mr**, Sres.

messy ['mesɪ] adj *(messier, messiest)* *(untidy)* desordenado,-a; *(confused)* enredado,-a; *(dirty)* sucio,-a.

met [met] pt & pp → **meet**.

metabolism [me'tæbəlɪzəm] n metabolismo m.

metal ['metəl] **I** n metal m. **II** adj metálico,-a.

metallic [mɪ'tælɪk] adj metálico,-a; **m. blue**, azul metalizado.

metallurgy [me'tælədʒɪ] n metalurgia f.

metalwork ['metəlwɜːk] n *(craft)* metalistería f; *(objects)* objetos mpl de metal.

metaphor ['metəfər, 'metəfɔːr] n metáfora f.

mete [miːt] vtr **to m. out**, imponer.

meteor ['miːtɪər] n bólido m.

meteoric [miːtɪ'ɒrɪk] adj meteórico,-a.

meteorite ['miːtɪəraɪt] n meteorito m.

meteorology [miːtɪə'rɒlədʒɪ] n meteorología f.

meter[1] ['miːtər] n contador m.

meter[2] ['miːtər] n *US* → **metre**.

method ['meθəd] n método m.

methodical [mɪ'θɒdɪkəl] adj metódico,-a.

Methodist ['meθədɪst] adj & n metodista *(mf)*.

meths [meθs] n fam abbr of **methylated spirits**.

methylated spirits [meθɪleɪtɪd'spɪrɪts] n alcohol metilado or desnaturalizado.

meticulous [mə'tɪkjuləs] adj meticuloso,-a.

metre ['miːtər] n metro m.

metric ['metrɪk] adj métrico,-a.

metropolis [mɪ'trɒpəlɪs] n metrópoli f.

metropolitan [metrə'pɒlɪtən] adj metropolitano,-a.

mettle ['metəl] n valor m.

mew [mjuː] vi *(cat)* maullar.

mews [mjuːz] n *(street)* callejuela f; **m. flat**, apartamento m de lujo en unas caballerizas reconvertidas.

Mexican ['meksɪkən] adj & n mejicano,-a *(m,f)*, mexicano,-a *(m,f)*.

Mexico |'meksɪkəʊ| n Méjico, México.
miaow |miː'aʊ| I vi maullar. II n maullido m.
mice |maɪs| npl → mouse.
mickey |'mɪkɪ| n fam to take the m. (out of sb), tomar el pelo (a algn).
microbe |'maɪkrəʊb| n microbio m.
microchip |'maɪkrəʊtʃɪp| n microplaqueta f, microchip m.
microcomputer |maɪkrəʊkəm'pjuːtər| n microordenador m.
microcosm |'maɪkrəʊkɒzəm| n microcosmo m.
microfilm |'maɪkrəʊfɪlm| n microfilm m.
microphone |'maɪkrəfəʊn| n micrófono m.
microprocessor |maɪkrəʊ'prəʊsesər| n microprocesador m.
microscope |'maɪkrəskəʊp| n microscopio m.
microwave |'maɪkrəʊweɪv| n microonda f; m. (oven), (horno m) microondas m inv.
mid |mɪd| adj (in) m. afternoon, a media tarde; (in) m. April, a mediados de abril; to be in one's m. thirties, tener unos treinta y cinco años.
midair |mɪd'eər| I adj (collision, explosion) en el aire. II n fig to leave sth in m., dejar algo en el aire.
midday |mɪd'deɪ| I n mediodía m. II adj de mediodía.
middle |'mɪdəl| I adj de en medio; m. age, mediana edad f; the M. Ages, la Edad Media; the m. class, la clase media. II n 1 centro m, medio m; in the m. of, en medio de; in the m. of winter, en pleno invierno; fam in the m. of nowhere, en el quinto pino. 2 fam (waist) cintura f.
middle-aged |mɪdəl'eɪdʒd| adj de mediana edad.
middle-class |mɪdəl'klɑːs| adj de clase media.
middleman |'mɪdəlmæn| n intermediario m.
middleweight |'mɪdəlweɪt| n peso medio.
middling |'mɪdlɪŋ| adj mediano,-a.
midfielder |mɪd'fiːldər| n Sport centrocampista mf.
midge |mɪdʒ| n mosca enana.
midget |'mɪdʒɪt| n enano,-a m,f.
Midlands |'mɪdləndz| npl the M., la región central de Inglaterra.
midnight |'mɪdnaɪt| n medianoche f.
midst |mɪdst| prep in the m. of, en medio de.
midsummer |mɪd'sʌmər| n pleno verano; M.'s Day, Día m de San Juan (24 de junio).
midway |'mɪdweɪ| adv a medio camino.
midweek |'mɪdwiːk| I adv entre semana. II adj de entre semana.

midwife |'mɪdwaɪf| n comadrona f, partera f.
midwifery |'mɪdwɪfərɪ| n obstetricia f.
midwinter |mɪd'wɪntər| n pleno invierno m.
might¹ |maɪt| v aux → may.
might² |maɪt| n fml fuerza f, poder m.
mighty |'maɪtɪ| I adj (mightier, mightiest) (strong) fuerte; (powerful) poderoso, -a; (great) enorme.
migraine |'miːɡreɪn, 'maɪɡreɪn| n jaqueca f.
migrant |'maɪɡrənt| I adj migratorio,-a. II n (person) emigrante mf; (bird) ave migratoria.
migrate |maɪ'ɡreɪt| vi emigrar.
migration |maɪ'ɡreɪʃən| n migración f.
mike |maɪk| n fam (abbr of **microphone**) micro m.
mild |maɪld| adj (person, character) apacible; (climate) templado,-a; (punishment) leve; (tobacco, taste) suave. ◆**mildly** adv (softly, gently) suavemente; (slightly) ligeramente; and that's putting it m., y esto es decir poco.
mildew |'mɪldjuː| n moho m; (on plants) añublo m.
mildness |'maɪldnɪs| n (of character) apacibilidad f; (of climate, taste) suavidad f; (of punishment) levedad f.
mile |maɪl| n milla f; fam miles better, muchísimo mejor.
mileage |'maɪlɪdʒ| n kilometraje m.
milestone |'maɪlstəʊn| n hito m.
milieu |'miːljɜː| n medio m ambiente.
militant |'mɪlɪtənt| adj & n militante (mf).
military |'mɪlɪtərɪ| adj militar; to do one's m. service, hacer el servicio militar.
militia |mɪ'lɪʃə| n milicia f.
milk |mɪlk| I n leche f; m. chocolate, chocolate m con leche; m. shake, batido m. II vtr 1 (cow, goat) ordeñar. 2 fam they milked him of all his money, le sangraron hasta la última peseta.
milkman |'mɪlkmən| n lechero m.
milky |'mɪlkɪ| adj (milkier, milkiest) lechoso,-a; (colour) pálido,-a; M. Way, Vía Láctea.
mill |mɪl| I n (grinder) molino m; (for coffee) molinillo m; (factory) fábrica f; cotton m., hilandería f. II vtr moler. ◆**mill about, mill around** vi arremolinarse.
millennium |mɪ'lenɪəm| n (pl **millenniums** or **milenia** |mɪ'lenɪə|) milenio m.
miller |'mɪlər| n molinero,-a m,f.
millet |'mɪlɪt| n mijo m.
milligram(me) |'mɪlɪɡræm| n miligramo m.
millilitre, US **milliliter** |'mɪlɪliːtər| n mililitro m.
millimetre, US **millimeter** |'mɪlɪmiːtər|

n milímetro *m*.

milliner ['mɪlɪnər] *n* sombrerero,-a *m,f*.

millinery ['mɪlɪnərɪ] *n* sombreros *mpl* de señora.

million ['mɪljən] *n* millón *m*.

millionaire [mɪljə'neər] *n* millonario,-a *m,f*.

millstone ['mɪlstəʊn] *n* muela *f*; *fig* carga *f*.

mime [maɪm] I *n* (*art*) mímica *f*; (*play*) pantomima *f*. II *vtr* representar con gestos.

mimic ['mɪmɪk] I *adj & n* mímico,-a (*m,f*). II *vtr* imitar.

mimicry ['mɪmɪkrɪ] *n* imitación *f*.

minaret ['mɪnəret] *n* alminar *m*, minarete *m*.

mince [mɪns] I *n GB* (*meat*) carne picada; **m. pie**, pastel *m* de picadillo de fruta. II *vtr* picar; *fig* **he doesn't m. his words**, no tiene pelos en la lengua. III *vi* (*walk*) **to m. (along)**, andar con pasos menuditos.

mincemeat ['mɪnsmiːt] *n* (*dried fruit*) conserva *f* de picadillo de fruta; (*meat*) carne picada.

mincer ['mɪnsər] *n* picadora *f* de carne.

mind [maɪnd] I *n* 1 (*intellect*) mente *f*; (*brain*) cabeza *f*; **what kind of car do you have in m.?**, ¿en qué clase de coche estás pensando?; **to lose one's m.**, perder el juicio; **it slipped my m.**, lo olvidé por completo; **to call sth to m.**, recordar algo. 2 (*opinion*) **to be in two minds about sth**, estar indeciso,-a; **to my m.**, a mi parecer. II *vtr* 1 (*child*) cuidar; (*house*) vigilar; (*be careful of*) tener cuidado con; **m. the step!**, ¡ojo con el escalón!; **m. your own business!**, ¡no te metas donde no te llaman! 2 (*object to*) tener inconveniente en; **I wouldn't m. a cup of coffee**, me vendría bien un café; **never m.**, no importa. III *vi* 1 **m. you, he is fifty**, ten en cuenta que tiene cincuenta años. 2 (*object*) importar; **do you m. if I open the window?**, ¿le importa que abra la ventana?

minder ['maɪndər] *n fam* (*bodyguard*) guardaespaldas *m inv*; (*for child*) niñera *f*; (*babysitter*) canguro *mf*.

mindful ['maɪndful] *adj* consciente.

mindless ['maɪndlɪs] *adj* (*task*) de autómata; (*violence*) injustificable.

mine¹ [maɪn] *poss pron* (el) mío,-a, (la) mía, (los) míos, (las) mías, lo mío; **a friend of m.**, un amigo mío; **these gloves are m.**, estos guantes son míos; **which is m.?**, ¿cuál es el mío?

mine² [maɪn] I *n* mina *f*; *fig* **a m. of information**, un pozo de información. II *vtr* (*coal etc*) extraer; *Mil* minar.

minefield ['maɪnfiːld] *n* campo *m* de minas.

miner ['maɪnər] *n* minero,-a *m,f*.

mineral ['mɪnərəl] I *adj* mineral; **m.**

water, agua *f* mineral. II *n* mineral *m*.

minesweeper ['maɪnswiːpər] *n* dragaminas *m inv*.

mingle ['mɪŋgəl] *vi* mezclarse.

miniature ['mɪnɪtʃər] I *n* miniatura *f*. II *adj* (*railway*) en miniatura; (*camera, garden*) diminuto,-a.

minibus ['mɪnɪbʌs] *n* microbús *m*.

minim ['mɪnɪm] *n Mus* blanca *f*.

minimal ['mɪnɪməl] *adj* mínimo,-a.

minimum ['mɪnɪməm] I *adj* mínimo,-a; **m. wage**, salario mínimo. II *n* mínimo *m*.

mining ['maɪnɪŋ] I *n* minería *f*, explotación *f* de minas; *Mil Naut* minado *m*. II *adj* minero,-a.

miniskirt ['mɪnɪskɜːt] *n* minifalda *f*.

minister ['mɪnɪstər] I *n* ministro,-a *m,f*; *Rel* pastor,-a *m,f*. II *vi* **to m. to sb**, atender a algn.

ministerial [mɪnɪ'stɪərɪəl] *adj Pol* ministerial.

ministry ['mɪnɪstrɪ] *n Pol* ministerio *m*; *Rel* sacerdocio *m*.

mink [mɪŋk] *n* visón *m*; **m. coat**, abrigo *m* de visón.

minnow ['mɪnəʊ] *n* piscardo *m*.

minor ['maɪnər] I *adj* (*lesser*) menor; (*unimportant*) sin importancia; (*role*) secundario,-a; *Mus* menor. II *n Jur* menor *mf* de edad.

Minorca [mɪ'nɔːkə] *n* Menorca *f*.

minority [maɪ'nɒrɪtɪ] *n* minoría *f*; **to be in the m.**, ser (la) minoría; *Pol* **m. party**, partido minoritario.

mint¹ [mɪnt] I *n Fin* **the M.**, la Casa de la Moneda; **in m. condition**, en perfecto estado. II *vtr* (*coin, words*) acuñar.

mint² [mɪnt] *n Bot* menta *f*; (*sweet*) pastilla *f* de menta.

minus ['maɪnəs] I *prep* **5 m. 3**, 5 menos 3; **m. 10 degrees**, 10 grados bajo cero. II *adj* negativo,-a. III *n* **m. (sign)**, signo *m* (de) menos.

minute¹ ['mɪnɪt] *n* 1 minuto *m*; **at the last m.**, a última hora; **just a m.**, (*espera*) un momento; **this very m.**, ahora mismo. 2 **minutes**, (*notes*) el acta.

minute² [maɪ'njuːt] *adj* (*tiny*) diminuto, -a; (*examination*) minucioso,-a.

miracle ['mɪrəkəl] *n* milagro *m*.

miraculous [mɪ'rækjʊləs] *adj* milagroso, -a.

mirage [mɪ'rɑːʒ] *n* espejismo *m*.

mire [maɪər] *n* fango *m*, lodo *m*; (*muddy place*) lodazal *m*.

mirror ['mɪrər] I *n* espejo *m*; *fig* reflejo *m*; **rear-view m.**, retrovisor *m*; **m. image**, réplica *f*. II *vtr* reflejar.

mirth [mɜːθ] *n* alegría *f*; (*laughter*) risas *fpl*.

misadventure [mɪsəd'ventʃər] *n* desgracia *f*; **death by m.**, muerte *f* accidental.

misanthropist [mɪ'zænθrəpɪst] *n* misántropo,-a *m,f*.

misapprehension |mɪsæprɪ'henʃən| *n* malentendido *m*.

misbehave |mɪsbɪ'heɪv| *vi* portarse mal.

miscalculate |mɪs'kælkjʊleɪt| *vtr & vi* calcular mal.

miscarriage |'mɪskærɪdʒ| *n Med* aborto *m* (espontáneo); **m. of justice**, error *m* judicial.

miscellaneous |mɪsɪ'leɪnɪəs| *adj* variado,-a; **m. expenses**, gastos diversos.

mischief |'mɪstʃɪf| *n* (*naughtiness*) travesura *f*; *fml* (*evil*) malicia *f*; *fam* (*harm*) daño *m*; **to get up to m.**, hacer travesuras.

mischievous |'mɪstʃɪvəs| *adj* (*naughty*) travieso,-a; (*playful*) juguetón,-ona; *fml* (*wicked*) malicioso,-a.

misconception |mɪskən'sepʃən| *n* concepto erróneo.

misconduct |mɪs'kɒndʌkt| *n* mala conducta; **professional m.**, error *m* profesional.

misconstrue |mɪskən'struː| *vtr* interpretar mal.

miscount |mɪs'kaʊnt| *vtr* (*votes etc*) contar mal.

misdeed |mɪs'diːd| *n* fechoría *f*.

misdemeanour, *US* **misdemeanor** |mɪsdɪ'miːnər| *n* (*misdeed*) fechoría *f*; *Jur* delito *m* menor.

miser |'maɪzər| *n* avaro,-a *m,f*.

miserable |'mɪzərəbəl| *adj* (*sad*) triste; (*unfortunate*) desgraciado,-a; (*wretched*) miserable.

miserly |'maɪzəlɪ| *adj* avaro,-a, tacaño,-a.

misery |'mɪzərɪ| *n* (*sadness*) tristeza *f*; (*wretchedness*) desgracia *f*; (*suffering*) sufrimiento *m*; (*poverty*) miseria *f*; *fam* (*person*) aguafiestas *mf*.

misfire |mɪs'faɪər| *vi* (*engine, plan etc*) fallar.

misfit |'mɪsfɪt| *n* (*person*) inadaptado,-a *m,f*.

misfortune |mɪs'fɔːtʃən| *n* desgracia *f*.

misgiving |mɪs'gɪvɪŋ| *n* (*doubt*) recelo *m*; (*fear*) temor *m*.

misguided |mɪs'gaɪdɪd| *adj* equivocado, -a.

mishandle |mɪs'hændəl| *vtr* llevar *or* manejar mal.

mishap |'mɪshæp| *n* contratiempo *m*.

misinform |mɪsɪn'fɔːm| *vtr* informar mal.

misinterpret |mɪsɪn'tɜːprɪt| *vtr* interpretar mal.

misjudge |mɪs'dʒʌdʒ| *vtr* juzgar mal.

mislay |mɪs'leɪ| *vtr* extraviar.

mislead |mɪs'liːd| *vtr* despistar; (*deliberately*) engañar.

misleading |mɪs'liːdɪŋ| *adj* (*erroneous*) erróneo,-a; (*deliberately*) engañoso,-a.

mismanagement |mɪs'mænɪdʒmənt| *n* mala administración *f*.

misnomer |mɪs'nəʊmər| *n* nombre equivocado.

misogynist |mɪ'sɒdʒɪnɪst| *n* misógino,-a

m,f.

misplace |mɪs'pleɪs| *vtr* (*trust*) encauzar mal; (*book, spectacles etc*) extraviar.

misprint |'mɪsprɪnt| *n* errata *f*, error *m* de imprenta.

misrepresent |mɪsreprɪ'zent| *vtr* (*facts*) desvirtuar; (*words*) tergiversar.

miss¹ |mɪs| *n* señorita *f*.

miss² |mɪs| **I** *n* (*throw etc*) fallo *m*; *fam* **to give sth a m.**, pasar de algo. **II** *vtr* **1** (*when throwing*) fallar; (*when shooting*) errar. **2** (*train etc*) perder; (*opportunity*) dejar pasar; **you have missed the point**, no has captado la idea; *fig* **to m. the boat**, perder el tren. **3** (*omit*) saltarse. **4 I m. you**, te echo de menos. **III** *vi* (*when throwing*) fallar; (*when shooting*) errar; **is anything missing?**, ¿falta algo? ◆**miss out I** *vtr* (*omit*) saltarse; (*on purpose*) pasar por alto. **II** *vtr* **to m. out on**, perderse.

misshapen |mɪs'ʃeɪpən| *adj* deforme.

missile |'mɪsaɪl| *US n Mil* misil *m*; (*object thrown*) proyectil *m*.

missing |'mɪsɪŋ| *adj* (*object*) perdido,-a; (*person*) desaparecido,-a; (*from meeting etc*) ausente; **m. person**, desaparecido,-a *m,f*; **three cups are m.**, faltan tres tazas.

mission |'mɪʃən| *n* misión *f*.

missionary |'mɪʃənərɪ| *n* misionero,-a *m,f*.

misspent |'mɪsspent| *adj* (*youth*) malgastado,-a.

mist |mɪst| *n* neblina *f*; (*thick*) niebla *f*; (*at sea*) bruma *f*. **II** *vi* **to m. over** *or* **up**, (*countryside*) cubrirse de neblina; (*window etc*) empañarse.

mistake |mɪ'steɪk| **I** *n* error *m*; **by m.**, por equivocación; **I hurt him by m.**, le golpeé sin querer; **to make a m.**, equivocarse, cometer un error. **II** *vtr* (*pt mistook; pp mistaken*) (*meaning*) malentender; **to m. Jack for Bill**, confundir a Jack con Bill.

mistaken |mɪ'steɪkən| *adj* equivocado,-a, erróneo,-a; **you are m.**, estás equivocado,-a.

mister |'mɪstər| *n* señor *m*.

mistletoe |'mɪsltəʊ| *n* muérdago *m*.

mistook |mɪ'stʊk| *pt* → **mistake**.

mistreat |mɪs'triːt| *vtr* tratar mal.

mistress |'mɪstrɪs| *n* (*of house*) señora *f*, ama *f*; (*lover*) amante *f*; *Educ* (*primary school*) maestra *f*; (*secondary school*) profesora *f*.

mistrust |mɪs'trʌst| **I** *n* recelo *m*. **II** *vtr* desconfiar de.

misty |'mɪstɪ| *adj* (*mistier, mistiest*) (*day*) de niebla; (*window etc*) empañado,-a.

misunderstand |mɪsʌndə'stænd| *vtr & vi* malentender.

misunderstanding |mɪsʌndə'stændɪŋ| *n* malentendido *m*; (*disagreement*) desavenencia *f*.

misuse [mɪs'juːs] **I** n mal uso m; (of funds) malversación f; (of power) abuso m. **II** [mɪs'juːz] vtr emplear mal; (funds) malversar; (power) abusar de.

miter ['maɪtər] n US → mitre.

mitigate ['mɪtɪgeɪt] vtr atenuar.

mitigating ['mɪtɪgeɪtɪŋ] adj **m. circumstances,** circunstancias fpl atenuantes.

mitre ['maɪtər] n mitra f.

mitten ['mɪtən] n manopla f; (fingerless) ·mitón m.

mix [mɪks] **I** n mezcla f. **II** vtr mezclar. **III** vi (blend) mezclarse (with, con); (go well together) ir bien juntos. ◆**mix up** vtr (confuse) confundir (with, con); (papers) revolver; **to be mixed up in sth,** estar involucrado,-a en algo.

mixed [mɪkst] adj (assorted) surtido,-a; (varied) variado,-a; (school) mixto,-a; (feelings) contradictorio,-a.

mixed-up [mɪkst'ʌp] adj (objects, papers etc) revuelto,-a; (person) confuso,-a.

mixer ['mɪksər] n **1** Culin batidora f. **2 to be a good m.,** (person) tener don de gentes.

mixture ['mɪkstʃər] n mezcla f.

mix-up ['mɪksʌp] n fam confusión f, lío m.

mm abbr of millimetre(s), mm.

moan [məʊn] **I** n (groan) gemido m, quejido m. **II** vi (groan) gemir; (complain) quejarse (about, de).

moat [məʊt] n foso m.

mob [mɒb] **I** n multitud f; (riff-raff) gentuza f; **the m.,** el populacho. **II** vtr acosar.

mobile ['məʊbaɪl, US 'məʊbəl] **I** adj móvil; **m. home,** caravana f. **II** n (hanging ornament) móvil m.

mobility [məʊ'bɪlɪtɪ] n movilidad f.

mobilize ['məʊbɪlaɪz] vtr movilizar.

mock [mɒk] **I** adj (sympathy etc) fingido, -a; (objects) de imitación. **II** vtr (make fun of) burlarse de. **III** vi burlarse (at, de).

mockery ['mɒkərɪ] n burla f.

mode [məʊd] n (manner) modo m, estilo m; (fashion) moda f.

model ['mɒdəl] **I** n modelo m; (fashion model) modelo mf; (scale) **m.,** maqueta f. **II** adj (railway) en miniatura; (pupil) ejemplar; (school) modelo. **III** vtr (clay etc) modelar; (clothes) presentar. **IV** vi (make models) modelar; (work as model) trabajar de modelo.

modem ['məʊdem] n Comput modem m.

moderate[1] ['mɒdərɪt] **I** adj moderado,-a; (reasonable) razonable; (average) regular; (ability) mediocre. **II** n Pol moderado,-a m,f. ◆**moderately** adv medianamente.

moderate[2] ['mɒdəreɪt] **I** vtr moderar. **II** vi moderarse; (wind) calmarse; (in debate) arbitrar.

moderation [mɒdə'reɪʃən] n moderación f; **in m.,** con moderación.

modern ['mɒdən] adj moderno,-a; (history) contemporáneo,-a; **m. languages,** lenguas modernas.

modernize ['mɒdənaɪz] vtr modernizar.

modest ['mɒdɪst] adj modesto,-a; (chaste) púdico,-a; (price) módico,-a; (success) discreto,-a.

modesty ['mɒdɪstɪ] n (humility) modestia f; (chastity) pudor m.

modification [mɒdɪfɪ'keɪʃən] n modificación f.

modify ['mɒdɪfaɪ] vtr modificar.

module ['mɒdjuːl] n módulo m.

mogul ['məʊgʌl] n magnate m.

mohair ['məʊheər] **I** n mohair m. **II** adj de mohair.

moist [mɔɪst] adj húmedo,-a.

moisten ['mɔɪsən] vtr humedecer.

moisture ['mɔɪstʃər] n humedad f.

moisturizer ['mɔɪstʃəraɪzər] n crema f or leche f hidratante.

molar ['məʊlər] n muela f.

molasses [mə'læsɪz] n melaza f.

mold [məʊld] n US → mould.

mole[1] [məʊl] n (beauty spot) lunar m.

mole[2] [məʊl] n (animal) topo m.

molecule ['mɒlɪkjuːl] n molécula f.

molest [mə'lest] vtr importunar; (sexually assault) acosar (sexualmente).

mollycoddle ['mɒlɪkɒdəl] vtr fam mimar, consentir.

molt [məʊlt] vi US → moult.

molten ['məʊltən] adj fundido,-a; (lava) líquido,-a.

mom [mɒm] n US fam mamá f.

moment ['məʊmənt] n momento m; **at the m.,** en este momento; **for the m.,** de momento; **in a m.,** dentro de un momento; **at any m.,** de un momento a otro.

momentary ['məʊməntərɪ] adj momentáneo,-a. ◆**momentarily** adv momentáneamente; US (soon) dentro de poco.

momentous [məʊ'mentəs] adj trascendental.

momentum [məʊ'mentəm] n Phys momento m; (speed) velocidad f; fig **to gather m.,** cobrar velocidad.

mommy ['mɒmɪ] n US fam mamá f.

Monaco ['mɒnəkəʊ] n Mónaco.

monarch ['mɒnək] n monarca m.

monarchy ['mɒnəkɪ] n monarquía f.

monastery ['mɒnəstərɪ] n monasterio m.

Monday ['mʌndɪ] n lunes m.

monetarism ['mʌnɪtərɪzəm] n monetarismo m.

monetary ['mʌnɪtərɪ] adj monetario,-a.

money ['mʌnɪ] n dinero m; (currency) moneda f; **to make m.,** ganar dinero; **to put m. on,** apostar por.

moneylender ['mʌnɪlendər] n prestamista mf.

money-spinner ['mʌnɪspɪnər] n fam negocio *m* rentable.

Mongolia [mɒŋˈgəʊlɪə] *n* Mongolia.

mongolism [ˈmɒŋgəlɪzəm] *n* mongolismo *m*.

mongrel [ˈmʌŋgrəl] *n* perro mestizo.

monitor [ˈmɒnɪtəʳ] **I** *n* (screen) monitor *m*; Educ delegado,-a *m,f*. **II** *vtr* (check) controlar; (progress, events) seguir de cerca.

monk [mʌŋk] *n* monje *m*.

monkey [ˈmʌŋkɪ] *n* mono *m*; **m. nut**, cacahuete *m*; **m. wrench**, llave inglesa.

monochrome [ˈmɒnəkrəʊm] *adj* monocromo,-a; (television, photo) en blanco y negro.

monocle [ˈmɒnəkəl] *n* monóculo *m*.

monologue, US **monolog** [ˈmɒnəlɒg] *n* monólogo *m*.

monopolize [məˈnɒpəlaɪz] *vtr* Fin monopolizar; (attention etc) acaparar.

monopoly [məˈnɒpəlɪ] *n* monopolio *m*.

monotone [ˈmɒnətəʊn] *n* **in a m.**, con una voz monótona.

monotonous [məˈnɒtənəs] *adj* monótono,-a.

monotony [məˈnɒtənɪ] *n* monotonía *f*.

monsoon [mɒnˈsuːn] *n* monzón *m*.

monster [ˈmɒnstəʳ] *n* monstruo *m*.

monstrosity [mɒnˈstrɒsɪtɪ] *n* monstruosidad *f*.

monstrous [ˈmɒnstrəs] *adj* (huge) enorme; (hideous) monstruoso,-a; (outrageous) escandaloso,-a.

montage [ˈmɒntɑːʒ] *n* montaje *m*.

month [mʌnθ] *n* mes *m*.

monthly [ˈmʌnθlɪ] **I** *adj* mensual; **m. instalment**, mensualidad *f*. **II** *n* (periodical) revista *f* mensual. **III** *adv* mensualmente, cada mes.

monument [ˈmɒnjʊmənt] *n* monumento *m*.

monumental [mɒnjʊˈmentəl] *adj* monumental; fam (huge) enorme.

moo [muː] **I** *n* mugido *m*. **II** *vi* mugir.

mood [muːd] *n* humor *m*; **to be in a good/bad m.**, estar de buen/mal humor; **to be in the m. for (doing) sth**, estar de humor para (hacer) algo.

moody [ˈmuːdɪ] *adj* (moodier, moodiest) (changeable) de humor variable; (badtempered) malhumorado,-a.

moon [muːn] *n* luna *f*; fam **over the m.**, en el séptimo cielo.

moonlight [ˈmuːnlaɪt] *n* luz *f* de la luna.

moonlighting [ˈmuːnlaɪtɪŋ] *n* fam pluriempleo *m*.

moonlit [ˈmuːnlɪt] *adj* (night) de luna.

moor¹ [mʊəʳ] *n* (heath) páramo *m*.

moor² [mʊəʳ, mɔːʳ] *vtr* Naut amarrar.

Moor [mʊəʳ] *n* moro,-a *m,f*.

Moorish [ˈmʊərɪʃ] *adj* moro,-a.

moorland [ˈmʊələnd] *n* páramo *m*.

moose [muːs] *n inv* alce *m*.

moot [muːt] *adj* **it's a m. point**, es discutible.

mop [mɒp] **I** *n* (for floor) fregona *f*; fam **m. of hair**, melena *f*. **II** *vtr* fregar.
◆**mop up** *vtr* (liquids) enjugar; (enemy forces) acabar con.

mope [məʊp] *vi* estar alicaído,-a.
◆**mope about, mope around** *vi* andar abatido,-a.

moped [ˈməʊped] *n* ciclomotor *m*, vespa *f*.

moral [ˈmɒrəl] **I** *adj* moral. **II** *n* moraleja *f*; **morals**, moral *f sing*, moralidad *f sing*.

morale [məˈrɑːl] *n* moral *f*, estado *m* de ánimo.

morality [məˈrælɪtɪ] *n* moralidad *f*.

morass [məˈræs] *n* pantano *m*; fig lío *m*.

morbid [ˈmɔːbɪd] *adj* Med mórbido,-a; (mind) morboso,-a.

more [mɔːʳ] **I** *adj* más; **and what is m.**, y lo que es más; **is there any m. tea?**, ¿queda más té?; **I've no m. money**, no me queda más dinero; **m. tourists**, más turistas. **II** *pron* más; **how many m.?**, ¿cuántos más?; **I need some m.**, necesito más; **it's m. than enough**, es más que suficiente; **many/much m.**, muchos,-as/mucho más; **m. than a hundred**, más de cien; **the m. he has, the m. he wants**, cuanto más tiene más quiere. **III** *adv* más; **I won't do it any m.**, no lo volveré a hacer; **she doesn't live here any m.**, ya no vive aquí; **m. and m. difficult**, cada vez más difícil; **m. or less**, más o menos; **once m.**, una vez más.

moreover [mɔːˈrəʊvəʳ] *adv* además.

morgue [mɔːg] *n* depósito *m* de cadáveres.

morning [ˈmɔːnɪŋ] **I** *n* mañana *f*; (before dawn) madrugada *f*; **in the m.**, por la mañana; **on Monday mornings**, los lunes por la mañana; **tomorrow m.**, mañana por la mañana. **II** *adj* matutino,-a.

Moroccan [məˈrɒkən] *adj & n* marroquí (mf).

Morocco [məˈrɒkəʊ] *n* Marruecos *m*.

moron [ˈmɔːrɒn] *n* fam imbécil *mf*.

morose [məˈrəʊs] *adj* malhumorado,-a, hosco,-a.

morphine [ˈmɔːfiːn] *n* morfina *f*.

Morse [mɔːs] *n* **M. (code)**, (alfabeto *m*) Morse *m*.

morsel [ˈmɔːsəl] *n* (of food) bocado *m*; fig trozo *m*.

mortal [ˈmɔːtəl] **I** *adj* mortal. **II** *n* mortal *mf*. ◆**mortally** *adv* mortalmente; **m. wounded**, herido,-a de muerte.

mortality [mɔːˈtælɪtɪ] *n* mortalidad *f*.

mortar [ˈmɔːtəʳ] *n* mortero *m*.

mortgage [ˈmɔːgɪdʒ] **I** *n* hipoteca *f*. **II** *vtr* hipotecar.

mortify [ˈmɔːtɪfaɪ] *vtr* mortificar; fam **I was mortified**, me sentí avergonzado,-a.

mortuary [ˈmɔːtʃʊərɪ] *n* depósito *m* de cadáveres.

mosaic [məˈzeɪɪk] *n* mosaico *m*.

Moscow ['mɒskəʊ, US 'mɒskaʊ] n
Moscú.
Moslem ['mɒzləm] adj & n musulmán,
-ana (m,f).
mosque [mɒsk] n mezquita f.
mosquito [mɒs'kiːtəʊ] n (pl **mosquitoes**)
mosquito m; **m. net**, mosquitero m.
moss [mɒs] n musgo m.
most [məʊst] I adj (superl of **much**,
many) 1 (greatest in quantity etc) más; **this
house suffered (the) m. damage**, esta
casa fue la más afectada; **who made (the)
m. mistakes?**, ¿quién cometió más errores? 2 (the majority of) la mayoría de, la
mayor parte de; **for the m. part**, por lo
general; **m. of the time**, la mayor parte
del tiempo; **m. people**, la mayoría de la
gente.
II pron (greatest part) la mayor parte;
(greatest number) lo máximo, lo más; (the
majority of people) la mayoría; **at the
(very) m.**, como máximo; **to make the
m. of sth**, aprovechar algo al máximo.
III adv (superl of **much**) 1 más; **the m.
intelligent student**, el estudiante más
inteligente; **what I like m.**, lo que más
me gusta. 2 (very) muy; **m. likely**, muy
probablemente; **m. of all**, sobre todo.
◆**mostly** adv (chiefly) en su mayor
parte; (generally) generalmente; (usually)
normalmente.
MOT [eməʊ'tiː] GB abbr of **Ministry of
Transport; MOT test**, inspección técnica de vehículos, ITV.
motel [məʊ'tel] n motel m.
moth [mɒθ] n mariposa nocturna; **clothes
m.**, polilla f.
mother ['mʌðər] I n madre f; **unmarried
m.**, madre soltera; **M.'s Day**, Día m de
la Madre; **m. tongue**, lengua materna. II
vtr cuidar maternalmente.
motherhood ['mʌðəhʊd] n maternidad f.
mother-in-law ['mʌðərɪnlɔː] n suegra f.
motherly ['mʌðəlɪ] adj maternal.
mother-of-pearl [mʌðərəv'pɜːl] n madreperla f, nácar m.
mother-to-be [mʌðətə'biː] n futura madre.
motif [məʊ'tiːf] n Art Mus motivo m; (embroidered etc) adorno m; fig (main subject)
tema m.
motion ['məʊʃən] I n (movement) movimiento m; (gesture) ademán m; (proposal)
moción f. II vtr & vi hacer señas; **to m.
(to) sb to do sth**, hacer señas a algn para
que haga algo.
motionless ['məʊʃənlɪs] adj inmóvil.
motivate ['məʊtɪveɪt] vtr motivar.
motivation [məʊtɪ'veɪʃən] n motivación
f.
motive ['məʊtɪv] I adj (force) motriz. II n
(reason) motivo m; **with the best of
motives**, con la mejor intención.
motley ['mɒtlɪ] adj (**motlier, motliest**)

(multicoloured) abigarrado,-a; (varied)
variado,-a.
motor ['məʊtər] n (engine) motor m; fam
(car) máquina f; **m. racing**, carreras fpl
de coches.
motorbike ['məʊtəbaɪk] n fam motocicleta f, moto f.
motorboat ['məʊtəbəʊt] n (lancha) motora f.
motorcar ['məʊtəkɑːr] n coche m, automóvil m.
motorcycle ['məʊtəsaɪkəl] n motocicleta
f.
motorcyclist ['məʊtəsaɪklɪst] n motociclista mf.
motoring ['məʊtərɪŋ] n automovilismo m.
motorist ['məʊtərɪst] n automovilista mf.
motorway ['məʊtəweɪ] n GB autopista f.
mottled ['mɒtəld] adj (skin, animal) con
manchas; (surface) moteado,-a.
motto ['mɒtəʊ] n lema m.
mould¹, US **mold** [məʊld] n (fungus)
moho m.
mould², US **mold** [məʊld] I n molde m.
II vtr moldear; (clay) modelar.
moulder, US **molder** ['məʊldər] vi **to m.
(away)**, desmoronarse.
moulding, US **molding** ['məʊldɪŋ] n
moldura f.
mouldy, US **moldy** ['məʊldɪ] adj
(**mouldier, mouldiest**) mohoso,-a; **to go
m.**, enmohecerse.
moult [məʊlt] vi mudar.
mound [maʊnd] n montón m; (small hill)
montículo m.
mount¹ [maʊnt] n monte m; **M. Everest**, (Monte) Everest m.
mount² [maʊnt] I n (horse) montura f;
(support) soporte m, base f; (for photograph) marco m; (for jewel) engaste m. II
vtr (horse) subirse o montar a; (campaign)
organizar; (photograph) enmarcar; (jewel)
engastar. III vi (go up) subir; (get on
horse, bike) montar; (increase) subir.
◆**mount up** vi (accumulate) acumularse.
mountain ['maʊntɪn] I n montaña f; fig
(pile) montón m. II adj de montaña,
montañés,-esa; **m. bike**, bicicleta f de
montaña; **m. range**, sierra f, cordillera f.
mountaineer [maʊntɪ'nɪər] n alpinista
mf, Am andinista mf.
mountaineering [maʊntɪ'nɪərɪŋ] n alpinismo m, Am andinismo m.
mountainous ['maʊntɪnəs] adj
montañoso,-a.
mourn [mɔːn] vtr & vi **to m. (for) sb**, llorar la muerte de algn.
mourner ['mɔːnər] n doliente mf.
mournful ['mɔːnfʊl] adj triste; (voice) lúgubre.
mourning ['mɔːnɪŋ] n luto m; **in m.**, de
luto.
mouse [maʊs] n (pl **mice**) also Comput ra-

tón *m*.

mousetrap |'maʊstræp| *n* ratonera *f*.

mousse |muːs| *n Culin* mousse *f*; *(for hair)* **(styling)** m., espuma *f* (moldeadora).

moustache |mə'stɑːʃ| *n* bigote(s) *m(pl)*.

mousy |'maʊsɪ| *adj* **(mousier, mousiest)** *(colour)* pardusco,-a; *(hair)* castaño claro; *(shy)* tímido,-a.

mouth |maʊθ| **I** *n (pl* **mouths** |maʊðz|) 1 boca *f*; *fam* **down in the m.**, deprimido, -a. 2 *(of cave etc)* entrada *f*; *(of river)* desembocadura *f*. **II** *vtr* |maʊð| pronunciar; *(insults)* proferir.

mouthful |'maʊθfʊl| *n (of food)* bocado *m*; *(of drink)* sorbo *m*; **to be a bit of a m.**, ser difícil de pronunciar.

mouth organ |'maʊθɔːgən| *n* armónica *f*.

mouthpiece |'maʊθpiːs| *n Mus* boquilla *f*; *(of telephone)* micrófono *m*; *fig* (spokesman) portavoz *m*.

mouthwash |'maʊθwɒʃ| *n* elixir *m*, enjuague *m* bucal.

mouthwatering |'maʊθwɔːtərɪŋ| *adj* muy apetitoso,-a, que le hace a uno la boca agua.

movable |'muːvəbəl| *adj* movible, móvil.

move |muːv| **I** *n* 1 *(movement)* movimiento *m*; **to be on the m.**, estar en marcha; **we must make a m.**, debemos irnos ya; *fam* **get a m. on!**, ¡date prisa! 2 *(in game)* jugada *f*; *(turn)* turno *m*. 3 *(course of action)* medida *f*; **to make the first m.**, dar el primer paso. 4 *(to new home)* mudanza *f*; *(to new job)* traslado *m*.
II *vtr* 1 mover; *(furniture etc)* cambiar de sitio; *(transfer)* trasladar; **to m. house**, mudarse (de casa). 2 *(in game)* mover. 3 *(motivate)* inducir; *(persuade)* persuadir; **I won't be moved**, no me harán cambiar de parecer. 4 *(affect emotionally)* conmover. 5 *(resolution etc)* proponer.
III *vi* 1 *(change position)* moverse, desplazarse; *(change house)* mudarse (de casa); *(change post)* trasladarse; **m. out of the way!**, ¡quítate de en medio! 2 *(train etc)* estar en marcha; **to start moving**, ponerse en marcha. 3 *(travel)* ir. 4 *(leave)* irse, marcharse. 5 *(in game)* hacer una jugada. 6 *(take action)* tomar medidas.
◆**move about, move around I** *vtr* cambiar de sitio. **II** *vi (be restless)* ir y venir; *(travel)* viajar de un lugar a otro.
◆**move along I** *vtr (move forward)* hacer avanzar; *(keep moving)* hacer circular. **II** *vi (move forward)* avanzar; *(keep moving)* circular; **m. along!**, *(to person on bench)* ¡haz sitio! ◆**move away I** *vtr* alejar, apartar *(from*, de). **II** *vi (move aside)* alejarse, apartarse; *(leave)* irse; *(change house)* mudarse (de casa).
◆**move back I** *vtr (to original place)* volver. **II** *vi (withdraw)* retirarse; *(to original place)* volver. ◆**move forward I**

vtr avanzar; *(clock)* adelantar. **II** *vi* avanzar, adelantarse. ◆**move in** *vi (into new home)* instalarse. ◆**move off** *vi (go away)* marcharse; *(train)* salir. ◆**move on** *vi (keep moving)* circular; *(go forward)* avanzar; *(time)* transcurrir. ◆**move out** *vi (leave)* irse, marcharse; *(leave house)* mudarse. ◆**move over** *vi* correrse. ◆**move up** *vi (go up)* subir; *fig (be promoted)* ser ascendido,-a, ascender; *(move along)* correrse, hacer sitio.

movement |'muːvmənt| *n* 1 movimiento *m*; *(gesture)* gesto *m*, ademán *m*. 2 *(of goods)* transporte *m*; *(of employees)* traslado *m*. 3 *(trend)* corriente *f*. 4 *(of machine)* mecanismo *m*. 5 *(of goods, capital)* circulación *f*.

movie |'muːvɪ| *n US* película *f*; **to go to the movies**, ir al cine; **m. star**, estrella *f* de cine.

moving |'muːvɪŋ| *adj (that moves)* móvil; *(car etc)* en marcha; *fig (touching)* conmovedor,-a.

mow |məʊ| *vtr (pt* **mowed**; *pp* **mown** *or* **mowed**) *(lawn)* cortar; *(corn, wheat)* segar; *fig* **to m. down**, segar.

mower |'məʊər| *n* cortacésped *m & f*.

MP |em'piː| *abbr of* **Member of Parliament**.

mph |empi'eɪtʃ| *abbr of* **miles per hour**, millas *fpl* por hora.

MPhil |em'fɪl| *abbr of* **Master of Philosophy**.

Mr |'mɪstər| *abbr of* **mister**, señor *m*, Sr.

Mrs |'mɪsɪs| *abbr* señora *f*, Sra.

Ms |məz| *abbr* señora *f*, Sra, señorita *f*, Srta.

MSc |emes'siː| *abbr of* **Master of Science**.

much |mʌtʃ| **I** *adj* mucho,-a; **as m. ... as**, tanto,-a ... como; **how m. chocolate?**, ¿cuánto chocolate?; **m. admiration**, mucha admiración; **so m.**, tanto,-a. **II** *adv* mucho; **as m. as**, tanto como; **as m. as possible**, todo lo posible; **how m.?**, ¿cuánto?; **how m. is it?**, ¿cuánto es?, ¿cuánto vale?; **m. better**, mucho mejor; **m. more**, mucho más; **so m. the better**, ¡tanto mejor!; **thank you very m.**, muchísimas gracias; **they are m. the same**, son más o menos iguales; **too m.**, demasiado; **without so m. as**, sin siquiera. **III** *pron* mucho; **I thought as m.**, lo suponía; **m. of the town was destroyed**, gran parte de la ciudad quedó destruida; **m. remains to be done**, queda mucho por hacer.

muck |mʌk| *n (dirt)* suciedad *f*; *(mud)* lodo *m*; *fig* porquería *f*. ◆**muck about, muck around** *fam* **I** *vi (idle)* perder el tiempo; *(play the fool)* hacer el tonto. **II** *vtr* **to m. sb about**, fastidiar a algn. ◆**muck up** *vtr (dirty)* ensuciar; *fig (spoil)* echar a perder.

mucky ['mʌkɪ] adj (**muckier, muckiest**) sucio,-a.

mucus ['mjuːkəs] n moco m, mucosidad f.

mud [mʌd] n lodo m, barro m; (thick) fango m; **to sling m. at sb**, poner a algn por los suelos; **m. flat**, marisma f.

muddle ['mʌdəl] I n desorden m; fig (mix-up) embrollo m, lío m; **to get into a m.**, hacerse un lío. II vtr **to m. (up)**, confundir. ◆**muddle through** vi arreglárselas, ingeniárselas.

muddy ['mʌdɪ] adj (**muddier, muddiest**) (lane) fangoso,-a; (hands) cubierto,-a de lodo; (liquid) turbio,-a.

mudguard ['mʌdgɑːd] n guardabarros m inv.

muff¹ [mʌf] n manguito m; **ear muffs**, orejeras fpl.

muff² [mʌf] vtr fam pifiar; **to m. it (up)**, estropearlo.

muffin ['mʌfɪn] n panecillo m.

muffle ['mʌfəl] vtr (sound) amortiguar; **to m. (up)**, (person) abrigar.

muffler ['mʌflər] n US Aut silenciador m.

mug¹ [mʌg] n (large cup) tazón m; (beer tankard) jarra f.

mug² [mʌg] I n fam (fool) tonto,-a m,f; (face) jeta f. II vtr atracar, asaltar.

mugging ['mʌgɪŋ] n asalto m.

muggy ['mʌgɪ] adj (**muggier, muggiest**) bochornoso,-a.

mule [mjuːl] n mulo,-a m,f.

mull [mʌl] vtr **mulled wine**, vino m caliente con especias. ◆**mull over** vtr **to m. over sth**, reflexionar sobre algo.

multicoloured, US **multicolored** ['mʌltɪkʌləd] adj multicolor.

multinational [mʌltɪˈnæʃənəl] adj & nf multinacional.

multiple ['mʌltɪpəl] I adj múltiple; **m. sclerosis**, esclerosis f múltiple. II n múltiplo m.

multiplication [mʌltɪplɪˈkeɪʃən] n multiplicación f; **m. sign**, signo m de multiplicar.

multiply ['mʌltɪplaɪ] I vtr multiplicar (by, por). II vi multiplicarse.

multipurpose [mʌltɪˈpɜːpəs] adj multiuso inv.

multistorey [mʌltɪˈstɔːrɪ] adj (building) de varios pisos; **m. car park**, parking m de varias plantas.

multitude ['mʌltɪtjuːd] n multitud f, muchedumbre f.

mum¹ [mʌm] n fam mamá f.

mum² [mʌm] adj **to keep m.**, no decir ni pío.

mumble ['mʌmbəl] I vi hablar entre dientes. II vtr decir entre dientes.

mummy¹ ['mʌmɪ] n fam (mother) mamá f, mami f.

mummy² ['mʌmɪ] n (body) momia f.

mumps [mʌmps] n paperas fpl.

munch [mʌntʃ] vtr & vi mascar.

mundane [mʌnˈdeɪn] adj pej (ordinary) banal; (job, life) rutinario,-a.

municipal [mjuːˈnɪsɪpəl] adj municipal.

municipality [mjuːnɪsɪˈpælɪtɪ] n municipio m.

mural ['mjuərəl] adj & nm mural.

Murcia [muːˈsiːə] n Murcia.

murder ['mɜːdər] I n asesinato m, homicidio m. II vtr asesinar.

murderer ['mɜːdərər] n asesino m.

murderess ['mɜːdərɪs] n asesina f.

murderous ['mɜːdərəs] adj homicida.

murky ['mɜːkɪ] adj (**murkier, murkiest**) oscuro,-a; (water) turbio,-a.

murmur ['mɜːmər] I n murmullo m; (of traffic) ruido m; (complaint) queja f. II vtr & vi murmurar.

muscle ['mʌsəl] I n músculo m. II vi fam **to m. in on sth**, entrometerse en asuntos ajenos.

muscular ['mʌskjʊlər] adj (pain, tissue) muscular; (person) musculoso,-a.

muse [mjuːz] vi **to m. on or about sth**, meditar algo.

Muse [mjuːz] n (in mythology) musa f.

museum [mjuːˈziːəm] n museo m.

mushroom ['mʌʃruːm] I n seta f, hongo m; Culin champiñón m. II vi fig crecer de la noche a la mañana.

music ['mjuːzɪk] n música f; **m. hall**, teatro m de variedades.

musical ['mjuːzɪkəl] I adj musical; **to be m.**, estar dotado,-a para la música. II n musical m.

musician [mjuːˈzɪʃən] n músico,-a m,f.

Muslim ['muzlɪm] adj & n musulmán, -ana (m,f).

muslin ['mʌzlɪn] n muselina f.

mussel ['mʌsəl] n mejillón m.

must [mʌst] I v aux 1 (obligation) deber, tener que; **you m. arrive on time**, tienes que or debes llegar a la hora. 2 (probability) deber de; **he m. be ill**, debe de estar enfermo. II n fam necesidad f.

mustard ['mʌstəd] n mostaza f.

muster ['mʌstər] I vtr fig **to m. (up) courage**, cobrar fuerzas. II vi reunirse, juntarse.

mustn't ['mʌsənt] = **must not**.

musty ['mʌstɪ] adj (**mustier, mustiest**) que huele a cerrado or a humedad.

mute [mjuːt] I adj mudo,-a. II n (person) mudo,-a m,f; Mus sordina f.

muted ['mjuːtɪd] adj (sound) sordo,-a; (colour) suave.

mutilate ['mjuːtɪleɪt] vtr mutilar.

mutiny ['mjuːtɪnɪ] I n motín m. II vi amotinarse.

mutter ['mʌtər] I n (mumble) murmullo m. II vtr murmurar, decir entre dientes. III vi (angrily) refunfuñar.

mutton ['mʌtən] n (carne f de) cordero m.

mutual ['mju:tʃʊəl] adj mutuo,-a; (shared) común.

muzzle ['mʌzəl] I n (snout) hocico m; (for dog) bozal m; (of gun) boca f. II vtr (dog) abozalar; fig amordazar.

my [maɪ] poss adj mi; **my cousins**, mis primos; **my father**, mi padre; **one of my friends**, un amigo mío; **I washed my hair**, me lavé el pelo; **I twisted my ankle**, me torcí el tobillo.

myriad ['mɪrɪəd] n lit miríada f.

myself [maɪ'self] pers pron 1 (emphatic) yo mismo,-a; **my husband and m.**, mi marido y yo. 2 (reflexive) me; **I hurt m.**, me hice daño. 3 (after prep) mí (mismo,-a).

mysterious [mɪ'stɪərɪəs] adj misterioso, -a.

mystery ['mɪstərɪ] n misterio m.

mystical ['mɪstɪkəl] adj místico,-a.

mystify ['mɪstɪfaɪ] vtr dejar perplejo,-a.

mystique [mɪ'sti:k] n mística f.

myth [mɪθ] n mito m; **it's a complete m.**, es pura fantasía.

mythology [mɪ'θɒlədʒɪ] n mitología f.

N

N, n [en] n (the letter) N, n f.

N abbr of **North**, Norte, N.

nab [næb] vtr fam pillar.

nag [næg] I vtr dar la tabarra a; **to n. sb to do sth**, dar la tabarra a algn para que haga algo. II vi quejarse.

nagging ['nægɪŋ] adj (persistent) continuo,-a.

nail [neɪl] I n 1 (of finger, toe) uña f; **n. clippers**, cortaúñas m inv; **n. polish, n. varnish**, esmalte m or laca f de uñas. 2 (metal) clavo m; fig **to hit the n. on the head**, dar en el clavo. II vtr 1 clavar. 2 fam (catch, trap) pillar, coger.

nailbrush ['neɪlbrʌʃ] n cepillo m de uñas.

nailfile ['neɪlfaɪl] n lima f de uñas.

nail-scissors ['neɪlsɪzəz] npl tijeras fpl de uñas.

naïve [naɪ'i:v] adj ingenuo,-a.

naked ['neɪkɪd] adj desnudo,-a; (flame) sin protección; **the n. truth**, la pura verdad.

name [neɪm] I n 1 nombre m; (surname) apellido m; **what's your n.?**, ¿cómo te llamas?; **to call sb names**, poner verde a algn. 2 (reputation) reputación f; **to have a bad/good n.**, tener mala/buena reputación; **to make a n. for oneself**, hacerse famoso,-a. II vtr 1 llamar. 2 (appoint) nombrar. 3 (refer to) mencionar.

nameless ['neɪmlɪs] adj anónimo,-a; **to remain n.**, permanecer en el anonimato.

namely ['neɪmlɪ] adv a saber.

namesake ['neɪmseɪk] n tocayo,-a m,f.

nanny ['nænɪ] n niñera f.

nap [næp] I n (sleep) siesta f; **to have a n.**, echar la or una siesta. II vi fig **to catch sb napping**, coger a algn desprevenido.

napalm ['neɪpɑ:m] n napalm m.

nape [neɪp] n nuca f, cogote m.

napkin ['næpkɪn] n (table) n., servilleta f.

Naples ['neɪpəlz] n Nápoles f.

nappy ['næpɪ] n GB pañal m.

narcissus [nɑ:'sɪsəs] n Bot narciso m.

narcotic [nɑ:'kɒtɪk] I adj narcótico,-a. II n (usu pl) narcótico m, estupefaciente m.

narrate [nə'reɪt] vtr narrar, relatar.

narration [nə'reɪʃən] n narración f, relato m.

narrative ['nærətɪv] I n Lit narrativa f; (story) narración f. II adj narrativo,-a.

narrator [nə'reɪtər] n narrador,-a m,f.

narrow ['nærəʊ] I adj 1 (passage, road etc) estrecho,-a, angosto,-a. 2 (restricted) reducido,-a; (sense) estricto,-a; **to have a n. escape**, librarse por los pelos. II vi estrecharse. ◆**narrowly** adv 1 (closely) de cerca. 2 (by a small margin) por poco. ◆**narrow down** I vtr reducir, limitar. II to n. down to, reducirse a.

narrow-minded [nærəʊ'maɪndɪd] adj de miras estrechas.

nasal ['neɪzəl] adj nasal; (voice) gangoso, -a.

nastiness ['nɑ:stɪnɪs] n 1 (unpleasantness) carácter m desagradable. 2 (maliciousness) mala intención.

nasty ['nɑ:stɪ] adj (nastier, nastiest) 1 (person) desagradable; **a n. business**, un asunto feo; **a n. trick**, una mala jugada or pasada; **cheap and n.**, hortera; **to turn n.**, (of weather, situation) ponerse feo. 2 (unfriendly) antipático,-a; (malicious) mal intencionado,-a; fam **he's a n. piece of work**, es un asco de tío. 3 (dirty) sucio,-a, asqueroso,-a. 4 (illness, accident) grave.

nation ['neɪʃən] n nación f.

national ['næʃənəl] I adj nacional; **n. anthem**, himno m nacional; **n. insurance**, seguridad f social; GB Mil **n. service**, servicio m militar. II n súbdito, -a m,f.

nationalism ['næʃnəlɪzəm] n nacionalismo m.

nationalist ['næʃnəlɪst] adj & n nacionalista (mf).

nationality [næʃə'nælɪtɪ] n nacionalidad f.

nationalization [næʃnəlaɪ'zeɪʃən] n nacionalización f.

nationalize ['næʃnəlaɪz] vtr nacionalizar.

nationwide ['neɪʃənwaɪd] adj de ámbito nacional.

native |'neɪtɪv| **I** adj **1** (place) natal; **n. land**, patria f; **n. language**, lengua materna. **2** (innate) innato,-a. **3** (plant, animal) originario,-a (**to**, de). **II** n nativo,-a m,f, natural mf; (original inhabitant) indígena mf.

NATO, Nato |'neɪtəʊ| abbr of **North Atlantic Treaty Organization**, Organización f del Tratado del Atlántico Norte, OTAN f.

natter |'nætər| fam **I** vi charlar. **II** n charla f.

natural |'nætʃərəl| **I** adj **1** natural. **2** (normal) normal; **it's only n. that ...**, es lógico que .... **3** (born) nato,-a. **II** n **1** **she's a n. for the job**, es la persona ideal para el trabajo. **2** Mus becuadro m. ◆**naturally** adv **1** (of course) naturalmente. **2** (by nature) por naturaleza. **3** (in a relaxed manner) con naturalidad.

naturalize |'nætʃərəlaɪz| vtr **to become naturalized**, naturalizarse.

nature |'neɪtʃər| n **1** naturaleza f. **2** (character) naturaleza f, carácter m; **by n.**, por naturaleza; **human n.**, la naturaleza humana. **3** (sort, kind) índole f, clase f.

naught |nɔːt| n arch nada f; **to come to n.**, fracasar.

naughty |'nɔːtɪ| adj (**naughtier, naughtiest**) **1** (child) travieso,-a. **2** (joke, story) atrevido,-a, picante. ◆**naughtily** adv **to behave n.**, portarse mal.

nausea |'nɔːzɪə| n Med (sickness) náusea f.

nauseate |'nɔːzɪeɪt| vtr (disgust) dar asco a.

nauseating |'nɔːzɪeɪtɪŋ| adj nauseabundo,-a.

nautical |'nɔːtɪkəl| adj náutico,-a; **n. mile**, milla marítima.

naval |'neɪvəl| adj naval; **n. officer**, oficial mf de marina; **n. power**, potencia marítima or naval.

Navarre |nə'vɑːr| n Navarra f.

nave |neɪv| n Arch nave f.

navel |'neɪvəl| n Anat ombligo m.

navigate |'nævɪgeɪt| **I** vtr (river) navegar por; Naut (ship) gobernar. **II** vi navegar; (in driving) indicar la dirección.

navigation |nævɪ'geɪʃən| n Naut navegación f.

navigator |'nævɪgeɪtər| n **1** Naut navegante mf, oficial mf de derrota. **2** Aut Av copiloto mf.

navvy |'nævɪ| n GB fam peón m.

navy |'neɪvɪ| n marina f; **n. blue**, azul marino.

Nazi |'nɑːtsɪ| adj & n nazi (mf).

Nazism |'nɑːtsɪzəm| n nazismo m.

NB, nb |en'biː| abbr of **nota bene** (note well), N.B.

neap |niːp| n **n. (tide)**, marea muerta.

near |nɪər| **I** adj (in space) cercano,-a; (in time) próximo,-a; **in the n. future**, en un futuro próximo; **it was a n. thing**, poco faltó. **II** adv (in space) cerca; **n. and far**, por todas partes; **that's n. enough**, (ya) vale, está bien. **III** prep cerca de; **n. the end of the film**, hacia el final de la película. **IV** vtr acercarse a. ◆**nearly** adv casi; **very n.**, casi, casi; **we haven't n. enough**, no alcanza ni con mucho.

nearby |nɪə'baɪ| **I** adj cercano,-a. **II** adv cerca.

nearside |'nɪəsaɪd| n Aut (with left-hand drive) lado izquierdo; (with right-hand drive) lado derecho.

near-sighted |nɪə'saɪtɪd| adj miope.

neat |niːt| adj **1** (room, habits etc) ordenado,-a; (handwriting) claro,-a; (appearance) pulcro,-a. **2** (idea) ingenioso,-a. **3** (whisky etc) solo,-a. **4** US fam (fine) chulísimo,-a. ◆**neatly** adv **1** (carefully) cuidadosamente. **2** (cleverly) hábilmente.

necessary |'nesɪsərɪ| **I** adj **1** (essential) necesario,-a; **to do what is n.**, hacer lo que haga falta; **if n.**, si es preciso. **2** (unavoidable) inevitable. **II** n lo necesario. ◆**necessarily** |nesɪ'serəlɪ| adv necesariamente, por fuerza.

necessitate |nɪ'sesɪteɪt| vtr necesitar, exigir.

necessity |nɪ'sesɪtɪ| n **1** necesidad f; **out of n.**, por necesidad. **2** (article) requisito m indispensable; **necessities**, artículos mpl de primera necesidad.

neck |nek| **I** n cuello m; (of animal) pescuezo m; **to be n. and n.**, ir parejos; **to be up to one's n. in debt**, estar hasta el cuello de deudas; **to risk one's n.**, jugarse el tipo; **to stick one's n. out**, arriesgarse; **to win/lose by a n.**, (in horse racing) ganar/perder por una cabeza; **low n.**, escote bajo. **II** vi fam magrearse.

necklace |'neklɪs| n collar m.

neckline |'neklaɪn| n (of dress) escote m.

necktie |'nektaɪ| n corbata f.

nectar |'nektər| n néctar m.

nectarine |'nektərɪn| n nectarina f.

née |neɪ| adj **n. Brown**, de soltera Brown.

need |niːd| **I** n **1** necesidad f; **if n. be**, si fuera necesario; **there's no n. for you to do that**, no hace falta que hagas eso. **2** (poverty) indigencia f; **to be in n.**, estar necesitado; **to help a friend in n.**, sacar a un amigo de un apuro. **II** vtr **1** necesitar; **I n. to see him**, tengo que verle; iron **that's all I n.**, sólo me faltaba eso. **2** (action, solution etc) requerir, exigir. **III** aux v tener que, deber; **n. he go?**, ¿tiene que ir?; **you needn't wait**, no hace falta que esperes.

needle |'niːdəl| **I** n **1** (for sewing, knitting) aguja f. **2** Bot hoja f. **3** GB fam **to get the n.**, picarse. **II** vtr fam pinchar.

needless |'niːdlɪs| adj innecesario,-a; **n. to say**, huelga decir. ◆**needlessly** adv innecesariamente.

needlework ['ni:dəlwɜ:k] *n (sewing)* costura *f; (embroidery)* bordado *m.*

needy ['ni:dɪ] *adj (needier, neediest)* necesitado,-a.

negate [nɪ'geɪt] *vtr* 1 *(deny)* negar. 2 *(nullify)* anular.

negative ['negətɪv] I *adj* negativo,-a. II *n* 1 *Ling* negación *f.* 2 *Phot* negativo *m.*

neglect [nɪ'glekt] I *vtr* 1 *(child, duty etc)* descuidar, desatender. 2 to n. to do sth, *(omit to do)* no hacer algo. II *n* dejadez *f;* n. of duty, incumplimiento *m* del deber.

neglectful [nɪ'glektfʊl] *adj* descuidado,-a, negligente.

negligée ['neglɪʒeɪ] *n* salto *m* de cama.

negligence ['neglɪdʒəns] *n* negligencia *f,* descuido *m.*

negligent ['neglɪdʒənt] *adj* negligente, descuidado,-a.

negligible ['neglɪdʒɪbəl] *adj* insignificante.

negotiate [nɪ'gəʊʃɪeɪt] I *vtr* 1 *(contract)* negociar. 2 *fig (obstacle)* salvar, franquear. II *vi* negociar.

negotiation [nɪgəʊʃɪ'eɪʃən] *n* negociación *f.*

negro ['ni:grəʊ] *n (pl negroes)* negro,-a *m,f.*

neigh [neɪ] I *n* relincho *m.* II *vi* relinchar.

neighbour, *US* **neighbor** ['neɪbər] *n* vecino,-a *m,f; Rel* prójimo *m.*

neighbourhood, *US* **neighborhood** ['neɪbəhʊd] *n (district)* vecindad *f,* barrio *m; (people)* vecindario *m.*

neighbouring, *US* **neighboring** ['neɪbərɪŋ] *adj* vecino,-a.

neither ['naɪðər, 'niːðər] I *adj & pron* ninguno de los dos, ninguna de las dos. II *adv & conj* 1 ni; ... **nor**, ni ... ni; *fig* it's n. here nor there, no viene al caso. 2 tampoco; **she was not there and n. was her sister,** ella no estaba, ni su hermana tampoco.

neon ['ni:ɒn] *n* neón *m;* n. **light,** luz *f* de neón.

nephew ['nevju:, 'nefju:] *n* sobrino *m.*

nerve [nɜ:v] I *n* 1 *Anat* nervio *m;* **to get on sb's nerves,** poner los nervios de punta a algn; **n. gas,** gas nervioso. 2 *(courage)* valor *m.* 3 *fam (cheek)* cara *f,* descaro *m;* **what a n.!,** ¡qué cara!

nerve-racking ['nɜ:vrækɪŋ] *adj* crispante, exasperante.

nervous ['nɜ:vəs] *adj* 1 nervioso,-a; n. **breakdown,** depresión nerviosa. 2 *(afraid)* miedoso,-a. 3 *(timid)* tímido,-a.

nest [nest] I *n Orn* nido *m; (hen's)* nidal *m; (animal's)* madriguera *f;* **n. egg,** ahorros *mpl.* II *vi (birds)* anidar.

nestle ['nesəl] I *vtr* recostar. II *vi (settle comfortably)* acomodarse.

net[1] [net] *n* red *f; GB* **n. curtains,** visillos *mpl.*

net[2] [net] I *adj* neto,-a; n. **weight,** peso neto. II *vtr (earn)* ganar neto.

netball ['netbɔ:l] *n Sport* baloncesto femenino.

Netherlands ['neðələndz] *npl* **the N.,** los Países Bajos.

netting ['netɪŋ] *n* redes *fpl,* malla *f.*

nettle ['netəl] I *n Bot* ortiga *f.* II *vtr fam* irritar.

network ['netwɜ:k] *n* red *f.*

neurosis [njʊ'rəʊsɪs] *n* neurosis *f.*

neurotic [njʊ'rɒtɪk] *adj & n* neurótico,-a *(m,f).*

neuter ['nju:tər] I *adj* neutro,-a. II *n Ling* neutro *m.* III *vtr (geld)* castrar.

neutral ['nju:trəl] I *adj* neutro,-a; *Pol* **to remain n.,** permanecer neutral. II *n Aut* punto muerto.

neutrality [nju:'trælɪtɪ] *n* neutralidad *f.*

neutralize ['nju:trəlaɪz] *vtr* neutralizar.

neutron ['nju:trɒn] *n Phys* neutrón *m;* n. **bomb,** bomba *f* de neutrones.

never ['nevər] *adv* nunca, jamás; **he n. complains,** nunca se queja, no se queja nunca; **n. again,** nunca (ja)más; **n. in all my life,** jamás en la vida; *fam* **n. mind,** da igual, no importa; *fam* **well, I n. (did)!,** ¡no me digas!

never-ending [nevər'endɪŋ] *adj* sin fin, interminable.

nevertheless [nevəðə'les] *adv* sin embargo, no obstante.

new [nju:] *adj* nuevo,-a; **as good as n.,** como nuevo; n. **baby,** recién nacido *m;* **n. moon,** luna nueva; **N. Year,** Año nuevo; **N. Year's Eve,** Nochevieja *f;* **N. York,** Nueva York; **N. Zealand,** Nueva Zelanda. ◆**newly** *adv* recién, recientemente.

newborn ['nju:bɔ:n] *adj* recién nacido,-a.

newcomer ['nju:kʌmər] *n* recién llegado,-a *m,f; (to job etc)* nuevo,-a *m,f.*

newfangled ['nju:fæŋgəld] *adj* novedoso,-a.

newlywed ['nju:lɪwed] *n* recién casado,-a *m,f.*

news [nju:z] *n* noticias *fpl;* **a piece of n.,** una noticia; *fam* **it's n. to me,** ahora me entero; **n. agency,** agencia *f* de información; **n. bulletin,** boletín informativo; **n. clipping,** recorte *m* de periódico.

newsagent ['nju:zeɪdʒənt] *n* vendedor,-a *m,f* de periódicos.

newsflash ['nju:zflæʃ] *n* noticia *f* de última hora.

newsletter ['nju:zletər] *n* hoja informativa.

newspaper ['nju:zpeɪpər] *n* periódico *m,* diario *m.*

newsprint ['nju:zprɪnt] *n* papel *m* de periódico.

newsreader ['nju:zri:dər] *n TV Rad* presentador,-a *m,f* de los informativos.

newsreel ['nju:zri:l] *n* noticiario *m.*

news-stand |'njuːzstænd| n quiosco m de periódicos.

newt |njuːt| n Zool tritón m.

next |nekst| I adj 1 (in place) de al lado. 2 (in time) próximo,-a; **the n. day**, el día siguiente; **n.** Friday, el viernes que viene; **the week after n.**, dentro de dos semanas. 3 (in order) siguiente, próximo,-a; **n. of kin**, pariente m más cercano. II adv 1 después, luego; **what shall we do n.?**, ¿qué hacemos ahora? 2 (next time) la próxima vez. III prep **n. to**, al lado de, junto a; **n. to nothing**, casi nada.

next door |neks'dɔːr| adj & adv de al lado; **our n.-d. neighbour**, el vecino or la vecina de al lado.

NHS |eneɪtʃ'es| GB abbr of National Health Service, ≈ Seguridad f Social, SS f.

nib |nɪb| n plumilla f.

nibble |'nɪbəl| vtr & vi mordisquear.

nice |naɪs| adj 1 (person) simpático,-a; (thing) agradable; **n. and cool**, fresquito,-a; **to smell/taste n.**, oler/saber bien. 2 (nice-looking) bonito,-a, Am lindo,-a. 3 iron menudo,-a; **a n. mess you've made!**, ¡menudo lío has hecho! 4 fml (subtle) sutil. ◆**nicely** adv muy bien.

niche |niːtʃ| n 1 hornacina f, nicho m. 2 fig hueco m.

nick |nɪk| I n 1 (notch) muesca f; (cut) herida pequeña; fam **in the n. of time**, en el momento preciso. 2 GB sl **the n.**, (prison) chirona f. II vtr GB sl 1 (steal) birlar. 2 (arrest) pillar.

nickel |'nɪkəl| n 1 níquel m; **n. silver**, alpaca f. 2 US moneda f de cinco centavos.

nickname |'nɪkneɪm| I n apodo m. II vtr apodar.

nicotine |'nɪkətiːn| n nicotina f.

niece |niːs| n sobrina f.

nifty |'nɪftɪ| adj (niftier, niftiest) 1 (quick) rápido,-a; (agile) ágil. 2 (ingenious) ingenioso,-a.

Nigeria |naɪ'dʒɪərɪə| n Nigeria.

nigger |'nɪgər| n offens negro,-a m,f.

niggling |'nɪglɪŋ| adj (trifling) insignificante; (irritating) molesto,-a.

night |naɪt| n noche f; **at n.**, de noche; **at twelve o'clock at n.**, a las doce de la noche; **last n.**, anoche; **to have a n. out**, salir por la noche; **n. life**, vida nocturna; fam **n. owl**, trasnochador,-a m,f; **n. school**, escuela nocturna; **n. shift**, turno m de noche.

nightclub |'naɪtklʌb| n sala f de fiestas; (disco) discoteca f.

nightdress |'naɪtdres| n camisón m.

nightfall |'naɪtfɔːl| n anochecer m.

nightgown |'naɪtgaʊn| n camisón m.

nightingale |'naɪtɪŋgeɪl| n ruiseñor m.

nightly |'naɪtlɪ| I adj de cada noche. II adv todas las noches.

nightmare |'naɪtmeər| n pesadilla f.

nightshade |'naɪtʃeɪd| n Bot deadly n., belladona f.

night-time |'naɪttaɪm| n noche f; **at n.**, por la noche.

nil |nɪl| n nada f; Sport cero m; **two n.**, dos a cero.

Nile |naɪl| n **the N.**, el Nilo.

nimble |'nɪmbəl| adj ágil, rápido,-a.

nine |naɪn| adj & n nueve (m) inv; fam **dressed up to the nines**, de punta en blanco.

nineteen |naɪn'tiːn| adj & n diecinueve (m) inv.

nineteenth |naɪn'tiːnθ| adj decimonoveno,-a.

ninety |'naɪntɪ| adj & n noventa (m) inv.

ninth |naɪnθ| I adj & n noveno,-a (m,f). II n (fraction) noveno m.

nip |nɪp| I vtr 1 (pinch) pellizcar. 2 (bite) morder; **to n. sth in the bud**, cortar algo de raíz. II n 1 (pinch) pellizco m. 2 (bite) mordisco m.

nipple |'nɪpəl| n Anat (female) pezón m; (male) tetilla f.

nippy |'nɪpɪ| adj (nippier, nippiest) fam 1 GB (quick) rápido,-a. 2 (cold) fresquito, -a.

nit |nɪt| n liendre f.

nitrogen |'naɪtrədʒən| n Chem nitrógeno m.

nitroglycerin(e) |naɪtrəʊ'glɪsəriːn| n Chem nitroglicerina f.

nitty-gritty |nɪtɪ'grɪtɪ| n fam **to get down to the n.-g.**, ir al grano.

nitwit |'nɪtwɪt| n fam imbécil mf.

no |nəʊ| I adv no; **come here! - no!**, ¡ven aquí! - ¡no!; **no longer**, ya no; **no less than**, no menos de. II adj ninguno,-a; **she has no children**, no tiene hijos; **I have no idea**, no tengo (ni) idea; **it's no good** or **use**, no vale la pena; Aut 'no parking', 'prohibido aparcar'; **no sensible person**, ninguna persona razonable; fam **no way!**, ¡ni hablar! III n no m; **she won't take no for an answer**, no se dará por vencida; **to say no**, decir que no.

no. (pl **nos.**) abbr of number, número m, nº, núm.

nobility |nəʊ'bɪlɪtɪ| n nobleza f.

noble |'nəʊbəl| adj noble.

nobleman |'nəʊbəlmən| n noble m.

noblewoman |'nəʊbəlwʊmən| n noble f.

nobody |'nəʊbədɪ| I pron nadie; **there was n. there**, no había nadie; **n. else**, nadie más. II n nadie m; **he's a n.**, es un don nadie.

nocturnal |nɒk'tɜːnəl| adj nocturno,-a.

nod |nɒd| I n (of greeting) saludo m con la cabeza; (of agreement) señal f de asentimiento. II vi (agree) asentir con la cabeza. III vtr **to n. one's head**, inclinar la cabeza. ◆**nod**

off *vi* dormirse.

no-go |nəʊ'gəʊ| *adj* no-go area, zona prohibida.

noise |nɔɪz| *n* ruido *m*; **to make a n.**, hacer ruido.

noiseless |'nɔɪzlɪs| *adj* silencioso,-a, sin ruido.

noisy |'nɔɪzɪ| *adj* (noisier, noisiest) ruidoso,-a.

nomad |'nəʊmæd| *n* nómada *mf*.

no-man's-land |'nəʊmænzlænd| *n* tierra *f* de nadie.

nominal |'nɒmɪnəl| *adj* nominal; (payment, rent) simbólico,-a.

nominate |'nɒmɪneɪt| *vtr* 1 (propose) designar, proponer. 2 (appoint) nombrar.

nomination |nɒmɪ'neɪʃən| *n* 1 (proposal) propuesta *f*. 2 (appointment) nombramiento *m*.

nominative |'nɒmɪnətɪv| *n* nominativo *m*.

nominee |nɒmɪ'niː| *n* persona propuesta.

non- |nɒn| *pref* no.

non-aggression |nɒnə'greʃən| *n* Pol no agresión *f*; **n.-a. pact**, pacto *m* de no agresión.

non-alcoholic |nɒnælkə'hɒlɪk| *adj* sin alcohol.

non-aligned |nɒnə'laɪnd| *adj* Pol no alineado,-a.

nonchalant |'nɒnʃələnt| *adj* (indifferent) indiferente; (calm) imperturbable, impasible.

noncommittal |'nɒnkəmɪtəl| *adj* (person) evasivo,-a; (answer) que no compromete (a nada).

nonconformist |nɒnkən'fɔːmɪst| *n* inconformista *mf*.

nondescript |'nɒndɪskrɪpt| *adj* indescriptible; (uninteresting) soso,-a.

none |nʌn| *pron* ninguno,-a; **I know n. of them**, no conozco a ninguno de ellos; **n. at all**, nada en absoluto; **n. other than ...**, nada menos que ...; **II** *adv* de ningún modo; **she's n. the worse for it**, no se ha visto afectada *or* perjudicada por ello; **n. too soon**, a buena hora.

nonentity |nɒ'nentɪtɪ| *n* (person) cero *m* a la izquierda.

nonetheless |nʌnðə'les| *adv* no obstante, sin embargo.

nonevent |nɒnɪ'vent| *n* fracaso *m*.

nonexistent |nɒnɪg'zɪstənt| *adj* inexistente.

nonfiction |nɒn'fɪkʃən| *n* literatura *f* no novelesca.

no-nonsense |nəʊ'nɒnsens| *adj* (person) recto,-a, serio,-a.

nonplussed |nɒn'plʌst| *adj* perplejo,-a.

non-profit(-making) |nɒn'prɒfɪt(meɪkɪŋ)| *adj* sin fin lucrativo.

nonreturnable |nɒnrɪ'tɜːnəbəl| *adj* no retornable.

nonsense |'nɒnsəns| *n* tonterías *fpl*, disparates *mpl*; **that's n.**, eso es absurdo.

nonsmoker |nɒn'sməʊkər| *n* no fumador,-a *m,f*, persona *f* que no fuma.

nonstarter |nɒn'stɑːtər| *n* fig **to be a n.**, (person) estar destinado a fracasar; (plan) ser irrealizable.

nonstick |nɒn'stɪk| *adj* antiadherente.

nonstop |nɒn'stɒp| **I** *adj* sin parar; (train) directo,-a. **II** *adv* sin parar.

noodles |'nuːdəlz| *npl* Culin fideos *mpl*.

nook |nʊk| *n* recoveco *m*, rincón *m*.

noon |nuːn| *n* mediodía *m*; **at n.**, a mediodía.

no-one |'nəʊwʌn| *pron* nadie; **n. came**, no vino nadie.

noose |nuːs| *n* lazo *m*; (hangman's) soga *f*.

nor |nɔːr| *conj* ni, ni tampoco; **neither ... n.**, ni ... ni; **neither you n. I**, ni tú ni yo; **n. do I**, (ni) yo tampoco.

norm |nɔːm| *n* norma *f*.

normal |'nɔːməl| *adj* normal.

normality |nɔː'mælɪtɪ| *n* normalidad *f*.

normally |'nɔːməlɪ| *adv* normalmente.

Normandy |'nɔːməndɪ| *n* Normandía.

north |nɔːθ| **I** *n* norte *m*; **the N.**, el norte; **N. America**, América del Norte, Norteamérica; **N. Pole**, Polo *m* Norte; **N. Sea**, Mar *m* del Norte. **II** *adv* hacia el norte, al norte. **III** *adj* del norte; **n. wind**, viento *m* del norte.

northeast |nɔːθ'iːst| *n* nor(d)este *m*.

northerly |'nɔːðəlɪ| *adj* norte, del norte.

northern |'nɔːðən| *adj* del norte, septentrional; **n. hemisphere**, hemisferio *m* norte; **N. Ireland**, Irlanda del Norte.

northerner |'nɔːðənər| *n* norteño,-a, *mf*.

northward |'nɔːθwəd| *adj & adv* hacia el norte.

northwest |nɔːθ'west| *n* noroeste *m*.

Norway |'nɔːweɪ| *n* Noruega.

Norwegian |nɔː'wiːdʒən| **I** *adj* noruego,-a. **II** *n* 1 (person) noruego,-a *m,f*. 2 (language) noruego *m*.

nose |nəʊz| *n* 1 nariz *f*; fig (right) under sb's n., delante de las propias narices de algn; GB fam **to get up sb's n.**, hincharle a algn las narices. 2 (sense of smell) olfato *m*. 3 (of car, plane) morro *m*. ◆**nose about, nose around** *vi* curiosear.

nosebleed |'nəʊzbliːd| *n* hemorragia *f* nasal.

nosedive |'nəʊzdaɪv| Av **I** *n* picado *m*. **II** *vi* descender en picado.

nostalgia |nɒ'stældʒə| *n* nostalgia *f*.

nostalgic |nɒ'stældʒɪk| *adj* nostálgico,-a.

nostril |'nɒstrɪl| *n* Anat orificio *m* nasal.

nosy |'nəʊzɪ| *adj* (nosier, nosiest) fam entrometido,-a.

not |nɒt| *adv* no; **he's n. in today**, hoy no está; **I'm n. sorry to leave**, no siento nada irme; **n. at all**, en absoluto; **thank you - n. at all**, gracias - no hay de qué; **n. one (of them) thanked me**, nadie me dio las gracias; **n. that I don't want to**

come, no es que no quiera ir; **n. too
well,** bastante mal; **n. without reason,**
no sin razón; *fam* **n. likely!,** ¡ni hablar!
notable ['nəʊtəbəl] *adj* notable.
◆**notably** *adv* notablemente.
notary ['nəʊtərɪ] *n* notario *m.*
notch [nɒtʃ] *n* muesca *f; (cut)* corte *m.*
◆**notch up** *vtr fig* to n. up a victory,
apuntarse una victoria.
note [nəʊt] I *n* 1 *Mus* nota *f; fig* **to strike
the right n.,** acertar. 2 *(on paper)* nota *f.*
3 **to take n. of,** *(notice)* prestar atención
a. 4 *Fin* billete *m* (de banco). 5 **notes,**
apuntes *mpl;* **to take n.,** tomar apuntes.
II *vtr* 1 *(write down)* apuntar, anotar. 2
(notice) notar, fijarse en.
notebook ['nəʊtbʊk] *n* cuaderno *m,* libreta *f.*
noted ['nəʊtɪd] *adj* notable, célebre.
notepad ['nəʊtpæd] *n* bloc *m* de notas.
notepaper ['nəʊtpeɪpər] *n* papel *m* de
carta.
noteworthy ['nəʊtwɜːðɪ] *adj* digno,-a de
mención.
nothing ['nʌθɪŋ] I *n* nada; **I saw n.,** no vi
nada; **for n.,** *(free of charge)* gratis; **it's
n.,** no es nada; **it's n. to do with you,** no
tiene nada que ver contigo; **n. else,** nada
más; **there's n. in it,** no es cierto; *fam* **n.
much,** poca cosa; *fam* **there's n. to it,** es
facilísimo. II *adv* **she looks n. like her
sister,** no se parece en nada a su hermana.
notice ['nəʊtɪs] I *n* 1 *(warning)* aviso *m;*
he gave a month's n., presentó la dimisión con un mes de antelación; **at short
n.,** con poca antelación; **until further n.,**
hasta nuevo aviso; **without n.,** sin previo
aviso. 2 *(attention)* atención *f;* **to take no
n. of sth,** no hacer caso de algo; **to take
n. of sth,** prestar atención a algo; **it
escaped my n.,** se me escapó; **to come
to one's n.,** llegar al conocimiento de
uno. 3 *(in newspaper etc)* anuncio *m.* 4
(sign) letrero *m,* aviso *m.* II *vtr* darse
cuenta de, notar.
noticeable ['nəʊtɪsəbəl] *adj* que se nota,
evidente.
noticeboard ['nəʊtɪsbɔːd] *n* tablón *m* de
anuncios.
notification [nəʊtɪfɪ'keɪʃən] *n* aviso *m.*
notify ['nəʊtɪfaɪ] *vtr* avisar.
notion ['nəʊʃən] *n* 1 idea *f,* concepto *m.*
2 *(whim)* capricho *m.* 3 *US Sew* **notions,**
artículos *mpl* de mercería.
notorious [nəʊ'tɔːrɪəs] *adj* muy
conocido,-a.
notwithstanding [nɒtwɪθ'stændɪŋ] I *prep*
a pesar de. II *adv* sin embargo, no
obstante.
nougat ['nuːgɑː] *n* turrón blando.
nought [nɔːt] *n* cero *m.*
noun [naʊn] *n* nombre *m,* sustantivo *m.*
nourish ['nʌrɪʃ] *vtr* nutrir; *fig (hopes)*

abrigar.
nourishing ['nʌrɪʃɪŋ] *adj* nutritivo,-a.
nourishment ['nʌrɪʃmənt] *n* alimentación
f, nutrición *f.*
novel[1] ['nɒvəl] *n* novela *f.*
novel[2] ['nɒvəl] *adj* original, novedoso,-a.
novelist ['nɒvəlɪst] *n* novelista *mf.*
novelty ['nɒvəltɪ] *n* novedad *f.*
November [nəʊ'vembər] *n* noviembre *m.*
novice ['nɒvɪs] *n* 1 *(beginner)* novato,-a
m,f, principiante *mf.* 2 *Rel* novicio,-a
m,f.
now [naʊ] I *adv* 1 *(at this moment)* ahora;
just n., right n., ahora mismo; **from n.
on,** de ahora en adelante; **n. and then, n.
and again,** de vez en cuando. 2 *(for
events in past)* entonces. 3 *(at present, these
days)* actualmente, hoy (en) día. 4 *(not related to time)* **n. (then),** ahora bien; **n.,
n.!,** ¡vamos!, ¡ya está bien!. II *conj* **n.
(that),** ahora que, ya que. III *n* **until n.,**
hasta ahora; **he'll be home by n.,** ya habrá llegado a casa.
nowadays ['naʊədeɪz] *adv* hoy (en) día,
actualmente.
nowhere ['nəʊweər] *adv* en ninguna
parte; **that will get you n.,** eso no te
servirá de nada; **n. near ready,** no
está preparado, ni mucho menos.
noxious ['nɒkʃəs] *adv* nocivo,- a.
nozzle ['nɒzəl] *n* boca *f,* boquilla *f.*
nuance [njuː'ɑːns] *n* matiz *m.*
nub [nʌb] *n* **the n. of the matter,** el quid
de la cuestión.
nuclear ['njuːklɪər] *adj* nuclear; **n. arms,**
armas *fpl* nucleares; **n. disarmament,**
desarme *m* nuclear; **n. energy,** energía *f*
nuclear; **n. power station,** central *f* nuclear.
nucleus ['njuːklɪəs] *n* núcleo *m.*
nude [njuːd] I *adj* desnudo,-a. II *n* Art
Phot desnudo *m;* **in the n.,** al desnudo.
nudge [nʌdʒ] I *vtr* dar un codazo a. II *n*
codazo *m.*
nudist ['njuːdɪst] *adj & n* nudista *(mf).*
nudity ['njuːdɪtɪ] *n* desnudez *f.*
nugget ['nʌgɪt] *n* Min pepita *f;* **gold n.,**
pepita de oro.
nuisance ['njuːsəns] *n* 1 molestia *f,* pesadez *f;* **what a n.!,** ¡qué lata! 2 *(person)*
pesado,-a *m,f.*
nuke [njuːk] *sl* I *n (bomb)* bomba *f* nuclear *or* atómica. II *vtr* atacar con armas
nucleares.
null [nʌl] *adj* nulo,-a; **n. and void,** nulo y
sin valor.
nullify ['nʌlɪfaɪ] *vtr (pt & pp* **nullified)**
anular.
numb [nʌm] I *adj (without feeling)*
entumecido,-a; *fig* paralizado,-a; **n. with
fear,** paralizado de miedo. II *vtr (with
cold)* entumecer (de frío); *(with anaesthetic)* adormecer.
number ['nʌmbər] I *n* 1 número *m; Tel*

have you got my n.?, ¿tienes mi (número de) teléfono?; *fam* to look after n. one, barrer para adentro. 2 *(quantity)* a n. of people, varias personas. II *vtr* 1 *(put a number on)* numerar. 2 *(count)* contar; his days are numbered, tiene los días contados.

numberplate ['nʌmbəpleɪt] *n GB Aut* matrícula *f*.

numeral ['njuːmərəl] *n* número *m*, cifra *f*.

numerate ['njuːmərət] *adj* to be n., tener un conocimiento básico de matemáticas.

numerical [njuːˈmerɪkəl] *adj* numérico,-a.
◆**numerically** *adv* numéricamente.

numerous ['njuːmərəs] *adj* numeroso,-a.

numismatics [njuːmɪzˈmætɪks] *n* numismática *f*.

nun [nʌn] *n* monja *f*.

nuptial ['nʌpʃəl] *adj* nupcial.

nurse [nɜːs] I *n* enfermera *f*; *(male)* enfermero *m*; children's n., niñera *f*. II *vtr* 1 *(look after)* cuidar, atender. 2 *(baby)* acunar. 3 *(suckle)* amamantar. 4 *fig (grudge etc)* guardar.

nursery ['nɜːsərɪ] *n* 1 *(institution)* guardería *f*; n. school, jardín *m* de infancia. 2 *(in house)* cuarto *m* de los niños; n.

rhyme, poema *m* infantil. 3 *(garden centre)* vivero *m*.

nursing ['nɜːsɪŋ] *n* n. home, clínica *f*.

nurture ['nɜːtʃər] *vtr (animal)* alimentar; *(feelings)* abrigar.

nut [nʌt] *n* 1 *(fruit)* fruto seco; *fig* a tough n. to crack, un hueso duro de roer. 2 *sl (head)* coco *m*. 3 *sl (mad person)* loco,-a *m,f*. 4 *Tech* tuerca *f*.

nutcracker ['nʌtkrækər] *n* cascanueces *m inv*.

nutmeg ['nʌtmeg] *n* nuez moscada *f*.

nutrition [njuːˈtrɪʃən] *n* nutrición *f*.

nutritious [njuːˈtrɪʃəs] *adj* nutritivo,-a, alimenticio,-a.

nuts [nʌts] *adj fam* chalado,-a; to go n., volverse loco; he's n. about motorbikes, las motos le chiflan.

nutshell ['nʌtʃel] *n* cáscara *f*; *fig* in a n., en pocas palabras.

nylon ['naɪlɒn] I *n* 1 nilón *m*, nailon *m*. 2 nylons, medias *fpl* de nilón. II *adj* de nilón.

nymph [nɪmf] *n* ninfa *f*.

nymphomaniac [nɪmfəˈmeɪnɪæk] *n* ninfómana *f*.

O

O, o [əʊ] *n* 1 *(the letter)* O, o *f*. 2 *Math Tel* cero *m*.

oak [əʊk] *n* roble *m*.

OAP [əʊeɪˈpiː] *GB fam abbr of* old-age pensioner.

oar [ɔːr] *n* remo *m*.

oarsman ['ɔːzmən] *n* remero *m*.

oasis [əʊˈeɪsɪs] *n (pl oases* [əʊˈeɪsiːz]*)* oasis *m inv*.

oat [əʊt] *n* avena *f*; rolled oats, copos *mpl* de avena.

oath [əʊθ] *n (pl oaths* [əʊðz]*)* 1 *Jur* juramento *m*; to take an o., prestar juramento; *fam* on my o., palabra de honor. 2 *(swearword)* palabrota *f*.

oatmeal ['əʊtmiːl] *n* harina *f* de avena.

obedience [əˈbiːdɪəns] *n* obediencia *f*.

obedient [əˈbiːdɪənt] *adj* obediente.

obese [əʊˈbiːs] *adj* obeso,-a.

obey [əˈbeɪ] *vtr* obedecer; *(law)* cumplir con.

obituary [əˈbɪtjʊərɪ] *n* necrología *f*.

object[1] ['ɒbdʒɪkt] *n* 1 *(thing)* objeto *m*. 2 *(aim, purpose)* fin *m*, objetivo *m*. 3 the o. of criticism, el blanco de las críticas. 4 *(obstacle)* inconveniente *m*. 5 *Ling* complemento *m*.

object[2] [əbˈdʒekt] *vi* oponerse (to, a); do you o. to my smoking?, ¿le molesta que fume?

objection [əbˈdʒekʃən] *n* 1 objeción *f*. 2 *(drawback)* inconveniente *m*; provided

there's no o., si no hay inconveniente.

objectionable [əbˈdʒekʃənəbəl] *adj (unacceptable)* inaceptable; *(unpleasant)* ofensivo,-a.

objective [əbˈdʒektɪv] I *adj* objetivo,-a. II *n* objetivo *m*.

objector [əbˈdʒektər] *n* objetor,-a *m,f*.

obligation [ɒblɪˈgeɪʃən] *n* obligación *f*; to be under an o. to sb, estarle muy agradecido,-a a algn.

obligatory [ɒˈblɪgətərɪ] *adj* obligatorio,-a.

oblige [əˈblaɪdʒ] *vtr* 1 *(compel)* obligar; I'm obliged to do it, me veo obligado,-a a hacerlo. 2 *(do a favour for)* hacer un favor a. 3 to be obliged, *(grateful)* estar agradecido,-a.

obliging [əˈblaɪdʒɪŋ] *adj* solícito,-a.

oblique [əˈbliːk] *adj* oblicuo,-a, inclinado,-a; *fig* an o. reference, una alusión indirecta.

obliterate [əˈblɪtəreɪt] *vtr* 1 *(memory)* borrar. 2 *(species, race)* eliminar; *(village)* arrasar.

oblivion [əˈblɪvɪən] *n* olvido *m*; to sink into o., caer en el olvido.

oblivious [əˈblɪvɪəs] *adj* inconsciente.

oblong ['ɒblɒŋ] 1 *adj* oblongo,-a. II *n* rectángulo *m*.

obnoxious [əbˈnɒkʃəs] *adj* repugnante.

oboe ['əʊbəʊ] *n* oboe *m*.

obscene [əbˈsiːn] *adj* obsceno,-a.

obscure [əbˈskjʊər] I *adj* 1 oscuro,-a;

(vague) vago,-a. 2 *(author, poet etc)* desconocido,-a. II *vtr (truth)* ocultar.

obsequious |əb'siːkwɪəs| *adj* servil.

observance |əb'zɜːvəns| *n* 1 observancia *f*. 2 *Rel* **observances**, prácticas religiosas.

observant |əb'zɜːvənt| *adj* observador,-a.

observation |ɒbzə'veɪʃən| *n* observación *f*; *(surveillance)* vigilancia *f*.

observatory |əb'zɜːvətərɪ| *n* observatorio *m*.

observe |əb'zɜːv| *vtr* 1 observar; *(in surveillance)* vigilar. 2 *(remark)* advertir. 3 *(obey)* respetar.

observer |əb'zɜːvər| *n* observador,-a *m,f*.

obsess |əb'ses| *vtr* obsesionar; **to be obsessed**, estar obsesionado,-a **(with, by, con)**.

obsession |əb'seʃən| *n* obsesión *f*.

obsessive |əb'sesɪv| *adj* obsesivo,-a.

obsolete |'ɒbsəliːt, ɒbsə'liːt| *adj* obsoleto,-a.

obstacle |'ɒbstəkəl| *n* obstáculo *m*; *fig* impedimento *m*; **o. race**, carrera *f* de obstáculos.

obstinate |'ɒbstɪnɪt| *adj* 1 *(person)* obstinado,-a, terco,-a. 2 *(pain)* persistente.

obstruct |əb'strʌkt| *vtr* 1 obstruir; *(pipe etc)* atascar; *(view)* tapar. 2 *(hinder)* estorbar; *(progress)* dificultar.

obstruction |əb'strʌkʃən| *n* 1 obstrucción *f*. 2 *(hindrance)* obstáculo *m*.

obtain |əb'teɪn| *vtr* obtener, conseguir.

obtainable |əb'teɪnəbəl| *adj* obtenible.

obtrusive |əb'truːsɪv| *adj* 1 *(interfering)* entrometido,-a. 2 *(noticeable)* llamativo, -a.

obtuse |əb'tjuːs| *adj* obtuso,-a.

obviate |'ɒbvɪeɪt| *vtr fml* obviar.

obvious |'ɒbvɪəs| *adj* obvio,-a, evidente. ◆**obviously** *adv* evidentemente; **o.!**, ¡claro!, ¡por supuesto!

occasion |ə'keɪʒən| I *n* 1 ocasión *f*; **on o.**, de vez en cuando; **on the o. of**, con motivo de. 2 *(event)* acontecimiento *m*. 3 *(cause)* motivo *m*. II *vtr fml* ocasionar.

occasional |ə'keɪʒənəl| *adj* 1 esporádico,-a, eventual. ◆**occasionally** *adv* de vez en cuando.

occupant |'ɒkjupənt| *n* ocupante *mf*; *(tenant)* inquilino,-a *m,f*.

occupation |ɒkjʊ'peɪʃən| *n* 1 *(job, profession)* profesión *f*, ocupación *f*. 2 *(pastime)* pasatiempo *m*. 3 *(of building, house, country)* ocupación *f*.

occupational |ɒkjʊ'peɪʃənəl| *adj* profesional, laboral; **o. hazards**, gajes *mpl* del oficio.

occupied |'ɒkjupaɪd| *adj* ocupado,-a.

occupier |'ɒkjupaɪər| *n GB* ocupante *mf*; *(tenant)* inquilino,-a *m,f*.

occupy |'ɒkjupaɪ| *vtr* 1 *(live in)* ocupar, habitar. 2 *(time)* pasar; **to o. one's time**

in doing sth, dedicar su tiempo a hacer algo. 3 *(building, factory etc in protest)* tomar posesión de.

occur |ə'kɜːr| *vi* 1 *(event)* suceder, acaecer; *(change)* producirse. 2 *(be found)* encontrarse. 3 **it occurred to me that ...**, se me ocurrió que ....

occurrence |ə'kʌrəns| *n* acontecimiento *m*.

ocean |'əʊʃən| *n* océano *m*.

ocean-going |'əʊʃəngəʊɪŋ| *adj* de alta mar.

ochre, *US* **ocher** |'əʊkər| I *n* ocre *m*; **red o.**, almagre *m*; **yellow o.**, ocre amarillo. II *adj* (de color) ocre.

o'clock |ə'klɒk| *adv* **(it's) one o'c.**, (es) la una; **(it's) two o'c.**, (son) las dos.

octave |'ɒktɪv| *n* octava *f*.

October |ɒk'təʊbər| *n* octubre *m*.

octogenarian |ɒktəʊdʒɪ'neərɪən| *adj & n* octogenario,-a *(m,f)*.

octopus |'ɒktəpəs| *n* pulpo *m*.

odd |ɒd| I *adj* 1 *(strange)* raro,-a, extraño,-a. 2 *(occasional)* esporádico,-a; **at o. times**, de vez en cuando; **the o. customer**, algún que otro cliente; **o. job**, trabajillo *m*. 3 **an o. number**, *(not even)* un impar. 4 *(unpaired)* desparejado,-a; **an o. sock**, un calcetín suelto; *fig* **to be the o. man out**, estar de más. II *adv* y pico; **twenty o. people**, veinte y pico *or* y tantas personas. ◆**oddly** *adv* extrañamente; **o. enough**, por extraño que parezca.

oddity |'ɒdɪtɪ| *n* 1 *(thing)* curiosidad *f*; *(person)* estrafalario,-a *m,f*. 2 *(quality)* rareza *f*.

odds |ɒdz| *npl* 1 *(chances)* probabilidades *fpl*; **he's fighting against the o.**, lleva las de perder; **the o. are that ...**, lo más probable es que ... (+ *subj*). 2 *(in betting)* puntos *mpl* de ventaja; **the o. are five to one**, las apuestas están cinco a uno. 3 *GB* **it makes no o.**, da lo mismo; *fig* **at o. with sb**, reñido,-a con algn. 4 **o. and ends**, *(small things)* cositas *fpl*; *(trinkets)* chucherías *fpl*.

odds-on |'ɒdzɒn| *adj* seguro,-a; **o.-on favourite**, *(horse)* caballo favorito.

ode |əʊd| *n* oda *f*.

odious |'əʊdɪəs| *adj* repugnante.

odour, *US* **odor** |'əʊdər| *n* olor *m*; *(fragrance)* perfume *m*.

OECD |əʊiːsiː'diː| *abbr of* **Organization for Economic Co-operation and Development**, ≈ Organización *f* para la Cooperación y el Desarrollo Económico, OCDE *f*.

of |ɒv, *unstressed* əv| *prep* 1 *(belonging to, part of)* de; **a friend of mine**, un amigo mío; **the end of the novel**, el final de la novela. 2 *(containing)* de; **a bottle of wine**, una botella de vino. 3 *(origin)* de; **of good family**, de buena familia. 4 *(by)* de, por; **beloved of all**, amado,-a por to-dos. **5** (*quantity*) de; **there are four of us**, somos cuatro; **two of them**, dos de ellos. **6** (*from*) de; **free of**, libre de; **south of**, al sur de. **7** (*material*) de; **a dress (made) of silk**, un vestido de seda. **8** (*apposition*) de; **the city of Lisbon**, la ciudad de Lisboa. **9** (*characteristic*) de; **that's typical of her**, es muy propio de ella; **that's very kind of you**, es usted muy amable. **10** (*with adj*) de; **hard of hearing**, duro,-a de oído. **11** (*after superlative*) de; **the thing she wanted most of all**, lo que más quería. **12** (*cause*) por, de; **because of**, a causa de; **of necessity**, por necesidad. **13** (*concerning, about*) de, sobre; **to dream of sth/sb**, soñar con algo/algn; **to think of sb**, pensar en algn. **14** (*with dates*) de; **the seventh of November**, el siete de noviembre.

off [ɒf] **I** *prep* **1** (*movement*) de; **she fell o. her horse**, se cayó del caballo. **2** (*removal*) de; **I'll take sth o. the price for you**, se lo rebajaré un poco. **3** (*distance, situation*) de; **a few kilometres o. the coast**, a unos kilómetros de la costa; **a house o. the road**, una casa apartada de la carretera. **4 the ship went o. course**, el barco se desvió; **to be o. form**, no estar en forma. **5 I'm o. wine**, he perdido el gusto al vino.
II *adv* **1 he turned o. the radio**, apagó la radio. **2** (*absent*) fuera; **I have a day o.**, tengo un día libre; **to be o. sick**, estar de baja por enfermedad. **3** (*completely*) completamente; **this will kill o. any germs**, esto rematará cualquier germen. **4 his arrival is three days o.**, faltan tres días para su llegada; **six miles o.**, a seis millas. **5 I'm o. to London**, me voy a Londres; **she ran o.**, se fue corriendo. **6 ten per cent o.**, un descuento del diez por ciento; **to take one's shoes o.**, quitarse los zapatos. **7 o. and on**, de vez en cuando.
III *adj* **1** (*gas etc*) apagado,-a; (*water*) cortado,-a. **2** (*cancelled*) cancelado,-a. **3** (*low*) bajo,-a; (*unsatisfactory*) malo,-a; **on the o. chance**, por si acaso; **the o. season**, la temporada baja. **4 you're better o. like that**, así estás mejor. **5** (*gone bad*) (*meat, fish*) malo,-a, pasado,-a; (*milk*) agrio,-a.

offal ['ɒfəl] *n* (*of chicken etc*) menudillos *mpl*; (*of cattle, pigs*) asaduras *fpl*.
off-colour, *US* **off-color** ['ɒfkʌlər] *adj* **1** *GB* (*ill*) indispuesto,-a. **2** (*joke, story*) indecente.
offence [ə'fens] *n* **1** *Jur* delito *m*. **2** (*insult*) ofensa *f*; **to give o.**, ofender; **to take o. at sth**, ofenderse por algo. **3** *Mil* (*attack*) ofensiva *f*.
offend [ə'fend] *vtr* ofender.
offender [ə'fendər] *n* (*criminal*) de-

lincuente *mf*.
offense [ə'fens] *n US* → **offence**.
offensive [ə'fensɪv] **I** *adj* **1** (*insulting*) ofensivo,-a. **2** (*repulsive*) repugnante. **II** *n Mil* ofensiva *f*; **to be on the o.**, estar a la ofensiva.
offer ['ɒfər] **I** *vtr* **1** ofrecer; **to o. to do a job**, ofrecerse para hacer un trabajo. **2** (*propose*) proponer. **II** *n* **1** oferta *f*; (*proposal*) propuesta *f*; **o. of marriage**, proposición *f* de matrimonio. **2** *Com* **on o.**, de oferta.
offering ['ɒfərɪŋ] *n* **1** ofrecimiento *m*. **2** *Rel* ofrenda *f*.
offhand [ɒf'hænd] **I** *adj* (*abrupt*) brusco, -a; (*inconsiderate*) descortés. **II** *adv* **I don't know o.**, así sin pensarlo, no lo sé.
office ['ɒfɪs] *n* **1** (*room*) despacho *m*; (*building*) oficina *f*; **o. hours**, horas *fpl* de oficina. **2** *GB Pol* ministerio *m*. **3** *US* (*federal agency*) agencia *f* gubernamental. **4** (*position*) cargo *m*; **to hold o.**, ocupar un cargo. **5** *Pol* **to be in o.**, estar en el poder.
officer ['ɒfɪsər] *n* **1** *Mil* oficial *mf*. **2** (*police*) **o.**, agente *mf* de policía. **3** (*government official*) funcionario,-a *m,f*. **4** (*of company, society*) director,-a *m,f*.
official [ə'fɪʃəl] **I** *adj* oficial. **II** *n* funcionario,-a *m,f*.
officiate [ə'fɪʃɪeɪt] *vi* **1** ejercer; **to o. as**, ejercer de. **2** *Rel* oficiar.
officious [ə'fɪʃəs] *adj pej* entrometido,-a.
off-line ['ɒflaɪn] *adj Comput* desconectado,-a.
off-licence ['ɒflaɪsəns] *n GB* tienda *f* de bebidas alcohólicas.
off-peak [ɒf'piːk] *adj* (*flight*) de temporada baja; (*rate*) de fuera de las horas punta.
off-putting ['ɒfputɪŋ] *adj GB fam* desconcertante.
offset [ɒf'set] *vtr* (*pt & pp* **offset**) (*balance out*) compensar.
offshoot ['ɒfʃuːt] *n* **1** *Bot* renuevo *m*. **2** *fig* (*of organization*) ramificación *f*.
offshore [ɒf'ʃɔːr] *adj* **1** (*breeze etc*) terral. **2** (*oil rig*) costa afuera. **3** (*overseas*) en el extranjero; **o. investment**, inversión *f* en el extranjero.
offside [ɒf'saɪd] **I** *adv Ftb* fuera de juego. **II** *n Aut* (*with left-hand drive*) lado derecho; (*with right-hand drive*) lado izquierdo.
offspring ['ɒfsprɪŋ] *n inv* (*child*) vástago *m*; (*children*) progenitura *f*.
offstage [ɒf'steɪdʒ] *adj & adv* entre bastidores.
often ['ɒfən, 'ɒftən] *adv* a menudo, con frecuencia; **every so o.**, de vez en cuando.
ogle ['əʊgəl] *vtr & vi* **to o. (at) sb**, comerse a algn con los ojos.
oh [əʊ] *interj* ¡oh!, ¡ay!; **oh, my God!**,

¡Dios mío!

oil [ɔɪl] **I** n 1 aceite m; **o. lamp**, lámpara f de aceite, quinqué m; **o. slick**, mancha f de aceite; **olive o.**, aceite de oliva. 2 *Petrol* petróleo m; **o. rig**, plataforma petrolera; **o. tanker**, petrolero m. 3 (*painting*) pintura f al óleo; **o. colour**, **o. paint**, óleo m. **II** vtr engrasar.

oilcan [ˈɔɪlkæn] n aceitera f.

oilfield [ˈɔɪlfiːld] n yacimiento petrolífero.

oilskin [ˈɔɪlskɪn] n 1 hule m. 2 **oilskins**, chubasquero m sing, impermeable m sing de hule.

oily [ˈɔɪlɪ] adj (**oilier**, **oiliest**) aceitoso,-a, grasiento,-a; (*hair, skin*) graso,-a.

ointment [ˈɔɪntmənt] n ungüento m, pomada f.

O.K., **okay** [əʊˈkeɪ] fam **I** interj ¡vale!, ¡de acuerdo!. **II** adj bien; **is it O.K. if …?**, ¿está bien si …? **III** vtr dar el visto bueno a.

old [əʊld] **I** adj 1 viejo,-a; **an o. man**, un anciano; **o. age**, vejez f; **o.-age pensioner**, pensionista mf; GB **o. boy**, antiguo alumno; **o. hand**, veterano,-a m,f; **good o. John!**, ¡el bueno de John! 2 **how o. are you?**, ¿cuántos años tienes?; **she's five years o.**, tiene cinco años. 3 (*previous*) antiguo,-a. **II n of o.**, de antaño.

old-fashioned [əʊldˈfæʃənd] (*outdated*) a la antigua; (*unfashionable*) anticuado,-a, pasado,-a de moda.

olive [ˈɒlɪv] n 1 (*tree*) olivo m; **o. grove**, olivar m. 2 (*fruit*) aceituna f, oliva f. 3 (*wood*) olivo m. 4 **o. (green)**, (*colour*) verde m oliva.

Olympic [əˈlɪmpɪk] **I** adj olímpico,-a; **O. Games**, Juegos Olímpicos. **II** npl **the Olympics**, las Olimpíadas.

omelette, US **omelet** [ˈɒmlɪt] n tortilla f; **Spanish o.**, tortilla española or de patatas.

omen [ˈəʊmen] n presagio m.

ominous [ˈɒmɪnəs] adj de mal agüero.

omission [əʊˈmɪʃən] n omisión f; fig olvido m.

omit [əʊˈmɪt] vtr omitir; (*accidentally*) pasar por alto; (*forget*) olvidarse (**to**, de).

omnipotent [ɒmˈnɪpətənt] **I** adj omnipotente. **II** n **the O.**, el Todopoderoso.

on [ɒn] **I** prep 1 (*location*) sobre, encima de, en; **I hit him on the head**, le di un golpe en la cabeza; **it's on the desk**, está encima de or sobre el escritorio; **hanging on the wall**, colgado de la pared; **on page four**, en la página cuatro; **have you got any money on you?**, ¿llevas dinero?; **the drinks are on me/the house**, invito yo/invita la casa. 2 (*alongside*) en; **a town on the coast**, un pueblo en la costa. 3 (*direction*) en, a; **on the right**, a la derecha; **on the way**, en el camino. 4 (*time*) **on April 3rd**, el tres de abril; **on a sunny day**, un día de sol; **on Monday**, el lunes;

on Mondays, los lunes; **on that occasion**, en aquella ocasión; **on the following day**, al día siguiente; **on time**, a tiempo. 5 en; **on TV/the radio**, en la tele/radio; **to play sth on the piano**, tocar algo al piano; **on the phone**, al teléfono. 6 (*at the time of*) a; **on his arrival**, a su llegada; **on second thoughts**, pensándolo bien; **on learning of this**, al conocer esto. 7 **she lives on bread**, vive de pan; **to depend on**, depender de. 8 (*transport*) en, a; **on foot**, a pie; **on the train/plane/bus**, en el tren/avión/autobús; (*travel by*) en tren/avión/autobús. 9 (*state, process*) en, de; **on holiday**, de vacaciones; **she is here on business**, está aquí de negocios. 10 (*regarding*) sobre; **a lecture on numismatics**, una conferencia sobre numismática; **they congratulated him on his success**, le felicitaron por su éxito. 11 **on condition that**, (*subject to*) bajo la condición de que. 12 (*against*) contra; **an attack on**, un ataque contra. 13 **he's on the Times**, (*working for*) trabaja para el Times.

II adv 1 (*covering*) encima, puesto; **she had a coat on**, llevaba puesto un abrigo. 2 fam **have you anything on tonight?**, ¿tienes algún plan para esta noche? 3 **and so on**, y así sucesivamente; **go on!**, ¡sigue!; **he talks on and on**, habla sin parar; **to work on**, seguir trabajando. 4 **from that day on**, a partir de aquel día; **later on**, más tarde.

III adj fam 1 **to be on**, (*TV, radio, light*) estar encendido,-a; (*engine*) estar en marcha; (*film, play*) en cartelera; **that film was on last week**, pusieron esa película la semana pasada. 2 *Theat TV* **you're on!**, ¡a escena! 3 (*definitely planned*) previsto,-a; **you're on!**, ¡trato hecho! **that isn't on**, eso no vale.

once [wʌns] **I** adv 1 (*one time*) una vez; **o. a week**, una vez por semana; **o. in a while**, de vez en cuando; **o. more**, una vez más; **o. or twice**, un par de veces; fig **o. and for all**, de una vez por todas. 2 (*formerly*) en otro tiempo; **o. (upon a time) there was**, érase una vez. 3 **at o.**, en seguida, inmediatamente; **don't all speak at o.**, no habléis todos a la vez. **II** conj una vez que (+ subj), en cuanto (+ subj).

oncoming [ˈɒnkʌmɪŋ] adj (*car, traffic*) que viene en dirección contraria.

one [wʌn] **I** adj 1 un, una; **for o. thing**, primero; **you're the o. person who knows**, tú eres el único que lo sabe; **the o. and only**, el único, la única; **o. and the same**, el mismo, la misma. 2 (*indefinite*) un, una; **he'll come back o. day**, un día volverá.

II dem pron any **o.**, cualquiera; **that o.**, ése, ésa; **this o.**, éste, ésta; (*distant*)

aquél, aquélla; **the blue ones**, los azules, las azules; **the o. on the table**, el *or* la que está encima de la mesa; **the ones that, the ones who,** los *or* las que.
III *indef pron* **1** uno,-a *m,f*; **I, for o.,** am against it, yo, por lo menos, estoy en contra; **I'm not o. to complain,** no soy de los que se quejan; **o. at a time,** de uno en uno; **o. by o.,** uno tras otro; *fig* **o. and all,** todo el mundo. **2** *(indefinite person)* uno,-a *m,f*; **o. has to fight,** hay que luchar; **o. hopes that will never happen,** esperemos que no ocurra; **to break o.'s leg/arm,** romperse la pierna/el brazo. **3 o. another,** el uno al otro; **they love o. another,** se aman.
IV *n (digit)* uno *m*; **o. hundred/thousand,** cien/mil.

one-armed ['wʌnɑːmd] *adj fig* **o.-a. bandit,** máquina *f* tragaperras.
one-man ['wʌnmæn] *adj* **a o.-m. show,** un espectáculo con un solo artista.
one-man band [wʌnmæn'bænd] *n* hombre *m* orquesta *(inv)*.
one-off ['wʌnɒf] *adj GB fam* único,-a, fuera de serie.
oneself [wʌn'self] *pron* **1** *(reflexive)* uno,-a mismo,-a *m,f*, sí mismo,-a *m,f*; **to talk to o.,** hablar para sí. **2** *(alone)* uno,-a mismo,-a *m,f*; **by o.,** solo,-a. **3** *(one's usual self)* el *or* la de siempre.
one-sided ['wʌnsaɪdɪd] *adj (bargain)* desigual; *(judgement)* parcial; *(decision)* unilateral.
one-to-one ['wʌntəwʌn] *adj* **o.-to-o. tuition,** clase *f* individual.
one-way ['wʌnweɪ] *adj* **1** *(ticket)* de ida. **2** *(street)* de dirección única.
ongoing ['ɒngəʊɪŋ] *adj* **1** *(in progress)* en curso, actual. **2** *(developing)* en desarrollo.
onion ['ʌnjən] *n* cebolla *f*.
on-line [ɒn'laɪn] *adj Comput* conectado,-a.
onlooker ['ɒnlʊkər] *n* espectador,-a *m,f*.
only ['əʊnlɪ] **I** *adj* único,-a; **o. son,** hijo único. **II** *adv* **1** solamente, sólo; **'staff o.', 'reservado al personal'. 2** *(not earlier than)* apenas; **he has o. just left,** acaba de marcharse hace un momento; **o. yesterday,** ayer mismo. **3 o. too glad!,** ¡con mucho gusto!. **III** *conj* pero.
onset ['ɒnset] *n (start)* comienzo *m*.
onslaught ['ɒnslɔːt] *n* embestida *f*.
onto ['ɒntʊ, *unstressed* 'ɒntə] *prep* → **on**.
onus ['əʊnəs] *n* responsabilidad *f*.
onward ['ɒnwəd] *adj* hacia adelante.
onward(s) ['ɒnwəd(z)] *adv* a partir de, en adelante; **from this time o.,** de ahora en adelante.
ooze [uːz] **I** *vi* rezumar. **II** *vtr* rebosar.
opaque [əʊ'peɪk] *adj* opaco,-a.
OPEC ['əʊpek] *abbr of* **Organization of Petroleum Exporting Countries,** Organización *f* de los Países Exportadores de

Petróleo, OPEP *f*.
open ['əʊpən] **I** *adj* **1** abierto,-a; **half o.,** entreabierto; **wide o.,** abierto de par en par; **in the o. air,** al aire libre; **to be o. with sb,** ser sincero,-a con algn; *fig* **with o. arms,** con los brazos abiertos; **to keep an o. mind,** no tener prejuicios; **I am o. to suggestions,** acepto cualquier sugerencia; **o. to criticism,** susceptible a la crítica; **o. admiration,** franca admiración; *US* **o. house,** fiesta *f* de inauguración de residencia; **an o. question,** una cuestión sin resolver; **o. season,** *(in hunting)* temporada *f* de caza; *Av Rail* **o. ticket,** billete abierto; *GB* **O. University,** Universidad *f* a Distancia; **o. verdict,** veredicto inconcluso. **2** *(car etc)* descubierto, -a. **3** *(opposition)* manifiesto,-a.
II *vtr* **1** abrir; **to o. fire,** abrir fuego; *fig* **to o. one's heart to sb,** sincerarse con algn. **2** *(exhibition etc)* inaugurar; *(negotiations, conversation)* entablar.
III *vi* **1** abrir, abrirse; **to o. onto,** *(of door, window)* dar a. **2** *(start)* empezar; *Theat Cin* estrenarse.
IV *n* **1 in the o.,** al aire libre; *fig* **to bring into the o.,** hacer público. **2** *Sport* open *m*.
◆**open out I** *vtr* abrir, desplegar. **II** *vi (flowers)* abrirse; *(view)* extenderse.
◆**open up I** *vtr (market etc)* abrir; *(possibilities)* crear. **II** *vi* **1** abrirse; *fam* **o. up!,** ¡abra la puerta! **2** *(start)* empezar.
◆**openly** *adv* abiertamente.
opener ['əʊpənər] *n* **tin o.,** *US* **can o.,** abrelatas *m inv*.
opening ['əʊpənɪŋ] *n* **1** *(act)* apertura *f*; **o. night,** noche *f* de estreno; *GB* **o. time,** hora *f* de apertura de los bares. **2** *(beginning)* comienzo *m*. **3** *(aperture)* abertura *f*; *(gap)* brecha *f*. **4** *Com* oportunidad *f*. **5** *(vacancy)* vacante *f*.
open-minded [əʊpən'maɪndɪd] *adj* sin prejuicios.
openness ['əʊpənnɪs] *n* franqueza *f*.
open-plan ['əʊpənplæn] *adj (office)* abierto,-a.
opera ['ɒpərə] *n* ópera *f*; **o. house,** ópera, teatro *m* de la ópera.
operate ['ɒpəreɪt] **I** *vi* **1** *(function)* funcionar. **2** *Med* operar; **to o. on sb for appendicitis,** operar a algn de apendicitis. **II** *vtr* **1** *(control)* manejar. **2** *(business)* dirigir.
operatic [ɒpə'rætɪk] *adj* de ópera.
operating ['ɒpəreɪtɪŋ] *n* **1 o. costs,** gastos *mpl* de funcionamiento. **2** *Med* **o. table,** mesa *f* de operaciones; **o. theatre,** *US* **o. theater,** quirófano *m*.
operation [ɒpə'reɪʃən] *n* **1** *(of machine)* funcionamiento *m*; *(by person)* manejo *m*. **2** *Mil* maniobra *f*. **3** *Med* operación *f*, intervención quirúrgica; **to undergo an o. for,** ser operado,-a de.

operational [ɒpə'reɪʃənəl] adj 1 (ready for use) operativo,-a. 2 Mil operacional.

operative ['ɒpərətɪv] adj 1 Jur (in force) vigente; **to become o.**, entrar en vigor. 2 (significant) clave, significativo,-a; **the o. word**, la palabra clave.

operator ['ɒpəreɪtər] n 1 Ind operario,-a m,f. 2 Tel operador,-a m,f. 3 (dealer) negociante mf, agente mf; **tour o.**, agente de viajes.

opinion [ə'pɪnjən] n opinión f; **in my o.**, en mi opinión, a mi juicio; **it's a matter of o.**, es cuestión de opiniones; **to have a high o. of sb**, tener buen concepto de algn; **o. poll**, encuesta f, sondeo m.

opinionated [ə'pɪnjəneɪtɪd] adj dogmático,-a.

opium ['əupɪəm] n opio m.

opponent [ə'pəunənt] n adversario,-a m,f.

opportune ['ɒpətjuːn] adj oportuno,-a.

opportunist [ɒpə'tjuːnɪst] adj & n oportunista (mf).

opportunity [ɒpə'tjuːnɪtɪ] n 1 oportunidad f, ocasión f. 2 (prospect) perspectiva f.

oppose [ə'pəuz] vtr oponerse a.

opposed [ə'pəuzd] adj opuesto,-a; **to be o. to sth**, estar en contra de algo; **as o. to**, comparado,-a con.

opposing [ə'pəuzɪŋ] adj adversario,-a.

opposite ['ɒpəzɪt, 'ɒpəsɪt] I adj 1 (facing) de enfrente; (page) contiguo,-a. 2 (contrary) opuesto,-a, contrario,-a; **in the o. direction**, en dirección contraria. II n lo contrario m; **quite the o.!**, ¡al contrario!. III prep enfrente de, frente a. IV adv enfrente.

opposition [ɒpə'zɪʃən] n 1 oposición f; **in o. to**, en contra de. 2 Pol **the o.**, la oposición.

oppress [ə'pres] vtr oprimir.

oppression [ə'preʃən] n opresión f.

oppressive [ə'presɪv] adj opresivo,-a; (atmosphere) agobiante; (heat) sofocante.

opt [ɒpt] vi optar; **to o. for**, optar por; **to o. to do sth**, optar por hacer algo.
◆**opt out** vi retirarse; **to o. out of doing sth**, decidir no hacer algo.

optical ['ɒptɪkəl] adj óptico,-a.

optician [ɒp'tɪʃən] n óptico,-a m,f.

optics ['ɒptɪks] n óptica f.

optimist ['ɒptɪmɪst] n optimista mf.

optimistic [ɒptɪ'mɪstɪk] adj optimista.
◆**optimistically** adv con optimismo.

optimum ['ɒptɪməm] I n grado óptimo. II adj óptimo,-a.

option ['ɒpʃən] n opción f; **I have no o.**, no tengo más remedio; **to keep one's options open**, no comprometerse; **with the o. of**, con opción a.

optional ['ɒpʃənəl] adj optativo,-a, facultativo,-a; Educ **o. subject**, (asignatura f) optativa f.

opulence ['ɒpjuləns] n opulencia f.

or [ɔːr, unstressed ə] conj 1 o; (before a word beginning with o or ho) u; **or else**, si no, o bien; **whether you like it or not**, tanto si te gusta como si no; **either a bun or a piece of cake**, (o) una madalena o un trozo de pastel. 2 (with negative) ni; **he can't read or write**, no sabe leer ni escribir; → **nor**.

oral ['ɔːrəl, 'ɒrəl] I adj oral. II n examen m oral. ◆**orally** adv **to be taken o.**, por vía oral.

orange ['ɒrɪndʒ] I n naranja f; **o. juice**, zumo m de naranja. II adj de color naranja.

orator ['ɒrətər] n orador,-a m,f.

oratory ['ɒrətərɪ] n oratoria f.

orbit ['ɔːbɪt] I n Astron órbita f. II vtr girar alrededor de. III vi girar.

orchard ['ɔːtʃəd] n huerto m.

orchestra ['ɔːkɪstrə] n orquesta f.

orchestral [ɔː'kestrəl] adj orquestal.

orchid ['ɔːkɪd] n orquídea f.

ordain [ɔː'deɪn] vtr 1 Rel ordenar; **to be ordained**, ordenarse. 2 (decree) decretar.

ordeal [ɔː'diːl] n mala experiencia.

order ['ɔːdər] I n 1 (sequence) orden m; **in alphabetical o.**, por orden alfabético; **to put in o.**, ordenar. 2 (condition) estado m; **is your passport in o.?**, ¿tienes el pasaporte en regla?; **'out of o.'**, averiado,-a. 3 (peace) orden m; **to restore o.**, reestablecer el orden público. 4 (command) orden f. 5 Com pedido m, encargo m; **to be on o.**, estar pedido; **to o.**, a la medida; **o. form**, hoja f de pedido. 6 Rel orden f. 7 **of the highest o.**, (quality) de primera calidad. 8 (kind) índole f, tipo m; Biol orden m. 9 **in the o. of**, del orden de. 10 **in o. that**, (so as) (+ subj), a fin de que (+ subj); **in o. to** (+ infin), para, a fin de (+ infin). II vtr 1 (command) ordenar, mandar; **to o. sb to do sth**, mandar a algn hacer algo. 2 Com pedir, encargar; **to o. a dish**, pedir un plato.

orderly ['ɔːdəlɪ] I adj (tidy etc) ordenado,-a. II n 1 Med enfermero m. 2 Mil ordenanza m.

ordinary ['ɔːdənrɪ] I adj usual, normal; (average) corriente, común; **the o. citizen**, el ciudadano de a pie. II n **the o.**, lo corriente, lo normal; **out of the o.**, fuera de lo común.

ordnance ['ɔːdnəns] n GB **O. Survey**, servicio m oficial de topografía y cartografía.

ore [ɔːr] n mineral m.

organ ['ɔːgən] n Mus Anat etc órgano m.

organic [ɔː'gænɪk] adj orgánico,-a.

organism ['ɔːgənɪzəm] n organismo m.

organization [ɔːgənaɪ'zeɪʃən] n organización f.

organize ['ɔːgənaɪz] vtr organizar.

organizer ['ɔːgənaɪzər] n organizador,-a

m,f.
orgasm ['ɔːgæzəm] *n* orgasmo *m.*
orgy ['ɔːdʒɪ] *n* orgía *f.*
Orient ['ɔːrɪənt] *n* the O., el Oriente.
Oriental [ɔːrɪ'entəl] *adj & n* oriental *(mf).*
origin ['ɒrɪdʒɪn] *n* origen *m;* **country of** o., país *m* natal *or* de origen.
original [ə'rɪdʒɪnəl] I *adj* 1 original; *(first)* primero,-a. 2 *(imaginative)* original. II *n* original *m.* ◆**originally** *adv* 1 *(at first)* en un principio. 2 *(with imagination)* con originalidad.
originality [ərɪdʒɪ'nælɪtɪ] *n* originalidad *f.*
originate [ə'rɪdʒɪneɪt] I *vtr* originar. II *vi* to o. from *or* in, tener su origen en.
Orkneys ['ɔːknɪz] *npl* (Islas) Órcadas.
ornament ['ɔːnəmənt] *n* ornamento *m,* adorno *m.*
ornamental [ɔːnə'mentəl] *adj* decorativo,-a.
ornate [ɔː'neɪt] *adj* vistoso,-a.
ornithology [ɔːnɪ'θɒlədʒɪ] *n* ornitología *f.*
orphan ['ɔːfən] I *n* huérfano,-a *m,f.* II *vtr* she was orphaned, quedó huérfana.
orphanage ['ɔːfənɪdʒ] *n* orfanato *m.*
orthodox ['ɔːθədɒks] *adj* ortodoxo,-a.
orthodoxy ['ɔːθədɒksɪ] *n* ortodoxia *f.*
orthopaedic, *US* **orthopedic** [ɔːθəʊ'piːdɪk] *adj* ortopédico,-a.
oscillate ['ɒsɪleɪt] *vi* oscilar.
ostensible [ɒ'stensɪbəl] *adj* 1 *(apparent)* ostensible. 2 *(pretended)* aparente.
ostentatious [ɒsten'teɪʃəs] *adj* ostentoso,-a.
osteopath ['ɒstɪəpæθ] *n* osteópata *mf.*
ostracize ['ɒstrəsaɪz] *vtr (from society)* condenar al ostracismo; *(from group)* aislar, excluir.
ostrich ['ɒstrɪtʃ] *n* avestruz *f.*
other ['ʌðər] I *adj* 1 otro,-a; **every** o. day, cada dos días; **on the** o. hand, por otra parte; o. people have seen it, otros lo han visto; the o. four, los otros cuatro; the o. one, el otro, la otra; the o. thing, lo otro. 2 he must be somewhere or o., debe de estar en alguna parte. II *pron* otro,-a *m,f;* many others, otros muchos; the others, los otros, los demás; we see each o. quite often, nos vemos con bastante frecuencia.
otherwise ['ʌðəwaɪz] I *adv* 1 *(if not)* si no. 2 *(differently)* de otra manera. 3 *(in other respects)* por lo demás. II *adj* distinto,-a.
otter ['ɒtər] *n* nutria *f.*
ought [ɔːt] *v aux* 1 *(obligation)* deber; I thought I o. to tell you, creí que debía decírtelo; she o. to do it, debería hacerlo. 2 *(vague desirability)* tener que, deber; you o. to see the exhibition, deberías ver la exposición. 3 *(expectation)* he o. to pass the exam, seguramente aprobará el examen; that o. to do, con eso bastará.

ounce [aʊns] *n* onza *f.*
our [aʊər] *poss adj* nuestro,-a.
ours [aʊəz] *poss pron* 1 (el) nuestro, (la) nuestra. 2 of o., nuestro,-a; **a friend of** o., un amigo nuestro.
ourselves [aʊə'selvz] *pers pron pl* 1 *(reflexive)* nos. 2 *(emphatic)* nosotros mismos, nosotras mismas. 3 by o., a solas.
oust [aʊst] *vtr* 1 *(from a post)* desbancar. 2 *(from property etc)* desalojar.
out [aʊt] I *adv* 1 *(outside, away)* fuera; o. there, ahí fuera; to go o., salir. 2 I told him straight o., se lo dije muy claramente; o. loud, en voz alta. 3 hear me o., escúchame hasta el final. 4 o. of, *(place)* fuera de; move o. of the way!, ¡quítate de en medio!; o. of danger, fuera de peligro; to go o. of the room, salir de la habitación; o. of control, fuera de control; o. of date, *(expired)* caducado,-a; *(old-fashioned)* pasado,-a de moda. 5 o. of, *(cause, motive)* por. 6 o. of, *(made from)* de. 7 o. of, *(short of, without)* sin; I'm o. of money, se me ha acabado el dinero; o. of breath, sin aliento. 8 o. of, *(among)* entre; forty o. of fifty, cuarenta de cada cincuenta; *(in exam etc)* cuarenta sobre cincuenta.
II *adj* 1 the sun is o., ha salido el sol. 2 *(unfashionable)* pasado,-a de moda. 3 *(fire)* apagado,-a. 4 *(not working)* estropeado,-a. 5 she's o., *(not in)* ha salido, no está. 6 to be o. for sth/to do sth, buscar algo. 7 the book is just o., el libro acaba de salir. 8 *(inaccurate)* equivocado,-a; to be o. in one's calculations, equivocarse en los cálculos. 9 before the week is o., antes de que acabe la semana.
III *prep (out of)* por; he jumped o. the window, saltó por la ventana.
out-and-out ['aʊtənaʊt] *adj* redomado,-a.
outboard ['aʊtbɔːd] *adj* o. motor, fuera-borda *m.*
outbreak ['aʊtbreɪk] *n (of war)* comienzo *m;* *(of spots)* erupción *f;* *(of disease)* brote *m;* *(of violence)* ola *f;* *(of anger)* arrebato *m;* at the o. of war, cuando estalló la guerra.
outbuilding ['aʊtbɪldɪŋ] *n* dependencia *f.*
outburst ['aʊtbɜːst] *n (of anger)* arrebato *m;* *(of generosity)* arranque *m.*
outcast ['aʊtkɑːst] *n* marginado,-a *m,f.*
outcome ['aʊtkʌm] *n* resultado *m.*
outcrop ['aʊtkrɒp] *n* Geol afloramiento *m.*
outcry ['aʊtkraɪ] *n* there was an o., hubo fuertes protestas.
outdated [aʊt'deɪtɪd] *adj* anticuado,-a, obsoleto,-a.
outdo [aʊt'duː] *vtr* to o. sb, superar a algn.
outdoor ['aʊtdɔːr] *adj* 1 al aire libre. 2 *(clothes)* de calle.
outdoors [aʊt'dɔːz] *adv* fuera, al aire li-

bre.

outer ['aʊtər] *adj* exterior, externo,-a.

outfit ['aʊtfɪt] *n* 1 (*kit, equipment*) equipo *m*. 2 (*set of clothes*) conjunto *m*. 3 *fam* (*group*) grupo *m*.

outgoing ['aʊtgəʊɪŋ] **I** *adj* 1 (*departing*) saliente. 2 (*sociable*) extrovertido,-a. **II** *npl* **outgoings,** gastos *mpl*.

outgrow [aʊt'grəʊ] *vtr* **he's outgrowing all his clothes,** toda la ropa se le está quedando pequeña; **she'll o. it,** se le pasará con la edad.

outhouse ['aʊthaʊs] *n* → **outbuilding**.

outing ['aʊtɪŋ] *n* excursión *f*.

outlandish [aʊt'lændɪʃ] *adj* estrafalario, -a.

outlast [aʊt'lɑːst] *vtr* durar más que.

outlaw ['aʊtlɔː] **I** *n* proscrito,-a *m,f*. **II** *vtr* prohibir.

outlet ['aʊtlet, 'aʊtlɪt] *n* 1 (*opening*) salida *f*. 2 (*for emotions*) válvula *f* de escape. 3 *Com* mercado *m*. 4 (*for water*) desagüe *m*.

outline ['aʊtlaɪn] **I** *n* 1 (*draft*) bosquejo *m*. 2 (*outer line*) contorno *m*; (*silhouette*) perfil *m*. **II** *vtr* 1 (*draw lines of*) perfilar. 2 (*summarize*) resumir. 3 (*describe roughly*) trazar las líneas generales de.

outlive [aʊt'lɪv] *vtr* sobrevivir a.

outlook ['aʊtlʊk] *n* 1 (*point of view*) punto *m* de vista. 2 (*prospect*) perspectiva *f*; *Meteor* previsión *f*.

outlying ['aʊtlaɪɪŋ] *adj* (*remote*) aislado,-a.

outmoded [aʊt'məʊdɪd] *adj* anticuado,-a.

outnumber [aʊt'nʌmbər] *vtr* exceder en número.

out-of-the-way [aʊtəvðə'weɪ] *adj* 1 (*distant*) apartado,-a, aislado,-a. 2 (*uncommon*) poco corriente.

outpatient ['aʊtpeɪʃənt] *n* paciente externo,-a; **outpatients' department,** departamento *m* de consulta externa.

outpost ['aʊtpəʊst] *n* avanzada *f*.

output ['aʊtpʊt] *n* 1 producción *f*; (*of machine*) rendimiento *m*. 2 *Elec* potencia *f*. 3 *Comput* salida *f*.

outrage ['aʊtreɪdʒ] **I** *n* ultraje *m*; **it's an o.!,** ¡es un escándalo!. **II** *vtr* **to be outraged by sth,** indignarse por algo.

outrageous [aʊt'reɪdʒəs] *adj* (*behaviour*) escandaloso,-a; (*clothes*) extravagante; (*price*) exorbitante.

outright ['aʊtraɪt] **I** *adj* (*absolute*) absoluto,-a. **II** [aʊt'raɪt] *adv* 1 (*completely*) por completo. 2 (*directly*) directamente, sin reserva. 3 (*immediately*) en el acto.

outset ['aʊtset] *n* comienzo *m*, principio *m*.

outside [aʊt'saɪd] **I** *prep* 1 fuera de. 2 (*beyond*) más allá de. 3 (*other than*) aparte de. **II** ['aʊtsaɪd] *adj* 1 (*exterior*) exterior, externo,-a. 2 (*remote*) remoto,-a. **III** [aʊt'saɪd] *adv* fuera, afuera. **IV** *n* exterior *m*; **on the o.,** por fuera; *fam* **at the o.,**

como mucho.

outsider [aʊt'saɪdər] *n* 1 (*stranger*) extraño,-a *m,f*, forastero,-a *m,f*. 2 *Pol* candidato,-a *m,f* con pocas posibilidades de ganar.

outsize(d) ['aʊtsaɪz(d)] *adj* (*clothes*) de talla muy grande.

outskirts ['aʊtskɜːts] *npl* afueras *fpl*.

outspoken [aʊt'spəʊkən] *adj* directo,-a, abierto,-a.

outstanding [aʊt'stændɪŋ] *adj* 1 (*exceptional*) destacado,-a. 2 (*unpaid, unresolved*) pendiente.

outstretched [aʊt'stretʃt] *adj* extendido,-a.

outward ['aʊtwəd] *adj* 1 (*external*) exterior, externo,-a. 2 **the o. journey,** el viaje de ida. ◆**outwardly** *adv* aparentemente.

outward(s) ['aʊtwəd(z)] *adv* hacia (a)fuera.

outweigh [aʊt'weɪ] *vtr* 1 (*prevail over*) prevalecer sobre. 2 (*weigh more than*) pesar más que.

oval ['əʊvəl] **I** *adj* oval, ovalado,-a. **II** *n* óvalo *m*.

ovary ['əʊvərɪ] *n* ovario *m*.

ovation [əʊ'veɪʃən] *n* ovación *f*.

oven ['ʌvən] *n* horno *m*.

ovenproof ['ʌvənpruːf] *adj* refractario,-a.

over ['əʊvər] **I** *prep* 1 (*above*) encima de. 2 (*on top of*) sobre, encima de. 3 (*across*) al otro lado de; **the bridge o. the river,** el puente que cruza el río. 4 (*during*) durante. 5 (*throughout*) por. 6 **all o.,** por todo,-a; **famous all o. the world,** famoso en el mundo entero. 7 (*by the agency of*) por; **o. the phone,** por teléfono. 8 (*more than*) más de; **men o. twenty-five,** hombres mayores de veinticinco años; **o. and above,** además de. 9 (*recovered from*) recuperado,-a de. **II** *adv* 1 **o. there,** allá; **why don't you come o. tomorrow?,** ¿por qué no vienes a casa mañana? 2 (*throughout*) por; **all o.,** por todas partes. 3 (*more*) más. 4 (*again*) otra vez; **o. and o.** (*again*), una y otra vez; **twice o.,** dos veces seguidas. 5 (*in excess*) de más. **III** *adj* (*finished*) acabado,-a; **it's (all) o.,** se acabó; **the danger is o.,** ha pasado el peligro.

overall ['əʊvərɔːl] **I** *adj* total, global. **II** [əʊvər'ɔːl] *adv* (*on the whole*) por lo general, en conjunto. **III** ['əʊvərɔːl] *n* 1 *GB* guardapolvo *m*. 2 **overalls,** mono *m sing*.

overawe [əʊvər'ɔː] *vtr* **to be overawed,** sobrecogerse.

overbearing [əʊvə'beərɪŋ] *adj* (*domineering*) dominante; (*important*) significativo, -a.

overboard ['əʊvəbɔːd] *adv* por la borda; **man o.!,** ¡hombre al agua!; *fam* **to go o.,** pasarse.

overcast ['əʊvəkɑːst] *adj* nublado,-a.

overcharge [əʊvə'tʃɑːdʒ] *vtr* **1** (*charge too much*) cobrar demasiado. **2** (*overload*) sobrecargar.

overcoat ['əʊvəkəʊt] *n* abrigo *m*.

overcome [əʊvə'kʌm] *vtr* **1** (*conquer*) vencer; **o. by grief,** deshecho por el dolor. **2** (*obstacle*) superar.

overconfident [əʊvə'kɒnfɪdənt] *adj* presumido,-a, creído,-a.

overcrowded [əʊvə'kraʊdɪd] *adj* (*room*) atestado,-a (de gente); (*country*) superpoblado,-a.

overcrowding [əʊvə'kraʊdɪŋ] *n* (*of prisons etc*) hacinamiento *m*; (*of country*) superpoblación *f*.

overdo [əʊvə'duː] *vtr* **1** (*carry too far*) exagerar; **don't o. it,** no te pases. **2** *Culin* cocer *or* asar demasiado.

overdose ['əʊvədəʊs] *n* sobredosis *f*.

overdraft ['əʊvədrɑːft] *n* giro *m* en descubierto; (*amount*) saldo *m* deudor.

overdraw [əʊvə'drɔː] *vtr* **to be overdrawn,** tener la cuenta en descubierto.

overdue [əʊvə'djuː] *adj* (*rent, train etc*) atrasado,-a; (*reform*) largamente esperado,-a.

overestimate [əʊvər'estɪmeɪt] *vtr* sobreestimar.

overflow [əʊvə'fləʊ] **I** *vi* (*river*) desbordarse; (*cup etc*) derramarse. **II** ['əʊvəfləʊ] *n* (*of river etc*) desbordamiento *m*; **o. pipe,** cañería *f* de desagüe.

overgrown [əʊvə'grəʊn] *adj* **1** (*with grass*) cubierto,-a (de hierba). **2** (*in size*) demasiado grande.

overhaul [əʊvə'hɔːl] **I** *vtr* revisar. **II** ['əʊvəhɔːl] *n* revisión *f* y reparación *f*.

overhead [əʊvə'hed] **I** *adj* (por) encima de la cabeza; **o. cable,** cable aéreo. **II** [əʊvə'hed] *adv* arriba, por encima de la cabeza.

overheads ['əʊvəhedz] *npl* gastos *mpl* generales.

overhear [əʊvə'hɪəʳ] *vtr* oír por casualidad.

overheat [əʊvə'hiːt] *vi* recalentarse.

overjoyed [əʊvə'dʒɔɪd] *adj* rebosante de alegría.

overlap [əʊvə'læp] *vi* superponerse; *fig* **our plans o.,** nuestros planes coinciden parcialmente.

overleaf [əʊvə'liːf] *adv* al dorso.

overload [əʊvə'ləʊd] **I** *vtr* sobrecargar. **II** *n* sobrecarga *f*.

overlook [əʊvə'lʊk] *vtr* **1** (*fail to notice*) saltarse. **2** (*ignore*) no hacer caso de; **we'll o. it this time,** esta vez haremos la vista gorda. **3** (*have a view of*) dar a, tener vista a.

overnight [əʊvə'naɪt] **I** *adv* **1** (*during the night*) por la noche; **we stayed there o.,** pasamos la noche allí. **2** (*suddenly*) de la noche a la mañana. **II** ['əʊvənaɪt] *adj* (*sudden*) repentino,-a.

overpay [əʊvə'peɪ] *vtr* pagar demasiado.

overpower [əʊvə'paʊəʳ] *vtr* **1** (*subdue*) dominar. **2** (*affect strongly*) abrumar.

overrate [əʊvə'reɪt] *vtr* sobreestimar, supervalorar.

override [əʊvə'raɪd] *vtr* **1** (*disregard*) hacer caso omiso de. **2** (*annul, cancel out*) anular. **3** (*be more important than*) contar más que.

overriding [əʊvə'raɪdɪŋ] *adj* principal; (*importance*) primordial; (*need*) imperioso,-a.

overrule [əʊvə'ruːl] *vtr* invalidar; *Jur* denegar.

overrun [əʊvə'rʌn] *vtr* **1** (*country*) invadir. **2** (*allotted time*) excederse de.

overseas [əʊvə'siːz] **I** *adv* en ultramar; **to live o.,** vivir en el extranjero. **II** ['əʊvəsiːz] *adj* de ultramar; (*person*) extranjero,-a; (*trade*) exterior.

oversee [əʊvə'siː] *vtr* supervisar.

overseer ['əʊvəsiːəʳ] *n* supervisor,-a *m,f*; (*foreman*) capataz *m*.

overshadow [əʊvə'ʃædəʊ] *vtr fig* eclipsar.

overshoot [əʊvə'ʃuːt] *vtr* **to o. a turning,** pasarse un cruce; *fig* **to o. the mark,** pasarse de la raya.

oversight ['əʊvəsaɪt] *n* descuido *m*.

oversleep [əʊvə'sliːp] *vi* quedarse dormido,-a.

overspill ['əʊvəspɪl] *n* exceso *m* de población.

overstate [əʊvə'steɪt] *vtr* exagerar.

overstep [əʊvə'step] *vtr fig* **to o. the mark,** pasarse de la raya.

overt ['əʊvɜːt, əʊ'vɜːt] *adj* patente.

overtake [əʊvə'teɪk] *vtr* **1** *GB Aut* adelantar. **2** (*surpass*) superar a. **3** (*of night*) sorprender.

overthrow [əʊvə'θrəʊ] *vtr* (*government*) derribar.

overtime ['əʊvətaɪm] *n* horas *fpl* extra.

overtone ['əʊvətəʊn] *n* matiz *m*.

overture ['əʊvətjʊəʳ] *n* **1** *Mus* obertura *f*; *fig* (*introduction*) introducción *f*. **2** (*proposal*) propuesta *f*.

overturn [əʊvə'tɜːn] *vtr & vi* volcar.

overweight [əʊvə'weɪt] *adj* demasiado pesado,-a.

overwhelm [əʊvə'welm] *vtr* **1** (*defeat*) aplastar; (*overpower*) abrumar; **I'm overwhelmed,** estoy abrumado. **2** (*with letters, work etc*) inundar.

overwhelming [əʊvə'welmɪŋ] *adj* (*defeat*) aplastante; (*desire etc*) irresistible.

overwork [əʊvə'wɜːk] **I** *vi* trabajar demasiado. **II** *vtr* (*person*) forzar; (*excuse etc*) abusar de.

overwrought [əʊvə'rɔːt] *adj* **1** (*tense*) muy nervioso,-a. **2** *lit* (*too elaborate*) forzado,-a.

owe [əʊ] *vtr* deber.

owing ['əʊɪŋ] *adj* **o. to,** debido a, a causa

de.

owl [aul] *n* lechuza *f*, búho *m*.

own [əun] **I** *adj* propio,-a; **it's his o. fault**, es culpa suya. **II** *pron* **1 my o., your o., his o. etc**, lo mío, lo tuyo, lo suyo, etc; *fig* **to come into one's o.**, realizarse; *fam* **to get one's o. back**, tomarse la revancha. **2 on one's o.**, *(without help)* uno,-a mismo,-a; *(alone)* solo,-a. **III** *vtr* poseer, ser dueño,-a de. ◆**own up** *vtr* **to o. up (to)**, confesar.

owner ['əunər] *n* propietario,-a *m*,*f*, dueño,-a *m*,*f*.

ownership ['əunəʃip] *n* propiedad *f*, posesión *f*.

ox [ɒks] *n* (*pl* **oxen**) buey *m*.

oxide ['ɒksaid] *n* *Chem* óxido *m*.

oxtail ['ɒksteil] *n* rabo *m* de buey.

oxygen ['ɒksidʒən] *n* oxígeno *m*; **o. mask**, máscara *f* de oxígeno.

oyster ['ɔistər] *n* ostra *f*.

ozone ['əuzəun] *n* ozono *m*; **o. layer**, capa *f* de ozono.

P

P, p [piː] *n* (*the letter*) P, p *f*.

p 1 (*pl* **pp**) *abbr of* **page**, pág., p. **2** [piː] *GB fam abbr of* **penny, pence**, penique(s) *m*(*pl*).

PA [piː'ei] *fam* **1** *abbr of* **personal assistant**, ayudante *m* personal. **2** *abbr of* **public-address (system)**.

pa *abbr of* **per annum** (per year), al año.

pace [peis] **I** *n* (*step*) paso *m*; (*speed*) ritmo *m*; **to keep p. with**, seguir a; *fig* avanzar al mismo ritmo que; **to set the p.**, marcar el paso a; *fig* marcar la pauta. **II** *vi* **to p. up and down**, ir de un lado a otro.

pacemaker ['peismeikər] *n* *Sport* liebre *f*; *Med* marcapasos *m inv*.

Pacific [pə'sifik] *adj* **the P. (Ocean)**, el (océano) Pacífico.

pacifist ['pæsifist] *adj & n* pacifista (*mf*).

pacify ['pæsifai] *vtr* (*person*) calmar; (*country*) pacificar.

pack¹ [pæk] **I** *n* (*parcel*) paquete *m*; (*bundle*) bulto *m*; *US* (*of cigarettes*) paquete *m*; *GB* (*of cards*) baraja *f*; (*of hounds*) jauría *f*. **II** *vtr* **1** (*goods*) embalar, envasar; (*in suitcase*) poner; **to p. one's bags**, hacer las maletas; *fig* marcharse. **2** (*fill*) atestar. **3** (*press down*) (*snow*) apretar. **II** *vi* **1** hacer las maletas; *fam* **to send sb packing**, mandar a paseo a algn. **2** (*of people*) apiñarse (**into**, en). ◆**pack in** *vtr GB fam* (*give up*) dejar. ◆**pack off** *vtr fam* mandar. ◆**pack up** *fam* **I** *vtr* (*give up*) dejar. **II** *vi* (*stop working*) terminar; (*machine etc*) estropearse.

pack² [pæk] *vtr* (*meeting*) llenar de partidarios.

package ['pækidʒ] **I** *n* **1** (*parcel*) paquete *m*; (*bundle*) bulto *m*; **p. tour**, viaje *m* todo incluido. **2** (*of proposals etc*) paquete *m*; (*agreement*) acuerdo *m*; **p. deal**, convenio *m* general. **II** *vtr* (*goods*) envasar, embalar.

packet ['pækit] *n* paquete *m*; *fam* (*fortune*) dineral *m*.

packing ['pækiŋ] *n* embalaje *m*; **p. case**, caja *f* de embalar; **to do one's p.**, hacer las maletas.

pact [pækt] *n* pacto *m*.

pad¹ [pæd] **I** *n* **1** almohadilla *f*; (*of paper*) bloc *m*, taco *m*. **2 launch p.**, plataforma *f* de lanzamiento. **3** *fam* (*flat*) piso *m*. **II** *vtr* (*chair*) acolchar. ◆**pad out** *vtr fig* meter paja en.

pad² [pæd] *vi* **to p. about** *or* **around**, andar silenciosamente.

padding ['pædiŋ] *n* (*material*) relleno *m*; *fig* (*in speech etc*) paja *f*.

paddle¹ ['pædəl] **I** *n* (*oar*) pala *f*; **p. boat** *or* **steamer**, vapor *m* de ruedas. **II** *vtr* (*boat*) remar con pala en. **III** *vi* (*in boat*) remar con pala.

paddle² ['pædəl] *vi* chapotear.

paddling pool ['pædəliŋpuːl] *n* piscina *f* para niños.

paddock ['pædək] *n* potrero *m*; (*in race course*) paddock *m*.

paddy ['pædi] *n* arrozal *m*.

padlock ['pædlɒk] **I** *n* candado *m*. **II** *vtr* cerrar con candado.

paediatrician [piːdiə'triʃən] *n* pediatra *mf*.

pagan ['peigən] *adj & n* pagano,-a (*m,f*).

page¹ [peidʒ] *n* página *f*.

page² [peidʒ] **I** *n* (*servant*) paje *m*; (*of knight*) escudero *m*; (*at club*) botones *m inv*. **II** *vtr* (*call*) llamar por altavoz.

pageant ['pædʒənt] *n* (*show*) espectáculo *m*; (*procession*) desfile *m*; (*on horses*) cabalgata *f*.

pageantry ['pædʒəntri] *n* pompa *f*, boato *m*.

paid [peid] *adj* pagado,-a; *fig* **to put p. to sth**, acabar con algo.

pail [peil] *n* cubo *m*; (*child's*) cubito *m*.

pain [pein] **I** *n* **1** dolor *m*; (*grief*) sufrimiento *m*; *fam* **he's a p. (in the neck)**, es un pelmazo; **on p. of death**, so pena de muerte. **2 to take pains over sth**, esmerarse en algo. **II** *vtr* (*grieve*) dar pena a.

pained [peind] *adj* de reproche.

painful ['peinful] *adj* doloroso,-a; *fam* (*very bad*) malísimo,-a. ◆**painfully** *adv* **1 p. shy**, lastimosamente tímido,-a. **2**

fam terriblemente.

painkiller ['peɪnkɪlər] *n* analgésico *m*.

painless ['peɪnlɪs] *adj* sin dolor; *fig* sin dificultades.

painstaking ['peɪnzteɪkɪŋ] *adj (person)* concienzudo,-a; *(care, research)* esmerado,-a.

paint [peɪnt] **I** *n* pintura *f*. **II** *vtr* pintar; **to p. sth white**, pintar algo de blanco. **III** *vi* pintar.

paintbrush ['peɪntbrʌʃ] *n Art* pincel *m*; *(for walls)* brocha *f*.

painter ['peɪntər] *n* pintor,-a *m,f*.

painting ['peɪntɪŋ] *n* cuadro *m*; *(activity)* pintura *f*.

paintwork ['peɪntwɜːk] *n* pintura *f*.

pair [peər] *n (of gloves, shoes)* par *m*; *(of people, cards)* pareja *f*; **a p. of scissors**, unas tijeras; **a p. of trousers**, un pantalón, unos pantalones.

pajamas [pəˈdʒæməz] *npl US* → **pyjamas**.

Pakistan [paːkɪˈstaɪn] *n* Paquistán.

Pakistani [paːkɪˈstaɪnɪ] *adj & n* paquistaní *(mf)*.

pal [pæl] *n fam* amigo,-a *m,f*, colega *mf*.

palace ['pælɪs] *n* palacio *m*.

palatable ['pælətəbəl] *adj (tasty)* sabroso,-a; *fig* aceptable.

palate ['pælɪt] *n* paladar *m*.

palatial [pəˈleɪʃəl] *adj* magnífico,-a, suntuoso,-a.

palaver [pəˈlɑːvər] *n fam* lío *m*, follón *m*.

pale¹ [peɪl] **I** *adj (skin)* pálido,-a; *(colour)* claro,-a; *(light)* tenue; **to turn p.**, palidecer. **II** *vi* palidecer.

pale² [peɪl] *n fig* **to be beyond the p.**, ser inaceptable.

Palestine ['pælɪstaɪn] *n* Palestina.

Palestinian [pælɪˈstɪnɪən] *adj & n* palestino,-a *(m,f)*.

palette ['pælɪt] *n* paleta *f*; **p. knife**, espátula *f*.

paling ['peɪlɪŋ] *n* valla *f*.

palisade [pælɪˈseɪd] *n* palizada *f*, estacada *f*.

pall¹ [pɔːl] *n fig* manto *m*; *(of smoke)* cortina *f*.

pall² [pɔːl] *vi* aburrir; **it never palls**, nunca cansa.

pallet ['pælɪt] *n* plataforma *f* de carga.

pallid ['pælɪd] *adj* pálido,-a.

pallor ['pælər] *n* palidez *f*.

palm¹ [paːm] *n (tree)* palmera *f*; *(leaf)* palma *f*; **date p.**, palma datilera; **P. Sunday**, domingo *m* de Ramos.

palm² [paːm] *n Anat* palma *f*. ◆**palm off** *vtr* **to p. sth off on sb**, colocar *or* endosar algo a algn.

palmistry ['paːmɪstrɪ] *n* quiromancia *f*.

palpable ['pælpəbəl] *adj* palpable.

palpitate ['pælpɪteɪt] *vi* palpitar.

palpitation [pælpɪˈteɪʃən] *n* palpitación *f*.

paltry ['pɔːltrɪ] *adj* **(paltrier, paltriest)**

insignificante.

pamper ['pæmpər] *vtr* mimar, consentir.

pamphlet ['pæmflɪt] *n* folleto *m*.

pan¹ [pæn] **I** *n* **1** *(saucepan)* cazuela *f*, cacerola *f*. **2** *(of scales)* platillo *m*. **3** *(of lavatory)* taza *f*. **II** *vtr fam (critize)* dejar por los suelos.

pan² [pæn] *vi Cin* tomar vistas panorámicas.

panacea [pænəˈsɪə] *n* panacea *f*.

panache [pəˈnæʃ] *n* garbo *m*, salero *m*.

Panama ['pænəmaː] *n* Panamá; **P. Canal**, Canal *m* de Panamá.

pancake ['pænkeɪk] *n* crepe *f*.

panda ['pændə] *n* panda *m*; *GB* **p. car**, coche *m* patrulla.

pandemonium [pændɪˈməʊnɪəm] *n* alboroto *m*.

pander ['pændər] *vi* **to p. to**, *(person)* complacer a; *(wishes)* acceder a.

pane [peɪn] *n* cristal *m*, vidrio *m*.

panel ['pænəl] *n* **1** *(of wall)* panel *m*; *(flat surface)* tabla *f*; *(of instruments)* tablero *m*; *(of ceiling)* artesón *m*. **2** *(jury)* jurado *m*; *Rad TV* concursantes *mpl*.

panelling, *US* **paneling** ['pænəlɪŋ] *n* paneles *mpl*.

pang [pæŋ] *n (of pain, hunger)* punzada *f*; *(of childbirth)* dolores *mpl*; *fig (of conscience)* remordimiento *m*.

panic ['pænɪk] **I** *n* pánico *m*; **to get into a p.**, ponerse histérico,-a. **II** *vi* aterrarse.

panicky ['pænɪkɪ] *adj* asustadizo,-a.

panic-stricken ['pænɪkstrɪkən] *adj* aterrado,-a.

panorama [pænəˈrɑːmə] *n* panorama *m*.

pansy ['pænzɪ] *n Bot* pensamiento *m*; *fam pej* mariquita *f*.

pant [pænt] **I** *n* jadeo *m*. **II** *vi* jadear.

panther ['pænθər] *n* pantera *f*.

panties ['pæntɪz] *npl* bragas *fpl*.

pantomime ['pæntəmaɪm] *n Theat (play)* función *f* musical navideña; *(mime)* pantomima *f*.

pantry ['pæntrɪ] *n* despensa *f*.

pants [pænts] *npl (underpants) (ladies')* bragas *fpl*; *(men's)* calzoncillos *mpl*; *US (trousers)* pantalones *mpl*, pantalón *m*.

papal ['peɪpəl] *adj* papal.

paper ['peɪpər] **I** *n* **1** papel *m*; *fig* **on p.**, en teoría; **p. money**, papel moneda; **writing p.**, papel de escribir. **2** *(exam)* examen *m*; *(essay)* trabajo *m* (escrito). **3** *Pol* libro *m*. **4** *(newspaper)* periódico *m*; **the papers**, la prensa. **5** **papers**, *(documents)* documentos *mpl*. **II** *vtr* empapelar.

paperback ['peɪpəbæk] *n* libro *m* en rústica.

paperclip ['peɪpəklɪp] *n* clip *m*, sujetapapeles *m inv*.

paperweight ['peɪpəweɪt] *n* pisapapeles *m inv*.

paperwork ['peɪpəwɜːk] *n* papeleo *m*.

papier-mâché [pæpɪeɪˈmæʃeɪ] *n* cartón *m*

piedra.

paprika ['pæprikə] n pimentón molido.

par [pɑ:r] n (parity) igualdad f; Golf par m; fig it's p. for the course, es lo normal en estos casos; fig to feel below p., estar en baja forma.

parable ['pærəbəl] n parábola f.

parachute ['pærəʃu:t] I n paracaídas m inv. II vi to p. (down), saltar or lanzarse en paracaídas.

parade [pə'reid] I n desfile m; Mil to be on p., pasar revista. II vtr Mil hacer desfilar; fig (flaunt) hacer alarde de. III vi (troops) pasar revista; (procession) desfilar.

paradise ['pærədais] n paraíso m.

paradox ['pærədɒks] n paradoja f.

paradoxical [pærə'dɒksɪkəl] adj paradójico,-a.

paraffin ['pærəfɪn] n parafina f; liquid p., aceite m de parafina; p. lamp, lámpara f de petróleo.

paragon ['pærəgən] n modelo m.

paragraph ['pærəgrɑ:f] n párrafo m.

Paraguay ['pærəgwaɪ] n Paraguay.

Paraguayan [pærə'gwaɪən] adj & n paraguayo,-a (m,f).

parallel ['pærəlel] I adj paralelo,-a (to, with, a); fig comparable (to, with, a). II n Geog paralelo m; Geom paralela f; fig paralelo. III vtr fig ser paralelo,-a a.

paralysis [pə'rælɪsɪs] n parálisis f.

paralyse, US **paralyze** ['pærəlaɪz] vtr paralizar.

parameter [pə'ræmɪtər] n parámetro m.

paramilitary [pærə'mɪlɪtərɪ] adj paramilitar.

paramount ['pærəmaunt] adj of p. importance, de suma importancia.

paranoid ['pærənɔɪd] adj & n paranoico,-a (m,f).

paraphernalia [pærəfə'neɪlɪə] n parafernalia f.

paraphrase ['pærəfreɪz] vtr parafrasear.

parasite ['pærəsaɪt] n parásito m.

parasol ['pærəsɒl] n sombrilla f.

paratrooper ['pærətru:pər] n paracaidista mf.

parcel ['pɑ:səl] I n paquete m; p. bomb, paquete bomba. II vtr to p. up, envolver, empaquetar.

parched [pɑ:tʃt] adj (land) reseco,-a; (lips, mouth) seco,-a; fig to be p., estar muerto,-a de sed.

parchment ['pɑ:tʃmənt] n pergamino m.

pardon ['pɑ:dən] I n perdón m; Jur indulto m; I beg your p., (Usted) perdone; (I beg your) p.?, ¿cómo (dice)? II vtr perdonar; Jur indultar; p. me!, ¡Usted perdone!

parent ['peərənt] n parents, padres mpl.

parental [pə'rentəl] adj paternal; p. guidance, consejos mpl paternales.

parenthesis [pə'renθɪsɪs] n (pl parentheses [pə'renθɪsi:z]) paréntesis m inv; in

p., entre paréntesis.

pariah [pə'raɪə] n paria mf.

Paris ['pærɪs] n París.

parish ['pærɪʃ] n parroquia f.

Parisian [pə'rɪzɪən] adj & n parisino,-a (m,f).

parity ['pærɪtɪ] n igualdad f; (of shares) paridad f.

park [pɑ:k] I n parque m. II vtr (car) aparcar, Am parquear.

parking ['pɑ:kɪŋ] n aparcamiento m, estacionamiento m; 'no p.', 'prohibido aparcar'; US p. lot, aparcamiento; p. meter, parquímetro m; p. space, aparcamiento.

parliament ['pɑ:ləmənt] n parlamento m.

parliamentary [pɑ:lə'mentərɪ] adj parlamentario,-a.

parlour, US **parlor** ['pɑ:lər] n salón m.

parochial [pə'rəukɪəl] adj parroquial; pej (narrow-minded) de miras estrechas.

parody ['pærədɪ] n parodia f.

parole [pə'rəul] n Jur libertad f condicional; on p., en libertad bajo palabra.

parquet ['pɑ:keɪ] n p. floor, suelo m de parqué.

parrot ['pærət] n loro m, papagayo m.

parry ['pærɪ] vtr parar.

parsimonious [pɑ:sɪ'məunɪəs] adj tacaño,-a.

parsley ['pɑ:slɪ] n perejil m.

parsnip ['pɑ:snɪp] n chirivía f.

parson ['pɑ:sən] n cura m.

part [pɑ:t] I n 1 parte f; (piece) trozo m; (episode) capítulo m; Tech pieza f; for the most p., en la mayor parte. 2 Cin Theat papel m; to play a p. in sth, desempeñar un papel en algo; to take p. in sth, participar en algo. 3 (place) lugar m; in these parts, por estos lugares. 4 for my p., por mi parte; to take sb's p., tomar partido por algn; to take sth in good p., tomarse bien algo. II adj (partial) parcial; in p. exchange, como parte del pago. III adv (partly) en parte. IV vtr (separate) separar; to p. company with sb, separarse de algn; to p. one's hair, hacerse la raya (en el pelo). V vi separarse; (say goodbye) despedirse. ◆part with vtr separarse de. ◆partly adv en parte.

partial ['pɑ:ʃəl] adj parcial; to be p. to sth, ser aficionado,-a a algo.

participant [pɑ:'tɪsɪpənt] n participante mf; (in competition) concursante mf.

participate [pɑ:'tɪsɪpeɪt] vi participar (in, en).

participation [pɑ:tɪsɪ'peɪʃən] n participación f.

participle ['pɑ:tɪsɪpəl] n participio m.

particle ['pɑ:tɪkəl] n partícula f.

particular [pə'tɪkjulər] I adj 1 (special) particular, especial; in this p. case, en este caso concreto; that p. person, esa persona en particular. 2 (fussy) exigente.

II *npl* **particulars**, pormenores *mpl*; **to take down sb's particulars**, anotar los datos personales de algn. ◆**particularly** *adv* particularmente, especialmente.

parting ['pɑːtɪŋ] I *n (separation)* separación *f*; *(farewell)* despedida *f*; *(in hair)* raya *f*. II *adj* de despedida.

partisan [pɑːtɪ'zæn, 'pɑːtɪzæn] I *n* Mil guerrillero,-a *m,f*; *(supporter)* partidario,-a *m,f*. II *adj (supporter)* a ultranza; *(of party)* partidista.

partition [pɑː'tɪʃən] I *n (wall)* tabique *m*; *(of country)* partición *f*. II *vtr* dividir.

partner ['pɑːtnəʳ] I *n* compañero,-a *m,f*; *(in dancing, tennis)* pareja *f*; *(husband)* marido *m*; *(wife)* mujer *f*; Com socio,-a *m,f*. II *vtr* acompañar.

partnership ['pɑːtnəʃɪp] *n (relationship)* vida *f* en común; Com sociedad *f*.

partridge ['pɑːtrɪdʒ] *n* perdiz pardilla.

part-time [pɑːt'taɪm] I *adj (work etc)* de tiempo parcial. II *adv* a tiempo parcial.

party ['pɑːtɪ] I *n* 1 *(celebration)* fiesta *f*. 2 *(group)* grupo *m*. 3 Pol partido *m*; **p. political broadcast**, espacio *m* electoral. 4 Jur parte *f*. II *adj* de fiesta; Tel **p. line**, línea compartida.

pass [pɑːs] I *n* 1 *(of mountain)* desfiladero *m*. 2 *(permit)* permiso *m*; **bus p.**, abono *m* de autobús. 3 Sport pase *m*. 4 *fam* **to make a p. at sb**, intentar ligar con algn.
II *vtr* 1 pasar; *(overtake)* adelantar. 2 *(exam, law)* aprobar; Jur **to p. sentence**, dictar sentencia.
III *vi* 1 pasar; *(procession)* desfilar; *(car)* adelantar; *(people)* cruzarse; Sport hacer un pase; **we passed on the stairs**, nos cruzamos en la escalera. 2 *(pain)* remitir; *(opportunity)* perderse; *(time)* pasar. 3 *(happen)* ocurrir, pasar. 4 *(in exam)* aprobar.
◆**pass away** *vi euph* pasar a mejor vida. ◆**pass by** I *vtr* pasar de largo. II *vi* pasar cerca (de). ◆**pass for** *vtr* pasar por. ◆**pass off** I *vtr* hacer pasar; **to p. oneself off as sth**, hacerse pasar por algo. II *vi (happen)* transcurrir. ◆**pass on** I *vtr (hand on)* transmitir. II *vi euph* pasar a mejor vida. ◆**pass out** *vi (faint)* desmayarse; Mil graduarse. ◆**pass over** *vtr* 1 *(aircraft)* volar por. 2 *(disregard)* pasar por alto. ◆**pass up** *vtr fam* *(opportunity)* renunciar; *(offer)* rechazar.

passable ['pɑːsəbəl] *adj (road)* transitable; *(acceptable)* pasable.

passage ['pæsɪdʒ] *n* 1 *(alleyway)* callejón *m*; *(hallway)* pasillo *m*. 2 *(movement)* tránsito *m*; Naut travesía *f*; Mus Lit pasaje *m*.

passageway ['pæsɪdʒweɪ] *n (interior)* pasillo *m*; *(exterior)* pasaje *m*.

passbook ['pɑːsbʊk] *n* libreta *f* de banco.

passenger ['pæsɪndʒəʳ] *n* pasajero,-a *m,f*.

passer-by [pɑːsə'baɪ] *n* transeúnte *mf*.

passing ['pɑːsɪŋ] I *n* 1 *(of time)* transcurso *m*; **in p.**, de pasada. 2 *(of law)* aprobación *f*. II *adj* que pasa; *(glance)* rápido,-a; *(thought)* pasajero,-a.

passion ['pæʃən] *n* pasión *f*; **p. fruit**, granadilla *f*.

passionate ['pæʃənɪt] *adj* apasionado,-a.

passive ['pæsɪv] *adj* pasivo,-a.

Passover ['pɑːsəʊvəʳ] *n* Pascua *f* de los judíos.

passport ['pɑːspɔːt] *n* pasaporte *m*.

password ['pɑːswɜːd] *n* contraseña *f*.

past [pɑːst] I *n* pasado *m*; **in the p.**, en el pasado; **to have a p.**, tener antecedentes. II *adj* pasado,-a; *(former)* anterior; **in the p. weeks**, en las últimas semanas. III *adv* por delante; **to run p.**, pasar corriendo. IV *prep (beyond)* más allá de; *(more than)* más de; **he's p. forty**, pasa de los cuarenta (años); **it's five p. ten**, son las diez y cinco; *fam* **to be p. it**, estar muy carroza.

pasta ['pæstə] *n* pasta *f*, pastas *fpl*.

paste [peɪst] I *n* pasta *f*; *(glue)* engrudo *m*. II *vtr (stick)* pegar; *(put paste on)* engomar.

pastel ['pæstəl] *adj & n* pastel (*m*).

pasteurized ['pæstjəraɪzd] *adj* pasteurizado,-a.

pastille ['pæstɪl] *n* pastilla *f*.

pastime ['pɑːstaɪm] *n* pasatiempo *m*.

pastor ['pɑːstəʳ] *n* pastor *m*.

pastoral ['pɑːstərəl] *adj* pastoral.

pastry ['peɪstrɪ] *n (dough)* pasta *f*; *(cake)* pastel *m*.

pasture ['pɑːstʃəʳ] *n* pasto *m*.

pasty¹ ['pæstɪ] *n* Culin empanada *f*, pastel *m* de carne.

pasty² ['peɪstɪ] *adj (pastier, pastiest)* *(complexion)* pálido,-a.

pat [pæt] I *n (caress)* caricia *f*; *(tap)* palmadita *f*; *fig* **to give sb a p. on the back**, felicitar a algn. II *vtr* acariciar; **to p. sb on the back**, dar a algn una palmadita en la espalda.

patch [pætʃ] I *n (of material)* parche *m*; *(of land)* terreno *m*; *(of colour)* mancha *f*; *fig* **to go through a bad p.**, pasar por una mala racha. ◆**patch up** *vtr (garment)* poner un parche en; **to p. things up**, *(after argument)* limar asperezas.

patchwork ['pætʃwɜːk] I *n* labor *f* de retales. II *adj (quilt etc)* hecho,-a con retales distintos.

patchy ['pætʃɪ] *adj (patchier, patchiest)* *(colour, performance)* desigual; *(knowledge)* incompleto,-a.

pâté ['pæteɪ] *n* paté *m*.

patent¹ ['peɪtənt] I *n* Com patente *f*. II *adj (obvious)* patente, evidente; **p. medicine**, medicamento *m*. III *vtr* Com patentar. ◆**patently** *adv* **it is p. obvious**, está clarísimo.

patent² ['peɪtənt] *n* **p. (leather)**, charol

m.

paternal [pə'tɜ:nəl] *adj* paternal; *(grandmother etc)* paterno,-a.

paternity [pə'tɜ:nɪtɪ] *n* paternidad *f.*

path [pɑ:θ] *n* camino *m*, sendero *m*; *(route)* ruta *f*; *(of missile)* trayectoria *f.*

pathetic [pə'θetɪk] *adj (pitiful)* patético, -a; *fam (hopeless)* malísimo,-a; **she was a p. sight,** daba lástima verla.

pathological [pæθə'lɒdʒɪkəl] *adj* patológico,-a.

pathologist [pə'θɒlədʒɪst] *n* patólogo,-a *m,f.*

pathology [pə'θɒlədʒɪ] *n* patología *f.*

pathos ['peɪθɒs] *n* patetismo *m.*

pathway ['pɑ:θweɪ] *n* camino *m*, sendero *m.*

patience ['peɪʃəns] *n* 1 paciencia *f*; **to lose one's p. with sb,** perder la paciencia con algn. 2 *GB Cards* solitario *m.*

patient ['peɪʃənt] I *adj* paciente; **to be p. with sb,** tener paciencia con algn. II *n Med* paciente *m.*

patio ['pætɪəʊ] *n* patio *m.*

patriotic [pætrɪ'ɒtɪk] *adj (person)* patriota; *(speech, act)* patriótico,-a.

patrol [pə'trəʊl] I *n* patrulla *f*; **p. car,** coche *m* patrulla. II *vtr* patrullar por.

patrolman [pə'trəʊlmən] *n US* policía *m.*

patron ['peɪtrən] *n* 1 *(of charity)* patrocinador,-a *m,f*; *(of arts)* mecenas *m inv*; **p. saint,** (santo,-a *m,f*) patrón,-ona *m,f.* 2 *(customer)* cliente,-a *m,f* habitual.

patronize ['pætrənaɪz] *vtr* 1 *(arts)* fomentar; *(shop)* ser cliente,-a *m,f* habitual de; *(club etc)* frecuentar. 2 *pej (person)* tratar con condescendencia.

patronizing ['pætrənaɪzɪŋ] *adj pej* condescendiente.

patter¹ ['pætər] I *n (of rain)* repiqueteo *m*; *(of feet)* pasito *m.* II *vi (rain)* repiquetear; *(feet)* hacer ruido sordo.

patter² ['pætər] *n fam* labia *f*; *(of salesman)* discursillo preparado.

pattern ['pætən] *n Sew* patrón *m*; *(design)* dibujo *m*; *(on material)* estampado *m*; *fig (of behaviour)* modelo *m.*

paunch [pɔ:ntʃ] *n* panza *f.*

pauper ['pɔ:pər] *n* pobre *mf.*

pause [pɔ:z] I *n* pausa *f*; *(silence)* silencio *m.* II *vi* hacer una pausa; *(be silent)* callarse.

pave [peɪv] *vtr* pavimentar; *(with stones)* empedrar; *fig* **to p. the way for sb/sth,** preparar el terreno para algn/algo.

pavement ['peɪvmənt] *n* acera *f*; *US (road surface)* calzada *f*, pavimento *m.*

pavilion [pə'vɪljən] *n* pabellón *m*; *GB Sport (changing rooms)* vestuarios *mpl.*

paving ['peɪvɪŋ] *n (on road)* pavimento *m*; *(on floor)* enlosado *m*; *(with stones)* empedrado *m*; **p. stone,** losa *f.*

paw [pɔ:] I *n (foot)* pata *f*; *(of cat)* garra *f*; *(of lion)* zarpa *f.* II *vtr (of lion)* dar zarpa-

zos a; *pej (of person)* manosear, sobar.

pawn¹ [pɔ:n] *n Chess* peón *m*; *fig* **to be sb's p.,** ser el juguete de algn.

pawn² [pɔ:n] *vtr* empeñar.

pawnbroker ['pɔ:nbrəʊkər] *n* prestamista *mf.*

pawnshop ['pɔ:nʃɒp] *n* casa *f* de empeños.

pay [peɪ] I *n (wages)* paga *f*, sueldo *m*; **p. packet,** sobre *m* de la paga; **p. rise,** aumento *m* del sueldo; **p. slip,** nómina *f.* II *vtr (pt & pp paid)* 1 pagar; **to be or get paid,** cobrar. 2 *(attention)* prestar; *(homage)* rendir; *(visit)* hacer; **to p. sb a compliment,** halagar a algn. 3 *(be profitable for)* compensar. III *vi* 1 pagar; **to p. for sth,** pagar (por) algo. 2 *(be profitable)* ser rentable. ◆**pay back** *vtr* reembolsar; *fig* **to p. sb back,** vengarse de algn. ◆**pay in** *vtr (money)* ingresar. ◆**pay off** I *vtr (debt)* liquidar; *(mortgage)* cancelar. II *vi (be successful)* dar resultado. ◆**pay out** *vtr (spend)* gastar (**on,** en). ◆**pay up** *vi* pagar.

payable ['peɪəbəl] *adj* pagadero,-a.

payday ['peɪdeɪ] *n* día *m* de pago.

payee [peɪ'i:] *n* portador,-a *m,f.*

payment ['peɪmənt] *n* pago *m*; *(of cheque)* cobro *m*; **advance p.,** anticipo *m*; **down p.,** entrada *f*; **monthly p.,** mensualidad *f.*

payoff ['peɪɒf] *n (reward)* recompensa *f*; *fam (bribe)* soborno *m.*

payroll ['peɪrəʊl] *n* nómina *f.*

pc *abbr of* **per cent,** p.c.; *abbr of* **personal computer,** PC.

PE [pi:'i:] *abbr of* **physical education.**

pea [pi:] *n* guisante *m.*

peace [pi:s] *n* paz *f*; *(calm)* tranquilidad *f*; **at** *or* **in p.,** en paz; **p. and quiet,** tranquilidad; **to make p.,** hacer las paces; *(of countries)* firmar la paz.

peaceable ['pi:səbəl] *adj* pacífico,-a.

peaceful ['pi:sful] *adj (demonstration)* pacífico,-a; *(place)* tranquilo,-a.

peace-keeping ['pi:ski:pɪŋ] *adj* pacificador,-a; **p.-k. forces,** fuerzas *fpl* de pacificación.

peach [pi:tʃ] *n* melocotón *m.*

peacock ['pi:kɒk] *n* pavo *m* real.

peak [pi:k] *n (of cap)* visera *f*; *(of mountain)* pico *m*; *(summit)* cima *f*; *fig* cumbre *f*; **p. hours,** horas *fpl* punta; **p. period,** horas de mayor consumo; **p. season,** temporada alta.

peal [pi:l] *n (of bells)* repique *m*; **p. of thunder,** trueno *m*; **peals of laughter,** carcajadas *fpl.*

peanut ['pi:nʌt] *n* cacahuete *m*; **p. butter,** mantequilla *f or* manteca *f* de cacahuete.

pear [peər] *n* pera *f.*

pearl [pɜ:l] *n* perla *f.*

peasant ['pezənt] *adj & n* campesino,-a *(m,f).*

peat [pi:t] *n* turba *f*; **p. bog,** turbera *f.*

pebble ['pebəl] *n* guijarro *m*; *(small)* china *f*.

pecan [pɪ'kæn] *n* (*nut*) pacana *f*.

peck [pek] I *n* (*of bird*) picotazo *m*; *fam* (*kiss*) besito *m*. II *vtr* (*bird*) picotear; *fam* (*kiss*) dar un besito a. III *vi* to p. at one's food, picar la comida.

pecking order ['pekɪŋɔːdər] *n fig* jerarquía *f*.

peckish ['pekɪʃ] *adj fam* to feel p., empezar a tener hambre.

peculiar [pɪ'kjuːlɪər] *adj* (*odd*) extraño,-a; (*particular*) característico,-a.

peculiarity [pɪkjuːlɪ'ærɪtɪ] *n* (*oddity*) rareza *f*; (*characteristic*) característica *f*, peculiaridad *f*.

pedal ['pedəl] I *n* pedal *m*. II *vi* pedalear.

pedantic [pɪ'dæntɪk] *adj* pedante.

peddle ['pedəl] *vtr & vi Com* vender de puerta en puerta; to p. drugs, traficar con drogas.

peddler ['pedlər] *n* (*of drugs*) traficante *mf*; *US* → pedlar.

pedestal ['pedɪstəl] *n* pedestal *m*; *fig* to put sb on a p., poner a algn sobre un pedestal.

pedestrian [pɪ'destrɪən] I *n* peatón,-ona *m,f*; p. crossing, paso *m* de peatones. II *adj pej* prosaico,-a.

pediatrician [piːdɪə'trɪʃən] *n US* → paediatrician.

pedigree ['pedɪgriː] I *n* linaje *m*; (*family tree*) árbol genealógico; (*of animal*) pedigrí *m*. II *adj* (*animal*) de raza.

pedlar ['pedlər] *n* vendedor,-a *m,f* ambulante.

pee [piː] *fam* I *n* pis *m*. II *vi* hacer pis.

peek [piːk] I *n* ojeada *f*. II *vi* to p. at sth, mirar algo a hurtadillas.

peel [piːl] I *n* piel *f*; (*of orange, lemon*) cáscara *f*. II *vtr* (*fruit*) pelar. III *vi* (*paint*) desconcharse; (*wallpaper*) despegarse; (*skin*) pelarse.

peeler ['piːlər] *n* potato p., pelapatatas *m inv*.

peelings ['piːlɪŋz] *npl* peladuras *fpl*, mondaduras *fpl*.

peep[1] [piːp] *n* (*sound*) pío *m*.

peep[2] [piːp] I *n* (*glance*) ojeada *f*; (*furtive look*) mirada furtiva. II *vi* to p. at sth, echar una ojeada a algo; to p. out from behind sth, dejarse ver detrás de algo.

peephole ['piːphəʊl] *n* mirilla *f*.

peer[1] [pɪər] *n* (*noble*) par *m*; (*equal*) igual *mf*; p. group, grupo parejo.

peer[2] [pɪər] *vi* mirar detenidamente; (*shortsightedly*) mirar con ojos de miope.

peerage ['pɪərɪdʒ] *n* título *m* de nobleza.

peeved [piːvd] *adj fam* fastidiado,-a, de mal humor.

peevish ['piːvɪʃ] *adj* malhumorado,-a.

peg [peg] I *n* clavija *f*; (*for coat, hat*) percha *f*. II *vtr* (*clothes*) tender; (*prices*) fijar.

pejorative [pɪ'dʒɒrətɪv] *adj* peyorativo,-a.

Pekinese [piːkə'niːz] *adj & n* pequinés, -esa (*m,f*).

Peking [piː'kɪŋ] *n* Pekín.

pelican ['pelɪkən] *n* pelícano *m*; *GB* p. crossing, paso *m* de peatones.

pellet ['pelɪt] *n* bolita *f*; (*for gun*) perdigón *m*.

pelt[1] [pelt] *n* (*skin*) pellejo *m*.

pelt[2] [pelt] I *vtr* to p. sb with sth, tirar algo a algn. II *vi fam* 1 it's pelting (down), (*raining*) llueve a cántaros. 2 to p. along, (*rush*) correr a toda prisa.

pelvis ['pelvɪs] *n* pelvis *f*.

pen[1] [pen] I *n* pluma *f*. II *vtr* escribir.

pen[2] [pen] I *n* (*enclosure*) corral *m*; (*for sheep*) redil *m*; (*for children*) corralito *m*. II *vtr* to p. in, acorralar.

penal ['piːnəl] *adj* penal.

penalize ['piːnəlaɪz] *vtr* castigar; *Sport* penalizar.

penalty ['penəltɪ] *n* (*punishment*) pena *f*; *Sport* castigo; *Ftb* penalti *m*; to pay the p. for sth, cargar con las consecuencias de algo; p. area, área *f* de castigo.

penance ['penəns] *n* penitencia *f*.

pence [pens] *npl* → penny.

pencil ['pensəl] *n* lápiz *m*; p. case, estuche *m* de lápices; p. sharpener, sacapuntas *m inv*.

pendant ['pendənt] *n* colgante *m*.

pending ['pendɪŋ] I *adj* pendiente. II *prep* (*while*) mientras; p. a decision, (*until*) hasta que se tome una decisión.

pendulum ['pendjʊləm] *n* péndulo *m*.

penetrate ['penɪtreɪt] I *vtr* penetrar; *fig* adentrarse en. II *vi* atravesar; (*get inside*) penetrar.

penetrating ['penɪtreɪtɪŋ] *adj* (*look*) penetrante; (*mind*) perspicaz; (*sound*) agudo, -a.

penfriend ['penfrend] *n* amigo,-a *m,f* por carta.

penguin ['pengwɪn] *n* pingüino *m*.

penicillin [penɪ'sɪlɪn] *n* penicilina *f*.

peninsula [pɪ'nɪnsjʊlə] *n* península *f*.

penis ['piːnɪs] *n* pene *m*.

penitent ['penɪtənt] *adj Rel* penitente; (*repentant*) arrepentido,-a.

penitentiary [penɪ'tenʃərɪ] *n US* cárcel *f*, penal *m*.

penknife ['pennaɪf] *n* navaja *f*, cortaplumas *m inv*.

penniless ['penɪlɪs] *adj* sin dinero.

penny ['penɪ] *n* (*pl* pennies, pence [pens]) penique *m*.

penpal ['penpæl] *n US* → penfriend.

pension ['penʃən] *n* pensión *f*; retirement p., jubilación *f*.

pensioner ['penʃənər] *n* jubilado,-a *m,f*.

pensive ['pensɪv] *adj* pensativo,-a.

pentagon ['pentəgən] *n US Pol* the P., el Pentágono.

Pentecost ['pentɪkɒst] *n* Pentecostés *m*.

penthouse ['penthaus] *n* ático *m*.
pent-up ['pentʌp] *adj* reprimido,-a.
penultimate [pɪ'nʌltɪmɪt] *adj* penúltimo,-a.
people ['piːpəl] *npl* 1 gente *f sing*; *(individuals)* personas *fpl*; **many p.,** mucha gente; **old p.'s home,** asilo *m* de ancianos; **p. say that ...,** se dice que ...; **some p.,** algunas personas. 2 *(citizens)* ciudadanos *mpl*; *(inhabitants)* habitantes *mpl*; **the p.,** el pueblo. 3 *(nation)* pueblo *m*, nación *f*.
pep [pep] *n fam* ánimo *m*, energía *f*; **p. talk,** discurso *m* enardecedor. ◆**pep up** *vtr fam* animar.
pepper ['pepər] I *n (spice)* pimienta *f*; *(fruit)* pimiento *m*; **black p.,** pimienta negra; **p. pot,** pimentero *m*; **red/green p.,** pimiento rojo/verde; **p. mill,** molinillo *m* de pimienta. II *vtr fig* **peppered with,** salpicado,-a de.
peppermint ['pepəmɪnt] *n (sweet)* menta *f*; *(sweet)* pastilla *f* de menta.
per [pɜːr] *prep* por; **5 times p. week,** 5 veces a la semana; **p. cent,** por ciento; **p. day/annum,** al *or* por día/año; **p. capita,** per cápita.
perceive [pə'siːv] *vtr (see)* percibir.
percentage [pə'sentɪdʒ] *n* porcentaje *m*.
perceptible [pə'septəbəl] *adj (visible)* perceptible; *(sound)* audible; *(improvement)* sensible.
perception [pə'sepʃən] *n* percepción *f*.
perceptive [pə'septɪv] *adj* perspicaz.
perch¹ [pɜːtʃ] *n (fish)* perca *f*.
perch² [pɜːtʃ] I *n (for bird)* percha *f*. II *vi (bird)* posarse **(on,** en).
percolate ['pɜːkəleɪt] I *vtr* filtrar; **percolated coffee,** café *m* filtro. II *vi* filtrarse.
percolator ['pɜːkəleɪtər] *n* cafetera *f* de filtro.
percussion [pə'kʌʃən] *n* percusión *f*.
perennial [pə'renɪəl] *adj Bot* perenne.
perfect ['pɜːfɪkt] I *adj* perfecto,-a; **he's a p. stranger to us,** nos es totalmente desconocido; **p. tense,** tiempo perfecto. II [pə'fekt] *vtr* perfeccionar. ◆**perfectly** *adv* perfectamente; *(absolutely)* completamente.
perfection [pə'fekʃən] *n* perfección *f*.
perforate ['pɜːfəreɪt] *vtr* perforar.
perforation [pɜːfə'reɪʃən] *n* perforación *f*; *(on stamps etc)* perforado *m*.
perform [pə'fɔːm] I *vtr (task)* ejecutar, realizar; *(piece of music)* interpretar; *Theat* representar. II *vi (machine)* funcionar; *Mus* interpretar; *Theat* actuar.
performance [pə'fɔːməns] *n (of task)* ejecución *f*, realización *f*; *Mus* interpretación *f*; *Theat* representación *f*; *Sport* actuación *f*; *(of machine etc)* rendimiento *m*.
performer [pə'fɔːmər] *n Mus* intérprete *mf*; *Theat* actor *m*, actriz *f*.

perfume ['pɜːfjuːm] *n* perfume *m*.
perfunctory [pə'fʌŋktəri] *adj* superficial.
perhaps [pə'hæps, præps] *adv* tal vez, quizá(s).
peril ['perɪl] *n (risk)* riesgo *m*; *(danger)* peligro *m*.
perilous ['perɪləs] *adj (risky)* arriesgado, -a; *(dangerous)* peligroso,-a. ◆**perilously** *adv* peligrosamente.
perimeter [pə'rɪmɪtər] *n* perímetro *m*.
period ['pɪərɪəd] I *n* 1 período *m*; *(stage)* etapa *f*. 2 *Educ* clase *f*. 3 *(full stop)* punto *m*. 4 *(menstruation)* regla *f*. II *adj (dress, furniture)* de época.
periodic [pɪərɪ'ɒdɪk] *adj* periódico,-a. ◆**periodically** *adv* de vez en cuando.
periodical [pɪərɪ'ɒdɪkəl] I *adj* periódico, -a. II *n* revista *f*.
peripheral [pə'rɪfərəl] I *adj* periférico,-a. II *n Comput* unidad periférica.
perish ['perɪʃ] *vi* perecer; *(material)* echarse a perder.
perishable ['perɪʃəbəl] *adj* perecedero,-a.
perjury ['pɜːdʒəri] *n* perjurio *m*.
perk [pɜːk] *n fam* extra *m*. ◆**perk up** *vi (person)* animarse; *(after illness)* reponerse.
perky ['pɜːki] *adj (perkier, perkiest)* animado,-a, alegre.
perm [pɜːm] I *n* permanente *f*. II *vtr* **to have one's hair permed,** hacerse la permanente.
permanent ['pɜːmənənt] *adj* permanente; *(address, job)* fijo,-a.
permeate ['pɜːmɪeɪt] *vtr & vi* penetrar; *fig* extenderse por.
permissible [pə'mɪsəbəl] *adj* admisible.
permission [pə'mɪʃən] *n* permiso *m*.
permissive [pə'mɪsɪv] *adj* permisivo,-a.
permit ['pɜːmɪt] I *n* permiso *m*; *Com* licencia *f*. II [pə'mɪt] *vtr* **to p. sb to do sth,** permitir a algn hacer algo.
pernicious [pə'nɪʃəs] *adj* pernicioso,-a.
perpendicular [pɜːpən'dɪkjulər] I *adj* perpendicular; *(cliff)* vertical. II *n* perpendicular *f*.
perpetrate ['pɜːpɪtreɪt] *vtr* cometer.
perpetual [pə'petʃuəl] *adj (noise)* continuo,-a; *(arguing)* interminable; *(snow)* perpetuo,-a.
perplex [pə'pleks] *vtr* dejar perplejo,-a.
perplexing [pə'pleksɪŋ] *adj* desconcertante.
persecute ['pɜːsɪkjuːt] *vtr* perseguir; *(harass)* acosar.
persecution [pɜːsɪ'kjuːʃən] *n* persecución *f*; *(harassment)* acoso *m*.
perseverance [pɜːsɪ'vɪərəns] *n* perseverancia *f*.
persevere [pɜːsɪ'vɪər] *vi* perseverar.
Persian ['pɜːʃən] *adj* persa *m*; **P. Gulf,** golfo Pérsico.
persist [pə'sɪst] *vi* empeñarse **(in,** en).
persistence [pə'sɪstəns] *n* empeño *m*.

persistent |pəˈsɪstənt| *adj (person)* perseverante; *(smell etc)* persistente; *(continual)* constante.

person |ˈpɜːsən| *n (pl* **people** |ˈpiːpəl|)* persona *f*; *(individual)* individuo *m*; **in p.**, en persona.

personable |ˈpɜːsənəbəl| *adj (handsome)* bien parecido,-a; *(pleasant)* amable.

personal |ˈpɜːsənəl| **1** *adj (private)* personal; *(friend)* íntimo,-a. **p. computer**, ordenador *m* personal; **p. column**, anuncios *mpl* personales; **p. pronoun**, pronombre *m* personal. **2** *(in person)* en persona; **he will make a p. appearance**, estará aquí en persona. **3** *pej (comment etc)* indiscreto,-a. ◆**personally** *adv (for my part)* personalmente; *(in person)* en persona.

personality |pɜːsəˈnælɪtɪ| *n* personalidad *f*.

personify |pɜːˈsɒnɪfaɪ| *vtr* personificar, encarnar.

personnel |pɜːsəˈnel| *n* personal *m*.

perspective |pəˈspektɪv| *n* perspectiva *f*.

Perspex® |ˈpɜːspeks| *n* plexiglás® *m*.

perspiration |pɜːspəˈreɪʃən| *n* transpiración *f*.

perspire |pəˈspaɪər| *vi* transpirar.

persuade |pəˈsweɪd| *vtr* persuadir; **to p. sb to do sth**, persuadir a algn para que haga algo.

persuasion |pəˈsweɪʒən| *n* persuasión *f*; *(opinion, belief)* credo *m*.

persuasive |pəˈsweɪsɪv| *adj* persuasivo,-a.

pert |pɜːt| *adj* pizpireta, coqueto,-a.

pertain |pəˈteɪn| *vi* estar relacionado,-a (to, con).

pertinent |ˈpɜːtɪnənt| *adj (relevant)* pertinente; **p. to**, relacionado,-a con, a propósito de

perturbing |pəˈtɜːbɪŋ| *adj* inquietante.

Peru |pəˈruː| *n* Perú.

peruse |pəˈruːz| *vtr fml* leer.

Peruvian |pəˈruːvɪən| *adj & n* peruano,-a *(m,f)*.

pervade |pɜːˈveɪd| *vtr (of smell)* penetrar. *(of light)* difundirse por; *fig (of influence)* extenderse por.

pervasive |pɜːˈveɪsɪv| *adj (smell)* penetrante; *(influence)* extendido,-a.

perverse |pəˈvɜːs| *adj (wicked)* perverso,-a; *(contrary)* contrario,-a a todo.

perversion |pəˈvɜːʃən| *n Med Psych* perversión *f*; *(of justice, truth)* desvirtuación *f*.

pervert |ˈpɜːvɜːt| **I** *n Med* pervertido,-a *m,f* (sexual). **II** |pəˈvɜːt| *vtr* pervertir; *(justice, truth)* desvirtuar.

pessimist |ˈpesɪmɪst| *n* pesimista *mf*.

pessimistic |pesɪˈmɪstɪk| *adj* pesimista.

pest |pest| *n* **1** *Zool* animal nocivo; *Bot* planta nociva. **2** *fam (person)* pelma *mf*; *(thing)* lata *f*.

pester |ˈpestər| *vtr* molestar, fastidiar.

pet |pet| **I** *n* **1** animal doméstico. **2** *(favourite)* preferido,-a *m,f*; *fam* cariño *m*. **II** *adj (favourite)* preferido,-a. **III** *vtr* acariciar. **IV** *vi (sexually)* besuquearse.

petal |ˈpetəl| *n* pétalo *m*.

peter |ˈpiːtər| *vi* **to p. out**, agotarse.

petite |pəˈtiːt| *adj* menuda, chiquita.

petition |pɪˈtɪʃən| *n* petición *f*.

petrify |ˈpetrɪfaɪ| *vtr lit* petrificar; *fig* **they were petrified**, se quedaron de piedra.

petrol |ˈpetrəl| *n* gasolina *f*; **p. can**, bidón *m* de gasolina; **p. pump**, surtidor *m* de gasolina; **p. station**, gasolinera *f*; **p. tank**, depósito *m* de gasolina.

petroleum |pəˈtrəʊlɪəm| *n* petróleo *m*.

petticoat |ˈpetɪkəʊt| *n* enaguas *fpl*.

petty |ˈpetɪ| *adj (pettier, pettiest) (trivial)* insignificante; *(small-minded)* mezquino,-a; **p. cash**, dinero *m* para gastos pequeños; *Naut* **p. officer**, sargento *m* de marina.

petulant |ˈpetjʊlənt| *adj* malhumorado,-a.

pew |pjuː| *n* banco *m* de iglesia; *fam* **take a p.!**, ¡siéntate!

pewter |ˈpjuːtər| *n* peltre *m*.

phantom |ˈfæntəm| *adj & n* fantasma *(m)*.

pharmaceutical |fɑːməˈsjuːtɪkəl| *adj* farmacéutico,-a.

pharmacist |ˈfɑːməsɪst| *n* farmacéutico,-a *m,f*.

pharmacy |ˈfɑːməsɪ| *n* farmacia *f*.

phase |feɪz| **I** *n* fase *f*. **II** *vtr* **to p. sth in/out**, introducir/retirar algo progresivamente.

PhD |piːeɪtʃˈdiː| *abbr of* **Doctor of Philosophy**, Doctor,-a *m,f* en Filosofía.

pheasant |ˈfezənt| *n* faisán *m* (vulgar).

phenomenal |fɪˈnɒmɪnəl| *adj* fenomenal.

phenomenon |fɪˈnɒmɪnən| *n (pl* **phenomena** |fɪˈnɒmɪnə|)* fenómeno *m*.

phial |faɪəl| *n* frasco *m*.

philanthropist |fɪˈlænθrəpɪst| *n* filántropo,-a *m,f*.

philately |fɪˈlætəlɪ| *n* filatelia *f*.

Philippines |ˈfɪlɪpiːnz| *n* **the P.**, las (Islas) Filipinas.

philosopher |fɪˈlɒsəfər| *n* filósofo,-a *m,f*.

philosophical |fɪləˈsɒfɪkəl| *adj* filosófico,-a.

philosophy |fɪˈlɒsəfɪ| *n* filosofía *f*.

phlegm |flem| *n* flema *f*.

phlegmatic |flegˈmætɪk| *adj* flemático,-a.

phobia |ˈfəʊbɪə| *n* fobia *f*.

phone |fəʊn| *n* → **telephone**.

phone-in |ˈfəʊnɪn| *n fam* programa *m* de radio *or* televisión con línea telefónica abierta.

phonetic |fəˈnetɪk| **I** *adj* fonético,-a. **II** *n* **phonetics**, fonética *f sing*.

phoney |ˈfəʊnɪ| *adj (phonier, phoniest) (thing)* falso,-a; *(person)* farsante. **II** *n (person)* farsante *mf*.

phonograph |ˈfəʊnəɡrɑːf| *n US* toca-

discos *m inv*.
phosphate ['fɒsfeɪt] n fosfato *m*.
photo ['fəʊtəʊ] *n (abbr of photograph)* foto *f*.
photocopier ['fəʊtəʊkɒpɪəʳ] *n* fotocopiadora *f*.
photocopy ['fəʊtəʊkɒpɪ] **I** *n* fotocopia *f*. **II** *vtr* fotocopiar.
photogenic [fəʊtəʊ'dʒenɪk] *adj* fotogénico,-a.
photograph ['fəʊtəgræf, 'fəʊtəgrɑːf] **I** *n* fotografía *f*; **black and white/colour p.**, fotografía en blanco y negro/en color. **II** *vtr* fotografiar.
photographer [fə'tɒgrəfəʳ] *n* fotógrafo,-a *m,f*.
photography [fə'tɒgrəfɪ] *n* fotografía *f*.
phrase [freɪz] **I** *n* frase *f*; **p. book**, libro *m* de frases. **II** *vtr* expresar.
physical ['fɪzɪkəl] *adj* físico,-a; **p. education**, educación física. ◆**physically** *adv* físicamente; **p. handicapped**, minusválido,-a; **to be p. fit**, estar en forma.
physician [fɪ'zɪʃən] *n* médico,-a *m,f*.
physicist ['fɪzɪsɪst] *n* físico,-a *m,f*.
physics ['fɪzɪks] *n* física *f*.
physiological [fɪzɪə'lɒdʒɪkəl] *adj* fisiológico,-a.
physiotherapist [fɪzɪəʊ'θerəpɪst] *n* fisioterapeuta *mf*.
physique [fɪ'ziːk] *n* físico *m*.
pianist ['pɪənɪst] *n* pianista *mf*.
piano [pɪ'ænəʊ] *n* piano *m*.
piccolo ['pɪkələʊ] *n* flautín *m*.
pick [pɪk] **I** *n* 1 *(tool)* pico *m*, piqueta *f*. 2 **take your p.**, *(choice)* elige el que quieras. **II** *vtr* 1 *(choose)* escoger; *(team)* seleccionar. 2 *(flowers, fruit)* coger, recoger. 3 *(scratch)* hurgar; **to p. one's nose**, hurgarse la nariz; **to p. one's teeth**, mondarse los dientes. 4 **to p. sb's pocket**, robar algo del bolsillo de algn. 5 *(lock)* forzar. **III** *vi* **to p. at one's food**, comer sin ganas. ◆**pick off** *vtr* 1 *(remove)* quitar. 2 *(shoot)* matar uno a uno. ◆**pick on** *vtr (persecute)* meterse con. ◆**pick out** *vtr (choose)* elegir; *(distinguish)* distinguir; *(identify)* identificar. ◆**pick up I** *vtr* 1 *(object on floor)* recoger; *(telephone)* descolgar; **to p. oneself up**, levantarse; *fig* reponerse. 2 *(collect)* recoger; *(shopping, person)* buscar; **to p. up speed**, ganar velocidad. 3 *(acquire)* conseguir; *(learn)* aprender. **II** *vi (improve)* mejorarse, ir mejorando; *(prices)* subir.
pickaxe, *US* **pickax** ['pɪkæks] *n* piqueta *f*.
picket ['pɪkɪt] **I** *n* piquete *m*; **p. line**, piquete *m*. **II** *vtr* piquetear. **III** *vi* hacer piquete.
pickle ['pɪkəl] **I** *n* 1 *Culin* salsa *f* picante. 2 *fam (mess)* lío *m*, apuro *m*. **II** *vtr Culin*

conservar en adobo *or* escabeche; **pickled onions**, cebollas *fpl* en vinagre.
pickpocket ['pɪkpɒkɪt] *n* carterista *mf*.
pick-up ['pɪkʌp] *n* **p.-up (arm)**, *(on record player)* brazo *m*; **p.-up (truck)**, furgoneta *f*.
picnic ['pɪknɪk] **I** *n* comida *f* de campo, picnic *m*. **II** *vi* hacer una comida de campo.
pictorial [pɪk'tɔːrɪəl] *adj* ilustrado,- a.
picture ['pɪktʃəʳ] **I** *n* 1 *(painting)* cuadro *m*; *(drawing)* dibujo *m*; *(portrait)* retrato *m*; *(photo)* foto *f*; *(illustration)* ilustración *f*; **p. book**, libro ilustrado; **p. postcard**, tarjeta *f* postal. 2 *TV* imagen *m*; *Cin* película *f*; **to go to the pictures**, ir al cine. **II** *vtr (imagine)* imaginarse.
picturesque [pɪktʃə'resk] *adj* pintoresco, -ca.
pie [paɪ] *n (of fruit)* tarta *f*, pastel *m*; *(of meat etc)* pastel, empanada *f*; *(pasty)* empanadilla *f*.
piece [piːs] *n* 1 *(of food)* pedazo *m*, trozo *m*; *(of paper)* trozo; *(part)* pieza *f*; **a p. of advice**, un consejo; **a p. of furniture**, un mueble; **a p. of land**, una parcela; **a p. of news**, una noticia; **to break sth into pieces**, hacer algo pedazos; *fig* **to go to pieces**, perder el control (de sí mismo). 2 *Lit Mus* obra *f*, pieza *f*. 3 *(coin)* moneda *f*. 4 *(in chess)* pieza *f*; *(in draughts)* ficha *f*. ◆**piece together** *vtr (facts)* reconstruir; *(jigsaw)* hacer.
piecemeal ['piːsmiːl] *adv (by degrees)* poco a poco, a etapas; *(unsystematically)* desordenadamente.
piecework ['piːswɜːk] *n* trabajo *m* a destajo; **to be on p.**, trabajar a destajo.
pier [pɪəʳ] *n* embarcadero *m*, muelle *m*; *(promenade)* paseo *m* de madera que entra en el mar.
pierce [pɪəs] *vtr* perforar; *(penetrate)* penetrar en.
piercing ['pɪəsɪŋ] *adj (sound etc)* penetrante.
piety ['paɪɪtɪ] *n* piedad *f*.
pig [pɪg] *n* cerdo *m*; *fam (person)* cochino *m*; *(glutton)* tragón,-ona *m,f*; *sl offens (policeman)* madero *m*.
pigeon ['pɪdʒɪn] *n* paloma *f*; *Culin Sport* pichón *m*.
pigeonhole ['pɪdʒɪnhəʊl] *n* casilla *f*.
piggy ['pɪgɪ] *n* **p. bank**, hucha *f* en forma de cerdito.
pigheaded [pɪg'hedɪd] *adj* terco,-a, cabezota.
piglet ['pɪglɪt] *n* cerdito *m*, lechón *m*.
pigment ['pɪgmənt] *n* pigmento *m*.
pigskin ['pɪgskɪn] *n* piel *f* de cerdo.
pigsty ['pɪgstaɪ] *n* pocilga *f*.
pigtail ['pɪgteɪl] *n* trenza *f*; *(bullfighter's)* coleta *f*.
pike [paɪk] *n (fish)* lucio *m*.
pilchard ['pɪltʃəd] *n* sardina *f*.

pile¹ [paɪl] **I** *n* montón *m*. **II** *vtr* amontonar. **III** *vi* **to p. into**, apiñarse en; **to p. on/off a bus**, subir a/bajar de un autobús en tropel. ◆**pile up I** *vtr (things)* amontonar; *(riches, debts)* acumular. **II** *vi* amontonarse.

pile² [paɪl] *n (on carpet)* pelo *m*; **thick p.**, pelo largo.

piles [paɪlz] *npl Med* almorranas *fpl*, hemorroides *fpl*.

pile-up ['paɪlʌp] *n Aut* choque *m* en cadena.

pilfer ['pɪlfər] *vtr & vi* hurtar.

pilgrim ['pɪlgrɪm] *n* peregrino,-a *m,f*.

pilgrimage ['pɪlgrɪmɪdʒ] *n* peregrinación *f*.

pill [pɪl] *n* píldora *f*, pastilla *f*; **to be on the p.**, estar tomando la píldora (anticonceptiva).

pillage ['pɪlɪdʒ] *vtr & vi* pillar, saquear.

pillar ['pɪlər] *n* pilar *m*, columna *f*; *GB* **p. box**, buzón *m*.

pillion ['pɪljən] *n* asiento trasero (de una moto).

pillow ['pɪləʊ] *n* almohada *f*.

pillowcase ['pɪləʊkeɪs] *n* funda *f* de almohada.

pilot ['paɪlət] **I** *n* piloto *m*. **II** *adj (trial)* piloto *inv*; **p. light**, piloto *m*; **p. scheme**, proyecto piloto. **III** *vtr* pilotar.

pimp [pɪmp] *n* chulo *m*.

pimple ['pɪmpəl] *n* grano *m*, espinilla *f*.

pin [pɪn] **I** *n* alfiler *m*; *Tech* clavija *f*; *(wooden)* espiga *f*; *(in plug)* polo *m*; *Bowling* bolo *m*; *US (brooch)* broche *m*; **pins and needles**, hormigueo *m*. **II** *vtr (on board)* clavar con chinchetas; *(garment etc)* sujetar con alfileres; **to p. sb against a wall**, tener a algn contra una pared; *fig* **to p. one's hopes on sth**, poner sus esperanzas en algo; *fam* **to p. a crime on sb**, endosar un delito a algn. ◆**pin down** *vtr fig* **to p. sb down**, hacer que algn se comprometa.

pinafore ['pɪnəfɔːr] *n (apron)* delantal *m*; **p. dress**, pichi *m*.

pinball ['pɪnbɔːl] *n* flipper *m*, máquina *f* de petacos.

pincers ['pɪnsəz] *npl (on crab)* pinzas *fpl*; *(tool)* tenazas *fpl*.

pinch [pɪntʃ] **I** *n (nip)* pellizco *m*; *fig* **at a p.**, en caso de apuro; **a p. of salt**, una pizca de sal. **II** *vtr* pellizcar; *fam (steal)* birlar. **III** *vi (shoes)* apretar.

pincushion ['pɪnkʊʃən] *n* acerico *m*.

pine¹ [paɪn] *n (tree)* pino *m*; **p. cone**, piña *f*.

pine² [paɪn] *vi* **to p. (away)**, consumirse, morirse de pena; **to p. for sth/sb**, añorar algo/a algn.

pineapple ['paɪnæpəl] *n* piña *f*.

ping [pɪŋ] *n* sonido metálico; *(of bullet)* silbido *m*.

ping-pong ['pɪŋpɒŋ] *n* ping-pong *m*.

pink [pɪŋk] **I** *n (colour)* rosa *m*; *Bot* clavel *m*. **II** *adj (colour)* rosa *inv*; *Pol fam* rojillo,-a.

pinnacle ['pɪnəkəl] *n (of building)* pináculo *m*; *(of mountain)* cima *f*, pico *m*; *fig (of success)* cumbre *f*.

pinpoint ['pɪnpɔɪnt] *vtr* señalar.

pinstripe ['pɪnstraɪp] *adj* a rayas.

pint [paɪnt] *n* pinta *f*; *GB fam* **a p. (of beer)**, una pinta (de cerveza).

pioneer [paɪə'nɪər] **I** *n (settler)* pionero,-a *m,f*; *(forerunner)* precursor,-a *m,f*. **II** *vtr* ser pionero,-a en.

pious ['paɪəs] *adj* piadoso,-a, devoto,-a; *pej* beato,-a.

pip¹ [pɪp] *n (seed)* pepita *f*.

pip² [pɪp] *n (sound)* señal *f* (corta); *(on dice)* punto *m*.

pipe [paɪp] **I** *n* **1** conducto *m*, tubería *f*; *(of organ)* caramillo *m*; **fam the pipes**, *(bagpipes)* la gaita. **2** *(for smoking)* pipa *f*; **p. cleaner**, limpiapipas *m inv*; *fig* **p. dream**, sueño *m* imposible. **II** *vtr (water)* llevar por tubería; *(oil)* transportar por oleoducto; **piped music**, hilo *m* musical. ◆**pipe down** *vi fam* callarse. ◆**pipe up** *vi fam* hacerse oír.

pipeline ['paɪplaɪn] *n* tubería *f*, cañería *f*; *(for gas)* gasoducto *m*; *(for oil)* oleoducto *m*.

piper ['paɪpər] *n* gaitero,-a *m,f*.

piping ['paɪpɪŋ] **I** *n (for water, gas etc)* tubería *f*, cañería *f*. **II** *adj* **p. hot**, bien caliente.

piquant ['piːkənt] *adj* picante; *(fig)* intrigante.

pique [piːk] **I** *n* enojo *m*. **II** *vtr* herir.

pirate ['paɪrɪt] *n* pirata *m*; **p. edition**, edición pirata; **p. radio**, emisora pirata; **p. ship**, barco *m* pirata.

pirouette [pɪrʊ'et] **I** *n* pirueta *f*. **II** *vi* hacer piruetas.

Pisces ['paɪsiːz] *n* Piscis *m*.

piss [pɪs] *sl* **I** *vi* mear. **II** *n* meada *f*.

pissed [pɪst] *adj GB sl (drunk)* borracho, -a.

pistachio [pɪs'tɑːʃɪəʊ] *n (nut)* pistacho *m*.

pistol ['pɪstəl] *n* pistola *f*.

piston ['pɪstən] *n* pistón *m*.

pit [pɪt] **I** *n* hoyo *m*; *(large)* hoya *f*; *(coal mine)* mina *f* de carbón; *Theat* platea *f*; *(in motor racing)* foso *m*, box *m*. **II** *vtr* **to p. one's wits against sb**, medirse con algn.

pitch¹ [pɪtʃ] **I** *vtr* **1** *Mus (sound)* entonar. **2** *(throw)* lanzar, arrojar. **3** *(tent)* armar. **II** *vi (ship)* cabecear; **to p. forward**, caerse hacia adelante. **III** *n* **1** *Mus (of sound)* tono *m* **2** *Sport* campo *m*, cancha *f*. **3** *(in market etc)* puesto *m*. **4** *(throw)* lanzamiento *m*.

pitch² [pɪtʃ] *n (tar)* brea *f*, pez *f*.

pitch-black [pɪtʃ'blæk], **pitch-dark** [pɪtʃ'dɑːk] *adj* negro,-a como la boca del lobo.

pitched [pɪtʃt] *adj* **p. battle**, batalla *f* campal.

pitcher ['pɪtʃər] *n (container)* cántaro *m*, jarro *m*.

pitchfork ['pɪtʃfɔːk] *n* horca *f*.

piteous ['pɪtɪəs] *adj* lastimoso,-a.

pitfall ['pɪtfɔːl] *n* dificultad *f*, obstáculo *m*.

pith [pɪθ] *n (of orange)* piel blanca; *fig* meollo *m*.

pithy ['pɪθɪ] *adj (pithier, pithiest) fig* contundente.

pitiful ['pɪtɪfʊl] *adj (producing pity)* lastimoso,-a, *(terrible)* lamentable.

pitiless ['pɪtɪlɪs] *adj* despiadado,-a, implacable.

pittance ['pɪtəns] *n* miseria *f*.

pity ['pɪtɪ] I *n* 1 *(compassion)* compasión *f*, piedad *f*; **to take p. on sb**, compadecerse de algn. 2 *(shame)* lástima *f*, pena *f*; **what a p.!**, ¡qué pena!, ¡qué lástima! II *vtr* compadecerse de; **I p. them**, me dan pena.

pivot ['pɪvət] I *n* pivote *m*. II *vi* girar sobre su eje.

pizza ['piːtsə] *n* pizza *f*; **p. parlour**, pizzería *f*.

placard ['plækɑːd] *n* pancarta *f*.

placate [plə'keɪt] *vtr* aplacar, apaciguar.

place [pleɪs] I *n* 1 sitio *m*, lugar *m*; **to be in/out of p.**, estar en/fuera de su sitio; **to take p.**, tener lugar. 2 *(seat)* sitio *m*; *(on bus)* asiento *m*; *(at university)* plaza *m*; **to change places with sb**, intercambiar el sitio con algn; **to feel out of p.**, encontrarse fuera de lugar; **to take sb's p.**, sustituir a algn. 3 *(position on scale)* posición *f*; *(social position)* rango *m*; **in the first p.**, en primer lugar; **to take first p.**, ganar el primer lugar. 4 *(house)* casa *f*; *(building)* lugar *m*; **we're going to his p.**, vamos a su casa. II *vtr* poner, colocar; **to p. a bet**, hacer una apuesta; **to p. an order with sb**, hacer un pedido a algn. 2 *(face, person)* recordar; *(in job)* colocar en un empleo.

placid ['plæsɪd] *adj* apacible.

plagiarize ['pleɪdʒəraɪz] *vtr* plagiar.

plague [pleɪg] I *n (of insects)* plaga *f*; *Med* peste *f*. II *vtr* **to p. sb with requests**, acosar a algn a peticiones.

plaice [pleɪs] *n inv (fish)* platija *f*.

plaid [plæd, pleɪd] *n (cloth)* tejido *m* escocés.

plain [pleɪn] I *adj* 1 *(clear)* claro,- a, evidente; *fig* **he likes p. speaking**, le gusta hablar con franqueza. 2 *(simple)* sencillo,-a; *(chocolate)* amargo,-a; *(flour)* sin levadura; **in p. clothes**, vestido,-a de paisano; **the p. truth**, la verdad lisa y llana. 3 *(unattractive)* poco atractivo,-a. II *n Geog* llanura *f*, llano *m*. ◆**plainly** *adv* claramente; *(simply)* sencillamente; **to**

speak p., hablar con franqueza.

plaintiff ['pleɪntɪf] *n* demandante *mf*.

plaintive ['pleɪntɪv] *adj* lastimero,-a.

plait [plæt] I *n* trenza *f*. II *vtr* trenzar.

plan [plæn] I *n (scheme)* plan *m*, proyecto *m*; *(drawing)* plano *m*. II *vtr* 1 *(for future)* planear, proyectar; *(economy)* planificar. 2 *(intend)* pensar, tener la intención de; **it wasn't planned**, no estaba previsto. III *vi* hacer planes; **to p. on doing sth**, tener la intención de hacer algo.

plane¹ [pleɪn] I *n* 1 *Math* plano *m*; *fig* nivel *m*. 2 *Av fam* avión *m*. II *adj Geom* plano,-a. III *vi (glide)* planear.

plane² [pleɪn] I *n (tool)* cepillo *m*. II *vtr* cepillar.

plane³ [pleɪn] *n Bot* **p. (tree)**, plátano *m*.

planet ['plænɪt] *n* planeta *m*.

plank [plæŋk] *n* tabla *f*, tablón *m*.

planner ['plænər] *n* planificador,-a *m,f*.

planning ['plænɪŋ] *n* planificación *f*; **family p.**, planificación familiar; **p. permission**, permiso *m* de obras.

plant¹ [plɑːnt] I *n* planta *f*. II *vtr (flowers)* plantar; *(seeds)* sembrar; *(bomb)* colocar.

plant² [plɑːnt] *n (factory)* planta *f*, fábrica *f*; *(machinery)* maquinaria *f*.

plantation [plæn'teɪʃən] *n* plantación *f*.

plaque [plæk] *n* placa *f*; *(on teeth)* sarro *m*.

plaster ['plɑːstər] I *n Constr* yeso *m*; *Med* escayola *f*; *GB* **sticking p.**, esparadrapo *m*, tirita *f*; **p. of Paris**, yeso mate. II *vtr Constr* enyesar; *fig (cover)* cubrir de.

plastered ['plɑːstəd] *adj sl* borracho,-a, trompa.

plasterer ['plɑːstərər] *n* yesero,-a *m,f*.

plastic ['plæstɪk, 'plɑːstɪk] I *n* plástico *m*. II *adj (cup, bag)* de plástico; **p. surgery**, cirugía plástica.

Plasticine® ['plæstɪsiːn] *n* plastilina *f*.

plate [pleɪt] I *n* 1 plato *m*. 2 *(sheet)* placa *f*; **gold p.**, chapa *f* de oro; **p. glass**, vidrio cilindrado. 3 *Print* grabado *m*, lámina *f*. II *vtr* chapar.

plateau ['plætəʊ] *n* meseta *f*.

platform ['plætfɔːm] *n* 1 plataforma *f*; *(stage)* estrado *m*; *(at meeting)* tribuna *f*. 2 *Rail* andén *m*; **p. ticket**, billete *m* de andén. 3 *Pol (programme)* programa *m*.

platinum ['plætɪnəm] *n* platino *m*.

platitude ['plætɪtjuːd] *n* lugar *m* común, tópico *m*.

platoon [plə'tuːn] *n Mil* pelotón *m*.

platter ['plætər] *n* fuente *f*.

plausible ['plɔːzəbəl] *adj* plausible.

play [pleɪ] I *vtr* 1 *(game)* jugar a. 2 *Sport (position)* jugar de; *(team)* jugar contra; **to p. a shot**, *(in golf, tennis)* golpear. 3 *(instrument, tune)* tocar; **to p. a record**, poner un disco. 4 *Theat (part)* hacer (el papel) de; *(play)* representar; *fig* **to p. a part in sth**, participar en algo; *fig* **to p.**

the fool, hacer el tonto. II *vi* 1 *(children)* jugar (with, con); *(animals)* juguetear. 2 *Sport* jugar; to p. fair, jugar limpio; *fig* to p. for time, tratar de ganar tiempo. 3 *(joke)* bromear. 4 *Mus* tocar; *(instrument)* sonar. III *n* 1 *Theat* obra *f* de teatro. 2 *Sport* juego *m*; fair/foul p., juego limpio/ sucio. 3 *Tech & fig (movement)* juego *m*; *fig* to bring sth into p., poner algo en juego; a p. on words, un juego de palabras. ◆play around *vi (waste time)* gandulear; *(be unfaithful)* tener líos. ◆play down *vtr* minimizar, quitar importancia a. ◆play on *vtr (take advantage of)* aprovecharse de; *(nerves etc)* exacerbar. ◆play up I *vtr (annoy)* dar la lata, fastidiar. II *vi (child etc)* dar guerra.

playboy ['pleɪbɔɪ] *n* playboy *m*.

player ['pleɪər] *n Sport* jugador,-a *m,f*; *Mus* músico,-a *m,f*; *Theat (man)* actor *m*; *(woman)* actriz *f*.

playful ['pleɪful] *adj* juguetón,-ona.

playground ['pleɪgraʊnd] *n* patio *m* de recreo.

playgroup ['pleɪgruːp] *n* jardín *m* de infancia.

playing ['pleɪɪŋ] *n* juego *m*; p. card, carta *f*, naipe *m*; p. field, campo *m* de deportes.

playmate ['pleɪmeɪt] *n* compañero,-a *m,f* de juego.

play-off ['pleɪɒf] *n Sport* partido *m* de desempate.

playpen ['pleɪpen] *n* corralito *m* or parque *m* (de niños).

playschool ['pleɪskuːl] *n* jardín *m* de infancia.

plaything ['pleɪθɪŋ] *n* juguete *m*.

playwright ['pleɪraɪt] *n* dramaturgo,-a *m,f*.

PLC, plc [piːelˈsiː] *GB abbr of* **Public Limited Company**, Sociedad *f* Anónima, S.A.

plea [pliː] *n* 1 *(request)* petición *f*, súplica *f*; *(excuse)* pretexto *m*, disculpa *f*. 2 *Jur* alegato *m*.

plead [pliːd] I *vtr* 1 *Jur fig* to p. sb's cause, defender la causa de algn. 2 to p. ignorance, *(give as excuse)* alegar ignorancia. II *vi* 1 *(beg)* rogar, suplicar; to p. with sb to do sth, suplicar a algn que haga algo. 2 *Jur* to p. guilty/not guilty, declararse culpable/inocente.

pleasant ['plezənt] *adj* agradable.

pleasantry ['plezəntrɪ] *n* cumplido *m*.

please [pliːz] I *vtr (give pleasure to)* agradar, complacer; *(satisfy)* satisfacer; *fam* p. yourself, como quieras. II *vi* complacer; *(give satisfaction)* satisfacer; easy/hard to p., poco/muy exigente. III *adv* por favor; may I? - yes, ¿me permite? - desde luego; 'p. do not smoke', 'se ruega no fumar'; yes, p., sí, por favor.

pleased [pliːzd] *adj (happy)* contento,-a;

(satisfied) satisfecho,-a; p. to meet you!, ¡encantado,-a!, ¡mucho gusto!; to be p. about sth, alegrarse de algo.

pleasing ['pliːzɪŋ] *adj (pleasant)* agradable, grato,-a; *(satisfactory)* satisfactorio,-a.

pleasure ['pleʒər] *n* placer *m*; it's a p. to talk to him, da gusto hablar con él; to take great p. in doing sth, disfrutar mucho haciendo algo; with p., con mucho gusto.

pleat [pliːt] I *n* pliegue *m*. II *vtr* hacer pliegues en.

pledge [pledʒ] I *n* promesa *f*; *(token of love etc)* señal *f*; *(guarantee)* prenda *f*. II *vtr (promise)* prometer; *(pawn)* empeñar.

plentiful ['plentɪful] *adj* abundante.

plenty ['plentɪ] *n* abundancia *f*; p. of potatoes, muchas patatas; p. of time, tiempo de sobra; we've got p., tenemos de sobra.

pliable ['plaɪəbəl] *adj* flexible.

pliers ['plaɪəz] *npl* alicates *mpl*, tenazas *fpl*.

plight [plaɪt] *n* situación *f* grave.

plimsolls ['plɪmsəlz] *npl GB* zapatos *mpl* de tenis.

plinth [plɪnθ] *n* plinto *m*.

plod [plɒd] *vi* andar con paso pesado; *fig* to p. on, perseverar; *fig* to p. through a report, estudiar laboriosamente un informe.

plodder ['plɒdər] *n* trabajador,-a *m,f or* estudiante *mf* tenaz.

plonk[1] [plɒŋk] *vtr fam* dejar caer.

plonk[2] [plɒŋk] *n GB fam (wine)* vinazo *m*.

plot[1] [plɒt] I *n* 1 *(conspiracy)* complot *m*. 2 *Theat Lit (story)* argumento *m*, trama *f*. II *vtr* 1 *(course, route)* trazar. 2 *(scheme)* fraguar. III *vi* conspirar, tramar.

plot[2] [plɒt] *n Agr* terreno *m*; *(for building)* solar *m*; vegetable p., campo *m* de hortalizas.

plough [plaʊ] I *n* arado *m*. II *vtr* arar. III *vi fig* the car ploughed through the fencing, el coche atravesó la valla; to p. into sth, chocar contra algo; *fig* to p. through a book, leer un libro con dificultad. ◆plough back *vtr (profits)* reinvertir.

plow [plaʊ] *n US* → **plough**.

ploy [plɔɪ] *n* estratagema *f*.

pluck [plʌk] I *vtr* 1 arrancar (out of, de). 2 *(flowers)* coger. 3 *(chicken)* desplumar. 4 *(guitar)* puntear. II *n (courage)* valor *m*, ánimo *m*. ◆pluck up *vtr* to p. up courage, armarse de valor.

plucky ['plʌkɪ] *adj (pluckier, pluckiest)* valiente.

plug [plʌg] I *n* 1 *(in bath etc)* tapón *m*. 2 *Elec* enchufe *m*, clavija *f*; 2/3 pin p., clavija bipolar/tripolar. II *vtr* 1 *(hole)* tapar. 2 *fam (publicize)* dar publicidad a; *(idea etc)* hacer hincapié en. ◆plug in *vtr &*

vi enchufar.

plum [plʌm] *n (fruit)* ciruela *f; fig* **a p. job**, un chollo.

plumage ['plu:mɪdʒ] *n* plumaje *m.*

plumb [plʌm] **I** *n* plomo *m;* **p. line**, plomada *f.* **II** *adj* vertical. **III** *adv US fam* **p. in the middle**, justo en medio. **IV** *vtr fig* **to p. the depths**, tocar fondo.

plumber ['plʌmər] *n* fontanero,-a *m,f.*

plumbing ['plʌmɪŋ] *n (occupation)* fontanería *f; (system)* tuberías *fpl*, cañerías *fpl.*

plume [plu:m] *n* penacho *m.*

plummet ['plʌmɪt] *vi (bird, plane)* caer en picado; *fig (prices)* bajar vertiginosamente; *(morale)* caer a plomo.

plump¹ [plʌmp] *adj (person)* relleno,-a; *(baby)* rechoncho,-a.

plump² [plʌmp] *vi* **to p. for sth**, optar por algo. ◆**plump down** *vtr* dejar caer. ◆**plump up** *vtr (cushions)* ahuecar.

plunder ['plʌndər] **I** *vtr* saquear. **II** *n (action)* saqueo *m*, pillaje *m; (loot)* botín *m.*

plunge [plʌndʒ] **I** *vtr (immerse)* sumergir; *(thrust)* arrojar. **II** *vi (fall)* lanzarse, zambullirse; *fig (fall)* caer, hundirse; *(prices)* desplomarse. **III** *n (dive)* zambullida *f; fig (fall)* desplome *m;* **to take the p.**, dar el paso decisivo.

plunger ['plʌndʒər] *n Tech* émbolo *m; (for pipes)* desatascador *m.*

pluperfect [plu:'pɜ:fɪkt] *n* pluscuamperfecto *m.*

plural ['plʊərəl] *adj & n* plural *(m).*

plus [plʌs] **I** *prep* más; **three p. four makes seven**, tres más cuatro hacen siete. **II** *n Math* signo *m* más; *fig (advantage)* ventaja *f.*

plush [plʌʃ] **I** *n* felpa *f.* **II** *adj fam* lujoso,-a.

plutonium [plu:'təʊnɪəm] *n* plutonio *m.*

ply [plaɪ] **I** *vtr* **to p. one's trade**, ejercer su oficio; **to p. sb with drinks**, no parar de ofrecer copas a algn. **II** *vi (ship)* ir y venir; **to p. for hire**, ir en busca de clientes.

plywood ['plaɪwʊd] *n* madera contrachapada.

p.m. [pi:'em] *abbr of* **post meridiem** *(after noon)*, después del mediodía; **at 2 p.m.**, a las dos de la tarde.

PM [pi:'em] *GB fam abbr of* **Prime Minister.**

PMT [pi:em'ti:] *fam abbr of* **premenstrual tension.**

pneumatic [nju'mætɪk] *adj* neumático,-a.

pneumonia [nju:'məʊnɪə] *n* pulmonía *f.*

PO [pi:'əʊ] *abbr of* **Post Office.**

poach [pəʊtʃ] *vtr* **1 to p. fish/game**, pescar/cazar furtivamente. **2** *fig fam (steal)* birlar.

poach² [pəʊtʃ] *vtr Culin (egg)* escalfar; *(fish)* hervir.

poacher ['pəʊtʃər] *n* pescador/cazador furtivo.

pocket ['pɒkɪt] **I** *n* **1** bolsillo *m; fig* **to be £10 in/out of p.**, salir ganando/perdiendo 10 libras; **p. money**, dinero *m* de bolsillo. **2** *(of air)* bolsa *f.* **3** *(of resistance)* foco *m.* **II** *vtr (money)* embolsar.

pocketbook ['pɒkɪtbʊk] *n US* bolso *m.*

pocketknife ['pɒkɪtnaɪf] *n* navaja *f.*

pod [pɒd] *n* vaina *f.*

podgy ['pɒdʒɪ] *adj (podgier, podgiest)* gordinflón,-ona, regordete.

podium ['pəʊdɪəm] *n* podio *m.*

poem ['pəʊɪm] *n* poema *m.*

poet ['pəʊɪt] *n* poeta *mf.*

poetic [pəʊ'etɪk] *adj* poético,-a.

poetry ['pəʊɪtrɪ] *n* poesía *f.*

poignant ['pɔɪnjənt] *adj* conmovedor,-a.

point [pɔɪnt] **I** *n* **1** *(sharp end)* punta *f.* **2** *(place)* punto *m; fig* **p. of no return**, punto sin retorno. **3** *(quality)* **good/bad p.**, cualidad buena/mala; **weak/strong p.**, punto débil/fuerte. **4** *(moment)* **at that p.**, en aquel momento; **from that p. onwards**, desde entonces; **to be on the p. of doing sth**, estar a punto de hacer algo. **5** *(score)* punto *m*, tanto *m;* **to win on points**, ganar por puntos; **match p.**, *(in tennis)* pelota *f* de match. **6** *(in argument)* punto *m;* **to make one's p.**, insistir en el argumento; **I take your p.**, entiendo lo que quieres decir. **7** *(purpose)* propósito *m;* **I don't see the p.**, no veo el sentido; **that isn't the p.**, **it's beside the p.**, eso no viene al caso; **there's no p. in going**, no merece la pena ir; **to come to the p.**, llegar al meollo de la cuestión. **8** *(on scale)* punto *m; (in share index)* entero *m;* **six p. three**, seis coma tres; *fig* **up to a p.**, hasta cierto punto. **9** *Geog* punta *f.* **10 power p.**, toma *f* de corriente. **11 points**, *Aut* platinos *mpl; Rail* agujas *fpl.* **II** *vtr (way etc)* señalar, indicar; **to p. a gun at sb**, apuntar a algn con una pistola. **III** *vi* señalar, indicar; **to p. at sth/sb**, señalar algo/a algn con el dedo. ◆**point out** *vtr* indicar, señalar; *(mention)* hacer resaltar.

point-blank [pɔɪnt'blæŋk] **I** *adj* a quemarropa; *(refusal)* rotundo,-a. **II** *adv (shoot)* a quemarropa; *(refuse)* rotundamente.

pointed ['pɔɪntɪd] *adj (sharp)* puntiagudo,-a; *fig (comment)* intencionado,-a; *(cutting)* mordaz. ◆**pointedly** *adv fig (significantly)* con intención; *(cuttingly)* con mordacidad.

pointer ['pɔɪntər] *n* **1** *(indicator)* indicador *m*, aguja *f; (for map)* puntero *m.* **2** *(dog)* perro *m* de muestra.

pointless ['pɔɪntlɪs] *adj* sin sentido.

poise [pɔɪz] **I** *n (bearing)* porte *m; (self-assurance)* aplomo *m.* **II** *vtr fig* **to be poised to do sth**, estar listo,-a para hacer algo.

poison ['pɔɪzən] **I** *n* veneno *m.* **II** *vtr* envenenar.

poisoning ['pɔɪzənɪŋ] *n* envenenamiento *m*; (*by food etc*) intoxicación *f*.

poisonous ['pɔɪzənəs] *adj* (*plant, snake*) venenoso,-a; (*gas*) tóxico,-a; *fig* (*rumour*) pernicioso,-a.

poke [pəʊk] *vtr* (*with finger or stick*) dar con la punta del dedo *or* del bastón a; **to p. one's head out**, asomar la cabeza; **to p. the fire**, atizar el fuego. ◆**poke about, poke around** *vi* fisgonear, hurgar en. ◆**poke out** *vtr* (*eye*) sacar.

poker¹ ['pəʊkər] *n* (*for fire*) atizador *m*.

poker² ['pəʊkər] *n* Cards póquer *m*.

poker-faced ['pəʊkəfeɪst] *adj fam* de cara impasible.

poky ['pəʊkɪ] *adj* (*pokier, pokiest*) US fam pej minúsculo,-a; **a p. little room**, un cuartucho.

Poland ['pəʊlənd] *n* Polonia.

polar ['pəʊlər] *adj* polar; **p. bear**, oso *m* polar.

Pole [pəʊl] *n* polaco,-a *m,f*.

pole¹ [pəʊl] *n* palo *m*; **p. vault**, salto *m* con pértiga.

pole² [pəʊl] *n* Geog polo *m*; *fig* **to be poles apart**, ser polos opuestos.

police [pə'liːs] I *npl* policía *f sing*; **p. car**, coche *m* patrulla; **p. constable**, policía *m*; **p. force**, cuerpo *m* de policía; **p. record**, antecedentes *mpl* penales; **p. state**, estado *m* policial; **p. station**, comisaría *f*. II *vtr* vigilar.

policeman [pə'liːsmən] *n* policía *m*.

policewoman [pə'liːswʊmən] *n* (mujer *f*) policía *f*.

policy ['pɒlɪsɪ] *n* Pol política *f*; (*of company*) norma *f*, principio *m*; Ins póliza *f* (de seguros).

polio ['pəʊlɪəʊ] *n* poliomielitis *f*.

polish ['pɒlɪʃ] I *vtr* pulir; (*furniture*) encerar; (*shoes*) limpiar; (*silver*) sacar brillo a. II *n* 1 (*for furniture*) cera *f*; (*for shoes*) betún *m*; (*for nails*) esmalte *m*. 2 (*shine*) brillo *m*; *fig* (*refinement*) refinamiento *m*. ◆**polish off** *vtr fam* (*work*) despachar; (*food*) zamparse. ◆**polish up** *vtr fig* perfeccionar.

Polish ['pəʊlɪʃ] I *adj* polaco,-a. II *n* 1 **the P.**, *pl* los polacos. 2 (*language*) polaco *m*.

polished ['pɒlɪʃt] *adj fig* (*manners*) refinado,-a; (*style*) pulido,-a; (*performance*) impecable.

polite [pə'laɪt] *adj* educado,-a.

politeness [pə'laɪtnɪs] *n* educación *f*.

politic ['pɒlɪtɪk] *adj* prudente.

political [pə'lɪtɪkəl] *adj* político,-a.

politician [pɒlɪ'tɪʃən] *n* político,-a *m,f*.

politics ['pɒlɪtɪks] *n* sing política *f*.

polka ['pɒlkə] *n* (*dance*) polca *f*; **p. dot**, lunar *m*.

poll [pəʊl] I *n* 1 votación *f*; **the polls**, las elecciones; **to go to the polls**, acudir a las urnas. 2 (*survey*) encuesta *f*; GB **p. tax**, contribución urbana. II *vtr* (*votes*)

obtener.

pollen ['pɒlən] *n* polen *m*.

polling ['pəʊlɪŋ] *n* votación *f*; **p. booth**, cabina *f* electoral; **p. station**, colegio *m* electoral.

pollute [pə'luːt] *vtr* contaminar.

pollution [pə'luːʃən] *n* contaminación *f*, polución *f*; **environmental p.**, contaminación ambiental.

polo ['pəʊləʊ] *n* Sport polo *m*; **p. neck** (*sweater*), jersey *m* de cuello vuelto.

polyester [pɒlɪ'estər] *n* poliéster *m*.

polymer ['pɒlɪmər] *n* Chem polímero *m*.

Polynesia [pɒlɪ'niːzɪə] *n* Polinesia.

polystyrene [pɒlɪ'staɪriːn] *n* poliestireno *m*.

polytechnic [pɒlɪ'teknɪk] *n* escuela politécnica, politécnico *m*.

polythene ['pɒlɪθiːn] *n* polietileno *m*.

pomegranate ['pɒmɪɡrænɪt] *n* granada *f*.

pomp [pɒmp] *n* pompa *f*.

pompom ['pɒmpɒm], **pompon** ['pɒmpɒn] *n* borla *f*, pompón *m*.

pompous ['pɒmpəs] *adj* (*person*) presumido,-a; (*speech*) rimbombante.

pond [pɒnd] *n* estanque *m*.

ponder ['pɒndər] I *vtr* considerar. II *vi* **to p. over sth**, meditar sobre algo.

ponderous ['pɒndərəs] *adj* pesado,-a.

pong [pɒŋ] *n* GB fam hedor *m*.

pontoon¹ [pɒn'tuːn] *n* Constr pontón *m*.

pontoon² [pɒn'tuːn] *n* Cards veintiuna *f*.

pony ['pəʊnɪ] *n* poney *m*.

ponytail ['pəʊnɪteɪl] *n* cola *f* de caballo.

poodle ['puːdəl] *n* caniche *m*.

poof [pʊf] *n* GB sl offens marica *m*.

pool¹ [puːl] *n* (*of water, oil etc*) charco *m*; (*pond*) estanque *m*; (*in river*) pozo *m*; **swimming p.**, piscina *f*.

pool² [puːl] I *n* 1 (*common fund*) fondo *m* común. 2 **typing p.**, servicio *m* de mecanografía. 3 US (*snooker*) billar americano. 4 GB **football pools**, quinielas *fpl*. II *vtr* (*funds*) reunir; (*ideas, resources*) juntar.

poor [pʊər, pɔːr] I *adj* pobre; (*quality*) malo,-a; *fam* **you p. thing!**, ¡pobrecito!. II *npl* **the p.**, los pobres.

poorly ['pʊəlɪ, 'pɔːlɪ] I *adv* (*badly*) mal. II *adj* (*poorlier, poorliest*) (*ill*) mal, malo,-a.

pop [pɒp] I *vtr* (*burst*) hacer reventar; (*cork*) hacer saltar. II *vi* (*burst*) reventar; (*cork*) saltar; *fam* **I'm just popping over to Ian's**, voy un momento a casa de Ian. III *n* 1 (*noise*) pequeña explosión. 2 *fam* (*drink*) gaseosa *f*. 3 *fam* (*father*) papá *m*. 4 Mus *fam* música *f* pop; **p. singer**, cantante *mf* pop. ◆**pop in** *vi fam* entrar un momento, pasar.

popcorn ['pɒpkɔːn] *n* palomitas *fpl*.

Pope [pəʊp] *n* **the P.**, el Papa.

poplar ['pɒplər] *n* álamo *m*.

poppy ['pɒpɪ] *n* amapola *f*.

populace ['pɒpjʊləs] *n* (*people*) pueblo *m*.

popular ['pɒpjʊlər] *adj* popular; *(fashionable)* de moda; *(common)* corriente.

popularity [pɒpjʊ'lærɪtɪ] *n* popularidad *f*.

popularize ['pɒpjʊləraɪz] *vtr* popularizar.

populate ['pɒpjʊleɪt] *vtr* poblar.

population [pɒpjʊ'leɪʃən] *n* población *f*; **the p. explosion**, la explosión demográfica.

porcelain ['pɔːslɪn] *n* porcelana *f*.

porch [pɔːtʃ] *n (of church)* pórtico *m*; *(of house)* porche *m*, entrada *f*; *US (veranda)* terraza *f*.

porcupine ['pɔːkjʊpaɪn] *n* puerco *m* espín.

pore¹ [pɔːr] *vi* **to p. over sth**, leer *or* estudiar algo detenidamente.

pore² [pɔːr] *n Anat* poro *m*.

pork [pɔːk] *n* carne *f* de cerdo.

pornography [pɔː'nɒgrəfɪ] *n* pornografía *f*.

porous ['pɔːrəs] *adj* poroso,-a.

porpoise ['pɔːpəs] *n* marsopa *f*.

porridge ['pɒrɪdʒ] *n* gachas *fpl* de avena.

port¹ [pɔːt] *n (harbour)* puerto *m*; **p. of call**, puerto de escala.

port² [pɔːt] *n Naut Av (larboard)* babor *m*.

port³ [pɔːt] *n (wine)* vino *m* de Oporto, oporto *m*.

portable ['pɔːtəbəl] *adj* portátil.

portent ['pɔːtent] *n fml* augurio *m*, presagio *m*.

porter ['pɔːtər] *n (in hotel etc)* portero,-a *m,f*; *Rail* mozo *m* de estación; *US* mozo de los coches-cama.

portfolio [pɔːt'fəʊlɪəʊ] *n (file)* carpeta *f*; *(of artist, politician)* cartera *f*.

porthole ['pɔːthəʊl] *n* portilla *f*.

portion ['pɔːʃən] *n (part, piece)* parte *f*, porción *f*; *(of food)* ración *f*. ◆**portion out** *vtr* repartir.

portly ['pɔːtlɪ] *adj (portlier, portliest)* corpulento,-a.

portrait ['pɔːtrɪt, 'pɔːtreɪt] *n* retrato *m*.

portray [pɔː'treɪ] *vtr (paint portrait of)* retratar; *(describe)* describir; *Theat* representar.

Portugal ['pɔːtjʊgəl] *n* Portugal.

Portuguese [pɔːtjʊ'giːz] **I** *adj* portugués,-esa. **II** *n (person)* portugués, -esa *m,f*; *(language)* portugués *m*.

pose [pəʊz] **I** *vtr (problem)* plantear; *(threat)* representar. **II** *vi (for painting)* posar; *pej (behave affectedly)* hacer pose; **to p. as**, hacerse pasar por. **III** *n (stance)* postura *f*; *pej (affectation)* pose *f*.

posh [pɒʃ] *GB fam* **I** *adj* elegante, de lujo; *(person)* presumido,-a; *(accent)* de clase alta.

position [pə'zɪʃən] **I** *n* **1** posición *f*; *(location)* situación *f*; *(rank)* rango *m*; **to be in a p. to do sth**, estar en condiciones de hacer algo. **2** *(opinion)* postura *f*. **3** *(job)* puesto *m*. **II** *vtr* colocar.

positive ['pɒzɪtɪv] *adj* positivo,-a; *(sign)* favorable; *(proof)* incontrovertible; *(sure)* seguro,-a; *fam (absolute)* auténtico,-a.

possess [pə'zes] *vtr* poseer; *(of fear)* apoderarse de.

possessed [pə'zest] *adj* poseído,-a.

possession [pə'zeʃən] *n* posesión *f*; **possessions**, bienes *mpl*.

possessive [pə'zesɪv] *adj* posesivo,-a.

possibility [pɒsɪ'bɪlɪtɪ] *n* posibilidad *f*; **possibilities**, *(potential)* potencial *m sing*.

possible ['pɒsɪbəl] *adj* posible; **as much as p.**, todo lo posible; **as often as p.**, cuanto más mejor; **as soon as p.**, cuanto antes. ◆**possibly** *adv* posiblemente; *(perhaps)* tal vez, quizás; **I can't p. come**, no puedo venir de ninguna manera.

post¹ [pəʊst] **I** *n (of wood)* poste *m*. **II** *(fix)* fijar.

post² [pəʊst] **I** *n (job)* puesto *m*; *US* **trading p.**, factoría *f*. **II** *vtr* enviar.

post³ [pəʊst] *GB* **I** *n (mail)* correo *m*; **by p.**, por correo; **p. office**, oficina *f* de correos; **P. Office Box**, apartado *m* de correos. **II** *vtr (letter)* echar al correo; **to p. sth to sb**, mandar algo por correo a algn.

postage ['pəʊstɪdʒ] *n* franqueo *m*.

postal ['pəʊstəl] *adj* postal, de correos; **p. order**, giro *m* postal; **p. vote**, voto *m* por correo.

postbox ['pəʊstbɒks] *n GB* buzón *m*.

postcard ['pəʊstkɑːd] *n* (tarjeta *f*) postal *f*.

postcode ['pəʊstkəʊd] *n GB* código *m* postal.

postdate [pəʊst'deɪt] *vtr* poner fecha adelantada a.

poster ['pəʊstər] *n* póster *m*; *(advertising)* cartel *m*.

posterior [pɒ'stɪərɪər] **I** *n hum* trasero *m*, pompis *m*. **II** *adj* posterior.

posterity [pɒ'sterɪtɪ] *n* posteridad *f*.

postgraduate [pəʊst'grædjʊɪt] **I** *n* posgraduado,-a *m,f*. **II** *adj* de posgraduado.

posthumous ['pɒstjʊməs] *adj* póstumo, -a.

postman ['pəʊstmən] *n GB* cartero *m*.

postmark ['pəʊstmɑːk] *n* matasellos *m inv*.

postmaster ['pəʊstmɑːstər] *n* administrador *m* de correos; **p. general**, director *m* general de correos.

postmortem [pəʊst'mɔːtəm] *n* autopsia *f*.

postpone [pəʊst'pəʊn, pə'spəʊn] *vtr* aplazar.

postscript ['pəʊskrɪpt] *n* posdata *f*.

posture ['pɒstʃər] **I** *n* postura *f*; *(affected)* pose *f*. **II** *vi* adoptar una pose.

postwar ['pəʊstwɔːr] *adj* de la posguerra.

posy ['pəʊzɪ] *n* ramillete *m*.

pot [pɒt] **I** *n (container)* tarro *m*, pote *m*; *(for cooking)* olla *f*; *(for flowers)* maceta *f*;

fam to go to p., irse al traste; **p. shot,** tiro *m* al azar. II *vtr (plant)* poner en una maceta.

potassium |pə'tæsiəm| *n* potasio *m*.

potato |pə'teɪtəʊ| *n (pl* **potatoes)** patata *f.*

potent |'pəʊtənt| *adj* potente.

potential |pə'tenʃəl| I *adj* potencial, posible. II *n* potencial *m*. ◆**potentially** *adv* en potencia.

pothole |'pɒthəʊl| *n Geol* cueva *f; (in road)* bache *m*.

potholing |'pɒthəʊlɪŋ| *n GB* espeleología *f.*

potion |'pəʊʃən| *n* poción *f*, pócima *f*.

potluck |pɒt'lʌk| *n fam* to take p., conformarse con lo que haya.

potted |'pɒtɪd| *adj (food)* en conserva; *(plant)* en maceta *or* tiesto.

potter¹ |'pɒtər| *n* alfarero,-a *m,f*.

potter² |'pɒtər| *vi GB* to p. about *or* **around,** entretenerse.

pottery |'pɒtərɪ| *n (craft, place)* alfarería *f; (objects)* cerámica *f.*

potty¹ |'pɒtɪ| *adj (pottier, pottiest) GB fam* chiflado,-a.

potty² |'pɒtɪ| *n fam* orinal *m*.

pouch |paʊtʃ| *n* 1 bolsa *f; (for ammunition)* morral *m; (for tobacco)* petaca *f*. 2 *Zool* bolsa *f* abdominal.

poultry |'pəʊltrɪ| *n (live)* aves *fpl* de corral; *(food)* pollos *mpl.*

pounce |paʊns| *vi* to p. on, abalanzarse encima de.

pound¹ |paʊnd| I *vtr (strike)* aporrear. II *vi (heart)* palpitar; *(walk heavily)* andar con paso pesado.

pound² |paʊnd| *n (money, weight)* libra *f*.

pound³ |paʊnd| *n (for dogs)* perrera *f; (for cars)* depósito *m* de coches.

pour |pɔːr| I *vtr* echar, verter; to p. sb a drink, servirle una copa a algn. II *vi* correr, fluir; it's pouring with rain, está lloviendo a cántaros. ◆**pour out** *vtr* echar, verter; *fig* to p. one's heart out to sb, desahogarse con algn.

pouring |'pɔːrɪŋ| *adj (rain)* torrencial.

pout |paʊt| I *vi* hacer pucheros. II *n* puchero *m*.

poverty |'pɒvətɪ| *n* pobreza *f*.

poverty-stricken |'pɒvətɪstrɪkən| *adj* necesitado,-a; **to be p.-s.,** vivir en la miseria.

powder |'paʊdər| I *n* polvo *m;* **p. compact,** polvera *f;* **p. keg,** polvorín *m;* **p. puff,** borla *f;* **p. room,** servicios *mpl* de señoras. II *vtr* to p. one's nose, ponerse polvos en la cara; *euph* ir a los servicios *or* al tocador.

powdered |'paʊdəd| *adj (milk)* en polvo.

power |'paʊər| I *n* 1 fuerza *f; (energy)* energía *f; Elec* **to cut off the p.,** cortar la corriente; **p. point,** enchufe *m;* **p. station,** central eléctrica. 2 *(ability)* poder

m. 3 *(authority)* poder *m; (nation)* potencia *f; (influence)* influencia *f;* **to be in p.,** estar en el poder; *Pol* **to come into p.,** subir al poder; **the p. of veto,** el derecho de veto. 4 *Tech* potencia *f; (output)* rendimiento *m*. II *vtr* propulsar, impulsar.

powerboat |'paʊəbəʊt| *n* lancha *f* (motora).

powerful |'paʊəfʊl| *adj (strong)* fuerte; *(influential)* poderoso,-a; *(remedy)* eficaz; *(engine, machine)* potente; *(emotion)* fuerte; *(speech)* conmovedor,-a.

powerless |'paʊəlɪs| *adj* impotente, ineficaz.

pp *abbr of* **pages,** págs., pp.

PR |piː'ɑːr| *abbr of* **public relations.**

practicable |'præktɪkəbəl| *adj* factible.

practical |'præktɪkəl| *adj* práctico,-a; *(useful)* útil; *(sensible)* adecuado,-a. ◆**practically** *adv (almost)* casi.

practicality |præktɪ'kælɪtɪ| *n (of suggestion, plan)* factibilidad *f;* **practicalities,** detalles prácticos.

practice |'præktɪs| I *n* 1 *(habit)* costumbre *f*. 2 *(exercise)* práctica *f; Sport* entrenamiento *m; Mus* ensayo *m;* **to be out of p.,** no estar en forma. 3 *(way of doing sth)* práctica *f;* **in p.,** en la práctica; **to put sth into p.,** poner algo en práctica. 4 *(of profession)* ejercicio *m*. 5 *(place) (of doctors)* consultorio *m; (of lawyers)* bufete *m*. 6 *(clients) (of doctors)* pacientes *mpl; (of lawyers)* clientela *f*. II *vtr & vi US →* **practise.**

practise |'præktɪs| I *vtr* practicar; *(method)* seguir; *(principle)* poner en práctica; *Mus* ensayar; *(profession)* ejercer. II *vi* practicar; *Sport* entrenar; *Mus* ensayar; *(doctor)* practicar; *(lawyer)* ejercer.

practising, *US* **practicing** |'præktɪsɪŋ| *adj (doctor etc)* en ejercicio; *(Christian etc)* practicante.

practitioner |præk'tɪʃənər| *n GB Med* **general p.,** médico,-a *m,f* de cabecera; **medical p.,** médico,-a *m,f.*

pragmatic |præg'mætɪk| *adj* pragmático,-a.

prairie |'preərɪ| *n* pradera *f; US* llanura *f*.

praise |preɪz| I *n* alabanza *f*. II *vtr* alabar, elogiar.

praiseworthy |'preɪzwɜːðɪ| *adj* loable.

pram |præm| *n GB* cochecito *m* de niño.

prance |prɑːns| *vi (horse)* encabritarse; **to p. about,** *(person)* pegar brincos.

prank |præŋk| *n* broma *f; (of child)* travesura *f*.

prawn |prɔːn| *n* gamba *f*.

pray |preɪ| *vi* rezar, orar.

prayer |preər| *n* rezo *m*, oración *f; (entreaty)* súplica *f;* **p. book,** misal *m*.

preach |priːtʃ| *vi* predicar.

preacher |'priːtʃər| *n* predicador,-a *m,f.*

precarious [prɪ'keərɪəs] *adj* precario,-a.
precaution [prɪ'kɔ:ʃən] *n* precaución *f.*
precede [prɪ'si:d] *vtr* preceder.
precedence ['presɪdəns] *n* preferencia *f,* prioridad *f;* **to take p. over sth/sb,** tener prioridad sobre algo/algn.
precedent ['presɪdənt] *n* precedente *m.*
preceding [prɪ'si:dɪŋ] *adj* precedente.
precinct [prɪ'sɪŋkt] *n* recinto *m; US (district)* distrito *m;* **pedestrian/shopping p.,** zona *f* peatonal/comercial.
precious ['preʃəs] I *adj* precioso,-a; **p. stones,** piedras preciosas. II *adv fam* **little/few,** muy poco/pocos.
precipice ['presɪpɪs] *n* precipicio *m.*
precipitate [prɪ'sɪpɪteɪt] I *vtr* precipitar; *fig* arrojar. II *adj* precipitado,-a.
precise [prɪ'saɪs] *adj* preciso,-a, exacto,-a; *(meticulous)* meticuloso,-a. ◆**precisely** *adv (exactly)* precisamente, exactamente; **p.!,** ¡eso es!, ¡exacto!
precision [prɪ'sɪʒən] *n* precisión *f.*
preclude [prɪ'klu:d] *vtr* excluir; *(misunderstanding)* evitar.
precocious [prɪ'kəʊʃəs] *adj* precoz.
preconceived [pri:kən'si:vd] *adj* preconcebido,-a.
precondition [pri:kən'dɪʃən] *n* condición previa.
precursor [prɪ'kɜ:sər] *n* precursor,-a *m,f.*
predator ['predətər] *n* depredador *m.*
predecessor ['pri:dɪsesər] *n* antecesor,-a *m,f.*
predetermine [pri:dɪ'tɜ:mɪn] *vtr* predeterminar.
predicament [prɪ'dɪkəmənt] *n* apuro *m,* aprieto *m.*
predict [prɪ'dɪkt] *vtr* predecir, pronosticar.
predictable [prɪ'dɪktəbəl] *adj* previsible.
prediction [prɪ'dɪkʃən] *n* pronóstico *m.*
predispose [pri:dɪs'pəʊz] *vtr* **to be predisposed to doing sth,** estar predispuesto,-a a hacer algo.
predominant [prɪ'dɒmɪnənt] *adj* predominante. ◆**predominantly** *adv* en su mayoría.
predominate [prɪ'dɒmɪneɪt] *vi* predominar.
pre-empt [prɪ'empt] *vtr* adelantarse a.
preen [pri:n] *vtr* **to p. oneself,** *(of bird)* arreglarse las plumas; *fig (of person)* pavonearse.
prefab ['pri:fæb] *n GB fam (house)* casa prefabricada.
prefabricated [pri:'fæbrɪkeɪtɪd] *adj* prefabricado,-a.
preface ['prefɪs] I *n* prefacio *m.* II *vtr* prologar.
prefect ['pri:fekt] *n GB Educ* monitor,-a *m,f.*
prefer [prɪ'fɜ:r] *vtr* preferir; **I p. coffee to tea,** prefiero el café al té.
preferable ['prefərəbəl] *adj* preferible

(to, a). ◆**preferably** *adv* preferentemente.
preference ['prefərəns] *n* preferencia *f; (priority)* prioridad *f;* **to give p. to sth,** dar prioridad a algo.
preferential [prefə'renʃəl] *adj* preferente.
prefix ['pri:fɪks] *n* prefijo *m.*
pregnancy ['pregnənsɪ] *n* embarazo *m.*
pregnant ['pregnənt] *adj (woman)* embarazada; *(animal)* preñada; *fig* **a p. pause,** una pausa cargada de significado.
prehistoric(al) [pri:hɪ'stɒrɪk(əl)] *adj* prehistórico,-a.
prejudice ['predʒʊdɪs] I *n (bias)* prejuicio *m; (harm)* perjuicio *m.* II *vtr (bias)* predisponer; *(harm)* perjudicar.
prejudiced ['predʒʊdɪst] *adj* parcial; **to be p. against/in favour of,** estar predispuesto,-a en contra/a favor de.
preliminary [prɪ'lɪmɪnərɪ] I *adj* preliminar; *Sport (round)* eliminatorio,-a. II *n* **preliminaries,** preliminares *mpl.*
prelude ['prelju:d] *n* preludio *m.*
premarital [pri:'mærɪtəl] *adj* prematrimonial.
premature [premə'tjʊər, 'premətjʊər] *adj* prematuro,-a. ◆**prematurely** *adv* antes de tiempo.
premeditate [prɪ'medɪteɪt] *vtr (crime)* premeditar.
premenstrual [pri:'menstrʊəl] *adj* **p. tension,** tensión *f* premenstrual.
premier ['premjər] I *n Pol* primer,-a ministro,-a *m,f.* II *adj* primer, primero, -a.
premiere ['premɪeər] *n Cin* estreno *m.*
premise ['premɪs] *n* premisa *f.*
premises ['premɪsɪz] *npl* local *m sing;* **on the p.,** en el local.
premium ['pri:mɪəm] *n Com Fin Ind* prima *f;* **to be at a p.,** tener sobreprecio; *fig* estar muy solicitado,-a; *GB* **p. bonds,** bonos cotizados sobre la par.
premonition [premə'nɪʃən] *n* presentimiento *m.*
preoccupied [pri:'ɒkjʊpaɪd] *adj* preocupado,-a; **to be p. with sth,** preocuparse por algo.
prep [prep] 1 *fam abbr of* **preparation,** deberes *mpl.* 2 *abbr of* **preparatory school.**
prepaid [pri:'peɪd] *adj* con el porte pagado.
preparation [prepə'reɪʃən] *n* preparación *f; (plan)* preparativo *m; GB Educ (homework)* deberes *mpl.*
preparatory [prɪ'pærətərɪ] *adj* preparatorio,-a, preliminar; **p. school,** escuela primaria privada.
prepare [prɪ'peər] I *vtr* preparar; **to p. to do sth,** prepararse para hacer algo. II *vi* prepararse (**for,** para).
prepared [prɪ'peəd] *adj (ready)* preparado,-a; **to be p. to do sth,** *(willing)*

estar dispuesto,-a a hacer algo.

preponderance [prɪ'pɒndərəns] n preponderancia f.

preposition [prepə'zɪʃən] n preposición f.

preposterous [prɪ'pɒstərəs] adj absurdo,-a, ridículo,-a.

prerequisite [priː'rekwɪzɪt] n condición f previa.

prerogative [prɪ'rɒgətɪv] n prerrogativa f.

preschool [priː'skuːl] adj preescolar.

prescribe [prɪ'skraɪb] vtr (set down) prescribir; Med recetar; fig (recommend) recomendar.

prescription [prɪ'skrɪpʃən] n Med receta f.

presence ['prezəns] n presencia f; (attendance) asistencia f; fig p. of mind, presencia de ánimo.

present¹ ['prezənt] I adj 1 (in attendance) presente; Ling p. tense, (tiempo m) presente m; to be p. at, estar presente en. 2 (current) actual. II n (time) presente m, actualidad f; at p., actualmente; for the p., de momento; up to the p., hasta ahora. ◆**presently** adv (soon) dentro de poco; US (now) ahora.

present² ['prezənt] I vtr 1 (give as gift) regalar; (medals, prizes etc) entregar; to p. sb with sth, obsequiar a algn con algo. 2 (report etc) presentar; (opportunity) ofrecer; (problems) plantear. 3 (introduce) (person, programme) presentar. II ['prezənt] n (gift) regalo m; (formal) obsequio m.

presentable [prɪ'zentəbəl] adj presentable; to make oneself p., arreglarse.

presentation [prezən'teɪʃən] n 1 presentación f; p. ceremony, ceremonia f de entrega. 2 Rad TV representación f.

present-day ['prezəntdeɪ] adj actual, de hoy en día.

presenter [prɪ'zentər] n Rad locutor,-a m,f; TV presentador,-a m,f.

preservation [prezə'veɪʃən] n conservación f.

preservative [prɪ'zɜːvətɪv] n conservante m.

preserve [prɪ'zɜːv] I vtr 1 (keep) mantener. 2 Culin conservar. II n 1 (hunting) coto m. 2 Culin conserva f.

preside [prɪ'zaɪd] vi presidir.

president ['prezɪdənt] n Pol presidente,-a m,f; US Com director,-a m,f, gerente mf.

presidential [prezɪ'denʃəl] adj presidencial.

press [pres] I vtr 1 apretar; (button) pulsar; (grapes) pisar; (trousers etc) planchar. 2 (urge) presionar; to p. sb to do sth, acosar a algn para que haga algo. II vi (push) apretar; to p. against sb/sth, apretarse contra algn/algo; to p. (down) on sth, hacer presión sobre algo. 2 (urge) apremiar; time presses, el tiempo apre-

mia. III n 1 p. stud, botón m de presión. 2 (machine) prensa f; to go to p., entrar en prensa. 3 Press prensa f; the p., la prensa; to get a good/bad p., tener buena/mala prensa; p. agency, agencia f de prensa; p. conference, rueda f de prensa; p. cutting, recorte m de prensa. ◆**press on** vi seguir adelante.

pressed [prest] adj to be (hard) p. for, andar escaso,-a de; I'd be hard p. to do it, me costaría mucho hacerlo.

pressing ['presɪŋ] adj apremiante, urgente.

pressure ['preʃər] n presión f; Med Meteor high/low p., altas/bajas presiones; p. cooker, olla f a presión; p. gauge, manómetro m; fig to bring p. (to bear) on sb, ejercer presión sobre algn.

pressurize ['preʃəraɪz] vtr fig presionar; pressurized cabin, cabina presurizada.

prestige [pre'stiːʒ] n prestigio m.

presumably [prɪ'zjuːməblɪ] adv es de suponer que.

presume [prɪ'zjuːm] I vtr suponer, presumir. II vi (suppose) suponer; we p. so/not, suponemos que sí/no.

presumption [prɪ'zʌmpʃən] n 1 (supposition) suposición f. 2 (boldness) osadía f; (conceit) presunción f.

presumptuous [prɪ'zʌmptjʊəs] adj presuntuoso,-a.

presuppose [priːsə'pəʊz] vtr presuponer.

pretence, US **pretense** [prɪ'tens] n 1 (deception) fingimiento m; false pretences, estafa f sing; under the p. of, so pretexto de. 2 (claim) pretensión f.

pretend [prɪ'tend] I vtr (feign) fingir, aparentar; (claim) pretender. II vi (feign) fingir.

pretense [prɪ'tens] n US → pretence.

pretention [prɪ'tenʃən] n pretensión f.

pretentious [prɪ'tenʃəs] adj presuntuoso,-a, pretencioso,-a.

pretext ['priːtekst] n pretexto m; on the p. of, so pretexto de.

pretty ['prɪtɪ] I adj (prettier, prettiest) bonito,-a, guapo,-a. II adv fam bastante; p. much the same, más o menos lo mismo.

prevail [prɪ'veɪl] vi 1 predominar. 2 (win through) prevalecer. 3 to p. upon or on sb to do sth, (persuade) persuadir or convencer a algn para que haga algo.

prevailing [prɪ'veɪlɪŋ] adj (wind) predominante; (opinion) general; (condition, fashion) actual.

prevalent ['prevələnt] adj predominante; (illness) extendido,-a.

prevaricate [prɪ'værɪkeɪt] vi andar con ambages.

prevent [prɪ'vent] vtr impedir; (accident) evitar; (illness) prevenir; to p. sb from doing sth, impedir a algn hacer algo; to p. sth from happening, evitar que pase algo.

prevention |prɪ'venʃən| n prevención f.

preventive |prɪ'ventɪv| adj preventivo,-a.

preview |'priːvjuː| n (of film etc) preestreno m.

previous |'priːvɪəs| I adj anterior, previo,-a; **p. conviction,** antecedente m penal. II adv **p. to going,** antes de ir. ◆**previously** adv anteriormente, previamente.

prewar |'priːwɔːr| adj de antes de la guerra.

prey |preɪ| I n presa f; fig víctima f. II vi **to p. on,** alimentarse de.

price |praɪs| I n precio m; **what p. is that coat?,** ¿cuánto cuesta el abrigo?; **p. list,** lista f de precios; **p. tag,** etiqueta f. II vtr (put price on) poner un precio a; (value) valorar.

priceless |'praɪslɪs| adj que no tiene precio.

prick |prɪk| I vtr picar; **to p. one's finger,** pincharse el dedo; fig **to p. up one's ears,** aguzar el oído. II n 1 (with pin) pinchazo m. 2 sl (penis) polla f. 3 sl offens (person) gilipollas mf inv.

prickle |'prɪkəl| I n espina f; (spike) pincho m; (sensation) picor m. II vtr & vi pinchar, picar.

prickly |'prɪklɪ| adj (pricklier, prickliest) espinoso,-a; fig (touchy) enojadizo,-a; **p. heat,** sarpullido m por causa del calor; **p. pear,** higo chumbo.

pride |praɪd| I n orgullo m; (arrogance) soberbia f; **to take p. in sth,** enorgullecerse de algo. II vtr **to p. oneself on,** enorgullecerse de.

priest |priːst| n sacerdote m, cura m.

priestess |'priːstɪs| n sacerdotisa f.

priesthood |'priːsthʊd| n (clergy) clero m; (office) sacerdocio m.

prig |prɪg| n gazmoño,-a m,f, mojigato,-a m,f.

prim |prɪm| adj (primmer, primmest) **p.** (and proper), remilgado,-a.

prim(a)eval |praɪ'miːvəl| adj primitivo,-a.

primary |'praɪmərɪ| I adj fundamental, principal; **of p. importance,** primordial; **p. colour,** color primario; **p. education/school,** enseñanza/escuela primaria. II n US Pol (elección f) primaria f. ◆**primarily** adv ante todo.

primate¹ |'praɪmeɪt| n Rel primado m.

primate² |'praɪmeɪt| n Zool primate m.

prime |praɪm| I adj 1 principal; (major) primordial; **P. Minister,** primer ministro,-a m,f. 2 (first-rate) de primera; **p. number,** número primo. II n in the **p. of life** en la flor de la vida. III vtr (pump, engine) cebar; (surface) imprimar; fig (prepare) preparar.

primer¹ |'praɪmər| n (textbook) cartilla f.

primer² |'praɪmər| n (paint) imprimación f.

primitive |'prɪmɪtɪv| adj primitivo,-a; (method, tool) rudimentario,-a.

primrose |'prɪmrəʊz| n primavera f.

Primus® |'praɪməs| n hornillo m de camping.

prince |prɪns| n príncipe m; **P. Charming,** Príncipe Azul.

princess |prɪn'ses| n princesa f.

principal |'prɪnsɪpəl| I adj principal. II n Educ director,-a m,f; Theat (in play) protagonista mf principal.

principle |'prɪnsɪpəl| n principio m; **in p.,** en principio; **on p.,** por principio.

print |prɪnt| I vtr 1 imprimir; (publish) publicar; fig grabar; **printed matter,** impresos mpl. 2 (write) escribir con letra de imprenta. II n 1 (of hand, foot) huella f; Print letra f; **out of p.,** agotado,-a. 2 Tex estampado m; **p. skirt,** falda estampada. 3 Art grabado m; Phot copia f. ◆**print out** vtr Comput imprimir.

printer |'prɪntər| n (person) impresor,-a m,f; (machine) impresora f.

printing |'prɪntɪŋ| n (industry) imprenta f; (process) impresión f; (print run) tirada f; **p. press,** prensa f.

print-out |'prɪntaʊt| n Comput impresión f; (copy) copia impresa.

prior |'praɪər| adj previo,-a, anterior; **p. to leaving,** antes de salir.

priority |praɪ'ɒrɪtɪ| n prioridad f.

prise |praɪz| vtr **to p. sth open/off,** abrir algo con palanca.

prism |'prɪzəm| n prisma f.

prison |'prɪzən| n cárcel f, prisión f.

prisoner |'prɪzənər| n preso,-a m,f; **to hold sb p.,** detener a algn; **p. of war,** prisionero,-a m,f de guerra.

privacy |'praɪvəsɪ, 'prɪvəsɪ| n intimidad f.

private |'praɪvɪt| I adj privado,-a; (secretary) particular; (matter) personal; (letter) confidencial; **one's p. life,** la vida privada de uno; **'P.',** (notice) (on road) 'carretera privada'; (on gate) 'propiedad privada'; (on envelope) 'confidencial'; **p. detective,** fam **p. eye,** detective mf privado,-a; **p. school,** escuela privada. II n Mil soldado raso. ◆**privately** adv en privado; (personally) personalmente.

privet |'prɪvɪt| n alheña f.

privilege |'prɪvɪlɪdʒ| n privilegio m.

privileged |'prɪvɪlɪdʒd| adj privilegiado,-a.

privy |'prɪvɪ| I adj GB **P. Council,** Consejo Privado; **to be p. to sth,** estar enterado,-a de algo. II n (lavatory) retrete m.

prize |praɪz| I n premio m. II adj (first-class) de primera (categoría or clase). III vtr (value) apreciar, valorar.

prize-giving |'praɪzgɪvɪŋ| n distribución f de premios.

prizewinner |'praɪzwɪnər| n premiado,-a m,f.

pro¹ [prəʊ] n pro m; **the pros and cons of an issue**, los pros y los contras de una cuestión.

pro² [prəʊ] n (abbr of **professional**) fam profesional mf.

pro-³ [prəʊ] pref (in favour of) pro-.

probability [prɒbə'bɪlɪtɪ] n probabilidad f.

probable ['prɒbəbəl] adj probable.
◆**probably** adv probablemente.

probation [prə'beɪʃən] n Jur to be on p., estar en libertad condicional; **to be on two months' p.**, (at work) trabajar dos meses de prueba.

probe [prəʊb] I n Med Astronaut sonda f; (investigation) sondeo m. II vtr Med sondar; (investigate) investigar. ◆**probe into** vtr investigar.

problem ['prɒbləm] n problema m.

problematic(al) [prɒblə'mætɪk(əl)] adj problemático,-a; **it's p.**, tiene sus problemas.

procedure [prə'siːdʒər] n procedimiento m; (legal, business) gestión f, trámite m.

proceed [prə'siːd] vi seguir, proceder; to **p. to do sth**, ponerse a hacer algo; to **p. to the next matter**, pasar a la siguiente cuestión.

proceedings [prə'siːdɪŋz] npl (of meeting) actas fpl; (measures) medidas fpl; Jur proceso m sing.

proceeds ['prəʊsiːdz] npl ganancias fpl.

process ['prəʊses] I n proceso m; (method) método m, sistema m; **in the p. of**, en vías de. II vtr (information) tramitar; (food) tratar; Comput procesar.

processing ['prəʊsesɪŋ] n (of information) evaluación f; Comput tratamiento m.

procession [prə'seʃən] n desfile m; Rel procesión f.

proclaim [prə'kleɪm] vtr proclamar, declarar.

proclamation [prɒklə'meɪʃən] n proclamación f.

procrastinate [prəʊ'kræstɪneɪt] vi dejar las cosas para después.

procure [prə'kjʊər] vtr conseguir, procurarse.

prod [prɒd] vtr (with stick etc) golpear; (push) empujar.

prodigal ['prɒdɪgəl] adj pródigo,-a.

prodigious [prə'dɪdʒəs] adj prodigioso,-a.

prodigy ['prɒdɪdʒɪ] n prodigio m.

produce [prə'djuːs] I vtr 1 producir; Ind fabricar. 2 Theat dirigir; Rad TV realizar; Cin producir. 3 (give birth to) dar a luz a. 4 (document) enseñar; (bring out) sacar. II ['prɒdjuːs] n productos mpl; **p. of Spain**, producto m de España.

producer [prə'djuːsər] n 1 productor,-a m,f; Ind fabricante mf. 2 Theat director, -a m,f de escena; Rad TV realizador,-a m,f; Cin productor,-a m,f.

product ['prɒdʌkt] n producto m.

production [prə'dʌkʃən] n 1 producción f; Ind fabricación f. 2 Theat representación f; Rad TV realización f, Cin producción f; **p. line**, cadena f de montaje.

productive [prə'dʌktɪv] adj productivo, -a.

productivity [prɒdʌk'tɪvɪtɪ] n productividad f.

profane [prə'feɪn] adj (secular) profano,-a; (language) blasfemo,-a.

profess [prə'fes] vtr (faith) profesar; (opinion) expresar; (claim) pretender.

profession [prə'feʃən] n profesión f.

professional [prə'feʃənəl] I adj profesional; (soldier) de profesión; (polished) de gran calidad. II n profesional mf.

professor [prə'fesər] n catedrático,-a m,f.

proficiency [prə'fɪʃənsɪ] n (in language) capacidad f; (in skill) pericia f.

proficient [prə'fɪʃənt] adj (in language) experto,-a; (in skill) hábil.

profile ['prəʊfaɪl] n perfil m; **in p.**, de perfil.

profit ['prɒfɪt] I n 1 beneficio m, ganancia f; **to make a p. on**, sacar beneficios de. 2 fml (benefit) provecho m. II vi fig sacar provecho; **to p. from**, aprovecharse de.

profitability [prɒfɪtə'bɪlɪtɪ] n rentabilidad f.

profitable ['prɒfɪtəbəl] adj Com rentable; fig (worthwhile) provechoso,-a.

profiteer [prɒfɪ'tɪər] I n especulador,-a m,f. II vi obtener beneficios excesivos.

profound [prə'faʊnd] adj profundo,-a.

profuse [prə'fjuːs] adj profuso,-a, abundante. ◆**profusely** adv con profusión; **to sweat p.**, sudar mucho.

profusion [prə'fjuːʒən] n profusión f, abundancia f.

prognosis [prɒg'nəʊsɪs] n Med pronóstico m; fig (prediction) augurio m.

program ['prəʊgræm] Comput I n programa m. II vi & vtr programar.

programme, US program ['prəʊgræm] I n programa m; (plan) plan m. II vtr 1 (plan) planear, planificar. 2 (computer) programar.

programmer, US programer ['prəʊgræmər] n programador,-a m,f.

progress ['prəʊgres] I n progreso m; (development) desarrollo m; Med mejora f; **to make p.**, hacer progresos; **in p.**, en curso. II [prəʊ'gres] vi avanzar; (develop) desarrollar; (improve) hacer progresos; Med mejorar.

progressive [prə'gresɪv] adj (increasing) progresivo,-a; Pol progresista. ◆**progressively** adv progresivamente.

prohibit [prə'hɪbɪt] vtr prohibir; **to p. sb from doing sth**, prohibir a algn hacer algo.

prohibitive [prə'hɪbɪtɪv] adj prohibitivo, -a.

project ['prɒdʒekt] I n proyecto m; (plan)

plan *m*; *Educ* trabajo *m*. II [prə'dʒekt] *vtr* proyectar, planear. III *vi* (*stick out*) sobresalir.

projectile [prə'dʒektaɪl] *n fml* proyectil *m*.

projection [prə'dʒekʃən] *n* 1 (*overhang*) saliente *m*. 2 *Cin* proyección *f*. 3 (*forecast*) proyección *f*.

projector [prə'dʒektər] *n Cin* proyector *m*.

proletariat [prəʊlɪ'eərɪət] *n* proletariado *m*.

prolific [prə'lɪfɪk] *adj* prolífico,-a.

prologue ['prəʊlɒg] *n* prólogo *m*.

prolong [prə'lɒŋ] *vtr* prolongar.

prom [prɒm] *n* (*abbr of* **promenade**) *GB fam* (*seafront*) paseo marítimo *m*; (*concert*) concierto sinfónico en que parte del público está de pie.

promenade [prɒmə'nɑːd] I *n* (*at seaside*) paseo marítimo. II *vi* pasearse.

prominence ['prɒmɪnəns] *n* prominencia *f*; *fig* (*importance*) importancia *f*.

prominent ['prɒmɪnənt] *adj* (*standing out*) saliente; *fig* (*important*) importante; (*famous*) eminente.

promiscuous [prə'mɪskjʊəs] *adj* promiscuo,-a.

promise ['prɒmɪs] I *n* promesa *f*; **to show p.**, ser prometedor,-a. II *vtr & vi* prometer.

promising ['prɒmɪsɪŋ] *adj* prometedor,-a.

promontory ['prɒməntərɪ] *n* promontorio *m*.

promote [prə'məʊt] *vtr* ascender; (*product*) promocionar; (*ideas*) fomentar; *Ftb* **they've been promoted**, han subido.

promoter [prə'məʊtər] *n* promotor,-a *m,f*.

promotion [prə'məʊʃən] *n* (*in rank*) promoción *f*, ascenso *m*; (*of product*) promoción *f*; (*of arts etc*) fomento *m*.

prompt [prɒmpt] I *adj* (*quick*) rápido,-a; (*punctual*) puntual. II *adv* **at 2 o'clock p.**, a las 2 en punto. III *vtr* 1 (*motivate*) incitar; **to p. sb to do sth**, instar a algn a hacer algo. 2 (*actor*) apuntar. ◆**promptly** *adv* (*quickly*) rápidamente; (*punctually*) puntualmente.

prone [prəʊn] *adj* 1 **to be p. to do sth**, ser propenso,-a a hacer algo. 2 *fml* (*face down*) prono,-a.

prong [prɒŋ] *n* punta *f*, diente *m*.

pronoun ['prəʊnaʊn] *n* pronombre *m*.

pronounce [prə'naʊns] I *vtr* pronunciar; *fml* (*declare*) declarar. II *vi fml* **to p. on sth**, opinar sobre algo.

pronounced [prə'naʊnst] *adj* pronunciado,-a.

pronouncement [prə'naʊnsmənt] *n fml* declaración *f*.

pronunciation [prənʌnsɪ'eɪʃən] *n* pronunciación *f*.

proof [pruːf] I *n* prueba *f*. II *adj* 1 (*secure*)

a prueba de. 2 **this rum is 70% p.**, este ron tiene 70 grados. III *vtr* impermeabilizar.

prop¹ [prɒp] I *n* (*support*) puntal *m*; *fig* sostén *m*. II *vtr* (*support*) apoyar; *fig* sostener. ◆**prop up** *vtr* apoyar.

prop² [prɒp] *n Theat fam* accesorio *m*.

propaganda [prɒpə'gændə] *n* propaganda *f*.

propel [prə'pel] *vtr* propulsar.

propeller [prə'pelər] *n* hélice *f*.

propelling pencil [prəpelɪŋ'pensəl] *n* portaminas *m inv*.

propensity [prə'pensɪtɪ] *n fml* propensión *f*.

proper ['prɒpər] *adj* 1 adecuado,-a, correcto,-a; **the p. time**, el momento oportuno. 2 (*real*) real, auténtico,-a; (*actual, exact*) propiamente dicho,-a. 3 (*characteristic*) propio,-a; *Ling* **p. noun**, nombre propio. ◆**properly** *adv* (*suitably, correctly, decently*) correctamente; **it wasn't p. closed**, no estaba bien cerrado,-a; **she refused, quite p.**, se negó, y con razón.

property ['prɒpətɪ] *n* 1 (*quality*) propiedad *f*. 2 (*possession*) propiedad *f*, posesión *f*; **personal p.**, bienes *mpl*; **public p.**, dominio público. 3 (*estate*) finca *f*.

prophecy ['prɒfɪsɪ] *n* profecía *f*.

prophesy ['prɒfɪsaɪ] *vtr* (*predict*) predecir; *Rel* profetizar.

prophet ['prɒfɪt] *n* profeta *mf*.

proportion [prə'pɔːʃən] *n* proporción *f*; (*part, quantity*) parte *f*; **in p. to** *or* **with**, en proporción a.

proportional [prə'pɔːʃənəl] *adj* proporcional (**to, a**); *Pol* **p. representation**, representación *f* proporcional.

proportionate [prə'pɔːʃənɪt] *adj* proporcional.

proposal [prə'pəʊzəl] *n* propuesta *f*; (*suggestion*) sugerencia *f*; **p. of marriage**, propuesta de matrimonio.

propose [prə'pəʊz] I *vtr* proponer; (*suggest*) sugerir; *fml* (*intend*) tener la intención de. II *vi* declararse.

proposition [prɒpə'zɪʃən] *n* propuesta *f*; *Math* proposición *f*.

proprietor [prə'praɪətər] *n* propietario,-a *m,f*.

propriety [prə'praɪətɪ] *n* (*decency*) decoro *m*.

propulsion [prə'pʌlʃən] *n* propulsión *f*.

prosaic [prəʊ'zeɪɪk] *adj* prosaico,-a.

prose [prəʊz] *n Lit* prosa *f*; *Educ* texto *m* para traducir.

prosecute ['prɒsɪkjuːt] *vtr* procesar.

prosecution [prɒsɪ'kjuːʃən] *n* (*action*) proceso *m*, juicio *m*; **the p.**, la acusación.

prosecutor ['prɒsɪkjuːtər] *n* acusador,-a *m,f*.

prospect ['prɒspekt] I *n* (*outlook*) perspectiva *f*; (*hope*) esperanza *f*; **the job has**

prospects, es un trabajo con porvenir. II [prə'spekt] *vtr* explorar. III *vi* to p. for gold/oil, buscar oro/petróleo.

prospective [prə'spektɪv] *adj (future)* futuro,-a; *(possible)* eventual, probable.

prospector [prə'spektər] *n* gold p., buscador,-a *m,f* del oro.

prospectus [prə'spektəs] *n* prospecto *m.*

prosper ['prɒspər] *vi* prosperar.

prosperity [prɒ'sperɪtɪ] *n* prosperidad *f.*

prosperous ['prɒspərəs] *adj* próspero,-a.

prostitute ['prɒstɪtjuːt] *n* prostituta *f.*

prostitution [prɒstɪ'tjuːʃən] *n* prostitución *f.*

prostrate ['prɒstreɪt] *adj (face down)* boca abajo; p. with grief, deshecho de dolor.

protagonist [prəʊ'tægənɪst] *n* protagonista *mf.*

protect [prə'tekt] *vtr* proteger; *(interests etc)* salvaguardar; **to p. sb from sth,** proteger a algn de algo.

protection [prə'tekʃən] *n* protección *f.*

protective [prə'tektɪv] *adj* protector,-a.

protégé(e) ['prɒteʒeɪ] *n* protegido,-a *m,f.*

protein ['prəʊtiːn] *n* proteína *f.*

protest ['prəʊtest] I *n* protesta *f; (complaint)* queja *f.* II [prə'test] *vtr* protestar de. III *vi* GB protestar.

Protestant ['prɒtɪstənt] *adj & n* protestante *(mf).*

protester [prə'testər] *n* manifestante *mf.*

protocol ['prəʊtəkɒl] *n* protocolo *m.*

prototype ['prəʊtətaɪp] *n* prototipo *m.*

protracted [prə'træktɪd] *adj* prolongado,-a.

protrude [prə'truːd] *vi fml* sobresalir.

protuberance [prə'tjuːbərəns] *n fml* protuberancia *f.*

proud [praʊd] *adj* orgulloso,-a; *(arrogant)* soberbio,-a.

prove [pruːv] I *vtr* 1 probar, demostrar; *Math* comprobar; **to p. oneself,** dar pruebas de valor. 2 it proved to be disastrous, *(turned out)* resultó ser desastroso,-a.

proverb ['prɒvɜːb] *n* refrán *m,* proverbio *m.*

provide [prə'vaɪd] I *vtr* proporcionar; *(supplies)* suministrar, proveer. II *vi* proveer; **to p. for sb,** mantener a algn.

provided [prə'vaɪdɪd] *conj* p. (that), con tal de que.

providing [prə'vaɪdɪŋ] *conj* → provided.

province ['prɒvɪns] *n* provincia *f; fig (field of knowledge)* campo *m.*

provincial [prə'vɪnʃəl] I *adj* provincial; *pej* provinciano,-a. II *n pej (person)* provinciano,-a *m,f.*

provision [prə'vɪʒən] *n* provisión *f; (supply)* suministro *m;* **provisions,** *(food)* provisiones *fpl,* víveres *mpl.*

provisional [prə'vɪʒənəl] *adj* provisional.

proviso [prə'vaɪzəʊ] *n* with the p. that, a

condición de que.

provocation [prɒvə'keɪʃən] *n* provocación *f.*

provocative [prə'vɒkətɪv] *adj* provocador,-a; *(flirtatious)* provocativo,-a.

provoke [prə'vəʊk] *vtr* provocar.

prow [praʊ] *n* proa *f.*

prowess ['praʊɪs] *n* destreza *f.*

prowl [praʊl] I *n* merodeo *m;* **to be on the p.,** merodear, rondar. II *vi* merodear; *fam* **to p. about** *or* **around,** rondar.

prowler ['praʊlər] *n fam* merodeador *m.*

proximity [prɒk'sɪmɪtɪ] *n* proximidad *f;* in p. to, in the p. of, cerca de.

proxy ['prɒksɪ] *n Jur (power)* poderes *mpl; (person)* apoderado,-a *m,f;* by p., por poderes.

prudence ['pruːdəns] *n* prudencia *f.*

prudent ['pruːdənt] *adj* prudente.

prudish ['pruːdɪʃ] *adj* remilgado,-a.

prune¹ [pruːn] *n* ciruela pasa.

prune² [pruːn] *vtr (roses etc)* podar; *fig* acortar.

pry [praɪ] *vi* curiosear, husmear; **to p. into sb's affairs,** meterse en asuntos ajenos.

PS, ps [piː'es] *abbr of* (postscript), P.S., P.D.

psalm [sɑːm] *n* salmo *m.*

pseudo- ['sjuːdəʊ] *pref* pseudo-, seudo-.

pseudonym ['sjuːdənɪm] *n* (p)seudónimo *m.*

psyche ['saɪkɪ] *n* psique *f.*

psychiatric [saɪkɪ'ætrɪk] *adj* psiquiátrico,-a.

psychiatrist [saɪ'kaɪətrɪst] *n* psiquiatra *mf.*

psychiatry [saɪ'kaɪətrɪ] *n* psiquiatría *f.*

psychic ['saɪkɪk] I *adj* psíquico,-a. II *n* médium *mf.*

psychoanalysis [saɪkəʊə'nælɪsɪs] *n* psicoanálisis *f.*

psychoanalyst [saɪkəʊ'ænəlɪst] *n* psicoanalista *mf.*

psychological [saɪkə'lɒdʒɪkəl] *adj* psicológico,-a.

psychologist [saɪ'kɒlədʒɪst] *n* psicólogo,-a *m,f.*

psychology [saɪ'kɒlədʒɪ] *n* psicología *f.*

psychopath ['saɪkəʊpæθ] *n* psicópata *mf.*

PTO, pto [piːtiː'əʊ] *abbr of* please turn over, sigue.

pub [pʌb] *n GB fam* bar *m,* pub *m.*

puberty ['pjuːbətɪ] *n* pubertad *f.*

pubic ['pjuːbɪk] *adj* púbico,-a.

public ['pʌblɪk] I *adj* público,-a; **to make sth p.,** hacer público algo; p. **company,** empresa pública; p. **convenience,** servicios *mpl,* aseos *mpl;* p. **holiday,** fiesta *f* nacional; p. **house,** pub *m,* taberna *f;* p. **opinion,** opinión pública; p. **relations,** relaciones públicas; *GB* p. **school,** colegio privado; p. **transport,** transporte público. II *n* the p., el público; **in p.,** en

público.
public-address system |pʌblɪkə'dres sɪstəm| n megafonía f.
publican |'pʌblɪkən| n tabernero,-a m,f.
publication |pʌblɪ'keɪʃən| n publicación f.
publicity |pʌ'blɪsɪtɪ| n publicidad f.
publicize |'pʌblɪsaɪz| vtr (make public) hacer público,-a; (advertise) hacer publicidad a.
public-spirited |pʌblɪk'spɪrɪtɪd| adj de espíritu cívico.
publish |'pʌblɪʃ| vtr publicar, editar.
publisher |'pʌblɪʃər| n (person) editor,-a m,f; (firm) (casa f) editorial f.
publishing |'pʌblɪʃɪŋ| n (business) industria f editorial; **p. company** or **house**, casa f editorial.
pucker |'pʌkər| vtr (lips, brow) fruncir, arrugar.
pudding |'pʊdɪŋ| n Culin pudín m; (dessert) postre m; **Christmas p.**, pudín a base de frutos secos típico de Navidad; **p. basin**, cuenco m; **steamed p.**, budín m.
puddle |'pʌdəl| n charco m.
puff |pʌf| I n (of wind) racha f; (of smoke) bocanada f; (of pastry, pasta f de hojaldre. II vi (person) jadear, resoplar; (train) echar humo; **to p. on one's pipe**, chupar la pipa. III vtr (cigarette) dar una calada a. ◆**puff up** vi hincharse.
puffy |'pʌfɪ| adj (puffier, puffiest) hinchado,-a.
pugnacious |pʌg'neɪʃəs| adj belicoso,-a.
pull |pʊl| I n 1 to give sth a p., (tug) dar un tirón a algo. 2 (of engine) tracción f; fig (attraction) atracción f; (influence) enchufe m. II vtr 1 (tug) dar un tirón a; to **p. a muscle**, sufrir un tirón en un músculo; **to p. the trigger**, apretar el gatillo; **to p. to pieces**, hacer pedazos; fig poner algo por los suelos; fig **to p. sb's leg**, tomar el pelo a algn. 2 (draw) tirar, arrastrar; fig **to p. one's weight**, hacer su parte del trabajo. 3 (draw out) sacar. 4 fam (people) atraer. III vi (drag) tirar; to **p. alongside sb**, acercarse a algn. ◆**pull apart** vtr desmontar; fig (criticize) poner por los suelos. ◆**pull down** vtr (building) derribar. ◆**pull in** I vtr (crowds) atraer. II vi (train) entrar en la estación; (stop) parar. ◆**pull off** I vtr fam (carry out) llevar a cabo. II vi (vehicle) arrancar. ◆**pull out** I vtr (withdraw) retirar. II vi Aut **to p. out to overtake**, salir para adelantar. ◆**pull over** vi hacerse a un lado. ◆**pull through** vi reponerse, restablecerse. ◆**pull together** vtr **to p. oneself together**, calmarse. ◆**pull up** I vtr 1 (uproot) desarraigar; **to p. up one's socks**, subirse los calcetines; fig espabilarse. 2 (chair) acercar. II vi (stop) pararse.

pulley |'pʊlɪ| n polea f.
pullover |'pʊləʊvər| n jersey m.
pulp |pʌlp| I n (of paper, wood) pasta f; (of fruit) pulpa f; fam fig (book etc) basura f. II vtr reducir a pulpa.
pulpit |'pʊlpɪt| n púlpito m.
pulsate |pʌl'seɪt| vi vibrar, palpitar.
pulse¹ |pʌls| n Anat pulso m.
pulse² |pʌls| n Bot Culin legumbre f.
pumice (stone) |'pʌmɪs(stəʊn)| n piedra f pómez.
pummel |'pʌməl| vtr aporrear.
pump¹ |pʌmp| I n bomba f. II vtr bombear; **to p. sth in/out**, meter/sacar algo con una bomba; fam fig **to p. sb for information**, sonsacar información a algn. ◆**pump out** vtr (empty) vaciar. ◆**pump up** vtr (tyre) inflar.
pump² |pʌmp| n (shoe) zapatilla f.
pumpkin |'pʌmpkɪn| n calabaza f.
pun |pʌn| n juego m de palabras.
punch¹ |pʌntʃ| I n (for making holes) perforadora f; (for tickets) taladradora f; (in leather etc) punzón m. II vtr (make hole in) perforar; (in ticket) picar; (in leather) punzar.
punch² |pʌntʃ| I n (blow) puñetazo m; (in boxing) pegada f; fig **it lacks p.**, le falta fuerza; **p. line**, remate m (de un chiste). II vtr (with fist) dar un puñetazo a.
punch³ |pʌntʃ| n (drink) ponche m.
punch-up |'pʌntʃʌp| n fam pelea f.
punctual |'pʌŋktjʊəl| adj puntual.
punctuate |'pʌŋktjʊeɪt| vtr puntuar; fig salpicar.
punctuation |pʌŋktjʊ'eɪʃən| n puntuación f.
puncture |'pʌŋktʃər| I n pinchazo m. II vtr (tyre) pinchar.
pundit |'pʌndɪt| n fam experto,-a m,f.
pungent |'pʌndʒənt| adj (smell) acre; (taste) fuerte.
punish |'pʌnɪʃ| vtr castigar.
punishable |'pʌnɪʃəbəl| adj castigable, punible.
punishment |'pʌnɪʃmənt| n castigo m.
punk |pʌŋk| n fam 1 punk mf; **p. music**, música f punk. 2 US mamón m.
punt |pʌnt| I n (boat) batea f. II vi ir en batea.
punter |'pʌntər| n GB (gambler) jugador,-a m,f; (customer) cliente,-a m,f.
puny |'pjuːnɪ| adj (punier, puniest) enclenque, endeble.
pup |pʌp| n cachorro,-a m,f.
pupil¹ |'pjuːpəl| n Educ alumno,-a m,f.
pupil² |'pjuːpəl| n Anat pupila f.
puppet |'pʌpɪt| n títere m.
puppy |'pʌpɪ| n cachorro,-a m,f, perrito m.
purchase |'pɜːtʃɪs| I n compra f. II vtr comprar; **purchasing power**, poder adquisitivo.

purchaser |'pɜːtʃɪsər| *n* comprador,-a *m,f*.

pure |pjuər| *adj* puro,-a. ◆**purely** *adv* simplemente.

purée |'pjuəreɪ| *n* puré *m*.

purge |pɜːdʒ| I *n* purga *f*. II *vtr* purgar.

purify |'pjuərɪfaɪ| *vtr* purificar.

purl |pɜːl| *vtr* (*in knitting*) hacer punto del revés.

purple |'pɜːpəl| *adj* morado,-a, purpúreo,-a; **to go p.** (**in the face**), ponerse morado,-a.

purport |pɜː'pɔːt| *vi fml* pretender; **to p. to be sth**, pretender ser algo.

purpose |'pɜːpəs| *n* 1 propósito *m*, intención *f*; **on p.**, a propósito. 2 (*use*) utilidad *f*.

purposeful |'pɜːpəsful| *adj* (*resolute*) decidido,-a, resoluto,-a.

purr |pɜːr| *vi* (*cat*) ronronear; (*engine*) zumbar.

purse |pɜːs| I *n GB* monedero *m*; *US* (*bag*) bolso *m*; (*prize money*) premio *m* en metálico *f*. II *vtr* **to p. one's lips**, apretarse los labios.

purser |'pɜːsər| *n* contador,-a *m,f*.

pursue |pə'sjuː| *vtr* (*criminal*) perseguir; (*person*) seguir; (*pleasure*) buscar; (*career*) ejercer.

pursuer |pə'sjuːər| *n fml* perseguidor,-a *m,f*.

pursuit |pə'sjuːt| *n* (*of criminal*) persecución *f*; (*of animal*) caza *f*; (*of pleasure*) búsqueda *f*; (*pastime*) pasatiempo *m*.

purveyor |pə'veɪər| *n fml* proveedor,-a *m,f*.

pus |pʌs| *n* pus *m*.

push |puʃ| I *n* empujón *m*; *fig* (*drive*) brío *m*, dinamismo *m*. II *vtr* 1 empujar; (*button*) pulsar, apretar; **to p. one's finger into a hole**, meter el dedo en un agujero. 2 *fig* (*pressurize*) instar; (*harass*) acosar; *fam* **to be** (**hard**) **pushed for time**, andar justo,-a de tiempo. 3 *fam* (*product*) promover; **to p. drugs**, pasar droga. III *vi* empujar. ◆**push aside** *vtr* (*object*) apartar. ◆**push in** *vi* colarse. ◆**push off** *vi* (*in boat*) desatracar; *fam* **p. off!**, ¡lárgate! ◆**push on** *vi* (*continue*) seguir adelante. ◆**push through** *vtr* abrirse paso entre.

pushchair |'puʃtʃeər| *n GB* sillita *f* (de ruedas).

pusher |'puʃər| *n sl* (*of drugs*) camello *m*.

pushover |'puʃəuvər| *n fam* **it's a p.**, está chupado; **she's a p.**, es un ligue fácil.

push-up |'puʃʌp| *n Gymn* flexión *f* (de brazos).

pushy |'puʃɪ| *adj* (**pushier, pushiest**) *fam* agresivo,-a.

puss |pus|, **pussy** |'pusɪ| *n fam* minino *m*.

put |put| I *vtr* (*pt & pp* **put**) 1 poner; (*place*) colocar; (*insert*) meter; **to p. to bed**, acostar a; **to p. a picture up on the wall**, colgar un cuadro en la pared; **to p. a stop to sth**, poner término a algo; *fig* **to p. one's foot in it**, meter la pata. 2 (*present*) presentar, exponer; **to p. a question to sb**, hacer una pregunta a algn. 3 (*express*) expresar, decir; **to p. it mildly**, y me quedo corto; **to p. sth simply**, explicar algo de manera sencilla. 4 (*estimate*) calcular. 5 (*money*) ingresar; (*invest*) invertir.
II *vi Naut* **to p. to sea**, zarpar.
III *adv* **to stay p.**, quedarse quieto,-a.
◆**put about** *vtr* (*rumour*) hacer correr. ◆**put across** *vtr* (*idea etc*) comunicar. ◆**put aside** *vtr* (*money*) ahorrar; (*time*) reservar. ◆**put away** *vtr* (*tidy away*) recoger; *fam* (*eat*) zamparse; (*save money*) ahorrar. ◆**put back** *vtr* (*postpone*) aplazar; **to p. the clock back**, retrasar la hora. ◆**put by** *vtr* (*money*) ahorrar. ◆**put down** *vtr* (*set down*) dejar; (*suppress*) sofocar; (*humiliate*) humillar; (*criticize*) criticar; (*animal*) provocar la muerte de; (*write down*) apuntar. ◆**put down to** *vtr* achacar a. ◆**put forward** *vtr* (*theory*) exponer; (*proposal*) hacer; **to p. one's name forward for sth**, presentarse como candidato,-a para algo. ◆**put in** I *vtr* (*install*) instalar; (*complaint, request*) presentar; (*time*) pasar. II *vi Naut* hacer escala (**at**, en). ◆**put off** *vtr* (*postpone*) aplazar; **to p. sb off** (**doing**) **sth**, (*dissuade*) disuadir a algn de (hacer) algo. ◆**put on** *vtr* (*clothes*) poner, ponerse; (*show*) montar; (*concert*) dar; (*switch on*) (*radio*) poner; (*light*) encender; (*water, gas*) abrir; **to p. on weight**, aumentar de peso; **to p. on the brakes**, frenar; *fig* **to p. on a straight face**, poner cara de serio,-a. ◆**put out** *vtr* (*light, fire*) apagar; (*place outside*) sacar; (*extend*) (*arm*) extender; (*tongue*) sacar; (*hand*) tender; (*spread*) (*rumour*) hacer correr; (*annoy*) molestar; (*inconvenience*) incordiar; (*anger*) **to be p. out by sth**, enojarse por algo. ◆**put through** *vtr Tel* **p. me through to Pat, please**, póngame con Pat, por favor. ◆**put together** *vtr* (*join*) unir, reunir; (*assemble*) armar, montar. ◆**put up** *vtr* (*raise*) levantar, subir; (*picture*) colocar; (*curtains*) colgar; (*building*) construir; (*tent*) armar; (*prices*) subir, aumentar; (*accommodate*) alojar, hospedar; **to p. up a fight**, ofrecer resistencia. ◆**put up to** *vtr* **to p. sb up to sth**, incitar a algn a hacer algo. ◆**put up with** *vtr* aguantar, soportar.

putrid |'pjuːtrɪd| *adj fml* putrefacto,-a.

putt |pʌt| I *n* tiro *m* al hoyo. II *vtr & vi* tirar al hoyo.

putting |'pʌtɪŋ| *n* **p. green**, minigolf *m*.

putty |'pʌtɪ| *n* masilla *f*.

puzzle |'pʌzəl| I *n* rompecabezas *m inv*;

(*crossword*) crucigrama *m*; *fig* (*mystery*) misterio *m*. **II** *vtr* dejar perplejo,-a; **to be puzzled about sth,** no entender algo. ◆**puzzle over** *vtr* **to p. over sth,** dar vueltas a algo (en la cabeza).

puzzling ['pʌzəlɪŋ] *adj* extraño,-a, curioso,-a.

pygmy ['pɪgmɪ] *n* pigmeo,-a *m,f*; *fig* enano,-a *m,f*.

pyjamas [pə'dʒɑːməz] *npl* pijama *m sing*.

pylon ['paɪlən] *n* torre *f* (de conducción eléctrica).

pyramid ['pɪrəmɪd] *n* pirámide *f*.

Pyrenees [pɪrə'niːz] *npl* **the P.,** los Pirineos.

Pyrex® ['paɪreks] *n* pírex® *m*.

python ['paɪθən] *n* pitón *m*.

Q

Q, q [kjuː] *n* (*the letter*) Q, q *f*.

quack [kwæk] **I** *n* **1** (*of duck*) graznido *m*. **2** *fam* (*doctor*) curandero,-a *m,f*. **II** *vi* graznar.

quad [kwɒd] *n fam* **1** *GB* (*of school, university*) patio *m* interior. **2** (*quadruplet*) cuatrillizo,-a *m,f*.

quadrangle ['kwɒdræŋgəl] *n* **1** *Geom* cuadrángulo *m*. **2** (*courtyard*) patio *m* interior.

quadruple ['kwɒdrʊpəl, kwɒ'druːpəl] **I** *n* cuádruplo *m*. **II** *adj* cuádruple. **III** *vtr* cuadruplicar. **IV** *vi* cuadruplicarse.

quadruplet ['kwɒdrʊplɪt, kwɒ'druːplɪt] *n* cuatrillizo,-a *m,f*.

quagmire ['kwægmaɪər, 'kwɒgmaɪər] *n* (*land*) cenagal *m*.

quail[1] [kweɪl] *n Orn* codorniz *f*.

quail[2] [kweɪl] *vi fig* encogerse.

quaint [kweɪnt] *adj* (*picturesque*) pintoresco,-a; (*original*) singular.

quake [kweɪk] **I** *vi* temblar. **II** *n fam* temblor *m* de tierra.

Quaker ['kweɪkər] *n* cuáquero,-a *m,f*.

qualification [kwɒlɪfɪ'keɪʃən] *n* **1** (*ability*) aptitud *f*. **2** (*requirement*) requisito *m*. **3** (*diploma etc*) título *m*. **4** (*reservation*) reserva *f*.

qualified ['kwɒlɪfaɪd] *adj* **1** capacitado,-a; **q. teacher,** profesor titulado. **2** (*e.g. approval,* (*modified*) aprobación condicional.

qualify ['kwɒlɪfaɪ] **I** *vtr* **1** (*entitle*) capacitar. **2** (*modify*) modificar; (*statement*) matizar; *Ling* calificar. **II** *vi* **1** **to q. as,** (*doctor etc*) sacar el título de; **when did you q.?,** ¿cuándo terminaste la carrera? **2** (*in competition*) quedar clasificado,-a.

qualifying ['kwɒlɪfaɪŋ] *adj* (*round, exam*) eliminatorio,-a.

quality ['kwɒlɪtɪ] *n* **1** (*excellence*) calidad *f*; **q. control,** control *m* de calidad; **q. newspapers,** prensa *f* no sensacionalista. **2** (*attribute*) cualidad *f*.

qualm [kwɑːm] *n* **1** (*scruple*) escrúpulo *m*. **2** (*doubt*) duda *f*.

quandary ['kwɒndərɪ, 'kwɒndrɪ] *n* **to be in a q.,** estar en un dilema.

quango ['kwæŋgəʊ] *n* organización semiautónoma paralela.

quantity ['kwɒntɪtɪ] *n* cantidad *f*.

quarantine ['kwɒrəntiːn] *n* cuarentena *f*.

quarrel ['kwɒrəl] **I** *n* (*argument*) riña *f*, pelea *f*; (*disagreement*) desacuerdo *m*. **II** *vi* (*argue*) pelearse, reñir; **to q. with sth,** discrepar de algo.

quarrelsome ['kwɒrəlsəm] *adj* camorrista.

quarry[1] ['kwɒrɪ] *Min* **I** *n* cantera *f*. **II** *vtr* extraer.

quarry[2] ['kwɒrɪ] *n* presa *f*.

quart [kwɔːt] *n* (*measurement*) cuarto *m* de galón (*GB approx* 1,13 litros; *US approx* 0,94 litros).

quarter ['kwɔːtər] **I** *n* **1** cuarto *m*, cuarta parte; **a q. of an hour,** un cuarto de hora; **a q. of a cake,** la cuarta parte de un pastel. **2** **it's a q. to three,** *US* **it's a q. of three,** son las tres menos cuarto. **3** (*three months*) trimestre *m*. **4** *GB* (*weight*) cuarto *m* de libra. **5** *US* (*coin*) cuarto *m* (de dólar). **6** (*district*) barrio *m*. **7** **there was criticism from all quarters,** (*areas, people*) todos lo criticaron. **8** (*of moon*) cuarto *m*. **9** **quarters,** (*lodgings*) alojamiento *m sing*; *Mil* **officers' q.,** residencia *f sing* de oficiales; **at close quarters,** muy cerca. **II** *vtr* **1** (*cut into quarters*) dividir en cuartos. **2** (*accommodate*) alojar.

quarterfinal ['kwɔːtəfaɪnəl] *n Sport* cuarto *m* de final.

quarterly ['kwɔːtəlɪ] **I** *adj* trimestral. **II** *n* publicación *f* trimestral. **III** *adv* trimestralmente.

quartermaster ['kwɔːtəmɑːstər] *n* **1** *Mil* oficial *m* de intendencia. **2** *Naut* cabo *m* de la Marina.

quartet(te) [kwɔː'tet] *n* cuarteto *m*.

quartz [kwɔːts] *n* cuarzo *m*; **q. watch,** reloj *m* de cuarzo.

quash [kwɒʃ] *vtr Jur* anular; (*uprising*) aplastar.

quasi ['kwɑːzɪ, 'kweɪzaɪ, 'kweɪsaɪ] *pref* cuasi.

quaver ['kweɪvər] **I** *n* **1** *Mus* corchea *f*. **2** (*in voice*) temblor *m*. **II** *vi* (*voice*) temblar.

quay(side) ['kiː(saɪd)] *n* muelle *m*.

queasy ['kwiːzɪ] *adj* (**queasier, queasiest**)

to feel q., *(ill)* tener náuseas.
queen |kwi:n| *n* 1 reina *f.* 2 *offens* loca *f*, marica *m.*
queer |kwɪər| I *adj* 1 *(strange)* extraño,-a, raro,-a. 2 *fam (mad)* loco,-a. 3 *fam (unwell)* mareado,-a. 4 *offens* maricón. II *n sl offens* marica *m*, maricón *m.*
quell |kwel| *vtr* reprimir.
quench |kwentʃ| *vtr* apagar.
querulous |'kwerʊləs, 'kwerjʊləs| *adj fml* quejumbroso,-a.
query |'kwɪərɪ| I *n (question)* pregunta *f.* II *vtr (ask questions about)* preguntar acerca de; *(have doubts about)* poner en duda.
quest |kwest| *n lit* búsqueda *f*, busca *f.*
question |'kwestʃən| I *n* 1 *(interrogative)* pregunta *f*; **to ask sb a q.,** hacer una pregunta a algn; **he did it without q.,** lo hizo sin rechistar; **q. mark,** signo *m* de interrogación; *fig* interrogante *m.* 2 *(problem, issue)* asunto *m*, cuestión *f*; **it's a q. of two hours,** es cuestión de dos horas. 3 *(doubt)* duda *f*; **beyond q.,** fuera de duda; **in q.,** en duda; **to call sth into q.,** poner algo en duda. 4 **out of the q.,** imposible; **that's out of the q.,** ¡ni hablar! 5 *Educ* problema *m.* II *vtr (ask questions of)* hacer preguntas a; *(interrogate)* interrogar; *(query)* poner en duda.
questionable |'kwestʃənəbəl| *adj (doubtful)* dudoso,-a; *(debatable)* discutible.
questionnaire |'kwestʃə'neər| *n* cuestionario *m.*
queue |kju:| *GB* I *n* cola *f.* II *vi* **to q. (up),** hacer cola.
quibble |'kwɪbəl| I *n* pega *f.* II *vi* poner pegas *(with,* a); *fam* buscarle tres pies al gato.
quick |kwɪk| *adj* 1 *(fast)* rápido,-a; **a q. look,** un vistazo; **a q. snack,** un bocado; **be q.!,** ¡date prisa! 2 *(clever)* espabilado, -a; *(wit)* agudo,-a. 3 **she has a q. temper,** se fada con nada. ◆**quickly** *adv* rápidamente, de prisa.
quicken |'kwɪkən| I *vtr* acelerar; **to q. one's pace,** acelerar el paso. II *vi (speed up)* acelerarse.
quickness |'kwɪknɪs| *n* 1 *(speed)* rapidez *f.* 2 *(of wit)* agudeza *f*, viveza *f.*
quicksand |'kwɪksænd| *n* arenas movedizas.
quicksilver |'kwɪksɪlvər| *n* mercurio *m.*
quick-witted |kwɪk'wɪtɪd| *adj* agudo,-a.
quid |kwɪd| *n GB sl* libra *f* (esterlina).
quiet |'kwaɪət| I *n* 1 *(silence)* silencio *m.* 2 *(calm)* tranquilidad *f.* II *adj* 1 *(silent)* silencioso,-a; *(street)* tranquilo,-a; **a q. voice,** una voz suave; **keep q.!,** ¡silencio! 2 *(calm)* tranquilo,-a. 3 *Com Fin* business is q. today, hoy hay poco negocio. 4 *(person)* reservado,-a. 5 *(secret)* confidencial. 6 *(not showy) (clothes)*

sobrio,-a; *(colours)* apagado,-a. 7 *(ceremony, dinner)* íntimo,-a. II *vtr US* calmar. III *vi US* calmarse. ◆**quietly** *adv* 1 *(silently)* silenciosamente; **he spoke q.,** habló en voz baja. 2 *(calmly)* tranquilamente. 3 *(discreetly)* discretamente.
quieten |'kwaɪətən| I *vtr (silence)* callar; *(calm)* calmar. II *vi (silence)* callarse; *(calm)* calmarse. ◆**quieten down** *GB* I *vtr* calmar. II *vi* calmarse.
quietness |'kwaɪətnɪs| *n* 1 *(silence)* silencio *m.* 2 *(calm)* tranquilidad *f.*
quill |kwɪl| *n (feather, pen)* pluma *f*; *(of porcupine)* púa *f.*
quilt |kwɪlt| I *n* edredón *m.* II *vtr* acolchar.
quin |kwɪn| *n* quintillizo,-a *m,f.*
quinine |'kwɪni:n, *US* 'kwaɪnaɪn| *n* quinina *f.*
quintessential |kwɪntɪ'senʃəl| *adj* fundamental.
quintet(te) |kwɪn'tet| *n* quinteto *m.*
quintuple |'kwɪntjʊpəl, kwɪn'tju:pəl| I *adj* quíntuplo,-a. II *n* quíntuplo *m.* III *vtr* quintuplicar.
quintuplet |'kwɪntjʊplɪt, kwɪn'tju:plɪt| *n* quintillizo,-a *m,f.*
quip |kwɪp| I *n* salida *f*; *(joke)* chiste *m.* II *vi* bromear.
quirk |kwɜ:k| *n* 1 *(peculiarity)* manía *f.* 2 *(of fate)* arbitrariedad *f.*
quit |kwɪt| I *vtr (pt & pp* quitted *or esp US* quit) 1 *(leave)* dejar, abandonar. 2 **q. making that noise!,** ¡deja de hacer ese ruido!. II *vi* 1 *(go)* irse; *(give up)* dimitir. 2 *(cease)* dejar de hacer algo. III *adj* let's call it quits, dejémoslo estar.
quite |kwaɪt| *adv* 1 *(entirely)* totalmente; **she's q. right,** tiene toda la razón. 2 *(rather)* bastante; **q. a few,** bastantes; **q. a while,** un buen rato; **q. often,** con bastante frecuencia; **that's q. enough!,** ¡ya está bien! 3 **he's q. a character,** es un tipo original; **to be q. sth,** es increíble. 4 *(exactly)* exactamente; **q. (so)!,** ¡en efecto!, ¡exacto!
quiver¹ |'kwɪvər| *vi* temblar.
quiver² |'kwɪvər| *n (for arrows)* aljaba *f*, carcaj *m.*
quiz |kwɪz| I *n Rad TV* **q. show,** concurso *m.* II *vtr* hacer preguntas a.
quizzical |'kwɪzɪkəl| *adj* 1 *(bemused)* burlón,-ona. 2 *(enquiring)* curioso,-a.
quota |'kwəʊtə| *n* 1 *(proportional share)* cuota *f*, parte *f.* 2 *(prescribed amount, number)* cupo *m.*
quotation |kwəʊ'teɪʃən| *n* 1 *Lit* cita *f*; **q. marks,** comillas *fpl.* 2 *Fin* cotización *f.*
quote |kwəʊt| I *vtr* 1 *Lit* citar. 2 *Com* **to q. a price,** dar un presupuesto. 3 *Fin* cotizar. II *n* 1 *Lit* cita *f.* 2 *Com* presupuesto *m.*
quotient |'kwəʊʃənt| *n* cociente *m.*

R

R, r [ɑ:r] *n* (*the letter*) R, r *f*.

rabbi ['ræbaɪ] *n* rabí *m*, rabino *m*.

rabbit ['ræbɪt] I *n* conejo,-a *m,f*; **r. hutch**, conejera *f*. II *vi fam* **to r. (on)**, enrollarse.

rabble ['ræbəl] *n pej* **the r.**, el populacho.

rabies ['reɪbi:z] *n* rabia *f*.

RAC [ɑ:reɪ'si:] *GB abbr of* **Royal Automobile Club**, ≈ Real Automóvil Club *m* de España, RACE.

race[1] [reɪs] I *n* 1 *Sport* carrera *f*. 2 *GB* **the races**, las carreras (de caballos). II *vtr* 1 **I'll r. you!**, ¡te echo una carrera! 2 (*car, horse*) hacer correr. 3 (*engine*) acelerar. III *vi* (*go quickly*) correr; (*pulse*) acelerarse.

race[2] [reɪs] *n* (*people*) raza *f*.

racecourse ['reɪskɔ:s] *n GB* hipódromo *m*.

racehorse ['reɪshɔ:s] *n* caballo *m* de carreras.

racer ['reɪsər] *n Sport* 1 (*person*) corredor,-a *m,f*. 2 (*bicycle*) bicicleta *f* de carreras; (*car*) coche *m* de carreras.

racetrack ['reɪstræk] *n* (*for cars, people, bikes*) pista *f*; *US* (*for horses*) hipódromo *m*.

racial ['reɪʃəl] *adj* racial.

racing ['reɪsɪŋ] I *n* carreras *fpl*. II *adj* de carreras; **r. car/bike**, coche *m*/moto *f* de carreras.

racism ['reɪsɪzəm] *n* racismo *m*.

racist ['reɪsɪst] *adj & n* racista (*mf*).

rack [ræk] I *n* 1 (*shelf*) estante *m*; (*for clothes*) percha *f*; **luggage r.**, portaequipajes *m inv*; **roof r.**, baca *f*. 2 (*for torture*) potro *m*. II *vtr lit* (*torment*) atormentar; *fam fig* **to r. one's brains**, devanarse los sesos.

racket[1] ['rækɪt] *n* 1 (*din*) ruído *m*, jaleo *m*. 2 (*swindle*) timo *m*; (*shady business*) chanchullo *m*.

racket[2] ['rækɪt] *n Sport* raqueta *f*.

racquet ['rækɪt] *n* → **racket**.

racy ['reɪsɪ] *adj* (**racier, raciest**) (*lively*) vivo,-a; (*risqué*) atrevido,-a.

radar ['reɪdɑ:r] *n* radar *m*.

radiance ['reɪdɪəns] *n* resplandor *m*.

radiant ['reɪdɪənt] *adj* radiante, resplandeciente.

radiate ['reɪdɪeɪt] *vtr* irradiar; *fig* **she radiated happiness**, rebosaba de alegría.

radiation [reɪdɪ'eɪʃən] *n* radiación *f*.

radiator ['reɪdɪeɪtər] *n* radiador *m*.

radical ['rædɪkəl] *adj* radical.

radio ['reɪdɪəʊ] *n* radio *f*; **on the r.**, en *or* por la radio; **r. station**, emisora *f* (de radio).

radioactive [reɪdɪəʊ'æktɪv] *adj* radiactivo,-a.

radio-controlled [reɪdɪəʊkən'trəʊld] *adj* teledirigido,-a.

radiography [reɪdɪ'ɒɡrəfɪ] *n* radiografía *f*.

radiology [reɪdɪ'ɒlədʒɪ] *n* radiología *f*.

radiotherapy [reɪdɪəʊ'θerəpɪ] *n* radioterapia *f*.

radish ['rædɪʃ] *n* rábano *m*.

radius ['reɪdɪəs] *n* radio *m*; **within a r. of**, en un radio de.

RAF [ɑ:reɪ'ef] *GB abbr of* **Royal Air Force**, fuerzas aéreas británicas.

raffle ['ræfəl] I *n* rifa *f*. II *vtr* rifar.

raft [rɑ:ft] *n* balsa *f*.

rafter ['rɑ:ftər] *n* viga *f* de madera.

rag[1] [ræɡ] I *n* 1 (*torn piece*) harapo *m*; **r. doll**, muñeca *f* de trapo. 2 (*for cleaning*) trapo *m*. 3 *fam* **rags**, (*clothes*) trapos *mpl*. 4 *Press pej* periodicucho *m*.

rag[2] [ræɡ] I *n GB Univ* función benéfica. II *vtr* gastar bromas a.

rag-and-bone [ræɡən'bəʊn] *adj GB* **r.-and-b. man**, trapero *m*.

rage [reɪdʒ] I *n* 1 (*fury*) cólera *f*. 2 *fam* **it's all the r.**, hace furor. II *vi* 1 (*person*) rabiar, estar furioso,-a. 2 *fig* (*storm, sea*) rugir; (*wind*) bramar.

ragged ['ræɡɪd] *adj* 1 (*clothes*) hecho,-a jirones. 2 (*person*) harapiento,-a. 3 (*edge*) mellado,-a. 4 *fig* (*uneven*) desigual.

raging ['reɪdʒɪŋ] *adj* 1 (*angry*) furioso,-a. 2 *fig* (*sea*) embravecido,-a. 3 (*intense*) feroz; (*storm*) violento,-a.

raid [reɪd] I *n Mil* incursión *f*; (*by police*) redada *f*; (*robbery etc*) atraco *m*. II *vtr Mil* hacer una incursión en; (*police*) hacer una redada en; (*rob*) asaltar; *fam* **to r. the larder**, vaciar la despensa.

raider ['reɪdər] *n* (*invader*) invasor,-a *m,f*.

rail [reɪl] *n* 1 barra *f*. 2 (*railing*) barandilla *f*. 3 *Rail* carril *f*; **by r.**, (*send sth*) por ferrocarril; (*travel*) en tren.

railcard ['reɪlkɑ:d] *n GB* abono *m*.

railing ['reɪlɪŋ] *n* (*usu pl*) verja *f*.

railroad ['reɪlrəʊd] *n US* ferrocarril *m*.

railway ['reɪlweɪ] *n GB* ferrocarril *m*; **r. line, r. track**, vía férrea; **r. station**, estación *f* de ferrocarril.

railwayman ['reɪlweɪmən] *n GB* ferroviario *m*.

rain [reɪn] I *n* lluvia *f*; **in the r.**, bajo la lluvia. II *vi* llover; **it's raining**, llueve.

rainbow ['reɪnbəʊ] *n* arco *m* iris.

raincoat ['reɪnkəʊt] *n* impermeable *m*.

raindrop ['reɪndrɒp] *n* gota *f* de lluvia.

rainfall ['reɪnfɔ:l] *n* (*falling of rain*) precipitación *f*; (*amount*) pluviosidad *f*.

rainforest ['reɪnfɒrɪst] *n* selva *f* tropical.

rainy ['reɪnɪ] *adj* (**rainier, rainiest**) lluvioso,-a.

raise [reɪz] I *n US* aumento *m* (de

sueldo). **II** vtr **1** levantar; (glass) brindar; (voice) subir; (building) erigir. **2** (prices) aumentar. **3** (money, help) reunir. **4** (issue) plantear. **5** (crops, children) criar. **6** Rad comunicar con. **7** (standards) mejorar. **8** (laugh) provocar.

raisin |'reɪzən| n pasa f.

rake¹ |reɪk| **I** n (garden tool) rastrillo m; (for fire) hurgón m. **II** vtr (leaves) rastrillar; (fire) hurgar; (with machine gun) barrer.

rake² |reɪk| n (dissolute man) calavera m, libertino m.

rally |'rælɪ| **I** n **1** (gathering) reunión f; Pol mitin m. **2** Aut rallye m. **3** Ten jugada f. **II** vtr (support) reunir. **III** vi recuperarse.
◆**rally round** vi formar una piña.

RAM |ræm| Comput abbr of **random access memory**, RAM.

ram |ræm| **I** n **1** Zool carnero m. **2** Tech maza f. **II** vtr **1** (drive into place) hincar; (cram) embutir; fam to r. sth home, hacer algo patente. **2** (crash into) chocar con.

ramble |'ræmbəl| **I** n (walk) caminata f. **II** vi **1** (walk) hacer una excursión a pie. **2** fig (digress) divagar.

rambler |'ræmblər| n **1** (person) excursionista mf. **2** Bot rosal m trepador.

rambling |'ræmblɪŋ| adj **1** (incoherent) incoherente. **2** (house) laberíntico,-a. **3** Bot trepador,-a.

ramp |ræmp| n **1** rampa f. **2** Av (movable stairway) escalerilla f.

rampage |ræm'peɪdʒ| **I** n to be on the r., desmandarse. **II** vi to r. about, comportarse como un loco.

rampant |'ræmpənt| adj incontrolado,-a; **corruption is r.**, la corrupción está muy extendida.

rampart |'ræmpɑːt| n muralla f.

ramshackle |'ræmʃækəl| adj destartalado,-a.

ran |ræn| pt → **run**.

ranch |rɑːntʃ| n US rancho m, hacienda f.

rancher |'rɑːntʃər| n US ranchero,-a m,f.

rancid |'rænsɪd| adj rancio,-a.

rancour, US **rancor** |'ræŋkər| n fml rencor m.

R&D |ɑːrən'diː| n abbr of **Research and Development**, I+D.

random |'rændəm| **I** n at r., al azar. **II** adj fortuito,-a; **r. selection**, selección hecha al azar.

randy |'rændɪ| adj (**randier, randiest**) GB fam cachondo,-a, caliente.

rang |ræŋ| pt → **ring**.

range |reɪndʒ| **I** n **1** (of mountains) cordillera f, sierra f. **2** US (open land) pradera f. **3** (choice) surtido m; (of products) gama f. **4** Mus registro m. **5 firing r.**, campo m de tiro. **6** (of missile) alcance m; **at close r.**, de cerca; **long-/short-r. missiles**, misiles mpl de largo/corto alcance. **7 r. of vision**, campo m de visión. **8** Culin coci-

na f de carbón. **II** vi (extend) extenderse (**to**, hasta); **prices r. from five to twenty pounds**, los precios oscilan entre cinco y veinte libras. **III** vtr lit (wander) vagar por.

ranger |'reɪndʒər| n **1** (forest) r., guardabosques mf inv. **2** US (mounted policeman) policía m montado.

rank¹ |ræŋk| **I** n **1** Mil (row) fila f; **the ranks**, los soldados rasos; **the r. and file**, la base. **2** (position in army) graduación f; (in society) rango m. **3** (taxi) r., parada f de taxis. **II** vtr (classify) clasificar. **III** vi (figure) figurar; **to r. above/below sb**, figurar por encima/debajo de algn; **to r. with**, estar al mismo nivel que.

rank² |ræŋk| adj fml **1** (vegetation) exuberante. **2** (foul-smelling) fétido,-a. **3** (thorough) total, absoluto,-a.

ransack |'rænsæk| vtr (plunder) saquear; (rummage in) registrar.

ransom |'rænsəm| n rescate m; **to hold sb to r.**, pedir rescate por algn; fig poner a algn entre la espada y la pared.

rant |rænt| vi vociferar; fam to r. and rave, pegar gritos.

rap |ræp| **I** n **1** (blow) golpe m seco; (on door) golpecito m. **2** Mus rap m. **II** vtr & vi (knock) golpear.

rape¹ |reɪp| Jur **I** n violación f. **II** vtr violar.

rape² |reɪp| n Bot colza f.

rapeseed |'reɪpsiːd| n r. oil, aceite m de colza.

rapid |'ræpɪd| **I** adj rápido,-a. **II** npl rapids, (in river) rápidos mpl.

rapidity |rə'pɪdɪtɪ| n rapidez f.

rapist |'reɪpɪst| n violador,-a m,f.

rapport |ræ'pɔːr| n compenetración f.

rapture |'ræptʃər| n éxtasis m.

rapturous |'ræptʃərəs| adj muy entusiasta.

rare¹ |reər| adj raro,-a, poco común.
◆**rarely** adv raras veces.

rare² |reər| adj (steak) poco hecho,-a.

rarefied |'reərɪfaɪd| adj enrarecido,-a.

raring |'reərɪŋ| adj fam to be r. to do sth, morirse de ganas de hacer algo.

rarity |'reərɪtɪ| n rareza f.

rascal |'rɑːskəl| n granuja mf.

rash¹ |ræʃ| n **1** Med erupción f, sarpullido m. **2** fig (of robberies etc) racha f.

rash² |ræʃ| adj (reckless) impetuoso,-a; (words, actions) precipitado,-a, imprudente.

rasher |'ræʃər| n loncha f.

rasping |'rɑːspɪŋ| adj áspero,-a.

raspberry |'rɑːzbərɪ| n frambuesa f.

rat |ræt| n rata f; **r. poison**, raticida m.

rate |reɪt| **I** n **1** (ratio) índice m, tasa f; **at any r.**, (at least) al menos; (anyway) en cualquier caso. **2** (cost) precio m; Fin (of interest, exchange) tipo m. **3 at the r. of**, (speed) a la velocidad de; (quantity) a ra-

zón de. **4 first r.**, de primera categoría. **5**
GB **rates,** impuestos *mpl* municipales. **II**
vtr **1** *(estimate)* estimar. **2** *(evaluate)* tasar.
3 *(consider)* considerar.

rateable |'reɪtəbəl| *adj GB* **r. value,** valor
m catastral.

ratepayer |'reɪtpeɪəʳ| *n GB* contribuyente
mf.

rather |'rɑːðəʳ| *adv* **1** *(quite)* más bien,
bastante; *(very much so)* muy. **2** *(more
accurately)* mejor dicho; **r. than,** *(instead
of)* en vez de; *(more than)* más que. **3 she
would r. stay here,** *(prefer to)* prefiere
quedarse aquí.

ratify |'rætɪfaɪ| *vtr* ratificar.

rating |'reɪtɪŋ| *n* **1** *(valuation)* tasación *f*;
(score) valoración *f*. **2** *TV* **(programme)
ratings,** índice *m sing* de audiencia. **3**
Naut marinero *m* sin graduación.

ratio |'reɪʃɪəʊ| *n* razón *f*; **in the r. of,** a
razón de.

ration |'ræʃən| **I** *n* **1** *(allowance)* ración *f*.
2 rations, víveres *mpl*. **II** *vtr* racionar.

rational |'ræʃənəl| *adj* racional.

rationale |ræʃə'nɑːl| *n* base *f*.

rationalize |'ræʃənəlaɪz| *vtr* racionalizar.

rattle |'rætəl| **I** *n* **1** *(of train, cart)* traque-
teo *m*; *(of metal)* repiqueteo *m*; *(of glass)*
tintineo *m*. **2** *(toy)* sonajero *m*; *(instrument)* carraca *f*. **II** *vtr* **1** *(keys etc)* hacer
sonar. **2** *fam (unsettle)* poner nervioso,-a.
III *vi* sonar; *(metal)* repiquetear; *(glass)*
tintinear.

rattlesnake |'rætəlsneɪk| *n* serpiente *f* de
cascabel.

raucous |'rɔːkəs| *adj* estridente.

ravage |'rævɪdʒ| *fml* **I** *n (usu pl)* estragos
mpl. **II** *vtr* asolar, devastar.

rave |reɪv| *vi* **1** *(be delirious)* delirar. **2**
(be angry) enfurecerse *(at,* con*)*. **3** *fam
(show enthusiasm)* entusiasmarse *(about,*
por*)*. **II** *n fam* **r. review,** crítica *f* muy favorable.

raven |'reɪvən| *n* cuervo *m*.

ravenous |'rævənəs| *adj* **I'm r.,** tengo un
hambre que no veo.

ravine |rə'viːn| *n* barranco *m*.

raving |'reɪvɪŋ| *n fam* **r. mad,** loco,-a de
atar.

ravishing |'rævɪʃɪŋ| *adj (person)*
encantador,-a.

raw |rɔː| **I** *adj* **1** *(uncooked)* crudo,-a. **2**
(not processed) bruto,-a; *(alcohol)* puro,-a;
r. material, materia prima. **3** *(emotion)*
instintivo,-a. **4** *(weather)* crudo,-a. **5 r.
deal,** trato injusto. **6** *(wound)* abierto,-a;
r. flesh, carne viva. **7** *US (inexperienced)*
novato,-a. **8** *(frank)* franco,-a.

ray¹ |reɪ| *n* rayo *m*; *fig* **r. of hope,** rayo
de esperanza.

ray² |reɪ| *n (fish)* raya *f*.

rayon |'reɪɒn| *n* rayón *m*.

raze |reɪz| *vtr* arrasar.

razor |'reɪzəʳ| *n (for shaving)* maquinilla *f*

de afeitar; **r. blade,** hoja *f* de afeitar.

Rd *abbr of* **Road,** calle *f*, c/.

re |riː| *prep* respecto a, con referencia a.

reach |riːtʃ| **I** *vtr* **1** *(arrive at)* llegar a. **2**
(contact) localizar. **II** *vi* alcanzar; **to r. for
sth,** intentar coger algo; **to r. out,**
extender la mano. **III** *n* **1** *(range)* alcance
m; **out of r.,** fuera del alcance; **within r.,**
al alcance. **2** *Box* extensión *f* del brazo. **3
reaches,** *(on a river)* recta *f sing.*

react |rɪ'ækt| *vi* reaccionar.

reaction |rɪ'ækʃən| *n* reacción *f*.

reactor |rɪ'æktəʳ| *n* reactor *m*.

read |riːd| **I** *vtr (pt & pp* **read** |red|) **1**
leer. **2** *(decipher)* descifrar. **3** *(understand)*
entender; *(interpret)* interpretar. **4** *Univ*
estudiar. **II** *vi* **1** *(dial)* marcar. **2** *(signpost,
text)* decir. ◆**read out** *vtr* leer en voz
alta.

readable |'riːdəbəl| *adj* **1** *(interesting)* inte-
resante. **2** *(legible)* legible.

reader |'riːdəʳ| *n* **1** lector,-a *m,f*. **2** *(book)*
libro *m* de lectura. **3** *GB Univ* profesor,-a
adjunto,-a.

readership |'riːdəʃɪp| *n Press* lectores
mpl.

readiness |'redɪnɪs| *n* **1** *(preparedness)*
preparación *f*. **2** *(willingness)* buena disposición.

reading |'riːdɪŋ| *n* **1** lectura *f*. **2** *fig* inter-
pretación *f*. **3** *(of laws, bill)* presentación
f.

readjust |riːə'dʒʌst| **I** *vtr* reajustar. **II** *vi*
(adapt oneself) adaptarse.

ready |'redɪ| *adj* **1** *(prepared)* listo,-a,
preparado,-a; **r., steady, go!,** ¡prepara-
dos, listos, ya! **2 r. to,** *(to hand)* a punto
de. **3** *(to hand)* a mano; **r. cash,** dinero *m*
en efectivo. **4** *(willing)* dispuesto,-a a.
◆**readily** *adv* **1** *(easily)* fácilmente; **r.
available,** disponible en el acto. **2** *(willingly)* de buena gana.

ready-cooked |redɪ'kʊkt| *adj*
precocinado,-a.

ready-made |redɪ'meɪd| *adj*
confeccionado,-a; *(food)* preparado,-a.

real |rɪəl| *adj* **1** real, verdadero,-a; *fam* **for
r.,** de veras. **2** *(genuine)* auténtico,-a; **r.
leather,** piel legítima. **3** *US Com* **r.
estate,** bienes *mpl* inmuebles; **r. estate
agent,** agente inmobiliario. ◆**really** *adv*
verdaderamente, realmente; **I r. don't
know,** no lo sé de verdad; **r.?,** ¿de veras?

realism |'rɪəlɪzəm| *n* realismo *m*.

realistic |rɪə'lɪstɪk| *adj* realista.

reality |rɪ'ælɪtɪ| *n* realidad *f*; **in r.,** en rea-
lidad.

realize |'rɪəlaɪz| *vtr* **1** *(become aware of)*
darse cuenta de. **2** *(assets, plan)* realizar.

realization |rɪəlaɪ'zeɪʃən| *n* **1** *(understand-
ing)* comprensión *f*. **2** *(of plan, assets)* realización *f.*

realm |relm| *n (kingdom)* reino *m*; *fig
(field)* terreno *m*.

ream |riːm| n (of paper) resma f.
reap |riːp| vtr Agr cosechar; fig **to r. the benefits**, llevarse los beneficios.
reappear |riːəˈpɪər| vi reaparecer.
reappraisal |riːəˈpreɪzəl| n revaluación f.
rear¹ |rɪər| I n 1 (back part) parte f de atrás. 2 fam (buttocks) trasero m. II adj trasero,-a; **r. entrance**, puerta f de atrás.
rear² |rɪər| I vtr 1 (breed, raise) criar. 2 (lift up) levantar. II vi **to r. up**, (horse) encabritarse.
rearguard |ˈrɪəɡɑːd| n retaguardia f.
rearmament |riːˈɑːməmənt| n rearme m.
rearrange |riːəˈreɪndʒ| vtr 1 (furniture) colocar de otra manera. 2 (appointment) fijar otra fecha para.
rear-view |ˈrɪəvjuː| adj r.-v. **mirror**, (espejo m) retrovisor m.
reason |ˈriːzən| I n 1 motivo m, razón f; **for no r.**, sin razón; **for some r.**, por algún motivo. 2 (good sense) razón f; **it stands to r.**, es lógico; **to listen to r.**, atender a razones. II vi 1 **to r. with sb**, convencer a algn. 2 (argue, work out) razonar.
reasonable |ˈriːzənəbəl| adj 1 (fair) razonable. 2 (sensible) sensato,-a. 3 (average) regular. ◆**reasonably** adv (fairly) bastante.
reasoning |ˈriːzənɪŋ| n razonamiento m.
reassurance |riːəˈʃʊərəns| n consuelo m.
reassure |riːəˈʃʊər| vtr 1 (comfort) tranquilizar. 2 (restore confidence) dar confianza a.
reassuring |riːəˈʃʊərɪŋ| adj consolador,-a.
rebate |ˈriːbeɪt| n devolución f; **tax r.**, devolución fiscal.
rebel |ˈrebəl| I adj & n rebelde (mf). II |rɪˈbel| vi rebelarse, sublevarse (**against**, contra).
rebellion |rɪˈbeljən| n rebelión f.
rebellious |rɪˈbeljəs| adj rebelde.
rebound |ˈriːbaʊnd| I n (of ball) rebote m; fig **on the r.**, de rebote. II |rɪˈbaʊnd| vi (ball) rebotar.
rebuff |rɪˈbʌf| I n desaire m. II vtr desairar.
rebuild |riːˈbɪld| vtr reconstruir.
rebuke |rɪˈbjuːk| I n reproche m. II vtr reprochar.
rebut |rɪˈbʌt| vtr refutar.
recalcitrant |rɪˈkælsɪtrənt| adj fml recalcitrante.
recall |rɪˈkɔːl| vtr 1 (soldiers, products) hacer volver; (ambassador) retirar. 2 (remember) recordar.
recant |rɪˈkænt| vi fml retractarse.
recap |ˈriːkæp| I vtr & vi resumir; **to r.**, en resumen. II |ˈriːkæp| n recapitulación f.
recapitulate |riːkəˈpɪtjʊleɪt| vtr & vi fml recapitular.
recapture |riːˈkæptʃər| vtr fig recuperar.
recd Com abbr of **received**, recibido, -a.

recede |rɪˈsiːd| vi retroceder; (fade) desvanecerse.
receipt |rɪˈsiːt| n 1 (act) recepción f; **to acknowledge r. of sth**, acusar recibo de algo. 2 Com (paper) recibo m. 3 **receipts**, (takings) recuadación f sing.
receive |rɪˈsiːv| vtr 1 recibir. 2 Jur (stolen goods) ocultar. 3 (welcome) acoger. 4 TV Rad captar.
receiver |rɪˈsiːvər| n 1 (person) receptor,-a m,f. 2 Jur (of stolen goods) perista mf. 3 GB Jur official r., síndico m. 4 Tel auricular m. 5 Rad receptor m.
recent |ˈriːsənt| adj reciente; **in r. years**, en los últimos años. ◆**recently** adv hace poco, recientemente.
receptacle |rɪˈseptəkəl| n receptáculo m.
reception |rɪˈsepʃən| n 1 (welcome) acogida f. 2 (party) recepción f; **wedding r.**, banquete m de bodas. 3 **r. (desk)**, recepción f. 4 Rad TV recepción f.
receptionist |rɪˈsepʃənɪst| n recepcionista mf.
recess |ˈriːses, rɪˈses| n 1 (in a wall) hueco m. 2 (secret place) escondrijo m. 3 US Educ recreo m; Parl período m de vacaciones.
recession |rɪˈseʃən| n recesión f.
recharge |riːˈtʃɑːdʒ| vtr (battery) recargar.
rechargeable |riːˈtʃɑːdʒəbəl| adj recargable.
recipe |ˈresɪpɪ| n Culin receta f; fig fórmula f.
recipient |rɪˈsɪpɪənt| n receptor,-a m,f; (of letter) destinatario,-a m,f.
reciprocate |rɪˈsɪprəkeɪt| I vtr (favour etc) devolver. II vi hacer lo mismo.
recital |rɪˈsaɪtəl| n recital m.
recite |rɪˈsaɪt| vtr & vi recitar.
reckless |ˈreklɪs| adj (unwise) imprudente; (fearless) temerario,-a.
reckon |ˈrekən| vtr & vi 1 (calculate) calcular; (count) contar. 2 fam (think) creer; (consider) considerar. ◆**reckon on** vtr contar con.
reckoner |ˈrekənər| n ready r., tabla f de cálculo.
reckoning |ˈrekənɪŋ| n cálculo m; **by my r. ...**, según mis cálculos ...; fig **day of r.**, día m del juicio final.
reclaim |rɪˈkleɪm| vtr 1 (recover) recuperar; (demand back) reclamar. 2 (marshland etc) convertir.
recline |rɪˈklaɪn| vi recostarse, reclinarse.
reclining |rɪˈklaɪnɪŋ| adj recostado,-a; **r. seat**, asiento m abatible.
recluse |rɪˈkluːs| n recluso,-a m,f.
recognition |rekəɡˈnɪʃən| n reconocimiento m; (appreciation) apreciación f; **changed beyond all r.**, irreconocible.
recognizable |rekəɡˈnaɪzəbəl| adj reconocible.
recognize |ˈrekəɡnaɪz| vtr reconocer.

recoil ['ri:kɔil] I *n (of gun)* culatazo *m; (of spring)* aflojamiento *m.* II [ri'kɔil] *vi* 1 *(gun)* dar un culatazo; *(spring)* aflojarse. 2 *(in fear)* espantarse.

recollect [rekə'lekt] *vtr* recordar.

recollection [rekə'lekʃən] *n* recuerdo *m.*

recommend [rekə'mend] *vtr* recomendar.

recommendation [rekəmen'deiʃən] *n* recomendación *f.*

recompense ['rekəmpens] I *n* recompensa *f; Jur* indemnización *f.* II *vtr* recompensar; *Jur* indemnizar.

reconcile ['rekənsail] *vtr (two people)* reconciliar; *(two ideas)* conciliar; **to r. one-self to**, resignarse a.

recondition [ri:kən'diʃən] *vtr (engine)* revisar.

reconnaissance [ri'kɒnisəns] *n Mil* reconocimiento *m.*

reconnoitre, *US* **reconnoiter** [rekə'nɔitər] *vtr Mil* reconocer.

reconsider [ri:kən'sidər] *vtr* reconsiderar.

reconstruct [ri:kən'strʌkt] *vtr* reconstruir.

reconstruction [ri:kən'strʌkʃən] *n* reconstrucción *f.*

record ['rekɔːd] I *n* 1 *(account)* relación *f; (of meeting)* actas *fpl;* **off the r.**, confidencialmente. 2 *(document)* documento *m;* **r. of attendance**, registro *m* de asistencia; **public records**, archivos *mpl.* 3 *Med* historial médico. 4 *Mus* disco *m;* **r. player**, tocadiscos *m inv.* 5 *Sport* récord *m.* II [ri'kɔːd] *vtr* 1 *(relate)* hacer constar; *(note down)* apuntar. 2 *(record, voice)* grabar. 3 *(of thermometer etc)* marcar.

recorded [ri'kɔːdid] *adj* **r. delivery**, correo certificado; **r. message**, mensaje grabado.

recorder [ri'kɔːdər] 1 *(person)* registrador,-a *m,f; Jur* magistrado,-a. 2 *Mus* flauta *f.*

recording [ri'kɔːdiŋ] *n (registering)* registro *m; (recorded music, message etc)* grabación *f.*

recount [ri'kaunt] *vtr (tell)* contar.

re-count [ri:'kaunt] I *vi Pol* hacer un recuento. II ['ri:kaunt] *n Pol* recuento *m.*

recoup [ri'ku:p] *vtr (losses etc)* recuperar.

recourse [ri'kɔːs] *n* **to have r. to**, recurrir a.

recover [ri'kʌvər] I *vtr (items, lost time)* recuperar; *(consciousness)* recobrar. II *vi (from illness etc)* reponerse.

recovery [ri'kʌvəri] *n* 1 *(retrieval)* recuperación *f.* 2 *(from illness)* restablecimiento *m.*

recreation [rekri'eiʃən] *n* 1 diversión *f.* 2 *Educ (playtime)* recreo *m;* **r. ground**, terreno *m* de juegos.

recreational [rekri'eiʃənəl] *adj* recreativo,-a.

recrimination [rikrimi'neiʃən] *n* reprochе *m.*

recruit [ri'kru:t] I *n* recluta *m.* II *vtr (soldiers)* reclutar; *(workers)* contratar.

recruitment [ri'kru:tmənt] *n (of soldiers)* reclutamiento *m; (of employees)* contratación *f.*

rectangle ['rektæŋgəl] *n* rectángulo *m.*

rectangular [rek'tæŋgjulər] *adj* rectangular.

rectify ['rektifai] *vtr* rectificar.

rector ['rektər] *n* 1 *Rel* párroco *m.* 2 *Scot Educ* director,-a *m,f.*

recuperate [ri'ku:pəreit] *vi* reponerse.

recur [ri'kɜːr] *vi* repetirse.

recurrence [ri'kʌrəns] *n* repetición *f*, reaparición *f.*

recurrent [ri'kʌrənt] *adj* constante; *Med* recurrente.

recycle [ri:'saikəl] *vtr* reciclar.

recycling [ri:'saikliŋ] *n* reciclaje *m.*

red [red] I *adj (redder, reddest)* rojo,-a; **r. light**, semáforo *m* en rojo; **r. wine**, vino tinto; **to go r.**, ponerse colorado,-a; **to have r. hair**, ser pelirrojo,-a; *fig* **r. herring**, truco *m* para despistar; *fam* **to roll out the r. carpet for sb**, recibir a algn con todos los honores; **R. Cross**, Cruz Roja; **R. Indian**, piel roja *mf;* **R. Riding Hood**, Caperucita Roja; **R. Sea**, Mar Rojo; **r. tape**, papeleo *m.* II *n* 1 *(colour)* rojo *m; Fin* **to be in the r.**, estar en números rojos.

redcurrant ['redkʌrənt] *n* grosella roja.

redden ['redən] I *vi (blush)* enrojecerse, ponerse colorado,-a. II *vtr (make red)* teñir de rojo.

reddish ['rediʃ] *adj* rojizo,-a.

redeem [ri'di:m] *vtr* 1 *(regain)* recobrar; *(from pawn)* desempeñar; *(voucher)* canjear. 2 *(debt)* amortizar. 3 *(film, novel etc)* salvar. 4 *Rel* redimir; *fig* **to r. one-self**, redimirse.

redeeming [ri'di:miŋ] *adj* compensatorio,-a; **his only r. feature**, lo único que le salva.

redemption [ri'dempʃən] *n fml* 1 *(of debt)* amortización *f.* 2 *Rel* redención *f;* **beyond r.**, sin remedio.

redeploy [ri:di'plɔi] *vtr* transferir.

red-handed [red'hændid] *adj* **to catch sb r.-h.**, coger a algn con las manos en la masa.

redhead ['redhed] *n* pelirrojo,-a *m,f.*

red-hot [red'hɒt] *adj* 1 candente; **r.-h. news**, noticia(s) *f(pl)* de última hora. 2 *fam (passionate)* ardiente.

redial [ri:'daiəl] *n Tel (facility)* rellamada *f.*

redirect [ri:di'rekt] *vtr* 1 *(funds)* redistribuir. 2 *(letter)* remitir a la nueva dirección.

red-light [red'lait] *adj fam* **r.-l. district**, barrio chino.

redouble [ri:'dʌbəl] *vtr* redoblar.

che *m.*

redress [rɪ'dres] *fml* **I** *n* reparación *f.* **II** *vtr* reparar.

redskin ['redskɪn] *n offens* piel roja *mf.*

reduce [rɪ'djuːs] *vtr* **1** reducir. **2** *(in rank)* degradar. **3** *Culin (sauce)* espesar. **4** *Med* recomponer.

reduction [rɪ'dʌkʃən] *n* reducción *f*; *Com (in purchase price)* descuento *m*, rebaja *f.*

redundancy [rɪ'dʌndənsɪ] *n* despido *m.*

redundant [rɪ'dʌndənt] *adj* **1** *(superfluous)* redundante. **2** *Ind* **to be made r.**, perder el empleo; **to make sb r.**, despedir a algn.

reed [riːd] *n* **1** *Bot* caña *f.* **2** *Mus* caramillo *m.*

reef [riːf] *n* arrecife *m.*

reek [riːk] **I** *n* tufo *m.* **II** *vi* apestar.

reel [riːl] **I** *n* **1** *(spool)* bobina *f*, carrete *m.* **2** *Scot Mus* danza *f* tradicional. **II** *vi (stagger)* tambalearse.

re-elect [riːɪ'lekt] *vtr* reelegir.

ref [ref] *n* **1** *Sport fam abbr of* **referee.** **2** *Com abbr of* **reference,** ref.

refectory [rɪ'fektərɪ] *n* refectorio *m.*

refer [rɪ'fɜːr] **I** *vtr* mandar, enviar; **to r. a matter to a tribunal,** remitir un asunto a un tribunal. **II** *vi* **1** *(allude)* referirse, aludir **(to, a). 2** *(consult)* consultar **(to, -).**

referee [refə'riː] **I** *n* **1** *Sport* árbitro,-a *m,f.* **2** *(for job application)* garante *mf.* **II** *vtr Sport* arbitrar.

reference ['refərəns] *n* **1** referencia *f*; **with r. to,** referente a, con referencia a; **r. book,** libro *m* de consulta; **r. library,** biblioteca *f* de consulta. **2** *(character report)* informe *m*, referencia *f.*

referendum [refə'rendəm] *n* referéndum *m.*

refill ['riːfɪl] **I** *n* **1** *(replacement)* recambio *m*, carga *f.* **2** *fam (drink)* otra copa. **II** [riː'fɪl] *vtr* rellenar.

refine [rɪ'faɪn] *vtr* refinar.

refined [rɪ'faɪnd] *adj* refinado,-a.

refinement [rɪ'faɪnmənt] *n* refinamiento *m.*

refinery [rɪ'faɪnərɪ] *n* refinería *f.*

reflect [rɪ'flekt] **I** *vtr (light, attitude)* reflejar. **II** *vi (think)* reflexionar; **to r. on sth,** meditar sobre algo.

reflection [rɪ'flekʃən] *n* **1** *(indication, mirror image)* reflejo *m.* **2** *(thought)* reflexión *f*; **on r.,** pensándolo bien. **3** *(criticism)* crítica *f.*

reflector [rɪ'flektər] *n* **1** *Astron* reflector *m.* **2** *(of vehicle)* catafaro *m.*

reflex ['riːfleks] *n* reflejo *m.*

reflexive [rɪ'fleksɪv] *adj* reflexivo,-a.

reform [rɪ'fɔːm] **I** *n* reforma *f.* **II** *vtr* reformar.

reformation [refə'meɪʃən] *n* reforma *f.*

reformatory [rɪ'fɔːmətərɪ] *n* reformatorio *m.*

reformer [rɪ'fɔːmər] *n* reformador,-a *m,f.*

refrain [rɪ'freɪn] **I** *n* *Mus* estribillo *m*; *fig* lema *m.* **II** *vi* abstenerse **(from,** de).

refresh [rɪ'freʃ] *vtr* refrescar.

refresher [rɪ'freʃər] *n* **r. course,** cursillo *m* de reciclaje.

refreshing [rɪ'freʃɪŋ] *adj* refrescante; **a r. change,** un cambio muy agradable.

refreshment [rɪ'freʃmənt] *n* refresco *m.*

refrigerator [rɪ'frɪdʒəreɪtər] *n* nevera *f*, frigorífico *m.*

refuel [riː'fjuːəl] *vi* repostar combustible.

refuge ['refjuːdʒ] *n* refugio *m*, cobijo *m*; **to take r.,** refugiarse.

refugee [refjuː'dʒiː] *n* refugiado,-a *m,f.*

refund ['riːfʌnd] **I** *n* reembolso *m.* **II** [rɪ'fʌnd] *vtr* reembolsar, devolver.

refurbish [riː'fɜːbɪʃ] *vtr* redecorar.

refusal [rɪ'fjuːzəl] *n* negativa *f*; **to have first r. on sth,** tener la primera opción en algo.

refuse¹ [rɪ'fjuːz] **I** *vtr* rechazar; **to r. sb sth,** negar algo a algn. **II** *vi* negarse.

refuse² ['refjuːs] *n* basura *f*; **r. collector,** basurero *m.*

refute [rɪ'fjuːt] *vtr* refutar, rebatir.

regain [rɪ'geɪn] *vtr* recuperar; *(consciousness)* recobrar.

regal ['riːgəl] *adj* regio,-a.

regard [rɪ'gɑːd] **I** *n* **1** *(concern)* consideración *f*, respeto *m*; **with r. to,** respecto a. **2** *(esteem)* estima *f.* **3 regards,** *(good wishes)* recuerdos *mpl*; **give him my regards,** dale recuerdos de mi parte. **II** *vtr* **1** *(consider)* considerar. **2 as regards,** *(regarding)* respecto a.

regarding [rɪ'gɑːdɪŋ] *prep* respecto a.

regardless [rɪ'gɑːdlɪs] **I** *prep* a pesar de; **r. of the outcome,** pase lo que pase. **II** *adv* a toda costa.

regime [reɪ'ʒiːm] *n* régimen *m.*

regiment ['redʒɪmənt] **I** *n* regimiento *m.* **II** *vtr* regimentar.

regimental [redʒɪ'mentəl] *adj* del regimiento.

region ['riːdʒən] *n* **1** región *f.* **2 in the r. of,** aproximadamente.

regional ['riːdʒənəl] *adj* regional.

regionalism ['riːdʒənəlɪzəm] *n* regionalismo *m.*

register ['redʒɪstər] *n* **1** registro *m.* **II** *vtr* **1** *(record)* registrar. **2** *(letter)* certificar. **3** *(show)* mostrar; **his face registered fear,** en su rostro se reflejaba el miedo. **III** *vi (for course)* inscribirse; *Univ* matricularse.

registered ['redʒɪstəd] *adj* certificado,-a; **r. letter,** carta certificada; **r. trademark,** marca registrada.

registrar [redʒɪ'strɑːr, 'redʒɪstrɑːr] *n* **1** *(record keeper)* registrador,-a *m,f.* **2** *GB Med* interno,-a *m,f.* **3** *Univ* secretario,-a *m,f* general.

registration [redʒɪ'streɪʃən] *n* inscripción *f*; *Univ* matrícula *f*; *GB Aut* **r. number,** matrícula *f.*

registry ['redʒɪstrɪ] *n* registro *m*; **to get**

married in a r. office, casarse por lo civil; r. office, registro civil.

regret [rɪ'gret] I *n* (*remorse*) remordimiento *m*; (*sadness*) pesar *m*; **regrets**, (*excuses*) excusas *fpl*; **to have no regrets**, no arrepentirse de nada. II *vtr* arrepentirse de, lamentar.

regretful [rɪ'gretful] *adj* arrepentido,-a.

regrettable [rɪ'gretəbəl] *adj* lamentable.

regroup [riː'gruːp] I *vtr* reagrupar. II *vi* reagruparse.

regular ['regjulər] I *adj* 1 regular. 2 (*usual*) normal. 3 (*staff*) permanente. 4 (*frequent*) frecuente. 5 **r. army**, tropas *fpl* regulares. II *n* 1 (*customer*) cliente *mf* habitual. 2 *Mil* militar *m* de carrera. ◆**regularly** *adv* con regularidad.

regularity [regjʊ'lærɪtɪ] *n* regularidad *f*.

regulate ['regjʊleɪt] *vtr* regular.

regulation [regjʊ'leɪʃən] I *n* 1 (*control*) regulación *f*. 2 (*rule*) regla *f*. II *adj* reglamentario,-a.

rehabilitation [riːəbɪlɪ'teɪʃən] *n* rehabilitación *f*; **r. centre**, centro *m* de reinserción.

rehearsal [rɪ'hɜːsəl] *n* ensayo *m*.

rehearse [rɪ'hɜːs] *vtr & vi* ensayar.

reign [reɪn] I *n* reinado *m*. II *vi* reinar.

reigning ['reɪnɪŋ] *adj* **r. champion**, campeón *m* actual.

reimburse [riːɪm'bɜːs] *vtr* reembolsar.

rein [reɪn] *n* (*for horse*) rienda *f*; *fig* **he gave free r. to his emotions**, dio rienda suelta a sus emociones.

reindeer ['reɪndɪər] *n* reno *m*.

reinforce [riːɪn'fɔːs] *vtr* (*strengthen*) reforzar; (*support*) apoyar; **reinforced concrete**, hormigón armado.

reinforcement [riːɪn'fɔːsmənt] *n* 1 refuerzo *m*; *Constr* armazón *m*. 2 *Mil* **reinforcements**, refuerzos *mpl*.

reinstate [riːɪn'steɪt] *vtr* (*to job*) reincorporar.

reiterate [riː'ɪtəreɪt] *vtr & vi* reiterar.

reject ['riːdʒekt] I *n* 1 desecho *m*. 2 *Com* **rejects**, artículos defectuosos. II [rɪ'dʒekt] *vtr* rechazar.

rejection [rɪ'dʒekʃən] *n* rechazo *m*.

rejoice [rɪ'dʒɔɪs] *vi* regocijarse (**at**, **over**, **de**).

rejuvenate [rɪ'dʒuːvɪneɪt] *vtr* rejuvenecer; *fig* revitalizar.

relapse [rɪ'læps] I *n* 1 *Med* recaída *f*; **to have a r.**, sufrir una recaída. 2 (*into crime, alcoholism*) reincidencia *f*. II *vi* recaer.

relate [rɪ'leɪt] I *vtr* 1 (*connect*) relacionar. 2 (*tell*) relatar. II *vi* relacionarse.

related [rɪ'leɪtɪd] *adj* 1 (*linked*) relacionado,-a (**to**, **con**). 2 **to be r. to sb**, ser pariente de algn.

relation [rɪ'leɪʃən] *n* 1 (*link*) relación *f*; **in** *or* **with r. to**, respecto a; **it bears no r. to what we said**, no tiene nada que ver con

lo que dijimos. 2 (*member of family*) pariente,-a *m,f*.

relationship [rɪ'leɪʃənʃɪp] *n* 1 (*link*) relación *f*. 2 (*between people*) relaciones *fpl*; **to have a good/bad r. with sb**, llevarse bien/mal con algn.

relative ['relətɪv] I *n* pariente *mf*. II *adj* 1 relativo,-a. ◆**relatively** *adv* relativamente.

relax [rɪ'læks] I *vtr* (*muscles, rules*) relajar. II *vi* relajarse.

relaxation [riːlæk'seɪʃən] *n* 1 (*rest*) descanso *m*, relajación *f*. 2 (*of rules*) relajación *f*. 3 (*pastime*) distracción *f*.

relaxed [rɪ'lækst] *adj* relajado,-a; (*peaceful*) tranquilo,-a.

relaxing [rɪ'læksɪŋ] *adj* relajante.

relay ['riːleɪ] I *m* 1 relevo *m*; **r. (race)**, carrera *f* de relevos. 2 *Rad TV* retransmisión *f*. II [rɪ'leɪ] *vtr* 1 (*pass on*) difundir. 2 *Rad TV* retransmitir.

release [rɪ'liːs] I *n* 1 (*of prisoner*) liberación *f*, puesta *f* en libertad; (*of gas*) escape *m*. 2 *Com* puesta *f* en venta. 3 *Cin* estreno *m*. 4 (*record*) disco *m*. 5 *Press* comunicado *m*. II *vtr* 1 (*let go*) soltar; (*prisoner*) poner en libertad; (*gas*) despedir. 2 *Com* poner en venta. 3 *Cin* estrenar. 4 (*record*) editar. 5 (*publish*) publicar.

relegate ['relɪgeɪt] *vtr* 1 relegar. 2 *Ftb* **to be relegated**, bajar a una división inferior.

relent [rɪ'lent] *vi* ceder; (*storm*) aplacarse.

relentless [rɪ'lentlɪs] *adj* implacable.

relevant ['relɪvənt] *adj* pertinente (**to**, **a**); **it is not r.**, no viene al caso.

reliable [rɪ'laɪəbəl] *adj* (*person*) de fiar; a **r. car**, un coche seguro; **a r. source**, una fuente fidedigna. ◆**reliably** *adv* **to be r. informed that**, saber de buena tinta que.

reliability [rɪlaɪə'bɪlɪtɪ] *n* 1 (*of person*) formalidad *f*. 2 (*of car, machine*) fiabilidad *f*.

reliant [rɪ'laɪənt] *adj* **to be r. on**, depender de.

relic ['relɪk] *n* 1 *Rel* reliquia *f*. 2 (*reminder of past*) vestigio *m*. 3 **relics**, (*human remains*) restos *mpl* mortales.

relief [rɪ'liːf] *n* 1 alivio *m*. 2 (*help*) auxilio *m*, ayuda *f*. 3 *Art Geog* relieve *m*.

relieve [rɪ'liːv] *vtr* 1 aliviar; (*monotony*) romper. 2 (*take over from*) relevar. 3 *euph* **to r. oneself**, hacer sus necesidades. 4 **to r. sb of sth**, coger algo a algn.

relieved [rɪ'liːvd] *adj* aliviado,-a, tranquilizado,-a.

religion [rɪ'lɪdʒən] *n* religión *f*.

religious [rɪ'lɪdʒəs] *adj* religioso,-a.

relinquish [rɪ'lɪŋkwɪʃ] *vtr* renunciar a; **to r. one's hold on sth**, soltar algo.

relish ['relɪʃ] I *n* 1 (*enjoyment*) deleite *m*. 2 *Culin* condimento *m*. II *vtr* agradar.

relocate [riːləʊ'keɪt] *vtr* trasladar.

reluctance [rɪˈlʌktəns] n desgana f.

reluctant [rɪˈlʌktənt] adj reacio,-a; **to be r. to do sth,** estar poco dispuesto,-a a hacer algo. ◆**reluctantly** adv de mala gana, a regañadientes.

rely [rɪˈlaɪ] vi contar (**on,** con), confiar (**on,** en).

remain [rɪˈmeɪn] I vi 1 (stay) permanecer, quedarse. 2 (be left) quedar; **it remains to be seen,** está por ver. II npl **remains,** restos mpl.

remainder [rɪˈmeɪndər] n resto m.

remaining [rɪˈmeɪnɪŋ] adj restante.

remand [rɪˈmɑːnd] Jur I vtr remitir; **remanded in custody,** en prevención. II n detención f; **on r.,** detenido,-a.

remark [rɪˈmɑːk] I n comentario m. II vtr comentar.

remarkable [rɪˈmɑːkəbəl] adj extraordinario,-a; (strange) curioso,-a.

remedial [rɪˈmiːdɪəl] adj reparador,-a; **r. classes,** clases fpl para niños atrasados en los estudios.

remedy [ˈremɪdɪ] I n remedio m. II vtr remediar.

remember [rɪˈmembər] I vtr 1 acordarse de, recordar. 2 **r. me to your mother,** dale recuerdos a tu madre. II vi acordarse, recordar; **I don't r.,** no me acuerdo.

remembrance [rɪˈmembrəns] n **in r. of,** en recuerdo de; **R. Day,** día m en que se conmemora el armisticio de 1918.

remind [rɪˈmaɪnd] vtr recordar; **r. me to do it,** recuérdame que lo haga; **she reminds me of your sister,** me recuerda a tu hermana; **that reminds me,** ahora que me acuerdo.

reminder [rɪˈmaɪndər] n recordatorio m, aviso m.

reminisce [remɪˈnɪs] vi rememorar.

reminiscent [remɪˈnɪsənt] adj fml nostálgico,-a; **to be r. of,** recordar.

remiss [rɪˈmɪs] adj (negligent) descuidado,-a.

remission [rɪˈmɪʃən] n 1 Med remisión f. 2 Jur perdón m.

remit [rɪˈmɪt] vtr 1 (send) remitir. 2 Jur referir a otro tribunal.

remittance [rɪˈmɪtəns] n 1 (sending) envío m. 2 (payment) giro m, pago m.

remnant [ˈremnənt] n resto m; **remnants,** (of cloth) retales mpl.

remorse [rɪˈmɔːs] n remordimiento m.

remorseful [rɪˈmɔːsfʌl] adj lleno,-a de remordimiento.

remorseless [rɪˈmɔːslɪs] adj despiadado, -a.

remote [rɪˈməut] adj 1 (far away) remoto,-a; **r. control,** mando m a distancia. 2 (isolated) aislado,-a. 3 **r. person,** persona reservada. 4 (possibility) remoto,-a; **I haven't the remotest idea,** no tengo la más mínima idea.

◆**remotely** adv 1 (vaguely) vagamente. 2 (distantly) en lugar aislado.

remote-controlled [rɪməutkɒnˈtrəuld] adj teledirigido,-a.

remould, US **remold** [ˈriːməuld] n Aut neumático recauchutado.

removable [rɪˈmuːvəbəl] adj (detachable) que se puede quitar.

removal [rɪˈmuːvəl] n 1 (moving house) mudanza f; **r. van,** camión m de mudanzas. 2 (of stain etc) eliminación f.

remove [rɪˈmuːv] vtr 1 (move) quitar; **to r. one's make-up,** desmaquillarse; **to r. one's name from a list,** tachar su nombre de una lista. 2 (from office) despedir.

removed [rɪˈmuːvd] adj **far r. from,** muy diferente de.

remover [rɪˈmuːvər] n **make-up r.,** desmaquillador m; **nail varnish r.,** quitaesmalte m; **stain r.,** quitamanchas m inv.

remuneration [rɪmjuːnəˈreɪʃən] n fml remuneración f.

renaissance [rəˈneɪsəns] I n renacimiento m; **the R.,** el Renacimiento. II adj renacentista.

rend [rend] vtr (pt & pp **rent**) fml rasgar.

render [ˈrendər] vtr fml 1 (give) dar. 2 (make) hacer. 3 Com presentar. 4 (translate) traducir.

rendering [ˈrendərɪŋ] n 1 (of song, piece of music) interpretación f. 2 (translation) traducción f.

rendezvous [ˈrɒndɪvuː] I n 1 (meeting) cita f. 2 (place) lugar m de reunión. II vi reunirse.

renegade [ˈrenɪɡeɪd] n renegado,-a m,f.

renew [rɪˈnjuː] vtr (contract etc) renovar; (talks etc) reanudar; **with renewed vigour,** con renovadas fuerzas.

renewal [rɪˈnjuːəl] n 1 (of contract etc) renovación f. 2 (of talks etc) reanudación f.

renounce [rɪˈnauns] vtr fml renunciar.

renovate [ˈrenəveɪt] vtr renovar, hacer reformas en.

renown [rɪˈnaun] n renombre m.

renowned [rɪˈnaund] adj renombrado,-a.

rent [rent] I n 1 (for building, car, TV) alquiler m. 2 (for land) arriendo m. II vtr 1 (building, car, TV) alquilar. 2 (land) arrendar.

rental [ˈrentəl] n (of house etc) alquiler m.

renunciation [rɪnʌnsɪˈeɪʃən] n fml renuncia f.

reorganize [riːˈɔːɡənaɪz] vtr reorganizar.

rep [rep] fam 1 Com representante mf. 2 Theat teatro m de repertorio.

repair [rɪˈpeər] I n reparación f, arreglo m; **in good/bad r.,** en buen/mal estado. II vtr 1 arreglar; (car) reparar; (clothes) remendar. 2 (make amends for) reparar.

repartee [repɑːˈtiː] n réplica aguda.

repatriate [riːˈpætrɪeɪt] vtr repatriar.

repay [riːˈpeɪ] vtr (pt & pp **repaid**) devolver; **to r. a debt,** liquidar una deuda; **to r. a kindness,** devolver un favor.

repayment [riː'peɪmənt] *n* pago *m*.

repeal [rɪ'piːl] *Jur* I *n* revocación *f*. II *vtr* revocar.

repeat [rɪ'piːt] I *vtr* repetir; **to r. oneself,** repetirse. II *n (repetition)* repitición *f*; *TV* reposición *f*.

repeated [rɪ'piːtɪd] *adj* repetido,-a. ◆**repeatedly** *adv* repetidas veces.

repel [rɪ'pel] *vtr* 1 *(fight off)* repeler. 2 *(disgust)* repugnar.

repellent [rɪ'pelənt] I *adj* repelente. II *n (insect)* r., loción *f* or spray *m* antiinsectos; **water-r.,** impermeable *m*.

repent [rɪ'pent] *vtr & vi* arrepentirse (de).

repentance [rɪ'pentəns] *n* arrepentimiento *m*.

repercussion [riːpə'kʌʃən] *n (usu pl)* repercusión *f*.

repertoire ['repətwɑːr] *n* repertorio *m*.

repertory ['repətərɪ] *n Theat* teatro *m* de repertorio.

repetition [repɪ'tɪʃən] *n* repetición *f*.

repetitive [rɪ'petɪtɪv] *adj* repetitivo,-a.

replace [rɪ'pleɪs] *vtr* 1 *(put back)* volver a poner en su sitio. 2 *(substitute for)* sustituir, reemplazar.

replacement [rɪ'pleɪsmənt] *n* 1 *(returning)* reemplazo *m*. 2 *(person)* sustituto,-a *m,f*. 3 *(part)* pieza *f* de recambio.

replay ['riːpleɪ] *n* repetición *f*.

replenish [rɪ'plenɪʃ] *vtr* 1 *(fill up)* rellenar. 2 **to r. stocks,** reponer las existencias.

replete [rɪ'pliːt] *adj fml* repleto,-a.

replica ['replɪkə] *n* réplica *f*.

reply [rɪ'plaɪ] I *n* respuesta *f*, contestación *f*. II *vi* responder, contestar.

report [rɪ'pɔːt] I *n* 1 informe *m*; **medical r.,** parte médico; *GB* **school r.,** informe escolar. 2 *(piece of news)* noticia *f*. 3 *Press Rad TV* reportaje *m*. 4 *(rumour)* rumor *m*. 5 *fml (of gun)* estampido *m*. II *vtr* 1 **it is reported that ...,** se dice que .... 2 *(tell authorities about)* denunciar. 3 *Press* hacer un reportaje sobre. III *vi (of committee member etc)* 1 hacer un informe. 2 *Press* hacer un reportaje. 3 *(for duty etc)* presentarse; *Mil* **to r. sick,** coger la baja por enfermedad.

reported [rɪ'pɔːtɪd] *adj* **r. speech,** estilo indirecto. ◆**reportedly** *adv fml* según se dice.

reporter [rɪ'pɔːtər] *n* periodista *mf*.

repose [rɪ'pəʊz] *fml* I *n* reposo *m*. II *vtr & vi* reposar.

repossess [riːpə'zes] *vtr* volver a tomar posesión.

reprehensible [reprɪ'hensəbəl] *adj* reprensible, censurable.

represent [reprɪ'zent] *vtr* representar.

representation [reprɪzen'teɪʃən] *n* 1 representación *f*. 2 *fml* **representations,** queja *f sing*.

representative [reprɪ'zentətɪv] I *adj* representativo,-a. II *n* 1 representante *mf*. 2 *US Pol* diputado,-a *m,f*; **House of Representatives,** Cámara *f* de Representantes.

repress [rɪ'pres] *vtr* reprimir, contener.

repression [rɪ'preʃən] *n* represión *f*.

repressive [rɪ'presɪv] *adj* represivo,-a.

reprieve [rɪ'priːv] I *n* 1 *Jur* indulto *m*. 2 *fig* alivio *m*. II *vtr* 1 *Jur* indultar. 2 *(give temporary relief to)* aliviar temporalmente.

reprimand ['reprɪmɑːnd] I *n* reprimenda *f*. II *vtr* reprender.

reprisal [rɪ'praɪzəl] *n* represalia *f*.

reproach [rɪ'prəʊtʃ] I *n* reproche *m*; **beyond r.,** intachable. II *vtr* reprochar.

reproachful [rɪ'prəʊtʃfʊl] *adj* reprobador,-a.

reproduce [riːprə'djuːs] I *vtr* reproducir. II *vi* reproducirse.

reproduction [riːprə'dʌkʃən] *n* reproducción *f*.

reproof [rɪ'pruːf] *n fml* reprobación *f*, censura *f*.

reprove [rɪ'pruːv] *vtr fml* reprobar, censurar.

reptile ['reptaɪl] *n* reptil *m*.

republic [rɪ'pʌblɪk] *n* república *f*.

republican [rɪ'pʌblɪkən] *adj & n* republicano,-a *(m,f)*; *US Pol* **R. Party,** Partido Republicano.

repudiate [rɪ'pjuːdɪeɪt] *vtr fml* 1 *(reject)* rechazar. 2 *(not acknowledge)* negarse a reconocer.

repugnant [rɪ'pʌgnənt] *adj* repugnante.

repulse [rɪ'pʌls] *vtr* rechazar.

repulsive [rɪ'pʌlsɪv] *adj* repulsivo,-a.

reputable ['repjʊtəbəl] *adj (company etc)* acreditado,-a; *(person, products)* de toda confianza.

reputation [repjʊ'teɪʃən] *n* reputación *f*.

repute [rɪ'pjuːt] *n fml* reputación *f*.

reputed [rɪ'pjuːtɪd] *adj* supuesto,-a; **to be r. to be,** ser considerado,-a como. ◆**reputedly** *adv* según se dice.

request [rɪ'kwest] I *n* petición *f*, solicitud *f*; **available on r.,** disponible a petición de los interesados; *GB* **r. stop,** *(for bus)* parada *f* discrecional. II *vtr* pedir, solicitar.

require [rɪ'kwaɪər] *vtr* 1 *(need)* necesitar, requerir. 2 *(demand)* exigir.

requirement [rɪ'kwaɪəmənt] *n* 1 *(need)* necesidad *f*. 2 *(demand)* requisito *m*.

requisite ['rekwɪzɪt] *fml* I *adj* requerido,-a. II *n* requisito *m*.

requisition [rekwɪ'zɪʃən] I *n* requisición *f*. II *vtr* requisar.

rescind [rɪ'sɪnd] *vtr fml (contract)* rescindir; *(law)* abrogar.

rescue ['reskjuː] I *n* rescate *m*; **r. team,** equipo *m* de rescate. II *vtr* rescatar.

rescuer ['reskjʊər] *n* rescatador,-a *m,f*.

research |rɪˈsɜːtʃ| I n investigación f; **R. and Development,** Investigación más Desarrollo. II vtr & vi investigar.

researcher |rɪˈsɜːtʃər| n investigador,-a m,f.

resemblance |rɪˈzembləns| n semejanza f.

resemble |rɪˈzembəl| vtr parecerse a.

resent |rɪˈzent| vtr ofenderse por.

resentful |rɪˈzentfʊl| adj ofendido,-a.

resentment |rɪˈzentmənt| n resentimiento m.

reservation |rezəˈveɪʃən| n reserva f.

reserve |rɪˈzɜːv| I n 1 reserva f; **to keep sth in r.,** guardar algo de reserva. 2 Sport suplente mf. 3 Mil **reserves,** reservas fpl. II vtr reservar.

reserved |rɪˈzɜːvd| adj reservado,-a.

reservoir |ˈrezəvwɑːr| n embalse m, pantano m; fig reserva f.

reshape |riːˈʃeɪp| vtr rehacer; fig reorganizar.

reshuffle |riːˈʃʌfəl| n Pol remodelación f.

reside |rɪˈzaɪd| vi fml residir.

residence |ˈrezɪdəns| n fml (home) residencia f; (address) domicilio m; (period of time) permanencia f.

resident |ˈrezɪdənt| adj & n residente (mf); **to be r. in,** estar domiciliado,-a en.

residential |rezɪˈdenʃəl| adj residencial.

residue |ˈrezɪdjuː| n residuo m.

resign |rɪˈzaɪn| I vtr 1 (give up) dimitir. 2 **to r. oneself to sth,** resignarse a algo. II vi (from job) dimitir.

resignation |rezɪgˈneɪʃən| n 1 (from a job) dimisión f. 2 (acceptance) resignación f.

resigned |rɪˈzaɪnd| adj resignado,-a.

resilience |rɪˈzɪliəns| n resistencia f.

resilient |rɪˈzɪliənt| adj (strong) resistente.

resin |ˈrezɪn| n resina f.

resist |rɪˈzɪst| vtr 1 (not yield to) resistir. 2 (oppose) oponerse a.

resistance |rɪˈzɪstəns| n resistencia f.

resit |riːˈsɪt| vtr (exam) volver a presentarse a.

resolute |ˈrezəluːt| adj resuelto,-a, decidido,-a.

resolution |rezəˈluːʃən| n resolución f.

resolve |rɪˈzɒlv| I n resolución f. II vtr resolver; **to r. to do,** resolverse a hacer. III vi resolverse.

resonant |ˈrezənənt| adj resonante.

resort |rɪˈzɔːt| I n 1 (place) lugar m de vacaciones; **tourist r.,** centro turístico. 2 (recourse) recurso m; **as a last r.,** como último recurso. II vi recurrir (**to,** a).

resound |rɪˈzaʊnd| vi resonar; fig tener resonancia.

resounding |rɪˈzaʊndɪŋ| adj a r. **failure,** un fracaso total; a r. **success,** un éxito rotundo.

resource |rɪˈsɔːs| n recurso m.

resourceful |rɪˈsɔːsfʊl| adj ingenioso,-a.

respect |rɪˈspekt| I n 1 (deference) respeto m; **to pay one's respects to sb,** presentar sus respetos a algn. 2 (relation, reference) respecto m; **in that r.,** a ese respecto; **with r. to,** con referencia a. II vtr respetar.

respectable |rɪˈspektəbəl| adj respetable; (clothes) decente.

respectful |rɪˈspektfʊl| adj respetuoso,-a.

respective |rɪˈspektɪv| adj respectivo,-a. ◆**respectively** adv respectivamente.

respite |ˈrespaɪt| n fml respiro m.

resplendent |rɪˈsplendənt| adj resplandeciente.

respond |rɪˈspɒnd| vi responder.

response |rɪˈspɒns| n 1 (reply) respuesta f. 2 (reaction) reacción f.

responsibility |rɪspɒnsəˈbɪlɪtɪ| n responsabilidad f.

responsible |rɪˈspɒnsəbəl| adj responsable (**for,** de); **to be r. to sb,** tener que dar cuentas a algn.

responsive |rɪˈspɒnsɪv| adj sensible.

rest¹ |rest| I n 1 (break) descanso m; **r. cure,** cura f de reposo; US **r. room,** aseos mpl. 2 (peace) tranquilidad f; **at r.** (object) inmóvil. 3 (support) apoyo m. 4 Mus pausa f. II vtr 1 descansar. 2 (lean) apoyar; **to r. a ladder against a wall,** apoyar una escalera contra una pared. III vi 1 descansar. 2 (be calm) quedarse tranquilo,-a. 3 **it doesn't r. with me,** no depende de mí; **we'll let the matter r.,** dejémoslo estar.

rest² |rest| n **the r.,** (remainder) el resto, lo demás; **the r. of the day,** el resto del día; **the r. of the girls,** las demás chicas; **the r. of us,** los demás.

restaurant |ˈrestərɒnt| n restaurante m; Rail **r. car,** coche m restaurante.

restful |ˈrestfʊl| adj relajante.

restitution |restɪˈtjuːʃən| n fml restitución f; **to make r.,** restituir.

restive |ˈrestɪv| adj inquieto,-a, nervioso,-a.

restless |ˈrestlɪs| adj agitado,-a, inquieto,-a.

restoration |restəˈreɪʃən| n 1 (giving back) devolución f. 2 GB Hist **the R.,** la Restauración. 3 (of building, piece of furniture) restauración f.

restore |rɪˈstɔːr| vtr 1 (give back) devolver. 2 (re-establish) restablecer. 3 (building etc) restaurar.

restrain |rɪˈstreɪn| vtr contener; **to r. one's anger,** reprimir la cólera; **to r. oneself,** contenerse.

restrained |rɪˈstreɪnd| adj (person) moderado,-a; (emotion) contenido,-a.

restraint |rɪˈstreɪnt| n 1 (restriction) restricción f; (hindrance) traba f. 2 (moderation) moderación f.

restrict |rɪˈstrɪkt| vtr restringir, limitar.

restriction |rɪˈstrɪkʃən| n restricción f, limitación f.

restrictive [rɪ'strɪktɪv] *adj* restrictivo,-a.

result [rɪ'zʌlt] I *n* 1 resultado *m*. 2 *(consequence)* consecuencia f; **as a r. of**, como consecuencia de. II *vi* 1 resultar; **to r. from**, resultar de. 2 **to r. in**, causar.

resume [rɪ'zju:m] I *vtr (journey, work, conversation)* reanudar; *(control)* reasumir. II *vi* recomenzar.

résumé ['rezjʊmeɪ] *n* resumen *m*.

resumption [rɪ'zʌmpʃən] *n (of journey, work, conversation)* reanudación f.

resurface [ri:'sɜ:fɪs] I *vtr (road)* rehacer el firme de. II *vi fig* resurgir.

resurgence [rɪ'sɜ:dʒəns] *n* resurgimiento *m*.

resurrection [rezə'rekʃən] *n* resurrección f.

resuscitate [rɪ'sʌsɪteɪt] *vtr Med* reanimar.

retail ['ri:teɪl] I *n* venta f al por menor; **r. outlet**, punto *m* de venta; **r. price**, precio *m* de venta al público; **R. Price Index**, Indice *m* de Precios al Consumo. II *vtr* vender al por menor. III *vi* venderse al por menor. IV *adv* al por menor.

retailer ['ri:teɪlər] *n* detallista *mf*.

retain [rɪ'teɪn] *vtr* 1 *(heat)* conservar; *(personal effects)* guardar. 2 *(water)* retener. 3 *(facts, information)* recordar. 4 **to r. the services of a lawyer**, contratar a un abogado.

retainer [rɪ'teɪnər] *n* 1 *(payment)* anticipo *m* sobre los honorarios. 2 *(servant)* criado,-a *m,f*.

retaliate [rɪ'tælieɪt] *vi* tomar represalias *(against, contra)*.

retaliation [rɪtælɪ'eɪʃən] *n* represalias *fpl*; **in r.**, en represalia.

retarded [rɪ'tɑ:dɪd] *adj* retrasado,-a.

retch [retʃ] *vi* tener náuseas.

retentive [rɪ'tentɪv] *adj* retentivo,-a.

rethink ['ri:θɪŋk] *n fam* **to have a r. about sth**, volver a reflexionar sobre algo.

reticent ['retɪsənt] *adj* reticente.

retina ['retɪnə] *n* retina f.

retinue ['retɪnju:] *n* séquito *m*.

retire [rɪ'taɪər] I *vtr* jubilar. II *vi* 1 *(stop working)* jubilarse. 2 *(from race)* retirarse; **to r. for the night**, irse a la cama, acostarse.

retired [rɪ'taɪəd] *adj* jubilado,-a.

retirement [rɪ'taɪəmənt] *n* jubilación f.

retiring [rɪ'taɪərɪŋ] *adj* 1 *(reserved)* reservado,-a. 2 *(official)* saliente.

retort [rɪ'tɔ:t] I *n* réplica f. II *vi* replicar.

retrace [rɪ'treɪs] *vtr (recall)* reconstruir; **to r. one's steps**, volver sobre sus pasos.

retract [rɪ'trækt] I *vtr* 1 *(claws)* retraer; *(landing gear)* replegar. 2 *(statement)* retirar. II *vi* 1 *(claws)* retraerse; *(landing gear)* replegarse. 2 *fml* retractarse.

retread ['ri:tred] *n Aut* neumático recauchutado.

retreat [rɪ'tri:t] I *n* 1 *Mil* retirada f. 2 *(shelter)* refugio *m*. 3 *Rel* retiro *m*. II *vi* retirarse **(from, de)**.

retribution [retrɪ'bju:ʃən] *n* merecido *m*.

retrieval [rɪ'tri:vəl] *n* recuperación f; *Comput* **information r. system**, sistema *m* de recuperación de datos.

retrieve [rɪ'tri:v] *vtr* 1 *(recover)* recuperar; *(of dog)* Comput recoger. 2 *(rescue)* salvar. 3 *Ten* devolver.

retriever [rɪ'tri:vər] *n* perro *m* cazador.

retrograde ['retrəʊgreɪd] *adj* retrógrado,-a.

retrospect ['retrəʊspekt] *n* **in r.**, retrospectivamente.

retrospective [retrəʊ'spektɪv] I *adj* retrospectivo,-a. II *n Art* (exposición f) retrospectiva f.

return [rɪ'tɜ:n] I *n* 1 *(of person)* regreso *m*, vuelta f; **by r. of post**, a vuelta de correo; **in r. for**, a cambio de; **many happy returns!**, ¡felicidades!; **r. match**, partido *m* de vuelta; **r. ticket**, billete *m* de ida y vuelta. 2 *(of sth borrowed, stolen)* devolución f. 3 *(profit)* beneficio *m*, ganancia f. 4 *(interest)* interés *m*. II *vtr* 1 *(give back)* devolver; **'r. to sender'**, 'devuélvase al remitente'; **to r. a favour/sb's love**, corresponder a un favor/al amor de algn. 2 *Pol* reelegir. 3 *Jur (verdict)* pronunciar. III *vi* 1 *(come or go back)* volver, regresar. 2 *(reappear)* reaparecer.

returnable [rɪ'tɜ:nəbəl] *adj (bottle)* retornable.

reunion [ri:'ju:njən] *n* reunión f.

reunite [ri:ju:'naɪt] *vtr* **to be reunited with**, *(after separation)* reunirse con.

rev [rev] *fam* I *n Aut* revolución f. II *vi* **to r. (up)**, acelerar el motor.

revamp [ri:'væmp] *vtr* modernizar, renovar.

reveal [rɪ'vi:l] *vtr (make known)* revelar; *(show)* dejar ver.

revealing [rɪ'vi:lɪŋ] *adj* revelador,-a.

reveille [rɪ'vælɪ] *n* diana f.

revel ['revəl] *vi* disfrutar **(in, con)**; **to r. in doing sth**, gozar muchísimo haciendo algo.

revelation [revə'leɪʃən] *n* revelación f.

revelry ['revəlrɪ] *n* jarana f, juerga f.

revenge [rɪ'vendʒ] *n* venganza f; **to take r. on sb for sth**, vengarse de algo en algn.

revenue ['revɪnju:] *n* renta f.

reverberate [rɪ'vɜ:bəreɪt] *vi* 1 *(sound)* reverberar. 2 *(ideas, news)* resonar.

reverberation [rɪvɜ:bə'reɪʃən] *n* resonancia f.

revere [rɪ'vɪər] *vtr* reverenciar.

reverence ['revərəns] *n* reverencia f.

reverend ['revərənd] *Rel* I *adj* reverendo,-a; **R. Mother**, reverenda madre. II *n (Protestant)* pastor *m*; *(Catholic)* padre *m*.

reverie ['revərɪ] *n* ensueño *m*.

reversal [rɪ'vɜːsəl] *n* 1 (*of order*) inversión *f*. 2 (*of attitude, policy*) cambio *m* total. 3 *Jur* revocación *f*.

reverse [rɪ'vɜːs] I *adj* inverso,-a. II *n* 1 quite the r., todo lo contrario. 2 (*other side*) (*of cloth*) revés *m*; (*of coin*) cruz *f*; (*of page*) dorso *m*. 3 *Aut* r. gear, marcha *f* atrás. III *vtr* 1 (*order*) invertir. 2 (*turn round*) volver del revés. 3 (*change*) cambiar totalmente. 4 *Jur* revocar. 5 *GB Tel* to r. the charges, poner una conferencia a cobro revertido. IV *vi Aut* dar marcha atrás.

revert [rɪ'vɜːt] *vi* volver (to, a).

review [rɪ'vjuː] I *n* 1 (*examination*) examen *m*. 2 *Mil* revista *f*. 3 *Press* crítica *f*, reseña *f*. 4 (*magazine*) revista *f*. II *vtr* 1 (*examine*) examinar. 2 *Mil* to r. the troops, pasar revista a las tropas. 3 (*book etc*) hacer una crítica de.

reviewer [rɪ'vjuːər] *n* crítico,-a *m,f*.

revile [rɪ'vaɪl] *vtr fml* injuriar.

revise [rɪ'vaɪz] *vtr* 1 (*look over*) revisar; (*at school*) repasar. 2 (*change*) modificar. 3 (*proofs*) corregir.

revision [rɪ'vɪʒən] *n* 1 revisión *f*; (*at school*) repaso *m*. 2 (*change*) modificación *f*. 3. (*of proofs*) corrección *f*.

revitalize [riː'vaɪtəlaɪz] *vtr* revivificar.

revival [rɪ'vaɪvəl] *n* 1 (*of interest*) renacimiento *m*; (*of the economy*) reactivación *f*; (*of a country*) resurgimiento *m*. 2 *Theat* reestreno *m*. 3 *Med* reanimación *f*.

revive [rɪ'vaɪv] I *vtr* 1 (*interest*) renovar; (*a law*) restablecer; (*the economy*) reactivar; (*hopes*) despertar. 2 *Theat* reestrenar. 3 *Med* reanimar. II *vi* 1 (*interest, hopes*) renacer. 2 *Med* volver en sí.

revoke [rɪ'vəʊk] *vtr* revocar; (*permission*) suspender.

revolt [rɪ'vəʊlt] I *n* rebelión *f*, sublevación *f*. II *vi* rebelarse, sublevarse. III *vtr* repugnar, dar asco a.

revolting [rɪ'vəʊltɪŋ] *adj* repugnante.

revolution [revə'luːʃən] *n* revolución *f*.

revolutionary [revə'luːʃənərɪ] *adj & n* revolucionario,-a (*m,f*).

revolve [rɪ'vɒlv] I *vi* girar; *fig* to r. around, girar en torno a. II *vtr* hacer girar.

revolver [rɪ'vɒlvər] *n* revólver *m*.

revolving [rɪ'vɒlvɪŋ] *adj* giratorio,-a.

revue [rɪ'vjuː] *n* revista *f*.

revulsion [rɪ'vʌlʃən] *n* repulsión *f*.

reward [rɪ'wɔːd] I *n* recompensa *f*. II *vtr* recompensar.

rewarding [rɪ'wɔːdɪŋ] *adj* provechoso,-a.

rewire [riː'waɪər] *vtr Elec* to r. a house, poner nueva instalación eléctrica a una casa.

reword [riː'wɜːd] *vtr* expresar con otras palabras.

rewrite [riː'raɪt] *vtr* (*pt* rewrote [riː'rəʊt] *pp* rewritten [riː'rɪtən]) escribir de nue-

vo.

rhapsody ['ræpsədɪ] *n Mus* rapsodia *f*.

rhetoric ['retərɪk] *n* retórica *f*.

rhetorical [rɪ'tɒrɪkəl] *adj* retórico,-a.

rheumatism ['ruːmətɪzəm] *n* reuma *m*.

rheumatoid ['ruːmətɔɪd] *adj* r. arthritis, reuma *m* articular.

Rhine [raɪn] *n* the R., el Rin.

rhinoceros [raɪ'nɒsərəs] *n* rinoceronte *m*.

rhododendron [rəʊdə'dendrən] *n* rododendro *m*.

Rhone [rəʊn] *n* the R., el Ródano.

rhubarb ['ruːbɑːb] *n* ruibarbo *m*.

rhyme [raɪm] I *n* rima *f*; (*poem*) poema *m*. II *vi* rimar.

rhythm ['rɪðəm] *n* ritmo *m*.

rib[1] [rɪb] *n* 1 *Anat* costilla *f*; r. cage, caja torácica. 2 *Knit* canalé *m*. 3 (*of umbrella*) varilla *f*. 4 *Bot* (*of leaf*) nervio *m*.

rib[2] [rɪb] *vtr fam* burlarse de.

ribald ['rɪbəld] *adj* (*humour*) verde.

ribbon ['rɪbən] *n* cinta *f*; (*in hair etc*) lazo *m*; torn to ribbons, hecho,-a jirones.

rice [raɪs] *n* arroz *m*; brown r., arroz integral; r. paper, papel de arroz; r. pudding, arroz con leche.

rich [rɪtʃ] I *adj* (*person, food*) rico,-a; (*soil*) fértil; (*voice*) sonoro,-a; (*colour*) vivo,-a. II *npl* the r., los ricos. ◆**richly** *adv* ricamente; r. deserved, bien merecido,-a.

riches ['rɪtʃɪz] *npl* riquezas *fpl*.

richness ['rɪtʃnɪs] *n* riqueza *f*; (*of soil*) fertilidad *f*; (*of voice*) sonoridad *f*; (*of colour*) viveza *f*.

rickets ['rɪkɪts] *n Med* raquitismo *m*.

rickety ['rɪkətɪ] *adj* (*chair etc*) cojo,-a; (*car*) desvencijado,-a.

ricochet ['rɪkəʃeɪ, 'rɪkəʃet] I *n* rebote *m*. II *vi* rebotar.

rid [rɪd] *vtr* (*pt & pp* rid) librar; to get r. of sth, deshacerse de algo; to r. oneself of, librarse de.

riddance ['rɪdəns] *n fam* good r.!, ¡ya era hora!

ridden ['rɪdən] *pp* → ride.

riddle[1] ['rɪdəl] *n* 1 (*puzzle*) acertijo *m*, adivinanza *f*. 2 (*mystery*) enigma *m*.

riddle[2] ['rɪdəl] *vtr* (*with bullets*) acribillar.

ride [raɪd] I *n* paseo *m*, vuelta *f*; a short bus r., un corto trayecto en autobús; *fam* to take sb for a r., tomar el pelo a algn; horse r., paseo a caballo. II *vtr* (*pt* rode; *pp* ridden) (*bicycle, horse*) montar en; can you r. a bike?, ¿sabes montar en bici? III *vi* 1 (*on horse*) montar a caballo. 2 (*travel*) (*in bus, train etc*) viajar. 3 *Naut* to r. at anchor, estar anclado,-a. ◆**ride out** *vtr* sobrevivir; to r. out the storm, capear el temporal.

rider ['raɪdər] *n* (*of horse*) (*man*) jinete *m*, (*woman*) amazona *f*; (*of bicycle*) ciclista *mf*; (*of motorbike*) motociclista *mf*.

ridge [rɪdʒ] *n* (*crest of a hill*) cresta *f*; (*hillock*) loma *f*; (*of roof*) caballete *m*; *Meteor* área *m*.

ridicule |'rɪdɪkjuːl| **I** *n* burla *f*. **II** *vtr* burlarse de.

ridiculous |rɪ'dɪkjʊləs| *adj* ridículo,-a.

riding |'raɪdɪŋ| *n* equitación *f*; **r. breeches**, pantalones *mpl* de montar; **r. school**, escuela hípica.

rife |raɪf| *adj* abundante; **rumour is r. that ...**, corre la voz de que ...; **to be r. with**, abundar en.

riffraff |'rɪfræf| *n fam* chusma *f*, gentuza *f*.

rifle[1] |'raɪfəl| *n* fusil *m*, rifle *m*; **r. range**, campo *m* de tiro.

rifle[2] |'raɪfəl| *vtr* desvalijar.

rift |rɪft| *n* **1** *Geol* falla *f*. **2** *fig* (*in friendship*) ruptura *f*; *Pol* (*in party*) escisión *f*; (*quarrel*) desavenencia *f*.

rig |rɪg| **I** *n* **1** *Naut* aparejo *m*. **2** (*oil*) **r.**, (*onshore*) torre *f* de perforación; (*offshore*) plataforma petrolífera. **II** *vtr pej* amañar. ◆**rig out** *vtr fam* ataviar. ◆**rig up** *vtr* improvisar.

rigging |'rɪgɪŋ| *n* aparejo *m*, jarcia *f*.

right |raɪt| **I** *adj* **1** (*not left*) derecho,-a; **the r. hand**, la mano derecha. **2** (*correct*) correcto,-a; (*time*) exacto,-a.; **to be r.**, tener razón; **all r.**, de acuerdo; **r.?**, ¿vale?; **that's r.**, eso es; **the r. word**, la palabra justa. **3** (*true*) cierto,-a. **4** (*suitable*) adecuado,-a; **the r. time**, el momento oportuno. **5** (*proper*) apropiado,-a. **6** *fam* (*healthy*) bien. **7** *fam* (*complete*) auténtico,-a. **8** (*in order*) en orden. **9 r. angle**, ángulo recto. **II** *n* **1** (*right side*) derecha *f*. **2** (*right hand*) mano derecha. **3** *Pol* **the R.**, la derecha. **4** (*lawful claim*) derecho *m*; **in one's own r.**, por derecho propio; **r. of way**, (*across land*) derecho de paso; (*on roads*) prioridad *f*; **civil rights**, derechos civiles. **5 r. and wrong**, el bien y el mal. **III** *adv* **1** (*correctly*) bien; **it's just r.**, es justo lo que hace falta. **2 r. away**, (*immediately*) en seguida. **3** (*to the right*) a la derecha; **r. and left**, a diestro y siniestro; **to turn r.**, girar a la derecha. **4** (*directly*) directamente; **go r. on**, sigue recto; **r. at the top**, en todo lo alto; **r. in the middle**, justo en medio; **r. to the end**, hasta el final. **IV** *vtr* **1** (*correct*) corregir. **2** (*put straight*) enderezar.

righteous |'raɪtʃəs| *adj* (*upright*) recto,-a.

rightful |'raɪtfʊl| *adj* legítimo,-a.

right-hand |raɪt'hænd| *adj* derecho,-a; **r.-h. drive**, conducción *f* por la derecha; **r.-h. side**, lado derecho; *fam* **r.-h. man**, brazo derecho.

right-handed |raɪt'hændɪd| *adj* (*person*) que usa la mano derecha; (*tool*) para la mano derecha.

rightly |'raɪtlɪ| *adv* debidamente; **and r. so**, y con razón.

right-wing |'raɪtwɪŋ| *adj* de derechas, derechista.

right-winger |raɪt'wɪŋər| *n* derechista *mf*.

rigid |'rɪdʒɪd| *adj* rígido,-a, inflexible.

rigidity |rɪ'dʒɪdɪtɪ| *n* rigidez *f*, inflexibilidad *f*.

rigmarole |'rɪgmərəʊl| *n fam* galimatías *m inv*.

rigorous |'rɪgərəs| *adj* riguroso,-a.

rigour, *US* **rigor** |'rɪgər| *n* rigor *m*, severidad *f*.

rile |raɪl| *vtr fam* irritar, sacar de quicio.

rim |rɪm| *n* (*edge*) borde *m*; (*of wheel*) llanta *f*; (*of spectacles*) montura *f*.

rind |raɪnd| *n* (*of fruit, cheese*) corteza *f*.

ring[1] |rɪŋ| **I** *n* **1** (*sound of bell*) toque *m*; (*of doorbell, alarm clock*) timbre *m*. **2** *Tel* llamada *f*. **II** *vtr* (*pt* **rang**; *pp* **rung**) **1** (*bell*) tocar; *fig* **it rings a bell**, me suena. **2** *GB Tel* llamar por teléfono. **III** *vi* **1** (*bell, phone etc*) sonar. **2 my ears are ringing**, tengo un pitido en los oídos. **3** *Tel* llamar. ◆**ring back** *vtr GB Tel* volver a llamar. ◆**ring off** *vi GB Tel* colgar. ◆**ring out** *vi* resonar. ◆**ring up** *vtr GB Tel* llamar por teléfono a.

ring[2] |rɪŋ| *n* **1** (*metal hoop*) aro *m*; **curtain r.**, anilla *f*; **r. binder**, carpeta *f* de anillas. **2** (*for finger*) anillo *m*, sortija *f*; **r. finger**, dedo *m* anular. **3** (*circle*) círculo *m*; **r. road**, carretera *f* de circunvalación. **4** *Gymn* **rings**, anillas *fpl*. **5** (*group of people*) corro *m*; (*of spies*) red *f*; (*of thieves*) banda *f*. **6** (*arena*) pista *f*; *Box* cuadrilátero *m*; (*for bullfights*) ruedo *m*; **circus r.**, pista de circo. **II** *vtr* **1** (*bird, animal*) anillar. **2** (*surround*) rodear.

ringing |'rɪŋɪŋ| *n* (*of bell*) toque *m*, repique *m*; (*in ears*) pitido *m*.

ringleader |'rɪŋliːdər| *n* cabecilla *mf*.

ringlet |'rɪŋlɪt| *n* tirabuzón *m*.

rink |rɪŋk| *n* pista *f*; **ice r.**, pista de hielo.

rinse |rɪns| **I** *n* **1** (*of clothes, hair*) aclarado *m*; (*of dishes*) enjuagado *m*. **2** (*tint for hair*) reflejo *m*. **II** *vtr* **1** aclarar; (*the dishes*) enjuagar. **2 to r. one's hair**, (*tint*) darse reflejos en el pelo.

Rioja |rɪ'ɒxə| *n* Rioja.

riot |'raɪət| **I** *n* **1** disturbio *m*, motín *m*; **to run r.**, desmandarse; **r. police**, policía *f* antidisturbios. **2** *fig* (*of colour*) profusión *f*. **II** *vi* amotinarse.

rioter |'raɪətər| *n* amotinado,-a *m,f*.

riotous |'raɪətəs| *adj* **1** amotinado,-a. **2** (*noisy*) bullicioso,-a. **3** (*unrestrained*) desenfrenado,-a.

rip |rɪp| **I** *n* (*tear*) rasgón *m*. **II** *vtr* rasgar, rajar; **to r. one's trousers**, rajarse los pantalones. **III** *vi* rasgarse, rajarse. ◆**rip off** *vtr fam* **to r. sb off**, timar a algn. ◆**rip up** *vtr* hacer pedacitos.

ripcord |'rɪpkɔːd| *n* cuerda *f* de apertura.

ripe |raɪp| *adj* **1** maduro,-a. **2** (*ready*) listo,-a; **the time is r.**, es el momento oportuno.

ripen ['raɪpən] *vtr & vi* madurar.

rip-off ['rɪpɒf] *n fam* timo *m*.

ripple ['rɪpəl] **I** *n* **1** (*on water, fabric*) onda *f*. **2** (*sound*) murmullo *m*. **II** *vtr* (*water*) ondular. **III** *vi* **1** (*water*) ondularse. **2** (*applause*) extenderse.

rise [raɪz] **I** *n* **1** (*of slope, hill*) cuesta *f*. **2** (*of waters*) crecida *f*. **3** (*in status*) ascenso *m*. **4** (*in prices, temperature*) subida *f*; (*in wages*) aumento *m*. **5** (*in sound*) aumento *m*. **6 to give r. to**, ocasionar. **II** *vi* (*pt* **rose**; *pp* **risen** ['rɪzən]) **1** (*land etc*) elevarse. **2** (*waters*) crecer; (*river*) nacer; (*tide*) subir; (*wind*) levantarse. **3** (*sun, moon*) salir. **4** (*voice*) alzarse. **5** (*in rank*) ascender. **6** (*prices, temperature*) subir; (*wages*) aumentar. **7** (*curtain*) subir. **8** (*from bed*) levantarse. **9** (*stand up*) levantarse; *fig* (*city, building*) erguirse. **10 to r. to a challenge**, aceptar un reto; **to r. to the occasion**, ponerse a la altura de las circunstancias. ◆**rise above** *vtr* estar por encima de. ◆**rise up** *vi* (*rebel*) sublevarse.

rising ['raɪzɪŋ] **I** *adj* (*sun*) naciente; (*prices*) en aumento; **r. damp**, humedad *f*. **II** *n* **1** (*of sun*) salida *f*. **2** (*rebellion*) levantamiento *m*.

risk [rɪsk] **I** *n* riesgo *m*; **at r.**, en peligro; **at your own r.**, por su cuenta y riesgo; **to take risks**, arriesgarse. **II** *vtr* arriesgar; **I'll r. it**, correré el riesgo.

risky ['rɪskɪ] *adj* (**riskier, riskiest**) arriesgado,-a.

risqué ['rɪskeɪ] *adj* atrevido,-a; (*joke*) picante.

rite [raɪt] *n* rito *m*; **the last rites**, la extremaunción.

ritual ['rɪtjʊəl] *adj & n* ritual (*m*).

rival ['raɪvəl] **I** *adj & n* rival (*m,f*). **II** *vtr* rivalizar con.

rivalry ['raɪvəlrɪ] *n* rivalidad *f*.

river ['rɪvər] *n* río *m*; **down/up r.**, río abajo/arriba.

river-bank ['rɪvəbæŋk] *n* orilla *f*, ribera *f*.

river-bed ['rɪvəbed] *n* lecho *m*.

rivet ['rɪvɪt] **I** *n Tech* remache *m*, roblón *m*. **II** *vtr Tech* remachar; *fig* cautivar.

riveting ['rɪvɪtɪŋ] *adj fig* fascinante.

road [rəʊd] *n* **1** carretera *f*; *GB* **A/B r.**, carretera nacional/secundaria; **main r.**, carretera principal; **r. accident**, accidente *m* de tráfico; **r. safety**, seguridad *f* vial; **r. sign**, señal *f* de tráfico; **r. works**, obras *fpl*. **2** (*street*) calle *f*. **3** (*way*) camino *m*.

roadblock ['rəʊdblɒk] *n* control *m* policial.

roadhog ['rəʊdhɒg] *n fam* loco,- a *m,f* del volante, dominguero,-a *m,f*.

roadside ['rəʊdsaɪd] *n* borde *m* de la carretera; **r. restaurant/café**, restaurante *m*/cafetería *m* de carretera.

roadway ['rəʊdweɪ] *n* calzada *f*.

roadworthy ['rəʊdwɜːðɪ] *adj* (*vehicle*) en buen estado.

roam [rəʊm] **I** *vtr* vagar por, rondar. **II** *vi* vagar.

roar [rɔːr] **I** *n* (*of lion*) rugido *m*; (*of bull, sea, wind*) bramido *m*; (*of crowd*) clamor *m*. **II** *vi* (*lion, crowd*) rugir; (*bull, sea, wind*) bramar; (*crowd*) clamar; *fig* **to r. with laughter**, reírse a carcajadas.

roaring ['rɔːrɪŋ] *adj fam fig* **a r. success**, un éxito clamoroso; **to do a r. trade**, hacer un negocio redondo.

roast [rəʊst] **I** *adj* (*meat*) asado,-a; **r. beef**, rosbif *m*. **II** *n Culin* asado *m*. **III** *vtr* (*meat*) asar; (*coffee, nuts*) tostar. **IV** *vi fam fig* **I'm roasting**, me aso de calor.

rob [rɒb] *vtr* robar; (*bank*) atracar.

robber ['rɒbər] *n* ladrón,-a *m,f*; **bank r.**, atracador,-a *m,f*.

robbery ['rɒbərɪ] *n* robo *m*.

robe [rəʊb] *n* (*ceremonial*) toga *f*; (*dressing gown*) bata *f*.

robin ['rɒbɪn] *n* petirrojo *m*.

robot ['rəʊbɒt] *n* robot *m*.

robust [rəʊ'bʌst] *adj* (*sturdy*) robusto,-a.

rock [rɒk] **I** *n* **1** roca *f*; *fig* **to be on the rocks**, (*of marriage*) estar a punto de fracasar; *fig* **whisky on the rocks**, whisky *m* con hielo. **2** *US* (*stone*) piedra *f*. **3** *GB* (*sweet*) **stick of r.**, barra *f* de caramelo. **4** *Mus* música *f* rock; **r. and roll**, rock and roll *m*. **II** *vtr* **1** (*chair*) mecer; (*baby*) acunar. **2** (*shake*) hacer temblar; *fig* (*shock*) conmover. **III** *vi* **1** (*move to and fro*) mecerse. **2** (*shake*) vibrar.

rock-bottom [rɒk'bɒtəm] *adj* bajísimo,-a; **r.-b. prices**, precios regalados.

rockery ['rɒkərɪ] *n* jardín *m* de rocas.

rocket ['rɒkɪt] **I** *n* cohete *m*; **r. launcher**, lanzacohetes *m inv*. **II** *vi fam* (*prices*) dispararse.

rocking-chair ['rɒkɪŋtʃeər] *n* mecedora *f*.

rocking-horse ['rɒkɪŋhɔːs] *n* caballito *m* de balancín.

rocky ['rɒkɪ] *adj* (**rockier, rockiest**) rocoso,-a; *fam fig* (*unsteady*) inseguro,- a; **the R. Mountains**, las Montañas Rocosas.

rod [rɒd] *n* (*of metal*) barra *f*; (*stick*) vara *f*; **fishing r.**, caña *f* de pescar.

rode [rəʊd] *pt* → **ride**.

rodent ['rəʊdənt] *n* roedor *m*.

roe[1] [rəʊ] *n Zool* **r. (deer)**, corzo,-a *m,f*.

roe[2] [rəʊ] *n* (*fish eggs*) hueva *f*.

rogue [rəʊg] *n* granuja *m*.

role *n*, **rôle** [rəʊl] *n* papel *m*; **to play a r.**, desempeñar un papel.

roll [rəʊl] **I** *n* **1** rollo *m*; **r. of banknotes**, fajo *m* de billetes; *fam fig* **rolls of fat**, michelines *mpl*. **2** (**bread**) **r.**, bollo *m*. **3** (*list of names*) lista *f*, nómina *f*; **to call the r.**, pasar lista. **4** (*of ship*) balanceo *m*. **5** (*of drum*) redoble *m*; (*of thunder*) fragor *m*. **II** *vtr* **1** (*ball*) hacer rodar. **2** (*cigarette*) liar.

3 (*move*) mover. 4 (*push*) empujar. 5 (*lawn, road*) allanar. III *vi* 1 (*ball*) rodar; *fam* **to be rolling in money**, estar forrado,-a. 2 (*animal*) revolcarse. 3 (*ship*) balancearse. 4 (*drum*) redoblar; (*thunder*) retumbar. ◆**roll about, roll around** *vi* rodar (de acá para allá). ◆**roll by** *vi* (*years*) pasar. ◆**roll in** *vi fam* 1 (*arrive*) llegar. 2 (*money*) llegar a raudales. ◆**roll over** *vi* dar una vuelta. ◆**roll up I** *vtr* enrollar; (*blinds*) subir; **to r. up one's sleeves**, (ar)remangarse. II *vi fam* (*arrive*) llegar.

roll-call |'rəʊlkɔ:l| *n* **to have a r.**, pasar lista.

roller |'rəʊlər| *n* 1 *Tech* rodillo *m*; **r. coaster**, montaña rusa; **r. skate**, patín *m* de ruedas. 2 (*large wave*) ola *f* grande. 3 *usu pl* (*for hair*) rulo *m*.

rolling |'rəʊlɪŋ| I *adj* 1 *Rail* **r. stock**, material *m* rodante. 2 (*countryside*) ondulado,-a. II *n* rodamiento *m*; (*of ground*) apisonamiento *m*; **r. pin**, rodillo *m* (de cocina).

ROM |rɒm| *Comput abbr of* **read only memory**, memoria *f* sólo de lectura, ROM *f*.

Roman |'rəʊmən| *adj & n* romano,-a (*m,f*); **R. Catholic**, católico,-a *m,f* (romano,-a); **R. law**, derecho romano; **R. numerals**, números romanos.

Romance |rəʊ'mæns| *adj* *Ling* románico,-a, romance; **R. languages**, lenguas románicas.

romance |rəʊ'mæns| I *n* 1 (*tale*) novela romántica. 2 (*love affair*) aventura amorosa. 3 (*romantic quality*) lo romántico. II *vi* fantasear.

Romania |rəʊ'meɪnɪə| *n* → **Rumania**.

romantic |rəʊ'mæntɪk| *adj & n* romántico,-a (*m,f*).

Rome |rəʊm| *n* Roma *f*.

romp |rɒmp| I *n* jugueteo *m*. II *vi* juguetear.

rompers |'rɒmpəz| *npl* pelele *m sing*.

roof |ru:f| I *n* (*pl* **roofs** |ru:fs, ru:vz|) 1 tejado *m*; *fam* **to go through the r.**, (*of prices*) estar por las nubes; (*with anger*) subirse por las paredes. 2 *Aut* techo *m*; **r. rack**, baca *f*. 3 (*of mouth*) cielo *m*. II *vtr* techar.

roofing |'ru:fɪŋ| *n* materiales *mpl* usados para techar.

rook |rʊk| *n* 1 *Orn* grajo *m*. 2 *Chess* torre *f*.

rookie |'rʊkɪ| *n* *US fam* (*novice*) novato,-a *m,f*.

room |ru:m| *n* 1 habitación *f*, cuarto *m*; **single r.**, habitación individual; **r. service**, servicio *m* de habitación. 2 (*space*) sitio *m*, espacio *m*; **make r. for me**, hazme sitio.

rooming-house |'ru:mɪŋhaʊs| *n* *US* pensión *f*.

roommate |'ru:mmeɪt| *n* compañero,-a *m,f* de habitación.

roomy |'ru:mɪ| *adj* (**roomier, roomiest**) amplio,-a.

roost |ru:st| I *n* palo *m*, percha *f*; (*hen*) **r.**, gallinero *m*; *fig* **to rule the r.**, llevar la batuta. II *vi* posarse.

rooster |'ru:stər| *n esp US* gallo *m*.

root¹ |ru:t| I *n* raíz *f*; **to take r.**, echar raíces. II *vtr* arraigar. III *vi* arraigar. ◆**root out, root up** *vtr* arrancar de raíz.

root² |ru:t| *vi* (*search*) buscar; **to r. about** *or* **around for sth**, hurgar en busca de algo.

root³ |ru:t| *vi fam* **to r. for a team**, animar a un equipo.

rope |rəʊp| I *n* 1 (*thin*) cuerda *f*; (*thick*) soga *f*; *Naut* cabo *m*. 2 *fig* **to have sb on the ropes**, tener a algn contra las cuerdas; *fam fig* **to know the ropes**, estar al tanto. II *vtr* (*package*) atar; (*climbers*) encordar. ◆**rope in** *vtr fam* enganchar. ◆**rope off** *vtr* acordonar.

rop(e)y |'rəʊpɪ| *adj* (**ropier, ropiest**) *GB fam* chungo,-a.

rosary |'rəʊzərɪ| *n* rosario *m*.

rose¹ |rəʊz| *pt* → **rise**.

rose² |rəʊz| *n* 1 *Bot* rosa *f*; **r. bed**, roseda *f*; **r. bush**, rosal *m*. 2 (*colour*) rosa *m*. 3 (*of watering can*) alcachofa *f*.

rosé |'rəʊzeɪ| *n* (*vino m*) rosado *m*.

rosebud |'rəʊzbʌd| *n* capullo *m* de rosa.

rosemary |'rəʊzmərɪ| *n* romero *m*.

rosette |rəʊ'zet| *n* (*of ribbons*) escarapela *f*.

roster |'rɒstər| *n* lista *f*.

rostrum |'rɒstrəm| *n* tribuna *f*.

rosy |'rəʊzɪ| *adj* (**rosier, rosiest**) 1 (*complexion*) sonrosado,-a. 2 *fig* (*future*) prometedor,-a.

rot |rɒt| I *n* 1 (*decay*) putrefacción *f*; **dry r.**, putrefacción *f* de la madera. 2 *fam* (*nonsense*) tonterías *fpl*. II *vtr* pudrir. ◆**rot away** *vi* pudrirse.

rota |'rəʊtə| *n usu GB* lista *f*.

rotary |'rəʊtərɪ| *adj* rotatorio,-a, giratorio,-a.

rotate |rəʊ'teɪt| I *vtr* 1 (*revolve*) hacer girar. 2 (*jobs, crops*) alternar. II *vi* (*revolve*) girar.

rotating |rəʊ'teɪtɪŋ| *adj* rotativo,-a.

rotation |rəʊ'teɪʃən| *n* rotación *f*.

rote |rəʊt| *n* **by r.**, de memoria.

rotten |'rɒtən| *adj* 1 (*decayed*) podrido,-a; (*tooth*) picado,-a. 2 *fam* (*very bad*) malísimo,-a; *fam* **I feel r.**, me encuentro fatal.

rouble |'ru:bəl| *n* rublo *m*.

rouge |ru:ʒ| I *n* colorete *m*. II *vtr* poner colorete a.

rough |rʌf| I *adj* 1 (*surface, skin*) áspero,-a; (*terrain*) accidentado,-a; (*road*) desigual; (*sea*) agitado,-a; (*weather*) tempestuoso,-a. 2 (*rude*) grosero,-a; (*vio-*

lent) violento,-a. **3** (*voice*) bronco,-a. **4** (*wine*) áspero,-a. **5** (*bad*) malo,-a; *fam* **to feel r.**, encontrarse fatal. **6** (*approximate*) aproximado,-a. **7** (*plan etc*) preliminar; **r. draft**, borrador *m*; **r. sketch**, esbozo *m*. **8** (*harsh*) severo,-a. **II** *adv* duramente; *fam* *fig* **to sleep r.**, dormir a la intemperie. **III** *n* **1** *fam* (*person*) matón *m*. **2** *Golf* **the r.**, la hierba alta. **IV** *vtr fam* **to r. it**, vivir sin comodidades. ◆**roughly** *adv* **1** (*crudely*) toscamente. **2** (*clumsily*) torpemente. **3** (*not gently*) bruscamente. **4** (*approximately*) aproximadamente.

roughage ['rʌfɪdʒ] *n* (*substance*) fibra *f*.
rough-and-ready ['rʌfən'redɪ] *adj* improvisado,-a.
roughcast ['rʌfkɑːst] *n* mortero grueso.
roughen ['rʌfən] *vtr* poner áspero,-a.
roulette [ruː'let] *n* ruleta *f*.
Roumania [ruː'meɪnɪə] *n* → **Rumania**.
round [raʊnd] **I** *adj* redondo,-a; **in r. figures**, en números redondos; **r. table**, mesa redonda; **r. trip**, viaje *m* de ida y vuelta. **II** *n* **1** (*circle*) círculo *m*. **2** (*series*) serie *f*; **r. of talks**, ronda *f* de negociaciones. **3** (*of ammunition*) cartucho *m*; (*salvo*) salva *f*. **4** **a r. of toast**, unas tostadas. **5** (*of drinks*) ronda *f*. **6** **the daily r.**, (*routine*) la rutina diaria. **7** *Golf* partido *m*; *Cards* partida *f*. **8** *Box* round *m*. **9** (*in a competition*) eliminatoria *f*. **10** **rounds**, (*doctor's*) visita *f sing*; (*of salesman*) recorrido *m sing*. **III** *adv* **all year r.**, durante todo el año; **to invite sb r.**, invitar a algn a casa. **IV** *prep* alrededor de; **r. here**, por aquí; **r. the clock**, día y noche; **r. the corner**, a la vuelta de la esquina. **V** *vtr* (*turn*) dar la vuelta a. ◆**round off** *vtr* acabar, concluir. ◆**round on** *vtr* (*attack*) atacar. ◆**round up** *vtr* (*cattle*) acorralar, rodear; (*people*) reunir. ◆**roundly** *adv* completamente, totalmente.
roundabout ['raʊndəbaʊt] **I** *n* **1** (*merry-go-round*) tiovivo *m*. **2** *GB Aut* rotonda *f*. **II** *adj* indirecto,-a.
rounders ['raʊndəz] *n GB* juego *m* parecido al béisbol.
round-shouldered [raʊnd'ʃəʊldəd] *adj* cargado,-a de espaldas.
round-up ['raʊndʌp] *n* **1** (*of cattle*) rodeo *m*; (*of suspects*) redada *f*. **2** (*summary*) resumen *m*.
rouse [raʊz] *vtr* despertar; (*stir up*) suscitar.
rousing ['raʊzɪŋ] *adj* (*cheer*) entusiasta; (*applause*) caluroso,-a; (*speech, song*) conmovedor,-a.
rout [raʊt] **I** *n* aniquilación *f*. **II** *vtr* aniquilar.
route [ruːt] **I** *n* **1** ruta *f*; (*of bus*) línea *f*; *Naut* derrota *f*; *fig* camino *m*; **r. map**, mapa *m* de carreteras. **2** *US* **R.**, ≈ carretera *f* nacional. **II** *vtr* encaminar.

routine [ruː'tiːn] **I** *n* **1** rutina *f*. **2** *Theat* número *m*. **II** *adj* rutinario,-a.
roving ['rəʊvɪŋ] *adj* errante; **r. reporter**, enviado,-a *m,f* especial.
row¹ [rəʊ] *n* fila *f*, hilera *f*; *fig* **three times in a r.**, tres veces seguidas.
row² [rəʊ] *vtr & vi* (*in a boat*) remar.
row³ [raʊ] **I** *n* **1** (*quarrel*) pelea *f*, bronca *f*. **2** (*noise*) jaleo *m*; (*protest*) escándalo *m*. **II** *vi* pelearse.
rowboat ['rəʊbəʊt] *n US* bote *m* de remos.
rowdy ['raʊdɪ] **I** *adj* (*rowdier, rowdiest*) **1** (*noisy*) ruidoso,-a; (*disorderly*) alborotador,-a. **2** (*quarrelsome*) camorrista. **II** *n* camorrista *mf*.
rowing ['rəʊɪŋ] *n* remo *m*; **r. boat**, bote *m* de remos.
royal ['rɔɪəl] **I** *adj* real; **r. blue**, azul marino; **the R. Family**, la Familia Real. **II** *npl* **the Royals**, los miembros de la Familia Real. ◆**royally** *adv fig* magníficamente.
royalty ['rɔɪəltɪ] *n* **1** (*royal persons*) miembro(s) *m(pl)* de la Familia Real. **2** **royalties**, derechos *mpl* de autor.
RPI [ɑːpiː'aɪ] *n abbr of* **Retail Price Index**, IPC.
rpm [ɑːpiː'em] *abbr* **revolutions per minute**, revoluciones *fpl* por minuto, r.p.m.
RSPCA [ɑːrespiːsiː'eɪ] *GB abbr of* **Royal Society for the Prevention of Cruelty to Animals**, ≈ Sociedad *f* Protectora de Animales, SPA.
RSVP [ɑːresviːpiː'piː] *abbr of* **répondez s'il vous plaît** (please reply), se ruega contestación, S.R.C.
Rt Hon *GB Pol abbr of* (the) **Right Honourable**, su Señoría.
rub [rʌb] **I** *n* **to give sth a r.**, frotar algo. **II** *vtr* frotar; (*hard*) restregar; (*massage*) friccionar. **III** *vi* rozar (*against*, contra). ◆**rub down** *vtr* rotar; (*horse*) almohazar; (*surface*) raspar. ◆**rub in** *vtr* **1** (*cream etc*) frotar con. **2** *fam* **don't r. it in**, no me lo refriegues. ◆**rub off** *vtr* (*erase*) borrar. **II** *vi fig* **to r. off on sb**, influir en algn. ◆**rub out** *vtr* borrar. ◆**rub up** *vtr fam fig* **to r. sb up the wrong way**, fastidiar a algn.
rubber¹ ['rʌbər] *n* **1** (*substance*) caucho *m*, goma *f*; **r. band**, goma *f*; **r. plant**, gomero *m*; **r. stamp**, tampón *m*. **2** *GB* (*eraser*) goma *f* (de borrar). **3** *sl* (*condom*) goma *f*.
rubber² ['rʌbər] *n Bridge* rubber *m*.
rubbery ['rʌbərɪ] *adj* (*elastic*) elástico,-a.
rubbish ['rʌbɪʃ] *n* **1** *GB* (*refuse*) basura *f*; **r. bin**, cubo *m* de la basura; **r. dump**, vertedero *m*. **2** *fam* (*worthless thing*) birria *f*. **3** *fam* (*nonsense*) tonterías *fpl*.
rubble ['rʌbəl] *n* escombros *mpl*.
rubric ['ruːbrɪk] *n* rúbrica *f*.
ruby ['ruːbɪ] *n* rubí *m*.

rucksack |'rʌksæk| n mochila f.
ructions |'rʌkʃənz| npl fam jaleo m sing.
rudder |'rʌdər| n timón m.
ruddy |'rʌdɪ| adj (**ruddier, ruddiest**) 1 (complexion) rojizo,-a, colorado,-a. 2 GB fam (damned) maldito,-a.
rude |ru:d| adj 1 (impolite) maleducado,-a; (foul-mouthed) grosero,-a; **don't be r. to your mother**, no le faltes al respeto a tu madre. 2 **a r. awakening**, un despertar repentino.
rudimentary |ru:dɪ'mentərɪ| adj rudimentario,-a.
rudiments |'ru:dɪmənts| npl rudimentos mpl.
rue |ru:| vtr arrepentirse de.
rueful |'ru:fʊl| adj (regretful) arrepentido,-a; (sad) triste.
ruff |rʌf| n 1 (on animal) collarín m. 2 (collar) gorguera f.
ruffian |'rʌfɪən| n canalla m.
ruffle |'rʌfəl| vtr 1 (water) agitar. 2 (feathers) encrespar; (hair) despeinar. 3 fig (annoy) hacer perder la calma a.
ruffled |'rʌfəld| adj 1 (hair) alborotado,-a; (clothes) en desorden. 2 (perturbed) perturbado,-a.
rug |rʌg| n alfombra f, alfombrilla f.
rugby |'rʌgbɪ| n rugby m; **r. league**, rugby a trece; **r. union**, rugby a quince.
rugged |'rʌgɪd| adj 1 (terrain) accidentado,-a. 2 (features) marcado,-a. 3 (character) vigoroso,-a.
rugger |'rʌgər| n fam rugby m.
ruin |'ru:ɪn| I n 1 ruina f. 2 **ruins**, ruinas fpl, restos mpl; **in r.**, en ruinas. II vtr arruinar; (spoil) estropear.
rule |ru:l| I n 1 regla f, norma f; **to work to r.**, hacer una huelga de celo; **as a r.**, por regla general. 2 (government) dominio m; (of monarch) reinado m; **r. of law**, imperio m de la ley. II vtr & vi 1 (govern) gobernar; (of monarch) reinar. 2 (decide) decidir; (decree) decretar. 3 (draw) tirar.
◆**rule out** vtr descartar.
ruled |ru:ld| adj rayado,-a.
ruler |'ru:lər| n 1 dirigente mf; (monarch) soberano,-a m,f. 2 (for measuring) regla f.
ruling |'ru:lɪŋ| I adj (in charge) dirigente; fig (predominant) predominante; **the r. party**, el partido en el poder. II n Jur fallo m.
rum |rʌm| n ron m.
Rumania |ru:'meɪnɪə| n Rumanía.
Rumanian |ru:'meɪnɪən| I adj rumano,-a. II n (person) rumano,-a m,f; (language) rumano m.
rumble |'rʌmbəl| I n 1 ruido sordo; (of thunder) estruendo m. 2 (of stomach) ruido m. II vi 1 hacer un ruido sordo; (thunder) retumbar. 2 (stomach etc) hacer ruidos.
ruminate |'ru:mɪneɪt| vi (chew, ponder) rumiar.

rummage |'rʌmɪdʒ| vi revolver (**through, en**).
rumour, US **rumor** |'ru:mər| I n rumor m; **r. has it that ...**, se dice que .... II vtr it is rumoured that, se rumorea que.
rump |rʌmp| n (of animal) ancas fpl; fam hum (of person) trasero m; **r. steak**, filete m de lomo.
rumpus |'rʌmpəs| n fam jaleo m.
run |rʌn| I n 1 carrera f; **on the r.**, fugado,-a; **to go for a r.**, hacer footing; fig **in the long r.**, a largo plazo. 2 (trip) paseo m, vuelta f. 3 (sequence) serie f. 4 **ski r.**, pista f de esquí. 5 (demand) gran demanda f; **a r. on**, una gran demanda de. 6 **to give sb the r. of a house**, poner una casa a disposición de algn. 7 Print tirada f. 8 (in stocking) carrera f.
II vtr (pt **ran**; pp **run**) 1 correr; **to r. a race**, correr en una carrera; **to r. errands**, hacer recados. 2 (drive) llevar. 3 (house, business) llevar; (company) dirigir; (organize) organizar. 4 (fingers) pasar. 5 **it's a cheap car to r.**, (operate) es un coche económico; Comput **to r. a program**, pasar un programa. 6 Press publicar.
III vi 1 correr. 2 (colour) desteñirse. 3 (water, river) correr; **to leave the tap running**, dejar el grifo abierto; fam **your nose is running**, se te caen los mocos. 4 (operate) funcionar; **trains r. every two hours**, hay trenes cada dos horas. 5 Naut **to r. aground**, encallar. 6 Pol **to r. for president**, presentarse como candidato a la presidencia. 7 **so the story runs**, según lo que se dice. 8 (range) oscilar (**between, entre**). 9 **we're running low on milk**, nos queda poca leche. 10 **shyness runs in the family**, la timidez le viene de familia. 11 Cin Theat estar en cartel. 12 (last) durar. 13 (stocking) tener una carrera.
◆**run about** vi corretear. ◆**run across** vtr (meet) tropezar con. ◆**run away** vi fugarse; (horse) desbocarse. ◆**run down I** vtr 1 (stairs) bajar corriendo. 2 (in car) atropellar. 3 (criticize) criticar. II vi (battery) agotarse; (clock) pararse. II n vtr Aut rodar. ◆**run into** vtr 1 (room) entrar corriendo en. 2 (people, problems) tropezar con. 3 (crash into) chocar contra. ◆**run off I** vtr Print (copies) tirar. II vi escaparse. ◆**run on I** vtr Typ enlazar. II vi (function) funcionar con. ◆**run out** vi 1 (exit) salir corriendo. 2 (come to an end) agotarse; (of contract) vencer; **to r. out of**, quedarse sin. ◆**run over I** vtr 1 (in car) atropellar. 2 (rehearse) ensayar. II vi (overflow) rebosar. ◆**run through** vtr 1 (of river) pasar por. 2 (read quickly) echar un vistazo a. 3 (rehearse) ensayar. ◆**run up** vtr 1 (flag) izar. 2 (debts) acumular. ◆**run up against** vtr tropezar con.
runaway |'rʌnəweɪ| I n fugitivo,-a m,f. II

adj (person) huido,-a; *(horse)* desbocado, -a; *(vehicle)* incontrolado,-a; *(inflation)* galopante; *(success)* clamoroso,-a.
rundown ['rʌndaʊn] *n fam* **to give sb a r.**, poner a algn al corriente.
run-down [rʌn'daʊn] *adj* 1 *(exhausted)* agotado,-a. 2 *(dilapidated)* ruinoso,-a.
rung[1] [rʌŋ] *pp* → **ring**.
rung[2] [rʌŋ] *n (of ladder)* escalón *m*, peldaño *m*.
runner ['rʌnər] *n* 1 corredor,-a *m,f*. 2 *(horse)* caballo *m* de carreras. 3 *(of skate)* cuchilla *f*. 4 *(on table)* tapete *m*. 5 **r. bean**, judía escarlata.
runner-up [rʌnər'ʌp] *n* subcampeón,-ona *m,f*.
running ['rʌnɪŋ] I *n* 1 **he likes running**, le gusta correr; *fig* **to be in the r. for sth**, tener posibilidades de conseguir algo. 2 *(of company)* dirección *f*. 3 *(of machine)* funcionamiento *m*. II *adj* 1 **r. commentary**, comentario *m* en directo; **r. costs**, gastos *mpl* de mantenimiento; *Pol* **r. mate**, candidato *m* a la vicepresidencia; **r. water**, agua *f* corriente. 2 **three weeks r.**, tres semanas seguidas.
runny ['rʌnɪ] *adj (runnier, runniest)* blando,-a; *(egg)* crudo,-a; *(butter)* derretido,-a; *(nose)* que moquea.
run-of-the-mill [rʌnəvðə'mɪl] *adj* corriente y moliente.
runt [rʌnt] *n fam* enano,-a *m,f*.
run-up ['rʌnʌp] *n (to elections)* preliminares *mpl*.
runway ['rʌnweɪ] *n Av* pista *f* (de aterrizaje y despegue).
rupee [ru:'pi:] *n* rupia *f*.
rupture ['rʌptʃər] I *n* 1 *Med* hernia *f*. 2 *fig* ruptura *f*. II *vtr* 1 **to r. oneself**, herniarse. 2 *(break)* romper.

rural ['rʊərəl] *adj* rural.
ruse [ru:z] *n* ardid *m*, astucia *f*.
rush[1] [rʌʃ] *n Bot* junco *m*.
rush[2] [rʌʃ] I *n* 1 *(hurry)* prisa *f*; *(hustle and bustle)* ajetreo *m*; **there's no r.**, no corre prisa; **r. hour**, hora punta. 2 *(demand)* demanda *f*. 3 *(of wind)* ráfaga *f*. 4 *(of water)* torrente *m*. 5 *Mil* ataque *m*. II *vtr* 1 *(task)* hacer de prisa; *(person)* meter prisa a; **to r. sb to hospital**, llevar a algn urgentemente al hospital. 2 *(attack)* abalanzarse sobre; *Mil* tomar por asalto. III *vi (go quickly)* precipitarse. ◆**rush about** *vi* correr de un lado a otro. ◆**rush into** *vtr fig* **to r. into sth**, hacer algo sin pensarlo bien. ◆**rush off** *vi* irse corriendo.
rusk [rʌsk] *n* galleta dura para niños.
Russia ['rʌʃə] *n* Rusia.
Russian ['rʌʃən] I *adj* ruso,-a. II *n* 1 *(person)* ruso,-a *m,f*. 2 *(language)* ruso *m*.
rust [rʌst] I *n* 1 *(substance)* herrumbre *f*. 2 *(colour)* pardo rojizo. II *vtr* oxidar. III *vi* oxidarse.
rustic ['rʌstɪk] *adj* rústico,-a.
rustle ['rʌsəl] I *n* crujido *m*. II *vtr (papers etc)* hacer crujir. III *vi (steal cattle)* robar ganado.
rustproof ['rʌstpru:f] *adj* inoxidable.
rusty ['rʌstɪ] *adj (rustier, rustiest)* oxidado,-a; *fam fig* **my French is a bit r.**, tengo el francés un poco oxidado.
rut [rʌt] *n* 1 *(furrow)* surco *m*; *(groove)* ranura *f*. 2 *fig* **to be in a r.**, ser esclavo de la rutina. 3 *Zool* celo *m*.
ruthless ['ru:θlɪs] *adj* despiadado,-a.
rye [raɪ] *n* centeno *m*; **r. bread**, pan *m* de centeno; **r. grass**, ballica *f*; *US* **r. (whiskey)**, whisky *m* de centeno.

S

S, s [es] *n (the letter)* S, s *f*.
Sabbath ['sæbəθ] *n (Jewish)* sábado *m*; *(Christian)* domingo *m*.
sabbatical [sə'bætɪkəl] *adj* sabático,-a.
sabotage ['sæbətɑ:ʒ] I *n* sabotaje *m*. II *vtr* sabotear.
saccharin ['sækərɪn] *n* sacarina *f*.
sachet ['sæʃeɪ] *n* bolsita *f*, sobrecito *m*.
sack [sæk] I *n* 1 *(bag)* saco *m*. 2 *fam* **to get the s.**, ser despedido,-a; *fam* **to give sb the s.**, despedir a algn. II *vtr* 1 *fam* despedir. 2 *Mil* saquear.
sacking ['sækɪŋ] *n Tex* arpillera *f*.
sacrament ['sækrəmənt] *n* sacramento *m*.
sacred ['seɪkrɪd] *adj* sagrado,-a.
sacrifice ['sækrɪfaɪs] I *n* sacrificio *m*. II *vtr* sacrificar.
sacrificial [sækrɪ'fɪʃəl] *adj* **s. lamb**, chivo expiatorio.

sacrilege ['sækrɪlɪdʒ] *n* sacrilegio *m*.
sacrosanct ['sækrəʊsæŋkt] *adj* sacrosanto,-a.
sad [sæd] *adj (sadder, saddest)* triste; **how s.!**, ¡qué pena!
sadden ['sædən] *vtr* entristecer.
saddle ['sædəl] I *n (for horse)* silla *f* (de montar); *(of bicycle etc)* sillín *m*. II *vtr (horse)* ensillar; *fam* **to s. sb with sth**, cargarle a algn con algo.
saddlebag ['sædəlbæg] *n* alforja *f*.
sadist ['seɪdɪst] *n* sádico,-a *m,f*.
sadistic [sə'dɪstɪk] *adj* sádico,-a.
sadness ['sædnɪs] *n* tristeza *f*.
sadomasochism [seɪdəʊ'mæsəkɪzəm] *n* sadomasoquismo *m*.
sae [eseɪ'i:] *abbr of* **stamped addressed envelope**, sobre franqueado.
safari [sə'fɑ:rɪ] *n* safari *m*; **s. park**, re-

serva *f*.

safe [seɪf] **I** *adj* **1** (*unharmed*) ileso,-a; (*out of danger*) a salvo; **s. and sound**, sano,-a y salvo,-a. **2** (*not dangerous*) inocuo,-a. **3** (*secure, sure*) seguro,-a; **to be on the s. side**, para mayor seguridad; **s. house**, (*for spies etc*) piso franco. **4** (*driver*) prudente. **II** *n* (*for money etc*) caja *f* fuerte.
◆**safely** *adv* **1** con toda seguridad. **2** to arrive s., llegar sin incidentes.

safe-conduct [seɪf'kɒndʌkt] *n* salvoconducto *m*.

safe-deposit [seɪfdɪ'pɒzɪt] *n* **s.-d. (box)**, cámara blindada.

safeguard ['seɪfɡɑːd] **I** *n* (*protection*) salvaguarda *f*; (*guarantee*) garantía *f*. **II** *vtr* proteger, salvaguardar.

safekeeping [seɪf'kiːpɪŋ] *n* custodia *f*.

safety ['seɪftɪ] *n* seguridad *f*; **s. first!**, ¡la seguridad ante todo!; **s. belt**, cinturón *m* de seguridad; **s. net**, red *f* de protección; **s. pin**, imperdible *m*.

saffron ['sæfrən] *n* azafrán *m*.

sag [sæɡ] *vi* **1** (*roof*) hundirse; (*wall*) pandear; (*wood, iron*) combarse; (*flesh*) colgar. **2** *fig* (*spirits*) flaquear.

sage¹ [seɪdʒ] **I** *adj* (*wise*) sabio,-a. **II** *n* (*person*) sabio,-a *m,f*.

sage² [seɪdʒ] *n* salvia *f*.

Sagittarius [sædʒɪ'teərɪəs] *n* Sagitario *m*.

Sahara [sə'hɑːrə] *n* the S., el Sahara.

Saharan [sə'hɑːrən] *adj* saharaui, sahariano,-a.

said [sed] *adj* dicho,-a.

sail [seɪl] **I** *n* **1** (*canvas*) vela *f*; **to set s.**, zarpar. **2** (*trip*) paseo *m* en barco. **II** *vtr* (*ship*) gobernar; *lit* navegar. **III** *vi* **1** ir en barco. **2** (*set sail*) zarpar. ◆**sail through** *vtr fam* **he sailed through university**, en la universidad todo le fue sobre ruedas.

sailing ['seɪlɪŋ] *n* navegación *f*; (*yachting*) vela *f*; *fam* **it's all plain s.**, es todo coser y cantar; **s. boat** or **ship**, velero *m*, barco *m* de vela.

sailor ['seɪlə'] *n* marinero *m*.

saint [seɪnt] *n* santo,-a *m,f*; (*before all masculine names except those beginning Do or To*) San; (*before feminine names*) Santa; **S. Dominic**, Santo Domingo; **S. Helen**, Santa Elena; **S. John**, San Juan; **All Saints' Day**, Día *m* de Todos los Santos.

saintly ['seɪntlɪ] *adj* (**saintlier, saintliest**) santo,-a.

sake [seɪk] *n* **for the s. of**, por (el bien de); **for your own s.**, por tu propio bien.

salad ['sæləd] *n* ensalada *f*; **potato s.**, ensaladilla *f* (rusa); **s. bowl**, ensaladera *f*; **s. cream**, salsa *f* tipo mahonesa; **s. dressing**, vinagreta *f*, aliño *m*.

salami [sə'lɑːmɪ] *n* salchichón *m*, salami *m*.

salary ['sælərɪ] *n* salario *m*, sueldo *m*.

sale [seɪl] *n* **1** venta *f*; **for** or **on s.**, en venta; **sales department**, departamento *m* comercial; **sales manager**, jefe,-a *m,f* de ventas. **2** (*at low prices*) rebajas *fpl*.

salesclerk ['seɪlzklɑːk] *n* dependiente,-a *m,f*.

salesman ['seɪlzmən] *n* **1** vendedor *m*; (*in shop*) dependiente *m*. **2** (*commercial traveller*) representante *m*.

salesroom ['seɪlzruːm] *n* sala *f* de subastas.

saleswoman ['seɪlzwʊmən] *n* **1** vendedora *f*; (*in shop*) dependienta *f*. **2** (*commercial traveller*) representante *f*.

salient ['seɪlɪənt] *adj fig* sobresaliente.

saliva [sə'laɪvə] *n* saliva *f*.

sallow ['sæləʊ] *adj* cetrino,-a.

salmon ['sæmən] **I** *n* salmón *m*. **II** *adj* (de color) salmón.

salmonella [sælmə'nelə] *n* Biol Med (*bacteria*) salmonela *f*; (*food poisoning*) salmonelosis *f*.

salon ['sælɒn] *n* salón *m*.

saloon [sə'luːn] *n* **1** (*on ship*) cámara *f*. **2** US (*bar*) taberna *f*, bar *m*; GB **s. (bar)**, bar de lujo. **3** (*car*) turismo *m*.

salt [sɔːlt] **I** *n* sal *f*; *fig* **to take sth with a pinch of s.**, creer algo con reservas; **bath salts**, sales de baño; **smelling salts**, sales aromáticas. **II** *adj* salado,-a. **III** *vtr* **1** (*cure*) salar. **2** (*add salt to*) echar sal a.

saltcellar ['sɔːltselə'] *n* salero *m*.

saltwater ['sɔːltwɔːtə'] *adj* de agua salada.

salty ['sɔːltɪ] *adj* (**saltier, saltiest**) salado,-a.

salubrious [sə'luːbrɪəs] *adj* salubre, sano,-a.

salutary ['sæljʊtərɪ] *adj* (*experience*) beneficioso,-a; (*warning*) útil.

salute [sə'luːt] **I** *n* (*greeting*) saludo *m*. **II** *vtr* **1** *Mil* saludar. **2** *fig* (*achievement etc*) aplaudir. **III** *vi Mil* saludar.

salvage ['sælvɪdʒ] **I** *n* **1** (*of ship etc*) salvamento *m*, rescate *m*. **2** (*objects recovered*) objetos recuperados. **II** *vtr* (*from ship etc*) rescatar.

salvation [sæl'veɪʃən] *n* salvación *f*; **S. Army**, Ejército *m* de Salvación.

Samaritan [sə'mærɪtən] *n* samaritano,-a *m,f*; **the Samaritans**, ≈ el teléfono de la Esperanza.

same [seɪm] **I** *adj* mismo,-a; **at that very s. moment**, en ese mismísimo momento; **at the s. time**, (*simultaneously*) al mismo tiempo; (*however*) sin embargo; **in the s. way**, del mismo modo; **the two cars are the s.**, los dos coches son iguales. **II** *pron* el mismo, la misma, lo mismo; *fam* **the s. here**, lo mismo digo yo; *fam* **the s. to you!**, ¡igualmente!. **III** *adv* del mismo modo, igual; **all the s., just the s.**, sin embargo, aun así; **it's all the s. to me**, (a mí) me da igual or lo mismo.

sample [sɑːmpəl] **I** *n* muestra *f*. **II** *vtr* (*wines*) catar; (*dish*) probar.

sanatorium [sænə'tɔ:rɪəm] *n* sanatorio *m*.

sanctimonious [sæŋktɪ'məʊnɪəs] *adj* beato,-a.

sanction ['sæŋkʃən] **I** *n* **1** (*authorization*) permiso *m*. **2** (*penalty*) sanción *f*. **3** *Pol* **sanctions**, sanciones *fpl*. **II** *vtr* sancionar.

sanctity ['sæŋktɪtɪ] *n* (*sacredness*) santidad *f*; (*of marriage*) indisolubilidad *f*.

sanctuary ['sæŋktjʊərɪ] *n* **1** *Rel* santuario *m*. **2** *Pol* asilo *m*. **3** (*for birds, animals*) reserva *f*.

sand [sænd] **I** *n* arena *f*; **s. castle**, castillo *m* de arena; **s. dune**, duna *f*. **II** *vtr* **to s. (down)**, lijar.

sandal ['sændəl] *n* sandalia *f*.

sandalwood ['sændəlwʊd] *n* sándalo *m*.

sandbag ['sændbæg] *n* saco terrero.

sandpaper ['sændpeɪpər] *n* papel *m* de lija.

sandpit ['sændpɪt] *n* (*in playground etc*) arenal *m*.

sandstone ['sændstəʊn] *n* arenisca *f*.

sandwich ['sænwɪdʒ, 'sænwɪtʃ] **I** *n* (*bread roll*) bocadillo *m*; (*sliced bread*) sandwich *m*; *Educ* **s. course**, curso teórico-práctico. **II** *vtr* intercalar; **it was sandwiched between two lorries**, quedó encajonado entre dos camiones.

sandy ['sændɪ] *adj* (**sandier, sandiest**) **1** (*earth, beach*) arenoso,-a. **2** (*hair*) rubio rojizo.

sane [seɪn] *adj* (*not mad*) cuerdo,-a; (*sensible*) sensato,-a.

sang [sæŋ] *pt* → **sing**.

sanitarium [sænɪ'teərɪəm] *n* US sanatorio *m*.

sanitary ['sænɪtərɪ] *adj* sanitario,-a; (*hygienic*) higiénico,-a; **s. towel**, US **s. napkin**, compresa *f*.

sanitation [sænɪ'teɪʃən] *n* sanidad *f* (pública); (*plumbing*) sistema *m* de saneamiento.

sanity ['sænɪtɪ] *n* cordura *f*, juicio *m*; (*good sense*) sensatez *f*.

sank [sæŋk] *pt* → **sink**.

Santa Claus [sæntə'klɔ:z] *n* Papá Noel *m*, San Nicolás *m*.

sap¹ [sæp] *n* *Bot* savia *f*.

sap² [sæp] *vtr* (*undermine*) minar; *fig* agotar.

sapling ['sæplɪŋ] *n* *Bot* árbol *m* joven.

sapphire ['sæfaɪər] *n* zafiro *m*.

sarcasm ['sɑ:kæzəm] *n* sarcasmo *m*.

sarcastic [sɑ:'kæstɪk] *adj* sarcástico,-a.

sardine [sɑ:'di:n] *n* sardina *f*.

Sardinia [sɑ:'dɪnɪə] *n* Cerdeña.

sardonic [sɑ:'dɒnɪk] *adj* sardónico,-a.

sash¹ [sæʃ] *n* faja *f*.

sash² [sæʃ] *n* **s. window**, ventana *f* de guillotina.

sat [sæt] *pt & pp* → **sit**.

Satan ['seɪtən] *n* Satán *m*, Satanás *m*.

satanic [sə'tænɪk] *adj* satánico,-a.

satchel ['sætʃəl] *n* cartera *f* de colegial.

satellite ['sætəlaɪt] *n* satélite *m*; **s. dish aerial**, antena parabólica.

satin ['sætɪn] *n* satén *m*; **s. finish**, (acabado *m*) satinado *m*.

satire ['sætaɪər] *n* sátira *f*.

satirical [sə'tɪrɪkəl] *adj* satírico,-a.

satisfaction [sætɪs'fækʃən] *n* satisfacción *f*.

satisfactory [sætɪs'fæktərɪ] *adj* satisfactorio,-a.

satisfied ['sætɪsfaɪd] *adj* satisfecho,-a.

satisfy ['sætɪsfaɪ] *vtr* **1** satisfacer. **2** (*fulfil*) cumplir con. **3** (*convince*) convencer.

satisfying ['sætɪsfaɪɪŋ] *adj* satisfactorio,-a; (*pleasing*) agradable; (*meal*) que llena.

saturate ['sætʃəreɪt] *vtr* saturar (**with**, de).

Saturday ['sætədɪ] *n* sábado *m*.

sauce [sɔ:s] *n* **1** salsa *f*. **2** *fam* (*impudence*) descaro *m*.

saucepan ['sɔ:spən] *n* cacerola *f*; (*large*) olla *f*.

saucer ['sɔ:sər] *n* platillo *m*.

saucy ['sɔ:sɪ] *adj* (**saucier, sauciest**) *fam* fresco,-a.

Saudi Arabia [saʊdɪə'reɪbɪə] *n* Arabia *f* Saudita *or* Saudí.

Saudi Arabian [saʊdɪə'reɪbɪən] *adj & n* saudita (*mf*), saudí (*mf*).

sauna ['sɔ:nə] *n* sauna *f*.

saunter ['sɔ:ntər] **I** *n* paseo *m*. **II** *vi* pasearse.

sausage ['sɒsɪdʒ] *n* (*frankfurter etc*) salchicha *f*; (*cured*) salchichón *m*; (*spicy*) chorizo *m*; *fam* **s. dog**, perro *m* salchicha; *GB* **s. roll**, empanada *f* de carne.

sauté ['səʊteɪ] **I** *adj* salteado,-a. **II** *vtr* saltear.

savage ['sævɪdʒ] **I** *adj* **1** (*ferocious*) feroz; (*cruel*) cruel; (*violent*) salvaje. **2** (*primitive*) salvaje. **II** *n* salvaje *mf*. **III** *vtr* (*attack*) embestir; *fig* (*criticize*) criticar despiadadamente.

save [seɪv] **I** *vtr* **1** (*rescue*) salvar, rescatar; *fig* **to s. face**, salvar las apariencias. **2** (*put by*) guardar; (*money, energy, time*) ahorrar; (*food*) almacenar; **it saved him a lot of trouble**, le evitó muchos problemas. **II** *vi* **1 to s. (up)**, ahorrar. **2 to s. on paper**, (*economize*) ahorrar papel. **III** *n* *Ftb* parada *f*. **IV** *prep arch* salvo, excepto.

saving ['seɪvɪŋ] **I** *n* **1** (*of time, money*) ahorro *m*. **2 savings**, ahorros *mpl*; **s. account**, cuenta *f* de ahorros; **s. bank**, caja *f* de ahorros. **II** *adj* **it's his only s. grace**, es el único mérito que tiene.

saviour, *US* **savior** ['seɪvjər] *n* salvador,-a *m,f*.

savour, *US* **savor** ['seɪvər] **I** *n* sabor *m*, gusto *m*. **II** *vi* saborear.

savoury, *US* **savory** ['seɪvərɪ] *adj* (*tasty*) sabroso,-a; (*salted*) salado,-a; (*spicy*) picante.

saw¹ [sɔ:] **I** *n* (*tool*) sierra *f*. **II** *vtr & vi*

(*pt* **sawed**; *pp* **sawed** *or* **sawn**) serrar.
◆**saw up** *vtr* serrar (**into**, en).
saw² [sɔː] *pt* → **see¹**.
sawdust ['sɔːdʌst] *n* (a)serrín *m*.
sawmill ['sɔːmɪl] *n* aserradero *m*, serrería *f*.
sawn-off ['sɔːnɒf] *adj* recortado,-a; **s.-o. shotgun**, escopeta *f* de cañones recortados.
saxophone ['sæksəfəʊn] *n* saxofón *m*.
say [seɪ] **I** *vtr* (*pt & pp* **said**) **1** decir; **it goes without saying that ...**, huelga decir que ...; **it is said that ...**, se dice que ...; **not to s. ...**, por no decir ...; **that is to s.**, es decir; **to s. yes/no**, decir que sí/no; *fam* **I s.!**, ¡oiga!; **what does the sign s.?**, ¿qué pone en el letrero? **2** (*think*) pensar. **3 shall we s. Friday then ?**, ¿quedamos el viernes, pues? **II** *n* **I have no s. in the matter**, no tengo ni voz ni voto en el asunto; **to have one's s.**, dar su opinión.
saying ['seɪɪŋ] *n* refrán *m*, dicho *m*.
scab [skæb] *n* **1** *Med* costra *f*. **2** *fam pej* esquirol *mf*.
scaffold ['skæfəld] *n* (*for execution*) patíbulo *m*.
scaffolding ['skæfəldɪŋ] *n* *Constr* andamio *n*.
scald [skɔːld] **I** *n* escaldadura *f*. **II** *vtr* escaldar.
scale¹ [skeɪl] *n* (*of fish, on skin*) escama *f*; (*in boiler*) incrustaciones *fpl*.
scale² [skeɪl] **I** *n* **1** escala *f*; **on a large s.**, a gran escala; **to s.**, a escala; **s. model**, maqueta *f*. **2** (*extent*) alcance *m*. **3** *Mus* escala *f*. **II** *vtr* (*climb*) escalar. ◆**scale down** *vtr* (*drawing*) reducir a escala; (*production*) reducir.
scales [skeɪlz] *npl* (**pair of**) **s.**, (*shop, kitchen*) balanza *f sing*; (*bathroom*) báscula *f sing*.
scallop ['skɒləp] *n* **1** (*mollusc*) vieira *f*. **2** (*shell*) venera *f*.
scalp [skælp] **I** *n* cuero cabelludo; (*head*) cabeza *f*. **II** *vtr* arrancar el cuero cabelludo a.
scalpel ['skælpəl] *n* bisturí *m*.
scamper ['skæmpər] *vi* corretear.
scampi ['skæmpɪ] *n* gambas empanadas.
scan [skæn] **I** *vtr* **1** (*scrutinize*) escrutar; (*horizon*) otear. **2** (*glance at*) ojear. **3** (*of radar*) explorar. **II** *n* *Med* exploración ultrasónica; (*in gynaecology etc*) ecografía *f*.
scandal ['skændəl] *n* **1** escándalo *m*; **what a s.!**, ¡qué vergüenza! **2** (*gossip*) chismes *mpl*.
Scandinavia [skændɪ'neɪvɪə] *n* Escandinavia.
Scandinavian [skændɪ'neɪvɪən] *adj & n* escandinavo,-a (*m,f*).
scanner ['skænər] *n* *Med* escáner *m*.
scant [skænt] *adj* escaso,-a.
scanty ['skæntɪ] *adj* (**scantier, scantiest**)

escaso,-a; (*meal*) insuficiente; (*clothes*) ligero,-a.
scapegoat ['skeɪpgəʊt] *n* chivo expiatorio.
scar [skɑːr] *n* cicatriz *f*.
scarce [skeəs] *adj* escaso,-a; *fig* **to make oneself s.**, largarse. ◆**scarcely** *adv* apenas.
scarcity ['skeəsɪtɪ] *n* escasez *f*; (*rarity*) rareza *f*.
scare [skeər] **I** *n* (*fright*) susto *m*; (*widespread alarm*) pánico *m*; **bomb s.**, amenaza *f* de bomba. **II** *vtr* asustar, espantar; *fam* **to be scared stiff**, estar muerto,-a de miedo. ◆**scare away**, **scare off** *vtr* ahuyentar.
scarecrow ['skeəkrəʊ] *n* espantapájaros *m inv*.
scarf [skɑːf] *n* (*pl* **scarfs** *or* **scarves** [skɑːvz]) (*long, woollen*) bufanda *f*; (*square*) pañuelo *m*; (*silk*) fular *m*.
scarlet ['skɑːlɪt] **I** *adj* escarlata. **II** *n* escarlata *f*; **s. fever**, escarlatina *f*.
scarves [skɑːvz] *npl* → **scarf**.
scathing ['skeɪðɪŋ] *adj* mordaz, cáustico,-a.
scatter ['skætər] **I** *vtr* **1** (*papers etc*) esparcir, desparramar. **2** (*crowd*) dispersar. **II** *vi* dispersarse.
scatterbrained ['skætəbreɪnd] *adj* *fam* ligero,-a de cascos; (*forgetful*) despistado,-a.
scattered ['skætəd] *adj* **s. showers**, chubascos aislados.
scavenger ['skævɪndʒər] *n* **1** (*person*) rebuscador,-a *m,f*, trapero *m*. **2** (*animal*) (animal *m*) carroñero,-a *mf*.
scenario [sɪ'nɑːrɪəʊ] *n* *Cin* guión *m*.
scene [siːn] *n* **1** *Theat Cin TV* escena *f*; **behind the scenes**, entre bastidores. **2** (*place*) lugar *m*, escenario *m*; **a change of s.**, un cambio de aires. **3** (*view*) panorama *m*. **4 to make a s.**, (*fuss*) montar un espectáculo.
scenery ['siːnərɪ] *n* **1** (*landscape*) paisaje *m*. **2** *Theat* decorado *m*.
scenic ['siːnɪk] *adj* (*picturesque*) pintoresco,-a.
scent [sent] **I** *n* **1** (*smell*) olor *m*; (*of food*) aroma *m*. **2** (*perfume*) perfume *m*. **3** (*in hunting*) pista *f*. **II** *vtr* (*add perfume to*) perfumar; (*smell*) olfatear; *fig* presentir.
sceptic ['skeptɪk] *n* escéptico,-a *m,f*.
sceptical ['skeptɪkəl] *adj* escéptico,-a.
scepticism ['skeptɪsɪzəm] *n* escepticismo *m*.
sceptre ['septər] *n* cetro *m*.
schedule ['ʃedjuːl, *US* 'skedʒʊəl] **I** *n* **1** (*plan, agenda*) programa *m*; (*timetable*) horario *m*; **on s.**, a la hora (prevista); **to be behind s.**, llevar retraso. **2** (*list*) lista *f*; (*inventory*) inventario *m*. **II** *vtr* (*plan*) programar, fijar.
scheduled ['ʃedjuːld, *US* 'skedʒʊəld] *adj*

scheme 527 scramble

previsto,-a, fijo,-a; **s. flight,** vuelo regular.

scheme [skiːm] **I** n **1** (plan) plan m; (project) proyecto m; (idea) idea f; **colour s.,** combinación f de colores. **2** (plot) intriga f; (trick) ardid m. **II** vi (plot) tramar, intrigar.

scheming ['skiːmɪŋ] adj intrigante, maquinador,-a.

schism ['sɪzəm] n cisma m.

schizophrenic [skɪtsəʊ'frenɪk] adj & n esquizofrénico,-a (m,f).

scholar ['skɒlər] n (learned person) erudito,-a m,f; (pupil) alumno,-a m,f.

scholarship ['skɒləʃɪp] n **1** (learning) erudición f. **2** (grant) beca f; **s. holder,** becario,-a m,f.

school [skuːl] **I** n **1** escuela f, colegio m; **drama s.,** academia f de arte dramático; **of s. age,** en edad escolar; **s. year,** año m escolar. **2** US (university) universidad f. **3** (university department) facultad f. **4** (group of artists) escuela f; **s. of thought,** corriente f de opinión. **II** vtr (teach) enseñar; (train) formar.

schoolbook ['skuːlbʊk] n libro m de texto.

schoolboy ['skuːlbɔɪ] n alumno m.

schoolchild ['skuːltʃaɪld] n alumno,-a m,f.

schooldays ['skuːldeɪz] npl años mpl de colegio.

schoolgirl ['skuːlgɜːl] n alumna f.

schooling ['skuːlɪŋ] n educación f, estudios mpl.

schoolmaster ['skuːlmɑːstər] n profesor m; (primary school) maestro m.

schoolmistress ['skuːlmɪstrɪs] n profesora f; (primary school) maestra f.

schoolteacher ['skuːltiːtʃər] n profesor,-a m,f; (primary school) maestro,-a m,f.

schooner ['skuːnər] n Naut goleta f.

sciatica [saɪ'ætɪkə] n ciática f.

science ['saɪəns] n ciencia f; (school subject) ciencias; **s. fiction,** ciencia-ficción f.

scientific [saɪən'tɪfɪk] adj científico,-a.

scientist ['saɪəntɪst] n científico,-a m,f.

scintillating ['sɪntɪleɪtɪŋ] adj brillante.

scissors ['sɪzəz] npl tijeras fpl; **a pair of s.,** unas tijeras.

scoff¹ [skɒf] vi (mock) mofarse (at, de).

scoff² [skɒf] vtr fam (eat) zamparse.

scold [skəʊld] vtr regañar, reñir.

scone [skəʊn, skɒn] n bollo m, pastelito m.

scoop [skuːp] n **1** (for flour) pala f; (for ice cream) cucharón m; (amount) palada f, cucharada f. **2** Press exclusiva f. ◆**scoop out** vtr (flour etc) sacar con pala; (water) (from boat) achicar. ◆**scoop up** vtr recoger.

scooter ['skuːtər] n (child's) patinete m; (adult's) Vespa® f.

scope [skəʊp] n **1** (range) alcance m; (of undertaking) ámbito m. **2** (freedom) libertad f.

scorch [skɔːtʃ] vtr (singe) chamuscar.

scorching ['skɔːtʃɪŋ] adj fam abrasador, -a.

score [skɔːr] **I** n **1** Sport tanteo m; Cards Golf puntuación f; (result) resultado m. **2** (notch) muesca f. **3 I have a s. to settle with you,** tengo que ajustar las cuentas contigo. **4 on that s.,** a ese respecto. **5** (twenty) veintena f. **6** Mus (of opera) partitura f; (of film) música f. **II** vtr **1** (goal) marcar; (points) conseguir. **2** (wood) hacer una muesca en; (paper) rayar. **III** vi **1** Sport marcar un tanto; Ftb marcar un gol; (keep the score) llevar el marcador. **2** (have success) tener éxito (with, con); sl ligar (with, con). ◆**score out** vtr (word etc) tachar.

scoreboard ['skɔːbɔːd] n marcador m.

scorer ['skɔːrər] n **1** (goal striker) goleador m. **2** (scorekeeper) encargado,-a m,f del marcador.

scorn [skɔːn] **I** n desprecio m. **II** vtr despreciar.

scornful ['skɔːnfʊl] adj desdeñoso,-a.

Scorpio ['skɔːpɪəʊ] n Escorpión m.

scorpion ['skɔːpɪən] n alacrán m, escorpión m.

Scot [skɒt] n escocés,-esa m,f.

scotch [skɒtʃ] vtr (plot) frustrar; (rumour) negar, desmentir.

Scotch [skɒtʃ] **I** adj escocés,-esa; **S. tape®,** cinta adhesiva, celo® m. **II** n (whisky) whisky m escocés.

scot-free [skɒt'friː] adj impune.

Scotland ['skɒtlənd] n Escocia.

Scots [skɒts] **I** adj escocés,-esa. **II** n the **S.,** pl los escoceses.

Scotsman ['skɒtsmən] n escocés m.

Scotswoman ['skɒtswʊmən] n escocesa f.

Scottish ['skɒtɪʃ] adj escocés,-esa.

scoundrel ['skaʊndrəl] n sinvergüenza mf, canalla m.

scour¹ [skaʊər] vtr (clean) fregar, restregar.

scour² [skaʊər] vtr (search) (countryside) rastrear; (building) registrar.

scourge [skɜːdʒ] fig n azote m.

scout [skaʊt] **I** n Mil explorador,-a m,f; Sport Cin cazatalentos m inv; **boy s.,** boy m scout. **II** vi Mil reconocer el terreno; **to s. around for sth,** andar en busca de algo.

scowl [skaʊl] **I** vi fruncir el ceño; **to s. at sb,** mirar a algn con ceño. **II** n ceño m.

scrabble ['skræbəl] **I** vi escarbar; fig **to s. around for sth,** revolver todo para encontrar algo. **II** n S.®, Scrabble® m.

scraggy ['skrægɪ] adj (scraggier, scraggiest) delgado,-a, flacucho,-a.

scramble ['skræmbəl] **I** vi trepar; **to s. for,** pelearse por; **to s. up a tree,** trepar a un árbol. II *vtr* 1 *Culin* **scrambled eggs,** huevos revueltos. 2 *Rad Tel (message)* codificar; *(broadcast)* interferir. III *n (climb)* subida *f*; *fig* **it's going to be a s.,** *(rush)* va a ser muy apresurado.

scrap¹ [skræp] I *n* 1 *(small piece)* pedazo *m*; **there isn't a s. of truth in it,** no tiene ni un ápice de verdad; **s. (metal),** chatarra *f*; **s. dealer** *or* **merchant,** chatarrero, -a *m,f*; **s. paper,** papel *m* de borrador; **s. yard,** *(for cars)* cementerio *m* de coches. 2 **scraps,** restos *mpl*; *(of food)* sobras *fpl*. II *vtr (discard)* desechar; *fig (idea)* descartar.

scrap² [skræp] *fam* I *n (fight)* pelea *f*. II *vi* pelearse **(with,** con).

scrapbook ['skræpbuk] *n* álbum *m* de recortes.

scrape [skreɪp] I *vtr (paint, wood)* raspar; *(knee)* arañarse, hacerse un rasguño en. II *vi (make noise)* chirriar; *(rub)* rozar. III *n fam (trouble)* lío *m*. ◆**scrape through** *vi fam (exam)* aprobar por los pelos. ◆**scrape together** *vtr* reunir a duras penas.

scraper ['skreɪpər] *n* rasqueta *f*.

scrapheap ['skræphi:p] *n (dump)* vertedero *m*.

scratch [skrætʃ] I *n* 1 *(on skin, paintwork)* arañazo *m*; *(on record)* raya *f*. 2 *(noise)* chirrido *m*. 3 *fig* **to be up to s.,** dar la talla; *fig* **to start from s.,** partir de cero. II *adj* **s. team,** equipo improvisado. III *vtr* 1 *(with nail, claw)* arañar, rasguñar; *(paintwork)* rayar. 2 *(to relieve itching)* rascarse.

scrawl [skrɔ:l] I *n* garabatos *mpl*. II *vtr (message etc)* garabatear. III *vi* hacer garabatos.

scrawny ['skrɔ:nɪ] *adj* **(scrawnier, scrawniest)** flaco,-a.

scream [skri:m] I *n* chillido *m*; **screams of laughter,** carcajadas *fpl*. II *vtr (insults etc)* gritar. III *vi* chillar; **to s. at sb,** chillar a algn.

scree [skri:] *n* pedregal *m*.

screech [skri:tʃ] I *n (of person)* chillido *m*; *(of tyres, brakes)* chirrido *m*. II *vi (person)* chillar; *(tyres)* chirriar.

screen [skri:n] I *n* 1 *(movable partition)* biombo *m*. 2 *fig* cortina *f*. 3 *Cin TV Comput* pantalla *f*; **s. test,** casting *m*. II *vtr* 1 *(protect)* proteger; *(conceal)* tapar. 2 *(sieve) (coal etc)* tamizar; *fig (candidates)* seleccionar. 3 *(show) (film)* proyectar; *(for first time)* estrenar. 4 *Med* examinar.

screening ['skri:nɪŋ] *n* 1 *(of film)* proyección *f*; *(for first time)* estreno *m*. 2 *Med* exploración *f*.

screenplay ['skri:npleɪ] *n* guión *m*.

screw [skru:] I *n* 1 tornillo *m*. 2 *(propeller)* hélice *f*. II *vtr* 1 atornillar; **s. sth down** *or* **in** *or* **on,** fijar algo con tornillos. 2 *vulg* joder. ◆**screw up** *vtr* 1 *(piece of paper)* arrugar; *(one's face)* torcer. 2 *sl*

(ruin) joder.

screwdriver ['skru:draɪvər] *n* destornillador *m*.

scribble ['skrɪbəl] I *n* garabatos *mpl*. II *vtr (message etc)* garabatear. III *vi* hacer garabatos.

script [skrɪpt] *n* 1 *(writing)* escritura *f*; *(handwriting)* letra *f*; *Typ* letra cursiva. 2 *(in exam)* escrito *m*. 3 *Cin* guión *m*.

Scripture ['skrɪptʃər] *n* **Holy S.,** Sagrada Escritura.

scroll [skrəʊl] *n* rollo *m* de pergamino.

scrounge [skraʊndʒ] *fam* I *vi* gorronear; **to s. (around) for,** buscar; **to s. off sb,** vivir a costa de algn. II *vtr* gorronear.

scrounger ['skraʊndʒər] *n fam* gorrón, -ona *m,f*.

scrub¹ [skrʌb] *n (undergrowth)* maleza *f*.

scrub² [skrʌb] I *vtr* 1 frotar. 2 *fam (cancel)* borrar. II *n (cleaning)* fregado *m*.

scruff [skrʌf] *n* pescuezo *m*, cogote *m*.

scruffy ['skrʌfɪ] *adj* **(scruffier, scruffiest)** *fam* desaliñado,-a.

scrum [skrʌm] *n Rugby* melée *f*; **s. half,** medio *m* melée.

scruple ['skru:pəl] *n* escrúpulo *m*.

scrupulous ['skru:pjʊləs] *adj* escrupuloso,-a. ◆**scrupulously** *adv* **s. honest,** sumamente honrado,-a.

scrutinize ['skru:tɪnaɪz] *vtr* escudriñar.

scrutiny ['skru:tɪnɪ] *n* escrutinio *m*.

scuff [skʌf] *vtr (the floor)* rayar; *(one's feet)* arrastrar.

scuffle ['skʌfəl] I *n* pelea *f*. II *vi* pelearse **(with,** con).

scullery ['skʌlərɪ] *n* cuarto *m* de pila.

sculptor ['skʌlptər] *n* escultor *m*.

sculpture ['skʌlptʃər] *n* escultura *f*.

scum [skʌm] *n* 1 *(on liquid)* espuma *f*. 2 *fig* escoria *f*.

scupper ['skʌpər] *vtr GB fam (plan etc)* desbaratar.

scurrilous ['skʌrɪləs] *adj (abusive)* difamatorio,-a.

scurry ['skʌrɪ] *vi (run)* corretear; *(hurry)* apresurarse; **to s. away** *or* **off,** escabullirse.

scuttle¹ ['skʌtəl] *n* cubo *m*; **coal s.,** cubo del carbón.

scuttle² ['skʌtəl] *vtr (ship)* barrenar.

scuttle³ ['skʌtəl] *vi* **to s. away** *or* **off,** escabullirse.

scythe [saɪð] I *n* guadaña *f*. II *vtr* guadañar.

SDI [esdi:'aɪ] *abbr of* **Strategic Defence Initiative,** Iniciativa *f* para la Defensa Estratégica.

sea [si:] *n* mar *mf*; **by the s.,** a orillas del mar; **out at s.,** en alta mar; **to go by s.,** ir en barco; **to put to s.,** zarpar; *fig* **to be all at s.,** estar desorientado,-a; **s. breeze,** brisa marina; *fig* **s. change,** metamorfosis *f*; **s. level,** nivel *m* del mar; **s. lion,** león marino; **s. water,** agua *f* de mar.

seabed ['si:bed] *n* fondo *m* del mar.
seaboard ['si:bɔ:d] *n US* costa *f*, litoral *m*.
seafood ['si:fu:d] *n* mariscos *mpl*.
seafront ['si:frʌnt] *n* paseo marítimo.
seagull ['si:gʌl] *n* gaviota *f*.
seal¹ [si:l] *n Zool* foca *f*.
seal² [si:l] **I** *n* 1 (*official stamp*) sello *m*. 2 (*airtight closure*) cierre hermético; (*on bottle*) precinto *m*. **II** *vtr* 1 (*with official stamp*) sellar; (*with wax*) lacrar. 2 (*close*) cerrar; (*make airtight*) cerrar herméticamente. 3 (*determine*) this sealed his fate, esto decidió su destino. ◆**seal off** *vtr* (*pipe etc*) cerrar; (*area*) acordonar.
seam [si:m] *n* 1 *Sew* costura *f*; *Tech* juntura *f*; *fam* **to be bursting at the seams**, (*room*) rebosar de gente. 2 *Geol Min* veta *f*, filón *m*.
seaman ['si:mən] *n* marinero *m*.
seamy ['si:mɪ] *adj* (**seamier, seamiest**) *fig* sórdido,-a.
séance ['seɪɑ:ns] *n* sesión *f* de espiritismo.
seaplane ['si:pleɪn] *n* hidroavión *m*.
seaport ['si:pɔ:t] *n* puerto marítimo.
search [sɜ:tʃ] **I** *vtr* (*files etc*) buscar en; (*building, suitcase*) registrar; (*person*) cachear; (*one's conscience*) examinar. **II** *vi* buscar; **to s. through**, registrar. **III** *n* búsqueda *f*; (*of building etc*) registro *m*; (*of person*) cacheo *m*; **in s. of**, en busca de; **s. party**, equipo *m* de salvamento; **s. warrant**, orden *f* de registro.
searching ['sɜ:tʃɪŋ] *adj* (*look*) penetrante; (*question*) indagatorio,-a.
searchlight ['sɜ:tʃlaɪt] *n* reflector *m*.
seashell ['si:ʃel] *n* concha marina.
seashore ['si:ʃɔ:r] *n* (*beach*) playa *f*.
seasick ['si:sɪk] *adj* mareado,-a; **to get s.**, marearse.
seaside ['si:saɪd] *n* playa *f*, costa *f*; **s. resort**, lugar turístico de veraneo; **s. town**, pueblo costero,-a.
season¹ ['si:zən] *n* época *f*; (*of year*) estación *f*; (*for sport etc*) temporada *f*; **the busy s.**, la temporada alta; **the rainy s.**, la estación de lluvias; **in s.**, (*fruit*) en sazón; (*animal*) en celo; *GB* **s. ticket**, abono *m*.
season² ['si:zən] *vtr Culin* sazonar.
seasonal ['si:zənəl] *adj* estacional.
seasoned ['si:zənd] *adj* 1 *Culin* sazonado,-a. 2 *fig* (*campaigner*) curtido,-a, avezado,-a.
seasoning ['si:zənɪŋ] *n* condimento *m*, aderezo *m*.
seat [si:t] **I** *n* 1 asiento *m*; (*place*) plaza *f*; *Cin Theat* localidad *f*; **to take a s.**, sentarse; *Aut* **s. belt**, cinturón *m* de seguridad. 2 (*of cycle*) sillín *m*; *fam* (*buttocks*) trasero *m*. 3 (*of power, learning*) centro *m*, sede *f*. 4 *Parl* escaño *m*. **II** *vtr* 1 (*guests etc*) sentar. 2 (*accommodate*) tener cabida

para.
seating ['si:tɪŋ] *n* asientos *mpl*; **s. capacity**, cabida *f*, aforo *m*.
seaweed ['si:wi:d] *n* alga *f* (marina).
seaworthy ['si:wɜ:ðɪ] *adj* en condiciones de navegar.
sec [sek] *n fam* (*abbr of* **second**) segundo *m*.
secede [sɪ'si:d] *vi* separarse (**from**, de).
secluded [sɪ'klu:dɪd] *adj* retirado,-a, apartado,-a.
second¹ ['sekənd] **I** *adj* segundo,-a; **every s. day**, cada dos días; **it's the s. highest mountain**, es la segunda montaña más alta; **on s. thought(s) ...**, pensándolo bien ...; **to have s. thoughts about sth**, dudar de algo; **to settle for s. best**, conformarse con lo que hay. **II** *n* 1 (*in series*) segundo,-a *m,f*; **Charles the S.**, Carlos Segundo; **the s. of October**, el dos de octubre. 2 *Aut* (*gear*) segunda *f*. 3 *Com* **seconds**, artículos defectuosos. **III** *vtr* (*motion*) apoyar. **IV** *adv* **to come s.**, terminar en segundo lugar. ◆**secondly** *adv* en segundo lugar.
second² ['sekənd] *n* (*time*) segundo *m*; *fam* **in a s.**, enseguida; *fam* **just a s.!**, ¡un momentito!; **s. hand**, (*of watch, clock*) segundero *m*.
secondary ['sekəndərɪ] *adj* secundario,-a; *GB* **s. school**, escuela secundaria.
second-class [sekənd'klɑ:s] **I** *adj* de segunda clase. **II** *adv* **to travel s.-c.**, viajar en segunda.
second-hand ['sekəndhænd] *adj & adv* de segunda mano.
secondment [sɪ'kɒndmənt] *n GB* traslado *m* temporal.
second-rate ['sekəndreɪt] *adj* de segunda categoría.
secrecy ['si:krəsɪ] *n* secreto *m*; **in s.**, en secreto.
secret ['si:krɪt] **I** *adj* secreto,-a; **to keep sth s.**, mantener algo en secreto; **s. ballot**, votación secreta. **II** *n* secreto *m*; *fig* clave *f*; **in s.**, en secreto; **to keep a s.**, guardar un secreto. ◆**secretly** *adv* en secreto.
secretarial [sekrɪ'teərɪəl] *adj* de secretario,-a.
secretary ['sekrətrɪ] *n* secretario,-a *m,f*; **S. of State**, *GB* ministro,-a *m,f* con cartera; *US* ministro,-a *m,f* de Asuntos Exteriores.
secretion [sɪ'kri:ʃən] *n* secreción *f*.
secretive ['si:krɪtɪv] *adj* reservado,-a.
sect [sekt] *n* secta *f*.
sectarian [sek'teərɪən] *adj & n* sectario,-a (*m,f*).
section ['sekʃən] *n* 1 (*part*) sección *f*, parte *f*; (*of law*) artículo *m*; (*of community*) sector *m*; (*of orchestra, department*) sección *f*. 2 (*cut*) corte *m*.
sector ['sektər] *n* sector *m*.

secular ['sɛkjʊləʳ] *adj (school, teaching)* laico,-a; *(music, art)* profano,-a; *(priest)* seglar, secular.

secure [sɪ'kjʊəʳ] **I** *adj* seguro,-a; *(window, door)* bien cerrado,-a; *(ladder etc)* firme. **II** *vtr* **1** *(make safe)* asegurar. **2** *(fix)* *(rope, knot)* sujetar, fijar; *(object to floor)* afianzar; *(window, door)* cerrar bien. **3** *(obtain)* conseguir, obtener. **4** *Fin (guarantee)* avalar.

security [sɪ'kjʊərɪtɪ] *n* **1** seguridad *f*; **national s.**, seguridad nacional; **S. Council**, *(of United Nations)* Consejo *m* de Seguridad. **2** *Fin (guarantee)* fianza *f*; *(guarantor)* fiador,-a *m,f*. **3** *Fin* **securities**, valores *mpl*.

sedan [sɪ'dæn] *n* **1** *(also* **s. chair)** silla *f* de manos. **2** *US Aut* turismo *m*.

sedate [sɪ'deɪt] **I** *adj* sosegado,-a. **II** *vtr* sedar.

sedation [sɪ'deɪʃən] *n* sedación *f*.

sedative ['sedətɪv] *adj & n* sedante *(m)*.

sediment ['sedɪmənt] *n* sedimento *m*; *(of wine)* poso *m*.

seduce [sɪ'djuːs] *vtr* seducir.

seduction [sɪ'dʌkʃən] *n* seducción *f*.

seductive [sɪ'dʌktɪv] *adj* seductor,-a.

see[1] [siː] *vtr & vi (pt* **saw**; *pp* **seen**) **1** ver; **I'll s. what can be done**, veré lo que se puede hacer; **let's s.**, a ver; **that remains to be seen**, eso queda por ver; **s. page 10**, véase la página 10; **s. you (later)/soon!**, ¡hasta luego/pronto! **2** *(meet with)* ver, tener cita con; **they are seeing each other**, *(of couple)* salen juntos. **3** *(visit)* ver; **to s. the world**, recorrer el mundo. **4** *(understand)* entender; **as far as I can s.**, por lo visto; **I s.**, ya veo; **you s.**, **he hasn't got a car**, es que no tiene coche, ¿sabes? **5** **he sees himself as a second Caruso**, se cree otro Caruso. **6** *(ensure)* asegurarse de. **7 to s. sb home**, acompañar a algn a casa. ◆**see about** *vtr (deal with)* ocuparse de. ◆**see off** *vtr (say goodbye to)* despedirse de. ◆**see out** *vtr* **1** *(show out)* acompañar hasta la puerta. **2** *(survive)* sobrevivir. ◆**see through** *vtr* **1** *fam* **to s. through sb**, verle el plumero a algn. **2 I'll s. you through**, puedes contar con mi ayuda; **£20 should s. me through**, con 20 libras me las apaño. **3 to s. sth through**, *(carry out)* llevar algo a cabo. ◆**see to** *vtr (deal with)* ocuparse de.

see[2] [siː] *n Rel* sede *f*; **the Holy S.**, la Santa Sede.

seed [siːd] **I** *n* **1** *Bot* semilla *f*; *(of fruit)* pepita *f*; **to go to s.**, *(of plant)* granar; *fig (of person)* descuidarse. **2** *Ten (player)* cabeza *mf* de serie. **II** *vtr* **1** *(sow with seed)* sembrar. **2** *(grapes)* despepitar. **3** *Ten* preseleccionar.

seedling ['siːdlɪŋ] *n* plantón *m*.

seedy ['siːdɪ] *adj (seedier, seediest)* fam

(bar etc) sórdido,-a; *(clothes)* raído,-a; *(appearance)* desaseado,-a.

seeing ['siːɪŋ] *conj* **s. that**, visto que, dado que.

seek [siːk] **I** *vtr (pt & pp* **sought**) **1** *(look for)* buscar. **2** *(advice, help)* solicitar. **II** *vtr* buscar; **to s. to do sth**, procurar hacer algo. ◆**seek after** *vtr* buscar; **much sought after**, *(person)* muy solicitado,-a; *(thing)* muy cotizado,-a.

seem [siːm] *vi* parecer; **I s. to remember his name was Colin**, creo recordar que su nombre era Colin; **it seems to me that**, me parece que; **so it seems**, eso parece.

seeming ['siːmɪŋ] *adj* aparente. ◆**seemingly** *adv* aparentemente, según parece.

seen [siːn] *pp* → **see**[1].

seep [siːp] *vi* **to s. through/into/out**, filtrarse por/en/de.

seesaw ['siːsɔː] **I** *n* balancín *m*, subibaja *m*. **II** *vi* **1** columpiarse, balancearse. **2** *fig* vacilar, oscilar.

seethe [siːð] *vi* bullir, hervir; *fig* **to s. with anger**, rabiar; **to s. with people**, rebosar de gente.

see-through ['siːθruː] *adj* transparente.

segment ['segmənt] *n* segmento *m*; *(of orange)* gajo *m*.

segregate ['segrɪgeɪt] *vtr* segregar (**from**, de).

segregation [segrɪ'geɪʃən] *n* segregación *f*.

seize [siːz] *vtr (grab)* agarrar, asir; *Jur (property, drugs)* incautar; *(assets)* secuestrar; *(territory)* tomar; *(arrest)* detener; **to s. an opportunity**, aprovechar una ocasión; **to s. power**, hacerse con el poder. ◆**seize on** *vtr (chance)* agarrar; *(idea)* aferrarse a. ◆**seize up** *vi* agarrotarse.

seizure ['siːʒəʳ] *n* **1** *Jur (of property, drugs)* incautación *f*; *(of newspaper)* secuestro *m*; *(arrest)* detención *f*. **2** *Med* ataque *m* (de apoplejía).

seldom ['seldəm] *adv* rara vez, raramente.

select [sɪ'lekt] **I** *vtr (thing)* escoger, elegir; *(team)* seleccionar. **II** *adj* selecto,-a.

selected [sɪ'lektɪd] *adj* selecto,-a, escogido,-a; *(team, player)* seleccionado,-a; *Lit* **s. works**, obras escogidas.

selection [sɪ'lekʃən] *n (choosing)* elección *f*; *(people or things chosen)* selección *f*; *(range)* surtido *m*.

selective [sɪ'lektɪv] *adj* selectivo,-a.

self [self] *n (pl* **selves** [selvz]) uno,-a mismo,-a, sí mismo,-a; *Psych* **the s.**, el yo.

self- [self] *pref* auto-.

self-adhesive [selfəd'hiːsɪv] *adj* autoadhesivo,-a.

self-assured [selfə'ʃʊəd] *adj* seguro,-a de sí mismo,-a.

self-catering [self'keɪtərɪŋ] *adj* sin servicio de comida.

self-centred, *US* **self-centered** [self'sentəd] *adj* egocéntrico,-a.

self-confessed [selfkən'fest] *adj* confeso,-a.

self-confidence [self'kɒnfɪdəns] *n* confianza *f* en sí mismo,-a.

self-confident [self'kɒnfɪdənt] *adj* seguro,-a de sí mismo,-a.

self-conscious [self'kɒnʃəs] *adj* cohibido,-a.

self-contained [selfkən'teɪnd] *adj* *(flat)* con entrada propia; *(person)* independiente.

self-control [selfkən'trəʊl] *n* autocontrol *m*.

self-defence, *US* **self-defense** [selfdɪ'fens] *n* autodefensa *f*.

self-discipline [self'dɪsɪplɪn] *n* autodisciplina *f*.

self-employed [selfɪm'plɔɪd] *adj* *(worker)* autónomo,-a.

self-esteem [selfɪ'stiːm] *n* amor propio, autoestima *f*.

self-evident [self'evɪdənt] *adj* evidente, patente.

self-governing [self'gʌvənɪŋ] *adj* autónomo,-a.

self-important [selfɪm'pɔːtənt] *adj* engreído,-a, presumido,-a.

self-indulgent [selfɪn'dʌldʒənt] *adj* inmoderado,-a.

self-interest [self'ɪntrɪst] *n* egoísmo *m*.

selfish ['selfɪʃ] *adj* egoísta.

selfishness ['selfɪʃnɪs] *n* egoísmo *m*.

selfless ['selflɪs] *adj* desinteresado,-a.

self-made ['selfmeɪd] *adj* **s.-m. man,** hombre *m* que se ha hecho a sí mismo.

self-pity [self'pɪtɪ] *n* lástima *f* de sí mismo,-a, autocompasión *f*.

self-portrait [self'pɔːtreɪt] *n* autorretrato *m*.

self-possessed [selfpə'zest] *adj* sereno, -a, dueño,-a de sí mismo,-a.

self-preservation [selfprezə'veɪʃən] *n* **(instinct of) s.-p.,** instinto *m* de conservación.

self-raising ['selfreɪzɪŋ] *adj* *GB* **s.-r. flour,** harina *f* con levadura.

self-reliant [selfrɪ'laɪənt] *adj* autosuficiente.

self-respect [selfrɪ'spekt] *n* amor *m* propio, dignidad *f*.

self-righteous [self'raɪtʃəs] *adj* santurrón,-ona.

self-satisfied [self'sætɪsfaɪd] *adj* satisfecho,-a de sí mismo,-a.

self-service [self'sɜːvɪs] **I** *n* *(in shop etc)* autoservicio *m*. **II** *adj* de autoservicio.

self-sufficient [selfsə'fɪʃənt] *adj* autosuficiente.

self-taught [self'tɔːt] *adj* autodidacta.

sell [sel] **I** *vtr (pt & pp* **sold)** vender. **II** *vi* venderse; **this record is selling well,** este disco se vende bien. **III** *n* **hard/soft s.,** *(in advertising)* publicidad agresiva/ discreta. ◆**sell off** *vtr* vender; *(goods)* liquidar. ◆**sell out I** *vi* **to s. out to the enemy,** claudicar ante el enemigo. **II** *vtr Com* **we're sold out of sugar,** se nos ha agotado el azúcar; *Theat* **'sold out',** 'agotadas las localidades'.

seller ['selər] *n* vendedor,-a *m,f*.

selling ['selɪŋ] *n* venta *f*; **s. point,** atractivo *m* comercial; **s. price,** precio *m* de venta.

sellotape® ['seləteɪp] **I** *n* celo® *m*, cinta adhesiva. **II** *vtr* pegar *or* fijar con celo®.

sell-out ['selaʊt] *n* **1** *Theat* éxito *m* de taquilla. **2** *(act of disloyalty)* claudicación *f*.

semaphore ['seməfɔːr] *n* semáforo *m*.

semblance ['sembləns] *n* apariencia *f*; **there was some s. of truth in it,** había algo de verdad en ello.

semen ['siːmen] *n* semen *m*.

semester [sɪ'mestər] *n* semestre *m*.

semi- ['semɪ] *pref* semi-.

semicircle ['semɪsɜːkəl] *n* semicírculo *m*.

semicolon [semɪ'kəʊlən] *n* punto y coma *m*.

semiconductor [semɪkən'dʌktər] *n* semiconductor *m*.

semidetached [semɪdɪ'tætʃt] *GB* **I** *adj* adosado,-a. **II** *n* chalé adosado, casa adosada.

semifinal [semɪ'faɪnəl] *n* semifinal *f*.

seminar ['semɪnɑːr] *n* seminario *m*.

seminary ['semɪnərɪ] *n* seminario *m*.

semolina [semə'liːnə] *n* sémola *f*.

senate ['senɪt] *n* **1** *Pol* senado *m*. **2** *Univ* claustro *m*.

senator ['senətər] *n* senador,-a *m,f*.

send [send] **I** *vtr (pt & pp* **sent) 1** *(letter)* enviar, mandar; *(radio signal)* transmitir; *(rocket, ball)* lanzar; **he was sent to prison,** lo mandaron a la cárcel; **to s. sth flying,** tirar algo. **2** **to s. sb mad,** *(cause to become)* volver loco,-a a algn. **II** *vi* **to s. for sb,** mandar llamar a algn; **to s. for sth,** encargar algo. ◆**send away I** *vtr (dismiss)* despedir. **II** *vi* **to s. away for sth,** escribir pidiendo algo. ◆**send back** *vtr (goods etc)* devolver; *(person)* hacer volver. ◆**send in** *vtr (application etc)* mandar; *(troops)* enviar. ◆**send off** *vtr* **1** *(letter etc)* enviar; *(goods)* despachar. **2** *Ftb (player)* expulsar. ◆**send on** *vtr (luggage) (ahead)* facturar; *(later)* mandar (más tarde). ◆**send out** *vtr* **1** *(person)* echar. **2** *(invitations)* enviar. **3** *(emit)* emitir. ◆**send up** *vtr* **1** hacer subir; *(rocket)* lanzar; *(smoke)* echar. **2** *GB fam (make fun of) (person)* burlarse de; *(book etc)* satirizar.

sender ['sendər] *n* remitente *mf*.

sendoff ['sendɒf] *n fam* despedida *f*.

senile ['siːnaɪl] *adj* senil.

senior ['siːnjər] **I** *adj* **1** (*in age*) mayor;
William Armstrong S., William Armstrong padre; **s. citizen**, jubilado,-a *m,f*. **2**
(*in rank*) superior; (*with longer service*)
más antiguo,-a; *Mil* **s. officer**, oficial *mf*
de alta graduación. **II** *n* **1** **she's three
years my s.**, (*in age*) me lleva tres años.
2 *GB Educ* mayor *mf*; *US Educ* estudiante *mf* del último curso.

seniority [siːnɪ'ɒrɪtɪ] *n* antigüedad *f*.

sensation [sen'seɪʃən] *n* sensación *f*; **to
be a s.**, ser un éxito; **to cause a s.**, causar sensación.

sensational [sen'seɪʃənəl] *adj*
(*marvellous*) sensacional; (*exaggerated*)
sensacionalista.

sense [sens] **I** *n* **1** (*faculty*) sentido *m*;
(*feeling*) sensación *f*; **s. of direction/
humour**, sentido *m* de la orientación/del
humor. **2** (*wisdom*) sentido *m* común, juicio *m*; **common s.**, sentido común. **3**
(*meaning*) sentido *m*; (*of word*) significado
m; **in a s.**, en cierto sentido; **it doesn't
make s.**, no tiene sentido. **4** **to come to
one's senses**, recobrar el juicio. **II** *vtr*
sentir, percatarse de.

senseless ['senslɪs] *adj* **1** (*absurd*)
insensato,-a, absurdo,-a. **2** (*unconscious*)
sin conocimiento.

sensibility [sensɪ'bɪlɪtɪ] *n* **1** (*sensitivity*)
sensibilidad *f*. **2** **sensibilities**, susceptibilidad *f sing*.

sensible ['sensɪbəl] *adj* **1** (*wise*) sensato,
-a. **2** (*choice*) acertado,-a. **3** (*clothes, shoes*)
práctico,-a, cómodo,-a. **4** *fml* (*difference*)
apreciable.

sensitive ['sensɪtɪv] *adj* **1** (*person*) sensible; (*touchy*) susceptible. **2** (*skin*)
delicado,-a; (*document*) confidencial.

sensor ['sensər] *n* sensor *m*.

sensual ['sensjuəl] *adj* sensual.

sensuous ['sensjuəs] *adj* sensual.

sent [sent] *pt & pp* → **send**.

sentence ['sentəns] **I** *n* **1** frase *f*; *Ling*
oración *f*. **2** *Jur* sentencia *f*; **to pass s. on
sb**, imponer una pena a algn; **life s.**, cadena perpetua. **II** *vtr* *Jur* condenar.

sentiment ['sentɪmənt] *n* **1** (*sentimentality*) sensiblería *f*. **2** (*feeling*) sentimiento
m. **3** (*opinion*) opinión *f*.

sentimental [sentɪ'mentəl] *adj* sentimental.

sentry ['sentrɪ] *n* centinela *m*.

separate ['sepəreɪt] **I** *vtr* separar (**from**,
de); (*divide*) dividir (**into**, en);
(*distinguish*) distinguir. **II** *vi* separarse. **III**
['sepərɪt] *adj* separado,-a; (*different*)
distinto,-a; (*entrance*) particular. **IV** *npl*
separates, (*clothes*) piezas *fpl*.
◆**separately** *adv* por separado.

separation [sepə'reɪʃən] *n* separación *f*.

separatist ['sepərətɪst] *n* separatista *mf*.

September [sep'tembər] *n* se(p)tiembre
m.

septic ['septɪk] *adj* séptico,-a; **to become
s.**, (*of wound*) infectarse; **s. tank**, fosa
séptica.

sequel ['siːkwəl] *n* secuela *f*; (*of film etc*)
continuación *f*.

sequence ['siːkwəns] *n* **1** (*order*) secuencia
f, orden *m*. **2** (*series*) serie *f*, sucesión *f*;
Cin **film s.**, secuencia *f*.

serenade [serɪ'neɪd] *n* serenata *f*.

serene [sɪ'riːn] *adj* sereno,-a, tranquilo,-a.

sergeant ['sɑːdʒənt] *n* *Mil* sargento *m*;
(*of police*) cabo *m*; **s. major**, sargento mayor, brigada *m*.

serial ['sɪərɪəl] *n* **1** *Rad TV* serial *m*; (*soap
opera*) radionovela *f*, telenovela *f*. **2** **s.
number**, número *m* de serie.

series ['sɪəriːz] *n inv* serie *f*; (*of books*) colección *f*; (*of concerts, lectures*) ciclo *m*.

serious ['sɪərɪəs] *adj* **1** (*solemn, earnest*)
serio,-a; **I am s.**, hablo en serio. **2** (*causing concern*) grave. ◆**seriously** *adv* **1** (*in
earnest*) en serio. **2** (*dangerously, severely*)
gravemente.

seriousness ['sɪərɪəsnɪs] *n* gravedad *f*, seriedad *f*; **in all s.**, hablando en serio.

sermon ['sɜːmən] *n* sermón *m*.

serpent ['sɜːpənt] *n* serpiente *f*.

serrated [sɪ'reɪtɪd] *adj* dentado,-a.

serum ['sɪərəm] *n* suero *m*.

servant ['sɜːvənt] *n* (*domestic*) criado,-a
m,f; *fig* servidor,-a *m,f*.

serve [sɜːv] **I** *vtr* **1** servir. **2** (*customer*)
atender a. **3** *Ten* servir. **4** **if my memory
serves me right**, si mal no recuerdo; **it
serves him right**, bien merecido lo tiene.
5 *fam* **to s. time**, cumplir una condena;
to s. one's apprenticeship, hacer el
aprendizaje. **II** *vi* **1** servir; **to s. on a
committee**, ser miembro de una comisión. **2** *Ten* servir. **3** (*be useful*) servir
(**as**, de). **III** *n* *Ten* servicio *m*. ◆**serve
out**, **serve up** *vtr* servir.

service ['sɜːvɪs] **I** *n* **1** servicio *m*; **at your
s.!**, ¡a sus órdenes!; **how can I be of s.
to you?**, ¿en qué puedo servirle?; **s.
(charge) included**, servicio incluido; **s.
area**, área *m* de servicio; **s. industry**,
sector *m* de servicios; **s. station**, estación
f de servicio. **2** **medical s.**, servicios médicos; *Mil* **the Services**, las Fuerzas
Armadas; **the train s. to Bristol**, la línea
de trenes a Bristol. **3** (*maintenance*)
mantenimiento *m*. **4** *Rel* oficio *m*; (*mass*)
misa *f*. **5** *Ten* servicio *m*; **s. line**, línea *f*
de saque. **6** (*set of dishes*) juego *m*. **II** *vtr*
(*car, machine*) revisar.

serviceable ['sɜːvɪsəbəl] *adj* **1** (*fit for use*)
útil, servible. **2** (*practical*) práctico,-a.

serviceman ['sɜːvɪsmən] *n* militar *m*.

serviette [sɜːvɪ'et] *n* *GB* servilleta *f*.

sesame ['sesəmɪ] *n* sésamo *m*.

session ['seʃən] *n* **1** sesión *f*; **to be in s.**,
estar reunido,-a; (*of Parliament, court*) celebrar una sesión. **2** *Educ* (*academic year*)

año académico.

set¹ [set] I *vtr* (*pt & pp* set) 1 (*put, place*) poner, colocar; (*trap*) poner (*for*, para); **the novel is s. in Moscow**, la novela se desarrolla en Moscú; **to s. fire to sth**, prender fuego a algo. 2 (*time, price*) fijar; (*record*) establecer; (*trend*) imponer. 3 (*mechanism etc*) ajustar; (*bone*) encajar; **to s. one's watch**, poner el reloj en hora. 4 (*arrange*) arreglar; **he s. the words to music**, puso música a la letra; **to s. the table**, poner la mesa. 5 (*exam, homework*) poner; (*example*) dar; (*precedent*) sentar. 6 **to s. sail**, zarpar; **to s. sb free**, poner en libertad a algn; **to s. sth going**, poner algo en marcha. 7 (*pearl, diamond etc*) engastar. 8 *Print* componer.

II *vi* 1 (*sun, moon*) ponerse. 2 (*jelly, jam*) cuajar; (*cement*) fraguar; (*bone*) encajarse. 3 **to s. to,** (*begin*) ponerse a.

III *n* 1 **shampoo and s.**, lavar y marcar. 2 (*stage*) *Cin* plató *m*; *Theat* escenario *m*; (*scenery*) decorado *m*.

IV *adj* 1 (*task, idea*) fijo,-a, (*date, time*) señalado,-a; (*opinion*) inflexible; (*smile*) rígido,-a, (*gaze*) fijo,-a; **s. phrase**, frase hecha; **to be s. on doing sth**, estar empeñado,-a en hacer algo; **s. square**, cartabón *m*. 2 (*ready*) listo,-a.

◆**set about** *vtr* 1 (*begin*) empezar. 2 (*attack*) agredir. ◆**set aside** *vtr* (*time, money*) reservar; (*differences*) dejar de lado. ◆**set back** *vtr* 1 (*delay*) retrasar; (*hinder*) entorpecer. 2 *fam* (*cost*) costar. ◆**set down** *vtr* (*luggage etc*) dejar (en el suelo); *GB* (*passengers*) dejar. ◆**set in** *vi* (*winter, rain*) comenzar; **panic s. in**, cundió el pánico. ◆**set off** I *vi* (*depart*) salir. II *vtr* 1 (*bomb*) hacer estallar; (*burglar alarm*) hacer sonar; (*reaction*) desencadenar. 2 (*enhance*) hacer resaltar. ◆**set out** I *vi* 1 (*depart*) salir; **to s. out for ...**, partir hacia .... 2 **to s. out to do sth**, proponerse hacer algo. II *vtr* (*arrange*) disponer; (*present*) presentar. ◆**set up** I *vtr* 1 (*position*) colocar; (*statue, camp*) levantar; (*tent, stall*) montar. 2 (*business etc*) establecer; *fam* montar; (*committee*) constituir; *fam* **you've been s. up!**, ¡te han timado!. II *vi* establecerse.

set² [set] *n* 1 (*series*) serie *f*; (*of golf clubs etc*) juego *m*; (*of tools*) estuche *m*; (*of turbines etc*) equipo *m*; (*of books, poems*) colección *f*; (*of teeth*) dentadura *f*; *chess* **s.**, juego de ajedrez; **s. of cutlery**, cubertería *f*; **s. of kitchen utensils**, batería *f* de cocina. 2 (*of people*) grupo *m*; *pej* (*clique*) camarilla *f*. 3 *Math* conjunto *m*. 4 *Ten* set *m*. 5 **TV s.**, televisor *m*.

setback ['setbæk] *n* revés *m*, contratiempo *m*.

settee [se'ti:] *n* sofá *m*.

setting ['setɪŋ] *n* 1 (*background*) marco *m*; (*of novel, film*) escenario *m*. 2 (*of jewel*)

engaste *m*.

settle ['setəl] I *vtr* 1 (*put in position*) colocar. 2 (*decide on*) acordar; (*date, price*) fijar; (*problem*) resolver; (*differences*) arreglar. 3 (*debt*) pagar; (*account*) saldar. 4 (*nerves*) calmar; (*stomach*) asentar. 5 *fam* (*put an end to*) acabar con. 6 (*establish*) (*person*) instalar. 7 (*colonize*) asentarse en. II *vi* 1 (*bird, insect*) posarse; (*dust*) depositarse; (*snow*) cuajar; (*sediment*) precipitarse; (*liquid*) asentarse; **to s. into an armchair**, acomodarse en un sillón. 2 (*put down roots*) afincarse; (*in a colony*) asentarse. 3 (*weather*) serenarse. 4 (*child, nerves*) calmarse. 5 (*pay*) pagar; **to s. out of court**, llegar a un acuerdo amistoso. ◆**settle down** *vi* 1 (*put down roots*) instalarse; (*marry*) casarse. 2 **to s. down to work**, ponerse a trabajar. 3 (*child*) calmarse; (*situation*) normalizarse. ◆**settle for** *vtr* conformarse con. ◆**settle in** *vi* (*move in*) instalarse; (*become adapted*) adaptarse. ◆**settle with** *vtr* (*pay debt to*) ajustar cuentas con.

settlement ['setəlmənt] *n* 1 (*agreement*) acuerdo *m*. 2 (*of debt*) pago *m*; (*of account*) liquidación *f*. 3 (*dowry*) dote *m*. 4 (*colonization*) colonización *f*. 5 (*colony*) asentamiento *m*; (*village*) poblado *m*.

settler ['setlə'] *n* colono *m*.

setup ['setʌp] *n* (*system*) sistema *m*; (*situation*) situación *f*; *sl* montaje *m*.

seven ['sevən] *adj & n* siete (*m*) *inv*.

seventeen [sevən'ti:n] *adj & n* diecisiete (*m*), diez y siete (*m*).

seventeenth [sevən'ti:nθ] I *adj & n* decimoséptimo,-a (*m,f*). II *n* (*fraction*) decimoséptima parte.

seventh ['sevənθ] I *adj & n* séptimo,-a (*m,f*). II *n* séptimo *m*.

seventy ['sevəntɪ] *adj & n* setenta (*m*) *inv*.

sever ['sevə'] *vtr* (*cut*) cortar; *fig* (*relations*) romper.

several ['sevərəl] I *adj* 1 (*more than a few*) varios,-as. 2 (*different*) distintos,-as; *fml* (*separate*) respectivos,-as. II *pron* algunos,-as.

severance ['sevərəns] *n* (*of relations etc*) ruptura *f*; **s. pay**, indemnización *f* por despido.

severe [sɪ'vɪə'] *adj* severo,-a; (*climate, blow*) duro,-a; (*illness, loss*) grave; (*pain*) intenso,-a.

severity [sɪ'verɪtɪ] *n* (*of person, criticism, punishment*) severidad *f*; (*of climate*) rigor *m*; (*of illness*) gravedad *f*; (*of pain*) intensidad *f*; (*of style*) austeridad *f*.

Seville [sə'vɪl] *n* Sevilla *f*.

sew [səʊ] *vtr & vi* (*pt* sewed; *pp* sewed *or* sewn) coser. ◆**sew up** *vtr* (*stitch together*) coser; (*mend*) remendar.

sewage ['su:ɪdʒ] *n* aguas *fpl* residuales.

sewer ['su:ə'] *n* alcantarilla *f*, cloaca *f*.

sewerage ['suːǝrɪdʒ] *n* alcantarillado *m*.

sewing ['sǝuɪŋ] *n* costura *f*; **s. machine**, máquina *f* de coser.

sewn [sǝun] *pp* → **sew**.

sex [seks] *n* sexo *m*; **s. education**, educación *f* sexual; **to have s. with sb**, tener relaciones sexuales con algn; **s. appeal**, sex-appeal *m*.

sexist ['seksɪst] *adj & n* sexista (*mf*).

sexual ['seksjuǝl] *adj* sexual.

sexuality [seksjʊ'ælɪtɪ] *n* sexualidad *f*.

sexy ['seksɪ] *adj* (**sexier, sexiest**) *fam* sexi, erótico,-a.

shabby ['ʃæbɪ] *adj* (**shabbier, shabbiest**) **1** (*garment*) raído,-a; (*house*) desvencijado,-a; (*person*) (*in rags*) harapiento,-a; (*unkempt*) desaseado,-a. **2** (*treatment*) mezquino,-a.

shack [ʃæk] *n* choza *f*.

shackles ['ʃækǝlz] *npl* grilletes *mpl*, grillos *mpl*; *fig* trabas *fpl*.

shade [ʃeɪd] **I** *n* **1** (*shadow*) sombra *f*; **in the s.**, a la sombra. **2** (*eyeshade*) visera *f*; (*lampshade*) pantalla *f*; *US* (*blind*) persiana *f*. **3** (*of colour*) tono *m*, matiz *m*; *fig* (*of meaning*) matiz *m*. **4** (*small amount*) poquito *m*. **5** *fam* **shades**, gafas *fpl* de sol. **II** *vtr* (*from sun*) proteger contra el sol.

shadow ['ʃædǝu] **I** *n* **1** (*shade*) sombra *f*; (*darkness*) oscuridad *f*; *fig* **without a s. of a doubt**, sin lugar a dudas. **2** *GB* **the s. cabinet**, el gabinete de la oposición. **II** *vtr fig* seguir la pista a.

shadowy ['ʃædǝuɪ] *adj* (*dark*) oscuro,-a; (*hazy*) vago,-a.

shady ['ʃeɪdɪ] *adj* (**shadier, shadiest**) (*place*) a la sombra; (*suspicious*) (*person*) sospechoso,-a; (*deal*) turbio,-a.

shaft [ʃɑːft] *n* **1** (*of tool, golf club*) mango *m*; (*of lance*) asta *f*; (*of arrow*) astil *m*. **2** *Tech* eje *m*. **3** (*of mine*) pozo *m*; (*of lift, elevator*) hueco *m*. **4** (*beam of light*) rayo *m*.

shaggy ['ʃægɪ] *adj* (**shaggier, shaggiest**) (*hairy*) peludo,-a; (*long-haired*) melenudo,-a; (*beard*) desgreñado,-a.

shake [ʃeɪk] **I** *n* sacudida *f*. **II** *vtr* (*pt shook; pp shaken*) (*carpet etc*) sacudir; (*bottle*) agitar; (*dice*) mover; (*building*) hacer temblar; **the news shook him**, la noticia le conmocionó; **to s. hands with sb**, estrechar la mano a algn; **to s. one's head**, negar con la cabeza. **III** *vi* (*person, building*) temblar; **to s. with cold**, tiritar de frío. ◆**shake off** *vtr* **1** (*dust etc*) sacudirse. **2** *fig* (*bad habit*) librarse de; (*cough, cold*) quitarse de encima; (*pursuer*) dar esquinazo a. ◆**shake up** *vtr fig* (*shock*) trastornar; (*reorganize*) reorganizar.

shake-up ['ʃeɪkʌp] *n fig* reorganización *f*.

shaken ['ʃeɪkǝn] *pp* → **shake**.

shaky ['ʃeɪkɪ] *adj* (**shakier, shakiest**) (*hand, voice*) tembloroso,-a; (*step*) inseguro,-a; (*handwriting*) temblón,-ona.

shall [ʃæl, *unstressed* ʃǝl] *v aux* **1** (*used to form future tense*) (*first person only*) **I s.** (*or* **I'll**) **buy it**, lo compraré; **I s. not** (*or* **I shan't**) **say anything**, no diré nada. **2** (*used to form questions*) (*usu first person*) **I close the door ?**, ¿cierro la puerta?; **s. I mend it for you?**, ¿quieres que te lo repare?; **s. we go?**, ¿nos vamos? **3** (*emphatic, command, threat*) (*all persons*) **we s. overcome**, venceremos; **you s. leave immediately**, te irás enseguida.

shallow ['ʃælǝu] *adj* poco profundo,-a; *fig* superficial.

sham [ʃæm] **I** *adj* falso,-a; (*illness etc*) fingido,-a. **II** *n* **1** (*pretence*) engaño *m*, farsa *f*. **2** (*person*) fantoche *m*. **III** *vtr* fingir, simular. **IV** *vi* fingir.

shambles ['ʃæmbǝlz] *n* confusión *f*; **the performance was a s.**, la función fue un desastre.

shame [ʃeɪm] **I** *n* **1** vergüenza *f*; **to put to s.**, (*far outdo*) eclipsar, sobrepasar. **2** (*pity*) pena *f*, lástima *f*; **what a s. !**, ¡qué pena!, ¡qué lástima!. **II** *vtr* avergonzar; (*disgrace*) deshonrar.

shamefaced ['ʃeɪmfeɪst] *adj* avergonzado,-a.

shameful ['ʃeɪmfʊl] *adj* vergonzoso,-a.

shameless ['ʃeɪmlɪs] *adj* descarado,-a.

shampoo [ʃæm'puː] **I** *n* champú *m*. **II** *vtr* lavar con champú; **to s. one's hair**, lavarse el pelo.

shamrock ['ʃæmrɒk] *n* trébol *m*.

shandy ['ʃændɪ] *n GB* clara *f*, cerveza *f* con gaseosa.

shantytown ['ʃæntɪtaʊn] *n* barrio *m* de chabolas.

shape [ʃeɪp] **I** *n* **1** (*portion*) parte *f*. **2** *Fin* acción *f*; **s. index**, índice *m* de la Bolsa; **s. prices**, cotizaciones *fpl*. **II** *vtr* **1** (*divide*) dividir. **2** (*have in common*) compartir. **III** *vi* compartir. ◆**share out** *vtr* repartir.

shapeless ['ʃeɪplɪs] *adj* amorfo,-a, informe.

shapely ['ʃeɪplɪ] *adj* (**shapelier, shapeliest**) escultural.

share [ʃeǝr] **I** *n* **1** forma *f*; (*shadow*) silueta *m*; **to take s.**, tomar forma. **2** **in good/bad s.**, (*condition*) en buen/ mal estado; **to be in good s.**, (*health*) estar en forma. **II** *vtr* dar forma a; (*clay*) modelar; (*stone*) tallar; (*character*) formar; (*destiny*) determinar; **star-shaped**, con forma de estrella. **III** *vi* (*also s. up*) tomar forma; **to s. up well**, (*events*) tomar buen cariz; (*person*) hacer progresos.

shareholder ['ʃeǝhǝuldǝr] *n* accionista *mf*.

shark [ʃɑːk] *n* **1** (*fish*) tiburón *m*. **2** *fam* (*swindler*) estafador,-a *m,f*; **loan s.**, usurero,-a *m,f*.

sharp [ʃɑːp] **I** *adj* **1** (*razor, knife*)

afilado,-a; *(needle, pencil)* puntiagudo,-a.
2 *(angle)* agudo,-a; *(features)* anguloso,-a;
(bend) cerrado,-a. 3 *(outline)* definido,-a;
(contrast) marcado,-a. 4 *(observant)* perspicaz; *(clever)* listo,-a; *(quick-witted)*
avispado,-a; *(cunning)* astuto,-a. 5
(sudden) brusco,-a. 6 *(pain, cry)* agudo,-a;
(wind) penetrante. 7 *(sour)* acre. 8 *(criticism)* mordaz; *(temper)* arisco,-a; *(tone)*
seco,-a. 9 *Mus* sostenido,-a; *(out of tune)*
desafinado,-a. II *adv* at 2 o'clock s.,
(exactly) a las dos en punto. III *n Mus*
sostenido *m*. ◆**sharply** *adv* 1 *(abruptly)*
bruscamente. 2 *(clearly)* marcadamente.

sharpen ['ʃɑːpən] *vtr* 1 *(knife)* afilar;
(pencil) sacar punta a. 2 *fig (desire, intelligence)* agudizar.

sharpener ['ʃɑːpənər] *n (for knife)* afila-
dor *m*; *(for pencil)* sacapuntas *m inv*.

sharp-eyed [ʃɑːpʹaɪd] *adj* con ojos de
lince.

shatter ['ʃætər] I *vtr* hacer añicos; *(nerves)*
destrozar; *(hopes)* frustrar. II *vi* hacerse
añicos.

shave [ʃeɪv] I *n* afeitado *m*; **to have a s.,**
afeitarse; *fig* **to have a close s.,** escaparse
por los pelos. II *vtr (pt* **shaved;** *pp*
shaved *or* **shaven** ['ʃeɪvən]) *(person)* afeitar; *(wood)* cepillar. III *vi* afeitarse.

shaver ['ʃeɪvər] *n* **(electric) s.,** máquina *f*
de afeitar.

shaving ['ʃeɪvɪŋ] *n* 1 *(of wood)* viruta *f*. 2
s. brush, brocha *f* de afeitar; **s. cream,**
crema *f* de afeitar; **s. foam,** espuma *f* de
afeitar.

shawl [ʃɔːl] *n* chal *m*.

she [ʃiː] *pers pron* ella.

she- [ʃiː] *pref (of animal)* hembra; **s.-cat,**
gata *f*.

sheaf [ʃiːf] *n (pl* **sheaves** [ʃiːvz]) *Agr* gavilla *f*; *(of arrows)* haz *m*; *(of papers,
banknotes)* fajo *m*.

shear [ʃɪər] I *vtr (pt* **sheared;** *pp* **shorn** *or*
sheared) *(sheep)* esquilar; **to s. off,**
cortar. II *vi* esquilar ovejas.

shears [ʃɪəz] *npl* tijeras *fpl* (grandes).

sheath [ʃiːθ] *n* 1 *(for sword)* vaina *f*; *(for
knife, scissors)* funda *f*. 2 *(contraceptive)*
preservativo *m*.

sheaves [ʃiːvz] *npl* → **sheaf.**

shed¹ [ʃed] *n (in garden)* cobertizo *m*;
(workmen's hut) barraca *f*; *(for cattle)* establo *m*; *(in factory)* nave *f*.

shed² [ʃed] *vtr (pt & pp* **shed)** 1 *(clothes)*
despojarse de; *(unwanted thing)* deshacerse de; **the snake s. its skin,** la
serpiente mudó de piel. 2 *(blood, tears)*
derramar.

sheen [ʃiːn] *n* brillo *m*.

sheep [ʃiːp] *n inv* oveja *f*.

sheepdog ['ʃiːpdɒg] *n* perro *m* pastor.

sheepish ['ʃiːpɪʃ] *adj* avergonzado,-a.

sheepskin ['ʃiːpskɪn] *n* piel *f* de carnero.

sheer [ʃɪər] *adj* 1 *(utter)* total, puro,-a. 2

(cliff) escarpado,-a; *(drop)* vertical. 3
(stockings, cloth) fino,-a.

sheet [ʃiːt] *n* 1 *(on bed)* sábana *f*. 2 *(of
paper)* hoja *f*; *(of tin, glass, plastic)* lámina
f; *(of ice)* capa *f*.

sheik(h) [ʃeɪk] *n* jeque *m*.

shelf [ʃelf] *n (pl* **shelves** [ʃelvz]) *(on bookcase)* estante *m*; *(in cupboard)* tabla *f*;
shelves, estantería *f*.

shell [ʃel] I *n* 1 *(of egg, nut)* cáscara *f*; *(of
pea)* vaina *f*; *(of tortoise etc)* caparazón *m*;
(of snail etc) concha *f*. 2 *(of building)*
armazón *m*. 3 *(mortar etc)* obús *m*, proyectil *m*; *(cartridge)* cartucho *m*; **s. shock,**
neurosis *f* de guerra. II *vtr* 1 *(peas)* des-
vainar; *(nuts)* pelar. 2 *Mil* bombardear.

shellfish ['ʃelfɪʃ] *n inv* marisco *m*, mariscos *mpl*.

shelter ['ʃeltər] I *n* 1 *(protection)* abrigo *m*,
amparo *m*; **to take s.,** refugiarse **(from,
de).** 2 *(place)* refugio *m*; *(for homeless)* asilo *m*; **bus s.,** marquesina *f*. II *vtr* 1 *(protect)* abrigar, proteger. 2 *(take into one's
home)* ocultar. III *vi* refugiarse.

sheltered ['ʃeltəd] *adj (place)* abrigado,-a;
to lead a s. life, vivir apartado,-a del
mundo.

shelve [ʃelv] *vtr fig (postpone)* dar carpetazo a.

shelves [ʃelvz] *npl* → **shelf.**

shepherd ['ʃepəd] I *n* pastor *m*; **s.'s pie,**
pastel *m* de carne picada con puré de patatas. II *vtr fig* **to s. sb in,** hacer entrar a
algn.

sheriff ['ʃerɪf] *n GB* gobernador *m* civil;
Scot juez *m* presidente; *US* sheriff *m*.

sherry ['ʃerɪ] *n* jerez *m*.

Shetland ['ʃetlənd] *n* **the S. Isles, S.,** las
Islas Shetland; **S. wool,** lana *f* Shetland.

shield [ʃiːld] I *n* 1 escudo *m*; *(of policeman)* placa *f*. 2 *(on machinery)* blindaje *m*.
II *vtr* proteger **(from, de).**

shift [ʃɪft] I *n* 1 *(change)* cambio *m*; *US
Aut (gear)* **s.,** cambio de velocidades. 2
(period of work, group of workers) turno *m*;
to be on the day s., hacer el turno de
día. II *vtr (change)* cambiar; *(move)*
cambiar de sitio, trasladar. III *vi (move)*
moverse; *(change place)* cambiar de sitio;
(opinion) cambiar; *(wind)* cambiar de dirección.

shiftless ['ʃɪftlɪs] *n* perezoso,-a, vago,-a.

shiftwork ['ʃɪftwɜːk] *n* trabajo *m* por
turnos.

shifty ['ʃɪftɪ] *adj (shiftier, shiftiest) (look)*
furtivo,-a; *(person)* sospechoso,-a.

shilling ['ʃɪlɪŋ] *n* chelín *m*.

shimmer ['ʃɪmər] I *vi* relucir; *(shine)* brillar. II *n* luz trémula, reflejo trémulo;
(shining) brillo *m*.

shin [ʃɪn] *n* espinilla *f*; **s. pad,** espinillera
f.

shine [ʃaɪn] I *vi (pt & pp* **shone)** 1 *(light)*
brillar; *(metal)* relucir. 2 *fig (excel)* sobre-

salir (**at, en**). **II** *vtr* **1** *(lamp)* dirigir. **2** *(pt & pp shined)* *(polish)* sacar brillo a; *(shoes)* limpiar. **III** *n* brillo *m*, lustre *m*.

shingle ['ʃɪŋgəl] *n* **1** *(pebbles)* guijarros *mpl*. **2** *(roof tile)* tablilla *f*.

shingles ['ʃɪŋgəlz] *npl Med* herpes *m*.

shining ['ʃaɪnɪŋ] *adj fig (outstanding)* ilustre.

shiny ['ʃaɪnɪ] *adj* (**shinier, shiniest**) brillante.

ship [ʃɪp] **I** *n* barco *m*, buque *m*. **II** *vtr* **1** *(take on board)* embarcar. **2** *(transport)* transportar (en barco); *(send)* enviar, mandar.

shipbuilding ['ʃɪpbɪldɪŋ] *n* construcción *f* naval.

shipment ['ʃɪpmənt] *n* **1** *(act)* transporte *m*. **2** *(load)* consignación *f*, envío *m*.

shipper ['ʃɪpər] *n (person)* cargador,-a *m,f*.

shipping ['ʃɪpɪŋ] *n* **1** *(ships)* barcos *mpl*; **s. lane**, vía *f* de navegación. **2** *(loading)* embarque *m*; *(transporting)* transporte *m* (en barco); **s. company**, compañía naviera.

shipshape ['ʃɪpʃeɪp] *adj & adv* en perfecto orden.

shipwreck ['ʃɪprek] **I** *n* naufragio *m*. **II** *vtr* **to be shipwrecked**, naufragar.

shipyard ['ʃɪpjɑːd] *n* astillero *m*.

shire [ʃaɪər] *n GB* condado *m*.

shirk [ʃɜːk] **I** *vtr (duty)* faltar a; *(problem)* eludir. **II** *vi* gandulear.

shirt [ʃɜːt] *n* camisa *f*; **in s. sleeves**, en mangas de camisa; *fam* **keep your s. on!**, ¡no te sulfures!

shit [ʃɪt] *vulg* **I** *n* mierda *f*; *sl* **in the s.**, jodido,-a. **II** *interj* ¡mierda!. **III** *vi* cagar.

shiver ['ʃɪvər] **I** *vi (with cold)* tiritar; *(with fear)* temblar, estremecerse. **II** *n (with cold, fear)* escalofrío *m*.

shoal [ʃəʊl] *n (of fish)* banco *m*.

shock [ʃɒk] **I** *n* **1** *(jolt)* choque *m*; **s. absorber**, amortiguador *m*; **s. wave**, onda expansiva. **2** *(upset)* conmoción *f*; *(scare)* susto *m*. **3** *Med* shock *m*. **II** *vtr (upset)* conmover; *(startle)* sobresaltar; *(scandalize)* escandalizar.

shocking ['ʃɒkɪŋ] *adj* **1** *(causing horror)* espantoso,-a; *fam (very bad)* horroroso,-a. **2** *(disgraceful)* escandaloso,-a. **3 s. pink**, rosa chillón.

shod [ʃɒd] *pt & pp* → **shoe**.

shoddy ['ʃɒdɪ] *adj* (**shoddier, shoddiest**) *(goods)* de mala calidad; *(work)* chapucero,-a.

shoe [ʃuː] **I** *n* **1** zapato *m*; *(for horse)* herradura *f*; **brake s.**, zapata *f*; **s. polish**, betún *m*; **s. repair (shop)**, remiendo *m* de zapatos; **s. shop**, *US* **s. store**, zapatería *f*. **2 shoes**, calzado *m sing*. **II** *vtr (pt & pp shod)* *(horse)* herrar.

shoebrush ['ʃuːbrʌʃ] *n* cepillo *m* para los zapatos.

shoehorn ['ʃuːhɔːn] *n* calzador *m*.

shoelace ['ʃuːleɪs] *n* cordón *m* (de zapatos).

shoestring ['ʃuːstrɪŋ] *n fig* **to do sth on a s.**, hacer algo con poquísimo dinero.

shone [ʃɒn, *US* ʃəʊn] *pt & pp* → **shine I & II**.

shoo [ʃuː] **I** *interj* ¡fuera!. **II** *vtr* **to s. (away)**, espantar.

shook [ʃʊk] *pt* → **shake**.

shoot [ʃuːt] **I** *n Bot* retoño *m*; *(of vine)* sarmiento *m*. **II** *vtr (pt & pp shot)* **1** pegar un tiro a; *(kill)* matar; *(execute)* fusilar; *(hunt)* cazar; **to s. dead**, matar a tiros. **2** *(missile, glance)* lanzar; *(bullet, ball)* disparar. **3** *(film)* rodar, filmar; *Phot* fotografiar. **4** *sl* **to s. (up)**, *(heroin etc)* chutarse. **III** *vi* **1** *(with gun)* disparar *(at sb,* sobre, *a algn)*; **to s. at a target**, tirar al blanco; *Ftb* **to s. at the goal**, chutar a puerta. **2** **to s. past** *or* **by**, pasar flechado,-a. ◆**shoot down** *vtr (aircraft)* derribar. ◆**shoot out** *vi (person)* salir disparado,-a; *(water)* brotar; *(flames)* salir. ◆**shoot up** *vi (flames)* salir; *(water)* brotar; *(prices)* dispararse.

shooting ['ʃuːtɪŋ] **I** *n* **1** *(shots)* tiros *mpl*; *(murder)* asesinato *m*; *(hunting)* caza *f*; **s. star**, estrella *f* fugaz. **2** *(of film)* rodaje *m*. **II** *adj (pain)* punzante.

shoot-out ['ʃuːtaʊt] *n* tiroteo *m*.

shop [ʃɒp] **I** *n* **1** tienda *f*; *(large store)* almacén *m*; **s. assistant**, dependiente,-a *m,f*; **s. window**, escaparate *m*. **2** *(workshop)* taller *m*; **s. floor**, *(place)* planta *f*; *(workers)* obreros *mpl*; *GB* **s. steward**, enlace *mf* sindical. **II** *vi* hacer compras; **to go shopping**, ir de compras.

shopkeeper ['ʃɒpkiːpər] *n* tendero,-a *m,f*.

shoplifter ['ʃɒplɪftər] *n* ladrón,-ona *m,f* (de tiendas).

shopper ['ʃɒpər] *n* comprador,-a *m,f*.

shopping ['ʃɒpɪŋ] *n (purchases)* compras *fpl*; **s. bag/basket**, bolsa *f*/cesta *f* de la compra; **s. centre** *or* **precinct**, centro *m* comercial.

shopsoiled ['ʃɒpsɔɪld], *US* **shopworn** ['ʃɒpwɔːn] *adj* deteriorado,-a.

shore[1] [ʃɔːr] *n (of sea, lake)* orilla *f*; *US (beach)* playa *f*; *(coast)* costa *f*; **to go on s.**, desembarcar.

shore[2] [ʃɔːr] *vtr* **to s. (up)**, apuntalar.

shorn [ʃɔːn] *pp* → **shear**.

short [ʃɔːt] **I** *adj* **1** corto,-a; *(not tall)* bajo,-a; **in a s. while**, dentro de un rato; **in the s. term**, a corto plazo; **s. circuit**, cortocircuito *m*; **s. cut**, atajo *m*; *GB* **s. list**, lista *f* de seleccionados; **s. story**, relato corto, cuento *m*; **s. wave**, onda corta. **2** *(brief)* corto,-a, breve; **'Bob' is s. for 'Robert'**, 'Bob' es el diminutivo de 'Robert'; **for s.**, para abreviar; **in s.**, en pocas palabras. **3** **to be s. of breath**, faltarle a uno la respiración; **to be s. of food**, andar escaso,-a de comida. **4** *(curt)* brusco,-a, seco,-a. **II** *adv* **1 to pull up s.**, pararse en seco. **2 to cut s.**, *(holiday)* interrumpir; *(meeting)* suspender; **we're running s. of coffee**, se nos está acabando el café. **3 s. of**, *(except)* excepto, menos. **III** *n* **1** *Cin* cortometraje *m*. **2** *fam (drink)* copa *f*. **IV** *vi* **to s.** (out), tener un cortocircuito. ◆**shortly** *adv (soon)* dentro de poco; **s. after**, poco después.

shortage ['ʃɔːtɪdʒ] *n* escasez *f*.

shortbread ['ʃɔːtbred] *n* mantecado *m*.

short-change [ʃɔːt'tʃeɪndʒ] *vtr* **to s.-c. sb**, no devolver el cambio completo a algn; *fig* timar a algn.

short-circuit [ʃɔːt'sɜːkɪt] **I** *vtr* provocar un cortocircuito en. **II** *vi* tener un cortocircuito.

shortcomings ['ʃɔːtkʌmɪŋz] *npl* defectos *mpl*.

shortcrust ['ʃɔːtkrʌst] *n* **s. pastry**, pasta brisa.

shorten ['ʃɔːtən] *vtr (skirt, visit)* acortar; *(word)* abreviar; *(text)* resumir.

shortfall ['ʃɔːtfɔːl] *n* déficit *m*.

shorthand ['ʃɔːthænd] *n* taquigrafía *f*; *GB* **s. typing**, taquimecanografía *f*; *GB* **s. typist**, taquimecanógrafo,-a *m,f*.

short-list ['ʃɔːtlɪst] *vtr* poner en la lista de seleccionados.

short-lived [ʃɔːt'lɪvd] *adv* efímero,-a.

short-range [ʃɔːt'reɪndʒ] *adj* de corto alcance.

shorts [ʃɔːts] *npl* **1** pantalones *mpl* cortos; **a pair of s.**, un pantalón corto. **2** *US (underpants)* calzoncillos *mpl*.

short-sighted [ʃɔːt'saɪtɪd] *adj (person)* miope; *fig (plan etc)* sin visión de futuro.

short-staffed [ʃɔːt'stɑːft] *adj* escaso,-a de personal.

short-tempered [ʃɔːt'tempəd] *adj* de mal genio.

short-term ['ʃɔːtɜːm] *adj* a corto plazo.

shot¹ [ʃɒt] **I** *n* **1** *(act, sound)* tiro *m*, disparo *m*. **2** *(projectile)* bala *f*; *(pellets)* perdigones *mpl*; *fig* **he was off like a s.**, salió disparado; *Sport* **s. put**, lanzamiento *m* de peso. **3** *(person)* tirador,-a *m,f*. **4** *Ftb (kick)* tiro *m* (a puerta); *(in billiards, cricket, golf)* golpe *m*. **5** *(attempt)* tentativa *f*; **to have a s. at sth**, intentar hacer algo. **6** *(injection)* inyección *f*; *fam* pinchazo *m*. **7** *(drink)* trago *m*. **8** *Phot* foto *f*; *Cin* toma *f*.

shot² [ʃɒt] *pt & pp* → **shoot**.

shotgun ['ʃɒtgʌn] *n* escopeta *f*.

should [ʃʊd, *unstressed* ʃəd] *v aux* **1** *(duty)* deber; **all employees s. wear helmets**, todos los empleados deben llevar casco; **he s. have been an architect**, debería haber sido arquitecto. **2** *(probability)* deber de; **he s. have finished by now**, ya debe de haber acabado; **this s. be interesting**, esto promete ser interesante. **3** *(conditional use)* **if anything strange s.**

happen, si pasara algo raro. **4 I s. like to ask a question**, quisiera hacer una pregunta.

shoulder ['ʃəʊldər] **I** *n* **1** hombro *m*; **s. blade**, omóplato *m*; **s. strap**, *(of garment)* tirante *m*; *(of bag)* correa *f*; *Aut* **hard s.**, arcén *m*. **2** *Culin* paletilla *f*. **II** *vtr fig (responsibilities)* cargar con.

shout [ʃaʊt] **I** *n* grito *m*. **II** *vtr* gritar. **III** *vi* gritar; **to s. at sb**, gritar a algn. ◆**shout down** *vtr* abuchear.

shouting ['ʃaʊtɪŋ] *n* gritos *mpl*, vocerío *m*.

shove [ʃʌv] **I** *n fam* empujón *m*. **II** *vtr* empujar; **to s. sth into one's pocket**, meterse algo en el bolsillo a empellones. **III** *vi* empujar; *(jostle)* dar empellones. ◆**shove off** *vi fam* largarse. ◆**shove up** *vi fam (move along)* correrse.

shovel ['ʃʌvəl] **I** *n* pala *f*; **mechanical s.**, excavadora *f*. **II** *vtr* mover con pala *or* a paladas.

show [ʃəʊ] **I** *vtr (pt* **showed**; *pp* **shown** *or* **showed**) **1** *(ticket etc)* mostrar; *(painting etc)* exponer; *(film)* poner; *(latest plans etc)* presentar. **2** *(display)* demostrar; **to s. oneself to be**, comportarse como. **3** *(teach)* enseñar; *(explain)* explicar. **4** *(temperature, way etc)* indicar; *(profit etc)* registrar. **5** *(prove)* demostrar. **6** *(conduct)* llevar; **to s. sb in**, hacer pasar a algn; **to s. sb to the door**, acompañar a algn hasta la puerta.

II *vi* **1** *(be visible)* notarse. **2** *fam (turn up)* aparecer. **3** *Cin* **what's showing?**, ¿qué ponen?

III *n* **1** *(display)* demostración *f*. **2** *(outward appearance)* apariencia *f*. **3** *(exhibition)* exposición *f*; **on s.**, expuesto,-a; **boat s.**, salón náutico; **motor s.**, salón del automóvil. **4** *Theat (entertainment)* espectáculo *m*; *(performance)* función *f*; *Rad TV* programa *m*; **s. business**, *fam* **s. biz**, el mundo del espectáculo. ◆**show off** *vtr* **1** *(highlight)* hacer resaltar. **2** *fam (flaunt)* hacer alarde de. **II** *vi fam* farolear. ◆**show up** *vtr* **1** *(reveal)* sacar a luz; *(highlight)* hacer resaltar. **2** *fam (embarrass)* dejar en evidencia. **II** *vi* **1** *(stand out)* destacarse. **2** *fam (arrive)* aparecer.

showdown ['ʃəʊdaʊn] *n* enfrentamiento *m*.

shower ['ʃaʊər] **I** *n* **1** *(rain)* chubasco *m*, chaparrón *m*. **2** *fig (of stones, blows etc)* lluvia *f*. **3** *(bath)* ducha *f*; **to have a s.**, ducharse. **II** *vtr* **1** *(spray)* rociar. **2** *fig* **to s. gifts/praise on sb**, colmar a algn de regalos/elogios. **III** *vi* ducharse.

showerproof ['ʃaʊəpruːf] *adj* impermeable.

showing ['ʃəʊɪŋ] *n (of film)* proyección *f*.

showjumping ['ʃəʊdʒʌmpɪŋ] *n* hípica *f*.

shown [ʃəʊn] *pp* → **show**.

show-off ['ʃəʊɒf] n fam farolero,-a m,f.

showpiece ['ʃəʊpiːs] n (in exhibition etc) obra maestra; fig (at school etc) modelo f.

showroom ['ʃəʊruːm] n Com exposición f; Art galería f.

shrank [ʃræŋk] pt → **shrink**.

shrapnel ['ʃræpnəl] n metralla f.

shred [ʃred] I n triza f; (of cloth) jirón m; (of paper) tira f. II vtr (paper) hacer trizas; (vegetables) rallar.

shredder ['ʃredər] n (for waste paper) trituradora f; (for vegetables) rallador m.

shrew [ʃruː] n 1 Zool musaraña f. 2 fig (woman) arpía f.

shrewd [ʃruːd] adj astuto,-a; (clear-sighted) perspicaz; (wise) sabio,-a; (decision) acertado,-a.

shriek [ʃriːk] I n chillido m; **shrieks of laughter**, carcajadas fpl. II vi chillar.

shrill [ʃrɪl] adj agudo,-a, estridente.

shrimp [ʃrɪmp] I n camarón m. II vi pescar camarones.

shrine [ʃraɪn] n (tomb) sepulcro m; (relic case) relicario m; (chapel) capilla f; (holy place) lugar sagrado.

shrink [ʃrɪŋk] I vtr (pt **shrank**; pp **shrunk**) encoger. II vi 1 (clothes) encoger(se). 2 (savings) disminuir. **3 to s. (back)**, echarse atrás; **to s. from doing sth**, no tener valor para hacer algo. II n fam (psychiatrist) psiquiatra m,f.

shrinkage ['ʃrɪŋkɪdʒ] n 1 (of cloth) encogimiento m; (of metal) contracción f. 2 (of savings etc) disminución f.

shrink-wrapped ['ʃrɪŋkræpt] adj envuelto,-a en plástico.

shrivel ['ʃrɪvəl] I vtr **to s. (up)**, encoger; (plant) secar; (skin) arrugar. II vi encogerse; (plant) secarse; (skin) arrugarse.

shroud [ʃraʊd] I n Rel sudario m. II vtr fig envolver.

Shrove Tuesday [ʃrəʊv'tjuːzdɪ] n martes m de carnaval.

shrub [ʃrʌb] n arbusto m.

shrubbery ['ʃrʌbərɪ] n arbustos mpl.

shrug [ʃrʌg] I vtr **to s. one's shoulders**, encogerse de hombros. II vi encogerse de hombros. III n encogimiento de hombros. ◆**shrug off** vtr no dejarse desanimar por.

shrunk [ʃrʌŋk] pp → **shrink**.

shudder ['ʃʌdər] I n 1 escalofrío m, estremecimiento m. 2 (of machinery) sacudida f. II vi 1 (person) estremecerse. 2 (machinery) dar sacudidas.

shuffle ['ʃʌfəl] I vtr 1 (feet) arrastrar. 2 (papers etc) revolver; (cards) barajar. II vi 1 (walk) andar arrastrando los pies. 2 Cards barajar.

shun [ʃʌn] vtr (person) esquivar; (responsibility) rehuir.

shunt [ʃʌnt] vtr Rail cambiar de vía; Elec derivar.

shut [ʃʌt] I vtr (pt & pp **shut**) cerrar. II vi

cerrarse. III adj cerrado,-a. ◆**shut down** I vtr (factory) cerrar. II vi (factory) cerrar. ◆**shut off** vtr (gas, water etc) cortar. ◆**shut out** vtr 1 (lock out) dejar fuera a. 2 (exclude) excluir. ◆**shut up** I vtr 1 (close) cerrar. 2 (imprison) encerrar. 3 fam (silence) callar. II vi fam (keep quiet) callarse.

shutdown ['ʃʌtdaʊn] n cierre m.

shutter ['ʃʌtər] n 1 (on window) contraventana f, postigo m. 2 Phot obturador m.

shuttle ['ʃʌtəl] I n 1 (in weaving) lanzadera f. 2 Av puente aéreo; (space) s., transbordador m espacial. II vi ir y venir.

shuttlecock ['ʃʌtəlkɒk] n volante m.

shy [ʃaɪ] I adj (shyer, shyest or shier, shiest) (timid) tímido,-a; (reserved) reservado,-a. II vi (horse) espantarse (at, de); fig **to s. away from doing sth**, negarse a hacer algo.

shyness ['ʃaɪnɪs] n timidez f.

Siberia [saɪ'bɪərɪə] n Siberia.

sibling ['sɪblɪŋ] n fml (brother) hermano m; (sister) hermana f; **siblings**, hermanos.

Sicily ['sɪsɪlɪ] n Sicilia.

sick [sɪk] adj 1 (ill) enfermo,-a; **s. leave**, baja f por enfermedad; **s. pay**, subsidio m de enfermedad. 2 **to feel s.**, (about to vomit) tener ganas de devolver; **to be s.**, devolver. 3 fam (fed up) harto,-a. 4 fam (mind, joke) morboso,-a; **s. humour**, humor negro.

sickbay ['sɪkbeɪ] n enfermería f.

sicken ['sɪkən] I vtr (make ill) poner enfermo; (revolt) dar asco a. II vi (fall ill) enfermar.

sickening ['sɪkənɪŋ] adj nauseabundo,-a; (revolting) repugnante; (horrifying) escalofriante.

sickle ['sɪkəl] n hoz f.

sickly ['sɪklɪ] adj (sicklier, sickliest) 1 (person) enfermizo,-a. 2 (taste) empalagoso,-a. 3 (smile) forzado,-a.

sickness ['sɪknɪs] n 1 (illness) enfermedad f. 2 (nausea) náuseas fpl.

side [saɪd] I n 1 lado m; (of coin etc) cara f; (of hill) ladera f; **by the s. of**, junto a. 2 (of body) costado m; (of animal) ijar m; **a s. of bacon**, una loncha de tocino; **by my s.**, a mi lado; **s. by s.**, juntos. 3 (edge) borde m; (of lake, river) orilla f. 4 fig (aspect) aspecto m. 5 (team) equipo m; Pol partido m; **she's on our s.**, está de nuestro lado; **to take sides with sb**, ponerse de parte de algn; **s. dish**, guarnición f; **s. effect**, efecto secundario; **s. entrance**, entrada f lateral; **s. street**, calle f lateral. II vi **to s. with sb**, ponerse de parte de algn.

sideboard ['saɪdbɔːd] n aparador m.

sideburns ['saɪdbɜːnz] npl patillas fpl.

sidelight ['saɪdlaɪt] n Aut luz f lateral, piloto m.

sideline ['saɪdlaɪn] n 1 Sport línea f de banda. 2 Com (product) línea suplementaria; (job) empleo suplementario.

sidelong ['saɪdlɒŋ] adj de reojo.

side-saddle ['saɪdsædəl] I n silla f de amazona. II adv to ride s., montar a la inglesa.

sideshow ['saɪdʃəʊ] n atracción secundaria.

sidestep ['saɪdstep] I vtr (issue) esquivar. II vi Box fintar.

sidetrack ['saɪdtræk] vtr fig (person) despistar.

sidewalk ['saɪdwɔːk] n US acera f.

sideways ['saɪdweɪz] I adj (movement) lateral; (look) de reojo. II adv de lado.

siding ['saɪdɪŋ] n Rail apartadero m, vía muerta.

sidle ['saɪdəl] vi to s. up to sb, acercarse furtivamente a algn.

siege [siːdʒ] n sitio m, cerco m; to lay s. to, sitiar.

sieve [sɪv] I n (fine) tamiz m; (coarse) criba f. II vtr (fine) tamizar; (coarse) cribar.

sift [sɪft] vtr (sieve) tamizar; fig to s. through, examinar cuidadosamente.

sigh [saɪ] I vi suspirar. II n suspiro m.

sight [saɪt] I n 1 (faculty) vista f; at first s., a primera vista; to catch s. of, divisar; to know by s., conocer de vista; to lose s. of sth/sb, perder algo/a algn de vista. 2 (range of vision) vista f; within s., a la vista; to come into s., aparecer. 3 (spectacle) espectáculo m. 4 (on gun) mira f; fig to set one's sights on, tener la mira puesta en. 5 sights, monumentos mpl. II vtr ver; (land) divisar.

sightseeing ['saɪtsiːɪŋ] n turismo m; to go s., hacer turismo.

sign [saɪn] I n 1 (symbol) signo m. 2 (gesture) gesto m, seña f; (signal) señal f. 3 (indication) señal f; (trace) rastro m, huella f; as a s. of, como muestra de. 4 (notice) anuncio m; (board) letrero m. II vtr 1 (letter etc) firmar. 2 Ftb firmar. III vi firmar. ◆sign on I vtr (worker) contratar. II vi (worker) firmar un contrato; GB fam apuntarse al paro; (regularly) firmar el paro. ◆sign up I vtr (soldier) reclutar; (worker) contratar. II vi (soldier) alistarse; (worker) firmar un contrato.

signal ['sɪgnəl] I n señal f; Rad TV sintonía f; Rail s. box, garita f de señales. II vtr (message) transmitir por señales. 2 (direction etc) indicar. III vi (with hands) hacer señales; (in car) señalar.

signalman ['sɪgnəlmən] n guardavía m.

signature ['sɪgnɪtʃər] n (name) firma f; Rad TV s. tune, sintonía f.

signet ['sɪgnɪt] n s. ring, (anillo m de) sello m.

significance [sɪg'nɪfɪkəns] n (meaning) significado m; (importance) importancia f.

significant [sɪg'nɪfɪkənt] adj (meaningful)

significativo,-a; (important) importante. ◆**significantly** adv (markedly) sensiblemente.

signify ['sɪgnɪfaɪ] vtr 1 (mean) significar. 2 (show, make known) indicar.

signpost ['saɪnpəʊst] n poste m indicador.

silence ['saɪləns] I n silencio m. II vtr acallar; (engine) silenciar.

silencer ['saɪlənsər] n silenciador m.

silent ['saɪlənt] adj silencioso,-a; (not talkative) callado,-a; (film) mudo,-a; be s.!, ¡cállate!; to remain s., guardar silencio. ◆**silently** adv silenciosamente.

silhouette [sɪluː'et] n silueta f.

silicon ['sɪlɪkən] n silicio m; s. chip, chip m (de silicio).

silk [sɪlk] I n seda f. II adj de seda.

silky ['sɪlkɪ] adj (silkier, silkiest) (cloth) sedoso,-a; (voice etc) aterciopelado,-a.

sill [sɪl] n (of window) alféizar m.

silly ['sɪlɪ] adj (sillier, silliest) tonto,-a.

silo ['saɪləʊ] n silo m.

silt [sɪlt] n cieno m. ◆**silt up** vi obstruirse con cieno.

silver ['sɪlvər] I n 1 (metal) plata f. 2 (coins) monedas fpl (de plata). 3 (tableware) vajilla f de plata. II adj de plata; s. foil, (tinfoil) papel m de aluminio; s. paper, papel de plata; s. wedding, bodas fpl de plata.

silver-plated [sɪlvə'pleɪtɪd] adj plateado,-a.

silversmith ['sɪlvəsmɪθ] n platero,-a m,f.

silverware ['sɪlvəweər] n vajilla f de plata.

silvery ['sɪlvərɪ] adj plateado,-a.

similar ['sɪmɪlər] adj parecido,-a, semejante (to, a); to be s., parecerse. ◆**similarly** adv 1 (as well) igualmente. 2 (likewise) del mismo modo, asimismo.

similarity [sɪmɪ'lærɪtɪ] n semejanza f.

simile ['sɪmɪlɪ] n símil m.

simmer ['sɪmər] I vtr cocer a fuego lento. II vi cocerse a fuego lento. ◆**simmer down** vi fam calmarse.

simpering ['sɪmpərɪŋ] adj melindroso,-a.

simple ['sɪmpəl] adj 1 sencillo,-a; s. interest, interés m simple. 2 (natural) natural. 3 (foolish) simple; (naïve) ingenuo,-a; (dim) de pocas luces. ◆**simply** adv 1 (plainly) sencillamente. 2 (only) simplemente, sólo.

simplicity [sɪm'plɪsɪtɪ] n 1 sencillez f. 2 (naïveté) ingenuidad f.

simplify ['sɪmplɪfaɪ] vtr simplificar.

simulate ['sɪmjʊleɪt] vtr simular.

simulator ['sɪmjʊleɪtər] n flight s., simulador de vuelo.

simultaneous [sɪməl'teɪnɪəs] adj simultáneo,-a. ◆**simultaneously** adv simultáneamente.

sin [sɪn] I n pecado m. II vi pecar.

since [sɪns] I adv (ever) s., desde

entonces; **long s.**, hace mucho tiempo; **it has s. come out that ...**, desde entonces se ha sabido que .... **II** *prep* desde; **she has been living here s.** 1975, vive aquí desde 1975. **III** *conj* **1** *(time)* desde que; **how long is it s. you last saw him?**, ¿cuánto tiempo hace que lo viste por última vez? **2** *(because, as)* ya que, puesto que.

sincere [sɪn'sɪər] *adj* sincero,-a. ◆**sincerely** *adv* sinceramente; **Yours s.**, *(in letter)* (le saluda) atentamente.

sincerity [sɪn'serɪtɪ] *n* sinceridad *f.*

sinew ['sɪnjuː] *n* *(tendon)* tendón *m*; *(in meat)* nervio *m.*

sinful ['sɪnful] *adj* *(person)* pecador,-a; *(act, thought)* pecaminoso,-a; *fig* *(waste etc)* escandaloso,-a.

sing [sɪŋ] **I** *vtr* *(pt* **sang**; *pp* **sung**) cantar. **II** *vi* *(person, bird)* cantar; *(kettle, bullets)* silbar.

singe [sɪndʒ] *vtr* chamuscar.

singer ['sɪŋər] *n* cantante *mf.*

singing ['sɪŋɪŋ] *n* *(art)* canto *m*; *(songs)* canciones *fpl*; *(of kettle)* silbido *m.*

single ['sɪŋgəl] **I** *adj* **1** *(solitary)* solo,-a. **2** *(only one)* único,-a. **3** *(not double)* sencillo,-a; **s. bed/room**, cama *fl* habitación *f* individual. **4** *(unmarried)* soltero,-a. **II** *n* **1** *Rail* billete *m* de ida. **2** *(record)* single *m*. **3** *Sport* **singles**, individuales *mpl*. ◆**single out** *vtr* *(choose)* escoger; *(distinguish)* distinguir. ◆**singly** *adv* *(individually)* por separado; *(one by one)* uno por uno.

single-breasted [sɪŋgəl'brestɪd] *adj* *(suit, jacket)* recto,-a.

single-handed [sɪŋgəl'hændɪd] *adj & adv* sin ayuda.

single-minded [sɪŋgəl'maɪndɪd] *adj* resuelto,-a.

singlet [sɪŋglɪt] *n GB* camiseta *f.*

singular ['sɪŋgjulər] **I** *adj* **1** *Ling* singular. **2** *fml* *(outstanding)* excepcional. **3** *fml* *(unique)* único,-a. **II** *n Ling* singular *m.* ◆**singularly** *adv* excepcionalmente.

sinister ['sɪnɪstər] *adj* siniestro,-a.

sink¹ [sɪŋk] *n* *(in kitchen)* fregadero *m.*

sink² [sɪŋk] **I** *vtr* *(pt* **sank**; *pp* **sunk**) **1** *(ship)* hundir, echar a pique; *fig* *(hopes)* acabar con. **2** *(hole, well)* cavar; *(post, knife, teeth)* hincar. **II** *vi* **1** *(ship)* hundirse. **2** *fig* **my heart sank**, se me cayó el alma a los pies. **3** *(sun)* ponerse. **4** **to s. to one's knees**, hincarse de rodillas. ◆**sink in** *vi* *(penetrate)* penetrar; *fig* **it hasn't sunk in yet**, todavía no me he/se ha *etc* hecho a la idea.

sinner ['sɪnər] *n* pecador,-a *m,f.*

sinus ['saɪnəs] *n* seno *m.*

sip [sɪp] **I** *n* sorbo *m*. **II** *vtr* sorber, beber a sorbos.

siphon ['saɪfən] *n* sifón *m*. ◆**siphon off** *vtr* *(liquid)* sacar con sifón; *fig* *(funds,*

traffic) desviar.

sir [sɜːr] *n fml* **1** señor *m*; **yes, s.**, sí, señor. **2** *(title)* sir; **S. Walter Raleigh**, Sir Walter Raleigh.

siren ['saɪərən] *n* sirena *f.*

sirloin ['sɜːlɔɪn] *n* solomillo *m.*

sissy ['sɪsɪ] *n fam* *(coward)* miedica *mf.*

sister ['sɪstər] *n* **1** *(relation)* hermana *f.* **2** *GB Med* enfermera *f* jefe. **3** *Rel* hermana *f*; *(before name)* sor.

sister-in-law ['sɪstərɪnlɔː] *n* cuñada *f.*

sit [sɪt] **I** *vtr* *(pt & pp* **sat**) **1** *(child etc)* sentar **(in, on, en)**. **2** *GB* *(exam)* presentar a. **II** *vi* **1** *(action)* sentarse. **2** *(be seated)* estar sentado,-a. **3** *(object)* estar; *(be situated)* hallarse; *(person)* quedarse. **4** *(assembly)* reunirse. ◆**sit back** *vi* recostarse. ◆**sit down** *vi* sentarse. ◆**sit in on** *vtr* asistir sin participar a. ◆**sit out** *vtr* aguantar hasta el final. ◆**sit through** *vtr* aguantar. ◆**sit up** *vi* **1** incorporarse. **2** *(stay up late)* quedarse levantado,-a.

site [saɪt] **I** *n* **1** *(area)* lugar *m*; **building s.**, solar *m*; *(under construction)* obra *f.* **2** *(location)* situación *f*; **nuclear testing s.**, zona *f* de pruebas nucleares. **II** *vtr* situar.

sit-in ['sɪtɪn] *n fam* *(demonstration)* sentada *f*; *(strike)* huelga *f* de brazos caídos.

sitting ['sɪtɪŋ] **I** *n* *(of committee)* sesión *f*; *(in canteen)* turno *m*. **II** *adj* **s. room**, sala *f* de estar.

situated ['sɪtjʊeɪtɪd] *adj* situado,-a, ubicado,-a.

situation [sɪtjʊ'eɪʃən] *n* **1** situación *f.* **2** *(job)* puesto *m*; *GB* **'situations vacant'**, *(in newspaper)* 'ofertas de trabajo'.

six [sɪks] *adj & n* seis *(m) inv.*

sixteen [sɪks'tiːn] *adj & n* dieciséis *(m) inv*, diez y seis *(m) inv.*

sixteenth [sɪks'tiːnθ] **I** *adj & n* decimosexto,-a *(m,f).* **II** *n* *(fraction)* dieciseisavo *m.*

sixth [sɪksθ] **I** *adj* sexto,-a; *GB Educ* **s. form**, ≈ COU; **s. former**, ≈ estudiante de COU. **II** *n* **1** *(in series)* sexto,-a *m,f.* **2** *(fraction)* sexto *m*, sexta parte *f.*

sixty ['sɪkstɪ] *adj & n* sesenta *(m) inv.*

size [saɪz] *n* tamaño *m*; *(of garment)* talla *f*; *(of shoes)* número *m*; *(of person)* estatura *f*; *(scope)* alcance *m*; **what s. do you take?**, *(garment)* ¿qué talla tienes?; *(shoes)* ¿qué número calzas? ◆**size up** *vtr* *(person)* juzgar; *(situation, problem)* evaluar.

siz(e)able ['saɪzəbəl] *adj* *(building etc)* *(bastante)* grande; *(sum)* considerable; *(problem)* importante.

sizzle ['sɪzəl] *vi* chisporrotear.

skate¹ [skeɪt] **I** *n* patín *m*. **II** *vtr* patinar.

skate² [skeɪt] *n* *(fish)* raya *f.*

skateboard ['skeɪtbɔːd] *n* monopatín *m.*

skater ['skeɪtər] *n* patinador,-a *m,f.*

skating ['skeɪtɪŋ] *n* patinaje *m*; **s. rink**,

pista *f* de patinaje.

skeleton ['skelɪtən] **I** *n* **1** esqueleto *m*. **2** *(of building)* armazón *m*. **3** *(outline)* esquema *m*. **II** *adj (staff, service)* reducido,-a; **s. key,** llave maestra.

skeptic ['skeptɪk] *n US* → **sceptic.**

sketch [sketʃ] **I** *n* **1** *(preliminary drawing)* bosquejo *m*, esbozo *m*; *(drawing)* dibujo *m*; *(outline)* esquema *m*; *(rough draft)* boceto *m*. **2** *Theat TV* sketch *m*. **II** *vtr (draw)* dibujar; *(preliminary drawing)* bosquejar, esbozar.

sketch-book ['sketʃbʊk], **sketch-pad** ['sketʃpæd] *n* bloc *m* de dibujo.

sketchy ['sketʃɪ] *adj* (**sketchier, sketchiest**) *(incomplete)* incompleto,-a; *(not detailed)* vago,-a.

skewer ['skjʊəʳ] *n* pincho *m*, broqueta *f*.

ski [skiː] **I** *n* esquí *m*. **II** *adj* de esquí; **s. boots,** botas *fpl* de esquiar; **s. jump,** *(action)* salto *m* con esquís; **s. lift,** telesquí *m*; *(with seats)* telesilla *f*; **s. pants,** pantalón *m sing* de esquiar; **s. resort,** estación *f* de esquí; **s. stick** *or* **pole,** bastón *m* de esquiar. **III** *vi* esquiar; **to go skiing,** ir a esquiar.

skid [skɪd] **I** *n* patinazo *m*. **II** *vi* patinar.

skier ['skiːəʳ] *n* esquiador,-a *m,f*.

skiing ['skiːɪŋ] *n* esquí *m*.

skilful, *US* **skillful** ['skɪlfʊl] *adj* hábil, diestro,-a.

skill [skɪl] *n* **1** *(ability)* habilidad *f*, destreza *f*; *(talent)* don *m*. **2** *(technique)* técnica *f*.

skilled [skɪld] *adj* **1** *(dextrous)* hábil, diestro,-a; *(expert)* experto,-a. **2** *(worker)* cualificado,-a.

skim [skɪm] **I** *vtr* **1** *(milk)* desnatar; **skimmed milk,** leche desnatada. **2** *(brush against)* rozar; **s. the ground,** *(bird, plane)* volar a ras de suelo. **II** *vi fig* to s. **through a book,** hojear un libro.

skimp [skɪmp] *vtr & vi (food, material)* escatimar; *(work)* chapucear.

skimpy ['skɪmpɪ] *adj* (**skimpier, skimpiest**) *(shorts)* muy corto,-a; *(meal)* escaso,-a.

skin [skɪn] **I** *n* **1** piel *f*; *(of face)* cutis *m*; *(complexion)* tez *f*; **s. cream,** crema *f* de belleza. **2** *(of fruit)* piel *f*; *(of lemon)* cáscara *f*; *(peeling)* mondadura *f*. **3** *(of sausage)* pellejo *m*. **4** *(on milk etc)* nata *f*. **II** *vtr* **1** *(animal)* despellejar. **2** *(graze)* arañar.

skin-deep [skɪn'diːp] *adj* superficial.

skin-diving ['skɪndaɪvɪŋ] *n* buceo *m*, submarinismo *m*.

skinhead ['skɪnhed] *n fam* cabeza *mf* rapada.

skinny ['skɪnɪ] *adj* (**skinnier, skinniest**) *fam* flaco,-a.

skin-tight ['skɪntaɪt] *adj (clothing)* muy ajustado,-a.

skip¹ [skɪp] **I** *n* *(jump)* salto *m*, brinco *m*.

II *vi (jump)* saltar, brincar; *(with rope)* saltar a la comba; *fig* **to s. over sth,** saltarse algo. **III** *vtr fig* saltarse.

skip² [skɪp] *n (container)* contenedor *m*.

skipper ['skɪpəʳ] *n Naut Sport fam* capitán,-ana *m,f*.

skipping ['skɪpɪŋ] *n* comba *f*; **s. rope,** comba .

skirmish ['skɜːmɪʃ] *n* escaramuza *f*.

skirt [skɜːt] **I** *n* falda *f*. **II** *vtr (town etc)* rodear; *(coast)* bordear; *fig (problem)* esquivar.

skirting ['skɜːtɪŋ] *GB n* **s. (board),** zócalo *m*.

skit [skɪt] *n* sátira *f*, parodia *f*.

skittle ['skɪtəl] *n* **1** *(pin)* bolo *m*. **2** **skittles,** *(game)* (juego *m* de los) bolos *mpl*, boliche *m*.

skive [skaɪv] *vi GB fam* escaquearse.

skulk [skʌlk] *vi (hide)* esconderse; *(prowl)* merodear; *(lie in wait)* estar al acecho.

skull [skʌl] *n Anat* cráneo *m*; *fam* calavera *f*.

skunk [skʌŋk] *n* mofeta *f*.

sky [skaɪ] *n* cielo *m*; **s. blue,** azul *m* celeste.

skylight ['skaɪlaɪt] *n* tragaluz *m*, claraboya *f*.

skyline ['skaɪlaɪn] *n (of city)* perfil *m*.

skyscraper ['skaɪskreɪpəʳ] *n* rascacielos *m inv*.

slab [slæb] *n (of stone)* losa *f*, *(of chocolate)* tableta *f*; *(of cake)* trozo *m*.

slack [slæk] **I** *adj* **1** *(not taut)* flojo,-a. **2** *(lax)* descuidado,-a; *(lazy)* vago,-a. **3** *(market)* flojo,-a; **business is s.,** hay poco negocio. **II** *n (in rope)* parte floja.

slacken ['slækən] **I** *vtr* **1** *(rope)* aflojar. **2** *(speed)* reducir. **II** *vi* **1** *(rope)* aflojarse; *(wind)* amainar. **2** *(trade)* aflojar.

◆**slacken off** *vi* disminuirse.

slacks [slæks] *npl dated* pantalones *mpl*, pantalón *m*.

slag [slæg] *n* **1** *Min* escoria *f*; **s. heap,** escorial *m*. **2** *GB sl (woman)* puta *f*.

◆**slag off** *vtr GB* poner verde a.

slain [sleɪn] *npl* **the s.,** los caídos.

slam [slæm] **I** *n (of door)* portazo *m*. **II** *vtr (bang)* cerrar de golpe; **to s. sth down on the table,** soltar algo sobre la mesa de un palmetazo; **to s. the door,** dar un portazo; **to s. on the brakes,** dar un frenazo. **III** *vi (door)* cerrarse de golpe.

slander ['slɑːndəʳ] **I** *n* difamación *f*, calumnia *f*. **II** *vtr* difamar, calumniar.

slang [slæŋ] *n* argot *m*, jerga *f*.

slant [slɑːnt] **I** *n* **1** inclinación *f*; *(slope)* pendiente *f*. **2** *fig (point of view)* punto *m* de vista. **II** *vtr fig (problem etc)* enfocar subjetivamente. **III** *vi* inclinarse.

slanting ['slɑːntɪŋ] *adj* inclinado,-a.

slap [slæp] **I** *n* palmada *f*; *(in face)* bofetada *f*. **II** *adv fam* **he ran s. into the fence,** se dio de lleno contra la valla; **s. in the**

middle of ..., justo en medio de .... III *vtr* pegar con la mano; *(hit in face)* dar una bofetada a; **to s. sb on the back**, dar a algn una palmada en la espalda.
slapdash ['slæp'dæʃ] *adj fam* descuidado,-a; *(work)* chapucero,-a.
slapstick ['slæpstɪk] *n* bufonadas *fpl*, payasadas *fpl*.
slap-up ['slæpʌp] *adj fam* **s.-up meal**, comilona *f*.
slash [slæʃ] I *n Typ fam* barra oblicua. II *vtr* 1 *(with knife)* acuchillar; *(with sword)* dar un tajo a. 2 *fig (prices)* rebajar.
slat [slæt] *n* tablilla *f*, listón *m*.
slate [sleɪt] I *n* pizarra *f*; *fig* **to wipe the s. clean**, hacer borrón y cuenta nueva. II *vtr GB fam* criticar duramente.
slaughter ['slɔːtər] I *n (of animals)* matanza *f*; *(of people)* carnicería *f*. II *vtr (animals)* matar; *(people)* matar brutalmente; *(in large numbers)* masacrar.
slaughterhouse ['slɔːtəhaʊs] *n* matadero *m*.
Slav [slɑːv] *adj & n* eslavo,-a *(m,f)*.
slave [sleɪv] I *n* esclavo,-a *m,f*; **s. trade**, trata *f* de esclavos. II *vi* **to s. (away)**, dar el callo.
slavery ['sleɪvərɪ] *n* esclavitud *f*.
Slavonic [slə'vɒnɪk] *adj* eslavo,-a.
slay [sleɪ] *vtr (pt* slew; *pp* slain) matar.
sleazy ['sliːzɪ] *adj (*sleazier, sleaziest) sórdido,-a.
sled [sled] I *n US* trineo *m*. II *vi* ir en trineo.
sledge [sledʒ] *n GB* trineo *m*.
sledgehammer ['sledʒhæmər] *n* almádena *f*.
sleek [sliːk] *adj (hair)* lustroso,-a; *(appearance)* impecable.
sleep [sliːp] I *n* sueño *m*. II *vi* 1 dormir; **to go to s.**, dormirse; *fig* **to send to s.**, *(hacer)* dormir; *fam* **to s. like a log**, dormir como un lirón. 2 **my foot has gone to s.**, se me ha dormido el pie. ◆**sleep in** *vi GB (oversleep)* quedarse dormido,-a; *(have a lie-in)* quedarse en la cama. ◆**sleep with** *vtr fam* **to s. with sb**, acostarse con algn.
sleeper ['sliːpər] *n* 1 *(person)* durmiente *mf*; **to be a heavy s.**, tener el sueño pesado. 2 *GB Rail (on track)* traviesa *f*. 3 *Rail (coach)* coche-cama *m*; *(berth)* litera *f*.
sleeping ['sliːpɪŋ] *adj* **s. bag**, saco *m* de dormir; **S. Beauty**, la Bella durmiente; **s. car**, coche-cama *m*; *GB Com* **s. partner**, socio,-a *m,f* comanditario,-a; **s. pill**, somnífero *m*.
sleepless ['sliːplɪs] *adj* **to have a s. night**, pasar la noche en blanco.
sleepwalker ['sliːpwɔːkər] *n* sonámbulo,-a *m,f*.
sleepy ['sliːpɪ] *adj (*sleepier, sleepiest) soñoliento,-a; **to be** *or* **feel s.**, tener sueño.

ño.
sleet [sliːt] I *n* aguanieve *f*. II *vi* **it's sleeting**, cae aguanieve.
sleeve [sliːv] *n (of garment)* manga *f*; *(of record)* funda *f*.
sleigh [sleɪ] *n* trineo *m*; **s. bell**, cascabel *m*.
sleight [slaɪt] *n* **s. of hand**, juego *m* de manos.
slender ['slendər] *adj* 1 *(thin)* delgado,-a. 2 *fig (hope, chance)* remoto.
slept [slept] *pt & pp* → **sleep**.
slew [sluː] *pt* → **slay**.
slice [slaɪs] I *n* 1 *(of bread)* rebanada *f*; *(of ham)* loncha *f*; *(of beef etc)* tajada *f*; *(of lemon etc)* rodaja *f*; *(of cake)* trozo *m*. 2 *(utensil)* pala *f*. II *vtr (food)* cortar a rebanadas *or* tajos *or* rodajas; *(divide)* partir.
slick [slɪk] I *adj* 1 *(programme, show)* logrado,-a. 2 *(skilful)* hábil, mañoso,-a. II *n (oil)* **s.**, marea negra.
slide [slaɪd] I *n* 1 *(act)* resbalón *m*. 2 *(in prices etc)* baja *f*. 3 *(in playground)* tobogán *m*. 4 *Phot* diapositiva *f*; **s. projector**, proyector *m* de diapositivas. 5 **s. rule**, regla *f* de cálculo. 6 *GB (for hair)* pasador *m*. II *vtr (pt & pp* slid) deslizar; *(furniture)* correr. III *vi (on purpose)* deslizarse; *(slip)* resbalar.
sliding ['slaɪdɪŋ] *adj (door, window)* corredizo,-a; **s. scale**, escala *f* móvil.
slight [slaɪt] I *adj* 1 *(small)* pequeño,-a; **not in the slightest**, en absoluto. 2 *(build)* menudo,-a; *(slim)* delgado,-a; *(frail)* delicado,-a. 3 *(trivial)* leve. II *n (affront)* desaire *m*. III *vtr* 1 *(scorn)* despreciar. 2 *(snub)* desairar. ◆**slightly** *adv (a little)* ligeramente, algo.
slim [slɪm] I *adj (*slimmer, slimmest) 1 *(person)* delgado,-a. 2 *fig (resources)* escaso,-a; *(hope, chance)* remoto,-a. II *vi* adelgazar.
slime [slaɪm] *n (mud)* lodo *m*, cieno *m*; *(of snail)* baba *f*.
slimming ['slɪmɪŋ] I *adj (diet, pills)* para adelgazar; *(food)* que no engorda. II *n (process)* adelgazamiento *m*.
slimy ['slaɪmɪ] *adj (*slimier, slimiest) 1 *(muddy)* lodoso,-a; *(snail)* baboso,-a. 2 *fig (person)* zalamero,-a.
sling [slɪŋ] I *n* 1 *(catapult)* honda *f*; *(child's)* tirador *m*. 2 *Med* cabestrillo *m*. II *vtr (pt & pp* slung) *(throw)* tirar.
slink [slɪŋk] *vi (pt & pp* slunk) **to s. off**, escabullirse.
slip [slɪp] I *n* 1 *(slide)* resbalón *m*; *fam fig* **to give sb the s.**, dar esquinazo a algn. 2 *(mistake)* error *m*; *(moral)* desliz *m*; **a s. of the tongue**, un lapsus linguae. 3 *(underskirt)* combinación *f*. 4 *(of paper)* trocito *m*. II *vi* 1 *(slide)* resbalar. 2 *Med* dislocarse; **slipped disc**, vértebra dislocada. 3 *(move quickly)* ir de prisa. 4

(standards etc) deteriorarse. **III** *vtr* **1** *(slide)* dar a escondidas. **2 it slipped my memory**, se me fue de la cabeza. ◆**slip away** *vi (person)* escabullirse. ◆**slip off** *vtr (clothes)* quitarse rápidamente. ◆**slip on** *vtr (clothes)* ponerse rápidamente. ◆**slip out** *vi* **1** *(leave)* salir. **2** *fig* **the secret slipped out**, se le escapó el secreto. ◆**slip up** *vi fam (blunder)* cometer un desliz.

slipper ['slɪpər] *n* zapatilla *f*.

slippery ['slɪpərɪ] *adj* resbaladizo,-a.

slip-road ['slɪprəʊd] *n GB* vía *f* de acceso.

slipshod ['slɪpʃɒd] *adj* descuidado,-a; *(work)* chapucero,-a.

slip-up ['slɪpʌp] *n fam (blunder)* desliz *m*.

slipway ['slɪpweɪ] *n* grada *f*.

slit [slɪt] **I** *n (opening)* hendidura *f*; *(cut)* corte *m*, raja *f*. **II** *vtr (pt & pp* **slit)** cortar, rajar.

slither ['slɪðər] *vi* deslizarse.

sliver ['slɪvər] *n (of wood, glass)* astilla *f*; *(of ham)* loncha *f*.

slob [slɒb] *n fam* dejado,-a *m,f*.

slog [slɒg] **I** *n fam* **it was a hard s.**, costó un montón. **II** *vi* **1** *fam* **to s. away**, sudar tinta. **2** *(walk)* caminar trabajosamente. **III** *vtr (hit)* golpear fuerte.

slogan ['sləʊgən] *n* (e)slogan *m*, lema *m*.

slop [slɒp] **I** *vi* **to s. (over)**, derramarse; **to s. about**, chapotear. **II** *vtr* derramar.

slope [sləʊp] **I** *n (incline)* cuesta *f*, pendiente *f*; *(up)* subida *f*; *(down)* bajada *f*; *(of mountain)* ladera *f*; *(of roof)* vertiente *f*. **II** *vi* inclinarse; **to s. up/down**, subir/bajar en pendiente. ◆**slope off** *vi fam* largarse.

sloping ['sləʊpɪŋ] *adj* inclinado,-a.

sloppy ['slɒpɪ] *adj (sloppier, sloppiest) fam* descuidado,-a; *(work)* chapucero,-a; *(appearance)* desaliñado,-a.

slot [slɒt] **I** *n* **1** *(for coin)* ranura *f*; *(opening)* rendija *f*; **s. machine**, *(for gambling)* (máquina *f*) tragaperras *f inv*; *(vending machine)* distribuidor automático. **2** *Rad TV* espacio *m*. **II** *vtr (place)* meter; *(put in)* introducir. **III** *vi* **to s. in** *or* **together**, encajar.

sloth [sləʊθ] *n fml (laziness)* pereza *f*.

slouch [slaʊtʃ] *vi* andar *or* sentarse con los hombros caídos.

slovenly ['slʌvənlɪ] *adj* descuidado,-a; *(appearance)* desaliñado,-a; *(work)* chapucero,-a.

slow [sləʊ] **I** *adj* **1** lento,-a; **in s. motion**, a cámara lenta; **to be s. to do sth**, tardar en hacer algo. **2** *(clock)* atrasado,-a. **3** *(stupid)* lento,-a, torpe. **II** *adv* despacio, lentamente. **III** *vtr (car)* reducir la marcha de; *(progress)* retrasar. **IV** *vi* **to s. down** *or* **up**, ir más despacio; *(in car)* reducir la velocidad. ◆**slowly** *adv* despacio, lentamente.

sludge [slʌdʒ] *n (mud)* fango *m*, lodo *m*.

slug [slʌg] **I** *n* **1** *Zool* babosa *f*. **2** *US fam (bullet)* posta *f*. **3** *fam (blow)* porrazo *m*. **II** *vtr fam (hit)* aporrear.

sluggish ['slʌgɪʃ] *adj* **1** *(river, engine)* lento,-a; *Com* flojo,-a. **2** *(lazy)* perezoso, -a.

sluice [slu:s] *n (waterway)* canal *m*.

sluicegate ['slu:sgeɪt] *n* esclusa *f*.

slum [slʌm] *n (usu pl)* barrios bajos.

slumber ['slʌmbər] *fml* **I** *n (sleep)* sueño *m*. **II** *vi* dormir.

slump [slʌmp] **I** *n* **1** *(drop in sales etc)* bajón *m*. **2** *(economic depression)* crisis económica. **II** *vi* **1** *(sales etc)* caer de repente; *(prices)* desplomarse; *(the economy)* hundirse; *fig (morale)* hundirse. **2** *(fall)* caer.

slung [slʌŋ] *pt & pp* → **sling**.

slur [slɜ:r] **I** *n (stigma)* mancha *f*; *(slanderous remark)* calumnia *f*. **II** *vtr (word)* tragarse.

slush [slʌʃ] *n* **1** *(melting snow)* nieve medio fundida. **2** *fam* sentimentalismo *m*. **3** *US fam* **s. fund**, fondos *mpl* para sobornos.

slut [slʌt] *n offens* **1** *(untidy woman)* marrana *f*. **2** *(whore)* fulana *f*.

sly [slaɪ] *adj (slyer, slyest* or **slier, sliest)** **1** *(cunning)* astuto,-a. **2** *(secretive)* furtivo,-a. **3** *(mischievous)* travieso,-a. **4** *(underhand)* malicioso,-a.

smack¹ [smæk] **I** *n* **1** *(slap)* bofetada *f*. **2** *(sharp noise)* ruido sonoro. **II** *vtr (hit)* dar una bofetada a. **2** *(hit)* golpear; *fig* **to s. one's lips**, relamerse.

smack² [smæk] *vi fig* **to s. of**, oler a.

small [smɔ:l] **I** *adj* **1** pequeño,-a; **a s. table**, una mesita; **in s. letters**, en minúsculas; **in the s. hours**, a altas horas de la noche; **s. ads**, anuncios *mpl* por palabras; *fig* **s. print**, letra pequeña. **2** *(in height)* bajo,-a. **3** *(scant)* escaso,-a; **s. change**, cambio *m*, suelto *m*. **4** *(minor)* insignificante; **s. businessmen**, pequeños comerciantes; **s. talk**, charloteo *m*. **5** *(increase)* ligero,-a. **II** *n* **1 s. of the back**, región *f* lumbar. **2** *GB fam* **smalls**, *(underwear)* paños *mpl* menores.

smallholder ['smɔ:lhəʊldər] *n* minifundista *mf*.

smallpox ['smɔ:lpɒks] *n* viruela *f*.

smarmy ['smɑ:mɪ] *adj (smarmier, smarmiest) fam* cobista, zalamero,-a.

smart [smɑ:t] **I** *adj* **1** *(elegant)* elegante. **2** *(clever)* listo,-a, inteligente; *fam* **s. alec(k)**, listillo. **3** *(quick)* rápido,-a; *(pace)* ligero,-a. **II** *vi* **1** *(sting)* picar, escocer. **2** *fig* sufrir.

smarten ['smɑ:tən] **I** *vtr* **to s. (up)**, arreglar. **II** *vi* **to s. oneself (up)**, arreglarse.

smash [smæʃ] **I** *n* **1** *(loud noise)* estrépito *m*; *(collision)* choque violento. **2** *Ten* smash *m*. **II** *vtr* **1** *(break)* romper; *(shatter)* hacer pedazos; (crush) aplastar. 2 (destroy) destrozar; (defeat) aplastar. 3 (record) fulminar. III vi (break) romperse; (shatter) hacerse pedazos; (crash) estrellarse; Ten hacer un mate. ◆smash up vtr fam (car) hacer pedazos; (place) destrozar.

smashing ['smæʃɪŋ] adj GB fam estupendo,-a.

smattering ['smætərɪŋ] n he had a s. of French, hablaba un poquito de francés.

smear [smɪər] I n 1 (smudge) mancha f; s. (test), citología f. 2 fig (defamation) calumnia f. II vtr 1 (butter etc) untar; (grease) embadurnar. 2 (make dirty) manchar. 3 fig (defame) calumniar, difamar.

smell [smel] I n 1 (sense) olfato m. 2 (odour) olor m. II vtr (pt & pp smelled or smelt) oler; fig olfatear. III vi oler (a); it smells good/like lavender, huele bien/a lavanda; he smelt of whisky, olía a whisky.

smelly ['smelɪ] adj (smellier, smelliest) fam maloliente, apestoso,-a.

smelt [smelt] vtr (ore) fundir.

smile [smaɪl] I n sonrisa f. II vi sonreír; to s. at sb, sonreír a algn; to s. at sth, reírse de algo.

smiling ['smaɪlɪŋ] adj sonriente, risueño,-a.

smirk [smɜːk] I n (conceited) sonrisa satisfecha; (foolish) sonrisa f boba. II vi (conceitedly) sonreír con satisfacción; (foolishly) sonreír bobamente.

smith [smɪθ] n herrero m.

smithy ['smɪðɪ] n herrería f.

smitten ['smɪtən] adj fam to be s. with sb, estar enamorado,-a de algn.

smock [smɒk] n (blouse) blusón m; (worn in pregnancy) blusón de premamá; (overall) bata f.

smog [smɒg] n niebla tóxica, smog m.

smoke [sməʊk] I n humo m; s. bomb, bomba f de humo; s. screen, cortina f de humo. II vi fumar; (chimney etc) echar humo. III vtr 1 (tobacco) fumar; to s. a pipe, fumar en pipa. 2 (fish, meat) ahumar.

smoked [sməʊkt] adj ahumado,-a.

smokeless ['sməʊklɪs] adj s. fuel, combustible sin humo; s. zone, zona libre de humos.

smoker ['sməʊkər] n 1 (person) fumador,-a m,f. 2 Rail vagón m de fumadores.

smoking ['sməʊkɪŋ] n 'no s.', 'prohibido fumar'.

smoky ['sməʊkɪ] adj (smokier, smokiest) 1 (chimney) humeante; (room) lleno,-a de humo; (atmosphere) cargado,-a (de humo); (food) ahumado,-a. 2 (colour) ahumado,-a.

smolder ['sməʊldər] vi US → smoulder.

smooth [smuːð] I adj 1 (surface) liso,-a; (skin) suave; (road) llano,-a; (sea)

tranquilo,-a. 2 (beer, wine) suave. 3 (flowing) fluido,-a. 4 (flight) tranquilo,-a; (transition) sin problemas. 5 pej (slick) zalamero,-a. II vtr 1 (hair etc) alisar. 2 (plane down) limar. ◆smooth out vtr (creases) alisar; fig (difficulties) allanar; (problems) resolver. ◆smooth over vtr fig to s. things over, limar asperezas. ◆smoothly adv sobre ruedas.

smother ['smʌðər] vtr 1 (asphyxiate) asfixiar; (suffocate) sofocar. 2 fig (cover) cubrir (with, de).

smoulder ['sməʊldər] vi (fire) arder sin llama; fig (passions) arder; smouldering hatred, odio latente.

smudge [smʌdʒ] I n (stain) mancha f; (of ink) borrón m. II vtr manchar; (piece of writing) emborronar.

smug [smʌg] adj (smugger, smuggest) engreído,-a.

smuggle ['smʌgəl] vtr pasar de contrabando.

smuggler ['smʌglər] n contrabandista mf.

smuggling ['smʌglɪŋ] n contrabando m.

smutty ['smʌtɪ] adj (smuttier, smuttiest) fam obsceno,-a; (joke) verde; (book, film etc) pornográfico,-a.

snack [snæk] n bocado m; s. bar, cafetería f.

snag [snæg] I n (difficulty) pega f, problemilla m. II vtr (clothing) enganchar.

snail [sneɪl] n caracol m.

snake [sneɪk] n (big) serpiente f; (small) culebra f.

snap [snæp] I n 1 (noise) ruido seco; (of branch, fingers) chasquido m. 2 (bite) mordisco m. 3 Phot (foto f) instantánea f. II adj (sudden) repentino,-a. III vtr 1 (branch etc) partir (en dos). 2 (make noise) hacer un ruido seco; to s. one's fingers, chasquear los dedos; to s. sth shut, cerrar algo de golpe. 3 Phot sacar una foto de. IV vi 1 (break) romperse. 2 (whip) chasquear; to s. shut, cerrarse de golpe. 3 (dog) amenazar; fam to s. at sb, regañar a algn. ◆snap off I vtr (branch etc) arrancar. II vi (branch etc) separarse. ◆snap up vtr fam to s. up a bargain, llevarse una ganga.

snappy ['snæpɪ] adj (snappier, snappiest) fam 1 (quick) rápido,-a; look s.!, make it s.!, ¡date prisa! 2 (stylish) elegante. 3 (short-tempered) irritable.

snapshot ['snæpʃɒt] n (foto f) instantánea f.

snare [sneər] I n trampa f. II vtr (animal) cazar con trampa; fig (person) hacer caer en la trampa.

snarl¹ [snɑːl] I n gruñido m. II vi gruñir.

snarl² [snɑːl] I n (in wool) maraña f. II vtr to s. (up), (wool) enmarañar; (traffic) atascar; (plans) enredar.

snatch [snætʃ] I n 1 fam (theft) robo m;

bag s., tirón m. 2 (fragment) fragmentos mpl. II vtr 1 (grab) arrebatar. 2 fam (steal) robar; (kidnap) secuestrar. III vi to s. at sth, intentar agarrar algo.

sneak [sniːk] I n fam chivato,-a m,f. II vtr to s. sth out of a place, sacar algo de un lugar a escondidas. III vi 1 to s. off, escabullirse; to s. in/out, entrar/salir a hurtadillas. 2 to s. on sb, (tell tales) chivarse de algn.

sneakers ['sniːkəz] npl US zapatillas fpl de deporte.

sneaky ['sniːkɪ] adj (sneakier, sneakiest) solapado,-a.

sneer [snɪəʳ] vi to s. at, hacer un gesto de desprecio a.

sneeze [sniːz] I n estornudo m. II vi estornudar.

sniff [snɪf] I n (by person) aspiración f; (by dog) husmeo m. II vtr (flower etc) oler; (suspiciously) husmear; (snuff etc) aspirar; (glue) esnifar. III vi aspirar por la nariz.

snigger ['snɪgəʳ] I n risa disimulada. II vi reír disimuladamente; to s. at sth, burlarse de algo.

snip [snɪp] I n 1 (cut) tijeretada f; (small piece) recorte m. 2 GB fam (bargain) ganga f. II vtr cortar a tijeretazos.

sniper ['snaɪpəʳ] n francotirador,-a m,f.

snippet ['snɪpɪt] n (of cloth, paper) recorte m; (of conversation) fragmento m.

snivel ['snɪvəl] vi lloriquear.

snivelling ['snɪvəlɪŋ] adj llorón,-ona.

snob [snɒb] n (e)snob mf.

snobbery ['snɒbərɪ] n (e)snobismo m.

snobbish ['snɒbɪʃ] adj (e)snob.

snooker ['snuːkəʳ] n snooker m, billar ruso.

snoop [snuːp] vi fisgar, fisgonear.

snooty ['snuːtɪ] adj (snootier, snootiest) fam (e)snob.

snooze [snuːz] fam I n cabezada f. II vi echar una cabezada.

snore [snɔːʳ] I n ronquido m. II vi roncar.

snoring ['snɔːrɪŋ] n ronquidos mpl.

snorkel ['snɔːkəl] n (of swimmer) tubo m de respiración; (of submarine) esnórquel m.

snort [snɔːt] I n resoplido m. II vi resoplar.

snout [snaʊt] n (of animal, gun etc) morro m.

snow [snəʊ] I n nieve f; s. shower, nevada f. II vi nevar; it's snowing, está nevando. III vtr fig to be snowed under with work, estar agobiado,-a de trabajo.

snowball ['snəʊbɔːl] I n bola f de nieve. II vi fig aumentar rápidamente.

snowbound ['snəʊbaʊnd] adj aislado,-a por la nieve.

snowdrift ['snəʊdrɪft] n ventisquero m.

snowdrop ['snəʊdrɒp] n campanilla f de invierno.

snowfall ['snəʊfɔːl] n nevada f.

snowflake ['snəʊfleɪk] n copo m de nieve.

snowman ['snəʊmæn] n hombre m de nieve.

snowplough, US **snowplow** ['snəʊplaʊ] n quitanieves m inv.

snowshoe ['snəʊʃuː] n raqueta f (de nieve).

snowstorm ['snəʊstɔːm] n nevasca f.

snowy ['snəʊɪ] adj (snowier, snowiest) (mountain) nevado,-a; (climate) nevoso,-a; (day) de nieve.

Snr, snr esp US abbr of senior.

snub [snʌb] I n (of person) desaire m; (of offer) rechazo m. II vtr (person) desairar; (offer) rechazar.

snub-nosed ['snʌbnəʊzd] adj de nariz respingona.

snuff [snʌf] n rapé m.

snug [snʌg] adj (snugger, snuggest) 1 (cosy) cómodo,-a. 2 (tightfitting) ajustado, -a. ◆**snugly** adv to fit s., (clothes) quedar ajustado,-a; (object in box etc) encajar.

snuggle ['snʌgəl] vi to s. down in bed, acurrucarse en la cama; to s. up to sb, arrimarse a algn.

so [səʊ] I adv 1 (to such an extent) tanto; he was so tired that ..., estaba tan cansado que ...; it's so long since ..., hace tanto tiempo que ...; he isn't so nice as his sister, no es tan agradable como su hermana; fam so long!, ¡hasta luego! 2 (degree) tanto; a week or so, una semana más o menos; twenty or so, una veintena; we loved her so (much), la queríamos tanto; so many books, tantos libros; fam he's ever so handsome!, ¡es tan guapo!; iron so much for that, ¿qué le vamos a hacer? 3 (thus, in this way) así, de esta manera; and so on, and so forth, y así sucesivamente; if so, en este caso; I think/hope so, creo/espero que sí; I told you so, ya te lo dije; it so happens that ..., da la casualidad de que ...; so be it!, ¡así sea!; so far, hasta ahora or allí; so it seems, eso parece; so they say, eso dicen; you're late! - so I am!, ¡llegas tarde! - ¡tienes razón! 4 (also) I'm going to Spain - so am I, voy a España - yo también.

II conj 1 (expresses result) así que; so you like England, do you?, ¿así que te gusta Inglaterra, pues?; fam so what?, ¿y qué? 2 (expresses purpose) para que; I'll put the key here so (that) everyone can see it, pongo la llave aquí para que todos la vean.

so-and-so ['səʊənsəʊ] n fam Mr So-and-so, Don Fulano de tal; pej an old so-and-so, un viejo imbécil.

soak [səʊk] I vtr (washing, food) remojar; (cotton, wool) empapar (in, en). II vi (washing, food) estar en remojo. ◆**soak in** vi penetrar. ◆**soak up** vtr absorber.

soaking ['səʊkɪŋ] adj (object) empapado,

-a; (person) calado,-a hasta los huesos.
soap [soup] I n 1 jabón m; **s. flakes**, jabón en escamas; **s. powder**, jabón en polvo. 2 TV **s. opera**, culebrón m. II vtr enjabonar.
soapy ['soupɪ] adj (soapier, soapiest) jabonoso,-a; (hands) cubierto,-a de jabón.
soar [sɔːr] vi (bird, plane) remontar el vuelo; fig (skyscraper) elevarse; (hopes, prices) aumentar.
sob [sɒb] I n sollozo m. II vi sollozar.
sober ['soubər] adj (not drunk, moderate) sobrio,-a; (sensible) sensato,-a; (serious) serio,-a; (colour) discreto,-a. ◆**sober up** vi he sobered up, se le pasó la borrachera.
so-called ['soukɔːld] adj supuesto,-a, llamado,-a.
soccer ['sɒkər] n fútbol m.
sociable ['soufəbəl] adj (gregarious) sociable; (friendly) amistoso,-a.
social ['soufəl] adj social; **s. class**, clase f social; **s. climber**, arribista mf; **S. Democratic**, socialdemócrata; US **s. insurance**, seguro m social; **s. security**, seguridad f social; **the s. services**, los servicios sociales; **s. welfare**, seguro social; **s. work**, asistencia f social; **s. worker**, asistente,-a m,f social. ◆**socially** adv socialmente.
socialist ['soufəlɪst] adj & n socialista (mf).
socialite ['soufəlaɪt] n vividor,-a m,f.
socialize ['soufəlaɪz] I vi alternar, mezclarse con la gente. II vtr socializar.
society [sə'saɪətɪ] I n 1 sociedad f; **the consumer s.**, la sociedad de consumo; (high) **s.**, la alta sociedad. 2 (club) asociación f. 3 (companionship) compañía f. II adj de sociedad; **s. column**, ecos mpl de sociedad.
sociologist [sousɪ'ɒlədʒɪst] n sociólogo,-a m,f.
sociology [sousɪ'ɒlədʒɪ] n sociología f.
sock [sɒk] n calcetín m.
socket ['sɒkɪt] n 1 (of eye) cuenca f. 2 Elec enchufe m.
sod¹ [sɒd] n fml (piece of turf) terrón m.
sod² [sɒd] vulg I n 1 offens (bastard) cabrón,-ona m,f; **the lazy s.!**, ¡qué tío más vago! 2 (wretch) desgraciado,-a m,f; **the poor s.**, el pobrecito. 3 vulg I've done s. all today, hoy no he pegado ni golpe. II vtr **s. it!**, ¡maldita sea!
soda ['soudə] n 1 Chem sosa f; **baking s.**, bicarbonato sódico. 2 **s. water**, soda f. 3 US (fizzy drink) gaseosa f.
sodden ['sɒdən] adj empapado,-a.
sodium ['soudɪəm] n sodio m.
sofa ['soufə] n sofá m; **s. bed**, sofá cama.
soft [sɒft] adj 1 (not hard) blando,-a; **s. toy**, muñeco m de peluche. 2 (skin, colour, hair, light, music) suave; (breeze, steps) ligero,-a. 3 (lenient) permisivo,-a. 4

(voice) bajo,-a. 5 (foolish) lelo,-a; **to be a s. touch**, ser fácil de engañar. 6 **to have a s. spot for sb**, tener debilidad por algn. 7 (easy) fácil; **s. job**, chollo m. 8 (drink) no alcohólico,-a; **s. drinks**, refrescos mpl. 9 **s. drugs**, drogas blandas; **s. porn**, pornografía blanda. ◆**softly** adv (gently) suavemente; (quietly) silenciosamente.
soften ['sɒfən] I vtr (leather, heart) ablandar; (skin) suavizar; fig (blow) amortiguar. II vi (leather, heart) ablandarse; (skin) suavizarse.
softness ['sɒftnɪs] n 1 blandura f. 2 (of hair, skin) suavidad f. 3 (foolishness) estupidez f.
software ['sɒftweər] n Comput software m; **s. package**, paquete m.
soggy ['sɒgɪ] adj (soggier, soggiest) empapado,-a; (bread) pastoso,-a.
soil [sɔɪl] I n (earth) tierra f. II vtr (dirty) ensuciar; fig (reputation) manchar.
soiled [sɔɪld] adj sucio,-a.
solace ['sɒlɪs] n fml consuelo m.
solar ['soulər] adj solar.
sold [sould] pt & pp → sell.
solder ['sɒldər] I n soldadura f. II vtr soldar.
soldier ['souldʒər] n soldado m; (military man) militar m; **toy s.**, soldadito m de plomo. ◆**soldier on** vi fig continuar contra viento y marea.
sole¹ [soul] n (of foot) planta f; (of shoe, sock) suela f.
sole² [soul] n (fish) lenguado m.
sole³ [soul] adj (only) único,-a.
solemn ['sɒləm] adj solemne.
solicit [sə'lɪsɪt] I vtr (request) solicitar. II vi (prostitute) abordar a los clientes.
solicitor [sə'lɪsɪtər] n abogado,-a m,f; (for wills) notario,-a m,f.
solid ['sɒlɪd] I adj 1 (not liquid) sólido,-a; (firm) firme. 2 (not hollow, pure) (metal) macizo,-a. 3 (fog etc) espeso,-a; (of strong material) resistente; **a man of s. build**, un hombre fornido. 4 (reliable) formal. 5 (unanimous) unánime. II n sólido m. ◆**solidly** adv sólidamente; **s. built**, (house etc) de construcción sólida; **to work s.**, trabajar sin descanso.
solidarity [sɒlɪ'dærɪtɪ] n solidaridad f.
solidify [sə'lɪdɪfaɪ] vi solidificarse.
soliloquy [sə'lɪləkwɪ] n soliloquio m.
solitaire ['sɒlɪteər] n solitario m.
solitary ['sɒlɪtərɪ] adj 1 (alone) solitario, -a; (secluded) apartado,-a. 2 (only) solo,-a.
solitude ['sɒlɪtjuːd] n soledad f.
solo ['souləu] n solo m.
soloist ['souləuɪst] n solista mf.
solstice ['sɒlstɪs] n solsticio m.
solution [sə'luːʃən] n solución f.
solve [sɒlv] vtr resolver, solucionar.
solvent ['sɒlvənt] adj & n solvente (m).
sombre, US **somber** ['sɒmbər] adj (dark)

sombrío,-a; (gloomy) lúgubre; (pessimistic) pesimista.

some [sʌm] **I** adj **1** (with plural nouns) unos,-as, algunos,-as; (several) varios,-as; (a few) unos,-as cuantos,-as; **did she bring s. flowers?**, ¿trajo flores?; **there were s. roses**, había unas rosas; **s. more peas**, más guisantes **2** (with singular nouns) algún, alguna; (a little) un poco de; **if you need s. help**, si necesitas ayuda; **there's s. wine left**, queda un poco de vino; **would you like s. coffee?**, ¿quiere café? **3** (certain) cierto,-a, alguno,-a; **in s. ways**, en cierto modo; **to s. extent**, hasta cierto punto; **s. people say that ...**, algunas personas dicen que .... **4** (unspecified) algún, alguna; **for s. reason or other**, por una razón o por otra; **in s. book or other**, en algún libro que otro; **s. other time**, otro día. **5** (quite a lot of) bastante; **it's s. distance away**, queda bastante lejos; **s. years ago**, hace algunos años.
II pron **1** (people) algunos,-as, unos,-as; **s. go by bus and s. by train**, unos van en autobús y otros en tren. **2** (objects) algunos,-as; (a few) unos,-as cuantos,-as; (a little) algo, un poco; (certain ones) algunos,-as.
III adv **s. thirty cars**, unos treinta coches.

somebody ['sʌmbədɪ] pron alguien; **s. else**, otro,-a.

somehow ['sʌmhaʊ] adv **1** (in some way) de alguna forma. **2** (for some reason) por alguna razón.

someone ['sʌmwʌn] pron & n → **somebody**.

someplace ['sʌmpleɪs] adv US → **somewhere**.

somersault ['sʌməsɔːlt] **I** n (by acrobat etc) salto m mortal; (by child) voltereta f; (by car) vuelta f de campana. **II** vi (acrobat etc) dar un salto mortal; (child) dar volteretas; (car) dar una vuelta de campana.

something ['sʌmθɪŋ] pron & n algo; **s. to eat/drink**, algo de comer/beber; **are you drunk or s.?**, ¿estás borracho o qué?; **s. must be done**, hay que hacer algo; **she has a certain s.**, tiene un no sé qué; **is s. the matter?**, ¿le pasa algo?; **s. else**, otra cosa; **s. of the kind**, algo por el estilo.

sometime ['sʌmtaɪm] adv algún día; **s. last week**, un día de la semana pasada; **s. next year**, durante el año que viene.

sometimes ['sʌmtaɪmz] adv a veces, de vez en cuando.

somewhat ['sʌmwɒt] adv fml algo, un tanto.

somewhere ['sʌmweəʳ] adv **1** (in some place) en alguna parte; (to some place) a alguna parte; **s. else**, (in some other place) en otra parte; (to some other place) a otra

parte; **s. or other**, no sé dónde. **2 s. in the region of**, (approximately) más o menos.

son [sʌn] n hijo m; **eldest/youngest s.**, hijo mayor/menor.

song [sɒŋ] n canción f; (of bird) canto m.

songwriter ['sɒŋraɪtəʳ] n compositor,-a m,f (de canciones).

sonic ['sɒnɪk] adj sónico,-a.

son-in-law ['sʌnɪnlɔː] n yerno m.

sonnet ['sɒnɪt] n soneto m.

sonny ['sʌnɪ] n fam hijo m, hijito m.

soon [suːn] adv **1** (within a short time) pronto, dentro de poco; (quickly) rápidamente; **see you s.!**, ¡hasta pronto!; **s. after midnight**, poco después de medianoche; **s. afterwards**, poco después. **2 as s. as I arrived**, en cuanto llegué; **as s. as possible**, cuanto antes. **3** (early) pronto; fig **don't speak too s.**, no cantes victoria. **4** (preference) **I would just as s. stay at home**, prefiero quedarme en casa. **5** (indifference) **I would (just) as s. read as watch TV**, tanto me da leer como ver la tele.

sooner ['suːnəʳ] adv **1** (earlier) más temprano; **s. or later**, tarde o temprano; **the s. the better**, cuanto antes mejor. **2 no s. had he finished than he fainted**, (immediately after) nada más acabar se desmayó. **3 I would s. do it alone**, (rather) prefiero hacerlo yo solo.

soot [sʊt] n hollín m.

soothe [suːð] vtr (calm) tranquilizar; (pain) aliviar.

sop [sɒp] n **1** fig (concession) favor m; (bribe) soborno m. **2 sops**, (food) sopa f sing. ◆**sop up** vtr empapar.

sophisticated [sə'fɪstɪkeɪtɪd] adj sofisticado,-a.

soporific [sɒpə'rɪfɪk] adj soporífero,-a.

sopping ['sɒpɪŋ] adj fam **s. (wet)**, como una sopa.

soppy ['sɒpɪ] adj (soppier, soppiest) fam sentimentaloide.

soprano [sə'prɑːnəʊ] n soprano mf.

sorcerer ['sɔːsərəʳ] n brujo m.

sorceress ['sɔːsərɪs] n bruja f.

sordid ['sɔːdɪd] adj sórdido,-a.

sore [sɔːʳ] **I** adj **1** dolorido,-a; **to have a s. throat**, tener dolor de garganta. **2** fam (angry) enfadado,-a; **to feel s. about sth**, estar resentido,-a por algo. **II** n llaga f. ◆**sorely** adv (very) muy; (a lot) mucho; (deeply) profundamente.

sorrow ['sɒrəʊ] n pena f, dolor m.

sorrowful ['sɒrəʊfʊl] adj afligido,-a.

sorry ['sɒrɪ] **I** adj (sorrier, sorriest) **1 I feel very s. for her**, me da mucha pena. **2** (pitiful) triste. **3 to be s. (about sth)**, sentir (algo); **I'm s. I'm late**, siento llegar tarde. **II** interj **1** (apology) ¡perdón! **2** GB (for repetition) ¿cómo?

sort [sɔːt] **I** n **1** (kind) clase f, tipo m;

(brand) marca *f*; **it's a s. of teapot**, es una especie de tetera. **2 he is a musician of sorts**, tiene algo de músico; **there's an office of sorts**, hay una especie de despacho. **3 s. of**, en cierto modo. II *vtr (classify)* clasificar. ◆**sort out** *vtr* 1 *(classify)* clasificar; *(put in order)* ordenar. 2 *(problem)* arreglar, solucionar.

sorting ['sɔ:tɪŋ] *n* **s. office**, sala *f* de batalla.

SOS [esəʊ'es] *abbr* **of save our souls**, S.O.S. *m*.

so-so ['səʊsəʊ] *adv fam* así así, regular.

soufflé ['su:fleɪ] *n* soufflé *m*, suflé *m*.

sought [sɔ:t] *pt & pp* → **seek**.

soul [səʊl] *n* 1 alma *f*. 2 **he's a good s.**, *(person)* es muy buena persona. 3 *Mus (música f)* soul *m*.

soul-destroying ['səʊldɪstrɔɪɪŋ] *adj (boring)* monótono,-a; *(demoralizing)* desmoralizador,-a.

soulful ['səʊlfʊl] *adj* conmovedor,-a.

sound¹ [saʊnd] I *n* sonido *m*; *(noise)* ruido *m*; *fig* **I don't like the s. of it**, no me gusta nada la idea; **s. barrier**, barrera *f* del sonido; **s. effects**, efectos sonoros. II *vtr (bell, trumpet)* tocar; **to s. the alarm**, dar la señal de alarma. III *vi* 1 *(trumpet, bell, alarm)* sonar. 2 *(give an impression)* parecer; **how does it s. to you?**, ¿qué te parece?; **it sounds interesting**, parece interesante.

sound² [saʊnd] I *adj* 1 *(healthy)* sano,-a; *(in good condition)* en buen estado. 2 *(safe, dependable)* seguro,-a; *(correct)* acertado,-a; *(logical)* lógico,-a. 3 *(basis etc)* sólido,-a. 4 *(defeat etc)* rotundo,-a; *(examination etc)* a fondo. 5 *(sleep)* profundo,-a. II *adv* **to be s. asleep**, estar profundamente dormido,-a.

sound³ [saʊnd] *vtr Naut Med* sondar. ◆**sound out** *vtr* sondear.

sound⁴ [saʊnd] *n Geog* estrecho *m*.

sounding ['saʊndɪŋ] *n Naut* sondeo *m*.

soundproof ['saʊndpru:f] *adj* insonorizado,-a.

soundtrack ['saʊndtræk] *n* banda sonora.

soup [su:p] *n* sopa *f*; *(thin, clear)* caldo *m*; *fam* **in the s.**, en un apuro; **s. dish**, plato hondo; **s. spoon**, cuchara *f* sopera.

sour [saʊər] *adj* 1 *(fruit, wine)* agrio,-a; *(milk)* cortado,-a; **to go s.**, *(milk)* cortarse; *(wine)* agriarse; *fig (situation)* empeorar; *fam fig* **s. grapes!**, ¡te aguantas! 2 *fig (person)* amargado,-a.

source [sɔ:s] *n* fuente *f*; *(of infection)* foco *m*.

south [saʊθ] I *n* sur *m*; **in the s. of England**, en el sur de Inglaterra; **to the s. of York**, al sur de York. II *adj* del sur; **S. Africa**, Sudáfrica; **S. African**, sudafricano,-a *(m,f)*; **S. Pole**, Polo *m* Sur. III *adv (location)* al sur; *(direction)* hacia el sur.

southeast [saʊθ'i:st] I *n* sudeste *m*. II *adv (location)* al sudeste; *(direction)* hacia el sudeste.

southeasterly [saʊθ'i:stəlɪ] *adj* del sudeste.

southerly ['sʌðəlɪ] *adj (direction)* hacia el sur; *(point)* al sur; *(wind)* del sur.

southern ['sʌðən] *adj* del sur, meridional; **S. Europe**, Europa del Sur; **the s. hemisphere**, el hemisferio sur.

southerner ['sʌðənər] *n* sureño,-a *m,f*.

southward ['saʊθwəd] *adj & adv* hacia el sur.

southwest [saʊθ'west] I *n* suroeste *m*. II *adj* suroeste. III *adv (location)* al suroeste; *(direction)* hacia el suroeste.

souvenir [su:və'nɪər] *n* recuerdo *m*, souvenir *m*.

sovereign ['sɒvrɪn] I *n* 1 *(monarch)* soberano,-a *m,f*. 2 *arch (coin)* soberano *m*. II *adj* soberano,-a.

soviet ['səʊvɪət] I *n* 1 *(council)* soviet *m*. 2 **the Soviets**, los soviéticos. II *adj* soviético,-a; *Hist* **S. Union**, Unión Soviética.

sow¹ [səʊ] *vtr (pt sowed; pp sowed or sown)* sembrar.

sow² [saʊ] *n Zool* cerda *f*.

soy [sɔɪ] *n US* soja *f*; **s. sauce**, salsa *f* de soja.

soya ['sɔɪə] *n GB* soja *f*.

spa [spɑ:] *n* balneario *m*.

space [speɪs] I *n* 1 espacio *m*; **s. age**, era *f* espacial; **s. shuttle**, transbordador *m* espacial; **s. station**, estación *f* espacial. 2 *(room)* sitio *m*; **in a confined s.**, en un espacio reducido. II *vtr (also s. out)* espaciar, separar.

spacecraft ['speɪskrɑ:ft] *n inv* nave *f* espacial.

spaceman ['speɪsmən] *n* astronauta *m*, cosmonauta *m*.

spacing ['speɪsɪŋ] *n* **double s.**, doble espacio.

spacious ['speɪʃəs] *adj* espacioso,-a, amplio,-a.

spade¹ [speɪd] *n (for digging)* pala *f*.

spade² [speɪd] *n Cards (international pack)* pica *f*; *(Spanish pack)* espada *f*.

spaghetti [spə'getɪ] *n* espaguetis *mpl*.

Spain [speɪn] *n* España.

span [spæn] I *n (of wing)* envergadura *f*; *(of hand)* palmo *m*; *(of arch)* luz *f*; *(of road)* tramo *m*; *(of time)* lapso *m*; **life s.**, vida *f*. II *vtr (river etc)* extenderse sobre, atravesar; *(period of time etc)* abarcar.

Spaniard ['spænjəd] *n* español,-a *m,f*.

spaniel ['spænjəl] *n* perro *m* de aguas.

Spanish ['spænɪʃ] I *adj* español,-a. II *n* 1 **the S.**, los españoles. 2 *(language)* español *m*, castellano *m*.

Spanish-speaking ['spænɪʃspi:kɪŋ] *adj* de habla española, hispanohablante.

spank [spæŋk] *vtr* zurrar.

spanner |'spænər| n llave f (para tuercas); *GB fam* **to throw a s. in the works**, estropear los planes.

spar¹ |spɑ:r| n *Naut* palo m, verga f.

spar² |spɑ:r| vi 1 *Box* entrenarse. 2 *(argue)* discutir.

spare |speər| I vtr 1 *(do without)* prescindir de; **can you s. me 10?**, ¿me puedes dejar 10?; **I can't s. the time**, no tengo tiempo; **there's none to s.**, no sobra nada. 2 *(begrudge)* escatimar. 3 *(show mercy to)* perdonar. 4 **s. me the details**, ahórrate los detalles. II adj 1 *(left over)* sobrante; *(surplus)* de sobra, de más; **a s. moment**, un momento libre; **s. part**, (pieza f de) recambio m; **s. room**, cuarto m de los invitados; **s. tyre**, *Aut* neumático m de recambio; *GB fam (on body)* michelines mpl; **s. wheel**, rueda f de recambio. 2 *(thin)* enjuto,-a. III n *Aut* (pieza f de) recambio m.

sparing |'speərɪŋ| adj **to be s. with praise**, escatimar elogios; **to be s. with words**, ser parco,-a en palabras. ◆**sparingly** adv en poca cantidad.

spark |spɑ:k| I n chispa f; *Aut* **s. plug**, bujía f. II vi echar chispas. ◆**spark off** vtr desatar.

sparking |'spɑ:kɪŋ| adj **s. plug**, bujía f.

sparkle |'spɑ:kəl| I vi *(diamond, glass)* centellear, destellar; *(eyes)* brillar. II n *(of diamond, glass)* centelleo m, destello m; *(of eyes)* brillo m.

sparkling |'spɑ:klɪŋ| adj 1 *(diamond, glass)* centelleante; *(eyes)* brillante; **s. wine**, vino espumoso. 2 *fig (person, conversation)* vivaz.

sparrow |'spærəʊ| n gorrión m.

sparse |spɑ:s| adj *(thin)* escaso,-a; *(scattered)* esparcido,-a; *(hair)* ralo,-a.

Spartan |'spɑ:tən| adj & n espartano,-a (m,f).

spasm |'spæzəm| n 1 *Med* espasmo m; *(of coughing)* acceso m. 2 *(of anger, activity)* arrebato m.

spasmodic |spæz'mɒdɪk| adj 1 *Med* espasmódico,-a. 2 *(irregular)* irregular.

spastic |'spæstɪk| adj & n *Med* espástico,-a (m,f).

spat |spæt| pt & pp → spit¹.

spate |speɪt| n 1 *(of letters)* avalancha f; *(of words)* torrente m; *(of accidents)* racha f. 2 *GB (river)* desbordamiento m; **to be in full s.**, estar crecido,-a.

spatter |'spætər| vtr salpicar (with, de).

spatula |'spætjʊlə| n espátula f.

spawn |spɔːn| I n *(of fish, frogs)* huevas fpl. II vi *(fish, frogs)* frezar. III vtr *fig pej* generar.

speak |spiːk| I vtr *(pt spoke; pp spoken)* 1 *(utter)* decir; **to s. the truth**, decir la verdad. 2 *(language)* hablar. II vi 1 *(gen)* hablar; **roughly speaking**, a grandes rasgos; **so to s.**, por así decirlo; **speaking**

of ..., a propósito de ...; **to s. to sb**, hablar con algn. 2 *(make a speech)* pronunciar un discurso; *(take the floor)* tomar la palabra. 3 *Tel* hablar; **speaking!**, ¡al habla!; **who's speaking, please?**, ¿de parte de quién? ◆**speak for** vtr *(person, group)* hablar en nombre de; **it speaks for itself**, es evidente. ◆**speak out** vi **to s. out against sth**, denunciar algo. ◆**speak up** vi hablar más fuerte; *fig* **to s. up for sb**, intervenir a favor de algn.

speaker |'spiːkər| n 1 *(in dialogue)* interlocutor,-a m,f; *(lecturer)* conferenciante mf; *(public)* s., orador,-a m,f. 2 *(of language)* hablante mf. 3 *GB Parl* **the S.**, el Presidente de la Cámara de los Comunes; *US* **the S. of the House**, el Presidente de la Cámara de los Representantes. 4 *(loudspeaker)* altavoz m.

spear |spɪər| n lanza f; *(javelin)* jabalina f; *(harpoon)* arpón m.

spearhead |'spɪəhed| vtr encabezar.

spec |spek| n *fam* **on s.**, sin garantías.

special |'speʃəl| I adj especial; *(specific)* específico,-a; *(exceptional)* extraordinario,-a; **s. delivery**, *(letter)* exprés; *(parcel)* de entrega inmediata; **s. edition**, número m especial; **s. effects**, efectos mpl especiales. II n *Rad TV* programa m especial. ◆**specially** adv *(specifically)* especialmente; *(on purpose)* a propósito.

specialist |'speʃəlɪst| n especialista mf.

speciality |speʃɪ'ælɪtɪ| n especialidad f.

specialize |'speʃəlaɪz| vi especializarse (in, en).

specialty |'speʃəltɪ| n *US* → speciality.

species |'spiːʃiːz| n *(pl species)* especie f.

specific |sprɪ'sɪfɪk| adj específico,-a; *(definite)* concreto,-a; *(precise)* preciso,-a; **to be s.**, concretar. ◆**specifically** adv *(exactly)* específicamente; *(expressly)* expresamente; *(namely)* en concreto.

specification |spesɪfɪ'keɪʃən| n specifications, datos específicos.

specify |'spesɪfaɪ| vtr especificar, precisar.

specimen |'spesɪmɪn| n *(sample)* muestra f; *(example)* ejemplar m; **urine/tissue s.**, espécimen de orina/tejido.

speck |spek| n *(of dust)* mota f; *(stain)* manchita f; *(small trace)* pizca f.

speckled |'spekəld| adj moteado,-a.

specs |speks| npl *fam abbr of* spectacles.

spectacle |'spektəkəl| n 1 *(display)* espectáculo m. 2 spectacles, *(glasses)* gafas fpl.

spectacular |spek'tækjʊlər| I adj espectacular, impresionante. II n *Cin TV* *(gran)* espectáculo m.

spectator |spek'teɪtər| n espectador,-a m,f.

spectre, *US* **specter** |'spektər| n espectro m, fantasma m.

spectrum |'spektrəm| n espectro m.

speculate |'spekjʊleɪt| *vi* especular.
speculation |spekjʊ'leɪʃən| *n* especulación *f*.
speech |spiːtʃ| *n* **1** *(faculty)* habla *f*; *(pronunciation)* pronunciación *f*; **freedom of s.**, libertad *f* de expresión. **2** *(address)* discurso *m*; **to give a s.**, pronunciar un discurso. **3** *Ling* **part of s.**, parte *f* de la oración.
speechless |'spiːtʃlɪs| *adj* mudo,-a, boquiabierto,-a.
speed |spiːd| **I** *n* **1** velocidad *f*; *(rapidity)* rapidez *f*; **at top s.**, a toda velocidad; **s. limit**, límite *m* de velocidad. **II** *vi* **1** *(pt & pp* **sped)** *(go fast)* ir corriendo; *(hurry)* apresurarse; **to s. along**, *(car etc)* ir a toda velocidad; **to s. past**, pasar volando. **2** *(pt & pp* **speeded)** *(exceed speed limit)* conducir con exceso de velocidad. ◆**speed up I** *vtr (pt & pp* **speeded up)** acelerar; *(person)* meter prisa a. **II** *vi (person)* darse prisa.
speedboat |'spiːdbəʊt| *n* lancha rápida.
speeding |'spiːdɪŋ| *n* exceso *m* de velocidad.
speedometer |spɪ'dɒmɪtər| *n* velocímetro *m*.
speedway |'spiːdweɪ| *n* **1** *(racing)* carreras *fpl* de motos. **2** *(track)* pista *f* de carreras.
speedy |'spiːdɪ| *adj* **(speedier, speediest)** veloz, rápido,-a.
spell¹ |spel| **I** *vtr (pt & pp* **spelt** *or* **spelled)** *(letter by letter)* deletrear; *fig (denote)* significar; **how do you s. your name?**, ¿cómo se escribe su nombre?. **II** *vi* **she can't s.**, comete faltas de ortografía. ◆**spell out** *vtr fig* explicar con detalle.
spell² |spel| *n (magical)* hechizo *m*, encanto *m*.
spell³ |spel| *n* **1** *(period)* período *m*; *(short period)* rato *m*; *Meteor* **cold s.**, ola *f* de frío. **2** *(shift)* turno *m*.
spellbound |'spelbaʊnd| *adj* hechizado, -a, embelesado,-a.
spelling |'spelɪŋ| *n* ortografía *f*.
spend |spend| *vtr (pt & pp* **spent)** **1** *(money)* gastar **(on**, en). **2** *(time)* pasar; **to s. time on sth**, dedicar tiempo a algo.
spending |'spendɪŋ| *n* gastos *mpl*; **s. money**, dinero *m* de bolsillo; **s. power**, poder adquisitivo.
spendthrift |'spendθrɪft| *adj & n* derrochador,-a *(m,f)*.
spent |spent| *adj* gastado,-a.
sperm |spɜːm| *n* esperma *m*; **s. bank**, banco *m* de esperma; **s. whale**, cachalote *m*.
spew |spjuː| *vtr* **to s. (up)**, vomitar.
sphere |sfɪər| *n* esfera *f*.
spice |spaɪs| **I** *n* **1** especia *f*. **2** *fig* sal *f*. **II** *vtr* **1** *Culin* sazonar. **2** **to s. (up)**, *(story etc)* salpimentar.
spic(k)-and-span |spɪkən'spæn| *adj (very clean)* limpísimo,-a; *(well-groomed)* acicalado,-a.
spicy |'spaɪsɪ| *adj* **(spicier, spiciest)** **1** *Culin* sazonado,-a; *(hot)* picante. **2** *fig (story etc)* picante.
spider |'spaɪdər| *n* araña *f*; **s.'s web**, telaraña *f*.
spike¹ |spaɪk| *n (sharp point)* punta *f*; *(metal rod)* pincho *m*; *(on railing)* barrote *m*; *Sport (on shoes)* clavo *m*.
spike² |spaɪk| *n Bot* espiga *f*.
spiky |'spaɪkɪ| *adj* **(spikier, spikiest)** puntiagudo,-a; *(hairstyle)* de punta.
spill |spɪl| **I** *vtr (pt & pp* **spilled** *or* **spilt)** derramar. **II** *vi (liquid)* derramarse. ◆**spill over** *vi* desbordarse.
spin |spɪn| **I** *vtr (pt & pp* **spun)** **1** *(wheel etc)* hacer girar; *(washing)* centrifugar. **2** *(cotton, wool)* hilar; *(spider's web)* tejer. **II** *vi (wheel etc)* girar; *Av* caer en barrena; *Aut* patinar. **III** *n* **1** *(turn)* vuelta *f*, giro *m*. **2** *Sport* efecto *m*. **3** *Av* barrena *f*; *Aut* patinazo *m*. **4** *GB* **to go for a s.**, *(ride)* dar una vuelta.
spinach |'spɪnɪtʃ| *n* espinacas *fpl*.
spinal |'spaɪnəl| *adj* espinal, vertebral; **s. column**, columna *f* vertebral; **s. cord**, médula *f* espinal.
spindly |'spɪndlɪ| *adj* **(spindlier, spindliest)** *fam (long-bodied)* larguirucho,-a; *(long-legged)* zanquilargo,-a.
spin-dryer |spɪn'draɪər| *n* secador centrífugo.
spine |spaɪn| *n* **1** *Anat* columna *f* vertebral, espinazo *m*; *(of book)* lomo *m*. **2** *Zool* púa *f*; *Bot* espina *f*.
spineless |'spaɪnlɪs| *adj fig (weak)* sin carácter.
spinning |'spɪnɪŋ| *n* **1** *(of cotton etc) (act)* hilado *m*; *(art)* hilandería *f*; **s. wheel**, rueca *f*. **2** **s. top**, peonza *f*.
spin-off |'spɪnɒf| *n (by-product)* derivado *m*; *fig* efecto secundario.
spinster |'spɪnstər| *n* soltera *f*.
spiral |'spaɪərəl| **I** *n* espiral *f*. **II** *adj* en espiral; **s. staircase**, escalera *f* de caracol.
spirit¹ |'spɪrɪt| *n* **1** *(soul)* espíritu *m*, alma *f*; *(ghost)* fantasma *m*. **2** *(attitude)* espíritu *m*; *(mood)* humor *m*; **to take sth in the right s.**, tomar algo a bien; **community s.**, civismo *m*. **3** *(courage)* valor *m*; *(liveliness)* ánimo *m*; *(vitality)* vigor *m*; **to break sb's s.**, quebrar la voluntad de algn. **5** **spirits**, *(mood)* humor *m sing*; **to be in good s.**, estar de buen humor; **to be in high/low s.**, estar muy animado/ desanimado.
spirit² |'spɪrɪt| *n* **1** *Chem* alcohol *m*; **s. level**, nivel *m* de aire. **2** **spirits**, *(alcoholic drinks)* licores *mpl*.
spirited |'spɪrɪtɪd| *adj (person, attempt)* valiente; *(horse)* fogoso,-a; *(attack)* enérgico,-a.

spiritual ['spɪrɪtjʊəl] *adj* espiritual.
spit¹ [spɪt] I *vtr* (*pt* & *pp* **spat**) escupir.
II *vi* escupir; *fam* **he's the spitting image
of his father**, es el vivo retrato de su padre. III *n* (*saliva*) saliva *f*.
spit² [spɪt] *n Culin* asador *m*.
spite [spaɪt] I *n* 1 (*ill will*) rencor *m*, ojeriza *f*. 2 **in s. of**, a pesar de, pese a; **in s.
of the fact that**, a pesar de que, pese a
que. II *vtr* (*annoy*) fastidiar.
spiteful ['spaɪtfʊl] *adj* (*person*)
rencoroso,-a; (*remark*) malévolo,-a;
(*tongue*) viperino,-a.
spittle ['spɪtəl] *n* saliva *f*.
splash [splæʃ] I *vtr* salpicar. II *vi* 1 **to s.
(about)**, (*in water*) chapotear. 2 (*water
etc*) salpicar. III *n* 1 (*noise*) chapoteo *m*. 2
(*spray*) salpicadura *f*; *fig* (*of colour*) mancha *f*. ◆**splash out** *vi fam* tirar la casa
por la ventana.
spleen [spliːn] *n Anat* bazo *m*.
splendid ['splendɪd] *adj* espléndido,-a.
splendour, *US* **splendor** ['splendər] *n*
esplendor *m*.
splint [splɪnt] *n* tablilla *f*.
splinter ['splɪntər] I *n* (*wood*) astilla *f*;
(*bone, stone*) esquirla *f*; (*glass*) fragmento
m; **s. group**, grupo *m* disidente. II *vi* 1
(*wood etc*) astillarse. 2 *Pol* escindirse.
split [splɪt] I *n* 1 (*crack*) grieta *f*, hendidura *f*; (*tear*) desgarrón *m*; *fig* (*division*)
cisma *m*; *Pol* escisión *f*. 2 *Gymn* **to do
the splits**, abrir las piernas en cruz. II
adj partido,-a; **in a s. second**, en una
fracción de segundo; **s. personality**, des-
doblamiento *m* de personalidad. III *vtr*
(*pt* & *pp* **split**) 1 (*crack*) agrietar; (*cut*)
partir; (*tear*) rajar; (*atom*) desintegrar; *fig*
to s. hairs, buscarle tres pies al gato. 2
(*divide*) dividir. 3 (*share out*) repartir. 4
Pol escindir. IV *vi* 1 (*crack*) agrietarse;
(*into two parts*) partirse; (*garment*) rajarse.
2 (*divide*) dividirse. 3 *Pol* escindirse.
◆**split up** I *vtr* (*break up*) partir; (*divide
up*) dividir; (*share out*) repartir. II *vi*
(*couple*) separarse.
splutter ['splʌtər] *vi* (*person*) balbucear;
(*candle, fat*) chisporrotear; (*engine*) petardear.
spoil [spɔɪl] I *vtr* (*pt* & *pp* **spoiled** *or*
spoilt) 1 (*ruin*) estropear, echar a perder.
2 (*child*) mimar a; **to be spoilt for
choice**, tener demasiadas cosas para elegir. II *vi* (*food*) estropearse.
spoilsport ['spɔɪlspɔːt] *n fam* aguafiestas
mf inv.
spoilt [spɔɪlt] *adj* 1 (*food, merchandise*)
estropeado,-a. 2 (*child*) mimado,-a.
spoke¹ [spəʊk] *pt* → **speak**.
spoke² [spəʊk] *n* (*of wheel*) radio *m*, rayo
m.
spoken ['spəʊkən] *pp* → **speak**.
spokesman ['spəʊksmən] *n* portavoz *m*.
spokeswoman ['spəʊkswʊmən] *n* porta-

voz *f*.
sponge [spʌndʒ] I *n* esponja *f*; *fig* **to
throw in the s.**, arrojar la toalla; *GB* **s.
cake**, bizcocho *m*. II *vtr* (*wash*) lavar con
esponja. III *vi fam* vivir de gorra.
◆**sponge off**, **sponge on** *vtr* vivir a
costa de.
spongy ['spʌndʒɪ] *adj* (**spongier, spongi-
est**) esponjoso,-a.
sponsor ['spɒnsər] I *vtr* patrocinar; *Fin*
avalar; (*support*) respaldar. II *n*
patrocinador,-a *m,f*; *Fin* avalador,-a *m,f*.
sponsorship ['spɒnsəʃɪp] *n* patrocinio *m*;
Fin aval *m*; (*support*) respaldo *m*.
spontaneous [spɒn'teɪnɪəs] *adj*
espontáneo,-a.
spoof [spuːf] *n fam* 1 (*parody*) burla *f*. 2
(*hoax*) engaño *m*.
spooky ['spuːkɪ] *adj* (**spookier, spooki-
est**) *fam* espeluznante.
spool [spuːl] *n* bobina *f*, carrete *m*.
spoon [spuːn] I *n* cuchara *f*; (*small*) cu-
charita *f*. II *vtr* sacar con cuchara; (*serve*)
servir con cuchara.
spoon-feed ['spuːnfiːd] *vtr* (*baby*) dar de
comer con cuchara a *fig* (*spoil*) mimar.
spoonful ['spuːnfʊl] *n* cucharada *f*.
sporadic [spə'rædɪk] *adj* esporádico,-a.
sport [spɔːt] I *n* 1 deporte *m*. 2 *fam* **he's
a good s.**, es buena persona; **be a s.!**, ¡sé
amable!. II *vtr* (*display*) lucir.
sporting ['spɔːtɪŋ] *adj* deportivo,-a.
sports [spɔːts] I *npl* deportes *mpl*, deporte
m sing. II *adj* **s. car**, coche deportivo; **s.
jacket**, chaqueta *f* (de) sport.
sportsman ['spɔːtsmən] *n* deportista *m*.
sportsmanlike ['spɔːtsmənlaɪk] *adj*
deportivo,-a.
sportsmanship ['spɔːtsmənʃɪp] *n* deportividad *f*.
sportswear ['spɔːtsweər] *n* (*for sport*) ropa
f de deporte; (*casual clothes*) ropa *f* (de)
sport.
sportswoman ['spɔːtswʊmən] *n* deportista *f*.
sporty ['spɔːtɪ] *adj* (**sportier, sportiest**)
fam deportivo,-a.
spot [spɒt] *n* 1 (*dot*) punto *m*; (*on fabric*)
lunar *m*. 2 (*stain*) mancha *f*. 3 (*pimple*)
grano *m*. 4 (*place*) sitio *m*, lugar *m*; **on
the s.**, (*person*) allí, presente; **to decide
sth on the s.**, decidir algo en el acto; **s.
check**, chequeo rápido; *fig* **weak s.**,
punto débil; **to be in a tight s.**, estar en
un apuro; **to put sb on the s.**, poner a
algn en un aprieto. 5 *fam* (*small amount*)
poquito *m*; **a s. of bother**, unos proble-
millas. 6 *Rad TV Theat* (*in show*) espacio
m; (*advertisement*) spot *m*, anuncio *m*. II
vtr (*notice*) darse cuenta de, notar; (*see*)
ver.
spotless ['spɒtlɪs] *adj* (*very clean*) impecable; *fig* (*reputation etc*) intachable.
spotlight ['spɒtlaɪt] *n* foco *m*; *Aut* faro *m*

auxiliar; *fig* **to be in the s.,** ser objeto de la atención pública.

spot-on [spɒt'ɒn] *adj fam* exacto,-a.

spotted ['spɒtɪd] *adj (with dots)* con puntos; *(fabric)* con lunares; *(speckled)* moteado,-a.

spotty ['spɒtɪ] *adj (spottier, spottiest) pej* con granos.

spouse [spaʊs] *n* cónyuge *mf*.

spout [spaʊt] **I** *n (of jug)* pico *m*; *(of teapot)* pitorro *m*. **II** *vtr fam (nonsense)* soltar. **III** *vi* **to s. out/up,** *(liquid)* brotar.

sprain [spreɪn] **I** *n* esguince *m*. **II** *vtr* torcer; **to s. one's ankle,** torcerse el tobillo.

sprang [spræŋ] *pt → spring²*.

sprawl [sprɔːl] **I** *vi* **1** *(sit, lie)* tumbarse. **2** *(city, plant)* extenderse. **II** *n (of city)* extensión *f*.

spray¹ [spreɪ] **I** *n* **1** *(of water)* rociada *f*; *(from sea)* espuma *f*; *(from aerosol)* pulverización *f*. **2** *(aerosol)* spray *m*; *(for plants)* pulverizador *m*; **s. can,** aerosol *m*. **II** *vtr* **1** *(water)* rociar; *(insecticide, perfume)* pulverizar.

spray² [spreɪ] *n (of flowers)* ramita *f*.

spread [spred] **I** *n* **1** extensión *f*; *(of ideas)* difusión *f*; *(of disease, fire)* propagación *f*; *(of terrorism)* generalización *f*. **2** *(range)* gama *f*. **3** *(of wings)* envergadura *f*. **4** *(for bread)* pasta *f*; **cheese s.,** queso para untar. **5** *fam (large meal)* banquetazo *m*. **6** *Press* **full-page s.,** plana entera; **two-page s.,** doble página *f*. **II** *vtr (pt & pp spread)* **1** *(unfold)* desplegar; *(lay out)* extender; *fig* **to s. one's wings,** desplegar las alas. **2** *(butter etc)* untar. **3** *(news)* difundir; *(rumour)* hacer correr; *(disease, fire)* propagar; *(panic)* sembrar. **III** *vi* **1** *(stretch out)* extenderse; *(unfold)* desplegarse. **2** *(news)* difundirse; *(rumour)* correr; *(disease)* propagarse.

spread-eagled [spred'iːgəld] *adj* despatarrado,-a.

spreadsheet ['spredʃiːt] *n Comput* hoja *f* de cálculo.

spree [spriː] *n* juerga *f*; **to go on a s.,** ir de juerga.

sprig [sprɪg] *n* ramita *f*.

sprightly ['spraɪtlɪ] *adj (sprightlier, sprightliest) (nimble)* ágil; *(energetic)* enérgico,-a; *(lively)* animado,-a.

spring¹ [sprɪŋ] **I** *n* **1** *(season)* primavera *f*. **II** *adj* primaveral; **s. onion,** cebolleta *f*; **s. roll,** rollo *m* de primavera.

spring² [sprɪŋ] **I** *n* **1** *(of water)* manantial *m*, fuente *f*. **2** *(of watch etc)* resorte *m*; *(of mattress)* muelle *m*; *Aut* ballesta *f*. **II** *vi* *(pt sprang; pp sprung)* **1** *(jump)* saltar; **the lid sprang open,** la tapa se abrió de golpe. **2** *(appear)* aparecer de repente). **III** *vtr* **1** **to s. a leak,** hacer agua. **2** *fig (news, surprise)* dar de golpe ◆**spring up** *vi* aparecer; *(plants)* brotar; *(buildings)*

elevarse; *(problems)* surgir.

springboard ['sprɪŋbɔːd] *n* trampolín *m*.

spring-clean [sprɪŋ'kliːn] *vtr* limpiar a fondo.

springtime ['sprɪŋtaɪm] *n* primavera *f*.

springy ['sprɪŋɪ] *adj (springier, springiest) (bouncy)* elástico,-a; *fig (step)* saltarín.

sprinkle ['sprɪŋkəl] *vtr (with water)* rociar **(with,** de); *(with sugar)* espolvorear **(with,** de).

sprint [sprɪnt] **I** *n* esprint *m*. **II** *vi* esprintar.

sprinter ['sprɪntər] *n* esprínter *mf*, velocista *mf*.

sprout [spraʊt] **I** *vi (bud)* brotar; *fig* crecer rápidamente. **II** *n* **(Brussels) sprouts,** coles *fpl* de Bruselas.

spruce¹ [spruːs] *n inv Bot* picea *f*.

spruce² [spruːs] *adj (neat)* pulcro,-a; *(smart)* apuesto,-a. ◆**spruce up** *vtr* acicalar.

sprung [sprʌŋ] *pp → spring²*.

spry [spraɪ] *adj (sprier, spriest) (nimble)* ágil; *(active)* activo,-a; *(lively)* vivaz.

spun [spʌn] *pt & pp → spin*.

spur [spɜːr] **I** *n* **1** espuela *f*. **2** *fig (stimulus)* acicate *m*; **on the s. of the moment,** sin pensarlo. **II** *vtr* **1** *(horse)* espolear. **2** *fig* incitar.

spurious ['spjʊərɪəs] *adj* falso,-a, espurio,-a.

spurn [spɜːn] *vtr fml* desdeñar, rechazar.

spurt [spɜːt] **I** *n* **1** *(of liquid)* chorro *m*. **2** *fig (of activity etc)* racha *f*; *(effort)* esfuerzo *m*. **II** *vi* **1** *(liquid)* chorrear. **2** *(make an effort)* hacer un último esfuerzo; *(accelerate)* acelerar.

spy [spaɪ] **I** *n* espía *mf*. **II** *vtr fml (see)* divisar. **III** *vi* espiar **(on, a)**.

spyhole ['spaɪhəʊl] *n* mirilla *f*.

spying ['spaɪɪŋ] *n* espionaje *m*.

squabble ['skwɒbəl] **I** *n* riña *f*, pelea *f*. **II** *vi* reñir, pelearse **(over, about,** por).

squad [skwɒd] *n Mil* pelotón *m*; *(of police)* brigada *f*; *Sport* equipo *m*; **drugs s.,** brigada antidroga.

squadron ['skwɒdrən] *n Mil* escuadrón *m*; *Av* escuadrilla *f*; *Naut* escuadra *f*.

squalid ['skwɒlɪd] *adj (very dirty)* asqueroso,-a; *(poor)* miserable; *(motive)* vil.

squall¹ [skwɔːl] *n (wind)* ráfaga *f*.

squall² [skwɔːl] *vi* chillar, berrear.

squalor ['skwɒlər] *n (dirtiness)* mugre *f*; *(poverty)* miseria *f*.

squander ['skwɒndər] *vtr (money)* derrochar, despilfarrar; *(time)* desperdiciar.

square [skweər] **I** *n* **1** cuadro *m*; *(on chessboard, crossword)* casilla *f*; *fig* **we're back to s. one!,** ¡volvemos a partir desde cero! **2** *(in town)* plaza *f*. **3** *Math* cuadrado *m*. **II** *adj* **1** *(in shape)* cuadrado,-a. **2** *Math* cuadrado,-a; **s. metre,** metro cuadrado;

s. **root**, raíz cuadrada. 3 *fam* (*fair*) justo,-a; **to be s. with sb**, (*honest*) ser franco,-a con algn. 4 **a s. meal**, una buena comida. 5 (*old-fashioned*) carroza; (*conservative*) carca. III *vtr* 1 (*make square*) cuadrar; **to s. one's shoulders**, sacar el pecho. 2 *Math* elevar al cuadrado. 3 (*settle*) arreglar. IV *vi* (*agree*) cuadrar (**with**, con). ◆**squarely** *adv* (*directly*) directamente, de lleno.

squash¹ [skwɒʃ] I *n GB* (*drink*) concentrado *m*. II *vtr* 1 (*crush*) aplastar. 2 *fig* (*objection*) echar por tierra. III *vi* (*crush*) aplastarse.

squash² [skwɒʃ] *n Sport* squash *m*.

squat [skwɒt] I *adj* (*person*) rechoncho,-a. II *vi* 1 (*crouch*) agacharse, sentarse en cuclillas. 2 (*in building*) ocupar ilegalmente. III *n* (*building*) edificio *m* ocupado ilegalmente.

squatter ['skwɒtəʳ] *n* ocupante *mf* ilegal, okupa *m,f*.

squawk [skwɔːk] I *n* graznido *m*. II *vi* graznar.

squeak [skwiːk] I *n* (*of mouse*) chillido *m*; (*of hinge, wheel*) chirrido *m*; (*of shoes*) crujido *m*. II *vi* (*mouse*) chillar; (*hinge, wheel*) chirriar, rechinar; (*shoes*) crujir.

squeaky ['skwiːkɪ] *adj* (*squeakier, squeakiest*) chirriante; (*voice*) chillón, -ona; (*shoes*) que crujen.

squeal [skwiːl] I *n* (*of animal, person*) chillido *m*. II *vi* 1 (*animal, person*) chillar. 2 *fam* (*inform*) chivarse.

squeamish ['skwiːmɪʃ] *adj* muy sensible.

squeeze [skwiːz] I *vtr* apretar; (*lemon etc*) exprimir; (*sponge*) estrujar; **to s. paste out of a tube**, sacar pasta de un tubo apretando. II *vi* **to s. in**, apretujarse. III *n* 1 (*pressure*) estrujón *m*; **a s. of lemon**, unas gotas de limón. 2 (*of hand*) apretón *m*; (*hug*) abrazo *m*; (*crush*) apiñamiento *m*; **credit s.**, reducción *f* de créditos.

squelch [skweltʃ] *vi* chapotear.

squid [skwɪd] *n* calamar *m*; (*small*) chipirón *m*.

squiggle ['skwɪgəl] *n* garabato *m*.

squint [skwɪnt] I *n* 1 bizquera *f*; **to have a s.**, ser bizco,-a. 2 *fig* (*quick look*) vistazo *m*. II *vi* ser bizco,-a. 2 **to s. at sth**, (*glance*) echar un vistazo a algo; (*with eyes half-closed*) mirar algo con los ojos entrecerrados.

squirm [skwɜːm] *vi* retorcerse; *fig* (*feel embarrassed*) sentirse incómodo,-a.

squirrel ['skwɪrəl] *n* ardilla *f*.

squirt [skwɜːt] I *n* (*of liquid*) chorro *m*. II *vtr* lanzar a chorro. III *vi* **to s. out**, salir a chorros.

Sr *abbr* → **Snr**.

Sri Lanka [sriːˈlæŋkə] *n* Sri Lanka.

St 1 *abbr of* **Saint**, San, Sto., Sta. 2 *abbr of* **Street**, c/.

st *GB abbr of* **stone**, peso que equivale a 6,350 kilogramos.

stab [stæb] I *n* (*with knife*) puñalada *f*; (*of pain*) punzada *f*; *fam fig* **to have a s. at doing sth**, intentar hacer algo. II *vtr* apuñalar.

stabbing ['stæbɪŋ] *adj* (*pain*) punzante.

stability [stəˈbɪlɪtɪ] *n* estabilidad *f*.

stable¹ ['steɪbəl] *adj* estable.

stable² ['steɪbəl] *n* cuadra *f*, caballeriza *f*.

stack [stæk] I *n* (*pile*) montón *m*; *fam* **he's got stacks of money**, está forrado. II *vtr* (*pile up*) amontonar, apilar; *fig* **the odds are stacked against us**, todo está en contra nuestra.

stadium ['steɪdɪəm] *n* estadio *m*.

staff [stɑːf] *n* 1 (*personnel*) personal *m*; *Mil* estado *m* mayor; **s. meeting**, claustro *m*; *GB* **s. nurse**, enfermera cualificada. 2 (*stick*) bastón *m*; (*of shepherd*) cayado *m*. II *vtr* proveer de personal.

staffroom ['stɑːfruːm] *n* sala *f* de profesores.

stag [stæg] *n* ciervo *m*, venado *m*; *fam* **s. party**, despedida *f* de soltero.

stage [steɪdʒ] I *n* 1 (*platform*) plataforma *f*. 2 (*in theatre*) escenario *m*; **s. door**, entrada *f* de artistas; **s. fright**, miedo escénico; **s. manager**, director,-a *m,f* de escena. 3 (*phase*) (*of development, journey, rocket*) etapa *f*; (*of road, pipeline*) tramo *m*; **at this s. of the negotiations**, a estas alturas de las negociaciones; **in stages**, por etapas. II *vtr* 1 (*play*) poner en escena, montar. 2 (*arrange*) organizar; (*carry out*) llevar a cabo.

stagecoach ['steɪdʒkəʊtʃ] *n* diligencia *f*.

stagger ['stægəʳ] I *vi* tambalearse. II *vtr* 1 (*amaze*) asombrar. 2 (*hours, work*) escalonar.

staggering ['stægərɪŋ] *adj* asombroso,-a.

stagnant ['stægnənt] *adj* estancado,-a.

stagnate [stægˈneɪt] *vi* estancarse.

staid [steɪd] *adj* (*person*) conservador,-a; (*manner, clothes*) serio,-a, formal.

stain [steɪn] I *n* 1 mancha *f*; **s. remover**, quitamanchas *m inv*. 2 (*dye*) tinte *m*. II *vtr* 1 manchar. 2 (*dye*) teñir. III *vi* mancharse.

stained [steɪnd] *adj* **s. glass window**, vidriera *f* de colores.

stainless ['steɪnlɪs] *adj* (*steel*) inoxidable.

stair [steəʳ] *n* escalón *m*, peldaño *m*; **stairs**, escalera *f sing*.

staircase ['steəkeɪs] *n* escalera *f*.

stake¹ [steɪk] I *n* (*stick*) estaca *f*; (*for plant*) rodrigón *m*; (*post*) poste *m*. II *vtr* **to s. (out)**, cercar con estacas.

stake² [steɪk] I *n* (*bet*) apuesta *f*; **the issue at s.**, el tema en cuestión; **to be at s.**, (*at risk*) estar en juego. 2 (*investment*) interés *m*. II *vtr* (*bet*) apostar; (*invest*) invertir; **to s. a claim to sth**, reivindicar algo.

stale [steɪl] *adj* (*food*) pasado,-a; (*bread*) duro,-a.

stalemate ['steɪlmeɪt] *n Chess* tablas *fpl*; *fig* to reach s., llegar a un punto muerto.

stalk¹ [stɔːk] *n* (*of plant*) tallo *m*; (*of fruit*) rabo *m*.

stalk² [stɔːk] I *vtr* (*of hunter*) cazar al acecho; (*of animal*) acechar. II *vi* he stalked out, salió airado.

stall¹ [stɔːl] I *n* 1 (*in market*) puesto *m*; (*at fair*) caseta *f*. 2 (*stable*) establo *m*; (*stable compartment*) casilla *f* de establo. 3 *Theat* stalls, platea *f sing*. II *vtr Aut* calar. III *vi Aut* calarse; *Av* perder velocidad.

stall² [stɔːl] *vi* dar largas a un asunto.

stallion ['stæljən] *n* semental *m*.

stalwart ['stɔːlwət] *n* incondicional *m,f*.

stamina ['stæmɪnə] *n* resistencia *f*.

stammer ['stæmər] I *n* tartamudeo *m*. II *vi* tartamudear.

stamp [stæmp] I *n* 1 (*postage stamp*) sello *m*; s. album, álbum *m* de sellos; s. collector, filatelista *mf*; *GB* s. duty, póliza *f*. 2 (*rubber stamp*) tampón *m*; (*for metals*) cuño *m*. 3 (*with foot*) patada *f*. II *vtr* 1 (*with postage stamp*) poner el sello a; stamped addressed envelope, sobre franqueado. 2 (*with rubber stamp*) sellar. 3 to s. one's feet, patear; (*in dancing*) zapatear. III *vi* patear. ◆**stamp out** *vtr fig* (*racism etc*) acabar con; (*rebellion*) sofocar.

stampede [stæm'piːd] I *n* estampida *f*; *fig* (*rush*) desbandada *f*. II *vi* desbandarse; *fig* (*rush*) precipitarse.

stance [stæns] *n* postura *f*.

stand [stænd] I *n* 1 (*position*) posición *f*, postura *f*; to make a s., resistir. 2 (*of lamp, sculpture*) pie *m*. 3 (*market stall*) puesto *m*; (*at fair*) caseta *f*; (*at exhibition*) stand *m*; newspaper s., quiosco *m*. 4 (*platform*) plataforma *f*; (*in stadium*) tribuna *f*; *US* (*witness box*) estrado *m*. II *vtr* (*pt & pp* stood) 1 (*place*) poner, colocar. 2 (*tolerate*) aguantar, soportar. 3 to s. one's ground, mantenerse firme. III *vi* 1 (*be upright*) estar de pie; (*get up*) levantarse; (*remain upright*) quedarse de pie; s. still!, ¡estáte quieto,-a! 2 (*measure*) medir. 3 (*be situated*) estar, encontrarse. 4 (*remain unchanged*) permanecer. 5 (*remain valid*) seguir vigente. 6 as things s., tal como están las cosas. 7 *Pol* presentarse. ◆**stand back** *vi* (*allow sb to pass*) abrir paso. ◆**stand by** I *vi* 1 (*do nothing*) quedarse sin hacer nada. 2 (*be ready*) estar listo,-a. II *vtr* (*person*) apoyar a; (*promise*) cumplir con; (*decision*) atenerse a. ◆**stand down** *vi fig* retirarse. ◆**stand for** *vtr* 1 (*mean*) significar. 2 (*represent*) representar. 3 (*tolerate*) aguantar. ◆**stand in** *vi* sustituir (for, -). ◆**stand out** *vi* (*mountain etc*) desta-

carse (against, contra); *fig* (*person*) destacar. ◆**stand up** *vi* (*get up*) ponerse de pie; (*be standing*) estar de pie; *fig* it will s. up to wear and tear, es muy resistente; *fig* to s. up for sb, defender a algn; *fig* to s. up to sb, hacer frente a algn.

standard ['stændəd] I *n* 1 (*level*) nivel *m*; s. of living, nivel de vida. 2 (*criterion*) criterio *m*. 3 (*norm*) norma *f*, estándar *m*. 4 (*flag*) estandarte *m*. II *adj* normal, estándar; s. lamp, lámpara *f* de pie.

standardize ['stændədaɪz] *vtr* normalizar.

standby ['stændbaɪ] *n* 1 (*thing*) recurso *m*. 2 (*person*) suplente *mf*; to be on s., *Mil* estar de retén; *Av* estar en la lista de espera; s. ticket, billete *m* sin reserva.

stand-in ['stændɪn] *n* suplente *mf*; *Cin* doble *mf*.

standing ['stændɪŋ] I *adj* 1 (*not sitting*) de pie; (*upright*) recto,-a; to give sb a s. ovation, ovacionar a algn de pie; there was s. room only, no quedaban asientos. 2 (*committee*) permanente; (*invitation*) permanente; *GB* s. order, pago fijo. II *n* 1 (*social position*) rango *m*. 2 (*duration*) duración *f*; (*in job*) antigüedad *f*.

stand-offish [stænd'ɒfɪʃ] *adj fam* distante.

standpoint ['stændpɔɪnt] *n* punto *m* de vista.

standstill ['stændstɪl] *n* at a s., (*car, traffic*) parado,-a; (*industry*) paralizado,-a; to come to a s., (*car, traffic*) pararse; (*industry*) paralizarse.

stank [stæŋk] *pt* → **stink**.

staple¹ ['steɪpl] I *n* (*fastener*) grapa *f*. II *vtr* grapar.

staple² ['steɪpəl] I *adj* (*food*) básico,-a; (*product*) de primera necesidad. II *n* (*food*) alimento básico.

stapler ['steɪplər] *n* grapadora *f*.

star [stɑːr] I *n* estrella *f*. II *adj* estelar. III *vtr Cin* tener como protagonista a. IV *vi Cin* to s. in a film, protagonizar una película.

starboard ['stɑːbəd] *n* estribor *m*.

starch [stɑːtʃ] I *n* almidón *m*. II *vtr* almidonar.

stardom ['stɑːdəm] *n* estrellato *m*.

stare [steər] I *n* mirada fija. II *vi* mirar fijamente.

starfish ['stɑːfɪʃ] *n* estrella *f* de mar.

stark [stɑːk] *adj* (*landscape*) desolado,-a; (*décor*) austero,-a; the s. truth, la dura realidad; s. poverty, la miseria.

stark-naked ['stɑːkneɪkɪd] *adj fam* en cueros.

starling ['stɑːlɪŋ] *n* estornino *m*.

starry ['stɑːrɪ] *adj* (starrier, starriest) estrellado,-a.

starry-eyed [stɑːrɪ'aɪd] *adj* (*idealistic*) idealista; (*in love*) enamorado,-a.

start [stɑːt] I *n* 1 (*beginning*) principio *m*,

comienzo *m; (of race)* salida *f;* **at the s.,** al principio; **for a s.,** para empezar; **from the s.,** desde el principio; **to make a fresh s.,** volver a empezar. 2 *(advantage)* ventaja *f.* 3 *(jump)* sobresalto *m.* **II** *vtr* 1 *(begin)* empezar, comenzar; **to s. doing sth,** empezar a hacer algo. 2 *(cause)* causar, provocar. 3 *(found)* fundar; **to s. a business,** montar un negocio. 4 *(set in motion)* arrancar. **III** *vi* 1 *(begin)* empezar, comenzar; *(engine)* arrancar; **starting from Monday,** a partir del lunes. 2 *(take fright)* asustarse, sobresaltarse. ◆**start off** *vi* 1 *(begin)* empezar; **to s. off by/with,** empezar por/con. 2 *(leave)* salir, ponerse en camino. ◆**start up** *vtr (engine)* arrancar. **II** *vi* empezar; *(car)* arrancar.

starter ['stɑːtər] *n* 1 *Sport (official)* juez *mf* de salida; *(competitor)* competidor,-a *m,f.* 2 *Aut* motor *m* de arranque. 3 *Culin fam* entrada *f.*

starting ['stɑːtɪŋ] *n* **s. block,** taco *m* de salida; **s. point,** punto *m* de partida; **s. post,** línea *f* de salida.

startle ['stɑːtəl] *vtr* asustar.

startling ['stɑːtlɪŋ] *adj* 1 *(frightening)* alarmante. 2 *(news etc)* asombroso,-a; *(coincidence)* extraordinario,-a.

starvation [stɑːˈveɪʃən] *n* hambre *f.*

starve [stɑːv] **I** *vtr* privar de comida; *fig* **he was starved of affection,** fue privado de cariño. **II** *vi* pasar hambre; **to s. to death,** morirse de hambre.

starving ['stɑːvɪŋ] *adj* hambriento,-a; *fam* **I'm s.!,** estoy muerto,-a de hambre.

state [steɪt] **I** *n* 1 estado *m;* **s. of emergency,** estado de emergencia; **s. of mind,** estado de ánimo; **to be in no fit s. to do sth,** no estar en condiciones de hacer algo; **the States,** los Estados Unidos; *US* **the S. Department,** el Ministerio de Asuntos Exteriores. **II** *adj* 1 *Pol* estatal; **s. education,** enseñanza pública; **s. ownership,** propiedad *f* del Estado. 2 *(ceremonial)* de gala; **s. visit,** visita *f* oficial. **III** *vtr* declarar, afirmar; *(case)* exponer; *(problem)* plantear.

stated ['steɪtɪd] *adj* indicado,-a.

stately ['steɪtlɪ] *adj (statelier, stateliest)* majestuoso,-a; **s. home,** casa solariega.

statement ['steɪtmənt] *n* 1 declaración *f;* **official s.,** comunicado *m* oficial; *Jur* **to make a s.,** prestar declaración. 2 *Fin* estado *m* de cuenta; **monthly s.,** balance *m* mensual.

statesman ['steɪtsmən] *n* estadista *m.*

static ['stætɪk] **I** *adj* estático,-a. **II** *n* *Rad* ruido.

station ['steɪʃən] **I** *n* 1 estación *f;* **s. wagon,** camioneta *f.* 2 *(position)* puesto *m.* 3 *(social standing)* rango *m.* **II** *vtr (place)* colocar; *Mil* apostar.

stationary ['steɪʃənərɪ] *adj (not moving)*

inmóvil; *(unchanging)* estacionario,-a.

stationer ['steɪʃənər] *n* papelero,-a *m,f;* **s.'s (shop),** papelería *f.*

stationery ['steɪʃənərɪ] *n (paper)* papel *m* de escribir; *(pens, ink etc)* artículos *mpl* de escritorio.

stationmaster ['steɪʃənmɑːstər] *n* jefe *m* de estación.

statistic [stəˈtɪstɪk] *n* estadística *f.*

statistical [stəˈtɪstɪkəl] *adj* estadístico,-a.

statistics [stəˈtɪstɪks] *npl (science)* estadística *f sing; (data)* estadísticas *fpl.*

statue ['stætjuː] *n* estatua *f.*

status ['steɪtəs] *n* estado *m;* **social s.,** estatus *m;* **s. symbol,** signo *m* de prestigio; **s. quo,** status quo *m.*

statute ['stætjuːt] *n* estatuto *m.*

statutory ['stætjʊtərɪ] *adj* reglamentario, -a; *(offence)* contemplado,-a por la ley; *(right)* legal; *(holiday)* oficial.

staunch [stɔːntʃ] *adj* incondicional, acérrimo.

stave [steɪv] *n* *Mus* pentagrama *m.* ◆**stave off** *vtr (repel)* rechazar; *(avoid)* evitar; *(delay)* aplazar.

stay¹ [steɪ] **I** *n* estancia *f.* **II** *vi* 1 *(remain)* quedarse, permanecer. 2 *(reside temporarily)* alojarse; **she's staying with us for a few days,** ha venido a pasar unos días con nosotros. **III** *vtr fig* **to s. the course,** aguantar hasta el final; **staying power,** resistencia *f.* ◆**stay in** *vi* quedarse en casa. ◆**stay on** *vi* quedarse. ◆**stay out** *vi* **to s. out all night,** no volver a casa en toda la noche. ◆**stay up** *vi* no acostarse.

stay² [steɪ] *n (rope)* estay *m,* viento *m.*

stead [sted] *n* **in sb's s.,** en lugar de algn; **to stand sb in good s.,** resultar muy útil a algn.

steadfast ['stedfəst, 'stedfɑːst] *adj* firme.

steady ['stedɪ] **I** *adj (steadier, steadiest)* firme, seguro,-a; *(gaze)* fijo,-a; *(prices)* estable; *(demand, speed)* constante; *(pace)* regular; *(worker)* aplicado,-a; **s. job,** empleo fijo. **II** *vtr (table etc)* estabilizar; *(nerves)* calmar. **III** *vi (market)* estabilizarse. ◆**steadily** *adv (improve)* constantemente; *(walk)* con paso seguro; *(gaze)* fijamente; *(rain, work)* sin parar.

steak [steɪk] *n* bistec *m.*

steal [stiːl] *(pt* **stole;** *pp* **stolen) I** *vtr* robar; **to s. a glance at sth,** echar una mirada furtiva a algo; **to s. the show,** llevarse todos los aplausos. **II** *vi* 1 *(rob)* robar. 2 *(move quietly)* moverse con sigilo; **to s. away,** escabullirse.

stealth [stelθ] *n* sigilo *m.*

stealthy ['stelθɪ] *adj (stealthier, stealthiest)* sigiloso,-a, furtivo,-a. ◆**stealthily** *adv* a hurtadillas.

steam [stiːm] **I** *n* vapor *m;* *fam* **to let off s.,** desahogarse; **s. engine,** máquina *f* de vapor. **II** *vtr* *Culin* cocer al vapor. **III** *vi* *(give off steam)* echar vapor; *(bowl of soup etc)* humear. ◆**steam up** *vi (window etc)* empañarse.

steamer |'sti:mər| *n Naut* vapor *m*.
steamroller |'sti:mrəʊlər| *n* apisonadora *f*.
steamship |'sti:mʃɪp| *n* vapor *m*.
steamy |'sti:mɪ| *adj (steamier, steamiest)* lleno,-a de vapor.
steel |sti:l| **I** *n* acero *m*; **s. industry**, industria siderúrgica. **II** *vtr fig* **to s. one-self to do sth**, armarse de valor para hacer algo.
steelworks |'sti:lwɜːks| *npl* acería *f sing*.
steep¹ |sti:p| *adj (hill etc)* empinado,-a; *fig (price, increase)* excesivo,-a.
steep² |sti:p| *vtr (washing)* remojar; *(food)* poner en remojo.
steeple |'sti:pəl| *n* aguja *f*.
steeplechase |'sti:pəltʃeɪs| *n* carrera *f* de obstáculos.
steer |stɪər| **I** *vtr* dirigir; *(car)* conducir; *(ship)* gobernar. **II** *vi (car)* conducirse; *fig* **to s. clear of sth**, evitar algo.
steering |'stɪərɪŋ| *n* dirección *f*; **assisted s.**, dirección asistida; **s. wheel**, volante *m*.
stem |stem| **I** *n* 1 *(of plant)* tallo *m*; *(of glass)* pie *m*; *(of pipe)* tubo *m*. 2 *(of word)* raíz *f*. **II** *vi* **to s. from**, derivarse de. **III** *vtr (blood)* restañar; *(flood, attack)* contener.
stench |stentʃ| *n* hedor *m*.
stencil |'stensəl| *n* 1 *(for artwork etc)* plantilla *f*. 2 *(for typing)* cliché *m*.
step |step| **I** *n* 1 paso *m*; *(sound)* paso, pisada *f*; **s. by s.**, poco a poco. 2 *(measure)* medida *f*; **a s. in the right direction**, un paso acertado. 3 *(stair)* peldaño *m*, escalón *m*. 4 **steps**, escalera *f*. **II** *vi* dar un paso; **s. this way, please**, haga el favor de pasar por aquí; **to s. aside**, apartarse. ◆**step down** *vi* dimitir. ◆**step forward** *vi (volunteer)* ofrecerse. ◆**step in** *vi* intervenir. ◆**step up** *vtr* aumentar.
stepbrother |'stepbrʌðər| *n* hermanastro *m*.
stepchild |'steptʃaɪld| *n* hijastro,-a *m,f*.
stepdaughter |'stepdɔ:tər| *n* hijastra *f*.
stepfather |'stepfɑ:ðər| *n* padrastro *m*.
stepladder |'steplædər| *n* escalera *f* de tijera.
stepmother |'stepmʌðər| *n* madrastra *f*.
stepping-stone |'stepɪŋstəʊn| *n* pasadera *f*; *fig* trampolín *m*.
stepsister |'stepsɪstər| *n* hermanastra *f*.
stepson |'stepsʌn| *n* hijastro *m*.
stereo |'sterɪəʊ| **I** *n* estéreo *m*. **II** *adj* estereo(fónico,-a.)
stereotype |'sterɪətaɪp| *n* estereotipo *m*.
sterile |'steraɪl| *adj (barren)* estéril.
sterilize |'sterɪlaɪz| *vtr* esterilizar.
sterling |'stɜːlɪŋ| **I** *n* libras *fpl* esterlinas; **s. silver**, plata *f* de ley; **the pound s.**, la

libra esterlina. **II** *adj (person, quality)* excelente.
stern¹ |stɜːn| *adj (severe)* severo,-a.
stern² |stɜːn| *n Naut* popa *f*.
steroid |'sterɔɪd| *n* esteroide *m*.
stethoscope |'steθəskəʊp| *n* estetoscopio *m*.
stew |stju:| **I** *n* estofado *m*, cocido *m*. **II** *vtr (meat)* guisar, estofar; *(fruit)* cocer.
steward |'stjuəd| *n (on estate)* administrador *m*; *(on ship)* camarero *m*; *(on plane)* auxiliar *m* de vuelo.
stewardess |'stjuədɪs| *n (on ship)* camarera *f*; *(on plane)* azafata *f*.
stick¹ |stɪk| *n* 1 palo *m*; *(walking stick)* bastón *m*; *(of dynamite)* cartucho *m*; *fam* **to give sb s.**, dar caña a algn. 2 *fam* **to live in the sticks**, vivir en el quinto pino.
stick² |stɪk| **I** *vtr (pt & pp stuck)* 1 *(push)* meter; *(knife)* clavar; **he stuck his head out of the window**, asomó la cabeza por la ventana. 2 *fam (put)* meter. 3 *(with glue etc)* pegar. 4 *fam (tolerate)* soportar, aguantar. **II** *vi* 1 *(become attached)* pegarse. 2 *(window, drawer)* atrancarse; *(machine part)* encasquillarse. ◆**stick at** *vtr* perseverar en. ◆**stick by** *vtr (friend)* ser fiel a; *(promise)* cumplir con. ◆**stick out** **I** *vi (project)* sobresalir; *(be noticeable)* resaltar. **II** *vtr (tongue)* sacar; *fig* **to s. one's neck out**, jugarse el tipo. ◆**stick to** *vtr (principles)* atenerse a. ◆**stick up** **I** *vi (project)* sobresalir; *(hair)* ponerse de punta. **II** *vtr* 1 *(poster)* fijar. 2 *(hand etc)* levantar. ◆**stick up for** *vtr* defender.
sticker |'stɪkər| *n (label)* etiqueta adhesiva; *(with slogan)* pegatina *f*.
stickler |'stɪklər| *n* meticuloso,-a; **to be a s. for detail**, ser muy detallista.
stick-up |'stɪkʌp| *n US fam* atraco *m*, asalto *m*.
sticky |'stɪkɪ| *adj (stickier, stickiest)* pegajoso,-a; *(label)* engomado,-a; *(weather)* bochornoso,-a; *fam (situation)* difícil.
stiff |stɪf| **I** *adj* 1 rígido,-a, tieso,-a; *(collar, lock)* duro,-a; *(joint)* entumecido,-a; *(machine part)* atascado,-a; **to have a s. neck**, tener tortícolis. 2 *fig (test)* difícil; *(punishment)* severo,-a; *(price)* excesivo,-a; *(drink)* fuerte; *(person) (unnatural)* estirado,-a. **II** *n* *fam (corpse)* fiambre *m*.
stiffen |'stɪfən| **I** *vtr* 1 *(fabric)* reforzar; *(collar)* almidonar; *fig (resistance)* fortalecer. **II** *vi (person)* ponerse tieso,-a; *(joints)* entumecerse; *fig (resistance)* fortalecerse.
stiffness |'stɪfnɪs| *n* rigidez *f*.
stifle |'staɪfəl| *vtr* sofocar; *(yawn)* reprimir. **II** *vi* ahogarse, sofocarse.
stifling |'staɪflɪŋ| *adj* sofocante, agobiante.
stigma |'stɪgmə| *n* estigma *m*.
stile |staɪl| *n* escalones *mpl* para pasar por encima de una valla.
stiletto |stɪ'letəʊ| *n* zapato *m* con tacón

de aguja.

still1 [stɪl] I *adv* 1 (*up to this time*) todavía, aún. 2 (*with comp adj & adv*) (*even*) aún; **s. colder**, aún más frío. 3 (*nonetheless*) no obstante, con todo. 4 (*however*) sin embargo. 5 (*motionless*) quieto; **to stand s.**, no moverse. II *adj* (*calm*) tranquilo,-a; (*peaceful*) sosegado,-a; (*silent*) silencioso,-a; (*motionless*) inmóvil. III *n Cin* fotograma *m*; *Art* **s. life**, naturaleza muerta. IV *vtr fml* (*fears etc*) calmar.

still2 [stɪl] *n* (*apparatus*) alambique *m*.

stillborn [ˈstɪlbɔːn] *adj* nacido,-a muerto,-a.

stillness [ˈstɪlnɪs] *n* calma *f*; (*silence*) silencio *m*.

stilt [stɪlt] *n* zanco *m*.

stilted [ˈstɪltɪd] *adj* afectado,-a.

stimulant [ˈstɪmjʊlənt] *n* estimulante *m*.

stimulate [ˈstɪmjʊleɪt] *vtr* estimular.

stimulating [ˈstɪmjʊleɪtɪŋ] *adj* estimulante.

stimulus [ˈstɪmjʊləs] *n* (*pl* **stimuli** [ˈstɪmjʊlaɪ]) estímulo *m*; *fig* incentivo *m*.

sting [stɪŋ] I *n* (*part of bee, wasp*) aguijón *m*; (*wound*) picadura *f*; (*burning*) escozor *m*; *fig* (*of remorse*) punzada *f*; *fig* (*of remark*) sarcasmo *m*. II *vtr* (*pt & pp* **stung**) picar; *fig* (*conscience*) remorder; *fig* (*remark*) herir en lo vivo. III *vi* picar.

stingy [ˈstɪndʒɪ] *adj* (**stingier, stingiest**) *fam* (*person*) tacaño,-a; (*amount*) escaso,-a; **to be s. with**, escatimar.

stink [stɪŋk] I *n* peste *m*, hedor *m*. II *vi* (*pt* **stank**; *pp* **stunk**) apestar, heder (**of**, a).

stinking [ˈstɪŋkɪŋ] I *adj* (*smelly*) apestoso,-a; *fam* **to have a s. cold**, tener un catarro bestial. II *adv fam* **he's s. rich**, está podrido de dinero.

stint [stɪnt] I *n* (*period*) período *m*, temporada *f*; (*shift*) turno *m*; **he did a two-year s. in the navy**, sirvió durante dos años en la Marina. II *vtr* escatimar.

stipulate [ˈstɪpjʊleɪt] *vtr* estipular.

stipulation [stɪpjʊˈleɪʃən] *n* estipulación *f*.

stir [stɜːr] I *n fig* revuelo *m*. II *vtr* 1 (*liquid*) remover. 2 (*move*) agitar. 3 *fig* (*curiosity, interest*) despertar; (*anger*) provocar. III *vi* (*move*) rebullirse. ◆**stir up** *vtr fig* (*memories, curiosity*) despertar; (*passions*) excitar; (*anger*) provocar; (*revolt*) fomentar.

stirring [ˈstɜːrɪŋ] *adj* conmovedor,-a.

stirrup [ˈstɪrəp] *n* estribo *m*.

stitch [stɪtʃ] I *n* 1 *Sew* puntada *f*; (*in knitting*) punto *m*; *Med* punto (de sutura); *fam* **we were in stitches**, nos tronchábamos de risa. 2 (*pain*) punzada *f*. II *vtr Sew* coser; *Med* suturar, dar puntos a.

stoat [stəʊt] *n* armiño *m*.

stock [stɒk] I *n* 1 (*supply*) reserva *f*; *Com* (*goods*) existencias *fpl*, stock *m*; (*selection*) surtido *m*; **out of s.**, agotado,-a; **to have sth in s.**, tener existencias de algo; *fig* **to take s. of**, evaluar. 2 *Fin* capital *m* social; **stocks and shares**, acciones *fpl*, valores *mpl*; **S. Exchange**, Bolsa *f* (de valores); **s. market**, bolsa. 3 *Agr* ganado *m*; **s. farming**, ganadería *f*. 4 *Culin* caldo *m*; **s. cube**, cubito *m* de caldo. 5 (*descent*) estirpe *f*. II *adj* 1 (*goods*) corriente. 2 (*excuse, response*) de siempre; (*phrase*) gastado,-a. III *vtr* 1 (*have in stock*) tener existencias de. 2 (*provide*) abastecer, surtir (**with**, de); (*cupboard*) llenar (**with**, de). ◆**stock up** *vi* abastecerse (**on**, with, de).

stockbroker [ˈstɒkbrəʊkər] *n* corredor,-a *m,f* de Bolsa.

stockholder [ˈstɒkhəʊldər] *n US* accionista *mf*.

stocking [ˈstɒkɪŋ] *n* media *f*; **a pair of stockings**, unas medias.

stockist [ˈstɒkɪst] *n* distribuidor,-a *m,f*.

stockpile [ˈstɒkpaɪl] I *n* reservas *fpl*. II *vtr* almacenar; (*accumulate*) acumular.

stocks [stɒks] *npl Hist* cepo *m sing*.

stocktaking [ˈstɒkteɪkɪŋ] *n Com* inventario *m*.

stocky [ˈstɒkɪ] *adj* (**stockier, stockiest**) (*squat*) rechoncho,-a; (*heavily built*) fornido,-a.

stodgy [ˈstɒdʒɪ] *adj* (**stodgier, stodgiest**) (*food*) indigesto,-a; *fig* (*book, person*) pesado,-a.

stoical [ˈstəʊɪkəl] *adj* estoico,-a.

stoke [stəʊk] *vtr* (*poke*) atizar; **to s. (up)**, (*feed*) alimentar.

stole1 [stəʊl] *pt* → **steal**.

stole2 [stəʊl] *n* estola *f*.

stolen [ˈstəʊlən] *pp* → **steal**.

stolid [ˈstɒlɪd] *adj* impasible.

stomach [ˈstʌmək] I *n* estómago *m*; **s. ache**, dolor *m* de estómago; **s. upset**, trastorno gástrico. II *vtr fig* aguantar.

stone [stəʊn] I *n* 1 piedra *f*; (*on grave*) lápida *f*; *fig* **at a s.'s throw**, a tiro de piedra. 2 *Med* cálculo *m*. 3 (*of fruit*) hueso *m*. 4 (*weight*) aprox 6.348 kg. II *adj* de piedra; **the S. Age**, la Edad de Piedra. III *vtr* (*kill*) lapidar.

stone-cold [stəʊnˈkəʊld] *adj* helado,-a.

stoned [stəʊnd] *adj sl* (*drugged*) colocado,-a; (*drunk*) como una cuba.

stone-deaf [stəʊnˈdef] *adj* sordo,-a como una tapia.

stonework [ˈstəʊnwɜːk] *n* mampostería *f*.

stony [ˈstəʊnɪ] *adj* (**stonier, stoniest**) (*ground*) pedregoso,-a; *fig* (*look, silence*) glacial.

stood [stʊd] *pt & pp* → **stand**.

stool [stuːl] *n* 1 (*seat*) taburete *m*. 2 *Med* heces *fpl*.

stoop [stuːp] *vi* 1 (*have a stoop*) andar encorvado,-a. 2 (*bend*) inclinarse, aga-

charse (**down**, -). **3** *fig* **to s. to**, rebajarse
a; **he wouldn't s. so low**, no se rebajaría
tanto.

stop [stɒp] **I** *n* **1** (*halt*) parada *f*, alto *m*;
to come to a s., pararse; **to put a s. to
sth**, poner fin a algo. **2** (*break*) pausa *f*;
(*for refuelling etc*) escala *f*. **3** (*for bus,
tram*) parada *f*. **4** (*punctuation mark*)
punto *m*. **II** *vtr* **1** (*halt*) parar;
interrumpir; (*pain, abuse etc*) poner fin a.
2 (*payments*) suspender; (*cheque*) anular. **3**
s. singing, deja de cantar; **s. it!**, ¡basta
ya! **4** (*prevent*) evitar; **to s. sb from doing
sth**, impedir a algn hacer algo. **5** (*hole*)
tapar; (*gap*) rellenar. **III** *vi* **1** (*person,
moving vehicle*) pararse, detenerse; **my
watch has stopped**, se me ha parado el
reloj; **to s. dead**, pararse en seco. **2**
(*cease*) acabarse, terminar. **3** *fam* (*stay*)
pararse. ◆**stop by** *vi fam* visitar.
◆**stop off** *vi* pararse un rato. ◆**stop
over** *vi* (*spend the night*) pasar la noche;
(*for refuelling etc*) hacer escala. ◆**stop
up** *vtr* (*hole*) tapar.

stopgap ['stɒpgæp] *n* (*thing*) medida *f*
provisional; (*person*) sustituto,-a *m,f*.

stopover ['stɒpəʊvər] *n* parada *f*; *Av*
escala *f*.

stoppage ['stɒpɪdʒ] *n* **1** (*of game, payments*) suspensión *f*; (*of work*) paro *m*;
(*strike*) huelga *f*; (*deduction*) deducción *f*.
2 (*blockage*) obstrucción *f*.

stopper ['stɒpər] *n* tapón *m*.

stop-press [stɒp'pres] *n* noticias *fpl* de
última hora.

stopwatch ['stɒpwɒtʃ] *n* cronómetro *m*.

storage ['stɔ:rɪdʒ] *n* almacenaje *m*, almacenamiento *m*; **s. battery**, acumulador *m*;
s. heater, placa acumuladora.

store [stɔ:r] **I** *n* **1** (*stock*) provisión *f*; *fig*
(*of wisdom*) reserva *f*. **2** **stores**, víveres
mpl. **3** (*warehouse*) almacén *m*. **4** *US*
(*shop*) tienda *f*; **department s.**, gran
almacén *m*. **II** *vtr* **1** (*furniture, computer
data*) almacenar; (*keep*) guardar. **2** **to s.**
(**up**), acumular.

storekeeper ['stɔ:ki:pər] *n US* tendero,-a
m,f.

storeroom ['stɔ:ru:m] *n* despensa *f*.

storey ['stɔ:rɪ] *n* piso *m*.

stork [stɔ:k] *n* cigüeña *f*.

storm [stɔ:m] **I** *n* tormenta *f*; (*with wind*)
vendaval *m*; *fig* (*uproar*) revuelo *m*; *fig* **she
has taken New York by s.**, ha cautivado
a todo Nueva York. **II** *vtr* tomar por
asalto. **III** *vi* (*with rage*) echar pestes.

stormy ['stɔ:mɪ] *adj* (**stormier, stormiest**)
(*weather*) tormentoso,-a; *fig* (*discussion*)
acalorado,-a; (*relationship*) tempestuoso,-a.

story¹ ['stɔ:rɪ] *n* historia *f*; (*tale, account*)
relato *m*; (*article*) artículo *m*; (*plot*) trama
f; (*joke*) chiste *m*; (*rumour*) rumor *m*; **it's
a long s.**, sería largo de contar; **tall s.**,

cuento chino.

story² ['stɔ:rɪ] *n US* → **storey.**

storybook ['stɔ:rɪbʊk] *n* libro *m* de
cuentos.

storyteller ['stɔ:rɪtelər] *n* cuentista *mf*.

stout [staʊt] **I** *adj* **1** (*fat*) gordo,-a,
corpulento,-a. **2** (*strong*) fuerte. **3** (*brave*)
valiente; (*determined*) firme. **II** *n* (*beer*)
cerveza negra. ◆**stoutly** *adv* resueltamente.

stove¹ [stəʊv] *n* **1** (*for heating*) estufa *f*. **2**
(*cooker*) cocina *f*.

stow [stəʊ] *vtr* **1** (*cargo*) estibar. **2** (*put
away*) guardar. ◆**stow away** *vi* (*on
ship, plane*) viajar de polizón.

stowaway ['stəʊəweɪ] *n* polizón *mf*.

straddle ['strædəl] *vtr* **1** (*horse etc*)
sentarse a horcajadas sobre. **2** *fig* (*embrace*) abarcar.

straggle ['strægəl] *vi* **1** (*lag behind*) rezagarse. **2** (*spread untidily*) desparramarse.

straggler ['stræglər] *n* rezagado,-a *m,f*.

straight [streɪt] **I** *adj* **1** (*not bent*) recto,-a,
derecho,-a; (*hair*) liso,-a; **to keep a s.
face**, contener la risa. **2** **I work eight
hours s.**, trabajo ocho horas seguidas. **3**
(*honest*) honrado,-a; (*answer*) sincero,-a;
(*refusal*) rotundo,-a; **let's get things s.**,
pongamos las cosas claras. **4** (*drink*)
solo,-a, sin mezcla. **II** *adv* **1** (*in a straight
line*) en línea recta. **2** (*directly*) directamente, derecho; **keep s. ahead**, sigue
todo recto; **she walked s. in**, entró sin
llamar. **3** **s. away**, en seguida; **s. off**, en
el acto. **4** (*frankly*) francamente. **III** *n GB
Sport* **the home s.**, la recta final.

straighten ['streɪtən] *vtr* (*sth bent*) enderezar, poner derecho,-a; (*tie, picture*) poner bien; (*hair*) alisar. ◆**straighten out**
vtr (*problem*) resolver.

straightforward [streɪt'fɔ:wəd] *adj* **1**
(*honest*) honrado,-a; (*sincere*) franco,-a. **2**
GB (*simple*) sencillo,-a.

strain¹ [streɪn] **I** *vtr* **1** (*rope etc*) estirar;
fig crear tensiones en. **2** *Med* torcer(se);
(*eyes, voice*) forzar; (*heart*) cansar. **3** (*liquid*) filtrar; (*vegetables, tea*) colar. **II** *vi*
(*pull*) tirar (**at**, de); *fig* **to s. to do sth**,
esforzarse por hacer algo. **III** *n* **1** tensión
f; (*effort*) esfuerzo *m*. **2** (*exhaustion*) agotamiento *m*. **3** *Med* torcedura *f*. **4** *Mus*
strains, son *m sing*.

strain² [streɪn] *n* **1** (*breed*) raza *f*. **2**
(*streak*) vena *f*.

strained ['streɪnd] **II** *adj* **1** (*muscle*)
torcido,-a; (*eyes*) cansado,-a; (*voice*)
forzado,-a. **2** (*atmosphere*) tenso,-a.

strainer ['streɪnər] *n* colador *m*.

strait [streɪt] *n* **1** (*usu pl*) *Geog* estrecho *m*.
2 (*usu pl*) (*difficulty*) aprieto *m*; **in dire
straits**, en un gran aprieto.

straitjacket ['streɪtdʒækɪt] *n* camisa *f* de
fuerza.

strait-laced [streɪt'leɪst] *adj* remilgado,-a.

strand¹ [strænd] *vtr fig (person)* abandonar; **to leave stranded,** dejar plantado,-a.

strand² [strænd] *n (of thread)* hebra *f*; *(of hair)* pelo *m*.

strange [streɪndʒ] *adj* 1 *(unknown)* desconocido,-a; *(unfamiliar)* nuevo,-a. 2 *(odd)* raro,-a, extraño,-a.

stranger ['streɪndʒər] *n (unknown person)* desconocido,-a *m,f*; *(outsider)* forastero,-a *m,f*.

strangle ['stræŋgəl] *vtr* estrangular.

stranglehold ['stræŋgəlhəʊld] *n* **to have a s. on sb,** tener a algn agarrado,-a por el cuello.

strangulation [stræŋgjʊ'leɪʃən] *n* estrangulación *f*.

strap [stræp] **I** *n (of leather)* correa *f*; *(on bag)* bandolera *f*; *(on dress)* tirante *m*. **II** *vtr* atar con correa.

strapping ['stræpɪŋ] *adj fam* fornido,-a, robusto,-a.

strategic [strə'tiːdʒɪk] *adj* estratégico,-a.

strategy ['strætɪdʒɪ] *n* estrategia *f*.

stratosphere ['strætəsfɪər] *n* estratosfera *f*.

stratum ['strɑːtəm] *n (pl strata)* estrato *m*.

straw [strɔː] *n* 1 paja *f*; *fig* **to clutch at straws,** agarrarse a un clavo ardiente; *fam* **that's the last s.!,** ¡eso ya es el colmo! 2 *(for drinking)* pajita *f*.

strawberry ['strɔːbərɪ] *n* fresa *f*; *(large)* fresón *m*.

stray [streɪ] **I** *vi (from path)* desviarse; *(get lost)* extraviarse. **II** *n* animal extraviado. **III** *adj (bullet)* perdido,-a; *(animal)* callejero,-a.

streak [striːk] **I** *n* 1 *(line)* raya *f*; **s. of lightning,** rayo *m*. 2 *(in hair)* reflejo *m*. 3 *fig (of genius etc)* vena *f*; *(of luck)* racha *f*. **II** *vtr* rayar **(with,** de). **III** *vi* **to s. past,** pasar como un rayo.

stream [striːm] **I** *n* 1 *(brook)* arroyo *m*, riachuelo *m*. 2 *(current)* corriente *f*. 3 *(of water, air)* flujo *m*; *(of tears)* torrente *m*; *(of blood)* chorro *m*; *(of light)* raudal *m*. 4 *fig (of abuse)* sarta *f*; *(of people)* oleada *f*. 3 *GB Educ* clase *f*. **II** *vtr GB Educ* poner en grupos. **III** *vi* 1 *(liquid)* correr. 2 *fig* **to s. in/out/past,** *(people etc)* entrar/salir/pasar en tropel. 3 *(hair, banner)* ondear.

streamer ['striːmər] *n (paper ribbon)* serpentina *f*.

streamlined ['striːmlaɪnd] *adj* 1 *(car)* aerodinámico,-a. 2 *(system, method)* racionalizado,-a.

street [striːt] *n* calle *f*; **the man in the s.,** el hombre de la calle; **s. map, s. plan,** (plano *m*) callejero *m*.

streetcar ['striːtkɑːr] *n US* tranvía *m*.

streetlamp ['striːtlæmp] *n* farol *m*.

streetwise ['striːtwaɪz] *adj* espabilado,-a.

strength [streŋθ] *n* 1 fuerza *f*; *(of rope etc)* resistencia *f*; *(of emotion, colour)* intensi-

dad *f*; *(of alcohol)* graduación *f*. 2 *(power)* poder *m*; **on the s. of,** a base de. 3 *(ability)* punto *m* fuerte. 4 **to be at full s./below s.,** tener/no tener completo el cupo.

strengthen ['streŋθən] **I** *vtr* 1 reforzar; *(character)* fortalecer. 2 *(intensify)* intensificar. **II** *vi* 1 *(gen)* reforzarse. 2 *(intensify)* intensificarse.

strenuous ['strenjʊəs] *adj* 1 *(denial)* enérgico,-a; *(effort, life)* intenso,-a. 2 *(exhausting)* fatigoso,-a, cansado,-a.

stress [stres] **I** *n* 1 *Tech* tensión *f*. 2 *Med* estrés *m*. 3 *(emphasis)* hincapié *m*; *(on word)* acento *m*. **II** *vtr* 1 *(emphasize)* subrayar; *(word)* acentuar.

stretch [stretʃ] **I** *vtr (elastic)* estirar; *(wings)* desplegar. **II** *vi (elastic)* estirarse; *fig* **my money won't s. to it,** mi dinero no me llegará para eso. **III** *n* 1 *(length)* trecho *m*, tramo *m*. 2 *(of land)* extensión *f*; *(of time)* intervalo *m*. ◆**stretch out I** *vtr (arm, hand)* alargar; *(legs)* estirar. **II** *vi* 1 *(person)* estirarse. 2 *(countryside, years etc)* extenderse.

stretcher ['stretʃər] *n* camilla *f*.

strew [struː] *vtr (pt strewed; pp strewed or strewn* [struːn]) esparcir.

stricken ['strɪkən] *adj (with grief)* afligido,-a; *(with illness)* aquejado,-a; *(by disaster etc)* afectado,-a; *(damaged)* dañado,-a.

strict [strɪkt] *adj* 1 estricto,-a. 2 *(absolute)* absoluto,-a. ◆**strictly** *adv* 1 *(categorically)* terminantemente. 2 *(precisely)* estrictamente; **s. speaking,** en sentido estricto.

stride [straɪd] **I** *n* zancada *f*, tranco *m*; *fig (progress)* progresos *mpl*. **II** *vi (pt strode; pp stridden* ['strɪdən]) **to s. (along),** andar a zancadas.

strident ['straɪdənt] *adj (voice, sound)* estridente; *(protest etc)* enérgico,-a.

strife [straɪf] *n* conflictos *mpl*.

strike [straɪk] **I** *vtr (pt & pp struck)* 1 *(hit)* pegar, golpear. 2 *(collide with)* chocar contra; *(bullet, lightning)* alcanzar. 3 *(match)* encender. 4 *(pose)* adoptar. 5 *(bargain)* cerrar; *(balance)* encontrar. 6 **the clock struck three,** el reloj dio las tres. 7 *(oil, gold)* descubrir; *fam* **to s. it lucky/rich,** tener suerte/hacerse rico,-a. 8 *(impress)* impresionar; **it strikes me ...,** me parece .... **II** *vi (pt & pp struck)* 1 *(attack)* atacar; *(disaster)* sobrevenir. 2 *(clock)* dar la hora. 3 *(workers)* declararse en huelga. **III** *n* 1 *(by workers)* huelga *f*; **on s.,** en huelga; **to call a s.,** convocar una huelga. 2 *(of oil, gold)* descubrimiento *m*. 3 *(blow)* golpe *m*. 4 *Mil* ataque *m*. ◆**strike back** *vi* devolver el golpe. ◆**strike down** *vtr* fulminar, abatir. ◆**strike out I** *vtr (cross out)* tachar. **II** *vi* **to s. out at sb,** arremeter contra algn.

◆**strike up** vtr 1 (friendship) trabar; (conversation) entablar. 2 (tune) empezar a tocar.

striker ['straɪkər] n 1 (worker) huelguista mf. 2 fam Ftb marcador,-a m,f.

striking ['straɪkɪŋ] adj (eye-catching) llamativo,-a; (noticeable) notable; (impressive) impresionante.

string [strɪŋ] I n 1 (cord) cuerda f; fig to **pull strings for sb**, enchufar a algn; s. **bean**, judía f verde. 2 (of events) cadena f; (of lies) sarta f. 3 (of racket, guitar) cuerda f; Mus **the strings**, los instrumentos de cuerda. II vtr (pt & pp **strung**) 1 (beads) ensartar. 2 (racket etc) encordar. 3 (beans) quitar la hebra a.

stringent ['strɪndʒənt] adj severo,-a, estricto,-a.

strip¹ [strɪp] I vtr 1 (person) desnudar; (bed) quitar la ropa de; (paint) quitar. 2 Tech to s. **(down)**, desmontar. II vi (undress) desnudarse; (perform striptease) hacer un striptease. ◆**strip off** I vtr quitar. II vi (undress) desnudarse.

strip² [strɪp] n tira f; (of land) franja f; (of metal) fleje m; s. **cartoon**, historieta f; s. **lighting**, alumbrado m fluorescente; to **tear sb off a s.**, echar una bronca a algn.

stripe [straɪp] n raya f; Mil galón m.

striped [straɪpt] adj rayado,-a, a rayas.

stripper ['strɪpər] n persona f que hace striptease.

strive [straɪv] vi (pt **strove**; pp **striven** ['strɪvən]) to s. **to do sth**, esforzarse por hacer algo.

strobe [strəʊb] n s. **lighting**, luces estroboscópicas.

strode [strəʊd] pt → **stride**.

stroke [strəʊk] I n 1 a s. **of luck**, un golpe de suerte. 2 (in golf, cricket) golpe m; (rowing) remada f; Swimming brazada f. 3 (of pen) trazo m; (of brush) pincelada f. 4 (caress) caricia f. 5 Med apoplejía f. II vtr acariciar.

stroll [strəʊl] I vi dar un paseo. II n paseo m.

stroller ['strəʊlər] n US (for baby) cochecito m.

strong [strɒŋ] I adj 1 fuerte. 2 (durable) sólido,-a. 3 (firm, resolute) firme. 4 (colour) intenso,-a; (light) brillante. 5 (incontestable) convincente. **6 to be 20 s.**, contar con 20 miembros. II adv fuerte; to **be going . s.**, (business) ir fuerte; (elderly person) conservarse bien. ◆**strongly** adv fuertemente.

strongbox ['strɒŋbɒks] n caja f fuerte.

stronghold ['strɒŋhəʊld] n Mil fortaleza f; fig baluarte m.

strongroom ['strɒŋruːm] n cámara acorazada.

stroppy ['strɒpɪ] adj (**stroppier**, **stroppiest**) GB fam de mala uva.

strove [strəʊv] pt → **strive**.

struck [strʌk] pt & pp → **strike**.

structural ['strʌktʃərəl] adj estructural.

structure ['strʌktʃər] n estructura f; (constructed thing) construcción f; (building) edificio m.

struggle ['strʌgəl] I vi luchar. II n lucha f; (physical fight) pelea f.

strum [strʌm] vtr (guitar) rasguear.

strung [strʌŋ] pt & pp → **string**.

strut [strʌt] vi pavonearse.

stub [stʌb] I n (of cigarette) colilla f; (of pencil) cabo m; (of cheque) matriz f. II vtr 1 (strike) golpear. 2 to s. **(out)**, apagar.

stubble ['stʌbəl] n (in field) rastrojo m; (on chin) barba f de tres días.

stubborn ['stʌbən] adj 1 terco,-a, testarudo,-a. 2 (stain) difícil. 3 (refusal) rotundo,-a.

stucco ['stʌkəʊ] n estuco m.

stuck [stʌk] pt & pp → **stick²**.

stuck-up [stʌk'ʌp] adj fam creído,-a.

stud¹ [stʌd] n 1 (on clothing) tachón m; (on football boots) taco m; (on shirt) botonadura f. II vtr (decorate) tachonar (**with**, de); fig (dot, cover) salpicar (**with**, de).

stud² [stʌd] n (horse) semental m.

student ['stjuːdənt] n estudiante mf; s. **teacher**, profesor,-a m,f en prácticas.

studio ['stjuːdɪəʊ] n TV Cin estudio m; (artist's) taller m; s. **apartment**, s. **flat**, estudio.

studious ['stjuːdɪəs] adj estudioso,-a. ◆**studiously** adv cuidadosamente.

study ['stʌdɪ] I vtr estudiar; (facts etc) examinar, investigar; (behaviour) observar. II vi estudiar; to s. **to be a doctor**, estudiar para médico. III n 1 estudio m; s. **group**, grupo m de trabajo. 2 (room) despacho m, estudio m.

stuff [stʌf] I vtr (container) llenar (**with**, de); Culin rellenar (**with**, con or de); (animal) disecar. 2 (cram) atiborrar (**with**, de). II n 1 fam (material) material m. 2 fam (things) cosas fpl; fam trastos mpl.

stuffing ['stʌfɪŋ] n Culin relleno m.

stuffy ['stʌfɪ] adj (**stuffier**, **stuffiest**) 1 (room) mal ventilado,-a; (atmosphere) cargado,-a. 2 (pompous) estirado,-a; (narrow-minded) de miras estrechas.

stumble ['stʌmbəl] vi tropezar, dar un traspié; fig to s. **across** or **on** or **upon**, tropezar or dar con.

stumbling ['stʌmblɪŋ] n s. **block**, escollo m.

stump [stʌmp] I n 1 (of pencil) cabo m; (of tree) tocón m; (of arm, leg) muñón m. 2 (in cricket) estaca f. II vtr (puzzle) confundir; to **be stumped**, estar perplejo,-a.

stun [stʌn] vtr (of blow) aturdir; fig (of news etc) sorprender.

stung [stʌŋ] pt & pp → **sting**.

stunk [stʌŋk] pt & pp → **stink**.

stunning ['stʌnɪŋ] adj (blow) duro,-a;

(news) sorprendente; *fam (woman, outfit)* fenomenal.

stunt¹ ['stʌnt] *vtr (growth)* atrofiar.

stunt² [stʌnt] *n* **1** *Av* acrobacia *f*. **2** publicity s., truco publicitario. **3** *Cin* escena peligrosa; **s. man**, doble *m*.

stunted ['stʌntɪd] *adj* enano,-a, mal desarrollado,-a.

stupefy ['stju:pɪfaɪ] *vtr (alcohol, drugs)* aturdir; *fig (news etc)* dejar pasmado,-a.

stupendous [stju:'pendəs] *adj (wonderful)* estupendo,-a.

stupid ['stju:pɪd] *adj* estúpido,-a, imbécil.

stupidity [stju:'pɪdɪtɪ] *n* estupidez *f*.

stupor ['stju:pər] *n* estupor *m*.

sturdy ['stɜ:dɪ] *adj (sturdier, sturdiest)* robusto,-a, fuerte; *(resistance)* enérgico,-a.

stutter ['stʌtər] **I** *vi* tartamudear. **II** *n* tartamudeo *m*.

sty [staɪ] *n (pen)* pocilga *f*.

sty(e) [staɪ] *n Med* orzuelo *m*.

style [staɪl] **I** *n* **1** estilo *m*; *(of dress)* modelo *m*. **2** *(fashion)* moda *f*. **3** **to live in s.**, *(elegance)* vivir a lo grande. **II** *vtr (hair)* marcar.

stylish ['staɪlɪʃ] *adj* con estilo.

stylist ['staɪlɪst] *n (hairdresser)* peluquero,-a *mf*.

stylus ['staɪləs] *n (of record player)* aguja *f*.

suave [swɑ:v] *adj* amable, afable; *pej* zalamero,-a.

sub [sʌb] *n fam* **1** *abbr of* **substitute**. **2** *abbr of* **subscription**.

sub- [sʌb] *pref* sub-.

subconscious [sʌb'kɒnʃəs] **I** *adj* subconsciente. **II** *n* **the s.**, el subconsciente.

subcontract [sʌbkən'trækt] *vtr* subcontratar.

subcontractor [sʌbkən'træktər] *n* subcontratista *mf*.

subdivide [sʌbdɪ'vaɪd] *vtr* subdividir *(into, en)*.

subdue [səb'dju:] *vtr* **1** *(nation, people)* sojuzgar. **2** *(feelings)* dominar. **3** *(colour, light)* atenuar.

subdued [səb'dju:d] *adj* **1** *(person, emotion)* callado,-a. **2** *(voice, tone)* bajo,-a. **3** *(light)* tenue; *(colour)* apagado,-a.

subject ['sʌbdʒɪkt] **I** *n* **1** *(citizen)* súbdito *m*. **2** *(topic)* tema *m*; **s. matter**, materia *f*; *(contents)* contenido *m*. **3** *Educ* asignatura *f*. **4** *Ling* sujeto *m*. **II** *adj* **s. to**, *(law, tax)* sujeto,-a a; *(charge)* expuesto,-a a; *(changes, delays)* susceptible de; *(illness)* propenso,-a a; *(conditional upon)* previo, -a. **III** [səb'dʒekt] *vtr* someter.

subjective [səb'dʒektɪv] *adj* subjetivo,-a.

subjunctive [səb'dʒʌŋktɪv] **I** *adj* subjuntivo,-a. **II** *n* subjuntivo *m*.

sublet [sʌb'let] *vtr & vi* subarrendar.

sublime [sə'blaɪm] *adj* sublime.

sub-machine-gun [sʌbmə'ʃi:ngʌn] *n* ametralladora *f*.

submarine ['sʌbməri:n] *n* submarino *m*.

submerge [səb'mɜ:dʒ] *vtr* sumergir; *(flood)* inundar; *fig* **submerged in ...**, sumido,-a en ....

submission [səb'mɪʃən] *n* **1** *(yielding)* sumisión *f*. **2** *(of documents)* presentación *f*. **3** *(report)* informe *m*.

submissive [səb'mɪsɪv] *adj* sumiso,-a.

submit [səb'mɪt] **I** *vtr* **1** *(present)* presentar. **2** *(subject)* someter **(to, a)**. **II** *vi (surrender)* rendirse.

subnormal [sʌb'nɔ:məl] *adj* subnormal.

subordinate [sə'bɔ:dɪnɪt] *adj & n* subordinado,-a *(m,f)*.

subpoena [səb'pi:nə] **I** *n* citación *f*. **II** *vtr* citar.

subscribe [səb'skraɪb] *vi (magazine)* suscribirse **(to, a)**; *(opinion, theory)* adherirse **(to, a)**.

subscriber [səb'skraɪbər] *n* abonado,-a *m,f*.

subscription [səb'skrɪpʃən] *n (to magazine)* abono *m*; *(to club)* cuota *f*.

subsequent ['sʌbsɪkwənt] *adj* subsiguiente. ◆**subsequently** *adv* posteriormente.

subside [səb'saɪd] *vi (land)* hundirse; *(floodwater)* bajar; *(wind, anger)* amainar.

subsidence [səb'saɪdəns] *n (of land)* hundimiento *m*; *(of floodwater)* bajada *f*; *(of wind)* amaine *m*.

subsidiary [sʌb'sɪdɪərɪ] **I** *adj (role)* secundario,-a. **II** *n Com* sucursal *f*, filial *f*.

subsidize ['sʌbsɪdaɪz] *vtr* subvencionar.

subsidy ['sʌbsɪdɪ] *n* subvención *f*.

subsistence [səb'sɪstəns] *n* subsistencia *f*.

substance ['sʌbstəns] *n* **1** sustancia *f*. **2** *(essence)* esencia *f*. **3** **a woman of s.**, *(wealth)* una mujer acaudalada.

substantial [səb'stænʃəl] *adj* **1** *(solid)* sólido,-a. **2** *(sum, loss)* importante; *(difference, improvement)* notable; *(meal)* abundante.

substantiate [səb'stænʃɪeɪt] *vtr* respaldar.

substitute ['sʌbstɪtju:t] **I** *vtr* sustituir; **to s. X for Y**, sustituir X por Y. **II** *n (person)* suplente *mf*; *(thing)* sucedáneo *m*.

subtitle ['sʌbtaɪtəl] *n* subtítulo *m*.

subtle ['sʌtəl] *adj* sutil; *(taste)* delicado,-a; *(remark)* ingenioso,-a; *(irony)* fino,-a.

subtlety ['sʌtəltɪ] *n* sutileza *f*; *(of remark)* ingeniosidad *f*; *(of irony, joke)* finura *f*.

subtract [səb'trækt] *vtr* restar.

subtraction [səb'trækʃən] *n* resta *f*.

suburb ['sʌbɜ:b] *n* barrio periférico; **the suburbs**, las afueras.

suburban [sə'bɜ:bən] *adj* suburbano,-a.

suburbia [sə'bɜ:bɪə] *n* barrios residenciales periféricos.

subversive [səb'vɜ:sɪv] *adj & n* subversivo,-a *(m,f)*.

subway ['sʌbweɪ] *n* **1** *GB (underpass)* paso subterráneo. **2** *US (underground railway)* metro *m*.

succeed |sək'si:d| I *vi* 1 *(person)* tener éxito; *(plan)* salir bien; **to s. in doing sth**, conseguir hacer algo. 2 *(follow after)* suceder; **to s. to**, *(throne)* suceder a. II *vtr (monarch)* suceder a.

succeeding |sək'si:dɪŋ| *adj* sucesivo,-a.

success |sək'ses| *n* éxito *m*.

successful |sək'sesful| *adj* de éxito, exitoso,-a; *(business)* próspero,-a; *(marriage)* feliz; **to be s. in doing sth**, lograr hacer algo. ◆**successfully** *adv* con éxito.

succession |sək'seʃən| *n* sucesión *f*, serie *f*; **in s.**, sucesivamente.

successive |sək'sesɪv| *adj* sucesivo,-a, consecutivo,-a.

successor |sək'sesər| *n* sucesor,-a *m,f*.

succinct |sək'sɪŋkt| *adj* sucinto,-a.

succumb |sə'kʌm| *vi* sucumbir (**to**, a).

such |sʌtʃ| I *adj* 1 *(of that sort)* tal, semejante; **artists s. as Monet**, artistas como Monet; **at s. and s. a time**, a tal hora; **in s. a way that**, de tal manera que. 2 *(so much, so great)* tanto,-a; **he's always in s. a hurry**, siempre anda con tanta prisa; **she was in s. pain**, sufría tanto; **s. a lot of books**, tantos libros. II *adv (so very)* tan; **it's s. a long time ago**, hace tanto tiempo; **she's s. a clever woman**, es una mujer tan inteligente; **we had s. good weather**, hizo un tiempo tan bueno.

suchlike |'sʌtʃlaɪk| I *adj* tal. II *n (things)* cosas *fpl* por el estilo; *(people)* gente *f* por el estilo.

suck |sʌk| I *vtr (by pump)* aspirar; *(liquid)* sorber; *(lollipop, blood)* chupar. II *vi (person)* chupar; *(baby)* mamar. ◆**suck in** *vtr (of whirlpool)* tragar.

sucker |'sʌkər| *n* 1 *fam* primo,-a *m,f*, bobo,-a *m,f*. 2 *Zool* ventosa *f*; *Bot* chupón *m*.

suckle |'sʌkəl| *vtr (mother)* amamantar.

suction |'sʌkʃən| *n* succión *f*.

sudden |'sʌdən| *adj* 1 *(hurried)* súbito,-a, repentino,-a. 2 *(unexpected)* imprevisto,-a. 3 *(abrupt)* brusco,-a; **all of a s.**, de repente. ◆**suddenly** *adv* de repente.

suds |sʌdz| *npl* espuma *f* de jabón, jabonaduras *fpl*.

sue |su:, sju:| *Jur* I *vtr* demandar. II *vi* presentar una demanda; **to s. for divorce**, solicitar el divorcio.

suede |sweɪd| *n* ante *m*, gamuza *f*; *(for gloves)* cabritilla *f*.

suet |'su:ɪt| *n* sebo *m*.

suffer |'sʌfər| I *vtr* 1 sufrir. 2 *(tolerate)* aguantar, soportar. II *vi* sufrir; **to s. from**, sufrir de.

sufferer |'sʌfərər| *n Med* enfermo,-a *m,f*.

suffering |'sʌfərɪŋ| *n (affliction)* sufrimiento *m*; *(pain, torment)* dolor *m*.

suffice |sə'faɪs| *vi fml* bastar, ser suficiente.

sufficient |sə'fɪʃənt| *adj* suficiente,

bastante. ◆**sufficiently** *adv* suficientemente, bastante.

suffocate |'sʌfəkeɪt| I *vtr* asfixiar. II *vi* asfixiarse.

suffocating |'sʌfəkeɪtɪŋ| *adj (heat)* agobiante, sofocante.

suffrage |'sʌfrɪdʒ| *n* sufragio *m*.

suffuse |sə'fju:z| *vtr lit* bañar, cubrir (**with**, de).

sugar |'ʃugər| I *n* azúcar *m & f*; **s. beet**, remolacha *f* (azucarera); **s. bowl**, azucarero *m*; **s. cane**, caña *f* de azúcar. II *vtr* azucarar, echar azúcar a.

sugary |'ʃugərɪ| *adj* 1 *(like sugar)* azucarado,-a. 2 *fig (insincere)* zalamero,-a; *(over-sentimental)* sentimentaloide.

suggest |sə'dʒest| *vtr* 1 *(propose)* sugerir. 2 *(advise)* aconsejar. 3 *(indicate, imply)* indicar.

suggestion |sə'dʒestʃən| *n* 1 *(proposal)* sugerencia *f*. 2 *(trace)* sombra *f*; *(small amount)* toque *m*.

suggestive |sə'dʒestɪv| *adj (remark)* indecente.

suicidal |sju:ɪ'saɪdəl| *adj* suicida.

suicide |'sju:ɪsaɪd| *n* suicidio *m*.

suit |su:t, sju:t| I *n* 1 traje *m* de chaqueta. 2 *Jur* pleito *m*. 3 *Cards* palo *m*; *fig* **to follow s.**, seguir el ejemplo. II *vtr* 1 *(be convenient to)* convenir a, venir bien a. 2 *(be right, appropriate for)* ir bien a; **red really suits you**, el rojo te favorece mucho; **they are well suited**, están hechos el uno para el otro. 3 *(adapt)* adaptar a. 4 *(please)* **s. yourself!**, ¡como quieras!

suitable |'sju:təbəl| *adj (convenient)* conveniente; *(appropriate)* adecuado,-a; **the most s. woman for the job**, la mujer más indicada para el puesto. ◆**suitably** *adv (correctly)* correctamente; *(properly)* adecuadamente.

suitcase |'su:tkeɪs| *n* maleta *f*.

suite |swi:t| *n* 1 *(of furniture)* juego *m*. 2 *(of hotel rooms, music)* suite *f*.

suitor |'sju:tər| *n Lit (wooer)* pretendiente *m*.

sulfur |'sʌlfər| *n US* → **sulphur**.

sulk |sʌlk| *vi* enfurruñarse.

sulky |'sʌlkɪ| *adj (sulkier, sulkiest)* malhumorado,-a, enfurruñado,-a.

sullen |'sʌlən| *adj* hosco,-a; *(sky)* plomizo,-a.

sulphur |'sʌlfər| *n* azufre *m*.

sulphuric |sʌl'fjʊərɪk| *adj* sulfúrico,-a.

sultan |'sʌltən| *n* sultán *m*.

sultana |sʌl'tɑ:nə| *n (raisin)* pasa *f* de Esmirna.

sultry |'sʌltrɪ| *adj (sultrier, sultriest)* 1 *(muggy)* bochornoso,-a. 2 *(seductive)* sensual.

sum |sʌm| *n* 1 *(arithmetic problem, amount)* suma *f*. 2 *(total amount)* total *m*; *(of money)* importe *m*. ◆**sum up** I *vtr* resumir. II *vi* resumir; **to s. up ...**, en resumidas cuentas ....

summarize ['sʌmǝraɪz] *vtr & vi* resumir.

summary ['sʌmǝrɪ] **I** *n* resumen *m*. **II** *adj* sumario,-a.

summer ['sʌmǝr] **I** *n* verano *m*. **II** *adj* (*holiday etc*) de verano; (*weather*) veraniego,-a; (*resort*) de veraneo.

summerhouse ['sʌmǝhaʊs] *n* cenador *m*, glorieta *f*.

summertime ['sʌmǝtaɪm] *n* verano *m*.

summit ['sʌmɪt] *n* **1** (*of mountain*) cima *f*, cumbre *f*. **2** *Pol* **s.** (**meeting**), cumbre *f*.

summon ['sʌmǝn] *vtr* **1** (*meeting, person*) convocar. **2** (*aid*) pedir. **3** *Jur* citar. ◆**summon up** *vtr* (*resources*) reunir; **to s. up one's courage,** armarse de valor.

summons ['sʌmǝnz] **I** *n* **1** (*call*) llamada *f*, llamamiento *m*. **2** *Jur* citación *f* judicial. **II** *vtr* *Jur* citar.

sumptuous ['sʌmptjʊǝs] *adj* suntuoso,-a.

sun [sʌn] **I** *n* sol *m*. **II** *vtr* **to s. oneself,** tomar el sol.

sunbathe ['sʌnbeɪð] *vi* tomar el sol.

sunbed ['sʌnbed] *n* (*in garden*) tumbona *f*; (*with sunlamp*) solario *m*.

sunburn ['sʌnbɜːn] *n* (*burn*) quemadura *f* de sol.

sunburnt ['sʌnbɜːnt] *adj* (*burnt*) quemado,-a por el sol; (*tanned*) bronceado,-a.

Sunday ['sʌndɪ] *n* domingo *m* *inv*; **S. newspaper,** periódico *m* del domingo; **S. school,** catequesis *f*.

sundial ['sʌndaɪǝl] *n* reloj *m* de sol.

sundown ['sʌndaʊn] *n* *US* anochecer *m*.

sundry ['sʌndrɪ] **I** *adj* diversos,-as, varios,-as; *fam* **all and s.,** todos sin excepción. **II** *npl* *Com* **sundries,** artículos *mpl* diversos; (*expenses*) gastos diversos.

sunflower ['sʌnflaʊǝr] *n* girasol *m*.

sung [sʌŋ] *pp* → **sing.**

sunglasses ['sʌnglɑːsɪz] *npl* gafas *fpl* de sol.

sunk [sʌŋk] *pp* → **sink.**

sunlamp ['sʌnlæmp] *n* lámpara *f* solar.

sunlight ['sʌnlaɪt] *n* sol *m*, luz *f* del sol.

sunlit ['sʌnlɪt] *adj* iluminado,-a por el sol.

sunny ['sʌnɪ] *adj* (**sunnier, sunniest**) **1** (*day*) de sol; (*place*) soleado,-a; **it is s.,** hace sol. **2** *fig* (*smile, disposition*) alegre; (*future*) prometedor,-a.

sunrise ['sʌnraɪz] *n* salida *f* del sol.

sunroof ['sʌnruːf] *n* *Aut* techo corredizo.

sunset ['sʌnset] *n* puesta *f* del sol.

sunshade ['sʌnʃeɪd] *n* sombrilla *f*.

sunshine ['sʌnʃaɪn] *n* sol *m*, luz *f* del sol.

sunstroke ['sʌnstrǝʊk] *n* insolación *f*.

suntan ['sʌntæn] *n* bronceado *m*; **s. oil** *or* **lotion,** (aceite *m*) bronceador *m*.

super ['suːpǝr] *adj* *fam* fenomenal.

super- ['suːpǝr] *pref* super-, sobre-.

superannuation [suːpǝrænjʊ'eɪʃǝn] *n* *GB* jubilación *f*, pensión *f*.

superb [suː'pɜːb] *adj* espléndido,-a.

supercilious [suːpǝ'sɪlɪǝs] *adj* (*condescending*) altanero,-a; (*disdainful*) desdeñoso,-a.

superficial [suːpǝ'fɪʃǝl] *adj* superficial.

superfluous [suː'pɜːflʊǝs] *adj* sobrante, superfluo,-a; **to be s.,** sobrar.

superhuman [suːpǝ'hjuːmǝn] *adj* sobrehumano,-a.

superimpose [suːpǝrɪm'pǝʊz] *vtr* sobreponer.

superintendent [suːpǝrɪn'tendǝnt] *n* director,-a *m,f*; **police s.,** subjefe,-a *m,f* de policía.

superior [suː'pɪǝrɪǝr] **I** *adj* **1** superior. **2** (*haughty*) altivo,-a. **II** *n* superior,-a *m,f*.

superiority [suːpɪǝrɪ'ɒrɪtɪ] *n* superioridad *f*.

superlative [suː'pɜːlǝtɪv] **I** *adj* superlativo,-a. **II** *n* *Ling* superlativo *m*.

superman ['suːpǝmæn] *n* superhombre *m*, supermán *m*.

supermarket ['suːpǝmɑːkɪt] *n* supermercado *m*.

supernatural [suːpǝ'nætʃǝrǝl] **I** *adj* sobrenatural. **II** *n* **the s.,** lo sobrenatural.

superpower ['suːpǝpaʊǝr] *n* *Pol* superpotencia *f*.

supersede [suːpǝ'siːd] *vtr* *fml* suplantar.

supersonic [suːpǝ'sɒnɪk] *adj* supersónico,-a.

superstitious [suːpǝ'stɪʃǝs] *adj* supersticioso,-a.

supertanker ['suːpǝtæŋkǝr] *n* superpetrolero *m*.

supervise ['suːpǝvaɪz] *vtr* supervisar; (*watch over*) vigilar.

supervision [suːpǝ'vɪʒǝn] *n* supervisión *f*.

supervisor ['suːpǝvaɪzǝr] *n* supervisor,-a *m,f*.

supper ['sʌpǝr] *n* cena *f*; **to have s.,** cenar.

supplant [sǝ'plɑːnt] *vtr* suplantar.

supple ['sʌpǝl] *adj* flexible.

supplement ['sʌplɪmǝnt] **I** *n* suplemento *m*. **II** ['sʌplɪment] *vtr* complementar.

supplementary [sʌplɪ'mentǝrɪ] *adj* adicional.

supplier [sǝ'plaɪǝr] *n* suministrador,-a *m,f*; *Com* proveedor,-a *m,f*.

supply [sǝ'plaɪ] **I** *n* **1** suministro *m*; *Com* provisión *f*; (*stock*) surtido *m*; **s. and demand,** oferta *f* y demanda. **2** **supplies,** (*food*) víveres *mpl*; *Mil* pertrechos *mpl*; **office supplies,** material *m* *sing* para oficina. **II** *vtr* **1** (*provide*) suministrar. **2** (*with provisions*) aprovisionar. **3** (*information*) facilitar. **4** *Com* surtir.

support [sǝ'pɔːt] **I** *n* **1** (*moral*) apoyo *m*. **2** (*funding*) ayuda económica. **II** *vtr* **1** (*weight etc*) sostener. **2** *fig* (*back*) apoyar; (*substantiate*) respaldar. **3** *Sport* ser (hincha) de. **4** (*sustain*) mantener; (*feed*) alimentar.

supporter [sǝ'pɔːtǝr] *n* *Pol* partidario,-a *m,f*; *Sport* hincha *mf*.

suppose [sə'pəʊz] vtr suponer; (presume) creer; **I s. not/so**, supongo que no/sí; **you're not supposed to smoke in here**, no está permitido fumar aquí dentro; **you're supposed to be in bed**, deberías estar acostado,-a ya.

supposed [sə'pəʊzd] adj supuesto,-a.
◆**supposedly** adv teóricamente.

suppress [sə'pres] vtr suprimir; (feelings, laugh etc) contener; (news, truth) callar; (revolt) sofocar.

supranational [su:prə'næʃənəl] adj supranacional.

supremacy [sʊ'preməsi] n supremacía f.

supreme [sʊ'pri:m] adj supremo,-a; **with s. indifference**, con total indiferencia.
◆**supremely** adv sumamente.

surcharge ['sɜ:tʃɑ:dʒ] n recargo m.

sure [ʃʊər] I adj 1 seguro,-a; **I'm s. (that) ...**, estoy seguro,-a de que ...; **make s. that it's ready**, asegúrate de que esté listo; **s. of oneself**, seguro,-a de sí mismo,-a. 2 US fam **s. thing!**, ¡claro!. II adv 1 (of course) claro. 2 (certainly) seguro. 3 **s. enough**, efectivamente. ◆**surely** adv (without a doubt) sin duda; **s. not!**, ¡no puede ser!

surety ['ʃʊərɪtɪ] n 1 (sum) fianza f. 2 (person) fiador,-a m,f; **to stand s. for sb**, ser fiador de algn.

surf [sɜ:f] I n (waves) oleaje m; (foam) espuma f. II vi Sport hacer surf.

surface ['sɜ:fɪs] I n superficie f; (of road) firme m. II adj superficial; **s. area**, área f de la superficie; **by s. mail**, por vía terrestre or marítima. III vtr (road) revestir. IV vi (submarine etc) salir a la superficie; fam (wake up) levantarse.

surface-to-air [sɜ:fɪstu'eər] adj **s.-to-a. missile**, misil m tierra-aire.

surfboard ['sɜ:fbɔ:d] n tabla f de surf.

surfeit ['sɜ:fɪt] n fml exceso m.

surfer ['sɜ:fər] n surfista mf.

surfing ['sɜ:fɪŋ] n surf m, surfing m.

surge [sɜ:dʒ] I n 1 (growth) alza f. 2 (of sea, sympathy) oleada f; fig (of anger, energy) arranque m. II vi **to s. forward**, (people) avanzar en tropel.

surgeon ['sɜ:dʒən] n cirujano,-a m,f.

surgery ['sɜ:dʒərɪ] n 1 (operation) cirujía f. 2 GB (consulting room) consultorio m; **s. hours**, horas fpl de consulta. 3 US (operating theatre) quirófano m.

surgical ['sɜ:dʒɪkəl] adj quirúrgico,-a; **s. spirit**, alcohol m de 90°.

surly ['sɜ:lɪ] adj (surlier, surliest) (bad-tempered) hosco,-a, malhumorado,-a; (rude) maleducado,-a.

surmount [sɜ:'maʊnt] vtr superar, vencer.

surname ['sɜ:neɪm] n apellido m.

surpass [sɜ:'pɑ:s] vtr superar.

surplus ['sɜ:pləs] I n (of goods) excedente m; (of budget) superávit m. II adj exce-

dente.

surprise [sə'praɪz] I n sorpresa f; **to take sb by s.**, coger desprevenido,-a a algn. II adj (visit) inesperado,-a; **s. attack**, ataque m sorpresa. III vtr sorprender.

surprising [sə'praɪzɪŋ] adj sorprendente.
◆**surprisingly** adv sorprendentemente, de modo sorprendente.

surrealist [sə'rɪəlɪst] adj & n surrealista (mf).

surrender [sə'rendər] I n Mil rendición f; (of weapons) entrega f; Ins rescate m. II vtr Mil rendir; (right) renunciar a. III vi (give in) rendirse.

surreptitious [sʌrəp'tɪʃəs] adj subrepticio,-a.

surrogate ['sʌrəgɪt] n fml sustituto,-a m,f; **s. mother**, madre f de alquiler.

surround [sə'raʊnd] I n marco m, borde m. II vtr rodear.

surrounding [sə'raʊndɪŋ] I adj circundante. II npl **surroundings**, (of place) alrededores mpl, cercanías fpl.

surveillance [sɜ:'veɪləns] n vigilancia f.

survey ['sɜ:veɪ] I n 1 (of building) inspección f; (of land) reconocimiento m. 2 (of trends etc) encuesta f. 3 (overall view) panorama m. II [sɜ:'veɪ] vtr 1 (building) inspeccionar; (land) medir. 2 (trends etc) hacer una encuesta sobre. 3 (look at) contemplar.

surveyor [sɜ:'veɪər] n agrimensor,-a m,f; **quantity s.**, aparejador,-a m,f.

survival [sə'vaɪvəl] n supervivencia f.

survive [sə'vaɪv] I vi sobrevivir; (remain) perdurar. II vtr sobrevivir a.

survivor [sə'vaɪvər] n superviviente mf.

susceptible [sə'septəbəl] adj (to attack) susceptible (**to**, a); (to illness) propenso,-a (**to**, a).

suspect ['sʌspekt] I adj (dubious) sospechoso,-a. II n sospechoso,-a m,f. III [sə'spekt] vtr 1 (person) sospechar (**of**, de); (plot, motives) recelar de. 2 (think likely) imaginar, creer.

suspend [sə'spend] vtr suspender; (pupil) expulsar por un tiempo.

suspended [sə'spendɪd] adj 1 suspendido,-a; Jur **s. sentence**, condena f condicional. 2 Sport sancionado,-a.

suspender [sə'spendər] n 1 (for stocking) liga f; **s. belt**, liguero m. 2 US **suspenders**, tirantes mpl.

suspense [sə'spens] n incertidumbre f; Cin Theat suspense m; **to keep sb in s.**, mantener a algn en la incertidumbre.

suspension [sə'spenʃən] n 1 suspensión f. 2 Sport sanción f. 3 (of pupil, employee) expulsión f temporal. 4 **s. bridge**, puente m colgante.

suspicion [sə'spɪʃən] n 1 sospecha f; (mistrust) recelo m; (doubt) duda f. 2 (trace) pizca f.

suspicious [sə'spɪʃəs] adj 1 (arousing

suspicion sospechoso,-a. 2 *(distrustful)* receloso,-a; **to be s. of sb,** desconfiar de algn.

sustain [sə'steɪn] *vtr* 1 sostener. 2 *(nourish)* sustentar. 3 *Jur (objection)* admitir. 4 *(injury etc)* sufrir.

sustained [sə'steɪnd] *adj* sostenido,-a.

sustenance ['sʌstənəns] *n* sustento *m*.

swab [swɒb] **I** *n (cotton wool)* algodón *m*; *(for specimen)* frotis *m*. **II** *vtr (wound)* limpiar.

swagger ['swægər] **I** *n* pavoneo *m*. **II** *vi* pavonearse.

swallow¹ ['swɒləʊ] **I** *n (of drink, food)* trago *m*. **II** *vtr* 1 *(drink, food)* tragar. 2 *fig (believe)* tragarse. **III** *vi* tragar. ◆**swallow up** *vtr fig* 1 *(engulf)* tragar. 2 *(eat up)* consumir.

swallow² ['swɒləʊ] *n Orn* golondrina *f*.

swam [swæm] *pt* → **swim**.

swamp [swɒmp] **I** *n* ciénaga *f*. **II** *vtr* 1 *(boat)* hundir. 2 *fig* inundar (**with**, **by**, de).

swan [swɒn] **I** *n* cisne *m*. **II** *vi fam* **to s. around,** pavonearse; **to s. around doing nothing,** hacer el vago.

swap [swɒp] **I** *n fam* intercambio *m*. **II** *vtr* cambiar. ◆**swap round, swap over** *vtr (switch)* cambiar.

swarm [swɔːm] **I** *n* enjambre *m*. **II** *vi (bees)* enjambrar; *fig* **Neath was swarming with tourists,** Neath estaba lleno de turistas.

swarthy ['swɔːðɪ] *adj (swarthier, swarthiest)* moreno,-a.

swastika ['swɒstɪkə] *n* esvástica *f*, cruz gamada.

swat [swɒt] *vtr* aplastar.

swathe [sweɪð] *vtr (bind up)* envolver.

sway [sweɪ] **I** *n* 1 *(movement)* balanceo *m*. 2 **to hold s. over sb,** dominar a algn. **II** *vi* 1 *(swing)* balancearse, mecerse. 2 *(totter)* tambalearse. **III** *vtr fig (persuade)* convencer.

swear [sweər] **I** *vtr (pt swore; pp sworn) (vow)* jurar; **to s. an oath,** prestar juramento. **II** *vi* 1 *(formally)* jurar, prestar juramento. 2 *(curse)* soltar tacos, decir palabrotas; *(blaspheme)* jurar; **to s. at sb,** echar pestes contra algn.

swear-word ['sweəwɜːd] *n* palabrota *f*.

sweat [swet] **I** *n (perspiration)* sudor *m*; *fam (hard work)* trabajo duro. **II** *vi (perspire)* sudar; *fig (work hard)* sudar la gota gorda. **III** *vtr fam* **to s. it out,** aguantar.

sweater ['swetər] *n* suéter *m*.

sweatshirt ['swetʃɜːt] *n* sudadera *f*.

sweaty ['swetɪ] *adj (sweatier, sweatiest)* sudoroso,-a.

swede [swiːd] *n Bot* nabo sueco.

Swede [swiːd] *n (person)* sueco,-a *m,f*.

Sweden ['swiːdən] *n* Suecia *f*.

Swedish ['swiːdɪʃ] **I** *adj* sueco,-a. **II** *n* 1 *(language)* sueco *m*. 2 **the S.,** *pl* los sue-

cos.

sweep [swiːp] **I** *n* 1 *(with broom)* barrido *m*; *fig* **to make a clean s. of things,** hacer tabla rasa. 2 *(of arm)* gesto amplio. 3 *(of river, road)* curva *f*. 4 *(chimney)* **s.,** deshollinador,-a *m,f*. **II** *vtr (pt & pp swept)* 1 *(floor etc)* barrer. 2 *(of searchlight)* recorrer; *(minefield)* rastrear. 3 *(spread throughout)* extenderse por. **III** *vi* 1 *(with broom)* barrer. **2 to s. in/out/past,** entrar/salir/pasar rápidamente. ◆**sweep aside** *vtr* apartar bruscamente; *fig (objections)* rechazar. ◆**sweep away** *vtr* 1 *(dust)* barrer. 2 *(of storm)* arrastrar. ◆**sweep up** *vi* barrer.

sweeper ['swiːpər] *n* 1 *(machine)* barredora *f*. 2 *Ftb* líbero *m*.

sweeping ['swiːpɪŋ] *adj* 1 *(broad)* amplio,-a; **a s. statement,** una declaración demasiado general. 2 *(victory)* aplastante. 3 *(reforms, changes etc)* radical.

sweet [swiːt] **I** *adj* 1 dulce; *(sugary)* azucarado,-a; **to have a s. tooth,** ser goloso,-a; **s. pea,** guisante *m* de olor; **s. shop,** bombonería *f*. 2 *(pleasant)* agradable; *(smell)* fragante; *(sound)* melodioso, -a. 3 *(person, animal)* encantador,-a. **II** *n* 1 GB caramelo *m*; *(chocolate)* bombón *m*. 2 *(dessert)* postre *m*.

sweet-and-sour ['swiːtənsaʊər] *adj* agridulce.

sweetcorn ['swiːtkɔːn] *n* maíz tierno.

sweeten ['swiːtən] *vtr* 1 *(tea etc)* azucarar. 2 *fig (temper)* aplacar; **to s. the pill,** suavizar el golpe.

sweetener ['swiːtənər] *n (for tea, coffee)* edulcorante *m*.

sweetheart ['swiːthɑːt] *n* 1 *(boyfriend)* novio *m*; *(girlfriend)* novia *f*. 2 *(dear, love)* cariño *m*, amor *m*.

sweetness ['swiːtnɪs] *n* dulzura *f*; *(of smell)* fragancia *f*; *(of sound)* suavidad *f*.

swell [swel] **I** *n (of sea)* marejada *f*, oleaje *m*. **II** *adj US fam* fenomenal. **III** *vi (pt swelled; pp swollen) (part of body)* hincharse; *(river)* subir. ◆**swell up** *vi* hincharse.

swelling ['swelɪŋ] *n* hinchazón *f*; *Med* tumefacción *f*.

sweltering ['sweltərɪŋ] *adj* agobiante.

swept [swept] *pt & pp* → **sweep.**

swerve [swɜːv] **I** *n* 1 *(by car)* viraje *m*. 2 *Sport (by player)* regate *m*. **II** *vi* 1 *(car)* dar un viraje brusco. 2 *Sport (player)* dar un regate.

swift [swɪft] **I** *adj* rápido,-a, veloz. **II** *n Orn* vencejo *m* (común). ◆**swiftly** *adv* rápidamente.

swig [swɪg] *fam* **I** *n* trago *m*. **II** *vtr* beber a tragos.

swill [swɪl] **I** *n* 1 bazofia *f*. 2 *(rinse)* enjuague *m*. **II** *vtr* 1 *(rinse)* enjuagar. 2 *fam (drink)* beber a grandes tragos. ◆**swill out** *vtr* enjuagar.

swim [swɪm] **I** vi (pt **swam**; pp **swum**) nadar; **to go swimming**, ir a nadar; fam **my head is swimming**, la cabeza me da vueltas. **II** vtr (the Channel) pasar a nado. **III** n baño m; **to go for a s.**, ir a nadar or bañarse.

swimmer ['swɪmər] n nadador,-a m,f.

swimming ['swɪmɪŋ] n natación f; **s. cap**, gorro m de baño; **s. costume**, traje m de baño, bañador m; **s. pool**, piscina f; **s. trunks**, bañador.

swimsuit ['swɪmsuːt] n traje m de baño, bañador m.

swindle ['swɪndəl] **I** n estafa f. **II** vtr estafar.

swindler ['swɪndlər] n estafador,-a m.

swine [swaɪn] n 1 (pl **swine**) (pig) cerdo m, puerco m. 2 (pl **swines**) fam (person) canalla mf, cochino,-a m,f.

swing [swɪŋ] **I** n 1 balanceo m, vaivén m; fig (in votes etc) viraje m; **s. bridge**, puente giratorio; **s. door**, puerta giratoria. 2 Box Golf swing m. 3 (plaything) columpio m. 4 (rhythm) ritmo m; (jazz style) swing m; **in full s.**, en plena marcha. **II** vi (pt & pp **swung**) 1 (move to and fro) balancearse; (arms, legs) menearse; (on swing) columpiarse; **to s. open/shut**, abrirse/cerrarse de golpe. 2 (turn) girar; **he swung round**, dio media vuelta. **III** vtr 1 (cause to move to and fro) balancear; (arms, legs) menear; (on swing) columpiar. 2 (turn) hacer girar; **she swung the sack onto her back**, se echó el saco a los hombros.

swingeing ['swɪndʒɪŋ] adj drástico,-a.

swipe [swaɪp] **I** n golpe m. **II** vtr 1 (hit) dar un tortazo a. 2 fam (steal) birlar.

swirl [swɜːl] **I** n remolino m; (of cream, smoke) voluta f. **II** vi arremolinarse.

swish [swɪʃ] **I** adj fam (smart) elegante. **II** vtr (tail) menear. **III** vi (whip) dar un chasquido; (skirt) crujir.

Swiss [swɪs] **I** adj suizo,-a. **II** n inv (person) suizo,-a m,f; **the S.**, pl los suizos.

switch [swɪtʃ] **I** n 1 Elec interruptor m. 2 (changeover) cambio repentino; (exchange) intercambio m. 3 (stick) vara f; (riding whip) fusta f. **II** vtr 1 (jobs, direction) cambiar de. 2 (allegiance) cambiar (to, por); (attention) desviar (to, hacia). ◆**switch off** vtr apagar. ◆**switch on** vtr encender. ◆**switch over** vi cambiar (to, a).

switchboard ['swɪtʃbɔːd] n centralita f.

Switzerland ['swɪtsələnd] n Suiza.

swivel ['swɪvəl] **I** n **s. chair**, silla giratoria. **II** vtr & vi girar.

swollen ['swəʊlən] adj (ankle, face) hinchado,-a; (river, lake) crecido,-a.

swoon [swuːn] arch **I** n desmayo m. **II** vi desmayarse.

swoop [swuːp] **I** n 1 (of bird) calada f; (of plane) descenso m en picado. 2 (by police) redada f. **II** vi 1 **to s. down**, (bird) abalanzarse (on, sobre); (plane) bajar en picado. 2 (police) hacer una redada.

swop [swɒp] vtr → **swap**.

sword [sɔːd] n espada f.

swordfish ['sɔːdfɪʃ] n pez m espada.

swore [swɔːr] pt → **swear**.

sworn [swɔːn] adj jurado,-a.

swot [swɒt] fam vi empollar.

swum [swʌm] pp → **swim**.

swung [swʌŋ] pt & pp → **swing**.

sycamore ['sɪkəmɔːr] n sicomoro m.

syllable ['sɪləbəl] n sílaba f.

syllabus ['sɪləbəs] n programa m de estudios.

symbol ['sɪmbəl] n símbolo m.

symbolic [sɪm'bɒlɪk] adj simbólico,-a.

symbolize ['sɪmbəlaɪz] vtr simbolizar.

symmetry ['sɪmɪtrɪ] n simetría f.

sympathetic [sɪmpə'θetɪk] adj 1 (showing pity) compasivo,-a. 2 (understanding) comprensivo,-a; (kind) amable.

sympathize ['sɪmpəθaɪz] vi 1 (show pity) compadecerse (**with**, de). 2 (understand) comprender.

sympathizer ['sɪmpəθaɪzər] n simpatizante mf.

sympathy ['sɪmpəθɪ] n 1 (pity) compasión f. 2 (condolences) pésame m; **letter of s.**, pésame; **to express one's s.**, dar el pésame. 3 (understanding) comprensión f.

symphony ['sɪmfənɪ] n sinfonía f.

symposium [sɪm'pəʊzɪəm] n simposio m.

symptom ['sɪmptəm] n síntoma m.

symptomatic [sɪmptə'mætɪk] adj sintomático,-a.

synagogue ['sɪnəgɒg] n sinagoga f.

synchronize ['sɪŋkrənaɪz] vtr sincronizar.

syndicate ['sɪndɪkɪt] n corporación f; **newspaper s.**, sindicato periodístico.

syndrome ['sɪndrəʊm] n síndrome m.

synonym ['sɪnənɪm] n sinónimo m.

synopsis [sɪ'nɒpsɪs] n sinopsis f inv.

syntax ['sɪntæks] n sintaxis f inv.

synthesis ['sɪnθɪsɪs] n (pl **syntheses** ['sɪnθɪsiːz]) síntesis f inv.

synthesizer ['sɪnθɪsaɪzər] n sintetizador m.

synthetic [sɪn'θetɪk] adj sintético,-a.

syphilis ['sɪfɪlɪs] n sífilis f.

syphon ['saɪfən] n → **siphon**.

Syria ['sɪrɪə] n Siria.

Syrian ['sɪrɪən] adj & n sirio,-a (m,f).

syringe [sɪ'rɪndʒ] n jeringa f, jeringuilla f.

syrup ['sɪrəp] n jarabe m, almíbar m.

system ['sɪstəm] n sistema m; fam **the s.**, el orden establecido; Comput **systems analyst**, analista mf de sistemas.

systematic [sɪstɪ'mætɪk] adj sistemático,-a.

T

T, t |tiː| *n (the letter)* T, t *f.*

t *abbr of* ton(s), **tonne(s),** t.

ta |tɑː| *interj GB fam* gracias.

tab |tæb| *n* 1 *(flap)* lengüeta *f; (label)* etiqueta *f; fam* **to keep tabs on sb,** vigilar a algn. 2 *US fam (bill)* cuenta *f.*

tabby |'tæbɪ| *n* t. **(cat),** gato,-a *m,f* romano,-a.

table |'teɪbəl| I *n* 1 mesa *f;* **to lay** *or* **set the t.,** poner la mesa; **t. lamp,** lámpara *f* de mesa; **t. mat,** salvamanteles *m inv;* **t. tennis,** ping-pong® *m,* tenis *m* de mesa; **t. wine,** vino *m* de mesa. 2 *(of figures)* tabla *f,* cuadro *m;* **t. of contents,** índice *m* de materias. II *vtr* presentar.

tablecloth |'teɪbəlklɒθ| *n* mantel *m.*

tablespoon |'teɪbəlspuːn| *n* cucharón *m.*

tablespoonful |'teɪbəlspuːnfʊl| *n* cucharada *f* grande.

tablet |'tæblɪt| *n* 1 *Med* pastilla *f.* 2 *(of stone)* lápida *f.* 3 *(of soap)* pastilla *f; (of chocolate)* tableta *f.* 4 *US (of writing paper)* bloc *m.*

tableware |'teɪbəlweər| *n* vajilla *f.*

tabloid |'tæblɔɪd| *n* periódico *m* de pequeño formato; **t. press,** prensa sensacionalista.

taboo |tə'buː| *adj & n* tabú *(m).*

tabulate |'tæbjʊleɪt| *vtr* disponer en listas.

tacit |'tæsɪt| *adj* tácito,-a.

taciturn |'tæsɪtɜːn| *adj* taciturno,-a.

tack |tæk| I *n* 1 *(small nail)* tachuela *f.* 2 *Sew* hilván *m.* 3 *Naut* amura *f; (distance)* bordada *f; fig* **to change t.,** cambiar de rumbo. II *vtr* 1 **to t. sth down,** clavar algo con tachuelas. 2 *Sew* hilvanar. III *vi Naut* virar de bordo. ◆**tack on** *vtr (add)* añadir.

tackle |'tækəl| I *n* 1 *(equipment)* aparejos *mpl; (fishing t.,* aparejos de pescar. 2 *Sport* placaje *m; Ftb* entrada *f.* II *vtr* agarrar; *(task)* emprender; *(problem)* abordar; *Sport* placar; *Ftb* entrar a.

tacky¹ |'tækɪ| *adj (tackier, tackiest)* pegajoso,-a.

tacky² |'tækɪ| *adj fam (shoddy)* cutre.

tact |tækt| *n* tacto *m,* diplomacia *f.*

tactful |'tæktfʊl| *adj* diplomático,-a.

tactical |'tæktɪkəl| *adj* táctico,-a.

tactic |'tæktɪk| *n* táctica *f;* **tactics,** táctica *f sing.*

tactless |'tæktlɪs| *adj (person)* poco diplomático,-a; *(question)* indiscreto,-a.

tadpole |'tædpəʊl| *n* renacuajo *m.*

tag |tæg| *n* 1 *(label)* etiqueta *f.* 2 *(saying)* coletilla *f.* ◆**tag along** *vi fam* pegarse. ◆**tag on** *vtr (add to end)* añadir.

tail |teɪl| I *n* 1 cola *f;* **t. end,** cola. 2 *(of shirt)* faldón *m;* **to wear tails,** ir de frac;

t. coat, frac *m.* 3 tails, *(of coin)* cruz *f sing.* II *vtr sl (follow)* seguir de cerca. ◆**tail away, tail off** *vi* desvanecerse.

tailback |'teɪlbæk| *n* caravana *f.*

tail-gate |'teɪlgeɪt| *n Aut* puerta trasera.

tailor |'teɪlər| I *n* sastre *m;* **t.'s (shop),** sastrería *f.* II *vtr (suit)* confeccionar; *fig* adaptar.

tailor-made |teɪlə'meɪd| *adj* hecho,-a a la medida.

tailwind |'teɪlwɪnd| *n* viento *m* de cola.

taint |teɪnt| *vtr* contaminar; *fig* corromper.

tainted |'teɪntɪd| *adj* contaminado,-a; *(reputation)* manchado,-a.

take |teɪk| I *vtr (pt* took; *pp* taken) 1 tomar, coger; **to t. an opportunity,** aprovechar una oportunidad; **to t. hold of sth,** agarrar algo; **to t. sth from one's pocket,** sacarse algo del bolsillo; **t. your time!,** ¡tómate el tiempo que quieras!; **to t. a bath,** bañarse; **to t. care,** cuidar; **his car takes six people,** caben seis personas en su coche; **is this seat taken?,** ¿está ocupado este asiento?; **to t. a decision,** tomar una decisión; **to t. a liking/dislike to sb,** tomar cariño/antipatía a algn; **to t. a photograph,** sacar una fotografía; **t. the first road on the left,** coja la primera a la izquierda; **to t. the train,** coger el tren. 2 *(accept)* aceptar; *(earn)* **to t. so much per week,** recaudar tanto por semana. 3 *(win)* ganar; *(prize)* llevarse. 4 *(eat, drink)* tomar; **to t. drugs,** drogarse. 5 **she's taking (a degree in) law,** estudia derecho; **to t. an exam (in ...),** examinarse (de ...). 6 *(person to a place)* llevar. 7 *(endure)* aguantar. 8 *(consider)* considerar. 9 **I t. it that ...,** supongo que ...; **what do you t. me for?,** ¿por quién me tomas? 10 *(require)* requerir; **it takes an hour to get there,** se tarda una hora en llegar hasta allí. 11 **to be taken ill,** enfermar.

II *n Cin* toma *f.*

◆**take after** *vtr* parecerse a. ◆**take apart** *vtr (machine)* desmontar. ◆**take away** *vtr* 1 *(carry off)* llevarse. 2 **to t. sth away from sb,** quitarle algo a algn. 3 *Math* restar. ◆**take back** *vtr* 1 *(give back)* devolver; *(receive back)* recuperar. 2 *(withdraw)* retractarse. ◆**take down** *vtr* 1 *(lower)* bajar. 2 *(demolish)* derribar. 3 *(write)* apuntar. ◆**take in** *vtr* 1 *(shelter, lodge)* alojar, acoger. 2 *Sew* meter. 3 *(include)* abarcar. 4 *(understand)* entender. 5 *(deceive)* engañar. ◆**take off** I *vtr* 1 quitar; **he took off his jacket,** se quitó la chaqueta. 2 *(lead or carry away)* llevarse. 3 *(deduct)* descontar. 4 *(imitate)* imitar burlonamente. II *vi Av* despegar.

◆**take on** vtr 1 (undertake) encargarse de. 2 (acquire) tomar. 3 (employ) contratar. 4 (compete with) competir con. ◆**take out** vtr sacar, quitar; **he's taking me out to dinner**, me ha invitado a cenar fuera. ◆**take over** I vtr Com Pol tomar posesión de; **the rebels took over the country**, los rebeldes se apoderaron del país. II vi to t. over from sb, relevar a algn. ◆**take to** vtr (become fond of) coger cariño a; **to t. to drink**, darse a la bebida. ◆**take up** vtr 1 Sew acortar. 2 (accept) aceptar; (adopt) adoptar. 3 I've taken up the piano/French, he empezado a tocar el piano/a aprender francés. 4 (occupy) ocupar.

takeaway ['teɪkəweɪ] GB I n (food) comida f para llevar; (restaurant) restaurante m que vende comida para llevar. II adj (food) para llevar.

take-home pay ['teɪkhəʊmpeɪ] n sueldo neto.

takeoff ['teɪkɒf] n 1 Av despegue m. 2 (imitation) imitación burlona.

takeover ['teɪkəʊvər] n Com absorción f; military t., golpe m de estado; t. bid, oferta pública de adquisición, OPA f.

takings ['teɪkɪŋz] npl Com recaudación f sing.

talc [tælk] n talco m.

talcum powder ['tælkəmpaʊdər] n (polvos mpl de) talco m.

tale [teɪl] n cuento m; to tell tales, contar chismes.

talent ['tælənt] n talento m.

talented ['tæləntɪd] adj dotado,-a.

talk [tɔːk] I vi hablar; (chat) charlar; (gossip) chismorrear; fam now you're talking!, ¡eso sí que me interesa!. II vtr to t. nonsense, decir tonterías; to t. sense, hablar con sentido común; to t. shop, hablar del trabajo. III n 1 (conversation) conversación f. 2 (words) palabras fpl; he's all t., no hace más que hablar. 3 (rumour) rumor m; (gossip) chismes mpl. 4 (lecture) charla f. ◆**talk into** vtr to t. sb into sth, convencer a algn para que haga algo. ◆**talk out of** vtr to t. sb out of sth, disuadir a algn de que haga algo. ◆**talk over** vtr discutir.

talkative ['tɔːkətɪv] adj hablador,-a.

talking ['tɔːkɪŋ] n no t. please!, ¡silencio, por favor!; t. point, tema m de conversación.

talking-to ['tɔːkɪŋtuː] n fam bronca f.

tall [tɔːl] adj alto,-a; a tree ten metres t., un árbol de diez metros (de alto); how t. are you?, ¿cuánto mides?; fig that's a t. order, eso es mucho pedir.

tally ['tælɪ] I vi to t. with sth, corresponderse con algo. II n Com apunte m; to keep a t. of, llevar la cuenta de.

talon ['tælən] n garra f.

tambourine [tæmbə'riːn] n pandereta f.

tame [teɪm] I adj 1 (animal) domado,-a; (by nature) manso,-a; (person) dócil. 2 (style) soso,-a. II vtr domar.

tamper ['tæmpər] vi to t. with, (text) adulterar; (records, an entry) falsificar; (lock) intentar forzar.

tampon ['tæmpɒn] n tampón m.

tan [tæn] I n 1 (colour) marrón rojizo. 2 (of skin) bronceado m. II adj (colour) marrón rojizo. III vtr 1 (leather) curtir. 2 (skin) broncear. IV vi ponerse moreno,-a.

tang [tæŋ] n sabor m fuerte.

tangent ['tændʒənt] n tangente f; fig to go off at a t., salirse por la tangente.

tangerine [tændʒə'riːn] n clementina f.

tangible ['tændʒəbəl] adj tangible.

tangle ['tæŋgəl] n (of thread) maraña f; fig lío m; fig to get into a t., hacerse un lío.

tank [tæŋk] n 1 (container) depósito m. 2 Mil tanque m.

tanker ['tæŋkər] n Naut tanque m; (for oil) petrolero m; Aut camión m cisterna.

Tannoy® ['tænɔɪ] n sistema m de megafonía.

tantalize ['tæntəlaɪz] vtr atormentar.

tantalizing ['tæntəlaɪzɪŋ] adj atormentador,-a.

tantamount ['tæntəmaʊnt] adj t. to, equivalente a.

tantrum ['tæntrəm] n rabieta f.

tap¹ [tæp] I vtr golpear suavemente; (with hand) dar una palmadita a. II vi to t. at the door, llamar suavemente a la puerta. III n golpecito m; t. dancing, claqué m.

tap² [tæp] I n (for water) grifo m; fig funds on t., fondos mpl disponibles. II vtr 1 (tree) sangrar; fig to t. new markets, explotar nuevos mercados. 2 (phone) pinchar.

tape [teɪp] I n 1 cinta f; sticky t., cinta adhesiva; t. measure, cinta métrica. 2 (for recording) cinta f (magnetofónica); t. recorder, magnetófono m, cassette m; t. recording, grabación f. II vtr 1 pegar (con cinta adhesiva). 2 (record) grabar (en cinta).

taper ['teɪpər] I vi estrecharse; (to a point) afilarse. II n (candle) vela f. ◆**taper off** vi ir disminuyendo.

tapestry ['tæpɪstrɪ] n tapiz m.

tapping ['tæpɪŋ] n (of tree) sangría f; (of resources) explotación f; Tel intervención f ilegal de un teléfono.

tar [tɑːr] n alquitrán m.

target ['tɑːgɪt] n 1 (object aimed at) blanco m; t. practice, tiro m al blanco. 2 (purpose) meta f.

tariff ['tærɪf] n tarifa f, arancel m.

tarmac® ['tɑːmæk] I n 1 (substance) alquitrán m. 2 Av pista f de aterrizaje. II vtr alquitranar.

tarnish ['tɑːnɪʃ] vtr deslustrar.

tarpaulin [tɑː'pɔːlɪn] n lona f.

tart¹ [tɑːt] n GB Culin tarta f.

tart² [tɑːt] adj (taste) ácido,-a, agrio,-a.

tart³ [tɑːt] fam I n puta f. II vtr GB to t. oneself up, emperifollarse.

tartan ['tɑːtən] n tartán m.

tartar ['tɑːtər] n 1 Chem tártaro m. 2 Culin t. sauce, salsa tártara.

task [tɑːsk] n tarea f; to take sb to t., reprender a algn; Mil t. force, destacamento m (de fuerzas).

tassel ['tæsəl] n borla f.

taste [teɪst] I n 1 (sense) gusto m; (flavour) sabor m; it has a burnt t., sabe a quemado. 2 (sample) (of food) bocado m; (of drink) trago m; to give sb a t. of his own medicine, pagar a algn con la misma moneda. 3 (liking) afición f; to have a t. for sth, gustarle a uno algo. 4 in bad t., de mal gusto; to have (good) t., tener (buen) gusto. II vtr (sample) probar. III vi to t. of sth, saber a algo.

tasteful ['teɪstful] adj de buen gusto.

tasteless ['teɪstlɪs] adj 1 (food) soso,-a. 2 (in bad taste) de mal gusto.

tasty ['teɪstɪ] adj (tastier, tastiest) sabroso,-a.

tattered ['tætəd] adj hecho,-a jirones.

tatters ['tætəz] npl in t., hecho,-a jirones.

tattoo¹ [tæ'tuː] n 1 Mil retreta f.

tattoo² [tæ'tuː] I vtr tatuar. II n (mark) tatuaje m.

tatty ['tætɪ] adj (tattier, tattiest) GB en mal estado; (material, clothing) raído,-a; (décor) deslustrado,-a.

taught [tɔːt] pt & pp → teach.

taunt [tɔːnt] I vtr to t. sb with sth, echar algo en cara a algn. II n pulla f.

Taurus ['tɔːrəs] n Tauro m.

taut [tɔːt] adj tenso,-a, tirante.

tavern ['tævən] n taberna f.

tawdry ['tɔːdrɪ] adj (tawdrier, tawdriest) hortera.

tawn(e)y ['tɔːnɪ] adj leonado,-a, rojizo,-a.

tax [tæks] I n impuesto m; t. free, exento,-a de impuestos; t. collector, recaudador,-a m,f (de impuestos); t. evasion, evasión f fiscal; t. return, declaración f de renta. II vtr 1 gravar. 2 (patience etc) poner a prueba.

taxable ['tæksəbəl] adj imponible.

taxation [tæk'seɪʃən] n impuestos mpl.

taxi ['tæksɪ] I n taxi m; t. driver, taxista mf; t. rank, parada f de taxis. II vi (aircraft) rodar por la pista.

taxidermy ['tæksɪdɜːmɪ] n taxidermia f.

taxing ['tæksɪŋ] adj exigente.

taxpayer ['tækspeɪər] n contribuyente mf.

TB, tb [tiː'biː] abbr of tuberculosis.

tea [tiː] n 1 té m; t. bag, bolsita f de té; t. break, descanso m; t. cosy, cubretetera f; t. leaf, hoja f de té; t. service or set, juego m de té; t. towel, paño m (de cocina). 2 (snack) merienda f; (high) t., merienda-cena f.

teach [tiːtʃ] I vtr (pt & pp taught) enseñar; (subject) dar clases de; to t. sb (how) to do sth, enseñar a algn a hacer algo. II vi dar clases, ser profesor,-a.

teacher ['tiːtʃər] n profesor,-a m,f; (in primary school) maestro,-a m,f.

teaching ['tiːtʃɪŋ] n enseñanza f.

teacup ['tiːkʌp] n taza f de té.

teak [tiːk] n teca f.

team [tiːm] n equipo m; (of oxen) yunta f.

team-mate ['tiːmmeɪt] n compañero,-a m,f de equipo.

teamwork ['tiːmwɜːk] n trabajo m en equipo.

teapot ['tiːpɒt] n tetera f.

tear¹ [tɪər] n lágrima f; to be in tears, estar llorando; t. gas, gas lacrimógeno.

tear² [teər] I vtr (pt tore; pp torn) 1 rajar, desgarrar. 2 to t. sth out of sb's hands, arrancarle algo de las manos a algn. II vi 1 (cloth) rajarse. 2 to t. along, ir a toda velocidad. III n desgarrón m; (in clothes) rasgón m. ◆tear down vtr derribar. ◆tear off vtr arrancar. ◆tear out vtr arrancar. ◆tear up vtr 1 romper, hacer pedazos. 2 (uproot) arrancar de raíz.

tearful ['tɪəful] adj lloroso,-a.

tearoom ['tiːruːm] n GB → teashop.

tease [tiːz] I vtr tomar el pelo a. II n bromista mf.

teashop ['tiːʃɒp] n GB salón m de té.

teaspoon ['tiːspuːn] n cucharilla f.

teaspoonful ['tiːspuːnful] n cucharadita f.

teat [tiːt] n (of animal) teta f; (of bottle) tetina f.

teatime ['tiːtaɪm] n hora f del té.

technical ['teknɪkəl] adj técnico,-a; t. college, instituto m de formación profesional. ◆technically adv (theoretically) en teoría.

technicality [teknɪ'kælɪtɪ] n detalle técnico.

technician [tek'nɪʃən] n técnico,-a m,f.

technique [tek'niːk] n técnica f.

technological [teknə'lɒdʒɪkəl] adj tecnológico,-a.

technology [tek'nɒlədʒɪ] n tecnología f.

teddy bear ['tedɪbeər] n oso m de felpa.

tedious ['tiːdɪəs] adj tedioso,-a, aburrido,-a.

tee [tiː] n Golf tee m.

teem [tiːm] vi to t. with, rebosar de; fam it was teeming down, llovía a cántaros.

teenage ['tiːneɪdʒ] adj adolescente.

teenager ['tiːneɪdʒər] n adolescente mf.

teens [tiːnz] npl adolescencia f sing.

tee-shirt ['tiːʃɜːt] n camiseta f.

teeter ['tiːtər] vi balancearse.

teeth [tiːθ] npl → tooth.

teethe [tiːð] vi echar los dientes.

teething ['tiːðɪŋ] n t. ring, chupador m; fig t. troubles, dificultades fpl iniciales.

teetotaller [tiː'təutələr] n abstemio,-a

m,f.

telecommunications ['telɪkəmjuːnɪ-'keɪʃənz] *n* telecomunicaciones *fpl.*

telegram ['telɪɡræm] *n* telegrama *m.*

telegraph ['telɪɡræf, 'telɪɡrɑːf] I *n* telégrafo *m*; **t. pole**, poste telegráfico. II *vtr & vi* telegrafiar.

telepathy [tɪ'lepəθɪ] *n* telepatía *f.*

telephone ['telɪfəʊn] I *n* teléfono *m*; *GB* **t. booth, t. box**, cabina *f* (telefónica); **t. call**, llamada telefónica; **t. directory**, guía telefónica; **t. number**, número *m* de teléfono. II *vtr* telefonear, llamar por teléfono.

telephonist [tɪ'lefənɪst] *n GB* telefonista *mf.*

telephoto ['telɪfəʊtəʊ] *adj* **t. lens**, teleobjetivo *m.*

teleprinter ['telɪprɪntər] *n* teletipo *m.*

telescope ['telɪskəʊp] I *n* telescopio *m.* II *vi* plegarse (como un catalejo). III *vtr* plegar.

telescopic [telɪ'skɒpɪk] *adj* (*umbrella*) plegable.

televise ['telɪvaɪz] *vtr* televisar.

television ['telɪvɪʒən] *n* televisión *f*; **t. programme**, programa *m* de televisión; **t. (set)**, televisor *m.*

telex ['teleks] I *n* télex *m.* II *vtr* enviar por télex.

tell [tel] I *vtr* (*pt & pp told*) 1 (*say*) decir; (*relate*) contar; (*inform*) comunicar; **to t. lies**, mentir; **to t. sb about sth**, contarle algo a algn; **you're telling me!**, ¡a mí me lo vas a contar! 2 (*order*) mandar; **to t. sb to do sth**, decir a algn que haga algo. 3 (*distinguish*) distinguir; **to know how to t. the time**, saber decir la hora. 4 **all told**, en total. II *vi* 1 (*reveal*) reflejar. 2 **who can t.?**, (*know*) ¿quién sabe? 3 (*have effect*) notarse; **the pressure is telling on her**, está acusando la presión. ◆**tell off** *vtr fam* regañar, reñir.

teller ['telər] *n* (*in bank etc*) cajero,-a *m,f.*

telling ['telɪŋ] *adj* (*action*) eficaz; (*blow, argument*) contundente.

telltale ['telteɪl] *n* chivato,-a *m,f*; **t. signs**, señales reveladoras.

telly ['telɪ] *n GB fam* **the t.**, la tele.

temp [temp] *n* (*abbr of* **temporary**) *fam* trabajador,-a *m,f* temporal.

temper ['tempər] I *n* 1 (*mood*) humor *m*; **to keep one's t.**, no perder la calma; **to lose one's t.**, perder los estribos. 2 (*temperament*) **to have a bad t.**, tener (mal) genio. II *vtr* (*in metallurgy*) templar; *fig* suavizar.

temperament ['tempərəmənt] *n* temperamento *m.*

temperamental [tempərə'mentəl] *adj* temperamental.

temperate ['tempərɪt] *adj* 1 mesurado,-a. 2 (*climate*) templado,-a.

temperature ['temprɪtʃər] *n* temperatura *f*; **to have a t.**, tener fiebre.

tempest ['tempɪst] *n* tempestad *f.*

temple¹ ['tempəl] *n Archit* templo *m.*

temple² ['tempəl] *n Anat* sien *f.*

tempo ['tempəʊ] *n* tiempo *m.*

temporary ['tempərərɪ] *adj* provisional; (*setback, improvement*) momentáneo,-a; (*staff*) temporal.

tempt [tempt] *vtr* tentar; **to t. providence**, tentar la suerte; **to t. sb to do sth**, incitar a algn a hacer algo.

temptation [temp'teɪʃən] *n* tentación *f.*

tempting ['temptɪŋ] *adj* tentador,-a.

ten [ten] *adj & n* diez (*m*) *inv.*

tenable ['tenəbəl] *adj* (*opinion*) sostenible.

tenacious [tɪ'neɪʃəs] *adj* tenaz.

tenancy ['tenənsɪ] *n* (*of house*) alquiler *m*; (*of land*) arrendamiento *m.*

tenant ['tenənt] *n* (*of house*) inquilino,-a *m,f*; (*of farm*) arrendatario,-a *m,f.*

tend¹ [tend] *vi* (*be inclined*) tender, tener tendencia (**to, a**).

tend² [tend] *vtr* (*care for*) cuidar.

tendency ['tendənsɪ] *n* tendencia *f.*

tender¹ ['tendər] *adj* (*affectionate*) cariñoso,-a; (*compassionate*) compasivo,-a; (*meat*) tierno,-a.

tender² ['tendər] I *vtr* ofrecer; **to t. one's resignation**, presentar la dimisión. II *vi Com* **to t. for**, sacar a concurso. III *n* 1 *Com* oferta *f.* 2 **legal t.**, moneda *f* de curso legal.

tenderness ['tendənɪs] *n* ternura *f.*

tendon ['tendən] *n* tendón *m.*

tenement ['tenɪmənt] *n* casa *f* de vecindad.

tenet ['tenɪt] *n* principio *m.*

tennis ['tenɪs] *n* tenis *m*; **t. ball**, pelota *f* de tenis; **t. court**, pista *f* de tenis; **t. player**, tenista *mf*; **t. racket** raqueta *f* de tenis; **t. shoe**, zapatilla *f* de tenis.

tenor ['tenər] *n Mus* tenor *m.*

tense¹ [tens] *adj* tenso,-a.

tense² [tens] *n Gram* tiempo *m.*

tension ['tenʃən] *n* tensión *f.*

tent [tent] *n* tienda *f* de campaña; **t. peg**, estaca *f.*

tentacle ['tentəkəl] *n* tentáculo *m.*

tentative ['tentətɪv] *adj* 1 (*not definite*) de prueba. 2 (*hesitant*) indeciso,-a.

tenterhooks ['tentəhʊks] *npl fig* **on t.**, sobre ascuas.

tenth [tenθ] I *adj & n* décimo,-a (*m,f*). II *n* (*fraction*) décimo *m.*

tenuous ['tenjʊəs] *adj* 1 tenue. 2 (*argument*) flojo,-a.

tenure ['tenjʊər] *n* 1 (*of office*) ocupación *f.* 2 (*of property*) arrendamiento *m.*

tepid ['tepɪd] *adj* tibio,-a.

term [tɜːm] I *n* 1 (*period*) período *m*; *Educ* trimestre *m*; **t. of office**, mandato *m*, legislatura *f*; **in the long/short t.**, a largo/corto plazo. 2 (*word*) término *m*; *fig* in

terms of money, en cuanto al dinero. **3 terms**, *(conditions)* condiciones *fpl*; **to come to terms with**, hacerse a la idea de. **4 to be on good/bad terms with sb**, tener buenas/malas relaciones con algn. **II** *vtr* calificar de.

terminal ['tɜ:mɪnəl] **I** *adj* terminal; **t. cancer**, cáncer incurable. **II** *n* terminal *f*.

terminate ['tɜ:mɪneɪt] **I** *vtr* terminar; **to t. a pregnancy**, abortar. **II** *vi* terminarse.

terminology [tɜ:mɪ'nɒlədʒɪ] *n* terminología *f*.

terminus ['tɜ:mɪnəs] *n* (*pl* **termini** ['tɜ:mɪnaɪ]) terminal *m*.

terrace ['terəs] *n* **1** *Agr* bancal *m*. **2** *GB* (*of houses*) hilera *f* de casas. **3** (*patio*) terraza *f*. **4** *Ftb* **the terraces**, las gradas.

terraced ['terəst] *adj* *GB* **t. houses**, casas *fpl* (de estilo uniforme) en hilera.

terrain [tə'reɪn] *n* terreno *m*.

terrible ['terəbəl] *adj* terrible; *fig* **I feel t.**, (*ill*) me encuentro fatal. ◆**terribly** *adv* terriblemente.

terrier ['terɪər] *n* terrier *m*.

terrific [tə'rɪfɪk] *adj* **1** *fam* (*excellent*) fenomenal. **2** (*extreme*) tremendo,-a.

terrify ['terɪfaɪ] *vtr* aterrorizar.

terrifying ['terɪfaɪɪŋ] *adj* aterrador,-a.

territory ['terɪtərɪ] *n* territorio *m*.

terror ['terər] *n* terror *m*.

terrorism ['terərɪzəm] *n* terrorismo *m*.

terrorist ['terərɪst] *adj & n* terrorista (*mf*).

terrorize ['terəraɪz] *vtr* aterrorizar.

terry ['terɪ] *n* **t. towel**, toalla *f* de rizo.

terse [tɜ:s] *adj* (*curt*) lacónico,-a.

test [test] **I** *vtr* probar, someter a una prueba; (*analyze*) analizar; *Med* hacer un análisis de. **II** *n* prueba *f*, examen *m*; **to put to the t.**, poner a prueba; **to stand the t.**, pasar la prueba; **t. match**, partido *m* internacional; **t. pilot**, piloto *m* de pruebas; **t. tube**, probeta *f*; **t.-tube baby**, niño *m* probeta.

testament ['testəmənt] *n* testamento *m*; **Old/New T.**, Antiguo/Nuevo Testamento.

testicle ['testɪkəl] *n* testículo *m*.

testify ['testɪfaɪ] **I** *vtr* declarar. **II** *vi* *fig* **to t. to sth**, atestiguar algo.

testimonial [testɪ'məʊnɪəl] *n* recomendación *f*.

testimony ['testɪmənɪ] *n* testimonio *m*, declaración *f*.

tetanus ['tetənəs] *n* tétano(s) *m inv*.

tether ['teðər] **I** *n* ronzal *m*; *fig* **to be at the end of one's t.**, estar hasta la coronilla. **II** *vtr* (*animal*) atar.

Texas ['teksəs] *n* Tejas.

text [tekst] *n* texto *m*.

textbook ['tekstbʊk] *n* libro *m* de texto.

textile ['tekstaɪl] **I** *n* tejido *m*. **II** *adj* textil.

texture ['tekstʃər] *n* textura *f*.

Thai [taɪ] *adj & n* tailandés,-esa (*m,f*).

Thailand ['taɪlænd] *n* Tailandia.

Thames [temz] *n* **the T.**, el Támesis.

than [ðæn, *unstressed* ðən] *conj* que; (*with numbers*) de; **he's older t. me**, es mayor que yo; **I have more/less t. you**, tengo más/menos que tú; **more interesting t. we thought**, más interesante de lo que creíamos; **more t. once**, más de una vez; **more t. ten people**, más de diez personas.

thank [θæŋk] *vtr* agradecer a; **t. you**, gracias.

thankful ['θæŋkfʊl] *adj* agradecido,-a.

thankless ['θæŋklɪs] *adj* (*task*) ingrato,-a.

thanks [θæŋks] *npl* gracias *fpl*; **no t.**, no gracias; **many t.**, muchas gracias; **t. for phoning**, gracias por llamar; **t. to**, gracias a.

thanksgiving [θæŋks'gɪvɪŋ] *n* *US* **T. Day**, Día *m* de Acción de Gracias.

that [ðæt, *unstressed* ðət] **I** *dem pron* (*pl* **those**) **1** ése *m*, ésa *f*; (*further away*) aquél *m*, aquélla *f*; **this one is new but t. is old**, éste es nuevo pero ése es viejo. **2** (*indefinite*) eso; (*remote*) aquello; **after t.**, después de eso; **like t.**, así; **t.'s right**, eso es; **t.'s where I live**, allí vivo yo; **what's t.?**, ¿qué es eso?; **who's t.?**, ¿quién es? **3** (*with relative*) el, la; **all those I saw**, todos los que vi.

II *dem adj* (*pl* **those**) (*masculine*) ese; (*feminine*) esa; (*further away*) (*masculine*) aquel; (*feminine*) aquella; **at t. time**, en aquella época; **t. book**, ese *or* aquel libro; **t. one**, ése, aquél.

III *rel pron* **1** (*subject, direct object*) que; **all (t.) you said**, todo lo que dijiste; **the letter (t.) I sent you**, la carta que te envié. **2** (*governed by preposition*) que, el/la que, los/las que, el/la cual, los/las cuales; **the car (t.) they came in**, el coche en el que vinieron. **3** (*when*) que, en que; **the moment (t.) you arrived**, el momento en que llegaste.

IV *conj* que; **come here so t. I can see you**, ven aquí (para) que te vea; **he said (t.) he would come**, dijo que vendría.

V *adv* así de, tanto, tan; **cut off t. much**, córteme un trozo así de grande; **I don't think it can be t. old**, no creo que sea tan viejo; **we haven't got t. much money**, no tenemos tanto dinero.

thatched [θætʃt] *adj* cubierto,-a con paja; **t. cottage**, casita *f* con techo de paja; **t. roof**, techo *m* de paja.

thaw [θɔ:] **I** *vtr* (*snow*) derretir; (*food, freezer*) descongelar. **II** *vi* descongelarse; (*snow*) derretirse. **III** *n* deshielo *m*.

the [ðə, *before vowel* ðɪ, *emphatic* ði:] **I** *def art* **1** el, la; *pl* los, las; **at** *or* **to t.**, al, a la; *pl* a los, a las; **of** *or* **from t.**, del, de la; *pl* de los, de las; **t. Alps**, los Alpes; **t. right time**, la hora exacta; **t. voice of t. people**, la voz del pueblo. **2** (*omitted*)

George t. Sixth, Jorge Sexto. **3 by t. day,** al día; **by t. dozen,** a docenas. **4** (with adjectives used as nouns) **t. elderly,** los ancianos. **5** (indicating kind) **he's not t. person to do that,** no es de los que hacen tales cosas. **6** (enough) **he hasn't t. patience to wait,** no tiene suficiente paciencia para esperar. **II** adv **t. more t. merrier,** cuantos más mejor; **t. sooner t. better,** cuanto antes mejor.

theatre, US **theater** [ˈθɪətər] n teatro m.

theatre-goer, US **theater-goer** [ˈθɪətəgəʊər] n aficionado,-a m,f, al teatro.

theatrical [θɪˈætrɪkəl] adj teatral.

theft [θeft] n robo m; **petty t.,** hurto m.

their [ðeər] poss adj (one thing) su; (various things) sus.

theirs [ðeəz] poss pron (el) suyo, (la) suya; pl (los) suyos, (las) suyas.

them [ðem] pers pron pl **1** (direct object) los, las; (indirect object) les; **I know t.,** los or las conozco; **I shall tell t. so,** se lo diré (a ellos or ellas); **it's t.!,** ¡son ellos!; **speak to t.,** hábleles. **2** (with preposition) ellos, ellas; **walk in front of t.,** camine delante de ellos; **they took the keys away with t.,** se llevaron las llaves; **both of t.,** los dos; **neither of t.,** ninguno de los dos; **none of t.,** ninguno de ellos.

theme [θiːm] n tema m; **t. tune,** sintonía f.

themselves [ðəmˈselvz] pers pron pl (as subject) ellos mismos, ellas mismas; (as direct or indirect object) se; (after a preposition) sí mismos, sí mismas; **they did it by t.,** lo hicieron ellos solos.

then [ðen] **I** adv **1** (at that time) entonces; **since t.,** desde entonces; **there and t.,** en el acto; **till t.,** hasta entonces. **2** (next, afterwards) luego. **3** (anyway) de todas formas. **4** (in that case) entonces; **go t.,** pues vete. **II** conj entonces. **III** adj **the t. president,** el entonces presidente.

theology [θɪˈɒlədʒɪ] n teología f.

theoretic(al) [θɪəˈretɪk(əl)] adj teórico,-a. ◆**theoretically** adv teóricamente.

theory [ˈθɪərɪ] n teoría f.

therapist [ˈθerəpɪst] n terapeuta mf.

therapy [ˈθerəpɪ] n terapia f.

there [ðeər] **I** adv **1** (indicating place) allí, allá; (nearer speaker) ahí; **here and t.,** acá y allá; **in t.,** ahí dentro; **is Peter t.?,** ¿está Peter? **2** (emphatic) **that man t.,** aquel hombre. **3** (unstressed) **t. is...,** **t. are...,** hay...; **t. were many cars,** había muchos coches; **t. were six of us,** éramos seis. **4** (in respect) **t.'s the difficulty,** ahí está la dificultad. **II** interj **so t.!,** ¡ea!; **t., t., bien, bien.

thereabouts [ˈðeərəbaʊts], US **thereabout** [ˈðeərəbaʊt] adv **in Cambridge or t.,** en Cambridge o por allí cerca; **at four o'clock or t.,** a las cuatro o así.

thereafter [ðeərˈɑːftər] adv a partir de entonces.

thereby [ˈðeəbaɪ] adv por eso o ello.

therefore [ˈðeəfɔːr] adv por lo tanto, por eso.

thermal [ˈθɜːməl] **I** adj (spring) termal; Phys térmico,-a. **II** n Meteor corriente térmica.

thermometer [θəˈmɒmɪtər] n termómetro m.

Thermos® [ˈθɜːməs] n **T. (flask),** termo m.

thermostat [ˈθɜːməstæt] n termostato m.

thesaurus [θɪˈsɔːrəs] n diccionario m de sinónimos.

these [ðiːz] **I** dem adj pl estos,-as. **II** dem pron pl éstos,-as; → **this.**

thesis [ˈθiːsɪs] n tesis f inv.

they [ðeɪ] pron pl **1** ellos, ellas; **t. are dancing,** están bailando; **t. are rich,** son ricos. **2** (stressed) **t. alone,** ellos solos; **t. themselves told me,** me lo dijeron ellos mismos. **3** (with relative) los, las. **4** (indefinite) **that's what t. say,** eso es lo que se dice; **t. say that ...,** se dice que ....

thick [θɪk] **I** adj **1** (book etc) grueso,-a; **a wall two metres t.,** un muro de dos metros de espesor. **2** (dense) espeso,-a. **3** fam (stupid) tonto,-a. **II** adv densamente. **III** n **to be in the t. of it,** estar metido,-a de lleno.

thicken [ˈθɪkən] **I** vtr espesar. **II** vi espesarse; fig (plot) complicarse.

thickness [ˈθɪknɪs] n (of wall etc) espesor m; (of wire, lips) grueso m; (of liquid, woodland) espesura f.

thickset [θɪkˈset] adj (person) rechoncho,-a.

thick-skinned [θɪkˈskɪnd] adj fig poco sensible.

thief [θiːf] n (pl **thieves** [θiːvz]) ladrón, -ona m,f.

thigh [θaɪ] n muslo m.

thimble [ˈθɪmbəl] n dedal m.

thin [θɪn] **I** adj (thinner, thinnest) **1** delgado,-a; **a t. slice,** una loncha fina. **2** (hair, vegetation) ralo,-a; (liquid) claro,-a; (population) escaso,-a. **3** fig (voice) débil; **a t. excuse,** un pobre pretexto. **II** vtr to **t. (down),** (paint) diluir. ◆**thinly** adv poco, ligeramente.

thing [θɪŋ] n **1** cosa f; **my things,** (clothing) mi ropa f sing; (possessions) mis cosas fpl; **for one t.,** en primer lugar; **the t. is ...,** resulta que ...; **what with one t. and another,** entre unas cosas y otras; **as things are,** tal como están las cosas. **2** **poor little t.!,** ¡pobrecito,-a!

think [θɪŋk] **I** vtr (pt & pp **thought**) **1** (believe) pensar, creer; **I t. so/not,** creo que sí/no. **2** **I thought as much,** yo me lo imaginaba. **II** vi **1** pensar (of, about; en); **give me time to t.,** dame tiempo para reflexionar; **to t. ahead,** prevenir. **2** (have *as opinion)* opinar, pensar; **to t. highly of sb,** apreciar a algn; **what do you t.?,** ¿a ti qué te parece? **3 just t.!,** ¡imagínate! ◆**think out** *vtr* meditar; **a carefully thought-out answer,** una respuesta razonada. ◆**think over** *vtr* reflexionar; **we'll have to t. it over,** lo tendremos que pensar. ◆**think up** *vtr* imaginar, idear.

thinking ['θɪŋkɪŋ] *adj* racional.

think-tank ['θɪŋktæŋk] *n fam* grupo *m* de expertos.

third [θɜːd] **I** *adj* tercero,-a; *(before masculine singular noun)* tercer; **(on) the t. of March,** el tres de marzo; **the T. World,** el Tercer Mundo; **t. party insurance,** seguro *m* a terceros. **II** *n* **1** *(in series)* tercero,-a *m,f.* **2** *(fraction)* tercio *m,* tercera parte. ◆**thirdly** *adv* en tercer lugar.

third-rate ['θɜːdreɪt] *adj* de calidad inferior.

thirst [θɜːst] *n* sed *f.*

thirsty ['θɜːstɪ] *adj* **(thirstier, thirstiest)** sediento,-a; **to be t.,** tener sed.

thirteen [θɜː'tiːn] *adj & n* trece *(m) inv.*

thirteenth [θɜː'tiːnθ] **I** *adj & n* decimotercero,-a *(m,f).* **II** *n* *(fraction)* decimotercera parte.

thirtieth ['θɜːtɪɪθ] **I** *adj & n* trigésimo,-a *(m,f).* **II** *n* *(fraction)* trigésima parte.

thirty ['θɜːtɪ] *adj & n* treinta *(m) inv.*

this [ðɪs] **I** *dem adj* (pl **these)** *(masculine)* este; *(feminine)* esta; **t. book/these books,** este libro/estos libros; **t. one,** éste, ésta. **II** *(pl* **these)** *dem pron* **1** *(indefinite)* esto; it was like t., fue así. **2** *(place)* **t. is where we met,** fue aquí donde nos conocimos. **3** *(time)* **it should have come before t.,** debería haber llegado ya. **4** *(specific person or thing)* éste *m,* ésta *f;* **I prefer these to those,** me gustan más éstos que aquéllos; *(introduction)* **t. is Mr Álvarez,** le presento al Sr. Álvarez; *Tel* **t. is Julia** (speaking), soy Julia. **III** *adv* **he got t. far,** llegó hasta aquí; **t. small/big,** así de pequeño/grande.

thistle ['θɪsəl] *n* cardo *m.*

thong [θɒŋ] *n* correa *f.*

thorax ['θɔːræks] *n* tórax *m.*

thorn [θɔːn] *n* espina *f.*

thorough ['θʌrə] *adj* *(careful)* minucioso,-a; *(work)* concienzudo,-a; *(knowledge)* profundo,-a; **to carry out a t. enquiry into a matter,** investigar a fondo un asunto. ◆**thoroughly** *adv (carefully)* a fondo; *(wholly)* completamente.

thoroughbred ['θʌrəbred] **I** *adj (horse)* de pura sangre. **II** *n (horse)* pura sangre *mf.*

thoroughfare ['θʌrəfeər] *n (road)* carretera *f; (street)* calle *f.*

those [ðəʊz] **I** *dem pron pl* ésos,-as; *(remote)* aquéllos,-as; **t. who,** los que, las que. **II** *dem adj pl* esos,-as; *(remote)* aquellos,-as; → **that I & II.**

though [ðəʊ] **I** *conj* **1** aunque; **strange t.**

it may seem, por (muy) extraño que parezca. **2 as t.,** como si; **it looks as t. he's gone,** parece que se ha ido. **II** *adv* sin embargo.

thought [θɔːt] *n* **1** *(act of thinking)* pensamiento *m;* **what a tempting t.!,** ¡qué idea más tentadora! **2** *(reflection)* reflexión *f.* **3** **it's the t. that counts,** *(intention)* lo que cuenta es la intención.

thoughtful ['θɔːtfʊl] *adj* *(pensive)* pensativo,-a; *(considerate)* atento,-a.

thoughtless ['θɔːtlɪs] *adj (person)* desconsiderado,-a; *(action)* irreflexivo,-a.

thousand ['θaʊzənd] *adj & n* mil *(m) inv;* **thousands of people,** miles de personas.

thousandth ['θaʊzənθ] **I** *adj* milésimo,-a. **II** *n* **1** *(in series)* milésimo,-a *m,f.* **2** *(fraction)* milésima parte.

thrash [θræʃ] **I** *vtr* dar una paliza a. **II** *vi* **to t. about** *o* **around,** agitarse. ◆**thrash out** *vtr* discutir a fondo.

thread [θred] **I** *n* **1** hilo *m;* **length of t.,** hebra *f.* **2** *(of screw)* rosca *f.* **II** *vtr* **1** *(needle)* enhebrar. **2** **to t. one's way,** colarse **(through,** por).

threadbare ['θredbeər] *adj* raído,-a.

threat [θret] *n* amenaza *f.*

threaten ['θretən] *vtr* amenazar; **to t. to do sth,** amenazar con hacer algo.

threatening ['θretənɪŋ] *adj* amenazador, -a. ◆**threateningly** *adv* de modo amenazador.

three [θriː] *adj & n* tres *(m).*

three-dimensional [θriːdɪ'menʃənəl] *adj* tridimensional.

threefold ['θriːfəʊld] **I** *adj* triple. **II** *adv* tres veces; **to increase t.,** triplicarse.

three-piece ['θriːpiːs] *adj* **t.-p. suit,** traje *m* de tres piezas; **t.-p. suite,** tresillo *m.*

three-ply ['θriːplaɪ] *adj* de tres hebras.

three-wheeler [θriː'wiːlər] *n Aut* coche *m* de tres ruedas; *(tricycle)* triciclo *m.*

thresh [θreʃ] *vtr* trillar.

threshold ['θreʃəʊld] *n* umbral *m; fig* **to be on the t. of,** estar a las puertas *o* en los umbrales de.

threw [θruː] *pt* → **throw.**

thrifty ['θrɪftɪ] *adj* **(thriftier, thriftiest)** económico,-a, ahorrador,-a.

thrill [θrɪl] **I** *n* **1** *(excitement)* emoción *f.* **2** *(quiver)* estremecimiento *m.* **II** *vtr (excite)* emocionar; *(audience)* entusiasmar.

thriller ['θrɪlər] *n* novela *f*/película *f* de suspense.

thrilling ['θrɪlɪŋ] *adj* emocionante.

thrive [θraɪv] *vi (pt* **thrived** *or* **throve;** *pp* **thrived** *or* **thriven** ['θrɪvən]) **1** *(person)* rebosar de salud. **2** *fig (business)* prosperar; **he thrives on it,** le viene de maravilla.

thriving ['θraɪvɪŋ] *adj fig* próspero,-a.

throat [θrəʊt] *n* garganta *f.*

throb [θrɒb] **I** *n (of heart)* latido *m; (of machine)* zumbido *m.* **II** *vi (heart)* latir; *(machine)* zumbar; **my head is throbbing,**

me va a estallar la cabeza.

throes [θrəʊz] *npl* to be in one's death t., estar agonizando; *fig* in the t. of ..., en pleno,- a ....

throne [θrəʊn] *n* trono *m*.

throng [θrɒŋ] I *n* multitud *f*, gentío *m*. II *vi* apiñarse. III *vtr* atestar.

throttle ['θrɒtəl] I *n* t. (valve), (of engine) válvula reguladora. II *vtr* (person) estrangular. ◆**throttle back** *vtr* (engine) desacelerar.

through [θru:] I *prep* 1 (place) a través de, por; to look t. the window, mirar por la ventana. 2 (time) a lo largo de; all t. his life, durante toda su vida. 3 (by means of) por, mediante; I learnt of it t. Jack, me enteré por Jack. 4 (because of) a or por causa de; t. ignorance, por ignorancia. II *adj* a t. train, un tren directo; t. traffic, tránsito *m*. III *adv* 1 (from one side to the other) de un lado a otro; to let sb t., dejar pasar a algn; *fig* socialist/ French t. and t., socialista/francés por los cuatro costados. 2 I'm t. with him, he terminado con él. 3 *Tel* to get t. to sb, comunicar con algn; you're t., ¡hablen!

throughout [θru:'aʊt] I *prep* por todo,-a; t. the year, durante todo el año. II *adv* (place) en todas partes; (time) todo el tiempo.

throve [θrəʊv] *pt* → thrive.

throw [θrəʊ] I *vtr* (pt threw; pp thrown) 1 tirar, arrojar; (to the ground) derribar; (rider) desmontar; *fig* he threw a fit, le dio un ataque; *fig* to t. a party, dar una fiesta. 2 (disconcert) desconcertar. II *n* tiro *m*, lanzamiento *m*; (in wrestling) derribo *m*. ◆**throw away** *vtr* (rubbish) tirar; (money) malgastar; (opportunity) perder. ◆**throw in** *vtr* 1 tirar; *Sport* sacar de banda; *fig* to t. in the towel, arrojar la toalla. 2 (include) añadir; (in deal) incluir (gratis). ◆**throw off** *vtr* (person, thing) deshacerse de; (clothes) quitarse. ◆**throw out** *vtr* (rubbish) tirar; (person) echar. ◆**throw up** I *vtr* 1 lanzar al aire. 2 *Constr* construir rápidamente. II *vi* fam vomitar, devolver.

throwaway ['θrəʊəweɪ] *adj* desechable.

throw-in ['θrəʊɪn] *n* Sport saque *m* de banda.

thrown [θrəʊn] *pp* → throw.

thru [θru:] *prep US* → through.

thrush [θrʌʃ] *n* Orn tordo *m*, zorzal *m*.

thrust [θrʌst] I *vtr* (pt & pp thrust) empujar con fuerza; he t. a letter into my hand, me puso una carta violentamente en la mano. II *n* (push) empujón *m*; Av Phys empuje *m*.

thud [θʌd] *n* ruido sordo.

thug [θʌg] *n* (lout) gamberro *m*; (criminal) criminal *m*.

thumb [θʌm] I *n* pulgar *m*. II *vtr* 1 manosear. 2 to t. a lift, hacer autostop.

◆**thumb through** *vtr* (book) hojear.

thumbtack ['θʌmtæk] *n US* chincheta *f*.

thump [θʌmp] I *n* 1 (sound) ruido sordo. 2 (blow) golpazo *m*; fam torta *f*. II *vtr* golpear. III *vi* 1 to t. on the table, golpear la mesa. 2 (heart) latir ruidosamente.

thunder ['θʌndər] I *n* trueno *m*; t. of applause, estruendo *m* de aplausos. II *vi* tronar.

thunderbolt ['θʌndəbəʊlt] *n* (lighting) rayo *m*; fig (news) bomba *f*.

thunderclap ['θʌndəklæp] *n* trueno *m*.

thunderous ['θʌndərəs] *adj* fig ensordecedor,-a.

thunderstorm ['θʌndəstɔ:m] *n* tormenta *f*.

thundery ['θʌndərɪ] *adj* (weather) tormentoso,-a.

Thursday ['θɜ:zdɪ] *n* jueves *m*.

thus [ðʌs] *adv* así, de esta manera; and t. ..., así que ....

thwart [θwɔ:t] *vtr* frustrar, desbaratar.

thyme [taɪm] *n* tomillo *m*.

thyroid ['θaɪrɔɪd] *n* tiroides *f inv*.

tiara [tɪ'ɑ:rə] *n* diadema *f*; Rel tiara *f*.

tic [tɪk] *n* tic *m*.

tick¹ [tɪk] I *n* 1 (sound) tic-tac *m*. 2 GB fam I'll do it in a t., ahora mismo lo hago. 3 (mark) marca *f* de visto bueno. II *vi* hacer tic-tac. III *vtr* marcar. ◆**tick off** *vtr* 1 (mark) marcar. 2 GB fam (reprimand) regañar. ◆**tick over** *vi* Aut funcionar al ralentí.

tick² [tɪk] *n* Ent garrapata *f*.

ticket ['tɪkɪt] *n* 1 (for bus etc) billete *m*; Theat entrada *f*; (for lottery) décimo *m*; t. collector, revisor,-a *m,f*; t. office, taquilla *f*. 2 (receipt) recibo *m*. 3 (label) etiqueta *f*. 4 Aut multa *f*.

tickle ['tɪkəl] I *vtr* hacer cosquillas. II *vi* hacer cosquillas. III *n* cosquillas *fpl*.

ticklish ['tɪklɪʃ] *adj* to be t., tener cosquillas.

tidal ['taɪdəl] *adj* de la marea; t. wave, ola *f* gigante.

tidbit ['tɪdbɪt] *n US* → titbit.

tiddlywinks ['tɪdlɪwɪŋks] *n* (game) pulga *f*.

tide [taɪd] *n* 1 marea *f*; high/low t., marea alta/baja. 2 fig (of events) curso *m*; the t. has turned, han cambiado las cosas; to go against the t., ir contra corriente.

tidings ['taɪdɪŋz] *npl fml* noticias *fpl*.

tidy ['taɪdɪ] I *adj* (tidier, tidiest) 1 (room, habits) ordenado,-a. 2 (appearance) arreglado,-a. II *vtr* arreglar; to t. away, poner en su sitio. III *vi* to t. (up), ordenar las cosas.

tie [taɪ] I *vtr* (shoelaces etc) atar; to t. a knot, hacer un nudo. II *vi* Sport empatar (with, con). II *n* 1 (bond) lazo *m*, vínculo *m*. 2 fig (hindrance) atadura *f*. 3 (clothing) corbata *f*. 4 Sport (match) partido *m*;

(draw) empate *m*. ◆**tie down** *vtr* sujetar; *fig* **to be tied down**, estar atado,- a; *fig* **to t. sb down to a promise**, obligar a algn a cumplir una promesa. ◆**tie up** *vtr* **1** *(parcel, dog)* atar. **2** *(deal)* concluir. **3** *(capital)* inmovilizar; *fig* **I'm tied up just now**, de momento estoy muy ocupado,-a.

tiebreaker ['taɪbreɪkə'] *n* tie-break *m*.

tiepin ['taɪpɪn] *n* alfiler *m* de corbata.

tier [tɪə'] *n (of seats)* fila *f*; *(in stadium)* grada *f*; **four-t. cake**, pastel *m* de cuatro pisos.

tiger ['taɪgə'] *n* tigre *m*.

tight [taɪt] **I** *adj* **1** apretado,-a; *(clothing)* ajustado,-a; *(seal)* hermético,-a; **my shoes are too t.**, me aprietan los zapatos; *fig* **to be in a t. corner**, estar en un apuro. **2** *(scarce)* escaso,-a; **money's a bit t.**, estamos escasos de dinero. **3** *(mean)* agarrado,-a. **4** *fam (drunk)* borracho,-a. **II** *adv* estrechamente; *(seal)* herméticamente; **hold t.**, agárrate fuerte; **shut t.**, bien cerrado,-a; **to sit t.**, no moverse de su sitio.

tighten ['taɪtən] **I** *vtr (screw)* apretar, *(rope)* tensar; *fig* **to t. (up) restrictions**, intensificar las restricciones. **II** *vi* apretarse; *(cable)* tensarse.

tightfisted [taɪt'fɪstɪd] *adj* tacaño,-a.

tightrope ['taɪtrəʊp] *n* cuerda floja; **t. walker**, funámbulo,-a *m,f*.

tights [taɪts] *npl (thin)* medias *fpl*, panties *mpl*; *(thick)* leotardos *mpl*; *(of dancer)* mallas *fpl*.

tile [taɪl] **I** *n (of roof)* teja *f*; *(glazed)* azulejo *m*; *(for floor)* baldosa *f*. **II** *vtr (roof)* tejar; *(wall)* azulejar; *(floor)* embaldosar.

tiled [taɪld] *adj (roof)* de *or* con tejas; *(wall)* revestido,-a de azulejos; *(floor)* embaldosado,-a.

till¹ [tɪl] *n (for cash)* caja *f*.

till² [tɪl] *vtr (field)* labrar, cultivar.

till³ [tɪl] **I** *prep* hasta; **from morning t. night**, de la mañana a la noche; **t. then**, hasta entonces. **II** *conj* hasta que.

tiller ['tɪlə'] *n Naut* caña *f* del timón.

tilt [tɪlt] **I** *n* **1** *(angle)* inclinación *f*. **2** *(at)* **full t.**, *(speed)* a toda velocidad. **II** *vi* **to t. over**, volcarse; **to t. (up)**, inclinarse. **III** *vtr* inclinar.

timber ['tɪmbə'] *n (wood)* madera *f* (de construcción); *(trees)* árboles *mpl*; **(piece of) t.**, viga *f*.

time [taɪm] **I** *n* **1** tiempo *m*; **all the t.**, todo el tiempo; **for some t. (past)**, desde hace algún tiempo; **I haven't seen him for a long t.**, hace mucho (tiempo) que no lo veo; **in a short t.**, en poco tiempo; **in no t.**, en un abrir y cerrar de ojos; **in t.**, a tiempo; **in three weeks' t.**, dentro de tres semanas; **to take one's t.**, hacer algo con calma; *fam* **to do t.**, cumplir una condena; **t. bomb**, bomba *f* de relojería; **t. limit**, límite *m* de tiempo; *(for payment etc)* plazo *m*; **t. switch**, interruptor *m* electrónico automático; **t. zone**, huso horario. **2** *(era)* época *f*, tiempos *mpl*; **a sign of the times**, un signo de los tiempos; **to be behind the times**, tener ideas anticuadas. **3** *(point in time)* momento *m*; **(at) any t. (you like)**, cuando quiera; **at no t.**, en ningún momento; **at that t.**, (en aquel) entonces; **at the same t.**, al mismo tiempo; **at times**, a veces; **from t. to t.**, de vez en cuando; **he may turn up at any t.**, puede llegar en cualquier momento. **4** *(time of day)* hora *f*; **and about t. too!**, ¡ya era hora!; **in good t.**, con anticipación; **on t.**, puntualmente; **what's the t.?**, ¿qué hora es? **5 t. of year**, época *f* del año. **6 to have a good/bad t.**, pasarlo bien/mal. **7** *(occasion)* vez *f*; **four at a t.**, cuatro a la vez; **next t.**, la próxima vez; **several times over**, varias veces; **three times running**, tres veces seguidas; **t. after t.**, una y otra vez. **8** *(in multiplication)* **three times four**, tres (multiplicado) por cuatro; **four times as big**, cuatro veces más grande. **9** *Mus* compás *m*; **in t.**, al compás.

II *vtr* **1** *(speech)* calcular la duración de; *Sport (race)* cronometrar. **2** *(choose the time of)* escoger el momento oportuno para.

time-consuming ['taɪmkənsjuːmɪŋ] *adj* que ocupa mucho tiempo.

time-lag ['taɪmlæg] *n* intervalo *m*.

timeless ['taɪmlɪs] *adj* eterno,-a.

timely ['taɪmlɪ] *adj (timelier, timeliest)* oportuno,-a.

timer ['taɪmə'] *n (device)* temporizador *m*.

timetable ['taɪmteɪbəl] *n* horario *m*.

timid ['tɪmɪd] *adj* tímido,-a.

timing ['taɪmɪŋ] *n* **1** *(timeliness)* oportunidad *f*; *(coordination)* coordinación *f*; **your t. was wrong**, no calculaste bien. **2** *Sport* cronometraje *m*.

tin [tɪn] **I** *n* **1** *(metal)* estaño *m*; **t. plate**, hojalata *f*. **2** *(container)* lata *f*. **II** *vtr (tins)* enlatar; **tinned food**, conservas *fpl*.

tinfoil ['tɪnfɔɪl] *n* papel *m* de estaño.

tinge [tɪndʒ] **I** *n* tinte *m*, matiz *m*. **II** *vtr* teñir.

tingle ['tɪngəl] *vi* **my feet are tingling**, siento un hormigueo en los pies.

tinker ['tɪŋkə'] **I** *n pej* calderero,-a *mf*. **II** *vi* **stop tinkering with the radio**, deja de toquetear la radio.

tinkle ['tɪŋkəl] *vi* tintinear.

tin-opener ['tɪnəʊpənə'] *n* abrelatas *m inv*.

tinsel ['tɪnsəl] *n* oropel *m*.

tint [tɪnt] **I** *n* tinte *m*, matiz *m*. **II** *vtr* teñir; **to t. one's hair**, teñirse el pelo.

tiny ['taɪnɪ] *adj (tinier, tiniest)* pequeñito,-a; **a t. bit**, un poquitín.

tip¹ [tɪp] **I** n (end) punta f; (of cigarette) colilla f; **it's on the t. of my tongue,** lo tengo en la punta de la lengua. **II** vtr poner cantera a; **tipped with steel,** con punta de acero.

tip² [tɪp] **I** n **1** (gratuity) propina f. **2** (advice) consejo m. **3** Sport (racing) pronóstico m. **II** vtr **1** dar una propina a. **2** Sport pronosticar. ◆**tip off** vtr (police) dar el chivatazo a.

tip³ [tɪp] **I** n GB rubbish t., vertedero m. **II** vtr inclinar; GB (rubbish) verter. **III** vi **to t. (up),** ladearse; (cart) bascular. ◆**tip over I** vtr volcar. **II** vi volcarse.

tipple ['tɪpəl] fam **I** vi empinar el codo. **II** n bebida alcohólica; **what's your t.?,** ¿qué te gusta beber?

tipsy ['tɪpsɪ] adj (tipsier, tipsiest) contentillo,-a.

tiptoe ['tɪptəʊ] **I** vi andar de puntillas; **to t. in/out,** entrar/salir de puntillas. **II** n **on t.,** de puntillas.

tiptop ['tɪptɒp] adj fam de primera.

tire¹ [taɪəʳ] n US → tyre.

tire² [taɪəʳ] **I** vtr cansar; **to t. sb out,** agotar a algn. **II** vi cansarse; **to t. of doing sth,** cansarse de hacer algo.

tired ['taɪəd] adj cansado,-a; **t. out,** rendido,-a; **to be t.,** estar cansado,-a; **to be t. of sth,** estar harto,-a de algo.

tireless ['taɪəlɪs] adj incansable.

tiresome ['taɪəsəm] adj pesado,-a.

tiring ['taɪərɪŋ] adj agotador,-a.

tissue ['tɪʃuː, 'tɪsjuː] n **1** Biol tejido m. **2** Tex tisú m; **t. paper,** papel m de seda. **3** (handkerchief) pañuelo m de papel, kleenex® m.

tit¹ [tɪt] n **to give t. for tat,** devolver la pelota.

tit² [tɪt] n sl (breast) teta f.

titbit ['tɪtbɪt] n golosina f.

titillate ['tɪtɪleɪt] vtr excitar.

tit(t)ivate ['tɪtɪveɪt] vtr emperifollar.

title ['taɪtəl] n **1** título m; Cin **credit titles,** ficha técnica; **t. page,** portada f; **t. role,** papel m principal. **2** Jur título m.

titter ['tɪtəʳ] **I** vi reírse nerviosamente; (foolishly) reírse tontamente. **II** n risa ahogada; (foolish) risilla tonta.

titular ['tɪtjʊləʳ] adj titular.

TM abbr of **trademark,** marca f (de fábrica).

to [tuː; unstressed before vowels tʊ, before consonants tə] **I** prep **1** (with place) a; (expressing direction) hacia; **from town to town,** de ciudad en ciudad; **he went to France/Japan,** fue a Francia/Japón; **I'm going to Mary's,** voy a casa de Mary; **it is thirty miles to London,** Londres está a treinta millas; **the train to Madrid,** el tren de Madrid; **to the east,** hacia el este; **to the right,** a la derecha; **what school do you go to?,** ¿a qué escuela vas? **2** (time) a; **from day to day,** de día

en día; **from two to four,** de dos a cuatro; **ten (minutes) to six,** las seis menos diez. **3** (as far as) hasta; **accurate to a millimetre,** exacto,-a hasta el milímetro. **4** (with indirect object) **he gave it to his cousin,** se lo dio a su primo; **what's that to you?,** ¿qué te importa a ti? **5** (towards a person) **he was very kind to me,** se portó muy bien conmigo. **6** (of) de; **heir to an estate,** heredero m de una propiedad; **adviser to the president,** consejero m del presidente. **7 to come to sb's assistance,** acudir en ayuda de algn; **to everyone's surprise,** para sorpresa de todos; **to this end,** con este fin. **8 to the best of my knowledge,** que yo sepa. **9** (compared to) **that's nothing to what I've seen,** eso no es nada en comparación con lo que he visto yo. **10** (in proportion) **one house to the square kilometre,** una casa por kilómetro cuadrado; **six votes to four,** seis votos contra cuatro. **11** (about) **what did he say to my suggestion?,** ¿qué contestó a mi sugerencia?

II with infin **1** with simple infinitives **to** is not translated but is shown by the verb endings; **to buy,** comprar; **to come,** venir. **2** (in order to) para; (with verbs of motion or purpose) a, por; **he did it to help me,** lo hizo para ayudarme; **he stopped to talk,** se detuvo a hablar; **he fought to convince them,** luchó por convencerlos. **3** various verbs followed by dependent infinitives take particular prepositions (a, de, en, por, con, para etc) and others take no preposition; → the entry of the verb in question. **4** (with adj and infin) a, de; **difficult to do,** difícil de hacer; **ready to listen,** dispuesto,-a a escuchar; **too hot to drink,** demasiado caliente para bebérselo. **5** (with noun and infin) **the first to complain,** el primero en quejarse; **this is the time to do it,** éste es el momento de hacerlo; **to have a great deal to do,** tener mucho que hacer. **6** (expressing following action) **he awoke to find the light still on,** al despertarse encontró la lámpara todavía encendida. **7** (with verbs of ordering, wishing etc) **he asked me to do it,** me pidió que lo hiciera. **8** (expressing obligation) **fifty employees are to go,** cincuenta empleados deben ser despedidos; **to have to do sth,** tener que hacer algo. **9** (replacing infin) **go if you want to,** váyase si quiere.

III adv **to go to and fro,** ir y venir; **to push the door to,** encajar la puerta.

toad [təʊd] n sapo m.

toadstool ['təʊdstuːl] n hongo m (venenoso).

toast¹ [təʊst] Culin **I** n pan tostado; **a slice of t.,** una tostada. **II** vtr tostar.

toast² [təʊst] **I** n (drink) brindis m inv; **to drink a t. to,** brindar por. **II** vtr brindar por.

toaster ['təʊstər] n tostador m (de pan).

tobacco [tə'bækəʊ] n tabaco m.

tobacconist [tə'bækənɪst] n GB estanquero,-a m,f; **t.'s (shop),** estanco m.

toboggan [tə'bɒgən] n tobogán m.

today [tə'deɪ] I n hoy m. II adv hoy; (nowadays) hoy en día; **a week t.,** justo dentro de una semana.

toddler ['tɒdlər] n niño,-a m,f que empieza a andar; **the toddlers,** los pequeñitos.

toddy ['tɒdɪ] n (drink) ponche m.

to-do [tə'duː] n lío m, jaleo m.

toe [təʊ] I n dedo m del pie; **big t.,** dedo gordo. II vtr **to t. the line,** conformarse.

toenail ['təʊneɪl] n uña f del dedo del pie.

toffee ['tɒfɪ] n caramelo m.

together [tə'geðər] adv junto, juntos,-as; **all t.,** todos juntos; **t. with,** junto con; **to bring t.,** reunir.

toil [tɔɪl] I n trabajo duro. II vi afanarse, trabajar (duro); **to t. up a hill,** subir penosamente una cuesta.

toilet ['tɔɪlɪt] n 1 wáter m, retrete m; (for public) servicios mpl; **t. paper o tissue,** papel higiénico; **t. roll,** rollo m de papel higiénico. 2 (washing etc) aseo m (personal); **t. bag,** neceser m; **t. soap,** jabón m de tocador.

toiletries ['tɔɪlɪtrɪz] npl artículos mpl de aseo.

token ['təʊkən] I n 1 (sign) señal f; **as a t. of respect,** en señal de respeto. 2 Com vale m; **book t.,** vale para comprar libros. II adj simbólico,-a.

told [təʊld] pt & pp → tell.

tolerable ['tɒlərəbəl] adj tolerable.

tolerance ['tɒlərəns] n tolerancia f.

tolerant ['tɒlərənt] adj tolerante.

tolerate ['tɒləreɪt] vtr tolerar.

toll[1] [təʊl] I vtr tocar. II vi doblar.

toll[2] [təʊl] n 1 Aut peaje m. 2 (loss) pérdidas fpl; **the death t.,** el número de víctimas mortales.

tomato [tə'mɑːtəʊ, US tə'meɪtəʊ] n (pl tomatoes) tomate m; **t. sauce,** salsa f de tomate.

tomb [tuːm] n tumba f, sepulcro m.

tomboy ['tɒmbɔɪ] n marimacho f.

tombstone ['tuːmstəʊn] n lápida f sepulcral.

tomcat ['tɒmkæt] n gato m (macho).

tomorrow [tə'mɒrəʊ] I n mañana m; **the day after t.,** pasado mañana; **t. night,** mañana por la noche. II adv mañana; **see you t.!,** ¡hasta mañana!; **t. week,** dentro de ocho días a partir de mañana.

ton [tʌn] n tonelada f; fam **tons of,** montones de.

tone [təʊn] I n tono m. II vi **to t. with sth,** armonizar con algo. ◆**tone down** vtr atenuar.

tone-deaf ['təʊndef] adj **to be t.-d.,** no

tener oído.

tongs [tɒŋz] npl (for sugar, hair) tenacillas fpl; (fire) t., tenazas fpl.

tongue [tʌŋ] n 1 lengua f; fig **to say sth t. in cheek,** decir algo con la boca pequeña; fig **t. twister,** trabalenguas m inv. 2 (of shoe) lengüeta f; (of bell) badajo m.

tongue-tied ['tʌŋtaɪd] adj mudo,-a (por la timidez).

tonic ['tɒnɪk] I n 1 Med tónico m. 2 (drink) tónica f. II adj tónico,-a; Mus **t. sol-fa,** solfeo m.

tonight [tə'naɪt] adv & n esta noche.

tonnage ['tʌnɪdʒ] n (of ship) tonelaje m.

tonne [tʌn] n → ton.

tonsil ['tɒnsəl] n amígdala f; **to have one's tonsils out,** ser operado,-a de las amígdalas.

tonsillitis [tɒnsɪ'laɪtɪs] n amigdalitis f.

too [tuː] adv 1 (besides) además. 2 (also) también. 3 (excessively) demasiado; **t. much money,** demasiado dinero; **ten pounds t. much,** diez libras de más; **t. frequently,** con demasiada frecuencia; **t. old,** demasiado viejo.

took [tʊk] pt → take.

tool [tuːl] n (utensil) herramienta f.

toolbox ['tuːlbɒks] n caja f de herramientas.

toot [tuːt] Aut I vtr tocar. II vi tocar la bocina.

tooth [tuːθ] n (pl teeth [tiːθ]) 1 diente m; (molar) muela f; fig **to fight t. and nail,** luchar a brazo partido. 2 (of saw) diente m; (of comb) púa f.

toothache ['tuːθeɪk] n dolor m de muelas.

toothbrush ['tuːθbrʌʃ] n cepillo m de dientes.

toothpaste ['tuːθpeɪst] n pasta dentífrica.

toothpick ['tuːθpɪk] n mondadientes m inv.

top[1] [tɒp] I n 1 (upper part) parte f de arriba; (of hill) cumbre f, cima f; (of tree) copa f; **from t. to bottom,** de arriba a abajo; **on t. of,** encima de; fig **on t. of it all ...,** para colmo ...; **t. hat,** sombrero m de copa. 2 (surface) superficie f. 3 (of list etc) cabeza f. 4 (of bottle etc) tapa f, tapón m. 5 (garment) camiseta f. 6 (best) lo mejor. 7 fig **at the t. of one's voice,** a voz en grito. II adj 1 (part) superior, de arriba; **the t. floor,** el último piso; **t. coat,** (of paint) última mano. 2 (highest) más alto,-a; Aut **t. gear,** directa f. 3 (best) mejor. III vtr 1 (place on top of) coronar. 2 Theat **to t. the bill,** encabezar el reparto. ◆**top up** vtr llenar hasta el tope; **to t. up the petrol tank,** llenar el depósito; fig **and to t. it all,** y para colmo.

top[2] [tɒp] n (toy) peonza f.

topic ['tɒpɪk] n tema m.

topical ['tɒpɪkəl] adj de actualidad.

top-level ['tɒplevəl] adj de alto nivel.

topmost ['tɒpməust] *adj* (el) más alto, (la) más alta.

topple ['tɒpəl] I *vi* (*building*) venirse abajo; **to t. (over)**, volcarse. II *vtr* volcar; *fig* (*government*) derrocar.

top-secret [tɒp'si:krɪt] *adj* de alto secreto.

topsy-turvy [tɒpsɪ'tɜ:vɪ] *adj & adv* al revés; (*in confusion*) en desorden, patas arriba.

torch [tɔ:tʃ] *n* (*electric*) linterna *f*.

tore [tɔ:r] *pt* → tear².

torment [tɔ:'ment] I *vtr* atormentar. II *n* ['tɔ:ment] tormento *m*, suplicio *m*.

torn [tɔ:n] *pp* → tear².

tornado [tɔ:'neɪdəu] *n* tornado *m*.

torpedo [tɔ:'pi:dəu] *n* torpedo *m*.

torrent ['tɒrənt] *n* torrente *m*.

torrential [tɒ'renʃəl] *adj* torrencial.

torrid ['tɒrɪd] *adj* tórrido,-a.

torso ['tɔ:səu] *n* torso *m*.

tortoise ['tɔ:təs] *n* tortuga *f* de tierra.

tortoiseshell ['tɔ:təsʃel] *adj* de carey.

torture ['tɔ:tʃər] I *vtr* torturar; *fig* atormentar. II *n* tortura *f*; *fig* tormento *m*.

Tory ['tɔ:rɪ] *adj & n GB Pol* conservador,-a (*m,f*).

toss [tɒs] I *vtr* 1 (*ball*) tirar; **to t. a coin**, echar a cara o cruz. 2 (*throw about*) sacudir. II *vi* 1 **to t. about**, agitarse; **to t. and turn**, dar vueltas en la cama. 2 *Sport* **to t. (up)**, sortear. III *n* 1 (*of ball*) lanzamiento *m*; (*of coin*) sorteo *m* (a cara o cruz). 2 (*of head*) sacudida *f*.

tot¹ [tɒt] *n* 1 (*tiny*) **t.**, (*child*) nene,-a *m,f*. 2 (*of whisky etc*) trago *m*.

tot² [tɒt] *GB vtr* **to t. up**, sumar.

total ['təutəl] I *n* total *m*; (*in bill*) importe *m*; **grand t.**, suma *f* total. II *adj* total. III *vtr* sumar. IV *vi* **to t. up to**, ascender a. ◆**totally** *adv* totalmente.

totalitarian [təutælɪ'teərɪən] *adj* totalitario,-a.

tote [təut] *n fam Sport* totalizador *m*.

tote bag ['təutbæg] *n* petate *m*.

totem ['təutəm] *n* tótem *m*.

totter ['tɒtər] *vi* tambalearse.

touch [tʌtʃ] I *vtr* 1 tocar; *fig* **to t. on a subject**, tocar un tema. 2 (*equal*) igualar. 3 (*move*) conmover. II *vi* tocarse; *fig* **it was t. and go whether we caught the train**, estuvimos a punto de perder el tren. III *n* 1 toque *m*. 2 (*sense of touch*) tacto *m*. 3 **it was a nice t. of his**, fue un detalle de su parte; **to put the finishing touches to sth**, dar los últimos toques a algo. 4 (*ability*) habilidad *f*. 5 (*contact*) contacto *m*; **to be/get/keep in t. with sb**, estar/ponerse/mantenerse en contacto con algn; **to be out of t. with sth**, no estar al tanto de algo. 6 (*small amount*) pizca *f*. 7 *Sport* **in t.**, fuera de banda. ◆**touch down** *vi* (*plane*) aterrizar. ◆**touch off**

vtr desencadenar. ◆**touch up** *vtr* (*picture*) retocar.

touchdown ['tʌtʃdaun] *n* 1 (*of plane*) aterrizaje *m*; (*of space capsule*) amerizaje *m*. 2 *Rugby* ensayo *m*.

touched [tʌtʃt] *adj* 1 (*moved*) emocionado,-a. 2 *fam* (*crazy*) tocado,-a.

touching ['tʌtʃɪŋ] *adj* conmovedor,-a.

touchline ['tʌtʃlaɪn] *n* línea *f* de banda.

touchy ['tʌtʃɪ] *adj* (**touchier, touchiest**) *fam* (*person*) susceptible; (*subject*) delicado,-a.

tough [tʌf] I *adj* (*material, competitor etc*) fuerte, resistente; (*test, criminal, meat*) duro,-a; (*punishment*) severo,-a; (*problem*) difícil. II *n* (*person*) matón *m*.

toughen ['tʌfən] *vtr* endurecer.

toupee ['tu:peɪ] *n* tupé *m*.

tour [tuər] I *n* 1 (*journey*) viaje *m*; **package t.**, viaje organizado. 2 (*of monument etc*) visita *f*; (*of city*) recorrido turístico. 3 *Sport Theat* gira *f*; **on t.**, de gira. II *vtr* 1 (*country*) viajar por. 2 (*building*) visitar. 3 *Theat* estar de gira en. III *vi* estar de viaje.

tourism ['tuərɪzəm] *n* turismo *m*.

tourist ['tuərɪst] *n* turista *mf*; **t. centre**, centro *m* de información turística; *Av* **t. class**, clase *f* turista.

tournament ['tuənəmənt] *n* torneo *m*.

tousled ['tauzəld] *adj* (*hair*) despeinado,-a.

tout [taut] I *vtr Com* tratar de vender; (*tickets*) revender. II *vi* salir a la caza y captura de compradores. III *n Com* gancho *m*; **ticket t.**, revendedor *m* de entradas.

tow [təu] I *n* **to take a car in t.**, remolcar un coche. II *vtr* remolcar.

towards [tə'wɔ:dz, tɔ:dz] *prep* 1 (*direction, time*) hacia. 2 (*with regard to*) hacia, (para) con; **our duty t. others**, nuestro deber para con los demás; **what is your attitude t. religion?**, ¿cuál es su actitud respecto a la religión?

towel ['tauəl] I *n* toalla *f*; **hand t.**, toallita *f*; **t. rail**, toallero *m*. II *vtr* **to t. dry**, secar con una toalla.

towelling ['tauəlɪŋ] *n* felpa *f*.

tower ['tauər] I *n* torre *f*. II *vi* **to t. over** *or* **above sth**, dominar algo.

towering ['tauərɪŋ] *adj* impresionante, enorme.

town [taun] *n* ciudad *f*; (*small*) pueblo *m*; **to go into t.**, ir al centro; *fam* **to go to t.**, tirar la casa por la ventana; **t. council**, ayuntamiento *m*; **t. councillor**, concejal,-a *m,f*; **t. hall**, ayuntamiento *m*; **t. planning**, urbanismo *m*.

townspeople ['taunzpi:pəl] *npl* ciudadanos *mpl*.

towpath ['təupɑ:θ] *n* sendero *m* a lo largo de un canal.

towrope ['təurəup] *n* cable *m* de remolque.

toxic ['tɒksɪk] *adj* tóxico,-a.

toy [tɔɪ] **I** *n* juguete *m*. **II** *vi* to t. with an idea, acariciar una idea; **to t. with one's food,** comer sin gana.

toyshop ['tɔɪʃɒp] *n* juguetería *f*.

trace [treɪs] **I** *n* 1 (*sign*) indicio *m*, vestigio *m*. 2 (*tracks*) huella(s) *f(pl)*. **II** *vtr* 1 (*drawing*) calcar. 2 (*plan*) bosquejar. 3 (*locate*) seguir la pista de.

tracing ['treɪsɪŋ] *n* t. paper, papel *m* de calco.

track [træk] **I** *n* 1 (*trail*) huellas *fpl*, pista *f*; **to keep/lose t. of sb,** no perder/perder de vista a algn. 2 (*pathway*) camino *m*; **to be on the right/wrong t.,** ir por el buen/ mal camino. 3 *Sport* pista *f*; (*for motor racing*) circuito *m*; *fig* t. **record,** historial *m*. 4 *Rail* vía *f*; *fig* **he has a one-t. mind,** tiene una única obsesión. 5 (*on record*) canción *f*. **II** *vtr* seguir la pista de; (*with radar*) seguir la trayectoria de. ◆**track down** *vtr* (*locate*) localizar.

tracksuit ['træksuːt] *n* chandal *m*.

tract¹ [trækt] *n* (*expanse*) extensión *f*.

tract² [trækt] *n* (*treatise*) tratado *m*; (*pamphlet*) folleto *m*.

traction ['trækʃən] *n* tracción *f*.

tractor ['træktər] *n* tractor *m*.

trade [treɪd] **I** *n* 1 (*profession*) oficio *m*; **by t.,** de oficio. 2 *Com* comercio *m*; **it's good for t.,** es bueno para los negocios; **the building t.,** (la industria de) la construcción; **t. name,** nombre *m* comercial; **t. union,** sindicato *m*; **t. unionist,** sindicalista *mf*. **II** *vi* comerciar (in, en). **III** *vtr* **to t. sth for sth,** trocar algo por algo. ◆**trade in** *vtr* dar como entrada.

trademark ['treɪdmɑːk] *n* marca *f* (de fábrica); **registered t.,** marca registrada.

trader ['treɪdər] *n* comerciante *mf*.

tradesman ['treɪdzmən] *n* (*shopkeeper*) tendero *m*.

trading ['treɪdɪŋ] *n* comercio *m*; *GB* t. **estate,** polígono *m* industrial.

tradition [trə'dɪʃən] *n* tradición *f*.

traditional [trə'dɪʃənəl] *adj* tradicional.

traffic ['træfɪk] **I** *n* 1 tráfico *m*, circulación *f*; **t. island,** isleta *f*; **t. jam,** atasco *m*; **t. lights,** semáforo *m sing*; **t. warden,** ≈ guardia *mf* urbano,-a. 2 (*trade*) tráfico *m*. **II** *vi* (*pt & pp* **trafficked**) **to t. in drugs,** traficar con droga.

trafficker ['træfɪkər] *n* traficante *mf*.

tragedy ['trædʒɪdɪ] *n* tragedia *f*.

tragic ['trædʒɪk] *adj* trágico,-a.

trail [treɪl] **I** *vtr* 1 (*drag*) arrastrar. 2 (*follow*) rastrear. **II** *vi* 1 (*drag*) arrastrarse. 2 **to t. behind,** rezagarse. **III** *n* 1 (*track*) pista *f*, rastro *m*. 2 (*path*) senda *f*, camino *m*. 3 (*of smoke*) estela *f*.

trailer ['treɪlər] *n* 1 *Aut* remolque *m*. 2 *US Aut* (*caravan*) caravana *f*. 3 *Cin* trailer *m*, avance *m*.

train [treɪn] **I** *n* 1 *Rail* tren *m*. 2 (*of vehicles*) convoy *m*; (*of followers*) séquito *m*; (*of events*) serie *f*. 3 (*of dress*) cola *f*. **II** *vtr* 1 (*teach*) formar; *Sport* entrenar; (*animal*) amaestrar; (*voice etc*) educar. 2 (*gun*) apuntar (on, a); (*camera*) enfocar (on, a). **III** *vi* prepararse; *Sport* entrenarse.

trainee [treɪ'niː] *n* aprendiz,-a *m,f*.

trainer ['treɪnər] *n* 1 *Sport* entrenador,-a *m,f*; (*of dogs*) amaestrador,-a *m,f*; (*of lions*) domador,-a *m,f*. 2 **trainers,** (*shoes*) zapatillas *fpl* de deporte.

training ['treɪnɪŋ] *n* (*instruction*) formación *f*; *Sport* entrenamiento *m*; (*of animals*) amaestramiento *m*; (*of lions*) doma *f*; **to go into t.,** empezar el entrenamiento; **vocational t.,** formación profesional.

traipse [treɪps] *vi fam* vagar.

trait [treɪt] *n* rasgo *m*.

traitor ['treɪtər] *n* traidor,-a *m,f*.

trajectory [trə'dʒektərɪ] *n* trayectoria *f*.

tram [træm], **tramcar** ['træmkɑːr] *n GB* tranvía *m*.

tramp [træmp] **I** *vi* 1 (*travel on foot*) caminar. 2 (*walk heavily*) andar con pasos pesados. **II** *n* (*person*) vagabundo,-a *m,f*; *pej* **she's a t.,** es una fulana.

trample ['træmpəl] *vtr* **to t. down the grass,** pisotear la hierba; **to t. sth underfoot,** pisotear algo.

trampoline ['træmpəliːn] *n* cama elástica.

trance [trɑːns] *n* trance *m*.

tranquil ['træŋkwɪl] *adj* tranquilo,-a.

tranquillity [træŋ'kwɪlɪtɪ] *n* tranquilidad *f*.

tranquillizer ['træŋkwɪlaɪzər] *n* tranquilizante *m*.

transact [træn'zækt] *vtr* negociar.

transaction [træn'zækʃən] *n* (*procedure*) tramitación *f*; (*deal*) transacción *f*.

transatlantic [trænzət'læntɪk] *adj* transatlántico,-a.

transcend [træn'send] *vtr* trascender.

transcribe [træn'skraɪb] *vtr* transcribir.

transcript ['trænskrɪpt] *n* transcripción *f*.

transcription [træn'skrɪpʃən] *n* transcripción *f*.

transfer [træns'fɜːr] **I** *vtr* trasladar; (*funds*) trasferir; *Jur* ceder; *Ftb* traspasar; *Tel* **to t. the charges,** hacer una llamada a cobro revertido. **II** ['trænsfɜːr] *n* 1 traslado *m*; (*of funds*) trasferencia *f*; *Jur* cesión *f*; *Ftb* traspaso *m*. 2 (*picture, design*) calcomanía *f*.

transform [træns'fɔːm] *vtr* trasformar.

transformation [trænsfə'meɪʃən] *n* trasformación *f*.

transfusion [træns'fjuːʒən] *n Med* transfusión *f* (de sangre).

transgress [trænz'gres] *vi fml* transgredir.

transient ['trænzɪənt] *adj* transitorio,-a.

transistor [træn'zɪstər] *n* transistor *m*.

transit ['trænzɪt] *n* tránsito *m*; **in t.,** de

tránsito.

transition [træn'zɪʃən] n transición f.

transitive ['trænzɪtɪv] adj transitivo,-a.

transitory ['trænzɪtərɪ] adj transitorio,-a.

translate [træns'leɪt] vtr traducir.

translation [træns'leɪʃən] n traducción f.

translator [træns'leɪtər] n traductor,-a m,f.

translucent [trænz'luːsənt] adj translúcido,-a.

transmission [trænz'mɪʃən] n transmisión f.

transmit [trænz'mɪt] vtr transmitir.

transmitter [trænz'mɪtər] n Rad (set) transmisor m; Rad TV (station) emisora f.

transparency [træns'pærənsɪ] n Phot diapositiva f.

transparent [træns'pærənt] adj transparente.

transpire [træn'spaɪər] vi (happen) ocurrir; it transpired that ..., ocurrió que ....

transplant [træns'plɑːnt] I vtr trasplantar. II ['trænsplɑːnt] n trasplante m.

transport [træns'pɔːt] I vtr transportar. II ['trænspɔːt] n transporte m; t. aircraft/ship, avión m/buque de transporte; GB t. café, bar m de carretera.

transportation [trænspɔː'teɪʃən] n transporte m.

transvestite [trænz'vestaɪt] n fam travestí mf.

trap [træp] I n trampa f; t. door, trampilla f; Theat escotillón m. II vtr atrapar.

trapeze [trə'piːz] n trapecio m.

trappings ['træpɪŋz] npl parafernalia f sing.

trash [træʃ] n (inferior goods) bazofia f; US (rubbish) basura f; fig to talk a lot of t., decir tonterías; US t. can, cubo m de la basura.

trashy ['træʃɪ] adj (trashier, trashiest) de ínfima calidad.

trauma ['trɔːmə] n trauma m.

traumatic [trɔː'mætɪk] adj traumático,-a.

travel ['trævəl] I vi 1 viajar; to t. through, recorrer. 2 (vehicle, electric current) ir; fig (news) propagarse. II vtr recorrer. III n viajar m; t. agency, agencia f de viajes.

traveller, US **traveler** ['trævələr] n viajero,-a m,f; t.'s cheque, cheque m de viaje.

travelling, US **traveling** ['trævəlɪŋ] I adj (salesman) ambulante. II n viajes mpl, (el) viajar m; I'm fond of t., me gusta viajar; t. expenses, gastos mpl de viaje.

travel-sick ['trævəlsɪk] adj to be t., estar mareado,-a.

travesty ['trævɪstɪ] n parodia f.

trawler ['trɔːlər] n barco m de arrastre.

tray [treɪ] n (for food) bandeja f; (for letters) cesta f (para la correspondencia).

treacherous ['tretʃərəs] adj 1 (person) traidor,-a; (action) traicionero,-a. 2 (dangerous) peligroso,-a.

treachery ['tretʃərɪ] n traición f.

treacle ['triːkəl] n GB melaza f.

tread [tred] I vi (pt trod; pp trod or trodden) pisar; to t. on, pisar. II vtr 1 (step on) pisar. 2 to t. water, mantenerse a flote verticalmente. III n 1 (step) paso m; (sound) ruido m de pasos. 2 (of tyre) banda f de rodadura.

treadmill ['tredmɪl] n fig rutina f.

treason ['triːzən] n traición f.

treasure ['treʒər] I n tesoro m. II vtr (keep) guardar como oro en paño; (value) apreciar muchísimo.

treasurer ['treʒərər] n tesorero,-a m,f.

treasury ['treʒərɪ] n Pol the T., ≈ Ministerio m de Hacienda; T. bill, bono m del Tesoro.

treat [triːt] I n 1 (present) regalo m. 2 (pleasure) placer m. II vtr 1 tratar; to t. badly, maltratar. 2 (regard) considerar. 3 he treated them to dinner, les invitó a cenar.

treatise ['triːtɪz] n tratado m.

treatment ['triːtmənt] n 1 (of person) trato m. 2 (of subject, of patient) tratamiento m.

treaty ['triːtɪ] n tratado m.

treble ['trebəl] I adj 1 (triple) triple; Mus t. clef, clave f de sol; Mus t. voice, voz f tiple. II vtr triplicar. III vi triplicarse.

tree [triː] n árbol m; apple/cherry t., manzano m/cerezo m.

treetop ['triːtɒp] n copa f.

trek [trek] I n (journey) viaje m (largo y difícil); fam (walk) caminata f. II vi (pt & pp trekked) hacer un viaje largo y difícil; fam (walk) ir caminando.

trellis ['trelɪs] n enrejado m.

tremble ['trembəl] vi temblar, estremecerse.

trembling ['tremblɪŋ] adj tembloroso,-a.

tremendous [trɪ'mendəs] adj (huge) enorme; (success) arrollador,-a; (shock etc) tremendo,-a; fam (marvellous) estupendo,-a.

tremor ['tremər] n temblor m.

trench [trentʃ] n 1 (ditch) zanja f; Mil trinchera f. 2 t. coat, trinchera f.

trend [trend] I n (tendency) tendencia f; (fashion) moda f. II vi tender (to, towards, hacia).

trendy ['trendɪ] adj (trendier, trendiest) fam (person) moderno,-a; (clothes) a la última.

trepidation [trepɪ'deɪʃən] n turbación f.

trespass ['trespəs] vi entrar sin autorización.

trespasser ['trespəsər] n intruso,-a m,f.

trestle ['tresəl] n caballete m.

trial ['traɪəl] n 1 Jur proceso m, juicio m. 2 (test) prueba f; on t., a prueba; by t. and error, a fuerza de equivocarse. 3 trials, (competition) concurso m sing. 4 trials, (suffering) sufrimiento m sing; t.

and tribulations, tribulaciones *fpl.*

triangle ['traɪæŋgəl] *n* triángulo *m.*

tribe [traɪb] *n* tribu *f.*

tribunal [traɪ'bjuːnəl] *n* tribunal *m.*

tributary ['trɪbjutərɪ] *n* (*river*) afluente *m.*

tribute ['trɪbjuːt] *n* 1 (*payment*) tributo *m.* 2 (*mark of respect*) homenaje *m*; **to pay t. to,** rendir homenaje a.

trice [traɪs] *n fam* **in a t.,** en un abrir y cerrar de ojos.

trick [trɪk] I *n* 1 (*ruse*) ardid *m*; (*dishonest*) engaño *m*; (*in question*) trampa *f.* 2 (*practical joke*) broma *f*; **to play a t. on sb,** gastarle una broma a algn; (*malicious*) jugar una mala pasada a algn. 3 (*of magic, knack*) truco *m*; **that'll do the t.!,** ¡eso es exactamente lo que hace falta! 4 *Cards* baza *f.* II *vtr* engañar; **to t. sb out of sth,** estafar algo a algn.

trickery ['trɪkərɪ] *n* engaños *mpl,* trampas *fpl.*

trickle ['trɪkəl] I *vi* discurrir; (*water*) gotear. II *n* hilo *m.*

tricky ['trɪkɪ] *adj* (*trickier, trickiest*) (*person*) astuto,-a; (*situation, mechanism*) delicado,-a.

tricycle ['traɪsɪkəl] *n* triciclo *m.*

tried [traɪd] *pt & pp →* **try.**

trifle ['traɪfəl] I *n* 1 (*insignificant thing*) bagatela *f*; **he's a t. optimistic,** es ligeramente optimista. 2 *GB Culin* postre *m* (de bizcocho, jerez, gelatina, frutas y nata). II *vi* **to t. with,** tomar a la ligera.

trifling ['traɪflɪŋ] *adj* insignificante, trivial.

trigger ['trɪgər] I *n* (*of gun*) gatillo *m*; (*of mechanism*) disparador *m.* II *vtr* **to t. (off),** desencadenar.

trill [trɪl] *n* (*of music, bird*) trino *m*; *Ling* vibración *f.*

trilogy ['trɪlədʒɪ] *n* trilogía *f.*

trim [trɪm] I *adj* (*trimmer, trimmest*) (*neat*) aseado,-a; **to have a t. figure,** tener buen tipo. II *vtr* 1 (*cut*) recortar; *fig* (*expenses*) disminuir. 2 (*decorate*) adornar. III *n* 1 (*condition*) estado *m*; *Naut* asiento *m.* 2 (*cut*) recorte *m.*

trimming ['trɪmɪŋ] *n* 1 (*cut*) recorte *m.* 2 (*on clothes*) adorno *m.* 3 *Culin* **trimmings,** guarnición *f sing.*

trinket ['trɪŋkɪt] *n* baratija *f.*

trio ['triːəʊ] *n* trío *m.*

trip [trɪp] I *n* 1 (*journey*) viaje *m*; (*excursion*) excursión *f*; **to go on a t.,** ir de excursión. 2 *sl* **to be on a t.,** (*on drugs*) estar colocado,-a. II *vi* 1 **to t. (up),** (*stumble*) tropezar (**over,** con); *fig* (*err*) equivocarse. 2 **to t. along,** ir con paso ligero. III *vtr* **to t. sb (up),** poner la zancadilla a algn; *fig* coger *or* pillar a algn.

tripe [traɪp] *n* 1 *Culin* callos *mpl.* 2 *fam* bobadas *fpl.*

triple ['trɪpəl] I *adj* triple. II *vtr* triplicar. III *vi* triplicarse.

triplet ['trɪplɪt] *n* trillizo,-a *m,f.*

triplicate ['trɪplɪkɪt] *adj* **in t.,** por triplicado.

tripod ['traɪpɒd] *n* trípode *m.*

trite [traɪt] *adj* (*sentiment*) banal; (*subject*) trillado,-a.

triumph ['traɪəmf] I *n* triunfo *m.* II *vi* triunfar.

triumphant [traɪ'ʌmfənt] *adj* triunfante.

trivia ['trɪvɪə] *npl* trivialidades *fpl.*

trivial ['trɪvɪəl] *adj* trivial, banal.

trod [trɒd] *pt & pp →* **tread.**

trodden ['trɒdən] *pp →* **tread.**

trolley ['trɒlɪ] *n GB* carro *m.*

trombone [trɒm'bəʊn] *n* trombón *m.*

troop [truːp] I *n* 1 (*of people*) grupo *m.* 2 *Mil* **troops,** tropas *fpl.* II *vi* **to t. in/out/off,** entrar/salir/marcharse en tropel.

trooper ['truːpər] *n* soldado *m* de caballería.

trooping ['truːpɪŋ] *n GB* **t. the colour,** ceremonia *f* de homenaje a la bandera de un regimiento.

trophy ['trəʊfɪ] *n* trofeo *m.*

tropic ['trɒpɪk] *n* trópico *m.*

tropical ['trɒpɪkəl] *adj* tropical.

trot [trɒt] I *vi* trotar. II *n* trote *m*; **to go at a t.,** ir al trote; *fam* **on the t.,** (*in succession*) seguidos,-as.

trouble ['trʌbəl] I *n* 1 (*misfortune*) desgracia *f.* 2 (*problems*) problemas *mpl*; **to be in t.,** estar en un lío; **to cause sb t.,** ocasionar problemas a algn; **to get sb out of t.,** sacar a algn de un apuro; **the t. is that ...,** lo que pasa es que .... 3 (*effort*) esfuerzo *m*; **it's no t.,** no es ninguna molestia; **it's not worth the t.,** no merece la pena; **to take the t. to do sth,** molestarse en hacer algo. 4 (*conflict*) conflicto *m.* 5 *Med* enfermedad *f*; **to have liver t.,** tener problemas de hígado. II *vtr* 1 (*affect*) afligir; (*worry*) preocupar; **that doesn't t. him at all,** eso le tiene sin cuidado. 2 (*bother*) molestar. III *vi* molestarse.

troubled ['trʌbəld] *adj* agitado,-a.

troublemaker ['trʌbəlmeɪkər] *n* alborotador,-a *m,f.*

troubleshooter ['trʌbəlʃuːtər] *n Ind* persona encargada de solucionar problemas.

troublesome ['trʌbəlsəm] *adj* molesto,-a.

trough [trɒf] *n* 1 (*drinking*) **t.,** abrevadero *m*; (*feeding*) **t.,** pesebre *m.* 2 (*of wave*) seno *m.* 3 *Geog Meteor* depresión *f.*

trounce [traʊns] *vtr* dar una paliza a.

troupe [truːp] *n Theat* compañía *f.*

trousers ['traʊzəz] *npl* pantalón *m sing,* pantalones *mpl.*

trousseau ['truːsəʊ] *n* ajuar *m.*

trout [traʊt] *n* trucha *f.*

trowel ['traʊəl] *n* 1 (*builder's*) palustre *m.* 2 (*for gardening*) desplantador *m.*

truant ['truːənt] *n* **to play t.,** hacer novillos.

truce [truːs] *n* tregua *f.*

truck¹ [trʌk] *n* 1 *GB Rail* vagón *m.* 2

US Aut camión *m*; **t. driver**, camionero,-a *m,f*.

truck² [trʌk] *n* **1 to have no t. with**, no estar dispuesto a toerar. **2** *US* verduras *fpl*; **t. farming**, cultivo *m* hortalizas.

truculent ['trʌkjʊlənt] *adj* truculento,-a.

trudge [trʌdʒ] *vi* caminar con dificultad.

true [truː] *adj* (**truer, truest**) **1** verdadero,-a; **it's t. that ...**, es verdad que ...; **to come t.**, cumplirse, hacerse realidad. **2** (*faithful*) fiel. **3** (*aim*) acertado,-a. ◆**truly** *adv* **1** de verdad; **really and t.?**, ¿de veras? **2** (*faithfully*) fielmente; **yours t.**, atentamente.

truffle ['trʌfəl] *n* trufa *f*.

trump [trʌmp] *Cards* I *n* triunfo *m*. II *vtr* fallar.

trumped-up ['trʌmptʌp] *adj* inventado,-a.

trumpet ['trʌmpɪt] *n* trompeta *f*.

trumpeting ['trʌmpɪtɪŋ] *n* (*of elephant*) berrido *m*.

truncheon ['trʌntʃən] *n* *GB* porra *f* (de policía).

trundle ['trʌndəl] *vi* rodar.

trunk [trʌŋk] *n* **1** (*of tree, body*) tronco *m*. **2** (*of elephant*) trompa *f*. **3** (*luggage*) baúl *m*. **4** *GB* *Tel* **t. call**, conferencia interurbana; *GB* **t. road**, carretera *f* principal.

trunks [trʌŋks] *npl* (**bathing**) **t.**, bañador *m* sing.

truss [trʌs] I *vtr* (*tie*) atar. II *n* **1** *Constr* cuchillo *m* de armadura. **2** *Med* braguero *m*.

trust [trʌst] I *n* **1** confianza *f*; **breach of t.**, abuso *m* de confianza. **2** *Jur* fideicomiso *m*. **3** *Fin* trust *m*. II *vtr* **1** (*hope*) esperar. **2** (*rely upon*) fiarse de; **to t. sb with sth**, confiar algo a algn. III *vi* confiar (**in**, en).

trusted ['trʌstɪd] *adj* de fiar.

trustee [trʌsˈtiː] *n* *Jur* fideicomisario,-a *m,f*; (*in bankruptcy*) síndico *m*.

trustful ['trʌstfʊl], **trusting** ['trʌstɪŋ] *adj* confiado,-a.

trustworthy ['trʌstwɜːði] *adj* (*person*) de confianza; (*information*) fidedigno,-a.

trusty ['trʌstɪ] *adj* (**trustier, trustiest**) fiel, leal.

truth [truːθ] *n* verdad *f*; **to tell the t.**, decir la verdad.

truthful ['truːθfʊl] *adj* (*person*) veraz, sincero,-a; (*testimony*) verídico,-a. ◆**truthfully** *adv* sinceramente.

try [traɪ] I *vtr* (*pt & pp* **tried**) **1** (*attempt*) intentar; **to t. do sth**, tratar de *or* intentar hacer algo. **2** (*test*) probar, ensayar; **to t. sb's patience**, poner a prueba la paciencia de algn. **3** *Jur* juzgar. II *vi* intenta. III *n* **1** (*attempt*) tentativa *f*, intento *m*. **2** *Sport* ensayo *m*. ◆**try on** *vtr* (*dress*) probarse. ◆**try out** *vtr* probar.

trying ['traɪɪŋ] *adj* (*person*) molesto,-a, pesado,-a; **to have a t. time**, pasar un mal rato.

tsar [zɑːr] *n* zar *m*.

T-shirt ['tiːʃɜːt] *n* camiseta *f*.

tub [tʌb] *n* **1** (*container*) tina *f*, cuba *f*. **2** (*bath*) bañera *f*.

tuba ['tjuːbə] *n* tuba *f*.

tubby ['tʌbɪ] *adj* (**tubbier, tubbiest**) rechoncho,-a.

tube [tjuːb] *n* **1** tubo *m*; *Anat* conducto *m*; (*of bicycle*) cámara *f* (de aire). **2** *GB* *fam* **the t.**, (*underground*) el metro.

tuberculosis [tjʊbɜːkjʊˈləʊsɪs] *n* tuberculosis *f*.

tubing ['tjuːbɪŋ] *n* tubería *f*; (**piece of**) **t.**, (trozo *m* de) tubo *m*.

tubular ['tjuːbjʊlər] *adj* tubular.

tuck [tʌk] I *vtr* **to t. in the bedclothes**, remeter la ropa de la cama; **to t. sb in**, arropar a algn; **to t. one's shirt into one's trousers**, meterse la camisa por dentro (de los pantalones). II *n* *Sew* pliegue *m*. ◆**tuck in** *vi* *fam* devorar.

Tuesday ['tjuːzdɪ] *n* martes *m*.

tuft [tʌft] *n* (*of hair*) mechón *m*.

tug [tʌg] I *vtr* (*pull at*) tirar de; (*haul along*) arrastrar; *Naut* remolcar. II *n* **1** (*pull*) tirón *m*; **t. of war**, (*game*) lucha *f* de la cuerda; *fig* lucha encarnizada. **2** *Naut* remolcador *m*.

tugboat ['tʌgbəʊt] *n* remolcador *m*.

tuition [tjuːˈɪʃən] *n* instrucción *f*; **private t.**, clases *fpl* particulares; **t. fees**, honorarios *mpl*.

tulip ['tjuːlɪp] *n* tulipán *m*.

tumble ['tʌmbəl] I *vi* (*person*) caerse; (*acrobat*) dar volteretas; (*building*) venirse abajo. II *vtr* volcar. III *n* **1** caída *f*. **2** **t. dryer**, secadora *f*.

tumbledown ['tʌmbəldaʊn] *adj* en ruinas.

tumbler ['tʌmblər] *n* vaso *m*.

tummy ['tʌmɪ] *n* *fam* estómago *m*, barriga *f*.

tumour, *US* **tumor** ['tjuːmər] *n* tumor *m*.

tumult ['tjuːmʌlt] *n* tumulto *m*.

tuna ['tjuːnə] *n* atún *m*, bonito *m*.

tune [tjuːn] *n* **1** (*melody*) melodía *f*; *fig* **to change one's t.**, cambiar de tono. **2** *Mus* tono *m*; **in/out of t.**, afinado/desafinado; **to sing out of t.**, desafinar. II *vtr* *Mus* afinar. III *vi* *Rad TV* **to t. in to a station**, sintonizar una emisora. ◆**tune up** *vi* afinar los instrumentos.

tuneful ['tjuːnfʊl] *adj* melodioso,-a.

tuner ['tjuːnər] *n* **1** (*of pianos*) afinador,-a *m,f*. **2** *Rad TV* (*knob*) sintonizador *m*.

tunic ['tjuːnɪk] *n* túnica *f*.

tuning ['tjuːnɪŋ] *n* **1** *Mus* afinación *f*; **t. fork**, diapasón *m*. **2** *Rad TV* **t. in**, sintonización *f*.

Tunisia [tjuːˈnɪzɪə] *n* Túnez.

Tunisian [tjuːˈnɪzɪən] *adj & n* tunecino,-a

(m,f).

tunnel ['tʌnəl] **I** *n* túnel *m; Min* galería *f.* **II** *vtr* **to t. through,** abrir un túnel a través de.

turban ['tɜːbən] *n* turbante *m.*

turbine ['tɜːbaɪn] *n* turbina *f.*

turbulent ['tɜːbjʊlənt] *adj* turbulento,-a.

tureen [təˈriːn] *n* sopera *f.*

turf [tɜːf] *n* **1** *(grass)* césped *m; (peat)* turba *f.* **2** *GB* **t. accountant,** *(in horse racing)* corredor,-a *m,f,* de apuestas. ◆**turf out** *vtr GB fam* **to t. sb out,** poner a algn de patitas en la calle.

Turk [tɜːk] *n* turco,-a *m,f.*

Turkey ['tɜːkɪ] *n* Turquía.

turkey ['tɜːkɪ] *n* pavo *m.*

Turkish ['tɜːkɪʃ] **I** *adj* turco,-a. **II** *n (language)* turco *m.*

turmoil ['tɜːmɔɪl] *n* confusión *f.*

turn [tɜːn] **I** *vtr* **1** volver; *(rotate)* girar, hacer girar; **to t. sth inside out,** volver algo del revés; **to t. a page,** volver una hoja; **to t. one's head/gaze,** volver la cabeza/mirada **(towards,** hacia); **to t. the corner,** doblar la esquina; *fig* **he's turned forty,** ha cumplido los cuarenta. **2** *(change)* transformar **(into,** en). **3** *(on lathe)* tornear.
II *vi* **1** *(rotate)* girar. **2** *(turn round)* volverse, dar la vuelta; **to t. to sb,** volverse hacia algn; *fig (for help)* acudir a algn; **to t. upside down,** volcarse; *fig* **to t. on sb,** volverse contra algn. **3** *(become)* volverse; **the milk has turned sour,** la leche se ha cortado.
III *n* **1** *(of wheel)* vuelta *f;* **meat done to a t.,** carne en su punto. **2** *(change of direction)* cambio *m* de dirección; *(in road)* curva *f;* **to take a t. for the better,** empezar a mejorar; **left/right t.,** giro *m* al izquierdo/a la derecha. **3 to do sb a good t.,** hacer un favor a algn. **4** *Med* ataque *m.* **5** *(in game, queue)* turno *m,* vez *f;* **it's your t.,** te toca a ti; **to take it in turns to do sth,** turnarse para hacer algo. **6** *Theat* número *m.* **7 t. of phrase,** giro *m.* ◆**turn aside I** *vtr* desviar. **II** *vi* desviarse. ◆**turn away I** *vtr (person)* rechazar. **II** *vi* volver la cabeza. ◆**turn back I** *vtr (person)* hacer retroceder; *(clock)* retrasar. **II** *vi* volverse. ◆**turn down I** *vtr* **1** *(gas, radio etc)* bajar. **2** *(reject)* rechazar. **3** *(fold)* doblar. ◆**turn in** *fam* **I** *vtr (person)* entregar a la policía. **II** *vi* acostarse. ◆**turn off I** *vtr (electricity)* desconectar; *(gas, light)* apagar; *(water)* cerrar. **II** *vi* desviarse. ◆**turn on** *vtr (electricity)* encender; *(tap, gas)* abrir; *(machine)* poner en marcha; *fam* **it turns me on,** me encanta. ◆**turn out I** *vtr* **1** *(extinguish)* apagar. **2** *(eject)* echar; *(empty)* vaciar. **3** *(produce)* producir. **II** *vi* **1** *(attend)* asistir. **2 it turns out that ...,** resulta que ...; **things have turned out well,** las cosas

han salido bien. ◆**turn over I** *vtr (turn upside down)* poner al revés; *(page)* dar la vuelta a. **II** *vi* volverse. ◆**turn round I** *vtr* volver. **II** *vi (rotate)* girar, dar vueltas. ◆**turn up I** *vtr* **1** *(collar)* levantar; **to t. up one's shirt sleeves,** arremangarse; **turned-up nose,** nariz respingona. **2** *Rad TV* subir. **II** *vi* **1** *fig* **something is sure to t. up,** algo saldrá. **2** *(arrive)* llegar, presentarse; **nobody turned up,** nadie se presentó. **3** *(attend)* asistir.

turning ['tɜːnɪŋ] *n* **1** *fig* **t. point,** punto decisivo. **2** *(in road)* salida *f.*

turnip ['tɜːnɪp] *n* nabo *m.*

turnout ['tɜːnaʊt] *n* asistencia *f.*

turnover ['tɜːnəʊvər] *n Com (sales)* facturación *f; (of goods)* movimiento *m.*

turnpike ['tɜːnpaɪk] *n US* autopista *f* de peaje.

turnstile ['tɜːnstaɪl] *n* torniquete *m.*

turntable ['tɜːnteɪbəl] *n (for record)* plato *m* (giratorio).

turn-up ['tɜːnʌp] *n GB* **1** *(of trousers)* vuelta *f.* **2** *fam* **what a t.-up for the books!,** ¡vaya sorpresa!

turpentine ['tɜːpəntaɪn] *n* (esencia *f* de) trementina *f.*

turquoise ['tɜːkwɔɪz] **I** *n (colour, stone)* turquesa *f.* **II** *adj* **t. (blue),** azul turquesa.

turret ['tʌrɪt] *n* torrecilla *f.*

turtle ['tɜːtəl] *n* tortuga *f.*

turtledove ['tɜːtldʌv] *n* tórtola *f.*

turtleneck ['tɜːtlnek] *n* a **t. (sweater),** un jersey de cuello alto.

tusk [tʌsk] *n* colmillo *m.*

tussle ['tʌsəl] *n* pelea *f,* lucha *f.*

tutor ['tjuːtər] *n Univ* tutor,-a *m,f;* **private t.,** profesor,-a *m,f* particular.

tutorial [tjuːˈtɔːrɪəl] *n Univ* tutoría *f,* seminario *m.*

tuxedo [tʌkˈsiːdəʊ] *n US* smoking *m.*

TV [tiːˈviː] *abbr of* **television,** TV.

twang [twæŋ] **I** *n* **1** *(of instrument)* sonido *m* vibrante. **2** *nasal* **t.,** gangueo *m.* **II** *vtr* puntear. **III** *vi (string)* vibrar.

tweak [twiːk] *vtr* pellizcar.

tweed [twiːd] *n* cheviot *m.*

tweezers ['twiːzəz] *npl* pinzas *fpl.*

twelfth [twelfθ] **I** *adj & n* duodécimo,-a *(m,f).* **II** *n (fraction)* duodécimo *m.*

twelve [twelv] *adj & n* doce *(m) inv.*

twentieth ['twentɪθ] **I** *adj & n* vigésimo,-a *(m,f).* **II** *n (fraction)* vigésimo *m.*

twenty ['twentɪ] *adj & n* veinte *(m) inv.*

twice [twaɪs] *adv* dos veces; **he's t. as old as I am,** tiene el doble de años que yo.

twiddle ['twɪdəl] **I** *vtr* dar vueltas a; **to t. one's moustache,** mesarse el bigote; **to t. one's thumbs,** estar mano sobre mano. **II** *vi* **to t. with sth,** juguetear con algo.

twig¹ [twɪg] *n* ramilla *f.*

twig² [twɪg] *vi GB fam* caer en la cuenta.

twilight ['twaɪlaɪt] n crepúsculo m.
twin [twɪn] I n mellizo,-a m,f; **identical twins,** gemelos (idénticos); **t. brother/ sister,** hermano gemelo/hermana gemela; **t. beds,** camas fpl gemelas. II vtr hermanar.
twine [twaɪn] I n bramante m. II vtr entretejer. III vi to **t. round sth,** enroscarse alrededor de algo.
twinge [twɪndʒ] n (of pain) punzada f; fig **t. of conscience,** remordimiento m.
twinkle ['twɪŋkəl] vi (stars) centellear; (eyes) brillar.
twinkling ['twɪŋklɪŋ] n (of stars) centelleo m; fig **in the t. of an eye,** en un abrir y cerrar de ojos.
twirl [twɜ:l] I vtr girar rápidamente. II vi (spin) girar rápidamente; (dancer) piruetear. III n (movement) giro rápido; (of dancer) pirueta f.
twist [twɪst] I vtr torcer; (sense) tergiversar; to **t. one's ankle,** torcerse el tobillo. II vi (smoke) formar volutas; (path) serpentear. III n 1 (of yarn) torzal m. 2 (movement) torsión f; Med torcedura f; fig **to give a new t. to sth,** dar un nuevo enfoque a algo. 3 (in road) vuelta f. 4 (dance) twist m.
twit [twɪt] n GB fam jilipollas mf inv.
twitch [twɪtʃ] I vtr dar un tirón a. II vi crisparse; **his face twitches,** tiene un tic en la cara.
twitter ['twɪtər] I vi gorjear. II n gorjeo m.
two [tu:] I adj dos inv; fig **to be in** or **of t. minds about sth,** estar indeciso,-a respecto a algo. II n dos m inv; fig **to put t. and t. together,** atar cabos.
two-faced ['tu:feɪst] adj hipócrita.
two-party ['tu:pɑ:tɪ] adj **t-p. system,** bi-

partidismo m.
twopence ['tʌpəns] n GB dos peniques.
two-piece ['tu:pi:s] I adj de dos piezas. II n (suit) traje m de dos piezas.
two-seater ['tu:si:tər] adj & n biplaza (f).
twosome ['tu:səm] n pareja f.
two-time ['tu:taɪm] vtr fam poner los cuernos a.
two-way ['tu:weɪ] adj 1 (street) de dos direcciones. 2 **t.-w. radio,** aparato m emisor y receptor.
tycoon [taɪ'ku:n] n magnate m.
type [taɪp] I n 1 (kind) tipo m, clase f; (brand) marca f; (of car) modelo m. 2 Typ carácter m; (print) caracteres mpl. II vtr & vi escribir a máquina.
typecast ['taɪpkɑ:st] vtr encasillar.
typescript ['taɪpskrɪpt] n texto m escrito a máquina.
typeset ['taɪpset] vtr componer.
typesetter ['taɪpsetər] n 1 (person) cajista mf. 2 (machine) máquina f para componer tipos.
typewriter ['taɪpraɪtər] n máquina f de escribir.
typewritten ['taɪprɪtən] adj escrito,-a a máquina.
typhoid ['taɪfɔɪd] n **t. (fever),** fiebre tifoidea.
typhoon [taɪ'fu:n] n tifón m.
typical ['tɪpɪkəl] adj típico,-a.
typify ['tɪpɪfaɪ] vtr tipificar.
typing ['taɪpɪŋ] n mecanografía f.
typist ['taɪpɪst] n mecanógrafo,-a m,f.
tyrannical [tɪ'rænɪkəl] adj tiránico,-a.
tyrannize ['tɪrənaɪz] vtr tiranizar.
tyranny ['tɪrənɪ] n tiranía f.
tyrant ['taɪrənt] n tirano,-a m,f.
tyre [taɪər] n neumático m; **t. pressure,** presión f de los neumáticos.

U

U, u [ju:] n (the letter) U, u f.
ubiquity [ju:'bɪkwɪtɪ] n ubicuidad f.
udder ['ʌdər] n ubre f.
UFO, ufo ['ju:efəʊ, 'ju:fəʊ] abbr of unidentified flying object, OVNI m, ovni m.
ugh [ux, uh, ʌh] interj ¡uf!, ¡puf!
ugly ['ʌglɪ] adj (uglier, ugliest) feo,-a; (situation) desagradable; fig **u. duckling,** patito feo.
UK [ju:'keɪ] abbr of United Kingdom, R.U. m.
Ukraine ['ju:kreɪn] n the U., Ucrania.
ulcer ['ʌlsər] n (sore) llaga f; (internal) úlcera f.
ulterior [ʌl'tɪərɪər] adj (motive) oculto,-a.
ultimate ['ʌltɪmɪt] adj 1 (final) último,-a; (aim) final. 2 (basic) esencial.
 ◆**ultimately** adv 1 (finally) finalmente. 2 (basically) en el fondo.

ultimatum [ʌltɪ'meɪtəm] n ultimátum m.
ultrasound [ʌltrə'saʊnd] n ultrasonido m.
ultraviolet [ʌltrə'vaɪəlɪt] adj ultravioleta.
umbilical [ʌm'bɪlɪkəl, ʌmbɪ'laɪkəl] adj **u. cord,** cordón m umbilical.
umbrella [ʌm'brelə] n paraguas m inv.
umpire ['ʌmpaɪər] I n árbitro m. II vtr arbitrar.
umpteen [ʌmp'ti:n] adj fam muchísimos,-as, la tira de.
umpteenth [ʌmp'ti:nθ] adj enésimo,-a.
UN [ju:'en] abbr of United Nations (Organization), ONU f sing.
unabashed [ʌnə'bæʃt] adj 1 (unperturbed) inmutable, imperturbable. 2 (shameless) desvergonzado,-a, descarado,-a.
unable [ʌn'eɪbəl] adj incapaz; **to be u. to do sth/anything,** no poder hacer algo/ nada.

unacceptable [ʌnəkˈseptəbəl] adj inaceptable.

unaccompanied [ʌnəˈkʌmpənɪd] adj solo,-a.

unaccountable [ʌnəˈkauntəbəl] adj inexplicable.

unaccounted-for [ʌnəˈkauntɪdfɔːr] adj to be u.-f., faltar.

unaccustomed [ʌnəˈkʌstəmd] adj he's u. to this climate, no está muy acostumbrado a este clima.

unaffected [ʌnəˈfektɪd] adj 1 no afectado,-a (by, por). 2 (indifferent) indiferente (by, a). 3 (natural) (person) natural; (style) llano,-a.

unaided [ʌnˈeɪdɪd] adj sin ayuda, solo,-a.

unanimous [juːˈnænɪməs] adj unánime.

unannounced [ʌnəˈnaunst] adj sin avisar.

unanswered [ʌnˈɑːnsəd] adj sin contestar.

unapproachable [ʌnəˈprəutʃəbəl] adj inabordable, inaccesible.

unarmed [ʌnˈɑːmd] adj desarmado,-a.

unashamed [ʌnəˈʃeɪmd] adj desvergonzado,-a.

unasked [ʌnˈɑːskt] adv u. (for), (unrequested) no solicitado,-a; (spontaneous) espontáneo,-a.

unassuming [ʌnəˈsjuːmɪŋ] adj sin pretensiones.

unattached [ʌnəˈtætʃt] adj 1 (independent) libre; (loose) suelto,-a. 2 (person) soltero,-a y sin compromiso.

unattended [ʌnəˈtendɪd] adj (counter etc) desatendido,-a; to leave a child u., dejar a un niño solo.

unauthorized [ʌnˈɔːθəraɪzd] adj 1 (person) no autorizado,-a. 2 (trade etc) ilícito,-a, ilegal.

unavoidable [ʌnəˈvɔɪdəbəl] adj inevitable; (accident) imprevisible.

unaware [ʌnəˈweər] adj to be u. of sth, ignorar algo.

unawares [ʌnəˈweəz] adv 1 (unexpectedly) desprevenido,-a. 2 (without knowing) inconscientemente.

unbalanced [ʌnˈbælənst] adj desequilibrado,-a.

unbearable [ʌnˈbeərəbəl] adj insoportable.

unbeatable [ʌnˈbiːtəbəl] adj (team) invencible; (price, quality) inmejorable.

unbelievable [ʌnbɪˈliːvəbəl] adj increíble.

unbend [ʌnˈbend] vi fam fig relajarse.

unbia(s)sed [ʌnˈbaɪəst] adj imparcial.

unborn [ʌnˈbɔːn] adj sin nacer, nonato, -a.

unbreakable [ʌnˈbreɪkəbəl] adj irrompible; fig inquebrantable.

unbroken [ʌnˈbrəukən] adj 1 (whole) intacto,-a. 2 (uninterrupted) continuo,-a. 3 (record) imbatido,-a.

unbutton [ʌnˈbʌtən] vtr desabrochar.

uncalled-for [ʌnˈkɔːldfɔːr] adj (inappropriate) insensato,-a; (unjustified) inmerecido,-a.

uncanny [ʌnˈkænɪ] adj misterioso,-a, extraño,-a.

unceasing [ʌnˈsiːsɪŋ] adj incesante.

uncertain [ʌnˈsɜːtən] adj 1 (not certain) incierto,-a; (doubtful) dudoso,-a; in no u. terms, claramente. 2 (hesitant) indeciso, -a.

uncertainty [ʌnˈsɜːtəntɪ] n incertidumbre f.

unchanged [ʌnˈtʃeɪndʒd] adj igual.

unchecked [ʌnˈtʃekt] adj 1 (unrestrained) desenfrenado,-a. 2 (not examined) no comprobado,-a.

uncivilized [ʌnˈsɪvɪlaɪzd] adj (tribe) incivilizado,-a, salvaje; (not cultured) inculto,-a.

uncle [ˈʌŋkəl] n tío m.

uncomfortable [ʌnˈkʌmftəbəl] adj incómodo,-a; to make things u. for, complicarle la vida a.

uncommon [ʌnˈkɒmən] adj 1 (rare) poco común; (unusual) extraordinario,-a. 2 (excessive) excesivo,-a. ◆**uncommonly** adv not u., con cierta frecuencia.

uncompromising [ʌnˈkɒmprəmaɪzɪŋ] adj intransigente; u. honesty, sinceridad absoluta.

unconcerned [ʌnkənˈsɜːnd] adj indiferente (about, a).

unconditional [ʌnkənˈdɪʃənəl] adj incondicional; u. refusal, negativa rotunda.

unconnected [ʌnkəˈnektɪd] adj no relacionado,-a.

unconscious [ʌnˈkɒnʃəs] I adj 1 inconsciente (of, de). 2 (unintentional) involuntario,-a. II n the u., el inconsciente.

unconsciousness [ʌnˈkɒnʃəsnɪs] n Med pérdida f del conocimiento.

uncontested [ʌnkənˈtestɪd] adj Pol u. seat, escaño m ganado sin oposición.

uncontrollable [ʌnkənˈtrəuləbəl] adj incontrolable; (desire) irresistible.

unconventional [ʌnkənˈvenʃənəl] adj poco convencional, original.

uncooperative [ʌnkəuˈɒpərətɪv] adj poco cooperativo,-a.

uncouth [ʌnˈkuːθ] adj (rude) grosero,-a.

uncover [ʌnˈkʌvər] vtr destapar; fig descubrir.

undamaged [ʌnˈdæmɪdʒd] adj (article etc) sin desperfectos; (person) indemne; (reputation) intacto,-a.

undaunted [ʌnˈdɔːntɪd] adj firme, impávido,-a.

undecided [ʌndɪˈsaɪdɪd] adj 1 (person) indeciso,-a. 2 (issue) pendiente; it's still u., está aún por decidir.

undefeated [ʌndɪˈfiːtɪd] adj invicto,-a.

undefined [ʌndɪˈfaɪnd] adj

indeterminado,-a.

undeniable [ʌndɪ'naɪəbəl] *adj* innegable.

under ['ʌndər] **I** *prep* **1** debajo de; **u. the sun**, bajo el sol. **2** (*less than*) menos de; **incomes u. £1,000**, ingresos inferiores a 1.000 libras; **u. age**, menor de edad. **3** (*of rank*) de rango inferior a. **4 u. Caesar**, bajo César. **5** (*subject to*) bajo; **u. arrest**, detenido,-a; **u. cover**, a cubierto; **u. obligation to**, en la obligación de; **u. the circumstances**, dadas las circunstancias; *fig* **I was u. the impression that ...**, tenía la impresión de que .... **6** (*according to*) según, conforme a. **II** *adv* abajo, debajo.

under- ['ʌndər] *pref* (*below*) sub-, infra-; (*insufficiently*) insuficientemente.

underarm ['ʌndərɑ:m] **I** *adj* **u. deodorant**, desodorante *m* para las axilas. **II** *adv* *Sport* por debajo del hombro.

undercarriage [ʌndə'kærɪdʒ] *n* tren *m* de aterrizaje.

undercharge [ʌndə'tʃɑːdʒ] *vtr* cobrar menos de lo debido.

underclothes ['ʌndəkləʊðz] *npl* ropa *f* sing interior.

undercoat ['ʌndəkəʊt] *n* (*of paint*) primera mano.

undercover [ʌndə'kʌvər] *adj* secreto,-a.

undercurrent ['ʌndəkʌrənt] *n* **1** (*in sea*) corriente submarina. **2** *fig* sentimiento *m* latente.

undercut [ʌndə'kʌt] *vtr* *Com* vender más barato que.

underdeveloped [ʌndədɪ'veləpt] *adj* subdesarrollado,-a.

underdog ['ʌndədɒg] *n* desvalido,-a *m,f*.

underestimate [ʌndər'estɪmeɪt] *vtr* infravalorar.

underexposure [ʌndərɪk'spəʊʒər] *n* *Phot* subexposición *f*.

underfed [ʌndə'fed] *adj* subalimentado, -a.

underfoot [ʌndə'fʊt] *adv* en el suelo.

undergo [ʌndə'gəʊ] *vtr* experimentar; (*change*) sufrir; (*test etc*) pasar por.

undergraduate [ʌndə'grædjʊɪt] *n* estudiante *mf* universitario,-a.

underground ['ʌndəgraʊnd] **I** *adj* subterráneo,-a; *fig* clandestino,-a. **II** [ʌndə'graʊnd] *adv* *fig* **to go u.**, pasar a la clandestinidad. **III** ['ʌndəgraʊnd] *n* **1** *Pol* movimiento clandestino. **2 the u.**, (*subway*) el metro.

undergrowth ['ʌndəgrəʊθ] *n* maleza *f*.

underhand ['ʌndəhænd] **I** *adj* (*method*) ilícito,-a; (*person*) solapado,-a. **II** *adv* bajo cuerda.

underline [ʌndə'laɪn] *vtr* subrayar.

underling ['ʌndəlɪŋ] *n* *pej* mandado,-a *m,f*.

underlying [ʌndə'laɪɪŋ] *adj* (*basic*) fundamental.

undermine [ʌndə'maɪn] *vtr* socavar, minar.

underneath [ʌndə'niːθ] **I** *prep* debajo de, bajo. **II** *adv* abajo, debajo. **III** *adj* de abajo. **IV** *n* parte *f* inferior.

undernourished [ʌndə'nʌrɪʃt] *adj* desnutrido,-a.

underpaid [ʌndə'peɪd] *adj* mal pagado,-a.

underpass ['ʌndəpɑːs] *n* paso subterráneo.

underprivileged [ʌndə'prɪvɪlɪdʒd] **I** *adj* desfavorecido,-a. **II** *npl* **the u.**, los menos favorecidos.

underrate [ʌndə'reɪt] *vtr* → **undervalue**.

undershirt ['ʌndəʃɜːt] *n* *US* camiseta *f*.

underskirt ['ʌndəskɜːt] *n* combinación *f*.

understand [ʌndə'stænd] *vtr & vi* (*pt & pp* **understood**) **1** (*comprehend*) entender, comprender; *fam* **do I make myself understood?**, ¿me explico? **2** (*assume, believe*) entender; **she gave me to u. that ...**, me dio a entender que .... **3** (*hear*) tener entendido. **4 to u. one another**, entenderse.

understandable [ʌndə'stændəbəl] *adj* comprensible.

understanding [ʌndə'stændɪŋ] **I** *n* **1** (*intellectual grasp*) entendimiento *m*, comprensión *f*. **2** (*interpretation*) intepretación *f*. **3** (*agreement*) acuerdo *m*. **4 on the u. that ...**, a condición de que .... **II** *adj* comprensivo,-a.

understatement [ʌndə'steɪtmənt] *n* **to make an u.**, minimizar, subestimar; **to say that the boy is rather clever is an u.**, decir que el chico es bastante listo es quedarse corto.

understood [ʌndə'stʊd] *adj* **1 I wish it to be u. that ...**, que conste que .... **2** (*agreed on*) convenido,-a. **3** (*implied*) sobreentendido,-a.

understudy ['ʌndəstʌdɪ] *n* suplente *mf*.

undertake [ʌndə'teɪk] *vtr* (*pt* **undertook**; *pp* **undertaken** [ʌndə'teɪkən]) **1** (*responsibility*) asumir; (*task, job*) encargarse de. **2** (*promise*) comprometerse a.

undertaker ['ʌndəteɪkər] *n* empresario,-a *m,f* de pompas fúnebres; **u.'s**, funeraria *f*.

undertaking [ʌndə'teɪkɪŋ] *n* **1** (*task*) empresa *f*. **2** (*guarantee*) garantía *f*.

undertone ['ʌndətəʊn] *n* **in an u.**, en voz baja.

underwater [ʌndə'wɔːtər] **I** *adj* submarino,-a. **II** *adv* bajo el agua.

underwear ['ʌndəweər] *n* *inv* ropa *f* interior.

underworld ['ʌndəwɜːld] *n* (*criminals*) hampa *f*, bajos fondos.

underwrite [ʌndə'raɪt] *vtr* (*pt* **underwrote**; *pp* **underwritten**) **1** (*guarantee*) garantizar, avalar. **2** (*insure*) asegurar.

underwriter ['ʌndəraɪtər] *n* **1** *Fin* suscriptor,-a *m,f*. **2** (*insurer*) asegurador,-a *m,f*.

undesirable |ʌndɪˈzaɪrəbəl| *adj & n* indeseable *(mf)*.

undeterred |ʌndɪˈtɜːd| *adj* sin inmutarse; **u. by**, sin arredrarse ante.

undies |ˈʌndɪz| *npl fam* bragas *fpl*.

undignified |ʌnˈdɪgnɪfaɪd| *adj (attitude etc)* indecoroso,-a.

undisciplined |ʌnˈdɪsɪplɪnd| *adj* indisciplinado,-a.

undisclosed |ʌndɪsˈkləʊzd| *adj* sin revelar.

undiscovered |ʌndɪsˈkʌvəd| *adj* sin descubrir.

undisguised |ʌndɪsˈgaɪzd| *adj fig* no disimulado,-a.

undisputed |ʌndɪsˈpjuːtɪd| *adj (unchallenged)* incontestable; *(unquestionable)* indiscutible.

undivided |ʌndɪˈvaɪdɪd| *adj* **to give one's u. attention**, prestar toda la atención.

undo |ʌnˈduː| *vtr (pt* **undid**; *pp* **undone**) 1 deshacer; *(button)* desabrochar. 2 *(put right)* enmendar.

undone¹ |ʌnˈdʌn| *adj (unfinished)* inacabado,-a.

undone² |ʌnˈdʌn| *adj (knot etc)* deshecho,-a; **to come u.**, *(shoelace)* desatarse; *(button, blouse)* desabrocharse; *(necklace etc)* soltarse.

undoubted |ʌnˈdaʊtɪd| *adj* indudable.

undress |ʌnˈdres| I *vtr* desnudar. II *vi* desnudarse.

undressed |ʌnˈdrest| *adj (naked)* desnudo,-a.

undue |ʌnˈdjuː| I *adj (excessive)* excesivo,-a. 2 *(improper)* indebido,-a.

undulate |ˈʌndjʊleɪt| *vi* ondular, ondear.

unearth |ʌnˈɜːθ| *vtr* desenterrar.

unearthly |ʌnˈɜːθlɪ| *adj* 1 *(being)* sobrenatural. 2 *fam (din)* espantoso,-a; **at an u. hour**, a una hora intempestiva.

uneasy |ʌnˈiːzɪ| *adj* 1 *(worried)* preocupado,-a; *(disturbing)* inquietante. 2 *(uncomfortable)* incómodo,-a.

uneconomic(al) |ʌniːkəˈnɒmɪk(əl)| *adj* poco económico,-a.

uneducated |ʌnˈedjʊkeɪtɪd| *adj* inculto, -a.

unemployed |ʌnɪmˈplɔɪd| I *adj* en paro, parado,-a; **to be u.**, estar en paro. II *npl* **the u.**, los parados.

unemployment |ʌnɪmˈplɔɪmənt| *n* paro *m*, desempleo *m*; **u. benefit**, *US* **u. compensation**, subsidio *m* de desempleo.

unending |ʌnˈendɪŋ| *adj* interminable.

unenviable |ʌnˈenvɪəbəl| *adj* poco enviable.

unequal |ʌnˈiːkwəl| *adj* desigual.

unequivocal |ʌnɪˈkwɪvəkəl| *adj* inequívoco,-a.

uneven |ʌnˈiːvən| *adj* 1 *(not level)* desigual; *(bumpy)* accidentado,-a. 2 *(variable)* irregular.

uneventful |ʌnɪˈventfʊl| *adj* sin aconteci-

mientos.

unexceptional |ʌnɪkˈsepʃənəl| *adj* ordinario,-a.

unexpected |ʌnɪkˈspektɪd| *adj (unhoped for)* inesperado,-a; *(event)* imprevisto,-a.

unfailing |ʌnˈfeɪlɪŋ| *adj* indefectible; *(incessant)* constante; *(patience)* inagotable.

unfair |ʌnˈfeər| *adj* injusto,-a; *Sport* sucio,-a.

unfaithful |ʌnˈfeɪθfʊl| *adj (friend)* desleal; *(husband, wife)* infiel.

unfamiliar |ʌnfəˈmɪljər| *adj (unknown)* desconocido,-a; *(not conversant)* no familiarizado,-a **(with**, con).

unfashionable |ʌnˈfæʃənəbəl| *adj* pasado,-a de moda; *(ideas etc)* poco popular.

unfasten |ʌnˈfɑːsən| *vtr (knot)* desatar; *(clothing, belt)* desabrochar.

unfavourable, *US* **unfavorable** |ʌnˈfeɪvərəbəl| *adj* desfavorable; *(criticism)* adverso,-a; *(winds)* contrario,-a.

unfeeling |ʌnˈfiːlɪŋ| *adj* insensible.

unfinished |ʌnˈfɪnɪʃt| *adj* inacabado,-a; **u. business**, un asunto pendiente.

unfit |ʌnˈfɪt| *adj* 1 *(thing)* inadecuado,-a; *(person)* no apto,-a **(for**, para). 2 *(incompetent)* incompetente. 3 *(physically)* incapacitado,-a; **to be u.**, no estar en forma.

unflinching |ʌnˈflɪntʃɪŋ| *adj* 1 *(determined)* resuelto,-a. 2 *(fearless)* impávido,-a.

unfold |ʌnˈfəʊld| I *vtr* 1 *(sheet)* desdoblar; *(newspaper)* abrir. 2 *(plan, secret)* revelar. II *vi* 1 *(open up)* abrirse; *(landscape)* extenderse. 2 *(plot)* desarrollarse. 3 *(secret)* descubrirse.

unforeseen |ʌnfɔːˈsiːn| *adj* imprevisto,-a.

unforgettable |ʌnfəˈgetəbəl| *adj* inolvidable.

unforgivable |ʌnfəˈgɪvəbəl| *adj* imperdonable.

unfortunate |ʌnˈfɔːtʃənɪt| *adj (person, event)* desgraciado,-a; *(remark)* desafortunado,-a; **how u.!**, ¡qué mala suerte! ◆**unfortunately** *adv* desgraciadamente, por desgracia.

unfounded |ʌnˈfaʊndɪd| *adj* infundado, -a.

unfriendly |ʌnˈfrendlɪ| *adj (unfriendlier, unfriendliest)* antipático,-a, poco amistoso,-a.

unfurl |ʌnˈfɜːl| *vi* desplegarse.

unfurnished |ʌnˈfɜːnɪʃt| *adj* sin amueblar.

ungainly |ʌnˈgeɪnlɪ| *adj (gait)* desgarbado,-a.

ungodly |ʌnˈgɒdlɪ| *adj (ungodlier, ungodliest) (behaviour)* impío,-a; *fam fig* **at an u. hour**, a una hora intempestiva.

ungrateful |ʌnˈgreɪtfʊl| *adj (person)* desagradecido,-a; *(task)* ingrato,-a.

unguarded |ʌnˈgɑːdɪd| *adj* 1 *(unprotected)*

desatendido,-a; *(imprudent)* desprevenido,-a. 2 *(frank)* franco,-a.
unhappiness |ʌn'hæpɪnɪs| *n* 1 *(sadness)*
tristeza *f*. 2 *(wretchedness)* desdicha *f*.
unhappy |ʌn'hæpɪ| *adj* (**unhappier, un-
happiest**) 1 *(sad)* triste. 2 *(wretched)*
desgraciado,-a, infeliz; *(unfortunate)*
desafortunado,-a.
unharmed |ʌn'hɑːmd| *adj* ileso,-a,
indemne.
unhealthy |ʌn'helθɪ| *adj* (**unhealthier,
unhealthiest**) 1 *(ill)* enfermizo,-a. 2 *(un-
wholesome)* malsano,-a.
unheard |ʌn'hɜːd| *adj* 1 her request went
u., su petición no fue atendida. 2 u. of,
(outrageous) inaudito,-a; *(without precedent)* sin precedente.
unhesitating |ʌn'hezɪteɪtɪŋ| *adj*
resuelto,-a.
unhook |ʌn'hʊk| *vtr (from hook)* des-
colgar; *(clothing)* desabrochar.
unhurt |ʌn'hɜːt| *adj* ileso,-a, indemne.
unhygienic |ʌnhaɪ'dʒiːnɪk| *adj*
antihigiénico,-a.
unidentified |ʌnaɪ'dentɪfaɪd| *adj* u. **flying
object**, objeto volador no identificado,
ovni *m*.
unification |juːnɪfɪ'keɪʃən| *n* unificación
f.
uniform |'juːnɪfɔːm| *adj & nm* uniforme.
uniformity |juːnɪ'fɔːmɪtɪ| *n* uniformidad
f.
unify |'juːnɪfaɪ| *vtr* unificar.
unilateral |juːnɪ'lætərəl| *adj* unilateral.
unimportant |ʌnɪm'pɔːtənt| *adj* poco
importante.
uninformed |ʌnɪn'fɔːmd| *adj (opinion)* sin
fundamento.
uninhabited |ʌnɪn'hæbɪtɪd| *adj*
despoblado,-a.
uninhibited |ʌnɪn'hɪbɪtɪd| *adj* sin inhibi-
ción.
uninspired |ʌnɪn'spaɪəd| *adj (person)*
falto,-a de inspiración; *(performance)*
insulso,-a.
uninspiring |ʌnɪn'spaɪərɪŋ| *adj* que no
inspira.
unintelligible |ʌnɪn'telɪdʒəbəl| *adj*
ininteligible, incomprensible.
unintentional |ʌnɪn'tenʃənəl| *adj*
involuntario,-a. ◆**unintentionally** *adv*
sin querer.
uninteresting |ʌn'ɪntrɪstɪŋ| *adj* poco
interesante.
uninterrupted |ʌnɪntə'rʌptɪd| *adj*
ininterrumpido,-a.
union |'juːnjən| I *n* 1 unión *f*. 2 *(organi-
zation)* sindicato *m*. 3 *US* the U., los
Estados Unidos; U. **Jack**, bandera *f* del
Reino Unido. II *adj* sindical.
unique |juː'niːk| *adj* único,-a.
unison |'juːnɪsən| *n Mus* unisonancia *f*;
fig (harmony) armonía *f*; in u., al unísono.
unit |'juːnɪt| *n* 1 unidad *f*; **monetary u.**,

unidad monetaria; *GB Fin* u. **trust**, sociedad *f* de inversiones. 2 *(piece of
furniture)* módulo *m*; **kitchen u.**, mueble
m de cocina. 3 *Tech* grupo *m*; *Comput*
central processing u., procesador *m* central; **visual display u.**, pantalla *f*. 4 *(department)* servicio *m*. 5 *(team)* equipo *m*.
unite |juː'naɪt| I *vtr* unir. II *vi* unirse.
united |juː'naɪtɪd| *adj* unido,-a; U. **King-
dom**, Reino Unido; U. **States (of America)**, Estados Unidos (de América); U.
Nations, Naciones Unidas.
unity |'juːnɪtɪ| *n* unidad *f*; *(harmony)*
armonía *f*.
universal |juːnɪ'vɜːsəl| *adj* universal.
universe |'juːnɪvɜːs| *n* universo *m*.
university |juːnɪ'vɜːsɪtɪ| I *n* universidad
f. II *adj* universitario,-a.
unjust |ʌn'dʒʌst| *adj* injusto,-a.
unkempt |ʌn'kempt| *adj* descuidado,-a;
(hair) despeinado,-a; *(appearance)*
desaliñado,-a.
unkind |ʌn'kaɪnd| *adj (not nice)* poco
amable; *(cruel)* despiadado,-a.
unknown |ʌn'nəʊn| I *adj* desconocido,-a;
u. **quantity**, incógnita *f*. II *n* the u., lo
desconocido.
unlawful |ʌn'lɔːfʊl| *adj (not legal)* ilegal.
unleash |ʌn'liːʃ| *vtr* 1 *(dog)* soltar. 2 *fig
(release)* liberar; *(provoke)* desencadenar.
unless |ʌn'les| *conj* a menos que, a no ser
que.
unlike |ʌn'laɪk| I *adj* diferente, distinto,
-a. II *prep* a diferencia de.
unlikely |ʌn'laɪklɪ| *adj* 1 *(improbable)*
poco probable. 2 *(unusual)* raro,-a.
unlimited |ʌn'lɪmɪtɪd| *adj* ilimitado,-a.
unload |ʌn'ləʊd| *vtr & vi* descargar.
unlock |ʌn'lɒk| *vtr* abrir (con llave).
unlucky |ʌn'lʌkɪ| *adj (**unluckier, unluck-
iest**) (unfortunate)* desgraciado,-a; to be
u., *(person)* tener mala suerte; *(thing)*
traer mala suerte. ◆**unluckily** *adv* de-
safortunadamente, por desgracia.
unmanageable |ʌn'mænɪdʒəbəl| *adj
(people)* ingobernable; *(child, hair)* incontrolable.
unmanned |ʌn'mænd| *adj (spacecraft etc)*
no tripulado,-a.
unmarried |ʌn'mærɪd| *adj* soltero,-a.
unmask |ʌn'mɑːsk| *vtr fig (plot)* descu-
brir.
unmistak(e)able |ʌnmɪs'teɪkəbəl| *adj*
inconfundible. ◆**unmistak(e)ably** *adv*
sin lugar a dudas.
unmitigated |ʌn'mɪtɪgeɪtɪd| *adj* 1 *(abso-
lute)* absoluto,-a; *(liar)* rematado,-a. 2
(grief) profundo,-a.
unnamed |ʌn'neɪmd| *adj (anonymous)*
anónimo,-a.
unnatural |ʌn'nætʃərəl| *adj* 1 *(against na-
ture)* antinatural; *(abnormal)* anormal. 2
(affected) afectado,-a.
unnecessary |ʌn'nesɪsərɪ| *adj*

innecesario,-a, inútil; **it's u. to add that ...**, sobra añadir que ....

unnoticed [ʌn'nəʊtɪst] *adj* desapercibido,-a; **to let sth pass u.**, pasar algo por alto.

unobserved [ʌnɒb'zɜːvd] *adj* inadvertido,-a.

unobtainable [ʌnəb'teɪnəbəl] *adj* inasequible, inalcanzable.

unobtrusive [ʌnəb'truːsɪv] *adj* discreto, -a.

unoccupied [ʌn'ɒkjʊpaɪd] *adj* (*house*) desocupado,-a; (*seat*) libre.

unofficial [ʌnə'fɪʃəl] *adj* no oficial.

unorthodox [ʌn'ɔːθədɒks] *adj* 1 (*behaviour etc*) poco ortodoxo,-a. 2 *Rel* heterodoxo,-a.

unpack [ʌn'pæk] I *vtr* (*boxes*) desembalar; (*suitcase*) deshacer. II *vi* deshacer la(s) maleta(s).

unpalatable [ʌn'pælətəbəl] *adj* desagradable.

unparalleled [ʌn'pærəleld] *adj* 1 (*in quality*) incomparable. 2 (*without precedent*) sin precedente.

unpardonable [ʌn'pɑːdənəbəl] *adj* imperdonable.

unperturbed [ʌnpə'tɜːbd] *adj* impasible.

unpleasant [ʌn'plezənt] *adj* desagradable (**to**, con).

unpleasantness [ʌn'plezəntnɪs] *n* disgusto *m*.

unplug [ʌn'plʌg] *vtr* desenchufar.

unpopular [ʌn'pɒpjʊlə^r] *adj* impopular; **to make oneself u.**, ganarse la antipatía de todos.

unprecedented [ʌn'presɪdentɪd] *adj* sin precedente.

unpredictable [ʌnprɪ'dɪktəbəl] *adj* imprevisible.

unprepared [ʌnprɪ'peəd] *adj* (*speech etc*) improvisado,-a; (*person*) desprevenido,-a.

unprincipled [ʌn'prɪnsɪpəld] *adj* sin escrúpulos.

unprintable [ʌn'prɪntəbəl] *adj* (*word, comment*) malsonante.

unproductive [ʌnprə'dʌktɪv] *adj* (*inefficient*) improductivo,-a; (*fruitless*) infructuoso,-a.

unprofessional [ʌnprə'feʃənəl] *adj* (*unethical*) poco profesional; (*substandard*) de aficionado,-a.

unprotected [ʌnprə'tektɪd] *adj* indefenso,-a.

unprovoked [ʌnprə'vəʊkt] *adj* gratuito, -a.

unpunished [ʌn'pʌnɪʃt] *adj* impune.

unqualified [ʌn'kwɒlɪfaɪd] *adj* 1 (*without qualification*) sin título; (*incompetent*) incompetente. 2 (*unconditional*) incondicional; (*denial*) rotundo,-a; (*endorsement*) sin reserva; (*success*) total.

unquestionable [ʌn'kwestʃənəbəl] *adj* indiscutible.

unquestioning [ʌn'kwestʃənɪŋ] *adj* incondicional; (*obedience*) ciego,-a.

unravel [ʌn'rævəl] I *vtr* desenmarañar. II *vi* desenmarañarse.

unreadable [ʌn'riːdəbəl] *adj* 1 (*handwriting*) ilegible. 2 (*book*) imposible de leer.

unreal [ʌn'rɪəl] *adj* irreal.

unrealistic [ʌnrɪə'lɪstɪk] *adj* poco realista.

unreasonable [ʌn'riːzənəbəl] *adj* poco razonable; (*demands*) desmedido,-a; (*prices*) exorbitante; (*hour*) inoportuno,-a.

unrefined [ʌnrɪ'faɪnd] *adj* 1 (*sugar, oil etc*) sin refinar. 2 (*person*) tosco,-a, basto,-a.

unrelated [ʌnrɪ'leɪtɪd] *adj* (*not connected*) no relacionado,-a.

unrelenting [ʌnrɪ'lentɪŋ] *adj* (*behaviour*) implacable; (*struggle*) encarnizado,-a.

unreliable [ʌnrɪ'laɪəbəl] *adj* 1 (*person*) de poca confianza. 2 (*information*) que no es de fiar; (*machine*) poco fiable.

unrelieved [ʌnrɪ'liːvd] *adj* (*boredom*) total.

unremitting [ʌnrɪ'mɪtɪŋ] *adj* 1 (*efforts etc*) incesante. 2 (*person*) incansable.

unrepentant [ʌnrɪ'pentənt] *adj* impenitente.

unreserved [ʌnrɪ'zɜːvd] *adj* (*praise, support*) sin reserva. ◆**unreservedly** *adv* sin reservas.

unrest [ʌn'rest] *n* (*social etc*) malestar *m*; **political u.**, agitación política.

unrivalled, *US* **unrivaled** [ʌn'raɪvəld] *adj* sin par, sin rival.

unroll [ʌn'rəʊl] *vtr* desenrollar.

unruffled [ʌn'rʌfəld] *adj fig* tranquilo,-a.

unruly [ʌn'ruːlɪ] *adj* (*unrulier, unruliest*) 1 (*child*) revoltoso,-a. 2 (*hair*) rebelde.

unsafe [ʌn'seɪf] *adj* (*dangerous*) peligroso,-a; (*risky*) inseguro,-a; **to feel u.**, sentirse expuesto,-a.

unsaid [ʌn'sed] *adj* **it's better left u.**, más vale no decir nada; **much was left u.**, quedó mucho por decir.

unsatisfactory [ʌnsætɪs'fæktərɪ] *adj* insatisfactorio,-a; **it's most u.**, deja mucho que desear.

unsavoury, *US* **unsavory** [ʌn'seɪvərɪ] *adj* desagradable.

unscathed [ʌn'skeɪðd] *adj* ileso,-a, indemne.

unscrew [ʌn'skruː] *vtr* destornillar.

unscrupulous [ʌn'skruːpjʊləs] *adj* sin escrúpulos.

unseemly [ʌn'siːmlɪ] *adj* impropio,-a.

unseen [ʌn'siːn] I *adj* invisible; (*unnoticed*) inadvertido,-a. II *n GB Educ* texto no trabajado en clase.

unselfish [ʌn'selfɪʃ] *adj* desinteresado,-a.

unsettle [ʌn'setəl] *vtr* perturbar.

unsettled [ʌn'setəld] *adj* 1 (*person*) nervioso,-a; (*situation*) inestable. 2 (*weather*) inestable. 3 (*matter, debt*) pendiente. 4 (*land*) sin colonizar.

unshaven |ʌnˈʃeɪvən| *adj* sin afeitar.

unsightly |ʌnˈsaɪtlɪ| *adj* feo,-a, desagradable.

unskilled |ʌnˈskɪld| *adj* (*worker*) no cualificado,-a; (*work*) no especializado,-a.

unsociable |ʌnˈsəʊʃəbəl| *adj* insociable, huraño,-a.

unsophisticated |ʌnsəˈfɪstɪkeɪtɪd| *adj* 1 (*naïve*) ingenuo,-a. 2 (*simple*) poco sofisticado,-a.

unsound |ʌnˈsaʊnd| *adj* 1 (*unstable*) inestable; **of u. mind**, demente. 2 (*fallacious*) falso,-a.

unspeakable |ʌnˈspiːkəbəl| *adj* 1 indecible. 2 *fig* (*evil*) atroz.

unspoken |ʌnˈspəʊkən| *adj* 1 (*tacit*) tácito,-a. 2 (*feeling*) interior, secreto,-a.

unstable |ʌnˈsteɪbəl| *adj* inestable.

unsteady |ʌnˈstedɪ| *adj* (*not firm*) inestable; (*table, chair*) cojo,-a; (*hand, voice*) tembloroso,-a.

unstinting |ʌnˈstɪntɪŋ| *adj* pródigo,-a (**in**, en, de).

unstuck |ʌnˈstʌk| *adj* **to come u.**, despegarse; *fig* venirse abajo.

unsuccessful |ʌnsəkˈsesfʊl| *adj* 1 (*fruitless*) fracasado,-a; (*useless*) vano,-a. 2 (*businessman etc*) fracasado,-a; (*candidate*) derrotado,-a; **to be u. at sth**, no tener éxito con algo. ◆**unsuccessfully** *adv* sin éxito, en vano.

unsuitable |ʌnˈsuːtəbəl| *adj* 1 (*person*) no apto,-a. 2 (*thing*) inadecuado,-a; (*remark*) inoportuno,-a; (*time*) inconveniente.

unsuited |ʌnˈsuːtɪd| *adj* 1 (*person*) no apto,-a; (*thing*) impropio,-a (**to**, para). 2 (*incompatible*) incompatible.

unsure |ʌnˈʃʊəʳ| *adj* poco seguro,-a.

unsuspecting |ʌnsəˈspektɪŋ| *adj* confiado,-a; **he went in u.**, entró sin sospechar nada.

unswerving |ʌnˈswɜːvɪŋ| *adj* firme.

unsympathetic |ʌnsɪmpəˈθetɪk| *adj* (*unfeeling*) impasible; (*not understanding*) poco comprensivo,-a.

untapped |ʌnˈtæpt| *adj* (*mine etc*) sin explotar.

untarnished |ʌnˈtɑːnɪʃt| *adj* *fig* sin mancha.

untenable |ʌnˈtenəbəl| *adj* insostenible.

unthinkable |ʌnˈθɪŋkəbəl| *adj* impensable, inconcebible.

untidy |ʌnˈtaɪdɪ| *adj* (*untidier, untidiest*) (*room, person*) desordenado,-a; (*hair*) despeinado,-a; (*appearance*) desaseado,-a.

untie |ʌnˈtaɪ| *vtr* desatar; (*free*) soltar.

until |ʌnˈtɪl| **I** *conj* hasta que; **she worked u. she collapsed**, trabajó hasta desfallecer; **u. she gets back**, hasta que vuelva. **II** *prep* hasta; **u. now**, hasta ahora; **u. ten o'clock**, hasta las diez; **not u. Monday**, hasta el lunes no.

untimely |ʌnˈtaɪmlɪ| *adj* 1 (*premature*) prematuro,-a. 2 (*inopportune*)

inoportuno,-a; (*hour*) intempestivo,-a.

untold |ʌnˈtəʊld| *adj* 1 (*indescribable*) indecible. 2 *fig* (*loss, wealth*) incalculable. 3 (*not told*) sin contar.

untouchable |ʌnˈtʌtʃəbəl| *adj & n* intocable (*mf*).

untoward |ʌntəˈwɔːd, ʌnˈtəʊəd| *adj* 1 (*unfortunate*) desafortunado,-a. 2 (*adverse*) adverso,-a.

untrained |ʌnˈtreɪnd| *adj* 1 (*unskilled*) sin preparación profesional. 2 (*inexpert*) inexperto,-a.

untrue |ʌnˈtruː| *adj* 1 (*false*) falso,-a. 2 (*unfaithful*) infiel. 3 (*inexact*) inexacto,-a.

untrustworthy |ʌnˈtrʌstwɜːðɪ| *adj* 1 (*person*) de poca confianza. 2 (*source*) no fidedigno,-a.

unused |ʌnˈjuːzd| *adj* 1 (*car*) sin usar; (*flat etc*) sin estrenar; (*stamp*) sin matar. 2 (*not in use*) que no ya se utiliza. 3 |ʌnˈjuːst| (*unaccustomed*) desacostumbrado,-a (**to**, a).

unusual |ʌnˈjuːʒʊəl| *adj* (*rare*) insólito,-a, poco común; (*original*) original; (*exceptional*) excepcional. ◆**unusually** *adv* excepcionalmente.

unveil |ʌnˈveɪl| *vtr* descubrir.

unwarranted |ʌnˈwɒrəntɪd| *adj* injustificado,-a; (*remark*) gratuito,-a.

unwavering |ʌnˈweɪvərɪŋ| *adj* (*loyalty*) constante, firme; (*courage*) inquebrantable.

unwelcome |ʌnˈwelkəm| *adj* (*visitor*) molesto,-a; (*visit*) inoportuno,-a; *fig* (*news etc*) desagradable.

unwell |ʌnˈwel| *adj* malo,-a, indispuesto,-a.

unwieldy |ʌnˈwiːldɪ| *adj* (*difficult to handle*) poco manejable; (*clumsy*) torpe.

unwilling |ʌnˈwɪlɪŋ| *adj* **to be u. to do sth**, no estar dispuesto a hacer algo. ◆**unwillingly** *adv* de mala gana.

unwind |ʌnˈwaɪnd| (*pt & pp* **unwound**) **I** *vtr* desenrollar. **II** *vi* 1 desenrollarse. 2 (*relax*) relajarse.

unwise |ʌnˈwaɪz| *adj* imprudente, desaconsejable.

unwitting |ʌnˈwɪtɪŋ| *adj* involuntario,-a.

unworkable |ʌnˈwɜːkəbəl| *adj* (*not feasible*) impracticable; (*suggestion*) irrealizable.

unworthy |ʌnˈwɜːðɪ| *adj* indigno,-a.

unwrap |ʌnˈræp| *vtr* (*gift*) desenvolver; (*package*) deshacer.

unwritten |ʌnˈrɪtən| *adj* no escrito,-a; (*agreement*) verbal.

unyielding |ʌnˈjiːldɪŋ| *adj* inflexible.

up |ʌp| **I** *prep* 1 (*movement*) **to climb up the mountain**, escalar la montaña; **to walk up the street**, ir calle arriba. 2 (*position*) en lo alto de; **further up the street**, más adelante (en la misma calle); **halfway up the ladder**, a mitad de la escalera.

II *adv* **1** (*upwards*) arriba, hacia arriba; (*position*) arriba; **from ten pounds up,** de diez libras para arriba; **halfway up,** a medio camino; **right up** (**to the top**), hasta arriba (del todo); **to go** *or* **come up,** subir; **'this side up',** 'este lado hacia arriba'. **2 the moon is up,** ha salido la luna. **3** (*towards*) hacia; **to come** *or* **go up to sb,** acercarse a algn; **to walk up and down,** ir de un lado a otro. **4** (*in, to*) **he's up in Yorkshire,** está en Yorkshire. **5** (*increased*) **bread is up,** el pan ha subido. **6 it's up for discussion,** se está discutiendo; **up for sale,** en venta. **7** *fam* **something's up,** pasa algo; **what's up** (**with you**)?, ¿qué pasa (contigo)? **8 to be up against sth,** enfrentarse con algo. **9 up to,** (*as far as, until*) hasta; **I can spend up to £5,** puedo gastar un máximo de cinco libras; **up to here,** hasta aquí; **up to now,** hasta ahora. **10 to be up to,** (*depend on*) depender de; (*be capable of*) estar a la altura de; **I don't feel up to doing it today,** hoy no me encuentro con fuerzas para hacerlo; **it's not up to much,** no vale gran cosa. **11 he's up to sth,** está tramando algo.

III *adj* **1** (*out of bed*) levantado,-a. **2** (*finished*) terminado,-a; **time's up,** (ya) es la hora.

IV *vtr fam* aumentar.

V *n fig* **ups and downs,** altibajos *mpl*.

up-and-coming |ʌpən'kʌmɪŋ| *adj* prometedor,-a.

upbringing |'ʌpbrɪŋɪŋ| *n* educación *f*.

update |ʌp'deɪt| *vtr* actualizar, poner al día.

upgrade |ʌp'greɪd| *vtr* **1** (*promote*) ascender. **2** (*improve*) mejorar la calidad de.

upheaval |ʌp'hiːvəl| *n* trastorno *m*.

uphill |'ʌphɪl| **I** *adj* ascendente; *fig* arduo,-a. **II** *adv* cuesta arriba.

uphold |ʌp'həʊld| *vtr* (*pt & pp* **upheld**) sostener.

upholstery |ʌp'həʊlstərɪ| *n* tapizado *m*, tapicería *f*.

upkeep |'ʌpkiːp| *n* mantenimiento *m*.

up-market |'ʌpmɑːkɪt| *adj* de categoría.

upon |ə'pɒn| *prep fml* en, sobre; **once u. a time ...,** érase una vez ...; **u. my word,** (mi) palabra de honor.

upper |'ʌpər| **I** *adj* **1** (*position*) superior; **u. storey,** piso de arriba; *fig* **to have the u. hand,** llevar la delantera. **2** (*in rank*) alto,-a; **the u. class,** la clase alta; **the U. House,** la Cámara Alta. **II** *n* (*of shoe*) pala *f*.

upper-class |'ʌpəklæs| *adj* de la clase alta.

uppermost |'ʌpəməʊst| *adj* más alto,-a; *fig* **it was u. in my mind,** era lo que me preocupaba más.

upright |'ʌpraɪt| **I** *adj* **1** (*vertical*) vertical.

2 (*honest*) honrado,-a. **II** *adv* derecho. **III** *n Ftb* (*post*) poste *m*.

uprising |'ʌpraɪzɪŋ| *n* sublevación *f*.

uproar |'ʌprɔːr| *n* tumulto *m*, alboroto *m*.

uproot |ʌp'ruːt| *vtr* (*plant*) arrancar de raíz.

upset |ʌp'set| **I** *vtr* (*pt & pp* **upset**) **1** (*overturn*) volcar; (*spill*) derramar. **2** (*shock*) trastornar; (*worry*) preocupar; (*displease*) disgustar. **3** (*spoil*) desbaratar. **4** (*make ill*) sentar mal a. **II** |'ʌpset| *n* **1** (*reversal*) revés *m*. **2** *Sport* resultado inesperado. **III** |ʌp'set| *adj* (*shocked*) alterado, -a; (*displeased*) disgustado,-a; **to have an u. stomach,** sentirse mal del estómago.

upshot |'ʌpʃɒt| *n* resultado *m*.

upside |'ʌpsaɪd| *n* **u. down,** al revés.

upstage |ʌp'steɪdʒ| *vtr fam* eclipsar.

upstairs |ʌp'steəz| **I** *adv* al piso de arriba; **she lives u.,** vive en el piso de arriba. **II** *n* piso *m* de arriba.

upstart |'ʌpstɑːt| *n* advenedizo,-a *m,f*.

upstream |ʌp'striːm| *adv* río arriba.

uptake |'ʌpteɪk| *n fam* **to be quick on the u.,** cogerlas al vuelo.

uptight |ʌp'taɪt| *adj fam* nervioso,-a.

up to date |ʌp tə 'deɪt| *adj* **1** (*current*) al día. **2** (*modern*) moderno,-a.

upturn |'ʌptɜːn| *n* mejora *f*.

upward |'ʌpwəd| *adj* ascendente.

upward(s) |'ʌpwəd(z)| *adv* hacia arriba; **from ten** (**years**) **u.,** a partir de los diez años; *fam* **u. of,** algo más de.

uranium |jʊ'reɪnɪəm| *n* uranio *m*.

urban |'ɜːbən| *adj* urbano,-a.

urbane |ɜː'beɪn| *adj* urbano,-a, cortés.

urchin |'ɜːtʃɪn| *n* **1** (*child*) pilluelo,-a *m,f*. **2 sea u.,** erizo *m* de mar.

urge |ɜːdʒ| **I** *vtr* **1** (*plead*) exhortar. **2** (*advocate*) preconizar; **to u. that sth should be done,** insistir en que se haga algo. **II** *n* impulso *m*. ◆ **urge on** *vtr* animar a.

urgency |'ɜːdʒənsɪ| *n* urgencia *f*.

urgent |'ɜːdʒənt| *adj* urgente; (*need, tone*) apremiante.

urinal |jʊ'raɪnəl| *n* (*toilet*) urinario *m*; (*bowl*) orinal *m*.

urinate |'jʊərɪneɪt| *vi* orinar.

urine |'jʊərɪn| *n* orina *f*.

urn |ɜːn| *n* **1** urna *f*. **2 tea u.,** tetera *f* grande.

Uruguay |'jʊərəɡwaɪ| *n* Uruguay.

Uruguayan |jʊərə'ɡwaɪən| *adj & n* uruguayo,-a *(m,f)*.

us |ʌs| *pers pron* **1** (*as object*) nos; **let's forget it,** olvidémoslo. **2** (*after prep*) nosotros,-as; **both of us,** nosotros dos; **he's one of us,** es de los nuestros. **3** (*after v to be*) nosotros,-as; **she wouldn't believe it was us,** no creía que fuéramos nosotros. **4** *fam* me; **give us a kiss!,** ¡dame un beso!

US |juː'es| *abbr of* **United States,**

EE.UU. *mpl.*

USA [juːesˈeɪ] *abbr of* **United States of America,** EE.UU. *mpl.*

usage [ˈjuːsɪdʒ] *n* 1 *(habit, custom)* costumbre *f.* 2 *Ling* uso *m.*

use [juːz] I *vtr* 1 emplear, utilizar; **what is it used for?,** ¿para qué sirve?; **to u. force,** hacer uso de la fuerza. 2 *(consume)* consumir, gastar. 3 *(take unfair advantage of)* aprovecharse de. 4 *fam* **I could u. a drink,** me vendría mal un trago. II *v aux (past tense only)* soler, acostumbrar; **where did you u. to live?,** ¿dónde vivías (antes)? III [juːs] *n* 1 uso *m,* empleo *m; (handling)* manejo *m;* **directions for u.,** modo de empleo; **in u.,** en uso; **'not in u.',** *(on lift)* 'no funciona'; **ready for u.,** listo para usar; **to make (good) u. of sth,** aprovechar algo; **to put to good u.,** sacar partido de. 2 *(application)* aplicación *f.* 3 *(usefulness)* utilidad *f;* **it's no u.,** es inútil; **what's the u.?,** ¿para qué?; *fam* **it's no u. crying,** no sirve de nada llorar; **of u.,** útil; **to be of u.,** servir. ◆ **use up** *vtr* acabar.

used [juːzd] *adj* 1 *(second-hand)* usado,-a. 2 [juːst] **to be u. to,** estar acostumbrado,-a a.

useful [ˈjuːsful] *adj* útil; *(practical)* práctico,-a; **to come in u.,** venir bien.

usefulness [ˈjuːsfʊlnɪs] *n* utilidad *f.*

useless [ˈjuːslɪs] *adj* inútil.

user [ˈjuːzəʳ] *n* 1 usuario,-a *m,f.* 2 *fam (of drugs)* drogadicto,-a *m,f.*

usher [ˈʌʃəʳ] I *n* 1 *Cin Theat* acomodador,-a *m,f.* 2 *(in court etc)* ujier

m. II *vtr* **to u. in,** *Cin Theat* acomodar; *(at home)* hacer pasar; **to u. out,** acompañar hasta la puerta.

USSR [juːesesˈɑːʳ] *Hist abbr of* **Union of Soviet Socialist Republics,** URSS *f.*

usual [ˈjuːʒʊəl] I *adj* corriente, normal; **as u.,** como siempre; **at the u. hour,** a la hora habitual; **earlier than u.,** más pronto que de costumbre; **the u. problems,** los problemas de siempre. II *n* lo habitual; **out of the u.,** fuera de lo común. ◆ **usually** *adv* normalmente.

usurpation [juːzɜːˈpeɪʃən] *n* usurpación *f.*

utensil [juːˈtensəl] *n* utensilio *m;* **kitchen utensils,** batería *f sing* de cocina.

uterus [ˈjuːtərəs] *n* útero *m.*

utilitarian [juːtɪlɪˈteərɪən] *adj* 1 *(in philosophy)* utilitarista. 2 *(useful)* utilitario,-a.

utility [juːˈtɪlɪtɪ] *n* 1 utilidad *f;* **u. room,** cuarto *m* de planchar; *(for storage)* trascocina *f.* 2 **(public) u.,** empresa *f* de servicio público.

utilize [ˈjuːtɪlaɪz] *vtr* utilizar.

utmost [ˈʌtməʊst] I *adj* sumo,-a; **of the u. importance,** de suma importancia. II *n* máximo *m;* **to do or try one's u.,** hacer todo lo posible; **to the u.,** al máximo, a más no poder.

utopian [juːˈtəʊpɪən] *adj* utópico,-a.

utter[1] [ˈʌtəʳ] *vtr (words)* pronunciar; *(sigh)* dar; *(cry, threat)* lanzar.

utter[2] [ˈʌtəʳ] *adj* total, completo,-a.

utterance [ˈʌtərəns] *n* declaración *f.*

U-turn [ˈjuːtɜːn] *n* cambio *m* de sentido; *Pol* giro *m* de 180° grados.

V

V, v [viː] *n (the letter)* V, v *f.*

V *abbr of* **volt(s),** V.

v 1 *abbr of* **verse,** v. 2 *(also* **vs)** *abbr of* **versus,** contra.

vacancy [ˈveɪkənsɪ] *n* 1 *(job)* vacante *f.* 2 *(room)* habitación *f* libre; **'no vacancies',** 'completo'.

vacant [ˈveɪkənt] *adj* 1 *(empty)* vacío,-a. 2 *(job)* vacante; *GB* **'situations v.',** 'ofertas de trabajo'. 3 *(free, not in use)* libre.

vacate [vəˈkeɪt] *vtr (flat)* desalojar.

vacation [vəˈkeɪʃən] I *n* vacaciones *fpl;* **on v.,** de vacaciones. II *vi US* pasar las vacaciones (**in, at,** en).

vacationer [vəˈkeɪʃənəʳ], **vacationist** [vəˈkeɪʃənɪst] *n US* **summer v.,** veraneante *mf.*

vaccinate [ˈvæksɪneɪt] *vtr* vacunar.

vaccine [ˈvæksiːn] *n* vacuna *f.*

vacuum [ˈvækjʊəm] I *n* vacío *m;* **v. cleaner,** aspiradora *f;* **v. flask,** termo *m.* II *vtr (carpet, room)* pasar la aspiradora por.

vacuum-packed [ˈvækjʊəmpækt] *adj*

envasado,-a al vacío.

vagina [vəˈdʒaɪnə] *n* vagina *f.*

vagrant [ˈveɪgrənt] *adj & n* vagabundo,-a *(m,f).*

vague [veɪg] *adj (imprecise)* vago,-a, impreciso,-a; *(indistinct)* borroso,-a.

vain [veɪn] *adj* 1 *(proud)* vanidoso,-a, presumido,-a. 2 *(hopeless)* vano,-a; **in v.,** en vano.

valentine [ˈvæləntaɪn] *n* 1 *(card)* tarjeta *f* que se manda el Día de los Enamorados. 2 *(sweetheart)* novio,-a *m,f.*

valet [ˈvælɪt, ˈvæleɪ] *n* ayuda *m* de cámara.

valiant [ˈvælɪənt] *adj* valiente.

valid [ˈvælɪd] *adj* válido,-a; **no longer v.,** caducado,-a.

valley [ˈvælɪ] *n* valle *m.*

valour, *US* **valor** [ˈvæləʳ] *n* valor *m,* valentía *f.*

valuable [ˈvæljʊəbəl] I *adj* valioso,-a, de valor. II *npl* **valuables,** objetos *mpl* de valor.

valuation [vælju'eɪʃən] n 1 (act) valoración f. 2 (price) valor m.

value ['vælju:] I n valor m; **50 pence is good v.**, 50 peniques es un buen precio; **to get good v. for money**, sacarle jugo al dinero; **v. added tax**, impuesto m sobre el valor añadido. II vtr valorar.

valve [vælv] n 1 Anat Tech válvula f. 2 Rad lámpara f.

vampire ['væmpaɪər] n vampiro m.

van [væn] n GB 1 Aut furgoneta f. 2 Rail furgón m.

vandal ['vændəl] n vándalo,-a m,f.

vandalism ['vændəlɪzəm] n vandalismo m.

vandalize ['vændəlaɪz] vtr destruir, destrozar.

vanguard ['væŋgɑːd] n vanguardia f.

vanilla [və'nɪlə] n vainilla f.

vanish ['vænɪʃ] vi desaparecer.

vanity ['vænɪtɪ] n vanidad f; **v. bag**, **v. case**, neceser m.

vantage ['vɑːntɪdʒ] n ventaja f; **v. point**, posición estratégica.

vaporizer ['veɪpəraɪzər] n (device) vaporizador m; (spray) pulverizador m.

vapour, US **vapor** ['veɪpər] n vapor m; (on windowpane) vaho m; **v. trail**, estela f de humo.

variable ['veərɪəbəl] adj & n variable (f).

variance ['veərɪəns] n fml **to be at v.**, no concordar; **to be at v. with sb**, estar en desacuerdo con algn.

variation [veərɪ'eɪʃən] n variación f.

varicose ['værɪkəʊs] adj **v. veins**, varices fpl.

varied ['veərɪd] adj variado,-a, diverso,-a.

variety [və'raɪɪtɪ] n 1 (diversity) variedad f; (assortment) surtido m; **for a v. of reasons**, por razones diversas. 2 **v. show**, espectáculo m de variedades.

various ['veərɪəs] adj diversos,-as, varios,-as.

varnish ['vɑːnɪʃ] I n barniz m; GB **nail v.**, esmalte m de uñas. II vtr barnizar; (nails) esmaltar.

vary ['veərɪ] vi variar; **prices v. from £2 to £4**, los precios oscilan entre 2 y 4 libras; **to v. in size**, variar de tamaño.

varying ['veərɪŋ] adj **with v. degrees of success**, con más o menos éxito.

vase [vɑːz] n florero m, jarrón m.

Vaseline® ['væsɪliːn] n vaselina f.

vast [vɑːst] adj vasto,-a; (majority) inmenso,-a.

VAT, Vat [viːeɪ'tiː, væt] abbr of **value added tax**, IVA m.

vat [væt] n cuba f, tina f.

Vatican ['vætɪkən] n **the V.**, el Vaticano.

vault¹ [vɔːlt] n bóveda f; (for wine) bodega f; (tomb) cripta f; (of bank) cámara acorazada.

vault² [vɔːlt] I vtr & vi saltar. II n Gymn salto m.

vaunt [vɔːnt] vtr fml jactarse de, hacer alarde de.

VCR [viːsiː'ɑːr] abbr of **video cassette recorder**, (grabador m de) video m.

VD [viː'diː] abbr of **venereal disease**, enfermedad venérea.

VDU [viːdiː'juː] abbr of **visual display unit**, pantalla f.

veal [viːl] n ternera f.

veer [vɪər] vi (ship) virar; (car) girar.

vegetable ['vedʒtəbəl] n (food) verdura f, hortaliza f; **v. garden**, huerta f, huerto m.

vegetarian [vedʒɪ'teərɪən] adj & n vegetariano,-a (m,f).

vegetation [vedʒɪ'teɪʃən] n vegetación f.

vehement ['viːɪmənt] adj vehemente.

vehicle ['viːɪkəl] n vehículo m.

veil [veɪl] I n velo m. II vtr velar.

vein [veɪn] n vena f.

velocity [vɪ'lɒsɪtɪ] n velocidad f.

velvet ['velvɪt] n terciopelo m.

velvety ['velvɪtɪ] adj aterciopelado,-a.

vendetta [ven'detə] n vendetta f.

vending ['vendɪŋ] n **v. machine**, máquina expendedora.

vendor ['vendɔːr] n vendedor,-a m,f.

veneer [vɪ'nɪər] n 1 (covering) chapa f. 2 fig apariencia f.

venerable ['venərəbəl] adj venerable.

venereal [vɪ'nɪərɪəl] adj venéreo,-a.

Venetian [vɪ'niːʃən] adj & n veneciano,-a (m,f); **v. blind**, persiana f graduable.

Venezuela [venɪ'zweɪlə] n Venezuela.

Venezuelan [venɪ'zweɪlən] adj & n venezolano,-a (m,f).

vengeance ['vendʒəns] n venganza f; fam **it was raining with a v.**, llovía con ganas.

Venice ['venɪs] n Venecia.

venison ['venzən, 'venɪsən] n carne f de venado.

venom ['venəm] n veneno m.

venomous ['venəməs] adj venenoso,-a; fig **v. tongue**, lengua viperina.

vent [vent] I n 1 (opening) abertura f, orificio m; (grille) rejilla f de ventilación; **air v.**, respiradero m. 2 (of volcano) chimenea f. II vtr fig (feelings) descargar.

ventilate ['ventɪleɪt] vtr ventilar.

ventilation [ventɪ'leɪʃən] n ventilación f.

ventilator ['ventɪleɪtər] n ventilador m.

ventriloquist [ven'trɪləkwɪst] n ventrílocuo,-a m,f.

venture ['ventʃər] I vtr arriesgar, aventurar; **he didn't v. to ask**, no se atrevió a preguntarlo. II vi arriesgarse; **to v. out of doors**, atreverse a salir. III n empresa arriesgada, aventura f; Com **business/joint v.**, empresa comercial/colectiva.

venue ['venjuː] n 1 (meeting place) lugar m de reunión. 2 (for concert etc) local m.

Venus ['viːnəs] n (goddess) Venus f; (planet) Venus m.

veranda(h) [vəˈrændə] *n* porche *m*, terraza *f*.

verb [vɜːb] *n* verbo *m*.

verbal [ˈvɜːbəl] *adj* verbal.

verbatim [vəˈbeɪtɪm] I *adj* textual. II *adv* textualmente.

verbose [vɜːˈbəʊs] *adj* prodigo,-a en palabras.

verdict [ˈvɜːdɪkt] *n* 1 *Jur* veredicto *m*, fallo *m*. 2 (*opinion*) opinión *f*, juicio *m*.

verge [vɜːdʒ] I *n* 1 (*margin*) borde *m*; *fig* **on the v. of**, al borde de; *fig* **to be on the v. of doing sth**, estar a punto de hacer algo. 2 *GB* (*of road*) arcén *m*. II *vi* rayar (**on**, en).

verification [verɪfɪˈkeɪʃən] *n* verificación *f*, comprobación *f*.

verify [ˈverɪfaɪ] *vtr* verificar, comprobar.

veritable [ˈverɪtəbəl] *adj* auténtico,-a.

vermicelli [vɜːmɪˈselɪ] *npl* fideos *mpl*.

vermin [ˈvɜːmɪn] *npl* 1 (*animals*) bichos *mpl*, sabandijas *fpl*. 2 *fig* gentuza *f sing*.

vermouth [ˈvɜːməθ] *n* vermú *m*, vermut *m*.

verrucca [vəˈruːkə] *n* verruga *f*.

versatile [ˈvɜːsətaɪl] *adj* (*person*) polifacético,-a; (*object*) versátil.

verse [vɜːs] *n* 1 (*stanza*) estrofa *f*. 2 (*poetry*) versos *mpl*, poesía *f*. 3 (*of song*) copla *f*. 4 (*of Bible*) versículo *m*.

versed [vɜːst] *adj* **to be (well) v. in**, ser (muy) versado en.

version [ˈvɜːʃən, ˈvɜːʒən] *n* 1 versión *f*; **stage v.**, adaptación *f* teatral. 2 *Aut* modelo *m*.

versus [ˈvɜːsəs] *prep* contra.

vertebra [ˈvɜːtɪbrə] *n* (*pl* **vertebras** *or* **vertebrae** [ˈvɜːtɪbriː]) vértebra *f*.

vertical [ˈvɜːtɪkəl] *adj & n* vertical (*f*).

vertigo [ˈvɜːtɪgəʊ] *n* vértigo *m*.

verve [vɜːv] *n* vigor *m*, brío *m*.

very [ˈverɪ] I *adv* 1 (*extremely*) muy; **to be v. hungry**, tener mucha hambre; **v. much**, muchísimo; **v. well**, muy bien. 2 (*emphatic*) **at the v. latest**, como máximo; **at the v. least**, como mínimo; **the v. best**, el mejor de todos; **the v. first/last**, el primero/último de todos; **the v. same day**, el mismo día. II *adj* 1 **at the v. end/beginning**, al final/principio de todo. 2 (*precise*) **at this v. moment**, en este mismo momento; **her v. words**, sus palabras exactas; **in the v. middle**, justo en medio. 3 (*mere*) **the v. thought of it!**, ¡sólo con pensarlo!

vespers [ˈvespəz] *npl* vísperas *fpl*.

vessel [ˈvesəl] *n* 1 (*container*) vasija *f*. 2 *Naut* buque *m*, nave *f*. 3 *Anat Bot* vaso *m*.

vest [vest] I *n* 1 (*undershirt*) camiseta *f* de tirantes. 2 *US* chaleco *m*. II *vtr Jur* conferir a (**with**, -).

vested [ˈvestɪd] *adj Jur Fin* **v. interests**, derechos adquiridos; *fig* intereses *mpl* personales.

vestibule [ˈvestɪbjuːl] *n* vestíbulo *m*.

vestige [ˈvestɪdʒ] *n* vestigio *m*.

vestry [ˈvestrɪ] *n* sacristía *f*.

vet [vet] I *n fam abbr of* **veterinary surgeon**. II *vtr GB* someter a investigación, examinar.

veteran [ˈvetərən] *n* 1 veterano,-a *m,f*. 2 *US* (*war*) v., ex combatiente *mf*.

veterinarian [vetərɪˈneərɪən] *n US* veterinario,-a *m,f*.

veterinary [ˈvetərɪnərɪ] *adj* veterinario,-a; **v. medicine**, veterinaria *f*; *GB* **v. surgeon**, veterinario,-a *m,f*.

veto [ˈviːtəʊ] I *n* (*pl* **vetoes**) veto *m*. II *vtr Pol* vetar; (*suggestion etc*) descartar.

vexed [vekst] *adj* 1 (*annoyed*) disgustado, -a. 2 (*debated*) controvertido, -a.

VHF [viːeɪtʃˈef] *abbr of* **very high frequency**, frecuencia muy alta, VHF.

via [ˈvaɪə] *prep* por, vía.

viable [ˈvaɪəbəl] *adj* viable, factible.

viaduct [ˈvaɪədʌkt] *n* viaducto *m*.

vibrant [ˈvaɪbrənt] *adj* 1 (*sound*) vibrante. 2 *fig* (*personality*) vital; (*city*) animado,-a.

vibrate [vaɪˈbreɪt] *vi* vibrar (**with**, de).

vibration [vaɪˈbreɪʃən] *n* vibración *f*.

vicar [ˈvɪkəʳ] *n* párroco *m*.

vicarage [ˈvɪkərɪdʒ] *n* casa *f* del párroco.

vicarious [vɪˈkeərɪəs] *adj* experimentado,-a por otro; (*punishment*) sufrido,-a por otro.

vice¹ [vaɪs] *n* vicio *m*.

vice² [vaɪs] *n* (*tool*) torno *m* de banco.

vice³ [vaɪs] *pref* vice-; **v. chancellor**, rector,-a *m,f*; **v. president**, vicepresidente,-a *m,f*.

vice-chairman [vaɪsˈtʃeəmən] *n* vicepresidente *m*.

vice versa [vaɪsɪˈvɜːsə] *adv* viceversa.

vicinity [vɪˈsɪnɪtɪ] *n* (*area*) vecindad *f*; **in the v. of**, (*geographic location*) cerca de; (*amount*) alrededor de.

vicious [ˈvɪʃəs] *adj* (*violent*) violento,-a; (*malicious*) malintencionado,-a; (*cruel*) cruel; **v. circle**, círculo vicioso.

victim [ˈvɪktɪm] *n* víctima *f*.

victimize [ˈvɪktɪmaɪz] *vtr* perseguir, tratar injustamente.

victor [ˈvɪktəʳ] *n* vencedor,-a *m,f*.

victorious [vɪkˈtɔːrɪəs] *adj* victorioso,-a.

victory [ˈvɪktərɪ] *n* victoria *f*.

video [ˈvɪdɪəʊ] *n* vídeo *m*; **v. camera**, videocámara *f*; **v. cassette**, videocasete *m*; **v. club**, videoclub *m*; **v. game**, videojuego *m*; **v. (cassette) recorder**, vídeo *m*; **v. tape**, cinta *f* de vídeo.

video-tape [ˈvɪdɪəʊteɪp] *vtr* grabar (en vídeo).

vie [vaɪ] *vi* competir (**against**, **with**, con).

Vienna [vɪˈenə] *n* Viena *f*.

Viennese [vɪəˈniːz] *adj & n* vienés,-esa

(m,f).

Vietnam |vjet'næm| n Vietnam.

view |vju:| I n 1 (sight) vista f, panorama m; **in full v.**, completamente visible; **on v.**, a la vista; **to come into v.**, aparecer; fig **in v. of the fact that ...**, dado que .... 2 (opinion) opinión f; **point of v.**, punto m de vista; **to take a dim v. of**, ver con malos ojos. 3 (aim) fin m; **with a v. to**, con la intención de. II vtr 1 (look at) mirar; (house etc) visitar. 2 (consider) contemplar; (topic, problem) enfocar.

viewer |'vju:ər| n 1 TV televidente mf. 2 Phot visionador m.

viewfinder |'vju:faɪndər| n visor m.

viewpoint |'vju:pɔɪnt| n punto m de vista.

vigil |'vɪdʒɪl| n vigilia f.

vigilante |vɪdʒɪ'læntɪ| n **v. group**, patrulla ciudadana.

vigorous |'vɪgərəs| adj vigoroso,-a, enérgico,-a.

vigour, US **vigor** |'vɪgər| n vigor m.

vile |vaɪl| adj 1 (evil) vil, infame. 2 (disgusting) repugnante. 3 fam (awful) horrible.

vilify |'vɪlɪfaɪ| vtr denigrar.

villa |'vɪlə| n 1 (in country) casa f de campo. 2 GB chalet m.

village |'vɪlɪdʒ| n (small) aldea f; (larger) pueblo m.

villager |'vɪlɪdʒər| n aldeano,-a m,f.

villain |'vɪlən| n villano,-a m,f; Cin Theat malo,-a m,f.

vinaigrette |vɪneɪ'gret| n vinagreta f.

vindicate |'vɪndɪkeɪt| vtr justificar, vindicar.

vindictive |vɪn'dɪktɪv| adj vengativo,-a.

vine |vaɪn| n vid f; (climbing) parra f.

vinegar |'vɪnɪgər| n vinagre m.

vineyard |'vɪnjəd| n niña f, viñedo m.

vintage |'vɪntɪdʒ| I n 1 (crop, year) cosecha f. 2 (season) vendimia f. 3 (era) era f. II adj 1 (wine) añejo,-a. 2 (classic) clásico,-a; **v. car**, coche m de época.

vinyl |'vaɪnɪl| n vinilo m.

viola |vɪ'əʊlə| n viola f.

violate |'vaɪəleɪt| vtr violar.

violence |'vaɪələns| n violencia f.

violent |'vaɪələnt| adj 1 violento,-a. 2 (intense) intenso,-a.

violet |'vaɪəlɪt| I n 1 Bot violeta f. 2 (colour) violeta m. II adj violeta.

violin |vaɪə'lɪn| n violín m.

violinist |vaɪə'lɪnɪst| n violinista mf.

VIP |vi:aɪ'pi:| fam abbr of **very important person**, personaje m muy importante.

viper |'vaɪpər| n víbora f.

virgin |'vɜ:dʒɪn| I n virgen f; **the V. Mary**, la Virgen María; **to be a v.**, ser virgen. II adj virgen.

virginity |və'dʒɪnɪtɪ| n virginidad f.

Virgo |'vɜ:gəʊ| n Virgo m.

virile |'vɪraɪl| adj viril.

virtual |'vɜ:tʃʊəl| adj virtual; Comput **v. reality**, realidad f virtual. ◆**virtually** adv (almost) prácticamente.

virtue |'vɜ:tju:, 'vɜ:tʃu:| n virtud f; **by v. of**, en virtud de.

virtuous |'vɜ:tʃʊəs| adj virtuoso,-a.

virulent |'vɪrʊlənt| adj virulento,-a.

virus |'vaɪrəs| n virus m inv.

visa |'vi:zə| n visado m, Am visa f.

vis-à-vis |vi:zɑː'vi:| prep 1 (regarding) respecto a. 2 (opposite) frente a.

viscose |'vɪskəʊs| n viscosa f.

viscount |'vaɪkaʊnt| n vizconde m.

visibility |vɪzɪ'bɪlɪtɪ| n visibilidad f.

visible |'vɪzɪbəl| adj visible.

vision |'vɪʒən| n 1 visión f. 2 (eyesight) vista f.

visit |'vɪzɪt| I vtr 1 (person) visitar, hacer una visita a. 2 (place) visitar, ir a. II n visita f; **to pay sb a v.**, hacerle una visita a algn.

visiting |'vɪzɪtɪŋ| adj GB **v. card**, tarjeta f de visita; Med **v. hours**, horas fpl de visita; Sport **v. team**, equipo m visitante.

visitor |'vɪzɪtər| n 1 (guest) invitado,-a m,f; **we've got visitors**, tenemos visita. 2 (in hotel) cliente,-a m,f. 3 (tourist) turista mf.

visor |'vaɪzər| n visera f.

vista |'vɪstə| n vista f, panorama m.

visual |'vɪʒʊəl, 'vɪzjʊəl| adj visual; **v. aids**, medios mpl visuales.

visualize |'vɪʒʊəlaɪz, 'vɪzjʊəlaɪz| vtr 1 (imagine) imaginar(se). 2 (foresee) prever.

vital |'vaɪtəl| adj 1 (lively) enérgico,-a. 2 (essential) fundamental. 3 (decisive) decisivo,-a; fam **v. statistics**, medidas fpl del cuerpo de la mujer. 4 Med (function, sign) vital. ◆**vitally** adv **it's v. important**, es de vital importancia.

vitality |vaɪ'tælɪtɪ| n vitalidad f.

vitamin |'vɪtəmɪn, US 'vaɪtəmɪn| n vitamina f.

viva |'vaɪvə| n (abbr of **viva voce**) GB examen m oral.

vivacious |vɪ'veɪʃəs| adj vivaz.

vivacity |vɪ'væsɪtɪ| n viveza f, vivacidad f.

vivid |'vɪvɪd| adj 1 (bright, lively) vivo,-a, intenso,-a. 2 (graphic) gráfico,-a.

vixen |'vɪksən| n zorra f.

V-neck(ed) |'vi:nek(t)| adj con el cuello en pico.

vocabulary |və'kæbjʊlərɪ| n vocabulario m.

vocal |'vəʊkəl| adj vocal; **v. cords**, cuerdas fpl vocales.

vocalist |'vəʊkəlɪst| n cantante mf.

vocation |vəʊ'keɪʃən| n vocación f.

vocational |vəʊ'keɪʃənəl| adj profesional; **v. training**, formación f profesional.

vociferous |vəʊ'sɪfərəs| adj 1 (protest) enérgico,-a. 2 (noisy) clamoroso,-a.

vodka |'vɒdkə| n vodka m & f.

vogue |vəʊg| n boga f, moda f; **in v.**, de

moda.
voice [vɔɪs] I *n* voz *f*; to lose one's v., quedarse afónico; *fig* at the top of one's v., a voz en grito. II *vtr* 1 (*express*) manifestar. 2 *Ling* sonorizar.
void [vɔɪd] I *adj* 1 v. of, sin. 2 *Jur* nulo, -a, inválido,-a. II *n* vacío *m*.
volatile ['vɒlətaɪl] *adj* volátil.
volcanic [vɒl'kænɪk] *adj* volcánico,-a.
volcano [vɒl'keɪnəʊ] *n* (*pl* **volcanoes**) volcán *m*.
volition [və'lɪʃən] *n fml* of one's own v., por voluntad propia.
volley ['vɒlɪ] I *n* 1 (*of shots*) descarga *f*. 2 *fig* (*of stones, insults*) lluvia *f*. 3 *Ten* volea *f*. II *vtr Ten* volear.
volleyball ['vɒlɪbɔːl] *n* voleibol *m*.
volt [vəʊlt] *n* voltio *m*.
voltage ['vəʊltɪdʒ] *n* voltaje *m*.
voluble ['vɒljʊbəl] *adj* locuaz, hablador,-a.
volume ['vɒljuːm] *n* 1 volumen *m*. 2 (*book*) volumen *m*, tomo *m*; *fig* to speak volumes, decirlo todo.
voluntary ['vɒləntərɪ] *adj* voluntario,-a; **v. organization**, organización benéfica.
volunteer [vɒlən'tɪər] I *n* voluntario,-a *m,f*. II *vtr* (*help etc*) ofrecer. III *vi* 1 ofrecerse (**for**, para). 2 *Mil* alistarse como voluntario.
voluptuous [və'lʌptjʊəs] *adj*
voluptuoso,-a.
vomit ['vɒmɪt] I *vtr & vi* vomitar. II *n* vómito *m*.
voracious [vɒ'reɪʃəs] *adj* voraz.
vortex ['vɔːteks] *n* (*pl* **vortices** ['vɔːtɪsiːz]) vórtice *m*; *fig* vorágine *f*.
vote [vəʊt] I *n* voto *m*; (*voting*) votación *f*; **v. of confidence**, voto de confianza; **to take a v. on sth**, someter algo a votación; **to have the v.**, tener derecho al voto. II *vtr* 1 votar. 2 (*elect*) elegir. 3 *fam* proponer. III *vi* votar; to v. for sb, votar a algn.
voter ['vəʊtər] *n* votante *mf*.
voting ['vəʊtɪŋ] *n* votación *f*.
vouch [vaʊtʃ] *vi* **to v. for sth/sb**, responder de algo/por algn.
voucher ['vaʊtʃər] *n GB* vale *m*.
vow [vaʊ] I *n* voto *m*. II *vtr* jurar.
vowel ['vaʊəl] *n* vocal *f*.
voyage ['vɔɪɪdʒ] *n* viaje *m*; (*crossing*) travesía *f*; to go on a v., hacer un viaje en (barco).
vulgar ['vʌlgər] *adj* (*coarse*) vulgar, ordinario,-a; (*in poor taste*) de mal gusto.
vulgarity [vʌl'gærɪtɪ] *n* (*coarseness*) vulgaridad *f*, ordinariez *f*; (*poor taste*) mal gusto *m*.
vulnerable ['vʌlnərəbəl] *adj* vulnerable.
vulture ['vʌltʃər] *n* buitre *m*.
vulva ['vʌlvə] *n* vulva *f*.

W

W, w ['dʌbəljuː] *n* (*the letter*) W, w *f*.
W 1 *abbr of* West, O. 2 *abbr of* Watt(s), W.
wad [wɒd] *n* (*of paper*) taco *m*; (*of cotton wool*) bolita *f*; (*of banknotes*) fajo *m*.
waddle ['wɒdəl] *vi* andar como los patos.
wade [weɪd] *vi* caminar por el agua; to w. across a river, vadear un río. ◆wade through *vtr* hacer con dificultad; I'm wading through the book, me cuesta mucho terminar el libro.
wafer ['weɪfər] *n* barquillo *m*; *Rel* hostia *f*.
waffle¹ ['wɒfəl] *n Culin* (tipo *m* de) barquillo *m*.
waffle² ['wɒfəl] *GB fam* I *vi* meter mucha paja; to w. on, parlotear. II *n* paja *f*.
waft [wɑːft, wɒft] I *vtr* llevar por el aire. II *vi* flotar (por *or* en el aire).
wag [wæg] I *vtr* menear. II *vi* (*tail*) menearse.
wage [weɪdʒ] I *n* (*also* **wages**) salario *m*, sueldo *m*; w. earner, asalariado,-a *m,f*. II *vtr* (*campaign*) realizar (**against**, contra); to w. war, hacer la guerra (**on**, a).
wage-packet ['weɪdʒpækɪt] *n* sueldo *m*.
wager ['weɪdʒər] I *n* apuesta *f*. II *vtr* apostar.
waggle ['wægəl] I *vtr* menear. II *vi* menearse.
wa(g)gon ['wægən] *n* (*horse-drawn*) carro *m*; *GB Rail* vagón *m*.
wail [weɪl] I *n* lamento *m*, gemido *m*. II *vi* (*person*) lamentar, gemir.
waist [weɪst] *n Anat* cintura *f*; *Sew* talle *m*.
waistcoat ['weɪstkəʊt] *n GB* chaleco *m*.
waistline ['weɪstlaɪn] *n Anat* cintura *f*; *Sew* talle *m*.
wait [weɪt] I *n* espera *f*; (*delay*) demora *f*; to lie in w., estar al acecho. II *vi* 1 esperar, aguardar; I can't w. to see her, me muero de ganas de verla; while you w., en el acto; to keep sb waiting, hacer esperar a algn. 2 to w. at table, servir la mesa. ◆wait about, wait around *vi* esperar. ◆wait on *vtr* servir.
waiter ['weɪtər] *n* camarero *m*.
waiting ['weɪtɪŋ] *n* 'No W.', 'Prohibido Aparcar'; w. list, lista *f* de espera; w. room, sala *f* de espera.
waitress ['weɪtrɪs] *n* camarera *f*.
waive [weɪv] *vtr fml* (*rule*) no aplicar.
wake¹ [weɪk] I *vtr* (*pt* **woke**; *pp* **woken**) to w. sb (up), despertar a algn. II *vi* to w. (up), despertar(se). III *n* (*for dead*) ve-

latorio m.
wake² [weɪk] n (in water) estela f; fig **in the w. of**, tras.
waken ['weɪkən] vtr lit despertar.
Wales [weɪlz] n (el país de) Gales.
walk [wɔːk] I n 1 (long) caminata m; (short) paseo m; **it's an hour's w.**, está a una hora de camino; **to go for a w.**, dar un paseo; **to take the dog for a w.**, sacar a pasear al perro. 2 (gait) modo m de andar. 3 **people from all walks of life**, gente f de toda condición. II vtr 1 **we walked her home**, la acompañamos a casa. 2 (dog) pasear. III vi 1 andar. 2 (go on foot) ir andando. ◆**walk away** vi alejarse; fig **to w. away with a prize**, llevarse un premio. ◆**walk into** vtr 1 (place) entrar en; fig (trap) caer en. 2 (bump into) chocarse contra. ◆**walk out** vi salir; Ind declararse en huelga; **to w. out on sb**, abandonar a algn. ◆**walk up** vi **to w. up to sb**, abordar a algn.
walkabout ['wɔːkəbaʊt] n (by Queen etc) paseo m informal entre la gente.
walker ['wɔːkər] n paseante mf; Sport marchador,-a m,f.
walkie-talkie [wɔːkɪ'tɔːkɪ] n walkie-talkie m.
walking ['wɔːkɪŋ] I n andar m; (hiking) excursionismo m. II adj **at w. pace**, a paso de marcha; **w. shoes**, zapatos mpl de andar; **w. stick**, bastón m.
Walkman® ['wɔːkmən] n (pl **Walkmans**) walkman® m.
walkout ['wɔːkaʊt] n Ind huelga f.
walkover ['wɔːkəʊvər] n **it was a w.**, fue pan comido.
walkway ['wɔːkweɪ] n esp US paso m de peatones.
wall [wɔːl] I n 1 (freestanding, exterior) muro m; fig **to have one's back to the w.**, estar entre la espada y la pared; **city w.**, muralla f; **garden w.**, tapia f. 2 (interior) pared f; **w. map**, mapa m mural. 3 Ftb barrera f. ◆**wall up** vtr (door, fireplace) tabicar.
walled [wɔːld] adj (city) amurallado,-a; (garden) cercado,-a con tapia.
wallet ['wɒlɪt] n cartera f.
wallflower ['wɔːlflaʊər] n 1 Bot alhelí m. 2 fam **to be a w.**, ser un convidado de piedra.
wallop ['wɒləp] fam I n golpazo m. II vtr 1 (hit) pegar fuerte. 2 (defeat) dar una paliza a.
wallow ['wɒləʊ] vi revolcarse (en, in); fig **to w. in self-pity**, sumirse en la autocompasión.
wallpaper ['wɔːlpeɪpər] I n papel pintado. II vtr empapelar.
wally ['wɒlɪ] n fam idiota mf.
walnut ['wɔːlnʌt] n nuez f; (tree, wood) nogal m.
walrus ['wɔːlrəs] n morsa f.

waltz [wɔːls] I n vals m. II vi bailar un vals.
wan [wɒn] adj (**wanner**, **wannest**) pálido,-a; (look, smile) apagado,-a.
wand [wɒnd] n (magic) w., varita f (mágica).
wander ['wɒndər] I vtr **to w. the streets**, vagar por las calles. II vi 1 (aimlessly) vagar, errar; **to w. about**, deambular; **to w. in/out**, entrar/salir sin prisas. 2 (stray) desviarse; (mind) divagar; **his glance wandered round the room**, recorrió el cuarto con la mirada.
wandering ['wɒndərɪŋ] adj errante; (tribe) nómada; (speech) divagador,-a.
wane [weɪn] vi menguar; (interest) decaer.
wangle ['wæŋgəl] vtr fam agenciarse.
wank [wæŋk] sl I n paja f. II vi hacerse una paja.
wanker ['wæŋkər] n sl mamón,-ona mf inv.
want [wɒnt] I n 1 (lack) falta f; **for w. of**, por falta de. 2 (poverty) miseria f. II vtr 1 (desire) querer, desear; **to w. to do sth**, querer hacer algo. 2 fam (need) necesitar; **the grass wants cutting**, hace falta cortar el césped. 3 (seek) buscar; **you're wanted on the phone**, te llaman al teléfono. ◆**want for** vtr carecer de; **to w. for nothing**, tenerlo todo.
wanting ['wɒntɪŋ] adj 1 **she is w. in tact**, le falta tacto. 2 **he was found w.**, no daba la talla.
wanton ['wɒntən] adj 1 (motiveless) sin motivo; **w. cruelty**, crueldad gratuita. 2 (unrestrained) desenfrenado,-a; (licentious) lascivo,-a.
war [wɔːr] n guerra f; **to be at w.**, estar en guerra (**with**, con); fig **to declare/wage w. on**, declarar/hacer la guerra a.
warble ['wɔːbəl] vi gorjear.
ward [wɔːd] I n 1 (of hospital) sala f. 2 Jur pupilo,-a m,f; **w. of court**, pupilo,-a bajo tutela judicial. 3 GB Pol distrito m electoral. ◆**ward off** vtr (blow) parar, desviar; (attack) rechazar; (danger) evitar; (illness) prevenir.
warden ['wɔːdən] n (of residence) guardián,-ana m,f; **game w.**, guardia m de coto.
warder ['wɔːdər] n GB carcelero,-a m,f.
wardrobe ['wɔːdrəʊb] n 1 armario m, ropero m. 2 (clothes) guardarropa m. 3 Theat vestuario m.
warehouse ['weəhaʊs] n almacén m.
wares [weəz] npl mercancías fpl.
warfare ['wɔːfeər] n guerra f.
warhead ['wɔːhed] n (nuclear) w., ojiva f nuclear.
warm [wɔːm] I adj 1 (water) tibio,-a; (hands) caliente; (climate) cálido,-a; **a w. day**, un día de calor; **I am w.**, tengo calor; **it is (very) w. today**, hoy hace (mucho) calor; **w. clothing**, ropa f de abrigo.

2 *(welcome, applause)* cálido,-a. II *vtr* calentar; *fig* alegrar. III *vi* calentarse; **to w. to sb**, cogerle simpatía a algn. ◆**warm up** I *vtr* 1 calentar; *(soup)* (re)calentar. 2 *(audience)* animar. II *vi* 1 calentarse; *(food)* (re)calentarse; *(person)* entrar en calor. 2 *(athlete)* hacer ejercicios de calentamiento. 3 *fig (audience, party)* animarse. ◆**warmly** *adv fig* calurosamente; *(thank)* con efusión.

warm-blooded [wɔːmˈblʌdɪd] *adj* de sangre caliente.

warm-hearted [wɔːmˈhɑːtɪd] *adj* afectuoso,-a.

warmth [wɔːmθ] *n (heat)* calor *m*; *fig* cordialidad *f*.

warn [wɔːn] *vtr* avisar *(of,* de), advertir *(about,* sobre; *against,* contra); **he warned me not to go**, me advirtió que no fuera; **to w. sb that**, advertir a algn que.

warning [ˈwɔːnɪŋ] I *adj* **w. light**, piloto *m*; **w. sign**, señal *f* de aviso. II *n* 1 *(of danger)* advertencia *f*, aviso *m*. 2 *(replacing punishment)* amonestación *f*. 3 *(notice)* aviso *m*; **without w.**, sin previo aviso.

warp [wɔːp] I *vtr* 1 *(wood)* alabear, combar. 2 *fig (mind)* pervertir. II *vi* alabearse, combarse.

warrant [ˈwɒrənt] I *n* 1 *Jur* orden *f* judicial; **death w.**, sentencia *f* de muerte. 2 *(authorization note)* cédula *f*; *Com* **bono m.** II *vtr* 1 *(justify)* justificar. 2 *(guarantee)* garantizar.

warranty [ˈwɒrəntɪ] *n Com* garantía *f*.

warren [ˈwɒrən] *n* conejera *f*; *fig* laberinto *m*.

warrior [ˈwɒrɪər] *n* guerrero,-a *m,f*.

Warsaw [ˈwɔːsɔː] *n* Varsovia.

warship [ˈwɔːʃɪp] *n* buque *m* o barco *m* de guerra.

wart [wɔːt] *n* verruga *f*.

wartime [ˈwɔːtaɪm] *n* tiempos *mpl* de guerra.

wary [ˈweərɪ] *adj (warier, wariest)* cauteloso,-a; **to be w. of doing sth**, dudar en hacer algo; **to be w. of sb/sth**, recelar de algo/algún.

was [wɒz] *pt* → **be**.

wash [wɒʃ] I *n* 1 lavado *m*; **to have a w.**, lavarse. 2 *(of ship)* estela *f; (sound)* chapoteo *m*. II *vtr* 1 lavar; *(dishes)* fregar; **to w. one's hair**, lavarse el pelo. 2 *(sea, river)* arrastrar. III *vi* 1 *(person)* lavarse; *(do the laundry)* hacer la colada. 2 *(lap)* batir. ◆**wash away** *vtr (of sea)* llevarse; *(traces)* borrar. ◆**wash off** *vi* quitarse lavando. ◆**wash out** I *vtr* 1 *(stain)* quitar lavando. 2 *(bottle)* enjuagar. II *vi* quitarse lavando. ◆**wash up** I *vtr GB (dishes)* fregar. II *vi* 1 *GB* fregar los platos. 2 *US* lavarse rápidamente.

washable [ˈwɒʃəbəl] *adj* lavable.

washbasin [ˈwɒʃbeɪsən], **washbowl**

[ˈwɒʃbəʊl] *n* palangana *f*.

washcloth [ˈwɒʃklɒθ] *n US* manopla *f*.

washer [ˈwɒʃər] *n (on tap)* junta *f*.

washing [ˈwɒʃɪŋ] *n* 1 *(action)* lavado *m*; *(of clothes)* colada *f; (dirty)* **w.**, ropa sucia; **to do the w.**, hacer la colada; **w. line**, tendedero *m*; **w. machine**, lavadora *f*; **w. powder**, detergente *m*.

washing-up [wɒʃɪŋˈʌp] *n GB* 1 *(action)* fregado *m*; **w.-up bowl**, barreño *m*; **w.-up liquid**, (detergente *m*) lavavajillas. 2 *(dishes)* platos *mpl* (para fregar).

washout [ˈwɒʃaʊt] *n fam* fracaso *m*.

washroom [ˈwɒʃruːm] *n US* servicios *mpl*.

wasp [wɒsp] *n* avispa *f*.

wastage [ˈweɪstɪdʒ] *n* pérdidas *fpl*.

waste [weɪst] I *adj* 1 *(unwanted)* desechado,-a; **w. food**, restos *mpl* de comida; **w. products**, productos *mpl* de desecho. 2 *(ground)* baldío,-a. II *n* 1 *(unnecessary use)* desperdicio *m; (of resources, effort, money)* derroche *m; (of time)* pérdida *f*; **to go to w.**, echarse a perder. 2 *(left-overs)* desperdicios *mpl; (rubbish)* basura *f*; **radio-active w.**, desechos radioactivos; **w. disposal unit**, trituradora *f* (de desperdicios); **w. pipe**, tubo *m* de desagüe. III *vtr (squander)* desperdiciar, malgastar; *(resources)* derrochar; *(money)* despilfarrar; *(time)* perder. ◆**waste away** *vi* consumirse.

wasteful [ˈweɪstful] *adj* derrochador,-a.

wasteland [ˈweɪstlænd] *n* baldío *m*.

wastepaper [weɪstˈpeɪpər] *n* papeles usados; **w. basket**, papelera *f*.

watch [wɒtʃ] I *n* 1 *(look-out)* vigilancia *f*; **to keep a close w. on sth/sb**, vigilar algo/a algn muy atentamente. 2 *Mil (body)* guardia *f; (individual)* centinela *m*; **to be on w.**, estar de guardia. 3 *(time-piece)* reloj *m*. II *vtr* 1 *(observe)* mirar, observar. 2 *(keep an eye on)* vigilar; *(with suspicion)* acechar. 3 *(be careful of)* cuidado con; *fig* **to w. one's step**, ir con pies de plomo. III *vi (look)* mirar, observar; **w. out!**, ¡cuidado! ◆**watch out for** *vtr (be careful of)* tener cuidado con.

watchband [ˈwɒtʃbænd] *n US* → **watch-strap**.

watchdog [ˈwɒtʃdɒg] *n* perro *m* guardián; *fig* guardián,-ana *m,f*.

watchful [ˈwɒtʃful] *adj* vigilante.

watchmaker [ˈwɒtʃmeɪkər] *n* relojero,-a *m,f*.

watchman [ˈwɒtʃmən] *n* vigilante *m*; **night w.**, *(of site)* vigilante nocturno.

watchstrap [ˈwɒtʃstræp] *n* correa *f* (de reloj).

watchtower [ˈwɒtʃtaʊər] *n* atalaya *f*.

water [ˈwɔːtər] I *n* 1 agua *f*; **w. bottle**, cantimplora *f*; **w. lily**, nenúfar *m*; **w. main**, conducción *f* de aguas; **w. polo**,

water polo *m*; **w. sports,** deportes acuáticos; **w. tank,** depósito *m* de agua; **territorial waters,** aguas jurisdiccionales; *fig* it's all w. under the bridge, ha llovido mucho desde entonces. **2 to pass w.,** orinar. **II** *vtr* (*plants*) regar. **III** *vi* my eyes are watering, me lloran los ojos; my mouth watered, se me hizo la boca agua.
◆**water down** (*drink*) aguar.

watercolour, *US* **watercolor** ['wɔːtəkʌlə] *n* acuarela *f.*

watercress ['wɔːtəkres] *n* berro *m.*

waterfall ['wɔːtəfɔːl] *n* cascada *f*; (*very big*) catarata *f.*

waterfront ['wɔːtəfrʌnt] *n* (*shore*) orilla *f* del agua; (*harbour*) puerto *m.*

watering ['wɔːtərɪŋ] *n* (*of plants*) riego *m*; **w. can,** regadera *f*; **w. place,** abrevadero *m.*

waterline ['wɔːtəlaɪn] *n* línea *f* de flotación.

waterlogged ['wɔːtəlɒgd] *adj* anegado,-a.

watermark ['wɔːtəmɑːk] *n* filigrana *f.*

watermelon ['wɔːtəmelən] *n* sandía *f.*

waterproof ['wɔːtəpruːf] **I** *adj* (*material*) impermeable; (*watch*) sumergible. **II** *n* (*coat*) impermeable *m.*

watershed ['wɔːtəʃed] *n* Geog línea divisoria de aguas; *fig* punto decisivo.

water-skiing ['wɔːtəskiːɪŋ] *n* esquí acuático.

watertight ['wɔːtətaɪt] *adj* hermético,-a.

waterway ['wɔːtəweɪ] *n* vía *f* fluvial.

waterworks ['wɔːtəwɜːks] *npl* central *f sing* de abastecimiento de agua; *fig* to turn on the w., empezar a llorar.

watery ['wɔːtərɪ] *adj* **1** (*soup*) aguado,-a; (*coffee*) flojo,-a. **2** (*eyes*) lacrimoso,-a. **3** (*pale*) pálido,-a.

watt [wɒt] *n* vatio *m.*

wave [weɪv] **I** *n* **1** (*at sea*) ola *f*. **2** (*in hair*) & Rad onda *f*. **3** *fig* (*of anger, strikes etc*) oleada *f*. **4** (*gesture*) saludo *m* con la mano. **II** *vtr* **1** agitar; (*brandish*) blandir. **2** (*hair*) ondular. **III** *vi* **1** agitar el brazo; **she waved (to me),** (*greeting*) me saludó con la mano; (*goodbye*) se despidió de mí) con la mano; (*signal*) me hizo señas con la mano. **2** (*flag*) ondear; (*corn*) ondular.

wavelength ['weɪvleŋθ] *n* longitud *f* de onda.

waver ['weɪvə'] *vi* (*hesitate*) vacilar; (*between,* entre); (*voice*) temblar; (*courage*) flaquear.

wavy ['weɪvɪ] *adj* (**wavier, waviest**) ondulado,-a.

wax[1] [wæks] **I** *n* cera *f*. **II** *vtr* encerar.

wax[2] [wæks] *vi* **1** (*moon*) crecer. **2 to w. lyrical,** exaltarse.

waxwork ['wækswɜːk] *n* **waxworks,** museo *m* de cera.

way [weɪ] **I** *n* **1** (*route*) camino *m*; (*road*) vía *f*, camino *m*; **a letter is on the w.,** una

carta está en camino; **on the w.,** en el camino; **on the w. here,** de camino para aquí; **out of the w.,** apartado,-a; **to ask the w.,** preguntar el camino; **to go the wrong w.,** ir por el camino equivocado; **to lose one's w.,** perderse; **to make one's w. through the crowd,** abrirse camino entre la multitud; **which is the w. to the station?,** ¿por dónde se va a la estación?; *fig* she went out of her w. to help, se desvivió por ayudar; **w. in,** entrada *f*; **w. out,** salida *f*; *fig* the easy w. out, la solución fácil; **I can't find my w. out,** no encuentro la salida; **on the w. back,** en el viaje de regreso; **on the w. up/down,** en la subida/bajada; **there's no w. through,** el paso está cerrado; **you're in the w.,** estás estorbando; **(get) out of the w.!,** ¡quítate de en medio!; *fig* to get sb/sth out of the w.,** desembarazarse de algn/algo; **I kept out of the w.,** me mantuve a distancia; *Aut* right of w.,** prioridad *f*; **there's a wall in the w.,** hay un muro en medio; **to give w.,** ceder; *Aut* ceder el paso. **2** (*direction*) dirección *f*; **come this w.,** venga por aquí; **which w. did he go?,** ¿por dónde se fue?; **that w.,** por allá; **the other w. round,** al revés. **3** (*distance*) distancia *f*; **a long w. off,** lejos; *fig* he'll go a long w.,** llegará lejos; *fig* we've come a long w.,** hemos hecho grandes progresos. **4 to get under w.,** (*travellers, work*) ponerse en marcha; (*meeting, match*) empezar. **5** (*means, method*) método *m*, manera *f*; **do it any w. you like,** hazlo como quieras; **I'll do it my w.,** lo haré a mi manera. **6** (*manner*) modo *m*, manera *f*; **in a friendly w.,** de modo amistoso; **one w. or another,** de un modo o de otro; **the French w. of life,** el estilo de vida francés; **the w. things are going,** tal como van las cosas; **to my w. of thinking,** a mi modo de ver; *fam* no w.!,** ¡ni hablar!; **she has a w. with children,** tiene un don para los niños; **by w. of,** a modo de; **either w.,** en cualquier caso; **in a w.,** en cierto sentido; **in many ways,** desde muchos puntos de vista; **in some ways,** en algunos aspectos; **in no w.,** de ninguna manera. **7** (*custom*) hábito *m*, costumbre *f*; **to be set in one's ways,** tener costumbres arraigadas. **8** (*state*) estado *m*; **leave it the w. it is,** déjalo tal como está; **he is in a bad w.,** está bastante mal. **9 by the w.,** a propósito; **in the w. of business,** en el curso de los negocios.

II *adv* *fam* mucho, muy; **it was w. off target,** cayó muy desviado del blanco; **w. back in 1940,** allá en 1940.

waylay [weɪ'leɪ] *vtr* (*pt* & *pp* **waylaid**) **1** (*attack*) atacar por sorpresa. **2** *fig* (*intercept*) salirle al paso a algn.

wayside ['weɪsaɪd] *n* *fig* to fall by the w.,

quedarse en el camino.

wayward |'weɪwəd| *adj* rebelde; *(capricious)* caprichoso,-a.

WC |dʌblju:'si:| *abbr of* **water closet**, wáter *m*, WC.

we |wi:| *pers pron* nosotros,-as.

weak |wi:k| *adj* débil; *(argument, excuse)* pobre; *(team, piece of work, tea)* flojo,-a.

weaken |'wi:kən| **I** *vtr* debilitar; *(argument)* quitar fuerza a. **II** *vi* **1** debilitarse. **2** *(concede ground)* ceder.

weakling |'wi:klɪŋ| *n* enclenque *mf*.

weakness |'wi:knɪs| *n* debilidad *f*; *(character flaw)* punto flaco.

wealth |welθ| *n* riqueza *f*; *fig* abundancia *f*.

wealthy |'welθɪ| *adj (wealthier, wealthiest)* rico,-a.

wean |wi:n| *vtr (child)* destetar; *fig* **to w. sb from the habit,** desacostumbrar (gradualmente) a algn de un hábito.

weapon |'wepən| *n* arma *f*.

wear |weər| **I** *vtr (pt* **wore**; *pp* **worn**) **1** *(clothes)* llevar puesto, vestir; *(shoes)* llevar puestos, calzar; **he wears glasses,** lleva gafas; **to w. black,** vestirse de negro. **2** *(erode)* desgastar. **II** *vi* **to w. (thin/smooth),** desgastarse (con el roce); *fig* **my patience is wearing thin,** se me está acabando la paciencia. **III** *n* **1** ropa *f*; **leisure w.,** ropa de sport. **2** *(use) (clothes)* uso *m*. **3** *(deterioration)* desgaste *m*; **normal w. and tear,** desgaste natural. ◆**wear away I** *vtr* erosionar. **II** *vi (stone etc)* erosionarse; *(inscription)* borrarse. ◆**wear down I** *vtr (heels)* desgastar; *fig* **to w. sb down,** vencer la resistencia de algn. **II** *vi* desgastarse. ◆**wear off** *vi (effect, pain)* pasar, desaparecer. ◆**wear out I** *vtr* gastar; *fig* agotar. **II** *vi* gastarse.

wearisome |'wɪərɪsəm| *adj* fatigoso,-a.

weary |'wɪərɪ| **I** *adj (wearier, weariest)* **1** *(tired)* cansado,-a. **2** *(fed up)* harto,-a. **II** *vtr* cansar. **III** *vi* cansarse (of, de). ◆**wearily** *adv* con cansancio.

weasel |'wi:zəl| *n* comadreja *f*.

weather |'weðər| **I** *n* tiempo *m*; **the w. is fine,** hace buen tiempo; *fig* **to feel under the w.,** no encontrarse bien; **w. chart,** mapa meteorológico; **w. forecast,** parte meteorológico; **w. vane,** veleta *f*. **II** *vtr fig (crisis)* aguantar; *fig* **to w. the storm,** capear el temporal.

weather-beaten |'weðəbi:tən| *adj* curtido,-a.

weathercock |'weðəkɒk| *n* veleta *f*.

weatherman |'weðəmæn| *n* hombre *m* del tiempo.

weave |wi:v| **I** *n* tejido *m*. **II** *vtr (pt* **wove**; *pp* **woven**) **1** *Tex* tejer. **2** *(interwine)* entretejer. **3** *(intrigues)* tramar. **III** *vi (person, road)* zigzaguear.

weaver |'wi:vər| *n* tejedor,-a *m,f*.

web |web| *n* **1** *(of spider)* telaraña *f*. **2** *(of*

lies) sarta *f*.

webbed |webd| *adj Orn* palmeado,-a.

wed |wed| *vtr arch (pt & pp* **wed** *or* **wedded**) casarse con.

wedding |'wedɪŋ| *n* boda *f*, casamiento *m*; **w. cake,** tarta *f* nupcial; **w. day,** día *m* de la boda; **w. dress,** traje *m* de novia; **w. present,** regalo *m* de boda; **w. ring,** alianza *f*.

wedge |wedʒ| **I** *n* **1** cuña *f*; *(for table leg)* calce *m*. **2** *(of cake, cheese)* trozo *m* grande. **II** *vtr* calzar; **to be wedged tight,** *(object)* estar completamente atrancado,-a.

Wednesday |'wenzdɪ| *n* miércoles *m*.

wee[1] |wi:| *adj esp Scot* pequeñito,-a.

wee[2] |wi:| *fam* **I** *n* pipí *m*. **II** *vi* hacer pipí.

weed |wi:d| *n* **1** *Bot* mala hierba. **II** *vtr* **1** *(garden)* escardar. **2** *fig* **to w. out,** eliminar. **III** *vi* escardar.

weedkiller |'wi:dkɪlə| *n* herbicida *m*.

weedy |'wi:dɪ| *adj (weeedier, weediest) pej* debilucho,-a.

week |wi:k| *n* semana *f*; **a w. (ago) today/yesterday,** hoy hace/ayer hizo una semana; **a w. today,** justo dentro de una semana; **last/next w.,** la semana pasada/que viene; **once a w.,** una vez por semana; **w. in, w. out,** semana tras semana.

weekday |'wi:kdeɪ| *n* día *m* laborable.

weekend |wi:k'end| *n* fin *m* de semana.

weekly |'wi:klɪ| **I** *adj* semanal. **II** *adv* semanalmente; **twice a w.,** dos veces por semana. **III** *Press* semanario *m*.

weep |wi:p| **I** *vi (pt & pp* **wept**) llorar; **to w. for sb,** llorar la muerte de algn. **II** *vtr (tears)* derramar.

weeping |'wi:pɪŋ| *adj* **w. willow,** sauce *m* llorón.

weigh |weɪ| **I** *vtr* **1** pesar. **2** *fig (consider)* ponderar. **3 to w. anchor,** levar anclas. **II** *vi* **1** pesar. **2** *fig (influence)* influir. ◆**weigh down** *vtr* sobrecargar. ◆**weigh in** *vi* **1** *Sport* pesarse. **2** *fam (join in)* intervenir. ◆**weigh up** *vtr (matter)* evaluar; *(person)* formar una opinión sobre; **to w. up the pros and cons,** sopesar los pros y los contras.

weight |weɪt| *n* **1** peso *m*; **to lose w.,** adelgazar; **to put on w.,** subir de peso; *fam fig* **to pull one's w.,** poner de su parte. **2** *(of clock, scales)* pesa *f*. **3** *fig* **that's a w. off my mind,** eso me quita un peso de encima.

weighting |'weɪtɪŋ| *n GB (on salary)* suplemento *m* de salario.

weightlifter |'weɪtlɪftər| *n* halterófilo,-a *m,f*.

weighty |'weɪtɪ| *adj (weightier, weightiest)* pesado,-a; *fig (problem, matter)* importante, grave; *(argument)* de peso.

weir |wɪər| *n* presa *f*.

weird |wɪəd| *adj* raro,-a, extraño,-a.

welcome |'welkəm| **I** *adj (person)*

bienvenido,-a; *(news)* grato,-a; *(change)* oportuno,-a; **to make sb w.**, acoger a algn calurosamente; **you're w.!**, ¡no hay de qué!. II *n (greeting)* bienvenida *f*. III *vtr* acoger; *(more formally)* darle la bienvenida a; *(news)* acoger con agrado; *(decision)* aplaudir.

welcoming ['welkəmɪŋ] *adj (person)* acogedor,-a; *(smile)* de bienvenida.

weld [weld] *vtr* soldar.

welfare ['welfeər] *n* **1** *(well-being)* bienestar *m*; **animal/child w.**, protección *f* de animales/de menores; **w. work**, asistencia *f* social; **w. worker**, asistente *mf* social. **2** *US (social security)* seguridad *f* social.

well¹ [wel] *n* **1** pozo *m*. **2** *(of staircase, lift)* hueco *m*. **3** *(of court, hall)* hemiciclo *m*. ◆**well up** *vi* brotar.

well² [wel] I *adj* **1** *(healthy)* bien; **are you keeping w.?**, estás bien de salud?; **to get w.**, reponerse. **2** *(satisfactory)* bien; **all is w.**, todo va bien; **it's just as w.**, menos mal. **3** **it is as w. to remember that**, conviene recordar que.
II *adv (better, best)* **1** *(properly)* bien; **he has done w.** (for himself), ha prosperado; **the business is doing w.**, el negocio marcha bien; **she did w. in the exam**, el examen le fue bien; **w. done!**, ¡muy bien! **he took it w.**, lo tomó a bien. **2** *(thoroughly)* bien; **I know it only too w.**, lo sé de sobra; *Culin* **w. done**, muy hecho,-a. **3** **he's w. over thirty**, tiene treinta años bien cumplidos; **w. after six o'clock**, mucho después de las seis. **4** *(easily, with good reason)* **he couldn't very w. say no**, difícilmente podía decir que no; **I may w. do that**, puede que haga eso. **5** **as w.**, también; **as w. as**, así como; **children as w. as adults**, tanto niños como adultos.
III *interj* **1** *(surprise)* ¡bueno!, ¡vaya!; **w. I never!**, ¡no me digas! **2** *(agreement, interrogation, resignation)* bueno; **very w.**, bueno; **w.?**, ¿y bien? **3** *(doubt)* pues; **w., I don't know**, pues no sé. **4** *(resumption)* **w., as I was saying**, pues (bien), como iba diciendo.

well-behaved ['welbɪheɪvd] *adj (child)* formal, educado,-a.

well-being ['welbi:ɪŋ] *n* bienestar *m*.

well-built ['welbɪlt] *adj (building etc)* de construcción sólida; *(person)* fornido,-a.

well-earned ['welɜːnd] *adj* merecido,-a.

well-educated [wel'edʊkeɪtɪd] *adj* culto,-a.

well-heeled ['welhi:ld] *adj fam* adinerado,-a.

wellingtons ['welɪŋtənz] *npl* botas *fpl* de goma.

well-informed ['welɪnfɔːmd] *adj* bien informado,-a.

well-known ['welnəʊn] *adj* (bien) conocido,-a.

well-mannered ['welmænəd] *adj* educado,-a.

well-meaning [wel'mi:nɪŋ] *adj* bien intencionado,-a.

well-off [wel'ɒf] *adj (rich)* acomodado,-a.

well-read [wel'red] *adj* culto,-a.

well-spoken [wel'spəʊkən] *adj* con acento culto.

well-to-do [weltə'du:] *adj* acomodado,-a.

well-wisher ['welwɪʃər] *n* admirador,-a *m,f*.

Welsh [welʃ] I *adj* galés,-esa; **W. rarebit**, tostada *f* con queso fundido. II *n* **1** *(language)* galés *m*. **2** **the W.**, *pl* los galeses.

Welshman ['welʃmən] *n* galés *m*.

Welshwoman ['welʃwʊmən] *n* galesa *f*.

welterweight ['welterweɪt] *n (peso m)* wélter *m*.

wench [wentʃ] *n dated pej* moza *f*.

went [went] *pt* → **go**.

wept [wept] *pt & pp* → **weep**.

were [wɜːr, *unstressed* wər] *pt* → **be**.

west [west] I *n* oeste *m*, occidente *m*; **in or to the w.**, al oeste; *Pol* **the W.**, los países occidentales. II *adj* del oeste, occidental; **the W. Indies**, las Antillas; **W. Indian**, antillano,-a. III *adv* al oeste, hacia el oeste.

westerly ['westəlɪ] *adj (wind)* del oeste.

western ['westən] I *adj* del oeste, occidental; **W. Europe**, Europa Occidental. II *n* *Cin* western *m*, película *f* del oeste.

westward ['westwəd] *adj* **in a w. direction**, hacia el oeste.

westwards ['westwədz] *adv* hacia el oeste.

wet [wet] I *adj (wetter, wettest)* **1** mojado,-a; *(slightly)* húmedo,-a; '**w. paint**', 'recién pintado'; **w. through**, *(person)* calado,-a hasta los huesos; *(thing)* empapado,-a; **w. suit**, traje isotérmico. **2** *(rainy)* lluvioso,-a. **3** *fam (person)* soso,-a; **w. blanket**, aguafiestas *mf inv*. II *n fam* apocado,-a *m,f*. III *vtr (pt & pp* **wet***)* mojar; **to w. oneself**, orinarse.

whack [wæk] I *vtr (hit hard)* golpear fuertemente. II *n* **1** *(blow)* porrazo *m*. **2** *fam (share)* paste *f*, porción *f*.

whale [weɪl] *n (pl* **whale** *or* **whales***)* ballena *f*.

wharf [wɔːf] *n (pl* **wharves** [wɔːvz]*)* muelle *m*.

what [wɒt, *unstressed* wət] I *adj* **1** *(direct question)* qué; **w. (sort of) bird is that?**, ¿qué tipo de ave es ésa?; **w. good is that?**, ¿para qué sirve eso? **2** *(indirect question)* qué; **ask her w. colour she likes**, pregúntale qué color le gusta.
II *pron* **1** *(direct question)* qué; **w. are you talking about?**, ¿de qué estás hablando?; **w. about your father?**, ¿y tu padre (qué)?; **w. about going tomorrow?**, ¿qué

te parece si vamos mañana?; **w. can I do for you?**, ¿en qué puedo servirle?; **w. did it cost?**, ¿cuánto costó?; **w. did you do that for?**, ¿por qué hiciste eso?; **w. (did you say)?**, ¿cómo?; **w. does it sound like?**, ¿cómo suena?; **w. is happening?**, ¿qué pasa?; **w. is it?**, *(definition)* ¿qué es?; *(what's the matter)* ¿qué pasa?; **w.'s it called?**, ¿cómo se llama?; **w.'s this for?**, ¿para qué sirve esto? **2** *(indirect question)* qué, lo que; **he asked me w. I thought**, me preguntó lo que pensaba; **I didn't know w. to say**, no sabía qué decir. **3** *(and)* **w.'s more**, y además; **come w. may**, pase lo que pase; **guess w.!**, ¿sabes qué?; **it's just w. I need**, es exactamente lo que necesito. **4** *exclam (surprise, indignation)* ¡cómo!; **w., no dessert!**, ¿cómo, no hay postre?
III *interj* **w. a goal!**, ¡qué *or* vaya golazo!; **w. a lovely picture!**, ¡qué cuadro más bonito!

whatever [wɒt'evə^r, *unstressed* wət'evə^r] **I** *adj* **1** *(any)* cualquiera que; **at w. time you like**, a la hora que quieras; **of w. colour**, no importa de qué color. **2** *(with negative)* **nothing w.**, nada en absoluto; **with no interest w.**, sin interés alguno. **II** *pron* **1** *(anything, all that)* (todo) lo que; **do w. you like**, haz lo que quieras. **2** *(no matter what)* **don't tell him w. you do**, no se le ocurra decírselo; **w. (else) you find**, cualquier (otra) cosa que encuentres; **he goes out w. the weather**, sale haga el tiempo que haga. **III** *interr* **w. happened?**, ¿qué pasó?

whatsoever [wɒtsəʊ'evə^r] *adj* **anything w.**, cualquier cosa; **nothing w.**, nada en absoluto.

wheat [wiːt] *n* trigo *m*; **w. germ**, germen *m* de trigo.

wheedle ['wiːdəl] *vtr* **to w. sb into doing sth**, engatusar a algn para que haga algo; **to w. sth out of sb**, sonsacar algo a algn halagándole.

wheel [wiːl] **I** *n* rueda *f*. **II** *vtr (bicycle)* empujar. **III** *vi* **1** *(bird)* revolotear. **2 to w. round**, girar sobre los talones.

wheelbarrow ['wiːlbærəʊ] *n* carretilla *f*.

wheelchair ['wiːltʃeə^r] *n* silla *f* de ruedas.

wheeze [wiːz] *vi* respirar con dificultad, resollar.

when [wen] **I** *adv* **1** *(direct question)* cuándo; **since w.?**, ¿desde cuándo?; **w. did he arrive?**, ¿cuándo llegó? **2** *(indirect question)* cuándo; **tell me w. to go**, dime cuándo debo irme. **3** *(on which)* en que; **the days w. I work**, los días en que trabajo. **II** *conj* **1** cuando; **I'll tell you w. she comes**, ya te diré cuando llegue; **w. he was a boy ...**, de niño .... **2** *(whenever)* cuando. **3** *(given that, if)* si. **4** *(although)* aunque.

whence [wens] *adv fml lit (from where)* de

dónde.

whenever [wen'evə^r] **I** *conj (when)* cuando; *(every time)* siempre que. **II** *adv* **w. that might be**, sea cuando sea.

where [weə^r] *adv* **1** *(direct question)* dónde; *(direction)* adónde; **w. are you going?**, ¿adónde vas?; **w. did we go wrong?**, ¿en qué nos equivocamos?; **w. do you come from?**, ¿de dónde es usted? **2** *(indirect question)* dónde; *(direction)* adónde; **tell me w. you went**, dime a-dónde fuiste. **3** *(at, in which)* donde; *(direction)* adonde, a donde. **4** *(when)* cuando.

whereabouts [weərə'baʊts] **I** *adv* **w. do you live?**, ¿por dónde vives? **II** ['weərəbaʊts] *n* paradero *m*.

whereas [weər'æz] *conj* **1** *(but, while)* mientras que. **2** *Jur* considerando que.

whereby [weə'baɪ] *adv* por el *or* la *or* lo cual.

whereupon [weərə'pɒn] *conj fml* después de lo cual.

wherever [weər'evə^r] **I** *conj* dondequiera que; **I'll find him w. he is**, le encontraré dondequiera que esté; **sit w. you like**, siéntate donde quieras. **II** *adv (direct question)* adónde.

wherewithal ['weəwɪðɔːl] *n fam* pelas *fpl*.

whet [wet] *vtr* **to w. sb's appetite**, abrir el apetito a algn.

whether ['weðə^r] *conj* **1** *(if)* si; **I don't know w. it is true**, no sé si es verdad; **I doubt w. he'll win**, dudo que gane. **2 w. he comes or not**, venga o no.

which [wɪtʃ] **I** *adj* **1** *(direct question)* qué; **w. colour do you prefer?**, ¿qué color prefieres?; **w. one?**, ¿cuál?; **w. way?**, ¿por dónde? **2** *(indirect question)* **tell me w. dress you like**, dime qué vestido te gusta. **3 w. time**, y para entonces; **in w. case**, en cuyo caso.
II *pron* **1** *(direct question)* cuál, cuáles; **w. of you did it?**, ¿quién de vosotros lo hizo? **2** *(indirect question)* cuál, cuáles; **I don't know w. I'd rather have**, no sé cuál prefiero. **3** *(defining relative)* que; *(after preposition)* que, el *or* la cual, los *or* las cuales, el *or* la que, los *or* las que; **here are the books (w.) I have read**, aquí están los libros que he leído; **the accident (w.) I told you about**, el accidente del que te hablé; **the car in w. he was travelling**, el coche en (el) que viajaba; **this is the one (w.) I like**, éste es el que me gusta. **4** *(non-defining relative)* el *or* la cual, los *or* las cuales; **I played three sets, all of w. I lost**, jugué tres sets, todos los cuales perdí. **5** *(referring to a clause)* lo cual, lo que; **he won w. made me very happy**, ganó, lo cual *or* lo que me alegró mucho.

whichever [wɪtʃ'evə^r] **I** *adj* el/la que, cualquiera que; **I'll take w. books you**

don't want, tomaré los libros que no quieras; **w. system you choose,** cualquiera que sea el sistema que elijas. **II** *pron* el que, la que.

whiff [wɪf] *n* **1** *(quick smell)* ráfaga *f*; *(of air, smoke)* bocanada *f*. **2** *fam (bad smell)* tufo *m*.

while [waɪl] **I** *n* **1** *(length of time)* rato *m*, tiempo *m*; **in a little w.,** dentro de poco; **once in a w.,** de vez en cuando. **2 it's not worth your w. staying,** no merece la pena que te quedes. **II** *conj* **1** *(time)* mientras; **he fell asleep w. driving,** se durmió mientras conducía. **2** *(although)* aunque. **3** *(whereas)* mientras que. ◆**while away** *vtr* to w. away the time, pasar el rato.

whilst [waɪlst] *conj* → while III.

whim [wɪm] *n* capricho *m*, antojo *m*.

whimper ['wɪmpər] **I** *n* quejido *m*. **II** *vi* lloriquear.

whine [waɪn] *vi* **1** *(child)* lloriquear; *(with pain)* gemir. **2** *(complain)* quejarse. **3** *(engine)* chirriar.

whip [wɪp] **I** *n* **1** *(for punishment)* látigo *m*; *(for riding)* fusta *f*. **2** *GB Parl* oficial *mf* encargado,-a de la disciplina de un partido. **II** *vtr* **1** *(as punishment)* azotar; *(horse)* fustigar. **2** *Culin* batir; **whipped cream,** nata montada. **3** *fam (steal)* mangar. ◆**whip away** *vtr* arrebatar. ◆**whip up** *vtr (passions, enthusiasm)* avivar; *(support)* incrementar.

whipping ['wɪpɪŋ] *n fig* **w. boy,** cabeza *f* de turco.

whip-round ['wɪpraund] *n fam* colecta *f*.

whirl [wɜːl] **I** *n* giro *m*; *fig* torbellino *m*. **II** *vtr* to w. sth round, dar vueltas a *or* hacer girar algo. **III** *vi* to w. round, girar con rapidez; *(leaves etc)* arremolinarse; **my head's whirling,** me está dando vueltas la cabeza.

whirlpool ['wɜːlpuːl] *n* remolino *m*.

whirlwind ['wɜːlwɪnd] *n* torbellino *m*.

whirr ['wɜːr] *vi* zumbar, runrunear.

whisk [wɪsk] **I** *n Culin* batidor *m*; *(electric)* batidora *f*. **II** *vtr Culin* batir. ◆**whisk away, whisk off** *vtr* quitar bruscamente, llevarse de repente.

whisker ['wɪskər] *n* whiskers, *(of person)* patillas *fpl*; *(of cat)* bigotes *mpl*.

whisky, US **whiskey** ['wɪskɪ] *n* whisky *m*.

whisper ['wɪspər] **I** *n* **1** *(sound)* susurro *m*. **2** *(rumour)* rumor *m*. **II** *vtr* decir en voz baja. **III** *vi* susurrar.

whistle ['wɪsəl] **I** *n* **1** *(instrument)* pito *m*. **2** *(sound)* silbido *m*, pitido *m*. **II** *vtr (tune)* silbar. **III** *vi* **1** *(person, kettle, wind)* silbar; *(train)* pitar.

white [waɪt] **I** *adj* blanco,-a; **to go w.,** *(face)* palidecer; *(hair)* encanecer; **w. coffee,** café *m* con leche; **w. hair,** pelo cano; **a w. Christmas,** una Navidad con nieve; *fig* **a w. lie,** una mentira piadosa;

US **the W. House,** la Casa Blanca; *Pol* **w. paper,** libro blanco; **w. sauce,** bechamel *f*. **II** *n* **1** *(colour, person, of eye)* blanco *m*. **2** *(of egg)* clara *f*. **3 whites,** ropa *f sing* blanca.

white-collar ['waɪtkɒlər] *adj* **w.-c. worker,** empleado *m* de oficina.

whiteness ['waɪtnɪs] *n* blancura *f*.

whitewash ['waɪtwɒʃ] **I** *n* **1** cal *f*. **2** *fig (cover-up)* encubrimiento *m*. **3** *fig (defeat)* paliza *f*. **II** *vtr* **1** *(wall)* enjalbegar, blanquear. **2** *fig* encubrir.

whiting ['waɪtɪŋ] *n inv (fish)* pescadilla *f*.

Whitsun(tide) ['wɪtsən(taɪd)] *n* pentecostés *m*.

whittle ['wɪtəl] *vtr* cortar en pedazos; **to w. away at,** roer; *fig* **to w. down,** reducir poco a poco.

whiz(z) [wɪz] *vi* **1** *(sound)* silbar. **2** **to w. past,** pasar volando; *fam* **w. kid,** joven *mf* dinámico,-a y emprendedor,-a.

who [huː] *pron* **1** *(direct question)* quién, quiénes; **w. are they?,** ¿quiénes son?; **w. is it?,** ¿quién es? **2** *(indirect question)* quién; **I don't know w. did it,** no sé quién lo hizo. **3** *rel (defining)* que; **those w. don't know,** los que no saben. **4** *rel (nondefining)* quien, quienes, el *or* la cual, los *or* las cuales; **Elena's mother, w. is very rich ...,** la madre de Elena, la cual es muy rica ....

whodun(n)it [huː'dʌnɪt] *n fam* novela *f or* obra *f* de teatro *or* película *f* de suspense.

whoever [huː'evər] *pron* **1** quienquiera que; **give it to w. you like,** dáselo a quien quieras; **w. said that is a fool,** el que dijo eso es un tonto; **w. you are,** quienquiera que seas. **2** *(direct question)* **w. told you that?,** ¿quién te dijo eso?

whole [həʊl] **I** *adj* **1** *(entire)* entero,-a, íntegro,-a; **a w. week,** una semana entera; **he took the w. lot,** se los llevó todos. **2** *(in one piece)* intacto,-a. **II** *n* **1** *(single unit)* todo *m*, conjunto *m*; **as a w.,** en su totalidad. **2** *(all)* totalidad *f*; **the w. of London,** todo Londres. **3 on the w.,** en general.

wholefood ['həʊlfuːd] *n* alimentos *mpl* integrales.

wholehearted [həʊl'hɑːtɪd] *adj (enthusiastic)* entusiasta; *(sincere)* sincero,-a; *(unreserved)* incondicional.

wholemeal ['həʊlmiːl] *adj* integral.

wholesale ['həʊlseɪl] *Com* **I** *n* venta *f* al por mayor. **II** *adj* al por mayor; *fig* total. **III** *adv* al por mayor; *fig* en su totalidad.

wholesaler ['həʊlseɪlər] *n* mayorista *mf*.

wholesome ['həʊlsəm] *adj* sano,-a.

wholly ['həʊlɪ] *adv* enteramente, completamente.

whom [huːm] *pron fml* **1** *(direct question) (accusative)* a quién; **w. did you talk to?,** ¿con quién hablaste?; *(after preposition)* **of/from w.?,** ¿de quién?; **to w. are you**

referring?, ¿a quién te refieres? 2 *rel (accusative)* que, a quien, a quienes; **those w. I have seen**, aquéllos a quien he visto. 3 *rel (after preposition)* quien, quienes, el *or* la cual, los *or* las cuales; **my brothers, both of w. are miners**, mis hermanos, que son mineros los dos.

whooping cough ['hu:pɪŋkɒf] *n* tos ferina.

whopping ['wɒpɪŋ] *adj fam* enorme.

whore [hɔːr] *n offens* puta *f*.

whose [hu:z] I *pron* 1 *(direct question)* de quién, de quiénes; **w. are these gloves?**, ¿de quién son estos guantes?; **w. is this?**, ¿de quién es esto? 2 *(indirect question)* de quién, de quiénes; **I don't know w. these coats are**, no sé de quién son estos abrigos. 3 *rel* cuyo(s), cuya(s); **the man w. children we saw**, el hombre a cuyos hijos vimos. II *adj* **w. car/house is this?**, ¿de quién es este coche/esta casa?.

why [waɪ] I *adv* por qué; *(for what purpose)* para qué; **w. did you do that?**, ¿por qué hiciste eso?; **w. not go to bed?**, ¿por qué no te acuestas?; **I don't know w. he did it**, no sé por qué lo hizo; **that is w. I didn't come**, por eso no vine; **there's no reason w. you shouldn't go**, no hay motivo para que no vayas. II *interj* 1 *(fancy that!)* ¡toma!, ¡vaya!; **w., it's David!**, ¡sí es David! 2 *(protest, assertion)* sí, vamos.

wick [wɪk] *n* mecha *f*.

wicked ['wɪkɪd] *adj* 1 malvado,-a. 2 *fam* malísimo,-a; *(temper)* de perros.

wicker ['wɪkər] I *n* mimbre *f*. II *adj* de mimbre.

wickerwork ['wɪkəwɜːk] *n (material)* mimbre *m*; *(articles)* artículos *mpl* de mimbre.

wicket ['wɪkɪt] *n Cricket (stumps)* palos *mpl*.

wide [waɪd] I *adj* 1 *(road, trousers)* ancho,-a; *(gap, interval)* grande; **it is ten metres w.**, tiene diez metros de ancho. 2 *(area, knowledge, support, range)* amplio,-a; **w. interests**, intereses muy diversos. 3 *(off target)* desviado,-a. II *adv* **from far and w.**, de todas partes; **to open one's eyes w.**, abrir los ojos de par en par; **w. apart**, muy separados,-as; **w. awake**, completamente despierto,-a; **w. open**, abierto,-a de par en par; **with mouth w. open**, boquiabierto,-a. ◆**widely** *adv (travel etc)* extensamente; *(believed)* generalmente; **he is w. known**, es muy conocido.

wide-angle ['waɪdæŋɡəl] *adj Phot* **w.-a. lens**, objetivo *m* gran angular.

widen ['waɪdən] I *vtr* ensanchar; *(interests)* ampliar. II *vi* ensancharse.

wide-ranging ['waɪdreɪndʒɪŋ] *adj (interests)* muy diversos,-as; *(discussion)* amplio,-a; *(study)* de gran alcance.

widespread ['waɪdspred] *adj (unrest, belief)* general; *(damage)* extenso,-a; **to become w.**, generalizarse.

widow ['wɪdəu] *n* viuda *f*.

widowed ['wɪdəud] *adj* enviudado,-a.

widower ['wɪdəuər] *n* viudo *m*.

width [wɪdθ] *n* 1 anchura *f*. 2 *(of material, swimming pool)* ancho *m*.

wield [wi:ld] *vtr (weapon)* blandir; *fig (power)* ejercer.

wife [waɪf] *n (pl wives)* mujer *f*, esposa *f*.

wig [wɪɡ] *n* peluca *f*.

wiggle ['wɪɡəl] I *vtr (finger etc)* menear; **to w. one's hips**, contonearse. II *vi* menearse.

Wight [waɪt] *n* **Isle of W.**, Isla *f* de Wight.

wild [waɪld] I *adj* 1 *(animal, tribe)* salvaje; **w. beast**, fiera *f*; *fig* **w. goose chase**, búsqueda *f* inútil. 2 *(plant)* silvestre. 3 *(landscape)* agreste; **the W. West**, el Salvaje Oeste. 4 *(temperament, behaviour)* alocado,-a; *(appearance)* desordenado,-a; *(passions etc)* desenfrenado,-a; *(laughter, thoughts)* loco,-a; *(applause)* fervoroso,-a; **to make a w. guess**, adivinar al azar; *fam fig* **she is w. about him/she is w. about tennis**, está loca por él/por el tenis. 5 *GB fam fig (angry)* furioso,-a. II *adv fig* **to run w.**, *(children)* desmandarse. III *n* **in the w.**, en el estado salvaje; *fig* **to live out in the wilds**, vivir en el quinto pino. ◆**wildly** *adv* 1 *(rush round etc)* como un,-a loco,-a; *(shoot)* sin apuntar; *(hit out)* a tontas y a locas. 2 **w. enthusiastic**, loco,-a de entusiasmo; **w. inaccurate**, totalmente erróneo,-a.

wildcat ['waɪldkæt] *n* **w. strike**, huelga *f* salvaje.

wilderness ['wɪldənɪs] *n* desierto *m*.

wildfire ['waɪldfaɪər] *n* **to spread like w.**, correr como la pólvora.

wildlife ['waɪldlaɪf] *n* fauna *f*; **w. park**, parque *m* natural.

wilful, US **wilfull** ['wɪlful] *adj* 1 *(stubborn)* terco,-a. 2 *Jur* premeditado,-a.

will¹ [wɪl] I *n* 1 voluntad *f*; **good/ill w.**, buena/mala voluntad; **of my own free w.**, por mi propia voluntad. 2 *Jur (testament)* testamento *m*; **to make one's w.**, hacer testamento. II *vtr* **fate willed that ...**, el destino quiso que ....

will² [wɪl] *v aux (pt would)* 1 *(future) (esp 2nd & 3rd person)* **they'll come**, vendrán; **w. he be there? - yes, he w.**, ¿estará allí? - sí, (estará); **you'll tell him, won't you?**, se lo dirás, ¿verdad?; **don't forget, w. you!**, ¡que no se te olvide, vale!; **she won't do it**, no lo hará. 2 *(command)* **you w. be here at eleven!**, ¡debes estar aquí a las once! 3 *(future perfect)* **they'll have finished by tomorrow**, habrán terminado para mañana. 4 *(willingness)* **be quiet, w. you! - no, I won't!**, ¿quiere callarse? -

no quiero; **I won't have it!**, ¡no lo permito!; **will you have a drink?** - **yes, I w.**, ¿quiere tomar algo? - sí, por favor; **won't you sit down?**, ¿quiere sentarse? 5 *(custom)* **accidents w. happen**, siempre habrá accidentes. 6 *(persistence)* **if you w. go out without a coat ...**, si te empeñas en salir sin abrigo .... 7 *(probability)* **he'll be on holiday now**, ahora estará de vacaciones. 8 *(ability)* **the lift w. hold ten people**, en el ascensor caben diez personas.

willing ['wɪlɪŋ] *adj (obliging)* complaciente; **I'm quite w. to do it**, lo haré con mucho gusto; **to be w. to do sth**, estar dispuesto,-a a hacer algo. ◆**willingly** *adv* de buena gana.

willingness ['wɪlɪŋnɪs] *n* buena voluntad.

willow ['wɪləʊ] *n w.* **(tree)**, sauce *m*.

willpower ['wɪlpaʊər] *n* (fuerza *f* de) voluntad *f*.

willy-nilly [wɪlɪ'nɪlɪ] *adv* por gusto o por fuerza.

wilt [wɪlt] *vi* marchitarse.

wily ['waɪlɪ] *adj (wilier, wiliest)* astuto,-a.

win [wɪn] **I** *n* victoria *f*. **II** *vtr (pt & pp* **won)** 1 ganar; *(prize)* llevarse; *(victory)* conseguir. 2 *fig (sympathy, friendship)* ganarse; *(praise)* cosechar; **to w. sb's love**, conquistar a algn. **III** *vi* ganar. ◆**win back** *vtr* recuperar. ◆**win over** *vtr (to cause, idea)* atraer **(to,** a, hacia); *(voters, support)* ganarse. ◆**win through** *vi* conseguir triunfar.

wince [wɪns] *vi* tener un rictus de dolor.

winch [wɪntʃ] *n* cigüeña *f*, torno *m*.

wind¹ [wɪnd] **I** *n* 1 viento *m*; *fig* **to get w. of sth**, olerse algo; **w. tunnel**, túnel aerodinámico. 2 *(breath)* aliento *m*; **to get one's second w.**, recobrar el aliento. 3 *Med* flato *m*, gases *mpl*. 4 **w. instrument**, instrumento *m* de viento. **II** *vtr* **to be winded**, quedarse sin aliento.

wind² [waɪnd] **I** *vtr (pt & pp* **wound)** 1 *(onto a reel)* enrollar; **to w. a bandage round one's finger**, vendarse el dedo. 2 **to w. on/back**, *(film, tape)* avanzar/ rebobinar. 3 *(clock)* dar cuerda a. **II** *vi (road, river)* serpentear. ◆**wind down I** *vtr (window)* bajar. **II** *vi fam (person)* relajarse. ◆**wind up I** *vtr* 1 *(roll up)* enrollar. 2 *(business etc)* cerrar; *(debate)* clausurar. 3 *(clock)* dar cuerda a. **II** *vi (meeting)* terminar.

windfall ['wɪndfɔːl] *n fig* ganancia inesperada.

winding ['waɪndɪŋ] *adj (road, river)* sinuoso,-a; *(staircase)* de caracol.

windmill ['wɪndmɪl] *n* molino *m* (de viento).

window ['wɪndəʊ] *n* ventana *f*; *(of vehicle, ticket office etc)* ventanilla *f*; *(shop)* **w.**, escaparate *m*; **to clean the windows**, limpiar los cristales; **w. box**, jardinera *f*;

w. cleaner, limpiacristales *mf inv*.

windowpane ['wɪndəʊpeɪn] *n* cristal *m*.

window-shopping ['wɪndəʊʃɒpɪŋ] *n* **to go w.-s.**, ir a mirar escaparates.

windowsill ['wɪndəʊsɪl] *n* alféizar *m*.

windpipe ['wɪndpaɪp] *n* tráquea *f*.

windscreen ['wɪndskriːn], *US* **windshield** ['wɪndfiːld] *n* parabrisas *m inv*; **w. washer**, lavaparabrisas *m inv*; **w. wiper**, limpiaparabrisas *m inv*.

windswept ['wɪndswept] *adj (landscape)* expuesto,-a a los vientos; *(person, hair)* despeinado,-a (por el viento).

windy ['wɪndɪ] *adj (windier, windiest)* *(weather)* ventoso,-a; *(place)* desprotegido,-a del viento; **it is very w. today**, hoy hace mucho viento.

wine [waɪn] *n* vino *m*; **w. cellar**, bodega *f*; **w. list**, lista *f* de vinos; **w. merchant**, vinatero,-a *m,f*; **w. tasting**, cata *f* de vinos; **w. vinegar**, vinagre *m* de vino.

wineglass ['waɪnglɑːs] *n* copa *f* (para vino).

wing [wɪŋ] *n* 1 *Orn Av* ala *f*. 2 *(of building)* ala *f*. 3 *Aut* aleta *f*; **w. mirror**, retrovisor *m* externo. 4 *Theat* **(in the) wings**, (entre) bastidores *mpl*. 5 *Ftb* banda *f*. 6 *Pol* ala *f*; **the left w.**, la izquierda.

winger ['wɪŋər] *n Ftb* extremo *m*.

wink [wɪŋk] **I** *n* guiño *m*; *fam fig* **I didn't get a w. (of sleep)**, no pegué ojo. **II** *vi* 1 *(person)* guiñar (el ojo). 2 *(light)* parpadear.

winner ['wɪnər] *n* ganador,-a *m,f*.

winning ['wɪnɪŋ] *adj (person, team)* ganador,-a; *(number)* premiado,-a; *(goal)* decisivo,-a; **w. post**, meta *f*.

winnings ['wɪnɪŋz] *npl* ganancias *fpl*.

winter ['wɪntər] **I** *n* invierno *m*. **II** *adj* de invierno; **w. sports**, deportes *mpl* de invierno. **III** *vi* invernar.

wintry ['wɪntrɪ] *adj (wintrier, wintriest)* invernal.

wipe [waɪp] **I** *vtr* limpiar; **to w. one's brow**, enjugarse la frente; **to w. one's feet/nose**, limpiarse los pies/las narices. ◆**wipe away** *vtr (tear)* enjugar. ◆**wipe off** *vtr* quitar frotando; **to w. sth off the blackboard/the tape**, borrar algo de la pizarra/de la cinta. ◆**wipe out** *vtr* 1 *(erase)* borrar. 2 *(army)* aniquilar; *(species etc)* exterminar. ◆**wipe up** *vtr* limpiar.

wire [waɪər] **I** *n* 1 alambre *m*; *Elec* cable *m*; *Tel* hilo; **w. cutters**, cizalla *f sing*. 2 *(telegram)* telegrama *m*. **II** *vtr* 1 **to w. (up) a house**, poner la instalación eléctrica de una casa; **to w. (up) an appliance to the mains**, conectar un aparato a la toma eléctrica. 2 *(information)* enviar por telegrama.

wireless ['waɪəlɪs] *n* radio *f*.

wiring ['waɪərɪŋ] *n (network)* cableado *m*; *(action)* instalación *f* del cableado.

wiry ['waɪərɪ] *adj* (**wirier, wiriest**) *(hair)* estropajoso,-a; *(person)* nervudo,-a.

wisdom ['wɪzdəm] *n* **1** *(learning)* sabiduría *f*, saber *m*. **2** *(good sense)* *(of person)* cordura *f*; *(of action)* sensatez *f*. **3** **w. tooth**, muela *f* del juicio.

wise [waɪz] *adj* **1** sabio,-a; **a w. man**, un sabio; **the Three W. Men**, los Reyes Magos. **2** *(remark)* juicioso,-a; *(decision)* acertado,-a; **it would be w. to keep quiet**, sería prudente callarse. ◆**wisely** *adv* *(with prudence)* prudentemente.

wisecrack ['waɪzkræk] *n fam* salida *f*, ocurrencia *f*.

wish [wɪʃ] **I** *n* **1** *(desire)* deseo *m* (**for**, de); **to make a w.**, pedir un deseo. **2 best wishes**, felicitaciones *fpl*; **give your mother my best wishes**, salude a su madre de mi parte; **with best wishes, Peter**, *(at end of letter)* saludos cordiales, Peter. **II** *vtr* **1** *(want)* querer, desear; **I w. I could stay longer**, me gustaría poder quedarme más tiempo; **I w. you had told me!**, ¡ojalá me lo hubieras dicho!; **to w. to do sth**, querer hacer algo. **2 to w. sb goodnight**, darle las buenas noches a algn; **to w. sb well**, desearle a algn mucha suerte. **III** *vi* *(want)* desear; **as you w.**, como quieras; **do as you w.**, haga lo que quiera; **to w. for sth**, desear algo.

wishful ['wɪʃful] *adj* **it's w. thinking**, es hacerse ilusiones.

wishy-washy ['wɪʃɪwɒʃɪ] *adj fam* *(person)* soso,-a; *(ideas)* poco definido,-a.

wisp [wɪsp] *n* *(of wool, hair)* mechón *m*; *(of smoke)* voluta *f*.

wistful ['wɪstful] *adj* melancólico,-a.

wit [wɪt] *n* **1** *(intelligence)* *(often pl)* inteligencia *f*; *fig* **to be at one's wits' end**, estar para volverse loco,-a; *fam fig* **to have one's wits about one**, ser despabilado,-a. **2** *(humour)* ingenio *m*. **3** *(person)* ingenioso,-a *m,f*.

witch [wɪtʃ] *n* bruja *f*; *fig* **w. hunt**, caza *f* de brujas.

witchcraft ['wɪtʃkrɑːft] *n* brujería *f*.

with [wɪð, wɪθ] *prep* con; **a room w. a bath**, un cuarto con baño; **do you have any money w. you?**, ¿traes dinero?; **the man w. the glasses**, el hombre de las gafas; **he went w. me/you**, fue conmigo/contigo; *fam* **w. (sugar) or without (sugar)?**, ¿con o sin azúcar?; **I have six w. this one**, con éste tengo seis; **w. all his faults, I admire him**, le admiro con todos sus defectos; **w. your permission**, con su permiso; **we're all w. you**, *(support)* todos estamos contigo; **you're not w. me, are you?** *(understand)* no me entiendes, ¿verdad?; **he's w. Lloyds**, trabaja para Lloyds; **she is popular w. her colleagues**, todos sus colegas la estiman mucho; **to fill a vase w. water**, llenar un jarrón de agua; **it is made w.**

butter, está hecho con mantequilla; **she put on weight w. so much eating**, engordó de tanto comer; **to be paralysed w. fear**, estar paralizado,-a de miedo; **w. experience**, con la experiencia.

withdraw [wɪð'drɔː] **I** *vtr* *(pt* **withdrew**; *pp* **withdrawn**) **1** retirar, sacar; **to w. money from the bank**, sacar dinero del banco. **2** *(go back on)* retirar; *(statement)* retractarse de; *(plan, claim)* renunciar a. **II** *vi* **1** retirarse. **2** *(drop out)* renunciar.

withdrawal [wɪð'drɔːəl] *n* retirada *f*; *(of statement)* retractación *f*; *(of complaint, plan)* renuncia *f*; **w. symptoms**, síndrome *m* de abstinencia.

withdrawn [wɪð'drɔːn] *adj* *(person)* introvertido,-a.

wither ['wɪðər] *vi* marchitarse.

withering ['wɪðərɪŋ] *adj* *(look)* fulminante; *(criticism)* mordaz.

withhold [wɪð'həʊld] *vtr* *(pt & pp* **withheld** [wɪð'held]) *(money)* retener; *(decision)* aplazar; *(consent)* negar; *(information)* ocultar.

within [wɪ'ðɪn] **I** *prep* **1** *(inside)* dentro de. **2** *(range)* **the house is w. walking distance**, se puede ir andando a la casa; **situated w. five kilometres of the town**, situado,-a a menos de cinco kilómetros de la ciudad; **w. sight of the sea**, con vistas al mar; *fig* **w. an inch of death**, a dos dedos de la muerte. **3** *(time)* **they arrived w. a few days of each other**, llegaron con pocos días de diferencia; **w. the hour**, dentro de una hora; **w. the next five years**, durante los cinco próximos años. **II** *adv* dentro; **from w.**, desde dentro.

with-it ['wɪðɪt] *adj fam* **she is very w. it**, tiene ideas muy modernas; **to get w. it**, ponerse de moda.

without [wɪ'ðaʊt] *prep* sin; **he did it w. my knowing**, lo hizo sin que lo supiera yo; *fig* **to do or go w. sth**, *(voluntarily)* prescindir de algo; *(forcibly)* pasar(se) sin algo.

withstand [wɪð'stænd] *vtr* *(pt & pp* **withstood**) resistir a; *(pain)* aguantar.

witness ['wɪtnɪs] **I** *n* **1** *(person)* testigo *mf*; **w. box**, *US* **w. stand**, barra *f* de los testigos. **2** *(evidence)* **to bear w. to sth**, dar fe de algo. **II** *vtr* **1** *(see)* presenciar, ser testigo de. **2** *fig (notice)* notar. **3** *Jur* **to w. a document**, firmar un documento como testigo.

witticism ['wɪtɪsɪzəm] *n* ocurrencia *f*, salida *f*.

witty ['wɪtɪ] *adj* (**wittier, wittiest**) ingenioso,-a, agudo,-a.

wives [waɪvz] *npl* → **wife**.

wizard ['wɪzəd] *n* hechicero *m*, mago *m*.

wizened ['wɪzənd] *adj* *(face)* arrugado,-a.

wobble ['wɒbəl] *vi* *(table, ladder etc)* tambalearse; *(jelly)* temblar.

woe [wəʊ] n *lit* infortunio m; **w. betide you if I catch you!**, ¡ay de ti si te cojo!

woeful ['wəʊfʊl] adj 1 (*person*) afligido,-a. 2 (*sight*) penoso,-a; **w. ignorance**, una ignorancia lamentable.

woke [wəʊk] pt → **wake**[1].

woken ['wəʊkən] pp → **wake**[1].

wolf [wʊlf] n (pl **wolves**) lobo m; *fig* **a w. in sheep's clothing**, un lobo con piel de cordero.

woman ['wʊmən] n (pl **women**) mujer f; **old w.**, vieja f; **women's libber**, feminista mf; *fam* **women's lib**, movimiento m feminista; **women's rights**, derechos mpl de la mujer.

womanhood ['wʊmənhʊd] n (*adult*) edad adulta de la mujer.

womanizer ['wʊmənaɪzər] n mujeriego m.

womanly ['wʊmənlɪ] adj femenino,-a.

womb [wu:m] n matriz f, útero m.

women ['wɪmɪn] npl → **woman**.

won [wʌn] pt & pp → **win**.

wonder ['wʌndər] I n 1 (*miracle*) milagro m; **no w. he hasn't come**, no es de extrañar que no haya venido. 2 (*amazement*) admiración f, asombro m. II vtr 1 (*be surprised*) sorprenderse. 2 (*ask oneself*) preguntarse; **I w. why**, ¿por qué será? III vi 1 (*marvel*) maravillarse; **to w. at sth**, admirarse de algo. 2 **it makes you w.**, (*reflect*) te da qué pensar.

wonderful ['wʌndəfʊl] adj maravilloso,-a. ◆**wonderfully** adv maravillosamente.

wont [wəʊnt] *fml* I adj **to be w. to**, soler. II n costumbre; **it is his w. to ...**, tiene la costumbre de ....

woo [wu:] vtr *lit* (*court*) cortejar; *fig* intentar congraciarse con.

wood [wʊd] n 1 (*forest*) bosque m. 2 (*material*) madera f; (*for fire*) leña f; *fam fig* **touch w.!**, ¡toca madera! 3 *Golf* palo m de madera. 4 (*bowling*) bola f.

woodcarving ['wʊdkɑːvɪŋ] n 1 (*craft*) tallado m en madera. 2 (*object*) talla f en madera.

woodcutter ['wʊdkʌtər] n leñador,-a m,f.

wooded ['wʊdɪd] adj arbolado,-a.

wooden ['wʊdən] adj 1 de madera; **w. spoon/leg**, cuchara f/pata f de palo. 2 *fig* rígido,-a; (*acting*) sin expresión.

woodlouse ['wʊdlaʊs] n cochinilla f.

woodpecker ['wʊdpekər] n pájaro carpintero.

woodwind ['wʊdwɪnd] n **w. (instruments)**, instrumentos mpl de viento de madera.

woodwork ['wʊdwɜːk] n 1 (*craft*) carpintería f. 2 (*of building*) maderaje m.

woodworm ['wʊdwɜːm] n carcoma f.

wool [wʊl] I n lana f; *fig* **to pull the w. over sb's eyes**, dar gato por liebre a algn. II adj de lana.

woollen, US **woolen** ['wʊlən] I adj 1 de lana. 2 (*industry*) lanero,-a. II npl **woollens**, géneros mpl de lana or de punto.

woolly, US **wooly** ['wʊlɪ] adj (**woollier, woolliest**, US **woolier, wooliest**) 1 (*made of wool*) de lana. 2 *fig* (*unclear*) confuso, -a.

word [wɜːd] I n 1 (*spoken, written*) palabra f; **in other words ...**, es decir ..., o sea ...; **words failed me**, me quedé sin habla; *fig* **a w. of advice**, un consejo; *fig* **I'd like a w. with you**, quiero hablar contigo un momento; *fig* **she didn't say it in so many words**, no lo dijo de modo tan explícito; **in the words of the poet ...**, como dice el poeta ...; *fig* **w. for w.**, palabra por palabra; **w. processing**, procesamiento m de textos; **w. processor**, procesador m de textos. 2 *fig* (*message*) mensaje m; **by w. of mouth**, de palabra; **is there any w. from him?**, ¿hay noticias de él?; **to send w.**, mandar recado. 3 *fig* (*rumour*) voz f, rumor m. 4 *fig* (*promise*) palabra f; **he's a man of his w.**, es hombre de palabra. II vtr (*express*) formular; **a badly worded letter**, una carta mal redactada.

wording ['wɜːdɪŋ] n expresión f; **I changed the w. slightly**, cambié algunas palabras.

word-perfect [wɜːd'pɜːfekt] adj **to be w.-p.**, saberse el papel perfectamente.

wore [wɔːr] pt → **wear**.

work [wɜːk] I n 1 trabajo m; **his w. in the field of physics**, su labor en el campo de la física; **it's hard w.**, cuesta trabajo. 2 (*employment*) trabajo m, empleo m; **out of w.**, parado,-a. 3 (*action*) obra f, acción f; **keep up the good w.!**, ¡que siga así! 4 **a piece of w.**, un trabajo; **a w. of art**, una obra de arte. 5 **works**, obras fpl; **public works**, obras (públicas). 6 **works**, (*machinery*) mecanismo m *sing*. 7 *GB* **works**, (*factory*) fábrica f.

II vtr 1 (*drive*) hacer trabajar; **to w. one's way up/down**, subir/bajar a duras penas; *fig* **to w. one's way up in a firm**, trabajarse el ascenso en una empresa. 2 (*machine*) manejar; (*mechanism*) accionar. 3 (*miracles, changes*) operar, hacer. 4 (*land*) cultivar; (*mine*) explotar. 5 (*wood, metal etc*) trabajar.

III vi 1 trabajar (**on, at, en**); **to w. as a gardener**, trabajar de jardinero. 2 (*machine*) funcionar; **it works on gas**, funciona con gas. 3 (*drug*) surtir efecto; (*system*) funcionar bien; (*plan, trick*) salir bien. 4 (*operate*) obrar; **to w. loose**, soltarse; **we have no data to w. on**, no tenemos datos en que basarnos.

◆**work off** vtr (*fat*) eliminar trabajando; (*anger*) desahogar. ◆**work out** I vtr 1 (*plan*) idear; (*itinerary*) planear; (*details*) desarrollar. 2 (*problem*) solucionar; (*solu-*

tion) encontrar; *(amount)* calcular; **I can't w. out how he did it**, no me explico cómo lo hizo. **II** *vi* **1 things didn't w. out for her**, las cosas no le salieron bien. **2 it works out at 5 each**, sale a 5 cada uno. **3** *Sport* hacer ejercicio. ◆**work through** *vi* penetrar (to, hasta). ◆**work up** *vtr (excite)* acalorar; **to get worked up**, excitarse; **to w. up enthusiasm**, entusiasmarse (for, con).

workable ['wɜːkəbəl] *adj* factible.

workaholic [wɜːkə'hɒlɪk] *n fam* trabajoadicto,-a.

workbench ['wɜːkbentʃ] *n* obrador *m*.

worker ['wɜːkər] *n* trabajador,-a *m,f*; *(manual)* obrero,-a *m,f*.

workforce ['wɜːkfɔːs] *n* mano *f* de obra.

working ['wɜːkɪŋ] **I** *adj* **1** *(population, capital)* activo,-a; **w. class**, clase obrera; **w. man**, obrero *m*. **2** *(clothes, conditions, hours)* de trabajo; **w. day**, día *m* laborable; *(number of hours)* jornada *f* laboral. **3 it is in w. order**, funciona. **4** *(majority)* suficiente; **w. knowledge**, conocimientos básicos. **II** *n* **workings**, *(mechanics)* funcionamiento *m sing*; *Min* explotación *f sing*.

workman ['wɜːkmən] *n (manual)* obrero *m*.

workmanship ['wɜːkmənʃɪp] *n (appearance)* acabado *m*; *(skill)* habilidad *f*, arte *m* **a fine piece of w.**, un trabajo excelente.

workmate ['wɜːkmeɪt] *n* compañero,-a *m,f* de trabajo.

work-out ['wɜːkaut] *n* entrenamiento *m*.

worksheet ['wɜːkʃiːt] *n* plan *m* de trabajo.

workshop ['wɜːkʃɒp] *n* taller *m*.

worktop ['wɜːktɒp] *n* encimera *f*.

work-to-rule [wɜːktə'ruːl] *n* huelga *f* de celo.

world [wɜːld] *n* mundo *m*; **all over the w.**, en todo el mundo; **the best in the w.**, el mejor del mundo; *fig* **there is a w. of difference between A and B**, hay un mundo de diferencia entre A y B; *fig* **to feel on top of the w.**, sentirse fenomenal; *fig* **to think the w. of sb**, adorar a algn; *fam fig* **it is out of this w.**, es una maravilla; **the W. Bank**, el Banco Mundial; *Ftb* **the W. Cup**, los Mundiales; **w. record**, récord *m* mundial; **w. war**, guerra *f* mundial.

world-class ['wɜːldklɑːs] *adj* de categoría mundial.

world-famous ['wɜːldfeɪməs] *adj* de fama mundial.

worldly ['wɜːldlɪ] *adj* mundano,-a.

worldwide ['wɜːldwaɪd] *adj* mundial.

worm [wɜːm] **I** *n* **1** gusano *m*; *(earth)* **w.**, lombriz *f*. **2** *Med* **worms**, lombrices *fpl*. **II** *vtr* **to w. a secret out of sb**, sonsacarle un secreto a algn.

worn [wɔːn] *adj* gastado, -a, usado,-a.

worn-out ['wɔːnaut] *adj (thing)* gastado, -a; *(person)* rendido,-a, agotado,-a.

worried ['wʌrɪd] *adj* inquieto,-a preocupado,-a.

worry ['wʌrɪ] **I** *vtr* **1** preocupar, inquietar; **it doesn't w. me**, me trae sin cuidado. **2** *(pester)* molestar. **II** *vi* preocuparse *(about, por)*; **don't w.**, no te preocupes. **III** *n (state)* inquietud *f*; *(cause)* preocupación *f*.

worrying ['wʌrɪɪŋ] *adj* inquietante, preocupante.

worse [wɜːs] **I** *adj (comp of bad)* peor; **he gets w. and w.**, va de mal en peor; **to get w.**, empeorar; *fam* **w. luck!**, ¡mala suerte!. **II** *n* **a change for the w.**, un empeoramiento; *fig* **to take a turn for the w.**, empeorar. **III** *adv (comp of badly)* peor; **w. than ever**, peor que nunca.

worship ['wɜːʃɪp] **I** *vtr* adorar. **II** *n* **1** adoración *f*. **2** *(ceremony)* culto *m*. **3** *GB* **his W. the Mayor**, el señor alcalde; *Jur* **your W.**, señoría.

worshipper ['wɜːʃɪpər] *n* devoto,-a *m,f*.

worst [wɜːst] **I** *adj (superl of bad)* peor; **the w. part about it is that ….**, lo peor es que ….. **II** *n* **1** *(person)* el *or* la peor, los *or* las peores. **2 the w. of the storm is over**, ya ha pasado lo peor de la tormenta. **III** *adv (superl of badly)* peor; *fig* **to come off w.**, salir perdiendo.

worth [wɜːθ] **I** *adj* **1 to be w. £3**, valer 3 libras; **a house w. £50,000**, una casa que vale 50.000 libras. **2** *(deserving of)* merecedor,-a de; **a book w. reading**, un libro que merece la pena leer; **for what it's w.**, por si sirve de algo; **it's w. your while**, it's w. it, vale *or* merece la pena; **it's w. mentioning**, es digno de mención. **II** *n* **1** *(in money)* valor *m*; **five pounds' w. of petrol**, gasolina por valor de 5 libras. **2** *(of person)* valía *f*.

worthless ['wɜːθlɪs] *adj* sin valor; *(person)* despreciable.

worthwhile [wɜːθ'waɪl] *adj* valioso,-a, que vale la pena.

worthy ['wɜːðɪ] *adj (worthier, worthiest)* **1** *(deserving)* digno,-a (of, de); *(winner, cause)* justo,-a. **2** *(citizen)* respetable; *(effort, motives, action)* loable.

would [wud, *unstressed* wəd] *v aux* **1** *(conditional)* **I w. go if I had time**, iría si tuviera tiempo; **he w. have won but for that**, habría ganado su no hubiera sido por eso; **we w. if we could**, lo haríamos si pudiéramos; **you would have to choose me!**, ¡tenías que elegirme precisamente a mí! **2** *(reported speech)* **he said that he w. come**, dijo que vendría. **3** *(willingness)* **the car wouldn't start**, el coche no arrancaba; **they asked him to come but he wouldn't**, le invitaron a venir pero no quiso; **w. you do me a fa-**

vour?, ¿quiere hacerme un favor? **4** *(wishing)* he w. like to know why, quisiera saber por qué; **I'd rather go home,** preferiría ir a casa; **w. you like a cigarette?**, ¿quiere un cigarrillo? **5** *(custom)* **we w. go for walks,** solíamos dar un paseo. **6** try as I w., por mucho que lo intentara. **7** *(conjecture)* it w. have been about three weeks ago, debe haber sido hace unas tres semanas; **w. this be your cousin?**, ¿será éste tu primo? **8** *(expectation)* so it w. appear, según parece.

would-be ['wudbi:] *adj* (*person)* en potencia; a **w.-be politician,** un aspirante a político; *pej* a **w.-be poet,** un supuesto poeta.

wound¹ [waund] *pt & pp* → **wind².**

wound² [wu:nd] *n* herida *f.* **II** *vtr* herir.

wove [wəuv] *pt* → **weave.**

woven ['wəuvən] *pp* → **weave.**

wow [wau] *fam* **I** *vtr* encandilar. **II** *interj* ¡caramba!

WP 1 *abbr of* **word processing. 2** *abbr of* **word processor.**

wrangle ['ræŋgəl] **I** *n* disputa *f.* **II** *vi* disputar (**over,** acerca de, por).

wrap [ræp] **I** *vtr* **1** *to* **w. (up),** envolver; **he wrapped his arms around her,** la estrechó entre sus brazos; *fam* **we wrapped up the deal,** concluimos el negocio. **II** *vi* *fam* **w. up well,** abrígate. **III** *n* *(shawl)* chal *m*; *(cape)* capa *f.*

wrapper ['ræpər] *n* *(of sweet)* envoltorio *m*; *(of book)* sobrecubierta *f.*

wrapping ['ræpɪŋ] *n* **w. paper,** papel *m* de envolver.

wreath [ri:θ] *n* (*pl* **wreaths** [ri:ðz, ri:θs]) *(of flowers)* corona *f*; **laurel w.,** corona de laurel.

wreck [rek] **I** *n* **1** *Naut* naufragio *m*; *(ship)* barco naufragado. **2** *(of car, plane)* restos *mpl*; *(of building)* ruinas *fpl.* **3** *fig (person)* ruina *f.* **II** *vtr* **1** *(ship)* hacer naufragar. **2** *(car, machine)* destrozar. **3** *fig (health, life)* arruinar; *(plans, hopes)* desbaratar; *(chances)* echar a perder.

wreckage ['rekɪdʒ] *n* *(of ship, car, plane)* restos *mpl*; *(of building)* ruinas *fpl.*

wren [ren] *n* chochín *m.*

wrench [rentʃ] **I** *n* **1** *(pull)* tirón *m.* **2** *Med* torcedura *f.* **3** *(tool)* *GB* llave inglesa; *US* llave. **II** *vtr* **to w. oneself free,** soltarse de un tirón; **to w. sth off sb,** arrebatarle algo a algn; **to w. sth off/open,** quitar/abrir algo de un tirón.

wrestle ['resəl] *vi* luchar.

wrestler ['reslər] *n* luchador,-a *m,f.*

wrestling ['reslɪŋ] *n* lucha *f.*

wretch [retʃ] *n* *(poor)* **w.,** desgraciado,-a *m,f.*

wretched ['retʃɪd] *adj* **1** desdichado,-a; *(conditions)* deplorable; *fam (bad, poor)* horrible. **2 I feel w.,** *(ill)* me siento fatal. **3** *(contemptible)* despreciable. **4** *fam*

(damned) maldito,-a, condenado,-a.

wriggle ['rɪgəl] **I** *vtr* menear. **II** *vi* **to w.** *(about)*, *(worm)* serpentear; *(restless child)* moverse nerviosamente; **to w. free,** escapar deslizándose.

wring [rɪŋ] *vtr* (*pt & pp* **wrung**) **1** *(clothes)* escurrir; *(hands)* retorcer. **2** *fig (extract)* arrancar, sacar.

wringing ['rɪŋɪŋ] *adj* **to be w. wet,** estar empapado,-a.

wrinkle ['rɪŋkəl] **I** *n* arruga *f.* **II** *vtr* arrugar. **III** *vi* arrugarse.

wrist [rɪst] *n* muñeca *f.*

wristwatch ['rɪstwɒtʃ] *n* reloj *m* de pulsera.

writ [rɪt] *n* orden *f* judicial.

write [raɪt] **I** *vtr* (*pt* **wrote**; *pp* **written**) escribir; *(article)* redactar; *(cheque)* extender. **II** *vi* escribir (**about,** sobre); **to w. for a paper,** colaborar en un periódico. ◆**write back** *vi* contestar. ◆**write down** *vtr* poner por escrito; *(note)* apuntar. ◆**write in** *vi* escribir. ◆**write off I** *vtr* *(debt)* condonar; *(car)* destrozar. **II** *vi* **to w. off for sth,** pedir algo por escrito. ◆**write out** *vtr* *(cheque, recipe)* extender. ◆**write up** *vtr* *(notes)* redactar; *(diary, journal)* poner al día.

write-off ['raɪtɒf] *n* **the car's a w.-o.,** el coche está hecho una ruina.

writer ['raɪtər] *n* *(by profession)* escritor,-a *m,f*; *(of book, letter)* autor,-a *m,f.*

writhe [raɪð] *vi* retorcerse.

writing ['raɪtɪŋ] *n* **1** *(script)* escritura *f*; *(handwriting)* letra *f*; **in w.,** por escrito. **2** **writings,** escritos *mpl.* **3** *(action)* escritura *f*; **w. desk,** escritorio *m.*

written ['rɪtən] *pp* → **write.**

wrong [rɒŋ] **I** *adj* **1** *(person)* equivocado,-a; **I was w. about that boy,** me equivoqué con ese chico; **to be w.,** no tener razón; **you're w. in thinking that ...,** te equivocas si piensas que .... **2** *(answer, way)* incorrecto,-a, equivocado,-a; **my watch is w.,** mi reloj anda mal; **to drive on the w. side of the road,** conducir por el lado contrario de la carretera; **to go the w. way,** equivocarse de camino; *Tel* **I've got the w. number,** me he confundido de número. **3** *(unsuitable)* impropio,-a inadecuado,-a; *(time)* inoportuno,-a; **to say the w. thing,** decir algo inoportuno. **4** *(immoral etc)* malo,-a; **there's nothing w. in that,** no hay nada malo en ello; **what's w. with smoking?,** ¿qué tiene de malo fumar? **5 is anything w.?,** ¿pasa algo?; **something's w.,** hay algo que no está bien; **what's w.?,** ¿qué pasa?; **what's w. with you?,** ¿qué te pasa?

II *adv* mal, incorrectamente; **to get it w.,** equivocarse; *fam* **to go w.,** *(plan)* fallar; salir mal.

III *n* **1** *(evil, bad action)* mal *m*; **you did w. to hit him,** hiciste mal en pegarle. **2**

(injustice) injusticia *f*; *(offence)* agravio *m*; **the rights and wrongs of a matter,** lo justo y lo injusto de un asunto. **3 to be in the w.,** *(to blame)* tener la culpa. **IV** *vtr (treat unfairly)* ser injusto,-a con; *(offend)* agraviar.
◆**wrongly** *adv* **1** *(incorrectly)* incorrectamente. **2** *(mistakenly)* equivocadamente. **3**

(unjustly) injustamente.
wrongdoing ['rɒŋduːɪŋ] *n* maldad *f*.
wrongful ['rɒŋful] *adj* injusto,-a.
wrote [rəut] *pt* → write.
wrung [rʌŋ] *pt & pp* → wring.
wry [raɪ] *adj* (**wrier, wriest** *or* **wryer, wryest**) sardónico,-a.

X

X, x [eks] *n (the letter)* X, x *f*.
xenophobia [zenə'fəubiə] *n* xenofobia *f*.
xenophobic [zenə'fəubɪk] *adj* xenófobo, -a.
Xerox® ['zɪərɒks] **I** *n* xerocopia *f*. **II** *vtr* xerocopiar.
Xmas ['eksməs, 'krɪsməs] *n abbr of*

Christmas.
X-ray [eks'reɪ] **I** *n* **1** *(beam)* rayo *m* X; **X-r. therapy,** radioterapia *f*. **2** *(picture)* radiografía *f*; **to have an X-r.,** hacerse una radiografía. **II** *vtr* radiografiar.
xylophone ['zaɪləfəun] *n* xilófono *m*.

Y

Y, y [waɪ] *n (the letter)* Y, y *f*.
yacht [jɒt] *n* yate *m*; **y. club,** club náutico.
yachting ['jɒtɪŋ] *n Sport* navegación *f* a vela; *(competition)* regatas *fpl*.
yachtsman ['jɒtsmən] *n* balandrista *m*.
yachtswoman ['jɒtswumən] *n* balandrista *f*.
yam [jæm] *n* **1** ñame *m*. **2** *US (sweet potato)* boniato *m*.
yank [jæŋk] *fam vtr* tirar; *(tooth)* arrancar.
Yank [jæŋk] *n GB pej* yanqui *mf*.
Yankee ['jæŋkɪ] *adj & n pej* yanqui *mf*.
yap [jæp] *vi (dog)* aullar; *fam (person)* darle al pico.
yard¹ [jɑːd] *n (measure)* yarda *f (aprox* 0.914 metros).
yard² [jɑːd] *n* patio *m*; *US* jardín *m*.
yardstick ['jɑːdstɪk] *n fig* criterio *m*, norma *f*.
yarn [jɑːn] *n* **1** *Sew* hilo *m*. **2** *(story)* historia *f*, cuento *m*; **to spin a y.,** *(lie)* inventarse una historia.
yawn [jɔːn] **I** *vi* bostezar. **II** *n* bostezo *m*.
yawning ['jɔːnɪŋ] *adj (gap)* profundo,-a.
yd *(pl yds) abbr of* yard.
yeah [jeə] *adv fam* sí.
year [jɪərʳ] *n* **1** año *m*; **all y. round,** durante todo el año; **last y.,** el año pasado; **next y.,** el año que viene; **y. in, y. out,** año tras año; **I'm ten years old,** tengo diez años. **2** *Educ* curso *m*; **first-y. student,** estudiante *m,f* de primero.
yearly ['jɪəlɪ] **I** *adj* anual. **II** *adv* anualmente, cada año.
yearn [jɜːn] *vi* **to y. for sth,** anhelar algo.
yearning ['jɜːnɪŋ] *n* anhelo *m* (**for,** de).
yeast [jiːst] *n* levadura *f*.
yell [jel] **I** *vi* gritar. **II** *n* grito *m*, alarido

m.
yellow ['jeləu] **I** *adj* amarillo,-a; *fam fig (cowardly)* cobarde; *Tel* **y. pages,** páginas amarillas. **II** *n* amarillo *m*.
yelp [jelp] **I** *vi* aullar. **II** *n* aullido *m*.
yen [jen] *n* **1** *(currency)* yen *m*. **2 to have a y. for sth,** tener ganas de algo.
yeoman ['jəumən] *n GB* **Y. of the Guard,** alabardero *m* de la Casa Real británica.
yes [jes] **I** *adv* sí; **you said y.,** dijiste que sí. **II** *n* sí *m*.
yesterday ['jestədeɪ] *adv & n* ayer *m*; **the day before y.,** anteayer; **y. morning,** ayer por la mañana.
yet [jet] **I** *adv* **1 not y.,** aún no, todavía no; **as y.,** hasta ahora; **I haven't eaten y.,** no he comido todavía. **2** *(in questions)* ya; **has he arrived y.?,** ¿ha venido ya? **3** *(even)* más; **y. again,** otra vez; **y. more,** todavía más. **4** *(eventually)* todavía, aún; **he'll win y.,** todavía puede ganar. **II** *conj* sin embargo.
yew [juː] *n* tejo *m*.
yield [jiːld] **I** *n* **1** rendimiento *m*. **2** *Agr* cosecha *f*. **3** *Fin* beneficio *m*. **II** *vtr* producir; *Agr* dar; *(money)* producir. **III** *vi* **1** *(surrender, break)* ceder. **3** *Aut* ceder el paso.
YMCA [waɪemsiː'eɪ] *abbr of* **Young Men's Christian Association,** albergue *m* para hombres jóvenes.
yob(bo) ['jɒb(əu)] *n fam* gamberro,-a *m,f*.
yoga ['jəugə] *n* yoga *m*.
yog(h)urt ['jɒgət] *n* yogur *m*.
yoke [jəuk] **I** *n* yugo *m*. **II** *vtr (oxen)* uncir; *fig* unir.
yokel ['jəukəl] *n pej* paleto,-a *m,f*.
yolk [jəuk] *n* yema *f*.

yonder ['jɒndər] adv más allá.
you [juː, unstressed jʊ] pers pron 1 (subject) (familiar use) (sing) tú; (pl) vosotros,-as; **how are y?**, ¿cómo estás?, ¿cómo estáis? 2 (subject) (polite use) (sing) usted; (pl) ustedes; **how are y.?**, ¿cómo está?, ¿cómo están? 3 (subject) (impers use) **y. never know**, nunca se sabe. 4 (object) (familiar use) (sing) (before verb) te; (after preposition) ti; (pl) (before verb) os; (after preposition) vosotros,-as; **I saw y.**, te vi, os vi; **it's for y.**, es para ti, es para vosotros,-as; **with you**, contigo, con vosotros,-as. 5 (object) (polite use) (sing) (before verb) le; (after preposition) usted; (pl) (before verb) les; (after preposition) ustedes; **I saw y.**, le vi, les vi; **it's for y.**, es para usted, es para ustedes; **with you**, con usted, con ustedes. 6 (object) (impers use) **alcohol makes you drunk**, el alcohol emborracha.
young [jʌŋ] I adj (age) joven; (brother etc) pequeño,-a; **y. lady**, señorita f; **y. man**, joven m. II n 1 (people) **the y.**, los jóvenes, la juventud. 2 (animals) crías fpl.
youngster ['jʌŋstər] n muchacho,-a m,f.
your [jɔː, unstressed jə] poss adj 1 (familiar use) (sing) tu, tus; (pl) vuestro,-a, vuestros,-as. 2 (polite use) su, sus. 3 (impers use) **the house is on y. right**, la casa queda a la derecha; **they clean y. shoes for you**, te limpian los zapatos. 4 (formal address) Su; **Y. Majesty**, Su Majestad.

yours [jɔːz] poss pron 1 (familiar use) (sing) el tuyo, la tuya, los tuyos, las tuyas; (pl) el vuestro, la vuestra, los vuestros, las vuestras; **the house is y.**, la casa es tuya. 2 (polite use) (sing) el suyo, la suya; (pl) los suyos, las suyas; **the house is y.**, la casa es suya. 3 (in letters) **y. faithfully**, le(s) saluda atentamente; **y. sincerely**, reciba un cordial saludo de.
yourself [jɔː'self, unstressed jə'self] (pl **yourselves** [jɔː'selvz] I pers pron 1 (familiar use) (sing) tú mismo,-a; (pl) vosotros,-as mismos,-as; **by y.**, (tú) solo; **by yourselves**, vosotros,-as solos, -as. 2 (polite use) (sing) usted mismo,-a; (pl) ustedes mismos,-as; **by y.**, (usted) solo, -a; **by yourselves**, (ustedes) solos, -as. II reflexive pron 1 (familiar use) (sing) te; pl (familiar use) os; **enjoy y.!**, ¡diviértete!; **enjoy yourselves**, ¡divertíos! 2 (polite use) se; **enjoy y.**, ¡diviértase!; **enjoy yourselves**, ¡diviértanse!
youth [juːθ] n 1 juventud f. 2 (young man) joven m; **y. club**, club m juvenil; **y. hostel**, albergue m juvenil.
youthful ['juːθfʊl] adj juvenil, joven.
Yugoslav ['juːgəʊslɑːv] adj & n yugoslavo,-a (m,f).
Yugoslavia [juːgəʊ'slɑːvɪə] n Yugoslavia.
Yugoslavian [juːgəʊ'slɑːvɪən] adj & n yugoslavo,-a (m,f).
YWCA [waɪdʌbəljuːsiː'eɪ] abbr of Young Women's Christian Association, albergue m para mujeres jóvenes.

Z

Z, z [zed, US ziː] n (the letter) Z, z f.
zany ['zeɪnɪ] adj (zanier, zaniest) fam 1 (mad) chiflado,-a. 2 (eccentric) estrafalario,-a.
zap [zæp] I interj ¡zas! II vtr sl 1 (hit) pegar. 2 fam (kill) cargarse a. III vi TV hacer zapping.
zeal [ziːl] n (enthusiasm) entusiasmo m.
zealous ['zeləs] adj (enthusiastic) entusiasta.
zebra ['ziːbrə, 'zebrə] n cebra f; GB **z. crossing**, paso m de peatones.
zenith ['zenɪθ] n Astron cenit m; fig apogeo m.
zero ['zɪərəʊ] n cero m; **z. hour**, hora f cero.
zest [zest] n (eagerness) entusiasmo m.
zigzag ['zɪgzæg] I n zigzag m. II vi zigzaguear.
Zimbabwe [zɪm'bɑːbweɪ] n Zimbabue.
zinc [zɪŋk] n cinc m, zinc m.
zip [zɪp] I n 1 **z. (fastener)**, cremallera f. 2 fam brío m; US **z. code**, código m

postal. II vi cerrarse con cremallera. ◆**zip by** vi pasar como un rayo. ◆**zip up** vtr cerrar con cremallera; **to z. sb up**, cerrar la cremallera a algn.
zipper ['zɪpər] n US cremallera f.
zodiac ['zəʊdɪæk] n zodiaco m, zodíaco m.
zombie ['zɒmbɪ] n zombie mf.
zone [zəʊn] I n zona f. II vtr dividir en zonas.
zoo [zuː] n zoo m.
zoological [zəʊə'lɒdʒɪkəl] adj zoológico,-a.
zoologist [zəʊ'ɒlədʒɪst] n zoólogo,-a m,f.
zoology [zəʊ'ɒlədʒɪ] n zoología f.
zoom [zuːm] I n 1 (buzz) zumbido m. 2 **z. lens**, zoom m, teleobjetivo m. II vi 1 (buzz) zumbar. 2 **to z. past**, pasar volando. ◆**zoom in** vi (camera) acercarse rápidamente.
zucchini [zuː'kiːnɪ] n US calabacín m.
Zulu ['zuːluː] adj & n zulú (mf).